DICTIONARY OF ISLAM

A CYCLOPAEDIA OF THE DOCTRINES, RITES, CEREMONIES, AND CUSTOMS, TOGETHER WITH THE TECHNICAL AND THEOLOGICAL TERMS OF THE MUSLIM RELIGION.

THOMAS PATRICK HUGHES, B.D., M.R.A.S.

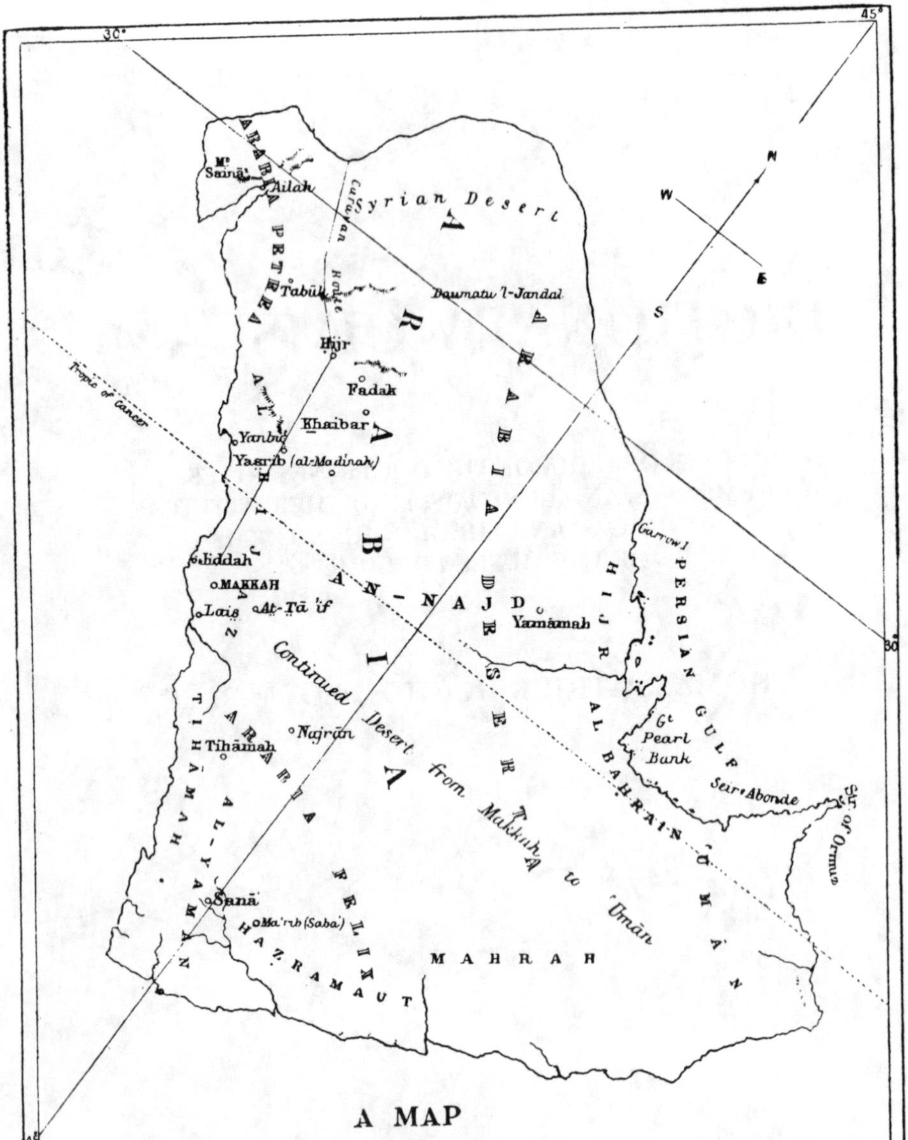

A MAP

OF THE

ARABIAN PENINSULA

During the Time of Prophet Muhammad (ص)

A DICTIONARY OF ISLAM

BEING

A CYCLOPAEDIA OF THE DOCTRINES, RITES, CEREMONIES, AND CUSTOMS, TOGETHER WITH THE TECHNICAL AND THEOLOGICAL TERMS OF THE MUSLIM RELIGION.

THOMAS PATRICK HUGHES, B.D., M.R.A.S.

WITH NUMEROUS ILLUSTRATIONS

KAZI Publications, Inc. (USA)

Cover Design by Liaquat Ali

Library of Congress Cataloging in Publication Data

Hughes, Thomas Patrick
Dictionary of Islam

Includes index.
1. Islam—Dictionaries.
I. Hughes, Thomas Patrick. II. Title.
[BP 40.G41 1993] 91-55138
ISBN 0-935782-70-2 CIP

PUBLISHED AND
DISTRIBUTED BY:

KAZI Publications, Inc.
3023-27 West Belmont Avenue
Chicago, IL 60618
(312) 267-7001

PREFACE

The increased interest manifested in relation to all matters affecting the East, and the great attention now given to the study of comparative religion, seem to indicate that the time has come when an attempt should be made to place before the English-speaking people of the world a systematic exposition of the doctrines of the Muslim Faith. The present work is intended to supply this want, by giving, in a tabulated form, a concise account of the doctrines, rites, ceremonies, and customs, together with the technical and theological terms, of the Muslim religion.

The *Dictionary* is, for the most part, an exposition of the opinions of the Sunni sect, with explanations of the chief points on which the Shiah and Wahhabi schools of thought differ from it. The present book does not profess to be a Biographical Dictionary but short biographical notices of persons connected with the early history of Islam have been given, inasmuch as many of these persons are connected with religious dogmas and ceremonies; the martyrdom of Husain, for instance, as being the foundation of the Muharram ceremonies; Abu Hanifah, as connected with a school of jurisprudence; and the Khalifah 'Umar as the real founder of the religious and political power of Islam. In the biographical notice of Muhammad, the Author has expressed his deep obligations to Sir William Muir' s great work, the *Life of Mahomet*.

It is impossible for anyone to write upon the subject of Islam without being largely indebted, not only to Sir William Muir's books, but also to the works of the late Mr. Lane, the author of *Modern Egyptians*, new editions of which have been edited by Mr. Stanley Lane Poole. Numerous quotations from these volumes will be found in the present work.

But whilst the Author has not hesitated in this compilation to avail himself of the above and similar works, he has, during a long residence amongst Muslim people, been able to consult very numerous Arabic and Persian works in their originals, and to obtain the assistance of very able Muslim scholars of all schools of thought in Islam.

He is specially indebted to Dr. F. Steingass of the University of Munich, the author of the *English—Arabic and Arabic-English Dictionaries,* for a careful revision of the whole work. The interesting article on writing is from the pen of this distinguished scholar, as well as some valuable criticisms on the compilation of the Quran and a biographical sketch of the Khalifah 'Umar.

Among the numerous suggestions which the Author received for the compilation of this Dictionary, was one from a well-known Arabic scholar, to the effect that the value of the work would be enhanced if the quotations from the Quran and from the Traditions, were given in their original Arabic. This, however, seemed incompatible with the general design of the book. The whole structure of the work is intended to be such as will make it available to English scholars unacquainted with the Arabic language and, consequently, most of the information given will be found under English words rather than under their Arabic equivalents. For example, for information regarding the attributes of the Divine Being, the reader must refer to the English GOD, and not to the Arabic ALLAH; or all the ritual and laws regarding the liturgical service, to the English PRAYER and not to the Arabic SALAT; for the marriage laws and ceremonies, to the English MARRIAGE, and not to the Arabic NIKAH. It is hoped that, in this way, the information given will be available to those who are entirely unacquainted with Oriental languages, or, indeed, with Eastern life.

The quotations from the Quran have been given chiefly from Palmer's and Rodwell's translations; and those in the Quranic narrative of Biblical characters (Moses, for example) have been taken from Mr. Stanley Lane Poole's edition of Lane's *Selections*. But, when needful, entirely new translations of quotations from the Quran have been given. The Dictionary of Islam has been compiled with very considerable study and labor, in the hope that it will be useful to many.

July 23rd, 1886

KAZI Publications, Inc. has reprinted this 19th century *Dictionary on Islam* with the author's preface for its readers because of the comprehensiveness and scope of the work. No similar work has been done over 100 years later. We do not agree with all of the entries or descriptions but felt that the knowledge should be made available to all to read and then to decide for himself or herself which descriptions are accurate of Muslim life and beliefs.

THE ARABIC LETTERS IN THIS VOLUME HAVE BEEN TRANSLITERATED AS FOLLOWS :—

Arabic.	Names.	Roman.	Pronunciation.
ا	Alif	A	*a*, *i*, *u*, at the beginning of a word.
ب	Bā	B	As in English.
ت	Tā	T	A soft dental, like the Italian *t*.
ث	S̤ā	S̤	Very nearly the sound of *th* in *thing*.
ج	Jīm	J	As in English.
ح	Ḥā	Ḥ	A strong aspirate.
خ	K͟hā	K͟h	Guttural, like the Scotch *ch* in *loch*.
د	Dāl	D	Soft dental.
ذ	Ẕāl	Ẕ	A sound between *dh* and *z*.
ر	Rā	R	
ز	Zā	Z	As in English.
س	Sīn	S	
ش	Shīn	Sh	
ص	Ṣād	Ṣ	A strongly articulated *s*; in Central Asia as *sw*.
ض	Ẓād	Ẓ	Something like the foreign pronunciation of the *th* in *that*; in Central Asia and India *z* or *zw*.
ط	Ṭā	Ṭ	A strongly articulated palatal *t*.
ظ	Z̤ā	Z̤	A strongly articulated *z*.
ع	‘Ain	‘	A guttural, the pronunciation of which must be learnt by ear.
غ	G͟hain	G͟h	A strong guttural *g͟h*.
ف	Fā	F	As in English.
ق	Qāf	Q	Like *ck* in *stuck*.
ك	Kāf	K	
ل	Lām	L	
م	Mīm	M	
ن	Nūn	N	As in English.
ه	Hā	H	
و	Wau	W	
ى	Yā	Y	
ـَ	Fatḥah	a	
ـِ	Kasrah	i	As in Italian.
ـُ	Ẓammah	u	
ء	Hamzah	’	Pronounced as *a*, *i*, *u*, preceded by a very slight aspiration.

DICTIONARY OF ISLĀM.

A.

AARON. Arabic *Hārūn* (هارون). The account given of Aaron in the Qur'ān will be found in the article on Moses. In Sūrah xix. 29, the Virgin Mary is addressed as "the Sister of Aaron." [MARY, MOSES.]

ABAD (ابد). Eternity; without end, as distinguished from Azal (ازل), without beginning.

'ABASA (عبس). "He frowned." The title of the LXXXth chapter of the Qur'ān. It is said that a blind man, named 'Abdu 'llāh ibn Umm Maktūm, once interrupted Muḥammad in conversation with certain chiefs of Quraish. The Prophet, however, took no notice of him, but frowned and turned away; and in the first verse of this Sūrah, he is represented as reproved by God for having done so:—"He frowned and turned his back, for that the blind man came unto him."

'ABBĀS (عباس). The son of 'Abdu 'l-Muṭṭalib, and consequently the paternal uncle of Muḥammad. The most celebrated of the "Companions," and the founder of the Abbaside dynasty, which held the Khalifate for a period of 509 years, namely, from A.D. 749 to A.D. 1258. He died in A.H. 32. His son Ibn-'Abbās was also a celebrated authority on Islamic traditions and law. [IBN 'ABBAS, ABBASIDES.]

ABBASIDES. Arabic *al-'Abbāsīyah* (العباسية). The name of a dynasty of Khalīfahs descended from al-'Abbās, the son of 'Abdu 'l-Muṭṭalib, and a paternal uncle of Muḥammad. On account of their descent from so near a relation of the Prophet, the Abbasides had, ever since the introduction of Islām, been very high in esteem amongst the Arabs, and had at an early period begun to excite the jealousy of the Umaiyade Khalīfahs, who after the defeat of 'Alī occupied the throne of the Arabian Empire. The Abbasides had for some time asserted their claims to the Khalifate, and in A.D. 746 they commenced open hostilities. In 749 the Abbaside Khalīifah Abū 'l-'Abbās, surnamed as-Saffāḥ, "the blood-shedder," was recognied as Khalīfah at al-Kūfah, and Marwān II., the last of the Umaiyade Khalīfahs, was defeated and slain.

Thirty-seven Khalīfahs of the Abbaside dynasty reigned over the Muḥammadan empire, extending over the period from A.H. 132 (A.D. 749–50) to A.H. 656 (A.D. 1258).

The names of the Abbaside Khalīfahs are:—Abū 'l-'Abbās as-Saffāḥ (A.D. 749), al-Manṣūr (A.D. 754), al-Mahdī (A.D. 775), al-Hādī (A.D. 785), Hārūn ar-Rashīd (A.D. 786), al-Amīn (A.D. 809), al-Ma'mūn (A.D. 813), al-Mu'taṣim (A.D. 833), al-Wāṣiq (A.D. 842), al-Mutawakkil (A.D. 847), al-Muntaṣir (A.D. 861), al-Musta'īn (A.D. 862), al-Mu'tazz (A.D. 866), al-Muhtadī (A.D. 869), al-Mu'tamid (A.D. 870), al-Mu'taẓid (A.D. 892)) al-Muktafī (A.D. 902), al-Muqtadir (A.D. 908), al-Qāhir (A.D. 932), ar-Rāẓī (A.D. 934), al-Muttaqī (A.D 940), al-Mustaqfī (A.D. 944), al-Muṭī' (A.D. 945), aṭ-Ṭāi' (A.D. 974), al-Qādir (A.D. 994), al-Qāim (A.D. 1031), al-Muqtadī (A.D. 1075), al-Mustaẓhir (A.D. 1094), al-Mustarshid (A.D. 1118), ar-Rāshid (A.D. 1135), al-Muqtafī (A.D. 1136), al-Mustanjid (A.D. 1160), al-Mustaẓī (A.D. 1170), an-Nāṣir (A.D. 1180), aẓ-Ẓāhir (A.D. 1225), al-Mustanṣir (A.D. 1226), al-Musta'ṣim (A.D. 1242 to A.D. 1258).

In the reign of al-Musta'ṣim Hūlākū, grandson of Jingīz Khān, entered Persia and became Sultan A.D. 1256. In 1258 he took Baghdād and put the Khalīfah al-Musta'ṣim to death. [KHALIFAH.]

ABDĀL (ابدال). "Substitutes," pl. of *Badal*. Certain persons by whom, it is said, God continues the world in existence. Their number is seventy, of whom forty reside in Syria, and thirty elsewhere. When one dies another takes his place, being so appointed by God. It is one of the signs of the last day that the *Abdāl* will come from Syria. (*Mishkāt*, xxiii. c. 3.) No one pretends to be able to identify these eminent persons in the world. God alone knows who they are, and where they are.

'ABDU 'LLĀH (عبدالله). The father of Muḥammad. He was the youngest son of 'Abdu 'l-Muṭṭalib. During the pregnancy of his wife Āminah, he set out on a mercantile expedition to Gaza in the south of Palestine, and on his way back he sickened and died at al-Madīnah, before the birth of his son Muḥammad. (*Kātibu 'l-Wāqidī*, p. 18; Muir's *Life of Mahomet*, vol. i. p. 11.)

'ABDU 'LLĀH IBN SA'D (عبدالله بن سعد). One of Muḥammad's secretaries. It is related that, when Muḥammad instructed 'Abdu 'llāh to write down the words (Sūrah xxiii. 12–14), "We (God) have created man from an extract of clay . . . then we produced it another creation," 'Abdu 'llāh exclaimed, "And blessed be God, the best of creators"; and Muḥammad told him to write that down also. Whereupon 'Abdu 'llāh boasted that he had been inspired with a sentence which the Prophet had acknowledged to be part of the Qur'ān. It is of him that it is written in the Qur'ān, Sūrah vi. 93, "Who is more unjust than he who devises against God a lie, or says, 'I am inspired,' when he is not inspired at all."

'ABDU 'L-MUṮṮALIB (عبدالمطلب). Muḥammad's grandfather and his guardian for two years. He died, aged 82, A.D. 578. His sons were 'Abdu 'llāh (Muḥammad's father), al-Hāris, az-Zuhair, Abū Ṭālib, Abū Lahab, al-'Abbās, and Hamza.

'ABDU 'L-QĀDIR AL-JĪLĀNĪ (عبدالقادر الجيلانى). The celebrated founder of the Qādiriyah order of darweshes, surnamed Pīr-Dastagīr. He died and was buried at Baghdād, A.H. 561.

'ABDU 'R-RAḤMĀN IBN 'AUF (عبدالرحمن بن عوف). One of the Companions who embraced Islām at a very early period, and was one of those who fled to Ethiopia. He also accompanied Muḥammad in all his battles, and received twenty wounds at Uhud. He died A.H. 32, aged 72 or 75, and was buried at Baqī'u 'l-Gharqad, the graveyard of al-Madīnah.

ABEL. Arabic *Hābīl* (هابيل), Heb. הֶבֶל *Hebel.* In the Qur'ān "the two sons of Adam" are called *Hābīl wa Qābīl*, and the following is the account given of them in that book (Sūrah v. 30–35), together with the remarks of the commentators in *italics* (as rendered in Mr. Lane's *Selections*, 2nd ed., p. 53), "Recite unto them the history of the two sons of Adam, *namely, Abel and Cain*, with truth. When they offered [their] offering *to God* (*Abel's being a ram, and Cain's being produce of the earth*), and it was accepted from one of them (*that is, from Abel; for fire descended from heaven, and devoured his offering*), and it was not accepted from the other, *Cain was enraged; but he concealed his envy until Adam performed a pilgrimage, when* he said *unto his brother*, I will assuredly slay thee. *Abel said, Wherefore? Cain answered, Because of the acceptance of thine offering to the exclusion of mine. Abel* replied, God only accepteth from the pious. If thou stretch forth to me thy hand to slay me, I will not stretch forth to thee my hand to slay thee; for I fear God, the Lord of the worlds. I desire that thou shouldst bear the sin [which thou intendest to commit] against me, *by slaying me*, and thy sin *which thou hast committed before*, and thou wilt be of the companions of the fire.—And that is the recompense of the offenders.—But his soul suffered him to slay his brother: so he slew him; and he became of [the number of] those who suffer loss. *And he knew not what to do with him; for he was the first dead person upon the face of the earth of the sons of Adam. So he carried him upon his back.* And God sent a raven, which scratched up the earth *with its bill and its talons and raised it over a dead raven that was with it until it hid it*, to show him how he should hide the corpse of his brother. He said, O my disgrace! Am I unable to be like this raven, and to hide the corpse of my brother?—And he became of [the number of] the repentant. *And he digged* [a grave] *for him and hid him.*—On account of this *which Cain did* We commanded the children of Israel that he who should slay a soul (not for *the latter's having slain* a soul or *committed* wickedness in the earth, *such as infidelity, or adultery, or intercepting the way, and the like*) [should be regarded] as though he had slain all mankind; and he who saveth it alive, *by abstaining from slaying it*, as though he had saved alive all mankind."

"The occasion of their making this offering is thus related, according to the common tradition in the East. Each of them being born with a twin-sister, when they were grown up, Adam, by God's direction, ordered Cain to marry Abel's twin-sister, and Abel to marry Cain's; (for it being the common opinion that marriages ought not to be had in the nearest degrees of consanguinity, since they must necessarily marry their sisters, it seemed reasonable to suppose they ought to take those of the remoter degree;) but this Cain refusing to agree to, because his own sister was the handsomest, Adam ordered them to make their offerings to God, thereby referring the dispute to His determination. The commentators say Cain's offering was a sheaf of the very worst of his corn, but Abel's a fat lamb of the best of his flock."—Sale's *Koran*, I., p. 122.

'ĀBID (عابد). "A worshipper [of God]." A term generally used for a devout person. The word frequently occurs in the Qur'ān; *e.g.* Sūrah ii. 132: "The baptism (*sibghah*) of God! And who is better than God at baptizing? We are the worshippers (*'ābidūn*) of God." The word *sibghah* is translated by Professor Palmer "dye" and "dyeing," but Sale, following the Muslim commentators, al-Baiẓāwī, Jalālu 'd-dīn, and Ḥusainī, who say it refers to the Christian rite, translates it "baptism." Others say that it means *fiṭrah* or *dīn*, the religion of God, with an adaptation to which mankind are created. See Lane's *Lexicon*. [BAPTISM.]

ĀBIQ (آبق). A runaway slave. [ABSCONDING OF SLAVES.]

ABJAD (ابجد). The name of an arithmetical arrangement of the alphabet, the letters of which have different powers from one to one thousand. It is in the order of the alphabet as used by the Jews as far as 400, the six remaining letters being added by the Arabians. The letters spell the words—

abjad hawwaz ḥuṭṭi kalaman
sa'faṣ qarashat s̤akhaẕ ẓaẓigh

The author of the Arabic Lexicon, *al-Qāmūs*, says that the first six words are the names of celebrated kings of Madyan (Midian), and that the last two words were added by the Arabians. Some say they are the names of the eight sons of the inventor of the Arabic character, Murāmir ibn Murra.

The following is a list of the letters with their English equivalents, and the power of each in numbers:—

1	*a* (*i*, *u*)	ا	60	*s*	س
2	*b*	ب	70	'	ع
3	*j*	ج	80	*f*	ف
4	*d*	د	90	*ṣ*	ص
5	*h*	ه	100	*q*	ق
6	*w*	و	200	*r*	ر
7	*z*	ز	300	*sh*	ش
8	*ḥ*	ح	400	*t*	ت
9	*ṭ*	ط	500	*s̤*	ث
10	*y*	ى	600	*kh*	خ
20	*k*	ك	700	*ẕ*	ذ
30	*l*	ل	800	*ẓ*	ض
40	*m*	م	900	*z̤*	ظ
50	*n*	ن	1000	*gh*	غ

[EXORCISM.]

ABLUTION. Arabic, *waẓū'*, *wuẓū'* (وضوء), Persian, *ābdast* (آبدست). Ablution is described by Muḥammad as "the half of faith and the key of prayer" (*Mishkāt*, iii. 3c), and is founded on the authority of the Qur'ān, sūrah v. 8, "O Believers! when ye prepare yourselves for prayer, wash your faces and hands up to the elbows, and wipe your heads and your feet to the ankles."

These ablutions are absolutely necessary as a preparation for the recital of the liturgical form of prayer, and are performed as follows: The worshipper, having tucked up his sleeves a little higher than his elbows, washes his hands three times; then he rinses his mouth three times, throwing the water into it with his right hand. After this, he, with his right hand, throws water up his nostrils, snuffing it up at the same time, and then blows it out, compressing his nostrils with the thumb and finger of the left hand—this being also performed three times. He then washes his face three times, throwing up the water with both hands. He next washes his right hand and arm, as high as the elbow, as many times, causing the water to run along his arm from the palm of the hand to the elbow, and in the same manner he washes the left. Then he draws his wetted right hand over the upper part of his head, raising his turban or cap with his left. If he has a beard, he then combs it with the wetted fingers of his right hand, holding his hand with the palm forwards, and passing the fingers through his beard from the throat upwards. He then puts the tips of his fore-fingers into his ears and twists them round, passing his thumbs at the same time round the back of the ears from the bottom upwards. Next, he wipes his neck with the back of the fingers of both hands, making the ends of his fingers meet behind his neck, and then drawing them forward. Lastly, he washes his feet, as high as the ankles, and passes his fingers between the toes. During this ceremony, which is generally performed in less than three minutes, the intending worshipper usually recites some pious ejaculations or prayers. For example:—

Before commencing the *waẓū'*:—"I am going to purify myself from all bodily uncleanness, preparatory to commencing prayer, that holy act of duty, which will draw my soul near to the throne of the Most High. In the name of God, the Great and Mighty. Praise be to God who has given us grace to be Muslims. Islām is a truth and infidelity a falsehood."

When washing the nostrils:—"O my God, if I am pleasing in Thy sight, perfume me with the odours of Paradise."

When washing the right hand:—"O my God, on the day of judgment, place the book of my actions in my right hand, and examine my account with favour."

When washing the left hand:—"O my God, place not at the resurrection the book of my actions in my left hand."

The Shiya'is, acting more in accordance with the text of the Qur'ān quoted above, only wipe, or rub (*masaḥ*) the feet, instead of washing them, as do the Sunnīs.

The ablution need not be performed before each of the five stated periods of prayer, when the person is conscious of having avoided every kind of impurity since the last performance of the ablution. The private parts of the body must also be purified when necessary. When water cannot be procured, or would be injurious to health, the ablution may be performed with dust or sand. This ceremony is called *Tayammum* (*q.v.*). The washing of the whole body is necessary after certain periods of impurity. [GHUSL.] The brushing of the teeth is also a religious duty. [MISWAK.] The benefits of ablution are highly extolled in the sayings of Muḥammad, *e.g.*, "He who performs the *waẓū'* thoroughly will extract all sin from his body, even though it may be lurking under his finger nails." "In the day of resurrection people shall come with bright faces, hands and feet, and there will be jewels in every place where the waters of the *wazū'* have reached." (*Mishkāt*, iii. 1.)

VESSELS FOR ABLUTIONS USED IN AFGHANISTAN AND INDIA

VESSELS FOR ABLUTIONS USED IN EGYPT. (LANE'S "EGYPTIANS.")

In all the principal mosques there are tanks, or wells, which supply water for the purposes of legal purification. [PURIFICATION.]

ABORTION. Arabic *Isqāṭ*. There is no mention of the subject in the Qur'ān, but according to the *Fatāwī 'Alamgīrī* (vol. iv. p. 238), it is forbidden after the child is formed in the womb. Muḥammad is related to have ordered prayers to be said over an abortion, when supplication should be made for the father and mother, for forgiveness and mercy. (*Mishkāt*, v. c. 2.)

ABRAHAM. Arabic *Ibrāhīm* (ابراهيم). One of the six great prophets to whom God delivered special laws. The "Friend of God," Khalīlu 'llāh, to whom were revealed twenty portions (*ṣaḥīfah*) of Scripture.

Abraham is very frequently mentioned in the Qur'ān, together with Ishmael and Isaac. The following are Mr. Lane's selections (giving in *italics* the remarks of Muslim commentators):—

"*Remember* when Abraham said to his father Āzar (*this was the surname of Terah*), Dost thou take images as deities? Verily I see thee and thy people to be in a manifest error.—(And thus, *as We showed him the error of his father and his people*, did We show Abraham the kingdom of the heavens and the earth, and [We did so] that he might be of [the number of] those who firmly believe.) And when the night overshadowed him, he saw a star (*it is said that it was Venus*), [and] he said *unto his people, who were astrologers*, This is my Lord, *according to your assertion*.—But when it set, he said, I like not those that set, *to take them as Lords, since it is not meet for a Lord to experience alteration and change of place, as they are of the nature of accidents. Yet this had no effect upon them.* And when he saw the moon rising, he said *unto them*, This is my Lord.—But when it set, he said, Verily if my Lord direct me not (*if He confirm me not in the right way*), I shall assuredly be of the erring people.—*This was a hint to his people that they were in error; but it had no effect upon them.* And when he saw the sun rising, he said, This is my Lord. This is greater *than the star and the moon*.—But when it set, *and the proof had been rendered more strong to them, yet they desisted not*, he said, O my people, verily I am clear of the [things] which ye associate *with God; namely, the images and the heavenly bodies. So they said unto him, What dost thou worship? He answered*, Verily I direct my face unto Him who hath created the heavens and the earth, following the right religion, and I am not of the polytheists.—And his people argued with him; [but] he said, Do ye argue with me respecting God, when He hath directed me, and I fear not what ye associate with Him unless my Lord will *that* aught *displeasing should befall me?* My Lord comprehendeth everything by *His* knowledge. Will ye not therefore consider? And wherefore should I fear what ye have associated *with God*, when ye fear not for your having associated with God that of which He hath not sent down unto you a proof? Then which of the two parties is the more worthy of safety? *Are we, or you?* If ye know *who is the more worthy of it, follow him.—God saith*, They who have believed, and not mixed their belief with injustice (*that is, polytheism*), for these shall be safety *from punishment*, and they are rightly directed." (Sūrah vi. 74–82.)

"Relate *unto them*, in the book (*that is, the Qur'ān*), *the history of* Abraham. Verily, he was a person of great veracity, a prophet. When he said unto his father *Āzar, who worshipped idols*, O my father, wherefore dost thou worship that which heareth not, nor seeth, nor averteth from thee aught, *whether of advantage or of injury?* O my father, verily [a degree] of knowledge hath come unto me, that hath not come unto thee: therefore follow me: I will direct thee into a right way. O my father, serve not the devil, *by obeying him in serving idols;* for the devil is very rebellious unto the Compassionate. O my father, verily I fear that a punishment will betide thee from the Compassionate, *if thou repent not,* and that thou wilt be unto the devil an aider, *and a companion in hell-fire.*—He replied, Art thou a rejector of my Gods, O Abraham, *and dost thou revile them?* If thou abstain not, I will assuredly assail thee *with stones or with ill words; therefore beware of me,* and leave me for a long time.—*Abraham* said, Peace *from me* be on thee! I will ask pardon for thee of my Lord; for He is gracious unto me: and I will separate myself from you and from what ye invoke instead of God; and I will call upon my Lord: perhaps I shall not be unsuccessful in calling upon my Lord, *as ye are in calling upon idols.*—And when he had separated himself from them, and from what they worshipped instead of God, *by going to the Holy Land,* We gave him *two sons, that he might cheer himself thereby, namely,* Isaac and Jacob; and each [of them] We made a prophet; and We bestowed upon them (*namely, the three*), of our mercy, *wealth and children;* and We caused them to receive high commendation." (Sūrah xix. 42–51.)

"We gave unto Abraham his direction formerly, *before he had attained to manhood;* and We knew him *to be worthy of it.* When he said unto his father and his people, What are these images, to *the worship of* which ye are devoted?—they answered, We found our fathers worshipping them, *and we have followed their example.* He said *unto them,* Verily ye and your fathers have been in a manifest error. They said, Hast thou come unto us with truth *in saying this,* or art thou of those who jest? He answered, Nay, your Lord (*the being who deserveth to be worshipped*) is the Lord of the heavens and the earth, who created them, *not after the similitude of anything pre-existing;* and I am of those who bear witness thereof. And, by God, I will assuredly devise a plot against your idols after ye shall have retired, turning your backs.—So, *after they had gone to their place of assembly, on a day when they held a festival,* he break them in pieces *with an axe,* except the chief of them, *upon whose neck he hung the axe;* that they might return unto it (*namely, the chief*) *and see what he had done with the others.* They said, *after they had returned and seen what he had done,* Who hath done this unto our gods? Verily he is of the unjust.—*And some of them* said, We heard a young man mention them *reproachfully:* he is called Abraham. They said, Then bring him before the eyes of the people, that they may bear witness *against him of his having done it.* They said *unto him, when he had been brought,* Hast thou done this unto our gods, O Abraham? He answered, Nay, this their chief did it: and ask ye them, if they [can] speak. And they returned unto themselves, *upon reflection,* and said *unto themselves,* Verily ye are the unjust, *in worshipping that which speaketh not.* Then they reverted to their obstinacy, *and said,* Verily thou knowest that these speak not: *then wherefore dost thou order us to ask them?* He said, Do ye then worship, instead of God, that which doth not profit you at all, nor injure you *if ye worship it not?* Fie on you, and on that which ye worship instead of God! Do ye not then understand?—They said, Burn ye him, and avenge your gods, if ye will do *so. So they collected abundance of firewood for him, and set fire to it; and they bound Abraham, and put him into an engine, and cast him into the fire. But, saith God,* We said, O fire, be thou cold, and a security unto Abraham! *So nought of him was burned save his bonds: the heat of the fire ceased, but its light remained; and by God's saying, Security,—Abraham was saved from dying by reason of its cold.* And they intended against him a plot; but he caused them to be the sufferers. And we delivered him and Lot, *the son of his brother Haran, from El-'Erāq,* [bringing them] unto the land which We blessed for the peoples, *by the abundance of its rivers and trees, namely, Syria. Abraham took up his abode in Palestine, and Lot in El-Mutefikeh, between which is a day's journey.* And *when Abraham had asked a son,* We gave unto him Isaac, and Jacob as an additional gift, *beyond what he had asked, being a son's son;* and all of them We made righteous persons *and prophets.* And We made them models of religion who directed *men* by Our command *unto Our religion;* and We commanded them by inspiration to do good works and to perform prayer and to give the appointed alms; and they served Us. And unto Lot We gave judgment and knowledge; and We delivered him from the city which committed filthy actions; for they were a people of evil, shameful doers; and We admitted him into our mercy; for he was [one] of the righteous." (Sūrah xxi. 52–75.)

"Hast thou not considered him who disputed with Abraham concerning his Lord, because God had given him the kingdom? *And he was Nimrod.* When Abraham said, (*upon his saying unto him, Who is thy Lord, unto whom thou invitest us?*), My Lord is He who giveth life and causeth to die,—he replied, I give life and cause to die.—*And he summoned two men, and slew one of them, and left the other. So when he saw that he understood not,* Abraham said, And verily God bringeth the sun from the east: now do thou bring it from the west.—And he who disbelieved was confounded; and God directeth not the offending people." (Sūrah ii. 260.)

"And Our messengers came formerly unto Abraham with good tidings *of Isaac and Jacob, who should be after him.* They said, Peace. He replied, Peace *be on you.* And he tarried not, but brought a roasted calf. And when he saw that their hands touched it not, he disliked them and conceived a fear of them. They said, Fear not: for we are sent unto the people of Lot, *that we may destroy them.* And his wife *Sarah* was standing *serving them,* and she laughed, *rejoicing at the tidings of their destruction.* And we gave her good tidings of Isaac; and after Isaac, Jacob.

She said, Alas! shall I bear a child when I am an old woman *of nine and ninety years*, and when this my husband is an old man *of a hundred or a hundred and twenty years?* Verily this [would be] a wonderful thing.—They said, Dost thou wonder at the command of God? The mercy of God and His blessings be on you, O people of the house (*of Abraham*)! for He is praiseworthy, glorious.—And when the terror had departed from Abraham, and the good tidings had come unto him, he disputed with Us (*that is, with Our messengers*) respecting the people of Lot; for Abraham was gentle, compassionate, repentant. *And he said unto them, Will ye destroy a city wherein are three hundred believers? They answered, No. He said, And will ye destroy a city wherein are two hundred believers? They answered, No. He said, And will ye destroy a city wherein are forty believers? They answered, No. He said, And will ye destroy a city wherein are fourteen believers? They answered, No. He said, And tell me, if there be in it one believer? They answered, No. He said, Verily in it is Lot. They replied, We know best who is in it. And when their dispute had become tedious, they said,* O Abraham, abstain from this *disputation;* for the command of thy Lord hath come *for their destruction*, and a punishment not [to be] averted is coming upon them." (Sūrah xi. 72–78.)

"And when Our decree *for the destruction of the people of Lot* came [to be executed], We turned them (*that is, their cities*) upside-down; *for Gabriel raised them to heaven, and let them fall upside-down to the earth;* and We rained upon them stones of baked clay, sent one after another, marked with thy Lord, *each with the name of him upon whom it should be cast:* and they [are] not far distant from the offenders; *that is, the stones are not, or the cities of the people of Lot were not, far distant from the people of Mekkeh.*" (Sūrah xi. 84.)

"And [Abraham] said [after his escape from Nimrod], Verily I am going unto my Lord, who will direct me *unto the place whither He hath commanded me to go, namely, Syria. And when he had arrived at the Holy Land, he said,* O my Lord, give me *a son* [who shall be one] of the righteous. Whereupon We gave him the glad tidings of a mild youth. And when he had attained to the age when he could work with him (*as some say, seven years; and some, thirteen*), he said, O my child, verily I have seen in a dream that I should sacrifice thee (*and the dreams of prophets are true; and their actions, by the command of God*); therefore consider what thou seest advisable *for me to do.* He replied, O my father, do what thou art commanded: thou shalt find me, if God please, [of the number] of the patient. And when they had resigned themselves, and he had laid him down on his temple, *in* [the valley of] *Minā, and had drawn the knife across his throat* (*but it produced no effect, by reason of an obstacle interposed by the divine power*), We called unto him, O Abraham, thou hast verified the vision. Verily thus do We reward the well-doers. Verily this was the manifest trial. And We ransomed him *whom he had been commanded to sacrifice (and he was Ishmael or Isaac; for there are two opinions)* with an excellent victim, *a ram from Paradise, the same that Abel had offered: Gabriel (on whom be peace!) brought it, and the lord Abraham sacrificed it, saying, God is most great!* And We left *this salutation* [to be bestowed] on him by the latter generations, Peace [be] on Abraham! Thus do We reward the well-doers: for he was of Our believing servants." (Sūrah xxxvii. 97–111.)

"*Remember* when Abraham said, O my Lord, show me how Thou will raise to life the dead.—He said, Hast thou not believed? He answered, Yea: but *I have asked Thee* that my heart may be at ease. He replied, Then take four birds and draw them towards thee, *and cut them in pieces and mingle together their flesh and their feathers;* then place upon each mountain *of thy land* a portion of them, then call them *unto thee:* they shall come unto thee quickly; and know thou that God is mighty [and] wise.—*And he took a peacock and a vulture and a raven and a cock, and did with them as hath been described, and kept their heads with him, and called them; whereupon the portions flew about, one to another, until they became complete: then they came to their heads.*" (Sūrah ii. 262.)

"*Remember*, when his Lord had tried Abraham by [certain] words, *commands and prohibitions*, and he fulfilled them, *God* said *unto him*, I constitute thee a model of religion unto men. He replied, And of my offspring *constitute models of religion.* [God] said, My covenant doth not apply to the offenders, *the unbelievers among them.*—And when We appointed the house (*that is, the Kaʿbah*) to be a place for the resort of men, and a place of security (*a man would meet the slayer of his father there and he would not provoke him* [to revenge],) and [said], Take, *O men*, the station of Abraham (*the stone upon which he stood at the time of building the House*) as a place of prayer, *that ye may perform behind it the prayers of the two rakʿahs* [which are ordained to be performed after the ceremony] *of the circuiting* [of the Kaʿbah].—And We commanded Abraham and Ishmael, [saying], Purify my House (*rid it of the idols*) for those who shall compass [it], and those who shall abide *there*, and those who shall bow down and prostrate themselves.—And when Abraham said, O my Lord, make this *place* a secure territory (*and God hath answered his prayer, and made it a sacred place, wherein the blood of man is not shed, nor is any one oppressed in it, nor is its game hunted* [or shot], *nor are its plants cut or pulled up*), and supply its inhabitants with fruits (*which hath been done by the transporting of aṭ-Ṭāʾif from Syria thither, when it* [that is, the territory of Makkah] *was desert, without sown land or water*, such of them as shall believe in God and the last day.—*He mentioned them peculiarly in the prayer agreeably with the saying of God, My covenant doth not apply to the offenders.—God* replied, And *I will supply* him who disbelieveth: I will make him to enjoy *a supply of food in this world*, a little *while*: then I will force him, *in the world to come*, to the punishment of the fire; and evil shall be the transit." (Sūrah ii. 118–120.)

"And *remember* when Abraham was raising the foundations of the House (*that is, building it*), together with Ishmael, *and they said*, O our Lord, accept of us *our building*; for Thou art the Hearer *of what is said*, the Knower *of what is done*. O our Lord, also make us resigned unto Thee, and *make* from among our offspring a people resigned unto Thee, and show us our rites (*the ordinances of our worship, or our pilgrimage*), and be propitious towards us; for Thou art the Very Propitious, the Merciful. (*They begged Him to be propitious to them, notwithstanding their honesty, from a motive of humility, and by way of instruction to their offspring.*) O our Lord, also send unto them (*that is, the people of the House*) an apostle from among them (*and God hath answered their prayer by sending Muḥammad*), who shall recite unto them Thy signs (*the Qur'ān*), and shall teach them the book (*the Qur'ān*), and the knowlege *that it containeth*, and shall purify them *from polytheism*; for Thou art the Mighty, the Wise.—And who will be averse from the religion of Abraham but he who maketh his soul foolish, *who is ignorant that it is God's creation, and that the worship of Him is incumbent on it; or who lightly esteemeth it and applieth it to vile purposes*; when We have chosen him in this world *as an apostle and a friend*, and he shall be in the world to come one of the righteous *for whom are high ranks?—And remember* when his Lord said unto him, Resign thyself:—he replied, I resign myself unto the Lord of the worlds.—And Abraham commanded his children to follow it (*namely, the religion*); and Jacob, *his children; saying*, O my children, verily God hath chosen for you the religion *of al-Islām*; therefore die not without your being Muslims.—*It was a prohibition from abandoning Islām and a command to persevere therein unto death.*" (Sūrah ii. 121–126.)

"*When the Jews said, Abraham was a Jew, and we are of his religion,—and the Christians said the like,* [the following] *was revealed*:— O people of the Scripture, wherefore do ye argue respecting Abraham, *asserting that he was of your religion*, when the Pentateuch and the Gospel were not sent down but after him *a long time?* Do ye not then understand *the falsity of your saying?* So ye, O people, have argued respecting that of which ye have knowledge, *concerning Moses and Jesus, and have asserted that ye are of their religion*: then wherefore do ye argue respecting that of which ye have no knowledge, *concerning Abraham?* But God knoweth *his case*, and ye know *it* not. Abraham was not a Jew nor a Christian: but he was orthodox, a Muslim [or one resigned], a Unitarian, and he was not of the polytheists." (Sūrah iii. 58–60.)

ABSCONDING OF SLAVES.

Arabic *Ibāq* (ابَاق). An absconded male or female slave is called *Ābiq*, but an infant slave who leaves his home is termed *ẓāll*, a word which is also used for an adult slave who has strayed. The apprehension of a fugitive slave is a laudable act, and the person who seizes him should bring him before the magistrate and receive a reward of forty dirhams. (Hamilton's *Hidāyah*, vol. ii. p. 278.)

ABSTINENCE.

Arabic *Taqwā* (تقوى). Is very frequently enjoined in the Qur'ān. The word generally applies to abstinence from idolatry in the first instance, but it is used to express a life of piety. An excessive abstinence and a life of asceticism are condemned in the Qur'ān, and the Christians are charged with the invention of the monastic life. (Sūrah lvii. 27.) "*As for the monastic life, they invented it themselves.*" [MONASTICISM, FASTING.]

ABŪ 'ABDI 'LLĀH (ابو عبدالله).

Muḥammad ibn Ismā'īl al-Bukhārī, the author of the well-known collection of traditions received by the Sunnīs. [BUKHARI.]

ABŪ 'ABDI 'LLĀH AḤMAD IBN ḤANBAL (ابو عبدالله احمد بن حنبل).

[HANBAL.]

ABŪ 'ABDI 'LLĀH IBN ANAS (ابوعبدالله مالك بن انس).

[MALIK.]

ABŪ 'ABDI 'LLĀH MUḤAMMAD IBN AL-ḤASAN (ابو عبدالله محمد بن الحسن).

Known as Imām Muḥammad. Born at Wāsiṭ, a city in Arabian 'Irāq, A.H. 132. He studied under the great Imām Abū Ḥanīfah, and had also studied under Imām Mālik for three years. He is celebrated as one of the disciples of the Imām Abū Ḥanīfah, from whom he occasionally differs, as is seen in the *Hidāyah*. He died at Rai, in Khurāsān, where his tomb is still to be seen, A.H. 189.

ABŪ BAKR (ابو بكر).

Of the origin of his name, there are various explanations. Some think that it means "the father of the maiden," and that he received this title because he was the father of 'Āyishah, whom Muḥammad married when she was only nine years old. His original name was 'Abdu 'l-Ka'bah (which the Prophet changed into 'Abdu 'llāh) Ibn Abī Quḥāfah. He was the first Khalīfah, or successor of Muḥammad. [SHI'AH.] Muḥammadan writers praise him for the purity of his life, and call him *aṣ-Ṣiddīq*, the Veracious. He only reigned two years, and died August 22nd, A.D. 634.

ABŪ DĀ'ŪD (ابو داود).

Sulaimān Ibn al-Ash'aṣ al-Sijistānī; born at al-Baṣrah A.H. 202, and died A.H. 275. The compiler of one of the six correct books of Sunnī traditions, called the *Sunnan Abī Dā'ūd*, which contains 4,008 traditions, said to have been carefully collated from 500,000. [TRADITIONS.]

ABŪ ḤANĪFAH (ابو حنيفة النعمان).

Abū Ḥanīfah an-Nu'mān is the great Sunnī Imām and jurisconsult, and the founder of the Ḥanīfī sect. His father, Ṣābit, was a silk dealer in the city of al-Kūfah, and it is said his grandfather, Zūṭa, was a native of Kābul. He was born at al-Kūfah, A.H. 80 (A.D. 700), and died at Baghdād, A.H. 150. He is regarded as the great oracle of Sunnī jurisprudence, and his doctrines, with those of his disciples, the Imām Abū Yūsuf and the Imām Muḥammad, are generally received throughout Turkey, Tartary, and Hindustan. It is related that Imām Mālik said that the Imām Abū Ḥanīfah was such a logician that, if he were to assert a wooden pillar was made of gold, he would prove it by argument.

ABŪ HURAIRAH (ابو هريرة). One of the most constant attendants of Muḥammad, who from his peculiar intimacy has related more traditions of the sayings and doings of the Prophet than any other individual. His real name is doubtful, but he was nicknamed Abū Hurairah on account of his fondness for a kitten. He embraced Islām in the year of the expedition to Khaibar, A.H. 7, and died in al-Madīnah, A.H. 57 or 59, aged 78.

ABŪ JAHL (ابو جهل). An implacable adversary of Muḥammad. His real name was 'Amr ibn Hishām, but he was surnamed, by the Muslims, Abū Jahl, or the "Father of Folly." He is supposed to be alluded to in the Qur'ān, Sūrah xxii. 8:—"There is a man who disputeth concerning God without either knowledge or direction." He was a boastful and debauched man, and was killed in the battle of Badr.

ABŪ LAHAB (ابو لهب). One of the sons of Abū Muṭṭalib, and an uncle to Muḥammad. He was a most bitter enemy to the Prophet, and opposed the establishment of Islām to the utmost of his power. His name was 'Abdu 'l- Uzza, but he was surnamed by Muḥammad, Abū Lahab, "The Father of the Flame." When Muḥammad received the command to admonish his relations, he called them all together, and told them he was a warner sent unto them before a grievous chastisement. Abū Lahab rejected his mission, and cried out, "Mayest thou perish! Hast thou called us together for this?" and took up a stone to cast at him; whereupon the cxith Sūrah of the Qur'ān was produced:—

"Let the hands of Abū Lahab perish, and let himself perish!
His wealth and his gains shall avail him naught.
Burned shall he be at a fiery flame,
And his wife laden with fire wood,
On her neck a rope of palm fibre."

Abū Lahab is said to have died of grief and vexation at the defeat which his friends had received at the battle of Badr, surviving that misfortune only seven days. His body was left unburied for several days.

Zaid and Abū Lahab are the only relatives or friends of Muḥammad mentioned by name in the Qur'ān

ABŪ 'L-HUẔAIL ZUFAR IBN AL-HUẔAIL (ابو الهذيل زفر بن الهذيل). Celebrated as the Imām Zufar, and as a contemporary and intimate friend of the great Imām Abū Ḥanīfah. He died at al-Baṣrah, A.H. 158.

ABŪ 'L-QĀSIM (ابو القاسم). "The father of Qāsim." One of the names of Muḥammad, assumed on the birth of his son Qāsim, who died in infancy. [MUHAMMAD.]

ABUSIVE LANGUAGE is forbidden by the Muslim law, and the offender must be punished according to the discretion of the Qāẓi. Abū Ḥanīfah says: "If a person abuse a Musalmān by calling him *an ass* or *a hog*, punishment is not incurred, because these expressions are in no respect defamatory of the person to whom they are used, it being evident that he is neither an ass nor a hog. But some allege that in *our* times chastisement is inflicted, since, in the modern acceptation, calling a man an ass or a hog is held to be abuse. Others, again, allege that it is esteemed only to be abuse when the person of whom it is said occupies a dignified position." According to Abū Ḥanīfah, the greatest number of stripes that can be inflicted for abusive language is thirty-nine. (Hamilton's *Hidāyah*, vol. ii. 78.)

Muḥammad is related to have said, "Abusing a Muslim is disobedience to God, and it is infidelity for anyone to join such an one in religious warfare." (*Mishkāt*, xxii. 2.)

ABŪ ṬĀLIB (ابو طالب). Muḥammad's uncle and guardian; the father of 'Alī. He is believed to have died as he had lived, an unbeliever in the Prophet's mission; but for forty years he had been his faithful friend and guardian. He died in the third year before the Hijrah.

ABŪ 'UBAIDAH (ابو عبيدة) **IBN AL-JARRAḤ** One of the Companions, who was with the Prophet in all his wars, and distinguished himself at the battle of Uḥud. He was highly esteemed by Muḥammad, who made him one of the *'Asharah al-Mubashsharah*, or ten patriarchs of the Muslim faith. He died A.H. 18, aged 58.

ABŪ YŪSUF (ابو يوسف). Known also as Ya'qūb ibn Ibrāhīm Born at Baghdād, A.H. 113. Studied under the Imām Abū Ḥanīfah, and is celebrated, together with the Imām Muḥammad and the Imām Zufar, as disciples of the great Imām; from whose opinions, however, the three disciples not unfrequently differ, as will be seen upon reference to the *Hidāyah*. He died A.H. 182.

'ĀD (عاد). A tribe located to the south of Arabia, to which the prophet Hūd is said to have been sent. See Qur'ān, vii. 63:—

"And to 'Ād we sent our brother Hūd, 'O my people,' said he, 'worship God: ye have no other god than Him: Will ye not then fear Him?'

"Said the unbelieving chiefs among his

people, 'We certainly perceive that thou art unsound of mind; and we surely deem thee an impostor.'

"He said, 'O my people! it is not unsoundness of mind in me, but I am an Apostle from the Lord of the Worlds.

"'The messages of my Lord do I announce to you, and I am your faithful counsellor.

"'Marvel ye that a warning hath come to you from your Lord through one of yourselves that He may warn you? Remember how he hath made you the successors of the people of Noah, and increased you in tallness of stature. Remember then the favours of God, that it may haply be well with you.'

"They said, 'Art thou come to us in order that we may worship one God alone, and leave what our fathers worshipped? Then bring that upon us with which thou threatenest us, if thou be a man of truth.'

"He said, 'Vengeance and wrath shall suddenly light on you from your Lord. Do ye dispute with me about names that you and your fathers have given your idols, and for which God hath sent you down no warranty? Wait ye then, and I too will wait with you.'

"And we delivered him, and those who were on his side, by our mercy, and we cut off, to the last man, those who had treated our signs as lies, and who were not believers."

Also, Sūrah lxxxix. 5: "Hast thou not seen how thy Lord dealt with 'Ād at Iram, adorned with pillars, whose like have not been reared in these lands." [HUD, IRAM.]

ADĀ' (اداء). Payment; satisfaction; completing (prayers, &c.).

ADAM. Arabic, *Ādam* (آدم). The first man. Reckoned by Muslim writers as the first prophet, to whom ten portions of scripture (*ṣahīfah*) are said to have been revealed. He is distinguished by the title of Ṣafīyu 'llāh, or, the "chosen one of God." He is mentioned in the Qur'ān in the following Sūrahs, which are taken from Mr. Lane's *Selections* (new edition, by Mr. Stanley Lane-Poole; Trübner, 1879), with the commentary in *italics*:—

"*Remember, O Muḥammad*, when thy Lord said unto the angels, I am about to place in the earth a vicegerent *to act for me in the execution of my ordinances therein, namely, Adam*,—they said, Wilt Thou place in it one who will corrupt in it *by disobediences*, and will shed blood (*as did the sons of El-Jānn, who were in it; where ore, when they acted corruptly, God sent to them the angels, who drove them away to the islands and the mountains*), when we [on the contrary] celebrate the divine perfection, *occupying ourselves* with Thy praise, and extol Thy holiness? *Therefore we are more worthy of the vicegerency.—God* replied, Verily I know that which ye know not, *as to the affair of appointing Adam vicegerent, and that among his posterity will be the obedient and the rebellious, and the just will be manifest among them. And he created Adam from the surface of the earth, taking a handful of every colour that it comprised, which was kneaded with various waters; and he completely formed it, and breathed into it the soul; so it became an animated sentient being.* And he taught Adam the names of all things, *infusing the knowledge of them into his heart.* Then He showed them (*namely, the things*) to the angels, and said, Declare unto me the names of these *things*, if ye say truth *in your assertion that I will not create any more knowing than ye, and that ye are more worthy of the vicegerency.* They replied, [*We extol*] Thy perfection! We have no knowledge excepting what Thou hast taught us; for Thou art the Knowing, the Wise.—*God* said, O Adam, tell them their names. And when he had told them their names, *God* said, Did I not say unto you that I know the secrets of the heavens and the earth, and know what ye reveal *of your words, saying, Wilt thou place in it*, etc., and what ye did conceal *of your words, saying, He will not create any more generous towards Him than we, nor any more knowing?*" (Sūrah ii. 28–31.)

"We created you; *that is, your father Adam:* then We formed you; *we formed him, and you in him:* then We said unto the angels, Prostrate yourselves unto Adam, *by way of salutation;* whereupon they prostrated themselves, except Iblees, *the father of the jinn, who was amid the angels:* he was not of those who prostrated themselves. *God* said, What hath hindered thee from prostrating thyself, when I commanded thee? He answered, I am better than he: Thou hast created me of fire, and Thou hast created him of earth. [God] said, Then descend thou from it; *that is, from Paradise; or, as some say, from the heavens;* for it is not fit for thee that thou behave thyself proudly therein: so go thou forth: verily thou shalt be of the contemptible. He replied, Grant me respite until the day when they (*that is, mankind*) shall be raised from the dead. He said, Thou shalt be of those [who are] respited: *and, in another verse* [in xv. 38, it is said], *until the day of the known period; that is, until the period of the first blast* [of the trumpet]. [And the devil] said, Now, as Thou hast led me into error, I will surely lay wait for them (*that is, for the sons of Adam*) in Thy right way, *the way that leadeth to Thee:* then I will surely come upon them, from before them, and from behind them, and from their right hands, and from their left, *and hinder them from pursuing the way* (*but, saith Ibn 'Abbās, he cannot come upon them above, lest he should intervene between the servant and God's mercy*), and Thou shalt not find the great number of them grateful, *or believing.* [God] said, Go forth from it, despised and driven away *from mercy.* Whosoever of them (*that is, of mankind*) shall follow thee, I will surely fill hell with you all; *with thee, and thy offspring, and with men.*" (Sūrah vii. 10–17.)

"And we said, O Adam, dwell thou and thy wife (*Howwā* [or Eve], *whom God created from a rib of his left side*) in the garden, and eat ye therefrom plentifully, wherever ye will; but approach ye not this tree, *to eat thereof; (and it was wheat, or the grape-vine, or some other tree;)* for *if ye do so*, ye will be of *the number of* the offenders. But the devil, *Iblees*, caused them to slip from it, *that is from the garden, by his saying unto them, Shall I show you the way to the tree of eternity? And he sware to them by God that he was one of the faithful advisers to them; so they ate of it*, and He ejected them from from that *state of delight* in which they were. And We said, Descend ye *to the earth, ye two with the offspring that ye comprise* [yet unborn], one of you (*that is, of your offspring*) an enemy to another; and there shall be for you, in the earth, a place of abode, and a provision, *of its vegetable produce*, for a time, *until the period of the expiration of your terms of life*. And Adam learned, from his Lord, words, *which were these:—O Lord, we have acted unjustly to our own souls, and if Thou do not forgive us, and be merciful unto us, we shall surely be of those who suffer loss. And he prayed in these words;* and He became propitious towards him, *accepting his repentance;* for He is the Very Propitious, the Merciful. We said, Descend ye from it (*from the garden*) altogether; and if there come unto you from Me a direction (*a book and an apostle*), those who follow my direction, *there shall come* no fear on them, nor shall they grieve *in the world to come; for they shall enter paradise:* but they who disbelieve and accuse our signs of falsehood, these shall be the companions of the fire: they shall remain therein for ever." (Sūrah ii. 33–37.)

The Muḥammadans say, that when they were cast down from Paradise [which is in the seventh heaven], Adam fell on the isle of Ceylon, or Sarandīb, and Eve near Jiddah (the port of Makkah) in Arabia; and that, after a separation of two hundred years, Adam was, on his repentance, conducted by the angel Gabriel to a mountain near Makkah, where he found and knew his wife, the mountain being then named ʻArafāt; and that he afterwards retired with her to Ceylon.—Sale.

ADAB (ادب). Discipline of the mind and manners; good education and good breeding; politeness; deportment; a mode of conduct or behaviour. A very long section of the Traditions is devoted to the sayings of Muḥammad regarding rules of conduct, and is found in the *Mishkātu 'l-Maṣābīḥ* under the title *Bābu 'l-Adab* (book xxii. Matthew's *Mishkāt*). It includes—(1) Salutations, (2) Asking permission to enter houses, (3) Shaking hands and embracing, (4) Rising up, (5) Sitting, sleeping and walking, (6) Sneezing and yawning, (7) Laughing, (8) Names, (9) Poetry and eloquence, (10) Backbiting and abuse, (11) Promises, (12) Joking, (13) Boasting and party spirit. The traditional sayings on these subjects will be found under their respective titles. *ʻIlmu 'l-Adab* is the science of Philology.

ʻĀDIYĀT (عاديات). "Swift horses." The title of the 100th Sūrah of the Qur'ān, the second verse of which is, "By the swift chargers and those who strike fire with their hoofs." Professor Palmer translates it "snorting chargers."

ADʻIYATU 'L-MĀṢŪRAH (ادعية المأثورة). "The prayers handed down by tradition." Those prayers which were said by Muḥammad, in addition to the regular liturgical prayers. They are found in different sections of the traditions or *Aḥādīs̤*.

ʻADL (عدل). Justice. Appointing what is just; equalising; making of the same weight. Ransom. The word occurs twelve times in the Qur'ān, *e.g.*, Sūrah iv. 128, "Ye are not able, it may be, *to act equitably* to your wives, even though ye covet it." Sūrah ii. 44, "Fear the day wherein no soul shall pay any *ransom* for another soul." Sūrah ii. 123, "And fear the day when no soul shall pay any *ransom* for a soul, nor shall an equivalent be received therefrom, nor any intercession avail; and they shall not be helped." Sūrah ii. 282, "Write it down *faithfully* . . . then let his agent dictate *faithfully*." Sūrah v. 105, "Let there be a testimony between you when any one of you is at the point of death—at the time he makes his will—two *equitable* persons from amongst you." Sūrah vi. 69, "And though it (soul) *compensate* with the fullest *compensation* it would not be accepted." Sūrah v. 115, "The words of thy Lord are fulfilled in truth and *justice*." Sūrah xvi., 78, "Is he to be held equal with him who bids what is *just*, and who is on the right way?" Sūrah xvi. 92, "Verily God bids you do justice." Sūrah xlix. 8, "Make peace with them with equity and be *just*." Sūrah lxxxii. 8, "Thy generous Lord, who created thee and moulded thee and disposed thee *aright*."

AL-ʻADL (العدل). One of the ninety-nine special names of God. It signifies "the Just." It does not occur in the Qur'ān as an attribute of the Divine Being, but it is in the list of attributes given in the Traditions. (*Mishkāt*, book x.)

ʻADN (عدن). The garden of Eden. *Jannatu ʻAdn*. The garden of perpetual abode. The term is used both for the garden of Eden, in which our first parents dwelt, and also for a place in celestial bliss. [JANNATU ʻADN.]

ADOPTION. Arabic *Tabannī* (تبنى). An adopted son, or daughter, of *known* descent, has no right to inherit from his, or her, adoptive parents and their relatives,—the filiation of this description being neither recommended nor recognised by Muḥammadan law. Such son or daughter is, however, entitled to what may be given under a valid deed in gift or will. In this particular the Muḥammadan agrees with the English, and the Hindu with the Roman law. (*Tagore Law Lectures*, 1873, p. 124.)

ADORATION. The acts and postures by which the Muslims express adoration at the time of prayer are similar to those used by the ancient Jews (*vide* Smith's *Dictionary of the Bible, in loco*), and consist of

Rukū', or the inclination of the body, the hands being placed on the knees; and *Sujūd*, or prostration upon the earth, the forehead touching the ground. [PRAYER.] The adoration of the black stone at Makkah forms an important feature in the ceremonies of the pilgrimage. [HAJJ.]

ADULTERY. Arabic *zinā'* (زناء). The term *zinā'* includes both adultery and fornication, but there is a difference in the punishment for these offences. [FORNICATION.]

Adultery is established before a Qāẓi, either by proof or confession. To establish it upon proof, four witnesses are required. (Qur'ān, Sūrah iv. 1.) When witnesses come forward, it is necessary that they should be examined particularly concerning the nature of the offence. When the witnesses shall have borne testimony completely, declaring that "they have seen the parties in the *very act* of carnal conjunction," the Qāẓi passes sentence.

A confession of adultery must be made by the person who has committed the sin, at four different times, although, according to the Imām ash-Shāfi'ī, one confession is sufficient. Some of the doctors hold that if a person retract his confession, his retraction must be credited, and he must be forthwith released.

At the commencement of Muḥammad's mission, women found guilty of adultery and fornication were punished by being literally immured—*Sūratu 'n-nisā* (iv.) 19, "Shut them up within their houses till death release them, or God make some way for them." This, however, was cancelled, and lapidation was substituted as the punishment for adultery, and 100 stripes and one year's banishment for fornication.

When an adulterer is to be stoned to death, he should be carried to some barren place, and the lapidation should be executed, first by the witnesses, then by the Qāẓi, and afterwards by the by-standers. When a woman is stoned, a hole or excavation should be dug to receive her, as deep as her waist, because Muhammad ordered such a hole to be dug for Ghandia.

It is lawful for a husband to slay his wife and her paramour, if he shall find them in the very act. If a supreme ruler, such as a Khalīfah, commit adultery, he is not subject to such punishment.

The state of marriage which subjects a whoremonger to lapidation, requires that he be *free* (*i.e.* not a slave), a Muslim, and one who has consummated a lawful marriage.

It will be seen that Muḥammadan law is almost identical with the divine law of the Jews with regard to adultery (Deut. xxiii. 22, Lev. xix. 20); but the Mosaic penalty applied as well to the betrothed as to the married woman.

AFFINITY. Arabic *Qarābah* (قرابة). The prohibited degrees (*ḥurmah*) with regard to marriages are as follows:—Mother, daughter, paternal aunt, maternal aunt, brother's or sister's daughter, grandmother, granddaughter, mother-in-law, step-mother, daughter-in-law, granddaughter-in-law. Nor can any man marry any who stand in any of these relationships from fosterage. The marriage of two sisters at the same time is forbidden, but the marriage of a *deceased* wife's sister is allowed. Marriage with a deceased brother's wife is very common in Muslim countries, such marriages being held to be a very honourable means of providing for a brother's widow. The marriage of cousins is also considered most desirable, as being the means of keeping families and tribes together. The passage of the Qur'ān on the subject of affinity, is as follows (Sūrah v. 27):—

"Marry not women whom your fathers have married: for this is a shame, and hateful, and an evil way:—though what is past (*i.e.* in times of ignorance) may be allowed.

"Forbidden to you are your mothers, and your daughters, and your sisters, and your aunts, both on the father and mother's side, and your nieces on the brother and sister's side, and your foster-mothers, and your foster-sisters, and the mothers of your wives, and your step-daughters who are your wards, born of your wives to whom ye have gone in: (but if ye have not gone in unto them, it shall be no sin in you to marry them;) and the wives of your sons who proceed out of your loins; and ye may not have two sisters; except where it is already done. Verily, God is Indulgent, Merciful!

"*Forbidden to you* also are married women, except those who are in your hands as slaves: This is the law of God for you. And it is allowed you, beside this, to seek out wives by means of your ealth, with wmodest conduct, and without fornication. And give those with whom ye have cohabited their dowry. This is the law. But it shall be no crime in you to make agreements over and above the law. Verily, God is Knowing, Wise!"

AFFLICTION. Arabic *ḥuzn* (حزن), *ghamm* (غم). The benefits of affliction are frequently expressed in both the Qu'rān and Traditions. For example: Sūrah ii. 150, "We will try you with something of fear, and hunger, and loss of wealth, and souls and fruit; but give good tidings to the patient who, when there falls on them a calamity, say, 'Verily we are God's and verily to Him we return.'" This formula is always used by Muḥammadans in any danger or sudden calamity, especially in the presence of death.

In the traditions (see *Mishkātu 'l-Maṣābiḥ*), Muḥammad is related to have said, "A Muslim is like unto standing green corn, which sometimes stands erect, but is sometimes cast down by the wind." "No affliction befals a servant of God but on account of the sins which he commits."

AFSŪN (افسون). The Persian term for *Da'wah* or exorcism. [EXORCISM.]

'AFŪ (عفو). *Lit.* "erasing, cancelling." The word is generally used in Muḥammadan books for pardon and forgiveness. It occurs eight times in the Qur'ān, *e.g.* Sūrah ii. 286, "Lord, make us not to carry what we have not strength for, but *forgive* us and pardon us and have mercy on us." Sūrah iv. 46, "Verily God *pardons* and forgives."

Al-'Afū is one of the ninety-nine special names of God. It means "one who erases or cancels;" "The Eraser (of sins)." See Qur'ān, Sūrah iv. 51.

AGENT. Arabic *wakīl* (وكيل). One legally appointed to act for another. For the Muḥammadan law regarding the appointment of agents to transact business, or to negotiate marriages, see Hamilton's *Hidāyah*, vol. iii. p. 1; Baillie's *Digest. Hanīfī Code*, p. 75; *Imāmīyah Code*, p. 29. The author of the *Hidāyah* says, "It is lawful for a person to appoint another his agent for the settlement, in his behalf, of every contract which he might lawfully have concluded himself, such as sale, marriage, and so forth;" and he then proceeds to lay down rules for guidance in such matters at great length. A woman who remains in privacy and is not accustomed to go into Court, ought, according to the saying of Abū Bakr, to appoint an agent and not appear herself. A slave or a minor may be appointed agent for a free man.

AL-AḤAD (الاحد). "The One." A title given to God. [NAMES OF GOD.]

AḤADĪYAH (احدية). Unity, concord. *Al-Aḥadīyah* is a term used by Ṣūfī mystics to express a condition of the mind, completely absorbed in a meditation on the Divine Unity. (*See* 'Abdu 'r-Razzāq's *Dictionary of the Technical Terms of the Ṣūfīs.* Sprenger's edition.)

AḤQĀF (احقاف). The name of a tract of land in Sihr in Yaman. The title of the XLVIth Sūrah of the Qur'ān.

AHLU 'L-BAIT (اهل البيت). "The people of the house." A term used in the Qur'ān (Sūrah xxxiii. 33), and in the Ḥadīs̤ (*Mishkāt*, xxiv. 21), for Muḥammad's household.

AHLU 'L-HAWĀ' (اهل الهواء). A visionary person; a libertine.

AHLU 'L-KITĀB (اهل الكتاب). *Lit.* "The people of the book." A term used in the Qur'ān for Jews and Christians, as believers in a revealed religion. Some sects of the Shī'ahs include the Majūsī (Magi) under this term.

AḤMAD (احمد). The name under which Muḥammad professes that Jesus Christ foretold his coming. *Vide* Qur'ān, Sūrah lxi. 6, "And remember when Jesus the son of Mary said, 'O children of Israel! of a truth I am God's Apostle to you to confirm the law which was given before me, and to announce an apostle that shall come after me, whose name shall be *Aḥmad.*'" Muḥammad had, no doubt, heard that Our Lord had promised a Paracletos (παρακλητος), John xvi. 7. This title, understood by him, probably from the similarity of sound, as equivalent to Periclytos (περικλυτος), he applied to himself with reference to his own name Muḥammad, the *praised* or *glorified one.* Muir thinks that in some imperfect Arabic translation of the Gospel of St. John, the word παρακλητος may have been translated *Aḥmad*, or *praised.* (*Life of Mahomet*, vol. i. 17.)

AḤZĀB (احزاب). "Confederates." The title of the XXXIIIrd Sūrah of the Qur'ān, which is said to have been written when al-Madīnah was besieged by a confederation of the Jewish tribes with the Arabs of Makkah. A.H. 5.

AIYŪB (ايوب). [JOB.]

AJAL (اجل). The appointed time of death, said to be ordained by God from the first. Qur'ān, Sūrah xxxv. 44, "He respites them until *the appointed time.* When their *appointed time* comes, verily God looks upon His servants." [DEATH.]

AJĪR (اجير). A term used in Muḥammadan law for a person hired for service. [IJARAH.]

AJNABĪ (اجنبى). A foreigner; any person not of Arabia.

ĀKHIR-I-CHAHĀR-I-SHAMBAH (آخر چهار شنبه). The last Wednesday of the month of Ṣafar. It is observed as a feast in commemoration of Muḥammad's having experienced some mitigation of his last illness, and having bathed. It was the last time he performed the legal bathing, for he died on the twelfth day of the next month. In some parts of Islām it is customary, in the early morning of this day to write verses of the Qur'ān, known as the *Seven Salāms* (q.v.), and then wash off the ink and drink it as a charm against evil. It is not observed by the Wahhābīs, nor is its observance universal in Islām.

AKHLĀQ (اخلاق). The plural of *Khulq.* Natures, dispositions, habits, manners. The general term for books on morality, *e.g.* *Akhlāq-i-Jalālī*, *Akhlāq-i-Muḥsinī*, the name of a dissertation on Ethics by Ḥusain Wā'iẓ Kāshifī, A.H. 910, which has been translated into English by the Rev. H. G. Keene (W. H. Allen & Co.).

ĀKHŪND (آخوند). A maulawī; a teacher. A title of respect given to eminent religious teachers. One of the most celebrated Muḥammadan teachers of modern times was the "Ākhūnd of Swāt," who died A.D. 1875. This great religious leader resided in the village of Saidū, in the district of Swāt, on the north-west frontier of India.

ĀKHŪNDZĀDAH (آخوندزاده). The son of an Ākhūnd. A title of respect given to the sons or descendants of celebrated religious teachers. [AKHUND.]

ĀL (آل). *Lit.* "offspring, or posterity." Used in Muslim works for the offspring of Muḥammad

AL-A'LA (الاعلى). "The Most High." The title of the LXXXVIIth Surah of the Qur'ān, in the second verse of which the word occurs: "The name of thy Lord *the Most High* is celebrated."

'ALAM (علم). A standard or ensign. A term used for the flags and standards paraded during the Muḥarram. [MUHARRAM, STANDARDS.]

'ĀLAM (عالم). The universe; world; condition, state of being.

'Ālamu 'l-arwāḥ .	The world of spirits.
'Ālamu 'l-khalq .	The world; this life.
'Ālamu 'l-bāqī .	The future state.
'Ālamu 'l-a'ẓamah .	The highest heaven.
'Ālamu 'sh-shahādah	The visible world.
'Ālamu 'l-ghaib .	The invisible world.
'Ālamu 'l-ma'qūl .	The rational world.

The four mystic stages of the Ṣūfīs are—

'Ālamu 'n-nāsūt .	The present world.
'Ālamu 'l-malakūt .	The state of angels.
'Ālamu 'l-jabarūt .	The state of power.
'Ālamu 'l-lāhūt .	The state of absorption into the Divinity.

[SUFIISM.]

'ALĀMĀT (علامات). The greater signs of the resurrection. ['ALAMATU 'S-SA'AH, RESURRECTION.]

'ALĀMĀTU 'N-NUBŪWAH (علامات النبوة). "The signs of Prophecy." A term used for the supposed miracles and other proofs of the mission of Muḥammad. The title of a chapter in the Traditions. (*Mishkāt*, xxi. c. vi.)

'ALĀMĀTU 'S-SĀ'AH (علامات الساعة). "The signs of the hour," *i.e.* the signs of the time of the Resurrection and of the Day of Judgment. The title of a section of the Traditions. (*Mishkāt*, xxiii. c. 3.) [RESURRECTION.]

'ALAQ (علق). "Congealed blood." The title of the XCVIth Sūrah, the first five verses of which are generally allowed to be the earliest portion of the Qur'ān.

AL-BALDAH (البلدة). "The City." A name sometimes used in the Ḥadīs̤ for Makkah.

ALCHEMY. Arabic *Kīmiyā* (كيمياء). According to the *Kashfu 'z-ẓunūn*, *in loco*, learned Muslims are not agreed as to the existence of this occult science, nor are they of one opinion as to its lawfulness, even if it should exist.

ALEXANDER THE GREAT. Mentioned in the Qur'ān as *Z̤ū 'l-Qarnain*, *i.e.* "He of the two horns," with which he is represented on his coins. (Sūrah xviii. 82.) He seems to have been regarded by Muḥammad as one invested with a divine commission:—"Verily we established his power upon earth"; but commentators are not agreed whether to assign to him the position of a Prophet. [ZU 'L-QARNAIN.]

AL-ḤAMD (الحمد). "Praise." A title given to the first Sūrah, so called because its first word is *Al-ḥamd*. This chapter is also called *Fātiḥah*, which term is used by modern Muslims for the Sūrah when it is said for the benefit of the dead, *Al-ḥamd* being its more usual title. [FATIHAH.]

AL-ḤAMDU-LI'LLĀH (الحمد لله). "Praise belongs to God." An ejaculation which is called *Taḥmīd*, and which occurs at the commencement of the first chapter of the Qur'ān. It is used as an ejaculation of thanksgiving—"Thank God!" It is very often recited with the addition of *Rabbi 'l-'ālamīn*, "Lord of the Universe." [TAHMID.]

AL-'ALĪ (العلى). One of the ninety-nine special names of God. It means "The Exalted One."

'ALĪ (على). The son of Abū-Ṭālib, and a cousin-german to Muḥammad, who adopted him as his son. He married Fāṭimah, the daughter of Muḥammad, and had by her three sons, Ḥasan, Ḥusain, and Muḥassin. He was the fourth Khalīfah, and reigned from A.H. 35 to A.H. 40. He was struck with a poisoned sword by Ibn Muljam, at al-Kūfah, and died after three days, aged fifty-nine years. The Shī'ahs hold that, on the death of Muḥammad, 'Alī was entitled to the Khalifate, and the respective claims of Abū Bakr, 'Umar, and 'Us̤mān on the one hand, and of 'Alī on the other, gave rise to the Shī'ah schism. 'Alī is surnamed by the Arabs *Asadu 'llāh*, and by the Persians *Sher-i-Khudā*, *i.e.* "The Lion of God." [SHI'AH.]

ALIF. The letter *Alif* (ا) is a monogram frequently placed at the head of letters, prescriptions, &c. It is the initial letter of the word *Allāh* (الله), "God."

ALIF LĀM MĪM. The Arabic letters الم, corresponding to *A L M*, which occur at the commencement of six Sūrahs, namely Sūratu 'l-Baqarah (II.), Sūratu Āli 'Imrān (III.), Sūratu 'l-'Ankabūt (XXIX.), Sūratu 'r-Rūm (XXX.), Sūratu Luqmān (XXXI.), and Sūratu 's-Sijdah (XXXII.). Muḥammad never explained the meaning of these mysterious letters, and consequently they are a fruitful source of perplexity to learned commentators. Jalālu 'd-dīn gives an exhaustive summary of the different views in his *Itqān* (p. 470). Some suppose they stand for the words *Allāh*, "God"; *Laṭīf*, "gracious"; *Majīd*, "glorious." Others say they stand for *Ana'llāhu a'lamu*, "I am the God who knoweth." Others maintain that they were not meant to be understood, and that they were inserted by the Divine command without explanation, in order to remind the reader that there were mysteries which his intellect would never fathom.

ĀLU 'IMRĀN (آل عمرآن). "The family of 'Imrān." The title of the third chapter of the Qur'ān.

'ĀLIM (عالم), pl. *'ulamā'*. A learned

man. The term usually includes all religious teachers, such as Imāms, Muftīs, Qāẓīs, and Maulawīes; and in Turkey it denotes the political party led by the religious teachers.

AL-'ALĪM (العليم). One of the ninety-nine special names of God. It frequently occurs in the Qur'ān, and means "The Wise One."

ALLĀH (الله). [GOD.]

ALLĀHU AKBAR (الله اكبر). "God is great," or "God is most great." An ejaculation which is called the *Takbīr*. It occurs frequently in the liturgical forms, and is used when slaying an animal for food. [TAKBIR.]

ALMSGIVING. The word generally used for alms is *Ṣadaqah*, or that which manifests righteousness; the word *zakāt*, or purification, being specially restricted to the legal alms. [ZAKAT.] *Ṣadaqātu 'l-Fiṭr* are the offerings given on the Lesser Festival. The duty of almsgiving is very frequently enjoined in the Qur'ān, *e.g.* Sūrah ii. 274–5, "What ye expend of good (*i.e.* of well-gotten wealth), it shall be paid to you again, and ye shall not be wronged. (Give your alms) unto the poor who are straitened in God's way and cannot traverse the earth. . . . Those who expend their wealth by night and by day, secretly and openly, they shall have their hire with their Lord."

The following are some of the sayings of Muḥammad on the subject of almsgiving, as they occur in the Traditions:—"The upper hand is better than the lower one. The upper hand is the giver of alms, and the lower hand is the poor beggar." "The best of alms are those given by a man of small means, who gives of that which he has earned by labour, and gives as much as he is able." "Begin by giving alms to your own relatives." "Doing justice between two people is alms; assisting a man on his beast is alms; good words are alms." "A camel lent out for milk is alms; a cup of milk every morning and evening is alms." "Your smiling in your brother's face is alms; assisting the blind is alms." "God says, Be thou liberal, thou child of Adam, that I may be liberal to thee." (See *Mishkāt*, Matthew's edition, vol. i. p. 429.)

ALWĀḤ (الواح), pl. of *Lauḥ*. "The tables" (of the Law). Mentioned in the Qur'ān, Sūrah vii. 142, "We wrote for him (Moses) upon the Tables (*al-Alwāḥ*) a monition concerning every matter."

Muslim divines are not agreed as to the number either of the tables, or of the Commandments. The commentators Jalālain say they were either seven or ten. [TEN COMMANDMENTS.]

'AMAL-NĀMAH (عمل نامه). The Persian word for *Ṣaḥīfatu 'l-A'māl*, or record of actions kept by the recording angels. [SAHIFATU 'L-A'MAL, KIRAMU 'L-KATIBIN.]

AMĀN (امان). Protection given by a Muslim conqueror to those who pay *Jizyah*, or poll tax. [JIHAD.]

AMBIYĀ (انبياء), pl. of *Nabī*. "Prophets." The title of the XXIst Sūrah. [PROPHETS.]

ĀMĪN (امين), Hebrew אָמֵן. An expression of assent used at the conclusion of prayers, very much as in our Christian worship. It is always used at the conclusion of the Sūratu 'l-Fātiḥah, or first chapter of the Qur'ān.

Amīn, "Faithful." *Al-Amīn* is the title which it is said was given to Muḥammad when a youth, on account of his fair and honourable bearing, which won the confidence of the people.

Amīnu 'l-Bait, one who wishes to perform the pilgrimage to Makkah.

ĀMINAH (آمنة). Muḥammad's mother. She was the wife of 'Abdu 'llāh, and the daughter of Wahb ibn 'Abdi Manāf. She died and was buried at al-Abwā, a place midway between Makkah and al-Madīnah, before her son claimed the position of a Prophet.

AMĪR (امير), *Anglicè*, Emir. "A ruler; a commander; a chief; a nobleman." It includes the various high offices in a Muslim state; the Imām, or Khalīfah, being styled *Amīru 'l-Umarā'*, the ruler of rulers; and *Amīru 'l-Mu'minīn*, the commander of the believers.

AMĪRU 'L-ḤAJJ (امير الحج). The chief of the pilgrimage." The officer in charge of the pilgrims to Makkah. [HAJJ.]

AMĪRU 'L-MU'MINĪN (امير المومنين). "The Commander of the Believers." A title which was first given to Abdu 'llāh ibn Jaḥsh after his expedition to Nakhlah, and which was afterwards assumed by the Khalīfahs (first by 'Umar) and the Sulṭāns of Turkey. [KHALIFAH.]

'AMR IBN AL-'ĀṢĪ (عمرو بن العاصى). One of the Companions, celebrated for his conquest of Syria, Palestine and Egypt, in the reigns of Abū Bakr and 'Umar. He died (according to an-Nawawī) A.H. 43.

AMULETS. Arabic *Ḥamā'il* (حمائل), "anything suspended"; *Ta'wīz*, "a refuge"; *Ḥijāb*, "a cover."

Amulets, although of heathen origin, are very common in Muḥammadan countries. The following are used as amulets: (1) a small Qur'ān, encased in silk or leather, and suspended from the shoulder; (2) a chapter or verse of the Qur'ān, written on paper and folded in leather or velvet; (3) some of the names of God, or the numerical power (see ABJAD) of these names; (4) the names of prophets, celebrated saints, or the numerical power of the same; (5) the Muḥammadan creed, engraven on stone or silver. The chapters of the Qur'ān generally selected for Amulets are: Sūrahs i., vi., xviii., xxxvi., xliv., lv., lxvii., lxxviii. Five verses known as the *Āyātu 'l-Ḥifẓ*, or "verses of protection," are also frequently inscribed on Amulets. They are Sūrahs ii. 256; xii. 64; xiii. 12; xv. 17: xxxvii. 7. [AYATU 'L-HIFZ.]

These charms are fastened on the arm or leg, or suspended round the neck, as a protection against evil. They are also put on houses and animals, and, in fact, upon anything from which evil is to be averted. Strictly, according to the principles of Islām, only the names of God, or verses from the Qur'ān, should be used for amulets. Information regarding the formation of magic squares and amulets will be found in the article on Exorcism. [EXORCISM, DA'WAH.]

ط	ف	ا	ح
ح	ط	ف	ا
ا	ح	ط	ف
ف	ا	ح	ط

AN AMULET OF THE ATTRIBUTE OF GOD—*Ḥāfiẓ*, "THE PROTECTOR."

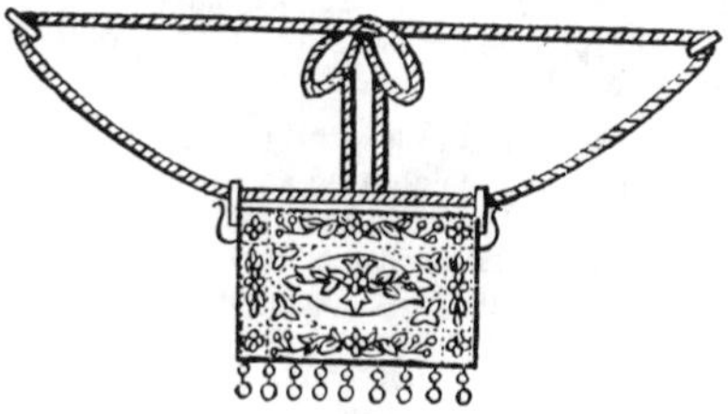

A SMALL QURAN SUSPENDED AS AN AMULET.

AL-AN'ĀM (الانعام). "The Cattle." The title of the VIth Sūrah, in verse 137 of which some superstitious customs of the Meccans, as to certain cattle, are incidentally mentioned.

ANĀNĪYAH (انانية). From *ana*, "I." "Egotism." *Al-anāniyah* is a term used by the Ṣūfīs to express the existence of man.

ANAS IBN MĀLIK (انس ابن مالك). The last of the Companions of Muḥammad, and the founder of the sect of the Mālikīs. He died at al-Baṣrah, A.H. 93, aged 103.

AL-ANFĀL (الانفال). "The Spoils." The title of the VIIIth Sūrah which was occasioned by a dispute regarding the spoils taken at the battle of Badr, between the young men who had fought and the old men who had stayed with the ensigns.

ANGEL. Arabic *mal'ak* or *malak* (ملاك، ملك). Persian *Firishtah* (فرشته). "It is believed," says Ibn Mājah, "that the angels are of a simple substance (created of light), endowed with life, and speech, and reason; and that the difference between them, the Jinn, and Shaiṭāns is a difference of species. Know," he adds, "that the angels are sanctified from carnal desire and the disturbance of anger: they disobey not God in what He hath commanded them, but do what they are commanded. Their food is the celebrating of His glory; their drink, the proclaiming of His holiness; their conversation, the commemoration of God, Whose name be exalted; their pleasure, His worship; and they are created in different forms and with different powers." (*Arabian Nights*, Lane's edition, Notes to the Introduction, p. 27.)

Four of them are archangels, or, as they are called in Arabic, *Karūbīyūn* (Cherubim), namely, *Jabra'īl*, or *Jibrīl*, (Gabriel), the angel of revelations; *Mīka'īl*, or *Mīkāl*, (Michael), the patron of the Israelites; *Isrāfīl*, the angel who will sound the trumpet at the last day; and *'Izrā'īl*, or *'Azrā'īl*, the angel of death. Angels are said to be inferior in dignity to human prophets, because all the angels were commanded to prostrate themselves before Adam (Sūrah ii. 32). Every believer is attended by two recording angels, called the *Kirāmu 'l-kātibīn*, one of whom records his good actions, and the other his evil actions. There are also two angels, called *Munkar* and *Nakīr*, who examine all the dead in their graves. The chief angel who has charge of hell is called *Mālik*, and his subordinates are named *Zabāniyah*, or guards. A more extended account of these angels will be found under their particular titles.

The angels intercede for man: "The angels celebrate the praise of their Lord, and ask forgiveness for the dwellers on earth." (Sūrah xlii. 3.) They also act as guardian angels: "Each hath a succession of angels before him and behind him, who watch over him by God's behest." (Sūrah xiii. 12.) "Is it not enough for you that your Lord aideth you with three thousand angels sent down (from on high)?" (Sūrah iii. 120.) "He is the supreme over His servants, and sendeth forth guardians who watch over you, until, when death overtaketh any one of you, our messengers receive him and fail not." (Sūrah vi. 61.)

There are eight angels who support the throne of God, "And the angels shall be on its sides, and over them on that day eight shall bear up the throne of thy Lord." (Sūrah lxix. 17.) Nineteen have charge of hell. "Over it are nineteen. None but angels have we made guardians of the fire." (Sūrah lxxiv. 30, 31.)

The names of the guardian angels given in the book on Exorcism (*da'wah*), entitled the *Jawāhiru 'l-Khamsah*, are Isrāfīl, Jibrā'īl, Kalkā'īl, Dardā'īl, Durbā'īl, Raftmā'īl, Sharkā'īl, Tankafīl, Ismā'īl, Sarakīkā'īl, Kharūrā'īl, Ṭaṭā'īl, Rūyā'īl, Hūlā'īl, Hamwākīl, 'Itrā'īl,

Amwākīl, 'Amrā'īl, 'Azrā'īl, Mīkā'īl, Mahkā'īl, Hartā'īl, 'Atā'īl, Nurā'īl, Nukhā'īl. [EXORCISM.]

ANIMALS. Arabic *Ḥayawān* (حيوان). According to the Qur'ān, Sūrah xxiv. 44, "God hath created every animal of water." "An idea," says Rodwell, "perhaps derived from Gen. i. 20, 21."

It is believed that at the Resurrection the irrational animals will be restored to life, that they may be brought to judgment, and then be annihilated. See Qur'ān, Sūrah vi. 38, "No kind of beast is there on the earth, nor fowl that flieth with its wings, but is a community like you; nothing have We passed over in the book (of the Eternal decrees): then unto their Lord shall they be gathered."

AL-'ANKABŪT (العنكبوت). "The Spider." The title of the XXIXth Sūrah, in which there is a passing reference to this insect in the 40th verse:—"The likeness for those who take to themselves guardians besides God is the likeness of the *spider* who buildeth her a house; but truly the frailest of all houses surely is the house of the spider."

AL-ANṢĀR (الانصار). "The Helpers," a term used for the early converts of al-Madīnah; but when all the citizens of al-Madīnah were ostensibly converted to Islām, they were all named *Anṣār*, while those Muslims who accompanied the Prophet from Makkah to al-Madīnah were called *Muhājirūn*, or exiles. (Muir's *Life of Mahomet*, vol iii. p. 26.) [MUHAMMAD.]

ANTICHRIST. [MASIHU 'D-DAJJAL.]

APOSTASY FROM ISLĀM. Arabic *irtidād* (ارتداد). According to Muslim law, a male apostate, or *Murtadd*, is liable to be put to death if he continue obstinate in his error; a female apostate is not subject to capital punishment, but she may be kept in confinement until she recant. (Hamilton's *Hidāyah*, vol. ii. p. 227.) If either the husband or wife apostatize from the faith of Islām, a divorce takes place *ipso facto;* the wife is entitled to her whole dower, but no sentence of divorce is necessary. If the husband and wife both apostatize together, their marriage is generally allowed to continue, although the Imām Zufar says it is annulled. But if, after their joint apostasy, either husband or wife were singly to return to Islām, then the marriage would be dissolved. (Hamilton's *Hidāyah*, vol. ii. p. 183.)

According to Abū Ḥanīfah, a male apostate is disabled from selling or otherwise disposing of his property. But Abū Yūsuf and Imām Muḥammad differ from their master upon this point, and consider a male apostate to be as competent to exercise every right as if he were still in the faith. (*Hidāyah*, vol. ii. p. 235.)

If a boy under age apostatize, he is not to be put to death, but to be imprisoned until he come to full age, when, if he continue in the state of unbelief, he must be put to death. Neither lunatics nor drunkards are held to be responsible for their apostasy from Islām. (*Hidāyah*, vol. ii. 246.) If a person *upon compulsion* become an apostate, his wife is not divorced, nor are his lands forfeited. If a person become a Musalmān upon compulsion, and afterwards apostatize, he is not to be put to death. (*Hidāyah*, vol. iii. 467.)

The will of a male apostate is not valid, but that of a female apostate is valid. (*Hidāyah*, vol. iv. 537.)

'Ikrimah relates that some apostates were brought to the Khalīfah 'Alī, and he burnt them alive; but Ibn 'Abbās heard of it, and said that the Khalīfah had not acted rightly, for the Prophet had said, "Punish not with God's punishment (*i.e.* fire), but whosoever changes his religion, kill him with the sword." (*Ṣaḥīḥu 'l-Bukhārī.*)

APOSTLE. Arabic *rasūl* (رسول), *ḥawārī* (حواری). The term *rasūl* (apostle or messenger) is applied to Muḥammad, that of *ḥawārī* being used in the Qur'ān (Sūrah iii. 4, 5; Sūrah iv. 111, 112; Sūrah lxi. 14) for the Apostles of Jesus. The word *ḥawārī* seems to be derived from the Æthiopic *ḥōra*, "to go"; *ḥawāryā*, "apostle"; although, according to al-Baiẓāwī, the commentator, it is derived from *ḥawira*, "to be white," in Syriac, *ḥewar*, and was given to the disciples of Jesus, he says, on account of their purity of life and sincerity, or because they were respectable men and wore white garments. In the Traditions (*Mishkāt*, book i. c. vi. part 2) *ḥawārī* is used for the followers of all the prophets. [PROPHETS.]

AL-'AQABAH (العقبة). A sheltered glen near Minā, celebrated as the scene of the two pledges, the first and second pledge of al-'Aqabah. The first pledge was made by ten men of the tribe of Khazraj and ten of Aus, when they plighted their faith to Muḥammad thus:—"We will not worship any but one God; we will not steal; nor commit adultery; nor kill our children; nor will we slander our neighbour; and we will obey the Prophet of God." The date assigned to this pledge by Sir W. Muir is April 21, A.D. 621. The second pledge was a few months afterwards, when seventy-three men and two women came forward, one by one, and took an oath of fealty to the Prophet. Muḥammad named twelve of the chief of these men, and said:—"Moses chose from amongst his people twelve leaders. Ye shall be sureties for the rest, even as were the Apostles of Jesus; and I am surety for my people. And the people answered, *Āmīn*, So be it." (Muir's *Life of Mahomet*, vol. ii. pp. 216, 232.)

'ĀQIB (عاقب). "A successor or deputy." "One who comes last." *Al-'āqib* is a title given to Muḥammad as being styled "the last of the prophets."

'ĀQILAH (عاقلة). The relatives who pay the expiatory mulct for manslaughter, or any other legal fine. They must be relatives descended from one common father. (Hamilton's *Hidāyah*, vol. iv. pages 449, 452; Baillie's *Law of Sale*, p. 214.)

'AQĪQAH (عقيقة). A custom observed by the Arabs on the birth of a child; namely, leaving the hair on the infant's head until the seventh day, when it is shaved, and animals are sacrificed, namely, two sheep for a boy and one for a girl. (*Mishkāt*, xviii. c. 3) It is enjoined by Muḥammadan law, and observed in all parts of Islām.

ARABIA. *Bilādu 'l-'Arab* (بلاد العرب), *Jazīratu 'l-'Arab* (جزيرة العرب), *'Arabistān* (عربستان). The peninsula bearing, amongst the Arabs, these names is the country situated on the east of the Red Sea, and extending as far as the Persian Gulf.

The word probably signifies a "barren place," "desert" (Heb. עֲרָבָה)

Ptolemy divides Arabia into three parts, Arabia Petræa, Arabia Felix, and Arabia Deserta; but Arabian geographers divide it into *Tihāmah*, *al-Ḥijāz*, *an-Najd*, *al-'Arūẓ*, and *al-Yaman*.

The races which have peopled Arabia are divided into three sections, *al-'Arabu 'l-Bā'idah*, *al-'Arabu 'l-'Āribah*, and *al-'Arabu 'l-Musta'ribah*.

I. *Al-'Arabu 'l-Bā'idah*, are the old "lost Arabs," of whom tradition has preserved the names of several tribes, as well as some memorable particulars regarding their extinction. This may well be called the fabulous period of Arabian history; but, as it has the sanction of the Qur'ān, it would be sacrilege in a Muslim to doubt its authenticity. According to this account, the most famous of the extinct tribes were those of 'Ād, Ṣamūd, Jadīs, and Ṭasm, all descended in the third or fourth generation from Shem. 'Ād, the father of his tribe, settled, according to tradition, in the Great Desert of al-Aḥqāf soon after the confusion of tongues. Shaddād his son succeeded him in the government, and greatly extended his dominions. He performed many fabulous exploits; among others, he erected a magnificent city in the desert of 'Adan, which had been begun by his father, and adorned it with a sumptuous palace and delightful gardens, in imitation of the celestial paradise, in order to inspire his subjects with a superstitious veneration for him as a god. This superb structure was built with bricks of gold and silver alternately disposed. The roof was of gold, inlaid with precious stones and pearls. The trees and shrubs were of the same precious materials. The fruits and flowers were rubies, and on the branches were perched birds of similar metals, the hollow parts of which were loaded with every species of the richest perfumes, so that every breeze that blew came charged with fragrance from the bills of these golden images. To this paradise he gave the name of Iram (see Qur'ān, Sūrah lxxxix. 6). On the completion of all this grandeur, Shaddād set out with a splendid retinue to admire its beauties. But heaven would not suffer his pride and impiety to go unpunished; for, when within a day's journey of the place, they were all destroyed by a terrible noise from the clouds. As a monument of Divine justice, the city, we are assured, still stands in the desert, though invisible. Southey, in his *Thalaba*, has viewed this and many of the other fables and superstitions of the Arabs with the eye of a poet, a philosopher, and an antiquary. According to aṭ-Ṭabarī, this legendary palace was discovered in the time of Mu'āwiyah, the first Khalīfah of Damascus, by a person in search of a stray camel. A fanciful tradition adds, that the Angel of death, on being asked whether, in the discharge of his duties, an instance had ever occurred in which he had felt some compassion towards his wretched victims, admitted that only twice had his sympathies been awakened—once towards a shipwrecked infant, which had been exposed on a solitary plank to struggle for existence with the winds and waves, and which he spared; and the second time in cutting off the unhappy Shaddād at the moment when almost within view of the glorious fabric which he had erected at so much expense. No sooner had the angel spoken, than a voice from heaven was heard to declare that the helpless innocent on the plank was no other than Shaddād himself; and that his punishment was a just retribution for his ingratitude to a merciful and kind Providence, which had not only saved his life, but raised him to unrivalled wealth and splendour. The whole fable seems to be a confused tradition of Belus and the ancient Babylon; or, rather, as the name would import, of Benhadad, mentioned in Scripture as one of the most famous of the Syrian kings, who, we are told, was worshipped by his subjects.

Of the 'Ādites and their succeeding princes, nothing certain is known, except that they were dispersed or destroyed in the course of a few centuries by the sovereigns of al-Yaman.

The tribe of Ṣamūd first settled in Arabia Felix, and on their expulsion they repaired to al-Ḥijr, on the confines of Syria. Like the 'Ādites, they are reported to have been of a most gigantic stature, the tallest being a hundred cubits high and the least sixty: and such was their muscular power, that, with a stamp of the foot in the driest soil, they could plant themselves knee-deep in the earth. They dwelt, the Qur'ān informs us, "in the caves of the rocks, and cut the mountains into houses, which remain to this day." In this tribe it is easy to discover the Thamudeni of Diodorus, Pliny, and Ptolemy.

The tribes of Ṭasm and Jadīs settled between Makkah and al-Madīnah, and occupied the whole level country of al-Yaman, living promiscuously under the same government. Their history is buried in darkness; and when the Arabs wish to denote anything of dubious authority, they call it a fable of Ṭasm.

The extinction of these tribes, according to the Qur'ān, was miraculous, and a signal example of Divine vengeance. The posterity of 'Ād and Ṣamūd had abandoned the worship of the true God, and lapsed into incorrigible idolatry. They had been chastised with a three years' drought, but their hearts remained hardened. To the former was sent the Prophet Hūd, to reclaim them and preach the unity of the Godhead. "O my people!" exclaimed the prophet, "ask pardon of your Lord; then turn unto Him with penitence, (and) He will send down the heavens upon you with copious rains, and with strength in addition to your strength will He increase you." Few believed, and the overthrow of the idolaters was effected by a hot and suffocating wind, that blew seven nights and eight days without intermission, accompanied with a terrible earthquake, by which their idols were broken to pieces, and their houses thrown to the ground. (See Qur'ān, Sūrah vii. 63, xi. 53.) Luqmān, who, according to some, was a famous king of the 'Ādites, and who lived to the age of seven eagles, escaped, with about sixty others, the common calamity. These few survivors gave rise to a tribe called the Latter 'Ād; but on account of their crimes they were transformed, as the Qur'ān states, into asses or monkeys. Hūd returned to Ḥazramaut, and was buried in the neighbourhood, where a small town, Qabr Hūd, still bears his name. Among the Arabs, 'Ād expresses the same remote age that Saturn or Ogyges did among the Greeks; anything of extreme antiquity is said to be "as old as King 'Ād."

The idolatrous tribe of Ṣamūd had the prophet Ṣāliḥ sent to them, whom D'Herbelot makes the son of Arphaxad, while Bochart and Sale suppose him to be Peleg, the brother of Joktan. His preaching had little effect. The fate of the 'Ādites, instead of being a warning, only set them to dig caverns in the rocks, where they hoped to escape the vengeance of winds and tempests. Others demanded a sign from the prophet in token of his mission. As a condition of their belief, they challenged him to a trial of power, similar to what took place between Elijah and the priests of Baal, and promised to follow the deity that should gain the triumph. From a certain rock a camel big with young was to come forth in their presence. The idolaters were foiled; for on Ṣāliḥ's pointing to the spot, a she-camel was produced, with a young one ready weaned. This miracle wrought conviction in a few; but the rest, far from believing, hamstrung the mother, killed her miraculous progeny, and divided the flesh among them. This act of impiety sealed their doom. "And a violent tempest overtook the wicked, and they were found prostrate on their breasts in their abodes." (Qur'ān, Sūrah vii. 71, xi. 64.)

The tribes of Jadīs and Ṭasm owe their extinction to a different cause. A certain despot, a Ṭasmite, but sovereign of both tribes, had rendered himself detested by a voluptuous law claiming for himself a priority of right over all the brides of the Jadīsites. This insult was not to be tolerated. A conspiracy was formed. The king and his chiefs were invited to an entertainment. The avengers had privately hidden their swords in the sand, and in the moment of mirth and festivity they fell upon the tyrant and his retinue, and finally extirpated the greater part of his subjects.

II.—The *pure* Arabs are those who claim to be descended from Joktan or Qaḥṭān, whom the present Arabs regard as their principal founder. The members of this genuine stock are styled al-'Arabu 'l-'Āribah, the genuine Arabs. According to their genealogy of this patriarch, his descendants formed two distinct branches. Ya'rub, one of his sons, founded the kingdom of al-Yaman, and Jurhum that of al-Ḥijāz. These two are the only sons spoken of by the Arabs. Their names do not occur in Scripture; but it has been conjectured that they were the Jerah and Hadoram mentioned by Moses as among the thirteen planters of Arabia (Gen. x. 26).

In the division of their nation into tribes the Arabs resemble the Jews. From an early era they have retained the distinction of separate and independent families. This partition was adverse to the consolidation of power or political influence, but it furnishes our chief guide into the dark abyss of their antiquities. The posterity of Ya'rub spread and multiplied into innumerable clans. New accessions rendered new subdivisions necessary. In the genealogical tables of Sale, Gagnier, and Saiyid Aḥmad K͟hān, are enumerated nearly three-score tribes of genuine Arabs, many of whom became celebrated long before the time of Muḥammad, and some of them retain their names even at the present day.

III.—The *'Arabu 'l-Musta'ribah*, the *mixed* Arabs, claim to be descended from Ishmael and the daughter of al-Muẓāẓ, King of al-Ḥijāz, whom he took to wife, and was of the ninth generation from Jurhum, the founder of that kingdom. Of the Jurhumites, till the time of Ishmael, little is recorded, except the names of their princes or chiefs, and that they had possession of the territory of al-Ḥijāz. But as Muḥammad traces his descent to this alliance, the Arabs have been more than usually careful to preserve and adorn his genealogy. The want of a pure ancestry is, in their estimation, more than compensated by the dignity of so sacred a connexion; for they boast as much as the Jews of being reckoned the children of Abraham. This circumstance will account for the preference with which they uniformly regard this branch of their pedigree, and for the many romantic legends they have grafted upon it. It is not improbable that the old giants and idolaters suffered an imaginary extinction to make way for a more favoured race, and that Divine chastisements always overtook those who dared to invade their consecrated territories.

The Scripture account of the expulsion and destiny of this venerated progenitor of the Arabs is brief, but simple and affecting. Ishmael was the son of Abraham by Hagar, an Egyptian slave. When fourteen years of age, he was supplanted in the hopes and affections of his father by the birth of Isaac, through whom the promises were to descend. This event made it necessary to remove the unhappy female and her child, who were accordingly sent forth to seek their fortune in some of the surrounding unoccupied districts. A small supply of provisions, and a bottle of water on her shoulder, was all she carried from the tent of her master. Directing her steps towards her native country, she wandered with the lad in the wilderness of Beer-sheba, which was destitute of springs. Here her stock failed, and it seemed impossible to avoid perishing by hunger or thirst. She resigned herself to her melancholy prospects, but the feelings of the mother were more acute than the agonies of want and despair. Unable to witness her son's death, she laid him under one of the shrubs, took an affecting leave of him, and retired to a distance. "And she went, and sat her down over against him, a good way off, as it were a bow-shot; for she said, Let me not see the death of the child. And she sat over against him, and lifted up her voice and wept." (Gen. xxi. 16.) At this moment an angel directed her to a well of water close at hand,—a discovery to which they owed the preservation of their lives. A promise formerly given was renewed, that sh mael was to become a great nation—that he was to be a wild man—his hand against every man, and every man's hand against him. The travellers continued their journey to the wilderness of Paran, and there took up their residence. In due time the lad grew to manhood, and greatly distinguished himself as an archer, and his mother took him a wife out of her own land. Here the sacred narrative breaks off abruptly, the main object of Moses being to follow the history of Abraham's descendants through the line of Isaac. The Arabs, in their version of Ishmael's history, have mixed a great deal of romance with the narrative of Scripture. They assert that al-Ḥijāz was the district where he settled, and that Makkah, then an arid wilderness, was the identical spot where his life was providentially saved, and where Hagar died and was buried. The well pointed out by the angel, they believe to be the famous Zamzam, of which all pious Muslims drink to this day. They make no allusion to his alliance with the Egyptian woman, by whom he had twelve sons (Gen. xxv. 12–18), the chiefs of as many nations, and the possessors of separate towns; but as polygamy was common in his age and country, it is not improbable he may have had more wives than one.

It was, say they, to commemorate the miraculous preservation of Ishmael that God commanded Abraham to build the Ka'bah, and his son to furnish the necessary materials.

Muḥammadan writers give the following account of Ishmael and his descendants:—Ishmael was constituted the prince and first high-priest of Makkah, and, during half a century he preached to the incredulous Arabs. At his death, which happened forty-eight years after that of Abraham, and in the 137th of his age, he was buried in the tomb of his mother Hagar. Between the erection of the Ka'bah and the birth of their Prophet, the Arabs reckon about 2,740 years. Ishmael was succeeded in the regal and sacerdotal office by his eldest son Nebat, although the pedigree of Muḥammad is traced from Kedar, a younger brother. But his family did not long enjoy this double authority; for, in progress of time, the Jurhumites seized the government and the guardianship of the temple, which they maintained about 300 years. These last, again, having corrupted the true worship, were assailed, as a punishment of their crimes, first by the scimitars of the Ishmaelites, who drove them from Makkah, and then by divers maladies, by which the whole race finally perished. Before quitting Makkah, however, they committed every kind of sacrilege and indignity. They filled up the Zamzam well, after having thrown into it the treasures and sacred utensils of the temple, the black stone, the swords and cuirasses of Qala'ah, the two golden gazelles presented by one of the kings of Arabia, the sacred image of the ram substituted for Isaac, and all the precious movables, forming at once the object and the workmanship of a superstitious devotion. For several centuries the posterity of Ishmael kept possession of the supreme dignity.

The following is the list of chiefs who are said to have ruled the Ḥijāz, and to have been the lineal ancestors of Muḥammad, as far as 'Adnān:—

A.D. 538 'Abdu 'llāh, the father of Muḥammad.
505 'Abdu 'l-Muṭṭalib.
472 Hāshim.
439 'Abd Manāf.
406 Quṣaiy.
373 Kilāb.
340 Murrah.
307 Ka'ab.
274 Luwaiy.
241 Ghālib.
208 Fihr or Quraish.
175 Mālik.
142 an-Naẓr.
109 Kinānah.
76 Khuzaimah.
43 Mudrikah.
10 al-Ya's.
B.C. 23 Muẓar.
56 Nizār.
89 Ma'add.
122 'Adnān.

The period between Ishmael and 'Adnān is variously estimated, some reckoning forty, others only seven, generations. The authority of Abu 'l-Fidā, who makes it ten, is that generally followed by the Arabs, being founded on a tradition of one of Muḥammad's wives. Making every allowance, however, for patriarchal longevity, even forty generations are insufficient to extend over a space of nearly 2,500 years. From 'Adnān to Muḥammad the genealogy is considered certain, comprehending twenty-one generations, and nearly

160 different tribes, all branching off from the same parent stem.

(See *Abū 'l-Fidā*; Gagnier's *Vie de Mahomet*; Pocock, *Specim. Arab. Hist.*; Saiyid Ahmad Khān's *Essays*; Sale's *Koran*, Prelim. Dis; Crichton's *Hist. Arabia*.)

ARABIC. *Lisānu-'l-'Arab; Lughatu 'l-'Arab.* The classical language of Arabia is held to be the language of the Qur'ān, and of the Traditions of Muḥammad, and by reason of its incomparable excellence is called اللغة *al-lughah*, or "the language." (See Qur'ān, Sūrah xvi. 105, "They say, Surely a person teacheth him [*i.e.* Muḥammad]. But the tongue of him at whom they hint is foreign, while this [*i.e.* the Qur'ān] is plain Arabic.")

This classical language is often termed, by the Arabians themselves, the language of Ma'add, and the language of Muẓar, and is a compound of many sister dialects, very often differing among themselves, which were spoken throughout the whole of the Peninsula before the religion of Muḥammad incited the nation to spread its conquering armies over foreign countries. Before that period, feuds among the tribes, throughout the whole extent of their territory, had prevented the blending of their dialects into one uniform language; but this effect of disunion was counteracted in a great measure by the institution of the sacred months, in which all acts of hostility were most strictly interdicted, and by the annual pilgrimage, and the yearly fair held at 'Ukāẓ, at which the poets of the various tribes contended for the meed of general admiration.

Qatādah says that the Quraish tribe used to cull what was most excellent in the dialects of Arabia, so that their dialect became the best of all. This assertion, however, is not altogether correct, for many of the children of the tribe of Quraish, in the time of Muḥammad, were sent into the desert to be there nursed, in order to acquire the utmost chasteness of speech. Muḥammad himself was sent to be brought up among the tribe of Sa'd ibn Bakr ibn Hawāzin, descendants of Muẓar, but not in the line of Quraish; and he is said to have urged the facts of his being a Quraish, and having also grown up among the tribe of Sa'd, as the grounds of his claim to be the most chaste in speech of the Arabs. Certain it is that the language of Ma'add was characterised by the highest degree of perfection, copiousness, and uniformity, in the time of Muḥammad, although it afterwards declined.

The language of the Qur'ān is universally acknowledged to be the most perfect form of Arabic speech. At the same time we must not forget that the acknowledged claims of the Qur'ān to be the direct utterance of the Divinity have made it impossible for any Muslim to criticise the work, and it has become the standard by which other literary compositions have to be judged. (See Lane's Introduction to his *Arabic Dictionary*, and Palmer's *Qur'ān*.)

ARABIC LEXICONS. The first Arabic lexicon is that which is generally ascribed to al-Khalīl, and entitled *Kitābu'l 'Ain.* The following are the most celebrated Arabic dictionaries composed after the *'Ain.*

The *Jamharah*, by Ibn Duraid, died A.H. 321.

The *Tahẕīb*, by al-Azharī, died A.H. 370.

The *Muḥīṭ*, by the Ṣāḥib Ibn 'Abbād, died A.H. 385.

The *Mujmal*, by Ibn Fāris, died A.H. 395.

The *Ṣiḥāḥ*, by al-Jauharī, died A.H. 398.

The *Jāmi'*, by al-Qazzāz, died A.H. 412.

The *Mū'ab*, by Abū Ghālib, died A.H. 436.

The *Muḥkam*, by Ibn Sīdah, died A.H. 458.

The *Asās*, by az-Zamakhsharī, died A.H. 538.

The *Mughrib*, by al-Muṭarrizī, died A.H. 610.

The *'Ubāb*, by aṣ-Ṣāghānī, died A.H. 660.

The *Lisānu 'l-'Arab*, by Ibn Mukarram, died A.H. 711.

The *Tahẕību 't-Tahẕīb*, by Maḥmūd at-Tanūkhi, died A.H. 723.

The *Miṣbāḥ*, by Aḥmad ibn Muḥammad al-Faiyūmī, compiled A.H. 734.

The *Mughni 'l-Labīb*, by Ibn Hishām, died A.H. 761.

The *Qāmūs*, by al-Fairūzābādī, died A.H. 816.

The *Ṣiḥāḥ* (says Mr. Lane in his Preface to his Dictionary), is among the books of lexicology like the *Ṣaḥīḥ of Al-Bukhārī* amongst the books of traditions; for the point on which turns the title to reliance is not the copiousness of the collection, but the condition of genuineness and correctness.

Two well-known dictionaries, compiled in modern times in Hindustān, are the *Ghiyāṣu 'l-Lughat*, by Maulawī Ghiyāṣu 'd-dīn of Rāmpūr, and the *Muntaha 'l-'Arab*, by 'Abdu 'r-Raḥīm ibn 'Abdu 'l-Karīm of Ṣafīpūr. These are both Arabic and Persian lexicons.

The Arabic-Latin dictionary of Jacob Golius, was printed at Leyden, A.D. 1653; that of Freytag at Halle, A.D. 1830-35.

The Arabic-English and English-Arabic dictionaries extant are—

Richardson's Persian-Arabic-English, A.D. 1777.

Richardson's English-Persian-Arabic, A.D. 1810.

Francis Johnson's Persian-Arabic-English, A.D. 1852.

Catafago's Arabic-English and English-Arabic, new edition, 1873.

Lane's Arabic-English, A.D. 1863 to 1882, imperfect.

Dr. Badger's English-Arabic, A.D. 1881.

Dr. Steingass's English-Arabic, A.D. 1882.

AL-A'RĀF (الاعراف). (1) The partition between heaven and hell, described in the Qur'ān, Sūrah vii. 44, "Betwixt the two (heaven and hell) there is a partition; and on al-A'rāf are men who know all by their marks; and they shall cry out to the inhabitants of Paradise, 'Peace be upon you!' (but) they have not (yet) entered it, although they so desire. And when their sight is turned towards the dwellers in the Fire, they say, 'O our Lord, place us not with the unjust people.'" According to Sale, *al-A'rāf* is derived from the verb *'arafa*, which signifies "to distinguish between things, or to part them"; though some commentators give another reason for the imposition of this name, because, say they, those who stand on this partition will *know* and *distinguish* the blessed from the damned by their respective marks or characteristics: and others say the word properly intends anything that is *elevated*, as such a wall of separation must be supposed to be. Some imagine it to be a sort of *limbo* for the patriarchs and prophets, or for the martyrs and those who have been most eminent for sanctity. Others place here those whose good and evil works are so equal that they exactly counterpoise each other, and therefore deserve neither reward nor punishment; and these, say they, will on the last day be admitted into Paradise, after they shall have performed an act of adoration, which will be imputed to them as a merit, and will make the scale of their good works to preponderate. Others suppose this intermediate space will be a receptacle for those who have gone to war, without their parents' leave, and therein suffered martyrdom; being excluded from Paradise for their disobedience, and escaping hell because they are martyrs. (2) The title of Sūrah vii. (3) A term used by Ṣūfī mystics to express a condition of the mind and soul when meditating on the existence of God in all things.

'ARAFAH (عرفة). The vigil of the 'Idu 'l-Azḥā, or Feast of Sacrifice, when the pilgrims proceed to Mount 'Arafāt. ['IDU 'L-AZHA.]

'ARAFĀT (عرفات), or *'Arafah.* The "Mount of Recognition," situated twelve miles from Makkah; the place where the pilgrims stay on the ninth day of the pilgrimage, and recite the mid-day and afternoon prayers, and hear the Khuṭbah or sermon. Hence it is a name given to the ninth day of the month Ẕu 'l-Ḥijjah. Upon the origin of the name given to this mountain, Burton says, "The Holy Hill owes its name to the following legend:—When our first parents forfeited heaven for eating wheat, which deprived them of their primeval purity, they were cast down upon earth. The serpent descended upon Ispahān, the peacock at Cābul; Satan at Bilbays (others say Semnān or Seistān), Eve upon 'Arafāt, and Adam at Ceylon (Sarandib). The latter, determining to seek his wife, began a journey, to which the earth owes its present mottled appearance. Wherever our first father placed his foot, which was large, a town afterwards arose; and between the strides will always be country. Wandering for many years, he came to the Mountain of Mercy, where our common mother was continually calling upon his name, and their *recognition* of each other gave the place the name of *'Arafah.*"

ARĀẒI (اراضى). *Lit.* "lands"; the sale of lands. Tombs are not included in the sale of lands. A place or station for casting the harvest is not considered to be amongst the rights and advantages of land, and therefore does not enter into the sale of it. (Baillie's *Law of Sale*, pages 54, 55.) [LAND.]

ARCHITECTURE. The term *Saracenic* is usually applied by English writers to Muḥammadan architecture. But though the style may be traced to the Arabians, they cannot themselves be considered the inventors of it. They had, in fact, no distinctive style of their own when they made their rapid conquests, but adapted existing styles of architecture to meet the religious and national feelings of the Muslims.

Muḥammad built a mosque at al-Madīnah, but it was an exceedingly simple structure, and he left no directions in the Qur'ān or in the Traditions on the subject.

The typical varieties of the earlier Muḥammadan architecture are those which appeared in Spain and in Egypt; its later form appeared in Constantinople. The oldest specimen of Saracenic architecture in Spain is the mosque of Cordova, which now serves as the cathedral of the city. It was commenced by the Khalīfah 'Abdu 'r-Raḥmān, 786 A.D.,

IN THE SANCTUARY OF THE CATHEDRAL OF CORDOVA.

with the avowed intention that it should be the finest mosque in the world, and Byzantine architects are said to have been specially invited to superintend its construction.

The earliest of the Muḥammedan buildings in Egypt, of which any portions still remain, is the Mosque of 'Amr at old Cairo, begun about A.D. 642, but greatly altered or rebuilt about sixty years later.

On the capture of Constantinople, St. Sophia was converted by the Muslim conquerors into their chief Mosque, and made their architectural model. The older Saracenic style, as seen at Cordova and old Cairo, continued to be the basis of the new, but it was modified throughout by Byzantine influence. In Persia we may clearly trace in Muḥammadan buildings the older Persian type, and in India

IN S. SOPHIA, CONSTANTINOPLE.

the Saracenic architects showed the same pliancy in adopting the styles of the various peoples amongst whom they settled. It thus happens (says Fergusson, in his *History of Indian Architecture*), that we have at least twelve or fifteen different styles of Muḥammadan architecture in Central Asia and in India.

IN THE TAJ MAHALL, AGRA.

A striking and distinctive feature in early Muḥammadan architecture is the horse-shoe arch, which in time gives way to a cusped or scalloped arch, strictly so termed, the outline being produced by intersecting semi-arches. Another variety of Saracenic arch is the circular-headed and stilted form. The pillars are commonly of exceedingly slender proportions, almost to apparent insecurity; but owing to the style of the embellishment, this lightness

IN THE MOTI MASJID, AGRA.

of particular forms tends to heighten the general luxuriance. Some have imagined that this element of slenderness in regard to pillars indicates a tent origin of the style. This tent-like character has been further kept up by concave ceilings and cupolas, emblazoned with painting and gilding. Decorations composed of animal and human figures, being interdicted by Muḥammadan law [PICTURES] are not found in Saracenic architecture; but their geometrical patterns exhibit singular beauty and complexity, inexhaustible variety of combinations, and a wonderful degree of harmonious intricacy, arising out of very simple elements. Lattice or open trellis

EARLY PATHAN STYLE IN THE QUTB BUILDINGS AT DELHI.

work is another fertile source of embellishment, and is similar to the tracery met with in Gothic buildings. Another characteristic of Saracenic style is that of the dome. For the most part domes occur in mosques and tombs, and are of Byzantine origin. Minarets are also a special feature in Muḥammadan mosques, and contribute much to the picturesqueness of these buildings. They are found in mosques of the later Saracenic style. (See Fergusson's *Indian and Eastern Architec-*

IN A HOUSE IN PESHAWAR.

ture, Mr. Owen Jones's *Alhambra Palace*, Hersemer's *Arabische Bauverzierungen*.)

‘ARĪYAH (عرية). A kind of sale permitted in Islām, namely, when a person computes what quantity of fruit there is on a tree and sells it before it is plucked. (*Mishkāt*, xii. c. v.)

‘ĀRĪYAH (عارية). (1) A loan for the use of anything of which *Qarẓ* cannot be made: *e.g.* the loan of a horse is *‘Āriyah*; the loan of money is *Qarẓ*. (2) A gift, of which the following is an example:—A person makes a gift to another of the dates of a palm-tree in his garden; but having afterwards some doubt of the propriety of that person coming daily to his garden where his family usually are, and being at the same time unwilling to depart from his promise, or to retract his gift, he gives some of the dates that have already been pulled in lieu of those upon the tree. (Baillie's *Law of Sale*, p. 300.)

ARK, NOAH'S (فلك نوح). It is mentioned in the history of the Deluge, as recorded in the Qur'ān, in two places—Sūrah xi. 39, "Build the ark under our eye and after our revelation," and Sūrah xxiii 27. There is also supposed to be an allusion to the ark in Sūrah xxxvi. 41, "And a sign to them is that we bare their offspring in the laden ship."

Al-Baiẓāwī says that Noah was two years building the ark, which was 300 cubits long, 50 wide, and 30 broad, and which was made of Indian plane-tree; that it consisted of three storeys, the lowest for beasts, the middle for men and women (who were separated from each other), and the highest for birds.

The ark is said to have rested on the mountain al-Jūdī. [NOAH.]

ARK OF THE COVENANT. The Hebrew word for "Ark" is תֵּבָה (*i.e.* a chest, a coffer), Chald. תֵּיבוּתָא, Arabic تابوت, تابوة. See Qur'ān, Sūrah ii. 249, "The sign of his (Saul's) kingdom is that there shall come unto you the ark (*Tābūt*); in it shall be security (*or* the Shechinah, *sakīnah*, Heb. שְׁכִינָה) from your Lord, and the relics of what the family of Moses and the family of Aaron left; the angels shall bear it." Jalālu 'd-dīn says this ark contained the images of the prophets, and was sent down from heaven to Adam, and at length came to the Israelites, who put great confidence therein, and continually carried it in front of their army, till it was taken by the Amalekites. But on this occasion the angels brought it back in the sight of all the people, and placed it at the feet of Saul (*Ṭālūt*), who was thereupon unanimously received as king.

ARMS, The Sale of. The sale of armour or warlike stores to rebels, or in their camp, is forbidden, because selling arms into the hands of rebels is an assistance to defection. But it is not forbidden to sell the materials for making arms to such persons. (Hamilton's *Hidāyah*, vol. ii. 225.)

ARSH (ارش). (1.) A legal term for compensation. (2.) A mulct; a fine; particularly that which is paid for shedding of blood. (3.) A gift for conciliating the favour of a judge; a bribe. (4.) Whatever a purchaser receives from a seller after discovering a fault in the article bought.

‘ARSH (عرش). The term used in the Qur'ān for the throne of God. Sūrah ix. 131, "He is the Lord of the *mighty throne*." Husainī, the commentator, says the throne has 8,000 pillars, and the distance between each pillar is 3,000,000 miles.

‘AṢABAH (عصبة). A legal term for male relatives by the father's side, agnates.

ĀṢAF (آصف). The *wazīr* or prime minister of Solomon. Alluded to in the Qur'ān, Sūrah xxvii. 40, as "He with whom was knowledge of the scripture." Muḥammadan commentators say he was the son of Barkhīya.

AṢAR (اثر). Relating; handing down by tradition. Generally used for a Ḥadīṣ related by one of the Companions, as distinguished from one of the Prophet's own.

AL-AṢARU 'SH-SHARĪF (الاثر الشريف). The sacred relic. A hair of either the beard or mustachios of Muḥammad, or a foot-print of the Prophet. One of these sacred relics (a hair of his beard) is exhibited in the great mosque at Delhi, another in a mosque in Cashmere.

AṢḤĀB (اصحاب), pl. of *Ṣāḥib*. The Companions or Associates of Muḥammad.

The term used for a single companion is *ṣaḥābī*. Concerning the title of "Companion," there is considerable controversy as to the persons to whom it can be applied. Sa'īd ibn al-Musaiyab reckoned none a "Companion," but those who had been a year or more with Muḥammad, and had gone on a warlike expedition with him. Some say that everyone who had attained puberty, had embraced Islām, and had seen the Prophet, was a "Companion," even though he had attended Muḥammad but an hour. Others, however, affirm that none could be a "Companion" unless Muḥammad chose him and he chose Muḥammad, and he adhered to the Prophet at all times. The general opinion is that every one who embraced Islām, saw the Prophet, and accompanied him, even for a short time, was a "Companion."

It is related that the Prophet marched to Makkah with 10,000 Muslims, to Ḥunain with 12,000, and that 40,000 accompanied him on the farewell pilgrimage. The number of the "Companions" at his death is said to have been 144,000.

In point of merit, the refugees (*Muhājirūn*) are more worthy than the auxiliaries (*Anṣār*); but by way of precedence, the auxiliaries are more worthy than the later refugees.

The "Companions" have been arranged in thirteen classes, which are given by Abū 'l-Fidā as follows:—1. Those who first embraced Islām, such as Khadījah, 'Alī, Zaid, and Abū Bakr, and those who did not delay till he had established his mission. II. The Companions who believed in him after his mission had been fully established, amongst whom was 'Umar. III. Those who fled to Abyssinia. IV. The first Companions of 'Aqabah, who preceeded the Auxiliaries. V. The second Companions of 'Aqabah. VI. The third Companions of 'Aqabah, who were seventy. VII. The refugees who went to the Prophet after his flight, when he was at Qubā, before the erection of the temple. VIII. The soldiers of the great battle of Badr. IX. Those who joined Islām between Badr and Hudaibiyah. X. Those who took the oath of fealty under the acacia tree at Hudaibiyah. XI. Those who joined after the treaty of Hudaibiyah, but before the conquest. XII. Those that embraced Islām on the day of conquest. XIII. Those who were children in the time of the Prophet, and had seen him.

Muḥammad frequently commended the "Companions," and spoke of their excellences and virtues, a chapter in the Traditions being devoted to this subject. (*Mishkāt*, xxiv. c. xiii.) He is related to have said, "My companions are like stars by which roads are found, for which ever companion you follow you will find the right road."

AL-AṢḤĀBU 'L-FĪL (اصحاب الفيل). "The Companions of the Elephant." A term used in the Chapter of the Elephant, or the cvth Sūrah:—"Hast thou not seen how thy Lord dealt with the *companions of the elephant*? Did He not cause their stratagem to miscarry? And He sent against them birds in flocks, small stones did they hurl down upon them, and he made them like stubble eaten down!"

This refers to the army of Abrahah, the Christian king of Abyssinia and Arabia Felix, said to have been lost, in the year of Muḥammad's birth, in an expedition against Makkah for the purpose of destroying the Ka'bah. This army was cut off by small-pox, and there is no doubt, as the Arabic word for small-pox also means "small stones," in reference to the hard gravelly feeling of the pustules, what is the true interpretation of the fourth verse of this Sūrah, which, like many other poetical passages in the Qur'ān, has formed the starting point for the most puerile and extravagant legends.

AṢḤĀBU 'L-KAHF (اصحاب الكهف). "The Companions of the Cave," *i.e.* the Seven Sleepers, mentioned in the Sūratu 'l-kahf, or Chapter xviii. of the Qur'ān. The story, as told by early Christian writers, is given by Gibbon (*Rise and Fall*, Chapter xxxi.). When the Emperor Decius persecuted the Christians, seven noble youths of Ephesus are said to have concealed themselves in a cave in the side of a mountain, where they were doomed to perish by the tyrant, who gave orders that the entrance should be firmly secured with a pile of huge stones. They immediately fell into a deep slumber, which was miraculously prolonged, without injuring the powers of life, during a period of 187 years. This popular tale, which Muḥammad must have heard when he drove his camels to the fairs of Syria, is introduced into the Qur'ān as a divine revelation.

AṢḤĀBU 'Ṣ-ṢUFFAH (اصحاب الصفة). "The sitters on the bench" of the temple at Makkah. They are thus described by Abū 'l-Fidā: "They were poor strangers, without friends or place of abode, who claimed the promises of the Apostle of God and implored his protection. Thus the porch of the temple became their mansion, and thence they obtained their name. When Muḥammad went to meals, he used to call some of them to partake with him; and he selected others to eat with his companions."

'ASHARAH MUBASHSHARAH (عشرة مبشرة). "The ten who received glad tidings." Ten of the most distinguished of Muḥammad's followers, whose certain entrance into Paradise he is said to have foretold. They are Abū Bakr, 'Umar, Usmān, 'Alī, Ṭalḥah, az-Zubair, 'Abdu 'r-Raḥmān, Sa'd-ibn-Abū-Waqqāṣ, Sa'īd ibn Zaid, Abū 'Ubaidah ibn al-Jarrāḥ. (*Mishkāt*, book xxiv. c. xx., part ii.) Muḥammad declared it presumption for anyone to count upon an entrance into heaven with absolute certainty, but he made an exception in favour of these ten distinguished persons.

AL-ASH'ARĪYAH (الاشعرية). A sect formed by Abu 'l-Ḥasan 'Alī ibn Ismā'īl al-Ash'arī, born A.H. 260 (A.D. 873–4).

They hold that the attributes of God are distinct from His essence, yet in such a way as to forbid any comparison being made between God and His creatures. They say they are not "*'ain* nor *ghair*:" not of His essence, nor distinct from it: *i.e.* they cannot be compared with any other things. They also hold that God has one eternal will, from which proceed all things, the good and the evil, the useful and the hurtful. The destiny of man was written on the eternal table before the world was created. So far they go with the Ṣifātīs, but in order to preserve the moral responsibility of man, they say that he has power to convert will into action. But this power cannot create anything new, for then God's sovereignty would be impaired; so they say that God in His providence so orders matters that whenever "a man desires to do a certain thing, good or bad, the action corresponding to the desire is, there and then, created by God, and, as it were, fitted on to the desire." Thus it seems as if it came naturally from the will of the man, whereas it does not. This action is called *Kasb* (acquisition), because it is acquired by a special creative act of God. It is an act directed to the obtaining of profit or the removing of injury: the term is therefore inapplicable to the Deity. Abū Bakr al-Bakillānī, a disciple of al-Ash'arī, says: 'The essence or substance of the action is the effect of the power of God, but its being an action of obedience, such as prayer, or an action of disobedience, such as fornication, are qualities of the action, which proceed from the power of man." The Imām Al-Ḥaramain (A.H. 419-478) held "that the actions of men were effected by the power which God has created in man." Abū Ishaq al-Isfarāyinī says: "That which maketh impression, or hath influence on action, is a compound of the power of God and the power of man." They also believe that the word of God is eternal, though they acknowledge that the vocal sounds used in the Qur'ān, which are the manifestation of that word, are created. They say, in short, that the Qur'ān contains (1) the eternal word which existed in the essence of God before time was; and (2) the word which consists of sounds and combinations of letters. This last they call the created word.

Thus Al-Ash'arī traversed the main positions of the Mutazilites, denying that man can, by the aid of his reason alone, rise to the knowledge of good and evil. He must exercise no judgment, but accept all that is revealed. He has no right to apply the moral laws which affect men to the actions of God. It cannot be asserted by the human reason that the good will be rewarded or the bad punished in a future world. Man must always approach God as a slave, in whom there is no light or knowledge to judge of the actions of the Supreme. Whether God will accept the penitent sinner or not cannot be asserted, for He is an absolute Sovereign, above all law. (Sale, from *Ibn Khaldun*; *Die Mu'taziliten oder die Freidenker in Islām*, von H. Steiner, 1865; *Zur Geschichte Abu 'l-Ḥasan al-ash'arish*, von W. Spitta, 1876; *De Strijd over het Dogma in den Islām tot op El-ash'arī*, door Dr. M. Th. Houtsma, Leiden, 1875; and *Exposé de la Réforme de l'Islamisme*, by M. A. F. Mehren Leiden, 1878.)

'ĀSHŪRĀ (عاشوراء). *Lit.* "the tenth." A voluntary fast day, observed on the tenth of the month of Muḥarram. It is related that Muḥammad observed it, and said it was a day respected by Jews and Christians. (*Mishkāt*, vii. c. vii. 1.)

It is the only day of Muḥarram observed by the Sunnī Muslims, being the day on which it is said God created Adam and Eve, heaven and hell, the tablet of decree, the pen, life, and death. It is kept by the Sunnīs as a fast. [MUHARRAM.]

ĀSIYAH (آسية). The wife of Pharaoh. One of the four perfect women (the Virgin Mary, Khadījah, and Fāṭimah, being the other three). See *Mishkātu 'l-Maṣābīḥ*, xxiv. c. 22. She is mentioned in the Qur'ān (Sūrah lxvi. 11): "And God striketh out a parable for those who believe: the wife of Pharaoh, when she said, 'My Lord, build for me a house with Thee in Paradise, and save me from Pharaoh and his works, and save me from the unjust people."

AṢL (اصل). Cause, first principle, foundation. *Aṣl-wafar'*, "cause and effect," "fundamental and derivative principle."

ASMĀ'U 'LLĀH (آسماء الله). [GOD, NAMES OF.]

'AṢR (عصر). The afternoon prayer. [PRAYERS.] The title of the CIIIrd Sūrah of the Qur'ān.

ASS. According to the Imām Abū Ḥanīfah, the ass is an unclean animal, and its flesh and milk are unlawful; nor is *zakāt* to be given on an ass. (Hamilton's *Hidāyah*, vol. i. 16, iv. 74, 86.)

ASSISTANTS. [ANSAR.]

ASTROLOGY. Arabic *'Ilmu 'n-nujūm.* Qatādah says, referring to the Qur'ān, that God has created stars for three uses: (1) as an ornament to the heavens (Sūrah lxvii. 5); (2) to stone the Devil with (Sūrah lxvii. 5); and (3) to direct travellers through the forests and on the sea (Sūrah xv. 16). Muḥammad condemns those who study the stars for any other purpose (*Mishkāt*, xxi. c. iii. pt. iii.), and consequently the science of Astrology is not considered lawful in Islām.

ASWAD (الاسود). An impostor who, in the time of Muḥammad, claimed the prophetic office. His name was 'Aihalah ibn Ka'b, and he belonged to the tribe of 'Aus, of which he was an influential chief. He was surnamed *Zu 'l-Ḥimār*, or "The Master of the Ass,"* because he used

* But another reading is *Zu 'l-Khimār*, or, "He with the veil."

frequently to say, "The master of the ass is coming unto me," and pretended to receive his revelations from two angels, named Suhaik and Shuraik. Being a good hand at legerdemain, and having a smooth tongue, he gained mightily on the multitude by the strange feats which he shewed them, and the eloquence of his discourse. By these means he greatly increased his power, and having made himself master of Najrān and the territory of Ṭā'if, on the death of Bādhān, the governor of Yaman for Muḥammad, he seized that province also, killing Shahr, the son of Bādhān, and taking to wife his widow Āzād, whose father he had also slain. The news being brought to Muḥammad, he sent to his friends and to the tribe of Hamdān, a party of whom conspiring with Qais ibn 'Abd Yaghūth, who bore Aswad a grudge, and with Fīrūz and Aswad's wife, broke by night into his house, where Fīrūz surprised him and cut off his head. While dying, it is said that he roared like a bull, at which his guards came to the chamber door, but were sent away by his wife, who told them that the prophet was only agitated by the divine inspiration. This was done the very night before Muḥammad died. The next morning the conspirators caused the following proclamation to be made, viz. "I bear witness that Muḥammad is the Apostle of God, and that 'Aihala is a liar"; and letters were immediately sent away to Muḥammad, with an account of what had been done; but a messenger from heaven outstripped them, and acquainted the prophet with the news, which he imparted to his Companions a little before his death, the letters themselves not arriving till Abū Bakr was chosen Khalif. It is said that Muḥammad on his occasion told those who attended him that before the Day of Judgment thirty more impostors, besides Musailimah and Aswad, should appear. The whole time from the beginning of Aswad's rebellion to his death was four months.

ATHEIST. [DAHRI.]

'ATĪRAH (عتيرة). The sacrifice offered by the idolatrous Arabs in the month of Rajab. It was allowed by the Prophet at the commencement of his mission, but was afterwards abolished. *Mishkāt*, book iv. c. 50, "Let there be no Fara' nor 'Atīrah."

AT-TAḤĪYĀT (التحيات). *Lit.* "the greetings." A part of the stated prayers, recited after the *Takbīru 'l-Qu'ūd*, after every two *rak'ahs*. It is recited whilst the worshipper kneels upon the ground. His left foot bent under him, he sits upon it, and places his hands upon his knees, and says:— "The adorations (*i.e. at-taḥīyātu*) of the tongue are for God, and also of the body and of alms-giving. Peace be on thee, O Prophet, with the mercy of God and His blessing. Peace be upon us, and upon God's righteous servants." (*Mishkāt*, iv., c. xvi.) [PRAYER.]

AUGURY. [FA'L.]

AULĪYĀ (اولياء), pl. of *walī*. "Favourites of God." The expression occurs in the Qurān in the following verse, "Are not the favourites of God those on whom no fear shall come, nor shall they be put to grief?" (Sūrah x. 63).

AUTĀD (اوتاد). *Lit.* "props or pillars." A term used by the Ṣūfīs for the four saints, by whom the four corners of the world are said to be supported.

A'ŪẔU BILLĀH (اعوذ بالله). Another name for the Ta'auwuẕ, or the prayer in the daily liturgy: "I seek refuge with God from the cursed Satan." [PRAYER.]

AVENGER OF BLOOD. In the Muḥammadan law, as in the Jewish, the punishment for wilful murder is left to the next of kin; but in the Jewish code the avenger of blood was compelled to take the life of the murderer, whilst in the Muslim code he may accept compensation, *vide* Qur'ān, Sūrah ii. 173, "O believers! retaliation (*Qiṣāṣ*) for blood-shedding is prescribed to you: the free man for the free, and the slave for the slave, and the woman for the woman; but he to whom his brother shall make any remission is to be dealt with equitably; and a payment should be made to him with liberality. This is a relaxation (*i.e.* of the stricter *lex talionis*) from your Lord, and a mercy." [QISAS.]

ĀYAH (آية). *Lit.* "a sign, or miracle." The term used for one of the smaller portions of the chapters of the Qur'ān, which we call verses. The number of verses is often set down after the title of the chapter, but the verses are not marked in the text as they are in our English Bibles. The number of verses in the Qur'ān is variously estimated, but they are generally said to be about six thousand two hundred. [QUR'AN.]

AL-A'YĀNU 'S-ṢĀBITAH (الاعيان الثابتة), pl. of *'ayn*, in the sense of "the essence" of a thing. The established essences. A term used by the Ṣūfī mystics to express figures emblematic of the names of God. ('Abdu 'r-Razzāq's *Dictionary of Technical Terms of the Ṣūfīs.* Sprenger's edition.)

ĀYATU 'L-FATḤ (اية الفتح). *Lit.* "The verse of victory." The fifty-ninth verse of the Sūratu 'l-An'ām (vi.) of the Qur'ān. The powers of this verse are said to be so great, that if a person constantly recite it he will obtain his desires. It is generally recited with this object forty times after each season of prayer. It is as follows:—"And with Him are the keys of the secret things; none knoweth them but He; and He knoweth whatever is on the land and in the sea; and no leaf falleth but He knoweth it; neither is there a grain in the darknesses of the earth, nor a green thing nor a dry thing, but it is noted in a clear book."

ĀYATU 'L-ḤIFẒ (ايات الحفظ). The verses of protection." Certain verses of the Qur'ān which are usually inscribed on amulets. They are:—Sūrah ii. 256, "And the preservation of both (heaven and earth) is no burden unto Him." Sūrah xii. 64, "God is the best protector." Sūrah xiii. 12, "They guard him by the command of God." Sūrah xv. 17, "We guard him from every devil driven away by stones." Sūrah xxxvii. 7, "A protection against every rebellious devil."

ĀYATU'L-KURSĪ (اية الكرسى). "The verse of the throne." Verse 256 of the Sūratu 'l-Baqarah, or chap. ii. of the Qur'ān. It is related (*Mishkāt*, book iv., c. xix., part iii.) that 'Alī heard Muḥammad say in the pulpit, "that person who repeats the *Āyatu 'l-Kursī* after every prayer, nothing prevents him entering into Paradise but life; and whoever says it when he goes to his bed-chamber, God will keep him in safety, together with his house and the house of his neighbour. The verse is as follows:—"God! There is no God but He; the Living, the Abiding. Neither slumber seizeth Him, nor sleep. To Him belongeth whatsoever is in heaven and whatsoever is in earth. Who is he that can intercede with Him but by His own permission? He knoweth what hath been before them, and what shall be after them; yet nought of His knowledge do they comprehend, save what He willeth. His THRONE reacheth over the heavens and the earth, and the upholding of both burdeneth Him not; and He is the High, the Great."

ĀYATU'L-MAWĀRĪS̤ (اية المواريث). "The verse of inheritances." The twelfth verse of the Sūratu 'n-nisā, or fourth chapter of the Qur'ān. It relates to inheritance, and is the foundation of the Muslim law on the subject. It is given in the article on Inheritance. [INHERITANCE.]

AYIMMATU'L-ASMĀ (ائمة الاسماء). "The leading names." The seven principal names or titles of God, namely:—

Al-Ḥayy . .	The Living.
Al-'Alīm . .	The Knowing.
Al-Murīd . .	The Purposer.
Al-Qādir . .	The Powerful.
As-Samī' . .	The Hearer.
Al-Baṣīr . .	The Seer.
Al-Mutakallim .	The Speaker.

'ĀYISHAH (عايشة). The daughter of Abū Bakr, and the favourite wife of Muḥammad, to whom she was married when only nine years of age. She survived her husband many years, and died at al-Madīnah, A.H. 58 (A.D. 678), aged sixty-seven, and obtained the title of *Ummu 'l-Mu'minīn*, "The Mother of the Believers."

AYMĀN (ايمان), pl. of *Yamīn*. [OATHS.]

AYYĀMU'L-BĪẒ (ايام البيض). "The days of the bright nights," mentioned in the *Mishkāt* (book vii. c. 7, part 3), as days on which Muḥammad did not eat, whether halting or marching. They are the 13th, 14th, and 15th nights of the month. (See Lane's *Dict.*, p. 284.)

AYYĀMU 'L-QARR (ايام القر). The day of rest after the day of sacrifice at the Pilgrimage. [HAJJ.]

AYYĀMU'N-NAḤR (ايام النحر). The season of sacrifice at the Pilgrimage. [HAJJ.]

AYYĀMU'T-TASHRĪQ (ايام التشريق). The three days after the feast of sacrifice at Minā during the Pilgrimage. So called because the flesh of the victims is then *dried*, or because they are not slain until after sun-rise. [HAJJ, PILGRIMAGE.]

AYYIM (ايم). A legal term for a woman having no husband, whether she be a virgin or a widow.

'AẒĀBU'L-QABR (عذاب القبر). "The punishment of the grave." That all persons, whether believers or not, undergo some punishment in their graves, is a fundamental article of the Muslim belief. These punishments are described in the following Ḥadīs̤ on the authority of Abū Hurairah:—

"The Prophet of God said, When a corpse is placed in its grave, two black angels come to it, with blue eyes. The name of the one is *Munkar* and of the other *Nakīr*, and they interrogate the dead person concerning the Prophet of God. If he be a Muslim, he will bear witness to the Unity of God and the mission of Muḥammad. The angels will then say, 'We knew thou wouldst say so'; and the grave will then expand seventy times seventy yards in length, and seventy times seventy in breadth. A light will then be given for the grave, and it will be said, 'Sleep.' Then the dead person will say, 'Shall I return to my brethren and inform them of this?' Then the angels will say, 'Sleep like the bridegroom, till God shall raise thee up from the grave on the Day of Resurrection.' But if the corpse be that of an unbeliever, it will be asked, 'What sayest thou about the Prophet?' and he will reply, 'I know him not.' And then the angels will say, 'We knew thou wouldst say so.' Then the ground will be ordered to close in upon him, and it will break his sides, and turn his right side to his left, and he will suffer perpetual punishment till God raise him therefrom." In another tradition, recorded by 'Anas, it is said, "The wicked will be struck with a rod (*miṭraqah*), and they will roar out, and their cries will be heard by all animals that may be near the grave excepting man and the genii." (*Mishkāt*, book i., c. v.).

All Muhammadan doctors of the orthodox schools (whether we apply the term orthodox to Sunnī or Shī'ah) believe in the literal interpretation of these punishments in the grave, which are said to take place as soon as the funeral party has left the grave-yard. A perusal of the various traditions on the subject must convince any unprejudiced mind that Muḥammad intended to teach a literal interpretation of his sayings on this subject. It is related that on one occasion, when the Prophet was riding through a grave-yard, his mule, hearing the groans of the dead, tried to throw his master. On that occasion, Muhammad said, "If I were not afraid that you would leave off burying, I would ask God to give you the power of hearing what I hear." Shaikh 'Abdu 'l-Ḥaqq, in his commentary on the *Mishkāt*, says, "The accounts which are here given of the punishment of the grave, are undoubtedly true, and they are not either imaginary or figurative." (*Mishkāt*, book i., chap. v.; see Persian edition with 'Abdu 'l-Ḥaqq's commentary.)

AZAL (ازل). Eternity with respect to the past, as distinguished from *abad* (ابد), eternity without end.

AZĀN (اذان). *Lit.* "announcement." The call or summons to public prayers proclaimed by the Mu'azzin (or crier)—in small mosques from the side of the building or at the door, and in large mosques from the minaret.

It is in Arabic as follows:—

الله اكبر – الله اكبر – الله اكبر – الله اكبر – اشهد ان لا اله الا الله – اشهد ان لا اله الا الله – اشهد ان محمدا رسول الله – اشهد ان محمدا رسول الله – حى على الصلوة – حى على الصلوة – حى على الفلاح – حى على الفلاح – الله اكبر – الله اكبر – لا اله الا الله.

Allāhu akbar! Allāhu akbar! Allāhu akbar! Allāhu akbar! Ashhadu an lā ilāha illa 'llāh! Ashhadu an lā ilāha illa 'llāh! Ashhadu anna Muḥammadan rasūlu-llāh! Ashhadu anna Muḥammadan rasūlu-llāh! Ḥayya 'ala 's-ṣalāti! Ḥayya 'ala 's-ṣalāti! Ḥayya 'ala 'l-falāḥ! Ḥayya 'ala 'l-falāḥ! Allāhu akbar! Allāhu akbar! Lā ilāha illa 'llāh!

Which is translated:—

"God is most great! God is most great! God is most great! God is most great! I testify that there is no god but God! I testify that there is no god but God! I testify that Muḥammad is the Apostle of God! I testify that Muḥammad is the Apostle of God! Come to prayer! Come to prayer! Come to salvation! Come to salvation! God is most great! God is most great! There is no god but God!"

In the Azān in the early morning, after the words, "Come to salvation!" is added الصلوة خير من النوم – الصلوة خير من النوم. *Aṣ-ṣalātu khairun mina 'n-naumi! Aṣ-ṣalātu khairun mina 'n-naumi!* "Prayer is better than sleep! Prayer is better than sleep!"

The Shī'ahs make a slight alteration in the Azān, by adding the words, حى على خير العمل – حى على خير العمل *Ḥayya 'alā khairi 'l-'amali! Ḥayya 'alā khairi 'l-'amali!* "Come to the best of works! Come to the best of works!" and by repeating the last sentence of the Azān, "There is no god but God," twice instead of once, as in the Sunnī Azān.

When the Azān is recited, it is usual for men of piety and religious feeling to respond to each call, as, for example, when the Mu'azzin cries:—

"Allāhu akbar! Allāhu akbar! Allāhu akbar! Allāhu akbar!"

Those who hear it repeat:—

"Allāhu akbar! Allāhu akbar! Allāhu akbar! Allāhu akbar!"

The Mu'azzin says—

"I testify that there is no god but God; I testify that there is no God but God."

They reply—

"I testify that there is no God but God; I testify that there is no god but God."

Mu'azzin.—"I testify that Muḥammad is the Apostle of God."

Reply.—"I testify that Muḥammad is the Apostle of God."

Mu'azzin.—"Come to prayer."

Reply.—"I have no power nor strength but from God the most High and Great."

Mu'azzin.—"Come to salvation."

Reply.—"What God willeth will be; what He willeth not willeth not be."

The recital of the Azān must be listened to with great reverence. If a person be walking at the time, he should stand still; if reclining, sit up. Mr. Lane, in his *Modern Egyptians*, says, "Most of the Mu'azzins of Cairo have harmonious and sonorous voices, which they strain to the utmost pitch; yet there is a simple and solemn melody in their chants which is very striking, particularly in the stillness of the night." But Vámbéry remarks that "the Turkistānees most carefully avoid all tune and melody. The manner in which the Azān is cried in the west is here (in Bokhārā) declared sinful, and the beautiful melancholy notes which, in the silent hour of a moonlit evening, are heard from the slender minarets on the Bosphorus, fascinating every hearer, would be listened to by the Bokhariot with feelings only of detestation."

The summons to prayer was at first the simple cry, "Come to public prayer." After the Qiblah was changed, Muḥammad bethought himself of a more formal call. Some suggested the Jewish trumpet, others the Christian bell; but neither was grateful to the Prophet's ear. The Azān, or call to prayer was then established. Tradition claims for it a supernatural origin, thus:—"While the matter was under discussion, 'Abdu 'llāh, a Khazrajite, dreamed that he met a man clad in green raiment, carrying a bell. 'Abdu 'llāh sought to buy it, saying that it would do well for bringing together the assembly of the faithful. "I will show thee a better way," replied the stranger; "let a crier cry aloud, 'God is most great,' &c." Waking from sleep, 'Abdu 'llah proceeded to Muḥammad, and told him his dream. (Muir, from *Kātibu 'l-Wākidī*.) Hishāmi recites the story as if 'Abdu'llāh had actually met the man.

Bingham, in his *Antiquities* (vol. ii., book

viii. chap. vii.), relates that, in the monastery of virgins which Paula, the famous Roman lady, set up and governed at Jerusalem, the signal for prayer was given by one going about and singing "Hallelujah!" for that was their call to church, as St. Jerome informs us.

The Azān is proclaimed before the stated times of prayer, either by one of the congregation, or by the Mu'azzin or crier, who is paid for the purpose. He must stand with his face towards Makkah, with the points of his forefingers in his ears, and recite the formula which has been given above.

It must not be recited by an unclean person, a drunkard, a madman, or a woman.

ĀZAR (آزر). Terah, the father of Abraham. Sūrah, vi. 74, "And when Ābrahīm said to his father Āzar, Takest thou images as gods?"

"The Eastern authors unanimously agree that he was a statuary, or carver of idols; and he is represented as the first who made images of clay, pictures only having been in use before, and taught that they were to be adored as gods. However, we are told his employment was a very honourable one, and that he was a great lord, and in high favour with Nimrod, whose son-in-law he was, because he made his idols for him, and was excellent in his art. Some of the Rabbins say Terah was a priest and chief of the order."—(Sale.)

AL-AZĀRIQAH (الازارقة). A sect of heretics founded by Nāfi' ibn al-Azraq, who say that 'Alī was an infidel, and that his assassin was right in killing him. (See *ash-Shahrastānī*, ed. Cureton, p. ٨٩, Haarbruecker's translation, I., p. 133.

AL-'AZBĀ' (العضباء). The slit-eared; one of Muḥammad's favourite camels.

AL-AẒḤĀ (الاضحى). ['IDU'L-AZHA.]

AL-'AẒĪM (العظيم). One of the ninety-nine special names of God. "The great One."

'AZĪMAH (عزيمة). An incantation. [EXORCISM.]

AL-'AZĪZ (العزيز). One of the ninety-nine special names of God. It frequently occurs in the Qur'ān. It means "the powerful, or the mighty One."

'AZRĀ'ĪL (عزرائيل). The angel of Death. Mentioned in the Qur'ān under the title of *Malaku 'l-Maut*, Sūrah xxxii. 11, "The angel of death who is charged with you shall cause you to die." [MALAKU 'L-MAUT.]

B

BABEL. Arabic بابل *Bābil*. Mentioned once in the Qur'ān, Sūrah ii. 96: "Sorcery did they teach to men, and what had been revealed to the two angels Hārūt and Mārūt at Bābil." Babel is regarded by the Muslims as the fountain-head of the science of magic. They suppose Hārūt and Mārūt to be two angels who, in consequence of their want of compassion for the frailties of mankind, were sent down to earth to be tempted. They both sinned, and, being permitted to choose whether they would be punished now or hereafter, chose the former, and are still suspended by the feet at Babel in a rocky pit, and are the great teachers of magic. (Lane's *Thousand and One Nights*, ch. iii. note 14.) *Vide Tafsīr-i-'Azīzī in loco.*

BĀBU 'L-ABWĀB (باب الابواب). *Lit.* "The door of doors." A term used by the Ṣūfīs for repentance. ('Abdu 'r-Razzāq's *Dictionary of Sufī Terms.*)

BĀBU 'S-SALĀM (باب السلام). "The Gate of Peace." The gateway in the sacred mosque at Makkah through which Muḥammad entered when he was elected by the Quraish to decide the question as to which section of the tribe should lift the Black Stone into its place. It was originally called the Bāb Banī Shaibah, "the Gate of the Banū Shaibah," the family of Shaibah ibn 'Usmān, to whom Muḥammad gave the key of the Ka'bah. Burkhardt says that there are now two gateways called by this name. Burton says, "The Bābu 's-Salām resembles in its isolation a triumphal arch, and is built of cut stone." (Burton's *Pilgrimage*, vol. ii. p. 174. See Muir's *Life of Mahomet*, pp. 28, 29.)

BĀBU 'N-NISĀ, (باب النسا). "The Women's Gate." In later years, as Muḥammad added to the number of his wives, he provided for each a room or house on the same side of the mosque at al-Madīnah. From these he had a private entrance into the mosque, used only by himself, and the eastern gate still bears in its name, Bābu 'n-Nisā', the memory of the arrangement. (Muir's *Life of Mahomet*, iii. p. 20.)

BACKBITING. Anything secretly whispered of an absent person which is calculated to injure him, and which is true, is called *Ghībah*, a false accusation being expressed by *Buhtān*. Abū Hurairah says, "The question was put to the Prophet, 'Do you know what backbiting is?' and he replied, 'It is saying anything bad of a Muslim.' It was then said, 'But what is it if it is true?'

And he said, 'If it is true it is *Ghībah*, and if it is a false accusation, it is *Buhtān* (*i.e.* slander).'" (*Mishkāt*, xxii. c. x.)

The following are sayings of Muḥammad on the subject:—"The best of God's servants are those who when you meet them speak of God. The worst of God's servants are those who carry tales about, to do mischief and separate friends, and seek out the defects of good people." "He who wears two faces in this world shall have two tongues of fire in the day of the Resurrection." "It is unworthy of a believer to injure people's reputations, or to curse anyone, or to abuse anyone, or to talk vainly." "The best atonement you can make for backbiting is to say, 'O God pardon me and him (whom I have injured).'" *Mishkāt*, xxii. c. x.

BADAWĪ (بدوى). A name given to the Bedouin Arabs, or the Arabs of the desert. *Bedouin* is only a corruption of the plural of this word, which is derived from *Badw* = *Bādiyah*, "a desert."

AL-BADĪʻ (البديع) is one of the ninety-nine special names of God. It means "He who originates." It occurs in the Qur'an, Sūrah ii. 111, "He is the wonderful originator of the heavens and the earth; when He decreeth a matter, He doth but say to it, 'Be,' and it is."

BADR, The battle of. Arabic, *Ghazwatu 'l-Badr*. The first battle of Badr was fought in the month of Ramaẓān, A.H. 2 (March, A.D. 624), between Muḥammad and the Quraish. Many of the principal men of the Quraish were slain, including Abū Jahl, whose head was brought to the Prophet, and when it was cast at his feet, he exclaimed, "It is more acceptable to me than the choicest camel of Arabia." After the battle was over, some of the prisoners were cruelly murdered. Ḥusain says the losses of the Quraish at Badr were seventy killed and seventy prisoners. This victory at Badr consolidated the power of Muḥammad, and it is regarded by Muslim historians as one of the most important events of history. An account of this celebrated battle will be found in the article on *Muḥammad*.

The second battle of Badr was a bloodless victory, and took place in the month Ẕu 'l-Qaʻdah, A.H. 4 (April, A.D. 626).

BAḤĪRĀ (بحيرا). A Nestorian monk whom Muḥammad met when he was journeying back from Syria to Makkah, and who is said to have perceived by various signs that he was a prophet. His Christian name is supposed to have been Sergius (or Georgius).

Sprenger thinks that Baḥīrā remained with Muḥammad, and it has been suggested that there is an allusion to this monk in the Qur'ān, Sūrah xvi. 105: "We know that they say, 'It is only a man who teacheth him.'" Ḥusain the commentator says on this passage that the Prophet was in the habit of going every evening to a Christian to hear the Taurāt and Injīl. *Tafsīr-i-Ḥusainī*; Sale, p. 223; Muir's *Life of Mahomet*, p. 72.)

BAḤIRAH (بحيرة). (1.) A she-camel, she-goat or ewe, which had given birth to a tenth young one. (2.) A she-camel, the mother of which had brought forth ten females consecutively before her.

In these and similar cases, the pagan Arabs observed certain religious ceremonies, such as slitting the animal's ear, &c., all of which are forbidden in the Qur'ān: "God hath not ordained any Baḥīrah." (Sūrah v. 102.)

BAIʻ (بيع, pl. بيوع *buyūʻ*). A sale; commercial dealing; barter. *Baiʻ*, or "sale," in the language of the law, signifies an exchange of property for property with the mutual consent of parties. For the rules concerning sales and barter, see Hamilton's *Hidāyah*, vol. ii. 360; Baillie's *Muḥammadan Law of Sale*; *The Fatāwā ʻĀlamgīrī*.

Sale, in its ordinary acceptation, is a transfer of property in consideration of a price in money. The word has a more comprehensive meaning in the Muḥammadan law, and is applied to every exchange of property for property with mutual consent. It, therefore, includes barter as well as sale, and also loan, when the articles lent are intended to be consumed, and replaced to the lender by a similar quantity of the same kind. This transaction, which is truly an exchange of property for property, is termed *qarẓ* in the Muḥammadan law.

Between barter and sale there is no essential distinction in most systems of law, and the joint subject may in general be considerably simplified by being treated of solely as a sale. A course has been adopted in the Muḥammadan law, which obliges the reader to fix his attention on both sides of the contract. This may at first appear to him to be an unnecessary complication of the subject, but when he becomes acquainted with the definition of price, and the rules for the prohibition of excess in the exchange of a large class of commodities, which apply to every form of the contract, he will probably be of opinion that to treat of the subject in any other way would be attended with at least equal difficulties.

The first point which seems to require his attention is the meaning of the word "property" as it occurs in the definition of sale. The original term (*māl*), which has been thus translated, is defined by Muḥammadan lawyers to be "that which can be taken possession of and secured." This definition seems to imply that it is tangible or corporeal, and things or substances are accordingly the proper subjects of sale. Mere rights are not *māl*, and cannot therefore be lawfully sold apart from the corporeal things with which they may happen to be connected. Of such rights one of the most important is the right of a creditor to exact payment of a debt, which is not a proper subject of sale. In other words, debts cannot, by the Muḥammadan law, any more than by the common laws of England and Scotland, be lawfully sold.

Things are commonly divided into moveable and immoveable, the latter comprehending land and things permanently attached to it. But the distinction is not of much importance in the Muḥammadan law, as the transfer of land is in nowise distinguished from that of other kinds of property.

A more important division of things is that into *misli* and *kammī*. The former are things which, when they happen to perish, are to be replaced by an equal quantity of something similar to them; and the latter are things which, in the same circumstances, are to be replaced by their value. These two classes have been aptly styled "similars" and "dissimilars" by Mr. Hamilton, in his translation of the *Hidāyah*. Similars are things which are usually sold or exchanged by weight, or by measurement of capacity, that is, by dry or liquid measure; and dissimilars are things which are not sold or exchanged in either of these ways. Articles which are nearly alike, and are commonly sold or exchanged by number or tale, are classed with the first division of things, and may be termed "similars of tale"; while articles which differ materially from each other, yet are still usually sold or exchanged by number, belong to the second division, and may be called "dissimilars of tale." *Dirhams* and *dīnārs*, the only coined money known to the old Arabs, are included among similars of weight.

Similars of weight and capacity are distinguished in the Muḥammadan law from all other descriptions of property in a very remarkable way. When one article of weight is sold or exchanged for another article of weight, or one of measure is sold or exchanged for another of measure, the delivery of both must be immediate from hand to hand, and any delay of delivery in one of them is unlawful and prohibited. Where, again, the articles exchanged are also of the same kind, as when wheat is sold for wheat, or silver for silver, there must not only be reciprocal and immediate delivery of both before the separation of the parties, but also absolute equality of weight or measure, according as the articles are weighable or measurable, and any excess on either side is also unlawful and prohibited. These two prohibitions constitute in brief the doctrine of *reba*, or "usury," which is a marked characteristic of the Muḥammadan law of sale. The word *reba* properly signifies "excess," and there are no terms in the Muḥammadan law which corresponds to tho words "interest" and "usury," in the sense attached to them in the English language; but it was expressly prohibited by Muḥammad to his followers to derive any advantage from loans, and that particular kind of advantage which is called by us interest, and consists in the receiving back from the borrower a larger quantity than was actually lent to him, was effectually prevented by the two rules above-mentioned. These, like some other principles of Muḥammadan law, are applied with a rigour and minuteness that may to us seem incommensurate with their importance, but are easily accounted for when we know that they are believed to be of divine origin.

Similars of weight and capacity have a common feature of resemblance, which distinguishes them in their own nature from other commodities, and marks with further peculiarity their treatment in the Muḥammadan law. They are aggregates of minute parts, which are either exactly alike, or so nearly resemble each other, that the difference between them may be safely disregarded. For this reason they are usually dealt with in bulk, regard being had only to the whole of a stipulated quantity, and not to the individual parts of which it is composed. When sold in this manner they are said to be indeterminate. They may, however, be rendered specific in several ways. Actual delivery, or production with distinct reference at the time of contract, seems to be sufficient for that purpose in all cases. But something short of this would suffice for all similars but money. Thus, flour, or any kind of grain, may be rendered specific by being enclosed in a sack; or oil, or any liquid, by being put into casks or jars; and though the vessels are not actually produced at the time of contract, their contents may be sufficiently particularised by description of the vessels and their locality. Money is not susceptible of being thus particularised, and *dirhams* and *dīnārs* are frequently referred to in the following pages as things which cannot be rendered specific by description, or specification, as it is more literally termed. Hence, money is said to be always indeterminate. Other similars, including similars of tale, are sometimes specific and sometimes indeterminate. Dissimilars, including those of tale, are always specific.

When similars are sold indeterminately, the purchaser has no right to any specific portion of them until it be separated from a general mass, and marked or identified as the subject of the contract. From the moment of offer till actual delivery, he has nothing to rely upon but the seller's obligation, which may, therefore, be considered the direct subject of the contract. Similars taken indeterminately are accordingly termed *dayn*, or "obligations," in the Muḥammadan law. When taken specifically, they are classed with dissimilars, under the general name of *'ayn*. The literal meaning of this term is "substance or thing"; but when opposed to *dayn* it means something determinate or specific. The subject of traffic may thus be divided into two classes, specific and indeterminate; or, if we substitute for the latter the word "obligation," and omit the word "specific" as unnecessary when not opposed to "indeterminate," these classes may, according to the view of Muḥammadan lawyers, be described as things and obligations.

There is some degree of presumption in using

a word in any other than its ordinary acceptation; and it is not without hesitation that (Mr. Baillie says) I have ventured to employ the word "obligation" to signify indeterminate things. My reasons for doing so are these: first it expresses the exact meaning of the Arabic word *dayn*, and yet distinguishes this use of it from another sense, in which it is also employed in the Muḥammadan law; second, it preserves consistency in the law. Thus, it will be found hereafter that the effect of sale is said to be to induce a right in the buyer to the thing sold, and in the seller to the price, and that this effect follows the contract immediately before reciprocal possession by the contracting parties. Now, it is obvious that this is impossible with regard to things that are indeterminate, if the things themselves are considered the subject of the contract, and cases are mentioned where it is expressly stated that there is no transfer of property to the purchaser, when similars of weight of capacity are sold without being distinctly specified, until actual possession take place. The difficulty disappears if we consider not the thing itself but the obligation to render it to be the subject of contract; for a right to the obligation passes immediately to the purchaser, and the seller may be compelled to perform it. If we now revert to the division of things into similars and dissimilars, money—which, it has been remarked, is always indeterminate—is therefore an obligation; dissimilars, which are always specific, are never obligations; and other similars, except money, being sometimes specific and sometimes indeterminate, are at one time obligations, and at another time things or substances.

Before proceeding farther it is necessary to advert more particularly to the other sense in which the word *dayn* is frequently employed in the Muḥammadan law. It means strictly "obligation," as already observed; but the obligation may be either that of the contracting party himself, or of another. In the former sense *deyn* is not only a proper subject of traffic, but forms the sole subject of one important kind of sale, hereafter to be noticed. But when *dayn* is used to signify the obligation of another than the contracting party, it is not a proper subject of traffic, and, as already observed, cannot be lawfully sold. In the following pages *dayn* has been always translated by the word "debt" when it signifies the obligation of a third party, and generally by the word "obligation," when it signifies the engagement of the contracting party himself, though when the things represented by the obligation are more prominently brought forward, it has sometimes been found necessary to substitute the expression, "indeterminate things."

Though barter and sale for a price, are confounded under one general name in the Muḥammadan law, it is sometimes necessary to consider one of the things exchanged as more strictly the subject of sale, or thing sold, and the other as the price. In this view the former is termed *mabīʿ*, and the latter *Ṣaman*. *Ṣaman*, or "price," is defined to be *dayn fī zimmah*, or, literally, an "obligation in responsibility." From which, unless the expression is a mere pleonasm, it would appear that the word *dayn* is sometimes used abstractly, and in a sense distinct from the idea of liability. That idea, however, is necessary to constitute price; for though cloth, when properly described, may, by reason of its divisibility and the similarity of its parts, be sometimes assumed to perform the function of price in a contract of sale, it is only when it is not immediately delivered, but is to remain for some time on the responsibility of the contracting party, that it can be adopted for that purpose.

It is a general principle of the Muḥammadan law of sale, founded on a declaration of the Prophet, that credit cannot be opposed to credit, that is, that both the things exchanged cannot be allowed to remain on the responsibility of the parties. Hence, it is only with regard to one of them that any stipulation for delay in its delivery is lawful. Price, from its definition above given, admits of being left on responsibility, and accordingly a stipulation for delay in the payment of the price is quite lawful and valid. It follows that a stipulation for delay in the delivery of the things sold cannot be lawful. And this is the case, with the exception of one particular kind of sale, hereafter to be noticed, in which the thing sold is always indeterminate, and the price is paid in advance. It may, therefore, be said of all specific things when the subject of sale, that a stipulation for delay in their delivery is illegal, and would invalidate a sale. The object of this rule may have been to prevent any change of the thing sold before delivery, and the disputes which might in consequence arise between the parties. But if they were allowed to select whichever they pleased of the articles exchanged to stand for the price, and the other for the thing sold, without any regard to their qualities, the object of the last-mentioned rule, whatever it may have been, might be defeated. This seems to have led to another arrangement of things into different classes, according to their capacities for supporting the functions of price or of the thing sold in a contract of sale. The first class comprehends *dirhams* and *dīnārs*, which are always price. The second class comprises the whole division of dissimilars (with the single exception of cloth), which are always the thing sold, or subject of sale, in a contract. The third class comprises, first, all similars of capacity; second, all similars of weight, except *dirhams* and *dīnārs*; and, third, all similars of tale. The whole of this class is capable of supporting both functions, and is sometimes the thing sold, and sometimes the price. The fourth class comprises cloth, and the copper coin called *fulūs*.

Sale implies a reciprocal vesting of the price in the seller and of the thing sold in the purchaser. This, as already remarked, is called its legal effect, and sale may be divided into different stages or degrees of completeness, according as this effect is immediate, suspended, invalid, or obligatory. Thus, sale must first of all be duly constituted or contracted. After that, there may still be some bar to its operation, which occasions a suspension of its effect. This generally arises from a defect of power in the seller, who may not be fully competent to act for himself, or may have insufficient authority, or no authority whatever, over the subject of sale. In this class of sales the effect is dependent on the assent or ratification of some other person than the party actually contracting. But whether the effect of a sale be immediate or suspended, there may be some taint of illegality in the mode of constituting it, or in its subject, or there may be other circumstances connected with it, which render it invalid. The causes of illegality are many and various. But even though a sale should be unimpeachable on the previous grounds, that is, though it should be duly constituted, operative or immediate in its effect, and free from any ground of illegality, still it may not be absolutely binding on the parties. This brings us to another remarkable peculiarity of the Muḥammadan law, viz. the doctrine of option, or right of cancellation. The Prophet himself recommended one of his followers to reserve a *locus penitentiæ*, or option, for three days in all his purchases. This has led to the option by stipulation, which may be reserved by either of the parties. But besides this, the purchaser has an option without any stipulation, with regard to things which he has purchased without seeing, and also on account of defects in the thing sold. The greatest of all defects is a want of title or right in the seller. The two last options to the purchase constitute a complete warranty of title and against all defects on the part of the seller, in which respect the Muḥammadan more nearly resembles the Scotch than the English law of sale.

There are many different kinds of sale. Twenty or more have been enumerated in the *Nihāyah*, of which eight are mentioned and explained. Four of these, which have reference to the thing sold, may require some notice in this place. The first, called *Muqāyaẓah*, is described as a sale of things for things, and corresponds nearly with barter; but the word "thing" (*ʻayn*) is here opposed to obligations, and *muqāyaẓah* is therefore properly an exchange of specific for specific things. So that if the goods exchanged were on both sides or on either side indeterminate, the transaction would not, I think, be a *muqāyaẓah*, though still barter. The second sale is called *ṣarf*, and is defined to be an exchange of obligations for obligations. The usual objects of this contract are *dirhams* and *dīnārs*, which being obligations, the definition is generally correct. But an exchange of money for bullion, or bullion for bullion, is also a *ṣarf*, and every sale of an obligation for an obligation is not a *ṣarf*, so that the definition is redundant as well as defective. It is essential to the legality of this kind of sale, that both the things exchanged should be delivered and taken possession of before the separation of the parties, and that when they are of the same kind, as silver for silver, or gold for gold, they should also be exactly equal by weight. These rules are necessary for the avoidance of *reba*, or "usury," as already explained; and the whole of *ṣarf*, which is treated of at a length quite disproportionate to its importance, may be considered as a continued illustration of the doctrine of *reba*. The third kind of sale is *salam*. It has been already observed that there can be no lawful stipulation for a postponement of the delivery of the thing sold, except under one particular form of sale. The form alluded to is *salam*. This word means, literally, "an advance"; and in a *salam* sale the price is immediately advanced for the goods to be delivered at a future fixed time. It is only things of the class of similars that can be sold in this way, and as they must necessarily be indeterminate, the proper subject of sale is an obligation; while, on the other hand, as the price must be actually paid or delivered at the time of the contract, before the separation of the parties, and must, therefore, even in the case of its being money, be produced, and in consequence be particularised or specific, a *salam* sale is strictly and properly the sale of an obligation for a thing, as defined above. Until actual payment or delivery of the price, however, it retains its character of an obligation, and for this reason the price and the goods are both termed "debts," and are adduced in the same chapter as examples of the principle that the sale of a debt, that is, of the money or goods which a person is under engagement to pay or deliver, before possession, is invalid. The last of the sales referred to is the ordinary exchange of goods for money, which being an obligation, the transaction is defined to be the sale of things for obligations.

There is another transaction which comes within the definition of sale, and has been already noticed, but may be further adverted to in this place. It is that which is called *Qarẓ* in the Arabic, and "loan" in the English language. The borrower acquires an absolute right of property in the things lent, and comes under an engagement to return an equal quantity of things of the same kind. The transaction is therefore necessarily limited to similars, whether of weight, capacity, or tale, and the things lent and repaid being of the same kind, the two rules already mentioned for the prevention of *reba*, or "usury," must be strictly observed. Hence it follows that any stipulation on the part of the borrower for delay or forbearance by the lender, or any stipulation by the lender for interest to be paid by the borrower are alike unlawful.

Notwithstanding the stringency of the rules for preventing usury, or the taking any interest on the loan of money, methods were found for evading them and still keeping within the letter of the law. It had always been considered lawful to take a pledge to secure the repayment of a debt. Pledges were ordinarily of movable property; when given as security for a debt, and the pledge happened to perish in the hands of the pawnee, the debt was held to be released to the extent of the value of the pledge. Land, though scarcely liable to this incident, was sometimes made the subject of pledge, and devices were adopted for enabling the lender to derive some advantage from its possession while in in the state of pledge. But the moderate advantage to be derived in this way does not seem to have contented the money-lenders, who in all ages and countries have been of a grasping disposition, and the expedient of a sale with a condition for redemption was adopted, which very closely resembles an English mortgage. In the latter, the condition is usually expressed in one of two ways, viz. either that the sale shall become void, or that the lender shall resell to the seller, on payment of principal and interest at an assigned term. The first of these forms would be inconsistent with the nature of sale under the Muḥammadan law, but a sale with a covenant by the lender to reconvey to the seller on repayment of the loan seems to have been in use probably long before the form was adopted in Europe. It is probable that a term was fixed within which the repayment should be made. If repayment were made at the assigned term, the lender was obliged to reconvey; but if not, the property would remain his own, and the difference between its value and the price or sum lent might have been made an ample compensation for the loss of interest. This form of sale, which was called *Baiʿu 'l-wafā*, seems to have been strictly legal according to the most approved authorities, though held to be what the law calls abominable, as a device for obtaining what it prohibits.

In constituting sale there is no material difference between the Muḥummadan and other systems of law. The offer and acceptance, which are expressed or implied in all cases, must be so connected as to obviate any doubt of the one being intended to apply to the other. For this purpose the Muḥammadan law requires that both shall be interchanged at the same meeting of the parties, and that no other business shall be suffered to intervene between an offer and its acceptance. A very slight interruption is sufficient to break the continuity of a negotiation, and to terminate the meeting in a technical sense, though the parties should still remain in personal communication. An acceptance after the interruption of an offer made before it would be insufficient to constitute a sale. This has led to distinctions of the meeting which may appear unnecessarily minute to a reader unacquainted with the manners of Eastern countries, where the people are often very dilatory in their bargains, interspersing them with conversation on indifferent topics. It is only when a meeting has reference to the act of contracting that its meaning is thus liable to be restricted; for when the word occurs in other parts of the law, as, for instance, when it is said of a *ṣarf* contract that the things exchanged must be taken possession of at the meeting, the whole period that the parties may remain together is to be understood. As personal communication may be inconvenient in some cases, and impossible in others, the integrity of the meeting is held to be sufficiently preserved when a party who receives an offer by message or letter declares his acceptance of it on receiving the communication and apprehending its contents.

When a sale is lawfully contracted, the property in the things exchanged passes immediately from and to the parties respectively. In a legal sale, delivery and possession are not necessary for this purpose. Until possession is taken, however, the purchaser is not liable for accidental loss, and the seller has a lien for the price on the thing sold. Delivery by one party is in general tantamount to possession taken by the other. It is, therefore, sometimes of great importance to ascertain when there is a sufficient delivery; and many cases, real or imaginary, on the subject, are inserted in the *Fatāwā ʿĀlamgīrī*. It sometimes happens that a person purchases a thing of which he is already in possession, and it then becomes important to determine in what cases his previous possession is convertible into a possession under the purchase. Unless so converted, it would be held that there is no delivery under the sale, and the seller would of course retain his lien and remain liable for accidental loss.

Though possession is not necessary to complete the transfer of property under a legal sale, the case is different where the contract is illegal; for here property does not pass till possession is taken. The sale, however, though so far effectual, is still invalid, and liable to be set aside by a judge, at the instance of either of the parties, without any reference to the fact of the person complaining being able to come before him with what in legal phraseology is termed clean hands. A Muḥammadan judge is obliged by his law to interfere for the sake of the law itself, or, as it is more solemnly termed, for the right of God, which it is the duty of the judge to vindicate, though by so doing he may afford assistance to a party who personally may have no just claim to his interference. (*The Muhammadan Law of Sale, according to the Haneefee Code, from the Fatawa Alamgiri*, by Neil B. E. Baillie. Smith, Elder & Co., London.)

BAIL. Arabic كفالة *kafālah*. Bail is of two descriptions: *Kafālah bi-'n-nafs*, or "security for the person"; *Kafālah bi-'l-māl*, or "security for property." In the English courts in India, bail for the person is termed *Ḥāẓir-ẓamānī*, and bail for property *Ẓamānah*, or "security." Bail for the person is lawful except in cases of punishment (*Ḥudūd*) and retaliation (*Qiṣāṣ*). (*Hidāyah*, vol. ii. p. 576.)

AL-BĀʿIṢ (الباعث). One of the ninety-nine special names of God. It means

"He who awakes"; "The Awakener" (in the Day of Resurrection).

BAITU 'L-ḤAMD (بيت الحمد). "The House of Praise." An expression which occurs in the Traditions (*Mishkāt* v. 7). When the soul of a child is taken, God says, "Build a house for my servant in Paradise and call it a *house of praise*."

BAITU 'L-ḤARĀM (بيت الحرام). "The Sacred House." A name given to the Meccan mosque. [MASJIDU 'L-HARAM.]

BAITU 'L-ḤIKMAH (بيت الحكمة). *Lit.* "The House of Wisdom." A term used by Ṣūfīs for the heart of the sincere seekers after God. ('Abdu 'r-Razzāq's *Dictionary of Ṣūfī Terms.*)

BAITU 'L-LĀH (بيت الله). "The House of God." A name given to the Meccan mosque. [MASJIDU 'L-HARAM.]

BAITU 'L-MĀL (بيت المال). *Lit.* "The House of Property." The public treasury of a Muslim state, which the ruler is not allowed to use for his personal expenses, but only for the public good.

The sources of income are: (1) *Zakāt*, or the legal tax raised upon land, personal property, and merchandise, which, after deducting the expense of collecting, should be expended in the support of the poor and destitute. (2) The fifth of all spoils and booty taken in war. (3) The produce of mines and of treasure-trove. (4) Property for which there is no owner. (5) The *Jizyah*, or tax levied on unbelievers. (*Hidāyah*, Arabic ed., vol. i. p. 452.)

AL-BAITU 'L-MA'MŪR (البيت المعمور). *Lit.* "The Inhabited House." A house in the seventh heaven, visited by Muḥammad during the Mi'rāj or night-journey. It is said to be immediately over the sacred temple at Makkah. [MI'RAJ.]

BAITU 'L-MIDRĀS (بيت المدراس). "The House of Instruction." A term (used in a tradition given by Abū Hurairah) for a Jewish school. (*Mishkāt*, xvii. c. xi.) In Heb. בֵּית הַמִּדְרָשׁ

AL-BAITU 'L-MUQADDAS (البيت المقدس). "The Holy House." A name given to the temple at Jerusalem. [AL-MASJIDU 'L-AQSA.]

BAITU 'L-QUDS (بيت القدس). *Lit.* "The House of Holiness." A term used by the Ṣūfīs for the heart of the true seeker after God when it is absorbed in meditation. ('Abdu 'r-Rāzzaq's *Dictionary of Ṣūfī Terms.*)

BAI'U 'L-WAFĀ (بيع الوفاء). The word *wafā* means the performance of a promise, and the *Bai'u 'l-Wafā* is a sale with a promise to be performed. It is, in fact, a pledge in the hands of the pawnee, who is not its propritor, nor is he free to make use of it without the permission of the owner. There are different opinions about the legality of this form of sale, but it is now the common form of mortgage in use in India, where it is usually styled *Bai' bi-'l-wafā*. (See Baillie's *Muḥammadan Law of Sale*, p. 303.)

al-BAIYINAH (البينة). *Lit.* "The Evidence." A title given to the XCVIIIth Sūrah of the Qur'ān, in which the word occurs.

BA'L (بعل), Heb. הַבַּעַל, *i.e.* "Lord." The chief deity worshipped by the Syro-Phœnician nations. It is known to the Muḥammadans as an idol worshipped in the days of the Prophet Elisha. (See *Ghiyāṣu 'l-Lughah.*)

BALAAM. There is said to be an allusion to Balaam in the Qur'ān, Sūrah vii. 174, "Recite to them the story of him to whom we gave our signs, and he departed therefrom, and Satan followed him, and he was of those who were beguiled."

The commentary of the Jalālain says that he was a learned man amongst the Israelites, who was requested by the Canaanites to curse Moses at the time when he was about to attack the *Jabbārūn* or "giants," a tribe of the Canaanites. Balaam at first refused to do so but at last yielded, when valuable presents were made to him. (See *Tafsīru 'l-Jalālain*, p. 142.)

BALAD (بلد). *Lit.* Any country, district, or town, regarded as an habitation. *Al-Balad*, the sacred territory of Makkah. A title given to the XCth Sūrah, in which the word occurs.

BĀLIGH (بالغ). "Of years of legal maturity; adult." [PUBERTY.]

BANISHMENT. Arabic تغريب *Taghrīb*. Expatriation for fornication is enjoined by Muḥammadan law, according to the Imām ash-Shāfi'ī, although it is not allowed by the other doctors of the law, and it is also a punishment inflicted upon highway robbers.

BANKRUPT. There is no provision in the Muḥammadan law for declaring a person bankrupt, and so placing him beyond the reach of his creditors; but the Qāẓī can declare a debtor insolvent, and free him from the obligation of *zakāt* and almsgiving.

BANŪ ISRĀ'ĪL (بنو اسرائيل). "The Children of Israel." A title of the XVIIth Sūrah or chapter of the Qur'ān, called also *Sūratu 'l-Mi'rāj*.

BANŪN (بنون). The plural of *ibn* (Heb. בָּנִים). "Sons; posterity; tribe." The word is more familiar to English readers in its inflected form *Banī*. The tribes whose names occur frequently in the early history of Islām, and are mentioned in the Traditions, are the *Banū-Quraish*, *Banu 'n-Najjār*, *Banū - Quraiẓah*, *Banū - Kinānah* *Banū 'n-Naẓr*, *Banū-Khuzā'ah*, *Banū-Bakr*,

Banū-'Āmir, *Banū - Asad*, *Banū - Fazārah*, *Banū-Liḥyān*, *Banū-Tamīm*, *Banū-Umaiyah*, *Banū-Zahrah*, and *Banū-Isrā'īl*.

BAPTISM. The only allusion to baptism in the Qur'ān is found in Sūrah ii. 132: "(We have) the baptism of God, and who is better to baptise than God?" The word here translated baptism is *ṣibghah*, *lit.* "dye," which, the commentators al-Jalālain and al-Baiẓāwī say, may, by comparison, refer to Christian baptism, "for," says al-Baiẓāwī, "the Naṣārā (Christians) were in the habit of dipping their offspring in a yellow water which they called *al-Ma'mūdiyah* and said it purified them and confirmed them as Christians." (See *Tafsīru 'l-Jalālain* and *Tafsīru 'l-Baiẓāwī*, *in loco.*)

AL-BĀQĪ (الباقى). One of the ninety-nine special names of God. It means "He who remains;" "The Everlasting One."

AL-BAQARAH (البقرة). "The Cow." The title of the second Sūrah of the Qur'ān, occasioned by the story of the red heifer mentioned in verse 63, "When Moses said to his people, God commandeth you to sacrifice a cow."

BAQĪ'U 'L-GHARQAD (بقيع الغرقد), or for shortness al-Baqī (البقيع). The burying-ground at al-Madīnah, which Muḥammad used to frequent at night to pray for forgiveness for the dead. (*Mishkāt*, iv. c. 28.)

BARĀ'AH (براءة). "Immunity, or security." A title given to the IXth Chapter of the Qur'ān, called also *Sūratu 't-Taubah*, "The Chapter of Repentance." It is remarkable as being the only Sūrah without the introductory form, "In the name of God, the Merciful, the Compassionate." Various reasons are assigned for this omission. Some commentators say that the prayer of mercy is not placed at the head of a chapter which speaks chiefly of God's wrath.

BĀRAH-I-WAFĀT (باره وفات). *Bārah* (Urdū) "twelve," and *Wafāt*. The twelfth day of the month Rabī'u 'l-Awwal, observed in commemoration of Muḥammad's death.

It seems to be a day instituted by the Muḥammadans of India, and is not observed universally amongst the Muslims of all countries. On this day *Fātiḥahs* are recited for Muḥammad's soul, and both in private houses and mosques portions of the Traditions and other works in praise of the Prophet's excellences are read.

The Wahhābīs do not observe this day, as it is believed to be an innovation, not having been kept by the early Muslims.

AL-BARĀ IBN 'ĀZIB (البراء بن عازب). One of the Companions who accompanied Muḥammad at the battle of the Ditch, and in most of his subsequent engagements. He assisted in conquering the district of Rai, A.H. 22, and was with the Khalīfah 'Alī at the battle of the Camel, A.H. 36.

AL-BĀRI' (البارى). "The Maker." One of the ninety-nine special names of God. It occurs in the Qur'ān, Sūrah lix. 24: "He is God the Creator, the Maker, the Fashioner. His are the excellent names."

BĀRIQAH (بارقة). *Lit.* "Refulgence, lightning." A term used by the Ṣūfīs for that enlightenment of the soul, which at first comes to the true Muslim as an earnest of greater enlightenment. ('Abdu 'r-Razzāq's *Dictionary of Ṣūfī Terms.*)

BARNABAS, the Gospel of. The Muḥammadans assert that a gospel of Barnabas existed in Arabic, and it is believed by some that Muḥammad obtained his account of Christianity from this spurious gospel.

"Of this gospel the Moriscoes in Africa have a translation in Spanish, and there is in the library of Prince Eugene of Savoy a manuscript of some antiquity, containing an Italian translation of the same gospel, made, it is supposed, for the use of renegades. This book appears to be no original forgery of the Muḥammadans, though they have no doubt interpolated and altered it since, the better to serve their purpose; and in particular, instead of the Paraclete or Comforter (St. John xiv. 16, 26; xv. 26; xvi. 7), they have in this apocryphal gospel inserted the word Periclyte, that is, "the famous or illustrious," by which they pretend their prophet was foretold by name, that being the signification of Muḥammad in Arabic; and this they say to justify that passage in the Qur'ān (Sūrah 61) where Jesus is formally asserted to have foretold his coming, under his other name of Aḥmad, which is derived from the same root as Muḥammad, and of the same import. From these or some other forgeries of the same stamp, it is that Muḥammadans quote several passages of which there are not the least footsteps in the New Testament." (Sale.)

After Mr. Sale had written the extract which we have quoted, he inspected a Spanish translation of the Italian copy of this apocryphal gospel, of which he gives the following account:—

"The book is a moderate quarto, in Spanish, written in a very legible hand, but a little damaged towards the latter end. It contains two hundred and twenty-two chapters of unequal length, and four hundred and twenty pages; and is said, in the front, to be translated from the Italian by an Aragonian Moslem named Moṣtafā de Aranda. There is a preface prefixed to it, wherein the discoverer of the original MS., who was a Christian monk called Fra Marino, tells us that, having accidentally met with a writing of Irenæus (among others), wherein he speaks against St. Paul, alleging for his authority the gospel of St. Barnabas, he became exceedingly desirous to find this gospel; and that God, of his mercy, having made him very intimate with Pope Sixtus V., one day, as they were together in that Pope's library, his Holiness fell asleep, and he, to employ himself, reaching down a book to read, the first he laid his hand on proved to be the very gospel he wanted; overjoyed at the discovery, he scrupled not to hide his prize in his sleeve, and on the Pope's awaking, took leave of him, carrying with him that celestial treasure, by reading of which he became a convert to Muḥammadanism.

"This Gospel of Barnabas contains a complete history of Jesus Christ, from His birth to His ascension, and most of the circumstances of the four real gospels are to be found therein, but many of them turned, and some artfully enough, to favour the Muḥammadan system. From the design of the whole, and the frequent interpolations of stories and passages, wherein Muḥammad is spoken of and foretold by name, as the messenger of God, and the great prophet who was to perfect the dispensation of Jesus, it appears to be a most bare-faced forgery. One particular I observe therein induces me to believe it to have been dressed up by a renegade Christian, slightly instructed in his new religion, and not educated as a Muḥammadan (unless the fault be imputed to the Spanish, or, perhaps, the Italian translator, and to the original compiler). I mean the giving to Muhammad the title of Messiah, and that not once or twice only, but in several places; whereas, the title of Messiah, or, as the Arabs write it, *al-Masīḥ*, *i.e.* Christ, is appropriated to Jesus in the Qur'ān, and is constantly applied by the Muḥammadans to him, and never to their own Prophet. The passages produced from the Italian MS. by M. de la Monnoye are to be seen in this Spanish version almost word for word."

The Rev. Joseph White, D.D., in his *Bampton Lectures* of 1784, gives a translation of those chapters in this spurious Gospel of Barnabas, which relate to the supposed crucifixion of Judas in the place of our Lord, and which we insert:—

"Judas came near to the people with whom Jesus was; and when He heard the noise He entered into the house where the disciples slept. And God, seeing the fear and danger of His servant, ordered Gabriel and Michael and Rafaīl and Azraīl to carry Him out of the world.

"And they came in all haste, and bare Him out of the window which looks towards the south. And they placed Him in the third heaven, where He will remain blessing God, in the company of angels, till near the end of the world." (Chapter 216.)

"And Judas the traitor entered before the rest into the place from which Jesus had just been taken up. And the disciples were sleeping. And the Wonderful God acted wonderfully, changing Judas into the same figure and speech with Jesus.

"We believing that it was He, said to him, Master, whom seekest thou? And he said to them, smiling, Ye have forgotten yourselves, since ye do not know Judas Iscariot.

"At this time the soldiery entered; and seeing Judas so like in every respect to Jesus, laid hands upon him," &c. (Chapter 217.)

"In which (Chap. 218) is related the passion of Judas the traitor.

"The soldiers afterwards took Judas and bound him, notwithstanding he said with truth to them that he was not Jesus. And soldiers mocked him saying, Sir, do not be afraid; for we are come to make thee King of Israel; and we have bound thee, because we know thou hast refused the kingdom. And Judas said, Ye have lost your senses.

"I came to show you Jesus, that ye might take Him; and ye have bound me, who am your guide. The soldiers lost their patience, hearing this, and they began to go with him, striking and buffeting him, till they reached Jerusalem," &c. &c. (Chapter 218.)

"They carried him to Mount Calvary, where they executed criminals, and crucified him, stripping him asked for the greater ignominy. Then he did nothing but cry out, O my God, why hast thou forsaken me, that I should die unjustly, when the real malefactor hath escaped? I say in truth that he was so like in person, figure, and gesture to Jesus, that as many as knew Him, believed firmly that it was He, except Peter; for which reason many left his doctrine, believing that it had been false; as He had said that He should not die till the end of the world.

"But those who stood firm were oppressed with grief, seeing him die whom they understood to be Jesus: not recollecting what He had told them. And in company with His mother, they were present at his death, weeping continually. And by means of Joseph Abarimatheas (*sic*), they obtained from the president the body of Judas. And they took him down from the cross, burying him with much lamentation in the new sepulchre of Joseph; having wrapped him up in linen and precious ointments." (Chapter 219.)

"They all returned, each man to his house: and he who writeth, with James and John, went with the mother of Jesus to Nazareth. And the disciples, who did not fear God with truth, went by night and stole the body of Judas, and hid it; spreading a report that He (*i.e.* Jesus) had risen again, from whence sprung great confusion among the people.

"And the High Priest commanded, under pain of anathema, that no one should talk of him; and on this account raised a great persecution, banishing some, tormenting others, and even stoning some to death: because it was not in the power of anyone to be silent on this subject. And then came news to Nazareth, that Jesus had risen again. And he that writeth desired the mother of Jesus to leave off her lamentation. And Mary said, Let us go to Jerusalem, to see if it is truth. If I see Him I shall die content. (Chapter 220).

"The Virgin returned to Jerusalem with him that writeth, and James and John, the same day that the decree of the High Priest came out.

"And as she feared God, though she knew

the command was unjust, she entreated those who talked with her not to speak of her Son. Who can say, how we were then affected? God, who knows the heart of man, knows that between the grief for the death of Judas, whom we understood to be Jesus, and the pleasure of seeing him risen again, we almost expired. And the angels who were the guardians of Mary went up to heaven the third day, and told Jesus what was passing. And He, moved with compassion for His mother, entreated of God that He might be seen by His disciples. And the Compassionate God ordered His four favourite angels to place Him within His own house, and to guard Him three days; that they and they only might see Him, who believed in His doctrine. Jesus descended, surrounded with light, into the house of His mother, where were the two sisters, Martha and Mary, and Lazarus, and he that writeth, and John and James, and Peter. And when they saw Him, they fell with their faces on the earth as if dead. And Jesus lifted them up, saying, Fear not, for I am your Master. Lament not henceforth, for I am alive. They were astonished at seeing Jesus, because they thought Him dead. And Mary weeping said, Tell me, my Son, why, if God gave Thee power to raise up the dead, did He consent that Thou shouldest die, with so much reproach and shame to Thy relations and friends, and so much hurt to Thy doctrine, leaving us all in desolation? Jesus replied, embracing His mother, Believe me, for I tell thee the truth, I have not been dead; for God has reserved Me for the end of the world. In saying this He desired the angels to manifest themselves, and to tell how He had passed through everything. At the instant they appeared like four suns; and all present prostrated themselves on the ground, overcome by the presence of the angels. And Jesus gave to all of them something to cover themselves with, that they might be able to hear the angels speak.

"And Jesus said to His mother, These are the Ministers of God. Gabriel knows His secrets; Michael fights with His enemies; Asrafiel will cite all to judgment; and Azrael receives the souls. And the holy angels told how they had, by the command of God, taken up Jesus, and transformed Judas, that he might suffer the punishment which he wished to bring on Jesus. And he that writeth said, Is it lawful for me to ask of Thee, in the same manner as when thou wast in the world? And Jesus answered, Speak, Barnabas, what thout wishest.

"And he said, I wish that Thou wouldest tell me how God, being so compassionate, could afflict us so much, in giving us to understand that Thou wast he that suffered, for we have been very near dying? And Thou being a prophet, why did He suffer Thee to fall under disgrace, by (apparently) placing Thee on a cross, and between two robbers? Jesus answered, Believe Me, Barnabas, let the fault be ever so small God chastiseth it with much punishment. And as my mother and faithful disciples loved me with a little earthly love, God chastised that love by this grief; that He might not chastise it in the other world. And though I was innocent, yet as they called Me God, and His Son, that the devils might not mock Me on the Day of Judgment, He has chosen that I should be mocked in this world.

"And this mocking shall last till the holy Messenger of God (*i.e.* Muḥammad) shall come, who shall undeceive all believers. And then He said, Just art Thou, O God! and to Thee only belongeth the honour and glory, with worship, for ever." (Chapter 221.)

"And then He said, Barnabas, that thou by all means write my gospel, relating everything which has happened in the world concerning Me; and let it be done exactly; in order that the faithful may be undeceived, knowing the truth. He that writeth said, Master, I will do it as Thou commandest me, God willing: but I did not see all that happened with Judas. Jesus answered, Here stand Peter and John, who saw it, and will relate it to thee.

"And He told James and John to call the seven apostles who were absent, and Nicodemus, and Joseph Abarimatheas (*sic*), and some of the seventy-two disciples. When they were come, they did eat with Him; and on the third day He commanded them all to go to the mount of Olives with His mother: because He was to return to heaven. All the apostles and disciples went, except twenty-five of the seventy-two, who had fled to Damascus with fear. And exactly at mid-day, while they were all in prayer, Jesus came with many angels (blessing God), with so much brightness that they all bent their faces to the ground. And Jesus raised them up, saying, Fear not your Master, who comes to take leave of you; and to recommend you to God our Lord, by the mercies received from His bounty: and be He with you!

"And upon this He disappeared with the angels; all of us remaining amazed at the great brightness in which he left us." (Chapter 222).

AL-BARR (البر). One of the ninety-nine special names of God. In its ordinary sense it means "pious," or "good." As applied to God, it means "The Beneficent One."

BARTER. [BAIʿ.]

BARZAKH (برزخ). (1) A thing that intervenes between any two things; a bar; an obstruction; or a thing that makes a separation between two things. In which sense it is used in the Qur'ān in two places. Sūrah xxv. 55, "He hath put an interspace between them (*i.e.* the two seas), and a barrier which it is forbidden them to pass." Sūrah lv. 20, "Yet between them (the two seas) is a *barrier*."

(2) The interval between the present life and that which is to come. See Qur'ān, Sūrah xxiii. 99, "And say, My Lord, I seek refuge with Thee from the incitings of the devils, and I seek refuge with Thee from their

presence. Until when death comes to any one of them, he says, My Lord! send me back (to life), if haply I may do right in that which I have left. Not so! A mere word that he speaks! But behind them there is *barzakh* (a bar), until the day when they shall be raised. And when the trumpet shall be blown, there shall be no relation between them on that day, nor shall they beg of each other then." Upon this verse the commentator Baizāwī says: "*Barzakh* is an intervening state (*ḥā'il*, 'a barrier') between death and the Day of Judgment, and whoever dies enters it." The commentator Ḥusain remarks: "*Barzakh* is a partition (*māni'*) between the living and the Day of Judgment, namely, the grave in which they will remain until the resurrection." The commentators al-Jalālain speak of it as a *ḥājiz*, or intervening state between death and judgment. 'Abdu 'r-Razzāq in his *Dictionary of Technical Terms of the Ṣūfīs* (Sprenger's Edition), gives a similar definition.

The word is employed by Muhammadan writers in at least two senses, some using it for the place of the dead, the grave, and others for the state of departed souls between death and judgment.

The condition of believers in the grave is held to be one of undisturbed rest, but that of unbelievers one of torment; for Muḥammad is related to have said, "There are appointed for the grave of the unbeliever ninety-nine serpents to bite him until the Day of Resurrection." (*Mishkāt*, i. c. 5, p. 12.) The word seems generally to be used in the sense of Hades, for every person who dies is said to enter *al-Barzakh*.

BA'Ṣ (بعث). *Lit.* "Raising." (1) The Day of Resurrection. (2) The office of a messenger or prophet.

BASE MONEY. The sale of one pure dirham and two base ones in exchange for two pure dirhams and one base one is lawful. By two base ones (*ghalaṭain*), are to be understood such as pass amongst merchants but are rejected at the public treasury. (*Hidāyah*, vol. ii. 560.)

al-BAṢĪR (البصير). One of the ninety-nine special names of God. It frequently occurs in the Qur'ān, and means "The All-seeing One."

BAṢĪRAH (بصيرة). *Lit.* "Penetration." The sight of the heart as distinguished from the sight of the eye (*Baṣārah* or *Baṣar*). A term used by theologians to express that enlightenment of the heart "whereby the spiritual man can understand spiritual things with as much certainty as the natural man can see objects with the sight of the eye." The word occurs twice in the Qur'ān, Sūrah xii. 108, "This is my way; I cry unto God, resting on *clear evidence*;" Sūrah lxxv. 14, "A man shall be *evidence* against himself."

AL-BĀSIṬ (الباسط). One of the ninety-nine special names of God. It means "He who spreads, or stretches out," and occurs in the Qur'ān, Sūrah xiii. 15. As applied to God, it means, "He who dispenses riches," &c.

BASTARD (ولد الزنا, *waladu 'z-zinā*). An illegitimate child has, according to Muḥammadan lȧw, no legal father, and consequently the law does not allow the father to interfere with his illegitimate child, even for the purposes of education. He cannot inherit the property of his father, but he is acknowledged as the rightful heir of his mother (Baillie's *Digest*, p. 432). The evidence of a bastard is valid, because he is innocent with respect to the immorality of his parents; but the Imām Mālik maintains that his testimony is not to be accepted with respect to a charge of whoredom. (*Hidāyah*, vol. ii. 692.)

BATHING. The Arabic term for ordinary bathing is (غسل) *ghasl*, and that for the religious purification of the whole body *ghusl*. In all large mosques, and in most respectable dwellings in Muḥammadan countries, there are bathing-rooms erected, both for the ordinary purposes of bathing and for the religious purification. An account of the legal purification will be found in the article GHUSL. Although purifications and bathing form so essential a part of the Muslim religion, cleanliness does not distinguish Muḥammadans, who are generally in this respect a striking contrast to their Hindū fellow subjects in India. According to the saying of Muḥammad, decency should be observed in bathing, and the clothes from the waist downwards should not be taken off at such times. (*Mishkāt*, ii. c. iv.)

BĀṬIL (باطل). That which is false in doctrine.

AL-BĀṬIN (الباطن). (1) One of the ninety-nine special names of God. It means "that which is hidden or concealed," "The Hidden One," or "He that knows hidden things." (2) A term used in theology for that which is hidden in its meaning, in contradistinction to that which is evident.

BATŪL (بتول). *Lit.* "A shoot or offset of a palm-tree cut off from its mother tree;" "a virgin" (as cut off or withheld from men). The term *al-Batūl* is applied to Fāṭimah, the daughter of Muḥammad, because she was separated from the other women of her age by her excellences. Heb. בְּתוּלָה *Bethūlāh*.

BĀ'ŪṢ (باعوث). A Syriac word, בָּעוּתָא (*i.e.* "petition, prayer"), which, in the dictionary *al-Qāmūs*, is said to mean the Christian Easter: and also prayers for rain, or the *Istisqā* of the Christians. (*Majmu 'l-Biḥār*, p. 101.)

BĀẒAQ or BĀẒIQ (باذق). A prohibited liquor. The juice of the grape boiled until a quantity less than two-thirds evaporates.

BEARD. Arabic لحية *liḥyah* or ذقن *zaqan*. The beard is regarded by Muslims as the badge of the dignity of manhood. The Prophet is related to have said, "Do the opposite of the polytheists and let your beard grow long." (*Mishkāt*, xx. iv.) And the growing of a beard is said to be *Fiṭrah*, or one of those customs which have been observed by every Prophet. [FITRAH.]

BEAUTY, Female. "The maiden, whose loveliness inspires the most impassioned expression in Arabic poetry and prose, is celebrated for her slender figure; she is like the cane among plants, and is elegant as the twig of the oriental willow. Her face is like the full moon, presenting the strongest contrast to the colour of her hair, which (to preserve the nature of the simile just employed) is of the deepest hue of night, and descends to the middle of her back. A rosy blush overspreads the centre of each cheek; and a mole is considered an additional charm. The Arabs, indeed, are particularly extravagant in their admiration of this natural beauty-spot, which, according to its place, is compared to a globule of ambergris upon a dish of alabaster, or upon the surface of a ruby. The eyes of the Arab beauty are intensely black, large, and long, of the form of an almond; they are full of brilliancy; but this is softened by a lid slightly depressed, and by long silken lashes, giving a tender and languid expression, which is full of enchantment, and scarcely to be improved by the adventitious aid of the black border of the *kuḥl*; for this the lovely maiden adds rather for the sake of fashion than necessity, having what the Arabs term natural *kuḥl*. The eye-brows are thin and arched, the forehead is wide, and fair as ivory; the nose straight, the mouth small; the lips are of a brilliant red, and the teeth "like pearls set in coral." The forms of the bosom are compared to two pomegranates; the waist is slender; the hips are wide and large; the feet and hands small; the fingers tapering, and their extremities dyed with the deep orange-red tint imparted by the leaves of *ḥinnā*.

The following is the most complete analysis of Arabian beauty, given by an unknown author, quoted by Al-Isḥāqī:—

"Four things in a woman should be *black*: the hair of the head, the eye-brows, the eye-lashes, and the dark part of the eyes; four *white*: the complexion of the skin, the white of the eyes, the teeth, and the legs; four *red*: the tongue, the lips, the middle of the cheeks, and the gumz; four *round*: the head, the neck, the fore-arms, and the ankles; four *long*: the back, the fingers, the arms, and the legs; four *wide*: the forehead, the eyes, the bosom, and the hips; four *fine*: the eye-brows, the nose, the lips, and the fingers; four *thick*: the lower part of the back, the thighs, the calves of the legs, and the knees; four *small*: the ears, the breasts, the hands, and the feet." (Lane's *Arabian Nights*, vol. i. p. 25.)

BEGGING. It is not lawful for any person possessing sufficient food for a day and night to beg (*Durru 'l-Mukhtār*, p. 108), and it is related that the Prophet said: "Acts of begging are scratches and wounds with which a man wounds his own face." "It is better for a man to take a rope and bring in a bundle of sticks to sell than to beg." "A man who continues to beg will appear in the Day of Judgment without any flesh on his face." (*Mishkāt*, Book vi. chap. v.)

BEINGS. According to Muḥammadan belief, there are three different species of created *intelligent* beings: (1) Angels (*Malāʼikah*), who are said to be created of light; (2) Genii (*Jinn*), who are created of fire; (3) Mankind (*Insān*), created of earth. These intelligent beings are called *Zawu 'l-'Uqūl*, or "Rational beings," whilst unintelligent beings" are called *Ghair Zawī 'l-'Uqūl*. *Ḥayawāni-Nāṭiq* is also a term used for rational beings (who can *speak*), and *Ḥayawāni-'Ajam* for all irrational creatures. [JINN.]

BELIEVERS. The terms used for believers are—*Mu'min*, pl. *Mu'minūn*; and *Muslim*, pl. *Muslimūn*. The difference expressed in these two words is explained in the Traditions, in a *Ḥadīs* given in the *Ṣaḥīḥ* of *Muslim* (p. 27), where it is recorded by 'Umar, as having been taught by Muḥammad, that a *Mu'min* is one who has *īmān*, or "faith;" Faith being a sincere belief in God, His angels, His inspired books, His prophets, the Day of Resurrection, and the predestination of good and evil; and that a *Muslim* is one who is resigned and obedient to the will of God, and bears witness that there is no god but God, and that Muḥammad is His Apostle, and is steadfast in prayer, and gives *zakāt*, or "legal alms," and fasts in the month of Ramaẓān, and makes a pilgrimage to the Temple (*Bait*) at Makkah, if he have the means.

The rewards in store for the believer are as follows (see *Sūratu 'l-Baqarah*, Sūrah ii. 76):—

"They who have believed and done the things that be right, they shall be the inmates of Paradise,—therein to abide for ever."

Sūrat 'n-Nisā, Sūrah iv. 60:—

"Those who have believed, and done the things that are right, we will bring them into gardens 'neath which the rivers flow—therein to abide eternally; therein shall they have wives of stainless purity: and we will bring them into shadowing shades."

Sūratu 'l-A'rāf, Sūrah vii. 40:—

"Those who have believed and done the things which are right, (we will lay on no one a burden beyond his power)—these shall be inmates of Paradise: for ever shall they abide therein;

"And will we remove whatever rancour was in their bosoms; rivers shall roll at their feet; and they shall say, 'Praise be to God who hath guided us hither! We had not been guided had not God guided us! Of a surety the Apostles of our Lord came to us with truth.' And a voice shall cry to them, 'This is Paradise, of which, as the meed of your works, ye are made heirs.'

"And the inmates of Paradise shall cry to the inmates of the Fire, "Now have we found what our Lord promised us to be true. Have ye too found what your Lord promised you to be true?' And they shall answer, 'Yes.' And a Herald shall proclaim between them: 'The curse of God be upon the evil doers,

"Who turn men aside from the way of God, and seek to make it crooked, and who believe not in the life to come!'

"And between them shall be a partition; and on *the wall* al-A'rāf, shall be men who will know all, by their tokens, and they shall cry to the inmates of Paradise, 'Peace be on you!' but they shall not *yet* enter it, although they long to do so.

"And when their eyes are turned towards the inmates of the Fire, they shall say, 'O our Lord! place us not with the offending people.'

"And they who are upon al-A'rāf shall cry to those whom they shall know by their tokens, 'Your amassings and your pride have availed you nothing.

"'Are these they on whom ye sware God would not bestow mercy? Enter ye into Paradise! where no fear shall be upon you, neither shall ye put to grief.'

"And the inmates of the fire shall cry to the inmates of Paradise: 'Pour upon us some water, or of the refreshments God hath given you?' They shall they, 'Truly God hath forbidden both to unbelievers."

For a further descriptions of the Muhammadan future state the reader is referred to the article PARADISE, which deals more directly with the sensual character of the heaven supposed to be in store for the believer in the mission of Muḥammad.

The following is a description of the believer which is given in the Qur'ān, *Sūratu 'l-Muminīn*, the XXIIIrd Sūrah, v. 1:—

"Happy now the Believers,
Who humble themselves in their prayer,
And who keep aloof from vain words,
And who are doers of alms-deeds (*zakāt*),
And who restrain their appetites,
(Save with their wives, or the slaves whom their right hands possess; for *in that case* they shall be free from blame:
But they whose desires reach further than this are transgressors:)
And who tend well their trusts and their covenants,
And who keep them strictly to their prayers:
These shall be the heritors, who shall inherit Paradise, to abide therein for ever."

BELLS. [NAQUS.]

BENEFICE. [WAQF.]

BENEFICENCE (Arabic سماحة *samāḥah*) is commended by Muhammad as one of the evidences of faith. (*Mishkāt*, Book i. c. i. part 3.)

Amr ibn 'Abaratah relates: "I came to the Prophet and said, 'O Prophet, what is Islām?' And he said, 'It is purity of speech and hospitality.' I then said, 'And what is faith?' And he said, 'Patience and *beneficence*."

BENJAMIN. Heb. בִּנְיָמִין, Arabic بنيامين *Binyāmīn*. The youngest of the children of Jacob. He is not mentioned by name in the Qur'ān, but he is referred to in Sūrah xii. 69, "And when they entered in unto Joseph, he took his brother (*i.e.* Benjamin) to stay with him. He said Verily I am thy brother, then take not that ill which they have been doing. And when he had equipped them with their equipment, he placed the drinking-cup in his brother's pack," &c. [JOSEPH.]

BEQUESTS. Arabic وصية *waṣīyah*, pl. *waṣāyā*. A bequest or will can be made verbally, although it is held to be better to execute it in writing. Two lawful witnesses are necessary to establish either a verbal bequest or a written will. A bequest in favour of a stranger to the amount of one-third of the whole property, is valid, but a bequest to any amount beyond that is invalid, unless the heirs give their consent. If a person make a bequest in favour of another from whom he has received a mortal wound, it is not valid, and if a legatee slay his testator the bequest in his favour is void. A bequest made to part of the heirs is not valid unless the other heirs give their consent. The bequest of a Muslim in favour of an unbeliever, or of an unbeliever in favour of a Muslim, is valid. If a person be involved in debt, legacies bequeathed by him are not lawful. A bequest in favour of a child yet unborn is valid, provided the fœtus happen to be less than six months old at the time of the making of the will.

If a testator deny his bequest, and the legatee produce witnesses to prove it, it is generally held not to be a retractation of it. If a person on his death-bed emancipate a slave, it takes effect after his death.

If a person will that "the pilgrimage incumbent on him be performed on his behalf after his death," his heirs must depute a person for the purpose, and supply him with the necessary expenses. (Hamilton's *Hidāyah*, vol. iv. 466.)

BESTIALITY is said by Muslim jurists to be the result of the most vitiated appetite and the utmost depravity of sentiment. But if a man commit it, he does not incur the *Ḥadd*, or stated punishment, as the act is not considered to have the properties of whoredom; the offender is to be punished by a discretionary correction (*Ta'zīr*). According to Muslim law, the beast should be killed, and if it be of an eatable species, it should be burnt. (*Hidāyah*, vol. ii. 27.) *Obs.* According to the Mosaic code, a man guilty of this crime was surely to be put to death. (Ex. xviii. 19.)

BETROTHAL. [KHITBAH.]

BĪʻAH (بيعة). A Christian church. The word occurs in a tradition in the *Mishkāt* (iv. c. vii. 2), and is translated by ʻAbdu 'l-Ḥaqq "*Kalīsah.*" [CHURCH.]

BIDʻAH (بدعة). A novelty or innovation in religion; heresy; schism.

BIER. Arabic جنازة *jināzah* and *janāzah.* The same word is used for the corpse, the bier, and the funeral. In most Muḥammadan countries the ordinary *charpoy*, or "bedstead," is used for the bier, which, in the case of a female, is covered with a canopy. [BURIAL.]

BIHISHT (بهشت). The Persian word for the celestial regions. [PARADISE, JANNAH, FIRDAUS.]

BILĀDU 'L-ISLĀM (بلاد الاسلام). "The countries of Islām." A term used in Muḥammadan law for Muslim countries. It is synonymous with the term Dāru 'l-Islām. [DARU 'L-ISLAM.]

BILĀL (بلال). The first *Muʻazzin* or caller to prayer appointed by Muḥammad. He was an Abyssinian slave who had been ransomed by Abū Bakr. He was tall, dark, and gaunt, with negro features and bushy hair. Muḥammad honoured and distinguished him as the "first fruits of Abyssinia." He survived the Prophet.

BILQĪS (بلقيس). The Queen of Saba', who visited Solomon and became one of his queens. An account of her, as it is given in the Qur'ān, will be found in the story of King Solomon. [SOLOMON.]

BINT LABŪN (بنت لبون). "The daughter of a milk-giver." A female camel two years old; so called because the mother is then suckling another foal. The proper age for a camel given in *zakāt*, or "legal alms," for camels from thirty-six in number up to forty-five.

BINT MAKHĀẒ (بنت مخاض). "The daughter of a pregnant." A female camel passed one year; so called because the mother is again pregnant. This is the proper age for a camel given in *zakāt*, or "alms," for camels from twenty-five in number up to thirty-five.

BIOGRAPHERS OF MUḤAMMAD. Although the Qur'ān may be said to be the key-stone to the biography of Muḥammad, yet it contains but comparatively few references to the personal history of the Prophet. The Traditions, or *Aḥādīs*, form the chief material for all biographical histories. [TRADITION.] The first who attempted to compile an account of Muḥammad in the form of a history, was az-Zuhrī, who died A.H. 124, and whose work, no longer extant, is mentioned by Ibn Khallikān. The earliest biographical writers whose works are extant are—Ibn Isḥāq, A.H 151; Al-Wāqidī, A.H. 207; Ibn Hishām, A.H. 218; Al-Bukhārī (history), A.H. 256; Aṭ-Ṭabari, A.H. 310. Amongst more recent biographies, the most noted are those by Ibnu 'l-Asīr, A.H. 630, and Ismāʻīl Abu 'l-fidā', A.H. 732. Abu 'l-fidā's work was translated into Latin by John Gagnier, Professor of Arabic at Oxford, A.D. 1723, and into English by the Rev. W. Murray, Episcopal clergymen at Duffus in Scotland, and published (without date) at Elgin. The first life of Muḥammad published in English is that by Dean Prideaux, which first appeared in 1723, and afterwards passed through several editions. Dr. Sprenger commenced a life of Muḥammad in English, and printed the first part at Allahabad, India, A.D. 1851; but it was never completed. The learned author afterwards published the whole of his work in German, at Berlin, 1869. The only complete life of Muḥammad in English which has any pretension to original research, is the well-known *Life of Mahomet*, by Sir William Muir, LL.D. (First Edition, four vols., London, 1858–61; Second Edition, one vol., London, 1877).

BIOGRAPHY. A Dictionary of Biography is called اسماء الرجال *asmā'u 'r-rijāl* (*lit.* "The Names of Men"). The most celebrated of these is, amongst Muslims, that by Ibn Khallikān, which has always been considered a work of the highest importance for the civil and literary history of the Muḥammadan people. Ibn Khallikān died A.H. 681 (A.D. 1282), but his dictionary received numerous additions from subsequent writers. It has been translated into English by MacGuckin De Slane (Paris, 1843).

BIRDS. It is commonly believed by the Muḥammadans that all kinds of birds, and many, if not all, beasts, have a language by which they communicate their thoughts to each other, and in the Qur'ān (Sūrah xxvii. 16) it is stated that King Solomon was taught the language of birds.

BI'R ZAMZAM (بئر زمزم). The well of Zamzam. [ZAM-ZAM.]

BI'R MAʻŪNAH (بئر معونة). The well of Maʻūnah. A celebrated spot four marches from Makkah, where a party of Muḥammad's followers were slain by the Banū ʻĀmir and Banū Sulaim. He professed to have received a special message from heaven regarding these martyrs, which runs thus:—"Acquaint our people that we have met our Lord. He is well pleased with us, and we are well pleased with Him." It is a remarkable verse, as having for some reason or other been cancelled, and removed from the Qur'ān. (Muir's *Life of Mahomet*, vol. iii. p. 207.)

BIRTH, Evidence of. According to the Imām Abu Ḥanīfah, if a married woman should claim to be the mother of a child, her claim is not to be valid unless the birth of of the child is attested by the testimony of *one woman.* But in the case of a father, inasmuch as the claim of parentage is a matter which relates purely to himself, his testimony alone is to be accepted.

The testimony of the midwife alone is sufficient with respect to *birth*, but with regard to *parentage*, it is established by the fact of the mother of the child being the wife of the husband.

If the woman be in her *'iddah* ['IDDAH] from a complete divorce, the testimony of the midwife is not sufficient with respect to birth, but the evidence of two men, or of one man and two women, is requisite. (Hamilton's *Hidāyah*, vol. iii. p. 134.)

It is also ruled that it is not lawful for a person to give evidence to anything which he has not seen, except in the cases of *birth, death*, and *marriage*. (Vol. ii. 676.)

BISHĀRAH (بشارة). [BUSHRA.]

BĪ-SHAR' (بی شرع). *Lit.* "Without the law." A term applied to those mystics who totally disregard the teaching of the Qur'ān. Antinomians. [SUFI.]

BISMILLĀH (بسم الله). *Lit.* "In the name of God." An ejaculation frequently used at the commencement of any undertaking. There are two forms of the Bismillah:—

1. *Bi-'smi 'llāhi 'r-raḥmāni 'r-raḥīm, i.e.* "In the name of God, the Compassionate, the Merciful." This is used at the commencement of meals, putting on new clothes, beginning any new work, and at the commencement of books. It occurs at the head of every chapter or sūrah in the Qur'ān, with the exception of the IXth (*i.e.* the *Sūratu 'l-Barā'ah*).

2. *Bi-'smi 'llāhi 'llāhi 'l-akbar, i.e.* "In the name of God, God the Most Great." Used at the time of slaughtering of animals, at the commencement of a battle, &c., the attribute of mercy being omitted on such occasions.

The formula *Bi-'smi 'llāhi 'r-raḥmāni 'r-raḥīm* is of Jewish origin. It was in the first instance taught to the Quraish by Umaiyah of Ṭā'if, the poet, who was a contemporary but somewhat older than, Muḥammad, and who, during his mercantile journeys into Arabia Petræa and Syria, had made himself acquainted with the sacred books and doctrines of Jews and Christians. (*Kitābu 'l-Aghānī*, 16, Delhi; quoted by Rodwell.)

BIẒĀ'AH (بضاعة). A share in a mercantile adventure. Property entrusted to another to be employed in trade.

BLACK STONE. [AL-HAJARU 'L-ASWAD.]

BLASPHEMY. Arabic كفر *kufr. Lit.* "to hide" (the truth). It includes a denial of any of the essential principles of Islām.

A Muslim convicted of blasphemy is sentenced to death in Muḥammadan countries. [APOSTASY.]

BLEEDING. Arabic حجامة *ḥijāmah.* The two great cures recommended by Muḥammad were blood-letting and drinking honey; and he taught that it was unlucky to be bled on a Friday, Saturday, or Sunday, the most lucky day being Tuesday, and the most lucky date the seventeenth of the month. (*Mishkāt*, xxi. c. 1.)

BLIND, The. Arabic *A'mā*, pl. *'Umyān.* It is not incumbent upon a blind man to engage in Jihād, or a religious war. And, according to the Imām Abū Ḥanīfah, the evidence of a blind person is not admissible, but the Imām Zufar maintains that such evidence is lawful when it affects a matter in which hearsay prevails. Sales and purchases made by a blind person are lawful. (Hamilton's *Hidāyah*, vol. ii., pp. 141, 402, 682.)

BLOOD. The sale of blood is unlawful. (Hamilton's *Hidāyah*, vol. ii. p. 428.)

BLOOD, The Avenger of. [QISAS.]

BLOOD, Issue of. [ISTIHAZAH.]

BOASTING. Arabic مفاخرة *mufākharah.* Muḥammad is related to have said, "I swear by God, a tribe must desist from boasting of their forefathers; for they are nothing more than coals from hell-fire (*i.e.* they were idolaters); and if you do not leave off boasting, verily you will be more hateful in the sight of God than a black-beetle. Mankind are all the sons of Adam, and Adam was of the earth." (*Mishkāt*, xxii. c. 13.)

BOOKS OF MOSES. [TAURAT.]

BOOKS, Stealing. The hand of a thief is not to be cut off for stealing a book, whatever be the subject of which it treats, because the object of the theft can only be the *contents* of the book, and not the book itself. But yet, it is to be observed, the hand is to be cut off for stealing "an *account* book," because in this case it is evident that the object of the theft is not the contents of the book, but the paper and material of which the book is made. (Hamilton's *Hidāyah*, vol. ii. 92.)

BOOTS. [SHOES.]

BREACH OF TRUST. Arabic خيانة *khiyānah.* The punishment of amputation of the hand is not inflicted for a breach of trust. And if a guest steal the property of his host whilst he is staying in his house, the hand is not cut off. Breach of trust in Muslim law being a less offence than ordinary theft, the punishment for breach of trust is left to the discretion of the judge. (Hamilton's *Hidāyah*, vol. ii. pp. 93–102.)

BRIBERY (Arabic رشوة *rishwah*) is not mentioned in the Qur'ān. In the *Fatāwā 'Alamgīrī* it is stated that presents to magistrates are of various kinds; for example, if a present be made in order to establish a friendship, it is lawful; but if it be given to influence the decision of the judge in the donor's favour, it is unlawful. It is also said, if a present be made to a judge from a sense of fear, it is lawful to give it, but unlawful to accept it. (Hamilton's *Hidāyah*, vol. iii. p. 332.)

BUʻĀṢ, Battle of. Arabic حرب بعاث *Ḥarb Buʻāṣ*. A battle fought between the Banū Khazraj and Banū Aus, about six years before the flight of Muḥammad from Makkah.

BUHTĀN (بهتان). A false accusation; calumny.

The word occurs twice in the Qur'ān:—

Sūrah iv. 112: "Whoso commits a fault or sin, and throws it upon one who is innocent, he hath to bear calumny (*buhtān*) and manifests in."

Sūrah xxiv. 15: "And why did ye not say when ye heard it, 'It is not for us to speak of this'? Celebrated be Thy praises, this is a mighty calumny (*buhtān*)." [BACKBITING.]

BUKĀ (بكاء). Heb. בָּכָה *he wept*. Weeping and lamentation for the dead. Immoderate weeping and lamentation over the graves of the dead is clearly forbidden by Muḥammad, who is related to have said, "Whatever is from the eyes (*i.e.* tears), and whatever is from the heart (*i.e.* sorrow), are from God; but what is from the hands and tongue is from the devil. Keep yourselves, O women, from wailing, which is the noise of the devil." (*Mishkāt*, v. c. vii.) The custom of wailing at the tombs of the dead is, however, common in all Muḥammadan countries. (See *Arabian Nights*, Lane's *Modern Egyptians*, Shaw's *Travels in Barbary*.) [BURIAL.]

AL-BUKHĀRĪ (البخاری). A short title given to the well-known collection of Sunni traditions by Abū ʻAbdu 'llāh Muḥammad ibn Ismāʻīl ibn Ibrāhīm ibn al-Mughirah al-Juʻfī al-Bukhari, who was born at Bukhārā, A.H. 194 (A.D. 810), and died at the village of Khartang near Samarqand, A.H. 256 (A.D. 870). His compilation comprises upwards of 7,000 traditions of the acts and sayings of the Prophet, selected from a mass of 600,000. His book is called the *Ṣaḥīḥ of al-Bukhārī*, and is said to have been the result of sixteen years labour. It is said that he was so anxious to record only trustworthy traditions that he performed a prostration in worship before the Almighty before he recorded each tradition.

BUKHTU NAṢṢAR (بخت نصر). "Nebuchadnezzar." It is thought by Jalālu 'd-dīn that there is a reference to his army taking Jerusalem in the Qur'ān, Sūrah xvii. 8, "And when the threat for the last (crime) came (to be inflicted, we sent an enemy) to harm your faces, and to enter the temple as they entered it the first time." The author of the *Qāmūs* says that *Bukht* is "son," and *Naṣṣar*, "an idol," *i.e.* "the son of Naṣṣar."

BŪLAS (بولس). "Despair." The name of one of the chambers of hell, where the proud will drink of the yellow water of the infernal regions. (*Mishkāt*, xxii. c. 20.)

BURĀQ (براق). *Lit.* "The bright one." The animal upon which Muḥammad is said to have performed the nocturnal journey called *Miʻrāj*. He was a white animal, between the size of a mule and an ass, having two wings. (*Majmaʻu 'l-Biḥār*, p. 89.) Muḥammad's conception of this mysterious animal is not unlike the Assyrian gryphon, of which Mr. Layard gives a sketch. [MIʻRAJ.]

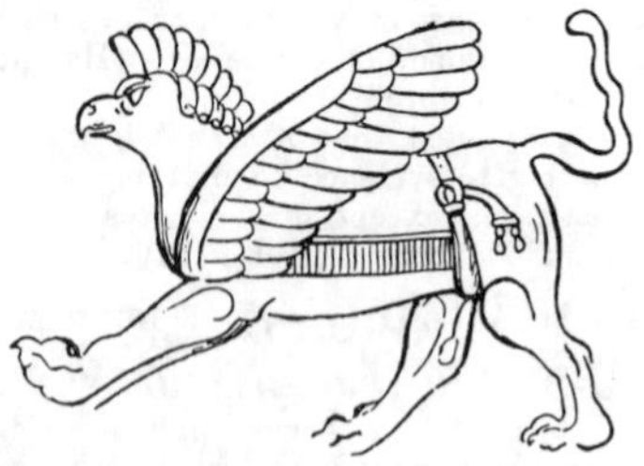

THE ASSYRIAN GRYPHON (Layard ii. 459).

BURGLARY is punished as an ordinary theft, namely by the amputation of the hand, but it is one of the niceties of Muḥammadan law, according to the Ḥanafī code, that if a thief break through the wall of the house, and enter therein, and take the property, and deliver it to an accomplice standing at the entrance of the breach, amputation of the hand is not incurred by either of the parties, because the thief who entered the house did not carry out the property. (*Hidāyah*, vol. ii. 103.)

BURIAL OF THE DEAD (جنازة *Jināzah* or *Janāzah*). The term *Janāzah* is used both for the bier and for the Muḥammadan funeral service. The burial service is founded upon the practice of Muḥammad, and varies but little in different countries, although the ceremonies connected with the funeral procession are diversified. In Egypt and Bukhārā, for instance, the male relations and friends of the deceased precede the corpse, whilst the female mourners follow behind. In India and Afghānistān, women do not usually attend funerals, and the friends and relatives of the deceased walk behind the bier. There is a tradition amongst some Muḥammadans that no one should precede the corpse, as the angels go before. Funeral processions in Afghānistān are usually very simple in their arrangements, and are said to be more in accordance with the practice of the Prophet, than those of Egypt and Turkey. It is considered a very meritorious act to carry the bier, and four from among the near relations, every now and then relieved by an equal number, carry it on their shoulders. Unlike our Christian custom of walking slowly to the grave, the Muḥammadans carry their dead quickly to the place of interment; for Muḥammad is related to have said, that it is good to carry the dead quickly to the grave, to cause the righteous person to arrive soon at happiness, and if he be a bad man, it is well to put wickedness away from one's shoulders. Funerals should always be attended on foot; for it is said that Muḥammad on one occasion rebuked his people for following on horseback. "Have you no shame?" said he, "since God's angels go on foot, and you go upon the backs of quadrupeds?" It is a highly meritorious act to attend a funeral, whether it be that of a Muslim, a Jew, or a Christian. There are, however, two traditions which appear to mark a change of feeling on the part of the Prophet of Arabia towards the Jews and Christians. "A bier passed by the Prophet, and he stood up; and it was said to the Prophet, this is the bier of a Jew. 'It is the holder of a soul,' he replied, 'from which we should take warning and fear.'" This rule is said to have been abrogated, for, "on one one occasion the Prophet sitting on the road when a bier passed, and the Prophet disliked that the bier of a Jew should be higher than his head, and he therefore stood up." (*Mishkāt*, v. c. v.) Notwithstanding these contradictory traditions, we believe that in all countries Muḥammadans are wont to pay great respect to the funerals of both Jews and Christians.

The Muḥammadan funeral service is not recited in the graveyard, it being too polluted a place for so sacred an office; but either in a mosque, or in some open space near the dwelling of the deceased person or the graveyard. The owner of the corpse, *i.e.* the nearest relative, is the proper person to recite the service; but it is usually said by the family Imām, or the Qāẓī.

The following is the order of the service:—

Some one present calls out,—

"Here begin the prayers for the dead."

Then those present arrange themselves in three, five, or seven rows opposite the corpse, with their faces Qiblah-wards (*i.e.* towards Makkah). The Imām stands in front of the ranks opposite the head (the Shī'ahs stand opposite the loins of a man) of the corpse, if it be that of male, or the waist, if it be that of a female.

The whole company having taken up the *Qiyām*, or standing position, the Imām recites the Nīyah.

"I purpose to perform prayers to God for this dead person, consisting of four *Takbīrs*."

Then placing his hands to the lobes of his ears, he says the first *Takbīr*.

"God is great!"

Then folding his hands, the right hand placed upon the left, below the navel, he recites the *Subḥān*:—

"Holiness to Thee, O God,
And to Thee be praise.
Great is Thy Name.
Great is Thy Greatness.
Great is Thy Praise.
There is no deity but Thee."

Then follows the second *Takbīr*:—

"God is great!"

Then the *Durūd*:—

"O God, have mercy on Muḥammad and upon his descendants, as Thou didst bestow mercy, and peace, and blessing, and compassion, and great kindness upon Abraham and upon his descendants.

"Thou art praised, and Thou art great!

"O God, bless Muḥammad and his descendants, as Thou didst bless and didst have compassion and great kindness upon Abraham and upon his descendants."

Then follows the third *Takbīr*:—

"God is great!"

After which the following prayer (*Du'ā*) is recited:—

"O God, forgive our living and our dead and those of us who are present, and those who are absent, and our children, and our full grown persons, our men and our women. O God, those whom Thou dost keep alive amongst us, keep alive in Islām, and those whom Thou causest to die, let them die in the Faith."

Then follows the fourth *Takbīr*:—

"God is great!"

Turning the head round to the right, he says:—

"Peace and mercy be to Thee."

Turning the head round to the left, he says:—

"Peace and mercy be to Thee."

The *Takbīr* is recited by the Imām aloud, but the *Subḥān*, the *Salām*, the *Durūd*, and the *Du'ā*, are recited by the Imām and the people in a low voice.

The people then seat themselves on the ground, and raise their hands in silent prayer in behalf of the deceased's soul, and afterwards addressing the relatives they say, "It is the decree of God." To which the chief mourner replies, "I am pleased with the will of God." He then gives permission to the people to retire by saying, "There is permission to depart."

Those who wish to return to their houses do so at this time, and the rest proceed to the grave. The corpse is then placed on its back in the grave, with the head to the north and feet to the south, the face being turned towards Makkah. The persons who place the corpse in the grave repeat the following sentence: "We commit thee to earth in the name of God and in the religion of the Prophet."

The bands of the shroud having been loosed, the recess, which is called the *laḥd*, is closed in with unburnt bricks and the grave filled in with earth. [GRAVE.] In some countries it is usual to recite verse 57 of the xxth Sūrah of the Qur'ān as the clods of earth are thrown into the grave; but this practice is objected to by the Wahhābīs, and by many learned divines. The verse is as follows:—

"From it (the earth) have We (God) created you, and unto it will We return you. and out of it will We bring you forth the second time."

After the burial, the people offer a *fātiḥah* (*i.e.* the first chapter of the Qur'ān) in the name of the deceased, and again when they have proceeded about forty paces from the grave they offer another *fātiḥah*; for at this juncture, it is said, the two angels Munkir and Nakir examine the deceased as to his faith. [PUNISHMENTS OF THE GRAVE.] After this, food is distributed to beggars and religious mendicants as a propitiatory offering to God, in the name of the deceased person.

If the grave be for the body of a woman, it should be to the height of a man's chest, if for a man, to the height of the waist. At the bottom of the grave the recess is made on the side to receive the corpse, which is called the *lāḥid* or *laḥd.* The dead are seldom interred in coffins, although they are not prohibited.

To build tombs with stones or burnt bricks, or to write a verse of the Qur'ān upon them, is forbidden in the Hadīs; but large stone and brick tombs are common to all Muḥammadan countries, and very frequently they bear inscriptions.

On the third day after the burial of the dead, it is usual for the relatives to visit the grave, and to recite selections from the Qur'ān. Those who can afford to pay Maulavīs, employ these learned men to recite the whole of the Qur'ān at the graves of their deceased relatives; and, the Qur'ān is divided into sections to admit of its being recited by the several Maulavīs at once. During the days of mourning the relatives abstain from wearing any article of dress of a bright colour, and their soiled garments remain unchanged.

A funeral procession in Egypt is graphically described by Mr. Lane in his *Modern Egyptians.* We give the account as it contrasts strikingly with the simple processions of Sunnī Muḥammadans in India.

"The first persons are about six or more poor men, called 'Yamanīyah,' mostly blind, who proceed two and two, or three and three, together. Walking at a moderate pace, or rather slowly, they chant incessantly, in a melancholy tone, the profession of faith ('There is no deity but God; Muhammad is God's Apostle; God favour and preserve him!'). They are followed by some male relations and friends of the deceased, and, in many cases, by two or more persons of some sect of darweshes, bearing the flags of their order. This is a general custom at the funeral of a darwesh. Next follow three or four or more schoolboys; one of them carries a *muṣḥaf* (or copy of the Qur'ān), or a volume consisting of one of the thirty sections of the Qur'ān, placed upon a kind of desk formed of palm-sticks, and covered over, generally with an embroidered kerchief. These boys chant, in a higher and livelier voice than the Yamanīyah, usually some words of a poem called the *Ḥashrīyah*, descriptive of the events of the last day, the judgment, &c. The schoolboys immediately precede the bier, which is borne head-foremost. Three or four friends of the deceased usually carry it for a short distance; then three or four other friends bear it a little further; and then these are in like manner relieved. Casual passengers, also, often take part in this service, which is esteemed highly meritorious. Behind the bier walk the female mourners; sometimes a group of more than a dozen, or twenty; with their hair dishevelled, though generally concealed by the head-veil; crying and shrieking, as before described; and often, the hired mourners accompany them, celebrating the praises of the deceased. Among the women, the relations and domestics of the deceased are distinguished by a strip of linen or cotton stuff or muslin, generally blue, bound round the head, and tied in a single knot behind: the ends hanging down a few inches. Each of these also carries a handkerchief, usually dyed blue, which she sometimes holds over her shoulders, and at other times twirls with both hands over her head, or before her face. The cries of the women, the lively chanting of the youths, and the deep tones uttered by the Yamanīyah, compose a strange discord.

"The funeral procession of a man of wealth, or of a person of the middle classes, is sometimes preceded by three or four or more camels, bearing bread and water to give to the poor at the tomb, and is composed of a more numerous and varied assemblage of persons. The foremost of these are the Yamanīyah, who chant the profession of the faith, as described above. They are generally followed by some male friends of the deceased, and some learned and devout persons who have been invited to attend the funeral. Next follows a group of four or more faqīhs, chanting the 'Sūratu 'l-An'ām' (the VIth chapter of the Qur'ān); and sometimes, another group, chanting the 'Sūrat Yā-sīn' (the XXXVIth chapter); another, chanting the 'Sūratu 'l-Kahf' (the XVIIIth chapter); and another chanting the 'Sūratu 'd-Dukhān' (the XLIVth chapter). These are followed by some munshids, singing the 'Burdah;' and these by certain persons called 'Aṣḥābu 'l-Aḥzāb,' who are members of religious orders founded by celebrated shaikhs. There are generally four or more of the order of the Hizbu 's-Sādāt, a similar group of the Ḥizbu 'sh-Shāzilī, and another of the Hizbu 'sh-Sha'rāwī; each group chants a particular form of prayer. After them are generally borne two or more half-furled flags, the banners of one or other of the principal orders of darweshes. Then follow the school-boys, the bier, and the female mourners, as in the procession before described, and, perhaps, the led horses of the bearers, if these be men of rank. A buffalo, to be sacrificed at the tomb, where its flesh is to be distributed to the poor, sometimes closes the procession.

"The funeral of a devout shaikh, or of one of the great 'Ulamā, is still more numerously attended, and the bier of such a person is not covered with a shawl. A 'walī' is further honoured in his funeral by a remarkable custom. Women follow his bier, but, instead of wailing, as they would after the corpse of an ordinary mortal, they rend the air with the shrill and quavering cries of joy called 'zaghārīṭ'; and if these cries are discontinued but for a minute, the bearers of the bier protest that they cannot proceed, that a supernatural power rivets them to the spot on which they stand. Very often, it is said, a 'walī' impels the bearers of his corpse to a particular spot. The following anecdote, describing an ingenious mode of puzzling a dead saint in a case of this kind, was related to me by one of my friends. Some men were lately bearing the corpse of a 'walī' to a tomb prepared for it in the great cemetery on the north of the metropolis, but on arriving at the gate called Bābu 'n-Naṣr, which leads to the cemetery, they found themselves unable to proceed further, from the cause above-mentioned. 'It seems,' said one of the bearers, 'that the shaikh is determined not to be buried in the cemetery of Bābu 'n-Naṣr, and what shall we do?' They were all much perplexed, but being as obstinate as the saint himself, they did not immediately yield to his caprice. Retreating a few paces, and then advancing with a quick step, they thought by such an impetus to force the corpse through the gateway; but their efforts were unsuccessful; and the same experiment they repeated in vain several times. They then placed the bier on the ground to rest and consult; and one of them, beckoning away his comrades to a distance beyond the hearing of the dead saint, said to them, 'Let us take up the bier again, and turn it round several times till the shaikh becomes giddy; he then will not know in what direction we are going, and we may take him easily through the gate.' This they did; the saint was puzzled as they expected, and quietly buried in the place which he had so striven to avoid.

"In the funerals of females and boys, the bier is usually only preceded by the Yamanīyah, chanting the profession of the faith, and by some male relations of the deceased; and followed by the female mourners; unless the deceased were of a family of wealth, or of considerable station in the world; in which case, the funeral procession is distinguished by some additional display. I shall give a short description of one of the most genteel and decorous funerals of this kind that I have witnessed: it was that of a young, unmarried lady. Two men, each bearing a large, furled, green flag, headed the procession, preceding the Yamanīyah, who chanted in an unusually low and solemn manner. These faqīrs, who were in number about eight, were followed by a group of fakihs, chanting a chapter of the Qur'ān. Next after the latter was a man bearing a large branch of 'Nabq' (or lote-tree), an emblem of the deceased. On each side of him walked a person bearing a tall staff or cane, to the top of which were attached several hoops ornamented with strips of various coloured paper. These were followed by two Turkish soldiers, side by side, one bearing, on a small round tray, a gilt silver 'qumqum' of rose-water, and the other bearing, on a similar tray, a 'mibkharah' of gilt silver, in which some odoriferous substance (as benzoin, or frankincense) was burning. These vessels diffused the odour of their contents on the way, and were afterwards used to perfume the sepulchral vault. Passengers were occasionally sprinkled with the rose-water. Next followed four men, each of whom bore, upon a small tray, several small lighted tapers of wax, stuck in lumps of paste of 'ḥinnā.' The bier was covered with rich shawls, and its shāhid was decorated with handsome ornaments of the head, having, besides the safā, a 'quṣṣah almās' (a long ornament of gold and diamonds worn over the forehead), and, upon its flat top, a rich diamond qurṣ. These were the jewels of the deceased, or were, perhaps, as is often the case, borrowed for the occasion. The female mourners, in number about seven or eight, clad in the usual manner of the ladies of Egypt (with the black silk covering, &c.), followed the bier, not on foot, as is the common custom in funerals in this country, but mounted on high-saddled asses; and only the last two or three of them were wailing; these being, probably, hired mourners. In another funeral-procession of a female, the daughter of a Turk of high rank, the Yamanīyah were followed by six slaves, walking two by two. The first two slaves bore each a silver qumqum of rose-water, which they sprinkled on the passengers; and one of them honoured me so profusely as to wet my dress very uncomfortably; after which, he poured a small quantity into my hands; and I wetted my face with it, according to custom. Each of the next two bore a silver mibkharah, with perfume; and the other two carried a silver 'āzqi (or hanging censer), with burning charcoal of frankincense. The jewels on the shāhid of the bier were of a costly description. Eleven ladies, mounted on high-saddled asses, together with several naddābahs, followed."

BURNING THE DEAD. There is no express injunction, in either the Qur'ān or the Traditions, regarding the burning of dead bodies, although the burning of the living is strictly forbidden. For Muḥammad said, "Punish not with God's punishment (which is fire), for it is not fit for anyone to punish with fire but God." (*Mishkāt*, xiv c. v. part 1.)

The teaching of the Traditions is that a dead body is as fully conscious of pain as a living body, for 'Āyishah said, that the Prophet said, "The breaking of the bones of a corpse is the same as doing it in life." (*Mishkāt*, v. c. vi. part 2.)

It is, therefore, pretty clearly established that cremation of the dead is strictly forbidden by the Muḥammadan religion. There is, however, nothing to confirm the impression that the burning of a corpse in any way prevents its soul entering paradise.

BURNING TO DEATH is strictly forbidden by Muslim law. 'Ikrimah relates that some apostates from Islām were brought to the Khalifah 'Alī, and he burnt them; and when Ibn 'Abbās heard of it, he said, "Had they been brought to me, I would not have burnt them; for the Prophet said, 'Punish not with God's punishment. Verily it is not fit for anyone to punish with fire but God.'" (*Mishkāt*, xiv. c. v. part 1.)

BURQA' (برقع). The veil or covering used for the seclusion of women when walking abroad. [VEILING OF WOMEN.]

BURŪJ (بروج). *Lit.* "Towers," which some interpret as real towers wherein the angels keep watch. A term used for the twelve signs of the zodiac. [SIGNS OF THE ZODIAC.] Al-Burūj is the title of the LXXXVth Sūrah of the Qur'ān.

BURYING OF THE DEAD. It is said by commentators that God taught mankind to bury their dead when "God sent a crow to scratch the earth, to show him (Cain) how he might hide his brother's body." (Qur'ān, Sūrah v. 34; *Tafsīr-i-Ḥusaini, in loco.*) The custom of burying their dead is universal in Islām. The ceremonies connected with funerals will be found in the article on Burial. [BURIAL.]

BURYING-GROUND. Arabic مقبرة *maqbarat* or *maqbarah*, "The place of graves." Persian *Qabr-gāh*, or *Qabristān*. They are sometimes spoken of by religious Muslims as *Marqad*, a "cemetery" or "sleeping-place," but the name has not obtained a general application to burial-grounds in the East as it has in the West. They are generally situated outside the city, the graves being covered with pebbles, and distinguished by headstones, those on the graves of men being with a turban-like head. The graves are dug from north to south. The grave-yards are usually much neglected. The Wahhābīs hold it to be a meritorious act, in accordance with the injunctions of the Prophet, to neglect the graves of the dead, the erection of brick tombs being forbidden. (*Hidāyah*, Arabic ed., vol. i. p. 90.) A grave-yard does not become public property until the proprietor formally makes a gift or bequest of it. (*Hidāyah*, vol ii., p. 357.)

BUSHRĀ (بشرى). "Good news;" "the gospel." A word used in the Traditions for the publication of Islām. (*Mishkāt*, xxiv. c. i.) "Accept good news, O ye sons of Tamim," which 'Abdu 'l-Ḥaqq says means "embrace Islām."

BUYING. [BAI'.]

BUZURG (بزرگ) *Lit.* "great." A Persian word used in the East for a saintly person, an old man, or a person of rank.

C.

CÆSAR. The Arabic and Persian form of the Latin Cæsar in *Qaiṣar*. The word occurs in the traditions of the *Ṣaḥiḥu 'l-Muslim* (vol. ii. p. 99), where it is applied to the Emperor Heraclius, who received a letter from Muḥammad inviting him to Islām, when he was at Edessa on his way to Jerusalem, August, A.D. 628. The origin of the title is uncertain. Spartianus, in his life of Aelius verus (c. ii.), mentions four different opinions respecting its origin: (1) That the word signified an elephant in the language of the Moors, and was given as a surname to one of the Julii because he had killed an elephant; or (2) That it was given to one of the Julii because he had been cut *(caesus)* out of his mother's womb after her death; or (3) Because he had been born with a great quantity of hair (*caesaries*) on his head; or (4) Because he had azure-coloured (*caesii*) eyes. Of these opinions the second is the one adopted by the Arabic-Persian Dictionary the *Ghiyāṣu 'l-Lughāt*.

The first of the Julian family who occurs in history as having obtained the surname of Cæsar is Sex. Julius Cæsar, prætor in B.C. 208. It was first assumed as an imperial title by Augustus as the adopted son of the dictator, and was by Augustus handed down to his adopted son Tiberius. It continued to be used by Caligula, Claudius, and Nero, as members, either by adoption or female descent, of Cæsar's family; but though the family became extinct with Nero, succeeding emperors still retained it as part of their titles, and it was the practice to prefix it to their own name, as, for instance, *Imperator Cæsar Domitianus Augustus*. The title was superseded in the Greek Empire under Alexis Commenus by that of Sebastocrator. In the west, it was conferred on Charles the Great, and was borne by those who succeeded him on the imperial throne. Although this dignity came to an end with the resignation of Francis II. in 1806, the title Kaiser is still assumed by the Emperors of Austria and Germany, and more recently by the Queen of England as *Qaiṣar-i-Hind*, or Empress of India.

CAIN. Arabic قابل *Qābil* (*Qābīl*). The account of Cain and Abel as given in the Qur'ān, Sūrah v. 30, will be found in the article ABEL. The Commentators say that the occasion of making the offering was as follows: Each of them being born with a twin sister, Adam by God's direction ordered Cain to marry Abel's twin sister, and Abel to marry Cain's, but that Cain refused. They were then ordered to submit the question by making a sacrifice, and Cain offered a sheaf of the very worst of his corn, whilst Abel offered the best fatted lamb of his flock. (*Tafsīru 'l-Baiẓāwī, in loco.*)

CALEB. Arabic *Kālab*. The son of Jephunneh (*Yūfannah*). He is not mentioned in the Qur'ān, but his name occurs in the *Tafsīru 'l-Baiẓāwī*, in Sūrah iv. 13.

CALF, GOLDEN, The, which the Israelites worshipped, is mentioned five times in the Qur'ān. Sūrahs ii. 48, 88; iv. 152; vii. 146; xx. 90. In Sūrah xx. 90, the person who made it is said to be as-Sāmirī. [MOSES.]

CALIPH. [KHALIFAH.]

CALUMNY is expressed by the word *Ghībah*, which means anything whispered to the detriment of an absent person, although it be true. *Buhtān*, expressing a false accusation. It is strictly forbidden in both the Qur'ān and Ḥadīs̤. [GHIBAH.]

CAMEL. Arabic *Ibil.* In the Qur'ān (Sūrah lxxxviii. 17), the institution of camels to ride upon is mentioned as an example of God's wisdom and kindness: "Do they not look then at the camel how she is created." As a proof of the great usefulness of the camel to the Arabian, and of the manner in which its very existence has influenced his language, it is remarkable that in almost every page of the Arabic Dictionary *Qāmūs* (as also in Richardson's edition), there is some reference to a camel.

Camels are a lawful sacrifice on the great festivals and on other occasions. And although it is lawful to slay a camel by *z̤abḥ*, or by merely cutting its throat, the most eligible method, according to Muslim law, is to slay a camel by *naḥr*, or by spearing it in the hollow of the throat near the breast-bone, because, says Abū Ḥanīfah, it is according to the *sunnah*, or practice of Muḥammad, and also because in that part of the throat three blood-vessels of a camel are combined. (Hamilton's *Hidāyah*, vol. iv. p. 72.) There is *zakāt*, or legal alms, on camels. [ZAKAT.] Muḥammadan law rules that the person who leads a string of camels is responsible for anything any one of the camels may injure or tread down. (*Ibid.*, iv. 379.)

CANAAN. Arabic *Kan'ān.* According to al-Jalālain and al-Baiẓāwī, the commentators, Canaan was the unbelieving son of Noah, but, according to the *Qāmus* dictionary, the grandson, who was drowned in the flood, and whose case is recorded in the Qur'ān (Sūrah xi. 44). He is said to be a son of Noah's wife Wā'ilah, who was an infidel. "And the Ark moved on them amid waves like mountains: and Noah called to his son—for he was apart—'Embark with us, O my child! and be not with the unbelievers.' He said, 'I will betake me to a mountain that shall secure me from the water.' He said, 'None shall be secure this day from the decree of God, save him on whom He shall have mercy.' And a wave passed between them, and he was among the drowned."

CAPTIVES. *Asīr*, pl. *Usārā* and *Usarā'*. With respect to captives, the Imām, or leader of the army, has it in his choice to slay them, "because the Prophet put captives to death, and also because slaying them terminates wickedness"; or, he may if he choose make them slaves. It is not lawful for the Imām to send captives back to their home and country, because that would be to strengthen the cause of infidelity against Islām. If they become Muslims after their capture, they must not be put to death, but they may be sold after their conversion. A converted captive must not be suffered to return to his country, and it is not lawful to release a captive gratuitously. The only method of dividing plunder which consists of slaves, is by selling them at the end of the expedition and then dividing the money. (*Hidāyah*, ii. 160.) [SLAVERY.]

CARAVAN. Persian *Kārwān*, Arabic *Qāfilah.* As the roads in the East are often unsafe and lead through dreary wastes, merchants and travellers associate together for mutual defence and comfort. These companies are called both *kārwān* and *qāfilah.* The party is always under the direction of a paid director, who is called Karwān- or Qāfilah-*Bāshī.* If a caravan is attacked on the road, the Muḥammadan law allows the punishment of crucifixion for the offence. (*Hidāyah*, vol. ii. 131.) But it is a curious provision of the Muslim law that if some of the travellers in a caravan commit a robbery upon others of the same caravan, punishment (*i.e.* of amputation) is not incurred by them. (Vol. ii. 137.)

CARRION (Arabic *Maitah*) is forbidden in the Qur'ān, Sūrah ii. 80. "*That which dieth of itself*, and blood, and swine's flesh, and that over which any other name than that of God hath been invoked, is forbidden. But he who shall partake of them by constraint, without lust or wilfulness, no sin shall be upon him."

CASTING LOTS. *Zalam*, or casting lots by shooting arrows, was an ancient Arabic custom, which is forbidden by Muḥammad in his Qur'ān, Sūrah v. 4; but *qur'ah*, or casting lots, in its ordinary sense, is not forbidden, for 'Āyishah relates that when the Prophet went on a journey, he used to cast lots as to which wife he should take with him. (*Mishkāt Bābu 'l-Qasam.*)

CATS. Arabic *Hirrah.* According to a Ḥadīs̤ of Abū Qutādah, who was one of the Companions, Muḥammad said, "Cats are not impure, they keep watch around us." He used water from which a cat had drunk for his purifications, and his wife 'Āyishah ate from a vessel from which a cat had eaten. (*Mishkāt*, book iii., c. 10, pt. 2.)

CATTLE. Arabic *An'ām.* They are said in the Qur'ān to be the gift of God, Sūrah xl. 79, "God it is who hath made for you cattle, that ye may ride on some and eat others."

Cattle kept for the purpose of labour, such as carrying burthens, drawing ploughs, &c., are not subject to *zakāt*, neither is there *zakāt* on cattle who are left to forage for one half year or more. (*Hidāyah*, i. 18.)

Al-An'ām is the title of the sixth Sūrah of the Qur'ān.

CAVE, The Companions of the (Arabic *Aṣḥābu 'l-kahf*), or the Seven Sleepers of Ephesus, form the subject of one of the chapters of the Qur'ān, Sūrah xviii. 6. [ASHABU 'L-KAHF.]

CELIBACY (Arabic *'Uzūbah*), although not absolutely condemned by Muḥammad, is held to be a lower form of life to that of marriage. It is related that 'Us̤mān ibn Maz̤'ūn wished to lead a celebate life, and the Prophet forbade him, for, said he, "When a Muslim marries he perfects his religion." (*Mishkāt*, book xii. c. xx.)

CEYLON. Arabic *Sarandīb*. The Commentators say that when Adam and Eve were cast out of Paradise, Adam fell on the island of Ceylon, and Eve near Jiddah in Arabia, and that after a separation of 200 years, Adam was, on his repentance, conducted by the angel Gabriel to a mountain near Makkah, where he found and knew his wife, the mountain being named 'Arafah; and that afterwards he retired with her to Ceylon, when they continued to propagate their species. (D'Herbelot, *Bibl. Orient.*, p. 55.)

CHASTITY. "Neither their (the Muslims') tenets nor their practice will in any respect bear to come into competition with Christian, or even with Jewish morality. . . . . For instance, we call the Muslims chaste because they abstained from indiscriminate profligacy, and kept carefully within the bounds prescribed as licit by their Prophet. But those bounds, besides the utmost freedom of divorce and change of wives, admitted an illimitable licence of cohabitation with 'all that the right hand of the believer might possess,' or, in other words, with any possible number of damsels he might choose to purchase, or receive in gift, or take captive in war." (Muir's *Life of Mahomet*, vol. i. 272. [CONCUBINAGE, SLAVES, MUT'AH, DIVORCE, MARRIAGE.]

CHARITY, as it implies tenderness and affection, is expressed by *ḥubb*, or *maḥabbah*; as it denotes almsgiving, it is *ṣadaqah*. He who is liberal and charitable to the poor is called *muḥibbu 'l-fuqarā'*.

CHERUBIM. Arabic *Karūbī*, pl. *Karūbīn*; *Lit.* "Those who are near." Heb. כְּרוּבִים. The word *karūbīn* is used by the commentator al-Baiẓāwī, for the angels mentioned in the Qur'ān, Sūrah xl. 70: "Those around it (the throne of God) celebrate the praise of their Lord, and believe in Him, and ask pardon for those who believe." Al-Baiẓāwī says the Karūbīn are the highest rank, and the first created angels. Ḥusain says there are 70,000 ranks of them round the throne of God. (*Tafsīru 'l-Baiẓāwī*, *Tafsīru Ḥusain*, *in loco.*)

CHESS. Arabic *Shaṭranj*. According to the Hidāyah, "It is an abomination to play at chess, dice, or any other game, for if anything be staked it is gambling (*maisir*), which is expressly forbidden in the Qur'ān; or if, on the other hand, nothing be hazarded, it is useless and vain. Besides, the Prophet has declared all the entertainments of a Muslim to be vain except three: the breaking in of his horse, the drawing of his bow, and playing and amusing himself with his wives. Several of the learned, however, deem the game at chess lawful as having a tendency to quicken the understanding. This is the opinion of *ash-Shāfi'ī*. If a man play at chess for a stake, it destroys the integrity of his character, but if he do not play for a stake, the integrity of his character is not affected. (Hamilton's *Hidāyah*, vol. iv. p. 122.)

CHILDREN. Arabic *Aulād*. There are no special injunctions in the Qur'ān regarding the customs to be observed at the birth of an infant (circumcision not being even once mentioned in that book), nor with reference to the training and instruction of the young; but the subject is frequently referred to in the Traditions and in Muḥammadan books on Ethics. Muḥammadans have so largely incorporated the customs of the Hindus in India with their own, especially those observed at the births of children, that it is sometimes difficult to distinguish those which are special characteristics of Islām; many of the customs recorded in Herklot's *Musalmans*, for example, being merely those common to Hindus as well as Muḥammadans. We shall, however, endeavour to describe those which are generally admitted to have some authority in the precepts of the Muslim religion.

(1.) *At the birth of a child*, after he has been properly washed with water and bound in swaddling clothes, he is carried by the midwife to the assembly of male relatives and friends, who have met on the occasion, when the chief Maulawī, or some person present, recites the *Az̤ān*, or summons to prayer [AZAN], in the infant's right ear, and the *Iqāmah*, which is the Az̤ān with the addition of the words, "We are standing up for prayers" [IQAMAH], in the left ear; a custom which is founded on the example of the Prophet, who is related to have done so at the birth of his grandson Ḥasan (*Mishkāt*, book xviii. c. iv. 2). The Maulawī then chews a little date fruit and inserts it into the infant's mouth, a custom also founded upon the example of Muḥammad. (*Mishkāt*, book xviii. c. iv. 1.) This ceremony being over, alms are distributed, and *fātiḥahs* are recited for the health and prosperity of the child. According to the traditions, the amount of silver given in alms should be of the same weight as the hair on the infant's head—the child's head being shaved for this purpose. (*Mishkāt*, *ibid.*, part 2.) The friends and neighbours then visit the home, and bring presents, and pay congratulatory compliments on the joyful occasion.

(2.) *The naming of the child* should, according to the Traditions (*Mishkāt*, *ibid.*), be given on the seventh day; the child being either named after some member of the family, or after some saint venerated by the family, or some name suggested by the auspicious hour, the planet, or the sign of the zodiac. [EXORCISM.]

(3.) On this, the seventh day, is observed also the *ceremony of 'Aqīqah*, established by Muḥammad himself (*Bābu 'l-'Aqīqah* in Arabic Ed. *Ṣaḥīḥ* of Abū Dāūd, vol. ii. p. 36) It consists of a sacrifice to God, in the name of the child, of two he-goats for a boy, and one he-goat for a girl. The goats must be not above a year old, and without spot or blemish. The animal is dressed and cooked, and whilst the friends eat of it they offer the following prayer:—"O God! I offer to thee instead of my own offspring, life for life, blood for blood, head for head, bone for bone, hair for hair, skin for skin. In the name of the great God, I do sacrifice this goat!"

(4.) The mother is purified on the *fortieth day*, when she is at liberty to go about as usual, and it is on this day that the infant is generally placed in the swinging cradle peculiar to eastern households. It is a day of some rejoicing amongst the members of the Ḥaram.

(5.) As soon as the child is able to talk, or when he has attained the age of four years, four months, and four days, he is taught the *Bismillah*; that is, to recite the inscription which occurs at the commencement of the Qur'ān: "*Bi-'smi 'llāhi 'r-raḥmāni 'r-raḥīm.*" In the name of God the Merciful, the Gracious. After this ceremony, the child is sent to school and taught the alphabet, and to recite certain chapters of the Qur'ān by rote.

(6.) According to the opinion of Sunnī doctors, the *circumcision* of the child should take place in his seventh year; the operation being generally performed by the barber. [CIRCUMCISION.] The child is not required to observe all the customs of the Muslim law until he has arrived at puberty [PUBERTY]; but it is held incumbent on parents and guardians to teach him the prayers as soon as he has been circumcised.

(7.) The time when the child has finished *reciting the whole of the Qur'ān*, once through, is also regarded as an important epoch in the life of a child. On this occasion the scholar makes his obeisance to his tutor and presents him with trays of sweetmeats, a suit of clothes, and money.

As we have already remarked, the instruction of youth is a frequent subject of discussion in books of Muslim Ethics. The following, which is taken from the *Akhlāq-i-Jalālī*, is an interesting specimen of Muḥammadan ideas on the subject:—The first requisite is to employ a proper nurse of a well-balanced temperament, for the qualities, both temperamental and spiritual, of the nurse are communicated to the infant. Next, since we are recommended by the Traditions to give the name on the seventh day (after birth), the precept had better be conformed to. In delaying it, however, there is this advantage, that time is given for a deliberate selection of an appropriate name. For, if we give the child an ill-assorted one. his whole life is embittered in consequence Hence caution in determining the name is one of the parent's obligations towards his offspring.

If we would prevent the child's acquiring culpable habits, we must apply ourselves to educate him as soon as weaned. For though men have a capacity for perfection, the tendency to vice is naturally implanted in the soul. The first requisite is to restrain him absolutely from all acquaintance with those excesses which are characterised as vice. For the mind of children is like a clear tablet, equally open to any inscription. Next to that, he should be taught the institutes of religion and rules of propriety, and, according as his power and capacity may admit, confined to their practice, and reprehended and restrained from their neglect. Thus, at the age of seven, we are told by the Traditions to enjoin him merely to say his prayers; at the age of ten, if he omits them, to admonish him by blows. By praising the good and censuring the bad, we should render him emulous of right and apprehensive of wrong. We should commend him when he performs a creditable action, and intimidate him when he commits a reprehensible one; and yet we should avoid, if possible, subjecting him to positive censure, imputing it rather to oversight, lest he grow audacious. If he keep his fault a secret, we are not to rend away the disguise; but if he do so repeatedly, we must rebuke him severely in private, aggravating the heinousness of such a practice, and intimidating him from its repetition. We must beware, however, of too much frequency of detection and reproof, for fear of his growing used to censure, and contracting a habit of recklessness; and thus, according to the proverb, "Men grow eager for that which is withheld," feeling a tendency to repeat the offence. For these reasons we should prefer to work by enhancing the attraction of virtue.

On meat, drink, and fine clothing, he must be taught to look with contempt, and deeply impressed with the conviction that it is the practice of women only to prize the colouring and figuring of dress; that men ought to hold themselves above it. The proprieties of meal-taking are those in which he should be earliest instructed, as far as he can acquire them. He should be made to understand that the proper end of eating is health and not gratification; that food and drink are a sort of medicine for the cure of hunger and thirst; and just as medicines are only to be taken in the measure of need, according as sickness may require their influence, food and drink are only to be used in quantity sufficient to satisfy hunger and remove thirst. He should be forbidden to vary his diet, and taught to prefer limiting himself to a single dish. His appetite should also be checked that he may be satisfied with meals at the stated hours. Let him not be a lover of delicacies. He should now and then be kept on dry bread only, in order that in time of need he may be able to subsist on that. Habits like these are better than riches. Let his principal meal be made in the evening rather than the morning, or he will be overpowered by drowsiness and lassitude during the day. Flesh let him have sparingly, or he will grow heavy and dull. Sweetmeats and other such aperient food should be forbidden him, as likewise all liquid at the time of meals. Incumbent as it is on all men to eschew strong drinks, there are obvious reasons why it is superlatively so on boys, impairing them both in mind and body, and leading to anger, rashness, audacity, and levity, qualities which such a practice is sure to confirm. Parties of this nature he should not be allowed unnecessarily to frequent, nor to listen to reprehensible conversation. His food should not be given to him till he has despatched his tasks, unless suffering from positive exhaustion. He must be forbidden to conceal any of his actions, lest he grow bold in impropriety; for, manifestly, the motive to concealment can be no other than an idea that they are culpable. Sleeping in the day and sleeping overmuch at night should be prohibited. Soft clothing and all the uses of luxury, such as cool retreats in the hot season, and fires and fur in the cold, he should be taught to abstain from; he should be inured to exercise, foot-walking, horse-riding, and all other appropriate accomplishments.

Next, let him learn the proprieties of conversation and behaviour. Let him not be tricked out with trimmings of the hair and womanly attention to dress, nor be presented with rings till the proper time for wearing them. Let him be forbidden to boast to his companions of his ancestry or worldly advantages. Let him be restrained from speaking untruths or from swearing in any case, whether true or false; for an oath is wrongful in anyone, and repugnant to the letter of the Traditions, saving when required by the interest of the public. And even though oaths may be requisite to men, to boys they never can be so. Let him be trained to silence, to speaking only when addressed, to listening in the presence of his elders, and expressing himself correctly.

For an instructor he should have a man of principle and intelligence, well acquainted with the discipline of morals, fond of cleanliness, noted for stateliness, dignity, and humanity, well acquainted with the dispositions of kings, with the etiquette of dining in their company, and with the terms of intercourse with all classes of mankind. It is desirable that others of his kind, and especially sons of noblemen, whose manners have always a distinguished elegance, should be at school with him, so that in their society he may escape lassitude, learn demeanour, and exert himself with emulation in his studies. If the instructor correct him with blows, he must be forbidden to cry, for that is the practice of slaves and imbeciles. On the other hand, the instructor must be careful not to resort to blows, except he is witness of an offence openly committed. When compelled to inflict them, it is desirable in the outset to make them small in number and great in pain; otherwise the warning is not so efficacious, and he may grow audacious enough to repeat the offence.

Let him be encouraged to liberality, and taught to look with contempt on the perishable things of this world; for more ill comes from the love of money than from the simoom of the desert or the serpent of the field. The Imām al-Ghazzālī, in commenting on the text, "Preserve me and them from idolatry," says that by idols is here meant gold and silver; and Abraham's prayer is that he and his descendants may be kept far removed from the worship of gold and silver, and from fixing their affections on them; because the love of these was the root of all evil. In his leisure hours he may be allowed to play, provided it does not lead to excess of fatigue or the commission of anything wrong.

When the discerning power begins to preponderate, it should be explained to him that the original object of worldly possessions is the maintenance of health; so that the body may be made to last the period requisite to the spirit's qualifying itself for the life eternal. Then, if he is to belong to the scientific classes, let him be instructed in the sciences. Let him be employed (as soon as disengaged from studying the essentials of the religion) in acquiring the sciences. The best course is to ascertain, by examination of the youth's character, for what science or art he is best qualified, and to employ him accordingly; for, agreeably to the proverb, "All facilities are not created to the same person"; everyone is not qualified for every profession, but each for a particular one.

This, indeed, is the expression of a principle by which the fortunes of man and of the world are regulated. With the old philosophers it was a practice to inspect the horoscope of nativity, and to devote the child to that profession which appeared from the planetary positions to be suitable to his nature. When a person is adapted to a profession, he can acquire it with little pains; and when unadapted, the utmost he can do is but to waste his time and defer his establishment in life. When a profession bears an incongruity with his nature, and means and appliances are unpropitious, we should not urge him to pursue it, but exchange it for some other, provided that there is no hope at all of succeeding with the first; otherwise it may lead to his perplexity. In the prosecution of every profession, let him adopt a system which will call into play the ardour of his nature, assist him in preserving health, and prevent obtusity and lassitude.

As soon as he is perfect in a profession, let him be required to gain his livelihood thereby; in order that, from an experience of its advantages, he may strive to master it completely, and make full progress in the minutiæ of its principles. And for this livelihood he must be trained to look to that honourable emolument which characterises the well-connected. He must not depend on the provision afforded by his father. For it generally happens, when the sons of the wealthy, by the pride of their parents' opulence, are debarred from acquiring a profession, that they sink by the vicissitudes of fortune into utter insignificance. Therefore, when he has so far mastered his profession as to earn a livelihood, it is expedient to provide him with a consort, and let him depend on his separate earning. The Kings of Fārs, forbearing to bring their sons up surrounded by domestics and retinue, sent them off to a distance, in order to habituate them to a life of hardship. The Dilemite chiefs had the same practice. A person bred upon the opposite principle can hardly be brought to good, especially if at all advanced in years; like hard wood which is with difficulty straightened. And this was the answer Socrates gave, when asked why his intimacies lay chiefly among the young.

In training daughters to that which befits them, domestic ministration, rigid seclusion, chastity, modesty, and the other qualities already appropriated to women—no care can be too great. They should be made emulous of acquiring the virtues of their sex, but must be altogether forbidden to read and write. When they reach the marriageable age, no time should be lost in marrying them to proper mates. (See *Akhlāq-i-Jalālī*, Thompson's ed.)

CHILD STEALING.

The hand of a thief is not to be cut off for stealing a *free-born* child, although there be ornaments upon it, because a free person is not property, and the ornaments are only appendages; and also because the thief may plead that he took the child up when it was crying, with a view to appease it, and to deliver it to the nurse. But Abū Yūsuf does not agree with Ḥanīfah; for he says where the value of the ornaments amounts to ten dirms, amputation is incurred. Amputation is also inflicted for stealing an infant slave, because a slave is property, although Abū Yūsuf says it is not. (*Hidāyah*, ii. 91.)

CHOSROES.

Arabic *Khusraw*. The King of Persia to whom Muḥammad sent a letter inviting him to Islām. He is said to be Nausherwān. (See *Ghiyāṣu 'l-Lughāt, in loco;* refer also to Muir's *Life of Mahomet*, vol. ii. 54 n.)

CHRIST.

[JESUS CHRIST.]

CHRISTIANITY and CHRISTIANS.

Arabic, *Naṣrānīyah*, "Christianity"; the terms used for Christians being *Naṣrān*, pl. *Naṣāra*, or *'Isawī*.

Christianity seems to have been widely diffused in Arabia at the time of Muḥammad. According to Caussin de Perceval, who quotes from Arabic writers, Christianity existed amongst the Banū Taghlib of Mesopotamia, the Banū 'Abdu 'l-Qais, the Banū Ḥāriṣ of Najrān, the Banū Ghassān of Syria, and other tribes between al-Madīnah and al-Kūfah.

The historian Philostorges (*Hist. Eccles.* lib. 1, c. 3) tells us that a monk named Theophilus, who was an Indian bishop, was sent by the Emperor Constance, A.D 342, to the Ḥimyarite King of Yaman, and obtained permission to build three Christian churches for those who professed Christianity; one at Zafār, another at 'Adan, and a third at Hurmuz on the Persian Gulf. According to the same author, the Christian religion was introduced into Najrān in the fifth century. A bishop sent by the Patriarch of Alexandria was established in the city of Zafār, and we are told by Muslim authors, quoted by Caussin de Perceval, that a Christian church was built at Ṣan'ā' which was the wonder of the age, the Roman Emperor and the Viceroy of Abyssinia furnishing the materials and workmen for the building. The Arabs of Yaman were ordered by the ruler of Abyssinia to perform a pilgrimage to this new church instead of to the Ka'bah; an edict which is said to have been resisted and to have given rise to the "War of the Elephant," when Abrahah, the Viceroy of Egypt, took an oath that he would destroy the Meccan temple, and marched at the head of an army of Abyssinians, mounted on an elephant. This "War of the Elephant" marks the period of Muḥammad's birth. [MUHAMMAD.]

The Christianity of this period is described by Mosheim as "expiring under a motley and enormous heap of superstitious inventions, with neither the courage nor the force to raise her head or display her national charms to a darkened and deluded world." Doubtless much of the success of Islām in its earlier stage was due to the state of degradation into which the Christian Church had fallen. The bitter dissensions of the Greeks, Nestorians, Eutychians, and Monophysites are matters of history, and must have held up the religion of Jesus to the ridicule of the heathen world. The controversies regarding the nature and person of our Divine Lord had begotten a sect of Tritheists, led by a Syrian philosopher named John Philoponus of Alexandria, and are sufficient to account for Muḥammad's conception of the Blessed Trinity. The worship of the Virgin Mary had also given rise to a religious controversy between the Antiduo-Marianites and the Collyridians; the former holding that the Virgin was not immaculate, and the latter raising her to a position of a goddess. Under the circumstances it is not surprising to find that the mind of the Arabian reformer turned away from Christianity and endeavoured to construct a religion on the lines of Judaism. [JUDAISM.]

Al-Baiẓāwī and other Muslim commentators, admit that Muḥammad received Christian instruction from learned Christians, named Jubrā and Yasāra (al-Baiẓāwī on Sūrah xvi. 105), and that on this account the Quraish said, "It is only some mortal that teaches him!" For the Traditions relate that Muḥammad used to stop and listen to these two Christians as they read aloud the Books of Moses (*Taurāt*) and the New Testament (*Injīl*). But it is remarkable that Muḥammad should, after all, have obtained such a cursory knowledge of Christianity. For from the text of the Qur'ān (extracts of which are subjoined), it is evident that he was under the impression that the Sacrament of Baptism was *Ṣibghah*, or the dyeing of the Christians' clothes; and if the Chapter of the Table refers to the Sacrament of the Lord's Supper (which is uncertain), it was "a table sent out of heaven that it may be a recurring festival." The doctrine of the Trinity is supposed to be a Tritheism of God, Jesus Christ, and the Virgin Mary; and a proof against the Divinity of Christ is urged from the fact that He and His mother "both ate food." The crucifixion is denied, and Mary the mother of Jesus is confounded with Mary the sister of Aaron. Such mistakes and omissions could only arise from a most imperfect acquaintance with the ordinary institutions and beliefs of the Christian communities, with whom Muḥammad must have been brought in contact. The gentler tone and spirit of the Christians seems to have won the sympathy of Muḥammad, and his expressions regarding them are less severe than with reference to the Jews; but the abstruse character of their creed, as shown in their endless schisms regarding the nature of the Trinity and the person of Christ, and the idolatrous character of their worship, as still seen in the ancient Syrian and Coptic churches, led him to turn from Christianity to Judaism as a model whereby to effect the reformation of a degraded and idolatrous people like the ancient Arabians. The Jewish and Mosaic character of Muḥammad's system will be treated of in another place. [JUDAISM.]

The following selections from the Qur'ān will show the actual teaching of that book regarding Christianity. In the whole of the Qur'ān there is not a single quotation from the New Testament, and it is noticeable that nearly all the allusions to Christianity are contained in Meccan Sūrahs; Sūrah ii. being according to Jalālu 'd-din Suyūṭī, one of the earliest chapters given at Makkah, and Sūrah v. the last.

Sūrah v. 85:—

"Of all men thou wilt certainly find the Jews, and those who join other gods with God, to be the most intense in hatred of those who believe; and thou shalt certainly find those to be nearest in affection to them who say, 'We are Christians.' This, because there are amongst them priests (*qissīsūn*) and monks, and because they are not proud."

Sūrah ii. 59:—

"Verily, they who believe (Muslims), and they who follow the Jewish religion, and the Christians, and the Sabeites—whoever of these believeth in God and the last day, and doeth that which is right, shall have their reward with their Lord: fear shall not come upon them, neither shall they be grieved."

(*The same verse occurs again in Sūrah* v. 74.)

Surah ii. 105:—

"And they say, 'None but Jews or Christians shall enter Paradise:' This is their wish. SAY: Give your proofs if ye speak the truth. But they who set their face with resignation Godward, and do what is right,—their reward is with their Lord; no fear shall come on them, neither shall they be grieved. Moreover, the Jews say, 'The Christians lean on naught:' 'On naught lean the Jews,' say the Christians. Yet both are readers of the Book. So with like words say they who have no knowledge. But on the resurrection day, God shall judge between them as to that in which they differ. And who committeth a greater wrong than he who hindereth God's name from being remembered in His temples, and who hasteth to ruin them? Such men cannot enter them but with fear. Theirs is shame in this world, and a severe torment in the next. The East and the West is God's: therefore, whichever way ye turn, there is the face of God. Truly God is immense and knoweth all. And they say, 'God hath a son:' No! Praise be to Him! But—His, whatever is in the Heavens and the Earth! All obeyeth Him, sole maker of the Heavens and of the Earth! And when He decreeth a thing, He only saith to it, 'Be,' and it is. And they who have no knowledge say, 'Unless God speak to us, or thou shew us a sign . . . .!' So, with like words, said those who were before them: their hearts are alike. Clear signs have we already shown for those who have firm faith. Verily, with the Truth have we sent thee, a bearer of good tidings and a warner: and of the people of Hell thou shalt not be questioned. But until thou follow their religion, neither Jews nor Christians will be satisfied with thee. SAY: Verily, guidance of God,—that is the guidance! And if, after 'the Knowledge,' which hath reached thee, thou follow their desires, thou shalt find neither helper nor protector against God."

Sūrah iv. 156:—

"Nay, but God hath sealed them up for their unbelief, so that but few believe. And for their unbelief,—and for their having spoken against Mary a grievous calumny,—and for their saying, 'Verily we have slain the Messiah (*Masīh*), Jesus (*'Isa*) the son of Mary, an Apostle of God.' Yet they slew him not, and they crucified him not, but they had only his likeness. And they who differed about him were in doubt concerning him. No sure knowledge had they about him, but followed only an opinion, and they did not really slay him, but God took him up to Himself. And God is Mighty, Wise!"

Sūrah ii. 130:—

"They say, moreover, 'Become Jews or Christians that ye may have the *true* guidance.' SAY: Nay! the religion of Abraham, the sound in faith, and not one of those who join gods with God!

Say ye: 'We believe in God, and that which hath been sent down to us, and that which hath been sent down to Abraham and Ishmael and Isaac and Jacob and the tribes: and that which hath been given to Moses and to Jesus, and that which was given to the prophets from their Lord. No difference do we make between any of them: and to God are we resigned (Muslims).' If, therefore, they believe even as ye believe, then have they true guidance; but if they turn back, then do they cut themselves off *from you:* and God will suffice *to protect* thee against them, for He is the Hearer, the Knower. The Baptism of God, and who is better to baptize than God? And Him do we serve."

Sūrah v. 75:—

"They surely are Infidels who say, 'God is the third of three:' for there is no God but one God: and if they refrain not from what they say, a grievous chastisement shall light on such of them as are Infidels. Will they not, therefore, be turned unto God, and ask pardon of Him? since God is Forgiving, Merciful! The Messiah, Son of Mary, is but an Apostle; other Apostles have flourished before him; and his mother was a just person: they both ate food. Behold! how we make clear to them the signs! then behold how they turn aside! SAY: Will ye worship, beside God, that which can neither hurt nor help? But God! He only Heareth, Knoweth. SAY: O people of the Book! outstep not bounds of truth in your religion; neither follow the desires of those who have already gone astray, and who have caused many to go astray, and have themselves gone astray from the evenness of the way. Those among the children of Israel who believed not were cursed by the tongue of David, and of Jesus, Son of Mary. This, because they were rebellious, and became transgressors: they forbade not one another the iniquity which they wrought! detestable are their actions!"

Sūrah v. 18:—

"And of those who say, 'We are Christians,' have we accepted the covenant. But they *too* have forgotten a part of what they were taught; wherefore we have stirred up enmity and hatred among them that shall last till the day of the Resurrection; and in the end will God tell them of their doings. O people of the Scriptures! now is our Apostle come to you to clear up to you much that ye concealed of those Scriptures, and to pass over many things. Now hath a light and a clear Book come to you from God, by which God will guide him who shall follow after His good pleasure to paths of peace, and will bring them out of the darkness to the light, by His will: and to the straight path will He guide them. Infidels now are they who say, 'Verily God is al-Masīḥ Ibn Maryam (the Messiah, son of Mary)! SAY: And who could aught obtain from God, if He chose to destroy al-Masīḥ Ibn Maryam, and his mother, and all who are on the earth together? For with God is the sovereignty of the Heavens and of the Earth, and of all that is between them! He createth what He will; and over all things is God potent. Say the Jews and Christians, 'Sons are we of God and His beloved.' SAY: Why then doth He chastise you for your sins? Nay! ye are but a part of the men whom He hath created!"

Sūrah v. 58:—

"O Believers! take not the Jews or Christians as friends. They are but one another's friends. If any one of you taketh them for his friends, he surely is one of them! God will not guide the evil-doers. So shalt thou see the diseased at heart speed away to them, and say, 'We fear lest a change of fortune befall us.' But haply God will of Himself bring about some victory or event of His own ordering: then soon will they repent them of their secret imaginings."

Sūrah xxii. 18:—

"As to those who believe, and the Jews, and the Sabeites, and the Christians, and the Magians, and those who join other gods with God, of a truth, God shall decide between them on the day of resurrection: for God is witness of all things."

Sūrah v. 112:—

"Remember when the Apostles said—'O Jesus, Son of Mary! is Thy Lord able to send down a furnished TABLE to us out of Heaven?' He said—'Fear God if ye be believers.' They said—'We desire to eat therefrom, and to have our hearts assured; and to know that thou hast indeed spoken truth to us, and to be witnesses thereof.' Jesus, Son of Mary, said—'O God, our Lord! send down a table to us out of Heaven, that it may become a recurring festival to us, to the first of us and to the last of us, and a sign from Thee; and do Thou nourish us, for Thou art the best of nourishers.' And God said—Verily, I will cause it to descend unto you; but whoever among you after that shall disbelieve, I will surely chastise him with a chastisement wherewith I will not chastise any other creature. And when God shall say—'O Jesus, Son of Mary, hast Thou said unto mankind—"Take me and my mother as two Gods, beside God?"' He shall say—'Glory be unto Thee! it is not for me to say that which I know to be not the truth; had I said that, verily Thou wouldest have known it: Thou knowest what is in me, but I know not what is in Thee; for Thou well knowest things unseen!"

Sūrah xix. 35:—

"This is Jesus, the son of Mary; this is a statement of the truth concerning which they doubt. It beseemeth not God to beget a son. Glory be to Him! when He decreeth a thing, He only saith to it, Be, and it is. And verily, God is my Lord and your Lord; adore Him then. This is the right way. But The Sects have fallen to variance among themselves *about Jesus:* but woe, because of the assembly of a great day, to those who believe not!"

The only New Testament saints mentioned by name in the Qur'ān, are John the Baptist, Zacharias, and the Virgin Mary.

In the *Mishkātu 'l-Maṣābīḥ*, there are recorded in the traditional sayings of Muḥammad, about six apparent plagiarisms from the New Testament; but whether they are the plagiarisms of Muḥammad himself or of those who profess to record his sayings, it is impossible to tell:—

Abū Hurairah says the Prophet said, "Of the seven persons whom God, in the last day, will draw to Himself, will be a man who has given alms and concealed it, so that his left hand knoweth not what the right hand doeth." (Book i. c. viii. pt. 1; comp. Matt. vi. 3.)

Again: "God accepts not the prayers of those who pray in long robes." (Book i. c. ix. pt. 2; comp. Matt. xii. 38.)

Again: "The doors of the celestial regions shall not open to them (the wicked) until a camel pass through the eye of a needle." (Book v. c. iii. pt. 3; comp. Mark x. 25.)

Abū Umamah relates that the Prophet said, "Blessed be Him who hath seen me. And blessed be him who hath not seen me and yet hath believed." (Book xxiv. c. xxvi. pt. 3; comp. John xx. 29.)

Mu'āz̤ relates that the Prophet said, "Do unto all men as you would they should do unto you, and reject for others what you would reject for yourself." (Book i. c. i. pt. 3; Matt. vii. 12.)

Abū Hurairah relates that the Prophet said, "Verily God will say in the day of resurrection, O ye sons of men! I was sick and ye did not visit me. And the sons of men will say, O Thou defender, how could we visit Thee, for Thou art the Lord of the universe, and art free from sickness? And God will say, O ye sons of men, did you not know that such a one of my servants was sick and ye did not visit him," &c. &c. (Book v. c. i. pt. 1; comp. Matt. xxv. 21.)

Although it would be difficult to prove it from the text of the Qur'ān, the general belief of Muḥammadans is that Christians are not in a state of salvation, and *Laẓa*, or the "blazing fire," mentioned in Sūrah lxx. 15, is, according to the Imām al-Baghawī, reserved for them.

The condition of a Christian in a Muslim state is that of a *Z̤immī*, or one who pays tribute to a Muḥammadan governor, for which he enjoys protection. He is allowed to repair any old church which may have been in existence at the time the country was subdued by Islām, but he is not allowed to erect new ones; "for," says Abū Ḥanīfah, "the construction of churches or synagogues in Muslim territory is unlawful, being forbidden in the Traditions." "It also behoves the Imām to make distinction between Muslims and *Z̤immīs* (*i.e.* Christians, Jews, and others paying tribute). It is therefore not allowable for them to ride upon horses or use armour, or to wear the same dresses as Muslims." The reason for this, says Abū Ḥanīfah, "is that Muḥammadans are to be held in honour and *Z̤immīs* are not."

The wives also of Z̤immīs are to be kept apart from those of Muslims on the public roads and baths. And it is also ordered that a mark should be placed on their doors, in order that when Muslim beggars come to them they should not pray for them!

The learned have ruled that a Z̤immī should not be allowed to ride at all, except in cases of necessity, and if he be thus of necessity allowed to ride, he should dismount when he meets a Muslim. (*Hidāyah*, vol. ii. 219.)

A judge when he administers an oath to a Christian, must direct him to say: "I swear by God who sent the Gospel to Jesus."

It is a singular ruling of the Muḥammadan law that a claim of *parentage* made by a Christian is preferable to a claim of *bondage* advanced by a Muslim. Abū Ḥanīfah says if a boy be in the possession of two men, the one a Muslim and the other a Christian, and the Christian assert that the boy is his son, and the Muslim assert that he is his slave, he must be decreed to be the son of the Christian and free, because although Islām is the superior religion, there can be no balance between the claim of offspring and the claim of bondage. (*Idem*, vol. iv. 133.)

Sir William Muir, referring to Muḥammad's reception of the Banū Ḥanīfah and other Christian tribes, A.H. 9, says, "On the departure of the embassy the Prophet gave them a vessel with some water in it running over from his own ablutions, and said to them, 'When ye reach your country break down your church, sprinkle its site with this water, and build a Masjid in its place.' These commands they carried into effect, and abandoned Christianity without compunction. To another Christian tribe he prohibited the practice of baptism; so that although the adults continued to be nominally Christian, their children grew up with no provision but that of the Qur'ān. . . . . It is no wonder that Christianity, thus insulted and trampled under foot, languished and soon disappeared from the peninsula." (*Life of Mahomet*, vol. iv. 219.)

CHURCHES.

CHURCHES. Arabic *Bīa'h* and *Kanīsah*, which terms include equally churches and synagogues. The construction of churches or synagogues in Muslim territory is unlawful, this being forbidden in the Traditions; but as for places of worship which belonged to the Jews or Christians before the country was conquered by the Muḥammadan power, they are at liberty to repair them, because the buildings cannot endure for ever, and, as the Imām of the Muslim army has left these people to the exercise of their own religion, it is a necessary inference that he has engaged not to prevent them from building or repairing their churches or synagogues. If, however, they attempt to remove these, and to build them in a place different from their former situation, the Imām must prevent them, since this is an actual construction. Monasteries and hermitages are under the same law. Places of prayer within their dwellings are allowed to be constructed, because they are merely an appurtenance to a private habitation. What is here said is held to be the rule with regard to cities, but not with respect to villages, because as the "tokens of Islām" (*i.e.* prayer, festivals, &c.) appear in cities, ẕimmīs (*i.e.* those paying tax for protection) should not be permitted to exhibit the tokens of their infidelity in the face of Islām. But as the tokens of Islām do not appear in villages, the erection of churches and synagogues is not prohibited there. But the Imām Abū Ḥanīfah held that this exemption merely applied to the village of Kusa, where the greater part of the inhabitants were ẕimmīs. He adds that in the country of Arabia, Jews and Christians are prohibited from constructing synagogues and churches, either in cities or villages, according to the saying of the Prophet, "*Two religions cannot exist in the country of Arabia.*" (*Hidāyah*, book ix. c. viii.)

If a Jew or a Christian, being in sound health, build a church or a synagogue and then die, such building is an inheritance, and descends to the heirs of the founder. According to Abū Ḥanīfah, it is a pious appropriation; but his two disciples hold such erections to be *sinful*, and only to be considered as ordinary property. If a Jew or a Christian will that his house after his death shall be converted into either a synagogue or church, the bequest is valid. (*Hidāyah*, book lii. c. vi.)

The following tradition related by Ṭalaq ibn 'Alī (*Mishkāt*, iv. c. viii. 2) exhibits Muḥammad's determination to destroy Christian churches: "We told the Prophet that there was a church on our ground; and we requested the favour of his giving us the water which remained after he had performed *waẓū*. And the Prophet called for water, performed *waẓū* and washed out his mouth; after which he poured the water for us into a vessel and ordered us to return, saying, 'When you arrive, destroy your church (Arabic *bī'ah*), and pour this water on the spot, and build a mosque there."

CIRCUMCISION. Arabic *Khitān*, *khitānah*, or *khatnah*. Circumcision is not once alluded to in the Qur'ān. The omission is remarkable, and Muslim writers do not attempt any explanation of it. It is held to be *sunnah*, or founded upon the customs of the Prophet (*Fatāwa 'Ālamgīrī*, vol. iv. p. 237), and dating its institution from the time of Abraham. There is no authentic account of the circumcision of Muḥammad, but it is asserted by some writers that he was born circumcised. This, however, is denied by the most eminent scholars. (*Raddu 'l-Mukhtār*, vol. v. p. 835.)

In the *Ṣaḥīḥu 'l-Bukhārī*, p. 931, a short chapter is devoted to the subject of *khitān*, or "circumcision," in which there are three traditions:—

Abū Hurairah relates that the Prophet said one of the observances of Fiṭrah is circumcision.

Abū Hurairah relates that the Prophet said that Abraham was circumcised when he was eighty years old.

Said ibn Jubair relates that it was asked of Ibn 'Abbās, "How old were you when the Prophet died?" He said, "I was circumcised in the days when it occurred." And Jubair says they did not circumcise in those days until men were full grown.

It is recommended to be performed upon a boy between the ages of seven and twelve, but it is lawful to circumcise a child seven days after his birth. In the case of a convert to Islām from some other creed, to whom the operation may be an occasion of great suffering, it can be dispensed with, although it is considered expedient and proper for all new converts to be circumcised. In all cases an *adult* is expected to circumcise himself, as it is a shame for an adult person to uncover himself to another.

The circumcision of females is also allowed, and is commonly practised in Arabia. (*Fatāwa 'Ālamgīrī*, vol. iv. p. 237.)

The barber is generally the person employed for the circumcision of boys, and the operation as practised by Muḥammadans in India is performed in the following manner. A bit of stick is used as a probe, and carried round and round between the glans and prepuce, to ascertain the exact extent of the frænum, and that no unnatural adhesions exist. The foreskin is then drawn forwards and a pair of forceps, consisting of a couple of pieces of split bamboo, five or six inches long and a quarter of an inch thick, tied firmly together at one end with a string to the extent of an inch, applied from above in an oblique direction, so as to exclude about an inch and a half of the prepuce above and three-quarters of an inch below. The forceps severely grasping it, causes a good deal of pain, but this state of suffering does not continue long, since the next thing to be done is the removal, which is done by one stroke of the razor drawn directly downwards. The hæmorrhage which follows is inconsiderable and easily stopped by the application of burnt rags and ashes.

According to several Muḥammadan doctors, there were seventeen of the prophets *born* in a circumcised state, namely, Zakarīyā, Shīs, Idrīs, Yūsuf, Ḥanẓalah, 'Īsa, Mūsa, Ādam, Nūḥ, Shu'aib, Sām, Lūṭ, Ṣāliḥ, Sulaimān, Yaḥya, Hūd, and Muḥammad. (*Durru 'l-Mukhtār*, p. 619.)

CLEAN AND UNCLEAN ANIMALS. All quadrupeds that seize their prey with their teeth, and all birds which seize it with their talons, are unlawful (*ḥarām*), the Prophet having prohibited mankind from eating them.

Hyenas and foxes, being both included under the class of animals of prey, are unlawful. (This is the doctrine of Abū Ḥanīfah, but ash-Shāfiʿī holds that they are lawful.) Elephants and weasels are also animals of prey. Pelicans and kites are abominable (*makrūh*), because they devour dead bodies.

Crows which feed on grain are *mubāḥ*, or indifferent, but carrion crows and ravens are unlawful. Abū Ḥanīfah says the magpie is indifferent (*mubāḥ*), but the Imām Yūsuf says it is abominable (*makrūh*).

Crocodiles and otters and wasps, and, in general, all insects are *makrūh*, or abominable. The ass and the mule are both unlawful. According to Abū Ḥanīfah and Mālik, horse-flesh is unlawful, but ash-Shāfiʿī says it is indifferent. The flesh of hares is also indifferent.

No animal that lives in the water, except fish, is lawful. But Mālik allows them.

Fishes dying of themselves are unlawful, and so are all animals who are *not* slain by *ẕabāḥ*. (*Hidāyah*, vol. iv. p. 74.) [ZABAH.]

It must be observed that in Muḥammadan law animals are either *ḥalāl*, "lawful," or *mubāḥ*, "indifferent," or *makrūh*, "abominable" (*i.e.* which is condemned but still is lawful), or *ḥarām*, "unlawful."

CLERGY. The Christian clergy are mentioned in the Qur'ān with expressions of comparative praise. Sūrah v. 85: "Thou wilt surely find that the strongest in enmity against those who believe are the Jews, and the idolaters; and thou wilt find those to be nearest in affection to them who say 'We are Christians'; that is because there are amongst them priests (*qissīsīn*) and monks, and because they are not proud."

The Muhammadans have no class of people occupying the precise position of priests or clergy, although the Imāms, or leaders of prayers in the public assembly, are persons of learning appointed by the congregation. In Central Asia, it is usual to set apart a learned man (well skilled in theology) by binding the turban round his head, the act being performed by a leading maulawī or scholar.

In Turkey and the western portion of Islām, those who are qualified to give an opinion in religious matters, and to take the lead in guiding the people in spiritual affairs, are called *ʿulamā'* (pl. of *ʿālim*), a term which has, in Hindustān and Central Asia, assumed the form of *maulawī*, a word derived from *maulā*, "lord."

The recognised offices in Islām corresponding to that of a priest or religious teacher, are, *Imām*, *Muftī*, and *Qāẓī*. Imām (in addition to its being used for the Khalīfah, or Caliph, in the Traditions), is the person who leads the public prayers, an office answering to the Latin *Antistes*. This official is appointed either by the congregation, or by the parish or section of the town or village, who frequent the mosque in which he leads the prayers. *Muftī* is the legal adviser, who decides difficult religious questions, and assists the *Qāẓī*, or judge. *Qāẓī* is the judge and the administrator of the law. The appointments of *Muftī* and *Qāẓī* are in the hands of the Muslim government of the place. It is usual for the Qāẓī to take the lead in prayers at funerals, whilst the Imām of the parish generally performs the *nikāḥ*, or religious service at marriages. [MARRIAGE.]

These offices are not necessarily hereditary, but it is usual in Muḥammadan countries for them to pass from father to son. In India at the present time there are families who retain the titles of *Muftī* and *Qāẓī*, although the duties connected with these offices are no longer performed by them.

CAUTION (Arabic *Ḥaẕar*) is enjoined by Muḥammad, who is related to have said, "A Muslim is not bitten twice at the same hole." "He is no perfect man who has not fallen into trouble, for there is no skilful physician but experience." "When a man has spoken, and has then looked first to his right and then to his left, what he has said is sacred to those present, and they must not disclose it to others." (*Mishkāt*, xxii. c. xviii.)

COINAGE. [MONEY.]

COLLECTOR OF TAXES. Arabic *ʿĀshir*, a collector of the tenths; and *ʿĀmil mutaṣaddiq*, a collector of alms.

The Khalīfah is to allow the officer employed in the collection of the *zakāt* as much out of it as is in proportion to his labour, and will remunerate himself and his assistants. (*Hidāyah*, vol. i. p. 54.)

COMMANDMENTS, The Ten. In the Qur'ān it is stated that God gave Moses certain monitions on tables (of stone), and also that he gave him nine clear signs. (See Sūrah vii. 142, and Sūrah xvii. 103.) These two statements have perplexed the commentators very much, and every effort is made by them to reconcile the nine signs with the Ten Commandments, although it is evident from the Qur'ān itself, that the nine clear signs refer to the miracles of Moses. [PLAGUES OF EGYPT.]

According to the Traditions, the Prophet himself was a little confused in the matter, and may to some extent be responsible for the mistakes of the commentators on his book, for it is related (*Mishkāt*, book i. c. ii. pt. 2) that a Jew came to the Prophet and asked him about the *nine* (*sic*) wonders which appeared by the hands of Moses. The Prophet said, "Do not associate anything with God, do not steal, do not commit adultery, do not kill, do not take an innocent before the king to be killed, do not practise magic, do not take interest, do not accuse an innocent woman of adultery, do not run away in battle, and especially for you, O Jews, not to work on the Sabbath." ʿAbdu 'l-Ḥaqq remarks on this tradition that the Jew asked about the nine (*sic*) miracles (or plagues) of Egypt, and the Prophet gave him the Ten Commandments.

A comparison of the Ten Commandments given by the great Jewish law-giver with those recorded in the above tradition and in the VIth Sūrah of the Qur'ān, verse 152, will show how imperfectly the Arabian Prophet was acquainted with the Old Testament scriptures.

The commentator Ḥusain, who wrote four hundred years ago, says the following verses in the Sūratu 'l-An'ām (vi.) are those Ten Commandments which in every dispensation are incumbent on mankind, and cannot be abrogated (meaning undoubtedly the Ten Commandments given to Moses).

"SAY: Come, I will rehearse what your Lord hath made binding on you—(1) that ye assign not aught to Him as partner: (2) and that ye be good to your parents: (3) and that ye slay not your children, because of poverty; for them and for you will we provide: (4) and that ye come not near to pollutions, outward or inward: (5) and that ye slay not anyone whom God hath forbidden you, unless for a just cause. This hath he enjoined on you, to the intent that ye may understand. (6) And come not nigh to the substance of the orphan, but to improve it, until he come of age: (7) and use a full measure, and a just balance: We will not task a soul beyond its ability. (8) And when ye give judgment, observe justice, even though it be the affair of a kinsman, (9) and fulfil the covenant of God. This hath God enjoined you for your monition — And, 'this is my right way.' Follow it then: (10) and follow not *other* paths lest ye be scattered from His path. This hath He enjoined you, that ye may fear Him." (Sūrah vi. 152.)

COMMANDER OF THE FAITHFUL. Arabic *Amīru 'l-Mu'minīn* (امير المومنين). A title given by the Muslims in the first instance to the first Khalīfah, Abū Bakr, and afterwards retained by succeeding Khalīfahs. It is assumed by almost any Muḥammadan ruler in the present day.

COMMENTARIES. [QUR'AN.]

COMMERCE. Arabic *Tijārah* (تجارة). Commerce and merchandise are said in the Qur'ān to be of God." Sūrah xvii. 68: "It is your Lord who drives the ships for you in the sea that ye may seek after plenty from Him; verily He is ever merciful to you. And when distress touches you in the sea, those whom ye call upon, except Him, stray away from you; but when He has brought you safe to shore, ye also turn away (from God); for man is ever ungrateful."

Zakāt is due on merchandise of every description, in proportion to 5 yer cent.

COMPANIONS, The. [ASHAB.]

COMPULSION. Arabic *Ikrāh* (اكراه). Muḥammadan law makes provision for persons acting under compulsion, when the person who compels has it in his power to execute what he orders, be he a king or a thief. (*Hidāyah*, vol. iii. p. 452.) *E.g.* a person forced into a contract may dissolve it. A Muslim may lawfully eat food which is prohibited if he be compelled to do so, being threatened with loss of life or limb. Nor is a Muslim guilty of sin who declares himself an unbeliever when the loss of a limb or of life is threatened. According to the Imām Abū Ḥanīfah, if a Muslim be compelled to divorce his wife, the divorce is valid; but with him the other three Imāms are not agreed in this ruling.

CONCUBINE. Arabic *Surrīyah* (سرية), pl. *sarārī*. The Muḥammadan religion appears to give almost unlimited license to concubinage, provided the woman be a slave, and not a free Muslim woman.

These female slaves must be either (1) taken captive in war, (2) or purchased by money, (3) or the descendants of slaves. Even married women, if taken in war, are, according to an injunction of the Qur'ān, Sūrah iv. 28, entirely at the disposal of the Muslim conqueror. "(Unlawful) to you are married women, *except* such as your right hand possess (*i.e.* taken in war, or purchased slaves)." This institution of concubinage is founded upon the example of Muḥammad himself, who took Rīḥānah the Jewess as his concubine after the battle with the Banū Quraizah (A.H. 5), and also Maria the Copt, who was sent him as a slave by the Governor of Egypt.

Should a concubine bear her master a child, the Muḥammadan law rules that she and her offspring are *ipso facto* free. For a further treatment of this subject, see article on SLAVES.

Amongst the Shī'ahs, the temporary marriage called Mut'ah exhibits the worst form of concubinage. [MUT'AH.]

It is interesting to compare the condition of the concubine under Muslim law and under the Mosaic. Under the law of Moses, a concubine would generally be either a Hebrew girl bought of her father, or a Gentile captive taken in war. So that whilst the Muḥammadan law forbids concubinage with a free woman, the Mosaic law permitted it and legislated for it. See Exodus xxi.: "If a man sell his daughter to be a maid-servant, she shall not go out as men-servants do. If she please not her master who hath betrothed her to himself, then shall he let her be redeemed; to sell her unto a strange nation he shall have no power, seeing he hath dealt deceitfully with her."

With regard to female slaves taken in war, the Mosaic law ruled. Deut. xxi. 10: "When thou goest to war against thine enemies, and the Lord thy God hath delivered them into thine hands, and thou hast taken them captive, and seest a beautiful woman, and hast a desire unto her, that thou wouldst have her to thy wife; then thou shalt bring her to thine home, &c. . . . And it shall be, if thou have no delight in her, then thou shalt let her go whither she will; but thou shalt not sell her," &c.

CONGREGATION. The Assembly of people in a mosque is called *Jam'ah* (جمعة), the term also being used in Afghanistan for the mosque itself.

There are special rewards for those Muḥammadans who assemble together for the stated prayers; for Muḥammad has said, "The prayers which are said in a congregation increase the rewards of the worshipper twenty-seven degrees." "Say your prayers in a congregation, far a wolf does not eat the sheep except one has strayed from the flock." (*Mishkāt*, book iv. ch. xxiv.)

The Sunni style themselves *Ahlu Sunnah wa Jam'ah, i.e.* "the people of the traditions and of the congregation," in contradistinction to the Shī'ahs, who do not worship in a congregation unless the Imām, or leader, be a man entirely free from sin. [IMAM.]

The word *jam'ah* is also used for an assembly of people collected to decide a question of law or theology, the *ijmā'* being their decision, more frequently called *ijmā'u 'l-ummah.*

CONSCIENCE. There is no word in the Qur'ān which exactly expresses the Christian conception of conscience. The word *nafs* (نفس), which, according to Arabic lexicons, expresses very much the same idea as the Hebrew נֶפֶשׁ *nephesh*, "life, animal spirit, *breath*" (Job xli. 21), seems to be used in the Qur'ān to convey the meaning of conscience, although English translators render it "soul." Muslim theologians say there are four kinds of consciences spoken of in the Qur'ān: (1) *Nafs lawwāmah*, the "self-accusing soul or conscience" (Sūrah lxxv. 3). (2) *Nafs ammārah*, the "soul or conscience prone to evil" (Sūrah xii. 53). (3) *Nafs muṭma'innah*, the "peaceful soul or conscience" (Sūrah lxxxix. 12). (4) *Nafs mulhammah*, the "soul or conscience in which is breathed both bad and good" (Sūrah lxxxiv. 27.)

It occurs also in the sense of conscience in the Traditions (*Mishkāt*, book i. ch. i. pt. 3): "When anything pricks your soul (*nafs*) forsake it." Abdu 'l-Ḥaqq, in his Persian commentary on the *Mishkāt*, renders it by *zāt*, but the English word conscience would seem to express the precise idea. In Persian Muḥammadan works, as well as in common conversation, the word *nafs* is now used in its evil sense, of desire or passion, but it must be evident that this is not its Qur'ānic meaning. The word ذمة *zimmah*, which in later Arabic, together with ضمير *ẓamīr*, is used to express conscience, has in the only passage where it occurs in the Qur'ān a decidedly different meaning, *e.g.* Sūrah ix. 8, 10, where it means clientship. Sale and Rodwell both translate it "faith," but Palmer more accurately renders it "ties of clientship."

CONVERSATION. The following instructions are given in the Qur'ān regarding talking and conversation. Sūrah xxxi. 17, "Be moderate in thy walk, and lower thy voice; verily the most disagreeable of voices is the voice of asses." Sūrah ii. 77, "Speak to men kindly." In the Traditions, Ibn Mas'ūd relates that Muḥammad said, "May those people go to the fire of hell who speak much."

On the subject of conversation, Faqīr Jani Muḥammad As'ad, the author of the celebrated ethical work entitled the *Akhlāk-i-Jalālī*, p. 288, says:—

"He should not talk much, for it is a sign of levity in feeling and weakness in judgment, and tends to lower him in point of consideration and position. We are told that the Prophet used to observe the strictest medium in his language; so much so, that, in the most protracted interviews, you might have counted the words he uttered. Buzurg Jamihr used to say, 'When you see a person talking much without occasion, be sure he is out of his senses.' Let him not give vent to expressions till he has determined in his own mind what he is going to say. When anyone is relating a story, however well known to the listener, the latter is not to intimate his acquaintance with it till the narrative is concluded. A question put to others he must not himself reply to; if put to a body of which he is a member, let him not prevent the others; and if another is engaged in answering what himself could answer better, let him keep silence till the other's statement is completed, and then give his own, but in such sort as not to annoy the former speaker. Let him not commence his reply till the querist's sentence is concluded. Conversations and discussions which do not concern him, although held in his presence, he is not to interfere in; and if people conceal what they are saying, he must not attempt furtively to overhear. To his elders he should speak with judgment, pitching his voice at a medium between high and low. Should any abstruse topic present itself, he should give it perspicuity by comparison. Prolixity he should never aim at, when not absolutely required; on the contrary, let it be his endeavour to compress all he has to say. Neither should he employ unusual terms or far-fetched figures. He should beware of obscenity and bad language; or if he must needs refer to an indecent subject, let him be content with allusion by metaphor. Of all things, let him keep clear of a taste for indelicacy, which tends to lower his breeding, degrade his respectability, and bring him into general disagreement and dislike. Let his language upon every occasion correspond with the exigency of his position; and if accompanied by gesticulation of the hand or eye or eyebrow, let it be only of that graceful sort which his situation calls for. Let him never, for right or wrong, engage in disputes with others of the company; least of all with the elders or the triflers of it: and when embarked in such dispute, let him be rigidly observant of the rules of candour.

"Let him not deal in profound observation beyond the intellect of those he is addressing, but adapt his discourse to the judgment of his hearers. Thus even the Prophet has declared—'We of the prophetic order are enjoined to address men in the measure of their understandings': and Jesus (blessed be he) said, 'Use not wisdom with the unwise to their annoyance' (St. Matthew vii. 6?). In all his conversation let him adhere to the ways of courtesy. Never let him mimic anyone's gestures, actions, or words, nor give utterance to the language of menace.

"When addressing a great person, let him begin with something ominous of good, as the permanence of his fortune, felicity, and so forth.

"From all back-biting, carping, slander, and falsehood, whether heard or spoken, let him hold it essential to keep clear; nay, even from any partnership with those addicted to such practices. Let him listen more than he speaks. It was the answer of a wise man to those who asked him why he did so, 'Because,' said he, 'God has given me two ears and only one tongue'; which was as much as to say, 'Hear twice as much as you speak.'"

CONVERTS TO THE MUḤAMMADAN RELIGION. According to the author of the *Hidāyah* (vol. ii. 170), if a hostile infidel embrace Islām in a hostile country, his person is his own, and he is not made a slave, nor can his children be enslaved. His property is also his own. But it is not so in the case of one who has been first conquered and then embraces Islām, for his own person and his children become slaves, and his wives are at the mercy of the victorious Muslim, whilst his lands also become the property of the State.

COVENANT. The word in the Qur'ān and the Traditions for God's Covenant with His people is *Mis̤āq*. Muḥammad taught, both in the Qur'ān and in the Traditions, that in the beginning God called all the souls of mankind together and took a promise (*wa'dah*) and a covenant (*mīs̤āq*) from them.

The account of this transaction is given as follows in the Qur'ān, Sūrah vii. 171:—

"Thy Lord brought forth their descendants from the reins of the sons of Adam and took them to witness against themselves, 'Am I not,' said He, 'your Lord?' They said, 'Yes, we witness it.' This we did, lest ye should say on the Day of Resurrection, 'Truly, of this were we heedless, because uninformed.'

"Or lest ye should say, 'Our fathers, indeed, aforetime joined other gods with our God, and we are their seed after them: wilt thou destroy us for the doings of vain men?'"

But the story as told in the Traditions is more graphic:—

"Ubai ibn Ka'b relates, in explanation of the verse in the Sūratu 'l-A'rāf (verse 171): When God created (the spirits of) the sons of Adam, he collected them together and made them of different tribes, and of different appearances, and gave them powers of speech. Then they began to speak, and God took from them a promise (*wa'dah*), and a covenant (*mīs̤āq*), and said, 'Am I not thy Lord?' They all answered and said, 'Thou art.' Then God said, 'Swear by the seven heavens and the seven earths, and by Adam your father, that you will not say in the resurrection, We did not understand this. Know ye therefore that there is no Deity but Me, and there is no God but Me. Do not associate anything with Me. I will verily send to you your own apostles who shall remind you of this Promise and of this Covenant, and I will send to you your own books.' The sons of Adam then replied, 'We are witnesses that Thou art our Lord (*Rabb*), and our God (*Allah*). There is no Lord but Thee and no God but Thee.' Then they confessed this and made it known to Adam. Then Adam looked at them and beheld that there were amongst them those that were rich and poor, handsome and ugly, and he said, 'O Lord why didst Thou not make them all alike?' And the Lord said, 'Truly I willed it thus in order that some of my servants may be thankful.' Then Adam saw amongst his posterity, prophets, like unto lamps, and upon these lamps there were lights, and they were appointed by special covenants of prophecy (*nabūwah*) and of apostleship (*rasālah*). And thus it is written in the Qur'ān (Sūrah xxxiii. 7), 'Remember we have entered into covenant with the Prophets, with thee Muḥammad, and with Noah, and with Abraham, and with Mūsa, and with Jesus the Son of Mary, and we made with them a covenant.' And (continues Ubai) Jesus was amongst the spirits." (*Mishkāt*, Arabic Ed. Bābu 'l-Qadr.)

COVERING THE HEAD. There is no injunction in either the Qur'ān or Traditions as to a man covering his head during prayers, although it is generally held to be more modest and correct for him to do so.

With reference to women, the law is imperative, for 'Āyishah relates that Muḥammad said, "God accepts not the prayer of an adult woman unless she cover her head." (*Mishkāt*, iv. c. ix.)

CORRUPTION OF THE SCRIPTURES. Muḥammadans charge the Jews and Christians with having altered their sacred books. The word used by Muḥammadan writers for this supposed corruption of the sacred Scriptures of the Jews and Christians is *Taḥrīf*.

The Imām Fak͟hru 'd-dīn Rāẕī, in his commentary, Tafsīr-i-Kabīr, explains *Taḥrīf* to mean "to change, alter, or turn aside anything from the truth." Muslim divines say there are two kinds of *taḥrīf*, namely, *taḥrīf-i-ma'nawī*, a corruption of the meaning; and *taḥrīf-i-lafẓī*, a corruption of the words.

Muḥammadan controversialists, when they become acquainted with the nature of the contents of the sacred books of the Jews and Christians, and of the impossibility of reconciling the contents of the Qur'ān with those of the sacred Scriptures, charge the Christians with the *taḥrīf-i-lafẓī*. They say the Christians have expunged the word *aḥmad* from the prophecies, and have inserted the expression "Son of God," and the story of the crucifixion, death, and resurrection of our blessed Lord. This view, however, is not the one held by the most celebrated of the Muslim commentators.

The Imām Muḥammad Ismā'īl al-Bukhārī (p. 1127, line 7), records that Ibn 'Abbās said that "the word *Taḥrīf* (corruption) signifies to change a thing from its original nature; and that there is no man who could corrupt a single word of what proceeded from God, so that the Jews and Christians could corrupt only by misrepresenting the *meaning* of the words of God."

Ibn Mazar and Ibn Abī Hātim state, in the commentary known as the *Tafsīr Durr-i-Manṣūr*, that they have it on the authority of Ibn Munīyah, that the *Taurāt* (*i.e.* the books of Moses), and the *Injīl* (*i.e.* the Gospels), are in the same state of purity in which they were sent down from heaven, and that no alterations had been made in them, but that the Jews were wont to deceive the people by unsound arguments, and by wresting the sense of Scripture.

Shāh Walīyu 'llāh, in his commentary, the *Fauzu 'l-Kabīr*, and also Ibn 'Abbās, support the same view.

This appears to be the correct interpretation of the various verses of the Qur'ān charging the Jews with having corrupted the meaning of the sacred Scriptures.

For example, Sūratu Āli 'Imrān (iii.), 72: "There are certainly some of them who read the Scriptures perversely, that ye may think what they read to be really in the Scriptures, yet it is not in the Scriptures; and they say this is from God, but it is not from God; and they speak that which is false concerning God against their own knowledge."

The Imām Fakhru 'd-dīn, in his commentary on this verse, and many others of the same character which occur in the Qur'ān, says it refers to a *taḥrīf-i-ma'nawī*, and that it does not mean that the Jews altered the text, but merely that they made alterations in the course of reading.

But whilst all the old commentators, who most probably had never seen a copy of the sacred books of the Jews and Christians, only charge them with a *taḥrīf-i-ma'nawī*, all modern controversialists amongst the Muḥammadans contend for a *taḥrīf-i-lafẓī*, as being the only solution of the difficulty.

In dealing with such opponents, the Christian divine will avail himself of the following arguments:—

1. The Qur'ān does not charge the Jews and Christians with corrupting the text of their sacred books; and many learned Muslim commentators admit that such is not the case.

2. The Qur'ān asserts that the Holy Scriptures of the Jews and Christians existed in the days of Muḥammad, who invariably speaks of them with reverence and respect.

3. There now exist manuscripts of the Old and New Testaments of an earlier date than that of Muḥammad (A.D. 610–632.)

4. There are versions of the Old and New Testament now extant, which existed before Muḥammad; for example, the Septuagint, the Latin Vulgate, the Syriac, the Coptic, and the Armenian versions.

5. The Hexapla, or Octapla of Origen, which dates four centuries before Muḥammad, gives various versions of the Old Testament Scriptures in parallel columns.

6. The Syrian Christians of St. Thomas, of Malabar and Travancore, in the south of India, who were separated from the western world for centuries, possess the same Scriptures.

7. In the works of Justin Martyr, who lived from A.D. 103 to 167, there are numerous quotations from our sacred books, which prove that they were exactly the same as those we have now. The same may be said of other early Christian writers.

Muḥammadan controversialists of the present day urge that the numerous readings which exist in the Christian books are a proof that they have been corrupted. But these do not affect, in the least, the main points at issue between the Christian and the Muslim. The Divine Sonship of Christ, the Fatherhood of God, the Crucifixion, Death, and Resurrection of Christ, and the Atonement, are all clearly stated in almost every book of the New Testament, whilst they are rejected by the Qur'ān.

The most plausible of modern objections urged by Muslim divines is, that the Christians have *lost* the *Injīl* which was sent down from heaven to Jesus; and that the New Testament contains merely the *Ḥadīṣ*, or *Sunnah* —the *traditions* handed down by Matthew, Mark, Luke, John, Paul, and others. It is, of course, a mere assertion, unsupported by any proof; but it appears to be a line of argument which commends itself to many modern Muslims.

CREATION. Arabic *Khalqah*.

The following are the allusions to the Creation which occur in the Qur'ān, Sūrah l. 37: "Of old We (God) created the heavens and the earth and all that is between them in six days, and no weariness touched Us." Sūrah xli. 8; "Do ye indeed disbelieve in Him who in two days created the earth? Do ye assign Him equals? The Lord of the World is He. And He hath placed on the earth the firm mountains which tower above it, and He hath blessed it, and distributed its nourishments throughout it (for the cravings of all are alike), in four days. Then He applied Himself to the heaven, which was but smoke: and to it and to the earth He said, "Come ye, in obedience or against your will?" and they both said, "We come obedient." And He completed them as seven heavens in two days, and in each heaven made known its office; and We furnished the lower heaven with lights and guardian angels. This is the disposition of the Almighty, the all-knowing one." Sūrah

xvi. 3: "He created the heavens and the earth to set forth his truth, high let Him be exalted above the gods they join with Him! Man hath He created out of a moist germ; yet lo! man is an open caviller. And the cattle! for you hath He created them, &c. . . . . Shall He who hath created be as he who hath not created? Will ye not consider?" Sūrah xiii. 2: "It is God who hath reared the heavens without pillars, thou canst behold; then seated Himself upon His throne, and imposed laws on the sun and moon; each travelleth to its appointeth goal. He ordereth all things. He maketh His signs clear. Haply ye will have firm faith in a meeting with your Lord. And He it is who hath outstretched the earth, and placed on it the firm mountains, and rivers; and of every fruit He hath placed on it two kinds. He causeth the night to enshroud the day." Sūrah xxxv. 12: "God created you of dust—then of the germs of life—then made you two sexes."

According to the Traditions (*Mishkāt*, xxiv. c. i. pt. 3), God created the earth on Saturday, the hills on Sunday, the trees on Monday, all unpleasant things on Tuesday, the light on Wednesday, the beasts on Thursday, and Adam, who was the last of Creation, was created after the time of afternoon prayers on Friday.

CREED. The Muḥammadan Creed, or *Kalimatu 'sh-shahādah* (shortly *Kalimah*) is the well-known formula:—

"I testify that there is no deity but God, and Muḥammad is the Apostle of God."

It is the belief of Muḥammadans that the first part of this creed, which is called the *nafi wa is̤bāt*, namely, "There is no deity but God," has been the expression of belief of every prophet since the days of Adam, and that the second portion has been changed according to the dispensation; for example, that in the days of Moses it would be: "There is no deity but God, and Moses is the Converser with God." In the Christian dispensation it was: "There is no deity but God, and Jesus is the Spirit of God."

Jābir relates that Muḥammad said "the keys of Paradise are bearing witness that there is no deity but God."

The recital of the *Kalimah*, or Creed, is the first of five pillars of practical religion in Islām; and when anyone is converted to Islām he is required to repeat this formula, and the following are the conditions required of every Muslim with reference to it:—

1. That it shall be repeated aloud, at least once in a life-time.
2. That the meaning of it shall be fully understood.
3. That it shall be believed in "by the heart."
4. That it shall be professed until death.
5. That it shall be recited correctly.
6. That it shall be always professed and declared without hesitation.

(*Sharḥu 'l-Wiqāyah.*)

CREMATION. [BURNING THE DEAD.]

CRESCENT. The figure of the crescent is the Turkish symbol, and hence it has been regarded by Europeans as the special emblem of the Muḥammadan religion, although it is unknown to the Muḥammadans of the East. This figure, however, did not originate with the Turks, but it was the symbol of sovereignty in the city of Byzantium previous to the Muslim conquest, as may be seen from the medals struck in honour of Augustus Trajan and others. The crescent has been the symbol of three different orders of knighthood; the first of which was instituted by Charles I., King of Naples, A.D. 1268; the second in 1448 by René of Anjou; the third by Sultan Selim in 1801. It must have been adopted by Muḥammadans for the first time upon the overthrow of the Byzantine Empire by Muḥammad II., and it is now generally used by the Turks as the insignia of their creed.

CROCODILE. Arabic *Timsāḥ*. The flesh of a crocodile is unlawful for food to a Muḥammadan. (Hamilton's *Hidāyah*, iv. 74.)

CROSS, The. Arabic *Aṣ-Ṣalīb*. The Qur'ān denies the crucifixion of our blessed Lord [CRUCIFIXION], and it is related by al-Wāqidī that Muḥammad had such a repugnance to the form of the cross that he broke everything brought into his house with that figure upon it. (Muir, iii. 61.) According to Abū Hurairah, the Prophet said, "I swear by heaven, it is near, when Jesus the Son of Mary will descend from heaven upon your people, a just king, and He will *break the cross*, and kill the swine. (*Mishkāt*, xxiii. c. vi.) The Imām Abū Yūsuf says that if a cross or a crucifix is stolen from a church, amputation (the punishment for theft) is not incurred; but if it is stolen from a private dwelling it is theft. (Hamilton's *Hidāyah*, vol. ii. p. 90.)

CRUCIFIXION. The Crucifixion of the Lord Jesus Christ is denied by the teaching of the Qur'ān. [JESUS CHRIST.] It is a punishment sanctioned by the Muḥammadan religion for highway robbers. (Hamilton's *Hidāyah*, vol. ii. 131.)

CRUELTY. A striking instance of the cruelty of Muḥammad's character occurs in a tradition given in the *Ṣaḥīḥu 'l-Bukhārī* (p. 1019). Anas relates, "Some of the people of the tribe of 'Ukl came to the Prophet and embraced Islām; but the air of al-Madīnah did not agree with them, and they wanted to leave the place. And the Prophet ordered them to go where the camels given in alms were assembled, and to drink their milk, which they did, and recovered from their sickness. But after this they became apostates, and renounced Islām, and stole the camels. Then the Prophet sent some people after them, and they were seized and brought back to al-Madīnah. Then the Prophet ordered their hands and their feet to be cut off as a punishment for theft, and their eyes to be pulled out. But the Prophet did not stop the bleeding, and they died." And in another it reads, "The Prophet ordered hot irons to be drawn across their eyes, and then to be cast on the plain of al-Madīnah; and when they asked for water it was not given them, and they died."

Sir William Muir (vol. iv. p. 307) says: "Magnanimity or moderation are nowhere discernible as features in the conduct of Muḥammad towards such of his enemies as failed to tender a timely allegiance. Over the bodies of the Quraish who fell at Badr he exulted with savage satisfaction; and several prisoners, accused of no crime but of scepticism and political opposition, were deliberately executed at his command. The Prince of Khaibar, after being subjected to inhuman torture for the purpose of discovering the treasures of his tribe, was, with his cousin, put to death on the pretext of having treacherously concealed them, and his wife was led away captive to the tent of the conqueror. Sentence of exile was enforced by Muḥammad with rigorous severity on two whole Jewish tribes at al-Madīnah; and of a third, likewise his neighbours, the women and children were sold into distant captivity, while the men, amounting to several hundreds, were butchered in cold blood before his eyes."

D.

DĀBBATU 'L-ARẔ (دابة الارض). *Lit.* "The Reptile of the Earth." A monster who shall arise in the last day, and shall cry unto the people of the earth that mankind have not believed in the revelations of God (*vide* Qur'ān, Sūrah xxvii. 84): "And when sentence falls upon them we will bring forth a *beast* out of the earth, that shall speak to them and say, 'Men of our signs would not be sure.'" According to the Traditions he will be the third sign of the coming resurrection, and will come forth from the mountain of Ṣufah. (*Mishkāt*, xxiii. c. iv.) Both Sale and Rodwell have confounded the Dābbatu 'l-Arẓ with Al-Jassāsah, the spy, mentioned in a tradition by Fāṭimah (*Mishkāt*, xxiii. c. iv.), and which is held to be a demon now in existence. [AL-JASSASAH.] For a description of the Dābbah, see the article on the RESURRECTION.

DABŪR (دبور). "The West wind." A term used by the Ṣūfīs to express the lust of the flesh, and its overwhelming power in the heart of man. (Abdu 'r-Razzāq's *Dictionary of Ṣūfī Terms.*)

DAHHĀ (دهها). Plural of the Persian ده, *ten.* The ten days of the Muharram, during which public mourning for 'Alī and his sons is observed by Shī'ah Muḥammadans. (Wilson's *Glossary of Indian Terms.*)

AD-DAHR (الدهر). "A long space of time." A title given to the LXXVIth chapter of the Qur'ān; called also Sūratu 'l-Insān, "The Chapter of Man." The title is taken from the first verse of the chapter: "Did not there pass over man a long space of time?"

DAHRĪ (دهری). One who believes in the eternity of matter, and asserts that the duration of this world is from eternity, and denies the Day of Resurrection and Judgment; an Atheist. (*Ghiyāsu 'l-Lughāt, in loco.*)

DAIN (دين). A debt contracted with some definite term fixed for repayment, as distinguished from *qarẓ*, which is used for a loan given without any fixed term for repayment. [DEBT.]

DAJJĀL (دجال). *Lit.* "false, lying." The name given in the Ḥadīs̤ to certain religious impostors who shall appear in the world; a term equivalent to our use of the word Antichrist. Muḥammad is related to have said there would be about thirty.

The *Masīḥu 'd-Dajjāl*, or "the lying Christ," it is said, will be the last of the *Dajjāls*, for an account of whom refer to article on MASIHU 'D-DAJJAL.

DALĪL (دليل). "An argument; a proof." *Dalīl burhānī*, "a convincing argument." *Dalīl qaṭ'ī*, "a decisive proof."

DAMASCUS. Arabic *Dimashq* According to Jalālu 'd-dīn Suyūṭī, Damascus is the second sacred city in Syria, Jerusalem being the first; and some have thought it must be the "Iram of the columns" mentioned in the Qur'ān, Sūrah lxxxix. 6, although this is not the view of most Muslim writers. [IRAM.] Damascus is not mentioned in the Qur'ān. With regard to the date of the erection of the city, Muḥammadan historians differ. Some say it was built by a slave named Dimashq, who belonged to Abraham, having been given to the patriarch by Nimrod; others say Dimashq was a slave belonging to Alexander the Great, and that the city was built in his day.

Damascus was taken by Khālid in the reign of the Khalīfah 'Umar, A.H. 13, and it became the capital of the Umaiyade Khalīfahs under Mu'āwiyah, A.H. 41, and remained the chief city of Islām until the fall of that dynasty, A.H. 132, when the Abbassides moved their capital first to al-Kūfah and then to Bagdād.

The great mosque at Damascus was erected by 'Abdu 'l-Malik ibn Marwān, the fifth Khalīfah of the Umaiyades. It was commenced A.H. 86, and finished in ten years, being erected on the ruins of an ancient Greek temple and of a Christian church.

The account, as given by Jalālu 'd-dīn Suyūṭī, in his *History of the Temple of Jerusalem*, is curious and interesting, showing that for a time the Muslims and Christians worshipped in the same building together.

"Here (in Damascus) all the servants of God joined, and built a church to worship God in. Some say, however, that this church was built by the Greeks: for 'Abdu 'llāh Ibn 'Abbās, having marched against Damascus and besieged it, demolished the walls, after he had entered the city by storm. Then there fell down a stone, having certain letters inscribed thereon in the Greek language. They therefore sent to bring a certain monk who could read Greek; but he said, 'Bring me in pitch the impression of the letters on the stone, which he found to be as follows: 'Woe unto thee, mother of shame! Pious is he who inflicts upon thee with usury the ill which God designs for thee in retribution. Woe unto thee from five eyes, who shall destroy thy wall after four thousand years.' Now, 'Abdu 'llāh's entire name was 'Abdu 'llāh Ibn 'Alī Ibn 'Abdi 'llāh Ibn 'Abbās Ibn 'Abdu 'l-Muqallib.

"Again, the historian Ibn Isahir says: When God had granted unto the Muslims the possession, as conquerors of the whole of Syria, He granted them among other cities that of Damascus with its dependencies. Thus God sent down His mercy upon them, and the commander-in-chief of the army (besieging Damascus), who was either Abū 'Ubaidah or, as some say, Khālid Ibn al-Walīd, wrote a treaty of capitulation and articles of surrender. By these he settled and appointed fourteen churches to remain in the hands of the Muslims. The church of which we have spoken above was left open and free for future consideration. This was on the plea that Khālid had entered the city at the sword's point by the eastern gate; but that the Christians at the same time were allowed to surrender by Abū 'Ubaidah, who entered at the western gate, opened under articles. This caused dissension; but at length it was agreed that half the place should be regarded as having capitulated and half as stormed.

"The Muslims therefore took this church, and Abū 'Ubaidah made it into a mosque. He was afterwards appointed Emir of Syria, and was the first who prayed here, all the company of Companions praying after him in the open area, now called the Companions' Tower; but the wall must then have been cut through, hard by the leaning tower, if the Companions really prayed in the 'blessed precinct.' At first the Christians and Muslims entered by the same gate, which was 'the gate of Adoration and Prayer,' over against the Qiblah, where the great tower now stands. Afterwards the Christians changed and went into their church by the gate facing the west; the Muslims taking the right-hand mosque. But the Christians were not suffered to chant aloud, or recite their books or strike their bells (or clappers), in order to honour the Companions with reverence and fear. Also, Mu'āwiyah built in his days a house for the Amīr, right opposite the mosque. Here he built a green chapel. This palace was noted for its perfection. Here Mu'āwiyah dwelt forty years; nor did this state of things change from A.H. 14 to A.H. 86. But Al-Walīd Ibn 'Abdu 'l-Malik began to think of destroying the churches, and of adding some to those already in the hands of the Muslims, so as to construct one great mosque; and this because some of the Muslims were sore troubled by hearing the recitations of the Christians from the Gospel, and their uplifted voices in prayer. He designed, therefore, to remove them from the Muslims and to annex this spot to the other, so as to make one great mosque. Therefore he called for the Christians, and asked them whether they would depart from those places which were in their hands, receiving in exchange greater portions in lieu thereof; and also retaining four churches not mentioned in the treaty—the Church of Maria, the Church of the Crucified, just within the eastern gate, the church Tallu 'l-Ḥabn, and the Church of the Glorious Mother, occupied previously by the burnishers. This, however, they vehemently refused to do. Thereupon the Khalīfah said, 'Bring me then the treaty which you possess since the time of the Companions.' They brought it, therefore, and it was read in al-Walīd's presence; when, lo! the Church of Thomas, outside the gate of Thomas, hard by the river, did not enter into the treaty, and was one of those called 'the greater of churches left upon' (for future disposal). 'There,' he said, 'this will I destroy and convert it into a mosque.' They said, 'Nay, let it alone, O commander of the Faithful, even although not mentioned among the churches, for we are content that you take the chapel of the church.' To this agreement, then, he held them, and received from them the Qubbah (or chapel vault, dome) of the church. Then he summoned workmen able to pull down, and assembled all the amīrs, chiefs, and great men. But the Christian bishops and priests coming, said, 'O commander of the Faithful, we find in our books that whosoever shall demolish this church will go mad.' Then said the Khalīfah, 'And I am very willing to be mad with God's inspiration; therefore no one shall demolish it before me.' Then he ascended the western tower, which had two spires, and contained a monastic cell. Here he found a monk, whom he ordered to descend. The monk making difficulties, and lingering, al-Walīd took him by the back of his neck, and ceased not pushing him until he had thrown him down stairs. Then he ascended to the most lofty spot in the church, above the great altar, called 'the Altar of the Martyrs.' Here he seized the ends of his sash, which was of a bright yellow colour, and fixed them into his belt. Taking, then, an axe into his hand, he struck against the very topmost stone, and brought it down. Then he called the amirs, and desired them to pull down the building as quickly as possible. Hereupon all the Muslims shouted, 'God is great!' three times; also the Christians loudly cried out with their wailing and woe upon the steps of Jairūn, where they had assembled. Al-Walīd therefore desired the commander of his guard to inflict blows upon them until they should depart, which he did. The Muslims then demolished all that the Christians had built in the great square here—altars and buildings and cloisters—until the whole square was one flat surface. He then resolved to build a splendid pile, unrivalled for beauty of architecture, which none could hereafter surpass. Al-Walīd therefore commissioned the most eminent architects and mathematicians to build the mosque, according to the model they most preferred. His brother chiefly moved and stirred him up to this undertaking, and next to him presided Sulaimān 'Abdu 'l-Malik. It is said that al-Walīd sent to the king of Greece to demand stone-masons and other workmen, for the purpose of building this mosque in the way he desired, sending word, that if the king refused, he would overrun his territory with his army, and reduce to utter ruin every church in his dominions, even the Church of the Holy City, and the Church of Edessa, and utterly destroy every vestige of the Greeks still remaining. The king of Greece, sent, therefore, numerous workmen. with a letter, expressing himself thus: 'If thy father knoweth what thou doest, and permits it, then truly I accuse him of disgraceful conduct, and blame him more than thee. If he understandeth it not, but thou only art conscious, then I blame thee above him.' When the letter came to al-Walīd, he wished to reply unto it, and assembled several persons for consultation. One of these was a well-known poet, who said, 'I will answer him, O Commander of the Faithful! out of the Book of God.' So said al-Walīd, 'Where, then, is that answer?' He replied this verse, 'David and Solomon, lo! they assume a right to the corn-field, a right to the place where the people are shearing their sheep. Also, we are witnesses of their decree; for Solomon hath given us to understand it, and both (David and Solomon) have come to us as judges and learned men.' Al-Walīd, by this reply, caused great surprise to the king of Greece. Al-Firsuk alludes to this in these verses:—

"I have made a separation between the Christians and their churches, and between the people who shine and those who are in darkness."

"I neglected for a season thus to apportion their happiness, I being a procrastinating vindicator of their grievances."

"Thy Lord hath made thee to resolve upon removing their churches from those mosques wherein good words are recited."

"Whilst they were together in one place, some were praying and prostrating themselves on their faces, slightly separated from others who, behold! were adoring God and idols."

"How shall the people of the Cross unite to ring their bells, when the reading of the Qur'ān is perpetually intermingled?"

"I resolved then to remove them, just as did those wise men when they decreed themselves a right to the seed-field and the flocks."

"When al-Walīd resolved to build the chapel which is in the midst of the cloister, called 'the Vulture's Chapel' (a name given to it by the country-people, because the porticos on each side look like two wings), he dug deep at the four corners of the intended chapel, until they came to sweet and limpid water. Here they first placed the foundation of the wall of the vineyard. Upon this they built with stone, and when the four corners were of sufficient height, they then built thereon the chapel; but it fell down again. Then said al-Walīd to some one of the mathematicians, who well knew the plan of the Vulture's Chapel, 'I wish you to build this chapel; for the injunction of God hath been given me, and I am confident that no one but thyself may build it.' He therefore built the four corners, and covered them with wicker, and disappeared for a whole year, al-Walīd not knowing where he was. After a year, al-Walīd dug down to the four corner foundations. Then he (*i.e.* the architect) said, 'Do not be in a hurry, O commander of the Faithful!' Then he found the mathematician, who had a man's head with him. He came to the four corners, and uncovered the wicker work, and lo! all that had been built above the earth had fallen down, until they were on a level with the earth. So he said, 'From this (work have I come).' Then he proceeded to build, and firmly fixed and supported a beautiful fabric.

"Some person also said al-Walīd wished to construct a brilliant chapel of pure gold, whereby the rank of the mosque might be magnified. Hereupon the superintendent said unto him, 'You cannot effect this.' Upon which al-Walīd struck him fifty blows with a whip, saying, 'Am I then incapable of effecting this?' The man replied, 'Certainly.' Then he said, 'I will, then, find out a way to know the truth. Bring forth all the gold thou hast'; which he did: and al-Walīd melted it, and formed it into one large brick, which contained one thousand pieces of gold. But the man said, 'O Commander of the Faithful! we shall require so many thousand bricks of this sort, if thou dost possess them; nor will this suffice for our work. Al-Walīd seeing that he was true and just, presented him with fifty dīnārs; and when al-Walīd roofed the great precinct, he adorned the roof, as well as the whole extent of the pavement, with a surface of gold. Some of al-Walīd's family also said unto him, 'They who come after thee will emulate thee in rendering the outer roof of this mosque more commodious every year.' Upon this al-Walīd ordered all the lead of the country to be collected together, in order to construct therewith an exterior outward covering, answering to the interior, which should be light upon the roof, and on the side-posts that supported the roof. So they collected lead throughout all Syria and many other countries; and whilst they were returning, they met with a certain woman who possessed a weight of lead—a weight of many talents. They began to chaffer with the woman for it; but she refused to sell it, except for its weight in silver. So they wrote to the Commander of the Faithful, informing him of this, who replied, 'Buy it from her, even for its weight in silver.' When, then, they offered this sum unto her, she said, 'Now that you have agreed to my proposal, and are satisfied to give the weight in silver, I give the weight as an offering unto God, to serve for the roof of the mosque.' Hereupon they marked one corner of the weight with the impression of a seal, 'This is God's.' Some say the woman was an Israelite; some say that they sought for lead in open ditches or holes, and came to a stone sepulchre, within which was a leaden sepulchre, whence they brought forth a dead body, and laid it on the ground. Whilst dragging it out, the head fell to the ground, and the neck being broken, much blood flowed forth from the mouth, which terrified them so much, that they rapidly fled away. This is said to have been the burial-place of King Saul. Also, the guardian of the mosque came unto al-Walīd and said, 'O Commander of the Faithful! men say that al-Walīd hath expended the money of the treasury unjustly.' Hereupon al-Walīd desired that all the people should be summoned to prayer. When all were assembled, al-Walīd mounted the pulpit, and said, 'Such and such reports have reached me.' Then he said, 'O 'Umar Ibn al-Muhājir! stand up and produce the money of the treasury.' Now it was carried upon mules. Therefore, pieces of hide being placed in the midst, beneath the chapel, he poured out all the gold and silver, to such a height, that those who stood on either side could not see one another. Scales being then brought out, the whole was weighed, when it was found that the amount would suffice for the public use for three years to come, even if nothing were added to the amount. Then all the people rejoiced, praising and glorifying God for this. Then said the Khalīfah, 'O people of Damascus! you boast among men of four things; of your air, of your water, of your cheerfulness, and of your gracefulness. Would that you would add to these a fifth, and become of the number of those who praise God, and are liberal in his service. Would that, thus changing, you would become thankful suppliants.'

"In the Qiblah of this mosque were three golden scimitars, enamelled in lapis lazuli. Upon each scimitar was engraved the following sentence: 'In the name of God, the Merciful and Compassionate! There is no god but God. He is the ever-living, the self-subsisting Being, who never slumbers nor sleeps. There is no god but God. He has no partner. We will never adore any but our Lord, the one God. Our faith is Islām, and our Prophet is Muḥammad. This mosque was built, and the churches which stood on the site of the chapel were demolished, by order of the servant of God, the Commander of the Faithful, al-Walīd Ibn 'Abdu 'l-Malik Ibn Marwān, in the month Ẕū 'l-Qa'dah, A.H. 86.' Upon another tablet was inscribed the whole of the first chapter of the Qur'ān. Here also were depicted the stars, then the morning twilight, then the spiral course of the sun, then the way of living which obtained after the arrival of the Faithful at Damascus. Also, it is said, that all the floor of this mosque was divided into small slabs, and that the stone (carving) of the walls extended to the utmost pinnacle. Above was a great golden vine, and above this were splendid enamelled knobs of green, red, blue, and white, whereby were figured and expressed all countries and regions, especially the Ka'bah, above the tower; also all the countries to the right and left (of Makkah), and all the most beautiful shrubs and trees of every region, famous either for their fruits or flowers. The roof had cornices of gold. Here was suspended a chain of gold and silver, which branched off into seven separate lights. In the tower of the Companions were two stones—beryls (some say they were the jewels called pearls); they were called 'The Little Ones.' When the candles were put out, they inflamed the eyes by their brilliant light. In the time of al-Amīn Ibn ar-Rashīd, Sulaimān, captain of the guard, was sent by that Khalīfah to Damascus, to steal those stones and bring them to him; which he did. When al-Ma'mūn discovered this, he sent them to Damascus, as a proof of his brother's misconduct. They afterwards again vanished, and in their place is a glass vessel. In this mosque all the gates, from the dome (gallery) unto the entrance, are open, and have no bars or locks. Over each is a loose curtain. In like manner there is a curtain upon all the walls as far as the bases of the golden vine, above which are the enamelled knobs. The capitals of the pillars were thickly covered with dead gilding. Here were also small galleries, to look down from, enclosed on the four sides of the skirting wall. Al-Walīd also built the northern minaret, now called 'the Bridegroom's Tower.' As to the western gallery, that existed many ages before, in each corner of this was a cell, raised upon very lofty walls, and used by the Greeks as an observatory. The two northern of these fell, and the two opposite remained. In the year 740, part of the eastern had been burnt. It then fell down, but was built up anew out of the Christians' money, because they had meditated the destruction (of it) by fire. It then was restored after a most beautiful plan. This is the tower (but God knows) upon which Jesus son of Maria will alight, for Muḥammad is reported to have said, 'I saw Jesus son of Maria come forth from near the white minaret, east of the mosque, placing his hands upon the wings of two angels, firmly bound to him. Upon him was the Divine glory (the Shechinah). He was marked by the red tinge of baptism. This is the mark of original sin.' Jesus (it is also said) shall come forth from the White Tower by the eastern gate, and shall enter the mosque. Then shall the word come forth for Jesus to fight with Antichrist at the corner of the city, as long as it shall please God. Now, when this mosque (the slaves' mosque) was completed, there was not to be found upon the face of the earth a building more beautiful, more splendid, more graceful, than this. On whatever side, or area, or place, the spectator looked, he still thought that side or spot the most preferable for beauty. In this mosque were certain talismans, placed therein since the time of the Greeks; so that no venomous or stinging creature could by any means obtain entrance into this enclosure, neither serpent, scorpion, beetle, nor spider. They say, also, that neither sparrows nor pigeons built their nests there, nor was anything to be found there which could annoy people. Most, or all, of those talismans were burnt by the fire that consumed the mosque, which fire took place in the night of Sha'bān, A.H. 461. Al-Walīd frequently prayed in the mosque. One night (it is related) he said to his people, 'I wish to pray to-night in the mosque; let no one remain there whilst I pray therein.' So when he came unto the gate of the Two Moments, he desired the gate to be opened, and entering in, he saw a man standing between the gate of the Two Moments and the gate of St. George, praying. He was rather nearer to the gate of St. George than to the other. So the Khalīfah said unto his people, 'Did I not charge you that no one should remain whilst I was praying in the mosque?' Then one of them said, 'O Commander of the Faithful! this is St George, who prays every night in the mosque.' Again, one prayer in this mosque equals thirty thousand prayers.

"Again. A certain man, going out of the gate of the mosque which is near the Jairūn, met Ka'b the scribe, who said, 'Whither bound?' He replied, 'To the Baitu 'l-Muqaddas, therein to pray.' Then said Ka'b, 'I will show you a spot wherein whosoever prayeth shall receive the same blessings as if he prayed in the Baitu 'l-Muqaddas.' The man, therefore, went with him. Then Ka'b showed him the space between the little gate from whence you go to Abyssinia, that is, the space covered by the arch of the gate, containing about one hundred yards, to the west, and said, 'Whoso prayeth within those two points shall be regarded as praying within the Baitu 'l-Muqaddas.' Now, this spot is said to be a spot fit to be sought by pilgrims. Here, it is asserted, is the head of John, son of Zacharias (Peace be with him!). For al-Walīd Ibn Muslim being desired to show where John's head was to be found, pointed with his hand to the plastered pillar—the fourth from the east corner. Zaid Ibn Wakad says, 'At the time it was proposed to build the mosque of Damascus, I saw the head of John, son of Zacharias, brought forth from underneath one of the corners of the chapel. The hair of the head was unchanged.' He says in another place, 'Being nominated by al-Walīd superintendent of the building, we found a cave, of which discovery we informed al-Walīd. He came, therefore, unto us at night, with a wax taper in his hand. Upon descending we found an elaborately carved little shrine, three within three (*i.e.* within the first a second, within the second a third). Within this last was a sarcophagus, and within this a casket; within which was the head of John, son of Zacharias. Over the casket was written, "Here is the head of John, son of Zacharias. Peace be with him!" By al-Walīd's command we restored the head to the spot whence it had been taken. The pillars which are above this spot are inclined obliquely to the others to distinguish the place. There is also over it a pillar with a head in plaster.' He asserts again, that when the happy event occurred of the conquest of Damascus, a certain person went up the stairs which led to the church, then standing where the mosque now stands. Here the blood of John, son of Zacharias was seen to flow in torrents and to boil up, nor did the blood sink down and become still until that seventy thousand had been slain over him. The spot where the head was found is now called al-Sakasak (perhaps, the Nail of the Narrow Cave).

"In the days of 'Umar, the Christians requested that he would confirm their claim to the right of meeting in those places which al-Walīd had taken from them and converted into mosques. They, therefore, claimed the whole inner area as their own from 'Umar. The latter thought it right to restore them what al-Walīd had taken from them, but upon examination he found that the churches without the suburbs were not comprehended in the articles of surrender by the Companions, such, for example, as the great Church of the Monastery of Observants or Carmelites, the Church of the Convent behind the Church of St. Thomas, and all the churches of the neighbouring villages. 'Umar therefore gave them the choice, either to restore them the churches they demanded, demolishing in that case all the other churches, or to leave those churches unmolested, and to receive from them a full consent to the free use of the open space by the Muslims. To this latter proposal they, after three days deliberation, agreed; and proper writings were drawn up on both sides. They gave the Muslims a deed of grant, and 'Umar gave them full security and assurance of protection. Nothing was to be compared to this mosque. It is said to be one of the strongholds of Paradise, and that no inhabitant of Damascus would long for Paradise when he looks upon his beautiful mosque. Al-Ma'mūn came to Damascus in company with his brother al-Mu'taṣim, and the Qāẓī Yaḥya Ibn Akṣam. Whilst viewing the mosque he said, 'What is the most wondrous sight here?' His brother said, 'These offerings and pledges.' The Qāẓī said, 'The marble and the columns.' Then said al-Ma'mūn, 'The most wondrous thing to me is, whether any other could be built at all like this.'" (*Hist. Temple of Jerusalem*, by Jalālu 'd-dīn, translated by Reynolds, p. 407.)

DANCING. Arabic *Raqs.* Dancing is generally held to be unlawful, although it does not appear to be forbidden in either the Qur'ān or the Traditions, but according to al-Bukhārī (Arabic ed., p. 135), the Prophet expressly permitted it on the day of the great festival. Those who hold it to be unlawful quote the following verse from the Qur'ān, Sūrah xvii. 39, "Walk not proudly on the earth," as a prohibition, although it does not seem to refer to the subject.

The Ṣūfīs make dancing a religious exercise, but the Sunnī Muslims consider it unlawful. (*Hidāyatu 's-Sā'il*, p. 107.)

DANIEL. Arabic *Dāniyāl.* A prophet celebrated amongst Muḥammadans as an interpreter of dreams. He is not mentioned in either the Qur'ān or the Traditions, but in the *Qaṣaṣu 'l-Ambiyā'*, p. 231, it is stated that in the reign of *Bukhtu Naṣṣar* (Nebuchadnezzer) he was imprisoned; and when he was in prison, the king had a dream which he had forgotten, and hearing that Daniel was an interpreter of dreams, he sent for him. When Daniel was in the presence of the King, he refused to prostrate, saying, it was lawful to prostrate alone to the Lord Almighty. For this he nearly lost his life, but was spared to interpret the king's dream, which was as follows: "He saw a great idol, the head of which was of gold, above the navel of silver, below the navel of copper, the legs of iron, and the feet of clay. And suddenly a stone fell from heaven upon the idol, and ground it to powder, and mixed all the substances, so that the wind blew them in all directions; but the stone grew gradually, and to such an extent that it covered the whole earth." The interpretation of it, as given by Daniel is said to be this: The idol represented different nations; the gold was the kingdom of Nebuchadnezzar, the silver the kingdom of his son, the copper the Romans, the iron the Persians, and the clay the tribe Zauzan, from which the kings of Persia and Rome should be descended; the great stone being a religion which should spread itself over the whole earth in the last day.

DĀR (دار). "A house, dwelling, habitation, land, country." A word which is used in various combinations, *e.g.*:—

ad-Dār	The abode—the city of al-Madīnah.
ad-Dārain	The two abodes—this world and the next.
Dāru 'l-adab	A seat of learning; a university.
Dāru 'l-baqā'	The abode which remaineth—heaven.
Dāru 'l-fanā	The abode which passeth away—earth.
Dāru 'l-ghurūr	The abode of delusion—the world.
Dāru 'l-ḥuzn	The vale of tears—the earth.
Dāru 'l-ibtilā'	The abode of temptation—the world.
Dāru 'l-khilāfah	The seat of the Imām or Khalīfah—capital
Dāru 'l-kutub	A library.
Dāru 'l-khuld	The home of eternity—Paradise.
ad-Dāru 'n-na'īm	The blessed abode—Paradise.
Dāru 'l-qaẓā'	The Qāẓī's court.
Dāru 'sh-shifā'	A hospital.
Dāru 's-surūr	The abode of joy—Paradise.
Dāru 'ẓ-ẓarb	A mint.
Dāru 'ẓ-ẓiyāfah	A banqueting-room.

[DARU 'L-BAWAR, DARU 'L-HARB, DARU 'L-ISLAM, DARU 'L-QARAR, DARU 'S-SALAM, DARU 'S-SALTANAH, DARU 'S-SAWAB.]

DARGĀH (درگاه). A royal court (Persian). In India it is a term used for a Muḥammadan shrine or tomb of some reputed holy person, and which is the object of pilgrimage and adoration. (Wilson's *Glossary of Indian Terms.*)

DĀRU 'L-BAWĀR (دار البوار). *Lit.* "The abode of perdition." A term used for hell in the Qur'ān, Sūrah xiv. 33: "And have made their people to alight at the *abode of perdition.*"

DĀRU 'L-ḤARB (دار الحرب). "The land of warfare." According to the Dictionary *Ghiyāṣu 'l-Lughāt*, *Dāru 'l-ḥārb* is "a country belonging to infidels which has not been subdued by Islām." According to the *Qāmūs*, it is "a country in which peace has not been proclaimed between Muslims and unbelievers."

In the *Fatāwa 'Ālamgiri*, vol. ii. p. 854, it is written that a *Dāru 'l-ḥarb* becomes a *Dāru 'l-Islām* on one condition, namely, the promulgation of the edicts of Islām. The Imām Muḥammad, in his book called the *Ziyādah*, says a *Dāru 'l-Islām* again becomes a *Daru 'l-ḥarb*, according to Abū Ḥanīfah, on three conditions, namely: (1) That the edicts of the unbelievers be promulgated, and the edicts of Islām be suppressed; (2) That the country in question be adjoining a *Dāru 'l-ḥarb* and no other Muslim country lie between them (that is, when the duty of Jihād or religious war becomes incumbent on them, and they have not the power to carry it on). (3) That no protection (*amān*) remains for either a Muslim or a *ẕimmī*; viz. that *amānu 'l-awwal*, or that first protection which was given them when the country was first conquered by Islām. The Imāms Yūsuf and Muḥammad both say that when the edicts of unbelievers are promulgated in a country, it is sufficient to constitute it a *Dāru 'l-ḥarb*.

In the *Raddu 'l-Mukhtār*, vol. iii. p. 391, it is stated, "If the edicts of Islām remain in force, together with the edicts of the unbelievers, then the country cannot be said to be a *Dāru 'l-ḥarb*." The important question as to whether a country in the position of Hindustān may be considered a *Dāru 'l-Islām* or a *Dāru 'l-ḥarb* has been fully discussed by Dr. W. W. Hunter, of the Bengal Civil Service, in his work entitled, *Indian Musulmāns*, which is the result of careful inquiry as to the necessary conditions of a Jihād, or a Crescentade, instituted at the time of the excitement which existed in India in 1870–71, in consequence of a Wahhābī conspiracy for the overthrow of Christian rule in that country. The whole matter, according to the Sunnī Musulmāns, hinges upon the question whether India is *Dāru 'l-ḥarb*, "a land of warfare," or *Dāru 'l-Islām*, "a land of Islām."

The Muftīs belonging to the Ḥanīfi and Shāfiʻī sects at Makkah decided that, "as long as even some of the peculiar observances of Islām prevail in a country, it is *Dāru 'l-Islām*."

The decision of the Muftī of the Mālikī sect was very similar, being to the following effect: "A country does not become *Dāru 'l-ḥarb* as soon as it passes into the hands of the infidels, but when all or most of the injunctions of Islām disappear therefrom."

The law doctors of North India decided that, "the absence of protection and liberty to Musulmāns is essential in a *Jihād*, or religious war, and also that there should be a probability of victory to the armies of Islām."

The Shīʻah decision on the subject was as follows: "A Jihād is lawful only when the armies of Islām are led by the rightful Imām, when arms and ammunitions of war and experienced warriors are ready, when it is against the enemies of God, when he who makes war is in possession of his reason, and when he has secured the permission of his parents, and has sufficient money to meet the expenses of his journey."

The Sunnīs and Shīʻahs alike believe in the eventual triumph of Islām, when the whole world shall become followers of the Prophet of Arabia; but whilst the Sunnīs are, of course, ready to undertake the accomplishment of this great end, "whenever there is a probability of victory to the Musulmāns," the Shīʻahs, true to the one great principle of their sect, must wait until the appearance of a rightful Imām. [JIHAD.]

DĀRU 'L-ISLĀM (دار الاسلام).

"Land of Islām." According to the *Raddu 'l-Mukhtār*, vol. iii. p. 391, it is a country in which the edicts of Islām are fully promulgated.

In a state brought under Muslims, all those who do not embrace the faith are placed under certain disabilities. They can worship God according to their own customs, *provided they are not idolaters*; but it must be done without any ostentation, and, whilst churches and synagogues may be repaired, *no new place of worship can be erected.* "The construction of churches, or synagogues, in Muslim territory is unlawful, this being forbidden in the Traditions; but if places of worship belonging to Jews, or Christians, be destroyed, or fall into decay, they are at liberty to repair them, because buildings cannot endure for ever."

Idol temples must be destroyed, and idolatry suppressed by force in all countries ruled according to strict Muslim law. (*Hidāyah*, vol. ii. p. 219.)

For further particulars, see article DARU 'L-HARB.

DĀRU 'L-QARĀR (دار القرار).

"The abode that abideth." An expression which occurs in the Qur'ān, Sūrah xl. 42: "O my people! this present life is only a passing joy, but the life to come is *the mansion that abideth.*"

DĀRU 'S-SALĀM (دار السلام).

"The abode of peace." An expression which occurs in the Qur'ān, Sūrah vi. 127: "For them is a *dwelling of peace* with their Lord! and in recompense for their works, shall He be their protector."

DĀRU 'S-SALṬANAH (دار السلطنة).

"The seat of government." A term given to the capital of a province, or a Muslim state.

DĀRU 'Ṣ-ṢAWĀB (دار الثواب).

"The house of recompense." A name given to the Jannatu ʻAdn, or Garden of Eden, by the commentator al-Baiẓāwī.

DARVESH, DARWĪSH (درويش).

A Persian word for a religious mendicant. A dervesh. It is derived from the word *dar*, "a door"; *lit.* one who goes from door to door. Amongst religious Muḥammadans, the darvesh is called a *faqir*, which is the word generally used for religious mendicant orders in Arabic books. The subject is, therefore, considered in the article on FAQIR.

DAUGHTERS. Arabic *Bint*, pl. *Banāt*; Heb. *Bath* (בַּת).

In the law of inheritance, the position of a daughter is secured by a verse in the Qur'ān, Sūrah iv. 12: "With regard to your children, God has commanded you to give the sons the portion of two daughters, and if there be daughters, more than two, then they shall have two-thirds of that which their father hath left, but if she be an only daughter she shall have the half."

The *Sirājīyah* explains the above as follows:—

"Daughters begotten by the deceased take in three cases: half goes to one only, and two-thirds to two or more: and, if there be a son, the male has the share of two females, and he makes them residuaries. The son's daughters are like the daughters begotten by the deceased; and they may be in six cases: half goes to one only, and two-thirds to two or more, on failure of daughters begotten by the deceased; with a single daughter of the deceased, they have a sixth, completing (with the daughter's half) two-thirds; but, with two daughters of the deceased, they have no share of the inheritance, unless there be, in an equal degree with, or in a lower degree than, them, a boy, who makes them residuaries. As to the remainder between them, the male has the portion of two females; and all of the son's daughters are excluded by the son himself.

"If a man leave three son's daughters, some of them in lower degrees than others, and three daughters of the son of another son, some of them in lower degree than others, and three daughters of the son's son of another son, some of them in lower degrees than others, as in the following table, this is called the case of *tashbīh*.

First set.	Second set.	Third set.
Son.	Son.	Son.
Son, daughter.	Son.	Son
Son, daughter.	Son, daughter.	Son.
Son, daughter.	Son, daughter.	Son, daughter.
	Son, daughter.	Son, daughter.
		Son, daughter.

"Here the eldest of the first line has none equal in degree with her; the middle one of the first line is equalled in degree by the eldest of the second, and the youngest of the first line is equalled by the middle one of the second, and by the eldest of the third line; the youngest of the second line is equalled by the middle one of the third line, and the youngest of the third set has no equal in degree. When thou hast comprehended this, then we say: the eldest of the first line has a moiety; the middle one of the first line has a sixth, together with her equal in degree, to make up two-thirds; and those in lower degrees never take anything, unless there be a son with them, who makes them residuaries, both her who is equal to him in degree, and her who is above him, but who is not entitled to a share; those below him are excluded." (Ramsay's ed. *As-Sirājīyah.*)

The age of puberty, or majority, of a daughter is established by the usual signs of womanhood; but in the absence of these signs, according to Abū Ḥanīfah, she is not of age until she is eighteen. But the two Imāms, Muḥammad and Yūsuf, fix the age at fifteen, and with this opinion the Imām ash-Shāfi'ī agrees.

With regard to a daughter's freedom in a marriage contract, Shaikh 'Abdu 'l-Ḥaqq, in his commentary on the Traditions (vol. iii. p. 105), says, "All the learned doctors are agreed that a virgin daughter, until she has arrived at the age of puberty, is entirely at the disposal of her father or lawful guardian, but that in the event of a woman having been left a widow after she has attained the age of puberty, she is entirely at liberty to marry whom she likes." There is, however, he says, some difference of opinion as to the freedom of a girl who has not been married and has *arrived at the age of puberty.* Abū Ḥanīfah rules that she is entirely free from the control of her guardian with regard to her marriage, but ash-Shāfi'ī rules otherwise. Again, as regards a widow who is not of age, Abū Ḥanīfah says she cannot marry without her guardian's permission, but ash-Shāfi'ī says she is free.

According to the teaching of the Prophet, "a virgin daughter gives her consent to marriage by silence." He also taught "that a woman ripe in years shall have her consent asked, and if she remain silent her silence is consent, but if she do not consent, she shall not be forced." But this tradition is also to be compared with another, in which he said, "There is no marriage without the permission of the guardians." (*Mishkāt*, xiii. c. iv. pt. 2.) Hence the difference between the learned doctors on this subject.

The author of the *Akhlāq-i-Jalālī* says it is not advisable to teach girls to read and write, and this is the general feeling amongst Muḥammadans in all parts of the world, although it is considered right to enable them to recite the Qur'ān and the liturgical prayers.

The father or guardian is to be blamed who does not marry his daughter at an early age, for Muḥammad is related to have said, "It is written in the Book of Moses, that whosoever does not marry his daughter when she hath reached the age of twelve years is responsible for any sin she may commit."

The ancient Arabs used to call the angels the "daughters of God," and objected strongly, as the Badāwīs do in the present day, to female offspring, and they used to bury their infant daughters alive. These practices Muḥammad reprobates in the Qur'an, Sūrah xvi. 59: "And they ascribe daughters unto God! Glory be to Him! But they desire them not for themselves. For when the birth of a daughter is announced to any one of them, dark shadows settle on his face, and he is sad; he hideth him from the people because of the ill tidings. Shall he keep it with disgrace, or bury it in the dust? Are not their judgments wrong?"

Mr. Rodwell remarks on this verse: "Thus Rabbinism teaches that to be a woman is a great degradation. The modern Jew says in his Daily Prayers, fol. 5, 6, "Blessed art thou, O Lord our God! King of the Universe! who hath not made me a woman."

DŪMAH (دومة). A fortified town held by the Christian chief Ukaidar, who was defeated by the Muslim general Khālid, and by him converted to Muḥammadanism, A.H. 9. But the mercenary character of Ukaidar's conversion led him to revolt after Muḥammad's death. (Muir's *Life of Mahomet*, vol. iv. p. 191.)

DAVID. Arabic *Dāwud*, or *Dāwūd*. A king of Israel and a Prophet, to whom God revealed the *Zabūr*, or Book of Psalms. [ZABUR.] He has no special title or *kalimah*, as all Muslims are agreed that he was not a law-giver or the founder of a dispensation. The account of him in the Qur'ān is exceedingly meagre. It is given as follows, with the commentator's remarks translated in italics by Mr. Lane:—

"And God gave him (*David*) the kingship *over the children of Israel*, and wisdom, *after the death of Samuel and Saul, and they* [namely these two gifts] *had not been given together to any one before him*; and He taught him what He pleased, *as the art of making coats of mail, and the language of birds.* And were it not for God's repelling men, one by another, surely the earth had become corrupt *by the predominance of the polytheists and the slaughter of the Muslims and the ruin of the places of worship*: but God is beneficent to the peoples, *and hath repelled some by others.*" (Sūrah ii. 227.)

"Hath the story of the two opposing parties come unto thee, when they ascended over the walls of the oratory *of David, having been prevented going in unto him by the door, because of his being engaged in devotion?* When they went in unto David, and he was frightened at them, they said, Fear not: *we are* two opposing parties. *It is said that they were two parties of more than one each; and it is said that they were two individuals, angels, who came as two litigants, to admonish David, who had ninety-nine wives, and had desired the wife of a person who had none but her, and married her and taken her as his wife.* [One of them said,] One of us hath wronged the other; therefore judge between us with truth, and be not unjust, but direct us into the right way. Verily this my brother *in religion* had nine-and-ninety ewes, and I had one ewe; and he said, Make me her keeper. And he overcame me in the dispute.—*And the other confessed him to have spoken truth.*—[David] said, Verily he hath wronged thee in demanding thy ewe *to add her* to his ewes; and verily many associates wrong one another, except those who believe and do righteous deeds: and few indeed are they.—*And the two angels said, ascending in their* [proper or assumed] *forms to heaven, The man hath passed sentence against himself. So David was admonished.* And David perceived that We had tried him *by his love of that woman;* wherefore he asked pardon of his Lord, and fell down bowing himself (*or prostrating himself*), and repented. So We forgave him that; and verily for him [was ordained] a high rank with Us (*that is, an increase of good fortune in this world*), and [there shall be for him] an excellent retreat *in the world to come.*" (Sūrah xxxviii. 20–24.)

"We compelled the mountains to glorify Us, with David, and the birds *also, on his commanding them to do so, when he experienced languor;* and We did *this.* And We taught him the art of making coats of mail (*for before his time plates of metal were used*) for you *among mankind in general*, that they might defend you from your suffering *in warring with your enemies.*—Will ye then, *O people of Mecca*, be thankful *for My favours, believing the apostles?*" (Sūrah xxi. 79, 80.)

Sale observes that Yaḥya the commentator, most rationally understands hereby the divine revelations which David received from God, and not the art of making coats of mail.—The cause of his applying himself to this art is thus related in the *Mirātu 'z-Zamān*:—He used to go forth in disguise; and when he found any people who knew him not, he approached them and asked them respecting the conduct of David, and they praised him and prayed for him; but one day, as he was asking questions respecting himself as usual, God sent to him an angel in the form of a human being, who said, "An excellent man were David if he did not take from the public treasury." Whereupon the heart of David was contracted, and he begged of God to render him independent: so He made iron soft to him, and it became in his hands as thread; and he used to sell a coat of mail for four thousand [pieces of money—whether gold or silver is not said], and with part of this he obtained food for himself, and part he gave in alms, and with part he fed his family. Hence an excellent coat of mail is often called by the Arabs "Dāwudī," *i.e.* "Davidean." (See Lane's translation of *The Thousand and One Nights*, chap. viii. note 5.)

David, it is said, divided his time regularly, setting apart one day for the service of God, another day for rendering justice to his people, another day for preaching to them, and another day for his own affairs.

DA'WA (دعوى). A claim in a lawsuit. A claim or demand. (See Hamilton's *Hidāyah*, vol. iii. p. 63.)

DA'WAH (دعوة). *Lit.* "A call, invocation (*i.e.* of God's help)." A term used to express a system of incantation which is held to be lawful by orthodox Muḥammadans; whilst *siḥr*, "magic," and *kahānah*, "fortune-telling," are said to be unlawful, the Prophet having forbidden both.

From the Muslim books it appears that Muḥammad is believed to have sanctioned the use of spells and incantations, so long as the words used were only those of the names of God, or of the good angels, and of the good genii; although the more strict amongst them (the Wahhābis, for example,) would say that only an invocation of God Himself was lawful—teaching which appears to be more in accordance with that of Muḥammad, who is related to have said, "There is nothing wrong in using spells so long as you do not associate anything with God." (*Mishkāt*, xxi. c. i.) It is therefore clearly lawful to use charms and amulets on which the name of God only is inscribed, and to invoke the help of God by any ceremony, provided no one is associated with Him.

The science of *da'wah* has, however, been very much elaborated, and in many respects its teachers seem to have departed from the original teaching of their Prophet on the subject.

In India, the most popular work on *da'wah* is the *Jawāhiru 'l-Khamsah*, by Shaikh Abū 'l-Muwayyid of Gujerat, A.H. 956, in which he says the science is used for the following purposes. (1) To establish friendship or enmity between two persons. (2) To cause the cure, or the sickness and death, of a person. (3) To secure the accomplishment of one's wishes, both temporal and spiritual. (4) To obtain defeat or victory in battle.

This book is largely made up of Hindu customs which, in India, have become part of Muḥammadanism; but we shall endeavour to confine ourselves to a consideration of those sections which exhibit the so-called science as it exists in its relation to Islām.

In order to explain this occult science, we shall consider it under the following divisions:

1. The qualifications necessary for the *'āmil*, or the person who practices it.

2. The tables required by the teacher, and their uses.

3. An explanation of the terms *niṣāb*, *zakāt*, *'ushr*, *qufl*, *daur*, *bazl*, *khatm*, and *sarī'u 'l-ijābah*, and their uses.

4. The methods employed for commanding the presence of the genii.

I. When anyone enters upon the study of the science, he must begin by paying the utmost attention to cleanliness. No dog, or cat, or any stranger, is allowed to enter his dwelling-place, and he must purify his house by burning wood-aloes, pastiles, and other sweet-scented perfumes. He must take the utmost care that his body is in no way defiled, and he must bathe and perform the legal ablutions constantly. A most important preparation for the exercise of the art is a forty-days' fast (*chilla*), when he must sleep on a mat spread on the ground, sleep as little as possible, and not enter into general conversation. Exorcists not unfrequently repair to some cave or retired spot in order to undergo complete abstinence.

The diet of the exorcist must depend upon the kind of *asmā*, or names of God he intends to recite. If they are the *asmā'u 'l-jalālīyah*, or "terrible attributes" of the Almighty, then he must refrain from the use of meat, fish, eggs, honey, and musk. If they are the *asmā'u 'l-jamālīyah*, or "amiable attributes," he must abstain from butter, curds, vinegar, salt, and ambergrise. If he intends to recite both attributes, he must then abstain from such things as garlic, onions, and assafœtida.

It is also of the utmost importance that the exorcist should eat things which are lawful, always speak the truth, and not cherish a proud or haughty spirit. He should be careful not to make a display of his powers before the world, but treasure up in his bosom the knowledge of his acquirements. It is considered very dangerous to his own life for a novice to practice the science of exorcism.

II. Previous to reciting any of the names or attributes of God for the establishment of friendship or enmity in behalf of any person, it is necessary to ascertain the initials of his or her name in the Arabic alphabet, which letters are considered by exorcists to be connected with the twelve signs of the zodiac, the seven planets, and the four elements. The following tables, which are taken from the *Jawāhiru 'l-Khamsah*, occur, in a similar form, in all books on exorcism, give the above combinations, together with the nature of the perfume to be burnt, and the names of the presiding genius and guardian angel. These tables may be considered the key to the whole science of exorcism.

Letters of the Alphabet arranged according to the *Abjad* [ABJAD], with their respective number.	1 ا	2 ب	3 ج	4 د	5 ه
The Special Attributes or Names of God.	الله *Allāh.*	باقي *Bāqi.*	جامع *Jāmi'.*	ديان *Dayyān.*	هادي *Hādī.*
The Number of the Attribute.	66	113	114	65	20
The Meaning of the Attribute.	God.	Eternal.	Assembler.	Reckoner.	Guide.
The Class of the Attribute.	Terrible.	Amiable.	Terrible & Amiable combined.	Terrible.	Amiable.
The Quality, Vice, or Virtue of the Letter.	Friendship.	Love.	Love.	Enmity.	Enmity.
The Elements. (*Arba'ah 'Anāṣir.*)	Fire.	Air.	Water.	Earth.	Fire.
The Perfume of the Letter.	Black Aloes	Sugar.	Cinnamon.	Red Sandal.	White Sandal.
The Signs of the Zodiac. (*Burūj.*)	*Ḥamal.* Ram.	*Jauzā'* Twins.	*Saraṭān.* Crab.	*Ṣaur.* Bull.	*Ḥamal.* Ram.
The Planets. (*Kawākib.*)	*Zuḥal.* Saturn.	*Mushtarī.* Jupiter.	*Mirrīkh.* Mars.	*Shams.* Sun.	*Zuhrah.* Venus.
The Genii. (*Jinn.*)	Qayupūsh.	Danūsh.	Nulūsh.	Ṭwayūsh.	Hūsh.
The Guardian Angels. (*Muwakkil.*)	Isrāfīl.	Jibrā'īl.	Kalkā'īl.	Dardā'īl.	Durbā'īl.

Letters of the Alphabet arranged according to the *Abjad* [ABJAD], with their respective number.	6 و	7 ز	8 ح	9 ط	10 ى
The Special Attributes or Names of God.	ولى *Walī*	زكى *Zakī.*	حق *Ḥaqq.*	طاهر *Ṭāhir.*	ياسين *Yāsīn.*
The Number of the Attribute.	46	37	108	215	130
The Meaning of the Attribute.	Friend.	Purifier.	Truth.	Holy.	Chief.
The Class of the Attribute.	Amiable.	Combined.	Combined.	Terrible.	Amiable.
The Quality, Vice, or Virtue of the Letter.	Love.	Love.	Hatred.	Desire.	Attraction.
The Elements. (*Arba'ah 'Anāṣir.*)	Air.	Water.	Earth.	Fire.	Air.
The Perfume of the Letter.	Camphor.	Honey.	Saffron.	Musk.	Rose Leaves.
The Signs of the Zodiac. (*Burūj.*)	*Jauzā'.* Twins.	*Saraṭān.* Crab.	*Jady.* Goat.	*Ḥamal.* Ram.	*Mīzān.* Scales.
The Planets. (*Kawākib*)	*'Uṭārid.* Mercury.	*Qamar.* Moon.	*Zuḥal.* Saturn.	*Mushtarī.* Jupiter.	*Mirrikh.* Mars.
The Genii. (*Jinn.*)	Puyūsh.	Kapūsh.	'Ayūsh.	Badyūsh.	Shahbūsh.
The Guardian Angel. (*Muwakkil.*)	Raftmā'īl.	Sharkā'īl.	Tankafīl.	Ishmā'īl.	Sarakīkā'īl.

Letters of the Alphabet arranged according to the *Abjad* [ABJAD], with their respective number.	20 ك	30 ل	40 م	50 ن	60 س
The Special Attributes or Names of God.	كافى *Kāfī.*	لطيف *Laṭīf.*	ملك *Malik.*	نور *Nūr.*	سميع *Samī'.*
The Number of the Attribute.	111	129	90	256	180
The Meaning of the Attribute.	Sufficient	Benignant.	King.	Light.	Hearer.
The Class of the Attribute.	Amiable.	Amiable.	Terrible.	Amiable.	Combined.
The Quality, Vice, or Virtue of the Letter.	Love.	Separation.	Love.	Hatred.	Desire.
The Elements. ('*Arba'ah 'Anāṣir.*)	Water.	Earth.	Fire.	Air.	Water.
The Perfume of the Letter.	White rose leaves.	Apples.	Quince.	Hyacinth.	Different kinds of Scents.
The Signs of the Zodiac. (*Burūj.*)	*'Aqrab.* Scorpion.	*Ṣaur.* Bull.	*Asad.* Lion.	*Mīzān.* Scales.	*Qaus.* Archer.
The Planets. (*Kawākib.*)	*Shams.* Sun.	*Zuhrah.* Venus.	*'Uṭārid.* Mercury.	*Qamar.* Moon.	*Zuḥal.* Saturn.
The Genii. (*Jinn.*)	Kadyūsh.	'Adyūsh.	Majbūsh.	Damalyūsh	Fa'yūsh.
The Guardian Angels. (*Muwakkil.*)	Kharurā'īl.	Ṭaṭā'īl.	Rūyā'īl.	Hūlā'īl.	Ham-wākīl.

Letters of the Alphabet arranged according to the *Abjad* [ABJAD], with their respective number.	70 ع	80 ف	90 ص	100 ق	200 ر
The Special Attributes or Names of God.	علی *'Alī.*	فتاح *Fattāḥ.*	صمد *Ṣamad.*	قادر *Qādir.*	رب *Rabb.*
The Number of the Attribute.	110	489	134	305	202
The Meaning of the Attribute.	Exalted.	Opener.	Established.	Powerful.	Lord.
The Class of the Attribute.	Terrible.	Amiable.	Terrible.	Combined.	Terrible.
The Quality, Vice, or Virtue of the Letter.	Riches.	Enmity.	Intimacy.	Desire.	Friendship.
The Elements. (*Arba'ah 'Anāṣir.*)	Earth.	Fire.	Air.	Water.	Earth.
The Perfume of the Letter.	White Pepper.	Walnut.	Nutmeg.	Orange.	Rosewater.
The Signs of the Zodiac. (*Burūj.*)	*Sumbulah.* Virgin.	*Asad.* Lion.	*Mīzān.* Scales.	*Ḥūt.* Fish.	*Sumbulah.* Virgin.
The Planets. (*Kawākib.*)	*Mushtarī.* Jupiter.	*Mirrīkh.* Mars.	*Shams.* Sun.	*Zuhrah.* Venus.	*'Uṭārid.* Mercury.
The Genii. (*Jinn.*)	Kashpūsh.	Laṭyūsh.	Kalapūsh.	Shamyūsh.	Rahūsh.
The Guardian Angels. (*Muwakkil.*)	Lumā'īl.	Sarhmā'īl.	Ahjmā'īl.	'Itrā'īl.	Amwākīl.

Letters of the Alphabet arranged according to the *Abjad* [ABJAD], with their respective number.	300 ش	400 ت	500 ث	600 خ
The Special Attributes or Names of God.	شفیع *Shafī'.*	تواب *Tawwāb.*	ثابت *Ṣābit.*	خالق *Khāliq.*
The Number of the Attribute.	460	409	903	731
The Meaning of the Attribute.	Accepter.	Forgiver.	Stable.	Creator.
The Class of the Attribute.	Amiable.	Amiable.	Terrible.	Combined.
The Quality, Vice, or Virtue of the Letter.	Enmity.	Sleeplessness.	Hatred.	Love.
The Elements. (*Arb'ah 'Anāṣir.*)	Fire.	Air.	Water.	Earth
The Perfume of the Letter.	White Aloes.	Amber.	White Aloes.	Violet.
The Signs of the Zodiac. (*Burūj.*)	*'Aqrab.* Scorpion.	*Dalw.* Watering Pot.	*Ḥūt.* Fish.	*Jady.* Goat.
The Planets. (*Kawākib.*)	*Qamar.* Moon.	*Zuḥal.* Saturn	*Mushtarī.* Jupiter.	*Mirrīkh.* Mars.
The Genii. (*Jinn.*)	Tashyūsh.	Laṭyūsh.	Ṭwahyūsh.	Dālāyūsh.
The Guardian Angels. (*Muwakkil.*)	Amrā'īl.	Azrā'īl.	Mīkā'īl.	Mahkā'īl.

Letters of the Alphabet arranged according to the *Abjad* [ABJAD], with their respective number.	700 ذ	800 ض	900 ظ	1000 غ
The Special Attributes or Names of God.	ذاكر *Ẕākir.*	ضار *Ẓārr.*	ظاهر *Ẕāhir.*	غفور *Ghafūr.*
The Number of the Attribute.	921	1001	1106	1285
The Meaning of the Attribute.	Rememberer.	Punisher.	Evident.	Great Forgiver.
The Class of the Attribute.	Combined.	Terrible.	Terrible.	Amiable.
The Quality, Vice, or Virtue of the Letter.	Hatred.	Hatred.	Enmity.	Convalescence.
The Elements. (*Arbaʿah ʿAnāṣir.*)	Fire.	Air.	Water.	Earth.
The Perfume of the Letter.	Sweet Basil.	Laburnam.	Jasmine.	Cloves.
The Signs of the Zodiac. (*Burūj.*)	*Qaus.* Archer.	*Dalw.* Watering Pot.	*Ḥūt.* Fish.	*Ḥūt.* Fish.
The Planets. (*Kawākib.*)	*Shams.* Sun.	*Zuhrah.* Venus.	*ʿUṭārid.* Mercury.	*Qamar.* Moon.
The Genii. (*Jinn.*)	Ṭwakapūsh.	Ghayūsh.	Ghafūpūsh.	ʿArkupūsh.
The Guardian Angel. (*Muwakkil.*)	Harṭāʾīl.	ʿAṭāʾīl.	Nurāʾīl.	Nukhāʾīl.

The sex of the signs of the Zodiac (*burūj*) has been determined as in the following table. Between males and females exists friendship; between males and hermaphrodites sometimes friendship sometimes enmity; between females and hermaphrodites the most inveterate enmity:—

MALES.		FEMALES.		HERMAPHRODITES.	
Ram	. *Burj-i-Ḥamal.*	Bull .	. *Burj-i-Ṡaur.*	Twins .	. *Burj-i-Jauzāʾ.*
Lion	. *Burj-i-Asad.*	Scales .	. *Burj-i-Mīzān.*	Virgin	. *Burj-i-Sumbulah.*
Scorpion	. *Burj-i-ʿAqrab.*	Crab .	. *Burj-i-Saraṭān.*	Goats .	. *Burj-i-Jady.*
Fish .	. *Burj-i-Ḥūt.*			Watering Pot .	. *Burj-i-Dalw.*
Archer	. *Burj-i-Qaus.*				

Astrologists have determined the relative dispositions of the planets (*kawākib*) to be as follows:—

Venus and Saturn.	Venus and Moon.	Jupiter and Venus.	Jupiter and Sun.	Sun and Moon.	Jupiter and Moon.	Sun and Venus.	Friendship.
Moon and Mercury.	Saturn and Mercury.	Jupiter and Mercury.	Mars and Mercury.	Venus and Mercury.	Mars and Venus.	Sun and Mercury.	Mixed Friendship and Enmity or Indifference.
Saturn and Sun.	Saturn and Moon.	Mars and Moon.	Mars and Sun.	Saturn and Sun.	Jupiter and Mars.	Jupiter and Saturn.	Enmity.

The four elements (*arba'ah 'anāṣir*) stand in relation to each other as follows :—

Water and Water. Fire and Fire.	Earth and Earth. Air and Air.	Friendship.
Fire and Air.	Air and Water.	Mixed Friendship and Enmity or Indifference.
Fire and Water. Fire and Earth.	Earth and Water.	Enmity.

As an illustration of the use of these tables, two persons, Akram and Raḥīmah, contemplate a matrimonial alliance, and wish to know if it will be a happy union or otherwise.

The exorcist must first ascertain if the elements (*arba'ah 'anāṣir*), the signs of the zodiac (*burūj*), and the planets (*kawākib*), are amicably or inimicably disposed to each other in the cases of these two individuals, and also if there is a combination expressed in the *ism* or name of God connected with their initial letters.

In the present instance the initial letter of Akram is *alif*, and that of Raḥīmah, *rā*, and a reference to the foregoing tables will produce the following results :—

	Akram. (اكرم).	*Raḥīmah.* (رحيمة).
Initial letter.	Alif ا.	Rā ر.
The quality of the letter.	Friendship.	Friendship.
The element.	Fire.	Earth.
The attribute.	Allāh.	Rabb.
The quality of the attribute.	Terrible.	Terrible.
The planet.	Saturn	Mercury.
The sign of the zodiac.	The ram.	The virgin.
The perfume.	Black aloes.	Rose water.
The genius.	Qayupūsh.	Rahūsh.
The angel.	Isrāfīl.	Amwākīl.

In considering this case, the exorcist will observe that there is a combination in the attributes of God, both belonging to the *asmā'u 'l-jalāliyah*, or terrible attributes. There is also a combination in the quality of the letters, both implying friendship. Their respective planets, Saturn and Mercury, show a combination of either mixed friendship and enmity, or, perhaps, indifference. The sign of the zodiac, the ram being a male, and that of the virgin a hermaphrodite, show a possible alternation of friendship and enmity between the parties. The elements, fire and earth, being opposed, imply enmity. It therefore appears that there will be nothing against these two persons, Akram and Raḥīmah forming a matrimonial alliance, and that they may reasonably expect as much happiness from their union as usually falls to the lot of the human race. Should the good offices of the exorcist be requested, he will, by incantation, according to the table given, appeal to the Almighty as Allāh and Rabb, call in the aid of the genii Qayupūsh and Rahūsh, and of the guardian angels, Isrāfīl and Amwākīl. The perfumes he will burn in his numerous recitals will be black aloes and rose-water, and so bring about a speedy increase in the happiness of the persons of Akram and Raḥīmah!

III. As we have already explained, the incantations used by exorcists consist in the recital of either the names or attributes of God, or of certain formulæ which are given in books on the subject. In the *Jawāhiru 'l-Khamsah*, there were many forms of incantation, but we select the following one to illustrate the subject :—

سبحانك لا اله الا انت رب كل شى و وارثه
ورازقه و راحمه

Subḥānaka! lā ilāha illā anta! Rabba-kulli-shai'in! wa wāriṣahu! wa rāziqahu! wa rāḥimahu!

Glory be to Thee! There is no deity but Thee! The Lord of All! and the Inheritor thereof! and the Provider therefor! and the Merciful thereon!

This incantation consists of forty-four letters, exclusive of vowel points, as is shown by the following table :—

1	س	Sīn	60
2	ب	Bā	2
3	ح	Ḥā	8
4	ا	Alif	1
5	ن	Nūn	50
6	ك	Kāf	20
7	ل	Lām	30
8	ا	Alif	1
9	ا	Alif	1
10	ل	Lām	30
11	ه	Hā	5
12	ا	Alif	1
13	ل	Lām	30
14	ل	Lām	30
15	ا	Alif	1
16	ا	Alif	1
17	ن	Nūn	50
18	ت	Tā	400

19	ر	Rā	200
20	ب	Bā	2
21	ب	Bā	2
22	ك	Kāf	20
23	ل	Lām	30
24	ل	Lām	30
25	ش	Shīn	300
26	ی	Ya	10
27	ء	Hamzah	1
28	و	Wau	6
29	و	Wau	6
30	ا	Alif	1
31	ر	Rā	200
32	ث	Ṣā	500
33	ه	Hā	5
34	و	Wau	6
35	ر	Rā	200
36	ا	Alif	1
37	ز	Zā	7
38	ق	Qāf	100
39	ه	Hā	5
40	و	Wau	6
41	ر	Rā	200
42	ا	Alif	1
43	ح	Ḥā	8
44	م	Mīm	40
45	ه	Hā	5
			2613

In reciting such an invocation, units are reckoned as hundreds, tens as thousands, hundreds as tens of thousands, and thousands as hundreds of thousands.

In the above formula—

Its *niṣāb*, or fixed estate, is the number of letters (*i.e.* 45) put into thousands = . . .	4,500
Its *zakāt*, or alms, is the half of the *niṣāb* added to itself, 4,500 and 2,250 = . . .	6,750
Its *ʻushr*, or tithes, is half of the above half added to the *zakāt*, 6,750 and 1,125 = . . .	7,875
Its *qufl*, or lock, is half of 1,125 =	563
Its *daur*, or circle, is obtained by adding to its *qufl* the sum of the *ʻushr* and then doubling the total :— 563 + 7,875 = 8,438; 8,438 + 8,438	16,876
Its *bazl*, or gift, is the fixed number	7,000
Its *khatm*, or seal, is the fixed number	1,200
Its *sariʻu 'l-ijābah*, or speedy answer, is the fixed number .	12,000
Total . . .	56,764

After the exorcist has recited the formula the above number of times, he should, in order to make a reply more certain, treble the *niṣāb*, making it 135,000, and then add 2,613, the value of the combined number of letters, making a total of 137,613 recitals. The number of these recitals should be divided as nearly as possible in equal parts for each day's reading, provided it be completed within forty days. By a rehearsal of these, says our author, the mind of the exorcist becomes completely transported, and, whether asleep or awake, he finds himself accompanied by spirits and genii (*jinn*) to the highest heavens and the lowest depths of earth. These spirits then reveal to him hidden mysteries, and render souls and spirits obedient to the will of the exorcist.

IV. If the exorcist wish to command the presence of genii in behalf of a certain person, it is generally supposed to be effected in the following manner. He must, first of all, shut himself up in a room and fast for forty days. He should besmear the chamber with red ochre, and, having purified himself, should sit on a small carpet, and proceed to call the genius or demon. He must, however, first find out what special genii are required to effect his purpose. If, for example, he is about to call in the aid of these spirits in behalf of a person named Bahrām (بهرام) he will find out, first, the special genii presiding over the name, the letters of which are, omitting the vowel points, B H R A M. Upon reference to the table it will be seen that they are Danush, Hūsh, Rahūsh, Qayupūsh, and Majbūsh. He must then find out what are the special names of God indicated by these letters, which we find in the table are *al-Bāqī*, "the Eternal," *al-Hādī*, "the Guide," *ar-Rabb*, "the Lord," *Allāh*, "God," *al-Malik*, "the King." He must then ascertain the power of the letters, indicating the number of times for the recital, which will be thus :—

B,	2	equal to	200
H,	5	,,	500
R,	200	,,	20,000
A,	1	,,	100
M,	40	,,	4,000
	Total		24,800

The exorcist should then, in order to call in the help of the genii, recite the following formula, not fewer than 24,800 times :—

Yā Danushu ! for the sake of the Eternal One !

Yā Hūshu ! for the sake of the Guide !

Yā Rahūshu ! for the sake of the Lord !

Yā Qayupūshu ! for the sake of Allāh !

Yā Majbūshu ! for the sake of the King !

The exorcist will perform this recital with his face turned towards the house of the object he wishes to affect, and burn the perfumes indicated according to the table for the letters of Bahrām's name.

There are very many other methods of performing this exorcism, but the foregoing will suffice as a specimen of the kind of service. [MAGIC.]

DAY. The Muḥammadan day commences at sun-set; our Thursday evening, for example, being the beginning of the Muslim Friday. The Arabic *Yaum* denotes the day of twenty-four hours, and *Nahār*, the day in contradistinction to the night (*lail*). The days of the week are as follows:—

Yaumu 'l-aḥad, first-day, Sunday.
Yaumu 'l-iṣnain, second day, Monday.
Yaumu 's-ṣalāsā', third day, Tuesday.
Yaumu 'l-arbā', fourth day, Wednesday.
Yaumu 'l-khamīs, Thursday.
Yaumu 'l-jum'ah, Day of Assembly, Friday.
Yaumu 's-sabt, Sabbath-day, Saturday.

Of the days of the week, Monday, Wednesday, Thursday, and Friday, are esteemed good and auspicious; the others evil. (*Qānūn-i-Islām*, p. 403.) Friday is the special day appointed by Muḥammad for meeting in the chief mosque for public worship. [FRIDAY.]

DAY OF JUDGMENT. [RESURRECTION.]

DEATH. Arabic *Maut; Wafāt.* It is distinctly taught in the Qur'ān that the hour of death is fixed for every living creature.

Sūrah xvi. 63: "If God were to punish men for their wrong-doing, He would not leave on the earth a single living creature; but He respites them until a stated time; and when their time comes they cannot delay it an hour, nor can they hasten it."

Sūrah iii. 182: "Every soul must taste death, and ye shall only be paid your hire on the day of resurrection."

Sūrah l. 17: "The agony of death shall come in truth, that is what thou didst shun."

In the Traditions, Muḥammad has taught that it is sinful to wish for death: "Wish not for death, not even if thou art a doer of good works, for peradventure thou mayest increase them with an increase of life. Nor even if thou art a sinner, for with increase of life thou mayest obtain God's pardon."

One day the Prophet said: "Whosoever loves to meet God, God will love to meet him, and whoever dislikes to meet God, God will dislike to meet him." Then 'Āyishah said, "Truly we all dislike death and consider it a great affliction." The Prophet replied, "Thou dost not understand me. When death comes near a believer, then God gives him a spirit of resignation, and so it is that there is nothing which a believer likes so much as death."

Al-Barā' ibn 'Āzib, one of the Companions, says:—

"I came out with the Prophet at the funeral of one of the assistants, and we arrived just at the grave, before they had interred the body, and the Prophet sat down, and we sat around him with our heads down, and were so silent, that you might say that birds were sitting upon our heads. And there was a stick in the Prophet's hand with which he kept striking the ground. Then he raised his head and said twice or thrice to his companions, 'Seek the protection of God from the punishments of the grave.' After that he said: 'Verily, when a Muslim separateth from the world and bringeth his soul to futurity, angels descend to him from the celestial regions, whose faces are white. You might say their faces are the sun, and they have a shroud of the shrouds of paradise, and perfumes therefrom. So they sit apart from the deceased, as far as the eyes can see. After which the Angel of Death (*Malaku 'l-Maut*) comes to the deceased and sits at his head, and says, "O pure soul, come forth to God's pardon and pleasure." Then the soul comes out, issuing like water from a bag, and the Angel of Death takes it; and when he takes it, the angels do not allow it to remain in his hands for the twinkling of an eye. But when the Angel of Death has taken the soul of a servant of God, he resigns it to his assistants, in whose hands is a shroud, and they put it into the shroud and with the perfumes, when a fragrance issues from the soul like the smell of the best musk that is to be found on the face of the earth. Then the angels carry it upwards, and they do not pass by any concourse of angels who do not say, "What is this pure soul, and who is owner of it?" And they say, "Such a one, the son of such a one," calling him by the best names by which he was known in the world, till they reach the lowest region of heaven with him. And the angels ask the door to be opened for him, which is done. Then angels follow it through each heaven, the angel of one region to those of the next, and so on till it reaches the seventh heaven, when God says, "Write the name of My servant in 'Illīyūn, and return him towards the earth, that is, to his body which is buried in the earth, because I have created man from earth and return him to it, and will bring him out from it again as I brought him out at first." Then the souls are returned into their bodies, when two angels [MUNKAR and NAKIR] come to the dead man and cause him to sit up, and say to him, "Who is thy Lord?" He replies, "My Lord is God." Then they say, "What is thy religion?" He says, "Islām." Then they say, "What is this man who is sent to you?" (*i.e.* the Prophet). He says, "He is the Prophet of God." Then they say, "What is your proof of his mission?" He says, "I read the book of God, and believed in it, and I proved it to be true." Then a voice calls out from the celestial regions, "My servant hath spoken true, therefore throw for him a bed from Paradise, and dress him in clothes from Paradise, and open a door for him towards Paradise." Then peace and perfumes come for him from Paradise, and his grave is enlarged for him as far as the eye can see. Then a man with a beautiful face comes to him, elegantly dressed, and perfumed, and he says, "Be joyful in that which hath made thee so, this is the day which was promised thee." Then the dead person says to him, "Who art thou, for thy face is perfectly beautiful?" And the man replies, "I am thy good deeds." Then the dead person cries out, "O Lord, hasten the resurrection for my sake!"'

"'But,' continued the Prophet, 'when an infidel dies, and is about to pass from the world and bring his soul to futurity, black-faced angels come down to him and with them sackcloths. Then they sit from the dead as far as the eye can see, after which the Angel of Death comes in order to sit at his head, and says, "O impure soul! come forth to the wrath of God." Then the soul is disturbed in the infidel's body. Then the Angel of Death draws it out as a hot spit is drawn out of wet wool.

"'Then the Angel of Death takes the soul of the infidel, and having taken it, the angels do not allow it to remain with him the twinkling of an eye, but they take it in the sackcloth, and a disagreeable smell issues from the soul, like that of the most fetid carcass that can be met with upon the face of the earth. Then the angels carry it upwards and do not pass by any assembly of angels who do not ask whose filthy soul is this. They answer such an one, the son of such an one, and they mention him by the worst names that he bore in the world, till they arrive with it at the lowest heaven, and call the door to be opened, but it cannot be done.' Then the Prophet repeated this verse: '*The doors of the celestial regions shall not be opened for them, nor shall they enter into paradise till a camel passes through the eye of a needle.*' Then God says, 'Write his history in Sijjīn,' which is the lowest earth; then his soul is thrown down with violence. Afterwards the Prophet repeated this verse: '*Unite no partner with God, for whoever uniteth gods with God is like that which falleth from high, and the birds snatch it away, or the wind wafteth it to a distant place.*' Then his soul is replaced in his body, and two angels [MUNKAR and NAKIR] come to him and set him up, and say, 'Who is thy Lord?' He says, 'Alas! alas! I do not know.' Then they say, 'What is thy religion?' He says, 'Alas! alas! I do not know.' And they say to him, 'What is the condition of the man who is sent down to you?' He says, 'Alas! alas! I do not know.' Then a voice comes from above, saying, 'He lieth; therefore spread a bed of fire for him and open a door for him towards hell.' Then the heat and hot winds of hell come to him, and his grave is made tight upon him, so as to squeeze his ribs. And a man with a hideous countenance comes to him shockingly dressed, of a vile smell, and he says, 'Be joyful in that which maketh thee miserable; this is the day that was promised thee.' Then the dead man says, 'Who art thou? Thy face is hideous, and brings wickedness.' He says, 'I am thy impure actions.' Then the dead person says, 'O Lord, delay the resurrection on my account!'"

The ceremonies attending the death of a Muslim are described as follows by Jāfir Shārīf in Herklot's *Qānūn-i-Islām*, as follows:—

Four or five days previous to a sick man's approaching his dissolution, he makes his will in favour of his son or any other person, in the presence of two or more witnesses, and either delivers it to others or retains it by him. In it he likewise appoints his executor. When about to expire, any learned reader of the Qur'ān is sent for, and requested to repeat with a loud voice the Sūrah Yā Sīn (or chap. xxxvi.), in order that the spirit of the man, by the hearing of its sound, may experience an easy concentration. It is said that when the spirit was commanded to enter the body of Adam, the soul having looked into it once, observed that it was a bad and dark place, and unworthy of its presence! Then the Just and Most Holy God illuminated the body of Adam with "lamps of light," and commanded the spirit to re-enter. It went in a second time, beheld the light, and saw the whole dwelling, and said, "There is no pleasing sound here for me to listen to." It is generally understood from the best works of the mystics of the East, that it was owing to this circumstance that the Almighty created music. The holy spirit, on hearing the sound of this music became so delighted that it entered Adam's body. Commentators on the Qur'ān, expositors of the Traditions and divines have written, that that sound resembled that produced by the repeating of the Sūratu Yā Sīn; it is therefore advisable to read at the hour of death this chapter for tranquillising the soul.

The Kalimatu 'sh-shahādah [CREED] is also read with an audible voice by those present. They do not require the patient to read it himself, as at such a time he is in a distressing situation, and not in a fit state of mind to repeat the Kalimah.

Most people lie insensible, and cannot even speak, but the pious retain their mental faculties and converse till the very last. The following is a most serious religious rule amongst us, viz. that if a person desire the patient to repeat the Kalimah, and the sick man expire without being able to do so, his faith is considered dubious; whilst the man who directed him so to do thereby incurs guilt. It is therefore best that the sitters-by read it, in anticipation of the hope that the sick man, by hearing the sound of it, may bring it to his recollection, and repeat it either aloud or in his own mind. In general, when a person is on the point of death, they pour *sharbat*, made of sugar and water, down his throat, to facilitate the exit of the vital spark, and some procure the holy water of the Zamzam well at Makkah. The moment the spirit has fled, the mouth is closed; because, if left open, it would present a disagreeable spectacle. The two great toes are brought in contact and fastened together with a thin slip of cloth, to prevent the legs remaining apart. They burn perfumes near the corpse. Should the individual have died in the evening, the shrouding and burial take place before midnight; if he die at a later hour, or should the articles required not be procurable at that late hour, he is buried early on the following morning. The sooner the sepulchral rites are performed the better, for it is not proper to keep a corpse long in the house, and for this reason the Prophet said that if he was a good man, the sooner he is buried the more quickly he will reach heaven; if a bad man, he should be speedily buried, in order that his unhappy lot may not fall upon others in the house; as also that the relatives of the deceased may not, by holding the corpse, weep too much or go without food. There are male and female washers, whose province it is to wash and shroud the corpse for payment. Sometimes, however, the relatives do it themselves. In undertaking the operation of washing, they dig a hole in the earth to receive the water used in the process, and prevent its spreading over a large surface, as some men and women consider it bad to tread on such water. Then they place the corpse on a bed, country-cot, plank, or straw. Some women, who are particular in these matters, are afraid even to venture near the place where the body has been washed. Having stripped the corpse and laid it on its back, with its head to the east and feet to the west, they cover it with a cloth—reaching, if it be a man, from the navel to the calves of the legs, if a woman, extending from the chest to the feet—and wash it with warm or with cold water. They raise the body gently and rub the abdomen four or five times, then pour plenty of water, and wash off all the dirt and filth with soap, &c., by means of flocks of cotton or cloth; after which, laying the body on the sides, they wash them; then the back, and the rest of the body; but gently, because, life having but just departed, the body is still warm and not insensible to pain. After this they wash and clean it well, so that no offensive smell may remain. They never throw water into the nostrils or mouth, but clean them with wicks of cloth or cotton. After that they perform *wuẓū'* for him, *i.e.* they wash his mouth, the two upper extremities up to the elbows, make *masaḥ* [MASAH] on his head, and throw water on his feet; these latter constituting the four parts of the *wuẓū* ceremony [ABLUTIONS]. They then put some camphor with water into a new large earthen pot, and with a new earthen pot they take out water and pour it three times, first from the head to the feet, then from the right shoulder to the feet, lastly from the left shoulder to the feet. Every time that a pot of water is poured the *Kalimatu 'sh-shahādah* is repeated, either by the person washing or another. Having bathed the body and wiped it dry with a new piece of cloth, they put on the shroud. The shroud consists of three pieces of cloth, if for a man, and five if for a woman.

Those for men comprise, 1st, a *lungī*, or *izār*, reaching from the navel down to the knees or ankle-joints; 2nd, a *qamīṣ*, or *kurta*, or *alfā*; its length is from the neck to the knees or ankles; 3rd, a *lifāfah*, or sheet, from above the head to below the feet. Women have two additional pieces of cloth: one a *sinah-band*, or breast-band, extending from the arm-pits to above the ankle-joints; the other a *damnī*, which encircles the head once and has its two ends dangling on each side. The manner of shrouding is as follows: having placed the shrouds on a new mat and fumigated them with the smoke of perfumes, the *lifāfah* is spread first on the mat, over it the *lungī* or *izār*, and above that the *qamīṣ*; and on the latter the *sīnah-band*, if it be a woman; the *damnī* is kept separate and tied on afterwards. The corpse must be carefully brought by itself from the place where it was bathed, and laid in the shrouds. *Surmah* is to be applied to the eyes with a tent made of paper rolled up, with a ring, or with a pice, and camphor to seven places, viz. on the forehead, including the nose, on the palms of the hands, on the knees and great toes, after which the different shrouds are to be properly put on one after another as they lay. The colour of the shroud is to be white; no other is admissible. It is of no consequence, however, if a coloured cloth is spread over the bier; which, after the funeral, or after the fortieth day, is given away to the *faqīr* who resides in the burying-ground, or to any other person, in charity. Previous to shrouding the body, they tear shreds from the cloths for the purpose of tying them on; and after shrouding the body, they tie one band above the head, a second below the feet, and a third about the chest, leaving about six or seven fingers' breadth of cloth above the head and below the feet, to admit of the ends being fastened. Should the relict of the deceased be present, they undo the cloth of the head and show her his face, and get her, in presence of two witnesses, to remit the dowry which he had settled upon her; but it is preferable that she remit it while he is still alive. Should the wife, owing to journeying, be at a distance from him, she is to remit it on receiving the intelligence of his demise.

Should his mother be present, she likewise says, "The milk with which I suckled thee I freely bestow on thee"; but this is merely a custom in India; it is neither enjoined in books of theology nor by the law of Islām. Then they place on the corpse a flower-sheet or merely wreaths of flowers. [GRAVE, BURIAL.]

DEATH, EVIDENCE OF. The Muḥammadan law admits of the evidence of death given in a court of justice being merely by report or hearsay. The reason of this is that death is an event of such a nature as to admit the privacy only of a few. But some have advanced that, in cases of death, the information of one man or woman is sufficient, "because death is not seen by many, since, as it occasions horror, the sight of it is avoided."

If a person say he was present at the burial of another, this amounts to the same as an actual sight of his death. (*Hidāyah*, vol. iv. p. 678.)

DEBT. In Muḥammadan law there are two words used for debt. *Dain* (دين), or money borrowed with some fixed term of payment, and *qarẓ* (قرض), or money lent without any definite understanding as to its repayment. Imprisonment for debt is allowed. (*Hidāyah*, vol. ii. p. 624.)

Upon the decease of a debtor, the law demands that after the payment of the funeral expenses, his just debts must be paid before payment of legacies.

To engage in a Jihād or religious war, is said by Muḥammad to remit every sin except that of being in debt. [JIHAD, DAIN, QARZ.]

DECORUM, or modesty of demeanour between the sexes, is strictly enjoined in Muslim law, and a special chapter is devoted to it in the *Durru 'l-Mukhtār* and other works on Muḥammadan law.

A man is not allowed to look at a woman except at her hands and face, nor is he allowed to touch her. But a physician is permitted to exercise the duties of his profession without restriction.

A judge in the exercise of his office may look in the face of a woman, and witnesses are under the same necessity.

DECREES OF GOD, The. Arabic *Qadar* or *Taqdīr*. [PREDESTINATION.]

DEEDS. Written deeds are, according to Muḥammadan law, of three kinds: I. *Mustabīn-i-marsūm*, or regular documents, such as are executed on paper, and have a regular title, superscription, &c., which are equivalent to oral declaration, whether the person be present or absent. II. *Mustabīn-i-ghair-i-marsūm*, or irregular documents, such as are *not* written on paper, but upon a wall or the leaf of a tree, or upon paper without any title or superscription or signature. III. *Ghair-i-mustabīn*, writings which are not documents in any sense, such as are delineated in the air or in the water by the motions of a dumb person.

DEFENDANT. Arabic *mudda'a 'alaihi* (مدعى عليه). *Lit.* "A claim upon him."

The author of the *Hidāyah* (vol. iii. p. 63) says a defendant is a person who, if he should wish to avoid the litigation, is compellable to sustain it. Some have defined a plaintiff, with respect to any article of property, to be a person who, from his being disseized of the said article, has no right to it but by the establishment of proof; and a defendant to be a person who has a plea of right to that article from his seizing or possession of it.

The Imām Muḥammad has said that a defendant is a person who denies. This is correct; but it requires a skill and knowledge of jurisprudence to distinguish the denier in a suit, as the reality and not the appearance is efficient, and it frequently happens that a person is in appearance the plaintiff, whilst in reality he is the defendant. Thus a trustee, when he says to the owner of the deposit, "I have restored to you your deposit," appears to be plaintiff, inasmuch as he pleads the return of the deposit; yet in reality he is the defendant, since he denies the obligation of responsibility, and hence his assertion, corroborated by an oath, must be credited.

DELIBERATION (Arabic *ta'annī* تانى) is enjoined by Muḥammad in the Traditions. He is related to have said, "Deliberation in your undertakings is pleasing to God, and hurry (*'ajalah*) is pleasing to the devil." "Deliberation is best in everything except in the things concerning eternity." (*Ḥadīs̤-i-Tirmiẕī.*)

DELUGE, The. Arabic *Ṭūfān* (طوفان). The story of the deluge is given by Muḥammad in his Qur'ān, to the Arabians as a "*secret history*, revealed to them (Sūrah xi. 51). The following are the allusions to it in the Qur'ān:—

Sūrah lxix. 11:—

"When the Flood rose high, we bare you in the Ark,

"That we might make that event a warning to you, and that the retaining ear might retain it."

Sūrah liv. 9:—

"Before them the people of Noah treated the truth as a lie, Our servant did they charge with falsehood, and said, 'Demoniac!' and he was rejected.

"Then cried he to his Lord, 'Verily, they prevail against me; come thou therefore to my succour.'

"So we opened the gates of Heaven with water which fell in torrents,

"And we caused the earth to break forth with springs, and their waters met by settled decree.

"And we bare him on a *vessel* made with planks and nails.

"Under our eyes it floated on: a recompense to him who had been rejected with unbelief.

"And we left it a sign: but, is there any one who receives the warning?

"And how great was my vengeance and my menace!"

Sūrah xi. 38:—

"And it was revealed unto Noah: 'Verily, none of thy people shall believe, save they who have believed already; therefore be not thou grieved at their doings.

"But build the Ark under our eye and after our revelation: and plead not with me for the evil-doers, for they are to be drowned.'

"So he built the Ark; and whenever the chiefs of his people passed by they laughed him to scorn: said he, 'Though ye laugh at us, we truly shall laugh at you, even as ye laugh at us; and in the end ye shall know

"On whom a punishment shall come that shall shame him; and on whom shall light a lasting punishment.'

"*Thus was it* until our sentence came to pass, and the earth's surface boiled up. We said, 'Carry into it one pair of every kind, and thy family, except him on whom sentence hath before been passed, and those who have believed.' But there believed not with him except a few.

"And he said, 'Embark ye therein. In the name of God be its course and its riding at anchor! Truly my Lord is right Gracious, Merciful.'

"And the Ark moved on with them amid waves like mountains: and Noah called to his son—for he was apart—'Embark with us, O my child! and be not with the unbelievers.'

"He said, 'I will betake me to a mountain that shall secure me from the water.' He said, 'None shall be secure this day from the decree of God, save him on whom He shall have mercy.' And a wave passed between them, and he was among the drowned.

"And it was said, 'O Earth! swallow up thy water'; and 'cease, O Heaven!' And the water abated, and the decree was fulfilled, and the Ark rested upon al-Jūdī; and it was said, 'Avaunt! ye tribe of the wicked!'

"And Noah called on his Lord and said, 'O Lord! verily my son is of my family: and thy promise is true, and thou art the most just of judges.'

"He said, 'O Noah! verily, he is not of thy family: in this thou actest not aright. Ask not of me that whereof thou knowest nought: I warn thee that thou become not of the ignorant.'

"He said, 'To thee verily, O my Lord, do I repair lest I ask that of thee wherein I have no knowledge: unless thou forgive me and be merciful to me I shall be one of the lost.'

"It was said to him, 'O Noah! debark with peace from Us, and with blessings on thee and on peoples from those who are with thee; but as for part, we will suffer them to enjoy themselves, but afterwards they shall suffer a grievous punishment from us to be inflicted.'

"This is a secret history which we reveal to thee. Thou didst not know them, thou nor thy people before this."

DEMONS. [DEVILS, GENII.]

DEPORTMENT.

Arabic *'ilmu 'l-mu'āsharah* (علم المعاشرة). Persian *nishast u barkhāst*. The Traditionists take some pains to explain the precise manner in which their Prophet walked, sat, slept, and rose, but their accounts are not always uniform and consistent. For example, whilst 'Abbād relates that he saw the Prophet sleeping on his back with one leg over the other, Jābir says the Prophet distinctly forbade it.

Modesty of deportment is enjoined in the Qur'ān, Sūrah xvii. 39: "Walk not proudly on the earth," which the commentators say means that the believer is not to toss his head or his arms as he walks. Sūrah xxv. 64: "The servants of the Merciful One are those who walk upon the earth lowly, and when the ignorant address them say, 'Peace!'"

Faqīr Jānī Muḥammad As'ad, the author of the celebrated ethical work, the *Akhlāq-i-Jalālī*, gives the following advice as regards general deportment:—

"He should not hurry as he walks, for that is a sign of levity; neither should he be unreasonably tardy, for that is a token of dulness. Let him neither stalk like the overbearing, nor agitate himself in the way of women and eunuchs; but constantly observe the middle course. Let him avoid going often backwards and forwards, for that betokens bewilderment; and holding his head downwards, for that indicates a mind overcome by sorrow and anxiety. In riding, no less, the same medium is to be observed. When he sits, let him not extend his feet, nor put one upon another. He must never kneel except in deference to his king, his preceptor, and his father, or other such person. Let him not rest his head on his knee or his hand, for that is a mark of dejection and indolence. Neither let him hold his neck awry, nor indulge in foolish tricks, such as playing with his fingers or other joints. Let him avoid twisting round or stretching himself. In spitting and blowing his nose, let him be careful that no one sees or hears him; that he blow it not towards the Qiblah, nor upon his hand, his skirt, or sleeve-lappet.

"When he enters an assembly, let him sit neither lower nor higher than his proper station. If he be himself the head of the party, he can sit as he likes, for his place must be the highest wherever it may be. If he has inadvertently taken a wrong place, let him exchange it for his own as soon as he discovers his mistake; should his own be occupied, he must return without disturbing others or annoying himself.

"In the presence of his male or female domestics, let him never bare anything but his hands and his face: the parts from his knee to his navel let him never expose at all; neither in public nor private, except on occasions of necessity for [ablution and the like. (*Vide* Gen. ix. 20; Lev. xvii. 6, xx. 11; Deut. xxii. 30.)

"He must not sleep in the presence of other persons, or lie on his back, particularly as the habit of snoring is thereby encouraged.

"Should sleep overpower him in the midst of a party, let him get up, if possible, or else dispel the drowsiness by relating some story, entering on some debate, and the like. But if he is with a set of persons who sleep themselves, let him either bear them company or leave them.

"The upshot of the whole is this: Let him so behave as not to incommode or disgust others; and should any of these observances appear troublesome, let him reflect, that to be formed to their contraries would be still more odious and still more unpleasant than any pains which their acquirement may cost him." *Akhlāq-i-Jalālī*, Thompson's Translation, p. 292.)

DEPOSIT

(Arabic *wadī'ah* وديعة, pl. *wadāi'*), in the language of the law, signifies a thing entrusted to the care of another. The proprietor of the thing is called *mūdi'*, or depositor; the person entrusted with it is *mūda'*, or trustee, and the property deposited is *wadī'ah*, which literally means the *leaving* of a thing with another.

According to the *Hidāyah*, the following are the rules of Islām regarding deposits.

A trustee is not responsible for deposit unless he transgress with respect to it. If therefore it be lost whilst it is in his care, and the loss has not been occasioned by any fault of his, the trustee has not to make good the loss, because the Prophet said, "*an honest trustee is not responsible.*"

A trustee may also keep the deposit himself or he may entrust it to another, provided the person is a member of his own family, but if he gives it to a stranger he renders himself responsible.

If the deposit is demanded by the depositor, and the trustee neglects to give it up, it is a transgression, and the trustee becomes responsible.

If the trustee mix the deposit (as of grain, oil, &c.) with his own property, in such a manner that the property cannot be separated, the depositor can claim to share equally in the whole property. But if the mixture be the result of accident, the proprietor becomes a proportionate sharer in the whole.

If the trustee deny the deposit upon demand, he is responsible in case of the loss of it. But not if the denial be made to a stranger, because (says Abū Yūsuf) the denial may be made for the sake of preserving it.

In the case of a deposit by two persons, the trustee cannot deliver to either his share, except it be in the presence of the other. And when two persons receive a divisible article in trust, each must keep one half, although these restrictions are not regarded when they are held to be inconvenient, or contrary to custom.

DEVIL, The. The devil is believed to be descended from Jānn, the progenitor of the evil genii. He is said to have been named 'Azāzīl, and to have possessed authority over the animal and spirit kingdom. But when God created Adam, the devil refused to prostrate before him, and he was therefore expelled from Eden. The sentence of death was then pronounced upon Satan; but upon seeking a respite, he obtained it until the Day of Judgment, when he will be destroyed. (*Vide* Qur'ān, Sūrah vii. 13.) According to the Qu'rān, the devil was created of fire, whilst Adam was created of clay. There are two words used in the Qur'ān to denote this great spirit of evil: (1) *Shaiṭān* (شيطان, שָׂטָן), an Arabic word derived from *shaṭn*, "opposition," *i.e.* "one who opposes; (2) *Iblīs* (ابليس, διάβολος), "devil," from *balas*, "a wicked or profligate person," *i.e.* "the wicked one." The former expression occurs in the Qur'ān fifty-two times, and the latter only nine, whilst in some verses (*e.g.* Sūrah ii. 32–34) the two words *Shaiṭān* and *Iblīs* occur for the same personality. According to the *Majma'u l-Biḥār*, *shaiṭān* denotes one who is far from the truth, and *iblīs* one who is without hope.

The following is the teaching of Muḥammad n the Traditions concerning the machinations of the devil (*Mishkāt*, book i. c. iii.):—

"'Verily, the devil enters into man as the blood into his body.

"'There is not one amongst you but has an angel and a devil appointed over him.' The Companions said, 'Do you include yourself in this?' He said, 'Yes, for me also; but God has given me victory over the devil, and he does not direct me except in what is good.'

"There is not one of the children of Adam, except Mary and her son (Jesus), but is touched by the devil at the time of its birth, hence the child makes a loud noise from the touch.

"Devil rests his throne upon the waters, and sends his armies to excite contention and strife amongst mankind; and those in his armies who are nearest to him in power and rank, are those who do the most mischief. One of them returns to the devil and says, 'I have done so and so,' and he says, 'You have done nothing'; after that another comes, and says. 'I did not quit him till I made a division between him and his wife'; then the devil appoints him a place near himself, and says, 'You are a good assistant.'

"The devil sticks close to the sons of Adam, and an angel also; the business of the devil is to do evil, and that of the angel to teach him the truth; and he who meets with truth and goodness in his mind, let him know it proceeds from God, and let him praise God; and he who finds the other, let him seek for an asylum from the devil in God.

"Then the Prophet read this verse of the Qur'ān: 'The devil threatens you with poverty if ye bestow in charity; and orders you to pursue avarice; but God promises you grace and abundance from charity.'

"'Usmān said, 'O Prophet of God! indeed the devil intrudes himself between me and my prayers, and my reading perplexes me.' Then the Prophet said, 'This is a demon called Khanzab, who casts doubt into prayer: when you are aware of it, take protection with God, and spit over your left arm three times.' 'Usmān said, 'Be it so'; and all doubt and perplexity was dispelled."

DEVIL, The Machinations of the. [WASWASAH.]

DIBĀGHAH (دباغة). "Tanning." According to the Traditions, the skins of animals are unclean until they are tanned. Muḥammad said, "Take nothing for any animals that shall have died until you tan their skins." And again, "Tanning purifies.' (*Mishkāt*, book iii. c. xi. 2.)

DIMASHQ (دمشق). [DAMASCUS.]

DĪN (دين). The Arabic word for "*religion.*" It is used especially for the religion of the Prophets and their inspired books, but it is also used for idolatrous religion. [RELIGION.]

DĪNĀR (دينار). Greek δηνάριον. A gold coin of one *misqāl* weight, or ninety-six barley grains, worth about ten shillings.

According to Mr. Hussey (*Ancient Weights*, p. 142), the average weight of the Roman denarii, at the end of the Commonwealth was sixty grains, whilst the English shilling contains eighty grains. Mr. Lane, in his Arabic dictionary, says, "its weight is seventy-one barley-corns and a half, nearly, reckoning the *dāniq* as eight grains of wheat and two-fifths; but if it be said that the *dāniq* is eight grains of wheat, then the *dīnār* is sixty-eight grains of wheat and four-sevenths. It is the same as the *misqāl*." The *dīnār* is only mentioned once in the Qur'ān, Sūrah ii. 66: "And some of them if thou entrust them with a *dīnār*, he will not give it back." It frequently occurs in books of law.

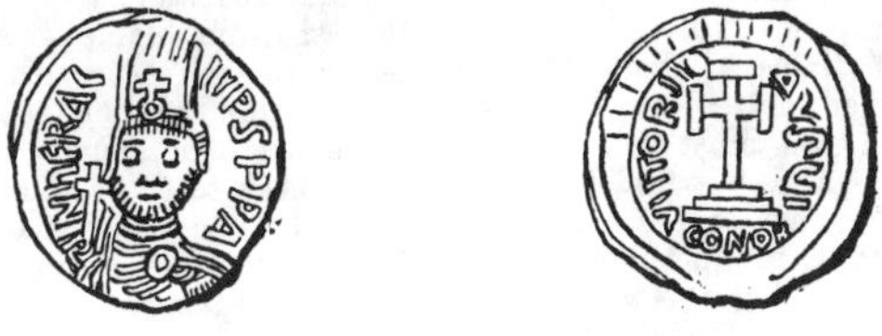

A GOLD DINAR OF HERACLIUS, A.D. 621. WEIGHT SIXTY GRAINS. ACTUAL SIZE.

A GOLD DINAR OF THE CITY OF GHAZNI, A.H. 616. ACTUAL SIZE

DIRHAM (درهم). Greek δραχμή. A silver coin, the shape of which resembled that of a date stone. During the caliphate of 'Umar, it was changed into a circular form; and in the time of Zubair, it was impressed with the words *Allāh*, "God," *barakah* "blessing." Ḥajjāj stamped upon it the chapter of the Qur'ān called Ikhlāṣ (cxii.), and others say he imprinted it with his own name. Various accounts are given of their weights; some saying that they were of ten, or nine, or six, or five *misqāls*; whilst others give the weights of twenty, twelve, and ten *qīrāṭs*, asserting at the same time that 'Umar had taken a *dirham* of each kind, and formed a coin of fourteen *qīrāṭs*, being the third part of the aggregate sum. (Blochmann's *Aīn-i-Akbari*, p. 36.)

The *dirham*, although it is frequently mentioned in books of law, only occurs once in the Qur'ān, Sūrah xii. 20, "And they sold him (Joseph) for a mean price, *dirhams* counted out, and they parted with him cheaply."

DIRRAH (درة). Vulg. *durrah*. A scourge made either of a flat piece of leather or of twisted thongs, and used by the public censor of morals and religion, called the *muḥtasib*. This scourge is inflicted either for the omission of the daily prayer, or for the committal of sins, which are punishable by the law with the infliction of stripes, such as fornication, scandal, and drunkenness. It is related that the Khalīfah 'Umar punished his son with the *dirrah* for drunkenness, and that he died from its effects. (*Tarikh-i-Khamīs*, vol. ii. p. 252.)

The word used in the Qur'ān and Ḥadīs for this scourge is *jaldah*, and in theological works, *sauṭ*; but *dirrah* is now the word generally used amongst modern Muslims.

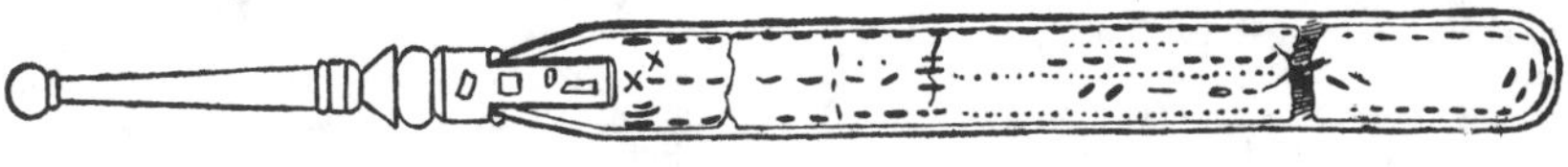

A DIRRAH USED BY A MUHTASIB IN THE PESHAWAR VALLEY.

DITCH, Battle of the. Arabic *Ghazwatu 'l-Khandaq* (غزوة الخندق). The defence of al-Madīnah against the Banū Quraiẓah, A.H. 5, when a trench was dug by the advice of Salmān, and the army of al-Madīnah was posted within it. After a month's siege, the enemy retired, and the almost bloodless victory is ascribed by Muhammad in the Qur'ān to the interposition of Providence. Sūrah xxxiii. 9: "Remember God's favours to you when hosts came to you and we sent against them a wind and hosts (of angels), that ye could not see, but God knew what ye were doing." (Muir's *Life of Mahomet*, vol. iii. p. 258.)

DIVINATION. *Kahānah*, or fortelling future events, is unlawful in Islām.

Mu'āwiyah ibn Ḥākim relates: "I said to the Prophet, 'O Messenger of God, we used to do some things in the time of ignorance of which we are not sure now. For example, we used to consult diviners about future events?' The Prophet said, 'Now that you have embraced Islām you must not consult them.' Then I said, 'And we used to take bad omens?' The Prophet said, 'If from a bad omen you are thrown into perplexity, let it not hinder you from doing the work you had intended to do.' Then I said, 'And we used to draw lines on the ground?' And the Prophet said, 'There was one of the Prophets who used to draw lines on the ground, therefore if you can draw a line like him it is good, otherwise it is vain.'"

'Āyishah says "the people asked the Prophet about diviners, whether they spoke true or not. And he said, 'You must not believe anything they say.' The people then said, 'But, O Prophet! they sometimes tell what is true?' The Prophet replied, 'Because one of the genii steals away the truth and carries it into the diviner's ear; and the diviners mix a hundred lies to one truth.'" [MAGIC.]

DIVORCE. Arabic *ṭalāq* (طلاق). In its primitive sense the word *ṭalāq* means dismission, but in law it signifies a release from the marriage tie.

The Muḥammadan law of divorce is founded upon express injunctions contained in the Qur'ān, as well as in the Traditions, and its rules occupy a very large section in all Muḥammadan works on jurisprudence.

I. *The teaching of the Qur'ān on the subject* is as follows:—

Sūrah ii. 226:—

"They who intend to abstain from their wives shall wait four months; but if they go back from their purpose, then verily God is Gracious, Merciful:

"And if they resolve on a divorce, then verily God is He who Heareth, Knoweth.

"The divorced shall wait the result, until they have had their courses thrice, nor ought they to conceal what God hath created in their wombs, if they believe in God and the last day; and it will be more just in their husbands to bring them back when in this state, if they desire what is right. And it is for the women to act as they (the husbands) act by them, in all fairness; but the men are a step above them. God is Mighty, Wise.

"Ye may give sentence of divorce to your wives twice: Keep them honourably, or put them away with kindness. But it is not allowed you to appropriate to yourselves aught of what ye have given to them, unless both fear that they cannot keep within the bounds set up by God. And if ye fear that they cannot observe the ordinances of God, no blame shall attach to either of you for what the wife shall herself give for her redemption. These are the bounds of God: therefore overstep them not; for whoever oversteppeth the bounds of God, they are evil doers.

"But if the husband give sentence of divorce to her *a third time*, it is not lawful for him to take her again, until she shall have married another husband; and if he also divorce her then shall no blame attach to them if they return to each other, thinking that they can keep within the bounds fixed by God. And these are the bounds of God; He maketh them clear to those who have knowledge.

"But when ye divorce women, and the time for sending them away is come, either retain them with generosity, or put them away with generosity: but retain them not by constraint so as to be unjust towards them. He who doth so, doth in fact injure himself. And make not the signs of God a jest; but remember God's favour towards you, and the Book and the Wisdom which He hath sent down to you for your warning, and fear God, and know that God's knowledge embraceth everything.

"And when ye divorce your wives, and they have waited the prescribed time, hinder them not from marrying the husbands when they have agreed among themselves in an honourable way. This warning is for him among you who believeth in God and in the last day. This is most pure for you, and most decent. God knoweth, but ye know not.

"Mothers, when divorced, shall give suck to their children two full years, if the father desire that the suckling be completed; and such maintenance and clothing as is fair for them, shall devolve on the father. No person shall be charged beyond his means. A mother shall not be pressed unfairly for her child, nor a father for his child: And the same with the father's heir. But if they choose to wean the child by consent and by bargain, it shall be no fault in them. And if ye choose to have a nurse for your children, it shall be no fault in you, in case ye pay what ye promised her according to that which is fair. Fear God, and know that God seeth what ye do.

* * * * *

"It shall be no crime in you if ye divorce your wives so long as ye have not consummated the marriage, nor settled any dowry on them. And provide what is needful for them —he who is in ample circumstances according to his means, and he who is straitened, according to his means—with fairness: This is binding on those who do what is right.

"But if ye divorce them before consummation, and have already settled a dowry on them, *ye shall give them* half of what ye have settled, unless they make a release, or he make a release in whose hand is the marriage tie. But if ye make a release, it will be nearer to piety."

Sūrah lxv. 1:—

"O Prophet! when ye divorce women,

divorce them at their special times. And reckon those times exactly, and fear God your Lord. Put them not forth from their houses, nor allow them to depart, unless they have committed a proven adultery. This is the precept of God; and whoso transgresseth the precept of God, assuredly imperilleth his own self. Thou knowest not whether, after this, God may not cause something new to occur *which may bring you together again.*

"And when they have reached their set time, then either keep them with kindness, or in kindness part from them. And take upright witnesses from among you, and bear witness as unto God. This is a caution for him who believeth in God and in the latter day. And whoso feareth God, to him will He grant a prosperous issue, and will provide for him whence he reckoned not upon it.

"And for him who putteth his trust in Him will God be all-sufficient. God truly will attain his purpose. For everything hath God assigned a period.

"As to such of your wives as have no hope of the recurrence of their times, if ye have doubts in regard to them, then reckon three months, and let the same be the term of those who have not yet had them. And as to those who are with child, their period shall be until they are delivered of their burden. God will make His command easy to Him who feareth Him.

* * * * *

"Lodge *the divorced* wherever ye lodge, according to your means; and distress them not by putting them to straits. And if they are pregnant, then be at charges for them till they are delivered of their burden; and if they suckle your children, then pay them their hire and consult among yourselves, and act generously: And if herein ye meet with obstacles, then let another female suckle for him."

II. *The teaching of Muḥammad on the general subject of Divorce is expressed in the Traditions as follows:—*

"The thing which is lawful but disliked by God is divorce."

"The woman who asks her husband to divorce her without a cause, the smell of Paradise is forbidden her."

"There are three things which, whether done in joke or in earnest, shall be considered serious and effectual, namely, marriage, divorce, and taking a wife back."

"Every divorce is lawful except a madman's."

"Cursed be the second husband who makes the wife (divorced) lawful for her first husband, and cursed be the first husband for whom she is made lawful."—(*Mishkāt*, xiii. c. xv.)

III. *Sunnī Muḥammadan Doctors are not agreed as to the Moral Status of Divorce.*

The Imām ash-Shāfiʿī, referring to the three kinds of divorce (which will be afterwards explained), says: "They are unexceptionable and legal because divorce is in itself a lawful act, whence it is that certain laws have been instituted respecting it; and this legality prevents any idea of danger being annexed to it. But, on the other hand, the Imām Abū Ḥanīfah and his disciples say that divorce is in itself a dangerous and disapproved procedure, as it dissolves marriage, an institution which involves many circumstances both of a spiritual as well as of a temporal nature. Nor is its propriety at all admitted, but on the ground of urgency of release from an unsuitable wife. And in reply to ash-Shāfiʿī, they say that the *legality* of divorce does not prevent its being considered dangerous, because it involves matters of both a spiritual and temporal character.

The author of the *Sharḥu 'l-Wiqāyah*, p. 108, says:—"Divorce is an abominable transaction in the sight of God, therefore such an act should only take place from necessity, and it is best to only make the one sentence of divorce (*i.e. ṭalāqu 'l-aḥsan*).

IV. *The Sunnī Law of Divorce*:—Divorce may be given either in the present time or may be referred to some future period. It may be pronounced by the husband either before or after the consummation of the marriage. It may be either given in writing or verbally.

The words by which divorce can be given are of two kinds:—*Ṣarīḥ*, or "express," as when the husband says, "Thou art divorced"; and *kināyah*, or "metaphorical," as when he says, "Thou art free; thou art cut off; veil yourself! Arise! seek for a mate," &c. &c.

Divorce is divided into *ṭalāqu 's-sunnah*, or that which is according to the Qur'ān and the Traditions, and *ṭalāqu 'l-badīʿ*, or a novel or heterodox divorce, which, although it is considered lawful, is not considered religious.

Ṭalāqu 's-sunnah is either the *aḥsan*, or "the most laudable," or *ḥasan*, the "laudable" method. *Ṭalāqu 'l-aḥsan*, or the "most laudable" method of divorce, is when the husband once expressly pronounces to his enjoyed but unpregnant wife the sentence, "Thou art divorced!" when she is in *ṭuhr* or a state of purity, during which he has had no carnal connection with her, and then leaves her to complete the prescribed *ʿiddah*, or "period of three months." Until the expiration of the *ʿiddah*, the divorce is revocable, but after the period is complete, it is irreversible, and if the husband wishes to take his wife back, they must go through the ceremony of marriage. But it must be observed that after the *ṭalāqu 'l-aḥsan*, the woman is not, as in the other kinds of divorce, compelled to marry another man, and be divorced before she can return to her former husband. All that is required is a re-marriage. The author of the *Hidāyah* says this mode of divorce is called *aḥsan*, or "most laudable," because it was usually adopted by the Companions of the Prophet, and also because it leaves it in the power of the husband to take his wife back, and she thus remains a lawful subject for re-marriage to him. Some European writers on Muḥammadanism have overlooked this fact in condemning the Muslim system of divorce.

The *ṭalāqu 'l-ḥasan*, or "laudable divorce,"

is when the husband repudiates an enjoyed wife by three sentences of divorce, either express or metaphorical, giving one sentence in each *ṭuhr*, or "period of purity." Imām Mālik condemns this kind of divorce, and says it is irregular. But Abū Ḥanīfah holds it to be *ḥasan*, or "good."

The *ṭalāqu 'l-badi'*, or "irregular form of divorce," is when the husband repudiates his wife by three sentences, either express or metaphorical, given them one at a time: "Thou art divorced! Thou art divorced! Thou art divorced!" Or, "Thou art free! Thou art free! Thou art free!" Even holding up three fingers, or dropping three stones, is held to be a sufficiently implied divorce to take legal effect. The Muslim who thus divorces his wife is held, in the *Hidāyah*, to be an offender against the law, but the divorce, however irregular, takes legal effect.

In both these kinds of divorce, *badi'* and *ḥasan*, the divorce is revocable (*rajī'*) after the first and second sentences, but it is irrevocable (*bā'in*) after the third sentence. After both *ḥasan* and *badi'* divorces, the divorced wife cannot, under any circumstances, return to her husband until she has been married, and enjoyed, and divorced by another husband. Muḥammadan doctors say the law has instituted this (somewhat disgraceful) arrangement in order to prevent divorces other than *ṭalāqu 'l-aḥsan.*

A husband may divorce his wife without any misbehaviour on her part, or without assigning any cause. The divorce of every husband is effective if he be of a sound understanding and of mature age; but that of a boy, or a lunatic, or one talking in his sleep, is not effective.

If a man pronounce a divorce whilst in a state of inebriety from drinking fermented liquor, such as wine, the divorce takes place. Repudiation by any husband who is sane and adult, is effective, whether he be free or a slave, willing, or acting under compulsion; and even though it were uttered in sport or jest, or by a mere slip of the tongue, instead of some other word. (*Fatāwa-i-'Ālamgīrī*, vol. i. p. 497.)

A sick man may divorce his wife, even though he be on his death-bed.

An agent or agents may be appointed by a husband to divorce his wife.

In addition to the will and caprice of the husband, there are also certain conditions which require a divorce.

The following are causes for divorce, but generally require to be ratified by a decree from the *Qāẓī* or "judge":—

(1.) *Jubb.* That is, when the husband has been by any cause deprived of his organ of generation. This condition is called *majbūb*. In this case the wife can obtain instant divorce if the defect occurred before marriage. Cases of evident madness and leprosy are treated in the same way. Divorce can be obtained at once.

(2.) *'Unnah*, or "impotence." (This includes *ratq*, "*vulva impervia cœunti*"; and *qarn*, "*vulva anteriore parte enascens.*") In cases of impotency in either husband or wife, a year of probation can be granted by the judge.

(3.) *Inequality of race or tribe.* A woman cannot be compelled to marry a man who belongs to an inferior tribe, and, in case of such a marriage, the elders of the superior tribe can demand a divorce; but if the divorce is not demanded, the marriage contract remains.

(4.) *Insufficient dower.* If the stipulated dowry is not given when demanded, divorce takes place.

(5.) *Refusal of Islām.* If one of the parties embrace Islām, the judge must offer it to the other three distinct times, and if he or she refuse to embrace the faith, divorce takes place.

(6.) *La'n*, or "imprecation." That is, when a husband charges his wife with adultery, the charge is investigated, but if there is no proof, and the man swears his wife is guilty, and the wife swears she is innocent, a divorce must be decreed.

(7.) *Īlā'*, or "vow." When a husband makes a vow not to have carnal intercourse with his wife for no less than four months, and keeps the vow inviolate, an irreversible divorce takes place.

(8.) *Reason of property.* If a husband become the proprietor of his wife (a slave), or the wife the proprietor of her husband (a slave), divorce takes place.

(9.) *An invalid marriage* of any kind, arising from incomplete *nikāḥ*, or "marriage ceremony," or from affinity, or from consanguinity.

(10.) *Difference of country* For example, if a husband flee from a *dāru 'l-ḥarb*, or "land of enmity," *i.e.* "a non-Muslim country," to a *dāru 'l-Islām*, or "country of Islām," and his wife refuse to perform *hijrah* (flight) and to accompany him, she is divorced.

(11.) *Apostasy from Islām.* The author of the *Raddu 'l-Mukhtār* (vol. ii. p. 643) says: "When a man or woman apostatises from Islām, then an immediate dissolution (*faskh*) of the marriage takes place, whether the apostasy be of the man or of the woman, without a decree from the *Qāẓī*." And again, (p. 645), "If both husband and wife apostatise at the same time, their marriage bond remains; and if at any future time the parties again return to Islām, no re-marriage is necessary to constitute them man and wife; but if one of the parties should apostatise before the other, a dissolution of the marriage takes place *ipso facto*."

Mr. J. B. S. Boyle, of Lahore, says: "As relevant to this subject, I give a quotation from Mr. Currie's excellent work on the *Indian Criminal Codes*, p. 445. The question is as to the effect of apostasy from Islām upon the marriage relation, and whether sexual intercourse with the apostate renders a person liable to be convicted for adultery under Section 497 of the Indian Penal Code. A. and B., Mahommedans, married under the Mahommedan law, are converted to Christianity. The wife, B., is first converted, but continues to live with her husband; subsequently the husband, A., is converted. Subsequent to the conversion of B., A. and B., still living together as husband and wife, both professing Christianity, B. has sexual intercourse with C. Will a conviction hold against C. under Section 497? Both Macnaghten and Baillie say the marriage becomes dissolved by apostasy of either party, and Grady, in his version of Hamilton's *Hidāyah*, p. 66, says: "If either husband or wife apostatize from the faith, a separation takes place, without divorce; according to Abū Haneefa and Abū Yoosuf. Imām Mahommed alleges if the apostasy is on the part of the husband.

"Apostasy annuls marriage in Haneefa's opinion, and in apostasy separation takes place without any decree of the magistrate. Cases which might decide this point have been lately tried both at Lucknow and Allahabad: at the former place *in re Afzul Hosein* v. *Hadee Begum*, and at the latter *Zuburdust Khan* v. *Wife*. But from certain remarks to be found in the judgment of the High Court, N. W. P., the Courts of Oudh and N. W. P., appear to differ on the most essential point. The point before the Oudh Court was (Hadee Begum's plea) that her marriage contract was dissolved by reason of her own apostasy, a sufficient answer to a suit brought by her Mahommedan husband for restitution of conjugal rights; *i.e.* Does the apostasy of a Mahommedan wife dissolve a marriage contract against the express wish of a Mahommedan husband in *dar-ool-harb* (land of war)? for India, it is contended, is not, under its present administration, *dar-ool-Islam* (land of safety). The Oudh Court held (admitting that apostasy by the husband dissolved the marriage and freed the wife) that apostasy by the wife did not free her if her husband sued for restitution of conjugal rights. They argued that apostasy by the wife, without the wish of the husband, could not be entertained; in fact, that as regards her husband's volition, the apostasy could not exist, and would not be recognised. That a suit for restitution of conjugal rights before the competent court of the time, seemed to them to be equivalent of the suit before the Cazee (Judge). The Oudh judges, in the absence of distinct precedent, say they fell back on the customs of the people amongst whom they lived. The Oudh Court evidently considered there was an essential difference between apostasy of a man and apostasy of a woman, of the husband or the wife; also between apostasy to a faith in a book and apostasy to the idol worship Mahommed and his followers renounce. Does such an essential difference exist? The point before the High Court N. W. P. was: Can a Mahommedan professing Christianity subsequent to his marriage with a Mussulmani, according to the Mahommedan law, obtain a decree for dissolution of that marriage under Act IV. of 1869, his wife having subsequently to him professed Christianity, and they under their new faith having lived together as man and wife? or whether the wife's contention is sound, that her marriage was cancelled by her husband's apostasy? They held the apostasy of the husband dissolved the marriage tie. This the Oudh Court admits, but the point before the Oudh Court was not before the High Court, N. W. P.; nevertheless from comments made by the High Court, N. W. P., on the Oudh decision, they evidently did not agree with the finding come to by the latter Court, on the point before it.

"Now, Mr. Currie asks in the above extract, does such an essential difference exist between apostasy to a book—that is, to a *kitabee* faith—and apostasy to idol worship? Answering this question necessitates a few remarks upon the judgments above mentioned. According to Mahommedan law, a man may lawfully marry a *kitabeeah*, but marriage with a Pagan or polytheist is unlawful. But the principle in Mahommedan law is, that when one of the parties turns to a state of religion that would render the marriage contract illegal if it were still to be entered into, what was legal before is made void. A Mahommedan woman, becoming a *kitabeeah*, does not render the marriage void, for there is nothing to render the marriage contract illegal if it were still to be entered into; but if the Mahommedan woman becomes an idolatress, the marriage is void, for the woman has turned to a state of religion that would render the marriage contract illegal if it were still to be entered into; a Mahommedan woman, becoming a Christian, consequently, would not be separated from her husband, because she belongs to the religion of the book, that is, a *kitabee* faith. If a *kitabeeah* becomes an idolatress, the marriage is dissolved, but if she change from one religion to another, and still remain a *kitabeeah*, the marriage is not vitiated. So far the Oudh Court is correct in its decision, that the Mahommedan wife's conversion to Christianity did not render the marriage null and void, but that a suit for restitution of conjugal rights would lie; and taking the case of C. having sexual intercourse with B. the wife of A. converted to Christianity, a conviction under Section 497, Indian Penal Code, would hold good. But with all deference, I do not think that the Oudh Court is correct when it states that 'apostasy by the wife without the wish of the husband could not be entertained; in fact, that as regards her husband's volition, the apostasy could not exist, and would not be recognised.'

"So far as regards a woman's apostatising to a *kitabee* faith, this holds good; but if a woman turns to Paganism, *ipso facto* the marriage is void, and does not depend upon the volition of the husband (having regard to the principle we have adverted to above), so that the husband under such circumstances could not maintain a suit for conjugal rights, nor would a conviction hold good against C., under Section 497, Indian Penal Code for sexual intercourse with B., the wife of A., who has apostatised to Paganism. The decisions of the two Courts, however, seem correct, on the principles of Mahommedan law, as to the effect of a husband apostatising from Islām.

By Mahommedan law, a marriage by a female Moslem with a man not of the Mahommedan faith is unlawful: applying the principle quoted before, the man having turned to a state of religion that would render the contract illegal if it were still to be entered into, the marriage is void. The apostasy of the husband dissolves the marriage tie; consequently there does exist an essential difference between apostasy of a man and of a woman, of the apostasy of the husband or the wife; also between apostasy to a faith in a book, that is, a revealed religion having a book of faith, and apostasy to the idol worship Mahommed and his followers renounce. The law allows a person the right to cease to be a Mahommedan in the fullest sense of the word, and to become a Christian, and to claim for himself and his descendants all the rights and obligations of a British subject." (*Hogg* v. *Greenway*, &c., 2, *Hyde's Reports*, 3. *Manual of Laws relating to Muḥammadans and their Relations of Life.*)

V. In addition to the forms of divorce already explained, there are three others of a peculiar nature, called *k͟hula'*, *mubāra'ah*, and *ẓihār*.

The form of divorce known as *k͟hula'*, is when, a husband and wife disagreeing, or for any other cause, the wife, on payment of a compensation or ransom to her husband, is permitted by the law to obtain from him a release from the marriage tie. The *k͟hula'* is generally effected by the husband giving back the dower or part thereof. When the aversion is on the part of the husband, it is generally held that he should grant his wife's request without compensation; but this is purely a matter of conscience, and not of law.

Mubāra'ah is a divorce which is effected by a mutual release.

Ẓihār, from *ẓahr*, "back," is a kind of divorce which is effected by a husband likening his wife to any part or member of the body of any of his kinswomen within the prohibited degree. As for example, if he were to say to his wife, "Thou art to me like the back of my mother." The motive of the husband in saying so must be examined, and if it appear that he meant divorce, his wife is not lawful to him until he have made expiation by freeing a slave, or by fasting two months, or by feeding sixty poor men. (See Qur'ān, Sūrah lviii. 4.)

(For the Sunnī Law of Divorce, see the *Hidāyah* and its Commentary, the *Kifāyah*; *Durru 'l-Muk͟htār* and its Commentary, the *Raddu l'-Muk͟htār*; the *Fatāwā-i-'Alamgīrī*; Hamilton's English Edition, *Hidāyah*; *Tagore Law Lectures, 1873.*)

VI. *The Shī'ah law of Divorce* differs only in a few particulars from that of the Sunnīs. According to Shī'ah law, a man must be an adult of understanding, of free choice and will, and of design and intention, when he divorces his wife. A marked contrast to the licence and liberty allowed by the Sunnī law. Nor can the Shīah divorce be effected in any language of a metaphorical kind. It must be express and be pronounced in Arabic (if the husband understand that language), and it must be spoken and not written. A divorce amongst the Shī'ahs does not take effect if given implicatively or ambiguously, whether intended or not. It is also absolutely necessary that the sentence should be pronounced by the husband in the presence of two just persons as witnesses, who shall hear and testify to the wording of the divorce.

(For the Shī'ah law of divorce, see *Shir'atu 'l-Islām*; *Taḥrīru 'l-Aḥkām*; *Mafātīḥ*; Mr. Neil Baillie's *Digest of Muḥammadan Law*; *Imamiah Code*; *Tagore Law Lectures, 1874.*)

VII *Compared with the Mosaic Law.* When compared with the Mosaic law, it will be seen that by the latter, divorce was only sanctioned when there was "*some uncleanness*" in the wife, and that whilst in Islām a husband can take back his divorced wife, in the law of God it was not permitted. See Deut. xxiv. 1–4.

"When a man hath taken a wife, and married her, and it come to pass that she find no favour in his eyes, because he hath found some uncleanness in her; then let him write her a bill of divorcement, and give *it* in her hand, and send her out of his house.

"And when she is departed out of his house, she may go and be another man's *wife.*

"And *if* the latter husband hate her, and write her a bill of divorcement, and giveth *it* in her hand, and sendeth her out of his house; or if the latter husband die, which took her *to be* his wife;

"Her former husband, which sent her away, may not take her again to be his wife, after that she is defiled; for that *is* abomination before the Lord: and thou shalt not cause the land to sin, which the Lord thy God giveth thee *for* an inheritance."

The ground of divorce in the Mosaic law was "some uncleanness in her." There were two interpretations of this by the Jewish doctors of the period of the New Testament. The School of Shammai seemed to limit it to a moral delinquency in the woman, whilst that of Hillel extended it to trifling causes. Our Lord appears to have regarded all the lesser causes than fornication as standing on too weak a ground.

Matt. v. 32: "But I say unto you, that whosoever shall put away his wife, saving for the cause of fornication, causeth her to commit adultery: and whosoever shall marry her that is divorced committeth adultery."

It will be seen that Muḥammad adopted the teaching of the School of Hillel, omitting the bill of divorcement, which was enjoined in Deut. xxiv. 3, thereby placing the woman entirely at the will and caprice of her husband.

Burkhardt tells us of an Arab, forty-five years old, who had had fifty wives, so that he must have divorced two wives and married two fresh ones on the average every year. We have cases of Muḥammad's own "Companions" not much better. This is the natural and legitimate effect of the law.

Sir William Muir (*Life of Mahomet*, vol iii. p. 305) says: "The idea of conjugal unity is utterly unknown to Mahometans, excepting when the Christian example is by chance followed; and even there, the continuance of the bond is purely dependent on the will of the husband. . . . I believe the *morale* of Hindu society, where polygamy is less encouraged, to be sounder, in a very marked degree, than that of Mahometan society."

DĪWĀN (ديوان). (1) In Muḥammadan law, the word signifies an account or record book, and also the bags in which the Qāẓī's records are kept. (2) It is also a court of justice, a royal court. (3) Also a minister of state; the chief officer in a Muḥammadan state; a finance minister. (4) In British courts a law-suit is called *diwānī*, when it refers to a civil suit, in contradistinction to *faujdārī*, or "criminal suit." (5) A collection of odes is called a *diwān*, *e.g.* *Diwān-i-Ḥāfiẓ*, "the Poems of Ḥāfiẓ."

DIYAH (دية). A pecuniary compensation for any offence upon the person. [FINES.]

DOGS (Arabic *kalb*, pl. *kilāb*; Heb. כֶּלֶב) are unclean animals; for according to a tradition by Abū Hurairah, Muḥammad said that when a dog drinks in a vessel, it must be washed seven times, and that the first cleansing should be with earth. (*Mishkāt*, book iii. c. ii. pt. 1.)

"Most people believe that when a dog howls near a house it forebodes death, for, it is said, a dog can distinguish the awful form of Azrā'īl, the Angel of Death." (Burton's *Arabia*, vol. i. p. 290.)

Ibn 'Umr says that dogs used to come into the Masjid at Makkah in the time of the Prophet, but the Companions never purified the mosque when the dog was dry.

The Imām Abū Yūsuf holds that the sale of a dog that bites is unlawful, whilst the Imām ash-Shāfi'ī has said that the sale of a dog is absolutely illegal, because the Prophet said the wages of whoredom and the price of a dog are forbidden. Abū Ḥanifah holds that dogs which are trained to hunt or watch may be lawfully sold. (Hamilton's *Hidāyah*, vol. ii. p. 543.)

It is lawful to hunt with a trained dog, and the sign of a dog being trained is that he catches game three times without killing it. The dog must be let slip with the ejaculation: *Bismillāhi 'llāhi Akbar*! "In the name of God, the great God!" when all game seized by him becomes lawful food. This custom is founded upon a verse in the Qur'ān, Sūrah v. 6: "Lawful for you are all good things and what ye have taught beasts of prey to catch, training them like dogs; ye teach them as God taught you. And mention the name of God over it."

Rules for hunting with dogs will be found in Hamilton's *Hidāyah*, vol. iv. p. 170.

DOG STAR. Sirius, or the dog star, was an object of worship amongst the ancient Arabs, and is mentioned in the Qur'ān, under the name of *ash-Shi'ra*, Sūrah liii. 50: "He (God) is the Lord of the Dog Star."

DOWER. Arabic, *mahr* (مهر), Heb. (מֹהַר). Dower is considered by some lawyers to be an effect of the marriage contract, imposed on the husband by the law as a mark of respect for the subject of the contract—the wife; while others consider that it is in exchange for the usufruct of the wife, and its payment is necessary, as upon the provision of a support to the wife depends the permanency of the matrimonial connection. Thus, it is indispensable *a fortiori*, so much so, that if it were not mentioned in the marriage contract, it would be still incumbent on the husband, as the law will presume it by virtue of the contract itself, and award it upon demand being made by the wife. In such case, the amount of dower will be to the extent of the dowers of the women of her rank and of the ladies of her father's family. Special beauty or accomplishments may, however, be pleaded for recovering a larger award than the customary dower, where the amount of dower is not mentioned in the contract. There is no limit to the amount of dower; it may be to a very large amount, considering the position and circumstance of the bridegroom, but its minimum is never less than ten dirhams; so where it is fixed at a lesser amount, the law will augment it up to ten dirhams. The dower need not invariably be in currency, or even in metal; everything, except carrion, blood, wine, and hog. Also the bridegroom's own labour, if he is a free man, being held by the law to be a good dower.

Dower is generally divided into two parts, termed *mu'ajjal*, "prompt," and *mu'ajjal*, "deferred." The *mu'ajjal* portion is exigible on entering into the contract, while the *mu'ajjal* part of the dower is payable upon dissolution of the contract. Although the first part is payable, and is sometimes paid, at the time the contract is entered into, yet it has been the general practice (at least in India) to leave it unpaid, and so like an on-demand obligation it remains due at all times—the wife's right to the same not being extinguished by lapse of time. The wife's (or her guardian's) object in leaving the exigible part of the dower unrealised, seems to be that there may always exist a valid guarantee for the good treatment of her by her husband. The women of the respectable classes reserve their right and power to demand their exigible dowers till such time as occasion should require the exercise thereof. The custom of fixing heavy dowers, generally beyond the husband's means, especially in India, seems to be based upon the intention of checking the husband from ill-treating his wife, and, above all, from his marrying another woman, as also from wrongfully or causelessly divorcing the former. For in the case of divorce the woman can demand the full payment of the dower. In the event of the death of the husband, the payment of the dower has the first claim on the estate after funeral expenses; the law regarding it as a just debt. (*Tagore Law Lectures, 1873*, p. 341; *Hidāyah*, vol. i. p. 122.)

DREAMS. Arabic *ḥulm* (حلم); *manām* (منام); *rūyā'* (رؤيا). The term used for a bad dream is *ḥulm*, and for an ordinary dream *manām*, *rūyā'* being used to express a heavenly vision. [RUYA.]

According to the traditions, the Prophet is related to have said, "A good dream is of God's favour and a bad dream is of the devil; therefore, when any of you dreams a dream which is such as he is pleased with, then he must not tell it to any but a beloved friend; and when he dreams a bad dream, then let him seek protection from God both from its evil and from the wickedness of Satan; and let him spit three times over his left shoulder, and not mention the dream to anyone; then, verily, no evil shall come nigh him." "The truest dream is the one which you have about day-break." "Good dreams are one of the parts of prophecy." (*Mishkāt*, xxi. c. iv.)

DRESS. Arabic *libās* (لباس). Decent apparel at the time of public worship is enjoined in the Qur'ān, Sūrah vii. 29: "O children of Adam! wear your goodly apparel when ye repair to any mosque." Excess in apparel and extravagance in dress are reproved, Sūrah vii. 25: "We (God) have sent down raiment to hide your nakedness, and splendid garments; but the raiment of piety, this is the best."

According to the *Hidāyah* (vol. iv. p. 92), a dress of silk is not lawful for men, but women are permitted to wear it. Men are prohibited from wearing gold ornaments, and also ornaments of silver, otherwise than a silver signet ring. The custom of keeping handkerchiefs in the hand, except for necessary use, is also forbidden.

The following are some of the sayings of the Prophet with regard to dress, as recorded in the Traditions. *Mishkāt*, xx. c. i.: "God will not look at him on the Day of Resurrection who shall wear long garments from pride." "Whoever wears a silken garment in this world shall not wear it in the next." "God will not have compassion upon him who wears long trousers (*i.e.* below the ankle) from pride." "It is lawful for the women of my people to wear silks and gold ornaments, but it is unlawful for the men." "Wear white clothes, because they are the cleanest, and the most agreeable; and bury your dead in white clothes."

According to the Traditions, the dress of Muḥammad was exceedingly simple. It is said he used to wear only two garments, the *izār*, or "under garment" which hung down three or four inches below his knees, and a mantle thrown over his shoulders. These two robes, with the turban, and white cotton drawers, completed the Prophet's wardrobe. His dress was generally of white, but he also wore green, red, and yellow, and sometimes a black woollen dress. It is said by some traditionists that in the taking of Makkah he wore a black turban. The end of his turban used to hang between his shoulders. And he used to wrap it many times round his head. It is said, "the edge of it appeared below like the soiled clothes of an oil dealer."

He was especially fond of white-striped yamanī cloth. He once prayed in a silken dress, but he cast it aside afterwards, saying, "it doth not become the faithful to wear silk." He once prayed in a spotted mantle, but the spots diverted his attention, and the garment was never again worn.

His sleeves, unlike those of the Eastern *choga* or *khaftān*, ended at the wrist, and he never wore long robes reaching to his ankles.

At first, he wore a gold ring with the stone inwards on his right hand, but it distracted his attention when preaching, and he changed it for a silver one. His shoes, which were often old and cobbled, were of the Ḥaẓramaut pattern, with two thongs. And he was in the habit of praying with his shoes on. [SHOES.]

The example of Muḥammad has doubtless influencd the customs of his followers in the matter of dress, the fashion of which has remained almost the same in eastern Muḥammadan countries centuries past; for although there are varieties of dress in Eastern as well as in European countries, still there are one or two characteristics of dress which are common to all oriental nations which have embraced Islām, namely, the turban folded round the head, the white cotton drawers, or full trousers, tied round the waist by a running string; the *qamis*, or "shirt," the *khaftān*, or "coat," and the *lungī*, or "scarf." The *qamiṣ* is the same as the *ketoneth* of the Hebrews, and the χίτων of the Greeks, a kind of long shirt with short sleeves, the ends of which extend over the trousers or drawers, reaching below the knees. The *khaftān* answers to the Hebrew מְעִיל *meil* (1 Sam. xviii 4), a tunic worn as an outer garment. The Jewish בֶּגֶד *beged*, or שִׂמְלָה *simlah*, must have been similar, to the quadrangular piece of cloth still worn as a scarf in Central Asia, and called a *lungī*, and similar to the *'abā'* of the Egyptians. It is worn in various ways, either wrapped round the body, or worn over the shoulders, and sometimes folded as a covering for the head.

The dress of Muḥammadans in Egypt is very minutely described by Mr. Lane in his *Modern Egyptians*, vol. i. p. 36.

The dress of the men of the middle and higher classes of Egypt consists of the following articles. First a pair of full drawers of linen or cotton tied round the body by a running string or band, the ends of which are embroidered with coloured silks, though concealed by the outer dress. The drawers descend a little below the knees or to the ankles; but many of the Arabs will not wear long drawers, because prohibited by the Prophet. Next is worn a *qamīs* or "shirt," with very full sleeves, reaching to the wrist; it is made of linen of a loose open texture, or of cotton stuff, or of muslin, or silk, or of a mixture of silk and cotton in strips, but all white. Over this, in winter, or in cool weather, most persons wear a *sudeyree*, which is a short vest of cloth, or of striped coloured silk, or cotton, without sleeves. Over the shirt and the *sudeyree*, or the former alone, is worn a long vest of striped silk or cotton (called *kaftān*) descending to the ankles, with long sleeves extending a few inches beyond the fingers' ends, but divided from a point a little above the wrist, or about the middle of the fore-arm, so that the hand is generally exposed, though it may be concealed by the sleeve when necessary, for it is customary to cover the hands in the presence of a person of high rank. Round this vest is wound the girdle, which is a coloured shawl, or a long piece of white-figured muslin.

The ordinary outer robe is a long cloth coat, of any colour, called by the Turks *jubbah*, but by the Egyptians *gibbeh*, the sleeves of which reach not quite to the wrist. Some persons also wear a *beneesh*, which is a robe of cloth with long sleeves, like those of the *kaftān*, but more ample; it is properly a robe of ceremony, and should be worn over the other cloth coat, but many persons wear it instead of the *gibbeh*.

Another robe, called *farageeyeh*, nearly resembles the *beneesh*; it has very long sleeves, but these are not slit, and it is chiefly worn by men of the learned professions. In cold or cool weather, a kind of black woollen cloak, called *abāyeh*, is commonly worn. Sometimes this is drawn over the head.

In winter, also, many persons wrap a muslin or other shawl (such as they use for a turban) about the head and shoulders. The head-dress consists, first, of a small close-fitting cotton cap, which is often changed; next a *tarboosh*, which is a red cloth cap, also fitting close to the head with a tassel of dark-blue silk at the crown; lastly, a long piece of white muslin, generally figured, or a kashmere shawl, which is wound round the *tarboosh*. Thus is formed the turban. The

AN EGYPTIAN MAULAWI (LANE).

kashmere shawl is seldom worn except in cool weather. Some persons wear two or three tarbooshes one over another. A shereef (or descendant of the Prophet) wears a green turban, or is privileged to do so, but no other person; and it is not common far any but a shereef to wear a bright green dress. Stockings are not in use, but some few persons in cold weather wear woollen or cotton socks. The shoes are of thick red morocco, pointed, and turning up at the toes. Some persons also wear inner shoes of soft yellow morocco, and with soles of the same; the outer shoes are taken off on stepping upon a carpet or mat, but not the inner; for this reason the former are often worn turned down at the heel.

The costume of the men of the lower orders is very simple. These, if not of the very poorest class, wear a pair of drawers, and a long and full shirt or gown of blue linen or cotton, or of brown woollen stuff, open from the neck nearly to the waist, and having wide sleeves. Over this some wear a white or red woollen girdle; for which servants often substitute a broad red belt of woollen stuff or of leather, generally containing a receptacle for money. Their turban is generally composed of a white, red, or yellow

AN EGYPTIAN PEASANT (LANE).

woollen shawl, or of a piece of coarse cotton or muslin wound round a tarboosh, under which is a white or brown felt cap; but many are so poor, as to have no other cap than the latter, no turban, nor even drawers, nor shoes, but only the blue or brown shirt, or merely a few rags, while many, on the other hand, wear a *sudeyree* under the blue shirt, and some, particularly servants in the houses of great men, wear a white shirt, a sudeyree, and a kaftān, or gibbeh, or both, and the blue shirt over all. The full sleeves of this shirt are sometimes drawn up by means of a cord, which passes round each shoulder and crosses behind, where it is tied in a knot. This custom is adopted by servants (particularly grooms), who have cords of crimson or dark blue silk for this purpose.

In cold weather, many persons of the lower classes wear an abayeh, like that before described, but coarser and sometimes (instead of being black) having broad stripes, brown and white, or blue and white, but the latter rarely. Another kind of cloak, more full than the abayeh, of black or deep blue woollen stuff, is also very commonly worn, it is called diffeeyeh. The shoes are of red or yellow morocco, or of sheep-skin. Those of the groom are of dark red morocco. Those of the door-keeper and the water-carrier of a private house, generally yellow.

The Muslims are distinguished by the colours of their turbans from the Copts and the Jews, who (as well as other subjects of the Turkish Sultān who are not Muslims) wear black, blue, gray, or light-brown turbans, and generally dull-coloured dresses.

The distinction of sects, families, dynasties, &c., among the Muslim Arabs by the colour of the turban and other articles of dress, is of very early origin. There are not many different forms of turbans now worn in Egypt; that worn by most of the servants is peculiarly formal, consisting of several spiral twists one above another like the threads of a screw. The kind common among the middle and higher classes of the tradesmen and other citizens of the metropolis and large towns is also very formal, but less so than that just before alluded to.

The Turkish turban worn in Egypt is of a more elegant fashion. The Syrian is distinguished by its width. The Ulama and men of religion and letters in general used to wear, as some do still, one particularly wide and formal called a mukleh. The turban is much respected. In the houses of the more wealthy classes, there is usually a chair on which it is placed at night. This is often sent with the furniture of a bride; as it is common for a lady to have one upon which to place her head-dress. It is never used for any other purpose.

The dress of the women of the middle and higher orders is handsome and elegant. Their shirt is very full, like that of the men, but shorter, not reaching to the knees; it is also, generally, of the same kind of material as the men's shirt, or of coloured crape, sometimes black. A pair of very wide trousers (called *shintiyān*) of a coloured striped stuff, of silk and cotton, or of printed or plain white muslin, is tied round the hips under the shirt, with a dikkeh; its lower extremities are drawn up and tied just below the knee with running strings, but it is sufficiently long to hang down to the feet, or almost to the ground, when attached in this manner. Over the shirt and shintiyān is worn a long vest (called *yelek*), of the same material as the latter; it nearly resembles the kaftān of the men, but is more tight to the body and arms; the sleeves also are longer, and it is made to button down the front from the bosom to a little below the girdle, instead of lapping over; it is open, likewise on each side, from the height of the hip downwards.

In general, the yelek is cut in such a manner as to leave half of the bosom uncovered, except by the shirt, but many ladies have it made more ample at that part, and according to the most approved fashion it should be of sufficient length to reach to the ground, or should exceed that length by two or three inches or more. A short vest (called *anteree*) reaching only a little below the waist, and exactly resembling a yelek of which the lower part has been cut off, is sometimes worn instead of the latter. A square shawl, or an embroidered kerchief, doubled diagonally, is put loosely round the waist as a girdle, the two corners that are folded together hanging down behind; or sometimes the lady's girdle is folded after the ordinary Turkish fashion, like that of the men, but more loosely.

Over the yelek is worn a gibbeh of cloth or velvet or silk, usually embroidered with gold or with coloured silk; it differs in form from the gibbeh of the men, chiefly in being not so wide, particularly in the fore part, and is of the same length as the yelek. Instead of this, a jacket (called *saltah*), generally of cloth or velvet, and embroidered in the same manner as the gibbeh, is often worn.

The head-dress consists of a takeeyeh and tarboosh, with a square kerchief (called *faroodeeyeh*) of printed or painted muslin or one of crape, wound tightly round, composing what is called a rabtah. Two or more such kerchiefs were commonly used a short time since, and still are sometimes to form the ladies'

AN EGYPTIAN LADY (LANE).

turban, but always wound in a high flat shape, very different from that of the turban of the men. A kind of crown, called *kurs*, and other ornaments, are attached to the ladies' head-dress. A long piece of white muslin, embroidered at each end with coloured silks and gold, or of coloured crape ornamented with gold thread, &c., and spangles, rests upon the head, and hangs down behind, nearly or quite to the ground; this is called *tarhah*, it is the head-veil; the face-veil I shall presently describe. The hair, except over the forehead and temples, is divided into numerous braids or plaits, generally from eleven to twenty-five in number, but always of an uneven number; these hang down the back. To each braid of hair are usually added three black silk cords with little ornaments of gold, &c., attached to them. Over the forehead the hair is cut rather short, but two full locks hang down on each side of the face; these are often curled in ringlets and sometimes plaited.

Few of the ladies of Egypt wear stockings or socks, but many of them wear mezz (or inner shoes) of yellow or red morocco, sometimes embroidered with gold. Over these, whenever they step off the matted or carpeted part of the floor, they put on baboog (or slippers) of yellow morocco, with high-pointed toes, or use high wooden clogs or pattens, generally from four to nine inches in height, and usually ornamented with mother-of-pearl or silver, &c.

The riding or walking attire is called *tezyeereh.* Whenever a lady leaves the house, she wears, in addition to what has been above

THE INDIAN BURKA. (*A. F. Hole.*)

described, first, a large, loose gown (called *tob* or *sebleh*), the sleeves of which are nearly equal in width to the whole length of the gown; it is of silk, generally of a pink or rose or violet colour. Next is put on the burka' or face-veil, which is a long strip of white muslin, concealing the whole of the face except the eyes, and reaching nearly to the feet. It is suspended at the top by a narrow band, which passes up the forehead, and which is sewed, as are also the two upper corners of the veil, to a band that is tied round the head. The lady then covers herself with a habarah, which, for a married lady, is composed of two breadths of glossy, black silk, each ell-wide, and three yards long; these are sewed together, at or near the selvages (according to the height of the person) the seam running horizontally, with respect to the manner in which it is worn; a piece of narrow black ribbon is sewed inside the upper part, about six inches from the edge, to tie round

THE EGYPTIAN HABARAH.

the head. But some of them imitate the Turkish ladies of Egypt in holding the front part so as to conceal all but that portion of the veil that is above the hands. The unmarried ladies wear a habarah of white silk, or a shawl. Some females of the middle classes, who cannot afford to purchase a habarah, wear instead of it an *eezār* (*izār*), which is a piece of white calico, of the same form and size as the former, and is worn in the same manner. On the feet are worn short boots or socks (called *khuff*), of yellow morocco, and over these the baboog. The dress of a large proportion of those women of the lower orders who are not of the poorest class, consists of a pair of trousers or drawers (similar in form to the shintiyān of the ladies, but generally of plain white cotton or linen), a blue linen or cotton shirt (not quite so full as that of the men), reaching to the feet, a burka' of a kind of coarse black crape, and a dark blue tarhah of muslin or linen. Some wear, over the long shirt, or instead of the latter, a linen tob, of the same form as that of the ladies; and within the long shirt, some wear a short white shirt; and some, a sudeyree also, or an anteree. The sleeves of the tob are often turned up over the head; either to prevent their being incommodious, or to supply the place of a tarhah. In addition to these articles of dress, many women who are not of the very poor classes wear, as a covering, a kind of plaid, similar in form to the habarah, composed of two pieces of cotton, woven in small chequers of blue and white, or cross stripes, with a mixture of red at each end. It is called *milayeh*; in general it is

AN INDIAN ZANANA LADY. (*A. F. Hole.*)

worn in the same manner as the habarah, but sometimes like the tarhah. The upper part of the black burka' is often ornamented with false pearls, small gold coins, and other little flat ornaments of the same metal (called bark); sometimes with a coral bead, and a gold coin beneath; also with some coins of base silver and more commonly with a pair of chain tassels of brass or silver (called *oyoon*) attached to the corners. A square black silk kerchief (called *asbeh*), with a border of red and yellow, is bound round the head, doubled diagonally, and tied with a single knot behind; or, instead of this, the tarboosh and faroodeeyeh are worn, though by very few women o the lower classes.

The best kind of shoes worn by the females of the lower orders are of red morocco, turned up, but generally round, at the toes. The burka' and shoes are most common in Cairo, and are also worn by many of the women throughout lower Egypt; but in Upper Egypt, the burka' is very seldom seen, and shoes are scarcely less uncommon. To supply the place of the former, when necessary, a portion of the tarhah is drawn before the face, so as to conceal nearly all the countenance except one eye.

Many of the women of the lower orders, even in the metropolis, never conceal their faces.

Throughout the greater part of Egypt, the most common dress of the women, merely consists of the blue shirt or tob and tarhah. In the southern parts of Upper Egypt chiefly above Akhmeem, most of the women envelop themselves in a large piece of dark-brown woollen stuff (called a *hulāleeyeh*), wrapping it round the body and attaching the upper parts together over each shoulder, and a piece of the same they use as a tarhah. This dull dress, though picturesque, is almost as disguising as the blue tinge which women in these parts of Egypt impart to their lips. Most of the women of the lower orders wear a variety of trumpery ornaments, such as ear-rings, necklaces, bracelets. &c., and sometimes a nose-ring.

The women of Egypt deem it more incumbent upon them to cover the upper and back part of the head than the face, and more requisite to conceal the face than most other parts of the person. I have often seen women but half covered with miserable rags, and several times females in the prime of womanhood, and others in more advanced age, with nothing on the body but a narrow strip of rag bound round the hips.

Mr. Burckhardt, in his *Notes on the Bedouins and Wahabys* (p. 47), thus describes the dress of the Badāwīs of the desert:—

In summer the men wear a coarse cotton shirt, over which the wealthy put a *kombar*, or "long gown," as it is worn in Turkish towns, of silk or cotton stuff. Most of them, however, do not wear the *kombar*, but simply wear over their shirt a woollen mantle. There are different sorts of mantles, one very thin, light, and white woollen, manufactured at Baghdād, and called *mesoumy*. A coarser and heavier kind, striped white and brown (worn over the mesoumy), is called *abba*. The Baghdād abbas are most esteemed, those made at Hamah, with short wide sleeves, are called *boush*. (In the northern parts of Syria, every kind of woollen mantle, whether white, black, or striped white and brown, or white and blue, are called *meshlakh*.) I have not seen any black abbas among the Aenezes, but frequently among the sheiks of Ahl el Shemal, sometimes interwoven with gold, and worth as much as ten pounds sterling. The Aenezes do not wear drawers; they walk and ride usually barefooted, even the richest of them, although they generally esteem yellow boots and red shoes. All the Bedouins wear on the head, instead of the red Turkish cap, a turban or square kerchief, of cotton or cotton and silk mixed; the turban is called *keffie*; this they fold about the head so that one corner falls backward, and two other corners hang over the fore part of the shoulders; with these two corners they cover their faces to protect them from the sun's rays, or hot wind, or rain, or to conceal their features if they wish to be unknown. The *keffie* is yellow or yellow mixed with green. Over the *keffie* the Aenezes tie, instead of a turban, a cord round the head; this cord is of camel's hair, and called *akal*. Some tie a handkerchief about the head, and it is then called *shutfe*. A few rich sheikhs wear shawls on their heads of Damascus or Baghdad manufacture, striped red and white; they sometimes also use red caps or *takie* (called in Syria *tarboush*), and under those they wear a smaller cap of camel's hair, called *maaraka* (in Syria *arkye*, where it is generally made of fine cotton stuff).

A BEDOUIN (BADAWI) OF THE DESERT.

The Aenezes are distinguished at first sight from all the Syrian Bedouins by the long tresses of their hair. They never shave their black hair, but cherish it from infancy, till they can twist it in tresses, that hang over the cheeks down to the breast: these tresses are called *keroun*. Some few Aenezes wear girdles of leather, others tie a cord or a piece of rag over the shirt Men and women wear from infancy a leather girdle around the naked waist, it consists of four or five thongs twisted together into a cord as thick as one's finger. I heard that the women tie their thongs separated from each other, round the waist. Both men and women adorn the girdles with pieces of ribands or amulets. The Aenezes called it *hhakou*; the Ahl el Shemal call it *bereim*. In summer the boys, until the age of seven or eight years, go stark naked; but I never saw any young girl in that state, although it was mentioned that in the interior of the desert the girls, at that early age, were not more encumbered by clothing than their little brothers. In winter, the Bedouins wear over the shirt a pelisse, made of several sheepskins stitched together; many wear these skins even in summer, because experience has taught them that the more warmly a person is clothed, the less he suffers from the sun. The Arabs endure the inclemency of the rainy season in a wonderful manner. While everything around them suffers from the cold, they sleep barefooted in an open tent, where the fire is not kept up beyond midnight. Yet in the middle of summer an Arab sleeps wrapt in his mantle upon the burning sand, and exposed to the rays of an intensely hot sun. The ladies' dress is a wide cotton gown of a dark colour, blue, brown, or black; on their heads they wear a kerchief called *shauber* or *mekroune*, the young females having it of a red colour, the old of black. All the Ranalla ladies wear black silk kerchiefs, two yards square, called *shale kās*; these are made at Damascus. Silver rings are much worn by the Aeneze ladies, both in the ears and noses; the ear-rings they call *terkie* (pl. *teraky*), the small nose-rings *shedre*, the larger (some of which are three inches and a half in diameter), *khezain*. All the women puncture their lips and dye them blue; this kind of tattooing they call *bertoum*, and apply it likewise in spotting their temples and foreheads. The Serhhān women puncture their cheeks, breasts, and arms, and the Ammour women their ankles. Several men also adorn their arms in the same manner. The Bedouin ladies half cover their faces with a dark-coloured veil, called *nekye*, which is so tied as to conceal the chin and mouth. The Egyptian women's veil (*berkoa*) is used by the Kebly Arabs. Round their wrists the Aeneze ladies wear glass bracelets of various colours; the rich also have silver bracelets and some wear silver chains about the neck Both in summer and winter the men and women go barefooted.

Captain Burton, in his account of *Zanzibar*, (vol. i. p. 382), says:—

The Arab's head-dress is a *kummeh* or *kofiyyāh* (red fez), a Surat *calotte* (*afiyyah*), or a white skull-cap, worn under a turban (*kilemba*) of Oman silk and cotton religiously mixed. Usually it is of fine blue and white cotton check, embroidered and fringed with a broad red border, with the ends hanging in unequal lengths over one shoulder. The coiffure is highly picturesque. The ruling family and grandees, however, have modified its vulgar folds, wearing it peaked in front, and somewhat resembling a *tiara*. The essential body-clothing, and the succedaneum for trousers is an *izor* (*nguo yaku Chini*), or loin-cloth, tucked in at the waist, six to seven feet long by two to three broad. The colours are brickdust and white, or blue and white, with a silk border striped red, black, and yellow. The very poor wear a dirty bit of cotton girdled by a *hakab* or *kundāvi*, a rope of plaited thongs; the rich prefer a fine embroidered stuff from Oman, supported at the waist by a silver chain. None but the western Arabs admit the innovation of drawers (*sūrūwali*). The *jama* or upper garment is a collarless coat, of the best broad-cloth, leek-green or some tender colour being preferred. It is secured over the left breast by a silken loop, and the straight wide sleeves are gaily lined. The *kizbāo* is a kind of waistcoat, covering only the bust; some wear it with sleeves, others without. The *dishdashes* (in Kisawahili Khanzu), a narrow-sleeved shirt buttoned at the throat, and extending to midshin, is made of calico (*baftah*), American drill and other stuffs called *doriyāh*, *tarabuzun*, and *jamdani*. Sailors are known by *khuzerangi*, a coarse cotton, stained dingy red-yellow, with henna or pomegranate rind, and rank with wars (bastard saffron) and shark's oil.

Respectable men guard the stomach with a *hizâm*, generally a Cashmere or Bombay shawl; others wear sashes of the dust-coloured raw silk, manufactured in Oman. The outer garment for chilly weather is the long tight-sleeved Persian *jubbeh*, *jokhah*, or *caftān*, of European broad-cloth. Most men shave their heads, and the Shafeis trim or entirely remove the moustaches.

The palms are reddened with henna, which is either brought from El Hejāz, or gathered in the plantations. The only ring is a plain cornelian seal and the sole other ornament is a talisman (*hirz*, in Kisawahili Hirizi). The eyes are blackened with *kohl*, or antimony of El Shām—here, not Syria, but the region about Meccah—and the mouth crimsoned by betel, looks as if a tooth had just been knocked out.

Dr. Eugene Schuyler, in his work on Turkestan (vol. i. p. 122), says :—

The dress of the Central Asiatic is very simple. He wears loose baggy trousers, usually made of coarse white cotton stuff fastened tightly round the waist, with a cord and tassel; this is a necessary article of dress, and is never or rarely taken off, at all events not in the presence of another. Frequently, when men are at work, this is the only garment, and in that case it is gradually turned up under the cord, or rolled up on the legs, so that the person is almost naked. Over this is worn a long shirt, either white or of some light-coloured print, reaching almost to the feet, and with a very narrow aperture for the neck, which renders it somewhat difficult to put the head through. The sleeves are long and loose. Beyond this there is nothing more but what is called the *chapan*, varying in number according to the weather, or the whim of the person. The *chapan* is a loose gown, cut very sloping in the neck, with strings to tie it together in front; and inordinately large sleeves, made with an immense gore, and about twice as long as is necessary; exceedingly inconvenient, but useful to conceal the hands, as Asiatic politeness dictates. In summer, these are usually made of Russian prints, or of the native alatcha, a striped cotton material, or of silk, either striped or with most gorgeous eastern patterns, in bright colours, especially red, yellow, and green. I have sometimes seen men with as many as four or five of these gowns, even in summer; they say that it keeps out the heat. In winter, one gown will frequently be made of cloth, and lined with fine lamb-skin or fur. The usual girdle is a large handkerchief, or a small shawl; at times, a long scarf wound several times tightly round the waist. The Jews in places under native rule are allowed no girdle, but a bit of rope or cord, as a mark of ignominy. From the girdle hang the accessory knives and several small bags and pouches, often prettily embroidered, for combs, money, &c. On the head there is a skull-cap; these in Tashkent are always embroidered with silk; in Būkhārā they are usually worked with silk, or worsted in cross-stitch in gay patterns. The turban, called *tchilpetch*, or "forty turns," is very long; and if the wearer has any pretence to elegance, it should be of fine thin material, which is chiefly imported from England. It requires considerable experience to wind one properly round the head, so that the folds will be well made and the appearance fashionable. One extremity is left to fall over the left shoulder, but is usually, except at prayer time, tucked in over the top. Should this end be on the right shoulder, it is said to be in the Afghān style. The majority of turbans are white particularly so in Tashkent, though white is

AN AFGHAN CHIEF. (*A. F. Hole.*)

especially the colour of the *mūllāhs* and religious people, whose learning is judged by the size of their turbans. In general, merchants prefer blue, striped, or chequered material.

AN AFGHAN MULLAH.

At home the men usually go barefooted, but on going out wear either a sort of slippers with pointed toes and very small high heels, or long soft boots, the sole and upper being made of the same material. In the street, one must in addition put on either a slipper or golosh, or wear riding-boots made of bright green horse hide, with turned-up pointed toes and very small high heels.

The dress of the women, in shape and fashion, differs but little from that of the men, as they wear similar trousers and shirts, though, in addition, they have long gowns, usually of bright-coloured silk, which extend from the neck to the ground. They wear an innumerable quantity of necklaces, and little amulets, pendents in their hair, and ear-rings, and occasionally even a nose-ring. This is by no means so ugly as is supposed: a pretty girl with a torquoise ring in one nostril is not at all unsightly. On the contrary, there is something piquant in it. Usually, when outside of the houses, all respectable women wear a heavy black veil, reaching to their waists, made of woven horse-hair, and over that is thrown a dark blue, or green *khalat*, the sleeves of which, tied together at the ends, dangle behind. The theory of this dull dress is, that the women desire to escape observation, and certainly for that purpose they have devised the most ugly and unseemly costume that could be imagined. They are, however, very inquisitive, and occasionally in bye-streets one is able to get a good glance at them before they pull down their veils.

The dress of the citizens of Persia has been often described, both by ancient and modern travellers. That of the men has changed very materially within the last century. The turban, as a head-dress, is now worn by none but the Arabian inhabitants of that country. The Persians wear a long cap covered with lamb's wool, the appearance of which is sometimes improved by being encircled with a cashmere shawl. The inhabitants of the principal towns are fond of dressing richly. Their upper garments are either made of chintz, silk, or cloth, and are often trimmed with gold or silver lace; they also wear brocade; and in winter their clothes are lined with furs, of which they import a great variety. It is not customary for any person, except the king, to wear jewels; but nothing can exceed the profusion which he displays of these ornaments; and his subjects seem peculiarly proud of this part of royal magnificence. They assert that when the monarch is dressed in his most splendid robes, and is seated in the sun, that the eye cannot gaze on the dazzling brilliancy of his attire.

DRINKABLES. Arabic *ashribah* (اشربة). There is a chapter in the Traditions devoted to this subject, and entitled *Bābu 'l-Ashribah.* The example of Muḥammad in his habit of drinking, having influenced the Eastern world in its habits, the following traditions are noticeable. Anas says "the Prophet has forbidden drinking water standing," and that he used to take breath three times in drinking; and would say drinking in this way cools the stomach, quenches the thirst, and gives health and vigour to the body.

Ibn 'Abbās says the Prophet forbade drinking water from the mouth of a leather bag.

Umm Salimah says "the Prophet said, He who drinks out of a silver cup drinks of hell fire." (*Mishkāt*, book xix. c. iii.)

DRINKING VESSELS. There are four drinking vessels which Muslims were forbidden by their Prophet to drink out of (*Mishkāt*, bk. i., c. i.) *ḥantam*, a "green vessel"; *dubbā'*, a large gourd hollowed out; *naqīr*, a cup made from the hollowed root of a tree; *muzaffat*, a vessel covered with pitch, or with a glutinous substance. These four kinds of vessels seem to have been used for drinking wine, hence the prohibition.

When a dog drinks from a vessel used by man, it should be washed seven times. (*Mishkāt*, book iii. c. ix. pt. i.)

DROWNING. Arabic *g͟haraq* (غرق). It is a strange anomaly in Muḥammadan law, according to the teaching of Abū Ḥanīfah, that if a person cause the death of another by immersing him under water until he die, the offence does not amount to murder, and retaliation (*qiṣāṣ*)is not incurred. The arguments of the learned divine are as follows: First, water is analogous to a small stick or rod, as is seldom or ever used in murder. Now, it is said in the Traditions that death produced by a rod is only manslaughter, and as in that a fine is merely incurred, so here likewise. Secondly, retaliation requires the observance of a perfect equality; but between drowning and wounding there is no equality, the former being short of the latter with regard to damaging the body. [MURDER.]

DRUNKENNESS. *Shurb* (شرب) denotes the state of a person who has taken intoxicating liquor, whilst *sukr* (سكر) implies a state of drunkenness. Wine of any kind being strictly forbidden by the Muslim law, no distinction is made in the punishment of a wine-drinker and a drunkard. If a Muslim drink wine, and two witnesses testify to his having done so, or if his breath smell of wine, or if he shall himself confess to having taken wine, or if he be found in a state of intoxication, he shall be beaten with eighty stripes, or, in the case of a slave, with forty stripes. (*Hidāyah*, vol. ii. p. 57; *Mishkāt*, bk. xv. c iv.) [KHAMR.]

DRUZES. A heretical mystic sect of Muḥammadans, which arose about the beginning of the eleventh century in the mountains of Syria. They are now chiefly found in the districts of Lebanon, and in the neighbourhood of Damascus. They were founded by al-Ḥakīm, the fanatical Khalīfah of the Fāṭimite race, who reigned at Cairo, assisted by two Persians named Hamzah and al-Darāzī, from the latter of whom the sect derives its name.

De Sacy, in his *Exposé de la Religion des Druzes*, gives the following summary of their belief:—

"To acknowledge only one God, without seeking to penetrate the nature of His being and of His attributes; to confess that He can neither be comprehended by the senses nor defined by words; to believe that the Divinity has shown itself to men at different epochs, under a human form, without participating in any of the weaknesses and imperfections of humanity; that it has shown itself at last, at the commencement of the fifth age of the Hejira, under the figure of Hakim Amr Allah; that that was the last of His manifestations, after which there is none other to be expected; that Hakim disappeared in the year 411 of the Hejira, to try the faith of His servants, to give room for the apostasy of hypocrites, and of those who had only embraced the true religion from the hope of worldly rewards; that in a short time he would appear again, full of glory and of majesty, to triumph over all his enemies, to extend His empire over all the earth, and to make His faithful worshippers happy for ever; to believe that Universal Intelligence is the first of God's creatures, the only direct production of His omnipotence; that it has appeared upon the earth at the epoch of each of the manifestations of the Divinity, and has finally appeared since the time of Hakim under the figure of Hamza, son of Ahmad; that it is by His ministry that all the other creatures have been produced; that Hamza only possesses the knowledge of all truth, that he is the prime minister of the true religion, and that he communicates, directly or indirectly, with the other ministers and with the faithful, but in different proportions, the knowledge and the grace which he receives directly from the Divinity, and of which he is the sole channel; that he only has immediate access to God, and acts as a mediator to the other worshippers of the Supreme Being; acknowledging that Hamza is he to whom Hakim will confide his sword, to make his religion triumph, to conquer all his rivals, and to distribute rewards and punishments according to the merits of each one; to know the other ministers of religion, and the rank which belongs to each of them; to give to each the obedience and submission which is their due; to confess that every soul has been created by the Universal Intelligence; that the number of men is always the same; and that souls pass successively into different bodies; that they are raised by their attachment to truth to a superior degree of excellence, or are degraded by neglecting or giving up religious meditation; to practise the seven commandments which the religion of Hamza imposes upon its followers, and which principally exacts from them the observance of truth, charity towards their brethren, the renunciation of their former religion, the most entire resignation and submission to the will of God; to confess that all preceding religions have only been types more or less perfect of true religion, that all their ceremonial observances are only allegories, and that the manifestation of true religion requires the abrogation of every other creed. Such is the abridgment of the religious system taught in the books of the Druzes, of which Hamza is the author, and whose followers are called Unitarians."

There is a very fnll and correct account of the religious belief of the Druzes in the *Researches into the Religions of Syria*, by the Rev. J. Wortabet, M.D. In this work Dr. Wortabet gives the following Catechism of the Druzes, which expresses their belief with regard to Christianity:—

"Q. What do ye say concerning the gospel which the Christians hold?

"A. That it is true; for it is the sayings of the Lord Christ, who was Salman el Pharisy during the life of Mohammed, and who is Hamzeh the son of Ali—not the false Christ who was born of Mary, for he was the son of Joseph.

"Q. Where was the true Christ when the false Christ was with the disciples?

"A. He was among the disciples. He uttered the truths of the gospel and taught Christ, the son of Joseph, the institutes of the Christian religion; but when Jesus disobeyed the true Christ, he put hatred into the hearts of the Jews, so that they crucified him.

"What became of him after the crucifixion?

"A. They put him into a grave, and the true Christ came and stole him, and gave out the report among men that Christ had risen out of the dead.

"Q. Why did he act in this manner?

"A. That he might establish the Christian religion, and confirm its followers in what he had taught them.

"Q. Why did he act in such a manner as to establish error?

"A. So that the Unitarians should be concealed in the religion of Jesus and none of them might be known.

"Q. Who was it that came from the grave and entered among the disciples when the doors were shut?

"A. The living Christ, who is immortal, even Hamzeh, the son and slave of our Lord.

"Q. Who brought the gospel to light, and preached it?

"A. Matthew, Mark, Luke, and John."

"Q. Why did not the Christians acknowledge the unity of God?

"A. Because God had not so decreed.

"Q. Why does God permit the introduction of evil and infidelity?

"A. Because He chooses to mislead some from, and to guide others, to the truth.

"Q. If infidelity and error proceed from Him, why does he punish those who follow them?

"A. Because when He deceived them, they did not obey Him.

"Q. How can a deluded man obey, when he is ignorant of the true state of the case?

"A. We are not bound to answer this question, for God is not accountable to his creatures for his dealings with them."

DU'Ā' (دعاء). "Prayer." The word *du'ā'* is generally used for supplication, as distinguished from *ṣalāt*, or the liturgical form of prayer, *e.g.* Qur'ān, Sūrah xiv. 42: "O my Lord! make me and my posterity to be constant in prayer (*ṣalāt*). O our Lord! and accept my supplication (*du'ā'*). [PRAYERS.]

DU'Ā'-I-MA'ṢŪR (دعاء ماثور). *Lit.* "Recorded prayer." A term used for prayers which were offered up by the Prophet, and have been handed down in the Traditions.

DU'Ā'U 'L-QUNŪT (دعاء القنوت), called also the *Qunūtu 'l-Witr*, "The prayer said standing." A form of prayer recited after the *qarā'ah* in the night prayer. Recited by some sects in the early morning. It is found in the Traditions. It is as follows:—

"O God, we seek help from Thee, and forgiveness of sins.

"We believe in Thee and trust in Thee.

"We praise Thee. We thank Thee. We are not unthankful.

"We expel, and we depart from him who does not obey Thee.

"We serve Thee only, and to Thee do we pray.

"We seek Thee, we prostrate ourselves and we serve Thee.

"We hope for Thy mercy. We fear Thy punishments.

"Surely Thy judgments are upon the infidels."

DUALISM. Professor Palmer, following the remarks of al-Baiẓāwī the commentator, says there is a protest against the dualistic doctrine that Light and Darkness were two co-eternal principles, in the Qur'ān, Sūrah vi. 1: "Praised be God who created the heavens and the earth, and brought into being the Darkness and the Light." (Palmer's *Qur'ān*, vol. i. p. 115; al-Baiẓāwī *in loco*.)

AD-DUKHĀN (الدخان). "The Smoke." The title of the XLIVth chapter of the Qur'ān, in which the words occur (9th verse): "Expect thou the day when the heaven shall bring a palpable *smoke*."

DULDUL (دلدل). The name of the Prophet's mule which he gave to 'Alī.

DUMB, The. Arabic *abkam* (ابكم), pl. *bukm*.

The intelligible signs of a dumb person suffice to verify his bequests and render them valid; he may also execute a marriage contract, or give a divorce, or execute a sale or purchase, or sue or incur punishment by signs, but he cannot sue in a case of *qiṣāṣ*, or retaliation for murder. This rule does not apply to a person who has been deprived of speech, but merely to one who has been born dumb. (*Hidāyah*, vol. iv. p. 568.) A dumb person can also acknowledge and deny the faith by a sign.

AD-DURRATU 'L-BAIẒĀ' (الدرة البيضاء). *Lit.* "The pearl of light." A term used by Ṣūfī mystics to express the *'āqlu 'l-awwal*, the first intelligence which God is said to have created at the beginning of the animate world. ('Abdu 'r-Razzāq's *Dictionary of Ṣūfī Terms*.)

DURŪD (درود; a Persian word. Arabic *aṣ-Ṣalāt* (الصلوة). A benediction; imploring mercy. A part of the stated prayer, recited immediately after the *Tashahhud*, whilst in the same posture. It is as follows: "O God, have mercy on Muḥammad and on his descendants, as Thou didst have mercy on Abraham and on his descendants! Thou art to be praised, and Thou art great! O God, bless Muḥammad and his descendants as Thou didst bless Abraham and his descendants. Thou art to be praised and Thou art great." The merits of this form of prayer are said to be very great; for, according to Anas, the Prophet said, "He who recites it will have blessings on his head ten times, ten sins will be forgiven, and he will be exalted ten steps." (*Mishkāt*, book iv. c. xvii.) [PRAYER.]

DŪZAKH (دوزخ). The Persian word for hell. [HELL.]

DYER. According to the Imām Abū Ḥanīfah, a dyer of cloth is at liberty to detain it until he receive his hire for dyeing it; and if the cloth perish in his hands whilst it is detained, he is not responsible. (*Hidāyah*, vol. iii. 320.)

DYING, The. Very special instructions are given in Muslim books as to the treatment of the dying. In the *Durru 'l-Mukhtār* (p. 88), the friends of the dying are recommended, if possible, to turn the head of the dying person towards Makkah; but if this be not convenient, his feet should be placed in that direction and his head slightly raised. The *Kalimatu 'sh-Shahādah* should then be recited, and the Sūrah Yā-Sīn (xxxvi.) and Sūratu 'r-Ra'd (xiii.) should be read from the Qur'ān. When the spirit has departed from the body, the mouth should be tied up and the eyes closed and the arms straightened, and the body should be perfumed, and no unclean person should be suffered to approach the corpse. Immediate steps should then be taken for the washing of the corpse. [DEATH.]

E.

EAR-RINGS; NOSE-RINGS. In the East it is the universal custom of Muḥammadan women to wear ear-rings, and they are not unfrequently worn by young men and children. Gold ear-rings are, however, forbidden in the Traditions; for Abū Hurairah relates that the Prophet said, "Whoever wishes to put into the ear or the nose of a friend a ring of hell fire, let him put in the ear or the nose of his friend a gold ring . . . . let your ornament be of silver." And Asmā' bint Yazīd relates the same tradition. (*Mishkāt*, book xx. c. 11, part 2.)

EAR AND NOSE RINGS.

EARTH, The. Arabic *arẓ* (ارض). Muḥammad taught his followers that just as there are seven heavens [HEAVEN] one above another, so there are seven earths one beneath another, the distance between each of these regions being five hundred years' journey. (*Mishkāt*, book xxiv. c. i. part 3.)

In the Qur'ān the earth is said to be stretched out like a carpet or bed (Sūrah ii. 20; xiii. 3; lxxviii. 6), which expression the ancient commentators understood to imply that the earth was a vast plane, but circular; and (Sūrah xxxix. 67) to be but a handful in the sight of God, which in the last day shall be changed into another earth (Sūrah xiv. 49).

The earth is believed by Muḥammadan writers to be surrounded by a great sea called *al-Baḥru 'l-Muḥīṭ*, or the circumambient ocean, which is bounded by the mountains of Qāf. The extent of the earth is said to be equal to a journey of five hundred years; two hundred years' journey being allotted to the sea, two hundred to the uninhabited desert, eighty to the country of Gog and Magog (*Yājūj wa Mājūj*) and the rest to the civilised world. Certain *terræ incognitæ* in the midst of the mountains of Qāf are said to be inhabited by the jinn, or genii. According to some, Makkah (or Jerusalem according to others) is situated in the centre of the earth. On the *Muḥīṭ* is the *'Arshu 'l-Iblīs*, or "Throne of Satan." The western portion of the *Muḥīṭ* is often called the *Baḥru 'ẓ-Ẓulmāt*, or "Sea of Darkness," and in the south-west corner of the earth is the Fountain of Life of which al-Khiẓr drank, and in virtue of which he still lives, and will live till the Day of Judgment. The mountains of Qāf which bound the great sea Muḥīṭ, form a circular barrier round the whole earth, and are said to be of green chrysolite, the colour of which the Prophet said imparts a greenish tint to the sky. The general opinion is that the mountains of Qāf bound our earth, but some say there are countries beyond, each country being a thousand years' journey.

The seven earths, which are five hundred years' journey from each other, are situated one beneath the other, and each of these seven regions has its special occupants. The occupants of the *first* are men, genii, and animals; the *second* is occupied by the suffocating wind which destroyed the infidel tribe of 'Ād (Sūrah lxix. 6); the *third* is filled with the stones of hell, mentioned in the Qur'ān (Sūrah ii. 22; lxvi. 6) as "the fuel of which is men and stones"; the *fourth* by the sulphur of hell; the *fifth* by the serpents of hell; the *sixth* by the scorpions of hell, which are in size and colour like black mules, and have tails like spears; and the *seventh* by the devil and his angels. Our earth is said to be supported on the shoulders of an angel, who stands upon a rock of ruby, which rock is supported on a huge bull with four thousand eyes, and the same number of ears, noses, mouths, tongues, and feet; between every one of each is a distance of five hundred years' journey. The name of this bull is *Kujūta*, who is supported by an enormous fish, the name of which is *Bahamūt*.

The above is but a brief outline of the Muḥammadan belief as regards the earth's formation; but the statements of Muḥammadan commentators are so wild on the subject, that it seems quite useless to quote them as authorities, for they contradict each other in endless variety.

EARTHQUAKE, The. Arabic *az-Zalzalah* (الزلزلة). The title of the xcixth Sūrah of the Qur'ān, in which it is stated that an earthquake will take place at the commencement of the signs of the last day:—

"When the Earth with her quaking shall quake

"And the Earth shall cast forth her burdens,

"And man shall say, What aileth her?

"On that day shall she tell out her tidings,

"Because thy Lord shall have inspired her.

"On that day shall men come forward in throngs to behold their works,

"And whosoever shall have wrought an atom's weight of good shall behold it,

"And whosoever shall have wrought an atom's weight of evil shall behold it."

EATING. According to the Traditions, Muḥammadans have been enjoined by their Prophet to eat in God's name, to return thanks, to eat with their right hand, and with their shoes off, and to lick the plate when the meal is finished. The following are some of Muḥammad's precepts on the subject:—

"The Devil has power over that food which is eaten without remembering God."

"Repeat the name of God. Eat with the right hand and eat from before you."

"When a man comes into a house at mealtime, and remembers the name of God, the devil says to his followers, 'There is no place here for you and me to-night, nor is there any supper for us."

"When anyone eats he must not wash his fingers until he has first licked them."

"Whoever eats a dish and licks it afterwards, the dish intercedes with God for him."

"When victuals are placed before you, eat them with your shoes off, because taking off your shoes will ease your feet." ('Abdu 'l-Ḥaqq adds, "and do it out of respect to the food.")

"Whoever eats from a plate and licks it afterwards, the dish says to him, 'May God free you from hell as you have freed me from the devils licking me.'"

Qatādah says that Anas said: "The Prophet did not eat off a table, as is the manner of proud men, who do it to avoid bending their backs." (*Mishkāt*, Arabic ed., *Bābu 'l-Aṭ'imah.*)

The following directions are given for eating, by Faqīr Muḥammad As'ad, the author of the *A<u>kh</u>lāq-i-Jalālī*. (Thompson's English Translation, p. 294):—

"First of all, he should wash his hands,

DINING

mouth, and nose. Before beginning he should say, 'In the name of God' (*Bismillāh*); and after ending he must say, 'Glory to God' (*Al-ḥamdu lillāh*). He is not to be in a hurry to begin, unless he is the master of the feast; he must not dirty his hands, or clothes, or the table-linen; he must not eat with more than three fingers, nor open his mouth wide; not take large mouthfuls, nor swallow them hastily, nor yet keep them too long unswallowed. He must not suck his fingers in the course of eating; but after he has eaten, he may, or rather ought, as there is scripture warrant for it.

"Let him not look from dish to dish, nor smell the food, nor pick and choose it. If there should be one dish better than the rest, let him not be greedy on his own account, but let him offer it to others. He must not spill the grease upon his fingers, or so as to wet his bread and salt. He must not eye his comrades in the midst of his mouthfuls. Let him eat from what is next him, unless of fruit, which it is allowable to eat from every quarter. What he has once put into his mouth (such as bones, &c.), he must not replace upon his bread, nor upon the table-cloth; if a bone has found its way there, let him remove it unseen. Let him beware of revolting gestures, and of letting anything drop from his mouth into the cup. Let him so behave, that, if anyone should wish to eat the relics of his repast, there may be nothing to revolt him.

"Where he is a guest, he must stay his hand sooner than the master of the feast; and whenever the rest discontinue eating, he must act in concert with them, except he be in his own house, or some other where he constitutes part of the family. Where he is himself the host, he must not continue eating when the rest have stayed their hands, so that something may be left for anyone who chances to fancy it.

"If he has occasion to drink in the course of his meal, let him do it softly, that no noise in his throat or mouth may be audible to others. He must not pick his teeth in the view of the company, nor swallow what his tongue may extract from between them; and so of what may be extracted by the toothpick, let him throw it aside so as to disgust no one.

"When the time comes for washing his hands, let him be exceedingly careful in cleansing his nails and fingers. Similar must be his particularity in washing his lips, mouth, and nostrils. He must not void his rheum into the basin; even the water in which his mouth has been rinsed, let him cover with his hand as he throws it away.

"Neither must he take the turn from others in washing his hands, saving when he is master of the entertainment, and then he should be the first to wash."

WASHING THE HANDS.

EATING WITH JEWS OR CHRISTIANS. In Muḥammadan countries, where the people have not been brought in contact with Hindus, with caste prejudices, Muslims never hesitate to eat with Jews and Christians, provided the drink and victuals are such as are lawful in Islām. Since the British occupation of India, the question has often been raised, and few Muḥammadans will eat with Englishmen. Syud Ahmad Khān, C.S.I., has written a book, in which he proves that it is lawful for Muḥammadans to eat with both Christians and Jews, and his arguments would seem to be in accordance with the teaching of the Qur'ān. Sūrah v. 7: "Lawful for you to-day are the good things, and the food of the people of the Book (*i.e.* Jews and Christians) is lawful for you, and your food is lawful for them."

Al-Baizāwī, commenting on this verse,

says: "This verse includes all kinds of food, that which is slain lawfully (*zabḥ*) or not, and this verse is of common application to all the people of the Book, whether Jews or Christians. But on one occasion Khalīfah 'Alī did not observe its injunctions with regard to the Banū Taghlib, a Christian tribe, because he said these people were not Christians, for they had not embraced anything of Christianity except wine-drinking. And he does not include amongst the people of the book, the Majūsīs, although he included the Majūsīs with the people of the Book when he took the poll-tax from them, according to a tradition which Muḥammad gave regarding the Majūsīs, viz. 'Treat the Majūsis as you would treat the people of the Book, but do not marry with them, nor eat what they slay." (*Tafsīru 'l-Baiẓāwī*, p. 216.)

The commentators, al-Kamālān, say the only question raised was that of animals slain by Jews and Christians, and the learned are all agreed that animals slain by them are lawful. (*Tafsīru 'l-Jalālain wa 'l-Kamālain*, p. 93.)

The following Ḥadīs̤ is given in the Ṣaḥiḥ Muslim on the subject: Abū Ṣa'labah related, "I said, O Prophet of God! Verily we live in a land belonging to the people of the Book (*i.e.* Jews or Christians); is it lawful for us to eat out of their dishes? The Prophet replied, The order for dishes is this: if you can get other dishes, then eat of them; but if ye cannot, then wash those of the people of the Book and eat from them."

The Imām Nawawī, the commentator on the Ṣaḥīḥ Muslim, says Abū Dā'ud has given this Ḥadīs̤ in a somewhat different form to that in the text. He says: "Abū Ṣa'labah relates, we were passing through the country of the people of the Book (*i.e.* Christians), and they were cooking pigs' flesh in their dishes, and drinking wine from their vessels." "For" (continues Nawawī), "the learned are all agreed that it is lawful to eat with Jews and Christians unless their vessels are polluted with wine or pork, in which case they must be washed before they are used." (*Ṣaḥīḥ Muslim wa Sharḥu Nawawī*, p. 146.)

ECLIPSE. The Arabic *khusūf* (خسوف) is used to denote either an eclipse of the sun or of the moon (*vide Mishkāt*, book iv. c. li.); but it is more specially applied to an eclipse of the moon; and *kusūf* (كسوف) for an eclipse of the sun (*vide* Richardson's Dictionary). Special prayers, consisting of two rak'ahs, are enjoined in the Traditions (*Mishkāt*, book iv. c. li.) at the time of an eclipse of either the sun or moon.

'Abdu 'llāh ibn 'Abbās says: "There was an eclipse of the sun in the time of the Prophet, and he recited prayers, and the people recited after him; and he stood up for a long time, as long as anyone would be repeating the Chapter of the Cow (*i.e.* Sūrah ii.). Then he performed a long rukū', after which he raised up his head and stood a long time, which was under the first standing; after which he did the second rukū', which was the same as the first in point of time; then he raised his head up from the second rukū'; and performed two prostrations, as is customary. Then he stood up a long time, in the second rak'ah, and this was shorter than the first standing, in the first rak'ah; after which he did a long rukū' in the second rak'ah, and this was under the first rukū', in the first rak'ah. After this, he raised up his head, and stood a long time; and this was shorter than the first, in the second rak'ah. Then he did a long rukū'; and this was not so great as the first, in the second rak'ah. Then he rose up, and performed two prostrations; and after repeating the creed, and giving the salām, he concluded his prayers. And the sun was bright. And the Prophet said, 'Verily, the sun and moon are two signs, amongst those which prove the existence of God, and are not eclipsed on account of the life or death of any person; and when ye see this, remember God.' The Companions said, 'O Prophet! We saw you about to take something in the place where you stood in prayer, after which we saw you draw back a little.' And the Prophet said, "I saw Paradise, and gathered a bunch of grapes from it; and if I had taken it and given it to you, verily you would have eaten of it as long as the world lasts. I also saw hell, and never saw such a horrid sight till this day; and I saw that they were mostly women there.' And the Companions said, 'O Prophet, why are most of the people of hell women?' He said, 'On account of their infidelity; not on account of their disobedience to God, but that they are ungrateful to their husbands, and hide the good things done them; and if you do good to one of them perpetually, after that, if they see the least fault in you, they will say, I never saw you perform a good work.'" (*Mishkāt*, book iv. c. ii.)

EDEN. Arabic *'Adn* (عدن), which al-Baiẓāwī says means "a fixed abode." The Hebrew עֵדֶן is generally understood by Hebrew scholars to mean "pleasure" or "delight."

The word *'Adn* is not used in the Qur'ān for the residence of our first parents, the term used being *al-jannah*, "the garden"; although the Muslim Commentators are agreed in calling it the *Jannatu 'Adn*, or "Garden of Eden." The expressions, *Jannatu 'Adn*, "the Garden of Eden," and *Jannātu 'Adn*, "the Gardens of Eden," occur ten times in the Qur'ān, but in each case they are used for the fourth heaven, or stage, of celestial bliss. [PARADISE.]

According to the Qur'ān, it seems clear that *Jannatu 'Adn* is considered to be a place in heaven. and not a terrestrial paradise, and hence a difficulty arises as to the locality of that Eden from which Adam fell. Is it the same place as the *fourth* abode of celestial bliss? or, was it a garden situated in some part of earth? Al-Baiẓāwī says that some people have thought this Eden was situated in the country of the Philistines, or between Fāris and Kirmān. But, he adds, the Garden of Eden is the *Dāru 's-Ṣawāb*, or "the House of Recompense," which is a stage in the paradise of the heavens; and that when Adam and Eve were cast out of Paradise, Adam fell on the isle of Ceylon, or *Sarandīb*, and Eve near Jiddah in Arabia; and after a separation of 200 years, Adam was, on his repentance, conducted by the Angel Gabriel to a mountain near Makkah, where he knew his wife Eve, the mountain being thence named 'Arafah (*i.e.* "the place of recognition); and that he afterwards retired with her to Ceylon, where they continued to propagate their species.

Muḥammad Ṭāhir (*Majma'u 'l-Biḥār*, p. 225), in remarking upon the fact that in the Traditions the rivers Jaihūn and Jaihān are said to be rivers in "the *garden*" (*al-Jannah*), says the terms are figurative, and mean that the faith extended to those regions and made them rivers of paradise. And in another place (*idem*, p. 164) the same author says the four rivers *Saiḥān* (Jaxartes), *Jaiḥān* (Jihon), *Furāt* (Euphrates), and *Nīl* (Nile), are the rivers of Paradise, and that the rivers Saiḥān and Jaiḥān are not the same as Jaihūn and Jaihān, but that these four rivers already mentioned originally came from Paradise to this earth of ours.

EDUCATION. Education without religion is to the Muḥammadan mind an anomaly. In all books of Traditions there are sections specially devoted to the consideration of knowledge, but only so far as it relates to a *knowledge of God*, and of "*God's Book*." (See *Ṣaḥīḥu 'l-Bukhārī*, *Bābu 'l-'Ilm.*) The people who read the "Book of God" are, according to the sayings of the Prophet, described as "assembling together in mosques, with light and comfort descending upon them, the grace of God covering them, and the angels of God encompassing them round about." The chief aim and object of education in Islām is, therefore, to obtain a knowledge of the religion of Muḥammad, and anything beyond this is considered superfluous, and even dangerous. Amongst Muḥammadan religious leaders there have always been two classes—those who affect the ascetic and strictly religious life of mortification, such as the Sūfī mystics and the Faqīrs [FAQIR]; and those who, by a careful study of the Qur'ān, the Traditions, and the numerous works on divinity, have attained to a high reputation for scholarship, and are known in Turkey as the '*Ulamā*', or "learned," and in India, as *Maulawīs*.

Amongst Muḥammadans generally, a knowledge of science and various branches of secular learning is considered dangerous to the faith, and it is discouraged by the religious, although some assert that Muḥammad has encouraged learning of all kinds in the Qur'ān, by the following verse, Sūrah ii. 272:—

"He giveth wisdom to whom He will, and He to whom wisdom is given hath had much good given him."

Mr. Lane, in his *Modern Egyptians*, says: "The parents seldom devote much of their time or attention to the intellectual education of their children; generally contenting themselves with instilling into their young minds a few principles of religion, and then submitting them, if they can afford to do so, to the instruction of a school. As early as possible, the child is taught to say, 'I testify that there is no deity but God, and I testify that Muḥammad is God's Apostle.' He receives also lessons of religious pride, and learns to hate the Christians, and all other sects but his own, as thoroughly as does the Muslim in advanced age."

In connection with all mosques of importance, in all parts of Islām whether in Turkey, Egypt, Persia, or India, there are small schools, either for the education of children, or for the training of students of divinity. The child who attends these seminaries is first taught his alphabet, which he learns from a small board, on which the letters are written by the teacher. He then becomes acquainted with the numerical value of each letter. [ABJAD.] After this he learns to write down the ninety-nine names of God, and other simple words taken from the Qur'ān. [GOD.] When he has mastered the spelling of words, he proceeds to learn the first chapter of the Qur'ān, then the last chapter, and gradually reads through the whole Qur'ān in Arabic, which he usually does without understanding a word of it. Having finished the Qur'ān, which is considered an incumbent religious duty, the pupil is instructed in the elements of grammar, and perhaps a few simple rules of arithmetic. To this is added a knowledge of one Hindustanī, or Persian book. The ability to read a single Persian book like the *Gulistān* or *Bostān*, is considered in Central Asia to be the sign of a liberal education. The ordinary schoolmaster is generally a man of little learning, the learned Maulawī usually devoting himself to the study of divinity, and not to the education of the young.

Amongst students of divinity, who are called *ṭalabatu* (sing. *ṭālib*) *'l-'ilm*, or "seekers after knowledge," the usual course of study is as follows: *aṣ-ṣarf*, grammatical inflection; *an-naḥw*, syntax; *al-manṭiq*, logic; *al-ḥisāb*, arithmetic; *al-jabr wa 'l-muqābalah*, algebra; *al-ma'na wa 'l-bayān*, rhetoric and versification; *al-fiqh*, jurisprudence; *al-'aqā'id*, scholastic theology; *at-tafsīr*, commentaries on the Qur'ān; *'ilmu 'l-uṣūl*, treatises on exegesis, and the principles and rules of interpretation of the laws of Islām; *al-aḥādīṣ*, the traditions and commentaries thereon. These are usually regarded as different branches of learning, and it is not often that a Maulawī, or *'Ālim*, attains to the knowledge of each section. For example, a scholar will be celebrated as being well educated in *al-aḥādīṣ*, but he may be weak in *al-fiqh*. The teacher, when instructing his pupils, seats himself on the ground with his hearers all seated round him in a ring. Instruction in mosques is usually given in the early morning, after the morning prayer, and continues some three or four hours. It is again renewed for a short time after the mid-day prayer.

Students in mosques are generally supported by the people of the *parish*, (each mosque having its section or parish), who can be called upon for food for all the inmates of a mosque every morning and evening. Not unfrequently mosques are endowed with land, or rents of shops and houses, for the payment of professors. Mr. Lane speaks of a mosque in Cairo, which had an endowment for the support of three hundred blind students. The great mosque *al-Azhar*, in Cairo, is the largest and most influential seat of learning in Islām. In 1875, when the present writer visited it, it had as many as 5,000 students gathered from all parts of the Muḥammadan world.

In India almost every mosque of importance has its class of students of divinity, but they are not established for the purposes of general education, but for the training of students of divinity who will in time become the Imāms of mosques. Some of the Maulawīs are men held in great reputation as Arabic scholars, but they are, as a rule, very deficient in general knowledge and information. Whether we look to India, or Persia, or Egypt, or Turkey, the attitude of Muḥammadanism is undoubtedly one in direct antagonism to the spread of secular education.

Much has been made by some writers of the liberal patronage extended to literature and science by ʻAbdu 'r-Raḥmān and his suc-

A MUSLIM SCHOOL.

cessors as Khalīfahs of Ca: dova in the Middle Ages. But there was nothing original, or Islāmic, in the literature thus patronised, for, as Professor Uerberweg remarks in his *History of Philosophy*, "the whole philosophy of the Arabians was a form of Aristotelianism, tempered more or less with Neo-Platonic conceptions." The philosophical works of the Greeks and their works of medical and physical science, were translated from Greek into Arabic by Syrian Christians, and not by Arabian Muslims. Muḥammadans cannot be altogether credited with these literary undertakings.

Al-Maqqarī, in his *History of the Dynasties of Spain*, has an interesting notice of education in that country, in which he writes:—

"Respecting the state of science among the Andalusians (Spaniards), we must own in justice that the people of that country were the most ardent lovers of knowledge, as well as those who best knew how to appreciate and distinguish a learned man and an ignorant one; indeed, science was so much esteemed by them, that whoever had not been endowed by God with the necessary qualifications to acquire it, did everything in his power to distinguish himself, and conceal from the people his want of instruction; for an ignorant man was at all times looked upon as an object of the greatest contempt, while the learned man, on the contrary, was not only respected by all, nobles and plebeians, but was trusted and consulted on every occasion; his name was in every mouth, his power and influence had no limits, and he was preferred and distinguished in all the occasions of life.

"Owing to this, rich men in Cordova, however illiterate they might be, encouraged letters, rewarded with the greatest munificence writers and poets, and spared neither trouble nor expense in forming large collections of books; so that, independently of the famous library founded by the Khalīfah al-Ḥākim, and which is said by writers worthy of credit to have contained no less than four hundred thousand volumes, there were in the capital many other libraries in the hands of wealthy individuals, where the studious could dive into the fathomless sea of knowledge, and bring up its inestimable pearls. Cordova was indeed, in the opinion of every author, the city in Andalus where most books were to be found, and its inhabitants were renowned for their passion for forming libraries. To such an extent did this rage for collection increase, says Ibn Sa'īd, that any man in power, or holding a situation under Government, considered himself obliged to have a library of his own, and would spare no trouble or expense in collecting books, merely in order that people might say,—Such a one has a very fine library, or, he possesses a unique copy of such a book, or, he has a copy of such a work in the hand-writing of such a one."

EGGS. According to the Imām Abū Ḥanīfah, if a person purchase eggs and after opening them discover them to be of bad quality and unfit for use, he is entitled to a complete restitution of the price from the seller. (*Hidāyah*, vol. ii. p. 415.)

EGYPT. Arabic *Miṣr* (مصر). The land of Egypt is mentioned several times in the Qur'ān in connection with the history of Joseph and Moses. In the year A.H. 7 (A.D. 628), Muḥammad sent an embassy to al-Muqauqis, the Roman Governor of Egypt, who received the embassy kindly and presented the Prophet with two female Coptic slaves.

ELEMENTS. Arabic *al-'Anāṣiru 'l-arba'ah* (العناصر الاربعة). "The four elements" of fire (*nār*), air (*hawā*), water (*mā'*), and earth (*arẓ*), from which all creation mineral, animal, and vegetable is produced.

The respective properties of these elements are said to be as follows: Fire, hot and dry; air, hot and cold; water, cold and wet; earth, cold and dry. A knowledge of the properties of the four elements is required in the so-called science of Da'wah. [DA'WAH.]

ELEPHANT, The year of. Arabic *'Āmu 'l-Fīl* (عام الفيل). The year in which Muḥammad was born. Being the year in which Abrahatu 'l-Ashram, an Abyssinian Christian and Viceroy of the King of Ṣan'ā' in Yaman marched with a large army and a number of elephants upon Makkah, with the intention of destroying the Ka'bah. He was defeated and his army destroyed in so sudden a manner, as to give rise to the legend embodied in the cvth Sūrah of the Qur'ān, which is known as the Chapter of the Elephant.

Professor Palmer says it is conjectured that small-pox broke out amongst the army. [ASHABU 'L-FIL.]

ELIJAH. Arabic *Ilyās* (الياس), *Ilyāsīn* (الياسين); Heb. אֵלִיָּהוּ; New Testament, 'Ηλίας. A prophet mentioned in the following verses in the Qur'ān:—

Sūrah xxxvii. 123: "Verily *Ilyās* (Elias) was of the Apostles; and when he said to his people, 'Will ye not fear, Do ye call upon Ba'l and leave the best of Creators, God your Lord, and the Lord of your fathers in the old time? But they called him a liar; verily, they shall surely be arraigned, save God's sincere servants. And we left him amongst posterity. Peace upon Ilyāsīn (Elias) verily, thus do we reward those who do well; verily he was of our servants who believe."

Sūrah vi. 85: "And Zachariah and John, and Jesus, and *Ilyās*, all righteous ones."

Al-Baiẓāwī says, "It has been said that this Ilyās, is the same as Idrīs, prefather of Noah, whilst others say he was the son of Yāsīn and descended from Aaron, the brother of Moses." [IDRIS.]

ELISHA. Arabic *al-Yasa'* (اليسع). Heb. אֱלִישָׁע. Elisha is mentioned twice in the Qur'ān, under the name *al-Yasa'*.

Sūrah xxxviii. 48: "And remember Ishmael and *Elisha*, and Zu 'l-kifl, for each was righteous."

Sūrah vi. 85, 86: "And Zachariah, and John, and Jesus, and Elias, all righteousness; and Ishmael and *Elisha* and Jonah and Lot, each have We preferred above the worlds."

The Commentators give no account of him except that he was the son of *Ukhtūb*, although the Bible says he was the son of Shaphat. Ḥusain says he was *Ibnu 'l-'ajūz* (the son of the old woman).

ELOQUENCE. The Arabic word *al-Bayān* (البيان), which is defined in the *Ghiyāṣu 'l-Lughah* as speaking fluently and eloquently, occurs once in the Qur'ān, Sūrah lv. 3: "He created man: he hath taught him *distinct speech*." The word also occurs in the Traditions, and it is remarkable that although the Qur'ān is written in rhythm, and in a grandiloquent style, that in the Traditions the Prophet seems to affect to despise eloquence, as will be seen from the following Aḥādīṣ:—Ibn 'Umar says the Prophet said, "May they go to hell who amplify their words." Abū Umāmah relates that the Prophet said, "Eloquence (*al-bayān*) is a kind of magic." Ibn Mas'ūd relates that the Prophet said, "Vain talking and embellishing (*bayān*) are two branches of hypocrisy." 'Amr ibn al-'Āṣī relates that the Prophet said, "I have been ordered to speak little, and verily it is best to speak little." (*Mishkāt*, book xxii. c. ix.)

EMANCIPATION OF SLAVES.

Arabic *I'tāq* (اعتاق). The emancipation of slaves is recommended by the Prophet, but the recommendation applies exclusively to slaves who are of the Muslim faith. He is related to have said: "Whoever frees a Muslim slave God will redeem that person from hell-fire member for member." (*Mishkāt*, book xiii. c. xix.) It is therefore laudable in a man to release his slave or for a woman to free her bond-woman, in order that they may secure freedom in the next world. (*Hidāyah*, vol. i. p. 420.)

ENFRANCHISEMENT.

In an orthodox Muḥammadan state, only those persons who have embraced the Muslim faith are enfranchised; all others are called upon to pay a poll tax (*jizyah*), for which they obtain security (*amān*). Those residents in a Muslim country who are not Muḥammadans are expected to wear a distinctive dress and to reside in a special part of the village or town in which they live. Slaves who may embrace the Muslim faith do not become *ipso facto* enfranchised, unless their master be an unbeliever, in which case their becoming Muslims secures their emancipation. *Zimmīs*, or persons not Muslims in a Muslim state, cannot give evidence against a Muslim. (See *Durru 'l-Mukhtār, in loco.*)

ENOCH.

[IDRIS.]

ENTERING INTO HOUSES.

To enter suddenly or abruptly into any person's home or apartment, is reckoned a great incivility in all eastern countries. With Muḥammadans it is a religious duty to give notice before you enter a house. The custom is founded upon an express injunction in the Qur'ān, Sūrah xxiv. 57–61:—

"O ye who believe! let your slaves and those of you who have not come of age, ask leave of you, three times a day, ere they come into your presence;—before the morning prayer, and when ye lay aside your garments at mid-day, and after the evening prayer. These are your three times of privacy. No blame shall attach to you or to them, *if* after these *times*, when ye go your rounds *of attendance* on one another, *they come in without permission.* Thus doth God make clear to you His signs: and God is Knowing, Wise!

"And when your children come of age, let them ask leave to come into your presence, as they who were before them asked it. Thus doth God make clear to you his signs: and God is Knowing, Wise.

"As to women who are past childbearing, and have no hope of marriage, no blame shall attach to them if they lay aside their *outer* garments, but so as not to shew their ornaments. Yet if they abstain from this, it will be better for them: and God Heareth, Knoweth.

"No crime shall it be in the blind, or in the lame, or in the sick, *to eat at your tables*: or in yourselves, if ye eat in your own houses, or in the houses of your fathers, or of your mothers, or of your brothers, or of your sisters, or of your uncles on the father's side, or of your aunts on the father's side, or of your uncles on the mother's side, or of your aunts on the mother's side, or in those of which ye possess the keys, or in the house of your friend. No blame shall attach to you whether ye eat together or apart.

"And when ye enter houses, salute one another with a good and blessed greeting as from God. Thus doth God make clear to you His signs, that haply ye may comprehend them."

The following are the traditions given in the *Mishkāt* on the subject (book xxii. c. ii.): Muḥammad is related to have said, "Do not permit anyone to enter your home unless he gives a salam first." 'Abdu 'llah ibn Mas'ūd says the Prophet said, "The signal for your permission to enter is that you lift up the curtain and enter until I prevent you." 'Abdu 'llah ibn Busr says, "Whenever the Prophet came to the door of a house, he would not stand in front of it, but on the side of the door, and say, 'The peace of God be with you.'" 'Aṭā' ibn Yasār says the Prophet told him to ask leave to enter even the room of his mother.

ENVY.

Arabic *Ḥasad* (حسد). The word occurs twice in the Qur'ān.

Sūrah ii. 103: "Many of those who have the Book would fain turn you again into unbelievers, even after ye have once believed, and that through *envy*."

Sūrah cxiii.: "I seek refuge . . . . . from the evil of the *envious* when he *envies*."

EPHESUS, The Seven Sleepers of.

[ASHABU 'L-KAHF.]

ESOP.

The Luqmān of the Qur'ān is generally supposed by European writers to be Esop. Sale is of opinion that Maximus Planudes borrowed the greater part of his life of Esop from the traditions he met with in the East concerning Luqmān. [LUQMAN.]

ETERNITY OF PUNISHMENT.

The Muḥammadan religion teaches that all Muslims (*i.e.* those who have embraced the religion of their Prophet) will be ultimately saved, although they will suffer for their actual sins in a purgatorial hell. But those who have not embraced Islām will suffer a never-ending torment in "the fire" (*an-nār*).

Sūrah ii. 37: "Those who misbelieve and call our signs lies, they are the fellows of hell, they shall dwell therein for ever" (*khālidūn*).

Sūrah xi. 108, 109: "And as for those who are wretched—why in the fire shall they groan and sob! to dwell therein for ever (*khālidūn*) as long as the heavens and the earth endure."

Al-Baiẓāwī says the expression "as long as the heavens and the earth endure," is an Arabic idiom expressing that which is eternal.

Ibn 'Arabī (died A.D. 638), in his book *Fuṣūṣu 'l-Ḥikam*, says the word *k͟hālid* in the verses quoted above does not imply eternal duration, but a period, or age, of long duration. Al-Baiẓāwī, the commentator, also admits that the literal meaning of the word only expresses a period of extended duration; but the Jalālān and Ḥusain both contend that its meaning is that of *abadī*, or "never ending," in which no being will be annihilated, and which no one can ever escape.

It is also to be observed that this word *k͟hālid* is that used for the eternity of bliss of those in Paradise:—

Sūrah xi. 110: "As for those who are glad —why in Paradise! to dwell therein for ever" (*k͟halidūn*).

EUCHARIST, OR LORD'S SUPPER.

It is a singular omission in the Qur'ān, that there is no direct allusion to this Christian institution.

Both Sale and Rodwell think that there is a reference to it in the following passages in the Qur'ān, Sūrah v. 112–114:—

"Remember when the Apostles said:—O Jesus, Son of Mary, is thy Lord able to send down a *table* (*mā'idah*, 'a table,' especially one covered with victuals) to us out of heaven? He said, Fear God if ye be believers. They said:—We desire to eat therefrom, and to have our hearts assured; and to know that thou hast indeed spoken truth to us, and we be witnesses thereof. Jesus, Son of Mary, said:—'O God, our Lord! send down a *table* to us out of heaven, that it may become a recurring festival to us, to the first of us, and to the last of us, and a sign from Thee; and do Thou nourish us, for Thou art the best of nourishers.'"

Muslim commentators are not agreed as to the meaning of these verses, but none of them suggest the institution of the Lord's Supper as an explanation. The interpretations are as confused as the revelation.

According to the Imām al-Bag͟hawī, 'Ammār ibn Yāsir said that the Prophet said it was *flesh and bread* which was sent down from heaven; but because the Christians to whom it was sent were unfaithful, it was taken away, and they became pigs and monkeys!

Ibn 'Abbās says that after a thirty days' fast, a table was sent down with seven loaves and seven fishes, and the whole company of disciples ate and were filled (St. Matt. xv. 34). The commentators al-Jalālān also give these two explanations, and the Sacrament of the Lord's Supper is never once suggested by any Muslim doctor in explanation of the above verses.

EUNUCH.

Arabic *k͟haṣī* (خصى). Although in all parts of the East it is usual for wealthy Muḥammadans to keep an establishment of eunuchs to guard the female members of the household, it has been strictly forbidden by Muḥammad for any of his followers to make themselves such, or to make others. 'Us̤mān ibn Maẓ'ūn came to him and said, "O Prophet! permit me to become a eunuch." But Muḥammad said, "He is not of my people who makes another a eunuch or becomes so himself. The manner in which my people become eunuchs is to exercise fasting." (*Mishkāt*, book iv. c. viii.)

EVE.

Arabic *Ḥawwā'* (حواء). [ADAM.]

EVIDENCE.

Arabic *Shahādah* (شهادة). The law of evidence is very clearly laid down in all Muhammadan books of law, especially in the *Hidāyah*, and the *Durru 'l-Muk͟htār*, and it is interesting to observe the difference between the law of evidence as provided for in the law of Moses, and that laid down in Muḥammadan books. In the Pentateuch two witnesses at least were required to establish any charge (Num. xxxv. 30), and the witness who withheld the truth was censured (Lev. v. 1), whilst slanderous reports and officious witnesses were discouraged (Ex. xxiii. 1; Lev. xix. 16), and false witnesses were punished with the punishment due to the offence they sought to establish (Deut. xix. 16). According to Josephus, women and slaves were not admitted to give evidence. (*Ant.* iv. c. 8, s. 15.)

The Sunnī law, as explained by the author of the *Hidāyah* (vol. iii. p. 664), is in many respects the same as the Jewish and is as follows:—

It is the duty of witnesses to bear testimony, and it is not lawful for them to conceal it, when the party concerned demands it from them. Because it is written in the Qur'ān, Sūrah ii. 282, "Let not witnesses withhold their evidence when it is demanded of them." And again, "Conceal not your testimony, for whoever conceals his testimony is an offender."

The requisition of the party is a condition, because the delivery of evidence is the right of the party requiring it, and therefore rests upon his requisition of it, as is the case with respect to all other rights.

In cases inducing corporal punishment, witnesses are at liberty either to give or withhold their testimony as they please; because in such case they are distracted between two laudable actions; namely, the establishment of the punishment, and the preservation of the criminal's character. The concealment of vice is, moreover, preferable; because the prophet said to a person that had borne testimony, "*Verily, it would have been better for you, if you had concealed it*"; and also because he elsewhere said, '*Whoever conceals the vices of his brother Muslim, shall have a veil drawn over his own crimes in both worlds by God.*" Besides, it has been inculcated both by the Prophet and his Companions as commendable to assist in the prevention of corporal punishment; and this is an evident argument for the concealment of such evidence as tends to establish it. It is incumbent, however, in the case of *theft*, to bear evidence to the *property*, by testifying that "a certain person *took* such property," in order to preserve the right of the proprietor; but the word *taken* must be used instead of *stolen*, to the end that the crime may be kept concealed; besides, if the word *stolen* were used, the thief would be rendered liable to amputation; and as, where amputation is incurred, there is no responsibility for the property, the proprietor's right would be destroyed.

The evidence required in a case of *whoredom* is that of four men, as has been ruled in the Qur'ān (Sūrah xxiv. 3); and the testimony of a woman in such a case is not admitted; because, az-Zuhrī says, "in the time of the Prophet and his two immediate successors, it was an invariable rule to exclude the evidence of women in all cases inducing punishment or retaliation," and also because the testimony of women involves a degree of doubt, as it is merely a *substitute* for evidence, being accepted only where the testimony of men cannot be had; and therefore it is not admitted in any matter liable to drop from the existence of a doubt.

The evidence required in other criminal cases is that of two men, according to the text of the Qur'ān; and the testimony of women is not admitted, on the strength of the tradition of az-Zuhrī above quoted. In all other cases the evidence required is that of two men, or of one man and two women, whether the case relate to property or to other rights, such as *marriage*, *divorce*, *agency*, *executorship*, or the like. Ash-Shāfiʿī has said that the evidence of one man and two women cannot be admitted, excepting in cases that relate to property, or its dependencies, such as *hire*, *bail*, and so forth; because the evidence of women is originally inadmissible on account of their defect of understanding, their want of memory and incapacity of governing, whence it is that their evidence is not admitted in *criminal* cases.

The evidence of one woman is admitted in cases of *birth* (as where one woman, for instance, declares that a certain woman brought forth a certain child). In the same manner also, the evidence, of one woman is sufficient with respect to virginity, or with respect to the defects of that part of a woman which is concealed from man. The principle of the law in these cases is derived from a traditional saying of the Prophet: "The evidence of women is valid with respect to such things as it is not fitting for man to behold." Ash-Shāfiʿī holds the evidence of *four* women to be a necessary condition in such cases.

The evidence of a woman with respect to *istihlāl* (the noise made by a child at its birth), is not admissible, in the opinion of Abū Ḥanīfah, so far as relates to the establishment of the right of heritage in the child; because this noise is of a nature to be known or discovered by men; but is admissible so far as relates to the necessity of reading funeral prayers over the child; because these prayers are merely a matter of religion: in consequence of her evidence, therefore, the funeral prayers are to be repeated over it. The two disciples, Muḥammad and Abū Yūsuf, maintain that the evidence of a woman is sufficient to establish the right of heritage also; because the noise in question being made *at the birth*, none but women can be supposed to be present when it is made. The evidence of a woman, therefore, to this noise, is the same as her evidence to a living birth; and as the evidence of women in the one case is admissible, so also is it in the other.

In all rights, whether of property or otherwise, the probity of the witness, and the use of the word *ashhadu*, "I bear witness," is absolutely requisite, even in the case of the evidence of women with respect to birth and the like. If, therefore, a witness should say, "I know," or "I know with certainty," without making use of the word *ashhadu*, in that case his evidence cannot be admitted. With respect to the *probity* of the witness, it is indispensable, because it is written in the Qur'ān, Sūrah lxv. 2, "Take the evidence of two just men"; and also because the probity of the witnesses induces a probability of the truth.

If the defendant throw a reproach on the witnesses, it is in that case incumbent on the Qāẓī to institute an enquiry into their character; because, in the same manner as it is probable that a Muslim abstains from falsehood as being a thing prohibited in the religion he professes, so also is it probable that one Muslim will not unjustly reproach another.

It is not lawful for a person to give evidence to such things as he has not actually seen, excepting in the cases of birth, death, marriage, and cohabitation.

But if a person, in any of the above cases, gives evidence from creditable hearsay, it is requisite that he give it in an *absolute* manner, by saying, for instance, "I bear testimony that A. is the son of B," and not, "I bear testimony so and so, *because I have heard it*," for in that case the Qāẓī cannot accept it.

The testimony of any person who is *property*—that is to say, a slave, male or female—is not admissible; because testimony is of an authoritative nature; and as a slave has no authority over his own person, it follows that he can have no authority over others, *a fortiori*.

The testimony of a person that has been punished for slander is inadmissible, because it is said in the Qur'ān, Sūrah xxiv. 4, "But as to those who accuse married persons of whoredom, and produce not four witnesses of the fact, scourge them with fourscore stripes, and receive not their testimony for ever; for such are infamous prevaricators,—excepting those who shall afterwards repent."

If an infidel who has suffered punishment for slander should afterwards become a Muslim, his evidence is then admissible; for although, on account of the said punishment, he had lost the degree in which he was before qualified to give evidence (that is, in all matters that related to his own sect), yet by his conversion to the Muslim faith he acquires a new competency in regard to evidence (namely, competency to give evidence relative to Muslims), which he did not possess before, and which is not affected by any matter that happened prior to the circumstance which gave birth to it.

Testimony in favour of a son or grandson, or in favour of a father or grandfather, is not admissible, because the Prophet has so ordained. Besides, as there is a kind of communion of benefits between these degrees of kindred, it follows that their testimony in matters relative to each other is in some degree a testimony in favour of themselves, and is therefore liable to suspicion.

So also the Prophet has said, "We are not to credit the evidence of a wife concerning her husband, or of a husband concerning his wife; or of a slave concerning his master; or of a master concerning his slave; or, lastly, of a hirer concerning his hireling."

The testimony of one partner in favour of another, in a matter relative to their joint property, is not admissible; because it is in some degree in favour of *himself*. The testimony, however, of partners, in favour of each other, in matters not relating to their joint property, is admissible, because in it there is no room for suspicion. The testimony of a person who has committed a great crime, such as induces punishment, is not admissible, because in consequence of such crime he is *unjust*. The testimony of a person who goes naked into the public bath is inadmissible, because of his committing a prohibited action in the exposure of his nakedness.

The testimony of a person who receives usury is inadmissible; and so, also, of one who plays for a stake at dice or chess. The evidence of a person guilty of base and low actions, such as making water or eating his victuals on the high road, is not admissible; because where a man is not refrained, by a sense of shame, from such actions as these, he exposes himself to a suspicion that he will not refrain from falsehood.

The evidence of a person who openly inveighs against the Companions of the Prophet and their disciples is not admissible, because of his apparent want of integrity. It is otherwise, however, where a person conceals his sentiments in regard to them, because in such case the want of integrity is not apparent.

The testimony of *ẕimmīs* with respect to each other is admissible, notwithstanding they be of different religions.

The Imām Abū Ḥanīfah is of opinion that a false witness must be stigmatised, but not chastised with blows. The two disciples are of opinion that he must be scourged and confined; and this also is the opinion of ash-Shāfiʻī.

The mode of stigmatising a false witness is this:—If the witness be a sojourner in any public street or market-place, let him be sent to that street or market place; or, if otherwise, let him be sent to his own tribe or kindred, after the evening prayers (as they are generally assembled in greater numbers at that time than any other); and let the stigmatiser inform the people that the Qāẓī salutes them, and informs them that he has detected this person in giving false evidence; that they must, therefore, beware of him themselves, and likewise desire others to beware of him.

If witnesses retract their testimony prior to the Qāẓī passing any decree, it becomes void; if, on the contrary, the Qāẓī pass a decree, and the witnesses afterwards retract their testimony, the decree is not thereby rendered void.

The retraction of evidence is not valid, unless it be made in the presence of the Qāẓī.

EVIL EYE. *Iṣābatu 'l-ʻAin* (اصابة العين). Muḥammad was a believer in the baneful influence of an evil eye. Asmā' bint ʻUmais relates that she said, "O Prophet, the family of Jaʻfar are affected by the baneful influences of an evil eye; may I use spells for them or not?" The Prophet said, "Yes, for if there were anything in the world which would overcome fate, it would be an evil eye." (*Mishkāt*, book xxi. c. i. part 2.)

EXECUTION. The Muḥammadan mode of execution is as follows:—The executioner (*jallād*) seizes the condemned culprit by the right hand, while with a sharp sword or axe he aims a blow at the back of the neck, and the head is detached at the first stroke. This mode of execution is still, or was till lately, practised in Muḥammadan states in India.

If a Qāẓī say, I have sentenced such a person to be stoned, or to have his hand cut off, or to be killed, do you therefore do it; it is lawful for that person to whom the Qāẓī has given the order to carry it out.

And according to Abū Ḥanīfah, if the Qāẓī order the executioner to cut off the right hand, and the executioner wilfully cut off the left, he is not liable to punishment. But other doctors do not agree with him.

EXECUTOR. Arabic *Waṣī* (وصى), a term also used for the testator; *wakīl ʻalā'l waṣīyah* (وكيل على الوصية). An executor having accepted his appointment in the presence of the testator, is not afterwards at liberty to withdraw, and any act indicative of his having accepted the position of executor binds him to fulfil his duties.

A Muslim may not appoint a slave, or a reprobate (*fāsiq*) or an infidel as his executor, and in the event of his doing so, the Qāẓī must nominate a proper substitute. But if none of the testator's heirs have attained their majority, a slave may be appointed as executor until they are of age.

If joint executors have been appointed and

one of them die, the Qāẓī must appoint a substitute in office.

In the cases of infants or absent heirs, the executor is entitled to possess himself *pro tem.* of their property, but he cannot trade with his ward's portion.

If a person die without appointing an executor, the next of kin administers the estate, and it is an arrangement of Muslim law that his father is his executor and not his eldest son. ((*Hidāyah*, vol. iv. p. 554.)

EXILES, The. [MUHAJIRUN.]

EXISTENCES.
The Arabic word *wujūd* (وجود), expresses a substance, or essence, or existence. According to Muḥammadan writers (see *Ghiyaṣu 'l-Lughah*), existences are of three kinds: *Wājibu 'l-wujūd*, "a necessary existence," *e.g.* Almighty God; *mumkinu 'l-wujūd*, "a possible existence," *e.g.* the human kind; *mumtani'u 'l-wujūd*, "an impossible existence," *e.g.* a partner with the Divine Being.

These terms are used by Muḥammadan scholars when discussing the doctrine of the Eternal Trinity with Christian Evangelists.

EXORCISM. [DA'WAH.]

EXPIATION.
The doctrine of expiation or atonement for neglected duties, sins of omission and commission, is distinguished in the Muslim religion from the doctrine of sacrifice; sacrifices being strictly confined to the 'Idu 'l-Aẓḥā', or Feast of Sacrifice in the month of pilgrimage.

There are two words employed in the Qur'ān to express the doctrine of expiation: *kaffārah* (كفارة), from *kafr*, "to hide"; and *fidyah* (فدية), from *fidā'*, "to exchange, or ransom."

(1) *Kaffārah* occurs in the following verses:—

Sūrah v. 49:—

"And therein (Ex. xxi. 23) have we enacted for them, 'Life for life, an eye for eye, and nose for nose, and ear for ear, and tooth for tooth, and for wounds retaliation:'—Whoso shall compromise it as alms shall have therein the *expiation of his sin*; and whoso will not judge by what God hath sent down—such are the transgressors."

Sūrah v. 91:—

"God will not punish you for a mistaken word in your oaths: but he will punish you in regard to an oath taken seriously. Its *expiation* shall be to feed ten poor persons with such middling food as ye feed your own families with, or to clothe them; or to set free a captive. But he who cannot find means, shall fast three days. This is the *expiation* of your oaths when ye shall have sworn."

Sūrah v. 96:—

"O believers! kill no game while ye are on pilgrimage. Whosoever among you shall purposely kill it, shall compensate for it in domestic animals of equal value (according to the judgment of two just persons among you), to be brought as an offering to the Ka'bah; or in *expiation* thereof shall feed the poor; or as the equivalent of this shall fast, that he may taste the ill consequence of his deed. God forgiveth what is past; but whoever doeth it again, God will take vengeance on him; for God is mighty and vengeance is His."

(2) *Fidyah* occurs in the following verses:—

Sūrah ii. 180:—

"But he amongst you who is ill, or on a journey, then let him fast another number of days; and those who are fit to fast and do not, the *expiation* of this shall be the maintenance of a poor man. And he who of his own accord performeth a good work, shall derive good from it: and good shall it be for you to fast—if ye knew it."

Surah ii. 192:—

"Accomplish the Pilgrimage and Visitation of the holy places in honour of God: and if ye be hemmed in by foes, send whatever offering shall be the easiest: and shave not your heads until the offering reach the place of sacrifice. But whoever among you is sick, or hath an ailment of the head, must *expiate* by fasting, or alms, or an offering."

Sūrah lvii. 13:—

"On that day the hypocrites, both men and women, shall say to those who believe, 'Tarry for us, that we may kindle our light at yours.' It shall be said, 'Return ye back, and seek light for yourselves.' But between them shall be set a wall with a gateway, within which shall be the Mercy, and in front, without it, the Torment. They shall cry to them, 'Were we not with you?' They shall say, 'Yes! but ye led yourselves into temptation, and ye delayed, and ye doubted, and the good things ye craved deceived you, till the doom of God arrived:—and the deceiver deceived you in regard to God.'

"On that day, therefore, no *expiation* shall be taken from you or from those who believe not:—your abode the fire!—This shall be your master! and wretched the journey thither!"

(3) In theological books the term *kaffāratu 'z-zunūb*, "the atonement for sins," is used for the duties of prayer, fasting, almsgiving, and pilgrimage. There is also a popular saying that *ziyāratu 'l-qubūr* is *kaffāratu 'z-zunūb*, *i.e.* the visiting of shrines of the saints is an atonement for sins.

Theologians define the terms *kaffārah* and *fidyah* as expressing that expiation which is due to God, whilst *diyah* and *qiṣāṣ* are that which is due to man. [FINES, SACRIFICES.]

For that expiation which is made by freeing a slave, the word, *taḥrīr* is used, a word which implies setting a slave free for God's sake, although the word does not in any sense mean a ransom or atonement for sin. It occurs in the Qur'ān, Sūrah iv. 94, "Whosoever kills a believer by mistake let him FREE a believing neck" (*i.e.* a Muslim slave).

EXTRAVAGANCE.
Arabic *Isrāf* (اسراف). An extravagant person or

prodigal is *musrif*, or *mubaẕẕir*, and is condemned in the Qur'ān:—

Sūrah xvii. 28, 29 : " Waste not wastefully, for the wasteful were ever the brothers of the devil ; and the devil is ever ungrateful to his Lord."

Sūrah vii. 29: " O sons of men, take your ornaments to every mosque ; and eat and drink, but be not extravagant, for He loves not the extravagant."

EYES. Arabic *'Ayn* (عين) ; pl. *Uyūn, A'yun, A'yān.* " If a person strike another in the eye, so as to force the member with its vessels out of the socket, there is no retaliation in this case, it being impossible to preserve a perfect equality in extracting an eye. But if the eye remain in its place, and the sight be destroyed, retaliation is to be inflicted, as in this case equality may be effected by extinguishing the sight of the offender's corresponding eye with a hot iron." (*Hidāyah*, iv. 294.)

There is a tradition by Mālik that the *diyah* or "fine" for blinding one eye is fifteen camels. (*Mishkāt*, book xiv. 167.)   [EVIL EYE.]

EZEKIEL. Arabic *Ḥizqīl.* Not mentioned by name, but there is generally supposed to be an allusion to Ezekiel's vision of the dry bones (Ezek. xxxvii. 1) in the Qur'ān, Sūrah ii. 244:—

" Dost thou not look at those who left their homes by thousands, for fear of death ; and God said to them 'Die,' and He then quickened them again ? "

Al-Baiẓāwī says that a number of Israelites fled from their villages either to join in a religious war, or for fear of the plague, and were struck dead, but Ezekiel raised them to life again.

The Kamālān say he is perhaps the same as Ẕū 'l-Kifl. [ZU 'L-KIFL.]

EZRA. Arabic *'Uzair.* The son of Sharaḥyā', the scribe. Mentioned only once by name in the Qur'ān, Sūrah ix. 30 :—

" The Jews say 'Uzair (Ezra) is a son of God."

Al-Baiẓāwī says that during the Babylonish captivity the *taurāt* (the law) was lost, and that as there was no one who remembered the law when the Jews returned from captivity, God raised up Ezra from the dead, although he had been buried a hundred years. And that when the Jews saw him thus raised from the dead, they said he must be the son of God.

This story is supposed to have been renvealed in the Qur'ān, Sūrah ii. 261 :—

" [Hast thou not considered] him who passed by a city (*which was Jerusalem*), *riding upon an ass, and having with him a basket of figs and a vessel of the juice of grapes and he was 'Uzair,* and it was falling down upon its roofs, *Nebuchadnezzar having ruined it ?* He said, *wondering at the power of God,* How will God quicken this after its death ? —And God caused him to die for a hundred years. Then He raised him to life: and He said *unto him,* How long hast thou tarried *here ?*—He answered I have tarried a day, or part of a day.—*For he slept in the first part of the day, and was deprived of his life, and was reanimated at sunset.* He said Nay, thou hast tarried a hundred years: but look at thy food and thy drink : they have not become changed by time: and look at thine ass.—*And he beheld it dead, and its bones white and shining.—We have done this that thou mayest know,* and that We may make thee a sign *of the resurrection* unto men. And look at the bones *of thine ass,* how We will raise them ; then We will clothe them with flesh. *So he looked at them, and they had become put together, and were clothed with flesh, and life was breathed into it, and it brayed.* Therefore when it had been made manifest to him he said, I know ˎthat God is able to accomplish everything."

F.

FAI' (فى). Booty obtained from infidels. According to Muḥammad ibn Ṭāhir, *fai'* is booty taken from a country which submits to Islām without resistance, as distinguished from *ghanīmah*, or plunder. The Khalīfah 'Umar said it was the special privilege of the Prophet to take booty as well as plunder, a privilege not permitted to any other prophet.

'Auf ibn Malik says the Prophet used to divide booty on the same day he took it, and would give two shares to a man with a wife, and only one share to a man without one. (*Mishkāt*, book xvii. c. xii.)

FAITH. [IMAN.]

FAIZ-I-AQDAS (فيض اقدس, Persian). Communications of *divine grace* made to angels and prophets and other superior intelligences.

AL-FAJR (الفجر), " The Daybreak." The title of the LXXXIXth Sūrah of the Qur'ān, in the first verse of which the word occurs.

FA'L (فال). A good omen, as distinguished from *ṭiyārah*, " a bad omen."

Muḥammad is related to have said, " Do not put faith in a bad omen, but rather take a good one." The people asked, " What is a good omen ? " And he replied, " Any good word which any of you may hear."

Ibn 'Abbās says, " The Prophet used to take good omens by men's names, but he would not take bad omens."

Qaṭ'ān ibn Qabīsah says, " The Prophet forbade taking omens from the running of animals, the flight of birds, and from throwing pebbles, which were done by the idolators of Arabia." (*Mishkāt*, book xxi. c. ii.)

It is, however, very commonly practised

amongst the Muhammadans of India. For example, if a person start out on an important journey, and he meet a woman first, he will take it as a bad omen, and if he meet a man he will regard it as a good one.

AL-FALAQ (الفلق), "The Daybreak." The title of the CXIIIth Sūrah of the Qur'ān. The word signifies *cleaving*, and denotes the breaking forth of the light from the darkness.

FALL, The (of Adam). Is known amongst Muslim writers as *zallatu Ādam*, "the fall," or *slip* of Adam. The term *zallah*, "a slip" or "error," being applied to prophets, but not *z̤amb*, "a sin," which they say Prophets do not commit.

The following is the account of Adam's "*slip*," as given in the Qur'ān, Sūrah ii. 33:—

"And we said, 'O Adam! dwell thou and thy wife in the Garden, and eat ye plentifully therefrom wherever ye list; but to this tree come not nigh, lest ye become of the transgressors.'

"But Satan made them slip (*azallahumā*) from it, and caused their banishment from the place in which they were. And we said, 'Get ye down, the one of you an enemy to the other: and there shall be for you in the earth a dwelling-place, and a provision for a time.'"

Sūrah vii. 18–24:—

"'And, O Adam! dwell thou and thy wife in Paradise, and eat ye whence ye will, but to this tree approach not, lest ye become of the unjust doers.'

"Then Satan whispered them to show them their nakedness, which had been hidden from them both. And he said, 'This tree hath your Lord forbidden you, only lest ye should become angels, or lest ye should become immortals.'

"And he sware to them both, 'Verily I am unto you one who counselleth aright.'

"So he beguiled them by deceits: and when they had tasted of the tree, their nakedness appeared to them, and they began to sew together upon themselves the leaves of the garden. And their Lord called to them, 'Did I not forbid you this tree, and did I not say to you, "Verily, Satan is your declared enemy"?'

"They said, 'O our Lord! With ourselves have we dealt unjustly: if thou forgive us not and have pity on us, we shall surely be of those who perish.'

"He said, 'Get ye down, the one of you an enemy to the other; and on earth shall be your dwelling, and your provision for a season.'

"He said, 'On it shall ye live, and on it shall ye die, and from it shall ye be taken forth.'"

Sūrah xx. 114–120:—

"And of old We made a covenant with Adam; but he forgat *it*; and we found no firmness *of purpose* in him.

"And when We said to the angels, 'Fall down and worship Adam,' they worshipped all, save Eblis, *who* refused: and We said, 'O Adam! this truly is a foe to thee and to thy wife. Let him not therefore drive you out of the garden, and ye become wretched;

"'For to thee *is it granted* that thou shalt not hunger therein, neither shalt thou be naked;

"'And that thou shalt not thirst therein, neither shalt thou parch with heat';

"But Satan whispered him: said he, 'O Adam! shall I shew thee the tree of Eternity, and the Kingdom that faileth not?'

"And they both ate thereof, and their nakedness appeared to them, and they began to sew of the leaves of the Garden to cover them, and Adam disobeyed his Lord and went astray.

"Afterwards his Lord chose him for himself, and was turned towards him, and guided him."

The Muslim Commentators are much perplexed as to the scene of the fall of Adam. From the text of the Qur'ān it would appear that the Paradise spoken of was in heaven and not on earth; and the tradition, that when Adam was cast forth he fell on the island of Ceylon, would support this view. But al-Baiẓāwī says some say the Garden of Eden was situated either in the country of the Philistines or in Fāris, and that Adam was cast out of it and sent in the direction of Hindustān. But this view he rejects, and maintains that the Garden of Eden was in the heavens, and that the fall occurred before Adam and Eve inhabited this earth of ours. [EDEN.]

The Muḥammadan commentators are silent as to the effects of Adam's fall upon the human race.

FALSE WITNESS. The Imām Abū Ḥanīfah is of opinion that a false witness must be publicly stigmatised, but not chastised with blows; but the Imāms ash-Shāfiʿī, Yūsuf, and Muḥammad are of opinion that he should be scourged and imprisoned.

In the Law of Moses, a false witness was punished with the punishment of the offence it sought to establish. Deut. xx. 19: "Thou shalt do unto him as he had thought to do unto his brother." [EVIDENCE.]

FANĀʾ (فناء). Extinction. The last stage in the Ṣufiistic journey. [SUFIISM.]

FAQĪH (فقيه). A Muḥammadan lawyer or theologian. The term is still retained in Spanish as *alfaqui*. [FIQH.]

FAQĪR (فقير). Persian *darwesh*. The Arabic word *faqīr* signifies "poor"; but it is used in the sense of being in need of mercy, and poor in the sight of God, rather than in need of worldly assistance. *Darwesh* is a Persian word, derived from *dar*, "a door," *i.e.* those who beg from door to door. The terms are generally used for those who lead a religious life. Religious faqirs are divided into two great classes, the *ba sharʿ* (with the law), or those who govern their conduct according to the principles of Islām;

and the *be shar'* (without the law), or those who do not rule their lives according to the principles of any religious creed, although they call themselves Musulmāns. The former are called *sālik*, or travellers on the pathway (*ṭarīqah*) to heaven; and the latter are either *āzād* (free), or *majẕūb* (abstracted). The *sālik* embrace the various religious orders who perform the *ẕikrs*, described in the article ZIKR.

The *Majẕūb* faqīrs are totally absorbed in religious reverie. The *Āzād* shave their beards, whiskers, moustachios, eye-brows, and eye-lashes, and lead lives of celibacy.

The *Āzād* and *Majẕūb* faqīrs can scarcely be said to be Muḥammadans, as they do not say the regular prayers or observe the ordinances of Islām, so that a description of their various sects does not fall within the limits of this work. The Sālik faqīrs are divided into very numerous orders; but their chief difference consists in their *silsilah*, or chain of succession, from their great teachers, the Khalīfahs Abū Bakr and 'Alī, who are said to have been the founders of the religious order of faqīrs.

It is impossible to become acquainted with all the rules and ceremonies of the numerous orders of faqīrs; for, like those of the Freemasons and other secret societies, they are not divulged to the uninitiated.

The doctrines of the darwesh orders are those of the Ṣūfī mystics, and their religious ceremonies consist of exercises called *ẕikrs*, or "recitals." [ZIKR, SUFIISM.]

M. D'Ohsson, in his celebrated work on the *Ottoman Empire*, traces the origin of the order of faqīrs to the time of Muḥammad himself:—

"In the first year of the Hijrah, forty-five citizens of Makkah joined themselves to as many others of al-Madīnah. They took an oath of fidelity to the doctrines of their Prophet, and formed a sect or fraternity, the object of which was to establish among themselves a community of property, and to perform every day certain religious practices in a spirit of penitence and mortification. To distinguish themselves from other Muḥammadans, they took the name of Sūfīs. [SUFIISM.] This name, which later was attributed to the most zealous partizans of Islām, is the same still in use to indicate any Musulmān who retires from the world to study, to lead a life of pious contemplation, and to follow the most painful exercises of an exaggerated devotion. To the name of Sūfī they added also that of faqīr, because their maxim was to renounce the goods of the earth, and to live in an entire abnegation of all worldly enjoyments, following thereby the words of the Prophet, *al-faqru fakhrī*, or 'Poverty is my pride.' Following their example, Abū Bakr and 'Alī established, even during the life-time of the Prophet and under his own eyes, religious orders, over which each presided, with Ẕikrs or peculiar religious exercises, established by them separately, and a vow taken by each of the voluntary disciples forming them. On his decease, Abū Bakr made over his office of president to one Salmānu 'l-Fārisī, and 'Alī to al-Ḥasanu 'l-Baṣrī, and each of these charges were consecrated under the title Khalīfah, or successor. The two first successors followed the example of the Khalīfahs of Islām, and transmitted it to their successors, and these in turn to others, the most aged and venerable of their fraternity. Some among them, led by the delirium of the imagination, wandered away from the primitive rules of their society, and converted, from time to time, these fraternities into a multitude of religious orders.

"They were doubtlessly emboldened in this enterprise by that of a recluse who, in the thirty-seventh year of the Hijrah (A.D. 657) formed the first order of anchorets of the greatest austerity, named Uwais al-Karānī, a native of Kārū, in Yaman, who one day announced that the archangel Gabriel had appeared to him in a dream, and in the name of the Eternal God commanded him to withdraw from the world, and to give himself up to a life of contemplation and penitence. This visionary pretended also to have received from that heavenly visitor the plan of his future conduct, and the rules of his institution. These consisted in a continual abstinence, in retirement from society, in an abandonment of the pleasures of innocent nature, and in the recital of an infinity of prayers day and night (*Ẕikrs*). Uwais even added to these practices. He went so far as to draw out his teeth, in honour, it is said, of the Prophet, who had lost two of his own in the celebrated battle of Uḥud. He required his disciples to make the same sacrifice. He pretended that all those who would be especially favoured by heaven, and really called to the exercises of his Order, should lose their teeth in a supernatural manner; that an angel should draw out their teeth whilst in the midst of a deep sleep; and that on awakening they should find them by their bedside. The experiences of such a vocation were doubtless too severe to attract many proselytes to the order; it only enjoyed a certain degree of attraction for fanatics and credulously ignorant people during the first days of Islām. Since then it has remained in Yaman, where it originated, and where its partisans were always but few in number."

It was about A.H. 49 (A.D. 766), that the Shaikh Alwān, a mystic renowned for his religious fervour, founded the first regular order of faqīrs, now known as the *Alwanīyah*, with its special rules and religious exercises, although similar associations of men without strict rules had existed from the days of Abū Bakr, the first Khalīfah. And although there is the formal declaration of Muḥammad, "Let there be no monasticism in Islām," still the inclinations of Eastern races to a solitary and a contemplative life, carried it even against the positive opposition of orthodox Islām, and now there is scarcely a maulāwī or learned man of reputation in Islām who is not a member of some religious order.

Each century gave birth to new orders, named after their respective founders, but in the present day there is no means of ascertaining the actual number of these associations of mystic Muslims. M. D'Ohsson, in the work already quoted, gives a list of thirty-two orders, but it is by no means comprehensive.

No.	Name of the Order.	Founder.	Place of the Founder's Shrine.	Date. A.H.	Date. A.D.
1	Alwaniyah	Shaikh Alwan	Jeddah	149	766
2	Adhamiyah	Ibrahim ibn Adham	Damascus	161	777
3	Bastamiyah	Bayazid Bastami	Jabal Bastam	261	874
4	Saqatiyah	Sirri Saqati	Baghdād	295	907
5	Qadiriyah	Abdu 'l-Qadir Jilani	Baghdād	561	1165
6	Rufaiyah	Saiyid Ahmad Rufai	Baghdād	576	1182
7	Suhrwardiyah	Shihabu 'd-Din	Baghdād	602	1205
8	Kabrawiyah	Najmu 'd-Din	Khawazim	617	1220
9	Shaziliyah	Abu 'l-Hasan	Makkah	656	1258
10	Maulawiyah	Jalalu 'd-Din Rumi	Conyah	672	1273
11	Badawiyah	Abu 'l-Fitan Ahmad	Tanta, Egypt	675	1276
12	Naqshbandiyah	Pir Muhammad	Qasri Arifan	719	1319
13	Sadiyah	Sadu 'd-Din	Damascus	736	1335
14	Bakhtashiyah	Haji Bakhtash	Kīr Sher	736	1357
15	Khalwatiyah	Umar Khalwati	Cæsarea	800	1397
16	Zainiyah	Zainu 'd-Din	Kufah	838	1438
17	Babaiyah	Abdu 'l-Ghani	Adrianople	870	1465
18	Bahramiyah	Haji Bahrami	Angora	876	1471
19	Ashrafiyah	Ashraf Rumi	Chīn Iznic	899	1493
20	Bakriyah	Abu Bakr Wafai	Aleppo	902	1496
21	Sunbuliyah	Sunbul Yusuf Bulawi	Constantinople	936	1529
22	Gulshaniyah	Ibrahim Gulshani	Cairo	940	1533
23	Ighit Bashiyah	Shamsu 'd-Din	Magnesia	951	1544
24	Umm Sunaniyah	Shaikh Umm Sunan	Constantinople	959	1552
25	Jalwatiyah	Pir Uftadi	Broosa	988	1580
26	Ashaqiyah	Hasanu 'd-Din	Constantinople	1001	1592
27	Shamsiyah	Shamsu 'd-Din	Madīnah	1010	1601
28	Sunan Ummiyah	Alim Sunan Ummi	Alwali	1079	1668
29	Niyaziyah	Muhammad Niyaz	Lemnos	1100	1694
30	Muradiyah	Murad Shami	Constantinople	1132	1719
31	Nuruddiniyah	Nuru 'd-Din	Constantinople	1146	1733
32	Jamaliyah	Jamalu 'd-Din	Constantinople	1164	1750

Three of these orders, the Basṭāmīyah, the Naqshbandīyah, and the Bakhtāshīyah, de-

A BASTAMI SHAIKH. (*Brown.*)

scend from the original order established by the first Khalīfah, Abū Bakr. The fourth Khalīfah, ʿAlī, gave birth to all the others. Each order has its *silsilah*, or chain of succession, from one of these two great founders.

The Naqshbandiyah, who are the followers of Khwajah Pīr Muḥammad Naqshband, are a very numerous order. They usually perform the *Zikr-i-Khafī*, or silent devotions, described in the account of ZIKR.

The first duty of the members of this Order is to recite, daily, particular prayers, called the *khātim khāwjagān*; once, at least, the *Istighfār* (Prayer for Forgiveness); seven times the *salāmāt*; seven times the *Fātiḥah* (first chapter of the Qur'ān); nine times the chapter of the Qur'ān called *Inshirāh* (Chapter xciv.); lastly, the *Ikhlāṣ* (Chapter cxii.). To these are added the ceremonies called Zikr. [ZIKR.]

For these recitals they meet together once a week. Ordinarily, this is on Thursday, and after the fifth prayer of the day, so that it occurs after night-fall. In each city, suburb, or quarter, the members of this association, divided into different bodies, assemble at the house of their respective pīr or shaikh, where, seated, they perform their pious exercises with the most perfect gravity. The shaikh, or any other brother in his stead, chants the prayers which constitute the association, and the assembly respond in chorus, "Hū (He)," or "Allāh!" In some cities, the Naqshbandīyah have especial halls, consecrated wholly to this purpose, and then the shaikh only is distinguished from the other brethren by a special turban.

The Bakhtāshīyah was founded by a native of Bukhārā, and is celebrated as being the order which eventually gave birth to the fanatical order of Janissaries. The symbol of their order is the mystic girdle, which they put off and on seven times, saying:—

1. "I tie up greediness, and unbind generosity."
2. "I tie up anger, and unbind meekness."
3. "I tie up avarice, and unbind piety."
4. "I tie up ignorance, and unbind the fear of God."
5. "I tie up passion, and unbind the love of God."
6. "I tie up hunger, and unbind (spiritual) contentment."
7. "I tie up Satanism and unbind Divineness."

The Maulawīyah are the most popular religious order of faqīrs in the Turkish empire.

THE MAULAWI OR DANCING DARWESH.

They are called by Europeans, who witness their zikrs and various religious performances at Constantinople and Cairo, the "dancing," or "whirling" darweshes. They were founded by the Maulawī Jalālu 'd-dīn ar-Rūmī, the renowned author of the *Masnawī*, a book much read in Persia, and, indeed, in all parts of Islām.

They have service at their *takyah*, or "convent," every Wednesday and Sunday at two o'clock. There are about twenty performers, with high round felt caps and brown mantles. At a given signal they all fall flat on their faces, and rise and walk slowly round and round with their arms folded, bowing and turning slowly several times. They then cast

THE MAULAWI OR DANCING DARWESH.

off their mantles and appear in long bell-shaped petticoats and jackets, and then begin to spin, revolving, dancing and turning with extraordinary velocity. [ZIKR.]

THE MAULAWI OR DANCING DARWESH.

The Qādirīyah sprang from the celebrated Saiyid 'Abdu 'l-Qādir, surnamed Pīr-i-Dastagīr, whose shrine is at Bagdad. They practise both the *Zikr-i-Jalī* and the *Zikr-i-Khafī*. Most of the Sunnī Maulawīs on the north-west frontier of India are members of this order. In Egypt it is most popular among fishermen.

The Chishtīyah are followers of Mu'īnu 'd-dīn Banda Nawāz, surnamed the *Gīsū darāz*, or the "long-ringletted." His shrine is at Calburgah.

The Shī'ahs generally become faqīrs of this order. They are partial to vocal music, for the founder of the order remarked that singing was the food and support of the soul. They perform the *Zikr-i-Jalī*, described in the article on ZIKR.

The Jalālīyah were founded by Saiyid Jalālu 'd-dīn, of Bukhārā. They are met with in Central Asia. Religious mendicants are often of this order.

The Suhrwardīyah are a popular order in Afghānistān, and comprise a number of learned men. They are the followers of Shihābu 'd-dīn of Suhrward of al-'Irāq. These are the most noted orders of *ba shar'* faqīrs.

The *be shar'* faqīrs are very numerous.

The most popular order in India is that of the Murdārīyah, founded by Zinda Shāh Murdār, of Syria, whose shrine is at Makanpur, in Oudh. From these have sprung the *Malang* faqīrs, who crowd the bazaars of India. They wear their hair matted and tied in a knot. The Rufā'īyah order is also a numerous one in some parts of India. They practise the most severe discipline, and mortify themselves by beating their bodies. They are known in Turkey and Egypt as the "Howling Darweshes."

Another well-known order of darweshes is the *Qalandarīyah*, or "Wandering Darweshes," founded by Qalandar Yūsuf al-Andalusī, a

A QALANDAR. (*Brown.*)

native of Spain. He was for a time a member of the Bakhtāshīs; but having been dismissed from the order, he established one of his own, with the obligation of perpetual travelling. The Qalandar faqīr is a prominent character in Eastern romance.

Each order is established on different principles, and has its rules and statutes and peculiar devotions. These characteristics extend even to the garments worn by their followers. Each order has, in fact, a particular dress, and amongst the greater part of them this is chosen so as to mark a difference in that of the shaikh from that of the ordinary members. It is perceived principally in the turbans, the shape of the coat, the colours, and the nature of the stuff of which the dresses are made. The shaikhs wear robes of green or white cloth; and any of those who in winter line them with fur, use that kind called petit gris and zibaline martin. Few darweshes use

A RUFA'I IN ECSTATICS. (*Brown.*)

cloth for their dress. Black or white felt dresses called *'abā'*, such as are made in some of the cities of Anatolia, are the most usual. Those

THE SHAIKH OF THE DANCING DARWESHES AT CAIRO. (*From a Photograph.*)

who wear black felt are the Jalwattis and the Qādirīs. The latter have adopted it for their boots, and muslin for their turbans.

Some, such as the Maulawīs and the Bakrīs, wear tall caps called *kulāhs*, made also of felt; and others, such as the Rufāʿīs, use short caps called Ṭāqīyah, to which is added a coarse cloth. The head-dress of almost all the darweshes is called *tāj*, which signifies a "crown." These turbans are of different forms, either from the manner in which the muslin is folded, or by the cut of the cloth which covers the top of the head. The cloth

AN EGYPTIAN FAKIR. (*From a Photograph.*)

is in several gores. Some have four, as the Adhamīs; some six, as the Qādirīs and the Saʿdīs; the Gulshanīs have eight; the Bakhtāshis twelve; and the Jalwatīs eighteen.

AN EGYPTIAN FAQIR. (*From a Photograph.*)

The darweshes carry about with them one or other of the following articles: a small crooked stick or iron, which the devotee places under his arm-pit or forehead, to lean upon when he meditates, or an iron or brass bar on which there is a little artificial hand wherewith to scratch his unwashed body, a bag made of lamb-skin, a *kashkūl* or beggar's wallet.

Generally, all the darweshes allow their beards and mustachios to grow. Some of the orders—the Qādirīs, Rufāʿīs, Khalwatīs, Gulshanīs, Jalwatīs, and the Nūru 'd-dīnīs—still wear long hair, in memory of the usage of the Prophet and several of his disciples. Some allow their hair to fall over their shoulders; others tie it up and put it under their turban.

Whilst private Musulmāns are in the habit of holding rosaries of beads as a pastime, the darweshes do the same, only in a spirit of religion and piety. These rosaries have thirty-three, sixty-six, or ninety-nine beads, which is the number of the attributes of the Divinity [GOD]. Some have them always in their hands, others in their girdles; and all are required to recite, several times during the day, the particular prayers of their order. [TASBIH.]

The individual who desires to enter an order is received in an assembly of the fraternity, presided over by the shaikh, who touches his hand and breathes in his ear three times the words, "*Lā ilāha illa 'llāh*" ("There is no god but God"), commanding him to repeat them 101, 151, or 301 times each day. This ceremony is called the *Talqīn*. The recipient, faithful to the orders of his chief, obligates himself to spend his time in perfect retirement, and to report to the shaikh the visions or dreams which he may have during the course of his novitiate. These dreams, besides characterising the sanctity of his vocation, and his spiritual advancement in the order, serve likewise as so many supernatural means to direct the shaikh regarding the periods when he may again breathe in the ear of the neophyte the second words of the initiation, "*Yā Allāh!*" ("O God!"), and successively all the others to the last, "*Yā Qahhār!*" ("O avengeful God!"). The full complement of this exercise is called *Chilleh*, or "forty days," a period sometimes even longer, according to the dispositions, more or less favourable, of the candidate. Arrived at the last grade of his novitiate, he is then supposed to have fully ended his career, called *Takmīlu 's-Sulūk*, and acquired the degree of perfection for his solemn admission into the corps to which he has devoted himself. During all his novitiate, the recipient bears the name of *Murīd*, or "Disciple," and the shaikh who directs him in this pretended celestial career takes the title of *Murshid*, or "Spiritual Guide."

The founder of the Alwānīs laid out the first rules of this novitiate; they were subsequently perfected by the institution of the Qādirīs, and more so by the Khalwatīs. The darweshes of these two last societies are distinguished in some countries by the decoration of their turban, on the top of which are embroidered the words "*Lā ilāha illā 'llāh*" (There is no god but God).

The tests of the novice among the Maulawīs seem to be still more severe, and the reception of these dervishes is attended with ceremonies peculiar to their order. The aspirant is required to labour in the convent or *takyah* 1,001 successive days in the lowest grade, on which account he is called the *kārrā kolak* (jackal). If he fails in this service only one day, or is absent one night, he is obliged to recommence his novitiate. The chief of the kitchen, or *ashjibāshī*, one of the most notable of the darweshes, presents him to the shaikh, who, seated in an angle of the sofā, receives him amid a general assembly of all the darweshes of the convent. The candidate kisses the hand of the shaikh, and takes a seat before him on a mat, which covers the floor of the hall. The chief of the kitchen places his right hand on the neck, and his left hand on the forehead of the novice, whilst the shaikh takes off his cap and holds it over his head, reciting the following Persian *distich*, the composition of the founder of the order:—

"It is true greatness and felicity to close the heart to all human passions; the abandonment of the vanities of this world is the happy effect of the victorious strength given by the grace of our Holy Prophet."

These verses are followed by the exordium of the Takbīr, "*Allāhu akbar*—God is great," after which the shaikh covers the head of the new darwesh, who now rises and places himself with the Ashjibāshī in the middle of the hall, where they assume the most humble posture, their hands crossed upon the breast, the left foot over the right foot, and the head inclined towards the left shoulder. The shaikh addresses these words to the head of the kitchen:—

"May the services of this darwesh, thy brother, be agreeable to the throne of the Eternal, and in the eyes of our Pīr (the founder of the order); may his satisfaction, his felicity, and his glory grow in this nest of the humble, in the cell of the poor; let us exclaim '*Hū!*' in honour of our Maulawī."

They answer "*Hū!*" and the accepted novice, arising from his place, kisses the hand of the shaikh, who at this moment addresses to him some paternal exhortations on the subject of the duties of his new condition, and closes by ordering all the darweshes of the meeting to recognise and embrace their new brother.

The following is said to be the usual method of admitting a Muḥammadan to the order of a *ba shar'* faqīr in India. Having first performed the legal ablutions, the *murīd* (disciple) seats himself before the *murshid* (spiritual guide). The murshid then takes the murīd's right hand, and requires of him a confession of sin according to the following form.—

"I ask forgiveness of the great God than Whom there is no other deity, the Eternal, the Everlasting, the Living One: I turn to Him for repentance, and beg His grace and forgiveness."

This, or a similar form of repentance, is repeated several times. The murīd then repeats after the murshid:—

"I beg for the favour of God and of the Prophet, and I take for my guide to God such a one (here naming the murshid) not to change or to separate from him. God is our witness. By the great God. There is no deity but God. Amen."

The murshid and the murīd then recite the first chapter of the Qur'ān, and the murīd concludes the ceremony by kissing the murshid's hand.

After the initiatory rite, the murīd undergoes a series of instructions, including the *ẕikrs*, which he is required to repeat daily. The murīd frequently visits his murshid, and sometimes the murshids proceed on a circuit of visitation to their disciples. The place where these "holy men" sit down to instruct the people is ever afterwards held sacred, a small flag is hoisted on a tree, and it is fenced in. Such places are called "*takyah*," and are protected and kept free from pollution by some faqīr engaged for the purpose.

Another account of the admission of a *murid*, or "disciple," into the order of Qādirīyah faqīrs, is given by Tawakkul Beg in the *Journal Asiatique*:—

"Having been introduced by Akhūnd Mullā Muḥammad to Shaikh Mulla Shāh, my heart, through frequent intercourse with him, was filled with such a burning desire to arrive at a true knowledge of the mystical science, that I found no sleep by night, nor rest by day. When the initiation commenced, I passed the whole night without sleep, and repeated innumerable times the Sūratu 'l-Ikhlāṣ:—

'Say: He is God alone;
God the eternal:
He begetteth not, and He is not begotten:
And there is none like unto Him.'
(Sūrah cxii.)

"Whosoever repeats this Sūrah one hundred times can accomplish all his vows. I desired that the shaikh should bestow on me his love. No sooner had I finished my task, than the heart of the shaikh became full of sympathy for me. On the following night I was conducted to his presence. During the whole of that night he concentrated his thoughts on me, whilst I gave myself up to inward meditation. Three nights passed in this way. On the fourth night the shaikh said:—'Let Mullā Sanghim and Ṣāliḥ Beg, who are very susceptible to ecstatic emotions, apply their spiritual energies to Tawakkul Beg.'

"They did so, whilst I passed the whole night in meditation, with my face turned toward Makkah. As the morning drew near, a little light came into my mind, but I could not distinguish form or colour. After the morning prayers, I was taken to the shaikh who bade me inform him of my mental state. I replied that I had seen a light with my inward eye. On hearing this, the shaikh became animated and said: 'Thy heart is dark, but the time is come when I will show myself clearly to thee.' He then ordered me to sit down in front of him, and to impress his features on my mind. Then having blindfolded me, he ordered me to concentrate all my thoughts upon him. I did so, and in an instant, by the spiritual help of the shaikh, my heart opened. He asked me what I saw. I said that I saw another Tawakkul Beg and another Mullā Shāh. The bandage was then removed, and I saw the shaikh in front of me. Again they covered my face, and again I saw him with my inward eye. Astonished, I cried: 'O master! whether I look with my bodily eye, or with my spiritual sight, it is always you I see.' I then saw a dazzling figure approach me. The shaikh told me to say to the apparition, 'What is your name?' In my spirit I put the question, and the figure answered to my heart: 'I am 'Abdu 'l-Qādir al-Jilānī, I have already aided thee, thy heart is opened.' Much affected, I vowed that in honour of the saint, I would repeat the whole Qur'ān every Friday night.

"Mullā Shāh then said: 'The spiritual world has been shown to thee in all its beauty.' I then rendered perfect obedience to the shaikh. The following day I saw the Prophet, the chief Companions, and legions of saints and angels. After three months I entered the cheerless region in which the figures appeared no more. During the whole of this time the shaikh continued to explain to me the mystery of the doctrine of the Unity and of the knowlege of God; but as yet he did not show me the absolute reality. It was not until a year had passed that I arrived at the true conception of unity. Then in words such as these I told the shaikh of my inspiration. 'I look upon the body as only dust and water, I regard neither my heart nor my soul, alas! that in separation from Thee (God) so much of my life has passed. *Thou wert I and I knew it not.*' The shaikh was delighted, and said that the truth of the union with God was now clearly revealed to me. Then addressing those who were present, he said:—

"'Tawakkul Beg learnt from me the doctrine of the Unity, his inward eye has been opened, the spheres of colours and of images have been shown to him. At length, he entered the colourless region. He has now attained to the Unity; doubt and scepticism henceforth have no power over him. No one sees the Unity with the outward eye, till the inward eye gains strength and power.'"

Each institution imposes on its darweshes the obligation to recite certain passages at different times of the day in private, as well as in common with others. Several have also practices which are peculiar to themselves, and which consist in dances, or rather religious circular movements. In each convent there is a room consecrated to these exercises. Nothing is simpler than its construction; it contains no ornaments of any nature; the middle of the room, turned towards Makkah, contains a niche or *miḥrāb*, in front of which is a small carpet, mostly made of the skin of a sheep, on which the shaikh of the community reclines; over the niche the name of the founder of the order is written. In some halls this inscription is surmounted by two others—one containing the Confession of Faith, and the other the words "Bismillāh," &c. ("In the name of God, the most Clement and Merciful.") In others are seen on the wall to the right and the left of the niche tablets, on which are written in large letters the name of God (Allāh), that of Muḥammad, and those of the four first Khalīfahs. At others are seen the names of al-Ḥasan and al-Ḥusain, grandsons of the Prophet, and some verses of the Qur'ān, or others of a moral character.

The exercises which are followed in these halls are of various kinds, a description of which is given in the account of ZIKR.

The more zealous faqīrs devote themselves to the most austere acts, and shut themselves up in their cells, so as to give themselves up for whole hours to prayer and meditation; the others pass very often a whole night in pronouncing the words *Hū* and *Allāh*, or rather the phrase, *Lā ilāha illā 'llāh.* So as to drive away sleep from their eyes, some of them stand for whole nights in very uncomfortable positions. They sit with their feet on the ground, the two hands resting upon their knees: they fasten themselves in this attitude by a band of leather passed over their neck and legs. Others tie their hair with a cord to the ceiling, and call this usage *Chilleh.* There are some, also, who devote themselves to an absolute retirement from the world, and to the most rigid abstinence, living only on bread and water for twelve days successively, in honour of the twelve Imāms of the race of 'Alī. This retirement is called *Khalwah.* They pretend that the shaikh 'Amr Khalwatī was the first to follow it, and that he often practised it. They add that one day, having left his retirement, he heard a celestial voice saying, "O 'Amr Khalwatī, why dost thou abandon us?" and that, faithful to this oracle, he felt himself obliged to consecrate the rest of his days to works of penitence, and even to institute an order under the name of Khalwatīs, a name signifying "living in retirement." For this reason, darweshes of this order consider it their duty, more than any others, to live in solitude and abstinence. The more devoted among them observe sometimes a painful fast of forty days consecutively, called by them *al-arb'aūn* (forty). Amongst them all their object is the expiation of their sins, the sanctification of their lives, and the glorification of Islām; the prosperity of the state, and the general salvation of the Muḥammadan people. The most ancient and the greatest of the orders, such as the Alwānīs the Adhamīs, the Qādirīs, the Rufa'īs, the Naqshbandīs, the Khalwatīs, &c., are considered as the cardinal orders; for which reason they call themselves the *Uṣūls*, or "Originals,"

They give to the others the names of the *Furū'*, or "Branches," signifying thereby secondary ones, to designate their filiation or emanation from the first. The order of the Naqshbandīs and Khalwatīs hold, however, the first rank in the temporal line; the one on account of the conformity of its statutes to the principles of the ten first confraternities, and to the lustre which causes the grandees and principal citizens of the empire to incorporate themselves in it; and the other, because of its being the source of the mother society which gave birth to many others. In the spiritual line, the order of the Qādirīs, Maulawīs, Bakhtāshīs, Rufa'īs, and the Sā'dīs, are the most distinguished, especially the three first, on account of the eminent sanctity of their founders, of the multitude of the miracles attributed to them, and of the superabundance of the merit which is deemed especially attached to them.

Although all of them are considered as mendicant orders, no darwesh is allowed to beg, especially in public. The only exception is among the Bakhtāshīs, who deem it meritorious to live by alms; and many of these visit not only private houses, but even the streets, public squares, bureaux, and public houses, for the purpose of recommending themselves to the charity of their brethren.

They only express their requests by the words "*Shayid Ullāh*," a corruption from "*Shayun li-'llāh*," which means, "Something for the love of God." Many of these make it a rule to live only by the labour of their hands, in imitation of Ḥājī Bakhtāsh, their founder; and, like him, they make spoons. ladles, graters, and other utensils, of wood or marble. It is these, also, who fashion the pieces of marble, white or veined, which are used as collars or buckles for the belts of all the darweshes of their order, and the *kashkūls*, or shell cups, in which they are obliged to ask alms.

Although in no wise bound by any oaths, all being free to change their community, and even to return to the world, and there to adopt any occupation which may please their fancy, it is rarely that anyone makes use of this liberty. Each one regards it as a sacred duty to end his days in the dress of his order. To this spirit of poverty and perseverance, in which they are so exemplary, must be added that of perfect submission to their superior. This latter is elevated by the deep humility which accompanies all their conduct, not only in the interior of the cloisters, but even in private life. One never meets them anywhere but with head bent and the most respectful countenance. They never salute anyone, particularly the Maulawīs, and the Bakhtāshīs, except by the exclamation, "*Yā Hū!*" The words *Ai bi-'llāh*, "thanks to God," frequently are used in their conversation; and the more devout or enthusiastic speak only of dreams, visions, celestial spirits, supernatural objects, &c.

They are seldom exposed to the trouble and vexations of ambition, because the most ancient darweshes are those who may aspire to the grade of shaikh, or superior of the convent. The shaikhs are named by their respective generals, called the Raisu 'l-Mashā'ikh (chief of shaikhs). Those of the Maulawīs have the distinctive title of Cheleby Efendi. All reside in the same cities which contain the ashes of the founders of their orders, called by the name of Āstāneh signifying "the court." They are subordinate to the Muftī of the capital, who exercises absolute jurisdiction over them. In the Turkish Empire the Shaikhu 'l-Islām has the right of removing all the generals of the various orders, even those of the Qādirīs, the Maulawīs, and of the Bakhtāshīs, although the dignity be hereditary in their family, on account of their all three being sprung from the blood of the same founders of their orders. The Muftī has likewise the right to confirm the shaikhs who may be nominated by any of the generals of the orders.

(See *The Dervishes or Oriental Spiritualism*, by John P. Brown; Malcolm's *Persia*; Lane's *Modern Egyptians*: D'Ohsson's *Ottoman Empire*; Ubicini's *Letters on Turkey*; Herklott's *Musalmans*; *Tazkiratu 'l-Auliyā*, by Shaikh Farīdu 'd-Dīn al-'Aṭṭār.)

FAQR (فقر). The life of a Faqīr or an ascetic.

FARA' (فرع). The first-born of either camels, sheep, or goats, which the Arab pagans used to offer to idols. This was allowed by the Prophet at the commencement of his mission, but afterwards abolished. (*Mishkāt*, book iv. c. 50.)

FARĀ'IẒ (فرائض), pl. of *Farīẓah*. "Inheritances." A term used for the law of inheritance, or *'Ilmu 'l-Farā'iẓ*. Farīẓah means literally an ordinance of God, and this branch of Muslim law is so called because it is established fully in the Qur'ān, Sūrah iv. [INHERITANCE.]

FARAQ (فرق). *Lit.* "Separation." *Faraq-i-Awwal* is a term used by Ṣūfī mystics to express that state of mind in which the soul is drawn away from a contemplation of God by a contemplation of his creation; and *faraq-i-ṣānī* (the second separation) is when the soul is constantly contemplating the stability of the creation with the eternity of the Creator. ('Abdu 'r-Razzāq's *Dictionary of Ṣūfī Terms.*)

FĀRAQLĪṬ (فارقليط). The Arabic rendering of the Greek παράκλητος, "Paraclete." Muḥammadan writers assert that it is the original of the word translated *Aḥmad* in the following verse in the Qur'ān, Sūrah lxi. v. 6:—

"And call to mind when Jesus, son of Mary, said:—'O children of Israel! Verily I am an Apostle of God unto you, attesting the *Taurāt* revealed before me, and giving good tidings of a Prophet that shall come after whose name is *Aḥmad*."

Aḥmad is another derivative of the root to which Muḥammad belongs, signifying, like it, "the Praised." It is not improbable that in some imperfect copies of St. John xvi. 7, παράκλητος may have been rendered περικλυτος, which in some early Arabic translation of the Gospel may have been translated *Aḥmad.* In the *Majma'u 'l-Biḥār*, a work written three hundred years ago, the word *fāraqlīṭ* is said to mean a distinguisher between truth and error The word also occurs several times in the well-known Shī'ah work, the *Ḥayatu 'l-Qulūb* (*vide* Merrick's translation, page 86). The author says, "It is well known that his (the Prophet's) name in the Taurāt is *Mūādmūād*, in the gospels (Injīl) *Tābtāb*, and in the Psalms (*Zabūr*) *Farakleet.*" And again (p. 308), "God said to Jesus, O Son of my handmaid . . . verily I will send the chosen of prophets, Aḥmad, whom I have selected of all my creatures, even *Farkaleet*, my friend and servant." [JESUS.]

FARSAKH (فرسخ). Persian *Farsang.* A land measure which occurs in Muḥammadan books of law. It is a league of 18,000 feet, or three and a half miles in length.

FARWAH (فروة). An Arab of the Banū Juẕām and Governor of 'Ammān, who is represented by tradition (upon imperfect evidence) as one of the early martyrs of Islām. Having been converted to Islām, the Roman authorities crucified him. (Muir's *Life of Mahomet*, vol. ii. p. 103.)

FARẒ (فرض). That which is obligatory. A term used for those rules and ordinances of religion which are said to have been established and enjoined by God Himself, as distinguished from those which are established upon the precept or practice of the Prophet, and which are called *sunnah.*

FARẒ KIFĀ'Ī (فرض كفائى). A command which is imperative (*farẓ*) upon all Muslims, but which if one person in eight or ten performs it, it is sufficient (*kifā'ī*), or equivalent to all having performed it.

They are generally held to be five in number: (1) To return a salutation; (2) To visit the sick and inquire after their welfare; (3) To follow a bier on foot to the grave; (4) To accept an invitation to dinner; (5) Replying to a sneeze. [SNEEZING.]

They are also said to be six or seven in number, when there are added one or two of the following: (1) To give advice when asked for it; (2) To help a Muslim to verify his oath; (3) To assist a person in distress. 'Abdu 'l-Ḥaqq says this last injunction applies to all cases, whether that of a Muslim or an infidel. (*Mishkāt*, book v. c. i. part 1.)

FARẒU 'L-'AIN (فرض العين). An injunction or ordinance the obligation of which extends to every Muslim, as prayer, fasting, &c.

FĀSID (فاسد). A seditious or rebellious person

FĀSIQ (فاسق). A term used in Muḥammadan law for a reprobate person who neglects decorum in his dress and behaviour. The acceptance of such a person's evidence is not admissible. He is not regarded as a Muslim citizen, although he may profess Islām.

FASTING. Arabic *Ṣaum* (صوم); Persian *Rozah* (روزه). Fasting was highly commended by Muḥammad as an atonement for sin. The following are the fasts founded upon the example of the Prophet and observed by devout Muslims:—

(1) The thirty-days of the month of *Ramaẓān.* This month's fast is regarded as a divine institution, being enjoined in the Qur'ān (Sūrah ii. 180) and is therefore compulsory. [RAMAZAN.]

(2) The day *'Ashūrā'.* The tenth day of the month Muḥarram. This is a voluntary fast, but it is pretty generally observed by all Muslims, for Abū Qatādah relates that the Prophet said he hoped that the fast of 'Āshūrā' would cover the sins of the coming year. (*Mishkāt*, book vii. ch. vii. pt. 1.) ['ASHURA'.]

(3) The six days following the *'Īdu 'l-Fiṭr.* Abū Aiyūb relates that the Prophet said, "The person who fasts the month of Ramaẓān, and follows it up with six days of the month of Shawwāl, will obtain the rewards of a continued fast." (*Mishkāt*, book vii. ch. vii. pt. 1.)

(4) The Monday and Thursday of every week are recommended as fast days, as distinguished from the Christian fast of Wednesday. Abū Hurairah relates that the Prophet said, "The actions of God's servants are represented at the throne of God on Mondays and Thursdays." (*Mishkāt*, book vii. ch. vii. pt. 2.) These days are only observed by strictly religious Muslims.

(5) The month of Sha'bān. 'Āyishah relates that "the Prophet used sometimes to fast part of this month and sometimes the whole." (*Mishkāt*, book vii. ch. vii. pt. 1.) It is seldom observed in the present day.

(6) The 13th, 14th, and 15th of each month. These days are termed *al-ayyāmu 'l-bīẓ. i.e.* the bright days, and were observed by Muḥammad himself as fasts. (*Mishkāt*, book vii. ch. vii. pt. 2) These are generally observed by devout Muslims.

(7) Fasting alternate days, which Muḥammad said was the fast observed by David, King of Israel. (*Mishkāt*, book vii. ch. vii. pt. 1.)

In the Traditions, fasting is commended by Muḥammad in the following words:—

"Every good act that a man does shall receive from ten to seven hundred rewards, but the rewards of fasting are beyond bounds, for fasting is for God alone, and He will give its rewards."

"He who fasts abandons the cravings of his appetites for God's sake."

"There are two pleasures in fasting, one when the person who fasts breaks it, and the other in the next world when he meets his

Lord. The very smell of the mouth of a keeper of a fast is more agreeable to God than the smell of musk."

"Fasting is a shield."

"When any of you fast utter no bad words, nor raise your voice in strife. If anyone abuse one who is fasting, let him refrain from replying; let him say that he is keeping a fast." (*Mishkāt*, book vii. ch. i. pt. 1.)

FATE. [PREDESTINATION.]

AL-FATḤ (الفتح), "The victory."

The title of the XLVIIIth Sūrah of the Qur'ān, in the first verse of which the word occurs. "Verily We (God) have given thee an obvious victory, that God may pardon thee thy former and later sin."

Professor Palmer says "Some of the commentators take this to mean sins committed by Muḥammad before his call and after it. Others refer the word to the *liaison* with the Coptic handmaiden Mary, and to his marriage with Zainab, the wife of his adopted son Zaid." None of the commentators we have consulted, including al-Baiẓāwī, al-Jalālān, al-Kamālān, and Ḥusain, give the last interpretation. They all say it refers to his sins before and after his call to the Apostleship.

FATHER. In the Sunnī law of

inheritance, a father is a sharer in the property of his son or son's son, taking one-sixth, but if his son die unmarried and without issue, the father is the residuary and takes the whole.

According to the law of *qiṣāṣ* or retaliation, if a father take the life of his son, he is not to be slain, for the Prophet has said, "Retaliation must not be executed upon the parent for his offspring"; and Abū Ḥanīfah adds, "because as the parent is the efficient cause of his child's existence, it is not proper that the child should require or be the occasion of his father's death"; whence it is that a son is forbidden to shoot his father, when in the army of the enemy, or to throw a stone at him, if suffering lapidation for adultery.

In the law of evidence, the testimony of a father for or against his child is not admitted in a court of law.

AL-FĀTIḤAH (الفاتحة). *Lit.* "The

opening one." The first chapter of the Qur'ān, called also the *Sūratu 'l-Ḥamd*, or the "Chapter of Praise." It is held in great veneration by Muḥammadans, and is used by them very much as the *Paternoster* is recited by Roman Catholics. It is repeated over sick persons as a means of healing and also recited as an intercession for the souls of the departed, and occurs in each *rak'ah* of the daily prayer. Muḥammad is related to have said it was the greatest Sūrah in the Qur'ān, and to have called it the *Qur'ānu 'l-Aẓīm*, or the "exalted reading." It is also entitled the *Sab'u 'l-Maṣānī*, or the "seven recitals," as it contains seven verses; also *Ummu 'l-Qur'ān*, the "Mother of the Qur'ān." According to a saying of the Prophet, the *fātiḥah* was revealed twice; once at Makkah and once at al-Madīnah. The *Amīn* is always said at the conclusion of this prayer.

The following transliteration of the Arabic of the Fātiḥah into English characters may give some idea of the rhythm in which the Qur'ān is written:—

"*Al-ḥamdu li-'llāhi Rabbi 'l-'ālamīn.*
Ar-raḥmāni 'r-raḥīm.
Māliki yaumi 'd-dīn.
Iyāka na'budu, wa-iyāka nasta'īn.
Ihdinā 'ṣ-ṣirāta 'l-mustaqīm.
Ṣirāṭa 'llaẕīna an'amta 'alaihim.
Ghairi 'l-maghẓūbi 'alaihim, walā 'ẓ-ẓāllīn.

Which is translated by Rodwell in his English Qur'ān as follows:—

"Praise be to God, Lord of all the worlds!
The Compassionate, the Merciful!
King on the Day of Judgment!
Thee do we worship, and to Thee do we cry for help!
Guide Thou us on the right path!
The path of those to whom Thou art gracious!
Not of those with whom Thou art angered, nor of those who go astray."

FĀṬIMAH (فاطمة). A daughter

of Muḥammad, by his first wife Khadījah. She married 'Alī the cousin of Muḥammad, by whom she had three sons, al-Ḥasan, al-Ḥusain, and al-Muḥsin; the latter died in infancy. From the two former are descended the posterity of the Prophet, known as Saiyids. Fāṭimah died six months after her father. She is spoken of by the Prophet as one of the four perfect women, and is called *al-Batūl*, or "the Virgin," by which is meant one who had renounced the World, also *Fāṭimatu 'z-zuhrā'*, or "the beautiful Fāṭimah."

There are three women of the name of Fāṭimah mentioned in the Traditions: (1) Fāṭimah, the daughter of Muḥammad; (2) The mother of 'Alī; (3) The daughter of Ḥamzah, the uncle of Muḥammad.

AL-FĀṬIMĪYAH (الفاطمية). "The

Fatimides." A dynasty of Khālīfahs who reigned over Egypt and North Africa from A.D. 908 to A.D. 1171. They obtained the name from the pretensions of the founder of their dynasty Abū Muḥammad 'Ubaidu 'llāh, who asserted that he was a Saiyid, and descended from Fāṭimah, the daughter of the Prophet and 'Alī. His opponents declared he was the grandson of a Jew of the Magian religion.

There were in all fourteen Khalīfahs of this dynasty:—

1. *'Ubaidu 'llāh*, the first Fatimide Khalīfah, was born A.D. 882. Having incurred the displeasure of al-Muktafī, the reigning Abasside Khalīfah, he was obliged to wander through various parts of Africa, till through fortunate circumstances he was raised in A.D. 910 from a dungeon in Segelmessa to sovereign power. He assumed the title of al-Mahdī, or "the Director of the Faithful."

[MAHDI.] He subdued the Amīrs in the north of Africa, who had become independent of the Abassides, and established his authority from the Atlantic to the borders of Egypt. He founded Mahadi on the site of the ancient Aphrodisium, a town on the coast of Africa, about a hundred miles south of Tunis, and made it his capital. He became the author of a great schism among the Muḥammadans by disowning the authority of the Abassides, and assuming the titles of Khalīfah and Amīru 'l-Mu'minīn, "Prince of the Faithful." His fleets ravaged the coasts of Italy and Sicily, and his armies frequently invaded Egypt, but without any permanent success.

(2) Al-Qā'im succeeded his father in A.D. 933. During his reign, an impostor, Abū Yazīd, originally an Ethiopian slave, advanced certain peculiar doctrines in religion, which he was enabled to propagate over the whole of the north of Africa, and was so successful in his military expeditions as to deprive al-Qā'im of all his dominions, and confine him to his capital, Mahadi, which he was besieging when al-Qā'im died.

(3) *Al-Manṣūr* succeeded his father in A.D. 946, when the kingdom was in a state of the greatest confusion. By his valour and prudence he regained the greater part of the dominions of his grandfather 'Ubaidu 'llah, defeated the usurper Abū Yazīd, and laid the foundation of that power which enabled his son al-Mu'izz to conquer Egypt.

(4) *Al-Mu'izz* (A.D. 955) was the most powerful of the Fatimide Khalīfahs. He was successful in a naval war with Spain, and took the island of Sicily; but his most celebrated conquest was that of Egypt, which was subdued in A.D. 972. Two years afterwards he removed his court to Egypt, and founded Cairo. The name of the Abasside Khalīfah was omitted in the Friday prayers, and his own substituted in its place; from which time the great schism of the Fatimide and Abasside Khalīfahs is more frequently dated than from the assumption of the title by 'Ubaidu 'llah. The armies of al-Mu'izz conquered the whole of Palestine and Syria as far as Damascus.

(5) *Al-'Azīz* (A.D. 978). The dominions recently acquired by al-Mu'izz were secured to the Fatimide Khalīfahs by the wise government of his son, al-'Azīz, who took several towns in Syria. He married a Christian woman, whose brothers he made patriarchs of Alexandria and Jerusalem.

(6) *Al-Ḥākim* was only eleven years of age when he succeeded his father in A.D. 996. He is distinguished even among Oriental despots by his cruelty and folly. His tyranny caused frequent insurrections in Cairo. He persecuted the Jews and Christians, and burnt their places of worship. By his order the Church of the Resurrection at Jerusalem was destroyed (A.D. 1009). His persecutions of the Christians induced them to appeal to their brethren in the West, and was one of the causes that led to the crusades. He carried his folly so far as to seek to become the founder of a new religion, and to assert that he was the express image of God. He was assassinated in A.D 1021, and was succeeded by his son.

(7) *Aẓ-Ẓāhir* (A.D. 1021) was not so cruel as his father, but was addicted to pleasure, and resigned all the cares of government to his Vizirs. In his reign the power of the Fatimide Khalīfahs began to decline. They possessed nothing but the external show of royalty; secluded in the harem, they were the slaves of their vizirs whom they could not remove, and dared not disobey. In addition to the evils of misgovernment, Egypt was afflicted in the reign of aẓ-Ẓāhir with one of the most dreadful famines that ever visited the country.

(8) *Al-Mustanṣir* (A.D. 1037) was only nine years old when he succeeded his father. The Turks invaded Syria and Palestine in his reign, took Damascus and Jerusalem (1076), where the princes of the house of Ortok, a Turkish family, established an independent kingdom. They advanced to the Nile with the intention of conquering Egypt, but were repulsed.

(9) *Al-Musta'lī* (A.D. 1094), the second son of al-Mustanṣir, was seated on the throne by the all-powerful Vizir Afẓal, in whose hands the entire power rested during the whole of al-Musta'lī's reign. The invasion of Asia Minor by the Crusaders in 1097 appeared to Afẓal a favourable opportunity for the recovery of Jerusalem. Refusing to assist the Turks against the Crusaders, he marched against Jerusalem, took it (1098), and deprived the Ortok princes of the sovereignty which they had oxercised for twenty years. His possession of Jerusalem was, however, of very short duration, for it was taken in the following year (1099) by the Crusaders. Anxious to recover his loss, he led an immense army in the same year against Jerusalem, but was entirely defeated by the Crusaders near Ascalon.

(10) *Al-Āmir* (A.D. 1101).
(11) *Al-Ḥāfiẓ* (A.D. 1129).
(12) *Aẓ-Ẓāfir* (A.D. 1149).
(13) *Al-Fā'iz* (A.D. 1154).

During these reigns the power of the Fatimides rapidly decayed.

(14) *Al-'Āẓid* (A.D. 1160) was the last Khalīfah of the Fatimide dynasty At the commencement of his reign Egypt was divided into two factions, the respective chiefs of which, Dargham and Shāwir, disputed for the dignity of Vizir. Shāwir implored the assistance of Nūru 'd-dīn, who sent an army into Egypt under the command of Shīrkūh, by means of which his rival was crushed. But becoming jealous of Nūru 'd-dīn's power in Egypt, he solicited the aid of Amauri, King of Jerusalem, who marched into Egypt and expelled Shīrkūh from the country. Nūru 'd-dīn soon sent another army into Egypt under the same commander, who was accompanied by his nephew, the celebrated Ṣalāḥu 'd-dīn (Saladin). Shīrkūh was again unsuccessful, and was obliged to retreat. The ambition of Amauri afforded

shortly afterwards a more favourable opportunity for the reduction of Egypt. Amauri, after driving Shīrkūh out of the country, meditated the design of reducing it to his own authority. Shāwir, alarmed at the success of Amauri, entreated the assistance of Nūru 'd-dīn, who sent Shīrkūh for the third time at the head of a numerous army. He repulsed the Christians, and afterwards put the treacherous Vizir to death. Shīrkūh succeeded to his dignity, but dying shortly after, Saladin obtained the post of Vizir. As Nūru 'd-dīn was attached to the interests of the Abassides, he gave orders for the proclamation of al-Mustahdī, the Abasside Khalīfah, and for depriving the Fatimides of the Khalifate. 'Āẓid, who was then on a sick-bed, died a few days afterwards. [KHALIFAH.]

FATQ (فتق). *Lit.* "Opening." A term used by Ṣūfī mystics to explain the eternity of matter, together with its development in creation. ('Abdu 'r-Razzāq's *Dict. of Ṣūfī Terms.*)

FATRAH (فترة). *Lit.* "Languor," or "Intermission." (1) The interval between the supposed revelation of the xcvith Sūrah of the Qur'ān and the lxxivth and xciiird Sūrahs. It is during this period that the powers of inspiration of the Prophet are said to have been suspended, and it was then that he contemplated suicide by intending to cast himself from Mount Ḥirā'. The accounts of this interval are confused and contradictory, and various are the periods assigned to it, viz. from seven months to seven years.

(2) The term is also used for the time which elapses between the disappearance of a prophet and the appearance of another. (*Ghiyāṣu 'l-Lughah in loco.*)

(3) A term used by Ṣūfī mystics for a declension in spiritual life. ('Abdu 'r-Razzāq's *Dict. of Ṣūfī Terms.*)

AL-**FATTĀḤ** (الفتاح), "The Opener" of that which is difficult.

One of the ninety-nine names or attributes of God. It occurs in the Qur'ān, Sūrah xxxiv., "For He is *the opener* who knows."

FATWĀ (فتوى). A religious or judicial sentence pronounced by the Khalīfah or by a Muftī, or Qāẓī. It is generally written. The following is a *fatwā* delivered by the present Muftī of the Ḥanafī sect at Makkah in reply to the question as to whether India is a *Dāru 'l-Islām*. Fatwās are generally written in a similar form to this, but in Arabic:—

"All praises are due to the Almighty, who is Lord of all the creation!

O Almighty, increase my knowledge!

As long as even some of the peculiar observances of Islām prevail in it, it is the Dāru 'l-Islām.

The Almighty is Omniscient, Pure and High!

This is the *Fatwā* passed by one who hopes for the secret favour of the Almighty, who praises God, and prays for blessings and peace on his Prophet.

(Signed) JAMAL IBN 'ABDU 'L-LAH SHAIKH 'UMARU 'L-ḤANAFI, the present Muftī of Makkah (the Honoured).

May God favour him and his father."

FAUJDĀR (فوجدار). An officer of the Moghul Government who was invested with the charge of the police, and jurisdiction in all criminal matters. A criminal judge. *Faujdārī* is a term now used in British courts for a criminal suit as opposed to *dīwānī*, or civil.

FAUTU 'L-ḤAJJ (فوت الحج). The end of the Pilgrimage. [PILGRIMAGE.]

FAẒL (فضل). *Lit.* "That which remains over and above; redundant." A word used in the Qur'ān for God's grace or kindness. Sūrah ii. 244: "God is Lord of *grace* to men, but most men give no thanks." The Christian idea of divine grace, as in the New Testament, seems to be better expressed by *fayẓ-i-aqdas*.

FAẒŪLĪ (فضولي). *Lit.* "That which is in excess." A term used in Muḥammadan law for anything unauthorised, *e.g.* *bai'-i-faẓūlī*, is an unauthorised sale. *Nikāḥ-i-faẓūlī* is an unauthorised marriage, when the contracts are made by an unauthorised agent.

FEAST DAYS. Arabic *'īd* (عيد); dual *'idān*; plural *a'yād*. The two great festivals of the Muḥammadans are, the *'Īdu 'l-Fiṭr*, and the *'Īdu 'l-Aẓḥā*. The other festivals which are celebrated as days of rejoicing are, the *Shab-i-Barāt*, or the fifteenth day of Sha'bān; the *Nau-Roz*, or New Year's day; the *Akhir-i-Chahār Shamba*, or the last Wednesday of the month of Ṣafar; the *Laylatu 'r-Raghā'ib*, or the first Friday in the month of the month Rajab; the *Maulūd*, or the birthday of Muḥammad.

An account of these feasts is given under their respective titles.

FEMALE INFANTICIDE, which existed amongst the ancient Arabians, was condemned by Muḥammad. *Vide* Qur'ān:—

Sūrah xvi. 60: "For when the birth of a daughter is announced to any one of them, dark shadows settle on his face, and he is sad. He hideth himself from the people because of the bad news: shall he keep it with disgrace or bury it in the dust? Are not their judgments wrong."

Sūrah xvii. 33: "Kill not your children for fear of want: for them and for you will We (God) provide."

Sūrah lxxxi. 8: ". . . And when the damsel that had been buried alive shall be asked (at the Day of Judgment) for what crime she was put to death."

FIDYAH (فدية). A ransom. From *fidā'*, "to ransom," "to exchange." An expiation for sin, or for duties unperformed. The word occurs three times in the Qur'ān :—

Sūrah ii. 180: "For those who are able to keep it (the fast) and yet break it, there shall be as an *expiation* the maintenance of a poor man."

Sūrah ii. 192: "Perform the pilgrimage and the visitation of the holy places. . . . But whoever among you is sick, or hath an ailment of the head, must *expiate* by fasting, or alms, or a sacrifice."

Sūrah lvii. 14: "On that day (the Day of Judgment) no *expiation* shall be taken from you (*i.e.* the hypocrites) or from those who do not believe; your abode is the fire."

The other word used in the Qur'ān for the same idea is *kaffārah*. [KAFFARAH, EXPIATION.]

FIG. Arabic *at-Tīn* (التين). The title of the xcvth Sūrah of the Qur'ān, so called because Muḥammad makes the Almighty swear by that fruit in the first verse. Al-Baiẓāwī says God swears by figs because of their great use. They are most excellent, because they can be eaten at once, having no stones, they are easy of digestion, and help to carry off the phlegm, and gravel in the kidneys or bladder, and remove obstructions of the liver, and also cure piles and gout. (*Tafsīru 'l-Baiẓāwī, in loco*).

FIJĀR (فجار). *Lit.* "That which is unlawful." A term given to a series of sacrilegious wars carried on between the Quraish, and the Banū Hawāzin, when Muḥammad was a youth, about A.D. 580–590. (Muir, vol. ii. 3.)

AL-FĪL (الفيل). The title of the cvth Sūrah of the Qur'ān, as it gives an account of the *Aṣḥābu 'l-Fīl*, or "People of the Elephant." [ELEPHANT.]

FINES. Arabic *Diyah* (دية). A term which, in its strictest sense, means a sum exacted for any offence upon the person, in consideration for the claim of *qiṣāṣ*, or retaliation, not being insisted upon. (This does not apply to wilful murder.) A full and complete fine is that levied upon a person for manslaughter, which consists of either one hundred female camels or ten thousand dirhams (silver), or one thousand dīnārs (gold).

The fine for slaying a woman is half that for slaying a man, "because the rank of a woman is lower than that of a man, so also her faculties and uses!" The fine for slaying a *z̤immī* (be he a Jew, Christian, or idolater) is the same as for slaying a Muslim.

A complete fine is also levied for the destruction of a nose, or a tongue, or a virile member, and, also, if a person tear out the beard, or the hair of the scalp, or the whiskers, or both eyebrows, so that they never grow again, "because the beauty of the countenance is thereby effaced."

A complete fine is due for any fellow parts, as for two eyes, two lips, &c., and one half the fine for one single member.

For each finger, a tenth of the complete fine is due, and as every finger has three joints, a third of the fine for the whole is due for each joint.

The fine for a tooth is a twentieth of the complete fine.

A half fine is due for merely destroying the *use* of a limb, but if a person strike another in any way so as to completely destroy the beauty of his person, a complete fine must be paid. Wounds on the face, viz. from the crown of the head to the chin, are specially treated, and are termed *shijāj*. Of *shijāj*, or "face wounds," there are ten: (1) *ḥārifah*, or such as draw no blood—a mere scratch; (2) *dāmiyah*, a scratch which draws blood, without causing it to flow; (3) *damīyah*, a scratch which causes blood to flow; (4) *bāẓi'ah*, a cut through the skin; (5) *mutalāḥimah*, a cut to the flesh; (6) *simḥāq*, a wound reaching into the pericranium; (7) *mūẓiḥah*, a wound which lays bare the bone; (8) *hāshimah*, a fracture of the skull; (9) *munākilah*, a fracture which causes the removal of part of the skull; (10) *āmmah*, a wound extending to the brain.

For an *āmmah* wound, a third of the complete fine is due. Fifteen camels are due for a *munākilah*, ten for a *hāshimah*, five for a *mūẓiḥah*, and so on.

All other wounds on other parts of the body may be adjusted for according to the above scale, but are left to the decision of the judge.

For further information on the subject see "Bābu 'l-Diyah" in the *Durru 'l-Mukhtār*, or the *Hidāyah*, or the *Fatāwā 'Ālamgīrī*, or the *Raddu 'l-Muḥtār*.

FIQH (فقه). The dogmatic theology of the Muslims. Works on Muḥammadan law, whether civil or religious. The books most read by the Sunnīs are the *Hidāyah*, written by a learned man named 'Alī ibn Abī Bakr, A.H. 593, part of which has been translated by the late Colonel Charles Hamilton; the *Durru 'l-Mukhtār*, by 'Alā'u 'd-dīn, A.H. 1088; the *Sharḥu 'l-Wiqāyah*, by 'Ubaidu 'llāh ibn Mas'ūd, A.H. 745; the *Raddu 'l-Muḥtār*, by Saiyid Muḥammad Amīn ibn 'Ābidi 'd-dīn, and the *Fatāwa 'Ālamgīrī* Amongst the Imāmīyah School, or Shī'ahs, the principal works are *Kitābu 'sh-Sharāi'*, by Abū 'l-Ḥasan 'Alī (A.H. 326); the *Muqni' fī 'l-Fiqh*, by Abū Ja'far (A.H. 360); the *Sharā'i'u 'l-Islām*, by Shaikh Najmu 'd-dīn (A.H. 679); and the *Jāmi'u 'l-'Abbāsi*, by Bahā'u 'd-dīn (A.H. 1031).

FĪRĀSAH (فراسة), or *farāsah*. A Ṣūfī term for the enlightenment of the heart. A penetration into the secrets of the unknown. *'Ilmu 'l-firāsah*, "The science of physiognomy."

FIRĀSH (فراش). *Lit.* "A couch." In Muḥammadan law "a wife."

FIR'AUN (فرعون). [PHAROAH.]

FIRDAUS (فردوس). The highest stage of celestial bliss. [PARADISE.]

FIRE. Arabic *nār* (نار). (1) The term *an-nār*, "the fire," is generally used in the Qur'ān and the Traditions for "hell." (2) In the Qur'ān (Sūrah xxxvii. 29) the power of God is declared as being able to "give fire out of a green tree." On which al-Baizāwī says "the usual way of getting fire is by rubbing two pieces of wood together, one of which is *markh* and the other *afār*, and they produce fire, although both the sticks are green. (3) The burning to death of human beings is condemned by Muḥammad, who said "Let no one punish with the punishment of fire but God."

FIRST-BORN. Although the Arabian legislator followed the Mosaic law in so many of his legal enactments, he has carefully avoided any legislation as to the rights of primogeniture, although it formed such a marked feature in the Pentateuch, in which the first-born of man and beast were devoted to God, and were redeemed with a price. In the Muslim law of inheritance, all the sons share equally, whilst in the Mosaic law the eldest son received a double portion of the father's inheritance. (Deut. xxi. 17.)

In cases of chiefship, or monarchy, the eldest son usually inherits, but it rests entirely upon his fitness for the position. Very often the eldest son is passed by and a younger brother selected as ruler. This was also the case amongst the Jews when Solomon succeeded his father in the kingdom. (1 Kings i. 30; ii. 22.)

The curious fact that Muḥammad made no provision for these rights of primogeniture, may have arisen from his having had no son to survive him.

FISH. Arabic *samak* (سمك). (1) Fish which, dying of themselves, float upon the surface of the water, are abominated, according to Abū Ḥanīfah. Ash-Shāfi'ī, and Mālik say they are indifferent. Abū Ḥanīfah teaches that fish which are killed by accident are lawful, but such as die of themselves without any accident are unlawful. There are, however, different opinions regarding those which die of extreme heat or cold.

(2) In the law of sale, it is not lawful to sell fish which is not yet caught, nor is it lawful to sell fish which the vendor may have caught and afterwards thrown into a large tank.

(3) Whilst the destruction of all animals, except noxious ones, is forbidden during the pilgrimage, fishing in the sea is permitted by the Qu'rān, Sūrah v. 97: "Lawful for you is the game of the sea."

FITAN (فتن), pl. of *fitnah*. Seditions; strifes; commotions.

A term specially used for those wars and commotions which shall precede the Resurrection. A chapter is devoted to the subject in all the books of traditions. (See *Ṣaḥīḥu 'l-Bukhārī*, p. 1045; *Ṣaḥīḥu Muslim*, p. 388.)

Muḥammad is related to have said, "There will be Khalīfahs after me that will not go the straight road in which I have gone, nor will follow my example, but in those times there will be the hearts of devils in the bodies of men." Ḥuzaifah then said to him, "O Prophet, what shall I do if I live to see those days?" And the Prophet said, "Obey him who has the rule over you, even though he flog your back and take your money."

Ṣafīyah, in a tradition (recorded in at-Tirmiẕī and Abū Dā'ud), said that Muḥammad said that the succession would last for thirty years, and that the "four rightly directed Khalīfahs" reigned exactly that time: Abū Bakr, two years; 'Umar, ten; 'Usman, twelve; and 'Alī, six.

A mover or leader of sedition is called a *baghī* or rebel. [REBELLION.]

FIṬRAH (فطرة). *Lit.* "Nature." Certain ancient practices of the prophets before the time of Muḥammad, which have not been forbidden by him.

'Āyishah relates that the Prophet said: "There are ten qualities of the prophets—clipping the mustachios, so that they do not enter the mouth, not cutting or shaving the beard, cleansing the teeth (*i.e. miswāk*), cleansing the nostrils with water at the usual ablutions, cutting the nails, cleaning the finger joints, pulling out the hairs under the arm-pits, shaving the hair of the privates, washing with water after passing urine, and cleansing the mouth with water at the time of ablution." (See *Ṣaḥīḥu Muslim.*)

The nose is to be washed out with water because it is supposed that the devil resides in the nose during the night. (See *Mishkāt.*)

There is a chapter in the *Avesta* of the Parsees, containing injunctions as to the paring of the nails of the hands and feet.

FIVE FOUNDATIONS OF ISLĀM. (1) *Shahādah*, or bearing witness that there is no deity but God; (2) *Ṣalāt*, or the observance of the five stated periods of prayer; (3) *Zakāt*, giving the legal alms once a year; (4) *Ṣaum*, fasting during the whole of the month of Ramaẓān; (5) *Ḥajj*, the pilgrimage to Makkah once in a life-time. They are also called the five foundations of *practice*, as distinguished from the six foundations of *faith*. [ISLAM, IMAN.]

FIVE KEYS OF SECRET KNOWLEDGE, which are with God alone, are said to be found in the last verse of the Sūrah Luqmān (xxxist, 34) of the Qur'ān: "God! with Him is (1) the Knowledge of the Hour; (2) and He sendeth down rain; (3) and He knoweth what is in the wombs; (4) but no soul knoweth what shall be on the morrow; (5) neither knoweth any soul in what land he shall die. Verily God is knowing and is informed of all."

FIVE SENSES, The. Arabic *al-ḥawāssul 'l-khamsah* (الحواسّ الخمسة). According to Muḥammadan writers, there are five external (*ẓāhirī*) senses, and five internal (*bāṭinī*) senses. The former being those five faculties known amongst European writers as seeing (*baṣīrah*), hearing (*sāmi'ah*), smelling (*shāmmah*), taste (*z̤āʼiqah*), touch (*lāmisah*). The latter: common sense (*ḥiss-i-mushtarak*), the imaginative faculty (*qūwat-i-k͟hayāl*), the thinking faculty (*qūwat-i-mutaṣarrifah*), the instinctive faculty (*qūwat-i-wāhimah*), the retentive faculty (*qūwat-i-ḥāfiz̤ah*).

FOOD. Arabic *ṭa'ām* (طعام), pl. *aṭ'imah.* The injunctions contained in the Qur'ān (Sūrah ii. 167) respecting food are as follows: "O ye who believe! eat of the good things with which we have supplied you, and give God thanks if ye are His worshippers. Only that which dieth of itself, and blood, and swine's flesh, and that over which any other name than that of God hath been invoked, hath God forbidden you. But he who shall partake of them by constraint, without desire, or of necessity, then no sin shall be upon him. Verily God is forgiving and merciful." Sūrah v. 92.: "O Believers! wine (*k͟hamr*) and games of chance, and statues, and divining-arrows are only an abomination of Satan's work! Avoid them that ye may prosper."

The other injunctions concerning food are found in the Traditions and sayings of Muḥammad.

No animal, except fish and locusts, is lawful food unless it be slaughtered according to the Muḥammadan law, namely, by drawing the knife across the throat and cutting the windpipe, the carotid arteries, and the gullet, repeating at the same time the words "*Bi'smi 'llāhi, Allāhu akbar*," *i.e.* "In the name of God, God is great." A *clean* animal, so slaughtered, becomes lawful food for Muslims, whether slaughtered by Jews, Christians, or Muḥammadans, but animals slaughtered by either an idolater, or an apostate from Islām, is not lawful.

Z̤abḥ, or the slaying of animals, is of two kinds. *Ik͟htiyārī*, or of choice, and *Iẓṭirārī*, or of necessity. The former being the slaughtering of animals in the name of God, the latter being the slaughter effected by a wound, as in shooting birds or animals, in which case the words *Bi'smi 'llāhi, Allāhu akbar* must be said at the time of the discharge of the arrow from the bow or the shot from the gun.

According to the *Hidāyah*, all quadrupeds that seize their prey with their teeth, and all birds which seize it with their talons are unlawful, because the Prophet has prohibited mankind from eating them. Hyenas, foxes, elephants, weasels, pelicans, kites, carrion crows, ravens, crocodiles, otters, asses, mules, wasps, and in general all insects, are forbidden. But there is some doubt as to the lawfulness of horses' flesh. Fishes dying of themselves are also forbidden.

The prohibition of wine in the Qur'ān under the word *k͟hamr* is held to exclude all things which have an intoxicating tendency, such as opium, chars, bhang, and tobacco.

A Muslim can have no religious scruples to eat with a Christian, as long as the food eaten is of a lawful kind. Saiyid Aḥmad Khān Bahādur, C.S.I., has written a treatise proving that Muḥammadans can eat with the *Ahl-i-Kitāb*, namely, Jews or Christians. The Muḥammadans of India, whilst they will eat food cooked by idolatrous Hindūs, refuse to touch that cooked either by Native or European Christians; and they often refuse to allow Christians to draw water from the public wells, although Hindūs are permitted to do so. Such objections arise solely from jealousy of race, and an unfriendly feeling towards the ruling power. In Afghanistan and Persia, no such objections exist; and no doubt much evil has been caused by Government allowing Hindūstānī Muslims to create a religious custom which has no foundation whatever, except that of national hatred to their English conquerors. [EATING.]

FORBIDDEN FRUIT, The. Mentioned in the Qur'ān, Sūrah ii. 33: "And we (God) said, 'O Adam, dwell thou and thy wife in Paradise and eat therefrom amply as you wish; but do not draw near this tree' (*shajarah*)."

Concerning this tree, the Commentators have various opinions. Ḥusain says some say it was a fig tree, or a vine, but most people think it was a grain of wheat (*ḥinṭah*) from a wheat stalk. [ADAM, FALL.]

FORGIVENESS. [PARDON, 'AFU.]

FORGIVENESS OF INJURIES. Enjoined in the Qur'ān in the following words (Sūrah xlii. 38): "Let the recompense of evil be only a like evil—but he who forgiveth and maketh peace, shall find his reward for it from God; verily He loveth not those who act unjustly. And there shall be no way open (*i.e.* no blame) against those who, after being wronged, avenge themselves. . . . . Whoso beareth wrongs and forgiveth—this is a bounden duty."

FORNICATION. Arabic *zinā'* (زناء). The word *zinā'* includes both fornication with an unmarried person, and adultery with a married person. [ADULTERY.]

The sin of fornication must be established, as in the case of adultery, either by *proofs* or by confession.

To establish it by proof, four witnesses are required, and if any person bring an accusation against a woman of chaste reputation and fail to establish it, he must be punished with eighty stripes. [QAZF.]

When a person for conscience sake confesses the sin of fornication, the confession must be repeated four times at four different appearances before a qāẓī, and the person confessing must be very exact and particular as to the circumstances, so that there can be no mistake. A self-accused person may also retract the confession at any period before, or during, the infliction of the punishment, and the retractation must be accepted.

The punishment for fornication is one hundred stripes (or fifty for a slave). The scourging to be inflicted upon a man standing and upon a woman sitting; and the woman is not to be stripped. It should be done with moderation, with a strap or whip, which has no knots upon it, and the stripes should be given not *all* upon the same part of the body. [DIRRAH.]

In some countries banishment is added to the punishment of scourging for fornication. especially if the sin is often repeated, so as to constitute common prostitution.

The law is founded upon the following verse in the Qur'ān, Sūrah xxiv. 2–5:—

"The whore and the whoremonger—scourge each of them with an hundred stripes; and let not compassion keep you from *carrying out* the sentence of God, if ye believe in God and the last day: And let some of the faithful witness their chastisement.

"The whoremonger shall not marry other than a whore or an idolatress; and the whore shall not marry other than a whoremonger or an idolater. Such *alliances* are forbidden to the faithful.

"They who defame virtuous women, and bring not four witnesses, scourge them with *fourscore* stripes, and receive ye not their testimony for ever, for these are perverse persons—

"Save those who afterwards repent and live virtuously; for truly God is Lenient, Merciful!"

The Muḥammadan law differs from Jewish law with regard to fornication; see Exodus xxii. 16, 17:—"If a man entice a maid that is not betrothed, and lie with her, he shall surely endow her to be his wife. If her father utterly refuse to give her unto him, he shall pay money according to the dowry of virgins." Deut. xxii. 25–29:—"If a damsel that is a virgin be betrothed unto a husband, and a man find her in the city and lie with her, then ye shall bring them out unto the gate of the city, and ye shall stone them with stones that they die: the damsel because she cried not, being in the city, and the man because he hath humbled his neighbour's wife; so shalt thou put away evil from among you. But if a man find a betrothed damsel in the field, and the man force her and lie with her, then the man only that lay with her shall die. But unto the damsel shalt thou do nothing: there is in the damsel no sin worthy of death. . . . If a man find a damsel that is a virgin, which is not betrothed, and lay hold on her, and lie with her, and they be found, then the man that lay with her shall give unto the damsel's father fifty shekels of silver, and she shall be his wife; because he hath humbled her, he may not put her away all his days."

FORTUNE-TELLING.

Arabic *kahānah* (كهانة). Mu'āwiyah ibn Ḥakam relates that he asked the Prophet if it were right to consult fortune-tellers about future events, and he replied, "Since you have embraced Islām, you must not consult them." [MAGIC.]

FOSTERAGE.

Arabic *raẓā'ah*, *riẓā'ah* (رضاعة). According to Abū Ḥanīfah, the period of fosterage is thirty months; but the two disciples, Yūsuf and Muḥammad, hold it to be two years, whilst Ẓufar maintains that it is three years. Fosterage with respect to the prohibitions attached to it is of two kinds; first, where a woman takes a strange child to nurse, by which all future matrimonial connection between that child and the woman, or her relations within the prohibited degrees, is rendered illegal; secondly, where a woman nurses two children, male and female, upon the same milk, which prohibits any future matrimonial connection between them. For further particulars on this subject, see Hamilton's *Hidāyah*, vol. i. page 187.

FOUNDLING.

Arabic *laqīṭ* (لقيط). *Lit.* "That which is picked up." The person who finds the child is called the *multaqiṭ*. The taking up of a foundling is said to be a laudable and generous act, and where the finder sees that the child's life is in peril, it is an incumbent religious duty. (*Hidāyah*, vol. ii. p. 252.)

The maintenance of a foundling is defrayed from the public treasury, but the finder is not to demand anything for his trouble and expense, but after the finding of the child has been reported to the magistrate, the child is legally placed under the care of the *multaqiṭ*, and supported by the state. A foundling is declared to be free, and not a slave, and unless he be found on the land or property of a Jew or Christian, he is declared a Muslim. But if the child be found on the property of a Jew or Christian, he will be declared a Jew or Christian as the case may be. The *multaqiṭ* cannot contract the foundling in marriage without the sanction of the magistrate, but he may send him to school and in every respect see to his education and training without consulting the magistrate.

FRIDAY.

Arabic *Jum'ah* (جمعة). "The Day of Assembly." The Muḥammadan Sabbath, on which they assemble in the *Jāmi' 'Masjid*, or chief mosque, and recite two rik'ahs of prayers and listen to the oration, or khuṭbah at the time of mid-day prayer. Muḥammad claims in the Traditions to have established Friday as a day of worship by divine command. He says, "Friday was ordered as a divine day of worship both for the Jew and Christian, but they have acted contrary to the command The Jew fixed Saturday and the Christian fixed Sunday."

According to the same traditions, Friday is "the best day on which the sun rises, the day on which Adam was taken into Paradise and turned out of it, the day on which he repented and on which he died. It will also be the Day of Resurrection."

There is also a certain hour on Friday (known only to God) on which a Muslim obtains all the good he asks of the Almighty. Muḥammad prayed that God may put a seal on the heart of every Muslim who through negligence omits prayer for three successive Fridays. Muḥammad said:—

"Whoever bathes on Friday and comes to prayers in the beginning and comes on foot and sets near the Imām and listens to the khuṭbah, and says nothing playful, but sits silent, every step he took will get the rewards of a whole year's worshipping and rewards of one year's fast and one year's prayings at night."

"There are three descriptions of people present on Friday, one of them who comes to the masjid talking triflingly, and this is what he gets instead of rewards; and there is a man who is present for making supplications, and he asks God, and if He wills He gives him, if not, refuses; the third a man who attends to hear the khuṭbah and is silent, and does not incommode anyone, and this Friday covers his sins till the next, and three days longer; for God says, Whoever doth one good act will receive ten in return." (*Mishkāt*, book iv. c. xliii.) [KHUTBAH.]

FRIENDSHIP with Jews and Christians is condemned in the Qur'ān, Sūrah v. 56: "O ye who believe! take not the Jews and Christians for your friends (or patrons); they are the friends of each other; but whoso amongst you takes them for friends, verily he is of them, and, verily, God guides not an unjust people."

FRUITS OF THE EARTH are described in the Qur'ān as evidences of God's love and care for his creatures.

Sūrah vi. 142:—

"He it is who produceth gardens of the vine trellised and untrellised, and the palm trees, and the corn of various food, and olives, and pomegranates, like and unlike. Eat of their fruit when they bear fruit, and pay the due thereof on the day of its ingathering: and be not prodigal, for God loveth not the prodigal."

Sūrah xiii. 3:—

"And He it is who hath outstretched the earth, and placed on it the firm mountains, and rivers: and of every fruit He hath placed on it two kinds: He causeth the night to enshroud the day. Verily in this are signs for those who reflect.

"And on the earth hard by each other are its various portions: gardens of grapes and corn, and palm trees single or clustered. Though watered by the same water, yet some make we more excellent as food than other: Verily in all this are signs for those who understand."

FUGITIVES. (1) A fugitive slave, either male or female, is called *ābiq* (آبق). The capture of a fugitive slave is a laudable act, and the captor is entitled to a reward of forty dirhams. (2) A fugitive on account of religion is called *muhājir* (مهاجر). Special blessings are promised to those who flee their country on account of their being Muslims.

Sūrah iv. 101: "Whosoever flees in the way of God shall find in the earth a spacious refuge."

Sūrah xxii. 57: "Those who flee in God's way and then are slain or die, God will provide them with a godly provision." [SLAVES, MUHAJIR.]

FULS (فلس). An idol (or an idol temple), belonging to the Banī Ṭaiy, a tribe divided between the profession of idolatry and Christianity. Destroyed by 'Alī by order of Muḥammad, A.H. 630. (Muir, vol. iv. p. 177.)

FUNERAL. Arabic *janāzah* (جنازة). [BURIAL.]

FURĀT (فرات). The river Euphrates, said to be one of the rivers of Eden. [EDEN.]

AL-FURQĀN (الفرقان). (1) The title of the xxvth Sūrah of the Qur'ān. (2) One of the titles of the Qur'ān (Sūrah ii. 181; iii. 2; xxv. 1). (3) The title given to the Taurāt revealed to Moses (Sūrah ii. 50; xxi. 49). (4) The victory on the day of the battle of Badr (Sūrah viii. 42). (5) A term used by Ṣūfī mystics for a distinguishing between truth and error.

Muḥammadan lexicographers are unanimous in interpretating the word *furqān* to mean that which distinguishes between good and evil, lawful and unlawful. The Jews use the word *perek*, or *pirka*, from the same root, to denote a section or portion of scripture.

FUṢṢILAT (فصلت). *Lit.* "Were made plain." A title of the XLIst Sūrah of the Qur'ān, from the word occurring in the second verse. The Sūrah is also known as the *Hāmīm as-Sajdah*, to distingush it from the Sūrah XXXIInd, which is also called *as-Sajdah*, or "Adoration."

FUTURE LIFE. The immortality of the soul and the reality of a future life are very distinctive doctrines of the religion of Muḥammad, and very numerous are the references to it in the Qur'ān. The whole system of Islām is based upon the belief in the future existence of the soul of man. A description of the special character of this future life will be found in the article on PARADISE.

The terms generally used to express a future life are *Dāru 'l-Akhirat*, *Dāru 'l-Baqā'* *Dāru 'l-Uqbā*.

G.

GABR (گبر). [MAJUS.]

GABRIEL. Arabic *Jibrāʾīl* (جبرائيل). In the Qurʾān *Jibrīl* (جبريل). The angelic being who is supposed to have been the medium of the revelation of the Qurʾān to Muḥammad. He is mentioned only twice in the Qurʾān by name. Sūratu 'l-Baqarah ii. 91: "Whoso is the enemy of Gabriel—for he hath by God's leave caused to descend on thy heart the confirmation of previous revelations," &c. And again in Sūratu 't-Taḥrīm, lxvi. 4: "God is his Protector, and Gabriel." He is, however, supposed to be spoken of in Sūrahs ii. 81, 254; v. 109; xvi. 104, as "the Holy Spirit," *Rūḥu 'l-Qudus*; in Sūrah xxvi. 193, as "the Faithful Spirit," *ar-Rūḥu 'l-Amīn*; and in liii. 5, as "one terrible in power," *Shadīdu 'l-Quwā*.

The account of Gabriel's first appearance to Muḥammad is related as follows by Abū 'l-Fidāʾ: "Muḥammad was wont to retire to Mount Ḥirā for a month every year. When the year of his mission came, he went to Mount Ḥirā in the month of Ramaẓān for the purpose of sojourning there, having his family with him; and there he abode until the night arrived in which God was pleased to bless him. Gabriel came to him, and said to him, 'Recite!' And he replied, 'What shall I recite?' And he said, 'Recite thou, in the name of thy Lord who created. Created man from clots of blood. Recite thou! For the Lord is most Beneficent. Who hath taught the use of the pen. Hath taught man that which he knoweth not.' After this the Prophet went to the middle of the mountain, and heard a voice from heaven which said, 'Thou art the Messenger of God and I am Gabriel.' He continued standing in his place to contemplate Gabriel until he withdrew." [QURAN.]

Sir William Muir says: "It is clear that at a later period at least, if not from the first, Mahomet confounded Gabriel with the Holy Ghost. The idea may have arisen from some such misapprehension as the following. Mary conceived Jesus by the power of the Holy Ghost, which overshadowed her. But it was Gabriel who visited Mary to announce the conception of the Saviour. The Holy Ghost was therefore another name for Gabriel. We need hardly wonder at this ignorance when Mahomet seems to have believed that Christians held Mary to be the third person in the Trinity!"

With reference to the verse quoted above, from the Sūratu 'l-Baqarah, Sale says the Commentators say that the Jews asked what angel it was that brought the Qurʾān to Muḥammad, and on being told that it was Gabriel, they replied that he was their enemy, and the messenger of wrath and judgment; but that if it had been Michael they would have believed on him, because that angel was their friend, and the messenger of peace and plenty.

It is also important to observe that the only distinct assertion of Gabriel being the medium of divine revelation, occurs in a Madanīyah Sūrah.

Gabriel is called in Muslim books *ar-Rūḥu 'l-Aʿẓam*, "The Supreme Spirit"; *ar-Rūḥu 'l-Mukarram*, "The Honoured Spirit"; *Rūḥu 'l-Ilqāʾ*, "The Spirit of casting into"; *Rūḥu 'l-Qudus*, "The Holy Spirit"; and *ar-Rūḥu 'l-Amīn*, "The Faithful Spirit."

GAMBLING (Arabic *maisir*, ميسر; *qimār* قمار) is forbidden in the Qurʾān.

Sūrah ii. 216: "They will ask thee concerning wine, and games of chance. Say both is a great sin, and advantage also, to men, but their sin is greater than their advantage."

Sūrah v. 93: "Only would Satan sow hatred and strife among you, by wine and games of chance, and turn you aside from the remembrance of God, and from prayer: will ye not, therefore, abstain from them?"

The evidence of a gambler is not admissible in a Muḥammadan court of law, because gaming is a great crime. (*Hidāyah* ii. p. 688.)

GARDEN. Arabic *jannah* (جنة); Heb. גַּן, pl. גַּנִּים. In the Qurʾān the residence of our first parents is called *Al-jannah*, "the garden," and not *Jannatu ʿAdn*, or the "Garden of Eden," *Jannatu ʿAdn* being the fourth stage of celestial bliss. *Al-jannāt*, "the gardens," is a term frequently used in the Qurʾān for the state of heavenly joy; and the stages of paradise, which are eight, are known as—(1) The *garden* of eternity, (2) The dwelling of peace, (3) The dwelling which abideth, (4) The *garden* of Eden, (5) The *garden* of refuge, (6) The *garden* of delight, (7) The *garden* of ʿIllīyūn, (8) The *garden* of Paradise. [PARADISE.]

GENII. Arabic *jinn* (جن), and *jānn* (جان). Muḥammad was a sincere believer in the existence of good and evil genii, and has left a record of his belief in the LXXIInd chapter of his Qurʾān, entitled the *Sūratu 'l-Jinn*. It opens thus:—

"SAY: It hath been revealed to me that a company of JINN listened and said,—Verily, we have heard a marvellous discourse (Qurʾān);

"It guideth to the truth; wherefore we believed in it, and we will not henceforth join any *being* with our Lord;

"And He,—may the majesty of our Lord be exalted!—hath taken no spouse neither hath he any offspring.

"But the foolish among us hath spoken of God that which is unjust:

"And we verily thought that no one amongst men or jinn would have uttered a lie against God.

"There are indeed people among men, who have sought for refuge unto people among jinn: but they only increased their folly:

"And they thought as ye think, that God would not raise any from the dead.

"And the Heavens did we essay, but found them filled with a mighty garrison, and with flaming darts;

"And we sat on some of the seats to listen, but whoever listeneth findeth an ambush *ready* for him of flaming darts."

The following exhaustive account of the Muḥammadan belief on the subject is taken from the writings of the late Mr. Lane (the learned author of the *Modern Egyptians* and of *Notes on the Arabian Nights*), but slightly altered to meet the requirements of the present work.

According to a tradition from the Prophet, this species consists of five orders, namely, Jānn (who are the least powerful of all), Jinn, Shaiṭāns (or devils), ʿIfrīts, and Marīds. The last, it is added, are the most powerful; and the Jānn are transformed Jinn, like as certain apes and swine were transformed men. It must, however, be remarked that the terms *Jinn* and *Jānn* are generally used indiscriminately as names of the whole species, whether good or bad, and that the former term is the more common. Also, that *Shaiṭān* is commonly used to signify any evil genius. An *ʿIfrīt* is a powerful evil genius; a *Marīd*, an evil genius of the most powerful class. The Jinn (but, generally speaking, evil ones) are called by the Persians *Deves*, the most powerful evil Jinn, *Narahs* (which signifies "males," though they are said to be males and females); the good Jinn, *Pīrīs*, though this term is commonly applied to females. In a tradition from the Prophet, it is said, "The Jānn were created of a smokeless fire." The word which signifies "a smokeless fire' has been misunderstood by some as meaning "the flame of fire." *Al-Jauharī* (in the *Ṣiḥāḥ*) renders it rightly; and says that of this fire was the Shaiṭān or Iblīs created. *Al-Jānn* is sometimes used as a name for Iblīs, as in the following verse of the Qur'ān (Sūrah xv. 27): "And the Jānn [the father of the Jinn, *i.e.* Iblīs] we had created before [*i.e.* before the creation of Adam] of the fire of the Samūm [*i.e.* of the fire without smoke]." *Jānn* also signifies "a serpent," as in other passages of the Qur'ān, and is used in the same book as synonymous with Jinn. In the last sense it is generally believed to be used in the tradition quoted in the commencement of this paragraph. There are several apparently contradictory traditions from the Prophet, which are reconciled by what has been above stated; in one it is said that Iblīs was the father of all the Jānn and Shaiṭān; Jānn being here synonymous with Jinn; in another, that Jānn was the father of all the Jinn, here Jānn being used as a name for *Iblīs.*

"It is held," says al-Qazwīnī, "that the Jinn are aerial animals, with transparent bodies, which can assume various forms. People differ in opinion respecting these beings; some consider the Jinn and Shaiṭāns as unruly men, but these persons are of the Muʿtazilahs [a sect of Muslim freethinkers], and some hold that God, whose name be exalted, created the angels of the light of fire, and the Jinn of its flame [but this is at variance with the general opinion], and the Shaiṭāns of its smoke [which is also at variance with the common opinion]; and that [all] these kinds of beings are [usually] invisible to men, but that they assume what forms they please, and when their form becomes condensed they are visible." This last remark illustrates several descriptions of genii in the *Arabian Nights*, where the form of the monster is at first undefined, or like an enormous pillar, and then gradually assumes a human shape and less gigantic size.

It is said that God created the Jānn [or Jinn] two thousand years before Adam [or, according to some writers, much earlier], and that there are believers and infidels and every sect among them, as among men. Some say that a prophet named Yūsuf was sent to the Jinn; others, that they had only preachers or admonishers; others, again, that seventy apostles were sent, before Muḥammad, to Jinn and men conjointly. It is commonly believed that the preadamite Jinn were governed by forty (or, according to some, seventy-two) kings, to each of whom the Arab writers give the name of Sulaiman (or Solomon); and that they derive their appellation from the last of these, who was called Jānn ibn Jānn, and who, some say, built the Pyramids of Egypt.

The following account of the preadamite Jinn is given by al-Qazwīnī:—

"It is related in histories that a race of Jinn in ancient times, before the creation of Adam, inhabited the earth, and covered it, the land and the sea, and the plains and the mountains; and the favours of God were multiplied upon them, and they had government, and prophecy, and religion and law; but they transgressed and offended, and opposed their prophets, and made wickedness to abound in the earth: whereupon God, whose name be exalted, sent against them an army of angels, who took possession of the earth, and drove away the Jinn to the regions of the islands, and made many of them prisoners; and of those who were made prisoners was ʿAzazīl (afterwards called Iblīs, from his despair), and a slaughter was made among them. At that time, ʿAzazīl was young; he grew up among the angels [and probably for that reason was called one of them], and became learned in their knowledge, and assumed the government of them; and his days were prolonged until he became their chief; and thus it continued for a long time, until the affair between him and Adam happened, as God, whose name be exalted, hath said, 'When we said unto the Angels, Worship ye Adam, and

[all] worshipped except Iblīs, [who] was [one] of the Jinn.' (Sūrah l. 49)."

Iblīs, we are told by another authority, was sent as a governor upon the earth, and judged among the Jinn a thousand years, after which he ascended into heaven, and remained employed in worship until the creation of Adam. The name of Iblīs was originally, according to some, 'Azazīl (as before mentioned), and according to others, al-Ḥāris̤; his patronymic is Abū Munnah or Abū 'l-G͟himr. It is disputed whether he was of the angels or of the Jinn. There are three opinions on this point: (1) That he was of the angels, from a tradition from Ibn 'Abbas; (2) That he was of the Shaiṭāns (or evil Jinn), as it is said in the Qur'ān, "Except Iblīs' [who] was [one] of the Jinn"; this was the opinion of al-Ḥasanu 'l-Baṣrī, and is that commonly held; (3) That he was neither of the angels nor of the Jinn, but created alone of fire. Ibn 'Abbās founds his opinion on the same text from which al-Ḥasanu 'l-Baṣrī derives his: "When we said unto the angels, worship ye Adam, and [all] worshipped except Iblīs, [who] was [one] of the Jinn" (before quoted); which he explains by saying that the most noble and honourable among the angels are called "the Jinn," because they are veiled from the eyes of the other angels on account of their superiority; and that Iblīs was one of these Jinn. He adds, that he had the government of the lowest heaven and of the earth, and was called the Ṭā'us (*lit.* "Peacock") of the angels; and that there was not a spot in the lowest heaven but he had prostrated himself upon it; but when the Jinn rebelled upon the earth, God sent a troop of angels, who drove them to the islands and mountains; and Iblīs being elated with pride, and refusing to prostrate himself before Adam, God transformed him into a Shaiṭān. But this reasoning is opposed by other verses, in which Iblis is represented as saying, "Thou hast created me of fire, and has created him [Adam] of earth." It is therefore argued, "If he were created originally of fire, how was he created of light? for the angels were [all] created of light." The former verse may be explained by the tradition that Iblīs, having been taken captive, was exalted among the angels; or, perhaps, there is an ellipsis after the word "Angels"; for it might be inferred that the command given to the Angels was also (and *a fortiori*) to be obeyed by the Jinn.

According to a tradition, Iblīs and all the Shaiṭāns are distinguished from the other Jinn by a longer existence. "The Shaiṭāns," it is added, "are the children of Iblīs, and die not but with him; whereas the [other] Jinn die before him, though they may live many centuries. But this is not altogether accordant with the popular belief: Iblīs and many other evil Jinn are to survive mankind, but they are to die before the general resurrection, as also even the angels, the last of whom will be the Angel of Death, 'Izrā'īl. Yet not all the evil Jinn are to live thus long. Many of them are killed by shooting stars, hurled at them from heaven; wherefore, the Arabs, when they see a shooting star (*shihāb*), often exclaim, 'May God transfix the enemy of the faith!' Many also are killed by other Jinn, and some even by men. The fire of which the Jinn is created circulates in his veins, in place of blood; therefore, when he receives a mortal wound, this fire, issuing from his veins, generally consumes him to ashes.

The Jinn, it has been already shown, are peaceable. They also eat and drink, and propagate their species, sometimes in conjunction with human beings; in which latter case, the offspring partakes of the nature of both parents. In all these respects they differ from the angels. Among the evil Jinn are distinguished the five sons of their chief, Iblīs; namely, Ṭīr, who brings about calamities, losses, and injuries; al-A'war, who encourages debauchery; Sūt, who suggests lies; Dāsim, who causes hatred between man and wife; and Zalambūr, who presides over places of traffic.

The most common forms and habitations or places of resort of the Jinn must now be described. The following traditions from the Prophet are to the purpose:—

The Jinn are of various shapes, having the forms of serpents, scorpions, lions, wolves, jackals, &c. The Jinn are of three kinds—one on the land, one on the sea, and one in the air. The Jinn consist of forty troops, each troop consisting of six hundred thousand. The Jinn are of three kinds—one have wings and fly; another are snakes and dogs; and the third move about from place to place like men. Domestic snakes are asserted to be Jinn on the same authority.

The Prophet ordered his followers to kill serpents and scorpions if they intruded at prayers; but on other occasions, he seems to have required first to admonish them to depart, and then, if they remained, to kill them. The Doctors, however, differ in opinion whether all kinds of snakes or serpents should be admonished first; or whether any should; for the Prophet, say they, took a covenant of the Jinn [probably after the above-mentioned command], that they should not enter the houses of the faithful; therefore, it is argued, if they enter, they break their covenant, and it becomes lawful to kill them without previous admonishment. Yet it is related that 'Āyishah, one of the Prophet's wives, having killed a serpent in her chamber, was alarmed by a dream, and fearing that it might have been a Muslim Jinnī, as it did not enter her chamber, when she was undressed, gave in alms, as an expiation, twelve thousand dirhams (about £300), the price of the blood of a Muslim.

The Jinn are said to appear to mankind most commonly in the shapes of serpents, dogs, cats, or human beings. In the last case they are sometimes of the stature of men, and sometimes of a size enormously gigantic. If good, they are generally resplendently handsome; if evil, horribly hideous. They become invisible at pleasure (by a rapid extension or rarefaction of the particles which compose them), or suddenly disappear in the earth or air, or through a solid wall. Many Muslims in the present day profess to have seen and held intercourse with them.

The *Zauba'ah*, which is a whirlwind that raises the sand or dust in the form of a pillar of prodigious height, often seen sweeping across the deserts and fields, is believed to be caused by the flight of an evil genii. To defend themselves from a Jinn thus "riding in the whirlwind," the Arabs often exclaim, "Iron! Iron!" (*Ḥadīd! Ḥadīd!*) or, "Iron! thou unlucky!" (*Ḥadīd! yā Mashūm!*), as the Jinn are supposed to have a great dread of that metal; or they exclaim, "God is most great!" (*Allāhu akbar!*) A similar superstition prevails with respect to the waterspout at sea.

It is believed that the chief abode of the Jinn is in the mountains of Qāf, which are supposed to encompass the whole of our earth. But they are also believed to pervade the solid body of our earth, and the firmament; and to choose, as their principal places of resort, or of occasional abode, baths, wells, the latrina, ovens, ruined houses, market-places, the junctures of roads, the sea, and rivers.

The Arabs, therefore, when they pour water, &c., on the ground, or enter a bath, or let down a bucket into a well, or visit the latrina, and on various other occasions, say, "Permission!" or "Permission, ye blessed!" (*Izn!* or *Izn yā Mubārakūn!*). The evil spirits (or evil *genii*), it is said, had liberty to enter any of the seven heavens till the birth of Jesus, when they were excluded from three of them. On the birth of Muḥammad, they were forbidden the other four. They continue, however, to ascend to the confines of the lowest heaven, and there listening to the conversation of the angels respecting things decreed by God, obtain knowledge of futurity, which they sometimes impart to men, who by means of talismans or certain invocations make them to serve the purposes of magical performances.

What the Prophet said of Iblīs in the following tradition, applies also to the evil Jinn over whom he presides: His chief abode [among men] is the bath; his chief places of resort are the markets and junctures of roads; his food is whatever is killed without the name of God being pronounced over it; his drink, whatever is intoxicating; his Mu'azzin, the mizmār (a musical pipe), *i.e.* any musical instrument); his Qur'ān, poetry; his written character, the marks made in geomancy; his speech, falsehood; his snares are women.

That particular genii presided over particular places, was the opinion of the early Arabs. It is said in the Qur'ān (Sūrah lxxii. 6), "And there were certain men who sought refuge with certain of the Jinn." In the commentary of the Jalālān, I find the following remark on these words:—"When they halted, on their journey, in a place of fear, each man said, 'I seek refuge with the lord of this place, from the mischief of his foolish ones!'" In illustration of this, I may insert the following tradition, translated from *al-Qazwīnī*:—"It is related by a certain narrator of traditions, that he descended into a valley with his sheep, and a wolf carried off a ewe from among them; and he arose, and raised his voice, and cried, 'O inhabitant of the valley!' whereupon he heard a voice saying, 'O wolf, restore to him his sheep!' and the wolf came with the ewe, and left her, and departed." The same opinion is held by the modern Arabs, though probably they do not use such an invocation.

A similar superstition, a relic of ancient Egyptian credulity, still prevails among the people of Cairo. It is believed that each quarter of this city has its peculiar guardian-genius, or Agathodæmon, which has the form of a serpent.

It has already been mentioned that some of the Jinn are Muslims, and others infidels. The good acquit themselves of the imperative duties of religion, namely, prayers, alms-giving, fasting during the month of Ramaẓān, and pilgrimage to Makkah and Mount 'Arafāt, but in the performance of these duties they are generally invisible to human beings.

No man, it is said, ever obtained such absolute power over the Jinn as Sulaimān ibn Dā'ud (Solomon, the son of David). This he did by virtue of a most wonderful talisman, which is said to have come down to him from heaven. It was a sealing ring, upon which was engraved "the most great name" of God [AL-ISMU 'L-A'ZAM], and was partly composed of brass and partly of iron. With the brass he stamped his written commands to the good Jinn; with the iron (for a reason before mentioned) those to the evil Jinn or devils. Over both orders he had unlimited power, as well as over the birds and the winds, and, as is generally said, the wild beasts. His wazīr, Aṣaf the son of Barkhīyah, is also said to have been acquainted with "the most great name," by uttering which the greatest miracles may be performed, even that of raising the dead. By virtue of this name, engraved on his ring, Sulaimān compelled the Jinn to assist in building the temple of Jerusalem, and in various other works. Many of the evil genii he converted to the true faith, and many others of this class, who remained obstinate in infidelity, he confined in prisons. He is said to have been monarch of the whole earth. Hence, perhaps, the name of Sulaimān is given to the universal monarchs of the preadamite Jinn; unless the story of his own universal dominion originated from confounding him with those kings of the Jinn.

The injuries related to have been inflicted upon human beings by evil genii are of various kinds. Genii are said to have often carried off beautiful women, whom they have forcibly kept as their wives or concubines. Malicious or disturbed genii are asserted often to station themselves on the roofs, or at the windows, of houses, and to throw down bricks and stones on persons passing by. When they take possession of an uninhabited house, they seldom fail to persecute terribly any person who goes to reside in it. They are also very apt to pilfer provisions, &c. Many learned and devout persons, to secure their property from such depredations, repeat the words, "In the name of God, the Compassionate, the Merciful!" on locking the doors of their houses, rooms, or closets, and on covering the bread-basket, or anything containing food. During the month of Ramaẓān, the evil genii are believed to be confined in prison; and, therefore, on the last night of that month, with the same view, women sometimes repeat the words above mentioned, and sprinkle salt upon the floors of the apartments of their houses.

To complete this sketch of Arabian mythology, an account must be added of several creatures generally believed to be of inferior orders of the Jinn. One of these is the Ghūl, which is commonly regarded as a kind of Shaiṭān, or evil genii, that eats men, and is also described by some as a Jinn, or an enchanter, who assumes various forms. The Ghūls are said to appear in the forms of various animals, and of human beings, and in many monstrous shapes; to haunt burial-grounds and other sequestered spots; to feed upon dead human bodies; and to kill and devour any human creature who has the misfortune to fall in their way; whence the term "Ghūl" is applied to any cannibal.

An opinion quoted by a celebrated author respecting the Ghūl is, that it is a demoniacal animal, which passes a solitary existence in the deserts, resembling both man and brute; that it appears to a person travelling alone in the night and in solitary places, and, being supposed by him to be itself a traveller, lures him out of his way. Another opinion stated by him is this: that, when the Shaiṭāns attempt to hear words by stealth [from the confines of the lowest heaven], they are struck by shooting stars, and some are burnt; some falling into a sea, or rather a large river *(baḥr)*, become converted into crocodiles; and some, falling upon the land, become Ghūls. The same author adds the following tradition: "The Ghūl is any Jinn that is opposed to travels, assuming various forms and appearances; and affirms that several of the Companions of the Prophet saw Ghūls in their travels; and that 'Umar among them saw a Ghūl while on a journey to Syria, before Islām, and struck it with his sword."

It appears that "Ghūl" is, properly speaking, a name only given to a female demon of the kind above described; the male is called 'Quṭrub." It is said that these beings, and the Ghaddār, or Gharrār, and other similar creatures, which will presently be mentioned, are the offspring of Iblīs and of a wife whom God created for him of the fire of the Samūm (which here signifies, as in an instance before mentioned, "a smokeless fire"); and that they sprang from an egg. The female Ghūl, it is added, appears to men in the deserts, in various forms, converses with them, and sometimes prostitutes herself to them.

The Si'lāt, or Si'lā', is another demoniacal creature, described by some [or rather, by most authors] as of the Jinn. It is said that it is mostly found in forests; and that when it captures a man, it makes him dance, and plays with him as the cat plays with the mouse. A man of Isfahan asserted that many beings of this kind abounded in his country; that sometime the wolf would hunt one of them by night, and devour it, and that, when it had seized it, the Si'lā' would cry out, "Come to my help, for the wolf devoureth me!" or it would cry, "Who will liberate me? I have a hundred dīnārs, and he shall receive them!" But the people knowing that it was the cry of the Si'lā', no one would liberate it; and so the wolf would eat it.

An island in the sea of China (Ṣīn) is called "the island of the Si'lā'," by Arab geographers, from its being said to be inhabited by the demons so named; they are described as creatures of hideous forms, supposed to be Shaiṭāns, the offspring of human beings and Jinn, who eat men.

The Ghaddār is another creature of a similar nature, described as being found in the borders of al-Yaman, and sometimes in Tihāmah, and in the upper parts of Egypt. It is said that it entices a man to it, and either tortures him in a manner not to be described, or merely terrifies him, and leaves him.

The Dalhān is also a demoniacal being, inhabiting the islands of the seas, having the form of a man, and riding on an ostrich. It eats the flesh of men whom the sea casts on the shore from wrecks. Some say that a Dalhān once attacked a ship on the sea, and desired to take the crew; but they contended with it; whereupon it uttered a cry which caused them to fall on their faces, and it took them.

The Shiqq is another demoniacal creature, having the form of half a human being (like a man divided longitudinally); and it is believed that the Nasnās is the offspring of a Shiqq and of a human being. The Shiqq appears to travellers; and it was a demon of this kind who killed, and was killed by 'Alqamah, the son of Safwān, the son of Umaiyah, of whom it is well known that he was killed by a Jinn. So says al-Qazwīnī.

The Nasnās (above mentioned) is described as resembling half a human being; having half a head, half a body, one arm, and one leg, with which it hops with much agility; as being found in the woods of al-Yaman, and being endowed with speech; "but God," it is added, "is all knowing." It is said that it is found in Ḥaẓramaut as well as al-Yaman; and that one was brought alive to al-Mutawakkil. It resembled a man in form, excepting that it had but half a face, which was in its breast, and a tail like that of a sheep. The people of Ḥaẓramaut, it is added, eat it; and its flesh is sweet. It is only generated in their country.

A man who went there asserted that he saw a captured Nasnās, which cried out for mercy, conjuring him by God and by himself.

A race of people whose head is in the breast, is described as inhabiting an island called Jabah (supposed to be Java), in the sea of Hind, or India. A kind of Nasnās is also described as inhabiting the island of Raij, in the sea of China, and having wings like those of the bat.

The Hātif is a being that is heard, but not seen; and is often mentioned by Arab writers. It is generally the communicator of some intelligence in the way of advice, or direction, or warning. (See Lane's *Modern Egyptians*; Lane's *Notes on the Arabian Nights.*)

GENTILES. Arabic *Ummī* (امى, from *umm*, "a mother"); pl. *ummīyūn*, *lit.* "Ignorant as new-born babes." Hebrew גּוֹיִם. According to al-Baiẓāwī, all the people of the earth who do not possess a divine Book. In the Qur'ān, the term is specially applied to the idolaters of Arabia.

Sūrah lxii. 2: "He (God) it is who sent unto the Gentiles a Prophet, amongst them to recite to them His signs and to purify them, and to teach them the Book, the wisdom, although they were before in obvious error."

GEORGE, St. [JIRJIS, AL-KHIZR.]

AL-GHĀBAH (الغابة). "The desert." A name given to the open plain near al-Madīnah.

GHABN (غبن). Fraud or deceit in sales.

GHADDĀR (غدار). A species of demon said to be found on the borders of al-Yaman. [GENII.]

GHADĪR (غدير). A festival of the Shī'ahs on the 18th of the month of Zū 'l-Ḥijjah, when three images of dough filled with honey are made to represent Abū Bakr, 'Umar, and 'Usmān, which are stuck with knives, and the honey is sipped as typical of the blood of the usurping Khalīfahs. The festival is named from *Ghadīr*, "a pool," and the festival commemorates, it is said, Muḥammad having declared 'Alī his successor at *Ghadīr Khūm*, a watering place midway between Makkah and al-Madīnah.

GHAIB (غيب). *Lit.* "Secret." The terms *Ghaibu 'l-Huwīyah*, "Secret essence," and *al-Ghaibu 'l-Mutlaq*, "the absolute unknowable," are used by Ṣūfī mystics to express the nature of God. ('Abdu 'r-Razzāq's *Dict. of Ṣūfī Terms.*)

GHAIRAH (غيرة). "Jealousy." Muḥammad is related to have said, "There is a kind of jealousy (*ghairah*) which God likes, and there is a kind of jealousy which he abominates. The jealousy which God likes is when a man has suspicion that his wife or slave girl comes and sits by a stranger; the jealousy which God abominates is when, without cause, a man harbours in his heart a bad opinion of his wife." (*Mishkāt*, book xiii. c. xv. pt. 2.)

GHAIR-I-MAHDI (غير مهدى). *Lit.* "Without Mahdī." A small sect who believe that the Imām Mahdī will not reappear. They say that one Saiyid Muḥammad of Jeypore was the real Mahdī, the twelfth Imām, and that he has now gone never more to return. They venerate him as highly as they do the Prophet, and consider all other Muslims to be unbelievers. On the night called Lailatu 'l-Qadr, in the month of Ramaẓān, they meet and repeat two rak'ah prayers. After that act of devotion is over, they say: "God is Almighty, Muḥammad is our Prophet, the Qur'ān and Mahdī are just and true. Imām Mahdī is come and gone. Whosoever disbelieves this is an infidel." They are a very fanatical sect. (See *Qanūn-i-Islām.*)

GHAMARĀT (غمرات), plural of *ghamrah*, "abyss." A word used to express the agonies of death. It occurs in the Qur'ān, Sūrah vi. 93: "But couldst thou see when the ungodly are in the *floods of death* (*ghamarātu 'l-maut*), and the angels reach forth their hands, saying, 'Yield up your souls:—this day shall ye be recompensed with a humiliating punishment.'"

AL-GHANĪ (الغنى). "The Independent One." One of the ninety-nine special names or attributes of God, expressing the superiority of the Almighty over the necessities and requirements of mankind. The word occurs in the Qur'ān, Sūrah lx. 6, and is translated by Palmer, "*He is rich.*"

GHAṢB (غصب). "Using by force; usurpation."

Ghaṣb, in its literal sense, means the forcibly taking a thing from another. In the language of the law it signifies the taking of the property of another which is valuable and sacred, without the consent of the proprietor, in such a manner as to destroy the proprietor's possession of it, whence it is that usurpation is established by exacting service from the slave of another, or by putting a burden upon the quadruped of another, but not by sitting upon the carpet of another; because by the use of the slave of another, and by loading the quadruped of another, the possession of the proprietor is destroyed, whereas by sitting upon the carpet of another the possession of the proprietor is not destroyed It is to be observed that if any person knowingly and wilfully usurp the property of another, he is held in law to be an offender, and becomes responsible for a compensation. If, on the contrary, he should not have made the usurpation knowingly and wilfully (as where a person destroys property on the supposition of its belonging to himself, and it afterwards proves the right of another), he is in that case also liable for a compensation, because a compensation is the right of men; but he is not an offender, as his erroneous offence is cancelled. (*Hidāyah*, vol. iii. p. 522.)

AL-GHĀSHIYAH (الغاشية). "The Covering, Overwhelming." A name given to the LXXXVIIIth Sūrah of the Qur'ān, the word occurring in the first verse for the Day of Judgment: "Has there come to thee the story of the *overwhelming*?"

GHĀSIL (غاسل). "A washer of the dead." An official is generally appointed for this purpose by the Imām of the parish.

GHASSĀN (غسان). A tribe of Arabs inhabiting the western side of the Syrian desert in the time of Muḥammad. (See Muir's *Life of Mahomet*, vol. i. p. clxxxiii.)

GHAṬAFĀN (غطفان). An Arabian tribe descended from Qais.

GHAUṢ (غوث). *Lit.* "One to whom we can cry for help." A mediator. A title given to a Muḥammadan saint. Some hold it to be the highest order of sanctity, whilst others regard it as second in rank to that of *Quṭb*. According to the *Ghiyāṣu 'l-Lughah* it is an inferior rank of sanctity to that of *Quṭb*.

GHAẒAB (غضب). "Anger," "wrath." A word used frequently in the Qur'ān for the wrath of God, *e.g.* Sūrah iv. 95: "God shall be angry with him."

GHĀZĪ (غازي). One who fights in the cause of Islām. A hero; a warrior. One who slays an infidel. It is also a title of distinction conferred by Muslim rulers upon generals and warriors of renown. In the Turkish Empire the title of *Ghāzī* implies something similar to our "Field Marshal." The Prophet is related to have said, "God is sponsor for him who goes forth to fight in the road of God, for His satisfaction and for that of His Prophet. He shall, if he be not killed, return to his home with plunder and rewards. And if he die, his reward is paradise." (*Mishkāt*, book xvii. c. 1.)

GHAZWAH (غزوة). A military force when it is lead by either an Apostle (*Rasūl*) or an Imām. A small force commanded by one of the Imām's lieutenants is a *sarīyah*, or brigade. (See *Ghiyāṣu 'l-Lughah, in loco.*)

AL-GHAZZĀLI (الغزالي). Abū Ḥamīd Muḥammad ibn Muḥammad ibn Aḥmad *al-Ghazzālī*, is a well known Sunnī doctor surnamed *Ḥujjatu 'l-Islām* ("the proof of Islām"). He was a native of Ṭūs, and for sometime a professor in the college at Naisāpūr. Born A.H. 450 (A.D. 1058), died A.H. 505 (A.D. 1111), at Ṭūs. His exposition on the nature of God will be found in the article GOD. His great theological work is the *Iḥyā'u 'Ulūmi 'd-Dīn.*

GHĪBAH (غيبة). "Slander; calumny." Anything whispered of an absent person to his detriment, although it be true. (*Buhtān* expressing a false accusation.) *Ghībah* is condemned in the Qur'ān (Sūrah xlix. 12): "O believers, avoid frequent suspicions, for some suspicions are a crime; neither let one of you traduce (*ghībah*) another in his absence." A chapter is devoted to the condemnation of backbiting and calumny in the Traditions (*vide Mishkāt*, book xxii. ch. x.)

GHIFĀR (غفار). An Arabian tribe in the time of Muḥammad who inhabited a tract of country in the vicinity of al-Madīnah. They were descendants of Abū Zarri 'l-Ghifārī.

GHISHĀWAH (غشاوة). *Lit.* "A covering." A dimness in the eye. A word used in the Qur'ān for spiritual blindness. Sūrah ii. 6: "Their hearts and their ears hath God sealed up, and over their eyes is a *covering.*"

GHISLĪN (غسلين). The water, blood, and matter, supposed by Muḥammadans to run down the skin and flesh of the damned in hell. See Qur'ān, Sūrah lxix. 36: "No friend shall he have here that day, nor food but *ghislīn.*"

GHŪL (غول). A man-devouring demon of the woods. A species of Jinn [GENII.]

GHULĀM (غلام), pl. *ghilmah*. A boy under age. A term used in modern Muslim for a slave, the legal word being *'abd.* It occurs in the Qur'ān for a son. Sūrah iii. 42: "She (Mary) said, 'How can I have a *son* when a man has not touched me?"

GHULĀT (غلاة). *Lit.* "The Zealots." A title given to a leading sect of the Shī'ahs who, through their excessive zeal for the Imāms, have raised them above the degree of human beings.

GHULŪL (غلول). Defrauding or purloining any part of the lawful plunder in a *jihād* or religious war. Forbidden in the Qur'ān, Sūrah iii. 155: "But he who shall *defraud*, shall come forth with his defraudings on the day of the resurrection: then shall every soul be paid what it hath merited, and they shall not be treated with injustice."

GHURĀB (غراب). *Lit.* "A crow." *Ghurābu 'l-Bain*: "The crow of separation." A term used by the Ṣūfī mystics for a certain state of separation from God. ('Abdu 'r-Razzāq's *Dict. of Ṣūfī Terms.*)

GHURRAH (غرة). A fine of five hundred dirhams. A slave of that value. It is the fine for a person striking a woman so as to occasion a miscarriage. (*Hidāyah*, vol. iv. p. 552.)

GHUSL (غسل), as distinguished from *ghasl* (washing) is the religious act of bathing the whole body after a legal impurity. It is founded upon the express injunction of the Qur'ān, Sūrah v. 9: "If ye are polluted then purify yourselves." And the

Traditions most minutely relate the occasions on which the Prophet performed the ceremony of *ghusl*, or bathing. The Muslim teachers of all sects are unanimous in prescribing the washing of the whole body after the following acts, which render the body *junub*, or impure: (1) *Ḥayẓ*, menses; (2) *nifās*, puerperium; (3) *jimā'*, coitus; (4) *iḥtilām*, pollutio nocturna. It is absolutely necessary that every part of the body should be washed, for 'Alī relates that the Prophet said, "He who leaves but one hair unwashed on his body, will be punished in hell accordingly." (*Mishkāt*, book ii. c. viii.)

GHUSL MASNŪN (غسل مسنون). *Lit.* "Washings which are Sunnah."

Such washings are founded upon the Sunnah, or precept and practice of Muḥammad, although they are not supposed to be of divine institution. They are four in number: (1) Upon the admission of a convert to Islām; (2) Before the Friday prayers and on the great festivals; (3) After washing the dead; (4) After blood-letting. (See *Ṣaḥīḥu 'l-Bukhārī*, p. 39, *Bābu 'l-Ghusl.*) Akrimah relates that people came from al-'Irāq and asked Ibn 'Abbās if he believed that bathing on Fridays was a divine institution, and Ibn 'Abbās replied, "No, but bathing is a great purifier, and I will tell you how the custom of bathing began. The people were engaged in daily labour and wore blankets, and the people sweated to such a degree as to cause a bad smell, so the Prophet said, 'O men! bathe ye on Fridays and put some scent on your clothes.'" (Matthew's *Mishkāt*, vol i. p. 120, from the Ḥadīs̤ of Abū Dā'ud.)

GIANTS. There is but one allusion to giants in the Qur'ān, namely, to the tribe 'Ād, who are spoken of as men "with lofty statures" (Sūrah lxxxix. 6), and the commentator, Shāh 'Abdu 'l-Azīz of Delhi, says they were men of not less than twelve yards in stature. According to a tradition in the *Kitābu 'sh-Shafah* by the Qāẓī 'Ayāẓ (p. 65), Adam was sixty yards in height. In the *Ghiyās̤u 'l-Lughah*, a giant named 'Ūj is mentioned, who was born in the days of Adam and lived until the time of Moses, a period of 3,500 years, and that he was so high, that the flood in the days of Noah only reached to his waist. There are traditions and stories of giants whose graves exist unto the present day, throughout the whole of Asia. Opposite the Church Mission House at Peshawur is a grave nine yards long, which is held in great reverence by both Muḥammadans and Hindus. De la Belle, in his *Travels in Persia*, vol ii. p. 89, mentions several which exist in Persia. Giant graves in Hindustan are numerous.

GIDEON. In the Qur'ān there is evidently a confusion in one passage between the story of Saul as told therein, and the account of Gideon given in the Old Testament, as the following extracts will show:—

"And when Saul marched forth with his forces, he said, 'God will test you by a river: He who drinketh of it shall not be of my band; but he who shall not taste it, drinking a drink out of the hand excepted, shall be of my band.' And, except a few of them, they drank of it. And when they had passed it, he and those who believed with him, the *former* said, 'We have no strength this day against Goliath (Jālūt) and his forces:' But they who held it as certain that they must meet God, said, 'How oft, by God's will, hath a small host vanquished a numerous host! and God is with the steadfastly enduring.'" (Sūrah ii. 250.)

Which compare with Judges vii. 5:—

"So they brought down the people unto the water; and the Lord said unto Gideon, Every one that lappeth of the water with his tongue, as a dog lappeth, him shalt thou set by himself; likewise every one that boweth down upon his knees to drink. . . . The Lord said, By the three hundred men that lapped will I save you, and deliver the Midianites into thine hand"

GIFTS. Arabic *hibah* (هبة), pl. *hibāt*. A deed of gift. The term *hibah* in the language of Muslim law means a transfer of property made immediately and without exchange. He who makes the gift is called the *wāhib*, or donor; the thing given, *mauhūb*; and the person to whom it is given is *mauhūb lahu*.

Muḥammad sanctioned the retraction of a gift when he said, "A donor preserves his right to his gift, so long as he does not obtain a return for it." Although there is another tradition which says: "Let not a donor retract his gift; but let a father if he pleases retract his gift to his son." Ash-Shāfi'ī maintains that it is not lawful to retract a gift, except it be from a father to a son. All the doctors are agreed that to retract a gift is an abomination, for Muḥammad said: "The retraction of a gift is like eating one's spittle." The general opinion is that a gift to a stranger may be retracted, but not a gift to a kinsman. A retracted gift, by the mutual consent of the parties, should be effected by a decree of the Qāẓī, or judge. (*Hidāyah*, vol. iii. p. 290.)

GIRDLE. Arabic *niṭāq* (نطاق). Amongst the Bakhtāshīs and several other orders of faqīrs, investiture with a girdle is the sign of incorporation into the order. The Bakhtāshīs say that Adam was the first to wear the girdle worn by them, and after him fifteen other prophets wore it in succession, viz. Seth, Noah, Shu'aib, Job, Joseph, Abraham, Husha', Yūsha', Jirjis, Jonas, Ṣāliḥ, Zakariah, al-Khiẓr, Ilyās, and Jesus. (Brown's *Dervishes*, p. 145.)

GNOSTICS. "The singular correspondence between the allusions to the crucifixion in the Corân, and the wild speculations of the early heretics, have led to the conjecture that Mahomet acquired his notions of Christianity from a Gnostic source. But Gnosticism had disappeared from Egypt before the sixth century, and there is no reason for supposing that it had at any time gained footing in Arabia. Besides, there is no affinity between the supernaturalism of the Gnostics and Docetæ, and the rationalism of the Corân. According to the former, the Deity must be removed far from the gross contact of evil matter; and the Æon Christ, which alighted upon Jesus at His baptism, must ascend to its native regions before the crucifixion. With Mahomet, on the contrary, Jesus Christ was a mere man—wonderfully born, indeed—but still an ordinary man, a servant of the Almighty, as others had been before him. But although there is no ground for believing that Gnostic doctrines were taught to Mahomet, yet some of the strange fancies of those heretics, preserved in Syrian tradition, may have come to the ears of his informants (the chief of whom, even on Christian topics, seem to have been Jews, unable probably to distinguish heretical fable from Christian doctrine), and have been by them adopted as a likely and convenient mode of explaining away that which formed the great barrier between Jews and Christians." (Muir's *Life of Mahomet*, new ed. p. 161.)

GOD.

The name of the Creator of the Universe in the Qur'ān is *Allāh*, which is the title given to the Supreme Being by Muḥammadans of every race and language.

Allāh is supposed to be derived from *ilāh*, a deity or god, with the addition of the definite article *al*—*Al-ilāh*, "the God"—or, according to some authorities, it is from *lāh*, *i.e.* *Al-lāh*, "the secret one." But Abū Ḥanīfah says that just as the essence of God is unchangeable, so is His name, and that *Allāh* has ever been the name of the Eternal Being. (See *Ghiyāṣu 'l-Lughah*.)

Allāh may be an Arabic rendering of the Hebrew אֵל *el*, and the unused root אוּל *ūl*, "to be strong," or from אֱלוֹהַ, the singular form of אֱלֹהִים. It is expressed in Persian and Hindustani by the word *Khudā*, derived from the Persian *khud*, self; the self-existing one.

Another word very frequently used for the Almighty in the Qur'ān is *Rabb*, which is generally translated in English versions of the Qur'ān, "Lord." It seems to stand in the relative position of the Jehovah of the Old Testament and the Κύριος of the New Testament. The word is understood by Muslims to mean "the sustainer," but it is probably derived from the Hebrew רַבָּה *rabbah*, "a stronghold," or from its root *rab*, which, according to Gesenius, means "a multitude," or anything of size or importance.

The title *Allāh* is called the *Ismu 'z-Z̤āt*, or, the essential name of God, all other titles, including *Rabb*, being considered *Asmā'u 'ṣ-Ṣifāt*, or "attributes" of the Divine Being. These attributes are called *al-Asmā'u 'l-ḥusnā*, or the "excellent names." The expression occurs in the Qur'ān (Sūrah vii. 179), "But God's are *excellent names*, call on Him thereby." This verse is commented upon in the Traditions, and Abū Hurairah says that Muḥammad said, "Verily, there are ninety-nine names of God, and whoever recites them shall enter into Paradise."

In the same tradition these names (or attributes) are given as follows:—

1.	*Ar-Raḥmān* .	The Merciful.
2.	*Ar-Raḥīm* .	The Compassionate.
3.	*Al-Malik* .	The King.
4.	*Al-Quddūs* .	The Holy.
5.	*As-Salām* .	The Peace.
6.	*Al-Mu'min* .	The Faithful.
7.	*Al-Muhaimin* .	The Protector.
8.	*Al-'Azīz* .	The Mighty.
9.	*Al-Jabbār* .	The Repairer.
10.	*Al-Mutakabbir* .	The Great.
11.	*Al-Khāliq* .	The Creator.
12.	*Al-Bārī* .	The Maker.
13.	*Al-Muṣawwir* .	The Fashioner.
14.	*Al-Ghaffār* .	The Forgiver.
15.	*Al-Qahhār* .	The Dominant.
16.	*Al-Wahhāb* .	The Bestower.
17.	*Ar-Razzāq* .	The Provider.
18.	*Al-Fattāḥ* .	The Opener.
19.	*Al-'Alīm* .	The Knower.
20.	*Al-Qābiẓ* .	The Restrainer.
21.	*Al-Bāsiṭ* .	The Spreader.
22.	*Al-Khāfiẓ* .	The Abaser.
23.	*Ar-Rāfi'* .	The Exalter.
24.	*Al-Mu'izz* .	The Honourer.
25.	*Al-Muzīl* .	The Destroyer.
26.	*As-Sāmi'* .	The Hearer.
27.	*Al-Baṣīr* .	The Seer.
28.	*Al-Ḥākim* .	The Ruler.
29.	*Al-'Adl* .	The Just.
30.	*Al-Laṭīf* .	The Subtle.
31.	*Al-Khabīr* .	The Aware.
32.	*Al-Ḥalīm* .	The Clement.
33.	*Al-'Aẓīm* .	The Grand.
34.	*Al-Ghafūr* .	The Forgiving.
35.	*Ash-Shakūr* .	The Grateful.
36.	*Al-'Alī* .	The Exalted.
37.	*Al-Kabīr* .	The Great.
38.	*Al-Ḥafīẓ* .	The Guardian.
39.	*Al-Muqīt* .	The Strengthener.
40.	*Al-Ḥasīb* .	The Reckoner.
41.	*Al-Jalīl* .	The Majestic.
42.	*Al-Karīm* .	The Generous
43.	*Ar-Raqīb* .	The Watcher.
44.	*Al-Mujīb* .	The Approver.
45.	*Al-Wāsi'* .	The Comprehensive.
46.	*Al-Ḥakīm* .	The Wise.
47.	*Al-Wadūd* .	The Loving.
48.	*Al-Majīd* .	The Glorious
49.	*Al-Bā'is̤* .	The Raiser.
50.	*Ash-Shahīd* .	The Witness.
51.	*Al-Ḥaqq* .	The Truth.
52.	*Al-Wakīl* .	The Advocate.
53.	*Al-Qawī* .	The Strong.
54.	*Al-Matīn* .	The Firm.
55.	*Al-Walī* .	The Patron.
56.	*Al-Ḥamīd* .	The Laudable.
57.	*Al-Muḥṣī* .	The Counter.
58.	*Al-Mubdī* .	The Beginner.
59.	*Al-Mu'īd* .	The Restorer.
60.	*Al-Muḥyī* .	The Quickener.

61.	*Al-Mumīt* .	The Killer.
62.	*Al-Ḥaiy* .	The Living.
63.	*Al-Qaiyūm*	The Subsisting.
64.	*Al-Wājid* .	The Finder.
65.	*Al-Majīd* .	The Glorious.
66.	*Al-Wāḥid* .	The One.
67.	*Ab-Samad* .	The Eternal.
68.	*Al-Qādir* .	The Powerful.
69.	*Al-Muqtadir* .	The Prevailing.
70.	*Al-Muqaddim* .	The Bringing forward.
71.	*Al-Mu'akhkhir* .	The Deferrer.
72.	*Al-Awwal* .	The First.
73.	*Al-Ākhir* .	The Last.
74.	*Aẓ-Ẓāhir* .	The Evident.
75.	*Al-Bāṭin* .	The Hidden.
76.	*Al-Wālī* .	The Governor.
77.	*Al-Muta'ālī* .	The Exalted.
78.	*Al-Barr* .	The Righteous.
79.	*At-Tauwāb* .	The Accepter of Repentance.
80.	*Al-Muntaqim* .	The Avenger.
81.	*Al-'Afūw* .	The Pardoner.
82.	*Ar-Ra'uf* .	The Kind.
83.	*Māliku 'l-Mulk* .	The Ruler of the Kingdom.
84.	*Ẕū 'l-Jalāli wa 'l-Ikrām* .	The Lord of Majesty and Liberality.
85.	*Al-Muqsiṭ* .	The Equitable.
86.	*Al-Jāmi'* .	The Collector.
87.	*Al-Ghanī* .	The Independent.
88.	*Al-Mughnī* .	The Enricher.
89.	*Al-Mu'ṭī* .	The Giver.
90.	*Al-Māni'* .	The Withholder.
91.	*Aẓ-Ẓārr* .	The Distresser.
92.	*An-Nāfi'* .	The Profiter.
93.	*An-Nūr* .	The Light.
94.	*Al-Hādī* .	The Guide.
95.	*Al-Badī'* .	The Incomparable.
96.	*Al-Bāqī* .	The Enduring.
97.	*Al-Wāris̤* .	The Inheritor.
98.	*Ar-Rashīd* .	The Director.
99.	*Aṣ-Ṣabūr* .	The Patient.

The list either begins or closes with *Allāh*, thus completing the number of one hundred names, which are usually recited on a rosary in the ceremony of Ẕikr [ZIKR], as well as at all leisure moments, by devout Muslims. The Wahhābīs do not use a rosary, but count the names on their fingers, which they say was the custom of the Prophet, for from the Traditions it appears that Muḥammad did not use a rosary.

According to the Traditions (*Mishkāt*, book x. c. i.), the Almighty has an "exalted name" known as the *Ismu 'l-A'ẓam*, which Muḥammad is related to have said was either in the *Sūratu 'l-Baqarah*, the second chapter of the Qur'ān, 158th verse, or in the *Sūratu Āli 'Imrān*, the third chapter, first verse. The names of God which occur in these two verses are *ar-Raḥmān*, "the Merciful," *ar-Raḥīm*, "The Compassionate," *al-Ḥaiy*, "the Living," and *al-Qaiyūm*, "the Subsisting." There is, however, another tradition, from which it would appear that the name may be either *al-Aḥad*, "the One," or *aṣ-Ṣamad*, "the Eternal."

'Abdu 'l-Ḥaqq, in his remarks on these traditions, says that it is generally held, according to a tradition by 'Ayishah, that this great name is known only to the prophets and other saintly persons. The compiler of the *Kitābu 't-Ta'rīfāt* says it is none other than the name of *Allāh*.

The Prophet having said that whoever calls upon God by this name shall obtain all his desires (*Mishkāt*, book x. c. i. pt. 2), the various sects of faqīrs and mystics spend much time in endeavouring to ascertain what the name really is [DA'WAH], and the person who is able to assert that he has obtained this secret knowledge possesses great influence over the minds of the superstitious.

There can be little doubt that the discussion regarding this exalted name has arisen from the circumstance that Muḥammad became aware of the fact that the Jews never recited the great name of Jehovah, and spoke of it as "the great and terrible name," "the peculiar name" of God.

The attributes of God as expressed in the ninety-nine names, are divided into the *asmā'u 'l-jalālīyah*, or the glorious attributes, and the *asmā'u 'l-jamālīyah*, or the terrible attributes. Such names as *ar-Raḥīm*, "the Merciful," *al-Karīm*, "the Kind," and *al 'Afūw*, "the Forgiver," belonging to the former; and *al-Qawī*, "the Strong," *al-Muntaqim*, "the Avenger," and *al-Qādir*, "the Powerful," to the latter.

In praying to God it is usual for the worshipper to address the Almighty by that name or attribute which he wishes to appeal to. For example, if praying for pardon, he will address God as either *al-'Afūw*, "the Pardoner," or *at-Tauwāb*, "the Receiver of repentance.'

A belief in the existence of God, His Unity, His Absolute Power, and in the other essential attributes of an Eternal and Almighty Being, is the most important part of the Muslim religion, and is supposed to be expressed in the two clauses of the well-known formula :—

لا اله الا الله

Lā ilāha Il-lā 'l-lahu.

There is no deity But Allāh.

The first clause, "There is no deity," is known as the *Nafī*, or that which is rejected, and the second clause, "But Allāh," as the *Is̤bāt*, or that which is established, the term *Nafī wa-Is̤bāt* being applied to the first two clauses of the Muslim's *Kalimah*, or creed.

The teaching of Muḥammad in his Qur'ān as to the nature of God, forms such an important consideration in an exposition of Islām, that no apology is needed for full and lengthy quotations from that book on the subject.

The following verses are arranged in chronological order according to *Jalālu 'd-dīn as-Suyūṭī's* list :—

Sūratu 'l-Ikhlāṣ. Chapter cxiii.

(One of the earliest chapters of the Qur'ān)

"Say, He is God, One [God]
"God, the Eternal.

"He begetteth not nor is begotten,
"And there is none equal unto Him."

Sūratu 'l-A'rāf. Chapter vii. 52.
(Given at al-Madinah.)

"Verily your Lord is God, who created the heavens and the earth in six days: then He ascended the throne. He causeth the night to cover the day; it followeth it swiftly: and *He created* the sun and the moon and the stars, made subject utterly to His command. Do not the *whole* creation and command belong to Him? Blessed be God, the Lord of the Worlds."

Sūratu Maryam. Chapter xix. 91–96.
(Given at Makkah.)

"They say, 'The Compassionate hath gotten offspring': Ye have done an impious thing.

"It wanteth little but that the heavens be rent thereat, and that the earth cleave asunder, and that the mountains fall down in pieces.

"*For* that they have attributed offspring to the Compassionate, when it beseemeth not the Compassionate to get offspring.

"There is none of all that are in the heavens and the earth but he shall come unto the Compassionate as a servant. He hath known them and numbered them with an *exact* numbering.

"And each of them shall come unto Him on the day of resurrection, alone.

"Verily those who have believed and have done the things that are right, on them the Compassionate will bestow [His] love."

Sūratu 'l-Ḥijr. Chapter xv. 16–25
(Given at Makkah.)

"We (God) have placed in heaven *the twelve* signs *of the Zodiac*, and adorned them for the beholders *with the constellations*;

"And We have guarded them (*by means of shooting stars*) from every accursed devil.

"Excepting him who listened by stealth, whom a manifest shooting star pursueth.

"We have also spread forth the earth, and thrown thereon firm *mountains*, and We have caused to spring forth in it every kind [of green thing] weighed.

"And We have provided for you therein necessaries of life, and *for* him whom ye do not sustain;

"And there is not a thing but the storehouses thereof are with Us, and We send it not down save in determined quantities.

"We also send the fertilizing winds, and We send down water from heaven, and give you to drink thereof; and ye are not the storers of it.

"And verily We give life and death, and We are the heirs *of all the creation.*

"We also know those who have gone before you, and We know those who follow after [you].

"And verily thy Lord will assemble them together: for He is Wise, Knowing."

Sūratu 'l-An'ām. Chapter vi. 59–64.
(Given at Makkah.)

"With Him are the keys of the hidden things: none knoweth them but He: and He knoweth whatsoever is on the land and in the sea, and there falleth not a leaf but He knoweth it, nor a grain in the dark parts of the earth, nor a moist thing nor a dry thing, but [it is noted] in a distinct writing.

"And it is He who taketh your souls at night, and knoweth what ye have gained in the day; then He reviveth you therein, that an appointed time may be fulfilled. Then unto Him shall ye return: then will He declare unto you what ye have done.

"And He is the Supreme over His servants, and He sendeth watchers over you, until when death cometh unto any one of you, Our messengers take his soul, and they fail not.

"Then are they returned unto God their Lord, the True. Doth not judgment belong to Him? And He is the most quick of reckoners.

"SAY, Who delivereth you from the darknesses of the land and of the sea, *when* ye supplicate Him humbly and in secret, *saying*, 'If Thou deliver us from these *dangers*, we will assuredly be of [the number of] the thankful'?

"SAY, God delivereth you from them and from every affliction."

Ib., 95–103:—

"Verily God causeth the grain to come forth, and the date-stone: He bringeth forth the living from the dead, and He bringeth forth the dead from the living: This is God; then wherefore are ye turned away?

"He causeth the dawn to appear, and hath ordained the night for rest, and the sun and the moon for reckoning *time:* this is the appointment of the Mighty, the Wise.

"And it is He who hath ordained for you the stars, that ye may be guided by them in the darkness of the land and of the sea: We have clearly shown the signs *of Our power* unto the people who know.

"And it is He who hath produced you from one soul, and *there is* a place of rest and of storing: We have clearly shown the signs to the people who understand.

"And it is He who hath sent down water from heaven, and We have produced thereby the germs of everything, and We have caused the green thing to come forth therefrom, from which We draw forth grains massed; and from the palm-tree, from its fruit-branch, clusters of dates heaped together: and gardens of grapes, and the olive and the pomegranate, like one another and not like. Look ye at their fruits when they bear fruit, and their ripening. Verily therein are signs unto the people who believe.

"Yet they have set up the Jinn as partners of God, though He hath created them, and without knowledge have they falsely attributed to Him sons and daughters. Extolled be His purity, and high be He exalted above that which they attribute [to Him]!

"*He is* the Author of the heavens and the earth. How then should He have offspring, when He hath no consort, and hath created everything and knoweth everything?

"This is God your Lord. There is no God but He, the Creator of everything: therefore worship ye Him; and He is guardian over everything.

"The eyes see Him not, but He seeth the eyes: and He is the Gracious, the Knowing."

Sūratu Banī Isra'īl. Chapter lxvii. 1–4.
(Given at Makkah.)

"Blessed be He in whose hand is the dominion and who is all powerful;

"Who hath created death and life, that He may prove you, which of you [will be] best in works: and He is the Mighty, the Very-Forgiving:

"Who hath created seven heavens, one above another. Thou seest not any fault in the creation of the Compassionate. But lift up the eyes again to *heaven.* Dost thou see any fissures?

"Then lift up the eyes again twice; the sight shall return unto thee dull and dim."

Sūratu 'l-'Ankabūt. Chapter xxix. 40–43.
(Given at Makkah.)

"The likeness of those who take to themselves Tutelars instead of God is as the likeness of the spider, which maketh for herself a dwelling; and the frailest of dwellings surely is the dwelling of the spider! If they knew ——!

"Verily God knoweth whatever thing they invoke in His stead; and He is the Mighty, the Wise.

"And these parables we propound unto men; but none understand them except the wise.

"God hath created the heavens and the earth in truth: verily therein is a sign unto the believers."

Sūratu 'l-Baqarah. Chapter ii. 157–160.
(Given at al-Madīnah.)

"And your God is One God: there is no god but He, the Compassionate, the Merciful.

"Verily in the creation of the heavens and the earth, and the varying of night and day, and the ships that course upon the sea *laden* with what is profitable to mankind, and the water that God hath sent down from heaven, quickening the earth thereby after its death, and scattering about it all kinds of beasts; and in the changing of the winds, and the clouds that are compelled to do service between heaven and earth, are signs unto a people who understand.

"Yet among men are those who take to themselves, beside God, idols, which they love as *with* the love of God: but those who have believed are more loving towards God *than these towards their idols.*"

Ib., 256:—

"God! There is no God but He, the Ever-Living, the Ever-Subsisting. Slumber seizeth Him not, nor sleep. To Him belongeth whatsoever is in the Heavens and whatsoever is in the Earth. Who is he that shall intercede with Him, unless by His permission? He knoweth what [hath been] before them and what [shall be] after them, and they shall not compass aught of His knowledge save what He willeth. His Throne comprehendeth the Heavens and the Earth, and the care of them burdeneth Him not. And He is the High, the Great.

Sūratu Āli 'Imrān, Chapter iii. 25.
(Given at al-Madīnah.)

"Say, O God, to whom belongeth dominion, Thou givest dominion to whom Thou wilt, and from whom Thou wilt Thou takest it away; Thou exaltest whom Thou wilt, and whom Thou wilt Thou humblest. In Thy hand is good. Verily Thou art all-powerful.

"Thou causest the night to pass into the day, and Thou causest the day to pass into the night; and Thou bringest forth the living from the dead, and Thou bringest forth the dead from the living; and Thou givest sustenance to whom Thou wilt without measure."

Sūratu 'r-Ra'd. Chapter xiii. 13.
(Given at al-Madīnah.)

"It is He who maketh the lightning to appear unto you, [causing] fear and hope *of rain*, and formeth the pregnant clouds.

"And the thunder proclaimeth His perfection with His praise; and [likewise] the angels, in fear of Him. And He sendeth the thunderbolts, and striketh with them whom He pleaseth, whilst they dispute concerning God; for He is mighty in power."

Sūratu 'n-Nisā'. Chapter iv. 51.
(Given at al-Madīnah.)

"Verily God will not forgive the associating with Him [any other being as a god], but will forgive other *sins* unto whom He pleaseth; and whoso associateth [another] with God hath wrought a great wickedness."

The following is an interpretation of the Muslim belief in the existence and nature of God, by the famous scholastic divine, the Imām al-Ghazzālī, in his book entitled *al-Maqṣadu 'l-asnā*, an extract from which Ockley has translated from *Pocock's Specimen Historiæ Arabum*:—

"Praise be to God the Creator and Restorer of all things; who does whatsoever He pleases, who is master of the glorious throne and mighty force, and directs His sincere servants into the right way and the straight path; who favoureth them, who have once borne testimony to the unity, by preserving their confessions from the darkness of doubt and hesitation; who directs them to follow His chosen apostle, upon whom be the blessing and peace of God; and to go after His most honourable companions, to whom he hath vouchsafed His assistance and direction which is revealed to them in His essence and operations by the excellencies of His attributes, to the knowledge whereof no man attains but he that hath been taught by hearing. To these, as touching His essence, He maketh known that He is one, and hath no partner; singular, without anything like Him; uniform, having no contrary; separate, having no equal. He is ancient, having no first; eternal, having no beginning; remaining for ever, having no end; continuing to eternity, without any termination. He persists, without ceasing to be; remains without failing, and never did cease, nor ever shall cease to be described by glorious attributes, nor is subject to any decree so as to be determined by any precise limits or set times, but is the First and the Last, and is within and without.

"(*What God is not.*) He, glorified be His name, is not a body endued with form, nor a substance circumscribed with limits or determined by measure; neither does He resemble bodies, as they are capable of being measured or divided. Neither is He a substance, neither do substances exist in Him; neither is He an accident, nor do accidents exist in Him. Neither is he like to anything that exists, neither is anything like to Him; nor is he determinate in quantity nor comprehended by bounds, nor circumscribed by the differences of situation, nor contained in the heavens. He sits upon the throne, after that manner which He Himself hath described, and in that same sense which He Himself means, which is a sitting far removed from any notion of contact, or resting upon, or local situation; but both the throne itself, and whatsoever is upon it, are sustained by the goodness of his power, and are subject to the grasp of His hand. But He is above the throne, and above all things, even to the utmost ends of the earth; but so above as at the same time not to be a whit nearer the throne and the heaven; since He is exalted by (infinite) degrees above the throne no less than He is exalted above the earth, and at the same time is near to everything that hath a being; nay, 'nearer to man than their jugular veins, and is witness to everything': though His nearness is not like the nearness of bodies, as neither is His essence like the essence of bodies. Neither doth He exist in anything, neither doth anything exist in Him; but He is too high to be contained in any place, and too holy to be determined by time; for He was before time and place were created, and is now after the same manner as He always was. He is also distinct from the creatures by His attributes, neither is there anything besides Himself in His essence, nor is His essence in any other besides Him. He is too holy to be subject to change, or any local motion; neither do any accidents dwell in Him, nor any contingencies befall Him; but He abides through all generations with His glorious attributes, free from all danger of dissolution. As to the attribute of perfection, He wants no addition of His perfection. As to being, He is known to exist by the apprehension of the understanding; and He is seen as He is by an ocular intuition, which will be vouchsafed out of His mercy and grace to the holy in the eternal mansion, completing their joy by the vision of His glorious presence.

"(*His power.*) He, praised be His name, is living, powerful, mighty, omnipotent, not liable to any defect or impotence; neither slumbering nor sleeping, nor being obnoxious to decay or death. To Him belongs the kingdom, and the power, and the might. His is the dominion, and the excellency, and the creation, and the command thereof. The heavens are folded up in His right hand, and all creatures are couched within His grasp. His excellency consists in His creating and producing, and His unity in communicating existence and a beginning of being. He created men and their works, and measured out their maintenance and their determined times. Nothing that is possible can escape His grasp, nor can the vicissitudes of things elude his power. The effects of his might are innumerable, and the objects of his knowledge infinite.

"(*His knowledge.*) He, praised be His name, knows all things that can be understood, and comprehends whatsoever comes to pass, from the extremities of the earth to the highest heavens. Even the weight of a pismire could not escape Him either in earth or heaven; but He would perceive the creeping of the black pismire in the dark night upon the hard stone, and discern the motion of an atom in the open air. He knows what is secret and conceals it, and views the conceptions of the minds, and the motions of the thoughts, and the inmost recesses of secrets, by a knowledge ancient and eternal, that never ceased to be His attribute from eternal eternity, and not by any new knowledge, superadded to His essence, either inhering or adventitious.

"(*His will.*) He, praised be His name, doth will those things to be that are, and disposes of all accidents. Nothing passes in the empire, nor the kingdom, neither little nor much, nor small nor great, nor good nor evil, nor profitable nor hurtful, nor faith nor infidelity, nor knowledge nor ignorance, nor prosperity nor adversity, nor increase nor decrease, nor obedience nor rebellion, but by His determinate counsel and decree, and His definite sentence and will. Nor doth the wink of him that seeth, nor the subtlety of him that thinketh, exceed the bounds of His will; but it is He who gave all things their beginning; He is the creator and restorer, the sole operator of what He pleases; there is no reversing His decree nor delaying what He hath determined, nor is there any refuge to man from his rebellion against Him, but only His help and mercy; nor hath any man any power to perform any duty towards Him, but through His love and will. Though men, genii, angels and devils, should conspire together either to put one single atom in motion, or cause it to cease its motion, without His will and approbation, they would not be able to do it. His will subsists in His essence amongst the rest of His attributes, and was from eternity one of His eternal attributes, by which He willed from eternity the existence of those things that He had decreed, which were produced in their proper seasons according to His eternal will, without any *before* or *after*, and in agreement both with His knowledge and will, and not by methodising of thoughts, nor waiting for a proper time, for which reason no one thing is in Him a hindrance from another.

"(*His hearing and sight.*) And He, praised be His name, is hearing and seeing, and heareth and seeth. No audible object, how still soever, escapeth His hearing; nor is any thing visible so small as to escape his sight;

for distance is no hindrance to His hearing, nor darkness to His sight. He sees without pupil or eye-lid, and hears without any passage or ear, even as He knoweth without a heart, and performs His actions without the assistance of any corporeal limb, and creates without any instrument, for His attributes (or properties) are not like those of men, any more than His essence is like theirs.

"(*His word.*) Furthermore, He doth speak, command, forbid, promise, and threaten by an eternal, ancient word, subsisting in His essence. Neither is it like to the word of the creatures, nor doth it consist in a voice arising from the commotion of the air and the collision of bodies, nor letters which are separated by the joining together of the lips or the motion of the tongue. The Qur'ān, the Law, the Gospel, and the Psalter, are books sent down by Him to His apostles, and the Qur'ān, indeed, is read with tongues, written in books, and kept in hearts: yet as subsisting in the essence of God, it doth not become liable to separation and division whilst it is transferred into the hearts and the papers. Thus Moses also heard the Word of God without voice or letter, even as the saints behold the essence of God without substance or accident. And since these are his attributes, He liveth and knoweth, is powerful and willeth and operateth, and seeth and speaketh, by life and knowledge, and will and hearing, and sight and word, not by His simple essence.

"(*His works.*) He, praised be His name, exists after such a manner that nothing besides Him hath any being but what is produced by His operation, and floweth from His justice after the best, most excellent, most perfect, and most just model. He is, moreover, wise in His works, and just in His decrees. But His justice is not to be compared with the justice of men. For a man may be supposed to act unjustly by invading the possession of another; but no injustice can be conceived by God, inasmuch as there is nothing that belongs to any other besides Himself, so that wrong is not imputable to Him as meddling with things not appertaining to Him. All things, Himself only excepted, genii, men, the devil, angels, heaven, earth, animals, plants, substance, accident, intelligible, sensible, were all created originally by Him. He created them by His power out of mere privation, and brought them into light, when as yet they were nothing at all, but He alone existing from eternity, neither was there any other with Him. Now He created all things in the beginning for the manifestation of His power, and His will, and the confirmation of His word, which was true from all eternity. Not that He stood in need of them, nor wanted them; but He manifestly declared His glory in creating and producing, and commanding, without being under any obligation, nor out of necessity. Loving kindness, the showing favour and grace, and beneficence, belong to Him; whereas it is in His power to pour forth upon men a variety of torments, and afflict them with various kinds of sorrows and diseases, which, if He were to do, His justice could not be arraigned, nor would he be chargeable with injustice. Yet he rewards those that worship Him for their obedience on account of his promise and beneficence, not of their merit nor of necessity, since there is nothing which He can be tied to perform; nor can any injustice be supposed in Him, nor can He be under any obligation to any person whatsoever. That His creatures, however, should be bound to serve Him, ariseth from His having declared by the tongues of the prophets that it was due to Him from them. The worship of Him is not simply the dictate of the understanding, but He sent messengers to carry to men His commands, and promises, and threats, whose veracity He proved by manifest miracles, whereby men are obliged to give credit to them in those things that they relate."

Included in the attributes of God as given in His ninety-nine titles or names, there are the *Haft ṣifāt*, or Seven Attributes; Muḥammad al-Barqawī has expressed them as follows:—

(1) *Ḥayāt*, or Life. God Most High is alone to be adored. He has neither associate nor equal. He is free from the imperfections of humanity. He is neither begotten nor does He beget. He is invisible. He is without figure, form, colour or parts. His existence has neither beginning nor end. He is immutable. If He so wills, He can annihilate the world in a moment of time and, if it seem good to Him, recreate it in an instant. Nothing is difficult to Him, whether it be the creation of a fly or that of the seven heavens. He receives neither profit nor loss from whatever may happen. If all the Infidels became believers and all the irreligious pious, He would gain no advantage. On the other hand, if all Believers became infidels, He would suffer no loss.

(2) *'Ilm*, or Knowledge. He has knowledge of all things hidden or manifest, whether in heaven or on earth. He knows the number of the leaves of the trees, of the grains of wheat and of sand. Events past and future are known to Him. He knows what enters into the heart of man and what He utters with His mouth. He alone, except those to whom He has revealed them, knows the invisible things. He is free from forgetfulness, negligence and error. His knowledge is eternal: it is not posterior to His essence.

(3) *Qudrah*, or Power. He is Almighty. If He wills, He can raise the dead, make stones talk, trees walk, annihilate the heavens and the earth, and recreate of gold or of silver thousands similar to those destroyed. He can transport a man in a moment of time from the east to the west, or from the west to the east, or to the seventh heaven. His power is eternal *a priori* and *a posteriori*. It is not posterior to His essence.

(4) *Irādah*, or Will. He can do what He wills, and whatever He wills comes to pass. He is not obliged to act. Everything, good or evil, in this world exists by His will. He wills the faith of the believer and the piety of the

religious. If He were to change His will there would be neither a true believer nor a pious man. He willeth also the unbelief of the unbeliever and the irreligion of the wicked and, without that will, there would neither be unbelief nor irreligion. All we do we do by His will: what He willeth not does not come to pass. If one should ask why God does not will that all men should believe, we answer: "We have no right to enquire about what God wills and does. He is perfectly free to will and to do what He pleases." In creating unbelievers, in willing that they should remain in that state; in making serpents, scorpions and pigs: in willing, in short, all that is evil, God has wise ends in view which it is not necessary that we should know. We must acknowledge that the will of God is eternal and that it is not posterior to His essence.

(5) *Sam'*, or Hearing. He hears all sounds whether low or loud. He hears without an ear, for His attributes are not like those of men.

(6) *Baṣar*, or Seeing. He sees all things, even the steps of a black ant on a black stone in a dark night; yet He has no eye as men have.

(7) *Kalām*, or Speech. He speaks, but not with a tongue as men do. He speaks to some of His servants without the intervention of another, even as He spoke to Moses, and to Muḥammad on the night of the ascension to heaven. He speaks to others by the instrumentality of Gabriel, and this is the usual way in which He communicates His will to the prophets. It follows from this that the Qur'ān is the word of God, and is eternal and uncreated. (Sale's *Faith of Islām.*)

With regard to the Muḥammadan belief in the Supreme Being, Mr. Palgrave, the well-known Oriental traveller, thus expresses himself:—

"'There is no god but God,' are words simply tantamount in English to the negation of any deity save one alone; and thus much they certainly mean in Arabic, but the imply much more also. Their full sense is, not only to deny absolutely and unreservedly all plurality, whether of nature or of person, in the Supreme Being, not only to establish the unity of the Unbegetting and Unbegot, in all its simple and uncommunicable Oneness; but besides this, the words in Arabic and among Arabs imply that this one Supreme Being is also the only Agent, the only Force, the only act existing throughout the universe, and leave to all beings else, matter or spirit, instinct or intelligence, physical or moral, nothing but pure unconditional passiveness, alike in movement or in quiescence, in action or in capacity. The sole power, the sole motor, movement, energy, and deed, is God; the rest is downright inertia and mere instrumentality, from the highest archangel down to the simplest atom of creation. Hence, in this one sentence, is summed up a system which, for want of a better name, I may be permitted to call the Pantheism of Force, or of Act, thus exclusively assigned to God, Who absorbs it all, exercises it all, and to Whom alone it can be ascribed, whether for preserving or for destroying, for relative evil or for equally relative good. I say 'relative,' because it is clear that in such a theology no place is left for absolute good or evil, reason or extravagance, all is abridged in the autocratical will of the One great Agent: '*sic volo, sic jubeo, stet pro ratione voluntas*'; or, more significantly still, in Arabic *Kema yeshao* (*ka-mā yashā'u*), 'as He wills it,' to quote the constantly recurring expression of the Coran.

"Thus immeasureably and eternally exalted above, and dissimilar from, all creatures, which lie levelled before Him on one common plane of instrumentality and inertness, God is One in the totality of omnipotent and omnipresent action, which acknowledges no rule, standard, or limit, save His own sole and absolute will. He communicates nothing to His creatures, for their seeming power and act ever remain His alone, and in return He receives nothing from them; for whatever they may be, that they are in Him, by Him, and from Him only. And, secondly, no superiority, no distinction, no pre-eminence, can be lawfully claimed by one creature over its fellow, in the utter equalisation of their unexceptional servitude and abasement; all are alike tools of the one solitary Force which employs them to crush or to benefit, to truth or to error, to honour or shame, to happiness or misery, quite independently of their individual fitness, deserts, or advantage, and simply because 'He wills it,' and 'as He wills it.'

"One might at first sight think that this tremendous Autocrat, this uncontrolled and unsympathising Power, would be far above anything like passions, desires, or inclinations. Yet such is not the case, for He has with respect to His creatures one main feeling and source of action, namely, jealousy of them, lest they should perchance attribute to themselves something of what is His alone, and thus encroach on His all-engrossing kingdom. Hence He is ever more prone to punish than to reward, to inflict pain than to bestow pleasure, to ruin than to build. It is His singular satisfaction to let created beings continually feel that they are nothing else than His slaves, His tools, and contemptible tools also, that thus they may the better acknowledge His superiority, and know His power to be above their power, His cunning above their cunning, His will above their will, His pride above their pride; or rather, that there is no power, cunning, will, or pride, save His own.

"But He Himself, sterile in His inaccessible height, neither loving nor enjoying aught save His own and self-measured decree, without son, companion, or counsellor, is no less barren of Himself than for His creatures, and His own barrenness and lone egoism in Himself is the cause and rule of His indifferent and unregarding despotism around. The first note is the key of the whole tune, and the primal idea of God runs through and modifies the whole system and creed that centres in Him.

"That the notion here given of the Deity, monstrous and blasphemous as it may appear, is exactly and literally that which the Coran conveys or intends to convey, I at present take for granted. But that it indeed is so, no one who has attentively perused and thought over the Arabic text (for mere cursory reading, especially in a translation, will not suffice), can hesitate to allow. In fact, every phrase of the preceding sentences, every touch in this odious portrait, has been taken, to the best of my ability, word for word, or at least meaning for meaning, from the 'Book,' the truest mirror of the mind and scope of its writer.

"And that such was in reality Mahomet's mind and idea, is fully confirmed by the witness-tongue of contemporary tradition. Of this we have many authentic samples: the *Saheeh* (*Ṣaḥīḥ*), the *Commentary of Beydāwi* (*al-Baiẓāwī*), the *Mishkat ul Masabih*, and fifty similar works, afford ample testimony on this point. But for the benefit of my readers in general, all of whom may not have drunk equally deep at the fountain-heads of Islamic dogma, I will subjoin a specimen, known perhaps to many Orientalists, yet too characteristic to be here omitted, a repetition of which I have endured times out of number from admiring and approving Wahhābīs in Nejed.

"'Accordingly, when God'—so runs the tradition: I had better said, the blasphemy—'resolved to create the human race, He took into His hands a mass of earth, the same whence all mankind were to be formed, and in which they after a manner pre-existed; and having then divided the clod into two equal portions, He threw the one half into hell, saying, "These to eternal fire, and I care not"; and projected the other half into heaven, adding, "and these to Paradise, I care not."' (See *Mishkātu 'l-Maṣābīḥ Bābu 'l-Qadr.*)

"Commentary would here be superfluous. But in this we have before us the adequate idea of predestination, or, to give it a truer name, pre-damnation, held and taught in the school of the Coran. Paradise and hell are at once totally independent of love or hatred on the part of the Deity, and of merits or demerits, of good or evil conduct, on the part of the creature; and, in the corresponding theory, rightly so, since the very actions which we call good or ill-deserving, right or wrong, wicked or virtuous, are in their essence all one and of one, and accordingly merit neither praise nor blame, punishment nor recompense, except and simply after the arbitrary value which the all-regulating will of the great despot may choose to assign or impute to them. In a word, He burns one individual through all eternity amid red-hot chains and seas of molten fire, and seats another in the plenary enjoyment of an everlasting brothel between forty celestial concubines, just and equally for His own good pleasure, and because He wills it.

"Men are thus all on one common level, here and hereafter, in their physical, social, and moral light—the level of slaves to one sole Master, of tools to one universal Agent. But the equalising process does not stop here: beasts, birds, fishes, insects, all participate of the same honour or debasement; all are, like man, the slaves of God, the tools and automata of His will; and hence Mahomet is simply logical and self-consistent when in the Coran he informs his followers, that birds, beasts, and the rest are 'nations' like themselves, nor does any intrinsic distinction exist between them and the human species, except what accidental diversity the 'King, the Proud One, the Mighty, the Giant,' &c., as he styles his God, may have been pleased to make, just as He willed it, and so long as He may will it.

"However, should any one think himself aggrieved by such association, he may console himself by reflecting that, on the other hand, angels, archangels, genii, devils, and whatever other spiritual beings may exist, are no less on his level also; and that if he himself be no better than a camel, he is, however, no worse than Gabriel or any seraph. And then, over all and above all, 'There is no god but God.'"—(*Central and Eastern Arabia*, vol. i. p. 365.)

GOG AND MAGOG.

GOG AND MAGOG. Arabic *Yājūj wa Mājūj*, also spelt *Ma'jūj wa Ya'jūj* (ياجوج وماجوج). A barbarous people of Central Asia, perhaps the Turkomans, who are in the Qur'ān represented as doing evil in the land in the days of Ẕū 'l-Qarnain (or Alexander). See Sūrah xviii. 93–97:—

"They said, 'O Ẕū 'l-Qarnain! verily Gog and Magog waste this land; shall we then pay thee tribute, so thou build a rampart between us and them?'

"He said, 'Better *than your tribute* is the might wherewith my Lord hath strengthened me; but help me strenuously, and I will set a barrier between you and them.

"'Bring me blocks of iron,'—until when it filled the space between the mountain sides—'Ply,' said he, 'your bellows,'—until when he had made it red with heat (fire), he said,—'Bring me molten brass that I may pour upon it.'

"And Gog and Magog were not able to scale it, neither were they able to dig through it.

"'This,' said he, 'is a mercy from my Lord.'"

They are also spoken of in Sūrah xxi. 95, 96, as a people who shall appear in the last days:—

"There is a ban on every city which we shall have destroyed, that they shall not arise again,

"Until a way is opened for Gog and Magog, and they shall hasten from every high land."

Al-Baiẓāwī says Yājūj and Mājūj are two tribes descended from Japheth the son of Noah, and some say Yājūj belong to the Turks and Mājūj to the Jīls. (Comp

Ezekiel xxxviii. 2; xxxix. 1; Rev. xvi. 14; xx. 8.)

GOLD. Arabic *zahab* (ذهب); Heb. זהב. The *zakāt* imposed upon gold is upon twenty *misqāls* one-half misqāl, and upon every four misqāls in excess, one qīrāt, because the alms upon gold is one fortieth of the whole. This is due upon all gold, whether it be in coin or in ornaments. But ash-Shāfi'ī says it is not due upon the ornaments of women or the rings of men. (*Hidāyah*, vol. i. p. 27.)

The sale of gold is only lawful when it is exactly equal in point of weight, for Muḥammad said, "Sell gold for gold, from hand to hand, at an equal rate according to weight, for any inequality in point of weight is usury." (*Idem*, vol. ii. 552.)

"It is not lawful for a man or woman to eat or drink out of gold or silver vessels." (*Idem*, vol. vi. 86.)

GOLIATH. Arabic *Jālūt* (جالوت). The giant whom King David slew. Mentioned in the Qur'ān, Sūrah ii. 251: "And when they went forth to battle against Jālūt and his army, they said, 'O Lord, give us patience, and strengthen our feet, and help us against the infidels!' Therefore they discomfited them by the will of God, and David slew Jālūt."

The commentators have not ventured to give any account of Jālūt.

GOMORRAH. Arabic *Ghamūrah* (غمورة). Not mentioned by name in the Qūr'ān; but *Sadūm wa Ghamūrah* are understood to be the "overturned cities" referred to in Sūrahs ix. 71, lxix. 9.

GOOD WORKS. Arabic *aṣ-Ṣāliḥāt* (الصالحات). According to the teaching of the Qur'ān, good works without faith will not save from the torments of hell.

Sūrah xviii. 103–5: "Shall we tell you who are they that have lost their labour most; whose efforts in the present life have been mistaken, and who deemed that what they did was right? They are those who believed not in the signs of the Lord, or that they should ever meet Him. Vain, therefore, are their works; and no weight will we allow them on the day of Resurrection."

Faith in the above is belief in the mission of Muḥammad: all Muslims being considered in a state of grace, no matter what their actions may be. With reference to the good deeds of Muslims, the following is the teaching of Muḥammad, as recorded in the Traditions (*Mishkāt*, book x. chap. iii.):—

"When a man is brought to Islām and he performs it well, God covers all his former sins, and he gets ten rewards for every good act, up to seven hundred, and even more than that, whereas the reward of misdeeds is as one to one, unless God passes that over likewise."

"There are three persons whose actions are not written; one a person asleep until he awakes; the second, a boy not arrived at puberty; the third, a madman until he recovers his reason."

"Verily, God recordeth both the good deeds and the evil deeds. He who has proposed to do evil and did not do it, for him God recordeth one perfectly good deed. And he who intended to do good and put his intentions into practice, for him God recordeth from ten to seven hundred good deeds (according to their merits). And he who intended to do evil but did it not, God recordeth one good act; but he who intendeth to do evil and doeth it, for him God recordeth one evil deed."

"Verily, the condition of that person who does evil and after that good deeds, is like the condition of a man with tight armour on, which has troubled him. He does one good deed and the rings of the armour become open. He does another good deed, and the armour falls from his body."

"Verily there was a man amongst those who were before you to whom the angel of death came to take his soul, and he was asked 'Have you done any good act?' He said in answer, 'I do not remember that I have done any good.' It was said to him, 'Look well into yourself, and consider if you have done any good work. He said, 'I do not find any good in myself, except that I used to buy and sell in the world and used to claim my right from the rich, but allowed them their leisure to pay me when they liked, and I forgave the poor.' Then God brought that man into paradise."

"An adulteress was forgiven, who passed by a dog at a well, and the dog was holding out his tongue from thirst, which was near killing him. The woman drew off her boot and tied it to the end of her veil, and drew water for the dog, and gave him to drink, and she was forgiven on account of that act. It was asked the Prophet, 'Verily, are there rewards for our doing good to quadrupeds, and giving them water to drink?' He said, 'There are rewards for benefiting every animal having a moist liver.'"

"Your smiling in your brother's face is alms; and your exhorting mankind to virtuous deeds is alms; and your prohibiting the forbidden is alms; and your showing men the road when they lose it is alms; and your assisting the blind is alms; and your removing stones, thorns, and bones, which are inconvenient to man is alms; and your pouring water from your bucket into that of your brother is alms for you."

GOSHAH-NISHĪN (گوشه نشين). *Lit.* "One who sits in a corner." A Persian term for a devout person who in retirement engages in the contemplation of the Deity.

GOSPEL. Arabic *Injīl* (انجيل). A term applied to the whole of the New Testament scriptures. [NEW TESTAMENT.]

GRAMMAR. [ILMU 'L-ADAB.]

GRANDFATHER. Arabic *jadd* (جد). If a father die without appointing an executor, the grandfather represents the father. And in making contracts of marriage, the grandfather has precedence of an executor, although the executor takes precedence in managing the property. (*Hidāyah*, vol. iv. p. 555.) In case of the father being poor, it is the duty of the grandfather to act for his grandchild in the distribution of alms, &c. (*Idem*, vol. ii. p. 244.)

GRANDMOTHER. Arabic *jaddah* (جدة). If the mother of an infant die, the right *ḥizānah*, or guardianship, rests with the maternal grandmother in preference to the paternal; but if she be not living, the paternal grandmother has the right prior to any other relation. The *paternal* grandmother is also entitled to a sixth of the effects of a child of her son, if the child's mother be dead, as being the mother's share. (*Hidāyah*, vol. i. p. 386.)

GRAVE. Arabic *qabr* (قبر); Heb. קבר. The graves of Muḥammadans are so dug as to allow the body to lie with its face towards Makkah; consequently in India they are dug from north to south. It is usual to dig a grave the depth equal to the height of the breast of a middle-sized man, and to make a recess at the bottom, which is called *laḥd*, in which the body is placed. The body having been placed in this recess, it is closed with unburnt bricks, and the grave is filled with earth and a mound raised over it.

The Traditions of Muḥammad, as well as the works of Muslim doctors, all teach that a dead body is conscious of pain, and therefore great care is taken to prevent any pressure upon the body.

'Āmir relates that his father Sa'd ibn Abī Waqqāṣ said on his death-bed, "Make a *laḥd* for me towards Makkah, and put unburnt bricks upon my grave, as was done in the case of the Prophet (*Ṣaḥīḥu Muslim*, p. 211).

Sufyān at-Tammār relates that he "saw the Prophet's grave, and the top of it was like a camel's back." (*Ṣaḥīḥu 'l-Bukhārī*.)

Ibn 'Abbās says "a red cloth was placed upon the Prophet's grave." (*Mishkāt*, book v. c. vi.)

Jābir says "the Prophet prohibited building with mortar on graves, and also placing inscriptions upon them." (*Mishkāt*, book v. c. vi.) But notwithstanding this tradition (which is acted upon by the Wahhābīs), masonry tombs are most common in all parts of Islām, and form some of the most striking specimens of Muḥammadan architecture. [TOMBS.]

GRAVE, The Punishments of the. ['AZABU 'L-QABR.]

GREEKS. Arabic *ar-Rūm* (الروم), by which is meant the Byzantine or Eastern Empire. In the xxxth chapter of the Qur'ān, entitled the *Sūratu 'r-Rūm*, or the "Chapter of the Greeks," there is a reference to the defeat of the Byzantine power by the Persians with a supposed prophecy of future successes. The chapter begins thus:—

"Alif. Lām. Mīm. THE GREEKS have been defeated

"In a land hard by: But after their defeat they shall defeat their foes,

"In a few years. First and last is the affair with God. And on that day shall the faithful rejoice

"In the aid of their God: He aideth whom He will; and He is the Mighty, the Merciful.

"It is the promise of God: To his promise God will not be untrue: but most men know if not."

Following al-Baiẓāwī, the Jalālān, and other commentators, Sale remarks that—

The accomplishment of the prophecy contained in this passage, which is very famous among the Muḥammadans, being insisted on by their doctors as a convincing proof that the Qur'ān really came down from heaven, it may be excusable to be a little particular.

The passage is said to have been revealed on occasion of a great victory obtained by the Persians over the Greeks, the news whereof coming to Makkah, the infidels became strangely elated, and began to abuse Muḥammad and his followers, imagining that this success of the Persians, who, like themselves, were idolators, and supposed to have no scriptures, against the Christians, who pretended as well as Muḥammad to worship one God, and to have divine scriptures, was an earnest of their own future successes against the Prophet, and those of his religion, to check which vain hopes it was foretold in the words of the text, that how improbable soever it might seem, yet the scale should be turned in a few years, and the vanquished Greeks prevail as remarkably against the Persians. That this prophecy was exactly fulfilled, the commentators fail not to observe, though they do not exactly agree in the accounts they give of its accomplishment, the number of years between the two actions being not precisely determined. Some place the victory gained by the Persians in the fifth year before the Hijrah, and their defeat by the Greeks in the second year after it, when the battle of Badr was fought; others place the former in the third or fourth year before the Hijrah, and the latter in the end of the sixth or beginning of the seventh year after it, when the expedition of al-Ḥudaibiyah was undertaken. The date of the victory gained by the Greeks in the first of these accounts, interferes with a story which the commentators tell, of a wager laid by Abū Bakr with Ubaiy ibn Khalf, who turned this prophecy into ridicule. Abū Bakr at first laid ten young camels that the Persians should receive an overthrow within three years, but on his acquainting Muḥammad with what he had done, that Prophet told him that the word *bi'z*, made use of in this passage, signified no determinate number of years, but any number from three to nine (though some suppose the tenth year is included), and therefore advised him to prolong the time and to raise the wager, which he accordingly proposed to Ubaiy, and they agreed that the time assigned should be nine years and the wager a hundred camels. Before the time was elapsed, Ubaiy died of a wound received at Uḥud, in the third year of the Hijrah; but the event afterwards showing that Abū Bakr had won, he received the camels of Ubay's heirs, and brought them in triumph to Muḥammad. History informs us that the successes of Khosru Parviz, King of Persia, who carried on a terrible war against the Greek empire, to revenge the death of Maurice, his father-in-law, slain by Phocas, were very great, and continued in an uninterrupted course for two-and-twenty years. Particularly in the year of Christ 615, about the beginning of the sixth year before the Hijrah, the Persians, having the preceding year conquered Syria, made themselves masters of Palestine and took Jerusalem, which seems to be that signal advantage gained over the Greeks mentioned in this passage, as agreeing best with the terms here used, and most likely to alarm the Arabs by reason of their vicinity to the scene of action; and there was so little probability at that time of the Greeks being able to retrieve their losses, much less to distress the Persians, that in the following years the arms of the latter made still farther and more considerable progresses, and at length they laid siege to Constantinople itself. But in the year 625, in which the fourth year of the Hijrah began, abut ten years after the taking of Jerusalem, the Greeks, when it was least expected, gained a remarkable victory over the Persians, and not only obliged them to quit the territories of the empire, by carrying the war into their own country, but drove them to the last extremity, and spoiled the capital city al-Madāyin; Heraclius enjoying thenceforward a continued series of good fortune, to the deposition and death of Khosrū. (Sale's *Koran*, *in loco.*)

GROVE, The. Arabic *Aikah* (ايكة). The *Aṣḥābu 'l-Aikah*, or "the people of the Grove," are mentioned four times in the Qur'ān, Sūrahs xv. 78, xxvi. 176, xxviii. 21, l. 13, as being a tribe or class of people who treated the prophets as liars. The following particulars regarding them are given in Sūrah xxvi. 170:—

"The people of the grove of Madyan treated the Apostles as liars.

"When Shu'aib their brother said to them, 'Will ye not fear God?

"I truly am your trustworthy Apostle.

"Fear God, then, and obey me:

"No reward ask I of you for this: my reward is of the Lord of the Worlds alone."

GUARDIANSHIP. Guardianship over a minor is of two kinds: *wilāyah* (ولاية), or guardianship of the property and education and marriage of the ward, and *ḥiẓānah* (حضانة), or guardianship over the rearing and bringing up of the child.

Guardians are either so by natural right or by testament, or by appointment by a judge.

The guardianship of a minor for the management and preservation of his property devolves first on his or her father, then on the father's executor, next on the paternal grandfather, then on his executor, then on the executors of such executors, next on the ruling power or his representative, the Qāẓī, or judge. In default of a father, father's father, and their executors, as above, all of whom are termed near guardians, it rests in the Qāẓī to appoint a guardian of an infant's property. The other paternal kinsmen who are termed remote kindred, and the mother succeed, according to proximity, to the guardianship of an infant for the purpose of education and marriage; they have no right to be guardians of his property, unless appointed to be so by the ruling authority, or in the original proprietor's will, proved by competent witnesses. The mother's right of guardianship is, however, forfeited upon her being remarried to a stranger, but regained when she is divorced by him, and has again become a widow.

In default of the mother as well as of the paternal kindred of a minor, his maternal relations are, according to proximity, entitled to guardianship for the purposes of education and marriage, and not for the management of his property, unless so appointed in the late owner's will or by the Qāẓī.

The general rule is that a guardian, executor, or anyone who has the care of the person and property of a minor, can enter into a contract which is or likely to be advantageous and not injurious to his ward.

A guardian may sell or purchase moveables on account of his ward, either for an equivalent or at such a rate as to occasion an inconsiderable loss, but not at such a rate as to make the loss great and apparent. (*Hidāyah*, vol. iv. p. 553.)

A guardian is allowed to borrow money for the support and education of his ward, even by pawning the minor's property; the debt so contracted must be paid out of his (the minor's) estate, or by him when he comes of age.

It is not lawful for a guardian to pledge into his own hands goods belonging to his ward on account of a debt due to him, or into the hands of his child being an infant, or into the hands of his slave being a merchant and free from debt. (*Hidāyah*, vol. iv. p. 214.)

A father can pawn the goods of his infant child into his own hands for a debt due from the child, or into the hands of another of his children being an infant.

A father may also pawn on account of his own debt the goods belonging to his minor son, who on coming of age will redeem the goods discharging the debt, and have a claim on the father for the sum.

The contract of pawn entered into by a father with respect to his minor child's goods cannot be annulled by the minor, even if it were not for his own debt or for his own benefit.

The mother is, of all the persons, the best entitled to the custody (*ḥiẓānah*) of her infant child during marriage and after separation from her husband, unless she be an apostate, or wicked, or unworthy to be trusted. (*Fatāwā-i-'Alamgīrī*, vol. i. p. 728.)

Next the mother's mother how high soever is entitled to the custody (*ḥiẓānah*) of a child; failing her by death, or marriage to a stranger, the full sister is entitled; failing her by death or marriage to a stranger, the half-sister by the mother. On failure of her in the same way the daughter of the full sister, then the daughter of the half-sister by the mother. Next the maternal aunt in the same way, and then the paternal aunts also in like manner. (*Fatāwā-i-'Ālamgīrī*, vol. i. p. 728.)

An *umm-i-walad* (or a female slave who has borne a child to her master), when emancipated, obtains the right of taking her child. (*Hidāyah*, vol. i. p. 389.)

When it is necessary to remove a boy from the custody of women, or there is no woman of his own people to take charge of him, he is to be given up to his agnate male relatives (*'aṣābah*). Of these the father is the first, then the paternal grandfather, how high soever, then the full brother, then the half-brother by the father, then the son of the full brother, then the son of the half-brother by the father, then the full paternal uncle, then the half paternal uncle by the father, then the sons of paternal uncles in the same order. But though a boy may be given up to the son of his paternal uncle, a girl should not be entrusted to him

No male has any right to the custody of a female child, but one who is within the prohibited degrees of relationship to her; and an *'aṣābah* who is profligate has no right to her custody. (*Fatāwā-i-'Ālamgīrī*, vol. i. p. 729.)

A female's custody of a boy terminates when he is seven years old, and of a girl at her puberty.

Male custody of a boy continues till puberty, of a female not only till puberty, but till she can be safely left to herself and trusted to take care of herself.

When a female has neither father nor grandfather nor any of her *'aṣābah* to take charge of her, or the *'aṣābah* is profligate, it is the duty of the judge to take cognizance of her condition; and if she can be trusted to take care of herself, he should allow her to live alone, whether she be a virgin or a *saiyidah*, and if not, he should place her with some female *amīn*, or trustee, in whom he has confidence; for he is the superintendent of all Muslims. (*Fatāwā-i-'Alamgīrī*, vol. i. p. 730.)

When a mother refuses to take charge of a child without hire, it may be committed to another.

A boy or girl having passed the period of *ḥiẓānah*, has no option to be with one parent in preference to the other, but must necessarily thenceforth remain in charge of the father. (*Hidāyah*, vol. i. p. 389.)

Before the completion of *'iddah*, or dissolution of marriage, the proper place of *ḥiẓānah* is that where the husband and wife live, and the former cannot take away the child out of the custody of the latter. After completion of her *'iddah*, and separation from her husband, a woman can take her child to the place of her nativity, provided the marriage had been contracted there, or it is so near from the place of separation or husband's residence, that if the husband should leave the latter in the morning to visit the child, he can return to his residence before night. There is also no objection to her removing with the child from a village to the city or chief town of the district, the same being advantageous to the child, and in no respect injurious to the father. If the child's mother be dead, and its *ḥiẓānah* or custody has passed to the maternal grandfather, she cannot remove the child to her own city, though the marriage had taken place there. Other women than the grandmother are like her in respect to the place of *ḥiẓānah*.

When an *umm-i-walad* has been emancipated, she has no right to take her child from the city in which the father is residing.

(*Hidāyah*, vol. i.; *Fatāwā-i-'Ālamgīrī*, vol. i.; *Durru 'l-Mukhtār*, p. 846; *Jāmi'u 'r-Rumūz*; *Tagore Lectures, 1879*; Bailie's *Digest*, p. 430.)

GUEST. Arabic *ẓaif* (ضيف).

[HOSPITALITY.]

GURZ (گرز). (1) The Persian word for the *miṭraqah*, or iron mace, wherewith the infidel dead are smitten in their graves by the angels Munkar and Nakīr. ['AZABU 'L-QABR.]

(2) An iron mace pointed at one end and having a knob at the other covered with spikes, and used by the Gurz Mār, or Rufa'ī faqīrs, for striking against their breasts in their devotional exercises. (*Qānūn-i-Islām*, p. 291.)

H.

HABĀ' (هباء). "Dust," especially the finer particles which fly about and are only conspicuous in the sun's rays.

A term used by the Ṣūfī mystics for those portions of matter (*hayūla*) which God has distributed in creation. ('Abdu 'r-Razzāq's *Dict. of Ṣūfī Terms.*)

ḤABĪB AN-NAJJĀR (حبيب النجار). "Ḥabīb the Carpenter," whose story is told in the Qur'ān (Sūrah xxxvi. 12), as follows:—

"Set forth to them the instance of the people of the city (*i.e.* of Antioch) when the Sent Ones came to it.

"When we sent two (*i.e.* John and Jude)

unto them and they charged them both with imposture—therefore with a third (*i.e.* Simon Peter) we strengthened them: and they said, 'Verily we are the Sent unto you *of God*.'

"They said, 'Ye are only men like us: Nought hath the God of Mercy sent down. Ye do nothing but lie.'

"They said, 'Our Lord knoweth that we are surely sent unto you;

"'To proclaim a clear message is our only duty.'

"They said, 'Of a truth we augur ill from you: if ye desist not we will surely stone you, and a grievous punishment will surely befall you from us.'

"They said, 'Your augury of ill is with yourselves. Will ye be warned? Nay, ye are an erring people.'

"Then from the end of the city a man (*i.e.* Ḥabīb, the carpenter) came running: He said, 'O my people! follow the Sent Ones;

"'Follow those who ask not of you a recompence, and who are rightly guided.

"'And why should I not worship Him who made me, and to whom ye shall be brought back?

"'Shall I take gods beside Him? If the God of mercy be pleased to afflict me, their intercession will not avert from me aught, nor will they deliver:

"'Truly then should I be in a manifest error.

"'Verily, in your Lord have I believed; therefore hear me.'

"—It was said to him, 'Enter thou into Paradise' (*i.e.* after they had stoned him to death). And he said, 'Oh that my people knew

"'How gracious God hath been to me, and that He hath made me one of *His* honoured ones.'

"But no army sent we down out of heaven after his *death*, nor were we then sending down *our angels*—

"There was but one shout *from Gabriel*, and lo! they were extinct.

"Oh! the misery *that rests* upon my servants! No apostle cometh to them but they laugh him to scorn."

Al-Baiẓāwī, the commentator, says the people of the City of Antioch were idolaters, and that Jesus sent two of his disciples, Yaḥya and Yūnas (John and Jude) to preach to them. And when they arrived, they met Ḥabīb, the carpenter, to whom they made known their mission. Ḥabīb said, "What signs can ye show that ye are sent of God?" And the disciples replied, "We can heal the sick and give sight to those who are born blind, and cure the leprosy." Then Ḥabīb brought his sick son to them, and they laid their hands upon him and he was healed. And Ḥabīb believed on Jesus, and he made known the gospel to the people of the city. Many of the people then came to the disciples and were also healed. The news then reached the ear of the governor of the city, and he sent for the two disciples and they preached to him. He replied, "Is your God different from our God?" They said, "Yes. He it is who made thee and thy gods." The governor then sent them away and put them in prison. When they were in prison, Jesus sent Sham'ūn (Simon Peter), and he came secretly and made friends with the servants of the governor, and in time gained access to the governor's presence, and performed a miracle in the presence of the governor by raising a child who had been dead seven days. The child when raised from the dead, said he had seen Jesus Christ in heaven, and that he had interceded for the three disciples in prison. The governor believed and many others with him. Those who did not believe raised a disturbance in the city, and Ḥabīb the carpenter exhorted them to believe. For this he was stoned, and, having died, entered into Paradise.

Ḥabīb's tomb is still seen at Antioch, and is visited by Muḥammadans as a shrine.

HABĪL (هبيل). [ABEL.]

ḤABWAH (حبوة). The posture of sitting with the legs and thighs contracted towards the belly, the back bent forwards, and supported in that position by the arms crossed over the knees. Muslims are forbidden to sit in this posture during the recital of the Khuṭbah on Fridays (*Mishkāt*, book iv. p. 45, pt. 2) as it inclines to drowsiness.

ḤADAS̤ (حدث). State of an unclean person, of one who has not performed the usual ablutions before prayer.

ḤADD (حد), pl. *ḥudūd*. In its primitive sense *ḥadd* signifies "obstruction," whence a porter or gate-keeper is called *ḥaddād*, or "obstructer," from his office of prohibiting people from entering. In law it expresses the punishments, the limits of which have been defined by Muḥammad either in the Qur'ān or in the Ḥadīs̤. These punishments are (1) For *adultery*, stoning; (2) For *fornication*, a hundred stripes; (3) For *the false accusation of a married person with adultery* (or *Qazf*), eighty stripes; (4) For *apostasy*, death; (5) For *drinking wine*, eighty stripes; (6) For *theft*, the cutting off of the right hand; (7) For *highway robbery*: for simple robbery on the highway, the loss of hands and feet; for robbery with murder, death, either by the sword or by crucifixion. (*Hidāyah*, vol. ii. p. 1. [PUNISHMENT.]

AL-ḤADĪD (الحديد). "Iron." The title of the LVIIth Sūrah of the Qur'ān, in which the word occurs (verse 25): "We sent down *iron* in which are both keen violence and advantages to men."

ḤĀDIS̤ (حادث). What happens for the first time; new, fresh. That which is born in time as opposed to *qadīm*, or that which is without a beginning, as God.

ḤADĪS̤ (حديث), pl. *aḥādīs̤*. [TRADITION.]

ḤADĪS̤ QUDSĪ (حديث قدسى). A divine saying. A term used for a *ḥadīs̤* which relates a revelation from God in the language of the Prophet. An example is found in the *Mishkāt* (book i. c. i. pt. 1): "Abū Hurairah said, 'The Prophet of God related these words of God, "The sons of Adam vex me, and abuse the age, whereas I am The AGE itself: In my hands are all events: I have made the day and night."'"

HADĪYAH (هدية). A present or offering made to persons of consequence, kings or rulers.

HADY (هدى). Cattle sacrificed at Makkah during the Pilgrimage, as distinguished from animals sacrificed on the Great Festival, which are called *uẓḥīyah*. These animals are branded and sent off with strings round their necks, as offerings to the sacred temple. They may be bullocks, or camels, or sheep, or goats. (*Mishkāt*, book xi. c. viii.)

ḤĀFIẒ (حافظ). *Lit.* "A guardian" or protector. (1) One of the names of God, *al-Ḥāfiẓ*. (2) A governor, *e.g. Ḥāfiẓu 'l-Bait;* the guardian of the Makkan temple. (3) One who has committed the whole of the Qur'ān to memory.

'Usmān relates that the Prophet said: "The best person amongst you is he who has learnt the Qur'ān and teaches it. (*Mishkāt*, book vii. c. i.) In the east it is usual for blind men to commit the Qur'ān to memory, and to thus obtain the honourable distinction of *Ḥāfiẓ*.

ḤAFṢAH (حفصة). One of Muḥammad's wives. She was the daughter of 'Umar, and the widow of Khunais, an early convert to Islām. She married Muḥammad about six months after her former husband's death. During the lifetime of the Prophet she was a person of considerable influence in his counsels, being the daughter of 'Umar. She survived Muḥammad some years, and has recorded several traditions of his sayings.

HAGAR. Arabic *Hājar* (هاجر). The slave wife of Abraham and the mother of Ishmael. Al-Baiẓāwī says that Hājar was the slave girl of Sarah, the wife of Abraham, and she admitted her to Abraham, and from her was born Ishmael. Sarah became jealous of Hājar (because she had a son), and she demanded of Abraham that he should put both the mother and child away, and he sent them away in the direction of Makkah, and at Makkah God produced for them the spring Zamzam [ZAMZAM]. When the tribe of Jurhum saw that there was water in that place, they said to Hājar, "If you will share with us the water of this spring, we will share with you the milk of our herds," and from that time Makkah became a place of importance. (*Tafsīru 'l-Baiẓāwī*, p. 424.)

HAIR. Arabic *sha'r, sha'ar* (شعر). Heb. שֵׂעָר.

The sale of human hair is unlawful in the same manner as the use of it for any purpose is unlawful. Being a part of the human body, it is necessary to preserve it from disgrace, to which an exposure of it to sale necessarily subjects it. It is related in the traditions that God has cursed women who use false hair. (*Hidāyah*, vol. ii. p. 439.) [HEAD.]

ḤĀ'IṬĪYAH (حائطية). A sect of Muslims founded by Aḥmad ibn Ḥā'iṭ, who said there were two Gods, one whose existence is from eternity (*qadīm*), *i.e.* Allāh, and the other who is created in time (*muḥaddaṣ*), *i.e.* al-Masīḥ (Christ), and that it is he who will judge the world in the last day. And he maintained that this is the meaning of the words which occur in the traditions: "God created man in his own image." (*Kitābu 'l-Ta'rīfāt, in loco.*)

ḤAIWĀN (حيوان). The animal creation; which is divided into *ḥaiwān nāṭiq*, or rational beings; and *ḥaiwān sākit*, or irrational beings. [ANIMALS, BEINGS.]

AL-ḤAIY (الحى); Heb. חַי. "The Living One." One of the ninety-nine attributes of God. The term frequently occurs in the Qur'ān.

ḤĀ'IẒAH (حائضة). A menstruous woman. [MENSTRUATION.]

ḤĀJAR (هاجر). [HAGAR.]

AL-ḤAJARU 'L-ASWAD (الحجر الاسود). *Lit.* "The Black Stone." The famous black stone which forms part of the sharp angle of the Ka'bah in the temple at Makkah. Mr. Burkhardt says, "It is an irregular oval, about seven inches in diameter, with an undulating surface, composed of about a dozen smaller stones of different sizes and shapes, well joined together with a small quantity of cement, and perfectly well smoothed; it looks as if the whole had been broken into as many pieces by a violent blow, and then united again. It is very difficult to determine accurately the quality of this stone, which has been worn to its present surface by the millions of touches and kisses it has received. It appeared to me like a lava, containing several small extraneous particles of a whitish and of a yellow substance. Its colour is now a deep reddish brown approaching to black. It is surrounded on all sides by a border composed of a substance which I took to be a close cement of pitch and gravel of a similar, but not quite the same, brownish colour. This border serves to support its detached pieces; it is two or three inches in breadth, and rises a little above the surface of the stone. Both the border and the stone itself are encircled by a silver band, broader below than above, and on the two sides, with a considerable swelling below, as if a part of the stone were hidden under it. The lower part of the border is studded with silver nails."

Captain Burton remarks, "The colour appeared to me black and metallic, and the centre of the stone was sunk about two inches below the metallic circle. Round the sides was a reddish brown cement, almost level with the metal, and sloping down to the middle of the stone. The band is now a massive arch of gold or silver gilt. I found the aperture in which the stone is, one span and three fingers broad."

According to Ibn 'Abbās, Muḥammad said

the black stone came down from Paradise, and at the time of its descent it was whiter than milk, but that the sins of the children of Adam have caused it to be black, by their touching it. That on the Day of Resurrection, when it will have two eyes, by which it will see and know all those who touched it and kissed it, and when it will have a tongue to speak, it will give evidence in favour of those who touched and kissed it.

Maximus Tyrius, who wrote in the second century, says "The Arabians pay homage to I know not what god, which they represent by a quadrangular stone," alluding to the Ka'bah or temple which contains the black stone. The Guebars or Ancient Persians, assert that the Black Stone was amongst the images and relics left by Mahabad and his successors in the Ka'bah, and that it was an emblem of Saturn. It is probably an aërolite, and owes its reputation, like many others, to its fall from the sky. Its existence as an object of adoration in an iconoclastic religious system, can only be accounted for by Muḥammad's attempt to conciliate the idolaters of Arabia.

A complete list of the falls of aërolites and meteoric stones through the atmosphere, is published in the *Edinburgh Philosophical Journal*, from a work by Chladni in German, in which the subject is ably and fully treated.

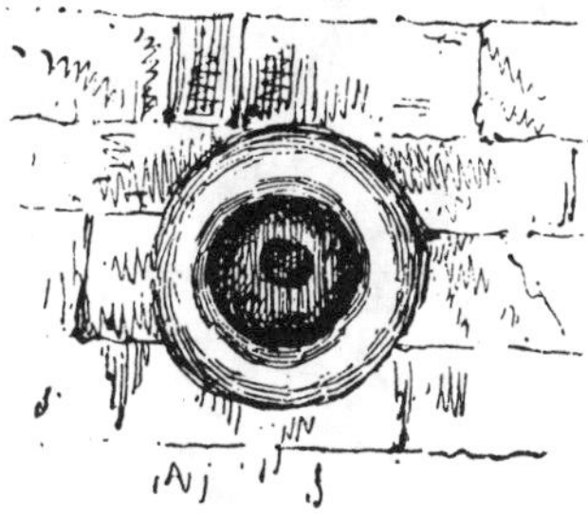

THE HAJARU 'L-ASWAD. (*Burton.*)

ḤAJB (حجب). A legal term in the Muḥammadan law of inheritance, signifying the cutting off of an heir from his portion.

ḤĀJĪ (حاجى), also *ḥājj*. A person who has performed the *ḥajj*, or pilgrimage to Makkah. It is retained as a title of honour by those who have performed the pilgrimage, *e.g.* *Ḥājī Qāsim*, *i.e.* "Qāsim the Pilgrim." [HAJJ.]

ḤAJJ (حج). *Lit.* "setting out," "tending towards." The pilgrimage to Makkah performed in the month of Ẕū 'l-Ḥijjah, or the twelfth month of the Muḥammadan year. It is the fifth pillar of Muḥammadan practical religion, and an incumbent religious duty, founded upon express injunctions in the Qur'ān. According to Muḥammad it is a divine institution, and has the following authority in the Qur'ān for its due observance:—

(*It is noticeable that all the verses in the Qur'ān with regard to the pilgrimage are in the later Sūrahs, when they are arranged in their chronological order.*)

Sūrah xxii. 28:—

"And proclaim to the peoples a PILGRIMAGE (*ḥajj*). Let them come to thee on foot and on every fleet camel, arriving by every deep defile:

"That they may bear witness of its benefits to them, and may make mention of God's name on the appointed days (*i.e.* the ten first days of Ẕū 'l-Ḥijjah), over the brute beasts with which He hath supplied them for sustenance: Therefore eat thereof yourselves, and feed the needy, the poor:

"Then let them bring the neglect of their persons to a close, and let them pay their vows, and circuit the ancient House.

"This *do*. And he that respecteth the sacred ordinances of God, this will be best for him with his Lord."

Sūrah ii. 153:—

"Verily, as-Ṣafā and al-Marwah are among the signs of God: whoever then maketh a pilgrimage (*ḥajj*) to the temple, or visiteth it, shall not be to blame if he go round about them both. And as for him who of his own accord doeth what is good—God is Grateful, Knowing."

Idem, 192:—

"Accomplish the pilgrimage (*ḥajj*), and the visitation (*'umrah*) for God: and if ye be hemmed in by foes, send whatever sacrifice shall be the easiest, and shave not your heads until the offering reach the place of sacrifice. But whoever among you is sick or has an ailment of the head, must expiate by fasting, alms, or an offering.

"And when ye are safe *from foes*, he who contents himself with the visitation (*'umrah*) until the pilgrimage (*ḥajj*), *shall bring* whatever offering shall be the easiest. But he who findeth nothing *to offer*, shall fast three days in the pilgrimage itself, and seven days when ye return: they shall be ten days in all. This is binding on him whose family shall not be present t the sacred Mosque (*al-Masjidu 'l-ḥarām*). And fear God, and know that God is terrible in punishing.

"*Let* the pilgrimage *be made* in the months already known (*i.e.* Shawwāl, Ẕū 'l-Qa'dah, and Ẕū 'l-Ḥijjah): whoever therefore undertaketh the pilgrimage therein, let him not know a woman, nor transgress, nor wrangle in the pilgrimage. The good which ye do, God knoweth it. And provide *for your journey;* but the best provision is the fear of God: fear me, then, O men of understanding!

"It shall be no crime in you if ye seek an increase from your Lord (*i.e.* to trade); and when ye pass swiftly on from 'Arafāt, then remember God near the holy temple (*al-Masjidu 'l-ḥarām*); and remember Him, because He hath guided you who before this were of those who went astray:

"Then pass on quickly where the people quickly pass (*i.e.* from 'Arafāt), and ask pardon of God, for God is Forgiving, Merciful.

"And when ye have finished your holy rites, remember God as ye remember your own fathers, or with a yet more intense remembrance! Some men there are who say, 'O our Lord! give us *our portion* in this world:' but such shall have no portion in the next life:

"And some say, 'O our Lord! give us good in this world and good in the next, and keep us from the torment of the fire.'

"They shall have the lot which they have merited: and God is swift to reckon.

"Bear God in mind during the stated days: but if any haste away in two days (*i.e.* after the *ḥajj*), it shall be no fault in him: And if any tarry longer, it shall be no fault in him, if he fear God. Fear God, then, and know that to Him shall ye be gathered."

Sūrah iii. 90:—

"The first temple that was founded for mankind, was that in Bakkah (*i.e.* Makkah)—Blessed, and a guidance to human beings.

"In it are evident signs, even the standing-place of Abraham (*Maqāmu Ibrahīm*): and he who entereth it is safe. And the pilgrimage to the temple, is a service due to God from those who are able to journey thither."

Sūrah v. 2:—

"O Believers! violate neither the rites of God, nor the sacred month, nor the offering, nor its ornaments, (*i.e.* on the necks of animals), nor those who press on to the sacred house (*al-Baitu 'l-Ḥarām*), seeking favour from their Lord and his good pleasure in them."

The performance of the pilgrimage is incumbent upon every Muslim, once in his lifetime, if he be an adult, free, sane, well in health, and has sufficient money for the expenses of the journey and for the support of his family during his absence.

If a woman perform the pilgrimage she must do it in company with her husband, or a near relative (*maḥram*). If she can obtain the protection of a near relative and has the necessary expenses for the journey, it is not lawful for her husband to prevent her performing the pilgrimage. This *maḥram* is a near relative whom it is not lawful for her to marry.

The Imām ash-Shāfiʻī denies the necessity of such attendance, stating that the Qur'ān makes no such restriction. His objection is, however, met by a Tradition. "A certain man came to the Prophet and said: 'My wife is about to make the ḥajj, but I am called to go on a warlike expedition.' The Prophet said: 'Turn away from the war and accompany thy wife in the ḥajj.'"

For a lawful ḥajj there are three actions which are *farẓ*, and five which are *wājib*; all the rest are *sunnah* or *mustaḥabb*. The *farẓ* are: to wear no other garment except the *iḥrām*; to stand in 'Arafāt; to make the *ṭawāf*, or circuit round the Kaʻbah.

The *wājib* duties are: to stay in al-Muzdalifah; to run between Mount aṣ-Ṣafā and Mount al-Marwah; to perform the Ramyu 'r-Rijām, or the casting of the pebbles; if the pilgrims are non-Meccans, to make an extra *ṭawāf*; to shave the head after the pilgrimage is over.

The ḥajj must be made at the appointed season. Sūrah ii. 193: "Let the pilgrimage be made in the months already known." These months are Shawwāl, Ẕū 'l-Qaʻdah, and the first ten days of Ẕū 'l-Ḥijjah. The actual ḥajj must be in the month Ẕū 'l-Ḥijjah, but the preparations for, and the *nīyah*, or intention of the ḥajj can be made in the two preceding months. The *'umrah*, or ordinary visitation ['UMRAH], can be done at any time of the year except on the ninth and four succeeding days of Ẕū 'l-Ḥijjah. On each of the various roads leading to Makkah, there are at a distance of about five or six miles from the city stages called Mīqāt. The following are the names. On the Madīnah road, the stage is called Ẕū 'l-Ḥalīfah; on the 'Irāq road, Ẕātu 'Arq; on the Syrian road, Hujfah; on the Najd road, Qarn; on the Yaman road, Yalamlam.

THE PILGRIM.

The following is the orthodox way of performing the pilgrimage, founded upon the example of the Prophet himself. (See *Ṣaḥīḥu 'l-Buk͟hārī, Kitābu 'l-Manāsik*, p. 205.)

Upon the pilgrim's arrival at the last stage near Makkah, he bathes himself, and performs two rakʻah prayers, and then divesting himself of his clothes, he assumes the pilgrim's sacred robe, which is called *iḥrām*. This garment consists of two seamless wrappers, one being wrapped round the waist, and the other thrown loosely over the shoulder, the head being left uncovered. Sandals may also be worn, but not shoes or boots. After he has assumed the pilgrim's garb, he must not anoint his head, shave any part of his body, pare his nails, nor wear any other garment than the *iḥrām*. The pilgrim having now entered upon the ḥajj, faces Makkah, and makes the *nīyah* (intention), and says: "O God, I purpose to make the ḥajj; make this service easy to me and accept it from me." He then proceeds on his journey to the sacred city and on his way, as well as at different periods in the pilgrimage, he recites, or sings with a loud voice, the pilgrim's song, called the *Talbiyah* (a word signifying waiting or standing for orders). In Arabic it runs thus (as given in the *Ṣaḥiḥu 'l-Bukhārī*, p. 210):—

"*Labbaika! Allāhumma! Labbaika!*
Labbaika! Lā Shārika laka! Labbaika!
Inna 'l-ḥamda wa 'n-ni'mata laka, wa 'l-mulku laka!
Lā shārika laka!"

Which, following the Persian commentator, 'Abdu 'l-Ḥaqq, may be translated as follows:—

"I stand up for Thy service, O God! I stand up!
I stand up! There is no partner with Thee! I stand up!
Verily Thine is the Praise, the Blessing and the Kingdom!
There is no partner with Thee!"

Immediately on his arrival at Makkah he performs legal ablutions in the Masjidu 'l-ḥarām, and then kisses the black stone (al-Ḥajaru 'l-aswad). He then encompasses the Ka'bah seven times; three times at a quick step or run, and four times at a slow pace. These acts are called the *ṭawāf* and are performed by commencing on the right and leaving the Ka'bah on the left. Each time as the pilgrim passes round the Ka'bah, he touches the Ruknu 'l-Yamānī, or the Yamānī corner, and kisses the sacred black stone. He then proceeds to the Maqāmu Ibrahīm (the place of Abraham), where he recites the 119th verse of the IInd Sūrah of the Qur'ān, "Take ye the station of Abraham for a place of prayer," and performs two rak'ah prayers, after which he returns to the black stone and kisses it. He then goes to the gate of the temple leading to Mount aṣ-Ṣafā, and from it ascends the hill, reciting the 153rd verse of the IInd Sūrah of the Qur'ān, "Verily as-Ṣafā and al-Marwah are the signs of God." Having arrived at the summit of the mount, turning towards the Ka'bah, he recites the following:—

"There is no deity but only God! God is great! There is no deity but God alone! He hath performed His promise, and hath aided His servant and hath put to flight the hosts of infidels by Himself alone!"

These words are recited thrice. He then runs from the top of Mount as-Ṣafā to the summit of Mount al-Marwah seven times, repeating the aforesaid prayers on the top of each hill. This is the sixth day, the evening of which is spent at Makkah, where he again encompasses the Ka'bah.

Upon the seventh day he listens to the khuṭbah, or oration, in the great mosque, in which are set forth the excellences of the pilgrimage and the necessary duties required of all true Muslims on the following days.

On the eighth day, which is called Tarwiyah, he proceeds with his fellow pilgrims to Mina, where he stays and performs the usual services of the Muslim ritual, and remains the night.

The next day (the ninth), after morning prayer, he proceeds to Mount 'Arafāt, where he recites the usual prayers and listens to another khuṭbah. He then leaves for al-Muzdalifah, a place midway between Mina and 'Arafāt, where he should arrive for the sunset prayer.

The next day, the tenth, is the *Yaumu 'n-Naḥr*, or the "Day of Sacrifice," known all through the Muslim world and celebrated as the *'Idu 'l-Aẓḥā*. Early in the morning, the pilgrims having said their prayers at Muzdalifah, then proceed in a body to three pillars in Mina, the first of which is called the *Shaiṭānu 'l-Kabīr*, or "Great Devil." The pilgrim casts seven stones at each of these pillars, the ceremony being called the *Ramyu 'r-Rijām*, or casting of stones. Holding the rajm, or pebble between the thumb and fore-finger of the right hand, the pilgrim throws it at a distance of not less than fifteen feet, and says—"In the name of God, the Almighty, I do this, and in hatred of the devil and his shame." The remaining six stones are thrown in the same way. It is said that this ceremony has been performed ever since the days of Abraham. The pilgrim then returns to Mina and performs the sacrifice of the *'Idu 'l-Aẓḥā*. The victim may be a sheep, or a goat, or a cow, or a camel, according to the means of the pilgrim.

Placing its head towards the Ka'bah, its fore-legs being bandaged together, the pilgrim stands on the right side of his victim and plunges the knife into its throat with great force, and cries with a loud voice, "*Allāhu Akbar!*" "God is great! O God, accept this sacrifice from me!"

This ceremony concludes the pilgrimage, and the *ḥājī* or pilgrim then gets himself shaved and his nails pared, and the *iḥrām* or pilgrim garment is removed. Although the pilgrimage is over, he should still rest at Makkah the three following days, which are known as the *Ayyāmu 't-Tashrīq*, or the days of drying up of the blood of the sacrifice. Three well-earned days of rest after the peripatetic performance of the last four days.

Before he leaves Makkah he should once more perform the circuits round the Ka'bah and throw stones at the Satanic pillars at Mina, seven times. He should also drink of the water of the *zamzam* well.

Most Muslims then go to al-Madīnah, and make their salutations at the shrine of Muḥammad. This is regarded as an incumbent duty by all except the Wahhābīs, who hold that to make the visitation of the Prophet's tomb a religious ceremony is *shirk*, or associating the creature with God.

From the time the pilgrim has assumed the iḥrām until he takes it off, he must abstain from worldly affairs and devote himself entirely to the duties of the ḥajj. He is not allowed to hunt, though he may catch fish if he can. "O Believers, kill no game while ye are on pilgrimage." (Sūrah v. 96.) The Prophet also said: "He who shows the place where game is to be found is equally as bad as the man who kills it." The ḥājī must not scratch himself, lest vermin be destroyed, or a hair be uprooted. Should he feel uncomfortable, he must rub himself with the open palm of his hand. The face and head must be left uncovered, the hair on the head and beard unwashed and uncut. "Shave not your heads until the offering reach the place of sacrifice."

(Sūrah ii. 192.) On arriving at an elevated place, on descending a valley, on meeting any one, on entering the city of Makkah or the sacred temple, the ḥājī should continually repeat the word "*Labbaika, Labbaika*"; and whenever he sees the Ka'bah he should recite the *Takbīr*, "God is great!" and the *Ta'līh* "There is no deity but God!"

The pilgrimage known as the ḥajj, as has been already stated, can only be made on the appointed days of the month of Z̲u 'l-Ḥijjah. A visit at any other time is called the 'Umrah. ['UMRAH.] If the pilgrim arrives as late as the ninth day, and is in time to spend that day, he can still perform the pilgrimage legally.

The pilgrimage cannot be performed by proxy by Sunnī Muslims, but is allowed by the Shī'ahs, and it is by both considered a meritorious act to pay the expenses of one who cannot afford to perform it. But if a Muḥammadan on his death-bed bequeath a sum of money to be paid to a certain person to perform the pilgrimage, it is considered to satisfy the claims of the Muslim law. If a Muslim have the means of performing the pilgrimage, and omit to do so, its omission is equal to a *kabīrah*, or mortal sin.

According to the saying of the Prophet (*Mishkāt*, book xi. ch. 1), the merits of a pilgrimage to Makkah are very great:—

"He who makes a pilgrimage for God's sake, and does not talk loosely, nor act wickedly, shall return as pure from sin as the day on which he was born." "Verily, they (the ḥajj and the 'umrah) put away poverty and sin like the fires of a forge removes dross. The reward of a pilgrimage is paradise." "When you see a pilgrim, salute and embrace him, and request him to ask pardon of God for you, for his own sins have been forgiven and his supplications will be accepted."

For a philological and technical explanation of the following terms which occur in this account of the ḥajj, refer to the words as they occur in this dictionary: 'ARAFAH, AYYAMU 'T-TASHRIQ, HAJARU 'L-ASWAD, HAJI, IHRAM, MARWAH, MASJIDU 'L-HARAM, MAQAMU IBRAHIM, MAHRAM, MIQAT, MUZDALIFAH, TAWAF, 'UMRAH, RAMYU 'L-JIMAR, ZAMZAM, TALBIYAH, RUK'NU 'L-YAMANI, TARWIAH, KHUTBAH, 'IDU 'L-AZHA, SAFA.

The Muslim who has performed the pilgrimage is called a ḥājī, which title he retains, *e.g. Ḥājī Qāsim*, the Pilgrim Qāsim.

Only five Englishmen are known to have visited Makkah, and to have witnessed the ceremonies of the pilgrimage:—Joseph Pitts, of Exeter, A.D. 1678; John Lewis Burckhardt, A.D. 1814; Lieutenant Richard Burton, of the Bombay Army, A.D. 1853; Mr. H. Bicknell, A.D. 1862; Mr. T. F. Keane, 1880. The narratives of each of these "pilgrims" have been published. The first account in English of the visit of a European to Makkah, is that of Lodovico Bartema, a gentleman of Rome, who visited Makkah in 1503. His narrative was published in Willes and Eden's Decades, A.D. 1555.

Professor Palmer ("Introduction" to the Qur'ān, p. liii.) says:—"The ceremonies of the pilgrimage could not be entirely done away with. The universal reverence of the Arab for the Kaabah was too favourable and obvious a means for uniting all the tribes into one confederation with one common purpose in view. The traditions of Abraham the father of their race, and the founder of Muhammad's own religion, as he always declared it to be, no doubt gave the ancient temple a peculiar sanctity in the Prophet's eyes, and although he first settled upon Jerusalem as his *qiblah*, he afterwards reverted to the Kaabah itself. Here, then, Muhammad found a shrine, to which, as well as *at* which, devotion had been paid from time immemorial; it was one thing which the scattered Arabian nation had in common—the one thing which gave them even the shadow of a national feeling; and to have dreamed of abolishing it, or even of diminishing the honours paid to it, would have been madness and ruin to his enterprise. He therefore did the next best thing, he cleared it of idols and dedicated it to the service of God."

Mr. Stanley Lane Poole (Introduction to Lane's *Selections*, p. lxxxiv.) remarks:—

"This same pilgrimage is often urged as a sign of Moḥammad's tendency to superstition and even idolatry. It is asked how the destroyer of idols could have reconciled his conscience to the circuits of the Ka'bah and the veneration of the black stone covered with adoring kisses. The rites of the pilgrimage cannot certainly be defended against the charge of superstition; but it is easy to see why Moḥammad enjoined them. They were hallowed to him by the memories of his ancestors, who had been the guardians of the sacred temple, and by the traditional reverence of all his people; and besides this tie of association, which in itself was enough to make it impossible for him to do away with the rites, Moḥammad perceived that the worship in the Ka'bah would prove of real value to his religion. He swept away the more idolatrous and immoral part of the ceremonies, but he retained the pilgrimage to Mekka and the old veneration of the temple for reasons of which it is impossible to dispute the wisdom He well knew the consolidating effect of forming a centre to which his followers should gather; and hence he reasserted the sanctity of the black stone that 'came down from heaven'; he ordained that everywhere throughout the world the Muslim should pray looking towards the Ka'bah, and he enjoined him to make the pilgrimage thither. Mekka is to the Muslim what Jerusalem is to the Jew. It bears with it all the influence of centuries of associations. It carries the Muslim back to the cradle of his faith, the childhood of his prophet; it reminds him of the struggle between the old faith and the new, of the overthrow of the idols, and the establishment of the worship of the One God. And, most of all, it bids him remember that all his brother Muslims are worshipping towards the same sacred spot; that he is one of a great company of believers, united by one faith, filled with the same hopes, reverencing the same thing, worshipping the same God. Moḥammad showed his knowledge of the religious emotions in man when he preserved the sanctity of the temple of Islām."

The Makkan pilgrimage admits of no other explanation than this, that the Prophet of Arabia found it expedient to compromise with Arabian idolatry. And hence we find the superstition and silly customs of the Ḥajj grafted on to a religion which professes to be both monotheistic in its principle, and iconoclastic in its practices.

A careful and critical study of Islām will, we think, convince any candid mind that at first Muḥammad intended to construct his religion on the lines of the Old Testament. Abraham, the true Muslim, was his prototype, Moses his law-giver, and Jerusalem his *Qiblah*. But circumstances were ever wont to change not only the Prophet's revelations, but also his moral standards. Makkah became the Qiblah; and the spectacle of the Muslim world bowing in the direction of a black stone, whilst they worship the one God, marks Islām, with its Makkan pilgrimage, as a religion of compromise.

Apologists of Islām have endeavoured to shield Muḥammad from the solemn charge of having "forged the name of God," but we know of nothing which can justify the act of giving the stupid and unmeaning ceremonies of the pilgrimage all the force and solemnity of a divine enactment.

The Wahhābīs, the Puritans of Islam, regard the circumambulation of the Prophet's tomb as superstitious (as *shirk*, or associating something with God, in fact), but how can they justify the foolish ceremonies of the ḥajj? If reverence for the Prophet's tomb is *shirk*, what are the runnings at aṣ-Ṣafā and al-Marwah, the stonings of the pillars, and the kissings of the black stone? No Muslim has ever yet attempted to give a spiritual explanation of the ceremonies of the Makkan pilgrimage, for in attempting to do so he would be charged with the heresy of *shirk!*

Mr. W. S. Blunt in his *Future of Islām*, has given some interesting statistics regarding the pilgrimage to Makkah in the year 1880, which he obtained during a residence at Cairo, Damascus, and Jiddah. The figures, he says, are taken principally from an official record kept for some years past at Jiddah, and checked as far as European subjects are concerned, by reference to the consular agents residing there.

TABLE OF THE MECCA PILGRIMAGE OF 1880.

Nationality of Pilgrims.	Arriving by Sea.	Arriving by Land.	Total of Mussulman population represented.
Ottoman subjects including pilgrims from Syria and Irak, but not from Egypt or Arabia proper	8,500	1,000	22,000,000
Egyptians	5,000	1,000	5,000,000
Mogrebbins ("people of the West"), that is to say, Arabic-speaking Mussalmans from the Barbary States, Tripoli, Tunis, Algiers, and Morocco. These are always classed together and are not easily distinguishable from each other	6,000	—	18,000,000
Arabs from Yemen	3,000	—	2,500,000
,, ,, Oman and Hadramaut	3,000	—	3,000,000
,, ,, Nejd, Assir, and Hasa, most of them Wahhabites	—	5,000	4,000,000
,, ,, Hejaz, of these perhaps 10.000 Meccans	—	22,000	2,000,000
Negroes from Soudan	2,000	—	10,000,000 (?)
,, ,, Zanzibar	1,000	—	1,500,000
Malabari from the Cape of Good Hope	150	—	
Persians	6,000	2,500	8,000,000
Indians (British subjects)	15,000	—	40,000,000
Malays, chiefly from Java and Dutch subjects	12,000	—	30,000,000
Chinese	100	—	15,000,000
Mongols from the Khanates, included in the Ottoman Haj	—	—	6,000,000
Lazis, Circassians, Tartars, &c. (Russian subjects), included in the Ottoman Haj	—	—	5,000,000
Independent Afghans and Beluchis, included in the Indian and Persian Hajs	—	—	3,000,000
Total of pilgrims present at Arafat	93,250.		
	Total Census of Islam		175,000,000

ḤAJJATU 'L-WADĀ' (حجة الوداع). The last or farewell pilgrimage performed by Muḥammad, and which is taken as the model of an orthodox ḥajj. It is called the *Ḥajju 'l-Akbar*, or Greater Pilgrimage, in the Qur'ān, Sūrah ix. 3. (See *Mishkāt*, book xi. ch. iii., and Muir's *Life of Mahomet.*) It is supposed to have commenced February 23, A.D. 632.

ḤAJJ MABRŪR (حج مبرور). An approved or accepted pilgrimage (*Mishkāt*, book xi. ch. i. pt. 2). A pilgrimmage to Makkah performed according to the conditions of Muslim law.

ḤAKAM (حكم). An arbitrator appointed by a qāẓī to settle disputes. It is not lawful to appoint either a slave or an unbeliever, or a slanderer, or an infant, as an arbitrator. (*Hidāyah*, vol. ii. p. 638.)

According to the Qur'ān, Sūrah iv. 39, domestic quarrels should be settled by an arbitrator:—"If ye fear a breach between the two (*i.e.* husband and wife) then appoint an arbitrator from his people, and an arbitrator from her people."

Al-Ḥakam, the Abitrator, is one of the ninety-nine attributes of God, although it is not so employed in the Qur'ān.

ḤĀKIM (حاكم). "A just ruler." The term *Aḥkamu 'l-Ḥākimīn*, "the Most Just of Rulers, is used for God, Qur'ān, Sūrah xcv. 8; also, *Khairu 'l-Ḥākimīn*, *i.e.* "Best of Rulers," Sūrah vii. 85.

ḤAKĪM (حكيم), pl. *ḥukamā'*; Heb. חָכָם. *Lit.* "A wise person." (1) A philosopher. (2) A doctor of medicine. (3) *Al-Ḥakīm*, "The Wise One." One of the ninety-nine attributes of God It frequently occurs in the Qur'ān, *e.g.* Sūrah ii. 123: "Thou art the Mighty and *the Wise!*"

ḤĀL (حال). A state, or condition. A term used by the Ṣūfī mystics for those thoughts and conditions which come upon the heart of man without his intention or desire, such as sorrow, or fear, or pleasure, or desire, or lust. If these conditions are stable and intransient, they are called *malkah* or *maqām*; but if they are transient and fleeting, they are called *ḥāl*. (Abdu 'r-Razzāq's *Dictionary of Ṣūfī Terms.*)

A state of ecstasy induced by continued contemplation of God. It is considered a divine gift and a sure prognostication of speedily arriving at "The Truth."

Professor Palmer says (*Oriental Mysticism*, p. 66), "This assiduous contemplation of startling metaphysical theories is exceedingly attractive to an Oriental mind, and not unfrequently produces a state of mental excitement akin to the phenomena observed during the recent religious revivals. Such ecstatic state is considered a sure prognostication of direct illumination of the heart by God, and constitutes the fifth stage (in the mystic journey) called *hāl* or ecstasy."

ḤALĀL (حلال). *Lit.* "That which is untied or loosed." That which is lawful, as distinguished from *ḥarām*, or that which is unlawful.

AL-ḤALĪM (حليم). "The Clement." One of the ninety-nine attributes of God. It occurs in the Qur'ān, *e.g.* Sūrah ii. 225: "God is forgiving and *clement.*"

ḤAMĀ'IL (حمائل). *Lit.* "Things suspended." An amulet or charm. [AMULET.]

ḤAMĀLAH (حمالة). Compensation for manslaughter or murder, called also *diyah*. [DIYAH.]

ḤAMALATU 'L-'ARSH (حملة العرش). *Lit.* "Those who bear the throne." Certain angels mentioned in the Qur'ān, Sūrah xl. 7: "*Those who bear the throne* (*i.e.* the Ḥamalatu 'l-'Arsh) and those around it (*i.e.* the Karūbīn) celebrate the praise of their Lord, and believe in Him, and ask pardon for those who believe."

Al-Baghawī, the commentator, says they are eight angels of the highest rank. They are so tall that their feet stand on the lowest strata of the earth and their heads reach the highest heavens, the universe does not reach up to their navels, and it is a journey of seven hundred years from their ears to their shoulders! (*Al-Baghawī*, Bombay edition, vol. ii. p. 23.)

HĀMĀN (هامان). The prime minister of Pharaoh. Mentioned in the Qur'ān in three different chapters.

Sūrah xxviii. 7: "For sinners were Pharaoh and Hāmān."

Sūrah xxix. 38: "Korah (Qārūn) and Pharaoh and Hāmān! with proofs of his mission did Moses come to them and they behaved proudly on the earth."

Sūrah xl. 38:—

"And Pharaoh said, 'O Hāmān, build for me a tower that I may reach the avenues,

"'The avenues of the heavens, and may mount to the God of Moses, for I verily deem him a liar.'"

Some European critics think that Muḥammad has here made Hāmān the favourite of Ahasuerus and the enemy of the Jews, the vizier of Pharaoh. The Rabbins make this vizier to have been Korah, Jethro, or Balaam. (*Midr. Jalkut on Ex.* ch. 1, Sect. 162–168.)

In the *Mishkāt* (book iv. ch. i. pt. 3), there is a tradition that Muḥammad said he who neglects prayers will be in hell with Korah, Pharaoh, Hāmān, and Ubaiy ibn Khalf (an infidel whom Muḥammad slew with his own hand at the battle of Uḥud.)

AL-ḤAMD (الحمد), the "Praise." A title of the first chapter of the Qur'ān. According to Kitābu 'l-Ta'rifāt, "praise" (*ḥamd*) of God is of three kinds:—

(1) *Al-ḥamdu 'l-Qaulī*, the praise of God with the tongue, with those attributes with which He has made known Himself. (2) *Al-ḥamdu 'l-Fi'lī*, the praise of God with the body according to the will of God. (3) *Al-ḥamdu 'l-Ḥālī*, the praise of God with the heart and spirit.

AL-ḤAMĪD (الحميد). "The Laudable." The One worthy of praise. One of the ninety-nine attributes of God. It frequently occurs in the Qur'ān, *e.g.* Sūrah xi. 76, "Verily He is *to be praised.*"

ḤĀ MĪM (حا ميم). Seven Sūrahs of the Qur'ān begin with the letters ح *ḥ*, م *m*, and are called *al-Ḥawāmīm.* They are the XL, XLI, XLII, XLIII, XLIV, XLV, and XLVI. Various opinions are held by Muḥammadan commentators as to the meaning of these mysterious letters. Jalālu 'd-dīn as-Suyūṭī in his *Itqān*, says these letters are simply initial letters, the meaning of which is known only to God, but Ibn 'Abbās says the letters ح *ḥ*, and م *m*, stand for الرحمان *ar-Raḥmān*, "the Merciful," one of the attributes of God.

Mr. Rodwell, in his Introduction to the Ḳorân, says, "Possibly the letters *Ha*, *Mim*, which are prefixed to numerous *successive* Suras were private marks, or initial letters, attached by their proprietor to the copies furnished to Said when effecting his recension of the text under Othman. In the same way, the letters prefixed to other Suras may be monograms, or abbreviations, or initial letters of the names of the persons to whom the copies of the respective Suras belonged."

ḤAMRĀU 'L-ĀSĀD (حمرا الاساد). A village or small town, the scene of one of Muḥammad's expeditions against the Quraish. Having reached this spot he kindled five hundred fires to make the Quraish believe that the pursuing force was very large, and, contenting himself with this demonstration, he returned to al-Madīnah, from which it was about 60 miles. According to Burton, it is the modern Wasitah.

"At Hamrâ al Asād, Mahomet made prisoner one of the enemy, the poet Abu Ozza, who had loitered behind the rest. He had been taken prisoner at Bedr, and, having five daughters dependent on him, had been freely released, on the promise that he would not again bear arms in the war against the Prophet. He now sought for mercy: 'O Mahomet!' he prayed, 'forgive me of thy grace.' 'Nay, verily,' said the Prophet, 'a believer may not be twice bitten from the same hole. Thou shalt never return to Mecca, stroke thy beard and say, I have again deceived Mahomet. Lead him forth to execution!' So saying, he motioned to a bystander, who with his sword struck off the captive's head." (Muir's *Life of Mahomet*, new ed. p. 276.)

ḤAMZAH (حمزة). Muḥammad's uncle, who embraced Islām and became one of its bravest champions. He was at the battle of Uḥud and slew 'Us̱mān, one of the leaders of the Quraish, but was soon afterwards himself killed by a wild negro named Waḥshī, and his dead body shamefully mutilated. At his death Muḥammad is recorded to have said that Ḥamzah was "the lion of God and of His Apostle." The warlike deeds of Ḥamzah are recorded in Persian poetry, in which he is celebrated as Amīr Ḥamzah.

ḤAMZĪYAH (حمزية). A sect of Muslims founded by Ḥamzah ibn Adrak, who say that the children (infants) of infidels will be consigned to the Fire of Hell, the general belief of Muḥammadans being that they will have a special place in al-A'rāf. (*Kitābu 't-Ta'rīfāt, in loco.*)

ḤANAFĪ (حنفى), ḤANĪFĪ (حنيفى). A member of the sect of Sunnīs founded by the Imām Abū Ḥanīfah. [ABU HANIFAH.]

ḤANBAL. [IBN H. .BAL.]

ḤANBALĪ (حنبلى). A member of the Ḥanbalī sect of Sunnī Muslims. [IBN HANBAL.]

HAND. Arabic *yad* (يد), pl. *ayādī.* Heb. יָד.

(1) It is a rule with Muslims to honour the right hand above the left; to use the right hand for all honourable purposes, and the left for actions which, though necessary, are unclean. The hands must be washed before prayers [ABLUTIONS] and before meals.

(2) The expression *yadu 'llāh*, the "hand of God," occurs in the Qur'ān:—

Sūrah v. 69: "The Jews say, '*God's hand* is fettered'; their hands are fettered, for they are cursed."

Sūrah xlviii. 10: "God's hand is above their hands."

There is a controversy between the orthodox Sunnīs and the Wahhābīs regarding the expression, "God's hand." The former maintaining that it is a figurative expression for the power of God, the latter holding that it is *literal*; but that it is impossible to say in what sense or manner God has a hand; for as the essence of God is not known, how can the manner of His existence be understood?

HANDKERCHIEFS. The custom of keeping a handkerchief in the hand, as is frequently practised, is said to be abominable (*makrūh*). Many, however, hold that it is allowable, if done from motives of necessity. This, says Abū Ḥanīfah, is approved; for the practice is abominable only when it is done ostentatiously. (*Hidāyah*, vol. iv. p. 95.)

ḤANĪF (حنيف), pl. *Ḥunafā'*. *Lit.* "One who is inclined." (1) Anyone sincere in his inclination to Islām. (2) One orthodox in the faith. (3) One who is of the religion of Abraham. (See *Majma'u 'l-Biḥār, in loco.*)

The word occurs *ten* times in the Qur'ān.

I.—Six times for the religion of Abraham:—

Sūrah ii. 129: "They say, 'Be ye Jews or Christians so shall ye be guided! Say: 'Not so!' but the faith of Abraham, the *Ḥanīf*, he was not of the idolaters."

Sūrah iii. 60: "Abraham was not a Jew nor yet a Christian, but he was a *Ḥanīf* resigned, and not of the idolaters."

Idem, 89: "Follow the faith of Abraham, a *Ḥanīf*, who was not of the idolaters."

Sūrah vi. 162: "The faith of Abraham, *the Ḥanīf*, he was not of the idolaters."

Sūrah xvi. 121: "Verily Abraham was an Imām, *a Ḥanīf*, and was not of the idolaters."

Sūrah vi. 79: (Abraham said) "I have turned my face to Him who originated the heaven and the earth as a *Ḥanif*, and I am not of the idolaters."

II.—*Four* times for one sound in the faith:—

Sūrah x. 105: "Make steadfast thy face to the religion as *a Ḥanīf*, and be not an idolater."

Sūrah xxii. 32: "Avoid speaking falsely being *Ḥanīfs* to God, not associating aught with Him."

Sūrah xcviii. 4: "Being sincere in religion unto Him, as *Ḥanīfs*, and to be steadfast in prayer."

Sūrah xxx. 29: "Set thy face steadfast towards the religion as a *Ḥanīf*."

III.—The term was also applied in the early stages of Islām, and before Muḥammad claimed the position of an inspired prophet, to those who had endeavoured to search for the truth among the mass of conflicting dogmas and superstitions of the religions that existed in Arabia. Amongst these Ḥanīfs were Waraqah, the Prophet's cousin, and Zaid ibn 'Amr, surnamed the Enquirer. They were known as Ḥanīfs, a word which originally meant "inclining one's steps toward anything," and therefore signified either a convert or a pervert. Muḥammad appears from the above verses (when chronologically arranged), to have first used it for the religion of Abraham, but afterwards for any sincere professor of Islām.

ḤAQĪQAH (حقيقة). "Truth; sincerity."

(1) The essence of a thing as meaning that by being which a thing is what it is. As when we say that a rational animal is the *ḥaqīqah* of a human being. (See *Kitābu 't-Ta'rifāt.*)

(2) A word or phrase used in its proper or original sense, as opposed to that which is figurative. A speech without trope or figure.

(3) The sixth stage in the mystic journey of the Ṣūfī, when he is supposed to receive a revelation of the true nature of the Godhead, and to have arrived at "the Truth."

AL-ḤAQĪQATU 'L-MUḤAMMADĪYAH (الحقيقة المحمدية). The original essence of Muḥammad, the *Nūr-i-Muḥammadīyah*, or the Light of Muḥammad, which is believed to have been created before all things. (*Kitābu 't-Ta'rifāt, in loco.*)

The Wahhābīs do not believe in the pre-existence of their Prophet, and the doctrine is most probably an invention of the Ṣūfī mystics in the early stages of Islām.

According to the Imām Qasṭalānī (*Muwahib-i-laduniya*, vol. i. p. 12), it is related by Jābir ibn 'Abdi 'llāh al-Anṣārī that the Prophet said, "The first thing created was the light of your Prophet, which was created from the light of God. This light of mine roamed about wherever God willed, and when the Almighty resolved to make the world, he divided this light of Muḥammad into four portions; from the first he created the Pen (*qalam*); from the second, the Tablet (*lauḥ*); from the third, the highest heaven and the throne of God (*'arsh*); the fourth portion was divided into four sections: from the first were created the *Ḥamalatu 'l-'Arsh*, or the eight angels who support the throne of God; from the second, the *kursī*, or lower throne of God; from the third, the angels; and the fourth, being divided into four subdivisions, from it were created (1) the firmaments or seven heavens, (2) the earth, (3) the seven paradises and seven hells, (4) and again from a fourth section were created (1) the light of the eyes, (2) the light of the mind, (3) the light of the love of the Unity of God, (4) the remaining portion of creation."

The author of the *Ḥayātu 'l-Qulūb*, a Shī'ah book of traditions (See Merrick's translation, p. 4), says the traditions respecting the creations from this Light of Muḥammad are numerous and discordant, but that the discrepancies may possibly be reconciled by referring the diverse dates to different eras in the process of creation. "The holy light of Muḥammad," he says, "dwelt under the empyrean seventy-three thousand years, and then resided seventy thousand years in Paradise. Afterwards it rested another period of seventy thousand years under the celestial tree called *Sidratu 'l-Muntahā*, and, emigrating from heaven to heaven, arrived at length in the lowest of these celestial mansions, where it remained until the Most High willed the creation of Adam."

(A very curious account of the absurd belief of the Shī'ahs on this subject will be found in Mr. Merrick's edition of the *Ḥiyātu 'l-Qulūb*; Boston, 1850.)

ḤAQĪQĪ (حقيقى). "Literal," as opposed to that which is *majāzī*, or figurative.

ḤAQQ (حق). "Truth, justice." A term used in theology for that which is true, *e g.* The word of God; religion. In law it implies that which is due. A thing decreed; a claim. By the Ṣūfī mystics it is always used for the Divine Essence; God.

Al-Ḥaqq, "The Truth." One of the ninety-nine attributes of God.

AL-ḤĀQQAH (الحاقة). *Lit.* "The surely Impending." The title of the LXIXth Sūrah of the Qur'ān, in which the word occurs in the opening verse: "The inevitable! (*al-Ḥāqqatu!*). What is the inevitable?" The word is understood by all commentators to mean the Day of Resurrection and Judgment. It does not occur in any other portion of the Qur'ān.

ḤAQQU 'L-'ABD (حق العبد). "The right of the slave (of God)." In law the right of an injured individual to demand redress and justice.

ḤAQQU 'LLĀH (حق الله). "The right of God." In law, the retributive chastisement which it is the duty of a magistrate to inflict for crime and offences against morality and religion. In theology it means prayer, alms, fasting, pilgrimage, and other religious duties.

ḤAQQU 'L-YAQĪN (حق اليقين). "A conviction of the truth." A term used by the Ṣūfī mystics for a state in which the seeker after truth has in thought and reflection a positive evidence of his extinction and of his being incorporated in the Essence of God. [YAQIN.]

ḤAQQU 'N-NĀS (حق الناس). "The right of men." A term in law implying the same as *Ḥaqqu 'l-'Abd.*

ḤARAM (حرم), pl. *Ḥuram.* "That which is sacred. (1) *Al-Ḥaram*, the sacred precincts of Makkah or al-Madīnah. (2) *Ḥaram*, the apartments of women in a Muḥammadan household. [HARIM.] (3) *Ḥuram*, wives.

ḤARĀM (حرام). *Lit.* "prohibited." That which is unlawful. The word is used in both a good and a bad sense, *e.g. Baitu 'l-ḥarām*, the sacred house; and *Mālu 'l-ḥarām*, unlawful possessions. *Ibnu 'l-ḥarām*, an illegitimate son; *Shahru 'l-ḥarām*, a sacred month.

A thing is said to be *ḥarām* when it is forbidden, as opposed to that which is *ḥalāl*, or lawful. A pilgrim is said to be *ḥarām* as soon as he has put on the pilgrim's garb.

Ḥarāmu 'llāh lâ afa'lu is a form of oath that a man will not do a thing.

ḤARAMU 'L-MĀDĪNAH (حرم المدينة). The sacred boundary of al-Madīnah within which certain acts are unlawful which are lawful elsewhere. The Imām Abū Ḥanifah says that although it is respectful to the position of the sacred city, as the birth-place of the Prophet, not to bear arms, or kill, or cut grass, &c., still it is not, as in the case of Makkah, an incumbent religious duty. According to a tradition by 'Alī ibn Abī Ṭālib (*Mishkāt*, book xi. ch. xvi.), the *Ḥudūdu 'l-Ḥaram*, or sacred limits of al-Madīnah are from Jabal 'Air to Ṣaur. According to Burton, the diameter of the Ḥaram is from ten to twelve miles. (*El Medinah and Meccah*, vol. i. p. 362.)

ḤARAMU MAKKAH (حرم مكة). The sacred boundary of Makkah within which certain acts are unlawful which are lawful elsewhere. It is not lawful to carry arms, or to fight within its limits. Its thorns must not be broken, nor its game molested, nor must anything be taken up which has fallen on the ground, unless it is done to restore it to its owner. Its fresh grass or even its dry grass must not be cut; except the bog rush (*izkhir*), because it is used for blacksmith's fires and for thatching houses. (A tradition by Ibn 'Abbās, *Mishkāt*, book xi. ch. xv. pt. 1). 'Abdu 'l-Ḥaqq says that when Abraham, "the friend of God," placed the black stone at the time of the building of the Ka'bah, its east, west, north, and south quarters became bright with light, and that wherever the brightness extended itself became the *Ḥudūdu 'l-Ḥaram*, or the limits of the sacred city. These limits are marked by *manārs* or pillars on all sides, except on the Jiddah and Jairānah roads, regarding which there is some dispute as to the exact distance.

HAREEM. [HARIM.]

HARES. Arabic *arnab*, pl. *arānib*. Heb. אַרְנֶבֶת. The flesh of the hare is lawful, for the Prophet ate it, and commanded his companions to do so (*Hidāyah*, vol. iv. p. 75). A difference of opinion has in all ages existed as to the value of the hare as an article of food. The Greeks and Romans ate it in spite of an opinion that prevailed that it was not wholesome. In the law of Moses, it is specified amongst the unclean animals (Lev. xi. 6; Deut xiv. 7). The Parsees do not eat hare's flesh, nor do the Armenians.

ḤARF (حرف). (1) An extremity, verge, or border. (2) A letter of the alphabet. (3) A particle in grammar. (4) A dialect of Arabia, or a mode of expression peculiar to certain Arabs. The Qur'ān is said to have been revealed in seven dialects (*sab'at aḥruf*). [QUR'AN.] (5) A term used by the Ṣūfī mystics for the particle of any true essence.

ḤARĪM, or HAREEM (حريم). A word used especially in Turkey, Egypt, and Syria, for the female apartments of a Muḥammadan household. In Persia, Afghanistan, and India, the terms *ḥaramgah*, *maḥall-sarāi* and *zanānah* are used for the same place.

The seclusion of women being enjoined in the Qur'ān (Sūrah xxxiii. 55), in all Muḥammadan countries it is the rule for respectable women to remain secluded at home, and not to travel abroad unveiled, nor to associate with men other than their husbands or such male relatives as are forbidden in marriage by reason of consanguinity. In consequence of these injunctions, which have all the force of a divine enactment, the female portion of a Muḥammadan family always resides in apartments which are in an inclosed courtyard and excluded from public view. This inclosure is called the *ḥarīm*, and sometimes *ḥaram*, or in Persian *zanānah*, from *zan*, a "woman"). Mr. Lane in his *Modern Egyptians*, has given a full account of the Egyptian ḥarīm. We are indebted to Mrs. Meer Ali for the following very graphic and interesting description of a Muḥammadan zanānah or ḥarīm in Lucknow.

Mrs. Meer Ali was an English lady who married a Muḥammadan gentleman, and reided amongst the people of Lucknow for twelve years. Upon the death of her husband, she returned to England, and published her *Observations on the Musalmans of India*, which was dedicated, with permission, to Queen Adelaide.

"The habitable buildings of a native Muḥammadan home are raised a few steps from the court; a line of pillars forms the front of the building, which has no upper rooms; the roof is flat, and the sides and back without windows, or any aperture through which air can be received. The sides and back are merely high walls, forming an enclosure, and the only air is admitted from the fronts of the dwelling-place facing the court-yard. The apartments are divided into long halls, the extreme corners having small rooms or dark closets purposely built for the repository of valuables or stores; doors are fixed to these closets, which are the only places I have seen with them in a zanānah or maḥall (house or palace occupied by females); the floor is either of beaten earth, bricks, or stones; boarded floors are not yet introduced. As they have neither doors nor windows to the halls, warmth or privacy is secured by means of thick wadded curtains, made to fit each opening between the pillars. Some zanānahs have two rows of pillars in the halls with wadded curtains to each, thus forming two distinct halls, as occasion may serve, or greater warmth be required; this is a convenient arrangement where the establishment of servants, slaves, &c. is extensive.

"The wadded curtains are called pardahs; these are sometimes made of woollen cloth, but more generally of coarse calico, of two colours, in patchwork style, striped, vandyked, or in some other ingeniously contrived and ornamented way, according to their individual taste.

"Besides the pardahs, the openings between the pillars have blinds neatly made of fine bamboo strips, woven together with coloured cords; these are called chicks. Many of them are painted green; others are more gaudy, both in colour and variety of patterns. These blinds constitute a real comfort to everyone in India, as they admit air when let down, and at the same time shut out flies and other annoying insects; besides which, the extreme glare is shaded by them—a desirable object to foreigners in particular.

"The floors of the halls are first matted with the coarse date-leaf matting of the country, over which are spread shaṭranjīs (thick cotton carpets, peculiarly the manufacture of the Upper Provinces of India, woven in stripes of blue and white, or shades of blue); a white calico carpet covers the shaṭranjī on which the females take their seat.

"The bedsteads of the family are placed, during the day, in lines at the back of the halls, to be moved at pleasure to any chosen spot for the night's repose; often into the open court-yard, for the benefit of the pure air. They are all formed on one principle, differing only in size and quality; they stand about half a yard from the floor, the legs round and broad at bottom, narrowing as they rise towards the frame, which is laced over with a thick cotton tape, made for the purpose, and plaited in chequers, and thus rendered soft, or rather elastic, and very pleasant to recline upon. The legs of these bedsteads are in some instances gold and silver gilt, or pure silver; others have enamel paintings on fine wood; the inferior grades have them merely of wood painted plain and varnished. The servants' bedsteads are of the common mango-wood without ornament, the lacing of these for the sacking being of elastic string manufactured from the fibre of the cocoa-nut.

"Such are the bedsteads of every class of people. They seldom have mattresses: a white quilt is spread on the lacing, over which a calico sheet, tied at each corner of the bedstead with cords and tassels; several thin flat pillows of beaten cotton for the head; a muslin sheet for warm weather, and a well wadded *razāī* (coverlid) for winter is all these children of Nature deem essential to their comfort in the way of sleeping. They have no idea of night-dresses; the same suit that adorns a lady, is retained both night and day, until a change be needed. The single article exchanged at night is the *ḍupaṭṭa* (a small shawl for the head), and that only when it happens to be of silver tissue or embroidery, for which a muslin or calico sheet is substituted.

"The very highest circles have the same habits in common with the meanest, but those who can afford shawls of Cashmere, prefer them for sleeping in, when the cold weather renders them bearable. Blankets are never used except by the poorest peasantry, who wear them in lieu of better garments night and day in the winter season; they are always black, the natural colour of the wool. The quilts of the higher orders are generally made of silk of the brightest hues, well wadded, and lined with dyed muslin of assimilating colour; they are usually bound with broad silver ribands, and sometimes bordered with gold brocaded trimmings. The middling classes have fine chintz quilts, and the servants and slaves coarse ones of the same material; but all are on the same plan, whether for a queen or the meanest of her slaves, differing only in the quality of the material. The mistress of the house is easily distinguished by her seat of honour in the hall of a zanānah, a *masnad* not being allowed to any other person but the lady of the mansion. The masnad carpet is spread on the floor, if possible near to a pillar about the centre of the hall, and is made of many varieties of fabric—gold cloth, quilted silk, brocaded silk, velvet, fine chintz, or whatever may suit the lady's taste, circumstances, or convenience. It is about two yards square, and generally bordered or fringed, on which is placed the all-important masnad. This article may be understood by those who have seen a lace-maker's pillow in England, excepting only that the masnad is about twenty times the size of that useful little article in the hands of our industrious villagers. The masnad is covered with gold cloth, silk, velvet, or calico, with square pillows' to correspond, for the elbows, the knees, &c. This is the seat of honour, to be invited to share which, with the lady-owner, is a mark of favour to an equal or inferior: when a superior pays a visit of honour, the prided seat is usually surrendered to her, and the lady of the house takes her place most humbly on the very edge of her own carpet. Looking-glasses or ornamental furniture are very rarely to be seen in the zanānah, even of the very richest females. Chairs and sofas are produced when English visitors are expected; but the ladies of Hīndustān prefer the usual mode of sitting and lounging on the carpet; and as for tables, I suppose not one gentlewoman of the whole country has ever been seated at one; and very few, perhaps, have any idea of their useful purposes, all their meals being served on the floor, where *dastarkhwans* (table-cloths we should call them) are spread, but neither knives, forks, spoons, glasses, nor napkins, so essential to the comfortable enjoyment of a meal amongst Europeans. But those who never knew such comforts have no desire for the indulgence, nor taste to appreciate them.

"On the several occasions, amongst native society, of assembling in large parties, as at births and marriages, the halls, although extensive, would be inadequate to accommodate the whole party. They then have awnings of white calico, neatly flounced with muslin, supported on poles fixed in the court-yard, and connecting the open space with the great hall, by wooden platforms which are brought to a line with the building, and covered with *shaṭranjī*, and white carpets to correspond with the floor-furniture of the hall; and here the ladies sit by day and sleep by night very comfortably, without feeling any great inconvenience from the absence of their bedsteads, which could never be arranged for the accommodation of so large an assemblage—nor is it ever expected.

"The usually barren look of these almost unfurnished halls, is on such occasions quite changed, when the ladies are assembled in their various dresses; the brilliant display of jewels, the glittering drapery of their dress, the various expressions of countenance, and different figures, the multitude of female attendants and slaves, the children of all ages and sizes in their variously ornamental dresses, are subjects to attract both the eye and the mind of an observing visitor; and the hall, which when empty appeared desolate and comfortless, thus filled, leaves nothing wanting to render the scene attractive.

"The buzz of human voices, the happy playfulness of the children, the chaste singing of the *ḍomnīs* fill up the animated picture. I have sometimes passed an hour or two in witnessing their innocent amusements, without any feeling of regret for the brief sacrifice of time I had made. I am free to confess, however, that I have returned to my tranquil home with increased delight after having witnessed the bustle of a zanānah assembly. At first I pitied the apparent monotony of their lives; but this feeling has worn away by intimacy with the people, who are thus precluded from mixing generally with the world. They are happy in their confinement; and never having felt the sweets of liberty, would not know how to use the boon if it were to be granted them. As the bird from the nest immured in a cage is both cheerful and contented, so are these females. They have not, it is true, many intellectual resources, but they have naturally good understandings, and having learned their duty they strive to fulfil it. So far as I have had any opportunity of making personal observations on their general character, they appear to me obedient wives, dutiful daughters, affectionate mothers, kind mistresses, sincere friends, and liberal benefactresses to the distressed poor. These are their moral qualifications, and in their religious duties, they are zealous in performing the several ordinances which they have been instructed by their parents or husbands to observe. If there be any merit in obeying the injunctions of their law-giver, those whom I have known most intimately, deserve praise since 'they are faithful in that they profess.'

"To ladies accustomed from infancy to confinement, this kind of life is by no means irksome; they have their employments and their amusements, and though these are not exactly to our taste, nor suited to our mode of education, they are not the less relished by those for whom they were invented. They perhaps wonder equally at some of our modes of dissipating time, and fancy we might spend it more profitably. Be that as it may, the Muslim ladies, with whom I have been long intimate, appear to me always happy, contented, and satisfied with the seclusion to which they were born; they desire no other, and I have ceased to regret they cannot be made partakers of that freedom of intercourse with the world; we deem so essential to our happiness, since their health suffers nothing from that confinement, by which they are preserved from a variety of snares and temptations; besides which, they would deem it disgraceful in the highest degree to mix indiscriminately with men who are not relations. They are educated from infancy for retirement, and they can have no wish that the custom should be changed, which keeps them apart from the society of men who are not very nearly related to them. Female society is unlimited, and that they enjoy without restraint.

"Those females who rank above peasants or inferior servants, are disposed from principle to keep themselves strictly from observation; all who have any regard for the character or the honour of their house, seclude themselves from the eye of strangers, carefully instructing their young daughters to a rigid observance of their own prudent example. Little girls, when four years old, are kept strictly behind the *pardah* (*lit.* "curtain"), and when they move abroad it is always in covered conveyances, and under the guardianship of a faithful female domestic, who is equally tenacious as the mother to preserve the young lady's reputation unblemished by concealing her from the gaze of men.

"The ladies of zanānah life are not restricted from the society of their own sex; they are, as I have before remarked, extravagantly fond of company, and equally as hospitable when entertained. To be alone is a trial to which they are seldom exposed, every lady having companions amongst her dependants; and according to her means the number in her establishment is regulated. Some ladies of rank have from two to ten companions, independent of slaves and domestics; and there are some of the royal family at Lucknow who entertain in their service two or three hundred female dependants, of all classes. A well-filled zanānah is a mark of gentility; and even the poorest lady in the country will retain a number of slaves and domestics, if she cannot afford companions; besides which they are miserable without society, the habit of associating with numbers having grown up with infancy to maturity: 'to be alone,' is considered, with women thus situated, a real calamity.

"On occasions of assembling in large parties, each lady takes with her a companion besides two or three slaves to attend upon her, no one expecting to be served by the servants of the house at which they are visiting. This swells the numbers to be provided for; and as the visit is always for three days and three nights (except on *'Īds*, when the visit is confined to one day), some forethought must be exercised by the lady of the house, that all may be accommodated in such a manner as may secure to her the reputation of hospitality.

"The kitchen and offices to the zanānah, I have remarked, occupy one side of the quadrangle; they face the great or centre hall appropriated to the assembly. These kitchens, however, are sufficiently distant to prevent any great annoyance from the smoke —I say smoke, because chimneys have not yet been introduced into the kitchens of the natives.

"The fire-places are all on the ground, something resembling stoves, each admitting one saucepan, the Asiatic style of cooking requiring no other contrivance. Roast or boiled joints are never seen at the dinner of a native; a leg of mutton or sirloin of beef would place the hostess under all sorts of difficulties, where knives and forks are not understood to be amongst the useful appendages of a meal. The varieties of their dishes are countless, but stews and curries are the chief; all the others are mere varieties. The only thing in the shape of roast meats are small lean cutlets bruised, seasoned and cemented with pounded poppy seed. Several being fastened together on skewers, they are grilled or roasted over a charcoal fire spread on the ground, and then called *kabāb*, which word implies roast meat.

"The kitchen of a zanānah would be inadequate to the business of cooking for a large assembly; the most choice dishes only (for the highly-favoured guests), are cooked by the servants of the establishment. The needed abundance required in entertaining a large party is provided by a regular bāzār cook, several of whom establish themselves in native cities, or wherever there is a Muslim population. Orders being previously given, the morning and evening dinners are punctually forwarded at the appointed hours in covered trays, each tray having portions of the several good things ordered, so that there is no confusion in serving out the feast on its arrival at the mansion. The food thus prepared by the bāzār cook (*nānbai*, he is called), is plain boiled rice, sweet rice, *khīr* (rice-milk), *mutanjan* (rice sweetened with the addition of preserved fruits, raisins, &c., coloured with saffron), *salans* (curries) of many varieties, some cooked with vegetables, others with unripe fruits with or without meat; *pulāos* of many sorts, *kabābs*, preserves, pickles, chatnīs, and many other things too tedious to admit of detail.

"The bread in general use amongst natives is chiefly unleavened: nothing in the likeness of English bread is to be seen at their meals; and many object to its being fermented with the intoxicating toddy (extracted from a tree). Most of the native bread is baked on iron plates over a charcoal fire. They have many varieties, both plain and rich, and some of the latter resembles our pastry, both in quality and flavour.

"The dinners, I have said, are brought into the zanānah, ready dished in the native earthenware, on trays; and as they neither use spoons nor forks, there is no great delay in setting out the meal where nothing is required for display or effect, beyond the excellent quality of the food and its being well cooked. In a large assembly all cannot dine at the *dastarkhwān* of the lady hostess, even if privileged by their rank; they are, therefore, accommodated in groups of ten, fifteen, or more, as may be convenient; each lady having her companion at the meal, and her slaves to brush off the intruding flies with a chaurī, to hand water, or to fetch or carry any article of delicacy from or to a neighbouring group. The slaves and servants dine in parties after their ladies have finished, in any retired corner of the court-yard—always avoiding as much as possible the presence of their superiors.

"Before anyone touches the meal, water is carried round for each lady to wash the hand and rinse the mouth. It is deemed unclean to eat without this form of ablution, and the person neglecting it would be held unholy. This done, the lady turns to her meal, saying, "Bismillāh!" (In the name or to the praise of God!), and with the right hand conveys the food to her mouth (the left hand is never used at meals); and although they partake of every variety of food placed before them with no other aid than their fingers, yet the mechanical habit is so perfect, that they neither drop a grain of rice, soil the dress, nor retain any of the food on their fingers. The custom must always be offensive to a foreign eye, and the habit none would wish to copy; yet everyone who witnesses must admire the neat way in which eating is accomplished by these really 'Children of Nature.'

"The repast concluded, the *lota* (vessel with water), and the *laggan* (to receive the water in after rinsing the hands and mouth), are passed round. To every person who, having announced by the '*Ash-Shukru li'llāh!*' (All thanks to God!) that she has finished, the attendants present first the powdered peas, called *besan*,—which answers the purpose of soap in removing grease, &c. from the fingers—and then the water in due course. Soap has not even yet been brought into fashion by the natives, except by the washermen; I have often been surprised that they have not found the use of soap a necessary article in the nursery, where the only substitute I have seen is the powdered pea.

"Lotas and laggans are articles in use with all classes of people; they must be poor indeed who do not boast of one, at least, in their family. They are always of metal, either brass, or copper lacquered over, or zinc; in some cases, as with the nobility, silver and even gold are converted into these useful articles of native comfort.

"China or glass is comparatively but little used; water is their only beverage, and this is preferred, in the absence of metal basins, out of the common red earthen *katora* (cup shaped like a vase).

"China dishes, bowls, and basins, are used for serving many of the savoury articles of food in; but it is as common in the privacy of the palace, as well as in the huts of the peasantry, to see many choice things introduced at meals served up in the rude red earthen platter; many of the delicacies of Asiatic cookery being esteemed more palatable from the earthen flavour of the new vessel in which it is served.

"China tea-sets are very rarely found in the zanānah, tea being used by the natives more as a medicine than a refreshment, except by such gentlemen as have frequent intercourse with the "Ṣāḥib Log" (English gentry), among whom they acquire a taste for this delightful beverage. The ladies, however, must have a severe cold to induce them to partake of the beverage even as a remedy, but by no means as a luxury. I imagined that the inhabitants of a zanānah were sadly deficient in actual comforts, when I found, upon my first arrival in India, that there were no preparations for breakfast going forward; everyone seemed engaged in pān-eating, and smoking the ḥuqqah, but no breakfast after the morning namāz. I was, however, soon satisfied that they felt no sort of privation, as the early meal so common in Europe has never been introduced in Eastern circles. Their first meal is a good substantial dinner, at ten, eleven, or twelve o'clock, after which follows pān and the ḥuqqah; to this succeeds a sleep of two or three hours, providing it does not impede the duty of prayer—the pious, I ought to remark, would give up every indulgence which would prevent the discharge of this duty. The second meal follows in twelve hours from the first, and consists of the same substantial fare; after which they usually sleep again until the dawn of day is near at hand.

"The *ḥuqqah* (pipe) is almost in general use with females. It is a common practice with the lady of the house to present the ḥuqqah she is smoking to her favoured guest. This mark of attention is always to be duly appreciated; but such is the deference paid to parents, that a son can rarely be persuaded by an indulgent father or mother to smoke a ḥuqqah in their revered presence; this praiseworthy feeling originates not in fear, but real genuine respect. The parents entertain for their son the most tender regard; and the father makes him both his companion and his friend; yet the most familiar endearments do not lessen the feeling of reverence a good son entertains for his father. This is one among the many samples of patriarchal life, and which I can never witness in real life, without feeling respect for the persons who follow up the patterns I have been taught to venerate in our Holy Scripture.

"The ḥuqqah (pipe) as an indulgence or a privilege, is a great definer of etiquette. In the presence of the king or reigning nawāb, no subject, however high he may rank in blood or royal favour, can presume to smoke. In native courts, on state occasions, ḥuqqahs are presented only to the Governor-General, the Commander-in-Chief, or the Resident at his court, who are considered equal in rank, and therefore entitled to the privilege of smoking with him; and they cannot consistently resist the intended honour. Should they dislike smoking, a hint is readily understood by the ḥuqqah bardār to bring the ḥuqqah, charged with the materials, without the addition of fire. Applications of the *munhnāl* (mouthpiece) to the mouth, indicates a sense of the honour conferred." (*Observations on the Musalmāns of India*, vol. i. p. 304.)

ḤĀRIS̤ (حارث). A surname which frequently occurs amongst "the Companions." In the *Taqrību 't-Tahẕib*, there are not fewer that sixty-five persons of this name, of whom short biographical notes are given.

Ḥāris̤ ibn Naufal ibn al-Ḥāris̤ ibn 'Abdi 'l-Muṭṭālib, was a Companion of some consequence; he lived close to the house of the Prophet, and had frequently to make room as the Prophet's Ḥarīm extended itself. [HOUSES.]

Ḥāris̤ ibn Hishām ibn al-Mug͟hīrah, is another Companion, who lived at Makkah.

Ḥāris̤ son of Suwaid ibn Ṣāmit, the poet, was executed at Uḥud.

ḤĀRIS̤ĪYAH (حارثية). A sect of Muslims founded by Abū 'l-Ḥāris̤, who in opposition to the sect Abāẓīyah, said it was not correct to say the acts of men were not the acts of God. (*Kitābu 't-Ta'rīfāt, in loco.*)

HĀRŪN (هارون). [AARON.]

HĀRŪT WA MĀRŪT (هاروت و ماروت). Two angels mentioned in

the Qur'ān. They are said to be two angels who, in consequence of their compassion for the frailties of mankind, were sent down to earth to be tempted. They both sinned, and being permitted to choose whether they would be punished now or hereafter, chose the former, and are still suspended by the feet at Babel in a rocky pit, where they are great teachers of magic.

The account of these two angels in the Qur'ān, is given in Sūrah ii. 96 :—

"They (the Jews) followed what the devils taught in the reign of Solomon: not that Solomon was unbelieving, but the devils were unbelieving. Sorcery did they teach to men, and what had been revealed to the two angels, Hārūt and Mārūt, at Babel. Yet no man did these two teach until they had said, 'We are only a temptation. Be not then an unbeliever.' From these two did men learn how to cause division between man and wife: but unless by leave of God, no man did they harm thereby. They learned, indeed, what would harm and not profit them; and yet they knew that he who bought that art should have no part in the life to come! And vile the price for which they have sold themselves, —if they had but known it!"

ḤASAD (حسد). "Envy, malevolence, malice." It occurs twice in the Qur'ān.

Sūrah ii. 103: "Many of the people of the Book (*i.e.* Jews and Christians) desire to bring you back to unbelief after ye have believed, out *of selfish envy*, even after the truth hath been clearly shewn them."

Sūrah cxiii. 5: "I seek refuge . . . . from the *envy* of the envious when he envies."

AL-ḤASAN (الحسن). The fifth Khalīfah. The eldest son of Fāṭimah, the daughter of Muḥammad, by her husband the Khalīfah 'Alī. Born A.H. 3. Died A.H. 49. He succeeded his father 'Alī as Khalīfah A.H. 41, and reigned about six months. He resigned the Caliphate in favour of Mu'āwiyah, and was eventually poisoned by his wife Ja'dah, who was suborned to commit the deed by Yazīd, the son of Mu'āwiyah, by a promise of marrying her, which promise he did not keep. Al-Ḥasan had twenty children, fifteen sons and five daughters, from whom are descended one section of the great family of Saiyids, or Lords, the descendants of the Prophet. The history of al-Ḥasan, together with the tragical death of his brother al-Ḥusain, form the plot of the miracle play of the Muḥarram. [HUSAIN, MUHARRAM, SAIYID.]

HĀSHIM (هاشم). The great grandfather of Muḥammad. Born, according to M. C. de Perceval, A.D. 464. Sprenger places his birth in A.D. 442. He married Salmah, by whom he had a son, 'Abdu 'l-Muṭṭalib. the father of 'Abdu 'llah, who was the father of Muḥammad. The author of the *Qāmūs* says Hāshim's original name was 'Amr, but he was surnamed Hāshim on account of his hospitality in distributing bread (*hashm*, to break bread) to the pilgrims at Makkah.

ḤASHR (حشر). *Lit.* "Going forth from one place, and assembling in another." Hence the word is used in the Qur'ān in two senses, viz. an emigration and an assembly, *e.g.* Sūrah lix. 2: "It was He who drove forth from their homes those people of the book (*i.e.* Jews) who misbelieved, at the first *emigration.*" (Hence al-Ḥashr is the title of the LIXth Sūrah of the Qur'ān) Sūrah xxvii. 17: "And his hosts of the jinn and men and birds were *assembled* for Solomon."

The term *Yaumu 'l-Ḥashr* is therefore used for the Day of Resurrection, or the day when the dead shall migrate from their graves and assemble for judgment. It occurs in this sense in the Qur'ān, Sūrah l. 42 :—

"Verily we cause to live, and we cause to die. To us shall all return.

"On the day when the earth shall swiftly cleave asunder over the *dead, will this gathering be easy* to Us.

AL-ḤASĪB (الحسيب). "The Reckoner," in the Day of Judgment. One of the ninety-nine attributes of God. The title occurs in the Qur'ān three times.

Sūrah iv. 7: "God sufficeth for taking account."

Idem, 88: "God of all things takes an account."

Sūrah xxxiii. 39: "God is good enough at reckoning up."

ḤASSĀN (حسان). The son of Ṣābit. A celebrated poet in the time of Muḥammad, who embraced Islām. He is said to have lived 120 years, 60 of which were passed in idolatry and 60 in Islām.

It is related in the Traditions that the Prophet on the day of battle with the Banū Quraiẓah, cried out, "O Hassān ibn Ṣābit, abuse the infidels in your verse, for verily Gabriel helps you!" (*Mishkāt*, book xxii. ch. ix. pt. 1.) [POETRY.]

ḤĀṬIB IBN 'AMR (حاطب بن عمرو). An early convert to Islām, and one of the most trusted of Muḥammad's followers. He distinguished himself at the taking of Makkah.

ḤAULĀNU 'L-ḤAUL (حولان الحول). "A complete year." A term used in Muḥammadan law for the period property must be in possession before *zakāt* is required of it. (*Hidāyah*, vol. i. p. 2.)

ḤAUẒU 'L-KAUṢAR (حوض الكوثر). A pond or river in Paradise. According to Muḥammad's sayings in the Traditions (*Mishkāt*, book xxiii. ch. xii.), it is more than a month's journey in circumference, its waters are whiter than snow and sweeter than honey mixed with milk, and those who drink of it shall never thirst. The word *kauṣar* occurs once in the Qur'ān, namely in Sūrah cviii., which derives therefrom its title, and where its translation and meaning is doubtful. "Verily, we have given thee *al-Kauṣar*." Al-Baiẓāwī, the commentator, says it either means that which is good or abundant; or the pond *al-Kauṣar* which is mentioned in the Traditions.

HAWĀ (هوا). "Desire, love; hankering after." A term used by the Ṣūfī mystics for lust, or unholy desire. *Hawā-i-Nafṣānī*, "the lust of the flesh"; *Ahl-i-Hawā*, "a sceptic, an unbeliever."

HAWĀJIM (هواجم). *Lit.* "Assaults, shocks." A term used by the Ṣūfī mystics for those thoughts of the heart which enter it without desire or intention. ('Abdu 'r-Razzāq's *Dict. of Ṣūfī Terms.*)

HAWĀJIS (هواجس). "Thoughts." A term used by the Ṣūfī mystics for the worldly thoughts of the heart. ('Abdu 'r-Razzāq's *Dict. of Ṣūfī Terms.*)

ḤAWĀLAH (حوالة). A legal term signifying the removal or transfer of a debt by way of security or corroboration from that of the original debtor to that person to whom it is transferred. (*Hidāyah*, vol. ii. p. 606.)

ḤAWĀMĪM (حواميم). A title given to the seven chapters of the Qur'ān which begin with the letters ح Ḥā م Mīm, namely, XL, Sūratu 'l-Mu'min; XLI, Sūratu Fuṣṣilat; XLII, Sūratu 'sh-Shūrā; XLIII, Sūratu 'l-Zukhruf; XLIV, Sūratu 'd-Dukhān; XLV, Sūratu 'l-Jāsīyah; XLVI, Sūratu 'l-Aḥqāf.

For an explanation of the letters H M at the commencement of these Sūrahs, *see* HA MIM.

It is related in the Traditions that a man said to the Prophet, "I am old, and my memory is imperfect, and my tongue is stiff;" and the Prophet replied, "Then repeat three of the Sūrahs beginning with Ḥā Mīm." (*Mishkāt*, book viii. ch. i. pt. 3.)

ḤAWĀRĪ (حواری). The word used in the Qur'ān (Sūrahs iii. 45; lxi. 14) for the Apostles of Jesus. Al-Baiẓāwī, the Muḥammadan commentator, says it is derived from *ḥawar*, "to be white," and was given to the disciples of Jesus, either on account of their purity of life and sincerity; or because they were respectable men and wore white garments. In the Traditions (*Mishkāt*, book i. ch. vi. pt. 1) it is used for the followers of all the Prophets. The word may be derived from the Æthiopic *hawryra*, "to go, to be sent."

AL-ḤAWĀSSU 'L-KHAMSAH (الحواس الخمسة). [FIVE SENSES.]

HAWĀZIN (هوازن). A great and warlike tribe of Arabia in the days of Muḥammad, who dwelt between Makkah and aṭ-Ṭā'if. Muḥammad defeated them at the battle of Ḥunain, A.H. 8, a victory which in the Qur'ān, Sūrah ix. 26, is ascribed to angelic aid. (See Muir's *Life of Mahomet*, new ed. p. 432.)

HĀWIYAH (هاوية). A division of hell. The bottomless pit for the hypocrites. Qur'ān, Sūrah ci. 6, "But as for him whose balance is light, his dwelling shall be *Hāwiyah*."

HAWK, The. Arabic *ba'z* (باز), *ṣaqr* (صقر). It is lawful to hunt with hawks provided they are trained. A hawk is held to be trained when she obeys the voice of her master. [HUNTING.]

ḤAYĀ' (حياء). "Shame, pudency, modesty." The word does not occur in the Qur'ān, but in the Traditions it is said, "*Allāhu ḥayīyun*," *i.e.* "God acts with modesty." By which is understood that God hates that which is immodest or shameless. Muḥammad is related to have said, "Modesty (*ḥayā'*) brings nothing but good." (*Mishkāt*, book xxii. ch. xix.)

ḤAYĀT (حيوة). "Life." The word frequently occurs in the Qur'ān, *e.g.* Sūrah xviii. 44, "Wealth and children are an adornment of the *life* of this world." Sūrah ii. 25, "For you in retaliation is there *life*, O ye possessors of mind!"

Al-Ḥayātu 'd-dunyā, "the worldly life," is a term used in the Qur'ān for those things in this world which prevent from attaining to the eternal life of the next world.

Sūrah ii. 80: "Those who have bought this *worldly life* with the future, the torment shall not be lightened from them nor shall they be helped."

HAYŪLĀ (هيولی). "Matter." The first principle of everything material. It does not occur in either the Qur'ān or the Ḥadīs̤.

ḤAYẒ (حيض). Menses. [MENSTRUATION.]

ḤAẔAR (حذر). According to Arabic lexicons, the word means vigilance or a cautious fear, but it only occurs twice in the Qur'ān, and in both instances it implies terror.

Sūrah ii. 18: "They put their fingers in their ears at the thunder-clap *for fear* of death." (*Ḥaẕara 'l-Maut.*) *Idem*, 244: "Dost thou not look at those who left their homes by thousands *for fear* of death."

AL-ḤAẒARĀTU 'L-KHAMS (الحضرات الخمس). According to the *Kitābu 't-Ta'rifāt*, *al-ḥaẓarātu 'l-Khamsu 'l-Ilāhiyah*, or "the five divine existences," is a term used by the Ṣūfī mystics for the following:—

1. *Ḥaẓratu 'l-ghaibi 'l-muṭlaq*, That existence which is absolutely unknown, *i.e.* God.

2. *Ḥaẓratu 'sh-shahādati 'l-muṭlaqah*, Those celestial (*ajrām*) and terrestrial (*ajsām*) existences which are evident to the senses.

3. *Ḥaẓratu 'ālami 'l-arwaḥ*, That existence which consists of the spiritual world of angels and spirits.

4. *Ḥaẓratu 'ālami 'l-miṡāl*, That existence, which is the unseen world, where there is the true likeness of everything which exists on the earth.

5. *Ḥaẓratu 'l-jāmi'ah*, The collective existence of the four already mentioned.

ḤĀẒIR ẒĀMINĪ (حاضر ضامنى). Bail for the person, which, according to the Imām Abu Ḥanīfah, is lawful. Bail for property is called *māl ẓāminī*.

HAẒRAH (حضرة). *Lit.* "Presence." This title of respect has no equivalent in English, as it is employed in a variety of acceptations. Applied to an officer of rank, it would mean "*your honour*"; to a clergyman, "*your reverence*"; to a king, "*your majesty*." When applied to the names of prophets, apostles, or saints, it expresses the sacredness of his office and character, *i.e.* our Saviour is called *Ḥaẓratu ʿIsa*, and the Virgin Mary, *Ḥaẓratu Maryam*. The word is much used in Persian theological works. It is seldom used in this sense in Arabic books. *Ḥaẓratu 'llāh*, "the presence of God," is an Arabic term in prayer.

HEAD. Arabic *ra's*, *rās* (راس). Heb. ראשׁ. The author of the *Raddu 'l-Muḥtār*, vol. i. p. 670, says: "It is abominable (*makrūh*) to say the prayers with the head uncovered, if it be done from laziness, but it is of no consequence if a Muslim say his prayers with his head uncovered from a sense of humility and unworthiness. But still it is better not to uncover the head, for humility is a matter connected with the heart."

Amongst Muḥammadans it is considered a sign of disrespect to receive a visitor with the head uncovered; consequently on the approach of a visitor the turban or cap is immediately placed on the head.

There is no general custom as to shaving the head or otherwise. In Afghanistan, Muḥammadans generally shave the head, but the Baluchīs and many other Muslim tribes wear long hair.

The Egyptians shave all the rest of the hair, or leave only a small tuft (called *shūshah*) upon the crown of the head. Mr. Lane says: This last custom (which is almost universal among them) is said to have originated in the fear that if the Muslim should fall into the hands of an infidel, and be slain, the latter might cut off the head of his victim, and finding no hair by which to hold it, put his impure hand into the mouth, in order to carry it, for the beard might not be sufficiently long; but was probably adopted from the Turks, for it is generally neglected by the Badāwīs, and the custom of shaving the head is of late origin among the Arabs in general, and practised for the sake of cleanliness.

HEAVEN. Arabic *Samā'* (سماء); Persian *Asmān* (اسمان); Heb. שָׁמַיִם, which expresses the firmament as distinguished from *Firdaus*, or Paradise, the abodes of bliss. [PARADISE.] In the Qur'ān it is stated that there are seven paths, or stages, in heaven. Sūrah xxiii. 17: "And we have created above you *seven paths*, nor are we heedless of the creation." By which the commentators understand that they are paths of the angels and of the celestial bodies. The creation of the heaven is declared to be for God's glory and not for His pastime. Sūrah xxi. 16: "We created not the heaven and the earth, and that which is between them, by way of sport."

It is the general belief that at the last day the heavens will fall, but that they are now upheld by God's power. Sūrah xxii. 64: "He holds up the heaven from falling on the earth save at His bidding."

According to the traditions (*Mishkāt*, book xxiv. ch. vii.), Muḥammad during the miʿrāj, or night journey, passed through these seven heavens, and they are stated to be as follows: (1) That which is of pure virgin silver and which is Adam's residence; (2) of pure gold, which is John the Baptist's and Jesus'; (3) of pearls, which is Joseph's; (4) of white gold, which is Enoch's; (5) of silver which is Aaron's; (6) of ruby and garnet, which is Moses'; (7) which is Abraham's. These accounts are, however, most confused; for in some books and according to popular tradition, the fourth and not the second heaven is assigned to Jesus.

This view is in harmony with the seven spheres of Ptolemy, the first of which is that of the moon, the second Mercury, the third Venus, the fourth the Sun, the fifth Mars, the sixth Jupiter, the seventh Saturn; each of which orbs was supposed by the ancients to revolve round the earth in its proper sphere. Muḥammad said the distance between each heavenly region is five hundred years' journey. (*Mishkāt*, book xxiv. ch. i. pt. 3).

The Rabbis spoke of two heavens (*cf.* Deut. x. 14), "The heaven and the heaven of heavens," or seven (ἑπτὰ οὐρανοὺς οὕς τινες ἀριθμοῦσι κατ' ἐπανάβασιν, *Clem. Alex. Strom.*, iv. 7, 636). "Resch Lakisch dixit septem esse cœlos, quorum nomina sunt, 1. velum; 2. expansum; 3. nubes; 4. habitaculum; 5. habitatio; 6. sedes fixa; 7. Araboth. (*See* Wetstein, ad. 2 Cor. xii. 2). St. Paul's expression, "ἕως τριτοῦ οὐρανοῦ," 2 Cor. xii. 2, has led to some discussion, for Grotius says the Jews divided the heaven into three parts, (1) *Nubiferum*, the atmosphere; (2) *Astriferum*, the firmament; and (3) *Empyreum*, the abode of God. But the statement, however, does not seem to be supported by any known Rabbinic authority.

HEBER. [HUD].

HEGIRA. [HIJRAH.]

HEIRS. Arabic *wāriṣ* (وارث), pl. *waraṣah*. [INHERITANCE.]

HELL. The place of torment is most frequently spoken of in the Qur'ān and Traditions as *an-Nār*, "the fire," but the word *Jahannam* occurs about thirty times. It is said to have seven portals or divisions. Sūrah xv. 44: "Verily, hell (*jahannam*) is promised to all together (who follow Satan). It has seven portals, and at every door there is a separate party of them."

The Persian word used for hell in books of theology is *dozakh*.

The seven divisions of hell are given by Muslim commentators as follows:—

1. *Jahannam* (جهنم), γέεννα, the purgatorial hell for all Muḥammadans. For according to the Qur'ān, all Muslims will pass through the regions of hell. Sūrah xix. 72: "There is not one of you who will not go down to it (hell), that is settled and decided by thy Lord."

3. *Laẓa* (لظى). Sūrah xcvii. 5: "For *Laẓā*, dragging by the scalp, shall claim him who turned his back and went away, and amassed and hoarded."

3. *Al-Ḥuṭamah* (الحطمة). Sūrah civ. 4:—

"Nay! for verily he shall be flung into *al-Ḥuṭamah*;

"And who shall teach thee what *al-Ḥuṭamah* is?

"It is God's kindled fire,

"Which shall mount above the hearts *of the damned;*

"It shall verily rise over them like a vault,

"On outstretched columns."

4. *Sa'īr* (سعير). Sūrah iv. 11: "Those who devour the property of orphans unjustly, only devour into their bellies fire, and they broil in *sa'īr*."

(The word occurs in fourteen other places.)

5. *Saqar* (سقر). Sūrah liv. 47: "The sinners are in error and excitement. On the day when they shall be dragged into the fire on their faces! Taste ye the touch of *saqar*!"

Sūrah lxxiv. 44: "What drove you into *saqar?*"

6. *Al-Jaḥīm* (الجحيم). Sūrah ii. 113: "Thou shalt not be questioned as to the fellows of *al-Jaḥīm*" (*Aṣḥābu 'l-Jaḥīm*).

(The word occurs in twenty other places).

7. *Hāwiyah* (هاوية). Sūrah ci. 8: "As for him whose balance is light, his dwelling shall be *Hāwiyah*."

The Muḥammadan commentators, with that utter recklessness which so characterizes their writings, distribute these seven stations as follows (see *al-Bag͟hawī*, *al-Baiẓāwī*, and others): (1) *Jahannam*, the purgatorial hell for Muslims. (2) *Laẓā*, a blazing fire for Christians. (3) *Al-Ḥuṭamah*, an intense fire for the Jews. (4) *Sa'īr*, a flaming fire for the Sabians. (5) *Saqar*, a scorching fire for the Magi. (6) *Al-Jaḥīm*, a huge hot fire for idolaters. (7) *Hāwiyah*, bottomless pit for the hypocrites. A reference to the Qur'ān will prove that there is not the least reason for assigning these regions to their respective tenants beyond the sentence already quoted: "At each portal a separate party."

The *teaching of the Qur'ān* (which is chiefly confined to those Sūrahs which, chronologically arranged, are the earliest), is as follows:—

Sūrah lxxiv. 26–34 (generally held to be the second Sūrah composed by Muḥammad, and relating to al-Walīd ibn al-Mug͟hīrah, a person of note amongst the unbelieving Makkans):—

"We will surely cast him into Saqar.

"And who shall teach thee what Saqar is?

"It leaveth nought, it spareth nought,

"Blackening the skin.

"Over it are nineteen *angels*.

"None but angels have we made guardians of the fire (*aṣḥābu 'n-nār*): nor have we made this to be their number but to perplex the unbelievers, and that they who possess the Scriptures may be certain of the Truth, and that they who believe may increase their faith;

"And that they to whom the Scriptures have been given, and the believers, may not doubt;

"And that the infirm of heart and the unbelievers may say, What meaneth God by this parable?

"Thus God misleadeth whom He will, and whom He will He doth guide aright: and none knoweth the armies of thy Lord but Himself: and this is no other than a warning to mankind."

Sūrah lxxxviii. 1–7:—

"Hath the tidings of the day that shall overshadow reached thee?

"Downcast on that day shall be the countenances of some,

"Travailing and worn,

"Burnt at the scorching fire,

"Made to drink from a fountain fiercely boiling.

"No food shall they have but the fruit of ẓarī' (a bitter thorn),

"Which shall not fatten nor appease their hunger."

Sūrah lxxviii. 21–30:—

"Hell (*Jahannam*) truly shall be a place of snares,

"The home of transgressors,

"To abide therein ages;

"No coolness shall they taste therein nor any drink,

"Save boiling water and running sores;

"Meet recompence!

"For they looked not forward to their account;

"And they gave the lie to our signs, charging them with falsehood;

"But we noted and wrote down all:

"'Taste this then: and we will give you increase of nought but torment.'"

The above are all Madīnah Sūrahs composed in the earlier stage of Muḥammad's mission. The allusions to hell in the Makkan Sūrahs are brief and are in every case directed against *unbelievers in the Prophet's mission*, and not against sin; *e.g.* Sūrah ix. 69, "God hath promised to the hypocrites (*i.e. dissemblers as far as Islām was concerned*), men and women, and unto the unbelievers, hell-fire to dwell therein for ever."

The teaching of Muḥammad in the Traditions is much more specific, but it is impossible to assign a date for these traditions, even assuming them to be authentic. They are given on the authority of al-Buk͟hārī and Muslim (*Mishkāt*, book xxiii. ch. xv.):—

"'The fire of the world is one part of seventy parts of hell fire.' It was said, 'O Prophet of God! verily the fire of the world would be sufficient for punishing.' The Prophet replied, 'Hell-fire has been made more than the fire of the world by sixty-nine parts, every part of which is like the fire of the world.'"

"Verily, the easiest of the infernals in punishment, is he who shall have both his shoes and thongs of them of fire, by which the brains of his head boil, like the boiling of a copper furnace; and he will not suppose that anyone is more severely punished than himself; whilst verily, he is the least so."

"On the Day of Resurrection, the most luxurious of the world will be brought, and dipped once into the fire; after that it will be said, 'O child of Adam, did you ever see any good, or did comfort ever pass by you in the world?' He will say, 'I swear by God I never saw any good, nor did comfort ever come near me.' And a man of the severest distresses and troubles in the world will be brought into paradise; and it will be said to him, 'O son of Adam, did you ever see any trouble, and did distress ever come to you in the world?' And he will say, 'I swear by God, O my Lord, I never suffered troubles in the world, nor did I ever see hardship.'"

"There are some of the infernals that will be taken by the fire up to their ankles, and some up to their knees, and some up to their waist, and some up to their necks."

"Hell-fire burnt a thousand years so that it became red, and burnt another thousand years till it became white; after that it burnt a thousand years till it became black; then hell fire is black and dark, and never has any light."

"Verily, hot water will be poured upon the heads of the infernals, and will penetrate into their bellies, and will cut to pieces everything within them; so that they will come out at their feet; and this is the meaning of the word of God, 'Boiling water shall be poured on their heads, and everything in their bellies shall be dissolved thereby,' after that, they will be made as they were."

"The infernals shall be drenched with yellow water, draught after draught, and it will be brought to their mouths and they will be disgusted at it; and when very near, it will scorch their faces, and when they drink it it will tear their entrails to pieces. God says, 'They who must dwell for ever in hell-fire, will have the boiling water given them to drink which shall burst their bowels'; and God will say, 'If the infidels complain of thirst, they shall be assisted with water like molten copper, which will fry their faces; it will be a shocking beverage.'"

For most of these circumstances relating to hell and the state of the damned, Muḥammad was in all probability indebted to the Jews and, in part, to the Magians, both of whom agree in making seven distinct apartments in hell. (*Nishmat hayim*, f. 32; *Gemar. Arubin*, f. 19; *Zohar. ad. Exod. xxvi. 2*, &c. and *Hyde de Rel. Vet. Pers.*, p. 245), though they vary in other particulars.

The former place an angel as a guard over each of these infernal apartments, and suppose he will intercede for the miserable wretches there imprisoned, who will openly acknowledge the justice of God in their condemnation. (*Midrash, Yalkut Shemuni*, pt. 11, f. 116.) They also teach that the wicked will suffer a diversity of punishments, and that by intolerable cold (*Zohar. ad. Exod. xix.*) as well as heat, and that their faces shall become black (*Yalkut Shemuni, ubi sup.* f. 86); and believe those of their own religion shall also be punished in hell hereafter according to their crimes (for they hold that few or none will be found exactly righteous as to deserve no punishment at all,) but will soon be delivered thence, when they shall be sufficiently purged from their sins by their father Abraham, or at the intercession of him or some other of the prophets. (*Nishmat hayim*, f. 82; *Gemar. Arubin*, f. 19.)

The Magians allow but one angel to preside over all the seven hells, who is named by them Vanānd Yezād, and, as they teach, assigns punishments proportionate to each person's crimes, restraining also the tyranny and excessive cruelty of the devil, who would, if left to himself, torment the damned beyond their sentence. (*Hyde, de Rel. Vet. Pers.* p. 182.) Those of this religion do also mention and describe various kinds of torments wherewith the wicked will be punished in the next life; among which, though they reckon extreme cold to be one, yet they do not admit fire, out of respect, as it seems, to that element, which they take to be the representation of the divine nature, and therefore they rather choose to describe the damned souls as suffering by other kinds of punishment, such as an intolerable stink, the stinging and biting of serpents and wild beasts, the cutting and tearing of the flesh by the devils, excessive hunger and thirst, and the like. (See *Eundem, ibid.*, p. 399; Sale's *Pre. Dis.*)

The author of the *Sharḥu 'l-Muwāqif*, p. 586, also says: "It is agreed amongst all orthodox Muslims that all unbelievers, without exception, will be consigned to the fire for ever, and that they will never be free from torment." "But," he adds, "there are certain heretics, who call themselves Muslims, who deny the eternity of the torments of the fire. For they say, it is an essential property of all things fleshly that they come to an end. And, moreover, it is not possible for a thing to exist which goes on burning for ever. But to this we reply that God is all powerful and can do as He likes."

The sect called as-Samāmīyah, founded by Samāmah ibn Ashras an-Numairī, say: "The Jews, and Christians, and Majūsī, and Zanādiqah, will, after the Day of Judgment, return to dust, just as the animals and the little children of unbelievers do." (*Sharḥu 'l-Muwāqif*, p. 633.)

The same writer says (p. 687): "Besides those who are unbelievers, all those (Muslims) who are sinners and have committed great sins (*kabā'ir*), will go to hell; but they will not remain there always, for it has been said in the Qur'ān (Sūrah xcix. 7), "He who does an atom of good shall see its reward."

With reference to the verse in the Qur'ān, which distinctly states that all Muslims shall enter hell (Sūrah xix. 73, "There is not one of you that shall not go down to it"), al-Kamālān, the commentators, say, that according to extant traditions, all Muslims will enter hell, but it will be cool and pleasant to those who have not committed great sins; or, according to some writers, they will simply pass along the bridge *Ṣirāt*, which is over the infernal regions.

HELPERS, The. [ANSAR.]

HERACLIUS. Arabic *Hiraql* (هرقل). The Roman Emperor to whom Muḥammad sent an embassy with a letter inviting him to Islām, A.H. 7, A.D. 628.

"In the autumn of this year (A.D. 628), Heraclius fulfilled his vow of thanksgiving for the wonderful success which had crowned his arms (in Persia); he performed on foot the pilgrimage from Edessa to Jerusalem, where the 'true cross,' recovered from the Persians, was with solemnity and pomp restored to the Holy Sepulchre. While preparing for this journey, or during the journey itself, an uncouth despatch in the Arabic character was laid before Heraclius. It was forwarded by the Governor of Bostra, into whose hands it had been delivered by an Arab chief. The epistle was addressed to the Emperor himself, from 'Mahomet the Apostle of God,' the rude impression of whose seal could be deciphered at the foot. In strange and simple accents like those of the Prophets of old, it summoned Heraclius to acknowledge the mission of Mahomet, to cast aside the idolatrous worship of Jesus and his Mother, and to return to the Catholic faith of the one only God. The letter was probably cast aside, or preserved, it may be, as a strange curiosity, the effusion of some harmless fanatic." (Muir's *Life of Mahomet*, new ed. p. 383.)

Tradition, of course, has another story. "Now the Emperor was at this time at Hims, performing a pedestrian journey, in fulfilment of the vow which he had made, that, if the Romans overcame the Persians, he would travel on foot from Constantinople to Aelia (Jerusalem). So having read the letter, he commanded his chief men to meet him in the royal camp at Hims. And thus he addressed them:—'Ye chiefs of Rome! Do you desire safety and guidance, so that your kingdom shall be firmly established, and that ye may follow the commands of Jesus, Son of Mary?' 'And what, O King! shall secure us this?' 'Even that ye follow the Arabian Prophet,' said Heraclius. Whereupon they all started aside like wild asses of the desert, each raising his cross and waving it aloft in the air. Whereupon Heraclius, despairing of their conversion, and unwilling to lose his kingdom, desisted, saying that he had only wished to test their constancy and faith, and that he was now satisfied by this display of firmness and devotion. The courtiers bowed their heads, and so the Prophet's despatch was rejected." (*Kātibu 'l-Wāqidī*, p. 50, quoted by Muir, in a note to the above passage.)

The letter written by Muḥammad to Heraclius is, according to a tradition by Ibn 'Abbās, as follows:—

"In the name of God the Merciful, the Compassionate. This letter is from Muḥammad the Messenger of God, to Hiraql, chief of ar-Rūm. Peace be upon whosoever has gone on the straight road! After this, I say, verily I call thee to Islām. Embrace Islām that ye may obtain peace. Embrace Islām and God will give thee a double reward If ye reject Islām, then on thee shall rest the sins of thy subjects and followers. O ye people of the Book (*i.e.* Christians) come to a creed which is laid down plainly between us and you, that we will not serve other than God, nor associate aught with Him, nor take each other for lords rather than God. But if they turn back, then say, 'Bear witness that we are Muslims.'" (*Qur'ān*, iii. 57.) (See *Ṣaḥīḥu Muslim*, p. 98.)

The Shī'ah traditions give the above letter almost *verbatim*. (See Merrick's *Ḥayātu 'l-Qulūb*, p. 89.)

"Not long after, another despatch, bearing the same seal, and couched in similar terms, reached the court of Heraclius. It was addressed to Hârith VII., Prince of the Bani Ghassân, who forwarded it to the Emperor, with an address from himself, soliciting permission to chastise the audacious impostor. But Heraclius regarding the ominous voice from Arabia beneath his notice, forbade the expedition, and desired that Hârith should be in attendance at Jerusalem, to swell the imperial train at the approaching visitation of the temple. Little did the Emperor imagine that the kingdom which, unperceived by the world, this obscure Pretender was founding in Arabia, would in a few short years wrest from his grasp that Holy City and the fair provinces which, with so much toil and so much glory, he had just recovered from the Persians!" (Muir's *Life of Mahomet*, p. 384.)

(For the Shī'ah account of the embassy to Heraclius, see Merrick's *Ḥayātu 'l-Qulūb*, p. 88.)

HERMAPHRODITE (Arabic خنثى, *Khunṣā*) is a person who is possessed of the organs of generation of both man and woman, and for whose spiritual existence the Muḥammadan law legislates (*vide Hidāyah*, vol. iv. p. 559). For example, it is a rule, with respect to equivocal hermaphrodites, that they are required to observe all the more comprehensive points of the spiritual law, but not those concerning the propriety of which, in regard to them, any doubt exists In public prayer they must take their station between the men and the women, but in other respects observe the customs of women. (*Idem*, p. 561.)

HIBAH (هبة). A legal term in Muḥammadan law, which signifies a deed of gift, a transfer of property, made immediately and without any exchange. [GIFTS.]

ḤIDĀD (حداد). "Mourning." The state of a widow who abstains from scents, ornaments, &c., on account of the death of her husband. *Ḥidād* must be observed for a period of four months and ten days. (*Hidāyah*, vol. i. p. 370.)

HIDĀYAH (هداية). *Lit.* "Guidance." The title of a well known book on Sunnī law, and frequently quoted in the present work. There are many Muḥammadan works entitled *al-Hidāyah*, but this is called *Hidāyah fi'l-furū'*, or "a guidance in particular points." It was composed by the Shaikh Burhānu 'd-dīn 'Alī, who was born at Marghīnān in Transoxania about A.H. 530 (A.D. 1135), and died A.H. 593.

There is an English translation of the *Hidāyah* (omitting the chapters on Prayer and Purification), by Charles Hamilton, four vols., London, A.D. 1791.

ḤIFẒU 'L-'AHD (حفظ العهد). *Lit.* "The guarding of the covenant." A term used by the Ṣūfī mystics for remaining firm in that state in which God has brought them. ('Abdu 'r-Razzāq's *Dict. of Ṣūfī Terms.*)

HIGHWAY ROBBERY. Arabic *qaṭ'u 't-ṭarīq* (قطع الطريق). Persian *rahzani*. Highway robbery is a very heinous offence according to Muḥammadan law, the punishment of which has been fixed by the Qur'ān (Sūrah v. 37): "The recompense of those who war against God and His apostle, and go about to enact violence on the earth, is that they be slain or crucified, or have their alternate hands and feet cut off, or be banished the land." According to the *Hidāyah*, highway robbers are of four kinds, viz. (1) Those who are seized before they have robbed or murdered any person, or put any person in fear. These are to be imprisoned by the magistrate until their repentance is evident. (2) Those who have robbed but have not murdered. These are to have their right hand and left foot struck off. (3) Those who have committed murder but have not robbed. These are punished with death. (4) Those who have committed both robbery and murder. These are punished according to the option of the magistrate. If he please, he can first cut off a hand and foot, and then put them to death by the sword, or by crucifixion; or he may kill them at once without inflicting amputation. If any one among a band of robbers be guilty of murder, the punishment of death must be inflicted upon the whole band.

ḤIJĀB (حجاب). A partition or curtain. Veiling or concealing.

(1) A term used for the seclusion of women enjoined in the Qur'ān, Sūrah xxxiii. 53: "And when ye ask them (the Prophet's wives) for an article, ask them from behind a curtain; that is purer for your hearts and for theirs."

(2) A term used by the Ṣūfī mystics for that which obscures the light of God in the soul of man. ('Abdu 'r-Razzāq's *Dict. of Ṣūfī Terms.*)

ḤIJĀZ (حجاز). *Lit.* "A barrier or anything similar by which two things are separated." The name *al-Ḥijāz* is given to that tract of country which separates Najd from Tahāmah, and is an irregular parallelogram about 250 miles long and 150 miles wide. It may be considered the holy land of the Muḥammadans, for within its limits are the sacred cities of al-Madīnah and Makkah, and most of its places are someway connected with the history of Muḥammad. It is a barren district consisting of sandy plains towards the shore and rocky hills in the interior; and so destitute of provisions as to depend, even for the necessaries of life, on the supplies of other countries. Among its fertile spots is Wādī Fāṭimah, which is well watered, and produces grain and vegetables. Sajrah abounds in date trees. Aṭ-Ṭa'if, seventy-two miles from Makkah, is celebrated for its gardens, and the neighbourhood of al-Madīnah has cultivated fields. The towns on the coast are Jiddah and Yambu', the former being considered the port of Makkah, from which it is distant about fifty-five miles, and the latter that of al-Madīnah. Al-Ḥijāz is bounded eastward by a lofty range of mountains, which, near at-Ṭā'if, take the name of Jabalu 'l-Qura. The scenery there is occasionally beautiful and picturesque; the small rivulets that descend from the rocks afford nourishment to the plains below, which are clothed with verdure and shady trees. The vicinity of Makkah is bleak and bare; for several miles it is surrounded with thousands of hills all nearly of one height; their dark and naked peaks rise one behind another, appearing at a distance like cocks of hay. The most celebrated of these are aṣ-Ṣafā, 'Arafah and al-Marwah, which have always been connected with the religious rites of the Muḥammadan pilgrimage.

ḤIJR (حجر). In its primitive sense means interdiction or prevention.

(1) In the language of the law it signifies an interdiction of action with respect to a particular person, who is either an infant, an idiot, or a slave. (*Hidāyah*, vol. iii. p. 468.)

(2) *Al-Hijr* is a territory in the province of al-Ḥijāz between al-Madīnah and Syria, where the tribe of Ṣamūd dwelt. It is the title of the xvth Sūrah of the Qur'ān, in the 80th verse of which the word occurs: "The inhabitants of al-Ḥijr likewise accused the messenger of God of imposture."

HIJRAH (هجرة). *Lit.* "migration." (1) The departure of Muḥammad from Makkah. (2) The Muslim era. (3) The act of a Muslim leaving a country under infidel rule. (4) Fleeing from sin.

The date of Muḥammad's flight from Makkah was the fourth day of the first month of Rabī', which by the calculation of M. Caussin de Perceval was June 20th, A.D. 622. The Hijrah, or the era of the "Hegira," was instituted seventeen years later by the Khalīfah 'Umar, which dates from the first day of the first lunar month of the year, viz. Muḥarram, which day in the year when the era was established fell on Thursday the 15th of July

A.D. 622. But although 'Umar instituted the official era, according to aṭ-Ṭabarī, the custom of referring to events as happening before or after the Hijrah originated with Muḥammad himself.

Professor H. H. Wilson in his *Glossary of Terms* gives the following method of ascertaining the Muḥammadan and Christian years:—

Multiply the Hijrah year by 2,977, the difference between 100 solar and as many lunar Muḥammadan years; divide the product by 100, and deduct the quotient from the Hijrah year; add to the result 621,569 (the decimal being the equivalent of the 15th July, plus 12 days for the change of the Kalendar); and the quotient will be the Christian year from the date at which the Muḥammadan year begins; thus, Hij. 1269 × 2·977 = 3777·8, which divided by 100 = 37·778 and 1269 − 37·778 = 1231·222; this + 621·569 = 1852·791, the decimals corresponding to 9 months and 15 days, *i.e.* the 15th of October, which is the commencement of the Hij. year 1269. The reverse formula for finding the corresponding Hijrah year to a given Christian year, is thus laid down: Subtract 622 from the current year; multiply the result by 1·0307; cut off two decimals and add ·46; the sum will be the year, which, when it has a surplus decimal, requires the addition of 1: thus, 1852 − 622 = 1230; 1230 × 1·0307 = 1267·761; 1267·76 + ·46 = 1268·22; add therefore 1, and we have the equivalent Hijrah year 1269.

The Persian era of Yezdegird commenced on June 16th, A.D. 632, or ten years later than the Ḥijrah.

ḤIKMAH (حكمة). *Al-ḥikmah*, "the wisdom," is a term used by the Ṣūfī mystics to express a knowledge of the essence, attributes, specialities, and results of things as they exist and are seen, with the study of their cause, effects, and uses. This is said to be the wisdom mentioned in the Qur'ān, Sūrah ii. 272: "He (God) bringeth the wisdom (*al-ḥikmah*) unto whom He willeth."

The Ṣūfīs say there are four kinds of wisdom expressed in the term *al-ḥikmah*:—

(1) *Al-ḥikmatu 'l-Manṭūqah*, "spoken wisdom," which is made known in the Qur'ān, or in the *Ṭarīqah*, "the Path" (*i.e.* the Ṣūfī path).

(2) *Al-ḥikmatu 'l-maskūtah*, "unspoken wisdom." Such as understood only by Ṣūfī mystics, and not by the natural man.

(3) *Al-ḥikmatu 'l-majhūlah*, "unknown wisdom," or those acts of the Creator the wisdom of which is unknown to the creature, such as the infliction of pain upon the creatures of God, the death of infants, or the eternal fire of hell. Things which we believe, but which we do not understand.

(4) *Al-ḥikmatu 'l-jāmi'ah*, "collective wisdom," or the knowledge of the truth (*ḥaqq*), and acting upon it, and the perception of error (*bāṭil*) and the rejection of it. ('Abdu 'r-Razzāq's *Dict. of Ṣūfī Terms.*)

HILĀL (هلال). The new moon. A term used for the first three days of the month.

ḤILF (حلف). An oath; a vow. An affidavit. *Hilf nāmah*, a written solemn declaration. *Ḥālif*, one who takes an oath.

ḤILFU 'L-FUẒŪL (حلف الفضول). A confederacy formed by the descendants of Hāshim, Zuhrah, and Taim, in the house of 'Abdu 'llah ibn Jud'ān at Makkah, for the suppression of violence and injustice at the restoration of peace after the Sacrilegious war. Muḥammad was then a youth, and Sir William Muir says this confederacy "aroused an enthusiasm in the mind of Mahomet, which the exploits of the sacrilegious war failed to kindle."

ḤILM (حلم). Being mild, gentle, clement. Restraining oneself at a time when the spirit is roused to anger. Delaying in punishing a tyrant. (*Kitābu 't-Ta'rīfāt.*) Hence *al-Ḥalīm*, the Clement, is one of the attributes of God.

ḤIMA (حمى). *Lit.* "guarded, forbidden." A portion of land reserved by the ruler of a country as a grazing ground. (See *Mishkāt*, book xii. ch. i. pt. i.) "Know ye that every prince has a grazing ground which is forbidden to the people, and know ye the grazing place (*ḥima*) is the thing forbidden by Him to men."

HIMMAH (همة). "Resolution, strength, ability." A term used by the Ṣūfī mystics for a determination of the heart to incline itself entirely to God. ('Abdu 'r-Razzāq's *Dict. of Ṣūfī Terms.*)

ḤINNA' (حناء). The *Lawsonia inermis*, or Eastern privet, used for dyeing the hands and feet on festive occasions. [MARRIAGE.] Muḥammad enjoined the use of ḥinnā', and approved of women staining their hands and feet with it. He also dyed his own beard with it, and recommended its use for this purpose (*Mishkāt*, book xx. c. 4.) It has therefore become a religious custom, and is *sunnah.*

ḤIQQAH (حقة). A female camel turned three years. The proger age for a camel to be given in *zakāt*, or legal alms, for camels from forty-six to sixty in number.

ḤIRĀ' (حراء). The name of a mountain near Makkah, said to have been the scene of the first revelation given to Muḥammad. [MUHAMMAD.]

HIRAQL (هرقل). Heraclius the Roman Emperor, to whom Muḥammad sent an embassy, A.H. 7, A.D. 628. [HERACLIUS.]

HIRE. The Arabic term *ijārah* (اجارة), which means the use and enjoyment of property for a time, includes hire, rental, and lease. The hirer is termed *ājir*, *or mu'jir*. The person who receives the rent is the *musta'jir*.

The following are some of the chief points in the Sunnī law with regard to *ijārah*, and for further particulars the reader must refer in English to Hamilton's *Hidāyah*, vol. iii. p 312, or in Arabic to such works as the *Durru 'l-Mukhtār*, *Fatāwā-i-'Ālamgīrī*, and the *Raddu 'l-Muḥtār*, in which works it is treated in the *Bābu 'l-Ijārah*.

A contract of hire, or rental, or lease, is not valid unless both the usufruct and the hire be particularly known and specified, because there is a traditional saying of the Prophet, "If a person hire another let him first inform him of the wages he is to receive."

A workman is not entitled to anything until his work is finished, but the article wrought upon may be detained until the workman be paid his full wages, and the workman is not responsible for any loss or damage in the article during such detention. If a person hire another to carry a letter to al-Baṣrah and bring back an answer, and he accordingly go to al-Baṣrah and there find the person dead to whom the letter was addressed, and come back, and return the letter, he is not entitled to any wages whatever! This strange ruling is according to Abū Ḥanīfah and two of his disciples, but the Imām Muḥammad says the messenger ought to be paid.

It is lawful to *hire a house or shop* for the purpose of residence, although no mention be made of the business to be followed in it, and the lessee is at liberty to carry on any business he pleases, unless it be injurious to the building. For example, a blacksmith or a fuller must not reside in the house, unless it is previously so agreed, since the exercise of those trades would shake the building.

It is lawful *to hire or lease land* for the purposes of cultivation, and in this case the hirer is entitled to the use of the road leading to the land, and likewise the water (*i.e.* his turn of water) although no mention of these be made in the contract.

A lease of land is not valid unless mention is made of the article to be raised on it, not only with a view to cultivation, but also for other purposes, such as building, and so forth. Or the lessor of the land may make declaration to the effect:—"I let the land on this occasion, that the lessee shall raise on it whatever he pleases."

If a person hire unoccupied land for the purposes of building or planting, it is lawful, but on the term of the lease expiring it is incumbent on the lessee to remove his buildings and trees, and to restore the land to the lessor in such a state as may leave him no claim upon it, because houses or trees have no specific limit of existence, and if they were left on the land it might be injurious to the proprietor. But it is otherwise when the land is hired or leased for the purpose of tillage, and the term of the lease expires at a time when the grain is yet unripe. In this case, the grain must be suffered to remain upon the ground at a proportionate rent, until it is fit for reaping.

The *hire of an animal* is lawful, either for carriage, or for riding, or for any use to which animals are applied. And if a person hire an animal to carry a burden, and the person who lets it to hire specify the nature and quantity of the article with which the hirer is to load the animal, the hirer is at liberty to load the animal with an equal quantity of any article not more troublesome or prejudicial in the carriage than wheat, such as barley, &c. The hirer is not at liberty to load the animal with a more prejudicial article than wheat (unless stipulated beforehand), such as salt or iron. For a hired animal perishing from ill-usage, the hirer is responsible.

(*For the sayings of Muḥammad on the subject of hire and leases, refer to the Mishkāt, Bābu 'l-Ijārah.*)

ḤIRṢ (حرص). "Avarice, greed, eagerness." Derivatives of the word occur three times in the Qur'ān. Sūrah ii. 90: "Thou wilt find them (the Jews) the *greediest* of men for life." Sūrah iv. 128: "And ye may not have it at all in your power to treat your wives with equal justice, even though *you be anxious* to do so." Sūrah xii. 104: "And yet most men, though *thou ardently desire it*, will not believe."

ḤISS (حس). "Understanding, sense." *Ḥiss bāṭin*, internal sense; *ḥiss ẓāhir*, external sense; *ḥiss mushtarik*, common sense.

ḤIẒĀNAH (حضانة). *Al-ḥiẓānah* is the right of a mother to the custody of her children. "The mother is of all persons the best entitled to the custody of her infant children during the connubial relationship as well as after its dissolution." (*Fatāwā-i-'Ālamgīrī*, vol. i. p. 728.)

When the children are no longer dependent on the mother's care, the father has a right to educate and take charge of them, and is entitled to the guardianship of their person in preference to the mother. Among the Ḥanafīs, the mother is entitled to the custody of her daughter until she arrives at puberty; but according to the other three Sunnī sects, the custody continues until she is married.

There is difference of opinion as to the extent of the period of the mother's custody over her male children. The Hanafīs limit it to the child's seventh year, but the Shāfi'īs and Malakīs allow the boy the option of remaining under his mother's guardianship until he has arrived at puberty. Among the Shī'ahs, the mother is entitled to the custody of her children until they are weaned, a period limited to two years. After the child is weaned, its custody, if a male, devolves on the father, if a female, on the mother. The mother's custody of the girl continues to the seventh year.

The right of *ḥiẓānah* is lost by the mother if she is married to a stranger, or if she misconducts herself, or if she changes her domicile so as to prevent the father or tutor from exercising the necessary supervision over the child.

Apostasy is also a bar to the exercise of the right of *ḥiẓānah*. A woman, consequently, who apostatizes from Islām, whether before or after the right vests in her, is disentitled from exercising or claiming the right of *ḥiẓānah* in respect to a Muslim child.

The custody of illegitimate children appertains exclusively to the mother and her relations. (*Personal Law of Muḥammadans*, by Syud Amīr Ali, p. 214.) [GUARDIANSHIP.]

HOLY SPIRIT. Arabic *Ruḥu 'l-Quds* (روح القدس). The Holy Spirit is mentioned three times in the Qur'ān. In the Sūratu 'n-Naḥl (xvith, 104), as the inspiring agent of the Qur'ān: "Say, The Holy Spirit brought it down from thy Lord in truth." And twice in the Sūratu 'l-Baqarah (iind, 81 and 254), as the divine power which aided the Lord Jesus: "and We strengthened him by the Holy Spirit" (in both verses).

The Jalālān, al-Baiẓāwī, and the Muslim commentators in general, say this Holy Spirit was the angel Gabriel who sanctified Jesus, and constantly aided Him, and who also brought the Qur'ān down from heaven and revealed it to Muḥammad.

For a further consideration of the subject, see SPIRIT.

HOMICIDE. [MURDER.]

HONEY. Arabic *'asal* (عسل). In the Qur'ān it is specially mentioned as the gift of God. Sūrah xvi. 70: "Thy Lord inspired the bee. 'Take to houses in the mountains, and in the trees, and in the hives they build. Then eat from every fruit and walk in the beaten paths of thy Lord.' There cometh forth from her body a draught varying in hue, in which is a cure for man."

HORSES. Arabic *faras* (فرس), *k͟hail* (خيل), pl. *k͟huyūl*. Muḥammad's affection for horses was very great, as was natural to an Arabian. Anas says there was nothing the Prophet was so fond of as women and horses. Abū Qatādah relates that Muḥammad said: "The best horses are black with white foreheads and having a white upper lip." But Abū Wahhāb says the Prophet considered a bay horse with white forehead, white fore and hind legs the best. An instance of the way in which the traditionists sometimes contradict each other! (*Mishkāt*, book xvii. c. ii.)

In the *Hidāyah* (Arabic edition, vol. ii. p. 432) it is said that horses are of four kinds: (1) *Birẓaun*, *Burẓūn*, a heavy draught horse brought from foreign countries. (2) *'Atīq*, a first blood horse of Arabia. (3) *Hajīn*, a half-bred horse whose mother is an Arab and father a foreigner. (4) A half-bred horse whose father is an Arab and whose mother is a foreigner.

In taking a share of plunder, a horseman is entitled to a double share, but he is not entitled to any more if he keep more horses than one.

HOSPITALITY. Arabic *ẓiyāfah* (ضيافة). It is related that Muḥammad said:—

"Whoever believes in God and in the Day of Resurrection must respect his guest."

"If a Muslim be the guest of a people and he spends the whole night without being entertained, it shall be lawful for every Muslim present to take money and grain necessary for the entertainment of the man."

"It is according to my practice that the host shall come out with his guest to the door of his house." (*Mishkāt*, book xix. ch. ii.)

Hospitality is enjoined in the Qur'ān. Sūrah iv. 40: "Show kindness to your parents, and to your kindred, and to orphans, and to the poor, and to your neighbour who is akin and to your neighbour who is a stranger, and the companion who is strange, and *to the son of the road*."

HOUR, The. Arabic *as-Sā'ah* (الساعة). A term frequently used in the Qur'ān for the Day of Judgment.

Sūrah vi. 31: "When *the hour* comes suddenly upon them."

Sūrah vii. 186: "They will ask you about *the hour* for what time it is fixed."

Sūrah xv. 85: "Verily *the hour* is surely coming."

Sūrah xvi. 79: "Nor is the matter of *the hour* aught but as the twinkling of an eye, or nigher still."

Sūrah xxii. 1: "Verily the earthquake of *the hour* is a mighty thing."

Sūrah liv. 46: "Nay *the hour* is their promised time! and *the hour* is most severe and bitter."

HOURS OF PRAYER. The terms "Hours of Prayer" and "Canonical Hours," being used in the Christian Church (see Johnson's *Engl. Canons and Canons of Cuthbert*, ch. 15), we shall consider under this title the stated periods of Muḥammadan prayer. [PRAYER.] They are five: (1) *Fajr* (فجر), daybreak; (2) *Ẓuhr* (ظهر), when the sun begins to decline at midday; (3) *'Aṣr* (عصر), midway between *ẓuhr* and *mag͟hrib*; (4) *Mag͟hrib* (مغرب), evening; (5) *'Ishā* (عشاء), when the night has closed in. According to the Traditions (*Mishkāt*, book xxiv. ch. vii. pt. 1), Muḥammad professed to have received his instructions to say prayer five times a day during the Mi'rāj, or the celebrated night journey to heaven. He said, God first ordered him to pray fifty times a day, but that Moses advised him to get the Almighty to reduce the number of canonical hours to five, he himself having tried fifty times for his own people with very ill success!

It is remarkable that there is but one passage in the Qur'ān, in which the stated hours of prayer are enjoined, and that it mentions only *four* and not five periods. *Sūratu 'r-Rūm*, xxx. 16, 17: "Glorify God when it is evening (*masā'*), and at morning (*ṣubḥ*),— and to Him be praise in the heavens and in the earth,—and at afternoon (*'ashī*), and at noon-tide (*ẕuhr*)." But al-Jalālān, the commentators, say all are agreed that the term, "when it is *masā'*" (evening or night), includes both sunset and after sunset, and therefore both the *maghrib* and *'ishā'* prayers are included.

Three hours of prayer were observed by the Jews. David says, "Evening, morning, and at noon will I pray." (Ps. lv. 17.) Daniel "kneeled upon his knees three times a day." These three hours of the Jews seem to have been continued by the Apostles (see Acts iii. 1), and were transmitted to the early church in succeeding ages, for Tertullian speaks of "those common hours which mark the divisions of the day, the third, sixth, and ninth, which we observe in scripture to be more solemn than the rest." (*De Orat.*, c. 25.) And Clement of Alexandria says, "If some fix stated hours of prayer, as the third, sixth, and ninth, the man of knowledge prays to God throughout his whole life." (*Stom.* l. vii. c. 7, sect. 40.) Jerome says, "There are three times in which the knees are bent to God. Tradition assigns the third, the sixth, and the ninth hour." (*Com. in Dan.*, c. vi. 10.)

In the third century there seems to have been *five* stated periods of prayer, for Basil of Cappadocia speaks of five hours as suitable for monks, namely, the morning, the third hour, the sixth, the ninth, and the evening. (*Regulæ fusius Tract. Resp. ad Qu.*, 37, sections 3-5.)

It is therefore probable that Muḥammad obtained his idea of *five* stated periods of prayer during his two journeys to Syria. But he changed the time, as will be seen from the table annexed, which was drawn up by Mr. Lane at Cairo, and shows the times of Muḥammadan prayer with the apparent European time of sunset, in or near the latitude of Cairo at the commencement of each zodiacal month:—

		Maghrib or Sunset.		*'Ishā* or Night.	*Fajr* or Daybreak.	*Ẕuhr* or Noon.	*'Aṣr* or Afternoon.
		Muslim Time.	European Time.	Muslim Time.	Muslim Time.	Muslim Time.	Muslim Time.
June 21		Sunset, or 12 o'clock Muslim Time.	7 4 P.M.	1 34	8 6	4 56	8 13
July 22	May 21		6 53 „	1 30	8 30	5 7	8 43
Aug. 23	Apl. 20		6 31 „	1 22	9 24	5 29	9 4
Sept. 23	Mar. 20		6 4 „	1 18	10 24	5 56	9 24
Oct. 23	Feb. 18		5 37 „	1 18	11 18	6 23	9 35
Nov. 22	Jan. 20		5 15 „	1 22	11 59	6 45	9 41
Dec. 21			5 4 „	1 24	12 15	6 56	9 43

N.B.—The time of noon, according to Muḥammadan reckoning, on any particular day, subtracted from twelve, gives the apparent time of sunset on that day according to European reckoning.

HOUSES. Arabic *bait* (بيت), pl. *buyūt*; *dār* (دار), pl. *diyâr*, *dūr*; Heb. בַּיִת. In the time of Muḥammad the houses of the Arabs were made of a framework of *jarīd*, or palm-sticks, covered over with a cloth of camel's hair, or a curtain of a similar stuff, forming the door. Those of the better class were made of walls of unbaked bricks, and date-leaf roofs plastered over with mud and clay. Of this description were the abodes of Muḥammad's family. (Burton, vol. i. p. 433.)

Sir William Muir, translating from the account given by the secretary of al-Wāqidī (*Life of Mahomet*, new ed., p. 546), says:—

"Abdallah ibn Yazîd relates, that he saw the house in which the wives of the Prophet dwelt at the time when Omar ibn ('Abd) al-Azîz, then governor of Medîna (about A.H. 100) demolished them. They were built of unburnt bricks, and had separate apartments made of palm branches, daubed (or built up) with mud; he counted nine houses, each having separate apartments in the space from the house of Ayesha, and the gate of Mahomet to the house of Asma, daughter of Hosein. Observing the dwelling-place of Omm Salma, he questioned her grandson concerning it; and he told him that when the Prophet was absent on the expedition to Dûma, Omm Salma built up an addition to her house with a wall of unburnt bricks. When Mahomet returned, he went in to her, and asked what new building this was. She replied, 'I purposed, O Prophet, to shut out the glances of men thereby!' Mahomet answered, 'O Omm Salma! verily the most unprofitable thing that eateth up the wealth of a believer is building.' A citizen of Medîna present at the time, confirmed this account, and added that the curtains (Anglo-Indice, *purdas*) of the doors were of black hair-cloth. He was present, he said, when the despatch of the Caliph Abd al Malîk (A.H. 86–88) was read aloud, commanding that these houses should be brought within the area of the Mosque, and he never witnessed sorer weeping than there was amongst the people that day. One exclaimed, 'I wish, by the Lord! that they would leave these houses alone thus as they are; then would those that spring up hereafter in Medîna, and strangers from the ends of the earth, come and see what kind of building sufficed for the Prophet's own abode, and the sight thereof would deter men from extravagance and pride.

"There were four houses of unburnt bricks, the apartments being of palm-branches; and

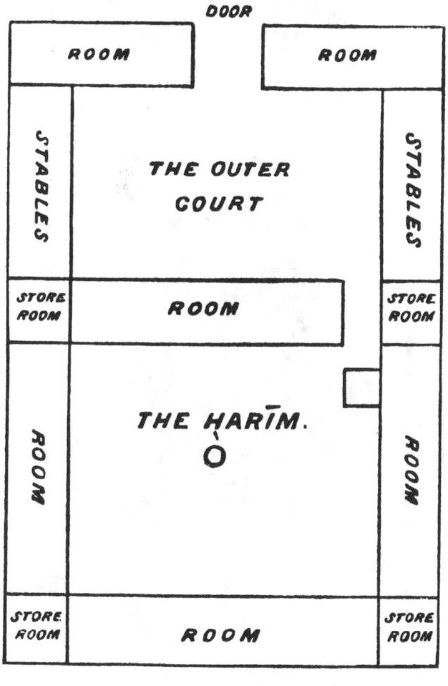

THE USUAL PLAN OF AN ORDINARY HOUSE IN CENTRAL ASIA.

five houses made of palm-branches built up with mud and without any separate apartments. Each was three Arabian yards in length. Some say that they had leather curtains for the doors. One could reach the roof with the hand. The house of Hâritha was next to that of Mahomet. Now, whenever Mahomet took to himself a new wife, he added another house to the row, and Haritha was obliged successively to remove his house and build on the space beyond. At last this was repeated so often, that the Prophet said to those about him, 'Verily, it shameth me to turn Haritha over and over again out of his house.'"

The houses of the rural poor in all parts of Islām, in Turkey, Egypt, Syria, Arabia. Persia, Afghānistān, and India, are usually bulit either of mud or of unburnt bricks. In mountainous parts of Aghānistān they are built of stones (collected from the beds of rivers) and mud. They are generally one storey high, and of one apartment in which the cattle are also housed. The roofs are flat and are formed of mud and straw laid upon branches of trees and rafters. The windows are small apertures, high up in the walls, and sometimes grated with wood.

A MUHAMMADAN HOUSE IN PESHAWUR.

There are no chimneys, but in the centre of the roof there is an opening to emit the smoke, the fire being lighted on the ground in the centre of the room. In front of the house there is an inclosure, either of thorns or a mud wall, which secures privacy to the dwelling. A separate building, called in Asia a *ḥujrah*, or guest chamber, is provided for male visitors or guests; this chamber being common property of the section of the village, except in the case of chiefs or wealthy land-owners, who keep ḥujrahs of their own. In towns the houses of the inferior kind do not differ much from those in the villages, except that there is sometimes an upper storey. In some parts of Afghānistān and Persia, it becomes necessary for each householder to protect his dwelling, in which case a watch tower, of mud, is erected close to the house.

The injunctions of Muḥammad regarding the seclusion of women have very greatly influenced the plan and arrangement of Muḥammadan dwelling-houses of the better class throughout the world, all respectable houses being so constructed as to seclude the female apartments from public view. In cities such as Cairo, Damascus, Delhi, Peshawur, and Cabul, the prevailing plan of dwelling-houses is an entrance through a blank wall, whose mean appearance is usually relieved by a handsome door-way and a few latticed windows. A respectable house usually consists

A MUHAMMADAN HOUSE IN CAIRO. (*Lane.*)

of two courts, the first being that used by the male visitors and guests, and the inner court is the *ḥarim* or *zanānah* reserved for the female members of the family. Facing the outer court will be an upper chamber, or *bālā k͟hānah* as it is called in Persian, the ὑπερῷον, or upper room of the New Testament, in which there will be a *dīwān*, or raised seat or sofa, upon which the inmates can sit, eat, or sleep. This is the usual reception room. In Asia, this bālā k͟hānah seems to take the place of the more elaborate *qāʿah* described by Mr. Lane in his *Modern Egyptians*, vol. i. p. 39, which is either on the ground or upper floor. Within the first enclosure will be the stables for horses and cattle, and in its centre a raised dais as seats for servants and attendants. It should be noticed that there are no special bed-rooms in Eastern houses. Male visitors and friends will sleep in the verandahs of the outer court, or on the dīwān in the upper court.

The ḥarīm or women's apartments in the inner court is entered by a small door. It is

INTERIOR OF A MUHAMMADAN HOUSE IN CAIRO. (*Lane.*)

a quadrangle with verandahs on each of the four sides, formed by a row of pillars, the apertures of which are usually closed by sliding shutters. The back of the rooms being without windows, the only air being admitted from the front of the dwelling-place. The apartments are divided into long rooms, usually four, the extreme corners having small closets purposely built as store-rooms. On festive occasions these verandah rooms will be spread with handsome carpets, carpets and pillows being almost the only furniture of an Eastern dwelling, chairs being a modern invention. The roofs of these rooms are flat, and as the top is fenced in with a barrier some four feet high, the female members of the household sleep on the top of the house in the hot weather. [HARIM.]

In no point do Oriental habits differ more from European than in the use of the roof. Its flat surface, in fine weather the usual place of resort, is made useful for various household purposes, as drying corn, hanging up linen, and drying fruit.

In the centre of the inner court or ḥarīm, there is usually a well, so that the female domestics are not obliged to leave the seclusion of the ḥarim for water-carrying. In a large court, of a wealthy person, there is usually a raised dais of either stone or wood, on which carpets are spread, and on which the ladies sit or recline. In the better class of dwellings, there are numerous courtyards, and special ones are devoted to winter and summer uses. In Peshawur, most respectable houses have an underground room, called a *taḥ khānah*, where the inmates in the hot weather sleep at mid-day. These rooms are exceedingly cool and pleasant on hot sultry days.

Over the entrance door of a Muḥammadan dwelling it is usual to put an inscription, either of the Kalimah, or Creed, or of some verse of the Qur'ān.

We have only attempted to describe, briefly, the ordinary dwelling-houses of Muḥammadans, which are common to all parts of the Eastern world; but in large wealthy cities, such as Damascus, Cairo, Delhi, and Lucknow, there are very handsome houses, which would require a longer description than our space admits of. For Mrs. Meer Ali's account of a Muḥammadan ḥarīm or zanānah, see HARIM

HOUSES, Permission to enter.

Arabic *isti'ẕān* (استئذان). To enter suddenly or abruptly into any person's house or apartments, is reckoned a great incivility in the East, and the law on this subject is very distinctly laid down in both the Qur'ān and the Traditions.

Sūrah xxiv. 27–29 :—

"O ye who believe! enter not into other houses than your own, until ye have asked leave, and have saluted its inmates. This will be best for you: haply ye will bear this in mind.

"And if ye find no one therein, then enter it not till leave be given you; and if it be said to you, 'Go ye back,' then go ye back. This will be more blameless in you, and God knoweth what ye do.

"There shall be no harm in your entering houses in which no one dwelleth, for the supply of your needs: and God knoweth what ye do openly and what ye hide."

The traditionists record numerous injunctions of Muḥammad on the subject. A man asked the Prophet, "Must I ask leave to go in to see my mother?" He said, "Yes." Then the man said, "But I stay in the same house with her!" The Prophet said: "But you must ask permission even if you stay in the same house." Then the man said, "But I wait upon her!" The Prophet said: "What! would you like to see her naked? You must ask permission."

The Khalīfah 'Umar said it was according to the teaching of the Prophet that if you salam three times and get no reply, you must then go away from the house.

Abū Hurairah says that the Prophet said: "When anyone sends to call you then you can return with the messenger and enter the house without permission." (*Mishkāt*, book xxii. ch. ii. pt. 2.)

HU, HUWA (هو).

The personal pronoun of the third person, singular, masculine, HE, *i.e.* God, or He is. It occurs in the Qur'ān in this sense, *e.g.* Sūrah iii. 1, الله لا اله الا هو *Allāhu lā ilāha illā Huwa*, "God, there is no god but HE," which sentence is called the *nafy wa is̤bāt* (or that which is rejected, "there is no god," and that which is affirmed, "but He." The word is often used by Ṣūfī mystics in this form: يا هو يا هو يا من لا يعلم ما هو الا هو *yā hū, yā hū, yā man lā ya'lamu mā hū illā hū*, "O He (who is), O He (who is), O He whom no one knows what He Himself is but Himself." Some commentators have supposed the word *Hū* to stand for the exalted name of God, the *Ismu 'l-a'ẓam*, which Muslim doctors say is only known to God. [JEHOVAH, ISMU 'L-A'ZAM.]

HUBAL or HOBAL (هبل).

The great image which stood over the well or hollow within the Ka'bah. In the cavity beneath were preserved the offerings and other treasures of the temple. (*Aṭ-Ṭabarī*, p. 6, quoted by Muir.) The idol was destroyed by Muḥammad at his final conquest of Makkah, A.H. 8, A.D. 630. "Mounted on (his camel) Al Caswa, he proceeded to the Káabah, reverently saluted with his staff the sacred stone and made the seven circuits of the temple. Then pointing with the staff one by one to the numerous idols placed around, he commanded that they should be hewn down. The great image of Hobal, reared as the tutelary deity of Mecca, in front of the Káabah, shared the common fate. 'Truth hath come,' exclaimed Mahomet, in words of the Corân, as it fell with a crash to the ground, 'and falsehood hath vanished; for falsehood is evanescent.'" (Sūrah xvii. 83). See Muir, *Life of Mahomet*, new ed. p. 422. It is remarkable that there is no distinct allusion to the idol in the whole of the Qur'ān

ḤUBS (حبس).

Any bequest for pious purposes. A term used in Shī'ah law for *waqf*. Anything devoted to the service of God. (See Baillie's *Imāmeea Code*, p. 227.)

HŪD (هود).

A prophet said to have been sent to the tribe of 'Ād. Al-

Baiẓāwī says he was, according to some, the son of ʻAbdu 'llah, the son of Rabāḥ, the son of Khalūd, the son of ʻĀd, the son of ʻAuṣ the son of Iram, the son of Sām, son of Noah, or, according to others, Hūd was the son of Shālaḥ, son of Arfakhshad, son of Sām, son of Noah. D'Herbelot thinks he must be the Heber of the Bible (Judges iv. 1.)

The following are the accounts given of him in the Qur'ān, Sūrah vii 63–70:—

"And to ʻĀd we sent their brother Hūd. 'O my people, said he, worship God: ye have no other God than Him: will ye not then fear Him?' Said the unbelieving chiefs among his people, 'We certainly perceive that thou art unsound of mind, and verily we deem thee an impostor.' He replied, 'O my people! there is no unsoundness of mind in me, but I am an apostle from the Lord of the worlds. The messages of my Lord do I announce to you, and I am your faithful counsellor. Marvel ye that a warning hath come to you from your Lord through one of yourselves that He may warn you? But remember when He made you the successors of the people of Noah, and increased you in tallness of stature. Remember then the favours of God; happily it shall be well with you.' They said, 'Art thou come to us in order that we may worship one God only, and desert what our fathers worshipped? Then bring that upon us with which thou threatenest us, if thou be a man of truth.' He replied, 'Vengeance and wrath shall suddenly light on you from your Lord. Do ye dispute with me about names that you and your fathers have given those idols, and for which God hath sent you down no warranty? Wait ye then, and I too will wait with you.' And We delivered him and those who were on his side by our mercy, and we cut off to the last man those who had treated our signs as lies and who were not believers."

Sūrah xi. 52–63:—

"And unto ʻĀd We sent their brother Hūd. He said, 'O my people, worship God. Ye have no God beside Him. Lo, ye are only devisers of a lie, O my people! I ask of you no recompense for this; verily my recompense is with Him only who hath made me. Will ye not then understand? And O my people! ask pardon of your Lord; then turn unto Him with penitence! He will send down the heavens upon you with copious rains. And with strength in addition to your strength will He increase you; but turn not back with deeds of evil.' They replied, 'O Hūd, thou hast not brought us proofs of thy mission, and we are not the persons to abandon our gods at thy word, and we believe thee not. We can only say that some of our gods have smitten thee with evil.' He said, 'Now take I God to witness, and do ye also witness, that I am innocent of that which ye associate (in worship with God) beside himself. Conspire then against me altogether and delay me not; Lo, I trust in God, my Lord and yours No moving creature is there which He holdeth not by its forelock. Right, truly, is the way in which my Lord goeth. So if ye turn back, then I have already declared to you that wherewith I was sent to you, and my Lord will put another people in your place, nor shall ye at all injure Him; verily, my Lord keepeth watch over all things.' And when our doom came to be inflicted, We rescued Hūd and those who had like faith with him, by our special mercy; and We rescued them from the rigorous chastisement. And these men of ʻĀd gainsaid the signs of their Lord, and rebelled against His messengers and followed the bidding of every proud contumacious person; followed therefore were they in this world by a curse; and in the day of the Resurrection it shall be said to them, 'Did not, verily, the people of ʻĀd disbelieve their Lord?' Was it not said, 'Away with ʻĀd, the people of Hūd?'"

Sūrah xxvi. 123–139:

"The people of ʻĀd treated the Sent Ones as liars. When their brother Hūd said to them, 'Will ye not fear God? I truly am your apostle, worthy of all credit; fear God then and obey me. I ask of you no reward for this, for my reward is of the Lord of the worlds alone. Build ye a landmark on every height, in pastime? And raise ye structures to be your lasting abodes? And when ye put forth your power, do ye put it forth with harshness? Fear ye God, then, and obey me; and fear ye Him who hath plenteously bestowed on you, ye well know what? Plenteously bestowed on you flocks and children, and gardens and fountains. Indeed, I fear for you the punishment of a great day.' They said, 'It is the same to us whether thou warn or warn us not; verily this is but a creation [tale] of the ancients, and we are not they who shall be punished.' So they charged him with imposture and We destroyed them. Verily in this was a sign: yet most of them believed not."

AL-ḤUDAIBIYAH (الحديبية). Al-Ḥudaibiyah, a well on an open space on the verge of the Ḥaram or sacred territory, which encircles Makkah. Celebrated as the scene of a truce between Muḥammad and the Quraish known as the *truce of al-Ḥudaibiyah*, when the Prophet agreed not to enter Makkah that year, but to defer his visit until the next, when they should not enter it with any weapons save those of the traveller, namely, to each a sheathed sword. (Muir, from *Kātibu 'l-Wāqidī.*)

The treaty is referred to in the Qur'ān as "a victory," in the XLVIIIth Sūrah, 1st verse: "We have given thee an obvious victory." A chapter which is said to have been revealed on this occasion and to have foretold the final taking of Makkah, which happened two years afterwards. (See *al-Baizāwī, in loco.*)

ḤUJJAH (حجة). "An argument; a proof." The word occurs in the Qur'ān.

Sūrah ii. 145: "Turn your faces towards it (the Kaʻbah) that men may have no *argument* against you, save only those of them who are unjust."

Sūrah vi. 84: "These are our *arguments* which we gave to Abraham against his people."

Sūrah vi. 150: "God's is the perfect argument (*hujjatu 'l-bālighah*).

ḤUJJATU 'L-ḤAQQI 'ALA 'L-KHALQ (حجة الحق على الخلق). *Lit.*

"The demonstration of truth upon the creature." A term used by the Ṣūfī mystics for the *Insānu 'l-kāmil*, or the "perfect man," as Adam was when he proceeded from the hand of his Maker, and when he became a demonstration of God's wisdom and power before the angels of heaven. As is stated in the Qur'ān, Sūrah ii. 29: "Thy Lord said I am about to place a vicegerent (*khalīfah*) in the earth. ('Abdu 'r-Razzāq's *Dict. of Ṣūfī Terms.*)

ḤUJRAH (حجرة). The "chamber"

in which Muḥammad died and was buried, which was originally the apartment allotted to 'Āyishah, the Prophet's favourite wife. It is situated behind the Masjidu 'n-Nabī, or Prophet's mosque, at al-Madīnah, and is an irregular square of fifty-five feet, separated from the mosque by a passage of about 26 feet. Inside the Ḥujrah are supposed to be the three tombs of Muḥammad, Abū Bakr, and 'Umar, facing the south, surrounded by stone walls, without any aperture, or, as others say, by strong planking. Whatever this material may be, it is hung outside with a curtain, somewhat like a four-post bed. The outer railing is separated by a darker passage from the inner, and is of iron filagree, painted green and gold. This fence, which connects the columns, forbids passage to all men. It has four gates, the Bābu 'l-Muwājihah (the Front Gate), the Bābu Fāṭimah (the Gate of Fāṭimah), the Bābu 'sh-Shām (the Syrian Gate), and the Bābu 't-Taubah (the Gate of Repentance). The Syrian Gate is the only one which is not kept closed, and is the passage which admits the officers in charge of the place. On the southern side of the fence there are three small windows about a foot square, which are said to be about three cubits from the head of the Prophet's tomb. Above the Ḥujrah is the green dome, surmounted by a large gilt crescent, springing from a series of globes. Within the building are the tombs of Muḥammad, Abū Bakr, and 'Umar, with a space reserved for the grave of our Lord Jesus Christ, whom Muslims say will again visit the earth, and die and be buried at al-Madīnah. The grave of Fāṭimah, the Prophet's daughter, is supposed to be in a separate part of the building, although some say she was buried in Baqī'. The Prophet's body is said to be stretched full length on the right side, with the right palm supporting the right cheek, the face fronting Makkah. Close behind him is placed Abū Bakr, whose face fronts Muḥammad's shoulder, and then 'Umar, who occupies the same position with respect to his predecessor. Amongst Christian historians there was a popular story to the effect that Muḥammadans believed the coffin of their Prophet to be suspended in the air, which has no foundation whatever in Muslim literature, and Niebuhr thinks the story must have arisen from the rude pictures sold to strangers. Captain Burton gives the annexed plan of the building.

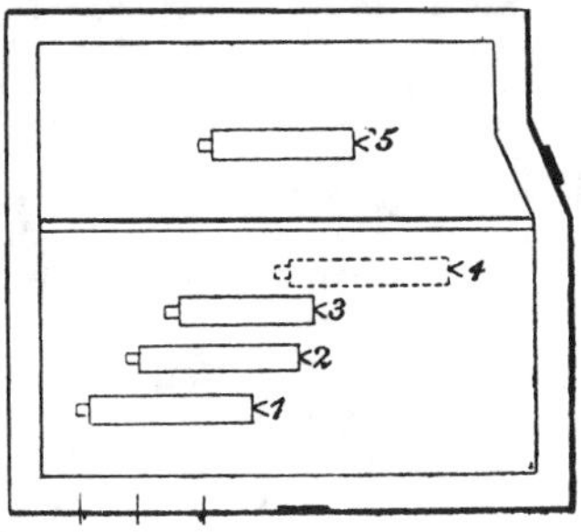

1. Muḥammad.
2. Abū Bakr.
3. 'Umar.
4. The space for the tomb of Jesus
5. Fāṭimah.

It is related that Muḥammad prayed that God would not allow his followers to make his tomb an object of idolatrous adoration, and consequently the adoration paid to the tomb at al-Madīnah has been condemned by the Wahhābīs and other Muslim reformers.

In A.D. 1804, when al-Madīnah was taken by the Wahhābīs, their chief, Sa'ūd, stripped the tomb of all its valuables, and proclaimed that all prayers and exclamations addressed to it were idolatrous. (See Burton's *Pilgrimage*, vol. ii.; Burckhardt's *Arabia and Wahhābīs.*)

The garden annexed to the tomb is called *ar-Rauẓah*, which is a title also given by some writers to the tomb itself.

Abū Dā'ud relates that al-Qāsim the grandson of Abū Bakr came to 'Āyishah and said, "O Mother, lift up the curtain of the Prophet's tomb and of his two friends, Abū Bakr and 'Umar, and she uncovered the graves, which were neither high nor low, but about one span in height, and were covered with red gravel. (*Mishkāt*, book v. ch. vi. pt. 2.)

AL-ḤUJURĀT (الحجرات).

"Chambers." The title of the XLIXth Sūrah of the Qur'ān, in which the word occurs.

ḤUKM (حكم), pl. *aḥkām*. "Order;

command; rule; sentence; judgment, of God, or of the prophets, or of a ruler or judge." It occurs in different senses in the Qur'ān, *e.g.*:—

Sūrah iii. 73: "It beseemeth not a man, that God should give him the Scriptures and the *Judgment* and the Prophecy, and that then he should say to his followers, 'Be ye worshippers of me, as well as of God'; but rather, 'Be ye perfect in things pertaining to God, since ye know the Scriptures and have studied deep.'"

(Both Sale and Rodwell translate the word *al-ḥukm*, "the wisdom," but Palmer renders it more correctly, "the judgment.")

Sūrah xii. 40: "Judgment is God's alone: He bids you worship only Him."

Sūrah xxi. 79: "To each (David and Solomon) we gave *judgment* and knowledge."

Al-ḥukmu 'sh-Shar'ī, "the injunction of the law," is a term used for a command of God, which relates to the life and conduct of an adult Muslim. (*Kitābu 't-Ta'rīfāt, in loco.*)

ḤULŪL (حلول). *Lit.* "descending; alighting; transmigration." A Ṣūfī term for the indwelling light in the soul of man.

HUMAN SACRIFICES. There is no trace in the Qur'ān or Traditions of the immolation of human beings to the Deity as a religious rite. But M. C. de Percival (vol. ii. p. 101) mentions a Ghassānide prince who was sacrificed to Venus by Munzir, King of Ḥirā'. Infanticide was common in ancient Arabia, but it seems to have been done either, as amongst the Rajputs of India, from a feeling of disappointment at the birth of female children, or to avoid the expense and trouble of rearing them. The latter seems to have been the ordinary reason; for we read in the Qur'ān, Sūrah xvii. 33: "Kill not your children for fear of poverty." [INFANTICIDE.]

AL-HUMAZAH (الهمزة). "The slanderer." The title of the CIVth Sūrah of the Qur'ān, so called because it commences with the words: "*Woe unto every slanderer.*" The passage is said to have been revealed against al-Akhnas ibn Sharīq, who had been guilty of slandering the Prophet.

ḤUNAIN (حنين). The name of a valley about three miles to the north-east of Makkah, where in the eighth year of the Hijrah a battle took place between Muḥammad and the Banū Hawāzin, when the latter were defeated. In the Qur'ān, the victory of Ḥunain is ascribed to angelic assistance.

Sūrah ix. 25: "Verily God hath assisted you in many battle-fields and on the day of Ḥunain."

HUNTING. Arabic *ṣaid* (صيد); Heb. צַיִד. There are special rules laid down n Muslim law with regard to hunting. (See Hamilton's *Hidāyah*, vol. iv. p. 170.)

It is lawful to hunt with a trained dog, or a panther (Arabic *fahd*, Persian *yūz*, which is an animal of the lynx species, hooded and trained like a hawk), or a hawk, or a falcon.

The sign of a dog being trained is his catching game three times without eating it. A hawk is trained when she attends to the call of her master. If the dog or panther eat any part of the game it is unlawful, but if a hawk eat of it, it is lawful; but if the dog merely eat the blood and not the flesh, it is lawful. If a hunter take game alive which his dog has wounded, he must slay it according to the law of *Zabḥ*, namely, by cutting its throat, with the head turned Makkah-wards, and reciting, "In the name of the Great God!" The law is the same with respect to game shot by an arrow.

If a sportsman let fly an arrow (or fire a gun) at game, he must repeat the invocation, "In the name of the Great God!"

And then the flesh becomes lawful if the game is killed by the shot. But if only wounded, the animal must be slain with the invocation. Game hit by an arrow which has not a sharp point is unlawful, and so is that killed by throwing pebbles.

Game killed by a Magian, or an apostate, or a worshipper of images is not lawful, because they are not allowed to perform *ẕabḥ*. But that slain by a Christian or a Jew is lawful.

Hunting is not allowed on the pilgrimage nor within the limits of the sacred cities of Makkah and al-Madīnah.

'Adī ibn Ḥātim (*Mishkāt*, book xviii. ch. i.) gives the following tradition on the subject of hunting:—

"The Prophet said to me, 'When you send your dog in pursuit of game, repeat the name of God, as at slaying an animal; then if your dog holds the game for you, and you find it alive, then slay it; but if you find your dog has killed it, and not eaten of it, then eat it; but if the dog has eaten any of it, do not you eat it, for then the dog has kept it for himself. Then if you find another dog along with yours, and the game is killed, do not eat of it; for verily you cannot know which of the dogs killed it; and if the other dog killed it, it might so be that when he was let loose after the game, the name of God might not have been repeated. And when you shoot an arrow at game, repeat the name of God, the same as in slaying an animal; then if you lose sight of the game, and on finding it perceive nothing but the impression of your own arrow, then eat it if you wish; but if you find the game drowned, do not eat of it, although the mark of your arrow should be in it.'"

ḤUR (حور), the plural of *ḥaura*. The women of Paradise described in the Qur'ān, *e.g.* Sūrah lv. 56-78:—

"Therein shall be the damsels with retiring glances, whom nor man nor djinn hath touched before them:

"Which then of the bounties of your Lord will ye twain deny?

"Like jacynths and pearls:

"Which, &c.

"Shall the reward of good be aught but good?

"Which, &c.

"And beside these shall be two other gardens:
"Which, &c.
"Of a dark green:
"Which, &c.
"With gushing fountains in each:
"Which, &c.
"In each fruits and the palm and the pomegranate:
"Which, &c.
"In each, the fair, the beauteous ones:
"Which, &c.
"With large dark eyeballs, kept close in their pavilions:
"Which, &c.
"Whom man hath never touched, nor any djinn:
"Which, &c.
"*Their spouses* on soft green cushions and on beautiful carpets shall recline:
"Which, &c.
"Blessed be the name of thy Lord, full of majesty and glory."

AL-ḤUSAIN (الحسين). The second son of Fāṭimah, the daughter of Muḥammad, by her husband 'Alī, the fourth Khalīfah. A brother to al-Ḥasan, the fifth Khalīfah. According to the Shī'ahs, he was the third Khalīfah. He was born A.H. 4, and died at Karbalā A.H. 61, being cruelly slain in his conflict with Yazīd, the seventh Khalīfah, according to the Sunnīs.

The martyrdom of al-Ḥusain is celebrated by the Shī'ahs every year during the first ten days of the Muḥarram [MUHARRAM]; an account of his tragic death is therefore necessary for understanding the intensity of feeling with which the scenes and incidents of the last days of the "Imām Ḥusain" are enacted in the "Miracle Play," a translation of which has been given in English by Sir Lewis Pelly. The following account is taken from the Preface to this work, p. xi. *seqq.*:—

"Shortly after the accession of Yezid (Yazīd), Ḥusain received at Mecca secret messages from the people of Cufa (al-Kūfah), entreating him to place himself at the head of the army of the faithful in Babylonia. Yezid, however, had full intimation of the intended revolt, and long before Ḥusain could reach Cufa, the too easy governor of that city had been replaced by Obaidallah ('Ubaidu 'llāh ibn Ziyād), the resolute ruler of Bussorah (al-Baṣrah), who by his rapid measures disconcerted the plans of the conspirators, and drove them to a premature outbreak, and the surrender of their leader Muslim. The latter foresaw the ruin which he had brought on Ḥusain, and shed bitter tears on that account when captured. His head was struck off and sent to Yezid. On Ḥusain arriving at the confines of Babylonia, he was met by Harro (al-Ḥurr), who had been sent out by Obaidallah with a body of horsemen to intercept his approach. Ḥusain, addressing them, asserted his title to the Califate, and invited them to submit to him. Harro replied, 'We are commanded as soon as we meet you to bring you directly to Cufa into the presence of Obaidallah, the son of Ziyad.' Ḥusain answered, 'I would sooner die than submit to that,' and gave the word to his men to ride on; but Harro wheeled about and intercepted them. At the same time, Harro said, 'I have no commission to fight with you, but I am commanded not to part with you until I have conducted you into Cufa'; but he bade Ḥusain to choose any road into that city 'that did not go directly back to Mecca,' and 'do you,' said he, 'write to Yezid or Obaidallah, and I will write to Obaidallah, and perhaps it may please God I may meet with something that may bring me off without my being forced to an extremity on your account.' Then he retreated his force a little to allow Ḥusain to lead the way towards Cufa, and Ḥusain took the road that leads by Adib and Cadisia. This was on Thursday the 1st of Mohurrum (Muḥarram), A.H. 61 (A.D. 680). When night came on, he still continued his march all through the night. As he rode on he nodded a little, and waking again, said, 'Men travel by night, and the destinies travel toward them; this I know to be a message of death.'

"In the morning, after prayers were over, he mended his pace, and as he rode on there came up a horseman, who took no notice of him, but saluted Harro, and delivered to him a letter, giving orders from Obaidallah to lead Ḥusain and his men into a place where was neither town nor fortifications, and there leave them till the Syrian forces should surround them.

"This was on Friday the 2nd of Mohurrum. The day after, Amer ('Umar ibn Sa'īd) came upon them with four thousand men, who were on their march to Dailam. They had been encamped without the walls of Cufa, and when Obaidallah heard of Ḥusain's coming, he commanded Amer to defer his march to Dailam and go against Ḥusain. But one and all dissuaded him. 'Beware that you go not against Ḥusain, and rebel against your Lord, and cut off mercy from you, for you had better be deprived of the dominion of the whole world than meet your Lord with the blood of Ḥusain upon you.' Amer was fain to acquiesce, but upon Obaidallah renewing his command with threats, he marched against Ḥusain, and came up with him, as aforesaid, on Saturday the 3rd of Mohurrum.

"On Amer sending to inquire of Ḥusain what brought him thither, the latter replied, 'The Cufans wrote to me; but since they reject me, I am willing to return to Mecca.' Amer was glad when he heard it, and said, 'I hope to God I may be excused from fighting against him.' Then he wrote to this purpose to Obaidallah; but Obaidallah sternly replied, 'Get between him and the river,' and Amer did so; and the name of the place where he cut Ḥusain off from the Euphrates was called Kerbela (Karbalā): '*Kerb* (anguish) and *belā* (vexation), Trouble and affliction,' said Ḥusain when he heard it.

"Then Ḥusain sought a conference with

Amer, in which he proposed either to go to Yezid, to return to Mecca, or, as some add, but others deny, to fight against the Turks. Obaidallah was at first inclined to accede to these conditions, until Shamer stood up and swore that no terms should be made with Ḥusain, adding significantly that he had been informed of a long conference between Ḥusain and Amer.

"Then Obaidallah sent Shamer with orders to Amer, that if Ḥusain would surrender unconditionally, he would be received; if not, Amer was to fall upon him and his men, and trample them under his feet. Should he refuse to do so, Shamer was to strike off Amer's head, and himself command the attack against Ḥusain.

"Thus passed Sunday, Monday, Tuesday, Wednesday, Thursday, and Friday, the 4th, 5th, 6th, 7th, 8th, and 9th of Mohurrum. On the evening of the 9th, Amer drew up his forces close to Ḥusain's camp, and himself rode up to Ḥusain as he was sitting in the door of his tent just after the evening prayer, and told him of the conditions offered by Obaidallah. Husain desired Amer to give him time until the next morning, when he would make his answer.

"In the night his sister came weeping to his bedside, and, awaking him, exclaimed, 'Alas for the desolation of my family! my mother Fatima is dead and my father Ali, and my brother Ḥasan. Alas for the destruction that is past! and alas for the destruction that is to come!' 'Sister,' Ḥusain replied, 'put your trust in God, and know that man is born to die, and that the heavens shall not remain; everything shall pass away but the presence of God, who created all things by His power, and shall make them by His power to pass away, and they shall return to Him alone. My father was better than me, and my mother was better than me; and my brother was better than me; and they and we and all Muslims have an example in the Apostle of God.' Then he told his men that Obaidallah wanted nobody but him, and that they should go away to their homes. But they said, 'God forbid that we should ever see the day wherein we survive you!' Then he commanded them to cord their tents close together, and make a line of them, so as to keep out the enemy's horse. And he digged a trench behind his camp, which he filled with wood to be set on fire, so that he could only be attacked in front. The rest of the night he spent in prayer and supplication, while the enemy's guard patrolled all night long round and round his camp.

"The next morning both sides prepared for the slaughter. Ḥusain first washed and anointed himself with musk, and several of his chief men did the like; and one asking them what it meant, Ḥusain replied pleasantly, 'Alas! there is nothing between us and the black-eyed girls of Paradise but that these troopers come down upon us and slay us!' Then he mounted his horse, and set the Coran before him, crying, 'O God, Thou art my confidence in every trouble and my hope in every adversity!' and submitted himself to the judgment of his companions before the opened pages of the sacred volume. At this his sisters and daughters began to weep, when he cried out in bitter anguish self-reproachfully, 'God reward the son of Abbas,' in allusion to advice which his cousin, Abdullah ibn Abbas, had given him, to leave the women behind in Mecca. At this moment a party of the enemy's horse wheeled about and came up to Ḥusain, who expected to be attacked by them. But it was Harro, who had quitted the ranks of the Syrian army, and had now come to die with Ḥusain, and testify his repentance before men and God. As Harro rode into the doomed camp, he shouted back to Amer, 'Alas for you!' Whereupon Amer commanded his men to 'bring up the colours.' As soon as they were set in front of the troops, Shamer shot an arrow into the camp, saying, 'Bear witness that I shot the first arrow,' and so the fight began on both sides. It raged, chiefly in a series of single combats, until noon-day, when both sides retired to prayer, Ḥusain adding to the usual office the 'Prayer of Fear,' never used but in cases of extremity. When shortly afterwards the fight was renewed, Ḥusain was struck on the head by a sword. Faint with the loss of blood, he sat down by his tent and took upon his lap his little son Abdullah, who was at once killed by a flying arrow. He placed the little corpse upon the ground, crying out, 'We come from God and we return to Him. O God, give me strength to bear these misfortunes.' Growing thirsty, he ran toward the Euphrates, where, as he stooped to drink, an arrow struck him in the mouth. Raising his hands, all besmeared and dripping with blood, to heaven, he stood for awhile and prayed earnestly. His little nephew, a beautiful child, who went up to kiss him, had his hand cut off with a sword, on which Ḥusain again wept, saying, 'Thy reward, dear child, is with thy forefathers in the realms of bliss.' Hounded on by Shamer, the Syrian troops now surrounded him; but Ḥusain, nothing daunted, charged them right and left. In the midst of the fighting, his sister came between him and his slayers, crying out to Amer, how he could stand by and see Ḥusain slain. Whereupon, with tears trickling down his beard, Amer turned his face away; but Shamer, with threats and curses, set on his soldiers again, and at last one wounded Ḥusain upon the hand, and a second gashed him on the neck, and a third thrust him through the body with a spear. No sooner had he fallen to the ground than Shamer rode a troop of horsemen over his corpse, backwards and forwards, over and over again, until it was trampled into the very ground, a scarcely recognisable mass of mangled flesh and mud.

"Thus, twelve years after the death of his brother Ḥasan, Ḥusain, the second son of Ali, met his own death on the bloody plain of Kerbela on Saturday the 10th day of Mohurrum, A.H. 61 (A.D. 680)."

From al-Ḥusain and his brother al-Ḥasan are derived the descendants of the Prophet known throughout Islām as Saiyids. [SAIYID, HASAN, MUHARRAM.]

HUSBAND. Arabic *zauj* (زوج). A husband is not guardian over his wife any further than respects the rights of marriage, nor does the provision for her rest upon him any further than with respect to food, clothing, and lodging (*Hidāyah*, vol. i. 63), but he may be imprisoned for the maintenance of his wife (*Ibidem*, vol. ii. p. 628). The evidence of a husband concerning his wife is not accepted by the Sunnīs, but it is allowed in Shī'ah law (*Ib.*, vol. ii. p. 685). The Muḥammadan law demands that a Muslim husband shall reside equally with each of his wives, unless one wife bestow her right upon another wife. (*Ib.*, vol. i. p. 184.)

ḤUSNU 'L-KHULQ (حسن الخلق). "A good disposition." Abū Hurairah relates that one of the Companions once asked Muḥammad, "What is the best thing that has been given to man?" and Muḥammad replied, "A good disposition." Muḥammad is also related to have said that the "heaviest thing which will be put in the scales of a Muslim in the Day of Judgment is a *good disposition*." (*Mishkāt*, book xxii. ch. xix. pt. 2.)

AL-ḤUṬAMAH (الحطمة). A division of Hell, mentioned in the Qur'ān, Sūrah civ. :—

"Woe to every backbiter,
"Who amasseth wealth and storeth it against the future!
"He thinketh surely that his wealth shall be with him for ever.
"Nay! for verily he shall be flung into *al-ḥuṭamah*,
"And who shall teach thee what *al-ḥuṭamah* is?
"It is God's kindled fire,
"Which shall mount above the hearts *of the damned;*
"It shall verily rise over them like a vault,
"On outstretched columns."

The Imām al-Baghawī says it is the division of Hell specially reserved for the Jews.

ḤUWAIRIṢ (حويرث). One of the citizens of Makkah, who was excluded from the general amnesty on the taking of Makkah, in consequence of his having pursued Zainab, Muḥammad's daughter, while endeavouring to effect her escape from Makkah. He was afterwards seized and slain by 'Alī.

ḤUẔAIFAH (حذيفة). The son of al-Yamān. He was a "sworn companion" of the Prophet, one of the most eminent of the Aṣḥāb, and it is recorded by Muslim the Traditionist, that he was specially instructed by the Prophet. His father, al-Yamān, also called Ḥisl or Ḥusail, was likewise a companion, who fell at Uḥud. Ḥuẕaifah died in the time of 'Alī's Khalīfate, A.H. 36. (See *Taqrību 't-Tahẕīb*, p. 51.) Sir William Muir says he was the Companion who first suggested to 'Uṣmān the necessity of the recension of the Qūr'ān, A.H. 33. (*Life of Mahomet*, new ed. p. 556.)

"Hodzeifa, who had warred both in Armenia and Adzerbâijan, and had observed the different readings of the Syrians, and of the men of Irâc, was alarmed at the number and extent of the variations, and warned Othmân to interpose and 'stop the people before they should differ regarding their scriptures, as did the Jews and Christians.'"

HUẔAIL (هذيل). The ancestor of the Banū Huẕail, a tribe distinguished in the annals of war and poetry, and, as we learn from Burckhardt, still occupying under the same name the environs of Makkah. (*Travels in Arabia*, vol. i. pp. 63, 66.)

HYPOCRISY. Arabic *riyā* (رياء), *nifāq* (نفاق), *makr* (مكر), *mudāhanat* (مداهنة). When there is an allusion to hypocrisy in the Qur'ān, it refers to that class of people known as *al-Munāfiqūn*, or the hypocrites of al-Madīnah, who in the days of the Prophet professed to follow him, whilst secretly they opposed him [MUNAFIQUN], *vide* Sūrahs ii. 7; xxxiii. 47; lvii. 13. But in the Traditions we have the following with reference to this sin, *Mishkāt*, book i. ch. iii. pt. 3):—

"The signs of hypocrisy are three: speaking falsely, promising and not performing, and being perfidious when trusted."

"There are four qualities, which being possessed by anyone, constitute a complete hypocrite; and whoever has one of the four has one hypocritical quality till he discards it: perfidy when trusted, the breaking of agreements, speaking falsely, and prosecuting hostility by treachery."

HYPOCRITES. Arabic *munāfiqūn* (منافقون). A term applied by Muḥammad to those residents of al-Madīnah who during his first stay in that city ostensibly joined Islām, but in secret were disaffected.

I.

IBĀḤĪYAH (اباحية). A sect of libertines who consider all things lawful.

IBĀQ (اباق). The absconding of slaves. The fugitive slave being termed *ābiq*, or, if he be an infant, *zāll*, or the strayed one. The restorer of a fugitive slave is entitled to a reward of forty dirhams, but no reward is given for the restoration of a strayed infant slave. [SLAVERY.]

IBĀẒĪYAH (اباضية). A sect of Muslims founded by 'Abdu 'llāh ibn Ibāẓ, who said that if a man commit a *kabīrah* or great sin, he is an infidel, and not a believer. (*Kitābu 't-Ta'rīfāt, in loco.*)

IBLĪS (ابليس). [DEVIL.]

IBN 'ABBĀS (ابن عباس). 'Abdu 'llāh, the eldest son of 'Abbās, and a cousin of Muḥammad. One of the most celebrated of the Companions, and the relator of numerous traditions. It is said that the angel Gabriel appeared to him, when he was only ten years old, and revealed to him the meaning of the Qur'ān, which accounted for his intimate acquaintance with the letter and meaning of the book. He was called *Tarjumānu 'l-Qur'ān*, or "the interpreter of the Qur'ān." He was appointed Governor of al-Baṣrah by the Khalīfah 'Alī, which office he held for some time. He returned to the Ḥijāz and died at aṭ-Ṭā'if A.H. 68 (A.D. 687), aged 72 years.

IBN ḤANBAL (ابن حنبل). The Imām Abū 'Abdi 'llāh Aḥmad ibn Ḥanbal, the founder of the fourth orthodox sect of the Sunnīs, was born at Baghdād A.H. 164, A.D. 780, where he received his education under Yazīd ibn Hārūn and Yaḥya ibn Sa'īd. On ash-Shāfi'ī coming to Baghdād (A.H. 195), Ibn Ḥanbal attended the lectures delivered there by that doctor, and was instructed by him in the traditions. In process of time he acquired a high reputation from his profound knowledge of both the civil and spiritual law, and particularly for the extent of his erudition with respect to the precepts of the Prophet, of which it is said that he could repeat above a million. His fame began to spread just at the time when the disputes ran highest concerning the nature of the Qur'ān, which some held to have existed from eternity, whilst others maintained it to be created. Unfortunately for Ibn Ḥanbal, the Khalīfah al-Mu'taṣim was of the latter opinion, to which this doctor refusing to subscribe, he was imprisoned and severely scourged by the Khalīfah's order.

For this hard usage, indeed, he afterwards received some satisfaction from al-Mutawakkil, the son of al-Mu'taṣim, who, upon succeeding to the throne, issued a decree of general toleration, leaving every person at liberty to judge for himself upon this point. This tolerant Khalifah set the persecuted doctor at liberty, receiving him at his Court with the most honourable marks of distinction, and offering him a compensatory present of 1,000 pieces of gold, which, however, he refused to accept. After having attained the rank of Imām, he retired from the world, and led a recluse life for several years. He died A.H 241 (A.D. 855), aged 75. He obtained so high a reputation for sanctity, that his funeral was attended by a train of 800,000 men and 60,000 women; and it is asserted as a kind of miracle, that on the day of his decease no fewer than 20,000 Jews and Christians embraced the faith. For about a century after his death, the sect of Ibn Ḥanbal were numerous and even powerful; and uniting to their zeal a large proportion of fanaticism, became at length so turbulent and troublesome as to require the strong arm of Government to keep them in order. Like most other fanatical sects, they dwindled away in process of time, and are now to be met with only in a few parts of Arabia. Although orthodox in their other tenets, there was one point on which they differed from the rest of the Muslims; for they asserted that God had actually set Muḥammad upon his throne, and constituted him his substitute in the government of the universe; an assertion which was regarded with horror, as an impious blasphemy, and which brought them into great disrepute. This, however, did not happen until many years after Ibn Ḥanbal's decease, and is in no degree attributed to him. He published only two works of note: one entitled the *Musnad*, which is said to contain above 30,000 traditions selected from 750,000; and another, a collection of apothegms, or proverbs, containing many admirable precepts upon the government of the passions. He had several eminent pupils, particularly Ismā'īl al-Bukhārī and Muslim Ibn Dā'ūd. His authority is but seldom quoted by any of the modern commentators on jurisprudence.

The modern Wahhābīs are supposed to follow (to some extent) the teachings of Aḥmad ibn Ḥanbal.

IBN KHALLIKĀN (ابن خلكان). The well-known Muḥammadan biographer. He drew his descent from a family of Balkh. He was born at Arbelah, but resided at Damascus, where he filled the office of chief Qaẓi, and died A.H. 681 (A.D. 1282). His biographical dictionary has been translated into English by Baron de Slane. (Paris 1843.) The biographical notes in the present work are chiefly from Ibn Khallikān's work.

IBN MĀJAH (ابن ماجة). Abū 'Abdi 'llāh Muḥammad Ibn Yazīd Ibn Mājah al-Qazwīnī was maulawī of the tribe of Rabī'ah, and a celebrated Ḥāfiẓ of the Qur'ān, and is known as the compiler of the *Kitābu 's-Sunan*, or "Book of Traditions." This work is counted one of the six *Ṣaḥīḥs*, or authentic collections of Ḥadīs̱. Born A.H. 209 (A.D. 824). Died A.H. 273 (A.D. 886).

IBN MAS'ŪD (ابن مسعود). 'Abdu 'llāh ibn Mas'ūd, "a companion" of considerable note. One of the illustrious "ten" (*'Asharah Mubashsharah*) to whom Muḥammad gave an assurance of Paradise. He was present at the battle of Badr and subsequent engagements. Died at al-Madīnah A.H. 32, aged 60.

IBN MULJAM (ابن ملجم). The Muslim who slew the Khalīfah 'Alī. The author of the *Ḥayātu 'l-Qulūb* (*Merrick's Translation*, p. 204) says when 'Alī was martyred by Ibn Muljam his celestial likeness (*i.e.* in the *'Ālamu 'l-Mis̤āl*) appeared wounded also; wherefore angels visit the similitude morning and evening and curse the name of Ibn Muljam.

IBN ṢAIYĀD (ابن صياد). A mysterious personage who lived in the time of Muḥammad, and who was mistaken by some people for ad-Dajjālu 'l-Masiḥ, or the Antichrist. 'Abdu 'l-Ḥaqq says some say he was a Jew of al-Madīnah named 'Abdu 'llāh.

Ibn 'Umar relates that the Prophet went to Ibn Ṣaiyād, accompanied by a party of his companions, and found him playing with boys; and at this time he had nearly reached puberty; and Ibn Ṣaiyād had no intimation of the coming of the Prophet and the companions, till the Prophet struck him upon the back, and said, "Do you bear witness that I am the Prophet of God?" Then Ibn Ṣaiyād looked at the Prophet and said, "I bear witness that you are the Prophet of the illiterate." After that he said to the Prophet, "Do you bear witness that I am the Prophet of God?" Then the Prophet pressed him with both his hands and said, "I believe in God and His Prophets"; and then said to Ibn Ṣaiyād, "What do you look at?" He said, "Sometimes a person comes to me telling the truth; and sometimes another person telling lies; like as magicians, to whom devils bring truth and falsehood." The Prophet said, "The Devil comes to you, and brings you news, false and true." After that, the Prophet said, 'Verily, I have concealed a revelation from you" (which was the one in which there is mention of the smoke); and Ibn Ṣaiyād said, "Is it the one with the smoke?" Then the Prophet said, "Begone! you cannot surpass your own degree!" Ibn 'Umar said, "O Prophet of God! do you permit me to strike off Ibn Ṣaiyād's head?" He said, "If Ibn Ṣaiyād be Dajjāl, you will not be able to kill him, because Jesus will be his slayer; and if he is not Dajjāl there can be no good in your killing him." After this the Prophet and Ubaiy ibn Ka'b al-Anṣārī went towards some date trees belonging to Ibn Ṣaiyād, and the Prophet hid himself behind the branches, to listen to what he would say, before Ibn Ṣaiyād discovered him. And at this time Ibn Ṣaiyād was lying upon his bed, with a sheet over his face, talking to himself; and his mother saw the Prophet standing behind the branches of the trees, and said to her son, "Muḥammad is standing." At this he became silent; and the Prophet said, "Had not his mother informed him he would have said something to have discovered what he is." Then the Prophet repeated, "Praised be God, by that which is worthy of him"; and then mentioned Dajjāl and said, "Verily, I fear for you from Dajjāl; there is no Prophet but he alarmed his people about him. Verily, Noah frightened his people about Dajjāl; but I will tell you a thing in the matter of Dajjāl, which no one Prophet ever told his people: know that he is blind, and that verily God is not blind."

Abū Sa'īd al-Khudri says: "Ibn Ṣaiyād asked the Prophet about the earth of Paradise; and he said, 'The earth of Paradise is in whiteness like flour twice sifted; and in smell like pure musk.' And I accompanied Ibn Ṣaiyād from al-Madīnah to Makkah; and he said to me, 'What trouble I have experienced from people's supposing me Dajjāl! Have you not heard, O Ibn Ṣaiyād, the Prophet of God say, "Verily, Dajjāl will have no children"? and I have; and verily, the Prophet has said, "Dajjāl is an infidel," and I am a Muslim'; and the Prophet said, "Dajjāl will neither enter al-Mādinah nor Makkah"; and verily, I am going from al-Madīnah and intend going to Makkah.' After that, Ibn Ṣaiyād said, in the latter part of his speech, 'Beware; I swear by God, I know the place of Dajjāl's birth, and where he stays; and I know his father and mother.' Then this made me doubtful; and I said, 'May the remainder of your days be lost to you.' A person present said to Ibn Ṣaiyād, 'Would you like to be Dajjāl?' He said, 'If I possessed what Dajjāl is described to have, such as the power of leading astray, I should not dislike it.'"

Ibn 'Umar says: "I met Ibn Ṣaiyād when he had swollen eyes, and I said, 'How long has this been?' He said, 'I do not know.' I said, 'Do not know, now that your eyes are in your head?' He said, 'If God pleased He could create eyes in your limbs, and they would not know anything about it; in this manner also, man is so employed as to be insensible to pains.' Then Ibn Ṣaiyād made a noise from his nose, louder than the braying of an ass." (*Mishkāt*, book xxiii. ch. v.)

IBN 'UMAR (ابن عمر). Abū 'Abdi 'r-Raḥmān 'Abdu 'llāh, son of 'Umar the celebrated Khalīfah, was one of the most eminent of the "companions" of Muḥammad. He embraced Islām with his father when he was only eight years old. For a period of sixty years he occupied the leading position as a traditionist, and al-Bukhārī, the collector of traditions, says the most authentic are those given on the authority of Ibn 'Umar. He died at Makkah A.H. 73 (A.D. 692), aged 84 years.

IBRĀHĪM (ابراهيم). The patriarch Abraham. [ABRAHAM.]

IBRĀHĪM (ابراهيم). The infant son of Muḥammad by his slave girl, Mary the Copt. Born A.H. 8, died A.H. 10 (A.D. 631).

ʿĪD (عيد). [FESTIVAL.]

ʿĪDĀN (عيدان). The Dual of ʿĪd, a festival. The two festivals, the ʿĪdu ʾl-Fiṭr, and the ʿĪdu ʾl-Aẓḥā.

ʿIDDAH (عدة). *Lit.* "Number." The term of probation incumbent upon a woman in consequence of a dissolution of marriage, either by divorce or the death of her husband. After a divorce the period is three months, and after the death of her husband, four months and ten days, both periods being enjoined by the Qurʾān (Sūrah lxv. 4; ii. 234.)

ʿĪDGĀH (عيدگاه). *Lit.* "A place of festival." A Persian term for the *muṣallā*, or praying-place, set apart for the public prayers said on the two chief festivals, viz. ʿĪdu ʾl-Fiṭr, and ʿĪdu ʾl-Aẓḥa. [ʿIDAN.]

IDIOTS. Arabic *majnūn* (مجنون), pl. *majānīn*. Mr. Lane, in his *Modern Egyptians*, vol. i. p. 288, says:—

"An idiot or a fool is vulgarly regarded by them as a being whose mind is in heaven, while his grosser part mingles among ordinary mortals; consequently he is considered an especial favourite of heaven. Whatever enormities a reputed saint may commit (and there are many who are constantly infringing precepts of their religion), such acts do not affect his fame for sanctity; for they are considered as the results of the abstraction of his mind from worldly things; his soul, or reasoning faculties, being wholly absorbed in devotion, so that his passions are left without control. Lunatics who are dangerous to society are kept in confinement; but those who are harmless are generally regarded as saints. Most of the reputed saints of Egypt are either lunatics, or idiots, or impostors."

IDOLATRY. The word used in the Qurʾān for idolatry is *shirk* (شرك), and for an idolater, *mushrik* (مشرك), pl. *mushrikūn*. In theological works the word *waṡanī* (وثنى) is used for an idolater (*waṡan*, an idol), and *ʿibādatu ʾl-auṡān* (عبادة الاوثان), for idolatry.

In one of the earliest Sūrahs of the Qurʾān (when chronologically arranged), lii. 35–43, idolatry is condemned in the following language:—

"Were they created by nothing? or were they the creators of themselves?

"Created they the Heavens and Earth? Nay, rather, they have no faith.

"Hold they thy Lord's treasures? Bear they the rule supreme?

"Have they a ladder for hearing the angels? Let anyone who hath heard them bring a clear proof of it.

"Hath God daughters and ye sons?

"Askest thou pay of them? They are themselves weighed down with debts.

"Have they such a knowledge of the secret things that they can write them down?

"Desire they to lay snares for thee? But the snared ones shall be they who do not believe.

"Have they any God beside God? Glory be to God above what they join with Him."

But they are. in a later Sūrah (nearly the last), ix. 28, declared unclean, and forbidden to enter the sacred temple at Makkah. That was after Muḥammad had destroyed the idols in his last pilgrimage to the Sacred House.

"O Believers! only they who join gods with God are unclean! Let them not, therefore, after this their year, come near the sacred temple. And if ye fear want, God, if He please, will enrich you of His abundance: for God is Knowing, Wise."

In a Sūrah given about the same time (iv. 51, 116), idolatry is declared to be the unpardonable sin:—

"Verily, God will not forgive the union of other gods with Himself! But other than this will He forgive to whom He pleaseth. And he who uniteh gods with God hath devised a great wickedness."

"God truly will not forgive the joining other gods with Himself. Other sins He will forgive to whom He will: but he who joineth gods with God, hath erred with far-gone error."

Nor is it lawful for Muslims to pray for the souls of idolaters, as is evident from Sūrah ix. 114:—

"It is not for the prophet or the faithful to pray for the forgiveness of those, even though they be of kin, who associate other beings with God, after it hath been made clear to them that they are to be the inmates of Hell.

"For neither did Abraham ask forgiveness for his father, but in pursuance of a promise which he had promised to him: but when it was shewn him that he was an enemy to God, he declared himself clear of him. Yet Abraham was pitiful, kind."

Sir William Muir says (Int. p. ccxii.) that "Mahomet is related to have said that Amr son of Lohai (the first Khozaite king, A.D. 200) was the earliest who dared to change the 'pure religion of Ishmael,' and set up idols brought from Syria. This, however, is a mere Muslim conceit. The practice of idolatry thickly overspread the whole peninsula from a much more remote period."

From the chapters from the Qurʾān, already quoted, it will be seen that from the very first Muḥammad denounced idolatry. But the weakness of his position compelled him to move cautiously. The expressions contained in the al-Madīnah Sūrahs, given when Muḥammad could not enter Makkah, are much more restrained than those in the Sūrahs given after the capture of Makkah and the destruction of the idols of the Kaʿbah.

At an early period (about the fifth year) of his mission, Muḥammad seems to have contemplated a compromise and reconciliation with Makkan idolatry. Sir William Muir (quoting from *aṭ-Ṭabarī*, pp. 140–142, and *Kātibu 'l-Waqidī*, p. 40), says:—

"On a certain day, the chief men of Mecca, assembled in a group beside the Káaba, discussed, as was their wont, the affairs of the city. Mahomet appeared, and, seating himself by them in a friendly manner, began to recite in their hearing Sura liii. The chapter opens with a description of the first visit of Gabriel to Mahomet, and then unfolds a second vision of that angel, in which certain heavenly mysteries were revealed. It then proceeds:—

And see ye not Lât and Ozza,
And Manât the third besides?

"When he had reached this verse, the devil suggested to Mahomet an expression of thoughts which had long possessed his soul, and put into his mouth words of reconciliation and compromise, the revelation of such as he had been yearning that God might send unto his people, namely:—

These are the exalted females,
And verily their intercession is to be hoped for.

"The Coreish were astonished and delighted with this acknowledgment of their deities; and as Mahomet wound up the Sura with the closing words,—

Wherefore bow down before God, and serve Him,

the whole assembly prostrated themselves with one accord on the ground and worshipped. Walîd alone, unable from the infirmities of age to bow down, took a handful of earth and worshipped, pressing it to his forehead.

"And all the people were pleased at that which Mahomet had spoken, and they began to say, 'Now we know that it is the Lord alone that giveth life and taketh it away, that createth and supporteth. And as for these our goddesses, make intercession with Him for us; wherefore, as thou hast conceded unto them a portion, we are content to follow thee.'

"But their words disquieted Mahomet, and he retired to his house. In the evening Gabriel visited him, and the Prophet (as was his wont) recited the Sura unto him. And Gabriel said, 'What is this that thou hast done? thou hast repeated before the people words that I never gave unto thee.' So Mahomet grieved sore, and feared the Lord greatly; and he said, 'I have spoken of God that which he hath not said.' But the Lord comforted His Prophet, and restored his confidence, and cancelled the verse, and revealed the true reading thereof (as it now stands), namely:—

And see ye not Lât and Ozza,
And Manât the third besides?
What! shall there be male progeny unto you, and female unto him?
That were indeed an unjust partition!
They are naught but names, which ye and your fathers have invented, &c.

"Now, when the Coreish heard this, they spoke among themselves, saying, 'Mahomet hath repented his favourable mention of the rank of our goddesses with the Lord. He hath changed the same, and brought other words instead.' So the two Satanic verses were in the mouth of every one of the unbelievers, and they increased their malice, and stirred them up to persecute the faithful with still greater severity." (Sir W. Muir's *Life of Mahomet*, new ed. p. 86, *seqq.*)

The Commentators do not refer to this circumstance, and pious Muḥammadans would reject the whole story, but, as Sir W. Muir says, "the authorities are too strong to be impugned."

These narratives of aṭ-Ṭabarī and the secretary of al-Wāqidī are fully borne out in the facts of Muḥammad's subsequent compromise with the idolatrous feelings of the people; for whilst he removed the images from the Ka'bah, he at the same time retained the *black stone* as an object of superstitious reverence, and although he destroyed *Isāf* and *Nā'ilah*, the deities of aṣ-Ṣafā and al-Marwah, he still retained the "runnings to and fro," and the "stonings of the pillars," as part of the sacred rites of what was intended to be a purely theistic and iconoclastic system. The most singular feature in the fetichism of Arabia was the adoration paid to unshapen stones, and Muḥammad found it impossible to construct his religion without some compromise with the popular form of idolatry. It is a curious circumstance that so much of the zeal and bigotry of the Wahhābī puritans is directed against the *shirk*, or idolatry, of the popular veneration for tombs and other objects of adoration, and yet they see no objection to the adoration of the black stone, and those other strange and peculiar customs which form part of the rites of the Makkan pilgrimage.

IDOLS. Arabic *waṣan* (وثن), pl. *auṣān*, also *ṣanam* (صنم), pl. *aṣnām*, both words being used in the Qur'ān. Ten of the idols of ancient Arabia are mentioned by name in the Qur'ān, viz.:—

Sūrah iv. 52: "Hast thou not observed those to whom a part of the Scriptures hath been given? They believe in *al-Jibt* and *aṭ-Ṭāghūt*, and say of the infidels, 'These are guided in a better path than those who hold the faith.'"

Sūrah liii. 19: "Have ye considered *al-Lāt*, *al-'Uzza*, and *Manāt* the third?"

Sūrah lxxi. 21: "They have plotted a great plot and said, "Ye shall surely not leave your gods: ye shall surely neither leave *Wadd*, nor *Suwā'*, nor *Yaghūṣ*, nor *Ya'ūq*, nor *Nasr*, and they led astray many."

Al-Jibt and aṭ-Ṭāghūt (the latter also mentioned in Sūrah ii. 257, 259) were, according to Jalālu 'd-dīn, two idols of the Quraish whom certain renegade Jews honoured in order to please the Quraish.

Al-Lāt was the chief idol of the Banū Ṣaqīf at aṭ-Ṭā'if. The name appears to be the feminine of *Allāh*, God.

Al-'Uzza has been identified with Venus, but it was worshipped under the form of an acacia tree, and was the deity of the Banū Ghaṭafān.

Manāt was a large sacrificial stone worshipped by the Banū Khuzā'ah and Banū Huzail.

The five idols, *Wadd*, *Suwā'*, *Yaghūs*, *Yā'ūq*, and *Nasr*, the commentators say, were originally five persons of eminence in the time of Adam, who after their deaths were worshipped in the form of idols.

Wadd was worshipped by the Banū Kalb in the form of a man, and is said to have represented heaven.

Suwā' was a female deity of the Banū Ḥamdān.

Yaghūṣ was a deity of the Banū Mazḥij and in the form of a lion.

Ya'ūq was an idol of the Banū Murād in the shape of a horse.

Nasr was, as its name implies, an image of an eagle, and worshipped by Ḥimyar.

It is said (according to Burkhardt, p. 164) that at the time of Muḥammad's suppression of idol worship in the Makkan temple, there were not fewer than 360 idols in existence.

The chief of the minor deities was *Hubal*, an image of a man, and said to have been originally brought from Syria. Other well-known idols were *Isāf*, an idol on Mount aṣ-Ṣafā, and *Nā'ilah*, an image on Mount al-Marwah, as part of the rites of the pilgrimage, the Prophet not being able to divert entirely the regard of the people for them.

Habhah was a large sacred stone on which camels were sacrificed, and the *Hajaru 'l-Aswad*, or Black Stone, was an object, as it still is, of idolatrous worship. In the Ka'bah there were also images representing Abraham and Ishmael, each with divining arrows in his hand.

The statement, made by some writers, that the image or picture of Jesus and Mary had a place in the Ka'bah, seems to be without any authority.

Although Herodotus does not refer to the Ka'bah, yet he mentions as one of the chief divinities of Arabia *Alilat*, which is strong evidence of the existence of an idol called *al-Lāt* at that time as an object of worship. (*Herod.* iii. 8.) [IDOLATRY.]

IDRĪS (ادريس).

A prophet mentioned twice in the Qur'ān, about whose identity there is some discussion.

Sūrah xix. 57: "Commemorate *Idrīs* in the Book; verily he was a man of truth and a Prophet, and we raised him to a lofty place."

Sūrah xxi. 85; "And Ishmael, and Idrīs, and Zū 'l-kifl—all steadfast in patience."

Al-Baiẓāwī says Idrīs was of the posterity of Shīṣ (Seth), and a forefather of Noah, and his name was Uḥnūkh (Enoch, Heb. חֲנוֹךְ, *Consecrated*). He was called *Idrīs* from *dars*, "to instruct," from his knowledge of divine mysteries, and thirty portions of God's sacred scriptures were revealed to him. He was the first person who learned to write, and he was the inventor of the science of astronomy and arithmetic.

Ḥusain says, "In the *Jāmi'u 'l-Uṣūl*, it is written that Idrīs was born one hundred years after the death of Adam."

The Jalālān say the meaning of the words in the Qur'ān, "*we raised him to a lofty place*," is that he liveth either in the fourth heaven, or in the sixth or seventh heaven, or that he was raised up from the dead and taken to Paradise.

The Kāmālān say, "In the book called the *Rauẓatu 'l-Aḥbāb*, Ibn Jarīr relates that Idrīs was the special friend of one of the angels of heaven, and that this angel took him up into the heavens, and when they arrived in the fourth heaven they met the Angel of Death. The angel asked the Angel of Death how many years there were remaining of the life of Idrīs; and the Angel of Death said, 'Where is Idrīs, for I have received orders to bring death to him?' Idrīs then remained in the fourth heaven, and he died in the wings of his angel friend who had taken him from earth."

Some of the Commentators think Idrīs and Elijah (Ilyās) are the same persons. But the accounts given seem to identify him with Enoch.

'ĪDU 'L-AẒḤĀ (عيدالاضحى).

Vulg. *'Id-i-Zuḥā*, "The feast of sacrifice." Called also *Yaumu 'n-Naḥr*; *Qurbān-'Id*; *Baqarah-'Id* (*i.e.* the cow festival); and in Turkey and Egypt *'Idu Bairām*. It is also called the *'Idu 'l-kabīr*, the great festival, as distinguished from the *'Idu 'l-Fiṭr*, which is called the minor festival, or *al-'Idu 'ṣ-ṣaghīr*.

It is celebrated on the tenth day of Zū 'l-Ḥijjah, and is part of the rites of the Makkan pilgrimage, although it is observed as well in all parts of Islām both as a day of sacrifice and as a great festival. It is founded on an injunction in the Qur'ān, Sūrah xxii. 33–38.

"This *do*. And they who respect the symbols of God, *perform an action* which proceedeth from piety of heart.

"Ye may obtain advantages from the *cattle* up to the set time *for slaying them*; then, the place for sacrificing them is at the ancient House.

"And to every people have we appointed symbols, that they may commemorate the name of God over the brute beasts which He hath provided for them. And your God is the one God. To Him, therefore, surrender yourselves: and bear thou good tidings to those who humble themselves,—

"Whose hearts, when mention is made of God, thrill with awe; and to those who remain steadfast under all that befalleth them, and observe prayer, and give alms of that with which we have supplied them.

"And the camels have we appointed you for the sacrifice to God: *much* good have ye in them. Make mention, therefore, of the name of God over them *when ye slay them*, as they stand in a row; and when they are fallen over on their sides, eat of them, and feed him who is content *and asketh not*, and him who asketh. Thus have We subjected them to you, to the intent ye should be thankful.

"By no means can their flesh reach unto God, neither their blood; but piety on your part reacheth Him. Thus hath He subjected them to you, that ye might magnify God for His guidance: moreover, announce glad tidings to those who do good deeds."

The institution of the sacrifice was as follows:—A few months after the Hijrah, or flight from Makkah, Muḥammad, dwelling in al-Madīnah, observed that the Jews kept, on the tenth day of the seventh month, the great fast of the Atonement. A tradition records that the Prophet asked them why they kept this fast. He was informed that it was a memorial of the deliverance of Moses and the children of Israel from the hands of Pharaoh. "We have a greater right in Moses than they," said Muḥammad, so he fasted with the Jews and commanded his followers to fast also. This was at the period of his mission when Muḥammad was friendly with the Jews of al-Madīnah, who occasionally came to hear him preach. The Prophet also occasionally attended the synagogue. Then came the change of the Qiblah from Jerusalem to Makkah, for the Jews were not so ready to change their creed as Muḥammad had at first hoped. In the second year of the Hijrah, Muḥammad and his followers did not participate in the Jewish fast, for the Prophet now instituted the 'Īdu 'l-Aẓḥā. The idolatrous Arabs had been in the habit of making an annual pilgrimage to Makkah at this season of the year. The offering of animals in sacrifice formed a part of the concluding ceremony of that pilgrimage. That portion — the sacrifice of animals — Muḥammad adopted in the feast which now, at al-Madīnah, he substituted for the Jewish fast. This was well calculated to attract the attention of the Makkans and to gain the goodwill of the Arabs. Muḥammad could not then make the pilgrimage to Makkah, for as yet there was a hostile feeling between the inhabitants of the two cities; but on the tenth day of the month Ẕū 'l-Ḥijjah, at the very time when the Arabs at Makkah were engaged in sacrificing victims, Muḥammad went forth from his house at al-Madīnah, and assembling his followers instituted the 'Īdu 'l-Aẓḥā. Two young kids were brought before him. One he sacrificed and said: "O Lord! I sacrifice this for my whole people, all those who bear witness to Thy unity and to my mission. O Lord! this is for Muḥammad and for the family of Muḥammad."

There is nothing in the Qur'ān to connect this sacrifice with the history of Ishmael, but it is generally held by Muḥammadans to have been instituted in commemoration of Abraham's willingness to offer up his son as a sacrifice. And Muḥammadan writers generally maintain that the son was Ishmael and not Isaac, and that the scene took place on Mount Mina near Makkah, and not in the land of Moriah, as is stated in Genesis.

The following is the account given by Muḥammadan writers:—"When Ibrahīm (the peace of God be upon him) founded Makkah, the Lord desired him to prepare a feast for Him. Upon Ibrahīm's (the friend of God) requesting to know what He would have on the occasion, the Lord replied, 'Offer up thy son Ismā'īl.' Agreeably to God's command he took Ismā'īl to the Ka'bah to sacrifice him, and having laid him down, he made several ineffectual strokes on his throat with a knife, on which Ismā'īl observed, 'Your eyes being uncovered, it is through pity and compassion for me you allow the knife to miss: it would be better if you blindfolded yourself with the end of your turban and then sacrificed me.' Ibrahīm acted upon his son's suggestion and having repeated the words '*Bi-smi 'llāhi, allāhu akbar*' (*i.e.* 'In the name of God! God is great!'), he drew the knife across his son's neck. In the meanwhile, however, Gabriel had substituted a broad-tailed sheep for the youth Ismā'īl, and Ibrahīm unfolding his eyes observed, to his surprise, the sheep slain, and his son standing behind him." (See *Qiṣaṣu 'l-Ambiyā'*.)

It is a notable fact that whilst Muḥammad professed to abrogate the Jewish ritual, and also ignored entirely the doctrine of the Atonement as taught in the New Testament, denying even the very fact of our Saviour's crucifixion, he made the "*day of sacrifice*" the great central festival of his religion.

There is a very remarkable Ḥadīs̤, related by 'Āyishah, who states that Muḥammad said, "Man hath not done anything on the 'Īdu 'l-Aẓḥā more pleasing to God than spilling blood; for verily the animal sacrificed will come, on the day of resurrection, with its horns, its hair, and its hoofs, and will make the scale of his (good) actions heavy. Verily its blood reacheth the acceptance of God, before it falleth upon the ground, therefore be joyful in it." (*Mishkāt*, book iv. ch. xlii. sec. 2.)

Muḥammad has thus become a witness to the doctrine of the Christian faith that "without shedding of blood, there is no remission." The animal sacrificed must be without blemish, and of full age; but it may be either a goat, a sheep, a cow, or a camel.

The religious part of the festival is observed as follows:—The people assemble in the morning for prayer, in the 'Īdgāh, or place erected outside the city for these special festival prayers. The whole congregation then standing in the usual order, the Imām takes his place in front of them and leads them in two rak'ahs of prayer. After prayers the Imām ascends the mimbar or pulpit and delivers a Khuṭbah, or oration, on the subject of the festival.

We are indebted to Mr. Sell for the following specimen of the Khuṭbah:—

"In the name of God, the Compassionate, the Merciful.

"God is Great. There is no God but God. God is Great! God is Great and worthy of all praise. He is Holy. Day and night we should praise Him. He is without partner, without equal. All praise be to Him. Holy is He, Who makes the rich generous, Who provides the sacrifice for the wise. He is Great, without an equal. All praise be to

Him. Listen! I testify that there is no God but God. He is alone, without partner. This testimony is as bright as the early dawn, as brilliant as the glorious feast day. Muḥammad is His servant who delivered His message. On Muḥammad, and on his family, and on his Companions may the peace of God rest. On you who are present, O congregation of Muslimīn, may the mercy of God for ever rest. O servants of God! our first duty is to fear God and to be kind. God has said, ‘I will be with those who fear Me and are kind.’

“Know, O servants of God! that to rejoice on the feast day is the sign and mark of the pure and good. Exalted will be the rank of such in Paradise, especially on the day of resurrection will they obtain dignity and honour. Do not on this day foolish acts. It is no time for amusements and negligence. This is the day on which to utter the praises of God. Read the Kalimah, the Takbīr and the Tamḥīd. This is a high festival season and the feast of sacrifice. Read now the Takbīru ’t-Tashrīq. God is great! God is great! There is no God but God! God is great! God is great! All praise be to Him! From the morning of the ‘Arafah, after every *farẓ rak‘ah*, it is good for a person to repeat the Takbīru ’t-Tashrīq. The woman before whom is a man as Imām, and the traveller whose Imām is a permanent resident, should also repeat this *Takbīr*. It should be said at each Namāz until the Ṣalātu ’l-‘Aṣr of the Feast day (10th). Some, however, say that it should be recited every day till the afternoon of the thirteenth day, as these are the days of the Tashrīq. If the Imām forgets to recite, let not the worshipper forget. Know, O believers, that every free man who is a Ṣāḥib-i-Niṣāb should offer sacrifice on this day, provided that this sum is exclusive of his horse, his clothes, his tools, and his household goods and slaves. It is wājib for everyone to offer sacrifice for himself, but it is not a wājib order that he should do it for his children. A goat, a ram, or a cow, should be offered in sacrifice for every seven persons. The victim must not be one-eyed, blind, lame, or very thin.

“If you sacrifice a fat animal it will serve you well, and carry you across the Ṣirāṭ. O Believers, thus said the Prophet, on whom be the mercy and peace of God, ‘Sacrifice the victim with your own hands, this was the Sunnah of Ibrahīm, on whom be peace.’

“In the Kitābu Zādi ’t-Taqwa it is said that, on the ‘Īdu ’l-Fiṭr and the ‘Īdu ’l-Aẓḥā, four *nafl rak‘ahs* should be said after the farẓ Namāz of the ‘Īd. In the first rak‘ah after the Sūratu ’l-Fātiḥah recite the Sūratu ’l-A‘la (Sūrah lxxvii); in the second, the Sūratu ’sh-Shams (Sūrah xci.); in the third, the Sūratu ’ẓ-Ẓuḥa (Sūrah xciii.); in the fourth, the Sūratu ’l-Ikhlāṣ (cxii.).

“O Believers, if ye do so, God will pardon the sins of fifty years which are past and of fifty years to come. The reading of these Sūrahs is equal, as an act of merit, to the reading of all the books God has sent by His prophets.

“May God include us amongst those who are accepted by Him, who act according to the Law, whose desire will be granted at the Last Day. To all such there will be no fear in the Day of Resurrection; no sorrow in the examination at the Day of Judgment. The best of all books is the Qur’ān. O believers! May God give to us and to you a blessing for ever, by the grace of the Noble Qur’ān. May its verses be our guide, and may its wise mention of God direct us aright. I desire that God may pardon all believers, male and female, the Muslimīn and the Muslimāt. O believers, also seek for pardon. Truly God is the Forgiver, the Merciful, the Eternal King, the Compassionate, the Clement. O believers, the Khuṭbah is over. Let all desire that on Muḥammad Muṣṭafa the mercy and peace of God may rest.”

The Khuṭbah being ended, the people all return to their homes. The head of the family then takes a sheep, or a cow, or a goat, or camel, and turning its head towards Makkah says:

“In the name of the great God.

“Verily, my prayers, my sacrifice, my life, my death, belong to God, the Lord of the worlds. He has no partner: that is what I am bidden: for I am first of those who are *Mūslim* (*i.e.* resigned).”

And then he slays the animal. The flesh of the animal is then divided into three portions, one third being given to relations, one third to the poor, and the remaining third reserved for the family. Quite apart from its religious ceremonies, the festival is observed as a great time of rejoicing, and the holiday is kept for two or three days in a similar way to that of the minor festival or the ‘Īdu ’l-Fiṭr. [HAJJ, ISHMAEL, SACRIFICE.]

‘ĪDU ’L-FITR (عيد الفطر). *Lit.* “The Festival of the Breaking of the Fast.” It is called also *‘Īdu Ramaẓān*, the *‘Īdu ’ṣ-Ṣadaqah* (Feast of Alms), and the *‘Īdu ’ṣ-ṣaghīr* (Minor Festival). It commences as soon as the month’s fast in Ramaẓān is over, and consequently on the first day of the month of Shawwāl. It is specially a feast of alms-giving. “Bring out your alms,” said Ibn ‘Abbās, “for the Prophet has ordained this as a divine institution, one Ṣā‘ of barley or dates, or a half Ṣā‘ of wheat: this is for every person, free or bond, man or woman, old or young, to purify thy fast (*i.e.* the month’s fast just concluded) of any obscene language, and to give victuals to the poor.” (*Mishkāt*, book vi. ch. iii.)

On this festival the people, having previously distributed the alms which are called the *Ṣadaqatu ’l-Fiṭr*, assemble in the vast assembly outside the city in the Īdgāh, and, being led by the Imām, recite two rak‘ahs of prayer. After prayers the Imām ascends the *mimbar*, or pulpit, and delivers the *khuṭbah*, or oration. We are indebted to Mr. Sell for the following specimen of one of these sermons:—

“In the name of God, the Compassionate, the Merciful.

"Holy is God who has opened the door of mercy for those who fast, and in mercy and kindness has granted them the right of entrance into heaven. God is greater than all. There is no God save Him. God is great! God is great! and worthy of praise. It is of His grace and favour that He rewards those who keep the fast. He has said: 'I will give in the future world houses and palaces, and many excellent blessings to those who fast. God is great! God is great! Holy is He who certainly sent the Qur'ān to our Prophet in the month of Ramaẓān, and who sends angels to grant peace to all true believers. God is great! and worthy of all praise. We praise and thank Him for the 'Īdu 'l-Fiṭr, that great blessing; and we testify that beside Him there is no God. He is alone. He has no partner. This witness which we give to His Unity will be a cause of our safety here, and finally gain us an entrance to Paradise. Muḥammad (on whom be the mercy and peace of God) and all famous prophets are His slaves. He is the Lord of genii and of men. From Him comes mercy and peace upon Muḥammad and his family, so long as the world shall last. God is greater than all. There is none beside Him. God is great! God is great! and worthy of all praise. O company of Believers, O congregation of Muslims, the mercy of the True One is on you. He says that this Feast day is a blessing to you, and a curse to the unbelievers. Your fasting will not be rewarded, and your prayers will be stayed in their flight to heaven until you have given the *ṣadaqah*. O congregation of Believers, to give alms is to you a wājib duty. Give to the poor some measures of grain or its money equivalent. Your duty in Ramaẓān was to say the Tarāwīḥ prayers, to make supplication to God, to sit and meditate (*i'tikāf*) and to read the Qur'ān. The religious duties of the first ten days of Ramaẓān gain the mercy of God, those of the second ten merit His pardon; whilst those of the last ten save those who do them from the punishment of hell. God has declared that Ramaẓān is a noble month, for is not one of its nights, the Lailatu 'l-Qadr, better than a thousand months? On that night Gabriel and the angels descended from heaven: till the morning breaks it is full of blessing. Its eloquent interpreter, and its clearest proof is the Qur'ān, the Word of God, most Gracious. Holy is God who says in the Qur'ān: 'This is a guide for men, a distinguisher between right and wrong.' O Believers, in such a month be present, obey the order of your God, and fast; but let the sick and the travellers substitute some other days on which to fast, so that no days be lost, and say: 'God is great!' and praise Him. God has made the fast easy for you. O Believers, God will bless you and us by the grace of the Holy Qur'ān. Every verse of it is a benefit to us and fills us with wisdom. God is the Bestower, the Holy King, the Munificent, the Kind, the Nourisher, the Merciful, the Clement."

The Khuṭbah being ended, the whole congregation raise their hands and offer a *munājāt* for the remission of sins, the recovery of the sick, increase of rain, abundance of corn, preservation from misfortune, and freedom from debt. The Imām then descends to the ground, and makes further supplication for the people, the congregation saying "*Amīn*" at the end of each supplication. At the close of the service the members of the congregation salute and embrace each other, and offer mutual congratulations, and then return to their homes, and spend the rest of the day in feasting and merriment.

Mrs. Meer Hasan Ali, in her *Observations on the Musalmans of India*, says:—

"The assemblies of the ladies on this festival are marked by all the amusements and indulgences they can possibly invent or enjoy in their secluded state. Some receiving, others paying visits in covered conveyances; all doing honour to the day by wearing their best jewellery and most splendid dress. The Zanānah rings with festive songs and loud music, the cheerful meeting of friends, the distribution of presents to dependants, and remembrances to the poor; all is life and joy, cheerful bustle and amusement, on this happy day of festival, when the good lady of the mansion sits in state to receive presents from inferiors and to grant proofs of her favour to others."

Mr. Lane, in his *Modern Egyptians*, vol. ii. p. 238, thus describes the 'Īdu 'l-Fiṭr, as kept in Egypt:—

"Soon after sunrise on the first day, the people having all dressed in new, or in their best clothes, the men assemble in the mosques, and perform the prayers of two rek'ahs, a Soonneh ordinance of the 'eed; after which, the Khateeb delivers an exhortation. Friends, meeting in the mosque, or in the street, or in each other's houses, congratulate and embrace and kiss each other. They generally visit each other for this purpose. Some, even of the lower classes, dress themselves entirely in a new suit of clothes, and almost everyone wears something new, if it be only a pair of shoes. The servant is presented with at least one new article of clothing by the master, and receives a few piasters from each of his master's friends, if they visit the house; or even goes to those friends to congratulate them, and receives his present; if he have served a former master, he also visits him, and is in like manner rewarded for his trouble; and sometimes he brings a present of a dish of sweet cakes, and obtains, in return, money of twice the value, or more. On the days of this 'eed, most of the people of Cairo eat salted fish, and thin, folded pancakes, and a kind of bun. Some families also prepare a dish consisting of stewed meat, with onions, and a quantity of treacle, vinegar, and coarse flour; and the master usually procures dried fruits, such as nuts, raisins, &c., for his family. Most of the shops in the metropolis are closed, except those at which eatables and sherbet are sold; but the streets present a gay appearance, from the crowds of passengers in their holiday clothes

"On one or more days of this festival, some or all of the members of most families, but chiefly the women, visit the tombs of their relatives. This they also do on the occasion of the other grand festival. ['IDU 'L-AZHA.] The visitors, or their servants, carry palm branches, and sometimes sweet basil, to lay upon the tomb which they go to visit. The palm-branch is broken into several pieces, and these, or the leaves only, are placed on the tomb.

"Numerous groups of women are seen on these occasions, bearing palm-branches, on their way to the cemeteries in the neighbourhood of the metropolis. They are also provided, according to their circumstances, with cakes, bread, dates, or some other kind of food, to distribute to the poor who resort to the burial-ground on these days. Sometimes tents are pitched for them; the tents surround the tomb which is the object of the visit. The visitors recite the Fat'hhah, or, if they can afford it, employ a person to recite first the Soorat Ya'-Seen, or a larger portion of the Kuran. Often a *khutmeh* (or recital of the whole of the Qurān) is performed at the tomb, or in the house, by several fickees. Then men generally return immediately after these rites have been performed, and the fragments or leaves of the palm-branch laid on the tomb: the women usually go to the tomb early in the morning, and do not return until the afternoon; some of them (but these are not generally esteemed women of correct conduct), if they have a tent, pass the night in it, and remain until the end of the festival, or until the afternoon of the following Friday; so, too, do the women of a family possessed of a private, enclosed burial-ground, with a house within it, for there are many such enclosures, and not a few with houses for the accommodation of the females in the midst of the public cemeteries of Cairo. Intrigues are said to be not uncommon with the females who spend the night in tents among the tombs. The great cemetery of Báb en-Nusr, in the desert tract immediately on the north of the metropolis, presents a remarkable scene on the two 'eeds. In a part next the city-gate from which the burial-ground takes its name, many swings and whirligigs are erected, and several large tents, in some of which dancers, reciters of Aboo-Zeyd, and other performers, amuse a dense crowd of spectators; and throughout the burial-ground are seen numerous tents for the reception of the visitors of the tombs. About two or three days after the 'eed above described, the 'Kisweh,' or covering of the Káabeh, which is sent annually with the great caravan of pilgrims, is conveyed in procession from the citadel of the metropolis, where it is manufactured at the Sooltán's expense, to the mosque of the Hhasaneyn, to be sewed together and lined, preparatively to the approaching pilgrimage." [KISWAH.]

The visiting of tombs on the occasion of the two festivals is not a custom in India. It is generally done in the Muḥarram, both by the Sunnīs and the Shī'ahs

'IFFAH (عفة). "Chastity, continence, purity." *Ahlu 'iffah*, "those who are chaste."

'IFRĪT (عفريت). A demon, or class of demons, mentioned in the Qur'ān (Sūrah xxvii. 39). They are said to be giants, and very malicious. The ghosts of the wicked dead are sometimes called by this name. [GENII.]

IFṬĀR (افطار). *Lit.* "Breaking." Breaking the month's fast on the evening of the 'Īdu 'l-Fiṭr, that is, at the first sight of the new moon, after sunset. It is also used for breaking the fast every evening after sunset during the month of Ramaẓān. It is, according to the example of the Prophet, to break the fast by eating either dates or salt.

IḤDĀD (احداد). The period of mourning observed by a widow for her husband, namely, four months and ten days. [MOURNING.]

IHLĀL (اهلال). *Lit.* "Raising the voice." A term used for the Talbiyah. [TALBIYAH.]

IḤRĀM (احرام). *Lit.* "Prohibiting." The pilgrim's dress, and also the state in which the pilgrim is held to be from the time he assumes this distinctive garb until he lays it aside. It consists of two new white cotton cloths, each six feet long by three and a half broad. One of these sheets, termed *ridā'* is thrown over the back, and, exposing the arm and shoulder, is knotted at the right side in the style called *wishaḥ*. The other, called *izār*, is wrapped round the loins from the waist to the knee, and knotted or tucked in at the middle.

In the state of iḥrām, the pilgrim is forbidden the following actions: connection with or kissing women, covering the face, perfumes, hunting or slaying animals, anointing the head with oil, cutting the beard or shaving the head, colouring the clothes, washing the head or beard with marsh mallows, cutting the nails, plucking a blade of grass, cutting a green tree. But although the pilgrim is not allowed to hunt or slay animals, he may kill the following noxious creatures: a lion, a biting dog, a snake or scorpion, a crow, a kite, and a rat. For each offence against the rules of iḥrām, special sacrifices are ordained, according to the offence. [HAJJ.]

IḤSĀN (احسان). *Lit.* "To confer favours, or to perform an action in a perfect manner." A term used in the Traditions for the sincere worship of God. Muḥammad said *Iḥsān* was "both to worship God as if thou sawest Him, and to remember that God seest thee." (*Mishkāt*, book i. ch. i. pt. 1.) The word is used in this sense by the Ṣūfī mystics. ('Abdu 'r-Razzāq's *Dict. of Ṣūfī Terms.*)

IḤṢĀN (احصان). *Lit.* "Keeping a wife secluded." A legal term for a married man. (*Hidāyah*, vol. ii. p. 49.)

IḤṢĀRU 'L-ḤAJJ (احصار الحج). The hindering of the Pilgrimage. For example: If a pilgrim be stopped on his way by any unforeseen circumstance, such as sickness or accident, he is required to send an animal to be sacrificed at the Sacred City. (*Hidāyah*, Arabic ed., vol. i. p. 184.) This injunction is founded upon the teaching of the Qur'ān, Sūrah ii. 192. "And if he be prevented, then send whatever offering shall be easiest: and shave not your heads until the offering reach the place of sacrifice. But whoever among you is sick, or hath an ailment of the head, must expiate by fasting, or alms, or a victim for sacrifice. And when ye are secure (from hindrances) then he who delights in the visitation (*'Umrah*) of the holy place until the Pilgrimage, shall bring whatever offering shall be the easiest. But he who hath nothing to offer shall fast three days in the Pilgrimage and seven days when ye return: they shall be ten days in all."

IḤTIKĀR (احتكار). Hoarding up grain with the object of raising the price. Used for monopoly of all kinds. Abū Ḥanīfah restricts its use to a monopoly of the necessaries of life. It is strictly forbidden by Muḥammad, who is related to have said: "Whoever monopoliseth is a sinner"; "Those who bring grain to a city to sell at a cheap rate are blessed, and they who keep it back in order to sell at a high rate are cursed." (*Mishkāt*, book xii. ch. viii.)

IḤTILAM (احتلام). *Pollutio nocturna*; after which *ghusl*, or legal bathing, is absolutely necessary. [PURIFICATION.]

IHTIMĀM (اهتمام). "Superintendence; care." The trust or jurisdiction of a landowner over certain portions of land.

IḤYĀU 'L-MAWĀT (احياء الموات). *Lit.* "The revival of dead lands." A legal term for the cultivation of wastes.

IḤẒĀR (احضار). A summons citing to appear before a Qāẓī or Judge.

ĪJĀB (ايجاب). The first proposal made by one of the parties in negociating or concluding a bargain. [MARRIAGE.]

IJĀRAH (اجارة). Price, hire, wages, rent, profit, emolument, according to the subject to which it applies. [HIRE.]

IJMĀ' (اجماع). The third foundation of Islām. It literally means "collecting," or "assembling," and in Muslim divinity it expresses the unanimous consent of the Mujtahidūn (learned doctors); or, as we should call it, "the unanimous consent of the Fathers." A Mujtahid is a Muslim divine of the highest degree of learning, a title usually conferred by Muslim rulers. [MUJTAHID.] There are three foundations of *Ijmā'*: (1) *Ittifāq-i-Qaulī*, unanimous consent expressed in declaration of *opinion*; (2) *Ittifāq-i-Fi'lī* expressed in unanimity of *practice*; (3) *Ittifāq-i-Sakūtī*, when the majority of the Mujtahidūn signified their tacit assent to the opinions of the minority by "*silence*" or non-interference.

The Mujtahidūn capable of making *Ijmā'* must be "men of learning and piety, not heretics, nor fools, but men of judgment."

There is great diversity of opinion as to up to what period in the history of Islām *Ijmā'* can be accepted. Some doctors assert that only the *Ijmā'* of the Mujtahidūn who were *Aṣḥāb* (companions); others, that of those who were not only "companions" but "descendants" of the "Prophet," can be accepted; whilst others accept the *Ijmā'* of the *Anṣārs* (helpers), and of the *Muhājirūn* (fugitives), who were dwellers in al-Madīnah with Muḥammad. The majority of learned Muslim divines, however, appear to think that *Ijmā'* may be collected in every age, although they admit that, owing to the numerous divisions which have arisen amongst Muḥammadans, it has not been possible since the days of the *Taba'u 't-Tābi'in* (*i.e.* the followers of the followers of the Companions).

The following is considered to be the relative value of *Ijmā'*:—

That of the *Aṣḥāb* (companions) is equal to *Ḥadīṣ Mutawātir*. That which was decided afterwards, but in accordance with the unanimous opinion of the Aṣḥāb, is equal to *Ḥadīṣ-i-Khabar-i-Mashhūr*, and that upon which there was diversity of opinion amongst the *Aṣḥāb*, but has since been decided by the later Mujtahidūn is equal to *Ḥadīṣ-i-Khabar-i-Wāḥid*. (See Syud Ahmad Khan's Essay.)

Some European writers confuse the term *Ijmā'* with *Ijtihād*. But *Ijtihād* is the deduction made by a single Mujtahid, whilst *Ijmā'* is the collective opinion of a council of Mujtahidūn, or enlightened doctors.

Amongst the Shī'ahs there are still Mujtahidūn whose *Ijmā'* is accepted, but the Sunnīs have four orthodox schools of interpretation, named after their respective founders—Ḥanafī, Shāfa'ī, Malakī, and Ḥambali. The Wahhābīs for the most part reject *Ijmā'* collected after the death of "the Companions."

It will be easily understood what a fruitful source of religious dissension and sectarian strife this third foundation of the rule of faith is. Divided as the Christian Church is by its numerous sects, it will compare favourably with Muḥammadanism even in this respect. Muḥammad, it is related, prophesied that, as the Jewish Church had been divided into seventy-one sects! and the Christians into seventy-two! so his followers would be divided into seventy-three sects! But every Muslim historian is obliged to admit that they have far exceeded the limits of Muḥammad's prophecy; for, according to 'Abdu 'l-Qādir al-Jīlānī, there are at least 150.

IJTIHĀD (اجتهاد). *Lit.* "Exertion." The logical deduction on a legal or theological question by a Mujtahid or learned and enlightened doctor, as distinguished from *Ijmā'*, which is the collective opinion of a council of divines.

This method of attaining to a certain degree of authority in searching into the principles of jurisprudence is sanctioned by the Traditions:—

"The Prophet wished to send a man named Mu'āẕ to al-Yaman to receive some money collected for alms, which he was then to distribute to the poor. On appointing him he said: 'O Mu'āẕ, by what rule will you act?' He replied, 'By the Law of the Qur'ān.' 'But if you find no direction therein?' 'Then I will act according to the Sunnah of the Prophet.' 'But what if that fails?' 'Then I will make an *Ijtihād*, and act on that.' The Prophet raised his hands and said, 'Praise be to God who guides the messenger of His Prophet in what He pleases.'"

The growth of this system of divinity is traced by a Sunnī writer, Mirza Qāṣim Beg, Professor in the University of St. Petersburg (extracts from which are given in Sell's *Faith of Islām*), as follows:—

1. God, the only legislator, has shown the way of felicity to the people whom He has chosen, and in order to enable them to walk in that way He has shown to them the precepts which are found partly in the eternal Qur'ān, and partly in the sayings of the Prophet transmitted to posterity by the Companions and preserved in the Sunnah. That way is called the Sharī'ah (law). The rules thereof are called Aḥkām (commandments).

2. The Qur'ān and the Sunnah, which since their manifestation are the primitive sources of the orders of the Law, form two branches of study, viz. 'Ilm-i-Tafsīr, or the interpretation of the Qur'ān, and 'Ilm-i-Ḥadīs̤, or the study of Tradition.

3. All the orders of the Law have regard either to the actions (*Dīn*), or to the belief (*Imān*) of the faithful (*Mukallif*).

4. As the Qur'ān and the Sunnah are the principal sources from whence the precepts of the Sharī'ah have been drawn, so the rules recognised as the principal elements of actual jurisprudence are the subject of 'Ilm-i-Fiqh, or the science of Law.

Fiqh in its root signifies "conception, comprehension." Thus Muḥammad prayed for Ibn Mas'ūd: "May God make him comprehend (*Faqqaha-hu*), and make him know the interpretation of the Qur'ān." Muḥammad in his quality of Judge and chief of the Believers decided, without appeal or contradiction, all the affairs of the people. His sayings served as a guide to the Companions. After the death of the Prophet the first Khalīfahs acted on the authority of the Traditions. Meanwhile the Qur'ān and the Sunnah, the principal elements of religion and legislation, became little by little the subject of controversy. It was then that men applied themselves vigorously to the task of learning by heart the Qur'ān and the Traditions, and then that jurisprudence became a separate science. No science had as yet been systematically taught, and the early Musalmāns did not possess books which would serve for such teaching. A change soon, however, took place. In the year in which the great jurisconsult of Syria died (A.H. 80), Nu'mān ibn S̤ābit, surnamed Abū Ḥanīfah, was born. He is the most celebrated of the founders of the schools of jurisprudence, a science which ranks first in all Muslim seats of learning. Until that time and for thirty years later the learned doctors had all their knowledge by heart, and those who possessed good memories were highly esteemed. Many of them knew by heart the whole Qur'ān with the comments made on it by the Prophet and by the Companions; they also knew the Traditions and their explanations, and all the commands which proceed from the Qur'ān and the Sunnah. Such men enjoyed the right of Mujtahidūn. They transmitted their knowledge to their scholars orally. It was not till towards the middle of the second century of the Hijrah that treatises on the different branches of the Law were written, after which six schools (*Maẕhabs*) of jurisprudence were formed. The founders (all Imāms of the first class) were Abū Ḥanīfah, the Imāmu 'l-A'ẓam or greatest Imām (A.H. 150), Sufyān as̤-S̤aurī (A.H. 161), Mālik (A.H. 179), ash-Shāfi'ī (A.H. 204), Ibn Ḥanbal (A.H. 241), and the Imām Dāwūd aẓ-Ẓāhirī (A.H. 270). The two sects founded by as-S̤aurī and aẓ-Ẓāhirī became extinct in the eighth century of the Hijrah. The other four still remain. These men venerated one another. The younger ones speak with great respect of the elder. Thus ash-Shāfi'ī says: "No one in the world was so well versed in jurisprudence as Abū Ḥanīfah was, and he who has read neither his works nor those of his disciples knows nothing of jurisprudence." Ibn Ḥanbal, when sick, wore a shirt which had belonged to ash-Shāfi'ī, in order that he might be cured of his malady; but all this did not prevent them starting schools of their own, for the right of *Ijtihād* is granted to those who are real Mujtahidūn.

There are three degrees of *Ijtihād*:

1. *Ijtihād fī'sh-Shar'*, absolute independence in legislation.

2. *Ijtihād fī 'l-Maẕhab*, authority in the judicial systems founded by the Mujtahidūn of the first class.

3. *Ijtihād fī'l-Masā'il*, authority in cases which have not been decided by the authors of the four systems of jurisprudence.

The first is called a complete and absolute authority, the second relative, the third special.

(1) *Ijtihād fī 'sh-Shar'*.

Absolute independence in legislation is the gift of God. He to whom it is given when seeking to discover the meaning of the Divine Law is not bound to follow any other teacher. He can use his own judgment. This gift was bestowed on the jurisconsults of the first, and to some of the second and third centuries. The Companions, however, who were closely connected with the Prophet, having transmitted immediately to their posterity the treasures of legislation, are looked upon as Mujtahidūn of much higher authority than those of the second and third centuries. Thus Abū Ḥanīfah says: "That which comes to us from the Companions is on our head and eyes (*i.e.* to be received with respect): as to that which comes from the Tābi'ūn, they are men and we are men."

Since the time of the Tābi'ūn this degree of Mujtahid has only been conferred on the six great Imāms before mentioned. Theoretically any Muslim can attain to this degree, but it is one of the principles of jurisprudence that the confirmation of this rank is dependent on many conditions, and so no one now gains the honour. These conditions are :—

1. The knowledge of the Qur'ān and all that is related to it; that is to say, a complete knowledge of Arabic literature, a profound acquaintance with the orders of the Qur'ān and all their sub-divisions, their relationship to each other and their connection with the orders of the Sunnah. The candidate should know when and why each verse of the Qur'ān was written, he should have a perfect acquaintance with the literal meaning of the words, the speciality or generality of each clause, the abrogating and abrogated sentences. He should be able to make clear the meaning of the "obscure" passages (*Mutashābih*), to discriminate between the literal and the allegorical, the universal and the particular.

2. He must know the Qur'ān by heart with all the Traditions and explanations.

3. He must have a perfect knowledge of the Traditions, or at least of three thousand of them.

He must know their source, history, object, and their connection with the laws of the Qur'ān. He should know by heart the most important Traditions.

4. A pious and austere life.

5. A profound knowledge of all the sciences of the Law.

Should anyone *now* aspire to such a degree another condition would be added, viz. :—

6. A complete knowledge of the four schools of jurisprudence.

The obstacles, then, are almost insurmountable. On the one hand, there is the severity of the 'Ulamā', which requires from the candidate things almost impossible; on the other, there is the attachment of the 'Ulamā' to their own Imāms, for should such a man arise no one is bound now to listen to him. The Imām Ibn Ḥanbal said: "Draw your knowledge from whence the Imāms drew theirs, and do not content yourself with following others, for that is certainly blindness of sight." Thus the schools of the four Imāms remain intact after a thousand years have passed, and so the 'Ulamā' recognise since the time of these Imāms no Mujtahid of the first degree. Ibn Ḥanbal was the last.

The rights of the man who attained to this degree were very important. He was not bound to be a disciple of another, he was a mediator between the Law and his followers, for whom he established a system of legislation, without anyone having the right to make any objection. He had the right to explain the Qur'ān, the Sunnah, and the Ijmā', according as he understood them. He used the Prophet's words, whilst his disciples only used his. Should a disciple find some discrepancy between a decision of his own Imām and the Qur'ān or Traditions, he must abide by the decision of the Imām. The Law does not permit him to interpret after his own fashion. When once the disciple has entered the sect of one Imām he cannot leave it and join another. He loses the right of private judgment, for only a Mujtahid of the first class can dispute the decision of one of the Imāms. Theoretically, such Mujtahidūn may still arise; but, as we have already shown, practically they do not.

(2.) *Ijtihād fī 'l-Maẕhab.*

This degree has been granted to the immediate disciples of the great Imāms who have elaborated the systems of their masters. They enjoyed the special consideration of the contemporary 'Ulamā', and of their respective Imāms who in some cases have allowed them to retain their own opinion. The most famous of these men are the two disciples of Abū Ḥanīfah, Abū Yūsuf, and Muḥammad ibn al-Ḥasan. In a secondary matter their opinion carries great weight. It is laid down as a rule that a Muftī may follow the unanimous opinion of these two even when it goes against that of Abū Ḥanīfah.

(3.) *Ijtihād fī 'l-Masā'il.*

This is the degree of special independence. The candidates for it should have a perfect knowledge of all the branches of jurisprudence according to the four schools of the Arabic language and literature. They can solve cases which come before them, giving reasons for their judgment, or decide on cases which have not been settled by previous Mujtahidūn; but in either case their decisions must always be in absolute accordance with the opinions of the Mujtahidūn of the first and second classes, and with the principles which guided them. Many of these men attained great celebrity during their lifetime, but to most of them this rank is not accorded till after their death. Since their Imām Qāẓī Khān died (A.H. 592), no one has been recognised by the Sunnīs as a Mujtahid even of the third class.

There are three other inferior classes of jurists, called Muqallidūn, or followers of the Mujtahidūn; but all that the highest in rank amongst them can do is to explain obscure passages in the writings of the older jurisconsults. By some of the 'Ulamā' they are considered to be equal to the Mujtahidūn of the third class. If there are several conflicting legal opinions on any point, they can select one opinion on which to base their decision. This a mere Qāẓī cannot do. In such a case he would have to refer to these men or to their writings for guidance. They seem to have written commentaries on the legal systems without originating anything new. The author of the *Hidāyah*, who lived at the end of the sixth century, was a Muqallid.

IKHLĀṢ (اخلاص). *Lit.* "Sincerity." (1) A theological term, implying that a Muslim performs his religious acts in the sight of God alone, and not to be seen of men. (2) Al-Ikhlāṣ, the title of the CXIIth Sūrah of the Qur'ān. A chapter which occurs in the daily prayer, and reads thus:—

"Say, 'He is God alone!
God the Eternal!
He begets not, and is not begotten!
Nor is there anyone like unto him!'"

Professor Palmer says this chapter is generally known as *al-Ikhlāṣ*, "clearing oneself," *i.e.* of belief in any but one God.

IKRĀH (اكراه). [COMPULSION.]

ʻIKRIMAH (عكرمة). *Lit.* "A hen pigeon." The son of Abū Jahl ibn Hishām. A "companion" of the Prophet. He embraced Islām after the final taking of Makkah. For some years he and his father, Abū Jahl, were determined opponents of Islām. He was one of the heroes of the Quraish at the battle of Badr, and commanded the left wing of the Quraish army at Uhud. He opposed the Prophet's advance on Makkah, and on defeat fled to Jiddah, intending to escape to Africa, but he was brought back by his wife to Makkah, and received pardon from Muḥammad, and embraced Islām. He became one of Abū Bakr's generals, and died in his reign.

ʻIKRIMAH (عكرمة). Abū ʻAbdi 'llāh ʻIkrimah ibn ʻAbdi 'llāh, was a slave belonging to Ibn ʻAbbās. His master took great pains to teach him the Qur'ān and the Traditions, and consequently he is known as a traditionist of some note. His master, Ibn ʻAbbās, died without giving him his liberty, and ʻAlī the son of Ibn ʻAbbās sold him to Khālid ibn Yazīd for four thousand dīnārs. But ʻIkrimah went to ʻAlī and said, "You have sold your father's learning for four thousand dīnārs!" Upon this, ʻAlī, being ashamed, obtained Khālid's consent to annul the bargain, and he granted ʻIkrimah his liberty. He died A.H. 107 (A.D. 725), aged 84.

ĪLĀ' (ايلاء). A form of divorce in which a man makes a vow that he will not have connection with his wife for not less than four months and observes it inviolate. The divorce is thereby effected *ipso facto*, without a decree of separation from the judge. See Qur'ān, Sūratu 'l-Baqarah, ii. 226: "Those who swear off from their women, they must wait four months; but if they break their vow, God is forgiving and merciful."

Sulaiman ibn Yasār says: "I was in company with about ten of the Prophet's Companions, and every one said, 'A man who swears that he will not go near his wife for four months shall be imprisoned until he return to her, or he shall divorce her.'" (*Mishkāt*, book xiii. ch. xiii.)

ILĀH (اله). An object of worship or adoration; *i.e.* a god, or deity. The term *Allāh*, "God," being *Ilāh* with the definite article ال *al*, *i e. al-ilāh*, "the God."

ILĀHĪ (الهى). From *Ilāh*, "God." (1) That which is divine, *e.g. ad-dīnu 'l-Ilāhī*, the divine religion. (2) *Ilāhī* is also used for the era instituted by the Emperor Akbar, commencing with the first year of his reign, A.H. 963, A.D. 1556. Although found on the coins of Akbar and his immediate successors, it never obtained currency, and is now obsolete.

IʻLĀN (اعلان). Publishing the notice of marriage by sending messengers to the houses of friends. A custom which is founded upon the express injunction of the Prophet, as reported by ʻĀyishah: "Give notice of marriages, perform them in mosques, and beat drums for them." (*Mishkāt*, book xiii. ch. iv. pt. 2.)

ILHĀM (الهام). [INSPIRATION.]

AL-ILHĀMU 'R-RABBĀNĪ (الالهام الربانى). [INSPIRATION.]

ILLEGITIMATE CHILDREN. An illegitimate child, Arabic *waladu 'z-zinā'* (ولد الزناء), has legally no father, and a putative father is, therefore, excluded from the custody of such a child. The child only inherits from its mother and the mother's relations, who in return inherit from him. (*Tagore Law Lectures, 1873*, pp. 123, 488.)

ʻILLĪYŪN (عليون). The seventh stage of celestial bliss. Also the register in which the good deeds of Muslims are said to be written. See Sūratu 't-Taṭfīf, lxxxiii. 18: "The register of the righteous is in ʻIllīyūn." See also *Mishkāt*, book v. ch. iii. pt. 3: "The angels follow it (the soul) through each heaven, and the angels of one region pass it on to the next until it reaches the seventh heaven, when God says, 'Write the name of my servant in *ʻIllīyūn*, and return him to the earth, that is, to his body which is buried in the earth."

ʻILM (علم). *Lit.* "To know; knowledge." In Muslim theology, the word *ʻIlm* is always used for *religious* knowledge. ʻAbdu 'l-Ḥaqq says it is the knowledge of religion as expressed in "the Book" (Qur'ān) and the "Sunnah" (Traditions), and is of two kinds, *ʻIlmu 'l-Mabādī*, elementary knowledge, or that relating to the words and sentences of the Qur'ān and Ḥadīṣ; and *ʻIlmu 'l-Maqāṣid*, perfected knowledge, or that relating to faith and works, as taught in the Qur'ān and Ḥadīṣ. There is also *ʻIlmu 'l-Mukāshafah*, revealed knowledge, or that secret knowledge, or light, which shines into the heart of the pious Muslim, whereby he becomes enlightened as to the truths of religion. This spiritual knowledge is also called *ʻIlmu 'l-Ḥaqīqah*, or the knowledge of the truth. It is related (*Mishkāt*, book ii. ch. i. Arabic ed.) that the Prophet said ʻIlm is of three kinds, viz. *Āyātu 'l-Muḥkam*, *Sunnatu 'l-Qā'im*, and *Farīẓatu 'l-ʻAdil*, and that whatever is beyond these three is not necessary. The learned doctors explain these terms as follows: *Ayātu 'l-Muḥkam*, the established text or verses of the Qur'ān; *Sunnatu 'l-Qā'im*, the correct Aḥādīs̤ or Traditions; and *Farīẓatu 'l-'Adil*, the lawful interpretation of the Qur'ān and the Traditions.

The acquisition and the imparting of religious knowledge is very highly commended by Muḥammad (see *Mishkātu 'l-Maṣābiḥ, in loco*):—

"The desire of knowledge is a divine commandment for every Muslim, and to instruct in knowledge those who are unworthy of it, is like putting pearls, jewels, and gold on the necks of swine."

"Whoever is asked about the knowledge which he hath, and concealeth it, will be reined with a bridle of fire on the Day of Resurrection."

"There are two avaricious persons that are never satisfied: one of them in knowledge, the more he attains the more he desires; the other of the world, with the things of which he is never satisfied."

"That person who will pursue the road of knowledge, God will direct him to the road of Paradise; and verily the angels spread their arms to receive him that seeketh after knowledge; and everything in heaven and earth will ask grace for him. Verily the superiority of a learned man over a worshipper is like that of the full moon over all the stars."

'ILMU 'L-ADAB (علم الادب). The science of Philology. In *Ḥājī Khalfah*, Lexicon, vol. i. p. 215, quoted by Lane, it is "the science by which one guards against error in the language of the Arabs, with respect to words and with respect to writing."

The science of polite writing is classed under twelve heads: 1, *lughah*, lexicology; 2, *ṣarf*, accidence; 3, *ishtiqāq*, derivation; 4, *naḥw*, syntax; 5, *ma'ānī*, sense or meaning; 6, *bayān*, eloquence; 7, *'arūẓ*, prosody; 8, *qāfiyah*, rhyme; 9, *rasmu 'l-khaṭṭ*, caligraphy; 10, *qarẓush-shi'r*, versification; 11, *inshā'u 'n-naṣr*, prose composition; 12, *muḥāẓarah*, dictation. These sections are regarded as distinct sciences.

'ILMU 'L-AKHLĀQ (علم الاخلاق). Ethics; morals. The best-known works on the subject are the Persian works—the *Akhlāq-i-Jalālī*, by Faqīr Jānī Muḥammad, A.H. 908, which has been translated into English, with references and notes, by W. F. Thompson, Esq. (London, 1839); the *Akhlāq-i-Naṣirī*, by Naṣīru 'd-dīn aṭ-Ṭūsī, A.H. 672; and the *Akhlāq-i-Muḥsinī* by the Maulawī Ḥusain al-Kāshifī (Ḥusain the commentator), A.H. 910.

'ILMU 'L-AKTĀF (علم الاكتاف). The science of divining by the shoulder-blades of sheep. It was the custom of the ancient Arabs to place the shoulder-bone of a sheep in the sun, and to examine it, and so divine by its marks future events, in the same way as by the science of palmistry. (*Kashfu 'ẓ-Ẓunūn, in loco.*)

'ILMU 'L-'AQĀ'ID (علم العقائد). ['ILMU 'L-KALAM.]

'ILMU 'L-ASMĀ' (علم الاسماء). The knowledge of the names, titles, or attributes of God. [GOD, ZIKR, SUFIISM.]

'ILMU 'L-BĀṮIN (علم الباطن). The mystic science; the same as Taṣawwuf. [SUFIISM.]

'ILMU 'L-FALAK (علم الفلك). The science of Astronomy. According to the Muhammadans the earth is the centre of the astronomical system. The seven planets, which are called the *nujūmu 's-saiyārāt* or wandering stars, as distinguished from fixed stars, are 1, *Qamar*, Moon; 2, *'Uṭārid*, Mercury; 3, *Zuhrah*, Venus; 4, *Shams*, Sun; 5, *Mirrīkh*, Mars; 6, *Mushtarī*, Jupiter; 7, *Zuḥal*, Saturn.

The Arabian arrangement of the planets is that of Ptolemy, who placed the earth in the centre of the universe, and nearest to it the moon, whose synodic revolution is the shortest of all, being performed in 29½ days. Next to the moon he placed Mercury, who returns to his conjunctions in 116 days. After Mercury followed Venus, whose periodic time is 584 days. Beyond Venus he placed the sun, then Mars, next Jupiter, and lastly Saturn, beyond which are the fixed stars.

The signs of the zodiac (*minṭaqatu 'l-burūj*) are called: 1, *Ḥamal*, Ram; 2, *Ṣaur*, Bull; 3, *Jauzā'*, Twins; 4, *Saraṭān*, Crab; 5, *Asad*, Lion; 6, *Sunbalah* (*lit.* an ear of corn), Virgin; 7, *Mīzān*, Scales; 8, *'Aqrab*, Scorpion; 9, *Qaus* (bow), Archer; 10, *Jady* (he-goat), Capricorn; 11, *Dalw* (watering-pot), Aquarius; 12, *Ḥūt*, Fish.

'ILMU 'L-FARĀ'IẒ (علم الفرائض). The law of inheritance. [INHERITANCE.]

'ILMU 'L-FIQH (علم الفقه). Jurisprudence; and the knowledge of all subjects connected with practical religion. In the first place, *Fiqh* deals with the five pillars of practical religion: 1, the recital of the creed; 2, prayer; 3, fasting; 4, *zakāt* or almsgiving; 5, *ḥajj* or pilgrimage: and in the second place with all questions of jurisprudence such as marriage, divorce, inheritance, sale, evidence, slavery, partnership, warfare, &c. &c.

The chief Sunnī works on the subject are: Of the Ḥanafī sect, the *Hidāyah*, the *Fatāwā-i-'Alamgīrī*, the *Durru 'l-Mukhhtar*, and *Raddu 'l-Muḥtār*; of the Shāfi'ī and Malakī sects, the *Kitābu 'l-Anwār*, the *Muḥarrar*, and the *Ikhtilāfu 'l-A'immah*. The best-known Shī'ah works on jurisprudence are the *Sharā'i'u 'l-Islām*, the *Mafātiḥ*, and the *Jāmi'u 'sh-Shatāt*.

'ILMU 'L-ḤADĪS̤ (علم الحديث). The science of the Traditions; *i.e.* the various canons which have been established for ascertaining the authenticity and genuineness of the Ḥadīs̤ or Traditions. The *Nukhbatu 'l-Fikar*, with its commentary the *Nuzhatu 'n-Naẓar* by Shahābu 'd-dīn Aḥmad al-'Asqalānī (Lee's ed. Calcutta, 1862), is a well-known work on the subject.

'ILMU 'L-HANDASAH (علم الهندسة). The science of Geometry.

'ILMU 'L-ḤIKMAH (علم الحكمة). Also *'Ilmu 'l-Falsafah* (علم الفلسفة). [PHILOSOPHY.]

'ILMU 'L-ḤISĀB (علم الحساب). Arithmetic.

'ILMU 'L-ILĀHĪYĀT (علم الالهيات). A knowledge of divinity. [THEOLOGY.]

'ILMU 'L-INSHĀ' (علم الانشاء). The art of literary composition. [INSHA'.]

'ILMU 'L-JABR (علم الجبر). Algebra.

'ILMU 'L-KAFF (علم الكف). The science of palmistry said to have been practised by Daniel.

'ILMU 'L-KALĀM (علم الكلام). Scholastic theology. It is also known as *'Ilmu 'l-'Aqā'id*, the science of the articles of belief. The author of the *Kashfu 'ẓ-Ẓunūn* defines it as "the science whereby we are able to bring forward proofs of our religious belief," and it includes the discussion of the nature of the existence and the attributes of God.

'Ilmu 'l-Kalām is the discussion of all subjects connected with the six articles of the Muslim Creed: 1, the Unity of God; 2, the Angels; 3, the Books; 4, the Prophets; 5, the Day of Judgment; 6, the Decrees of God, as distinguished from *al-Fiqh*, which is an exposition of the five foundations of practical religion--1, recital of the Creed; 2, prayer; 3, fasting; 4, zakāt; 5, ḥajj.

The most celebrated works on the subject of 'Aqā'id or 'Ilmu 'l-Kalām are: *Sharḥu 'l-'Aqā'id*, by the Maulāwī Mas'ūd Sa'du 'd-dīn at-Taftazānī, A.H. 792; the *Sharḥu 'l-Muwāqif*, by Saiyid Sharīf Jurjānī.

'ILMU 'L-LUGHAH (علم اللغة). Lexicography. [ARABIC LEXICONS.]

'ILMU 'L-MANṬIQ (علم المنطق). Logical science. [LOGIC.]

'ILMU 'L-MASĀḤAH (علم المساحة). Mensuration.

'ILMU 'L-MILĀḤAH (علم الملاحة). The nautical art. The science of making and navigating ships.

'ILMU 'L-MŪSIQA (علم الموسيقى). The science of Music. [MUSIC.]

'ILMU 'L-UṢŪL (علم الاصول). The science of the "roots," or fundamentals of the religion of Muḥammad, namely, of the Qur'ān, Aḥādīs̤, Ijmā', and Qiyās. The science of exegesis, or the rules of interpretation of these four roots of Islām. An explanation of the methods of this science will be found in the article on QUR'AN, Sect. viii., the same principles applying to the other three fundamentals.

The best known works on the 'Ilmu 'l-Uṣū are the *Manār*, by 'Abdu 'llāh ibn Aḥmad an-Nasafī, A.H. 710, and its commentary, the *Nūru 'l-Anwār*; also *at-Tanqīḥ*, by 'Ubaidu 'llāh ibn Mas'ūd, A.H. 747, with its commentary, *at-Tauẓiḥ*, by the same author, and a super-commentary, the *Talwiḥu 't-Tauẓiḥ*, by Sa'du 'd-dīn Mas'ūd ibn 'Umar at-Taftāzānī, A.H. 792.

AL-'ILMU 'L-YAQĪN (العلم اليقين). Certain knowledge; demonstration; a religious life; a knowledge of the truth.

'ILMU 'N-NABĀTĀT (علم النباتات). Botany. The knowledge of the use of herbs.

'ILMU 'N-NUJŪM (علم النجوم). Astrology. "The science by which are discovered the events both of the present and of the future by means of the position of the stars." (*Kashfu 'ẓ-Ẓunūn, in loco.*) [ASTROLOGY.]

'ILMU 'R-RAML (علم الرمل). Geomancy. A pretended divination by means of lines on the sand (*raml*). It is said to have been practised as a miracle by six prophets, viz. Adam, Idrīs, Luqmān, Armiyā (Jeremiah), Sha'yā' (Isaiah), Daniel. (See *Kashfu 'ẓ-Ẓunūn, in loco.*)

'ILMU 'R-RIYĀẒAH (علم الرياضة). Mathematics. The author of the *Kashfu 'ẓ-Ẓunūn* says the science of *Riyāẓah* is divided into four sections: 1, *handasah*, geometry; 2, *hi'ah*, astronomy; 3, *ḥisāb*, arithmetic; 4, *mūsīqā*, music.

'ILMU 'SH-SHI'R (علم الشعر). [POETRY.]

'ILMU 'S-SIḤR (علم السحر). The science of magic. [MAGIC.]

'ILMU 'S-SĪMIYĀ' (علم السيمياء). Natural magic, chiromancy, palmistry.

AL-'ILMU 'Ṭ-ṬABĪ'Ī (العلم الطبيعى). Natural philosophy.

'ILMU 'T-TAJWĪD (علم التجويد), called also *'Ilmu 'l-Qirā'ah*. The science of reading the Qur'ān correctly. The most popular work on the subject is *al-Muqaddamatu 'l-Jazarīyah*, by the Shaikh Muḥammad ibn Muḥammad al-Jazarī (A.H. 833).

'ILMU 'T-TAṢAWWUF (علم التصوف). The mystic or contemplative science. [SUFIISM.]

'ILMU 'T-TASHRĪḤ (علم التشريح). The science of anatomy.

'ILMU 'T-TAWĀRĪKH (علم التواريخ), or *'Ilmu 't-Ta'rīkh*. Chronology, history. For a complete list of Muhammadan histories of an early date, see *Kashfu 'ẓ-Ẓunūn in loco.*

'ILMU 'Ṭ-ṬIBB (علم الطب). The science of Medicine. For a list of medical books of an early date, see *Kashfu 'ẓ-Ẓunūn, in loco.*

ILQĀ' (القاء). *Lit.* "Injecting; infusing." A theological term used for the teaching of the heart by the power of God. Inspiration of soul in that which is good.

IMAGES. It is unlawful for a Muḥammadan to have an image of any kind in his house. (*Mishkāt*, book xx. ch. v.) [PICTURES, IDOLS.]

IMĀM (امام). One whose leadership or example is to be followed. A pattern; a model; an example of evil. The term is used in the Qur'ān in these senses.

Sūrah ii. 118: "Verily I have set thee (Abraham) as an *Imām* (or a leader) for mankind."

Sūrah xvii. 73: "The day when we will call all men by their *Imām* (or leader)."

Sūrah xxxvi. 11: "Everything we have set down in a *clear model*."

Sūrah xv. 79: "They (Sodom and Midian) are an obvious *example*."

Sūrah xxv 74: "Make us a *model* to the pious"

Muḥammadans use the term in the following senses:—

(1) The Imām, or Khalīfah, of the Muslim people. The author of the *Hidāyah* says, by the rightful Imām is understood a person in whom all the qualities essential to magistracy are united, such as Islāmism, freedom, sanity of intellect, and maturity of age, and who has been elected into his office by any tribe of Muslims, with their general consent; whose view and intention is the advancement of the true religion, and the strengthening of the Muslims, and under whom the Muslims enjoy security in person and property; one who levies title and tribute according to law; who, out of the public treasury, pays what is due to learned men preachers, qāẓīs, muftīs, philosophers, public teachers, and so forth; and who is just in all his dealings with Muslims; for whoever does not answer this description is not the right Imām, whence it is not incumbent to support such a one, but rather it is incumbent to oppose him, and make war upon him until such time as he either adopt a proper mode of conduct, or be slain; as is written in the *Ma'dinu 'l-Ḥaqā'iq*, copied from the *Fawā'id*. (*Hidāyah*, vol. ii. p. 248.)

THE IMAM LEADING PRAYERS AND RECITING THE FATIHAH OR FIRST SURAH OF THE QUR'AN. (*E. Campbell.*)

For a discussion of this meaning of the title, refer to the article on KHALIFAH, which is the term used for the Imām of the Sunnī Muslims.

(2) The Shī'ahs apply the term *Imām* to the twelve leaders of their sect whom they call the true Imāms [SHI'AH], and not using the term Khalīfah for this office as the Sunnīs do. The Shī'ah traditions are very wild on the subject of the Imāmate, and contrast unfavourably with those of the Sunnīs.

In the *Ḥayātu 'l-Qulūb* (Merrick's edition, p. 203), Muḥammad is said to have related: "On the night of the ascension, the Most High commanded me to inquire of the past prophets for what reason they were exalted to that rank, and they all testified, We were raised up on account of your prophetical office, and the Imāmate of 'Alī ibn Abī Ṭālib, and of the Imāms of your posterity. A divine voice then commanded, 'Look on the right side of the empyrean.' I looked and saw the similitude of 'Alī and al-Ḥasan, and al-Ḥusain, and 'Alī ibn al-Ḥusain (*alias* Zainu 'l-'Abidīn), and Muḥammad al-Bāqir, and Ja'far aṣ-Ṣādiq, and Mūsā al-Kāẓim, and 'Alī ibn Mūsā ar-Riẓā, and Muḥammad at-Jaqı, and 'Alī an-Naqī, and al-Ḥasan al-'Askarī, and al-Mahdī, all performing prayers in a sea of light. These, said the Most High, are my proofs, vicegerents, and friends, and the last of them will take vengeance on my enemies."

(3) The Imām, or leader, of any system of theology or law. Abū Ḥanīfah and the other three doctors of the Sunnīs are called *Imāms*, and so are other leading doctors of divinity.

The term is still used for a religious leader. For example, the head of the Wahhābīs on the North-West frontier of India is called the Imām, and so is the chief of Najd.

(4) The Imām or leader of prayers in any Masjid. Mr. Sale says it answers to the Latin *Antistes*. Each mosque, however small, has its Imām, or priest, who is supported by endowments. The office is not in any sense a sacerdotal one, the Imām not being set apart with any ceremony, as in the case of a Christian presbyter, nor the office being hereditary, as in the case of the Hindu Brahmins. The position of *Imām* in this sense is not unlike the *sheliach*, or *legatus*, of the Jewish synagogue, who acted as the delegate of the congregation, and was the chief reader of prayers in their name. But quite independent of the duly appointed minister of a mosque, who is responsible for its services, and receives its revenues, no congregation of Muslim worshippers can assemble without one of the party taking the lead in the prayers by standing in front, and who is said "*to act as Imām*" for the assembly.

The rules laid down on this subject, as given in the Traditions, are as follows (*Mishkāt*, book iv. ch. xxvii., xxviii.):—

Abū Saʿīd al-Khudrī says the Prophet said: "When there are three persons, one of them must act as Imām and the other two follow him, and the most worthy of them to act as such is he who repeats the Qur'ān best."

Abū Maʿsūd al-Anṣārī says the Prophet said: "Let him act as Imām to a congregation who knows the Qur'ān thoroughly; and if all present should be equal in that respect, then let him perform who is best informed in the rules of prayer; and if they are equal in this respect also, let him act as Imām who has fled for the sake of Islām; and if equal in this likewise, let that person act who is oldest; but the governed must not act as Imām to the governor."

Abū Hurairah relates that the Prophet said: "When any of you acts as Imām to others, he must be concise in his prayers, because there are decrepit, aged, and sick persons amongst them, and when any one of you says his prayers alone, he may be as prolix as he pleases. [MASJID.]

IMĀM-BĀRAH (امام باره). A building in which the festival of the Muḥarram is celebrated, and service held in commemoration of the deaths of ʿAlī and his sons, al-Ḥasan and al-Ḥusain. At other times, the *tāzias*, or shrines, are preserved in it; sometimes it is used as the mausoleum of the founder of the family. [MUHARRAM.]

IMĀMĪYAH (اماميه). *Lit.* "The followers of the Imām." The chief sect of the Shīʿas, namely, those who acknowledge the twelve Imāms. [SHIʿAH.]

IMĀM MUBĪN (امام مبين). "The clear prototype or model." The expression occurs twice in the Qur'ān, Sūrah xxxvi. 11, "Everything we do set down in a clear prototype" (*fī Imāmin Mubīnin*). Here it appears to be used for the Qur'ān as an inspired record. Sūrah xv. 79, "Verily they became both, Sodom and Midian, a clear example" (*labi - Imāmin Mubīnin*). Muḥammadan teachers use the word for the *Lahwu 'l-Maḥfūẓ*, or the Tablet of Decrees.

AL-IMĀMU 'L-MAHDĪ (الامام المهدى). *Lit.* "The well-guided Leader." Umm Salmah relates that the Prophet said, "Strife and disputations will be created among men when a Khalīfah shall die: and this shall be in the last days. And a man of the people of al-Madīnah will come forth and will flee from al-Madīnah to Makkah, and the men of Makkah will come and try to make him *Imām* by flattery, but he will not be pleased. Then men shall acknowledge him as *Imām*. Then an army from Syria shall advance against him, and this army shall be engulphed in an earthquake at Badāʾah, between Makkah and al-Madīnah. Then when the people shall see this the Abdāl, *i.e.* the Substitutes or good people [ABDAL], will come from Syria, and a multitude from al-ʿIrāq. And after that a man shall be born of the Quraish, of the tribe of Kalb, who will also send an army against him *i.e.* al-Mahdī; but he shall be victorious. Then he will rule people according to the laws of Muḥammad, and will give strength to Islām upon the earth, and he will remain on the earth seven years. Then will he die, and Muslims will say prayers in his behalf."

The Shīʿahs believe that al-Mahdī has already come and is still concealed in some part of the earth. For they suppose him to be the last of the twelve Imāms, named Muḥammad ʿAbdu 'l-Qāṣim [SHIʿAHS], who will again appear in the last days. The Shīʿahs say that Muḥammad said, "O ye people, I am the Prophet and ʿAlī is my heir, and from us will descend al-Mahdī, the seal of the Imāms, who will conquer all religions and will take vengeance on the wicked." (*Ḥarjātu 'l-Qulūb*, p. 342.)

I'MĀN, ĪMĀN (ايمان). "Faith," which, according to the Muḥammadan doctors, is the belief of the heart and the confession of the lips to the truth of the Muslim religion. Faith is of two kinds: *I'mān Mujmal*, or the simple expression of faith in the teaching of the Qur'ān and the *Aḥādīṣ*, or Traditions; and *I'mān Mufaṣṣal*, or a formal declaration of belief in the six articles of the Muslim Creed: 1, in God; 2, the Angels of God; 3, the Books of God; 4, the Prophets of God; 5, the Day of Judgment; 6, Predestination to good and evil. In the Traditions, I'mām includes practice (*ʿAmal*), and all that belongs to the religious life of the Muslim. It is related (*Mishkāt*, book i. ch. i.) that Muḥammad said, "That person has tasted the sweets of faith who is pleased with God as his Lord, with Islām as his religion, and with Muḥammad as the Prophet of God." And again (*ib.*), "The most excellent faith is to love him who loves God, and to hate him who hates God, to keep the tongue employed in repeating the name of God [ZIKR], and to do unto men as you would wish them to do unto you, and to reject for others what you would reject for yourself."

Salvation by faith without works is clearly taught (*Mishkāt*, book i. ch. i.) by Muḥammad, *e.g.* "When anyone of you shall have believed truly and sincerely, then whatever good action that person may do will be rewarded from ten to seven hundred fold, and every sin he may commit will be expiated one by one before he dies." Good works, however, are the test of faith. A man asked the Prophet what was the sign whereby he might know the reality of his faith. He said, "If thou dost derive pleasure from the good that thou hast done, and art grieved for the evil which thou hast committed, then thou art a true believer" (*Mishkāt*, book i. ch. i.). Some of the Prophet's friends came to him and said, "Verily, we find in our minds such wicked propensities, that we think it even a sin to speak of them." The Prophet said, "Do you find them really bad?" They said, "Yes." He said, "This is an evidence of faith." By which he meant, if the man had not faith he would not have felt the wickedness of his heart.

'IMLĪQ (عمليق). The grandson of Shem, the son of Noah. The progenitor of the 'Amāliqah, the Amalekites of Scripture. They are said to be some of the earliest inhabitants of Makkah and al-Madīnah.

IMMACULATE CONCEPTION of the Virgin Mary. This doctrine was asserted by Muḥammad (*Mishkāt*, book i. ch. iii. pt. 1). The Prophet said, "There is not of the sons of Adam, except Mary and her Son, one born but is touched by the Devil at the time of his birth, and the child makes a loud noise from the touch."

When or where the doctrine of the Immaculate Conception was first taught is quite unknown. Perrone says that some writers have ascribed its origin to France, *and he himself is of opinion that it came from the East*, and was recognized in Naples in the ninth century. (Blunt's *Dictionary of Doctrinal and Historical Theology, in loco.*)

The doctrine of the Immaculate Conception was finally imposed as an Article of Faith in the Romish Church, by Pius IX., Dec. 8th, 1854.

IMMODESTY. [MODESTY.]

IMPOSTURE. The Quraish charged Muḥammad, at the early period of his preaching, with imposture. The following Sūrahs were given in answer to these charges:—

Sūrah xxv. 5–7: "Those who misbelieve say, 'This is nothing but a lie which he has forged, and another people hath helped him at it'; but they have wrought an injustice and a falsehood. And they say, 'They are old folk's tales which he has got written down while they are dictated to him morning and evening. Say He sent it down who knows the secrets of heaven and earth."

Sūrah lxix. 40–43: "Verily it is the speech of a noble Apostle, and it is not the speech of a poet:—little is it ye believe!

"And it is not the speech of a soothsayer, —little is it that ye mind! It is a revelation from the Lord, the Lord of all the worlds."

IMPOTENCY. Arabic *'Anānah* (عنانة), *'Innīnah* (عنينة). Both according to Sunnī and Shī'ah law it cancels the marriage contract, but the decree of the Qāẓī is necessary before it can take effect. [DIVORCE.]

IMPRISONMENT. Arabic *Sijn* (سجن), *Habs* (حبس). According to the Ḥanīfī school of jurisprudence, the person upon whom punishment or retaliation is claimed, must not be imprisoned until evidence be given, either by two people of unknown character (that is, of whom it is not known whether they be just or unjust), or by one just man who is known to the Qāẓī; because the imprisonment, in this case, is founded on suspicion, and suspicion cannot be confirmed but by the evidence of two men of unknown character, or of one just man. It is otherwise in imprisonment on account of property; because the defendant, in that instance, cannot be imprisoned but upon the evidence of two just men; for imprisonment on such an account is a grievous oppression, and, therefore, requires to be grounded on complete proof. In the Mabsūṭ, under the head of duties of the Qāẓī, it is mentioned that, according to the two disciples, the defendant, in a case of punishment for slander, or of retaliation, is not to be imprisoned on the evidence of one just man, because, as the exaction of bail is in such case (in their opinion) lawful, bail is, therefore to be taken from him. When a claimant establishes his right before the Qāẓī, and demands of him the imprisonment of his debtor, the Qāẓī must not precipitately comply, but must first order the debtor to render the right; after which, if he should attempt to delay, the Qāẓī may imprison him. If a defendant, after the decree of the Qāẓī against him, delay the payment in a case where the debt due was contracted for some equivalent (as in the case of goods purchased for a price, or of money, or of goods borrowed on promise of a return), the Qāẓī must immediately imprison him, because the property he received is a proof of his being possessed of wealth. In the same manner, the Qāẓī must imprison a refractory defendant who has undertaken an obligation in virtue of some contract, such as marriage or bail, because his voluntary engagement in an obligation is an argument of his possession of wealth, since no one is supposed to undertake what he is not competent to fulfil.

A husband may be imprisoned for the maintenance of his wife, because in withholding it he is guilty of oppression; but a father cannot be imprisoned for a debt due to his son, because imprisonment is a species of severity which a son has no right to be the cause of inflicting on his father; in the same manner as in cases of retaliation or punishment. If, however, a father withhold maintenance from an infant son, who has no property of his own, he must be imprisoned; because this tends to preserve the life of the child. (*Hidāyah*, vol. ii.)

'IMRĀN (عمران). According to Muḥammadan writers the name of two different persons. The one the father of Moses and Aaron, and the other the father of the Virgin Mary. Christian writers imagine that the Qur'ān confounds Mary, the mother of Jesus, with Mary or Maryam, the sister of Moses and Aaron. The verses are as follows:—

Sūrah iii. 30: "Verily, above all human beings did God choose Adam and Noah, and the family of 'Imrān, the one the posterity of the other; and God heareth and knoweth. Remember when the wife of 'Imrān said, 'O my Lord, I vow to Thee what is in my womb, for Thy special service. . . . And I have named her Mary, and I commend her and her offspring to Thy special protection.'"

Sūrah lxvi. 12: "And Mary the daughter of 'Imrān, ever virgin, and into whose womb We breathed Our spirit."

Sūrah xix. 29: "'O sister of Aaron! thy father was not a wicked man, nor unchaste thy mother.' And she made a sign unto them pointing towards the babe."

Al-Baiẓāwī the commentator, says the 'Imrān first mentioned in Sūrah iii. is the father of Moses, and the second the father of Mary the Virgin. He attempts to explain the anachronism in Sūrah xix. by stating that (1) Mary is called the sister of Aaron by way of comparison; (2) or because she was of the Levitical race; (3) or, as some have said, there was a man of the name of Aaron, renowned either for piety or wickedness, who lived at the time, and she is said, by way of derision, to be like him!

IMSĀK (امساك). *Lit.* "Keeping back." The word occurs only once in the Qur'ān, Sūrah ii. 228: "Divorce (may happen) twice; then, *keep them* in reason or let them go in kindness."

The word is used in theological works for being miserly in charity, and in giving in God's service, in opposition to *Infāq.*

IN'ĀM (انعام). A gift; a benefaction in general. A gift by a superior to an inferior. In India, the term is especially applied to grants of land held rent-free, and in hereditary and perpetual occupation; the tenure came in time to be qualified by the reservation of a portion of the assessable revenue, or by the exaction of all proceeds exceeding the intended value of the original assignment; the term is also vaguely applied to grants of rent-free land without reference to perpetuity or any specified conditions. The grants are also distinguishable by their origin from the ruling authorities, or from the village communities, and are again distinguishable by peculiar reservations, or by their being applicable to different objects.

Sanad-i-In'ām is a grant emanating from the ruling power of the time of the grant, free from all Government exactions, in perpetuity, and validified by a Sanad, or official deed of grant; it usually comprises land included in the village area, but which is uncultivated, or has been abandoned; and it is subject to the village functionaries.

Nisbat-i-In'ām (from *nisbah*, "a portion"), are lands granted rent-free by the village out of its own lands; the loss or deduction thence accruing to the Government, assessment being made good by the village community. (Wilson's *Glossary of Indian Terms.*)

INCANTATION. [DA'WAH, MAGIC.]

INCENSE. Arabic *Bakhūr* (بخور), *Lubān* (لبان). Heb. לְבוֹנָה, in Isaiah xliii. 23, &c. The use of incense forms no part of the religious customs of the Muslim, although its use as a perfume for a corpse is permitted by the Traditions. It is, however, much used as an offering at the shrines of the Muḥammadan saints, and forms an important item in the so-called science of Da'wah. [DA'WAH.]

INFANTS, The Religion of. The general rule is that the religion of an infant is the same as that of its parents. But where one of the parents is a Muḥammadan, and the other of a different persuasion (as a Jew or a Christian), the infant must be accounted a Muḥammadan, on the principle that where the reasons are equally balanced, the preference is to be given to that religion. (*Hidāyah*, vol. i. p. 177. *Sharīfīyah*, Appendix No 71. Baillie's *Inheritance*, p. 28.)

INFANT SALVATION. The author of *Durru 'l-Mukhtār*, vol. i. p. 891, says: Abū Ḥanīfah gave no answer to the question whether the infants of *mushrikūn* (those who associate another with God) will have to answer for themselves in the Day of Judgment or not; or whether they will inherit the *Fire* (*i.e.* Hell), or go to Paradise (*Jannah*) or not. But Ibn al-Humām has said, the learned are not agreed upon these questions, and it is evident that Abū Ḥanīfah and others are at a loss to answer them; and, moreover, there are contradictory traditions recorded regarding them. So it is evident that in the matter of salvation, they (the infants) will be committed to God, and we are not able to say anything regarding this matter. Muḥammad ibn al-Ḥasan (the disciple of Abū Ḥanifah), has said, "I am certain God will not commit anyone to the punishment (of hell) until he has committed sin." And Ibn Abī Sharīf (a disciple of Ibn al-Ḥasan, says the Companions were silent regarding the question of the future of infants; but it is related by the Imām Nawawī (commentator on the *Ṣaḥīḥ Muslim*) that there are three views regarding the salvation of infants. Some say they will go to hell, some do not venture an opinion on the subject, and some say they will enter Paradise; and the last view he considers the correct one, in accordance with the tradition which says, "Every child is born according to the law of God."

INFĀQ (انفاق). *Lit.* "Giving forth; expending." The word occurs once in the Qur'ān, Sūrah xvii. 102: "Did ye control the treasuries of the mercy of my Lord, then ye would hold them through fear of expending (*infāq*), for man is ever niggardly."

The word is used for giving in charity and in God's service, in opposition to *imsāk*.

INFIDEL. There are several words used for those in a state of infidelity: 1, *kāfir* (كافر), one who *hides* or *denies* the truth; 2, *mushrik* (مشرك), one who gives *companions* to God; 3, *mulḥid* (ملحد), one who has *deviated* from the truth; 4, *zandīq* (زنديق), an infidel or a zend-worshipper; 5, *munāfiq* (منافق), one who secretly disbelieves in the mission of Muḥammad; 6, *murtadd* (مرتد), an apostate from Islām; 7, *dahrī* (دهرى), an atheist; 8, *waṡanīy* (وثنى), a pagan or idolater.

AL-INFIṬĀR (الانفطار). "The cleaving asunder." The title of the LXXXIInd Sūrah of the Qur'ān, in which the word occurs. *Zamakhsharī*, according to Savary, says that "the Muslims who shall recite this chapter shall receive a divine favour for every drop of water that drops from the clouds, and another for each grave on the face of the earth."

INHERITANCE. Arabic *Farā'iẓ* (فرائض), *Mīrāṡ* (ميراث). The law of inheritance is called *'ilmu 'l-farā'iẓ*, or *'ilm-i-mīrāṡ*. The verses in the Qur'ān upon which the law of inheritance is founded are called *Ayātu 'l-Mawāriṡ*, the Verses of Inheritance; they begin at the 12th verse of Sūratu 'n-Nisā', or the IVth chapter of the Qur'ān, and are as follows:—

"With regard to your children, God commandeth you to give the male the portion of two females; and if they be females more than two, then they shall have two-thirds of that which *their father* hath left: but if she be an only daughter, she shall have the half; and the father and mother of the deceased shall each of them have a sixth part of what he hath left, if he have a child; but if he have no child, and his parents be his heirs, then his mother shall have the third; and if he have brethren, his mother shall have the sixth, after paying the bequests he shall have bequeathed, and his debts. As to your fathers, or your children, ye know not which of them is the most advantageous to you. This is the law of God. Verily, God is Knowing, Wise!

"Half of what your wives leave shall be yours, if they have no issue; but if they have issue, then a fourth of what they leave shall be yours, after paying the bequests they shall bequeath, and debts.

"And your wives shall have a fourth part of what ye leave, if ye have no issue; but if ye have issue, then they shall have an eighth part of what ye leave, after paying the bequests ye shall bequeath, and debts.

"If a man or woman make a distant relation their heir, and he or she have a brother or a sister, each of these two shall have a sixth; but if there are more than this, then shall they be sharers in a third, after payment of the bequests he shall have bequeathed, and debts,

"Without loss to any one. This is the ordinance of God, and God is Knowing, Gracious!"

The earliest authority in the Traditions on the subject of inheritance is Zaid ibn Ṣābit, and the present law is chiefly collected from his sayings, as recorded in the *Ḥadīṡ*. There are no very important differences between the Sunnī and Shīa'h law with reference to this question. The highest authority amongst the former is the book *as-Sirājīyah*, by Sirāju 'd-dīn Muḥammad, A.H. 600, which has been published with a commentary entitled *Mamzūj*, by Sir W. Jones, Calcutta, 1792.

The Shī'ah law of inheritance will be found in the *Mafātīḥ* and the *Jāmi'u 'sh-Shatāt*.

The property of a deceased Muslim is applicable, in the first place, to the payment of his funeral expenses; secondly, to the discharge of his debts; and, thirdly, to the payment of legacies as far as one-third of the residue. The remaining two-thirds, with so much of the third as is not absorbed by legacies are the patrimony of the heirs. A Muḥammadan is therefore disabled from disposing of more than a third of his property by will. (See *As-Sirajīyah.*)

The clear residue of the estate after the payment of funeral expenses, debts, and legacies, descends to the heirs; and among these the first are persons for whom the law has provided certain specific shares or portions, and who are thence denominated *Sharers*, or *ẕawū 'l-furūẓ*.

In most cases there must be a residue after the shares have been satisfied; and this passes to another class of persons who from that circumstance may be termed *Residuaries*, or *'aṣabah*.

It can seldom happen that the deceased should have no individual connected with him who would fall under these two classes; but to guard against this possible contingency, the law has provided another class of persons, who, though many of them may be nearly related to the deceased, by reason of their remote position with respect to the inheritance, have been denominated *Distant kindred*, or *ẕawū 'l-arḥām*.

"As a general rule," says Mr. Ameer Ali, "the law of succession, both among the Shiahs (Shī'ahs) and the Sunnis, proceeds on the assumption of intestacy. During his lifetime a Mussulman has absolute power over his property, whether it is ancestral or self-acquired, or whether it is real or personal. He may dispose of it in whatever way he likes. But such dispositions in order to be valid and effective, are required to have operation given to them during the lifetime of the owner. If a gift be made, the subject matter of the gift must be made over to the donee during the lifetime of the donor; he must, in fact, divest himself of all proprietary rights in it, and place the donee in possession. To make the operation of the gift dependent upon the donor's death, would invalidate the donation. So also in the case of endowments for charitable or religious purposes. A disposition in favour of a charity, in order to be valid, should be accompanied by the complete divestment of all proprietary rights. As regards testamentary dispositions, the power is limited to one-third of the property, provided it is not in favour of one who is entitled to share in the inheritance. For example, the proprietor may devise by will one-third of his property to a stranger; should the devise, however, relate to more than one-third, or should it be in favour of an heir, it would be invalid.

"This restriction on the testamentary powers of a Mussulman, which is not without analogy in some of the Western systems, leads to the consequence that, as far as the major portion of the estate and effects of a deceased propositus is concerned, the distribution takes place as if he had died intestate.

"Intestacy is accordingly the general rule among the Mussulmans; and as almost in every case there are more heirs than one entitled to share in the inheritance of the deceased, it is important to bear in mind the points of contact as well as of divergence between the Shiah and the Sunni schools.

"As regards the points of contact, it may be stated generally that both the Sunnis and the Shiahs are agreed on the principle by which the individuals who are entitled to an inheritance in the estate of the deceased can be distinguished from those who have no right. For example, a Mussulman upon his death, may leave behind him a numerous body of relations. In the absence of certain determinate rules, it would be extremely difficult to distinguish between the inheriting and the non-inheriting relations. In order to obviate this difficulty and to render it easy to distinguish between the two classes of heirs, it is recognized by both the schools as a general rule, and one capable of universal application, that when a deceased Mussulman leaves behind him two relations, one of whom is connected with him through the other, the former shall not succeed whilst the intermediate person is alive. For example, if a person on his death leave behind him a son and that son's son, this latter will not succeed to his grandfather's estate while his father is alive. The other rule, which is also framed with the object of discovering the heirs of a deceased individual, is adopted with some modification by the two schools. For example, on the succession of male agnates, the Sunnis prefer the nearer in degree to the more remote, whilst the Shiahs apply the rule of nearness or propinquity to all cases, without distinction of class or sex. If a person die leaving behind him a brother's son, and a brother's grandson, and his own daughter's son, among the Sunnis, the brother's son being a male agnate and nearer to the deceased than the brother's grandson, takes the inheritance in preference to the others; whilst among the Shiahs, the daughter's son, being nearer in blood, would exclude the others." (*Personal Law*, by Ameer Ali, p. 41.)

The law of inheritance, even according to Muslim doctors of law, is acknowledged to be an exceedingly difficult object of study; it will, therefore, be impossible to follow it out in all its intricacies, but we give a carefully-drawn table by Mr. A. Ramsey, on the Sunnī law, and a more simple one on Shīʿah inheritance by Mr. Ameer Ali.

I.—SHARERS.

* Are always entitled to some shares.
† Are liable to exclusion by others who are nearer.
R Denotes those who benefit by the return.

* 1° **Father.** (α).—As mere *sharer*, when a son or a son's son, how low soever, he takes $\frac{1}{6}$. (β).—As mere *residuary*, when no successor but himself, he takes the whole: or with a sharer, not a child or son's child, how low soever, he takes what is left by such sharer. (γ).—As sharer and residuary, as when there are daughters and son's daughter, but no son or son's son, he, as sharer, takes $\frac{1}{6}$; daughter takes $\frac{1}{2}$, or two or more daughters, $\frac{2}{3}$; son's daughter $\frac{1}{6}$; and father the remainder as residuary.

† 2° **True Grandfather,** *i.e.* father's father, his father and so forth, into whose line of relationship to deceased no mother enters, is excluded by father, and excludes brothers and sisters; comes into father's place when no father, but does not, like father, reduce mother's share to $\frac{1}{3}$ of residue, nor entirely exclude paternal grandmother.

† 3° **Half Brothers by same Mother,** take, in the absence of children, or son's descendants, and father and true grandfather, one $\frac{1}{6}$, two or more between them $\frac{1}{3}$. R

* 4° **Daughters**; when no sons, take, one $\frac{1}{2}$; two or more, $\frac{2}{3}$ between them: with sons become residuaries and take each half a son's share. R

† 5° **Son's Daughters**; take as daughters, when there is no child; take nothing when there is a son or more daughters than one; take $\frac{1}{6}$ when only one daughter; are made residuaries by brother or male cousin how low soever. R

* 6° **Mother**: takes $\frac{1}{6}$, when there is a child or son's child, how low soever, or two or more brothers or sisters of whole or half blood; takes $\frac{1}{3}$, when none of these: when husband or wife and both parents, takes $\frac{1}{3}$ of remainder after deducting their shares, the residue going to father: if no father, but grandfather, takes $\frac{1}{3}$ of the whole. R

† 7° **True Grandmother,** *i.e.* father's or mother's mother, how high soever; when no mother, takes $\frac{1}{6}$: if more than one, $\frac{1}{6}$ between them. Paternal grandmother is excluded by both father and mother; maternal grandmother by mother only. R

† 8° Full Sisters, take as daughters when no children, son's children, how low soever, father, true grandfather or full brother: with full brother, take half share of male: when daughters or son's daughters, how low soever, but neither sons, nor sons' sons, nor father, nor true grandfather, nor brothers, the full sisters take as residuaries what remains after daughter or son's daughter have had their share. R

† 9° Half Sisters by same Father: as full sisters, when there are none: with one full sister, take $\frac{1}{6}$; when two full sisters, take nothing, unless they have a brother who makes them residuaries, and then they take half a male's share. R

† 10° Half Sisters by Mother only: when no children or son's children how low soever, or father or true grandfather, take, one $\frac{1}{6}$; two or more $\frac{1}{3}$ between them. R

* 11° Husband: if no child or son's child, how low soever, takes $\frac{1}{2}$; otherwise $\frac{1}{4}$.

* 12° Wife: if no child or son's child, how low soever, takes $\frac{1}{4}$: if otherwise, $\frac{1}{8}$. Several widows share equally.

Corollary.—*All* brothers and sisters are excluded by son, son's son, how low soever, father or true grandfather. Half brothers and sisters, on father's side, are excluded by these and also by full brother. Half brothers and sisters on mother's side are excluded by *any* child or son's child, by father and true grandfather.

II.—RESIDUARIES.

A.—Residuaries in their own right, being *males* into whose line of relationship to the deceased no *female* enters.

(*a.*) *Descendants.*

1. Son.
2. Son's son.
3. Son's son's son.
4. Son of No. 3.
   4A. Son of No. 4.
   4B. And so on, how low soever.

(*b*) *Ascendants.*

5. Father.
6. Father's father.
7. Father of No. 6.
8. Father of No. 7.
   8A. Father of No. 8.
   8B. And so on, how high soever.

(*c.*) *Collaterals.*

9. Full brother.
10. Half brother by father.
11. Son of No. 9.
12. Son of No. 10.
    11A. Son of No. 11.
    12A. Son of No. 12.
    11B. Son of No. 11A.
    12B. Son of No. 12A.
    And so on, how low soever.
13. Full paternal uncle by father.
14. Half paternal uncle by father.
15. Son of No. 13.
16. Son of No. 14.
    15A. Son of No. 15.
    16A. Son of No. 16.
    And so on, how low soever.
17. Father's full paternal uncle by father's side.
18. Father's half paternal uncle by father's side.
19. Son of No. 17.
20. Son of No. 18.
    19A. Son of No. 19.
    20A. Son of No. 20.
    And so on, how low soever.
21. Grandfather's full paternal uncle by father's side.
22. Grandfather's half paternal uncle by father's side.
23. Son of No. 21.
24. Son of No. 22.
    23A. Son of No. 23.
    24A. Son of No. 24.
    And so on, how low soever.

N.B.—*a.* A nearer Residuary in the above Table is preferred to and excludes a more remote.

β. Where several Residuaries are in the same degree, they take *per capita*, not *per stirpes*, *i.e.* they share equally.

γ. The whole blood is preferred to and excludes the half blood at each stage.

B.—Residuaries in another's right, being certain females, who are made residuaries by males parallel to them; but who, in the absence of such males, are only entitled to legal shares. These female Residuaries take each half as much as the parallel male who makes them Residuaries.

1. Daughter made Residuary by son.
2. Son's daughter made Residuary by son's son.
3. Full sister made Residuary by full brother.
4. Half sister by father made Residuary by *her* brother.

C. Residuaries with another, being certain females who become residuaries with other females.

1. Full sisters with daughters or daughters' sons.
2. Half sisters by father.

N.B.—When there are several Residuaries of different kinds or classes, *e.g.* residuaries in their own right and residuaries with another, propinquity to deceased gives a preference: so that the residuary with another, when nearer to the deceased than the residuary in himself, is the first.

If there be Residuaries and no Sharers, the Residuaries take all the property.

It there be Sharers, and no Residuaries, the Sharers take all the property by the doctrine of the "Return." Seven persons are entitled to the Return. 1*st*, mother; 2*nd*, grandmother; 3*rd*, daughter; 4*th*, son's daughter; 5*th*, full sister; 6*th*, half sister by father; 7*th*, half brother or sister by mother.

A posthumous child inherits. There is no presumption as to commorients, who are supposed to die at the same time unless there be proof otherwise.

If there be neither Sharers nor Residuaries, the property will go to the following class (Distant Kindred).

III.—DISTANT KINDRED.

Comprising all relatives, who are neither Shares nor Residuaries.

Class 1.

Descendants: Children of daughters and son's daughters.

1. Daughter's son.
2. Daughter's daughter.
3. Son of No. 1.
4. Daughter of No. 1.
5. Son of No. 2.
6. Daughter of No. 2, and so on, how low soever, and whether male or female.
7. Son's daughter's son.
8. Son's daughter's daughter.
9. Son of No. 7.
10. Daughter of No. 7.
11. Son of No. 8.
12. Daughter of No. 8, and so on, how low soever, and whether male or female.

N.B.—(α)—Distant kindred of the first class take according to proximity of degree: but, when equal in this respect, those who claim through an heir, *i.e.* sharer or residuary, have a preference over those who claim through one not an heir.

(β)—When the sexes of their ancestors differ, distribution is made having regard to such difference of sex, *e.g.* daughter of daughter's son gets a portion double that of son of daughter's daughter, and when the claimants are equal in degree, but different in sex, males take twice as much as females.

Class 2.

Ascendants: False grandfathers and false grandmothers.

13. Maternal grandfather.
14. Father of No. 13, father of No. 14, and so on, how high soever (*i.e.* all false grandfathers).
15. Maternal grandfather's mother.
16. Mother of No. 15, and so on, how high soever (*i.e.* all false grandmothers).

N.B.—Rules (α) and (β), applicable to class 1, apply also to class 2. *Further* (γ) when the sides of relation differ, the claimant by the *paternal* side gets twice as much as the claimant by the *maternal* side.

Class 3.

Parents' Descendants.

17. Full brother's daughter and her descendants.
18. Full sister's son.
19. Full sister's daughters and their descendants, how low soever.
20. Daughter of half brother by father, and her descendants.
21. Son of half sister by father.
22. Daughter of half sister by father, and their descendants, how low soever.
23. Son of half brother by mother.
24. Daughter of half brother by mother and their descendants, how low soever.
25. Son of half sister by mother.
26. Daughter of half sister by mother, and their descendants, how low soever.

N.B.—Rules (α) and (β) applicable to class 1, apply also to class 3. *Further* (δ) when two claimants are equal in respect of proximity, one who claims through a residuary is preferred to one who cannot so claim.

Class 4.

Descendants of the two grandfathers and the two grandmothers.

27. Full paternal aunt and her descendants.*
28. Half paternal aunt and her descendants.*
29. Father's half brother by mother and his descendants.*
30. Father's half sister by mother and her descendants.*
31. Maternal uncle and his descendants.*
32. Maternal aunt and her descendants.*

* Male or Female, and how low soever.

N.B. (ε)—The *sides* of relation being equal, uncles and aunts of the whole blood are preferred to those of the half, and those connected by same father only, whether males or females, are preferred to those connected by the same mother only. (η) Where sides of relation differ, the claimant by paternal relation gets twice as much as the claimant by maternal relation. (θ) Where sides and strength of relation are equal, the male gets twice as much as the female.

General Rule.—Each of these classes excludes the next following class.

IV.—Successor by Contract or Mutual Friendship.

V.—Successor of acknowledged Kindred.

VI.—Universal Legatee.

VII.—Public Treasury.

A Synoptical Table of Shi'ah Inheritance.

I.—Consanguinity, or *Nasab*

- First Class.
  - (1) Immediate ascendants, viz. father and mother.
  - (2) Lineal descendants, sons and daughters and grandchildren.
- Second Class.
  - (1) Ascendants of second and third degrees viz. grand-parents and their parents,
  - (2) Brothers and sisters and their children.
- Third Class
  - (1) Paternal uncles and aunts and their children.
  - (2) Maternal uncles and aunts and their children.

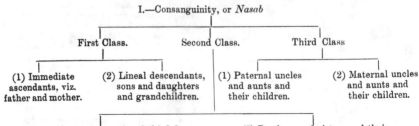

II.—Special Cause, or *Sabab*.

Matrimony.

Husband or Wife.

Walā'.

(1) Emancipation. (2) Suretyship. (3) Spiritual Headship.

[For the Muḥammadan law of inheritance in English, refer to Sir William Jones' translation of the *Sirājīyah* (Calcutta, A.D. 1792), reprinted by Mr. Almaric Ramsey, A.D. 1869. *The Muḥammadan Law of Inheritance*, by Mr. N. B. E. Baillie, A.D. 1832; by Mr. S. G. Grady, A.D. 1869; also *Personal Law of the Muḥammadans*, by Mr. Ameer Ali, 1880. The Arabic works on the subject are: For Sunnī law, *as-Sirājīyah, ash-Sharīfīyah, Hidāyah, Durru 'l-Mukhtār*; for Shīʻah law, *Jāmiʻu 'sh-Shatāt, Mafātīḥ, Sharāʼiʻu 'l-Islām, Irshād-i-Allāmah.*]

INHIBITION. Arabic *ḥijr* (حجر), which, in its primitive sense, means "interdiction or prevention." In the language of the law it signifies an interdiction of action with respect to a particular person; the causes of inhibition being three: infancy, insanity, and servitude.

The acts of an infant, *i.e.* one under puberty, are unlawful, unless sanctioned by his guardian. The acts of a lunatic who has no lucid intervals are not at all lawful; and so are those of a male or female slave. (*Hidāyah*, iii. p. 468.)

INITIAL LETTERS of the Qur'ān. [QUR'AN.]

INJĪL (انجيل). Gr. Εὐαγγέλιον. Evangel. *Injīl* is used in the Qur'ān, and in the Traditions, and in all Muḥammadan theological works of an early date, for the revelations made by God to Jesus. But in recent works it is applied by Muḥammadans to the New Testament. The word occurs twelve times in the Qur'ān, as in the following Sūrahs, which we have arranged *chronologically*, and not as they occur in the Qur'ān. (It will be seen that the expression *Injīl* is not mentioned in the earlier Sūrahs. See chronological table of Sūrahs in article QUR'AN.)

Sūrah vii. 156: "Who follow the Apostle—the illiterate Prophet, whom they find written down with them in the Law (*Taurāt*) and the *Gospel* (*Injīl*)."

Sūrah iii. 2: "He has sent thee a book (*i.e.* the Qur'ān) confirming what was before it, and has revealed the Law, and the *Gospel* before, for the guidance of men."

Sūrah iii. 43: "He will teach him the Book and Wisdom, and the Law and the *Gospel*."

Sūrah iii. 58: "Why do ye dispute about Abraham, when the Law and the *Gospel* were not revealed until after him."

Sūrah lvii. 27: "We gave him (Jesus) the *Gospel*, and we placed in the hearts of those who followed him kindness and compassion."

Sūrah xlviii. 29: "Their marks are in their faces from the effects of adoration: that is their similitude in the Law, and their similitude in the *Gospel*."

Sūrah ix. 112: "Promised in truth in the Law, in the *Gospel*, and in the Qur'ān."

Sūrah v. 50: "We brought him (Jesus) the *Gospel*."

Sūrah v. 51: "Then let the people of the *Gospel* judge by what is revealed therein."

Sūrah v. 70: "And were they steadfast in the Law and in the *Gospel?*"

Sūrah v. 72: "Ye rest on nought until ye stand fast by the Law and the *Gospel* and what is revealed to you from your Lord."

Sūrah v. 110: "When I taught thee the Book, and Wisdom, and the Law, and the Gospel."

There are also allusions to the Christian Scriptures in the following verses:—

Sūrah xix. 31. (The infant Jesus said,) "Verily, I am the servant of God: He hath given me *the book*, and He hath made me a prophet."

Muḥammad was much more indebted to Judaism than Christianity for the teaching he received, which enabled him to overthrow Arabian idolatry and to establish the worship of the One True God [CHRISTIANITY, JUDAISM], and consequently we find more frequent allusions to the Law of Moses than to the Gospel of Christ; and, as it has been already stated, the references to the Gospel as a revelation are in the later Sūrahs. But in all references to the Injīl as an inspired record, there is not one single statement to the effect that the Christians of Muḥammad's day did not possess the genuine Scriptures. In Sūrah iv. 169, (which is an al-Madīnah Sūrah), the Christians are charged with *extravagance*, or error in doctrine, but not with not possessing the true Gospels:—

"Ye people of the Book! commit not extravagance in your religion; and say not of God other than the truth. For verily the Messiah, Jesus, the son of Mary, is an apostle of God, and His word which He placed in Mary, and a spirit from Him. Wherefore, believe in God, and in His apostle; and say not,—'the Trinity';—refrain; it will be better for you. For verily God is one God; far exalted is He above the possibility that there should be unto Him progeny! to Him belongeth whatever is in the heavens and in the earth, and He sufficeth as a guardian."

In Sūrah lxi. 6, there is an appeal to the Gospel in support of Muḥammad's mission, and the appeal is made without any doubt that he was referring to a genuine saying of Christ, well known to the Christians of that day. The verse is as follows:—

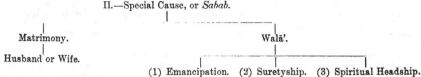

"When Jesus, the son of Mary, said: 'O children of Israel! verily, I am the apostle of God to you, verifying the law that was before me, and giving you glad tidings of an apostle who shall come after me, whose name shall be Aḥmad!' But when he did come to them with manifest signs, they said, 'This is manifest sorcery!'"

The allusion is to the promise of the Paraclete in John xvi. 7, the Muslims declaring that the word παράκλητος has been substituted for the Greek περικλυτός, the word Aḥmad, which is equivalent to Muḥammad, meaning "Praised." The charge which modern Muslims bring against the Christians of having either lost, or changed the original Scriptures, is treated of under the head of CORRUPTION OF THE SCRIPTURES; but some curious statements on the subject will be found in an article in the *Kashfu 'z-Ẓunūn.* It is a Bibliographical Dictionary, compiled by Ḥājjī Khalīfah about 200 years ago. The statements in its article on INJIL are such a strange mixture of fact and fiction that we translate the article from the Arabic *in extenso*:—

"The *Injīl* is a book which God revealed to 'Īsa ibn Maryam. In the work entitled *al-Muwāhib* (by Shihābu 'd-Dīn Aḥmad al-Qasṭalānī, died A.H. 923), it is recorded that the *Injīl* was first revealed in the Syriac tongue, and has since been translated into seventeen languages. But in the *Ṣaḥiḥu 'l-Bukhārī* (A.H. 256), in the story of Waraqah ibn Naufal, it is related that the *Injīl* was revealed in Hebrew. According to Wahb ibn Munabbih, as quoted by Zamakhsharī (A.H. 538) in the *Kashshāf*, the *Injīl* was revealed to Jesus on the 13th day of the month Ramaẓān, although some say it was on the 18th day of that month, 1200 years after the revelation of the Zabūr (Psalms) to Moses.

"It is a disputed question whether or not the *Injīl* abrogates the Law of Moses (*Taurāt*). Some say that Jesus was not a *Sāḥibu 'sh-Sharī'ah* (a law-giver); for it is said in the *Injīl*:—

قال عيسى انى ما جئت لتبديل شرع موسى
عليه السلام بل لتكميله

'I am not come to abrogate (*tabdil*) the Law of Moses, but to fulfil it (*takmīl*).'

"But al-Baiẓāwī (A.H. 685), in his commentary the *Anwāru 't-Tanzīl*, seems to prove that the Law of Jesus does abrogate the Law of Moses (*Shar'u Mūsā*), for there are certain things revealed to Jesus which were not revealed to Moses.

"At the commencement of the *Injīl* is inscribed باسم الاب و الابن الخم, 'In the name of the Father and of the Son,' &c. And the *Injīl*, which is now in the hands of the Christians, is merely a history of the Christ (*Sīratu 'l-Masīḥ*), collected by his four companions Matta, Lūqā, Marqūṣ and Yūḥannā.

"In the book entitled the *Tuḥfatu 'l-Adīb fī Raddi 'alā Ahli 'ṣ-Ṣalīb*, or 'A refutation of the servants of the Cross' (written by 'Abdu 'llāh, a pervert from Christianity to Islām, A.H. 823), it is said that these four Companions are they who corrupted the religion of Jesus, and have added to it. And that they were not of the *Ḥawārīyūn*, or Apostles, mentioned in the Qur'ān. Matta did not see Jesus until the year he was taken up to heaven; and after the Ascension of Jesus he wrote in the city of Alexandria, with his own hand, his *Injīl*, in which he gives an account of the birth and life of Jesus, mentioning several circumstances which are not mentioned by others. Luqā also did not see Jesus, but he was converted to Christianity by one *Būlis* (Paul), who was an Israelite, who himself had not seen Jesus, but was converted by *Anānīyā* (Ananias). Marqūṣ also did not see Jesus at all, but was converted to Christianity, after the Ascension of Jesus, by the Apostle *Bītrū*, and received the *Injīl* (Gospel) from that Apostle in the city of Rome. And his Gospel in many respects contradicts the statements of the other three. Yūḥannā was the son of the sister of Maryam, the mother of Jesus, and the Christians assert that Jesus was present at the marriage of Yūḥannā, when Jesus changed the water into wine. It was the first miracle performed by Jesus.

"When Yūḥannā saw the miracle, he was converted to Christianity, and left his wife and followed Jesus. He was the writer of the fourth *Injīl* (Gospel). It was written in Greek, in the city of Ephesus. These are the four persons who altered and changed the true *Injīl*, for there was only one *Injīl* revealed to Jesus, in which there was no contradiction or discrepancy. These people have invented lies concerning God and His Prophet Jesus, upon whom be peace, as it is a well known fact, although the Christians (*Naṣāra*) deny it. For example, Marqūṣ has written in the first chapter of his Gospel that in the book of the Prophet Isaiah it is said by God, 'I have sent an angel before thy face, namely, before the face of Jesus,' whereas the words are not in the book of Isaiah but in that of Malachi. [See Mark i. 2. In the Received Version the words are "in the Prophets"; but in the Revised Version we have "in Isaiah the prophet."]

"Again, it is related by Matta, in the first or rather thirteenth chapter of his Gospel [*sic*; see, however, Matt. xii. 40], that Jesus said, 'My body will remain in the belly of the earth three days and three nights after my death, just as Jonas was in the whale's belly;' and it is evident it was not true, for Matta agrees with the three other writers of the Gospels that Jesus died in the sixth hour on Friday, and was buried in the first hour of the night on Saturday, and rose from the dead early on Sunday morning, so that he remained in the belly of the earth one day and two nights. So there remains no doubt that the writers of the Gospels told the untruth. For neither Jesus said of himself, nor did God in his *Injīl* say of him, that Jesus will be killed or buried in the earth, for God has said (*i.e.* in the Qur'ān, Sūrah iv. 156), 'They slew him not, for certain! Nay, God raised him up unto Himself.' For this cause there were various divisions amongst the

Christians. Other circumstances similar to these are mentioned in the *Tuḥfatu 'l-Adīb*. Then there are the fundamental rules and doctrines (*al-Qawā'id*), upon which the Christians are, *with very few exceptions*, universally agreed, namely: (1) *At-Taghṭīs* (Baptism); (2) Faith in the *Taṡlīṡ*, or Trinity; (3) the Incarnation of the *Uqnūm* (*i.e.* the essence) of the Son in the womb of Mary; (4) a belief in the *Fiṭrah* (*i.e.* the Holy Communion); (5) the Confession of all sins to the Priest (*Qisīs*). These five foundations also are full of falsehood, corruption, and ignorance."

"In the work entitled *al-Insānu 'l-Kāmil* (written by the Shaikh 'Abdu 'l-Karīm ibn Ibrahīm al-Jīlī, lived A.H. 767–811) it is said that when the Christians found that there was at the commencement of the *Injīl* the superscription باسم الاب و الابن, *i.e.* 'in the name of the Father and Son,' they took the words in their natural meaning, and [thinking it ought to be *Ab*, father, *Umm*, mother, and *Ibn*, son] understood by *Ab*, the Spirit, by *Umm*, Mary, and by *Ibn*, Jesus; and on this account they said, *Ṣāliṡu Ṡalāṡatin*, *i.e.* '(God is) the third of three.' (Sūrah v. 77.) But they did not understand that by *Ab* is meant God Most High, by *Umm*, the *Mahīyatu 'l-Ḥaqā'iq*, or 'Essence of Truth" (*Quidditas veritatum*), and by *Ibn*, the Book of God, which is called the *Wujūdu 'l-Muṭlaq*, or 'Absolute Existence,' being an emanation of the Essence of Truth, as it is implied in the words of the Qur'ān, Sūrah xiii. 9: 'And with him is the *Ummu 'l-Kitāb*, or the Mother of the Book.'"

AL-INSĀN (الانسان). "Man." The title of the LXXVIth Sūrah of the Qur'ān, called also Sūratu 'd-Dahr, both words occurring in the first verse: "Did there not pass over man (*insān*) a long space of time (*dahr*), during which he was a thing not worthy of remembrance."

Some take these words to be spoken of Adam, whose body, according to tradition, was first a figure of clay, and was left for forty years to dry, before God breathed into it; but others understand them of man in general and of the time he lies in the womb. (See *al-Baiẓāwī, in loco*.)

AL-INSĀNU 'L-KĀMIL (الانسان الكامل). "The perfect man." A term used by the Ṣūfī mystics for one in whom are combined all the attributes of divinity and of humanity. (*Kitābu 't-Ta'rīfāt, in loco*). Also title of a mystic work by 'Abdu 'l-Karīm ibn Ibrahīm al-Jīlī (lived A.H. 767–811).

INSHĀ (انشاء). *Lit.* "Constructing; raising-up." The term is particularly applied to literary compositions and forms of letter-writing.

Mr. Lane, in his *Modern Egyptians*, vol. i. p. 272, mentions the Shaikh of the great Mosque, the Azhar, as the author of a collection of Arabic letters on various subjects, which are intended as models of epistolary style, such a collection being called an *Inshā'*.

INSHĀ'A 'LLĀHU TA'ĀLA (ان شاء الله تعالى). "If it should please God Almighty." A very frequent ejaculation amongst Muslims. [ISTISNA'.]

AL-INSHIRĀḤ (الانشراح). "Expanding." The title of the XCIVth Sūrah of the Qur'ān, which opens with the words "Have we not expanded thy breast." It is supposed to allude to the opening of Muḥammad's heart in his infancy, when it is said to have been taken out and cleansed of original sin. (See *al-Baiẓāwī, in loco.*)

INSOLVENCY of a debtor is established by a judicial decree; and after such a declaration a bequest by such a person is void. If, however, the creditors relinquish their claim, the bequest is then valid. (*Hidāyah*, iv. p. 475.)

INSPIRATION. Arabic *waḥy* (وحى). According to the *Nūru 'l-Anwār*, by Shaikh Jīwan Aḥmad (A.H. 1130), inspiration is of two kinds. *Waḥy ẓāhir*, external inspiration, or *Waḥy bāṭin*, internal inspiration.

I.—*External Inspiration* is of three kinds:—

(1) *Waḥyu Qur'ān*, or that which was received from the mouth of the angel Gabriel, and reached the ear of the Prophet, after he knew beyond doubt that it was the angel who spoke to him. This is the only kind of inspiration admitted to be in the Qur'ān. It is sometimes called the *Waḥy matlū*.

(2) *Ishāratu 'l-Malak*, or that which was received from the angel but not by word of mouth, as when the Prophet said, "the Holy Ghost has breathed into my heart."

(3) *Ilhām* or *Waḥyu qalb*, or that which was made known to the Prophet by the "light of prophecy." This kind of inspiration is said to be possessed by *Walīs* or saints, in which case it may be either true or false.

II.—*Internal Inspiration* is that which the Prophet obtained by thought and analogical reasoning, just as the *Mujtahidūn*, or enlightened doctors of the law obtain it. It is the belief of all orthodox Muslims that their Prophet always spoke on matters of religion by the lower forms of inspiration (*i.e. Ishāratu 'l-Malak*, *Ilhām*, or *Waḥyu qalb*); and, consequently a Ḥadīṡ is held to be inspired in as great a degree, although not in the same manner as the Qur'ān itself. The inspiration of the Ḥadīṡ is called the *Waḥy ghair matlū*. (See *Nūru 'l-Anwār*, p. 181; *Mishkāt*, book i. ch. vi. pt. 2.)

Sūratu 'n-Najm, liii. 2: "Your lord (*ṣāḥib*) erreth not, nor is he led astray, neither speaketh he from impulse."

According to the strict Muḥammadan doctrine, every syllable of the Qur'ān is of a directly divine origin, although wild rhapsodical Sūrahs first composed by Muḥammad (as xci., c., cii., ciii). do not at all bear marks of such an assumption, and were not probably intended to be clothed in the dress of a message from the Most High, which characterizes the rest of the Qur'ān. But when Muhammad's die was cast (the turning point in his career) of assuming that Great Name as the speaker of His revelations, then these earlier Sūrahs also came to be regarded as emanating directly from the Deity. Hence it arises that Muḥammadans rigidly include every word of the Qur'ān, at whatever stage delivered, in the category of *Qāla 'llāhu*, or "Thus saith the Lord," and it is one of their arguments against our Christian scriptures that they are not entirely cast in the same mould—not exclusively oracles from the mouth, and spoken in the person of God. (Muir's *Life of Mahomet.*)

The following is a description of inspiration as given by Ibn Khaldūn, "The sign that a man is inspired," he says, "is, that he is at times completely absent, though in the society of others. His respiration is stentorious and he seems to be in a cataleptic fit, or in a swoon. This, however, is merely apparent; for in reality such an *ecstasis* is an absorption into the invisible world; and he has within his grasp what he alone is able to conceive, which is above the conception of others. Subsequently these spiritual visions descend and become perceptible to the faculties of man. They are either whispered to him in a low tone, or an angel appears to him in human shape and tells him what he brings from God. Then the ecstasis ceases, and the prophet remembers what he has heard."

INTELLECT. Arabic *'aql* (عقل), *fahm* (فهم), *idrāk* (ادراك).

The Faqīr Jānī Muhammad ibn As'ad, in his work the *Akhlāq-i-Jalālī*, says: "The reasonable mind has two powers, (1) the power of *perceiving*, and (2) the power of *impelling*; and each of these powers has two divisions: in the percipient power, 1st, an *observative intellect*, which is the source of impression from the celestial sources, by the reception of those ideas which are the materials of knowledge; 2nd, an *active intellect*, which, through thought and reflection, is the remote source of motion to the body in its separate actions. Combined with the appetent and vindictive powers, this division originates the occurrence of many states productive of action or impact, as shame, laughing, crying; in its operation on imgination and supposition, it leads to the accession of ideas and arts in the partial state; and in its relation with the observative sense and the connection maintained between them, it is the means of originating general ideas relating to actions, as the beauty of truth, the odiousness of falsehood, and the like. The *impelling power* has likewise two divisions: 1st, the *vindictive power*, which is the source of forcibly repelling what is disagreeable; 2nd, the *appetent power*, which is the source of acquiring what is agreeable." (Thompson's ed. p. 52.)

INTERCALATION of the Year.

Arabic *nasī'*. The privilege of commuting the last of the three continuous sacred months for the one succeeding it, the month Ṣafar, in which case *Muharram* became secular, and *Ṣafar* sacred. M. Caussin de Perceval supposes that this innovation was introduced by Quṣaiy, an ancestor sixth in ascent from Muḥammad, who lived in the middle of the fifth century. Dr. Sprenger thinks that intercalation in the ordinary sense of the word was not practised at Makkah, and that the Arab year was a purely lunar one, performing its cycle regularly, and losing one year in every thirty-three.

The custom of *nasī'* was abolished by Muḥammad, at the farewell pilgrimage, A.H. 10, as is stated in the Qur'ān, Sūrah ix. 36, 37:—

"Twelve months is the number of months with God, according to God's book, *since* the day when He created the heavens and the earth: of these four are sacred; this is the right usage. But wrong not yourselves therein; attack those who join gods with God in all, as they attack you in all: and know that God is with those who fear Him.

"To carry over a sacred month to another, is only a growth of infidelity. The Infidels are led into error by it. They allow it one year, and forbid it another, that they may make good the number of months which God hath hallowed, and they allow that which God hath prohibited."

INTERCESSION. Arabic *Shafā'ah* (شفاعة).

There is a general belief amongst Muḥammadans that their Prophet is a living intercessor for them at the throne of God; but the Wahhābīs state that the intercession of their Prophet will only be by the permission (*Izn*) of God at the *last day*, and that there is no intercession for sins until the Day of Judgment. The teaching of the Qur'ān and the Traditions seems to be in favour of this view.

Sūrah ii. 256: "Who is he that can intercede with Him but by His own permission?"

Sūrah xix. 90: "None shall meet (in the Day of Judgment) with intercession save he who hath entered into covenant with the God of mercy."

Sūrah xx. 108: "No intercession shall avail on that day, save his whom the Merciful shall allow, and whose words He shall approve."

Sūrah xxxiv. 22: "No intercession shall avail with him but that which He Himself alloweth."

Sūrah xxxix. 45: "Intercession is wholly with God."

Sūrah lxxviii. 38: "On the day whereon the spirit (*Rūḥ*) and the angels shall stand ranged in order they shall not utter a word, save he whom the God of mercy permits, and who shall say what is right."

The statements of Muḥammad, as contained in the Traditions, are as follows:—

"He is most fortunate in my intercession in the Day of Judgment, who shall have said from his heart, without any mixture of hypocrisy, 'There is no deity but God.'"

"I will intercede for those who shall have committed great sins."

"Three classes will intercede on the Day of Judgment, the Prophets, the Learned, the Martyrs." (*Mishkāt*, book xxxiii. ch. xii.)

The author of the *Sharḥ-i-Muwāqif* says (p. 588): According to the Sunnīs, the intercession of Muḥammad is specially for those who have committed great sins (*ahlu 'l-kabā'ir*), for the purpose of removing punishment; for Muḥammad has said, "My intercession is for those who have committed great sins." But the Mu'tazilahs say the intercession of Muḥammad is for the increase of merit, and not for the prevention of punishment; for it is said in the Qur'ān, Sūrah ii. 45: "Fear the day wherein no soul shall pay recompense for another soul. Nor shall intercession be accepted for it, nor shall compensation be taken from it, nor shall they be helped."

INTERMEDIATE STATE. The state of the soul between the time of death and the resurrection is generally expressed by the term *'Ālam-i-Barzakh*, for an explanation of which refer to the article BARZAKH Ṣūfī writers use the term *'Ālam-i-Arwāḥ*, "The world of spirits."

From the Traditions it would appear that Muḥammad taught that the intermediate state is not one of unconsciousness. To the wicked it is certainly not; but inasmuch as the Muslim is encouraged to "*sleep like the bridegroom*," it may be inferred that the intermediate state of the Muslim is held to be one of absolute repose." [PUNISHMENTS OF THE GRAVE.]

INZĀR (انظار). Listening or lending an ear to the bankrupt's statement or petition.

INZI'ĀJ (انزعاج). *Lit.* "Being disturbed and moved from its place." A term used by the Ṣūfī mystics for the movement and excitement of the heart in the direction of God, through the effect either of a sermon, or of music and singing. ('Abdu 'r-Razzāq's *Dict. of Ṣūfī Terms.*)

IQĀLAH (اقالة). "Cancelling." In law, the cancelling or dissolution of sale, or any other contract.

IQĀMAH (اقامة). *Lit.* "Causing to stand." A recitation at the commencement of the stated prayers when said in a congregation, after the worshippers have taken up their position. It is the same as the I'zān, with the addition of the sentence, "Verily prayers are now ready" (*Qad qāmati 'ṣ-ṣalāt*). The sentences are, however, recited singly by all the sects except the Ḥanafīs who give it exactly as the I'zān. It is not recited by the Imām, but by the person who stands behind him, who is called the *Muqtadī*, or "follower." In large mosques it is usual for the *Mu'azzin*, or caller to prayer, to take this office. But in his absence the person who happens to be behind the Imām recites the *Iqāmah*. [IMAM.]

IQRĀR (اقرار). Acknowledgment; confession.

(1) A legal term used for the avowal of the right of another upon one's self in sales, contracts, and divorce. (2) A theological term used for a confession of the Muslim faith, or a confession of sin. (3) *Iqrār-nāmah*, a legal deed of acknowledgment. (4) *Iqrār-nāmah ṣalāṣī*, a deed of arbitration by a third party. (5) *Iqrāru 'l-aṣām*, a confession of guilt by a prisoner. (6) *Iqrār 'āmm*, a public acknowledgment.

IQTIZĀ (اقتضاء). *Lit.* "Demanding." A term used in the exegesis of the Qur'ān for sentences which demand certain conditions, *e.g.* Sūrah iv. 94: "Whoso killeth a Mu'min (a believer) by mischance shall be bound to free a slave." Here the condition demanded is that the slave shall be the property of the person who frees him, and if he have not a slave to free, then some other expiation is required.

IRĀDAH (ارادة). Purpose, will, intention. (1) A word used for the intention, or will of man. (2) *Irādatu 'llah*, the will of God. (3) According to the Ṣūfī mystics, it is "a flame of love in the heart which desires God and longs to be united with Him. ('Abdu 'r-Razzāq's *Dict. of Ṣūfī Terms.*)

IRAM (ارم). A place mentioned in the Qur'ān, Sūrah lxxxix. 6: "Iram of the columns, the like of which has not been created in these lands."

It is related that ash-Shaddād, the son of 'Ād, ordered the construction of a terrestial paradise in the desert of 'Adan, ostensibly to rival the celestial one, and to be called Iram after his great grandfather. On going to take possession of it, he and all his people were struck dead by a noise from heaven, and the paradise disappeared.

AL-'IRĀQ (العراق). *Lit.* "A side, or shore." A country frequently mentioned in the Traditions, which extends from 'Abbadān to al-Mauṣil in length, and from al-Qādisīyah to Ḥalwān in breadth. Said to be so named because it was on the "shore" of the rivers Tigris and Euphrates. Its principal cities were al-Baṣrah and al-Kūfah, and were called *al-'Irāqān*, or the Two 'Irāqs.

'IRBĀN (عربان). Earnest-money paid in any legal transaction.

IRHAṢ (ارهاص). *Lit.* "Laying the Foundation." A term used for any wonder wrought in behalf of a Prophet before he assumes the prophetic office; for example, the existence of a light on the forehead of Muḥammad's ancestors is an *Irhāṣ*. (*Kitābu 't-Ta'rīfāt.*)

IRON. Arabic *al-Ḥadīd* (الحديد). The title of Sūrah lvii. in the Qur'ān, in the 25th verse of which it is said: "We (God) sent down *iron*, in which are both keen violence and advantages to men." Zamakhsharī says that Adam brought down with him from Paradise five things made of iron, viz. an anvil, a pair of tongs, two hammers, a greater and lesser, and a needle.

IRTIDĀD (ارتداد). [APOSTASY.]

'ĪSA (عيسى). The name given to Jesus in the Qur'ān and all Muḥammadan writings. [JESUS CHRIST.]

ISAAC. Arabic *Isḥāq* (اسحاق). The son of Abraham. He is mentioned in the Qur'ān as specially the child of promise, and a gift from God to Abraham; and also as an inspired prophet.

Sūrah xxi. 72: "And We (God) gave him (Abraham) *Isaac* and Jacob as a farther gift; and we made them all righteous."

Sūrah xix. 50:

"And when he had separated himself from them and that which they worshipped beside God, we bestowed on him *Isaac* and Jacob; and each of them we made a prophet.

"And we bestowed gifts on them in our mercy, and gave them the lofty tongue of truth."

The birth of Isaac as a child of promise to Abraham is related in Sūrah xi. 72–77:—

"And our messengers came formerly to Abraham with glad tidings. 'Peace,' said they. He said, 'Peace,' and he tarried not, but brought a roasted calf.

"And when he saw that their hands touched it not, he misliked them, and grew fearful of them. They said, 'Fear not, for we are sent to the people of Lot.'

"His wife was standing by and laughed; and we announced *Isaac* to her; and after *Isaac*, Jacob.

"She said, 'Ah, woe is me! shall I bear a son when I am old, and when this my husband is an old man? This truly would be a marvellous thing.'

"They said, 'Marvellest thou at the command of God? God's mercy and blessing be upon you, O people of this house; praise and glory are His due?'

"And when Abraham's fear had passed away, and these glad tidings had reached him, he pleaded with us for the people of Lot. Verily, Abraham was right kind, pitiful, relenting."

Abraham's willingness to offer up his son is told in the Qur'ān, and from the text there would seem little doubt but Isaac was intended, although al-Baiẓāwī and many commentators declare it was Ishmael. The account runs thus (Sūrah xxxvii. 97–113):—

"And he said, 'Verily, I repair to my Lord who will guide me.

"'O Lord give me *a son*, of the righteous.'

"We announced to him a youth of meekness.

"And when he became a full-grown youth,

"His father said to him, 'My son, I have seen in a dream that I should sacrifice thee; therefore, consider what thou seest *right*.'

"He said, 'My father, do what thou art bidden; of the patient, if God please, shalt thou find me.'

"And when they had surrendered them to the will of God, he laid him down upon his forehead.

"We cried unto him, 'O Abraham!

"'Now hast thou satisfied the vision. See how we recompense the righteous.

"This was indeed a decisive test.

"And we ransomed his *son* with a costly victim,

"And we left this for him among posterity,

"'PEACE BE ON ABRAHAM!'

"Thus do we reward the well-doers,

"For he was of our believing servants.

"And we announced Isaac to him—a righteous prophet—

"And on him and on Isaac we bestowed our blessing. And among their offspring were well-doers, and others, to their own hurt undoubted sinners."

The feast of sacrifice, the 'Īdu 'l-Aẓḥā, is said to have been instituted in commemoration of this event. ['IDU 'L-AZHA.]

Syud Ahmad Khan Bahadur, in his *Essays on Arabia*, remarks that learned Muḥammadan theologians distinctly say it was Isaac and not Ishmael who was to have been offered up; but our researches scarcely confirm the learned Syud's statement. Ismā'īl al-Bukhārī, no mean authority, says it was Ishmael, and so does al-Baiẓāwī.

The weight of traditional authority seems to be in favour of Isaac, and so does the text of the Qur'ān, which we have explained in the account of Ishmael; and yet amongst both the Sunnīs and the Shī'ahs the opinion is now almost universal that it was Ishmael. [ISHMAEL.]

ISAIAH. Arabic *Sha'yā'* (شعياء). The name is not mentioned in the Qur'ān, but al-Baiẓāwī, the commentator, in remarking on Sūratu 'l-Mi'rāj, xvii. 4:—"We decreed to the children of Isrā'īl in the Book, 'Ye shall verily do evil in the earth twice,'"—says the *two sins* committed by the Israelites were first the murder of Sha'yā ibn Amsiyā (*i.e.* Isaiah, son of Amoz) or Armiyā (*i.e.* Jeremiah); and the second, the murder of Zakariā and John the Baptist, and the intention of killing Jesus.

I'ṢĀR (ايثار). Honouring another above oneself. Thinking of another's gain rather than one's own. The highest form of human friendship.

'ISHĀ' (عشاء). The Night Prayer. The liturgical prayer recited after the night has well set in. [PRAYER.]

ISḤĀQ (اسحاق). [ISAAC.]

ISḤĀQĪYAH (اسحاقية). A Shī'ah sect founded by a person named Isḥāq, who held that the Spirit of God existed in the Khalīfah 'Alī.

ISHĀRATU 'L-MALAK (اشارة الملك). [INSPIRATION.]

ISHMAEL. Arabic *Ismā'īl* (اسماعيل). The eldest son of Abraham, by his "*wife*" Hagar. [HAJAR].

(1) The progenitor of the Arabian race, and, according to the Qur'ān, an inspired prophet. Sūrah xix. 55:—

"And commemorate *Ishmael* in 'the Book;' for he was true to his promise, and was an Apostle, a prophet;

"And he enjoined prayer and almsgiving on his people, and was well-pleasing to his Lord."

(2) Said to have assisted his father in the construction of the Ka'bah. Sūrah ii. 119, 121:—

"And remember when we appointed the Holy House as man's resort and safe retreat, and said, 'Take ye the station of Abraham for a place of prayer.' And we commanded Abraham and *Ishmael*, 'Purify my house for those who shall go in procession round it, and those who shall abide there for devotion, and those who shall bow down and prostrate themselves.'

* * * * *

"And when Abraham, with *Ishmael*, raised the foundations of the House, *they said*, 'O our Lord! accept *it* from us; for Thou art the Hearer, the Knower.'"

(3) Also mentioned in six other places.

Sūrah ii. 134: "Do ye say that Abraham and *Ishmael*, and Isaac and Jacob, and the Tribes were Jews, or Christians?"

Sūrah iii. 78: "And what was revealed to Abraham and *Ishmael* and Isaac and Jacob and the Tribes."

Sūrah iv. 161: "And we inspired Abraham and *Ishmael*, and Jacob and the Tribes."

Sūrah vi. 86: "And *Ishmael* and Elisha, and Jonah, and Lot."

Sūrah xxi. 85: "And *Ishmael*, and Idrīs, and Zu 'l-Kifl, all these were of the patient."

Sūrah xxxviii. 48: "And remember *Ishmael*, and Elisha, and Zū 'l-Kifl, for each was righteous."

(4) According to the Old Testament, Ishmael had twelve sons, and Muḥammadan tradition also agrees with this:—

Genesis xxv. 12: "Now these are the generations of Ishmael, Abraham's son, whom Hagar the Egyptian, Sarah's handmaid, bare unto Abraham. And these are the names of the sons of Ishmael, according to their generations: the first-born of Ishmael, Nebajoth; and Kedar, and Adbeel, and Mibsam, and Mishma, and Dumah, and Massa, and Hadar, and Tema, and Jetur, and Naphish, and Kedemah. These are the sons of Ishmael, and these are their names by their castles, twelve princes according to their nations."

The names of these sons of Ishmael can still be distinguished amongst the tribes, the names of which occur in Muḥammadan history: Nebajoth (*Nabayuṣ*), the founder of the Nabathean nation, who succeeded the Idumeans in Arabia, and were an important people in Northern Arabia. Kedar (*Qaidar*) was also a famous tribe, so famous that the Badawīs of the desert applied the name to all Jews. Dumah is still preserved in the name Dūmatu 'l-Jandal. Tema corresponds with Taimah, and Jetur with the Jadūr of modern Arabia. Muḥammad is said to have been descended from Ishmael's second son Kedar (Qaidar), through one named 'Adnān. The period between 'Adnān and Ishmael is doubtful. Some reckon forty generations, others only four. Umm Salmah, one of the Prophet's wives, said 'Adnān was the son of 'Adad, the son of Humaisa, son of Nabat, son of Ishmael. (See *Abū 'l-Fidā'*, p. 62.) Muslim historians, however, admit that the pedigree of Muḥammad beyond 'Adnān is uncertain; but they are unanimous in tracing his descent to 'Adnān in the following line: (1) Muḥammad, (2) 'Abdu 'llāh, (3) Abū Muṭṭalib, (4) Hāshim, (5) 'Abdu Manāf, (6) Quṣaiy, (7) Kilāb, (8) Murrah, (9) Ka'b, (10) Luwaiy, (11) Ghālib, (12) Fihr, (13) Mālik, (14) An-Naẓr, (15) Kinānah, (16) Khuzaimah, (17) Mudrikah, (18) Al-Ya's, (19) Muẓar, (20) Nizār, (21) Ma'add, (22) 'Adnān.

Syud Ahmad Khan Bahadur, traces the descent of Muḥammad to Kedar, the son of Ishmael, and the view is one in accordance with that of most Muslim writers. In the time of Isaiah the two chief Arabian tribes seem to have been the descendants of Nebajoth and Kedar. (See Isaiah lx. 7.) "All the flocks of Kedar shall be gathered unto thee, the rams of Nebajoth shall minister unto thee."

(5) The account of Hagar leaving Abraham's home is given in numerous traditions. But there are two traditions given by Ibn 'Abbās, and recorded in the *Ṣaḥīḥ* of al-Bukhārī, which are the foundation of Muḥammadan history on the subject. We give them as they have been translated by Syud Ahmad Khan, and afterwards append the Scripture narrative, which can be compared with the traditions of Islām:—

Tradition I.

For reasons known only to Abraham and his wife, Sarah, the former took Ishmael, his son, and the boy's mother (Hagar), and left his country.

And they had with them a skin full of water.

Ishmael's mother drank from out the skin, suckling her child.

Upon her arriving at the place where Mecca now stands, she placed the child under a bush.

Then Abraham returned to come back to his wife, and the mother of Ishmael followed him,

Until she reached Keda.

And she called out, "O Abraham, with whom leavest thou me?"

He answered, "With God."

She replied, "I am satisfied with my God."

Then she returned, and commenced drinking out of the skin, and suckled her infant until the water was consumed.

And she thought that if she went and looked around, she might, perhaps, see someone; and she went.

She ascended Mount Safā, and looked around to see whether or not there was anyone in sight; then hastily returning through the wilderness, she ascended the mountain of Marvā.

Then she said, "I must now go and see how my child is." And she went, and saw that he was at the point of death; but not being able to compose her mind, she said, "If I go and look around, peradventure I may see someone." And accordingly she ascended the mountain of Safā, but could descry no one.

And this she repeated seven times.

She then said, "It will be better for me to go and see my child." But she suddenly heard a voice.

And she replied, "Kindly assist me, if you have any compassion"

The angel was Gabriel.

The narrator of the tradition, stamping the earth with his foot, said, this was exactly what the angel did, and that water issued from the spot; and she began to widen the hole.

It is related by Ibn 'Abbās, that the Prophet said that had she (Hagar) allowed the water to remain in its former state, the water would then have continued issuing forth for ever.

She used to drink that water and suckle her child.

Tradition II.

Abraham brought with him his wife (Hagar) and his son (Ishmael),

Whom she (Hagar) suckled.

And they both placed the child close by the spot where the Kaaba now stands under a bush.

Near the well of Zamzem, near the lofty side of the temple—and in those days Mecca was uninhabited and without water—and they deposited the child in the above place.

And Abraham placed beside them a bag full of dates,

And a skin full of water.

Then returned Abraham, and Ishmael's mother ran after him,

And said, "Abraham, whither goest thou, and wherefore leavest thou me here?

"In this wilderness, where there is no one to pity me, neither is there anything to eat?" This she repeated several times, but Abraham hearkened not unto her. Then she asked him, "Has God commanded thee to do this?"

He answered, "Yes."

"Then," said she, "God will cause no harm to come unto me."

Thereupon she returned back.

And Abraham went away, and when he reached Saneoa, he could not see those he had left behind him.

Then he turned towards Mecca, and prayed thus: "O Lord, I have caused some of my offspring to settle in an unfruitful valley, near thy holy house, O Lord, that they may be constant in prayer. Grant, therefore, that the hearts of some men may be affected with kindness towards them; and do thou bestow on them all sorts of fruits, that they may give thanks."

And the mother of Ishmael began to suckle her child, and to drink water out of the skin until it was emptied,

And she and her son felt thirsty. And when she saw that her child was suffering from thirst, she could not bear to see it in such a plight, and retired, and reached the mountain of Safā, that was near, and ascending it, looked at the plain, in the hope of seeing someone; but, not perceiving anyone, she came down from the mountain.

When she reached the desert, she girded up her loins and ran as one mad, until she crossed the desert, and ascended Mount Marvā; but she could not see anyone.

She repeated the same seven times.

It is related by Ibn 'Abbās, that the Prophet said that this was the origin of the custom of true believers running between these mountains during the Haj.

And when she ascended the Marvā mountain, she heard a voice.

She was startled thereat; and upon hearing it again, she said, "Wherefore callest thou on me? Assist me if thou canst."

She then saw an angel near the Zamzem.

He (the angel) made a hollow place, either by his foot or with his wing, and the water issued forth; and the mother of Ishmael commenced widening it.

She filled the skin with water, which came out of it as from a fountain.

It is related by Ibn 'Abbās that the Prophet said, "May God bless the mother of Ishmael. Had she left the Zamzem as it was, or had she not filled her skin with water, then the Zamzem would always have remained an overflowing fountain."

Then she drank the water, and suckled her child.

The account as given in the Bible, Genesis xxii. 9, is as follows:—

"And Sarah saw the son of Hagar the Egyptian, which she had borne unto Abraham, mocking. Wherefore she said unto Abraham, Cast out this bondwoman and her son; for the son of this bondwoman shall not he heir with my son, even with Isaac. And this thing was very grievous in Abraham's sight, because of his son. And God said unto Abraham, Let it not be grievous in thy sight because of the lad, and because of thy bondwoman; in all that Sarah hath said unto thee, hearken unto her voice; for in Isaac shall thy seed be called. And also of the son of the bondwoman will I make a nation, because he is thy seed. And Abraham rose up early in the morning, and took bread, and a bottle of water, and gave it unto Hagar, putting it on her shoulder, and the child, and sent her away; and she departed, and wandered in the wilderness of Beersheba. And the water was spent in the bottle, and she cast the child under one of the shrubs. And she went, and set her down over against him a good way off, as it were a bow shot; for she said, Let me not see the death of the child. And she sat over against him, and lifted up her voice, and wept. And God heard the voice of the lad, and the angel of God called to Hagar out of heaven, and said unto her,

What aileth thee, Hagar? Fear not; for God hath heard the voice of the lad where he is. Arise, lift up the lad, and hold him in thine hand, for I will make him a great nation. And God opened her eyes, and she saw a well of water; and she went, and filled the bottle with water, and gave the lad drink. And God was with the lad; and he grew, and dwelt in the wilderness, and became an archer. And he dwelt in the wilderness of Paran; and his mother took him a wife out of the land of Egypt."

With reference to the above account, as given in Holy Scripture, Syud Ahmad Khān remarks:—

"Notwithstanding the perfect coincidence of the facts taken from the Scriptures with those from the Koran, as above shown, there are, nevertheless, three very important questions which suggest themselves respecting Ishmael's settlement.

"First. Where did Abraham leave Ishmael and his mother after expelling them from his home?

"Secondly. Where did Ishmael and Hagar settle after their wanderings in the desert?

"Thirdly. Was it in the very spot where they had rested for the first time, or in some other place?

"The Koran mentions nothing on the subject; but there are some local traditions, and also a few Hadeeses, which treat of it, the latter, however, by reason of their not possessing sufficient authority, and from their not being traced up to the Prophet, are as little to be relied on as the former. The local traditions being deemed unworthy of credit, from their mixing up together occurrences that had happened on various and different occasions, we do not think it necessary to dwell on the first question more than has been done by the Scriptures themselves, which say that 'He (Abraham) sent her (Hagar) away; and she departed, and wandered in the wilderness of Beersheba.'

"As for the two remaining questions, although the language of Scripture is not very clear—since, in one place it says, 'And he (Ishmael) grew, and dwelt in the wilderness, and became an archer' (Gen. xxi. 20), and in another, 'He (Ishmael) dwelt in the wilderness of Paran' (Gen. xxi. 21), passages which would certainly lead us to infer that Ishmael had changed the place of his abode; yet, as no Christian commentator represents him as having removed from one place to another, and as, moreover, neither the religious nor the local traditions of the Mohammedans in any way confirm the above, it may be safely asserted that Ishmael and his mother did not change the place where they dwelt, and that by the word 'wilderness' alone the sacred writer meant the wilderness of Paran. The solving of the whole question depends, therefore, upon ascertaining and fixing the position of the said wilderness of Paran, where Ishmael is said to have settled.

"Oriental geographers mention three places as known by the appellation of Paran. First, that wilderness wherein the city of Mecca now stands, and the mountains in its vicinity; secondly, those mountains and a village which are situated in Eastern Egypt, or Arabia Petræa; and thirdly, a district in the province of Samarcand."

(6) Al-Baiẓāwī says it was Ishmael, and not Isaac, whom Abraham was willing to offer up as a sacrifice; but this view is neither supported by the text of the Qur'ān nor by the preponderance of traditional testimony. If we compare Sūrah xi. 74: "And We announced Isaac (as the child of promise) to her," with Sūrah xxxvii. 99: "We announced (as a child of promise) to him a youth of meekness; and when he became a full-grown youth, his father said to him, 'My son, I have seen in a dream that I should sacrifice thee'"—there can be no doubt in any candid mind that, as far as the Qur'ān is concerned, Isaac and not Ishmael is intended. [ISAAC.]

The two commentators al-Kamālān quote a number of traditions on the subject. They say Ibn 'Umar, Ibn 'Abbās, Ḥasan, and 'Abdu 'llāh ibn Aḥmad, relate that it was Isaac; whilst Ibn Mas'ūd, Mujāhid, 'Ikrimah, Qatādah, and Ibn Isḥāq say it was Ishmael. But whatever may be the real facts of the case, it is certain that popular tradition amongst both Sunnīs and Shī'ahs assigns the honour to Ishmael, and believe the great Festival of Sacrifice, the 'Īdu 'l-Aẓḥa, to have been established to commemorate the event. ['IDU 'L-AZHA.]

The author of the Shī'ah work, the *Ḥayātu 'l-Qulūb* (Merrick's ed. p. 28) says: "On a certain occasion when this illustrious father (Abraham) was performing the rites of the pilgrimage at Mecca, Abraham said to his beloved child, 'I dreamed that I must sacrifice you; now consider what is to be done with reference to such an admonition.' Ishmael replied, 'Do as you shall be commanded of God. Verify your dream. You will find me endure patiently.' But when Abraham was about to sacrifice Ishmael, the Most High God made a black and white sheep his substitute, a sheep which had been pasturing forty years in Paradise, and was created by the direct power of God for this event. Now every sheep offered on Mount Minā, until the Day of Judgment is a substitute, or a commemoration of the substitute for Ishmael."

The idea is universal amongst Muḥammadans that the incident took place on Mount Minā near Makkah, and not in the "land of Moriah," as stated in Genesis xxii. 3. (For a discussion on the site of Mount Moriah, see Mr. George Grove's article in Smith's *Dict. of the Bible.*)

Sir William Muir says (*Life of Mahomet*, new ed. p. xvii.): "By a summary adjustment, the story of Palestine became the story of the Hejâz. The precincts of the Káaba were hallowed as the scene of Hagar's distress, and the sacred well Zamzem as the source of her relief. The pilgrims hasted to and fro between Safa and Marwa in memory of her hurried steps in search of water. It was Abraham and Ishmael who built the (Meccan) temple, placed in it the black stone, and established for all mankind the pilgrimage to Arafât. In imitation of him it was that stones were flung by pilgrims at Satan; and sacrifices were offered at Minâ in remembrance of the vicarious sacrifice by Abraham instead of his son. And thus, although the indigenous rites may have been little if at all altered, by the adoption of the Abrahamic legends, they came to be viewed in a totally different light, and to be connected in the Arab imagination with something of the sanctity of Abraham, the Friend of God. The gulf between the gross idolatry of Arabia and the pure theism of the Jews was bridged over. Upon this common ground Mahomet took his stand, and proclaimed to his people a new and a spiritual system, in accents to which all Arabia could respond. The rites of the Káaba were retained, but stripped by him of every idolatrous tendency; and they still hang, a strange unmeaning shroud, around the living theism of Islâm."

'ISHQ (عشق). "Love." A word used by mystic writers to express a divine love. The word, however, preferred by orthodox Muslim writers for the love of God, or love to God, is *hubb* (حب).

ISLĀM (اسلام). Resignation to the will of God. The word generally used by Muḥammadans themselves for their religion. 'Abdu 'l-Ḥaqq says it implies submission to the divine will; and Muḥammad explained it to mean the observance of the five duties: (1) Bearing witness that there is but one God; (2) Reciting the daily prayers; (3) Giving the legal alms; (4) Observing the Ramaẓān or month's fast; (5) Making the pilgrimage to Makkah once in a lifetime.

In the Qur'ān the word is used for doing homage to God. Islām is said to be the religion of all the prophets from the time of Abraham, as will appear from the following verses (Sūrah iii. 78, 79):—"SAY: We believe in God and in what hath been sent down to Abraham, and Ishmael, and Isaac, and Jacob, and the Tribes, and in what was given to Moses, and Jesus and the Prophets from their Lord. We make no difference between them, and to Him are we resigned (*i.e.* Muslims). Whoso desireth any other religion than Islām, that religion shall never be accepted of Him, and in the next world he shall be lost."

There are three words used by Muḥammadan writers for religion, namely *Dīn*, *Millah*, and *Maẕhab*; and in the *Kitābu 't-Ta'rīfāt*, the difference implied in these words is said to be as follows:—*Dīn*, as it stands in its relation to God, *e.g. Dīnu 'llāh*, the religion of God; *Millah*, as it stands in relation to a prophet or lawgiver, *e.g. Millatu Ibrahīm*, the religion of Abraham; and *Maẕhab*, as it stands in relation to the divines of Islām, *e.g. Maẕhab Ḥanafī*, the religion or religious teaching of Abu Ḥanīfah. The expression *Dīn*, however, is of general application. [RELIGION.]

Those who profess the religion of Islām are called Musalmāns, Muslims, or Mu'mins.

Ahlu 'l-Kitāb, "the people of the Book," is used for Muḥammadans, Jews, and Christians.

IS̱M (اثم). A sin; anything forbidden by the law.

'IṢMAH (عصمة). *Lit.* "Keeping back from sin." The continence and freedom from sin which Muḥammadans say was the state of each Prophet, and which is that of nfant children.

ISMĀ'ĪL (اسماعيل). [ISHMAEL.]

ISMĀ'ĪL (اسمائيل). The name of the angel who is said to have accompanied the angel Gabriel in his last visit to the Prophet on his death-bed. He is said to command one hundred thousand angels. (*Mishkāt*, book xxiv. ch. x. pt. 3.)

ISMĀ'ĪLĪYAH (اسماعيلية). A Shī'ah sect who said that Ismā'īl ibn Ja'far aṣ-Ṣādiq was the true Imām and not Mūsā al-Kāẓim, and who held that God was neither existent nor non-existent, nor intelligent nor unintelligent, nor powerful nor helpless, &c.; for, they said, it is not possible for any thing or attribute to be associated with God, for He is the maker of all things, even of names and attributes. (*Kitābu 't-Ta'rīfāt, in loco.*)

ISM-I-JALĀLĪ (اسم جلالى). Any of the attributes of God which express His power and greatness, *e.g. al-Ḥākim*, the Judge; *al-Ādil*, the Just; *al-Kabīr*, the Great. [GOD.]

ISM-I-JAMĀLĪ (اسم جمالى). Any of the attributes of God which express His mercy or condescension, *e.g. ar-Raḥīm*, the Compassionate; *as-Samī'*, the Hearer; *al-Ḥāfiẓ*, the Guardian.

ISM-I-ṢIFAH (اسم صفة). Name of a divine attribute.

AL-ISMU 'L-A'ẒAM (الاسم الاعظم). The exalted name of God, which is generally believed to be known only to the Prophets. Muḥammad is related to have said that it occurs in either the Sūratu 'l-Baqarah, ii. 256: "God (Allah) there is no God but He (*Hū*), the Living (*al-Ḥaiy*), the Self-subsistent (*al-Qaiyūm*)"; or in the Sūratu 'Āli 'Imrān, iii. 1, which contains the same words; or in the Suratu Ṭā Hā, xx. 110: "Faces shall be humbled before the Living (*al-Ḥaiy*) and the Self-subsistent (*al-Qaiyūm*)."

It is therefore generally held to be either *Allah*, or *Hū*, or *al-Ḥaiy*, or *al-Qaiyūm*

It is very probable that the mysterious title of the Divine Being refers to the great name of Jehovah, the superstitious reverence for which on the part of the Jews must have been well known to Muḥammad.

ISMU 'Ẕ-ẔĀT (اسم الذات). Name of the Divine Essence; the essential name of God, *i.e.* Allāh, or *Hū*, as distinguished from His attributes. [ALLAH.]

IS̱NĀ-'ISHARĪYAH (اثناعشرية). *Lit.* "The twelve eans." Those Shī'ahs who acknowledge the twelve Imāms. [SHI'AH.]

ISQĀṬ (اسقاط). [ABORTION.]

ISRĀ (اسرای). [MI'RAJ.]

ISRAEL. Arabic *Isrā'īl* (اسرائيل). The surname of Ya'qūb (Jacob). Al-Baiẓāwī says the meaning of Isrā'īl in Hebrew is *Ṣufwatu 'llāh, i.e.* "the sincere friend of God"; or, as some say, *'Abdu 'llāh*, "the servant of God. *Banū Isrā'īl*, "the children of Israel," is a term that frequently occurs in the Qur'ān. The XVIIth chapter of the Qur'ān, known as the *Sūratu 'l-Mi'rāj*, is also called the *Sūratu Banī Isrā'īl.*

ISRĀF (اسراف). *Lit.* "Wasting." Extravagance in religious duties, *i.e.* doing more than is required by the law.

ISRĀFĪL (اسرافيل). The Archangel who will sound the trumpet at the Day of Resurrection. His name, however, does not occur in either the Qur'ān, or the Traditions.

IṢRĀR (اصرار). A word used by the Arabs for a horse pricking up his ears, and not obeying the rein. A term in Muḥammadan theology for persisting in any sin, and being determined to commit the sin in future.

ISSUE OF BLOOD. Arabic *Istiḥāẓah* (استحاضة). [MUSTAHAZAH.]

ISTI'ĀNAH (استعانة). *Lit.* "Seeking aid." Imploring help from God. The word occurs in the Sūratu 'l-Fātiḥah, or the first chapter of the Qur'ān, which is part of the liturgical prayer: واياك نستعين *wa-iyāka nasta'īn*, "Of Thee only do we seek help."

ISTIBRA' (استبراء). The purification of the womb. The period of probation, of one menses, to be observed after the purchase of a female slave (or in the case of a virgin under age), the period of one month before she is taken to her master's bed.

ISTIBṢĀR (استبصار). A Book of Muḥammadan traditions, received by the Shī'ahs, compiled by Shaikh Naṣiru 'd-Dīn Abū Ja'far Muḥammad aṭ-Ṭūsī, A.H. 672.

ISTIDLĀL (استدلال). A term used in the science of exegesis for those sentences which require certain proofs. [QUR'AN.]

ISTIDRĀJ (استدراج). *Lit.* "Promoting by degrees, step by step." The word occurs in the Qur'ān for an unbeliever being brought by degrees to hell and destruction.

Sūrah vii. 181: "They who say our signs are lies, We (God) will bring them down *step by step* from whence they know not."

Sūrah lxviii. 44: "We (God) will surely bring them down *step by step* from whence they do not know, and I (God) will let them have their way; for My device is sure."

(In this verse the sudden transition from the first person plural to the first person singular, for the Almighty, is peculiar; it is, however, of frequent occurrence in the Qur'ān.)

ISTIGHFĀR (استغفار). Seeking forgiveness of God. It is related of Muḥammad that he said:—

"I swear by God that I ask pardon of God, and repent before Him more than seventy times daily.

"O men, repent and turn to God, for verily I repent before Him one hundred times a day." (*Mishkāt*, book x. ch. iii.)

ISTIḤĀẒAH (استحاضة). The issue of blood of women; during which time they are ceremonially unclean. (*Vide Mishkāt*, book iii. ch. xvi.)

ISTIḤSĀN (استحسان). *Lit.* "Approving." A term used in the exegesis of the Qur'ān and of the Ḥadīs̤. It implies the rejection of Qiyāṣ [QIYAS], and the admission of the law of expediency.

For example, it is a law of Islām that everything that is washed must be squeezed like a cloth; but, as it is impossible to squeeze a vessel, it is evident that it must be cleansed without squeezing. (*Nūru 'l-Anwār*, p. 208.)

ISTIKHĀRAH (استخارة). *Lit.* "Asking favours." A prayer for special favours and blessings, consisting of the recital of two *rak'ah* prayers. (*Mishkāt*, book iv. ch. xl.)

Jābir says: "The Prophet taught the *Istikhārah*, as he also did a chapter of the Qur'ān; and he said, 'When anyone of you intends doing a thing, he must perform two *rak'ah* prayers expressly for *Istikhārah*, and afterwards recite the following supplication: O God, I supplicate Thy help, in Thy great wisdom; and I pray for ability through Thy power. I ask a thing of Thy bounty. Thou knowest all, but I do not. Thou art powerful, and I am not. Thou knowest the secrets of men. O God! if the matter I am about to undertake is good for my faith, my life, and my futurity, then make it easy for me, and give me success in it. But if it is bad for my faith, my life, and my futurity, then put it away from me, and show me what is good, and satisfy me. And the person praying shall mention in his prayer the business which he has in hand.'"

This very simple and commendable injunction has, however, been perverted to superstitious uses.

Mr. Lane, in his *Modern Egyptians*, says:—

"Some persons have recourse to the Qur'ān for an answer to their doubts. This they call making an "*istikhárah*," or application for the favour of Heaven, or for direction in the right course. Repeating three times the opening chapter, the 112th chapter, and the fifty-eighth verse of the sixth chapter, they let the book fall open, or open it at random, and, from the seventh line of the right-hand page, draw their answer.

"The words often will not convey a direct answer, but are taken as affirmative or negative according as their general tenour is good or bad, promising a blessing, or denouncing a threat, &c. Instead of reading the seventh line of this page, some count the number of letters *kha* and *sheen* which occur in the whole page; and if the *kha's* predominate, the inference is favourable. *Kha* represents *kheyr*, or *good*; *sheen, shur*, or *evil*. There is another mode of *istikhárah*; which is, to take hold of any two points of a *sebhhah* (or rosary), after reciting the Fat'hhah three times, and then to count the beads between these two points, saying, in passing the first bead through the fingers, '[I assert] the absolute glory of God;' in passing the second, 'Praise be to God;' in passing the third, 'There is no deity but God;' and repeating these expressions in the same order, to the last bead. If the first expression fall to the last bead, the answer is affirmative and favourable; if the second, indifferent; if the last, negative. This is practised by many persons.

"Some, again, in similar cases, on lying down to sleep at night, beg of God to direct them by a dream; by causing them to see something white or green, or water, if the action which they contemplate be approved, or if they are to expect approaching good fortune; and if not, by causing them to see something black or red, or fire; they then recite the *Fat'hhah* ten times, and continue to repeat these words: 'O God, favour our lord Mohammad!' — until they fall asleep." (*Modern Egyptians*, vol. i. 338.)

Amongst pious Muslims in Asia it is usual to recite the two *rak'ah* prayers before retiring to rest, in the hope that God will reveal His will in a dream during the night.

ISTĪLĀD (استيلاد). Claim of offspring. A legal term signifying the act of a Muslim, having a child born to him of a female slave, which he acknowledges as his own, whereby the slave becomes free. (*Hidāyah*, vol. i. p. 478.)

IṢṬILĀḤ (اصطلاح), pl. *Iṣṭilāḥāt*. A phrase; a term; idiom. A theological term. The author of the *Kitābu 't-Ta'rīfāt* says it is the agreement of a tribe, or sect, or party, to give a special meaning to a word, over and above that which it has in its literal sense, but which is in accordance with it.

ISTINJĀ' (استنجاء). Abstersion; concerning which there are most minute instructions in the Traditions and in other books of Muslim divinity. Such acts of cleansing must be performed with the left hand, with not less than three handfuls of water, or with three of dry earth. (*Mishkāt*, book ii. 1.)

ISTINSHĀQ (استنشاق). The act of throwing water up into the nostrils, which is part of the religious ablution or *wazū*. [ABLUTION.]

ISTIQĀMAH (استقامة). *Lit.* "Standing erect." A term (1) used by the Ṣūfī mystics for rectitude of life, purity of life; (2) being constant in religion according to the rules of the Qur'ān.

ISTIQBĀL (استقبال). *Lit.* "Going forth to meet." (1) A custom amongst Orientals of going out to meet a friend or guest on his arrival; (2) turning the face towards Makkah for prayer; (3) a coming era or period; the future.

ISTIRJĀ' (استرجاع). *Lit.* "Returning." A term used for the act of appealing to God for help in the time of affliction by repeating the following ejaculation from the Qur'ān, Sūrah ii. 150: *Innā li'llāhi wa innā ilaihi raji'ūn*, "Verily, we belong to God, and verily we shall return to God." This formula is used by Muḥammadans in any danger or sudden calamity, especially in the presence of death.

ISTIṢḤĀB (استصحاب). A law or injunction contained in a previous revelation (*e.g.* the Law of Moses) and not abrogated by the succeeding law-giver.

ISTIṢNĀ' (استثناء). *Lit.* "Excepting or excluding." A term used for the custom of exclaiming, "If God will." It is in accordance with the injunctions of the Qur'ān, Sūrah xviii. 23: "And never say of anything, 'Verily, I am going to do that to-morrow,' without, 'If God will.'" (Compare James iv. 15: "For ye ought to say, If the Lord will.")

ISTISQĀ' (استسقاء). Prayers for rain, consisting of two *rak'ah* prayers. (*Mishkāt*, book iv. ch. liii.)

I'TAQ (اعتاق). *Lit.* "Setting free." The manumission of slaves. [SLAVERY.]

IṬFĪR (اطفير). [POTIPHAR.]

I'TIKĀF (اعتكاف). Seeking retirement in a mosque during the last ten days of the Fast of Ramaẓān; during which time the worshipper does not leave the place, except for necessary purposes. The time is spent in reciting the Qur'ān and in performing the ceremony of Ẕikr, or the recital of the names and praises of the Deity.

'ITQ (عتق). "Being free." In the language of the law it signifies the power given to a person by the extinction of bondage. Hence the emancipation of slaves. (*Hidāyah*, vol. i. p. 413.)

ITTIḤAD (اتحاد). Union; concord; intimate friendship. A term used by the Ṣūfī mystics for "seeing the existence of all things visible as only existing in God." ('Abdu 'r-Razzāq's *Dict. of Ṣūfī Terms.*)

IẒN (اذن). Permission. [INTERCESSION.]

'IZRĀ'ĪL (عزرائيل). The Angel of Death, or the *Malaku 'l-Maut*, who comes to a man at the hour of death to carry his soul away from the body. See Qur'ān, Sūrah xxxii. 11: "The *Angel of Death* shall take you away, he who is given charge of you. Then unto your Lord shall ye return."

Muḥammad is related to have said that when the Angel of Death approaches a believer he sits at his head and says, "O pure soul, come forth to God's pardon and pleasure!" And then the soul comes out as gently as water from a bag. But, in the case of an infidel, the Angel of Death sits at his head and says, "O impure soul, come forth to the wrath of God!" And then the Angel of Death draws it out as a hot spit is drawn out of wet wool. (*Mishkāt*, book v. ch. iii.)

J.

JABALU MŪSA (جبل موسى). The Mount of Moses; Mount Sinai. It is called in the Qur'ān, Sūrah ii. 60, *aṭ-Ṭūr*, "The Mountain."

AL-JABARĪYAH (الجبرية). *Lit.* "The Necessitarians." A sect of Muḥammadans who deny free agency in man.

They take their denomination from *Jabr*, which signifies "necessity or compulsion;" because they hold man to be necessarily and inevitably constrained to act as he does by force of God's eternal and immutable decree. This sect is distinguished into two species, some being more rigid and extreme in their opinion, who are thence called pure Jabarīyahs; and others, more moderate, who are therefore called middle Jabarīyahs. The former will not allow men to be said either to act, or to have any power at all, either operative or acquiring, asserting that man can do nothing, but produces all his actions by necessity, having neither power, nor will, nor choice, any more than an inanimate agent. They also declare that rewarding and punishing are also the effects of necessity; and the same they say of the imposing of commands. This was the doctrine of the Jahmīyahs, the followers of Jahm ibn Sufwān, who likewise held that Paradise and Hell will vanish, or be annihilated, after those who are destined thereto respectively shall have entered them, so that at last there will remain no existing being besides God, supposing those words of the Qur'ān which declare that the inhabitants of Paradise and of Hell shall remain therein for ever, to be hyperbolical only, and intended for corroboration, and not to denote an eternal duration in reality. The moderate Jabarīyahs are they who ascribe some power to man, but such a power as hath no influence on the action; for as to those who grant the power of man to have a certain influence on the action, which influence is called Acquisition, some will not admit them to be called Jabarīyahs, though others reckon those also to be called middle Jabarīyahs, and to contend for the middle opinion between absolute necessity and absolute liberty, who attribute to man acquisition, or concurrence, in producing the action, whereby he gaineth commendation or blame (yet without admitting it to have any influence on the action), and, therefore, make the Ashārians a branch of this sect. (Sale's *Koran*, Introd.)

JABARŪT (جبروت). The possession of power, of omnipotence. One of the mystic stages of the Ṣūfī. [SUFIISM.]

JABBAR (جبار). Omnipotent; an absolute sovereign. *Al-Jabbār*, "The Absolute." One of the ninety-nine names or attributes of God.

Sūrah lix. 23: "The King, the Holy, the Peaceful, the Faithful, the Protector, the Mighty, *the Absolute*, the Great.

JABĪL (جبيل). The Angel of the Mountains; mentioned in the Shi'ah work, *Ḥayātu 'l-Qulūb*. (Merrick's ed. p. 128.)

JĀBIR (جابر). The son of a poor citizen of al-Madīnah, slain at Uḥud. He embraced Islām and accompanied Muḥammad in numerous battles. He lived to a great age, for he died at al-Medīnah A.H. 78, aged 94 years.

JABR (جبر). A Christian servant of a family from Ḥaẓramaut—a convert to Islām—accused by the Quraish with having instructed the Prophet.

Sūrah xvi. 105: "We knew that they said, 'It is only some mortal that teaches him.' The tongue of him they incline towards is barbarous, this is plain Arabic."

Ḥusain says Jabr was one of the *Ahlu 'l-Kitāb*, and was well read in the *Taurāt* and *Injīl*, and Muḥammad used to hear him read these books as he passed by his house.

JACOB. Arabic *Ya'qūb* (يعقوب). The son of Isaac; an inspired prophet. There are frequent but brief allusions to the Patriarch Jacob in the Qur'ān in connection with Abraham and Isaac. The story of his journey to Egypt will be found in the account of Joseph as given in the XIIth Sūrah of the Qur'ān. [JOSEPH.]

A brief reference to his death is made in Sūrah ii. ch. 127:—

"Were ye present when Jacob was at the point of death? when he said to his sons, 'Whom will ye worship when I am gone?' They said, 'We will worship thy God and the God of thy fathers Abraham and Ismael and Isaac, one God, and to Him are we surrendered (Muslims).' That people have now passed away; they have the reward of their deeds and ye shall have the meed of yours: but of their doings ye shall not be questioned. They say, moreover, 'Become Jews or Christians that ye may have the *true* guidance.' Say: Nay! the religion of Abraham, the sound in faith, and not one of those who join gods with God!"

JADD (جد). A term used in Muḥammadan law for either a paternal or a maternal grandfather. The word has also the meaning *greatness*, *majesty*, as in Sūrah lxxii. 3: "May the Majesty of our Lord be exalted." [GRANDFATHER.]

JA'FAR (جعفر). A son of Abū Ṭālib and a cousin to Muḥammad. He was a great friend to the poor, and was called by Muḥammad *Abū 'l-Masākīn*, "the father of the poor." He fell bravely at the battle of Mu'tah, A.H. 8.

JA'FARU 'Ṣ-ṢĀDIQ (جعفر الصادق). Abū 'Abdi'llah Ja'far ibn Muḥammad ibn 'Alī ibn al-Ḥusain ibn 'Alī ibn Abī Ṭālib, was one of the twelve persons who, according to the Shī'ahs, are considered the rightful Imāms [SHI'AH]. He was surnamed aṣ-Ṣādiq, "The Veracious," on account of his uprightness of character. He was a learned man, and his pupil, Abū Mūsā, is said to have composed a work of two thousand pages containing the problems of his master Ja'faru 'ṣ-Ṣādiq. Ja'far was born A.H 80, and died A.H. 148, and was buried in the cemetery al-Bakī' at al-Madīnah.

JĀGĪR (جاگير). Persian *Jā*, "A place;" *Gīr*, "Occupying." A tenure common under the Muḥammadan Government, in which the public revenues of a given tract of land were made over to a servant of the State, together with the powers requisite to enable him to collect and appropriate such revenue, and administer the general government of the district. The assignment was either conditional or unconditional; in the former case, some public service, as the levy and maintenance of troops, or other specified duty, was engaged for; the latter was left to the entire disposal of the grantee. The assignment was either for a stated term, or, more usually, for the lifetime of the holder, lapsing, on his death, to the State, although not unusually renewed to his heir, on payment of a *nazarāna* or fine, and sometimes specified to be a hereditary assignment, without which specification it was held to be a life-tenure only. (*Ben. Reg.* xxxvii. 1723, cl. 15.) A Jāgīr was also liable to forfeiture on failure of performance of the conditions on which it was granted, or on the holder's incurring the displeasure of the Emperor. On the other hand, in the inability of the State to vindicate its rights, a Jāgīr was sometimes converted into a perpetual and transferable estate; and the same consequence has resulted from the recognition of sundry Jāgīr as hereditary by the British Government after the extinction of the Native Governments by which they were originally granted; so that they have now come to be considered as family properties, of which the holders could not be rightfully dispossessed, and to which their legal heirs succeed, as a matter of course, without fine or *nazarāna*, such having been silently dispensed with. (Wilson's *Glossary of Indian Terms.*)

JAHANNAM (جهنم). [HELL.]

JAHL (جهل). "Ignorance." A term used by theologians for an ignorance of religious truths, which they say is of two kinds: *Jahl-i-Basīṭ*, simple ignorance; and *Jahl-i-Murakkab*, or complicated ignorance, or confirmed error.

JAIFAR (جيفر). A king of 'Umān to whom Muḥammad sent a despatch inviting him to Islām, which event led eventually to the conversion of that province.

"On his return from the siege of Tâyif, towards the close of the eighth year of the Hegira, Mahomet sent Amru with a despatch to Jeyfar, King of Omân, summoning him and his brother to make profession of the true faith. At first they gave answer 'that they would be the weakest among the Arabs, if they made another man possessor of their property.' But as Amru was about to depart, they repented, and, calling him back, embraced Islâm. The people followed their example, and without demur paid their tithes to Amru, who continued till the Prophet's death to be his representative in Omân." (Muir's *Life of Mahomet*, new ed. p. 471.)

JAIḤŪN (جيحون). The river Jihon, or Bactrus, said to be one of the rivers of Eden. [EDEN.]

JĀ'-I-NAMĀZ (جاى نماز). Persian. "The place of prayer." A term used in Asia for the small mat or carpet on which a Muslim prays. It is called in Arabic *Sujjādah* and *Muṣallā*.

The carpet is about five feet in length, and has a point or *Qiblah* worked in the pattern to mark the place for prostration.

A JA-I-NAMAZ, OR PRAYER CARPET, AS USED IN PESHAWAR.

JAIYID (جيد). Pure money; current coin. A term used in Muslim law. (*Hidāyah*, vol. iii. p. 152.)

JALĀL (جلال). Being glorious or mighty. *Ẕū 'l-Jalāl*, "The Glorious One," is an attribute of God. See Qur'ān, Sūrah lv. 78: "Blessed be the name of thy Lord who is possessed of *glory* and honour."

Al-Jalāl is a term used by Ṣūfī mystics to express that state of the Almighty which places Him beyond the understanding of His creatures. ('Abdu 'r-Razzāq's *Dictionary of Ṣūfī Terms.*)

AL-JALĀLĀN (الجلالان). "The two Jalāls." A term given to two commentators of the name of Jalālu 'd-dīn, whose joint work is called the *Tafsīru 'l-Jalālain*; the first half of which was compiled by the Shaikh Jalālu'd-dīn al-Maḥallī, died A.H. 864, and the rest by Jalālu 'd-dīn as-Suyūṭī, died A.H. 911.

Jalālu 'd-dīn as-Suyūṭī was a prolific author. Grammar, rhetoric, dogmatical and practical theology, history, criticism, medicine, and anatomy, comprise some of the subjects on which he wrote. His *Itqān*, which is an explanatory work on the Qur'ān, has been published by the Asiatic Society of Bengal, and edited by Dr. Sprenger (A.D. 1857), and his *History of the Temple of Jerusalem* has been translated by the Rev. James Reynolds for the Oriental Translation Society (A.D. 1836). [JERUSALEM.]

JA'LU 'L-JAUF (جعل الجوف). Another name for Dūmatu 'l-Jandal, a place near Tabūk. [DUMAH.]

JĀLŪT (جالوت). [GOLIATH.]

JAMRAH (جمرة). *Lit.* "Gravel, or small pebbles." (1) The three pillars at Minā, at which the Makkan pilgrims throw seven pebbles. They are known as al-Ūlā, the first; al-Wusṭā, the middle; and al-'Āqibah, the last. According to Muslim writers these pillars mark the successive spots where the Devil, in the shape of an old Shaikh, appeared to Adam, Abraham, and Ishmael, and was driven away by the simple process which Gabriel taught them of throwing seven small pebbles. The *Jamratu 'l-'Āqibah*, is known as the *Shaiṭānu 'l-Kabīr*, or the "Great Devil."

Captain Burton, in his *El Medinah and Mecca*, vol. ii. 227, says:—

"The '*Shaiṭānu 'l-Kabīr*' is a dwarf buttress of rude masonry, about eight feet high by two and a half broad, placed against a rough wall of stones, at the Meccan entrance to Muna. As the ceremony of 'Ramy,' or Lapidation, must be performed on the first day by all pilgrims between sunrise and sunset, and as the fiend was malicious enough to appear in a rugged pass, the crowd makes the place dangerous. On one side of the road, which is not forty feet broad, stood a row of shops, belonging principally to barbers. On the other side is the rugged wall of the pillar, with a *chevaux de frise* of Bedouins and naked boys. The narrow space was crowded with pilgrims, all struggling like drowning men to approach as near as possible to the Devil."

THE SHAITANU 'L-KABIR. (*Burton.*)

(2) *Jamrah* also means a "live coal," and is an astronomical or meteorological term used to signify the infusion of vital heat into the elements in spring, or rather, at the end of winter. According to this theory there are three Jamarāt: one, the infusion of heat into the air, occurs thirty days before the vernal equinox; the second, affecting the waters, seven days later; and the third, vivifying the earth, sixteen days before the equinox. (Catafago's *Dictionary*, *in loco.*)

JAM'U 'L-JAM' (جمع الجمع). *Lit.* "The plural of a plural." A term used by the Ṣūfī mystics for the high position of the Perfect Man or *al-Insānu 'l-Kāmil.*

JANĀB (جناب). "Majesty." A term of respect used in India in addressing a person of rank or office, whether Native or European. *Janāb-i-'alī*, "Your high eminence."

JANĀBAH (جنابة). A state of uncleanness. The *Niddoh*, or separation, of Leviticus xii. 5. The menses, coitus, childbirth, pollutio nocturna, contact with the dead, or having performed the offices of nature, place the person in a state of Janābah or separation. [PURIFICATION.]

JANĀZAH, JINĀZAH (جنازة). A term used both for the *bier*, and for the *funeral service* of a Muslim, also for the corpse itself. [BURIAL.]

JĀNN (جان). The father of the Jinn. [JINN.]

JANNAH (جنة), pl. *Jannāt.* *Lit.* "A garden." (1) A term used for the regions of celestial bliss. [PARADISE.] (2) A term used by Ṣūfī mystics to express different stages of the spiritual life: *Jannatu 'l-Af'āl*, the paradise of works, or that enjoyment which is derived from sensual pleasures, such as eating, drinking, &c.; *Jannatu 'l-Wirāsah*, the paradise of inheritance, which is a disposition like that of the saints and prophets; *Jannatu 'ṣ-Ṣifāt*, the paradise of attributes, becoming like God; *Jannatu 'z-Zāt*, the paradise of essence, being united with God (*i.e.* absorption into the divine essence). ('Abdu 'r-Razzāq's *Dictionary of Ṣūfī Terms.*)

JANNATU 'ADN (جنات عدن). The Gardens of Eden. (Sūrah ix. 73, *et alias.*) [PARADISE.]

JANNĀTU 'L-FIRDAUS (جنات الفردوس). The Gardens of Paradise. (Sūrah xviii. 107.) [PARADISE.]

JANNATU' L-KHULD (جنة الخلد). The Garden of Eternity. (Sūrah xxv. 16.) [PARADISE.]

JANNĀTU 'L-MA'WA (جنات الماوى). The Gardens of Refuge. (Sūrah xxxii. 19.) [PARADISE.]

JANNĀTU'N-NA'ĪM (جنات النعيم). The Gardens of Delight. (Sūrah v. 70.) [PARADISE.]

JĀR MULĀṢIQ (جار ملاصق). "A next-door neighbour." A term used in Muḥammadan law for a joint proprietor in a house, or room or wall of the house. (*Hidāyah*, vol. iii. p. 565.)

JARR (جر). "Dragging." A degree of chastisement practised according to Muḥammadan law, namely, by *dragging* the offender to the door and exposing him to scorn. (Hamilton's *Hidāyah*, vol. ii. p. 76.)

AL-JĀṢIYAH (الجاثية). *Lit.* "The Kneeling." A title given to the XLVth Sūrah of the Qur'ān, in which the expression occurs (verse 26):—

"And God's is the kingdom of the Heavens and of the Earth; and on the day when the Hour shall arrive, on that day shall the despisers perish. And thou shalt see every nation *kneeling*; to its own book shall every nation be summoned:—'This day shall ye be repaid as ye have wrought.'"

JĀṢULĪQ (جاثليق). An Arabicized word from the Greek Καθολικὸς. The *Catholicos*, or Primate of the Christians. In the *Ghiyāṣu 'l-Lughah* he is said to be the chief of the Christians, and under him is the *Miṭrān* (Metropolitan), and then the *Usquf* (Bishop), and then *Qasīs* (Presbyter), and then *Shammās* (Deacon)."

Mr. Lane, in his Dictionary, gives the Order of *Biṭrāq* (Patriarch) as under the *Jāṣulīq*, which term we understand to mean, in Muḥammadan works, none other than the Patriarch, *e.g.* of Jerusalem, or Antioch, &c.

JAWĀMI'U 'L-KALIM (جوامع الكلم). *Lit.* "Comprehending many significations." A title given to the Qur'ān and to certain traditions, because it is related that the Prophet said that has been revealed to me which comprehends many significations. (*Kashfu 'l-Iṣṭilāḥāt, in loco.*)

JAZ'AH (جذعة). A female camel in her fifth year. The proper age for a camel given in zakāt or legal alms for camels from sixty-one to seventy-five in number. [ZAKAT.]

JAZBAH (جذبة). "Attraction." A term used by the Ṣūfī mystics to express a yearning after the Divine Being. The nearer approach of man to his Maker through God's grace. ('Abdu 'r-Razzāq's *Dictionary of Ṣūfī Terms.*)

JEDDAH. Arabic *Jiddah* (جدة). The principal seaport of Arabia, and one of the *Mīqāt* or stages where the Makkan pilgrims put on the *Iḥrām* or pilgrim's robe. It is also celebrated as the place of Eve's sepulchre. She is said to measure 120 paces from head to waist, and 80 paces from waist to heel. (*Burton.*)

JEHOVAH. Heb. יְהֹוָה. In the Old Testament it is usually with the vowel points of אֲדֹנָי; but when the two occur together, the former is pointed יֱהֹוִה, that is, with the vowels of אֱלֹהִים, as in Obad. i. 1; Heb. iii. 19. The LXX. generally render it by Κύριος, the vulgate by *Dominus*; and in this respect they have been followed by the A.V. where it is translated "The Lord." The true pronunciation of this name, by which God was known to the Hebrews, has been entirely lost, the Jews themselves scrupulously avoiding every mention of it, and substituting in its stead one or other of the words with whose proper vowel-points it may happen to be written. This custom, which had its origin in reverence, and has almost degenerated into a superstition, was founded upon an erroneous rendering of Lev. xxiv. 16, "He that blasphemeth the name of God shall surely be put to death"; from which it was inferred that the mere utterance of the name constituted a capital offence. In the Rabbinical writings it is distinguished by various euphemistic expressions; as simply "the name," or "the name of four letters" (the Greek *tetragrammaton*); "the great and terrible name"; "the peculiar name," *i.e.* appropriated to God alone; "the separate name," *i.e.* either the name which is separated or removed from human knowledge, or, as some render, "the name which has been interpreted or revealed." (Professor W. A. Wright, M.A., Smith's *Dictionary of the Bible, in loco.*)

This superstitious reverence for the word Jehovah must have been the origin of the *Ismu 'l-A'ẓam*, or "exalted name," which Muḥammad is related to have said was known only to God and His prophets; but which, he said, occurs in one of three verses in the Qur'ān, namely: Sūratu 'l-Baqarah ii. 256: "God! (*Allāh*) there is no God but He (*Hū*) the Living One (*al-Ḥaiy*), the Self-Subsisting One (*al-Qaiyūm*)"; or, in the Sūratu Āli 'Imrān iii. 1, which contains the same words; or, in the Sūratu Ṭā Hā xx. 110: "Faces shall be humbled before the Living One (*al-Ḥaiy*), the Self-Subsistent One (*al-Qaiyūm*)."

Some European scholars (see Catafago's *Arabic Dictionary*) have fancied the *Yahūh* יהוה, or Yahovah of the Hebrews, is identical with the ejaculation of the Muslim devotee, *Yā Hū*, "O He!" (*i.e.* God). Al-Baiẓāwī says the word *Hū* (better *Huwa*), *i.e.* HE (God), may be the *Ismu 'l-A'ẓam*, or Exalted Name of the Almighty, especially as it occurs in two of the verses of the Qur'ān indicated by Muḥammad, namely, Sūrahs ii. 256, iii. 1. [HUWA, GOD.]

JEREMIAH. Arabic *Armiyā* (ارميا). The prophet is not mentioned in the Qur'ān, but Muslim historians say he was contemporary with Ma'add, the son of 'Adnān, the renowned ancestor of Muḥammad. The *Kātibu 'l-Wāqidī* says: "God watched over 'Adnān's son Ma'add, who was by the command of the Lord taken by Armiyā and Abrakhā (Jeremiah and Baruch) into the land of Harram and nurtured safely." According to the *Ghiyāṣu 'l-Lughah*, he is the same as al-Khiẓr. [AL-KHIZR.]

JERUSALEM. Arabic *al-Baitu 'l-Muqaddas* (البيت المقدس), "the Holy House," or *Baitu 'l-Maqdis* (بيت المقدس), "the House of the Sanctuary"; *Aurashalīm* (اورشليم); *Iliyā'* (ايلياء), *i.e.* *Aelia Capitolina.*

In the Qur'ān Jerusalem is never mentioned by name, and in the Traditions and other Muslim works, it is always called *al-Baitu 'l-Muqaddas*, "the Holy House," as referring to the Temple of Jerusalem, or *Iliyā'*. The allusions to it in the Qur'ān, are as follows:—

Sūrah ii. 55 (where God, after giving the manna and quails, is represented as saying to the children of Israel): "Enter the city and eat therefrom as plentifully as ye wish." Al-Baiẓāwī the commentator says this city was the the *Baitu 'l-Maqdis* (Jerusalem), or *Arīḥā* (Jericho).

Sūrah ii. 261: "Like him who passed by a city when it was desolate, and as he walked over its roofs said, 'How will God revive this after its destruction?" Commentators say Elias or *al-Khiẓr* visited the city of Jerusalem after its destruction by Nebuchadnezzar.

Sūrah xxx. opens with a reference to the Persians conquering Syria and taking Jerusalem.

In Sūrah xvii. 1, Muḥammad is represented as having taken his flight from Makkah to Jerusalem. "Celebrated be the praises of Him who by night took his servant from the *Masjidu 'l-Ḥarām* (the Sacred Mosque) to the *Masjidu 'l-Aqṣā* (the Remote Mosque), the precinct of which we have blessed."

And in Sūrah l. 40, one of the signs of the approach of the last day will be: "The crier (to prayer) shall cry from a near place" (*i.e.* a place from which all men shall hear). Ḥusain says this "near place" is the Temple at Jerusalem.

A curious account of Jerusalem and its temple, the Masjidu 'l-Aqṣā, or Distant Mosque (so called because it is a distant object of pilgrimage), has been written by Jalālu 'd-dīn as-Suyūṭī, one of the commentators on the Qur'ān, known as the Jalālān. It was written in the year A.H. 848, A.D. 1444, and the special object of the book appears to be to exalt the merits of Jerusalem as a place of prayer and pilgrimage. [For an account of the Temple, see MASJIDU 'L-AQSA.] He says Jerusalem is specially honoured as being the scene of the repentance of David and Solomon. The place where God sent His angel to Solomon, announced glad tidings to Zacharias and John, showed David a plan of the Temple, and put all the beasts of the earth and fowls of the air in subjection to him. It was at Jerusalem that the prophets sacrificed; that Jesus was born and spoke in his cradle; and it was at Jerusalem that Jesus ascended to heaven; and it will be there that He will again descend. Gog and Magog shall subdue every place on the earth but Jerusalem, and it will be there that God Almighty will destroy them. It is in the holy land of Jerusalem that Adam and Abraham, and Isaac and Mary, are buried. And in the last days there will be a general flight to Jerusalem, and the Ark and the Shechinah will be again restored to the Temple. There will all mankind be gathered at the Resurrection for judgment, and God will enter, surrounded by His angels, into the Holy Temple, when He comes to judge the earth. (See Reynolds' Translation, p. 16.)

The peculiar reference paid to the Sacred Rock (*aṣ-Ṣakhrah*) seems to be one of the many instances of afterthought and addition to Islām since the time of Muḥammad. Mu'āwiyah seems to have encouraged it in order to direct the affections and fanaticism of his subjects into a new channel, and to withdraw their *exclusive* attention from Makkah and al-Madīnah, where the rival family of 'Alī resided.

In the same book there is a desultory account of the taking of Jerusalem by the Khalīfah 'Umar.

After the conclusion of the battle of Yarmūk (Hieromax), the whole army of the Muslims marched into the territory of Palestine and Jordan. Then they closely besieged the city. The conquest was attended with difficulty until the arrival of the Khalīfah 'Umar with four thousand horse. He came upon the holy place on the eastern side, and then encircled the city. They fought for a long time, until at last the inhabitants sent a party to the walls with a flag of truce, asking for a parley. The Patriarch (Sophronius) then demanded the safe conduct of a messenger to 'Umar. The envoy came without hindrance and requested 'Umar to make peace and to accept tribute.

Jalālu 'd-dīn gives a copy of the treaty which the Muslims compelled the people of Jerusalem to sign. It reads as follows:—

"In the name of God, the Merciful and Compassionate! This is the writing from the Christians of the Holy City to 'Umar ibn al-

Khaṭṭāb, the Commander of the Faithful. When you came down upon us, we asked of you a capitulation for ourselves and our possessions, and our children, and the people of our religion; and we have stipulated with you, that we shall not be polluted by interruption in our places of worship, or whatever chapels, or churches, or cells, or monasteries of monks, may be therein; and that no one shall live therein who may have the impress of Muslims (by long residence), and that we will not prohibit the Muslims from entering them, by night or by day; and that we will open the gates wide to passengers and to travellers; and if any Muslim passing by shall take up his lodging with us three nights, we shall give him food, and not entertain in our churches a spy, nor conceal him unknown to the Muslims; and not teach our children the Qur'ān; and not publicly exhibit the Associating or Christian religion, and not beg any one to embrace it; and not hinder anyone of our relations from entering the Muslim religion, if he will, and that we should honour the Muslims and make much of them, and place them in our assemblies, if anyone of them will, and give them the chief seats, and not imitate them in our dress, neither in girdles, nor in the turban, nor the slipper, nor the parting of the hair, and never write in their language, nor call ourselves by their surnames; and that we should never ride upon great saddles, nor suspend our swords by belts, and never accept arms (the bow, sword, and club), nor carry them with us; and that we should never engrave upon our signet-rings in the Arabic language; and that we should not sell wine, and that we should shave the front of our heads, and tie up our dress, wherever we may be, and not wear wide girdles at our waist; and that we should never publicly exhibit the cross upon our churches, nor expose our crosses, nor ever inscribe them in the path of the Muslims, nor in their market places, and never strike our bells the (quick) stroke, nor raise our voices over the dead, nor publicly expose the lights, or anything else, in the roads and markets of the Muslims, and never come near them with our dead, and never receive any slave who has drawn upon himself familiarity with Muslims, and never look upon them in their houses."

We learn moreover, from the same authority, as follows:—

"When 'Umar ratified the treaty, he added thereto,—'And that we will not strike anyone of the Muslims. We stipulate this with you for ourselves and the people of our religion; and we accept these terms of capitulation: and if we subsequently violate a point of that which we have stipulated, upon our lives be it, and let there be no faith with us and may it be allowed you to do to us whatever is lawful against rebellious and revolting subjects.'" (*Hist. of Jerusalem*, by Jalālu 'd-dīn, Reynolds' Translation.)

There were within the city 12,000 Greeks and 50,000 natives, and the Khalīfah 'Umar insisted that all the Greeks depart within three days, and that the natives should pay tribute. Five dīnārs were imposed upon the rich, four upon the middle classes, and three upon the lower classes; very old and very young persons paid nothing.

When 'Umar entered the Holy City, his first object was to find the Sacred Rock (*aṣ-Ṣakhrah*), the site of the Masjidu 'l-Aqṣā, to which Muḥammad said he was carried on Burāq on the night of the Mi'rāj [MIRAJ], and he therefore requested the Patriarch to direct him to the spot. They first went to the Church of the Resurrection, and the Patriarch said, "This is the Mosque of David." But 'Umar said, "Thou hast spoken falsely, for the Apostle of God (Muḥammad) described the place to me, and it was not like this." They then went to the church on Zion, and the Patriarch said, "This is the Mosque of David." But 'Umar said, "Thou hast spoken falsely." And in this manner the Patriarch took 'Umar to every church in the city. At last they came to a gate, which is now called *Bābu 'l-Muḥammad*, or the Gate of Muḥammad, and clearing away the filth on the steps, they came to a narrow passage, and the Khalīfah, creeping on his knees, came to the central sewer. Here, standing up, 'Umar looked at the rock (*aṣ-Ṣakhrah*), and then exclaimed, "By Him in whose hand is my life, this is the place which the Apostle of God (upon whom be peace and blessing) described to us." 'Umar then ordered a mosque to be built thereon. And 'Abdu 'l-Malik ibn Marwān built the mosque of the Baitu 'l-Muquddas (now known as the Mosque of 'Umar). He spent upon it the produce of seven years' tax upon Egypt. He began it in A.H. 69 and finished it in A.H. 72.

Some authority quoted by Jalālu 'd-dīn says the Holy City did not cease to be in the hands of the Muslims from its surrender to 'Umar until the year A.H. 491, when it was taken by the Franks, who killed therein a vast number of Muslims in the space of seven days. In the Masjidu 'l-Aqṣa alone, they killed 70,000, and they took from aṣ-Sakhrah the vessels of gold and silver and the wealth which was preserved in strong boxes. "But," he adds, "Ṣalāḥu 'd-dīn (Saladin) was raised up for the complete deliverance of the Holy City; for he was the most renowned of Lions, and the very brightness of Fire."

(For a further account of the taking of the city by Saladin, see Reynolds' translation of Jalālu 'd-dīn's *History of the Temple of Jerusalem*, p. 199.)

A brief outline of the History of Jerusalem from the Time of Christ.

A.D.

33. The crucifixion, death resurrection, and ascension of Jesus Christ at Jerusalem.
43. St. Paul's first visit to Jerusalem after his conversion to Christianity.
69. Taken by Titus.
136. The Emperor Hadrian bestows on the city the name of Aelia Capitolina.

A.D. (This name is used by Jalālu 'd-dīn in his book, A.D. 1444.)

336. Jerusalem under Christian rule, the *Martyrion* and the Church of the Resurrection built.

614. The city invested and taken by the Persians under Chosroes II. (See Qur'ān, Sūrah xxx.)

621. The era of the flight of Muḥammad.

628. The Emperor Heraclius enters Jerusalem in triumph.

637. The patriarch Sophronius surrenders the Holy City to the Khalīfah 'Umar. Liberty of worship secured to the Christians in churches which already existed, but they are prohibited the erection of new churches. A mosque built on the reputed site of Jacob's vision, now known as the mosque of 'Umar. Said to be on the site of the temple called by Muslims Masjidu 'l-Aqṣā, the Remote Mosque, or aṣ-Ṣakhrah, the Rock.

800. Ambassadors sent by the Emperor Charlemagne to distribute alms in the Holy City. The Khalīfah Harūn ar-Rashīd sends back as a present to the Emperor the keys of Calvary and the Holy Sepulchre.

820. Held for a time by the rebel chief Tamum Abū Ḥarab.

969. Falls into the hands of the Fāṭimate Khalīfah Mu'izz. The Church of the Holy Sepulchre burnt.

1035. The pilgrimage of Robert of Normandy.

1054. The pilgrimage of Lietbert of Cambray.

1065. The pilgrimage of the German bishops.

1077. Jerusalem pillaged by the army of Malik Shah.

1084. The Turkoman chief Urtok becomes ruler of the Holy City. The Christians suffer.

1098. The city retaken by the Fāṭimate Khalīfah.

1099. 40,000 Crusaders appear before its walls. The city taken by the Crusaders. 10,000 Muslims slain. Godfrey of Bouillon made King. (For eighty years the city remained in the hands of the Christians.)

1187. Retaken by Saladin (Ṣalāhu 'd-dīn), the Muslim general.

1219. Ceded to the Christians by virtue of a treaty with the Emperor Frederick II.

1239. Taken by the Muslims.

1243. Again ceded to the Christians.

1244. The Christians defeated at Gaza, and Jerusalem occupied by the Muslims.

1277. Nominally annexed to the kingdom of Sicily.

1517. Becomes part of the Empire of the Ottoman Sultān Selim I.

1542. Sultān Sulaiman I. builds the present walls.

A.D.

1832. Muḥammad 'Alī Pasha of Egypt takes the city.

1840. Restored to the Sultān of Turkey.

[AS-SAKHRAH, MASJIDU 'L-AQSA.]

JESUS CHRIST. Arabic *'Īsā 'l-Masīḥ* (عيسى المسيح). In the Qur'ān, the Lord Jesus Christ is spoken of under the following names and titles:—

(1) *'Īsā* (عيسى), "Jesus." Al-Baiẓāwī says it is the same as the Hebrew *Ishū'*, (ايشوع), and derived from *al-'ayas*, "white mingled with red," without, however, explaining this derivation.

(2) *'Īsā ibn Maryam* (عيسى بن مريم), "Jesus the son of Mary," from whom He was born by the power of God.

(3) *Al-Masīḥ* (المسيح), "the Messiah." Sūrah iii. 40: "His name shall be Messiah Jesus." Al-Kamālān, the commentators, say he is called al-Masīḥ either because he was both blessed and anointed by the angel Gabriel, or because whomsoever Jesus touched was healed.

(4) *Kalimatu 'llāh* (كلمة الله), "the Word of God." Sūrah iv. 169: "His word." Ḥusain says by this expression is meant he who was born at the express fiat of God. (Sūrah xix. 36: "He says only to it BE and it is.")

(5) *Qaulu 'l-Ḥaqq* (قول الحق). "The Word of Truth." Surah xix. 35. Some commentators take the expression *qaulu 'l-ḥaqq* as referring to the statement made being "the word of truth," whilst others take it as referring to Christ Himself, "The Word of Truth."

(6) *Rūḥun min Allāh* (روح من الله), "A Spirit from God." Sūrah iv. 169: "A Spirit from Him." Al-Baiẓāwī says it is a spirit which proceedeth from God. The title *Rūḥu 'llāh* is the special Kalimah for Jesus Christ. [PROPHETS.]

(7) *Rasūlu 'llāh* (رسول الله), "The Messenger of God." Sūrah iv. 169. It is the same title as Muḥammad assumed for himself, *i.e.* the Prophet, or Apostle, or Messenger of God.

(8) *'Abdu 'llāh* (عبد الله), "The Servant of God." Sūrah xix. 31: "Verily, I am the servant of God."

(9) *Nabīyu 'llāh* (نبى الله), "The Prophet of God." Sūrah xix. 31: "He hath made me a Prophet."

(10) *Wajīhun fī 'd-dunyā wa 'l-ākhirah* (وجيه فى الدنيا والاخرة), "Illustrious in this world and in the next," namely, as al-Baiẓāwī explains it, "in this world as a Prophet, in the next as an Intercessor." Sūrah iii. 40.

In order to present the somewhat incoherent narrative of the Qur'ān in a systematic form, we shall arrange its history of the Lord Jesus into (1) The Annunciation of the Virgin, (2) The Birth of Jesus, (3) His Miracles, (4) His Mission, (5) His Crucifixion, (6) His Divinity and Sinlessness, (7) The Trinity, (8) His Second Coming (as taught in the Traditions), (9) His Exaltation in Heaven. From a perusal of these selections it will be seen that Muḥammad taught that Jesus was miraculously born of the Virgin Mary, who was sister of Aaron and the daughter of 'Imrān, near the trunk of a palm tree. That the Jews charged the Virgin with being unchaste; but the babe, speaking in his cradle, vindicated his mother's honour. That Jesus performed miracles, giving life to a clay figure of a bird, healing the blind, curing the leper, quickening the dead, and bringing down a table from heaven "as a festival and a sign." That he (Jesus) was specially commissioned as the Apostle or Prophet of God to confirm the Law and to reveal the Gospel. That he proclaimed his mission with many manifest signs, being strengthened by the Holy Spirit. That he foretold the advent of another Prophet, whose name should be Aḥmad. That the Jews intended to crucify him, but God deceived them, for they did not crucify Jesus, but only his likeness. That he is now in one of the stages of celestial bliss. That after he left this earth his disciples disputed amongst themselves, some calling him a God, and making him one of a Trinity of the "Father, the Mother, and the Son." That he will come again at the last day, and will slay Antichrist, kill all the swine, break the Cross, remove the poll-tax from the infidels. That he will reign as a just king for forty-five years, marry, and have children, and die and be buried near Muḥammad at al-Madīnah, between the graves of Abū Bakr and 'Umar.

I.—The Annunciation of the Virgin.

Surah iii. 37–43: "And remember when the angels said, 'O Mary! verily hath God chosen thee, and purified thee, and chosen thee above the women of the worlds! O Mary! be devout towards thy Lord, and prostrate thyself, and bow down with those who bow.' This is one of the announcements of things unseen by thee: To thee, *O Muḥammad!* do we reveal it; for thou wast not with them when they cast lots with reeds which of them should rear Mary; nor wast thou with them when they disputed about it. *Remember* when the angel said, 'O Mary! Verily God announceth to thee the Word from Him: His name shall be, Messiah Jesus the son of Mary, illustrious in this world, and in the next, and one of those who have near access to God; and he shall speak to men alike when in the cradle and when grown up; and he shall be one of the just.' She said, 'How, O my Lord! shall I have a son, when man hath not touched me?' He said, 'Thus: God will create what He will; when He decreeth a thing, He only saith, "Be," and it is.' And He will teach him the Book, and the Wisdom, and the Law, and the Evangel; and he shall be an apostle to the chilren of Israel."

Sūrah xix. 16–21: "And make mention in the Book, of Mary, when she went apart from her family, eastward, and took a veil *to shroud herself* from them: and We sent Our spirit to her, and he took before her the form of a perfect man. She said: 'I fly for refuge from thee to the God of Mercy! If thou fearest Him, *begone from me.*' He said: 'I am only a messenger of thy Lord, that I may bestow on thee a holy son.' She said: 'How shall I have a son, when man hath never touched me? and I am not unchaste.' He said: 'So shall it be. Thy Lord hath said: "Easy is this with me; and we will make him a sign to mankind, and a mercy from us. For it is a thing decreed."'"

[In the earlier part of Sūrah iii. the Virgin Mary is spoken of as the daughter of 'Imrān. Commentators say that 'Imrān died before Mary was born. In the traditions it is stated "that the only two persons born into the world who have not been touched of the Devil are Mary and her son Jesus." Thus teaching not only the Immaculate Conception of Mary, but also of her mother. "*When she went eastward*"; Ḥusain says, she went out of her house in an eastward direction, in order to perform her ablutions, when Gabriel appeared to her.]

II.—The Birth of Jesus.

Sūrah xix. 22–34: "And she conceived him, and retired with him to a far-off place. And the throes came upon her by the trunk of a palm. She said: 'Oh, would that I had died ere this, and been a thing forgotten, forgotten quite!' And one cried to her from below her: 'Grieve not thou, thy Lord hath provided a streamlet at thy feet:—And shake the trunk of the palm-tree toward thee: it will drop fresh ripe dates upon thee. Eat then and drink, and be of cheerful eye: and shouldst thou see a man, say,—Verily, I have vowed abstinence to the God of mercy.—To no one will I speak this day.' Then came she with the babe to her people, bearing him. They said, 'O Mary! now hast thou done a strange thing! O sister of Aaron! Thy father was not a man of wickedness, nor unchaste thy mother.' And she made a sign *to them, pointing* towards the babe. They said, 'How shall we speak with him who is in the cradle, an infant?' It said, 'Verily, I am the servant of God; He hath given me the Book, and He hath made me a prophet; and He hath made me blessed wherever I may be, and hath enjoined me prayer and almsgiving so long as I shall live; and to be dutiful to her that bare me: and he hath not made me proud, depraved. And the peace of God was on me the day I was born, and will be the day I shall die, and the day I shall be raised to life."

Sūrah xxiii. 52: "And we appointed the Son and his Mother for a sign; and we prepared an abode in a lofty spot, quiet and watered with springs."

[Professor Wahl understands this last verse to refer to Paradise, but the Muslim commentators all refer it to the place of abode; and al-Baiẓāwī and Ḥusain say it was either in Jerusalem, or Damascus, or Ramleh! Ḥusain says Jesus was born in Bethlehem. The expression, "*O sister of Aaron,*" as applied to the Virgin Mary, suggests an anachronism of some consequence, but the commentators get over the difficulty. The Kamālān say it is a figurative expression implying that she was pure and righteous like a sister of Aaron. But al-Baiẓāwī says it means that she was of the tribe of Aaron. European authors suggest that there was a confusion between Miriam the Virgin and Miriam the sister of Moses. Al-Baiẓāwī says: "The palm to which she fled, that she might lean on it in her travail, was a withered trunk, without any head or verdure; and this happened in the winter season, notwithstanding which, it miraculously supplied her with fruits for her refreshment, as is mentioned immediately." Mr. Sale says: "It has been observed, that the Mohammedan account of the delivery of the Virgin Mary very much resembles that of Latona, as described by the poets, not only in this circumstance of their laying hold on a palm-tree (though some say Latona embraced an olive-tree, or an olive and a palm, or else two laurels), but also in that of their infants speaking; which Apollo is fabled to have done in the womb." (See Homer, *Hymn. in Apoll.*; Callimach, *Hymn. in Delum.*)

III.—The Miracles of Jesus.

Sūrah iii. 43–46: "And He will teach him the Book, and the Wisdom, and the Law, and the Evangel; and he shall be an apostle to the children of Israel. 'Now have I come,' *he will say*, 'to you with a sign from your Lord: Out of clay will I make for you, as it were, the figure of a bird: and I will breathe into it, and it shall become, by God's leave, a bird. And I will heal the blind, and the leper; and by God's leave will I quicken the dead; and I will tell you what ye eat, and what ye store up in your houses! Truly in this will be a sign for you, if ye are believers.' And when Jesus perceived unbelief on their part, He said, 'Who my helpers with God?' The apostles said, 'We *will be* God's helpers! We believe in God, and bear thou witness that we are Muslims. O our Lord! we believe in what thou hast sent down, and we follow the apostle; write us up, then, with those who bear witness *to him.*'"

[The commentators al-Jalālān say Jesus made for his disciples a bat, for it is the most perfect of birds in make, and it flew while they looked at it; but when it had gone out of their sight, it fell down dead. That he cured in one day fifty thousand persons, and that he raised Lazarus ('Āzar) from the dead; also Shem, the son of Noah, who had been dead 4,000 years, but he died immediately; also the son of an old woman, and the daughter of a tax-collector.]

Sūrah v. 112–115: "Remember when the Apostles said: 'O Jesus, Son of Mary! is thy Lord able to send down a furnished table to us out of Heaven?' He said: 'Fear God if ye be believers.' They said: 'We desire to eat therefrom, and to have our hearts assured; and to know that thou hast indeed spoken truth to us, and to be witnesses thereof.' Jesus, Son of Mary, said: 'O God, our Lord! send down a table to us out of Heaven, that it may become a recurring festival to us, to the first of us and to the last of us, and a sign from thee; and do thou nourish us, for thou art the best of nourishers.' And God said: 'Verily, I will cause it to descend unto you; but whoever among you after that shall disbelieve, I will surely chastise him with a chastisement wherewith I will not chastise any other creature.'"

[Mr. Sale, in his commentary on this miracle, says (quoting from al-Baiẓāwī):—"This miracle is thus related by the commentators. Jesus having, at the request of his followers, asked it of God, a red table immediately descended in their sight, between two clouds, and was set before them. Whereupon he rose up, and having made the ablution, prayed, and then took off the cloth which covered the table, saying, 'In the name of God, the best provider of food!' What the provisions were, with which this table was furnished, is a matter wherein the expositors are not agreed. One will have them to be nine cakes of bread and nine fishes; another, bread and flesh; another, all sorts of food, except flesh; another, all sorts of food, except bread and flesh; another, all except bread and fish; another, one fish, which had the taste of all manner of food; and another, fruits of paradise; but the most received tradition is, that when the table was uncovered, there appeared a fish ready dressed, without scales or prickly fins, dropping with fat, having salt placed at its head, and vinegar at its tail, and round it all sorts of herbs, except leeks, and five loaves of bread, on one of which there were olives; on the second, honey; on the third, butter; on the fourth, cheese; and on the fifth, dried flesh. They add, that Jesus, at the request of the apostles, showed them another miracle, by restoring the fish to life, and causing its scales and fins to return to it; at which the standers-by, being affrighted, he caused it to become as it was before: that one thousand three hundred men and women, all afflicted with bodily infirmities or poverty, ate of these provisions, and were satisfied, the fish remaining whole as it was at first; that then the table flew up to heaven in the sight of all; and everyone who had partaken of this food were delivered from their infirmities and misfortunes; and that it continued to descend for forty days together, at dinner-time, and stood on the ground till the sun declined, and was then taken up into the clouds. Some of the Mohammedan writers are of opinion that this table did not really descend, but that it was only a parable; but most think the words of the Koran are plain to the contrary. A further tradition is, that several men were changed into swine for disbelieving this miracle, and attributing it to magic art; or, as others pretend, for stealing some of the victuals from off it."]

IV.—The Mission of Jesus.

Sūrah lvii. 26, 27: "And of old sent we Noah and Abraham, and on their seed conferred the gift of prophecy, and the Book; and some of them we guided aright; but many were evil doers. Then we caused our apostles to follow in their footsteps; and we caused Jesus the son of Mary to follow them; and we gave him the Evangel and we put into the hearts of those who followed him kindness and compassion: but as to the monastic life, they invented it themselves. The desire only of pleasing God did we prescribe to them, and this they observed not as it ought to have been observed: but to such of them as believed gave we their reward, though many of them were perverse."

Sūrah v. 50, 51: "And in the footsteps of the prophets caused we Jesus, the son of Mary, to follow, confirming the law which was before him: and we gave him the Evangel with its guidance and light, confirmatory of the preceding Law; a guidance and warning to those who fear God;—And that the people of the Evangel may judge according to what God hath sent down therein. And whoso will not judge by what God hath sent down—such are the perverse."

Sūrah ii. 81: "Moreover, to Moses gave we 'the Book,' and we raised up apostles after him; and to Jesus, son of Mary, gave we clear proofs *of his mission*, and strengthened him by the Holy Spirit. So oft then as an apostle cometh to you with that which your souls desire not, swell ye with pride, and treat some as impostors, and slay others?"

Sūrah ii. 254: "Some of the apostles we have endowed more highly than others: Those to whom God hath spoken, He hath raised to the loftiest grade, and to Jesus the Son of Mary we gave manifest signs, and we strengthened him with the Holy Spirit. And if God had pleased, they who came after them would not have wrangled, after the clear signs had reached them. But into disputes they fell: some of them believed, and some were infidels; yet if God had pleased, they would not have thus wrangled: but God doth what he will."

Sūrah lxi. 6: "And *remember* when Jesus the son of Mary said, 'O children of Israel! of a truth I am God's apostle to you to confirm the law which was given before me, and to announce an apostle that shall come after me whose name shall be Aḥmad!' But when he (Aḥmad) presented himself with clear proofs of his mission, they said, 'This is manifest sorcery!'"

Sūrah vi. 85: "And Zachariah, John, Jesus, and Elias: all were just persons."

Sūrah iv. 157: "And there shall not be one of the people of the Book but shall believe in him (Jesus) before his death, and in the day of judgment he shall be a witness against them."

Sūrah iii. 44: "And I have come to attest the law which was before me; and to allow you part of that which had been forbidden you; and I come to you with a sign from your Lord: Fear God, then, and obey me; of a truth God is my Lord, and your Lord: Therefore worship Him. This is a right way."

V.—The Crucifixion of Jesus.

Sūrah iii. 47–50: "And the Jews plotted, and God plotted: But of those who plot is God the best. Remember when God said, 'O Jesus! verily I will cause thee to die, and will take thee up to myself and deliver thee from those who believe not; and I will place those who follow thee above those who believe not, until the Day of Resurrection. Then, to me is your return, and wherein ye differ will I decide between you. And as to those who believe not, I will chastise them with a terrible chastisement in this world and in the next; and none shall they have to help them.' But as to those who believe, and do the things that are right, He will pay them their recompense. God loveth not the doers of evil."

Sūrah iv. 155, 156: "And for their unbelief [are the Jews cursed]—and for their having spoken against Mary a grievous calumny,—And for their saying, 'Verily we have slain the Messiah, Jesus the son of Mary, an Apostle of God.' Yet they slew him not, and they crucified him not, but they had only his likeness. And they who differed about him were in doubt concerning him: No sure knowledge had they about him, but followed only an opinion, and they really did not slay him, but God took him up to Himself. And God is Mighty, Wise!"

[Sale, in his notes on the Qur'ān, says: "The person crucified some will have to be a spy that was sent to entrap him; others that it was one Titian, who by the direction of Judas entered in at a window of the house where Jesus was, to kill him; and others that it was Judas himself, who agreed with the rulers of the Jews to betray him for thirty pieces of silver, and led those who were sent to take him. They add, that Jesus, after his crucifixion in *effigy*, was sent down again to the earth to comfort his mother and disciples and acquaint them how the Jews were deceived, and was then taken up a second time into heaven. It is supposed by several that this story was an original invention of Moḥammad's; but they are certainly mistaken: for several sectaries held the same opinion long before his time. The Basilidians, in the very beginning of Christianity, denied that Christ himself suffered, but [asserted] that Simon the Cirenean was crucified in his place. The Corinthians before them, and the Carpocratians next (to name no more of those who affirmed Jesus to have been a mere man), did believe the same thing, that it was not himself, but one of his followers, very like him, that was crucified. Photius tells us that he read a book entitled *The Journeys of the Apostles*, relating the acts of Peter, John, Andrew, Thomas, and Paul; and among other things contained therein this was one, that Christ was not crucified, but another in his stead, and that therefore he laughed at his crucifiers, or those who thought they had crucified him." The "Cross of Christ" is the missing link in the Muslim's creed; for we have in Islām the great anomaly of a religion which rejects the doctrine of a sacrifice for sin, whilst its great central feast is *a Feast of Sacrifice.* It is related by the Muslim historian al-Wāqidī, that Muḥammad had such repugnance to the sign of the cross that he destroyed everything brought to his house with that figure upon it.]

VI.—Divinity and Sonship of Christ, and His Sinlessness.

Sūrah xix. 35, 36: "That is Jesus the son of Mary, the word of truth (*Qaulu 'l-Ḥaqq*), whereon ye do dispute! God could not take to Himself a son! Celebrated be His praise! When He decrees a matter He only says to it, 'BE,' and it is; and verily God is my Lord and your Lord, so worship Him: this is the right way. But the sects have differed among themselves."

Sūrah iii. 51, 52: "These signs, and this wise warning do we rehearse to thee. Verily, Jesus is as Adam in the sight of God. He created Him of dust: He then said to him, 'Be'—and he was."

Sūrah xliii. 57-65: "And when the Son of Mary was set forth as an instance *of divine power*, lo! thy people cried out for *joy* thereat: And they said, 'Are our gods or is he the better?' They put this forth to thee only in the spirit of dispute. Yea, they are a contentious people. Jesus is no more than a servant whom we favoured, and proposed as an instance *of divine power* to the children of Israel; and if we pleased, we could from yourselves bring forth Angels to succeed you on earth: and he shall be a sign of the *last* hour; doubt not then of it, and follow ye me: this is the right way; and let not Satan turn you aside from it, for he is your manifest foe. And when Jesus came with manifest proofs, he said, 'Now am I come to you with wisdom; and a part of those things about which ye are at variance I will clear up to you; fear ye God, therefore, and obey me. Verily, God is my Lord and your Lord; wherefore, worship ye him: this is a right way.' But the different parties fell into disputes among themselves; but woe to those who thus transgressed, because of the punishment of an afflictive day!"

Sūrah ix. 30: "The Jews say Ezra is the Son of God; and the Christians say that the Messiah is the Son of God; that is what they say with their mouths imitating the sayings of those who misbelieved before—God fight them!—How they lie!"

Sūrah iii. 72, 73: "And some truly are there among them who torture the Scriptures with their tongues, in order that ye may suppose it to be from the Scripture, yet it is not from the Scripture. And they say, 'This is from God'; yet it is not from God: and they utter a lie against God, and they know they do so. It beseemeth not a man, that God should give him the Scriptures and the Wisdom, and the gift of prophecy, and that then he should say to his followers, 'Be ye worshippers of me, as well as of God'; but rather, 'Be ye perfect in things pertaining to God, since ye know' the Scriptures, and have studied deep.'"

Sūrah v. 19: "Infidels now are they who say, 'Verily God is the Messiah Ibn Maryam (son of Mary)! Say: And who could aught obtain from God, if he chose to destroy the Messiah Ibn Maryam, and his mother, and all who are on the earth together?'"

There is a remarkable Ḥadīs̤ related by Anas, which inadvertently proves that, whilst Muḥammad admitted his own sinfulness, as well as that of other prophets, he could not charge our Lord with sin. It is as follows: "The Prophet of God said, 'In the Day of Resurrection Muslims will not be able to move, and they will be greatly distressed, and will say, "Would to God that we had asked Him to create some one to intercede for us, that we might be taken from this place, and be delivered from tribulation and sorrow?" Then these men will go to Adam, and will say, "Thou art the father of all men, God created thee with His hand, and made thee a dweller in Paradise, and ordered His angels to prostrate themselves before thee, and taught thee the names of all things. Ask grace for us we pray thee!" And Adam will say, "I am not of that degree of eminence you suppose, for I committed a sin in eating of the grain which was forbidden. Go to Noah, the Prophet, he was the first who was sent by God to the unbelievers on the face of the earth." Then they will go to Noah and ask for intercession, and he will say, "I am not of that degree which ye suppose." And he will remember the sin which he committed in asking the Lord for the deliverance of his son (Hūd), not knowing whether it was a right request or not; and he will say, "Go to Abraham, who is the Friend of God." Then they will go to Abraham, and he will say, "I am not of that degree which ye suppose." And he will remember the three occasions upon which he told lies in the world; and he will say, "Go to Moses, who is the servant to whom God gave His law, and whom He allowed to converse with Him." And they will go to Moses, and Moses will say, "I am not of that degree which ye suppose." And he will remember the sin which he committed in slaying a man, and he will say, "Go to Jesus, He is the servant of God, the Apostle of God, the Spirit of God, and the Word of God." Then they will go to Jesus, and He will say, "Go to Muḥammad who is a servant, whose sins God has forgiven both first and last." Then the Muslims will come to me, and I will ask permission to go into God's presence and intercede for them.'" (*Mishkāt*, book xxiii. ch. xii.)

[In dealing with Muḥammadans the Christian missionary must not treat their system as though the teachings of Islām were precisely those of the modern Socinians (we speak of the *modern* Socinians, for both the Socini, uncle and nephew, admitted the miraculous conception of Christ, and said he ought to be worshipped.) Islām admits of the miraculous conception of Christ, and that He is the "*Word*" which God "conveyed into Mary"; and whilst the other five great prophets are but "the chosen," "the preacher," "the friend," "the converser with," and "the messenger of" God, Jesus is admitted to be the "*Spirit of God.*" He is the greatest miracle worker of all the prophets; and whilst Muḥammad is dead and buried, and saw corruption, all Muslim divines admit that Jesus "saw no corruption," and still lives with a human body in Paradise.

Moreover, it is said in the Ḥadīs̤ that the *Ḥaqīqatu'l-Muḥammadīyah* or the *Nūr-i-Muḥammad*, "the essence, or light of Muḥammad," was created before all things which were made by God. The pre-existence of the divine "Word which was made flesh and dwelt amongst us" is not, therefore, an idea foreign to the Muslim mind.]

VII.—The Trinity.

Sūrah v. 76–79: "They misbelieve who say, 'Verily, God is the Messiah, the son of Mary'; but the Messiah said, 'O children of Israel! worship God, my Lord and your Lord; verily, he who associates aught with God, God hath forbidden him Paradise, and his resort is the Fire, and the unjust shall have none to help them. They misbelieve who say, 'Verily, God is the third of three, for there is no God but one; and if they do not desist from what they say, there shall touch those who misbelieve amongst them grievous woe. Will they not turn again towards God and ask pardon of Him? for God is forgiving and merciful.' The Messiah, the son of Mary, is only a prophet! Prophets before him have passed away; and his mother was a confessor; they used both to eat food. See how we explain to them the signs, yet see how they turn aside!"

Sūrah iv. 169: "O ye people of the Book! overstep not bounds in your religion; and of God, speak only truth. The Messiah, Jesus, son of Mary, is only an apostle of God, and His Word which he conveyed into Mary, and a Spirit from Him. Believe, therefore, in God and His apostles, and say not, 'Three': (*i.e. there is a Trinity*)—Forbear—it will be better for you. God is only one God! Far be it from His glory that He should have a son! His, whatever is in the Heavens, and whatever is in the Earth! And God is a sufficient Guardian."

Sūrah v. 116, 117: "And when God shall say —'O Jesus, Son of Mary: hast thou said unto mankind—"Take me and my mother as two Gods, beside God?"' He shall say—'Glory be unto Thee! it is not for me to say that which I know to be not the truth; had I said that, verily thou wouldest have known it: Thou knowest what is in me, but I know not what is in Thee; for Thou well knowest things unseen! I spake not to them aught but that which thou didst bid me—"Worship God, my Lord and your Lord"; and I was a witness against them so long as I was amongst them: but when Thou didst take me away to Thyself Thou wert the watcher over them, for Thou art witness over all.'"

[From the text of the Qur'ān it appears that Muḥammad thought the Holy Trinity of the Christians consisted of the Father, the Son, and the Virgin; and historians tell us that there existed in Arabia a sect called Collyridians, who considered the Virgin Mary a divine person, and offered in worship to her a cake called Collyris; it is, therefore, not improbable that Muḥammad obtained his perverted notion of the Holy Trinity from the existence of this sect. From the expression "they both ate food," we must conclude that Muḥammad had but a sensuous idea of the Trinity in Unity, and had never been instructed in the orthodox faith with reference to this dogma.

Al-Baiẓāwī (A.H. 685), in his commentary on Sūrah iv. 169, says: "Say not there are Three," that is, "Do not say there are three Gods," namely, *Allāh* and *al-Masīḥ* and *Maryam*; or "Do not say God is Three," meaning that there are Three *Aqānīm* (اقانيم) or Essences —*Ab* (Father), *Ibn* (Son), and *Rūḥu'l-Quds* (Holy Spirit), and interpreting it thus: *Ab*, the *Ẕāt* or Essence; *Ibn*, the *'Ilm* or Knowledge; and *Rūhu 'l-Qud*, the Ḥayāt or Life of God.

Ḥusain (A.H. 900) quotes al-Baiẓāwī, and offers no opinion of his own.

The Jalālān (A.H. 911) say "Three" means Allāh and 'Īsa and his Mother.

The word generally used by Muḥammadan writers for the Trinity is *at-Tas̤līs̤* (التثليث). [TRINITY.]

VIII.—The Second Coming of Jesus.

The Qur'ān has no definite teaching on the subject, but the Traditions have. See *Mishkātu 'l-Maṣābīḥ*, book xxiii. ch. vi.)

Abū Hurairah relates that the Prophet said, "I swear by God, it is near, when Jesus, son of Mary, will descend from the heavens upon your people, a just king, and he will break the cross, and will kill the swine, and will remove the poll-tax from the unenfranchised; and there will be great wealth in his time, so much that nobody will accept of it; and in that time, one prostration in prayer will be better than the world and everything in it."

And Abū Hurairah said, "If ye doubt about this coming to pass, then read this verse (Sūrah iv. 157), and there shall not be one of those who have received the Scriptures who shall not believe in Him (Jesus) before His death."

Abū Hurairah again relates that the Prophet said, "I swear by God, Jesus son of Mary will come down, a just king; he will kill the swine, and break the cross, and remove the poll-tax from the unenfranchised; and camels will not be rode in his time on account of the immensity of wealth, and man's being in want of nothing; and verily enmity, hatred and malice will go from man; and verily, Jesus will call people to wealth, and nobody will take it."

Jābir relates that the Prophet said: "A section of my people will always fight for the true religion, and will be victorious, unto the resurrection. Then Jesus son of Mary will come down; and the prince of my people will say to him, 'Come in front, and say prayers for us.' And he will say to him, 'I shall not act as Imām, because some of you are princes over others.' And Jesus will say this from respect to my people."

'Abdu'llāh ibn 'Amr relates that the Prophet said: "Jesus will come down to the earth, and will marry and have children, and will stay on the earth forty-five years, and then die, and be buried in my place of burial; and I and Jesus shall rise up from one place, between Abū-Bakr and 'Umar." [HUJRAH.]

IX.—His Exaltation in Heaven.

There is some difference of opinion as to where Jesus Christ now is. All Muslim divines agree that "he saw no corruption," but they differ as to the exact stage of celestial bliss in which he resides in the body. According to a tradition by Qatādah (*Mishkāt*, book xxiv. ch. vii.), Muḥammad said, on the night of the Mī'rāj or celestial journey, he saw John and Jesus in the second heaven. The Jalalān agree with this tradition. But in the commentary known as the *Jāmi'u 'l-Bayān* (vol. i. 656) it is said he is in the third region of bliss; whilst some say he is in the fourth.

X.—The Disciples of Jesus.

The disciples of Jesus are called in the Qur'ān *al-Ḥawāriyūn*, a word which seems to be derived from an Ethiopic root, signifying "to send," but which al-Baiẓāwī says means "white ones," and that it was given to the disciples of Jesus either because they were holy and sincere men or because they wore white clothes. It is noticeable that not one of the twelve apostles is mentioned by name in the Qur'ān. In the story told of disciples visiting the city (of Antioch), three disciples are mentioned, and commentators say they were John, Jude and Simon. [See Sūrah xxxvi. 13, 19—HABIB THE CARPENTER.] John the Baptist and his father Zacharias are mentioned. (Sūrahs xix. 7, xxi. 90.)

JETHRO. [SHU'AIB.]

JEWELS.

JEWELS. Arabic *Jauhar* (جوهر), pl. *Jawāhir*. According to the *Hidāyah* a thief is liable to suffer amputation of the hand for stealing jewels, such as a ring set with emerald, ruby, or chrysolite, as such are rare articles, and are not held to be of an indifferent nature, neither are they undesirable. (Vol. ii. p. 93.)

A *sillim* sale [SILLIM], or a sale in trust, of jewels and marine shells, is not lawful, because the unities of these vary in their value. (Vol. ii p. 539.) In the partition of property, jewels must not be divided by the Qāẓī, but by mutual arrangement in the family, because of the great difference in the actual value of jewels. (Vol. iv. 13.)

JEWS, JUDAISM.

JEWS, JUDAISM. The Jews are mentioned in the Qur'ān and Traditions under the names of *Yahūdī* (يهودى), pl. *Yahūd*, and *Banū Isrā'īl* (بنو اسرائيل), "Children of Israel." No distinction is made between Jews and Israelites. They are acknowledged to be a people in possession of a divine book, and are called *Ahlu 'l-Kitāb*, or "people of the book." Moses is their special law-giver (Abraham not having been a Jew, but a "*Ḥanīf Muslim*"); they are a people highly-favoured of God, but are said to have perverted the meaning of Scripture, and to have called Ezra "the Son of God." They have an intense hatred of all true Muslims; and, as a punishment for their sins, some of them in times past had been changed into apes and swine, and others will have their hands tied to their necks and be cast into the Fire at the Day of Judgment.

The following are the selections from the Qur'ān relating to the Jews:—

Sūrah ii. 116: "O children of Israel! remember my favour wherewith I have favoured you, and that high above all mankind have I raised you."

Sūrah v. 48, 49: "Verily, we have sent down the law (*Taurāt*) wherein are guidance and light. By it did the prophets who professed Islām judge the Jews; and the doctors and the teachers *judged* by that portion of the Book of God, of which they were the keepers and the witnesses. Therefore, *O Jews*! fear not men but fear Me; and barter not away my signs for a mean price! And whoso will not judge by what God hath sent down—such are the Infidels. And therein have we enacted for them, 'Life for life, an eye for eye, and nose for nose, and ear for ear, and tooth for tooth, and for wounds retaliation':—Whoso shall compromise it as alms shall have therein the expiation *of his sin*; and whoso will not judge by what God hath sent down—such are the transgressors."

Sūrah iii. 60: "Abraham was not a Jew, nor yet a Christian. He was a Ḥanīf Muslim, and not an idolater."

Sūrah ix. 30: "The Jews say, 'Ezra ('Uzair) is a son of God'; and the Christians say, 'The Messiah is a son of God.' Such the saying in their mouths! They resemble the saying of the Infidels of old! God do battle with them! How are they misguided!"

Sūrah vi. 147: "To the Jews did we forbid every beast having an entire hoof, and of both bullocks and sheep we forbade them the fat, save what might be on their backs, or their entrails, and the fat attached to the bone. With this have we recompensed them, because of their transgression: and verily, we are indeed equitable."

Sūrah iv. 48, 49: "Among the Jews are those who displace the words of their Scriptures, and say, 'We have heard, and we have not obeyed. Hear thou, but as one that heareth not; and LOOK AT US'; perplexing with their tongues, and wounding the Faith by their revilings. But if they would say, 'We have heard, and we obey; hear thou, and REGARD US'; it were better for them, and more right. But God hath cursed them for their unbelief. Few only of them are believers!"

Sūrah ii. 70–73: "Desire ye then that for your sakes *the Jews* should believe? Yet a part of them heard the word of God, and then, after they had understood it, perverted it, and knew that they did so. And when they fall in with the faithful, they say, 'We believe'; but when they are apart one with another, they say, 'Will ye acquaint them with what God hath revealed to you, that they may dispute with you about it in the presence of your Lord?' Understand ye their aim? Know they not that God knoweth what they hide, as well as what they bring to light? But there are illiterates among them who are not acquainted with the Book, but with lies only, and have but vague fancies. Woe to those who with their own hands transcribe the Book corruptly, and then say, 'This is from God,' that they may sell it for some mean price! Woe then to them for that which their hands have written! and, Woe to them for the gains which they have made!"

Sūrah v. 64–69: "SAY: O people of the Book! do ye not disavow us only because we believe in God, and in what He hath sent down to us, and in what He hath sent down aforetime, and because most of you are doers of ill? SAY: Can I announce to you any retribution worse than that *which awaiteth them* with God? They whom God hath cursed and with whom He hath been angry—some of them hath He changed into apes and swine; and they who worship Ṭagūt are in evil plight, and have gone far astray from the right path! When they presented themselves to you they said, 'We believe'; but Infidels they came in unto you, and Infidels they went forth! God well knew what they concealed. Many of them shalt thou see hastening together to wickedness and malice, and to eat unlawful things. Shame on them for what they have done! Had not their doctors and teachers forbidden their uttering wickedness, and their eating unlawful food, bad indeed would have been their doings! 'The hand of God,' say the Jews, 'is chained up.' Their own hands shall be chained up—and for that which they have said shall they be cursed. Nay! outstretched are both His hands! At His own pleasure does He bestow gifts. That which hath been sent down to thee from thy Lord will surely increase the rebellion and unbelief of many of them; and we have put enmity and hatred between them that shall last till the day of the Resurrection. Oft as they kindle *a beacon* fire for war shall God quench it! and their aim will be to abet disorder on the earth: but God loveth not the abettors of disorder."

Nearly all the leading scripture characters connected with Old Testament history are either mentioned by name in the Qur'ān or are referred to in the Traditions and commentaries

(*a*) In the Qur'ān we have Adam (*Adam*), Abel (*Hābīl*), Cain (*Qābīl*), Enoch (*Idrīs*), Noah (*Nūḥ*), Abraham (*Ibrahīm*), Lot (*Lūt*), Isaac (*Isḥāq*), Ishmael (*Ismā'īl*), Jacob (*Ya'qūb*), Joseph (*Yūsuf*), Job (*Aiyūb*), Moses (*Mūsā*), Aaron (*Hārūn*), Korah (*Qārūn*), Pharaoh (*Fir'aūn*), Haman (*Hāmān*), David (*Dā'ūd*), Goliath (*Jālūt*), Solomon (*Sulaimān*), Saul (*Ṭālūt*), Jonah (*Yūnas*), Elisha (*Al-yasa'*).

(*b*) In the Traditions and in the earliest commentaries on the Qur'ān, are mentioned: Eve (*Ḥawwā'*), Hagar (*Hājar*), Nebuchadnezzar (*Bukhtnaṣṣar*), Joshua (*Yūsha'*), Jeremiah (*Armiyā*), Isaiah (*Sha'yā'*), Benjamin (*Binyāmīn*), Ezekiel (*Ḥizqīl*), Baalam (*Bal'am*), Daniel (*Dāniyāl*), Sarah (*Sārah*), and many others. But it is remarkable that after Solomon, there is no mention of the Kings of Israel and Judah.

(*c*) The chief incidents of Jewish history are recorded in the Qur'ān with a strange and curious admixture of Rabbinical fable. The creation of the world, the formation of Adam and Eve, the fall, the expulsion from Eden, Cain's and Abel's sacrifices, the death of Abel; Noah's preaching, the Ark built, the deluge, the tower of Babel; Abraham, the friend of God, his call from idolatry, Isaac the son of promise, Sarah's incredulity, Hagar and Ishmael, the willingness of Abraham to sacrifice his son, Lot and the cities of the plain; Jacob and the tribes, Joseph sold into Egypt, Potiphar's wife, Joseph tempted, the dreams of the baker and butler, and of the king; Moses, his preservation in infancy, kills an Egyptian, flies to Midian, works miracles in the presence of Pharaoh, manna from heaven, the giving of the law, Aaron's rod, the golden calf, the passage of the Red Sea; Job's patience; Balaam cursing the Israelites; David's psalms, his sin and repentance; Solomon's wisdom, the Queen of Sheba, the building of the temple; Jonah's preaching, his escape from the fish: these and many other incidents, evidently taken from the Old Testament, and worked up into a narrative with the assistance of Talmudic interpretations, form the chief historical portion of the Qur'ān.

(*d*) Many of the doctrines and social precepts of the Qur'ān are also from Judaism. The Unity of God, the ministry of angels, the inspired law, the law of marriage and divorce, domestic slavery, the day of Sacrifice, prayer and ablution, the lex talionis, the degrees of affinity, the stoning of the adulterer, and many other injunctions, are precisely those of the Mosaic code, with some modifications to meet the requirements of Arabian social life.

Whilst, therefore, Muḥammad took little of his religious system from Christianity, he was vastly indebted to Judaism both for his historical narratives and his doctrines and precepts. Islām is nothing more nor less than Judaism plus the Apostleship of Muḥammad. The teachings of Jesus form no part of his religious system. [CHRISTIANITY.]

(*e*) The Quraish charged Muḥammad with want of originality in his revelations. For even at the end of his career, and when he was uttering his latest Sūrahs, "they said, as our verses were rehearsed to them—'This is nothing but tales of yore.'" (Sūrah viii. 31.) "And when it was said to them, What is it your Lord sent down? They said, 'Old folk's tales.'" (Sūrah xvi. 25.) The

Quraish even charged him with having obtained assistance, "They said it is only some mortal who teaches him." And Muḥammad admits there was someone who might be suspected of helping him, for he replies, "The tongue of him whom they lean towards is barbarous and this (Qur'ān) is plain Arabic." (Sūrah xvi. 105.) Ḥusain, the commentator, in remarking upon this verse, says, "It is related that there was a slave belonging to 'Amr ibn 'Abdi 'llāh al-Ḥaẓramī, named Jabr (and according to some a second slave named Yasār), who used to read the Law and the Gospel, and Muḥammad used, when he passed, to stand and listen."

And the whole construction of the Qur'ān bears out the supposition that its subject matter was received orally and worked into poetical Arabic by a man of genius. Whatever he may have heard from the readings of Jabr and Yasār of the text of the Old and New Testament scriptures, it is very evident that he obtained his explanations from one well versed in Talmudic lore. A Jewish Rabbi, Abraham Geiger, in A.D. 1833, wrote a prize essay in answer to the question put by the university: "Inquiratur in fontes Alcorani seu legis Muhammedicæ eos, qui ex Judæismo derivandi sunt." His essay in reply is entitled, "Was hat Mohammed aus dem Judenthume aufgenommen?" In this treatise it is clearly demonstrated how much the whole system of Islām is indebted to Talmudic Judaism for its teachings. Its narratives, its doctrines, and its theological terms, are chiefly derived from those of the Talmud.

The works of Geiger, J. M. Arnold, Hershom, McCaul, Bishop Barclay, Deutsch, Lightfoot, Schottgen, Ugolini, Meuschen (which pending a complete translation of the Talmud, can be consulted), will, upon comparison with the teachings of the Qur'ān, reveal how entirely Muḥammad constructed his religious system on the lines of Talmudic Judaism. We are indebted to the late Dr. J. M. Arnold's *Islam and Christianity*, for the following review of the subject, he having largely availed himself of the facts given in Geiger's celebrated essay, already referred to.

The seven heavens and the seven earths which are held in the Talmud, have found their way into the Qur'ān.[1] During the creation, God's glorious throne was placed in the air upon the water.[2] According to the Talmud, "the world is the sixtieth part of the garden, the garden is the sixtieth part of Eden"; and Muḥammad states that the breadth of the garden is that of heaven and earth.[3] Both in the Qur'ān and Talmud we find seven hells as the appointed abode for the damned, and each hell has seven gates in both documents.[4] The entrance of *Jahannam* is marked, according to the Sukkah, by two date-trees, between which smoke issues; and the Qur'ān speaks of a tree in hell [ZAQQUM] of which the damned are to eat, and of which many terrible things are related.[1] In the Talmud the prince of hell demands supply for his domain, and a similar request is made in the Qur'ān.[2] Between the seven heavens and the seven hells is an intermediate place [A'RAF], for those who are too good to be cast into hell and too imperfect to be admitted into heaven.[3] This intermediate abode is, however, so narrow, that the conversations of the blessed and the damned on either side may be overheard. Again, the happiness of Paradise [PARADISE] is similarly described in both Talmud and Qur'ān;[4] also the difficulty of attaining it. The Talmud declares that it is as easy for an elephant to enter through the eye of a needle; the Qur'ān substituting a camel for an elephant.[5] That the dead live in the sight of God is stated in both documents in the same terms, and that there is no admission to the actual presence of the Almighty before the Day of Judgment and the resurrection of the dead.[6] The signs of the last day as given in the Qur'ān are borrowed equally from the Scriptures and the Talmud.[7] [RESURRECTION.]

The lengthened descriptions in the Qur'ān of the future resurrection and judgment are also tinged with a Talmudical colouring. That the several members of the human body shall bear witness against the damned, and that idols shall share in the punishment of their worshippers, is stated in both the Talmud and Qur'ān.[8] The time of the last judgment Muḥammad declined to fix, resting upon the Jewish or Scriptural sentence, that "one day with God is like a thousand."[9] The Jews, in speaking of the resurrection of the dead, allude to the sending down of rain; the Qur'ān also affirms that this means of quickening the dead will be employed.[10] Further still, the Talmudical idea that the dead will rise in the garments in which they were buried, likewise has been adopted by Islām.[11] The Jewish opinion was that "all the prophets saw in a dark, but Moses in a clear mirror."[12] In the Qur'ān, God sends down His angelic messenger, Gabriel, as "the Holy Ghost," with revelations; and this very

[1] Chagiga, ix. 2.
[2] Rashi on Gen. i. 2; and Sūrahs xi. 9; xxvii. 26; xxiii. 117 lxxxv. 15.
[3] Thaanith, x.; Pesashim, xciv.; and Sūrah iii. 127.
[4] Talmud Eurbin, xix. 1; Midrash on Ps. xi.; and Sūrah xv. 44.

[1] Sukkah xxxvii.; and Sūrahs xxxvii. 60; xliv. 43.
[2] Othioth by Rabbi Akiba, viii. 1; and Sūrah l. 29.
[3] Midrash on Eccles. vii. 14; and Sūrah vii. 44–47.
[4] Mishnah Aboth, iv. 17; and Sūrahs ix. 38; xiii. 26.
[5] Sūrah vii. 38.
[6] Sūrahs lxxv. 23; lxxxix. 27.
[7] Sūrahs xxi. 104; xxxix. 67; xliv. 9; xvii. 60; xxi. 98; xxii. 2; xxvii. 89. Compared with Isa. xxxiv. 4; Ezek. xxxviii., xxxix.
[8] Chagiga, xxvi.; Thaanith xi.; and Sūrahs xxiv. 24; xxxvi. 65; xli. 19; Sukkah, xxix.; and Sūrah xxi. 98.
[9] Ps. xc. 4; Sanhedrin, xcv. 2; and Sūrah xxii. 46; xxxii. 4; Ezek. xxxvii. 13; and Sūrah c. 9.
[10] Thaanith, at the beginning; and Sūrahs vi. 95; xxx. 49; xxxvi. 33; xli. 39; xliii. 10.
[11] Sanhedrin, xc. 2; Khethubhoth, cxi. 2.
[12] Jebhamoth, xlix.; and Sūrah xlii. 50.

notion of Gabriel being considered the Spirit of God seems to be borrowed from the Jews.[1]

Again, the demonology of the Qur'ān is chiefly taken from the Talmud. Three properties the demons have in common with angels, and three with men—they have wings like angels, they can fly from one end of the world to the other, and know things to come. But do they know future events? No, but they listen behind the veil. The three properties in common with men are: they eat and drink, indulge in physical love, and die.[2] This Jewish idea was adopted in the Qur'ān, and spun out *ad libitum*; for instance, whilst listening once to the angelic conversations, they were hunted away with stones. Their presence in places of worship is admitted both in the Talmud and the Qur'ān; thus it happened that "when the servant of God stood up to invoke Him, the Jinns all but pressed on him in the crowd."[3] [GENII.]

Amongst the moral precepts which are borrowed from the Talmud, we may mention that children are not to obey their parents when the latter demand that which is evil.[4] Prayer may be performed standing, walking, or even riding;[5] devotions may be shortened in urgent cases, without committing sin;[6] drunken persons are not to engage in acts of worship;[7] ablutions before prayer are in special cases enforced, but generally required both in the Talmud and the Qur'ān;[8] each permit the use of sand instead of water [TAYAMMUM], when the latter is not to be procured.[9] The Talmud prohibits loud and noisy prayers, and Muḥammad gives this short injunction:—"Cry not in your prayers";[10] in addition to this secret prayer, public worship is equally commended. The Shema prayer of the Jews is to be performed "when one is able to distinguish a blue from a white thread," and this is precisely the criterion of the commencement of the fast in the Qur'ān.[11] [RAMAZAN.]

The following social precepts are likewise copied from Judaism: a divorced woman must wait three months before marrying again[12] [DIVORCE]; mothers are to nurse their children two full years; and the degrees of affinity within which marriages are lawful.[13] [MARRIAGE.] The historical incidents which Muḥammad borrowed from Judaism are embodied, regardless of the sources from which he gleaned them, and indifferent to all order or system. Ignorant of Jewish history, Muḥammad appropriates none of the historical way-marks which determine the great epochs recorded in the Old Testament, but confines himself to certain occurrences in the lives of single individuals. At the head of the antediluvian patriarchs stands the primogenitor of the human race. In Sūrah, ii. 28–33 we read, "When thy Lord said to the angels, Verily I am going to place a substitute on earth, they said, Wilt thou place there one who will do evil therein and shed blood? but we celebrate Thy praise and sanctify Thee. God answered, Verily I know that which ye know not; and He taught Adam the names of all things, and then proposed them to the angels, and said, Declare unto me the names of these things if ye say truth. They answered, Praise be unto Thee, we have no knowledge but what Thou teachest us, for Thou art knowing and wise. God said, O, Adam, tell them their names. And when he had told them their names, God said, Did I not tell you that I know the secrets of heaven and earth, and know that which ye discover, and that which ye conceal?" Let us examine whence the Qur'ān obtained this information. "When God intended to create man, He advised with the angels and said unto them, We will make man in our own image (Gen. i. 26). Then said they, What is man, that Thou rememberest him (Psalm viii. 5), what shall be his peculiarity? He answered, His wisdom is superior to yours. Then brought He before them cattle, animals, and birds, and asked for their names, but they knew it not. After man was created, He caused them to pass before Him, and asked for their names and he answered, This is an ox, that an ass, this a horse, and that a camel. But what is thy name? To me it becomes to be called 'earthly,' for from 'earth' I am created."[1] To this may be added the fable that God commanded the angels to worship Adam,[2] which is likewise appropriated from Talmudic writings. Some Jewish fables record that the angels contemplated worshipping man, but were prevented by God; others precisely agree with the Qur'ān,[3] that God commanded the angels to worship man, and that they obeyed with the exception of Satan.

The Sunnah informs us that Adam was sixty yards high, and Rabinnical fables make him extend from one end of the world to the other; but upon the angels esteeming him a second deity, God put His hand upon him and reduced him to a thousand yards![4] [ADAM.]

The account given in the Qur'ān of Cain's murder is borrowed from the Bible, and his conversation with Abel, before he slew him,[5] is the same as that in the Targum of Jerusalem, generally called pseudo-Jonathan. After the murder, Cain sees a raven burying

1 1 Kings xxii. 21.
2 Chagiga xvi. 1; and Sūrahs xv. 17, 34; xxxvii. 78; lxxxi. 24; lxvii. 5; xxxvii. 7; lxxii.
3 Sūrah lxxii. 19.
4 Jebhamoth, vi.; and Sūrah xxix. 7.
5 Berachoth, x.; and Sūrahs ii. 230; iii. 188; x. 13.
6 Mishnah Berachoth, iv. 4; and Sūrah iv. 102.
7 Berachoth, xxxi. 2; and Sūrah iv. 46.
8 Mishnah Berachoth, iii. 4; and Sūrahs iv. 46; v. 9.
9 Berachoth, xlvi.; and Sūrah v. 8.
10 Berachoth xxxi. 2; and Surah xvii. 110.
11 Mishnah Berachoth, i. 2; and Sūrah ii. 183.
12 Mishnah Jebhamoth, iv. 10; and Sūrah ii. 228.
13 Talmud Kethuboth, lx. 1; and Sūrahs ii. 233; xxxi. 13; xxiv. 31; Joseph., *Antiq.* ii. 9.

1 Midrash Rabbah on Leviticus, Parashah xix.; and Genesis, Parashah viii.; and Sanhedrin, xxxviii.
2 Sūrahs vii. 10–26; xv. 28–44; xvi. 63–69; xviii. 48; xx. 115; xxxvii. 71–86.
3 Midrash of Rabbi Moses, examined by Zunz, p. 296.
4 Eisenmenger, *Judenthum*, vol. i. p. 365.
5 Sūrah v. 30.

another, and from this sight gains the idea of interring Abel. The Jewish fable differs only in ascribing the interment to the parents: "Adam and his wife sat weeping and lamenting him, not knowing what to do with the body, as they were unacquainted with burying. Then came a raven, whose fellow was dead: he took and buried it in the earth, hiding it before their eyes. Then said Adam, I shall do like this raven, and, taking Abel's corpse, he dug in the earth and hid it."[1] The sentence following in the Qur'ān—"Wherefore we commanded the children of Israel, that he who slayeth a soul, not by way of retaliation, or because he doeth corruptly in the earth, shall be as if he had slain all mankind; but he who saveth a soul alive shall be as if he saved all souls alive," would have no connection with what precedes or follows, were it not for the Targum of Onkelos, in the paraphrase of Gen. iv. 10, where it is said that the blood of Cain's brother cried to God from the earth, thus implying that Abel's posterity were also cut off. And in the Mishnah Sanhedrin, we find the very words which the Qur'ān attaches to the murder, apparently with sense or connection.[2] [ABEL, CAIN.]

Noah stands forth as the preacher of righteousness, builds the ark, and is saved, with his family;[3] his character is, however, drawn more from Rabbinical than Biblical sources. The conversations of Noah with the people, and the words with which they mocked him whilst building the ark,[4] are the same in Talmudical writings as in the Qur'ān; and both declare that the generation of the flood was punished with boiling water.[5] [NOAH.]

The next patriarch after the flood is Hūd, who is none other than Eber; another sample of the ignorance of Muḥammad. In the days of Hūd the tower is constructed; the "obstinate hero," probably Nimrod, takes the lead; the sin of idolatry is abounding; an idol is contemplated as the crowning of the tower; but the building is overthrown, the tribes are dispersed, and punished in this world and in the world to come.[6] These particulars are evidently borrowed from scripture and Rabbinical writings. In the Qur'ān, however, the dispersion is caused by a poisonous wind, and not by the confusion of tongues. The significance which the Qur'ān gives to Hūd is again in perfect accordance with Rabbinical Judaism: "Eber was a great prophet, for he prophetically called his son Peleg (dispersion), by the help of the Holy Ghost, because the earth was to be dispersed."[7] Among all the patriarchs, Abraham was most esteemed by Muḥammad, as being neither Jew nor Christian, but a Muslim. That he wrote books is also the belief of the Jewish

[1] Pirke Rabbi Elieser, xxi.; and Sūrah v. 34.
[2] Mishnah Sanhedrin, iv. 5.
[3] Geiger's Essay, p. 109; and Sūrahs vii. 57; x. 72; xxii. 43; xxiii. 23; xxv. 39; xxvi. 105; xxix. 13; xxxvii. 73; liv. 9; lxxi. 1.
[4] Sanhedrin, cviii.
[5] Rosh Hashanah, xvi. 2; Sanhedrin, cviii.; and Sūrahs xi. 42; xxiii. 27.
[6] Mishnah Sanhedrin, x. 3; and Sūrah xi. 63.
[7] Seder Olam, quoted Midrash Jalkut, lxii.

doctors.[1] His attaining the knowledge of the true faith, his zeal to convert his generation; his destruction of the idols; the fury of the people; their insisting on his being burned, and his marvellous deliverance: all these particulars in the life of Abraham, as given by the Qur'ān, are minutely copied from Jewish fictions.[2] [HUD, ABRAHAM.]

The Qur'ān states that the angels whom Abraham received appeared as ordinary Arabs, and he was astonished when they declined to eat. According to the Talmud, they also "appeared to him no more than Arabs;"[3] but another passage adds: "The angels descended and did eat. Are they, then, said to have really eaten? No! but they appeared as if they did eat and drink." As a proof of Muḥammad's uncertainty respecting the history of Abraham, we add, that the doubt regarding their having a son in their old age is expressed in the Qur'ān by Abraham instead of Sarah, and she is made to laugh at the promise of a son, before it was given. Again, the command to offer his son is given to Abraham before Isaac is born or promised, so that the son who was to be offered up could be none other than Ishmael, who was spoken of immediately before as the "meek youth!" Muḥammadan divines are, however, not agreed whether Ishmael was to be offered up, although it is reported by some that the horns of the ram, which was sacrificed in his stead, were preserved at Makkah, his dwelling-place! [ISHMAEL.] We may account for Muḥammad's reckoning Ishmael among the prophets and patriarchs, from his being considered the patriarch of the Arabs and the founder of the Ka'bah.

Among the sons of Jacob, Joseph occupies the pre-eminence. His history is mainly the same as in the Bible, embellished with the fabulous tradition of the Jews. Among these is the assumption that Joseph "would have sinned had he not seen the evident demonstration of his Lord." That this is borrowed is clear from the following fable: Rabbi Jochanan saith, "Both intended to commit sin: seizing him by the garment, she said, Lie with me. . . . Then appeared to him the form of his father at the window, who called to him, Joseph! Joseph! the names of thy brothers shall be engraven upon the stones of the Ephod, also thine own: wilt thou that it shall be erased?"[4] This is almost literally repeated by a Muslim commentary to the Sūrah xii. 24. The fable of Potiphar's wife inviting the Egyptian ladies to a feast, to see Joseph, because they had laughed at her, and of their being so overcome with admiration of Joseph,[5] that they accidentally cut their hands in eating fruit, is exactly so related in a very ancient Hebrew book, from which Muḥammad doubtless derived it. The story about the garment being rent, and the setting

[1] The Jews ascribe to him the *Sepher Jezirah*.
[2] Midrash Rabbah on Genesis, Parash. xvii.
[3] Kiddushin, lii.
[4] Sotah, xxxvi. 2.
[5] Sūrah xii. 26; and the Commentary of al-Farrār.

up of an evidence of guilt or innocence respecting it, is also borrowed, to the very letter from the same source.[1] In this Sūrah it is also stated, that "the devil made him (Joseph) forget the remembrance of his Lord," in perfect harmony with the Jewish tradition, "Vain speech tendeth to destruction; though Joseph twice urged the chief butler to remember him, yet he had to remain two years longer in prison."[2] The seeking protection from man is here represented as the instigation of Satan. [JOSEPH.]

The Qur'ān causes Jacob to tell his sons to enter at different gates, and the same injunction is given by the Patriarch in the Jewish writings: "Jacob said to them, Enter not through one and the same gate."[3] The exclamation of the sons of Israel, when they found the cup in Benjamin's sack—"Has he stolen? so has his brother also"—are clearly a perversion of the words which the Jewish traditions put into their mouths: "Behold a thief, son of a female thief!" referring to the stealing of the Seraphim by Rachel.[4] Muḥammad, again, acquaints us that Jacob knew by divine revelation that his son Joseph was still alive, and Jewish tradition enables us to point out whence he obtained the information. We read in the Midrash Jalkut, "An unbeliever asked our master, Do the dead continue to live? your parents do not believe it, and will ye receive it? Of Jacob, it is said, he refused to be comforted; had he believed that the dead still lived, would he not have been comforted? But he answered, Fool, he knew by the Holy Ghost that he still really lived, and about a living person people need no comfort."[5]

Muḥammad made but scanty allusions to the early patriarchs, Joseph only excepted; but concerning Moses, it was his interest to be more profuse in his communications, possibly from the desire to be considered like him, as he is generally thought to have taken that prophet as his model. Among the oppressions which Pharaoh exercised towards the Jews, are named his ordering their children to be cast into the water. Moses, the son of 'Imrān was put into an ark by his mother; Pharaoh's wife, observing the child, rescues him from death, and gives him back to his mother to nurse. When Moses was grown up, he sought to assist his oppressed brethren, and kills an Egyptian; being the next day reminded of this deed by an Hebrew, he flees to Midian, and marries the daughter of an inhabitant of that country.[6] When about to leave Midian, he sees a burning bush, and, approaching it, receives a call to go to Egypt to exhort Pharaoh, and perform miracles; he accepts the mission, but requests the aid of his brother Aaron.[1] Pharaoh, however remains an infidel, and gathers his sorcerers together, who perform only inferior miracles; and, in spite of Pharaoh's threats, they become believers.[2] Judgment falls upon the Egyptians; they are drowned, whilst the Israelites are saved.[3] A rock yields water. Moses receives the law,[4] and desires to see the glory of God.[5] During Moses' absence, the Israelites make a golden calf, which he destroys, and reducing it to powder, makes them drink it.[6] After this, Moses chooses seventy men as assistants.[7] The spies sent to Canaan are all wicked with the exception of two: the people being deceived by them, must wander forty years in the desert.[8] Korah, on quarrelling with Moses, is swallowed up by the earth.[9] [KORAH.] The marvellous journey of Moses with his servant is not to be omitted in this summary of events.[10] Among the details deserve to be mentioned, that Hāmān and Korah were counsellors of Pharaoh.[11] It is not surprising that Muḥammad should associate Hāmān with Pharaoh as an enemy of the Jews, since he cared little when individuals lived, provided they could be introduced with advantage. Korah, according to Jewish tradition, was chief agent or treasurer to Pharaoh.[12] The ante-exodus persecution of the Jews is ascribed to a dream of Pharaoh.[13] This is in exact accordance with Jewish tradition, which, as Canon Churton remarks, has in part the sanction of Acts vii. and Hebrews xi., though not found in Exodus: "The sorcerers said to Pharaoh, A boy shall be born who will lead the Israelites out of Egypt. Then thought he, Cast all male children into the river, and he will be cast in among them."[14] The words (Exod. xi. 7), "I will call one of the Hebrew women," produced the Rabbinical fiction, "Why just a Hebrew woman? This shows that he was handed to all the Egyptian women; but he would not drink, for God said, The mouth which shall once speak with me, should it drink what is unclean?"[15] This was too valuable for Muḥammad to omit from the Qur'ān.[16] Although it is nowhere said in the Bible that the sign of the leprous hand was wrought in the presence of Pharaoh, yet the Qur'ān relates it as having there taken place.[17] And in this also it was preceded by Jewish tradition—"He put his hand into his bosom, and withdrew it leprous, white as snow; they also put their hands into their

[1] Midrash Jalkut, cxlvi.
[2] Midrash Rabbah on Gen. xl. 14; Geiger, p. 146; and Sūrah xii. 42.
[3] Midrash Rabbah on Genesis, Parash. xci.; and Sūrah xii. 67.
[4] Midrash Rabbah, xcii.; Gen. xxxi. 19; and Sūrah xii. 77.
[5] Midrash Jalkut, cxliii.; and Sūrah xii. 86.
[6] Sūrahs xx. 37; xxviii. 2.

[1] Sūrahs xx. 8; xxvi. 9; xxxviii. 29; lxxix. 15.
[2] Sūrahs vii. 101; x. 76; xi. 99; xx. 50.
[3] Sūrahs ii. 46; vii. 127; x. 90; xx. 79; xxvi. 52 xxviii. 40; xliii. 55.
[4] Sūrah vii. 143.
[5] Sūrahs vii. 135; ii. 52; ix. 152.
[6] Sūrahs ii. 48; vii. 147; xx. 82.
[7] Sūrah vii. 155.
[8] Sūrah v. 23.
[9] Sūrah xxviii. 16.
[10] Sūrah xviii. 59.
[11] Sūrah xxviii. 38; xxix. 38; xl. 25.
Midrash on Numbers, Parash. xiv.
[13] Sūrah xxviii. 5.
[14] Pirke Rabbi Elieser, xlviii.
[15] Sotah xii. 2.
[16] Sūrah xxiii. 11.
[17] Sūrahs vii. 105; xxv. 32.

bosoms and withdrew them leprous, white as snow."[1] Again, among Moses' own people, none but his own tribe believed him.[2] This Muḥammad doubtless inferred from the statement of the Rabbis: "The tribe of Levi was exempted from hard labour."[3] Among the sorcerers of Egypt, who first asked for their wages, and then became believers, when their serpents were swallowed by that of Moses,[4] Pharaoh himself was chief.[5] Here, again, Muḥammad is indebted to Judaism: "Pharaoh, who lived in the days of Moses, was a great sorcerer."[6] In other places of the Qur'ān, Pharaoh claims divinity,[7] and Jewish tradition makes him declare, "Already from the beginning ye speak falsehood, for I am Lord of the world, I have made myself as well as the Nile"; as it is said of him (Ezek. xxix. 3), "Mine is the river, and I have made it."[8] The Arab prophet was much confused with regard to the plagues; in some places he enumerates nine,[9] in others only five, the first of which is said to be the Flood![10] As the drowning in the Red Sea happened after the plagues, he can only allude to the Deluge.

The following somewhat dark and uncertain passage[11] concerning Pharaoh has caused commentators great perplexity. It is stated that Pharaoh pursued the Israelites until actually drowning, when, confessing himself a Muslim, he was saved alive from the bottom of the sea, to be a "witness for ages to come."[12] But we find that it is merely a version of a Jewish fable: "Perceive the great power of repentance! Pharaoh, King of Egypt, uttered very wicked words—Who is the God whose voice I shall obey? (Exod. v. 2.) Yet as he repented, saying, 'Who is like unto thee among the gods?' (xv. 2) God saved him from death; for it saith, Almost had I stretched out my hands and destroyed; but God let him live, that he might declare his power and strength."[13]

As Jewish commentators add to Exod. xv. 27, where we read of twelve fountains being found near Elim, that each of the tribes had a well,[14] so Muḥammad transposes the statement, and declares that twelve fountains sprang from the rock which had been smitten by Moses at Rephidim.[15] The Rabbinical fable, that God covered the Israelites with Mount Sinai, on the occasion of the lawgiving,[16] is thus amplified in the Qur'ān: "We shook the mountain over them, as though it had been a covering, and they imagined that it was falling upon them; and we said, "Receive the law which we have brought unto you with reverence."[1] The Qur'ān adds that the Israelites, now demanding to see God, die, and are raised again.[2] It will not be difficult to trace the origin of this figment. When the Israelites demanded two things from God—that they might see his glory and hear his voice—both were granted to them. Then it is added, "These things, however, they had no power to resist; as they came to Mount Sinai, and He appeared unto them, their souls escaped by His speaking, as it is said, 'My soul escaped as He spake.' The Torah, however, interceded for them, saying, 'Does a king give his daughter to marriage and kill his household? The whole world rejoices (at my appearance), and thy children (the Israelites) shall they die?' At once their souls returned; therefore it is said, The doctrine of God is perfect, and brings back the soul."[3] In the matter of the golden calf, the Qur'ān follows as usual the fabulous account of the Rabbinical traditions. Both represent Aaron as having been nearly killed when at first resisting the entreaty of the people. The Sanhedrin relates: "Aaron saw Chur slaughtered before his eyes (who opposed them), and he thought, If I do not yield to them they will deal with me as they dealt with Chur."[4] According to another passage in the Qur'ān, an Israelite named as-Sāmirī enticed them, and made the calf.[5] Like the wandering Jew in Christian fable, as-Sāmirī is punished by Moses with endless wandering, and he is compelled to repeat the words, "Touch me not."[6] Jewish traditions make Mikah assist in manufacturing the idol calf;[7] but Muḥammad either derived as-Sāmirī from Samael, or, as the Samaritans are stated by the Arab writers to have said, "Touch me not," he may have considered as-Sāmirī as the author of the sect of the Samaritans. That the calf thus produced by as-Sāmirī from the ornaments of the people, lowed on being finished,[8] is evidently a repetition of the following Jewish tradition: "The calf came forth (Exod. xxii. 24) roaring, and the Israelites saw it. Rabbi Jehuda says, Samael entered the calf and roared to deceive the Israelites." The addition, that the tribe of Levi remained faithful to God, is both Scriptural and Rabbinical.[9] The matter of Korah is honoured with singular embellishments; for instance, Korah had such riches, that from ten to forty strong men were required to carry the keys of his treasures.[10] Abū 'l-Fidā, says forty mules were required to convey the keys. Jewish tradition is still more extra-

[1] Pirke Rabbi Elieser, xlviii.
[2] Sūrah x. 23.
[3] Midrash Rabbah, Parash. v.
[4] Sūrahs vii. 11; xxvi. 40.
[5] Sūrahs xx. 47; xxvi. 48.
[6] Midrash Jalkut, clxxxii.
[7] Sūrahs xxviii. 38; xliii. 50.
[8] Rab. Exodus, Parash. v.
[9] Sūrahs xvii. 103; xxvii. 112.
[10] Sūrah vii. 130.
[11] Sūrah x. 90.
[12] See al-Baiẓāwī, Husain, al-Jalālān, and others.
[13] Pirke Rabbi Elieser, xliii.; Midrash Jalkut, ccxxxviii.
[14] Rashi on Exodus, xv. 27.
[15] Canon Churton pointed out to Dr. J. M. Arnold that the statement of twelve streams flowing from the rock occurs in the Liturgy of St. Thomas (*vide* Howard's *Christ. of St. Thomas*, p. 224).
[16] Aboda Sarah, ii. 2.

[1] Sūrah vii. 170.
[2] Sūrahs ii. 52; iv. 152.
[3] Aboda Sarah, ii. 2.
[4] Sanhedrin, v.; and Sūrah vii. 150.
[5] Sūrah xx. 87, 90, 96.
[6] Sūrah xx. 97.
[7] Rashi to Sanhedrin, ci. 2.
[8] Pirke Rabbi Elieser, clix.; and Sūrah vii. 147; xx. 90.
[9] Pirke Rabbi Elieser, xlv.; and Sūrah vii. 159; see Exodus xxxii. 26.
[10] Sūrah xxviii. 76.

vagant: "Joseph buried three treasures in Egypt, one of which became known to Korah. Riches are turned to destruction to him that possesses them (Eccles. v. 12), and this may well be applied to Korah. The keys to the treasures of Korah made a burden for 300 white mules."[1]

The accusation from which God cleared his servant Moses, of which the Qur'ān makes mention, was occasioned by Korah. "Abu Aliah says it refers to Korah hiring a harlot to reproach Moses before all the people, upon which God struck her dumb, and destroyed Korah, which cleared Moses from the charge."[2] This is unquestionably an amplification of the following passage: "Moses heard, and fell on his face. What was it he heard? That they accused him of having to do with another man's wife."[3] Others conceive the unjust charge from which Moses was cleared, to have been that of murdering Aaron on Mount Hor, because he and Eleazar only were present when Aaron died! That they had recourse to Jewish tradition, will appear from the subjoined extract: "The whole congregation saw that Aaron was dead; and when Moses and Eleazar came down from the mountain, the whole congregation gathered together, asking, Where is Aaron? But they said, He is dead. How can the Angel of Death touch a man, by whom he was resisted and restrained, as it is said, He stood between the dead and the living, and the plague was stayed? If ye bring him, it is well; if not, we will stone you. Moses prayed, Lord of the World, remove from me this suspicion! Then God opened and showed them Aaron's body." And to this the passage applies: "The whole congregation saw," &c. (Numb. xx. 29, 75.) [MOSES.]

The time of the Judges is passed over unnoticed, and from the manner in which the election of a king is introduced,[4] it would appear that Muḥammad was ignorant of the long interval between Moses and Saul.[5] [SAUL.] Of David's history, only his victory over Goliath and his fall through Bathsheba are recorded. [DAVID.] The Traditions make mention of the brevity of his slumbers, and commentators of the Qur'ān affirm the same: "The Apostle of God said David slept half the night; he then rose for a third part, and slept again a sixth part." This is derived from the Rabbis, who assert that the king slept only for the term of "sixty breathings."[6] Of the wisdom of Solomon, the Qur'ān makes particular mention; and to support the statement, adds, that he understood the language of birds; this was also the opinion of the Jewish doctors. The winds, or, more probable, spirits, obeyed him; and demons, birds, and beasts, formed part of his standing army.[1] Jewish commentators record that "demons of various kinds, and evil spirits were subject to him."[2] The story of the Queen of Sheba, and the adventures of the lapwing,[3] are only abridgments from Jewish traditions. With regard to the fable, that demons assisted Solomon in the building of the Temple, and, being deceived, continued it after his death, we may here add that Muḥammad borrowed it directly from the Jews.[4] When Solomon became haughty, one of his many demons ruled in his stead, till he repented. The Sanhedrin also refers to this degradation: "In the beginning Solomon reigned also over the upper worlds"; as it is said, "Solomon sat on the throne of God"; after that only over his staff, as it is said, "What profit hath a man of all his labour?" and still later, "This is my portion of all my labour."[5] On repenting, he maimed his horses, considering them a useless luxury. In the Talmud and the Scriptures, we find allusion to his obtaining them as well as to their being prohibited.[6] [SOLOMON.]

Elijah is among the few characters which Muḥammad notices after Solomon; nothing, indeed, is mentioned of his rapture to heaven, yet he is considered a great prophet.[7] Among the Jews, Elijah appears in human form to the pious on earth, he visits them in their places of worship, and communicates revelations from God to eminent Rabbis. In this charater Elijah also appears in Muslim divinity. [ELIJAH.] Jonah is the "man of the fish";[8] Muḥammad relates his history in his usual style, not omitting his journey to Nineveh, or the gourd which afforded him shade. [JONAH.] Job, too, with his suffering and cure is noticed[9] [JOB]; also the three men who were cast into a burning fiery furnace[10] (Dan. iii. 8); the turning back of the shadow of degrees on the occasion of Hezekiah's recovery.[11]

(See Arnold's *Islam and Christianity*, Longmans, London, 1874; p. 116, *seqq.* Dr. J. M. Arnold gives in many instances the original Hebrew of his quotations from the Talmud.)

In the Qur'ān there are several Hebrew and Talmudic terms which seem to indicate that its author had become familiar with Talmudic teaching. The following are the most noticeable:—

(1) The *Qur'ān*, قرآن, from *qara'*, "to read," Heb. קָרָא, and equivalent to מִקְרָא, "reading." See Neh. viii. 8: "And caused them to understand *the reading*."

[1] Pirke Rabbi Elieser, xlv.
[2] Al-Farrār on Sūrah xxiii. 69.
[3] Pirke Rabbi Elieser, xlv.
[4] Sūrah ii. 247: "Dost thou not look at a crowd of the children of Israel after Moses' time, when they said to a prophet of theirs, Raise up for us a king, and we will fight in God's way."
[5] Muḥammad ascribes to Saul what the Scriptures relate of Gideon. Judges vii. 5.
[6] See Berachoth.

[1] Sūrahs xxi. 81; xxvii. 15; xxxiv. 11; xxxviii. 35.
[2] The second Targum on Esther i. 2.
[3] Dr. J. M. Arnold gives a translation of the story from the Targum. (See *Islam and Christianity*, p. 146.)
[4] Gittin, lxviii.; and Sūrah xxxiv.
[5] Sanhedrin, xx.; also Mid. Rab. on Numbers, Parash. xi.
[6] Sanhedrin, xxi.; and Sūrah xxxviii. 29.
[7] Sūrah vi. 85; xxxvii. 123, 130.
[8] Sūrah vi. 85; x. 98; xxi. 87; lxviii. 48.
[9] Sūrah xxi. 83; xxxviii. 40.
[10] Sūrah lxxxv. 4.
[11] Sūrah xxv. 47; and 2 Kings xx. 9.

(2) The *Maṣānī*, مثانی, "repetitions," Sūrah xv. 86, which is the Talmudic מִשְׁנָה.

(3) The *Taurāt*, توراة, used for the Books of Moses, the Heb. תּוֹרָה of the Old Testament.

(4) The *Shechinah*, or *Sakīnah*, سكينة, Sūrah ii. 249: "The sign of his kingdom is that there shall come to you the ARK (*Tābūt*), and SHECHINA (*Sakīnah*) in it from the Lord." Heb. שְׁכִינָה. A term not used in the Bible, but used by the Rabbinical writers to express the visible presence of God between the Cherubim on the Mercy seat of the Tabernacle.

(5) The Ark, *Tābūt*, تابوت. In Sūrah ii. 249, for the Ark of the Covenant, and in Sūrah xx. 39, for Noah's Ark. The Heb. תֵּבָה (which is used in the Bible for Noah's Ark and the ark of bulrushes), and not the Heb. אָרוֹן; the former being Rabbinical.

(6) Angel, *Malak*, ملك, Heb. מַלְאָךְ, an angel or messenger of God.

(7) Spirit, *Ruḥ*, روح, Heb. רוּחַ. A term used both for the angel Gabriel and for Jesus Christ.

(8) The Sabbath, *Sabt*, سبت. Sūrah vii. 164; ii. 62. Heb. שַׁבָּת.

(9) *Jahannam*, γέεννα, hell, جهنم. The Rabbinical גֵּיהִנֹּם, and not the שְׁאוֹל, of the Old Testament. The final letter م proves that it was adopted from the Talmudic Hebrew and not from the Greek.

JIBRĀ'ĪL (جبرائيل). The angel Gabriel. [GABRIEL.]

JIBT (جبت). An idol of the Quraish mentioned in the Qur'ān, Sūrah iv. 54: "They (certain renegade Jews) believe in *Jibt* and *Ṭāghūt*, and say of the infidels, These are guided in a better path than those who hold the faith." The Jalālān say certain Jews used to do homage to these idols in order to please the Quraish.

JIHĀD (جهاد). *Lit.* "An effort, or a striving." A religious war with those who are unbelievers in the mission of Muḥammad. It is an incumbent religious duty, established in the Qur'ān and in the Traditions as a divine institution, and enjoined specially for the purpose of advancing Islām and of repelling evil from Muslims.

When an infidel's country is conquered by a Muslim ruler, its inhabitants are offered three alternatives:—

(1) *The reception of Islām*, in which case the conquered become enfranchised citizens of the Muslim state.

(2) *The payment of a poll-tax* (*Jizyah*), by which unbelievers in Islam obtain protection, and become *Zimmīs*, provided they are not the idolaters of Arabia.

(3) *Death by the sword*, to those who will not pay the poll tax.

Ṣūfī writers say that there are two Jihāds: *al-Jihādu 'l-Akbar*, or "the greater warfare," which is against one's own lusts; and *al-Jihādu 'l-Aṣghar*, or "the lesser warfare," against infidels.

The duty of religious war (which all commentators agree is a duty extending to all time) is laid down in the Qur'ān in the following verses, and it is remarkable that all the verses occur in the al-Madīnah Sūrahs, being those given after Muḥammad had established himself as a paramount ruler, and was in a position to dictate terms to his enemies.

Sūrah ix. 5, 6: "And when the sacred months are passed, kill those who join other gods with God wherever ye shall find them; and seize them, besiege them, and lay wait for them with every kind of ambush: but if they shall convert, and observe prayer, and pay the obligatory alms, then let them go their way, for God is Gracious, Merciful. If any one of those who join gods with God ask an asylum of thee, grant him an asylum, that he may hear the Word of God, and then let him reach his place of safety. This, for that they are people devoid of knowledge."

Sūrah ix. 29: "Make war upon such of those to whom the Scriptures have been given as believe not in God, or in the last day, and who forbid not that which God and His Apostle have forbidden, and who profess not the profession of the truth, until they pay tribute (*jizyah*) out of hand, and they be humbled."

Sūrah iv. 76–79: "Let those then fight on the path of God, who exchange this present life for that which is to come; for whoever fighteth on God's path, whether he be slain or conquer, we will in the end give him a great reward. But what hath come to you that ye fight not on the path of God, and for the weak among men, women, and children, who say, 'O our Lord! bring us forth from this city whose inhabitants are oppressors; give us a champion from Thy presence; and give us from thy presence a defender.' They who believe, fight on the path of God; and they who believe not, fight on the path of Ṭāgūt: Fight therefore against the friends of Satan. Verily the craft of Satan shall be powerless! Hast thou not marked those to whom it was said, 'Withhold your hands awhile *from war*; and observe prayer, and pay the stated alms.' But when war is commanded them, lo! a portion of them fear men as with the fear of God, or with a yet greater fear, and say: 'O our Lord! why hast Thou commanded us war? Couldst thou not have given us respite till our not distant end?' SAY: Small the fruition of this world; but the next life is the *true* good for him who feareth God! and ye shall not be wronged so much as the skin of a date-stone."

Sūrah ii. 214, 215: "They will ask thee concerning war in the Sacred Month. SAY: To war therein is bad, but to turn aside from the cause of God, and to have no faith in Him, and in the Sacred Temple, and to drive out its people, is worse in the sight of God; and civil strife is worse than bloodshed. They will not cease to war against you until they turn you from your religion, if they be able: but whoever of you shall turn from his religion and die an infidel, their works shall be fruitless in this world, and in the next: they shall be consigned to the fire; therein to abide for aye. But they who believe, and who fly their country, and fight in the cause of God may hope for God's mercy: and God is Gracious, Merciful.

Sūrah viii. 39–42: "SAY to the infidels: If they desist *from their unbelief*, what is now past shall be forgiven them; but if they return *to it*, they have already before them the doom of the ancients! Fight then against them till strife be at an end, and the religion be all of it God's. If they desist, verily God beholdeth what they do: but if they turn their back, know ye that God is your protector: Excellent protector! excellent helper! And know ye, that when ye have taken any booty, a fifth part belongeth to God and to the Apostle, and to the near of kin, and to orphans, and to the poor, and to the wayfarer.

Long chapters in the Traditions are devoted to the subject of Jihād (see *Ṣaḥīḥu 'l-Bukhārī* and *Ṣaḥīḥu Muslim*, Arabic editions, Bābu 'l-Jihād), from which the following are quotations of the sayings of the Prophet:—

"God is sponsor for him who goeth forth to fight on the road of God (*Sabīlu 'llāh*). If he be not killed, he shall return to his house with rewards and booty, but if he be slain, he shall be taken to Paradise."

"I swear by God I should like to be killed on the road of God, then be killed and brought to life again, then killed again and then brought to life again, so that I may obtain new rewards every time."

"Guarding the frontiers of Islām for even one day is worth more than the whole world and all that is in it."

"The fire of hell shall not touch the legs of him who shall be covered with the dust of battle in the road of God."

"He who assists another with arms to fight in the way of God, is as the champion, and is a sharer of the rewards. And he who stayeth behind to take charge of the family of a warrior is even as a champion in war."

"This religion will ever be established, even to the Day of Resurrection, as long as Muslims fight for it."

"In the last day the wounds of those who have been wounded in the way of God will be evident, and will drop with blood, but their smell will be as the perfume of musk."

"Being killed in the road of God covers all sins, but the sin of debt."

"He who dies and has not fought for the religion of Islām, nor has even said in his heart, 'Would to God I were a champion that could die in the road of God,' is even as a hypocrite."

"Fighting in the road of God, or resolving to do so, is a divine duty. When your Imām orders you to go forth to fight, then obey him."

The following is the teaching of the Ḥanafī school of Sunnīs on the subject of Jihād, as given in the *Hidāyah*, vol. ii. p. 140:—

"The sacred injunction concerning war is sufficiently observed when it is carried on by any one party or tribe of Muslims, and it is then no longer of any force with respect to the rest. It is established as a divine ordinance, by the word of God, who said in the Qur'ān, 'Slay the infidels,' and also by a saying of the Prophet, 'War is permanently established until the Day of Judgment' (meaning the ordinance respecting war). The observance, however, in the degree above mentioned, suffices, because war is not a positive injunction, as it is in its nature murderous and destructive, and is enjoined only for the purpose of advancing the true faith or repelling evil from the servants of God; and when this end is answered by any single tribe or party of Muslims making war, the obligation is no longer binding upon the rest, in the same manner as in the prayers for the dead—(if, however, no one Muslim were to make war, the whole of the Muslim, would incur the criminality of neglecting it)—and also because if the injunction were positive, the whole of the Muslims must consequently engage in war, in which case the materials for war (such as horses, armour, and so forth) could not be procured. Thus it appears that the observance of war as aforesaid suffices, except where there is a general summons (that is, where the infidels invade a Muslim territory, and the Imām for the time being issues a general proclamation requiring all persons to go forth to fight), for in this case war becomes a positive injunction with respect to the whole of the inhabitants, whether men or women, and whether the Imām be a just or an unjust person; and if the people of that territory be unable to repulse the infidels, then war becomes a positive injunction with respect to all in that neighbourhood; and if these also do not suffice it, then comes a positive injunction with respect to the next neighbours; and in same manner with respect to all the Muslims from east to west.

"The destruction of the sword is incurred by infidels, although they be not the first aggressors, as appears fram various passages in the traditions which are generally received to this effect.

"It is not incumbent upon infants to make war, as they are objects of compassion; neither is it incumbent upon slaves or women, as the rights of the master, or of the husband, have precedence; nor is it so upon the blind, the maimed, or the decrepid, as such are incapable. If, however, the infidels make an attack upon a city or territory, in this case the repulsion of them is incumbent upon all Muslims, insomuch that a wife may go forth without the consent of her husband, and a slave without the leave of his master, because war then becomes a positive injunction; and possession, either by bondage or by marriage, cannot come in competition with a positive injunction, as in prayer (for instance) or fasting. This is supposing a general summons; for without that it is not lawful for a woman or slave to go forth to make war without the consent of the husband or master, as there is in this case no necessity for their assistance, since others suffice, and hence no reason exists for destroying the right of the husband or master on that account. If there be any fund in the public treasury, so long as the fund lasts any extraordinary exaction for the support of the warriors is abominable, because such exaction resembles a hire for that which is a service of God as much as prayer or fasting, and, hire being forbidden in these instances, so is it in that which resembles them. In this case, moreover, there is no occasion for any extraordinary exactions, since the funds of the public treasury are prepared to answer all emergencies of the Muslims, such as war, and so forth. If, however, there be no funds in the public treasury, in this case the Imām need not hesitate to levy contributions for the better support of the warriors, because in levying a contribution the greater evil (namely, the destruction of the person) is repelled, and the contribution is the smaller evil, and the imposition of a smaller evil to remedy a greater is of no consequence. A confirmation of this is found in what is related of the Prophet, that he took various articles of armour, and so forth, from Ṣafwān and 'Umar; in the same manner also he took property from married men, and bestowed it upon the unmarried, in order to encourage them and enable them to go forth to fight with cheerfulness; and he also used to take the horses from those who remained at home, and bestowed them upon those who went forth to fight on foot. When the Muslims enter the enemy's country and besiege the cities or strongholds of the infidels, it is necessary to invite them to embrace the faith, because Ibn 'Abbās relates of the Prophet that he never destroyed any without previously inviting them to embrace the faith. If, therefore, they embrace the faith, it is unnecessary to war with them, because that which was the design of the war is then obtained without war. The Prophet, moreover, has said we are directed to make war upon men only until such time as they shall confess, 'There is no God but one God.' But when they repeat this creed, their persons and properties are in protection (*amān*). If they do not accept the call to the faith, they must then be called upon to pay *jizyah*, or capitation tax, because the Prophet directed the commanders of his armies so to do, and also because by submitting to this tax war is forbidden and terminated upon the authority of the Qur'ān. (This call to pay capitation tax, however, respects only those from whom the capitation tax is acceptable, for, as to apostates and the idolaters of Arabia, to call upon them to pay the tax is useless, since nothing is accepted from them but embracing the faith, as it is thus commanded in the Qur'ān). If those who are called upon to pay capitation tax consent to do so, they then become entitled to the same protection and subject to the same rules as Muslims, because 'Alī has declared infidels agree to a capitation tax only in order to render their blood the same as Muslims' blood, and their property the same as Muslims' property.

"It is not lawful to make war upon any people who have never before been called to the faith, without previously requiring them to embrace it, because the Prophet so instructed his commanders, directing them to call the infidels to the faith, and also because the people will hence perceive that they are attacked for the sake of religion, and not for the sake of taking their property, or making slaves of their children, and on this consideration it is possible that they may be induced to agree to the call, in order to save themselves from the troubles of war.

"If a Muslim attack infidels without previously calling them to the faith, he is an offender, because this is forbidden; but yet if he do attack them before thus inviting them and slay them, and take their property, neither fine, expiation, nor atonement are due, because that which protects (namely, Islām) does not exist in them, nor are they under protection by place (namely, the *Dāru 'l-Islām*, or Muslim territory), and the mere prohibition of the act is not sufficient to sanction the exaction either of fine or of atonement for property; in the same manner as the slaying of the women or infant children of infidels is forbidden, but if, notwithstanding, a person were to slay such, he is not liable to a fine. It is laudable to call to the faith a people to whom a call has already come, in order that they may have the more full and ample warning; but yet this is not incumbent, as it appears in the Traditions that the Prophet plundered and despoiled the tribe of al-Muṣṭaliq by surprise, and he also agreed with Asāmah to make a predatory attack upon Qubnā at an early hour, and to set it on fire, and such attacks are not preceded by a call. (Qubnā is a place in Syria: some assert it is the name of a tribe).

"If the infidels, upon receiving the call, neither consent to it nor agree to pay capitation tax, it is then incumbent on the Muslims to call upon God for assistance, and to make war upon them, because God is the assistant of those who serve Him, and the destroyer of His enemies, the infidels, and it is necessary to implore His aid upon every occasion; the Prophet, moreover, commands us so to do. And having so done, the Muslims must then with God's assistance attack the infidels with all manner of warlike engines (as the Prophet did by the people of Ṭā'if), and must also set fire to their habitations (in the same manner as the Prophet fired Baweera), and must inundate them with water and tear up their plantations and tread down their grain because by these means they will become weakened, and their resolution will fail and their force be broken; these means are, therefore, all sanctified by the law.

"It is no objection to shooting arrows or other missiles against the infidels that there may chance to be among them a Muslim in the way either of bondage or of traffic, because the shooting of arrows and so forth among the infidels remedies a general evil in the repulsion thereof from the whole body of Muslims, whereas the slaying of a Muslim slave or trader is only a particular evil, and to repel a general evil a particular evil must be adopted, and also because it seldom happens that the strongholds of the infidels are destitute of Muslims, since it is most probable that there are Muslims residing in them, either in the way of bondage or of traffic, and hence, if the use of missile weapons were prohibited on account of these Muslims, war would be obstructed. If the infidels in time of battle should make shields of Muslim children, or of Muslims, who are prisoners in their hands, yet there is no need on that account to refrain from the use of missile weapons, for the reason already mentioned. It is requisite, however, that the Muslims in using such weapons aim at the infidels, and not at the children or the Muslim captives, because, as it is impossible in shooting to distinguish precisely between them and the infidels, the person who discharges the weapon must make this distinction in his intention and design by aiming at the infidels, and not at the others, since thus much is practicable, and the distinction must be made as far as is practicable.

"There is also neither fine nor expiation upon the warriors on account of such of their arrows or other missiles as happen to hit the children or the Muslims, because the war is in observance of a divine ordinance, and atonement is not due for anything which may happen in the fulfilment of a divine ordinance, for otherwise men would neglect the fulfilment of the ordinance from an apprehension of becoming liable to atonement. It is otherwise in the case of a person eating the bread of another when perishing for hunger, as in that instance atonement is due; although eating the bread of other people, in such a situation, be a divine ordinance, because a person perishing for hunger will not refrain from eating the provision of another, from the apprehension of atonement, since his life depends upon it; whereas war is attended with trouble and dangerous to life, whence men would be deterred, by apprehension of atonement, from engaging in it. There is no objection to the warriors carrying their Qur'āns and their women along with them, where the Muslim force is considerable, to such a degree as to afford a protection from the enemy, and not to admit of any apprehension from them, because in that case safety is most probable, and a thing which is most probable stands and is accounted as a thing certain. If the force of the warriors be small (such as is termed a *Sarrīyah*), so as not to afford security from the enemy, in this case their carrying their women or Qur'āns along with them is reprobated, because in such a situation taking those with them is exposing them to dishonour; and taking the Qur'ān with them, in particular, is exposing it to contempt, since infidels scoff at the Qur'ān, with a view of insulting the Muslims; and this is the true meaning of the saying of the Prophet, 'Carry not the Qur'ān along with you into the territory of the enemy' (that is, of the infidels). If a Muslim go into an infidel camp under a protection, there is no objection to his taking his Qur'ān along with him, provided these infidels be such as observe their engagements, because from these no violence is to be apprehended.

"It is lawful for aged women to accompany an army, for the performance of such business as suits them, such as dressing victuals, administering water, and preparing medicines for the sick and wounded; but with respect to young women, it is better that they stay at home, as this may prevent perplexity or disturbance. The women, however, must not engage in fight, as this argues weakness in the Muslims. Women, therefore, must not take any personal concern in battle unless in a case of absolute necessity; and it is not laudable to carry young women along with the army, either for the purpose of carnal gratification, or for service; if, however, the necessity be very urgent, female slaves may be taken, but not wives. A wife must not engage in a fight but with the consent of her husband, nor a slave but with the consent of his owner (according to what was already stated, that the right of the husband and the master has precedence), unless from necessity where an attack is made by the enemy.

"It does not become Muslims to break treaties or to act unfairly with respect to plunder or to disfigure people (by cutting off their ears and noses, and so forth); for as to what is related of the Prophet, that he disfigured the Oorneans, it is abrogated by subsequent prohibitions. In the same manner it does not become Muslims to slay women or children, or men aged, bedridden, or blind, because opposition and fighting are the only occasions which make slaughter allowable (according to our doctors), and such persons are incapable of these. For the same reason also the paralytic are not to be slain, nor those who are dismembered of the right hand, or of the right hand and left foot. Ash-Shāfi'ī maintains that aged men, or persons bedridden or blind, may be slain, because (according to him) infidelity is an occasion of slaughter being allowable, and this appears in these persons. What was before observed, however, that the paralytic or dismembered are not to be slain, is in proof against him, as infidelity appears in these also, yet still they are not slain, whence it is evident that mere infidelity is not a justifiable occasion of slaughter. The Prophet, moreover, forbade the slaying of infants or single persons, and once, when the Prophet saw a woman who was slain, he said, 'Alas! this woman did not fight, why, therefore, was she slain?' But yet, if any of these persons be killed in war, or if a woman be a queen or chief, in this case it is allowable to slay them, they being qualified to molest the servants of God. So, also, if such persons as the above should attempt to fight, they may be slain, for the purpose of removing evil, and because fighting renders slaying allowable.

"A lunatic must not be slain unless he fight, as such a person is not responsible for his faith, but yet where he is found fighting it is necessary to slay him, for the removal of evil. It is also to be observed that infants or lunatics may be slain so long as they are actually engaged in fight, but it is not allowed to kill them after they are taken prisoners, contrary to the case of others, who may be slain even after they are taken, as they are liable to punishment because they are responsible for their faith.

"A person who is insane occasionally stands, during his lucid intervals, in the same predicament as a sane person.

"It is abominable in a Muslim to begin fighting with his father, who happens to be among the infidels, nor must he slay him, because God has said in the Qur'ān, 'Honour thy father and thy mother,' and also because the preservation of the father's life is incumbent upon the son, according to all the doctors, and the permission to fight with him would be repugnant to that sentiment. If, also, the son should find the father, he must not slay him himself, but must hold him in view until some other come and slay him: for thus the end is answered without the son slaying his father, which is an offence.

"If, however, the father attempt to slay the son, insomuch that the son is unable to repel him but by killing him, in this case the son need not hesitate to slay him, because the design of the son is merely to repel him, which is lawful; for if a Muslim were to draw his sword with a design of killing his son, in such a way that the son is unable to repel him but by killing him, it is then lawful for the son to slay his father, because his design is merely repulsion. In a case, therefore, where the father is an infidel, and attempts to slay his son, it is lawful for the son to slay the father in self-defence *à fortiori*.

"If the Imām make peace with aliens, or with any particular tribe or body of them, and perceive it to be eligible for the Muslims, there need be no hesitation, because it is said in the Qur'ān: 'If the infidels be inclined to peace do ye likewise consent thereto,' and also because the Prophet in the year of the punishment of Eubea, made a peace between the Muslims and the people of Mecca for the space of ten years; peace, moreover is war in effect where the interest of the Muslims requires it, since the design of war is the removal of evil, and this is obtained by means of peace: contrary to where peace is not to the interest of the Muslims, for it is not in that case lawful, as this would be abandoning war both apparently and in effect. It is here, however, proper to observe that it is not absolutely necessary to restrict a peace to the term above recorded (namely, ten years), because the end for which peace is made may be sometimes more effectually obtained by extending it to a longer term. If the Imām make peace with the aliens for a single term (namely, ten years), and afterwards perceive that it is most advantageous for the Muslim's interest to break it, he may in that case lawfully renew the war after giving them due notice, because, upon a change of the circumstances which rendered peace advisable, the breach of peace is war, and the observance of it a desertion of war, both in appearance and also in effect, and war is an ordinance of God, and the forsaking of it is not becoming (to Muslims). It is to be observed that giving due notice to the enemy is in this case indispensably requisite in such a manner that treachery may not be induced, since this is forbidden. It is also requisite that such a delay be made in renewing the war with them, as may allow intelligence of the peace being broken off to be universally received among them, and for this such a time suffices as may admit of the king or chief of the enemy communicating the same to the different parts of their dominion, since by such a delay the charge of treachery is avoided.

"If the infidels act with perfidy in a peace, it is in such case lawful for the Imām to attack them without any previous notice, since the breach of treaty in this instance originates with them, whence there is no occasion to commence the war on the part of the Muslims by giving them notice. It would be otherwise, however, if only a small party of them were to violate the treaty by entering the Muslim territory and there committing robberies upon the Muslims, since this does not amount to a breach of treaty. If, moreover, this party be in force so as to be capable of opposition, and openly fight with the Muslims, this is a breach of treaty with respect to that party only, but not with respect to the rest of their nation or tribe, because, as this party have violated the treaty without any permission from their prince, the rest are not answerable for their act; whereas if they made their attack by permission of their prince, the breach of treaty would be regarded as by the whole, all being virtually implicated in it.

"If the Imām make peace with the aliens in return for property, there is no scruple; because since peace may be lawfully made without any such gratification, it is also lawful in return for a gratification. This, however, is only where the Muslims stand in need of the property thus to be acquired; for if they be not in necessity, making peace for property is not lawful, since peace is a desertion of war both in appearance and in effect. It is to be observed that if the Imām receive this property by sending a messenger and making peace without the Muslim troops entering the enemy's territory, the object of disbursement of it is the same as that of *jizyah* or capitation-tax; that is, it is to be expended upon the warriors and not upon the poor. If, however, the property be taken after the Muslims have invaded the enemy, in this case it is as plunder, one-fifth going to the Imām and the remainder to be divided among the troops, as the property has in fact been taken by force in this instance. It is incumbent on the Imām to keep peace with apostates, and not to make war upon them, in order that they may have time to consider their situation, since it is to be hoped that they may again return to the faith. It is, therefore, lawful to delay fighting with them in a hope that they may again embrace Islām; but it is not lawful to take property from them. If, however, the Imām should take property from them, it is not incumbent upon him to return it, as such property is not in protection. If infidels harass the Muslims, and offer them peace in return for property, the Imām must not accede thereto, as this would be a degradation of the Muslim honour, and disgrace would be attached to all the parties concerned in it; this, therefore, is not lawful except where destruction is to be apprehended, in which case the purchasing a peace with property is lawful, because it is a duty to repel destruction in every possible mode."

[For Khalīfah 'Umar's treatment of the garrison of Jerusalem when captured, see the treaty given in the article JERUSALEM.]

JIHĀZ (جهاز). (1) The wedding trousseau of a Muḥammadan wife. Those vestments and furniture which a bride brings to her husband's house, and which ever remain the property of the wife. (*Hidāyah*, vol. iii. p. 100.) (2) The word is also used for the shroud of a dead Muslim.

JINĀYAH (جناية), pl. *Jināyāt*. The legal term for all offences committed against the person, such as murder, wounding, drowning, &c.

JINN (جن). [GENII.]

JĪRĀN (جيران). "Neighbours." "If a person make a bequest to his neighbours (*jīrān*) it includes, according to some doctors, all those houses which are within forty cubits of his house in every direction. Some say it is forty houses on either side of his." (See Baillie's *Digest of Imāmīyah Law*, pp. 216, 246.) [NEIGHBOURS.]

JIRJĪS (جرجيس). George. St. George of England. The author of the *Ghiyāṣu 'l-Lughah* says that, "Jirgīs Bāqiyā is the name of a prophet who was on several occasions killed by his people, and was again raised to life by God, and over and over again instructed and preached the way of God. He is called Bāqiyā on account of his being raised up from the dead." This seems to be a wild and exaggerated account of the story of George of Cappadocia, who suffered death in the first year of the reign of Julian. It is a mystery how this George ever was admitted into the Christian Calendar at all, and still more marvellous how he became a Muḥammadan prophet as well as the patron saint of England. Jalālu 'd-dīn as-Suyūṭī, in his *History of the Temple of Jerusalem*, says Jirjīs was at Damascus in the time of Mu'āwiyah the Khalīfah. [AL-KHIZR.]

JIZYAH (جزية). The capitation tax, which is levied by Muḥammadan rulers upon subjects who are of a different faith, but claim protection (*amān*). It is founded upon a direct injunction of the Qur'ān: "Make war upon such of those, to whom the Scriptures have been given, as believe not in God or in the last day, and forbid not that which God and his Apostles have forbidden, and who profess not the profession of truth, until they pay *tribute* (*jizyah*) out of their hand, and they be humbled."

According to the *Hidāyah* (vol. ii. p. 211), *jizyah* is of two kinds: that which is established voluntarily, and that which is enforced. The usual rate is one dīnār for every male person, females and children being exempt according to Abū Ḥanīfah, but included by Ash-Shāfi'ī. It should be imposed upon Jews, and Christians, and Magians, but it should not be accepted from the Arabian idolators, or from apostates, who should be killed. But from idolators of other countries than Arabia it may be accepted. It should not be levied upon monks, or hermits, or paupers, or slaves. He who pays the capitation tax and obtains protection from the Muḥammadan state is called a *zimmī*.

JOB. Arabic *Aiyūb* (ايوب). Mentioned in the Qur'ān as a prophet and an example of patience.

Sūrah xxi. 83, 84: "And *remember* Job: when he cried to his Lord, 'Truly evil hath touched me: but Thou art the most merciful of those who show mercy.' So we heard him, and lightened the burden of his woe; and we gave him back his family, and as many more with them,—a mercy from us, and a memorial for those who serve us."

Sūrah xxxviii. 40-44: "And remember our servant Job when he cried to his Lord, 'Verily, Satan hath laid on me disease and pain.' 'Stamp,' said we, 'with thy foot. This is to wash with; cool, and to drink.' And we gave him back his family, and as many more with them in our mercy; and for a monition to men of judgment. And *we said*, 'Take in thine hand a rod, and strike with it, nor break thine oath.' Verily, we found him patient! How excellent a servant, one who turned to us, was he!"

Sūrah iv. 161: "And we have inspired thee as we inspired . . . . Jesus and Job and Jonah, and Aaron, and Solomon."

Sūrah vi. 84: "And we have guided . . . . David and Solomon, and Job, and Joseph."

Mr. Sale, following the commentators al-Jalālān and al-Baiẓāwī, says: "The Muḥammadan writers tell us that Job was of the race of Esau, and was blessed with a numerous family and abundant riches; but that God proved him by taking away all that he had, even his children, who were killed by the fall of a house: notwithstanding which, he continued to serve God and to return Him thanks as usual; that he was then struck with a filthy disease, his body being full of worms and so offensive that as he lay on the dunghill none could bear to come near him: that his wife, however (whom some call Raḥmeh the daughter of Ephraim the son of Joseph, and others Makhir the daughter of Manasses), attended him with great patience, supporting him with what she earned by her labour; but that the devil appearing to her one day, after having reminded her of her past prosperity, promised her that if she would worship him he would restore all they had lost: whereupon she asked her husband's consent, who was so angry at the proposal, that he swore, if he recovered, to give his wife a hundred stripes; and that after his affliction his wealth increased, his wife also becoming young and handsome again, and bearing him twenty-six sons. Some, to express the great riches which were bestowed on Job after his sufferings, say he had two threshing-floors, one for wheat and the other for barley, and that God sent two clouds, which rained gold on the one and silver on the other till they ran over. The traditions differ as to the continuance of Job's calamities: one will have it to be eighteen years: another, thirteen; another, three; and another, exactly seven years seven months and seven hours.

JOHN BAPTIST. Arabic *Yaḥya* (يحيى). Mentioned three times in the Qur'ān.

The XIXth Sūrah opens with an account of the Birth of John the Baptist:—

"A recital of thy Lord's mercy to his servant Zacharias; when he called upon his Lord with secret calling, and said: 'O Lord, verily my bones are weakened, and the hoar hairs glisten on my head, and never, Lord, have I prayed to Thee with ill success. But now I have fears for my kindred after me; and my wife is barren: give me, then, a successor as Thy special gift, who shall be my heir and an heir of the family of Jacob: and make him, Lord, well pleasing to Thee. 'O Zacharias! verily we announce to thee a son,—his name John: that name We have given to none before him.' He said: 'O my Lord! how when my wife is barren shall I have a son, and when I have now reached old age, failing in my powers?' He said: 'So shall it be. Thy Lord hath said, Easy is this to me, for I created thee aforetime when thou wast nothing.' He said: 'Vouchsafe me, O my Lord! a sign.' He said: 'Thy sign shall be that for three nights, though sound in health, thou speakest not to man.' And he came forth from the sanctuary to his people, and made signs to them to sing praises morn and even. *We said:* 'O John! receive the Book with purpose of heart':—and We bestowed on him wisdom while yet a child; and mercifulness from Ourself, and purity; and pious was he, and duteous to his parents; and not proud, rebellious. And peace was on him on the day he was born, and the day of his death, and *shall be* on the day when he shall be raised to life!"

Sūrah xxi. 89: "And Zacharias; when he called upon his Lord saying, 'O my Lord, leave me not childless: but there is no better heir than Thyself.' So we heard him, and gave him John, and we made his wife fit for child-bearing. Verily, these vied in goodness, and called upon us with love and fear, and humbled themselves before us."

Sūrah vi. 85: "And we guided . . . . Zacharias, and *John*, and Jesus, and Elias, all righteous ones."

JOKING. Arabic *Mizāḥ* (مزاح). It is said Muḥammad was fond of jesting, but Ibn 'Abbās relates that the Prophet said, "Do not joke with your brother Muslim to hurt him."

Anas relates that the Prophet said to an old woman, "No old woman will enter Paradise." The old woman said "Why?" And the Prophet said, "Because it is written in the Qur'ān (Sūrah lvi. 35) 'We have made them virgins.' There will be no old women in heaven." (*Mishkāt*, book xxii. ch. xii.)

JONAH. Arabic *Yūnus* (يونس). Mentioned in the Qur'ān as a prophet, and as *Ṣāḥibu 'l-Ḥūt* and *Ẕū 'n-Nūn*, "He of the Fish."

Sūrah xxxvii. 139–148: "Jonas, too, was one of the Apostles (*mursalīn*), when he fled unto the laden ship, and lots were cast, and he was doomed, and the fish swallowed him, for he was blameworthy. But had he not been of those who praise Us, in its belly had he surely remained, till the day of resurrection. And we cast him on the bare *shore*—and he was sick;—and we caused a gourd-plant to grow up over him, and we sent him to a hundred thousand persons, or even more, and because they believed, we continued their enjoyments for a season."

Sūrah lxviii. 48–50: "Patiently then await the judgment of thy Lord, and be not like him who was in the fish (*Ṣāḥibu 'l-Ḥūt*), when in deep distress he cried *to God.* Had not favour from his Lord reached him, cast forth would he have been on the naked shore, overwhelmed with shame: but his Lord chose him and made him of the just."

Sūrah x. 98 (*called the Sūratu Yūnus*): "Verily they against whom the decree of thy Lord is pronounced, shall not believe, even though every kind of sign come unto them, till they behold the dolorous torment! Were it otherwise, any city, had it believed, might have found its safety in its faith. But it was so, only with the people of Jonas. When they believed, we delivered them from the penalty of shame in this world, and provided for them for a time. But if thy Lord had pleased, verily all who are in the earth would have believed together. What! wilt thou compel men to become believers?"

Sūrah vi. 86: "We guided . . . . Ishmael and Elisha, and Jonah, and Lot."

Sūrah xxi. 87: "And *Ẕū 'n-Nūn* (he of the fish), when he went on his way in anger, and thought that we had no power over him. But in the darkness he cried, 'There is no

God but Thou: Glory be unto Thee! Verily, I have been one of the evil doers': so we heard him and rescued him from misery: for thus rescue we the faithful."

[Sale, in his *Notes on the Qur'ān*, quoting from al-Jalālān and al-Baiẓāwī, says: "When Jonah first began to exhort the people to repentance, instead of hearkening to him, they used him very ill, so that he was obliged to leave the city, threatening them at his departure that they should be destroyed within three days, or, as others say, within forty. But when the time drew near, and they saw the heavens overcast with a black cloud which shot forth fire and filled the air with smoke and hung directly over the city, they were in a terrible consternation, and getting into the fields, with their families and cattle, they put on sackcloth and humbled themselves before God, calling aloud for pardon and sincerely repenting of their past wickedness. Whereupon God was pleased to forgive them, and the storm blew over. It is said that the fish, after it had swallowed Jonah, swam after the ship with its head above water, that the prophet might breathe; who continued to praise God till the fish came to land and vomited him out. Some imagine Jonah's plant to have been a fig; and others, the mōz (or banana), which bears very large leaves and excellent fruit, and that this plant withered the next morning, and that Jonah being much concerned at it God made a remonstrance to him in behalf of the Ninevites, agreeably to what is recorded in Scripture."]

JORDAN. Arabic *Ardan, Urdunn* (اردن). Referring to Sūrah iii. 39, the legend is that the priests threw lots, by casting arrows into the river Jordan, as to which should take charge of the Virgin Mary after the Annunciation. "Thou wert not by them when they threw their lots which of them should take care of Mary, nor wert thou by them when they did dispute."

JOSEPH. Arabic *Yūsuf* (يوسف). The son of Jacob, and, according to the Qur'ān, an inspired prophet. (Sūrahs vi. 84; xl. 36.)

The account of Joseph occupies a whole chapter in the Qur'ān, entitled the Chapter of Yūsuf (Sūrah xii.). Al-Baiẓāwī says that certain Jews instigated the Quraish to inquire of Muḥammad the story of Joseph and his family going into Egypt, and that in order to prove the truth of his mission, God sent Muḥammad this chapter, the *Sūratu Yūsuf*, from heaven. The same writer says it is a most meritorious chapter, for whosoever shall read it and teach it to others shall have an easy death. (See al-Baiẓāwī *in loco*.)

The story of *Yūsuf wa Zulaikhah* is one of the most popular love songs in the East. It was produced in Persian verse by Nūru 'd-dīn 'Abdu 'r-Raḥmān ibn Aḥmad Jāmī, A.H. 898. And the Shaikh Ḥamdu 'llāh ibn Shamsi 'd-dīn Muḥammad (A.H. 909), rendered it into Turkī verse.

The author of the *Akhlāq-i-Jalālī* says: "We have it amongst the sayings of Muḥammad that women should be forbidden to read or listen to the history of Joseph (*as told in the Qur'ān*), lest it lead to their swerving from the rule of chastity." (Thompson's edition.)

We give the account as told in the Qur'ān, with the commentators' remarks in *italics*, as rendered by Mr. Lane in his *Selections from the Kuran* (new ed. by Mr. S. Lane Poole), the account of Joseph's temptation, which Mr. Lane omits, being added from Rodwell's translation of the Qur'ān:—

"*Remember*, when Joseph said unto his father, O my father, verily I saw *in sleep* eleven stars and the sun and the moon: I saw them making obeisance unto me. He replied, O my child, relate not thy vision to thy brethren, lest they contrive a plot against thee, *knowing its interpretation to be that they are the stars and that the sun is thy mother and the moon thy father*; for the devil is unto man a manifest enemy. And thus, *as thou sawest*, thy Lord will choose thee, and teach thee the interpretation of events, *or dreams*, and will accomplish his favour upon thee *by the gift of prophecy*, and upon the family of Jacob, as He accomplished it upon thy fathers before, Abraham and Isaac; for thy Lord is knowing and wise.—Verily in *the history of* Joseph and his brethren are signs to the inquirers.—When they (*the brethren of Joseph*) said, *one to another*, Verily Joseph and his brother *Benjamin* are dearer unto our father than we, and we are a number of men; verily our father is in a manifest error; slay ye Joseph, or drive him away into a *distant* land; so the face of your father shall be directed alone unto you, *regarding no other*, and ye shall be after it a just people:—a speaker among them, *namely, Judah*, said, Slay not Joseph, but throw him to the bottom of the well; then some of the travellers may light upon him, if ye do *this. And they were satisfied therewith.* They said, O our father, wherefore dost thou not intrust us with Joseph, when verily we are faithful unto him? Send him with us to-morrow *into the plain*, that he may divert himself and sport; and we will surely take care of him.—He replied, Verily your taking him away will grieve me, and I fear lest the wolf devour him while ye are heedless of him. They said, Surely if the wolf devour him, when we are a number of men, we shall in that case be indeed weak. *So he sent him with them.* And when they went away with him, and agreed to put him at the bottom of the well, *they did so. They pulled off his shirt, after they had beaten him, and had treated him with contempt and had desired to slay him; and they let him down; and when he had arrived half-way down the well they let him fall, that he might die; and he fell into the water. He then betook himself to a mass of rock; and they called to him; so he answered them, imagining that they would have mercy upon him. They however desired to crush him with a piece of rock; but Judah prevented them.* And We said unto him by revelation, *while he was in the well (and he was seventeen years of age, or less), to quiet his heart*, Thou shalt assuredly declare unto them this their action, and they shall not know *thee at the time.* And they came to their father at nightfall weeping. They said, O our father, we went to run races, and left Joseph with our clothes, and the wolf devoured him; and thou wilt not believe us, though we speak truth. And they brought false blood upon his shirt. *Jacob* said *unto them*, Nay, your minds have made a thing seem pleasant unto you, *and ye have done it;* but patience is seemly, and God's assistance is implored with respect to that which ye relate.

"And travellers came *on their way from Midian to Egypt, and alighted near the well;* and they sent their drawer of water, and he let down his bucket *into the well: so Joseph caught hold upon it, and the man drew him forth; and when he saw him*, he said, O good news! This is a young man!—*And his brethren thereupon knew his case: wherefore they came unto him*, and they concealed his case, *making him* as a piece of merchandise; *for they said, He is our slave who hath absconded. And Joseph was silent, fearing lest they should slay him.* And God knew that which they did. And they sold him for a mean price, [for] some dirhems counted down, *twenty, or two-and-twenty;* and they were indifferent to him. *The travellers then brought him to Egypt, and he who had bought him sold him for twenty deenárs and a pair of shoes and two garments.* And the Egyptian who bought him, *namely, Kiṭfeer* (*Qiṭfīr* or *Iṭfīr*), said unto his wife *Zeleekha* (*Zalīkhā*), Treat him hospitably; peradventure he may be advantageous to us or we may adopt him as a son. *For he was childless.* And thus We prepared an establishment for Joseph in the land *of Egypt*, to teach him the interpretation of events, *or dreams;* for God is well able to effect His purpose; but the greater number of men, *namely, the unbelievers*, know not *this.* And when he had attained his age of strength (*thirty years, or three-and-thirty*), We bestowed on him wisdom and knowledge *in matters of religion, before he was sent as a prophet;* for thus do We recompense the well-doers." (Sūrah xii. 4–22.)

"And she in whose house he was, conceived a passion for him, and she shut the doors and said, 'Come hither.' He said, 'God keep me! Verily, my lord hath given me a good home: and the injurious shall not prosper.'

"But she longed for him; and he had longed for her had he not seen a token from his Lord. Thus we averted evil and defilement from him, for he was one of our sincere servants.

"And they both made for the door, and she rent his shirt behind; and at the door they met her lord. 'What,' said she, 'shall be the recompense of him who would do evil to thy family, but a prison or a sore punishment?'

"He said, 'She solicited me to evil.' And a witness out of her own family witnessed: 'If his shirt be rent in front she speaketh truth, and he is a liar:

"'But if his shirt be rent behind, she lieth and he is true.'

"And when his lord saw his shirt torn behind, he said, 'This is one of your devices! verily your devices are great!

"'Joseph! leave this affair. And thou, *O wife*, ask pardon for thy crime, for thou hast sinned.'

"And in the city, the women said, 'The wife of the Prince hath solicited her servant: he hath fired her with his love: but we clearly see her manifest error.'

"And when she heard of their cabal, she sent to them and got ready a banquet for them, and gave each one of them a knife, and said, '*Joseph* shew thyself to them.' And when they saw him they were amazed at him, and cut their hands, and said, 'God keep us! This is no man! This is no other than a noble angel!'

"She said, 'This is he about whom ye blamed me. I wished him to yield to my desires, but he stood firm. But if he obey not my command, he shall surely be cast into prison, and become one of the despised.'

"He said, 'O my Lord! I prefer the prison to compliance with their bidding: but unless thou turn away their snares from me, I shall play the youth with them, and become one of the unwise.'

"And his Lord heard him and turned aside their snares from him: for He is the Hearer, the Knower." (Rodwell, Sūrah xii. 23-34.)

"Then it seemed good unto them, after they had seen the signs *of his innocence, to imprison him.* They will assuredly imprison him for a time, *until the talk of the people respecting him cease. So they imprisoned him.* And there entered with him into the prison two young men, *servants of the king, one of whom was his cup-bearer and the other was his victualler. And they found that he interpreted dreams; wherefore* one of them, *namely, the cup-bearer*, said, I dreamed that I was pressing grapes: and the other said, I dreamed that I was carrying upon my head some bread, whereof the birds did eat: acquaint us with the interpretation thereof; for we see thee to be one of the beneficent.—He replied, There shall not come unto you any food wherewith ye shall be fed *in a dream*, but I will acquaint you with the interpretation thereof *when ye are awake*, before *the interpretation of* it come unto you. This is *a part* of that which my Lord hath taught me. Verily I have abandoned the religion of a people who believe not in God and who disbelieve in the world to come; and I follow the religion of my fathers, Abraham and Isaac and Jacob. It is not *fit* for us to associate anything with God. This *knowledge of the unity* hath been given us of the bounty of God towards us and towards mankind; but the greater number of men are not thankful. O ye two companions (*or inmates*) of the prison, are sundry lords better, or is God, the One, the Almighty? Ye worship not, beside Him, aught save names which ye and your fathers have given *to idols*, concerning which God hath not sent down any convincing proof. Judgment belongeth not [unto any] save unto God *alone.* He hath commanded that ye worship not any but Him. This is the right religion; but the greater number of men know not. O ye two companions of the prison, as to one of you, *namely, the cup-bearer,* he will serve wine unto his lord *as formerly;* and as to the other, he will be crucified, and the birds will eat from off his head.—*Upon this they said, We dreamed not aught. He replied,* The thing is decreed concerning which ye [did] ask a determination, *whether ye have spoken truth or have lied.* And he said unto him whom he judged to be the person who should escape of them two, *namely the cup-bearer,* Mention me unto thy lord, *and say unto him, In the prison is a young man imprisoned unjustly.—And he went forth.* But the devil caused him to forget to mention *Joseph* unto his lord: so he remained in the prison some years: *it is said, seven; and it is said, twelve.*

"And the king *of Egypt, Er Reiyán the son of El-Weleed* (*Raiyān ibn al-Walīd al-'Imlīqī*) said, Verily I saw in a dream seven fat kine which seven lean *kine* devoured, and seven green ears of corn and *seven* other *ears* dried up. O ye nobles, explain unto me my dream, if ye interpret a dream.—They replied, *These are* confused dreams, and we know not the interpretation of dreams. And he who had escaped, of the two *young men, namely the cup-bearer,* said (for he remembered after a time *the condition of Joseph*), I will acquaint you with the interpretation thereof; wherefore send me. *So they sent him; and he came unto Joseph, and said,* O Joseph, O thou of great veracity, give us an explanation respecting seven fat kine which seven lean kine devoured, and seven green ears of corn and other seven dried up, that I may return unto the men (*the king and his companions*), that they may know *the interpretation thereof.* He replied, Ye shall sow seven years as usual: (*this is the interpretation of the seven fat kine:*) and what ye reap do ye leave in its ear, *lest it spoil;* except a little, whereof ye shall eat. Then there shall come, after that, seven grievous [years]: (*this is the in-interpretation of the seven lean kine:*) they shall consume what ye shall have provided for them, *of the grain sown in the seven years of plenty,* except a little which ye shall have kept. Then there shall come, after that, a year wherein men shall be aided *with rain,* and wherein they shall press *grapes and other fruits.*—And the king said, *when the messenger came unto him and acquainted him with the interpretation of the dream,* Bring unto me him *who hath interpreted it.*" (Sūrah xii. 35–50.)

"And when the messenger came to Joseph, he said, 'Go back to thy lord, and ask him what meant the women who cut their hands, verily my lord knoweth the snare they laid.' *Then,* said *the Prince to the women,* 'What was your purpose when ye solicited Joseph?' They said, 'God keep us! we know not any ill of him.' The wife of the Prince said, 'Now doth the truth appear. It was I who would have led him into unlawful love, and he is assuredly one of the truthful.' 'This,' said Joseph, 'that *my lord* may learn that I did not in his absence play him false, and that God guideth not the machinations of deceivers. Yet do I not absolve myself: verily the heart is prone to evil, save those on which my Lord has mercy. Lo! my Lord is Gracious, Forgiving, Merciful.' And the King said, 'Bring him to me: I will take him for my special service.'" (Rodwell, Sūrah xii. 50–54.)

"And when he had spoken unto him, he said *unto him,* Thou art this day firmly established with us, and intrusted *with our affairs. What then seest thou fit for us to do?—He answered, Collect provision, and sow abundant seed in these plentiful years, and store up the grain in its ear: then the people will come unto thee that they may obtain provision from thee. The king said, And who will act for me in this affair? Joseph* said, Set me over the granaries of the land; for I am careful and knowing.—Thus did We prepare an establishment for Joseph in the land, that he might take for himself a dwelling therein wherever he pleased.—*And it is related that the king crowned him, and put a ring on his finger, and instated him in the place of Kiṭfeer, whom he dismissed from his office; after which, Kiṭfeer died, and thereupon the king married him to his wife Zeleekha, and she bore him two sons.* We bestow Our mercy on whom We please, and We cause not the reward of the well-doers to perish: and certainly the reward of the world to come is better for those who have believed and have feared.

"*And the years of scarcity began, and afflicted the land of Canaan and Syria,* and the brethren of Joseph came, *except Benjamin, to procure provision, having heard that the governor of Egypt gave food for its price.* And they went in unto him, and he knew them; but they knew him not; *and they spake unto him in the Hebrew language; whereupon he said, as one who distrusted them, What hath brought you to my country? So they answered, For corn. But he said, Perhaps ye are spies. They replied, God preserve us from being spies! He said, Then whence are ye? They answered, From the land of Canaan, and our father is Jacob the prophet of God. He said, And hath he sons beside you? They answered, Yea: we were twelve; but the youngest of us went away, and perished in the desert, and he was the dearest of us unto him; and his uterine brother remained, and he retained him that he might console himself thereby for the loss of the other. And Joseph gave orders to lodge them, and to treat them generously.* And when he had furnished them with their provision, *and given them their full measure,* he said, Bring me your brother from your father, *namely, Benjamin, that I may know your veracity in that ye have said.* Do ye not see that I give full measure, and that I am the most hospitable of the receivers of guests? But if ye bring him not, there shall be no measuring *of corn* for you from me, nor shall ye approach me.—They replied, We will solicit his father for him, and we will surely perform *that.* And he said unto his young men, Put their money, *which they brought as the price of the corn,* in their sacks, that they may know it when they have returned to their family: peradventure they will return *to us; for they will not deem it lawful to keep it.*—And when they returned to their father, they said, O our father, the measuring of corn is denied us *if thou send not our brother unto him;* therefore send with us our brother, that we may obtain measure; and we will surely take care of him. He said, Shall I intrust you with him otherwise than as I intrusted you with his brother *Joseph* before? But God is the best guardian, and He is the most merciful of those who show mercy.—And when they opened their goods, they found their money had been returned unto them. They said, O our father, what desire we *of the generosity of the king greater than this?* This our money hath been returned unto us; and we will provide corn for our family, and will take care of our brother, and shall receive a camel-load more, *for our brother.* This is a quantity easy *unto the king, by reason of his munificence.*—He said, I will by no means send him with you until ye give me a solemn promise by God that ye will assuredly bring him back unto me unless *an inevitable and insuperable impediment* encompass you. *And they complied with this his desire.* And when they had given him their solemn promise, he said, God is witness of what we say. *And he sent him with them;* and he said, O my sons, enter not *the city of Miṣr* by one gate; but enter by different gates; *lest the evil eye fall upon you.* But I shall not avert from you, *by my saying this,* anything *decreed to befall you* from God: *I only say this from a feeling of compassion.* Judgment belongeth not unto any save unto God *alone.* On Him do I rely, and on Him let those rely who rely.

"And when they entered as their father had commanded them, *separately,* it did not avert from them anything *decreed to befall them* from God, but only satisfied a desire in the soul of Jacob, which he accomplished; *that is, the desire of averting the evil eye, arising from a feeling of compassion:* and he was endowed with knowledge, because We had taught him: but the greater number of men, *namely the unbelievers,* know not *God's inspiration of his saints.* And when they went in unto Joseph, he received unto him (*or pressed unto him*) his brother. He said, Verily, I am thy brother: therefore be not sorrowful for that which they did *from envy to us. And he commanded him that he should not inform them, and agree with him that he should employ a stratagem to retain him with him.* And when he had furnished them with their provision, he put the cup, *which was a measure made of gold set with jewels,* in the sack of his brother *Benjamin.* Then a crier cried, *after they had gone forth from the chamber of Joseph,* O company of travellers, ye are surely thieves. They said (and turned unto them), What is it that ye miss? They answered, We miss the king's measure; and to him who shall bring it shall be given a camel-load *of corn,* and I am surety for it, *namely the load.* They replied, By God! ye well know that we have not come to act corruptly in the land, and we have not been thieves. *The crier and his companions* said, Then what shall be the recompense of him *who hath stolen it,* if ye be liars *in your saying, We have not been thieves,—and it be found among you?* They answered, His recompense shall be that he in whose sack it shall be found *shall be made a slave:* he, *the thief,* shall be compensation for it; *namely, for the thing stolen. Such was the usage of the family of Jacob.* Thus do We recompense the offenders *who are guilty of theft.—So they turned towards Joseph, that he might search their sacks.* And he began with their sacks, *and searched them* before the sack of his brother *Benjamin, lest he should be suspected.* Then he took it forth (*namely the measure*) from the sack of his brother. Thus, *saith God,* did We contrive a stratagem for Joseph. It was not lawful for him to take his brother *as a slave for theft* by the law of the king *of Egypt* (*for his recompense by his law was beating, and a fine of twice the value of the thing stolen; not the being made a slave*), unless God had pleased, *by inspiring him to inquire of his brethren and inspiring them to reply according to their usage.* We exalt unto degrees of knowledge and honour whom We please, *as Joseph;* and there is who is knowing about everyone else endowed with knowledge.—They said, If he steal, a brother of his hath stolen before; *namely, Joseph; for he stole an idol of gold belonging to the father of his mother, and broke it, that he might not worship it.* And Joseph concealed it in his mind, and did not discover it to them. He said *within himself,* Ye are in a worse condition *than Joseph and his brother, by reason of your having stolen your brother from your father and your having treated him unjustly;* and God well knoweth what ye state *concerning him.*—They said, O prince, verily he hath a father, a very old man, *who loveth him more than us, and consoleth himself by him for the loss of his son who hath perished, and the separation of him grieveth him;* therefore take one of us *as a slave* in his stead; for we see thee [to be one] of the beneficent. He replied, God preserve us from taking [any] save him in whose possession we found our property; for then (*if we took another*), we [should be] unjust.

And when they despaired of obtaining him, they retired to confer privately together. The chief of them *in age* (*namely, Reuben, or in judgment, namely, Judah*), said, Do ye not know that your father hath obtained of you a solemn promise in the name of God, *with respect of your brother,* and how ye formerly failed of your duty with respect to Joseph? Therefore I will by no means depart from the land *of Egypt* until my father give me permission *to return to him,* or God decide for me *by the delivery of my brother;* and He is the best, *the most just,* of those who decide. Return ye to your father, and say, O our father verily thy son hath committed theft, and we bore not testimony *against him* save according to that which we knew *of a certainty, by our seeing the cup in his sack;* and we were not acquainted with what was unseen *by us when we gave the solemn promise: had we known that he would commit theft, we had not taken him. And send thou*, and ask *the people of* the city in which we have been (*namely, Miṣr*) and the company of travellers with whom we have arrived (*who were a people of Canaan*): and we are surely speakers of truth.—*So they returned to him, and said unto him those words.* He replied, Nay, your minds have made a thing seem pleasant unto you, *and ye have done it* (*he suspected them, on account of their former conduct in the case of Joseph*); but patience is seemly: peradventure God will bring them back (*namely, Joseph and his brother*) unto me, together; for He is the Knowing *with respect to my case*, the Wise *in His acts.* And he turned from them, and said, O! my sorrow for Joseph! And his eyes became white in consequence of mourning, and he was oppressed with silent grief. They said, By God, thou wilt not cease to think upon Joseph until thou be at the point of death, or be of the number of the dead. He replied, I only complain of my great and unconcealable grief and my sorrow unto God; *not unto any beside Him; for He it is unto whom complaint is made with advantage;* and I know by revelation from God what ye know not; *namely, that the dream of Joseph was true, and that he is living. Then he said*, O my sons, go and seek news of Joseph and his brother; and despair not of the mercy of God; for none despaireth of the mercy of God except the unbelieving people.

"*So they departed towards Egypt, unto Joseph;* and when they went in unto him, they said, O Prince, distress (*that is, hunger*) hath affected us and our family, and we have come with paltry money (*it was base money, or some other sort*): yet give us full measure, and be charitable to us, *by excusing the badness of our money;* for God recompenseth those who act charitably. *And he had pity upon them, and compassion affected him, and he lifted up the curtain that was between him and them: then* he said *unto them in reproach*, Do ye know what ye did unto Joseph, *in beating and selling and other actions*, and his brother, *by your injurious conduct to him after the separation of his brother*, when ye were ignorant *of what would be the result of the case of Joseph?* They replied, *after they had recognised him* (*desiring confirmation*), Art thou indeed Joseph? He answered, I am Joseph, and this is my brother. God hath been gracious unto us, *by bringing us together;* for whosoever feareth *God* and is patient [will be rewarded]: God will not suffer the reward of the well-doers to perish. They replied, By God, verily God hath preferred thee above us, and we have been indeed sinners. He said, There shall be no reproach cast on you this day: God forgive you; for He is the most merciful of those that show mercy. *And he asked them respecting his father: so they answered, His eyes are gone. And he said*, Go ye with this my shirt (*it was the shirt of Abraham, which he wore when he was cast into the fire: it was on his*, that is, Joseph's *neck*, appended as an amulet, *in the well; and it was from paradise: Gabriel commanded him to send it, and said, In it is its odour*, that is, the odour of paradise, *and it shall not be cast upon any one afflicted* with a disease *but he shall be restored to health*), and cast it, said Joseph, upon the face of my father: he shall recover his sight; and bring unto me all your family. —And when the company of travellers had gone forth *from El-'Areesh of Egypt*, their father said, *unto those who were present of his offspring*, Verily I perceive the smell of Joseph (*for the zephyr had conveyed it to him, by permission of Him whose name be exalted, from the distance of three days' journey, or eight, or more*): were it not that ye think I dote, *ye would believe me.* They replied, By God, thou art surely in thine old error. And when the messenger of good tidings (*namely, Judah*) came *with the shirt* (*and he had borne the bloody shirt; wherefore he desired to rejoice him, as he had grieved him*), he cast it upon his face, and he recovered his sight Thereupon Jacob said, Did I not say unto you, I know, from God, what ye know not? They said, O our father, ask pardon of our crimes for us; for we have been sinners. He replied, I will ask pardon for you of my Lord; for He is the Very forgiving, the Merciful.—*He delayed doing so until the first appearance of the dawn, that the prayer might be more likely to be answered; or, as some say, until the night of* [that is, preceding] *Friday.*

"*They then repaired to Egypt, and Joseph and the great men came forth to meet them;* and when they went in unto Joseph, *in his pavilion or tent*, he received unto him (*or pressed unto him*) his parents (*his father and his mother and his maternal aunt*), and said unto *them*, Enter ye Miṣr, if God please, in safety. *So they entered; and Joseph seated himself upon his couch*, and he caused his parents to ascend upon the seat of state, and they (*that is, his parents and his brethren*) fell down, bowing themselves unto him (*bending, but not putting the forehead*) upon the ground: *such being their mode of obeisance in that time.* And he said, O my father, this is the interpretation of my dream of former times: my Lord hath made it true; and He hath shown favour unto me, since He took me forth from the prison (*he said not, from the well,—from a motive of generosity, that his brethren might not be abashed*), and hath brought you from the desert, after that the devil had excited discord between me and my brethren; for my Lord is gracious unto whom He pleaseth; for He is the Knowing, the Wise.—*And his father resided with him four and twenty years, or seventeen; and the period of his separation was eighteen, or forty, or eighty years. And death came unto him; and thereupon he charged Joseph that he should carry him and bury him by his fathers. So he went himself and buried him. Then he returned to Egypt and remained after him three and twenty years; and when his case was ended, and he knew that he should not last upon earth, and his soul desired the lasting possession, he said,* O my Lord, Thou hast given me dominion, and taught me the interpretation of events (*or dreams*): Creator of the heavens and the earth, Thou art my guardian in this world and in the world to come. Make me to die a Muslim, and join me with the righteous *among my forefathers. And he lived after that a week, or more, and died a hundred and twenty years old. And the Egyptians disputed concerning his burial: so they put him in a chest of marble, and buried him in the upper part of the Nile, that the blessing resulting from him might be general to the tracts on each side of it. Extolled be the perfection of Him to whose dominion there is no end!* (Sūrah xii. 54 to the end.)

For the Talmudic origin of this account, see JUDAISM.

JOSHUA. Arabic *Yūsha'* (يوشع). Son of Nūn. Not mentioned by name in the Qur'ān, but is most probably "the servant" mentioned in Sūrah xviii. 59: "When Moses said to his servant, 'I will not stop until I reach the confluence of the two seas, or for years I will journey on.'" (*Vide* al-Baizāwī *in loco.*) Some say he is the Ẕū 'l-Kifl of Sūrah xxi. 85. [ZU 'L-KIFL.]

JUBAIR (جبير). Jubair ibn Muṭ'im an-Naufalī. One of the Companions, and acknowledged as a traditionist by al-Bukhārī and Muslim. He was one of the most learned of the Quraish chiefs. Died at Makkah A.H. 54. Ibn Jubair, his son, was an Imām of great renown, he died A.H. 99.

JUBBU 'L-ḤUZN (جب الحزن). "The pit of sorrow," which Muḥammad said was a desert in hell, from which hell itself calls for protection, and which is reserved for readers of the Qur'ān who are haughty in their behaviour. (*Mishkāt*, book ii. ch. iii.)

JUDGE. Arabic *Qāẓī* (قاضى). A magistrate or judge appointed by the ruler of a Muḥammadan country. He should be an adult, a free man, a Muslim, sane, and unconvicted of slander (*qazf*). It becomes a Muslim not to covet the appointment of Qāẓī, for the Prophet has said: "Whoever seeks the appointment of Qāẓī shall be left alone, but to him who accepts the office on compulsion, an angel shall descend and guide him." (*Mishkāt*, book xvi. ch. iii.)

The Qāẓī must exercise his office in some public place, the chief mosque being recommended, or, if in his own house, he should see that the public have free access. He must not accept any presents except from relatives and old friends, nor should he attend feasts and entertainments given by others than his relatives and friends. In addition to his duties as magistrate, it is his duty to attend funerals and weddings, and when present it is his right and office to perform the ceremonies. A woman may exercise the office of a Qāẓī, except in the administration of punishment (*ḥadd*) or retaliation (*qiṣāṣ*). (*Hidāyah*, vol. ii. p. 613.)

JUDGMENT-DAY. Arabic *Qiyāmah* (قيامة). [RESURRECTION.]

AL-JŪDĪ (الجودى). Mount Ararat, upon which the ark of Noah rested. Mentioned in the Qur'ān, Sūrah xi. 46: "And it (the ark) settled on *al-Jūdī*."

Jūdī is a corruption apparently for Mount Giordi, the Gordyœi of the Greeks, situated between Armenia and Mesopotamia.

Ainsworth, in his *Travels in the Track of the Ten Thousand*, says tradition still points to Jabal Judī as the scene of the event, and maintains the belief that fragments of the ark exist on its summit.

Whiston, in his *History of Armenia*, p. 361, says *Araratia* is the name of a province and not of a mountain in Armenia.

JU'L (جعل). The hire or reward of labour. An extraordinary pay or donation. In the language of the law, a reward for bringing back a fugitive slave.

JUMĀDĀ 'L-UKHRĀ (جمادى الاخرى). The sixth month of the Muḥammadan year. [MONTHS.]

JUMĀDĀ 'L-ŪLĀ (جمادى الاولى). The fifth month of the Muḥammadan year. [MONTHS.]

JUM'AH (جمعة). [FRIDAY.]

JUNUB (جنب). *Lit.* "One who is separated." The unclean. A person who is in a state of uncleanness [JANABAH] whereby he or she cannot perform any religious act or join in religious assemblies. [PURIFICATION.]

JURF (جرف). *Lit.* "A wasted river-bank." A place three miles from al-Madīnah, celebrated in Muḥammadan history.

JUSTIFIABLE HOMICIDE. The Muḥammadan law on the subject is as follows:—

"If any person draw a sword upon a Muslim he (the Muslim) is at liberty to kill him in self-defence, because the Prophet has said, 'He who draws a sword upon a Muslim renders his blood liable to be shed with impunity'; and also, because a person who thus draws a sword is a rebel, and guilty of sedition; and it is lawful to slay such, God having said, in the Qur'ān, 'Slay those who are guilty of sedition, to the end that it may be prevented.' Besides, it is indispensably requisite that a man repel murder from himself and as, in the present instance, there is no method of effecting this but by slaying the person, it is consequently lawful so to do. If however, it be possible to effect the self-defence without slaying the person, it is not lawful to slay him. It is written in the *Jama Sagheer* (*al-Jâmi'u 's-Saghīr*), that if a person strike at another with a sword, during either night or day, or lift a club against another in the night in a city, or in the day-time in the highway out of the city; and the person so threatened kill him who thus strikes with the sword, or lifts the club, nothing is incurred; because, as striking with a sword affords no room for delay or deliberation, it is in this case necessary to kill the person in order to repel him; and although, in the case of a club, there be more room for deliberation, yet in the night-time assistance cannot be obtained, and hence the person threatened is in a manner forced, in repelling the other's attack, to kill him. (And so likewise where the attack is made during the day-time in the highway, as there assistance cannot readily be obtained). Where, therefore, a person thus slays another, the blood of the slain is of no account. If a lunatic draw a sword upon a person, and the person slay him, the fine of blood is due from his property, and does not fall upon his Akilas (*Aqilah*). As-Shāfi'ī maintains that nothing whatever is incurred in this instance. In the same manner, also, if an infant draw a sword and make an attack upon a person, or if an animal attack anyone, and the person so attacked slay the infant, or the animal, a fine is due on account of the infant, or the value on account of the animal, according to Abū Ḥanīfah, but not according to ash-Shāfi'ī.

"If a person draw a sword upon another, and strike him, and then go away, and the person struck, or any other, afterwards kill this person, he is liable to retaliation. This is where the striker retires in such a way as indicates that he will not strike again, for as, upon his so retiring, he no longer continues an assailant, and the protection of his blood (which had been forfeited by the assault) reverts, retaliation is consequently incurred by killing him.

"If a person come in the night to a stranger, and carry off his goods by theft, and the owner of the goods follow and slay him, nothing whatever is incurred, the Prophet having said, 'Ye may kill in preservation of your property.' It is to be observed, however, that this is only where the owner cannot recover his property but by killing the thief; for if he know that upon his calling out the thief would relinquish the goods, and he notwithstanding neglect calling out, and slay him, retaliation is incurred upon him, since he in this case slays the person unrighteously." (*Hidāyah*, vol. iv. p. 291.)

JUWAIRĪYAH (جويرية). One of Muḥammad's wives. She was the daughter of the chief of the Banī 'l-Musṭaliq. She survived the Prophet some years.

Sir William Muir writes (*Life of Mahomet*, new ed. p. 309): "The captives of the Bani Mustalick having been carried to Medîna with the rest of the booty, men from their tribe soon arrived to make terms for their release. One of them was Juweiria, a damsel about twenty years of age, full of grace and beauty, the daughter of a chief, and married to one of her own tribe. She fell to the lot of a citizen, who, taking advantage of her rank and comeliness, fixed her ransom at nine ounces of gold. Despairing to raise so large a sum, she ventured into the presence of the Prophet, while seated in the apartment of Ayesha, and pleaded for some remission of the heavy price demanded for her freedom. Ayesha no sooner saw that she was fair to look upon, and of a sprightly winning carriage, than her jealousy prognosticated what was about to come to pass. Mahomet listened to her supplications. 'Wilt thou hearken,' he said, 'to something better than that thou askest of me?' Surprised by his gentle accents, she inquired what that might be: 'Even that I should pay thy ransom, and marry thee myself!' The damsel forthwith expressed her consent, the ransom was paid, and Mahomet, taking her at once to wife, built a seventh house for her reception. As soon as the marriage was noised abroad, the people said that the Bani Mustalick having now become their relatives, they would let the rest of the prisoners go free as Juweiria's dower; 'and thus no woman,' said Ayesha, telling the story in after days, 'was ever a greater blessing to her people than this Juweiria.'"

JUZ' (جزء). One of the thirty portions into which the Qur'ān is divided. [SIPARA.]

K.

KA'BAH (كعبة). *Lit.* "A cube." The cube-like building in the centre of the mosque at Makkah, which contains the Ḥajaru 'l-Aswad, or black stone.

I. *A Description of the Ka'bah.*—It is, according to Burckhardt and Burton, an oblong massive structure, 18 paces in length, 14 in breadth, and about 35 feet in height. It is constructed of grey Makkan stone, in large blocks of different sizes, joined together in a very rough manner, with cement. (Burton says it is excellent mortar, like Roman cement.) The Ka'bah stands upon a base two feet in height, which presents a sharp inclined plane; its roof being flat, it has, at a distance, the appearance of a perfect cube. The only door which affords entrance, and which is opened but two or three times in the year (Burton says it can be entered by pilgrims, by paying the guardian a liberal fee), is on the east side, and about seven feet above the ground. At the south-east corner of the Ka'bah, near the door, is the famous black stone [HAJARU 'L-ASWAD], which forms a part of the sharp angle of the building, at four or five feet above the ground The black stone is an irregular oval, about seven inches in diameter, with an undulating surface, composed of about a dozen smaller stones of different shapes and sizes. It is surrounded on all sides by a border of reddish brown cement, both the stone and the border being encircled by a band of a massive arch of gold or silver gilt, the aperture of the stone being one span and three fingers broad. In the corner facing the south, there is another stone about five feet from the ground. It is one foot and a half in length, and two inches in breadth, placed upright, and of common Makkan stone. According to the rites of the pilgrimage, this stone, which is called ar-Ruknu 'l-Yamānī, or Yaman pillar, should only be touched with the right hand as the pilgrim passes it, but Captain Burton says he frequently saw it kissed by the pilgrims. Just by the door of the Ka'bah, and close to the wall, is a slight hollow in the ground, lined with marble and sufficiently large to admit of three persons sitting, which is called al-Mi'jan, and supposed to be the place where Abraham and his son Ishmael kneaded the

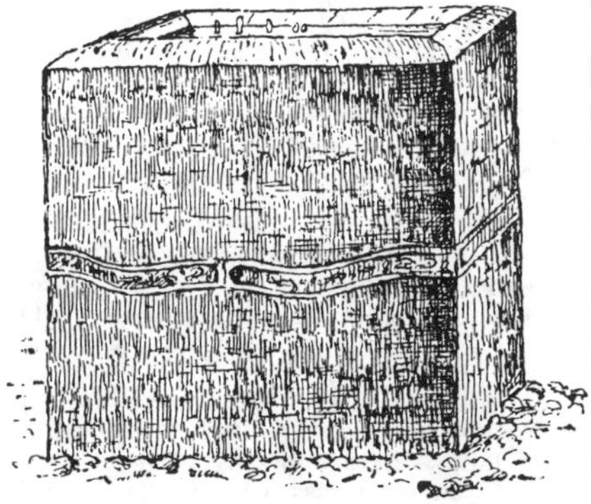

THE KA'BAH. (*From a Photograph.*)

chalk and mud which they used to build the Ka'bah. Here it is thought meritorious to pray. On the basis of the Ka'bah, just above the Mi'jan, is an ancient Kufic inscription, which neither Burckhardt nor Burton were able to decipher or to copy. On the north-west side of the Ka'bah, about two feet below its summit, is the water-spout, which is called the Mi'zābu' r-Raḥmah, or the water-spout of mercy. This spout is of gold, and was sent hither from Constantinople in A.H. 981. It carries rain from the roof, and discharges it upon Ishmael's grave. There are two large green marble slabs, which are said to have been presents from Cairo, A.H. 241, which are supposed to mark the graves of Hagar and Ishmael. The pavement round the Ka'bah consists of a very handsome mosaic of various coloured stones, and is said to have been laid down A.H. 826. On one side of the Ka'bah is a semicircular wall, the extremities of which are in a line with the sides of the Ka'bah, and distant about six feet, leaving an opening which leads to the grave of Ishmael. The wall is called al-Ḥaṭīm, "the broken," and the enclosed area al-Ḥijr, "the enclosure." The Ka'bah is covered with a coarse tissue of mixed silk and cotton, being of a brilliant black colour, and with a gold band round it, upon which is inscribed the ninetieth verse of the third chapter of the Qu'rān: "Verily the first home founded for mankind was surely that at Bakkah, for a blessing and a guidance to mankind." The inscription being in large Kufic characters. For a further account of this cover, see KISWAH.

THE KA'BAH. (*Burton.*)

II. *The History of the Ka'bah*, is embraced in the history of the Baitu 'llāh or MASJIDU 'L-HARAM.

According to the Traditions and the inventive genius of Muslim writers, the Ka'bah was first constructed in heaven (where a model of it still remains, called the *Baitu'l-Ma'mūr*) two thousand years before the creation of the world. Adam erected the Ka'bah on earth exactly below the spot its perfect model occupies in heaven, and selected the stones from the five sacred mountains, Sinai, al-Jūdī, Ḥirā', Olivet, and Lebanon. Ten thousand angels were appointed to guard the structure, but, as Burckhardt remarks, they appear to have been often most remiss in their duty! At the Deluge the Sacred House was destroyed. But the Almighty is said to have instructed Abraham to rebuild it. In its reconstruction Abraham was assisted by his son Ishmael, who with his mother Hagar were at the time residents of Makkah, Abraham having journeyed from Syria in order to obey the commands of God.

Upon digging they found the original foundations of the building. But wanting a stone to mark the corner of the building, Ishmael started in search of one, and as he was going in the direction of Jabal Qubais, the angel Gabriel met him, and gave him the famous black stone. Ibn 'Abbās relates that the Prophet said, the black stone when it came down from Paradise was whiter than milk, but that it has become black from the sins of those who have touched it. (*Mishkāt*, book xi. ch. iv. pt. 2.)

Upon the death of Ishmael, the Ka'bah fell into the possession of the Banū Jurhum, and remained in their hands for a thousand years. It then became the property of the Banū Khuzā'ah, who held it for three hundred years. But being constantly exposed to torrents, it was destroyed, and was rebuilt by Qusaiy ibn Kilāb, who put a top to it. Up to this time it is said to have been open at the roof.

It is said, by Muḥammadan historians, that 'Amr ibn Luḥaiy was the first who introduced idolatry into Arabia, and that he brought the great idol Hubal from Hait in Mesopotamia and placed it in the sacred house. It then became a Pantheon common to all the tribes. [IDOLS.] The tribe of Quṣaiy were the first who built dwelling-houses round the Ka'bah. The successors of the Banū Quṣaiy were the Quraish. Soon after they came into possession, the Ka'bah was destroyed by fire, and they rebuilt it of wood and of a smaller size, than it had been in the time of the Banū Quṣaiy. The roof was supported within by six pillars, and the statue of Hubal was placed over a wall then existing within the Ka'bah. This took place during the youth of Muḥammad. Al-Azraqī, quoted by Burckhardt, says that the figure of the Virgin Mary and the infant Jesus was sculptured as a deity upon one of the six pillars nearest the gate.

The grandfather of Muḥammad, 'Abdu 'l-Muṭṭalib, the son of Hāshim, became the custodian of the Sacred House; and during his time, the Ka'bah being considered too low in its structure, the Quraish wished to raise it; so they demolished it and then they rebuilt till the work reached the place of the black stone. Each tribe wishing to have the honour of raising the black stone into its place, they quarrelled amongst themselves. But they at last agreed that the first man who should enter the gate of the enclosure should be umpire. Muḥammad was the first to enter, and he was appointed umpire. He thereupon ordered them to place the stone upon a cloth and each tribe by its representative to take hold of the cloth and lift it into its place. The dispute was thus ended, and when the stone had reached its proper place, Muḥammad fixed it in its situation with his own hand.

At the commencement of Muḥammad's mission, it is remarkable that there is scarcely an allusion to the Ka'bah, and this fact, taken with the circumstance that the earliest Qiblah or direction for prayer, was Jerusalem, and not the Ka'bah, seems to imply that Muḥammad's strong iconoclastic tendencies did not incline his sympathies to this ancient idol temple with its superstitious ceremonies. Had the Jews favourably received the new prophet as one who taught the religion of Abraham, to the abrogation of that of Moses and Jesus, Jerusalem and not Makkah would have been the sacred city, and the ancient Rock [SAKHRAH] and not the Ka'bah would have been the object of superstitious reverence.

Taking the Sūrahs chronologically, the earliest reference in the Qur'ān to the Ka'bah occurs in Sūrah lii. 4, where the Prophet swears by the *frequented house* (*al-Baitu 'l-Ma'mūr*), but commentators are not agreed whether it refers to the Ka'bah in Makkah, or its heavenly model above, which is said to be frequented by the angels. We then come to Sūrah xvii. 1, where Muḥammad refers to his celebrated night dream of his journey from the Sacred Mosque (*al-Masjidu 'l-Ḥarām*) at Makkah to the Remote Mosque (*al-Masjidu 'l-Aqṣā*) at Jerusalem. And in this verse we find the Rock at Jerusalem spoken of as "the precinct of which We (God) have blessed, to show him (Muḥammad) of our signs," proving that even then the Prophet of Arabia had his heart fixed on Mount Zion, and not on the Ka'bah.

When Muḥammad found himself established in al-Madīnah, with a very good prospect of his obtaining possession of Makkah, and its historic associations, he seems to have withdrawn his thoughts from Jerusalem, and its Sacred Rock and to fix them on the house at Bakkah as the home founded for mankind,—Blessed, and a guidance to all creatures. (Sūrah iii. 90). The Jews proving obdurate, and there being little chance of his succeeding in establishing his claim as their prophet spoken of by Moses, he changes the Qiblah, or direction for prayer, from Jerusalem to Makkah. The house at Makkah is made "a place of resort unto men and a sanctuary" (Sūrah ii. 119).

The Qiblah is changed by an express command of the Almighty, and the whole passage is remarkable as exhibiting a decided concession on the part of Muḥammad to the claims of the Ka'bah as a central object of adoration. (Sūrah iii. 138-145.)

"We appointed the Qiblah which thou formerly hadst, only that we might know him who followeth the apostle, from him who turneth on his heels: The change is a difficulty, but not to those whom God hath guided. But God will not let your faith be fruitless; for unto man is God Merciful, Gracious. We have seen thee turning thy face towards every part of Heaven; but we will have thee turn to a Qiblah which shall please thee. Turn then thy face towards the sacred Mosque, and wherever ye be, turn your faces towards that part. They, verily, to whom 'the Book' hath been given, know this to be the truth from their Lord: and God is not regardless of what ye do. Even though thou shouldest bring every kind of sign to those who have received the Scriptures, yet thy Qiblah they will not adopt; nor shalt thou adopt their Qiblah; nor will one part of them adopt the Qiblah of the other. And if, after the knowledge which hath come to thee, thou follow their wishes, verily then wilt thou become of the unrighteous. They to whom we have given the Scriptures know him—*the apostle*—even as they know their own children: but truly a part of them do conceal the truth, though acquainted with it. The truth is from thy Lord. Be not then of those who doubt. All have a quarter of the Heavens to which they turn them; but wherever ye be, hasten emulously after good: God will one day bring you all together; verily, God is all-powerful. And from whatever place thou comest forth, turn thy face toward the sacred Mosque; for this is the truth from thy Lord; and God is not inattentive to your doings. And from whatever place thou comest forth, turn thy face toward the sacred Mosque; and wherever ye be, to that part turn your faces, lest men have cause of dispute against you: but as for the impious among them, fear them not; but fear me, that I may perfect my favours on you, and that ye may be guided aright."

The verses of the second Sūrah of the Qur'ān are, according to Jalālu 'd-dīn and other commentators, not in their chronological order. It is therefore difficult to fix the precise date of the following verse:—

Sūrah ii. 108: "Who is more unjust than he who prohibits God's mosques, that His name should not be worshipped there, and who strives to ruin them."

According to al-Baiẓāwī, the verse either refers to the sacking of Jerusalem by Titus, or to the Quraish who, at al-Ḥudaibiyah, had prevented the Prophet from entering Makkah until the following year.

In the seventh year of the Hijrah, Muḥammad was, according to the treaty with the Quraish at al-Ḥudaibiyah in the previous year, allowed to enter Makkah, and perform the circuit of the Ka'bah. Hubal and the other idols of the Arabian pantheon were still within the sacred building, but, as Muḥammad's visit was limited to three days, he confined himself to the ordinary rites of the '*Umrah*, or visitation, without interfering with the idolatrous arrangement of the Ka'bah itself. Before he left, at the hour of midday prayer, Bilāl ascended the holy house, and from its summit gave the first call to Muslim prayers, which were afterwards led by the Prophet in the usual form.

The following year Muḥammad occupied Makkah by force of arms. The idols in the Ka'bah were destroyed, and the rites of the pilgrimage were established as by divine enactment. From this time the history of the Ka'bah becomes part of the history of Islām.

The Khalīfah 'Umar first built a mosque round the Ka'bah, A.H. 17.

For a history of the sacred mosque at Makkah, see MASJIDU 'L-HARAM.

KA'B IBN MĀLIK (كعب بن مالك). A companion of the Prophet and one of the Anṣārs of the tribe of Khazraj. He was celebrated as a poet, and embraced Islām after the second pledge of 'Akabah. He was one of the three companions who refused to accompany Muḥammad on the expedition to Tabūk (Hilāl and Marārah being the other two), and who are referred to in the Qur'ān, Sūrah ix. 118, 119: "Verily He is kind to them, unto the three who were left behind." For a time Muḥammad was displeased with them, but he afterwards became reconciled. Ka'b became a companion of some note, and died during the reign of 'Alī.

AL-KABĪR (الكبير). "The Great One." One of the ninety-nine attributes of God, Sūrah xxxiv. 22: "He is the High (*al-'Alī*) and the Great (*al-Kabīr*)."

KABĪRAH (كبيرة). The fem. of *kabīr*, "great." A term used in theological books for *Gunāh-i-Kabīrah*, "a great sin"; namely, that sin which is clearly forbidden in the law, and for which punishment has been ordained of God. [SIN.]

KA'BĪYAH (كعبية). A sect of Muslims founded by Abū Qāsim Muḥammad ibn al-Ka'bī, who was a Mu'tazilī of Bagdād, who said the acts of God were without purpose, will, or desire.

KACHKŪL (كچكول). Persian (vulg. *kachkol*). The begging bowl of a religious mendicant. [FAQIR.]

KAFĀLAH (كفالة). [BAIL.]

KAFAN (كفن). The shroud for the dead. It usually consists of three pieces of cloth for a man and five for a woman. Those for a man: 1, An *izār*, or piece of cloth, reaching from the navel to the knees or ankle joints; 2, A *qamīṣ*, or shirt, from the neck to the knees; 3, A sheet to cover the whole corpse. For a woman there are also a breast band and head band. The whole being of white. [BURIAL.]

KAFFĀRAH (كفارة), from *kafr*, "to hide." Heb. כִּפֻּרִים. *Lit.* "Coverings; atonements; expiation."

The word occurs four times in the Qur'ān:—

Sūrah v. 49: "Whoso remitteth it as alms shall have *expiation* for his sins."

Sūrah v. 91: "Its *expiation* shall be to feed ten persons." "This is the *expiation* for your oaths."

Sūrah v. 96: "In *expiation* thereof shall ye feed the poor."

The other word used is *fidyah* [FIDYAH]. The expression *kaffāratu 'z-ẕunūb*, "atonement for sins," is used for expiation by prayer, alms, fasting, and pilgrimage. [EXPIATION.]

AL-KĀFĪ (الكافى). "The Sufficient One." An attribute of God mentioned in the Qur'ān, Sūrah xxxix. 37: "Is not God *sufficient* for His servant."

AL-KĀFĪ (الكافى). The title of a collection of traditions by Abū Ja'far Muḥammad ibn Ya'qūb al-Kulīnī (A.H. 328) received by the Shī'ahs.

KĀFIR (كافر), pl. *kāfirūn*. *Lit.* "The coverer." One who hides or covers up the truth.

The word is generally used by Muḥammadans to define one who is an unbeliever in the ministry of Muḥammad and his Qur'ān, and in this sense it seems to have been used by Muḥammad himself. Sūrah ii. 37: "Those who misbelieve (*wa'llaẕīna kafarū*), and call our signs lies, they are fellows of the Fire, they shall dwell within for ever."

It is also used for those who believe in the Divinity of the Lord Jesus, and the Holy Trinity. Sūrah v. 76: "They indeed are infidels (*la-qad kafara 'llazīna*), who say God is al-Masīḥu ibn Maryam. . . . Verily him who associates anything with God, hath God forbidden Paradise, and his resort is the Fire."

Sūrah v. 77: "They are infidels who say Verily God is the third of three."

[On this passage the Kamālān say it refers to the Nestorians and to the Malakā'īyah, who believe that God is one of three, the other two being the mother and son.]

According to the *Raddu 'l-Muḥtār* (vol. iii. p. 442), there are five classes of kāfirs or infidels: (1) Those who do not believe in the Great First Cause; (2) Those who do not believe in the Unity of God, as the Ṣanawīyah who believe in the two eternal principles of light and darkness; (3) Those who believe in the Unity of God, but do not believe in a revelation; (4) Those who are idolaters; (5) Those who believe in God and in a revelation, but do not believe in the general mission of Muḥammad to the whole of mankind, as the Christians, a sect of the Jews (*sic*).

Saiyid Sharīf Jurjānī says: "Mankind are divided into two parties, namely, those who acknowledge the mission of Muḥammad, or those who do not believe in it. Those who do not believe in his mission are either those who reject it and yet believe in the inspiration and divine mission of other prophets, as the Jews or Christians, and also the *Majūsī* (Fire Worshippers); or those who do not believe in any revelation of God's will. Those who do not believe in any revelation from God, are either those who acknowledge the existence of God, as the *Brāhmā* (Buddhists?), or those who deny the existence of a Supreme Ruler, as the *Dahrī*, or Atheists."

"Those who do not acknowledge Muḥammad as an inspired prophet are either those who do it wilfully and from mere enmity, or those who do not acknowledge it from reflection and due study of the subject. For the former is eternal punishment, and for the latter that punishment which is not eternal. There are also those who, whilst they are Muslims, are not orthodox in their belief; these are heretics, but they are not kāfirs. Those who are orthodox are *an-Nājī* or the salvationists." (*Sharḥu 'l-Muwāqif*, p. 597.)

KAFŪR (كفور). The unthankful, or ungrateful. Condemned in the Qur'ān, Sūrah xxii. 39: "God loveth not the false, the *unthankful*."

KĀFŪR (كافور). *Lit.* "Camphor." A fountain in Paradise mentioned in the Qur'ān (Sūrah lxxvi. 5) as the fountain whereof the servants of the Lord shall drink. But al-Baiẓāwī, the commentator, takes it for an appellative, and believes that the wine of Paradise will be mixed with *camphor* because of its agreeable coolness and smell.

AL-KAHF (الكهف). "The Cave." The title of the XVIIIth chapter of the Qur'ān, in which is related the story of the Seven Sleepers of Ephesus, known as the *Aṣḥābu 'l-Kahf*.

KĀHIN (كاهن), pl. *kahanah* and *kuhhān*. A soothsayer, or augur. The word occurs only twice in the Qur'ān; and in both instances it is used for "a soothsayer."

Sūrah lii. 29: "For thou (Muḥammad), by the favour of thy Lord, art neither a soothsayer (*kāhin*), nor one possessed (*majnūn*)."

Sūrah lxix. 42: "Neither is it (the Qur'ān) the word of a soothsayer (*kāhin*)."

The word is used in the Traditions in the same sense only:—

Mishkāt, book iv. chap. i.: "The Prophet said, believe in Islām, and put not your trust in soothsayers (*kahanah*)."

Mishkāt, book xxi. ch. ii.: "'Āyishah relates that the Prophet was asked about *kahanah*, fortune-tellers, and he said, 'You must not believe anything they say.' It was then said, 'O Prophet, why do they then sometimes tell lies?' And the Prophet said: 'Because one of the jinn steals away the truth and carries it to the magician's ear, and the magicians (*kuhhān*) mix a hundred lies with it.'"

The Hebrew כֹּהֵן *Kohain*, ἱερεύς, is applied in the Old Testament not only to the Jewish priests, but also to Melchizedek (Gen. xiv. 18), Potipher (Gen. xli. 45; see marginal reading in our English version), and to Jethro (Ex. ii. 16).

KAHRUBĀ (كهربا). *Lit.* "Attracting Straws." Electricity, or the power of attraction. A Ṣūfī term.

KAIFĪYAH (كيفية). "Detailed circumstances." A term used in Muḥammadan books for a statement or account of anything, *e.g.* *kaifīyat-i-taskhīr*, "the manner of attack"; *kaifīyat-i-rāsikhah*, "a fixed or permanent quality"; *kaifīyat-i-'āriẓah*, "a moveable or accidental quality."

KA'LAH (كالة). A kind of sale which is prohibited. *Mishkāt*, book xii. ch. v. pt. 2: "The Prophet has forbidden selling on credit for credit."

'Abdu 'l-Ḥaqq explains it thus: "If 'Amr owe Zaid a piece of cloth, and Bakr ten dirhams, and Zaid say to Bakr, I have sold you the piece of cloth, which is with 'Amr for ten dirhams"—this sale is forbidden.

KALĀM (كلام). "A word; speech." *'Ilmu 'l-kalām*, "scholastic theology"; *fasīḥu 'l-kalām*, "eloquent"; *muḥaṣṣalu 'l-kalām*, "the substance of a discourse."

KALAMU 'LLĀH (كلام الله). "The Word of God." A title given to the Qur'ān. Sūrah ii. 70: "Already a sect of them have heard the *Word of God*."

KALIMAH (كلمة). *Lit.* "The Word." The Creed of the Muslim.

لا اله الا الله محمد رسول الله

Lā Ilāha illā 'llāhu: Muḥammadun Rasūlu 'llāh.

"There is no deity but God: Muḥammad is the Apostle of God."

The whole sentence as it stands does not occur in the Qur'ān; but the first part of the creed, "There is no deity but God," is in the Sūratu Muḥammad, or XLVIIth chapter of the Qur'ān, verse 21; and the second part, "Muḥammad is the Apostle of God," is in the Sūratu 'l-Fatḥ, or XLVIIIth chapter, verse 29. The first sentence is known as the *Nafy* and the *Iṣbāt*, or the rejection (*there is no deity*) and the affirmation (*but God*), and is recited often as a religious office by the Ṣūfī faqīrs.

The whole creed frequently occurs in the Traditions, and is an oft-recurring clause in the daily prayer.

This *Kalimah* occupies a similar place in the Muslim religion to the "*Shema' Israil*" of the Hebrew Bible in the Jews' religion. The *Shema'* ("Hear") is the fourth verse of Deut. vi.: "Hear, O Israil, *Jehovah our Elohīm is one Jehovah*"; which is frequently used in daily morning and evening service of the Jews. From the Traditions (*Mishkāt*, book xi. ch. 2, pt. 1) it appears that a something similar to this well known symbol of the Muslim creed, was in use amongst the ancient Arabians, and is still recited by Muslims, amongst whom it is known as the *Talbiyah*: "I stand up for Thy service, O God! There is no partner with Thee." [TALBIYAH.]

The recital of the *kalimah* is the first of the five foundations or pillars of practice, and, according to the *Fawā'idu 'sh-Sharī'ah*, every Muslim should recite it *aloud* at least once in his lifetime, and he should understand its meaning. [RECITAL OF THE CREED.]

KALIMATU 'L-ḤAẒRAH (كلمة الحضرة). The fiat of God when He said "Be," and it was created. The word كن, *kun*, is therefore called the *Kalimatu 'l-Ḥaẓrah*. It occurs in the Qur'ān, Sūrah xxxvi. 82: "His bidding is only when He desires anything to say to it 'BE,' and it is." And in about eleven other places.

KALIMATU 'SH-SHAHĀDAT (كلمة الشهادة). "The word of testimony." The following expression of belief; "I bear witness that there is no deity but God, and that Muḥammad is His Apostle." [PRAYER.]

KALĪMU 'LLĀH (كليم الله). "The Converser with God." A title given to the Prophet Moses (*vide Mishkāt*, book xxii. ch. xii.). It is also referred to in the Qur'ān, Sūrah iv. 162: "Moses did God speak to—conversing."

KALĪSAH, KILĪSAH (كليسة). A Christian Church. Ἐκκλησία. The word is used in books of Muḥammadan law for both Christian and Jewish places of worship. The word *kanīsah* is also used. [KANISAH.]

KĀMIL (كامل). "Perfect; complete." *Al-Insānu 'l-Kāmil*, "the perfect man." A mystic term. [INSANU 'L-KAMIL.]

KAMILĪYAH (كاملية). A sect of Shī'ah Muslims founded by Abū 'l-Kāmil, who said the Aṣāḥīb, or Companions of the Prophet, were infidels, because they rejected the house of 'Alī in forming the Khalīfate, and he even called the Khalīfah 'Alī an infidel because he did not claim his rights when Muḥammad died. (*Kitābu 't-Ta'rīfāt, in loco.*)

KAN'ĀN (كنعان). "Canaan." Not mentioned by name in the Qur'ān. The Commentators al-Baiẓāwī and Jalālu 'd-dīn, say he was the son of Noah; but the author of the Qāmūs dictionary says he was the son of Shem. (According to the Old Testament, he was the son of Ham, Gen. x. 6; 1 Chron. i. 8.)

He is said to be that son of Noah who was drowned, through unbelief, in the deluge. See Qur'ān, Sūrah xi. 44. [NOAH.]

KANĪSAH (كنيسة). A Christian church, a Jewish synagogue, or a pagan temple. It is used in the *Hidāyah* (vol. ii p. 219) for a synagogue. [CHURCHES.]

AL-KANZU 'L-MAKHFĪ (الكنز المخفي). *Lit.* "The Secret Treasure." A term used by the Ṣūfīs for the essence and personality of God.

KĀRAWĀN (كاروان). Persian. "A caravan." The Arabic term is *Qāfilah*. A party of merchants proceeding on a journey under the direction of a leader who is called a *Qāfilah Bāshī*.

KARBALĀ' (كربلاء), or **MASHHADU 'L-ḤUSAIN**. A city in al-'Irāq, celebrated as the scene of the martyrdom of al-Ḥusain [AL-HUSAIN] and the place of his sepulchre. It is fifty miles south-west of Baghdād, and about six miles west of the Euphrates.

AL-KARĪM (الكريم). "The Generous One." One of the ninety-nine attributes of God.

KARŪBĪN (كروبين). [CHERUBIM.]

KASHF (كشف). The uncovering of anything covered; manifestation. A mystic term used for a revelation of any secret truth to the mind of man, by the grace and power of God.

KĀTIB (كاتب). An Amanuensis; a clerk; a secretary. In the latter sense it is used for Muḥammad ibn Sa'd ibn Manī' az-Zuhrī, the secretary to al-Wāqidī. [KATIBU 'L-WAQIDI.]

KĀTIBU 'L-WĀQIDI (كاتب الواقدي). The secretary of al-Wāqidī. A Muslim historian, largely quoted by Sir William Muir in his *Life of Mahomet*, and also by Sprenger, and often given as an authority in the present work.

Mr. Ameer Ali in his *Life of Muḥammad* (London, 1873), couples the name of *Kātibu l-Wāqidī* with that of *al-Waqidī* himself, as regarded by "the Muḥammadan as the least trustworthy and most careless biographers of Muḥammad," and quotes Ibn Khallikān in support of his opinion. It is quite true that Ibn Khallikān does speak of the traditions received by al-Wāqidī as "of feeble authority," but he bears testimony to the trustworthiness of *al-Wāqidī's secretary* in the strongest terms, as will be seen in the following quotation, and it is manifestly unfair of Mr. Ameer Ali to couple the two names together in his preface:—

"Abû Abd Allah Muhammad Ibn Saad Ibn Manî az-Zuhri, was a man of the highest talents, merit, and eminence. He lived for some time with al-Wakidi [WAQIDI] in the character of a secretary, and for this reason he became known by the appellation of Katibu-l-Wakidi. Amongst the masters under whom he studied was Sofyân Ibn Oyaina. Traditional information was delivered on his own authority by Abû Bakr Ibn Abid-Dunyâ and Abû Muhammad al-Hârith Ibn Abi Osâma at-Tamîmi. He composed an excellent work, in fifteen volumes, on the different classes (*tabakât*) of Muhammad's companions and of the Tâbis. It contains also a history of the khalifs brought down to his own time. He left also a smaller *Tabakât*. *His character as a veracious and trustworthy historian is universally admitted.* It is said that the complete collection of al-Wakidi's works remained in the possession of four persons, the first of whom was his secretary, Muhammad ibn Saad. This distinguished writer displayed great acquirements in the sciences, the traditions, and traditional literature; most of his books treat of the traditions and law. The Khatîb Abû Bakr, author of the history of Baghdad, speaks of him in these terms: 'We consider Muhammad ibn Saad as a *man of unimpeached integrity, and the Traditions which he delivered are a proof of his veracity*, for in the greater part of the information handed down by him, we find him discussing it, passage by passage.' He was a *mawla* (slave) to al-Husain Ibn Abd Allah Ibn Obaid Allah Ibn al-Abbâs Ibn Abd al-Muttalib. He died at Baghdad on Sunday the 4th of the latter Jumâda, A.H. 203 (December, A.D. 818), at the age of sixty-two years, and was interred in the cemetery outside the Damascus gate (Bâb as-Shâm.)"—(Ibn Khallikān, *Biog. Dict., in loco.*)

AL-KAUSAR (الكوثر). *Lit.* "Abundance." A pond in Muḥammad's paradise known as the *Ḥauẓu 'l-Kauṣar*, or "The Pond of Abundance."

The word occurs once in the Qur'ān, Sūrah cviii. 1–3:—

"Truly we have given thee an *abundance* (*i.e. al-Kauṣar*);

"Pray therefore to the Lord, and slay the victims.

"Verily whoso hateth thee shall be childless."

But it is not clear whether the pond is intended in this verse. Al-Baiẓāwī thinks it refers to abundance of blessings and not to the pond.

Anas relates that the Prophet said the prophet saw the pond al-Kauṣar in the night of his Mi'rāj or heavenly journey [MI'RAJ] and that it "was a river of water on each side of which there were domes, each formed of a hollow pearl."

'Abdu 'llāh ibn 'Amr relates that the Prophet said "the circumference of *al-Kauṣar* is a month's journey, and it is a square, its water whiter than milk, its smell sweeter than musk, and its cups for drinking sparkle like the stars of heaven. He who drinks of its waters shall never thirst." (*Mishkāt*, book xxiii. ch. xii.)

KHABAR-I-WĀḤID (خبر واحد). A term used in the Traditions for a tradition related by one person and handed down by one chain of narrators. [TRADITION.]

KHABAR MUTAWĀTIR (خبر متواتر). A term used for a tradition which is handed down by very many distinct chains of narrators, and which has been always accepted as authentic and genuine, no doubt ever having been raised against it.

Syud Ahmad Khan says all learned Muslims of every period have declared the Qur'ān is the only Ḥadīṣ Mutawātir, but some have declared certain Aḥādīṣ also to be Mutawātir, the number of such not exceeding five. (*Essay on the Traditions*, p. 15.) [TRADITIONS.]

KHABĪṢ (خبيث). "Impure; base; wicked."

Qur'ān viii. 38: "That God may distinguish the *vile* from the good, and may put the vile one on the top of the other, and heap all up together, and put them into hell."

KHADĪJAH (خديجة). Known as *Khadījatu 'l-Kubrā*, "Khadījah the Great." The first wife of Muḥammad, and the first convert to a belief in his mission.

She was a Quraish lady of good fortune, the daughter of Khuwailid, who was the great grandson of Quṣaiy. Before she married Muḥammad, she was a widow who had been twice married, and had borne two sons and a daughter. Upon her marriage with Muḥammad, she had attained her fortieth year, whilst he was only twenty-five years of age. She continued to be his only wife until the day of her death. She died December, A.D. 619, aged 65; having been his counsellor and support for five-and-twenty years. She had borne Muḥammad two sons and four daughters: al-Qāṣim, and 'Abdu 'llāh, also called aṭ-Ṭaiyib and aṭ-Ṭāhir, Zainab, Ruqaiyah, Fāṭimah, and Umm Kulṣūm. Of those, only Fāṭimah survived the Prophet, and from her and her husband 'Alī are descended that posterity of Saiyids who are the subjects of such frequent petitions in the khuṭbahs and the liturgical prayers in all parts of the Muḥammadan world.

Muḥammad ever retained his affection for Khadījah. 'Āyishah said: "I was never so jealous of any one of the Prophet's wives as I was of Khadījah, although I never saw her. The Prophet was always talking of her, and he would very often slay goats and cut them up, and send pieces of them as presents to Khadījah's female friends. I often said to him, 'One might suppose there had not been such another woman as Khadījah in the world!' And the Prophet would then praise her and say she was so and so, and I had children by her." (*Mishkāt*, book xxix. ch. xxii.)

According to a traditional saying of Muḥammad, Khadijah, Fāṭimah, the Virgin Mary, and Āsiyah the wife of Pharaoh, were the four perfect women. (*Mishkāt*, book xxiv. ch. xxix. pt. 2.) [MUHAMMAD.]

KHAFĪ (خفى). "Hidden." A term used in works on exegesis for that which is hidden in its meaning, as compared with that which is obvious. [QURAN.]

KHAIBAR (خيبر). A rich and populous valley, eight stages from al-Madīnah, inhabited by Jews. It is celebrated in the history of Islām as the scene of one of Muḥammad's expeditions, A.H. 7, when the chief Kinānah was slain and the whole valley conquered. (See Muir's *Life of Mahomet*, new ed., p. 388, *seqq.*)

Here the Prophet instituted mut'ah, or temporary marriage. [MUT'AH.] Here were the special orders regarding clean and unclean animals promulgated. Here Muḥammad married Ṣafīyah, the widow of the chief of Khaibar. Here Zainab, the sister of the warrior Marhab, who had lost her husband, her father, and her brother in battle, tried to poison the Prophet with a poisoned kid. The campaign of Khaibar, therefore, marks an epoch in the Prophet's history. [MUHAMMAD.]

KHAIRĀT (خيرات). The plural of *Khair*. "Charity; good deeds." The word occurs in the Qur'ān in its singular form (*khair*), but in modern theological works it is more frequently used in its plural form.

KHAIRU 'L-QURŪN (خير القرون). The best generations. A term used for the first three generations of Muslims from the time of the Prophet. Muḥammad is related to have said there would be three virtuous generations, the one in which he lived and the two following it.

KHALFĪYAH (خلفية). A sect of Muslims founded by Khalfu 'l-Khāriji, who maintained, contrary to the general belief, that the children of idolaters will be eternally damned.

KHĀLID (خالد). Son of al-Walīd. The famous Muḥammadan general. He fought against Muḥammad at Uḥud and defeated the Muslim army. The Prophet married Maimūnah, who was an aunt to Khālid, a lady fifty-one years of age, and soon afterwards Khālid himself embraced Islām and became one of its most powerful champions. He led the Bedouin converts in the advance on Makkah, and was present as one of the chief leaders of the Muslim army at the battle of Ḥunain, and subsequent expeditions. In the reign of Abū Bakr, he murdered Malik Ibn Nuwairah, an eminent Arab chief, and married his widow. The murder greatly displeased the Khalīfah Abū Bākr, and he would have ordered Khālid to be put to death, but 'Umar interceded for him. He afterwards took the lead in various expeditions. He invaded al-'Irāq and Syria, took Bustrah, defeated the Christians at Ajnadin, commanded the Muslim army at Yarmūk, and subdued the country as far as the Euphrates. After the taking of Damascus, he was recalled by 'Umar, and sent to Ḥimṣ and Ba'labakk. He died at Ḥimṣ A.H. 18, A.D. 639.

KHĀLIDŪN (خالدون), pl. of *khālid*, "Everlasting." A term used to express the everlasting character of the joys of heaven and the torments of hell. It is used fifty times in the Qur'ān in this sense. [ETERNAL PUNISHMENT.]

KHALĪFAH (خليفة), pl. *Khulafā'*, from *khalf*, "to leave behind." *Anglice*, "Caliph." A successor; a lieutenant; a vicegerent, or deputy. The word is used in the Qur'ān for Adam, as the vicegerent of the Almighty on earth.

Sūrah ii. 28: "And when thy Lord said to the angels, 'I am about to place a vicegerent (*khalīfah*) on the earth,' they said, 'Wilt Thou place therein one who will do evil therein and shed blood?'"

And also for David:—

Sūrah xxxviii. 25: "O David! verily We have made thee a vicegerent (*khalīfah*); judge then between men with truth."

In Muḥammadanism it is the title given to the successor of Muḥammad, who is vested with absolute authority in all matters of state, both civil and religious, as long as he rules in conformity with the law of the Qur'ān and Ḥadīṣ. The word more frequently used for the office in Muhammadan works of jurisprudence, is *Imām* (leader), or *al-Imāmu 'l-A'ẓam* (the great leader). It is held to be an essential principle in the establishment of the office, that there shall be only one Khalīfah at the same time; for the Prophet said: "When two Khalīfahs have been set up, put the last to death and preserve the other, for the last is a rebel." (*Mishkāt*, book xvi. ch. i.)

According to all Sunnī Muḥammadan books, it is absolutely necessary that the Khalīfah be "a man, an adult, a sane person, a free man, a learned divine, a powerful ruler, a just person, and one of the *Quraish* (*i.e.* of the tribe to which the Prophet himself belonged).

The Shī'ahs hold that he should be one of the descendants of the Prophet's own family;

but this is rejected by the Sunnīs and Wahhābīs.

The condition that the Khalīfah should be of the Quraish is very important, for thereby the present Ottoman Sultāns fail to establish their claims to the Khalīfate (Arabic *Khilāfah*). The four immediate successors of Muḥammad are entitled the *Khulafā'u 'r-Rāshidūn*, or "the well-directed Khalīfahs." According to the *Baghyatu 'r-Raid*, only the first five Khalīfahs, Abū Bakr, 'Umar, 'Usmān, 'Alī, and al-Ḥasan, are entitled to the distinction of Khalīfah, the others being merely *Amīrs*, or Governors. After the deaths of the first five Khalīfahs, the Khalīfate, which is allowed by all parties to be elective and not hereditary, passed successively to the Umayades (*Banū Umayah*). The first Khalīfah of this dynasty was Mu'āwiyah, the grandson of Umaiyah of the Quraish tribe, who received the Khalīfate from al-Ḥasan. Of the Umayades, there were fourteen Khalīfahs who reigned at Damascus, extending over a period from A.H. 41 to A.H. 132 (A.D. 661 to A.D. 750). The title then passed to Abū 'l-'Abbās, the fourth in descent from al-'Abbās, the uncle of Muḥammad, and the Abbaside Khalīfahs, thirty-seven in number, who reigned at Baghdād from A.H. 132 to A.H. 656 (A.D. 750 to A.D. 1258).

The temporal power of the Abbaside Khalīfahs was overthrown by Halāk Khān, grandson of the celebrated Chenjiz Kkan, A.D. 1258; but for three centuries, certain descendants of the Abbaside, or Baghdād Khalīfahs, resided in Egypt, and asserted their claim to the spiritual power. The founder of the present dynasty of Turkish Sultans was 'Usman (Othmān), a chieftain descended from the Orghuz Turks (born at Sakut, A.D. 1259), who was at first the ruler of a small territory in Bithynia, but who in 1299 invaded the whole country of Makkah, and subsequently extended his conquests to the Black Sea, and whose successor, Salīm (ninth in descent), obtained the title of Khalīfah from one of the Abbaside Khalīfahs in Egypt. About the year A.D. 1515 (A.H. 921), Salīm I., ruler of the Ottoman Turks and Emperor of Constantinople, finding himself the most powerful prince of his day in Islām, and wishing still further to consolidate his rule, conceived the idea of reviving in his own person the extinct glories of the Khalīfate. He had more than one claim to be considered their champion by orthodox Muḥammadans, for he was the grandson of that Muḥammad II. who had finally extinguished the Roman Empire of the East; and he had himself just ended a successful campaign against the heretical Shah of Persia. His only rivals among Sunnī princes were the Muslim Emperors in India, the Emperor of Morocco, and the Mameluke ruler of Egypt, then known to the world as *par excellence*, "the Sultan." With the two former, as rulers of what were remote lands of Islām, Salim seems to have troubled himself little, but he made war on Egypt. In A.D. 1516 he invaded Syria, its outlying province, and in A.D. 1517 he entered Cairo. There he made prisoner the reigning Mameluke, Qansau 'l-Ghaurī, and had him publicly beheaded.

He then, in virtue of a very doubtful cession made to him of his rights by one Mutawakkil Ibn 'Amri 'l-Ḥākim, a descendant of the house of al-'Abbās, whom he found living as titular Khalīfah in Cairo, took to himself the following style and title: *Sulṭānu 's-Salāṭīn wa Ḥākimu 'l-Ḥākimīn, Maliku 'l-Baḥrain wa Ḥāmīyu 'l-Barrain, Khalīfatu 'r-Rasūli 'llāh, Amīru 'l-Mu'minīn, wa Sulṭān, wa Khān*; that is: "King of kings and Ruler of rulers, Monarch of the two seas (the Mediterranean and the Red Sea) and Protector of the two lands (al-Ḥijāz and Syria, the holy lands of Islām), Successor (Khalīfah) of the Apostle of God, Ruler of the Faithful, King and Chief." It is said that he first had the satisfaction of hearing his name mentioned in the public prayers as Khalīfah when he visited the Great Mosque of Zacharias at Aleppo, on his return northwards in 1519.

Such are the titles still claimed by the Ottoman Sulṭāns, who arrogate to themselves the position of Khalīfahs and Successors to the Prophet. It is, however, a mere assertion; for the title and office being elective and not hereditary, it was not in the power of any Khalīfah to transfer it to another. Force of circumstances alone has compelled the ruler of the Ottoman Empire to assume the position, and has induced his subjects to acquiesce in the usurpation. We have not seen a single work of authority, nor met with a single man of learning, attempting to prove that the Sulṭāns of Turkey are rightful Khalīfahs; for the assumption of the title by anyone who is not of the Quraish tribe is undoubtedly illegal and heretical, as will be seen from the following authorities:—

Mishkātu 'l-Maṣābīḥ, book xxiv. ch. xii.: "Ibn 'Amr relates that the Prophet of God said: 'The Khalīfah shall be in the Quraish tribe as long as there are two persons in it, one to rule and another to serve.'"

Sharḥu 'l-Muwāqif, p. 606, Arabic edition, Egypt: "It is a condition that the Khalīfah (Imām) be of the Quraish tribe. All admit this except the Khawārij and certain Mu'tazilahs. We all say with the Prophet: 'Let the Khalīfah be of the Quraish'; and it is certain that the Companions acted upon this injunction, for Abū Bakr urged it as an authority upon the Anṣārs, on the day of Sakhifah, when the Companions were present and agreed. It is, therefore, for a certainty established that the Khalīfah must be of the Quraish."

The Ḥujjatu 'llāhi 'l-Balāghah, p. 335, Arabic edition, Delhi: "It is a necessary condition that the Khalīfah (Imām) be of the Quraish tribe."

The Kash'hāfu 'l-Iṣṭilāḥāt; A Dictionary of Technical Terms. Edited by Colonel N. Lees, *in loco*: "The Khalīfah (Imām) must be a Quraish."

It is a matter of history that the Wahhābīs regarded the Turkish Sulṭān as a usurper, when Sa'ūd took Makkah and al-Madīnah in 1804; and to the present day, in countries not under Turkish rule, the khuṭbah is recited in behalf of the Amīr, or ruler of the Muslim state, iustead of the Ottoman Sulṭān, which would not be the case if he were acknowledged as a lawful Khalīfah. In a collection of khuṭbahs, entitled the *Majma'u Khuṭab*, the name of the Sulṭān of Turkey does not once occur, although this collection is much used in Muḥammadan states. We have seen it stated that the Sulṭān is prayed for in Hyderabad and Bengal; but we believe it will be found, upon careful inquiry, that he was not mentioned by name, until very recently, in any of the mosques of India. khuṭbahs, in which there are prayers for the Ottoman Sulṭān by name, have been imported from Constantinople.

According to Mr. W. S. Blunt, the chief arguments of the Hanifite 'Ulamā' in support of the claims of the present Ottoman dynasty are:—

(1) *The right of the Sword.*—The Khalīfate being a necessity (and this all Muslims admit), it was also a necessity that the *de facto* holder of the title should be recognised until a claimant with a better title should appear. Now, the first qualification of a claimant was, that he should make the claim, and the second, that he should be supported by a party; and Salīm had both claimed the Khalīfate and supported his pretensions at the head of an army. He challenged the world to produce a rival, and no rival had been found.

(2) *Election*, that is, the sanction of a legal body of elders. It was argued that, as the *ahlu 'aqd* (or council), had been removed from al-Madīnah to Damascus, and from Damascus to Baghdād, and from Baghdād to Cairo, so it had been once more legally removed from Cairo to Constantinople. Salīm had brought with him to St. Sophia's some of the 'Ulamā' (learned men) of the Azhar mosque in Cairo, and these in conjunction with the Turkish 'Ulamā had elected him or ratified his election. A form of election is to the present day observed at Constantinople in token of this right, and each new Sulṭān of the house of 'Usmān, as he succeeds to the temporal sovereignty of Turkey, must wait before being recognised as Khalīfah till he has received the sword of office at the hands of the 'Ulamā'. This ceremony it is customary to perform in the mosque of Aiyūb.

(3) *Nomination.*—Sulṭān Salīm, as has been already said, obtained from Mutawakkil, a descendant of the Abbasides, and himself titularly Khalīfah, a full cession of all the Khalīfah rights of that family. The fact, as far as it goes, is historical, and the only flaw in the argument would seem to be that Mutawakkil had no right thus to dispose of a title to an alien, which was his own only in virtue of his birth. As a precedent for nomination, they cite the act of Abū Bakr, who on his death-bed recommended 'Umar as his successor in the Khalīfate.

(4) *The Guardianship of the Two Shrines* (*Ḥaraman*), that is to say, of Makkah and Jerusalem, but especially of Makkah. It has been asserted by some of the 'Ulamā', and it is certainly a common opinion at the present day, that the sovereignty of al-Ḥijāz is in itself sufficient title to the Khalīfate. It seems certainly to have been so considered in the first age of Islām, and many a bloody war was then fought for the right of protecting the *Baitu 'llāh*, but the connection of al-Ḥijāz with the empire of the Khalīfahs has been too often broken to make this a very tenable argument. In the tenth century, Makkah was held by the Karmathian heretics, in the thirteenth by the Imāms of Ṣan'ā', and for seven years in the present century by the Wahhābīs. Still the *de facto* sovereignty of the Ḥaramain, or two shrines, was one of Salīm's pleas; and it is one which has reappeared in modern arguments respecting the Khalīfal rights of his descendants.

(5) *Possession of the Amānāt*, or sacred relics. This last is a plea addressed to the vulgar rather than to the learned; but it is one which cannot be passed by unnoticed here, for it exercises a powerful influence at the present day over the ignorant mass of Muslims. It was asserted, and is still a pious belief, that from the sack of Baghdād in A.D. 1258, certain relicts of the Prophet and his Companions were saved and brought to Cairo, and thence transferred by Salīm to Constantinople. These were represented as constituting the imperial insignia of office, and their possession as giving a title to the succession. They consisted of the cloak of the Prophet, borne by his soldiers as a standard, of some hairs of the Prophet's beard, and of the sword of 'Umar. The vulgar still believe them to be preserved in the mosque of Aiyūb at Constantinople. (See *The Future of Islām*, by Wilfrid Scawen Blunt, London, 1882, p. 66.)

On the general question as to whether or not an Imām, or Khalīfah, is necessary for Islām, the author of the *Sharḥu 'l-Muwāqif* says, "The appointment of an Imām (*i.e.* Khalīfah) is incumbent upon the united body of Muslims, according to the orthodox law of the Sunnīs, although the Mu'tazilahs and Zaidīyahs say it is merely expedient, but not ordered by the law, whilst the Ishmailīyahs and the Imāmīyahs say God will Himself appoint an Imām for the establishment of sound doctrine. Some say the appointment of an Imām is only necessary when Muslims are at peace amongst themselves and united, and not when they are in a state of rebellion.

The arguments in favour of the absolute necessity of an Imām, or Khalīfah, being appointed, are that in the time of Abū Bakr, the first Khalīfah, it was established by general consent; and Abū Bakr, in his first khuṭbah after the death of Muḥammad, said: "Beware! Muḥammad is certainly dead, and it is necessary for this religion that some one should be appointed for its protection." And all the Muslims at that time consented to this saying of Abū Bakr, and consequently in all ages Muslims have had an Imām. And it is well known that without such an officer Islām cannot be protected from evil, for without him it is impossible to maintain the orders of the Muslim law, such as marriage, Jihād, punishment, and the various ordinances of Islām. (*Sharḥu 'l-Muwāqif*, p. 603.)

The following are some of the injunctions of Muḥammad regarding the Imām or Khalīfah:—

"When two Khalīfahs have been set up, put the last of them to death and preserve the other, for the second is a rebel."

"He who acknowledges an Imām must obey him as far as he can, and if a pretender comes, kill him."

"Whomever God appoints as Imām, and he does not protect his people, shall never smell the smells of paradise."

"It is indispensable for every Muslim to listen to, and approve the orders of the Imām, whether he likes or dislikes, so long as he is not ordered to sin and act contrary to law; then when he is ordered to sin, he must neither attend to it nor obey it."

"Whoever quits obedience to the Imām and divides a body of Muslims, dies like the people in ignorance; and whoever takes a part in an affray, without knowing the true from the false, does not fight to show his religion, but to aid oppression; and if he is slain, then he dies as the people of ignorance; and that person who shall draw his sword upon my people, and kill the virtuous and the vicious, and not fear the killing of Muslims or those protected by them, is not of me nor am I of him."

"The Companions said, 'O Prophet! when they are our enemies and we theirs, may we not fight with them?' He said, 'No, so long as they keep on foot the prayers amongst you'; this he repeated, 'Beware! he who shall be constituted your prince, see if he does anything in disobedience to God; and if he does, hold it in displeasure, but do not withdraw yourselves from his obedience."

"He who forsakes obedience to the Imām, will come before God on the Day of Resurrection without a proof of his faith; and he who dies without having professed to the Imām, dies as the people of ignorance."

"Prophets were the governors of the children of Israel; when one died, another supplied his place; and verily there is no prophet after me, and the time is near when there will be after me a great many Khalīfahs. The Companions said, 'Then what do you order us?' The Prophet said, 'Obey the Khalīfah, and give him his due; for verily God will ask about the duty of the subject.'"

"Beware! you are all guardians, and you will all be asked about your subjects; then the Imām is the guardian of the subject, and he will be asked respecting the subject; and a man is as a shepherd to his own family, and will be asked how they behaved, and his conduct to them; and a wife is a guardian to her husband's house and children, and will be interrogated about them; and a slave is a shepherd to his master's property, and will be asked about it whether he took good care of it or not."

"God never sent any prophet, nor ever made any Khalīfah, but had two counsellors with him; one of them directing lawful deeds, and that is an angel, and the other, in sin, and that is the devil; and he is guarded from sin whom God has guarded." (*Mishkāt*, book xvi. ch. i.)

I.—*The Khalīfahs of the Sunnīs*, from the death of Muḥammad to the present time.

(1) The four rightly directed Khalifahs, and al-Ḥasan (at Makkah):—

1. Abū Bakr, A.H. 11 (A.D. 632).
(Collected the Qur'ān into one volume.)
2. 'Umar, A.H. 13 (A.D. 634).
(Conquered Egypt, Syria, and Persia.)
3. 'Us̤man, A.H. 23 (A.D. 643).
(Invades Cyprus; revolt at al-Kūfah.)
4. 'Alī, A.H. 35 (A.D. 655).
(Revolt of Mu'āwiyah; 'Alī assassinated.)
5. Al-Ḥasan, A.H. 40 (A.D. 660).
(Resigns; poisoned.)

(2) Umaiyade dynasty. The Banū Umaiyah (at Damascus):—

1. Mu'āwiyah I., A.H. 41 (A.D. 661).
(Siege of Constantinople; makes Damascus the capital.)
2. Yazīd I., A.H. 60 (A.D. 679).
(Destruction of al-Ḥusain's party and his death.)
3. Mu'āwiyah II., A.H. 64. (A.D. 683).
(Deposed.)
4. Marwān I., A.H. 64 (A.D. 683).
(Poisoned.)
5. 'Abdu 'l-Malik, A.H. 65 (A.D. 684).
(Arabian money first coined.)
6. Al-Walīd I., A.H. 86 (A.D. 705).
(Conquest of Africa, Spain, Bukhārah.)
7. Sulaimān, A.H. 96 (A.D. 715).
(Defeated before Constantinople; dies of grief.)
8. 'Umar (Omer), A.H. 99 (A.D. 717).
(Poisoned.)
9. Yazīd II., A.H. 101 (A.D. 720).
(His generals successful in war.)
10. Hishām, A.H. 105 (A.D. 724).
(Charles Martel checks the conquest of the Arabs in the West; rise of the Abbasides.)
11. Al-Walīd II., A.H. 125 (A.D. 743).
(Slain by conspirators.)
12. Yazīd III., A.H. 126 (A.D. 744).
(Died of the plague.)
13. Ibrahīm, A.H. 126 (A.D. 744).
(Deposed.)
14. Marwān, A.H. 127 (A.D. 744).
(Defeated by the Abbasides, pursued to Egypt, and slain on the banks of the Nile.)

The end of the Umayah dynasty, A.H. 132 (A.D. 749).

(3) The Abbāside dynasty. Ad-Daulatu 'l-'Abbāsīyah (at Baghdād and Saumara).

1. Abū 'l-'Abbās as-Saffāḥ, A.H. 132 (A.D. 750).
(Resides at al-Kūfah.)
2. Al-Manṣūr, A.H. 136 (A.D. 754).
(Abdu 'r-Raḥmān, the Umaiyah Khalīfah seizes Spain; Baghdād founded).

3. Al-Mahdī, A.H. 158 (A.D. 775).
(Conquers Nicomedia on Sea of Marmora, making the Empress Irene pay tribute.)
4. Al-Hādī, A.H. 169 (A.D. 785).
5. Harūnu 'r-Rashīd, A.H. 170 (A.H. 786).
(The hero of Arabian Nights; a flourishing period of Arabian literature.)
6. Al-Amīn, A.H. 193 (A.D. 809).
7. Al-Ma'mūn, A.H. 198 (A.D. 813).
(The Augustan period of Arabian letters.)
8. Al-Mu'taṣim, A.H. 218 (A.D. 833).
(Makes the city of Saumara his capital; decline of the Khalifate.)
9. Al-Wāṣiq, A.H. 227 (A.D. 841).
10. Al-Mutawakkil, A.H. 232 (A.D. 847).
(A persecutor of the Jews and Christians; murdered.)
11. Al-Muntaṣir, A H. 247 (A.D. 861).
12. Al-Musta'īn, A.H. 248 (A.D. 862).
13. Al-Mu'tazz, A.H. 252 (A.D. 866).
14. Al-Muhtadī, A.A. 255 (A.D. 869).
15. Al-Mu'tamid, A.H. 256 (A.D. 870).
(Re-establishes the capital at Baghdād.)
16. Mu'taẓid, A.H. 279 (A.D. 892).
(Conquers Persia; Ismail Samain seizes Turkistan from the Khalīfah.)
17. Al-Muktafī I., A.H. 289 (A.D. 902).
(Ismail Samain seizes Persia from the Khalīfah.)
18. Al-Muqtadir, A.H. 295 (A.D. 908).
(The Fāṭimites in Egypt.)
19. Al-Qāhir, A.H. 320 (A.D. 932).
(Blinded and deposed.)
20. Ar-Rāẓi, A.H. 322 (A.D. 934).
(The last of the Khalīfahs who ever recited the khuṭbah.)
21. Al-Mūttaqī, A.H. 329 (A.D. 940).
(Decline of the Abbasides.)
22. Al-Mustakfī, A.H. 333 (A.D. 944).
23. Al-Muṭī', A.H. 334 (A.D. 945).
(The Faṭimate Khalīfahs seize all North Africa and Egypt.)
24. Aṭ-Ṭāi', A.H. 363 (A.D. 974).
(Deposed.)
25. Al-Qādir, A.H. 381 (A.D. 991).
(Mahmūd of Ghazni conquers India.)
26. Al-Qā'im, A.H. 422 (A.D. 1031).
(Rise of the Seljukian Turks.)
27. Al-Muqtadī, A.H. 467 (A.D. 1075).
(The first crusade; rise of Ḥasan Jubah, and his followers the Assassins.)
28. Al-Musta'ẓir, A.H. 487 (A.D. 1094).
(Jerusalem taken by the Fāṭimites.)
29. Al-Mustarshid, A.H. 512 (A.D. 1118).
(Murdered by the Assassins.)
30. Ar-Rāshid, A.H. 529 (A.D. 1135).
(Murdered by the Assassins.)
31. Al-Muktafī II., A.H. 530 (A.D. 1136).
(Defeated by the Turks; second crusade, A.D. 1146.)
32. Al-Mustanjid, A.H. 555 (A.D. 1160).
(Disorders in Persia.)
33. Al-Mustahdī, A.H. 566 (A.D. 1170).
(Saladin, the Sulṭān of Egypt, conquers Syria.)
34. An-Nāṣir, A.H. 575 (A.D. 1180).
(Conquests of Jengiz Khān; third crusade, A.D. 1189.)
35. Aẓ-Ẓāhir, A.H. 622 (A.D. 1225).
36. Al-Mustanṣir, A.H. 623 (A.D. 1226).
(Persia subject to the Moghuls.)
37. Al-Musta'ṣim, A.H. 640 (A.D. 1240).
(Halaku, the Turk, a grandson of Jengiz Khān, takes Baghdād and puts the Khalīfah to death, A.H. 656 (A.D. 1258). The uncle of the last Khalīfah goes to Egypt, while the Khalīfate continues only as a spiritual power.

(4) The 'Uṣmān, or Turk Dynasty (at Constantinople).

1. 'Uṣmān I. (Othmān), A.D. 1299.
2. Ūrkhān, A.D. 1326.
3. Murād (Amurath), A.D. 1360.
4. Bayāzīd I., A.D. 1389.
5. Sulaimān I., A.D. 1402.
6. Mūsa, A.D. 1410.
7. Muḥammad I., A.D. 1413.
8. Murād II., A.D. 1421.
9. Muḥammad II., A.D. 1451.
10. Bayāzīd II., A.D. 1481.
11. Salīm I. (Selim), A.D. 1512.
(Assumes the title of Khalīfah.)
12. Sulaimān II., A.D. 1520.
13. Salīm II., A.D. 1566.
14. Murād III., A.D. 1574.
15. Muḥammad III., A.D. 1595.
16. Aḥmad I., A.D. 1603.
17. Muṣṭafa I., A.D. 1617.
(Deposed in favour of his nephew.)
18. 'Uṣman II., A.D. 1618.
19. Muṣṭafa I., A.D. 1622.
(Restored and again deposed.)
20. Murād IV., A.D. 1623.
21. Ibrahīm, A.D. 1640.
22. Muḥammad IV., A.D. 1649.
23. Sulaimān III., A.D. 1687.
24. Aḥmad II., A.D. 1691.
25. Muṣṭafa II., A.D. 1695.
26. Aḥmad III., A.D. 1703.
27. Maḥmūd I., A.D. 1730.
28. 'Uṣmān III., A D. 1754.
29. Muṣṭafa III., A.D. 1757.
30. 'Abdu 'l-Ḥamīd I., 1774.
31. Salīm III., A.D 1788.
32. Muṣṭafa IV., A.D. 1807.
33. Maḥmūd II., 1808.
34. 'Abdu 'l-Majīd, A.D. 1839.
35. 'Abdu 'l-'Azīz, A.D. 1861.
36. Murād V., A.D. 1876.
37. 'Abdu 'l-Ḥamīd, A.D. 1876.

II.—*The Shī'ahs* only regard those as rightful *Imāms* (they do not use the word *Khalīfah*) who are descended from 'Alī (the son-in-law of the Prophet) and his wife Fāṭimah, the Prophet's daughter. According to their traditions, Muḥammad distinctly nominated 'Alī as his successor when he was returning from his farewell pilgrimage. They say, that on his way to al-Madīnah, the Prophet, with 'Alī and certain other of the Companions stayed at a place called Ghadīri-i-Khūm. And that it was here revealed by Gabriel that he should nominate 'Alī as his successor. He is related to have said, "O ye people, I am your Prophet and 'Alī is my successor. From us (*i.e.* 'Alī and my daughter) shall descend al-Mahdī, the seal of the Imāms." (See *Ḥayātu 'l-Qulūb*, p. 334.)

According to the Shī'ahs, there have only been twelve lawful Imāms:—

1. 'Alī, son-in-law of Muḥammad.
2. Al-Ḥasan, eldest son of 'Alī and Fāṭimah.
3. Al-Ḥusain, the second son of 'Alī and Fāṭimah.
4. Zainu 'l-'Ābidīn, son of al-Ḥusain.
5. Muḥammad al-Bāqir, son of Zainu 'l-'Ābidīn.
6. Ja'faru 'ṣ-Ṣādiq, son of Muḥammad al-Bāqir.
7. Musā 'l-Kāẓim, son of Ja'far.
8. 'Alī ar-Raẓā, son of Mūsā.
9. Muḥammad at-Taqī, son of 'Ali ar-Raẓā.
10. 'Alī an-Naqi, son of at-Taqī.
11. Al-Ḥasan al-'Askarī, son of 'Alī.
12. Muḥammad, son of al- Askarī, or the Imām Mahdī, who is supposed to be still alive, although he has withdrawn himself from the world, and that he will appear again as *al-Mahdī*, the Director, in the last days. [AL-MAHDI.]

The Kings of Persia have never claimed to be in any sense the successors of the Prophet.

Sulṭān Maḥmūd 'Abdu 'llah (A.H. 706, A.D. 1306), was the first monarch of Persia who proclaimed himself a Shī'ah.

III.—*The Fāṭimide Khalīfahs* were a dynasty who claimed the Khalīfate in the reign of the Abbaside Khalīfah Muqtadir, their founder, 'Ubaidu 'llāh, pretending to be al-Mahdī, "The Director," and a descendant of Fāṭimah, the daughter of the Prophet. They reigned over Egypt and North Africa from A.D. 910 to A.D. 1171, and were in all fourteen Khalīfahs.

1. 'Ubaidu 'llāh, A.D. 910.
   (Ravaged the coasts of Italy and invaded Egypt several times.)
2. Al-Qā'im, A.D. 933.
3. Al-Manṣūr, A.D. 946.
4. Al-Mu'izz, A.D. 955.
   (Established the Khalīfate of the Fāṭimides in Egypt; defeated in Spain; took Sicily; founded Cairo; conquered Syria and Palestine.)
5. Al-'Azīz, A.D. 978.
   (Married a Christian woman, whose brothers he made Patriarchs of Alexandria and Jerusalem.)
6. Al-Ḥākim, A.D. 996.
   (Persecuted Jews and Christians.)
7. Aẓ-Ẓāhir, A.D. 1021.
   (The power of the Fāṭimides declines.)
8. Al-Mustanṣir, A.D. 1037.
   (The rise of the Turks.)
9. Al-Musta'lī, A.D. 1094.
   (Defeated by the Crusaders.)
10. Al-Amīr, A.D. 1101.
11. Al-Ḥāfiẓ, A.D. 1129.
12. Aẓ-Ẓafīr, A.D. 1149.
13. Al-Fā'iz, A.D. 1154.
14. Al-Āẓid, A.D. 1160.
    (The last of the Fāṭimide Khalīfahs. His Wazīr, Nūru 'd-dīn, on the death of his master, submits to the Abbaside Khalīfah Mustahdī, A.D. 1171.)

[FATIMIYAH.]

IV.—*The Khalīfate of Cordova* in Spain was founded by a descendant of the deposed Umaiyah dynasty, 'Abdu 'r-Raḥmān ibn Mu'āwiyah. Muslim Amīrs had ruled at Cordova from A.D. 711, when Ṭārik and Mūsā came over from Africa and invaded Spain. But 'Abdu 'r-Raḥmān was the first to assume the title of Khalīfah.

The following is a list of the Khalīfahs of Cordova and Granada from A.D. 755 to the fall of Granada, A.D. 1492:—

1. 'Abdu 'r-Raḥmān I., A.D. 755.
   (Cordova embellished and the Mazquita erected.)
2. Hishām I., A.D. 786.
3. 'Abdu 'r-Raḥmān II., A.D. 786.
4. Al-Ḥakam I., A.D. 796.
   (Surnamed "The Cruel.")
5. 'Abdu 'r-Raḥmān III., A.D. 821.
   (Christians persecuted.)
6. Muḥammad I., A.D. 852.
   (Alfonso the Great obtains victories.)
7. Al-Munayyir, A.D. 886.
8. 'Abdu 'llāh, A.D. 888.
   (Flourishing period of literature and science at Cordova.)
9. 'Abdu 'r-Raḥmān IV., A.D. 912.
   (The heroic age of Spain.)
10. Al-Ḥakam II., A.D. 961.
11. Hishām II., A.D. 976.
12. Sulaimān, A.D. 1012.
    (Defeated and executed by 'Alī.)
13. 'Alī, A.D. 1015.
14. 'Abdu 'r-Raḥmān V., A.D. 1017.
15. Al-Qāsim, A.D. 1018.
16. 'Abdu 'r-Raḥmān VI., A.D. 1023.
17. Muḥammad II., A.D. 1023.
18. Hishām III., A.D. 1026.
    (Esteemed for his equitable and humane government.)
19. Jawāhir, A.D. 1031.
20. Muḥammad III., A.D. 1044.
21. Muḥammad IV., A.D. 1060.
22. Muḥammad V., A.D. 1069.
    (Siege of Toledo, A.D. 1082.)
23. Yūsuf I., A.D. 1094.
24. 'Alī, A.D. 1107.
25. Tāshifīn, A.D. 1144.
26. 'Abdu 'l-Mun'im, A.D. 1147.
27. Yūsuf II., A.D. 1163.
28. Ya'qūb I., A.D. 1178.
29. Muḥammad VI., A.D. 1199.
30. Ya'qūb II., A.D. 1213.
31. Abū Ya'qūb, A.D. 1213.
32. Abū Mālik, A.D. 1223.
33. Al-Ma'nūn, A.D. 1225.
    (Died in Morocco.)
34. Abū 'Alī, A.D. 1225.
    (Cordova surprised by Ferdinand of Leon and Castile, and taken. The fall of the Khalīfate of Cordova, A.D. 1236. A Khalīfate established by the Moors at Granada.)

The Khalīfahs or Sulṭāns of Granada.

35. Muḥammad I., A.D. 1238.
    (Encourages literature.)
36. Muḥammad II., A.D. 1273.
37. Muḥammad III., A.D. 1302.

38. An-Nāṣir, A.D. 1309.
39. Ismā'īl I., A.D. 1313.
40. Muḥammad IV., A.D. 1325.
41. Yūsuf I., A.D. 1333.
42. Muḥammad V., A.D. 1354.
43. Ismā'īl II., A.D. 1359.
44. Abū Sa'īd, A.D. 1360.
45. Yūsuf II., A.D. 1391.
46. Muḥammad VI., A.D. 1396.
47. Yūsuf III., A.D. 1408.
48. Muḥammad VII., A.D. 1423.
49. Muḥammad VIII., A.D. 1427.
50. Muḥammad VII. (restored), A.D. 1429.
51. Yūsuf IV., A.D. 1432.
52. Muḥammad VII. (again restored), A.D. 1432.
53. Muḥammad IX., A.D. 1445.
54. Muḥammad X., A.D. 1454.
55. 'Alī, A.D. 1463.
56. Abū 'Abdi 'llāh, A.D. 1483.
57. 'Abdu 'llāh az-Zaggâl, A.D. 1484.
    (The fall of Granada, and the consolidation of the Spanish Monarchy, A.D. 1492.)

Thus, amidst the acclammations of Christendom, Ferdinand and Isabella planted the symbol of Christian faith on the walls of Granada, and proclaimed the destruction of Muḥammadan rule in Spain.

KHALĪLU 'LLĀH (خليل الله). "The friend of God." A title given to Abraham in the Qur'ān, Sūrah iv. 124: "For God took Abraham as his friend."

With regard to this verse, al-Baiẓāwī says: "Abraham in a time of dearth sent to a friend of his in Egypt for a supply of corn: but the friend denied him, saying, in his excuse, that though there was a famine in their country also, yet, had it been for Abraham's own family, he would have sent what he desired, but he knew he wanted it only to entertain his guests, and give away to the poor, according to his usual hospitality. The servants whom Abraham had sent on this message, being ashamed to return empty, to conceal the matter from their neighbours, filled their sacks with fine white sand, which in the East pretty much resembles meal. Abraham being informed by his servants on their return of their ill success, the concern he was under threw him into a sleep, and in the meantime Sarah, knowing nothing of what had happened, opening one of the sacks, found good flour in it, and immediately set to making bread. Abraham awaking, and smelling the new bread, asked her whence she had the flour. 'Why,' says she, 'from your friend in Egypt.' 'Nay,' replied the patriarch, 'it must have come from no other than *my friend*, God Almighty.'" [ABRAHAM.]

KHAMR (خمر). The word used in the Qur'ān for wine or anything that intoxicates.

Sūrah ii. 216: "They will ask thee about wine (*khamr*), and games of chance: say in both is sin and profit to men, but the sin of both is greater than the profit of the same."

By the orthodox, the term *khamr* is generally held to include not only alcoholic drinks, but opium and other narcotics. Some understand it to include tobacco; hence the destruction of tobacco pipes in the streets of Makkah by the Wahhābīs. [WAHHABI.]

KHĀN (خان). Persian. "A ruler; a chief." A term used for the supreme ruler of small countries or provinces. The Khān of the Tartars. It is also one of the titles of the Sulṭān of Turkey. It is also used for a caravansary or inn, being a corruption of the Persian *khanah*, "a home."

AL-KHANNĀS (الخناس). A demon mentioned in the Qur'ān, Sūrah cxiv. (the last chapter):—

"SAY: I betake me for refuge to the Lord of men,
"The King of men,
"The God of men,
"Against the mischief of the stealthily withdrawing whisperer (*al-khannās*),
"Who whispereth in man's breast—
"Against genii and men."

KHANZAB (خنزب). A demon who casts doubt at the time of prayer. 'Uṣmān ibn Abī 'l-'Āṣī relates that he came to the Prophet and complained that he was disturbed by the devil during prayers. The Prophet said, "This is a demon called Khanzab who disturbs prayer. When you are aware of any such disturbance, seek protection of God and spit over your left shoulder three times." 'Uṣmān did so, and all doubt and perplexity was dispelled.

KHARĀBĀT (خرابات). "A wine-shop or tavern." A mystic term for the society of the Murshid, or inspired teacher. See *Dīwān-i-Ḥāfiz* (Bicknell's edition, p. 212):—

"Within the Magian's *house of wine* our Maker's light I see."
"Behold this marvel, what a light and where that sight I see."

KHARĀJ (خراج). A tax, or tribute on land. This was originally applied to a land tribute from non-Muslim tribes (*Hidāyah*, vol. ii. p. 204), but it is now used for a tax, or land-rent due to the State. *Lā-kharāj* is a term used for lands exempt from any such payment.

KHARQU 'L-'ĀDAH (خرق العادة). *Lit.* "The splitting of Nature." That which is contrary to the usual course of nature. A term use for miracles. Either (1) *Mu'jizah*, miracles worked by Prophets; or (2) *Karāmah*, wonders performed by walīs or saints; or (3) *Istidrāj*, wonders worked by the power of Satan. [MIRACLES.]

KHASHYAH (خشية). "Fear." *Khashyatu 'llāh*, "The fear of God," is an expression which occurs in the Qur'ān.

Sūrah ii. 69: "There are some that fall down for fear of God."

Sūrah iv. 79: "A portion of them fear men as with the fear of God, or with a yet greater fear."

KHAṢR (خصر). *Lit.* "The middle or waist." An act forbidden in prayer, as related by Abū Hurairah, who said: "The Prophet forbade *Khaṣr* in prayer." (*Mishkāt*, book iv. ch. xx.) It is generally held to be the act of holding the waist with the hands to relieve the sensation of fatigue experienced in the position of standing. Some divines believe it to be a prohibition to lean on a *mikhṣarah*, or staff, in prayer, whilst others give to it the sense of cutting short the verbal forms of prayer, or remaining too short a time in the prescribed attitude. (*Shaikh 'Abdu 'l-Ḥaqq.*)

KHĀṢṢ (خاص). "Special" as distinguished from *'Āmm*, "general." A term frequently used by Muḥammadan writers and in treatises on exegesis.

KHATIMU 'N-NABĪYĪN (خاتم النبيين). "The seal of the Prophets." A title assumed by Muḥammad in the Qur'ān. Sūrah xxxiii. 40: "He is the Apostle of God and the *seal of the Prophets*." By which is meant, that he is the last of the Prophets.

KHĀTIMU 'N-NABŪWAH (خاتم النبوة). "The seal of prophecy." A term used for the large mole or fleshy protuberance on Muḥammad's back, which is said to have been a divine sign of his prophetic office.

'Abdu 'llāh ibn Sarjis describes it as being as large as his closed fist, with moles round about it. Abū Ramṣah wanted to remove it, but Muḥammad refused saying, "The Physician thereof is He who placed it there."

KHĀṬIR (خاطر). "Mind; conscience." A term used by mystic teachers. *Khāṭir* is said to be of four kinds: *Al-Khāṭiru 'r-Rabbānī*, "conscience inspired of God"; *al-Khāṭiru 'l-Malakī*, "conscience inspired by angels"; *al-Khāṭiru 'n-Nafsānī*, "a conscience inspired by the flesh"; *al-Khāṭiru 'sh-Shaiṭānī*, "a conscience inspired by the devil." (*Kitābu 't-Ta'rīfāt, in loco.*)

KHATMAH (ختمة). An epilogue, but more generally a recitation of the whole of the Qur'ān. (*Khatm*, "concluding.")

Mr. Lane in his *Arabian Nights* (vol. i. p. 382), says the most approved and common mode of entertaining guests at modern private festivities, is by a *khatmah*, which is the recitation of the whole of the Qur'ān. Their mode of recitation is a peculiar chanting.

KHATN (ختن). A legal term for the husbands of female relations within the prohibited degrees. It likewise includes all the relations of these husbands. (*Hidāyah*, vol. iv. p. 518.)

KHATNAH (ختنة). [CIRCUMCISION.]

KHAṬṬ (خط). A line; a letter of the alphabet; an epistle. (1) A figure drawn by exorcists making an incantation. (2) *Khaṭṭ-i-Sharīf*, "royal letters; a diploma." (3) 'Abdu 'llāh ibn 'Abbās says a *khaṭṭ*, or "letter," is the language of the hand, and its divine origin is stated in the Qur'ān, Sūrah xcvi. 4: "Who hath taught us the use of the pen." It is said Adam first wrote with his finger in the dust, but others say it was Idrīs. The same traditionist says the first who invented the Arabic character, were three persons of the tribe of Bulān of the race of Banū Ṭaiy.

Ibn Isḥāq says there are four classes of Arabic writing: the Makkī, the Madanī, the Baṣrī, and the Kūfī; and the first who wrote the Qur'ān in a clear and elegant writing, was Khālid ibn Abī 'l-Haiyāj, and that he was set to the work by Sa'd, who employed him as a caligraphist for the Khalīfah Walīd ibn 'Abdi 'l-Malik, A.H. 86, and that Khālid wrote it in what is now called the Kufic character. (*Khashfu 'z-Ẓunūn*, Flügel's ed., vol. iii. p. 149.)

KHAUF (خوف). "Fear." Generally used for the fear of God. 'Abdu 'llāh ibn Mas'ūd relates that Muḥammad said: "There is no Muslim whose eyes shed tears, although they be as small as the head of a fly, from *fear* of God, but shall escape hell fire." (*Mishkāt*, book xxii. ch. xxix. pt. 3.)

KHAWĀRIJ (خوارج). *Lit.* "The Revolters." A sect of Muslims who affirm that any man may be promoted to the dignity of Khalīfah, even though he be not of the Quraish tribe, provided he be elected by the Muḥammadan nation. The first who were so-called were the 12,000 men who revolted from 'Alī after they had fought under him at the battle of Ṣiffīn, and took offence at his submitting the decision of his right to the Khalīfate to the arbitration of men when, in their opinion, it ought to have been submitted to the judgment of God They affirmed that a man might be appointed Khalīfah, no matter of what tribe or nation, provided he were a just and pious person, and that if the Khalīfah turned away from the truth, he might be put to death or deposed. They also held that there was no absolute necessity for a Khalīfah at all. In A.H. 38, large numbers of this sect were killed, but a few escaped, and propagated their schism in different parts of the world. [KHALIFAH.]

KHAZRAJ (خزرج). An Arabic tribe who, at an early period of Muḥammad's mission, submitted to his authority. They are supposed to have settled in al-Madīnah early in the fourth century.

KHIBRAH (خبرة). A proof; an experiment. Practical knowledge. *Ahlu 'l-Khibrah*, persons practically acquainted with any subject.

KHILĀFAH (خلافة). The office of Khalīfah. [KHALIFAH.]

KHIL'AH or KHIL'AT (خلعة). A dress of honour presented by a ruler to an inferior, as a mark of distinction. A complete *khil'ah* may include arms, or a horse, or an elephant.

K͟HILWAH (خلوة). "Privacy; retirement." A term used by the Ṣūfīs for retirement from the world for the purposes of worship and meditation.

K͟HIRQAH (خرقة). The robe of the faqīr or ascetic. A religious habit made of shreds and patches, worn by darveshes.

K͟HIṬBAH (خطبة). "Betrothal." Called in Hindūstānī *mangnī*. No religious ceremony is enjoined by Muḥammadan law, but it is usual for the Maulawī or Qāẓī to be invited to be present to offer up a prayer for a blessing on the proceeding.

The ceremony is usually accompanied with great rejoicings. The following is Mrs. Meer Hassan Ali's account of a betrothal in the neighbourhood of Lucknow:—

"A very intimate friend of mine was seeking for a suitable match for her son, and, being much in her confidence, I was initiated in all the mysteries and arrangements (according to Musalman rule) of the affair, pending the marriage of her son.

"The young lady to be sought (wooed we have it), had been described as amiable and pretty—advantages as much esteemed as her rank; fortune she had none worth mentioning, but it was what is termed in Indian society a good and equal match. The overture was, therefore, to be made from the youth's family in the following manner:—

"On a silver tray covered with gold brocade, and fringed with silver, was laid the youth's pedigree, traced by a neat writer in the Persian character, on richly embossed paper, ornamented and emblazoned with gold figures. The youth being a Saiyid, his pedigree was traced up to Muhammad, in both paternal and maternal lines, and many a hero and begum of their noble blood filled up the space from the Prophet down to the youthful Mir Muhammad, my friend's son.

"On the tray, with the pedigree, was laid a *nazr*, or offering of five gold mohurs, and twenty-one (the lucky number) rupees; a brocaded cover, fringed with silver, was spread over the whole, and this was conveyed by the male agent to the young begum's father. The tray and its contents are retained for ever, if the proposal is accepted; if rejected, the parties return the whole without delay, which is received as a tacit proof that the suitor is rejected: no further explanation is ever given or required.

"In the present instance the tray was detained, and in a few days after a female from their family was sent to my friend's house, to make a general scrutiny of the zanánah and its inmates. This female was pressed to stay a day or two, and in that time many important subjects underwent discussion. The youth was introduced, and, everything according with the views entertained by both parties, the fathers met, and the marriage, it was decided, should take place within a twelvemonth, when the young lady would have accomplished her thirteenth year.

"'Do you decide on having *mangnī* performed?' is the question proposed by the father of the youth to the father of the young maiden. In the present case it was chosen, and great were the preparations of my friend to do all possible honour to the future bride of her son.

"*Mangnī* is the first contract, by which the parties are bound to fulfil their engagement at an appointed time.

"The dress for a bride differs in one material point from the general style of Hindustani costume: a sort of gown is worn, made of silver tissue, or some equally expensive article, about the walking length of an English dress; the skirt is open in front, and contains about twenty breadths of the material, a tight body, and long sleeves. The whole dress is trimmed very richly with embroidered trimming and silver riband; the *deputtah* (drapery) is made to correspond. This style of dress is the original Hindoo fashion, and was worn at the Court of Delhi for many centuries; but of late years it has been used only on marriage festivals amongst the better sort of people in Hindustán, except kings or náwábs sending khillauts to females, when this dress, called a jhammah, is invariably one of the articles.

"The costly dresses for the present mangnī my friend prepared at great expense, and with much good taste; to which were added a ruby ring of great value, large gold earrings, offerings of money, the flower-garlands for the head, neck, wrists, and ancles, formed of the sweet-scented jessamine; choice confectionery set out in trays with the pawns and fruits; the whole conveyed under an escort of soldiers and servants, with a band of music, from the residence of Mir Muhammad to that of his bride elect, accompanied by many friends of the family. These offerings from the youth bind the contract with the young lady, who wears his ring from that day to the end of her life.

"The poorer sort of people perform mangnī by the youth simply sending a rupee in a silk band, to be tied on the girl's arm.

"Being curious to know the whole business of a wedding ceremony amongst the Musalmán people, I was allowed to perform the part of 'officiating friend' on this occasion of celebrating the mangnī. The parents of the young lady having been consulted, my visit was a source of solicitude to the whole family, who made every possible preparation to receive me with becoming respect. I went just in time to reach the gate at the moment the parade arrived. I was handed to the door of the zanánah by the girl's father, and was soon surrounded by the young members of the family, together with many lady-visitors, slaves, and women-servants of the establishment. They had never before seen an English woman, and the novelty, I fancy, surprised the whole group; they examined my dress, my complexion, hair, hands, &c., and looked the wonder they could not express in words. The young begum was not amongst the gazing throng; some preliminary customs detained her behind the purdah, where it may be supposed she endured all the agony of suspense and curiosity by her compliance with the prescribed forms.

"The lady of the mansion waited my approach to the great hall, with all due etiquette, standing to receive and embrace me on my advancing towards her. This ceremony performed, I was invited to take a seat on the carpet with her on the ground; a chair had been provided for me, but I chose to respect the lady's preference, and the seat on the floor suited me for the time without much inconvenience.

"After some time had been passed in conversation on such subjects as suited the tastes of the lady of the house, I was surprised at the servants entering with trays, which they placed immediately before me, containing a full-dress suit in the costume of Hindustán. The hostess told me she had prepared this dress for me, and I must condescend to wear it. I would have declined the gaudy array, but one of her friends whispered me, 'The custom is of long standing; when the face of a stranger is first seen, a dress is always presented; I should displease Sumdun Begum by my refusal; besides, it would be deemed an ill omen at the mangnī of the young Bohur Begum if I did not put on the native dress before I saw the face of the bride elect.' These I found to be weighty arguments, and felt constrained to quiet their apprehensions of ill-luck by compliance; I therefore forced the gold dress and the glittering drapery over my other clothes, at the expense of some suffering from the heat, for it was at the very hottest season of the year, and the hall was crowded with visitors.

"This important point conceded to them, I was led to a side hall, where the little girl was seated on her carpet of rich embroidery, her face resting on her knees in apparent bashfulness. I could not directly ascertain whether she was plain, or pretty, as the female agent had represented. I was allowed the privilege of decorating the young lady with the sweet jessamine guinahs, and placing the ring on the fore-finger of the right hand; after which, the ear-rings, the gold-tissue dress, the deputtah, were all in their turn put on, the offering of money presented, and then I had the first embrace before her mother. She looked very pretty, just turned twelve. If I could have prevailed on her to be cheerful, I should have been much gratified to have extended my visit in her apartment, but the poor child seemed ready to sink with timidity; and out of compassion to the dear girl, I hurried away from the hall, to relieve her from the burden my presence seemed to inflict, the moment I had accomplished my last duty, which was to feed her with my own hands, giving her seven pieces of sugar-candy; seven, on this occasion, is the lucky number, I presume, as I was particularly cautioned to feed her with exactly that number of pieces.

"Returning to the assembly in the dalhána; I would have gladly taken leave, but there was yet one other custom to be observed to secure a happy omen to the young people's union. Once again seated on the musnud with Sumdun Begum, the female slaves entered with sherbert in silver basins. Each person taking sherbert is expected to deposit gold or silver coins in the tray; the sherbert-money at this house is collected for the bride; and when, during the three days' performance of the marriage ceremony at the bridegroom's house, sherbert is presented to the guests, the money collected there is reserved for him. The produce of the two houses is afterwards compared, and conclusions drawn as to the greatest portion of respect paid by the friends on either side. The poor people find the sherbert-money a useful fund to help them to keep house; but with the rich it is a mere matter to boast of, that so much money was collected in consequence of the number of visitors who attended the nuptials." (Mrs. Meer Hasan Ali's *Indian Musalmáns*, vol. i. p. 362.)

KHIYĀNAH (خيانة). Breach of trust. Amputation is not incurred by a breach of trust, as in the case of ordinary theft, according to a saying of the Prophet recorded in the *Hidāyah* (vol. ii. p. 93).

KHIYĀR (خيار). "Option." A term used to express a certain period after the conclusion of a bargain, during which either of the parties may cancel it. According to 'Abdu 'l-Haqq, it is of five kinds: (1) *Khiyāru 'sh-Shart*, optional condition; where one of the parties stipulates for a period of three days or less. (2) *Khiyāru 'l-'Aib*, option from defect; the option of dissolving the contract on discovery of defect. (3) *Khiyāru 'r-Ru'yah*, option of inspection; the option of rejecting the thing purchased after sight. (4) *Khiyāru 't-Ta'yīn*, option of determination; where a person, having purchased two or three things of the same kind, stipulates a period to make his selection. (5) *Khiyāru 'l-Majlis*, the option of withdrawing from the contract as long as the meeting of the parties continues. The Hanafiyah doctors do not accept the last, but it is allowed by the other sects.

KHIZLĀN (خذلان). "Abandonment." The abandonment of a Muslim by God. The word occurs once in the Qur'ān, Sūrah iii. 154: "If then God help you, none shall overcome you, but if He *abandon* you, who is he that shall help you."

Used by a Christian, it would imply the state of a person fallen from grace.

AL-KHIZR (الخضر). *Lit.* "The green one." The Maulāwī Muhammad Tāhir says the learned are not agreed as to whether he is a prophet or not. His real name is, according to al-Baizāwī, Balyā ibn Malkān. Some say he lived in the time of Abraham, and that he is still alive in the flesh, and most of the religious and Sūfī mystics are agreed upon this point, and some have declared that they have seen him; and they say he is still to be seen in sacred places, such as Makkah or Jerusalem. Some few traditionists deny his existence. Others say he is of the family of Noah, and the son of a king. (*Majma'u 'l-Biḥār*, p. 250.)

His name does not occur in the Qur'ān, but Ḥusain, Jalālu 'd-dīn, al-Baiẓāwī, and nearly all the commentators, believe that al-Khizr is the mysterious individual referred to in the following narrative in the Qur'ān:—

Sūrah xviii. 59–81: "*Remember* when Moses said to his servant, 'I will not stop till I reach the confluence of the two seas (*i.e.* the sea of Greece and the sea of Persia), or for years will I journey on.' But when they reached their confluence, they forgot their fish, and it took its way in the sea at will. And when they had passed on, said Moses to his servant, 'Bring us our morning meal; for now have we incurred weariness from this journey.' He said, 'What thinkest thou? When we repaired to the rock for rest I forgot the fish; and none but Satan made me forget it, so as not to mention it; and it hath taken its way in the sea in a wondrous sort.' He said, 'It is this we were in quest of.' And they both went back retracing their footsteps. Then found they one of our servants to whom we had vouchsafed our mercy, and whom we had instructed with our knowledge. And Moses said to him, 'Shall I follow thee that thou teach me, for guidance, of that which thou too hast been taught?' He said, 'Verily, thou canst not have patience with me; how canst thou be patient in matters whose meaning thou comprehendest not?' He said, 'Thou shalt find me patient if God please, nor will I disobey thy bidding.' He said, 'Then, if thou follow me, ask me not of aught until I have given thee an account thereof.' So they both went on till they embarked in a ship, and he (*the unknown*) staved it in. 'What!' said *Moses*, 'hast thou staved it in that thou mayest drown its crew? a strange thing now hast thou done!' He said, 'Did I not tell thee that thou couldst not have patience with me?' He said, 'Chide me not that I forgat, nor lay on me a hard command.' Then went they on till they met a youth, and he slew him. Said Moses, 'Hast thou slain him who is free from guilt of blood? Now hast thou wrought a grievous thing!' He said, 'Did I not tell thee that thou couldst not have patience with me?' Moses said, 'If after this I ask thee aught, then let me be thy comrade no longer; but now hast thou my excuse.' They went on till they came to the people of a city. Of this people they asked food, but they refused them for guests. And they found in it a wall that was about to fall, and he set it upright. Said Moses, 'If thou hadst wished, for this thou mightest have obtained pay.' He said, 'This is the parting point between me and thee. But I will first tell thee the meaning of that which thou couldst not await with patience. As to the vessel, it belonged to poor men who toiled upon the sea, and I was minded to damage it, for in their rear was a king who seized every ship by force. As to the youth, his parents were believers, and we feared lest he should trouble them by error and infidelity. And we desired that their Lord might give them in his place a child, better than he in virtue, and nearer to filial piety. And as to the wall, it belonged to two orphan youths in the city, and beneath it was their treasure: and their father was a righteous man: and thy Lord desired that they should reach the age of strength, and take forth their treasure through the mercy of thy Lord. And not of mine own will have I done this. This is the interpretation of that which thou couldst not bear with patience."

In some Muslim books he seems to be confounded with Elias, and in others with St. George, the patron saint of England. In the above quotation he is represented as the companion of Moses, and the commentator Ḥusain says he was a general in the army of Ẕū 'l-Qarnain (Alexander the Great). But as al-Khizr is supposed to have discovered and drunk of the fountain of life, he may be contemporary with any age!

KHUBĀB or KHABBĀB (خباب).

The son of al-Araṣṣ, the blacksmith. A slave converted in the early history of Islām, and one who suffered much persecution from the Quraish on account of his religious opinions.

When 'Umar was Khalīfah, Khubāb ibn al-Araṣṣ showed him the scars of the stripes he had received from the unbelieving Makkans twenty or thirty years before, 'Umar seated him upon his masnad, saying that there was but one man who was more worthy of this favour than Khubāb, namely, Bilāl, who had also been sorely persecuted by the unbelievers. But Khubāb replied: "Why is he more worthy than I am? He had his friends among the idolators, whom the Lord raised up to help him. But I had none to help me. And I well remember one day they took me and kindled a fire for me, and threw me therein upon my back, and a man stamped with his foot upon my chest, my back being towards the ground. And when they uncovered my back, lo! it was blistered and white." (*Kātibu 'l-Wāqidī*, quoted by Sir W. Muir.)

KHUBAIB (خبيب). Son of 'Ada.

One of the early martyrs of Islām. Being perfidiously sold to the Quraish, he was by them put to death in a most cruel manner, being mutilated and impaled. When at the stake and in the midst of his tortures, he was asked whether he did not wish Muḥammad was in his place, and he answered, "I would not wish to be with my family, my substance, and my children, on condition that Muḥammad was only pricked with a thorn." When bound to the stake, his enemies said, "Now abjure Islām, and we will let you go." He replied, "Not for the whole world."

Sir William Muir says: "I see no reason to doubt the main facts of the story." (*Life of Mahomet*, new ed. p. 286.)

KHUDAI (خداى), also KHUDĀ (خدا).

From the Persian خود *khūd*,

"self," and ای *āi*, "coming." The Supreme Being; the Self-Existing God. [GOD.] *Khudā-parast*, "a God worshipper"; *Khudā-tars*, "a God fearer"; *Khudā-shinās*, "a God knower"; *Khudā-faroshān*, "God sellers," *i.e.* hypocrites.

KHUDĀWAND (خداوند). A Persian word, signifying, "lord," "prince," "master." A possessor: a man of authority. It is used as a title of the Deity, and by Christian missionaries in India it is generally employed as a translation of the Greek Κύριος, "Lord." In the *Ghiyāṣū 'l-Lughah*, it is derived from *Khudā*, "God"; and *wand*, "like"; *i.e.* one like unto God.

KHUL' (خلع). An agreement entered into for the purpose of dissolving marriage. The release from the marriage tie obtained by a wife upon payment of a compensation or consideration. In the *Hidāyah* it is said: "Whenever enmity takes place between husband and wife, and they both see reason to apprehend the ends of marriage are not likely to be answered by a continuance of their union, the woman need not scruple to release herself from the power of her husband, by offering such a compensation as may induce him to liberate her." In the event of a woman desiring this form of divorce, she is not entitled to the repayment of her dower. This law is laid down in the Qur'ān: "If ye fear that they cannot observe the ordinances of God, then no blame shall attach to either of you for what the wife shall herself give for her redemption." (Sūrah ii. 229.)

AL-KHULAFĀ'U 'R-RĀSHIDŪN (الخلفاء الراشدون). "The well-directed Khalīfahs." A title given to the first four successors of Muḥammad—Abū Bakr, 'Umar (Omar), 'Uṣmān, and 'Alī. It is generally held by the Sunnīs that after these four reigns, Islām became corrupted, and the succession in the office of Khalīfah uncertain. [KHALIFAH.]

KHULQ (خلق). "Disposition; temper; nature." Qur'ān, Sūrah lxviii. 4: "Verily thou art of a noble *nature*."

KHULṬĪN (خلطين). An infusion of dates and raisins, boiled together until they ferment and become spirituous, but of which a Muslim can drink without impropriety or sin. This is grounded on a circumstance relative to Ibn Ziyād, which is thus related by himself: "'Abdu 'llāh, the son of 'Umar, having given me some sherbet to drink, I became intoxicated to such a degree that I knew not my own house. I went to him next morning, and, having informed him of the circumstance, he acquainted me that he had given me nothing but a drink composed of dates and raisins. Now this was certainly *khulṭīn*, which had undergone the operation of boiling; because it is elsewhere related by 'Umar that it is unlawful in its crude state." (*Hidāyah*, vol. iv. p. 161.)

KHULŪD (خلود). "Eternity." [ETERNAL PUNISHMENT.]

KHUMS (خمس). "A fifth." The fifth of property which is given to the Baitu 'l-Māl, or public treasury.

KHUNṢĀ (خنثى). [HERMAPHRODITE.]

KHUSŪF (خسوف). [ECLIPSE OF THE MOON.]

KHUṬBAH (خطبة). The sermon or oration delivered on Fridays at the time of *ẓuhr*, or meridian prayer. It is also recited on the two great festivals in the morning after sunrise. ['IDU 'L-FITR, 'IDU 'L-AZHA.] The Friday prayer and sermon are established by an injunction in the Qur'ān, Sūrah lxii. 9: "O ye who believe! when the call to prayer is made upon the congregation day (*yaumu 'l-jum'ah*), then hasten to the remembrance of God, and leave off traffic." By the words "remembrance of God," most commentators understand the khuṭbah or sermon.

From the Traditions, it appears that Muḥammad used frequently to deliver a khuṭbah, and that it was not the studied and formal oration which it has become in more recent times.

Jābir says: "When the Prophet delivered the khuṭbah, his eyes used to be red, and his voice high, and his anger raged so that you would say he was warning a tribe of the approach of a hostile army, and frightening them with apprehensions of its arrival thus: It is at hand! In the evening or morning it will come down upon you and plunder you! And the Prophet would say, I have been sent, and the Resurrection is like these two fingers, and he used to join his fore-finger with the next to it, as an explanation of the semblance that the Resurrection was not farther off than the difference of length in the two fingers." (*Mishkāt*, book iv. ch. xlvi.)

On Fridays, after the usual ablutions, the four Sunnah prayers are recited, and the preacher, or *khaṭīb*, then seats himself on the pulpit, or *mimbar*, whilst the Mu'azzin proclaims azān; after which he stands up on the second step and delivers the khuṭbah. It must be in Arabic, and must include prayers for Muḥammad, the Companions, and the king, but its composition and general structure is left to the discretion of the preacher. In some countries, Egypt for example (Lane's *Egyptians*, vol. i. p. 107), the khatīb holds a wooden sword in his hand, whilst he delivers the exhortation. The khuṭbah is divided into two sections, the *khuṭbatu 'l-wa'z*, and the *khuṭbatu 'n-na't*, supplications being made between the two sections. The following is a translation of a khuṭbah, as delivered in India in the present day, from which the name and titles of the reigning monarch are omitted. It is the third of a series of sermons published at Lucknow in a volume entitled *Majma'u Khutab*:—

"In the name of God, the Compassionate, the Merciful.

"Praised be God. Praised be that God who hath shown us the way in this religion. If He had not guided us into the path we should not have found it.

"I bear witness that there is no deity but God. He is one. He has no associate. I bear witness that Muḥammad is, of a truth, His servant and His Apostle. May God have mercy upon him, and upon his descendants, and upon his companions, and give them peace.

"Fear God, O ye people, and fear that day, the Day of Judgment, when a father will not be able to answer for his son, nor the son for the father. Of a truth God's promises are true. Let not this present life make you proud. Let not the deceiver (Satan) lead you astray.

"O ye people who have believed, turn ye to God, as Naṣūḥ* did turn to God. Verily God doth forgive all sin, verily He is the merciful, the forgiver of sins. Verily He is the most munificent, and bountiful, the King, the Holy One, the Clement, the Most Merciful."

(*The preacher then descends from the pulpit, and sitting on the floor of the mosque, offers up a silent prayer. He then again ascends the mimbar, as before, and proceeds.*)

"In the name of God, the Compassionate, the Merciful.

"Praised be God. We praise Him. We seek help from Him. We ask forgiveness of sins. We trust in Him. We seek refuge in Him from evil desires and from former sinful actions. He who has God for His guide is never lost; and whomsoever He leadeth aside none can guide into the right path.

"We bear witness that there is no deity but God. He is one. He hath no partner.

"Verily we bear witness that Muḥammad is the servant and apostle of God, and may God have mercy upon him, who is more exalted than any being. May God have mercy upon his descendants, and upon his companions! May God give them peace! Especially upon Amīru 'l-Mu'minīn Abū Bakr aṣ-Ṣiddīq (may God be pleased with him). And upon him who was the most temperate of the 'friends,' Amīru 'l-Mu'minīn 'Umar Ibn al-Khattāb (may God be pleased with him). And upon him whose modesty and faith were perfect, Amīru 'l-Mu'minīn 'Usmān (may God be pleased with him). And upon the Lion of the powerful God, Amīru 'l-Mu'minīn 'Alī ibn Abī-Ṭālib (may God be pleased with him). And upon the two Imāms, the holy ones, the two martyrs, Amīru 'l-Mu'minīn Abū Muḥammad al-Ḥasan and Abū 'Abdi 'llāh al-Ḥusain (may God be pleased with both of them). And upon the mother of these two persons, the chief of women, Fāṭimatu 'z-Zuhrā' (may God be pleased with her). And upon his (Muḥammad's) two uncles, Ḥamzah and al-'Abbās (may God be pleased with them). And upon the rest of the 'companions,' and upon the 'followers' (may God be pleased with all of them). Of Thy mercy, O most merciful of all merciful ones, O God, forgive all Muslim men and Muslim women, all male believers and all female believers. Of a truth Thou art He who wilt receive our prayers.

"O God, help those who help the religion of Muḥammad. May we also exert ourselves to help those who help Islām. Make those weak, who weaken the religion of Muḥammad.

"O God, bless the ruler of the age, and make him kind and favourable to the people.

"O servants of God, may God have mercy upon you. Verily, God enjoineth justice and the doing of good, and gifts to kindred; and He forbiddeth wickedness, and wrong, and oppression. He warneth you that haply ye may be mindful. (Sūrah cxvi. 92.)

"O ye people, remember the great and exalted God. He will also remember you. He will answer your prayers. The remembrance of God is great, and good, and honourable, and noble, and meritorious, and worthy, and sublime."

A more eloquent and strikingly characteristic khuṭbah has been translated by Mr. Lane in his *Modern Egyptians* (vol. i. p. 107). It is a New Year's Day sermon, delivered in the great mosque at Cairo, on the first Friday in the year, on the occasion of Mr. Lane's first visit, and is as follows:—

"In the name of God, the Compassionate, the Merciful.

"Praise be to God, the Renewer of Years, and the Multiplier of favours, and the Creator of months and days, according to the most perfect wisdom and most admirable regulation; who hath dignified the months of the Arabs above all other months, and hath pronounced that among the more excellent of them is al-Muḥarram the Sacred, and hath commenced with it the year, as He hath closed it with Ẕū 'l-Ḥijjah. How propitious is the beginning, and how good is the end! I extol His perfection, exempting Him from the association of any other deity with Him He hath well considered what He hath formed and established what He hath contrived, and He alone hath the power to create and to annihilate. I praise Him, extolling His perfection, and exalting His name, for the knowledge and inspiration which He hath graciously vouchsafed; and I testify that there is no deity but God alone; He hath no companion; He is the Most Holy King; the God of Peace; and I testify that our lord and our Prophet and our friend Muḥammad is His servant and His Apostle, and His elect, and His friend, the Guide of the Way, and the lamp of the dark. O God, bless and save and beautify this noble Prophet, and chief and excellent apostle, the merciful-hearted, our Lord Muḥammad, and his family and his companions, and his wives, and his posterity, and the people of his house, the

* *Naṣūḥ*, is a word which occurs in the eighth verse of the Sūratu 't-Taḥrīm (lxvi.) in the Qur'ān; it is translated "true repentance" by Sale and Rodwell, but it is supposed to be a person's name by several commentators.

noble persons, and grant them ample salvation.

"O servants of God, your lives have been gradually curtailed, and year after year hath passed away, and ye are sleeping on the bed of indolence, and on the pillow of iniquity. Ye pass by the tombs of your predecessors, and fear not the assault of destiny and destruction, as if others departed from the world and ye must of necessity remain in it. Ye rejoice at the arrival of new years, as if they brought an increase to the term of life, and swim in the seas of desires, and enlarge your hopes, and in every way exceed other people in presumption; and ye are sluggish in doing good. O how great a calamity is this! God teacheth by an allegory. Know ye not that in the curtailment of time by indolence and sleep there is very great trouble? Know ye not that in the cutting short of lives by the termination of years is a very great warning? Know ye not that the night and day divide the lives of numerous souls? Know ye not that health and capacity are two blessings coveted by many men? But the truth hath become manifest to him who hath eyes. Ye are now between two years: one year hath passed away, and come to an end, with its evils; and ye have entered upon another year, in which, if it please God, mankind shall be relieved. Is any of you determining upon diligence in doing good in the year to come? or repenting of his failings in the times that are passed? The happy one is he who maketh amends for the time past in the time to come; and the miserable one is he whose days pass away and he is careless of his time. This new year hath arrived, and the sacred month of God hath come with blessings to you, the first of the months of the year, and of the four sacred months, as hath been said, and the most worthy of preference and honour and reverence. Its fast is the most excellent of fasts after that which is obligatory, and the doing of good in it is among the most excellent of the objects of desire. Whosoever desireth to reap advantage from it, let him fast the ninth and tenth days, looking for aid. Abstain not from the fast through indolence, and esteeming it a hardship; but comply with it, in the best manner, and honour it with the best of honours, and improve your time by the worship of God morning and evening. Turn unto God with repentance, before the assault of death: He is the God who accepteth repentance of His servants, and pardoneth sins. The Apostle of God (God bless and save him) hath said, 'The most excellent prayer, after the prescribed, is the prayer that is said in the last third of the night; and the most excellent fast, after Ramaẓān, is that of the month of God, al-Muharram.'

(*The khaṭīb, having concluded his exhortation, says to the congregation, "Supplicate God." He then sits down and prays privately; and each member of the congregation at the same time offers up some private petition, as after the ordinary prayers, holding his hands before him (looking at the palms), and then drawing them down his face. The khaṭīb then rises again, and recites the following*):

"Praise be to God, abundant praise, as He hath commanded. I testify that there is no deity but God alone: He hath no companion: affirming His supremacy, and condemning him who denieth and disbelieveth: and I testify that our Lord and our Prophet Muḥammad is His servant and His apostle, the lord of mankind, the intercessor, the accepted intercessor, on the Day of Assembling: God bless him and his family as long as the eye seeth and the ear heareth. O people, reverence God by doing what He hath commanded, and abstain from that which He hath forbidden and prohibited. The happy one is he who obeyeth, and the miserable one is he who opposeth and sinneth. Know that the present world is a transitory abode, and that the world to come is a lasting abode. Make provision, therefore, in your transitory state for your lasting state, and prepare for your reckoning and standing before your Lord: for know that ye shall tomorrow be placed before God, and reckoned with according to your deeds; and before the Lord of Might ye shall be present, 'and those who acted unjustly shall know with what an overthrowal they shall be overthrown.' Know that God, whose perfection I extol, and whose name be exalted, hath said and ceaseth not to say wisely, and to command judiciously, warning you, and teaching, and honouring the dignity of your Prophet, extolling and magnifying him. Verily, God and His angels bless the Prophet: 'O ye who believe, bless him, and greet him with a salutation.' O God bless Muḥammad and the family of Muḥammad, as Thou blessedst Ibrahīm and the family of Ibrahīm among all creatures, for Thou art praiseworthy and glorious. O God, do Thou also be well pleased with the four Khalīfahs, the orthodox lords, of high dignity and illustrious honour, Abū Bakr, aṣ-Ṣiddīq, and 'Umar, and 'Us̤mān, and 'Alī; and be Thou well pleased, O God, with the six who remained of the ten noble and just persons who swore allegiance to Thy Prophet Muḥammad (God bless him and save him) under the tree (for Thou art the Lord of piety and the Lord of pardon); those persons of excellence and clemency, and rectitude and prosperity, Ṭalḥah, and Zubair, and Ṣa'd, and Sa'īd, and 'Abdu 'r-Raḥmān ibn 'Auf, and Abū 'Ubaidah Āmir ibn al-Jarrāh; and with all the Companions of the Apostle of God (God bless and save him); and be Thou well pleased, O God, with the two martyred descendants, the two bright moons, the 'two lords of the youths of the people of Paradise in Paradise,' the two sweet-smelling flowers of the Prophet of this nation, Abū Muḥammad al-Ḥasan and Abū 'Abdi 'llāh al-Ḥusain; and be Thou well pleased, O God, with their mother, the daughter of the Apostle of God (God bless and save him), Fāṭimatu 'z-Zahrā', and with their grandmother Khadījah al-Kubra, and with 'Āyishah, the mother of the faithful, and with the rest of the pure wives, and with the generation which succeeded the Companions, and with the generation which succeeded that, with beneficence to the Day of Judgment. O God, pardon the believing men and the believing women, and the Muslim men and the Muslim women, those who are living, and the dead; for Thou art a hearer near, an answerer of prayers, O Lord, of the beings of the whole world. O God, aid Islām, and strengthen its pillars, and make infidelity to tremble, and destroy its might, by the preservation of Thy servant, and the son of Thy servant, the submissive to the Might of Thy Majesty and Glory, whom God hath aided, by the care of the Adored King, our master the Sulṭān, son of the Sulṭān, the Sulṭān Maḥmūd Khān; may God assist him, and prolong [his reign]. O God, assist him, and assist his armies, O Thou Lord of the religion, and the world present, and the world to come, O Lord of the beings of the whole world.

"O God, assist the forces of the Muslims, and the armies of the Unitarians. O God, frustrate the infidels and polytheists, thine enemies, the enemies of the religion. O God, invert their banners, and ruin their habitations, and give them and their wealth as booty to the Muslims. O God, unloose the captivity of the captives, and annul the debts of the debtors; and make this town to be safe and secure, and blessed with wealth and plenty, and all the towns of the Muslims, O Lord of the beings of the whole world. And decree safety and health to us and to all travellers, and pilgrims, and warriors, and wanderers, upon Thy earth, and upon Thy sea, such as are Muslims, O Lord of the beings of the whole world.

"'O Lord, we have acted unjustly towards our own souls, and if Thou do not forgive us and be merciful unto us, we shall surely be of those who perish.' I beg of God, the Great, that He may forgive me and you, and all the people of Muḥammad, the servants of God. 'Verily God commandeth justice, and the doing of good, and giving what is due to kindred; and forbiddeth wickedness, and iniquity, and oppression: He admonisheth you that ye may reflect. Remember God; He will remember you: and thank Him; He will increase to you your blessings. Praise be to God, the Lord of the beings of the whole world!"

The khuṭbah being ended, the khaṭīb then descends from the pulpit, and, if he officiate as Imām, takes his position and leads the people in a two-rak'ah prayer. The khaṭīb, however, does not always officiate as Imām. The Prophet is related to have said that the length of a man's prayers and the shortness of his sermon, are signs of a man's common sense.

According to the best authorities, the name of the reigning Khalīfah ought to be recited in the khuṭbah, and the fact that it is not so recited in independent Muḥammadan kingdoms, but the name of the Sulṭān or Amīr is substituted for the Khalīfah, has its significance, for it is a question whether the Sulṭān of Turkey, has any real claim to the spiritual headship of Islām. [KHALIFAH.] In India the name of the king is omitted and the expression "Ruler of the Age" is used.

In India, the recital of the khuṭbah serves to remind every Muḥammadan priest, at least once a week, that he is in a *Dāru 'l-Ḥarb*, "a land of enmity." Still the fact that he can recite his khuṭbah at all in a country not under Muslim rule, must also assure him that he is in a *Dāru 'l-Amān*, or "land of protection."

KHUṬBATU 'L-WAQFAH (خطبة الوقفة). The "sermon of standing." The sermon or oration recited on Mount 'Arafāt at the mid-day prayer on the ninth day of the pilgrimage. (Burton's *Pilgrimage*, vol. ii. p. 219.) [KHUTBAH.]

KHUZĀ'AH (خزاعة). *Lit.* "A remnant." A part of the Banū 'l-Azd who were left behind when the tribe migrated, and who settled down permanently near Makkah. They were from the first friendly to Muḥammad, and made a treaty with him soon after that of al-Ḥudaibiyah. They were an important portion of the army which marched to Makkah with the Prophet.

KHUZAIMAH (خزيمة). An Arabian tribe were expelled by the Yaman tribes and afterwards settled in the Ḥijāz, where they bore a prominent part in opposing the army of Muḥammad.

KHUZAIMAH IBN ṢĀBIT (خزيمة بن ثابت). A Companion of some renown. He was present at the battle of Badr. He was killed at the same time as the Khalīfah 'Alī, A.H. 37.

KHWĀJAH (خواجة). Persian. A rich or respectable man; a gentleman. An opulent merchant.

KIBR (كبر). "Pride; haughtiness." With regard to mortal man, it is considered a vice, but with regard to the Infinite God, it is held to be one of His attributes. *Al-Kabīr*, "the Great One."

AL-KĪMIYĀ' (الكيمياء). "Alchemy." The word is supposed to be derived from the Greek χυμὸς, which signifies "juice," and to be properly confined to the study of extracts and essences of plants. It is now, however, applied more especially to a pretended science, which had for its object the transmutation of the baser materials into gold or silver, or the discovery of a panacea or universal remedy for diseases. Although this so-called science has now fallen into deserved contempt, it was held in high repute, and much cultivated from the 13th to the 17th century, especially amongst the Saracens. The first Muslim of reputation who is said to have given his attention to the subject, was Khālid, a son of the Khalīfah Yazīd (A.D. 683), and the first who wrote on the subject was Jābir ibn Abbān aṣ-Ṣūfī, who was a disciple of Khālid.

Ḥājī Khalfah, the celebrated author of the *Kashfu 'z-Ẓunūn*, says "the word *Kīmiyah* comes from the Hebrew, *kīm* and *yah* and means 'from God.' There is some discussion regarding this science. Many people do not believe in its existence, amongst others the celebrated philosopher Shaikh 'Alī ibn Sīnā', who wrote against it in his book, the *Kitābu 'sh-Shafā'*: also Ya'qūb al-Kindī, and many others. But, on the other hand, many learned men have believed in its existence; for example, Imām Fakhru 'd-dīn ar-Rāzi, and Shaikh Najmu 'd-dīn al-Baghdādī." (*Kashfu 'z-Ẓunūn, in loco.*)

Ahlu Kīmiyā', is a term used not only for an alchymist, but for a deceiver, and also a lover.

Al-Kīmiyā'u 'l-Akbar, the philosopher's stone, or some celebrated tincture.

Kīmiyāu 'l-Ma'ānī, the chemistry of meanings, that is, the study of truth.

II.—Amongst the Ṣūfī mystics, the term *al-Kīmiyā'* is used for being satisfied with the things in possession, and not yearning after things which we do not possess. *Kīmiyā'u 'l-'Awām*, the alchymistry of the ordinary people, is the exchange of spiritual things for the things which perish. *Kīmiyā'u 'l-'Khawāṣṣ*, the alchymistry of special people, is the emptying of the heart of everything except God. *Kīmiyā'u 's-Sa'ādah*, the alchymistry of felicity, is the purification of one's heart from all things that are evil by the attainment of special graces. ('Abdu 'r-Razzāq's *Dict. of Ṣūfī Terms.*)

KINĀNAH (كنانة). (1) The name of the ancestor and founder of the Arabian tribe, the Banū Kinānah, the father of an-Naẓr, the grandfather of Fihr, who was surnamed Quraish. [QURAISH.]

(2) The name of the Jewish chief of Khaibar who defended the fortress of Qamuṣ against Muḥammad. He was slain by order of the Prophet, who afterwards took Kinānah's bride, Ṣafīyah, to his home and married her. [SAFIYAH.]

KINAYAH (كناية). "A metaphor." A word used in the science of exegesis, *e.g.* "Thou art separated," by which may be meant, "Thou art divorced," which is called *Ṭalāqu 'l-Kināyah*, or a divorce in metaphor.

KINDAH (كندة). A tribe of al-Yaman, and the descendants of Ḥimyar. They are admitted to be one of the noblest of the Arab tribes. One of the remarkable descendants of this tribe was al-Kindi the philosopher. [KINDI.]

AL-KINDĪ (الكندى), the philosopher. Abū Yūsuf Ya'qūb ibn Isḥāq ibn aṣ-Ṣabbāḥ al-Kindi, who flourished at the court of the Khalīfah Ma'mūm, A.D. 833, and who translated numerous classical and philosophical works for the Abbaside Government. De Slane says his father Isḥāq was Amīr of al-Kūfah, and his great grandfather was one of the Prophet's Companions. It was at one time supposed he was a Jew or a convert to the Jewish religion, while others tried to identify him with the author of an Apology for Christianity, entitled *Risālatu 'Abdi 'l-Masīḥ ibn Isḥāq al-Kindī*, in which the writer explains to a Muslim friend his reasons for holding the Christian faith, in preference to Islām, whose acceptance the latter had pressed upon him. But it has been proved that al-Kindī, the philosopher, and al-Kindī, the author of the said treatise, are two distinct persons, although both living at the court of al-Ma'mūn and belonging to the same tribe.

Dr. J. M. Arnold, in his *Islām and Christianity*, p. 372, says the *Risālah*, or treatise of al-Kindī, is quoted as a genuine production by the celebrated historian, Muḥammad ibn Aḥmad al-Bīrūnī (died A.H. 430), in one of his works in confirmation of his statement that there were human sacrifices offered up in Arabia prior to the time of Muḥammad.

The Apology of al-Kindi has been rendered into English by Sir William Muir, from an edition in Arabic published by the Turkish Missions Aid Society.

KINDRED. [INHERITANCE, MARRIAGE.]

KING. The term used in the Qur'ān for a king is generally *malik* (ملك), Heb. מֶלֶךְ, *e.g.* when the Israelites "said to a prophet of theirs, 'Raise up for us a king.'" (Surah ii. 246.)

(1) The word *malik* is now merely used in Arabia and in Central Asia for a petty chief.

(2) *Sulṭān* occurs in the Qur'ān for "authority," or "power," and not for a king. Sūrah lxix. 29, "My authority has perished from me." But it is now the title assumed by the Emperor of Turkey.

(3) *Pādshāh* and *Shāh* are Persian words, the ruler of Persia having assumed the title of Shāh or King. The word *Pādshāh* is derived from *pād*, "a throne," and *shāh*, "a lord or possessor," *i.e.* "the lord of the throne." In Hindustani it is *Bādshah.*

(4) *Wālī*, is a title assumed by Muḥammadan rulers, the title being held by the Barakzai rulers of Afghānistan in all legal documents. The word simply means a possessor, or one in authority.

(5) *Amīr* has a similar meaning to *Wālī*, and is a title which is assumed by Muslim rulers, as the Amīrs of Bukharah and of Kabūl. It is derived from *'amr*, "to rule."

(6) *Saiyid*, "a lord," is a title given to the descendants of Muḥammad, and is a regal title assumed by the ruler of Zanzibār.

(7) *Imām*, "a leader," is the legal title of the head of the Muslims, and it is that given to the successors of Muḥammad, who are so called in the Traditions and in Muḥammadan works of law. [IMAM.]

(8) *Khalīfah*, "a vicegerent." Khalīfah, or Caliph, is used for the same regal personage as Imām. [KHALIFAH, RULERS.]

KIRĀMAH (كرامة). The miracles of any saint other than a Prophet, as distinguished from *mu'jizah*, which is always used for the miracles of an apostle or prophet. [MIRACLES.]

KIRĀMĪYAH (كراميه). A sect of Muslims founded by Muḥammad ibn Karīm, and called also the Mujassīyah, or Corporealists, because they admitted not only a resemblance between God and created beings, but declared him to be corporeal in substance.

"The more sober among them, indeed, when they applied the word body to God, would be understood to mean that He is a self-subsisting being, which with them is the definition of body; but yet some of them affirmed him to be finite, and circumscribed either on all sides, or on some only (as beneath, for example), according to different opinions; and others allowed that He might be felt by the hand, and seen by the eye. Nay, one David al-Jawâri went so far as to say that His deity was a body composed of flesh and blood, and that He had members, as hands, feet, a head, a tongue, eyes, and ears; but that he was a body, however, not like other bodies, neither was he like to any created being. He is also said, further, to have affirmed that from the crown of the head to the breast he was hollow, and from the breast downward solid, and that He had black curled hair. These most blasphemous and monstrous notions were the consequence of the literal acceptation of those passages in the Koran (Sūrahs xl. 10; xx. 4; ii. 109), which figuratively attribute corporeal actions to God, and of the words of Muḥammad, when he said that God created man in His own image, and that he himself had felt the fingers of God, which He laid on his back, to be cold; besides which, this sect are charged with fathering on their Prophet a great number of spurious and forged traditions to support their opinion, the greater part whereof they borrowed from the Jews, who are accused as naturally prone to assimilate God to men, so that they describe Him as weeping for Noah's flood till His eyes were sore." (Sale.)

KIRĀMUN KĀTIBŪN (كرام كاتبون). *Lit.* "Illustrious writers." The two recording angels who are said to be with every man, one on the right hand to record his good deeds, and one on his left to record the evil deeds. They are mentioned in the Qur'ān, Sūratu 'l-Infiṭār (lxxxii.): "Yet truly there are guardians over you, *illustrious recorders* (*kirāman kātibīn*) cognizant of your actions."

It is related that the Prophet enjoined his people not to spit in front, or on the right, but on the left, as on that side stands the recording angel of evil. (*Mishkāt*, book iv. ch. viii. pt. 1.)

As these angels are supposed to be changed every day, they are called the *mu'aqqibāt*, or those who succeed each other.

KISRĀ (كسرى), pl. *Akāsirah*. The Chosroes, or Cyrus, a name given to almost every king of Persia of the Sassānian dynasty (like Cæsar among the Romans and Pharaoh among the Egyptians). The kings of Persia, prior to Islām, according to Arab historians, composed four dynasties, namely, the Peshdādians, the chronology of which is unknown; the Kayānians, which ended B.C. 331, when Persia was conquered by Alexander the Great; the Ashkānians, which terminated A.D. 202; and the Sassānians, the last of whom was overcome by the Arabs, A.D. 636.

From the Qur'ān, Sūrah xxx. 1, it appears that after the taking of Jerusalem by Chosroes, the sympathies of Muḥammad were all enlisted on the side of the Cæsar, and he foretells his ultimate victory over the king of Persia:—

"The Greeks have been conquered in the neighbouring coast, but in a few years after their defeat they shall again be victorious."

In the sixth year of the Hijrah, Muhammad sent a despatch to Chosroes, inviting him to Islām. Sir William Muir says (*Life of Mahomet*, new ed. p. 384):—

"The despatch for the King of Persia reached the Court probably some months after the accession of Siroes. It was delivered to the Monarch, who, on hearing the contents, tore it in pieces. When this was reported to Mahomet, he prayed and said: 'Even thus, O Lord! rend Thou his kingdom from him.' Connected with the court of Persia, but of date somewhat earlier than the despatch sent to it, is a remarkable incident, which was followed by results of considerable importance.

"A few months before his overthrow, the Chosroes, receiving strange reports of the prophetical claims of Mahomet, and of the depredations committed on the Syrian border by his marauding bands, sent order to Bâdzân, the Persian Governor of Yemen, to despatch two trusty men to Medîna, and procure for him certain information regarding the Pretender. Bâdzân obeyed, and with the messengers sent a courteous despatch to Mahomet. By the time they arrived at Medîna, tidings had reached the Prophet of the deposition and death of Chosroes. When the despatch, therefore, was read before him, he smiled at its contents, and summoned the ambassadors to embrace Islâm. He then apprised them of the murder of the Chosroes and the accession of his son. 'Go,' said he, 'inform your master of this, and require him to tender his submission to the Prophet of the Lord.' The glory of Persia had now departed. She had long ago relaxed her grasp upon Arabia; and the Governor of Yemen was free to choose a protectorate more congenial to his people. Bâdzân, therefore, gladly recognised the rising fortunes of Islām, and signified his adhesion to the Prophet. From the distance of this province, its allegiance was at the first little more than nominal; but the accession served as a point for further action, and meanwhile added new prestige to the Prophet's name."

KISWAH (كسوة). *Lit.* "A robe." The covering of the Ka'abah, or cube-like building, at Makkah. [KA'BAH.]

When Captain Burton visited Makkah in 1853, he found it to be a coarse tissue of mixed silk and cotton, and of eight pieces, two for each face of the building, the seams being concealed by the broad gilt band called the *ḥizām*. It is lined with white calico, and has cotton ropes to secure the covering to metal rings at the basement. But on the occasion of Captain Burton's visit, the kiswah was tucked up by ropes from the roof. The whole is of a brilliant black, with the gold band running round it.

The *burqa'*, or veil, is a curtain hung before the door of the Ka'bah, also of black brocade, embroidered with inscriptions, in letters of gold, of verses from the Qur'ān, and lined with green silk.

According to Burton, the inscription on the gold band of the kiswah is the ninetieth verse of the third Sūrah of the Qur'ān: "Verily, the first House founded for mankind was surely that at Bakkah, for a blessing and a guidance to the worlds." The whole of the kiswah is covered with seven Sūrahs of the Qur'ān, namely, xviiith, xixth, iiird, ixth, xxth, xxxixth, and lxviith (*i.e.* al-Kahf, Maryam, Ālu 'Imrān, at-Taubah, Ṭā Ḥā, Yā Sīn, and al-Mulk). The character is the ancient Kufic, and legible from a considerable distance.

Mr. Lane says that the kiswah is made of a mixture of silk and *cotton*, because the Prophet expressly forbade silk as an article of dress.

The kiswah and burqa' are now manufactured at Cairo, at a manufactory called the Khurunfīsh, and is made by a family who possess the hereditary right, and who are called the *Baitu 's-Sa'd*. When they are completed, they are taken to the mosque known as the Sulṭān Ḥasan, and there kept until they are sent off with a caravan of pilgrims to Makkah. This usually takes place a few days after the 'Īdu 'l-Fiṭr, generally about the 6th day of the month of Shawwāl, and two or three weeks before the departure of the regal canopy or Maḥmal. [MAHMAL.] The procession of the kiswah is similar to that of the Maḥmal, and therefore requires no separate description.

According to Muslim historians, the Ka'bah was first dressed with a kiswah or robe by a Ḥimyarite chief, named Tubba'u 'l-Arqān. From the time of Quṣaiy it was veiled by subscriptions collected from Pagan Arabs, until Abū Rabiyah ibn al-Mughīrah ibn 'Abdi 'llāh provided the covering, whereby he obtained the title of *al-'Adl*, "the Just." When Muhammad obtained possession, he ordered it to be covered with fine Yamānī cloth, and ordered the expense to be defrayed from the public treasury. The Khalīfah 'Umar chose Egyptian linen, and ordered the robe to be renewed every year. Khalīfah 'Usmān, being a man of eminent piety ordered it to be clothed twice a year. For the winter it had a robe of brocade silk, and in the summer a suit of fine linen. Mu'āwiyah, the Umaiyah Khalīfah, was the first to establish the present kiswah of silk and linen tissue, but being reminded of the Prophet's well-known dislike to silken robes he changed it again to the more orthodox covering of Yamānī cloth. The Khalīfah Ma'mūn (A.D. 813) ordered the dress to be changed three times a year, the fine Yamānī cloth on the 1st of Rajab, white brocade on the 1st of Shuwwāl, for the pilgrimage two months later, and rich red brocade on the 10th of Muḥarram. The Khalīfah al-Mutawakkil (A.D. 847) sent a new robe every two months. During the Abbaside dynasty, the investing of the Ka'bah with the kiswah was regarded as a sign of sovereignty over the holy places. The later Khalīfahs of Baghdād are said to have sent a kiswah of green and gold. The Fāṭimide Khalīfahs made the kiswah at Cairo of black brocade of mixed silk and cotton; and when Sulṭān Salīm assumed the power of the Khalīfate (A.D. 1512), the kiswah still continued to be supplied from Cairo, as is now the case under the Ottoman rule.

(Burckhardt's *Arabia*, Lane's *Egyptians*, Ali Bey's *Pilgrimage*, Burton's *Mecca and Medina.*) [KA'BAH, MASJIDU 'L-HARAM.]

AL-KITĀB (الكتاب). "The Book." A term used for the Qur'ān, and extended to all inspired books of the Jews and Christians, who are called *Ahlu 'l-Kitāb*, or believers in the book.

KITĀBĪ (كتابى). A term used for one of the *Ahlu 'l-Kitāb*, "the people of the Book," or those in possession of the inspired word of God, as Jews or Christians.

KITĀBĪYAH (كتابية). Fem. of *Kitābī*. A female of the *Ahlu 'l-Kitāb*, or those who possess an inspired book, Jews or Christians.

KITĀBU 'L-A'MĀL (كتاب الاعمال). [SAHIFATU 'L-A'MAL.]

AL-KITĀBU 'L-ḤUKMĪ (الكتاب الحكمى). A letter transmissible from one Qāẓi to another when the defendant in a suit resides at a distance. Such letter must be a transcript of real evidence.

AL-KITABU 'L-MUBĪN (الكتاب المبين). *Lit.* "The Manifest or clear book." The term is used in the Qur'ān both for the Tablet of Decrees (*Lauḥu 'l-Maḥfūẓ*, and for the Qur'ān itself.

Sūrah vi. 59: "No leaf falleth but He knoweth it; neither is there a grain in the darkness of the earth, nor a green thing or sere, but it is noted in the *clear book*."

Sūrah iv. 18: "Now hath a light and a *clear book* come to you from God."

KITMĀN (كتمان). "Concealing; keeping secret." The injunction of the Qur'ān is: "*Hide* not the truth while ye know it"; and yet the art of concealing profane religious beliefs has been a special characteristic of the Eastern mystics.

KNEELING. The attitude of kneeling amongst Muhammadans consists of placing the two knees on the ground and sitting on the feet behind. Kneeling as practised by Christians in the present day, does not exist amongst Muslims as an attidude of worship.

The word *jāṡī*, which occurs in the Qur'ān, Sūrah xlv. 27: "And thou shalt see each nation *kneeling* (*jāṡiyatan*), each nation summoned to the book," expresses an attitude of fear and not of worship.

KNOWLEDGE. ['ilm.]

KORAH. Arabic *Qārūn* (قارون). Heb. קֹרַח. The son of *Yaṣhar* (Izhar), son of Qāhis (Kohath), son of Lāwī (Levi). The leader of the rebellion against Moses. Num. xvi. 1; Jude 11 (where he is coupled with Cain and Balaam). He is mentioned three times in the Qur'ān.

Sūrah xl. 24, 25: "Moreover we had sent Moses of old, with our signs and with clear authority, to Pharaoh, and Haman, and Korah; and they said, 'Sorcerer, impostor.'"

Sūrah xxix. 38: "And Korah and Pharaoh and Haman. With proofs of his mission did Moses come to them, and they behaved proudly on the earth; but us they could not outstrip; for every one of them did we seize in his sin. Against some of them did we send a stone-charged wind; some of them did the terrible cry of Gabriel surprise; for some of them we cleaved the earth; and some of them we drowned."

Sūrah xxviii. 76–82: "Now Korah was of the people of Moses: but he behaved haughtily toward them; for we had given him such treasure that its keys would have burdened a company of men of strength. When his people said to him, 'Exult not, for God loveth not those who exult; but seek by means of what God hath given thee, to attain the future Mansion; and neglect not thy part in this world, but be bounteous to others as God hath been bounteous to thee, and seek not to commit excesses on the earth; for God loveth not those who commit excesses:' he said, 'It hath been given me only on account of the knowledge that is in me.' Did he not know that God had destroyed before him generations that were mightier than he in strength and had amassed more abundant wealth? But the wicked shall not be asked of their crimes. And Korah went forth to his people in his pomp. Those who were greedy for this present life said, 'Oh that we had the like of that which hath been bestowed on Korah! Truly he is possessed of great good fortune.' But they to whom knowledge had been given said, 'Woe to you! the reward of God is better for him who believeth and worketh righteousness, and none shall win it but those who have patiently endured.' And we clave the earth for him and for his palace, and he had no forces, in the place of God, to help him, nor was he among those who are succoured. And in the morning those who the day before had coveted his lot said, 'Aha! God enlargeth supplies to whom He pleaseth of His servants, or is sparing. Had not God been gracious to us, He had caused it to cleave for us. Aha! the ungrateful can never prosper."

Al-Baiẓāwī says Korah brought a false accusation of immorality against Moses, and Moses complained to God, and God directed him to command the earth what he pleased, and it should obey him; whereupon he said, "O earth, swallow them up"; and immediately the earth opened under Korah and his confederates, and swallowed them up, with his palace and all his riches.—There is a tradition that as Korah sank gradually into the ground, first to his knees, then to his waist, then to his neck, he cried out four several times, "O Moses, have mercy on me!" but that Moses continued to say, "O earth, swallow them up!" till at last he wholly disappeared: upon which God said to Moses, "Thou hadst no mercy on Korah, though he asked pardon of thee four times; but I would have had compassion on him if he had asked pardon of Me but once."

He is represented by Jalālu 'd-dīn as the most beautiful of the Israelites of his time. His opulence and avarice have become a proverb for those who amass wealth without giving away in alms and charity.

In the Talmud it is said that "Joseph concealed three treasures in Egypt, one of which became known to Korah . . . . the keys of Korah's treasure chambers were a burden for 300 white mules." *Midr. Jalkut on Eccl.* v. 12: "Riches kept for the owners thereof to their hurt,"—which may have furnished Muḥammad with the nucleus of this story. Compare also *Tract. Psachim*, fol. 119*a*.

AL-KŪFAH (الكوفة). A city on the west bank of the river Euphrates, about four days march from Baghdād, but which has now entirely disappeared.

The city of al-Kūfah was founded soon after the Arabs conquered Persia, A.D. 636, and in the reign of the Khalīfah 'Umar. It was built opposite the ancient town of Madain, on the other side of the river. The first Abbaside Khalīfah, Abū 'l-'Abbas, A.D. 750, made it his capital, and it was then a flourishing city, but when the Khalīfah al-Manṣūr built Baghdād, al-Kūfah decreased in importance, and gradually fell into decay. It was much famed for its learned men, and especially for its grammarians. Two sects of rival grammarians were named respectively from al-Baṣrah and al-Kūfah, and the more ancient characters of Arabic writing are called Kūfī or Kufic, after this seat of learning. The Kufic-Arabic letters resemble the Syriac, being square and heavy. The ancient copies of the Qur'ān are written in Kufic.

KUFR (كفر). *Lit.* "That which covers the truth." Infidelity; blasphemy. Disbelieving in the Qur'ān or in any of the tenets of the Muslim religion. [KAFIR.]

KULĀH (كلاه). The Persian for a cap, or cowl, especially worn by Muḥammadan faqīrs or darweshes. The faqīrs generally call it their *tāj* or crown, and it is one of the distinguishing marks of their order.

KULAHS. (*E. Campbell.*)

KULṢŪM (كلثوم). Kulṣūm ibn Hadam, the name of a hospitable but blind chief, with whom Muḥammad stayed at Qubā' upon his arrival in that place after his flight from Makkah. It was whilst he was staying with Kulṣūm that Muḥammad built his first mosque at Qubā'. Kulṣūm died soon afterwards.

KURZ IBN JABIR (كرز بن جابر). A Quraish chieftain who committed a raid near al-Madīnah, and carried off some of the flocks and herds of the Muslims. He was afterwards converted to Islām, and fell under Khālid at the taking of Makkah.

KUSŪF (كسوف). [ECLIPSE OF THE SUN.]

L.

LĀĀDRĪYAH (لاادرية). A sect of heretics who say it is impossible for mortal man to be certain of any fact, even of man's own identity.

LABBAIKA (لبيك). [TALBIYAH.]

LABĪD (لبيد). The son of Rabī'ah ibn Ja'far al-'Āmirī, a celebrated poet in the time of Muḥammad who embraced Islām, and who is said to have died at al-Kūfah at the advanced age of 157 years. The Prophet is related to have said, "The truest words ever uttered by a poet are those of Labīd,—'Know that everything is vanity but God.'" (*Mishkāt*, book xxxii. ch. x. pt. 1.) [POETRY.]

LAḤD (لحد). The hollow made in a grave on the Qiblah side, in which the corpse is placed. It is made the same length as the grave, and is as high as would allow a person to sit up in it.

LĀHŪT (لاهوت). *Lit.* "Extinction" or "absorption." (1) The last stage of the mystic journey. (2) Divinity. (3) Life penetrating all things. [SUFIISM.]

LAḤYĀN (لحيان). A branch of the Huzail tribe, which inhabited, in the days of Muḥammad, as they still do, the vicinity of Makkah. Muhammad formed an expedition against them, A.H. 6, on account of their treacherous attack on a small party of Muslims at Rajī.

LAILATU 'L - BARĀ'AH (ليلة البراءة). [SHAB-I-BARA'AH.]

al-LAILATU 'L-MUBĀRAKAH (الليلة المباركة). *Lit.* "The Blessed Night." [LAILATU 'L-QADR.]

LAILATU 'L-QADR (ليلة القدر). "The night of power." A mysterious night, in the month of Ramaẓān, the precise date of which is said to have been known only to the Prophet and a few of the Companions. The following is the allusion to it in the Qur'ān. Sūratu 'l-Qadr (xcvii.):—

"Verily we have caused it (the Qur'ān) to descend on the *Lailatu 'l-Qadr*.

"Who shall teach thee what the Lailatu 'l-Qadr is?

"The Lailatu 'l-Qadr excelleth a thousand months:

"Therein descend the angels, and the spirit by permission

"Of their Lord in every matter;

"And all is peace until the breaking of the dawn."

This night must not be confounded, as it often is, with the Shab-i-Barā'ah, which is generally called Shab-i-Qadr, or the night of power, but which occurs on the 15th of Sha'bān. [SHAB-I-BARA'AH.]

The excellences of the Lailatu 'l-Qadr are said to be innumerable, and it is believed that during its solemn hours the whole animal and vegetable creation bow down in humble adoration to the Almighty.

LAILATU 'R-RAGHĀ'IB (ليلة الرغائب).

The "night of supererogatory devotions." A festival observed on the first Friday in the month Rajab, by certain mystic leaders who affirm that it was established by the Prophet; but it is generally rejected by orthodox Sunnīs. (See *Raddu 'l-Muḥtār*, vol. i. p. 717.)

LAIS̤ (ليث).

An Arabic tribe descended from Kinānah. Al-Baiẓāwī says they thought it unlawful for a man to eat alone, and were the cause of the verse in the Qur'ān, Sūrah xxiv. 60: "There is no crime in you, whether ye eat together or separately."

LAMENTATION. [BUKA'.]

LA'NAH (لعنة).

"Imprecation; curse; anathema." A word used thirteen times in the Qur'ān, *e.g.* Sūrah ii. 83: "The curse of God is on the infidels."

LAND. Arabic *arẓ* (ارض), *balad* (بلد), *mulk* (ملك).

The following are some of the principal rules of Muslim law relating to land:—

(1) *Tithes or Zakāt on lands.*—Upon every thing produced from the ground there is due a tenth, or *'āshir*, *'ushr* (Heb. מַעֲשֵׂר), whether the soil be watered by the annual overflow of great rivers, or by periodical rains; excepting upon articles of wood, bamboos, and grass, which are not subject to tithe. Land watered by means of buckets or machinery, such as Persian wheels, or by watering camels, are subject to only *half* tithes. (*Hidāyah*, vol. i. p. 44.)

(2) *Conquered lands* become the property of the state. Those of idolaters remain so. Those belonging to Jews, Christians, or Fire worshippers, are secured to the owners on payment of tribute. Those who afterwards embrace Islām recover their property, according to ash-Shāfi'ī, but not according to the Ḥanīfah school. Upon the Muslim army evacuating an enemy's country, it becomes unlawful for the troops to feed their cattle on the land without due payment. (*Hidāyah*, vol. ii. p. 170.)

(3) *Appropriation for religious uses.*—Land may be so appropriated; but if a person appropriate land for such a purpose and it should afterwards be discovered that an indefinite portion of it was the property of another person, the appropriation is void with respect to the remainder also. The appropriation must also be of a *perpetual* and not of a temporary nature. (*Hidāyah*, vol. ii. p. 340.)

(4) *The sale of land is lawful.* In such sales the trees upon the land are included in the sale, whether specified or not; but neither the grain growing on the ground, nor the fruit growing on the trees, are included, unless specified. But in the case of the fruit or corn being purchased with the land, it must be gathered or cleared away at once. In the sale of ground, the seed sown in the ground is not included. Land may be resold previous to seizin' or possession, by the first purchaser, according to Abū Ḥanīfah, but the Imām Muḥammad says it is unlawful. Wells and watercourses are not included in the sale of lands unless specified. (*Hidāyah*, vol. ii. pp. 372, 481, 503.)

(5) *Claims against land* must be made by the plaintiff, defining the four boundaries and specifying the names of each possessor, and the demand for the land must be made in explicit terms. And if the land has been resold, a decree must be given either for or against the last possessor, according to some doctors. (*Hidāyah*, vol. iii. p. 65.)

(6) *Land can be lent*, and the borrower can build upon it, but when the lender receives back his land, he can compel the borrower to remove his houses and trees. Land lent for tillage cannot be resumed by the lender until the crops sown have been reaped.' Abū Ḥanīfah maintains that when land is lent to another, the contract should be in these words, "You have given me to eat of this land." (*Hidāyah*, vol. iii. p. 284, 288.)

(7) *A gift of land* which is uncultivated cannot be retracted after houses have been built on it or trees planted. If the donee sell half of the granted land, the donor in that case may, if he wishes, resume the other half. If a person make a gift of land to his relative within the prohibited degrees it is not lawful for him to resume it. (*Hidāyah*, vol. iii. p. 302.)

(8) *The Ijārah, or rental of land, is lawful*, but the period must be specified, otherwise the rent may be demanded from day to day. But a lease of land is not lawful unless mention is made of the article to be raised upon it, and at the expiration of the lease the land must be restored in its original state. A hirer of land is not responsible for accidents; for example, if in burning off the stubble he happen to burn other property, he is not responsible for loss incurred. (*Hidāyah*, vol. iii. p. 314, &c.)

(9) *The cultivation of waste and unclaimed lands* is lawful, when it is done with the permission of the ruler of the country, and the act of cultivation invests the cultivator with a right of property in them. But if the land be not cultivated for three years after it has been allotted, it may again be claimed by the state. (*Hidāyah*, vol. iv. p. 128.)

(10) *If a person be slain on lands* belonging to anyone, and situated near a village, and the proprietor of the land be not an inhabitant of the village, he is responsible for the murder, as the regulation and protection of those lands rest upon him. (*Hidāyah*, vol. iv. p. 447.)

LAPIDATION. [STONING.]

LAPWING. Arabic *hudhud* (هدهد).

The name in the Qur'ān, Sūrah xxvii. 20, for the bird which carried the letter from King

Solomon to the Queen of Sheba. [SOLOMON.] It is the דּוּכִיפַת of the Old Testament, Lev. xi. 19, Deut. xiv. 18. Greek ἔποψ. The modern Hoopoe.

The commentators al-Jalālān and al-Baiẓāwī say that Solomon, having finished the temple of Jerusalem, went in pilgrimage to Makkah, whence, having stayed as long as he pleased, he proceeded towards al-Yaman; leaving Makkah in the morning, he arrived by noon at Ṣan‘ā’, and being extremely delighted with the country, rested there. But wanting water to make the ablution, he looked among the birds for the lapwing, whose business it was to find it; for it is pretended she was sagacious or sharp-sighted to discover water underground, which the devils used to draw, after she had marked the place by digging with her bill. They add that this bird was then taking a tour in the air, whence, seeing one of her companions alighting, she descended also, and having had a description given her by the other of the city of Saba’, whence she was just arrived, they both went together to take a view of the place, and returned soon after Solomon had made the inquiry given in the Qur’ān: "He reviewed the birds and said, 'How is it I do not see *al-Hudhud?* Is he, then, amongst the absent?'"

LAQAB (لقب). A surname. Either a title of honour or a nickname; *e.g.* Al-Ḥusain ibn Mas‘ūd *al-Farrā*, "the tanner"; Abū Sa‘īd *Tāju 'l-Mulūk*, "the crown of kings"; Ibn Muḥammad *at-Taghlabī*, "of the tribe of Taghlab." [NAMES.]

LAQĪṬ (لقيط), in its primitive sense, signifies anything lifted from the ground, but in the language of the law it signifies a child abandoned by those to whom it properly belongs. The person who finds the child is termed the *multaqiṭ*, or the taker up. [FOUNDLING.]

LARCENY. Arabic *sariqah* (سرقة). In the language of the law, *sariqah* signifies the taking away the property of another in a secret manner, at a time when such property is in custody. Custody is of two kinds: 1st, by place, for example, a house or a shop; and, 2nd, by personal guard, which is by means of a personal watch over the property. If an adult of sound understanding steal out of undoubted custody ten dirhams, or property to the value of ten dirhams, the Muḥammadan law awards the amputation of a hand, for it is said in the Qur’ān, Sūrah v. 42: "If a man or woman steal, cut off their hands."

With regard to the amount of the value which constitutes a theft, there is some difference of opinion. According to Abū Ḥanīfah, it is ten dirhams; according to ash-Shāfi‘ī, it is the fourth of a dīnār, or twelve dirhams; whilst Mālik holds that the sum is three dirhams.

The freeman and the slave are on equal footing with respect to punishment for theft, and the hand of the slave is to be struck off in the same manner as the hand of a free Muslim.

The theft must be established upon the testimony of two witnesses, but the magistrate must examine the witnesses as to the manner, time, and place of the theft. The thief must also be held in confinement, or suspicion, until the witnesses be fully examined.

If a party commit a theft, and each of the party receive ten dirhams, the hand of each is to be cut off; but if they receive less than ten dirhams each, they are not liable to amputation.

Amputation is not incurred by the theft of anything of a trifling nature, such as wood, bamboos, grass, fish, fowls, and garden stuff.

Amputation is not incurred by the theft of such things as quickly decay and spoil, such as milk or fruit, nor for stealing fruit whilst upon the tree, or grain which has not been reaped, these not being considered as in custody.

The hand of a thief is not struck off for stealing any fermented liquor, because he may explain his intention in taking it, by saying, "I took it with a view to spill it"; and also because some fermented liquors are not lawful property.

The hand is not to be cut off for stealing a guitar or tabor, these being of use merely as idle amusements.

Amputation is not incurred by stealing a Qur’ān, although ash-Shāfi‘ī maintains that it is.

There is no amputation for stealing the door of a mosque. Nor is the hand struck off for stealing a crucifix or a chess board, as it is in the thief's power to excuse himself by saying, "I took them with a view to break and destroy them, as things prohibited." It is otherwise with a coin bearing the impression of an idol, by the theft of which amputation is incurred; because the money is not an object of worship.

The hand is not to be struck off for stealing a free-born infant, although there be ornaments upon it, because a free person is not property; but amputation is incurred by stealing an infant slave, although the stealing of an adult slave does not incur amputation, as such an act does not come under the description of theft, being an usurpation or a fraud.

Amputation is not incurred for stealing a book, because the object of the thief can only be its contents and not the property.

The hand is not cut off for stealing a cur-dog, because such an animal is common property; nor for stealing utensils made of wood.

There is no amputation for stealing from the public treasury, because everything there is the common property of all Muslims, and in which the thief, as a member of the community has a share. And if a person steal from property of which he is in part owner, amputation is not inflicted. Nor if a creditor steal from his debt is the hand cut off.

The right hand of the thief is to be cut off at the joint of the wrist and the stump afterwards cauterised, and for the second theft the left foot, and for any theft beyond that he must suffer imprisonment.

AL-LĀT (اللات). The name of an idol worshipped by the ancient Arabians, probably the *Alilat* of Herodotus. The idol Lāt is mentioned in the Qur'ān in conjunction with the two other idols, *al-'Uzzā* and *Manāt*. See Sūrah liii. 19: "What think ye, then, of al-Lāt and al-'Uzzā, and Manāt, the third idol besides?"

In connection with this verse there is an interesting discussion. (See Muir, new ed. p. 86.) Al-Wāqidī and aṭ-Ṭabarī both relate that, on a certain day, the chief men of Makkah assembled in a group beside the Ka'bah, discussed, as was their wont, the affairs of the city, when the Prophet appeared, and seating himself by them in a friendly manner, began to recite the 53rd chapter of the Qur'ān; and when he had reached the verse "What think ye then of al-Lāt, and al-'Uzzā, and Manāt, the third idol besides?" the Devil suggested words of reconciliation and compromise with idolatry, namely, "These are exalted females, and verily their intercession is to be hoped for." These words, however, which were received by the idolaters with great delight, were afterwards disavowed by the Prophet, for Gabriel revealed to him the true reading, namely, "What think ye then of al-Lāt, and al-'Uzzā, and Manāt, the third idol besides? Shall ye have male progeny and God female? This, then, were an unjust partition! Verily, these are mere names which ye and your fathers have given them."

The narrative thus related by al-Wāqidī and aṭ-Ṭabarī is given as an explanation of Sūrah xxii. 51: "Nor have we sent any apostle or prophet before thee into whose readings Satan hath not injected some wrong desire."

AL-LATĪF (اللطيف). "The Mysterious or the Subtle One." One of the ninety-nine attributes of God. Sūrah vi. 103: "For He is the Subtle (*al-Laṭīf*), the All-informed (*al-Khabīr*).

LAṬĪFAH (لطيفة). A term used by Ṣūfī mystics for any sign or influence in the soul, derived from God, which has such a mysterious effect on the heart that mortal man cannot express it in language, just as a delicious taste in the mouth cannot be exactly expressed by the tongue. (*Kitābu 't-Ta'rīfāt, in loco.*)

LAUGHING. Arabic *ẓaḥk*, *ẓiḥk* (ضحك). Heb. צָחַק. (Gen. xviii. 13.) Immoderate laughing is generally condemned by Muḥammadan teachers, for 'Āyishah relates that Muḥammad "never laughed a full laugh so that the inside of his mouth could be seen; he only smiled." (*Mishkāt*, book xxii. ch. vii.)

AL-LAUḤU 'L-MAḤFŪẒ (اللوح المحفوظ). "The preserved tablet." In the Ḥadīs̤ and in theological works it is used to denote the tablet on which the decrees of God were recorded with reference to mankind. In the Qur'ān it only occurs once, when it refers to the Qur'ān itself. Sūrah lxxxv. 21, 22: "It is a glorious Qur'ān written on the *preserved table*." The plural *alwāḥ* occurs in Sūrah vii. 142, for the tables of the law given to Moses.

LAW, The. The words used by Muslims to express "the law," are *ash-Sharī'ah* (الشريعة) and *ash-Shar'* (الشرع), the meaning of which is "the way." The compiler of the *Ghiyās̤u'l-Lughah* defines it as "the *way* or *road* in the religion of Muḥammad, which God has established for the guidance of His people, both for the worship of God and for the duties of life." The term *ash-Sharī'ah* occurs once in the Qur'ān, Sūrah xlv. 17: "We (God) put thee (Muḥammad) in the *right way* concerning the affair." The term *ash-Shir'ah* is almost obsolete in books on Muslim theology, but it occurs once in the Qur'ān, Sūrah v. 52: "To every one have we given a *right way*."

In the Traditions and theological works, the word *ash-Shar'* is generally used to express the law of Muhammad. The Hebrew תּוֹרָה occurs in the Qur'ān as *Taurāt*, and is always used for the law of Moses. [TAURAT.]

According to Muslim doctors, *ash-Shar'*, or "the Law," may be divided into five sections: *I'tiqādāt*, "belief"; *Ādāb*, "moralities"; *'Ibādāt*, "devotions"; *Mu'āmalāt*, "transactions"; and *'Uqūbāt*, "punishments."

(1) *I'tiqādāt*, embraces all that is contained in the six articles of the Muslim faith, namely, Belief in (*a*) God; (*b*) His angels; (*c*) His Books; (*d*) His Prophets; (*e*) The Day of Judgment; (*f*) The Decrees of God. This section of Muslim law is termed *'Ilmu 'l-'Aqā'id*, or, "The Science of the Articles of Belief," and includes all branches of scholastic theology. The books chiefly consulted on this subject in the present work are the *Sharḥu 'l-Muwāqif*, by Saiyid Sharīf-al-Jurjānī, and the *Sharḥu 'l-'Aqā'id*, by Mas'ūd Sa'du 'd-dīn at-Taftāzānī.

(2) *Ādāb* embraces the consideration of all

those moral excellences which are enjoined in the Qur'ān and Traditions, as *Ikhlāṣ*, "sincerity"; *Tawwakkul*, "confidence in God"; *Tawāẓuʻ*, "humility"; *Tafwīẓ*, "resignation"; *Qaṣru 'l-ʻAmal*, "keeping down one's expectation"; *Zuhd fī 'd-dunyā*, "renunciation of the world"; *Naṣīḥah*, "giving good counsel and advice"; *Qanāʻah*, "contentment;" *Sakhāwah*, "liberality;" *Ḥubb*, "love to God and man"; *Ṣabr*, "patience"; &c. (See *Majmaʻu 'l-Biḥār*, vol. ii. p. 422.)

(3) *ʻIbādāt*, includes all acts of devotion to God, such as are included in the five pillars of practice: (*a*) Recital of the Creed; (*b*) Prayer; (*c*) *Zakāt*, or "legal alms"; (*d*) *Saum*, or "fasting"; (*e*) The pilgrimage to Makkah. It will also embrace such religious acts as *Jihād*, or warfare for the propagation of the religion of Islām.

(4) *Muʻāmalāt*, includes such duties as are required between man and man, and is divided into *Mukhāṣamāt*, "altercations"; *Munākaḥāt*, "nuptials"; *Amānāt*, "securities." Under these three heads are embraced all the various sections of civil jurisprudence such as barter, sale, agency, larceny, marriage, divorce, dower, partnership, claims, &c.

(5) *ʻUqūbāt*, denotes the punishments instituted in the Qur'ān and Traditions, namely, (*a*) *Qiṣāṣ*, "retaliation"; (*b*) *Ḥaddu 's-sariqah*, punishment for theft by the loss of a hand; (*c*) *Ḥaddu 'z-zinā'*, punishment for fornication and adultery, stoning for a married person and one hundred lashes for an unmarried person; (*e*) *Ḥaddu 'l-qazf*, or punishment of eighty lashes for slander; *Ḥaddu 'r-riddah*, or punishment by death for apostasy; *Ḥaddu 'sh-shurb*, or punishment with eighty lashes for wine-drinking.

The two common divisions of Muḥammadan law are *ʻIlmu 'l-Kalām*, or *ʻAqā'id*, embracing all matters of faith; and *ʻIlmu 'l-Fiqh*, which includes all matters of practice as distinguished from articles of faith.

Muslim law is also divided into two great distinctions of *Mashrūʻ*, "lawful," and *Ghairu 'l-mashrūʻ*, unlawful," or, as it is expressed in Persian, *Rawā* and *Nārawā*.

That which is lawful is graded into five classes. (1) *Farẓ*, that which is proved beyond all doubt to have been enjoined either in the Qur'ān or in a tradition of undoubted authority, and the denial or disobedience of which is positive infidelity. (2) *Wājib*, that which is obligatory, but of which there is some doubt whether or not it was enjoined in the Qur'ān or in a tradition of undoubted authority. (3) *Sunnah*, that which was practised by Muḥammad; (4) *Mustāḥabb*, that which Muḥammad and his Companions sometimes did and sometimes omitted; (5) *Mubāḥ*, that which is desirable, but which may be omitted without fear of sin.

Things which are unlawful are graded into three classes: (1) *Mufsid*, that which is most vicious and corrupting, a mortal sin; (2) *Ḥarām*, that which is distinctly forbidden; (3) *Makrūh*, that which is generally held to be unclean.

These distinctions of lawful and unlawful, with their various subdivisions, apply to all branches of Muslim law, whether it relate to ordinary duties of life, or of devotion to God.

It will be seen how important a place the example, practices, and sayings of Muḥammad occupy in the moral law of Islām. This branch of Muslim law is called *as-Sunnah*, or the custom of Muḥammad, and is distinguished as—

(1) *Sunnatu 'l-fiʻlī*, that which Muḥammad himself *did*.

(2) *Sunnatu 'l-qaulī*, that which Muḥammad *said* should be practised.

(3) *Sunnatu 't-taqrīrī*, that which was done in the presence of Muḥammad, and which he appears to have sanctioned.

It is therefore a serious mistake to suppose that the Qur'ān contains all that is esteemed necessary for faith and practice in Islām; the example of Muḥammad is as binding upon the Muslim as any injunction contained in the Qur'ān itself, for neither that which is *Farẓ* nor that which is *Sunnah* can be omitted without sin.

The true origin and fountain of all law is the Qur'ān and the Traditions, and no Muslim school of theology has ever rejected the Traditions. They are binding upon Sunnī, and Shīʻah, and Wahhābī; the only difference between the Sunnī and Shīʻah being that they receive different collections of Traditions. The Wahhābīs receive those of the Sunnīs, and call themselves *Muḥaddiṣin*, or traditionists.

In addition to the Qur'ān and Hadīṣ (or Traditions), both Sunnī and Shīʻah Muslims acknowledge the concurrence of the learned, called *Ijmāʻ*, the Shīʻahs believing that they still possess Mujtahids capable of giving an infallible interpretation of the law; the Sunnīs, on the other hand, confessing that, since the days of the four great doctors (Abū Ḥanīfah, Mālik, ash-Shāfiʻī, and Ibn Ḥanbal), *Ijmāʻ* has not been possible; whilst the Wahhābīs accept only the *Ijmāʻ* of those who conversed with the Prophet himself. The fourth foundation of orthodoxy in both Sunnī and Shīʻah schools is the system of interpretation called *Qiyāṣ*, or ratiocination.

I. *The Sunnīs* all receive the same collections of traditions, especially those which are known as the "six correct books," the *Ṣaḥīḥu 'l-Bukhārī*, the *Saḥīḥu Muslim*, the *Sunanu 't-Tirmiẓī*, *Sunanu Abī Dā'ūd*, *Sunanu an-Nasafī*, and *Sunanu Ibn Mājah*. The compilation by the Imām Mālik, which is first in order of date, is also a collection of traditions of very great authority. [TRADITIONS.]

These different sects of Sunnīs do not differ in *uṣūl*, or fundamentals of religious belief, but in minor rules of practice, and in certain legal interpretations; but being of different opinions and broaching in some respects separate doctrines, four schools of jurisprudence have been established, known as *Ḥanafī*, *Shāfiʻī*, *Ḥanbalī*, and *Mālikī*.

The differences amongst these four Sunnī schools are based either upon different traditions or upon different interpretations of the same traditions, also upon the various ways in which the liberty of *qiyāṣ*, or ratiocination, has been exercised. Consequently the number of works which have appeared on the subjects of scholastic science and jurisprudence, has been very great indeed.

We are indebted to Mr. Shama Churun Sircar, the learned and able Tagore Professor of Law in Calcutta, for the following *résumé* of the principal Sunnī writings on *ash-Shar'*.

"The chief works that treat generally of the doctrines of the four principal sects of the Sunnís, are mentioned by Hájí Khalífah to be the *Jámi-ul-Mazáhib* (*Jāmi'u 'l-Maẕā-hib*), the *Majmaa-ul-Khiláfíyat*, the *Yanábiya-ul-Ahkám* (*Yanābī'u 'l-Aḥkām*), the *Uyún*, and the *Zubdat-ul-Ahkám*. The *Kanz-ud-Dakáik* (*Kanzu 'd-Daqā'iq*), by An-Nasafí, is a book of great reputation, principally derived from the *Wáfí*; and containing questions and decisions according to the doctrines of Abú-Hanífah, Abú-Yusuf, Imám Muhammad, Zufar, Sháfií, Málik, and others. Many commentaries have been written on the last mentioned work; the most famous of them is the *Bahr-ur-Ráik* (*al-Baḥru 'r-Rā'iq*), which may, indeed, almost be said to have superseded its original, at least in India. The *Bahr-ur-Ráik* is by Zainu-ul-Áábidín Bin Nujaim-ul Misrí (Ibn Najīm), A.H. 970. The *Multaka-al-Abhár* (*Multaqa 'l-Abḥār*), by Shaikh Ibráhím Bin Muhammad al-Halabí, who died A.H. 956, is a universal code of Muhammadan law. It gives the different opinions or doctrines of Abú Hanífah, Málik, Sháfií, and Hanbal, the chief Mujtahid Imáms and the founders of the four great sects of Sunnís, and illustrates them by those of the principal jurisconsults of the school of Abú Hanífah. It is more frequently referred to as an authority throughout Turkey, than any other treatise on jurisprudence.

"The digests inculcating exclusively the doctrines of each of the said four great sects are, indeed, numerous, though a very few of them which maintain the doctrines of the Málikí, or Sháfií, or Hanbalí sects are used in India. Digests written by Málik or any of his followers are scarcely found in India.

"Of the digests maintaining the Málikí doctrines, two have lately appeared in France (by M. Vincent, 1842; M. Perron, 1843). The first work of Sháfií, entitled the *Usúl* (*Uṣūl*), or fundamentals, which contains the principles of the Muhammadan civil and canon law, may be classed as a digest. The *Mukhtasar*, the *Mansúr*, the *Rasáil-ul-Muatabirah* (*ar-Rasā'ilu 'l-Mu'tabarah*), and the *Kitáb-ul-Wasáik*, are amongst the other works written by Abú Ibráhím Bin Yahiyá-al-Muzani, a distinguished disciple of Sháfií, and a native of Egypt (A.H. 264), and are according to the doctrines of Sháfií. The works by Ibnu Hambal and his followers are few in number, and rare.

"The followers of the Haníff sect, which obtains most commonly amongst the Muhammadans of India, have, like others, divided their law into two general branches or parts, respectively called the Fikah (law, religious and secular), and Faráïz (the succession to, and division of, inheritance).

"The works which are on Fikah (*Fiqh*), and which are considered as the chief authorities of the Haníff sect, are the following:—Abú Hanífah's own digest of law, entitled the *Fikah-ul-Akbar* (*al-Fiqhu'l-Akbar*). This is the first in rank, and has been commented upon by various writers, many of whom are mentioned by Hájí Khalífah. The doctrines of that great lawyer, however, are sometimes qualified or dissented from by his two famous pupils, Abú Yusuf and Imám Muhammad. The work entitled *Adab-ul-Kází*, which treats of the duties of a magistrate, is known to have been written by Abú Yusuf. Save and except this, no other work appears to have been composed by him. He, however, is said to have supplied his notes to his pupil Imám Muhammad, who made use of them in the composition of his own works. The works of Imám Muhammad are six in number, five of which are, in common, entitled the *Záhir-ur-Rawáyát* (*Ẓāhiru 'r-Rawāyāt*, conspicuous traditions or reports). They are: 1. The *Jámi-ul-Kabír* (*al-Jāmi'u 'l-Kabīr*); 2. *Jámi-us-Saghír* (*al-Jāmi'u 's-Ṣaghīr*); 3. *Mabsút fí Farú-ul-Haníflyát*; 4. *Ziyádát fi Farú-ul-Haníflyát*; and 5. *Siyar al-Kabír wa Saghír*. The *Nawádir*, the sixth and last of the known compositions of Imám Muhammad, though not so highly esteemed as the others, is still greatly respected as an authority.

"The next authorities among the Hanafís, after the founder of their sect and his two disciples, are the Imám Zufar Bin al-Hazíl who was chief judge at Basrah, where he died (A.H. 158), and Hasan Bin Ziyád. These lawyers are said to have been contemporaries, friends, and scholars of Abú-Hanífah, and their works are quoted here as authorities for Abú Hanífah's doctrines, more especially when the two disciples are silent. The most celebrated of the several treatises known by the name of *Adáb-ul Kází* was written by Abú Bakr Ahmad Bin 'Umar ul-Khassáf (A.H. 261). An abridgement of the Hanafí doctrines, called the *Mukhtasar ut-Tahaví*, was written by Abú Jaafar Ahmad Bin Muhammad at-Tahaví (A.H. 331), who wrote also a commentary on the *Jámi us-Saghír* of Imám Muhammad.

"The *Mukhtasar lil-Kudúrí*, by Abú ul-Husain Ahmad Bin Muhammad al-Kudúrí (A.H. 228) is among the most esteemed of the works which follow the doctrines of Abú Hanífah. There is a well-known commentary on the *Mukhtasar lil-Kudúrí*, entitled *Al-Jauharat un-Nayyirah*, which is sometimes called *Al-Jauharat ul-Munírah*. The digest, entitled the *Mabsút* (*al-Mabsūṭ*), was composed by Shams-ul-Aïmmah Abú Bakr Muhammad as-Sarakhsi whilst in prison at U'zjand. This is a work of great extent and authority. He was also the author of the most celebrated work entitled *Al-Muhít* (*al-Muḥīṭ*), which is derived in a great measure from the *Mabsút*, the *Ziyádát*, and the *Nawádir* of Imám Muhammad. The work entitled the *Muhít*, by Burhán-ud-dín Mahmúd Bin Ahmad, already spoken of, is not so greatly esteemed as the *Muhít as-Sarakhsi* (*Muḥīṭu 'ṣ-Ṣarakhsī*). A compendium of Al-Kudúrí's *Mukhtasar*, which he entitled the *Tuhfat-ul-Fukahá* (*Tuḥfatu 'l-Fuqahā'*), was composed by Shaikh Alá-ud-dín Muhammad as-Samarkandí. The work of Alá-ud-dín was commented upon by his pupil Abú Bakr Bin Masuúd.

"There are several Arabic works on philosophical and theological subjects which bear the name of *Al-Hidáyah* (the guide). The work entitled *Al-Hidáyah fí-al-Farú*, or the guide in particular points, is a digest of law according to the doctrines of Abú Hanífah and his disciples Abú Yusuf and Imám Muhammad. The author of this work is Shaikh Burhán-ud-dín Alí (A.H. 593), whose reputation as a lawyer was beyond that of all his contemporaries. This *Hidáyah* is a commentary on the *Badáya-ul-Mubtadá*, an introduction to the study of law, written by the same author in a style exceedingly concise and close. In praise of the *Hidáyah*, Hájí Khalífah says, 'It has been declared, like the *Kurán*, to have superseded all previous books on the law; that all persons should remember the rules prescribed in it, and that it should be followed as a guide through life.' The *Hidáyah* has, besides the *Kifáyah*, many other commentaries, as a work of so great celebrity and authority is expected to have. The principal ones are the *Ináyah* (*'Ināyah*), the *Niháyah*, and the *Fath-ul-Kabír*.

"The name *Ináyah*, however, is given to two commentaries on the *Hidáyah*. Of these, the one composed by Shaikh Kamál-ud-dín Muhammad Bin Mahmúd, who died A.H. 786, is highly esteemed and useful. Supplying by way of innuendoes what was omitted or left to implication, also expressing what was understood in the *Hidáyah*, and explaining the words and expounding the passages of the original by the insertion of explanatory phrases, the author of the *Ináyah* has rendered the work such as to be considered of itself one of his own principal works, with citations of passages from the *Hidáyah*.

"The *Niháyah* is composed by Husám-ud-dín Husain Bin Alí, who is said to have been a pupil of Burhán-ud-dín Alí. This is said to be the first commentary composed on the *Hidáyah*; and it is important for having added the law of inheritance to the *Hidáyah*, which treats only of the Fikah. The commentary, entitled the *Kifáyah*, is by Imám-ud-dín Amír Kátib Bin Amír Umar, who had previously written another explanatory gloss of the same work, and entitled it the *Ghávat-ul-Bayán* The *Kifáyah* was finished A.H. 747, and, besides the author's own observations, it gives concisely the substance of other commentaries.

"The *Fath-ul-Kabír lil-Aájiz ul-Fakír*, by Kamál-ud-dín Muhammad as-Siwásí, commonly called Ibnu Hammám, who died A.H. 861, is the most comprehensive of all the comments on the *Hidáyah*, and includes a collection of decisions which render it extremely useful. The short commentary entitled the *Fawáid*, written by Hamíd-ud-dín Alí, Al-Bukhárí, who died A.H. 667, is said to be the first of all the commentaries on the *Hidáyah*. The *Wáfí*, by Abú-ul-Barakát Abd ullah Bin Ahmad, commonly called Háfiz-ud-dín an-Nasafí, and its commentary the *Káfí*, by the same author, are works of authority. An-Nasafí died A.H. 710.

"The *Vikáyah* (*al-Wiqāyah*), which was written in the seventh century of the Hijrah by Burhán ash-Shariyat Mahmúd, is an elementary work to enable the student to study and understand the *Hidáyah*. The *Vikáyah* is printed, and invariably studied, with its celebrated commentary, the *Sharh ul-Vikáyah*, written by Ubaidullah Bin Masuúd, who died A.H. 745. The *Sharh-ul-Vikáyah* contains the text of the *Vikáyah*, with a gloss most perspicuously explanatory and illustrative; so much so, that those chapters of it which treat of marriage, dower, and divorce, are studied in the Madrassahs of India in preference to the *Hidáyah* itself. There are also other commentaries on the *Vikáyah*, but not so useful as the above. On the *Sharh-ul-Vikáyah*, again, there is an excellent commentary, entitled the *Chalpí*, written by Akhí Yusuf Bin Juníd, who was one of the then eight professors at Constantinople. This work was commenced to be written about A.H. 891, and completed A.H. 901; and the whole of it was published in Calcutta A.H. 1245, and extracts therefrom have been printed.

"The *Nikáyah* (*an-Niqāyah*), another elementary law book, is the work of the author of the *Sharh-ul-Vikáyah*. It is sometimes called the *Mukhtasar ul-Vikáyah*, being, in fact, an abridgment of that work. Three comments on the *Nikayah* are much esteemed; they were written respectively by Abú ul-Makárim Bin Abd-ullah (A.H. 907), Abú Alí Bin Muhammad al-Birjindí (A.H. 935), and Shams ud-dín Muhammad al-Khurásání Al-Kohistání (A.H. 941). The last commentary is entitled the *Jámi-ur-Rumūz* (*Jāmi'u 'r-Rumūz*), which is the fullest and the clearest of the lot, as well as one of the most useful law books.

"The *Ashbah wa an-Nazáïr* (*al-Ashbāh wa 'n-Naẓā'ir*) is also an elementary work of great reputation. It was composed by Zain-al-Aábidín, the author of the *Bahr-ur-Ráïk* already mentioned. Hájí Khalífah speaks of this work in high terms, and enumerates several appendices to it that have been composed at different times. The treatise on exegesis entitled the *Núr-ul-Anwár fi Sharah ul-Manár* (*Nūru 'l-Anwār fī Sharḥi 'l-Manār*), by Shaikh Jún Bin Abú Sayyid Al-Makkí (Shaikh Jīwan ibn Abū Sa'īd), was printed in Calcutta (A.D. 1819), and is frequently referred to as a book of authority. A small tract on the sources of the Sharaa, entitled the *Usúl-ush-Sháshí*, together with an explanatory commentary, was printed in lithography, at Delhi, in the year A.D. 1847.

"The *Tanvír-ul-Absár* (*Tanwīru 'l-Abṣār*), composed by Shaikh Shams-ud-dín Muhammad Bin Abd-ullah-al-Ghazzí (A.H. 995), is one of the most celebrated and useful books according to the Haníf í doctrines. This work has many commentaries. One of them, entitled the *Manh-ul-Ghaffár* (*Manḥu 'l-G͟haffār*), which is written by the author himself, is a work of considerable extent.

"The *Durr-ul-Mukhtár*, which is another commentary on the *Tanvír-ul-Absár*, is a work of great celebrity. This work was written (A.H. 1071) by Muhammad Alá-ud-Dín Bin Shaikh Alí al-Hiskafí. Though a commentary, it is virtually a digest, which of itself has several commentaries, the most celebrated of them is the *Tahtáví*, a work used in India. Another commentary on the *Durr-ul-Mukhtár* is the *Radd-ul-Muhtár*. This is a very copious work, comprising an immense number of cases and decisions illustrative of the principles contained in the principal work. The *Durr-ul-Mukhtár* treats not only of the Fikah but also of the Faráïz. It is used by the followers of the Haníf í doctrines wherever they are, but it is most highly esteemed in Arabia, where it is studied and referred to in preference to other books of law.

"Many works have been written according to the doctrines of Abú Haníffah in the Turkish Empire, and are received there as authorities. The most celebrated of those is the *Multaka-ul-Abhár*, by Shaikh Ibráhím Bin Muhammad al-Halabí, the *Durr-ul-Hukkám*, by Mullah Khusrú, *Kánún-námai-Jazá*, a tract on penal laws, &c.

"The treatises on the laws of inheritance, according to the doctrines of Sháfií, are the *Faráïz-ul-Mutawallí*, by Abú Sayíd Abd-ur-Rahmān Bin Mamun-ul-Mutawalli (who died A.H. 478), the *Faráïz-ul-Mukuddasí*, by Abú-ul-Fazl Abd-ul-Malik Bin Ibráhím al-Hamadání Al-Mukuddasí, and Abú Munsúr Abd-ul-Kahír Al-Baghdádí (who died respectively A.H. 489 and 429); *Al-Faraïz-ul-Fazárí*, by Burhán-ud-dín Abú Isháq Al-Fazárí, commonly called Ibnu Firkáh (who died in A.H. 729), and *Al-Faráïz ul-Farikiyah*, by Shams-ud-dín Muhammad Bin Killáyí (who died A.H. 777).

"Of the books on the law of inheritance according to the Haníf í doctrines, the most celebrated, and the one invariably consulted in India, is the *Sirájiyyah* (*as-Sirājīyah*), which is also called the *Faráïz-us-Sajáwandí*, being, as it is, composed by Siráj-ud-Dín Muhammad bin Abd-ur-Rashíd as-Sajáwandí. This work has been commented upon by a vast number of writers, upwards of forty being enumerated in the *Kashf-uz-Zunún* by Hájí Khalífah. The most celebrated of these commentaries, and the most generally used to explain the text of the *Sirajiyyah*, is the *Sharífiyyah* (*ash-Sharīfiyah*), by Sayyid Sharif Ali Bin Muhammad Al-Jurjání (who died A.H. 814).

"There is another kind of digest which treats of the *Ilm-ul-Fatáwá* (the science of decisions). The works of this nature are also very numerous, and are, for the most part, called *Fatáwá* (decisions), with the names of their authors; and, though called *Fatáwá*, most of them contain also the rules of law as well as legal decisions. Of those again, some treat of the Fikah alone, others of the Faráïz (inheritance) also; some of them, moreover, treat of the decisions of particular lawyers, or those found in particular books; others treat of those which tend to illustrate the doctrines of the several sects; whilst the rest of them are devoted to recording the opinions of learned jurists.

"There are several collections of decisions, according to the doctrines of Sháfií. The one most esteemed seems to be the *Fatáwá Ibn us-Saláh*, by Abú Amru-Usmán Bin Abd-ur Rahmán ash-Sháhrazúrí, commonly called Ibn us-Saláh, who died in A.H. 642. Ibnu Firkáh, the author of the *Faráïz-ul-Fazárí* (a treatise on inheritance), also made a collection of decisions according to the same doctrines, which is called, after his name, the *Fatáwá-i-Ibnu Firkáh*.

"Of the Fatáwás of the Haníf í doctrines the following are generally known in India. The *Khulásat ul-Fatáwá* (*K͟hulāṣatu 'l-Fatāwā*), by Imám Iftikhar-ud-Dín Tahir Bin Ahmad Al-Bukhárí, who died A.H 542, is a select collection of decisions of great authority. The *Zakhírat-ul-Fatáwá* (*Ẕak͟hīratu 'l-Fatāwā*), sometimes called the *Zakhírat-ul-Burhániyah*, by Burhán-ud-Dín Bin Mázah al-Bukhárí, the author of the *Muhít-ul-Burhání*, is also a celebrated, though not a large, collection of decisions, principally taken from the *Muhít*. The *Fatáwá-i-Kází Khán*, by Imám Fakhr-ud-Dín Hasan Bin Mansúr al-U'zjandí al-Farghání, commonly called Kází Khán, who died A.H. 592, is a work held in very high authority. It is replete with cases of common occurence, and is, therefore, of great practical utility, more especially as many of the decisions are illustrated by proofs and reasoning on which they are founded. The two works entitled the *Fusúl-ul-Isturúshí* and *Fusúl-ul-Imádíah*, were incorporated in a collection entitled the *Jámi-ul-Fusúlain*, which is a work of some celebrity. It was compiled by Badr-ud-Dín Muhammad, known by the name of Ibn-ul-Kází Simáwanah (A.H. 823). The *Fatáwá az-Zahíriyah*, which contains decisions collected partly from the *Khizánat-ul-Wákiyát*, was written by Jahír-ud-Dín Abú Bakr Muhammad Bin Ahmad al-Bukhárí (A.H. 619). The *Kuniyat-ul-Muniyat* is a collection of decisions of considerable authority by Mukhtár Bin Mahmúd Bin Muhammad as-Záhidí Abú-ur-Rijá al-Ghazmíní, surnamed Najm-ud-Dín, who died A.H. 658. An-Navaví, the author of the biographical dictionary entitled the *Tahzíb-ul-Asmá* (*Tahẕību 'l-Asmā'*), who died A.H. 677, made a collection of decisions of some note, which is called the *Fatáwá an-Navaví*. He also composed a smaller work of the same nature, entitled *al-Masáïl-ul-Muhimmat* (*'Uyūn al-Masā'ili 'l-Muhimmah*), arranged in the manner of question and answer. The *Khizánat-ul-Muftiyín*, by Imám Husain Bin Muhammad as-Samaání, who completed his work in A.H. 740, contains a large collection of decisions, and is a book of some authority in India. The *Khizánat-ul-Fatáwá*, by Ahmad

Bin Muhammad Abú Bakr al-Hanafí, is a collection of decisions made towards the end of the eighth century of the Hijrah, and comprises questions of rare occurrence. The *Fatáwá Tátár-Kháníyah* was originally a large collection of Fatáwás, in several volumes, by Imám Aálim Bin Alá al-Hanafí, taken from the *Muhít-ul-Burhání*, the *Zakhírat*, the *Kháníyah*, and the *Zahíriyah*. Afterwards, however, a selection was made from these decisions by Imám Ibráhím Bin Muhammad al-Halabí, who died A.H 956, and an epitome was thus formed, which is in one volume, and still retains the title of *Tátár-Kháníyah*. The *Fatáwá-i-Ahl-us-Samarkand*, is a collection of the decisions of those learned men of the city of Samarkand who are omitted, or lightly passed over, in the *Fatáwá-Tátár Kháníyah* and the *Jámi-ul-Fusúlain*, to both of which works it may be considered a supplement. The *Fatáwá az-Zainíyah* contains decisions by Zain ul-Aabidín Ibráhím Bin Nujaim al-Misrí, the author of the *Bahr-ur-Ráik* and the *Ashbah wa-an-Nazáïr*. They were collected by his son Ahmad (about A.H. 970). The *Fatáwá al-Ankiraví*, a collection of decisions of al-Ankiraví by Shaikh-ul-Islám Muhammad Bin al-Husain, who died A.H. 1098, is a work of authority. The *Fatáwá Hammádiyah*, though it seems to be a modern compilation, is a work of considerable authority.

"Tipú Sultán ordered a collection of Fatáwás to be made in Persian by a society of the learned of Mysore. It comprises three hundred and thirteen chapters, and is entitled the *Fatáwá-i-Muhammadí*.

"Mr. Harrington, in his analysis (vol. i. 2nd ed.), mentions a few other books of Fatáwá, viz. the *Fatáwá Bazázíah*, the *Fatáwá Nakshbandiyah*, the *Mukhtár-ul-Fatáwá*, and the *Fatáwá Karákhání*. The last of these he describes to be a Persian compilation, the cases included in which were collected by Mullah Sadar-ud-Dín Bin Yakúb, and arranged some years after his death by Kará Khán, in the reign of Sultán Alá-ud-Dín.

"The following works of the present class, published at Constantinople, and containing decisions according to the doctrines of Abú Hanífah, may be noticed. A collection of Fatwas in the Turkish and Arabic languages, entitled the *Kitáb fi al-Fikah al-Kadúsí*, composed by Hafiz Muhammad Bin Ahmad al-Kadúsí A.H. 1226. The *Fatáwá-i-Abd-ur-Rahím Effendí*, is a collection of judgments pronounced at various times in Turkey, and collected by the Muftí Abd-ur-Rahím. It was printed in the year 1827. Dabagzadeh Nuamán Effendí is the author of a collection of six hundred and seventy decisions, which is entitled the *Tuhfat us-Sukúk*, and was published in the year 1832.

"The *Jámi-ul-Ijáratín (Jámi'u'l-Ijárát)* is a collection of decisions relating to the law of farming and the tenure of land, by Muhammad Aarif. It was printed in the year 1836.

"A collection of Fatwás relating to leases was published at Constantinople by M. D'Adelbourg, in the year 1838. Prefixed to this collection are the principles of the law of lease, according to the *Multaka*; and it is followed by an analytical table, facilitating reference to the various decisions.

"Of the Fatwás which treat both of the Fikah and Faráïz, two are most generally used in India. These are the *Fatáwá Sirujiyyah* and *Fatáwá Alamgírí*. The *Fatáwá Sirájiyyah*, with some principles, contains a collection of decisions on cases which do not generally occur in other books. The *Fatáwá Alamgírí*, with opinions and precepts of law, contains an immense number of law cases. This work, from its comprehensive nature, is applicable to almost every case that arises involving points of the Hanífí doctrines. Although opinions of modern compilers are not esteemed as of equal authority with those of the older writers on jurisprudence, yet being composed by a great number of the most learned lawyers of the age, and by order of the then greatest person of the realm, the Emperor Aurungzeb Alamgir (by whose name the book is designated), the *Fatáwá Alamgírí* is esteemed as a very high authority in India; and containing, as it does, decisions on cases of any shape based upon unquestionable authorities, this book is here referred to more frequently than any other work of a similar nature, and has not up to this day been surpassed by any work, except perhaps, by the *Radd-ul-Muhtár*, already spoken of. During the long rule of the Muhammadans in India, the *Fatáwá Alamgírí* alone appears to have been translated into Persian, by order of Zéb-un-nisá, daughter of the Emperor Arungzeb Alamgír. Since the establishment of the British Government in India, the books of Jináyah and Hudúd from the *Futáwá Alamgírí* were translated into Persian, under the direction of the Council of the College of Fort William in Calcutta, by the then Kází-ul-Kuzzát, Muhammad Najm ud-Dín Khán, and were published in the year 1813, together with a Persian treatise on *Tázírát*, by the same author.

"In the same year the book on *Tázírát* from the *Durr-ul-Mukhtár* was translated, printed, and published, by Moulavi Muhammad Khalíl-ud-Dín, under the orders of Mr. Harrington, the then Chief Judge of the late Sudder Dewany Adawlut.

"The *Hidáyah* was translated into Persian by four of the most learned Moulavis of that time and of this country (India). Unfortunately, however, the learned translators have, in the body of the book, inserted many things by way of explanatory remarks and illustrative expositions, instead of subjoining them in the form of notes. Furthermore, they have, in a considerable degree, deviated from the original. For all these reasons, we are warranted to say, that the Persian version of the *Hidáyah* does not represent a true picture of the original.

"Macnaghten's *Principles of Muhammadan Law* were translated into Urdu and lithographed, many years ago, in Dehli. Another translation of the same work was made and published in Calcutta a few years ago.

"The work entitled the *Bighyat-i-Báhis*, by Al-Mutakannah, which is a tract treating of Zaid's system of Faráïz, was translated into English by Sir William Jones. A translation of the *Sirájiyyah* also was made by Sir William Jones, who at the same time made an abstract translation of its celebrated commentary (the *Sharífiyyah*), with the addition of illustrations and exemplifications from his own brain and pen. A translation of the selected portions from the two books of the *Fatáwá-i-Alamgírí*, which comprise the subject of sale, was published by Mr. Neil Baillie.

"The Persian version of the *Hidáyah*, already noticed, was, by order of Warren Hastings, commenced to be translated into English by Mr. James Anderson, but shortly after, he being engaged in an important foreign employment, the translation was finished, and revised by his colleague, Mr. Charles Hamilton. It is a matter of regret that the translation in question was not executed from the original *Hidáyah* itself, instead of from its Persian translation, which contains frequent explanatory remarks and illustrative expositions interpolated in the book itself, instead of being subjoined by way of notes. Added to this, the Persian translators have, in a considerable degree, deviated from the original.

"Of the digests of Muhammadan law in English, the first appears to be the chapter on criminal law of the Muhammadans as modified by regulations. This is incorporated in Harrington's *Analysis of Bengal Regulations*. An abstract of Muhammadan law, which is from the pen of Lieutenant-Colonel Vans Kennedy, will be found in the *Journal of the Royal Asiatic Society*. 'This work,' says Mr. Morley, 'is well worthy the attention of the student.' The work entitled the *Principles and Precedents of Mudammadan Law*, written by Mr. (afterwards Sir) William Hay Macnaghten, is the clearest or easiest, if not the amplest or sufficient, work on that law hitherto written in English. Mr. Neil Baillie's *Muhammadan Law of Inheritance*, according to Abú Hanífah and his followers, with appendix containing authorities from the original Arabic, is an excellent work of the kind. The treatise on inheritance, gift, will, sale, and mortgage, compiled by Mr. F. E. Elberling, a Danish judge at Serampore, in the year 1844, contains principles of Muhammadan law, with those of the other laws, as used in India.

"In the year 1865, Mr. Neil Baillie, the author of the work already mentioned, completed and published a digest of Muhammadan law on all the subjects to which the Muhammadan law is usually applied by the British Courts of Justice in India. It gives translations of almost all the principles and some of the cases contained in the *Fatáwá Alamgírí*, the great digest of Muhammadan law in India, and quotes occasionally other available authorities. Being generally close to the original, and fully dealing with the subjects it treats of, this work must be said to be authentic, as well as the amplest of the digests of Muhammadan law hitherto written in English according to the doctrines of the Hanifi sect." (See the *Tagore Law Lectures, 1873*, by Shama Churan Sircār; Thacker, Spink & Co., Calcutta.)

II.—*The Shīʿahs*, although they are divided amongst themselves into numerous sects which differ from each other in various points of religious belief, are unanimous in rejecting the collections of Traditions of the Sunnīs. The Sunnīs arrogate to themselves the title of Traditionists, but this does not imply that the Shīʿahs do not receive the Ḥadīs̤, but merely that they reject the "six correct books" of their opponents.

The works on Ḥadīs̤ compiled by the Shīʿahs are very numerous, and they maintain that they have earlier and more authentic collections than those of the Sunnīs. They say that in the time of al-Ḥasan and al-Ḥusain, a certain person who was grandfather to ʿAbdu ʾllāh ibn ʿAlī ibn Abī Shuʿbah al-Ḥalabī, collected traditions and gave them to his grandson for careful record. This record was verified and corrected by Imām Jaʿfar aṣ-Ṣadiq. The Sunnī doctor, Abū Ḥanīfah, was a pupil of this distinguished personage in his earlier days, but afterwards separated from him and established a school of his own.

There are four books of traditions, known as the *Kutub-i-Arbaʿah*, which seem to be held in the same estimation by the Shīʿahs, as the six *Ṣaḥīḥs* of the Sunnīs. They are entitled the *Tahẕīb*, the *Istibṣār*, the *Kāfī*, and *Man lā Yastaḥẓirah al-Faqīh*. [TRADITIONS.]

Mr. Shama Churun Sircar, Tagore Professor of Law, has also reviewed the Shīʿah, or Imamīyah, law books, and we are indebted to him for the following *résumé*:—

"One of the earliest works on civil and criminal laws was written by Abdullah Bin Alí al Halabí. But it does not appear that any of his legal compositions are extant.

"A number of law-treatises of the present class was composed by Yunas Bin Abd ur-Rahmán (already spoken of as a writer on traditions). The most famous of these treatises is entitled the *Jámi-ul-Kabír*.

"Several works on law were written by Abú al-Hasan Alí Bin al-Hasan al-Kumí, commonly called Ibnu Bábavaih, one of which works is entitled the *Kitábu ash-Sharáyah*. The *Maknaa fi al-Fikah* (*Muqnaʿ fī ʾl-Fiqh*) is the best known of the law books of the present class composed by Abú Jaafar.

"Abú Abdullah Muhammad an-Nuamání, surnamed the Shaikh Mufíd, and Ibnu Muallim, a renowned Shíah lawyer, is stated to have written two hundred works, amongst which one called the *Irshád* is well known. When Shaikh Mufíd is quoted in conjunction with Abú Jaafar at-Túsí, they also are spoken of as 'the two Shaikhs' (Shaikhain).

"The chief works on law, written by Abú Jaafar Muhammad at-Túsí (Abū Jaʿfar Muḥammad aṭ-Ṭūsī), are the *Mabsút*, the *Khiláf*, the *Nihāyah*, and the *Muhít*. These works are held in great estimation, and he is considered one of the highest authorities in law. The *Risálat-i-Jaafariyah* is likewise a legal treatise by at-Túsí, which is frequently quoted.

"The *Sharáya ul-Islám*, written by Shaikh Najm ud-dín Abú ul-Kásim Jaafar Bin Muayyid al-Hillí, commonly called Shaikh Muayyid, is a work of the highest authority, at least in India, and is more universally referred to than any other Shíah law book, and is the chief authority for the law of the Shíahs in India. A copious and valuable commentary upon the *Sharáya ul-Islám*, entitled the *Masálik ul-Afhám*, was written by Zayin-ud-dín Alí as-Sáilí, commonly called the 'Shahíd-i-Sání, (second martyr). There are two other commentaries on the *Sharáya ul-Islám*, respectively entitled the *Madár ul-Ahkám* and *Jawáhir ul-Kalám*, the latter of which was written by Shaikh Muhammad Hasan an-Najafí.

"Of the works on jurisprudence written by Yahiyah Bin Ahmad al-Hillí, who was celebrated for his knowledge of traditions, and is well known amongst the Imámiyah sects for his works, the *Jámi ash-Sharáya* and the *Mudkhal dar Usúl-i-Fikah* are held in the greatest repute.

"Of the numerous law books written by Shaikh Allámah Jamál-ud-dín Hasan Bin Yusuf Bin al-Mutahhir al-Hillí, who is called the chief of the lawyers of Hilliah, and whose works are frequently referred to as authorities of undisputed merit, the most famous are the *Talkhís ul-Marám*, the *Gháyit ul-Ahkám*, and the *Tahrír ul-Ahkám*, which last is a justly celebrated work. The *Mukhtalaf-ush-Shíah* is also a well-known composition of this great lawyer, and his *Irshád ul-Azhán* is constantly quoted as an authority under the name of the *Irshád-i-Allámáh*.

"The *Jámi-ul-Abbási* is a concise and comprehensive treatise on Shíah law, in twenty books or chapters. It is generally considered as the work of Bahá-ud-dín Muhammad Aámilí, who died A.H. 1031.

"The *Mafátíh*, by Muhammad Bin Murtazá, surnamed Muhsan, and the commentary on the book by his nephew, who was of the same name, but surnamed Hádí, are modern works deserving of notice.

"The *Rouzat ul-Ahkám*, written in Persian by the third Mujtahid of Oudh, consists of four chapters. The first of these is on Inheritance, which is treated of therein most fully and perspicuously. This work was lithographed at Lucknow, first in A.H. 1257, and again in A.H. 1264.

"A general digest of the Imámiyah law in temporal matters was compiled under the superintendence of Sir William Jones. This book is composed of extracts from the work called the *Káfí*, which is a commentary on the *Mafátíh*, as well as from the *Sharáyá ul-Islám*. The manuscript of this digest still remains in the possession of the High Court of Judicature at Calcutta.

"The earliest treatises on the Faráïz, or Inheritance, of the Shíahs appear to have been written by Abdul Azíz Bin Ahmad al-Azádí, and Abú Muhammad al-Kindí, the latter of whom is said to have lived in the reign of Hárún ur-Rashíd.

"A work on the law of inheritance, entitled the al-Ijáz fí al-Faráïz has been left by Abú Jaafar Muhammad at-Túsí in addition to his general works on the Kurán, the Hadís and jurisprudence.

"The best known and most esteemed works on the law of inheritance are the *Ihtijáj ush-Shíah*, by Saád Bin Abd-ullah al-Asharí, the *Kítáb ul-Mawáris*, by Abú al-Hasan Alí Bábavaih; the *Hamal ul-Faráïz* and the *Faráïz ush-Shariyah*, by Shaikh Mufíd. The *Sharáya ul-Islám*, which, as already stated, is one of the highest authorities on the Shíah law, contains also a chapter on Inheritance.

Of all the above-mentioned books on civil and criminal laws, those that are commonly referred to in India are the following: The *Sharáya ul-Islám*, *Rouzat-ul-Ahkám*, *Sharah-i-Lumá*, *Mafátíh*, *Tahrír*, and *Irshád ul-Azhán*.

"Of the books on this branch of Muhammadan law, only that part of the *Sharáyah ul-Islám* which treats of the forensic law has been translated, though not fully, by Mr. Neil Baillie. A considerable part of the digest compiled under the superintendence of Sir William Jones (as already noticed) was translated by Colonel Baillie, out of which the chapter on Inheritance has been printed by Mr. Neil Baillie at the end of the second part of his digest of Muhammadan law. Although the chapter above alluded to is copious, yet it must be remarked that it is not so clear and useful as the *Sharáya-ul-Islám* and *Rouzat ul-Ahkám*." (See *Tagore Law Lectures, 1874, the Imámiyah Code*, by Shama Churun Sircar; Thacker, Spink and Co., Calcutta.)

LAẔĀ (لظى). "Fire, flame." A division, or stage in hell, mentioned in the Qur'ān, Sūrah lxx. 15. Al-Baghawī, the commentator, says it is that portion of hell which is reserved for the Christians who have not believed in Muḥammad. [HELL.]

LAZARUS. Arabic *al-'Āzar* (العازر). Not mentioned by name in the Qur'ān, but Jalālu 'd-dīn, in remarking on Sūrah iii. 43: "I will bring the dead to life by God's permission," says, amongst those whom Jesus raised from the dead was al-'Āzar, who was his special friend and companion. The account given by the commentators al-Kamālān of the raising of Lazarus, is very similar to that given in the New Testament.

LEASE. Arabic *ijārah* (اجارة). [HIRE.]

LEBANON. Arabic *Lubnān* (لبنان). Not mentioned in the Qur'ān, but tradition has it that Ishmael collected the stones for the Ka'bah from five sacred mountains, one of which was Mount Libanus. The followers of Ismā'ilu 'd-Darāzī, known as the Druses, a fanatical sect of Muslims, reside on the southern range of the Lebanon chain. [DRUSES.]

LEGACY. [WILLS.]

LEGITIMACY. *Waladu 'l-ḥalāl* (ولد الحلال), "a legitimate child"; *waladu 'z-zinā'* (ولد الزناء), "an illegitimate child."

The Muḥammadan law, unlike the law of England, makes legitimacy depend, not merely upon the fact of the child being born in "lawful wedlock," but also *conceived* after lawful marriage.

According to the Sunnīs and Shī'ahs, and according to the teaching of the Qur'ān itself, the shortest period of gestation recognised by law is *six months*, and consequently a child born any time after six months from the date of marriage has a claim to legitimacy. Amongst the Sunnīs, a simple denial of the paternity of the child so born would not take away its status of legitimacy. But the Shī'ahs hold that if a man get a woman with child and then marry her, and she give birth to the child within six months after marriage, legitimacy is not established.

As to the longest period of pregnancy, there are some strange rulings in Muslim law. The Shīa'hs, upon the basis of a decision pronounced by 'Alī, recognise ten lunar months as the longest period of gestation, and this is now regarded as the longest legal period by both Shī'ahs and Sunnīs. But Abū Ḥanīfah and his two disciples, upon the authority of a tradition reported by 'Āyishah, regard two years as the longest period of gestation, and the Imām ash-Shāfi'ī extended it to four, and the Imām Mālik to five and even seven years! It is said these Sunnī doctors based their opinions on the legendary birth of Zuhak Tāzi and others, who were born, so it is related, in the fourth year of conception! But Muslim divines say that the old jurisconsults of the Sunnī school were actuated by a sentiment of humanity, and not by any indifference as to the laws of nature, their chief desire being to prevent an abuse of the provisions of the law regarding divorce and the disavowal of children. The general concensus of Muslim doctors points to ten months as the longest period of pregnancy which can be recognised by any court of justice.

[Under the old Roman law, it was ten months. In the *Code Napoleon*, article 312, it is three hundred days. Under the Jewish law, the husband had the absolute right of disavowal. See *Code Rabbinique*, vol. ii. p. 63.]

The Muḥammadan law, like the English law, does not recognise the legitimation of antenuptial children. Whereas, according to French and Scotch law, such children are legitimated by the subsequent marriage of the parents.

In Sunnī law, an invalid marriage does not affect the legitimacy of children born from it, Nor does it in Shī'ah law; but the Shī'ah law demands proof that such a marriage was a *bona fide* one, whilst the Ḥanafī code is not strict on this point.

In the case of a divorce by *li'ān* [LI'AN], the *waladu 'l-mulā'anah*, or "child of imprecation," is cut off from his right of inheritance from his father.

(See Syud Ameer Ali's *Personal Law of Muhammadans*, p. 160; *Fatāwā-i-'Alamghīri*, p. 210; *Sharā'i'u 'l-Islām*, p. 301.) [PARENTAGE.]

LETTERS. The letters of Muslims are distinguished by several peculiarities, dictated by the rule of politeness. "The paper is thick, white, and highly polished; sometimes it is ornamented with flowers of gold; and the edges are always cut straight with scissors. The upper half is generally left blank; and the writing never occupies any portion of the second side. The name of the person to whom the letter is addressed, when the writer is an inferior or an equal, and even in some other cases, commonly occurs in the first sentence, preceded by several titles of honour; and is often written a little above the line to which it appertains, the space beneath it in that line being left blank; sometimes it is written in letters of gold, or red ink. A king, writing to a subject, or a great man to a dependant, usually places his name and seal at the head of his letter. The seal is the impression of a signet (generally a ring, worn on the little finger of the right hand), upon which is engraved the name of the person, commonly accompanied by the word 'His (*i.e.* God's) servant,' or some other words expressive of trust in God, &c. Its impression is considered more valid than the sign-manual, and is indispensable to give authority to the letter. It is made by dabbing some ink on the surface of the signet, and pressing this upon the paper: the place which is to be stamped being first moistened, by touching the tongue with a finger of the right hand, and then gently rubbing the part with that finger. A person writing to a superior, or to an equal, or even an inferior to whom he wishes to show respect, signs his name at the bottom of his letter, next the left side or corner, and places the seal immediately to the right of this; but if he particularly desire to testify his humility, he places it beneath his name, or even partly over the lower edge of the paper, which consequently does not receive the whole of the impression." (Lane's *Arabian Nights*, vol. i. p. 23.)

LI'ĀN (لعان). *Lit.* "Mutual cursing." A form of divorce which takes place under the following circumstances. "If a man accuses his wife of adultery, and does not prove it by four witnesses, he must swear before God that he is the teller of truth four times, and then add: 'If I am a liar, may God curse me.' The wife then says four times, 'I swear before God that my husband lies'; and then adds: 'May God's anger be upon me if this man be a teller of truth.' After this a divorce takes place *ipso facto*." (See Sūratu 'n-Nūr, xxiv. 6; *Mishkāt*, book xiii. ch. xv.).

In the case of Li'ān, as in the other forms of divorce, the woman can claim her dower.

Li'ān is not allowed in four cases, viz. a Christian woman married to a Muslim, a Jewess married to a Muslim, a free woman married to a slave, and a slave girl married to a free man.

The children of a woman divorced by Li'ān are illegitimate.

LIBĀS (لباس). [APPAREL.]

LIBERALITY. Arabic *sak͟hāwah* (سخاوة), "hospitality"; *infāq* (انفاق), "general liberality in everything."

Liberality is specially commended by Muḥammad in the Traditions:—

"The liberal man is near to God, near to Paradise, near to men, and distant from hell. The miser is far from God, far from Paradise, far from man, and near the fire. Truly an ignorant but liberal man is more beloved by God, than a miser who is a worshipper of God."

"Three people will not enter Paradise: a deceiver, a miser, and one who reproaches others with obligation after giving."

"Every morning God sends two angels, and one of them says, 'O God, give to the liberal man something in lieu of that which he has given away!' and the other says, 'O God, ruin the property of the miser!'"

"The miser and the liberal man are like two men dressed in coats of mail, their arms glued to their breasts and collar bones, on account of the tightness of the coats of mail. The liberal man stands up when giving alms, and the coat of mail expands for him. The miser stands up when intending alms; the coat of mail becomes tight, and every ring of it sticks fast to its place."

LIḤYAH (لحية). [BEARD.]

LISĀNU 'L-ḤAQQ (لسان الحق). *Lit.* "The language of truth." The *Insānu 'l-Kāmil*, or "perfect man," in which the secret influences of al-Mutakallim, "the Speaker" (*i.e.* God), are evident.

LITERATURE, MUSLIM. Arabic *'Ilmu 'l-Adab* (علم الادب). The oldest specimens of Arabic literature now extant were composed in the century which preceded the birth of Muḥammad. They consist of short extemporaneous elegies, afterwards committed to writing, or narratives of combats of hostile tribes written in rhythmical prose, similar to that which we find in the Qur'ān.

Baron De Slane says the *Ḥamāsah*, the *Kitābu 'l-Ag͟hānī*, and the *Amālī* of Abū 'Alīyu 'l-Kālī, furnish a copious supply of examples, which prove that the art of composing in rhythmical prose not only existed before Muḥammad's time, but was even then generally practised, and had been brought to a high degree of perfection. The variety of its inflections, the regularity of its syntax, and the harmony of its prosody, furnish in themselves a proof of the high degree of culture which the language of the pre-Islamic Arabians had attained. The annual meetings of the poets at the fair of 'Ukāz encouraged literature, and tended to give regularity of formation and elegance of style to these early poetic effusions.

The appearance of the Qur'ān brought about a gradual, but remarkable change in tone and spirit of Arabic literature. An extraordinary admixture of falsehood and truth, it was given to the world by its author as the uncreated and Eternal Word, and as a standing miracle not only of sound doctrine, but of literary style and language. This strange assertion, of course, deterred nearly every attempt at imitation, although it is related that Ibn al-Muqaffa', al-Mutanabbi, and a few others, of a sceptical turn of mind, essayed in some of their writings to surpass the style of the Qur'ān. But as the Muslims in all ages have drawn their principles of grammar and rhetoric from the Qur'ān itself, we need not be surprised that these and every other attempt to surpass its excellences have been considered failures.

One circumstance in the earliest history of Islām was of itself instrumental in giving rise to a most extensive literature of a special class. The Qur'ān (unlike the Pentateuch and New Testament) was not a narrative of the life of its author. And yet, at the same time, Muḥammad had left very special injunctions as to the transmission of his precepts and actions. [TRADITION.] The study of these traditional sayings, together with that of the Qur'ān, gave rise to all the branches of Arabic learning.

The *Aḥādīs̤*, or "the sayings of Muḥammad," were considered by his followers as the result of divine inspiration, and they were therefore treasured up in the memories of his followers with the same care which they had taken in learning by heart the chapters of the Qur'ān. They recorded not only what the Prophet said and did, but also what he refrained from saying and doing, his very silence (*sunnatu 's-sukūt*) on questions of doctrine or rule of life being also regarded as the result of divine guidance. It therefore became of paramount importance, to those who were sincere followers of Muḥammad, that they should be in possession of his precepts and practices, and even of the most trifling circumstances of his daily life. The mass of traditions increased rapidly, and became so great that it was quite impossible for any one single person to recollect them.

According to Jalālu 'd-dīn as-Suyūṭī, the first who wrote down the traditional sayings of the Prophet was Ibn Shihāb az-Zuhrī, during the reign of the K͟halīfah 'Umar II. ibn 'Abdi 'l-'Azīz (A.H. 99–101); but the Imām Mālik (A.H. 95–179), the compiler of the book known as *al-Muwaṭṭā* is generally held to be the author of the earliest collection of Traditions. (See *Kashfu 'z̤-Z̤unūn, in loco.*)

So rapidly did this branch of Muslim learning increase, that when al-Buk͟hārī (A.H. 194–256) determined to make a careful collation of trustworthy traditions, he found not fewer than 300,000 extant, from which he selected 7,275.

The necessity of distinguishing the genuine

traditions from the false gave rise to new branches of literature. A just appreciation of the credit to which each traditionist was entitled, could only be formed from a knowledge of the details of his history, and of the moral character of his life. Hence numerous biographical works, arranged in chronological order, containing short accounts of the principal persons connected with the early history of Islām, were compiled. The necessity for tracing the places of their birth and the race from which they sprang, led Muslim critics to the study of genealogy and geography

The sense of the Qur'ān, with its casual references to contemporaneous as well as to past history, was felt to be difficult and obscure, in many places; and this led the learned Muslims to study not only the traditional sayings of Muḥammad already alluded to, but any historical or geographical works which would help them in understanding the text of "the Book."

In the early days of Islām, general history was regarded with little favour as a subject for study, and many orthodox doctors of Muslim law were led by religious scruples to condemn the study of secular history; and the works of Grecian and Latin poets, philologists, grammarians, and historians, only received their approval in so far as they served to explain the text of the Qur'ān and the traditional records of Muḥammad's followers.

The real attitude of the leaders of Islām was decidedly hostile towards all literature which was not in strict harmony with the teachings of their religion. If in succeeding ages the Saracens became, as they undoubtedly did, the liberal patrons of literature and science, there cannot be a doubt that in the earliest ages of Islām, in the days of the four "*well-directed*" Khalīfahs, not merely the greatest indifference, but the most bigoted opposition was shown to all literary effort which had not emanated from the fountain of Islām itself. And consequently the wild uncivilized conquerors of Jerusalem, Cæsarea, Damascus, and Alexandria, viewed the destruction of the literary lore of ages which was stored up in those ancient cities with indifference, if not with unmitigated satisfaction. Everything, science, history, and religion, must be brought down to the level and standard of the teaching of the Qur'ān and the life of the Prophet of Arabia, and whatever differed therefrom was from the Devil himself, and deserved the pious condemnation of every true child of the faith.

But the possession of power and riches gave rise to new feelings, and the pious aversion to intellectual pursuits gradually relaxed in proportion as their empire extended itself. The possession of those countries, which had for so long been the seats of ancient literature and art, naturally introduced among the Muslims a spirit of refinement, and the love of learning. But it was not the outcome of their religious belief, it was the result of the peculiar circumstances which surrounded their unparalleled conquest of a civilized world. Their stern fanaticism yielded to the mild influence of letters, and, "by a singular anomaly," says Andrew Crichton, "in the history of nations, Europe became indebted to the implacable enemies of her religion and her liberties for her most valuable lessons in science and arts." In this they present a marked contrast to the Goths and Huns; and what is most remarkable is, not that succesful conquerors should encourage literature, but that, within a single century, a race of religionists should pass from a period of the deepest barbarism to that of the universal diffusion of science. In A.D. 641, the Khalīfah ʻUmar is said to have destroyed the Alexandrian library. In A.D. 750, the Khalīfahs of Baghdad, the munificent patrons of literature, mounted the throne. Eight centuries elapsed from the foundation of Rome to the age of Augustus, whilst one century alone marks the transition from the wild barbarism of the Khalīfahs of Makkah to the intellectual refinement of the Khalīfahs of al-Kūfah and Baghdād. The Saracens, when they conquered the cities of the West, came into possession of the richest legacies of intellectual wealth, and they used these legacies in such a manner as to earn for themselves the most prominent place in the page of history as patrons of learning. But the truth is, the literature of the great Byzantine empire exercised a kind of patronage over Saracenic kings. If the Saracens produced not many original works on science, philosophy, or art, they had the energy and good sense to translate those of Greece and Rome. (See the list of Arabic works in the *Kashfu 'z-Ẓunūn.*)

Under the Umaiyah Khalīfahs, the genius of Greece began to obtain an influence over the minds of the Muslims.

ʻAbdu 'l-Malik, the fifth Khalīfah of the Umaiyah dynasty (A.H. 65), was himself a poet, and assembled around him at his court the most distinguished poets of his time. Even the Christian poet, al-Akhṭal took his place in the front rank of the literary favorites of the Court.

But it was especially under al-Manṣūr, the Abbasside Khalīfah (A.H. 136), that the golden age of Arabian literature in the East commenced. Accident brought him acquainted with a Greek physician named George, who was invited to court, and to whom the Saracens are indebted for the study of medicine.

The celebrated Hārūnu 'r-Rashīd, the hero of the Arabian Nights, was specially the patron of learning. He was always surrounded by learned men, and whenever he erected a mosque he always established and endowed a school of learning in connection with it. It is related that amongst the presents he sent to the Emperor Charlemagne was an hydraulic clock. The head of his schools and the chief director of the education of his empire, was John ibn Massua, a Nestorian Christian of Damascus.

The reign of Ma'mūn (A.H. 198) has been called the Augustan period of Arabian literature. The Khalifah Ma'mūn himself was a scholar, and he selected for his companions the most eminent scholars from the East and West. Baghdād became the resort of poets, philosophers, historians, and mathematicians from every country and every creed. Amongst the scholars of his court was al-Kindī, the Christian author of a remarkable treatise in defence of Christianity against Islām, side by side with al-Kindī, the philosopher, who translated numerous classical and philosophical works for his munificent and generous patron, and wrote a letter to refute the doctrine of the Trinity. [KINDI.] It is said that in the time of Ma'mūn, "literary relics of conquered provinces, which his generals amassed with infinite care, were brought to the foot of the throne as the most precious tribute he could demand. Hundreds of camels might be seen entering the gates of Baghdād, laden with no other freight than volumes of Greek, Hebrew, and Persian literature." Masters, instructors, translators, and commentators, formed the court of Baghdād, which appeared rather to be a learned academy than the capital of a great nation of conquerors. When a treaty of peace was concluded with the Grecian Emperor Michael III., it was stipulated that a large and valuable collection of books should be sent to Baghdād from the libraries of Constantinople, which were translated by the *savans* of his court into the Arabic tongue; and it is stated that the original manuscripts were destroyed, in order that the learning of the world might be retained in the "divine language of the Prophet!"

The Khalīfah al-Wāṣiq (A.H. 227), whose residence had been removed by his predecessor, al-Mu'taṣim, from Baghdād to Saumara, was also a patron of letters. He especially patronised poetry and music.

Under al-Mu'tamid (A.H. 256), Baghdād again became the seat of learning.

Al-Mustanṣir (A.H. 623), the last but one of the Abbaside Khalīfahs, adorned Baghdād by erecting a mosque and college, which bore his name, and which historians tell us had no equal in the Muslim world. Whilst the city of Baghdād, in the time of the Abbaside dynasty, was the great centre of learning, al-Baṣrah and al-Kūfah almost equalled the capital itself in reputation, and in the number of celebrated authors and treatises which they produced. Damascus, Aleppo, Balkh, Ispahan, and Samarcand, also became renowned as seats of learning. It is said that a certain doctor of science was once obliged to decline an invitation to settle in the city of Samarcand, because the transport of his books would have required 400 camels!

Under the Fāṭimide Khalīfahs (A.D. 910 to 1160), Egypt became for the second time the asylum of literature. Alexandria had more than twnnty schools of learning, and Cairo, which was founded by al-Mu'izz (A.D. 955), soon possessed a royal library of 100,000 manuscripts. A *Dāru 'l-Ḥikmah*, or school of science, was founded by the Khalīfah al-Ḥākim (A.D. 996), in the city of Cairo, with an annual revenue of 2,570 dinārs. The institution combined all the advantages of a free school and a free library.

But it was in Spain (Arabic *Andalus*) that Arabian literature continued to flourish to a later period than in the schools of Cairo and Baghdād. The cities of Cordova, Seville, and Granada, which were under Muslim rule for several centuries (Cordova, from A.D. 755 to 1236; Granada, to A.D. 1484), rivalled each other in the magnificence of their academies, colleges, and libraries. Muslim historians say that Cordova alone has produced not fewer than 170 eminent men, and its library, founded by al-Ḥakam II. (A.D. 961), contained 400,000 volumes; and the Khalīfah himself was so eminent a scholar, that he had carefully examined each of these books himself, and with his own hand had written in each book the genealogies, births and deaths of their respective authors.

Muḥammad, the first Khalīfah of Granada, was a patron of literature, and the celebrated academy of that city was long under the direction of Shamsu 'd-dīn of Murcia, so famous among the Arabs for his skill in polite literature. Kasīrī has recorded the names of 120 authors whose talents conferred dignity and fame on the Muslim University of Granada.

So universal was the patronage of literature in Spain, that in the cities of the Andalusian kingdom, there were as many as seventy free libraries open to the public, as well as seventeen distinguished colleges of learning.

(For an interesting account of the state of literature in Spain under the Moors, the English reader can refer to Pascual de Gayango's translation of al-Makkari's *History of the Muhammadan Dynasties in Spain*, London, 1840.)

History, which was so neglected amongst the ancient Arabs, was cultivated with assiduity by the Muslim. There is extant an immense number of works in this department of literature. The compiler of the Bibliographical Dictionary, the *Kashfu 'z-Ẓunūn*, gives a list of the names and titles of 1,300 works of history, comprising annals, chronicles, and memoirs. As might be expected, the earliest Muslim histories were compiled with the special object of giving to the world the history of the Prophet of Arabia and his immediate successors. The earliest historian of whom we have any extensive remains is Ibn Isḥāq, who died A.H. 151, or fifteen years after the overthrow of the Umaiyah dynasty. He was succeeded by Ibn Hishām, who died A.H. 213, and who made the labours of Ibn Isḥāq the basis of his history. Another celebrated Muslim historian is Ibn Sa'd, who is generally known as Kātibu 'l-Wāqidī, or al-Wāqidī's secretary, and is supposed to have even surpassed his master in historical accuracy.

Abū Ja'far ibn Jarīr aṭ-Ṭabarī flourished in the latter part of the third century of the Muslim era, and has been styled by Gibbon, "the Livy of the Arabians." He flourished in the city of Baghdād, where he died A.H. 310. Aṭ-Ṭabarī compiled not only annals of Muḥammad's life, but he wrote a history of the progress of Islām under the earlier Khalīfahs. Abū 'l-Faraj, a Christian physician of Malatia in Armenia, Abū 'l-fidā, Prince of Hamah, and Ibn Kātib of Granada, are amongst the celebrated historians of later times. The writings of Ibn Ḥusain of Cordova are said to contain 160,000 pages!

Biographical works, and memoirs of men specially distinguished for their achievements, were innumerable. The most notable work of the kind is Ibn Khallikān's Bibliographical Dictionary, which has been translated into English by De Slane (Paris, 1843). The Dictionary of the Sciences by Muḥammad Abū 'Abdi 'llāh of Granada is an elaborate work. The Bibliographical Dictionary, entitled the *Kashfu 'ẓ-Ẓunūn* (often quoted in the present work), is a laborious compilation, giving the names of several thousands of well-known books and authors in every department of literature. 'Abdu 'l-Munẓar of Valencia wrote a genealogical history of celebrated horses, and another celebrity wrote one of camels. The encyclopædians, gazetteers, and other similar compilations, are very numerous.

Arabic lexicons have been compiled in regular succession from the first appearance of the work supposed to have been compiled by Khalīl ibn Aḥmad, entitled *Kitābu 'l-'Ayn*, which must have been written about A.H. 170, to the most recent publications which have issued from the presses of Lucknow, Bombay, and Cairo. [ARABIC LEXICONS.]

Poetry was, of old, a favourite occupation of the Arab people, and was, after the introduction of learning by the Khalīfahs of Baghdād, cultivated with enthusiasm. Al-Mutanabbī of al-Kūfah, Khalīl ibn Aḥmad, and others, are poets of note in the time of the Abbasside Khalīfahs. So great was the number of Arabic poets, that an abridgement, or dictionary, of the lives of the most celebrated of them, compiled by Abū 'l-'Abbās, son of the Khalīfah al-Mu'taṣim, contains notices of 130. [POETRY.]

With Numismatics the Saracens of Spain were well acquainted, and Maqrīzī and Namarī wrote histories of Arabian money. The study of geography was not neglected. The library of Cairo had two massive globes, and the Sharīf Idrīsī of Cordova made a silver globe for Roger II., King of Sicily. Ibn Rashīd, a distinguished geographer, journeyed through Africa, Egypt, and Syria, in the interests of geographical science. But to reconcile some of the statements of Muḥammadan tradition with geographical discoveries must have required a strong effort of the imagination. [QAF.]

To the study of medicine the Arabs paid particular attention. Many of our modern pharmaceutical terms, such as camphor, jalap, and syrup, are of Arabian origin. The Christian physician, George, introduced the study of medicine at the court of Khalīfah al-Manṣūr. [MEDICINE.]

The superstitious feeling of the Muslim as to the polluted touch of the dead, debarred the orthodox from attempting the study of anatomy. The doctrine that even at death the soul does not depart from the body, and the popular belief that both soul and body must appear entire to undergo the examination by Munkar and Nakīr in the grave, were sufficient reasons why the dissection of the dead body should not be attempted.

Operation for cataract in the eye was an Arabian practice, and the celebrated philosopher, Avicenna (Abū 'Alī ibn Sīnā') wrote in defence of depression instead of extraction, which he considered a dangerous experiment.

Botany, as subsidiary to medicine, was studied by the Saracens; and it is said the Arabian botanists discovered several herbal remedies, which were not known to the Greeks. Ibn al-Baiṭār, a native of Malaga, who died at Damascus A.D. 1248, was the most distinguished Arabian botanist. Al-Birūnī, who died A.D. 941, resided in India for nearly forty years in order to study botany and chemistry.

The first great Arabic chemist was Jābir, a native of Ḥarrān in Mesopotamia. He lived in the eighth century, and only some 150 years after the flight of Muḥammad. He is credited with the discovery of sulphuric acid, nitric acid, and aqua regia. D'Herbelot states that he wrote 500 works on chemistry. The nomenclature of science demonstrates how much it owes to the Arabs—alcohol, alembic, alkali, and other similar terms, being derived from the Saracens.

The science of astronomy, insomuch as it was necessary for the study of the occult science of astrology, was cultivated with great zeal. The Khalīfah Ma'mūn was himself devoted to this study Under his patronage, the astronomers of Baghdād and al-Kūfah accurately measured a degree of the great circle of the earth, and determined at 24,000 miles the entire circumference of the globe. (See *Abū 'l-Fidā'* and *Ibn Khallikān*.) The obliquity of the ecliptic was calculated at about twenty-three degrees and a half, "but," as Andrew Crichton remarks, "not a single step was made towards the discovery of the solar system beyond the hypothesis of Ptolemy." Modern astronomy is indebted to the Saracens for the introduction of observatories. The celebrated astronomer and mathematician Jābir (A.D. 1196), erected one at Seville, which may still be seen. Bailly, in his *Hist. de l'Astronomie*, affirms that Kepler drew the ideas that led to his discovery of the elliptical orbits of planets from the Saracen, Nūru 'd-dīn, whose treatise on the sphere is preserved in the Escurial library.

Algebra, though not the invention of the Arabs, received valuable accessions from their talents, and Ibn Mūsā and Jābir composed original works on spherical trigonometry. Al-Kindī translated Autolycus' *De Sphæra Mota*, and wrote a treatise of his own *De Sex Quantitatibus*.

Architecture was an art in which the Saracens excelled, but their buildings were erected on the wrecks of cities, castles, and fortresses, which they had destroyed, and the Saracenic style is merely a copy of the Byzantine. [ARCHITECTURE.]

To the early Muslims, pictures and sculpture were considered impious and contrary to divine law, and it is to these strong religious feelings that we owe the introduction of that peculiar style of embellishment which is called the *Arabesque*, which rejects all representations of human and animal figures.

In caligraphy or ornamental writing, the Muslims excel even to the present day, although it is to the Chinese that they are indebted for the purity and elegance of their paper.

Music is generally understood to have been forbidden in the Muḥammadan religion, but both at Bag͟hdād and Cordova were established schools for the cultivation of this art. [MUSIC.]

Much more might be written on the subject of Muslim or Saracenic literature, but it would exceed the limits of our present work. Enough has been said to show that, notwithstanding their barbarous origin, they in due time became the patrons of literature and science. They cannot, however, claim a high rank as inventors and discoverers, for many of their best and most useful works were but translations from the Greek. Too much has been made of the debt which the Western world owes, or is supposed to owe, to its Saracen conquerors for their patronage of literature. It would have been strange if a race of conquerors, who came suddenly and rapidly into possession of some of the most cultivated and refined regions of the earth, had not kindled new lights at those ancient beacons of literature and science which smouldered beneath their feet.

In the *Kashfu 'ẓ-Ẓunūn*, it is related that when Sa'd ibn Abū Waqqāṣ conquered Persia, he wrote to the K͟halīfah 'Umar and asked him what he should do with the philosophical works which they had found in the libraries of the cities of Persia, whether he should keep them or send them to Makkah; then 'Umar replied, "Cast them into the rivers, for if in these books there is a guidance (of life), then we have a still better guidance in the book of God (the Qur'ān), and if, on the contrary, there is in them that which will lead us astray, then God protect us from them"; so, according to these instructions, Sa'd cast some into the rivers and some into the fire. So was lost to us the Philosophy of Persia! (*Kashfu 'ẓ-Ẓunūn*, p. 341.)

Such was the spirit in which the early Muslims regarded the literature of the countries they conquered, and which gave rise to the frequently repeated story that 'Umar ordered the destruction of the libraries of Alexandria, Cæsarea, and Ispahan, while even the enlightened Ma'mūn is said to have committed to the flames the Greek and Latin originals of the books he caused to be translated. It therefore seems probable that the world of literature lost quite as much as it gained by the Saracen conquest of the West. What the attitude of the Muslim world now is towards science and literature, the condition of the Muslim in North Africa, in Turkey, in Afghanistan, and in India, will declare. A condition of things arising from peculiarities of religious belief. If we study carefully the peculiar structure of Islām as a religious system, and become acquainted with the actual state of things amongst Muḥammadan nations now existing, we shall feel compelled to admit that the patronage of literature by the Muslim K͟halīfahs of Cordova, Cairo, and Bag͟hdād, must have been the outcome of impulses derived from other sources than the example and precept of the Arabian legislator or the teachings of the Qur'ān.

(See Ibn K͟hallikān's *Biographical Dict.*; Crichton's *Arabia*; D'Herbelot's *Bibl. Orient.*; Al-Makkari's *Muhammadan Dynasties in Spain*; Pocock; Muir's *Mahomet*; Abū 'l-Fidā'; Toderini's *Lit. des Turcs*; Kashfu 'z-Zunūn; Sir William Jones's *Asiatic Res.*; Schnurrer's *Bibl. Arab.*; Ibn al-Jazwī's *Talqīḥ*; M. de Sacey; Ṭabaqātu 'sh-Shāfi'īyīn.)

LITURGY. [PRAYER.]

LIWĀ' (لواء). A banner; a standard. [STANDARDS.]

LOCUSTS (Arabic *jarād*, جراد) are lawful food for Muslims without being killed by *ẕabḥ*. [FOOD.]

LOGIC. Arabic *'Ilmu 'l-manṭiq* (علم المنطق), "the science of rational speech," from *naṭaq*, "to speak"; *'Ilmu 'l-mīzān* (علم الميزان), "the science of weighing" (evidence), from *mīzān*, "scales."

The author of the *Ak͟hlāq-i-Jalālī* says "the ancient sages, whose wisdom had borrowed its lustre from the loop-hole of prophecy, always directed the seeker after excellence to cultivate first *'Ilmu 'l-ak͟hlāq*, 'the science of moral culture,' then *'Ilmu 'l-manṭiq*, 'the science of logic,' then *'Ilmu 'l-riyāẓīyāt*, 'mathematics,' then *'Ilmu 'l-ḥikmah*, 'physics,' and, lastly, *'Ilmu 'l-Ilāhī*, 'theology.' But Ḥakīm Abū 'Alī al-Maṣqawī (A.D. 10), would place mathematics before logic, which seems the preferable course. This will explain the inscription placed by Plato over the door of his house, 'He who knows not geometry, let him not enter here.'" (See Thompson's ed. p. 31.)

The Arabs, being suddenly called from the desert of Arabia to all the duties and dignities of civilized life, were at first much pressed to reconcile the simplicity of the precepts of their Prophet with the surroundings of their new state of existence; and consequently the multitude of distinctions, both in morals and jurisprudence, they were obliged to adopt, gave the study of dialectics an importance in the religion of Islām which it never lost. The Imām Mālik said of the great teacher Abū Ḥanīfah, that he was such a master of logic, that if he were to assert that a pillar of wood was made of gold, he would prove it to you by the rules of logic.

The first Muslim of note who gave his attention to the study of logic was Khālid ibn Yazīd (A.H. 60), who is reported to have been a man of great learning, and who ordered certain Greek works on logic to be translated into Arabic. The Khalīfah Ma'mūn (A.H. 198) gave great attention to this and to every other branch of learning, and ordered the translation of several Greek books of logic, brought from the library of Constantinople, into the Arabic tongue. Mulla Kātib Chalpi gives a long list of those who have translated works on logic. Stephen, named Istifānu 'l-Qadīm, translated a book for Khālid ibn Yazīd. Batrīq did one for the Khalīfah al-Manṣūr. Ibn Yaḥya rendered a Persian book on logic into Arabic for the Khalīfah al-Ma'mūn, also Ibn Na'imah 'Abdu 'l-Masīḥ (a Christian), Ḥusain bin Bahrīq, Hilāl ibn Abī Hilāl of Ḥimṣ, and many others translated books on logic from the Persian. Mūsā and Yūsuf, two sons of Khālid, and Ḥasan ibn Sahl are mentioned as having translated from the language of Hind (India) into Arabic. Amongst the philosophers who rendered Greek books on logic into Arabic are mentioned Ḥunain, Abū 'l-Faraj, Abū 'l-Sulaiman as-Sanjari, Yahya an-Naḥwī, Ya'qūb ibn Isḥāq al-Kindī, Abū Zaid Aḥmad ibn Sahl al-Balkhī, Ibn Sīnā' (Avicenna), and very many others.

An Arabic treatise of logic has been translated into English by the Bengal Asiatic Society.

LORD'S SUPPER. [EUCHARIST.]

LOT. Arabic *Lūṭ* (لوط). Heb. לוֹט.

Held by Muḥammadans as "a righteous man," specially sent as a prophet to the city of Sodom.

The commentator, al-Baiẓāwī, says that Lot was the son of Hārān, the son of Āzar, or Tarāḥ, and consequently Abraham's nephew, who brought him with him from Chaldea into Palestine, where, they say, he was sent by God, to reclaim the inhabitants of Sodom and the other neighbouring cities, which were overthrown with it, from the unnatural vice to which they were addicted. And this Muḥammadan tradition seems to be countenanced by the words of the apostle, that this righteous man dwelling among them, in seeing and hearing, "vexed his righteous soul from day to day with their unlawful deeds," whence it is probable that he omitted no opportunity of endeavouring their reformation. His name frequently occurs in the Qur'ān, as will be seen from the following selections:—

Sūrah vii. 72–82: "We also *sent* Lot, when he said to his people, Commit ye this filthy deed in which no creature hath gone before you? Come ye to men, instead of women, lustfully? Ye are indeed a people given up to excess. But the only answer of his people was to say, 'Turn them out of your city, for they are men who vaunt them pure.' And we delivered him and his family, except his wife; she was of those who lingered: and we rained a rain upon them: and see what was the end of the wicked!"

Sūrah xxi. 74, 75: "And unto Lot we gave wisdom and knowledge; and we rescued him from the city which wrought filthiness; for they were a people, evil, perverse: and we caused him to enter into our mercy, for he was of the righteous."

Sūrah xxix. 27–34: "*We sent* also Lot: when he said to his people, 'Proceed ye to a filthiness in which no people in the world hath ever gone before you? Proceed ye even to men? attack ye them on the highway? and proceed ye to the crime in your assemblies?' But the only answer of his people was to say, 'Bring God's chastisement upon us, if thou art a man of truth.' He cried: My Lord! help me against this polluted people. And when our messengers came to Abraham with the tidings *of a son*, they said, 'Of a truth we will destroy the in-dwellers in this city, for its in-dwellers are evil doers.' He said, 'Lot is therein.' They said, 'We know full well who therein is. Him and his family will we save, except his wife; she will be of those who linger.' And when our messengers came to Lot, he was troubled for them, and his arm was too weak to protect them; and they said, 'Fear not, and distress not thyself, for thee and thy family will we save, except thy wife; she will be of those who linger. We will surely bring down upon the dwellers in this city vengeance from heaven for the excesses they have committed.' And in what we have left of it is a clear sign to men of understanding."

Sūrah xxvi. 160–175: "The people of Lot treated their apostles as liars, when their brother Lot said to them, 'Will ye not fear God? I am your Apostle worthy of all credit: fear God, then, and obey me. For this I ask you no reward: my reward is of the Lord of the worlds alone. What! with men, of all creatures, will ye have commerce? And leave ye your wives whom your Lord hath created for you? Ah! ye are an erring people!' They said, 'O Lot, if thou desist not, one of the banished shalt thou surely be.' He said, 'I utterly abhor your doings: My Lord! deliver me and my family from what they do.' So we delivered him and his whole family—save an aged one among those who tarried—then we destroyed the rest—and we rained a rain upon them, and fatal was the rain to those whom we had warned. In this truly was a sign; but most of them did not believe. But thy Lord! He is the Powerful, the Merciful!"

Sūrah xxvii. 55–59: "And Lot, when he said to his people, 'What! proceed ye to such filthiness with your eyes open? What! come ye with lust unto men rather than to women? Surely ye are an ignorant people.' And the answer of his people was but to say, 'Cast out the family of Lot from your city: they, forsooth, are men of purity!' So we rescued him and his family: but as for his wife, we decreed her to be of them that lingered: and we rained a rain upon them, and fatal was the rain to those who had had their warning."

LOTS, Drawing of.

There are two words used to express drawing of lots—

maisir (ميسر) and (قرعة) *qur'ah.* The former is used for games of chance, which are condemned in the Qur'ān (Sūrahs ii. 216; v. 92); the latter the casting of lots in the division of land or property. (*Hidāyah*, vol. iv. p. 17.)

LOVE. The words used in the Qur'ān for love and its synonyms are *wudd* (ود), *ḥubb* (حب), *maḥabbah* (محبة), and *mawaddah* (مودة).

(1) *Wudd.* Sūrah xix. 96: "Verily those who believe and act aright, to them the Merciful One will give *love.*"

(2) *Ḥubb.* Sūrah v. 59: "God will bring a people whom He will *love*, and who will *love* him."

Sūrah ii. 160: "They *love* them (idols) as they should *love* God, whilst those who believe *love* God more."

Sūrah lxxxix. 21: "Ye *love* wealth with a complete *love.*"

Sūrah xii. 30: "He (Joseph) has infatuated her (Zulaik͟hah) with *love.*"

(3) *Maḥabbah.* Sūrah xx. 39: "For on thee (Moses) have I (God) cast my *love.*"

(4) *Mawaddah.* Sūrah iv. 75: "As though there were no *friendship* between you and him."

Sūrah v. 85: "Thou will find the nearest in *friendship* to those who believe to be those who say We are Christians."

Sūrah xxix. 24. "Verily, ye take idols beside God through mutual *friendship* in the affairs of this world."

Sūrah xxx. 20: "He has caused between you *affection* and pity."

Sūrah xli. 22: "Say! I do not ask for it hire, only the *affection* of my kinsfolk."

Sūrah lx. 1: "O ye who believe! take not my enemy and your enemy for patrons encountering them with *affection.*"

Sūrah lx. 7: "Mayhap God will place *affection* between you."

From the above quotations, it will be seen that in the Qur'ān, the word *mawaddah* is used for friendship and affection only, but that the other terms are synonymous, and are used for both divine and human love.

In the traditions, *ḥubb* is also used for both kinds of love (see *Mishkāt*, book xxii. ch. xvi.), and a section of the Ḥadīs̤ is devoted to the consideration of "Brotherly love for God's pleasure."

'Āyishah relates that the Prophet said, "Souls were at the first collected together (in the spirit-world) like assembled armies, and then they were dispersed and sent into bodies; and that consequently those who had been acquainted with each other in the spirit world, became so in this, and those who had been strangers there would be strangers here."

The author of the *Ak͟hlāq-i-Jalālī* distinguishes between *animal* love and *spiritual* love. Animal love, he says, takes its rise from excess of appetite. But spiritual love, which arises from harmony of souls, is not to be reckoned a vice, but, on the contrary, a species of virtue:—

"Let love be thy master, all masters above,
For the good and the great are all prentice to love."

The cause of love, he says, is excessive eagerness either for *pleasure* or for *good*; the first is *animal love*, and is culpable; the second is *spiritual love*, and is a praiseworthy virtue. (See Thompson's ed., pp. 227–234.)

The term more generally used in Oriental writings for the passion of love is *'Ishq* (عشق), a word which az-Zamak͟hsharī, in his work the *Asās* (quoted by Lane), says is derived from the word *al-'ashaqah*, a species of ivy which twines upon trees and cleaves to them. But it seems not improbable that it is connected with the Hebrew אִשָּׁה "a woman," or is derived from חָשַׁק "to desire." (See Deut. vii. 7: "The Lord hath set his *love* upon thee"; and Ps. xci. 14: "Because he hath set his *love* upon me.") The philosopher Ibn Sīnā' (Avicenna), in a treatise on *al-'Ishq* (regarding it as the passion of the natural propensities), says it is a passion not merely peculiar to the human species, but that it pervades all existing things, both in heaven and earth, in the animal, the vegetable, and even in the mineral kingdom; and that its meaning is not perceived or known, and is rendered all the more obscure by the explanation thereof. (See *Tāju 'l-'Arūs*, by Saiyid Murtada.)

Mīr Abū 'l-Baqā, in his work entitled the *Kullīyāt*, thus defines the various degrees of love, which are supposed to represent not only intensity of natural love between man and woman, but also the Sufiistic or divine love, which is the subject of so many mystic works:—First, *hawā*, the inclining of the soul or mind to the object of love; then, *'Ilāqah*, love cleaving to the heart; then, *kalaf*, violent and intense love, accompanied by perplexity; then *'ishq*, amorous desire, accompanied by melancholy; then, *shaghaf*, ardour of love, accompanied by pleasure; then, *jawā*, inward love, accompanied by amorous desire, or grief and sorrow; then, *tatāyum*, a state of enslavement; then, *tabl*, love sickness; then, *walah*, distraction, accompanied with loss of reason; and, lastly, *huyām*, overpowering love, with a wandering about at random.

In Professor Palmer's little work on Oriental mysticism, founded on a Persian MS. by 'Azīz ibn Muḥammad an-Nafsānī, and entitled the *Maksad i Aksā* (*Maqṣad-i-Aqṣā*), or the "Remotest Aim," we read, "Man sets his face towards this world, and is entangled in the love of wealth and dignity, until the grace of God steps in and turns his heart towards God. The tendency which proceeds from God is called Attraction; that which proceeds from man is called Inclination, Desire, and LOVE. As the inclination increases its name changes, and it causes the Traveller to renounce everything else but God (who becomes his *Qibla*), and thus setting his face God-wards, and forgetting everything but God, it is developed into LOVE."

This is by no means the last and ultimate stage of the journey, but most men are said to be content to pass their lives therein and to leave the world without making any further progress therein [SUFIISM]. Such a person the Ṣūfīs call *Majẕūb*, or, Attracted. And it is in this state that *'Ishq*, or spiritual love, becomes the subject of religious contemplation just as it is in the Song of Solomon. "Let him kiss me with the kisses of his mouth, for thy *love* is better than wine." But whilst the lover in the Song of Solomon is supposed to represent the Almighty God, and the loved one the Church, in Eastern Ṣūfī poetry the *'āshiq*, or lover, is man, and the *mash'ūq*, or the Beloved One, is God.

The Ṣūfī poet Jāmī, in his *Salaman and Absal*, thus writes of the joy of Divine love; and his prologue to the Deity, as rendered into English, will illustrate the mystic conception of love.

"Time it is
To unfold Thy perfect beauty. I would be
Thy lover, and Thine only—I, mine eyes
Sealed in the light of Thee, to all but Thee,
Yea, in the revelation of Thyself
Self-lost, and conscience-quit of good and evil,
Thou movest under all the forms of truth,
Under the forms of all created things;
Look whence I will, still nothing I discern
But Thee in all the universe, in which
Thyself Thou dost invest, and through the eyes
Of man, the subtle censor scrutinize.
To thy *Harīm* Dividuality,
No entrance finds—no word of *this* and *that*;
Do Thou my separate and derived self
Make one with Thy essential! Leave me room
On that *divan* (sofa) which leaves no room for two:
Lest, like the simple Kurd of whom they tell,
I grow perplext, O God, 'twixt 'I' and 'Thou.'
If 'I'—this dignity and wisdom whence?
If 'Thou'—then what is this abject impotence?"

[The fable of the Kurd, which is also told in verse, is this. A Kurd left the solitude of the desert for the bustle of a busy city. Being tired of the commotion around him, he lay down to sleep. But fearing he might not know himself when he arose, in the midst of so much commotion, he tied a pumpkin round his foot. A knave, who heard him deliberating about the difficulty of knowing himself again, took the pumpkin off the Kurd's foot, and tied it round his own. When the Kurd awoke, he was bewildered, and exclaimed—

"Whether I be I or no,
If I—the pumpkin why on you?
If you—then where am I, and who?"]

For further information on the subject of mystic love, see SUFIISM.

LUBB (لب). The heart or soul of man. That faculty of the mind which is enlightened and purified by the Holy Light, *i.e. Nūru 'l-Quds* (the Light of God). (*Kitābu 't-Ta'rīfāt, in loco.*)

LUDD (لد). A small town in Palestine, where it is said Jesus will find ad-Dajjālu 'l-Masīḥ, and will kill him. (*Mishkāt*, book xxiii. ch. iv.) The ancient Lydda, nine miles from Joppa. (See Acts ix. 32, 38.) It is the modern Diospolis, which in Jerome's time was an episcopal see. The remains of the ancient church are still seen. It is said to be the native town of St. George.

LUNATIC. The Arabic *majnūn* (مجنون) includes all mad persons, whether born idiots, or persons who have become insane. According to Muḥammadan law, a lunatic is not liable to punishment for robbery, or to retaliation for murder. *Zakāt* (legal alms) is not to be taken from him, nor is he to be slain in war. The apostasy of a lunatic does not amount to a change of faith, as in all matters, both civil and religious, he is not to be held responsible to either God or man. An idiot or fool is generally regarded in the East by the common people, as an inspired being. Mr. Lane, in his *Modern Egyptians*, says, "Most of the reputed saints of Egypt are either lunatics, or idiots, or impostors." A remark which will equally apply to India and Central Asia.

LUQMĀN (لقمان). A person of eminence, known as *Luqmānu 'l-Ḥakīm*, or Luqmān the Philosopher, mentioned in the Qur'ān as one upon whom God had bestowed wisdom.

Sūrah xxxi. 11–19: "Of old we bestowed wisdom upon Luqmān, *and taught him thus*—'Be thankful to God: for whoever is thankful, is thankful to his own behoof; and if any shall be thankless. . . . God truly is self-sufficient, worthy of all praise!' And *bear in mind* when Luqmān said to his son by way of warning, 'O my son! join not other gods with God, for the joining gods with God is the great impiety. O my son! observe prayer, and enjoin the right and forbid the wrong, and be patient under whatever shall betide thee: for this is a bounden duty. And distort not thy face at men; nor walk thou loftily on the earth; for God loveth no arrogant vain-glorious one. But let thy pace be middling; and lower thy voice: for the least pleasing of voices is surely the voice of asses.' See ye not how that God hath put under you all that is in the heavens and all that is on the earth, and hath been bounteous to you of his favours, both for soul and body. But some are there who dispute of God without knowledge, and have no guidance and no illuminating Book."

Commentators are not agreed as to whether Luqmān is an inspired prophet or not. Ḥusain says most of the learned think he was a philosopher, and not a prophet. Some say he was the son of Bā'ūr, and a nephew of

Job, being his sister's son; others that he was a nephew of Abraham; others that he was born in the time of King David, and lived until the time of Jonah, being one thousand years of age. Others, that he was an African slave and a shepherd amongst the Israelites. Some say he was a tailor, others a carpenter. He is admitted by all Arabian historians to have been a fabulist and a writer of proverbs, and consequently European authors have concluded that he must be the same person whom the Greeks, not knowing his real name, have called Æsop, *i.e.* Æthiops.

Mr. Sale says: "The commentators mention several quick repartees of Luqmān, which (together with the circumstances above mentioned) agrees so well with what Maximus Planudes has written of Æsop, that from thence, and from the fables attributed to Luqmān by the Orientals, the latter has been generally thought to be no other than the Æsop of the Greeks. However that be (for I think the matter will bear a dispute), I am of opinion that Planudes borrowed a great part of his life of Æsop from the traditions he met with in the East concerning Luqmān, concluding them to have been the same person, because they were both slaves, and supposed to be the writers of those fables which go under their respective names, and bear a great resemblance to one another; for it has long since been observed by learned men, that the greater part of that monk's performance is an absurd romance, and suported by no evidence of the ancient writers."

Dr. Spenger thinks Luqmān is identical with the Elxai of the Ebionites (*Das Leben und die Lehre des Mohammad*, vol. i. p. 34).

Luqmān is the title of the xxist Sūrah of the Qur'ān.

LUQṬAH (لقطة). "Troves." Property which a person finds and takes away to preserve it in trust. In English law, trover (from the French *trouver*) is an action which a man has against another who has found or obtained possession of his goods, and refuses to deliver them on demand. (Se *Blackstone.*) According to Muḥammadan law, the finder of lost property is obliged to advertise it for the space of a year before he can claim it as his own. If the finder be a wealthy person, he should give it to the poor. (*Hidāyah*, vol. ii. p. 277.) [TROVES.]

LŪṬ (لوط). [LOT.]

LUXURY. Arabic *tana"um* (تنعم). In the training of children, the author of the *Akhlāq-i-Jalālī* condemns luxury. He says, "Sleeping in the day and sleeping overmuch at night should be prohibited. Soft clothing and all uses of luxury, such as cool retreats in the hot weather, and fires and furs in the cold, they should be taught to abstain from. They should be inured to exercise, foot-walking, horse-riding, and all other appropriate accomplishments." (*Akhlāq-i-Jalālī*, p. 280.)

LYING. Arabic *kiẕẕāb* (كذاب). A pretty general infirmity of nature in the East, which still remains uncorrected by the modern influences of Islām. But Muḥammad is related to have said: "When a servant of God tells a lie, his guardian angels move away from him to the distance of a mile, because of the badness of its smell." (*Mishkāt*, book xxii. ch. ii.)

M.

MA'ĀQIL (معاقل). The fines for murder, manslaughter, &c. (*Hidāyah*, vol. iv. p. 448.) [DIYAH.]

AL-MA'ĀRIJ (المعارج). *Lit.* "The Ascents." The title of the LXXth chapter of the Qur'ān, in the second verse of which occurs the sentence, "God, the possessor of the Ascents (or Steps) by which the angels ascend unto Him, and the Spirit (*i.e.* Gabriel), in a day whose space is fifty thousand years."

Sale, translating from al-Baiẓāwī and Zamakhsharī, says: "This is supposed to be the space which would be required for their ascent from the lowest part of the creation to the throne of God, if it were to be measured, or the time which it would take a man to perform a journey; and this is not contradictory to what is said elsewhere (if it be to be interpreted of the ascent of the angels), that the length of the day whereon they ascend is 1,000 years, because that is meant only of their ascent from earth to the lower heaven, including also the time of their descent.

"But the commentators, generally taking the day spoken of in both these passages to be the Day of Judgment, have recourse to several expedients to reconcile them, and as both passages seem to contradict what Muḥamman doctors teach, that God will judge all creatures in the space of half-a-day, they suppose those large numbers of years are designed to express the time of the previous attendance of those who are to be judged, or else to the space wherein God will judge the unbelieving nations, of which, they say, there will be fifty, the trial of each nation taking up 1,000 years, though that of the true believers will be over in the short space above mentioned."

MABNĀ 'T-TAṢAWWUF (مبنى التصوف). *Lit.* "The Foundation of Ṣūfiism." A term used by the Ṣūfīs to embrace the three principles of their system. (1) The choice of the ascetic life; (2) The intention to bestow freely upon others; (3) The giving up of one's own will and desires, and desiring only the will of God. (See 'Abdu 'r-Razzāq's *Dict. of Ṣūfī Terms.*)

AL-MADĪNAH (المدينة). *Lit.* "The city." The city celebrated as the burial place of Muḥammad. It was called Yasrib (see Qur'ān, Sūrah xxxiii. 13), but was distinguished as *al-Madīnah*, "the city," and *Madīnatu 'n-Nabī*, "the city of the Prophet," after it had become famous by giving shelter to Muḥammad. It is esteemed only second to Makkah in point of sanctity. Muḥammad is related to have said, "There are angels guarding the roads to al-Madīnah, on account of which neither plague, or the Dajjāl (Antichrist) can enter it." "I was ordered," he said, "to flee to a city which shall eat up (conquer) all other cities, and its name is now *al-Madīnah* (*the* city); verily she puts away evil from man, like as the forge purifies iron." "God has made the name of al-Madīnah both *ṭābah* and *ṭaiyibah*," *i.e.* both good and odoriferous.

Al-Madīnah is built on the elevated plain of Arabia, not far from the eastern base of the ridge of mountains which divide the table-land from the lower country between it and the Red Sea. The town stands on the lowest part, on the plain where the water-courses unite, which produce in the rainy season numerous pools of stagnant water, and render the climate unhealthy. Gardens and date-plantations, interspersed with fields, inclose the town on three sides; on the side towards Makkah the rocky nature of the soil renders cultivation impossible. The city forms an oval about 2,800 paces in circuit, ending in a point. The castle is built at the point on a small rocky elevation. The whole is inclosed by a thick wall of stone, between 35 and 40 feet high, flanked by about 30 towers and surrounded by a ditch. Three well-built gates lead into the town. The houses are well built of stone, and generally two stories high. As this stone is of a dark colour, the streets have a gloomy aspect, and are for the most part very narrow, often only two or three paces across; a few of the principal streets are paved with stone. There are only two large streets which contain shops. The principal buildings within the city are the great mosque containing the tomb of Muḥammad, two fine colleges, and the castle, standing at the western extremity of the city, which is surrounded by strong walls and several high and solid towers, and contains a deep well of good water.

The town is well supplied with sweet water by a subterraneous canal which runs from the village of Qubā', about three-quarters of a mile distant in a southern direction. In several parts of the town steps are made down to the canal, where the inhabitants supply themselves with water which, however, contains nitre, and produces indigestion in persons not accustomed to it. There are also many wells scattered over the town; every garden has one by which it is irrigated; and when the ground is bored to the depth of twenty-five or thirty feet, water is found in plenty. During the rainy season, many torrents descend from the higher grounds to the lower depression in which al-Madīnah is built, and part of the city is inundated. This plentiful supply of water made this site a considerable settlement of Arabs long before it became sacred among the Muḥammadans, by the flight, residence, and death of the Prophet, to which it owes its name of Madīnatu 'n-Nabī, or the City of the Prophet. (See Burckhardt's *Travels in Arabia.*)

An account of the Prophet's mosque is given under MASJIDU 'N-NABI, and of the burial chamber of Muḥammad under HUJRAH.

MADRASAH (مدرسة). A school. [EDUCATION.]

MADYAN (مدين). Midian. The descendants of Midian, the son of Abraham and Keturah, and a city and district bearing his name, situated on the Red Sea, south-east of Mount Sinai.

Mentioned in the Qur'ān, Sūrah vii. 83: "We sent to Madyan their brother Shu'aib." [SHUAIB.]

MAFQŪD (مفقود). A legal term for a person who is lost, and of whom no information can be obtained. He is not considered legally dead until the period expires when he would be ninety years old.

MAGIANS. [MAJUS.]

MAGIC. Arabic *siḥr* (سحر). A belief in the magical art is entertained by almost all Muḥammadans, and there is a large number of persons who study it.

Although magic (*as-siḥr*) is condemned in the Qur'ān (Sūrah ii. 96) and in the Traditions (*Mishkāt*, book xxi. ch. iii. pt. 1), there are still many superstitious practices resembling this occult science, which are clearly permitted according to the sayings of Muḥammad.

Anas says, "The Prophet permitted a spell (*ruqyah*) being used to counteract the ill effects of the evil eye; and on those bitten by snakes or scorpions." (*Ṣaḥīḥu Muslim*, p. 233.)

Umm Salmah relates "that the Prophet allowed a spell to be used for the removal of yellowness in the eye, which, he said, proceeded from the malignant eye." (*Ṣaḥīḥu 'l-Bukhārī*, p. 854.)

'Auf ibn Mālik says "the Prophet said there is nothing wrong in using spells, provided the use of them does not associate anything with God." (*Mishkāt*, book xxi. ch. i.)

The terms used to express the magical arts are, *da'wah*, *lit.* "an invitation of the spirits," exorcism; *'azīmah*, an incantation; *kihānah*, divination, or fortune-telling; *ruqyah*, a spell; and *siḥr*, magic.

The term *da'wah* is held to imply a lawful incantation, in which only the assistance of God is invited by the use of either the *Ismu 'l-A'ẓam*, or great and unknown name of God, or the recital of the ninety-nine names or attributes of the Almighty. *As-Siḥr*, or the magical use of evil spirits: and *kihānah*, fortune-telling, are held to be strictly unlawful.

Incantation and exorcism as practised by Muḥammadans is treated of in the article on DA'WAH.

Mr. Lane, in his annotated edition of the *Arabian Nights*, says:—

There are two descriptions of magic, one is spiritual, regarded by all but freethinkers as true; the other, natural, and denounced by the more religious and enlightened as deceptive.

I. Spiritual magic, which is termed "er Roohanee" (*ar-rūḥānī*), chiefly depends upon the virtues of certain names of God, and passages from the Kurán, and the agency of angels, and jinn, or genii. It is of two kinds, Divine and Satanic ("Rahmanee," *i.e.* relating to "the Compassionate" [who is God], and "Sheytanee," relating to the Devil.)

1. Divine magic is regarded as a sublime science, and is studied only by good men, and practised only for good purposes. Perfection in this branch of magic consists in the knowledge of the most great name of God [ISMU 'L-AZAM]; but this knowledge is imparted to none but the peculiar favourites of heaven. By virtue of this name, which was engraved on his seal ring, Solomon subjected to his dominion the jinn and the birds and the winds. By pronouncing it, his minister Asaf (*Āṣaf*), also, transported in an instant, to the presence of his sovereign, in Jerusalem, the throne of the Queen of Sheba. But this was a small miracle to effect by such means, for, by uttering this name, a man may even raise the dead. Other names of the Deity, commonly known, are believed to have particular efficacies when uttered or written; as also are the names of the Prophet, and angels and good jinn are said to be rendered subservient to the purposes of divine magic by means of certain invocations. Of such names and invocations, together with words unintelligible to the uninitiated in this science, passages from the Kurán, mysterious combinations of numbers, and peculiar diagrams and figures, are chiefly composed written charms employed for good purposes. Enchantment, when used for benevolent purposes, is regarded by the vulgar as a branch of lawful or divine magic; but not so by the learned, and the same remark applies to the science of divination.

2. Satanic magic, as its name implies, is a science depending on the agency of the Devil and the inferior evil jinn, whose services are obtained by means similar to those which propitiate, or render subservient, the good jinn. It is condemned by the Prophet and all good Muslims, and only practised for bad purposes. Es sehr (*as-Siḥr*), or enchantment, is almost universally acknowledged to be a branch of Satanic magic, but some few persons assert (agreeably with several tales in the *Arabian Nights*), that it may be, and by some has been, studied with good intentions, and practised by the aid of good jinn; consequently, that there is such a science as good enchantment, which is to be regarded as a branch of divine or lawful magic. The metamorphoses are said to be generally effected by means of spells, or invocations to jinn, accompanied by the sprinkling of water or dust, &c., on the object to be transformed. Persons are said to be enchanted in various ways; some paralyzed, or even deprived of life, others, affected with irresistible passion for certain objects, others, again, rendered demoniacs, and some, transformed into brutes, birds, &c. The evil eye is believed to enchant in a very powerful and distressing manner. This was acknowledged even by the Prophet. Diseases and death are often attributed to its influence. Amulets are worn by many Muslims with the view of counteracting or preserving from enchantment; and for the same purpose many ridiculous ceremonies are practised. Divination, which is termed El-Kihaneh (*al-Kihānah*), is pronounced on the highest authority to be a branch of Satanic magic; though not believed to be so by all Muslims. According to an assertion of the Prophet, what a fortuneteller says may sometimes be true; because one of the jinn steals away the truth, and carries it to the magician's ear; for the angels come down to the region next the earth (the lowest heaven), and mention the works that have been pre-ordained in heaven; and the devils (or evil jinn) listen to what the angels say, and hear the orders predestined in heaven, and carry them to the fortune-tellers. It is on such occasions that shooting stars are hurled at the devils. It is said that, "the diviner obtains the services of the Sheytan (*Shaiṭān*) by magic arts, and by names invoked, and by the burning of perfumes, and he informs him of secret things; for the devils, before the mission of the Apostle of God, it is added, used to ascend to heaven, and hear words by stealth. That the evil jinn are believed still to ascend sufficiently near to the lowest heaven to hear the conversation of the angels, and so to assist magicians, appears from the former quotation, and is asserted by all Muslims. The discovery of hidden treasures is one of the objects for which divination is most studied. The mode of divination called "Darb-el-Mendel" (*Ẓarbu 'l-Mandal*), is by some supposed to be effected by the aid of evil jinn; but the more enlightened of the Muslims regard it as a branch of natural magic. Some curious performances of this kind, by means of a fluid mirror of ink, have been described in the *Account of the Manners and Customs of the Modern Egyptians*, and in No. 117 of the *Quarterly Review*.

There are certain modes of divination which cannot properly be classed under the head of spiritual magic, but require a place between the account of this science and that of natural magic. The most important of these branches of Kihaneh is Astrology, which is called *Ilm en Nujoom* (*'Ilmu 'n-Nujūm*). This is studied by many Muslims in the present day, and its professors are often employed by the Arabs to determine a fortunate period for laying the foundation of a building, commencing a journey, &c.; but more frequently by the Persians and Turks. The Prophet pronounced Astrology to be a branch of magic. Another branch of Kihaneh is Geomancy, called "Darb er Ramal" (*Ẓarbu Raml*); a mode of divination from certain marks made on sand (whence its appellation), or on paper; and said to be chiefly founded on astrology. The science called "ez Zijr," or "el Eyafeh" (*al-'Iyāfah*), is a third branch of Kihaneh, being divination or auguration, chiefly from the motions and positions, or postures, of birds, or of gazelles and other beasts of the chase. Thus what was termed a "Saneh" (*Sāniḥ*), that is, such an animal standing or passing with its right side towards the spectator, was esteemed among the Arabs as of good omen; and a "Bareh" (*Bāriḥ*), or an animal of this kind, with its left side towards the spectator, was held as inauspicious. "El Kiyafeh" (*al-Qiyāfah*), under which term are included Chiromancy and its kindred sciences, is a fourth branch of Kihaneh, "El Tefaul" (*at-Tafawwul*), or the taking an omen, particularly a good one, from a name or words accidentally heard or seen, or chosen from a book belonging to the same science. The taking a "fál," or omen, from the Kurán, is generally held to be lawful. Various trifling events are considered as ominous. For instance, a Sultan quitting his palace with his troops, a standard happened to strike a "thureiya" (*ṡurayyā*, a cluster of lamps so called from resembling the Pleiades), and broke them: he drew from this an evil omen, and would have relinquished the expedition; but one of his chief officers said to him, "O our Lord, thy standard has reached the Pleiades," and being relieved by this remark, he proceeded, and returned victorious.

(See *The Thousand and One Nights*, a new translation, with copious notes, by Edward W. Lane; new ed. by E. S. Poole, vol. i. p. 60.)

MAGISTRATES. [QAZI.]

MAGPIE. Arabic *'aq'aq* (عقعق).

According to Abū Ḥanīfah, the flesh of the magpie is *mubāḥ*, or indifferent; but the Imām Yūsuf held it to be *makrūh*, or reprobated, because it frequently feeds on dead bodies. (*Hidāyah*, vol. iv. p. 74.)

AL-MAHDĪ (المهدى). *Lit.* "The Directed One,"

hence, "who is fit to direct others, Guide, Leader." A ruler who shall in the last days appear upon the earth. According to the Shī'ahs, he has already appeared in the person of Muḥammad Abu 'l-Qāsim, the twelfth Imām, who is believed to be concealed in some secret place until the day of his manifestation before the end of the world. But the Sunnis say he has not yet appeared. In the history of Muḥammadanism, there are numerous instances of impostors having assumed the character of this mysterious personage, amongst others, Saiyid Aḥmad, who fought against the Sikhs on the North-West frontier of the Panjāb, A.D. 1826, and still more recently, the Muḥammadan who has claimed to be *al-Mahdī* in the Sudān in Egypt.

The sayings of the Prophet on the subject, according to al-Bukhārī, and other traditionists, are as follows:—

"The world will not come to an end until a man of my tribe and of my name shall be master of Arabia."

"When you see black ensigns coming from the direction of Khorosān, then join them, for the Imām of God will be with the standards, whose name is *al-Mahdī*."

"The *Mahdī* will be descended from me, he will be a man with an open countenance and with a high nose. He will fill the earth with equity and justice, even as it has been filled with tyranny and oppression, and he will reign over the earth seven years."

"Quarrelling and disputation shall exist amongst men, and then shall a man of the people of al-Madīnah come forth, and shall go from al-Madīnah to Makkah, and the people of Makkah shall make him Imām. Then shall the ruler of Syria send an army against the *Mahdī*, but the Syrian army shall perish by an earthquake near Badā', between al-Madīnah and Makkah. And when the people shall see this, the Abdāl [ABDAL] will come from Syria, and also a multitude from al-'Irāq. After this an enemy to the *Mahdī* shall arise from the Quraish tribe, whose uncles shall be of the tribe of Kalb, and this man shall send an army against the *Mahdī*. The *Mahdī* shall rule according to the example of your Prophet, and shall give strength and stability to Islām. He shall reign for seven years, and then die."

"There shall be much rain in the days of the *Mahdī* and the inhabitants both of heaven and earth shall be pleased with him. Men's lives shall pass so pleasantly, that they will wish even the dead were alive again." (*Mishkātu 'l-Maṣābiḥ*, book xxiii. ch. 3.)

According to Shī'ah traditions, Muḥammad is related to have said: "O ye people! I am the Prophet and 'Alī is my heir, and from us will descend *al-Mahdī*, the seal (*i.e.* the last) of the Imāms, who will conquer all religions and take vengeance on the wicked. He will take fortresses and will destroy them, and slay every tribe of idolaters, and he will avenge the deaths of the martyrs of God. He will be the champion of the Faith, and a drawer of water at the fountain of divine knowledge. He will reward merit and requite every fool according to his folly. He will be the approved and chosen of God, and the heir of all knowledge. He will be the valiant in doing right, and one to whom the Most High has entrusted Islām. . . . O ye people, I have explained to you, and 'Alī also will make you understand it." (*Ḥiyātu 'l-Qulūb*, Merrick's ed., p. 342.)

It is probable that it is from these traditions that the opinion became current amongst the Christians that the Muḥammadans expected their Prophet would rise again.

MAḤJŪR (محجور). A slave inhibited

by the ruler from exercising any office or agency. (*Hidāyah*, vol. iii. 5.)

MAHMAL, MAHMIL (محمل). A covered litter borne on a camel, both from Cairo and from Damascus, to Makkah, as an emblem of royalty at the time of the pilgrimage.

It is said that Sultan Az-Zāhir Beybars, King of Egypt, was the first who sent a mahmal with the caravan of pilgrims to Makkah in A.D. 1272, but that it had its origin a few years before his accession to the throne, under the following circumstances:—

Shaghru 'd-Durr, a beautiful Turkish

THE MAHMAL. (*From an Original Picture.*)

female slave, who became the favourite wife of Sultān aṣ-Ṣālih Najmu 'd-dīn, and who on the death of his son (with whom terminated the dynasty of Aiyūb) caused herself to be acknowledged Queen of Egypt, performed the ḥajj in a magnificent litter borne by a camel. And for successive years her empty litter was sent yearly to Makkah, as an emblem of state. After her death, a similar litter was sent each year with the caravan of pilgrims from Cairo and Damascus, and is called *maḥmal* or *maḥmil*, a word signifying that by which anything is supported.

Mr. Lane, in his *Modern Egyptians*, vol. ii. p. 162, thus describes the maḥmal :—

"It is a square skeleton frame of wood with a pyramidal top, and has a covering of black brocade richly worked with inscriptions and ornamental embroidery in gold, in some parts upon a ground of green or red silk, and bordered with a fringe of silk, with tassels, surmounted by silver balls. Its covering is not always made after the same pattern with regard to the decorations ; but in every cover that I have seen, I have remarked on the upper part of the front a view of the Temple of Makkah, worked in gold, and over it the Sultan's cipher. It contains nothing ; but has two copies of the Kurán, one on a small scroll, and the other in the usual form of a book, also small, each inclosed in a case of

THE MAHMAL. (*Lane.*)

gilt silver, attached externally at the top. The five balls with crescents, which ornament the maḥmal, are of gilt silver. The maḥmal is borne by a fine tall camel, which is generally indulged with exemption from every kind of labour during the remainder of its life."

Eastern travellers often confuse the maḥmal with the kiswah, or covering for the Ka'bah, which is a totally distinct thing, although it is made in Cairo and sent at the same time as the maḥmal. [KISWAH.]

The Wahhābīs prohibited the maḥmal as an object of vain pomp, and on one occasion intercepted the caravan which escorted it.

Captain Burton saw both the Egyptian and the Damascus maḥmals on the plain below 'Arafah at the time of the pilgrimage.

MAḤMŪDĪYAH (محمودية). A Shī'ah sect founded by Mīr Sharīf, who in the reign of Akbar held a military appointment in Bengal. He was a disciple of Maḥmūd of Busakhwān, the founder of the Nuqtawīyah sect. Maḥmūd lived in the reign of Timur, and professed to be al-Mahdī. He also called himself the Shakhs-i-Waḥīd—the Individual one. He used to quote the verse, "It may be that thy Lord will raise thee up to a glorious (*maḥmūd*) station" (Sūrah xvii. 81). From this he argued that the body of man had been advancing in purity since the creation, and that on its reaching to a certain degree, one Maḥmūd (glorious) would arise, and that then the dispensation of Muhammad would come to an end. He claimed to be the Maḥmūd. He also taught the doctrine of transmigration, and that the beginning of everything was the earth atom (*nuqṭah*). It is on this account that they are called in Persian the Nuqtawīyah sect. They are also known by the names Maḥmūdīyah and Waḥīdīyah. Shah 'Abbās, King of Persia, expelled them from his dominions, but Akbar received the fugitives kindly, and promoted some amongst them to high offices of State.

MAHR (مهر). Heb. מֹהַר. The dower or settlement of money or property on the wife, without which a marriage is not legal, for an explanation of which see the article on DOWER.

The Hebrew word occurs three times in the old Testament, viz. Gen. xxxiv. 12; Ex. xxii. 17; 1 Sam. xviii. 25. [DOWER and MARRIAGE.]

MAḤRAM (محرم). *Lit.* "Unlawful." A near relative with whom it is unlawful to marry. Muḥammad enjoined that every woman performing pilgrimage should have a maḥram with her night and day, to prevent scandal. (*Mishkāt*, book xi. ch. i.)

AL-MĀ'IDAH (المائدة). *Lit.* "The table." The title of the vth Sūrah of the Qur'ān, in the 114th verse of which the word occurs: "O Jesus, son of Mary! is thy Lord able to send down to us a *table*?"

"This miracle is thus related by the commentators. Jesus having at the request of his followers asked it of God, a red table immediately descended, in their sight, between two clouds, and was set before them; whereupon he rose up, and, having made the ablution, prayed, and then took off the cloth which covered the table, saying, 'In the name of God, the best provider of food!' What the provisions were with which this table was furnished, is a matter wherein the expositors are not agreed. One will have them to be nine cakes of bread and nine fishes; another, bread and flesh; another, all sorts of food except flesh; another, all sorts of food except bread and flesh; another, all except bread and fish; another, one fish which had the taste of all manner of food; and another, fruits of paradise; but the most received tradition is that when the table was uncovered, there appeared a fish ready dressed, without scales or prickly fins, dropping with fat, having salt placed at its head and vinegar at its tail, and round it all sorts of herbs except leeks, and fine loaves of bread, on one of which there were olives, on the second honey, on the third butter, on the fourth cheese, and on the fifth dried flesh. They add that Jesus, at the request of the Apostles, showed them another miracle, by restoring the fish to life, and causing its scales and fins to return to it, at which the standers-by being affrighted, he caused it to become as it was before; that one thousand three hundred men and women, all afflicted with bodily infirmities or poverty, ate of these provisions, and were satisfied, the fish remaining whole as it was at first; that then the table flew up to heaven in the sight of all; and every one who had partaken of this food were delivered from their infirmities and misfortunes; and that it continued to descend for forty days together, at dinner-time, and stood on the ground till the sun declined, and was then taken up into the clouds. Some of the Muḥammadan writers are of opinion that this table did not really descend, but that it was only a parable; but most think the words of the Qur'ān are plain to the contrary. A further tradition is that several men were changed into swine for disbelieving this miracle, and attributing it to magic art; or, as others pretend, for stealing some of the victuals from off it. Several other fabulous circumstances are also told, which are scarce worth transcribing. Some say the table descended on a Sunday, which was the reason of the Christians observing that day as sacred. Others pretend that this day is still kept among them as a very great festival, and it seems as if the story had its rise from an imperfect notion of Christ's last supper and the institution of the Eucharist." (Sale's Qur'ān.)

MAIMŪNAH (ميمونة). The last of Muḥammad's wives. A sister to Ummu 'l-Fazl, the wife of al-'Abbās, and consequently related to the Prophet. She was a widow, 51 years of age, when Muḥammad married her. She survived him, and died at the age of 81, being buried on the very spot on which she had celebrated her marriage. (Muir's *Life of Mahomet*, new ed. p. 403.)

MAINTENANCE. Arabic *nafaqah* (نفقة), which, in the language of the law, signifies all those things which are necessary to the support of life, such as food, clothes, and lodging, although many confine it solely to food. (*Durru 'l-Mukhtār*, p. 283.)

There are three causes of maintenance established by law. (1) Marriage; (2) Relaionship; (3) Property (*i.e.* in case of a lave)

A husband is bound to give proper maintenance to his wife or wives, provided she or they have not become refractory or rebellious, but have surrendered herself or themselves to the custody of their husband.

Maintenance may be decreed out of the property of an absent husband, whether it be held in trust, or deposit, or *muẓārabah* for him.

If the husband become poor to such a degree as to be unable to provide his wife her maintenance, still they are not to be separated on this account, but the Qāẓī shall direct the woman to procure necessaries for herself upon her husband's credit, the amount remaining a debt upon him.

A divorced wife is entitled to food, clothing, and lodging during the period of her *'iddah*, and until her delivery, if she be pregnant. No maintenance is, however, due to a woman, whether pregnant or not, for the *'iddah* observed upon the death of her husband. No maintenance is due to a woman upon separation caused by her own fault.

A father is bound to support his infant children; and no one shares the obligation with him.

A mother, who is a married wife, cannot be compelled to suckle her infant, except where a nurse cannot be procured, or the child refuses to take the milk of any other than of the mother, who in that case is bound to suckle it, unless incapacitated for want of health, or other sufficient cause.

If neither the father nor the child has any property, the mother may be compelled to suckle it.

The maintenance of an infant child is incumbent upon the father, although he be of a different religion; and, in the same manner, the maintenance of a wife is incumbent upon her husband, notwithstanding this circumstance.

Maintenance of children becomes, however, incumbent upon the father only where they possess no independent property.

When the father is poor and the child's paternal grandfather is rich, and the child's own property is unavailable, the grandfather may be directed to maintain him, and the amount will be a debt due to him from the father, for which the grandfather may have recourse against him; after which the father may reimburse himself by having recourse against the child's property, if there is any.

When the father is infirm and the child has no property of his own, the paternal grandfather may be ordered to maintain him, without right of recourse against anyone; and, in like manner, if the child's mother be rich, or the grandmother rich, while its father is poor, she may be ordered to maintain the child, and the maintenance will be a debt against the child if he be not infirm, but if he be so, he is not liable.

If the father is poor and the mother is rich, and the young child has also a rich grandfather, the mother should be ordered to maintain the child out of her own property, with a right of recourse against the father and the grandfather is not to be called upon to do so. When the father is poor, and has a rich brother, he may be ordered to maintain the child, with right of recourse against the father.

When male children have strength enough to work for their livelihood, though not actually adult, the father may set them to work for their own maintenance, or hire them out, and maintain them out of their wages; but he has no power to hire females out for work or service.

A father must maintain his female children absolutely until they are married, when they have no property of their own. But he is not obliged to maintain his adult male children unless they are disabled by infirmity or disease.

It is also incumbent on a father to maintain his son's wife, when the son is young, poor, or infirm.

The maintenance to an adult daughter, or to an adult son who is disabled, rests upon the parents in three equal parts, two-thirds being furnished by the father, and one-third by the mother.

A child in easy circumstances may be compelled to maintain his poor parents, whether they be Muslim or not, or whether by their own industry they be able to earn anything for subsistence or not.

Where there are male and female children, or children only of the male sex, or only of the female sex, the maintenance of both parents is alike incumbent upon them.

Where there is a mixture of male and female children, the maintenance of both parents is incumbent on them alike.

When a mother is poor, her son is bound to maintain her, though he be in straitened circumstances himself, and she not infirm. When a son is able to maintain only one of his parents, the mother has the better right; and if he have both parents and a minor son, and is able to maintain only one of them, the son has the preferable right. When he has both parents, and cannot afford maintenance to either of them, he should take them to live with him, that they may participate in what food he has for himself. When the son, though poor, is earning something, and his father is infirm, the son should allow the father to share his food with him.

As of a father and mother, so the maintenance of grandfathers and grandmothers, if they be indigent, is incumbent upon their grandchildren, though the former be of different religion.

It is a man's duty to provide maintenance for all his infant male relations within prohibited degrees who are in poverty; and also to all female relations within the same degrees, whether infants or adults, where they are in necessity; and also to all adult male relations within the same degrees who are poor, disabled, or blind; but the obligation does not extend beyond those relations.

No adult male, if in health, is entitled to maintenance, though he is poor; but a person is obliged to maintain his adult female relatives, though in health of body, if they require it. The maintenance of a mere relative is not incumbent on any poor person; contrary to the maintenance of a wife and child, for whom poor and rich are equally liable.

When a poor person has a father and a son's son, both in easy circumstances, the father is liable for his maintenance; and when there is a daughter and a son's son, the daughter only is liable, though they both divide the inheritance between them. So also, when there is a daughter's daughter, or daughter's son, and a full brother, the child of the daughter, whether male or female, is liable, though the brother is entitled to the inheritance. When a person has a parent and a child, both in easy circumstances, the latter is liable, though both are equally near to him. But if he have a grandfather and a son's son, they are liable for his maintenance in proportion to their shares in the inheritance, that is, the grandfather for a sixth, and the son's son for the remainder. If a poor person has a Christian son and a Muslim brother, both in easy circumstances, the son is liable for the maintenance, though the brother would take the inheritance. If he has a mother and grandfather, they are both liable in proportion to their shares as heirs, that is, the mother in one-third, and the grandfather in two-thirds. So, also, when with the mother there is a full brother, or the son of a full brother, or a full paternal uncle, or any other of the *'aṣabah* or residuaries the maintenance is on them, by thirds according to the rules of inheritance. When there is a maternal uncle, and the son of a full paternal uncle, the liability for maintenance is on the former, though the latter would have the inheritance; because the condition of liability is wanting on the latter, who is not within the forbidden degrees.

If a man have a paternal uncle and aunt, and a maternal aunt, his maintenance is on the uncle; and if the uncle be in straitened circumstances, it is on both the others. The principle in this case is, that when a person who takes the whole of the inheritance is in straitened circumstances, his inability is the same as death, and being as it were dead, the maintenance is cast on the remaining relatives in the same proportions as they would be entitled to in the inheritance of the person to be maintained, if the other were not in existence; and that when one who takes only a part of the inheritance is in straitened circumstances, he is to be treated as if he were dead, and the maintenance is cast on the others, according to the shares of the inheritance to which they would be entitled if they should succeed together with him. (See *Durru 'l-Mukhtār, Bābu 'n-Nafaqah.*)

AL-MAISIR (الميسر). A game of chance forbidden in the Qur'ān. Sūrahs ii. 216; v. 92, 93. It signifies a game performed with arrows, and much in use with pagan Arabs. But the term *al-maisar* is now understood to include all games of chance or hazard.

MAJBŪB (مجبوب). A complete eunuch, as distinguished from *khaṣī*, or one who is simply castrated. (*Hidāyah*, vol. i. p. 356.)

AL-MAJĪD (المجيد). "The Glorious One." One of the ninety-nine names or attributes of God. It occurs in the Qur'ān. Sūrah xi. 76: "Verily He is to be praised and *glorified*."

MAJORITY. [PUBERTY.]

MĀJŪJ (ماجوج). [YAJUJ.]

AL-MAJŪS (المجوس), pl. of *Majūsī*. The Magians. Mentioned in the Qur'ān only once, Sūrah xxii. 17: "As to those who believe, and the Jews, and the Sabeites, and the Christians, and the Magians, and those who join other gods with God, of a truth, God shall decide between them on the Day of Resurrection: for God is witness of all things."

Most Muḥammadan writers (especially amongst the Shī'ahs) believe them to have formerly possessed a revelation from God which they have since lost.

The Magians were a sect of ancient philosophers which arose in the East at a very early period, devoting much of their time to the study of the heavenly bodies. They were the learned men of their time, and we find Daniel the Prophet promoted to the head of this sect in Chaldea. (Dan v. 11.) They are supposed to have worshipped the Deity under the emblem of fire; whilst the Sabians, to whom they were opposed, worshipped the heavenly bodies. They held in the greatest abhorrence the worship of images, and considered fire the purest symbol of the Divine Being. This religious sect was reformed by Zoroaster in the sixth century before Christ, and it was the national religion of Persia until it was supplanted by Muḥammadanism. The Magians are now known in Persia as *Gabrs*, and in India as *Pārsīs*. Their sacred book is the *Zend Avesta*, an English translation of which has been published by Mr. A. H. Bleeck (Hertford, 1864), from Professor Spiegel's German translation. There is an able refutation of the Pārsī religion by the late Rev. John Wilson, D.D. (Bombay, 1843).

MAJZŪB (مجذوب). *Lit.* "Attracted." A term used by the Ṣūfīs for a person whom God has chosen for Himself, for a manifestation of His love, and who is thus enabled to attain to all the stages of Ṣūfīism without any effort or trouble. (See ('Abdu 'r-Razzāq's *Dict. of Ṣūfī Terms.*)

MAKKAH (مكة). The capital of Arabia, and the most sacred city of the Muslims. It is celebrated as the birth-place of Muḥammad, and as the site of the Ka'bah, or Sacred Cube, building. Muḥammad is related to have said of Makkah, "What a splendid city thou art! If I had not been driven out of thee by my tribe, I would dwell in no other place but in thee." "It is not man but God who has made Makkah sacred." "My people will be always safe in this world and the next as long as they respect Makkah." (*Mishkāt*, book xl. ch. xv.)

Makkah (the ancient name of which was Bakkah) is situated in about 21° 30′ N. lat., 40° 20′ E. long., and 70 miles from the Red Sea, in a sandy valley running north and south, and from 100 to 70 paces broad. The chief part of the city is placed where the valley is widest. In the narrower part there are single rows of houses only, or detached shops. The town itself covers a space of about 1,500 paces in length, but the whole extent of ground comprehended under the denomination of Makkah, amounts to 3,500 paces in length. The surrounding rocky hills are from 200 to 500 feet in height, barren, and destitute of trees. Most of the town is situated in the valley itself, but there are some parts built on the sides of the hills. The streets are in general broader than those of Eastern cities, for the purpose of accommodating the vast number of pilgrims who resort to it. The houses are lofty and of stone, and the numerous windows that face the streets give to these quite a European aspect. Many of the houses are three stories high.

The only public place in the body of the town is the large square of the great mosque, which is enlivened during the Ḥajj (Pilgrimage) by a great number of well-stored shops. The streets are all unpaved, and in summer the sand and dust are as great a nuisance as the mud is in the rainy season, during which they are scarcely passable after a storm.

Makkah is badly provided with water. There are a few cisterns for receiving rain, and the well-water is brackish. The famous well of Zamzam, in the great mosque, is indeed copious enough to supply the whole town, but the water is not well tasted. The best water is brought by an aqueduct from the vicinity of 'Arafah, six or seven miles distant. There are two places in the interior of the city, where the aqueduct runs above ground, and in these parts it is let off into small channels or fountains, at which some slaves of the Sharīf (the ruler of the city) are stationed to exact a toll from persons who fill their water-skins.

All the houses in Makkah except those of the principal and richest inhabitants, are constructed for the accommodation of lodgers, and divided into numerous separate apartments, each consisting of a sitting-room and a small kitchen. Except four or five houses belonging to the Sharīf, two colleges, and the sacred mosque, Makkah has no public edifices of any importance.

The inhabitants of Makkah, with few exceptions, are Arabians. They have two kinds of employment, trade and the service of the temple. During the Ḥajj, Makkah becomes one of the largest fairs in the East, and certainly the most interesting, from the variety of nations which frequent it. The merchants of the place make large profits during this time by their merchandise. They have also a considerable trade with the Beduins and with other parts of Arabia. The greatest profit, however, is derived from supplying food for 60,000 pilgrims and 20,000 camels. The only articles of manufacture are some pottery and beads; there are a few dyeing-houses in the city.

Makkah is governed by a Sharīf, who is chosen from the Saiyids (or descendants of the Prophet) settled in the Ḥijāz, who were once numerous, but are now reduced to a few families in Makkah. Although he obtains his office by the choice of his people, or by force, he holds his authority from the Turkish Sultan.

Makkah was the seat of government during the reigns of the first five Khalīfahs.

(For an account of the sacred temple, see the article on MASJIDU 'L-HARAM.)

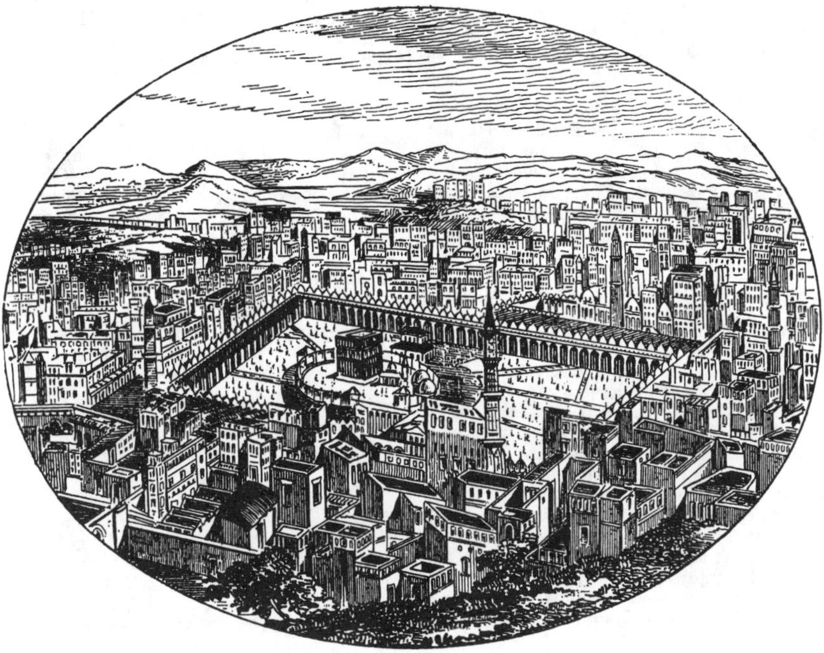

MAKKAH. *(From Stanley Lane-Poole's edition of Lane's "Selections.")*

MAKRŪH (مكروه). *Lit.* "That which is hateful and unbecoming." A term used in the religious, civil, and ceremonial law of Islām, for an act the unlawfulness of which is not absolutely certain, but which is considered improper and unbecoming.

The author of the *Hidāyah* remarks that the doctors of the Ḥanafī sect have disagreed as to the extent to which the term can be received.

The Imām Muḥammad is of opinion that *makrūh* is unlawful, but as he could not draw any convincing argument in favour of his opinion from either the Qur'ān or Traditions, he renounced the general application of "unlawfulness" with respect to such things or acts, and classed them under those which are merely improper.

The Imāms Abū Ḥanīfah and Abū Yūsuf hold that the term applies to that which in its qualities nearly approaches to unlawful, without it being actually so. (*Hidāyah*, vol. iv. p. 86.)

In the *Kitābu 't-Ta'rifāt*, that which is *makrūh* is divided into *makrūh taḥrīmī*, "that which is nearly unlawful"; and *makrūh tanzīhī*, "that which approaches the lawful."

In all works on Muḥammadan law, a section is devoted to the consideration of things which are held to be *makrūh*.

AL-MALĀ'IKAH (الملائكة). *Lit.* "The Angels." The title of the xxxvth Chapter of the Qur'ān in the first verse of which the word occurs:—"Who employeth the *angels* as envoys." It is also called *Sūratu 'l-Fāṭir*, the "Chapter of the Originator."

MALAK (ملك). [ANGEL.]

MALAKU 'L-MAUT (ملك الموت). "The Angel of Death." See Qur'ān, Sūrah xxxii. 11: "The angel of death who is charged with you shall cause you to die: then ye shall be returned to your Lord." He is also called *ʿIzrāʾīl*.

MALANG (ملنگ). An order of Muḥammadan faqīrs or darveshes, who are the descendants and followers of Jaman Juti, a follower of Zindu Shah Madār. They usually wear the hair of the head very full and matted and formed into a knot behind. The order is a very common one in India. (Herklot's *Musalmans*, p. 290.)

AL-MĀLIK (المالك). "The Possessor, lord, ruler." One of the ninety-nine names or attributes of God. It frequently occurs in the Qur'ān, *e.g.* in the first Sūrah, "*Ruler* of the Day of Judgment."

MĀLIK (مالك). *Lit.* "One in authority, a possessor." The angel who is said to preside over hell, and superintend the torments of the damned. He is mentioned in the Qur'ān, Sūrah xliii. 77: "And they shall cry out, O Mālik! let thy Lord make an end of us; he shall say, Verily, tarry here." Perhaps the same as מֹלֶךְ *Molech*, the fire-god and tutelary deity of the children of Ammon.

MĀLIK (مالك). The founder of a sect of Sunnī Muslims.

The Imām Abū ʿAbdi 'llāh Mālik ibn Anas, the founder of one of the four orthodox sects of Sunnīs, was born at al-Madīnah, A.H. 94 (A.D. 716). He lived in the same place and received his earliest impressions of Islām from Sahl ibn Saʿd, the almost sole survivor of the Companions of the Prophet. He was considered to be the most learned man of his time, and his self-denial and abstinence were such that he usually fasted four days in the week. He enjoyed the advantages of a personal acquaintance and familiar intercourse with the Imām Abū Ḥanīfah, although differing from him on many important questions regarding the authority of the Traditions. His pride, however, was at least equal to his literary endowments. In proof of this, it is related of him that when the great Khalīfah Harūnu 'r-Rashīd came to al-Madīnah to visit the tomb of the Prophet, Mālik having gone forth to meet him, the Khalīfah addressed him, "O Mālik! I entreat as a favour that you will come every day to me and my two sons, Amīn and Ma'mūn, and instruct us in traditional knowledge." To which the sage haughtily replied, "O Khalīfah, science is of a dignified nature, and instead of going to any person, requires that all should come to it." The story further says that the sovereign, with much humility, asked his pardon, acknowledged the truth of his remark, and sent both his sons to Mālik, who seated them among his other scholars without any distinction.

With regard to the Traditions, his authority is generally quoted as decisive; in fact, he considered them as altogether superseding the judgment of a man, and on his death-bed severely condemned himself for the many decisions he had presumed to give on the mere suggestion of his own reason. The Qur'ān and the Sunnah excepted, the only study to which he applied himself in his latter days, was the contemplation of the Deity; and his mind was at length so much absorbed in the immensity of the Divine attributes and perfections, as to lose sight of all more insignificant objects! Hence he gradually withdrew himself from the world, became indifferent to its concerns, and after some years of complete retirement, died at al-Madīnah, A.H. 179 (A.D. 795). His authority is at present chiefly received in Barbary and the other northern states of Africa. Of his works, the only one upon record is one of tradition, known as the *Muwaṭṭa'*. His principal pupil was ash-Shāfiʿī, who afterwards himself gave the name to a sect.

MĀLIKU 'L-MULK (مالك الملك). "The Lord of the Kingdom." One of the ninety-nine names or attributes of God. It occurs once in the Qur'ān, Sūrah iii. 25: "Say, O God, *Lord of the Kingdom*, Thou givest the kingdom to whomsoever Thou pleasest, and strippest the kingdom from whomsoever Thou pleasest."

MĀL ẒĀMINĪ (مال ضامنى). Bail for property. A legal term. (*Hidāyah*, vol. ii. p. 568). Bail for the person is *ḥāẓir ẓāminī*.

MAMĀT (ممات). "Death"; *e.g.* Sūrah vi. 163: "My prayers, my sacrifice, my life, and my *death*, belong to God." [MAUT.]

MAMLŪK (مملوك), pl. *mamālīk*. "A slave." A term used in Muslim law for a bond-slave, the word *ʿabd* signifying both "a slave" and "a servant of God." It occurs only once in the Qur'ān, Sūrah xvi. 77: "God propounds a comparison between a slave (*mamlūk*) and the property of his master."

This word has become historic in the *Mamlukes*, or that military body of slaves who for a long time ruled Egypt. These military slaves were first organized by Mālik aṣ-Ṣāliḥ, who purchased many thousands of slaves in the markets of Asia, and brought them to Egypt in the 13th century. They were by him embodied into a corps of 12,000 men, but in A.D. 1254, they revolted, and killed Turan Shah, the last prince of the Aiyūb dynasty. They then raised to the throne of Egypt al-Muʿizz, who was himself a Turkoman slave. The Mamlukes continued the ruling power in Egypt till A.D. 1517, when Salīm I. defeated them and put to death Tumaun Bey, the last of the Mamluke dynasty. They were, however, maintained in Egypt as a military aristocracy, and were a powerful body at the time of the French invasion. Muḥammad ʿAlī Pasha of Egypt destroyed their power and influence by murdering many of them in A.D. 1811.

MAʿMŪDĪYAH (معمودية). A word used by the commentator al-Baiẓāwī for Christian Baptism In remarking on Sūrah

ii. 132, "the baptism of God" (*Ṣibghatu 'llāh*), he says, "The Nazarenes used to dip their children in yellow water, and they called it *Ma'mūdīyah*; and they said, whoever was dipped in *Ma'mūdiyah* was purified, and that it was a sign of his becoming a Nazarene." (See *Tafsīru 'l-Baiẓāwī, in loco.*)

MANĀRAH (منارة). Anglice *minaret.* From *manār*, "a place were a fire is lit, lighthouse, pillar." The lofty turret of a mosque, from which the Mu'aẕẕin, or "caller to prayer," invites the people to prayer. In the early days of Islām there were no minarets to the mosques, those at Qūbā' and al-Madīnah being erected by 'Umar ibn 'Abdi 'l-'Azīz, A.H. 86. [MOSQUE.]

MANĀSIK (مناسك). From *mansik*, "a place of sacrifice." The sacred rites and ceremonies attending the pilgrimage. [HAJJ.]

MANĀT (منات). An idol mentioned in the Qur'ān, Sūrah liii. 19, 20: "What think ye, then, of al-Lāt and al-'Uzzā, and Manāt, the third idol besides."

According to Ḥusain, it was an idol of the tribes of Huẕail and Khazā'ah. For a discussion of the subject, see the article on LAT.

AL-MĀNI' (المانع). "The Withholder." One of the ninety-nine names or attributes of God. It does not occur in the Qur'ān, but is given in the Ḥadīs̤.

MANĪḤAH (منيحة). A legal term for a camel lent, with permission to use its milk, its hair, and its young, but on condition of returning the camel itself. Such an animal cannot be sacrificed. (*Mishkāt*, book iv. ch. 50.)

MANLĀ (منلا). A learned man. A Muhammadan priest. The Egyptian form of Maulavī or Mulla.

MAN-LĀ-YASTAḤẒIRAHU 'L-FAQĪH (من لا يستحضره الفقيه). A book of Shī'ah traditions compiled by Saiyid Rāzī, A.H. 406.

MANNA. Arabic *mann* (من); Heb. מָן *mān*; Greek *μάννα*. The giving of manna to the children of Israel is mentioned three times in the Qur'ān.

Sūrah ii. 54: "And we overshadowed them with the cloud, and sent down manna and the quails."

Sūrah xx. 82: "We caused the manna and the quails to descend upon you."

Sūrah vii. 160: "We caused clouds to overshadow them, and sent down upon them the manna and the quails."

'Abdu 'l-'Azīz, in his commentary, says it was like white sugar.

MANSLAUGHTER. [MURDER.]

MANUMISSION. Arabic *'Itq* (عتق). [SLAVERY.]

MAQĀM MAḤMŪD (مقام محمود). "A glorious station," or place in heaven, said to be reserved for Muḥammad. It is mentioned in the XVIIth chapter of the Qur'ān, verse 81; "It may be that thy Lord will raise thee to *a glorious station.*"

Religious Muslims always pray that God will grant the *Maqām Maḥmud* to their Prophet, when they hear the Aẕān recited. [AZAN.]

MAQĀMU IBRAHĪM (مقام ابرهيم). "The place or station of Abraham." Mentioned twice in the Qur'ān.

Sūrah iii. 91: "In it (Makkah) are evident signs, even the *place of Abraham.*"

Sūrah ii. 119: "Take ye the *station of Abraham* for a place of prayer."

It is a place at Makkah within the Masjid boundary, supposed to have the impression of the foot-marks of Abraham. Burckhardt says this is a small building, supported by six pillars about eight feet high, four of which are surrounded from the top to bottom by a fine iron railing, while they leave the space behind the two hind pillars open. Within the railing is a frame about five feet square, terminating in a pyramidal top, and said to contain the sacred stone upon which Abraham stood when he built the Ka'bah.

MAQSŪRAH (مقصورة). A closet or place of retirement. A place set apart in mosques, enclosed with curtains, where devout men recite their supererogatory prayers, and perform *ẕikr*. [ZIKR.]

MARIYATU 'L-QIBṬĪYAH (مارية القبطية). [MARY THE COPT.]

MARRIAGE. The celebration of the marriage contract is called *nikāh* (نكاح). The festive rejoicings *'urs* (عرس); Persian *shādī*). Marriage is enjoined upon every Muslim, and celibacy is frequently condemned by Muḥammad. It is related in the Traditions that Muḥammad said: "When the servant of God marries, he perfects half of his religion;" and that "on one occasion Muḥammad asked a man if he was married, and being answered in the negative, he said, 'Art thou sound and healthy?' Upon the man replying that he was, Muḥammad said, 'Then thou art one of the brothers of the devil.'" (*Mishkāt*, book xiii. ch. i.) Consequently in Islām, even the ascetic orders are rather married than single.

It is related that one of the Companions, named 'Us̤mān ibn Maẓ'ūn, wished to lead a life of celibacy, but Muḥammad forbade him.

The following are some of the sayings of Muḥammad on the subject of marriage (see *Mishkātu 'l-Masābīḥ*, book xiii.):—

"The best wedding is that upon which the least trouble and expense is bestowed."

"The worst of feasts are marriage feasts, to which the rich are invited and the poor left out, and he who abandons the acceptation of an invitation, then verily disobeys God and His Prophet."

"Matrimonial alliances (between two families or tribes) increase friendship more than anything else."

"Marry women who will love their husbands and be very prolific, for I wish you to be more numerous than any other people."

"When anyone demands your daughter in marriage, and you are pleased with his disposition and his faith, then give her to him; for if you do not so, then there will be strife and contention in the world."

"A woman may be married either for her money, her reputation, her beauty, or her religion; then look out for a religious woman, for if you do marry other than a religious woman, may your hands be rubbed with dirt."

"All young men who have arrived at the age of puberty should marry, for marriage prevents sins. He who cannot marry should fast."

"When a Muslim marries he perfects half his religion, and he should practise abstinence for the remaining half."

"Beware! make not large settlements upon women; because, if great settlements were a cause of greatness in the world and of righteousness before God, surely it would be most proper for the Prophet of God to make them."

"When any of you wishes to demand a woman in marriage, if he can arrange it, let him see her first."

"A woman ripe in years shall have her consent asked in marriage, and if she remain silent her silence is her consent, and if she refuse she shall not be married by force."

"A widow shall not be married until she be consulted, nor shall a virgin be married until her consent be asked." The Companions said, "In what manner is the permission of a virgin?" He replied, "Her consent is by her silence."

"If a woman marries without the consent of her guardian, her marriage is null and void, is null and void, is null and void; then, if her marriage hath been consummated, the woman shall take her dower; if her guardians dispute about her marriage, then the king is her guardian."

The subject of Muslim marriages will now be treated in the present article under the headings—I. The Validity of Marriage; II. The Legal Disablities to Marriage; III. The Religious Ceremony; IV. The Marriage Festivities.

I.—The Validity of Marriage.

Muslims are permitted to marry four free women, and to have as many slaves for concubines as they may have acquired. See Qur'ān, Sūrah iv. 3: "Of women who seem good in your eyes, marry two, or three, or four; and if ye still fear that ye shall not act equitably, then one only; or the slaves whom ye have acquired." [WIVES.]

Usufructory or temporary marriages were sanctioned by the Prophet, but this law is said by the Sunnīs to have been abrogated, although it is allowed by the Shīʿahs, and is practised in Persia in the present day. [MUTʿAH.] These temporary marriages are undoubtedly the greatest blot in Muḥammad's moral legislation, and admit of no satisfactory apology.

Marriage, according to Muḥammadan law, is simply a civil contract, and its validity does not depend upon any religious ceremony. Though the civil contract is not positively prescribed to be reduced to writing, its validity depends upon the consent of the parties, which is called *ījāb* and *qabūl*, "declaration" and "acceptance"; the presence of two male witnesses (or one male and two female witnesses); and a dower of not less than ten dirhams, to be settled upon the woman. The omission of the settlement does not, however, invalidate the contract, for under any circumstances, the woman becomes entitled to her dower of ten dirhams or more. (A dower suitable to the position of the woman is called *Mahru 'l-miṣl.*)

Liberty is allowed a woman who has reached the age of puberty, to marry or refuse to marry a particular man, independent of her guardian, who has no power to dispose of her in marriage without her consent or against her will; while the objection is reserved for the girl, married by her guardian during her infancy, to ratify or dissolve the contract immediately on reaching her majority. When a woman, adult and sane, elects to be married through an agent (*wakīl*), she empowers him, in the presence of competent witnesses, to convey her consent to the bridegroom. The agent, if a stranger, need not see her, and it is sufficient that the witnesses, who see her, satisfy him that she, expressly or *impliedly*, consents to the proposition of which he is the bearer. The law respects the modesty of the sex, and allows the expression of consent on the part of the lady by indirect ways, even without words. With a virgin, silence is taken as consent, and so is a smile or laugh.

Mr. Syed Ameer Ali says:—

"The validity of a marriage under the Muhammadan law depends on two conditions: first, on the capacity of the parties to marry each other; secondly, on the celebration of the marriage according to the forms prescribed in the place where the marriage is celebrated, or which are recognised as legal by the customary law of the Mussalmans. It is a recognised principle that the capacity of each of the parties to a marriage is to be judged of by their respective *lex domicilii* 'If they are each, whether belonging to the same country or to different countries, capable according to their *lex domicilii* of marriage with the other, they have the capacity required by the rule under consideration. In short, as in other contracts, so in that of marriage, personal capacity must depend on the law of domicil.'

"The capacity of a Mussalman domiciled in England will be regulated by the English law, but the capacity of one who is domiciled in the

Belâd-ul-Islâm (*i.e.* a Muhammadan country), by the provisions of the Mussalman law. It is, therefore, important to consider what the requisite conditions are to vest in an individual the capacity to enter into a valid contract of marriage. As a general rule, it may be remarked, that under the Islâmic law, the capacity to contract a valid marriage rests on the same basis as the capacity to enter into any other contract. 'Among the conditions which are requisite for the validity of a contract of marriage (says the *Fatâwa-i-Alamgîrî*, p. 377), are understanding, puberty, and freedom, in the contracting parties, with this difference, that whilst the first requisite is essentially necessary for the validity of the marriage, as a marriage cannot be contracted by a *majnûn* (*non compos mentis*), or a boy without understanding, the other two conditions are required only to give operation to the contract, as the marriage contracted by a (minor) boy (possessed) of understanding is dependent for its operation on the consent of his guardian.' Puberty and discretion constitute, accordingly, the essential conditions of the capacity to enter into a valid contract of marriage. A person who is an infant in the eye of the law is disqualified from entering into any legal transactions (*tassarufât-i-shariyeh—taṣarrufāt-i-shar'iah*), and is consequently incompetent to contract a marriage. Like the English common law, however, the Muhammadan law makes a distinction between a contract made by a minor possessed of discretion or understanding and one made by a child who does not possess understanding. A marriage contracted by a minor who has not arrived at the age of discretion, or who does not possess understanding, or who cannot comprehend the consequences of the act, is a mere nullity.

"The Mohammadan law fixes no particular age when discretion should be presumed. Under the English law, however, the age of seven marks the difference between want of understanding in children and capacity to comprehend the legal effects of particular acts. The Indian Penal Code also has fixed the age of seven as the period when the liability for offences should commence. It may be assumed, perhaps not without some reason, that the same principle ought to govern cases under the Muhammadan law, that is, when a contract of marriage is entered into by a child under the age of seven, it will be regarded as a nullity. It is otherwise, however, in the case of a marriage contracted by a person of understanding. 'It is valid,' says the *Fatâwa*, 'though dependent for its operation on the consent of the guardian.'

"A contract entered into by a person who is insane is null and void, unless it is made during a lucid interval. A slave cannot enter into a contract of marriage without the consent of his master. The Mussalman lawyers, therefore, add freedom (*hurriyet*) as one of the conditions to the capacity for marriage.

"Majority is presumed, among the Hanafis and the Shiahs, on the completion of the fifteenth year, in the case of both males and females, unless there is any evidence to show that puberty was attained earlier.

"Besides puberty and discretion, the capacity to marry requires that there should be no legal disability or bar to the union of the parties; that in fact they should not be within the prohibited degrees, or so related to or connected with each other as to make their union unlawful." (See Syed Ameer Ali's *Personal Law of the Muhammadans*, p. 216.)

With regard to the consent of the woman, Mr. Syed Ameer Ali remarks :—

"No contract can be said to be complete unless the contracting parties understand its nature and mutually consent to it. A contract of marriage also implies mutual consent, and when the parties see one another, and of their own accord agree to bind themselves, both having the capacity to do so, there is no doubt as to the validity of the marriage. Owing, however, to the privacy in which Eastern women generally live, and the difficulties under which they labour in the exercise of their own choice in matrimonial matters, the Mohammadan law, with somewhat wearying particularity, lays down the principle by which they may not only protect themselves from the cupidity of their natural guardians, but may also have a certain scope in the selection of their husbands.

"For example, when a marriage is contracted on behalf of an adult person of either sex, it is an essential condition to its validity that such person should consent thereto, or, in other words, marriage contracted without his or her authority or consent is null, by whomsoever it may have been entered into.

"Among the Hanafis and the Shiahs, the capacity of a woman, who is adult and sane, to contract herself in marriage is absolute. The Shiah law is most explicit on this point. It expressly declares that, in the marriage of a discreet female (*rashîdah*) who is adult, no guardian is required. The *Hidâya* holds the same opinion. A woman (it says) who is adult and of sound mind, may be married by virtue of her own consent, although the contract may not have been made or acceded to by her guardians, and this whether she be a virgin or *saibbah*. Among the Shafais and the Malikis, although the consent of the adult virgin is an essential to the validity of a contract of marriage entered into on her behalf, as among the Hanafis and the Shiahs, she cannot contract herself in marriage without the intervention of a *walî*. (Hamilton's *Hidāyah*, vol. i. p. 95.)

"Among the Shafais, a woman cannot personally consent to the marriage. The presence of the *walî*, or guardian, is essentially necessary to give validity to the contract. The *walî*'s intervention is required by the Shafais and the Malikis to supplement the presumed incapacity of the woman to understand the nature of the contract, to settle the terms and other matters of a similar import, and to guard the girl from being victimised by an unscrupulous adventurer, or from marrying a person morally or socially unfitted for her. It is owing to the importance and multifariousness of the duties with which a *walî* is charged, that the Sunni law is particular in ascertaining the order in which the right of guardianship is possessed by the different individuals who may be entitled to it. The schools are not in accord with reference to the order. The Hanafis entrust the office first to the agnates in the order of succession; then to the mother, the sister, the relatives on the mother's side, and lastly to the Kazi. The Shafais adopt the following order: The father, the father's father, the son (by a previous marriage), the full brother, the consanguinous brother, the nephew, the uncle, the cousin, the tutor, and lastly the Kazi; thus entirely excluding the female relations from the *wilayet*. The Malikis agree with the Shafais in confiding the office of guardian only to men, but they adopt an order slightly different. They assign the first rank to the sons of the woman (by a former marriage), the second to the father; and then successively to the full brother, nephew, paternal grandfather, paternal uncle, cousin, manumittor, and lastly to the Kazi. Among the Malikis and the Shafais, where the presence of the guardian at a marriage is always necessary, the question has given birth to two different systems. The first of these considers the guardian to derive his powers entirely from the law. It consequently insists not only on his presence at the marriage, but on his actual participation in giving the consent. According to this view, not only is a marriage contracted through a more distant guardian invalid, whilst one more nearly connected is present, but the latter cannot validate a marriage contracted at the time without his consent, by according his consent subsequently. This harsh doctrine, however, does not appear to be forced in any community following the Maliki or Shafai tenets. The second system is diametrically opposed to the first, and seems to have been enunciated by Shaikh Ziâd as the doctrine taught by Malik. According to this system the right of the guardian, though no doubt a creation of the law, is exercised only in virtue of the power or special authorisation granted by the woman; for the woman once emancipated from the *patria potestas* is mistress of her own actions. She is not only entitled to consult her own interests in matrimony, but can appoint whomsoever she chooses to represent her and protect her legitimate interests. If she think the nearer guardian inimically inclined towards her, she may appoint one more remote to act for her during her marriage. Under this view of the law, the guardian acts as an attorney on behalf of the woman, deriving all his powers from her and acting solely for her benefit. This doctrine has been adopted by Al-Karkhi, Ibn al-Kâsim, and Ibn-i-Salamun, and has been formally enunciated by the Algerian Kazis in several consecutive judgments. When the *wali* preferentially entitled to act is absent, and his whereabouts unknown, when he is a prisoner or has been reduced to slavery, or is absent more than ten days' journey from the place where the woman is residing, or is insane or an infant, then the *wilayet* passes to the person next in order to him. The Hanafis hold that the woman is always entitled to give her consent without the intervention of a guardian. When a guardian is employed and found acting on her behalf, he is presumed to derive his power solely from her, so that he cannot act in any circumstances in contravention of his authority or instructions. When the woman has authorised her guardian to marry her to a particular individual, or has consented to a marriage proposed to her by a specific person, the guardian has no power to marry her to another. Under the Shiah law, a woman who is 'adult and discreet,' is herself competent to enter into a contract of marriage. She requires no representative or intermediary, through whom to give her consent. 'If her guardians,' says the *Sharâya*, 'refuse to marry her to an equal when desired by her to do so, there is no doubt that she is entitled to contract herself, even against their wish.' The Shiahs agree with the Hanafis in giving to females the power of representing others in matrimonial contracts. In a contract of marriage, full regard is to be paid to the words of a female who is adult and sane, that is, possessed of sound understanding; she is, accordingly, not only qualified to contract herself, but also to act as the agent of another in giving expression either to the declaration or to the consent. The *Mafâtih* and the *Jama-ush-Shattât*, also declare 'that it is not requisite that the parties through whom a contract is entered into should both be males, since with us (the Shiahs) a contract made through (the agency or intermediation of) a female is valid.' To recapitulate. Under the Maliki and Shafai law, the marriage of an adult girl is not valid unless her consent is obtained to it, but such consent must be given through a legally authorised *wali*, who would act as her representative. Under the Hanafi and Shiah law, the woman can consent to her own marriage, either with or without a guardian or agent." (*Personal Law of the Muhammadans*, p. 233.)

II.—The Legal Disabilities to Marriage.

There are nine prohibitions to marriage, namely:—

1. *Consanguinity*, which includes mother, grandmother, sister, niece, aunt, &c.

2. *Affinity*, which includes mother-in-law, step-grandmother, daughter-in-law, step-granddaughter, &c.

3. *Fosterage*. A man cannot marry his foster mother, nor foster sister, unless the foster brother and sister were nursed by the same mother at intervals widely separated. But a man may marry the mother of his foster sister, or the foster mother of his sister.

4. A man may not marry his wife's sister during his wife's lifetime, unless she be divorced.

5. A man married to a free woman cannot marry a slave.

6. It is not lawful for a man to marry the wife or *mu'taddah* of another, whether the *'iddah* be on account of repudiation or death. That is, he cannot marry until the expiration of the woman's *'iddah*, or period of probation.

7. A Muslim cannot marry a polytheist, or Majūsīyah. But he may marry a Jewess, or a Christian, or a Sabean.

8. A woman is prohibited by reason of property. For example, it is not lawful for a man to marry his own slave, or a woman her bondsman.

9. A woman is prohibited by repudiation or divorce. If a man pronounces three divorces upon a wife who is free, or two upon a slave, she is not lawful to him until she shall have been regularly espoused by another man, who having duly consummated the marriage, afterwards divorces her, or dies, and her *'iddah* from him be accomplished.

Mr. Syed Ameer Ali says:—

"The prohibitions may be divided into four heads, viz. *relative* or *absolute*, *prohibitive* or *directory*. They arise in the first place from legitimate and illegitimate relationship of blood (consanguinity); secondly, from alliance or affinity (*al-muṣāḥarat*); thirdly, from fosterage (*ar-riẓā'*); and, fourthly, from completion of number (*i.e.* four). The ancient Arabs permitted the union of step-mothers and mothers-in-law on one side, and step-sons and sons-in-law on the other. The Kurân expressly forbids this custom: 'Marry not women whom your fathers have had to wife (except what is already past), for this is an uncleanliness and abomination, and an evil way.' (Sūrah iv. 26.) Then come the more definite prohibitions in the next verse: 'Ye are forbidden to marry your mothers, your daughters, your sisters, and your aunts, both on the father's and on the mother's side; your brothers' daughters and your sister's daughters; your mothers who have given you suck and your foster-sisters; your wives' mothers, your daughters-in-law, born of your wives with whom ye have cohabited. Ye are also prohibited to take to wife two sisters (except what is already past), nor to marry women who are already married.' (Sūrah iv. 27.)

"The prohibitions founded on consanguinity (*taḥrīmu 'n-nasab*) are the same among the Sunnis as among the Shiahs. No marriage can be contracted with the ascendants, with the descendants, with relations of the second rank, such as brothers and sisters or their descendants, with paternal and maternal uncles and aunts. Nor can a marriage be contracted with a natural offspring or his or her descendants. Among the Shiahs, marriage is forbidden for fosterage in the same order as in the case of *nasab*. The Sunnis, however, permit marriage in spite of fosterage in the following cases: The marriage of the father of the child with the mother of his child's foster-mother, or with her daughter; the marriage of the foster-mother with the brother of the child whom she has fostered; the marriage with the foster-mother of an uncle or aunt. The relationship by fosterage arises among the Shiahs when the child has been really nourished at the breast of the foster-mother. Among the Sunnis, it is required that the child should have been suckled at least fifteen times, or at least a day and night. Among the Hanafis, it is enough if it have been suckled only once. Among the Shafais it is necessary that it should have been suckled four times. There is no difference among the Sunnis and the Shiahs regarding the prohibitions arising from alliance. Under the Shiah law, a woman against whom a proceeding by *laân* (*li'ân*) has taken place on the ground of her adultery, and who is thereby divorced from her husband, cannot under any circumstance re-marry him. The Shafais and Malikis agree in this opinion with the Shiahs. The Hanafis, however, allow a re-marriage with a woman divorced by *laân*. The Shiahs as well as the Shafais, Malikis, and Hanbalis, hold that a marriage with a woman who is already pregnant (by another) is absolutely illegal. According to the *Hidâya*, however, it would appear that Abu Hanifah and his disciple Muhammad were of opinion that such a marriage was allowable. The practice among the Indian Hanifis is variable. But generally speaking, such marriages are regarded with extreme disapprobation. Among the Shafais, Malikis and Hanbalis, marriages are prohibited during the state of *ihrâm* (pilgrimage to Makkah), so that when a marriage is contracted by two persons, either of whom is a follower of the doctrines of the above-mentioned schools whilst on the pilgrimage, it is illegal. The Hanafis regard such marriages to be legal. With the Shiahs, though a marriage in a state of *ihrâm* is, in any case, illegal, the woman is not prohibited to the man always, unless he was aware of the illegality of the union. All the schools prohibit contemporaneous marriages with two women so related to each other that, supposing either of them to be a male a marriage between them would be illegal. Illicit intercourse between a man and a woman, according to the Hanafis and Shiahs, prohibits the man from marrying the woman's mother as well as her daughter. The observant student of the law of the two principal sects which divide the world of Islâm, cannot fail to notice the distinctive peculiarity existing between them in respect to their attitude to outside people. The nations who adopted the Shiah doctrines never seem to have come into contact with the Christian races of the West to any marked extent; whilst their relations with the Mago-Zoroastrians of the East were both intimate and lasting. The Sunnis, on the other hand, seem always to have been more or less influenced by the Western nations. In consequence of the different positions which the followers of the sects occupied towards non-Muslims, a wide divergence exists between the Shiah and Sunni schools of law regarding intermarriages between Muslims and non-Muslims. It has already been pointed out that the Kurân, for political reasons, forbade all unions between Mussalmans and idolaters. It said in explicit terms, 'Marry not a woman of the Polytheists (*Mushrikin*) until she embraces Islâm.' But it also declared that 'such women as are *muhsinas* (of chaste reputation) belonging to the scriptural sects,' or believing in a revealed or moral religion, 'are lawful to Muslims.'

"From these and similar directions, two somewhat divergent conclusions have been drawn by the lawyers of the two schools. The Sunnis recognise as legal and valid a marriage contracted between a Muslim on one side, and a Hebrew or a Christian woman on the other. They hold, however, that a marriage between a Mussalman and a Magian or a Hindu woman is invalid. The Akhbari Shiahs and the Mutazalas agree with the Sunni doctors. The Usuli Shiahs do not recognise as legal a permanent contract of marriage between Muslims and the followers of any other creed. They allow, however, temporary contracts extending over a term of years, or a certain specified period, with a Christian, Jew, or a Magian female. Abu Hanifah permits a Mussalman to marry a Sabean woman, but Abu Yusuf and Muhammad and the other Sunni Imâms, hold such unions illegal.

"A female Muslim cannot under any circumstances marry a non-Muslim. Both schools prohibit a Muhammadan from marrying an idolatrous female, or one who worships the stars or any kind of fetish whatsoever.

"These prohibitions are relative in their nature and in their effect. They do not imply the absolute nullity of the marriage. For example, when a Muhammadan marries a Hindu woman in a place where the laws of Islâm are in force, the marriage only is invalid, and does not affect the status of legitimacy of the offspring." (See *Personal Law of the Muhammadans*, p. 220.)

III.—The Religious Ceremony.

The Muḥammadan law appoints no specific religious ceremony, nor are any religious rites necessary for the contraction of a valid marriage. Legally, a marriage contracted between two persons possessing the capacity to enter into the contract, is valid and binding, if entered into by mutual consent in the presence of witnesses. And the Shīʻah law even dispenses with witnesses.

In India there is little difference between the rites that are practised at the marriage ceremonies of the Shīʻahs and Sunnīs.

In all cases the religious ceremony is left entirely to the discretion of the Qāẓī or person who performs the ceremony, and consequently there is no uniformity of ritual. Some Qāẓīs merely recite the *Fātiḥah* (the first chapter of the Qur'ān), and the *durūd*, or blessing. The following is the more common order of performing the service. The Qāẓī, the bridegroom, and the bride's attorney, with the witnesses, having assembled in some convenient place (but not in a mosque), arrangements are made as to the amount of dower or *mahr*. The bridegroom then repeats after the Qāẓī the following:—

1. The *Istighfār*. "I desire forgiveness from God."

2. The four *Quls*. The four chapters of the Qur'ān commencing with the word "*Qul*" (cix., cxii., cxiii., cxiv.). These chapters have nothing in them connected with the subject of marriage, and appear to be selected on account of their brevity.

3. The *Kalimah*, or Creed. "There is no Deity but God, and Muḥammad is the Prophet of God."

4. The *Ṣifwatu 'l-Imān*. A profession of belief in God, the Angels, the Scriptures, the Prophets, the Resurrection, and the Absolute Decree of good and evil.

The Qāẓī then requests the bride's attorney to take the hand of the bridegroom, and to say, "Such an one's daughter, by the agency of her attorney and by the testimony of two witnesses, has, in your marriage with her, had such a dower settled upon her; do you consent to it?" To which the bridegroom replies, "With my whole heart and soul, to my marriage with this woman, as well as to the dower already settled upon her, I consent, I consent, I consent."

After this the Qāẓī raises his hands and offers the following prayer: "O great God! grant that mutual love may reign between this couple, as it existed between Adam and Eve, Abraham and Sarah, Joseph and Zalîkha, Moses and Zipporah, his highness Muḥammad and ʻĀyishah, and his highness ʻAlī al-Murtaẓā and Fāṭimatu 'z-Zahrā."

The ceremony being over, the bridegroom embraces his friends and receives their congratulations.

According to the *Durru 'l-Mukhtār*, p. 196, and all schools of Muslim law, the bridegroom is entitled to see his wife before the marriage, but Eastern customs very rarely allow the exercise of this right, and the husband, generally speaking, sees his wife for the first time when leading her to the nuptial chamber.

IV.—The Marriage Festivities.

Nikāḥ is preceded and followed by festive rejoicings which have been variously described by Oriental travellers, but they are not parts of either the civil or religious ceremonies.

The following account of a *shādī* or wedding in Hiudustan is abridged (with some correction) from Mrs. Meer Hasan Alī's *Musalmāns of India*.

The marriage ceremony usually occupies three days and three nights. The day being fixed, the mother of the bride actively employs the intervening time in finishing her preparations for the young lady's departure from the paternal roof with suitable articles, which might prove the bride was not sent forth to her new family without proper provision: A silver-gilt bedstead with the necessary furniture; a silver pawn-dān, shaped very like an English spice-box; a chillumchi or wash-hand basin; a lota or water-jug, resembling an old-fashioned coffee-pot; a silver luggun, or spittoon; a surai, or water-bottle; silver basins for water; several dozens of copper pots, plates, and spoons for cooking; dishes, plates and platters in endless variety; and numerous other articles needful for housekeeping, including a looking-glass for the bride's toilette, masnads, cushions, and carpets.

On the first day the ladies' apartments of both houses are completely filled with visitors of all grades, from the wives and mothers of noblemen, down to the humblest acquaintance of the family, and to do honour to the hostess, the guests appear in their best attire and most valuable ornaments. The poor bride is kept in strict confinement in a dark closet or room during the whole three days' merriment, whilst the happy bridegroom is the most prominent person in the assembly of the males, where amusements are contrived to please and divert him, the whole party vying in personal attentions to him. The ladies are occupied in conversations and merriment, and amused with native songs and music of the domnis, smoking the huqqa, eating pawn, dinner, &c. Company is their delight and time passes pleasantly with them in such an assembly.

The second day is one of bustle and preparation in the bride's home; it is spent in arranging the various articles that are to accompany the bride's *mayndī* or *ḥinnā'* (the *Lawsonia inermis*), which is forwarded in the evening to the bridegroom's house with great parade. The herb *mayndī* or *hinnā* is in general request amongst the natives of India, for the purpose of dyeing the hands and feet; and is considered by them an indispensable article to their comfort, keeping those members cool, and a great ornament to the person. Long established custom obliges the bride to send *mayndī* on the second night of the nuptials to the bridegroom; and to make the event more conspicuous, presents proportioned to the means of the party accompany the trays of prepared *mayndī*.

The female friends of the bride's family attend the procession in covered conveyances, and the male guests on horses, elephants, and in palkies; trains of servants and bands of music swell the procession (amongst persons of distinction) to a magnitude inconceivable to those who have not visited the large native cities of India.

Amongst the bride's presents with *mayndī* may be noticed everything requisite for a full-dress suit for the bridegroom, and the etcetras of his toilette; confectionery, dried fruits, preserves, the prepared pawns, and a multitude of trifles too tedious to enumerate, but which are nevertheless esteemed luxuries with the native young people, and are considered essential to the occasion. One thing I must not omit, the sugar-candy, which forms the source of amusement when the bridegroom is under the dominion of the females in his mother's zanānah. The fireworks sent with the presents are concealed in flowers formed of the transparent uberuck; these flowers are set out in frames, and represent beds of flowers in their varied forms and colours; these in their number and gay appearance have a pretty effect in the procession, interspersed with the trays containing the dresses, &c. All the trays are first covered with basketwork raised in domes, and over these are thrown draperies of broadcloth, gold cloth, and brocade, neatly fringed in bright colours.

The *mayndī* procession having reached the bridegroom's house, bustle and excitement pervade through every department of the mansion. The gentlemen are introduced to the father's hall; the ladies to the youth's mother, who in all possible state is prepared to receive the bride's friends.

The ladies crowd into the centre hall to witness, through the blinds of bamboo, the important process of dressing the bridegroom in his bride's presents. The centre purdah is let down, in which are openings to admit the hands and feet; and close to this purdah a low stool is placed. When all these preliminary preparations are made, and the ladies securely under cover, notice is sent to the male assembly that "the bridegroom is wanted"; and he then enters the zanānah courtyard, amidst the deafening sounds of trumpets and drums from without, and a serenade from the female singers within. He seats himself on the stool placed for him close to the purdah, and obeys the several commands he receives from the hidden females, with childlike docility. The moist *mayndī* is then tied on with bandages by hands he cannot see, and, if time admits, one hour is requisite to fix the dye bright and permanent on the hands and feet. During this delay, the hour is passed in lively dialogues with the several purdahed dames, who have all the advantages of seeing though themselves unseen; the singers occasionally lauding his praise in extempore strains, after describing the loveliness of his bride (whom they know nothing about), and foretelling the happiness which awaits him in his marriage, but which, in the lottery, may perhaps prove a blank. The sugar-candy, broken into small lumps, is presented by the ladies whilst his hands and feet are fast bound in the bandages of *mayndī*; but as he cannot help himself, and it is an omen of good to eat the bride's sweets at this ceremony, they are sure he will try to catch the morsels which they present to his mouth and then draw back, teasing the youth with their banterings, until at last he may successfully snap at the candy, and seize the fingers also with the dainty, to the general amusement of the whole party and the youth's entire satisfaction.

The *mayndī* supposed to have done its duty the bandages are removed, the old nurse of his infancy (always retained for life), assists him with water to wash off the leaves, dries his feet and hands, rubs him with perfumes, and robes him in his bride's presents. Thus attired, he takes leave of his tormentors, sends respectful messages to his bride's family, and bows his way from their guardianship to the male apartment, where he is greeted by a flourish of trumpets and the congratulations of the guests, many of whom make him presents and embrace him cordially.

The dinner is introduced at twelve, amongst the bridegroom's guests, and the night passed in good-humoured conviviality, although the strongest beverage at the feast consists of sugar and water sherbet. The dancing-women's performances, the displays of fireworks, the dinner, pawn, and ḥuqqah, form the chief amusements of the night, and they break up only when the dawn of morning approaches.

The bride's female friends take sherbet and pawn after the bridegroom's departure from the zanānah, after which they hasten away to the bride's assembly, to detail the whole business of their mission.

BRINGING HOME THE BRIDE IN AFGHANISTAN. (*A. F. Hole.*)

The third day, the eventful *barāt*, arrives to awaken in the heart of a tender mother all the good feelings of fond affection; she is, perhaps, about to part with the great solace of her life under many domestic trials; at any rate, she transfers her beloved child to another protection. All marriages are not equally happy in their termination; it is a lottery, a fate, in the good mother's calculation. Her darling child may be the favoured of Heaven, for which she prays; she may be however, the miserable first wife of a licentious pluralist; nothing is certain, but she will strive to trust in God's mercy, that the event prove a happy one to her dearly-loved girl.

The young bride is in close confinement during the days of celebrating her nuptials; on the third, she is tormented with the preparations for her departure. The *mayndī* must be applied to her hands and feet, the formidable operations of bathing, drying her hair, oiling and dressing her head, dyeing her lips, gums, and teeth with antimony, fixing on her the wedding ornaments, the nose-ring presented by her husband's family; the many rings to be placed on her fingers and toes, the rings fixed in her ears, are all so many new trials to her, which though a complication of inconvenience, she cannot venture to murmur at, and therefore submits to with the passive weakness of a lamb.

Towards the close of the evening, all these preparations being fulfilled, the marriage portion is set in order to accompany the bride. The guests make their own amusements for the day: the mother is too much occupied with her daughter's affairs to give much of her time or attention to them; nor do they expect it, for they all know by experience the nature of a mother's duties at such an interesting period.

The bridegroom's house is nearly in the same state of bustle as the bride's, though of a very different description, as the preparing for the reception of a bride is an event of vast importance in the opinion of a Musalman. The gentlemen assemble in the evening, and are regaled with sherbet and the ḥuqqah, and entertained with the *nauch*-singing and fireworks, until the appointed hour for setting out in the procession to fetch the bride to her new home.

The procession is on a grand scale; every friend or acquaintance, together with their elephants, are pressed into the service of the bridegroom on this night of Barāt. The young man himself is mounted on a handsome charger, the legs, tail, and mane of which are dyed with *mayndī*, whilst the ornamental furniture of the horse is splendid with spangles and embroidery. The dress of the bridegroom is of gold cloth, richly trimmed, with a turban to correspond, to the top of which is fastened an immense bunch of silver trimming, that falls over his face to his waist, and answers the purpose of a veil (this is in strict keeping with the Hindu custom at their marriage processions). A select few of the females from the bridegroom's house attend in his train to bring home the bride, accompanied by innumerable torches, with bands of music, soldiers, and servants, to give effect to the procession. On their arrival at the gate of the bride's residence, the gentlemen are introduced to the father's apartments, where fire-works, music, and singing, occupy their time and attention until the hour for departure arrives.

The marriage ceremony is performed in the presence of witnesses, although the bride is not seen by any of the males at the time, not even by her husband, until they have been lawfully united according to the common form.

The Maulawī commences by calling on the young maiden by name, to answer to his demand, "Is it by your own consent this marriage takes place with ——?" naming the person who is the bridegroom; the bride answers, "It is by my consent." The Maulawī then explains the law of Muḥammad, and reads a certain chapter from that portion of the Qur'ān which binds the parties in holy wedlock. He then turns to the young man, and asks him to name the sum he proposes as his wife's dowry. The bridegroom thus called upon, names ten, twenty, or, perhaps, a hundred lacs of rupees; the Maulawī repeats to all present the amount proposed, and then prays that the young couple thus united may be blessed in this world and in eternity. All the gentlemen then retire except the bridegroom, who is delayed entering the hall until the bride's guests have retreated into the side rooms; as soon as this is accomplished he is introduced into the presence of his mother-in-law and her daughter by the women servants. He studiously avoids looking up as he enters the hall, because, according to the custom of this people, he must first see his wife's face in a looking-glass, which is placed before the young couple, when he is seated on the masnad by his bride. Happy for him if he then beholds a face that bespeaks the gentle being he hopes Fate has destined to make him happy. If otherwise, he must submit; there is no untying the sacred contract.

Many absurd customs follow this first introduction of the bride and bridegroom. When the procession is all formed, the goods and chattels of the bride are loaded on the heads of the carriers; the bridegroom conveys his young wife in his arms to the covered palankeen, which is in readiness within the court, and the procession moves off in grand style, with a perpetual din of noisy music, until they arrive at the bridegroom's mansion.

The poor mother has, perhaps, had many struggles with her own heart to save her daughter's feelings during the preparation for departure; but when the separation takes place, the scene is affecting beyond description. I never witnessed anything equal to it in other societies; indeed, so powerfully are the feelings of the mother excited, that she rarely acquires her usual composure until her daughter is allowed to revisit her, which is generally within a week after her marriage. (See Mrs. Meer Hasan Ali's *Indian Musalmans*, vol. i. p. 46.)

The above description of a wedding in India has been selected as representative of such ceremonies; but there is no uniform custom of celebrating Muslim nuptials, the nuptial ceremonies in Afghanistan being much more simple in their character, as will be seen by the illustration given on the preceding page.

Mr. Lane, in his *Modern Egyptians*, gives the following interesting account of a wedding in Egypt:—

"Marriages in Cairo are generally conducted, in the case of a virgin, in the following manner; but in that of a widow, or a divorced woman, with little ceremony. Most commonly, the mother, or some other near female relation, of the youth or man who is desirous of obtaining a wife, describes to him the personal and other qualifications of the young women with whom she is acquainted, and directs his choice; or he employs a 'khat'beh,' or 'khatibeh' (*khāṭibah*), a woman whose regular business it is to assist men in such cases. Sometimes two or more women of this profession are employed. A khat'beh gives her report confidentially, describing one girl as being like a gazelle, pretty and elegant and young; and another as not pretty, but rich, and so forth. If the man have a mother and other near female relations, two or three of these usually go with a khat'beh to pay visits to several hareems, to which she has access in her professional character of a match-maker; for she is employed as much by the women as the men. She sometimes, also, exercises the trade of a 'dellaleh' (or broker), for the sale of ornaments, clothing, &c., which procures her admission into almost every hareem. The women who accompany her in search of a wife for their relation, are introduced to the different hareems merely as ordinary visitors; and as such, if disappointed, they soon take their leave, though the object of their visit is, of course, well understood by the other party; but if they find among the females of a family (and they are sure to see all who are marriageable) a girl or young woman having the necessary personal qualifications, they state the motives of their visit, and ask, if the proposed match be not at once disapproved of, what property, ornaments, &c., the objects of their wishes may possess. If the father of the intended bride be dead, she may perhaps possess one or more houses, shops, &c.; and in almost every case, a marriageable girl of the middle or higher ranks has a set of ornaments of gold and jewels. The women visitors, having asked these and other questions, bring their report to the expectant youth or man. If satisfied with their report, he gives a present to the khat'beh, and sends her again to the family of his intended wife, to make known to them his wishes. She generally gives an exaggerated description of his personal attractions, wealth, &c. For instance, she will say of a very ordinary young man, of scarcely any property, and of whose disposition she knows nothing. 'My daughter, the youth who wishes to marry you is young, graceful, elegant, beardless, has plenty of money, dresses handsomely, is fond of delicacies, but cannot enjoy his luxuries alone; he wants you as his companion; he will give you everything that money can procure; he is a stayer at home, and will spend his whole time with you, caressing and fondling you.'

"The parents may betroth their daughter to whom they please, and marry her to him without her consent, if she be not arrived at the age of puberty; but after she has attained that age, she may choose a husband for herself, and appoint any man to arrange and effect her marriage. In the former case, however, the khat'beh and the relations of a girl sought in marriage usually endeavour to obtain her consent to the proposed union. Very often a father objects to giving a daughter in marriage to a man who is not of the same profession or trade as himself; and to marrying a younger daughter before an elder! The bridegroom can scarcely ever obtain even a surreptitious glance at the features of his bride, until he finds her in his absolute possession, unless she belong to the lower classes of society; in which case it is easy enough for him to see her face.

"When a female is about to marry, she should have a 'wekeel' (*wakīl*, or deputy), to settle the compact and conclude the contract, for her, with her proposed husband. If she be under the age of puberty, this is absolutely necessary; and in this case, her father, if living, or (if he be dead) her nearest adult male relation, or a guardian appointed by will, or by the Kadee, performs the office of wekeel; but if she be of age, she appoints her own wekeel, or may even make the contract herself; though this is seldom done.

"After a youth or man has made choice of a female to demand in marriage, on the report of his female relations, or that of the khat'beh, and, by proxy, made the preliminary arrangements before described with her and her relations in the hareem, he repairs with two or three of his friends to her wekeel. Having obtained the wekeel's consent to the union, if the intended bride be under age, he asks what is the amount of the required *mahr* (or dowry).

"The giving of a dowry is indispensable. The usual amount of the dowry, if the parties be in possession of a moderately good income, is about a thousand riyals (or twenty-two pounds ten shillings); or, sometimes, not more than half that sum. The wealthy calculate the dowry in purses, of five hundred piasters (about five pounds sterling) each; and fix its amount at ten purses or more.

"It must be borne in mind that we are considering the case of a virgin bride; the dowry of a widow or divorced woman is much less. In settling the amount of the dowry, as in other pecuniary transactions, a little haggling frequently takes place; if a thousand riyals be demanded through the wekeel, the party of the intended bridegroom will probably make an offer of six hundred; the former party then gradually lowering the demand, and the other increasing the offer, they at length agree to fix it at eight hundred. It is generally stipulated that two-thirds of the dowry shall be paid immediately before the marriage-contract is made; and the remaining third held in reserve, to be paid to the wife in case of divorcing her against her own consent, or in case of the husband's death.

"This affair being settled, and confirmed by all persons present reciting the opening chapter of the Kuran (the Fat'hah), an early day (perhaps the day next following) is appointed for paying the money, and performing the ceremony of the marriage-contract, which is properly called 'akd en-nikah' (*'aqdu 'n-nikāḥ*). The making this contract is commonly called 'ketb el-kitáb' (*katbu 'l-kitāb*, or the writing of the writ); but it is very seldom the case that any document is written to confirm the marriage, unless the bridegroom is about to travel to another place, and fears that he may have occasion to prove his marriage where witnesses of the contract cannot be procured. Sometimes the marriage-contract is concluded immediately after the arrangement respecting the dowry, but more generally a day or two after.

"On the day appointed for this ceremony, the bridegroom, again accompanied by two or three of his friends, goes to the house of his bride, usually about noon, taking with him that portion of the dowry which he has promised to pay on this occasion. He and his companions are received by the bride's wekeel, and two or more friends of the latter are usually present. It is necessary that there be two witnesses (and those must be Muslims) to the marriage-contract, unless in a situation where witnesses cannot be procured. All persons present recite the Fat'hah; and the bridegroom then pays the money. After this, the marriage-contract is performed. It is very simple. The bridegroom and the bride's wekeel sit upon the ground, face to face, with one knee upon the ground, and grasp each other's right hand, raising the thumbs, and pressing them against each other. A 'fekeeh' (*faqih*) is generally employed to instruct them what they are to say. Having placed a handkerchief over their joined hands, he usually prefaces the words of the contract with a khutbeh (*khuṭbah*), consisting of a few words of exhortation and prayer, with quotations from the Kuran and Traditions, on the excellence and advantages of marriage. He then desires the bride's wekeel to say, 'I betroth (or marry) to thee my daughter (or the female who has appointed me her wekeel), such a one (naming the bride), the virgin [or the adult], for a dowry of such an amount.' (The words 'for a dowry,' &c., are sometimes omitted.) The bride's wekeel having said this, the bridegroom says, 'I accept from thee her betrothal [or marriage] to myself, and take her under my care, and myself to afford her my protection; and ye who are present bear witness of this.' The wekeel addresses the bridegroom in the same manner a second and a third time; and each time, the latter replies as before. Both then generally add, 'And blessing be on the Apostles: and praise be to God, the Lord of the beings of the whole world. Amen.' After which all present again repeat the Fat'hah. It is not always the same form of khutbeh that is recited on these occasions; any form may be used, and it may be repeated by any person; it is not even necessary, and is often altogether omitted.

"The contract concluded, the bridegroom sometimes (but seldom, unless he be a person of the lower orders) kisses the hands of his friends and others there present; and they are presented with sharbat, and generally remain to dinner. Each of them receives an embroidered handkerchief, provided by the family of the bride; except the fekeeh, who receives a similar handkerchief, with a small gold coin tied up in it, from the bridegroom. Before the persons assembled on this occasion disperse, they settle when the 'leylet ed-dakhleh' is to be. This is the night when the bride is brought to the house of the bridegroom, and the latter, for the first time, visits her.

"The bridegroom should receive his bride on the eve of Friday, or that of Monday; but the former is generally esteemed the more fortunate period. Let us say, for instance, that the bride is to be conducted to him on the eve of Friday.

"During two or three or more preceding nights, the street or quarter in which the bridegroom lives is illuminated with chandeliers and lanterns, or with lanterns and small lamps, some suspended from cords drawn across from the bridegroom's and several other houses on each side to the houses opposite; and several small silk flags, each of two colours, generally red and green, are attached to these or other cords.

"An entertainment is also given on each of these nights, particularly on the last night before that on which the wedding is concluded, at the bridegroom's house. On these occasions, it is customary for the persons invited, and for all intimate friends, to send presents to his house, a day or two before the feast which they purpose or expect to attend. They generally send sugar, coffee, rice, wax candles, or a lamb. The former articles are usually placed upon a tray of copper or wood, and covered with a silk or embroidered kerchief. The guests are entertained on these occasions by musicians and male or female singers, by dancing girls, or by the performance of a 'khatmeh' (*khatmah*), or a 'zikr' (*ẕikr*).

"The customs which I am now about to describe are observed by those classes that compose the main bulk of the population of Cairo.

"On the preceding Wednesday (or on the Saturday if the wedding be to conclude on the eve of Monday), at about the hour of noon, or a little later, the bride goes in state to the bath. The procession to the bath is called 'Zeffet el-Hammām.' It is headed by a party of musicians, with a hautboy or two, and drums of different kinds. Sometimes at the head of the bride's party, are two men, who carry the utensils and linen used in the bath, upon two round trays, each of which is covered with an embroidered or a plain silk kerchief; also a sakka (*saqqā*) who gives water to any of the passengers, if asked; and two other persons, one of whom bears a 'kamkam,' or bottle, of plain or gilt silver, or of china, containing rose-water, or orange-flower water, which he occasionally sprinkles on the passengers; and the other, a 'mibkharah' (or perfuming vessel) of silver, with aloes-wood, or some other odoriferous substance, burning in it; but it is seldom that the procession is thus attended. In general, the first persons among the bride's party are several of her married female relations and friends, walking in pairs; and next, a number of young virgins. The former are dressed in the usual manner, covered with the black silk ḥabarah; the latter have white silk ḥabarahs, or shawls. Then follows the bride, walking under a canopy of silk, of some gay colour, as pink, rose-colour, or yellow; or of two colours, composing wide stripes, often rose-colour and yellow. It is carried by four men, by means of a pole at each corner, and is open only in front; and at the top of each of the four poles is attached an embroidered handkerchief.

A BRIDAL PROCESSION IN CAIRO. (*From Lane's "Egyptians."*)

"The dress of the bride, during this procession, entirely conceals her person. She is generally covered from head to foot with a red kashmere shawl; or with a white or yellow shawl, though rarely. Upon her head is placed a small pasteboard cap, or crown. The shawl is placed over this, and conceals from the view of the public the richer articles of her dress, her face, and her jewels, &c., except one or two 'kussahs' (and sometimes other ornaments), generally of diamonds and emeralds, attached to that part of the shawl which covers her forehead.

"She is accompanied by two or three of her female relations within the canopy; and often, when in hot weather, a woman, walking backwards before her, is constantly employed in fanning her, with a large fan of black ostrich-feathers, the lower part of the front of which is usually ornamented with a piece of looking-glass. Sometimes one zeffeh, with a single canopy, serves for two brides, who walk side by side. The procession moves very slowly, and generally pursues a circuitous route, for the sake of greater display. On leaving the house, it turns to the right. It is closed by a second party of musicians, similar to the first, or by two or three drummers.

"In the bridal processions of the lower orders, which are often conducted in the same manner as that above described, the women of the party frequently utter, at intervals, those shrill cries of joy called 'zaghareet'; and females of the poorer classes, when merely spectators of a zeffeh, often do the same. The whole bath is sometimes hired for the bride and her party exclusively.

"They pass several hours, or seldom less than two, occupied in washing, sporting, and feasting; and frequently ''al'mehs,' or female singers, are hired to amuse them in the bath; they then return in the same order in which they came.

"The expense of the zeffeh falls on the relations of the bride, but the feast that follows it is supplied by the bridegroom.

"Having returned from the bath to the house of her family, the bride and her companions sup together. If 'al'mehs have contributed to the festivity in the bath, they, also, return with the bride, to renew their concert. Their songs are always on the subject of love, and of the joyous event which occasions their presence. After the company have been thus entertained, a large quantity of henná having been prepared, mixed into a paste, the bride takes a lump of it in her hand, and receives contributions (called 'nukoot') from her guests; each of them sticks a coin (usually of gold) in the henná which she holds upon her hand; and when the lump is closely stuck with these coins, she scrapes it off her hand upon the edge of a basin of water. Having collected in this manner from all her guests, some more henná is applied to her hands and feet, which are then bound with pieces of linen; and in this state they remain until the next morning, when they are found to be sufficiently dyed with its deep orange red tint. Her guests make use of the remainder of the dye for their own hands This night is called 'Leylet el-Henná,' or, 'the Night of the Ḥenná.'

"It is on this night, and sometimes also during the latter half of the preceding day, that the bridegroom gives his chief entertainment.

"'Mohabbazeen' (or low farce-players) often perform on this occasion before the house, or, if it be large enough, in the court. The other and more common performances by which the guests are amused, have been before mentioned.

"On the following day, the bride goes in procession to the house of the bridegroom. The procession before described is called 'the zeffeh of the bath,' to distinguish it from this, which is the more important, and which is therefore particularly called 'Zeffet el-'Arooseh,' or 'the Zeffeh of the Bride.' In some cases, to diminish the expenses of the marriage ceremonies, the bride is conducted privately to the bath, and only honoured with a zeffeh to the bridegroom's house. This procession is exactly similar to the former. The bride and her party, after breakfasting together, generally set out a little after midday.

"They proceed in the same order, and at the same slow pace, as in the zeffeh of the bath; and, if the house of the bridegroom is near, they follow a circuitous route, through several principal streets, for the sake of display. The ceremony usually occupies three or more hours.

"Sometimes, before bridal processions of this kind, two swordsmen, clad in nothing but their drawers, engage each other in a mock combat; or two peasants cudgel each other with nebboots or long staves. In the procession of a bride of a wealthy family, any person who has the art of performing some extraordinary feat to amuse the spectators is almost sure of being a welcome assistant, and of receiving a handsome present. When the Seyyid Omar, the Nakeel el-Ashraf (or chief of the descendants of the Prophet), who was the main instrument of advancing Mohammad 'Alee to the dignity of Basha of Egypt, married a daughter, about forty-five years since, there walked before the procession a young man who had made an incision in his abdomen, and drawn out a large portion of his intestines, which he carried before him on a silver tray. After the procession he restored them to their proper place, and remained in bed many days before he recovered from the effects of this foolish and disgusting act. Another man, on the same occasion, ran a sword through his arm, before the crowding spectators, and then bound over the wound, without withdrawing the sword, several handkerchiefs, which were soaked with the blood. These facts were described to me by an eye-witness. A spectacle of a more singular and more disgusting nature used to be not uncommon on similar occasions, but is now very seldom witnessed. Sometimes, also, 'hawees' (or conjurors and sleight-of-hand performers) exhibit a variety of tricks on these occasions. But the most common of all the performances here mentioned are the mock fights. Similar exhibitions are also sometimes witnessed on the occasion of a circumcision Grand zeffehs are sometimes accompanied by a numbers of cars, each bearing a group of persons of some manufacture or trade, performing the usual work of their craft; even such as builders, whitewashers, &c., including members of all, or almost all, the arts and manufactures practised in the metropolis. In one car there are generally some men making coffee, which they occasionally present to spectators; in another, instrumental musicians, and in another, 'al'mehs (or female singers).

"The bride, in zeffehs of this kind, is sometimes conveyed in a close European carriage, but more frequently, she and her female relations and friends are mounted on high-saddled asses, and, with musicians and female singers, before and behind them, close the procession.

"The bride and her party, having arrived at the bridegroom's house, sit down to a repast. Her friends shortly after take their departure, leaving with her only her mother and sister, or other near female relations, and one or two other women; usually the belláneh. The ensuing night is called 'Leylet ed-Dakhleh,' or 'the Night of the Entrance.'

"The bridegroom sits below. Before sunset he goes to the bath, and there changes his clothes, or he merely does the latter at home; and, after having supped with a party of his friends, waits till a little before the night prayer, or until the third or fourth hour of the night, when, according to general custom, he should repair to some celebrated mosque, and there say his prayers. If young, he is generally honoured with a zeffeh on this occasion. In this case he goes to the mosque preceded by musicians with drums and a hautboy or two, and accompanied by a number of friends, and by several men bearing 'mashals' (*mash'als*). The mashals are a kind of cresset, that is, a staff with a cylindrical frame of iron at the top, filled with flaming wood, or having two, three, four, or five of these receptacles for fire. The party usually proceeds to the mosque with a quick pace, and without much order. A second group of musicians, with the same instruments, or with drums only, closes the procession.

"The bridegroom is generally dressed in a kuftán with red stripes, and a red gibbeh, with a kashmere shawl of the same colour for his turban, and walks between two friends similarly dressed. The prayers are commonly performed merely as a matter of ceremony, and it is frequently the case that the bridegroom does not pray at all, or prays without having previously performed the wudoo, like memlooks, who say their prayers only because they fear their master. The procession returns from the mosque with more order and display, and very slowly; perhaps because it would be considered unbecoming in the bridegroom to hasten home to take possession of his bride. It is headed, as before, by musicians, and two or more bearers of mashals. These are generally followed by two men, bearing, by means of a pole resting horizontally upon their shoulders, a hanging frame, to which are attached about sixty or more small lamps, in four circles, one above another, the uppermost of which circles is made to revolve, being turned round occasionally by one of the two bearers. These numerous lamps, and several mashals besides those before mentioned, brilliantly illumine the streets through which the procession passes, and produce a remarkably picturesque effect. The bridegroom and his friends and other attendants follow, advancing in the form of an oblong ring, all facing the interior of the ring, and each bearing in his hand one or more wax candles, and sometimes a sprig of henná or some other flower, except the bridegroom and the friend on either side of him. These three form the latter part of the ring, which generally consists of twenty or more persons.

"At frequent intervals, the party stops for a few minutes, and during each of the pauses, a boy or a man, one of the persons who compose the ring, sings a few words of an epithalamium. The sounds of the drums, and the shrill notes of the hautboy (which the bride hears half an hour or more before the procession arrives at the house), cease during these songs. The train is closed, as in the former case (when on the way to the mosque) by a second group of musicians.

"In the manner above described, the bridegroom's zeffeh is most commonly conducted; but there is another mode that is more respectable, called 'zeffeh sádátee,' which signifies the 'gentlemen's zeffeh.' In this, the bridegroom is accompanied by his friends in the manner described above, and attended and preceded by men bearing mashals, but not by musicians; in the place of these are about six or eight men, who, from their being employed as singers on occasions of this kind, are called 'wilad el-layalee,' or 'sons of the nights.' Thus attended, he goes to the mosque; and while he returns slowly thence to his house, the singers above mentioned chant, or rather sing, 'muweshshahs' (lyric odes) in praise of the Prophet. Having returned to the house, these same persons chant portions of the Kuran, one after another, for the amusement of the guests; then, all together, recite the opening chapter (the Fat'hah); after which, one of them sings a 'kaseedeh' (or short poem), in praise of the Prophet; lastly, all of them again sing muweshshahs. After having thus performed, they receive 'nukoot' (or contributions of money) from the bridegroom and his friends.

"Soon after his return from the mosque, the bridegroom leaves his friends in a lower apartment, enjoying their pipes and coffee and sharbat. The bride's mother and sister, or whatever other female relations were left with her, are above, and the bride herself and the belláneh, in a separate apartment. If the bridegroom is a youth or young man, it is considered proper that he as well as the bride should exhibit some degree of bashfulness; one of his friends, therefore, carries him a part of the way up to the hareem. Sometimes, when the parties are persons of wealth, the bride is displayed before the bridegroom in different dresses, to the number of seven; but generally he finds her with the belláneh alone, and on entering the apartment he gives a present to this attendant, and she at once retires.

"The bride has a shawl thrown over her head, and the bridegroom must give her a present of money, which is called 'the price of the uncovering' of the face, before he attempts to remove this, which she does not allow him to do without some apparent reluctance, if not violent resistance, in order to show her maiden modesty. On removing the covering, he says, 'In the name of God, the Compassionate, the Merciful,' and then greets her with this compliment: 'The night be blessed,' or '—— is blessed,' to which she replies, if timidity do not choke her utterance, 'God bless thee.' The bridegroom now, in most cases, sees the face of his bride for the first time, and generally finds her nearly what he has been led to expect. Often, but not always, a curious ceremony is then performed.

"The bridegroom takes off every article of the bride's clothing except her shirt, seats her upon a mattress or bed, the head of which is turned towards the direction of Makkah, placing her so that her back is also turned in that direction, and draws forward and spreads upon the bed, the lower part of the front of her shirt; having done this, he stands at the distance of rather less than three feet before her, and performs the prayers of two rak'ahs; laying his head and hands in prostration upon the part of her shirt that is extended before her lap. He remains with her but a few minutes longer. Having satisfied his curiosity respecting her personal charms, he calls to the women (who generally collect at the door, where they wait in anxious suspense) to raise their cries of joy, or zaghareet, and the shrill sounds make known to the persons below and in the neighbourhood, and often, responded to by other women, spread still further the news that he has acknowledged himself satisfied with his bride. He soon after descends to rejoin his friends, and remains with them an hour, before he returns to his wife. It very seldom happens that the husband, if disappointed in his bride, immediately disgraces and divorces her; in general, he retains her in this case a week or more.

"Marriages, among the Egyptians, are sometimes conducted without any pomp or ceremony, even in the case of virgins, by mutual consent of the bridegroom and the bride's family, or the bride herself; and widows and divorced women are never honoured with a zeffeh on marrying again. The mere sentence, 'I give myself up to thee,' uttered by a female to a man who proposes to become her husband (even without the presence of witnesses, if none can easily be procured), renders her his legal wife, if arrived at puberty; and marriages with widows and divorced women, among the Muslims of Egypt, and other Arabs, are sometimes concluded in this simple manner. The dowry of widows and divorced women is generally one quarter or third or half the amount of that of a virgin.

"In Cairo, among persons not of the lowest order, though in very humble life, the marriage ceremonies are conducted in the same manner as among the middle orders. But when the expenses of such zeffehs as I have described cannot by any means be paid, the bride is paraded in a very simple manner, covered with a shawl (generally red), and surrounded by a group of her female relations and friends, dressed in their best, or in borrowed clothes, and enlivened by no other sounds of joy than their zaghareet, which they repeat at frequent intervals." (Lane's *Modern Egyptians.*)

(For the law of marriage in Ḥanafī law, see *Fatāwā-i-ʿĀlamgīrī*, p. 377; *Fatāwā-i-Qāẓī Ḵẖān*, p. 380; Hamilton's *Hidāyah*, vol. i. p. 89; *Durru 'l-Muḵẖtār*, p. 196. In Shīʿah law, *Jāmiʿu 'sh-Shattāt*; *Sharāʾiʿu 'l-Islām*, p. 260. For marriage ceremonies, Lane's *Egyptians*; Herklott's *Musalmans*; Mrs. Meer Hasan Ali's *Musalmans*; M. C. de Perceval, *Hist. des Arabes.*)

MARṢĪYAH (مرثية). A funeral elegy. Especially applied to those sung during the Muḥarram in commemoration of al-Hasan and al-Husain.

MARTYR. The Arabic word for "martyr" in the Qur'ān, and in Muslim theology, is *shāhid* (شاهد), pl. *shuhūd*, or *shahīd* (شهيد), pl. *shuhadā'*, the literal meaning of which is "present as a witness." It implies all that is understood by the Greek μάρτυς, and the English martyr; but it is also a much more comprehensive term, for, according to Muḥammadan law, not only those who die in witness of, or in defence of the faith, are martyrs, but all those who die such deaths as are calculated to excite the compassion and pity of their fellow men.

The word occurs in the Qur'ān, Sūrah iv. 71: "Whoso obeys God and the Apostle, these are with those with whom God has been well pleased—with prophets (*nabīyīn*), and confessors (*ṣiddīqīn*), and martyrs (*shuhadā'*), and the righteous (*ṣāliḥīn*): a fair company are they."

A perfect martyr, or *ash-shahīdu 'l-kāmil*, is one who has either been slain in a religious war, or who has been killed unjustly. But the schools of divinity are not agreed as to whether it is necessary, or not, that such persons should be in a state of ceremonial purity at the time of their death, to entitle them to such a high rank.

A special blessing is promised to those who die in a *jihād*, or religious war, see Qur'ān, Sūrah iii. 163: "Count not those who are killed in the way of God as dead, but living with their Lord." And according to Muslim law, all persons who have died in defence of the faith, or have been slain unjustly, are entitled to Muslim burial without the usual ablution or any change of clothes, such as are necessary in the case of ordinary persons, the rank of martyrdom being such as to render the corpse legally pure.

But in addition to these two classes of persons, namely those who are slain in religious war, and those who have been killed unjustly, the rank of *shahīd* is given, in a figurative sense, to any who die in such a manner as to excite the sympathy and pity of mankind, such as by sudden death, or from some malignant disease, or in childbirth, or in the acquirement of knowledge, or a stranger in a foreign country, or dying on Thursday night. These persons are entitled to the rank of martyr, but not to the honour of being buried without legal washing and purification. (See *Raddu 'l-Muḥtār*, vol. i. p. 952; *Kashshāf Iṣṭilāḥātu 'l-Funūn*, vol. i. p. 747; *G͟hiyāṣu 'l-Lug͟hah, in loco.*)

MĀRŪT (ماروت). [HARUT.]

MARWAH (مروة). A hill near Makkah, connected with the rites of the pilgrimage. According to Burton, it means "hard, white flints, full of fire." [HAJJ.]

MARYAM (مريم). [MARY.]

MARY THE VIRGIN. Arabic *Maryam* (مريم). Heb. מִרְיָם. The mother of Jesus. According to Muḥammadan tradition, and the Qur'ān, she was the daughter of 'Imrān and his wife Ḥannah, and the sister of Aaron.

The account of her birth as given in the Qur'ān is in Sūrah iii. 31:—

"Remember when the wife of Imran said, 'O my Lord! I vow to Thee what is in my womb, for thy special service. Accept it from me, for Thou Hearest, Knowest!' And when she had given birth to it, she said, 'O my Lord! Verily I have brought forth a female,'—God knew what she had brought forth: a male is not as a female—'and I have named her Mary, and I take refuge with Thee for her and for her offspring, from Satan the stoned.' So with goodly acceptance did her Lord accept her, and with goodly growth did he make her grow. Zacharias reared her. So oft as Zacharias went in to Mary at the sanctuary, he found her supplied with food. 'Oh Mary!' said he, 'whence hast thou this?' She said, 'It is from God; for God supplieth whom He will, without reckoning!'"

In Sūrah xix. 28, is the story of her giving birth to Jesus. [JESUS CHRIST.] And when she brought the child to the people, they exclaimed, "O sister of Aaron! Thy father was not a bad man, nor was thy mother a harlot."

Christian critics have assumed, and not without much reason, that Muḥammad has confused the Mary of the New Testament with the Miriam of the Old, by representing her as the daughter of 'Imrān and the sister of Aaron. It is certainly a cause of some perplexity to the commentators. Al-Baiẓāwī says she was called "sister of Aaron" because she was of the Levitical race; but Ḥusain says that the Aaron mentioned in the verse is not the same person as the brother of Moses.

Muḥammad is related to have said that "no child is born but the devil hath touched it, except Mary and her son Jesus."

MARY THE COPT. Arabic *Māriyatu 'l-Qibṭīyah* (مارية القبطية). A concubine of Muḥammad's, and the mother of his son Ibrāhīm, who died in infancy. She was a Christian slave girl presented to Muḥammad by the Roman governor of Egypt. [MUHAMMAD.]

MASAḤ (مسح). The act of touching the boots or the turban for purification, by drawing the three central fingers over the boot or turban at once, whereby they become ceremonially clean. (*Mishkāt*, book ii. ch. vii.; book iii. ch. x.)

AL-MAS̤ĀNĪ (المثانى). From *Mas̤na*, "two-and-two." A title given to the Qur'ān on account of its numerous repetitions.

AL-MASĪḤ (المسيح). An evident corruption of the Heb. מָשִׁיחַ, which answers to the Χριστὸς of the New Testament, and our English Christ. It occurs seven times in the Qur'ān as the surname of Jesus. Al-Baiẓāwī the commentator says, "It is originally a Hebrew word, signifying 'the blessed one,' although some have (erroneously, as he thinks) held it to come from *Masah*, 'to anoint,' either because Jesus healed people with his touch, or because he had been anointed by Gabriel as a prophet." [JESUS.]

AL-MASĪḤU 'D-DAJJĀL (المسيح الدجال). "The lying Christ." The Antichrist which Muḥammad said would appear before the Day of Resurrection. He is generally called ad-Dajjāl, but in the Traditions he is called *al-Masīḥu'd-Dajjāl*, and very many have been the speculations as to why he is called *al-Masīḥ*. The compiler of the *Qāmūs* says there have been at least fifty reasons assigned for his being called *al-Masīḥ*. Some say it is because he will have his eyes touched (*masaḥ*) and be rendered blind; others, that the word was originally *masīk͟h*, a "monster." (See *Ḥujaju 'l-Kalimah*, p. 401.) Sale, in the preface to his translation of the Qur'ān, says Muslim writers state that the Jews will give him the name of *al-Masīḥ*, because they will mistake him for the true Messiah, who has come to restore the kingdom of Israel to them.

Regarding this personage, Abū Hurairah relates that Muḥammad said:—

"The Resurrection will not be until the Grecians shall attack 'Amāq and Dābiq. Then an army will come out from al-Madīnah against them, the best of men on that day; and when the lines of battle shall be drawn up, the Grecians will say, 'Vacate a place between us and those who made captives a tribe of ours' (and their design will be to separate the Musalmāns). And the Musalmāns will say, 'By God! we will not clear a place between you and our brother Musalmāns.' And the Musalmāns will fight the Grecians and a third of the Musalmāns will be defeated; and God will not accept their repentance. And a third of the Musalmāns will be slain, and they will be the best of martyrs before God. And a third of them will conquer the countries of Greece; after which they will be thrown into commotions, and Constantinople will be taken. And whilst the Musalmāns shall be dividing the plunder, having hung up their swords upon the olive tree, all on a sudden the Devil will call out, 'Verily, Dajjāl has attacked your wives and children in your absence.' Then, on hearing this, the Musalmāns will come out of the city; and this information of devils will be false, but when they enter Syria, Dajjāl will come out, and whilst the Musalmāns shall be preparing their implements of war, and dressing their ranks, all on a sudden prayers will begin, and Jesus Son of Mary will come down, and act as Imām to them. And when Dajjāl, this enemy of God, shall see Jesus, he will fear to be near, dissolving away like salt in water. And if Jesus lets him alone, verily he will melt and perish, and God will kill him by the hand of Jesus, who will show to the people the blood of Dajjāl upon his lance." (*Mishkāt*, book xxiii. ch. ii.)

In other traditions, Muḥammad is related to have said that ad-Dajjāl will be a young man with long hair and blind in the one eye, and on his forehead will be the three letters K F R, signifying *kāfir* or infidel. He will first appear midway between Syria and 'Irāq, and will do many wonders and perform many miracles, and will eventually be slain by Jesus.

MASJID (مسجد). *Lit.* "The place of prostration." The mosque, or place of public prayer. Mosques are generally built of stone or brick, in the form of a square, in the centre of which is an open court-yard, surrounded with cloisters for students. In the centre of the wall facing Makkah is the *miḥrāb* or niche, which marks the direction of the Ka'bah at Makkah, and to the right of this niche is the *mimbar* or pulpit, from which the khuṭbah, or Friday oration, is recited In the centre of the open court-yard there is usually a large tank, in which the worshippers perform their ablutions (*waẓu'*), and adjoining the mosque are latrines, in which the legal washings (*ghusl*) can be performed. Along the front within the doorway is a low barrier, a few inches high, which denotes the sacred part of the mosque.

The mosques in India and Central Asia are generally constructed on the following plan:—

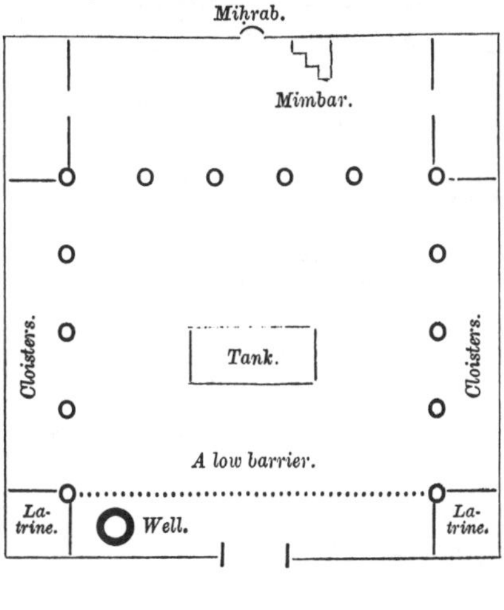

The mosques in Turkey, Syria, and Egypt are often covered buildings, not unlike Christian churches.

The first mosque erected by Muḥammad was at Qubā', near al-Madīnah. It was without cupola, niche, or minaret, these being added by al-Walīd about eighty years afterwards, nor were there arches supported by pillars, nor cloisters. An ordinary mosque in an Afghan village is still of this description.

The Muslim as he enters the mosque stops at the barrier and takes off his shoes, carries them in his left hand, sole to sole, and puts his right foot first as he passes into the square devoted to prayer. If he have not previously performed the ablution, he repairs

INTERIOR OF A MOSQUE IN CAIRO.
(*Lane.*)

at once to the tank or well to perform the necessary duty, and before he commences his prayers he places his shoes and his sword and pistol, if he be thus armed, a little before the spot where his head will touch the ground as he prostrates; his shoes must be put one upon the other, sole to sole.

The chief officer of a mosque is the Imām, or leader of prayers, but there are generally Maulawīs, or learned men, attached to mosques for the instruction of the students. Sometimes the Imām and Maulawī are combined in one, and sometimes a learned Maulawī will possess the mosque, but pay an Imām as his curate to say the stated prayers. There is also a *Mu'aẓẓin*, or "caller to prayer," whose duty it is to give the Azān. The trustee or superintendent of a mosque is called *mutāwallī*.

Although mosques are esteemed sacred buildings, they are also places of general resort, and persons may be seen in them lounging and chattering together on secular topics, and eating and sleeping, although such things were forbidden by Muḥammad. They are, in all parts of Islām, used as rest-houses for strangers and travellers.

The Imām, or priest, of the mosque, is supported by endowments, or offerings, the Maulawīs, or professors of divinity by fees, or offerings, and the students of a mosque are supported either by endowments, or the benefactions of the people. In towns and villages there is a parish allotted to each mosque, and the people within the section of the parish claim the services of the Imām at their marriages and funerals, and they pay to him the usual offerings made on the two festivals.

In a large mosque, known as the *Masjidu 'l-Jāmi'*, where the khuṭbah, or Friday oration is delivered, a person known as the khāṭib (also *khaṭīb*), or preacher, is appointed, whose duty it is to lead the Friday prayer and to preach the sermon.

Muḥammad did not forbid women to attend public prayers in a mosque, but it is pronounced better for them to pray in private.

The following injunctions are given in the Qur'ān regarding mosques :—

Sūrah vii. 29: "O children of Adam! wear your goodly apparel when ye repair to any mosque."

Sūrah ix. 18: "He only should visit the Masjids of God who believeth in God and the last day, and observeth prayer, and payeth the legal alms, and dreadeth none but God."

THE JAMA' MASJID AT DELHI. (*A. F. Hole.*)

Muḥammad's injunctions regarding mosques, as handed down in the Traditions, are as follows :—

"When you enter a Masjid, you must say, 'O Creator! open on us the doors of Thy compassion'; and when you leave the Masjid, say, 'O Lord! we supplicate thy munificence.'"

"It is a sin to spit in a Masjid, and the removal of the sin is to cover it over."

"Whoever shall enter a Masjid, let him enter it for a good object, namely, to learn something himself or to teach others. For he ranks as an equal with him who fights in the cause of God, who thus enters a Masjid; but he who enters a Masjid on any other account, is like unto a man who covets the property of another. Verily, a time will come when men will attend to worldly matters in a Masjid. But sit ye not with such."

"Do not prevent your women from coming to the Masjids, but their homes are better for them."

"Do not read poetry in a Masjid, and do not buy and sell there, nor sit in a circle talking before prayers on a Friday."

"The prayers of a man in his own house are equal to the reward of one prayer, but prayers in a Masjid near his home are equal to twenty-five prayers, and in a Jāmi' (or central mosque), they are equal to five hundred prayers, and in Jerusalem to fifty thousand, and in my Masjid (at al-Madīnah) fifty thousand, and at the Ka'bah, one hundred thousand."

The Muslim law regarding the erection and endowment (*waqf*) *of Masjids*, as contained in

Sunnī and Shīʿah works, is as follows. According to the Sunnīs:—

When a person has erected a Masjid, his right therein does not cease until he has separated both the area occupied by the Masjid and also the road and entrance thereunto from his own private property.

If a person build a Masjid, his right of property in it does not cease so long as he does not separate it from his private property, and give general permission to the people to come and worship in it. But as soon as he separates it from his property and allows even a single person to say his prayers in it, his right to the property devoted to God as a mosque ceases.

When a trustee or superintendent (*mutawallī*) has been appointed for a Masjid, and delivery of the property has been made to him, the Masjid ceases to be private property. So, also, when delivery of it is made to the Qāẓī, or his deputy.

If a person appropriate ground for the purpose of erecting a Masjid, he cannot afterwards resume or sell it, neither can it be claimed by his heirs and inherited, because this ground is altogether alienated from the right of the individual, and appertains solely to God.

When a man has an unoccupied space of ground fit for building upon, and has directed a body of persons to assemble on it for prayers, the space becomes a Masjid, if the permission were given expressly to pray on it for ever; or, in absolute terms, intending that it should be for ever; and the property does not go to his heirs at his death. But if the permission were given for a day, or a month, or a year, the space would not become a Masjid, and on his death it would be the property of his heirs.

A MOSQUE IN AFGHANISTAN. (*A. F. Hole.*)

If a man during his sickness has made his own house a Masjid, and died, and it neither falls within a third of his property nor is allowed by his heirs, the whole of it is heritage, and the act of making it a Masjid is void, because, the heirs having a right in it, there has been no separation from the rights of mankind, and an undefined portion has been made a Masjid, which is void. In the same way as if he should make his land a Masjid, and another person should establish an undefined right, in which case the remainder would revert to the property of the appropriator; contrary to the case of a person making a bequest that a third of his residence shall be made a Masjid, which would be valid; for in such a case there is a separation, as the house may be divided and a third of it converted into a Masjid. (A third of a man's property being the extent to which he can bequeath to other than his heirs.)

When a man has made his land a Masjid, and stipulated for something out of it for himself, it is not valid, according to all the jurists.

It is also generally agreed that if a man make a Masjid on condition that he shall have an option, the waqf is lawful and the condition is void.

When a man has built a Masjid and called persons to witness that he shall have the power to cancel and sell it, the condition is void, and the Masjid is as if he had erected a Masjid for the people of the street, saying, "It is for this street especially," when it would, notwithstanding, be for others as well as for them to worship in.

When a Masjid has fallen into decay and is no longer used for prayers, nor required by the people, it does not revert to the appropriator or his heirs, and cannot be sold according to the most correct opinions.

When of two Masjids one is old and gone to decay, the people cannot use its materials to repair the more recent one, according to either the Imām Muḥammad or Imām Abū Yūsuf. Because though the former thought that the materials may be so applied, he held that it is the original appropriator or his heirs, to whom the property reverts, that can so apply them, and because Abū Yūsuf was of opinion that the property in a Masjid never reverts to the original appropriator, though it should fall to ruin and be no longer used by the people.

INTERIOR OF A MOSQUE AT CAIRO. (*Dr. Ebers.*)

If a man appropriate his land for the benefit of a Masjid, and to provide for its repairs and necessaries, such as oil, &c., and when nothing more is required for the Masjid, to apply what remains to poor Muslims the appropriation is lawful.

If a man has appropriated his land for the benefit of a Masjid, without any ultimate destination for the poor, the appropriation is lawful, according to all opinions.

If a man gives money for the repairs of a Masjid, also for its maintenance and for its benefit, it is valid. For if it cannot operate as a waqf, it operates as a transfer by way of gift to the Masjid, and the establishing of property in this manner to a Masjid is valid, being completed by taking possession.

If a person should say, "I have bequeathed a third of my property to the Masjid," it would not be lawful, unless he say "to expend on the Masjid." So if he were to say, "I have bequeathed a third of my property to the lamps of the Masjid," it would not be lawful unless he say, "to give light with it in the Masjid." If he say, "I have given my house for a Masjid," it is valid as a transfer, requiring delivery. (*Fatāwā-i-'Ālamgīrī*, vol. ii. p. 545; *Hidāyah*, vol. ii. p. 356; Baillie's *Digest*, pp. 504–605.)

The Shī'ah law regarding the endowment of Masjids, or land for the benefit of Masjids, does not differ in any important particular from that of the Sunnīs. But there is a provision in the Shī'ah law regarding the sale of an endowment which is important.

If dissensions arise among the persons in whose favour the waqf is made, and there is apprehension of the property being destroyed, while on the other hand the sale thereof is productive of benefit, then, in that case, its sale is lawful.

If a house belonging to a waqf should fall into ruins, the space would not cease to be waqf, nor would its sale be lawful. If, however, dissensions should arise among the persons for whom it was appropriated, insomuch as to give room for apprehension that it will be destroyed, its sale would be lawful.

And even if there should be no such difference, nor any room for such apprehensions, but the sale would be more for the advantage of the parties interested, some are of opinion that the sale would be lawful; but the approved doctrine is to forbid it. (*Mafātiḥ*; *Sharā'i'u 'l-Islām*, p. 239.)

AL-MASJIDU 'L-ĀQṢĀ (المسجد الاقصى). *Lit.* "The Most Distant Mosque." The temple at Jerusalem erected by Solomon, called also *al-Baitu 'l-Muqaddas*, or "the Holy House." Known also in Muḥammadan literature as *aṣ-Ṣakhrah*, "the Rock," from which it is believed Muḥammad ascended to heaven on the occasion of his celestial journey. (See Qur'ān, Sūrah xvii.)

Jalālu 'd-dīn as-Suyūṭy has devoted a whole volume to the consideration of the superabundant merits existing in the Masjidu 'l-Aqṣā, which work has been translated into English by the Rev. James Reynolds (Oriental Translation Fund, 1836). He says it is called *al-Aqṣā*, because it is the most distant mosque to which pilgrimage is directed. [JERUSALEM, AS-SAKHRAH.]

MASJIDU 'L-ḤARĀM (مسجد الحرام). "The Sacred Mosque." The temple at Makkah which contains the Ka'bah, or Cube-house, in which is placed the *Ḥajaru 'l-Aswad*, or "Black Stone." The term *Baitu 'llāh*, or "House of God," is applied to the whole enclosure, although it more specially denotes the Ka'bah itself.

The following graphic account of this celebrated building is given by the traveller Burckhardt, who visited it in A.D. 1814. Captain R. Burton, who visited the temple thirty-eight years later, testifies to the great accuracy of Burckhardt's description, and quotes his description *in extenso.* The account by Burckhardt is given in the present article, with some slight corrections.

The Ka'bah stands in an oblong square, two hundred and fifty paces long, and two hundred broad, none of the sides of which runs quite in a straight line, though at first sight the whole appears to be of a regular shape. This open square is enclosed on the eastern side by a colonnade; the pillars stand in a quadruple row; they are three deep on the other sides, and united by pointed arches, every four of which support a small dome, plastered and whitened on the outside. These domes, according to Quṭbu 'd-dīn, are one hundred and fifty-two in number. Along the whole colonnade, on the four sides, lamps are suspended from the arches. Some are lighted every night, and all during the nights of Ramaẓān. The pillars are above twenty feet in height, and generally from one foot and a half to one foot and three quarters in diameter; but little regularity has been observed in regard to them. Some are of white marble, granite, or porphyry, but the greater number are of common stone of the Makkah mountains. Fasy states the whole at five hundred and eighty-nine, and says they are all of marble excepting one hundred and twenty-six, which are of common stone, and three of composition. Quṭbu 'd-dīn reckons five hundred and fifty-five, of which, according to him, three hundred and eleven are of marble, and the rest of stone taken from the neighbouring mountains; but neither of these authors lived to see the latest repairs of the mosque, after the destruction occasioned by a torrent, in A.D. 1626. Between every three or four columns stands an octagonal one, about four feet in thickness. On the east side are two shafts of reddish gray granite, in one piece, and one fine gray porphyry column with slabs of white feldspath. On the north side is one red granite column, and one of fine-grained red porphyry; these are probably the columns which Quṭbu 'd-dīn states to have been brought from Egypt, and principally from Akhinim (Panopolis), when the chief Mahdī enlarged the mosque, in A.H. 163. Among the four hundred and fifty or five hundred columns, which form the enclosure, I found not any two capitals or bases exactly alike. The capitals are of coarse Saracenic workmanship; some of them, which had served for former buildings, by the ignorance

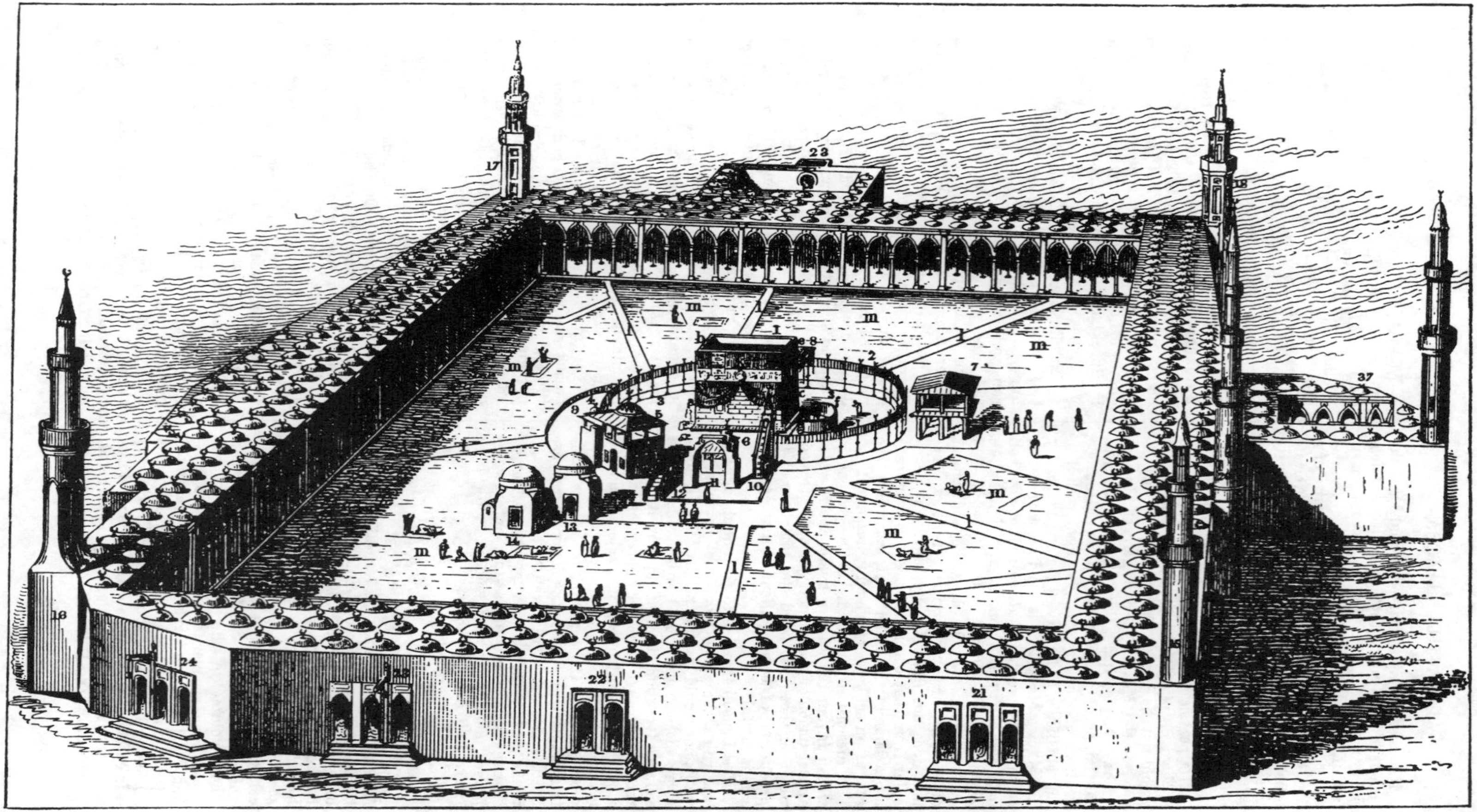

THE SACRED MOSQUE, THE MASJIDU 'L-HARAM AT MAKKAH.

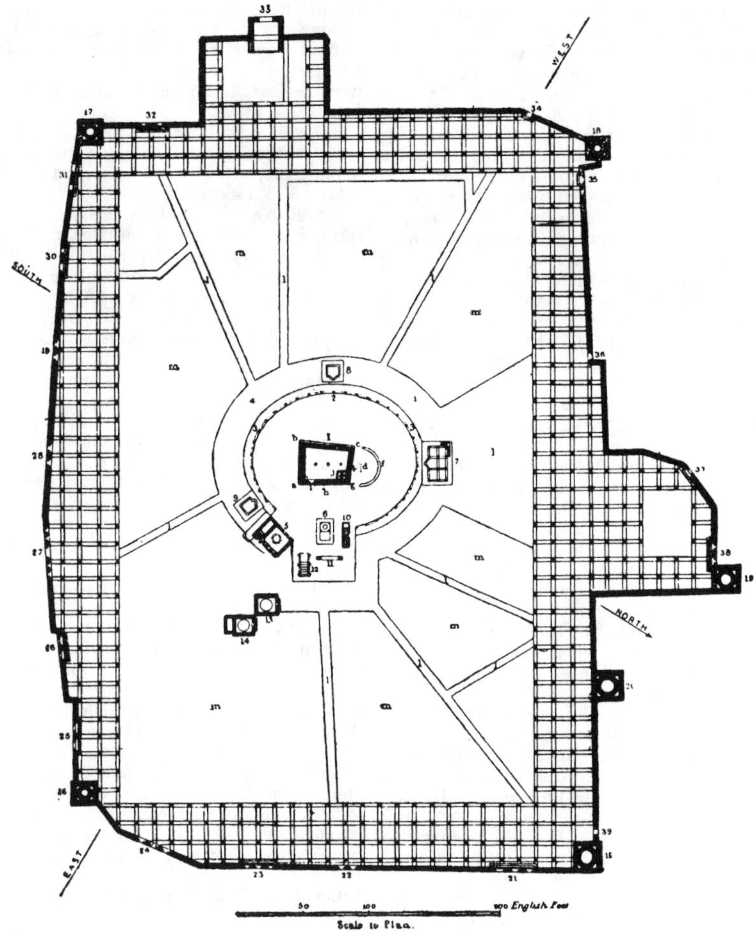

THE MASJIDU 'L-HARAM.

REFERENCES TO THE PLAN AND VIEW.

1 *The Ka'bah.*
a *The Black Stone.*
b *Ruknu 'l-Yamānī.*
c *Ruknu 'sh-Shāmī.*
d *Tombs of Ismā'īl and his mother.*
e *The Mi'zāb.*
f *The Wall of Ḥaṭīm.*
g *Ruknu 'l-Irāk.*
h *Spot called Mi'jan.*
i *Door.*
j *Staircase to Roof.*
k *The Kiswah, or silk covering with the golden band.*
2 *Pillars suspending lamps.*
3 & 4 *Outer and Inner steps.*
5 *Building over the Well Zamzam.*
6 *Praying station, or Maqāmu 'l-Ibrāhīm of the Shāfi'īs.*
7 *Maqāmu 'l-Ḥanafī.*
8 *Maqāmu 'l-Malakī.*
9 *Maqāmu 'l-Ḥanbalī.*
10 *Mimbar or Pulpit.*
11 *Bābu 's-Salām or Shaibar.*
12 *Ad-Daraj or Staircase for the Ka'bah.*
13 *Qubbatu 's-Sa'b.*
14 *Qubbatu 'l-'Abbās.*
1 1 *Paved causeways, &c.*
m m *Gravelled spaces.*
15 *Minaret of Bābu 's-Salām.*
16 ,, ,, *Bābu 'Alī.*
17 ,, ,, *Bābu 'l-Wadā'.*
18 ,, ,, *Bābu 'l-'Umrah.*
19 ,, ,, *Bābu 'z-Ziyādah.*
20 ,, ,, *Madrasah Kail Beg.*

GATES.

21 *Bābu 's-Salām.*
22 ,, *'n-Nabī.*
23 ,, *'l-'Abbās.*
24 ,, *'Alī or Binī Hashim.*
25 ,, *'z-Zait or Bābu 'l-'Ashrah.*
26 ,, *'l-Baghlah.*
27 ,, *'ṣ-Ṣafā.*
28 *Bābu 'r-Raḥmah.*
29 ,, *'l-Jiyād.*
30 ,, *'l-Ujlān or Bābu 'sh-Sharīf.*
31 ,, *'l-Umm Hani.*
32 ,, *'l-Wadā'.*
33 ,, *Ibrāhīm or the Tailors.*
34 ,, *Binī Saham, or Bābu 'l-'Umrah.*
35 *Bābu 'l-Atik.*
36 ,, *'l-Ajlah or Bābu 'l-Basitiyah.*
37 ,, *Kutubi.*
38 ,, *'z-Ziyādah or Bābu 'l-Nadwah.*
39 ,, *Paraibah.*

of the workmen have been placed upside down upon the shafts. I observed about half-a-dozen marble bases of good Grecian workmanship. A few of the marble columns bear Arabic or Cufic inscriptions, in which I read the dates A.H. 863 and A.H. 762. A column on the east side exhibits a very ancient Cufic inscription, somewhat defaced, which I could neither read nor copy. Those shafts, formed of the Makkan stone, cut principally from the side of the mountain near the Shubaikah quarter, are mostly in three pieces; but the marble shafts are in one piece.

Some of the columns are strengthened with broad iron rings or bands, as in many other Saracen buildings of the East; they were first employed here by Ibn Dhaher Berkouk, King of Egypt, in rebuilding the mosque, which had been destroyed by fire in A.H. 802.

This temple has been so often ruined and repaired, that no traces of remote antiquity are to be found about it. On the inside of the great wall which encloses the colonnades, a single Arabic inscription is seen, in large characters, but containing merely the names of Muḥammad and his immediate successors, Abū Bakr, 'Umar, 'Us̱mān, and 'Alī. The name of Allah, in large characters, occurs also in several places. On the outside, over the gates, are long inscriptions, in the Ṡuluṡī character, commemorating the names of those by whom the gates were built, long and minute details of which are given by the historians of Makkah.

The inscription on the south side, over Bābu Ibrahīm, is most conspicuous; all that side was rebuilt by the Egyptian Sultān al-G͟haurī, A.H. 906. Over the Bābu 'Alī and Bābu 'l-'Abbās is a long inscription, also in the Ṡuluṡī character, placed there by Sultān Murād ibn Sulaimān, A.H. 984, after he had repaired the whole building. Quṭbu 'd-dīn has given this inscription at length; it occupies several pages in his history, and is a monument of the Sultān's vanity. This side of the mosque having escaped destruction in A.D. 1626, the inscription remains uninjured.

Some parts of the walls and arches are gaudily painted, in stripes of yellow, red, and blue, as are also the minarets. Paintings of flowers, in the usual Muslim style, are nowhere seen; the floors of the colonnades are paved with large stones badly cemented together.

Seven paved causeways lead from the colonnades towards the Ka'bah, or holy house, in the centre. They are of sufficient breadth to admit four or five persons to walk abreast, and they are elevated about nine inches above the ground. Between these causeways, which are covered with fine gravel or sand, grass appears growing in several places, produced by the zamzam water oozing out of the jars, which are placed in the ground in long rows during the day. The whole area of the mosque is upon a lower level than any of the streets surrounding it. There is a descent of eight or ten steps from the gates on the north side into the platform of the colonnade, and of three or four steps from the gates, on the south side.

Towards the middle of this area stands the Ka'bah; it is one hundred and fifteen paces from the north colonnade, and eighty-eight from the south.

For this want of symmetry we may readily account, the Ka'bah having existed prior to the mosque, which was built around it, and enlarged at different periods.

The Ka'bah is an oblong massive structure, eighteen paces in length, fourteen in breadth, and from thirty-five to forty feet in height. I took the bearing of one of its longest sides, and found it to be N.N.W. ½ W. It is constructed of the grey Makkan stone, in large blocks of different sizes, joined together in a very rough manner, and with bad cement. It was entirely rebuilt as it now stands in A.D. 1627: the torrent, in the preceding year, had thrown down three of its sides; and, preparatory to its re-erection, the fourth side was, according to Assamī, pulled down, after the 'Ulamā', or learned divines, had been consulted on the question, whether mortals might be permitted to destroy any part of the holy edifice without incurring the charge of sacrilege and infidelity.

The Ka'bah stands upon a base two feet in height, which presents a sharp inclined plane; its roof being flat, it has at a distance the appearance of a perfect cube. The only door which affords entrance, and which is opened but two or three times in the year, is on the north side, and about seven feet above the ground. In entering it, therefore, wooden steps are used; of them I shall speak hereafter. In the first periods of Islām, however, when it was rebuilt in A.H. 64, by Ibn Zubair, Chief of Makkah, the nephew of 'Āyishah, it had two doors even with the ground-floor of the mosque. The present door (which, according to Azraqī, was brought hither from Constantinople in A.D. 1633), is wholly coated with silver, and has several gilt ornaments. Upon its threshold are placed every night various small lighted wax candles, and perfuming pans, filled with musk, aloe-wood, &c.

At the north-east corner of the Ka'bah, near the door, is the famous "Black Stone"; it forms a part of the sharp angle of the building, at four or five feet above the ground. It is an irregular oval, about seven inches in diameter, with an undulated surface, composed of about a dozen smaller stones of different sizes and shapes, well joined together with a small quantity of cement, and perfectly smoothed; it looks as if the whole had been broken into many pieces by a violent blow, and then united again. It is very difficult to determine accurately the quality of this stone, which has been worn to its present surface by the millions of touches and kisses it has received. It appeared to me like a lava, containing several small extraneous particles, of a whitish and of a yellowish substance. Its colour is now a deep reddish brown, approaching to black; it is surrounded on all sides by a border, composed of a substance which I took to be a close cement of pitch and gravel, of a similar, but not quite the same brownish colour. This border serves to support its detached pieces; it is two or three inches in breadth, and rises a little above the surface of the stone. Both the border and the stone itself are encircled by a silver band, broader below than above and on the two sides, with a considerable swelling below, as if a part of the stone were hidden under it. The lower part of the border is studded with silver nails.

In the south-east corner of the Ka'bah, or, as the Arabs call it, Ruknu 'l-Yamānī, there is another stone, about five feet from the ground; it is one foot and a half in length, and two inches in breadth, placed upright and of the common Makkah stone. This the people walking round the Ka'bah touch only with the right hand; they do not kiss it.

On the north side of the Ka'bah just by its door, and close to the wall, is a slight hollow in the ground, lined with marble, and sufficiently large to admit of three persons sitting. Here it is thought meritorious to pray. The spot is called Mi'jan, and supposed to be that where Abraham and his son Ishmael kneaded the chalk and mud which they used in building the Ka'bah; and near this Mi'jan the former is said to have placed the large stone upon which he stood while working at the masonry. On the basis of the Ka'bah, just over the Mi'jan, is an ancient Cufic inscription, but this I was unable to decipher, and had no opportunity of copying it. I do not find it mentioned by any of the historians.

On the west side of the Ka'bah, about two feet below its summit, is the famous Mi'zāb, or water-spout, through which the rain-water collected on the roof of the building is discharged so as to fall upon the ground. It is about four feet in length and six inches in breadth, as well as I could judge from below, with borders equal in height to its breadth. At the mouth hangs what is called the beard of the Mi'zāb, a gilt board, over which the water falls. This spout was sent hither from Constantinople in A.H. 981, and is reported to be of pure gold. The pavement round the Ka'bah, below the Mi'zāb, was laid down in A.H. 826, and consists of various coloured stones, forming a very handsome specimen of mosaic. There are two large slabs of fine verde-antico in the centre, which, according to Makrīzī, were sent thither as presents from Cairo in A.H. 241. This is the spot where, according to Muhammadan tradition, Ishmael, the son of Abraham, and his mother Hagar, are buried; and here it is meritorious for the pilgrim to recite a prayer of two rak'ahs.

On this west side is a semi-circular wall, the two extremities of which are in a line with the sides of the Ka'bah, and distant from it three or four feet, leaving an opening which leads to the burying-place of Ishmael. The wall bears the name of Ḥaṭīm, and the area which it encloses is called Ḥijr, or Ḥijru Ismā'īl, on account of its being "*separated*" from the Ka'bah; the wall itself, also, is sometimes so called; and the name Ḥaṭīm is given by the historians to the space of ground between the Ka'bah and the wall on one side, and the Bi'ru 'z-Zamzam and Maqāmu Ibrāhīm on the other. The present Makkans, however, apply the name Ḥaṭīm to the wall only.

Tradition says that the Ka'bah once extended as far as the Ḥaṭīm, and that this side having fallen down just at the time of the Ḥajj, the expenses of repairing it were demanded from the pilgrims, under a pretence that the revenues of government were not acquired in a manner sufficiently pure to admit of their application towards a purpose so sacred, whilst the money of the pilgrims would possess the requisite sanctity. The sum, however, obtained from them, proved very inadequate: all that could be done, therefore, was to raise a wall, which marked the space formerly occupied by the Ka'bah. This tradition, although current among the Makkans, is at variance with history, which declares that the Ḥijr was built by the Banū Quraish, who contracted the dimensions of the Ka'bah, that it was united to the building by Ḥajjāj, and again separated from it by Ibn Zubair.

It is asserted by Fasy, that a part of the Ḥijr, as it now stands, was never comprehended within the Ka'bah. The law regards it as a portion of the Ka'bah, inasmuch as it is esteemed equally meritorious to pray in the Ḥijr as in the Ka'bah itself; and the pilgrims who have not an opportunity of entering the latter, are permitted to affirm upon oath that they have prayed in the Ka'bah, although they may have only prostrated themselves within the enclosure of the Ḥaṭīm. The wall is built of solid stone, about five feet in height, and four in thickness, cased all over with white marble, and inscribed with prayers and invocations, neatly sculptured upon the stone in modern characters. These and the casing are the work of al-Ghaurī, the Egyptian Sultān, in A.H. 917, as we learn from Quṭbu 'd-dīn.

The walk round the Ka'bah is performed on the outside of the wall—the nearer to it the better. The four sides of the Ka'bah are covered with a black silk stuff, hanging down, and leaving the roof bare. This curtain, or veil, is called *kiswah*, and renewed annually at the time of the Ḥajj, being brought from Cairo, where it is manufactured at the Sultān's expense. On it are various prayers, interwoven in the same colour as the stuff, and it is, therefore, extremely difficult to read them. A little above the middle, and running round the whole building, is a line of similar inscriptions, worked in gold thread. That part of the kiswah which covers the door is richly embroidered with silver. Openings are left for the black stone, and the other in the south-east corner, which thus remain uncovered.

The kiswah is always of the same form and pattern; that which I saw on my first visit to the mosque was in a decayed state, and full of holes. On the 25th of the month Ẕū 'l-Qadah, the old one is taken away, and the Ka'bah continues without a cover for fifteen days. It is then said that "The Ka'bah has assumed the *iḥrām*," which lasts until the tenth of Ẕū 'l-Ḥijjah, the day of the return of the pilgrims from 'Arafah to Wādī Minā, when the new kiswah is put on. During the first days, the new covering is tucked up by cords fastened on the roof, so as to leave the lower part of the building exposed; having remained thus for many days, it is let down, and covers the whole structure, being then tied to strong brass wings in the basis of the Ka'bah. The removal of the old kiswah was performed in a very indecorous manner; and a contest ensued among the pilgrims and the people of Makkah, both young and old, about a few rags of it. The pilgrims even collect the dust which sticks to the walls of the Ka'bah, under the kiswah, and sell it, on their return, as a sacred relic. [KISWAH.]

At the moment the building is uncovered and completely bare (*'uryān*), a crowd of women assemble round it, rejoicing with cries called *walwalah*.

The black colour of the kiswah, covering a large cube in the midst of a vast square, gives to the Ka'bah, at first sight, a very singular and imposing appearance; as it is not fastened down tightly, the slightest breeze causes it to move in slow undulations, which are hailed with prayers by the congregation assembled round the building, as a sign of the presence of its guardian angels, whose wings, by their motion, are supposed to be the cause of the waving of the covering. Seventy thousand angels have the Ka'bah in their holy care, and are ordered to transport it to Paradise, when the trumpet of the Last Judgment shall be sounded.

The clothing of the Ka'bah was an ancient custom of the Pagan Arabs. The first kiswah, says Azraqī, was put on by Asad Tubba', one of the Ḥimyarite kings of Yaman; before Islām, it had two coverings, one for winter and the other for summer. In the early ages of Islām, it was sometimes white and sometimes red, and consisted of the richest brocade. In subsequent times it was furnished by the different Sultāns of Baghdad, Egypt, or Yaman, according to their respective influence over Makkah prevailed; for the clothing of the Ka'bah appears to have always been considered as a proof of sovereignty over the Ḥijāz. Kalaun, Sultān of Egypt, assumed to himself and successors the exclusive right, and from them the Sultāns at Constantinople have inherited it. Kalaun appropriated the revenue of the two large villages, Bisaus and Sandabair, in Lower Egypt, to the expense of the kiswah, and Sultān Sulaiman ibn Salīm subsequently added several others; but the Ka'bah has long been deprived of this resource.

Round the Ka'bah is a good pavement of marble, about eight inches below the level of the great square; it was laid in A.H. 981, by order of the Sultān, and describes an irregular oval; it is surrounded by thirty-two slender gilt pillars, or rather poles, between every two of which are suspended seven glass lamps, always lighted after sunset. Beyond the poles is a second pavement, about eight paces broad, somewhat elevated above the first, but of coarser work; then another, six inches higher, and eighteen paces broad, upon which stand several small buildings; beyond this is the gravelled ground, so that two broad steps may be said to lead from the square down to the Ka'bah. The small buildings just mentioned, which surround the Ka'bah, are the five Maqāms, with the well of Zamzam, the arch called Bābu 's-Salām (the Gate of Peace), and the mimbar (pulpit).

Opposite the four sides of the Ka'bah stand four other small buildings, where the Imāms of the four orthodox Muḥammadan sects, the Ḥanafī, Shāfi'ī, Ḥanbalī, and Malakī, take their station, and guide the congregation in their prayers. The Maqāmu 'l-Malakī, on the south, and that of Ḥanbalī, opposite the Black Stone, are small pavilions, open on all sides, and supported by four slender pillars, with a light sloping roof, terminating in a point, exactly in the style of Indian pagodas.

The Maqāmu 'l-Ḥanafī, which is the largest, being fifteen paces by eight, is open on all sides, and supported by twelve small pillars; it has an upper storey, also open, where the Mu'aẕẕin, who calls to prayers, takes his stand. This was first built in A.H. 923, by Sultān Salīm I.; it was afterwards rebuilt by Khushgildī, Governor of Jiddah, in A.H. 947; but all the four Maqāms, as they now stand, were built in A.H. 1074. The Maqāmu 'sh-Shāfi'ī is over the well Zamzam, to which it serves as an upper chamber.

Near their respective Maqāms, the adherents of the four different sects seat themselves for prayers. During my stay at Makkah, the Ḥanafīs always began their prayer first; but, according to Muslim custom, the Shāfi'īs should pray first in the mosque, then the Ḥanafīs, Malakīs, and Ḥanbalīs. The evening prayer is an exception, which they are all enjoined to utter together. The Maqāmu 'l-Ḥanbalī is the place where the officers of government and other great people are seated during prayers; here the Pasha and the Sharīf are placed, and, in their absence the eunuchs of the temple. These fill the space under this Maqām in front, and behind it the female pilgrims who visit the temple have their places assigned, to which they repair principally for the two evening prayers, few of them being seen in the mosque at the three other daily prayers. They also perform the ṭawāf, or walk round the Ka'bah, but generally at night, though it is not uncommon to see them walking in the daytime among the men.

The present building which encloses Zamzam, stands close by the Maqāmu 'l-Ḥanbalī, and was erected in A.H. 1072; it is of a square shape, and of massive construction, with an entrance to the north, opening into the room which contains the well. This room is beautifully ornamented with marbles of various colours; and adjoining to it, but having a separate door, is a small room with a stone reservoir, which is always full of Zamzam water; this the pilgrims get to drink by passing their hand with a cup through an iron grated opening, which serves as a window, into the reservoir, without entering the room.

The mouth of the well is surrounded by a wall five feet in height, and about ten feet in diameter. Upon this the people stand who draw up the water, in leathern buckets, an iron railing being so placed as to prevent their falling in. In Fasy's time, there were eight marble basins in this room for the purpose of ablution.

From before dawn to near midnight, the well-room is constantly crowded with visitors Everyone is at liberty to draw up the water for himself, but the labour is generally performed by persons placed there on purpose, and paid by the mosque; they expect also a trifle from those who come to drink, though they dare not demand it. I have been more than once in the room a quarter of an hour before I could get a draught of water, so great was the crowd. Devout pilgrims sometimes mount the wall and draw the bucket for several hours, in the hope of thus expiating their evil deeds.

Before the Wahhābī invasion, the well Zamzam belonged to the Sharīf, and the water becoming thus a monopoly, was only to be purchased at a high price; but one of Sa'ūd's first orders, on his arrival at Makkah, was to abolish this traffic, and the holy water is now dispensed gratis. The Turks consider it a miracle that the water of this well never diminishes, notwithstanding the continual draught from it. There is certainly no diminution in its depth, for, by an accurate inspection of the rope by which the buckets are drawn up, I found that the same length was required both at morning and evening, to reach the surface of the water. Upon inquiry, I learned from one of the persons who had descended in the time of the Wahhābīs to repair the masonry, that the water was flowing at the bottom, and that the well is therefore supplied by a subterraneous rivulet. The water is heavy to the taste, and sometimes in its colour resembles milk; but it is perfectly sweet, and differs very much from that of the brackish wells dispersed over the town. When first drawn up, it is slightly tepid, resembling, in this respect, many other fountains of the Ḥijāz.

Zamzam supplies the whole town, and there is scarcely one family that does not daily fill a jar with the water. This only serves, however, for drinking or for ablution, as it is thought impious to employ water so sacred for culinary purposes or on common occasions. Almost every pilgrim when he repairs to the mosque for evening prayer, has a jar of the water placed before him by those who earn their livelihood by performing this service.

The water is distributed in the mosque to all who are thirsty for a trifling fee, by water-carriers, with large jars upon their backs; these men are also paid by charitable pilgrims for supplying the poorer ones with this holy beverage immediately before or after prayers.

The water is regarded as an infallible cure for all diseases; and the devotees believe that the more they drink of it, the better their health will be, and their prayers the more acceptable to the Deity. I have seen some of them at the well swallowing such a quantity of it, as I should hardly have thought possible. A man who lived in the same house with me, and was ill of an intermittent fever, repaired every evening to Zamzam, and drank of the water till he was almost fainting; after which he lay for several hours extended upon his back, on the pavement near the Ka'bah, and then returned to renew his draught. When by this practice he was brought to the verge of death, he declared himself fully convinced that the increase of his illness proceeded wholly from his being unable to swallow a sufficient quantity of the water. Many pilgrims, not content with drinking it merely, strip themselves in the room, and have buckets of it thrown over them, by which they believe that the heart is purified as well as the outer body.

Few pilgrims quit Makkah without carrying away some of this water in copper or tin bottles, either for the purpose of making presents, or for their own use in case of illness, when they drink it, or for ablution after death. I carried away four small bottles, with the intention of offering them as presents to the Muḥammadan kings in the black countries. I have seen it sold at Suez by pilgrims returning from Makkah, at the rate of one piastre for the quantity that filled a coffee-cup.

The chief of Zamzam is one of the principal 'Ulamā' of Makkah. I need not remind the reader that Zamzam is supposed to be the spring found in the wilderness by Hagar, at the moment when her infant son Ishmael was dying of thirst. It seems probable that the town of Makkah owes its origin to this well. For many miles round, no sweet water is found, nor is there found in any part of the adjacent country so copious a supply.

On the north-east side of Zamzam stand two small buildings, one behind the other, called al-Qubbatain; they are covered by domes painted in the same manner as the mosque, and in them are kept water-jars, lamps, carpets, mats, brooms, and other articles used in the very mosque. These two ugly buildings are injurious to the interior appearance of the building, their heavy forms and structure being very disadvantageously contrasted with the light and airy shape of the Maqāms. I heard some pilgrims from Greece, men of better taste than the Arabs, express their regret that the Qubbatain should be allowed to disfigure the mosque. Their contents might be deposited in some of the buildings adjoining the mosque, of which they form no essential part, no religious importance being attached to them. They were built by Khushgildī, Governor of Jiddah, A.H. 947;

one is called Qubbatu 'l-'Abbās, from having been placed on the site of a small tank, said to have been formed by al-'Abbās, the uncle of Muḥammad.

A few paces west of Zamzam, and directly opposite to the door of the Ka'bah, stands a ladder or staircase, which is moved up to the wall of the Ka'bah, on the days when that building is opened, and by which the visitors ascend to the door; it is of wood, with some carved ornaments, moves on low wheels, and is sufficiently broad to admit of four persons ascending abreast. The first ladder was sent hither from Cairo in A.H. 818, by Mu'yad Abū 'n-Nāṣir, King of Egypt; for in the Ḥijāz, it seems, there has always been so great a want of artizans, that whenever the mosque required any work, it was necessary to have mechanics brought from Cairo, and even sometimes from Constantinople.

In the same line with the ladder, and close by it stands a lightly-built, insulated, and circular arch, about fifteen feet wide and eighteen feet high, called Bābu 's-Salām, which must not be confounded with the great gate of the mosque bearing the same name. Those who enter the Baitu 'llāh for the first time, are enjoined to do so by the outer and inner Bābu 's-Salām; in passing under the latter, they are to exclaim, "O God, may it be a happy entrance!" I do not know by whom this arch was built, but it appears to be modern.

Nearly in front of the Bābu 's-Salām, and nearer to the Ka'bah than any of the other surrounding buildings, stands the Maqāmu Ibrāhīm. This is a small building, supported by six pillars about eight feet high, four of which are surrounded from top to bottom by a fine iron railing, which thus leaves the space beyond the two hind pillars open; within the railing is a frame about five feet square, terminating in a pyramidal top, and said to contain the sacred stone upon which Abraham stood when he built the Ka'bah, and which, with the help of his son Ishmael, he had removed from hence to the place called Mi'jan, already mentioned. The stone is said to have yielded under the weight of the Patriarch, and to preserve the impression of his foot still visible upon it; but no pilgrim has ever seen it, as the frame is always entirely covered with a brocade of red silk richly embroidered. Persons are constantly seen before the railing, invoking the good offices of Abraham, and a short prayer must be uttered by the side of the Maqām, after the walk round the Ka'bah is completed. It is said that many of the Companions, or first adherents of Muḥammad, were interred in the open space between this Maqām and Zamzam, from which circumstance it is one of the most favourite places of prayer in the mosque. In this part of the area, the Khalīfah Sulaimān ibn 'Abdi 'l-Malik, brother of al-Walīd, built a fine reservoir, in A.H. 97, which was filled from a spring east of 'Arafāt; but the Makkans destroyed it after his death, on the pretence that the water of Zamzam was preferable.

On the side of Maqāmu Ibrāhīm, facing the middle part of the front of the Ka'bah, stands the Mimbar, or pulpit, of the mosque; it is elegantly formed of fine white marble, with many sculptured ornaments, and was sent as a present to the mosque in A.H. 969, by Sultān Sulaimān ibn Salīm. A straight narrow staircase leads up to the post of the khaṭīb, or preacher, which is surmounted by a gilt polygonal pointed steeple, resembling an obelisk. Here a sermon is preached on Fridays, and on certain festivals; these, like the Friday sermons of all mosques in the Muḥammadan countries, are usually of the same tenour, with some slight alterations upon extraordinary occasions. Before the Wahhābīs invaded Makkah, prayers were added for the Sultān and the Sharīf; but these were forbidden by Sa'ūd. Since the Turkish conquest, however, the ancient custom has been restored. The right of preaching in the Mimbar is vested in several of the first 'Ulamā' in Makkah; they are always elderly persons, and officiate in rotation. In ancient times Muḥammad himself, his successors, and the Khalīfahs, whenever they came to Makkah, mounted the pulpit, and preached to the people.

The khaṭīb, or preacher, appears in the Mimbar wrapped in a white cloak, which covers his head and body, and with a stick in hand; a practice observed also in Egypt and Syria, in memory of the first age of Islām, when the preachers found it necessary to be armed, from fear of being surprised. As in other mosques, two green flags are placed on each side of him.

About the Mimbar, the visitors of the Ka'bah deposit their shoes; as it is neither permitted to walk round the Ka'bah with covered feet, nor thought decent to carry the shoes in the hand, as is done in other mosques. Several persons keep watch over the shoes, for which they expect a small present; but the vicinity of the holy temple does not intimidate the dishonest, for I lost successively from this spot three new pairs of shoes; and the same thing happens to many pilgrims.

I have now described all the buildings within the enclosure of the temple.

The gravel-ground, and part of the adjoining outer pavement of the Ka'bah is covered, at the time of evening prayers, with carpets of from sixty to eighty feet in length, and four feet in breadth, of Egyptian manufacture, which are rolled up after prayers. The greater part of the pilgrims bring their own carpets with them. The more distant parts of the area, and the floor under the colonnade, are spread with mats brought from Souakin; the latter situation being the usual place for the performance of the mid-day and afternoon prayers. Many of these mats are presented to the mosque by the pilgrims, for which they have in return the satisfaction of seeing their names inscribed on them in large characters.

At sunset, great numbers assemble for the first evening prayer; they form themselves into several wide circles, sometimes as many as twenty, around the Ka'bah, as a common centre before which every person makes his prostration; and thus, as the Muhammadan doctors observe, Makkah is the only spot throughout the world in which the true believer can, with propriety, turn during his prayers towards any point of the compass. The Imām takes his post near the gate of the Ka'bah, and his genuflexions are imitated by the whole assembled multitude. The effect of the joint prostrations of six or eight thousand persons, added to the recollection of the distance and various quarters from whence they come, or for what purpose, cannot fail to impress the most cool-minded spectator with some degree of awe. At night, when the lamps are lighted, and numbers of devotees are performing the Ṭawāf round the Ka'bah, the sight of the busy crowds, the voices of the Muṭawwifs, intent upon making themselves heard by those to whom they recite their prayers, the loud conversation of many idle persons, the running, playing, and laughing of boys, give to the whole a very different appearance, and one more resembling that of a place of public amusement. The crowd, however, leaves the mosque about nine o'clock, when it again becomes the place of silent meditation and prayer to the few visitors who are led to the spot by sincere piety, and not worldly motives or fashion.

There is an opinion prevalent at Makkah, founded on holy tradition, that the mosque will contain any number of the faithful; and that if even the whole Muḥammadan community were to enter at once, they would all find room in it to pray. The guardian angels, it is said, would invisibly extend the dimensions of the building, and diminish the size of each individual. The fact is, that during the most numerous pilgrimages, the mosque, which can contain, I believe, about thirty-five thousand persons in the act of prayer, is never half-filled. Even on Fridays, the greater part of the Makkans, contrary to the injunctions of the law, pray at home, if at all, and many pilgrims follow their example. I could never count more than ten thousand individuals in the mosque at one time, even after the return from 'Arafāt, when the whole body of pilgrims was collected for a few days in and about the city.

At every hour of the day persons may be seen under the colonnade, occupied in reading the Qur'ān and other religious books; and here many poor Indians, or negroes, spread their mats, and pass the whole period of their residence at Makkah. Here they both eat and sleep; but cooking is not allowed. During the hours of noon, many persons come to repose beneath the cool shade of the vaulted roof of the colonnade; a custom which not only accounts for the mode of construction observed in the old Muḥammadan temples of Egypt and Arabia, but for that also of the ancient Egyptian temples, the immense porticoes of which were probably left open to the idolatrous natives, whose mud-built houses could afford them but an imperfect refuge against the mid-day heats.

It is only during the hours of prayer that the great mosques of these countries partake of the sanctity of prayer, or in any degree seem to be regarded as consecrated places. In al-Azhar, the first mosque at Cairo, I have seen boys crying pancakes for sale, barbers shaving their customers, and many of the lower orders eating their dinners, where, during prayers, not the slightest motion, nor even whisper, diverts the attention of the congregation. Not a sound but the voice of the Imām, is heard during prayers in the great mosque at Makkah, which at other times is the place of meeting for men of business to converse on their affairs, and is sometimes so full of poor pilgrims, or of diseased persons lying about under the colonnade, in midst of their miserable baggage, as to have the appearance of a hospital rather than a temple. Boys play in the great square, and servants carry luggage across it, to pass by the nearest route from one part of the town to the other. In these respects, the temple of Makkah resembles the other great mosques of the East. But the holy Ka'bah is rendered the scene of such indecencies and criminal acts, as cannot with propriety be more particularly noticed. They are not only practised here with impunity, but, it may be said, almost publicly; and my indignation has often been excited, on witnessing abominations which called forth from other passing spectators nothing more than a laugh or a slight reprimand.

In several parts of the colonnade, public schools are held, where young children are taught to spell and read; they are most noisy groups, and the schoolmaster's stick is in constant action. Some learned men of Makkah deliver lectures on religious subjects every afternoon under the colonnade, but the auditors are seldom numerous. On Fridays, after prayer, some Turkish 'Ulamā' explain to their countrymen assembled around them a few chapters of the Qur'ān, after which each of the audience kisses the hand of the expositor, and drops money into his cap. I particularly admired the fluency of speech of one of these 'Ulamā', although I did not understand him, the lecture being delivered in the Turkish language. His gesticulations, and the inflexions of his voice, were most expressive; but, like an actor on the stage, he would laugh and cry in the same minute, and adapt his features to his purpose in the most skilful manner. He was a native of Brusa, and amassed a considerable sum of money.

Near the gate of the mosque called Bābu 's-Salām, a few Arab shaikhs daily take their seat, with their inkstand and paper, ready to write, for any applicant, letters, accounts, contracts, or any similar document.

They also deal in written charms, like those current in the Black countries, such as amulets, love-receipts, &c. They are principally employed by Bedouins, and demand an exorbitant remuneration.

Winding sheets (*kafan*) and other linen washed in the waters of Zamzam, are constantly seen hanging to dry between the columns. Many pilgrims purchase at Makkah the shroud in which they wish to be buried, and wash it themselves at the well of Zamzam, supposing that, if the corpse be wrapped in linen which has been wetted with this holy water, the peace of the soul after death will be more effectually secured. Some pilgrims make this linen an article of traffic.

Makkah generally, but the mosque in particular, abounds in flocks of wild pigeons, which are considered to be the inviolable property of the temple, and are called the pigeons of the Baitu 'llāh. Nobody dares to kill any of them, even when they enter the private houses. In the square of the mosque, several small stone basins are regularly filled with water for their use; here, also, Arab women expose for sale, upon small straw mats, corn and durrah, which the pilgrims purchase, and throw to the pigeons. I have seen some of the public women take this mode of exhibiting themselves, and of bargaining with the pilgrims, under pretence of selling them corn for the sacred pigeons.

The gates of the mosque are nineteen in number, and are distributed about it, without any order or symmetry. The principal of these gates are: on the north side, Bābu 's-Salām, by which every pilgrim enters the mosque; Bābu 'l-'Abbās; Bābu 'n-Nabī, by which Muḥammad is said to have always entered the mosque; Bābu 'Alī. On the east side: Bābu Zai, or Bābu 'l-'Ashrah, through which the ten first adherents of Muḥammad used to enter; Bābu 'ṣ-Ṣafā; two gates called Bībānu 'sh-Sharīf, opposite the palaces of the Sharīf. On the south side: Bābu Ibrāhīm, where the colonnade projects beyond the straight line of the columns, and forms a small square; Bābu 'l-'Umrah, through which it is necessary to pass, on visiting the 'Umrah. On the west side: Bābu 'z-Ziyādah, forming a projecting square similar to that at Bābu Ibrāhīm, but larger.

Most of these gates have high-pointed arches, but a few round arches are seen among them, which, like all the arches of this kind in the Ḥijāz, are nearly semicircular. They are without any ornament, except the inscription on the exterior, which commemorates the name of the builder; and they are all posterior in date to the fourteenth century. As each gate consists of two or three arches, or divisions, separated by narrow walls, these divisions are counted in the enumeration of the gates leading into the Ka'bah, and thus make up the number thirty-nine.

There being no doors to the gates, the mosque is consequently open at all times. I have crossed at every hour of the night, and always found people there, either at prayers or walking about.

The outside walls of the mosque are those of the houses which surround it on all sides. These houses belonged originally to the mosque; the greater part are now the property of individuals, who have purchased them. They are let out to the richest pilgrims, at very high prices, as much as five hundred piastres being given, during the pilgrimage, for a good apartment, with windows opening into the mosque. Windows have, in consequence, been opened in many parts of the walls, on a level with the street, and above that of the floor of the colonnades. Pilgrims living in these apartments are allowed to perform the Friday's prayers at home, because, having the Ka'bah in view from the windows, they are supposed to be in the mosque itself, and to join in prayer those assembled within the temple. Upon a level with the ground-floor of the colonnades, and opening into them, are small apartments formed in the walls, having the appearance of dungeons; these have remained the property of the mosque, while the houses above them belong to private individuals. They are let out to watermen, who deposit in them the Zamzam jars, or to less opulent pilgrims who wish to live in the mosque. Some of the surrounding houses still belong to the mosque, and were originally intended for public schools, as their name of Madrasah implies; they are now all let out to pilgrims. In one of the largest of them, Muḥammad 'Alī Pasha lived; in another Ḥasan Pasha.

Close to Bābu Ibrāhīm is a large madrasah, now the property of Saiyid Ageyl, one of the principal merchants of the town, whose warehouse opens into the mosque. This person, who is aged, has the reputation of great sanctity; and it is said that the hand of the Sharīf Ghālib, when once in the act of collaring him for refusing to advance some money, was momentarily struck with palsy. He has evening assemblies in his house, where theological books are read, and religious topics discussed.

Among other buildings forming the enclosure of the mosque, is the Miḥkam, or house of justice, close by the Bābu 'z-Ziyādah; it is a fine, firmly-built structure, with lofty arches in the interior, and has a row of high windows looking into the mosque. It is inhabited by the Qāẓī. Adjoining to it stands a large Madrasah, enclosing a square, known by the name of Madrasah Sulaimān, built by Sultān Sulaimān and his son Salīm II., in A.H. 973. It is always well filled with Turkish pilgrims, the friends of the Qāẓī, who disposes of the lodgings.

The exterior of the mosque is adorned with seven minarets, irregularly distributed: 1. Minaret of Bābu 'l-'Umrah; 2. of Bābu 's-Salām; 3. of Bābu 'Alī; 4. of Bābu 'l-Wadā'; 5. of Madrasah Kail Beg; 6. of Bābu 'z-Ziyādah; 7. of Madrasah Sultān Sulaiman. They are quadrangular or round steeples, in no way differing from other minarets. The entrance to them is from the different buildings round the mosque, which they adjoin. A beautiful view of the busy crowd below is obtained by ascending the most northern one. (Taken, with slight alterations, chiefly in the spelling of Arabic words and names, from Burckhardt's *Travels in Arabia*, vol. i. p. 243.)

Mr. Sale says: "The temple of Mecca was a place of worship, and in singular veneration with the Arabs from great antiquity, and many centuries before Muhammad. Though it was most probably dedicated at first to an idolatrous use, yet the Muhammadans are generally persuaded that the Ka'bah is almost coeval with the world; for they say that Adam, after his expulsion from Paradise, begged of God that he might erect a building like that he had seen there, called Baitu 'l-Ma'mūr, or the frequented house, and al Durah, towards which he might direct his prayers, and which he might compass, as the angels do the celestial one. Whereupon God let down a representation of that house in curtains of light, and set it in Mecca, perpendicularly under its original, ordering the patriarch to turn towards it when he prayed, and to compass it by way of devotion. After Adam's death, his son Seth built a house in the same form, of stone and clay, which being destroyed by the Deluge, was rebuilt by Abraham and Ishmael at God's command, in the place where the former had stood, and after the same model, they being directed therein by revelation.

"After this edifice had undergone several reparations, it was, a few years after the birth of Muhammad, rebuilt by the Quraish on the old foundation, and afterwards repaired by Abdullah Ibn Zubair, the Khalif of Mecca; and at length again rebuilt by Yusuf, surnamed al Hijaj Ibn Yusuf, in the seventy-fourth year of the Hijrah, with some alterations, in the form wherein it now remains. Some years after, however, the Khalif Harun al Rashid (or, as others write, his father al Mahdi, or his grandfather al Mansur) intended again to change what had been altered by al Hijaj, and to reduce the Ka'bah to the old form in which it was left by Abdullah, but was dissuaded from meddling with it, lest so holy a place should become the sport of princes, and being new-modelled after everyone's fancy, should lose that reverence which was justly paid it. But notwithstanding the antiquity and holiness of this building, they have a prophecy by tradition from Muhammad, that in the last times the Ethiopians shall come and utterly demolish it, after which it will not be rebuilt again for ever." (*Prel. Dis.*, p. 83).

The following are the references to the Sacred Mosque in the Qur'ān:—

Sūrah ii. 144, 145: "From whatever place thou comest forth, then turn your face towards the Sacred Mosque; for this is a duty enjoined by thy Lord; and God is not inattentive to your doings. And from whatever place thou comest forth, then turn thy face toward the Sacred Mosque: and wherever ye be, to that part turn your faces, that men have no cause of dispute against you."

Sūrah v. 2: "O Believers! violate neither the rites of God, nor the sacred month, nor the offering, nor its ornaments, nor those who press on to the Sacred Mosque, seeking favour from their Lord and His good pleasure in them."

Sūrah viii. 33–35: "But God chose not to chastise them while thou wast with them, nor would God chastise them when they sued for pardon. But because they debarred the faithful from the Sacred Mosque, albeit they are not its guardians, nothing is there on their part why God should not chastise them. The God-fearing only are its guardians; but most of them know it not. And their prayer at the house is no other than whistling through the fingers and clapping of the hands—'Taste then the torment, for that ye have been unbelievers.'"

Sūrah ix. 7: "How shall they who add gods to God be in league with God and with His Apostle, save those with whom ye made a league at the Sacred Mosque? So long as they are true to you, be ye true to them; for God loveth those who fear Him."

Sūrah ix. 28: "O Believers! only they who join gods with God are unclean! Let them not, therefore, after this their year, come near the Sacred Mosque. And if ye fear want, God, if He please, will enrich you of His abundance: for God is Knowing, Wise."

Sūrah xvii. 1: "Glory be to Him who carried his servant by night from the Sacred Mosque to the temple that is more remote (*i.e.* Jerusalem), whose precinct we have blessed, that we might show him of our signs! for He is the Hearer, the Seer."

Sūrah xxii. 25: "From the Sacred Mosque which we have appointed to all men, alike for those who abide therein, and for the stranger."

Sūrah xlviii. 25: "These are they who believed not, and kept you away from the Sacred Mosque, as well as the offering which was prevented from reaching the place of sacrifice."

Sūrah xlviii. 27: "Now hath God in truth made good to His Apostle the dream *in which he said*, 'Ye shall surely enter the Sacred Mosque, if God will, in full security, having your heads shaved and your hair cut: ye shall not fear; for He knoweth what ye know not; and He hath ordained you, beside this, a speedy victory."

AL-MASJIDU 'L-JĀMI' (المسجد الجامع). *Lit.* "The collecting mosque." A title given to the chief mosque of any city in which people assemble for the Friday prayer and khutbah. [KHUTBAH.]

MASJIDU 'L-KHAIF (مسجد الخيف). A mosque at Minā, three miles from Makkah. Here, according to the Arabs, Adam is buried, "his head being at one end of a long wall, and his feet at another, whilst the dome covers his omphalic region." (Burton's *Pilgrimage*, vol. ii. p. 203.)

MASJIDU 'N-NABĪ (مسجد النبى). "The Prophet's Mosque" at al-Madīnah. It is held to be the second mosque in Islām in point of seniority, and the same, or, according to others the first, in dignity, ranking with the Sacred Mosque at Makkah.

The following is Captain R. F. Burton's account of its history:—

"Muḥammad ordered to erect a place of worship there, sent for the youths to whom it belonged and certain Anṣār, or auxiliaries, their guardians; the ground was offered to him in free gift, but he insisted upon purchasing it, paying more than its value. Having caused the soil to be levelled and the trees to be felled, he laid the foundation of the first mosque.

"In those times of primitive simplicity its walls were made of rough stone and unbaked bricks, and trunks of date-trees supported a palm-stick roof, concerning which the Archangel Gabriel delivered an order that it should not be higher than seven cubits, the elevation of Solomon's temple. All ornament was strictly forbidden. The Anṣār, or men of Medinah, and the Muhājirīn, or fugitives from Mecca, carried the building materials in their arms from the cemetery Baki', near the well

of Aiyūb, north of the spot where Ibrahīm's mosque now stands, and the Prophet was to be seen aiding them in their labours, and reciting for their encouragement:

'O Allah! there is no good but the good of futurity;
Then have mercy upon my Anṣār and Muhājirīn."

"The length of this mosque was fifty-four cubits from north to south, and sixty-three in breadth, and it was hemmed in by houses on all sides save the western. Till the seventeenth month of the new era, the congregation faced towards the northern wall. After that time a fresh 'revelation' turned them in the direction of Makkah—southwards; on which occasion the Archangel Gabriel descended and miraculously opened through the hills and wilds a view of the Ka'bah, that

MASJIDU 'N-NABI AT AL-MADINAH.   (*Captain R. Burton.*)

there might be no difficulty in ascertaining its true position.

"After the capture of Khaibar in A.H. 7, the Prophet and his first three successors restored the mosque, but Muslim historians do not consider this a second foundation. Muḥammad laid the first brick, and Abu-Hurayrah declares that he saw him carry heaps of building material piled up to his breast. The Khalīfahs, each in the turn of his succession, placed a brick close to that laid by the Prophet, and aided him in raising the walls. Tabrāni relates that one of the Anṣār had a house adjacent, which Muḥammad wished to make part of the place of prayer; the proprietor was offered in exchange for it a home in Paradise, which he gently rejected, pleading poverty. His excuse was admitted, and 'Uṣmān, after purchasing the place for 10,000 dirhams, gave it

to the Prophet on the long credit originally offered. The mosque was a square of 100 cubits. Like the former building, it had three doors: one on the south side, where the *Miḥrābu 'n-Nabawi*, or the 'Prophet's niche," now is, another in the place of the present *Bābu 'r-Raḥmah*, and the third at the *Bābu 'Uṣmān*, now called the "Gate of Gabriel." Instead of a miḥrāb or prayer niche, a large block of stone, directed the congregation. At first it was placed against the northern wall of the mosque, and it was removed to the southern when Makkah became the Qiblah. In the beginning the Prophet, whilst preaching the khutbah or Friday sermon, leaned, when fatigued, against a post. The mimbar, or pulpit, was the invention of a Madīnah man of the Banū Najjār. It was a wooden frame, two cubits long by one broad, with three steps, each one span high; on the topmost of these the Prophet sat when he required rest. The pulpit assumed its present form about A.H. 90, during the artistic reign of Walīd.

"In this mosque Muḥammad spent the greater part of the day with his companions, conversing, instructing, and comforting the poor. Hard by were the abodes of his wives, his family, and his principal friends. Here he prayed, hearkening to the Azān, or devotion call, from the roof. Here he received worldly envoys and embassies, and the heavenly messages conveyed by the Archangel Gabriel. And within a few yards of the hallowed spot, he died, and found, it is supposed, a grave.

"The theatre of events so important to Islām, could not be allowed—especially as no divine decree forbade the change—to remain in its pristine lowliness. The first Khalīfah contented himself with merely restoring some of the palm pillars, which had fallen to the ground. 'Umar, the second successor, surrounded the Ḥujrah, or 'Āyishah's chamber, in which the Prophet was buried, with a mud wall, and in A.H. 17, he enlarged the mosque to 140 cubits by 120, taking in ground on all sides except the eastern, where stood the abodes of the 'Mothers of the Moslems' (*Ummu 'l-Mu'minīn*). Outside the northern wall he erected a ṣuffah, called Batha—a raised bench of wood, earth, or stone, upon which the people might recreate themselves with conversation and quoting poetry, for the mosque was now becoming a place of peculiar reverence to men.

"The second Masjid was erected A.H. 29 by the third Khalīfah, 'Usmān, who, regardless of the clamours of the people, overthrew the old one, and extended the building greatly towards the north, and a little towards the west; but he did not remove the eastern limit on account of the private houses. He made the roof of Indian teak, and erected walls of hewn and carved stone. These innovations caused some excitement, which he allayed by quoting a tradition of the Prophet, with one of which he appears perpetually to have been prepared. The saying in question was, according to some, 'Were this my mosque extended to Ṣafā, it verily would still be my mosque'; according to others, 'Were the Prophet's mosque extended to Zū 'l-Ḥulafā', it would still be his.' But 'Usmān's skill in the quotation of tradition did not prevent the new building being in part a cause of his death. It was finished on the 1st Muḥarram, A.H. 30.

"At length, Islām, grown splendid and powerful, determined to surpass other nations in the magnificence of its public buildings. In A.H. 88, al-Walid the First, twelfth Khalīfah of the Banī Umayah race, after building the noble Jāmi'-Masjid of the Ommiades at Damascus, determined to display his liberality at al-Madīnah. The governor of the place, 'Umar ibn 'Abdu 'l-Azīz, was directed to buy for 7,000 dinars all the hovels of raw brick that hedged in the eastern side of the old mosque. They were inhabited by descendants of the Prophet and of the early Khalīfahs, and in more than one case, the ejection of the holy tenantry was effected with considerable difficulty. Some of the women (ever the most obstinate on such occasions) refused to take money, and 'Umar was forced to the objectionable measure of turning them out of doors with exposed faces in full day. The Greek Emperor, applied to by the magnificent Khalīfah, sent immense presents, silver lamp chains, valuable curiosities, forty loads of small cut stones for pietra-dura, and a sum of 80,000 dinars, or, as others say, 40,000 mishkals of gold. He also despatched forty Coptic and forty Greek artists to carve the marble pillars and the casings of the walls, and to superintend the gilding and the mosaic work.

"One of these Christians was beheaded for sculpturing a hog on the Qiblah wall, and another, in an attempt to defile the roof, fell to the ground, and his brains were dashed out. The remainder apostatized, but this did not prevent the older Arabs murmuring that their mosque had been turned into a kanīsah (or Church). The Ḥujrah, or chamber, where, by Muḥammad's permission, 'Izrā'īl, the Angel of Death, separated his soul from his body, whilst his head was lying in the lap of 'Āyishah, his favourite wife, was now for the first time taken into the mosque. The raw brick enceinte which surrounded the three graves was exchanged for one of carved stone, enclosed by an outer precinct with a narrow passage between. These double walls were either without a door, or had only a small blocked-up wicket on the northern side, and from that day (A.H. 90), no one has been able to approach the sepulchre. A minaret was erected at each corner of the mosque. The building was enlarged to 200 cubits by 167, and was finished in A.H. 91. When Walīd, the Khalīfah, visited it in state, he inquired of his lieutenant why greater magnificence had not been displayed in the erection; upon which 'Umar informed him, to his astonishment, that the walls alone had cost 45,000 dinars.

"The fourth mosque was erected in A.H. 191, by al-Mahdī, third prince of the Banū 'Abbās or Baghdad Khalīfahs—celebrated in history only for spending enormous sums upon a pilgrimage. He enlarged the building by adding ten handsome pillars of carved marble, with gilt capitals, on the northern side. In A.H. 202, al-Ma'mūn made further additions to this mosque.

"It was from al-Mahdī's Masjid that Ḥakīm ibn Amri 'llah, the third Fāṭimite Khalīfah of Egypt, and the deity of the Druse sect, determined to steal the bodies of the Prophet and his two companions. About A.H. 412, he sent emissaries to al-Madīnah; the attempt, however, failed, and the would be violators of the tomb lost their lives. It is generally supposed that Ḥakīm's object was to transfer the visitation to his own capital; but in one so manifestly insane it is difficult to discover the spring of action. Two Christians, habited like Maghrabī pilgrims, in A.H. 550, dug a mine from a neighbouring house into the temple. They were discovered, beheaded, and burned to ashes. In relating these events, the Muslim historians mix up many foolish preternaturalisms with credible matter. At last, to prevent a recurrence of such sacrilegious attempts, Māliku 'l-'Ādil Nūru 'd-dīn, of the Baharite Mamluk Sultans, or, according to others, Sultan Nūru 'd-dīn Shāhid Maḥmūd bin Zengi, who, warned by a vision of the Prophet, had started for al-Madīnah only in time to discover the two Christians, surrounded the holy place with a deep trench, filled with molten lead. By this means Abū Bakr and 'Umar, who had run considerable risks of their own, have ever since been enabled to occupy their last home undisturbed.

"In A.H. 654, the fifth mosque was erected in consequence of a fire, which some authors attribute to a volcano that broke out close to the town in terrible eruption; others, with more fanaticism and less probability, to the schismatic Banū Ḥusain, then the guardians of the tomb. On this occasion the Ḥujrah was saved, together with the old and venerable copies of the Qur'ān there deposited, especially the Cufic MSS., written by Uṣmān, the third Khalīfah. The piety of three sovereigns, Musta'ṣim (last Khalīfah of Baghdad) Muẓaffir Shems-ud-dīn-Yūsuf, chief of Yaman, and Ẓāhir Beybars, Baharite Sultan of Egypt, completed the work in A.H. 688. This building was enlarged and beautified by the princes of Egypt, and lasted upwards of 200 years.

"The sixth mosque was built, almost as it now stands, by Kaid Bey, nineteenth Sultan of the Circasian Mamluk kings of Egypt, in A.H. 888. Musta'ṣim's mosque had been struck by lightning during a storm; thirteen men were killed at prayers, and the destroying element spared nothing but the interior of the Ḥujrah. The railing and dome were restored; niches and a pulpit were sent from Cairo, and the gates and minarets were distributed as they are now. Not content with this, Kaid Bey established 'waqf' (bequests) and pensions, and introduced order among the attendants on the tomb. In the tenth century, Sultan Sulaiman the Magnificent paved with fine white marble the Rauẓah or garden, which Kaid Bey, not daring to alter, had left of earth, and erected the fine minaret that bears his name. During the dominion of the later Sultans and of Mohammad Ali, a few trifling presents of lamps, carpets, wax candles, and chandeliers, and a few immaterial alterations have been made." (See *Personal Narrative of a Pilgrimage to El Medinah and Meccah*, by Richard F. Burton, 2nd edition, vol. i. p. 345.)

MASJIDU 'T-TAQWĀ (مسجد التقوى). *Lit.* "The Mosque of Piety." The mosque at Qubā', a place about three miles south-east of al-Madīnah. It was here that it is said that the Prophet's camel, al-Qaṣwā rested on its way from Makkah to al-Madīnah, on the occasion of the Flight. And when Muḥammad desired the Companions to mount the camel, Abū Bakr and 'Umar did so, but she still remained on the ground; but when 'Alī obeyed the order, she arose. Here the Prophet decided to erect a place for prayer. It was the first mosque erected in Islām. Muḥammad laid the first brick, and with an iron javelin marked out the direction for prayer. The Prophet, during his residence at al-Madīnah, used to visit it once a week on foot, and he always made a point of praying there the morning prayer on the 17th of Ramaẓān. A prayer in the mosque of Qubā' is said to be equal in merit to a Lesser Pilgrimage to Makkah, and the place itself bears rank after the mosques of Makkah and al-Madinah and before that of Jerusalem. It was originally a square building of very small size, but the Khalīfah 'Uṣman enlarged it. Sultān 'Abdu 'l-Ḥamīd rebuilt the place, but it has no pretensions to grandeur. (See Burton's *Pilgrimage*, vol. i. p. 390.)

MASNŪN (مسنون). That which is founded upon the precept or practice of Muḥammad. [SUNNAH.]

AL-MATĪN (المتين). "The Strong" (as a fortification is strong). One of the ninety-nine names or attributes of God. It occurs in the Qur'ān, Sūrah li. 58: "God is the provider, endowed with power, the *Strong*."

MATN (متن). The text of a book. The notes, or commentary upon the text are called the *sharḥ*. A word frequently used by Muḥammadans in theological books.

MA'ŪDAH (موءودة). From *wa'ad*, "to bury alive." A damsel buried alive. A custom which existed before the time of Muḥammad in ancient Arabia, but which was forbidden by him. Sūrah xvii. 33: "Kill not your children from fear of want." See also Sūrahs xvi. 61; lxxxi. 8.

MAULĀ (مولى), pl. *mawālī*. A term used in Muslim law for a slave, but in the Qur'ān for "a protector or helper," *i.e.* God Almighty.

Sūrah viii. 41: "Know ye that God is your *protector*."

Sūrah ii. 386: "Thou (God) art our *protector*."

Sūrah xlvii. 12: "God is the *protector* of those who believe."

The plural form occurs in the Qur'ān, Sūrah iv. 37, where it is translated by Palmer thus: "To everyone have we appointed *kinsfolk*" (*mawālī*).

MAULAWĪ (مولوى). From *maulā*, "a lord or master." A term generally used for a learned man.

MAULID (مولد). The birthday, especially of a prophet or saint. The birthday of Muḥammad, which is known as *Maulidu 'n-Nabī*, is celebrated on the 12th of Rabī'u 'l-Awwal. It is a day observed in Turkey and Egypt and in some parts of Hindustān, but not in Central Asia, by the recital of numerous *ẕikrs*, and by distribution of alms.

Mr. Lane, in his *Modern Egyptians*, vol. ii. p. 171, gives the following specimen of a *zikr* recited in the Maulidu 'n-Nabī: "O God bless our lord Muḥammad among the latter generations; and bless our lord Muḥammad in every time and period, and bless our lord Muḥammad among the most exalted princes, unto the Day of Judgment; and bless all the prophets and apostles among the inhabitants of the heavens, and of the earth, and may God (whose name be blessed and exalted) be well pleased with our lords and our masters, those persons of illustrious estimation, Abū Bakr, and 'Umar, and 'Us̤mān, and 'Alī, and with all the other favourites of God. God is our sufficiency, excellent is the Guardian. And there is no strength nor power but in God, the High, the Great. O God, O our Lord, O Thou liberal of pardon, O Thou most bountiful of the most bountiful, O God. Amīn."

MĀ'U 'L-QUDS (ماء القدس). *Lit.* "Water of Holiness." A term used by the Ṣūfīs for such holy influences on the soul of man as enable him to overcome the lusts of the flesh, and to become holy. (See 'Abdu 'r-Razzāq's *Dict. of Ṣūfī Terms*.)

AL-MĀ'ŪN (الماعون). *Lit.* "Necessaries." The title of the CVIIth Sūrah of the Qur'ān, in the last verse of which the word occurs.

MAUT (موت). "Death." Heb. מָוֶת. The word is always used in the Qur'ān in its literal sense, meaning the departure of the spirit from the body, *e.g.* Sūrah ii. 182: "Every soul must taste of *death*." But amongst the Ṣūfīs it is employed in a figurative sense, *e.g. al-mautu 'l-abyaẓ*, or "the white death," is held to mean abstinence from food, or that feeling of hunger which purifies the soul. A person who frequently abstains from food is said to have entered this state of death. *Al-mautu 'l-akhẓar*, "the green death," the wearing of old clothes in a state of voluntary poverty. When a person has given up wearing purple and fine linen, and has chosen the garments of poverty, he is said to have entered this state of death. *Al-mautu 'l-aswad*, "the black death," the voluntary taking up of trouble, and submitting to be evil spoken of for the truth's sake. When a Muslim has learnt to submit to such troubles and persecutions, he is said to have entered into this state of death. (See 'Abdu 'r-Razzāq's *Dict. of Ṣūfī Terms*.) [MAMAT.]

MA'ZŪN (مأذون). A licensed or privileged slave. A slave who has received a remission of all the inhibitions attending his state of bondage.

MEAT. [FOOD.]

MECCA. [MAKKAH.]

MEDICINE. Arabic *dawā'* (دوا). The only medicine recommended in the Qu'rān is honey. See Sūrah xvi. 71: "From its (the bee's) belly cometh forth a fluid of varying hues, which yieldeth medicine to man."

MEDINA. [AL-MADĪNAH.]

MEDITATION. [MURAQABAH.]

MENSTRUATION. Arabic *maḥīẓ* (محيض). The *catamenia*, or menses, is termed *ḥayẓ*. The woman in this condition is called *ḥā'iẓ* or *ḥā'iẓah*. All books of Muḥammadan theology contain a chapter devoted to the treatment of women in this condition. During the period of menstruation, women are not permitted to say their prayers, or to touch or read the Qur'ān, or enter a mosque, and are forbidden to their husbands. But it is related in the traditions that Muḥammad abrogated the law of Moses which set a menstruous woman entirely apart for seven days. (Leviticus xv. 19). And Anas says that when the Jews heard this they said, "This man opposes our customs in everything."

(See Qur'ān, Sūrah ii. 222; *Mishkātu 'l-Maṣābiḥ*, Hamilton's ed. vol. i. p. 121; Arabic ed. *Bābu 'l-Ḥaiẓ*.)

When the period of menses ceases, bathing must be performed and prayer said.

MERCY. Arabic *Raḥmah* (رحمة). Heb. רחם. The attribute of mercy is specially mentioned in the Qur'ān as one which characterizes the Divine Being; each chapter of that book (with the exception of the IXth), beginning with the superscription, *Bismillāhi 'r-Raḥmāni 'r-Raḥīm*, "In the name of God the Merciful, the Compassionate." In the *Tafsīr-i-Raufī* it is said that *ar-Raḥmān* is only applicable to God, whilst *ar-Raḥīm* may be applied to the creature as well as to God; but the Jalālān say the two terms are synonymous, and on this account they are used together. Al-Baiẓāwī remarks that the attribute of mercy expresses "softness of heart" (*riqqatu 'l-qalb*), and "a turning with kindness and favour towards a person," and in this way it expresses God's sympathy with mankind, although the terms are not strictly applicable to an unchangeable Being. In the Qur'ān, Job is described as speaking of God as "the most merciful of merciful ones." (Sūrah xxi. 83). And the angels who bear the throne, and those around it who celebrate God's praises, cry out: "Our Lord! thou dost embrace all things in mercy and knowledge!" (Sūrah xl. 7.) The "Treasuries of the mercies of the Lord," are often referred to in the Qur'ān (*e.g.* Sūrahs xvii. 102; xviii. 81). The word *Raḥmah*, "a mercy," is a term used for a divine book; it is frequently applied to the Qur'ān, which is called "a mercy and a guidance" (Sūrahs x. 58; xvii. 84), and also to the books of Moses (Sūrahs xi. 20; xii. 111). In one place it is used for Paradise, "They are in God's mercy" (Sūrah iii. 103). The bounty of God's mercy is the constant theme both of the Qur'ān and the Traditions; *e.g.* Sūrah vii. 155: "My mercy embraceth everything." To despair of God's mercy is a cardinal sin. Sūrah xxxix. 54: "Be not in despair of the mercy of God; verily, God forgives sins, all of them." Sūrah xv. 56: "Only those who err despair of the mercy of their Lord."

In the Traditions, Muḥammad is related to have said: "When God created the world He wrote a book, which is with Him on the exalted throne, and therein is written, 'Verily my mercy overcomes my anger.'" And, again, "Verily, God has one hundred mercies; one mercy hath he sent down to men and genii, but He hath reserved ninety-nine mercies, by which He will be gracious to His people." (*Mishkāt*, book x. ch. 4.)

The LVth Sūrah of the Qur'ān is entitled the *Sūratu 'r-Raḥmān*, or the "Chapter of the Merciful," in which are set forth the "bounties of the Lord." It is a chapter which is sadly marred by its concluding description of the sensual enjoyments of Muḥammad's paradise.

The Christians are spoken of in the Qur'ān, Sūrah lvii. 27, as those in whose hearts God "placed mercy (*raḥmah*) and compassion (*ra'fah*)."

MICHAEL. In Muḥammadan works generally, the Archangel Michael is called *Mīkā'īl* (ميكائيل), Heb. מִיכָאֵל; but in the Qur'ān, in which his name once occurs, he is called *Mīkāl* (ميكال). Al-Baiẓāwī says that a Jew named 'Abdu 'llāh ibn Ṣūrīyā', objected to Muḥammad's assertion that the Archangel Gabriel revealed the Qur'ān to him, because he was an avenging angel, and said that if it had been sent by Michael, their own guardian angel (Daniel xii. 1), they might have believed. This assertion called forth the following verses from Muḥammad in Sūrah ii. 92:—

"Whoso is the enemy of Gabriel—For he it is who by God's leave hath caused *the Qur'ān* to descend on thy heart, the confirmation of previous revelations, and guidance, and good tidings to the faithful—Whoso is an enemy to God or his angels, or to Gabriel, or to Michael, *shall have God as his enemy*: for verily God is an enemy to the infidels. Moreover, clear signs have we sent down to thee, and none will disbelieve them but the perverse."

MIDIAN. [MADYAN.]

MIFTĀḤU 'L-JANNAH (مفتاح الجنة). "The Key of Paradise." A term used by Muḥammad for prayer. (*Mishkāt*, book iii. ch. i.)

MIḤJAN (محجن). A hook-headed stick about four feet long, which, it is said, the Prophet always carried; now carried by men of religious pretensions.

MIḤRĀB (محراب). A niche in the centre of a wall of a mosque, which marks the direction of Makkah, and before which the Imām takes his position when he leads the congregation in prayer. In the Masjidu 'n-Nabī, or Prophet's mosque, at al-Madīnah, a large black stone, placed against the northern wall, facing Jerusalem, directed the congregation, but it was removed to the southern side when the Qiblah was changed to Makkah.

The Miḥrāb, as it now exists, dates from the days of al-Walīd (A.H. 90), and it seems probable that the Khalīfah borrowed the idea

A MIHRAB.

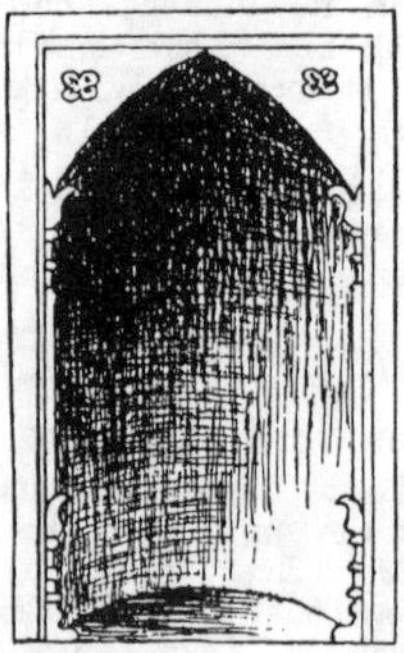

A MIHRAB. (*W. S. Chadwick.*)

from the Hindus, such a niche being a peculiarly Hindu feature in sacred buildings.

The word occurs four times in the Qur'ān, where it is used for a chamber (Sūrahs iii. 32, 33; xix. 12; xxxviii. 20), and its plural, *maḥārīb*, once (Sūrah xxxiv. 12).

MĪKĀ'ĪL (ميكائيل). [MICHAEL.]

MILLAH (ملة). A word which occurs in the Qur'ān fifteen times. *Eight* times for the religion of Abraham (Sūrahs ii. 124, 129; iii. 89; iv. 124; vi. 162; xii. 38; xvi. 124; xxii. 77); *twice* for the religion of former prophets (Sūrahs xiv. 16; xxxviii. 6); *once* for the religion of the seven children of the cave (Sūrah xviii. 19); *three* times for idolatrous religions (Sūrahs xii. 37; vii. 86, 87); and *once* for the religion of Jews and Christians (Sūrah ii. 114). The word is used in the Traditions for the religion of Abraham (*Mishkāt*, book x. ch. v.).

According to the *Kitābu 't-Ta'rīfāt*, it is expressive of religion as it stands in relation to the prophets, as distinguished from *Dīn* (دين), which signifies religion as it stands in relation to God, or from *Mazhab* (مذهب), which signifies religion with reference to the learned doctors. [RELIGION.] Sprenger and Deutsch have invested the origin and meaning of this word with a certain amount of mystery, which is interesting.

Dr. Sprenger says (*Das Leben und die Lehre des Mohammad*, vol. ii. p. 276 *n*):—"When Mohammad speaks of the religion of Abraham, he generally uses the word *Milla* (*Millah*) and not *Dīn*. Arabian philologists have tried to trace the meaning of the word from their mother tongue, thus, *Malla* (*Mallah*) signifies *fire* or *hot ashes* in Arabic and Zaggag says (*Thālaby*, vol. ii. p. 114), that religion is called *Milla* because of the impression which it makes, and which may be compared to that which fire makes upon the bread baked in ashes. Since the Arabs are unable to give a better explanation, we must presume that *milla* is a foreign word, imported by the teachers of the 'Milla of Abraham" in the Hijāz. Philo considered Abraham the chief promoter of the doctrine of the Unity of God, and doubtless, even before Philo, Jewish thought, in tracing the doctrine of the true religion, not only as far back as Moses, but even to the father of their nation, emancipated the indispensability of the form of the law, and so prepared the road to Essaism and Christianity."

Mr. Emanuel Deutsch, in his article on Islām (*Literary Remains*, p 130), says: "The word used in the Qurān for the religion of Abraham is generally *Milla*. Sprenger, after ridiculing the indeed absurd attempts made to derive it from an Arabic root, concludes that it must be a foreign word introduced by the teachers of the 'Milla of Abraham' into the Hijāz. He is perfectly right. Milla = Memra = Logos, are identical; being the Hebrew, Chaldee (Targum, Peshito in slightly varied spelling), and Greek terms respectively for the 'Word,' that surrogate for the Divine name used by the Targum, by Philo, by St. John. This Milla or 'Word,' which Abraham proclaimed, he, 'who was not an astrologer but a prophet,' teaches according to the Haggadah, first of all, the existence of one God, the Creator of the Universe, who rules this universe with mercy and lovingkindness."

MILK. Arabic *laban* (لبن). The sale of milk in the udder is unlawful (*Hidāyah*, vol. ii. p. 433). In the Qur'ān it is mentioned as one of God's special gifts. "Verily, ye have in cattle a lesson: we give you to drink from that which is in their bellies betwixt chyme and blood—pure milk—easy to swallow for those who drink." (Sūrah xvi. 68.)

MINĀ (منى). *Lit.* "A wish." A sacred valley near Makkah, in which part of the Pilgrimage ceremonies take place. According to 'Abdu 'l-Ḥaqq, it was so called because Adam *wished* for paradise in this valley.

MINARET. [MANARAH.]

MINBAR. Generally pronounced *mimbar* (منبر). The pulpit in a mosque from which the khuṭbah (or sermon) is recited. It consists of three steps, and is sometimes a moveable wooden structure, and sometimes a fixture of brick or stone built against the wall. Muḥammad, in addressing the congregation, stood on the uppermost

A MIMBAR IN AN INDIAN MOSQUE.
(*W. S. Chadwick.*)

step, Abū Bakr on the second, and 'Umar on the third or lowest. 'Usmān fixed upon the middle step, and since then it has been the custom to preach from that step. The Shī'ahs have four steps to their mimbars.

The mimbars in the mosques of Cairo are

A MIMBAR IN AN EGYPTIAN MOSQUE.
(*W. S. Chadwick.*)

elevated structures, but in Asia they are of a more primitive character.

Burton says: "In the beginning the Prophet leaned, when fatigued, against a post, whilst preaching the khuṭbah or Friday sermon. The mimbar, or pulpit, was an invention of a Madinah man of the Banū Najjār. It was a wooden frame, two cubits long by one broad, with three steps, each one span high; on the topmost of these the Prophet sat when he required rest. The pulpit assumed its present form about A.H. 90, during the artistic reign of El Walid."

A MIMBAR IN MOSQUES AT PESHAWAR.

MINES. Arabic *ma'din* (معدن), pl. *ma'ādin*. In Zakāt, mines are subject to a payment of one fifth. (*Hidāyah*, vol. i. 39.)

MINḤAH (منحة). A legal term for a portion of camel's or sheep's milk which another is allowed to draw, but afterwards to restore the animal to its original owner.

MINORITY. [PUBERTY.]

MĪQAT (ميقات). *Lit.* "A stated time, or place." The stations at which Makkan pilgrims assume the *iḥrām* or "pilgrim's garment." Five of these stations were established by Muḥammad (*Mishkāt*, book xi. ch. i. pt. 1), and the sixth has been added since to suit the convenience of travellers from the East. They are as follows: (1) *Zu 'l-Ḥulafā'*, for the pilgrims from al-Madīnah; (2) *Juḥfah*, for Syria; (3) *Qarnu 'l-Manāzil*, for Najd; (4) *Yaulamlam*, for Yaman; (5) *Ẕāt-i-'Irq*, for 'Irāq; (6) *Ibrahīm Mursīa*, for those who arrive by sea from India and the east.

The putting on of the iḥrām at Jerusalem is highly meritorious, according to a tradition, which says, "The Prophet said, Whoever wears the iḥrām for ḥajj or 'umrah, from the Masjidu 'l-Aqṣā (*i.e.* the Temple at Jerusalem) to the Masjidu 'l-Ḥarām, shall be forgiven for all his past and future sins." (*Mishkāt*, book xi. ch. i. pt. 2.)

MĪR (مير). A title of respect used for the descendants of celebrated Muḥammadan saints. More generally used for Saiyids, or descendants of Fāṭimah, the Prophet's daughter.

MIRACLES. Supernatural powers given to men are spoken of by Muslim lexicographers as *khāriqu 'l-'ādat* (خارق العادة), or "things contrary to custom." In Muslim theology, they are expressed by eight terms: (1) *Ayah* (آية), pl. *āyāt*, "a sign"; the only word used in the Qur'ān for a miracle (see Sūrahs xiii. 27; xxix. 49; liv. 2). (2) *Mu'jizah* (معجزة), pl. *mu'jizāt*, "making weak or feeble," or that which renders the adversaries to the truth weak and feeble; a term used only for miracles prformed by prophets. (3) *Irhāṣ* (ارهاص), pl. *irhāṣāt*, *lit.* "laying a foundation"; used for any miracle performed by a prophet before his assumption of the prophetical office. (4) *'Alāmah* (علامة), pl. *'alāmāt*, "a sign," the same as *āyah*, and used for the signs of the coming Resurrection. (5) *Karāmah* (كرامة), pl. *karāmāt*, *lit.* "beneficence"; wonders wrought by saints for the good of the people as well as in proof of their own saintship. (6) *Ma'ūnah* (معونة), pl. *ma'wanāt*, *lit.* "help or assistance;" used also for the wonders wrought by saints. (7) *Istidrāj* (استدراج), *lit.* "promoting by degrees"; a term employed to express the miracles wrought by the assistance of the Devil with the permission of God. (8) *Ihānah* (اهانة), pl. *ihānāt*, *lit.* "contempt"; miracles wrought by the assistance of the Devil, but when they turn out to the disdain and contempt of the worker.

It does not appear from the Qur'ān that Muḥammad ever claimed the power of working miracles, but, on the contrary, he asserted that it was not his mission to work signs and wonders in proof of his apostleship. This seems to be evident from the following verses in the Qur'ān:—

Sūrah xxix. 49: "They say, Why are not signs (*āyāt*) sent down to him from his Lord? Say: Signs are in the power of God alone, and I am only an open warner."

Sūrah xiii. 27–30: "And they who believe not say, Why is not a sign (*āyah*) sent down to him from his Lord? Say: God truly misleadeth whom He will, and guideth to Himself him who turneth to Him. . . . If there were a Qur'ān by which the mountains would be set in motion, or the earth cleft by it, or the dead be addressed by it, they would not believe."

Sūrah xvii. 92–97: "And they say, By no means will we believe on thee till thou cause a fountain to gush forth for us from the earth, or till thou have a garden of palm trees and grapes, and thou cause gushing rivers to gush forth in its midst, or till thou make heaven to fall upon us, as thou hast given out in pieces; or thou bring God and the angels to vouch for thee; or thou have a house of God, or thou mount up into heaven; nor will we believe in thy mounting up until thou send us down a book which we may read. Say: Praise be to my Lord! Am I more than a man, and an apostle? And what hindereth men from believing, when the guidance hath come to them, but that they say, Hath God sent a mere man as an apostle? Say: Did angels walk the earth as its familiars, we had surely sent them an angel-apostle out of heaven."

But notwithstanding these positive assertions on the part of their Prophet against his ability to work miracles, there are at least four places in the Qur'ān where the Muḥammadans believe that miracles are referred to

1. The clefting of the moon (Sūrah liv. 1, 2):

"The hour hath approached, and the moon hath been cleft. But if the unbelievers see a sign (*āyah*), they turn aside and say, Magic ! that shall pass away ! "

Al-Baiẓāwī says, in his commentary on this verse, "Some say that the unbelievers demanded this sign of the Prophet, and the moon was cleft in two; but others say it refers to a sign of the coming Resurrection, the words 'will be cleft' being expressed in the prophetic preterite."

Rodwell renders it "hath been cleft," as he thinks Muḥammad may possibly allude to some meteor or comet which he fancied to be part of the moon.

2. The assistance given to the Muslims at the battle of Badr. Sūrah iii. 120, 121: "When thou didst say to the faithful: 'Is it not enough for you that your Lord aideth you with three thousand angels sent down from on high?' Nay; but if ye be steadfast, and fear God, and the foe come upon you in hot haste, your Lord will help you with five thousand angels with their distinguishing marks."

These "distinguishing marks," say the commentators, were when the angels rode on black and white horses, and .had on their heads white and yellow turbans, the ends of which hung down between their shoulders.

3. The celebrated night journey. Sūrah xvii. 1: "We declare the glory of Him who transports his servant by night from the Masjidu 'l-Ḥaram to the Masjidu 'l-Aqṣā (*i.e.* from Makkah to Jerusalem)."

4. The Qur'ān itself, which the Muḥammadans say is the great miracle of Islām, the like of which has not been created, nor ever will be, by the power of man. In proof of this they quote Sūrah xxix. 48: "It is a clear sign (*āyah*) in the hearts of whom the knowledge hath reached."

Although these very doubtful assertions in the Qur'ān fail to establish the miraculous powers of the Prophet, the Traditions record numerous occasions when he worked miracles in the presence of his people.

The following are recorded in the traditions of al-Bukhārī and Muslim:—

(1) On the flight from Makkah, Surāqah being cursed by the Prophet, his horse sank up to its belly in the hard ground.

(2) The Prophet marked out at Badr the exact spot on which each of the idolaters should be slain, and Anas says not one of them passed alive beyond the spot marked by the Prophet.

(3) He cured the broken leg of 'Abdu 'llāh ibn Atiq by a touch.

(4) He converted hard ground into a heap of sand by one stroke of an axe.

(5) He fed a l thousand people upon one kid and a *ṣā'* of barley.

(6) He gave a miraculous supply of water at the battle of al-Ḥudaibiyah.

(7) Two trees miraculously moved to form a shade for the Prophet.

(8) He made *Jābir* a good horseman by his prayers.

(9) A wooden pillar wept to such an extent that it nearly rent in two parts, because the Prophet desisted from leaning against it.

(10) A sluggish horse became swift from being ridden by the Prophet.

(11) Seventy or eighty people miraculously fed on a few barley loaves and a little butter.

(12) Three hundred men fed from a single cake.

The following are recorded by various writers :—

(1) The Prophet was saluted by the hills and trees near Makkah, with the salutation, "Peace be to thee, O Messenger of God ! "

(2) A tree moved from its place to the shade when the Prophet slept under it.

(3) The Prophet cured a maniacal boy by saying. "Come out of him."

(4) A wolf was made to speak by the Prophet.

(For further information, see *Kitābu 'l-Mu'jizāt, Ṣaḥīḥu 'l-Bukhārī, Mishkātu 'l-Maṣābiḥ, Ṣaḥīḥu Muslim.*)

MI'RĀJ (معراج). *Lit.* "An ascent."

Muḥammad's supposed journey to heaven; called also *Isrā* (اسری), "the nocturnal journey." It is said to have taken place in the twelfth year of the Prophet's mission, in the month of Rabī'u 'l-Awwal.

According to 'Abdu 'l-Ḥaqq, there are some divines who have regarded this miraculous event as a mere vision, but, he adds, the majority hold it to be a literal journey.

The only mention of the vision in the Qur'ān is contained in Sūrah xvii. 1 : "Praise be to Him who carried His servant by night from the Masjidu 'l-Ḥarām (*i.e.* the Makkan temple) to the Masjidu 'l-Aqṣā (*i.e.* the Temple of Jerusalem)."

The following is the description of the supposed journey given in the *Mishkātu 'l-Maṣābiḥ.* Muḥammad is related to have said :—

"Whilst I was sleeping upon my side, he (Gabriel) came to me, and cut me open from my breast to below my navel, and took out my heart, and washed the cavity with Zamzam water, and then filled my heart with Faith and Science. After this, a white animal was brought for me to ride upon. Its size was between that of a mule and an ass, and it stretched as far as the eye could see. The name of the animal was Burāq. Then I mounted the animal, and ascended until we arrived at the lowest heaven, and Gabriel demanded that the door should be opened. And it was asked, 'Who is it?' and he said, 'I am Gabriel.' And they then said, 'Who is with you?' and he answered, 'It is Muḥammad.' They said, 'Has Muḥammad been called to the office of a prophet?' He said, 'Yes.' They said, 'Welcome Muḥammmad; his coming is well.' Then the door was opened; and when I arrived in the first heaven, behold, I saw Adam. And Gabriel said to me, 'This is your father Adam, salute him.' Then I saluted Adam, and he answered it, and said, 'You are welcome, O good son, and good Prophet !' After that Gabriel took me above, and we reached the second heaven; and he asked the door to be opened, and it was said, 'Who is it?' He said, 'I am Gabriel.' It was said, 'Who is with you?' He said, 'Muḥammad.' It was said, 'Was he called?' He said, 'Yes.' It was said, 'Welcome Muḥammad; his coming is well.' Then the door was opened; and when I arrived in the second region, behold, I saw John and Jesus (sisters' sons). And Gabriel said, 'This is John, and this is Jesus; salute both of them.' Then I saluted them, and they returned it. After that they said, 'Welcome good brother and Prophet.' After that we went up to the third heaven, and asked the door to be opened; and it was said, 'Who is it?' Gabriel said, 'I am Gabriel.' They said, 'Who is with you?' He said, 'Muḥammad.' They said, 'Was he called?' Gabriel said, 'Yes.' They said, 'Welcome Muḥammad; his coming is well.' Then the door was opened; and when I entered the third heaven, behold, I saw Joseph. And Gabriel said, 'This is Joseph, salute him.' Then I did so, and he answered it, and said, 'Welcome, good brother and good Prophet.' After that Gabriel took me to the fourth heaven, and asked the door to be opened; it was said, 'Who is that?' He said, 'I am Gabriel.' It was said, 'Who is with you?' He said, 'Muḥammad.' It was said, 'Was he called?' He said, 'Yes.' They said, 'Welcome Muḥammad; his coming his well.' And the door was opened; and when I entered the fourth heaven, behold, I saw Enoch. And Gabriel said, 'This is Enoch, salute him.' And I did so, and he answered it, and said, 'Welcome, good brother and Prophet.' After that Gabriel took me to the fifth heaven, and asked the door to be opened; and it was said, 'Who is there?' He said, 'I am Gabriel.' It was said, 'Who is with you?' He said, 'Muḥammad.' They said, 'Was he called?' He said, 'Yes.' They said, 'Welcome Muḥammad; his coming is well.' Then the door was opened; and when I arrived in the fifth region, behold, I saw Aaron. And Gabriel said, 'This is Aaron, salute him.' And I did so, and he returned it, and said, 'Welcome, good brother and Prophet.' After that Gabriel took me to the sixth heaven, and asked the door to be opened; and they said, 'Who is there?' He said, 'I am Gabriel.' They said, 'And who is with you?' He said, 'Muḥammad.' They said, 'Is he called?' He said, 'Yes.' They said, 'Welcome Muḥammad; his coming is well.' Then the door was opened; and when I entered the sixth heaven, behold, I saw Moses. And Gabriel said, 'This is Moses, salute him.' And I did so; and he returned it, and said, 'Welcome, good brother and Prophet.' And when I passed him, he wept. And I said to him, 'What makes you weep?' He said, 'Because one is sent after me, of whose people more will enter Paradise than of mine.' After that Gabriel took me up to the seventh heaven, and asked the door to be opened; and it was said, 'Who is it?' He said, 'I am Gabriel.' And it was said, 'Who is with you?' He said, 'Muḥammad.' They said, 'Was he called?' He said, 'Yes.' They said, 'Welcome Muḥammad; his coming is well.' Then I entered the seventh heaven, and behold, I saw Abraham. And Gabriel said, 'This is Abraham, your father, salute him'; which I did, and he returned it, and said, 'Welcome good son and good Prophet.' After that I was taken up to the tree called Sidratu 'l-Muntahā; and behold its fruits were like water-pots, and its leaves like elephant's ears. And Gabriel said, 'This is Sidratu 'l-Muntahā.' And I saw four rivers there; two of them hidden, and two manifest. I said to Gabriel, 'What are these?' He said, 'These two concealed rivers are in Paradise; and the two manifest are the Nile and the Euphrates.' After that, I was shown the Baitu 'l-M'amūr. After that, a vessel full of wine, another full of milk, and another of honey, were brought to me; and I took the milk and drank it. And Gabriel said, 'Milk is religion; you and your people will be of it." After that the divine orders for prayers were fifty every day. Then I returned, and passed by Moses; and he said, 'What have you been ordered?' I said, 'Fifty prayers every day.' Then Moses said, 'Verily, your people will not be able to perform fifty prayers every day; and verily, I swear by God, I tried men before you; I applied a remedy to the sons of Israel, but it had not the desired effect. Then return to your Lord, and ask your people to be released from that. And I returned; and ten prayers were taken off. Then I went to Moses, and he said as before; and I returned to God's court, and ten prayers more were curtailed. Then I retuned to Moses, and he said as before; then I returned to God's court, and ten more were taken off. And I went to Moses, and he said as before; then I returned to God, and ten more were lessened. Then I went to Moses, and he said as before; then I went to God's court, and was ordered five prayers every day. Then I went to Moses, and he said, 'How many have you been ordered?' I said, 'Five prayers every day.' He said, 'Verily, your people will not be able to perform five prayers every day; for, verily, I tried men before you, and applied the severest remedy to the sons of Israel. Then return to your Lord, and ask them to be lightened.' I said, 'I have asked Him till I am quite ashamed; I cannot return to Him again. But I am satisfied, and resign the work of my people to God.' Then, when I passed from that place, a crier called out, 'I have established My divine commandments, and have made them easy to My servants."

Sūratu 'l-Mi'rāj is a title of the XVIIth chapter of the Qur'ān, in the first verse of which there is a reference to the night journey of Muḥammad. It is called also the Suratu Banī Isrā'īl, or the Chapter of the Children of Israel.

MĪRĀṢ (ميراث). [INHERITANCE.]

MĪRZĀ (ميرزا). A title of respect given to persons of good family.

MIRZABAH, MIRZABBAH (مرزبة). "A clod-crusher." The iron hammer with which the dead are beaten who cannot reply satisfactorily to the questions put to them by Munkar and Nakīr. Called also *Mitraqah* (مطرقة). [PUNISHMENTS OF THE GRAVE.]

MĪṢĀQ (ميثاق). "A covenant." A word used in the Qur'ān for God's covenant with his people. [COVENANT.]

MISHKĀTU 'L-MAṢABĪḤ (مشكوة المصابيح). A well-known book of Sunnī tradition, much used by Sunnī Muslims in India, and frequently quoted in the present work. It was originally compiled by the Imām Ḥusain al-Baghawī, the celebrated commentator, who died A.H. 510 or 516, and called the *Maṣābiḥu 's-Sunnah*, or the "Lamps of the Traditions." In the year A.H. 737, Shaikh Walīyu 'd-dīn revised the work of al-Baghawī, adding an additional chapter to each section, and called it the *Mishkātu 'l-Maṣābīḥ*, or the "Niche for lamps." In the time of the Emperor Akbar, Shaikh 'Abdu 'l-Ḥaqq translated the work into Persian, and added a commentary. (See *Kashfu 'z-Ẓunūn, in loco.*)

MISKĪN (مسكين). "A poor person." Heb. Eccles. ix. 15, מִסְכֵּן. According to Muslim law, a person who has no property whatever, as distinguished from a *faqīr* (فقير), or a person who possesses a little property, but is poor. (*Hidāyah*, vol. i. p. 54.)

MIṢQĀL (مثقال). An Arabic weight, which frequently occurs in Muhammadan law books. Richardson gives it at a dram and three-sevenths. It is also used for a gold coin of that weight. [MONEY.]

MIṢR (مصر). [EGYPT.]

MISWĀK (مسواك). (1) A tooth-cleaner made of wood, about a span long. It is preferred when made of a wood which has a bitter flavour. The *Salvadora Indica* is the tree, the wood of which is used in India.

(2) The act of cleaning the teeth, which is a religious ceremony founded upon the example of Muḥammad, and forms the first part of the *waẓū'*, or "ablution before prayer."

The Prophet was particularly careful in the observance of *miswāk* (see *Mishkāt*, book iii. ch. 4.) It is amongst those things which are called *fiṭrah* (*q.v.*).

MIṬRAQAH (مطرقة). The iron hammer or mace with which the infidels will be smitten in their graves by the angels Munkar and Nakīr. Persian *gurz.* [PUNISHMENTS OF THE GRAVE.]

MIYĀN (ميان). A Persian word, used as a title of respect for the descendants of celebrated Muḥammadan saints.

MĪZĀN (ميزان), pl. *mawāzīn.* Heb. pl. מאֹזְנַיִם. *Lit.* "A balance."

(1) The law contained in the Qur'ān, Sūrah xlii. 16: "God is He who hath sent down the Book with truth and the *balance.*"

(2) The scales in which the actions of all men shall be weighed. Sūrah xxi. 47: "Just balances will be set up for the Day of the Resurrection, neither shall any soul be wronged in aught; though, were a work but the weight of a grain of mustard seed, we would bring it forth *to be weighed*: and our reckoning will suffice."

Muḥammad is related by 'Abdu 'llāh ibn 'Amr to have said: "Verily, God will bring a Muslim into the presence of all men on the Day of Judgment, and will show him ninety-nine large books, and each book as long as the eye can reach. Then God will say to him, 'Do you deny anything in these books? Have my writers injured you?' And the Muslim will say, 'O my Lord, I deny nothing that is in them.' Then God will say, 'Have you any excuse?' And he will say, 'No.' Then God will say, 'I have good news for you, for there is no oppression in this day.' Then God will bring forth a piece of paper, on which is written: 'I bear witness that there is no deity but God, and I bear witness that Muḥammad is His servant and apostle.' And God will say, 'Go and weigh your actions.' And the Muslim will say, 'What is this bit of paper compared with those large books?' And God will say, 'This bit of paper is heavy, weigh it.' Then the books will be put in the scale, and the bit of paper in the other, and the books containing the actions will be light, and the bit of paper, whereon is written the creed of the Muslim, will be heavy." (See Collection of Ḥadīs by at-Tirmiẕī.)

The commentators say that the scales will be held by the angel Gabriel, and that they are of so vast a size, one hangs over Paradise, and the other over Hell, and they are capacious enough to contain both heaven and earth. Though some are willing to understand what is said in the Traditions concerning this balance allegorically, and only as a figurative representation of God's equity, yet the more ancient and orthodox opinion is that it is to be taken literally; and since words and actions, being mere accidents, are not capable of being themselves weighed, they say that the books wherein they are written will be thrown into the scales, and according as those wherein the good or the evil actions are recorded shall preponderate, sentence will be given; those whose balances laden with their good works shall be heavy, will be saved; but those whose balances are light, will be condemned. Nor will anyone have cause to complain that God suffers any good actions to pass unrewarded, because the wicked obtain rewards for the good they do in the present life, and therefore can expect no favour in the next.

The old Jewish writers make mention of the books to be produced at the Last Day, wherein men's actions are registered, as of the balance wherein they shall be weighed, and the Bible itself seems to have given the first notion of both. But what the Persian Magi believe of the balance comes nearest to the Muhammadan opinion. They hold that on the Day of Judgment, two angels, named Mihr and

Sorush, will stand on the bridge between heaven and hell, and examine every person as he passes; that the former, who represents the divine mercy, will hold a balance in his hand, to weigh the actions of men; that, according to the report he shall make thereof to God, sentence will be pronounced, and those whose good works are found more ponderous, if they turn the scale but by the weight of a hair, will be permitted to pass forward to Paradise; but those whose good works shall be found light, will be, by the other angel, who represents God's justice, precipitated from the bridge into hell.

MODERATION. Arabic *iqtiṣād* (اقتصاد). According to Muḥammad's teaching, moderation in all religious matters is better than excessive piety, and a chapter in the Traditions is devoted to the subject. He is related to have said:—

"The best act in God's sight is that which is constantly attended to, although in a small degree."

"Do what you are able conveniently; because God will not be tired of rewarding as long as you are not tired of doing."

"You must continue at your prayers as long as it is agreeable to you, and when you are tired sit down."

"Verily, religion is easy, therefore hold it firm." (See *Mishkāt*, *Bābu 'l-Iqtiṣād*.)

MODESTY (Arabic *hayā'* حياء) is frequently commended in the traditional sayings of Muḥammad, who is related to have said:—

"Modesty is a branch of faith."

"Verily, modesty and faith are joined together." (*Mishkāt*, book xxii. ch. xix.)

MONASTICISM (Arabic *rahbānīyah* رهبانية) was forbidden by Muḥammad. It is related in the Traditions that 'Uṣmān ibn Maẓ'ūn came to the Prophet with the request that he might retire from society and become a monk (*rāhib*). The Prophet replied, "The retirement which becomes my people is to sit in the corner of a mosque and wait for the time of prayer." (*Mishkāt*, book iv. ch. 8.)

In the Qur'ān, the Christians are charged with inventing the monastic life. Sūrah lvii. 27: "We gave them the Gospel, and we put into the hearts of those who follow him, kindness and compassion; *but as to the monastic life, they invented it themselves.*"

According to the *Hidāyah* (vol. ii. p. 215), capitation-tax is not to be imposed upon Rāhibs, whether Christian or Pagan, but this is a matter of dispute.

MONEY. There are three coins mentioned in the Qur'ān, (1) *Qinṭār* (قنطار), (2) *Dīnār* (دينار), (3) *Dirham* (درهم), pl. *Darāhim.*

(1) *Qinṭār.* Sūrah iii. 68: "Among the people of the Book are those to one of whom, if you entrust a *qinṭār*, he will restore it."

In the *Qāmūs*, it is said that a *qinṭār* was a gold coin of the value of 200 *dīnārs*, but Muḥammad Ṭāhir, the author of the *Majma'u 'l-Biḥār* (p. 173), says it implies a very considerable sum of money, as much gold as will go into the hide of a cow. It is generally translated talent.

(2) *Dīnār.* Sūrah iii. 68: "There are those to whom, if thou entrust a *dīnār*, they will not restore it to thee." It was the denarius, or a small gold coin.

(3) *Dirham.* Sūrah xii. 20: "And they sold him for a mean price, *dirhams* counted out." A silver drachma. [QINTAR, DINAR, DIRHAM, WEIGHTS.]

Mr. Prinsep says: "The silver rupee (*rupya*, silver piece), now current in Muslim countries, was introduced, according to Abulfazel, by Sher Shah, who usurped the throne of Delhi from Humayoon in the year 1542. Previous to his time, the Arabic dirhim (silver drachma), the gold dinar (*denarius auri*), and the copper fuloos (*follis*), formed the currency of the Moghul dominions. Sher Shah's rupee had on one side the Muḥammadan creed, on the other the emperor's name and the date in Persian, both encircled in an annular Hindee inscription. Since 'the same coin was revived and made more pure,' in Akber's reign, we may assume the original weight of the rupee, from Abulfazel's statement, to have been 11¼ máshas. Akber's square rupee, called from its inscription the jilály, was of the same weight and value. This coin was also called the chahár-yáree, from the four friends of the Prophet, Abubekr, Omar, Osman, Ali, whose names are inscribed on the margin. This rupee is supposed by the vulgar to have talismanic power."

MONOGAMY. Although polygamy is sanctioned in the Qur'ān, the words, "*and if ye fear that ye cannot be equitable, then only one*" (Sūrah iv. 3), would seem to imply a leaning to monogamy, as the safest and most discreet form of matrimony. The author of the *Akhlāq-i-Jalālī* says: "Excepting, indeed, in the case of kings, who marry to multiply offspring, and towards whom the wife has no alternative but obedience, plurality of wives is not defensible. Even in their case it were better to be cautious; for husband and wife are like heart and body, and like as one heart cannot supply life to two bodies, one man can hardly provide for the management of two homes." (Thompson's English Translation, p. 266.)

MONOPOLY. Arabic *iḥtikār* (احتكار). A monopoly of the necessaries of life (as, for example, the hoarding up of grain with the object of raising its price) is forbidden in Muḥammadan law. For the Prophet has said:—

"Whoever monopolizeth is a sinner."

"Whosoever keepeth back grain forty days, in order to increase its price, is both a forsaker of God, and is forsaken of God." (*Mishkāt*, book xii. ch. x.; *Hidāyah*, vol. iv. p. 114.)

MONTH. Arabic *shahr* (شهر), pl. *shuhūr.* The months of the Muḥammadan year are lunar, and the first of the month is reckoned from the sunset immediately succeeding the *appearance* of the new moon (*hilāl*). The names of the months are: (1) Muḥarram محرّم; (2) Ṣafar سفر; (3) Rabīʿu 'l-Awwal ربيع الاول; (4) Rabīʿu 'l-Ākhir ربيع الاخر; (5) Jumādā 'l-Ūlā جمادى الاولى; (6) Jumādā 'l-Ukhrā جمادى الاخرى; (7) Rajab رجب; (8) Shaʿbān شعبان; (9) Ramaẓān رمضان; (10) Shawwāl شوّال; (11) Ẕū 'l-Qaʿdah ذو القعدة; (12) Ẕū 'l-Ḥijjah ذو الحجة.

Four of these months are held to be sacred, namely, Muḥarram, Rajab, Ẕū 'l-Qaʿdah, Ẕū 'l-Ḥijjah, and according to the teaching of the Qur'ān (Sūrah ix. 36), it is not lawful for Muslims to fight during these months, except when they attack those "who join other gods with God, even as they attack you one and all."

The names of the months seem to have been given at a time when the intercalary year was in force, although Muslim writers assume that the names were merely given to the months as they then stood at the time when they were so named. For a discussion of the formation of the Muḥammadan year, the reader is referred to that article. [YEAR.]

(1) *Muḥarram* is the first month in the Muḥammadan calendar, and is so called because, both in the pagan age and in the time of Muḥammad, it was held unlawful (*ḥarām*) to go to war in this month. It is considered a most auspicious month, and Muḥammad is related to have said, "Whosoever shall fast on Thursday, Friday, and Saturday in this month, shall be removed from hell fire a distance of seven hundred years journey; and that he who shall keep awake the first night of this month, shall be forgiven all the sins of the past year; and he who shall fast the whole of the first day, shall be kept from sin for the next two years." (*Hanīsu 'l-Waizīn*, p. 154.) The first ten days of this month are observed in commemoration of the martyrdom of al-Ḥusain, and the tenth day is the ʿĀshūrā' fast.

(2) *Ṣafar*, the second month, is supposed to derive its name from *ṣafir*, "empty," either because in it the Arabians went forth to war and left their homes empty, or, according to Rubeh, because they left whom they attacked empty. According to some writers, it was so named from *ṣufār*, "yellowness," because when it was first so called, it was autumn, when the leaves bore a yellowish tint. (*Vide* Lane's *Arabic Dict.*; *Ghiyāṣu 'l-Lughah.*) It is held to be the most unlucky and inauspicious month in the whole year, for in it, it is said, Adam was turned out of Eden. (See *Hanīsu 'l-Waizīn.*) It was during this month that the Prophet was taken ill, but his partial recovery took place on the last Wednesday.

(3) *Rabīʿu 'l-Awwal*, and (4) *Rabīʿu 'l-Ākhir*, the first and second spring months, are said to have been so named when the calendar was first formed, and when these months occurred in the spring. Muḥammad died on the 12th day of the Rabīʿu 'l-Awwal.

(5) *Jumādā 'l-Ūlā*, and (6) *Jumādā 'l-Ukhrā*, are the fifth and sixth months, about which there is some discussion as to the origin of the name. Mr. Lane, in his Dictionary, says the two months to which the name *Jamādā* (freezing) is applied, are said to be so called because, when they were so named, they fell in the season of freezing water; but this derivation seems to have been invented when the two months thus named had fallen back into, or beyond, the winter, for when they received this appellation, the former of them evidently commenced in March, and the latter ended in May. Therefore, I hold the opinion of M. Caussin de Perceval, that they were thus called because falling in a period when the earth had become dry and hard, by reason of paucity of rain, *jamād* being an epithet applied to land upon which rain has not fallen, which opinion is confirmed by the obvious derivation of the names of other months. (See Lane's *Arabic Dict. in loco.*)

(7) *Rajab*, the "honoured" month, so called because of the honour in which the month was held in the Times of Ignorance, inasmuch as war was not permitted during this month. The Prophet is related to have said that the month Rajab was like a snowy white fountain flowing from heaven itself, and that he who fasts on this month will drink of the waters of life. It is called *Rajab-i-Muẓar*, because the Muẓar tribe held it in high esteem. It is usual for religious Muslims to spend the first Friday night (*i.e.* our Thursday night) of this month in prayer.

(8) *Shaʿbān*, the month of separation (called also the *Shahru 'n-Nabī*, "the Prophet's month"), is so called because the ancient Arabians used to separate, or disperse themselves, in this month in search of water (for when the months were regulated by the solar year, this month corresponded partly to June and partly to July), or, as some say, for predatory expeditions. On the fifteenth day of this month is the *Shab-i-Barāt*, or "Night of Record," upon which it is said that God registers annually all the actions of mankind which they are to perform during the year, and upon which Muḥammad enjoined his followers to keep awake the whole night and to repeat one hundred rakʿah prayers. [SHAB-I-BARAT.]

(9) *Ramaẓān*, the ninth month of the Muḥammadan year, is that which is observed as a strict fast. The word is derived from *ramẓ*, "to burn," because it is said that, when the month was first named, it occurred in the hot season; or because the month's fast is supposed to burn away the sins of men. (See *Ghiyāṣu 'l-Lughah.*) The excellence of this month is much extolled by Muḥammad, who said that during this month the gates of Paradise are opened, and the gates of Hell shut. (*Mishkāt*, book vii. chap. i. sec. 1.) [RAMAZAN.]

(10) *Shawwāl*, *lit.* "a tail," is the tenth month of the lunar year, and, according to Arabic lexicons (see *Ghiyāṣu 'l-Lughah*, *Qāmūs*, &c.), it is so called because, when first named, it coincided with the season when the she-camels, being seven or eight

months gone with young, raised their tails; or, because it was the month for hunting. The Arabs used to say that it was an unlucky month in which to make marriage contracts, but the Prophet ignored their thus auguring, and married ʿĀyishah in this month. The *ʿĪdu 'l-Fitr*, or "the Feast of Breaking the Fast," occurs on the first of this month.

(11) *Z̲ū 'l-Qaʿdah*, or the month of truce, is the eleventh month, and so called by the ancient Arabs, because it was a month in which warfare was not conducted, and in which the people were engaged in peaceful occupations.

(12) *Z̲ū 'l-Ḥijjah*, the month of the Pilgrimage, is the last month of the Muḥammadan calendar. It is the month in which the pilgrimage to Makkah must be made, a visit to the sacred city at another time having in no way the merits of a pilgrimage. The *Ḥajj*, or "Pilgrimage," is performed upon the seventh, eighth, ninth, and tenth of this month. The *ʿĪdu 'l-Aẓḥā*, or "Feast of Sacrifice," is held on the tenth. [HAJJ.]

MORTGAGE. [IJARAH.]

MOON. Arabic *qamar* (قمر). The moon is frequently mentioned in the Qur'ān. Muḥammad on three occasions swears by it (Sūrahs lxxiv. 35; lxxxiv. 18; xci. 2), and it is said to have been set in the heavens for a light (Sūrahs x. 5; lxxi. 15), to run to its appointed goal (Sūrahs xxxv. 14; xxxix. 7), and that it will be eclipsed at the Day of Judgment (Sūrah lxxv. 8). The LIVth Sūrah of the Qur'ān, which is entitled the *Sūratu 'l-Qamar*, begins with a reference to the splitting of the moon, which is a matter of controversy. It reads: "The hour draws nigh and the moon is split asunder. But if they see a sign, they turn aside and say magic continues."

Al-Baiẓāwī refers it to a miracle, and says the unbelievers having asked Muḥammad for a sign, the moon appeared to be cloven in twain. But the most natural explanation of the passage is, that the expression refers to one of the signs of the Resurrection.

At an eclipse of the moon, a devout Muslim is expected to recite a two rakʿah prayer.

MOORS. The name given to the Muḥammadan conquerors of Spain, on account of their having come from the ancient Mauri, or Mauretania, now known as the Empire of Morocco. The word *Mauri* is supposed to have been derived from the Alexandrian word μαυροί, "blacks." (See Smith's *Dict. of Greek and Roman Geography: Mauretania.*)

MOSES. Arabic *Mūsā* (موسى). Heb. מֹשֶׁה. According to Muḥammadanism, he is one of the six great prophets who founded dispensations, and to whom the *Taurāt* was revealed. His special title, or kalimah, is *Kalīmu 'llāh*, "One who conversed with God." A lengthy account is given of his intercourse with Pharaoh and his dealings with the Children of Israel in the Qur'ān, which we take from Mr. Lane's *Selections*, together with the remarks of the Jalālān, al-Baiẓāwī, and other commentators, in *italics*. (Stanley Lane-Poole's new ed. of Lane's *Selections*, p. 97.)

"We will rehearse unto thee of the history of Moses and Pharaoh with truth, for *the sake of* people who believe. Verily Pharaoh exalted himself in the land *of Egypt*, and divided its inhabitants into parties *to serve him*. He rendered weak one class of them, *namely the children of Israel*, slaughtering their male children, and preserving alive their females, *because one of the diviners said unto him, A child will be born among the children of Israel, who will be the means of the loss of thy kingdom;*—for he was one of the corrupt doers. And We desired to be gracious unto those who had been deemed weak in the land, and to make them models of religion, and to make them the heirs *of the possessions of Pharaoh*, and to establish them in the land *of Egypt, and in Syria*, and to show Pharaoh and Hāmān and their forces what they feared from them. And We said, by revelation, unto the mother of Moses, *the child abovementioned, of whose birth none knew save his sister*, Suckle him; and when thou fearest for him cast him in the river *Nile*, and fear not *his being drowned*, nor mourn *for his separation;* for We will restore him unto thee, and will make him one of the apostles. *So she suckled him three months, during which he wept not; and then she feared for him, wherefore she put him into an ark pitched within and furnished with a bed for him, and she closed it and cast it in the river Nile by night.* And the family of Pharaoh lighted upon him *in the ark on the morrow of that night; so they put it before him, and it was opened, and Moses was taken forth from it, sucking milk from his thumb:* that he might be unto them *eventually* an enemy and an affliction; for Pharaoh and Hāmān (*his Wezeer*) and their forces were sinners; *wherefore they were punished by his hand.* And the wife of Pharaoh said, *when he and his servants had proposed to kill him, He is* delight of the eye unto me and unto thee: do not ye kill him: peradventure he may be serviceable unto us, or we may adopt him as a son. *And they complied with her desire;* and they knew not *the consequence.*

"And the heart of the mother of Moses, *when she knew of his having been lighted upon*, became disquieted; and she had almost made him known *to be her son*, had We not fortified her heart with patience, that she might be one of the believers *in Our promise.* And she said unto his sister *Maryam* (Mary), Trace him, *that thou mayest know his case.* And she watched him from a distance, while they knew not *that she was his sister and that she was watching him.* And We forbade him the breasts, *preventing him from taking the breast of any nurse except his mother*, before *his restoration to her;* so *his sister* said, Shall I direct you unto the people of a house who will nurse him for you, and who will be faithful unto him? *And her offer was accepted; therefore she brought his mother, and he took her breast: so she returned with him to her house, as God hath said,*—And We restored him to his mother, that her eye might be cheerful and that she might not grieve, and that she might know that the promise of God *to restore him unto her* was true: but the greater number of them (*that is, of mankind*) know not *this. And it appeared not that this was his sister and this his mother; and he remained with her until she had weaned him; and her hire was paid her, for every day a deenár, which she took because it was the wealth of a hostile person. She then brought him unto Pharaoh, and he was brought up in his abode, as God hath related of him in the Chapter of the Poets* (Sūrah xxvi. 17), *where Pharaoh said unto Moses, Have we not brought thee up among us a child, and hast thou not dwelt among us* thirty *years of thy life?*

"And when he had attained his age of strength (*thirty years or thirty and three*), and had become of full age (*forty years*), We bestowed on him wisdom and knowledge *in religion, before he was sent as a prophet;* and thus do We reward the well-doers. And he entered the city *of Pharaoh, which was Munf* [Memphis], *after he had been absent from him a while,* at a time when its inhabitants were inadvertent, *at the hour of the noon-sleep*, and he found therein two men fighting; this being of his party (*namely an Israelite*), and this of his enemies, *an Egyptian, who was compelling the Israelite to carry firewood to the kitchen of Pharaoh without pay:* and he who was of his party begged him to aid him against him who was of his enemies. *So Moses said unto the latter, Let him go. And it is said that he replied to Moses, I have a mind to put the burden on thee.* And Moses struck him with his fist, and killed him. *But he intended not to kill him; and he buried him in the sand.* He said, This is of the work of the devil, *who hath excited my anger;* for he is an enemy *unto the son of Adam*, a manifest misleader *of him.* He said, *in repentance*, O my Lord, verily I have acted injuriously unto mine own soul, *by killing him;* therefore forgive me. So He forgave him: for He is the Very Forgiving, the Merciful.—He said, O my Lord, by the *favours* with which Thou hast favoured me, *defend me*, and I will by no means be an assistant to the sinners *after this.*—And the next morning he was afraid in the city, watching *for what might happen unto him on account of the slain man;* and lo, he who had begged his assistance the day before was crying out to him for aid *against another Egyptian.* Moses said unto him, Verily thou art a person manifestly in error, *because of that which thou hast done yesterday and to-day.* But when he was about to lay violent hands upon him who was an enemy unto them both (*namely unto Moses and him who begged his aid*), *the latter* said, *imagining that he would lay violent hands upon him, because of that which he had said unto him,* O Moses, dost thou desire to kill me, as thou killedst a soul yesterday? Thou desirest not aught but to be an oppressor in the land, and thou desirest not to be [one] of the reconcilers.—*And the Egyptian heard that: so he knew that the killer was Moses; wherefore he departed unto Pharaoh and acquainted him therewith, and Pharaoh commanded the executioners to slay Moses, and they betook themselves to seek him.* But a man *who was a believer, of the family of Pharaoh,* came from the furthest part of the city, running *by a way that was nearer than the way by which they had come:* he said, O Moses, verily the chiefs *of the people of Pharaoh* are consulting respecting thee, to slay thee; therefore go forth *from the city:* verily I am unto thee one of the admonishers. So he went forth from it in fear, watching *in fear of pursuer, or for the aid of God.* He said, O my Lord, deliver me from the unjust people *of Pharaoh!*

"And when he was journeying towards Medyen, *which was the city of Sho'eyb (Shu'aib), eight days journey from Miṣr (named after Medyen [Madyan] the son of Abraham), and he knew not the way unto it,* he said, Peradventure my Lord will direct me unto the right way, *or the middle way. And God sent unto him an angel, having in his hand a short spear; and he went with him thither.* And when he came unto the water (*or well*) of Medyen, he found at it a company of men watering *their animals;* and he found besides them two women keeping away *their sheep from the water.* He said *unto them (namely the two women)*, What is the matter with you *that ye water not?* They answered, We shall not water until the pastors shall have driven away *their animals;* and our father is a very old man, *who cannot water the sheep.* And he watered for them *from another well near unto them, from which he lifted a stone that none could lift but ten persons.* Then he retired to the shade *of an Egyptian thorn-tree on account of the violence of the heat of the sun: and he was hungry,* and he said, O my Lord, verily I am in need of the good *provision* which Thou shalt send down unto me. *And the two women returned unto their father in less time than they were accustomed to do: so he asked them the reason thereof; and they informed him of the person who had watered for them; whereupon he said unto one of them, Call him unto me.*

"And one of them came unto him, walking bashfully, *with the sleeve of her shift over her face, by reason of her abashment at him:* she said, My father calleth thee, that he may recompense thee with the reward of thy having watered for us. *And he assented to her call, disliking in his mind the receiving of the reward: but it seemeth that she intended the compensation if he were of such as desired it. And she walked before him; and the wind blew her garment, and her legs were discovered: so he said unto her, Walk behind me and direct me in the way. And she did so, until she came unto her father, who was Sho'eyb, on whom be peace! and with him was prepared a supper. He said unto him, Sit and sup. But he replied, I fear lest it be a compensation for my having watered for them, and we are a family who seek not a compensation for doing good. He said, Nay, it is my custom and hath been the custom of my fathers to entertain the guest and to give food. So he ate; and acquainted him with his case.* And when he had come unto him, and had related to him the story *of his having killed the Egyptian and their intention to kill him and his fear of Pharaoh*, he replied, Fear not: thou hast escaped from the unjust people. (*For Pharaoh had no dominion over Medyen.*) One of them [namely of the women] said (*and she was the one who had been sent*), O my father, hire him *to tend our sheep in our stead;* for the best whom thou canst hire is the strong, the trustworthy. *So he asked her respecting him, and she acquainted him with what hath been above related, his lifting up the stone of the well, and his saying unto her, Walk behind me;—and moreover, that when she had come unto him, and he knew of her presence, he hung down his head and raised it not.* He *therefore* said, Verily I desire to marry thee unto one of these my two daughters, on the condition that thou shalt be a hired servant to me, *to tend my sheep*, eight years; and if thou fulfil ten *years*, it shall be of thine own will; and I desire not to lay a difficulty upon thee *by imposing as a condition the ten years:* thou shalt find me, if God, please, one of the just, *who are faithful to their covenants.* He replied, This be the covenant between me and thee; whichever of the two terms I fulfil, there shall be no injustice against me *by demanding an addition thereto;* and God is witness of what we say. *And the marriage-contract was concluded according to this; and Sho'eyb ordered his daughter to give unto Moses a rod wherewith to drive away the wild beasts from his sheep: and the rods of the prophets were in his possession; and the rod of Adam, of the myrtle of paradise, fell into her hand; and Moses took it, with the knowledge of Sho'eyb.* (Sūrah xxviii. 21–28.)

"Hath the history of Moses been related to thee? when he saw fire, *during his journey from Medyen on his way to Egypt*, and said unto his family, *or his wife*, Tarry ye *here;* for I have seen fire: perhaps I may bring you a brand from it, or find at the fire a guide *to direct me in the way. For he had missed the way in consequence of the darkness of the night.* And when he came unto it (*and it was a bramble bush*), he was called to by a voice saying, O Moses, verily I am thy Lord; therefore pull off thy shoes; for thou art in the holy valley of Tuwa. And I have chosen thee *from among thy people;* wherefore hearken attentively unto that which is revealed *unto thee by Me.* Verily I am God: there is no Deity except Me; therefore worship Me, and perform prayer in remembrance of Me. Verily the hour is coming: I will manifest it *unto mankind, and its nearness shall appear unto them by its signs*, that every soul may be recompensed *therein* for its *good and evil* work: therefore let not him who believeth not in it, and followeth his lust, hinder thee from *believing in* it, lest thou perish. And what is that in thy right hand, O Moses?—He answered, It is my rod, whereon I lean and wherewith I beat down leaves for my sheep *that they may eat them;* and I have other uses for it, *as the carrying of provision and the water-skin, and the driving away of reptiles.* He said, Cast it down, O Moses. So he cast it down; and lo, it was a serpent running along. *God* said, Take it, and fear *it* not: we will restore it to its former state. *And he put his hand into its mouth; whereupon it became again a rod.* And God said, And put thy *right* hand to thy *left* arm-pit, *and take it forth:* it shall come forth white, without evil, (*that is without leprosy; shining like the rays of the sun, dazzling the sight,*) as another sign, that We may show thee the greatest of our signs *of thine apostleship.* (*And when he desired to restore his hand to its first state, he put it as before described, and drew it forth.*) Go *as an apostle* unto Pharaoh *and those who are with him;* for he hath acted with exceeding impiety *by arrogating to himself divinity.*—*Moses* said, O my Lord, dilate my bosom, *that it may bear the message*, and make my affair easy unto me, and loose the knot of my tongue (*this had arisen from his having been burned in his mouth by a live coal when he was a child*), that they may understand my speech *when I deliver the message.* And appoint unto me a Wezeer of my family, *namely* Aaron [Haroon] my brother. Strengthen my back by him, and make him a colleague in my affair, that we may glorify Thee much, and remember Thee much; for Thou knowest us.

"God replied, Thou hast obtained thy petition, O Moses, and We have been gracious unto thee another time: forasmuch as We revealed unto thy mother what was revealed, *when she gave birth to thee and feared that Pharaoh would kill thee among the others that were born*, saying, Cast him into the ark, and then cast him, *in the ark*, into the river *Nile*, and the river shall throw him on the shore; then an enemy unto Me and an enemy unto him (*namely Pharaoh*) shall take him. And I bestowed on thee, *after he had taken thee*, love from Me, *that thou mightest be loved by men, so that Pharaoh and all that saw thee loved thee;* and that thou mightest be bred up in Mine eye. Also forasmuch as thy sister *Maryam* went *that she might learn what became of thee, after they had brought nurses and thou hadst refused to take the breast of any one of them*, and she said, Shall I direct you unto one who will nurse him? (*whereupon her proposal was accepted, and she brought his mother*): so We restored thee to thy mother, that her eye might become cheerful and that she might not grieve. And thou slewest a soul, *namely the Copt in Egypt, and wast sorry for his slaughter, on account of Pharaoh*, and We delivered thee from sorrow; and We tried thee with *other* trial, *and delivered thee from it.* And thou stayedst *ten* years among the people of Medyen, *after thou hadst come thither from Egypt, at the abode of Sho'eyb the prophet, and he married thee to his daughter.* Then thou camest according to *My* decree, *as to the time of thy mission, when thou hadst attained the age of forty years*, O Moses; and I have chosen thee for Myself. Go thou and thy brother *unto the people*, with My *nine* signs, and cease ye not to remember Me. Go ye unto Pharaoh; for he hath acted with exceeding impiety, *by arrogating to himself divinity*, and speak unto him with gentle speech, *exhorting him to relinquish that conduct:* peradventure he will consider, or will fear *God, and repent.* (*The* [mere] *hope with respect to the two* [result is expressed] *because of God's knowledge that he would not repent.*)—They replied, O our Lord, verily we fear that he may be precipitately violent against us, *hastening to punish us*, or that he may act with exceeding injustice *towards us.* He said, Fear ye not; for I am with you: I will hear and will see. Therefore go ye unto him, and say, Verily we are the apostles of thy Lord: therefore send with us the children of Israel *unto Syria*, and do not afflict them, *but cease to employ them in thy difficult works, such as digging and building, and carrying the heavy burden.* We have come unto thee with a sign from thy Lord, *attesting our veracity in asserting ourselves apostles:* and peace be on him who followeth the right direction:—*that is, he shall be secure from punishment.* Verily it hath been revealed unto us that punishment [shall be inflicted] upon him who chargeth with falsehood *that wherewith we have come*, and turneth away *from it.* (Sūrah xx. 8–50.)

"Then We sent after them, *namely the apostles before mentioned* [who were Sho'eyb and his predecessors], Moses, with Our signs unto Pharaoh and his nobles, and they acted unjustly with respect to them, *disbelieving in the signs:* but see what was the end of the corrupt doers. And Moses said, O Pharaoh, verily I am an apostle from the Lord of the world *unto thee. But he charged him with falsehood: so he said, I am* right not to say of God aught but the truth. I have come unto you with a proof from your Lord: therefore send with me *to Syria* the children of Israel.—*Pharaoh* said *unto him*, If thou hast come with a sign *confirmatory of thy pretension*, produce it, if thou be of those who speak truth. So he cast down his rod; and lo, it was a manifest serpent. And he drew forth his hand *from his bosom;* and lo, it was white *and radiant* unto the beholders. The nobles of the people of Pharaoh said, Verily this is a knowing enchanter: he desireth to expel you from your land. What then do ye command?—They answered, Put off for a time him and his brother, and send unto the cities collectors [of the inhabitants], that they may bring unto thee every knowing enchanter. And the enchanters came unto Pharaoh. They said, Shall we surely have a reward if we be the party who overcome? He answered, Yea; and verily ye shall be of those who are admitted near unto my person. They said, O Moses, either do thou cast down *thy rod*, or we will cast down *what we have with us.* He replied, Cast ye. And when they cast down *their cords and their rods*, they enchanted the eyes of the men, *diverting them from the true perception of them;* and they terrified them; *for they imagined them to be serpents running;* and they performed a great enchantment. And We spake by revelation unto Moses, [saying,] Cast down thy rod. And lo, it swallowed up what they had caused to appear changed. So the truth was confirmed, and that which they had wrought became vain; and they were overcome there, and were rendered contemptible. And the enchanters cast themselves down prostrate: they said, We believe in the Lord of the worlds, the Lord of Moses and Aaron. Pharaoh said, Have ye believed in Him before I have given you permission? Verily this is a plot that ye have contrived in the city, that ye may cause its inhabitants to go forth from it. But ye shall know *what shall happen unto you at my hand.* I will assuredly cut off your hands and your feet on the opposite sides—*the right hand of each and his left foot:* then I will crucify you all.—They replied, Verily unto our Lord shall we return, *after our death, of whatever kind it be;* and thou dost not take vengeance on us but because we believed in the signs of our Lord when they came unto us. O our Lord, pour upon us patience, and cause us to die Muslims! (Sūrah vii. 101–123).

"And Pharaoh said, Let me alone that I may kill Moses, (*for they had diverted him from killing him,*) and let him call upon his Lord *to defend him from me.* Verily I fear lest he change your religion, *and prevent your worshipping me*, or that he may cause corruption to appear in the earth (*that is, slaughter, and other offences*).—And Moses said *unto his people, having heard this*, Verily, I have recourse for defence unto my Lord and your Lord from every proud person who believeth not in the day of account. And a man who was a believer, of the family of Pharaoh (*it is said that he was the son of his paternal uncle,*) who concealed his faith, said, Will ye kill a man because he saith, My Lord is God,—when he hath come unto you with evident proofs from your Lord? And if he be a liar, on him [will be] *the evil consequence of* his lie; but if he be a speaker of truth, somewhat of that *punishment with* which he threateneth you will befall you *speedily.* Verily God directeth not him who is a transgressor, *or polytheist*, [and] a liar. O my people, ye have the dominion to-day, being overcomers in the land *of Egypt;* but who will defend us from the punishment of God *if ye kill his favourite servants*, if it come unto us?—Pharaoh said, I will not advise you to do [aught] save what I see to be advisable, *which is, to kill Moses;* and I will not direct you save into the right way. And he who had believed said, O my people, verily I fear for you the like of the day of the confederates, the like of the condition of the people of Noah and 'A'd and Thamood and those who have lived after them: and God willeth not injustice unto His servants. And, O my people, verily I fear for you the day of calling (*that is, the day of resurrection, when the people of Paradise and those of Hell shall often call one to another*). On the day when ye shall turn back *from the place of reckoning unto hell*, ye shall have no protector against God. And he whom God shall cause to err shall have no director. Moreover, Joseph (*who was*

Joseph the son of Jacob according to one opinion, and who lived unto the time of Moses; and Joseph the son of Abraham the son of Joseph the son of Jacob, according to another opinion) came unto you before *Moses*, with evident *miraculous* proofs; but ye ceased not to be in doubt respecting that wherewith he came unto you, until, when he died, ye said *without proof* God will by no means send an apostle after him. Thus God causeth to err him who is a transgressor, *or polytheist*, [and] a sceptic. They who dispute respecting the signs of God, without any convincing proof having come unto them, *their disputing* is very hateful with God and with those who have believed. Thus God sealeth every heart (*or the whole heart*) of a proud contumacious person.

"And Pharaoh said, O Hámán, build for me a tower, that I may reach the avenues, the avenues of the heavens, and ascend unto the God of Moses; but verily I think him, *namely Moses*, a liar *in his assertion that he hath any god but myself*. And thus the wickedness of his deed was made to seem comely unto Pharaoh, and he was turned away from the path *of rectitude;* and the artifice of Pharaoh [ended] not save in loss. And he who had believed said, O my people, follow me: I will direct you into the right way. O my people, this present life is only a temporary enjoyment; but the world to come is the mansion of firm continuance. Whosoever doeth evil, he shall not be recompensed save with the like of it; and whosoever doeth good, whether male or female, and is a believer, these shall enter Paradise; they shall be provided for therein without reckoning. And, O my people, how is it that I invite you unto salvation, and ye invite me unto the Fire? Ye invite me to deny God, and to associate with Him that of which I have no knowledge; but I invite you unto the Mighty, the Very Forgiving. [There is] no doubt but that the false gods to *the worship of* which ye invite me are not to be invoked in this world, nor in the world to come, and that our return [shall be] unto God, and that the transgressors shall be the companions of the Fire. And ye shall remember, *when ye see the punishment*, what I say unto you; and I commit my case unto God; for God seeth His servants.—*This he said when they threatened him for opposing their religion.* Therefore God preserved him from the evils which they had artfully devised (*namely slaughter*), and a most evil punishment encompassed the people of Pharaoh, *with Pharaoh himself* (*namely the drowning*); *then* they shall be exposed to the Fire morning and evening; and on the day when the hour [of judgment] shall come, *it shall be said unto the angels*, Introduce the people of Pharaoh into the most severe punishment. (Sūrah xl. 27–49.)

"And the nobles of the people of Pharaoh said *unto him*, Will thou let Moses and his people go that they may act corruptly in the earth, *by inviting to disobey thee*, and leave thee and thy gods? (*For he had made for them little idols for them to worship, and he said, I am your Lord and their Lord;—and therefore he said, I am your Lord the Most High.*) He answered, We will slaughter their male children and will suffer their females to live: and verily we shall prevail over them. *And thus they did unto them; wherefore the children of Israel complained, and* Moses said unto his people, Seek aid of God, and be patient; for the earth belongeth unto God: He causeth whomsoever He will of His servants to inherit it; and the *prosperous* end is for those who fear *God*. They replied, We have been afflicted before thou camest unto us and since thou hast come unto us. He said, Perhaps your Lord will destroy your enemy and cause you to succeed [him] in the earth, and He will see how ye will act *therein.*—And We had punished the family of Pharaoh with dearth and with scarcity of fruits, that they might be admonished *and might believe*. But when good betided them, they said, This is ours:—*that is, we deserve it;—and they were not grateful for it;* and if evil befell them, they ascribed it to the ill luck of Moses and those *believers* who were with him. Nay, their ill-luck was only with God, *He brought it upon them:* but the greater number of them know not *this*. And they said *unto Moses*, Whatsoever sign thou bring unto us, to enchant us therewith, we will not believe in thee. *So he uttered an imprecation upon them*, and We sent upon them the flood, *which entered their houses and reached to the throats of the persons sitting, seven days*, and the locusts, *which ate their corn and their fruits*, and the kummal, *or grubs, or a kind of tick, which sought after what the locusts had left*, and the frogs, *which filled their houses and their food*, and the blood *in their waters;* distinct signs: but they were proud, *refusing to believe in them*, and were a wicked people. And when the punishment fell upon them, they said, O Moses, supplicate for us thy Lord, according to that which He hath covenanted with thee, *namely, that He will withdraw from us the punishment if we believe:* verily, if thou remove from us the punishment, we will assuredly believe thee, and we will assuredly send with thee the children of Israel. But when We removed from them the punishment until a period at which they should arrive, lo, they brake their promise. Wherefore we took vengeance on them, and drowned them in the sea, because they charged our signs with falsehood and were heedless of them. And We caused the people who had been rendered weak, *by being enslaved*, to inherit the eastern parts of the earth and its western parts, which we blessed *with water and trees*, (*namely Syria*); and the gracious word of thy Lord was fulfilled on the children of Israel, because they had been patient; and We destroyed the *structures* which Pharaoh and his people had built and what they had erected." (Sūrah vii. 124–133.)

"We brought the children of Israel across the sea, and Pharaoh and his troops pursued them with violence and hostility, until, when drowning overtook him, he said, I believe that there is no deity but He in whom the children of Israel believe, and I am one of the Muslims. *But Gabriel thrust into his mouth some of the mire of the sea, lest mercy should be granted him, and said,* Now *thou believest,* and thou hast been rebellious hitherto, and wast [one] of the corrupters. But to-day we will raise thee with thy lifeless body *from the sea,* that thou mayest be a sign unto those who shall come after thee. (*It is related, on the authority of Ibn-'Abbás, that some of the children of Israel doubted his death; wherefore he was brought forth to them that they might see him.*) But verily many men are heedless of Our signs. (Sūrah x. 90–92.)

"And We brought the children of Israel across the sea; and they came unto a people who gave themselves up to *the worship of* idols belonging to them; [whereupon] they said, O Moses, make for us a god (*an idol for us to worship*), like as they have gods. He replied, Verily ye are a people who are ignorant, *since ye have requited God's favour towards you with that which ye have said;* for that [religion] in which these are [occupied shall be] destroyed, and vain is that which they do. He said, Shall I seek for you any other deity than God, when He hath preferred you above the peoples *of your time.* (Sūrah vii. 134–136.)

"And We caused the thin clouds to shade you *from the heat of the sun in the desert,* and caused the manna and the quails to descend upon you, *and said,* Eat of the good things which We have given you for food, *and store not up.—But they were ungrateful for the benefit, and stored up; wherefore it was cut off from them.* And they injured not Us *thereby;* but they did injure their own souls." (Sūrah ii. 54.)

"Remember, O children of Israel, when ye said, O Moses, we will not bear patiently the having one *kind of* food, *the manna and the quails;* therefore supplicate for us thy Lord, that He may produce for us *somewhat* of that which the earth bringeth forth, of its herbs and its cucumbers and its wheat and its lentils and its onions:—he said *unto them,* Will ye take in exchange that which is worse for that which is better?—*But they refused to recede; therefore he supplicated God, and He said,* Get ye down into a great city; for ye shall have *therein* what ye have asked.—And *the marks of* abjection and poverty were stamped upon them: *so these characteristics necessarily belong to them, even if they are rich, as necessarily as the stamped coin belongeth to its die;* and they returned with indignation from God. This was because they did disbelieve in the signs of God, and slay the prophets (*as Zechariah and John*) unjustly: this was because they rebelled and did transgress." (Sūrah ii. 58.)

"And *remember* when Moses asked drink for his people, *who had become thirsty in the desert,* and We said, Strike with thy rod the stone. (*It was the stone that fled away with his garment: it was light, square, like the head of a man, marble or kedhdhán.*) *Accordingly he struck it;* and there gushed out from it twelve fountains, *according to the number of the tribes,* all men (*each tribe of them*) knowing their drinking-place. *And We said unto them,* Eat ye and drink of the supply of God, and commit not evil in the earth, acting corruptly. (Sūrah ii. 57.)

"*Remember* also when We obtained your bond *that ye would do according to that which is contained in the Law,* and *had* lifted up over you the mountain, namely Mount Sinai, *pulled it up by the roots and raised it over you when ye had refused to accept the Law, and We said,* Receive that which We have given you, with resolution, and remember that which is contained in it, *to do according thereto:* peradventure ye will fear *the Fire, or acts of disobedience.*—Then ye turned back after that; and had it not been for the grace of God towards you and His mercy, ye had certainly been of those who perish. And ye know those of you who transgressed on the Sabbath, *by catching fish, when We had forbidden them to do so, and they were the people of Eyleh,* and We said unto them, Be ye apes, driven away from the society of men.—*Thereupon they became such, and they perished after three days.*—And We made it (*namely that punishment*) an example unto those who were contemporary with them and those who came after them, and a warning to the pious. (Sūrah ii. 60–62.)

"And We appointed unto Moses thirty nights, *at the expiration of which We would speak to him, on the condition of his fasting during them; and they were* [the nights of the month of] *Dhu-l-Kaadeh; and he fasted during them: but when they were ended, he disliked the smell of his breath; so he used a tooth-stick; whereupon God commanded him to fast ten other nights, that He might speak to Him with the odour of his breath, as He whose name be exalted hath said,* and We completed them by adding ten *nights of Dhu-l-Ḥijjeh:* so the stated time of his Lord was completed, forty nights. And Moses said unto his brother Aaron, *at his departure to the mountain for the private collocution,* Be thou my deputy among my people, and act rightly, and follow not the way of the corrupt doers *by agreeing with them in acts of disobedience.* And when Moses came at Our appointed time, and his Lord spake unto him *without an intermediary,* he said, O my Lord, show me *Thyself,* that I may see Thee. He replied, Thou shalt not see Me: but look at the mountain, *which is stronger than thou;* and if it remain firm in its place, then shalt thou see Me. And when his Lord displayed Himself to the mountain (*that is, when there appeared, of His light, half of the tip of His little finger, as related in a tradition which El-Ḥákim hath verified*), He reduced it to powder, *levelling it even with the ground around it;* and Moses fell down in a swoon. And when he recovered, he said, Extolled be Thy perfection! I turn unto Thee repenting, and I am the first of the believers *in my time.*—*God* said *unto him,* O Moses, I have chosen thee above the people *of thy time* by honouring thee, by My commissions and by My speaking *unto thee:* therefore receive what I have given thee, and be of those who are grateful. And We wrote for him upon the tables *of the Law* (*which were of the lote-tree of Paradise, or of chrysolite, or of emerald; in number seven, or ten*) an admonition concerning every *requisite* matter *of religion*, and a distinct explanation of everything; *and said*, Therefore receive it with resolution, and command thy people to act according to the most excellent [precepts] thereof. (Sūrah vii. 138–142.)

"And the people of Moses, after it (*that is, after his departure for the private collocution*), made of their ornaments (*which they had borrowed of the people of Pharaoh*), a corporeal calf *which Es-Sámiree cast for them, and* which lowed; *for he had the faculty of doing so in consequence of their having put into its mouth some dust taken from* beneath *the hoof of the horse of Gabriel; and they took it as a god.* Did they not see that it spake not to them, nor directed them in the way? They took it *as a god*, and were offenders. But when they repented, and saw that they had erred, *which was after the return of Moses*, they said, Verily if our Lord do not have mercy upon us and forgive us, we shall assuredly be of those who perish. (Sūrah vii. 146–148.)

"And Moses returned unto his people enraged *against them*, exceedingly sorrowful. He said, O my people, did not your Lord promise you a good *true* promise, *that He would give you the Law?* But did the time *of my absence* seem tedious to you, or did ye desire that indignation from your Lord should befall you, and therefore did ye break your promise to me, *and abstain from coming after me?*—They answered, We did not break our promise to thee of our own authority; but we were made to carry loads of the ornaments of the people *of Pharaoh* (*which the children of Israel had borrowed of them under pretence of* [requiring them for] *a wedding, and which remained in their possession*), and we cast them *into the fire, by order of Es-Sámiree.* And in like manner also Es-Sámiree cast *their ornaments which he had, and some of the dust which he had taken from the traces of the hoofs of the horse of Gabriel;* and he produced unto them a corporeal calf, *of flesh and blood*, which lowed, *by reason of the dust, the property of which is to give life to that into which it is put; and he had put it, after he had moulded the calf, into its mouth.* And they (*namely Es-Sámiree and his followers*) said, This is your god, and the god of Moses; but he hath forgotten *his lord here, and gone to seek him. God saith*, But did they not see that it returned them not an answer, nor was able to cause them hurt or profit? And Aaron had said unto them, before *the return of Moses*, O my people, ye are only tried by it; and verily your Lord is the Compassionate; therefore follow me, *by worshipping Him*, and obey my command. They replied, We will by no means cease to be devoted to *the worship of* it until Moses return unto us. *Moses* said *after his return*, O Aaron, what hindered thee, when thou sawest that they had gone astray, from following me? Hast thou then been disobedient to my command *by remaining among them who worshipped another than God?*—He answered, O son of my mother, seize me not by my beard (*for he had taken hold of his beard with his left hand*), nor by [the hair of] my head (*for he had taken hold of his hair with his right hand, in anger*). Verily I feared *lest if I followed thee* (*for a company of those who worshipped the calf would inevitably have followed me*) thou shouldst say, Thou hast made a division among the children of Israel, and hast not waited for my sentence. *Moses* said, And what was thy motive *for doing as thou hast*, O Sámiree? He answered, I saw that which they saw not; therefore I took a handful *of dust* from the foot-marks *of the horse* of the apostle *Gabriel*, and cast it *into the molten calf;* and thus my soul allured me *to take a handful of the dust above-mentioned, and to cast it upon that which had no life, that it might have life; and I saw that thy people had demanded of thee that thou wouldst make them a god; so my soul suggested to me that this calf should be their god. Moses* said *unto him*, Then get thee gone *from among us*, and [the punishment] for thee during *the period of thy* life [shall be], that thou shalt say *unto whomsoever thou shalt see*, Touch *me* not:—(*so he used to wander about the desert, and when he touched anyone, or anyone touched him, they both became affected with a burning fever:*) and verily for thee is a threat which thou shalt by no means find to be false. And look at thy god, to *the worship of* which thou hast continued devoted. We will assuredly burn it: then we will assuredly reduce it to powder and scatter it in the sea. (*And Moses, after he had slaughtered it, did this.*) Your deity is God only, except whom there is no deity. He comprehendeth all things by *His* knowledge.—Thus, *O Moḥammad*, do We relate unto thee accounts of what hath happened heretofore; and We have given thee, from Us, an admonition; *namely the Kur-án.* (Sūrah xx. 88-99.)

"And they were made to drink down the calf into their hearts (*that is, the love of it mingled with their hearts as drink mingleth,*) because of their unbelief. (Sūrah ii. 87.)

"Remember, O children of Israel, when Moses said unto his people *who worshipped the calf*, O my people, verily ye have injured your own souls by your taking to yourselves the calf *as a god;* therefore turn with repentance unto your Creator *from the worship of it*, and slay one another: (*that is, let the innocent among you slay the criminal:*) this will be best for you in the estimation of your Creator. *And he aided you to do that, sending upon you a black cloud, lest one of you should see another and have compassion on him, until there were slain of you about seventy thousand.* And *thereupon* He became propitious towards you, *accepting your repentance;* for He is the Very Propitious, the Merciful. (Sūrah ii. 51.)

"Remember, also, O children of Israel, when ye said, *having gone forth with Moses to beg pardon of God for your worship of the calf, and having heard his words*, O Moses, we will not believe thee until we see God manifestly:—whereupon the vehement sound assailed you, *and ye died*, while ye beheld *what happened to you*. Then We raised you to life after ye had been dead, that peradventure ye might give thanks. (Sūrah ii. 52, 53.)

"And Moses chose *from* his people seventy men, *of those who had not worshipped the calf, by the command of God*, at the time appointed by Us *for their coming to ask pardon for their companions' worship of the calf; and he went forth with them;* and when the convulsion (*the violent earthquake*) took them away (*because, saith Ibn-'Abbás, they did not separate themselves from their people when the latter worshipped the calf*), *Moses* said, O my Lord, if Thou hadst pleased, Thou hadst destroyed them before *my going forth with them, that the children of Israel might have beheld it and might not suspect me;* and me [also]. Wilt Thou destroy us for that which the foolish among us have done? It is naught but Thy trial: Thou wilt cause to err thereby whom Thou pleasest, and Thou wilt rightly guide whom Thou pleasest. Thou art our guardian; and do Thou forgive us and have mercy upon us; for Thou art the best of those who forgive: and appoint for us in this world what is good, and in the world to come; for unto Thee have we turned with repentance. —*God* replied, I will afflict with My punishment whom I please, and My mercy extendeth over everything *in the world;* and I will appoint it, *in the world to come*, for those who fear and give the legal alms, and those who believe on Our signs, who shall follow the apostle, the illiterate prophet, *Moḥammad*, whom they shall find written down with them in the Pentateuch and the Gospel, *by his name and his description*. He will command them that which is right, and forbid them that which is evil; and will allow them as lawful the good things *among those forbidden in their law*, and prohibit them the impure, *as carrion and other things*, and will take off from them their burden and the yokes that were upon them, *as the slaying of a soul* [for an atonement] *in repentance, and the cutting off of the mark left by impurity*. And those who shall believe in him and honour him and assist him and follow the light which shall be sent down with him, *namely the Kur-án*, these shall be the prosperous. (Sūrah vii. 154–156.)

"And *remember* when Moses said unto his people, O my people, remember the favour of God towards you, since He hath appointed prophets from among you, and made you princes (*masters of servants and other attendants*), and given you what He hath not given any [other] of the peoples (*as the manna and the quails and other things*). O my people, enter the Holy Land which God hath decreed for you (*namely Syria*), and turn not back, lest ye turn losers.—They replied, O Moses, verily there is in it a gigantic people, *of the remains of the tribe of 'A'd*, and we will not enter it until they go forth from it; but if they go forth from it, then we will enter. —Thereupon two men, of those who feared *to disobey God, namely Joshua and Caleb, of the chiefs whom Moses sent to discover the circumstances of the giants, and* upon whom God had conferred favour, *and who had concealed what they had seen of the state of the giants, excepting from Moses, wherefore the other chiefs became cowardly*, said *unto them*, Enter ye upon them through the gate *of the city, and fear them not; for they are bodies without hearts;* and when ye enter it, ye overcome; and upon God place your dependence, if ye be believers. —But they said, O Moses, we will never enter it while they remain therein. Therefore go thou and thy Lord, and fight: for we remain here.—*Then Moses* said, O my Lord, verily I am not master of any but myself and my brother: therefore distinguish between us and the unrighteous people.—*God* replied, Verily it (*namely the Holy Land*) shall be forbidden them forty years; they shall wander in perplexity in the land: and be not thou solicitous for the unrighteous people.—*The land* through which they wandered *was* only *nine leagues* in extent. *They used to journey during the night with diligence; but in the morning they found themselves in the place whence they had set forth; and they journeyed during the day in like manner. Thus they did until all of them had become extinct, excepting those who had not attained the age of twenty years; and it is said that they were six hundred thousand. Aaron and Moses died in the desert; and mercy was their lot: but punishment was the lot of those. And Moses begged his Lord, when he was about to die, that He would bring him as near as a stone's throw to the Holy Land: wherefore He did so. And Joshua was made a prophet after the forty* [years], *and he gave orders to fight against the giants. So he went with those who were with him, and fought against them: and it was Friday; and the sun stood still for him awhile, until he had made an end of fighting against them.* (Sūrah v, 23–29.)

"Ḳároon [or Korah] was of the people of Moses (*he was the son of his paternal uncle, and the son of his maternal aunt, and he believed in him*); but he behaved insolently towards them; for We had bestowed upon him such treasures that their keys were heavy burdens for a company of men endowed with strength, *in number, as some say, seventy; and some, forty; and some, ten; and some, another number. Remember* when his people (*the believers among the children of Israel*) said unto him, Rejoice not *exultingly in the abundance of thy wealth;* for God loveth not those who *so* rejoice; but seek to attain, by means of the *wealth* which God hath given thee, the latter abode [of Paradise], *by expanding thy wealth in the service of God;* and neglect not thy part in this world, *to work therein for the world to come;* but be beneficent *unto mankind, by bestowing alms*, as God hath been beneficent unto thee; and seek not to act corruptly in the earth; for God loveth not the corrupt doers. He replied, I have only been given it on account of the knowledge that I possess. *For he was the most learned of the children of Israel in the Law, after Moses and Aaron. God saith*, Did he not know that God had destroyed before him, of the generations, those that were mightier than he in strength, and who had amassed more abundance *of wealth?* And the wicked shall not be asked respecting their sins, *because God knoweth them: therefore they shall be sent into the Fire without a reckoning.* And *Ḳároon* went forth unto his people in his pomp, *with his many dependants mounted, adorned with garments of gold and silk, upon decked horses and mules.* Those who desired the present life said, O would that we had the like of that which hath been bestowed on Ḳároon *in this world!* Verily he is possessed of great good fortune!—But those unto whom knowledge *of what God hath promised in the world to come* had been given, said *unto them,* Woe to you! The reward of God *in the world to come* (*which is Paradise*) is better for him who believeth and worketh righteousness *than that which hath been bestowed on Ḳároon in the present world;* and none shall receive it but the patient *in the service of God.* And We caused the earth to cleave asunder and swallow up him and his mansion, and he had no forces to defend him, in the place of God, nor was he of the [number of the] saved. And the next morning, those who had wished for his place the day before said, Aha! God enlargeth provision unto whom He pleaseth of His servants, and is sparing *of it unto whom He pleaseth!* Had not God been gracious unto us, He had caused [the earth] to cleave asunder and swallow up us! Aha! the ungrateful *for His benefits* do not prosper! (Sūrah xxviii. 76–82.)

"*Remember*, when Moses said unto his people (*when one of them had been slain, whose murderer was not known, and they asked him to beg God that He would discover him to them, wherefore he supplicated Him*), Verily God commandeth you to sacrifice a cow. They said, Dost thou make a jest of us? He said, I beg God to preserve me from being *one* of the foolish. *So when they knew that he decidedly intended* what he had ordered, they said, Supplicate for us thy Lord, that He may manifest to us what she is; *that is, what is her age. Moses* replied, He saith, She is a cow neither old nor young; *but* of a middle age, between those *two:* therefore do as ye are commanded. They said, Supplicate for us thy Lord, that He may manifest to us what is her colour. He replied, He saith, She is a red cow: her colour is very bright: she rejoiceth the beholders. They said, Supplicate for us thy Lord, that He may manifest to us what she is, *whether she be a pasturing or a working cow;* for cows *of the description mentioned* are to us like one another; and we, if God please, shall indeed be rightly directed *to her.* (*In a tradition it is said, Had they not said, 'If God please,'—she had not ever been manifested to them.*) He replied, He saith, She is a cow not subdued *by work* that plougheth the ground, nor doth she water the field: [she is] free *from defects and the marks of work;* there is no colour in her different from the rest of her colour. They said, Now thou hast brought the truth. *And they sought her, and found her in the possession of the young man who acted piously towards his mother, and they bought her for as much gold as her hide would contain.* Then they sacrificed her; but they were near to leaving it undone, *on account of the greatness of her price.* (*And in a tradition it is said, Had they sacrificed any cow whatever, He had satisfied them: but they acted hardly towards themselves; so God acted hardly towards them.*) And when ye slew a soul, and contended together respecting it, (and God brought forth [to light] that which ye did conceal—*this is the beginning of the story* [and was the occasion of the order to sacrifice this particular cow,]) We said, Strike him (*that is, the slain person*) with part of her. *So he was struck with her tongue, or the root of her tail, or, as some say, with her right thigh; whereupon he came to life, and said, Such-a-one and such-a-one slew me,—to the two sons of his uncle. And he died.* *They two* [the murderers] *were therefore deprived of the inheritance, and were slain.* Thus God raiseth to life the dead, and showeth you His signs (*the proof of His power*), that peradventure ye may understand, *and know that He who is able to raise to life one soul is able to raise to life many souls.* Then your hearts became hard, *O ye Jews, so as not to accept the truth,* after that, and they [were] as stones, or more hard: for of stones there are indeed some from which rivers gush forth; and of them there are indeed some that cleave asunder and water issueth from them; and of them there are indeed some that fall down through fear of God; *whereas your hearts are not impressed, nor do they grow soft, nor do they become humble.* But God is not heedless of that which ye do: *He only reserveth you unto your time.* (Sūrah ii. 63–69.)

"*Remember* when Moses said to his young man *Joshua the son of Nun, who served him and acquired knowledge from him,* I will not cease *to go forward* until I reach the place where the two seas (*the Sea of Greece and the Sea of Persia*) meet, or travel for a long space of time. And when they reached the place where they (*the two seas*) met they forgot their fish: *Joshua forgot to take it up, on their departure; and Moses forgot to remind him;* and it made its way in the sea by a hollow passage, *God withholding the water from it.* And when they had passed beyond *that place, and proceeded until the time of the morning-meal on the following day,* [Moses] said unto his young man, Bring us our morning-meal: we have experienced fatigue from this our journey. He replied, What thinkest thou? When we repaired to the rock to rest *at that place,* I forgot the fish, and none made me forget to mention it but the Devil; and it made its way in the sea in a wonderful manner.—*Moses* said, That (*namely our loss of the fish*) is what we were desiring: *for it is a sign unto us of our finding him whom we seek.* And they returned by the way that they had come, following the footsteps, *and came to the rock.* And they found one of Our servants (*namely El-Khiḍr*) unto whom We had granted mercy from Us (*that is, the gift of prophecy in the opinion of some, and the rank of a saint according to another opinion, which most of the learned hold*), and whom We had taught knowledge from Us *respecting things unseen.—El-Bukhâree hath related a tradition that Moses performed the office of a preacher among the children of Israel, and was asked who was the most knowing of men; to which he answered, I:—whereupon God blamed him for this, because he did not refer the knowledge thereof to Him. And God said unto him by revelation, Verily I have a servant at the place where the two seas meet, and he is more knowing than thou. Moses said, O my Lord, and how shall I meet with him? He answered, Thou shalt take with thee a fish, and put it into a measuring vessel, and where thou shalt lose the fish, there is he. So he took a fish, and put it into a vessel. Then he departed, and Joshua the son of Nun departed with him, until they came to the rock, where they laid down their heads and slept. And the fish became agitated in the vessel, and escaped from it, and fell into the sea, and it made its way in the sea by a hollow passage, God withholding the water from the fish so that it became like a vault over it: and when Moses' companion awoke, he forgot to inform him of the fish.*

"Moses said unto him [namely El-Khiḍr], Shall I follow thee, that thou mayest teach me [part] of that which thou hast been taught, for a direction *unto me?* He answered, Verily thou canst not have patience with me. For how canst thou be patient with respect to that whereof thou comprehendest not the knowledge?—He replied, Thou shalt find me, if God please, patient; and I will not disobey any command of thine. He said, Then if thou follow me, ask me not respecting anything: *but be patient* until I give thee an account thereof. *And Moses assented to his condition.* And they departed, *walking along the shore of the sea*, until, when they embarked in the ship *that passed by them*, he, *El-Khiḍr*, made a hole in it, *by pulling out a plank or two planks from it on the outside by means of an axe when it reached the middle of the sea. Moses* said *unto him*, Hast thou made a hole in it that thou mayest drown its people? Thou hast done a grievous thing.—(*But it is related that the water entered not the hole.*) He replied, Did I not say that thou couldst not have patience with me? [Moses] said, Chastise me not for my forgetfulness, nor impose on me a difficulty in my case.—And they departed, *after they had gone forth from the vessel, walking on*, until, when they found a boy *who had not attained the age of knowing right and wrong, playing with other children, and he was the most beautiful of them in countenance*, and he (*El-Khiḍr*) slew him, *Moses* said *unto him*, Hast thou slain an innocent soul, without *his having slain* a soul? Thou hast done an iniquitous thing.—He replied, Did I not say that thou couldst not have patience with me? [Moses] said, If I ask thee concerning anything after this *time*, suffer me not to accompany thee. Now hast thou received from me an excuse *for thy separating thyself from me.*—And they departed [and proceeded] until, when they came to the people of a city (*which was Antioch*), they asked food of its people; but they refused to entertain them: and they found therein a wall, *the height whereof was a hundred cubits*, which was about to fall down; whereupon he (*El-Khiḍr*) set it upright *with his hand. Moses* said *unto him*, If thou wouldst, thou mightest have obtained pay for it, *since they did not entertain us, notwithstanding our want of food. El-Khiḍr* said *unto him*, This shall be a separation between me and thee; *but before my separation from thee*, I will declare unto thee the interpretation of that which thou couldst not bear with patience.

"As to the vessel, it belonged to *ten* poor men, who pursued their business on the sea; and I desired to render it unsound; for there was behind them a king, *an unbeliever*, who took every *sound* vessel by force. And as to the boy, his parents were believers, and we feared that he would transgress against them rebelliously and impiously: *for, according to a tradition related by Muslim, he was constituted by nature an unbeliever, and had he lived he had so acted;* wherefore we desired that their Lord should create for them a better than he in virtue, and [one] more disposed than he to filial piety. *And God created for them a daughter, who married a prophet, and gave birth to a prophet, by means of whom God directed a people to the right way.* And as to the wall, it belonged to two orphan youths in the city, and beneath it was a treasure *buried, of gold and silver*, belonging to them; and their father was a righteous man; and thy Lord desired that they should attain their age of strength and take forth their treasure through the mercy of thy Lord. And I did it not (*namely what hath been mentioned*) of mine own will, *but by direction of God.* This is the interpretation of that which thou couldst not bear with patience. (Sūrah xviii. 59–81.)"

The following remarks are taken from Sale's notes of al-Baiẓāwī and other commentators:—

"There is a tradition that Moses was a very swarthy man; and that when he put his hand into his bosom, and drew it out again, it became extremely white and splendid, surpassing the brightness of the sun.

"Moses had an impediment in his speech, which was occasioned by the following accident. Pharaoh one day carrying him in his arms when a child, he suddenly laid hold of his beard and plucked it in a very rough manner, which put Pharaoh into such a passion, that he ordered him to be put to death: but A'siyeh, his wife, representing to him that he was but a child, who could not distinguish between a burning coal and a ruby, he ordered the experiment to be made; and a live coal and a ruby being set before Moses, he took the coal and put it into his mouth, and burnt his tongue; and thereupon he was pardoned.—This is a Jewish story a little altered.

"It is related that the midwife appointed to attend the Hebrew women, terrified by a light which appeared between the eyes of Moses at his birth, and touched with extraordinary affection for the child, did not discover him to the officers, so that her mother kept him in her house, and nursed him three months; after which it was impossible for her to conceal him any longer, the king then giving orders to make the searches more strictly.

"The commentators say that the mother of Moses made an ark of the papyrus, and pitched it, and put in some cotton; and having laid the child therein, committed it to the river, a branch of which went into Pharaoh's garden: that the stream carried the ark thither into a fishpond, at the head of which Pharaoh was then sitting with his wife A'siyeh, the daughter of Muzáhem; and that the king, having commanded it to be taken up and opened, and finding in it a beautiful child, took a fancy to it, and ordered it to be brought up. Some writers mention a miraculous preservation of Moses before he was put into the ark; and tell us, that his mother having hid him from Pharaoh's officers in an oven, his sister, in her mother's absence, kindled a large fire in the oven to heat it, not knowing the child was there; but that he was afterwards taken out unhurt."

MOSQUE. The Muḥammadan place of worship, which is called in Arabic *masjid* (مسجد). The term "mosque" is found in all European languages, and must have been derived from the Arabic form of the word, *e.g.* Spanish, *mesquita*; Italian, *moschea*; German, *Moschee*; French, *mosquée*; English, *mosque* or *mosk*.

For an account of these buildings, see MASJID.

MOTHER. (1) Kindness towards a mother is enjoined in the Qur'ān. Sūrah xlvi. 14: "We have prescribed for man kindness towards his parents. His mother bore him with trouble, and brought him forth with trouble."

(2) Mothers cannot be compelled to nurse their children.

(3) They are not, without their husband's permission, allowed to move them to a strange place. (*Hidāyah*, vol. i. pp. 386, 390.)

MOURNING. The period of mourning for the dead is restricted to three days, during which time the friends and relatives are expected to visit the bereaved family, and offer up prayers for the departed (*fātiḥah*), and speak words of consolation (*ta'ziyah*). But a widow must observe the custom of mourning for a period of four months and ten days, which period is called *iḥdād*. During these periods of mourning, it is the duty of all concerned to abstain from the use of perfumes and ornaments, and to wear soiled garments. Lamentation, *bukā'* (Heb. *bokhoh*), for the dead is strictly forbidden by the Prophet (*Mishkāt*, book v. ch. vii.), but it is nevertheless a common custom in the East, amongst all sects of Muḥammadans. (See *Arabian Nights*; Lane's *Modern Egyptians*; Shaw's *Travels in Barbary*.)

MU'AHID (معاهد). One who enters into covenant (*'ahd*) with another. An infidel who is permitted by a Muslim Government to enter its towns and carry on traffic, *i.e.* a *ẕimmī*. [ZIMMI.]

AL-MU'AKHKHIR (الموخر). "The Deferrer." One of the ninety-nine names or attributes of God. It does not occur in the Qur'ān, but is given in the Ḥadīs̤.

MU'ALLIM (معلم). A teacher in a school or mosque. *Al-Mu'allimu 'l-Awwal*, "The first teacher," is a term used by philosophers for Aristotle. Amongst the Ṣūfīs it is used for Adam, who is said to be the first prophet. *Mu'allimu 'l-Malā'ikah*, "The teacher of angels," is also used by the Ṣūfīs for Adam, because it is said in the Qur'ān, Sūrah ii. 31: "O Adam, declare unto them (the angels) their names."

MU'ĀNAQAH (معانقة). Embracing, or throwing oneself on the neck of one's friend. A custom especially enjoined by Muḥammad. (*Mishkāt*, book xxii. ch. iii. pt. 2.)

AL-MU'AQQIBĀT (المعقبات). *Lit.* "The succeeding ones." A title given to the recording angels. [KIRAMU 'L-KATIBIN.]

MU'ĀWIYAH (معاوية). The sixth Khalīfah, and the founder of the Umaiyah dynasty (the Ommiades). He was the son of Abū Sufyān, one of the leading Companions of Muḥammad, and became Khalīfah on the death of al-Ḥasan, and is regarded with great hatred by the Shī'ahs. He died A.H. 60. He was the first Khalīfah who made the Khalīfate hereditary.

AL-MU'AWWIẔĀT (المعوذات). *Lit.* "The seekers of refuge." The two last chapters of the Qur'ān.

Sūratu 'l-Falaq (cxiii.), beginning with, "Say: I flee for refuge to the Lord of the Daybreak."

Sūratu 'n-Nās (cxiv.) beginning, "Say: I flee for refuge to the Lord of men."

These chapters were ordered by Muḥammad to be recited after each stated prayer. (*Mishkāt*, book iv. ch. xix. pt. 2.)

MU'AẔ IBN JABAL (معاذ بن جبل). One of the most famous of the "Companions." He was of the Banū Khazraj, and was only twenty years of age at the battle of Badr. Being well skilled in the Qur'ān, he was left at Makkah to instruct the people in the principles of Islām. He was also sent as the head of a band of collectors of taxes to south Arabia, and became Qāẓī of al-Yaman. After Muḥammad's death, he became a leading person in the counsels of Abū Bakr and 'Umar, and was placed in charge of Syria by the latter Khalīfah. He died at Ṭā'ūn 'Amawās.

MU'AẔẔIN (موذن). The caller of the *azān*, or "summons to prayer." In small mosques, the azān is given by the Imām, but in the larger ones, an official is specially appointed for the purpose. When the mosque has a minaret, he calls from the top of it, but in smaller places of worship, from the side of the mosque. The first mu'azzin was Bilāl, the son of an Abyssinian slave-girl, and Muḥammad is related to have said, "The callers to prayer may expect Paradise, and whoever serves in the office for seven years shall be saved from hell fire." (*Mishkāt*, book iv. ch. vi.) [AZAN.]

MUBĀḤ (مباح). *Lit.* "Allowed." A term used in the religious and ceremonial law of Islām for an action which a person may do or let alone, being attended with neither praise nor blame.

MUBĀRĀT (مباراة). "Mutual discharge." A term used in the law of divorce when a man says to his wife, "I am discharged from the marriage between you and me," and she consents thereto. It is the same as *khul'*.

AL-MUBDI' (المبدئ). "The Producer or Beginner." One of the ninety-nine names or attributes of God. It does not occur in the Qur'ān, but the idea is expressed in Sūrah lxxxv. 13: "He produces and restores."

MUBTADI' (مبتدع). *Lit.* "An inventor." A heretic, or a broacher of new opinions.

MUDABBAR (مدبر). A slave who has received his freedom in consequence of the master's death, in accordance with a previous promise.

MUDDA'Ī (مدعى). A plaintiff in a law-suit.

MUDDA'Ī-'ALAIH (مدعى عليه). A defendant in a law-suit.

AL-MUDDAṢṢIR (المدثر). *Lit.* "The Enwrapped." The title of the LXXIVth Sūrah of the Qur'ān, in the first verse of which the word occurs. "O Thou, enwrapped in thy mantle, arise and preach." This is considered by some to be the earliest Sūrah in the Qur'ān, but others think it was the XCVIth. [MUHAMMAD.]

MUFARRIḤU 'L-AḤZAN (مفرح الاحزان). *Lit.* "The making cheerful under affliction." A term used by pious Muslims for a spirit of resignation in affliction, which, they say, is to be produced by possessing faith with a firm belief in the decrees of fate. ('Abdu 'r-Razzāq's *Dict. of Ṣūfī Terms.*)

MUFSID (مفسد). "A pernicious person." It occurs in the Qur'ān frequently, *e.g.* Sūrah ii. 219: "God knoweth the foul dealer (*mufsid*) from the fair dealer (*muṣliḥ*)."

MUFTĪ (مفتى). The officer who expounds the law. He assists the Qāẓī, or judge, and supplies him with *fatwās*, or decisions. He must be learned in the Qur'ān and Ḥadīṣ, and in the Muslim works of law.

AL-MUGHNI (المغنى). "The Enricher." One of the ninety-nine names or attributes of God. It is referred to in the Qur'ān, Sūrah iv. 129: "God can make both independent (*lit.* 'enrich') out of His abundance."

MUḤĀDAṢAH (محادثة). *Lit.* "Discoursing together." A term used by the Ṣūfīs for the calling of a person by God through some outward means, as when, according to the Qur'ān, Sūrah xxviii. 30, God spoke to Moses out of a tree. ('Abdu 'r-Razzāq's *Dict. of Ṣūfī Terms.*)

MUḤADDIṢ (محدث). (1) The narrator of a Ḥadīṣ or acts and words of Muḥammad. (2) One learned in the Traditions.

AL-MUHAIMIN (المهيمن). "The Protector." One of the ninety-nine names or attributes of God. It occurs in the Qur'ān, Sūrah lix. 23, "He is . . . the *Protector.*"

MUHĀJIR (مهاجر). From *hijrah*, "flight." One who performs *hijrah* either by (1) leaving Makkah in company with the Prophet, or (2) leaving a country ruled by an infidel power, or (3) by fleeing from what God has forbidden.

MUHĀJIRŪN (مهاجرون). The pl. of *Muhājir*. The exiles or refugees. A term used for all those converts to Islām who fled with their Prophet from Makkah. Under the title are also included all who from time to time joined Muḥammad at al-Madīnah, either from Makkah or from any other quarter, up to the taking of Makkah in A.H. 8. They rank first in order amongst the Companions of the Prophet.

MUḤALLIL (محلل). *Lit.* "One who makes lawful." The man who marries a divorced wife in order to make her lawful for her former husband if he wish to marry her. [DIVORCE.]

MUḤAMMAD (محمد). *Lit.* "The Praised One." Sometimes spelt *Mohammed*, *Mohomed*, or *Mahomet*.

Muḥammad, the founder of the religion generally known as Muḥammadanism, but called by its own adherents Islām [ISLAM], was the posthumous son of 'Abdu 'llāh, by his wife Āminah. 'Abdu 'llāh belonged to the family of Hāshim, which was the noblest tribe of the Quraish section of the Arabian race, and said to be directly descended from Ishmael. The father of 'Abdu 'llāh and the grandfather of Muḥammad, was 'Abdu 'l-Muṭṭalib, who held the high office of custodian of the Ka'bah. [KA'BAH.] The same year which saw the destruction of the Abyssinian invader, and formed an epoch in the history of Arabia, known as the Era of the Elephant, on account of the vast array of elephants the invaders brought with them, witnessed the birth of Muḥammad. Muhammad is said to have been born about fifty-five days after the attack of Abrahah, or on the 12th day of the month Rabīu 'l-Awwal of the first year of the Era of the Elephant, which M. Caussin de Perceval believes to have been the fortieth year of the reign of Chosroes the Great (*Kasra Anushirwan*), and calculates the date to have been August 20th, A.D. 570 (see vol. i. pp. 282, 283). According to Sprenger, it was April 20th, A.D. 571 (*Das Leben und die Lehre des Mohammad*, vol. i. p. 138.)

Muḥammad was born at Makkah. And immediately upon his birth, his mother, Āminah, sent a special messenger to inform 'Abdu 'l-Muṭṭalib of the news. The messenger reached the chief as he sat within the sacred enclosure of the Ka'bah, in the midst of his sons and principal men, and he arose with joy and went to the house of Āminah. He then took the child in his arms, and went to the Ka'bah, and gave thanks to God. The Quraish tribe begged the grandfather to name the child after some member of the family, but 'Abdu 'l-Muṭṭalib said, "I desire that the God who has created the child on earth may be glorified in heaven, and he called him Muḥammad, "the praised one."

Al-Ḥāfiẓ, on the authority of Makhzūm (quoted by Abū 'l-Fidā', p. 59), says that on the night that Muḥammad was born, the palace of Chosroes was shaken, and fourteen of its turrets fell; the fires of the Persians were extinguished, which had not been extinguished before for a thousand years; and the lake Sāwah sank.

It was not the custom of the better class of women amongst the Arabians to nurse their children, and consequently the infant, soon after his birth, was made over to Ṣuwaibah, a slave-girl of his uncle Abū Lahab. Ṣuwaibah had a son, whose name was Masrūḥ, whom she nursed at the same time, and she had also nursed Ḥamzāh, Muḥammad's uncle, and Abū Salimah; so that these three men were his foster-brothers. Ṣuwaibah only suckled Muḥammad for a few days, when the child was made over to Ḥalīmah, a woman of the tribe of the Banū Sa'd. Ḥalīmah was the daughter of 'Abdu 'llāh Abū Zu'aib, the son of al-Ḥāriṣ, and she took Muḥammad to her desert home, amongst the Banū Sa'd, where he remained for a period of two years. The foster-brother suckled by Ḥalīmah was 'Abdu 'llāh, and his foster-sisters Anisah and Ḥarāmah.

The following story connected with Muḥammad's stay with Ḥalīmah is related by Abū 'l-Fidā' (p. 64). When some time passed, Muḥammad and his foster-brother went out to a distance from the house, when Ḥalīmah's son came to his mother and said, "Two men clothed in white raiments have taken hold of the Quraish boy, and have thrown him down and have ripped open his belly." So Ḥalīmah and her husband went to the place where the child was, but found him standing on his feet. And they said, "What has happened to thee child?" And he answered and said, "Two men came to me, and threw me down and ripped up my belly." Then Ḥalīmah's husband said to her, "I greatly fear that this boy has got the epilepsy." So they took him to his mother Āminah. And Ḥalīmah said to Āminah, "I am afraid he is possessed of a devil." But Āminah said, "What in the world can Satan have to do with my son that he should be his enemy?"

This circumstance has been regarded as the miracle when Gabriel came and took out the heart of the child and washed it from the stains of original sin. And some commentators say the first verse of the xcivth Sūrah of the Qur'ān alludes to it: "Have we not opened thy breast?"

Muḥammad ever retained a most grateful recollection of the kindness he had received from the Banū Sa'd, and, in after years, he used to say, "Verily I am the most perfect Arab amongst you. My descent is from the Quraish, and my speech is the tongue of the Banū Sa'd."

In his sixth year, Muḥammad was taken by his mother to al-Madīnah, but on the return journey she fell sick, and died at a place called al-Abwā', where her body was buried. In subsequent years, Muḥammad visited his mother's tomb at al-Abwā', and wept over it, saying, "This is the grave of my mother; the Lord hath permitted me to visit it, and I sought leave to pray for her salvation, but it was not granted. So I called my mother to remembrance, and the tender memory of her overcame me, and I wept."

The little orphan was then carried on to Makkah by Umm Aiman, who, although young in years, became his faithful nurse and companion. The charge of Muḥammad was now undertaken by 'Abdu 'l-Muṭṭalib, but the old chief died two years afterwards, and the child was committed to the care of his paternal uncle, Abū Ṭālib. When Muḥammad was twelve years old, he was taken by his uncle on a mercantile journey to Syria, and proceeded as far as Buṣrā. The expedition lasted for some months. According to the Muslim historian, Abū 'l-Fidā', it was at Buṣrā that Muḥammad met the Christian monk Buḥaira', who is related to have said to Abū Ṭālib, "Return with this youth, and guard him from the hatred of the Jews; for great dignity awaits this your brother's son." It was on this journey that Muḥammad was brought in contact with the profession of Christianity in Syria, and had an opportunity of obtaining some information as to the national and social customs of Christians. He must have also passed through many Jewish settlements. It is, therefore, highly probable that it was on the occasion of this journey that Muḥammad's mind became first impressed with the absolute necessity of reforming, not only the gross idolatry of Makkah, but the degrading social habits of the Arabian people.

After this journey, the youth of Muḥammad seems to have been passed uneventfully, but all authorities agree in ascribing to him a correctness of manner, and a purity of morals, which were at that time rare amongst the people of Makkah. The fair character and honourable bearing of the unobtrusive youth won the approbation of the citizens of Makkah, and by common consent he received the title of *al-Amīn*, "The Faithful."

Between the years A.D. 580–590, the sacrilegious war broke out between the Quraish and the Banū Hawāzin, which lasted for nearly ten years. In two of the contests, Muḥammad, though only a lad, accompanied his uncles in their local wars. They were called "sacrilegious" because they were carried on during the sacred months, when fighting was forbidden.

The youth of Muḥammad passed away without any other incidents of interest. At this period he was employed, like other lads, in tending the sheep and goats of Makkah upon the neighbouring hills and valleys. He used afterwards to allude to his shepherd life, and say it comported with his prophetic office, even as it did with that of Moses and David: "Verily there hath been no prophet who hath not performed the work of a shepherd."

When Muḥammad had reached his twenty-fifth year, on the recommendation of his uncle, Abū Ṭālib, he entered the service of Khadījah, a rich widow of Makkah. She was of the Quraish tribe, the daughter of Khuwailid ibn Asad. With Maisarah, her servant, Muḥammad was placed in charge of the widow's merchandise, and he again travelled the same route which he had traversed thirteen years before with his uncle. His journey again extended as far as Buṣrā, a city about sixty miles to the east of the river Jordan. He visited Aleppo and Damascus, and was doubtless brought in frequent contact with both Jews and Christians, and had another opportunity of obtaining that superficial acquaintance with the Jewish and Christian faiths, which enabled him in after years to embody so much of the teaching of the Bible in the verses of the Qur'ān. "The mutual animosity of Jew towards Christian," says Mr. Stobart, "though they professed to worship the true God, though they appealed to the old Testament, and both equally revered the name of Abraham, and professed to abhor that idolatry in which he had been bred, may have led Muḥammad to think that possibly more divine truth lay hid in both these systems of belief, though covered and concealed by human inventions, and may have suggested to him the possibility of forming out of these conflicting elements one single simple catholic creed, and of thus uniting mankind in the worship and love of the great Father of all." (Stobart's *Islām*, p. 56.)

Muḥammad having proved himself faithful in the commercial interests of his mistress, was soon rewarded with her hand in marriage. When Muḥammad married her she was a widow of forty years of age, and had been already twice married, and had borne to her former husbands, two sons and a daughter. The house of Muḥammad and Khadījah was a bright and happy one, and their marriage fortunate and fruitful. Two sons and four daughters were its issue. Their eldest son was al-Qāsim, who died at the age of two years, whence Muḥammad was sometimes called *Abū 'l-Qāsim*, or the father of al-Qāsim. The other son, 'Abdu 'llāh, surnamed aṭ-Ṭāhir and aṭ-Ṭaiyib, died in infancy. The four daughters were Zainab, Ruqaiyah, Umm Qulsūm, and Fāṭimah. [FATIMAH.]

During her lifetime, Khadījah was Muḥammad's only wife, and he always looked back to this period of his life with fond remembrance. When the world called him an impostor and a cheat, Khadījah was the first to acknowledge him to be the "Apostle of God." Indeed, so much did he dwell upon the mutual love of Khadījah and himself, that the envious 'Āyishah declared herself more jealous of this rival, who was dead, than of all the living rivals who contested with her the affection of the Prophet.

As yet Muḥammad was almost a stranger to the outside world, but he now obtained some reputation among his fellow men, by taking a prominent part in the resuscitation of an old league, called the Federation of the Fuẓūl [HILFU 'L-FUZUL], formed in ancient times for the repression of acts of lawlessness within the walls of Makkah. A new compact was formed between four or five of the chief families of Makkah for the protection of the weak and oppressed, and Muḥammad was one of the most prominent movers in this federation, the revival of which resulted mainly from his efforts.

In his thirty-fifth year, he settled by his decision a grave difficulty, which had sprung up during the reconstructien of the Ka'bah, regarding the placing of the sacred stone, and which almost threatened to plunge the whole of Arabia into another of their oft-recurring wars.

The Ka'bah was too low in the building, and the Quraish wished to raise it higher, and so they demolished it. When it was rebuilt as far as the position of the Black Stone, the question arose, who should be the honoured instrument of raising the sacred relic into its place, for each tribe claimed the honour. Then the oldest citizen arose and said, "My advice is that the man who first entereth by the gate of the Banū Shaibah, shall be selected umpire in this difficult question, or shall himself place the stone." The proposal was agreed upon, and the first man who entered the gate was he who was known as *al-Amīn*, "The Faithful," Muḥammad, the son of 'Abdu 'llāh. Muḥammad decided upon an expedient, which served to satisfy the contending parties. The stone was placed on a cloth, and each tribe shared in the honour of raising it, by taking hold of the cloth. The stone being thus deposited in its proper place, the Quraish built on without interruption, and the great idol Hubal was placed in the centre of the sacred edifice, and around were ranged the various other idols of the Arabian people. "This circumstance," says Sir William Muir, "strikingly illustrates the absence of any paramount authority at Mecca at this time.

A curious story is related of an attempt made about this period to gain the rule of Mecca. The aspirant was Othmân, first cousin of Khadîja's father. He was dissatisfied, as the legend goes, with the idolatrous system of Mecca, and travelled to the court of the Roman Emperor, where he was honourably entertained, and admitted to Christian baptism. He returned to Mecca, and on the strength of an imperial grant, real or pretended, laid claim to the government of the city. But his claim was rejected, and he fled to Syria, where he found a refuge with the Ghassânide prince. But emissaries from Mecca, by the aid of gifts, counteracted his authority with the prince, and at last procured his death."—Muir's *Life of Mahomet*, new ed. p. 31.)

Shortly after the rebuilding of the Ka'bah, Muḥammad adopted 'Alī, the son of his friend and former guardian, Abū Ṭālib. 'Alī was at this time only six years old. About this period he admitted to his closest intimacy another person, unconnected with him by family ties, but of more equal age. This was Zaid, a slave-boy belonging to Khadījah, who, to gratify her husband, made him a present of the slave. Zaid was the son of Ḥāris̤ah, of the Banū 'Uẕrah, a tribe which occupied the region of South Syria, and had been taken captive and sold to Khadījah's grandfather as a slave. When Ḥāris̤ah heard that Muḥammad possessed Zaid, he came to Makkah and offered a large payment for his release. Muḥammad summoned Zaid, and gave him the option to go or stay. Zaid elected to stay, and Muḥammad, delighted with his faithfulness, gave him his liberty, and adopted him as his son. The freed man was henceforth known as *Zaid ibn Muḥammad*.

" Muḥammad was now approaching his fortieth year, and increased contemplation and reflection engaged his mind. The idolatry and moral debasement of his people pressed heavily upon him, and the dim and imperfect shadows of Judaism and Christianity excited doubts without satisfying them; and his mind was perplexed with uncertainty as to what was the true religion." (Muir's *Life of Mahomet*, new ed. p. 35.)

It is probable that it was at this time Muḥammad composed those Sūrahs of the Qur'ān which express the anxious yearning of an inquirer rather than the more positive teaching of an Apostle, and we would assign to this period the following verses of the Qur'ān, which, according to Muḥammadan commentators, are admitted to be of a very early date. (See Jalālu 'd-dīn's *Itqān*.)

Sūratu 'l-'Aṣr (ciii.):—

" I swear by the declining day!

" Verily, man's lot is cast amid destruction,

" Save those who believe and do the things which be right, and enjoin truth and enjoin each other to be patient."

Sūratu 'l-'Ādiyāt (c.):—

" By the snorting chargers!

" And those that dash off sparks of fire!

" And those that scour to the attack at morn!

" And stir therein the dust aloft;

" And cleave therein their midway through a host!

" Truly, man is to his Lord ungrateful,

" And of this he is himself a witness;

" And truly, he is vehement in the love of this world's good.

" Ah! knoweth he not, that when that which is in the graves shall be laid bare,

" And that which is in men's breasts shall be brought forth,

" Verily their Lord shall on that day be informed concerning them?"

Sūratu 'l-Fātiḥah (i.):—

" Praise be to God, Lord of all the worlds,

" The compassionate, the merciful!

" King of the day of reckoning!

" Thee *only* do we worship, and to Thee do we cry for help.

" Guide Thou us on the straight path,

" The path of those to whom Thou hast been gracious;—with whom thou art not angry, and who go not astray."

The latter Sūrah is the Fātiḥah, or initial prayer, &c., often recited in public worship, and it appears to contain, if not the very words, at all events the gist of the daily prayer of an anxious and inquiring soul.

These Sūrahs were most probably followed by others of a similar character, being poetical effusions rather than express enunciations of any definite teaching. For example, Sūrahs ci., xcv., civ., xcii., xci., cvi.

Muḥammad seems to have employed himself in such meditations as find expression in these Sūrahs, some years before he assumed the office of a divine teacher, for it was but slowly and by degrees that he was led on to believe that he was really called of God, to preach a reformation both to his own people and to all mankind.

Bewildered by his own speculations amidst uncertain flickerings of spiritual light, Muḥammad spent some time in retirement, and in the agonies of distress repeatedly meditated suicide. Perplexed with the mysterious destiny of man and the failure of repeated revelations, he would fall into ecstatic reveries, and it was during one of these seasons of retirement, in the cave of Ḥirā', that he believed an angel appeared to him in a dream, and that the first revelation came. According to the traditions collected by al-Bukhārī and Muslim (see Arabic edition, as Matthew's translation in the *Mishkāt* is defective in several very important particulars), the first communication was made to Muḥammad in a dream.

'Āyishah relates: " The first revelations which the Prophet of God received were in true dreams. He never dreamed but it came to pass as regularly as the dawn of day After this the Prophet went into retirement, and he used to seclude himself in a cave in Mount Ḥirā', and worship there day and night. He would, whenever he wished, return to his family at Makkah, and then go back again, taking with him the necessaries of life. Thus he continued to return to Khadījah from time to time, until one day the revelation came down to him, and the angel (*Malak*) came to him and said, 'Read' (*iqra'*); but the Prophet said, 'I am not a reader.' And the Prophet related that the angel took hold of him, and squeezed him as much as he could bear, and then said again, 'Read'; and the Prophet said, 'I am not a reader.' Then the angel took hold of him a second time, and squeezed him as much as he could bear, and then let him go, and said, 'Read'; then the Prophet said, 'I am not a reader.' Then the angel again seized the Prophet, and squeezed him, and said:—

'Read thou, in the name of thy Lord who created;—

'Created man out of clots of blood:—

'Read thou! For thy Lord is the most Beneficent,

'Who hath taught the use of the pen;—

'Hath taught man that which he knoweth not.'

(See Qur'ān, Sūratu 'l-'Alaq (xcvi.), the first five verses.)

Then the Prophet repeated the words with a trembling heart. And he returned (*i.e.* from Ḥirā' to Makkah) to Khadījah, and said, 'Wrap me up, wrap me up.' And they wrapped him up in a garment until his fear was dispelled; and he told Khadījah what had occurred, and he said to Khadījah, 'I was afraid I should die.' Then Khadījah said, 'No, it will not be so, I swear by God. He will never make thee melancholy or sad. For you are kind to your relatives, you speak the truth, you are faithful in trust, you bear the afflictions of the people, you spend in good works what you gain in trade, you are hospitable, and you assist your fellow men.' After this Khadījah took the Prophet to Waraqah, who was the son of her uncle, and said to him, 'O son of my uncle, hear what your brother's son says to you.' Then Waraqah said to the Prophet, 'O son of my uncle, what do you see?' Then the Prophet told Waraqah what he had seen; and Waraqah said, 'This is the *Nāmūs* [NAMUS] which God sent to Moses. O would to God I were young in this time! and would to God I were living at the time of your people turning you out!' The Prophet said, 'Will my people turn me out?' And Waraqah said, 'Yes. No man has ever come as you have come, and not been held in enmity; but if I should live to that day, I will give you great help.' Waraqah soon died, and after that the revelation ceased (*i.e.* for a time)."

The first vision was followed by a considerable period, during which no further revelation was given, and during which Muḥammad suffered much mental depression. [FITRAH.]

"During this period," al-Bukhārī says, "the Prophet was very sorrowful, so much so that he wished to throw himself from the top of a hill to destroy himself."

But after a lapse of time, as he was wrapped up in his garments and lay stretched upon his carpet, the angel is said to have again addressed him, in the chapter which begins (Sūrah lxxiv.)—

"O thou enwrapped in thy mantle,
Arise and preach!"

Muḥammad then believed himself to be a commissioned Apostle, the messenger and the prophet of God, sent to reclaim a fallen people to the knowledge and service of their God. His revelations were God's Book, and his sayings the utterances of inspiration.

The first convert to Islām was his faithful wife Khadījah, the two next, 'Alī and Zaid, his adopted children, and afterwards his old trusted friend, Abū Bakr, "the True." Then followed 'Usmān, who was a grandson of 'Abdu 'l-Muṭṭalib; Ṭalḥah, the renowned warrior of after days; and 'Abdu 'r-Raḥmān, a merchant of some consequence. The new converts soon numbered some fifty souls, either members of the Prophet's family or his dearest friends.

An important change now occurred in the relations of Muḥammad with the citizens of Makkah. Their hostility was aroused, and the Muslims were subjected to some persecution and indignity. It was not, however, until some three years of his ministration had elapsed that any general opposition was organized. Hostility once excited soon showed itself in acts of violence. Sa'īd, a youthful convert, was attacked whilst leading a party of Muslims in prayer. He defended himself, and struck one of his opponents with a camel goad. It was, says Sir William Muir, "the first blood spilt in the cause of Islām."

In the fourth year of his mission, Muḥammad took possession of the house of Arqam (a recent convert), and there held meetings for those who wished to know the teaching of the Prophet more perfectly.

The house of Arqam was in front of the Ka'bah, and was therefore in a convenient position. So famous did it become as the birth-place of believers, that it was afterwards styled the "House of Islām."

As the number of believers increased, so did the enmity of the persecutor, and in order to escape the danger of perversion, Muḥammad recommended such of his followers who were without protection to seek an asylum in a foreign land. Eleven men, accompanied by their families, set out for the port of Shueiba, where, finding two vessels about to sail, they embarked in haste, and were conveyed to Abyssinia.

Here they met with a kind reception from the Negus, or king, and their period of exile was passed in peace and comfort. This is termed the first *hijrah*, or "flight," to Abyssinia, as distinguished from the later and more extensive emigration to the same land. In three months the refugees returned to Makkah.

About this time a strange episode occurred, in which Muḥammad sought a compromise with his people, by admitting their gods into his system as intercessors with the Supreme Being. While the Quraish sat beneath the Ka'bah, he recited the following Sūrah as an inspired message (liii.):—

"And see ye not Lāt and 'Uzzā,
And Manāt the third besides?

These are exalted females,
And verily their intercession is to be hoped for."

The idolaters were reconciled, and bowed before the God of Muḥammad. But his heart smote him, and not long after the obnoxious lines (those in italics) were said to be recalled by Gabriel, as suggested by the Evil One, and there was substituted the uncompromising denunciation of idolatry, from which he never after swerved:—

"What! shall there be male progeny unto you, and females unto him?

"That indeed were an unjust partition.

"They are naught but names which ye and your fathers have invented."

In the sixth year of his mission, the cause of Muḥammad was strengthened by the accession of two powerful citizens, Ḥamzah and ʿUmar. Ḥamzah was the uncle and also the foster-brother of the Prophet, a man of distinguished bravery, whose heroism earned for him the title of the "Lion of God." ʿUmar was a bold impulsive spirit, the very man needed to give strength to a cause, one who in a remarkable manner left the impress of his character upon the religious system he embraced. He succeeded Abū Bakr in the Khalīfate, and left the stamp of his fierce warlike spirit upon Islām. [UMAR.]

Alarmed at the bold part which Muḥammad and his followers were now able to assume, the Quraish formed a hostile confederacy, by which all intercourse with the Muslims and their supporters was suspended. The severity of the ban at last overreached its object, for the sympathies of the people were enlisted by their privation in favour of Muḥammad and his followers. The interdict was cancelled and the Hāshimites restored to freedom.

In the beginning of the tenth year of his mission, and in the fiftieth of his life, Muḥammad lost his faithful and devoted wife Khadījah. For twenty-five years she had been his counsellor and support, and his grief at her death at first was inconsolable. She was sixty-five years old when she died. Abū Ṭālib, the Prophet's uncle and guardian, died a few weeks afterwards. His conversion to Islām is a matter of uncertainty. Within two months of the death of Khadījah (who was his only wife during her lifetime), the Prophet married Saudah, the widow of one of the Abyssinian emigrants, and also betrothed himself to ʿĀyishah, the daughter of his friend Abū Bakr, then but a girl of seven years.

Abū Ṭālib had hardly been buried a fortnight when Muḥammad, followed only by his faithful attendants, set out on an adventurous mission to aṭ-Ṭāʾif, a place sixty miles to the east of Makkah, and the nearest city of importance. He went first to the three principal men of the city, and explained the object of his mission, and invited them to the honour of supporting him in sustaining the new faith. But he failed in producing conviction. Muḥammad remained at aṭ-Ṭāʾif ten days, but with no success. The mob, stirred up to hasten the departure of the unwelcome visitor, hooted at him in the streets, and pelted him with stones, and at last compelled him to flee out of the city. They chased him fully two miles across the sandy plain, until wearied and mortified, he took refuge for the night in a neighbouring garden, where he spent some time in earnest prayer. (Muir, 2nd ed., p. 114.)

Reinvigorated by the rest, he set forth on the return journey to Makkah.

Repulsed from aṭ-Ṭāʾif, and utterly hopeless at home, the fortunes of Muḥammad seemed dark, but hope dawned at last from an unexpected quarter. At the yearly pilgrimage, a little group of worshippers from al-Madīnah was attracted and won over at Minā by the preaching of Islām, joined his mission, and the following year they met Muḥammad and took the oath of allegiance which is known as the first *Pledge of ʿAqabah.* This little party consisted of twelve men, ten were of the Khazraj and two of the Aus tribe. They plighted their faith to Muḥammad as follows:—"We will not worship any but one God, we will not steal, neither will we commit adultery, nor will we kill our children; we will not slander in anywise; and we will obey the Prophet in everything that is just."

At al-Madīnah the claims of the new Prophet found a ready response. A teacher was deputed from Makkah to al-Madīnah, and the new faith spread with marvellous rapidity.

The hopes of Muḥammad were now fixed on al-Madīnah, visions of his journey northwards doubtless flitted before his imagination and the musing of the day, reappeared in his midnight slumbers.

He dreamed that he was swiftly carried by Gabriel on a winged steed past al-Madīnah to the Temple of Jerusalem, where he was welcomed by the former Prophets all assembled in solemn conclave. From Jerusalem he seemed to mount upwards, and to ascend from one heaven to another, until he found himself in the awful presence of his Maker, who dismissed him with the order that he should command his followers to pray five times a day. [MIʿRAJ, BURAQ.]

When the time of pilgrimage again arrived, Muḥammad found himself surrounded by an enthusiastic band of seventy disciples from al-Madīnah, who in a secret defile at Minā plighted their faith, the second *Pledge of Aqabah,* whereby they promised to receive and defend the Faith at the risk of their own lives. After this Muḥammad determined to quit Makkah, and the command was given, "Depart unto al-Madīnah, for the Lord hath verily given you brethren in that city, and a house in which ye may find refuge." And so, abandoning house and home, the Muslims set out secretly in little parties for al-Madīnah, where the numbers soon reached to about one hundred and fifty, counting women and children. Muḥammad, with Abū Bakr and ʿAlī, with their families, were left almost alone in Makkah. The Quraish held a council, and determined to slay Muḥammad; but being warned of their designs, he escaped to Mount Ṣaur, near Makkah, where he hid himself three days in a cave, and after three more days he reached al-Madīnah.

The day of his flight, or *hijrah*, marks the Muḥammadan era, or Hegira. The date of the flight was the 4th of Rabīʿu 'l-Awwal, and by the calculations of M. Caussin de Perceval, the 20th of June, A.D. 622. [HIJRAH.]

The flight to al-Madīnah changes the scene, and with it the character of the portions of the Qur'ān revealed there. He who at Makkah is the admonisher and persuader, at al-Madīnah is the legislator and the warrior, and the verses of the Qur'ān assume a more didactic tone. Poetry makes way for prose, and he openly assumes the office of a public warner and prophet.

The idolaters of Makkah disappear and their place is taken by the hypocrites [MUNAFIQUN] of al-Madīnah. Here at al-Madīnah there was no opposition to Muḥammad and his doctrines; but, nevertheless, an undercurrent of disaffection prevailed. The head of the party was ʿAbdu 'llāh ibn Ubaiy, who, but for the new turn in the fortunes of the city was on the point of being its chief. These disaffected citizens, the *munāfiqūn*, or "hypocrites," as they are called, continued to be the objects of bitter denunciation in the Qur'ān till near the close of the Prophet's career. But before the success of Islām they too vanish from the scene.

The first year of Muḥammad's residence at al-Madīnah was chiefly occupied in building the great mosque [MASJIDU 'N-NABI], and in providing houses for himself and his followers. In a short time he became the recognised chief of the city. The mosque and the houses were finished within seven months of Muḥammad's arrival. About the middle of the winter he left the house of Abū Aiyūb, with whom he had been staying, and installed Saudah in her new residence. Shortly afterwards he celebrated his nuptials with ʿĀyishah, who, though she had been three years affianced, was but a girl of ten years.

Thus, at the age of fifty-three, a new phase commenced in the life of Muḥammad. Hitherto limiting himself to a single wife, he had shunned the indulgence, but he now surrounds himself with the cares and discord, of polygamy. The unity of his family was now broken, never again to be restored. Thenceforward his love was to be claimed, his attentions shared by a plurality of wives, and his days spent between their houses, for Muḥammad had no separate apartments of his own.

Those Muslims who had left Makkah with the Prophet and settled in al-Madīnah, were now known as the Refugees [MUHAJIRUN] whilst those who embraced the faith at al-Madīnah, were designated the Assistants or Allies [ANSAR]. Both these names in time became titles of distinguished honour.

In the second year of the Ḥijrah, Muḥammad commenced hostilities against the Quraish, and the first pitched battle took place at Badr. With an army of 305 followers, of whom two-thirds were citizens of al-Madīnah, Muḥammad routed a force three times the number. The following graphic description of the battle of Badr is given by Sir William Muir. (New ed. p. 230.)

"The valley of Badr consists of a plain, with steep hills to the north and east; on the south is a low rocky range; and on the west rise a succession of sandy hillocks. A rivulet, rising in the inland mountains, runs through the valley, producing along its course numerous springs, which here and there were dug into cisterns for the accommodation of travellers. At the nearest of these springs, the army of Mahomet halted. Habâl, a citizen of Medîna, advised him to proceed onwards. 'Let us go,' he said, 'to the farthest spring, on the side of the enemy. I know a never-failing fountain of sweet water there; let us make that our reservoir, and destroy the other wells.' The advice was good. It was at once adopted, and the command of the water thus secured.

"The night was drawing on. So they hastily constructed near the well a hut of palm branches, in which Mahomet and Abu Bakr slept. Sâd ibn Muâdz (Saʿd ibn Muʿāẕ) kept watch by the entrance with his drawn sword. It rained during the night, but more heavily towards the camp of the Coreish. The Moslim army, wearied with its long march, enjoyed sound and refreshing sleep. The dreams of Mahomet turned upon his enemies, and they were pictured to his imagination as a weak and contemptible force.

"In the morning he drew up his little army, and, pointing with an arrow which he held in his hand, arranged the ranks. The previous day he had placed the chief banner, that of the Refugees, in the hands of Musâl, who nobly proved his right to the distinction. The Khazrajite ensign was committed to Hobâb; that of the Bani Aus, to Sâd ibn Muâdz.

"Meanwhile, dissension again broke out in the camp of the Coreish, on the policy of fighting against their kinsmen. Shaiba and Otba (ʿUtbah), two chiefs of rank, influenced, it is said, by their slave Addâs (the same who comforted the Prophet on his flight from Tâyif), strongly urged that the attack should be abandoned. Just then, Omeir, a diviner by arrows, having ridden hastily round the valley, returned to report the result of his reconnaisance. 'Ye Coreish,' he said, after telling them his estimate of the enemy's number, 'calamities approach you, fraught with destruction. Inevitable death rideth upon the camels of Yathreb (Yaṣrib). It is a people that hath neither defence nor refuge but in their swords. They are dumb as the grave; their tongues they put forth with the serpent's deadly aim. Not a man of them shall we kill, but in his stead one of ourselves also will be slain; and when there shall have been slaughtered amongst us a number equal unto them, of what avail will life be to us after that?' These words began to produce a pacific effect, when Abu Jahl, as before, loudly opposed the proposals for peace. Turning to Amir the Hadhramite, he bade him call to mind the blood of his brother slain at Nakhla. The flame was rekindled. Amir threw off his clothes, cast dust upon his body, and began frantically to cry aloud his brother's name. The deceased had been a confederate of the family of Shaiba and Otba ('Utbah). Their pride and honour were affected. They saw that thoughts of peace must now be scattered to the winds; and they resolved signally to vindicate themselves from the imputation of cowardice cast on them by Abu Jahl. The army was drawn up in line. The three standards for the centre and wings were borne, according to ancient privilege, by members of the house of Abd al Dar. They moved forward but slowly over the intervening sand-hills, which the rain had made heavy and fatiguing. The same cause, acting with less intensity, had rendered the ground in front of Mahomet lighter and more firm to walk upon. The Coreish laboured under another disadvantage; they had the rising sun before them, while the army of Medina faced the west.

"Mahomet had barely arrayed his line of battle, when the advanced column of the enemy was discerned over the rising sands in front. Their greatly superior numbers were concealed by the fall of the ground behind, and this imparted confidence to the Moslems. But Mahomet was fully alive to the critical position. The fate of Islam hung upon the issue of the approaching battle. Followed by Abu Bakr, he hastened for a moment into the little hut, and raising his hands, poured forth these earnest petitions, "O Lord, I beseech Thee, forget not Thy promise of assistance and of victory. O Lord! if this little band be vanquished, idolatry will prevail, and the pure worship of thee cease from off the earth!' 'The Lord,' said Abu Bakr, comforting him, 'will surely come to thine aid, and will lighten thy countenance with the joy of victory.'

"The time for action had arrived. Mahomet again came forth. The enemy was already close; but the army of Medîna remained still. Mahomet had no cavalry to cover an advance, and before superior numbers he must keep close his ranks. Accordingly the Prophet had strictly forbidden his followers to stir till he should give the order for advance; only they were to check any flank movement of the Coreish by the discharge of arrows. The cistern was guarded as their palladium. Certain desperate warriors of the Coreish swore that they would drink water from it, destroy it, or perish in the attempt. Scarcely one returned from the rash enterprise. With signal gallantry, Aswad advanced close to the brink, when a blow from Hamza's sword fell upon his leg, and nearly severed it from his body. Still defending himself, he crawled inwards and made good his vow; for he drank of the water, and with his remaining leg demolished part of the cistern before the sword of Hamza put an end to his life.

"Already, after the fashion of Arabian warfare, single combats had been fought at various points, when the two brothers Shaiba and Otba, and Walîd the son of Otba, still smarting from the words of Abu Jahl, advanced into the space between the armies, and defied three champions from the army of Mahomet to meet them singly. Three citizens of Medîna stepped forward; but Mahomet, unwilling either that the glory or the burden of the opening conflict should rest with his allies, called them back; and, turning to his kinsmen said: 'Ye sons of Hâshim! arise and fight, according to your right.' Then Obeida ('Ubaidah), Hamza, and Ali, the uncle and cousins of the Prophet, went forth. Hamza wore an ostrich feather in his breast, and a white plume distinguished the helmet of Ali. But their features were hid by their armour. Otba, therefore, not knowing who his opponents might be, cried aloud, 'Speak, that we may recognise you! If ye be equals, we shall fight with you.' Hamza answered, 'I am the son of Abd al Muttalib —Hamza, the Lion of God, and the Lion of His Prophet.' 'A worthy foe,' exclaimed, Otba; 'but who are these others with thee?' Hamza repeated their names. Otba replied, 'Meet foes, every one!'

"Then Otba called to his son Walîd, 'Arise and fight.' So Walîd stepped forth and Ali came out against him. They were the youngest of the six. The combat was short; Walîd fell mortally wounded by the sword of Ali. Eager to avenge his son's death, Otba hastened forward, and Hamza advanced to meet him. The swords gleamed quick, and again the Coreishite warrior was slain by the Moslim lion. Shaiba alone remained of the three champions of Mecca; and Obeida, the veteran of the Moslems, threescore years and five, now drew near to fight with him. Both being well advanced in years, the conflict was less decisive than before. At last, Shaiba dealt a sword-cut on the leg of Obeida with such force as to sever the tendon, and bring him to the ground. Seeing this, Hamza and Ali both rushed on Shaiba and despatched him. Obeida survived but for a few days, and was buried on the march back at Safra.

"The fate of their champions was ominous for the Coreish, and their spirits sank. The ranks began to close, with the battle-cry on the Moslem side of, 'Ye conquerors, strike!' and the fighting became general. But there were still many of those scenes of individual bravery which characterise the irregular warfare of Asiatic armies, and often impart to them a Homeric interest. Prodigies of valour were exhibited on both sides; but the army of the Faithful was borne forward by an enthusiasm which the half-hearted Coreish were unable to withstand.

"What part Mahomet himself took in the battle is not clear. Some traditions represent him moving along the ranks with a drawn sword. It is more likely (according to others) that he contented himself with inciting his followers by the promise of divine assistance, and by holding out the prospect of Paradise to those who fell The spirit of Omeir, a lad of but sixteen years, was kindled within him as he listened to the Prophet's words. Tradition delights to tell of the ardour with which the stripling threw away a handful of dates which he was eating. 'Is it these,' he exclaimed, 'that hold me back from Paradise? Verily I will taste no more of them until I meet my Lord!' With such words, he drew his sword, and, casting himself upon the enemy, soon obtained the fate he coveted.

"It was a stormy wintry day. A piercing blast swept across the valley. 'That,' said Mahomet, 'is Gabriel with a thousand angels flying as a whirlwind at our foe.' Another, and yet another blast:—it was Michael, and after him, Seraphîl, each with a like angelic troop. The battle raged. The Prophet stooped, and lifting a handful of gravel, cast it towards the Coreish, and cried, 'Confusion seize their faces!' The action was well timed. The line of the Coreish began to waver. Their movements were impeded by the heavy sands on which they stood; and, when the ranks gave way, their numbers added but confusion. The Moslems followed eagerly on their retreating steps, slaying or taking captive all that fell within their reach. Retreat soon turned into ignominious flight. The Coreish, in their haste to escape, cast away their armour and abandoned their beasts of burden with the camp and equipage. Forty-nine were killed, and about the same number taken prisoners. Mahomet lost only fourteen, of whom eight were citizens of Medîna, and six Refugees.

"Many of the principal men of the Coreish, and some of Mahomet's bitterest opponents, were slain. Chief amongst these was Abu Jahl. Muâdz brought him to the ground by a blow which cut his leg in two. Muâdz, in his turn, was attacked by Ikrima ('Ikrimah), the son of Abu Jahl, and his arm nearly severed from his shoulder. As the mutilated limb hanging by the skin impeded his action, Muâdz put his foot upon it, pulled it off, and went on his way fighting. Such were the heroes of Bedr. Abu Jahl was yet breathing when Abdallah, Mahomet's servant, ran up, and cutting off his head, carried it to his master. 'The head of the enemy of God!' exclaimed Mahomet. 'God! There is none other God but He!' 'There is no other!' responded Abdallah, as he cast the bloody head at the Prophet's feet. 'It is more acceptable to me,' cried Mahomet, 'than the choicest camel in all Arabia.'

"But there were others whose death caused no gratification to Mahomet. Abdul Bokhtari had shown him special kindness at the time when he was shut up in the quarter of Abu Tâlib; Mahomet, mindful of this favour, had commanded that he should not be harmed. Abdul Bokhtari had a companion seated on his camel behind him. A warrior, riding up, told him of the quarter given by Mahomet; but added, 'I cannot spare the man behind thee.' 'The women of Mecca,' Abdul Bokhtari exclaimed, 'shall never say that I abandoned my comrade through love of life. Do thy work upon us.' So they were killed, both he and his companion.

"After the battle was over, some of the prisoners were cruelly put to death. The following incident illustrates the savage spirit already characteristic of the faith. Omeya ibn Khalf and his son were unable to escape with the fugitive Coreish, and, seeing Abdal Rahmân pass, implored that he would make them his prisoners. Abdal Rahmân, mindful of an ancient friendship, cast away the plunder he was carrying, and, making both his prisoners, was proceeding with them to the Moslim camp. As the party passed, Bilâl espied his old enemy—for Omeya had used to persecute him—and he screamed aloud, 'Slay him. This man is the head of the unbelievers. I am lost, I am lost, if he lives!' From all sides the infuriated soldiers, hearing Bilâl's appeal, poured in upon the wretched captives; and Abdal Rahmân, finding resistance impossible, bade them save their lives as best they could. Defence was vain; and the two prisoners were immediately cut in pieces.

"When the enemy had disappeared, the army of Medîna was for some time engaged in gathering the spoil. Every man was allowed to retain the plunder of anyone whom he himself had slain. The rest was thrown into a common stock. The booty consisted of one hundred and fifteen camels, fourteen horses, carpets and other articles of fine leather, vestments, and much equipage and armour. A diversity of opinion arose about the distribution. Those who had hotly pursued the enemy and exposed their lives in securing the spoil, claimed the whole, or at the least a superior portion; while such as had remained behind upon the field of battle for the safety of the Prophet and of the camp, urged that they had equally with the others fulfilled the part assigned to them, and that, having been restrained by duty from the pursuit, they were entitled to a full share of the prey. The contention was so sharp, that Mahomet interposed with a message from heaven, and assumed possession of the whole booty. It was God who had given the victory, and to God the spoil belonged: 'They will ask thee concerning the prey. Say, the prey is God's and his Prophet's. Wherefore fear God, and dispose of the matter rightly among youselves; and be obedient unto God and His Prophet, if ye be true Believers'—and so on in the same strain. Shortly afterwards, the following ordinance, which the Mussulman law of prize recognises to the present day, was given forth: 'And know that whatsoever thing ye plunder, verily one fifth thereof is for God and for the Prophet, and for him that is of kin (unto the Prophet), and for the orphans, and the poor, and the wayfarer—if ye be they that believe in God, and in that which We sent down to our Servant on the Day of Discrimination, the day on which the two armies met; and God is over all things powerful.' (See Qur'ān, Sūrah viii.)

"In accordance with the divine command,

the booty was gathered together on the field, and placed under a special officer, a citizen of Medîna. The next day it was divided, near Safra, in equal allotments, among the whole army, after the Prophet's fifth had been set apart. All shared alike, excepting that the horsemen received each two extra portions for their horses. To the lot of every man fell a camel, with its gear; or two camels unaccoutred; or a leathern couch, or some such equivalent. Mahomet obtained the famous camel of Abu Jahl, and a sword known by the name of Dzul Ficâr (Ẕū 'l-Fiqār). The sword was selected by him beyond his share, according to a custom which allowed him, in virtue of the prophetic dignity, to choose from the booty, before division, whatever thing might please him most.

"The sun was now declining, so they hastily dug a pit on the battle-field, and cast the enemy's dead into it. Mahomet looked on, as the bodies were brought up and cast in. Abu Bakr, too, stood by, and, examining their features, called aloud their names. 'Otba! Shaiba! Omeyya! Abu Jahl!' exclaimed Mahomet, as one by one the corpses were, without ceremony, thrown into the common grave. 'Have ye now found that which your Lord promised you true? What my Lord promised me, that verily have I found to be true. Woe unto this people! Ye have rejected me, your Prophet! Ye cast me forth, and others gave me refuge; ye fought against me, and others came to my help!' 'O Prophet!' said the bystanders, 'dost thou speak unto the dead?' 'Yea, verily,' replied Mahomet, 'for they well know that the promise of their Lord unto them hath fully come to pass.'

"At the moment when the corpse of Otba was tossed into a pit, a look of distress overcast the countenance of his son, Abu Hodzeifa (Abū Ḥuẕaifah). Mahomet turned kindly to him, and said, 'Perhaps thou art distressed for thy father's fate?' 'Not so, O Prophet of the Lord! I do not doubt the justice of my father's fate; but I knew well his wise and generous heart, and I had trusted that the Lord would have led him to the faith. But now that I see him slain, and my hope destroyed, it is for that I grieve.' So the Prophet comforted Abu Hodzeifa, and blessed him, and said, 'It is well.'

"The army of Medîna, carrying their dead and wounded, retired in the evening to the valley of Otheil, several miles from Bedr; and there Mahomet passed the night. On the morrow the prisoners were brought up before him. As he scrutinised each, his eye fell fiercely on Nadhr, son of Hârish (al-Naẓr ibn al-Ḥāriṡ). 'There was death in that glance,' whispered Nadhr, trembling, to a bystander. 'Not so,' replied the other, 'it is but thine own imagination.' The unfortunate prisoner thought otherwise, and besought Musâb to intercede for him. Musâb reminded him that he had denied the faith and persecuted Believers. 'Ah!' said Nadhr, 'had the Coreish made thee a prisoner, they would never have put thee to death!' 'Even were it so,' Musâb scornfully replied, 'I am not as thou art; Islâm hath rent all bonds asunder.' Micdâd, the captor, fearing lest the prisoner, and with him the chance of a rich ransom, was about to slip from his hands, cried out, 'The prisoner is mine!' But at this moment the command to 'Strike off his head!' was interposed by Mahomet, who had been watching what passed. 'And, O Lord!' he added, 'do thou of thy bounty grant unto Micdâd a better prey than this.' Nadhr was forthwith beheaded by Ali.

"Two days afterwards, about half-way to Medîna, Ocba, another prisoner, was ordered out for execution. He ventured to expostulate and demand why he should be treated more rigorously than the other captives. 'Because of thy enmity to God and to His Prophet,' replied Mahomet. 'And my little girl!' cried Ocba, in the bitterness of his soul, 'who will take care of her?' 'Hell-fire!' exclaimed the heartless conqueror, and on the instant his victim was hewn to the ground. 'Wretch that thou wast!' continued Mahomet, 'and persecutor! unbeliever in God, in His Prophet, and in His Book! I give thanks unto the Lord that hath slain thee, and comforted mine eyes thereby.'"

Such was the battle of Badr Insignificant in numbers, but most memorable in the annals of Islām on account of its important results. It was at Badr that "the Prophet" first drew the sword in the assertion of his claim as a commissioned apostle of the Most High God, and the victory is attributed in the Qur'ān to the direct intervention of the Almighty. See Sūrah iii. 11:—

"Ye have already had a sign in the meeting of the two hosts. The one host fought in the cause of God, and the other was infidel To their own eye-sight, the infidels saw you twice as many as themselves: And God aided with His succour whom He would: And in this truly was a lesson for men endued with discernment."

Al-Baiẓāwī, the commentator, says 3,000 angels fought for the Muslims on the battle-field of Badr.

Muḥammad was received in triumph at al-Madīnah, but his joy was interrupted by the death of his daughter Ruqaiyah, the divorced wife of 'Utbah ibn Lahab, but who had been afterwards married to Uṣmān ibn 'Affān. On his return to al-Madīnah (A.H. 3), Muḥammad found his position much strengthened, and from this time the Qur'ān assumes a rude dictatorial tone. He who at one time only spoke as a searcher after truth, now demands unhesitating obedience from the whole country of Arabia.

The Jews, however, were still unimpressed and were slow to acknowledge Muḥammad, although he claimed to be but the teacher of the creed of Abraham. Muḥammad sought but a plausible excuse for a rupture with the sons of Israel, and an opportunity soon presented itself. A Muslim girl was insulted by a youth of a Jewish tribe, and, taking advantage of the circumstance, the whole tribe was attacked, proscribed, and banished. Their houses and lands were confiscated and divided amongst the Faithful. In the course of the same year, Ka'b ibn al-Ashraf, a Jew, was assassinated because he annoyed the Muslims with his verses. About this time, Muḥammad married his fourth wife, Ḥafṣah, the daughter of 'Umar the celebrated Ḵẖalīfah. In the early part of the year, al-Ḥasan, the son of Fāṭimah and 'Alī, was born.

The tidings of the defeat at Badr aroused the bitterest feelings of the Quraish. They advanced upon al-Madīnah 3,000 strong. In ten days the Makkan army reached Ẕū 'l-halfah, four miles south of al-Madīnah, and then moving northwards, they encamped at Uḥud, an isolated mountain three miles north-east of the city. Muḥammad, clad in armour, led out his army of 1,000 men, and halted for the night; and at early dawn advanced on Uḥud. He was soon abandoned by 'Abdu 'llāh, the chief of the Hypocrites [MUNAFI-QUN] with 300 of his followers.

Ḵẖālid ibn al-Walīd, a name afterwards famous in Muslim history, commanding the right wing of the Quraish, attacked the Muslims, and raised the cry, " Muḥammad is slain ! " The confusion of the Faithful was great, and defied all the efforts of Muḥammad to rally them. The Prophet himself was wounded in the face by two arrows. The Muslims were completely defeated, but the retreat was ably conducted by Abū Bakr, 'Umar, and 'Uṣmān, and the victorious Quraish did not attempt a pursuit.

Abū 'l-Fidā' gives the following quaint account of the battle :—

" When the two armies engaged and approached each other, Hind, daughter of 'Utbah, the wife of Abū Sufyān, arose with the women that were with her, and they beat upon the tabors as they followed the men to battle. And Hind said, ' Well done, ye sons of 'Abdu 'd-Dār, well done ? Strike ye with every weapon ye possess." And Ḥamzah, the Prophet's uncle, fought most valiantly that day; and he slew Artah, the standard-bearer of the unbelievers."

" And Abū Kamiyah, the Laiṣite slew Muṣ'ab, the standard-bearer of the Muslims, and when Muṣ'ab was slain, the Prophet gave the standard of Islām to 'Alī, the son of Abū Ṭālib. Now, the archers were too eager for the spoil, and they left the position in which Muḥammad had posted them. And Ḵẖālid, the leader of the unbelievers, came with the cavalry to the rear of the Muslims, and raised a cry that Muḥammad was slain. So the Muslims were overcome by the unbelievers, and the Quraish gained the victory. The number of martyrs in the cause of Islām who fell at Uḥud was seventy. The number of the slain amongst the unbelievers was twenty-two. The enemy even struck Muḥammad. Their stones hit him and he fell. His foreteeth were struck out, and he was wounded in the face. Two nails of the helmet entered the face of Muḥammad. And Abū 'Ubaidah pulled one of the nails out of his face and

one tooth dropped out ; and he pulled out another nail and another tooth dropped out. And when Abū 'Ubaidah was taking out the teeth, Sunān Abū Sa'īd sucked the blood from Muḥammad's face and swallowed it. Upon which the Prophet said, ' Whosoever toucheth my blood, him shall the fire of hell never touch.'

" Then Hind and her companions fell on the Muslims who were slain, and cut off their noses and their ears. And Hind cut a slice from Ḥamzah's liver and ate it. Then Abū Sufyān, the husband of Hind, stuck his spear into Ḥamzah's body, and cried with a loud voice, ' The fortunes of war are uncertain ! The day of Uḥud for the day of Badr ! Let the idol of Hubal be exalted ! ' Then Muḥammad sought for the body of his uncle, and he found it lying on the ground with the belly ripped open and the ears and nose cut off. And the Prophet said, ' God hath revealed to me concerning the Quraish. Verily, retaliation shall be made on thirty of them for the death of Ḥamzah, and verily Ḥamzah is now in the seventh heaven.' Then Muḥammad prayed for Ḥamzah, and went to each of the bodies of the slain and prayed for them. Some of the Muslims wanted ‚to carry their dead to al-Madīnah, but the Prophet said, ' Bury them where they fell.' "

There is an allusion to the defeat at Uḥud in the third Sūrah of the Qur'ān : " What befell you when the two armies met by God's permission. Count not those who are killed in the way of God as dead. They are living with their Lord."

The fourth year of the Hijrah (A.D. 625) opened with the despatch of 500 Muslims against the tribe of Asd, who were making preparations to invade al-Madīnah. The enemy fled at the appearance of the Muslim troops, and the place was sacked.

During this year there were several expeditions. Amongst others, one against the Jewish tribe Banū Naẓīr, whose homes were spoiled, and the people banished, because they would not accept the mission of the " Apostle of God." There is an allusion to this event in the second Sūrah of the Qur'ān. A second expedition was also made to Badr, but there was no fighting, although the event is known as the second battle of Badr ; for after waiting eight days for an engagement with the Quraish, the Muslims returned in triumph to al-Madīnah.

It was about this time that Muḥammad made two additions to his ḥaram, by marrying Zaināb, the widow of 'Ubaidah, who fell at Badr, as his fifth wife, and Ummu Salimah, the widow of Abū Salimah, who fell at the battle of Uḥud, for his sixth ; thus exceeding the legal number of four wives, to which he restricted his followers.

Muḥammad being threatened by combined contingents of the Quraish, the Banū Ḡẖaṭfān and the Jewish tribes of Naẓīr and Quraizah, who advanced upon al-Madīnah with an army of 12,000 men, he, at the advice of a Persian named Salmān, caused a trench to be dug round the city, and then issued forth to defend it at the head of 3,000 Muslims. Both sides remained inactive for nearly a month, when, at last, the Quraish and their allies broke up the siege. This engagement is known in Muslim history as *Gazwatu 'l-Khandaq*, or the "Battle of the Ditch." Special reference is made to this event in the Qur'ān, Sūrah xxxiii. 9, where the success of the Muslims is attributed to the intervention of God, "who sent a blast and a host that were not seen."

The next expedition was against the Jewish tribe, the Banū Quraiẓah, when Muḥammad led an army of three thousand men with thirty-six horse. The Jews sustained a siege of some twenty-five days, but were at last compelled to capitulate. Their fate was left to the decision of the Prophet's companion, Sa'd, whose sentence was that the male captives should be slain, the female captives and children sold into slavery, and the spoils divided amongst the army. The Prophet commended the cruel judgment of Sa'd, as a decision according to the judgment of God, given on high from the seven heavens; and about 700 captives were deliberately beheaded, in parties in the presence of Muḥammad. One of the female captives, Rīḥānah, whose husband and male relatives had perished in the massacre, the Prophet reserved for himself. This cruel massacre of the Banū Quraiẓah is commended in the XXXIIIrd Sūrah of the Qur'ān, verse 25.

Before the close of this year, Muḥammad married his cousin Zainab. The Prophet had previously given her in marriage to Zaid ibn Ḥāriṣah, his freed man and adopted son. But upon visiting the house of Zaid, and not finding him at home, the Prophet accidentally cast his eyes on Zainab, and was so smitten with her beauty, that he exclaimed, "Praise belongeth unto God, who turneth the hearts of men even as He will." Zainab saw that she had made an impression on the Prophet's heart, and when her husband returned, recounted the circumstances to him. Zaid determined to part with her in favour of his friend and benefactor, and offered to divorce her. But the relations of the Arabs to their adopted children were so strict, that nothing but a revelation from heaven could settle the difficulty. It was to meet this domestic emergency that the Prophet produced the following verses of the Qur'ān, Sūrah xxxiii. 36–38, to sanction his own heart's desire:—

"And it is not for a believer, man or woman, to have any choice in their affairs, when God and His Apostle have decreed a matter: and whoever disobeyeth God and His Apostle, erreth with palpable error. And, *remember*, when thou saidst to him unto whom God had shown favour, and to whom thou also hadst shown favour, 'Keep thy wife to thyself, and fear God;' and thou didst hide in thy mind what God would bring to light, and thou didst fear man; but more right had it been to fear God. And when Zaid had settled concerning her to divorce her, we married her to thee, that it might not be a crime in the faithful to marry the wives of their adopted sons, when they have settled the affair concerning them. And the behest of God is to be performed. No blame attacheth to the Prophet where God hath given him a permission. Such was the way of God with those prophets who flourished before thee."

The scandal of the marriage was removed by the pretended revelation, and according to the Traditions, Zainab used to vaunt herself as the one wife of the Prophet's harīm who had been given in marriage by God Himself. At all events, she exchanged a husband who had a pug nose and was short and ill-favoured for one who was the leading chief of Arabia!

Muḥammad's numerous marriages (four being the legal number—Sūrah iv. 3) were likely to excite the jealousy and opposition of less favoured Muslims, but an additional chapter of the Qur'ān avoided complications, and allowed the "Prophet of God" greater liberty in this respect! See Sūrah xxxiii. 49: "O Prophet, we have allowed thee thy wives whom thou hast dowered, and the slaves whom thy right hand possesseth . . . and any believing woman who has given herself up to the Prophet, if the Prophet desireth to wed her; a privilege for thee above the rest of the Faithful."

About this time certain injunctions were issued for the seclusion of women, and for the regulation of social and domestic intercourse (Sūrah xxv.). These rules were made more stringent in the case of the Prophet's own wives, who, in the case of incontinence, are threatened with double punishment (Sūrah xxxiii.). The jealousy of the Prophet, who was now getting old, was allayed by the Divine command, that his wives should, in the event of his death, never marry again. The obligation devolving on believers, to consort equally with their several wives, was also relaxed specially in the Prophet's favour (Sūrah xlviii.).

In the sixth year of the Hijrah several military expeditions were made. Amongst others, to the Banū Quraiẓah and the Banū Laḥyān. On his return from the last expedition Muḥammad stopped for a few moments to visit the grave of his mother, and desired to pray for her soul. But a verse from the Qur'ān, alleged to have been revealed on this occasion, forbade his praying for the forgiveness of one who died an infidel. Sūrah ix. 114, 115:—

"It is not for the Prophet or the Faithful to pray for the forgiveness of those, even though they be of kin, who associate other beings with God, after it hath been made clear to them that they are to be the inmates of Hell. For neither did Abraham ask forgiveness for his father, but in pursuance of a promise which he had promised to him: but when it was shown him that he was an enemy to God, he declared himself clear of him. Yet Abraham was pitiful, kind."

Muḥammad marched in person against the Banū 'l-Musṭaliq, and completely surprised and routed them. One thousand camels, five thousand sheep, and a great many women and children, became the spoil of the

Muslims. One of the female captives, named Juwairīyah, fell to the lot of Ṣābit ibn Qais, who, as a meritorious act, offered to release her and give her her liberty, for a certain sum. On applying to Muḥammad to help her with the money to pay the ransom, he readily agreed to do so, and when she was freed he married her. Thereupon, the Muslims recognised the Banū 'l-Muṣṭaliq as allies. Juwairīyah survived Muḥammad forty-five years.

At the last stage, returning from the campaign against the Banū 'l-Muṣṭaliq, 'Āyishah's tent and litter were by inadvertence carried away, while she was for a moment absent, and on her return she found herself in the dark alone. Expecting the mistake to be discovered, she sat down to await the issue, when, after some delay, one of the followers came up, and finding her in this plight, bade her mount his camel, and so conducted her to al-Madīnah. The citizens drew sinister conclusions from the circumstance, and Muḥammad himself became estranged from 'Āyishah, and she retired to her father's home. Several weeks elapsed, when, at length, the Prophet was supernaturally informed of her innocence (Sūrah xxiv.). The law was then promulgated which requires four eye-witnesses to establish the charge of adultery, in default of which the imputation is to be punished as a slander, with eighty lashes. [QAZAF.] 'Āyishah was taken back to her home, and her accusers were beaten.

It was during the year A.H. 6, that Muḥammad conceived the idea of addressing foreign sovereigns and princes, and of inviting them to embrace Islām. His letter to the Emperor Heraclius has been handed down by Ibn 'Abbās (*Mishkāt*, book xvii. ch. civ.), and is as follows:—

"In the name of God, the Compassionate, the Merciful, Muḥammad, who is the servant of God, and His Apostle, to Haraql, the Qaiṣar of Rūm. Peace be on whoever has gone on the straight road. After this I say, Verily, I call you to Islām. Embrace Islām, and God will reward you twofold. If you turn away from the offer of Islām, then on you be the sins of your people. O people of the Book (*i.e.* Christians), come towards a creed which is fit both for us and for you. It is this, to worship none but God, and not to associate anything with God, and not to call others God. Therefore, O ye people of the Book, if ye refuse, beware! We are Muslims, and our religion is Islām.

(Seal.)

"MUHAMMAD, the Apostle of God."

The letter was sent to the Governor of Buṣrā that he might convey it to Cæsar, but we have no record of a reply having been received.

He also wrote to Kasra-Parwiz, King of Persia, but Kasra tore the letter in pieces. On hearing the fate of his letter, Muḥammad said, "Even so shall his kingdom be shattered to pieces." His third embassy was to Najasih, the King of Abyssinia, who received the message with honour. The fourth was to Jarīḥ ibn Matta, the Muqauqis, or Governor, of Egypt. Jarīḥ sent a polite reply, and begged the Prophet's acceptance of two beautiful Coptic slave girls. One of these, Shirīn, the Prophet gave to Ḥassān the poet, but he reserved the other Māriyah, for himself. In due time, Māriyah presented the Prophet with a son, who was named Ibrāhīm, the birth of which made the mother a free woman, and placed her in the honourable position of the wife. But the Prophet's extreme fondness for the recent addition to his already extensive ḥarīm was resented by his numerous wives. 'Āyishah and Ḥafṣah were especially enraged, for the Prophet was in the habit of visiting Māriyah on the day due to one of these ladies. Ḥafṣah, who, being the daughter of 'Umar, was a person of great political importance, took up the matter, and in order to pacify her the Prophet swore solemnly that he would never visit Māriyah again, and enjoined Ḥafṣah to keep the secret from the rest of his wives. She, however, revealed it in confidence to 'Āyishah! Muḥammad was annoyed at finding his confidence betrayed, and separated himself for a whole month from his wives, and spent his time in Māriyah's apartment. The situation was a difficult one, not merely on account of the complications caused in his own domestic circle, but because 'Umar, the father of Ḥafṣah, was a most important political personage in those days. The only way out of the difficulty was to produce a third direct revelation from heaven, which appeared in the Sūratu 't-Taḥrīm, or the "Chapter of Prohibition" (lxvi.), of the Qur'ān, and reads as follows:—

"Why, O Prophet! dost thou hold that to be forbidden which God hath made lawful to thee, from a desire to please thy wives, since God is Lenient, Merciful? God hath allowed you release from your oaths; and God is your master; and He is the Knowing, Wise. When the Prophet told a recent occurrence as a secret to one of his wives (*i.e.* Ḥafṣah), and when she divulged it and God informed him of this, he acquainted her with part and withheld part. And when he had told her of it, she said, 'Who told thee this?' He said, 'The Knowing, the Sage hath told it me. If ye both be turned to God in penitence, for now have your hearts gone astray . . . but if ye conspire against the Prophet, then *know* that God is his Protector, and Gabriel, and every just man among the faithful; and the angels are his helpers besides. Haply if he put you both (*i.e.* Ḥafṣah and 'Āyishah) away, his Lord will give him in exchange other wives better than you, Muslims, believers, devout, penitent, obedient, observant of fasting, both known of men and virgins.'"

In the Muḥarram of A.H. 7, Muḥammad assembled a force of 1,600 men, and marched against Khaibar, a fertile district inhabited by the Jews, and situated about six days' march to the north-east of al-Madīnah. The attack on Khaibar taxed both the energy and skill of the Warrior Prophet, for it was defended by several fortresses. The fort

Qamuṣ was defended by Kinānah, a powerful Jewish chief, who claimed for himself the title of "King of the Jews." Several assaults were made and vigorously repulsed by the besieged. Both Abū Bakr and 'Umar were equally unsuccessful in their attempts to take the position, when the Prophet selected 'Alī to lead a detachment of picked men. A famous Jewish warrior named Marhab, now presented himself, and challenged 'Alī to single combat. The challenge was accepted, and 'Alī, armed with his famous sword "Zu 'l-Fiqār," given to him by the Prophet, cleft the head of his adversary in twain, and secured a victory. In a few days all the fortresses of the district were taken, and Khaibar was subjugated to Islām.

Amongst the female captives was Ṣafīyah, the widow of the chief Kinānah, who had fallen at Qamuṣ. One of Muḥammad's followers begged her for himself, but the Prophet, struck with her beauty, threw his mantle over her, and took her to his ḥarīm.

The booty taken at Khaibar was very considerable, and in order to secure the district to Muslim rule, the Jews of the district were exiled to the banks of the Jordan.

It was during the Khaibar expedition that Muḥammad instituted Mut'ah, an abominable temporary marriage, to meet the demands of his army. This is an institution still observed by the Shī'ahs, but said by the Sunnīs to have been abolished by Muḥammad. [MUT'AH.] It was at Khaibar that an attempt was made, by a Jewess named Zainab, to poison Muḥammad. She dressed a kid, and having steeped it in deadly poison, placed it before the Prophet, who ate but a mouthful of the poisoned kid when the deed was discovered. Zainab was immediately put to death.

The subjugation of the Jewish districts of Fadak, Wādī 'l-Qurā and Tannah, on the confines of Syria, followed that of Khaibar. This year, in the sacred month of Zu 'l-Qa'dah, Muḥammad decided to perform the 'Umrah, or religious vistation of Makkah ['UMRAH], and for this purpose he left al-Madīnah with a following of some 4,400 men. When they were within two days' march of Makkah, their advance was checked by the hostile Quraish, and Muḥammad, turning to the west from 'Usfān, encamped at al-Ḥudaibiyah, within seven miles of the sacred city. At this spot a truce was made, which is known as the treaty of al-Ḥudaibiyah, in which it was stipulated that all hostilities should cease for ten years, and that for the future the Muslims should have the privilege, unmolested, of paying a yearly visit of three days to the Ka'bah.

After sacrificing the victims at al-Ḥudaibiyah, Muḥammad and his followers returned to al-Madīnah.

The advent of the holy month Zū 'l-Qa'dah, of the next year (A.H. 8), was eagerly expected by Muḥammad and his followers, for then, according to the terms of the truce of al-Ḥudaibiyah, they might, without molestation, visit the holy city, and spend three days in the performance of the accustomed rites. The number of the faithful swelled on the approach to nearly 2,000 men, and the Quraish thought it best to retire with their forces to the heights overlooking the valley. Seated on his camel al-Qaṣwā, which eight years before had borne him in his flight from the cave of Ṣaur a hunted fugitive, the Prophet, now surrounded by joyous crowds of disciples, the companions of his exile, approached and saluted the holy shrine. Eagerly did he press forward to the Ka'bah, touched with his staff the Black Stone, seven times made the circuit of the holy house, seven times journeyed between aṣ-Ṣafā and al-Marwah, sacrificed the victims, and fulfilled all the ceremonies of the lesser pilgrimage.

While at Makkah he negotiated an alliance with Maimūnah, his eleventh and last wife. His marriage gained him two most important converts—Khālid, the "Sword of God," who before this had turned the tide of battle at Uḥud; and 'Amr, destined afterwards to carry to foreign lands the victorious standards of Islām.

The services of these two important converts were quickly utilised. An envoy from Muḥammad to the Christian Prince of Bostra, in Syria, having been slain by the chief of Mūtah—a village to the south-east of the Dead Sea—a force of 3,000 men, under his adopted son Zaid, was sent to exact retribution, and to call the offending tribe to the faith. On the northward march, though they learnt that an overwhelming force of Arabs and Romans—the latter of whom met the Muslims for the first time—was assembling to oppose them, they resolved resolutely to push forward. The result was their disastrous defeat and repulse. Zaid and Ja'far, a brother of 'Alī, fell defending the white banner of the Prophet. Khālid, by a series of manœuvres, succeeded in drawing off the army, and conducting it without further loss to al-Madīnah. A month later, however, 'Amr marched unopposed through the lands of the hostile tribes, received their submission, and restored the prestige of Islām on the Syrian frontier. Muḥammad deeply felt the loss of Zaid and Ja'far, and exhibited the tenderest sympathy for their widows and orphans.

The defeat at Mūtah was followed, in the south, by events of the greatest moment to Muḥammad. Certain smouldering hostilities between tribes inhabiting the neighbourhood of Makkah broke forth about the end of the year. These were judged to be infractions of the treaty (some of these tribes being in league with the Quraish), and were eagerly seized upon by Muḥammad, as justifying those designs upon Makkah which the success of his arms, and the dominion he possessed over numberless tribes in the north, in the Ḥijāz, and Najd, now made it easy for him to carry out.

Having, therefore, determined to attack his native city, he announced his intention to his followers, and directed his allies among the Bedouin tribe, to join him on the march to Makkah. Although he took every precaution to prevent his preparations becoming known, the news reached the ears of the Quraish, who sent Abū Sufyān to deprecate his anger and to ask him to abandon his purpose. Humiliation and failure were the only result of this mission.

On the 1st January, A.D. 630, Muḥammad's march commenced, and after eight days, through unfrequented roads and defiles, the army, swelled to the number of 10,000 men, halted and lighted their camp fires on the heights of Marru 'z-Ẓahrān, a day's march from the sacred city. The Prophet had been joined on his march by his uncle al-'Abbās, and on the night of his arrival Abū Sufyān again presented himself, and besought an interview. On the morrow it was granted. "Has the time not yet come, O Abū Sufyān," cried Muḥammad, "for thee to acknowledge that there is but one God, and that I am his Apostle." He answered that his heart still felt some hesitancy; but seeing the threatening sword of al-'Abbās, and knowing that Makkah was at the mercy of the Prophet, he repeated the prescribed formula of belief, and was sent to prepare the city for his approach.

The Prophet made his public entry into Makkah on his favourite camel, having Abū Bakr on his right hand, Usaid on his left, and Usāmah walking behind him. On his way he recited the XLVIIIth Sūrah of the Qur'ān, known as the "Chapter of Victory." He then entered the Sacred Mosque and circuited the Ka'bah seven times, touching the Black Stone as he passed with his stick. Observing several pictures of angels inside the Ka'bah, he ordered them to be removed, at the same time crying out with a loud voice, "God is great! God is great!" He then fixed the Qiblah [QIBLAH] at Makkah, and ordered the destruction of the 360 idols which the Makkan temple contained, himself destroying a wooden pigeon suspended from the roof, and regarded as one of the deities of the Quraish.

On the 11th day of the month of Ramaẓān, he repaired to Mount aṣ-Ṣafā, where all the people of Makkah had been assembled in order to take the oath of allegiance to him. 'Umar, acting as his deputy, administered the oath, whereby the people bound themselves to obey Muḥammad, to abstain from theft, adultery, infanticide, lying, and backbiting.

During his stay at Makkah, Muḥammad sent small detachments of troops into the district, who destroyed the temples of al-'Uzza, Suwa', and Manāt, the three famous idol-temples of the neighbouring tribes. The Prophet had given strict orders that these expeditions should be carried out in a peaceable manner, and that only in cases of necessity should force of arms be used. Khālid ibn al-Walīd, however, who commanded 350 men, found himself opposed by the Jazimah tribe, for instead of saying as they were commanded, "We are Muslims," they said, "We are Sabians"; and the impetuous general, whose name afterwards became so celebrated in history, ordered the whole tribe to be slain. Muḥammad, when he heard of this barbarity, exclaimed, "Oh! my God, I am innocent of this"; and he despatched a large sum of money for the widows and orphans of the slain, and severely rebuked Khālid.

The Prophet left Makkah after a fortnight's residence, and at the head of 12,000 men attacked the Banī Ṣaqīf and the Banī Hawāzin. Mālik ibn Ans, the chief of the Ṣaqīf, made a bold stand, and the Prophet rallied his forces with the utmost difficulty, but having thrown a handful of dust in the direction of the enemy as a signal of victory, the Muslims renewed the charge, and 700 of the tribe were left dead on the field. This victory was followed immediately by one over the Banū Hawāzin, in the valley of Auṭās. (See Sūrah ix. 25, 26.)

The ninth year of the Hijrah is known as the year of deputations, as being the year in which the various tribes of Arabia submitted to the claim of the Prophet, and sent embassies of peace to him. It is also remarkable for numerous minor expeditions.

Hearing that the Romans were assembling in large force on their frontier, Muḥammad determined to attack them at Tabūk (a city between al-Madīnah and Damascus). The army sent to Tabūk was the largest employed in the time of the Prophet, for it is said to have numbered 20,000, and 10,000 cavalry. By the time the army had arrived at Tabūk, the rumoured invasion had been proved unfounded. Muḥammad, however, utilised a portion of the force by sending it, under the command of Khālid, to Dūmah, where he received the submission of the Jewish and Christian tribes. A treaty with John, the Christian Prince of Ailah, was made, and Ukaidar, the Christian chief of Dūmah was converted to Islām.

The gradual submission of Arabia, and the acknowledgment of the spiritual and temporal supremacy of the Prophet throughout the entire peninsula, followed. Indeed, in the complex system which he had established, the spiritual and secular functions were intimately blended, and involved in each other, and whilst in his humble home at al-Madīnah he retained still the simple manners of his earlier years, which, at his time of life, he had probably no inclination to alter, he exercised all those regal and sacerdotal powers which the victorious arms of his lieutenants, or the voluntary submission of the most distant provinces of Arabia, had caused to be universally acknowledged. Tax-collectors were appointed to receive the prescribed offerings or tithes, which generally amounted to "a tenth part of the increase."

The city of aṭ-Ṭā'if, trusting to its natural strength, constituted itself a centre of disaffection; but at last, driven to extremities, and seeing that all the neighbouring tribes had one by one submitted, its chief, after a vain attempt to obtain some relaxation in the rules of Islām, consented to the destruction of the adored idol al-Lāt, and adopted the new faith.

It was during the time of the next yearly pilgrimage (March, A.D. 631), that Muḥammad issued an important command, the crowning stone of the system he had raised, which shows at once the power he wielded, and the strong hold his doctrines had already taken throughout Arabia. Refusing to be present himself during the ceremonies of the pilgrimage, he commissioned ʿAlī to announce to the assembled multitudes in the valley of Minā, that, at the expiration of the four sacred months, the Prophet would hold himself absolved from every obligation or league with idolaters; that after that year no unbeliever would be allowed to perform the pilgrimage, or to visit the holy places; and further, he gave directions that either within or without the sacred territory, war was to be waged with them, that they were to be killed, besieged, and laid in wait for "wheresoever found." He ordains, however, that if they repent and pay the legal alms, they are to be dismissed freely; but as regards "those unto whom the Scriptures have been delivered" (Jews and Christians, &c.), "they are to be fought against until they pay tribute by right of subjection, and are reduced low."

"Such, then," says Sir William Muir, "is the declared mission of Islam, arrived at by slow, though inevitable steps, and now imprinted unchangeably upon its banners. The Jews and Christians, and perhaps the Magians,—'people of the book'—are to be tolerated, but held in subjection, and under tribute; but for the rest, the sword is not to be sheathed till they are exterminated, or submit to the faith which is to become 'superior to every other religion.'"

About the middle of the year, a heavy grief fell upon Muḥammad, in the death of his little son Ibrāhīm.

On the return of the sacred month (March, A.D. 632), Muḥammad, accompanied by all his wives, selected his victims, assumed the pilgrim garb, and set out on what is called *Ḥajjatu 'l-Wadāʿ*, or "The Valedictory Pilgrimage," to the holy places, from which every trace of the old superstition had been removed, and which, in accordance with his orders of the previous year, no idolater was to visit. Approaching the Kaʿbah by the gate of the Banū Shaibah, he carefully performed all the ceremonies of the *ʿUmrah*, or "lesser Pilgrimage," and then proceeded to consummate those of the greater. On the 8th of the holy month Ẕu 'l-Ḥijjah, he rode to the Wādī Minā, some three miles east of Makkah, and rested there for the night. Next day, passing Muzdalifah, the midway station, he reached in the evening the valley in which stands the granite hill of ʿArafah. From the "summit he spoke to the pilgrims regarding its sacred precincts, announced to them the perfecting of their religion," offered up the prescribed prayers, and hurried back to Muzdalifah for the night. On the 10th, proceeding to Minā, he cast the accustomed stones, slew the victims brought for sacrifice, had his head shaved and his nails pared, ordering the hair, &c., to be burnt; and, the ceremonies ended, laid aside the pilgrim garb. At Minā, during his three days' stay, he preached to the pilgrims, called them to witness that he had faithfully fulfilled his mission, and urged them not to depart from the exact observances of the religion which he had appointed. Returning to Makkah, he again went through the ceremonies of the ʿUmrah, made the circuit of the temple, drank of the well Zamzam, prayed in the Kaʿbah, and thus, having rigorously performed all the ceremonies, that his example might serve as a model for all succeeding time, he turned to al-Madīnah.

The excitement and fatigue of his journey to the holy places told sensibly on his health, which for some time had shown indications of increasing infirmity. In the death of Ibrāhīm he had received a blow which weighed down his spirit; the poison of Ḵẖaibar still rankled in his veins, afflicted him at times with excruciating pain, and bowed him to the grave. His life had been a hard and a stirring one, and now the important affairs of his spiritual and temporal kingdom, and the cares of his large domestic circle, denied him that quiet and seclusion for which he longed.

The news of the Prophet's failing health was soon noised abroad, and tended to encourage his rivals to increased energy of action. Three different revolts, each headed by a dangerous competitor, were now on the point of breaking out. The first of these was led by Musailimah, a rival prophet, who now stated that Muḥammad had distinctly nominated him as his successor [MUSAILIMAH]; the second, by Aswad, a wealthy and eloquent rival, with a considerable following [ASWAD]; and the third, by Ṭulaiḥah, a famous warrior of Najd, who claimed the prophetic office.

In the Traditions it is related that Musailimah addressed a letter to Muḥammad, which ran:—

"Musailimah, the Prophet of God, to Muḥammad, the Prophet of God. Peace be to you. I am your associate. Let the exercise of authority be divided between us. Half the earth is mine, and half belongs to the Quraish. But the Quraish are a greedy people, and will not be satisfied with a fair division."

To this presumptuous epistle Muḥammad replied:—

"Muḥammad, the Prophet of God, to Musailimah, the Liar. Peace be on those who follow the straight road. The earth is God's, and He giveth it to whom He will. Those only prosper who fear the Lord."

The opposition of Musailimah was, however, a formidable one, and after Muḥammad's death he was slain by Ḵẖālid during the reign of Abū Bakr.

The health of Muḥammad grew worse, and he now requested that he might be permitted to remain in the home of ʿĀyishah, his beloved wife, an arrangement to which his other wives assented.

The account we now give of the closing scenes of Muḥammad's life, is from the graphic pen of Sir William Muir (*Life of Mahomet*, new ed., p. 501 *et seq.*), and founded on the traditional histories of al-Wāqidī's secretary, and Ibn Hishām.

"On the night of Saturday (11 Rabī'u 'l-Awwal, 6th June, A.D. 632), the sickness assumed a very serious aspect. The fever rose to such a pitch that the hand could hardly be kept upon his skin from its burning heat. His body was racked with pain; restless and moaning, he tossed about upon his bed. Alarmed at a severe paroxysm of the disease, Omm Salma, one of his wives, screamed aloud. Mahomet rebuked her:—'Quiet!' he said. 'No one crieth out thus but an unbeliever.' During the night, Ayesha sought to comfort him, and suggested that he should seek for consolation in the same lessons he had so often taught to others when in sickness: 'O Prophet!' she said, 'if one of us had moaned thus, thou would'st surely have found fault with it.' 'Yes,' he replied, 'but I burn with the fever-heat of any two of you together.' 'Then,' exclaimed one, 'thou shalt surely have a double reward.' 'Yes,' he answered, 'I swear by Him in whose hands is my life, that there is not upon the earth a believer afflicted with any calamity or disease, but the Lord thereby causeth his sins to fall from him, even as leaves are shed in autumn from a tree.' At another time he said, 'Suffering is an expiation for sin. Verily, if the believer suffer but the scratch of a thorn, the Lord raiseth his rank thereby, and wipeth away from him a sin.' 'Believers,' he would affirm, 'are tried according to their faith. If a man's faith be strong, so are his sufferings; if he be weak, they are proportioned thereunto. Yet in any case, the suffering shall not be remitted until he walk upon the earth without the guilt of a single transgression cleaving unto him.'

"Omar, approaching the bed, placed his hand on Mahomet's forehead, and suddenly withdrew it, from the greatness of the heat: 'O Prophet!' he said, 'how violent is the fever on thee!' 'Yea, verily,' replied Mahomet, 'but I have been during the night season repeating in praise of the Lord seventy Suras, and among them the seven long ones.' Omar answered: 'But the Lord hath forgiven thee all thy sins, the former and the latter; now, then, why not rest and take thine ease?' 'Nay,' replied Mahomet, 'for wherefore should I not be a faithful servant unto Him?'

"An attendant, while Mahomet lay covered up, put his hand below the sheet, and feeling the excessive heat, made a remark similar to that of Omar. Mahomet replied: 'Even as this affliction prevaileth now against me, so shall my reward hereafter be enhanced.' 'And who are they,' asked another, 'that suffer the severest trials?' 'The prophets and the righteous,' said Mahomet; and then he made mention of one prophet having been destroyed by lice, and of another who was tried with poverty, so that he had but a rag to cover his nakedness withal; 'yet each of them rejoiced exceedingly in his affliction, even as one of you in great spoil would rejoice.'

"On the Sunday, Mahomet lay in a very weak and helpless state. Osâma, who had delayed his departure to see what the issue of the sickness might be, came in from Jorf to visit him. Removing the clothes from the Prophet's face, he stooped down and kissed him, but there was no audible response. Mahomet only raised his hands to heaven in the attidude of blessing, and then placed them upon Osâma. So he returned to the camp.

"During some part of this day Mahomet complained of pain in his side, and the suffering became so great, that he fell into a state of unconsciousness. Omm Salma advised that physic should be given him. Asma, the sister of Meimûna, prepared a draught after an Abyssinian recipe, and they forced it into his mouth. Reviving from its effects, he felt the unpleasant taste in his mouth, and cried, 'What is this that ye have done to me? Ye have even given me physic!' They confessed that they had done so, and enumerated the ingredients of which Asma had compounded it. 'Out upon you!' he angrily exclaimed; 'this is a remedy for the pleurisy, which she hath learned in the land of Abyssinia; but that is not a disease which the Lord will suffer to attack me. Now shall ye all partake of the same dose. Let not one remain in the house without being physicked, even as ye have physicked me, excepting only my uncle Abbâs.' So all the women arose, and they poured the physic, in presence of the dying Prophet, into each other's mouths.

"After this, the conversation turning upon Abyssinia, Omm Salma and Omm Habiba, who had both been exiles there, spoke of the beauty of a cathedral in that country, called the Church of Maria, and of the wonderful pictures on its walls. Mahomet listened quietly to them, and then said, 'These, verily, are the people who, when a good man hath lived amongst them, build over his tomb a place of worship, and they adorn it with their pictures. These, in the eyes of the Lord, are the worst part of all the creation.' He stopped, and covered himself with the bed-clothes; then casting them off in the restlessness and perhaps delirium of the fever, he said: 'The Lord destroy the Jews and Christians! Let His anger be kindled against those that turn the tombs of their prophets into places of worship. O Lord, let not my tomb be an object of worship. Let there not remain any faith but that of Islam throughout the whole land of Arabia!'

"About this time, recognising Omar and some other chief men in the room, he called out, 'Bring hither to me ink and paper, that I may record for you a writing which shall prevent your going astray for ever.' Omar said, 'He wandereth in his mind. Is not the Corân sufficient for us?' But the women wished that the writing materials should be brought; and a discussion ensued. Thereupon one said, 'What is his condition at this present moment? Come, let us see whether he speaketh deliriously or not.' So they went and asked him what his wishes were regarding the writing he had spoken of; but he no longer desired to indite it. 'Leave me thus alone,' he said, 'for my present state is better than that ye call me to,'

"In the course of this day, Mahomet called Ayesha to him, and said, 'Where is that gold which I gave unto thee to keep?' On her replying that it was by her, he desired that she should spend it at once in charity. Then he dozed off in a half-conscious state; and some time after asked if she had done as he desired her. On her saying that she had not yet done so, he called for the money (which was apparently a portion of the tithe income); she placed it in his hand, and counted six golden dinars. He directed that it should be divided among certain indigent families; and then lying down, he said, 'Now I am at peace. Verily it would not have become me to meet my Lord, and this gold in my possession.'

"All Sunday night the illness of Mahomet continued unabated. He was overheard praying: one of the ejaculations was to this effect: 'O my soul! Why seekest thou for refuge elsewhere than in God alone?' The morning brought some measure of relief. The fever and the pain abated; and there was an apparent return of strength.

"The dangerous crisis of the Prophet's sickness on the preceding night having become known throughout the city, the mosque was crowded in the morning, at the hour of prayer, by men and women, who came seeking anxiously for tidings. Abu Bakr, as usual, led the devotions; as Imâm he stood in the place of Mahomet before the congregation, his back turned towards them. He had ended the first Rakáat, or series of prostrations, and the people had stood up again for a second, when the curtain of Ayesha's door (to the left of the audience, and a little way behind Abu Bakr) slowly moved aside, and Mahomet himself appeared. As he entered the assembly, he whispered in the ear of Fadhl (Fazl), son of Abbas, who with a servant supported him: 'The Lord verily hath granted unto me refreshment in prayer'; and he looked around with a gladsome smile, marked by all who at the moment caught a glimpse of his countenance. That smile no doubt was the index of deep emotion in his heart. What doubts or fears may have crossed the mind of Mahomet, as he lay on the bed of death, and felt that the time was drawing nigh when he must render an account to that God whose messenger he professed to be, tradition affords us no grounds even to conjecture. The rival claims of Aswad and Museilama had, perhaps, suggested misgivings, such as those which had long ago distracted his soul. What if he, too, were an impostor, deceiving himself and deceiving others also! If any doubts and questionings of this nature had arisen in his mind, the sight of the great congregation, in attitude devout and earnest, may have caused him comfort and reassurance. That which brings forth good fruit must itself be good. The mission which had transferred gross and debased idolaters into spiritual worshippers such as these, resigning every faculty to the service of the one great God; and which, wherever accepted and believed in, was daily producing the same wonderful change, that mission must be divine, and the voice from within which prompted him to undertake it must have been the voice of the Almighty, revealed through His ministering spirit. Perhaps it was a thought like this which passed at the moment through the mind of the Prophet, and lighted up his countenance with that smile of joy, diffusing gladness over the crowded courts of the mosque.

"Having paused thus for a moment at the door, Mahomet, supported as before, walked softly to the front, where Abu Bakr stood. The people made way for him, opening their ranks as he advanced. Abu Bakr heard the rustle (for he never when at prayer turned himself or looked to the right hand or the left), and, apprehending the cause which alone at that time could create so great sensation, stepped backwards to join the congregation and vacate the place of leader for the Prophet. But Mahomet motioned him to resume the post, and taking his hand, moved forward to the pulpit. There he sat on the ground by the side of Abu Bakr, who resumed the service, and finished it in customary form.

"When the prayers were ended, Abu Bakr entered into conversation with Mahomet. He rejoiced to find him to all appearance convalescent. 'O Prophet,' he said, 'I perceive that, by the grace of God, thou art better today, even as we desire to see thee. Now this day is the turn of my wife, the daughter of Khârija; shall I go and visit her?' Mahomet gave him permission. So he departed to her house at Al Sunh, a suburb of the upper city.

"Mahomet then sat himself down for a little while in the court-yard of the mosque, near the door of Ayesha's apartment, and addressed the people, who, overjoyed to find him again in their midst, crowded round. He spoke with emotion, and with a voice still so powerful as to reach beyond the outer doors of the mosque. 'By the Lord,' he said, 'as for myself, verily, no man can lay hold of me in any matter; I have not made lawful anything excepting what God hath made lawful; nor have I prohibited aught but that which God in His book hath prohibited.' Osâma was there; when he came to bid farewell (before starting on an expedition against the Roman border), Mahomet said to him, 'Go forward with the army; and the blessing of the Lord be with thee!' Then turning to the women who sat close by, 'O Fâtima!' he exclaimed, 'my daughter, and Safiâ, my aunt! Work ye both that which shall procure you acceptance with the Lord; for verily I have no power with him to save you in anywise. Having said this, he arose and re-entered the room of Ayesha.

"Mahomet, exhausted by the exertion he had undergone, lay down upon his bed; and Ayesha, seeing him to be very weak, raised his head from the pillow, and laid it tenderly upon her bosom. At that moment one of her relatives entered with a green tooth-pick in his hand. Ayesha observed that the eye of

Mahomet rested on it, and, knowing it to be such as he liked, asked whether he wished to have it. He signified assent. Chewing it a little to make it soft and pliable, she placed it in his hand. This pleased him; for he took up the tooth-pick and used it, rubbing his teeth with his ordinary vigour; then he put it down.

"His strength now rapidly sank. He seemed to be aware that death was drawing near. He called for a pitcher of water, and, wetting his face, prayed thus: 'O Lord, I beseech thee to assist me in the agonies of death!' Then three times he ejaculated earnestly, 'Gabriel, come close unto me!'

"At this time he began to blow upon himself, perhaps in the half-consciousness of delirium, repeating the while an ejaculatory form which he had been in the habit of praying over persons who were very sick. When he ceased, from weakness, Ayesha took up the task, and continued to blow upon him and recite the same prayer. Then, seeing that he was very low, she seized his right hand and rubbed it (another practice of the Prophet when visiting the sick), repeating all the while the earnest invocation. But Mahomet was too far gone to bear even this. He now wished to be in perfect quiet: 'Take off thy hand from me,' he said, 'that cannot benefit me now.' After a little he prayed in a whisper, 'Lord grant me pardon; and join me to the companionship on high!' Then at intervals: 'Eternity in Paradise!' 'Pardon!' 'Yes; the blessed companionship on high!' He stretched himself gently. Then all was still. His head grew heavy on the breast of Ayesha. The Prophet of Arabia was dead.

"Softly removing his head from her bosom, Ayesha placed it on the pillow, and rising up joined the other women, who were beating their faces in bitter lamentation.

"The sun had but shortly passed the meridian. It was only an hour or two since Mahomet had entered the mosque cheerful, and seemingly convalescent. He now lay cold in death."

As soon as the intelligence of the Prophet's death was published a crowd of people assembled at the door of the house of 'Āyishah, exclaiming, "How can our Apostle be dead; he who was to be our witness in the Day of Judgment?" "No," said 'Umar, "he is not dead; he has gone to visit his Lord as the Prophet Moses did, when, after an absence of forty days, he reappeared to his people. Our Prophet will be restored to us, and those are traitors to the cause of Islām who say he is dead. If they say so, let them be cut in pieces." But Abū Bakr entered the house at this juncture, and after viewing the body of the Prophet with touching demonstrations of affection, he appeared at the door and addressed the crowd thus: "O Muslims, if ye adore Muḥammad, know that Muḥammad is dead. If ye adore God, God is alive, and cannot die. Do ye forget the verse in the Qur'ān: 'Muḥammad is no more than an apostle. Other apostles have already passed before him?' (see Sūrah iii. 138), and also the other verse, 'Thou shalt surely die, O Muḥammad, and they also shall die?'" (see Sūrah xxxix. 31). 'Umar acknowledged his error, and the crowd was satisfied and dispersed.

Al-'Abbās presided at the preparations for the burial, and the body was duly washed and perfumed. There was some dispute between the Quraish and the Anṣār as to the place of burial; but Abū Bakr silenced them, affirming that he had heard Muḥammad say that a prophet should be buried on the spot where he died. A grave was accordingly dug in the ground within the house of 'Āyishah, and under the bed on which the Prophet died. This spot is now known as the Ḥujrah, or chamber, at al-Madīnah. The last rites were performed by 'Alī and the two sons of al-'Abbās. [HUJRAH.]

The foregoing account of Muḥammad's death is that of Sunnī traditionists. The Shī'ahs deny almost every word of it, and give the following as an authentic narrative of the Prophet's death. The manifest object being to establish the claim of 'Alī to be Muḥammad's successor. It is translated from the Shī'ah book entitled the *Ḥayātu 'l-Qulūb* (see Merrick's translation, p. 368):—

"The Prophet returned to his house, and in the space of three days his sickness became severe. He then tied a bandage on his head, and leaning on the Commander of the Faithful (*i.e.* 'Alī) and Fazl-ibn-Abbâs, went to the mesjed and ascended the mimber (or pulpit), and, sitting down, addressed the people thus: 'The time is near when I shall be concealed from you. Whoever has any claim on me, let him now declare it. Verily, none can claim favour at the hand of God but by obeying Him, and none can expect to be safe without good works, or to enjoy the favour of God without obedience. Nothing but good works will deliver from divine wrath, and verily, if I should sin, I should go to hell. O Lord, I have delivered thy message.' He then came down from the mimber and performed short prayers with the people, and returned to the house of Ummsalmah, where he remained one or two days. That cursed woman Auyeshah, having satisfied his other wives on the subject, came to the Prophet, and induced him by entreaties to go to her house, where his sickness became very oppressive. At the hour for morning prayers Bilâl shouted the azân, but the Prophet, near his departure to the holy world, heard it not. Auyeshah then sent to her father, Abubekr, to go to the mesjed, and lead the devotions of the people, and Hafsah sent the same message to Omar. As these two women were conversing about the matter before the Prophet, not seeming to suppose that he understood them, he interrupted them, saying, 'Quit such talk; you are like the women that tried to lead Yusuf astray.' Finding that, contrary to his orders, Abubekr and Omar were in the city with seditious designs, he was very sorrowful; and oppressed as he was with a severe disease, he rose, and leaning on Aly and Fazl-bin-Abbâs, with extreme difficulty went to the mesjed, lest Abubekr or Omar should perform prayers, and the people doubt who should be his successor. On arriving at the mesjed, he found that the cursed Abubekr had occupied the place of the leader of prayers, and already begun the devotions with the people. The Prophet, with his blessed hand, signed to Abubekr to remove, and he took his place, and from weakness sat down to perform prayers, which he began anew, regardless of Abubekr's commencement.

"On returning to his house Muhammad summoned Abubekr, Omar, and some others, and demanded if he had not ordered them to depart with the army of Asâmeh. They replied that he had. Abubekr said that he had gone and returned again; and Omar said that he did not go, for he did not wish to hear of the Prophet's sickness from another. Muhammad then told them to go with the army of Asâmah, and three times pronounced a curse on any who should disobey. His exertions produced such exhaustion that he swooned, on which the Musalmans present and his wives and children wept and lamented aloud. At length the Prophet opened his blessed eyes, and said, 'Bring me an inkstand and a sheep's shoulder-blade, that I may write a direction which will prevent your going astray.' One of the Companions of the Prophet rose to bring what he had ordered, but Omar said, 'Come back, he speaks deliriously; disease has overcome him, and the book of God is sufficient for us.' It is, however, a disputed matter whether Omar said this. However, they said to the Prophet, 'Shall we bring what you ordered.' He replied, 'After what I have heard from you I do not need them, but I give you a dying charge to treat my family well, and not turn from them. [The compiler observes that this tradition about the inkstand and shoulder-blade is mentioned in several Sunnī books.]

"During the last sickness of the Prophet, while he was lying with his head in Aly's lap, and Abbâs was standing before him and brushing away the flies with his cloak, he opened his eyes and asked Abbâs to become his executor, pay his debts, and support his family. Abbâs said he was an old man with a large family, and could not do it. Muhammad then proferred the same to Aly, who was so much affected that he could not command utterance for some time, but as soon as he could speak, promised with the greatest devotion to perform the Prophet's request. Muhammad, after being raised into a sitting posture, in which he was supported by Aly, ordered Bilâl to bring his helmet, called *Zool-jabeen* (*Z̲ū 'l-jabīn*); his coat of mail, *Zatûl-Fazool* (*Z̲ātu 'l-Fuẓūl*); his banner, *Akab*; his sword, *Zool-fakâr* (*Z̲ū 'l-fiqār*); his turbans, *Sahâb* and *Tahmeeah*; his two party-coloured garments, his little staff, and his walking cane, *Mamshook*. In relating the story, Abbâs remarked that he had never before seen the party-coloured scarf, which was so lustrous as nearly to blind the eyes. The Prophet now addressed Aly, saying, 'Jibraeel brought me this article and told me to put it into the rings of my mail, and bind it on me for a girdle.' He then called for his two pairs of Arab shoes, one pair of which had been patched. Next he ordered the shirt he wore on the night of the Marâj, or ascent to heaven, and the shirt he wore at the battle of Ohod. He then called for his three caps, one of which he wore in journeying, another on festivals, and the third when sitting among his Companions. He then told Bilâl to bring his two mules, Shahba and Duldul, his two she-camels, Ghazbâ and Sahbâ, and his two horses, Jinah and Khyrdam.

"Jinah was kept at the door of the mesjed for the use of a messenger, and Khyrdam was mounted by the Prophet at the battle of Ohod, where Jibraeel cried, 'Advance, Khyrdam.' Last, he called for his ass Yafoor. Muhammad now directed Abbâs to take Aly's place, and support his back. He then said, 'Rise, O Aly, and take these my property, while I yet live, that no one may quarrel with you about them after I am gone.'

"When I rose,' said Aly, 'my feet were so cramped that it was with the utmost difficulty that I could move. Having taken the articles and animals to my house, I returned and stood before the Prophet, who on seeing me took his ring from his right hand, pointing the way of truth, and put it on my right hand, the house being full of the Benu Hâshim and other Musulmans, and while from weakness his head nodded to the right and left, he cried aloud, 'O company of Musulmans, Aly is my brother, my successor, and Khaleefah among my people and sect, he will pay my debts and cancel my engagements. O ye sons of Hâshim and Abdul-mutalib, and ye other Musulmans, be not hostile to Aly, and do not oppose him, lest ye be led astray, and do not envy him, nor incline from him to another, lest ye become infidels. He then ordered Abbâs to give his place to Aly. Abbâs replied, 'Do you remove an old man to seat a child in his place?' The Prophet repeated the order; and the third time Abbâs rose in anger, and Aly took his place. Muhammad, finding his uncle angry, said to him, 'Do nothing to cause me to leave the world offended with you, and my wrath send you to hell.' On hearing this, Abbâs went back to his place, and Muhammad directed Aly to lay him down.

"The Prophet said to Bilâl, 'Bring my two sons Hasan and Husain.' When they were presented he pressed them to his bosom, smelt and kissed those two flowers of the garden of prophecy. Aly, fearing they would trouble the Prophet, was about to take them away; but he said, 'Let them be, that I may smell them, and they smell me, and we prepare to meet each other; for after I am gone great calamities will befall them, but may God curse those that cause them to fear and do them injustice. O Lord, I commit them to Thee and to the worthy of the Faithful, namely, Aly-bin-Abutalib. The Prophet then dismissed the people and they went away, but Abbâs and his son Fazl, and Aly-bin-Abutalib, and those belonging to the household of the Prophet, remained. Abbâs then said to the Prophet, 'If the Khalâfat (Khilāfah) is established among us, the Benu Hâshim, assure us of it, that we may rejoice; but if you foresee that they will treat us unjustly and deprive us of the Khalâfat, commit us to your Companions.' Muhammad replied, 'After I am gone they will weaken and overcome you,' at which declaration all the family wept, and, moreover, despaired of the Prophet's life.

"Aly continued to attend Muhammad night and day, never leaving him except from the most imperative necessity. On one of these occasions, when Aly was absent, the Prophet said, 'Call my friend and brother.' Auyeshah and Hafsah sent for their fathers, Abubekr and Omar, but he turned from them and covered his face, on which they remarked, 'He does not want us, he wants Aly,' whom Fatimah called; and Muhammad pressed him to his bosom, and they mingled their perspiration together, and the Prophet communicated to him a thousand chapters of knowledge, each opening to a thousand more. One tradition declares that Muhammad kept Aly in his bed till his pure spirit left his body, his arm meanwhile embracing Aly."

[In compiling this account of the life of Muḥammad, we must express our deep obligations to Sir William Muir's *Life of Mahomet* (1st ed., 4 vols.; 2nd ed., 1 vol.; Smith, Elder and Co., London). In many cases we have given the *ipsissima verba* of his narrative, with his kind permission. The chief literature on the subject, in addition to Sir William Muir's work, is: *Das Leben und die Lehre des Moḥammad*, A. Sprenger, Berlin, 1869; *Specimen Historiæ Arabum*, E. Pocock, Oxon. 1650; *Ismael Abulfeda De Vita et Rebus gestis Mohamedis*, J. Gagnier, Oxon. 1723; *Life of Mahomet*, Washington Irving, London, 1850: *Life of Mahomed from Original Sources*, A. Sprenger, Allahabad, 1851: *Essays on the Life of Muhammad*, Syud Ahmad Khan, C.S.I., London; *A Critical Examination of the Life and Teachings of Muhammad*, Syud Ameer Ali Moulla, LL.D., London, 1873; *Islam and its Founder*, S.P.C.K., 1878; *Mahomet et le Coran*, T. Barthelemy de St. Hilaire, 1865; *The True Nature of the Imposture Fully Explained*, H. Prideaux, London, 1718; the first three volumes of the modern part of *An Universal History*, London, 1770 (specially recommended by Dr. Badger); *Tareek-i-Tabari*, Zotenberg; *Das Leben Mohammed's nach Ibn Ishāk, bearbeitet von Ibn Hischam*, G. Weil, 2 vols., 1864. The earliest biographers whose works are extant in Arabic, are Ibn Isḥāq (A.H. 151), Ibn Hishām (A.H. 218), al-Wāqidī (A.H. 207), aṭ-Ṭabarī (A.H. 310).]

Muḥammad is referred to by name in four places in the Qur'ān:—

Sūrah iii. 138: "Muḥammad is but an apostle: apostles have passed away before his time; what if he die, or is killed, will ye retreat upon your heels?"

Sūrah xxxiii. 40: "Muḥammad is not the father of any of your men, but the Apostle of God, and the Seal of the Prophets."

Sūrah xlvii. 2: "Those who believe and do right and believe in what is revealed to Muḥammad,—and it is the truth from their Lord,—He will cover for them their offences and set right their mind."

Sūrah xlviii. 29: "Muḥammad is the Apostle of God."

He is said to have been foretold by Jesus under the name of Aḥmad. Sūrah lxi. 6: "Giving you glad tidings of an Apostle who shall come after me whose name shall be Aḥmad." [AHMAD.]

According to a tradition of Ibn 'Abbās, the Prophet said: "My name in the Qur'ān is Muḥammad, and in the Injīl Aḥmad, and in the Taurāt Aḥyad (from the root حيد, "to shun"), and I am called Aḥyad because I shun hell-fire more than any of my people." (*An-Nawawī*, Wüstenfeld's edition, p. 28.)

MUḤAMMAD, The Character of.

(1) Sir William Muir (*Life of Mahomet*, new ed. p. 537 *et seqq.*), has carefully collated from the traditions embodied by the secretary of al-Wāqidī, an account of the person and character of Muḥammad. "This account," as Sir William Muir remarks, "illustates generally the style and contents of the Muslim biographies of their Prophet."

"When Ayesha was questioned about Mahomet she used to say: 'He was a man just such as yourselves; he laughed often and smiled much.' 'But how would he occupy himself at home?' 'Even as any of you occupy yourselves. He would mend his clothes, and cobble his shoes. He used to help me in my household duties; but what he did oftenest was to sew. If he had the choice between two matters, he would choose the easiest, so as that no sin accrued therefrom. He never took revenge excepting where the honour of God was concerned. When angry with any person, he would say, "What hath taken such a one that he should soil his forehead in the mud!"'

"His humility was shown by his riding upon asses, by his accepting the invitation even of slaves, and when mounted, by his taking another behind him. He would say· 'I sit at meals as a servant doeth, and I eat like a servant: for I really am a servant'; and he would sit as one that was always ready to rise. He discouraged (supererogatory) fasting, and works of mortification. When seated with his followers, he would remain long silent at a time. In the mosque at Medîna they used to repeat pieces of poetry, and tell stories regarding the incidents that occurred in the 'days of ignorance,' and laugh; and Mahomet listening to them, would smile at what they said.

"Mahomet hated nothing more than lying; and whenever he knew that any of his followers had erred in this respect, he would hold himself aloof from them until he was assured of their repentance.

"*His Speech.*

"He did not speak rapidly, running his words into one another, but enunciated each syllable distinctly, so that what he said was imprinted in the memory of every one who heard him. When at public prayers, it might be known from a distance that he was reading by the motion of his beard. He never read in a singing or chanting style; but he would draw out his voice, resting at certain places. Thus, in the prefatory words of a Sura, he would pause after *bismillâhi*, after *al Rahmân*, and again after *al Rahîm*.

"*Gait.*

"He used to walk so rapidly that the people half ran behind him, and could hardly keep up with him.

"*Habits in Eating.*

"He never ate reclining, for Gabriel had told him that such was the manner of kings; nor had he ever two men to walk behind him. He used to eat with his thumb and his two forefingers; and when he had done, he would lick them, beginning with the middle one. When offered by Gabriel the valley of Mecca full of gold, he preferred to forego it; saying that when he was hungry he would come before the Lord lowly, and when full, with praise.

"*Moderation.*

"A servant-maid being once long in returning from an errand, Mahomet was annoyed, and said; 'If it were not for the law of retaliation, I should have punished you with this tooth-pick' (*i.e.* with an inappreciably light punishment).

"*Customs at Prayer.*

"He used to stand for such a length of time at prayer that his legs would swell. When remonstrated with, he said: 'What! shall I not behave as a thankful servant should?' He never yawned at prayer. When he sneezed, he did so with a subdued voice, covering his face. At funerals he never rode: he would remain silent on such occasions, as if conversing with himself, so that the people used to think he was holding communication with the dead.

"*Refusal to make Personal Use of Tithes.*

"While he accepted presents he refused to use anything that had been offered as alms; neither would he allow anyone in his family to use what had been brought as alms; 'For,' said he, 'alms are the impurity of mankind' (*i.e.* that which cleanses their impurity). His scruples on this point were so strong that he would not eat even a date picked up on the road, lest perchance it might have dropped from a tithe load.

"*Food Relished.*

"Mahomet had a special liking for sweetmeats and honey. He was also fond of cucumbers and of undried dates. When a lamb or a kid was being cooked, Mahomet would go to the pot, take out the shoulder, and eat it. He used to eat moist dates and cooked food together. What he most relished was a mess of bread cooked with meat, and a dish of dates dressed with butter and milk.

"Mahomet used to have sweet (rain) water kept for his use.

"*Women and Scents.*

"A great array of traditions are produced to prove that the Prophet was fond of women and scents, and liked these of all things in the world the best. Ayesha used to say: 'The Prophet loved three things—women, scents, and food; he had his heart's desire of the two first, but not of the last.'

"*Straitened means at Medina.*

"Ayesha tells us that for months together Mahomet did not get a full meal. 'Months used to pass,' she says again, 'and no fire would be lighted in Mahomet's house, either for baking bread or cooking meat.' 'How, then, did ye live?' 'By the "two black things" (dates and water), and by what the citizens used to send unto us; the Lord requite them! Such of them as had milch cattle would send us a little milk. The Prophet never enjoyed the luxury of two kinds of food the same day; if he had flesh there was nothing else; and so if he had dates; so likewise if he had bread.'

"'We possessed no sieves, but used to bruise the grain and blow off the husks.'

"*Appearance, Habits, &c.*

"He used to wear two garments. His *izâr* (under-garment) hung down three or four inches below his knees. His mantle was not wrapped round him so as to cover his body, but he would draw the end of it under his shoulder.

"He used to divide his time into three parts: one was given to God, the second allotted to his family, the third to himself. When public business began to press upon him, he gave up one half of the latter portion to the service of others.

"When he pointed he did so with his whole hand; and when he was astonished he turned his hand over (with the palm upwards). In speaking with another, he brought his hand near to the person addressed; and he would strike the palm of the left in the thumb of the right hand. Angry, he would avert his face; joyful, he would look downwards. He often smiled, and, when he laughed, his teeth used to appear white as hailstones.

"In the interval allotted to others, he received all that came to him, listened to their representations, and occupied himself in disposing of their business and in hearing what they had to tell him. He would say on such occasions: 'Let those that are here give information regarding that which passeth to them that are absent; and they that cannot themselves appear to make known their necessities, let others report them to me in their stead; the Lord will establish the feet of such in the Day of Judgment.'

"Seal of Prophecy.

"This, says one, was a protuberance on the Prophet's back of the size and appearance of a pigeon's egg. It is said to have been the divine seal which, according to the predictions of the Scriptures, marked Mahomet as the last of the Prophets. How far Mahomet himself encouraged this idea it is impossible to say. From the traditions it would seem to have been nothing more than a mole of unusual size; and the saying of Mahomet, that 'God had placed it there,' was probably the germ of supernatural associations which grew up concerning it.

"Hair.

"His hair used to be combed; it was neither curling nor smooth. He had, says one, four curled locks. His hair was ordinarily parted, but he did not care if it was not so. According to another tradition, 'The Jews and Christians used to let their hair fall down, while the heathen parted it. Now Mahomet loved to follow the people of the Book in matters concerning which he had no express command. So he used to let down his hair without parting it. Subsequently, however, he fell into the habit of parting it.'

"Moustache.

"Mahomet used to clip his moustache. A Magian once came to him and said: 'You ought to clip your beard and allow your moustaches to grow.' 'Nay,' said the Prophet, 'for my Lord hath commanded me to clip the moustaches and allow the beard to grow.'

"Dress.

"Various traditions are quoted on the different colours he used to wear—white chiefly, but also red, yellow, and green. He sometimes put on woollen clothes. Ayesha, it is said, exhibited a piece of woollen stuff in which she swore that Mahomet died. She adds that he once had a black woollen dress; and she still remembered, as she spoke, the contrast between the Prophet's fair skin and the black cloth. 'The odour of it, however, becoming unpleasant, he cast it off, for he loved sweet odours.'

"He entered Mecca on the taking of the city (some say) with a black turban. He had also a black standard. The end of his turban used to hang down between his shoulders. He once received the present of a scarf for a turban, which had a figured or spotted fringe; and this he cut off before wearing it. He was very fond of striped Yemen stuffs. He used to wrap his turban many times round his head, and 'the lower edge of it used to appear like the soiled clothes of an oil-dealer.'

"He once prayed in a silken dress, and then cast it aside with abhorrence, saying: 'Such stuff it doth not become the pious to wear.' On another occasion, as he prayed in a figured or spotted mantle, the spots attracted his notice; when he had ended, he said: 'Take away that mantle, for verily it hath distracted me in my prayers, and bring me a common one.' His sleeve ended at the wrist. The robes in which he was in the habit of receiving embassies, and his fine Hadhramaut mantle, remained with the Caliphs; when worn or rent, these garments were mended with fresh cloth; and in after times, the Caliphs used to wear them at the festivals. When he put on new clothes (either an under-garment, a girdle, or a turban), the Prophet would offer up a prayer such as this: 'Praise be to the Lord who hath clothed me with that which shall hide my nakedness and adorn me while I live. I pray Thee for the good that is in this, and the good that hath been made for it; and I seek refuge from the evil that is in the same, and from the evil that hath been made for it.'

"Shoes.

"His servant, Anas, had charge of his shoes and of his water-pot. After his master's death, Anas used to show his shoes. They were after the Hadhramaut pattern, with two thongs. In the year 100 or 110 A.H., one went to buy shoes at Mecca, and tells us that the shoemaker offered to make them exactly after the model of Mahomet's, which he said he had seen in the possession of Fâtima, granddaughter of Abbâs. His shoes used to be cobbled. He was in the habit of praying with his shoes on. On one occasion, having taken them off at prayers, all the people did likewise, but Mahomet told them there was no necessity, for he had merely taken off his own because Gabriel had apprised him that there was some dirty substance attaching to them (cleanliness being required in all the surroundings at prayer). The thongs of his shoes once broke, and they mended them for him by adding a new piece; after the service, Mahomet desired his shoes to be taken away and the thongs restored as they were; 'For,' said he, 'I was distracted at prayer thereby.'

"Tooth-picks.

"Ayesha tells us that Mahomet never lay down, by night or by day, but on waking he applied the tooth-pick to his teeth before he performed ablution. He used it so much as to wear away his gums. The tooth-pick was always placed conveniently for him at night, so that, when he got up in the night to pray, he might use it before his lustrations. One says that he saw him with the toothpick in his mouth, and that he kept saying áâ, áâ, as if about to vomit. His tooth-picks were made of the green wood of the palm-tree. He never travelled without one.

"Articles of Toilet.

"He very frequently oiled his hair, poured water on his beard, and applied antimony to his eyes.

"Armour.

"Four sections are devoted to the description of Mahomet's armour,—his swords, coats of mail, shields, lances, and bows.

"*Miscellaneous.*

"The Prophet used to snuff simsim (sesamum), and wash his hands in a decoction of the wild plum-tree. When he was afraid of forgetting anything, he would tie a thread on his finger or his ring.

"*Horses.*

"The first horse which Mahomet ever possessed was one he purchased of the Bani Fazâra, for ten owckeas (ounces of silver); and he called its name *sakb* (running water), from the easiness of its paces. Mahomet was mounted on it at the battle of Ohod, when there was but one other horse from Medîna on the field. He had also a horse called *Sabáha* (*Shamjah?*); he raced it and it won, and he was greatly rejoiced thereat. He had a third horse, named *Murtajis* (neigher).

"*Riding Camels.*

"Besides Al Caswa (al-Qaṣwā), Mahomet had a camel called Adhba (al-'Aẓbā), which in speed outstripped all others. Yet one day an Arab passed it when at its fleetest pace. The Moslems were chagrined at this; but Mahomet reproved them, saying, 'It is the property of the Lord, that whensoever men exalt anything, or seek to exalt it, then the Lord putteth down the same.

"*Milch Camels.*

"Mahomet had twenty milch camels, the same that were plundered at Al Ghâba. Their milk was for the support of his family: every evening they gave two large skinsful. Omm Salmah relates: 'Our chief food when we lived with Mahomet was milk. The camels used to be brought from Al Ghâba every evening. I had one called Arîs, and Ayesha one called Al Samra. The herdman fed them at Al Jûania, and brought them to our homes in the evening. There was also one for Mahomet.

"*Milch Flocks.*

"Mahomet had seven goats which Omm Ayman used to tend (this probably refers to an early period of his residence at Medîna). His flocks grazed at Ohod and Himna alternately, and were brought back to the house of that wife whose turn it was for Mahomet to be in her abode. A favourite goat having died, the Prophet desired its skin to be tanned.

"Mahomet attached a peculiar blessing to the possession of goats. 'There is no house,' he would say, 'possessing a goat, but a blessing abideth thereon; and there is no house possessing three goats, but the angels pass the night there praying for its inmates until the morning.'

"*Servants.*

"Fourteen or fifteen persons are mentioned who served the Prophet at various times. His slaves he always freed.

"*Houses.*

"Abdallah ibn Yazîd relates that he saw the houses in which the wives of the Prophet dwelt, at the time when Omar ibn Al Azîz, Governor of Medîna (about A.H. 100) demolished them. They were built of unburnt bricks, and had separate apartments made of palm-branches, daubed (or built-up) with mud; he counted nine houses, each having separate apartments, in the space extending from the house of Ayesha and the gate of Mahomet to the house of Asma, daughter of Hosein. Observing the dwelling-place of Omm Salma, he questioned her grandson concerning it, and he told him that when the Prophet was absent on the expedition to Dûma, Omm Salma built up an addition to her house with a wall of unburnt bricks. When Mahomet returned, he went in to her, and asked what new building this was. She replied, 'I purposed, O Prophet, to shut out the glances of men thereby!' Mahomet answered: 'O Omm Salma! verily, the most unprofitable thing that eateth up the wealth of the Believer is building.' A citizen of Medîna present at the time, confirmed this account, and added that the curtains of the door were of black hair-cloth. He was present, he said, when the despatch of the Caliph Abd al Malîk (A.H. 86–88) was read aloud, commanding that these houses should be brought within the area of the mosque, and he never witnessed sorer weeping than there was amongst the people that day. One exclaimed: 'I wish, by the Lord! that they would leave these houses alone thus as they are; then would those that spring up hereafter in Medîna, and strangers from the ends of the earth, come and see what kind of building sufficed for the Prophet's own abode, and the sight thereof would deter men from extravagance and pride.'

"There were four houses of unburnt bricks, the apartments being of palm-branches; and five houses made of palm-branches built up with mud and without any separate apartments. Each was three Arabian yards in length. Some say they had leather curtains for the doors. One could reach the roof with the hand.

"The house of Hâritha (Ḥāriṣah) was next to that of Mahomet. Now whenever Mahomet took to himself a new wife, he added another house to the row, and Hâritha was obliged successively to remove his house, and to build on the space beyond. At last this was repeated so often, that the Prophet said to those about him: 'Verily, it shameth me to turn Hâritha over and over again out of his house.'

"*Properties.*

"There were seven gardens which Mukheirîck the Jew left to Mahomet. Omar ibn Al Azîz, the Caliph, said that, when Governor of Medîna, he ate of the fruit of these, and never tasted sweeter dates. Others say that these gardens formed a portion of the confiscated estates of the Bani Nadhîr. They were afterwards dedicated perpetually to pious purposes.

"Mahomet had three other properties:—

"I. The confiscated lands of the Bani

Nadhîr. The produce of these was appropriated to his own wants. One of the plots was called Mashruba Omm Ibrahîm, the 'summer garden of (Mary) the mother of Ibrahîm,' where the Prophet used to visit her.

"II. Fadak; the fruits of this were reserved as a fund for indigent travellers.

"III. The fifth share, and the lands received by capitulation, in Kheibar. This was divided into three parts. Two were devoted for the benefit of the Moslems generally (*i.e.* for State purposes); the proceeds of the third, Mahomet assigned for the support of his own family; and what remained over he added to the fund for the use of the Moslems." (*The Life of Mahomet*, by William Muir, Esq., London, 1861, vol. iv., p. 325.)

(2) Dr. A. Sprenger, Persian translator of the Government of India, and Principal of the Calcutta Madrasah, gives the following valuable review of the character of Muḥammad, as regards his assumption of the prophetic office:—

"Up to his fortieth year, Mohammad devoutly worshipped the gods of his fathers. The predominance of his imaginative powers, and his peculiar position, gave him a turn for religious meditation. He annually spent the month of Ramazan in seclusion in a cave of Mount Hirá, where the Qorayshites used to devote themselves to ascetic exercises. In this retreat he passed a certain number of nights in prayers, fasted, fed the poor, and gave himself up to meditation; and on his return to Makkah he walked seven times round the Ka'bah before he went to his own house.

"When he was forty years of age, the first doubts concerning idolatry arose in his mind. The true believers ascribe this crisis to a divine revelation, and therefore carefully conceal the circumstances which may have given the first impulse. It is likely that the eccentric Zaid, whom he must have met in Mount Hirá, first instilled purer notions respecting God into his mind, and induced him to read the Biblical history. To abjure the gods, from whom he had hoped for salvation, caused a great struggle to Mohammad, and he became dejected and fond of solitude. He spent the greater part of his time in Hirá, and came only occasionally to Makkah for new provisions.

"Undisturbed meditation increased his excitement, and his overstrained brains were, even in sleep, occupied with doubts and speculations. In one of his visions he saw an angel, who said to him, 'Read.' He answered, 'I am not reading.' The angel laid hold of him and squeezed him, until Mohammad succeeded in making an effort. Then he released him, and said again, 'Read.' Mohammad answered, 'I am not reading.' This was repeated three times; and at length the angel said, 'Read in the name of thy Lord, the Creator, who has created man of congealed blood;—read, for thy Lord is most beneficent. It is He who has taught by the pen (has revealed the Scriptures); it is He who has taught man what he does not know' These are the initial words of a Surah of the Quran, and the first revelation which Mohammad received. If this dream was as momentous as authentic traditions make it, it must have been the crisis, which caused Mohammad to seek for truth in the books of the Jews and Christians. The words of the angel admit hardly any other sense After much hesitation he determines to study the tenets of another faith, which was hostile to that of his fathers. His resolve is sanctioned by a vision, and he thanks the Creator, whom the Qorayshites always considered the greatest among their gods, for having sent a revelation to direct man.

"It is certain, however, that no Musalman will admit the sense which I give to these verses of the Quran; and Mohammad himself, in the progress of his career, formally denied having read any part of the Scriptures before the Quran had been revealed to him. This, however, can only be true if he meant the first verses of the Quran, that is to say, those mentioned above; for in the following revelations he introduces the names of most prophets, he holds up their history as an example to the Makkians, he borrows expressions from the Bible which he admired for their sublimity, he betrays his acquaintance with the gospels by referring to an erroneously translated verse of St. John, for a proof of his mission, and he frequently alludes to the legends of the Rabbins and Christians. Whence has the Prophet of the Gentiles obtained his knowledge of the Biblical history? He answers the question himself: It is God who has revealed it to me. This assertion satisfies the believer, and is a hint to the inquirer in tracing the sources of his information. He would hardly have hazarded it had he not obtained his instruction under considerable secresy. The spirit of persecution at Makkah, which manifested itself against Zaid, made caution necessary for Mohammad, though originally he may have had no ulterior views, in making himself acquainted with another faith. Yet with all his precautions, the Qorayshites knew enough of his history to disprove his pretensions. He himself confesses, in a Surah revealed at Makkah (Sūrah xxv. 5), that they said that the Quran was a tissue of falsehood; that several people had assisted him; and that he preached nothing more than what was contained in the "Asátyr of the Ancients," which he used to write, from the dictation of his teachers, morning and evening. Who were the men who instructed Mohammad? It is not likely that he would have dared to declare before them, that the doctrines which he had received from them had been revealed to him; nor is it likely that, had they been alive after the new religion had become triumphant, they would have allowed him to take all the credit to himself. Those who exercised an influence upon Mohammad were his disciples; but we find no instance in which he appeared to buy secresy by submitting to the dictation of others. I am inclined to think, therefore, that his instructors died during his early career; and this supposition enables us to ascertain the names of some of them. The few specimens of the sayings of Zaid, which have been preserved, prove that Mohammad borrowed freely from him, not only his tenets, but even his expressions; and Zaid did not long survive Mohammad's assumption of his office. It is likely that Waraqah, the cousin of Khadyjah, who, it would appear, brought about her marriage with Mohammad, who was the first to declare that the Great Law [NAMUS] would be revaled to him, and who expressed a wish to assist him during the persecutions to which every prophet was subject, was one of his teachers. Waraqah died shortly before the time when he publicly proclaimed his mission. The defence of the Prophet, that the man, of whom his countrymen said that he assisted him in writing the Quran, was a foreigner (Sūrah xvi. 105), and unable to write so pure Arabic as the language of the Quran was, leads us to suspect that one of his chief authorities for the Biblical legends was 'Addas, a monk of Nineveh, who was settled at Makkah. (See *Tafsīru 'l-Baiẓāwī* on Sūrah xxv. 6.) And there can be no doubt that the Rabbins of the Hijaz communicated to Mohammad their legends. The commentators upon the Quran inform us further, that he used to listen to Jabr and Yasár, two sword-manufacturers at Makkah, when they read the scriptures; and Ibn Isháq says, that he had intercourse with 'Abdal-Rahmán, a Christian of Zamámah; but we must never forget that the object of these authorities, in such matters, is not to instruct their readers, but to mislead them.

"It is certain, from the context, where the expression occurs, and from the commentators on the Quran, that '*Asátyr of the Ancients*' is the name of a book; but we have very little information as to its origin and contents. (See the Commentaries of al-Baiẓāwī and the Jalālān on Sūrah xxv.) That dogmas were propounded in it, besides Biblical legends, appears from several passages of the Quran, where it is said that it contained the doctrine of the Resurrection. (Sūrahs xxvii. 70, xlvi. 16.) It is also clear that it was known at Makkah before Mohammad; for the Qorayshites told him that they and their fathers had been acquainted with it before he taught it, and that all that he taught was contained in it. (Sūrah lxviii. 15.) Mohammad had, in all likelihood, besides, a version of portions of the scriptures, both of the genuine and some of the apocryphal works; for he refers his audience to them without reserve. Tabary informs us that when Mohammad first entered on his office, even his wife Khadyjah had read the scriptures, and was acquainted with the history of the prophets. (See Bal'āmy's translation of Tabary in Persian.)

"In spite of three passages of the Quran quoted above, the meaning of which they clumsily pervert, almost all modern Musalman writers, and many of the old ones, deny that Mohammad knew reading or writing. Good authors, however, particularly among the Shiahs, admit that he knew reading; but they say he was not a skilful penman. The only support of the opinion of the former is one passage of the Quran, Sūrah vii. 156, in which Mohammad says that he was the Prophet of the Ummis, and an Ummi himself. This word, they say, means illiterate; but others say it means a man who is not skilful in writing; and others suppose it to mean a Makkian or an Arab. It is clear that they merely guess, from the context, at the meaning of the word. *Ummi* is derived from *ummah*, 'nation' (Latin *gens*, Greek *ethnos*), and on comparing the passages of the Quran, in which it occurs, it appears that it means *gentile* (Greek *ethnicos*). It is said in the Quran, that some Jews are honest, but others think there is no harm in wronging the Ummis. Imám Sadiq observes (*Hiyatu 'l-Qulub*, vol. ii. chapter 6, p. 2) on this passage, that the Arabs are meant under Ummis, and that they are called so, though they knew writing, because God had revealed no book to them, and had sent them no prophet. Several instances in which Mohammad did read and write are recorded by Bokhary, Nasay, and others. It is, however, certain that he wished to appear ignorant, in order to raise the elegance of the composition of the Quran into a miracle.

* * * * *

"According to one record, the doubts, indecision, and preparation of the Prophet for his office lasted seven years; and so sincere and intense were his meditations on matters of religion, that they brought him to the brink of madness. In the Quran we can trace three phases in the progress of the mind of Mohammad from idolatry to the formation of a new creed. First, the religion of the Kab'ah, in which he sincerely believed, seems to have formed the principal subject of his meditations. The contemplation of nature, probably assisted by instruction, led him to the knowledge of the unity of God; and there is hardly a verse in the Quran which does not shew how forcibly he was struck with this truth. By satisfying the faith of his fathers, he tried to reconcile it with the belief in one God; and for some time he considered the idols round the Ka'bah daughters of God, who intercede with Him for their worshippers. But he gave up this belief, chiefly because he could not reconcile himself to the idea that God should have only daughters, which was ignominious in the eyes of an Arab; and that men should have sons, who reflect honour on a family. He also connected the idolatrous worship of the black stone, and the ceremonies of the Hajj, and almost all the other pagan usages of the Haramites, with their Abraham. This idea was not his own. The sceptics who preceded him held the same opinion; yet it was neither ancient nor general among the pagan Arabs. We find no connexion between the tenets of Moses and those of the Haramites; and though Biblical names are very frequent among the Musalmans, we do not find one instance of their occurrence among the pagans of the Hijaz before Mohammad.

"It has been mentioned that the vision in which he was ordered to read, caused him finally to renounce idolatry; we are told that after this vision an intermission of revelation, called *fatrah*, took place, which lasted upwards of two years. The meaning of *fatrah* is simply that, though this vision was a revelation, he did not assume his office for two or three years. It is certain that he composed many Surahs of the Quran during this time; and it must have been during this period that the tenets of the Jews and Christians seriously occupied his mind. Before the vision he was an idolater; and after the *fatrah* he possessed the acquaintance with the scriptural history which we find in the Quran. Even after he had declared himself a prophet, he shewed, during the beginning of his career, a strong leaning towards, and a sincere belief in, the scriptures and Biblical legends; but in proportion to his success he separated himself from the Bible.

"This is the second phase in the progress of the Prophet's mind. His belief in the scriptures does not imply that he ever belonged to the Christian or Jewish Church. He never could reconcile his notions of God with the doctrine of the Trinity, and with the Divinity of Christ, and he was disgusted with the monkish institutions and sectarian disputes of the Christians. His creed was: 'He is God alone, the Eternal God; He has not begotten, and is not begotten; and none is His equal.' (See Sūrah cxii.) Nothing, however, can be more erroneous than to suppose that Mohammad was, at any period of his early career, a deist. Faith, when once extinct, cannot be revived; and it was his enthusiastic faith in inspiration that made him a prophet. Disappointed with the Jewish and Christian religions, he began to form a system of faith of his own; and this is the third phase of the transition period. For some time, it seems, he had no intention to preach it publicly, but circumstances, as well as the warm conviction of the truth of his creed, at length prevailed upon him to spread it beyond the circle of his family and friends.

"The mental excitement of the Prophet was much increased during the *fatrah*, and like the ardent scholar in one of Schiller's poems, who dared to lift the veil of truth, he was nearly annihilated by the light which broke in upon him. He usually wandered about in the hills near Makkah, and was so long absent, that on one occasion, his wife being afraid that he was lost, sent men in search of him. He suffered from hallucinations of his senses, and, to finish his sufferings, he several times contemplated suicide by throwing himself down from a precipice. His friends were alarmed at his state of mind. Some considered it as the eccentricities of a poetical genius; others thought that he was a *kahin*, or soothsayer; but the majority took a less charitable view (see Sūrah lxix. 40, xx. 5), and declared that he was insane; and, as madness and melancholy are ascribed to supernatural influence in the East, they said that he was in the power of Satan and his agents, the jinn. They called in exorcists; and he himself doubted the soundness of his mind. 'I hear a sound,' he said to his wife, 'and see a light. I am afraid there are jinn in me.' And on other occasions he said, 'I am afraid I am a *kahin*.' 'God will never allow that such should befall thee,' said Khadyjah; 'for thou keepest thy engagements, and assistest thy relations.' According to some accounts, she added, 'Thou wilt be the prophet of thy nation.' And, in order to remove every doubt, she took him to her cousin Waraqah; and he said to her, 'I see thou (*i.e.* thy explanation) art correct; the cause of the excitement of thy husband is the coming to him of the great nomos, law, which is like the nomos of Moses. If I should be alive when he receives his mission, I would assist him; for I believe in him.' After this Khadyjah went to the monk, 'Addas, and he confirmed what Waraqah had said. Waraqah died soon after, before Mohammad entered on his mission.

"The words of Mohammad, 'I am afraid I am a kahin,' require some explanation. The Arabs, previous to the promulgation of Islam, believed in *kahins*, soothsayers; and even in our days they have greater faith in saints and inspired persons than other equally uncivilized nations. Such a belief is so necessary a limitation of the personal freedom of the Bedouins, which knows no other bounds, that I consider it as the offspring of liberty. Even the most refractory spirit sees no humiliation in confessing his wrong-doings to a helpless seer, and in submitting to his decisions; and by doing so, if he has embroiled himself, he can return to peace with himself and with society. We find, therefore, in the ancient history of Arabia, that litigations were frequently referred to celebrated kahins. These, it would appear, were eccentric persons, of great cunning, and not without genius. The specimens which we have of their oracles are obscure, and usually in rhymed prose and incoherent sentences; and they are frequently preceded by a heavy oath to the truth of what they say, like some of the Surahs of the Quran. It was believed that they knew what was concealed from the eyes of the common mortals; but they were looked upon with awe; for the Arabs conceived that they were possessed by, or allied with, Satan and the jinn. The evil spirits used to approach the gates of heaven by stealth, to pry into the secrets which were being transacted between God and the angels, and to convey them to the kahins. Existing prejudices left no alternative to Mohammad but to proclaim himself a prophet who was inspired by God and His angels, or to be considered a kahin possessed by Satan and his agents the jinn.

"Khadyjah and her friends advised him to adopt the former course; and, after some hesitation, he followed their advice, as it would appear, with his own conviction. His purer notions of the Deity, his moral conduct, his predilection for religious speculations, and his piety, were proofs sufficiently strong to convince an affectionate wife that the supernatural influence, under which he was, came from heaven. But, as the pagan Arabs had very imperfect notions of divine inspiration, it was necessary for him to prove to them, by the history of the prophets, that some seers were inspired by God; and to this end, he devoted more than two-thirds of the Quran to Biblical legends, most of which he has so well adapted to his own case, that if we substitute the name of Mohammad for Moses and Abraham, we have his own views, fate, and tendency. And, in order to remove every doubt as to the cause of his excitement, Mohammad subsequently maintained, that since he had assumed his office, heaven was surrounded by a strong guard of angels; and if the jinn venture to ascend to its precincts, a flaming dart, that is to say, a shooting star, is thrown at them, and they are precipitated to the lower regions; and, therefore, the kahins ceased with the commencement of his mission.

"The declaration of Waraqah, and of the monk 'Addas, that the great nomos would descend upon him, and the faith of his wife, neither conveyed full conviction nor gave they sufficient courage to Mohammad to declare himself publicly the messenger of God; on the contrary, they increased the morbid state of his mind. A fatalist, as he was, it was a hallucination and a fit which decided him to follow their advice. One day, whilst he was wandering about in the hills near Makkah, with the intention to destroy himself, he heard a voice; and, on raising his head, he beheld Gabriel, between heaven and earth; and the angel assured him that he was the prophet of God. This hallucination is one of the few clearly stated miracles to which he appeals in the Quran. Not even an allusion is made, in that book, to his fits, during which his followers believe that he received the revelations. This bears out the account of Wáqidy, which I have followed, and proves that it was rather the exalted state of his mind, than his fits, which caused his friends to believe in his mission. Frightened by this apparition, he retuned home; and, feeling unwell, he called for covering. He had a fit, and they poured cold water upon him; and when he was recovering from it, he received the revelation, 'O thou covered, arise and preach, and magnify thy Lord, and cleanse thy garment, and fly every abomination'; and henceforth, we are told, he received revelations without intermission; that is to say, the fatrah was at an end, and he assumed his office.

"This crisis of Mohammad's struggles bears a strange resemblance to the opening scene of Goethe's *Faust*. He paints, in that admirable drama, the struggles of mind which attend the transition, in men of genius, from the ideal to the real—from youth to manhood. Both in Mohammad and in Faust the anguish of the mind, distracted by doubts, is dispelled by the song of angels, which rises from their own bosoms, and is the voice of the consciousness of their sincerity and warmth in seeking for truth; and in both, after this crisis, the enthusiasm ebbs gradually down to calm design, and they now blasphemously sacrifice their faith in God to self-aggrandisement. In this respect the resemblance of the second part of *Faust* to Mohammad's career at Madinah is complete. As the period of transition in the life of the Prophet has hitherto been completely unknown in Europe, Goethe's general picture of this period, in the life of enthusiasts, is like a prediction in reference to the individual case of Mohammad.

"Some authors consider the fits of the Prophet as the principal evidence of his mission, and it is therefore necessary to say a few words on them. They were preceded by a great depression of spirits; he was despondent, and his face was clouded; and they were ushered in by coldness of the extremities and shivering. He shook, as if he were suffering of ague, and called out for covering. His mind was in a most painfully excited state. He heard a tinkling in his ears, as if bells were ringing; or a humming, as if bees were swarming round his head; and his lips quivered; but this motion was under the control of volition. If the attack proceeded beyond this stage, his eyes became fixed and staring, and the motions of his head became convulsive and automatic. At length, perspiration broke out, which covered his face in large drops; and with this ended the attack. Sometimes, however, if he had a violent fit, he fell comatose to the ground, like a person who is intoxicated; and (at least at a latter period of his life) his face was flushed, and his respiration stertorous, and he remained in that state for some time. The bystanders sprinkled water in his face; but he himself fancied that he would derive a great benefit from being cupped on the head. This is all the information which I have been able to collect concerning the fits of Mohammad. It will be observed that we have no distinct account of a paroxysm between the one which he had in his infancy, and the one after which he assumed his office. It is likely that up to his forty-fourth year they were not habitual. The alarm of the nurse, under whose care he had been two years before he had the former of these two fits, shews that it was the first, and the age and circumstances under which he had it, render it likely that it was solitary, and caused by the heat of the sun and gastric irritation. The fit after which he assumed his office was undoubtedly brought on by long-continued and increasing mental excitement, and by his ascetic exercises. We know that he used frequently to fast, and that he sometimes devoted the greater part of the night to prayer. The bias of the Musalmans is to gloss over the aberration of mind, and the intention to commit suicide, of their prophet Most of his biographers pass over the transition period in silence. We may, therefore, be justified in stretching the scanty information which we can glean from them to the utmost extent, and in supposing that he was for some time a complete maniac; and that the fit after which he assumed his office was a paroxysm of cataleptic insanity. This disease is sometimes accompanied by such interesting psychical phenomena, that even in modern times it has given rise to many superstitious opinions. After this paroxysm the fits became habitual, though the moral excitement cooled down, and they assumed more and more an epileptic character." (*The Life of Mohammad from Original Sources*, by A. Sprenger, M.D., part i., Allahabad, 1851, p. 949.)

(3) Dr. Marcus Dodds, in his *Mohammed, Buddha, and Christ*," says:—

"But is Mohammed in no sense a prophet? Certainly he had two of the most important characteristics of the prophetic order. He saw truth about God which his fellow-men did not see, and he had an irresistible inward impulse to publish this truth. In respect of this latter qualification, Mohammed may stand comparison with the most courageous of the heroic prophets of Israel. For the truth's sake he risked his life, he suffered daily persecution for years, and eventually banishment, the loss of property, of the goodwill of his fellow-citizens, and of the confidence of his friends; he suffered, in short, as much as any man can suffer short of death, which he only escaped by flight, and yet he unflinchingly proclaimed his message. No bribe, threat, or inducement, could silence him. 'Though they array against me the sun on the right-hand and the moon on the left, I cannot renounce my purpose.' And it was this persistency, this belief in his call, to proclaim the unity of God, which was the making of Islam.

"Other men have been monotheists in the midst of idolaters, but no other man has founded a strong and enduring monotheistic religion. The distinction in his case was his resolution that other men should believe. If we ask what it was that made Mohammed aggressive and proselytizing, where other men had been content to cherish a solitary faith, we must answer that it was nothing else than the depth and force of his own conviction of the truth. To himself the difference between one God and many, between the unseen Creator and these ugly lumps of stone or wood, was simply infinite. The one creed was death and darkness to him, the other life and light. It is useless seeking for motives in such a case—for ends to serve and selfish reasons for his speaking; the impossibility with Mohammed was to keep silence. His acceptance of the office of teacher of his people was anything but the ill-advised and sudden impulse of a light-minded vanity or ambition. His own convictions had been reached only after long years of lonely mental agony, and of a doubt and distraction bordering on madness. Who can doubt the earnestness of that search after truth and the living God, that drove the affluent merchant from his comfortable home and his fond wife, to make his abode for months at a time in the dismal cave on Mount Hira? If we respect the shrinking of Isaiah or Jeremiah from the heavy task of proclaiming unwelcome truth, we must also respect the keen sensitiveness of Mohammed, who was so burdened by this same responsibility, and so persuaded of his incompetency for the task, that at times he thought his new feelings and thoughts were a snare of the Devil, and at times he would fain have rid himself of all further struggle by casting himself from a friendly precipice. His rolling his head in his mantle, the sound of the ringing of bells in his ears, his sobbing like a young camel, the sudden grey hairs which he himself ascribed to the terrific Suras—what were all these but so many physical signs of nervous organization overstrained by anxiety and thought?

"His giving himself out as a prophet of God was, in the first instance, not only sincere, but probably correct in the sense in which he himself understood it. He felt that he had thoughts of God which it deeply concerned all around him to receive, and he knew that these thoughts were given him by God, although not, as we shall see, a revelation strictly so called. His mistake by no means lay in his supposing himself to be called upon by God to speak for Him and introduce a better religion, but it lay in his gradually coming to insist quite as much on men's accepting him as a prophet as on their accepting the great truth he preached. He was a prophet to his countrymen in so far as he proclaimed the unity of God, but this was no sufficient ground for his claiming to be their guide in all matters of religion, still less for his assuming the lordship over them in all matters civil as well. The modesty and humility apparent in him, so long as his mind was possessed with objective truth, gradually gives way to the presumptuousness and arrogance of a mind turned more to a sense of its own importance. To put the second article of the Mohammedan creed on the same level as the first, to make it as essential that men should believe in the mission of Mohammed as in the unity of God, was an ignorant, incongruous, and false combination. Had Mohammed known his own ignorance as well as his knowledge, the world would have had one religion the less, and Christianity would have had one more reformer." (*Mohammed, Buddha, and Christ*, p. 17.)

(4) Thomas Carlyle, in his lecture, "The Hero as Prophet," says:—

"Mahomet himself, after all that can be said about him, was not a sensual man. We shall err widely if we consider this man as a common voluptuary, intent mainly on base enjoyments—nay, on enjoyments of any kind. His household was of the frugalest, his common diet barley-bread and water; sometimes for months there was not a fire once lighted on his hearth. They record with just pride that he would mend his own shoes, patch his own cloak. A poor hard-toiling, ill-provided man; careless of what vulgar men toil for. Not a bad man, I should say; something better in him than hunger of any sort—or these wild Arab men fighting and jostling three and twenty years at his hand, in close contact with him always, would not have reverenced him so! These were wild men, bursting ever and anon into quarrel, into all kinds of fierce sincerity; without right, worth, and manhood, no man could have commanded them. They called him Prophet, you say? Why, he stood there face to face with them; bare, not enshrined in any mystery, visibly clouting his own cloak, cobbling his own shoes, fighting, counselling, ordering in the midst of them, they must have seen what kind of a man he was, let him be called what you like! No emperor with his tiaras was obeyed as this man in a cloak of his own clouting. During three and twenty years of rough actual trial, I find something of a veritable Hero necessary for that of itself.

"His last words are a prayer, broken ejaculations of a heart struggling-up in trembling hope towards its Maker. We cannot say his religion made him worse; it made him better; good, not bad. Generous things are recorded of him; when he lost his daughter, the thing he answers is, in his own dialect, everyway sincere, and yet equivalent to that of Christians: 'The Lord giveth and the Lord taketh away; blessed be the name of the Lord.' He answered in like manner of Said, his emancipated well-beloved slave, the second of the believers. Said had fallen in the war of Tâbûc, the first of Mahomet's fightings with the Greeks. Mahomet said it was well, Said had done his Master's work, Said had now gone to his Master; it was all well with Said. Yet Said's daughter found him weeping over the body; the old gray-haired man melting in tears! What do I see? said she. You see a friend weeping over his friend. He went out for the last time into the mosque two days before his death; asked, If he had injured any man? Let his own back bear the stripes. If he owed any man? A voice answered, 'Yes, me; three drachms, borrowed on such an occasion.' Mahomet ordered them to be paid. 'Better be in shame now,' said he, 'than at the Day of Judgment.' You remember Kadîjah, and the 'No by Allah!' Traits of this kind show us the genuine man, the brother of us all, brought visible through twelve centuries, the veritable son of our common Mother." (*Lectures on Heroes*, p. 66.)

(5) The Rev. Dr. Badger remarks:—

"With respect to the private as distinct from the public character of Muhammad, from the time of his settlement at al-Madinah, it does not appear to have deteriorated, except in one particular, from what it had been prior to the flight from Mecca. He was still frugal in his habits, generous and liberal, faithful to his associates, treasured up the loving memory of absent and departed friends, and awaited his last summons with fortitude and submission. That he entertained an excessive passion for women, was lustful, if you will, cannot be denied; but the fourteen wives whom from first to last he married, and his eleven (? two: see MUHAMMAD'S WIVES) concubines, figure favourably by the side of David's six wives and numerous concubines (2 Sam. v. 13; 1 Chron. iii. 1–9; xiv. 3), Solomon's 700 wives and 300 concubines (1 Kings xi. 3), and Rehoboam's eighteen wives and sixty concubines (2 Chron. xi. 21), a plurality expressly forbidden to the sovereign of Israel, who was commanded not to multiply wives to himself. (Deut. xvii. 17.)

"It is not so much his polygamy, considering all the circumstances of the case, which justly lays Muhammad open to reproach, but his having deliberately infringed one of his own alleged divine revelations, which restricted the number of wives to 'four and no more' (Sura iv. 3); also, for having in the first instance dallied with Zainab, the wife of his freedman and adopted son Zaid-ibn-Harithah, who complacently divorced her in order that she might espouse the Prophet. In this case, moreover, as has already been related, he adduced the authority of God as sanctioning on his behoof first, and thenceforth in the behoof of all Muslims, the marriage of a man with the divorced wife of his adopted son, which up to that time had been considered incestuous. Whatever apology may be adduced for Muhammad in this matter of polygamy, there is no valid plea to justify his improbity and impiety in the case of Zainab."

(6) Sir William Muir says:—

"I would warn the reader against seeking to portray in his mind a character in all its parts consistent with itself as the character of Mahomet. The truth is, that the strangest inconsistencies blended together (according to the wont of human nature) throughout the life of the Prophet. The student of the history will trace for himself how the pure and lofty aspirations of Mahomet were first tinged, and then gradually debased by a half-unconscious self-deception, and how in this process truth merged into falsehood, sincerity into guile, these opposite principles often co-existing even as active agencies in his conduct. The reader will observe that simultaneously with the anxious desire to extinguish idolatry, and to promote religion and virtue in the world, there was nurtured by the Prophet in his own heart, a licentious self-indulgence, till in the end, assuming to be the favourite of Heaven, he justified himself by 'revelations' from God in the most flagrant breaches of morality. He will remark that while Mahomet cherished a kind and tender disposition, 'weeping with them that wept,' and binding to his person the hearts of his followers by the ready and self-denying offices of love and friendship, he could yet take pleasure in cruel and perfidious assassination, could gloat over the massacre of an entire tribe, and savagely consign the innocent babe to the fires of hell. Inconsistencies such as these continually present themselves from the period of Mahomet's arrival at Medîna, and it is by the study of these inconsistencies that his character must be rightly comprehended. The key to many difficulties of this description may be found, I believe, in the chapter 'on the belief of Mahomet in his own inspiration.' When once he had dared to forge the name of the Most High God as the seal and authority of his own words and actions, the germ was laid from which the errors of his after life freely and fatally developed themselves." (*Life of Mahomet*, new ed. p. 535.)

(7) Mr. Bosworth Smith, in his *Mohammed and Mohammedanism*, says :—

"Mohammed did not, indeed, himself conquer a world like Alexander, or Cæsar, or Napoleon. He did not himself weld together into a homogeneous whole a vast system of states like Charles the Great. He was not a philosophic king, like Marcus Aurelius, nor philosopher like Aristotle or like Bacon, ruling by pure reason the world of thought for centuries with a more than kingly power; he was not a legislator for all mankind, nor even the highest part of it, like Justinian; nor did he cheaply earn the title of the Great by being the first among rulers to turn, like Constantine, from the setting to the rising sun. He was not a universal philanthropist, like the greatest of the Stoics.

"Nor was he the apostle of the highest form of religion and civilisation combined, like Gregory or Boniface, like Leo or Alfred the Great. He was less, indeed, than most of these in one or two of the elements that go to make up human greatness, but he was also greater. Half Christian and half Pagan, half civilised and half barbarian, it was given to him in a marvellous degree to unite the peculiar excellences of the one with the peculiar excellences of the other. 'I have seen,' said the ambassador sent by the triumphant Quraish to the despised exile at Medina—'I have seen the Persian Chosroes and the Greek Heraclius sitting upon their thrones; but never did I see a man ruling his equals as does Mohammed.'

"Head of the State as well as of the Church, he was Cæsar and Pope in one; but he was Pope without the Pope's pretensions, Cæsar without the legions of Cæsar. Without a standing army, without a body-guard, without a palace, without a fixed revenue; if ever any man had the right to say that he ruled by a right divine, it was Mohammed, for he had all the power without its instruments, and without its supports.

* * * * *

"By a fortune absolutely unique in history, Mohammed is a three-fold founder—of a nation, of an empire, and of a religion. Illiterate himself, scarcely able to read or write, he was yet the author of a book which is a poem, a code of laws, a Book of Common Prayer, and a Bible in one, and is reverenced to this day by a sixth of the whole human race, as a miracle of purity of style, of wisdom, and of truth. It was the one miracle claimed by Mohammed—his standing miracle he called it; and a miracle indeed it is. But looking at the circumstances of the time, at the unbounded reverence of his followers, and comparing him with the Fathers of the Church or with mediæval saints, to my mind the most miraculous thing about Mohammed is, that he never claimed the power of working miracles. Whatever he had said he could do, his disciples would straightway have seen him do. They could not help attributing to him miraculous acts which he never did, and which he always denied he could do. What more crowning proof of his sincerity is needed? Mohammed to the end of his life claimed for himself that title only with which he had begun, and which the highest philosophy and the truest Christianity will one day, I venture to believe, agree in yielding to him, that of a Prophet, a very Prophet of God." (*Mohammed and Mohammedanism*, p. 340.)

(8) Major Robert Durie Osborn, in his *Islām under the Arabs*, says :—

"He (Muḥammad) was brought face to face with the question which every spiritual reformer has to meet and consider, against which so many noble spirits have gone to ruin. Will not the end justify the means? 'Here am I a faithful servant of God, eager only to enthrone Him in the hearts of men, and at the very goal and termination of my labours I am thwarted by this incapacity to work a miracle. It is true, as these infidels allege, that the older prophets did possess this power, and I, unless the very reason and purpose of my existence is to be made a blank, must also do something wonderful. But what kind of miracle? In his despair, Muḥammad declared that the Qur'ān itself was that constantly-recurring miracle they were seeking after. Had they ever heard these stories of Noah, Lot, Abraham, Joseph, Zacharias, Jesus, and others? No; neither had he. They were transcripts made from the 'preserved Table,' that stood before the throne of God. The archangel Gabriel had revealed them to Muḥammad, written in pure Arabic, for the spiritual edification of the Quraish. Thus in the twelfth Sūrah, where he details at great length an exceedingly ridiculous history of Joseph, he commences the narrative with these words, as spoken by God :—

'These are signs of the clear Book.
An Arabic Qur'ān have we sent it down, that ye might understand it.'

And at the close of the Sūrah, we are told :—

'This is one of the secret histories which we reveal unto thee. Thou wast not present with Joseph's brethren when they conceived their design and laid their plot: but the greater part of men, though thou long for it, will not believe. Thou shalt not ask of them any recompense for this *message*. It is simply an instruction for all mankind.'

And, again, in the LXVIIth Sūrah, he declares respecting the Qur'ān :—

'It is a missive from the Lord of the worlds.
But if Muḥammad had fabricated concerning us any sayings,
We had surely seized him by the right hand,
And had cut through the vein of his neck.

"It would be easy to multiply extracts of similar purport; but the above will suffice by way of illustration. There are modern biographers of the Prophet who would have us believe that he was not conscious of falsehood when making these assertions. He was under a hallucination, of course, but he believed what he said. *This to me is incredible.* The legends in the Qur'ān are derived chiefly from Talmudic sources. Muḥammad must have learned them from some Jew resident in or near Mekka. To work them up into the form of rhymed Sūrahs, to put his own peculiar doctrines in the mouth of Jewish patriarchs, the Virgin Mary, and the infant Jesus (who talks like a good Moslem the moment after his birth), must have required time, thought, and labour. It is not possible that the man who had done this could have forgotten all about it, and believed that these legends had been brought to him ready prepared by an angelic visitor. Muḥammad was guilty of falsehood under circumstances where he deemed the end justified the means." (*Islām under the Arabs*, p. 21.)

(9) The character of Muḥammad is a historic problem, and many have been the conjectures as to his motives and designs. Was he an impostor, a fanatic, or an honest man —"a very prophet of God"? And the problem might have for ever remained unsolved, had not the Prophet himself appealed to the Old and New Testaments in proof of his mission. This is the crucial test, established by the Prophet himself. He claims to be weighed in the balance with the divine Jesus.

Objection has often been made to the manner in which Christian divines have attacked the private character of Muḥammad. Why reject the prophetic mission of Muḥammad on account of his private vices, when you receive as inspired the sayings of a Balaam, a David, or a Solomon? Missionaries should not, as a rule, attack the character of Muḥammad in dealing with Islām; it rouses opposition, and is an offensive line of argument. Still, in forming an estimate of his prophetic claims, we maintain that the character of Muḥammad is an important consideration. We readily admit that bad men have sometimes been, like Balaam and others, the divinely appointed organs of inspiration; but in the case of Muḥammad, his professed inspiration sanctioned and encouraged his own vices. That which ought to have been the fountain of purity was, in fact, the cover of the Prophet's depravity. But how different it is in the case of the true prophet David, where, in the words of inspiration, he lays bare to public gaze the enormity of his own crimes. The deep contrition of his inmost soul is manifest in every line— "I acknowledge my transgression, and my sin is ever before me: against Thee, Thee only, have I sinned, and done this evil in Thy sight."

The best defenders of the Arabian Prophet are obliged to admit that the matter of Zainab, the wife of Zaid, and again, of Mary, the Coptic slave, are "an indelible stain" upon his memory; that "he is once or twice untrue to the kind and forgiving disposition of his best nature; that he is once or twice unrelenting in the punishment of his personal enemies; and that he is guilty even more than once of conniving at the assassination of inveterate opponents"; *but they give no satisfactory explanation or apology for all this being done under the supposed sanction of God* in the Qur'ān.

In forming an estimate of Muḥammad's prophetical pretensions, it must be remembered that he did not claim to be the founder of a new religion, but merely of a new covenant. He is the last and greatest of all God's prophets. He is sent to convert the world to the one true religion which God had before revealed to the five great lawgivers—Adam, Noah, Abraham, Moses, and Jesus! The creed of Muḥammad, therefore, claims to supersede that of the Lord Jesus. And it is here that we take our stand. We give Muḥammad credit as a warrior, as a legislator, as a poet, as a man of uncommon genius raising himself amidst great opposition to the pinnacle of renown; we admit that he is, without doubt, one of the greatest heroes the world has ever seen; but when we consider his claims to *supersede* the mission of the divine Jesus, we strip him of his borrowed plumes, and reduce him to the condition of an impostor! For whilst he has adopted and avowed his belief in the sacred books of the Jew and the Christian, and has given them all the stamp and currency which his authority and influence could impart, he has attempted to rob Christianity of every distinctive truth which it possesses—its divine Saviour, its Heavenly Comforter, its two Sacraments, its pure code of social morals, its spirit of love and truth—and has written his own refutation and condemnation with his own hand, by professing to confirm the divine oracles which sap the very foundations of his religious system. We follow the Prophet in his self-asserted mission from the cave of Ḥirā' to the closing scene, when he dies in the midst of the lamentations of his ḥarīm, and the contentions of his friends—the visions of Gabriel, the period of mental depression, the contemplated suicide, the assumption of the prophetic office, his struggles with Makkan unbelief, his flight to al-Madīnah, his triumphant entry into Makkah—and whilst we wonder at the genius of the hero, we pause at every stage and inquire, "Is this the Apostle of God, whose mission is to claim universal dominion, to the suppression not merely of idolatry, but of Christianity itself?" Then it is that the divine and holy character of Jesus rises to our view, and the inquiring mind sickens at the thought of the beloved, the pure, the lowly Jesus giving place to that of the ambitious, the sensual, the *time-serving* hero of Arabia. In the study of Islām, the character of Muḥammad needs an apology or a defence at every stage; but in the contemplation of the Christian system, whilst we everywhere read of Jesus, and see the reflection of His image in everything we read, the heart revels in the contemplation, the inner pulsations of our spiritual life bound within us at the study of a character so divine, so pure.

We are not insensible to the beauties of the Qur'ān as a literary production (although they have, without doubt, been overrated); but as we admire its conceptions of the Divine nature, its deep and fervent trust in the power of God, its frequent deep moral earnestness, and its sententious wisdom, we would gladly rid ourselves of our recollections of the Prophet, his licentious ḥarīm, his sanguinary battle-fields, his ambitious schemes; whilst as we peruse the Christian Scriptures, we find the grand central charm in the divine character of its Founder. It is the divine character of Jesus which gives fragrance to His words; it is the divine form of Jesus which shines through all He says or does; it is the divine life of Jesus which is the great central point in Gospel history. How, then, we ask, can the creed of Muḥammad, the son of 'Abdu 'llāh, supersede and abrogate that of Jesus, the Son of God? And it is a remarkable coincidence that, whilst the founder of Islām died feeling that he had but imperfectly fulfilled his mission, the Founder of Christianity died in the full consciousness that His work was done—"It is finished." It was in professing to produce a revelation which should supersede that of Jesus, that Muḥammad set the seal of his own refutation. (Hughes, *Notes on Muhammadanism*, p. 2.)

MUḤAMMAD (محمد).

The title of the XLVIIth Sūrah of the Qur'ān, in the second verse of which the word occurs: "Believe in what hath been revealed to Muḥammad."

The name Muḥammad occurs only in three more places in the Qur'ān:—

Sūrah iii. 138: "Muḥammad is but an apostle of God."

Sūrah xxxiii. 40: "Muḥammad is not the father of any of your men, but the Apostle of God, and the Seal of the Prophets."

Sūrah xlviii. 29: "Muḥammad is the Apostle of God."

MUḤAMMAD, The Wives of.

Arabic *al-azwāju 'l-muṭahharāt* (الازواج المطهرات), *i.e.* "The pure wives." According to the Traditions, Muḥammad took to himself eleven lawful wives, and two concubines. (See *Majma'u 'l-Biḥār*, p. 528.)

(1) *Khadījah* (خديجة), a Quraish lady, the daughter of Khuwailid ibn Asad. She was a rich widow lady, who had been twice married. She was married to Muḥammad when he was 25 years old, and she was 40 years, and remained his only wife for twenty-five years, until she died (A.D. 619), aged 65, Muḥammad being 50 years old. She bore Muḥammad two sons, al-Qāsim and 'Abdu 'llāh, surnamed aṭ-Ṭāhir and aṭ-Ṭaiyib, and four daughters, Zainab, Ruqaiyah, Fāṭimah, and Ummu Kulṣūm. Of these children, only Faṭīmah (the wife of 'Alī) survived Muḥammad.

(2) *Saudah* (سودة), daughter of Zama'ah, the widow of as-Sakrān (a Quraish and one of the Companions). Married about two months after the death of Khadījah.

(3) *'Āyishah* (عائشة), the daughter of Abū Bakr. She was betrothed when she was only 7 years old, and was married at 10, about the ninth month after the flight to al-Madīnah.

(4) *Juwairīyah* (جويرية), a widow, the daughter of al-Ḥāriṣ ibn Abī Ẓirār, the chief of the Banū Muṣṭaliq. Muḥammad ransomed her from a citizen who had fixed her ransom at nine ounces of gold. It is related that 'Āyishah said, "No woman was ever a greater blessing to her people than this Juwairīyah."

(5) *Ḥafṣah* (حفصة), the daughter of 'Umar. She was the widow of Khunais, an early convert to Islām. Muḥammad married her about six months after her former husband's death.

(6) *Zainab*, the daughter of Khuzaimah (زينب بنت خزيمة), the widow of Muḥammad's cousin 'Ubaidah, who was killed at the battle of Badr. She was called the "Mother of the Poor," *Ummu 'l-Masākīn*, on account of her care of destitute converts. She died before Muḥammad.

(7) *Ummu Salimah* (ام سلمة), the widow of Abū Salimah, one of the Refugees, who was wounded at the battle of Uḥud, and afterwards died of his wounds.

(8) *Zainab* the daughter of Jaḥsh (زينب بنت جحش), the wife of Muḥammad's adopted son Zaid. Zaid divorced her to please the Prophet. She was (being the wife of an adopted son) unlawful to him, but Sūrah xxxiii. 36 was produced to settle the difficulty.

(9) *Ṣafīyah* (صفية), daughter of Ḥayī ibn Akhṭab, the widow of Kinānah, the Khaibar chief, who was cruelly put to death. It was said that Muḥammad wished to divorce her, but she begged that her turn might be given to 'Āyishah.

(10) *Ummu Ḥabībah* (ام حبيبة), the daughter of Abū Sufyān and the widow of 'Ubaidu 'llāh, one of the "Four Enquirers," who, after emigrating as a Muslim to Abyssinia, had embraced Christianity there, and died in the profession of that faith.

(11) *Maimūnah* (ميمونة), the daughter of al-Ḥāriṣ and widowed kinswoman of Muḥammad, and the sister-in-law of al-'Abbās. She is said to have been 51 years of age when she married Muḥammad.

Muḥammad's concubines were:—

(1) *Mary the Copt* (مارية القبطية). A Christian slave-girl sent to Muḥammad by al-Muqauqis, the Roman Governor in Egypt. She became the mother of a son by Muḥammad, named Ibrāhīm, who died young.

(2) *Riḥānah* (ريحانة), a Jewess, whose husband had perished in the massacre of the Banū Quraiẓah. She declined the summons to conversion, and continued a Jew; but it is said she embraced Islām before her death.

At the time of Muḥammad's death, he had nine wives and two concubines living, (*Ṣaḥīḥu 'l-Bukhārī*, p. 798), Khadījah and Zainab bint Khuzaimah having died before him.

According to the Shī'ahs, Muḥammad had, in all, twenty-two wives. Eight of these never consummated the marriage. Their names are 'Alīyah bint Zabyān, Fatīlah bint Qais, Fāṭimah bint Ẓaḥḥāf, Asmā' bint Kana'ān, Mulaikah bint Suwaid, Lailah bint Khāṭib, and Shabah bint Ṣilah. Twelve were duly married. Their names are Khadījah, Saudah, Hind (or Ummu Salimah), 'Āyishah, Ḥafṣah, Zainab bint Jaḥsh, Ramalah bint Abī Sufyān (or Ummu Ḥabībah), Maimūnah, Zainab bint 'Umais, Juwairīyah bint al-Ḥāriṣ of the Banū Muṣṭaliq, Ṣafīyah, Khaulah bint Ḥakīm, and Ummiāni, a sister to 'Alī. Two were bondwomen: Māriyatu 'l-Qibṭīyah and Rīḥānah. (See *Jannātu 'l-Khulūd*, p. 14.)

MUḤAMMAD, The Children of.

According to the *Majma'u 'l-Biḥār*, p. 538, Muḥammad had seven children. Two sons and four daughters by Khadījah, and one son by Mary, his Coptic slave.

The two sons by Khadījah were al-Qāsim and 'Abdu 'llāh (called also aṭ-Ṭāhir and aṭ-Ṭaiyib); and the four daughters were Zainab, Ruqaiyah, Fāṭimah, and Ummu Kulṣūm. The son by his bondwoman Mary was Ibrāhīm. All these children died before Muḥammad, with the exception of Fāṭimah, who married 'Alī, the fourth Khalīfah, and from whom are descended the Saiyids. [SAIYID.]

Zainab married 'Abū 'l-'Āṣ bnu 'r-Rabī'. Ruqaiyah married 'Utbah ibn Abū Lahab, by whom she was divorced. She afterwards married 'Uṣmān, the third Khalīfah.

MUḤAMMAD'S GRAVE. [HUJRAH.]

MUḤAMMADAN.

Arabic *Muḥammadī* (محمدى). A name seldom used in Muḥammadan works for the followers of Muḥammad, who call themselves either Mu'mins, Muslims, or Musalmāns. It is, however, sometimes used in Indian papers and other popular publications, and it is *not*, as many European scholars suppose, an offensive term to Muslims.

MUḤAMMADANISM.

The religion of Muḥammad is called by its followers *al-Islām* (الاسلام), a word which implies the entire *surrender* of the will of man to God. [ISLAM.] Its adherents speak of themselves as *Muslims*, pl. *Muslimūn*, or *Mu'min*, pl. *Mu'minūn*; a Mu'min being a "believer." In Persian these terms are rendered by the word *Musalmān*, pl. *Musalmānān*.

The principles of Islām were first enunciated in portions of the Qur'ān, as they were revealed piecemeal by Muḥammad, together with such verbal explanations as were given by him to his followers; but when the final recension of the Qur'ān was produced by the Khalīfah 'Uṣmān, about twenty-two years after Muḥammad's death, the Muslims possessed a complete book, which they regarded as the inspired and infallible word of God. [QUR'AN.] But as an interpretation of its precepts, and as a supplement to its teachings, there also existed, side by side with the Qur'ān, the sayings, and practice of Muḥammad, called the *Aḥādīṣ* and *Sunnah*. These traditions of what the Prophet "did and said," gradually laid the foundations of what is now called Islām. For whilst it is a canon in Islām that nothing can be received or taught which is contrary to the literal injunctions of the Qur'ān, it is to the Traditions rather than to the Qur'ān that we must refer for Muḥammadan law on the subject of faith, knowledge, purification, prayer, almsgiving, fasting, marriage, barter, inheritance, punishments, fate, duties of magistrates, religious warfare, lawful food, death, Day of Judgment, &c., and each collection of traditions has sections devoted to these subjects; so that it is upon these traditional sayings, quite as much as upon the Qur'ān itfelf, that the religious and civil law of the Muslims is based, both Shī'ah and Sunnī appealing alike to Tradition in support of their views.

When the Prophet was alive, men could go direct to him with their doubts and difficulties; and an infallible authority was always present to give "inspired" directions. But after the deaths of all those who knew Muḥammad personally, it became absolutely necessary to systematise the great mass of traditional sayings then afloat amongst Muslims, and thus various schools of jurisprudence were formed; the concurrent opinion of those learned regarding matters of dispute in Muslim law being called *Ijmā'* [IJMA']. Upon this naturally followed the system of analogical reasoning called *Qiyās* [QIYAS]; thus constituting the four "pillars" or foundations of Islām, known as the *Qur'ān, Ḥadīṣ, Ijmā', and Qiyās*.

Islām, whether it be Shī'ah, Sunnī, or Wahhābī, is founded upon these four authorities, and it is not true, as is so frequently asserted, that the Shī'ahs reject the Traditions. They merely accept different *collections* of Aḥādīṣ to those received by the Sunnīs and Wahhābīs. Nor do the Wahhābīs reject Ijmā' and Qiyās, but they assert that *Ijmā'* was only possible in the earliest stages of Islām.

A study of the present work will show what an elaborate system of dogma Muḥammadanism is. This system of dogma, together with the liturgical form of worship, has been formulated from the traditional sayings of Muḥammad rather than from the Qur'ān itself. For example, the daily ritual, with its purifications, which are such a prominent feature in Islām, is entirely founded on the Traditions. [PRAYER.] Circumcision is not once mentioned in the Qur'ān.

The *Dīn*, or religion of the Muslim, is divided into *Īmān*, or "Faith," and *'Amal*, or "Practice."

Faith consists in the acceptance of six articles of belief:—

1. The Unity of God.
2. The Angels.
3. The Inspired Books.

4. The Inspired Prophets.
5. The Day of Judgment.
6. The Decrees of God.

Practical Religion consists in the observance of—

1. The recital of the Creed—" There is no deity but God, and Muḥammad is the Prophet of God."
2. The five stated periods of prayer.
3. The thirty days fast in the month Ramaẓān.
4. The payment of Zakāt, or the legal alms.
5. The Ḥajj, or Pilgrimage to Makkah.

A belief in these six articles of faith, and the observance of these five practical duties, constitute Islām. He who thus believes and acts is called a *Mu'min*, or " believer "; but he who rejects any article of faith or practice is a *Kāfir*, or " infidel."

Muḥammadan theology, which is very extensive, is divided into—

1. The Qur'ān and its commentaries.
2. The Traditions and their commentaries.
3. *Uṣūl*, or expositions on the principles of exegesis.
4. *'Aqā'id*, or expositions of scholastic theology founded on the six articles of faith.
5. *Fiqh*, or works on both civil and religious law. [THEOLOGY.]

Muḥammadanism is, therefore, a system which affords a large field for patient study and research, and much of its present energy and vitality is to be attributed to the fact that, in all parts of Islām, there are in the various mosques students who devote their whole lives to the study of Muslim divinity.

The two leading principles of Islām are those expressed in its well-known creed, or *kalimah*, namely, a belief in the absolute unity of the Divine Being, and in the mission of Muḥammad as the Messenger of the Almighty. [KALIMAH.]

" The faith," says Gibbon, " which he (Muḥammad) preached to his family and nation, is compounded of an eternal truth and a necessary fiction: That there is only one God, and that Muḥammad is the Apostle of God." (*Roman Empire*, vol. vi. p. 222.)

" Moḥammad's conception of God," says Mr. Stanley Lane-Poole, " has, I think, been misunderstood, and its effect upon the people consequently under-estimated. The God of Islám is commonly represented as a pitiless tyrant, who plays with humanity as on a chessboard, and works out his game without regard to the sacrifice of the pieces ; and there is a certain truth in the figure. There is more in Islám of the potter who shapes the clay than of the father pitying his children. Moḥammad conceived of God as the Semitic mind has always preferred to think of Him : his God is the All-Mighty, the All-Knowing, the All-Just. Irresistible Power is the first attribute he thinks of: the Lord of the Worlds, the Author of the Heavens and the Earth, who hath created Life and Death, in whose hand is Dominion, who maketh the Dawn to appear and causeth the Night to cover the Day, the Great, All-Powerful Lord of the Glorious Throne; the thunder proclaimeth His perfection, the whole earth is His handful, and the heavens shall be folded together in His right hand. And with the Power He conceives the Knowledge that directs it to right ends. God is the Wise, the Just, the True, the Swift in reckoning, who knoweth every ant's weight of good and of ill that each man hath done, and who suffereth not the reward of the faithful to perish.

"' God! There is no God but He, the Ever-Living, the Ever-Subsisting. Slumber seizeth Him not nor sleep. To Him belongeth whatsoever is in the Heavens and whatsoever is in the Earth. Who is he that shall intercede with Him, save by his permission? He knoweth the things that have gone before and the things that follow after, and men shall not compass aught of His knowledge, save what He willeth. His throne comprehendeth the Heavens and the Earth, and the care of them burdeneth Him not. And He is the High, the Great.'—*Ḳur-án*, ii. 256.

" But with this Power there is also the gentleness that belongs only to great strength. God is the Guardian over His servants, the Shelterer of the orphan, the Guider of the erring, the Deliverer from every affliction; in His hand is Good, and He is the Generous Lord, the Gracious, the Hearer, the Near-at-Hand. Every soorah of the Kur-án begins with the words, 'In the Name of God, the Compassionate, the Merciful,' and Moḥammad was never tired of telling the people how God was Very-Forgiving, that His love for man was more tender than the mother-bird for her young.

" It is too often forgotten how much there is in the Ḳur-án of the loving-kindness of God, but it must be allowed that these are not the main thoughts in Moḥammad's teaching. It is the doctrine of the Might of God that most held his imagination, and that has impressed itself most strongly upon Muslims of all ages. The fear rather than the love of God is the spur of Islám. There can be no question which is the higher incentive to good; but it is nearly certain that the love of God is an idea absolutely foreign to most of the races that have accepted Islám, and to preach such a doctrine would have been to mistake the leaning of the Semitic mind.

" The leading doctrine of Moḥammad, then, is the belief in One All-Powerful God. Islám is the self-surrender of every man to the will of God. Its danger lies in the stress laid on the power of God, which has brought about the stifling effects of fatalism. Moḥammad taught the foreknowledge of God, but he did not lay down precisely the doctrine of Predestination. He found it, as all have found it, a stumbling-block in the way of man's progress. It perplexed him, and he spoke of it, but often contradicted himself; and he would become angry if the subject were mooted in his presence: 'Sit not with a disputer about fate,' he said, 'nor begin a conversation with him.' Moḥammad vaguely recognised that little margin of Free Will which makes life not wholly mechanical.

'This doctrine of one Supreme God, to whose will it is the duty of every man to surrender himself, is the kernel of Islám, the truth for which Moḥammad lived and suffered and triumphed. But it was no new teaching, as he himself was constantly saying. His was only the last of revelations. Many prophets—Abraham, Moses, and Christ—had taught the same faith before; but people had hearkened little to their words. So Moḥammad was sent, not different from them, only a messenger, yet the last and greatest of them, the 'seal of prophecy,' the 'most excellent of the creation of God.' This is the second dogma of Islám: Moḥammad is the Apostle of God. It is well worthy of notice that it is not said, 'Moḥammad is the only apostle of God.' Islám is more tolerant in this matter than other religions. Its prophet is not the sole commissioner of the Most High, nor is his teaching the only true teaching the world has ever received. Many other messengers had been sent by God to guide men to the right, and these taught the same religion that was in the mouth of the preacher of Islám. Hence Muslims reverence Moses and Christ only next to Moḥammad. All they claim for their founder is that he was the last and best of the messengers of the one God." (Introduction to Lane's *Selections*, 2nd ed., p. lxxix. *et seqq.*)

Islām does not profess to be a new religion, formulated by Muḥammad (nor indeed is it), but a continuation of the religious principles established by Adam, by Naoh, by Abraham, by Moses, and by Jesus, as well as by other inspired teachers, for it is said that God sent not fewer than 313 apostles into the world to reclaim it from superstition and infidelity. The revelations of these great prophets are generally supposed to have been lost, but God, it is asserted, had retained all that is necessary for man's guidance in the Qur'ān, although, as a matter of fact, a very large proportion of the ethical, devotional, and dogmatic teaching in Islām, comes from the traditional sayings of Muḥammad and not from the Qur'ān itself. [TRADITIONS.]

In reading the different articles in the present work, the reader cannot fail to be struck with the great indebtedness of Muḥammad to the Jewish religion for the chief elements of his system. Mr. Emanuel Deutsch has truly remarked "that Muḥammadanism owes more to Judaism than either to Heathenism or to Christianity. It is not merely parallelisms, reminiscences, allusions, technical terms, and the like of Judaism, its lore and dogma and ceremony, its *Halacha*, and its *Hagyadah*, its Law and Legend, which we find in the Qur'ān; but we think Islām neither more nor less than Judaism—as adapted to Arabia—*plus* the Apostleship of Jesus and Muḥammad. Nay, we verily believe that a great deal of such Christianity as has found its way into the Qur'ān, has found it through Jewish channels." (*Literary Remains*, p. 64.)

Its conception of God, its prophets, its seven heavens and seven hells, its law of marriage and divorce, its law of oaths, its purifications and ritual, its festivals, are all of marked Jewish origin, and prove that Talmudic Judaism forms the kernel of Muḥammadanism, which even according to the words of the founder, professed to be the "religion of Abraham." See Sūrah iii. 60: "Abraham was neither a Jew nor Christian, but he was a *Ḥanīf*, a Muslim." Nevertheless, Muḥammad, although he professed to take his legislation from Abraham, incorporated into his system a vast amount of the law of Moses.

The sects of Islām have become numerous; indeed, the Prophet is related to have predicted that his followers would be divided into seventy-three. They have far exceeded the limits of that prophecy, for, according to 'Abdu 'l-Qādir al-Jilāni, there are at least 150. The chief sect is the Sunnī, which is divided into four schools of interpretation, known after their respective founders, Ḥanafī, Shāfi'ī, Malakī, Ḥanbalī. The Shī'ahs, who separated from the so-called orthodox Sunnīs on the question of the Khalīfate, maintaining that 'Alī and not Abū Bakr was the rightful successor to Muḥammad, are divided also into numerous sects. [SHI'AH.] The Wahhābīs are a comparatively modern sect, who are the Puritans of Islām, maintaining that Islām has very far departed from the original teaching of Muḥammad, as expressed in the Traditions. They consequently reject very many of the so-called Ijtihād of the Sunnīs, and take the literal meaning of the Traditional sayings of the Prophet as the best exposition of the Qur'ān.

The Shī'ah sect is almost entirely confined to Persia, although there are a few thousand in Lucknow and other parts of India. Of the Sunnīs, the Ḥanafīs are found chiefly in Turkey, Arabia, India, and Central Asia, the Shāfi'īs in Egypt, and the Malakīs in Marrocco and Tunis. The Ḥanbalī are a small sect found in Arabia. Wahhabīism, as will be seen upon reference to the article on the subject, is a principle of reform which has extended itself to all parts of Islām. It is scarcely to be called a sect, but a school of thought in Sunnī Islām.

One hundred and seventy millions of the human race are said to profess the religion of Muḥammad; and, according to the late Mr. Keith Johnstone's computations, they are distributed as follows:—In Europe, 5,974,000; in Africa, 50,416,000; in Asia, 112,739,000.

Mr. W. S. Blunt divides 175 millions as follows:—Turkey, Syria, and 'Irāq, 22 millions; Egypt, 5 millions; North Africa, 18 millions; Arabia, 11½ millions; Central Africa, 11½ millions; Persia, 8 milllions; India, 40 millions; Malays (Java), 30 millions; China, 15 millions; Central Asia, 11 millions; Afghanistan, 3 millions. No census having been taken of any of these countries, except India, the numbers are merely an approximation. Out of this supposed population of Islām, 93,250 pilgrims were present at Makkah in the year 1880. (Blunt's *Future of Islam*, p. 10.)

In some parts of the world—in Africa for

example — Muḥammadanism is spreading; and even in Borneo, and in other islands of the Indian Archipelago, we are told that it has supplanted Hinduism. In Central Asia, within the last twenty years, numerous villages of Shiaposh Kafirs have been forcibly converted to Islām, and in Santalia and other parts of India, the converts to Islām from the aboriginal tribes are not inconsiderable.

But, although Muḥammadanism has, perhaps, gained in numerical strength within the last few years, no candid Muslim will deny that it has lost, and is still losing, its vital power. Indeed, "this want of faith and decline in vitality" are regarded as the signs of the last days by many a devout Muslim.

In no Muḥammadan state is Muslim law administered in its strict integrity, and even in the Sultan's own dominion, some of the most sacred principles of the Prophet's religion are set at naught by the civil power; and, as far as we can ascertain (and we speak after a good deal of personal research), the prevalence of downright infidelity amongst educated Muslims is unmistakable. "No intelligent man believes in the teaching of the Muslim divines," said a highly educated Muḥammadan Egyptian not long ago; "for our religion is not in keeping with the progress of thought." The truth is, the Arabian Prophet over-legislated, and, as we now see in Turkey, it is impossible for civilised Muḥammadans to be tied hand and foot by laws and social customs which were intended for Arabian society as it existed 1,200 years ago; whilst, on the contrary, Christianity legislates in spirit, and can therefore be adapted to the spiritual and social necessities of mankind in the various stages of human thought and civilisation.

Mr. Palgrave, in his *Central and Eastern Arabia*, remarks:—

"Islam is in its essence stationary, and was framed thus to remain. Sterile like its God, lifeless like its first principle and supreme original in all that constitutes true life—for life is love, participation, and progress, and of these, the Coranic Deity has none—it justly repudiates all change, all advance, all development. To borrow the forcible words of Lord Houghton, the 'written book' is there, the 'dead man's hand,' stiff and motionless; whatever savours of vitality is by that alone convicted of heresy and defection.

"But Christianity with its living and loving God, Begetter and Begotten, Spirit and Movement, nay more, a Creator made creature, the Maker and the made existing in One, a Divinity communicating itself by uninterrupted gradation and degree, from the most intimate union far off to the faintest irradiation, through all that it has made for love and governs in love; One who calls His creatures not slaves, not servants, but friends, nay sons, nay gods —to sum up, a religion in whose seal and secret 'God in man is one with man in God,' must also be necessarily a religion of vitality, of progress, of advancement. The contrast between it and Islam is that of movement with fixedness, of participation with sterility, of development with barrenness, of life with petrifaction. The first vital principle and the animating spirit of its birth must indeed abide ever the same, but the outer form must change with the changing days, and new offshoots of fresh sap and greenness be continually thrown out as witnesses to the vitality within, else were the vine withered and the branches dead.

"I have no intention here — it would be extremely out of place — of entering on the maze of controversy, or discussing whether any dogmatic attempt to reproduce the religious phase of a former age is likely to succeed. I only say that life supposes movement and growth, and both imply change; that to censure a living thing for growing and changing is absurd; and that to attempt to hinder it from so doing, by pinning it down on a written label, or nailing it to a Procrustean framework, is tantamount to killing it altogether.

"Now Christianity is living, and because living must grow, must advance, must change, and was meant to do so; onwards and forwards is a condition of its very existence; and I cannot but think that those who do not recongnize this, show themselves so far ignorant of its true nature and essence. On the other hand, Islam is lifeless, and because lifeless cannot grow, cannot advance, cannot change, and was never intended so to do; 'Stand still' is its motto and its most essential condition." (*Central and Eastern Arabia*, vol. i. p. 372.)

Mr. Stanley Lane Poole, in his Introduction to Lane's *Selections*, says:—

"Islám is unfortunately a social system as well as a religion; and herein lies the great difficulty of fairly estimating its good and its bad influence on the world. It is but in the nature of things that the teacher who lays down the law of the relation of man to God should also endeavour to appoint the proper relation between man and his neighbour.

* * * * *

"Moḥammad not only promulgated a religion; he laid down a complete social system, containing minute regulations for a man's conduct in all circumstances of life, with due rewards or penalties according to his fulfilment of these rules. As a religion, Islám is great: it has taught men to worship one God with a pure worship who formerly worshipped many gods impurely. As a social system, Islám is a complete failure: it has misunderstood the relations of the sexes, upon which the whole character of a nation's life hangs, and, by degrading women, has degraded each successive generation of their children down an increasing scale of infamy and corruption, until it seems almost impossible to reach a lower level of vice."

Mr. W. E. H. Lecky remarks:—

"In the first place, then, it must be observed that the enthusiasm by which Mahometanism conquered the world, was mainly a military enthusiasm. Men were drawn to it at once, and without conditions, by the splendour of the achievements of its disciples, and it declared an absolute war against all the religions it encountered. Its history, therefore, exhibits nothing of the process of gradual absorption, persuasion, compromise, and assimilation, that are exhibited in the dealings of Christianity with the barbarians. In the next place, one of the great characteristics of the Koran is the extreme care and skill with which it labours to assist men in realising the unseen. Descriptions, the most minutely detailed, and at the same time the most vivid, are mingled with powerful appeals to those sensual passions by which the imagination in all countries, but especially in those in which Mahometanism has taken root, is most forcibly influenced. In no other religion that prohibits idols is the strain upon the imagination so slight." (*History of the Rise and Influence of Rationalism*, vol. i. p. 223.)

"This great religion, which so long rivalled the influence of Christianity, had indeed spread the deepest and most justifiable panic through Christendom. Without any of those aids to the imagination which pictures and images can furnish, without any elaborate sacerdotal organization, preaching the purest Monotheism among ignorant and barbarous men, and inculcating, on the whole, an extremely high aud noble system of morals, it spread with a rapidity, and it acquired a hold over the minds of its votaries, which it is probable that no other religion has altogether equalled. It borrowed from Christianity that doctrine of salvation by belief, which is perhaps the most powerful impulse that can be applied to the characters of masses of men, and it elaborated so minutely the charms of its sensual heavens and the terrors of its material hell, as to cause the alternative to appeal with unrivalled force to the gross imaginations of the people. It possessed a book which, however inferior to that of the opposing religion, has nevertheless been the consolation and the support of millions in many ages. It taught a fatalism which, in its first age, nerved its adherents with a matchless military courage, and which, though in later days it has often paralysed their active energies, has also rarely failed to support them under the pressure of inevitable calamity. But, above all, it discovered the great though fatal secret, of uniting indissolubly the passion of the soldier with the passion of the devotee. Making the conquest of the infidel the first of duties, and proposing heaven as the certain reward of the valiant soldier, it created a blended enthusiasm that soon overpowered the divided counsels and the voluptuous governments of the East, and within a century of the death of Muḥammad, his followers had almost extirpated Christianity from its original home, founded great monarchies in Asia and Africa, planted a noble, though transient and exotic, civilisation in Spain, menaced the capital of the Eastern empire, and but for the issue of a single battle, they would probably have extended their sceptre over the energetic and progressive races of Central Europe. The wave was broken by Charles Martel, at the battle of Poictiers, and it is now useless to speculate what might have been the consequences, had Muḥammadanism unfurled its triumphant banner among those Teutonic tribes, who have so often changed their creed, and on whom the course of civilisation has so largely depended." (*Hist. of European Morals*, vol. ii. p. 266.)

"The influence of Chatholicism was seconded by Muḥammadanism, which on this (suicide), as on many other points, borrowed its teaching from the Christian Church, and even intensified it; for suicide, which is never expressly condemned in the Bible, is more than once forbidden in the Qur'ān, and the Christian duty of resignation was exaggerated by the Moslem into a complete fatalism. Under the empire of Catholicism and Muḥammadanism, suicide, during many centuries, almost absolutely ceased in all the civilised, active and progressive part of mankind. When we recollect how warmly it was applauded, or how faintly it was condemned in the civilisations of Greece and Rome, when we remember, too, that there was scarcely a barbarous tribe from Denmark to Spain who did not habitually practise it, we may realise the complete revolution which was effected in this sphere by the influence of Christianity." (*Hist. of European Morals*, vol. ii. p. 56.)

Major Durie Osborn says:—

"When Islam penetrates to countries lower in the scale of humanity than were the Arabs of Muhammad's day, it suffices to elevate them to that level. But it does so at a tremendous cost. It reproduces in its new converts the characteristics of its first—their impenetrable self-esteem, their unintelligent scorn, and blind hatred of all other creeds. And thus the capacity for all further advance is destroyed; the mind is obdurately shut to the entrance of any purer light. But it is a grievous error to confound that transient gleam of culture which illuminated Baghdad under the first Abbaside khalifs with the legitimate fruits of Islam. When the Arabs conquered Syria and Persia, they brought with them no new knowledge to take the place of that which had preceded them. Mere Bedouins of the desert, they found themselves all at once the masters of vast countries, with everything to learn. They were compelled to put themselves to school under the very people they had vanquished. Thus the Persians and Syrians, conquered though they were and tributary, from the ignorance of their masters, retained in their hands the control of the administrative machinery. The Abbaside khalifs were borne into power by means of a Persian revolution, headed by a Persian slave. Then began the endeavour to root the old Greek philosophy, and the deep and beautiful thoughts of Zoroaster, on the hard and barren soil of Muhammadanism. It was an impossible attempt to make a frail exotic flourish on uncongenial soil. It has imparted, indeed, a deceptive lustre to this period of Muhammadan history; but the orthodox Muhammadans knew that their faith and the wisdom of the Greeks could not amalgamate, and they fought fiercely against the innovators. Successive storms of barbarians sweeping down from the north of Asia, tore up the fragile plant by the roots, and scattered its blossoms to the winds. The new comers embraced the creed of the Koran in its primitive simplicity; they hated and repudiated the refinements which the Persians would fain have engrafted on it. And they won the day. The present condition of Central Asia is the legitimate fruit of Islam; not the glories of Baghdad, which were but the afterglow of the thought and culture which sank with the fall of the Sassanides, and the expulsion of the Byzantine emperors. So also in Moorish Spain. The blossom and the fruitage which Muhammadanism seemed to put forth there were, in fact, due to influences alien to Islam—to the intimate contact, namely, with Jewish and Christian thought; for when the Moors were driven back into northern Africa, all that blossom and fruitage withered away, and Northern Africa sank into the intellectual darkness and political anarchy in which it lies at the present time. There are to be found in Muhammadan history all the elements of greatness—faith, courage, endurance, self-sacrifice; but, closed within the narrow walls of a rude theology and barbarous polity, from which the capacity to grow and the liberty to modify have been sternly cut off, they work no deliverance upon the earth. They are strong only for destruction. When that work is over, they either prey upon each other, or beat themselves to death against the bars of their prison-house. No permanent dwelling-place can be erected on a foundation of sand; and no durable or humanising polity upon a foundation of fatalism, despotism, polygamy and slavery. When Muhammadan states cease to be racked by revolutions, they succumb to the poison diffused by a corrupt moral atmosphere. A Darwesh, ejaculating 'Allah!' and revolving in a series of rapid gyrations until he drops senseless, is an exact image of the course of their history." (*Islam under the Arabs*, p. 93.)

Lieutenant-Colonel W. F. Butler, C.B., remarks:—

"The Goth might ravage Italy, but the Goth came forth purified from the flames which he himself had kindled. The Saxon swept Britain, but the music of the Celtic heart softened his rough nature, and wooed him into less churlish habits. Visigoth and Frank, Heruli and Vandal, blotted out their verocity in the very light of the civilisation they had striven to extinguish. Even the Hun, wildest Tartar from the Scythian waste, was touched and softened in his wicker encampment amid Pannonian plains; but the Turk—wherever his scymitar reached—degraded, defiled, and defamed; blasting into eternal decay Greek, Roman and Latin civilisation, until, when all had gone, he sat down, satiated with savagery, to doze for two hundred years into hopeless decrepitude." (*Good Words* for September 1880.)

Literature on the subject of Muḥammadanism:—

Muhamedis Imposturæ. W. Bedwell. London 1615

A Lytell Treatyse of the Turkes Law called Alcoran. W. De Worde. London. No date.

Mahomet Unmasked. W. Bedwell. London 1642

The Alcoran of Mahomet. Alex. Ross. London 1642

Religion and Manners of Mahometans. Joseph Pitts. Exon . . . 1704

History of the Saracens. S. Ockley. London 1708

Four Treatises by Reland and others. London 1712

The True Nature of the Imposture. Dean Prideaux. London . . . 1718

Abulfeda. Translated into Latin. J. Gagnier. London 1723

Muhammadanism Explained. Joseph Morgan. London 1723

Life of Mahomet. Count Boulainvilliers. Translated. London . . 1731

Translation of Koran and Preliminary Discourse. G. Sale. London . 1734

Reflections on Mohammedism (sic.) Anon. London 1735

The Morality of the East, extracted from the Koran. Anon. London. . 1766

Roman Empire. E. Gibbon. London 1776

The Koran. Translated. Savary . 1782

Bampton Lectures. Rev. J. White. Oxford 1784

The Hidayah. Translated by C. Hamilton. London 1791

The Rise of Mahomet accounted for. N. Alcock. London 1796

Life of Mahomet. Anon. London . 1799

The Mishkāt. Translated by Mathews. Calcutta 1809

History of Muhammedanism. C. Mills. London 1817

Christianity compared with Hinduism and Muhamadanism. London . . 1823

The Muhammedan System. Rev. W. H. Mills 1828

Mahometanism Unveiled. Rev. C. Forster. London 1829

An Apology for the Life of Mohammed. G. Higgins. London . . . 1829

A Reply to Higgins. R. M. Beverley. Beverley 1829

Travels in Arabia. J. L. Burckhardt. London 1829

Controversial Tracts. Rev. H. Martyn. Edited by S. Lee. No date or place.

Animadversions on Higgins. Rev. P. Inchbald. Doncaster 1830

Notes on Bedouins and Wahhabis. J. L. Burckhardt. London . . . 1830

Observations on the Musulmans. Mrs. Meer Hasan Ali. London . . . 1832

Qanoon-e-Islam. Dr. Herklots. London 1832

History of Muhammadanism. W. C. Taylor. London 1834

History of the Wahhabies. Sir H. J. Brydges. London 1834

Muhammedan Dynasties in Spain. Al Makkari. Translated. London . 1840

The Hero as Prophet. Thomas Carlyle. London 1840

Manners and Customs of the Modern Egyptians. E. W. Lane. London . 1842

Ibn 'Khallikan's Biographical Dictionary. M. G. De Slane Translated. London 1843

Selections from the Kur-án. E. W. Lane. London 1843

Life of Mohammed. Rev. George Bush. New York 1844

The Relation of Islam to the Gospel. Dr. J. A. Moehler. Translated by J. P. Menge. Calcutta 1847

Life of Mahomet. Washington Irving. London 1850

Life of Mohammed. By Abulfeda. Translated by Rev. W. Murray. Elgin. No date.

Muhammadan Law of Sale. N. B. E. Baillie. London 1850

Life of Mohammad. A Sprenger. Calcutta 1851

Islamism, its Rise and Progress. F. A. Neale. London 1854

Pilgrimage to El Medinah and Mecca. R. F. Burton. London 1855

Life of Mahomet. W. Muir. London 1858

Mohammedan Religion Explained. Rev. J. D. Macbride. London . . 1859

Ishmael. Rev. J. M. Arnold. London 1859

Arabian Nights with Notes. E. W. Lane. London 1859

Imposture instanced in the Life of Mahomet. Rev. G. Akehurst. London 1859

Testimony borne by the Koran. W. Muir. Allahabad 1860

Religions of Syria. Rev. John Wortabet. London 1860

Muhammedan Commentary on the Bible. Syed Ahmad. Ghazeepur . 1862

Digest of Muhammadan Law. Hanifi Code. N. B. E. Baillie. London . 1865

Food for Reflection. Rev. Dr. Koelle. London 1865

Central and Eastern Arabia. W. G. Palgrave. London 1865

The Mizān ul Haqq. Dr. Pfander. Translated. London 1867

Aīn i Akbari of Abul Fazl. Translated. H. Blochman. Calcutta . . 1868

Notes on Islam. Rev. A. Brinckman. London 1868

Digest of Muhammadan Law. Imameea Code. N. B. E. Baillie. London 1869

Law of Inheritance. S. G. Grady. London 1869

Al Sirajiyyah. Translated. A. Rumsey. London 1869

Apology for Muhammad. John Davenport. London 1869

Pilgrimage to Mecca. Begum of Bhopal. London 1870

Our Indian Musulmans. W. W. Hunter. London 1871

On Dr. Hunter's "Indian Musulmans." Syed Ahmed Khan . . 1871

The Koran Translated. Rev. J. M. Rodwell. London 1871

Essays on the Life of Muhammad. Syed Ahmed Khan. London . . . 1871

Essays on Eastern Questions. W. G. Palgrave. London 1872

Manual of Laws. J. B. S. Boyle. Lahore 1873

Life of Muhammad. Syed Ameer Ali. London 1873

Tagore Lectures. Shama Churun Sircar. Calcutta 1873

Tagore Lectures. Shama Churun Sircar. Calcutta 1874

Islām and Christianity. Rev. J. M. Arnold. London 1874

Mohammed and Mohammedanism. R. Bosworth Smith. London 1874

Essay on Islam. Emanuel Deutsch. London 1874

Islam under the Arabs. R. D. Osborn. London 1876

Notes on Muhammadanism. Rev. T. P. Hughes. London. 2nd ed. . 1877

Christianity and Islam. Rev. W. R. W. Stephens. London . . . 1877

Islam and its Founder. J. W. H. Stobart. London 1878

Mohammed, Buddha, and Christ. Marcus Dods. London 1878

Islam, its Origin, Genius, and Mission. J. J. Lake. London 1878

Islam under the Khalifs of Baghdad. R. D. Osborn. London 1878

Lane's Selections from the Kurān. New ed. S. L. Poole. London . . 1879

The Miracle Play of Hasan and Husain. Sir Lewis Pelly. London . 1879

The Personal Law of Muhammedans. Syed Ameer Ali. London . . . 1880

The Faith of Islam. Rev. E. Sell. Madras 1880

The Future of Islam. W. S. Blunt. London 1880

The Quran. Translated. 2 vols. Prof. E. H. Palmer. Oxford . . 1880

Commentary on the Qurān. Rev. E. M. Wherry. London . . . 1882

Reforms in Mohammadan States. Moulvie Cheragh Ali. Bombay . 1883

Annals of the Early Caliphate. Sir W. Muir. London 1883

Religio Turcia Mahometis vita. J. Wallich. Stadae Suecorum . . . 1659

Refutatio Al Corani. L. Marracio. Patavii 1698

Specimen Historiæ Arabum. E. Pocock. Oxon 1750

Recueil des Rites et Cérémonies du Pélerinage de la Mecque. Galland. Amsterdam 1754

Bibliothèque Orientale. D'Herbelot. Maestricht 1776

Lettres sur l'Histoire des Arabes avant l'Islamisme 1836

Essai sur l'Histoire des Arabes avant l'Islamisme. A. P. Caussin de Perceval 1848

Die Geisterlehre der Moslimen. Von Hammer Purgstall. Wien 1852
Geshichte des Qorans. T. Nöldeke . 1860
Das Leben Mohammed's nach Ibn Ishak. Bearbeitet von Ibn Hischam, by Weil 1864
Mahomet et le Coran. T. B. de St. Hilaire. Paris 1865
Geshichte der herrschenden Ideen des Islams. A. von Kremer . . . 1868
Das Leben und die Lehre des Mohammad. A. Sprenger. Berlin . . 1869
L'Islamisme d'après le Coran, Garcin de Tassy. Paris 1874
Essai sur l'Histoire de l'Islamisme. R. Dozy 1879

MUḤARRAM (محرم). *Lit.* "That which is forbidden." Anything sacred. (1) The first month of the Muḥammadan year [MONTHS.] (2) The first ten days of the month, observed in commemoration of the martyrdom of al-Ḥusain, the second son of Fāṭimah, the Prophet's daughter, by ʿAlī. [AL-HUSAIN.] These days of lamentation are only observed by the Shīʿah Muslims, but the tenth day of Muḥarram is observed by the Sunnīs in commemoration of its having been the day on which Adam and Eve, heaven and hell, the pen, fate, life and death, were created. [ASHURA'.]

The ceremonies of the Muḥarram differ much in different places and countries. The following is a graphic description of the observance of the Muḥarram at Ispahan in the year 1811, which has been taken, with some slight alterations from Morier's *Second Journey through Persia* :—

The tragical termination of al-Ḥusain's life, commencing with his flight from al-Madīnah and terminating with his death on the plain of Karbalā', has been drawn up in the form of a drama, consisting of several parts, of which one is performed by actors on each successive day of the mourning. The last part, which is appointed for the Roz-i-Qatl, comprises the events of the day on which he met his death, and is acted with great pomp before the King, in the largest square of the city. The subject, which is full of affecting incidents, would of itself excite great interest in the breasts of a Christian audience; but allied as it is with all the religious and national feelings of the Persians, it awakens their strongest passions. Al-Husain would be a hero in our eyes; in theirs he is a martyr. The vicissitudes of his life, his dangers in the desert, his fortitude, his invincible courage, and his devotedness at the hour of his death, are all circumstances upon which the Persians dwell with rapture, and which excite in them an enthusiasm not to be diminished by lapse of time. The celebration of this mourning keeps up in their minds the remembrance of those who destroyed him, and consequently their hatred for all Musalmāns who do not partake of their feelings. They execrate Yazīd and curse ʿUmar with such rancour, that it is necessary to have witnessed the scenes that are exhibited in their cities to judge of the degree of fanaticism which possesses them at this time. I have seen some of the most violent of them, as they vociferated, "O Ḥusain!" walk about the streets almost naked, with only their loins covered, and their bodies streaming with blood, by the voluntary cuts which they have given to themselves, either as acts of love, anguish, or mortification. Such must have been the cuttings of which we read in Holy Writ, which were forbidden to the Israelites by Moses (Lev. xix. 28, Deut. xiv. 1), and these extravagances, I conjecture, must resemble the practices of the priests of Baal, who cried aloud and cut themselves after this manner with knives and lancets, till the blood gushed out upon them. 1 Kings xviii. 28; see also Jeremiah xvi. 5, 6, and 7.

The preparations which were made throughout the city consisted in erecting large tents, that are there called *takiyah*, in the streets and open places, in fitting them up with black linen, and furnishing them with objects emblematical of the mourning. These tents are erected either at the joint expense of the district, or by men of consequence, as an act of devotion; and all ranks of people have a free access to them. The expense of a *takiyah* consists in the hire of a *mulla*, or priest, of actors and their clothes, and in the purchase of lights. Many there are who seize this opportunity of atoning for past sins, or of rendering thanks to heaven for some blessing, by adding charity to the good act of erecting a *takiyah*, and distribute gratuitous food to those who attend it.

Our neighbour Muḥammad Khān had a *takiyah* in his house, to which all the people of the district flocked in great numbers. During the time of this assemblage we heard a constant noise of drums, cymbals, and trumpets. We remarked that besides the *takiyah* in different open places and streets of the town, a wooden pulpit, without any appendage, was erected, upon which a *mulla*, or priest, was mounted, preaching to the people who were collected around him. A European ambassador, who is said to have intrigued with Yazīd in favour of al-Ḥusain, was brought forward to be an actor in one of the parts of the tragedy, and the populace were in consequence inclined to look favourably upon us. Notwithstanding the excitation of the public mind, we did not cease to take our usual rides, and we generally passed unmolested through the middle of congregations, during the time of their devotions. Such little scruples have they at our seeing their religious ceremonies, that on the eighth night of the Muḥarram the Grand Vizier invited the whole of the embassy to attend his *takiyah*. On entering the room we found a large assembly of Persians clad in dark-coloured clothes, which, accompanied with their black caps, their black beards, and their dismal faces, really looked as if they were afflicting their souls. They neither wore their dagggers, nor any parts of their dress which they look upon as ornamental. A mulla of high consideration sat next to the

Grand Vizier, and kept him in serious conversation, whilst the remaining part of the society communicated with each other in whispers. After we had sat some time, the windows of the room in which we were seated were thrown open, and we then discovered a priest placed on a high chair, under the covering of a tent, surrounded by a crowd of the populace; the whole of the scene being lighted up with candles. He commenced by an exordium, in which he reminded them of the great value of each tear shed for the sake of the Imām al-Ḥusain, which would be an atonement for a past life of wickedness; and also informed them with much solemnity, that whatsoever soul it be that shall not be afflicted in the same day, shall be cut off from among the people. He then began to read from a book, with a sort of nasal chaunt, that part of the tragic history of al-Ḥusain appointed for the day, which soon produced its effect upon his audience, for he scarcely had turned over three leaves, before the Grand Vizier commenced to shake his head to and fro, to utter in a most piteous voice the usual Persian exclamation of grief, "*Wahi! Wahi! Wahi!*" both of which acts were followed in a more or less violent manner by the rest of the audience. The chaunting of the mulla lasted nearly an hour, and some parts of his story were indeed pathetic, and well calculated to rouse the feelings of a superstitious and lively people. In one part of it, all the company stood up, and I observed that the Grand Vizier turned himself towards the wall, with his hand extended before him, and prayed. After the mulla had finished, a company of actors appeared, some dressed as women, who chaunted forth their parts from slips of paper, in a sort of recitative, that was not unpleasing even to our ears. In the very tragical parts, most of them appeared to cry very unaffectedly; and as I sat near the Grand Vizier, and to his neighbour the priest, I was witness to many real tears that fell from them. In some of these mournful assemblies, it is the custom for a mulla to

A MUHARRAM PROCESSION IN INDIA. (*By a Native Artist.*)

go about to each person at the height of his grief, with a piece of cotton in his hand, with which he carefully collects the falling tears, and which he then squeezes into a bottle, preserving them with the greatest caution. This practically illustrates that passage in the 56th Psalm, verse 8, "Put thou my tears into thy bottle." Some Persians believe that in the agony of death, when all medicines have failed, a drop of tears so collected, put into the mouth of a dying man, has been known to revive him; and it is for such use, that they are collected.

On the Roz-i-Qatl, or day of martyrdom, the tenth day, the Ambassador was invited by the King to be present at the termination of the ceremonies, in which the death of al-Ḥusain was to be represented. We set off after breakfast, and placed ourselves in a small tent, that was pitched for our accommodation over an arched gateway, which was situated close to the room in which His Majesty was to be seated.

We looked upon the great square which is in front of the palace, at the entrance of which we perceived a circle of Cajars, or people of the King's own tribe, who were standing barefooted, and beating their breasts in cadence to the chaunting of one who stood in the centre, and with whom they now and then joined their voices in chorus. Smiting the breast is a universal act throughout the mourning; and the breast is made bare for that purpose, by unbuttoning the top of the shirt. The King, in order to show his humility, ordered the Cajars, among whom were many of his own relations, to walk about without either shoes or stockings, to superintend the order of the different ceremonies about to be performed, and they were to be seen stepping tenderly over the stones, with sticks in their hands, doing the duties of menials, now keeping back a crowd, then dealing out blows with their sticks, and settling the order of the processions.

Part of the square was partitioned off by an enclosure, which was to represent the town of Karbalā', near which al-Ḥusain was put to death; and close to this were two small tents, which were to represent his encampment in the desert with his family. A wooden platform covered with carpets, upon which the actors were to perform, completed all the scenery used on the occasion.

A short time after we had reached our tent, the King appeared, and although we could not see him, yet we were soon apprised of his presence by all the people standing up, and by the bowing of his officers. The procession then commenced as follows:—First came a stout man, naked from the waist upwards, balancing in his girdle a long thick pole, surmounted by an ornament made of tin, curiously wrought with devices from the Qur'ān, in height altogether about thirty feet. Then another, naked like the former, balanced an ornamental pole in his girdle still more ponderous, though not so high, upon which a young darvesh resting his feet upon the bearer's girdle had placed himself, chaunting verses with all his might in praise of the King. After him a person of more strength and more nakedness, a water carrier, walked forwards, bearing an immense leather sack filled with water slung over his back. This personage, we were told, was emblematical of the great thirst which al-Ḥusain suffered in the desert.

A litter in the shape of a sarcophagus, which was called *Qabr-i-Husain*, or the tomb of al-Ḥusain (a *Tāʿziyah*) succeeded, borne on the shoulders of eight men. On its front was a large oval ornament entirely covered with precious stones, and just above it, a great diamond star. On a small projection were two tapers placed on candlesticks enriched with jewels. The top and sides were covered with Cashmere shawls, and on

THE MUHARRAM CEREMONIES IN THE IMAMBARAH OR TAKIAH IN INDIA.
(By a Native Artist.)

the summit rested a turban, intended to represent the head-dress of the Khalīfah. On each side walked two men bearing poles, from which a variety of beautiful shawls were suspended. At the top of which were representations of al-Husain's hand studded with jewellery.

After this came four led horses, caparisoned in the richest manner. The fronts of their heads were ornamented with plates, entirely covered with diamonds, that emitted a thousand beautiful rays. Their bodies were dressed with shawls and gold stuffs; and on their saddles were placed some objects emblematical of the death of al-Ḥusain. When all these had passed, they arranged themselves in a row to the right of the King's apartment.

After a short pause, a body of fierce-looking men, with only a loose white sheet thrown over their naked bodies, marched forwards. They were all begrimed with blood; and each brandishing a sword, they sang a sort of a hymn, the tones of which were very wild. These represented the sixty-two relations, or the Martyrs, as the Persians call them, who accompanied al-Ḥusain, and were slain in defending him. Close after them was led a white horse, covered with artificial wounds, with arrows stuck all about him, and caparisoned in black, representing the horse upon which al-Ḥusain was mounted when he was killed. A band of about fifty men, striking two pieces of wood together in their hands, completed the procession. They arranged themselves in rows before the King, and marshalled by a *maître de ballet*, who stood in the middle to regulate their movements, they performed a dance, clapping their hands in the best possible time. The *maître de ballet* all this time sang in recitative, to which the dancers joined at different intervals with loud shouts and reiterated clapping of their pieces of wood.

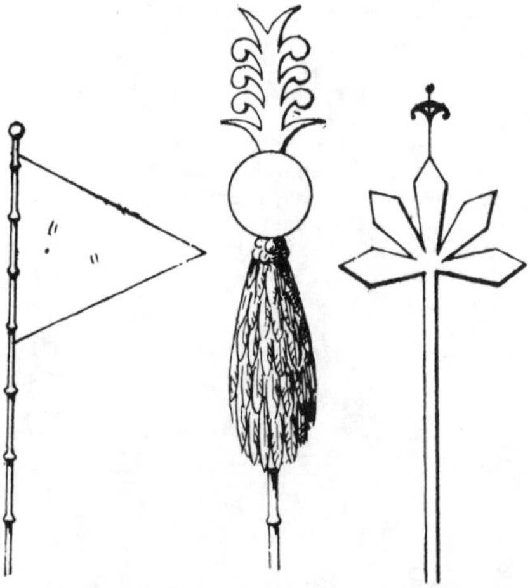

MUHARRAM STANDARDS.

The two processions were succeeded by the tragedians. Al-Ḥusain came forward, followed by his wives, sisters, and first relatives. They performed many long and

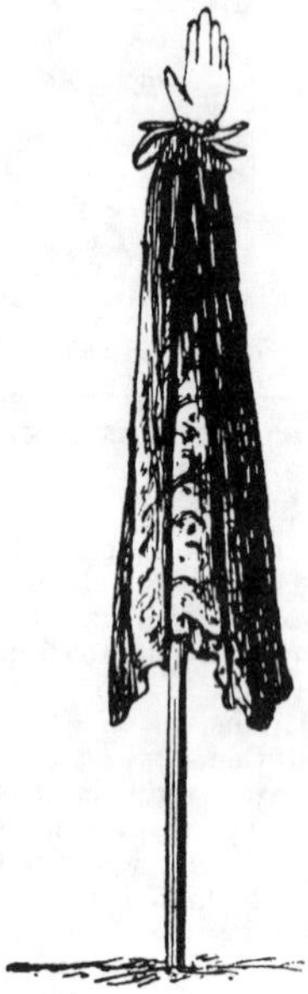

HUSAIN'S HAND AND STANDARD.

tedious acts; but as our distance from the stage was too great to hear the many affecting things which they no doubt said to each other, we will proceed at once to where the unfortunate al-Ḥusain lay extended on the ground, ready to receive the death-stroke from a ruffian dressed in armour, who acted the part of executioner. At this moment a burst of lamentation issued from the multitude, and heavy sobs and real tears came from almost every one of those who were near enough to come under our inspection. The indignation of the populace wanted some object upon which to vent itself, and it fell upon those of the actors who had performed the part of Yazīd's soldiers. No sooner was al-Ḥusain killed, than they were driven off the ground by a volley of stones, followed by shouts of abuse. We were informed that it is so difficult to procure performers to fill these characters, that on the present occasion a party of Russian prisoners were pressed into the army of Yazīd, and they made as speedy an exit after the catastrophe as it was in their power.

The scene terminated by the burning of Karbalā'. Several reed huts had been constructed behind the enclosure before mentioned, which of a sudden were set on fire. The tomb of al-Ḥusain was seen covered with black cloth, and upon it sat a figure disguised in a tiger's skin, which was intended to represent the miraculous lion, recorded to have kept watch over his remains after he had been buried. The most extraordinary part of the whole exhibition was the representation of the dead bodies of the martyrs; who having been decapitated, were all placed in a row, each body with a head close to it. To effect this, several Persians buried themselves alive, leaving the head out just above ground; whilst others put their heads under ground, leaving out the body. The heads and bodies were placed in such relative positions to each other, as to make it appear that they had been severed. This is done by way of penance; but in hot weather, the violence of the exertion has been known to produce death. The whole ceremony was terminated by a k͟huṭbah, or oration, in praise of al-Ḥusain. (Morier's *Second Journey through Persia.*)

"The martyrdom of Hasan and Husain is celebrated by the Shiahs all over India, during the first ten days of the month of Mohurrum. Attached to every Shiah's house is an Imambarrah, a hall or inclosure built expressly for the celebration of the anniversary of the death of Husain. The enclosure is generally arcaded along its side, and in most instances it is covered in with a domed roof. Against the side of the Imambarrah, directed towards Mecca, is set the *tabut*—also called *tazia* (*ta'ziyah*), or model of the tombs at Kerbela. In the houses of the wealthier Shiahs, these *tabuts* are fixtures, and are beautifully fashioned of silver and gold, or of ivory and ebony, embellished all over with inlaid work. The poorer Shiahs provide themselves with a *tabut* made for the occasion of lath and plaster, tricked out in mica and tinsel. A week before the new moon of the Mohurrum, they enclose a space, called the *tabut khana*, in which the *tabut* is prepared; and the very moment the new moon is seen, a spade is struck into the ground before "the enclosure of the tombs," where a pit is afterwards dug, in which a bonfire is lighted, and kept burning through all the ten days of the Mohurrum solemnities. Those who cannot afford to erect a *tabut khana*, or even to put up a little *tabut* or *taziah* in their dwelling-house, always have a Mohurrum fire lighted, if it consist only of a night-light floating at the bottom of an earthen pot or basin sunk in the ground. It is doubtful whether this custom refers to the trench of fire Husain set blazing behind his camp, or is a survival from the older Ashura (ten days) festival, which is said to have been instituted in commemoration of the deliverance of the Hebrew Arabs from Pharaoh and his host at the Red Sea; or from the yet more ancient Bael fire. But, in India, these Mohurrum fires, especially among the more ignorant populace, Hindus as well as Mohammedans, are regarded with the most superstitious reverence, and have a greater hold on them even than the *tabuts*. All day long the passers by stop before the

A MUHARRAM TABUT. (*A. F. Hole.*)

fires and make their vows over them, and all night long the crowds dance round them, and leap through the flames and scatter about the burning brands snatched from them. The *tabut* is lighted up like an altar, with innumerable green wax candles, and nothing can be more brilliant than the appearance of an Imambarrah of white stone, or polished white stucco, picked out in green, lighted up with glass chandeliers, sconces, and oil-lamps, arranged along the leading architectural lines of the building, with its *tabut* on one side, dazzling to blindness. Before the *tabut* are placed the "properties" to be used by the celebrants in the "Passion Play," the bows and arrows, the sword and spear, and the banners of Husain, &c.; and in front of it is set a movable pulpit, also made of the richest materials, and covered with rich brocades in green and gold. Such is the theatre in which twice daily during the first ten days of the month of Mohurrum, the deaths of the first martyrs of Islam are yearly commemorated in India. Each day has its special solemnity, corresponding with the succession of events during the ten days that Husain was encamped on the fatal plain of Kerbela; but the prescribed order of the services in the daily development of the great Shiah function of the Mohurrum would appear not to be always strictly observed in Bombay." (Pelly's *Miracle Play of Hasan and Husain*, Preface, p. xvii.)

The drama, or "Miracle Play" which is recited in Persia during the Muḥarram, has been rendered into English by Colonel Sir Lewis Pelly, K.C.B. (Allen & Co., 1879), from which we take the death scene of al-Ḥusain on the battle-field of Karbalā', a scene which, the historian Gibbon (*Decline and Fall*, vol. ix. ch. 341) says, "in a distant age and climate, will awaken the sympathy of the coldest reader."

"*Husain.*—I am sore distressed at the unkind treatment received at the hands of the cruel heavens. Pitiful tyranny is exercised towards me by a cruel, unbelieving army! All the sorrows and troubles of this world have overwhelmed me! I am become a butt for the arrow of affliction and trouble. I am a holy bird stript of its quills and feathers by the hand of the archer of tyranny, and am become, O friends, utterly disabled, and unable to fly to my sacred nest. They are going to kill me mercilessly, for no other crime or guilt except that I happen to be a prophet's grandson.

"*Shimar (challenging him).*—O Husain, why dost thou not appear in the field? Why dost not thy majesty show thy face in battle? How long art thou going to sit still without displaying thy valour in war? Why dost thou not put on thy robe of martyrdom and come forth? If thou art indeed so magnanimous as not to fear death, if thou carest not about the whistling sounds of the arrows when let fly from the bow, mount thou, quickly, thy swift horse named Zú'l janáh, and deliver thy soul from so many troubles. Yea, come to the field of battle, be it as it may. Enter soon among thy women, and with tears bid them a last farewell; then come forth to war, and show us thy great fortitude.

"*Husain (talking to himself).*—Although the accursed fellow, Shimar, will put me to death in an hour's time, yet the reproachful language of the enemy seems to be worse than destruction itself. It is better that the foe should sever my head cruelly from the body, than make me hear these abusive words. What can I do? I have no one left to help me, no Kásim to hold my stirrup for a minute when about to mount All are gone! Look around if thou canst find anyone to defend the descendant of Muhammad, the chosen of God—if thou canst see any ready to assist the holy family of God's Prophet! In this land of trials there is no kind protector to have compassion on the household of the Apostle of God, and befriend them.

"*Zainab.*—May I be offered for the sad tones of thy voice, dear brother! Time has thrown on my head the black earth of sorrow. It has grieved me to the quick. Wait, brother, do not go till thy Kásim arrives. Have patience for a minute, my 'Alí Akbar is coming.

"*Husain (looking around).*—Is there one who wishes to please God, his Maker? Is there any willing to behave faithfully towards his real friends? Is there a person ready to give up his life for our sake, to save us, to defend us in this dreadful struggle of Karbalá?

"*Zainab.*—O Lord, Zainab's brother has no one to assist or support him! Occasions of his sorrows are innumerable, without anyone to sympathise with him in the least? Sad and desolate, he is leaning on his spear! He has bent his neck in a calamitous manner; he has no famous 'Alí Akbar, no renowned 'Abbás any more!

"*Husain.*—Is there anyone to pity our condition, to help us in this terrible conflict of Karbalá? Is there a kind soul to give us a hand of assistance for God's sake?

"*Zainab.*—Brave cavalier of Karbalá, it is not fitting for thee to be so hurried. Go a little more slowly; troubles will come quickly enough. Didst thou ever say thou hadst a Zainab in the tent? Is not this poor creature weeping and mourning for thee?

"*The Imam Husain.*—Dear sister, thou rest of my disquieted, broken heart, smite on thy head and mourn, thou thousand-noted nightingale. To-day I shall be killed by the ignoble Shimar. To-day shall the rose be turned out of its delightful spot by the tyranny of the thistle. Dear sister, if any dust happen to settle on the rosy cheeks of my lovely daughter Sukainah, be pleased to wash it away most tenderly with the rose-water of thy tears? My daughter has been accustomed to sit always in the dear lap of her father whenever she wished to rest; for my sake, receive and caress her in thy bosom.

"*Zainab.*—O thou intimate friend of this assembly of poor afflicted strangers, the flaming effect of thy speech has left no rest in my mind. Tell me, what have we done that thou shouldest so reward us? Who is the criminal among us for whose sake we must suffer thus? Take us back, brother, to Madínah, to the sacred monument of our noble grandfather; let us go home, and live like queens in our own country.

"*Husain.*—O my afflicted, distressed, tormented sister, would to God there were a way of escape for me! Notwithstanding they have cruelly cut down the cypress-like stature of my dear son 'Alí Akbar; notwithstanding Kásim my lovely nephew tinged himself with his own blood; still they are intent to kill me also. They do not allow me to go back from 'Irák, nor do they let me turn elsewhere. They will neither permit me to go to India, nor the capital of China. I cannot set out for the territory of Abyssinia, or take refuge in Zanzibar.

"*Zainab.*—Oh, how am I vexed in my mind, dear brother, on hearing these sad things! May I die, rather than listen to such affecting words any more! What shall we, an assembly of desolate widows and orphans, do after thou art gone? Oh! how can we live?

"*Husain.*—O miserable creature, weep not now, nor be so very much upset; thou shalt cry plentifully hereafter, owing to the wickedness of time. When the wicked Shimar shall sever my head from the body; when thou shalt be made a captive prisoner, and forced to ride on an unsaddled camel; when my body shall be trampled under foot by the enemy's horses, and trodden under their hoofs; when my beloved Sukainah shall be cruelly struck by Shimar, my wicked murderer; when they shall lead thee away captive from Karbalá to Shám; and when they shall make thee and others live there in a horrible, ruined place; yea, when thou shalt see all this, then thou mayest, and verily wilt, cry. But I admonish thee, sister, since this sad case has no remedy but patience, to resign the whole matter, submissively, to the Lord, the good Maker of all! Mourn not for my misfortune, but bear it patiently, without giving occasion to the enemy to rejoice triumphantly on this account, or speak reproachfully concerning us.

"*Kulsúm.*—Thou struttest about gaily, O Husain, thou beloved of my heart. Look a little behind thee; see how Kulsúm is sighing after thee with tearful eyes! I am strewing pearls in thy way, precious jewels from the sea of my eyes! Let me put my head on the hoof of thy winged steed, Zú'l janáh.

"*Husain.*—Beloved sister, kindle not a fire in my heart by so doing. Take away thy head from under the hoof of my steed. O thousand-noted nightingale, sing not such a sad-toned melody. I am going away; be thou the kind keeper of my helpless ones.

"*Kulsúm.*—Behold what the heavens have at length brought on me! what they have done also to my brother! Him they have made to have parched lips through thirst, and me they have caused to melt into water, and gush out like tears from the eyes! Harsh severity is mingled with tyrannous cruelty.

"*Husain.*—Trials, afflictions, and pains, the thicker they fall on man, the better, dear sister, do they prepare him for his journey heavenward. We rejoice in tribulations, seeing they are but temporary, and yet they work out an eternal and blissful end. Though it is predestined that I should suffer martyrdom in this shameful manner, yet the treasury of everlasting happiness shall be at my disposal as a consequent reward. Thou must think of that, and be no longer sorry. The dust raised in the field of such battles is as highly esteemed by me, O sister, as the philosopher's stone was, in former times, by the alchemists; and the soil of Karbalá is the sure remedy of my inward pains.

"*Kulsúm.*—May I be sacrificed for thee! Since this occurrence is thus inevitable, I pray thee describe to thy poor sister Kulsúm her duty after thy death. Tell me, where shall I go, or in what direction set my face? What am I to do? and which of thy orphan children am I to caress most?

"*Husain.*—Show thy utmost kindness, good sister, to Sukainah, my darling girl, for the pain of being fatherless is most severely felt by children too much fondled by their parents, especially girls. I have regard to all my children, to be sure, but I love Sukainah most.

"*An old Female Slave of Husain's mother.*—Dignified master, I am sick and weary in heart at the bare idea of separation from thee. Have a kind regard to me, an old slave, much stricken with age! Master, by thy soul do I swear that I am altogether weary of life. I have grown old in thy service; pardon me, please, all the faults ever committed by me.

"*Husain.*—Yes, thou hast served us, indeed, for a very long time. Thou hast shown much affection and love toward me and my children, O handmaid of my dear mother Fátimah; thou hast verily suffered much in our house: how often didst thou grind corn with thine own hand for my mother! Thou hast also dandled Husain most caressingly in thy arms. Thou art black-faced, that is true, but thou hast, I opine, a pure white heart, and art much esteemed by us. To-day I am about to leave thee, owing thee, at the same time, innumerable thanks for the good services thou hast performed; but I beg thy pardon for all inconsiderate actions on my part.

"*The Maid.*—May I be a sacrifice for thee, thou royal ruler of the capital of faith! turn not my days black, like my face, thou benevolent master. Truly I have had many troubles on thy behalf. How many nights have I spent in watchfulness at thy cradle! At one moment I would caress thee in my arms, at another I would fondle thee in my bosom. I became prematurely old by my diligent service, O Husain! Is it proper now that thou shouldst put round my poor neck the heavy chain of thy intolerable absence? Is this, dear master, the reward of the services I have done thee?

"*Husain.*—Though thy body, O maid, is now broken down by age and infirmity, yet thou hast served us all the days of thy life with sincerity and love; thou must know, therefore, that thy diligence and vigilance will never be disregarded by us. Excuse me to-day, when I am offering my body and soul in the cause of God, and cannot help thee at all; but be sure I will fully pay the reward of thy services in the day of universal account.

"*The Maid.*—Dost thou remember, good sir, how many troubles I have suffered with thee for the dear sake of 'Alí Akbar, the light of thine eyes? Though I have not suckled him with my own breasts, to be sure, yet I laboured hard for him till he reached the age of eighteen years and came here to Karbalá. But, alas! dear flourishing 'Alí Akbar has been this day cruelly killed—what a pity! and I strove so much for his sake, yet all, as it were, in vain. Yea, what a sad loss!

"*Husain.*—Speak not of my 'Alí Akbar any more, O maiden, nor set fire to the granary of my patience and make it flame. (*Turning to his sister.*) Poor distressed Zainab, have the goodness to be kind always to my mother's old maid, for she has experienced many troubles in our family; she has laboured hard in training 'Alí Akbar my son.

"*Umm Lailah* (*the mother of 'Alí Akbar*).—The elegant stature of my Akbar fell on the ground; like as a beautiful cypress tree it was forcibly felled! Alas for the memory of thy upright stature! Alas, O my youthful son of handsome form and appearance! Alas my troubles at night-time for thee! How often did I watch thy bed, singing lullabies for thee until the morning! How sweet is the memory of those times! yea, how pleasant the very thought of those days! Alas! where art thou now, dear child? O thou who art ever remembered by me, come and see thy mother's wretched condition, come!

"*Husain.*—O Lord, why is this mournful voice so affecting? Methinks the owner of it, the bemoaning person, has a flame in her heart. It resembles the doleful tone of a lapwing whose wings are burned! like as when a miraculous lapwing, the companion of Solomon the wise, the king of God's holy people, received intelligence suddenly about the death of its royal guardian!

"*Umm Lailah.*—Again I am put in mind of my dear son! O my heart, melted into blood, pour thyself forth! Dear son, whilst thou wast alive, I had some honour and respect, everybody had some regard for me; but since thou art gone, I am altogether abandoned. Woe be to me! woe be to me! I am despised and rejected. Woe unto me! woe unto me!

"*Husain.*—Do not set fire to the harvest of my soul any further. Husain is, before God, greatly ashamed of his shortcomings towards thee. Come out from the tent, for it is the last meeting previous to separating from one another for ever; thy distress is an additional weight to the heavy burden of my grief.

"*The Mother of 'Alí Akbar.*—I humbly state it, O glory of all ages, that I did not expect from thy saintship that thou wouldest disregard thy handmaid in such a way. Thou dost show thy kind regard and favour to all except me. Dost thou not remember my sincere services done to thee? Am I not by birth a descendant of the glorious kings of Persia, brought as a captive to Arabia when the former empire fell and gave place to the new-born monarchy of the latter kingdom? The Judge, the living Creator, was pleased to grant me an offspring, whom we called 'Alí Akbar, this day lost to us for ever. May I be offered for thee! While 'Alí Akbar my son was alive, I had indeed a sort of esteem and credit with thee; but now that my cypress, my newly-sprung-up cedar, is unjustly felled, I have fallen from credit too, and must therefore shed tears.

"*Husain.*—Be it known unto thee, O thou violet of the flower-garden of modesty, that thou art altogether mistaken. I swear by the holy enlightened dust of my mother Zahrah's grave, that thou art more honourable and dearer now than ever. I well remember the affectionate recommendations of 'Alí Akbar, our son, concerning thee. How much he was mindful of thee at the moment of his parting! How tenderly he cared for thee, and spoke concerning thee to every one of his family!

"*'Alí Akbar's Mother.*—O gracious Lord, I adjure thee, by the merit of my son, 'Alí Akbar, never to lessen the shadow of Husain from over my head. May no one ever be in my miserable condition—never be a desolate, homeless woman, like me!

"*Husain.*—O thou unfortunate Zainab, my sister, the hour of separation is come! The day of joy is gone for ever! the night of affliction has drawn near! Drooping, withering sister, yet most blest in thy temper, I have a request from thee which I fear to make known.

"*Zainab.*—May I be a sacrifice for thy heart, thou moon-faced, glorious sun! there is nobody here, if thou hast a private matter to disclose to thy sister.

"*Husain.*—Dear unfortunate sister, who art already severely vexed in heart, if I tell thee what my request is, what will be thy condition then? Though I cannot restrain myself from speaking, still I am in doubt as to which is better, to speak, or to forbear.

"*Zainab.*—My breast is pierced! My heart boils within me like a cauldron, owing to this thy conversation. Thou soul of thy sister, hold not back from Zainab what thou hast in thy mind.

"*Husain.*—My poor sister, I am covered with shame before thee, I cannot lift up my head. Though the request is a trifle, yet I know it is grievous to thee to grant. It is this; bring me an old, dirty, ragged garment to put on. But do not ask me, I pray thee, the reason why, until I myself think it proper to tell thee.

"*Zainab.*—I am now going to the tent to fetch thee what thou seekest; but I am utterly astonished, brother, as to why thou dost want this loathsome thing. (*Returning with a tattered shirt.*) Take it, here is the ragged robe for which thou didst ask. I wonder what thou wilt do with it.

"*Husain.*—Do not remain here, dear sister. Go for awhile to thine own tent; for if thou see that which I am about to do, thou wilt be grievously disturbed. Turn to thy tent, poor miserable sister, listen to what I say, and leave me, I pray thee, alone.

"*Zainab (going away).*—I am gone, but I am sorry I cannot tell what this enigma means. It is puzzling indeed! Remain thou with thy mysterious coat, O Husain! May all of us be offered as a ransom for thee, dear brother! Thou art without any to assist or befriend thee! Thou art surrounded by the wicked enemy! Yes, thy kind helpers have all been killed by the unbelieving nation!

"*Husain (putting on the garment).*—The term of life has no perpetual duration in itself. Who ever saw in a flower-garden a rose without its thorn! I will put on this old robe close to my skin, and place over it my new apparel, though neither the old nor the new of this world can be depended on. I hope Zainab has not been observing what I have been doing, for, poor creature, she can scarcely bear the sight of any such like thing.

"*Zainab.*—Alas! I do not know what is the matter with Husain, my brother. What has an old garment to do with being a king? Dost thou desire, O Husain, that the enemy should come to know this thing and reproach thy sister about it? Put off, I pray thee, this old ragged garment, otherwise I shall pull off my head-dress, and uncover my head for shame.

"*Husain.*—Rend not thy dress, modest sister, nor pull off thy head-covering. There is a mystery involved in my action. Know that what Husain has done has a good meaning in it. His putting on an old garment is not without its signification.

"*Zainab.*—What mystery can be in this work, thou perfect high priest of faith? I will never admit any until thou shalt have fully explained the thing according to my capacity.

"*The Imám.*—To-day, dear sister, Shimar will behave cruelly towards me. He will sever my dear head from the body. His dagger not cutting my throat, he will be obliged to sever my head from behind. After he has killed me, when he begins to strip me of my clothes, he may perchance be ashamed to take off this ragged robe and thereby leave my body naked on the ground.

"*Zainab.*—O Lord, have mercy on my distracted heart! Thou alone art aware of the state of my mind. Gracious Creator, preserve the soul of Husain! Let not heaven pull down my house over me!

"*Sukainah.*—Dear father, by our Lord it is a painful thing to be fatherless; a misery, a great calamity to be helpless, bleeding in the heart, and an outcast! Dismount from the saddle, and make me sit by thy side. To pass over me or neglect me at such a time is very distressing. Let me put my head on thy dear lap, O father. It is sad thou shouldst not be aware of thy dear child's condition.

"*Husain.*—Bend not thy neck on one side, thou my beloved child; nor weep so sadly, like an orphan. Neither moan so melodiously, like a disconsolate nightingale. Come, lay thy dear head on my knees once more, and shed not so copiously a flood of tears from thine eyes, thou spirit of my life.

"*Sukainah.*—Dear father, thou whose lot is but grief, have mercy on me, mercy! O thou my physician in every pain and trouble, have pity on me! have pity on me! Alas, my heart, for the mention of the word separation! Alas, my grievance, for what is unbearable!

"*Husain.*—Groan not, wail not, my dear Sukainah, my poor oppressed, distressed girl. Go to thy tent and sleep soundly in thy bed until thy father gets thee some water to drink.

"*Zainab.*—Alas! alas! woe to me! my Husain is gone from me! Alas! alas! the arrow of my heart is shot away from the hand! Woe unto me, a thousand woes! I am to remain without Husain! The worshipper of truth is gone to meet his destined fate with a blood-stained shroud!

"*Husain.*—My disconsolate Zainab, be not so impatient. My homeless sister, show not thyself so fretful. Have patience, sister, the reward of the patient believers is the best of all. Render God thanks, the crown of intercession is fitted for our head only.

"*Zainab.*—O my afflicted mother, thou best of all women, pass a minute by those in Karbalá! see thy daughters prisoners of sorrow! behold them amidst strangers and foreigners. Come out awhile from thy pavilion in Paradise, O Fátimah, and weep affectionately over the state of us, thy children!

"*Husain.*—I have become friendless and without any helper, in a most strange manner. I have lost my troop and army in a wonderful way. Where is Akbar my son? let him come to me and hold the bridle of my horse, that I may mount. Where is Kásim my nephew? will he not help me and get ready my stirrup to make me cheerful? Why should I not shed much blood from mine eyes, seeing I cannot behold 'Abbás my standard-bearer? A brother is for the day of misfortune and calamity! A brother is better than a hundred diadems and thrones! A brother is the essence of life in the world! He who has a brother, though he be old, yet is young. Who is there to bring my horse for me? there is none. There is none even to weep for me in this state of misery!

"*Kulsúm.*—Because there is no 'Alí Akbar, dear brother, to help thee, Zainab, thy sister, will hold the horse for thee; and seeing 'Abbás, thy brother, is no longer to be found, I myself will bear the standard before thy winged steed instead of him.

"*Zainab.*—Let Zainab mourn bitterly for her brother's desolation. Who ever saw a woman, a gentlewoman, doing the duty of a groom or servant? Who can know, O Lord, besides Thee, the sad state of Husain in Karbalá, where his people so deserted him that a woman like myself is obliged to act as a servant for him?

"*Kulsúm.*—I am a standard-bearer for Husain, the martyr of Karbalá, O Lord God. I am the sister of 'Abbás; yea, the miserable sister of both. O friends, it being the tenth day of Muharram, I am therefore assisting Husain. I am bearing the ensign for him instead of 'Abbás my brother, his standard-bearer.

"*Zainab.*—Uncover your breasts a minute, O ye tear-shedding people, for it is time to beat the drum, seeing the king is going to ride. O Solomon the Prophet, where is thy glory? what has become of thy pompous retinue? Where are thy brothers, nephews, and companions?

"*Husain.*—There are none left to help me. My sister Zainab holds the bridle of the horse, and walks before me. Who ever saw a lady acting thus?

"*Zainab.*—Thou art going all alone! May the souls of all be a ransom for thee! and may thy departure make souls quit their bodies! A resurrection will be produced in thy tent by the cry of orphans and widows.

"*Husain.*—Sister, though it grieves me to go, yet I do it; peradventure I may see the face of Ashgar and the countenance of Akbar, those cypresses, those roses of Paradise.

"*Zainab.*—Would to God Zainab had died this very minute before thy face, in thy sight, that she might not behold such elegant bodies, such beautiful forms, rolling in their own blood!

"*Husain.*—O poor sister, if thou die here in this land in that sudden way that thou desirest, then who will ride in thy stead, in the city of Kúfah, on the camel's back?

"*Zainab.*—Slight not my pain, dear brother, for Zainab is somewhat alarmed as to the import of thy speech. What shall I do with thy family—with the poor widows and young children?

"*Husain.*—O afflicted one, it is decreed I should be killed by means of daggers and swords; henceforth, dear sister, thou shalt not see me. Behold, this is separation between me and thee!

"*The nephew of Husain.*—Dear uncle, thou hast resolved to journey. Thou art going once again to make me an orphan. To whom else wilt thou entrust us? Who is expected to take care of us? Thou wast, dear uncle, instead of my father Hasan, a defence to this helpless exiled creature.

"*Husain.*—Sorrow not, thou faithful child, thou shalt be killed too in this plain of trials. Return thou now to thy tent in peace, without grieving my soul any further, poor orphan!

"*The Darwísh from Kábul.*—O Lord God, wherefore is the outward appearance of a man of God usually without decoration or ornament? And why is the lap of the man of this world generally full of gold and jewels? On what account is the pillow of this great person the black dust of the road? and for what reason are the bed and the cushion of the rebellious made of velvet and stuffed with down? Either Islám, the religion of peace and charity, has no true foundation in the world, or this young man, who is so wounded and suffers from thirst, is still an infidel.

"*Husain.*—Why are thine eyes pouring down tears, young darwísh? Hast thou also lost an Akbar in the prime of his youth? Thou art immersed, as a water-fowl, in thy tears. Has thine 'Abbás been slain, thirsting, on the bank of the River Euphrates, that thou cryest so piteously? But if thou art sad only on account of my misfortune, then it matters not. Let me know whence comest thou, and whither is thy face set?

"*The Darwísh.*—It happened, young man, that last night I arrived in this valley, and made my lodging there. When one-half of the night had passed, of a sudden a great difficulty befell me, for I heard a child bemoaning and complaining of thirst, having given up altogether the idea of living any longer in this world. Sometimes it would beat its head and cry out for water; at other times it appeared to fall on the ground, fainting and motionless. I have, therefore, brought some water in this cup for that poor child, that it may drink and be refreshed a little. So I humbly beg thee, dear sir, to direct me to the place where the young child may be found, and tell me what is its name.

"*Husain.*—O God, let no man be ever in my pitiful condition, nor any family in this sad and deplorable state to which I am reduced. O young man, the child mentioned by thee is the peace of my troubled mind; it is my poor, miserable little girl.

"*The Darwísh.*—May I be offered for thee, dear sir, and for thy tearful eyes! Why should thy daughter be so sadly mourning and complaining? My heart is overwhelmed with grief for the abundance of tears running down thy cheeks. Why should the daughter of one like thee, a generous soul, suffer from thirst?

Husain.—Know, O young man, that we are never in need of the water of this life. Thou art quite mistaken if thou hast supposed us to be of this world. If I will, I can make the moon, or any other celestial orb, fall down on the earth; how much more can I get water for my children. Look at the hollow made in the ground with my spear; water would gush out of it if I were to like. I voluntarily die of thirst to obtain a crown of glory from God. I die parched, and offer myself a sacrifice for the sins of my people, that they should be saved from the wrath to come.

"*The Darwísh.*—What is thy name, sir? I perceive that thou art one of the chief saints of the most beneficent God. It is evident to me that thou art the brightness of the Lord's image, but I cannot tell to which sacred garden thy holy rose belongs.

"*Husain.*—O darwish, thou wilt soon be informed of the whole matter, for thou shalt be a martyr thyself; for thy plans and the result thereof have been revealed to me. Tell me, O darwísh, what is the end thou hast in view in this thy hazardous enterprise? When thou shalt have told me that, I will disclose to thee who I am.

"*The Darwísh.*—I intend, noble sir, after I have known the mystery of thy affairs, to set out, if God wills, from Karbalá to Najaf, namely, to the place where 'Alí, the highly exalted king of religion, the sovereign lord of the empire of existence, the supreme master of all the darwíshes, is buried. Yea, I am going to visit the tomb of 'Alí, the successor of the chosen of God, the son-in-law of the Prophet, the lion of the true Lord, the prince of believers, Haidar, the champion of faith.

"*Husain.*—Be it known unto the, O darwísh, that I, who am so sad and sorrowful, am the rose of the garden of that prince. I am of the family of the believers thou hast mentioned. I am Husain, the intercessor on the Day of Resurrection, the rose of the garden of glory.

"*The Darwísh.*—May I be offered a sacrifice for thy blessed arrival! Pardon me my fault, and give me permission to fight the battle of faith, for I am weary of life. It is better for me to be killed, and delivered at once from so many vexations of spirit. Martyrdom is, in fact, one of the glories of my faith.

"*Husain.*—Go forth, O atom, which aspirest to the glory of the sun; go forth, thou hast become at last worthy to know the hidden mysteries of faith. He who is slain for the sake of Husain shall have an abundant reward from God; yea, he shall be raised to life with 'Alí Akbar the sweet son of Husain.

"*The Darwísh (addressing Husain's antagonists).*—You cruel people have no religion at all. You are fire-worshippers, ignorant of God and His law. How long will you act unjustly towards the offspring of the priesthood? Is the account of the Day of Resurrection all false?

"*Ibn Sa'd (the general of Yazíd's army).*—O ye brave soldiers of Yazíd, deprive this fellow of his fund of life. Make his friends ready to mourn for him.

"*Husain.*—Is there anyone to help me? Is there any assistant to lend me his aid?

"*Ja'far (the king of jinns, with his troops, coming to Husain's assistance).*—O king of men and jinns, O Husain, peace be on thee! O judge of corporeal and spiritual beings, peace be on thee!

"*Husain.*—On thee be peace, thou handsome youth! Who art thou, that salutest us at such a time? Though thine affairs are not hidden from me at all, still it is advisable to ask thy name.

"*Ja'far.*—O lord of men and jinns, I am the least of thy servants, and my name is Ja'far, the chief ruler of all the tribes of jinns. To-day, while I was sitting on the glorious throne of my majesty, easy in mind, without any sad idea or thought whatever, I suddenly heard thy voice, when thou didst sadly implore assistance; and on hearing thee I lost my patience and senses. And, behold, I have come out with troops of jinns, of various abilities and qualifications, to lend thee help if necessary.

"*Husain.*—In the old abbey of this perishable kingdom, none can ever, O Ja'far, attain to immortality. What can I do with the empire of the world, or its tempting glories, after my dear ones have all died and gone? Is it proper that I, an old man, should live, and Akbar, a blooming youth, die in the prime of age? Return thou, Ja'far, to thy home, and weep for me as much as thou canst.

"*Ja'far (returning).*—Alas for Husain's exile and helplessness! Alas for his continual groans and sighs!

"*Husain (coming back from the field, dismounts his horse, and making a heap of dust, lays his head on it).*—O earth of Karbalá, do thou assist me, I pray! since I have no mother, be thou to me instead of one.

"*Ibn Sa'd orders the army to stone Husain.*—O ye men of valour, Husain the son of 'Alí has tumbled down from the winged horse; if I be not mistaken, heaven has fallen to earth! It is better for you to stone him most cruelly. Dispatch him soon, with stones, to his companions.

"*Husain.*—Ah, woe to me! my forehead is broken; blood runs down my luminous face.

"*Ibn Sa'd.*—Who is that brave soldier, who, in order to show his gratitude to Yazíd his sovereign lord, will step forward and, with a blow of his scymetar, slay Husain the son of 'Alí?

"*Shimar.*—I am he whose dagger is famous for bloodshed. My mother has borne me for this work alone. I care not about the conflict of the Day of Judgment; I am a worshipper of Yazíd, and have no fear of God. I can make the great throne of the Lord to shake and tremble. I alone can sever from the body the head of Husain the son of 'Alí. I am he who has no share in Islám. I will strike the chest of Husain, the ark of God's knowledge, with my boots, without any fear of punishment.

"*Husain.*—Oh, how wounds caused by arrows and daggers do smart! O God, have mercy in the Day of Judgment on my people for my sake. The time of death has arrived, but I have not my Akbar with me. Would to God my grandfather the Prophet were now here to see me!

"*The Prophet (appearing).*—Dear Husain, thy grandfather the Prophet of God has come to see thee. I am here to behold the mortal wounds of thy delicate body. Dear child, thou hast at length suffered martyrdom by the cruel hand of my own people! This was the reward I expected from them; thanks be to God! Open thine eyes, dear son, and behold thy grandfather with dishevelled hair. If thou hast any desire in thy heart, speak it out to me.

"*Husain.*—Dear grandfather, I abhor life; I would rather go and visit my dear ones in the next world. I earnestly desire to see my companions and friends—above all, my dearly beloved son 'Alí Akbar.

"*The Prophet.*—Be not grieved that 'Alí Akbar thy son was killed, since it tends to the good of my sinful people on the day of universal gathering.

"*Husain.*—Seeing 'Alí Akbar's martyrdom contributes to the happiness of thy people, seeing my own sufferings give validity to thy office of mediation, and seeing thy rest consists in my being troubled in this way, I would offer my soul, not once or twice, but a thousand times, for the salvation of thy people!

"*The Prophet.*—Sorrow not, dear grandchild; thou shalt be a mediator, too, in that day. At present thou art thirsty, but to-morrow thou shalt be the distributor of the water of Al Kausar.

"*Husain.*—O Lord God, besides Husain, who has happened to be thus situated? Every one when he dies has at least a mother at his head. But my mother is not here to rend her garments for me; she is not alive, that she might close my eyes when I die.

"*Fátimah, his mother (appearing).*—I am come to see thee, my child, my child! May I die another time, my child, my child! How shall I see thee slain, my son, my son! Rolling in thine own blood, my child, my child!

Husain.—Come, dear mother, I am anxiously waiting for thee. Come, come! I have partly to complain of thee. How is it that thou hast altogether forsaken thy son? How is it thou camest so late to visit me?

"*Fátimah.*—May I be offered for thy wounded, defaced body! Tell me, what dost thou wish thy mother to do now for thee?

"*Husain.*—I am now, dear mother, at the point of death. The ark of life is going to be cast on shore, mother. It is time that my soul should leave the body. Come, mother, close my eyes with thy kind hand.

"*Fátimah.*—O Lord, how difficult for a mother to see her dear child dying! I am Zahrah who am making this sad noise, because I have to close the eyes of my son Husain, who is on the point of death. Oh, tell me if thou hast any desire long cherished in thy heart, for I am distressed in mind owing to thy sad sighs!

"*Husain.*—Go, mother, my soul is come to my throat; go, I had no other desire except one, with which I must rise in the Day of Resurrection, namely, to see 'Alí Akbar's wedding.

"*Shimar.*—Make thy confession, for I want to sever thy head, and cause a perpetual separation between it and the body.

"*Zainab.*—O Shimar, do not go beyond thy limit; let me bind something on my brother's eyes.

"*Husain.*—Go to thy tent, sister, I am already undone. Go away; Zahrah my mother has already closed my eyes. Show to Sukainah my daughter always the tenderness of a mother. Be very kind to my child after me.

"*Shimar (addressing Husain).*—Stretch forth thy feet toward the holy Kiblah, the sacred temple of Makkah. See how my dagger waves over thee! It is time to cut thy throat.

"*Husain.*—O Lord, for the merit of me, the dear child of thy Prophet; O Lord, for the sad groaning of my miserable sister; O Lord, for the sake of young 'Abbás rolling in his blood, even that young brother of mine that was equal to my soul, I pray thee, in the Day of Judgment, forgive, O merciful Lord, the sins of my grandfather's people, and grant me, bountifully, the key of the treasure of intercession. (*Dies.*)"—(Pelly's *Miracle Play.* vol. ii. p. 81 *seqq.*)

MUHARRAMĀT (محرمات), pl. of

Muḥarramah. Those persons with whom it is not lawful to contract marriage. [MARRIAGE.]

MUHAYĀT (مهاياة). A legal term

used for the partition of usufruct. According to the *Hidāyah*, vol. iv. 31:—

Partition of property is more effectual than partition of usufruct in accomplishing the enjoyment of the use; for which reason, if one partner apply for a partition of property, and another for a partition of usufruct, the Qāẓī must grant the request of the former, and if a partition of usufruct should have taken place with respect to a thing capable of a partition of property (such as a house or a piece of ground), and afterwards one of the partners apply for a partition of property, the Qāẓī must grant a partition of property and annul the partition of usufruct.

MUḤĀẒARAH (محاضرة). *Lit.* "Being present." A term used by the Ṣūfīs for presenting of the soul to God in the service of *ẕikr* in order to obtain all the spiritual blessing possible from a contemplation of the ninety-nine attributes and titles of God. [ZIKR, GOD.]

MUḤRIM (محرم). The pilgrim in a state of Iḥrām, that is, after he has assumed the pilgrim's dress. [PILGRIMAGE.]

AL-MUḤṢĪ (المحصى). "The Counter." One of the ninety-nine names or attributes of God. "It is referred to in the Qur'ān, Sūrah xxxvi. 11: "Verily We quicken the dead and write down what they have done before, and the traces which they leave behind, and everything do We *set down* (*lit.* reckon up) in the clear Book of our decrees."

MUḤTAKIR (محتكر). *Lit.* "A forestaller." One who monopolises grain and other necessaries of life, which is unlawful. [MONOPOLY.]

MUḤTASIB (محتسب). The public censor of religion and morals, who is appointed by a Muslim ruler, to punish Muslims for neglecting the rites of their religion.

Sir Alexander Burnes, in his *Travels in Bokhara* (vol. i. p. 313), relates that he saw persons publicly scourged because they had slept during prayer-time and smoked on Friday. [DIRRAH.]

Burckhardt, in his account of the Wahhābīs (vol. ii. p. 146), says, the neglect of religious duty is always severely punished. . . . When Sa'ūd took al-Madīnah, he ordered some of his people after prayers in the mosque to call over the names of all the grown up inhabitants of the town who were to answer individually. He then commanded them to attend prayers regularly; and if any, one absented himself two or three times, Sa'ūd sent some of his Arabs to beat the man in his own house. At Makkah, when the hour of prayer arrived, he ordered the people to patrol the streets, armed with large sticks, and to drive all the inhabitants by force into the mosque; a harsh proceeding, but justified by the notorious irreligion of the Makkans.

Dr. Bellew, in his *Kashmīr and Kashgār* (p. 281), gives an animated account of the way in which the Muḥtasib performed his duties in the streets of Kashgār.

AL-MUḤYĪ (المحيى). "The giver of life." One of the ninety-nine names or attributes of God. It occurs twice in the Qur'ān:—

Sūrah xxx. 49: "Look then to the vestiges of God's mercy, how he quickens the earth after its death; verily He is the *quickener* of the dead."

Sūrah xli. 39: "Verily, he who quickens (the earth) will surely *quicken* the dead."

AL-MU'ĪD (المعيد). "The Restorer" (to life). One of the ninety-nine names or attributes of God. The word does not occur in the Qur'ān, but the idea is expressed in Sūrah lxxxv. 13, and many other places, "Verily He produces and *restores*."

AL-MU'IZZ (المعز). "The One who giveth honour." One of the ninety-nine names or attributes of God. The word does not occur in the Qur'ān, but the attribute is referred to in Sūrah iii. 25: "Thou *honourest* whom Thou pleasest."

AL-MUJĀDILAH (المجادلة). *Lit.* "She who disputed." The title of the LVIIIth Sūrah of the Qur'ān, in which the expression occurs: "Now hath God heard the speech of her who *disputed* with thee concerning her husband." Which refers to Khaulah bint Ṣa'labah, the wife of Aus ibn Ṣāmit, who being divorced by her husband in the "time of ignorance," came to ask whether the divorce was lawful.

MUJĀHID (مجاهد). A warrior in the cause of religion. [JIHAD.]

AL-MUJĪB (المجيب). "The One who answers to" (a prayer). One of the ninety-nine names or attributes of God. It occurs in the Qur'ān. Sūrah xi. 64: "Verily my Lord is nigh and *answers*" (prayer).

MU'JIZAH (معجزة). [MIRACLES.]

MUJTAHID (مجتهد), pl. *mujtahidūn*. *Lit.*, "One who strives" to attain to a high position of scholarship and learning.

The highest degree amongst Muḥammadan divines which is conferred either by the people or the ruler of a Muslim country upon eminent persons. The four doctors of the Sunnīs and their disciples were of this degree, but there are none of these enlightened teachers amongst the Sunnīs of the present day. They still exist in Persia, and are appointed by the people, the appointment being confirmed by the king. Malcolm, in his account of Persia, says:—

"There are seldom more than three or four priests of the dignity of Mujtahid in Persia. Their conduct is expected to be exemplary, and to show no wordly bias; neither must they connect themselves with the king or the officers of Government. They seldom depart from that character to which they owe their rank. The reason is obvious; the moment they deviate, the charm is broken which constitutes their power; men no longer solicit their advice or implore their protection; nor can they hope to see the monarch of the country courting popularity by walking to their humble dwellings, and placing them on the seat of honour when they condescend to visit his court. When a Mujtahid dies, his successor is always a person of the most eminent rank in the ecclesiastical order; and, though he may be pointed out to the populace by others of the same class seeking him as an associate, it is rare to hear of any intrigues being employed to obtain this enviable dignity.

"The Mujtahids of Persia exercise a great, though undefined, power over the courts of law, the judges of which constantly submit cases to their superior knowledge; and their sentence is deemed irrevocable, unless by a Mujtahid whose learning and sanctity are of acknowledged higher repute than that of the person by whom judgment has been pronounced. But the benefits which the inhabitants of Persia derive from the influence of these high priests, is not limited to their occasional aid of the courts of justice. The law is respected on account of the character of its ministers; kings fear to attack the decrees of tribunals over which they may be said to preside, and frequently endeavour to obtain popularity by referring cases to their decision. The sovereign, when no others dare approach him, cannot refuse to listen to a revered Mujtahid when he becomes an intercessor for the guilty. The habitations of this high order of priesthood are deemed sanctuaries for the oppressed; and the hand of despotic power is sometimes taken off a city, because the monarch will not offend a Mujtahid who has chosen it for his residence, but who refuses to dwell amid violence and injustice."

There is a common opinion that the title of *Mujtahid* can only be granted to those who are masters of seventy sciences. For a full account of the conditions of obtaining this rank, as expressed by a modern Muslim writer, will be found in the article on Ijmāʻ. [IJMAʻ.]

MUKĀRĪ (مكارى). A legal term for a person who lets horses, camels, &c., to hire. (*Hidāyah*, vol. iii. p. 371.)

MUKĀTAB (مكاتب). A slave who ransoms himself or herself, with the permission of the owner. [SLAVERY.]

MUKHADDARAH (مخدرة). A legal term for a woman in a state of purity. It is also used for a veiled woman, the word being derived from *khidr*, a "curtain or veil."

MUKHĀLAṬAH (مخالطة). *Lit.* "Intermingling," or mixing together. A term used for general intercourse, but specially applied to intercouse with those who are ceremonially unclean.

MULES. Arabic *baghl* (بغل), pl. *bighāl.*

Muḥammad forbade the breeding of mules, for Ibn ʻAbbās says the three special injunctions which he received were (1) to perform the ablutions thoroughly, (2) not to take alms, (3) not to breed mules. (*Mishkāt*, book xvii. ch. ii.)

The flesh of a mule is unlawful. (*Hidāyah*, vol. iv. p. 74.)

They are not liable to *zakāt*. (*Hidāyah*, vol. i. p. 16.)

MULḤAQ (ملحق). *Lit.* "Joined." A term used by the Ṣūfīs for the condition of the human soul when "it is absorbed into the essence of God." (ʻAbdu 'r-Razzāq's *Dictionary of Ṣūfi Terms.*)

MULḤID (ملحد). An infidel. *Lit.* "One who has *deviated*, or turned aside from the truth."

AL-MULK (الملك). *Lit.* "The Kingdom." The title of the LXVIIth Sūrah of the Qur'ān in the first verse of which the word occurs: "Blessed is He in whose hand is the *kingdom.*"

MULLĀ (ملا). A Persian form used for the Arabic *Maulawī*, "a learned man, a scholar."

In the *Ghiyāṣu 'l-Lughah* it is said that a learned man is called a *Mullā* because he is "filled" with knowledge; from *mala'*, "to fill."

MU'MIN (مومن), pl. *Mu'minūn*; from *Imān*, "faith." One who believes.

(1) A term generally used for Muḥammadans in the Qur'ān and in all Muslim books.

(2) *Al-Mu'min.* The title of the XLth Sūrah of the Qur'ān, in the 29th verse of which the word occurs: "A man of the family of Pharaoh who was a *believer*, but hid his faith."

(3) *Al-Mu'min*, "The Faithful." One of the ninety-nine names or attributes of God. It occurs in the Qur'ān, Sūrah lix. 28: "He is . . . the Faithful."

AL-MU'MINŪN (المومنون). *Lit.* "The Believers." The title of the XXIIIrd Sūrah of the Qur'ān, in the first verse of which the word occurs: "Prosperous are the *believers.*"

AL-MUMĪT (المميت). "The Killer." One of the ninety-nine names or attributes of God. It is referred to in the Qur'ān, Sūrah ii. 26: "He will kill you and then make you alive."

MUMSIK (ممسك). *Lit.* "One who withholds, a miser." Used for a miserly person in contradistinction to *munfiq*, "a liberal person." [MUNFIQ.]

AL-MUMTAḤINAH (الممتحنة). *Lit.* "She who is tried." The title of the LXth Sūrah of the Qur'ān, from the expression in the 10th verse: "O believers! when believing women come over to you as refugees, then make *trial* of them."

Al-Baiẓāwī says: "When such women sought an asylum at al-Madīnah, Muḥammad obliged them to swear that they were prompted only by a desire of embracing Islām, and that hatred of their husbands, or love of some Muslim, had not any influence on their conduct."

MUNĀFIQ (منافق), pl. *munāfiqūn.* "Hypocrite." A term especially given to those who in the time of the Prophet, whilst outwardly professing to believe in his mission, secretly denied the faith. They form the subject of the LXIIIrd Sūrah of the

Qur'ān, which hence is termed the *Sūratu 'l-Munāfiqīn.*

AL-MUNĀFIQŪN (المنافقون). "The Hypocrites." Title of the LXIIIrd Sūrah of the Qūr'ān, whose opening verses are:—

"When the Hypocrites come to thee, they say, 'We bear witness that thou art the Sent One of God.' God knoweth that thou art His Sent One: but God beareth witness that the *hypocrites* do surely lie. Their faith have they used as a cloak, and they turn aside others from the way of God! Evil are all their doings. This, for that they believed, then became unbelievers! Therefore hath a seal been set upon their hearts, and they understand not."

MUNĀJĀT (مناجاة). *Lit.* "Whispering to, confidential talk." Generally used for the extempore prayer offered after the usual liturgical form has been recited. [PRAYERS.]

MUNAṢṢAF (منصف). *Lit.* "Reduced to one-half." A species of prohibited liquor. The juice of grapes boiled until a quantity less than two-thirds evaporates. (*Hidāyah*, vol. iv. 158.)

MUNF, MANF (منف). The ancient Memphis. Mentioned in the Commentary of the Jalālān on the Qur'ān, Sūrah xxviii. 14, as the city in which Moses killed the Egyptian.

MUNFIQ (منفق). *Lit.* "One who spends." A charitable person. Qur'ān, Sūrah iii. 15: "Upon the patient, the truthful, the devout, the charitable, and those who ask for pardon at the dawn." [MUMSIK.]

MUNKAR and NAKĪR (منكر و نكير). "The Unknown" and "The Repudiating." The two angels who are said by Muḥammad to visit the dead in their graves and to interrogate them as to their belief in the Prophet and his religion.

They are described as two black angels with blue eyes. (*Mishkāt*, book i. ch. v.) [PUNISHMENTS OF THE GRAVE.]

AL-MUNTAQIM (المنتقم). "The Avenger." One of the ninety-nine names or attributes of God. It is referred to in the Qur'ān, Sūrah xxxii. 22: "Verily We will take *vengeance* on the sinners." Also Sūrahs xliii. 40, and xliv. 15.

AL-MUQADDIM (المقدم). "The Bringer-forward." One of the ninety-nine names or attributes of God. It does not occur in the Qur'ān, but is given in the Ḥadīs.

MUQAUQIS (مقوقس). The Roman Viceroy of Egypt; al-Muqauqis being his official title.

Muḥammad, in the year A.H. 7 (A.D. 628), sent an embassy to this official, inviting him to Islām. The Governor received the embassy kindly, and sent the following reply, "I am aware that a prophet is yet to arise; but I am of opinion he will appear in Syria. Thy messenger hath been received with honour. I send for thine acceptance two female slaves, who are much admired by the Copts, and also a present of raiment, and a mule for thee to ride on."

Mary, the fairest of the Coptic damsels, Muḥammad kept for himself, and gave the other to Ḥassān the poet. [MUHAMMAD, MARY THE COPT.]

MUQĀYAẒAH (مقايضة). Exchanging, bartering, giving an equivalent in anything but money. (*Hidāyah*, Arabic ed., vol. iii. p. 8.)

AL-MUQĪT (المقيت). "The Mighty or Guardian." One of the ninety-nine names or attributes of God. Sūrah iv. 88: "Verily God keepeth watch over everything."

AL-MUQSIṬ (المقسط). "The Equitable." One of the ninety-nine names or attributes of God. It does not occur in the Qu'rān, but is given in the Ḥadīṣ.

MUQTADA (مقتدى). *Lit.* "Followed, worthy to be followed." An exemplary person, as being eminent for sanctity of character.

MUQTADĪ (مقتدى). "Follower." The person who stands behind the Imām in the usual prayers and recites the *Iqāmah*. [IQAMAH.]

AL-MUQTADIR (المقتدر). "The Powerful or Prevailing." One of the ninety-nine names or attributes of God. It occurs three times in the Qur'ān:—

Sūrah xviii. 43: "For God is *powerful* over all."

Sūrah liv. 42: "As he only can punish, who is the Mighty, the *Strong*."

Sūrah v. 55: "With the *powerful* king."

MURĀBAḤAH (مرابحة). A legal term for selling a thing for a profit, when the seller distinctly states that he purchased it for so much and sells it for so much.

MURĀHAQAH (مراهقة). Arriving at Makkah when the ceremonies of the *ḥajj* are nearly finished. [HAJJ.]

MURĀHIQ (مراهق). A legal term for a boy or girl who is near the age of puberty.

MURĀQABAH (مراقبة). Meditation; contemplation. An act of devotion performed by the Ṣūfīs. [SUFI.]

MURDER. Arabic *qatl* (قتل). Homicide of which Muḥammadan law takes cognisance is of five kinds: (1) *Qatlu 'l-'Amd:*

(2) *Qatl shibhu 'l-'Amd*; (3) *Qatlu 'l-Khaṭā'*; (4) *Qatl qā'im maqāma 'l-Khaṭā'*; (5) *Qatl bi-Sabab*.

(1) *Qatlu 'l-'Amd* (قتل العمد), or "wilful murder," is where the perpetrator wilfully kills a person with a weapon, or something that serves for a weapon, such as a club, a sharp stone, or fire. If a person commit wilful murder, two points are established: first, that the murderer is a sinner deserving of hell, for it is written in the Qur'ān (Sūrah iv. 95), "Whosoever slayeth a believer purposely, his reward is hell"; and, secondly, that he is liable to retaliation, because it is written in the Qur'ān (Sūrah ii. 173), "It is incumbent on you to execute retaliation (*Qiṣāṣ*) for murder." But although retaliation is the punishment for wilful murder, still the heir or next of kin can either forgive or compound the offence; as the verse already quoted continues—"Yet he who is pardoned at all by his brother must be prosecuted in reason, and made to pay with kindness." In this respect Muḥammad departed from the Old Testament law, which made the retaliation compulsory on the next of kin.

One effect of wilful murder is that the murderer is excluded from being heir to the murdered person.

According to Abū Ḥanīfah, there is no *expiation* for wilful murder, but ash-Shāfi'ī maintains that expiation is incumbent as an act of piety.

(2) *Qatl shibhu 'l-'Amd* (قتل شبه العمد), or "manslaughter," or, as Hamilton more correctly renders it, "A semblance of wilful murder, is when the perpetrator strike a man with something which is neither a weapon nor serves as such."

The argument adduced by Abū Ḥanīfah is a saying of the Prophet: "Killing with a rod or stick is not murder, but only manslaughter, and the fine for it is a hundred camels, payable within three years."

Manslaughter is held to be sinful and to require expiation, and it excludes the manslayer from inheriting the property of the slain.

(3) *Qatlu 'l-Khaṭā'* (قتل الخطا), or "homicide by misadventure," is of two kinds: error in *intention*, and error in the *act*. Error in the act is where a person intends a particular act, and another act is thereby occasioned; as where, for instance, a person shoots an arrow at a mark and it hits a man. Error in intention, on the other hand, is where the mistake occurs not in the act, but with respect to the subject; as where a person shoots an arrow at a man supposing him to be game; or at a Muslim, supposing him to be a hostile infidel. The slayer by misadventure is required to free a Muslim slave, or fast two months successively, and to pay a fine within three years. He is also excluded from inheriting the property of the slain.

(4) *Qatl qā'im maqāma 'l-Khaṭā* (قتل قائم مقام الخطا), or "homicide of a similar nature to homicide by misadventure," is where, for example, a person walking in his sleep falls upon another, so as to kill him by the fall. It is subject to the same rules with homicide by misadventure.

(5) *Qatl bi-Sabab* (قتل بسبب), or, "homicide by intermediate cause," is where, for instance, a man digs a well, or sets up a stone, and another falls into the well, or over the stone, and dies. In this case a fine must be paid, but it does not exclude from inheritance, nor does it require expiation.

No special mention is made in either the Qur'ān or in Muḥammadan law books, of taking the life by poison. (The same remark applies to the Mosaic law. See Smith's *Dictionary of the Bible*, Article "Murder.")

With regard to retaliation, a freeman is slain for a freeman, and a slave for a slave; a freeman is also slain for the wilful murder of a slave the property of another.

According to Abū Ḥanīfah, a Muslim is put to death for killing an unbeliever, but ash-Shāfi'ī maintains otherwise, because the Prophet said, "A Muslim shall not suffer death for an unbeliever."

A man is slain for a woman; a father is not slain for his child, but a child is slain for the murder of his father; a master is not slain for the murder of his own slave, or for the slave of his child.

If a person immerse another into water whence it is impossible for him to escape by swimming, according to Abū Ḥanīfah, retaliation is not incurred, but ash-Shāfi'ī maintains that the murderer should be drowned.

Al-Baiẓāwī the commentator, in writing on Sūrah ii. 174, "This is an alleviation from your Lord and a mercy," says that in the Jewish law retaliation for murder was compulsory, but in the law of Christ the Christians were enjoined to forgive the murderer, whilst in the Qur'ān the choice is given of either retaliation or forgiveness.

MURĪD (مريد). *Lit.* "One who is desirous or willing." A disciple of some *murshid*, or leader, of a mystic order. Any student of divinity. [SUFI.]

MURJĪYAH, MURJI'AH (مرجية). *Lit.* "The Procrastinators." A sect of Muslims who teach that the judgment of every true believer, who hath been guilty of a grievous sin, will be deferred till the Resurrection; for which reason they pass no sentence on him in this world, either of absolution or condemnation. They also hold that disobedience with faith hurteth not, and that, on the other hand, obedience with infidelity profiteth not. As to the reason of their name the learned differ, because of the different significations of its root, each of which they accommodate to some opinion of the sect. Some think them so called because they postpone works to intention, that is, esteem works to be inferior in degree to intention, and profession of the faith; others, because they allow hope, by asserting that disobedience with faith hurteth not, &c.; others take the reason of the name to be, their deferring the sentence of the heinous sinner till the Resurrection; and others, their degrading of 'Alī, or removing him from the first degree to the fourths for the Murjīyahs in some points relating to the office of Imām, agree with the Khārijīyahs. This sect is divided into four classes, three of which, according as they happen to agree in particular dogmas with the Kharijīyahs, the Qādirīyahs, or the Jabarīyahs, are distinguished as Murjīyahs of those sects, and the fourth is that of the pure Murjīyahs, which last class is again subdivided into five others. The opinions of Mukātil and Bashar, both of a sect of the Murjīyahs called Ṣaubanians, should not be omitted. The former asserted that disobedience hurts not him who professes the unity of God, and is endued with faith; and that no true believer shall be cast into hell; he also thought that God will surely forgive all crimes except infidelity; and that a disobedient believer will be punished at the Day of Resurrection, on the bridge Sirāṭ, laid over the midst of hell, where the flames of hell-fire shall catch hold on him, and torment him in proportion to his disobedience, and that he shall then be admitted into Paradise.

The latter held, that if God do cast the believers guilty of grievous sins into hell, yet they will be delivered thence after they shall have been sufficiently punished; but that it is neither possible nor consistent with justice that they should remain therein for ever.

MURSAL (مرسل), pl. *mursalūn*. A messenger or apostle. A term frequently used in the Qur'ān for the prophets. It is only applied to those who are said to bringers of inspired books. [PROPHET.]

AL-MURSALĀT (المرسلات). *Lit.* "Those who are sent." The title of the LXXVIIth Sūrah of the Qur'ān, in the first verse of which the word occurs. "By the angels who are *sent* by God, following one another."

MURSHID (مرشد). A guide. From *rashād*, "a straight road." The title given to the spiritual director of any religious order. [SUFI.]

MURTADD (مرتد). [APOSTATE.]

AL-MUSABBIḤĀT (المسبحات). "The Praisers." A title given to those Sūrahs of the Qur'ān, which begin with *Subḥāna* (Glory to), or *Sabbaḥa* (he glorified), or *Yusabbiḥu* (he glorifies), or *Sabbiḥ* (glorify thou), viz. Sūrahs xvii., lvii., lix., lxi., lxii., lxiv., lxxxvii.

'Irbāẓ ibn Sāriyah relates that Muḥammad used to repeat the *Musabbiḥāt* before going to sleep, and that he said, "In them there is a verse which is better than a thousand." Most writers say this verse is concealed like the *Lailatu 'l-Qadr* (the night of power), or the *Sā'atu 'l-Jum'ah* (the hour on Friday), but 'Abdu 'l-Ḥaqq says it is most probably either the last verse of the Sūratu 'l-Ḥashr (lix.), "He is God, the Pardoner, the Maker, the Fashioner! To him are ascribed excellent titles," &c. Or, the first verse of the Sūratu 'l-Ḥadīd (lvii.), "All that is in the Heavens and in the Earth praiseth God." (See *Majma'u 'l-Biḥār*, p. 86; *Mishkāt*, book viii. ch. i.)

MUṢADDIQ (مصدق). The collector of the *zakāt* and *ṣadaqah*, or legal alms. In Muḥammadan states he is appointed by the state. This officer does not now exist in Hindustan under British rule.

MUṢĀFAḤAH (مصافحة). Taking the hand. Joining or shaking hands. A custom expressly enjoined by Muḥammad, who said, "If two Muslims meet and join hands (*i.e.* shake hands), their sins will be forgiven before they separate." (*Mishkāt*, book xxii. ch. iii. pt. 2.)

MUSAILAMAH (مسيلمة). An impostor who appeared in the time of Muḥammad, and claimed the Prophetic office, surnamed *Musailamatu 'l-Kazzāb*, or, "Musailamah the Liar." He headed an embassy sent by his tribe to Muḥammad in the ninth year of the Hijrah, and professed himself a Muslim; but on his return home, considering that he might possibly share with Muḥammad in his power, the next year he set up for a prophet also, pretending to join with him in the commission to recall mankind from idolatry to the worship of the true God; and he published written revelations, in imitation of the Qur'ān, of which Abū 'l-Faraj has preserved the following passage, viz. "Now hath God been gracious unto her that was with child, and hath brought forth from her the soul which runneth between the peritonœum and the bowels."

Musailamah, having formed a considerable party, began to think himself upon equal terms with Muḥammad, and sent him a letter, offering to go halves with him, in these words: "From Musailamah, the Apostle of God, to Muḥammad, the Apostle of God. Now let the earth be half mine and half thine." But Muḥammad, thinking himself too well established to need a partner, wrote him this answer: "From Muḥammad, the Apostle of God, to Musailamah, the Liar. The earth is God's; He giveth the same for inheritance unto such of His servants as He pleaseth; and the happy issue shall attend those who fear Him."

During the few months which Muḥammad lived after this revolt, Musailamah rather gained than lost ground, and grew very formidable; but Abū Bakr, in the eleventh year of the Hijrah, sent a great army against him, under the command of that consummate general Khālid ibn al-Walīd, who engaged Musailamah in a bloody battle, wherein the false prophet happening to be slain by Waḥshī, the negro slave who had killed Ḥamzah at Uḥud, and by the same lance, the Muslims gained an entire victory, ten thousand of the apostates being left dead on the spot, and the rest returning to Muḥammadanism.

MUṢALLĀ (مصلى). The small mat, cloth, or carpet on which a Muslim prays. The term *sajjādah* is used in Egypt. In Persia *Jai-namaz.*

A MUSALLA.

MUṢALLAṢ (مثلث). *Lit.* "Made into three, or into a third." An aromatic wine composed of new wine boiled to a third part and then mixed with sweet herbs. It is said by Abū Ḥanīfah to be a lawful drink. (*Hidāyah*, vol. iv. p. 162.)

MUSALMĀN (مسلمان). The Persian form of the word Muslim. A Muḥammadan. [MUHAMMADANISM.]

MUSĀMARAH (مسامرة). *Lit.* "Holding night conversations." A term used by the Ṣūfīs for God's converse with the heart of man. ('Abdu'r-Razzāq's *Dict. of Ṣūfī Terms.*)

MUSAQĀT (مساقاة). A compact entered into by two persons, by which it is agreed that the one shall deliver over to the other his fruit trees, on condition that the other shall take care of them, and whatever is produced shall belong to them both, in the proportions of one half, one third, or the like, as may be stipulated. (*Hidāyah*, vol. iv., p. 54.)

AL-MUṢAWWIR (المصور). "The Fashioner." One of the ninety-nine names or attributes of God. It occurs once in the Qur'ān, Sūrah lix. 24: "He is God, the Creator, the Maker, the *Fashioner.*"

MUSHABBIHAH (مشبهة). *Lit.* "The Assimilators." A sect of Muḥammadans who allowed a resemblance between God and His creatures, supposing Him to be a figure composed of members or parts, and capable of local motion. Some of the Shī'ahs belong to this sect.

MUSHĀHADAH (مشاهدة). A vision or revelation. A Ṣūfīistic expression for spiritual enlightenment.

MUSHRIK (مشرك), pl. *mushrikūn.* Those who give companions to God. It is used by modern Muslims for both Christians and idolaters, for those who believe in the Holy Trinity as well as for those who worship idols. The Wahhābīs also call their religious opponents *Mushrikūn*, because they pray to saints for assistance. In the Qur'ān the term is always used for the Makkan idolaters, and the Imām al-Baghawī says, in his commentary on Sūrah xcviii. 1, that the term *Ahlu 'l-Kitāb* is always used for the Jews and Christians and *Mushrikūn* for those who worship idols.

MUSHROOMS. Arabic *kam'* (كمء), pl. *akmu', kam'ah.* Abū Hurairah relates that Muḥammad said: "Mushrooms are a kind of manna which God sent to Moses, and its water is a cure for sore eyes.' (*Mishkāt*, book xxi. ch. i.)

MUSIC. Arabic *musīqā* (موسيقا), *mūsīqī* (موسيقى), which the author of the *Ghiyāṣu 'l-Lughah* says is a Syriac word. It is generally held by Muḥammadans to be contrary to the teachings of the Prophet; for Nāfi' relates that when he was walking with Ibn 'Umar on a road, they heard the music of a pipe, and that Ibn 'Umar put his fingers into his ears, and went on another road. Nāfi' then asked Ibn 'Umar why he did so, and he said, "I was with the Prophet, and when he heard the noise of a musical pipe, he put his fingers into his ears; and this happened when I was a child." (*Mishkāt*, book xxii. ch. ix., pt. 3.)

Muḥammadan doctors, however, are not agreed on the subject, for Abū Ḥanīfah says, "If a person break a lute or tabor, or pipe, or cymbal belonging to a Muslim, he is responsible, because the sale of such articles is lawful." But his two disciples, Imāms Muḥammad and Abū Yūsuf, do not agree with him. (*Hidāyah*, vol. iii. p. 558.)

MUṢLAH (مثلة). The mutilation of the body, which is forbidden by Muslim law, except in the case of retaliation. (*Mishkāt*, book xii. ch. ii.)

MUSLIM (مسلم), from *Islām.* One who has received Islām. A Muḥammadan. [MUHAMMADANISM, ISLAM.]

MUSLIM (مسلم). Abū 'l-Ḥusain Muslim, son of al-Ḥajjāj al-Qushairī, the compiler of the collection of the Traditions known as the *Ṣaḥīḥu Muslim*, was born at Naishapūr, A.H. 204, and died A.H. 261. His book of traditions ranks amongst the Sunnīs as but second in authority to the *Ṣaḥīḥu 'l-Bukhārī.* The two works being styled the *Ṣaḥīḥân*, or the "two authentics." It is said to contain 3,000 authentic traditions. [TRADITIONS.]

MUSTAḤĀẒAH (مستحاضة). A woman who has an issue of blood (*istiḥāẓah*), independent of the menses or of the cleansings after parturition. A *mustaḥāẓah* is not considered *junub*, or unclean, but may say her prayers and perform the other religious offices. Compare Leviticus xv. 3.

MUṢṬALIQ (مصطلق). Banū Muṣṭaliq. An Arabian tribe in the time of Muḥammad. He attacked the Banū Muṣṭaliq in A.H. 5, and took many of them prisoners.

(Muir's *Life of Mahomet*, vol. iii. p. 237). They embraced Islām at an early period.

MUSTA'MIN (مستامن). *Lit.* "One who seeks security." One who, being a foreigner, and not a Muslim, enters Muḥammadan territory, and claims safe conduct and immunity from hostilities.

AL-MUTA'ĀLĪ (المتعالى). "The Exalted." One of the ninety-nine names or attributes of God. It occurs in the Qur'ān, Sūrah xiii. 10: "He knows the unseen, and the visible,—the Great, the *Lofty One*."

MU'TADDAH (معتدة). A woman in her *'iddah*, or period of probation, after the death of her husband, or after her divorce.

MUT'AH (متعة). *Lit.* "Usufruct, enjoyment." A marriage contracted for a limited period, for a certain sum of money. Such marriages are still legal amongst the Shī'ahs, and exist in Persia (Malcolm's *Persia*, vol. ii. p. 591) to the present day, but they are said to be unlawful by the Sunnīs. They were permitted by the Arabian Prophet at Auṭās, and are undoubtedly the greatest stain upon his moral legislation; but the Sunnīs say that he afterwards prohibited a *mut'ah* marriage at Khaibar. (*Vide Mishkāt*, book xiii. ch. iv. pt. 2.)

The Shī'ahs establish the legality of *mut'ah* not only upon the traditions, but also upon the following verse in the Qur'ān, the meaning of which, according to the commentary *Tafsīr-i-Maẓharī*, is disputed. Sūrah iv. 28: "Forbidden to you also are married women, except those who are in your hands as slaves. This is the law of God for you. And it is allowed you, beside this, to seek out wives by means of your wealth, with modest conduct, and without fornication. And give those with whom ye have cohabited their dowry. This is the law. But it shall be no crime in you to make agreements over and above the law. Verily, God is Knowing, Wise!"

According to the Imāmīyah Code of Jurisprudence, the following are the conditions of *Mut'ah*, or "temporary marriages." There must be declaration and acceptance, as in the case of *nikāḥ*, and the subject of the contract must be either a Muslimah, a Christian, or a Jewess, or (according to some) a Majūsī; she should be chaste, and due inquiries should be made into her conduct, as it is abominable to enter into contract with a woman addicted to fornication, nor is it lawful to make such a contract with a virgin who has *no father*. Some dower must be specified, and if there is a failure in this respect, the contract is void. There must also be a fixed period, but its extent is left entirely to the parties: it may be a year, a month, or a day, only some limit must be distinctly specified, so as to guard the period from any extension or diminution. The practice of *'azl* (*extrahere ante emissionem seminis*) is lawful, but if, notwithstanding this the woman becomes pregnant, the child is the temporary husband's; but if he should deny the child, the denial is sustained by the law. Mut'ah marriages do not admit of divorce or repudiation, but the parties become absolutely separated on the expiration of the period. (Baillie's Digest.)

There is a curious account of a discussion at the Court of the Emperor Akbar with reference to the subject of Mut'ah marriages in the *'Aīn-i-Akbari* (Translation by H. Blochman, M.A., p. 173). At one of the meetings for discussion, the Emperor asked how many free-born women a man may legally marry. The lawyers answered that *four* was the limit fixed by the Prophet. His Majesty thereupon remarked that, from the time he had come of age he had not restricted himself to that number, and in justice to his wives, of whom he had a large number, both free-born and slaves, he now wanted to know what remedy the law provided for his case. Most of the Maulawīs present expressed their opinions, when the Emperor remarked that Shaikh 'Abdu 'n-Nabī had once told him that one of the Mujtahids had had as many as nine wives. Some of those present said that some learned men had allowed even eighteen from a too literal translation of the second verse of Sūratu 'n-Nisā' in the Qur'ān. [MARRIAGE.] After much discussion, the learned men present, having collected every tradition on the subject, decreed, first, that by *mut'ah* a man may marry any number of wives; and, secondly, that *mut'ah* marriages were sanctioned by the Imām Mālik; but a copy of the *Muwaṭṭa*, of the Imām Mālik was brought, and a passage cited from that collection of traditions against the legality of *mut'ah* marriages.

The disputation was again revived at a subsequent meeting, when at the request of the Emperor, Badā'onī gave the following summary of the discussion: "Imām Mālik, and the Shī'ahs are unanimous in looking upon *mut'ah* marriages as legal; Imām ash-Shāfi'ī and the great Imām Abū Ḥanīfah look upon *mut'ah* marriages as illegal. But should at any time a Qāẓī of the Malakī sect decide that *mut'ah* is legal, it is legal, according to the common belief, even for Shāfi'īs and Ḥanafīs. Every other opinion on this subject is idle talk." This saying pleased the Emperor, and he at once appointed a Qāẓī, who gave a decree which made *mut'ah* marriages legal.

In permitting these usufructuary marriages Muḥammad appears but to have given *Divine* (?) sanction to one of the abominable practices of ancient Arabia, for Burckhardt (vol. ii. p. 378) says, it was a custom of their forefathers to assign to a traveller who became their guest for the night, some female of the family, most commonly the host's own wife!

AL-MUTAKABBIR (المتكبر). "The Great." (When used of a human being it implies haughtiness.) One of the ninety-nine names or attributes of God. It occurs in the Qur'ān, Sūrah lix. 23: "He is . . . the Great One!"

MU'TAMIR (معتمر). A performer of the 'Umrah. [UMRAH.]

MU'TAQ (معتق). An emancipated slave. [SLAVERY.]

MUTAQĀDIM (متقادم). Such a distance of time as suffices to prevent punishment. It operates in a way somewhat similar to the English *statutary limitations.*

MUTAWALLĪ (متولى). *Lit.* "A person endowed with authority." A legal term used for a person entrusted with the management of a religious foundation. [MASJID.]

MU'TAZILAH (معتزلة). *Lit.* "The Separatists." A sect of Muḥammadans founded by Wāṣil ibn 'Aṭā', who separated from the school of Ḥasan al-Baṣrī (A.H. 110). The following are their chief tenets: (1) They entirely reject all eternal attributes of God, to avoid the distinction of persons made by the Christians; saying that eternity is the proper or formal attribute of his essence; that God knows by His essence, and not by His knowledge: and the same they affirm of His other attributes (though all the Mu'tazilahs do not understand these words in one sense). Hence this sect is also named Mu'aṭṭilī, from their divesting God of His attributes; for they went so far as to say, that to affirm these attributes is the same thing as to make more eternals than one, and that the unity of God is inconsistent with such an opinion. This was the true doctrine of Wāṣil, their master, who declared that whoever asserted an eternal attribute asserted there were two gods. This point of speculation concerning the divine attributes was not ripe at first, but was at length brought to maturity by Wāsil's followers, after they had read the books of the philosophers. (2) They believe the word of God to have been created *in subjecto* (as the schoolmen term it), and to consist of letters and sound; copies thereof being written in books, to express or imitate the original. (3) They also go farther, and affirm that whatever was created *in subjecto* is also an accident, and liable to perish. They deny absolute predestination, holding that God is not the author of evil, but of good only; and that man is a free agent; which is the opinion of the Qadarīyah sect. On account of this tenet and the first, the Mu'tazilahs look on themselves as the defenders of the unity and justice of God. (4) They hold that if a professor of the true religion be guilty of a grievous sin, and die without repentance, he will be eternally damned, though his punishment will be lighter than that of the infidels. (5) They deny all vision of God in Paradise by the corporeal eye, and reject all comparisons or similitudes applied to God.

According to Shahrastānī, the Mu'tazilah hold:—

"That God is eternal; and that eternity is the peculiar property of His essence; but they deny the existence of any eternal attributes (as distinct from His nature). For they say, He is Omniscient as to His nature; Living as to His nature; Almighty as to His nature; but not through any knowledge, power or life existing in Him as eternal attributes; for knowledge, power and life are part of His essence, otherwise, if they are to be looked upon as eternal attributes of the Deity, it will give rise to a multiplicity of eternal entities.

"They maintain that the knowledge of God is as much within the province of reason as that of any other entity; that He cannot be beheld with the corporeal sight; and, with the exception of Himself, everything else is liable to change or to suffer extinction. They also maintain that Justice is the animating principle of human actions: Justice according to them being the dictates of Reason and the concordance of the ultimate results of this conduct of man with such dictates.

"Again, they hold that there is no eternal law as regards human actions; that the divine ordinances which regulate the conduct of men are the results of growth and development; that God has commanded and forbidden, promised and threatened by a law which grew gradually. At the same time, say they, he who works righteousness merits rewards, and he who works evil deserves punishment. They also say that all knowledge is attained through reason, and must necessarily be so obtained. They hold that the cognition of good and evil is also within the province of reason; that nothing is known to be right or wrong until reason has enlightened us as to the distinction; and that thankfulness for the blessings of the Benefactor is made obligatory by reason, even before the promulgation of any law upon the subject. They also maintain that man has perfect freedom; is the author of his actions both good and evil, and deserves reward or punishment hereafter accordingly."

During the reigns of the Abbaside Khalīfahs al-Ma'mūn, al-Mu'taṣim, and al-Wāṣiq (A.H. 198–228) at Baghdād, the Mu'tazilah were in high favour. Mr. Syed Ameer Ali Moulvi, M.A., LL.B., in the preface to his book, *The Personal Law of the Mahommedans* (W. H. Allen and Co.), claims to belong to "the little known, though not unimportant philosophical and legal school of the Mutazalas," and he adds, "the young generation is tending unconsciously toward the Mutazalite doctrines."

According to the *Sharḥu 'l-Muwāqif*, the Mu'tazilah are divided into twenty sects, viz.: Waṣilīyah, 'Umarīyah, Huzailīyah, Naẓāmiyah, Aswārīyah, Askāfiyah, Jāfarīyah, Basharīyah, Mazdārīyah, Hishāmīyah, Ṣālhīyah, Hābiṭīyah, Hadbīyah, Ma'marīyah, Ṣamāmīyah, Khaiyāṭīyah, Jāhiẓīyah, Ka'bīyah, Jubā'īyah, and Buhshamīyah.

AL-MU'ṬĪ (المعطى). "The Giver." One of the ninety-nine names or attributes of God. It is referred to in the Qur'ān, Sūrah cviii. verse 1: "Verily we have *given* thee al-Kausar."

MUTILATION. [THEFT.]

MU'TIQ (معتق). The master who emancipates a slave. [SLAVERY.]

MUWAHHID (موحد), pl. *muwaḥhidūn.* A believer in one God. A term often used by Muslims to express their belief as as Unitarians.

MUWATTA' (موطا). *Lit.* "That which has been compiled." A title given to the book of traditions compiled by the Imām Mālik (died A.H. 179). It is the earliest compilation of traditions, and is placed by some amongst the Kutubu 's-Ṣittah, or the "six (correct) books." [TRADITIONS.]

MUZĀBANAH (مزابنة). *Lit.* "Repelling or pushing back." Selling without measure, for example, selling green dates upon trees in exchange for dry ones in the house, and the seller saying that the loss or gain rests with him. This kind of sale is forbidden. (*Mishkāt*, book xii. ch. 5.)

MUZĀRA'AH (مزارعة). Giving over land to the charge of another party on condition of receiving a fixed proportion of its produce.

MUẒĀRABAH (مضاربة). In the language of the law, Muẓārabah signifies a contract of copartnership, of which the one party (namely, the proprietor) is entitled to a profit on account of the stock, he being denominated *Rabbu 'l-Māl*, or proprietor of the stock (which is termed *Rāsu 'l-Māl*), and the other party is entitled to a profit on account of his labour, and this last is denominated the *muẓārib* (or manager), inasmuch as he derives a benefit from his own labour and endeavours. A contract of *muẓārabah*, therefore, cannot be established without a participation in the profit, for if the whole of the profit be stipulated to the proprietor of the stock, then it is considered as a *biẓā'ah*; or, if the whole be stipulated to the immediate manager, it must be considered as a loan.

AL-MUẒILL (المذل). "The One who abases." One of the ninety-nine names or attributes of God referred to in the Qur'ān, Sūrah iii. 25: "Thou honourest whom Thou pleasest and *abasest* whom Thou pleasest."

AL-MUZZAMMIL (المزمل). *Lit.* "The Wrapped up." The title of the LXXIVth Sūrah of the Qur'ān, in the first verse of which the word occurs. "O Thou, *enwrapped*, arise to prayer." It is said the chapter was revealed to Muḥammad when he was wrapped up in a blanket at night.

MYSTICISM. The word mysticism is of a vague signification, but it is generally applied to all those tendencies in religion which aspire to a direct communication between man and his God, not through the medium of the senses, but through the inward perception of the mind. Consequently the term is applied to the Pantheism of the ancient Hindu, to the Gnosticism of the ancient Greek, to the Quietism of Madame Guyon and Fénélon, to the Pietism of Molinos, to the doctrines of the Illuminati of Germany, to the visions of Swedenborg, as well as to the peculiar manifestations of mystic views amongst some modern Christian sects. It is a form of error which mistakes the operations of a merely human faculty for a divine manifestation, although it is often but a blind protest in behalf of what is highest and best in human nature.

The earliest mystics known are those of India, the best exposition of their system being the *Bhāgavad-gītā* (see Wilkins' translation). Sir William Jones says:—"A figurative mode of expressing the fervour of devotion, the ardent love of created spirits, toward their Beneficent Creator, has prevailed from time immemorial in Asia; particularly among the Persian Theists, both ancient Hushangis and modern Sufis, who seem to have borrowed it from the Indian philosophers of the Vedanta School, and their doctrines are also believed to be the source of that sublime but poetical theology which glows and sparkles in the writings of the old Academics. 'Plato travelled into Italy and Egypt,' says Blande Fleury, 'to learn the Theology of the Pagans at its fountain head.' Its true fountain, however, was neither in Italy nor in Egypt though considerable streams of it had been conducted thither by Pythagoras, and by the family of Misra, but in *Persia or India*, which the founder of the Italic sect had visited with a similar design."

Almost the only religion in the world in which we should have concluded, before examination, that the Pantheistic and mystic spirit of Hinduism was impossible, is the stern unbending religious system of Muḥammad and his followers. But even amongst Muslims there have ever been those who seek for divine intuition in individual souls, to the partial or entire rejection of the demands of creeds and ceremonies. These mystics are called Ṣūfīs, and have always included the philosophers, the poets, and the enthusiasts of Islām. For an account of these Muslims, see the article on SUFIISM.

N.

AN-NABA' (النبا). "The information.' The title of the LXXVIIIth Sūrah of the Qur'ān, in the second verse of which the word occurs: "Of the mighty *information* whereon they do dispute."

NĀBĀLIGH (نابالغ). A Persian term used for a minor. [PUBERTY.]

NABBĀSH (نباش). A plunderer or stripper of the dead. According to the Imāms Abū Yūsuf and ash-Shāfiʿī, the hand of a plunderer of the dead should be struck off, but Abū Ḥanīfah and the Imām Muḥammad are of the contrary opinion. (*Hidāyah*, vol. ii. p. 94.)

NABĪ (نبى). Heb. נָבִיא. A prophet. One who has received direct inspiration (*waḥy*) by means of an angel, or by the inspiration of the heart (*ilhām*); or has seen the things of God in a dream. (*Vide Kitābu 't-Taʿrīfāt.*) A *rasūl*, or "messenger," is one who has received *a book* through the angel Gabriel. [PROPHETS.]

NABĪZ (نبيذ). A kind of wine made from dates, which is lawful. (*Hidāyah*, vol. iv. p. 155.)

NĀD-I-ʿALĪ (ناد على). Persian. An amulet on which is inscribed a prayer to ʿAlī. It is much used by the Shīʿahs, and runs thus:—

> "Cry aloud to ʿAlī, who is the possessor of wonders!
> From him you will find help from trouble!
> He takes away very quickly all grief and anxiety!
> By the mission of Muḥammad and his own sanctity!"

NAFAQAH (نـفـقـة). [MAINTENANCE.]

AN-NĀFIʿ (النافع). "The Profiter." One of the ninety-nine names or attributes of God. It does not occur in the Qur'ān.

NĀFIʿ (نافع). A slave belonging to Ibn ʿUmar. Many traditions have been handed down by him, and his authority is highly respected. Died, A.H. 117.

NAFKH (نفخ). "Blowing." The blast on the Day of Judgment which will be sounded by Isrāfīl.

NAFL (نفل). "A voluntary act." A term applied to such acts of devotion as are not enjoined by the teaching of Muḥammad, or by his example. A work of supererogation. [PRAYER.]

NAFS̤ (نفث). Blowing as a necromancer when making incantations.

(1) It occurs in this sense in the Qur'ān, Sūrah cxiii. 4: "I seek refuge . . . from the evil of the blowers upon knots." Referring to those witches who make knots in a string and blow upon them, uttering some incantation.

(2) It is also used for the inspiration which Muḥammad professed to have received from Gabriel. (*Majmaʿu 'l-Biḥār*, p. 376.)

NAFS (نفس). Animal life; soul; substance; desire. A word which occurs in the Qur'ān and the Traditions for the human conscience. [CONSCIENCE.]

NAFSĀ' (نفساء). A woman in the condition of *nifās*, or the period after childbirth.

NAHJU 'L-BALĀGHAH (نـهـج البلاغة). "The Road of Eloquence." A celebrated book of Muḥammadan traditions compiled by ash-Sharīf Abū 'l-Qāṣim al-Murtaẓā, A.H. 406, or his brother ash-Sharīf ar-Raẓī al-Baghdādī. (See *Kashfu 'z-Ẓunūn*, vol. vi. p. 406.)

AN-NAḤL (النحل). "The Bee." The title of the XVIth Sūrah of the Qūr'ān, in the 70th verse of which the word occurs: "And thy Lord inspired the bee."

NAḤR (نحر). The lawful slaughtering of a camel, namely, by spearing it in the hollow of the throat, near the breastbone. (*Hidāyah*, vol. iv. p. 72.)

NĀ'IB (نائب). A deputy, a lieutenant. A Khalīfah is the *nā'ib*, or lieutenant, of Muḥammad. It is also used for the Viceroy of Egypt, who is the *nā'ib*, or deputy, of the Sulṭān. (Lane's *Arabian Nights*, Intro. p. 8.)

NAJĀSAH (نجاسة). A legal term for an impurity of any kind.

NAJĀSHĪ (نجاشى). Negus. The King of Abyssinia, often mentioned in the history of Muḥammad. Aṭ-Ṭabarī, in his history, p. 127, say: "Now a just king was there (Abyssinia) named an-Najāshī. It was a land where the Quraish used to do merchandise, because they found abundance of food, protection, and good traffic." (Muir's *Life of Mahomet*, vol. ii. p. 133.)

NAJD (نجد). "High." The highlands of Arabia. The name of the central province of Arabia. One of its cities, Riyāẓ, is celebrated as the seat of the Wahhābīs. (See *Central and Eastern Arabia*, by W. G. Palgrave, London, 1865; *Journey to the Wahabee Capital*, by Colonel Lewis Pelly, Bombay, 1866.)

AN-NĀJIYAH (الناجية). "The Saved." A term given to the *orthodox* sect of Muḥammadans, and consequently each sect arrogates to itself the title of *an-Nājiyah*, or "the saved."

AN-NAJJĀRĪYAH (النجارية). A sect of Muḥammadans founded by Muḥammad ibn Ḥusain an-Najjār, who agreed with the Mu'tazilah in rejecting all *eternal* attributes of God, to avoid distinction of persons as taught by the Christians, and in holding that the Word of God was created *in subjecto* (as the schoolmen term it), and to consist of letters and sound, and that God will not be seen in Paradise with the corporeal eye; but they did not receive the doctrines of that sect with regard to the decrees and predestination of God, but held the views of the orthodox party on this subject. According to the *Sharḥu 'l-Muwāqif*, they are divided into three sects, viz.: Burghūṣīyah, Za'farānīyah, and Mustadrikah.

AN-NAJM (النجم). "The Star." The title of the LIIIrd Sūrah of the Qur'ān, which begins with the words, "By the star when it falls."

NAJRĀN (نجران). A district between Yaman and Najd, inhabited by a Christian tribe, whose endurance and constancy in their Christian belief are the subject of the following verses in the Qur'ān. Sūrah lxxxv. 4–11. (The verses are said to have been revealed at an early date, and indicate Muḥammad's kind feeling towards the Christians):—

"Cursed be the diggers of the pit,
"Of the fuel-fed fire,
"When they sat around it
"Witnesses of what they inflicted on the believers!
"Nor did they torment them but for their faith in God, the Mighty, the Praiseworthy:
"His the kingdom of the Heavens and of the Earth; and God is the witness of everything.
"Verily, those who vexed the believers, men and women, and repented not, doth the torment of Hell, and the torment of the burning, await.
"But for those who shall have believed and done the things that be right, are the Gardens beneath whose shades the rivers flow. This is the immense bliss!"

Sir William Muir gives the following account of the persecution:—

"Dzu Nowâs was a votary of Judaism, which he is said to have embraced on a visit to Medîna. This creed he supported with an intolerant and proselytizing adherence, which at last proved fatal to his kingdom. His bigotry was aroused by the prevalence and success of Christianity in the neighbouring province of Najrân; and he invaded it with a large army. The Christians offered a strenuous resistance, but yielded at length to the treacherous promise that no ill would be done to them. They were offered the choice of Judaism or death, and those who remained constant to the faith of Jesus were cruelly massacred. Deep trenches were dug and filled with combustible materials; the pile was lighted, and the Christian martyrs cast headlong into the flame. The number thus miserably burned, or slain by the sword, is stated at no less than twenty thousand.

"However much the account of this melancholy carnage may have been exaggerated, there can be no doubt of the cruel and bloody character of the tyrant's administration in Najrân.

"News of the proceedings reached the Emperor Justin I., through his ambassador at Hîra, to which court Dzu Nowâs had exultingly communicated tidings of his triumph. One of the intended victims, Dous dzu Tholabân, also escaped to Constantinople, and holding up a half-burnt gospel, invoked, in the name of outraged Christendom, retribution upon the oppressor. The Emperor was moved, and indited a despatch to the Najâshi, or Prince of the Abyssinians, desiring him to take vengeance upon the barbarous Nimyarite. Immediately an armament was set on foot, and in a short time seventy thousand warriors embarked in thirteen hundred merchant ships or transports, crossed the narrow gulph which separates Yemen from Adulis. Dzu Nowâs was defeated. In despair, he urged his horse into the sea, and expiated in the waves the inhumanities of his career. The Abyssinian victory occurred in 525 A.D." (*Life of Mahomet*, 1st ed., Intro., p. clxii.)

NAJSH (نجش). "Exciting; stirring up." The practice of enhancing the price of goods, by making a tender for them without any intention of buying, but merely to incite others to offer a higher price. It is forbidden by Muḥammadan law. (Hamilton's *Hidāyah*, vol. ii. p. 46.)

NAKH̲' (نخع). The Banū 'n-Nakh̲', an Arabian tribe, the descendants of Qahlān, subdued by 'Alī during the lifetime of Muḥammad, A.H. 10. Two hundred of this tribe came to tender their allegiance to the Prophet, it being the last deputation received by him. (Muir's *Life of Mahomet*, new ed., p. 477.)

NAKH̲LAH (نخلة). A valley about midway between Makkah and aṭ-Ṭā'if, famous as the scene of the first expedition planned by Muḥammad against Makkah in which blood was shed. (See Muir's *Life of Mahomet*, new ed., p. 216 *et seq.*)

NĀKIḤ (ناكح). A legal term for a married man; a married woman is termed *mankūḥah* (منكوحة). The legal term for an unmarried person is *'azab* (عزب).

NAKĪR (نكير). One of the angels who interrogate the dead. [MUNKAR AND NAKIR.]

NAMĀZ (نماز). The Persian and Hindustāni term for *ṣalāt*, the Muḥammadan liturgical prayer. [PRAYER.]

NAMES, SURNAMES.

Arabic *Ism* (اسم), *Laqab* (لقب), *Kunyah* (كنية). The teaching of Muḥammad very greatly influenced the nomenclature of his followers, as is evident from the chapter devoted to the Traditions on the subject in the *Mishkātu 'l-Maṣābiḥ*, entitled "Bābu 'l-Asāmī," book xxii. ch. viii., from which are extracted the following traditional sayings of Muḥammad:—

"The best names in the sight of God are *'Abdu 'llāh* (the servant of God), *'Abdu 'r-Raḥmān* (the servant of the Merciful One)."

"You must not name your slaves *Yasār* (abundance), *Rabāḥ* (gain), *Najīḥ* (prosperous), *Aflaḥ* (felicitous), because if you ask after one of these your domestic servants, and he be not present, the negative reply will express that abundance, or gain, or prosperity, or felicity, are not in your dwelling."

"The vilest name you can give a human being is *Maliku 'l-Amlāk*, or 'King of Kings,' because no one can be such but God Himself."

"You must not say to your slaves, 'My slave,' or 'My slave girl,' for all your slaves are God's, but say, 'My boy,' or 'My girl,' or 'My youth,' or 'My lass." And a slave must not say to his master, *Yā Rabbī!* (*i.e.* My Lord!), but he may say to him *Yā Saiyidī!* (My Chief!)."

"Call your children after your Prophet (*i.e.* Muḥammad), but the names God likes best are *'Abdu 'llāh* (servant of God), *'Abdu 'r-Raḥmān*, and the next best names are *Ḥāris* (husbandman), and *Humām* (high-minded). The worst of names is *Ḥarb* (enmity), or *Murrah* (bitterness)." [Heb. מָרָה, see Ruth i. 20.]

Shuraiḥ ibn Hānī' relates that his father came to the Prophet with his tribe, and the Prophet heard them calling him *Abū 'l-Ḥakam*. When the Prophet said, "Why do you call him so? *Ḥakam*, 'Ruler,' is an attribute of God." And the Prophet ordered him to call himself *Abū Shuraiḥ*, *i.e.* the father of Shuraiḥ, his eldest son.

Modified, somewhat, by these iujunctions of the Prophet, Muḥammadan names have still continued to be ordered amongst learned Muslims according to the ancient custom of Arabia. Persons are often named—

(1) By a single name, as Muḥammad, Mūsā (Moses), Dā'ūd (David), Ibrāhīm (Abraham), Ḥasan, Aḥmad.

(2) As the father or mother of certain persons, *e.g.* Abū Dā'ūd, the father of David; or Ummu Salimah, the mother of Salimah.

(3) As the son of a certain one, *e.g.* Ibn 'Umar, the son of 'Umar; Ibn 'Abbās, the son of Abbās, &c.

(4) By a combination of words, *e.g. Nūru 'd-dīn*, "Light of Religion"; *'Abdu 'llāh*, "Servant of God."

(5) By a nickname of harmless signification, *e.g. Abū Hurairah*, "the kitten's father."

(6) By the trade or profession, *e.g. al-Manṣūr al-Ḥallāj*, Mansūr the dresser of cotton.

(7) By the name of his birth-place, *e.g. al-Bukhārī*, the native of Bukhārah.

These rules, guiding the nomenclature of the Arabians, give a strange sound to western ears in the names of celebrated authors. For instance, the celebrated compiler of the chief book of authentic traditions is known as "*Abū 'Abdi 'llāh, Muḥammad, ibn Ismā'īl ibn Ibrāhīm ibn Mughīrah al-Ju'fī, al-Bukhārī*, which means that his name is Muḥammad and that he is the father of a son named 'Abdu 'llāh, and that his own father's name was Ismā'īl, the son of Ibrāhīm, the son of Mughīrah, of the tribe of Ju'fī, and that he himself was born in Bukhārā.

Arabic names have undergone strange modifications when brought in contact with western languages, *e.g.* Averroës, the philosopher, is a corruption of *Ibn Rashīd*; Avicenna, of *Ibn Sīnā*; Achmet, the Sultan, of *Aḥmad*; Amurath, of *al-Murād*; Saladin, the celebrated warrior of the twelth century, of the Arabic *Ṣalāḥu 'd-dīn*, "the peace of religion."

AN-NAML (النمل). "The Ants."

The title of the XXVIIth Sūrah of the Qur'ān, in the 18th verse of which the word occurs: "They came upon the valley of the ants."

NĀMŪS (ناموس).

The angel, spirit, or being, which Waraqah is related to have said appeared to Moses. See *Ṣaḥīḥu 'l-Bukhārī*, p. 3, where it is said, when Muḥammad told Waraqah, the Jew, what he had seen on Mount Ḥirā', Waraqah exclaimed, "It is the *Nāmūs* who appeared from God to Moses."

'Abdu 'l-Ḥaqq says *Nāmūs* means one who can take knowledge of the secret thoughts of a man, and is used in contradistinction to the word *Jāsūs*, "a spy," who seeks to know the evil deeds of another.

According to the *Kitābu 't-Ta'rīfāt*, it is the law of God.

Mr. Emanuel Deutsch says: "The *nāmūs* is a hermaphrodite in words. It is Arabic and also Greek. It is Talmudic. It is, in the first instance, νόμος, 'law,' that which by 'custom and common consent' has become so. In Talmudic phraseology it stands for the Thorah or Revealed Law. In Arabic it further means one who communicates a secret message. And all these different significations were conveyed by Waraqah to Muhammad." (*Literary Remains*, p. 78.)

The word *nāmūs* occurs in the ethical work known as the *Akhlāq-i-Jalālī*, in the following passage:—

"The maintenance of equity, then, is realised by three things: (1) The holy institute of God, (2) The equitable Prince, (3) Money, or, as the old philosophers laid it down, the foremost νόμος is the institute, the second νόμος is the Prince who conforms to the institute (for religion and government are twins); and the third νόμος is money (νόμος in their language meaning discipline and correction). Thus the institute or greatest arbitrator is obeyed of all; to this even the Prince or secondary arbitrator is bound to conform. While the third arbitrator, which is money, should be invariably under the authority of the second, which is the Prince. An intimation of this principle we have in the Qur'ān, Sūra lvii. 25: "We have sent down the book, and the balance along with it, that man might stand by the right, and we have sent down steel (*ḥadīd*), wherein is mighty power and advantages to man." The book in this passage alludes to the institute; the balance to that which tests the quantities of things, in fact any instrument for ascertaining the value of heterogeneous objects (money being such an one), and steel to the sword, which is grasped by the might of the wrath-exerting doom-pronouncing Prince." (*Akhlāq-i-Jalālī*, Thompson's ed., p. 127.)

NAQL ṢAḤĪḤ (نقل صحيح). "Correct relation." A term used for a Ḥadīs, or tradition, related by a person of authority. [TRADITIONS.]

AN-NAQSHBANDĪYAH (النقشبندية). An ascetic order of Faqīrs, the followers of Khwājah Pīr Muḥammad Naqshband. They are a very numerous sect, and perform the *Zikr-i-Khafī*, or silent religious devotion described in the article on ZIKR.

NĀQŪS (ناقوس). A thin oblong piece of wood, which is beaten with a flexible rod called *wabīl* (وبيل), used by the Christians of Muḥammad's time to summon the people to worship. At first "the Companions" suggested either a lighted fire or the *nāqūs* as the call to prayer, but Muḥammad decided upon the *azān*. (*Mishkāt*, book iv. ch. v. pt. i.) This method of calling Christian people to prayer still exists in some Greek monasteries, and was seen and illustrated by the Hon. R. Curzon in 1833 (*Visits to the Monasteries of the Lavant*). It is called the *simandro* (σιμανδρο) and is generally beaten by one of the monks. [AZAN.]

THE NAQUS AS USED IN A MONASTERY

AN-NĀR (النار), "the fire," occurs in the Qur'ān very frequently for hell, *e.g.* Sūrah ii. 22: "Fear *the fire* whose fuel is men and stones."

All Sunnī commentators understand the fire of hell in its literal sense. (See al-Baiẓāwī on the above verse.) But Ṣūfī writers understand it to be merely figurative.

NARAWĀ (نارِوا). "Unlawful." A Persian word for those things which are expressly forbidden by the Qur'ān and Ḥadīs. It corresponds with the Arabic *Ḥarām*. [LAW.]

AN-NĀS (الناس). "Mankind." The title of the last Sūrah of the Qur'ān. The word occurs in this Sūrah, and is the last word in the Qur'ān, "from genii and *men*."

NASA' (نسا). "To omit." A term used in the Qur'ān for the system of intercalation of the year practised by the ancient Arabs, and which was abolished in the Qur'ān. (Sūrah ix. 37.) [INTERCALATION OF THE YEAR.]

NASAB (نسب). Family, race, lineage. The term, in its legal sense, is generally restricted to the descent of a child from his father, but it is sometimes applied to descent from the mother, and is generally employed in a larger sense to embrace other relationships. (Baillie's *Dig. Muh. Law*, p. 389.)

AN-NASĀ'Ī (النسائى). "Sunanu 'n-Nasā'ī," or *al-Mujtaba* (the selected), a name given to the collection of traditions by Abū 'Abdi 'r-Raḥmān Aḥmad an-Nasā'ī. Born A.H. 215, died A.H. 303. He first compiled a large collection of traditions called the *Sunanu 'l-Kubrā*, but he afterwards revised the whole and admitted only those traditions which were of authority. This collection (*Sunanu 's-Ṣughrā*) is one of the *Kutubu 's-Sittah*, or "six (correct) books." [TRADITIONS.]

NAṢĀRĀ (نصارى), pl. of *Naṣrān*. Nazarenes. The name given to professors of the Christian faith, both in the Qur'ān and the Traditions, and also in the theological works of the Muḥammadans. Christians are never called either *'Isawī* or *Masīḥī*, in Muḥammadan books written before the existence of modern missions; these titles having been applied to Christians by our own missionaries. [CHRISTIANITY.]

NASIKH (ناسخ). "One who cancels." A term used for a verse or sentence of the Qur'ān or Ḥadīs̤, which abrogates a previous one. The one abrogated being called *mansūkh*. [QUR'AN.]

NASR (نسر). One of the idols of ancient Arabia, mentioned in the Qur'ān, Sūrah lxxi. 23. It was an idol which, as its name implies, was worshipped under the form of *an eagle*.

AN-NAṢR (النصر). "Help." The title of the cxth Sūrah of the Qur'ān, in the first verse of which the word occurs: "When there comes God's help and victory."

NAṢṢ (نص). "A demonstration." A legal term used for the express law of the Qur'ān or Ḥadīs.

NAṢṢ-I-KARĪM (نص كريم). "Gracious revelation." A title given to the Qur'ān.

NAṢŪḤ (نصوح). "Sincere in friendship or repentance." In the latter sense the word occurs once in the Qur'ān, Sūrah lxvi. 8: "O Believers! turn to God with the turning of *true repentance*."

NĀSŪT (ناسوت). "Human nature." A term used by the Ṣūfīs to express the natural state of every man before he enters upon the mystic journey. They say the law has been specially revealed for the guidance of people in this condition, but that the law is not necessary for the higher states. [SUFI.]

NAUḤAH (نوحة). "Lamentations for the dead." The employment of paid mourners is forbidden by the Sunnī law, for Abū Sa'īdu 'l-Khudrī says, "The Prophet cursed both the paid mourner and him that listened to her lamentations." (*Mishkāt*, book v. ch viii. pt. 2.)

NAU ROZ (نو روز). "New Year's Day." Chiefly observed amongst the Persians. In Persia it is a day of great festivity. It is observed the first day after the sun has crossed the vernal equinox, and the festivities last for a week or more.

NAWA'IB (نوائب), pl. of *nā'ibah*. "Adversities." A legal term used for any special tax levied by the sovereign of a country. The ruling of the Sunnī law regarding it is as follows:—

"If it extend only to what is just (such as exactions for digging a canal, for the wages of safe guards, for the equipment of an army to fight against the infidels, for the release of Muslim captives, or for the digging of a ditch, the mending of a fort, or the construction of a bridge), the tax is lawful in the opinion of the whole of our doctors. But if it extend to exactions wrongfully imposed, that is, to such as tyrants extort from their subjects, in that case, concerning the validity of security for it, there is a difference of opinion amongst our modern doctors." (Hamilton's *Hidāyah*, vol. ii. p. 594.)

NAZARENES. [NASARA.]

AN-NAZI'ĀT (النازعات). "Those who tear out." The title of the LXXIXth Sūrah of the Qur'ān, which opens with the verse, "By those who tear out violently," referring to the Angel of Death and his assistants, who tear away the souls of the wicked violently, and gently release the souls of the good.

AN-NAẒĪR (النضير). A Jewish tribe residing in the vicinity of al-Madīnah, and known as the Banū 'n-Naẓīr, or Nadhīr. They are celebrated in Muḥammadan history, as having accepted the Prophet's mission after the battle of Badr, but when he met with reverses at Uḥud they forsook him, but they were afterwards defeated by the Prophet and exiled, some to Khaibar, and some to Ḥirā'. They were the occasion of the LIXth Sūrah of the Qur'ān, known as the *Sūratu 'l-Ḥashr*, or "Chapter of Emigration." (See *al-Baiẓāwī in loco*.)

NAẔR WA NIYĀZ (نذر و نياز). "Vows and oblations." These are given in the name of God, or in the name of the Prophet, or in the name of some Muslim saint. [VOWS.]

NEBUCHADNEZZAR. [BUKHT NASSAR.]

NECKLACE. Arabic *qilādah* (قلادة). The wearing of necklaces (among men) is forbidden in the Ḥadīs̤ (*Mishkāt*, Arabic edition, vol. ii. 5), although it is a custom very common amongst the Musalmāns of India.

NEGUS. [NAJASHI.]

NEHEMIAH. Not mentioned in the Qur'ān or in Muslim commentaries. But the following legend given in the Qur'ān

Sūrah ii. 261, seems to have its origin in the circuit made by Nehemiah (Neh. ii. 13):—

"Hast thou considered *him* who passed by a city which had been laid in ruins. 'How,' said he, 'shall God give life to this city, after she hath been dead?' And God caused him to die for an hundred years, and then raised him to life. *And God* said, 'How long hast thou waited?' He said, 'I have waited a day or part of a day.' He said, 'Nay, thou hast waited an hundred years. Look on thy food and thy drink; they are not corrupted; and look on thine ass; we would make thee a sign unto men: And look on the bones *of thine ass*, how we will raise them, then clothe them with flesh.' And when this was shown to him, he said, 'I acknowledge that God hath power to do all things.'"

The commentators, al-Kamālān, say it was either Jeremiah, or Khiẓr, or Ezekiel.

NEIGHBOURS. Arabic *jār* (جار), pl. *jīrān*. The Sunnīs hold that neighbours are those who worship in the same mosque, but some Shī'ah doctors say that a neighbour is anyone whose house is within forty cubits, whilst others maintain that the term extends to all the occupants of forty houses on either side. (Baillie's *Digest*, *Sunni Code*, p. 579; *Im. Code*, p. 216.)

A neighbour has the next right of pre-emption to a partner in the sale and purchase of houses and lands. (*Hidāyah*, vol. iii. p. 562.)

The rights of a neighbour in case of the sale of property, are established by the Muḥammadan law, for the Prophet has said that the neighbour of a house has a superior right to the purchase of that house (*i.e.* next to immediate relatives), and the neighbour of lands has a prior claim to the purchase of those lands, and if he be absent, the seller must wait his return. (*Hidāyah*, vol. iv. p. 562.)

Muslims are enjoined in the Qur'ān (Sūrah iv. 40) to be kind to their neighbours. In the Traditions, it is said that Muḥammad was so frequently advised by the angel Gabriel to order his people to be kind to their neighbours, that he almost imagined that he (the angel) wished to make neighbours heirs to each other. It is also related that the Prophet said, "He is not a perfect Muslim who eats to his full and leaves his neighbour hungry."

Abū Hurairah says that a man once said to the Prophet, "There is a woman who worships God a great deal, but she is very abusive to her neighbours." And the Prophet said "She will be in the fire." The man then said, "But there is another woman who worships little and gives but little in alms, but she does not annoy her neighbours with her tongue?" The Prophet said, "She will be in Paradise." (*Mishkāt*, book xxii. ch. xv.)

NESTOR. Arabic *Naṣṭūr* (نصطور). A Christian monk who resided in Syria, who is said to have borne witness to Muḥammad. The legend is not accepted by Sunnī writers, and Sir William Muir (*Life of Mahomet*, new ed., p. 21), says it is to be rejected as a puerile fabrication. It is, however, believed by the Shī'ahs, and the following is the story as given in the Shī'ah work entitled the *Ḥayātu 'l-Qulūb*, on the supposed authority of Abū Ṭālib, Muḥammad's uncle:—

"As we approached Shâm (Syria)," continued Abutâlib), I saw the houses of that country in motion, and light above the brightness of the sun beaming from them. The crowd that collected to see Mohammed, that Yusoof of Misree perfection, made the Bâzârs impassable wherever we went, and so loud were exclamations at his beauty and excellence altogether, that the sound reached the frontiers of Shâm. Every monk and learned man came to see him. The wisest of the wise among the people of the Book, who was called Nestoor, visited him, and for three days was in his company without speaking a word. At the close of the third day, apparently overwhelmed with emotion, he came near and walked around the Prophet, upon which I said unto him, 'O monk what do you want of the child?' He said, 'I wish to know his name.' I told him it was Mohammed-bin-Abdullah. At the mention of the name the monk's colour changed, and he requested to be allowed to see the shoulders of the Prophet. No sooner did he behold the seal of prophecy [SEAL OF PROPHECY], than he cast himself down, kissed it, and wept, saying, 'Carry back this sun of prophecy quickly to the place of his nativity. Verily, if you had known what enemies he has here, you would not have brought him with you.' The learned man continued his visit to the Prophet, treated him with the greatest reverence, and when we left the country gave him a shirt as a memento of his friendship. I carried Mohammed home with the utmost expedition, and when the news of our happy return reached Mekkah, great and small came out to welcome the Prophet, except Abujahl, who was intoxicated and ignorant of the event."

Other traditions respecting this journey into Syria inform us that many more miracles attended it. Savage animals and birds of the air rendered the most obsequious homage to the Prophet. And when the party reached the bâzârs of Buṣrā they met a company of monks, who immediately changed colour, as if their faces had been rubbed over with saffron, while their bodies shook as in an ague. "They besought us to visit their chief in their great church. We replied, What have you to do with us? On which they said, What harm is there in your coming to our place of worship? Accordingly we went with them, they supposing that Mohammed was in our company, and entered a very large and lofty church, where we saw their great wise man sitting among his disciples with a book in his hand. After looking at the book and scrutinizing us, he said to his people, 'You have accomplished nothing, the object of our inquiry is not here.' He then asked who we were, to which we replied that we were Koraysh. 'Of what family of that tribe?'

he further demanded. We answered that we were of the Benee Abdulshems. He then demanded if there was no other person belonging to our party besides those present. We told him there was a youth of the Benee Hâshim belonging to our company, who was called the orphan grandson of Abdulmutalib. On hearing this he shrieked, nearly swooned away, sprang up and cried, 'Alas! alas! the Nasarânee religion is ruined!' He then leaned on his crosier and fell into profound thought for a long time, with eight of his patriarchs and disciples standing around him. At last he said, 'Can you show me that youth?' We answered in the affirmative.

"He then accompanied us to the bâzâr, where we found the Prophet, with light beaming from the radiant moon of his face, and a great crowd of people around him, who had been attracted by his extraordinary beauty, and were buying his goods at the highest prices, while they sold their own to him at the cheapest rate. With the view of proving the knowledge of the wise man, we pointed out another individual as the object of his inquiry, but presently he recognised the Prophet himself, and shouted, 'By the truth of the Lord Meseeh, I have found him!' and overpowered with emotion, came and kissed his blessed head, saying, 'Thou art holy!' He then asked Mohammed many things concerning himself, all of which he satisfactorily answered. The wise man affirmed that if he were to live in the time of Mohammed's prophecy, he would fight for him in the cause of truth, declaring that whoever obeyed him would gain everlasting life, and whoever rejected him would die eternal death." (Merrick's translation of *Ḥayātu 'l-Qulūb*, p. 64.)

NEW MOON. Arabic *Hilāl* (هلال). The term is used for the first three days of the new moon.

NEW TESTAMENT. Arabic *al-'Ahdu 'l-Jadīd* (العهد الجديد). There is no evidence in the Qur'ān, or in the Traditions, that Muḥammad had ever seen, or was acquainted with, the New Testament. The Christian scriptures are spoken of in the Qur'ān as the *Injīl*, εὐαγγέλιον, "which was given to Jesus"; by which Muḥammadans understand a complete book somewhat similar to the Qur'ān. See Sūrah lvii. 27; "We caused our Apostles to follow in their footsteps (*i.e.* of Noah and Abraham), and We caused Jesus the son of Mary to follow them, and We gave him the *Injīl*, and We put into the hearts of those who followed him kindness and compassion; but as to the monastic life, they invented it themselves." The only New Testament characters mentioned by name in the Qur'ān are Jesus, Mary, Zacharias, John, and Gabriel, and there is no *direct* reference to the Sacraments of Baptism and the Lord's Supper, nor to the miracles or parables of Jesus. This is all the more remarkable, because the Old Testament history and its leading characters, are frequently mentioned in the Qur'ān. [INJIL, CHRISTIANITY.]

NEW YEAR. [NAUROZ.]

NICKNAME. Arabic *nabaz* (نبز), pl. *anbāz*. The calling of nicknames is forbidden in the Qur'ān, Sūrah xlix. 11: "O Believers, let not men laugh men to scorn who haply may be better than themselves. Neither let women laugh women to scorn, who haply may be better than themselves. Neither defame one another, nor call one another by nicknames."

This verse is said to have been given when Ṣafīyah, one of the Prophet's wives, complained that she had been taunted by the other women with her Jewish origin. Muḥammad answered her, "Canst thou not say, 'Aaron is my father, Moses is my uncle, and Muḥammad is my husband.'" (See *al-Baiẓāwi, in loco.*)

NIFĀQ (نفاق). Hypocrisy, or professing with the lips to believe and hiding infidelity in one's heart. (*Kitābu 't-Ta'rīfāt, in loco.*)

NIFĀS (نفاس). The condition of a woman after the birth of a child, during which period she is unclean and is not permitted to perform the usual prayers. According to the Sunnīs, it is a period of forty days, but according to the Shī'ahs, only ten.

NIGHT JOURNEY OF MUḤAMMAD. [MI'RAJ.]

NIGHT PRAYERS. Arabic *ṣalātu 'l-layl* (صلوة الليل), or *ṣalātu 't-tahajjud* (صلوة التهجد). From eight to twelve *rak'ah* prayers recited during the night, in addition to the *witr* prayers, which consist of an odd number of rak'ahs. These prayers are Sunnah, *i.e.* established according to the custom of the Prophet, but they are voluntary acts of devotion. (*Mishkāt*, book iv. ch. xxxii.)

NIKĀḤ (نكاح). A word which, in its literal sense signifies conjunction, but which in the language of the law implies the marriage contract. [MARRIAGE.]

NIMROD. Arabic *Numrūd* (نمرود). Heb. נִמְרוֹד. All Muḥammadan commentators say he was the son of Canaan (Kan'ān), and not, as stated in Genesis x. 8, the son of Cush.

He is referred to in the Qur'ān in the following passage:—

Sūrah ii. 260: "Hast thou not thought on him who disputed with Abraham about his Lord, because God had given him the kingdom? When Abraham said, 'My Lord is He who maketh alive and causeth to die:' He said, 'It is I who make alive and cause to die!' Abraham said, 'Since God bringeth the sun from the East, do thou, then bring it from the West.' The infidel was confounded; for God guideth not the evil doers."

Sūrah xxi. 68, 69: "They said: 'Burn him, and come to the succour of your gods: if ye will do *anything at all.*' We said, 'O fire! be thou cold, and to Abraham a safety!'"

The Rabbins make Nimrod to have been the persecutor of Abraham (comp. Targ. Jon. on Gen. xv. 7; Tr. Bava Bathra, fol. 91*a.*; Maimon. More Nevochim, iii. 29; Weil, *Legenden*, p. 74), and the Muḥammadan commentators say, that by Nimrod's order a large space was inclosed at Kūṣā, and filled with a vast quantity of wood, which being set on fire, burned so fiercely that none dared to venture near it; then they bound Abraham, and putting him into an engine (which some suppose to have been of the Devil's invention), shot him into the midst of the fire, from which he was preserved by the angel Gabriel, who was sent to his assistance, the fire burning only the cords with which he was bound. They add that the fire, having miraculously lost its heat in respect to Abraham, became an odoriferous air, and that the pile changed to a pleasant meadow, though it raged so furiously otherwise, that, according to some writers, about two thousand of the idolaters were consumed by it.

This story seems to have had no other foundation than that passage of Moses, where God is said to have brought Abraham out of Ur of the Chaldees, misunderstood; which word the Jews, the most trifling interpreters of scripture, and some moderns who have followed them, have translated out of the fire of the Chaldees; taking the word Ur, not for the proper name of a city, as it really is, but for an appellative signifying "fire." However, it is a fable of some antiquity, and credited not only by the Jews, but by several of the eastern Christians; the twenty-fifth of the second Kānūn, or January, being set apart in the Syrian calendar for the commemoration of Abraham's being cast into the fire.

The Jews also mention some other persecutions which Abraham underwent on account of his religion, particularly a ten years' imprisonment, some saying he was imprisoned by Nimrod, and others by his father Terah. Some tell us that Nimrod, on seeing this miraculous deliverance from his palace, cried out that he would make an offering to the God of Abraham; and that he accordingly sacrificed four thousand kine. But if he ever relented, he soon relapsed into his former infidelity, for he built a tower that he might ascend to heaven to see Abraham's God, which being overthrown, still persisting in his design, he would be carried to heaven in a chest borne by four monstrous birds; but after wandering for some time through the air, he fell down on a mountain with such force that he made it shake, whereto (as some fancy) a passage in the Qur'ān alludes (Sūrah xiv. 47), which may be translated, "Although their contrivances be such as to make the mountains tremble." Nimrod, disappointed in his design of making war with God, turns his arms against Abraham, who being a great prince, raised forces to defend himself; but God, dividing Nimrod's subjects, and confounding their language, deprived him of the greater part of his people, and plagued those who adhered to him by swarms of gnats, which destroyed almost all of them; and one of those gnats having entered into the nostril, or ear, of Nimrod, penetrated to one of the membranes of his brain, where growing bigger every day, it gave him such intolerable pain that he was obliged to cause his head to be beaten with a mallet, in order to procure some ease, which torture he suffered four hundred years; God being willing to punish by one of the smallest of his creatures him who insolently boasted himself to be lord of all. A Syrian calendar places the death of Nimrod, as if the time were well known, on the 8th of Tamūz, or July. (See Sale's *Koran*; D'Herbelot's *Bibl. Orient.*; al-Baiẓāwī's Com.)

NĪNAWĀ (نينوى). [NINEVEH.]

NINEVEH. Arabic *Nīnawā* (نينوى). Heb. נִינְוֵה. Not mentioned by name in the Qur'ān, but according to al-Baiẓāwī it is the city of "a hundred thousand persons, or even more," to whom Jonah was sent. See Qur'ān, Sūrah xxxvii. 147.

AN-NISĀ (النساء). "Women." The title of the IVth Sūrah of the Qur'ān, in the first verse of which the word occurs, and which treats to a great extent the subject of women.

NIṢĀB (نصاب). An estate or property for which *zakāt*, or legal alms, must be paid. [ZAKAT.]

NĪYAH (نية). A vow; intention; purpose. A term used for the vow or declaration of the intention to perform prayers. 'I have purposed to offer up to God only with a sincere heart this *morning* (or, as the case may be), with my face Qiblah-wards *two* (or, as the case may be) rak'ah prayers *farẓ* (*sunnah*, *nafl*, or *witr*).' It is also used by a Muslim about to perform the pilgrimage or the month's fast. The formula is necessary to render an act of devotion acceptable. [PRAYER.]

NIYĀZ-I-ALLĀH (نياز الله). A Persian term for offerings in the name of God.

NIYĀZ-I-RASŪL (نياز رسول). A Persian term for offerings in the name of the Prophet.

NOAH. Arabic *Nūḥ* (نوح). Heb. נֹחַ. A prophet to whom Muḥammadans give the Kalimah, or title, of *Nabīyu 'llāh*, "the Prophet of God." He is not supposed to have been the inspired author of "a *Book*."

The following is the account given of him and of the flood in the Qur'ān (with Mr. Lane's annotations in *italics*: see second edition, by Mr. Stanley Lane-Poole):—

"We formerly sent Noah unto his people, *saying*, Verily I am unto you a plain admonisher that ye worship not [any] but God. Verily I fear for you, *if ye worship any other*, the punishment of an afflictive day *in this world and the world to come.*—But the chiefs who disbelieved among his people replied, We see thee not to be other than a man, like unto us; and we see not any to have followed thee except the meanest of us, *as the weavers and the cobblers*, at first thought (*or rashly*), nor do we see you to have any excellence above us: nay, we imagine you to be liars *in your claim to the apostolic commission.* He said, O my people, tell me, if I have an evident proof from my Lord and He hath bestowed on me mercy (*the gift of prophecy*) from Himself which is hidden from you, shall we compel you to *receive* it when ye are averse thereto? *We cannot do so.* And, O my people, I ask not of you any riches for it; *namely, for delivering my message.* My reward is not due from any but God; and I will not drive away those who have believed *as ye have commanded me* [because they are poor people]. Verily they shall meet their Lord *at the resurrection, and He will recompense them, and will exact for them* [reparation] *from those who have treated them with injustice, and driven them away.* But I see you [to be] a people who are ignorant *of the end of your case.* And, O my people, who will defend me against God if I drive them away? Will ye not then consider? And I do not say unto you, I have the treasures of God; nor [do I say], I know the things unseen; nor do I say, Verily I am an angel; nor do I say, of those whom your eyes contemn, God will by no means bestow on them good: (God best knoweth what is in their minds:) verily I should in that case be [one] of the offenders.—They replied, O Noah, thou hast disputed with us and multiplied disputes with us: now bring upon us that *punishment* wherewith thou threatenest us, if thou be of those that speak truth. He said, Only God will bring it upon you, if He please *to hasten it unto you; for it is His affair, not mine;* and ye shall not escape *God:* nor will my counsel profit you, if I desire to counsel you, if God desire to lead you into error. He is your Lord; and unto Him shall ye be brought back." (Sūrah xi. 27–36.)

"And it was said by revelation unto Noah, Verily there shall not believe of thy people [any] but they who have already believed; therefore be not grieved for that which they have done." (Sūrah xi. 38.)

"*And he uttered an imprecation upon them, saying,* O my Lord, leave not upon the earth any one of the unbelievers; for if Thou leave them, they will lead Thy servants into error, and will not beget [any] but a wicked, ungrateful [offspring]. O my Lord, forgive me and my parents (*for they were believers*), and whomsoever entereth my house (*my abode, or my place of worship*), being a believer, and the believing men, and the believing women, (*to the day of resurrection,*) and add not to the offenders [aught] save destruction." (Sūrah lxxi. 27–29.)

"*And God answered his prayer, and said,* Construct the ark in our sight and according to our revelation, and speak not unto Me concerning those who have offended, *to beg Me not to destroy them;* for they [shall be] drowned. And he constructed the ark; and whenever a company of his people passed by him, they derided him. He said, If ye deride us, we will deride you, like as ye deride, *when we are saved and ye are drowned,* and ye shall know on whom shall come a punishment which shall render him vile, and whom shall befall a lasting punishment. [Thus he was employed] until when Our decree *for their destruction* came to pass, and the *baker's* oven overflowed *with water* (*for this was a signal unto Noah*), We said, Carry into it (*that is, into the ark*) of every pair, *male and female, of each of these descriptions,* two (*and it is related that God assembled for Noah the wild beasts and the birds and other creatures, and he proceeded to put his hands upon each kind, and his right hand fell always upon the male, and his left upon the female, and he carried them into the ark*), and thy family (excepting him upon whom the sentence *of destruction* hath already been pronounced, *namely, Noah's wife, and his son Canaan: but Shem and Ham and Japheth and their three wives he took*), and those who have believed; but there believed not with him save a few: *they were six men and their wives: and it is said that all who were in the ark were eighty, half of whom were men and half women.* And *Noah* said, Embark ye therein. In the name of God [be] its course and its mooring. Verily my Lord is very forgiving [and] merciful.—And it moved along with them amid waves like mountains; and Noah called unto his son, *Canaan,* who was apart *from the ark,* O my child, embark with us, and be not with the unbelievers! He replied, I will betake me to a mountain which will secure me from the water. [Noah] said, There is nought that will secure to-day from the decree of God [any] but him on whom He hath mercy. And the waves intervened between them; so he became [one] of the drowned. And it was said, O earth, swallow up thy water (*whereupon it drank it up, except what had descended from heaven, which became rivers and seas*), and, O heaven, cease *from raining;*—and the water abated, and the decree was fulfilled, and it (*namely, the ark*), rested on El-Joodee (*a mountain of El-Jezeereh, near El-Mósil*); and it was said, Perdition to the offending people!" (Sūrah xi. 39–46.)

"And Noah called upon his Lord, and said, O my Lord, verily my son is of my family, *and Thou hast promised me to save them,* and verily Thy promise is true, and Thou art the most just of those who exercise judgment. *God* replied, O Noah, verily he is not of thy family *who should be saved, or of the people of thy religion* Verily it (*namely, thine asking Me to save him*) is not a righteous act; *for he was an unbeliever, and there is no safety for the unbelievers;* therefore ask not of Me that wherein thou hast no knowledge. I admonish thee, lest thou become [one] of the ignorant.—*Noah* said, O my Lord, I beg Thee to preserve me from asking Thee that wherein I have no knowledge; and if Thou do not forgive me and have mercy upon me, I shall be of those who suffer loss.

—It was said, O Noah, descend *from the ark*, with peace from Us, and blessings, upon thee and upon peoples [that shall proceed] from those who are with thee *in the ark* (*that is, their believing posterity*); but peoples [that shall proceed] *from those who are with thee* We will permit to enjoy *the provisions of this world*; then a painful punishment shall befall them from Us, *in the world to come; they being unbelievers*." (Sūrah xi. 47–50.)

The commentator, al-Baiẓāwī, says that Noah went into the ark on the tenth of Rajab, and came out of it on the tenth of Muḥarram; which therefore became a fast; so that the whole time of Noah's being in the ark, according to him, was six months; and that Noah was two years in building the ark, which was framed of Indian plane-tree; that it was divided into three stories, of which the lower was designed for the beasts, the middle one for the men and women, and the upper for the birds; and the men were separated from the women by the body of Adam, which Noah had taken into the ark.

NOMOS. Greek νόμος. [NAMUS.]

NOSE, Cutting off. There is retaliation for cutting off a nose: a nose for a nose. (*Hidāyah*, vol. iv. p. 294.)

NUBŪWAH (نبوة). "Prophecy." The office or work of a *nabi* or prophet. [PROPHETS.]

NUḤ (نوح). [NOAH.]

AN-NUJABĀ' (النجباء), the pl. of *Najīb*. "The Excellent ones." According to the Ṣūfīs, forty saintly characters who always exist on earth for the benefit of its people. (See *Kashshāfu 'l-Iṣṭilaḥāt in loco*.) [ABDAL.]

NU'MĀN (نعمان). The name of several of the Kings of Ḥirā'. Nu'mān V. is celebrated in the annals of the history of Arabia, because his reign approached close upon the rise of Islām, and he was the patron of several poets of renown, who have celebrated his name. (See Muir's *Life of Mahomet*, 1st ed., Intro. p. clxxxi.)

Nu'mān is also the popular title of the Imām Abū Ḥanīfah. [HANIFAH.]

NUMRŪD (نمرود). [NIMROD.]

NŪN (نون). The letter *N* ن, which occurs at the commencement of the LXVIIIth Sūrah of the Qur'ān. The meaning of which is acknowledged by all commentators to be a mystery.

Al-Baiẓāwī says it is supposed that *nūn* either means an inkstand, referring to the pen of the first verse, or a fish, referring to that which swallowed Jonah mentioned in the 48th verse of this Sūrah, but he thinks it is merely an initial letter, the meaning of which is unknown to mortal man.

NUPTIAL FEAST. [WALIMAH, MARRIAGE.]

AN-NUQABĀ' (النقباء), the pl. of *Naqib*. "The Watchmen." According to the Ṣūfīs, they are three hundred persons who are ever to be found in the world, and who are engaged in its enlightenment. (See *Kitābu 't-Ta'rīfāt, in loco*.) [ABDAL.]

NUQŪ'U 'Z-ZABĪB (نقوع الزبيب). "Infusion of raisins." Water in which raisins are steeped until it becomes sweet and is affected in its substance. It is a prohibited. liquor. (Hamilton's *Hidāyah*, vol. iv. p. 159.)

AN-NŪR (النور). "The Light." One of the ninety-nine names or attributes of God. It occurs in the Qur'ān, Sūrah xxiv. 35:—

"God is the *Light* of the Heavens and of the Earth. His Light is like a niche in which is a lamp—the lamp encased in glass—the glass, as it were, a glistening star. From a blessed tree is it lighted, the olive neither of the East nor the West, whose oil would well nigh shine out, even though fire touched it not! It is light upon light. God guideth whom He will to His light, and God setteth forth parables to men, for God Knoweth all things."

NŪR-I-MUḤAMMADĪ (نورمحمدى). Persian for "The Light of Muḥammad." The original essence of Muḥammad, known in Arabic as the *Haqīqatu 'l-Muḥammadīyah*, under which title the subject is discussed in this dictionary. [HAQIQATU 'L-MUHAMMADIYAH.]

NŪRU 'L-ANWĀR (نور الانوار). "The Light of Lights." A title given to the Divine Being. (See 'Abdu 'r-Razzāq's *Dict. of Ṣūfī Terms*.)

NUZŪL (نزول). "Descent." (1) The portions of the Qur'ān as they were declared by Muḥammad to have descended from heaven by the hand of Gabriel.

(2) Property which falls to the state from default of heir, or which has been confiscated.

O.

OATH. Arabic *yamīn* (يمين), pl. *yamīnāt*, *aimān*. The teaching of the Qur'ān with reference to an oath, is expressed in the following verses:—

Sūrah ii. 225: "God will not punish you for an inconsiderate word in your oath, but he will punish you for that which your hearts have assented to."

Sūrah v. 91: "God will not punish you for an inconsiderate word in your oaths, but he will punish you in regard to an oath taken seriously. Its expiation shall be to feed ten poor persons with such moderate food as ye feed your own families with, or to clothe them; or to set free a captive. But he who cannot find means shall fast three days."

Sūrah xvi. 96: "Take not your oaths between you deceitfully."

The following is the teaching of Muḥammad, as given in the Traditions:—

"Whoever swears to a thing and says, 'If it please God,' and acts contrary to his oath, it is no sin."

"Swear not by idols or by your own fathers."

"Swear not by God except it be to the truth."

"Whoever swears by the prayers or by the fast, or by the pilgrimage, is not a Muslim."

The Prophet used generally to swear in these words: "No, by the Turner of Hearts."

According to the *Hidāyah* (Hamilton's ed., vol. vi., pp. 1, 2), *yamīn* is constituted by the use of the name of Almighty God, or by any of those appellations by which the Deity is generally known or understood.

False oaths are of three kinds:—

(1) *Al-Yamīnu 'l-Ghamūs* (اليمين الغموس). An oath taken concerning a thing already past, in which is conveyed an *intentional falsehood* on the part of the swearer: such an oath is highly sinful, the Prophet having declared —'Whosoever sweareth falsely, the same shall be condemned to hell."

(2) *Al-Yamīnu 'l-mun'aqid* (اليمين المنعقد). An oath taken concerning a matter which is to come. Thus, a man swears that he will do such a thing, or he will not do such a thing, and where he fails in this, expiation is incumbent upon him, which expiation is established on the authority of the sacred writings.

(3) *Yamīnu 'l-Laghw* (يمين اللغو). An oath taken concerning an incident or transaction already past, where the swearer believes that the matter to which he thus bears testimony accords with what he swears, though it should happen to be actually otherwise; in which case it may be hoped from the divine mercy that the swearer will not be condemned for such an oath.

The expiation, or *kaffārah*, is of no avail for the *Yamīnu 'l-Ghamūs*, but it is necessary for the *Yamīnu 'l-mun'aqid*. It consists of either feeding or clothing ten poor persons, or releasing a Muslim captive.

The Muslim law with regard to oaths is a modification of the Talmudic law, for from the Divine law the Jewish doctors deduced many special cases of perjury, which are thus classified:—

(1) *Jus jurandum promissorium*, a rash or inconsiderate oath for the future, or a false assertion respecting the past (Lev. v. 4).

(2) *Vanum*, an absurd contradictory assertion.

(3) *Depositi*, breach of contract denied (Lev. xix. 11).

(4) *Testimonii*, judicial perjury (Lev. v. 1). (H. W. P. in Smith's *Dict. of the Bible.*)

The Mosaic law admitted expiation in the case of rash or forgotten oaths, *vide* Lev. v. 4, but the *Yamīnu 'l-mun'aqid* of Muḥammadan law allows a much greater latitude, for it applies to *all* vows or oaths excepting those *intentionally* false made with regard to future events.

The teaching of Muḥammadan jurists on the subject of oaths and vows, exhibits that *reservatio mentalis* of Muḥammadan morality which is so similar to that of the Jewish Rabbis, and which was condemned by Jesus Christ in St. Matt. xxiii. 16.

Sunnī writers on jurisprudence say that an oath should be expressed by such attributes of the Deity as are commonly used in swearing, such as the *power*, or the *glory*, or the *might* of God, because an oath is usually expressed under one or other of those qualities; and the sense of *yamīn*, viz. "strength," is by this means obtained, since as the swearer believes in the power, glory, and might, and other attributes of the Deity, it follows that the mention of these attributes only is sufficient to strengthen the resolution in the performance of the act vowed, or the avoidance thereof.

If a man swear "by the knowledge of God," it does not constitute an oath, because an oath expressed by the knowledge of God is not in use; moreover, by "knowledge" is frequently implied merely that which is known; and in this sense the word knowledge is not expressive either of the name of God, or of any of His attributes. In the same manner, should a person swear "by the wrath of God," or "by the mercy of God," it does not constitute an oath, because an oath is not commonly expressed by any of these attributes; moreover, by the word *raḥmah* is sometimes understood "rain," and "heaven" is also occasionally expressed by that term; and by the word *Ghaiẓ* is understood "punishment"; and none of these are either appellations or attributes of the Deity.

If a person swear by another name than that of God,—such as "the Prophet," or "the Holy Temple," this does not constitute an oath, as the Prophet has said, "if any man among you take an oath, he must swear "by the name of God, or else his oath is void." If a person swear by the Qur'ān, it does not constitute an oath, although the Qur'ān be the word of God, because men do not swear by the Qur'ān. The compiler of the *Hidāyah* observes that this is where the swearer only says, "by the Prophet," or "by the Temple," or "by the Qur'ān," but if the swearer say, "If I act contrary to what I now say, may I be deprived 'of the Prophet,'" or "of the temple," or "of the Qur'ān," this constitutes an oath, because such privation would reduce the swearer to the state of an infidel, and the suspension of infidelity upon a condition amounts to *yamīn*.

Abū Ḥanīfah alleges that if a man should swear "by the truth of God," this does not constitute an oath, and in this Imām Muḥammad coincides. There are two opinions of Abū Yūsuf recorded on this point. According to one, it is *not* an oath; but according to the other it *is* an oath, because truth is one of the attributes of the Deity, signifying the certainty of the divine existence, and hence it is the same as if the swearer were to say, "by God, the truth!" and as oaths are common under this mode of expression, so an oath is hereby constituted. The argument of Imām Muḥammad and Abū Ḥanīfah is that the term "the truth," as here expressed, relates merely to the identity of the godhead as the object of obedience, and hence an oath thus expressed appears to be taken by that which is neither an appellation nor an attribute of God. The learned jurists, however, say that if a person express himself thus, "by the truth I will do so and so," this constitutes an oath, because the *truth* is one of the appellatives or proper names of God. But if a person were to say, "I will do this truly," it does not amount to an oath, because the word *truly* can only be taken, in this case, as a corroboration or confirmation of the promise contained in the speech, being the same as if he were to say, "I shall do this *indeed*." If a man say, "I swear," or "I vow," or "I testify," whether the words "by God" be superadded or not, it constitutes an oath, because such words are commonly used in swearing; the use of them in the *present* tense is undisputed; and they are also sometimes used in the *future* tense, where the context admits of a construction in the *present*; and attestation amounts to an oath, as in that sense it occurs in the sacred writings. Now swearing "*by the name* of God" is both customary and conformable to the divine ordinances, but *without* the name of God it is forbidden. When it so occurs, therefore, it must be construed into a lawful oath; hence some say that intention is not requisite in it; others, however, allege that the intention is essential, because the words here recited bear the construction of a *promise*, that is, they admit of being received as applying *to the future*, and also of being taken as a vow without the name of God.

If a person, speaking in the Persian language, were to say, "I swear by God," it amounts to an oath, because here the idiom confines the expression solely to the present; but if he were to say simply, "I swear," some allege that this does not constitute an oath. If he were to say, "I swear by the divorce of my wife," this is not an oath, as an oath is not so expressed in practice.

If a man in swearing say "by the age" or "the existence of God," it constitutes an oath, because the age or existence of God signifies his eternity, which is one of his attributes.

If a person should say, "If I do this may I be a Jew, or a Christian, or an infidel," it constitutes an oath; because, as the swearer has made the condition a sign of infidelity, it follows that he is conscious of his obligation to avoid the condition; and this obligation is possible, by making it an oath, in such a way as to render unlawful to himself that which is lawful. And if the oath relate to anything which he has done in the time past, as if he were to say, "If I have done so may I be a Jew or an infidel," and so forth, this is *yaminu 'l-Ghamūs*, or "perjury." The swearer is not, however, in this case made a Jew or an infidel, because the words "may I be an infidel," and so forth, relate to some future indefinite period. Some, on the contrary, have alleged that he becomes actually as an infidel," because the penalty which the swearer imprecates upon himself relates to the present instant of his testimony, being the same as if he were to say, "I am a Jew," &c. But the majority of doctors say, the swearer does not become a Jew or infidel in either of the cases, either in that of a vow with respect to the *future*, or an oath regarding the past, provided he consider this merely as a form of swearing. But if he believe that by thus swearing he fully subjects himself to the penalty expressed, he suffers accordingly, in either instance, because he appears consenting to infidelity, on account of having ventured upon a thing by the commission of which he conceives that he may be rendered an infidel.

If a person say, "If I do this, may the anger of God fall upon me," this does not constitute a vow, as not being a customary mode of expression for that purpose. And so also, if a person were to say, "May I be an adulterer or a drunkard or an usurer," because these are not generally understood or received as forms of swearing.

The following are considered the most solemn and binding methods of taking an oath:—

1. Saying three times "by the Great God."
2. Taking the Qur'ān and saying, "by what this contains of the word of God."
3. By placing a sword on the Qur'ān.
4. By saying, "I impose upon myself divorcement."

Muḥammad himself was rather given to

swearing, and the Qur'ān is full of wild oaths, one of the most terrible of which, according to the Prophet's own words, is to "swear by the setting stars." (Sūrah lvi. 74.)

Burckhardt, in his notes on the Bedouin Arabs, says that these children of the desert often take hold of the middle of a tent pole and swear by the life of the tent and its owners.

As might be expected, from the example set them by their Prophet, Muḥammadans are commonly guilty of taking God's name in vain by swearing upon every petty occasion. Like the μα Δία of the Greeks, the word is hardly ever out of their mouths.

[For further information on the subject of Oaths, see Hamilton's *Hidāyah*, book vi.; the *Durru 'l-Mukhtār*, the *Raddu 'l-Muḥtār*, and the *Fatāwā-i-'Alamgīrī, in loco*, in which there are chapters devoted to the consideration of oaths and vows made under all circumstances of life, *e.g.* with respect to entering places of residence; with regard to actions; with respect to eating and drinking, speaking and conversing; of vows in manumission and divorce; with respect to buying and selling, marriage, clothing, wearing ornaments, striking, killing, the payment of money, &c. &c.]

OATH, The administration of an.

An oath in a court of justice is not worthy of credit unless it be taken in the name of God, because Muḥammad said, "Whosoever takes an oath otherwise than in the name of God, is most certainly a polytheist." It is incumbent upon the Qāẓī, or judge, to request the swearer to corroborate his oath by reciting some of the attributes of God. For example, "I swear by God, the Righteous, the Knower of Secrets," &c. A defendant must not be required to swear by divorce or emancipation, as if he should say: "If it be true my wife is divorced, or my slave is free."

If an oath be administered to a Jew, he should say, "I swear by God who revealed the *Taurāt* to Moses."

If to a Christian, he should say, "I swear by God who revealed the *Injīl* to Jesus."

If to a Majūsī or fire-worshipper, he should say, "I swear by God who created fire."

An oath cannot be administered to an idolater otherwise than in the name of God, in accordance with this verse in the Qur'ān, "If ye ask of them who hath created you, verily they will say God Almighty." (Sūrah xxxix. 39.)

An oath cannot be administered to infidels in their places of worship, because the Qāẓī is not allowed to enter such a place. This applies to the places of worship of the Jews and Christians as well as of idolaters. (*Hidāyah*, vol. ii. p. 77.)

Women are not in Muslim law (as in Jewish, *Mishna Sheb.* iv. 1), forbidden to bear witness on oath.

OBSEQUIES OF THE DEAD.

[JANAZAH.]

OFFENCE AGAINST THE PERSON.

[JINAYAH.]

OFFERINGS.

The Arabic word *nazr* (نذر) is often used for an offering, but in its strict theological meaning it expresses a vow. *Khairāt* (خيرات), pl. of *Khair*, is used for ordinary acts of charity. *Ṣadaqah* (صدقة) also expresses the same meaning. *Niyāz* (نياز) is an offering to a saint. *Zakāt* (زكوة), the legal alms.

[For an account of these offerings refer to the words.]

OHUD.

[UHUD.]

OLD TESTAMENT.

Al-'Ahdu 'l-'Atīq (العهد العتيق.) Muḥammad, in his Qur'ān, professes to receive all the inspired books of the Old Testament. (See Sūrah ii. 130: "We believe in God, and what has been revealed to us, and what has been revealed to Abraham, and Ishmael, and Isaac, and Jacob, and the Tribes, *and what was brought unto the Prophets from their Lord:* and we will not distinguish between any of them, and unto Him are we resigned" (*i.e.* Muslims). But there is no evidence that Muḥammad had ever seen the Jewish Scriptures, as now received by both Jews and Christians. In the Qur'ān, he mentions the *Taurāt* of Moses, the *Zabūr* (Psalms) of David, and makes several references to the historical portions of the Old Testament; but Jonah is the only name amongst the writers of the prophetical books (either greater or minor), of the Old Testament scriptures, mentioned in the Qur'ān.

Muḥammadan writers say there have been 124,000 prophets, but only eight of these have been apostles to whom the Almighty has revealed books, and that only one hundred portions, or *ṣuhuf*, and four books, or *kutub*, have been given to mankind. Ten portions to Adam, the first of the prophets, fifty to Seth (not once mentioned in the Qur'ān), thirty to Idrīs or Enoch, and ten to Abraham. One book to Moses, another to David, another to Jesus, and the fourth to Muḥammad.

Six of the prophets are said to have brought in new laws which successively abrogated the preceding, namely Adam, Noah, Abraham, Moses, Jesus, and Muḥammad.

It is impossible to read the Qur'ān carefully without arriving at the conclusion that Muḥammad derived his knowledge of the events of Old Testament scriptures rather from the Rabbins and their Talmudic teaching, than from the inspired text itself. Mr. Emanuel Deutsch truly says: "Judaism forms the kernel of Muḥammadanism, both general and special. It seems as if he (Muḥammad) had breathed from his childhood almost the air of contemporary Judaism, such Judaism as is found by us crystallised in the Talmud, the Targum, and the Midras." (*Literary Remains*, p. 89.)

The following Old Testament characters are mentioned by name in the Qur'ān:—

Aaron, *Hārūn*; Abel, *Hābīl*; Cain, *Qābīl*; Abraham, *Ibrāhīm*; Adam, *Ādam*; Terah, *Āzar*; Korah, *Qārūn*; David, *Dā'ūd*; Goliath, *Jālūt*; Enoch, *Idrīs*; Elias, *Ilyās*; Elijah *Alyasa'* (*al-Yasa'*); Ezra, *'Uzair*; Gabriel, *Jibrīl*; Gog, *Yājūj*; Magog, *Mājūj*; Isaac, *Isḥāq*; Ishmael, *Ismā'īl*; Jacob, *Ya'qūb*; Joseph, *Yūsuf*; Job, *Aiyūb*; Jonah, *Yūnus*; Joshua, *Yūsha'*; Korah, *Qārūn*; Lot, *Lūṭ*; Michael, *Mīkā'īl*; Moses, *Mūsā*; Noah, *Nūḥ*; Pharaoh, *Firaun*; Solomon, *Sulaimān*; Saul, *Ṭālūt*.

The following incidents of Old Testament history are related in the Qur'ān, with a strange want of accuracy and a large admixture of Talmudic fable:—

Aaron makes a calf. Sūrah xx. 90.

Cain and Abel. Sūrah v. 30.

Abraham visited by Angels. Sūrah xi. 72, xv. 51.

Abraham ready to sacrifice his son. Sūrah xxxvii. 101.

Adam, his fall. Sūrah vii. 18, ii. 34.

Korah and his company. Sūrah xxviii. 76, xxix. 38, xl. 25.

Creation of the world. Sūrah xvi. 3, xiii. 3, xxxv. 1, 12.

David's praise of God. Sūrah xxxiv. 10.

Deluge. Sūrah liv. 9, lxix. 11, xi. 42.

Jacob goes to Egypt. Sūrah xii. 100.

Jonah and the fish. Sūrah vi. 86, x. 98, xxxvii. 139, lxviii. 48.

Joseph's history. Sūrah vi. 84, xii. 1, xl. 36.

Manna and quails given. Sūrah vii. 160, xx. 82.

Moses strikes the rock. Sūrah vii. 160.

Noah's ark. Sūrah xi. 40.

Pharoah. Sūrah ii. 46, x. 76, xliii. 45, xl. 38.

Solomon's judgment. Sūrah xxi. 78.

Queen of Sheba. Sūrah xxvii. 22.

The compiler of the *Kashfu 'z-Ẓunūn* (ed. Flügel, vol. ii. p. 458, article, *Taurāt*) attempts an account of the Old Testament scriptures.

He divides the whole into four sections, and gives the names of the books as follows:—

(1) The *Taurāt*, or the Five Books of Moses.

(2) *Yūsha'* (Joshua).
Sifru 'l-Ḥukkām (Judges).
Shamū'īl (Samuel).
Sifru 'l-Mulūk (Kings).

(3) *Sha'yā* (Isaiah).
Irmiyā (Jeremiah).
Ḥizqīl (Ezekiel).
Yūnus (Jonah).

(4) *Ta'rīkh*. A history from Adam to the building of the Temple.
Mazāmīr (Psalms).
Aiyūb (Job).
Amsāl (Proverbs).
Aḥbāru 'l-Hukkām qabla 'l-Mulūk (Ecclesiastes).
Nashā'id li-Sulaimān (Song of Solomon).
Ḥikmah (Wisdom).
An-Nawāḥ (Lamentations).
Urdshair (Esther).
Dānyāl (Daniel).
'Uzair (Esdras).

[PROPHETS, TAURAT, ZABUR.]

OLD AND NEW TESTAMENTS,

The testimony of the Qur'ān to the. The references in the Qur'ān to the sacred scriptures of the Jews and Christians are very many, and in all cases Muḥammad refers to these sacred writings with the highest respect and veneration. He acknowledges their inspiration, admits the existence of such documents in his own day, and appeals to them in support of his own mission.

The following verses of the Qur'ān, in which there are references to the Old and New Testament, have been placed in chronological order, and the translations given are for the *most part* from Sir William Muir's Manual on "The Coran," published by the Society for Promoting Christian Knowledge:—

Sūrah lxxxvii. 18: "Verily this is in the books of yore; the books of Abraham and Moses."

Sūrah liii. 37–40: "Hath he not been told of that which is in the pages of Moses, and of Abraham who acted faithfully? That a burdened soul shall not bear another's burden, and that there shall be nothing (*imputed*) to a man, but that which he himself hath wrought," &c.

Sūrah xxxii. 23–25: "And verily We gave Moses the book: wherefore be not in doubt as to the reception thereof, and We made it a direction to the Israelites. And We made from among them leaders who should direct according to Our command, when they were steadfast, and believed in Our signs. Verily thy Lord, he will judge between hem on the Day of Resurrection as to that concerning which they disagree."

Sūrah liv. 43: "Are your unbelievers (*Ye Makkans*) better than those (*i.e. of the days of Noah, Lot, Moses, &c., just referred to;*) or is there an immunity for you in the Scriptures?"

Sūrah xxxiv. 30: "And the unbelievers say:—We will not believe in this Qurān, nor in that (*which was revealed*) before it."

Sūrah xli. 45: "And verily We gave Moses the book, and they fell to variance concerning it."

Sūrah xlv. 15, 16: "And verily We gave the children of Israel the book, and wisdom, and prophecy, and We nourished them with pleasant food, and We exalted them above the rest of the world; and We gave them plain directions in the matter (*of religion;*) and they fell not to variance until after divine knowledge (*or* the Revelation,) had come unto them, out of jealousy among themselves. Verily, thy Lord will decide between them on the Day of Judgment, concerning that about which they disagree."

Sūrah xxxvii. 34: "Verily when it is said unto them:—There is no God but the Lord; they arrogantly reply,—What! shall we give up our gods for a phrenzied poet? Nay, he cometh with the truth, and attesteth (*the Revelations,*) of the (*former*) apostles."

Sūrah xxxvii. 114: "And verily we were gracious to Moses and Aaron, and saved them and their people from great tribulation; and We brought them assistance, and they were the conquerors; and We gave them the perspicuous book, and directed them into the right way."

Sūrah xxvi. 194: "Verily it (the Qur'ān) is a revelation from the Lord of creation; the faithful Spirit hath caused it to descend on thy heart, that thou mightest be one of the warners, in the plain Arabic tongue. And verily it is in the former Scriptures. What! is it not a sign unto them that the wise men of the Children of Israel recognize it?"

Sūrah xlvi. 12: "And when they refuse to be guided thereby, they say;—this is an antiquated lie. Yet preceding it there is the Book of Moses, a guide and a mercy; and this Qur'ān is a book attesting (*previous Revelation*), in the Arabic tongue, to warn the transgressors, and glad tidings to the righteous."

Sūrah xlvi. 30: "And (*call to mind*) when We caused a company of the Genii to turn aside unto thee that they might hear the Qur'ān; And, when they were present thereat, they said,—Give ear. And when it was ended, they returned to their people as warners; they said,—Oh our people! verily we have heard a book revealed after Moses, attesting the revelation that precedeth it; it leadeth to the truth, and unto the straight path."

Sūrah xxxv. 25: "And if they reject thee, verily they who preceded them rejected (their prophets), who brought them clear signs, and writings, and the enlightening book."

Sūrah xxxv. 31: "And that which We have revealed unto thee is the truth, attesting that which precedeth it."

Sūrah xix. 11: "Oh John! take the book (the Taurāt) with power;—and We gave him wisdom while a child."

Sūrah xix. 28, 29: "And she (*Mary*) pointed to him (*the infant Jesus:*) they said, —How shall we speak with a child in the cradle? (*The infant Jesus*) said,—verily I am the servant of God; he hath given me the book (*i.e. the Gospel*), and made me a prophet."

Sūrah xlii. 1: "Thus doth God, the glorious and the wise, communicate inspiration unto thee, as he did unto those that preceded thee."

Sūrah xlii. 12: "He hath ordained unto you the religion which he commanded unto Noah, and which We have revealed unto thee, and which We commanded unto Abraham, Moses, and Jesus;—saying, Maintain the (*true*) religion, and be not at variance therein."

Sūrah xlii. 14, 15: "And they did not differ until after the knowledge (*of Divine Revelation*) came unto them, rebelliously among themselves: and unless the word had gone forth from thy Lord (*respiting them*) until a fixed time, verily the matter had been decided between them. And verily they that have inherited the book after them are in a perplexing doubt respecting the same. Wherefore invite (*men unto the true faith*), and stand fast as thou hast been commanded, and follow not their desires. And say, I believe in whatever books God hath revealed, and I am commanded to decide between you: God is our Lord, and your Lord. To us will (*be reckoned*) our works—to you, yours. There is no ground of dispute between us and you. God will gather us together, and to Him shall be the return."

Sūrah xl. 55, 56: "And verily We gave unto Moses guidance, and We caused the Children of Israel to inherit the book,—a guide and an admonition unto people of understanding hearts. Wherefore be patient, for the promise of God is true, and ask pardon for thy sin," &c.

Sūrah xl. 72: "They who reject the book and that which We have sent our messengers with (*the Old and New Testament*),—they shall know; when the collars shall be on their necks, and the chains by which they shall be dragged into hell;—then shall they be burned in the fire."

Sūrah xxv. 36: "And verily We gave Moses the book, and We appointed his brother Aaron his helper."

Sūrah xx. 132: "And they (*the Quraish*) say,—'If he doth not bring us a sign from his Lord (*we will not believe*).' What! hath not an evident demonstration come unto them in the former pages?"

Sūrah xliii. 43: "And ask those of Our Apostles whom We have sent before thee, whether We have appointed any besides the Merciful, as a God whom they should worship."

Sūrah xii. 111: "It is not a story fabricated, but an attestation of (the revelation) which is before it, and an explanation of every matter, a guide and a mercy to the people that believe."

Sūrah xi. 17, 18: "These are they for whom there is no portion in the next life but fire: and that which they have done shall perish therein; vain will that be which they have wrought. What! (*shall such a one be equal unto him*) who proceedeth upon a plain direction from his Lord; and a witness from him (*i.e. from the Lord*) attendeth him, and before him (*or* it) is the Book of Moses a guide and a mercy."

Sūrah xi. 3: "And verily We gave Moses the book, and they fell to variance regarding it. And had not the word gone forth from thy Lord, surely the matter had been decided between them; and verily they are in perplexing doubt concerning the same."

Sūrah x. 37: "And this Qur'ān is not such that it could have been fabricated by other than God; but it is an attestation of that (*i.e. of those Scriptures*) which precede it, and an explanation of the book,—there is no doubt therein,—from the Lord of creation. What! will they say, he (*Muḥammad*) hath forged it? Say,—then bring a Surah like unto it."

Sūrah x. 93: "If thou art in doubt regarding that which We have sent down unto thee, then ask those who read the book (*revealed*) before thee. Verily the truth hath come unto thee from thy Lord; be not therefore amongst those that doubt."

Sūrah vi. 20: "Those to whom We have given the book recognize him as they recognise their own sons. They that have destroyed their own souls, these believe not."

Sūrah vi. 90: "These are they to whom We have given the book, and wisdom, and prophecy, and if these (*the Quraish*) disbelieve the same, verily We have given it in trust unto a people who are not disbelievers therein. These are they whom God hath guided; wherefore persevere in the guidance of them."

Sūrah vi. 92: "And they do not estimate God with a just estimation, when they say,—God hath not sent down—(*i.e. revealed*, anything to Man. Say, who sent down the book, which Moses brought, a light and a direction to mankind? Ye (*var. read.* they) make (*or* transcribe) it upon sheets of paper which ye (*or* they) show, and ye (*or* they) conceal much: and ye are taught that which ye knew not, neither did your fathers. Say, —God: then leave them to sport in their follies."

Sūrah vi. 93: "And this book We have revealed,—blessed,—certifying the truth of that (*revelation*) which precedeth it, and that thou mightest admonish the people of the city (Makkah) and those around it."

Sūrah vi. 114: "He it is that hath sent down to you the book, explaining (*all things*;) and those to whom We have given the book know that it (*the Qur'ān*) hath been sent down from thy Lord in truth. Wherefore, be not thou (*O Muḥammad*) among those that doubt."

Sūrah vi. 124: "And when a verse cometh unto them, they say,—We will not believe until there is brought unto us (*a revelation*) like unto that which the apostles of God brought."

Sūrah vi. 154: "Then We gave Moses the book complete as to whatever is excellent, and an explanation of every matter, and a direction and a mercy, if haply they might believe in the meeting of their Lord."

Sūrah vi. 155: "And this book (*the Qur'ān*) We have sent down,—blessed; wherefore follow it, and fear God, if haply ye may find mercy; lest ye should say,—Verily the Scripture hath been revealed to two people (*the Jews and Christians*) before us, and we are ignorant of their reading;—or lest ye should say,—If the Scripture had been revealed to us, we surely would have followed its direction better than they; and now verily a clear exposition hath come unto you from your Lord, a direction and mercy," &c.

Sūrah xxviii. 44: "And verily We gave Moses the book, after that We had destroyed the former generations,—an enlightenment unto mankind, and a direction, and a mercy, if haply they might be admonished."

Sūrah xxviii. 47: "And thou wert not on the side of Mount Sinai, when We called out (*to Moses*;) but (*thou art*) a mercy from thy Lord, that thou mayest admonish a people unto whom no warner hath come before thee, if perchance they may receive admonition;—and lest, if there befall them a calamity for the evil works they have committed, they should say,—Oh Lord! if thou hadst sent unto us a prophet, we had followed thy revelations, and been of the number of the believers. And now that the truth hath come unto them from us, they say,—if there were to come (*a revelation*) like unto that which came unto Moses (*we should believe*). What! do they not disbelieve in that which was given unto Moses heretofore; they say,—two impostures that mutually assist one another; and they say,—verily we reject them both. Say,—bring a book from God that guideth more aright than these two, if ye be true; and if they answer not," &c.

Sūrah xxviii. 53: "Those to whom We have given the Scripture before it (*i.e. before the Qur'ān*,) believe therein; and when it (*the Qur'ān*) is read unto them, they say,—We believe in it; verily it is the truth from our Lord, surely we were Muslims from before."

Sūrah xxiii. 25: "And verily We gave Moses the book, if haply they might be directed; and We made the son of Mary and his mother a sign," &c.

Sūrah xxi. 7: "And We sent not before thee (*as Apostles*) other than men whom We inspired: ask, therefore, the people of the Scripture, if ye know it not."

Sūrah xxi. 49: "And verily We gave Moses and Aaron the distinction (*al-Furqān*), and a light, and an admonition to the pious,—those who fear their Lord in secret, and who tremble for the hour (*of Judgment*). This blessed admonition also We have sent down; will ye therefore deny it?"

Sūrah xxi. 105: "And verily We have written in the Psalms, after the Law, that 'my servants, the righteous, shall inherit the earth."

Sūrah xvii. 2: "And We gave Moses the book, and made it a direction to the Children of Israel, (*saying*)—Take ye not other than Me for a patron."

Sūrah xvii. 4, 5, and 7: "And We declared in the book, in respect of the Children of Israel,—saying, Ye shall surely work corruptly on the earth twice, and ye shall be elated with great arrogance. And when the threat of the first of these two (*visitations*) came to pass, We sent against you our servants of terrible strength, &c., and when the threat of the second (*visitation*) came to pass," &c.

Sūrah xvii. 55: "And verily We have bestowed favour upon some of the prophets more than upon others, and We gave David the Psalms," &c.

Sūrah xvii. 108: "Say,—Believe in it (*the Qur'ān*), or believe not;—verily they unto whom the knowledge (*of Divine Revelation*) hath been given anterior to it, when they hear it recited unto them, fall down upon their faces worshipping: and they say,—Praised be our Lord; verily the promise of our Lord is fulfilled. And they fall down on their faces weeping, and it increaseth their humility."

Sūrah xvi. 43: "And We have not sent before thee other than men whom We have inspired;—wherefore ask the people of the Scripture if ye know not. (*We sent them*) with evident signs and books, and We have sent down unto thee the revelation, that thou mightest make known to mankind that which hath been revealed to them, that haply they might reflect."

Sūrah xiii. 45: "And those who disbelieve say,—Thou art not sent;—say,—God sufficeth for a witness between me and between you, and also he with whom is the knowledge of the book."

Sūrah xxix. 27: "And We gave to him (*i.e. to Abraham*) Isaac and Jacob, and We placed among his descendants prophecy and the book."

Sūrah xxix. 46: "And contend not with the people of the book (*Jews and Christians*) but in a generous manner, excepting those of them who act wickedly; and say,—We believe in that which hath been revealed to us, and in that which hath been revealed to you: and your God and our God is one, and we are to Him resigned."

Sūrah xxix. 47: "And thus have We sent down to thee the book (*the Qur'ān,*) and those to whom We have given the Scripture believe in it."

Sūrah vii. 158: "And I will shortly write down it (*i.e. my mercy,*) for those who fear the Lord and give alms, and those who believe in our signs: those who shall follow the apostle,—the illiterate prophet,—whom they shall find written (*i.e. described*) in the Pentateuch and in the Gospel among them; he shall command them to do that which is excellent," &c.

Sūrah vii. 168: "And (*call to mind*) when thy Lord commanded that there should certainly be sent against them (*i.e. the Jews*) until the day of resurrection those that would afflict them with grievous distress;—verily thy Lord is swift in vengeance, and he is surely forgiving and merciful. And We dispersed them in the earth amongst the nations; there are of them that are virtuous, and there are of them that are not so. And We proved them with blessings, and with adversities, if perchance they might return. And there succeeded after them a generation that inherited the book, who receive the temporal advantage of this world, and say,—It will be forgiven unto us. And if there come unto them an advantage the like thereof, they accept it. What! hath there not been taken from them the covenant of the book, that they should not say of God other than the truth, and they diligently study that which is therein."

Sūrah lxxiv. 30: "Over it (*Hell*) are nineteen angels; and We have not made the guardians of the fire other than angels; and We have not expressed their number, except as a trial to those who disbelieve, and in order that those to whom We have given the book may firmly believe, and that they who believe may increase in faith; and that those to whom We have given the book may not doubt, nor the believers."

Sūrah ii. 1–5: "This is the book in which there is no doubt,—a guide to the pious;—they who believe in the Unseen, and observe prayer, and spend out of that which we have provided them with;—and they who believe in that which hath been revealed unto thee, and that which hath been revealed before thee, and have faith in the life to come. These walk according to the direction of their Lord, and these are the blessed."

Sūrah ii. 36: "Oh Children of Israel! remember My favour wherewith I have favoured you, and fulfil My covenant,—I likewise will fulfil your covenant; and fear Me, and believe in that which I have revealed, attesting the truth of the (*Scripture*) which is with you: and be not the first to reject the same; and sell not my revelation for a small price; and clothe not the truth with error, and do not conceal the truth while ye know it."

Sūrah ii. 50: "And when We gave Moses the book and the distinction (*between good and evil,—Furqān,*)—if haply ye might be directed."

Sūrah ii. 71: "And when they (*the Jews of al-Madīnah,*) meet the believers, they say,—We believe; but when they retire privately one with the other, they say,—Why do ye acquaint them with what God hath revealed to you, that they may therewith dispute with you before your Lord? What do ye not understand? Do they not know that God knoweth what they conceal as well as that which they make public."

Sūrah ii. 79: "What do ye (*the Jews*) believe in part of the book, and reject part thereof? But whosoever amongst you doeth this, his reward shall be none other than disgrace in the present life, and in the Day of Judgment they shall be cast into a more awful torment."

Sūrah ii. 81: "And verily We gave Moses the Book, and caused prophets to arise after him, and We gave to Jesus, the Son of Mary, evident signs, and strengthened him with the Holy Spirit."

Sūrah ii. 89: "And when a Book (*i.e. the Qur'ān*) came unto them from God, attesting the truth of that (*Scripture*) which is with them, (although they had from before been praying for victory over those who disbelieve); yet when that came unto them which they recognised, they rejected the same."

Sūrah ii. 83: "And when it is said unto them;—Believe in that which God hath revealed; they say;—We believe in that which hath been revealed unto us; and they reject that which (*hath been revealed*) after it, although it be the truth attesting that which is with them."

Sūrah ii. 85: "And verily Moses came unto you with evident signs (*or* revelations); then ye took the calf," &c.

Sūrah ii. 86: "For he (*Gabriel*) hath caused it (*the Qur'ān*) to descend upon thy heart, by the command of God, attesting that

(*Scripture*) which is before it, and a direction and good tidings to the believers."

Sūrah ii. 95: "And when a prophet came unto them from God, attesting that (*Scripture*) which is with them, a party of those who have received the Scripture cast the Book of God behind their backs, as if they knew it not."

Sūrah ii. 107: "The Jews say, the Christians are not (*founded*) upon anything; and the Christians say the Jews are not (*founded*) upon anything; and yet they read the Scripture."

Sūrah ii. 130 (see also Sūrah iii. 79): "Say, —We believe in God and in what hath been revealed unto us, and in what hath been revealed unto Abraham, and Ishmael, and Isaac, and Jacob, and the Tribes; and in what hath been given unto Moses and unto Jesus, and in what hath been given unto the prophets from their Lord: we make no distinction between any of them; and unto Him we are resigned."

Sūrah ii. 139; "Verily We saw thee turn about thy face into the Heavens; wherefore We will cause thee to turn towards a qiblah that will please thee—turn therefore thy face towards the holy temple: wheresoever thou art, turn thy face towards it. And verily those to whom the Scripture hath been given, they know that this is the truth from their Lord, and God is not unmindful of that which they do. And if thou broughtest unto those to whom the Scripture hath been given, every kind of sign, they would not follow thy qiblah, nor wilt thou follow their qiblah," &c.

Sūrah ii. 142: "Those to whom We have given the Scripture recognise him as they recognise their own sons; but verily a section of them hide the truth, although they know it."

Sūrah ii. 169: "Verily they that conceal the Scripture which God hath revealed, and sell it for a small price;—these shall eat nought but the fire in their bellies, and God shall not speak unto them on the Day of Judgment, neither shall He purify them; they shall have bitter torment. These are they that have bought error at the price of direction, and punishment at the price of pardon:—how shall they endure the fire!—this because God hath sent down the Book in truth; and they that dispute regarding the Book are in a grievous error."

Sūrah ii. 209: "Mankind was one people, and God sent prophets as preachers of good tidings, and warners: and He sent down the Scripture with them in truth, that it might decide between men in that in which they differed:—and they differed not therein, excepting those to whom it was given, after there came to them clear demonstrations, wickedly amongst themselves; and God guided those that believed to the truth concerning which they disputed, by His will," &c.

Sūrah ii. 254: "Of these prophets We have preferred some above others. Some of them hath God spoken unto, and He hath raised some of them to high dignity. And We gave unto Jesus, the Son of Mary, evident signs, and We strengthened Him by the Holy Spirit. And if God had pleased, those that came after them would not have contended with one another, after the evident signs (*or* plain revelations) had come unto them. Yet they fell to variance. And amongst them were those that believed: and amongst them were those that disbelieved. And if God had wished, they had not contended with one another; but God doeth that which pleaseth Him."

Sūrah ii. 286: "The apostle believeth in that which hath been revealed unto him from his Lord: and the faithful, everyone of them, believeth in God, and in His angels, and in His books, and in His apostles; we make no distinction between any one of his apostles."

Sūrah lvii. 18: "And those that believe in God, and in His apostles, these are the righteous, and the witnesses with their Lord; they have their reward and their light; but they that disbelieve, and accuse Our revelations of falsehood, these are the companions of hell-fire."

Sūrah lvii. 25: "We have verily sent Our apostles with evident demonstrations; and We revealed unto them the Scripture, and the Balance, that men might observe justice; and We revealed (the use of) Iron wherein is great strength, and advantages to mankind, and in order that God might know who assisteth him and his apostles in secret,—for God is mighty and glorious. And verily We sent Noah and Abraham; and We placed amongst their posterity, prophecy and the Scripture: and amongst them were those that were rightly directed, but many of them were evil-doers. Afterwards We caused Our apostles to follow in their footsteps; and We caused Jesus, the Son of Mary, to succeed them, and We gave him the Gospel: and We put into the hearts of his followers compassion and mercy; and as to Monasticism they invented the same,—[We did not prescribe it unto them,]—simply out of a desire to please God, but they have not observed it with a right observance. And We have given those of them that believe, their reward, but many of them are evil-doers. Oh ye that believe! fear God, and believe in His prophet. He will give you a double portion of His mercy, and will create for you a Light wherein ye shall walk, and forgive you, for the Lord is forgiving and merciful."

Sūrah xcviii. 1: "The unbelievers from amongst the people of the Book, and the idolaters, did not waver until there came unto them a clear—a prophet from God reading pure pages, containing right Scriptures. And those to whom the Scriptures have been givon did not fall to variance, until after a clear (*Revelation*) had come unto them: and they are not commanded (*in their own Scriptures*) otherwise than that they should worship God, rendering unto Him the orthodox worship, and that they should observe prayer, and give alms; and this is the right faith."

Sūrah lxii. 5: "The likeness of those who are charged with the Law (the *Tourāt*), and do not discharge (*the obligations of*) it, is as the likeness of the Ass laden with books. Evil is the likeness of the people which rejecteth the signs of God: and God doth not guide the unjust people."

Sūrah xlviii. 29: "Muhammad is the prophet of God; and those who follow him are fierce against the unbelievers, but compassionate among themselves. Thou mayest see them bowing down, prostrating themselves, seeking the favour of God and his pleasure. Their signs are in their faces from the marks of their prostration. This is the likeness of them in the Pentateuch and the likeness of them in the Gospel,—as a seed which putteth forth its stalk and strengtheneth it, and swelleth and riseth on its stem, and delighteth the sower thereof,—that the unbelievers may be indignant thereat."

Sūrah lxi. 6: "And when Jesus, the Son of Mary, said:—O children of Israel, verily I am an Apostle of God unto you, attesting that which is before me of the Tourât, and giving glad tidings of an apostle that shall come after me, whose name is Ahmad (*the Praised*)."

Sūrah iv. 43: "Hast thou not seen those to whom We have given a portion of the Scripture?—they buy error, and desire that ye may err from the way: and God best knoweth your enemies. God sufficeth for a patron, and God sufficeth for a helper. Of those who profess Judaism there are that dislocate words from their places, and say—'we have heard,—and, have disobeyed'; and, 'do thou hearken without hearing;' and, 'look upon us'; twisting with their tongues, and reviling the faith. And if they had said, 'we have heard and obeyed'; and, 'hearken'; and, 'look upon us'; it had been better for them and more upright: but God hath cursed them for their unbelief, and they shall not believe, excepting a few. O ye unto whom the Scriptures have been given! believe in what We have revealed attesting that (*Scripture*) which is with you, before We deface your countenances, and turn them front backwards, or curse them as We cursed those who (*broke*) the Sabbath; and the command of the Lord was fulfilled."

Sūrah iv. 49: "Hast thou not seen those to whom a portion of the Scripture hath been given? they believe in false gods and idols, and they say to the unbelievers, These are better directed in the way than those who believe."

Sūrah iv. 52: "Do they envy mankind that which God hath given them of His bounty? And verily We gave to the children of Abraham the book and wisdom, and We gave them a mighty kingdom. Amongst them are those that believe in Him and those also that turn away from Him."

Sūrah iv. 58: "Hast thou not seen those who fancy that they believe in that which hath been revealed unto thee, and in that which hath been revealed before thee? They desire to go for a mutual decision unto the idol Jaghût: yet verily they have been commanded to disbelieve therein, and Satan desireth to deceive them into a wide deception."

Sūrah iv 130: "To God belongs whatever is in the heavens and in the earth, and verily We commanded those to whom the Scripture was given before you, and you likewise,—Fear God, and, if ye disbelieve, verily to God belongeth whatsoever is in the heavens and in the earth."

Sūrah iv. 135: "O ye that believe! believe in God and in His prophet, and in the book which He hath revealed to His prophet, and in the book which He revealed from before; and whoever disbelieves in God, and in His angels, and in His books, and in His prophets, and in the last day, verily he hath wandered into a wide error."

Sūrah iv. 149; "Verily they that reject God and His apostles, and seek to make a distinction between God and His apostles; and say,—We believe in a part, and we reject a part; and seek to take a path between the same; these are infidels in reality, and We have prepared for the infidels an ignominious punishment. But they that believe in God and in His apostles, and make no distinction between any of them, to these We shall surely give their reward, and God is forgiving and merciful. The people of the book will ask thee that thou cause a book to descend upon them from the heavens, and verily they asked Moses for a greater thing than that," &c.

Sūrah iv. 161: "But those of them that are grounded in knowledge, and the faithful, believe in that which hath been revealed unto thee, and in that which hath been revealed before thee. And those that observe prayer, and give alms, and the believers in God and in the last day, unto these shall We give a great reward. Verily We have revealed our will unto thee, as We revealed our will unto Abraham, and Ishmael, and Isaac, and Jacob, and the Tribes, and Jesus, and Job, and Jonas, and Aaron, and Solomon, and We gave unto David the Psalms; and Apostles, whom We have already made mention of unto thee; and Apostles, of whom We have not made mention unto thee; and God spake with Moses in open discourse," &c.

Sūrah iv. 169: "Ye people of the book! commit not extravagance in your religion; and say not of God other than the truth. For verily the Messiah, Jesus, the Son of Mary, is an apostle of God, and His word which he placed in Mary, and a spirit from Him. Wherefore believe in God, and in His apostle; and say not,—"the Trinity";—refrain; it will be better for you. For verily God is one God;—far exalted is He above the possibility that there should be unto Him progeny! to Him belongeth whatever is in the heavens and in the earth, and He sufficeth as a guardian."

Sūrah iii. 2: "God! there is no God but He, the living, the eternal. He hath caused to descend upon thee the Scripture in truth, attesting that which is before it: and He sent down the Tourât and the Gospel from before for the guidance of mankind: and He sent down the Furqān. Verily they that reject the signs of God, to them shall be a fearful punishment. And God is mighty, a God of vengeance."

Sūrah iii. 19: "And those to whom the book was given, did not fall to variance until after that the knowledge came unto them, wickedly among themselves."

Sūrah iii. 23: "Seest thou not those to whom a portion of the Scripture hath been given? They were called unto the book of God, that it might decide between them. Then a party of them turned away, and went aside. That was because they say,—the fire shall not touch us, but for a limited number of days. And that which they have devised hath deceived them in their religion."

Sūrah iii. 48: "And (*God*) shall teach Him (*Jesus*) the Scripture, and wisdom, and the Tourât, and the Gospel;—and (*shall send Him as*) an Apostle unto the Children of Israel. (*Jesus shall say*) Verily I have come unto you— . . . attesting the truth of that which (*Scripture revealed*) before me in the Tourât, and that I may make lawful unto you a part of that which is forbidden unto you."

Sūrah iii. 64: "O ye people of the Book! why do ye dispute concerning Abraham?—seeing that neither the Tourât nor the Gospel was revealed until after him; do ye not understand? Ah! ye are they which dispute concerning that of which ye have knowledge: why, therefore, do ye dispute concerning that of which ye have no knowledge? and God knoweth, but ye know not."

Sūrah iii. 68: "A party of the People of the Book desire to cause thee to go astray: but they shall not cause (*any*) to go astray, excepting their own souls, and they perceive it not. Oh People of the Book! why do ye reject the signs of God, while ye bear testimony (*thereto*)? O people of the Book! why do ye clothe the truth with that which is false, and hide the truth, while ye know (*it*)? and a party of the people of the book say,—Believe in that which is sent down unto those that believe, in the early part of the day; and reject (*it, in*) the latter part thereof; if haply they may turn back: and, believe not (*any*) excepting him that followeth your religion. Say,—Verily the direction is the direction of God, that there should be given unto one (*i.e. to Muḥammad, a revelation*) like unto that which hath been given unto you. Or, will they dispute with you before your Lord? say,—Verily favour is in the hand of God: He giveth it unto whomsoever He pleaseth; and God is widely comprehensive (*in His mercy*) and wise."

Sūrah iii. 77: "And verily amongst them is a party that twist their tongues in (reading) the book, that ye may think it is out of the book, though it is not out of the book; and they say,—'it is from God,' and it is not from God; and they speak a falsehood concerning God, knowingly."

Sūrah iii. 78: "It becometh not a man that God should give him a book, and wisdom, and prophecy, and that he should then say to mankind, Be worshippers of me besides God; but rather, Be ye perfect, inasmuch as ye know the book, and inasmuch as ye study it."

Sūrah iii. 80: "And (*call to mind*) when God made a covenant with the prophets, (*saying*) This verily is the book and the wisdom which I have given unto you; thereafter shall come an Apostle attesting the truth of that (*Scripture*) which is with you; ye shall surely believe in him, and assist him."

Sūrah iii. 93: "All food was lawful to the Children of Israel, excepting that which Israel made unlawful to himself, before the Tourât was revealed. Say,—Bring hither the Tourât, and read it, if ye be true. And whoever contriveth a lie concerning God after that, surely they are the transgressors."

Sūrah iii. 99: "Say; O ye People of the Book! why do ye disbelieve in the signs of God, and God is witness of that which ye do? Say, O ye People of the Book! why do ye hinder from the way of God him that believeth, desiring to make it (*the way of God*) crooked, while ye are witnesses?"

Sūrah iii. 113: "They are not all alike. Amongst the People of the Book there is an upright race that read the signs (*or* revelations) of God in the night season, and they bow down worshipping. They believe in God and the last day, and command that which is just and dissuade from that which is wicked, and they make haste in doing good works. These are the virtuous ones."

Sūrah iii. 119: "Behold, ye are they that love them (*the Jews*) and they do not love you, and ye believe in the entire Scripture."

Sūrah iii. 184: "They who say that God hath made a covenant with us, to the effect that we should not believe on an apostle until he cometh unto us with a sacrifice to be consumed by fire;—say,—Verily apostles have come unto you before me, with evident demonstrations, and with that of which ye speak. Why, therefore, have ye slain them, if ye be true? and if they accuse thee of imposture, verily the apostles before thee have been accused of imposture, who came with evident demonstrations, and the Scriptures, and the enlightening book."

Sūrah iii. 188: "And when God took a covenant from those to whom the book was given,—that they should unfold the same to mankind, and that they should not conceal it, and they threw it (*the covenant*) behind their backs, and sold it for a small price, and woeful is that which they have sold it for; think not that they who rejoice in that which they have done, and desire to be praised for that which they have not done, shall escape from punishment. To them shall be a grievous punishment."

Sūrah iii. 199: "And verily of the People of the Book there are those who believe in God, and in that which hath been revealed to you, and in that which hath been revealed to them, submissive unto God; they sell not the signs of God for a small price. These are they who have their reward with their Lord; for God is swift in taking account."

Sūrah v. 14-16: "And for that they have broken their covenant, We have cursed them, and We have made their hearts hard; they dislocate the word from its place, and they have forgotten a part of that whereby they were admonished. Thou wilt not cease to discover deceit in them, excepting a few of them. But pardon them, and forgive, for God loveth the beneficent. And of those that say, We are Christians, we have taken a covenant from them, and they have forgotten a part of that whereby they were admonished. Wherefore We have placed enmity and hatred between them, until the Day of Judgment; and God will surely then declare unto them that which they have wrought. O people of the Book! verily our apostle hath come unto you; he shall make manifest unto you much of that which ye have hidden of the book, and he shall pass over much."

Sūrah v. 47: "O thou apostle! let not those grieve thee who make haste after infidelity from amongst them that say, 'We believe,' with their mouths, but their hearts believe not. And from amongst the Jews there are that spy out in order to tell a falsehood; they spy out for another people that come not unto thee. They dislocate the word from out of its place. They say, 'If this be given you, then receive it—but if it be not given you, then beware.'"

Sūrah v. 50: "And how will they make thee their judge, since they have beside them the Tourât, in which is the command of God? Then they will turn their back after that, and these are not believers. Verily We have revealed the Tourât; therein is guidance and light. The prophets that submitted themselves to God judged thereby those that were Jews; and the doctors and priests *(did the same)*, in accordance with that which was confided to their charge of the book of God, and they were witnesses thereof. Wherefore fear not man, but fear Me, and sell not thou the signs of God for a small price. And he that doth not judge by that which God hath revealed, verily they are the unbelievers. And We have written for them,—verily life for life, and eye for eye, and nose for nose, and ear for ear, and tooth for tooth; and for wounding retaliation; and he that remitteth the same as alms it shall be an atonement unto him. And he that judgeth not by that which God hath sent down, they are the transgressors. And We caused Jesus, the Son of Mary, to follow in their footsteps, attesting the Scripture of the Tourât which preceded it; and We gave Him the Gospel, wherein is guidance and light, which attests the Tourāt that preceded it, and a direction and an admonition to the pious;—that the people of the Gospel might judge according to that which God hath revealed therein, and he that doth not judge according to that which God hath revealed, verily they are the flagitious ones. And We have revealed unto thee the book in truth, attesting that *(Scripture)* which precedeth it, and a custodian *(or* a witness) thereof. Wherefore judge between them in accordance with that which God hath revealed, and follow not their vain desires *(by swerving)* away from that which hath come unto thee. To every one of you have We given a law and a way; and if God had pleased, He had made you all of one faith;—but *(He hath not done so, in order)* that He might try you in that which He hath given you."

Sūrah v. 68: "Say,—O people of the Book! is there any other cause of your enmity against us, but that we believe in God, and in that which hath been revealed unto us, and in that which hath been revealed from before?—but the most of you are evil doers."

Sūrah v. 77: "Say:—O ye people of the Book! ye are not grounded upon anything, until ye set up *(or* observe) the Tourât and the Gospel, and that which hath been revealed unto you from your Lord."

Sūrah v. 91: "Thou wilt surely find the most bitter amongst mankind in their hatred towards those that believe to be the Jews and the idolaters. And thou wilt surely find the most friendly inclined amongst them towards the believers, to be those who say, We are Christians. That is because there are amongst them clergy and monks, and they are not arrogant. When they hear that which hath been revealed to the prophet, thou wilt see their eyes flowing with tears because of that which they recognise of the truth. They say, O our Lord! we believe; write us down with the witnesses; and what should hinder us that we should not believe in God, and in that which hath come unto us of the truth? and we desire that our Lord should introduce us amongst the righteous. God hath rewarded them for that which they have said, with gardens through which flow rivulets. They shall be for ever therein and that is the reward of the virtuous."

Sūrah v. 119: "And *(call to mind)* when God said,—O Jesus, Son of Mary! remember My favour towards thee, and towards thy Mother, when I strengthened thee with the Holy Spirit, that thou shouldest speak unto man, in the cradle, and also in mature age; and I taught thee the Scriptures, and wisdom, and the Tourāt, and the Gospel; and when thou madest of clay in the form of a bird by My command, and thou blewest thereupon, and it became a bird by My command; and thou healedst the blind and the leper by My command; and when thou didst raise the dead by My command. . . . And when I spake by inspiration unto the apostles, saying,—Believe in Me, and in My apostle *(i.e. Jesus;)* they said,—We believe; bear witness that we are true believers."

Sūrah lxvi. 13: "And Mary the daughter of Imrān, who preserved her virginity; and We breathed into her of Our spirit, and she attested the words of her Lord and His Scriptures, and was amongst the pious."

Sūrah ix. 113: "Verily, God hath bought from the believers their selves and their wealth, on the condition of paradise for them if they fight in the ways of God:—and whether they slay or be slain, the promise of God thereupon is true in the Tourāt, and in the Gospel, and in the Qur'ān." [CHRISTIANITY, JEWS, JUDAISM.]

OMER. ['UMAR.]

OMMIADES.

OMMIADES. Arabic *Banū Umaiyah* (بنو اميـة), or *ad-Daulatu 'l-Umawīyah* (الدولة الاموية). The dynasty of Khalīfahs who reigned from A.H. 41 (A.D. 661) to A.H. 132 (A.D. 750), descended from Mu'āwiyah, who was the great grandson of Umaiyah of the Quraish tribe. Mu'āwiyah, the son of Abū Sufyān, took possession of the Khalīfate on the death of al-Ḥasan, and established his capital at Damascus. The dynasty includes the names of fourteen Khalīfahs.

1. Mu'āwiyah, A.H. 41.
2. Yazīd (son of Mu'āwiyah), A.H. 60.
3. Mu'āwiyah II. (son of Yazīd), A.H. 64.
4. Marwān I. (son of al-Ḥakam), A.H. 64.
5. 'Abdu 'l Malik (son of Marwān), A.H. 65.
6. Al-Walīd (son of 'Abdu 'l-Malik), A.H. 86.
7. Sulaimān (son of 'Abdu 'l-Malik), A.H. 96.
8. 'Umar II. (son of 'Abdu 'l-'Azīz, son of Marwān), A.H. 99.
9. Yazīd II. (son of 'Abdu 'l-Malik), A.H. 101.
10. Hishām (son of 'Abdu 'l-Malik), A.H. 105.
11. Al-Walīd II. (son of Yazīd), A.H. 125.
12. Yazīd III. (son of al-Walīd), A.H. 126.
13. Ibrāhīm (son of al-Walīd), A.H. 126.
14. Marwān II. (son of Muḥammad, son of Marwān), A.H. 127–132.

The Abbasides conquered Khorasan under the brothers Ibrāhīm and 'Abū 'l-'Abbās, and refused to acknowledge Marwān. Marwān was afterwards defeated on the banks of the Zab, and fled to Egypt, where he was again defeated and slain, A.H. 132 (A.D. 750), and Abū 'l-'Abbās was proclaimed Khalīfah. [KHALIFAH.]

OPTION. [KHIYAR.]

ORDINATION.

ORDINATION. There is no ceremony in Islām corresponding to the Christian ordination. Sometimes the Imām of a mosque is appointed by the chief man of position binding a turban round his head. In Central Asia, Maulawīs of reputation certify as to the learning and ability of their disciples by binding a turban on their heads and authorizing them to teach. But it is not a custom of the Muslim religion.

ORNAMENTS.

ORNAMENTS. Men are prohibited from the use of ornaments of gold, such as rings and the like, because they are expressly forbidden by the Prophet. Ornaments of silver are likewise unlawful, but exceptions are made with respect to signet rings, girdles, or swords, which may be ornamented with silver. (*Hidāyah*, vol. iv. p. 92). Ibn Zubair says the Prophet condemned the use of little bells as ornaments for children, for he said there was a devil in every bell. Ibn Mālik says the Prophet forbade the wearing of gold rings, and he considered it just as bad to use gold ornaments. (*Mishkāt*, book xx. ch. ii.)

The Wahhābīs condemn the use of ornaments and silk dresses.

ORPHANS.

ORPHANS. Arabic *yatīm* (يتيم), pl. *yatāmā*. In Muḥammadan law, the term is used for a child whose father is dead.

Muḥammad gave very special instructions in the Qur'ān as to the treatment of orphans. See Sūrah iv. 2–7:—

"And give to the orphans their property and substitute not worthless things of your own for their valuable ones, and enjoy not their property in addition to your own; verily this is a great crime: and if ye are apprehensive that ye shall not deal fairly with orphans, then, of other women who seem good in your eyes, marry but two, or three, or four; and if ye still fear that ye shall not act equitably, then one only, or the slaves whom ye have acquired; this will make justice on your part easier. And give women their dowry as a free gift; but if of their own free will they kindly give up aught thereof to you, then enjoy it as convenient and profitable. And entrust not to the incapable the substance which God hath placed with you as a means of support, but maintain them therewith; and clothe them, and speak to them with kindly speech. And make trial of orphans until they reach the age of marriage; and if ye perceive in them a sound judgment, then hand over their substance to them; but consume ye it not profusely and hastily. Only because they have attained their majority. And let the rich guardian not even touch it; and let him who is poor, then use it for his support with discretion. And when ye make over their substance to them, then take witnesses in their presence. God also taketh a sufficient account."

According to al-Baizāwī and the Jalālān, the Muslim commentators understand these verses differently. Mr. Sale says the true meaning seems to be: Muḥammad, advising his followers that if they found they should wrong the female orphans under their care, either by marrying them against their inclinations, for the sake of their riches or beauty, or by not using or maintaining them so well as they ought by reason of their having already several wives, they should rather choose to marry other women, to avoid all occasion of sin. Others say that when this passage was revealed, many of the Arabians, fearing trouble and temptation, refused to take upon them the charge of orphans, and yet multiplied wives to a great excess and used them ill or, as others write, gave themselves up to fornication, which occasioned the passage. And according to these, its meaning must be either that if they feared they could not act justly towards orphans, they had as great reason to apprehend they could not deal equitably with so many wives, and therefore are commanded to marry but a certain number; or else, that since fornication was a crime as well as a wronging of orphans, they ought to avoid that also by marrying according to their abilities.

OTHMAN. [‘USMAN.]

OUTLAWS. (1) An Apostate, if he escapes to another country, is an outlaw. (2) A fornicator should be expelled from his country and be an outlaw for a whole year.

P.

PAIGHĀMBAR (پيغامبر). The Persian and Hindustānī translation of the Arabic *Rasūl* (رسول), and *Nabi* (نبى). [PROPHET.]

PARACLETE. [FARAQLIT.]

PARADISE. The Muḥammadan Paradise is called *al-Jannah* (الجنّة), "the garden," pl. *jannāt*, in Arabic; and *Bihisht* (بهشت), in Persian; the word *al-Firdaus* (الفردوس), or Paradise, being restricted to one region in the celestial abodes of bliss. There are eight heavens or paradises mentioned in the Qur'ān, and although they appear to be but eight different names for the place of bliss, Muḥammadan divines have held them to be eight different stages.

They are as follows (see *Ghiyāṣu 'l-Lughah*):—

1. Jannatu 'l-Khuld (Sūratu 'l-Furqān, xxv. 16), The Garden of Eternity.
2. Dāru 's-Salām (Sūratu 'l-An'ām, vi. 127), The Dwelling of Peace.
3. Dāru 'l-Qarār (Sūratu 'l-Mu'min, xl. 42), The Dwelling which abideth.
4. Jannātu 'l-'Adn (Sūratu 'l-Barā'ah, ix. 73), The Gardens of Eden.
5. Jannātu 'l-Ma'wā (Sūratu 's-Sajdah, xxxii. 19), The Gardens of Refuge.
6. Jannātu 'n-Na'īm (Sūratu l-Mā'idah, v. 70), The Gardens of Delight.
7. 'Illīyūn (Sūratu 't-Taṭfīf, lxxxiii. 18).
8. Jannātu 'l-Firdaus (Sūratu 'l-Kahf, xviii. 107), The Gardens of Paradise.

These eight stages are spoken of as eight doors in the *Mishkāt*, book ii. ch. i.)

The sensual delights of Muḥammad's Paradise are proverbial, and they must have exercised a considerable influence upon the minds of the people to whom he made known his mission. There are frequent allusions to them in the Qur'ān. The following are specimen passages:—

Sūratu 'l-Insān (lxxvi.), 12–22:—"God hath rewarded their constancy, with Paradise, and silken robes, reclining therein on bridal couches; nought shall they know of sun or piercing cold: its shades shall close over them, and low shall its fruits hang down: and vessels of silver and goblets like flagons shall be borne round among them: flagons of silver whose measure themselves shall mete. And there shall they be given to drink of the cup tempered with zanjabil (ginger) from the fount therein whose name is Salsabīl (*i.e.* the softly flowing). Blooming youths go round among them. When thou lookest at them, thou wouldst deem them scattered pearls; and when thou seest this, thou wilt see delights and a vast kingdom; their clothing green silk robes and rich brocade: with silver bracelets shall they be adorned; and drink of a pure beverage shall their Lord give them. This shall be your recompense."

Sūratu 'l-Wāqi'ah (lvi.), 12–39: "In gardens of delight, a crowd of the former and a few of the later generations; on inwrought couches reclining on them face to face, blooming youths go round about them with goblets and ewers and a cup of flowing wine; their brows ache not from it, nor fails the sense: and with such fruits as shall please them best, and with flesh of such birds as they shall long for; and theirs shall be the Houris (Arabic *ḥūr*), with large dark eyes, like pearls hidden in their shells, in recompense for their labours past. No vain discourse shall they hear therein, nor charge of sin, but only cry 'Peace! Peace!' . . . . Unfailing, unforbidden, and on lofty couches and of a rare creation have we made the Houris, and we have made them ever virgins, dear to their spouses and of equal age, for the people of the right hand, a crowd of the former, and a crowd of the later generations."

Sūratu 'r-Raḥmān (lv.), 54–56: "On couches with linings of brocade shall they recline, and the fruit of the two gardens shall be within their easy reach. . . . . Therein shall be the damsels with retiring glances, whom neither man nor jinn hath touched before them."

Sūratu 'l-Muḥammad (xlvii.) 16, 17: "Therein are rivers of water which corrupt not: rivers of milk, whose taste changeth not: and rivers of wine, delicious to those who quaff it; and rivers of clarified honey: and therein are all kinds of fruit for them from their Lord."

The descriptions of the celestial regions and the enjoyments promised to the faithful are still more minutely given in the traditional sayings of the Prophet; see the *Mishkāt*, book xxiii. ch. xiii.

Abū Mūsā relates that "the Apostle of God said, Verily there is a tent for every Muslim in Paradise, it is made of one pearl, its interior empty, its breadth 60 kos, and in every corner of it will be his wives: and they shall not see one another. The Muslim shall love them alternately," &c.

Abū Sa'īd relates that "the Apostle of God said, 'He who is least amongst the people of Paradise, shall have eighty thousand slaves, and seventy-two women, and has a tent pitched for him of pearls, rubies, and emeralds. . . . . Those who die in the world, young or old, are made of thirty years of age, and not more, when they enter Paradise.'"

Abu Sa'īd also relates that "the Apostle of God said, 'Verily a man in Paradise reclines upon seventy cushions, before he turns on his other side. Then a woman of Paradise comes to him and pats him on the shoulder, and the man sees his face in her cheek, which is brighter than a looking-glass, and verily her most inferior pearl brightens the east and west. Then the woman makes a *salām* to him, which he returns; and the man says, "Who are you?" and she replies, "I am of the number promised of God for the virtuous." And verily she will have seventy garments, and the man's eyes will be fixed on them, till he will see the marrow of the bones of her legs through the calves of them, and she will have crowns on her head, the meanest pearl of which would give light between the east and west.'"

One of the attractions of Paradise is the river Kauṡar. [KAUSAR.] According to Anas, "the Apostle of God said, it is a river which God has given me in Paradise, its water is whiter than milk, and sweeter than honey, and on its waters are birds whose necks are like the necks of camels."

The following is an instance of the way in which the Prophet endeavoured to suit his paradise to the tastes of the people:—

Abū Aiyūb says, "An Arab came to the Prophet and said, 'O Apostle of God! I am fond of horses; are there any in Paradise?' The Prophet replied, 'If you are taken into Paradise, you will get a ruby horse, with two wings, and you will mount him, and he will carry you wherever you wish.'"

Abū Hurairah said, "Verily the Apostle of God said, when an Arab was sitting near him, that a man of the people of Paradise will ask permission of his Lord to cultivate land, and God will say, 'Have you not everything you could wish for? What will you cultivate?' The man will say, 'Yes, everything is present, but I am fond of cultivating.' Then he will be permitted to cultivate, and he will sow, and, quicker than the twinkling of an eye, it will grow, become ripe, and be reaped, and it will stand in sheaves like mountains."

The apologists for Islām, Carlyle for example, have suggested that the sensual delights of Muḥammad's paradise may, after all, be taken in a figurative sense, as the Revelation of St. John or the Song of Solomon. It is quite true that such an interpretation is hinted at in the *Akhlāq-i-Jalālī* (Thompson's translation, p. 102), and Mr. Lane in his *Egyptians* (vol. i. p. 84) says that a Muslim of some learning considered the descriptions of Paradise figurative, but such is not the view held by Muḥammadan doctors, whether Sunnī, Shī'ah, or Wahhābī. They are all agreed as to the *literal* interpretation of the sensual enjoyments of the Muslim paradise, and very many are the books written giving minute particulars of the joys in store for the faithful.

Islām, true to its anti-Christian character, preaches a sensual abode of bliss, in opposition to the express teaching of our Lord in Matt. xxii. 30: "They neither marry nor are given in marriage, but are as the angels of God in heaven."

Were proof needed, to show that the Prophet taught a real and literal interpretation of the sensual delights of the abodes of bliss, a tradition of high authority is found in the *Ṣaḥīḥu Muslim* (p. 379), *vide* also *Mishkāt*, book xxiii. ch. 13), in which the Prophet goes to some trouble to explain the sanitary laws of the heavenly kingdom, in the most literal manner possible.

Sir William Muir says: "It is remarkable that the notices in the Corân of this voluptuous Paradise are almost entirely confined to a time when, whatever the tendency of his desires, Mahomet was living chaste and temperate with a single wife of threescore years of age. Gibbon characteristically observes that 'Mahomet has not specified the male companions of the female elect, lest he should either alarm the jealousy of the former husbands, or disturb their felicity by the suspicion of an everlasting marriage.' The remark, made in raillery, is pregnant with reason, and aims a fatal blow at the Paradise of Islām. Faithful women will renew their youth in heaven as well as faithful men: why should not their good works merit an equal and analogous reward? But Mahomet shrank from this legitimate conclusion. It is noteworthy that in the Medîna Suras—that is in all the voluminous revelations of the ten years following the Hégira—women are only twice referred to as one of the delights of Paradise; and on both occasions in these simple words:—'*and to them* (believers) there shall be therein pure wives.' (Sūrah ii. 23, Sūrah iv. 60.) Was it that satiety had then left no longings unfulfilled; or that a closer contact with Judaism had repressed the budding pruriency of his revelation, and covered with confusion the picture of a sensual Paradise which had been drawn at Mecca?" (*Life of Mahomet*, new ed. p. 82 and note.)

Sir W. Muir has omitted a third passage, Sūrah iii. 13, where "women of stainless purity" are spoken of, but it is remarkable how much more restrained are the Prophet's descriptions of Paradise in his later revelations. For example, Sūrah xiii. 23, 24, 35:— "Gardens of Eden—into which they shall enter together with the just of their fathers, and their wives and their descendants, and the angels shall go in unto them at every portal: Peace be with you, say they, because ye have endured all things . . . . The rivers flow beneath its bowers; its food and its shades are perpetual."

PARDON FOR SIN. The words used to express pardon for sins on the part of the Almighty, are *'Afw* (عفو), *Maghfirah* (مغفرة), and *Ghufrān* (غفران). The act of seeking pardon is *Istighfār* (استغفار).

The following is the teaching of the Qur'ān on the subject:—

Sūrah liii. 32, 33: "God's is what is in the heavens and what is in the earth, that He may reward those who do evil with evil, and those who do good with good. Those who shun great sins and iniquities—all but venial sins,—verily thy Lord is of ample forgiveness."

Sūrah lxvii. 12: "Verily those who fear their Lord in secret, for them is forgiveness and a great reward."

Sūrah xxxiii. 71: "He (God) will correct you for your works and pardon you for your sins; for he who obeys God and His Apostle has attained a mighty happiness."

Sūrah xxxv. 8: "Those who believe and do right, for them is forgiveness."

Sūrah viii. 29: "O ye who believe! if ye fear God, He will make for you a discrimination, and will cover your offences and will forgive you; for God is the Lord of mighty grace."

Repentance is expressed in the Qur'ān by the word *Taubah* (توبة), which the Imām an-Nawawī says means "turning the heart from sin." (*Commentary on Ṣaḥīḥu Muslim*, vol. ii. p. 354.) The word frequently occurs in the Qur'ān. For example:—

Sūrah iv. 20: "If they *repent* and amend, then let them be. Verily God relenteth. He is merciful."

Sūrah xxv. 71: "Whoso hath repented and hath done what is right, verily it is he who turneth to God with a true conversion" (*matāb*).

The teaching of the traditions on the subject of repentance and pardon for sin is in some places exceedingly wild, as will be seen from the following selections taken from the sayings of the Prophet given in the *Mishkāt*, book x. ch. iii:—

"There was a man of the children of Israel, who killed ninety-nine people, after which he came out, asking if his repentance would be accepted; and having met a monk, he asked him, 'Is there acceptance for my repentance?' The monk said, 'No.' Then the man killed the monk, and stood asking people about the approval of his repentance. And a man said to him, 'Come to such a village.' Then the signs of immediate death were upon him, and he tried to reach the village upon his knees, and died on the way. Then the angels of mercy and punishment disputed about him. Then God ordered the village towards which the man had attempted to go to be near to the corpse; and the village which he had fled from to be far away from him. Then God said to the angels, 'Compute, and measure the distance between the two villages.' And it was found that the village towards which he was going was nearer to him by one span. And he was pardoned."

"An incessant sinner has not sinned that has asked pardon, although he may have sinned seventy times a day, because asking pardon is the coverer of sin."

"God has said, 'Verily if you come before Me with sins equal to the dust of the earth, and then come before Me without associating anything with Me, verily I will come before you with the pardon equal to the dust of the earth."

"Verily God accepts of the repentance of His servant as long as is soul does not come into his throat."

"I swear by God that verily I ask pardon of God and repent before Him more than seventy times daily."

"Verily my heart is veiled with melancholy, and verily I ask pardon of God one hundred times a day."

"Verily, when a true believer commits a sin, a black spot is created in his heart; and if he repents and asks pardon of God, the black spot is rubbed off his heart; but if he increases his sins, the black spot increases, so that it takes hold of the whole heart. Then this spot is a rust which God has mentioned in the Qur'ān, 'their hearts became rusty from their works.'"

"Verily there were two men of the children of Israel who had a friendship for each other. One of them was a worshipper of God, and the other a sinner. The worshipper of God said to the sinner, 'Give up sinning.' He said, 'Leave me to my Lord.' At length he found him committing a very great sin, and said, 'Give up sinning' The sinner said, 'Leave me to my Lord. Were you sent as a guard over me?' The worshipper said, 'I swear by God He will not always forgive your sins, nor will He bring you into Paradise.' Then God sent an angel to them, who took both their souls, and they both appeared before God together. And God said to the sinner, 'Come into Paradise.' And he said to the other: 'What, can you prevent My compassion on my servant?' He said, 'I cannot, O my Lord.' And God said to the angels, 'Carry him to the fire.'"

PARENTAGE. The periods of six months and of two years are fixed as the shortest and longest periods of pregnancy, and consequently any child born within those periods is assumed to be the child of the woman's husband, even though she be either a widow or divorced. This strange ruling of Muslim law is founded on a declaration of 'Āyishah, who is related to have said, "The child does not remain in the womb of the mother beyond two years."

The Imām ash-Shāfi'ī has said the longest period of pregnancy extends to four years. (Hamilton's *Hidāyah*, vol. i. p. 383.)

If a person acknowledge the parentage of a child who is able to give an account of himself, and the ages of the parties are such as to admit of the one being the child of the other, and the parentage of the child be not well known to any person, and the child himself verify the statement, the parentage is established. (*Ibid.*, vol. iii. p. 169.)

PARENTS, Duty to, is frequently enjoined in the Qur'ān; for example, Sūrah xvii. 24, 25: "Thy Lord hath decreed that ye shall not serve other than Him, and that ye shall be kind to your parents, whether one or both of them reach old age with thee; and ye must not say, 'Fie!' (*Uff*) nor grumble at them, but speak to them a generous speech. And lower to them the wing of humility out of compassion, and say, 'O Lord! have compassion on them, as they brought me up when I was little!'"

PARISH. In connection with the mosques of cities and villages there are appointed districts not unlike English parishes. Within these districts the Imām of the mosque is held responsible for the marriages and burials of the people, and his services can be claimed for these ceremonies, for which he receives customary fees. Any other Maulawī performing marriages or burials, is expected to obtain the permission of the Imām of the parish. In fact, the position of the Imām of a mosque is similar to that of a beneficed clergyman. He receives the marriage and burial fees, fees at the ceremony of circumcision, thank offerings on the birth of a child, or on recovery from sickness, presents on the festival days, &c., as well as the *waqf*, or endowment, of the mosque.

PARSĪ. [MAJUS.]

PARTURITION. [NIFAS.]

PATIENCE. Arabic *ṣabr* (صبر), is frequently enjoined in the Qur'ān, *e.g.* Sūrah ii. 148: "O ye who believe! seek help through patience and prayer; verily God is with the patient."

PAWNING. [RAHN.]

PEN, The, of Fate. [QALAM.]

PENTATEUCH. [TAURAT.]

PESTILENCE. Arabic *ṭā'ūn* (طاعون), *wabā'* (وباء). According to the teaching of Muḥammad in the traditions, a pestilence is a punishment sent by God, it is also an occasion of martyrdom, and that Muslim who abides in the place where he is at the time of a pestilence, and dies of it, is admitted to the rank of a martyr. It is also enjoined that Musalmāns shall not enter a place where there is a pestilence raging, but remain where they are until it is passed. (*Mishkāt*, book v. ch. 1.)

PHARAOH. Arabic *Fir'aun* (فرعون). Heb. פַּרְעֹה. The King of Egypt in the time of Moses. Considered by all Muḥammadans to be the very personification of wickedness.

Al-Baiẓāwī says Fir'aun was the common title of the kings of Egypt, just as Cæsar was that of the Roman Emperors, and that the name of Pharaoh, according to some, was al-Walīd ibn Muṣ'ab, and according to others Muṣ'ab ibn Raiyām, and according to others Qābūs, and that he lived 620 years. Abū'l-fidā' says that Muṣ'ab being 170 years old, and having no child, whilst he kept his herds, he saw a cow calf, and heard her say at the same time, "O Muṣ'ab, be not grieved, thou shalt have a son, a wicked son, who shall be cast into hell," and that this son was the wicked Fir'aun of the time of Moses.

In the Qur'ān, Sūrah xxxviii. 11, he is surnamed *Fir'aun Ẕū 'l-Autād*, or "Pharaoh the master of the Stakes, who called the Apostles liars." Some say the stakes refer to the strength of his kingdom, others that they were instruments of torture and death which he used.

Pharaoh was drowned in the Red Sea, and the commentators say that Gabriel would not let his body sink, but that it floated as a sign and a warning to the children of Israel. (See Qur'ān, Sūrah x. 90–92.)

A further account of Pharaoh, as given in the Qur'ān, will be found in the article on Moses. The Pharaoh of Joseph's time is said to be Raiyān ibn al-Walīd al-'Amlīqī, the ancestor of the renowned Pharaoh in the time of Moses. [MOSES.]

PHILOSOPHY, MUSLIM. Arabic *falsafah* (فلسفة), or *'ilmu 'l-ḥikmah* (علم الحكمة). The following account of Arabian philosophy is taken with permission from Professor Ueberweg's *History of Philosophy*, translated by G. S. Morris, M.A. (Hodder and Stoughton), vol. i. p. 405:—

"The whole philsophy of the Arabians was only a form of Aristotelianism, tempered more or less with Neo-Platonic conceptions. The medical and physical science of the Greeks and Greek philosophy became known to the Arabs especially under the rule of the Abassidæ (from A.D. 750 on), when medical, and afterwards (from the time of the reign of Almamun, in the first half of the ninth century) philosophical works were translated from Greek into Syriac and Arabic by Syriac Christians. The tradition of Greek philosophy was associated with that combination of Platonism and Aristotelianism which prevailed among the last philosophers of antiquity, and with the study by Christian theologians of the Aristotelian logic as a formal organon of dogmatics; but in view of the rigid monotheism of the Mohammedan religion, it was necessary that the Aristotelian metaphysics, and especially the Aristotelian theology, should be more fully adopted among the Arabs than among the Neo-Platonists and Christians, and that in consequence of the union among the former of philosophical with medical studies, the works of Aristotle on natural science should be studied by them with especial zeal.

"Of the Arabian philosophers in the East, the most important were Alkendi (al-Kindī), who was still more renowned as a mathematician and astrologer; Alfarabi (al-Fārābī), who adopted the Neo-Platonic doctrine of emanation; Avicenna (Abū Sīnā), the representative of a purer Aristotelianism and a man who for centuries, even among the Christian scholars of the later mediæval centuries, stood in the highest consideration as a philosopher, and, still more, as a teacher of medicine; and, finally, Algazel (al-Ghazzālī), who maintained a philosophical skepticism in the interest of theological orthodoxy.

"The most important Arabian philosophers in the West were Avempace (Ibn Badja), Abubacer (Abū Bakr Ibn Ṭufail), and Averroës (Ibn Rashīd). Avempace and Abubacer dwell in their works on the idea of the independent and gradual development of man. Abubacer (in his 'Natural Man') develops this idea in a spirit of opposition to positive religion, although he affirms that positive religion and philosophical doctrine pursue the same end, namely, the union of the human intellect with the divine. Averroës, the celebrated commentator of Aristotle, interprets the doctrine of the latter respecting the active and the passive intellect in a sense which is nearly pantheistic and which excludes the idea of individual immortality. He admits the existence of only one active intellect, and affirms that this belongs in common to the whole human race, that it becomes temporarily particularized in individuals, but that each of its emanations becomes finally reabsorbed in the original whole, in which alone, therefore, they possess immortality.

"The acquaintance of the Mohammedan Arabs with the writings of Aristotle was brought about through the agency of Syrian Christians. Before the time of Mohammed, many Nestorian Syrians lived among the Arabs as physicians. Mohammed also had intercourse with Nestorian monks. Hareth Ibn Calda, the friend and physician of the Prophet, was a Nestorian. It was not, however, until after the extension of the Mohammedan rule over Syria and Persia, and chiefly after the Abassidæ had commenced to reign (A.D. 750), that foreign learning, especially in medicine and philosophy, became generally known among the Arabs. Philosophy had already been cultivated in those countries during the last days of Neo-Platonism, by David the Armenian (about 500 A.D.; his *Prolog.* to *Philos.* and to the *Isagoge*, and his commentary on the *Categ*, in Brandis' Collection of Scholia to Arist.; his works, Venice, 1823; on him *cf.* C. F. Neumann, Paris, 1829) and afterwards by the Syrians, especially Christian Syrians, translated Greek authors, particularly medical, but afterward philosophical authors also, first into Syriac, and then from Syriac into Arabic (or they, perhaps, made use also of earlier Syriac translations some of which are to-day extant).

"During the reign and at the instance of Almamun (A.D. 813–833), the first translations of works of Aristotle into Arabic were made, under the direction of Johannes Ibn-al-Batrik (*i.e.* the son of the Patriarch, who, according to Renan [l.l., p. 57], is to be distinguished from Johannes Mesue, the physician), these translations, in part still extant, were regarded (according to Abulfaragius, *Histor. Dynast.*. p. 153 *et al.*) as faithful but inelegant.

"A man more worthy of mention is Honein Ibn Ishak (Johannitius), a Nestorian, who flourished under Motewakkel, and died in 876. Acquainted with the Syriac, Arabic, and Greek languages, he was at the head of a school of interpreters at Bagdâd, to which his son Ishak Ben Honein and his nephew Hobeisch-el-Asam also belonged. The works not only of Aristotle himself, but also of several ancient Aristotelians (Alexander Aphrodisiensis, Themistius, and also Neo-Platonic exegetes, such as Porphyry and Ammonius), and of Galenus and others, were translated into (Syriac and) Arabic. Of these translations, also, some of those in Arabic are still existing, but the Syriac translations are all lost. (Honein's Arabic translation of the *Categories* has been edited by Jul. Theod. Zenker, Leips. 1846) In the tenth century new translations, not only of the works of Aristotle, but also of Theophrastus, Alexander of Aphrodisias, Theomistius, Syrianus, Ammonius, etc., were produced by Syrian Christians, of whom the most important were the Nestorians, Abu Baschar Mata and Jahja ben Adi, the Tagritan, as also Isa Ben Zaraa. The Syriac translations (or revisions of earlier translations) by these men have been lost, but the Arabic translations were widely circulated and have in large measure been preserved; they were used by Alfarabi, Avicenna, Averroës, and the other Arabian philosophers. The *Republic*, *Timæus*, and *Laws* of Plato, were also translated into Arabic. Averroës (in Spain, about 1150) possessed and paraphrased the *Rep.*, but he did not the *Politics* of Aristotle; the book existing in MS. at Paris, entitled *Siaset* (Siyāsah), *i.e. Politica*, is the spurious work *De Regimine Principum s. Secretum Secretorum;* the *Politics* of Aristotle is not known to exist in Arabic. Farther, extracts from the Neo-Platonists, especially from Proclus, were translated into Arabic. The Syrians were led, especially in consequence of their contact with the Arabs, to extend their studies beyond the *Organon*; they began to cultivate in the Arabic language all the branches of philosophy on the basis of Aristotle's works, and in this they were afterwards followed by the Arabs themselves, who soon surpassed their Syrian teachers. Alfarabi and Avicenna were the scholars of Syrian and Christian physicians. The later Syrian philosophy bears the type of the Arabian philosophy. The most important representative of the former was Gregorius Barhebræus or Abulfaragius, the Jacobite, who lived in the thirteenth century, and was descended from Jewish parents, and whose compendium of the Peripatetic philosophy (*Butyrum Sapientiæ*) is still of great authority among the Syrians.

"Alkendi (Abu Jusuf Jacub Ibn Eshak al Kendi, *i.e.* the father of Joseph, Jacob, son of Isaac, the Kendæan, of the district of Kendah) was born at Busra on the Persian Gulf, where later, in the tenth century, the

'Brothers of Purity' or the 'Sincere Brethren,' who collected in an Encyclopedia the learning then acceptable to the Arabians, were located. He lived during and after the first half of the ninth century, dying about 870. He was renowned as a mathematician, astrologer, physician, and philosopher. He composed commentaries on the logical writings of Aristotle, and wrote also on metaphysical problems. In theology he was a rationalist. His astrology was founded on the hypothesis that all things are so bound together by harmonious causal relations, that each, when completely conceived, must represent as in a mirror the whole universe

"Alfarabi (Abu Nasr Mohammed ben Mohammed ben Tarkhan of Farab), born near the end of the ninth century, received his philosophical training mainly at Bagdad, where he also began to teach. Attached to the mystical sect of the Sûfi, which Said Abul Chair had founded about A.D. 820 (under the unmistakable influence of Buddhism, although Tholuck ["*Ssufismus.*" Berlin, 1821, and *Blüthensammlung aus der Morgenländ. Mystik*, Berlin, 1825] assigns to it a purely Mohammedan origin), Alfarabi went at a later epoch to Aleppo and Damascus, where he died A.D. 950. In logic Alfarabi follows Aristotle almost without exception. Whether logic is to be regarded as a part of philosophy or not, depends, according to Alfarabi, on the greater or less extension given to the conception of philosophy, and is therefore a useless question. Argumentation is the instrument by which to develop the unknown from the known; it is employed by the *utens logicus*; *logica docens* is the theory which relates to this instrument, argumentation, or which treats of it as its subject (*subjectum*). Yet logic also treats of single concepts (*incomplexa*) as elements of judgments and argumentations (according to Alfarabi, as reported by Albertus M., *De Prædicabil.* i. 2 *seq.*, *cf.* Prantl, *Gesch. der Log.*, ii. p. 302 *seq.*). Alfarabi defines the universal (see Alb. M., *De Praed.*, ii. 5) as the *unum de multis et in multis*, which definition is followed immediately by the inference that the universal has no existence apart from the individual (*non habet esse separatum a multis*). It is worthy of notice that Alfarabi does not admit in its absolute sense the aphorism: *singulare sentitur, universale intelligitur*, but teaches that the singular, although in its material aspect an object of sensible perception, exists in its formal aspect in the intellect, and, on the other hand, that the universal, although as such belonging to the intellect, exists also *in sensu*, in so far as it exists blended with the individual (Alb., *An. post.* i. 1, 3). Among the contents of the Metaphysics of Alfarabi, mention should be made of his proof of the existence of God, which was employed by Albertus Magnus and later philosophers. This proof is founded on Plat., *Tim.*, p. 28: τῷ γενομένῳ φαμὲν ὑπ' αἰτίου τινὸς ἀνάγκην εἶναι γενέσθαι, and Arist., *Metaph.*, xii. 7: ἐστι τοίνυν τι καὶ ὃ κινεῖ, etc., or on the principle that all change and all development must have a cause. Alfarabi distinguishes (*Fontes Quæstionum*, ch. 3 *seq.*, in Schmölders *Doc. Phil. Ar.*, p. 44), between that which has a possible and that which has a necessary existence, just as Plato and Aristotle distinguish between the changeable and the eternal). If the possible is to exist in reality, a cause is necessary thereto. The world is composite, hence it had a beginning or was caused (ch. 2). But the series of causes and effects can neither recede *in infinitum*, nor return like a circle into itself: it must, therefore, depend upon some necessary link, and this link is the first being (*ens primum*). This first being exists necessarily; the supposition of its non-existence involves a contradiction. It is uncaused, and needs in order to its existence no cause external to itself. It is the cause of all that exists. Its eternity implies its perfection. It is free from all accidents. It is simple and unchangeable. As the absolutely Good it is at once absolute thought, absolute object of thought, and absolute thinking being (*intelligentia*, *intelligible*, *intelligens*). It has wisdom, life, insight, might, and will, beauty, excellence, brightness; it enjoys the highest happiness, is the first willing being and the first object of will (desire). In the knowledge of this being, Alfarabi (*De rebus studio Arist. phil. præmitt. Comm.*, ch. 4, *ap.* Schmölders, *Doc. ph. Arab.*, p. 22), sees the end of philosophy, and he defines the practical duty of man as consisting in rising, so far as human force permits it, into likeness with God. In his teachings respecting that which is caused by or derived from God (*Fontes Quæst*, ch. 6 *seq*,), Alfarabi follows the Neo-Platonists. His fundamental conception is expressed by the word *emanation*. The first created thing was the Intellect, which came forth from the first being (the Νοῦς of Plotinus; this doctrine was logically consistent only for Plotinus, not for Alfarabi, since the former represented his One as superior to all predicates, while Alfarabi, in agreement with Aristotle and with religious dogmatics, recognized in his first being intelligence). From this intellect flowed forth, as a new emanation, the Cosmical Soul, in the complication and combination of whose ideas the basis of corporeality is to be found. Emanation proceeds from the higher or outer spheres to the lower or inner ones. In bodies, matter and form are necessarily combined with each other. Terrestrial bodies are composed of the four elements. The lower physical powers, up to the potential intellect, are dependent on matter. The potential intellect, through the operation (in-beaming) of the active divine intellect, is made actual (*intellectus in actu* or *in effectu*), and this actual intellect, as resulting from development, may be called acquired intellect (*intellectus acquisitus*, after the doctrine of Alexander of Aphrodisias, concerning the νοῦς ἐπίκτητος). The actual human intellect is free from matter, and is a simple substance, which alone survives the death of the body and remains indestructible. Evil is a necessary condition of good in a finite world. All things are under divine guidance and are good, since all was created by God. Between the human understanding and the things which it seeks to know there exists (as Alfarabi teaches, *De Intellecto et Intellectu*, p. 48 *seq.*) a similarity of form, which arises from their having both been formed by the same first being, and which makes knowledge possible.

"Avicenna (Abu Ali Al Hosaiṇ Abdallah Ibn Sina) was born at Afsenna, in the province of Bokhara, in the year 980. His mind was early developed by the study of theology, philosophy, and medicine, and in his youth he had already written a scientific encyclopedia. He taught medicine and philosophy in Ispahan. He died at Hamadan in the fifty-eighth year of his life. His medical *Canon* was employed for centuries as the basis of instruction. In philosophy he set out from the doctrines of Alfarabi, but modified them by omitting many Neo-Platonic theorems and approximating more nearly to the real doctrine of Aristotle. The principle on which his logic was founded, and which Averroës adopted and Albertus Magnus often cites, was destined to exert a great influence. It was worded thus: *Intellectus in formis agit universalitatem* (Alb., *De Prœdicab*, ii. 3 and 6). The genus, as also the species, the differentia the accidens, and the proprium, are in themselves neither universal nor singular. But the thinking mind, by comparing the similar forms, forms the *genus logicum*, which answers to the definition of the genus, viz.: that it is predicated of many objects specifically different, and answers the question, 'What is it?' (tells the *quiditas*). It is the *genus naturale* which furnishes the basis of comparison. When the mind adds to the generic and specific the individual accidents, the singular is formed (Avic., *Log.*, Venice edition, 1508, f. 12, *ap.* Prantl, *Geschichte der Logik*, ii. 347 *seq.*) Only figuratively, according to Avicenna, can the genus be called matter and the specific difference form; such phraseology (frequent in Aristotle) is not strictly correct. Avicenna distinguishes several modes of generic existence, viz.: *ante res*, *in rebus*, and *post res*. Genera are *ante res* in the mind of God; for all that exists is related to God as a work of art is related to an artist; it existed in his wisdom and will before its entrance into the world of manifold existence; in this sense, and only in this sense, is the universal before the individual. Realized with its accidents in matter, the genus constitutes the natural thing, *res naturalis*, in which the universal essence is immanent. The third mode of the existence of the genus is that which it has in being conceived by the human intellect; when the latter abstracts the form and then compares it again with the individual objects to which by one and the same definition it belongs, in this comparison (*respectus*) is contained the universal (Avic., *Log.*, f. 12; *Metaph.*, v. 1, 2, f. 87, in Prantl, ii. p. 349). Our thought, which is directed to things, contains nevertheless dispositions which are peculiar to itself; when things are thought, there is added in thought something which does not exist outside of thought. Thus universality as such, the generic concept and the specific difference, the subject and predicate, and other similar elements, belong only to thought. Now it is possible to direct the attention, not merely to things, but also to the dispositions which are peculiar to thought, and this takes place in logic (*Metaph.*, i. 2; iii. 10, in Prantl, ii. p. 320 *seq.*). On this is based the distinction of 'first' and 'second intentions.' The direction of attention to things is the first intention (*intentio prima*); the second intention (*intentio secunda*) is directed to the dispositions which are peculiar to our thinking concerning things. Since the universal as such belongs not to things, but to thought, it belongs to the second intention. The principle of individual plurality, according to Avicenna, is matter, which he regards, not with Alfarabi as an emanation from the Cosmical Soul, but with Aristotle as eternal and uncreated; all potentiality is grounded in it, as actuality is in God. Nothing changeable can come forth directly from the unchangeable first cause. His first and only direct product is the *intelligentia prima* (the νοῦς of Plotinus, as with Alfarabi); from it the chain of emanations extends through the various celestial spheres down to our earth. But the issuing of the lower from the higher is to be conceived, not as a single, temporal act, but as an eternal act, in which cause and effect are synchronous. The cause which gave to things their existence must continually maintain them in existence; it is an error to imagine that things once brought into existence continue therein of themselves. Notwithstanding its dependence on God, the world has existed from eternity. Time and motion always were (Avic. *Metaph.*, vi. 2, *et al*; *cf.* the account in the *Tractatus de Erroribus*, *ap.* Hauréau, *Ph. Sc.*, i. p. 368). Avicenna distinguishes a twofold development of our potential understanding into actuality, the one common, depending on instruction, the other rare, and dependent on immediate divine illumination. According to a report transmitted to us by Averroës, Avicenna, in his *Philosophia Orientalis*, which has not come down to us, contradicted his Aristotelian principles, and conceived God as a heavenly body.

"Algazel (Abu Hamed Mohammed Ibn Achmed Al-Ghazzâli), born A.D. 1059 at Ghazzâlah in Khorasan, taught first at Bagdad, and afterwards, having become a Sûfi, resided in Syria. He died A.D. 1111 at Tus. He was a sceptic in philosophy, but only that his faith might be all the stronger in the doctrines of theology. His course in this respect marked a reaction of the exclusively religious principle of Mohammedanism against philosophical speculation—which in spite of all accommodation had not made itself fully orthodox—and particularly against Aristotelianism; between the mysticism of the Neo-Platonists, on the contrary, and the Sûfism of Algazel, there existed an essential affinity. In his *Makacid al filasifu* (*Maqāṣidu 'l-Falā-*

sifah), 'The Aims of the Philosophers,' Algazel sets forth the doctrines of philosophy following essentially Alfarabi and particularly Avicenna. These doctrines are then subjected by him to a hostile criticism in his *Tehafot al filasifa* (*Tahāfutu 'l-Falāsifah*), 'Against the Philosophers,' while in his 'Fundamental Principles of Faith,' he presents positively his own views. Averroës wrote by way of rejoinder his *Destructio Destructionis Philosophorum*. Algazel exerted himself especially to excite a fear of the chastisements of God, since in his opinion the men of his times were living in too great assurance. Against the philosophers he defended particularly the religious dogmas of the creation of the world in time and out of nothing, the reality of the divine attributes, and the resurrection of the body, as also the power of God to work miracles, in opposition to the supposed law of cause and effect. In the Middle Ages, his exposition of logic, metaphysics, and physics, as given in the *Makacid*, was much read.

"The result of the scepticism of Algazel was in the East the triumph of an unphilosophical orthodoxy; after him there arose in that quarter no philosopher worthy of mention. On the other hand, the Arabian philosophy began to flourish in Spain, where a succession of thinkers cultivated its various branches.

"Avempace (Abu Bekr Mohammed ben Jahja Ibn Badja), born at Saragossa near the end of the eleventh century, was celebrated as a physician, mathematician, astronomer, and philosopher. About 1118 he wrote, at Seville, a number of logical treatises. At a later period he lived in Granada, and afterwards also in Africa. He died at a not very advanced age in 1138, without having completed any extensive works; yet he wrote several smaller (mostly lost) treatises, among which, according to Munk (*Mélanges*, p. 386), were *Logical Tractates* (still existing, according to Casiri, *Biblioth. Arabico-Hisp. Escurialensis*, i. p. 179, in the library of the Escurial), a work on the soul, another on the conduct of the solitary (*régime du solitaire*), also on the union of the universal intellect with man, and a farewell letter; to these may be added commentaries on the *Physics*, *Meteorology*, and other works of Aristotle relating to physical science. Munk gives the substance of the 'Conduct of the Solitary,' as reported by a Jewish philosopher of the fourteenth century, Moses of Narbonne (*Mél.*, pp. 389-409). This work treats of the degrees by which the soul rises from that instinctive life which it shares with the lower animals, through gradual emancipation from materiality and potentiality to the acquired intellect (*intellectus acquisitus*) which is an emanation from the active intellect or Deity. Avempace seems (according to Averroës, *De Anima*, fol. 168A) to have identified the *intellectus materialis* with the imaginative faculty. In the highest grade of knowledge (in self-consciousness) thought is identical with its object.

"Abubacer (Abu Bakr Mohammed ben Abd al Malic Ibn Tophail al Keisi) was born in about the year 1100, at Wadi-Asch (Guadix), in Andalusia, and died in 1185, in Morocco. He was celebrated as a physician, mathematician, philosopher, and poet, and pursued still further the path of speculation opened up by Ibn Badja. His chief work, that has come down to us, is entitled *Haji Ibn Jakdhan* (*Ḥaiyu bnu Yaqẓān*), *i.e.* the Living One, the Son of the Waking One. The fundamental idea is the same as in Ibn Badja's 'Conduct of the Solitary'; it is an exposition of the gradual development of the capacities of man to the point where his intellect becomes one with the Divine. But Ibn Tophail goes considerably farther than his predecessor in maintaining the independence of man in opposition to the institutions and opinions of human society. In his theory he represents the individual as developing himself without external aid. That independence of thought and will, which man now owes to the whole course of the previous history of the human race, is regarded by him as existing in the natural man, out of whom he makes an extra historical ideal (like Rousseau in the eighteenth century). Ibn Tophail regards positive religion, with its law founded on reward and punishment, as only a necessary means of discipline for the multitude; religious conceptions are in his view only types or envelopes of that truth to the logical comprehension of which the philosopher gradually approaches.

"Averroës (Abul Walid Mohammed Ibn Achmed Ibn Roschd), born A.D. 1126, at Cordova, where his grandfather and father filled high judicial offices, studied first positive theology and jurisprudence, and then medicine, mathematics, and philosophy. He obtained subsequently the office of judge at Seville, and afterwards at Cordova. He was a junior contemporary and friend of Ibn Tophail, who presented him to Calif Abu Jacub Jusuf, soon after the latter's ascent of the throne (1163), and recommended him, in place of himself, for the work of preparing an analysis of the works of Aristotle. Ibn Roschd won the favour of this prince, who was quite familiar with the problems of philosophy, and at a later epoch he became his physician in ordinary (1182). For a time also he was in favour with a son of the prince, Jacub Almansur, who succeeded to his father's rule in 1184, and he was still honoured by him in 1195. But soon after this date he was accused of cultivating the philosophy and science of antiquity to the prejudice of the Mohammedan religion, and was robbed by Almansur of his dignities and banished to Elisana (Lucena) near Cordova; he was afterwards tolerated in Morocco. A strict prohibition was issued against the study of Greek philosophy, and whatever works on logic and metaphysics were discovered were delivered to the flames. Averroës died in 1198, in his seventy-third year Soon after, the rule of the Moors in Spain came to an end. The Arabian philosophy was extinguished, and liberal culture sunk under the exclusive rule of the Koran and of dogmatics.

"Averroës shows for Aristotle the most unconditional reverence, going in this respect much farther than Avicenna; he considers him, as the founders of religion are wont to be considered, as the man whom alone, among all men, God permitted to reach the highest summit of perfection. Aristotle was, in his opinion, the founder and perfecter of scientific knowledge. In logic, Averroës everywhere limits himself to merely annotating Aristotle. The principle of Avicenna: *intellectus in formis agit universalitatem*, is also his (Averr., *De An.*, i. 8., *cf.* Alb. M., *De Prœdicab.*, ii. ch. 6). Science treats not of universal things, but of individuals under their universal aspect, which the understanding recognises after making abstraction of their common nature (Destr. destr. fol. 17: *Scientia autem non est scientia rei universalis, sed est scientia particularium modo universali, quem facit intellectus in particularibus, quum abstrahit ab iis naturam unam communem, quæ divisa est in materiis.*) *The forms, which are developed through the influence of higher forms, and in the last resort through the influence of Deity, are contained embryonically in matter.*

"The most noticeable thing in his psychology is the explanation which he gives of the Aristotelian distinction between the active and the passive intellect (νοῦς παθητικός and ποιητικός). Thomas Aquinas, who opposes the explanation, gives it in these words: *Intellectum substantiam esse omnino ab anima separatam, esseque unum in omnibus hominibus;—nec Deum facere posse quod sint plures intellectus;* but, he says, Averroës added: *per rationem concludo de necessitate quod intellectus est unus numero, firmiter tamen teneo oppositum per fidem.* In his commentary to the twelfth book of the Metaphysics, Averroës compares the relation of the active reason to man with that of the sun to vision; as the sun, by its light, brings about the act of seeing, so the active reason enables us to know; hereby the rational capacity in man is developed into actual reason, which is one with the active reason. Averroës attempts to recognise two opinions, the one of which he ascribes to Alexander of Aphrodisias, and the other to Themistius and the other commentators. Alexander, he says, had held the passive intellect (νοῦς παθητικός) to be a mere 'disposition' connected with the animal faculties, and, in order that it might be able perfectly to receive all forms, absolutely formless; this disposition was in us, but the active intellect (νοῦς ποιητικός), was without us; after our death our individual intellects no longer existed. Themistius, on the contrary, and the other commentators, had regarded the passive intellect not as a mere disposition connected with the lower psychical powers, but as inhering in the same substratum to which the active intellect belonged; this substratum, according to them, was distinct from those animal powers of the soul which depend on material organs, and as it was immaterial, immortality was to be predicated of the individual intellect inhering in it. Averroës, on the other hand, held that the passive intellect (νοῦς παθητικός) was, indeed, more than a mere disposition, and assumed (with Themistius and most of the other Commentators, except Alexander) that the same substance was passive and active intellect (namely, the former in so far as it received forms, the latter in so far as it constructed forms); but he denied that the same substance in itself and in its individual existence was both passive and active, assuming (with Alexander) that there existed only one active intellect in the world, and that man had only the 'disposition' in virtue of which he could be affected by the active intellect; when the active intellect came in contact with this disposition there arose in us the passive or material intellect, the one active intellect becoming on its entrance into the plurality of souls particularized in them, just as light is decomposed into the different colours in bodies. The passive intellect was (according to Munk's translation): '*Une chose composée de la disposition qui existe en nous et d'un intellect qui se joint à cette disposition, et qui, en tant qu'il y est joint, est un intellect prédisposé (en puissance) et non pas un intellect en acte, mais qui est intellect en acte en tant qu'il n'est plus joint à la disposition*' (from the *Commentaire moyen sur le traité de l'Âme*, in Munk's *Mél.*, p. 447); the active intellect worked first upon the passive, so as to develop it into actual and acquired intellect, and then on this latter, which it absorbed into itself, so that after our death it could be said that our νοῦς, mind, continued to exist—though not as an individual substance, but only as an element of the universal mind. But Averroës did not identify this universal mind (as Alexander of Aphrodisias identified the νοῦς ποιητικός) with the Deity himself, but conceived it (following in this the earlier Arabian commentators and directly the Neo-Platonists) as an emanation from the Deity, and as the mover of the lowest of the celestial circles, *i.e.* the sphere of the moon. This doctrine was developed by Averroës, particularly in his commentaries on the *De Anima*, whereas, in the *Paraphrase* (written earlier) he had expressed himself in a more individualistic sense (Averr., *ap.* Munk, *Mélanges*, p. 442 *seq.*). The psychological teaching of Averroës resembled, therefore, in the character of its definitions, that of Themistius, but in its real content that of Alexander Aphrodisiensis, since both Averroës and Alexander limited the individual existence of the human intellect (νοῦς) to the period proceding death, and recognized the eternity only of the one universal active intellect (νοῦς ποιητικός). For this reason the doctrine of the Alexandrists and of the Averroists were both condemned by the Catholic Church.

"Averroës professed himself in no sense hostile to religion, least of all to Mohammedanism, which he regarded as the most perfect of all religions He demanded in the philosopher a grateful adherence to the religion of his people, the religion in which he was educated. But by this 'adherence' he meant only a skilful accommodation of his views and life to the requirements of positive religion—a course which could not but fail to satisfy the real defenders of the religious principle. Averroës considered religion as containing philosophical truth under the veil of figurative representation; by allegorical interpretation one might advance to purer knowledge, while the masses held to the literal sense. The highest grade of intelligence was philosophical knowledge; the peculiar religion of the philosopher consisted in the deepening of his knowledge; for man could offer to God no worthier cultus than that of the knowledge of his works, through which we attain to the knowlege of God himself in the fulness of His essence. (Averroës in the larger Commentary on the *Metaph.*, *ap.* Munk, *Mélanges*, p. 455 *seq.*)"

Dr. Marcus Dods remarks that "in philosophy the attainments of the Arabians have probably been overrated (see *Lit. Hist. of Middle Ages*, by Berrington, p. 445) rather than depreciated. As middle-men or transmitters, indeed, their importance can scarcely be too highly estimated. They were keen students of Aristotle when the very language in which he wrote was unknown in Roman Christendom: and the commentaries of Averroës on the most exact of Greek philosophers are said to be worthy of the text. It was at the Mohammedan university in his native city of Cordova, and from Arabian teachers, that this precursor of Spinoza derived those germs of thought whose fruit may be seen in the whole history of scholastic theology. And just before Averroes entered these learned halls, a young man passed from them, equipped with the same learning, and gifted with genius and penetration of judgment which have made his opinions final wherever the name of Memonides is known. Undoubtedly these two fellow-citizens—the Mohammedan Arab and the Arabic-speaking Jew—have left their mark deep on all subsequent Jewish and Christian learning. And even though it be doubted whether their influence has been wholly beneficial, they may well be claimed as instances of the intellectual ardour which Mohammedan learning could inspire or awaken. A recent writer of great promise in the philosophy of religion has assigned to the Arab thinkers the honourable function of creating modern philosophy. 'Theology and philosophy became in the hands of the Moors fused and blended; the Greek scientific theory as to the origin of things interwound with the Hebrew faith in a Creator. And so speculation became in a new and higher sense theistic; and the interpretation of the universe, the explication of God's relation to it and its relation to God.' (Fairbairn's *Studies*, p. 398.) But speculation had become theistic long before there was an Arab philosophy. The same questions which form the staple of modern philosophy were discussed at Alexandria three centuries before Mohammed; and there is scarcely a Christian thinker of the third or fourth century who does not write in presence of the great problem of God's connection with the world, the relation of the Infinite to the finite, of the unseen intangible Spirit to the crass material universe. What we have here to do with, however, is not to ascertain whether modern philosophy be truly the offspring of the unexpected marriage of Aristotle and the Koran, but whether the religion promulgated in the latter is or is not obstructive of intellectual effort and enlightenment. And enough has been said to show that there is nothing in the religion which necessarily and directly tends to obstruct either philosophy or science; though when we consider the history and achievements of that race which has for six centuries been the leading representative of Islam, we are inclined to add that there is nothing in the religion which necessarily leads on the mind to the highest intellectual effort. Voltaire, in his own nervous way, exclaims, 'I detest the Turks, as the tyrants of their wives and the enemies of the arts.' And the religion has shown an affinity for such uncivilised races. It has not taken captive any race which possesses a rich literature, nor has it given birth to any work of which the world demands a translation; and precisely in so far as individuals have shown themselves possessed of great speculative and creative genius, have they departed from the rigid orthodoxy of the Koran. We should conclude, therefore, that the outburst of literary and scientific enthusiasm in the eighth century was due, not directly to the influence of the Mohammedan religion, but to the mental awakening and exultant consciousness of power and widened horizon that came to the conquering Saracens. At first their newly-awakened energy found scope in other fields than that of philosophy. '*Marte undique obstrepenti, musis vix erat locus.*' But when the din of war died down, the voice of the Muses was heard, and the same fervour which had made the Saracen arms irresistible, was spent now in the acquirement of knowledge."—*Mohammed, Buddha, and Christ*, p. 113.)

PICTURES.

Muḥammad cursed the painter or drawer of men and animals (*Mishkāt*, book xii, ch. i. pt. 1), and consequently they are held to be unlawful.

PILGRIMAGES TO MAKKAH

are of two kinds: the *Ḥajj* or special pilgrimage performed in the month of Z̲u 'l-Ḥijjah, and the '*Umrah*, or visitation, which may be performed at any time of the year. [HAJJ, 'UMRAH.]

PĪR (پیر).

The Persian word for an elder. A term used for a *murshid*, or religious leader. [SUFIISM.]

PLAGUES OF EGYPT.

The following references occur to the ten plagues of Egypt in the Qur'ān,

Sūrah viii. 127–135: "Already had we chastised the people of Pharaoh with dearth and scarcity of fruits, that haply they might take warning: and when good fell to their lot they said, 'This is our due.' But if ill befell them, they regarded Moses and his partizans as (the birds) of ill omen. *Yet*, was not their evil omen from God? But most of them knew it not. And they said, 'Whatever sign thou bring us for our enchantment, we will not believe on thee. And we sent upon them the flood and the locusts and the qummal (lice) and the frogs and the blood, —clear signs—but they behaved proudly, and were a sinful people. And when any plague fell upon them, they said, 'O Moses! pray for us to thy Lord, according to that which he hath covenanted with thee: Truly if thou take off the plague from us, we will surely believe thee, and will surely send the children of Israel with thee.' But when we had taken off the plague from them, and the time which God had granted them had expired, behold! they broke their promise. Therefore we took vengeance on them and drowned them in the sea, because they treated our signs as falsehoods and were heedless of them. And we gave to the people who had been brought so low, the eastern and the western lands, which we had blessed as an heritage: and the good word of thy Lord was fulfilled on the children of Israel because they had borne up with patience: and we destroyed the works and the structures of Pharaoh and his people: And we brought the children of Israel across the sea, and they came to a people who gave themselves up to their idols. They said, 'O Moses! make us a god, as they have gods.' He said, 'Verily, ye are an ignorant people: for the worship they practice will be destroyed, and that which they do is vanity!'"

In the Sūrah xvii. 103–104, they are referred to as "nine clear signs," which some commentators understand to be the commandments of Moses.

"We heretofore gave to Moses nine clear signs. Ask thou, therefore, the children of Israel how it was when he came unto them, and Pharaoh said to him, 'Verily, I deem thee, O Moses, a man enchanted.'

"Said Moses, 'Thou knowest that none hath sent down these clear signs but the Lord of the Heavens and of the Earth; and I surely deem thee, O Pharaoh, a person lost.'"

Mr. Sale, translating from the Jalālān and al-Baiẓāwī, says: "These were, the changing his rod into a serpent, the making his hand white and shining, the producing locusts, lice, frogs, and blood, the dividing of the Red Sea, the bringing water out of the rock, and the shaking of Mount Sinai over the children of Israel. In lieu of the three last, some reckon the inundation of the Nile, the blasting of the corn and scarcity of the fruits of the earth. These words, however, are interpreted by others not of nine miracles, but of nine commandments, which Moses gave his people, and were thus numbered up by Muhammad himself to a Jew, who asked him the question, viz. That they should not be guilty of idolatry, nor steal, nor commit adultery or murder, nor practise sorcery or usury, nor accuse an innocent man to take away his life, or a modest woman of whoredom, nor desert the army, to which he added the observing of the Sabbath as a tenth commandment, but which peculiarly regarded the Jews, upon which answer, it is said, the Jew kissed the Prophet's hand and feet."

PLANETS.

PLANETS. Arabic *as-sayyārah* (السيارة). According to Arabic writers, there are seven planets, called *an-Najūmu 's-Sayyārāt* (النجوم السيارات), or, collectively, *as-Sayyārah*, the wandering stars, as distinguished from fixed stars, or *an-Najūmu 's-ṡawābit* (النجوم الثوابت). These planets are said to be situated in the seven firmaments in the following order: (1) *Al-Qamar*, Moon; (2) *'Uṭārid*, Mercury; (3) *Zuhrah*, Venus; (4) *ash-Shams*, Sun; (5) *al-Mirrīkh*, Mars; (6) *al-Mushtarī*, Jupiter; (7) *Zuḥal*, Saturn. (*Vide Kashshāf-i-Iṣṭilaḥāt, in loco.*)

It will be seen that the Arabian arrangement of the planets is that of Ptolemy, who placed the earth in the centre of the universe, and nearest to it the moon, whose synodic revolution is the shortest of all, being performed in 29½ days. Next to the moon he placed Mercury, who returns to his conjunctions in 116 days. After Mercury followed Venus, whose periodic time is 584 days. Beyond Venus he placed the Sun, then Mars, next Jupiter, and lastly Saturn, beyond which are the fixed stars.

PLUNDER. Arabic *ghanīmah* (غنيمة), *fay'* (فيء). If the Imām, or leader of the Muslim army, conquer a country by force of arms, he is at liberty to leave the land in possession of the original proprietors, provided they pay tribute, or he may divide it amongst the Muslims; but with regard to movable property, it is unlawful for him to leave it in possession of the infidels, but he must bring it away with the army and divide it amongst the soldiers. Four-fifths of the spoils belong to the troops, and the remaining one-fifth must be divided into three equal portions for the relief of orphans, the feeding of the poor, and the entertainment of travellers. Captives form part of the plunder. All cattle and baggage which cannot be carried away upon a retreat, must be destroyed. (*Hidāyah*, vol. ii. p. 159; *Mishkāt*, book xvii. ch. viii. pt. 1.)

POETS. Arabic *shā'ir* (شاعر), pl. *shu'arā'*. Poetry, *shi'r* (شعر). Muḥammad repudiated the idea of being a poet. See Qur'ān.

Sūrah xxxvi. 69: "We have not taught him poetry, nor was it proper for him; it is but a reminder and a plain Qur'ān."

Sūrah lxix. 40, 41: "Verily it is the speech of a noble apostle; and it is not the speech of a poet."

The Qur'ān being in manifest rhythm, and

in some places actual poetry, the declaration of the Prophet, that he was not a poet has much perplexed the commentators But the Imām Fak͟hru 'd Dīn ar-Rāzī, has hit upon the following clever explanation of the difficulty. He says, that in order to be a poet it is absolutely necessary that the poems should not be impromptu verses, but deliberately framed, and that, therefore, although the Qur'ān contains poetry (for example, in Sūrah xciv., which begins thus :—

الم نشرح لك صدرك
ووضعنا عنك وزرك

Alam nashraḥ laka ṣadraka
Wa waẓaʻnā ʻanka wizraka.

"Have we not opened thy breast for thee?
And taken off from thee thy burden?")

it is not really poetry, because the writer did not deliberately intend to produce the rhythm!

The same excuse is urged for the lines which Muḥammad is related to have uttered impromptu when his toe was wounded in battle :—

هل انت الا اصبع دميت
وفى سبيل الله ما لقيت

Hal anti illā iṣbaʻun damīti?
Wa fī sabīli 'llāhi mā laqīti.

"Art thou anything but a toe covered with blood?
"What has happened to thee has been in the road of God."

Arabic scholars (see *Kashfu Iṣṭilāḥāti 'l-Funūn, in loco*) divide the Arabic poets into six periods :—

(1) *Al-Jāhilīyūn*, those in the time of *ignorance*, or before Islām, such as the ancient Arabic poets Zuhair, Ṭarafah, Imru 'l-Qais, ʻAmr ibn Kulṣūm, al-Ḥāriṣ, and ʻAntarah.

(2) *Al-Muk͟hzaramūn* (*lit.* "spurious"), those born in the time of ignorance, but who embraced Islām, as Labīd and Ḥassān, whose names occur in the traditions.

(3) *Al-Mutaqaddimūn* (*lit.* "first"), those who were born in the time of Islām, of parents who were converts to Islām, as Jarīr and Farazdaq.

(4) *Al-Muwalladūn*, those who were born of true-born Muslims, as Bashār.

(5) *Al-Muḥdiṣūn*, the third generation of Muslim poets, as Abū Tammām, and Buk͟htari.

(6) *Al-Mutaʼak͟hk͟hirūn* (*lit.* "the last"), all succeeding poets.

The *Mutaqaddimūm*, the *Muwalladun*, and the *Muḥdiṣūn*, correspond with the *Aṣḥāb*, the *Tābiʻūn*, and the *Tābi ʻTābiʻūn*, or the three first generations of Muslims.

There are seven poems of ancient Arabia, who are known in history as the *Muʻallaqāt*, or "suspended," because they had been in turn suspended on the walls of the Makkan temple. They are also known as *Muzahhabāt*, or the "golden" poems, because they were written in gold. The names of their authors are Zuhair, Ṭarafah, Imru 'l-Qais, ʻAmru ibn Kulṣūm, al-Hāriṣ, ʻAntarah, and Labīd. The last of the seven embraced Islām. It is related that Labīd had posted up in the Kaʻbah his poem, beginning :—

الا كل شى ما خلا الله باطل

Alā kulla sha'in mā k͟halā 'llāha bāṭilu.

"Know that everything is vanity but God."

But that when he saw the first verses of the Sūratu 'l-Baqarah (ii.) of the Qur'ān posted up, he withdrew his verses and embraced Islām. Muḥammad repaid Labīd with the compliment that the words, "Know that everything is vanity but God," were the truest words ever uttered by a poet. (*Mishkāt*, book xxii. ch. x.)

In the earlier part of his mission, Muḥammad affected to despise the poets, and in the Qur'ān we find him saying (Sūrah xxvi. 224), "Those who go astray follow the poets"; and in the Traditions, *Mishkāt*, book xxii ch. x.: "A belly full of purulent matter is better than a belly full of poetry." But when Labīd and Ḥassān embraced Islām, the poets rise into favour, and the Prophet utters the wise but cautious saying, that "poetry is a kind of composition, which if it is good it is good, and if it is bad it is bad." In the battle with the Banū Quraiẓah, the Prophet called out to Ḥassān the poet, "Abuse the infidels in your verse, for truly the Holy Spirit (in the Ḥadīṣ it is Gabriel) will help you." Ịt is also related that the Prophet used to say, "O Lord! help Ḥassān the poet by the Holy Spirit (or Gabriel)."

It is generally admitted by Arabic scholars that the golden age of Arabic poetry was that immediately preceding or contemporaneous with Muḥammad, and that from the time of Muḥammad there was a gradual decline. This is not surprising, inasmuch as the Qur'ān is considered the most perfect model of composition ever revealed to mankind, and to be written in the language of Paradise.

Baron MacGuckin de Slane, in his Introduction to Ibn K͟hallikān's Dictionary, says :—

"The oldest monuments of Arabic literature which we still possess were composed within the century which preceded the birth of Muḥammad. They consist in short pieces of verse uttered on the spur of the moment, narrations of combats between hostile tribes, passages in rhythmical prose and kasîdas (qaṣīdahs), or elegies. The study of these remains reveals the existence of a language perfect in its form and application, admirably suited to express the various ideas which the aspect of nature could suggest to a pastoral people, and as equally adapted to portray the fiercer passions of the mind. The variety of its inflections, the regularity of its syntax, and the harmony of its prosody, are not less striking, and they furnish in themselves a sufficient proof of the high degree of culture which the language of the Arabic nation had already attained. The superior merit of this early literature was ever afterwards acknowledged by the Arabs themselves. It furnished them not only with models, but ideas for their poetical productions, and its influence has always continued perceptible in the Kasîda, which still contains the same thoughts, the same allusions as of old, and drags its slow length along in monotonous dignity. . . . (p. xv.)

"The decline of Arabic poetry can be easily traced down from the accession of the Abbasides to the time of the Aiyubites: for many centuries the patrons of the *belles-lettres* were of foreign extraction, and writers who sought their favour were obliged to conform their own judgment to that of persons who were in general unable to appreciate the true beauties of literary compositions. Works which had obtained the patronage of the prince could not fail to fix the attention of other poets, who took them as models which they strove to imitate and to surpass. The opinion held in the schools that the ancient *kasîdas* were masterpieces of art, contributed also to the perversion of good taste, their plan and ideas were servilely copied, and it was by refinement of expression alone that writers could display their talent; verbal quibbles, far-fetched allusions, thoughts borrowed from the old writers, and strained so as to be hardly recognisable, such were the means by which they strove to attain originality; sense was sacrificed to sound, the most discordant ideas were linked together for the futile advantage of obtaining a recurrence of words having a similar written form or a similar pronunciation; poets wrote for the ear and the eye, not for the mind, and yet the high estimation in which their productions were held may be judged from the readiness of Ibn Khallikân to quote them. His taste was that of the age in which he lived, and the extracts which he gives enable the reader to form an idea of the Arab mind at the period of the Crusades. The same feeling of impartiality which induces me to express so severe a censure on the generality of the Islamic poets, obliges me also to make some exceptions. The kasîdas of al-Mutanabbi are full of fire, daring originality, and depth of thought; he often reaches the sublime, and his style, though blemished by occasional faults, is very fine; al-Bohtori is remarkable for grace and elegance; Abû-l-Alâ for dignity and beauty; but Ibn-al-Fârid seems superior to them all, his pieces teem with sentiment and poetry, in his mystic reveries he soars towards the confines of another world pervaded with spiritual beauty, and glides with the reader from one enchanting scene to another; the judgment is captivated by the genius of the poet, and can hardly perceive the traits of false taste which disfigure, from time to time, his admirable style. Having pointed out the influence of the kasîda, or elegy, it may not be amiss to sketch the plan generally followed in this species of composition. The poet, accompanied by two friends, approaches, after a long journey through the desert, to the place where he saw his mistress the year before, and where he hopes to meet her again. At his request, they direct the camels on which they are mounted towards the spot, but the ruins of the rustic dwellings, the withered moss, brushwood, and branches of trees, with which were formed the frail abodes where the tribe had passed the summer, the hearthstones blackened by the fire, the solitary raven hovering around in search of a scanty nourishment, every object he perceives strikes him with the conviction that his beloved and her family have removed to some other region in the desert. Overcome with grief, heedless of the consolations of his friends, who exhort him to be firm, he long remains plunged in silent affliction; at length he finds relief in a torrent of tears, and, raising up his head, he extemporizes a mournful elegy. He commences by mentioning the places which he had already visited in hopes of finding her whom he loved, and calls to mind the dangers which he had encountered in the desert. He describes the camel which, though fatigued, still full of ardour, had borne him into the depths of the wilderness, he vaunts his own courage and extols the glory of his tribe. An adventure which happened on the previous night then comes to his memory: a fire blazing on a lofty hill, had attracted their attention and guided them to the tent of a generous Arab, where they found shelter and hospitality. He then praises the charms of his mistress, and complains of the pains of love and absence, whilst his companions hurry him away. He casts a parting look towards the place where she had resided, and lo! a dark cloud, fringed with rain, and rent with lightnings, overhangs the spot. This sight fills his heart with joy! an abundant shower is about to shed new life upon the parched soil, and thus ensure a rich herbage for the flocks; the family of his beloved will then soon return, and settle again in their former habitation.

"Such may be considered as the outline of the pastoral kasîda. In these productions the same ideas almost constantly recur, and the same words frequently serve to express them. The eulogistic kasîda, or poem in praise of some great man, assumes also the same form, with the sole difference that in place of a mistress it is a generous patron whom the poet goes to visit, or else, after praising the object of his passion, he celebrates the noble qualities of the man who is always ready, with abundant gifts, to bestow consolation on the afflicted lover.

"It results from this that a person familiar with the mode of composition followed in the kasîda, can often, from a single word in a verse, perceive the drift of the poet, and discover, almost intuitively, the thoughts which are to follow. He has thus a means of determining the true readings amidst the mass of errors with which copyists usually disfigure Arabic poetry knowing what the poet intends to say, he feels no longer any difficulty in disengaging the author's words from the faults of a corrupted text. The same peculiarity is frequently perceptible in pieces of a few verses; these generally reproduce some of the ideas contained in the kasîda, and for this reason they are justly styled fragments by Arabic writers.

"There exist, also, some compositions of an original form: such are the *dûbait*, or distich, and the *mawâlia*, both borrowed from the Persians, and the *muwashshaha*, invented in Spain by Ibn Abd Rabbîh. Pieces of this kind became general favourites by the novelty of their form and matter; the mawâlia was adopted by the dervishes, and the muwashshaha was cultivated with passion and attained its perfection in Andalusia, whence it was transported to the East. It cannot be denied that the Moorish poets, with all their extravagance of thought and expression, were far superior in their perception of the beauties of nature and the delicacies of sentiment, to their brethren of the East, and the European reader will often discover in their poems, with some surprise, the same ideas, metaphors, and systems of versification, which characterise the works of the troubadours and the early Italian poets.

"An idea borrowed from the ante-Islamic poets, and of frequent recurrence in the kasidas of later authors, is the *taif al-khiâl* (*ṭā'ifu 'l-khiyāl*), or phantom. The lover journeys with a caravan through the desert; for many nights his grief at being separated from his beloved prevents him from sleeping, but at length he yields to fatigue and closes his eyes. A phantom then approaches towards him, unseen by all but himself, and in it he recognises the image of his mistress, come to visit and console him. It was sent to him by the beloved, or rather it is herself in spirit, who has crossed the dreary waste and fleeted towards his couch; she, too, had slept, but it was to go and see her lover in her dreams. They thus meet in spite of the foes and spies who always surround the poet, ready to betray him if he obtain an interview with the beloved, and who are so jealous, that they hinder him from sleeping, lest he should see her image in his dream; it is only when they slumber that he dare close his eyes.

"The figurative language of the Muslim poets is often difficult to be understood. The narcissus is the eye; the feeble stem of that plant bends languidly under its flower, and thus recalls to mind the languor of the eyes. Pearls signify both tears and teeth, the latter are sometimes called hailstones, from their whiteness and moisture; the lips are cornelians or rubies; the gums a pomegranate flower; the dark foliage of the myrtle is synonymous with the black hair of the beloved, or with the first down which appears on the cheeks of youths at the period of puberty. The down itself is called the *izâr* or head-stall of the bridle, and the curve of the izâr is compared to the letters *lâm* and *nûn*. Ringlets trace on the cheek or neck the letter *wâw*; they are also called scorpions, either for their dark colour or their agitated movements; the eye is a sword; the eyelids, scabbards; the whiteness of the complexion, camphor; and a mole or beauty-spot, musk, which term denotes also dark hair. A mole is sometimes compared also to an ant creeping on the cheek towards the honey of the mouth; a handsome face is both a full-moon and day; black hair is night; the waist is a willow-branch, or a lance; the water of the face is self-respect; a poet sells the water of his face when he bestows mercenary praises on a rich patron devoid of every noble quality.

"Some of the verses in Arabic poetry (as in all Eastern poetry) are of a nature such as precludes translation. Had they been composed by a female on a youth whom she loved, they would seldom offer anything objectionable; but as the case is not so, they are utterly repugnant to European readers. It must not, however, be supposed that they are always the produce of a degraded passion; in many cases they were the usual expression of simple friendship and affection, or of those platonic attachments which the translated works of some Greek philosophers first taught the Moslims. Indeed, love and friendship are so closely confounded by them, that they designate both feelings by the same word, and it is not uncommon to meet epistles addressed by one aged doctor to another, and containing sentiments of the strongest kind, but which are the expression of friendship only. It often happens, also, that a poet describes his mistress under the attributes of the other sex, lest he should offend that excessive prudery of Oriental feelings which, since the fourth century of Islamism, scarcely allows an allusion to women, and more particularly in poetry, and this rigidness is still carried so far, that at Cairo public singers dare not amuse their auditors with a song in which the beloved is indicated as a female. Some of those pieces have also a mystic import, as the commentators of Hafiz, Saadi, and Shebisteri, have not failed to observe." (*Ib.*, p. xxxiii. *et seq.*)

POLL-TAX. [JIZYAH.]

POLYGAMY. In Muḥammadanism, polygamy has the express sanction of the Qur'ān, and is, therefore, held to be a divine institution. *Vide* Sūratu 'n-Nisā', or Chapter iv. 3:—

"But if ye cannot do justice between orphans, then marry what seems good to you of women, by twos, or threes, or fours: and if ye fear that ye cannot be equitable, then only one, or what your right hand possesses" (*i.e* female slaves).

Compare this with the teaching of the Talmud:—

"A man may marry many wives, for Rabba saith it is lawful to do so, if he can provide for them. Nevertheless, the wise men have given good advice, that a man should not marry more than four wives." (*Arbah. Turim. Ev. Hazaer*, 1.)

But although permission to indulge in polygamy is clear and unmistakable, the opening verse of the Sūrah from which the above is taken, seems to imply some slight leaning to monogamy as the highest form of married life, for it reads thus:—

"O ye men! fear your Lord, who created you from *one soul*, and created therefrom its mate, and diffused from them twain numerous men and women."

In the *Ain-i-Akbari*, it is related that a certain Mujtahid, or enlightened doctor, married eighteen wives, for he rendered the Arabic word *maṣna*, "double," and read the text already quoted, "Marry whatever women you like two and two, three and three, and four and four." And in the same work it is said that another learned Maulawī married eight wives, because he read the verse—"two + three + four = nine"!

Al-Baiẓāwī, the Jalālān, and other Sunnī commentators, are all agreed that the true reading of the verse limits the number of lawful wives to four. The Shī'ahs also hold the same opinion, but they sanction *Mut'ah*, or "temporary marriages." [MU'TAH.]

In the face of the united testimony of Islām founded upon the express injunctions of the Qur'ān, Syed Ameer Ali has the audacity to state in his *Critical Examination of the Life and Teachings of Muhammad*, p. 223, that "the greatest and most reprehensible mistake committed by Christian writers, is to suppose that Muhammad either adopted or legalised polygamy. The old idea of his having introduced it—a sign only of the ignorance of those who hold it—is by this time exploded, but the opinion that he adopted and legalised the custom is still maintained by the common masses as by many learned in Christendom. No belief can be more false"!

In his more recent work on the *Personal Law of the Muḥammadans*, the same writer remarks:—

"Muhammad restrained polygamy by limiting the maximum number of contemporaneous marriages, and by making absolute equity towards all obligatory on the man. It is worthy of note that the clause in the Qurán, which contains the permission to contract four contemporaneous marriages is immediately followed by a sentence which cuts down the significance of the preceding passage to its normal and legitimate dimensions. The former passage says, 'You may marry two, three, or four wives, but not more. The subsequent lines declare, 'but if you cannot deal equitably and justly with all you shall marry only one.' The extreme importance of this proviso, bearing especially in mind the meaning which is attached to the word 'equity' (*'adl*) in the Quranic teachings, has not been lost sight of by the great thinkers of the Moslem world. Even so early as the third century of the era of the Hijra during the reign of al-Mâmûn, the first Motazalite doctors taught that the developed Quranic laws inculcated monogamy. And though the cruel persecutions of the mad bigot, Mutawwakil, prevented the general diffusion of their teachings, the conviction is gradually forcing itself on all sides, in all advanced Moslem communities, that polygamy is as much opposed to the Islâmic laws as it is to the general progress of civilised society and true culture. In India especially, this idea is becoming a strong moral, if not a religious conviction, and many extraneous circumstances in combination with this growing feeling are tending to root out the existence of polygamy from among the Mussulmans. A custom has grown up in that country, which is largely followed by all classes of the community, of drawing up a marriage deed containing a formal renunciation, on the part of the future husband, of any right or semblance of right which he might possess or claim to possess to contract a second marriage during the existence of the first. This custom serves as a most efficacious check upon the growth and the perpetuation of the institution of polygamy. In India more than ninety-five per cent. of Muhammadans are at the present moment, either by conviction or necessity, monogamists. Among the educated classes, versed in the history of their ancestors, and able to compare it with the records of other nations, the custom is regarded with disapprobation, amounting almost to disgust. In Persia, according to Colonel Macgregor's statement, only two per cent. of the population enjoy the questionable luxury of plurality of wives. It is earnestly to be hoped that before long a general synod of Moslem doctors will authoritatively declare that polygamy, like slavery, is abhorrent to the laws of Islam." (*Personal Law of the Muhammadans*, p. 28.)

Syud Ahmad Khan Bahadur, in his essay, *Whether Islam has been beneficial or injurious to Society in general*, on the contrary, defends the institution of polygamy as divine, and quotes John Milton, Mr. Davenport, and Mr. Higgins, as Christian writers who defended the practice.

The Prophet claimed considerable indulgence for himself in the matter, and married eleven wives. [WIVES OF THE PROPHET.]

The views of Dr. Marcus Dods in his *Mohammed, Buddha, and Christ* (p. 55), give an able and interesting summary of the subject:—

"The defence of polygamy has been undertaken from various points of view, and with varying degrees of insight and of earnestness. But one cannot detect much progress among its defenders. F. W. Newman has nothing to say in its favour which had not previously been suggested by Voltaire; nothing, we may say, which does not occur to anyone who wishes to present the argument for a plurality of wives. It is somewhat late in the day to be called upon to argue for monogamy as abstractly right. Speculators like Aristotle (Econ. i. 2, 8), who have viewed the subject both as statesmen having a regard to what is practicable and will conduce to social prosperity, and as philosophers reasoning from first principles, have long ago demanded for their ideal society, not only monogamy, but also that mutual respect and love, and that strict purity and modesty, which polygamy kills. Let us say briefly that the only ground conscience recognises as warranting two persons to become one in flesh is that they be, first of all, one in spirit. That absolute surrender of the person which constitutes marriage is justified only by the circumstances that it is a surrender of the heart as well, and that it is mutual. To an ideal love, polygamy is abhorrent and impossible. As Mohammed himself, in another connection, and with more than his usual profundity, said, 'God has not put two hearts in you.' This is the grand law imbedded in our nature, and by which it is secured that the children born into the world be the fruit of the devoted surrender of one human spirit to another; by which, in other words, it is secured that love, the root principle of all human virtue and duty, be transmitted to the child and born in it. This is the beneficent law expressed in monogamy, and this law is traversed and robbed of its effects precisely in so far as even monogamous marriages are prompted by fleshly or worldly rather than by spiritual motives. The utilitarian argument Mr. Lecky (*Hist. European Morals*, vol. ii. p. 295) has summed up in three sentences: 'Nature, by making the number of males and females nearly equal, indicates it as natural. In no other form of marriage can the government of the family, which is one of the chief ends of marriage, be so happily sustained; and in no other does the woman assume the position of the equal of man.' But we have here to do only with Mohammedan apologists, and their reasonings are somewhat perplexing; for they first maintain that nature intended us to be polygamists (see Syud Ahmad's Essay, p. 8; Syud Ameer Ali's *Crit. Exam.*, p. 225), and then, secondly, declare that the greatest and most reprehensible mistake committed by Christian writers is to suppose that Mohammed either adopted or legalised polygamy." Probably the most that can be said for Mohammed in regard to this matter, is that he restricted polygamy, and that its abolition was impossible and unsuitable to the population he had to do with.

"The allegation, however, that Mohammed confined polygamy within narrower limits than the Arabs had previously recognised, though true, is immaterial. For, in the first place, he restricted polygamy indeed in others, but not in his own case; and thus left upon the minds of his followers the inevitable impression that an unrestricted polygamy was the higher state of the two.

"In the second place, while he restricted the number of lawful wives, he did not restrict the number of slave-concubines. In the third place, his restriction was practically of little value, because very few men could afford to keep more than four wives. And, lastly, as to the principle, he left it precisely where it was, for as Mr. Freeman justly observes (Lectures, p. 69): 'This is one of the cases in which the first step is everything. The difference between one wife and two is everything; that between four and five thousand is comparatively nothing.'

"And if the principle be defended as at least relatively good, nothing is to be urged against this as matter of fact; although the circumstance has been overlooked, that already very many thousands of Christian Arabs had found it quite possible to live in monogamy. But that polygamy is not incompatible with a sound, if not perfectly developed, morality, and with the highest tone of feeling, no one who has read the history of Israel will be disposed to deny. That it may suit a race in a certain stage of its development, and may in that stage lead to purer living and surer moral growth than its prohibition would, may be granted. But necessarily the religion which incorporates in its code of morals such allowances, stamps itself as something short of the final religion."

[MARRIAGE, MUT'AH, WIVES, WOMEN.]

POTIPHAR. Arabic *Qiṭfīr* (قطفير), or *Iṭfīr* (اطفير). The treasurer of Egypt in the time of Joseph, and the husband of Zulaik̲h̲ah. [JOSEPH.]

PRAYER. Arabic *ṣalāt* (صلوة), pl. *ṣalawāt*. Persian *namāz* (نماز), pl. *namāzhā*.

Prayer is the second of the five foundations, or pillars, of pratical religion in Islām, and is a devotional exercise which every Muslim is required to render to God at least five times a day, namely, at the early morning, midday, afternoon, evening, and night.

The general duty of prayer is frequently enjoined in the Qur'ān, but it is remarkable that in no single passage are the five periods mentioned.

See Sūratu 'r-Rūm (xxx.), 17: "Glorify God when it is evening (*masā'*) and at morning (*ṣubḥ*),—and to Him be praise in the heavens and the earth,—and at afternoon (*'ashī*), and at noon-tide (*ẓuhr*)." (But all commentators are agreed that *masā'* includes both sunset and after sunset; and, therefore, both the *Mag̲h̲rib* and *'Ashīyah* prayers.)

Sūrah xi. 116: "Observe prayer at early morning, at the close of the day, and at the approach of night; for the good deeds drive away the evil deeds."

Sūrah xx. 130: "Put up then with what they say; and celebrate the praise of thy Lord before the sunrise, and before its setting; and some time in the night do thou praise Him, and in the extremes of the day, that thou haply mayest please Him."

Sūrah xvii. 80: "Observe prayer at sunset, till the first darkening of the night, and the daybreak reading—for the daybreak reading hath its witnesses, and watch unto it in the night: this shall be an excess in service."

Sūrah ii. 42: "Seek aid with patience and prayer."

Sūrah iv. 1-4: "When ye have fulfilled your prayer, remember God standing and sitting, and lying on your sides; and when ye are in safety, then be steadfast in prayer. Verily prayer is for the believers prescribed and timed."

According to the Traditions, Muḥammad professed to have received instructions to recite prayers *five* times a day, during his *mi'rāj*, or ascent to heaven. The tradition runs thus:—

"The divine injunctions for prayer were

originally fifty times a day. And as I passed Moses (in heaven, during my ascent), Moses said to me, 'What have you been ordered?' I replied, 'Fifty times!' Then Moses said, 'Verily your people will never be able to bear it, for I tried the children of Israel with fifty times a day, but they could not manage it.' Then I returned to the Lord and asked for some remission. And ten prayers were taken off. Then I pleaded again and ten more were remitted. And so on until at last they were reduced to five times. Then I went to Moses, and he said, 'And how many prayers have you been ordered?' And I replied 'Five.' And Moses said, 'Verily I tried the children of Israel with even five, but it did not succeed. Return to your Lord, and ask for a further remission.' But I said, 'I have asked until I am quite ashamed, and I cannot ask again.'" (See *Ṣaḥīḥu Muslim*, vol. i. p. 91.)

This *Ṣalāt*, or liturgical service, has thus become one of the most prominent features of the Muḥammadan religion, and very numerous are the injunctions regarding it which have been handed down in the traditions. There are various minor differences amongst the numerous sects of Islām regarding the formula, but its main features are alike in all countries.

We shall describe prayer according to the Ḥanafī sect of Sunnī Muslims.

It is absolutely necessary that the service should be performed in Arabic; and that the clothes and body of the worshipper should be clean, and that the praying-place should be free from all impurity. It may be said either privately, or in company, or in a mosque—although services in a mosque are more meritorious than those elsewhere.

The stated prayers are always preceded by the ablution of the face, hands, and feet. [ABLUTION.]

At the time of public prayer, the *mu'aẕẕin*, or "crier," ascends the minaret, or stands at the side of the mosque nearest the public thoroughfare, and gives the *azān*, or "call to prayer," as follows:—

"God is great! God is great! God is great! God is great!
I bear witness that there is no god but God!
I bear witness that there is no god but God!
I bear witness that Muḥammad is the Apostle of God!
I bear witness that Muḥammad is the Apostle of God!
Come to prayers! Come to prayers!
Come to salvation! Come to salvation!

(*The Shīʻahs add "Come to good works!"*)

There is no other god but God!"

(*The Shīʻahs recite the last sentence twice.*)

In the early morning the following sentence is added: "Prayers are better than sleep!"

THE MU'AZZIN CALLING THE AZAN FROM A MINARET. (*A. F. Hole.*)

When the prayers are said in a congregation or in the mosque, they begin with the *Iqāmah*, which is a recitation of the same words as the *azān*, with the addition of the sentence, "Prayers are now ready!" The

THE NIYAH.

regular form of prayer then begins with the *Nīyah*, which is said standing, with the hands on either side:—

"I have purposed to offer up to God only,

with a sincere heart this morning (or, as the case may be), with my face Qiblah-wards, two (or, as the case may be) rak'ah prayers *Farẓ* (*Sunnah*, or *Nafl*)."

THE TAKBIR-I-TAHRIMAH.

Then follows the Takbīr-i-Taḥrīmah, said with the thumbs touching the lobules of the ears and the open hands on each side of the face:—

"God is great!"

THE QIYAM

The Qiyām, or standing position. The right hand placed upon the left, below the navel (the Shafi'is, and the two other orthodox sects, place their hands on their breasts, as also the Wahhābīs; the Shī'ahs keep their hands on either side. In all the sects the women perform the Qiyām with their hands on their breasts), and the eyes looking to the ground in self-abasement. During which is said the Subḥān (the Shī'ahs omit the Subḥān):—

"Holiness to Thee, O God!
And praise be to Thee!
Great is Thy name!
Great is Thy greatness!
There is no deity but Thee!"

The Ta'awwuẕ, or A'ūẕubillah, is then said as follows:—

"I seek refuge from God from cursed Satan."

After which the Tasmiyah is repeated:—

"In the name of God, the compassionate, the merciful."

Then follows the Fātiḥah, viz. the first chapter of the Qur'ān:—

"Praise be to God, Lord of all the worlds!
The compassionate, the merciful!
King of the day of reckoning!
Thee only do we worship, and to Thee only do we cry for help.
Guide Thou us in the straight path,
The path of those to whom Thou hast been gracious;
With whom Thou art not angry,
And who go not astray.—Amen."

After this the worshipper can repeat as many chapters of the Qur'ān as he may wish; he should, at least, recite one long or two short verses. The following chapter is usually recited, namely, the Sūratu 'l-Ikhlāṣ, or the 112th chapter:

"Say: He is God alone:
God the Eternal!
He begetteth not,
And is not begotten;
And there is none like unto Him."

THE RUKU'.

The Takbīr-i-Rukū', said whilst making an inclination of the head and body and placing the hands upon the knees, separating the fingers a little.

"God is great!"

The Tasbīḥ-i-Rukū', said in the same posture.

"I extol the holiness of my Lord, the Great!

(The Shī'ahs here add "and with His praise." This is also added by the Shī'ahs to the Tasbīḥ-i-Sijdah.)

"I extol the holiness of my Lord, the Great!

"I extol the holiness of my Lord, the Great!"

The Qiyām-i-Samī' Ullah or Tasmī', said with the body erect, but, unlike the former Qiyām, the hands being placed on either

THE TASMI'.

side. The Imām says aloud (when the prayers are said by a person alone, he recites both sentences):—

"God hears him who praises Him."

The people then respond in a low voice—

"O Lord, Thou art praised."

TAKBIRU 'S-SIJDAH.

Takbīr-i-Sijdah, said as the worshipper drops on his knees.

"God is great!"

Tasbīḥ-i-Sijdah, recited as the worshipper puts first his nose and then his forehead to the ground.

THE TASBIH-I-SIJDAH.

"I extol the holiness of my Lord, the most High!

"I extol the holiness of my Lord, the most High!

"I extol the holiness of my Lord, the most High!"

Then raising his head and body and sinking backward upon his heels, and placing his hands upon his thighs, he says the Takbīr-i-Jalsah (the Shī'ahs here omit the Takbīr, and say instead, "I rise and sit by the power of God!"

"God is great!"

THE TAKBIR-I-JALSAH.

Then, whilst prostrating as before, he says the Takbīr-i-Sijdah.

"God is great!"

And then during the prostration the Tasbīḥ-i-Sijdah as before.

"I extol the holiness of my Lord, the most High!"

"I extol the holiness of my Lord, the most High!"

"I extol the holiness of my Lord, the most High!"

Then, if at the close of one rak'ah, he repeats the Takbīr standing, when it is called Takbīr-i-Qiyām; but at the end of two rak'ahs, and at the close of the prayer, he repeats it sitting, when it is called Takbīr-i-Qu'ūd. (The Shī'ahs here recite the

Takbīr:—"*God is great!*" *with the thumbs touching the lobules of the ear, and add,* "*I seek forgiveness from God, my Lord, and I repent before Him!*"

"God is great!"

Here ends one rak'ah or form of prayer. The next rak'ah begins with the Fātihah or 1st chapter of the Qur'ān. At the close of every two rak'ahs he recites the Taḥīyah,

THE TAHIYAH.

which is said whilst kneeling upon the ground. His left foot bent under him he sits upon it, and places his hands upon his knees and says (the Shī'ahs omit the Taḥīyah):—

"The adorations of the tongue are for God, and also the adorations of the body, and alms-giving!

"Peace be on thee, O Prophet, with the mercy of God and His blessing!

"Peace be upon us and upon God's righteous servants!"

THE TASHAHHUD.

Then raising the first finger of the right hand he recites the Tashahhūd:—

"I testify that there is no deity but God (*the Shī'ahs add,* "*who has no partner*"); and I testify that Muḥammad is the servant of God, and the messenger of God!"

(*Every two rak'ahs close with the Tashahhud. The Darūd is said whilst in the same posture.*)

"O God, have mercy on Muḥammad and on his descendants (*the Shī'ahs merely recite:* "*God have mercy on Muḥammad and his descendants*"; *and omit the rest*), as Thou didst have mercy on Abraham and on his descendants. Thou art to be praised, and Thou art great. O God, bless Muḥammad and his descendants, as Thou didst bless Abraham and his descendants!

"Thou art to be praised, and Thou art great!"

Then the Du'ā':—

"O God our Lord, give us the blessings of this life, and also the blessings of life everlasting. Save us from the torments of fire."

(*The Du'ā' is omitted by the Shī'ahs, who recite the following instead;* "*Peace be on thee, O Prophet, with the mercy of God and His blessing! Peace be upon us, and upon God's righteous servants!*"

He then closes with the Salām.

THE SALAM.

Turning the head round to the right; he says:—

"The peace and mercy of God be with you."

THE SALAM.

Turning the head round to the left, he says—

"The peace and mercy of God be with you."

At the close of the whole set of prayers, that is of *Farẓ*, *Sunnah*, *Nafl*, or *Witr*, the worshipper raises his hands and offers up a *Munājāt*, or "supplication." This usually

THE MUNAJAT.

consists of prayers selected from the Qur'ān or Ḥadīs̤. They ought to be said in Arabic, although they are frequently offered up in the vernacular.

Such supplications were highly commended by Muḥammad, who is related to have said :—

"Supplication is the marrow of worship."

"There is nothing better before God than supplication."

"Supplicate God when ye are certain of its approval, and know that God accepts not the supplication of a negligent heart."

"Verily your Lord is ashamed of his servants when they raise up their hands to Him in supplication to return them empty."

These daily prayers are either *Farẓ*, *Sunnah*, *Nafl*, or *Witr*. *Farẓ*, are those rak'ahs (or forms of prayer), said to be enjoined by God. *Sunnah*, those founded on the practice of Muḥammad. *Nafl*, the voluntary performance of two rak'ahs, or more, which may be omitted without sin. *Witr*, an odd number of rak'ahs, either one, three, five, or seven, said after the night prayer. These divisions of prayer are entirely distinct from each other. They each begin afresh with the *Nīyah*, and worshippers may rest for awhile between them, but not converse on worldly subjects. The Wahhābīs think it correct to say the *Sunnah* prayers in their houses and only the *Farẓ* prayers in the mosque.

The five times of prayer are known as *Ẓuhr*, *'Aṣr*, *Maghrib*, *'Ishā'*, and *Fajr*. There are also three voluntary periods called *Ishrāq*, *Ẓuḥā*, and *Tahajjud*.

The following is a table showing the exact number of rak'ahs to be performed at each service :—

	No.	Time.	The Names of the Time of Prayer. Arabic.	Persian.	Urdu.	The Number of Rak'ahs said. Sunnat-i-ghair-i-mu'akkadah.	Sunnat-i-mu'akkadah.	Farz.	Sunnah after Farz.	Nafl.	Witr.
The five periods of prayer.	1	From dawn to sunrise.	Ṣalātu 'l-Fajr.	Namāz-i-Subḥ.	Fajr Kī Namāz.		2	2			
	2	When the sun has begun to decline.	Ṣalātu 'ẓ-Ẓuhr.	Namāz-i-Peshīn.	Ẓuhr Kī Namāz.		4	4	2	2	
	3	Midway between No. 2 and 4.	Ṣalātu 'l-'Aṣr.	Namāz-i-Dīgar.	'Aṣr Kī Namāz.	4		4			
	4	A few minutes after sunset.	Ṣalātu 'l-Maghrib.	Namāz-i-Shām.	Maghrib Kī Namāz.			3	2	2	
	5	When the night has closed in.	Ṣalātu 'l-'Ishā.	Namāz-i-Khuftan.	'Ishā' Kī Namāz.	4		4	2	2	7
Three periods which are voluntary.	1	When the sun has well risen.	Ṣalātu 'l-'Ishrāq.	Namāz-i-'Ishrāq.	Ishrāq Kī Namāz.					8	
	2	About 11 o'clock A.M.	Ṣalātu 'ẓ-Ẓuḥā.	Namāz-i-Chast.	Ẓuḥā Kī Namāz.					8	
	3	After midnight.	Ṣalātu 't-Tahajjud.	Namāz-i-Tahajjud.	Tahajjud Kī Namāz.					9	

According to the above table, a devout Muslim recites the same form of prayer at least seventy-five times in the day.

ᵕ 'Abdu 'llāh ibn 'Umar relates that the Prophet said, " The time for *Ẕuhr* prayers begins from the inclination of the sun towards the west and closes at the time when the shadow of a person shall be the length of his own stature, which time marks the beginning of the *'Aṣr* prayers, and the time of the *'Aṣr* prayers is from that time till the sun assumes a yellow appearance. The time of *Maghrib* prayers is from sunset as long as the red appearance in the horizon remains. The time of *'Ishā'* prayers is from that time till midnight. And the time of the *Fajr* prayers is from the break of day till the sun rises. Therefore, when the sun has risen you must not recite the morning prayer, for the sun rises between the horns of the devil." (*Mishkāt*, book iv. ch. ii.)

It is the ordinary custom of Muslims to say their prayers with their feet uncovered, but strictly according to the Traditions it is lawful to cover the feet with boots or shoes during prayer, provided they are free from impurity.

Shaddād ibn Aus relates that Muḥammad said, " Act the reverse of the Jews in your prayer, for they do not pray in boots and shoes."

Abū Saʻīd al-Ḵhudrī relates that " the Prophet said prayers with his companions, and all on a sudden took off his shoes, and put them down on his left side, and when the people observed it, they took off theirs also ; and when the Prophet had finished the prayers, he said, ' What caused you to take off your shoes ? ' They replied, ' We did so in order to follow your example.' And the Prophet said, ' Verily Gabriel came to me and told me there was a little filth upon my shoes ; therefore, when any one of you goes into a Masjid, look well at your shoes first ; and if you perceive any dirt, wipe it off, and then say your prayers in them.'" (*Mishkāt*, book iv. ch. ix. pt. 2.)

Any wandering of the eyes, or of the mind, a coughing or the like, answering a question, or any action not prescribed to be performed, must be strictly avoided (unless it is between the Sunnah prayers and the *farz*, or be difficult to avoid ; for it is held allowable to make three slight irregular motions, or deviations from correct deportment) ; otherwise, the worshipper must begin again and recite his prayers with due reverence.

If a person arrive late, he merely recites the Nīyah and Takbīr, and then joins the congregation in that part of the service in which they are engaged.

The Muslim may say his five daily prayers in his home, or shop, or in the street or road, but there are said to be special blessings attending prayer recited in a congregation.

In addition to the daily prayers, the following are special services for special occasions :—

Ṣalātu 'l-Jumʻah.—" The Friday Prayer."

It consists of two rakʻahs after the daily meridian prayer.

Ṣalātu 'l-Musāfir.—" Prayers for a traveller." Two rakʻahs instead of the usual number at the meridian, afternoon, and night prayers.

Ṣalātu 'l-Ḵhauf.—" The prayers of fear " Said in time of war. They are two rakʻahs recited first by one regiment or company and then by the other.

Ṣalātu 'l-Tarāwiḥ.—Twenty rakʻahs recited every evening during the Ramaẓān, immediately after the fifth daily prayer.

Ṣalātu 'l-Istiḵhārah.—Prayers for success or guidance. The person who is about to undertake any special business performs two rakʻah prayers and then goes to sleep. During his slumbers he may expect to have " *ilhām*," or inspiration, as to the undertaking for which he seeks guidance !

Ṣalātu 'l-Ḵhusūf.—Two rakʻahs said at the time of an eclipse of the moon.

Ṣalātu 'l-Kusūf.—Two rakʻahs said at the time of an eclipse of the sun.

Ṣalātu 'l-Istisqā'.—Prayer in time of drought, consisting of two rakʻahs.

Ṣalātu 'l-Janāzah.—Prayers at a funeral. [JANAZAH.]

The liturgical service of the Muslim is not given in the Qurʼān, but is founded upon very minute instructions given by the Prophet, and which are recorded in the Traditions, and for which the Arabic scholar can refer to *Ṣaḥīḥu 'l-Buḵhārī*, vol. i. p. 50 ; *Ṣaḥīḥu Muslim*, vol. i. p. 164 ; *Sunanu 't-Tirmiẕī*, p. 22 ; *Sunanu Abū Dāʼūd*, p. 56 : *Sunanu Muwatta'*, p. 50 ; and the English reader to Matthew's *Mishkāt*, book iv.

The following are selections from the sayings of Muḥammad with reference to the Liturgical prayers (*vide Mishkāt*, book iv.) :—

" That which leads a creature into infidelity is neglect of prayers."

" Not one of you must say your prayers in a garment without covering your whole body."

" God accepts not the prayers of a woman arrived at puberty unless she covers her head."

" People must not lift up their eyes whilst saying their prayers, or they will become blind."

" The prayers which are said in congregation increase the rewards of those said alone by twenty seven degrees." [MOSQUE.]

" The five stated prayers erase the sins which have been committed during the intervals between them, if they have not been mortal sins."

" That prayer preparatory to which the teeth shall have been cleaned with the Miswāk is more excellent than the prayer without Miswāk by seventy." [MISWAK.]

" The prayers of a person will not be accepted who has broken his ablution until he completes another ablution."

" That person who leaves even one hair without washing after uncleanness, will be punished in hell accordingly."

" When any one of you stands up for

prayer, he must not smooth the ground by wiping away pebbles, because the compassion of God descends upon him at that time."

"Order your children to say the stated prayers when they are seven years of age, and beat them if they do not do so when they are ten years old; and when they reach ten years, divide their beds."

"When you stand up to prayer, spit not in front, because you are then in God's presence; neither spit on your right side, because an angel is there. Spit, therefore either on your left side or under your feet, and then throw earth over it."

"Whoever says twelve rak'ahs of Sunnah prayers in the day and night, will have a house built for him in Paradise; four rak'ahs before the noon-day prayer, and two rak'ahs after it, and two after sunset prayer, and two rak'ahs after evening prayer, and two before morning prayer."

"'Tell me if any one of you had a rivulet before his door and bathed five times a day in it, whether any dirt would remain upon his body.' The Companions said, 'Nothing would remain.' The Prophet said, 'In this manner will the five daily prayers as ordered by God erase all little sins.'"

"When any one of you says his prayers, he must have something in front of him, but if he cannot find anything for that purpose, he must put his walking-stick into the ground; but if the ground be hard, then let him place it lengthways in front of him; but if he has no staff, he must draw a line on the ground, after which there will be no detriment in the prayers from anyone passing in front of it." [SUTRAH.]

"The best prayers for God were those of David the prophet, and the best fast are his also. David used to sleep half the night and would be woke, and in prayer a third part of the night and would fast one day and eat another."

The form of prayer, or rak'ahs, as given above, admit of no variations whether they are used in private or public, and consequently, notwithstanding the beauty of its devotional language, it is simply a superstitious act, having very little in common with the Christian idea of prayer.

We translate the Arabic *Ṣalāt*, and the Persian *Namāz* by the English word *prayer*, although this "second foundation" of the religion of Muḥammad is something quite distinct from that prayer which the Christian poet so well describes as the "soul's sincere desire uttered or unexpressed." It would be more correct to speak of the Muḥammadan *Ṣalāt* as a *service*; "prayer" being more correctly rendered by the Arabic *du'ā'*. In Islām prayer is reduced to a mechanical act, as distinct from a mental act; and in judging of the spiritual character of Muḥammadanism, we must take into careful consideration the precise character of that devotional service which every Muslim is required to render to God at least *five* times a day, and which undoubtedly, exercises so great an influence upon the character of the followers of Muḥammad.

The devotions of Islām are essentially "vain repetitions," for they must be said in the Arabic language, and admit of no change or variety. The effect of such a constant round of devotional forms, which are but the service of the lips, on the vast majority of Muḥammadans, can be easily imagined. The absence of anything like *true* devotion from these services, accounts for the fact that religion and true piety stand so far apart in the practice of Islām.

The late Dean Stanley remarks (*Eastern Church*, p. 279), "The ceremonial character of the religion of Musalmāns is, in spite of its simplicity, carried to a pitch beyond the utmost demands either of Rome or of Russia. . . . Prayer is reduced to a mechanical act as distinct from a mental act, beyond any ritual observances in the West. It is striking to see the figures along the banks of the Nile going through their prostrations, at the rising of the sun, with the uniformity and regularity of clockwork; but it resembles the worship of machines rather than of reasonable beings."

PRAYERS FOR THE DEAD.

According to the teaching of Muḥammad, it is the duty of all true Muslims to pray for the dead. (*Durru 'l-Mukhtār*, p. 135.) See also *Mishkāt*, book v. chap. iii.

"God most certainly exalts the degree of a virtuous servant in Paradise, and the virtuous servant says, 'O my Lord, from whence is this exalted degree for me?' and God says, 'It is on account of your children asking pardon for you."

"The Prophet passed by graves in al-Madīnah and turned his face towards them, and said, 'Peace be to you, O inhabitants of the graves! may God forgive us and you. Ye have passed on before us, and we are following you."

"A dead person in the grave is like one over his head in water, who calls to somebody to take him by the hand. For he has hope that his father or mother, or his brother, or his friend will pray for him. For when the prayer reaches the dead person, it is more esteemed by him than the whole world, and all that is in it; and verily God most certainly gives to the dead, on account of the prayers of the people of the earth, rewards like mountains, for verily the offerings of the living for the dead are asking forgiveness for them."

Sūrah lxxi. 29: "And Noah said, O my God, forgive me and my parents."

Sūrah ix. 114, 115: "It is not for the Prophet to pray for the forgiveness of those, who, even though they be near of kin, associate other gods with God, after it hath been made clear to them that they are to be the inmates of hell. For neither did Abraham ask forgiveness for his father, but in pursuance of a promise which he had promised him, and when it was shown him that he was an enemy of God, he declared himself clear of him: yet Abraham was pitiful and kind."

It is related in the Traditions that the Prophet visited his mother's grave, and wept in such a way as to cause those who were standing around him to weep also. And the Prophet said, "I have asked my benefactor permission to ask pardon for my mother, which was not granted then. I asked my Lord's permission to visit her grave and it was granted, therefore do ye visit graves, because they remind you of death."

PREACHER. Preaching. There are four words generally used for a preacher: *khaṭīb* (خطيب), *muẕakkir* (مذكر), *wāʿiẓ* (واعظ), and *nāṣiḥ* (ناصح).

Khaṭīb is always applied to the official who recites the khuṭbah, or oration, in the Friday service. The other three terms are applied generally to preachers.

In the present day, preaching seldom takes place in a mosque except on Fridays, when the khuṭbah is recited, although it is not forbidden, and Muḥammad was frequently in the habit of addressing his people after the prayers were over.

No Maulawī of reputation preaches in the street, but paid preachers sometimes undertake the office.

PREDESTINATION. Arabic *qadar* (قدر), the word generally used in the Ḥadīṣ; *taqdīr* (تقدير), the word usually employed in theological works. Expressions which mean "measuring out," or "preordering."

Taqdīr, or the absolute decree of good and evil, is the sixth article of the Muḥammadan creed, and the orthodox believe that whatever has, or shall come to pass in this world, whether it be good or bad, proceeds entirely from the Divine Will, and has been irrevocably fixed and recorded on a preserved tablet by the pen of fate. The doctrine, which forms a very important feature in the Muslim system, is thus taught in the Qur'ān:—

Sūrah liv. 49: "All things have been created after fixed decree" (*qadar*).

Sūrah iii. 139: "No one can die except by God's permission according to the book that fixeth the term of life.'

Sūrah lxxxvii. 2: "The Lord hath created and balanced all things and hath fixed their destinies and guided them."

Sūrah viii. 17: "God slew them, and those shafts were God's, not thine."

Sūrah ix. 51: "By no means can aught befall us but what God has destined for us."

Sūrah xiii. 30: "All sovereignty is in the hands of God."

Sūrah xiv. 4: "God misleadeth whom He will, and whom He will He guideth."

Sūrah xviii. 101: "The infidels whose eyes were veiled from my warning and had no power to hear."

The teaching of Muḥammad, as given in the Traditions handed down by al-Bukhārī and Muslim, is as follows:—

"God created Adam, and touched his back with his right hand, and brought forth from it a family; and God said to Adam, 'I have created this family for Paradise, and their actions will be like unto those of the people of Paradise.' Then God touched the back of Adam, and brought forth another family, and said, 'I have created this for hell, and their actions will be like unto those of the people of hell.' Then a man said to the Prophet, 'Of what use will deeds of any kind be?' He said, 'When God createth His servant for Paradise, his actions will be deserving of it until he die, when he will enter therein; and when God createth one for the fire, his actions will be like those of the people of hell till he die, when he will enter therein.'"

"'There is not one amongst you whose place is not written by God, whether in the fire or in Paradise.' The Companions said, 'O Prophet! since God hath appointed our places, may we confide in this and abandon our religious and moral duties?' He said, 'No; because the righteous will do good works and the wicked will do bad works.' After which the Prophet read this verse from the Qur'ān: 'To him who giveth alms, and feareth God, and yieldeth assent to the excellent creed, to him will we make easy the path to happiness. But to him who is worldly and is indifferent, and who does not believe in the excellent creed, to him will we make easy the path of misery.'"

"The first thing which God created was a pen, and He said to it 'Write'; it said, 'What shall I write?' And God said, 'Write down the quantity of every individual thing to be created,' and it wrote all that was and that will be, to eternity."

"God hath pre-ordained five things on his servants; the duration of life, their actions, their dwelling-places, their travels, and their portions."

"When God hath ordered a creature to die in any particular place, he causeth his wants to direct him to that."

"There is not one born but is created to Islām, but it is their fathers and mothers who make them Jews and Christians and Majūsī."

"It was said, 'O Prophet of God! inform me respecting charms, and the medicines which I swallow, and the shields which I make use of for protection, whether they prevent any of the decrees of God?' Muḥammad said, 'These also are by the decree of God.'"

"Verily God created Adam from a handful of earth, taken from all parts, and the children of Adam became different, like the earth; some of them red, some white, and some black, some between red, white and black, some gentle, and some severe, some impure and some pure."

"The Prophet of God was asked about the children of polytheists who might die in their infancy, whether they would go to heaven or hell. He said, 'God knoweth best what their actions would have been had they lived; it depends on this.'"

"The Prophet of God came out of his

house when the Companions were debating about fate, and he was angry, and became red in the face, to such a degree that you would say the seeds of a pomegranate had been bruised on it. And he said, 'Hath God ordered you to debate of fate? Was I sent to you for this? Your forefathers were destroyed for debating about fate and destiny; I adjure you not to argue on those points.'"

(See *Aḥādīṣu 'l-Buk͟hārī* and *Muslim, in loco.*) [PRESERVED TABLET.]

The doctrine is expressed in an Arabic treatise on the subject, as follows:—

"Faith in the decrees of God, is that we believe in our heart and confess with our tongue that the Most High God hath decreed all things; so that nothing can happen in the world, whether it respects the conditions and operations of things, or good or evil, or obedience and disobedience, or faith and infidelity, or sickness and health, or riches and poverty, or life and death, that is not contained in the written tablet of the decrees of God. But God hath so decreed good works, obedience, and faith, that He ordains and wills them, and that they may be under His decree, His salutary direction, His good pleasure and command. On the contrary, God hath decreed, and does ordain and determine evil, disobedience and infidelity; yet without His salutary direction, good pleasure, and command; but being only by way of seduction, indignation, and prohibition. But whosoever shall say that God is not delighted with good faith, or that God hath not an indignation against evil and unbelief, he is certainly an infidel."

The Rev. E. Sell, in his *Faith of Islám*, page 173, says:—

"There are three well-defined schools of thought on the subject.

"First.—The Jabríans (*Jabarīyūn*), so called from the word "*jabr*" compulsion, deny all free agency in man and say that man is necessarily constrained by the force of God's eternal and immutable decree to act as he does. They hold that as God is the absolute Lord, He can, if He so wills, admit all men into Paradise, or cast all into hell. This sect is one of the branches of the Ash'aríans with whom on most points they agree.

"Secondly.—The Qadríans (*Qadarīyūn*), who deny *Al-Qadr*, or God's absolute decree, say that evil and injustice ought not to be attributed to God but to man, who is altogether a free agent. God has given him the power to do or not to do an act. This sect is generally considered to be a branch of the Mutazilite body (*Mu'tazilah*), though in reality it existed before Wásil quitted the school of his master Hasan. As Wásil, however, followed the opinions of Mábad-al-Johní, the leading Qadrían divine, the Mutazilites and Qadríans are practically one and the same.

"Thirdly.—The Ash'aríans maintain that God has one eternal will which is applied to whatsoever He willeth, both of His own actions and those of men; that He willeth that which He knoweth and what is written on the *preserved table;* that He willeth both good and evil. So far they agree with the Jabríans; but then they seem to allow some power to man. The orthodox, or Sunní belief is theoretically Ash'arían, but practically the Sunnís are confirmed Jabríans. The Mutazilite doctrines are looked upon as quite heretical.

"No subject has been more warmly discussed in Islám than that of predestination. The following abstract of some lengthy discussions will present the points of difference.

"The Ash'aríans, who in this matter represent in the main orthodox views, formulate their objections to the Mutazilite system thus:—

"(i.) If man is the causer of an action by the force of his own will, then he should also have the power of controlling the result of that action.

"(ii.) If it be granted that man has the power to *originate* an act, it is necessary that he should know all acts, because a creator should be independent in act and choice. Intention must be conditioned by knowledge. To this the Mutazilites well reply that a man need not know the length of a road before he walks, or the structure of the throat before he talks.

"(iii.) Suppose a man wills to move his body and God at the same time wills it to be steady, then if both intentions come to pass there will be a collection of opposites; if neither, a removal of opposites; if the exaltation of the first, an unreasonable preference.

"(iv.) If man can create an act, some of his works will be better than some of the works of God, *e.g.* a man determines to have faith: now faith is a better thing than reptiles, which are created by God.

"(v.) If man is free to act, why can he not make at once a human body; why does he need to thank God for grace and faith?

"(vi.) But better far than all argument, the orthodox say, is the testimony of the Book. 'All things have we created under a fixed decree.' (Súra liv. 49.) 'When God created you and *that ye make.*' (Súra xxxvii. 94.) 'Some of them there were whom God guided and there were others decreed to err.' (Súra xvi. 38.) As God decrees faith and obedience He must be the causer of it, for 'on the hearts of these hath God graven the Faith.' (Súra lviii. 22.) 'It is he who causeth you to laugh and weep, to die and make alive.' (Súra liii. 44.) 'If God pleased He would surely bring them, one and all, to the guidance.' (Súra vi. 36.) 'Had God pleased, He had guided you all aright.' (Súra vi. 150.) 'Had the Lord pleased, He would have made mankind of one religion.' (Súra xi. 120.) 'God will mislead whom He pleaseth, and whom He pleaseth He will place upon the straight path.' (Súrah vi. 39.) Tradition records that the Prophet said. 'God is the maker of all makers and of their actions.'

"The Mutazilites took up the opposite side of this great question and said:—

"(i) If man has no power to will or to do, then what is the difference between praising

God and sinning against Him; between faith and infidelity; good and evil; what is the use of commands and prohibitions; rewards and punishments; promises and threats; what is the use of prophets, books, &c.

"(ii.) Some acts of men are bad, such as tyranny and polytheism. If these are created by God, it follows that to tyrannise and to ascribe plurality to the Deity is to render obedience. To this the Ash'aríans reply that orders are of two kinds, immediate and mediate. The former, which they call 'Amr-i-takwíní,' is the order, 'Be and it was.' This comprehends all existences and according to it whatever is ordered must come to pass. The latter they call 'Amr-i-tashrí'í,' an order given in the Law. This comes to men through prophets and thus is to be obeyed. True obedience is to act according to that which is revealed, not according to the secret intention of God, for that we know not.

"(iii.) If God decrees the acts of men, He should bear the name of that which he decrees. Thus the causer of infidelity is an infidel; of tyranny a tyrant, and so on; but to speak thus of God is blasphemy.

"(iv.) If infidelity is decreed by God He must wish it; but a prophet desires faith and obedience and so is opposed to God. To this the orthodox reply, that God knows by His eternal knowledge that such a man will die an infidel. If a prophet intends by bringing the message of salvation to such an one to make God's knowledge become ignorance, he would be doing wrong; but as he does not know the secret decrees of God, his duty is to deliver his message according to the Hadís: 'A prophet has only to deliver the clear message.'

"(v.) The Mutazilites claimed as on their side all verses of the Qurán, in which the words to do, to construct, to renew, to create, &c., are applied to men. Such are the verses: 'Whatever is in the heavens and the earth is God's that He may reward those who *do* evil according to their deeds: and those who *do* good will He reward with good things.' (Súra liii. 32.) 'Whoso shall have *wrought* evil shall not be recompensed but with its like: but whoso shall have *done* the things that are right, whether male or female and is a believer, these shall enter Paradise.' (Súra xl. 43.) 'Say: the truth is from the Lord; let him then who will, believe; and let him who will, be an infidel.' (Súra xviii. 28.) 'Those who add gods to God will say: 'If God had pleased neither we nor our fathers had given Him companions.' 'Say: Verily ye follow only a conceit, ye utter lies.' (Súra vi. 149.) The Hadís is also very plain. 'All good is in Thy hands and evil is not to Thee.'

"The Ash'aríans have one famous text which they bring to bear against all this reasoning and evidence. It is: 'This truly is a warning; and whoso willeth, taketh the way of his Lord; but *will it ye shall not*, unless God will it, for God is knowing, wise.' (Súra lxxvi. 29, 30.) To the Hadís they reply (1) that there is a difference between acquiescence in evil and decreeing it. Thus the expression 'God willeth not tyranny for His servants,' does not mean that God hath not decreed it, but that tyranny is not one of His attributes: so 'evil is not to Thee' means it is not an attribute of God; and (2) the Hadís must be explained in accordance with the teaching of the Qurán

"The Muslim philosophers tried to find a way out of the difficulty. Averhoes says: 'We are free to act in this way or that, but our will is always determined by some exterior cause. For example, we see something which pleases us, we are drawn to it in spite of ourselves. Our will is thus bound by exterior causes. These causes exist according to a certain order of things which is founded on the general laws of nature. God alone knows beforehand the necessary connection which to us is a mystery. The connection of our will with exterior causes is determined by the laws of nature. It is this which in theology we call, 'decrees and predestination.'" (*Mélanges de Philosophie Juive et Arabe*, par S. Munk, p. 458.)

PRE-EMPTION. Arabic *Shuf'ah* (شفعة). *Lit.* "Adjunction." The right of pre-emption is a power of possessing property which is for sale, and is established upon the teaching of Muḥammad. It applies *not* to movable property but to immovable property (*'aqār*). This right of pre-emption appertains in the first place to the co-sharer or partner in the property; secondly, to a sharer in the immunities and appendages of the property, such as the right to water, or to roads; and thirdly, to the neighbour. (*Hidāyah*, vol. iii. p. 594.)

PRE-EXISTENCE OF SOULS is taught both in the Qur'ān and the Traditions.

'Āyishah relates that Muḥammad said, "Souls before they became united with bodies were like assembled armies, and afterwards they were dispersed and sent into the bodies of mankind." (*Mishkāt*, book xxii. ch. xvi.)

There is said to be a reference to this doctrine in the Qur'ān:—

Sūrah vii. 171: "And when the Lord drew forth their posterity from the loins of the sons of Adam . . . ."

The commentator, al-Baiẓāwī, says God stroked Adam's back and extracted from his loins his whole posterity, which should come into the world until the Resurrection, one generation after another; and that these souls were all assembled together like small ants, and after they had in the presence of the angels confessed their dependence upon God, they were again caused to return into the loins of Adam." (See *Tafsīru 'l-Baiẓāwī, in loco.*)

PRESERVED TABLET. According to the teaching of Muḥammad, both the actions of men and the Qur'ān were recorded before creation upon a preserved tablet called *Lauḥ Maḥfuẓ* (لوح محفوظ), Sūrah xxxv. 22: "And if they treat thee as a liar, so did those who were before them treat their Apostles who came to them with the proofs *of their mission*, and with the Scriptures and with the clear Book"; and *Imām Mubīn* (امام مبين), Sūrah xxxvi. 11: "Verily, it is We who will quicken the dead, and write down the works which they have sent on before them, and the traces which they shall have left behind them: and everything have we set down in the clear Book of our decrees. [PREDESTINATION, QURAN.]

PRIDE, Arabic *kibr* (كبر), is forbidden in the Qur'ān, see Sūrah xvii. 39: "Walk not proudly on the earth; truly thou canst by no means cleave the earth, neither canst thou reach the mountains in height: all this is evil with thy Lord and odious."

PRIEST. There is no sacerdotal class of ministers in the Muḥammadan religion. The leader of the daily prayers is called an Imām. [IMAM.]

PRIVACY OF DWELLINGS is established by the teaching of Muḥammad, and it is therefore unlawful to enter the house without *Isti'zān*, or "asking permission." The injunction is given in the Qur'ān, Sūrah xxiv. 27–29:—

"O ye who believe! enter not into other houses than your own, until ye have asked leave, and have saluted its inmates. This will be best for you: haply ye will bear this in mind. And if ye find no one therein, then enter it not till leave be given you; and if it be said to you, 'Go ye back,' then go ye back. This will be more blameless in you, and God knoweth what ye do. There shall be no harm in your entering houses in which no one dwelleth, for the supply of your needs: and God knoweth what ye do openly and what ye hide."

'Atā' ibn Yasār relates that "A man once asked the Prophet, 'Must I ask leave to go into the room of my mother?' The Prophet said, 'Yes.' Then the man said, 'But I live in the same home.' The Prophet said, 'Yes, even if you live in the same home.' The man said, 'But I wait upon her!' The Prophet, 'But you must ask permission; for, what! would you like to see your mother naked?'"

It is further related that Muḥammad always went first to the right and then to the left of a door which had no curtain, and salamed several times before he entered. (*Mishkāt*, book xxii. ch. ii.)

This has become an established rule in the East, and it is considered very rude to enter any dwelling without first giving notice.

PROHIBITED DEGREES OF MARRIAGE. According to the Qur'ān they are seven: 1, mother; 2, daughter; 3, sister; 4, paternal aunt; 5, maternal aunt; 6, sister's daughter; 7, brother's daughter. And the same with regard to the other sex. It is also unlawful for a Muslim to marry his wife's sister (see Lev. xviii. 18) or his wife's aunt during the lifetime of his wife. Fosterage in Muslim law establishes relationship, and therefore a foster-sister or a foster-brother is unlawful in marriage. [MARRIAGE.]

PROPHET. The Arabic words used to express the prophetic office are *nabī* (نبى), pl. *ambiyā'*; *rasūl* (رسول), pl. *rusul*; and *mursal* (مرسل), pl. *mursalūn*. In Persian, the three titles are invariably translated by the word *paighambar* (پيغمبر) (*i.e.* a messenger).

Nabī is the Hebrew *nābī* נָבִיא, which Gesenius says means "one who bubbles forth" as a fountain. The Arabic lexicon, the *Qāmūs*, derives the word from *nubū'*, "to be exalted."

According to Muḥammadan writers a *nabī* is anyone directly inspired by God, and *rasūl* and *mursal*, one to whom a special mission has been entrusted.

Muḥammad is related to have said (*Mishkāt*, book xxiv. ch. i. pt. 3) that there were 124,000 *ambiyā'*, or prophets, and 315 apostles or messengers. Nine of these special messengers are entitled *Ūlū 'l-'Azm*, or "possessors of constancy, namely, Noah, Abraham, David, Jacob, Joseph, Job, Moses, Jesus, and Muḥammad. Six are dignified with special titles: Adam, *Ṣafīyu 'llāh*, the Chosen of God; Noah, *Nabīyu 'llāh*, the Preacher of God; Abraham, *Khalīlu 'llāh*, the Friend of God; Moses, *Kalīmu 'llāh*, the Converser with God; Jesus, *Rūḥu 'llāh*, the Spirit of God; Muḥammad, *Rasūlu 'llāh*, the Messenger of God.

The number of sacred books delivered to mankind is said to have been 104 (see *Majālisu 'l-Abrār*, p. 55); of these, ten were given to Adam, fifty to Seth (a name not mentioned in the Qur'ān), thirty to Enoch, ten to Abraham, the Taurāt to Moses, the Zabūr to David, the Injīl to Jesus, and the Qur'ān to Muḥammad.

The one hundred scriptures given to Adam, Seth, Enoch, and Abraham are termed *Ṣaḥīfah* (a pamphlet), and the other four *Kitāb* (a book); but all that is necessary for the Muslim to know of these inspired records is supposed to have been retained in the Qur'ān.

Muḥammad's enumeration of the Old and New Testament prophets, both as to name and chronological order, is exceedingly confused, and it is acknowledged to be a matter of doubt amongst Muslim commentators whether or not Alexander the Great and Æsop were inspired prophets.

The names of twenty-eight prophets are said to occur in the Qur'ān:—

Adam, Adam; *Idrīs*, Enoch; *Nūḥ*, Noah; *Hūd*, Heber?; *Ṣāliḥ*, Methusaleh; *Ibrāhīm*, Abraham; *Ismā'īl*, Ishmael; *Isḥāq*, Isaac; *Ya'qūb*, Jacob; *Yūsuf*, Joseph; *Lūṭ*, Lot; *Mūsā*, Moses; *Hārūn*, Aaron; *Shu'aib*, Jethro?; *Zakarīyā*, Zacharias, the father of John the Baptist; *Yaḥyā*, John Baptist; *'Isā*, Jesus; *Dā'ūd*, David; *Sulaimān*, Solomon; *Ilyās*, Elias; *Alyasa'*, Elisha; *Aiyūb*, Job; *Yūnus*, Jonah; *'Uzair*, Ezra; *Luqmān*, Æsop? more likely Balaam; *Ẕū 'l-Kifl*, Isaiah or Obadiah?; *Ẕū 'l-Qarnain*, Alexander the Great.

An account of these prophets will be found under their respective names.

A Persian book, entitled the *Qiṣaṣu 'l-Ambiyā'*, the "Tales of the Prophets," professes to give an account of the prophets mentioned in the Qur'ān, but the utter recklessness of the writer passes all description; for example, it is a matter of uncertainty whether Zu 'l-Qarnain is Alexander the Great or some celebrity who lived in the days of Abraham!

PROPHETESSES. It is said that only three women have been prophetesses: Sarah, the mother of Moses, and Mary, the daughter of 'Imrān; for Sarah received by revelation the news of Isaac's birth, the birth of Moses was divinely communicated to his mother, and Mary received from an angel the happy tidings of the birth of Jesus. (See *Hist. of Temple of Jerusalem*, translated from the Arabic.)

PSALMS OF DAVID, The. [ZABUR.]

PUBERTY. Arabic *bulūgh* (بلوغ), *bulughīyat* (بلوغية). The puberty of a boy is established as soon as the usual signs of manhood are known to exist; but if none of these signs exist, his puberty is not clearly established until he have completed his eighteenth year. The puberty of a girl is established in the same way; but if the usual signs of womanhood are known not to exist, her puberty is not established until her seventeenth year has been completed. This is according to the teaching of the Imām Abū Ḥanīfah. But his two disciples maintain that upon either a boy or girl *completing* the fifteenth year, they are to be declared adult. The Imām ash-Shāfi'ī concurs in this opinion, and it is said there is also a report of Abū Ḥanīfah to the same effect. The earliest period of puberty with respect to a boy is twelve years, and with respect to a girl nine years.

When a boy or girl approaches the age of puberty and they declare themselves adult, their declaration must be credited, and they then become subject to all the laws affecting adults, and must observe all the ordinances of the Muslim faith. (*Hidāyah*, Hamilton's Translation, vol. iii. p. 483; *Jāmiu 'r-Rumūz*, *Durru 'l-Mukhtār*.)

Syed Ameer Ali says:—

"The validity of marriages contracted for minors by any guardian other than the father or the grandfather, is not established until ratified by the parties on arriving at puberty. Such ratification in the case of males must be express, and in the case of females may be either express or implied. On arriving at puberty, both the parties have the right of either ratifying the contract entered into during their minority or of cancelling it. According to the Sunnis, in order to effect a dissolution of the matrimonial tie, in exercise of the right of option reserved to the parties, it is necessary that there should be a decree of the judge; and until such decree is made, the marriage remains intact. If before a decree has been obtained one of the parties should die, the survivor would be entitled to inherit from the deceased.

"The Shiahs differ materially from the Sunnis on this. They hold that a marriage contracted on behalf of minors by any unauthorised person (*fazūlī*), *i.e.* any person other than a father or a grandfather, remains in absolute suspension or abeyance until assented to by the parties on arriving at puberty; that, in fact, no legal effect arises from it until such ratification, and if in the interval previous to ratification, one of the parties should die, the contract would fall to the ground and there would be no right of inheritance in the survivor." (*Personal Law of the Mahommedans*, p. 269.)

PULPIT. The pulpit or *mimbar* (منبر), used for the recital of the *khuṭbah* on Fridays in the chief mosque is usually a wooden structure of three steps and movable, but in the large mosques of Turkey and Egypt it is a fixture of brick or stone.

It is related that the Prophet, when addressing the people, stood on the uttermost step, Abū Bakr on the second, and 'Umar on

A MIMBAR.
(*W. S. Chadwick.*)

the third or lowest. 'Usmān being the most humble of men, would gladly have descended lower, but this being impossible, he fixed upon the second step, from which it is now usual to recite the khuṭbah on Fridays and on the two great festivals. [MOSQUE, MIMBAR.]

PUNISHMENT is divided into three classes: (1) *Ḥadd* (حد), (2) *Qiṣāṣ* (قصاص), (3) *Ta'zīb* (تعذيب).

(1) *Ḥadd* (حد), pl. *Ḥudūd* (*lit.* "That which is defined"), is that punishment the limits of which have been defined in the Qur'ān and Ḥadīs. The following belong to this class:—

(*a*) Adultery, *zinā'* (زناء), for which the adulterer must be stoned, *rajm* (رجم). (*Mishkāt*, book xv. ch. 1.)

(*b*) Fornication, *zinā'* (زناء), for which the guilty persons must receive one hundred stripes. (Qur'ān, Sūrah xxiv. 2.)

(*c*) The false accusation of a married person with adultery, *qazf* (قذف), for which the offender must receive eighty stripes (Qur'ān, Sūrah xxiv. 4.)

(*d*) Apostacy, *irtidād* (ارتداد), which is punishable with death. (*Mishkāt*, book xiv. ch. v.)

(*e*) Drinking wine, *shurb* (شرب), for which the offender must receive eighty lashes. (*Mishkāt*, book xv. ch. iv.)

(*f*) Theft, *sariqah* (سرقة), which is punished by cutting off the right hand. (Qur'ān, Sūrah v. 42.)

(*g*) Highway robbery, *qaṭ'u 't-ṭarīq* (قطع الطريق): for robbery only, the loss of hands and feet, and for robbery with murder, death, either by the sword or crucifixion. (Qur'ān, Sūrah v. 37.)

(2) *Qiṣāṣ* (قصاص), *lit.* "retaliation," is that punishment which, although fixed by the law, can be remitted by the person offended against, or, in the case of a murdered person, by his heirs. It is applicable to cases of murder and of wounding. *Qiṣāṣ* is the *lex talionis* of Moses: "Eye for eye, tooth for tooth, burning for burning, wound for wound, stripe for stripe (Exodus xxi. 24); but in allowing a money compensation, Muḥammad departed from the Jewish Code. (Qur'ān, Sūrah ii. 173.)

(3) *Ta'zīb* (تعذيب), is the punishment which is left to the discretion of the Qāẓī or Judge. [HADD, QISAS, TA'ZIB.]

PUNISHMENTS OF THE GRAVE. [AZABU 'L-QABR.]

PURGATORY. [BARZAKH.]

PURIFICATIONS. Arabic *ṭahārah* (طهارة). The legal methods of purification under the Muḥammadan law vary but slightly from those which were enjoined in the Talmudic law of the Jews; with the remarkable difference that whilst with the Muslim the simple act of purification suffices, the Jew was taught by the use of expiatory offering to discern to its full extent the connection between the outward sign and the inward fount of impurity.

The most minute regulations with reference to the subject of legal purification, were laid down in the Jewish law, and are found in a treatise of the *Mishna* entitled *Yadaim.* See also Leviticus xv.

The following are the different acts of purification existing in Muḥammadan law:—

1. *Ghusl* (غسل). The washing of the whole body to absolve it from uncleanliness and to prepare it for the exercise of prayer, after the following acts: *pollutio nocturna, menses, coitus, puerperium.* [GHUSL.]

2. *Ghusl-masnūn* (غسل مسنون). Such washings of the whole body as are founded upon the *sunnah* or practice and precept of Muḥammad, although they are not supposed to be of divine institution, namely, upon the admission of a convert to Islām; before the Friday prayer, on the festivals; after washing the dead; and after blood-letting. [GHUSL MASNUN.]

3. *Waẓū'* (وضوء), or the simple ablution of hands, arms, ears, face, mouth, &c., before the recital of the usual prayers. [ABLUTION.]

4. *Tayyammum* (تيمم), or the use of sand or dust instead of water for the *waẓū'*. [TAYAMMUM.]

5. *Istinjā'* (استنجاء), or the abstersion of the private parts. [ISTINJA'.]

6. *Miswāk* (مسواك), or the cleansing of the teeth. [MISWAK.]

7. *Masḥ* (مسح), or the touching of the boots whereby they become purified for prayer. [MASAH.]

8. *Taṭhīr* (تطهير), or the cleansing of vessels, articles of clothing, &c., from impurity, which is generally done by applying either water, or sand and dust, the mere sprinkling being sufficient. [TATHIR.]

Q.

QABĀLAH, QIBĀLAH (قبالة). A deed of conveyance or transfer of right or property. Any contract or bargain or sale signed by a judge. (*Hidāyah*, vol. ii. p. 569.)

QĀBA QAUSAIN (قاب قوسين). *Lit.* "Two bows' length." An expression which occurs in the Qur'ān, Sūrah liii. 8–10: "Then he drew near and hovered o'er; until he was two bows' length off or nigher still. Then he revealed to his servant what he revealed him." Commentators understand this to refer to the angel Gabriel. Mystic writers use the term to express a state of nearness to God. (See 'Abdu 'r-Razzāq's *Dict. of Ṣūfī Terms.*)

QĀBĪL (قابيل). [CAIN.]

AL-QĀBIẒ (القابض). "The Restrainer." One of the ninety-nine attributes of God. But the word does not occur in the Qur'ān.

QABR (قبر). A grave. [GRAVE, TOMB.]

QABŪL (قبول). "Consent." A term in the Muḥammadan law of marriage, contracts, &c.

QABẒ WA BASṬ (قبض و بسط). Two terms which are employed to express two opposite states of the heart; *qabẓ* being a contraction, and *basṭ*, an expansion, of the spiritual state. (See 'Abdu 'r-Razzāq's *Dict. of Ṣūfī Terms.*)

QA'DAH (قعدة). The sitting posture in the daily prayer, when the *tashahhūd* is recited. [TASHAHHUD.]

QADAR (قدر). *Lit.* "Measuring." (1) The word generally used in the Ḥadīs̤ for fate, or predestination. (2) *Al-Qadar*, the title of the XCVIIth Sūrah of the Qur'ān. [TAQDIR, PREDESTINATION.]

QADARĪYAH (قدرية). A sect of Muḥammadans who deny absolute predestination and believe in the power (*qadr*) of man's free will. They were the ancient Mu'tazilahs before al-Wāṣil separated from the school of Ḥasan al-Baṣrī.

QADĪM (قديم). "Ancient; old." *Al-Qadīm*, "The one without beginning." *Qadīmu 'l-Aiyām*, "Ancient of days." God.

AL-QĀDIR (القادر). "The Powerful." One of the ninety-nine attributes of God. The word occurs in the Qur'ān, at Sūrah ii. 19, "God is *mighty* over all," and in many other passages.

QĀDIRĪYAH (قادرية). An ascetic order of Faqīrs instituted A.H. 561, by Saiyid 'Abdu 'l-Qādir al-Jilānī, surnamed Pīr Dastagīr, whose shrine is at Baghdād. It is the most popular religious order amongst the Sunnīs of Asia. [FAQIR, ZIKR.]

QĀF (قاف). (1) The twenty-first letter of the Arabic alphabet. (2) The title of the Lth Sūrah of the Qur'ān. (3) The circle of mountains which Easterns fancy encompass the world. The Muḥammadan belief being that they are inhabited by demons and jinn, and that the mountain range is of emerald which gives an azure hue to the sky. Hence in Persian *az qāf tā qāf* means the whole world. The name is also used for Mount Caucasus.

AL-QAHHAR (القهار). "The Dominant." One of the ninety-nine names of God. It occurs in the Qur'ān, Sūrah xiii. 17: "He is the One, the *Dominant*."

QĀ'IF (قائف). *Lit.* "Skilful in knowing footsteps." One who can judge of character from the outward appearance.

One instance of the kind is related in the Traditions, namely, 'Āyishah relates, "One day the Prophet came home in high spirits, and said, 'O 'Āyishah, verily Mujazziz al-Mudliji came and saw Usāmah and Zaid covered over with a cloth, except their feet; and he said, 'Verily, I know from these feet the relationship of father and son." (*Mishkāt*, book xiii. ch. xv. pt. 1.) This knowledge is called *'Ilmu 'l-Qiyāfah.*)

QAINUQĀ' (قينقاع). A Jewish tribe near al-Madīnah in the time of Muḥammad. He besieged them in their stronghold in the second year of the Hijrah, and, having conquered them, sent most of them into exile. (See Muir's *Life of Mahomet*, vol. iii. p. 134.)

QAIṢAR (قيصر). [CÆSAR.]

QAIS IBN SA'D (قيس بن سعد). One of the leading companions. He was of the tribe Khazraj and the son of Sa'd, a Companion of note. He was a man of large stature and corpulent, emiment for learning, wisdom, and courage. He commanded the Prophet's body-guard, and under the Khalīfah 'Alī he was made Governor of Egypt. Died at al-Madīnah, A.H. 60.

AL-QAIYŪM (القيوم). "The Self-Subsisting." One of the ninety-nine attributes of God. It occurs in the Qur'ān, Sūrah iii. 1: "There is no deity but God, the living, the self-subsisting."

QALAM (قلم). *Lit.* "A (reed) pen." (1) The pen with which God is said to have pre-recorded the actions of men. The Prophet said the first thing which God created was the *Pen* (*qalam*), and that it wrote down the quantity of every individual thing to be created, all that was and all that will be to all eternity. (See *Mishkāt.*) (2) *Al-Qalam*, the title of the LXVIIIth Sūrah of the Qur'ān.

QALANDAR (قلندر). A Persian title to an order of faqīrs or darwīshes. An Ascetic.

AL-QAMAR (القمر). "The moon." The title of the LIVth Sūrah of the Qur'ān, in the first verse of which the word occurs. "And the moon hath been split in sunder." [MOON, SHAQQU 'L-QAMAR.]

QANĀ'AH (قناعة). Contentment; resignation.

QĀNIT (قانت). *Lit.* "One who stands in prayer or in the service of God. Godly, devout, prayerful. The term is used twice in the Qur'ān:—

Sūrah xvi. 121: "Verily, Abraham was a leader in religion and obedient to God."

Sūrah xxxix. 12: "He who observeth the hours of the night in devotion."

QĀNŪN (قانون). Κάνων. Canon; a rule, a regulation, a law, a statute.

QARĀBAH (قرابة). *Lit.* "Proximity." A legal term in Muḥammadan law for relationship.

QĀRI' (قارى), pl. *qurrā'*. "A reader." A term used for one who reads the Qur'ān correctly, and is acqnainted with the *'Ilmu 't-Tajwīd*, or the science of reading the Qur'ān. In the history of Islām there are *seven* celebrated *Qurrā'*, or "readers," who are known as *al-Qurrā'u 's-Sab'ah*, or "the seven readers." They are—

1. Imām Ibn Kas̤īr. Died at Makkah, A.H. 120.

2. Imām 'Āsim of al-Kūfah, who learnt the way of reading the Qur'ān from 'Abdu 'r-Raḥmān as-Salāmī, who was taught by the Khalīfahs 'Us̤mān and 'Alī. He died at al-Kūfah, A.H. 127.

3. Imām Abū 'Umr was born at Makkah, A.H. 70, and died at al-Kūfah, A.H. 154. It is on his authority that the following important statement has been handed down: "When the first copy of the Qur'ān was written out

and presented to the Khalīfah 'Usmān, he said, 'There are faults of language in it; let the Arabs of the desert rectify them with their tongues." The meaning of this is that they should pronounce the words correctly but not alter the written copy.

4. Imām Ḥamzah of al-Kūfah was born A.H. 80, and died A.H. 156.

5. Imām al-Kisā'ī who had a great reputation as a Qāri', but none as a poet. It was a common saying, among the learned in grammar, that there was no one who knew so little poetry as al-Kisā'ī. He is said to have died at Ṭūs about the year A.H. 182.

6. Imām Nāfi', a native of al-Madīnah, who died A.H. 169.

7. Imām Ibn 'Āmir, who was a native of Syria. His date is uncertain.

AL-QĀRI'AH (القارعة). "The Striking." The title of the CIst Sūrah of the Qur'ān, which begins with the words, "The Striking! What is the Striking? And what shall make thee understand how terrible the striking will be."

Jalālu 'd-dīn says it is one of the epithets given to the last day, because it will *strike* the hearts of all creatures with terror.

QARĪN (قرين). *Lit.* "The one united." The demon which is said to be indissolubly united with every man. (See *Mishkāt*, book xiii. ch. xv.; also Qur'ān, Sūrah xli. 24; Sūrah xliii. 35; Sūrah l. 22.)

QARĪNAH (قرينة). The context. A term used in theological and exegetical works.

QĀRŪN (قارون). [KORAH.]

QARẒ (قرض). *Lit.* "Cutting." (1) A word used in the Qur'ān for good deeds done for God, for which a future recompense will be awarded, *e.g.* Sūrah v. 15: "Lend God a *liberal loan* and I will surely put away from you your evil deeds, and will cause you to enter gardens through which rivers flow."

(2) Money advanced as a loan without interest, to be repaid at the pleasure of the borrower.

(3) The word is used in Persian, Urdū, and Pushtoo for money lent at interest, but the legal term for such a debt is *ribā*.

QASAM (قسم). [OATH.]

QASĀMAH (قسامة). *Lit.* "Taking an oath." An oath under the following circumstances:—

When a person is found slain in a place, and it is not known who was the murderer, and his heirs demand satisfaction for his blood from the inhabitants of the district, then fifty of the inhabitants selected by the next of kin, must be put to their oaths and depose to this effect: "I swear by God that I did not kill him, nor do I know the murderer."

This custom is founded upon the Mosaic law. See Deut. xxi. 1–9.

AL-QAṢAṢ (القصص). "The narrative." The title of the XXVIIIth Sūrah of the Qur'ān. So called because in the 25th verse of this chapter Moses is said to have related the *narrative* of his adventures to Shu'aib.

QASM (قسم). *Lit.* "To divide." A division of conjugal rights, which is enjoined by the Muslim law. (See *Mishkāt*, book xiii. ch. x.)

AL-QAṢWĀ' (القصواء). *Lit.* "One whose ears are cropt." Muḥammad's celebrated she-camel who conveyed him in the flight from Makkah.

QATL (قتل). [MURDER.]

QATTĀT (قتات). A slanderer. A tale-bearer, who, according to the Traditions, will not enter the kingdom of heaven; for the Prophet has said, "A tale-bearer shall not enter Paradise." (*Mishkāt*, book xxii. ch. x. pt. 1.)

QAṬ'U 'Ṭ-ṬARĪQ (قطع الطريق). [HIGHWAY ROBBERY.]

QAUL (قول). A saying; a promise; a covenant. The word occurs in the Qur'ān frequently in these senses.

QAULU 'L-ḤAQQ (قول الحق). "The Word of Truth." A title given to Jesus Christ in the Qur'ān, Surah xix. 35: "This was Jesus the son of Mary, *the word of truth* concerning whom they doubt." By the commentators Ḥusain, al-Kamālān, and 'Abdu 'l-Qādir, the words are understood to refer to the statement made, but al-Baiẓāwī says it is a title applied to Jesus the son of Mary. [JESUS CHRIST.]

QAWAD (قود). "Retaliation." *Lex talionis.* [MURDER, QISAS, RETALIATION.]

AL-QAWĪ (قوى). "The Strong." One of the ninety-nine attributes of God. It occurs in the Qur'ān, Sūrah xi. 69: "Thy Lord is *the Strong*, the Mighty."

QAẒĀ' (قضاء), pl. *aqẓiyah*. *Lit.* "Consummating." (1) The office of a Qāẓī, or judge. (2) The sentence of a Qāẓī. (3) Repeating prayers to make up for having omitted them at the appointed time. (4) Making up for an omission in religious duties, such as fasting, &c. (5) The decree existing in the Divine mind from all eternity, and the execution and declaration of a decree at the appointed time. (6) Sudden death.

QAẒF (قذف). *Lit.* "Throwing at." Accusing a virtuous man or woman of adultery; the punishment for which is eighty lashes, or, in the case of a slave, forty lashes. This punishment was established by a supposed revelation from heaven, when the Prophet's favourite wife, 'Āyishah, was accused of improper intimacy with Ṣafwān Ibnu 'l-Mu'aṭṭil. *Vide* Qur'ān, Sūratu 'n-Nūr (xxiv.), 4: "But to those who accuse married persons of adultery and produce not four witnesses, them shall ye scourge with four-score stripes." (*Hidāyah*, vol. ii. p. 58.)

QIBLAH (قبلة). "Anything opposite." The direction in which all Muḥammadans must pray, whether in their public or in their private devotions, namely, towards Makkah. It is established by the express injunction of the Qur'ān, contained in the Sūratu l-Baqarah (ii.), 136–145:—

"Fools among men will say, What has turned them from their Qiblah on which they were agreed? Say, God's is the east and the west, He guides whom He will unto the right path. Thus have we made you a middle nation to be witnesses against men, and that the apostle may be a witness against you. We have not appointed the qiblah on which thou wert agreed, save that we might know who follows the Apostle from him who turns upon his heels, although it is a great thing save to those whom God doth guide. But God will not waste your faith, for verily God with men is kind and merciful. We see thee often turn about thy face in the heavens, but we will surely turn thee to a qiblah thou shalt like. Turn, then, thy face towards the Sacred Mosque, wherever ye be turn your faces towards it, for verily those who have the Book know that it is the truth from their Lord. God is not careless of that which ye do. And if thou shouldst bring to those who have been given the Book every sign, they would not follow your qiblah, nor do some of them follow the qiblah of the others; and if thou followest their lusts after the knowledge that has come to thee, then art thou of the evil-doers. Those whom we have given the Book know him as they know their sons, although a sect of them do surely hide the truth the while they know. The truth (is) from thy Lord, be not therefore one of those who doubt thereof. Every sect has some one side to which they turn (in prayer), but do ye hasten onwards to good works, wherever ye are, God will bring you all together. Verily, God is mighty over all. From whencesoever thou comest forth, there turn thy face towards the Sacred Mosque; for it is surely truth from thy Lord, God is not careless about what ye do. And from whencesoever thou comest forth, there turn thy face towards the Sacred Mosque, and wheresoever ye are, turn your faces towards it, that men may have no argument against you, save only those of them who are unjust, and fear them not, but fear me, and I will fulfil my favour to you; perchance ye may be guided yet."

In explanation of these verses (which are allowed to be of different periods), and the change of Qiblah, al-Baiẓāwī, the commentator, remarks that when Muḥammad was in Makkah he always worshipped towards the Ka'bah; but after the flight to al-Madīnah, he was ordered by God to change his Qiblah towards *aṣ-Ṣakhrah*, the rock at Jerusalem on which the Temple was formerly erected, in order to conciliate the Jews, but that, about sixteen months after his arrival in al-Madīnah, Muḥammad longed once more to pray towards Makkah, and he besought the Lord to this effect, and then the instructions were revealed, "Verily we have seen thee turning thy face," &c., as given above. (See *al-Baiẓāwī, in loco.*)

This temporary change of the Qiblah to Jerusalem is now regarded as "a trial of faith," and it is asserted that Makkah was always the true Qiblah. But it is impossible for any non-Muslim not to see in this transaction a piece of worldly wisdom on the part of the Prophet.

Jalālu 'd-dīn as-Suyūṭī admits that the 110th verse of the IInd Sūrah—which reads: "The east and the west is God's, therefore whichever way ye turn is the face of God"—has been abrogated by a more recent verse, and that at one time in the history of Muḥammad's mission there was no Qiblah at all.

Major Osborne remarks in his *Islām under the Arabs*, p. 58:—

"There have been few incidents more disastrous in their consequences to the human race than this decree of Muhammad, changing the Kibla from Jerusalem to Mekka. Had he remained true to his earlier and better faith, the Arabs would have entered the religious community of the nations as peace-makers, not as enemies and destroyers. To all alike—Jews, Christians, and Muhammadans—there would have been a single centre of holiness and devotion; but the Arab would have brought with him just that element of conviction which was needed to enlarge and vivify the preceding religions. To the Jew he would have been a living witness that the God who spake in times past to his fathers by the prophets still sent messengers to men, though not taken from the chosen seeds—the very testimony which they needed to rise out of the conception of a national deity to that of a God of all men.

"To the Christians, his deep and ardent conviction of God as a present living and working power, would have been a voice recalling them from their petty sectarian squabbles and virtual idolatry, to the presence of the living Christ. By the change of the Kibla, Islam was placed in direct antagonism to Judaism and Christianity. It became a rival faith, possessing an independent centre of existence. It ceased to draw its authenticity from the same wells of inspiration. Jew and Christian could learn nothing from a creed which they knew only as an exterminator; and the Muhammadan was condemned to a moral and intellectual isolation. And so long as he remains true to his creed, he cannot participate in the onward march of men. The keystone of that creed is a black pebble in a heathen temple. All the ordinances of his faith, all the history of it, are so grouped round and connected with this stone, that were the odour of sanctity dispelled which surrounds it, the whole religion would inevitably perish. The farther and the faster men progress elsewhere, the more hopeless becomes the position of the Muslim. He can only hate the knowledge which would gently lead him to the light. Chained to a black stone in a barren wilderness, the heart and reason of the Muhammadan world would seem to have taken the similitude of the objects they reverence; and the refreshing dews and genial sunshines which fertilise all else, seek in vain for anything to quicken there." (*Islam under the Arabs*, p. 58.)

QIBṬĪ (قبطى). Copt. The Christian descendants of the Ancient Egyptians, derived from Coptos, a great city in Upper Egypt now called Gooft. The favourite slave of Muḥammad, Māriyah, was a Copt, and is known in Muslim history as Māriyatu 'l-Qibṭīyah. [MUHAMMAD, WIVES OF.]

For an account of the manners and customs of the Coptic Christians, see Lane's *Modern Egyptians*.

QIMĀR (قمار). Dice or any game at chance. It is forbidden by the Muhammadan religion. (*Mishkāt*, book xvii. ch. ii. pt. 2.)

QINN (قن). A slave, especially one born in the family and whose father and mother are slaves.

QINṬĀR (قنطار). A talent. A sum of money mentioned in the Qur'ān, Sūrah ii. 67: "And of the people of the Book there are some of them who if thou entrust them with *a qinṭār* give it back to you."

Muḥammad Ṭāhir, the author of the *Majma'u 'l-Biḥār*, p. 173, says a *qinṭār* is a very large sum of money. As much gold as will go into the hide of a cow! or, according to others, 4,000 dinārs. Others say it is an unlimited sum, which implies a considerable amount of money.

QIRĀ'AH (قراءة). *Lit.* "Reading." A term given to the different methods of reading the Qur'ān. A science which is termed *'Ilmu 't-Tajwīd*. [QUR'AN.]

QIRĀN (قران). *Lit.* "Conjunction." (1) The conjunction of two planets. (2) The performance of the Ḥajj and the 'Umrah at the same time.

QIṢĀṢ (قصاص). From *qaṣaṣ*. *Lit.* "Tracking the footsteps of an enemy." The law of retaliation. The *lex talionis* of the Mosaic law, with the important difference that in the Muslim law the next of kin can accept a money compensation for wilful murder.

The subject of retaliation must be considered, first, as to occasions affecting life, and, secondly, as to retaliation in matters short of life.

(1) In occasions affecting life, retaliation is incurred by wilfully killing a person whose blood is under continual protection, such as a Muslim or a Z̤immī, in opposition to aliens who have only an occasional or temporary protection. A freeman is to be slain for a freeman, and a slave for a slave; but according t. Abū Ḥanīfah, a freeman is to be slain for the murder of a slave *if the slave be the property of another*. A Muslim is also slain for the murder of a z̤immī, according to Abū Ḥanīfah, but ash-Shāfi'ī disputes this, because the Prophet said a Muslim is not to be put to death for an infidel. A man is slain for a woman, an adult for an infant, and a sound person for one who is blind, infirm, dismembered, lame, or insane. A father is not to be slain for his child, because the Prophet has said, "Retaliation must not be executed upon the parent for his offspring"; but a child is slain for the murder of his parent. A master is not slain for his slave, and if one of two partners in a slave kill such a slave, retaliation is not incurred. If a person inherit the right of retaliating upon his parent, the retaliation fails. Retaliation is to be executed by the next of kin with some mortal weapon or sharp instrument capable of inflicting a mortal wound.

If a person immerse another, whether an infant or an adult, into water from which it is impossible to escape, retaliation, according to Abū Ḥanīfah, is not incurred, but his two disciples maintain otherwise.

(2) *Of retaliation short of life.* If a person wilfully strike off the hand of another, his hand is to be struck off in return, because it is said in the Qur'ān (Sūrah v. 49), "There is retaliation in case of wounds." If a person strike off the foot of another, or cut off the nose, retaliation is inflicted in return. If a person strike another on the eye, so as to force the member, with its vessels, out of the socket, there is no retaliation; it is impossible to preserve a perfect equality in extracting an eye. If, on the contrary, the eye remain in its place, but the faculty of seeing be destroyed, retaliation is to be inflicted, as in this case equality may be effected by extinguishing the sight of the offender's corresponding eye with a hot iron. If a person strike out the teeth of another, he incurs retaliation; for it is said in the Qur'ān, "A tooth for a tooth." (Sūrah v. 49.)

Retaliation is not to be inflicted in the case of breaking any bones except teeth, because it is impossible to observe an equality in other fractures. There is no retaliation, in offences short of life, between a man and a woman, a free person and a slave, or one slave and another slave; but ash-Shāfi'ī maintains that retaliation holds in these cases. Retaliation for parts of the body holds between a Muslim and an unbeliever, both being upon an equality between each other with respect to fines for the offences in question.

If the corresponding member of the maimer be defective, nothing more than retaliation on that defective member, or a fine; and if such member be in the meantime lost, nothing whatever is due.

There is no retaliation for the tongue or the virile member.

(3) *Retaliation may be commuted for a sum of money.* When the heirs of a murdered person enter into a composition with the murderer for a certain sum, retaliation is remitted, and the sum agreed to is due, to whatever amount. This is founded upon an express injunction of the Qur'ān: "Where the heir of the murdered person is offered anything, by way of compensation, out of

the property of the murderer, let him take it." And also in the Traditions, it is related that Muḥammad said (*Mishkāt*, book xiv.): "The heir of the murdered person is at liberty either to take retaliation, or a fine with the murderer's consent." Moreover, it is maintained by Muḥammadan jurists that retaliation is purely a matter which rests with the next of kin, who are at liberty to remit entirely by pardon, and that therefore a compensation can be accepted which is advantageous to the heirs and also to the murderer.

When a person who has incurred retaliation dies, the right to retaliation necessarily ceases, and consequently no fine is due from the murderer's estate. [MURDER.]

QISSĪS (قسيس). Persian *kashīsh*. A Christian presbyter or priest. The word occurs once in the Qur'ān, Sūrah v. 85: "Thou shalt certainly find those to be nearest in affection to them who say, 'We are Christians.' This because some of them are priests (*qissīsūn*) and monks (*ruhbān*), and because they are free from pride."

QIṬFĪR (قطفير). Potiphar. Alluded to in the Qur'ān, Sūrah xii. 21, as "the man from Egypt who had bought him" (Joseph). Al-Baiẓāwī, the commentator, says his name was Qiṭfīr.

QIYĀM (قيام). *Lit.* "Standing." (1) The standing in the Muḥammadan prayers when the *Subḥān*, the *Ta'awwuz*, the *Tasmiyah*, the *Fātiḥah*, and certain portions of the Qur'ān, are recited. [PRAYER.] (2) *Yaumu 'l-Qiyām*, the Day of Judgment.

AL-QIYĀMAH (القيامة). *Lit.* "The Standing up. (1) The Day of Resurrection. [RESURRECTION.] (2) The title of the LXXVth Sūrah of the Qur'ān. (3) The Ṣūfīs use the term in a spiritual sense for the state of a man who, having counted himself dead to the world, "stands up" in a new life in God. (See 'Abdu 'r-Razzāq's *Dict. of Ṣūfī Terms.*)

QIYĀS (قياس). *Lit.* "To compare." The fourth foundation of Islām, that is to say, the anological reasoning of the learned with regard to the teaching of the Qur'ān, Ḥadīs, and Ijmā'.

There are four conditions of *Qiyās*: (1) That the precept or practice upon which it is founded must be of common (*'āmm*) and not of special (*khāṣṣ*) application; (2) The cause (*'illah*) of the injunction must be known and understood; (3) The decision must be based upon either the Qur'ān, the Ḥadīs, or the Ijmā'; (4) The decision arrived at must not be contrary to anything declared elsewhere in the Qur'ān and Ḥadīs.

Qiyās is of two kinds, *Qiyās-i-Jalī*, or evident, and *Qiyās-i-Khafī*, or hidden.

An example of *Qiyās-i-Jalī* is as follows: Wine is forbidden in the Qur'ān under the word *khamr*, which literally means anything intoxicating; it is, therefore, evident that opium and all intoxicating drugs are also forbidden.

Qiyās-i-Khafī is seen in the following example:—In the Ḥadīs it is enjoined that one goat in forty must be given to God. To some poor persons the money may be more acceptable; therefore, the value of the goat may be given instead of the goat.

QUBĀ' (قباء). A place three miles from al-Madīnah, where the Prophet's she-camel, al-Qaṣwā' knelt down as she brought her master on his flight from Makkah, and where Muḥammad laid the foundations of a mosque. This was the first place of public prayer in Islām. Muḥammad laid the first brick with his javelin, and marked out the direction of prayer. It is this mosque which is mentioned in the Qur'ān, Sūrah ix. 109:—"There is a mosque founded from its first day in piety. More worthy is it that thou enter therein: therein are men who aspire to purity, and God loveth the purified."

It is esteemed the fourth mosque in rank, being next to that of Makkah, al-Madīnah, and Jerusalem, and tradition relates that the Prophet said one prayer in it was equal to a a lesser pilgrimage to Makkah. [UMRAH.] Captain Burton says:—

"It was originally a square building of very small size; Osman enlarged it in the direction of the minaret, making it sixty-six cubits each way. It is no longer 'mean and decayed' as in Burckhardt's time. The Sultan Abdel Hamid, father of Mahmud, created a neat structure of cut stone, whose crenelles make it look more like a place of defence than of prayer. It has, however, no pretensions to grandeur. The minaret is of Turkish shape. To the south, a small and narrow Riwak (*riwāq*), or raised hypo-style, with unpretending columns, looks out northwards upon a little open area simply sanded over: and this is the whole building."

AL-QUDDŪS (القدوس). "The Holy." One of the ninety-nine names of God. It occurs in the Qur'ān, Sūrah lix. 23: "He is God beside whom there is no deity, the King, *the Holy*."

QUDRAH (قدرة). Power. Omnipotence. One of the attributes of God. *al-Qudratu 'l-ḥalwā'*, The sweet cake of God, *i.e.* The manna of Israel. The word *Qudrah* does not occur in the Qur'ān.

QUNŪTU 'L-WITR (قنوت الوتر). A special supplication said after the *Witr* prayers, or, according to some, after the morning prayers. It was at such times that the Prophet would pray for the liberation of his friends and for the destruction of his enemies.

For the different forms of supplication, see *Mishkāt*, book iv. chapters xxxvi. and xxxvii

The following is the one usually recited. "O God! direct me amongst those to whom Thou hast shown the right road, and keep me in safety from the calamities of this world and the next, and love me amongst those Thou hast befriended. Increase Thy favours on me, and preserve me from ill; for verily Thou canst order at Thy will, and canst not be ordered. Verily none are ruined that Thou befriendest, nor are any made great with whom Thou art at enmity."

QURAISH (قريش). The Arabian tribe from which Muḥammad was descended, and of which his grandfather, 'Abdu 'l-Muṭṭalib was chief or prince. This tribe occupies a very prominent place in the Qur'ān and in Muḥammadan history. In the Traditions, a special section is set apart for a record of the sayings of the Prophet regarding the good qualities of this tribe.

Muḥammad is related to have said: "Whosoever wishes for the destruction of the Quraish, him may God destroy."

Ibn 'Umar relates that the Prophet said, "The office of Khalīfah should be in the Quraish as long as there are two persons left in the tribe, one to be ruler and the other to be ruled." (*Mishkāt*, book xxiv. c. xii.)

The Sharīf, or Sheriff of Makkah, is always of the Quraish tribe, but ever since the extinction of the Abbaside Khalīfahs, the Sultāns of Turkey have held the office of Khalīfah, who are not of this tribe. [KHALIFAH.]

For an account of the Quraish, refer to Sir William Muir's *Life of Mahomet*, vol. i. Intro. cxcv. See also article ARABIA.

Muḥammad Ṭāhir, in his *Majma'u 'l-Biḥār*, vol. ii., p. 133, says *Quraish* is the name of a great marine monster which preys on fish, and was given to this tribe on account of its strength and importance amongst the tribes of Arabia. *Quraish* is the title of the CVIth Sūrah of the Qur'ān.

QURAIẒAH (قريظة). A tribe of Jews located near al-Madīnah in the time of Muḥammad. They at first professed to support his mission, but afterwards became disaffected. The Prophet asserted that he had been commanded by God to destroy them, and a complete massacre of the men took place, and the women and children were taken captive. The event is referred to at length in the XXXIIIrd Sūrah of the Qur'ān.

Sir William Muir thus records the event:—

"The men and women were penned up for the night in separate yards; they were supplied with dates, and spent the night in prayer, repeating passages from their Scriptures, and exhorting one another in constancy. During the night graves or trenches sufficient to contain the dead bodies of the men were dug in the chief market-place of the city. When these were ready in the morning, Mahomet, himself a spectator of the tragedy, gave command that the captives should be brought forth in companies of five or six at a time. Each company was made to sit down by the brink of the trench destined for its grave, and there beheaded. Party after party they were thus led out, and butchered in cold blood, till the whole were slain. One woman alone was put to death. It was she who threw the millstone from the battlements. For Zoheir, an aged Jew, who had saved some of his allies of the Bani Aus in the battle of Boâth, Thâbit interceded and procured a pardon, including the freedom of his family and restoration of his property. 'But what hath become of all our chiefs,—of Kâb, of Huwey, of Ozzâl, the son of Samuel?' asked the old man. As one after another he named the leading chiefs of his tribe, he received to each inquiry the same reply,—they had all been slain already. 'Then of what use is life to me any longer? Leave me not to that bloodthirsty man who has killed all that are dear to me in cold blood. But slay me also, I entreat thee. Here, take my sword, it is sharp; strike high and hard.' Thâbit refused, and gave him over to another, who, under Ali's orders, beheaded the aged man, but attended to his last request in obtaining freedom for his family. When Mahomet was told of his saying, 'Slay me also, that I may go to my home and join those that have preceded me,' he answered, 'Yea, he shall join them in the fire of hell?'

"Having sated his revenge, and drenched the market-place with the blood of eight hundred victims, and having given command for the earth to be smoothed over their remains, Mahomet returned from the horrid spectacle to solace himself with the charms of Rîhâna, whose husband and all whose male relatives had just perished in the massacre. He invited her to be his wife, but she declined, and chose to remain (as, indeed, having refused marriage, she had no alternative) his slave or concubine. She also declined the summons to conversion, and continued in the Jewish faith, at which the Prophet was much concerned. It is said, however, that she afterwards embraced Islâm. She lived with Mahomet till his death.

"The booty was divided into four classes—lands, chattels, cattle, and slaves; and Mahomet took a fifth of each. There were (besides little children who counted with their mothers) a thousand captives; from his share of these, Mahomet made certain presents to his friends of slave girls and female servants. The rest of the women and children he sent to be sold among the Bedouin tribes of Najd, in exchange for horses and arms; for he kept steadily in view the advantage of raising around him a body of efficient horse." (*Life of Mahomet*, vol. iii. p. 276.)

QUR'ĀN (قران). The sacred book of the Muḥammadans, and believed by them to be the inspired word of God. It is written in the Arabic language.

The word *Qur'ān* is derived from the Arabic *Qara'*, which occurs at the commencement of Sūrah xcv., which is said to have been the first chapter revealed to Muḥammad, and has the same meaning as the Heb. קְרָא *kārā*, "to read," or "to recite," which is frequently used in Jeremiah xxxvi., as well as in other places in the Old Testament. It is, therefore, equivalent to the Heb. מִקְרָא *mikrā*, rendered in Nehemiah viii. 8, "the reading." It is the title given to the Muḥammadan Scriptures which are usually appealed to and quoted from as *al-Qur'ān al-Majīd*, the "Glorious Qur'ān"; *al-Qur'ān ash-Sharīf*, the "Noble Qur'ān"; and is also called the *Fūrqān*, "Distinguisher"; *Kalāmu 'llāh*, the "Word of God"; and *al-Kitāb*, "the Book."

According to Jalālu 'd-dīn as-Suyūṭī, in his *Itqān*, p. 117, the Qur'ān is distinguished in the text of the book by the following fifty-five special titles:—

1.	*Al-Kitāb*	The Book.
2.	*Al-Mubīn*	The Enlightener.
3.	*Al-Qur'ān*	The Reading.
4.	*Al-Karīm*	The Good.
5.	*Al-Kalām*	The Word.
6.	*Al-Burhān*	The Proof.
7.	*An-Nūr*	The Light.
8.	*Al-Hudā*	The Guidance.
9.	*Ar-Raḥmah*	The Mercy.
10.	*Al-Furqān*	The Distinguisher.
11.	*Ash-Shifā'*	The Health.
12.	*Al-Mu'iẓah*	The Sermon.
13.	*Az-Zikr*	The Reminder.
14.	*Al-Mubārak*	The Blessed.
15.	*Al-'Alī*	The Lofty.
16.	*Al-Ḥikmah*	The Wisdom.
17.	*Al-Ḥakīm*	The Philosopher.
18.	*Al-Muhaimin*	The Preserver.
19.	*Al-Muṣaddiq*	The Establisher of Truth.
20.	*Al-Ḥabl*	The Rope.
21.	*Aṣ-Ṣirāṭu 'l-Mustaqīm.*	The Straight Path.
22.	*Al-Qaiyim*	The Strong.
23.	*Al-Qaulu 'l-Faṣl*	The Distinguishing Speech.
24.	*An-Naba'u 'l-'Aẓīm.*	The Exalted News.
25.	*Al-Ḥasanu 'l-Ḥadīṣ.*	The Good Saying.
26.	*Al-Maṣānī*	The Repetition.
27.	*Al-Mutashābih*	The Uniform.
28.	*At-Tanzil*	The Revelation.
29.	*Ar-Rūḥ*	The Spirit.
30.	*Al-Waḥy*	The Inspiration.
31.	*Al-'Arabī*	The Arabic
32.	*Al-Baṣā'ir*	The Enlightenment.
33.	*Al-Bayān*	The Explanation.
34.	*Al-'Ilm*	The Knowledge.
35.	*Al-Ḥaqq*	The Truth.
36.	*Al-Hādī*	The Guide.
37.	*Al-'Ajab*	The Wonderful.
38.	*At-Tazkirah*	The Exhortation.
39.	*Al-'Urwatu 'l-Wuṣqā.*	The Firm Handle.
40.	*Aṣ-Ṣidq*	The Righteous.
41.	*Al-'Adl*	The Justice.
42.	*Al-Amr*	The Order.
43.	*Al-Munādī*	The Preacher.
44.	*Al-Bushrā*	The Glad Tidings.
45.	*Al-Majīd*	The Exalted.
46	*Az-Zabūr*	The Psalm.
47.	*Al-Bashīr*	The Herald of Glad Tidings.
48.	*An-Naẓīr*	The Warner.
49.	*Al-'Azīz*	The Mighty.
50.	*Al-Balāgh*	The Message.
51.	*Al-Qaṣaṣ*	The Narrative.
52.	*As-Ṣuḥuf*	The Pamphlets.
53.	*Al-Mukarramah*	The Excellent.
54.	*Al-Marfū'ah*	The Exalted.
55.	*Al-Muṭaharah*	The Purified.

I.—The Inspiration of the Qur'ān.

According to Abū Ḥanīfah, the great Sunnī Imām, the Qur'ān is eternal in its original essence. He says, "The Qur'ān is the Word of God, and is His inspired Word and Revelation. It is a necessary attribute (*ṣifah*) of God. It is not God, but still it is inseparable from God. It is written in a volume, it is read in a language, it is remembered in the heart, and its letters and its vowel points, and its writing are all created, for these are the works of man, but *God's word is uncreated* (*ghairu 'l-makhlūq*). Its words, its writing, its letters, and its verses, are for the necessities of man, for its meaning is arrived at by their use, but the Word of God is fixed in the essence (*zāt*) of God, and he who says that the word of God is created is an infidel." (See *Kitābu 'l-Waṣīyah*, p. 77.)

Muḥammadans believe the Qur'ān to have been written by "the hands of noble, righteous scribes," mentioned in the Sūratu 'Abasa (lxxx.) 15, and to have been sent down to the lowest heaven complete, from whence it was revealed from time to time to the Prophet by the angel Gabriel. [GABRIEL.]

There is, however, only one distinct assertion in the Qur'ān of Gabriel having been the medium of inspiration, namely, Sūratu 'l-Baqarah (ii.), 91; and this occurs in a Medinah Sūrah revealed about seven years after the Prophet's rule had been established. In the Sūratu 'sh-Shu'arā' (xxvi.), 193, the Qur'ān is said to have been given by the *Rūhu 'l-Amīn*, or "Faithful Spirit"; and in the Sūratu 'n-Najm (liii.), 5, Muḥammad claims to have been taught by the *Shadīdu 'l-Quwā*, or "One terrible in power"; and in the Traditions the agent of inspiration is generally spoken of as "an angel" (*malak*). It is, therefore, not quite certain through what agency Muḥammad believed himself to be inspired of God, the Holy Spirit or the angel Gabriel.

According to the traditions, the revelation was first communicated in dreams. 'Āyishah, one of the Prophet's wives, relates (*Mishkāt*, xxiv. 5):—

"The first revelations which the Prophet received were in true dreams; and he never dreamt but it came to pass as regularly as the dawn of day. After this the Prophet was fond of retirement, and used to seclude himself in a cave in Mount Ḥirā' and worship there day and night. He would, whenever he wished, return to his family at Makkah, and then go back again, taking with him the necessaries of life. Thus he continued to return to Khadījah from time to time, until one day the revelation came down to him, and the angel (Arabic *malak*, Heb. *malakh*, "an angel; a prophet"; a name of office, not of nature [See Wilson's Hebrew Lexicon, p. 13]) came to him and said, 'Read' (*iqra'*); but the Prophet said, 'I am not a reader.' And the Prophet related that he (*i.e.* the angel) took hold of me and squeezed me as much as I could bear, and he then let me go and said again, 'Read!' And I said, 'I am not a reader.' Then he took hold of me a second time, and squeezed me as much as I could bear, and then let me go, and said, 'Read!' And I said, 'I am not a reader.' Then he took hold of me a third time and squeezed me as much as I could bear, and said:—

"'Read! in the name of Thy Lord who created;
Created man from a clot of blood in the womb.
Read! for thy Lord is the most beneficent,
He hath taught men the use of the pen;
He hath taught man that which he knoweth not.'

(*These are the first five verses of the* XCVIth *Sūrah of the Qur'ān. The other verses of the Sūrah being of a later date.*)

"Then the Prophet repeated the words himself, and with his heart trembling he returned (*i.e.* from Ḥirā' to Makkah) to Khadījah, and said, 'Wrap me up, wrap me up.' And they wrapped him up in a garment till his fear was dispelled, and he told Khadījah what had passed, and he said: 'Verily, I was afraid I should have died.' Then Khadījah said, 'No, it will not be so. I swear by God, He will never make you melancholy or sad. For verily you are kind to your relatives, you speak the truth, you are faithful in trust, you bear the afflictions of the people, you spend in good works what you gain in trade, you are hospitable, and you assist your fellow men.' After this Khadījah took the Prophet to Waraqah, who was the son of her uncle, and she said to him, 'O son of my uncle! hear what your brother's son says.' Then Waraqah said to the Prophet, 'O son of my brother! what do you see?' Then the Prophet told Waraqah what he saw, and Waraqah said, 'That is the Nāmūs [NAMUS] which God sent to Moses.' 'Āyishah also relates that Ḥāris̤ ibn Hishām asked the Prophet, 'How did the revelation come to you?' and the Prophet said, 'Sometimes like the noise of a bell, and sometimes the angel would come and converse with me in the shape of a man.'"

According to 'Āyishah's statement, the Sūratu 'l-'Alaq (xcvi.) was the first portion of the Qur'ān revealed; but it is more probable that the poetical Sūrahs, in which there is no express declaration of the prophetic office, or of a divine commission, were composed at an earlier period. Internal evidence would assign the earliest date to the Sūrahs az-Zalzalah (xcix.), al-'Aṣr (ciii.), al-'Ādiyāt (c.), and al-Fātiḥah (i.), which are rather the utterances of a searcher after truth than of an Apostle of God.

Although the Qur'ān now appears as one book, the Muslim admits that it was not all made known to the Prophet in one and the same manner.

Mr. Sell, in his *Faith of Islām*, quoting from the *Mudāriju 'n-Nubūwah*, p. 509, gives the following as some of the modes of inspiration:—

"1. It is recorded on the authority of 'A'yesha, one of Muhammad's wives, that a brightness like the brightness of the morning came upon the Prophet. According to some commentators, this brightness remained six months. In some mysterious way Gabriel, through this brightness or vision, made known the will of God.

"2. Gabriel appeared in the form of Dahiah (Daḥyah), one of the Companions of the Prophet, renowned for his beauty and gracefulness. A learned dispute has arisen with regard to the abode of the soul of Gabriel when he assumed the bodily form of Dahiah. At times, the angelic nature of Gabriel overcame Muhammad, who was then translated to the world of angels. This always happened when the revelation was one of bad news, such as denunciations or predictions of woe. At other times, when the message brought by Gabriel was one of consolation and comfort, the human nature of the Prophet overcame the angelic nature of the angel, who, in such case, having assumed a human form, proceeded to deliver the message.

"3. The Prophet heard at times the noise of the tinkling of a bell. To him alone was known the meaning of the sound. He alone could distinguish in, and through it, the words which Gabriel wished him to understand. The effect of this mode of Wahí (*Waḥy*) was more marvellous than that of any of the other ways. When his ear caught the sound his whole frame became agitated On the coldest day, the perspiration, like beads of silver, would roll down his face. The glorious brightness of his countenance gave place to a ghastly hue, whilst the way in which he bent down his head showed the intensity of the emotion through which he was passing. If riding, the camel on which he sat would fall to the ground. The Prophet one day, when reclining with his head on the lap of Zeid, heard the well-known sound: Zeid, too, knew that something unusual was happening, for so heavy became the head of Muhammad that it was with the greatest difficulty he could support the weight.

"4. At the time of the Mi'ráj, or night ascent into heaven, God spoke to the Prophet without the intervention of an angel. It is a disputed point whether the face of the Lord was veiled or not.

"5. God sometimes appeared in a dream, and placing his hands on the Prophet's shoulders made known his will.

"6. Twice, angels having each six hundred wings, appeared and brought the message from God.

"7. Gabriel, though not appearing in bodily form, so inspired the heart of the Prophet, that the words he uttered under its influence were the words of God. This is technically called Ilka (Ilqā'), and is by some supposed to be the degree of inspiration to which the Traditions belong. (See *as-Suyūṭis Itqān*, p. 103.)

"Above all, the Prophet was not allowed to remain in any error; if, by any chance, he had made a wrong deduction from any previous revelation, another was always sent to rectify it. This idea has been worked up to a science of abrogation, according to which some verses of the Qurán abrogate others. Muhammad found it necessary to shift his stand-point more than once, and thus it became necessary to annul earlier portions of his revelation. [MANSUKH.]

"Thus in various ways was the revelation made known to Muhammad. At first there seems to have been a season of doubt, the dread lest after all it might be a mockery. But as years rolled on, confidence in himself and in his mission came. At times, too, there is a joyousness in his utterances as he swears by heaven and earth, by God and man; but more often the visions were weird and terrible. Tradition says:—"He roared like a camel, the sound as of bells well-nigh rent his heart in pieces." Some strange power moved him, his fear was uncontrollable. For twenty years or more the revelations came, a direction on things of heaven and of earth, to the Prophet as the spiritual guide of all men, to the Warrior-Chief, as the founder of political unity among the Arab tribes."

A SPECIMEN OF THE FIRST TWO PAGES OF A QUR'AN.

II.—The Collation of the Qur'ān.

The whole book was not arranged until after Muḥammad's death, but it is believed that the Prophet himself divided the Sūrahs [SURAH] and gave most of them their present titles, which are chosen from some word which occurs in the chapter. The following is the account of the collection and arrangement of the Qur'ān, as it stands at present, as given in traditions recorded by al-Bukhārī (see *Ṣaḥīḥu 'l-Bukhārī*, Arabic ed., p. 745.)

"Zaid ibn Ṣābit relates:—'Abu Bakr sent a person to me, and called me to him, at the time of the battle with the people of Yamāmah; and I went to him, and 'Umar was with him; and Abu Bakr said to me, "'Umar came to me and said, 'Verily a great many of the readers of the Qur'ān were slain on the day of the battle with the people of Yamāmah; and really I am afraid that if the slaughter should be great, much will be lost from the Qur'ān, because every person remembers something of it; and, verily, I see it advisable for you to order the Qur'ān to be collected into one book.' I said to 'Umar, 'How can I do a thing which the Prophet has not done?' He said, 'I swear by God, this collecting of the Qur'ān is a good thing.' And 'Umar used to be constantly returning to me and saying: 'You must collect the Qur'ān,' till at length God opened my breast so to do, and I saw what 'Umar had been advising.' And Zaid ibn Ṣābit says that, 'Abū Bakr said to me, "You are a young and sensible man, and I do not suspect you of forgetfulness, negligence, or perfidy; and, verily, you used to write for the Prophet his instructions from above; then look for the Qur'ān in every place and collect it.' I said, "I swear by God, that if people had ordered me to carry a mountain about from one place to another, it would not be heavier upon me than the order which Abū Bakr has given for collecting the Qur'ān." I said to Abū Bakr, "How do you do a thing which the Prophet of God did not?" He said, "By God, this collecting of the Qur'ān is a good act." And he used perpetually to return to me, until God put it into my heart to do the thing which the heart of Abu Bakr had been set upon. Then I sought for the Qur'ān, and collected it from the leaves of the date, and white stones, and the breasts of people that remembered it, till I found the last part of the chapter entitled *Tauba* (Repentance), with Abū Khuzaimah al-Anṣārī, and with no other person. These leaves were in the possession of Abū Bakr, until God caused him to die; after which 'Umar had them in his life-time; after that, they remained with his daughter, Ḥafṣah; after that, 'Uṣmān compiled them into one book.'

"Anas ibn Mālik relates: 'Huzaifah came to 'Uṣmān, and he had fought with the people of Syria in the conquest of Armenia; and had fought in Azurbaijān, with the people of al-'Irāq, and he was shocked at the different ways of people reading the Qur'ān. And Huzaifah said to 'Uṣmān, "O 'Uṣmān, assist this people, before they differ in the Book of God, just as the Jews and Christians differ in their books." Then 'Uṣmān sent a person to Ḥafṣah, ordering her to send those portions which she had, and saying, "I shall have a number of copies of them taken, and will then return them to you." And Ḥafṣah sent the portions to 'Uṣmān, and 'Uṣman ordered Zaid ibn Ṣābit, Ansārī, and Abdu 'llāh ibn az-Zubair, and Sa'īd ibn Al'ās, and 'Abdu 'r-Raḥmān ibn al-Ḥāris ibn Hishām; and these were all of the Quraish tribe, except Zaid ibn Sābit and 'Uṣmān. And he said to the three Quraishites, "When you and Zaid ibn-Ṣābit differ about any part of the dialect of the Qur'ān, then do ye write it in the Quraish dialect, because it came not down in the language of any tribe but theirs." Then they did as 'Uṣmān had ordered; and when a number of copies had been taken, 'Uṣmān returned the leaves to Ḥafṣah. And 'Uṣmān sent a copy to every quarter of the countries of Islām, and ordered all other leaves to be burnt, and Ibn Shahāb said, "Khārījah, son of Zaid ibn Ṣābit, informed me, saying, 'I could not find one verse when I was writing the Qur'ān, which, verily, I heard from the Prophet; then I looked for it, and found it with Khuzaimah, and entered it into the Sūratu 'l-Aḥzāb.'"

This recension of the Qur'ān produced by the Khalīfah 'Uṣmān has been handed down to us unaltered; and there is probably no other book in the world which has remained twelve centuries with so pure a text.

Sir William Muir remarks in his *Life of Mahomet*:—

"The original copy of the first edition was obtained from Haphsa's (Ḥafṣah) depository, and a careful recension of the whole set on foot. In case of difference between Zaid and his coadjutors, the voice of the latter, as demonstrative of the Coreishite idiom, was to preponderate; and the new collation was thus assimilated to the Meccan dialect, in which the Prophet had given utterance to his inspiration. Transcripts were multiplied and forwarded to the chief cities in the empire, and the previously existing copies were all, by the Caliph's command, committed to the flames. The old original was returned to Haphsa's custody.

"The recension of Othmân ('Uṣmān) has been handed down to us unaltered. So carefully, indeed, has it been preserved, that there are no variations of importance,—we might almost say no variations at all, amongst the innumerable copies of the Coran scattered throughout the vast bounds of the empire of Islâm.

"Contending and embittered factions, taking their rise in the murder of Othmân himself within a quarter of a century from the death of Mahomet, have ever since rent the Mahometan world. Yet but one Corân has been current amongst them; and the consentaneous use by them all in every age up to the present day of the same Scripture, is an irrefragable proof that we have now before us the very text prepared by command of the unfortunate Caliph. There is probably in the world no other work which has remained twelve centuries with so pure a text. The various readings are wonderfully few in number, and are chiefly confined to differences in the vowel points and diacritical signs. But these marks were invented at a later date.

"They did not exist at all in the early copies, and can hardly be said to affect the text of Othmân. Since, then, we possess the undoubted text of Othmân's recension, it remains to be inquired whether that text was an honest reproduction of Abu Bakr's edition, with the simple reconcilement of unimportant variations. There is the fullest ground for believing that it was so. No early or trustworthy traditions throw suspicion of tampering with the Corân in order to support his own claims upon Othmân. The

Sheeahs (Shī'ahs)* of later times, indeed, pretend that Othmân left out certain Suras or passages which favoured Ali. But this is incredible. He could not possibly have done so without it being observed at the time; and it cannot be imagined that Ali and his followers (not to mention the whole body of the Mussulmans who fondly regarded the Corân as the word of God, would have permitted such a proceeding.

"In support of this position, the following arguments may be adduced. First: When Othmân's edition was prepared, no open breach had yet taken place between the Omeyads and the Alyites. The unity of Islâm was still complete and unthreatened. Ali's pretensions were as yet undeveloped. No sufficient object can, therefore, be assigned for the perpetration by Othmân of an offence which Moslems regard as one of the blackest dye. Second: On the other hand, Ali, from the very commencement of Othmân's reign, had an influential party of adherents, strong enough in the end to depose the Caliph, to storm his palace in the heart of Medîna, and to put an end to his life. Can we conceive that these men would have remained quiet, when the very evidence of their leader's superior claims was being openly expunged from the book of God. Third: At the time of the recension, there were still multitudes alive who had the Corân, as originally delivered, by heart; and of the supposed passages favouring Ali—had any ever existed—there would have been numerous transcripts in the hands of his family and followers. Both of these sources must have proved an effectual check upon any attempt at suppression. Fourth: The party of Ali shortly after assumed an independent attitude, and he himself succeeded to the Caliphate. Is it possible that either Ali, or his party, when thus arrived at power, would have tolerated a mutilated Corân—mutilated expressly to destroy his claims Yet we find that they used the same Corân as their opponents, and raised no shadow of an objection against it.

"The insurgents are indeed said to have made it one of their complaints against Othmân that he had caused a new edition to be made of the Corân, and had committed all the old copies to the flames; but these proceedings were objected to simply as unauthorised and sacreligious. No hint was dropped of any alteration or omission. Such a supposition, palpably absurd at the time, is altogether an after-thought of the modern Sheeas.

"We may, then, safely conclude that Othmân's recension was, what it professed to be, a reproduction of Abu Bakr's edition, with a more perfect conformity to the dialect of Mecca, and possibly a more uniform arrangement of its parts,—but still a faithful reproduction.

"The most important question yet remains, viz. *Whether Abu Bakr's edition was itself an authentic and complete collection of Mahomet's Revelations.* The following considerations warrant the belief that it was authentic and, in the main, as complete as at the time was possible.

"First.—We have no reason to doubt that Abu Bakr was a sincere follower of Mahomet, and an earnest believer in the divine origin of the Corân. His faithful attachment to the Prophet's person, conspicuous for the last twenty years of his life, and his simple, consistent, and unambitious deportment as Caliph, admit no other supposition. Firmly believing the revelations of his friend to be the revelations of God himself, his first object would be to secure a pure and complete transcript of them. A similar argument applies with almost equal force to Omar, and the other agents in the revision. The great mass of Mussulmans were undoubtedly sincere in their belief. From the scribes themselves, employed in the compilation, down to the humblest believer who brought his little store of writing on stones or palm-leaves, all would be influenced by the same earnest desire to reproduce the very words which their Prophet had declared as his message from the Lord. And a similar guarantee existed in the feelings of the people at large, in whose soul no principle was more deeply rooted than an awful reverence for the supposed word of God. The Corân itself contains frequent denunciations against those who should presume to 'fabricate anything in the name of the Lord,' or conceal any part of that which He had revealed. Such an action, represented as the very worst description of crime, we cannot believe that the first Moslems, in the early ardour of their faith and love, would have dared to contemplate.

"Second. — The compilation was made within two years of Mahomet's death. We have seen that several of his followers had the entire revelation (excepting, perhaps, some obsolete fragments) by heart; that *every* Moslem treasured up more or less some portions in his memory; and that there were official Reciters of it, for public worship and tuition, in all countries to which Islâm extended. These formed an unbroken link between the Revelation fresh from Mahomet's lips, and the edition of it by Zeid. Thus the people were not only sincere and fervent in wishing for a faithful copy of the Corân; they were also in possession of ample means for realising their desire, and for testing the accuracy and completeness of the volume placed in their hands by Abu Bakr.

"Third.—A still greater security would be obtained from the fragmentary transcripts which existed in Mahomet's life-time, and which must have greatly multiplied before the Corân was compiled. These were in the possession, probably, of all who could read. And as we know that the compilation of Abu Bakr came into immediate and unquestioned

* *Hayātu 'l-Qulūb*, leaf 420: "The Ansars were ordained to oppose the claims of the family of Muḥammad, and this was the reason why the other wretches took the office of Khalifah by force. After thus treating one Khalifah of God, they then mutilated and changed the other Khalifah, which is the book of God."

use, it is reasonable to conclude that it embraced and corresponded with every extant fragment, and *therefore* by common consent, superseded them. We hear of no fragments, sentences, or words, intentionally omitted by the compilers, nor of any that differed from the received edition. Had any such been discoverable, they would undoubtedly have been preserved and noticed in those traditional repositories which treasured up the minutest and most trivial acts and sayings of the Prophet.

"Fourth.—The contents and the arrangement of the Corân speak forcibly for its authenticity. All the fragments that could possibly be obtained have with artless simplicity been joined together. The patchwork bears no marks of a designing genius or a moulding hand. It testifies to the faith and reverence of the compilers, and proves that they dared no more than simply collect the sacred fragments and place them in juxtaposition. Hence the interminable repetitions; the palling reiteration of the same ideas, truths, and doctrines; hence, scriptural stories and Arab legends, told over and over again with little verbal variation; hence the pervading want of connection, and the startling chasms between adjacent passages. Again, the frailties of Mahomet, supposed to have been noticed by the Deity, are all with evident faithfulness entered in the Corân. Not less undisguised are the frequent verses which are contradicted or abrogated by later revelations. The editor plainly contented himself with compiling and copying out in a continuous form, but with scrupulous accuracy, the fragmentary materials within his reach. He neither ventured to select from repeated versions of the same incident, nor to reconcile differences, nor by the alteration of a single letter to connect abrupt transitions of context, nor by tampering with the text to soften discreditable appearances. Thus we possess every internal guarantee of confidence.

"But it may be objected,—if the text of Abu Bakr's Corân was pure and universally received, how came it to be so soon corrupted, and to require, in consequence of its variations, an extensive recension? Tradition does not afford sufficient light to determine the cause of these discrepancies. They may have been owing to various readings in the older fragmentary transcripts which remained in the possession of the people; they may have originated in the diverse dialects of Arabia, and the different modes of pronunciation and orthography; or they may have sprung up naturally in the already vast domains of Islâm, before strict uniformity was officially enforced. It is sufficient for us to know that in Othmân's revision recourse was had to the *original* exemplar of the first compilation, and that there is otherwise every security, internal and external, that we possess a text the same as that which Mahomet himself gave forth and used." (*Life of Mahomet*, new ed., p. 557 *et seqq.*)

The various readings (*qirā'ah*) in the Qur'ān are not such as are usually understood by the term in English authors, but different *dialects* of the Arabic language. Ibn 'Abbās says the Prophet said, "Gabriel taught me to read the Qur'ān in one dialect, and when I recited it he taught me to recite it in another dialect, and so on until the number of dialects increased to seven." (*Mishkāt*, book ii. ch. ii.)

Muḥammad seems to have adopted this expedient to satisfy the desire of the leading tribes to have a Qur'ān in their own dialect; for 'Abdu 'l-Ḥaqq says, "The Qur'ān was first revealed in the dialect of the Quaraish, which was the Prophet's native tongue; but when the Prophet saw that the people of other tribes recited it with difficulty, then he obtained permission from God to extend its currency by allowing it to be recited in all the chief dialects of Arabia, which were seven:—Quraish, Taiy, Hawāzin, Yaman, Ṣaqīf, Huẕail, and Banū Tamīm. Every one of these tribes accordingly read the Qur'ān in its own dialect, till the time of 'Usmān, when these differences of reading were prohibited."

These seven dialects are called in Arabic *Saba'tu Aḥruf*, and in Persian *Haft Qirā'āt.*

III.—The Divisions of the Qur'ān.

The Qur'ān, which is written in the Arabic language, is divided into: *Ḥarf, Kalimah, Āyah, Sūrah, Rukū', Rub', Niṣf, Ṣulṣ, Juz', Manzal.*

1. *Ḥarf* (pl. *Ḥurūf*), Letters; of which there are said to be 323,671, or according to some authorities, 338,606.

2. *Kalimah* (pl. *Kalimāt*), Words; of which there are 77,934, or, according to some writers 79,934.

3. *Āyah* (pl. *Āyāt*), Verses. *Āyah* (Heb. אוֹת) is a word which signifies "sign." It was used by Muḥammad for short sections or verses of his supposed revelation. The division of verses differs in different editions of the Arabic Qur'ān. The number of verses in the Arabic Qur'āns are recorded after the title of the Sūrah, and the verses distinguished in the text by a small cypher or circle. The early readers of the Qur'ān did not agree as to the original position of these circles, and so it happens that there are five different systems of numbering the verses.

(*a*) *Kūfah* verses. The Readers in the city of al-Kūfah say that they followed the custom of 'Alī. Their way of reckoning is generally adopted in India. They reckon 6,239 verses.

(*b*) *Baṣrah* verses. The Readers of al-Baṣrah follow 'Āṣim ibn Ḥajjāj, a Companion. They reckon 6,204.

(*c*) *Shāmī* verses, The Readers in Syria (Shām) followed 'Abdu 'llāh ibn 'Umar, a Companion. They reckon 6,225 verses.

(*d*) *Makkah* verses. According to this arrangement, there are 6,219 verses.

(*e*) *Madīnah* verses. This way of reading contains 6,211 verses.

4. *Sūrah* (pl. *Suwar*), Chapters A word which signifies a row or series, but which

is now used exclusively for the chapters of the Qur'ān, which are one hundred and fourteen in number. These chapters are called after some word which occurs in the text, and, if the Traditions are to be trusted, they were so named by Muḥammad himself, although the verses of their respective Sūrahs were undoubtedly arranged after his death, and sometimes with little regard to their sequence. Muslim doctors admit that the Khalīfah 'Uṣmān arranged the chapters in the order in which they now stand in the Qur'ān.

The Sūrahs of the Muḥammadan Qur'ān are similar to the forty-three divisions of the Law amongst the Jews known as סְדָרִים *Sidārim*, or "orders." These were likewise named after a word in the section, *e.g.* The first is Bereshith, the second Noah, &c. (See Buxtorf's *Tiberias*, p. 181.)

Each Sūrah of the Qur'ān, with the exception of the IXth, begins with the words—

بسم الله الرحمن الرحيم

"In the name of the Merciful, the Compassionate."

The Sūrahs, as they stand in Arabic editions of the Qur'ān, are as follows:—

No.	Title of Sūrah.	Meaning in English.	The Chronological Order. According to Jalālu 'd-dīn.	According to Rev. J. M. Rodwell.	According to Sir W. Muir.
1	Fātiḥah	Preface	uncertain	8	6
2	Baqarah	Cow	86	91	uncertain
3	Ālu 'Imrān	Family of 'Imrān ...	88	97	A.H. 2 to 10
4	Nisā'	Women	91	100	uncertain
5	Mā'idah	Table	112	114	A.H. 6 to 10
6	An'ām	Cattle	54	89	81
7	A'rāf	Arāf	38	87	91
8	Anfāl	Spoils	87	95	A.H. 2
9	Taubah	Repentance	113	113	The last.
10	Yūnus	Jonah	50	84	79
11	Hūd	Hud	51	75	78
12	Yūsuf	Joseph	52	77	77
13	Ra'd	Thunder	95	90	89
14	Ibrāhīm	Abraham	71	76	80
15	Ḥijr	Hijr	53	57	62
16	Naḥl	Bee	69	73	88
17	Banū Isrā'īl	Children of Israel ...	49	67	87
18	Kahf	Cave	68	69	69
19	Maryam	Mary	43	58	68
20	Ṭā Ḥā	Ṭā Hā	44	55	75
21	Ambiyā'	Prophets	72	65	86
22	Ḥajj	Pilgrimage	103	107	85
23	Mu'minūn	Believers	73	64	84
24	Nūr	Light	102	105	A.H. 5
25	Furqān	Qur'ān	41	66	74
26	Shu'arā'	Poets	46	56	61
27	Naml	Ant	47	68	70
28	Qaṣaṣ...	Story	48	79	83
29	'Ankabūt	Spider	84	81	90
30	Rūm	Greeks	83	74	60
31	Luqmān	Luqmān	56	82	50
32	Sajdah	Prostration	74	70	44
33	Aḥzāb	Confederates	89	103	uncertain
34	Saba'	Saba	57	85	79
35	Malā'ikah	Angels	42	86	66
36	Yā Sīn	Yā Sīn	40	60	67
37	Ṣāffāt	Ranks	55	50	59
38	Ṣād	Ṣād	37	59	73
39	Zumar	Troops	58	80	45
40	Mu'min	Believer...	59	78	72
41	Fuṣṣilat	Explanation	60	71	53
42	Shūrā	Council	61	83	71
43	Zukhrūf	Ornaments	62	61	76
44	Dukhān	Smoke	63	53	58
45	Jāṣiyah	Kneeling	64	72	57
46	Aḥqāf	Aḥqāf	65	88	64

No.	Title of Sūrah.	Meaning in English.	The Chronological Order. According to Jalālu 'd-dīn.	According to Rev. J. M. Rodwell.	According to Sir W. Muir.
47	Muḥammad	Muḥammad	94	96	uncertain
48	Fatḥ	Victory	111	108	A.H. 6
49	Ḥujurāt	Chambers	106	112	uncertain
50	Qāf	Qāf	33	54	56
51	Ẕāriyāt	Scattering Winds ...	66	43	63
52	Ṯūr	Mountain	75	44	55
53	Najm	Star	22	46	43
54	Qamar	Moon	36	49	48
55	Raḥmān	Merciful	96	48	40
56	Wāqi'ah	Inevitable	45	45	41
57	Ḥadīd	Iron	93	99	uncertain
58	Mujādilah	Disputer	105	106	uncertain
59	Ḥashr	Assembly	101	102	A.H. 4
60	Mumtaḥinah ...	Proved	90	110	A.H. 7
61	Ṣaff	Array	110	98	uncertain
62	Jamu'ah	Assembly	108	94	uncertain
63	Munāfiqīn	Hypocrites	104	104	A.H. 65
64	Taghābun	Mutual Deceit	109	93	82
65	Ṯalāq	Divorce	108	101	uncertain
66	Taḥrīm	Prohibition	107	109	A.H. 7 to 8
67	Mulk	Kingdom	76	63	42
68	Qalam	Pen	2	17	52
69	Ḥāqqah	Inevitable Day	77	42	51
70	Ma'ārij	Steps	78	47	37
71	Nūḥ	Noah	70	51	54
72	Jinn	Genii	39	62	65
73	Muzzammil	Wrapped up	3	3	46
74	Muddaṣṣir	Enfolded	4	2	21
75	Qiyāmah	Resurrection	30	40	36
76	Dahr	Time	97	52	35
77	Mursalāt	Messengers	32	36	34
78	Naba'	News	79	37	33
79	Nāzi'āt	Those who drag ...	80	35	47
80	'Abasa	He frowned	23	24	26
81	Takwīr	Folding up	6	32	27
82	Infiṯār	Cleaving asunder ...	81	31	11
83	Taṯfīf	Short Measure	85	41	32
84	Inshiqāq	Rending in sunder ...	82	33	28
85	Burūj	Celestial Signs... ...	26	28	31
86	Ṯāriq	Night Star	35	22	29
87	A'la	Most High	7	25	25
88	Ghāshiyah	Overwhelming	67	38	25
89	Fajr	Day-break	9	39	14
90	Balad	City	34	18	15
91	Shams	Sun	25	23	4
92	Lail	Night	8	16	12
93	Ẕuḥā	Sun in his meridian ...	10	4	16
94	Inshirāḥ	Expanding	11	5	17
95	Tīn	Fig	27	26	8
96	'Alaq	Congealed blood ...	1	1	19
97	Qadr	(Night of) Power ...	24	92	24
98	Baiyinah	Evidence	99	21	uncertain
99	Zalzalah	Earthquake	92	30	3
100	'Ādiyāt	Swift horses	13	34	2
101	Qāri'ah	Striking	29	29	7
102	Takāṣur	Multiplying	15	14	9
103	'Aṣr	Afternoon	12	27	1
104	Humazah	Slanderer	31	13	10
105	Fīl	Elephant	18	19	13
106	Quraish	Quraish	28	20	5
107	Mā'ūn	Necessaries	16	15	39

No.	Title of Sūrah.	Meaning in English.	The Chronological Order. According to Jalālu 'd-dīn.	According to Rev. J. M. Rodwell.	According to Sir W. Muir.
108	Kauṣar	Kausar	14	9	18
109	Kāfirūn	Infidels	17	12	38
110	Naṣr	Assistance	101	111	30
111	Abū Lahab	Abū Lahab	5	11	22
112	Ikhlāṣ	Unity	21	10	20
113	Falaq	Day-break	19	6	uncertain
114	Nās	Men	20	7	uncertain

5. *Rukū'* (pl. *Rukū'āt*), an inclination of the head or bow. These are sections of about ten verses or less, at which the devout Muslim makes a bow of reverence; they are marked on the margin of the Qur'ān with the letter *'ain* ع, with the number of the *rukū'* over it. Muḥammadans generally quote their Qur'ān by the *Juz'* or *Sīpārah* and the *Rukū'*.

6. *Rub'*. The quarter of a *Juz'*, or *Sīpārah*.

7. *Niṣf*. The half of a *Sīpārah*.

8. *Ṣulṣ*. The three-quarters of a *Sīpārah*. These three divisions are denoted by the words being written on the margin.

9. *Juz'* (pl. *Ajzā'*). Persian *Sīpārah*. Thirty divisions of the Qur'ān, which have been made to enable the devout Muslim to recite the whole of the Qur'ān in the thirty days of Ramaẓān. Muḥammadans usually quote their Qur'ān by the *Sīpārah* or *Juz'* and not by the *Sūrah*.

10. *Manzil* (pl. *Manāzil*, Stages). These are seven in number, and are marked by the letters ف م ی ب ش و ق, which are said to spell *Famī bi Shauq*, "My mouth with desire." This arrangement is to enable the Muslim to recite the whole in the course of a week.

IV.—The Contents of the Qur'ān and the Chronological Arrangement of its Chapters.

In the Arabic Qur'ān, the Sūrahs are placed as they were arranged by Zaid ibn Ṣābit, who seems to have put them together regardless of any chronological sequence. The initial, or opening prayer, stands first, and then the longest chapters. But the Muḥammadan commentators admit that the Qur'ān is not chronologically arranged; and Jalālu 'd-dīn, in his *Itqān*, has given a list of them as they are supposed to have been revealed. This list will be found under the *Divisions of the Qur'ān* in the present article. And, what is still more confusing, all Muḥammadan doctors allow that in some of the Sūrahs there are verses which belong to a different date from that of other portions of the chapter; for example, in the Sūratu 'l-'Alaq, the first five verses belong to a much earlier date than the others; and in Sūratu 'l-Baqarah, verse 234 is acknowledged by all commentators to have been revealed after verse 240, which it abrogates.

If we arrange the Sūrahs or Chapters according to the order given in Suyūṭī's *Itqān*, or by Sir William Muir, or by Mr Rodwell, we cannot fail to mark the gradual development of Muḥammad's mind from that of a mere moral teacher and reformer to that of a prophet and warrior-chief. The contrast between the earlier, middle, and later Sūrahs is very instructive and interesting.

In the earlier Sūrahs we observe a predominance of a poetical element, a deep appreciation of the beauty of natural objects, fragmentary and impassioned utterances; denunciation of woe and punishment being expressed in these earlier Sūrahs with extreme brevity.

"With a change, however, in the position of Muḥammad when he openly assumes the office of 'public warner,' the Sūrahs begin to wear a more prosaic and didactic tone, though the poetical ornament of rhyme is preserved throughout. We lose the poet in the missionary aiming to convert, and in the warm asserter of dogmatic truths; the descriptions of natural objects, of the Judgment, of Heaven and Hell, make way for gradually increasing historical statements, first from Jewish, and subsequently from Christian histories; while in the twenty-nine (thirty?) Sūrahs revealed at Medina we no longer listen to vague words, often, as it would seem, without defininite aim, but to the earnest disputant with the opponents of the new faith, the Apostle pleading the cause of what he believes to be the truth of God. He who at Mecca is the admonisher and persuader, at Medina is the legislator and the warrior dictating obedience, and who uses other weapons than the pen of the poet and the scribe; while we are startled by finding obedience to God and the Apostle, God's gifts and the Apostle's, God's pleasure and the Apostle's, spoken of in the same breath, and epithets and attributes elsewhere applied to Allah openly applied to himself. 'Whoso obeyeth the Apostle obeyeth Allah.'

"The Suras, viewed as a whole, will thus appear to be the work of one who began his career as a thoughtful inquirer after truth, and as an earnest asserter of it in such rhetorical and poetical forms as he deemed most likely to win and attract his countrymen, but who gradually proceeded from the dogmatic teacher to the political founder of a system for which laws and regulations had to be provided as occasions arose. And of all the Suras, it must be remarked that they were intended not only for readers but for hearers—that they were all promulgated by public recital—and that much was left, as the imperfect sentences show, to the manner and suggestive action of the reciter." (Rodwell's *Preface to the Qur'ān.*)

The absence of the historical element from the Qur'ān, as regards the details of Muḥammad's daily life, may be judged of by the fact that only two of his contemporaries (Abū Lahab and Zaid) are mentioned in the entire volume, and that Muḥammad's name occurs but five times, although he is all the way through addressed by the angel Gabriel as the recipient of the divine revelations, with the word "Say." Perhaps also such passages as Sūrah ii., verses 5, 246, and 274, and the constant mention of guidance, direction, wandering, may have been suggested by reminiscences of his mercantile journeys in his earlier years.

Sir William Muir has very skilfully arranged the Sūrahs into six periods. (See *Corân*, S. P. C. K. ed.), and although they are not precisely in the chronological order given by Jalālu 'd-Dīn in his *Itqān*, the arrangement seeems to be fully borne out by internal evidence. With the assistance of Prof. Palmer's "Table of Contents" slightly altered (*The Qur'ān*, Oxford ed. 1880), we shall arrange the contents of the Qur'ān according to these periods.

THE FIRST PERIOD.

Eighteen Sūrahs, consisting of short rhapsodies, may have been composed by Muḥammad before he conceived the idea of a divine mission, none of which are in the form of a message from the Deity.

Chapter CIII.

Sūratu 'l-'Aṣr.

The Chapter of the Afternoon.

A short chapter of one verse as follows :—

"By the afternoon! Verily, man is in loss! Save those who believe and do right and bid each other be true, and bid each other be patient."

Chapter C.

Sūratu 'l-'Ādiyāt.

The Chapter of the Chargers.

Oath by the charging of war-horses.
Man is ungrateful.
Certainty of the Judgment.

Chapter XCIX.

Sūratu 'z-Zalzalah.

The Chapter of the Earthquake.

The earthquake preceding the Judgment Day.

Chapter XCI.

Suratu 'sh-Shams.

The Chapter of the Sun.

Purity of the soul brings happiness.
Example of Ṣamūd.
(*The latter verses are clearly of a later date than the first ten.*)

Chapter CVI.

Sūratu 'l-Quraish.

The Chapter of the Quraish.

The Quraish are bidden to give thanks to God for the trade of their two yearly caravans.

Chapter I.

Sūratu 'l-Fātiḥah.

The Opening Chapter.

A prayer for guidance.
(*This short chapter, which is the opening chapter of the Qur'ān, is recited in the liturgy.*)

"Praise be to God, Lord of all the worlds!
The compassionate, the merciful!
King of the day of reckoning!
Thee only do we worship, and to Thee only do we cry for help.
Guide Thou us in the straight path,
The path of those to whom Thou hast been gracious;
With whom Thou art not angry,
And who go not astray.."

Chapter CI.

Sūratu 'l-Qāri'ah.

The Chapter of the Smiting.

The terrors of the last day and of hell-fire (*al-Hāwiyah*)

Chapter XCV.

Sūratu 't-Tīn.

The Chapter of the Fig.

The degradation of man.
Future reward and punishment.

Chapter CII.

Sūratu 't-Takāṣur.

The Chapter of the Contention about Numbers.

Two families of the Arabs rebuked for contending which was the more numerous.
Warning of the punishment of hell.

Chapter CIV.

Sūratu 'l-Humazah.

The Chapter of the Backbiter.

Backbiters shall be cast into hell.

Chapter LXXXII.

Sūratu 'l-Infiṭār.

The Chapter of the Cleaving Asunder.

Signs of the Judgment Day.
Guardian angels.

Chapter XCII.

Sūratu 'l-Lail.

The Chapter of the Night.

Promise of reward to those who give alms and fear God and "believe in the best."

CHAPTER CV.

Sūratu 'l-Fīl.

The Chapter of the Elephant.

The miraculous destruction of the Abyssinian army under Abrahatu 'l-Ashram by birds when invading Makkah with elephants, in the year that Muḥammad was born.

CHAPTER LXXXIX.

Sūratu 'l-Fajr.

The Chapter of the Dawn.

Fate of previous nations who rejected their teachers.

Admonition to those who rely too much on their prosperity.

CHAPTER XC.

Sūratu 'l-Balad.

The Chapter of the City.

Exhortation to practise charity.

CHAPTER XCIII.

Sūratu 'ẓ-Ẓuḥā.

The Chapter of the Forenoon.

Muḥammad encouraged and bidden to remember how God has cared for him hitherto; he is to be charitable in return, and to publish God's goodness.

CHAPTER XCIV.

Sūratu 'l-Inshirāḥ.

The Chapter of "Have we not Expanded?"

God has made Muḥammad's mission easier to him.

CHAPTER CVIII.

Sūratu 'l-Kauṣar.

The Chapter of al-Kauṣar.

Muḥammad is commanded to offer the sacrifices out of his abundance.

Threat that his enemies shall be childless.

THE SECOND PERIOD.

Four Sūrahs. The opening of Muḥammad's Ministry. Sūrah xcvi. contains the command to recite, and, according to the Traditions, it was the first revelation.

CHAPTER XCVI.

Sūratu 'l-'Alaq.

The Chapter of Congealed Blood.

Muḥammad's first call to read the Qur'ān.

Denunciation of Abū Lahab for his opposition.

(*The latter verses of this Sūrah are admitted to be of a later date than the former.*)

CHAPTER CXII.

Sūratu 'l-Ikhlāṣ.

The Chapter of the Unity.

Declaration of God's unity.

(*This short Sūrah is highly esteemed, and is recited in the daily liturgy.*)

"Say: He is God alone:
God the Eternal!
He begetteth not,
And is not begotten;
And there is none like unto Him."

CHAPTER LXXIV.

Sūratu 'l-Muddaṣṣir.

The Chapter of the Covered.

Muḥammad while covered up is bidden to arise and preach.

Denunciation of a rich infidel who mocks at the revelation.

Hell and its nineteen angels.

The infidels rebuked for demanding material scriptures as a proof of Muḥammad's mission.

CHAPTER CXI.

Sūratu Tabbat.

The Chapter of "Let Perish."

Denunciation of Abū Lahab and his wife, who are threatened with hell fire.

THE THIRD PERIOD.

Nineteen Sūrahs, chiefly descriptions of the Resurrection, Paradise, and Hell, with reference to the growing opposition of the Quraish, given from the commencement of Muḥammud's public ministry to the Abyssinian emigration.

CHAPTER LXXXVII.

Sūratu 'l-A'lā.

The Chapter of the Most High.

Muḥammad shall not forget any of the revelation save what God pleases.

The revelation is the same as that given to Abraham and Moses.

CHAPTER XCVII.

Sūratu 'l-Qadr.

The Chapter of Power.

The Qur'ān revealed on the night of power

Its excellence.

Angels descend thereon.

CHAPTER LXXXVIII

Sūratu 'l-Ghāshiyah.

The Chapter of the Overwhelming.

Description of the Last Day, Heaven and Hell.

CHAPTER LXXX.

Sūratu 'Abasa.

The Chapter "he Frowned."

The Prophet rebuked for frowning on a poor blind believer.

The Creation and Resurrection.

CHAPTER LXXXIV.

Sūratu 'l-Inshiqāq.

The Chapter of the Rending Asunder

Signs of the Judgment Day.

The books of men's actions.

The Resurrection.

Denunciation of misbelievers.

CHAPTER LXXXI.

Sūratu 'l-Takwīr.

The Chapter of the Folding-up.

Terrors of the Judgment Day.

The female child who has been buried alive will demand vengeance.

Allusion to the Prophet's vision of Gabriel on Mount Ḥirā'.

He is vindicated from the charge of madness.

CHAPTER LXXXVI.

Sūratu 'uṭ-Ṭāriq.

The Chapter of the Night Star.

By the night-star, every soul has a guardian angel.

Creation and resurrection of man.

The plot of the infidels shall be frustrated.

CHAPTER CX.

Sūratu 'n-Naṣr.

The Chapter of Help.

Prophecy that men shall join Islām by troops.

CHAPTER LXXXV

Sūratu 'l-Burūj.

The Chapter of the Zodiacal Signs.

Denunciation of those who persecute believers.

Example of the fate of Pharaoh and S̤amūd.

CHAPTER LXXXIII.

Sūratu 't-Taṭfīf.

The Chapter of those who give Short Weight.

Fraudulent traders are warned.

Sijjīn, the register of the acts of the wicked.

Hell and heaven.

CHAPTER LXXVIII.

Sūratu 'n-Naba'.

The Chapter of the Information.

Description of the Day of Judgment, hell, and heaven.

CHAPTER LXXVII.

Sūratu 'l-Mursalāt.

The Chapter of Messengers.

Oath by the angels who execute God's behests.

Terrors of the Last Day.

Hell and Heaven.

CHAPTER LXXVI.

Sūratu 'd-Dahr.

The Chapter of Time.

Man's conception and birth

Unbelievers warned and believers promised a reward.

Exhortation to charity.

Bliss of the charitable in Paradise.

The Qur'ān revealed by degrees.

Only those believe whom God wills.

CHAPTER LXXV.

Sūratu 'l-Qiyāmah.

The Chapter of Resurrection.

The Resurrection.

Muḥammad is bidden not to be hurried in repeating the Qur'ān so as to commit it to memory.

Dying agony of an infidel.

CHAPTER LXX.

Sūratu 'l-Ma'ārij.

The Chapter of the Ascents.

An unbeliever mockingly calls for a judgment on himself and his companions.

The terrors of the Judgment Day.

Man's ingratitude.

Adultery denounced.

Certainty of the Judgment Day.

CHAPTER CIX.

Sūratu 'l-Kāfirūn.

The Chapter of the Misbelievers.

The Prophet will not follow the religion of the misbelievers.

CHAPTER CVII.

Sūratu 'l-Mā'ūn.

The Chapter of Necessaries.

Denunciation of the unbelieving and uncharitable.

CHAPTER LV.

Sūratu 'r-Raḥmān.

The Chapter of the Merciful.

An enumeration of the works of the Lord ending with a description of Paradise and Hell.

A refrain runs throughout this chapter :—

"Which then of your Lord's bounties do ye twain deny?"

CHAPTER LVI.

Sūratu 'l- Wāqi'ah.

The Chapter of the Inevitable.

Terrors of the inevitable Day of Judgment.

Description of Paradise and Hell.

Proofs in Nature.

None but the clean may touch the Qur'ān.

The condition of a dying man.

THE FOURTH PERIOD.

Twenty-two Sūrahs, given from the sixth to the tenth year of Muḥammad's ministry. With this period begin the narratives of the Jewish Scriptures, and Rabbinical and Arab legends. The temporary compromise with idolatry is connected with Sūrah liii.

CHAPTER LXVII.

Sūratu 'l-Mulk.

The Chapter of the Kingdom.

God the Lord of heavens.

The marvels thereof.

The discomfiture of the misbelievers in Hell.

The power of God exhibited in Nature.

Warnings and threats of punishment.

CHAPTER LIII.

Sūratu 'n-Najm.

The Chapter of the Star.

Oath by the star that Muḥammad's vision of his ascent to heaven was not a delusion.

Description of the same.

The amended passage relating to idolatry.

Wickedness of asserting the angels to be females.

God's Omniscience.

Rebuke of an apostle who paid another to take upon him his burden at the Judgment Day.

Definition of true religion.

God's attributes.

CHAPTER XXXII.

Sūratu 's-Sajdah.

The Chapter of Adoration.

The Qur'ān is truth from the Lord.

God the Creator and Governor.

The Resurrection.

Conduct of true believers when they hear the word.

Their reward.

The punishment of misbelievers.

Description of Hell.

The people are exhorted to believe and are admonished by the fate of the ruined cities they see around them.

They are warned of the Judgment Day.

CHAPTER XXXIX.

Sūratu 'z-Zumar.

The Chapter of the Troops.

Rebuke to the idolaters who say they serve false gods as a means of access to God himself.

The unity of God, the Creator and Controller of the universe.

His independence and omnipotence.

Ingratitude of man for God's help.

Difference between the believers and unbelievers.

Muḥammad is called to sincerity of religion and to Islām.

He is to fear the torment at the Judgment Day if he disobeys the call.

Hell-fire is prepared for the infidels.

Paradise promised to those who avoid idolatry.

The irrigation of the soil and the growth of corn are signs.

The Qur'ān makes the skin of those who fear God creep.

Threat of the Judgment Day.

The Makkans are warned by the fate of their predecessors not to reject the Qur'ān.

Parable showing the uncertain position of the idolaters.

Muḥammad not immortal.

Warning to those who lie against God, and promise of reward to those who assert the truth.

Muḥammad is not to be frightened with the idols of the Makkans.

Their helplessness demonstrated.

The Qur'ān is a guide, but the Prophet cannot compel men to follow it.

Human souls are taken to God during sleep, and those who are destined to live on are sent back.

No intercession allowed with God.

The doctrine of the unity of God terrifies the idolaters.

Prayer to God to decide between them

The infidels will regret on the Resurrection Day.

Ingratitude of man for God's help in trouble.

The Makkans are warned by the fate of their predecessors.

Exhortation to repentance before it is too late.

Salvation of the God-fearing.

God the creator and controller of everything.

Description of the Last Judgment.

All souls driven in troops to heaven or to hell.

CHAPTER LXXIII.

Sūratu 'l-Muzzammil.

The Chapter of the Enwrapped.

Muḥammad, when wrapped up in his mantle, is bidden to arise and pray.

Is bidden to repeat the Qur'ān and to practice devotion by night.

He is to bear with the unbelievers for a while.

Pharaoh rejected the apostle sent to him.

Stated times for prayer prescribed.

Almsgiving prescribed.

CHAPTER LXXIX.

Sūratu 'n-Nāzi'āt.

The Chapter of those who Tear Out.

The coming of the Day of Judgment.

The call of Moses.

His interview with Pharaoh.

Chastisement of the latter.

The Creation and Resurrection.

CHAPTER LIV.

Sūratu 'l-Qamar.

The Chapter of the Moon.

The splitting asunder of the moon.

Muḥammad accused of imposture.

The Makkans warned by the stories of Noah and the Deluge, of Ṣamūd, the people of Sodom, and Pharaoh.

The sure coming of the Judgment.

CHAPTER XXXIV.

Sūratu Saba'.

The Chapter of Saba'.

The omniscience of God.

Those who have received knowledge recognise the revelation.

The unbelievers mock at Muḥammad for preaching the Resurrection.

The birds and mountains sing praises with David.

Iron softened for him.

He makes coats of mail.

The wind subjected to Solomon.

A fountain of brass made to flow for him.

The jinns compelled to work for him.

His death only discovered by means of the worm that gnawed.

The staff that supported his corpse.

The prosperity of Saba'.

Bursting of the dyke (al-'Arim) and ruin of the town.

Helplessness of the false gods.

They cannot intercede for their worshippers when assembled at the Last Day.

Fate of the misbelievers on that day.

The proud and the weak shall dispute as to which misled the others.

The affluence of the Makkans will only increase their ruin.

The angels shall disown the worshippers of false gods.

The Makkans accuse Muḥammad of imposture.

So did other nations deal with their Prophets and were punished for it.

Muḥammad is cleared of the suspicion of insanity.

The wretched plight of the misbelievers on the Last Day.

CHAPTER XXXI.

Sūratu Luqmān.

The Chapter of Luqmān.

The Qur'ān a guidance to believers.

Denunciation of one who purchased Persian legends and preferred them to the Qur'ān.

God in Nature.

Other gods can create nothing.

Wisdom granted to Luqmān.

His advice to his son.

The obstinacy of the infidels rebuked.

If the sea were ink and the trees pens, they would not suffice to write the words of the Lord.

God manifest in the night and day, in the sun and moon, and in rescuing men from dangers by sea.

God only knows the future.

CHAPTER LXIX.

Sūratu 'l-Ḥāqqah.

The Chapter of the Inevitable.

The inevitable judgment.

Fate of those who denied it, of Ād, Ṣamūd, and Pharaoh.

The Deluge and the Last Judgment.

Vindication of Muḥammad from the charge of having forged the Qur'ān.

CHAPTER LXVIII.

Sūratu 'l-Qalam.

The Chapter of the Pen.

Muḥammad is neither mad nor an impostor.

Denounced by an insolent opponent

Example from the fate of the owner of the gardens.

Unbelievers threatened.

Muḥammad exhorted to be patient and not to follow the example of Jonah.

CHAPTER XLI.

Sūratu Fuṣṣilat.

The Chapter "Are Detailed."

The Makkans are called on to believe the Qur'ān.

The creation of the heavens and the earth.

Warning from the fate of 'Ād and Ṣamūd.

The very skins of the unbelievers shall bear witness against them on the Day of Judgment.

Punishment of those who reject the Qur'ān.

The angels descend and encourage those who believe.

Precept to return good for evil.

Refuge to be sought with God against temptation from the devil.

Against sun and moon worship.

The angels praise God, though the idolators are too proud to do so.

The quickening of the earth with rain is a sign.

The Qur'ān a confirmation of previous scriptures.

If it had been revealed in a foreign tongue the people would have objected that they could not understand it, and that the Prophet, being an Arab, should have had a revelation in his own language.

Moses' scripture was also the subject of dispute.

God is omniscient.

The false gods will desert their worshippers at the Resurrection.

Man's ingratitude for God's help in trouble.

God is sufficient witness of the truth.

CHAPTER LXXI.

Sūratu Nūḥ.

The Chapter of Noah.

Noah's preaching to the Antediluvians.

Their five idols also worshipped by the Arabs.

Their fate.

CHAPTER LII.

Sūratu 'ṭ-Ṭūr.

The Chapter of the Mount.

Oath by Mount Sinai and other things.

Terrors of the Last Day.

Bliss of Paradise.

Muḥammad is neither a madman, soothsayer, poet, nor impostor.

Reproof of the Makkans for their superstitions, and for proudly rejecting the Prophet.

CHAPTER L.

Sūratu Qāf.

The Chapter of Qāf.

Proofs in nature of a future life.

Example of the fate of the nations of old who rejected the apostles.

Creation of man.

God's proximity to him.

The two recording angels.

Death and Resurrection.

The Last Judgment and exhortation to believe.

CHAPTER XLV.

Sūratu 'l-Jāṣiyah.

The Chapter of the Kneeling.

God revealed in nature.

Denunciation of the infidels.

Trading by sea a sign of God's providence.

The law first given to Israel, then to Muḥammad in the Qur'ān.

Answer to the infidels who deny the Resurrection, and warning of their fate on that day.

CHAPTER XLIV.

Sūratu 'd-Dukhān.

The Chapter of the Smoke.

Night of the revelation of the Qur'ān.

Unity of God.

Threat of the Last Day, when a smoke shall cover the heavens, and the unbelievers shall be punished for rejecting the Prophet, and saying he is taught by others or distracted.

Fate of Pharaoh for rejecting Moses.

Fate of the people of Jubba'.

The Judgment Day.

The tree Zaqqūm and the punishment of hell.

Paradise and the virgins thereof.

The Qur'ān revealed in Arabic for an admonition.

Chapter XXXVII.

Sūratu 'ṣ-Ṣāffāt.

The Chapter of the Ranged.

Oath by the angels ranged in rank, by those who drive the clouds, and by those who rehearse the Qur'ān, that God is one alone!

They guard the gates of heaven, and pelt the devils, who would listen there, with shooting-stars.

Do the Makkans imagine themselves stronger than the angels, that they mock of God's signs and deny the Resurrection?

The false gods and the Makkans shall recriminate each other at the Judgment Day.

They say now, "Shall we leave our gods for a mad poet?"

They shall taste hell-fire for their unbelief, while the believers are in Paradise.

Description of the delights thereof.

The maidens there.

The blessed shall see their unbelieving former comrades in hell.

Immortality of the blessed.

Az-Zaqqūm the accursed tree in hell.

Horrors of that place.

The posterity of Noah were blessed.

Abraham mocks at and breaks the idols.

He is condemned to be burnt alive, but is delivered.

Is commanded to offer up his son as a sacrifice; obeys, but his son is spared.

His posterity is blessed.

Moses and Aaron, too, left a good report behind them; so, too, did Elias, who protested against the worship of Baal.

Lot was saved.

Jonah was delivered after having been thrown overboard and swallowed by a fish.

The gourd.

Jonah is sent to preach to the people of the city (of Nineveh).

The Makkans rebuked for saying that God has daughters, and for saying that He is akin to the jinns.

The angels declare that they are but the humble servants of God.

The success of the Prophet and the confusion of the infidels foretold.

Chapter XXX.

Sūratu 'r-Rūm.

The Chapter of the Greeks.

Victory of the Persians over the Greeks.

Prophecy of the coming triumph of the latter.

The Makkans warned by the fate of former cities.

The idols shall forsake them at the Resurrection.

The believers shall enter Paradise.

God is to be praised in the morning and evening and at noon and sunset.

His creation of man and of the universe and His providence are signs.

He is the incomparable Lord of all.

Warning against idolatry and schism.

Honesty inculcated and usury reproved.

God only creates and kills.

Corruption in the earth through sin.

The fate of former idolaters.

Exhortation to believe before the sudden coming of the Judgment Day.

God's sending rain to quicken the earth is a sign of His power.

Muḥammad cannot make the deaf hear his message.

Warning of the Last Day.

Chapter XXVI.

Sūratu 'sh-Shu'arā'.

The Chapter of the Poets.

Muḥammad is not to be vexed by the people's unbelief.

Though called a liar now, his cause shall triumph in the end.

Moses and Pharaoh.

He fears lest he may be killed for slaying the Egyptian.

Pharaoh charges him with ingratitude.

Their dispute about God.

Pharaoh claims to be God himself.

The miracles of the rod and the white hand.

Moses' contest with the magicians.

The magicians are conquered and believe.

Pharaoh threatens them with condign punishment.

The Israelites leave Egypt and are pursued.

The passing of the Red Sea and destruction of Pharaoh and his hosts.

The history of Abraham.

He preaches against idolatry.

Noah is called a liar and vindicated.

Hūd preaches to the people of 'Ād and Ṣāliḥ to Ṣamūd.

The latter hamstring the she-camel and perish.

The crime and punishment of the people of Sodom.

The people of the Grove and the prophet Shu'aib.

The Qur'ān revealed through the instrumentality of the Faithful Spirit (Gabriel) in plain Arabic.

The learned Jews recognise its truth from the prophecies in their own scriptures.

The devils could not have brought it.

Muḥammad is to be meek towards believers and to warn his clansmen.

Those upon whom the devils descend, namely, the poets who wander distraught in every vale.

CHAPTER XV.

Sūratu 'l-Ḥijr.

The Chapter of al-Ḥijr.

Misbelievers will one day regret their misbelief.

No city was ever destroyed without warning.

The infidels mockingly ask Muḥammad to bring down angels to punish them.

So did the sinners of old act towards their apostles.

There are signs enough in the zodiac, guarded as they are from the devils who are pelted with shooting-stars if they attempt to listen.

All nature is under God's control.

Man created from clay, and jinn from smokeless fire.

The angels bidden to adore Adam.

The devil refuses, is cursed and expelled, but respited until the Day of Judgment.

Is allowed to seduce mankind.

Hell, with its seven doors, promised to misbelievers, and Paradise to believers.

Story of Abraham's angelic guests.

They announce to him the birth of a son.

They proceed to Lot's family.

The crime and punishment of the people of Sodom.

The ruined cities still remain to tell the tale.

Similar fate of the people of the Grove and of al-Ḥijr.

The hour draws nigh.

The Lord Omniscient Creator has sent the Qur'ān and the seven verses of repetition.

Muḥammad is not to grieve at the worldly success of unbelievers.

Those who dismember the Qur'ān are threatened with punishment.

Muḥammad is encouraged against the misbelievers.

CHAPTER LI.

Sūratu 'z-Ẕāriyāt.

The Chapter of the Scatterers.

Oaths by different natural phenomena that the Judgment Day will come.

Story of Abraham's entertaining the angels.

The destruction of Sodom.

Fate of Pharaoh, of 'Ād, of Ṣamūd, and of the people of Noah.

Vindication of Muḥammad against the charges of imposture or madness.

THE FIFTH PERIOD.

Thirty-one Sūrahs. From the tenth year of Muḥammad's ministry to the flight from Makkah.

The Sūrahs of this period contain some narratives from the gospel. The rites of pilgrimage are enjoined. The cavillings of the Quraish are refuted; and we have vivid picturings of the Resurrection and Judgment, of Heaven and Hell, with proof's of God's unity, power and providence.

From stage to stage the Sūrahs become, on the average, longer, and some of them now fill many pages. In the latter Sūrahs of this period, we meet not unfrequently with Madīnah passages, which have been interpolated as bearing on some connected subject. As examples may be taken, verse 40 of Sūrah xxii., in which permission is given to bear arms against the Makkans; verse 33, Sūrah xvii., containing rules for the administration of justice; verse 111, Sūrah xvi., referring to such believers as had fled their country and fought for the faith; being all passages which could have been promulgated only after the Flight to al-Madīnah.

CHAPTER XLVI.

Sūratu 'l-Aḥqāf.

The Chapter of al-Aḥqāf.

God the only God and Creator.

The unbelievers call Muḥammad a sorcerer or a forger.

The book of Moses was revealed before, and the Qur'ān is a confirmation of it in Arabic.

Conception, birth, and life of man.

Kindness to parents and acceptance of Islām enjoined.

The misbelievers are warned by the example of 'Ād, who dwell in Aḥqāf, and by that of the cities whose ruins lie around Makkah.

Allusion to the jinns who listened to Muḥammad's preaching at Makkah on his return from aṭ-Ṭā'if.

Warning to unbelievers of the punishment of the Last Day.

CHAPTER LXXII.

Sūratu 'l-Jinn.

The Chapter of the Jinn.

A crowd of jinns listen to Muḥammad's teaching at Nakhlah.

Their account of themselves.

Muhammad exhorted to persevere in preaching.

CHAPTER XXXV.

Sūratu 'l-Malā'ikah.

The Chapter of the Angels.

Praise of God, who makes the Angels his messengers.

God's unity.

Apostles before Muḥammad were accused of imposture.

Punishment in store for the unbelievers.

Muḥammad is not to be vexed on their account.

God sends rain to quicken the dead earth.

This is a sign of the Resurrection.

The power of God shown in all nature.

The helplessness of the idols.

They will disclaim their worshippers at the Resurrection.

No soul shall bear the burden of another.

Muḥammad cannot compel people to believe.

He is only a warner.

Other nations have accused their prophets of imposture and perished.

Reward of the God-fearing of believers, and of those who read and follow the Qur'ān.

Punishment of hell for the infidels.

The idolaters shall be confounded on the Judgment Day.

The Quraish, in spite of their promises and of the examples around them, are more arrogant and unbelieving than other people.

If God were to punish men as they deserve, he would not leave so much as a beast on the earth; but He respites them for a time.

Chapter XXXVI.

Sūratu Yā Sīn.

The Chapter of Yā Sīn.

Muḥammad is God's messenger, and the Qur'ān is a revelation from God to warn a heedless people.

The infidels are predestined not to believe.

All men's work shall be recorded.

The apostles of Jesus rejected at Antioch.

Ḥabību 'n-Najjār exhorts the people to follow their advice.

He is stoned to death by the populace.

Gabriel cries out and the sinful people are destroyed.

Men will laugh at the apostles who come to them, but they have an example in the nations who have perished before them.

The quickening of the dead earth is a sign of the Resurrection.

God's power shown in the procreation of species.

The alternation of night and day, the phases of the moon, the sun and moon in their orbits, are signs of God's power.

So, too, the preservation of men in ships at sea.

Almsgiving enjoined.

The unbelievers jeer at the command.

The sudden coming of the Judgment Day.

Blessed state of the believers in Paradise, and misery of the unbelievers in hell.

Muḥammad is no mere poet.

The Qur'ān an admonition.

God's providence.

The false gods will not be able to help their worshippers.

Proofs of the Resurrection.

Chapter XIX.

Sūratu Maryam.

The Chapter of Mary.

Zachariah prays for an heir.

He is promised a son, who is to be called John.

Is struck dumb for three days as a sign.

John is born and given the Book, Judgment, grace, and purity.

Story of Mary.

The annunciation.

Her delivery beneath a palm-tree.

The infant Jesus in the cradle testifies to her innocence and to his own mission.

Warning of the Day of Judgment.

Story of Abraham.

He reproves his father, who threatens to stone him.

Abraham prays for him.

Isaac and Jacob are born to him.

Moses communes with God and has Aaron for a help.

Ishmael and Idrīs mentioned as Prophets.

Their seed, when the signs of the Merciful are read, fall down adoring.

The Makkans, their successors, are promised reward in Paradise, if they repent and believe.

The angels only descend at the bidding of the Lord.

Certainty of the Resurrection.

Punishment of those who have rebelled against the Merciful.

Reproof of one who said he should have wealth and children on the Judgment Day.

The false gods shall deny their worshippers then.

The devils sent to tempt unbelievers.

The gathering of the Judgment Day.

All nature is convulsed at the imputation that the Merciful has begotten a son.

This revelation is only to warn mankind by the example of the generations who have passed away.

Chapter XVIII.

Sūratu 'l-Kahf.

The Chapter of the Cave.

The Qur'ān is a warning especially to those who say God has begotten a son.

Muḥammad is not to grieve if they refuse to believe.

Story of the Fellows of the Cave.

Their number known only to God.

Muḥammad rebuked for promising a revelation on the subject.

He is enjoined to obey God in all things, and not to be induced to give up his poorer followers.

Hell-fire threatened for the unbelievers and Paradise promised to the good.

Parable of the proud man's garden which was destroyed, while that of the humble man flourished.

This life is like the herb that springs up and perishes.

Good works are more lasting than wealth and children.

The Last Day.

The devil refuses to adore Adam.

The men are not to take him for a patron

They shall be forsaken by their patrons at the Last Day.

Men would believe, but that the example of those of yore must be repeated.

Misbelievers are unjust, and shall not be allowed to understand, or be guided.

But God is merciful.

Story of Moses and his servant in search of al-Khiẓr.

They lose their fish at the confluence of the two seas.

They meet a strange prophet, who bids Moses not question anything he may do.

He scuttles a ship, kills a boy, and builds up a tottering wall.

Moses desires an explanation, which the stranger gives, and leaves him.

Story of Ẕū 'l-Qarnain.

He travels to the ocean of the setting sun.

Builds a rampart to keep in Gog and Magog.

These are to be let loose again before the Judgment Day.

Reward and punishment on that day.

Were the sea ink, it would not suffice for the words of the Lord.

The Prophet is only a mortal.

CHAPTER XXVII.

Ṣūratu 'n-Naml.

The Chapter of the Ant.

The Qur'ān a guidance to believers.

God appears to Moses in the fire.

Moses is sent to Pharaoh with signs, but is called a sorcerer.

David and Solomon endowed with knowledge.

Solomon taught the speech of birds.

His army of men, jinns, and birds, marches through the valley of the ant.

One ant bids the rest retire to their holes lest Solomon and his hosts crush them.

Solomon smiles and answers her.

He reviews the birds and misses the hoopoe, who, returning, brings news of the magnificence of the Queen of Sheba.

Solomon sends him back with a letter to the Queen.

A demon brings him her throne.

She comes to Solomon, recognises her throne; marvels at the palace with the glass floor, which she mistakes for water.

Becomes a Muslim.

Ṣamūd reject Ṣāliḥ and perish.

Lot is saved, while the people of Sodom are destroyed.

The Lord, the God of nature; the only God and Creator.

Certainty of the Resurrection.

The ruins of ancient cities an example,

The Qur'ān decides disputed points for the Jews.

Muḥammad bidden to trust in God, for he cannot make the deaf to hear his message.

The beast that shall appear at the Resurrection.

Terrors of the Last Day.

The Prophet bidden to worship the Lord of this land, to recite the Qur'ān, and to become a Muslim.

CHAPTER XLII.

Sūratu 'sh-Shūrā.

The Chapter of Counsel.

The Qur'ān inspired by God to warn the Mother of cities of the judgment to come.

God is one, the Creator of all things, who provides for all.

He calls men to the same religion as that of the prophets of old, which men have broken up into sects.

Muḥammad has only to proclaim his message.

Those who argue about God shall be confuted.

None knows when the hour shall come but God.

The idolaters shall only have their portion in this life.

God will vindicate the truth of His revelation.

His creation and providence signs of His power.

Men's misfortunes by land and sea are due to their own sins.

The provision of the next world is best for the righteous.

It is not sinful to retaliate if wronged, though forgiveness is a duty.

The sinners shall have none to help them on the Day of Judgment.

They are exhorted to repent before it comes.

Ingratitude of man.

God controls all.

No mortal has ever seen God face to face.

He speaks to men only through inspiration of His apostles.

This Qur'ān was revealed by a spirit to guide into the right way.

CHAPTER XL.

Sūratu 'l-Mu'min.

The Chapter of the Believer.

Attributes of God.

Muḥammad encouraged by the fate of other nations who rejected their apostles.

The angels' prayer for the believers.

Despair in hell of the idolaters.

The terrors of the Judgment Day.

God alone the Omniscient Judge.

The vestiges of former nations are still visible in the land to warn the people.

The story of Moses and Pharaoh.

The latter wishes to kill Moses, but a secret believer makes a long appeal.

Pharaoh bids Hāmān construct a tower to mount up to the God of Moses.

God saves the believer, and Pharaoh is ruined by his own devices.

Mutual recrimination of the damned.

Exhortation to patience and praise.

Those who wrangle about God rebuked.

The certain coming of the Hour.

The unity of God asserted and His attributes enumerated.

Idolatry forbidden.

The conception, birth, life, and death of man.

Idolaters shall find out their error in hell.

Muḥammad encouraged to wait for the issue.

Cattle to ride on and to eat are signs of God's providence.

The example of the nations who perished of old for rejecting the apostles.

CHAPTER XXXVIII.

Sūratu 's-Ṣād.

The Chapter of Ṣād.

Oath by the Qur'ān.

Example of former generations who perished for unbelief, and for saying that their prophets were sorcerers and the Scriptures forgeries.

The Makkans are warned thereby.

Any hosts of the confederates shall be routed.

Fate of the people of Noah, 'Ād, Pharaoh, Ṣamūd, and Lot.

The Makkans must expect the same.

Muḥammad exhorted to be patient of what they say.

He is reminded of the powers bestowed on David.

The parable of the ewe lambs proposed to David by the two antagonists.

David exhorted not to follow lust.

The heaven and earth were not created in vain, as the misbelievers think.

The Qur'ān a reminder.

Solomon, lost in admiration of his horses, neglects his devotions, but, repenting, slays them.

A jinn in Solomon's likeness is set on his throne to punish him.

He repents and prays God for a kingdom such as no one should ever possess again.

The wind and the devils made subject to him.

The patience of Job.

Abraham, Isaac, and Jacob.

Elisha and Ẕū 'l-Kifl.

Happiness of the righteous in Paradise.

Misery and mutual recrimination of the wicked in hell.

Muḥammad only sent to warn people and proclaim God's unity.

The creation of man and disobedience of Iblīs, who is expelled.

He is respited till the Judgment Day, that he may seduce people to misbelief.

But he and those who follow him shall fill hell.

Chapter XXV.

Sūratu 'l-Furqān.

The Chapter of the Discrimination.

The Discrimination sent down as a warning that God is one, the Creator and Governor of all; yet the Makkans call it old folks' tales.

They object that the Prophet acts and lives as a mere mortal or is crazy.

Hell-fire shall be the punishment of those who disbelieve in the Resurrection.

Description of the Judgment Day.

The Quraish object that the Qur'ān was revealed piecemeal.

Moses and Aaron and Noah were treated like Muḥammad, but those who called them liars were punished.

'Ād and Ṣamūd perished for the same sin.

The ruins of the cities of the plain are existing examples.

Yet they will not accept the Prophet.

God controls the shadow, gives night for a repose, quickens the dead earth with rain.

He lets loose the two seas, but places a barrier between them.

He has created man.

He is the loving and merciful God.

The Quraish object to the Merciful as a new God.

The lowly and moderate are His servants.

They abstain from idolatry, murder, false witness, and frivolous discourse.

These shall be rewarded.

God cares nothing for the rejection of his message by the infidels.

Their punishment shall be lasting.

Chapter XX.

Sūratu Ṭā Hā.

The Chapter of Ṭā Hā.

The Qur'ān a reminder from the Merciful, who owns all things and knows all things.

There is no god but He.

His are the excellent names.

Story of Moses.

He perceives the fire and is addressed from it by God in the holy valley Ṭuvan.

God shows him the miracle of the staff turned to a snake and of the white hand.

Sends him to Pharaoh.

Moses excuses himself because of the impediment in his speech.

Aaron is given him as a minister.

Moses' mother throws him into the sea.

His sister watches him.

He is restored to his mother.

Slays an Egyptian and flees to Midian.

Moses and Aaron go to Pharaoh and call on him to believe.

Pharaoh charges them with being magicians.

Their contest with the Egyptian magicians, who believe, and are threatened with punishment by Pharaoh.

Moses leads the children of Israel across the sea, by a dry road.

Pharaoh and his people are overwhelmed.

The covenant on Mount Sinai.

The miracle of the manna and quails.

As-Sāmirī makes the calf in Moses absence.

Moses seizes his brother angrily by the beard and destroys the calf.

Misbelievers threatened with the terrors of the Resurrection Day.

Fate of the mountains on that day.

All men shall be summoned to judgment.

No intercession shall avail except from such as the Merciful permits.

The Qur'ān is in Arabic that people may fear and remember.

Muḥammad is not to hasten on its revelation.

Adam broke his covenant with God

Angels bidden to adore Adam.

Iblīs refuses.

Tempts Adam.

Adam, Eve, and the Devil expelled from Paradise.

Misbelievers shall be gathered together blind on the Resurrection Day.

The Makkans pass by the ruined dwellings of the generations who have been aforetime destroyed for unbelief.

But for the Lord's word being passed, they would have perished too.

Muḥammad is exhorted to bear their insults patiently and to praise God through the day.

Prayer enjoined.

The fate of those of yore a sufficient sign.

Let them wait and see the issue.

CHAPTER XLIII.

Sūratu 'z-Zukhruf.

The Chapter of Gilding.

The original of the Qur'ān is with God

The example of the nations of old who mocked at the prophets.

God the Creator.

Men are biddon to praise Him who provides man with ships and cattle whereon to ride.

The Arabs are rebuked for attributing female offspring to God, when they themselves repine when a female child is born to any one of them.

They are also blamed for asserting that the angels are female.

The excuse that this was the religion of their fathers, will not avail

It is the same as older nations made.

Their fate.

Abraham disclaimed idolatry.

The Makkans were permitted to enjoy prosperity only until the Apostle came, and now that he has come they reject him.

The are reproved for saying that had the Prophet been a man of consideration at Makkah and aṭ-Ṭā'if, they would have owned him.

Misbelievers would have had still more wealth and enjoyment, but that men would have then all become infidels.

Those who turn from the admonition shall be chained to devils, who shall mislead them.

God will take vengeance on them, whether Muḥammad live to see it or not.

He is encouraged to persevere.

Moses was mocked by Pharaoh, whom he was sent to warn.

But Pharaoh and his people were drowned.

Answer to the Arabs, who objected that Jesus, too, must come under the ban against false gods.

But Jesus did not assume to be a god.

Threat of the coming of the Hour.

The joys of Paradise and the terrors of Hell.

The damned shall beg Mālik to make an end of them.

The recording angels note down the secret plots of the infidels.

God has no son.

He is the Lord of all.

CHAPTER XII.

Sūratu Yūsuf.

The Chapter of Joseph.

The Qur'ān revealed in Arabic that the Makkans may understand.

It contains the best of stories.

Story of Joseph.

He tells his father his dream.

Jacob advises him to keep it to himself.

Jealousy of Joseph's brethren.

They conspire to throw him in a pit.

Induce his father to let him go with them.

They cast him in the pit, and bring home his shirt covered with lying blood.

Travellers discover him and sell him into Egypt.

He is adopted by his master.

His mistress endeavours to seduce him.

His innocence proved.

His mistress shows him to the women of the city to excuse her conduct.

Their amazement at his beauty.

He is imprisoned.

Interprets the dreams of the baker and the cupbearer.

Pharaoh's dream.

Joseph is sent for to expound it.

He is appointed to a situation of trust in the land.

His brethren arrive and do not recognise him.

They ask for corn and he requires them to bring their youngest brother as the condition of his giving it to them.

The goods they had brought to barter are returned to their sacks.

Benjamin is sent back.

Joseph discovers himself to him.

Joseph places the king's drinking-cup in his brother's pack.

Accuses them all of the theft.

Takes Benjamin as a bondsman for the theft.

They return to Jacob, who, in great grief, sends them back again, to bring him news.

Joseph discovers himself to them and sends back his shirt.

Jacob recognises it by the smell.

Jacob goes back with them to Egypt.

This story appealed to as a proof of the truth of the Revelation.

CHAPTER XI.

Sūratu Hūd.

The Chapter of Hūd.

The Qur'ān a book calling men to believe in the unity of God.

Nothing is hidden from Him.

He is the Creator of all.

Men will not believe, and deem themselves secure, because their punishment is deferred.

They demand a sign, or say the Qur'ān is invented by the Prophet; but they and their false gods together cannot bring ten such Sūrahs.

Misbelievers threatened with future punishment, while believers are promised Paradise.

Noah was likewise sent, but his people objected that he was a mere mortal like themselves, and only followed by the meaner sort of men.

He also is accused of having invented his revelation.

He is saved in the ark and the unbelievers drowned.

He endeavours to save his son.

The ark settles on Mount al-Jūdī.

Hūd was sent to 'Ād.

His people plotted against him and were destroyed, while he was saved.

Ṣāliḥ was sent to Ṣamūd.

The she-camel given for a sign.

The people hamstring her and perish.

Abraham entertains the angels who are sent to the people of Lot.

He pleads for them.

Lot offers his daughters to the people of Sodom, to spare the angels.

He escapes by night, and Sodom is destroyed.

Shu'aib is sent to Midian, and his people, rejecting his mission, perish too.

Moses sent to Pharaoh, who shall be punished at the Resurrection.

The Makkans, too, shall be punished.

They are threatened with the Judgment Day, when they shall be sent to hell, while the believers are in Paradise.

The Makkans are bidden to take warning by the fate of the cities whose stories are related above.

These stories are intended to strengthen the Prophet's heart.

He is bidden to wait and leave the issue to God.

Chapter X.

Sūratu Yūnus.

The Chapter of Jonah.

No wonder that the Qur'ān was revealed to a mere man.

Misbelievers deem him a sorcerer.

God the Creator and Ruler.

No one can intercede with Him except by His permission.

Creation is a sign of His power.

Reward hereafter for the believers.

Man calls on God in distress, but forgets Him when deliverance comes.

Warning from the fall of former generations.

The infidels are not satisfied with the Qur'ān.

Muḥammad dare not invent a false revelation.

False gods can neither harm nor profit them.

People require a sign.

God saves people in dangers by land and sea.

This life is like grass.

Promise of Paradise and threat of Hell.

Fate of the idolaters and false gods at the Last Day.

God the Lord of all.

Other religions are mere conjecture.

The Qur'ān could only have been devised by God.

The Makkans are challenged to produce a single Sūrah like it.

Unbelievers warned of the Last Day by the fate of previous nations.

Reproval of those who prohibit lawful things.

God is ever watchful over the Prophet's actions.

Happiness of the believers.

The infidels cannot harm the Prophet.

Refutation of those who ascribe offspring to God.

Muḥammad encouraged by the story of Noah and the other prophets of old.

Fate of Pharaoh and vindication of Moses and Aaron.

The people of the Book (Jews and Christians) appealed to in confirmation of the truth of the Qur'ān.

The story of Jonah.

The people of Nineveh saved by repenting and believing in time.

The people are exhorted to embrace Islām, the faith of the Ḥanīf.

God alone is powerful.

Belief or unbelief affect only the individual himself.

Resignation and patience inculcated.

Chapter XIV.

Sūratu Ibrāhīm.

The Chapter of Abraham.

The Qur'ān revealed to bring men from darkness into light.

God is Lord of all.

No apostle sent except with the language of his own people.

Moses sent to Pharaoh.

The people of Noah.

'Ād and Ṣamūd objected that their prophets were mortals like themselves.

The prophets relied on God, who vindicated them.

Frightful description of hell.

Misbelievers are like ashes blown away by the stormy wind.

Helplessness of the damned.

But believers are in Paradise.

A good word is like a good tree whose root is in the earth and whose branches are in the sky, and which gives fruit in all seasons.

A bad word is as a tree that is felled.

God's word is sure.

Idolaters are threatened with hell-fire.

God is the Creator of all.

He subjects all things to man's use.

Abraham prayed that the territory of Makkah might be a sanctuary.

The unjust are only respited till the Judgment Day.

The ruins of the dwellings of those who have perished for the denying the mission of their apostles, are a proof of the truth of Muḥammad's mission.

The Lord will take vengeance on the Last Day, when sinners shall burn in hell with shirts of pitch to cover them.

The Qur'ān is a warning and an admonition.

Chapter VI.

Sūratu 'l-An'ām.

The Chapter of Cattle.

Light and darkness are both created by God.

Rebuke to idolaters.

They are exhorted to take warning by the fate of those of old who rejected the prophets.

Had the revelation been a material book, they would have disbelieved it.

If the Prophet had been an angel, he would have come in the guise of a man.

Attributes of God.

Muḥammad bidden to become a Muslim.

Those who have the Scriptures ought to recognise Muḥammad as the one foretold in them.

The idolaters will be disappointed of the intercession of their gods on the Judgment Day.

They deny the Resurrection Day now, but hereafter they will have awful proof of its truth.

The next world is preferable to this.

Prophets aforetime were also mocked at, and they were patient.

God could send them a sign if He pleased.

Beasts, birds, and the like, are communities like men.

Their fate is all written in the book.

They, too, shall be gathered on the Judgment Day.

Arguments in proof of the supreme power of God.

Muḥammad is only a messenger.

He is to disclaim miraculous power.

Is not to repulse believers.

He is bidden to abjure idolatry and not follow the lusts of the Makkans.

God's omniscience.

He takes men's souls to Himself during sleep.

Sends guardian angels to watch over them.

Preserves men in danger by land and sea.

Muḥammad is not to join in discussions on religion with idolaters, nor to associate with those who make a sport of it.

Folly of idolatry set forth.

God the Creator.

Abraham's perplexity in seeking after the true God.

Worships successively the stars, the moon, and the sun, but is convinced that they are not gods by seeing them set.

Turns to God and becomes a Ḥanīf.

Other prophets of old were inspired.

The Qur'ān is also a special revelation from God to the Makkans, fulfilling their Scriptures, but the Jews have perverted or suppressed parts of them.

Denunciation of one who falsely pretended to be inspired.

The Creation a proof of God's unity.

Rebuke to those who call the jinn His partners, or attribute offspring to Him.

Idolaters are not to be abused, lest they, too, speak ill of God.

The Makkans would not have believed even if a sign had been given them.

Muḥammad is to trust to God alone.

Men are not to abstain from food over which God's name has been pronounced.

God will vindicate His messenger.

Belief or the reverse depends on God's grace.

The jinns and false gods, together with their worshippers, will be condemned to everlasting torment.

God never punishes without first sending an apostle with warning.

The threatened doom cannot be averted.

Denunciation of the idolatrous practices of the Arabs.

Setting apart portions of the produce of the land for God and for the idols, and defrauding God of His portion.

Infanticide.

Declaring cattle and tilth inviolable.

God created all fruits and all cattle, both are therefore lawful.

Argument proving the absurdity of some of these customs.

Enumeration of the only kinds of food that are unlawful.

The prohibition to the Jews of certain food was only on account of their sins.

God's revealed word is the only certain argument.

Declaration of things really forbidden, namely, harshness to parents, infanticide, abominable sins, and murder.

The property of orphans is to be respected and fair-dealing to be practised.

No soul compelled beyond its capacity.

The Qur'ān to be accepted on the same authority as the Book of Moses was.

Faith required now without signs.

No latter profession on the Judgment Day shall profit them.

Good works to be rewarded tenfold, but evil works only by the same amount.

Islām is the religion of Abraham the Ḥanīf.

A belief in one God, to whom all prayer and devotion is due.

Each soul shall bear its own burden.

The high rank of some of the Makkans is only a trial from the Lord whereby to prove them.

CHAPTER LXIV.
Sūratu 't-Taghābun.
The Chapter of Mutual Deceit.

God the Creator.

The Resurrection.

The Unity of God.

Wealth and children must not distract men from the service of God.

CHAPTER XXVIII.
Sūratu 'l-Qaṣaṣ.
The Chapter of the Story.

The history of Moses and Pharaoh.

The latter and his vizier.

Hāmān oppresses the children of Israel.

Moses is exposed on the river by his mother.

He is adopted by Pharaoh.

His sister watches him, and his mother is engaged to nurse him.

He grows up and slays the Egyptian.

Flees to Midian.

Helps the two Midianites to draw water.

Serves their father Shohaib for ten years and then marries his daughter.

God appears to him in the fire.

Is sent with his brother Aaron to Pharaoh.

Hāmān builds Pharaoh a high tower to ascend to the God of Moses.

His punishment.
Moses gives the Law.
These stories are proofs of Muḥammad's mission.
The Arabs reject the Book of Moses and the Qur'ān as two impostures.
Those who have the Scriptures recognise the truth of the Qur'ān.
The Makkans warned by the example of the cities of old that have perished.
Disappointment of the idolaters at the Day of Judgment.
Helplessness of the idols before God.
Qārūn's great wealth.
The earth opens and swallows him up for his pride and his insolence to Moses.
Muḥammad encouraged in his faith and purpose.

Chapter XXIII.

Sūratu 'l-Mu'minīn.

The Chapter of Believers.

The humble, chaste, and honest, shall prosper.
The creation, birth, death, and resurrection of man.
God's goodness in providing for men's sustenance.
Noah sent to his people, who reject him because he is a mere mortal.
They are drowned, and he is saved in the ark.
Moses and Aaron were also called liars.
Mary and her son the cause of their followers division into sects.
The God-fearing encouraged.
The Quraish rebuked for their pride, and for denying Muḥammad, and calling him possessed.
They are reminded of the famine and defeat they have already experienced.
Doctrine of the Resurrection.
The unity of God.
He has no offspring.
Is omniscient.
Muḥammad is encouraged not to care for the false accusations of the Makkans, but to seek refuge in God.
Punishment, on the Day of Resurrection, of those who mocked at the little party of believers.

Chapter XXII.

Sūratu 'l-Ḥajj.

The Chapter of the Pilgrimage.

Terrors of the Last Day, yet men dispute about God and follow devils.
The conception, birth, growth, and death of men, and the growth of herbs in the ground are proofs of the Resurrection.
But some dispute, others waver between two opinions.
The most desperate means cannot thwart the divine decrees.
God will decide between the Jews, Christians, Sabians, Magians, and idolaters on the Judgment Day.
All nature adores God.
The misbelievers are threatened with hell-fire, and the believers promised Paradise.
Punishment threatened to those who prohibit men from visiting the Sacred Mosque.
Abraham, when bidden to cleanse the Ka'bah, was told to proclaim the pilgrimage.
The rules of the Ḥajj enjoined.
Cattle are lawful food.
Warning against idolatry and exhortation to become Ḥanīfs.
Sacrifices at the Ka'bah are enjoined.
All men have their appointed rites.
The name of God is to be mentioned over cattle when slaughtered.
Camels may be sacrificed and eaten.
God will defend believers, but loves not misbelieving traitors.
Those who have been driven from their homes for acknowledging God's unity are allowed to fight.
If men did not fight for such a cause, all places of worship would be destroyed.
The people of Noah, 'Ād, Ṣamūd, Abraham, and Lot, called their prophets liars, and were allowed to range at large, but at last they were punished.
Their cities were destroyed, and the ruins are visible to travellers still.
Muḥammad is only sent to warn the Makkans of a like fate.
Satan contrives to suggest a wrong reading to the Prophet while reading the Qur'ān.
The Kingdom shall be God's upon the Judgment Day.
Those who flee or are slain in the cause, shall be provided for and rewarded.
Believers who take revenge and are again attacked, will be helped.
All nature is subject to God.
Every nation has its rites to observe.
The idolaters treat the revelation with scorn.
The false gods could not even create a fly.
Exhortation to worship God and fight for the faith of Abraham, whose religion the Muslims profess.
God is the Sovereign and Helper.

Chapter XXI.

Sūratu 'l-Ambiyā'.

The Chapter of the Prophets.

Men mock at the revelation.
They say it is a jumble of dreams, and that Muḥammad is a poet, and they ask for a sign.
The prophets of old were but mortal.
The people who rejected them perished.
Heaven and earth were not created in sport.
Truth shall crush falsehood.
All things praise God.
If there were other gods than He, heaven and earth would be corrupted.
All former prophets were taught there is no god but God.
The Merciful has not begotten children.
The angels are only His servants.
The separation of earth from heaven, the creation of living things from water, the steadying of the earth by mountains, and placing the sky as a roof over it, and the

creation of the night and day, and of the sun and moon, are signs.

No one was ever granted immortality.

Every soul must taste of death.

The unbelievers mock at Muḥammad and disbelieve in the Merciful.

Man is hasty.

The infidels are threatened with punishment in the next world.

Those who mocked at the prophets of old perished.

No one shall be wronged on the Last Day.

Moses and Aaron received a scripture.

Abraham destroys the images which his people worshipped.

He tells them that it was the largest idol which did it.

He is condemned to be burnt alive, but the fire is miraculously made cool and safe.

Abraham, Lot, Isaac, and Jacob, all inspired.

Lot was brought safely out of a city of wrong-doers.

Noah also was saved.

David and Solomon give judgment about a field.

The mountains and birds are made subject to David.

He is taught the art of making coats of mail.

The wind and the demons are subjected to Solomon.

Job was saved.

Ishmail, Idrīs, and Z̲ū 'l-Kifl were patient, and entered into the mercy of the Lord.

Z̲ū 'n-Nūn (Jonah) was saved in the fish's belly.

Zachariah had his prayer granted and a son (John) given him.

The spirit was breathed into the Virgin Mary.

But their followers have divided into sects.

A city once destroyed for unbelief shall not be restored till Gog and Magog are let loose.

The promise draws nigh.

Idolaters shall be the pebbles of hell.

But the elect shall be rolled up as as-Sijill rolls up a book.

As is written in the Psalms, "The righteous shall inherit the earth."

Muḥammad sent as a mercy to the worlds.

God is one God.

He knows all.

He is the Merciful.

Chapter XVII.

Sūratu Banī Isrā'īl.

The Chapter of the Children of Israel.

Allusion to the night journey from the Sacred Mosque (at Makkah) to the Remote Mosque (at Jerusalem).

Moses received the book.

Noah was a faithful servant.

Israel's two sins and their punishment.

The Qur'ān a guide and a good tidings.

Man prays for evil and is hasty.

Night and day are two signs.

Every man's augury is round his neck.

Each one shall have a book on the Resurrection Day with an account of his deeds.

Each is to bear the burden of his own sins.

No city is destroyed till warned by an apostle.

Choice of good in this world or the next.

Muḥammad is not to associate others with God.

Kindness to parents enjoined.

Moderation to be practised.

Infanticide and fornication are sins.

Homicide is not to be avenged except for just cause.

Honesty and humility inculcated.

The angels are not the daughters of God.

If there were other gods, they would rebel against God.

All in the heavens praise Him.

Unbelievers cannot understand the Qur'ān.

The unity of God unacceptable to the Makkans.

The Resurrection.

Idolaters not to be provoked.

Some prophets preferred over others.

False gods themselves have recourse to God.

All cities to be destroyed before the Judgment Day.

Had Muḥammad been sent with signs, the Makkans would have disbelieved them like Ṣamūd.

The vision (of the Night Journey) and the Zaqqūm tree of hell, are causes of contention.

Iblīs' disobedience and fall.

He is given permission to delude men.

Safety by land and sea a special mercy from God.

All shall have justice at the Last Day.

The Ṣaqīf tribe at aṭ-Ṭā'if nearly seduced Muḥammad into promulgating an unauthorised sentence.

Injunction to pray.

Man is ungrateful.

Departure of the spirit.

Mankind and jinns together could not produce the like of the Qur'ān.

Signs demanded of Muḥammad.

He is only a mortal.

Fate of those who disbelieve in the Resurrection.

Moses brought nine signs, but Pharaoh disbelieved in them.

His fate.

The children of Israel succeeded him in his possessions.

The Qur'ān was revealed as occasion required.

Those who believe the scripture recognise it.

God and the Merciful One are not two gods, for God has no partner.

Chapter XVI.

Sūratu 'n-Naḥl.

The Chapter of the Bee.

God's decree will come to pass.

He sends the angels to instruct his servants to give warning that there is no other God.

The creation and ordering of all natural objects are signs of His power.

The false gods are inanimate and powerless.

God is but one.

The unbelievers who call the revelation old folks' tales, must bear the burden of their own sins.

On the Resurrection Day, their associates will disown them.

Reception by the angels of the wicked and the good in Hell and in Paradise.

The infidels strenuously deny the Resurrection.

The Muhājirūn are promised a good reward.

The Jews and Christians to be asked to confirm the Qur'ān.

All nature adores God.

Unity of God affirmed.

When in distress, men turn to God, but forget Him and become idolaters when deliverance comes.

The practice of setting aside part of their produce for the idols reproved.

The practice of female infanticide, while they ascribe daughters to God, is reproved, and disbelief in the future life also rebuked.

Satan is the patron of the infidels.

The Qur'ān sent down as a guidance and mercy.

The rain which quickens the dead earth, and the cattle which give milk, and the vines which give fruit and wine are signs.

The bee is inspired from the Lord to build hives and to use those made first by men.

Its honey is lawful.

The rich Arabs are reproved for their treatment of their slaves.

Helplessness of the false gods illustrated by the parable of the slave and of the dumb man.

Goodness of God in providing food and shelter for men.

Idolaters shall be disowned by the false gods at the Resurrection.

Every nation shall have a witness against it on that day.

Justice and good faith inculcated, especially the duty of keeping to a treaty once made.

Satan has no power over believers.

Verses of the Qur'ān abrogated.

The Holy Spirit (Gabriel) is the instrument of the revelation.

Suggestion that Muḥammad is helped by some mortal to compose the Qur'ān.

This cannot be, as the person hinted at speaks a foreign language and the Qur'ān is in Arabic.

Denunciation of misbelievers.

Warning of the fate Makkah is to expect if its inhabitants continue to disbelieve.

Unlawful foods.

God will forgive wrong done through ignorance.

Abraham was Ḥanīf.

The ordinance of the Sabbath.

Muḥammad is to dispute with his opponents kindly.

The believers are not to take too savage revenge.

They are exhorted to patience and trust in God.

Chapter XIII.

Sūratu 'r-Ra'd.

The Chapter of Thunder.

The Qur'ān a revelation from the Lord, the Creator and Governor of all.

Misbelievers are threatened.

God knows all, and the recording angels are ever present.

Lightning and thunder celebrate God's praises.

All in heaven and earth acknowledge Him.

God sends rain and causes the torrents to flow.

The scum thereof is like the dross on smelted ore.

The righteous and the believers are promised Paradise, and the misbelievers are threatened with hell-fire.

Exhortation to believe in the Merciful.

Were the Qur'ān to convulse nature, they would not believe.

Further threats against misbelievers.

God notes the deeds of every soul.

Stratagem unavailing against Him.

Paradise and Hell.

Muḥammad bidden to persevere in asserting the unity of God.

Had he not followed the Qur'ān, God would have forsaken him.

Other apostles have had wives and children.

None could bring a sign without God's permission.

For every period there is a revelation.

God can annul or confirm any part of His revelation which He pleases.

He has the Mother of the Book (*i.e* the Eternal Original).

Whether Muḥammad live to see his predictions fulfilled or not, God only knows.

His duty is only to preach the message.

The conquests of Islām pointed to.

God will support the prophets against misbelievers.

Chapter XXIX.

Sūratu 'l-'Ankabūt.

The Chapter of the Spider.

Believers must be proved.

Kindness to be shown to parents; but they are not to be obeyed if they endeavour to lead their children to idolatry.

The hypocrites stand by the Muslims only in success.

The unbelievers try to seduce the believers by offering to bear their sins.

Noah delivered from the deluge.

Abraham preaches against idolatry.

Is cast into the fire, but saved.

Flees from his native land.

Isaac and Jakob born to him.

Lot and the fate of the inhabitants of Sodom.

Midian and their prophet Shu'aib.

'Ād and Ṣamūd.
Fate of Qārūn, Pharaoh, and Hāmān.
Similitude of the spider.
Muḥammad bidden to rehearse the Qur'ān.
Prayer enjoined.
Those who have scriptures are to be mildly dealt with in disputation.
They believe in the Qur'ān.
Muḥammad unable to read.
Signs are only in the power of God.
The idolaters reproved, and threatened with punishment.
The believers promised reward.
God provides for all.
This world is but a sport.
God saves men in dangers by sea, yet they are ungrateful.
The territory of Makkah inviolable.
Exhortation to strive for the faith

Chapter VII.

Sūratu 'l-A'rāf

The Chapter of al-A'rāf.

Muḥammad is bidden to accept the Qur'ān fearlessly.
The Makkans must take warning by the fate of those who rejected the prophets of old.
The creation and fall of Adam.
Iblīs allowed to tempt mankind.
Men are to go to mosque decently clad.
God has only prohibited sinful actions.
Men are warned not to reject the mission of the apostles.
Their punishment at and after death if they do so.
The happiness of believers in Paradise.
Description of al-A'rāf, the partition between heaven and hell.
Immediate belief in the Qur'ān required.
God the Creator.
Humble and secret prayer enjoined.
Proofs of God's goodness.
Noah sent to warn his people.
He is saved in the ark while they are drowned.
Hūd sent to 'Ād.
They reject his preaching and are punished.
Ṣāliḥ sent to Ṣamūd.
Produces the she-camel as a sign.
The people hamstring her and are punished.
Lot sent to the people of Sodom.
Their punishment.
Shu'aib sent to Midian.
His people reject him and are destroyed.
Thus city after city was destroyed for rejecting the apostles.
Moses sent to Pharaoh.
The miracles of the snake and the white hand.
The magicians contend with Moses, are overcome and believe.
Pharaoh punishes them.
The slaughter of the first-born.
The plagues of Egypt.
The Israelites are delivered.
Moses communes with God, who appears to him on the mount.
The giving of the Law.
The golden calf.
Moses' wrath against Aaron.
The seventy elders.
The coming of Muḥammad, the illiterate Prophet, foretold.
Some Jews are just and rightly guided.
The division into twelve tribes.
The miracle of smiting the rock.
The manna and quails.
The command to enter the city, saying, "Ḥiṭṭatun," and punishment for disobedience.
The Sabbath-breaking city.
The transformation of the wicked inhabitants into apes.
The dispersion of the Jews.
The mountain held over the Jews.
The covenant of God with the posterity of Adam.
Am I not your Lord?
Humiliation of one who, having foretold the coming of a prophet in the time of Muḥammad, would not acknowledge the latter as such.
Many, both of the jinn and of mankind, predestined to hell.
The names of God are not to be perverted.
Muḥammad is not possessed.
The coming of the Hour.
Creation of Adam and Eve.
Conception and birth of their first child, 'Abdu 'l-Hāriṣ.
Their idolatry.
Idols are themselves servants of God.
They have neither life nor senses.
Muḥammad is bidden to treat his opponents with mildness.
The mention of God's name repels devilish influences.
Men are recommended to listen to the Qur'ān and to humble themselves before God, whom the angels adore.

Chapter CXIII.

Sūrātu 'l-Falaq.

The Chapter of the Daybreak.

The Prophet seeks refuge in God from evil influences.

Chapter CXIV.

Sūratu 'n-Nās.

The Chapter of Men.

The Prophet seeks refuge in God from the devil and his evil suggestions.

THE SIXTH AND LAST PERIOD.

Twenty Sūrahs given at al-Madīnah.

Chapter XCVIII.

Sūratu 'l-Baiyinah.

The Chapter of the Manifest Sign.

Rebuke to Jews and Christians for doubting the manifest sign of Muḥammad's mission.

Chapter II.

Sūratu 'l-Baqarah.

The Chapter of the Heifer.

The Qur'ān a guidance.
Rebuke to unbelievers.

A parable of one who kindles fire.
God is not ashamed of trifling similitudes.
The creation of man.
Adam taught the names.
Iblīs refuses to adore him.
The temptation and fall.
The Children of Israel.
Their trials in Egypt.
The golden calf.
The manna and quails.
Bidden to enter the city and say, "Ḥiṭṭatun."
Moses strikes the rock.
He bids the people slaughter a dun cow to discover a murder.
Charge against the Jews of corrupting the Scriptures.
The golden calf.
The mountain held over them.
Gabriel reveals the Qur'ān.
Hārūt and Mārūt.
Believers are not to say "Rā'inā," but "Unẓurnā."
Verses which are annulled will be replaced by better ones.
Paradise not exclusively for Jews and Christians.
Mosques to be free.
Story of Abraham.
He rebuilds the Ka'bah.
Was a Ḥanīf.
The qiblah free.
Aṣ-Ṣafā and al-Marwah may be compassed.
Proofs of God's unity.
Lawful and unlawful food.
The law of retaliation for homicide.
Testators.
The fast of Ramaẓān.
Rites of the pilgrimage.
Its duration.
Fighting for religion lawful during the sacred months.
Wine and gaming forbidden.
Marriage with idolaters unlawful.
The law of divorce.
Of suckling children.
The Muhājirūn to be rewarded.
The Children of Israel demand a king
Saul (Ṭālūt).
The shechina.
The ark.
Saul and Gideon confounded.
Goliath.
Jesus.
The *Ayatu 'l-kursī* (verse of the throne), asserting the self-subsistence and omnipresence of God.
Nimrod and Abraham.
Almsgiving.
No compulsion in religion.
Proofs of the Resurrection.
Ezekiel's vision of the dry bones referred to.
Abraham and the birds.
Almsgiving recommended.
Usurers denounced.
Laws relating to debt and trading.
Persons mentally incapable are to act by agents.
The believer's prayer.

CHAPTER III.

Sūratu Āli 'Imrān.

The Chapter of 'Imrān's Family.

God's unity and self-subsistence.
The Qur'ān confirmatory of previous scripture.
The verses are either decisive or ambiguous.
Example of Pharaoh's punishment.
The battle of Badr.
Islām the true religion.
Future torment eternal.
Obedience to God and the Apostle enjoined.
Conception of the Virgin Mary.
She is brought up by Zachariah.
Birth of John.
The annunciation of the Virgin.
Birth and infancy of Jesus.
The miracle of the birds of clay.
The disciples.
Allusion to Muḥammad's dispute with a Christian deputation from Najrān.
Abraham a Ḥanīf.
Reproof to Jews who pretend to believe and then recant, and who pervert the scriptures.
No distinction to be made between the prophets.
The Jews rebuked for prohibiting certain kinds of food.
The foundation of the Ka'bah.
Abraham's station.
Pilgrimage enjoined.
Schism and misbelief reproved.
Battle of Uḥud referred to.
The victory at Badr due to angelic aid.
Usury denounced.
Fate of those who rejected the prophets of old.
Muḥammad's death must not divert the believers from their faith.
Promise of God's help.
Further account of the battle of Badr.
The Muslim martyrs to enter Paradise.
The victory of Badr more than counterbalanced the defeat at Uḥud.
The hypocrites detected and reproved.
Death the common lot, even of apostles.
Prayer for the believers.
Exhortation to vie in good works and be patient.

CHAPTER VIII.

Sūratu 'l-Anfāl.

The Chapter of the Spoils.

Spoils belong to God and the Apostle.
Who are the true believers?
The expedition of Muḥammad against the caravan from Syria under Abū Sufyān.
The miraculous victory at Badr.
Address to the Makkans who, fearing an attack from Muḥammad, took sanctuary in the Ka'bah, and prayed to God to decide between themselves and him.
Exhortation to believe and avoid treachery.
Plots against Muḥammad frustrated by Divine interference.
The revelation treated as old folks' tales.

Rebuke of the idolaters for mocking the Muslims at prayer.
Offer of an amnesty to those who will believe.
Exhortation to fight the infidels.
Division of the spoils.
Description of the battle.
The enemy made to seem few in the Muslim's eyes, while they seemed more numerous than they really were.
The infidels forsaken by Satan, their leader, on the day of battle.
Fate of the hypocrites.
Warning from Pharaoh's fate.
The infidels who break their treaty.
Treachery to be met with the like.
God will help the Prophet against the traitors.
A few enduring believers shall conquer a multitude of infidels.
The Muslims are reproved for accepting ransom for the captives taken at Badr.
The spoils are lawful.
The Muhājirūn who fled with Muḥammad, and the inhabitants of al-Madīnah who gave him refuge, are to form ties of brotherhood.

Chapter XLVII.

Sūratu Muḥammad.
The Chapter of Muḥammad.

Promise of reward to believers.
Exhortation to deal severely with the enemy.
Description of Paradise and of Hell.
Reproof to some pretended believers and hypocrites who hesitate to obey the command to make war against the unbelievers.
Their secret malice shall be revealed.
Exhortation to believe, and to obey God and the Apostles, and sacrifice all for the faith.

Chapter LXII.

Sūratu 'l-Juma'ah.
The Chapter of the Congregation.

God has sent the illiterate prophet.
The Jews rebuked for unbelief.
Muslims are not to leave the congregation during divine service for the sake of merchandise.

Chapter V.

Sūratu 'l-Mā'idah.
The Chapter of the Table.

Believers are to fulfil their compacts.
Brute beasts, except those hereafter mentioned, are lawful, but chase during the pilgrimage is unlawful.
The rites and sacrifices of the Pilgrimage are lawful.
The Muslims are not to bear ill-will against the Quraish, who prevented them at Ḥudaibiyah from making the Pilgrimage.
Forbidden meats.
The food of Jews and Christians is lawful to Muslims.
So, too, their women.
Ablutions before prayers.
Rules for purification in cases of pollution.
The Muslims are bidden to remember the oath of fealty (at 'Aqabah), and how God made a similar covenant with the children of Israel, and chose twelve wardens.
Muḥammad is warned against their treachery, as well as against the Christians.
Refutation of the doctrine that Christ is God, and of the idea that the Jews and Christians are the sons of God and His beloved.
Muḥammad sent as a warner and herald of glad tidings.
Moses bade the children of Israel invade the Holy Land, and they were punished for hesitating.
Story of the two sons of Adam.
The crow shows Cain how to bury the body of Abel.
Gravity of homicide.
Those who make war against God and His Apostle are not to receive quarter.
Punishment for theft.
Muḥammad is to judge both Jews and Christians by the Qur'ān, in accordance with their own Scriptures, but not according to their lusts.
Or would they prefer to be judged according to the unjust laws of the time of the pagan Arabs?
The Muslims are not to take Jews and Christians for patrons.
The hypocrites hesitate to join the believers.
They are threatened.
Further appeals to the Jews and Christians.
Fate of those before them who were transformed for their sins.
The Jews reproved for saying that God's hand is fettered.
Some of them are moderate, but the greater part are misbelievers.
The Prophet is bound to preach his message.
Sabians, Jews, and Christians appealed to as believers.
Prophets of old were rejected.
Against the worship of the Messiah and the doctrine of the Trinity.
Jews and idolaters are the most hostile to the Muslims, and the Christians are nearest in love to them.
Expiation for an inconsiderate oath.
Wine and gambling forbidden.
Game not to be hunted or eaten during pilgrimage.
Expiation for violating this precept.
Fish is lawful at this time.
Rites of the Ḥajj to be observed.
Believers must not ask about painful things till the whole Qur'ān is revealed.
Denunciation of the superstitious practices of the Pagan Arabs with respect to certain cattle.
Witnesses required when a dying man makes his testament.
The mission of Jesus.
The miracles of the infancy.

The Apostles ask for a table from heaven as a sign.

Jesus denies commanding men to worship him and his mother as gods.

CHAPTER LIX.

Sūratu 'l-Ḥashr.

The Chapter of Assembly.

The chastisements of the Jews who would not believe in the Qur'ān.

The divisions of the spoils.

The treacherous conduct of the hypocrites.

CHAPTER IV.

Sūratu 'n-Nisā'.

The Chapter of Women.

God creates and watches over man.

Women's dowries.

Administration of the property of orphans and idiots.

Distribution of property among the heirs.

Witnesses required to prove adultery.

Believers are not to inherit women's estates against their will.

No false charge of adultery to be made with a view of keeping a woman's dowry.

Women whom it is unlawful to marry.

Men are superior to women.

Punishment of refractory wives.

Arbitration between man and wife.

Duty towards parents, kinsmen, orphans, the poor, neighbours, &c.

Almsgiving for appearance sake a crime.

Believers must not pray when drunk or polluted.

Sand may be used for purification when water is not to be had.

Charge against Jews of perverting the Scriptures and saying, "Rā'inā."

They are threatened with transformation, like those who broke the Sabbath, for their unbelief.

Idolatry the unpardonable sin.

Some who have Scriptures believe.

Trusts to be paid back.

Quarrels to be referred to God and the apostles only.

The Apostle will intercede for the believers.

Muḥammad commanded to settle their differences.

Believers to take precautions in sallying forth to battle.

They are exhorted to fight, and promised Paradise if they fall.

Obedience to the Prophet is obedience to God.

Salutation to be returned.

The hypocrites.

Deserters are to be slain, unless they have taken refuge with a tribe in league with the Muslims.

Penalty for killing a believer by mistake.

Believers are not to plunder others on the mere pretence that they are infidels.

Fate of the half-hearted Muslims who fell at Badr.

Precautions to be taken against an attack during prayers.

Exhortation to sincerity in supporting the faith.

Rebuke to the pagan Arabs for their idolatry and superstitious practices.

Islām the best religion, being that of Abraham the Ḥanīf.

Laws respecting women and orphans.

Equity and kindness recommended.

Partiality to one wife rather than another reproved.

Fear of God inculcated.

God does not pardon the unstable in faith or the hypocrites.

No middle course is allowed.

The Jews were punished for demanding a book from heaven.

Of old they asked Moses to show them God openly, and were punished.

They are reproached for breaking their covenant with God, for calumniating Mary, and for pretending that they killed Jesus, whereas they only killed his similitude, for God took him to Himself.

Certain lawful foods forbidden the Jews for their injustice and usury.

Muḥammad is inspired in the same manner as the other apostles and prophets.

Jesus is only an apostle of God and His Word, and a spirit from Him.

Doctrine of the Trinity denounced.

God has not begotten a son.

The law of inheritance in the case of remote kinship.

CHAPTER LVIII.

Sūratu 'l-Mujādilah.

The Chapter of the Disputer.

Abolition of the idolatrous custom of divorcing women with the formula, "Thou art to me as my mother's back."

God's omniscience and omnipresence.

He knows the secret plottings of the disaffected.

Discourse on the duties of true believers.

Denunciation of those who oppose the Apostle.

CHAPTER LXV.

Sūratu 'ṭ-Ṭalāq.

The Chapter of Divorce.

The laws of divorce.

The Arabs are admonished by the fate of former nations to believe in God.

The seven stories of heaven and earth.

CHAPTER LXIII.

Sūratu 'l-Munāfiqīn.

The Chapter of the Hypocrites.

The treacherous designs of the hypocrites revealed.

CHAPTER XXIV.

Sūratu 'n-Nūr.

The Chapter of Light.

(This chapter deals with the accusation of unchastity against 'Āyishah.)

Punishment of the whore and the whoremonger.

Witnesses required in the case of an imputation of unchastity to a wife.

Vindication of 'Āyishah's character and denunciation of the accusers.

Scandalmongers rebuked and threatened with punishment at the Last Day.

Believers are not to enter other persons' houses without permission, or in the absence of the owners.

Chastity and modest deportment enjoined, particularly upon women.

Those by whom women may be seen unveiled.

Slaves to be allowed to purchase their freedom.

Slave-girls not to be compelled to prostitute themselves.

God the Light of the Heavens.

Nothing keeps the believers from the service of God, but the unbeliever's works are like the mirage on a plain, or like darkness on a deep sea.

All nature is subject to God's control.

Reproof to a sect who would not accept the Prophet's arbitration.

Actual obedience required rather than an oath that they will be obedient.

Belief in the unity of God, steadfastness in prayer, and the giving of alms enjoined.

Slaves and children not to be admitted into an apartment without asking permission, when the occupant is likely to be undressed.

Rules for the social intercourse of women past child-bearing, and of the blind, lame, or sick.

Persons in whose houses it is lawful to eat food.

Salutations to be exchanged on entering houses.

Behaviour of the Muslims towards the Apostle.

He is to be more respectfully addressed than other people.

Chapter XXXIII.

Sūratu 'l-Aḥzāb.

The Chapter of the Confederates.

Muḥammad is warned against the hypocrites.

Wives divorced by the formula, "Thou art henceforth to me like my mother's back," are not to be considered as real mothers, and as such regarded as unlawful.

Neither are adopted sons to be looked upon as real sons.

The real ties of kinship and consanguinity are to supersede the tie of sworn brotherhood.

God's covenant with the Prophet.

Miraculous interference in favour of the Muslims when besieged by the confederate army at al-Madīnah.

Conduct of the hypocrites on the occasion.

Departure of the invaders.

Siege and defeat of the Banū Quraiẓah Jews.

The men are executed.

Their women and children are sold into slavery and their property confiscated.

Laws for the Prophet's wives.

They are to be discreet and avoid ostentation.

Encouragement to the good and true believers of either sex.

Vindication of Muḥammad's conduct in marrying Zainab, the divorced wife of his freed man and adopted son Zaid (who is mentioned by name).

No term need be observed in the case of women divorced before cohabitation.

Peculiar privileges granted to Muḥammad in the matter of women.

Limitation of his licence to take wives.

Muslims are not to enter the Prophet's house without permission.

After, they are to retire without inconveniencing him by familiar discourse.

Are to be very modest in their demeanour to his wives.

Are not to marry any of his wives after him.

Those relations who are permitted to see them unveiled.

God and His angels bless the Prophet.

Slander of misbelievers will be punished.

The women are to dress modestly.

Warning to the hypocrites and disaffected at al-Madīnah.

The fate of the infidels at the Last Judgment.

Man alone of all creation undertook the responsibility of faith.

Chapter LVII.

Sūratu 'l-Ḥadīd.

The Chapter of Iron.

God the controller of all nature.

Exhortation to embrace Islām.

Those who do so before the taking of Makkah are to have the precedence.

Discomfiture of the hypocrites and unbelievers at the Last Day.

The powers vouchsafed to former apostles.

Chapter LXI.

Sūratu 'ṣ-Ṣaff.

The Chapter of the Ranks.

Believers are bidden to keep their word and to fight for the faith.

Moses was disobeyed by his people.

Jesus prophesied the coming of Aḥmad.

The Christians rebuked.

Chapter XLVIII.

Sūratu 'l-Fatḥ.

The Chapter of Victory.

Announcement of a victory.

God comforts the believers and punishes the hypocrites and idolaters.

The oath of fealty.

The cowardice and excuses of the desert Arabs.

Those left behind wish to share the spoil gained at Khaibar.

The incapacitated alone are to be excused.

The oath of fealty at the tree.

God prevented a collision between the Makkans and the Muslims, when the latter were prohibited from making the pilgrimage.

Prophecy of the pilgrimage to be completed the next year.

Chapter LX.

Sūratu 'l-Mumtaḥinah.

The Chapter of the Tried.

Exhortations to the Muslims not to treat secretly with the Quraish.

Abraham's example.

Other idolaters who have not borne arms against them may be made friends of.

Women who desert from the infidels are to be tried before being received into Islām.

If they are really believers, they are, *ipso facto*, divorced.

The husbands are to be recompensed to the amount of the women's dowries.

Chapter LXVI.

Sūratu 't-Taḥrīm.

The Chapter of Prohibition.

The Prophet is relieved from a vow he had made to please his wives.

The jealousies in his ḥaram occasioned by his intrigue with the Coptic slave-girl, Mary.

Exhortation to hostilities against the infidels.

The example of the disobedient wives of Noah and Lot.

And of the good wife of Pharaoh.

And of the Virgin Mary.

Chapter IX.

Sūratu 't-Taubah.

The Chapter of Repentance.

(This chapter is without the initial formula, " In the name of the Merciful," &c.)

An immunity for four months proclaimed to such of the idolaters as have made a league with the Prophet, but they are to be killed wherever found when the sacred months have expired.

An idolater seeking refuge is to be helped, in order that he may hear the word of God.

None are to be included in the immunity but those with whom the league was made at the Sacred Mosque.

They are not to be trusted.

Exhortation to fight against the Makkans.

Idolaters may not repair to the mosques of God.

Reproof to al-'Abbās, the Prophet's uncle, who, while refusing to believe, claimed to have done enough in supplying water to the pilgrims and in making the pilgrimage himself.

Chapter XLIX.

Sūratu 'l-Ḥujurāt.

The Chapter of the Inner Chambers.

Rebuke to some of the Muslims who had presumed too much in the presence of the Apostle, and of the others who had called out rudely to him.

Also of a man who had nearly induced Muḥammad to attack a tribe who were still obedient.

Of certain Muslims who contended together.

Of others who use epithets of abuse against each other.

Who entertain unfounded suspicions.

Exhortation to obedience and reproof of the hypocrites.

The Muhājirūn are to hold the first rank.

Infidels are not to be taken for patrons, even when they are fathers or brothers.

Religion is to be preferred to ties of kinship.

The victory of Ḥunain.

The idolaters are not to be allowed to enter the Sacred Mosque at Makkah another year.

The infidels are to be attacked.

The Jews denounced for saying that Ezra is the son of God.

The assumption of the title Rabbi reproved.

Diatribe against Jewish doctors and Christian monks.

Of the sacred months and the sin of deferring them.

Exhortation to the Muslims to march forth to battle.

Allusions to the escape of Muḥammad and Abū Bakr from Makkah, and their concealment in a cave.

Rebuke to those who seek to be excused from fighting and to those who sought to excite sedition in the Muslim ranks.

Reproof to the hypocrites and half-hearted and to those who found fault with the Prophet for his use of the alms (*zakāt*).

Proper destination of the alms.

Hypocrites and renegades denounced.

They are warned by the example of the people of old who rejected the Prophets.

Rewards promised to the true believers.

Continued denunciation of the hypocrites and of those who held back from the fight.

Muḥammad is not to pray at the grave of any one of them who dies.

Their seeming prosperity is not to deceive him.

Happiness in store for the Apostle, the believers, and the Muhājirūn.

Those who may lawfully be excused military service.

The desert Arabs are among the worst of the hypocrites, though some believe.

Some people of al-Madīnah also denounced as hypocrites.

Others have sinned but confessed.

Others wait for God's pleasure.

Denunciation of some who had set up a mosque from motives of political opposition.

Muḥammad is not to sanction this mosque, but rather to use that of Qubā', founded by him while on his way from Makkah to al-Madīnah during the Flight.

God has bought the persons and wealth of the believers at the price of Paradise.

The Prophet and the believers must not ask forgiveness for the idolaters, however near of kin.

Abraham only asked pardon for his idolatrous father in fulfilment of a promise.

The three Anṣārs who refused to accompany Muḥammad to Tabūk are forgiven.

The people of al-Madīnah and the neighbouring Arabs blamed for holding back on the occasion.

All sacrifices for the sake of the religion are counted to them.

Exhortation to fight rigorously against the infidels.

Reproof to those who receive the revelation suspiciously.

God will stand by his Apostle.

V.—Sources of the Qur'ān.

Muḥammadanism owes more to Judaism (see a book by M. Geiger, entitled, *Was hat Muhammed aus dem Judenthume aufgenommen*, in which that learned Jew has traced all the leading features of Islām to Talmudic sources; also *Literary Remains of Emanuel Deutsch*, Essay on Islām; also article on JUDAISM in the present work) than it does to either Christianity or Sabeanism, for it is simply Talmudic Judaism adapted to Arabia, plus the Apostleship of Jesus and Muḥammad; and wherever Muḥammad departs from the monotheistic principles of Judaism, as in the idolatrous practices of the Pilgrimage to the Ka'bah, it is evident that it is done as a necessary concession to the national feelings and sympathies of the people of Arabia, and it is absolutely impossible for Muḥammadan divines to reconcile the idolatrous rites of the Ka'bah with that simple monotheism which it was evidently Muḥammad's intention to establish in Arabia.

"The sources (says Mr. Rodwell) whence Muhammad derived the materials of his Korân, are, over and above the more poetical parts which are his own creation, the legends of his time and country, Jewish traditions based upon the Talmud, and the Christian traditions of Arabia and of S. Syria. At a later period of his career, no one would venture to doubt the divine origin of his whole book. But at its commencement the case was different. The people of Mecca spoke openly and tauntingly of it as the work of a poet, as a collection of antiquated or fabulous legends, or as palpable sorcery. They accused him of having confederates, and even specified foreigners who had been his coadjutors. Such were Salman the Persian (Salmān al-Fārisī), to whom he may have owed the descriptions of heaven and hell, which are analogous to those of the Zendavesta; and the Christian monk Sergius, or, as the Muhammadans term him, Boheira (Buḥairah). From the latter, and perhaps from other Christians, especially slaves naturalized at Mecca, Muhammad obtained access to the teaching of the Apocryphal Gospels, and to many popular traditions of which those gospels are the concrete expression. His wife Chadijah (Khadījah), as well as her cousin Waraka (Waraqah), a reputed convert to Christianity, and Muhammad's intimate friend, are said to have been well acquainted with the doctrines and sacred books, both of Jews and Christians. And not only were several Arab tribes in the neighbourhood of Mecca converts to the Christian faith, but on two occasions Muhammad had travelled with his uncle Abu Talib, as far as Bostra, where he must have had opportunities of learning the general outlines of Oriental Christian doctrine, and perhaps of witnessing the ceremonial of their worship.

* * * * *

"It has been supposed that Muhammad derived many of his notions concerning Christianity from Gnosticism and that it is to the numerous Gnostic sects the Korân alludes when it reproaches the Christians with having 'split up their religion into parties.' But for Muhammad thus to have confounded Gnosticism with Christianity itself, its prevalence in Arabia must have been far more universal than we have reason to believe that it really was. In fact, we have no historical authority for supposing that the doctrines of these heretics were taught or professed in Arabia at all. It is certain, on the other hand, that the Basilidans, Valentinians, and other Gnostic sects had either died out, or been reabsorbed into the Orthodox Church, towards the middle of the fifth century, and had disappeared from Egypt before the sixth. It remains possible, however, that the Gnostic doctrine concerning the Crucifixion may have been adopted by Muhammad as likely to reconcile the Jews to Islam, as a religion embracing both Judaism and Christianity, if they might believe that Jesus had not been put to death, and thus find the stumbling-block of the Atonement removed out of their path. The Jews would, in this case, have simply been called upon to believe in Jesus as a divinely born and inspired teacher, who, like the patriarch Enoch, or the prophet Elijah, had been miraculously taken from the earth. But, in all other respects, the sober and matter-of-fact statements of the Korân, relative to the family and history of Jesus, are opposed to the wild and fantastic doctrines of Gnostic emanations, and especially to the manner in which they supposed Jesus, at his baptism, to have been brought into union with a higher nature. It is more clear that Muhammad borrowed in several points from the doctrines of the Ebionites, Essenes, and Sabeites. Epiphanius describes the notions of the Ebionites of Nabathæa, Moabites, and Basanites, with regard to Adam Jesus, almost in the very words of Sura iii. 52. He tells us that they observed *circumcision*, were *opposed to celibacy*, forbade turning to the sunrise, but *enjoined Jerusalem as their Kebla* (Qiblah), (as did Muhammad during twelve years), that they prescribed (as did the Sabeites) *washings*, very similar to those enjoined in the Korân, and allowed oaths (by certain natural objects, as *clouds*, *signs of the Zodiac*, *oil*, *the winds*, etc.), which also we find adopted therein. These points of contact with Islam, knowing as we do Muhammad's eclecticism, can hardly be accidental.

"We have no *evidence* that Muhammad had access to the Christian scriptures, though it is just possible that fragments of the Old or New Testament may have reached him through Chadijah or Waraka, or other Meccan Christians, possessing MSS. of our sacred volume. There is but one direct quotation

(Sura xxi. 105) in the whole Korân from the Scriptures; and though there are a few passages, as where *alms*, are said to be given *to be seen of men*, and as, *none forgiveth sins but God only*, which might seem to be identical with texts of the New Testament, yet this similarity is probably merely accidental. It is, however, curious to compare such passages as Deut. xxvi. 14, 17, and 1 Peter v. 2, with Sura xxiv. 50, and Sura x. 73—John vii. 15, with the '*illiterate*' prophet—Matt. xxiv. 36, and John xii. 27, with the use of the word *hour*, as meaning any judgment or crisis, and the *last* Judgment—*the voice of the Son of God* which the dead are to hear, with the exterminating or awakening *cry of Gabriel*, etc. The passages of this kind, with which the Korân abounds, result from Muhammad's general acquaintance with scriptural phraseology, partly through the popular legends, partly from personal intercourse with Jews and Christians. And we may be quite certain that, whatever materials Muhammad may have derived from our Scriptures, directly or indirectly, were carefully recast.

"It should also be borne in mind that we have no clear traces of the existence of Arabic versions of the Old or New Testament previous to the time of Muhammad. The passage of St. Jerome—'Hæc autem translatio nullum de veteribus sequitur interpretem; sed ex ipso Hebraico, *Arabicoque* sermone, et interdum Syro, nunc verba, nunc sensum, nunc simul utrumque resonabit' (Prol. Gal.), obviously does not refer to *versions*, but to *idiom*. The earliest Ar. version of the Old Testament of which we have any knowledge is that of R. Saadias Gaon, A.D. 900: and the oldest Ar. version of the New Testament is that published by Erpenius in 1616, and transcribed in the Thebais, in the year 1271, by a Coptic bishop, from a copy made by a person whose name is known, but whose date is uncertain. Michaelis thinks that the Arabic versions of the New Testament were made between the Saracen conquests in the seventh century and the Crusades in the eleventh century—an opinion in which he follows, or coincides with, Walton (Prol. in Polygl. § xiv.), who remarks—'Plane constat versionem Arabicam apud eas (ecclesias orientales) factam esse postquam lingua Arabica per victorias et religionem Muhammedanicam per Orientem propagata fuerat, et in multis locis facta esset vernacula.' If, indeed, in these comparatively late versions, the general phraseology, especially in the histories common to the Scriptures and to the Korân, bore any similarity to each other, and if the orthography of the proper names had been the same in each, it might have been fair to suppose that such versions had been made, more or less, upon the basis of others, which, though now lost, existed in the ages prior to Muhammad, and influenced, if they did not directly form, his sources of information. But this does not appear to be the case. The phraseology of our existing versions is not that of the Korân, and the versions as a whole appear to have been made from the Septuagint, the Vulgate, Syriac, Coptic, and Greek; Tischendorf, indeed, says that the four Gospels *originem mixtam habere videntur*; but the internal evidence is clearly in favour of the Greek origin of the Arabic Gospels. This can be seen in part even from the order of the words, which was retained, like that of the Greek, so far as possible, even in such constructions and transpositions of words as violate the rules of Arabic Syntax.

"From the Arab Jews, Muhammad would be enabled to derive an abundant though distorted knowledge of the Scripture histories. The secrecy in which he received his instructions from them and from his Christian informants, enabled him boldly to declare to the ignorant pagan Meccans that God had revealed those Biblical histories to him. But there can be no doubt, from the constant identity between the Talmudic perversions of Scripture histories and the statements of the Korân, that the Rabbis of Hejaz communicated their legends to Muhammad. And it should be remembered that the Talmud was completed a century previous to the era of Muhammad, and cannot fail to have extensively influenced the religious creed of all the Jews of the Arabian peninsula. In one passage, Muhammad speaks of an individual Jew—perhaps some one of note among his professed followers, as *a witness* to his mission; and there can be no doubt that his relations with the Jews were, at one time, those of friendship and intimacy, when we find him speaking of their recognizing him as they do their own children, and blaming their most colloquial expressions. It is impossible, however, for us at this distance of time to penetrate the mystery in which this subject is involved. Yet certain it is, that, although their testimony against Muhammad was speedily silenced, the Koreish knew enough of his private history to disbelieve and to disprove his pretensions of being the recipient of a divine revelation, and to accuse him of writing from the dictation of teachers morning and evening. And it is equally certain that all the information received by Muhammad was embellished and recast in his own mind and with his own words. There is a unity of thought, a directness and simplicity of purpose, a peculiar and laboured style, a uniformity of diction, coupled with a certain deficiency of imaginative power, which indicate that the ayats (signs or verses) of the Korân are the product of a single mind. The longer narratives were, probably, elaborated in his leisure hours, while the shorter verses, each proclaiming to be a *sign* or miracle, were promulgated as occasion required them. And, whatever Muhammad may himself profess in the Korân as to his ignorance even of reading and writing, and however strongly modern Muhammadans may insist upon the same point—an assertion, by the way, contradicted by many good authors—there can be no doubt that to assimilate and work up his materials, to fashion them into elaborate Suras, and to fit them for public recital, must have been a work requiring much time, study, and meditation, and presumes a far greater degree of general culture than any orthodox Muslim will be disposed to admit." (The Preface to Rodwell's El-Korân, p. xvi. *et seq.*)

VI.—The Recital and Reading of the Qur'ān.

Tilāwah (تلاوة), or "the recital of the Qur'ān," has been developed into a science known as *'Ilmu 'l-Tajwīd* (علم التجويد), which includes a knowledge of the peculiarities of the spelling of many words in the Qur'ān; of the *qirā'āt* (قراءات), or various readings; of the ejaculations, responses, and prayers to be said at the close of appointed passages; of the various divisions, punctuations, and marginal instructions; of the proper pronunciation of the Arabic words; and of the correct intonation of different passages.

The reading or recital of the Qur'ān should commence with legal ablution and prayer. The usual prayer is, "I seek protection from God against the cursed Satan!" which is followed by the invocation. "In the name of God the Merciful, the Compassionate!"

The mosque is considered the most suitable of all places in which to read the Qur'ān, and the most auspicious days of the week are Friday, Monday, and Thursday. The ordinary time allowed for reading the Qur'ān through is forty days, although by reciting a *juz'* or *sīpārah* daily, it can be done in thirty days, which is said to have been the custom of the Prophet. Some read it through by *manzils*, or stages, of which there are seven, which is done in a week. On no account should it be read through in less than three days, for which there is a three-fold division, known in Persian as the *Khatam-i-Manzil-i-Fīl*, the initial letters of each portion (فی ا ل) forming the word *fīl*.

Ejaculations, or responses, are made at certain places. For example, at the end of the Sūratu 'l-Fātiḥah (i.) and of the Sūratu 'l-Baqarah (ii.), say, "Amen!" At the end of the Sūratu Banī Isrā'īl (xvii.), say, "God is great!" After the last verse of the Sūratu 'l-Qiyāmah (lxxv.), say, "Is He not powerful enough to raise the dead? Say, Yes, for He is my Lord Most High!" At the end of the Sūratu 'l-Mulk (lxvii.), say, "God brings it (clear water) to us and He is Lord of all the Worlds!"

In addition to responses to be made after each Sūrah, or Chapter, there are certain ejaculations to be made after certain verses, for example, after the sixteenth verse of the third Sūrah, "There is no God but He, the Mighty, the Wise!" say, "I am a witness to this!"

There are fourteen verses hnown as the *Āyātu 's-Sajdah*, after which a prostration is made. They are Sūrahs vii. 205; xiii. 16; xvi. 51; vii. 109; xix. 59; xxii. 19; xxv. 61; xxvii. 26; xxxii. 15; xxxviii. 24; xli. 38; liii. 62; lxxxiv. 20; xcvi. 18.

There are numerous instructions given as to pronunciation, and there have arisen seven schools of pronunciation, which are known as those of the *Qurrā'u 's-Sab'ah*, or "seven readers (for a list of these readers, see QARI). It is considered quite lawful to recite the Qur'ān according to the pronunciation established by any one of these seven worthies.

There are many marks and symbols on the margin of an Arabic Qur'ān. Mr. Sell, in his *Ilm i Tajwid*, gives them in detail. (*Ilm i Tajwid*, Keys & Co., Madras, 1852.) The symbol for full stop is o, when the reader should take breath The word سكتة is written when a slight pause is made, but no breath taken. There are also signs which are known as *waqf*, or pause They were originally of five kinds, but many more have been added in modern times. They are distinguished by letters and words. [WAQF.]

There are twenty-nine Sūrahs of the Qur'ān which begin with certain letters of the alphabet. These letters, the learned say, have some profound meaning, known only to the Prophet himself, although it seems probable that they are simply marks recorded by the amanuensis.

(1) Six Sūrahs begin with the letters *Alif, Lām, Mīm.* الم *ALM*, viz. Sūrahs al-Baqarah (ii.), Ālu 'Imrān (iii.), al-'Ankabūt (xxix.), al-Rūm (xxx.), Luqmān (xxxi.), as-Sajdah (xxxii.). Golius thinks that they probably stand for *Amr li-Muḥammad*, "At the command of Muḥammad," and to have been written by the amanuensis. Jalālu 'd-dīn as-Suyūṭī says that Ibn 'Abbās said that they stood for *Anā 'llāhu a'limu*, "I, God, know" (that this is true). Al-Baiẓāwī thinks *A* stands for "Allāh," *L* for "Gabriel," and *M* for "Muḥammad." Mr. Sale gives the meaning as *Allāhu Laṭīfun Majīdun*, "God is gracious and exalted"; others have suggested *Allāhu li-Muḥammad*, "God to Muḥammad." But the general belief is that the letters have a hidden meaning.

(2) At the commencement of Sūratu 'l-A'rāf (vii.), there is *Alif, Lām, Mīm, Ṣād.* المص *ALMṢ*, which may mean: *A*, "Anā"; *L*, "Allah"; *M*, "Raḥmān"; *Ṣ*, "Ṣamad"; *i.e.* "I am God, the Merciful, the Eternal."

(3) The Sūratu 'r-Ra'd (xiii.) begins with the letters *Alif, Lām, Mīm, Rā.* المر *ALMR*, which al-Baiẓāwī takes to mean, *A*, "Anā"; *L*, "Allāhū"; *M*, "A'limu"; *R*, "Arā." "I, God, both know and see."

(4) Five Sūrahs begin with *Alif, Lām, Rā.* الر *ALR*, which some understand to mean *Amara lī Rabbī*, "My Lord hath said to me," or *Anā 'llāhu arā*, "I, God, see." These Sūrahs are Yūnus (x.), Hūd (xi.), Yūsuf (xii.), Ibrahīm (xiv.), al-Ḥijr (xv.).

(5) The Sūratu Maryam (xix.) begins with the letters *Kāf, Hā, Yā, 'Ain, Ṣād.* كهيعص *KHY'AṢ*, which Ibn 'Abbās says stand for five attributes of the Almighty: *Karīm*. "Gracious"; *Hādi*, "Guide"; *Ḥakīm* (taking the middle letter), "Wise"; *'Alīm*, "Learned"; *Ṣādiq*, "Righteous."

(6) The Sūratu ṬH (xx.), as its title implies, begins with the letters *Ṭā Hā* طه, which Ḥusain says may signify *Ṭāhir*,

"Pure"; *Hādi*, "Guide"; being attributes of God.

(7) Six Sūrahs commence with the letters *Ḥā Mīm* حم, *ḤM*, namely, Sūrahs al-Mu'min (xl.), Fuṣṣilat (xli.), az-Zukhruf (xliii.), ad-Dukhān (xliv.), al-Jāṣiyah (xlv.), al-Aḥqāf (xlvi.). Ibn 'Abbās says they indicate the attribute. *Raḥmān*, "Merciful."

(8) The Sūratu 'sh-Shūrā (xlii.) begins with *Ḥa Mīm 'Ain Sīn Qāf.* حمعسق *HM'ASQ*, which Muḥammad ibn Ka'b understood to mean *Ḥ* for *Raḥmān*, "Merciful"; *M* for *Raḥīm*, "Gracious"; *'A*, *'Alīm*, "Learned"; *S*, *Quddūs*, "Holy"; *Q*, *Qahhār*, "Dominant"; being attributes of God.

(9) The Sūratu YS (xxxvi.), as its title implies, begins with the letters *Yā Sīn* يس, which is supposed to stand for *Yā insān*, "O man!"

(10) The Sūratu Ṣ (xxxviii.), as its title signifies, begins with the letter *Ṣād* ص, which some say means *Ṣidq*, "Truth."

(11) The Sūratu Q (l.), as its name implies, begins with the letter *Qaf* ق, which Jalālu 'd-Dīn as-Suyūṭī says stands for *Qādir*, "Powerful," an attribute of God. Others think it means the mountain of Qāf.

(12) The Sūratu 'l-Naml (xxvii.) begins with the letters *Ṭā Sīn* طس, which Muḥammad ibn Ka'b says stand for *Zū't-ṭaul*, "Most Powerful," and *Quddūs*, "Holy," being attributes of the Almighty."

(13) Two Sūrahs, namely ash-Shu'arā' (xxvi.), and al-Qaṣaṣ (xxviii.), begin with *Ṭā Sīn Mīm* طسم, which supplies the addition of the attribute *Raḥmān*, "Merciful," to those of the former section, indicated by *ṬS*.

(14) The Sūratu 'l-Qalam (lxviii.) begins with *Nūn*, ن *N*, which some say stands for an ink-horn, others for a fish, and some for the attribute of *Nūr*, or "Light."

VII.—The Interpretation of the Qur'ān.

'Ilmu 'l-Uṣūl (علم الاصول), or the Exegesis of the Qur'ān, is a very important science, and is used by the Muslim divine to explain away many apparent or real contradictions. The most authoritative works on the *'Ilmu 'l-Uṣūl* of the Qur'ān, are *Manāru 'l-Uṣūl* and its commentary, the *Nūru 'l-Anwār*, and as-Suyūṭī's *Itqān* (ed. by Sprenger). The various laws of interpretation laid down in these books are very complicated, requiring the most careful study. We have only space for a mere outline of the system.

The words (*alfāẓ*) of the Qur'ān are of four classes: *Khāṣṣ*, *'Āmm*, *Mushtarak*, and *Mu'awwal.*

(1) *Khāṣṣ*, Words used in a special sense. This speciality of sense is of three kinds: *Khuṣūṣu 'l-jins*, Speciality of genus, *e.g.* mankind; *Khuṣūṣu 'n-nau'*, Speciality of species, *e.g.* a man; *khuṣūṣu 'l-'ain*, Speciality of an individual, *e.g.* Muḥammad.

(2) *'Āmm*, Collective or common, which embrace many individuals or things, *e.g.* people.

(3) *Mushtarak*, Complex words which have several significations; *e.g. 'ain*, a word which signifies an Eye, a Fountain, the Knee, or the Sun.

(4.) *Mu'awwal*, words which have several significations, all of which are possible, and so a special explanation is required. For example, Sūrah cviii. 2, reads thus in Sale's translation. "Wherefore pray unto the Lord and *slay* (the victims)." The word translated "slay" is in Arabic *inḥar*, from the root *naḥr*, which has several meanings. The followers of the great Legist, Abū Ḥanīfah, render it "sacrifice," and add the words (the "victims"). The followers of Ibn Ash-Shāfi'ī say it means "placing the hands on the breast in prayer."

II. The Sentences (*'Ibārah*) of the Qur'ān are either *Ẓāhir* or *Khafī*, *i.e.* either Obvious or Hidden.

Obvious sentences are of four classes:—*Ẓāhir*, *Naṣṣ*, *Mufassar*, *Muḥkam.*

(1.) *Ẓāhir.*—Those sentences, the meaning of which is *Obvious* or clear, without any assistance from the context (*qarīnah*).

(2.) *Naṣṣ*, a word commonly used for a text of the Qur'ān, but in its technical meaning here expressing what is meant by a sentence, the meaning of which is made clear by some word which occurs in it. The following sentence illustrates both *Ẓāhir* and *Naṣṣ*: "Take in marriage of such other women as please you, two, three, four." This sentence is *Ẓāhir*, because marriage is here declared lawful; it is *Naṣṣ*, because the words "one, two, three, four," which occur in the sentence, show the unlawfulness of having more than four wives.

(3.) *Mufassar*, or explained. A sentence which needs some word in it to explain it and make it clear. Thus: "And the angels prostrated themselves, all of them with one accord, save Iblīs (Satan)." Here the words "save Iblīs" show that he did not prostrate himself. This kind of sentence may be abrogated.

(4.) *Muḥkam*, or perspicuous. A sentence as to the meaning of which there can be no doubt, and which cannot be controverted, thus: "God knoweth all things." This kind of sentence cannot be abrogated. To act on such sentences without departing from the literal sense is the highest degree of obedience to God's command.

The difference between these sentences is seen when there is a real or apparent contradiction between them. If such should occur, the first must give place to the second, and so on. Thus Muḥkam cannot be abrogated or changed by any of the preceding, or Mufassar by Naṣṣ, &c.

Hidden sentences are either *Khafī*, *Mushkil*, *Mujmal*, or *Mutashābih.*

(1.) *Khafī.*—Sentences in which other persons or things are hidden beneath the plain meaning of a word or expression contained therein: *e.g.* Sūratu 'l-Mā'idah (v.), 42, "As for a thief whether male or female cut ye off their hands in recompense for their doings." In this sentence the word *sāriq*, "thief," is understood to have *hidden* beneath its literal meaning, both pickpockets and highway robbers.

(2.) *Mushkil.*—Sentences which are *ambiguous; e.g.* Sūratu 'd-Dahr (lxxvi.), 15, "And (their attendants) shall go round about them with vessels of silver and goblets. The bottles shall be bottles of silver." The difficulty here is that bottles are not made of silver, but of glass. The commentators say, however, that glass is dull in colour, though it has some lustre, whilst silver is white, and not so bright as glass. Now it may be, that the bottles of Paradise will be like glass bottles as regards their lustre, and like silver as regards their colour. But anyhow, it is very difficult to ascertain the meaning.

(3.) *Mujmal.*—Sentences which may have a variety of interpretations, owing to the words in them being capable of several meanings; in that case the meaning which is given to the sentence in the Traditions relating to it should be acted on and accepted; or which may contain some very rare word, and thus its meaning may be doubtful, as: "Man truly is by creation hasty" (Sūrah lxx. 19). In this verse the word *halū'*, "hasty," occurs. It is very rarely used, and had it not been for the following words, "when evil toucheth him, he is full of complaint; but when good befalleth him, he becometh niggardly," its meaning would not have been at all easy to understand.

The following is an illustration of the first kind of *Mujmal* sentences: "Stand for prayer (*ṣalāt*) and give alms (*zakāt*)." Both *ṣalāt* and *zakāt* are "Mushtarak" words. The people, therefore, did not understand this verse, so they applied to Muḥammad for an explanation. He explained to them that *ṣalāt* might mean the ritual of public prayer, standing to say the words "God is great," or standing to repeat a few verses of the Qur'ān; or it might mean private prayer. The primitive meaning of *zakāt* is "growing." The Prophet, however, fixed the meaning here to that of "almsgiving," and said, "Give of your substance one-fortieth part."

(4.) *Mutashābih.*—*Intricate* sentences, or expressions, the exact meaning of which it is impossible for man to ascertain until the day of resurrection, but which was known to the Prophet: *e.g.* the letters Alif, Lām, Mīm (A. L. M.); Alif, Lām, Rā' (A. L. R.); Alif, Lām, Mīm, Rā' (A. L. M. R.), &c., at the commencement of different Sūrahs or chapters. Also Sūratu 'l-Mulk (lxvii.) 1, "In whose hand is the Kingdom," *i.e.* God's *hand* (Arabic, *yad*); and Sūratu ṬH (xx.), "He is most merciful and sitteth on His throne," *i.e.* God *sitteth* (Arabic, *istawā*); and Sūratu 'l-Baqarah (ii.), 115, "The face of God" (Arabic, *wajhu 'llāh*).

III. The use (*isti'māl*) of words in the Qur'ān is divided into four classes. They are either *Ḥaqīqah*, *Majāz*, *Ṣarīḥ*, or *Kināyah*.

(1.) *Ḥaqīqah.*—Words which are used in their *literal* meaning: *e.g. rukū'*, "a prostration"; *zinā*, "adultery."

(2.) *Majāz.*—Words which are *figurative*; as *ṣalāt* in the sense of *namāz*, or the liturgical prayers.

(3.) *Ṣarīḥ.*—Words the meaning of which is *clear* and *palpable*: *e.g.* "Thou art *free*," "Thou art *divorced*."

(4.) *Kināyah.*—Words which are *metaphorical* in their meaning: *e.g.* "Thou art *separated*"; by which may be meant, "thou art *divorced*."

IV. The deduction of arguments, or *istidlāl*, as expressed in the Qur'ān, is divided into four sections: *'Ibārah*, *Ishārah*, *Dalālah*, and *Iqtiẓā*.

(1.) *'Ibārah*, or the plain sentence. "Mothers, after they are divorced, shall give suck unto their children two full years, and the father shall be obliged to maintain them and clothe them according to that which is reasonable." (Sūrah ii. 233.) From this verse two deductions are made. First, from the fact that the word "them" is in the feminine plural, it must refer to the mothers and not to the children; secondly, as the duty of supporting the mother is incumbent on the father, it shows that the relationship of the child is closer with the father than with the mother. Penal laws may be based on a deduction of this kind.

(2.) *Ishārah*, that is, a sign or hint which may be given from the order in which the words are placed; *e.g.* "Born of him," meaning, of course, the father.

(3.) *Dalālah*, or the argument which may be deducted from the use of some special word in the verse, as: "say not to your parents, 'Fie!' (Arabic, *uff*)." (Sūrah xvii. 23.) From the use of the word *uff*, it is argued that children may not beat or abuse their parents. Penal laws may be based on *dalālah*, thus: "And they strive after violence on the earth; but God loveth not the abettors of violence." (Sūrah v. 69.) The word translated "strive" is in Arabic literally *yas'auna*, "they run." From this the argument is deduced that as highwaymen wander about, they are included amongst those whom "God loveth not," and that, therefore, the severest punishment may be given to them, for any deduction that comes under the head of *dalālah* is a sufficient basis for the formation of the severest penal laws.

(4.) *Iqtiẓā.* This is a deduction which demands certain conditions: "whosoever killeth a believer by mischance, shall be bound to free a believer from slavery." (Sūrah iv. 94.) As a man has no authority to free his neighbour's slave, the condition here required, though not expressed, is that the slave should be his own property.

VIII.—The Abrogation of Passages in the Qur'ān.

Some passages of the Qur'ān are contradictory, and are often made the subject of attack; but it is part of the theological belief of the Muslim doctors that certain passages of the Qur'ān are *mansūkh* (منسوخ), or abrogated by verses revealed afterwards. entitled *nāsikh* (ناسخ). This was the doctrine taught by Muḥammad in the Sūratu 'l-Baqarah (ii.) 105: "Whatever verses we (*i.e.* God) cancel or cause thee to forget, we bring a better or its like." This convenient doctrine fell in with that law of expediency which appears to be the salient feature in Muḥammad's prophetical career.

In the *Tafsīr-i-'Azīzī*, it is written, that abrogated (*mansūkh*) verses of the Qur'ān are of three kinds: (1) Where the verse has been removed from the Qur'ān and another given in its place; (2) Where the injunction is abrogated and the letters of the verse remain; (3) Where both the verse and its injunction are removed from the text. This is also the view of Jalālu 'd-Dīn, who says that the number of abrogated verses has been variously estimated from five to five hundred.

The Greek verb καταλύω, in St. Matthew v. 17, has been translated in some of the versions of the New Testament by *mansūkh*; but it conveys a wrong impression to the Muḥammadan mind as to the Christian view regarding this question. According to most Greek lexicons, the Greek word means *to throw down*, or *to destroy* (as of a building), which is the meaning given to the word in our authorised English translation. Christ did not come to destroy, or to pull down, the Law and the Prophets; but we all admit that certain precepts of the Old Testament were abrogated by those of the New Testament. Indeed, we further admit that the old covenant was abrogated by the new covenant of grace. "He taketh away the first that he may establish the second," Heb. x. 9.

In the Arabic translation of the New Testament, printed at Beyrut A.D. 1869, καταλύω is translated by *naqẓ*, "to demolish"; in Mr. Loewenthal's Pushto translation, A.D. 1863, by *bāṭilawal*, "to destroy," or "render void"; and in Henry Martyn's Persian Testament, A.D. 1837, it is also translated by the Arabic *ibṭāl*, *i.e.* "making void." In both the Arabic-Urdū and Roman-Urdū it is unfortunately rendered *mansūkh*, a word which has a technical meaning in Muḥammadan theology contrary to that implied in the word used by our Lord in Matthew v. 17.

Jalālu 'd-Dīn in his *Itqān*, gives the following list of twenty verses which are acknowledged by all commentators to be abrogated. The verses are given as numbered in the *Itqān*.

No.	Mansūkh, or abrogated verses.	Nāsikh, or abrogating verses.	The Subject abrogated.
1	Sūratu 'l-Baqarah (ii.), 119.	Sūratu 'l-Baqarah (ii.), 145.	The Qiblah.
2	Sūratu 'l-Baqarah (ii.), 178.	Sūratu 'l-Mā'idah (v.), 49. Sūratu Banī Isrā'īl, (xvii.), 35.	Qiṣāṣ, or Retaliation.
3	Sūratu 'l-Baqarah (ii.), 183.	Sūratu 'l-Baqarah (ii.), 187.	The Fast of Ramaẓān.
4	Sūratu 'l-Baqarah (ii.), 184.	Sūratu 'l-Baqarah (ii.), 185.	Fidyah, or Expiation.
5	Sūratu Āli 'Imrān (iii.), 102.	Sūratu 't-Taghābun (lxiv.), 16.	The fear of God.
6	Sūratu 'n-Nisā' (iv.), 88.	Sūratu 'n-Nisā' (iv.), 89. Sūratu 't-Taubah (ix.), 5.	Jihād, or war with infidels.
7	Sūratu 'l-Baqarah (ii.), 216.	Sūratu 't-Taubah (ix.), 36.	Jihād in the Sacred months.
8	Sūratu 'l-Baqarah (ii.), 240.	Sūratu 'l-Baqarah (ii.), 234.	Provision for widows.
9	Sūratu 'l-Baqarah (ii.), 191.	Suratu 't-Taubah (ix.), 5.	Slaying enemies in the Sacred Mosque.
10	Sūratu 'n-Nisā' (iv.), 14.	Suratu 'n-Nūr (xxiv.), 2.	Imprisonment of the adulteress.
11	Sūratu 'l-Mā'idah (v.), 105.	Sūratu 'ṭ-Ṭalāq (lxv.), 2.	Witnesses.
12	Sūratu 'l-Anfāl (vii.), 66.	Sūratu 'l-Anfāl (vii.), 67.	Jihād, or war with infidels.
13	Sūratu 'n-Nūr (xxiv.), 3.	Sūratu 'n-Nūr (xxiv.), 32.	The marriage of adulterers.
14	Sūratu 'l-Aḥzāb (xxxiii.), 52.	Sūratu 'l-Aḥzāb (xxxiii.), 49.	The Prophet's wives.
15	Sūratu 'l-Mujādilah (lviii.), 13, first part of verse.	Sūratu 'l-Mujādilah (lviii)., 13, latter part of verse.	Giving alms before assembling a council.
16	Sūratu 'l-Mumtaḥinah (lx.), 11.	Sūratu 't-Taubah (ix.), 1.	Giving money to infidels for women taken in marriage.
17	Sūratu 't-Taubah (ix.), 39	Sūratu 't-Taubah (ix.), 92	Jihād, or war with infidels.
18	Sūratu 'l-Muzzammil (lxxiii.), 2.	Sūratu 'l-Muzzammil (lxxiii.), 20.	The night prayer.
19	Sūratu 'n-Nūr (xxiv.), 57.	Sūratu 'n-Nūr (xxiv.), 58.	Permission to young children to enter a house.
20	Sūratu 'n-Nisā' (iv.), 7.	Sūratu 'n-Nisā' (iv.), 11.	Division of property.

IX.—The Reputed Excellence of the Qur'ān, and its Miraculous Character.

Copies of the Qur'ān are held in the greatest esteem and reverence amongst Muḥammadans. They dare not to touch it without being first washed and purified, and they read it with the greatest care and respect, never holding it below their girdles. They swear by it, consult it on all occasions, carry it with them to war, write sentences of it on their banners, suspend it from their necks as a charm, and always place it on the highest shelf or in some place of honour in their houses. Muḥammadans, as we have already remarked, believe the Qur'ān to be uncreated and eternal, subsisting in the very essence of God. There have, however, been great differences of opinion on this subject. It was a point controverted with so much heat that it occasioned many calamities under the Abbaside Khalīfahs. Al-Ma'mūn (A.H. 218) made a public edict declaring the Qur'ān to be created, which was confirmed by his successors al-Mu'taṣim and al-Wāṣiq, who whipped and imprisoned and put to death those of the contrary opinion. But at length al-Mutawakkil, who succeeded al-Wāṣiq, put an end to these persecutions by revoking the former edicts, releasing those that were imprisoned on that account, and leaving every man at liberty as to his belief on this point. (*Abū 'l-Faraj*, p. 262.) The Qur'ān is, however, generally held to be a standing miracle, indeed, the one miracle which bears witness to the truth of Muḥammad's mission, an assumption which is based upon the Prophet's own statements in the Qur'ān (Sūrah x. 39, xi. 16, lii. 34), where he calls upon the people who charge him with having invented it to procure a single chapter like it. But the Mu'tazalites have asserted that there is nothing miraculous in its style and composition (*vide Sharḥu 'l-Muwāqif*). The excellences of the Qur'ān, as explained by the Prophet himself, claim a very important place in the traditions (see *Faẓā'ilu 'l-Qur'ān*, in the Traditions of al-Bukhārī and Muslim), from which the following are a few extracts:—

"The best person amongst you is he who has learnt the Qu'rān, and teaches it."

"Read the Qur'ān as long as you feel a pleasure in it, and when tired leave off."

"If the Qur'ān were wrapped in a skin and thrown into a fire, it would not burn."

"He who is an expert in the Qur'ān shall rank with the 'Honoured Righteous Scribes,' and he who reads the Qur'ān with difficulty and gets tired over it shall receive double rewards."

"The state of a Musulman who reads the Qur'ān is like the orange fruit whose smell and taste are pleasant."

"The person who repeats three verses from the beginning of the chapter of the Cave (Sūrah xviii.) shall be guarded from the strife of ad-Dajjāl"

"Everything has a heart, and the heart of the Qur'ān is the chapter Yā-sīn (Sūrah xxxvi.); and he who reads it, God will write for him rewards equal to those for reading the whole Qur'ān ten times."

"There is a Sūrah in the Qur'ān of thirty verses which intercedes for a man until he is pardoned, and it is that commencing with the words, 'Blessed is he in whose hands is the kingdom.'" (Sūrah lxvii.)

"God wrote a book two thousand years before creating the heavens and the earth, and sent two verses down from it, which are the two last verses of the chapter of the Cow (Sūrah ii.); and if they are not repeated in a house for three nights, the devil will be near that house."

"Verily the devil runs away from the house in which the chapter entitled the Cow is read."

"The chapter commencing with these words, 'Say God is one God' (Sūrah cxii.), is equal to a third of the Qur'ān."

"The person that repeats the chapter of the Cave (Sūrah xviii.) on Friday, the light of faith brightens him between two Fridays."

In the Qur'ān there are many assertions of its excellence; the following are a few selected verses:—

Sūrah iv. 94: "Can they not consider the Qur'ān? Were it from any other than God, they would assuredly have found in it many contradictions."

Sūrah ix. 16: "If they shall say, 'The Qur'ān is his own device.' Then bring ten Sūrahs like it of your devising."

Sūrah xlvi. 7: "Will they say, 'He hath devised it'? Say, If I have devised it, then not one single thing can ye ever obtain for me from God."

Sūrah liii. 4: "Verily the Qur'ān is none other than a revelation. One terrible in power taught it him."

Maracci, von Hammer, and other Orientalists, have selected the XCIst chapter of the Qur'ān, entitled the Sūratu 'sh-Shams, or the Chapter of the Sun, as a favourable specimen of the best style of the Qur'ān. It begins in Arabic thus:—

١ وَالشَّمْسِ وَضُحَاهَا ٢ وَالْقَمَرِ اذَا تَلَاهَا
٣ وَالنَّهَارِ اذَا جَلَّاهَا ۴ وَاللَّيْلِ اذَا يَغْشَاهَا
٥ وَالسَّمَاءِ وَمَا بَنَاهَا ٦ وَالْأَرْضِ وَمَا طَحَاهَا
٧ وَنَفْسٍ وَمَا سَوَّاهَا ٨ فَأَلْهَمَهَا فُجُورَهَا وَتَقْوَاهَا
٩ قَدْ أَفْلَحَ مَنْ زَكَّاهَا ١٠ وَقَدْ خَابَ مَنْ دَسَّاهَا

Which Mr. Rodwell translates as follows:—

1 By the Sun and his noonday brightness!
2 By the Moon when she followeth him!
3 By the Day when it revealeth his glory!
4 By the Night when it enshroudeth him!
5 By the Heaven and Him who built it!
6 By the Earth and Him who spread it forth!
7 By a soul and Him who balanced it,
8 And breathed into it its wickedness and its piety,

9 Blessed now is he who hath kept it pure,
10 And undone is he who hath corrupted it!

Baron von Hammer rendered it in German thus:—

1 Bey der Sonne, und ihrem schimmer;
2 Bey dem Mond der ihr folget immer;
3 Bey dem Tag der sie zeigt in vollem glanz;
4 Bey der Nacht, die sie verfinstert ganz;
5 Bey den Himmeln und dem der sie gemacht;
6 Bey der Erde und dem der sie schuf eben;
7 Bey der Seele und dem der sie ins gleichgewicht gebracht,
8 Bey dem der ihr das bewusstseyn des guten und bösen gegeben,
9 Selig wer seine Seele reinigt;
10 Wer dieselbe verdunklet wird auf ewig gepeinigt.

The renowned Orientalist, Sir William Jones, praised the following account of the drowning of Noah's sons as truly magnificent, and inferior in sublimity only to the simple declaration of the creation of light in Genesis. D'Herbelot also considers it one of the finest passages in the Qur'ān (Sūrah xi. 44–46):—

وَهِيَ تَجْرِي بِهِمْ فِي مَوْجٍ كَالْجِبَالِ وَنَادَى نُوحٌ
ٱبْنَهُ وَكَانَ فِي مَعْزِلٍ يَا بُنَيَّ ٱرْكَبْ مَعَنَا وَلَا تَكُنْ
مَعَ ٱلْكَافِرِينَ قَالَ سَآوِي إِلَى جَبَلٍ يَعْصِمُنِي مِنَ
ٱلْمَاءِ قَالَ لَا عَاصِمَ ٱلْيَوْمَ مِنْ أَمْرِ ٱللّٰهِ إِلَّا مَنْ
رَحِمَ وَحَالَ بَيْنَهُمَا ٱلْمَوْجُ فَكَانَ مِنَ ٱلْمُغْرَقِينَ
وَقِيلَ يَا أَرْضُ ٱبْلَعِي مَاءَكِ وَيَا سَمَاءُ أَقْلِعِي وَغِيضَ
ٱلْمَاءُ وَقُضِيَ ٱلْأَمْرُ وَٱسْتَوَتْ عَلَى ٱلْجُودِيِّ وَقِيلَ
بُعْداً لِلْقَوْمِ ٱلظَّالِمِينَ

It may be rendered as follows:—

"And the ark moved on with them amid waves like mountains:

"And Noah called to his son—for he was apart—

"'Embark with us, O my child! and stay not with the unbelievers.'

"He said, 'I will betake myself to a mountain that shall save me from the water.'

"He said, 'None shall be saved this day from God's decree, save him on whom He shall have mercy.'

"And a wave passed between them and he was drowned.

"And it was said, 'O earth! swallow up thy water! and O heaven! withhold thy rain!' And the water abated, and God's decree was fulfilled, and the ark rested on al-Jūdī.

"And it was said, 'Avaunt, ye tribe of the wicked!'"

X.—Commentaries on the Qur'ān.

In the earliest ages of Islām the expositions of the Qur'ān were handed down in the traditional sayings of the companions and their successors, but we have it on the authority of the *Kashfu 'z-Ẓunūn* that one Qutaibah ibn Aḥmad, who died A.H. 316, compiled a systematic commentary on the whole of the Qur'ān. The work is not now extant.

Muslim commentaries are very numerous. Dr. M. Arnold (*Islam and Christianity*, p. 81) says there are no less than 20,000 in the Library at Tripolis.

The best known commentaries amongst the Sunnīs are those of:—

Al-Baghawī, A.H. 515.
Az-Zamakhsharī, A.H. 604.
At-Tafsīru 'l-Kabīr, A.H. 606.
Ibnu 'l-'Arabi, A.H. 628.
Al-Baiẓāwī, A.H. 685.
Al-Mudārik, A.H. 701.
Ḥusain, A.H. 900.
Al-Jalālān, A.H. 864, A.H. 911.
Al-Mazharī, A.H. 1225.
'Azīzī, A.H. 1239.

Amongst the Shī'ahs the following are works of reputation:—

Shaikh Ṣadūq, A.H. 381.
At-Tafsīru 'l-Kabīr, by Saiyid Muḥammad ar-Rāzī, 30 volumes, A.H. 606.
Aṣ-Ṣāfī, A.H. 668.
As-Sirru 'l-Wajīz, A.H. 715.
Sidratu 'l-Muntahā, by Mīr Bakir, A.H. 1041.
Al-Burhān, by Saiyid Hasham, A.H. 1160.

XI.—Editions and Translations of the Qur'ān.

The Qur'ān was first printed in Arabic at Rome by Pagninus Brixiensis, Romæ, 1530, but it was either burned or remained unpublished. Since then the following editions of the Arabic text have appeared in Europe:—

Al-Coranus, seu lex Islamitica, &c., the Arabic text of the Qur'ān, published by A. Hinkelmann, Hamburg, 1649, 4to.

Alcorani textus universus, &c., the Arabic text with a Latin translation and numerous extracts from the principal commentaries, and preceded by a Prodromus, containing a "refutation" of the Qur'ān, by Maracci, Padua, 1698, folio.

القرآن, an anotated text of the Qur'ān, published by order and at the cost of the Empress Catherine II. of Russia, at St. Petersburgh in 1787, 1 vol. in folio. This edition was reprinted at St. Petersburgh in 1790, 1793, 1796, and 1798, and without any change at Kasan in 1803, 1809, and 1839. Another edition, in two vols, 4to, without notes, was published at Kasan, 1817, reprinted 1821 and 1843, and a third edition, in 6 vols. 8vo, at the same place, 1819.

Corani textus arabicus, &c., the first critical edition of the text, by G. Flügel, Leipzig, 1834, 4to. Second edition, 1842; third edition, 1869.

Coranus arabice, &c., revised republication of Flügel's text, by G. M. Redslob, Leipzig, 1837, 8vo.

Beidhawii commentarius in Coranum, &c., the text of the Qur'ān with al-Baiẓāwī's Commentary, by H. O. Fleisher, two vols. 4to, Leipzig, 1846.

The Muḥammadans, so far from thinking the Qur'ān profaned by a translation, as some authors have written (*Marracci de Alcoran.* p. 33), have taken care to have it translated into various languages, although these translations are always interlineary with the original text. Translations exist in Persian, Urdū, Pushto, Turkish, Javan, Malayan, and other languages, which have been made by Muḥammadans themselves.

The first translation atttempted by Europeans was a Latin version translated by an Englishman, Robert of Retina, and a German, Hermann of Dalmatia. This translation, which was done at the request of Peter, Abbot of the Monastery of Clugny, A.D. 1143, remained hidden nearly 400 years till it was published at Basle, 1543, by Theodore Bibliander, and was afterwards rendered into Italian, German, and Dutch. The next translation in German was by Schweigger, at Nurnberg, in 1616. This was followed by the above-mentioned work of Maracci, consisting of the Qur'ān, in Arabic, with a Latin version with notes and refutations, A.D. 1698.

The oldest French translation was done by M. Du Ryer (Paris, 1647). A Russian version appeared at St. Petersburg in 1776. M. Savary translated the Qur'ān into French in 1783. There have also been more recent French translations by Kasimirski (Paris, 1st ed. 1840, 2nd ed. 1841, 3rd ed. 1857).

The first English Qur'ān was Alexander Ross's translation of Du Ryer's French version (1649–1688). Sale's well-known work first appeared in 1734, and has since passed through numerous editions. A translation by the Rev. J. M. Rodwell, with the Sūrahs arranged in chronological order, was printed in 1861 (2nd ed. 1876). Professor Palmer, of Cambridge, translated the Qur'ān in 1880 (Oxford Press). A Roman-Urdū edition of the Qur'ān was published at Allahabad in 1844, and a second and revised edition at Ludianah in 1876 (both these being a transliteration of 'Abdu 'l-Qādir's well-known Urdū translation).

The best known translations in German are those by Boysen, published in 1773, with an Introduction and notes, and again revised and corrected from the Arabic by G. Wahl in 1828, and another by Dr. L. Ullmann, which has passed through two editions (1840, 1853).

XI.—The Opinions of European Writers on the Qur'ān.

Mr. Sale, in his Preliminary Discourse, remarks :—

"The style of the Korân is generally beautiful and fluent, especially where it imitates the prophetic manner, and scripture phrases. It is concise, and often obscure, adorned with bold figures after the Eastern taste, enlivened with florid and sententious expressions, and in many places, especially where the majesty and attributes of God are described, sublime and magnificent; of which the reader cannot but observe several instances, though he must not imagine the translation comes up to the original, notwithstanding my endeavours to do it justice.

"Though it be written in prose, yet the sentences generally conclude in a long continued rhyme, for the sake of which the sense is often interrupted, and unnecessary repetitions too frequently made, which appear still more ridiculous in a translation, where the ornament, such as it is, for whose sake they were made, cannot be perceived. However, the Arabians are so mightily delighted with this jingling that they employ it in their most elaborate compositions, which they also embellish with frequent passages of and allusions to the Korân, so that it is next to impossible to understand them without being well versed in this book.

"It is probable the harmony of expression which the Arabians find in the Korân might contribute not a little to make them relish the doctrine therein taught, and give an efficacy to arguments, which, had they been nakedly proposed without this rhetorical dress, might not have so easily prevailed. Very extraordinary effects are related of the power of words well chosen and artfully placed, which are no less powerful either to ravish or amaze than music itself; wherefore as much as has been ascribed by the best orators to this part of rhetoric as to any other. He must have a very bad ear, who is not uncommonly moved with the very cadence of a well-turned sentence; and Mohammed seems not to have been ignorant of the enthusiastic operation of rhetoric on the minds of men; for which reason he has not only employed his utmost skill in these his pretended revelations, to preserve that dignity and sublimity of style, which might seem not unworthy of the majesty of that Being, whom he gave out to be the author of them, and to imitate the prophetic manner of the Old Testament; but he has not neglected even the other arts of oratory; wherein he succeeded so well, and so strangely captivated the minds of his audience, that several of his opponents thought it the effect of witchcraft and enchantment, as he sometimes complains (Sūrah xv. 21, &c.)."

The late Professor Palmer, in his Introduction to the Qur'an, remarks :—

"The Arabs made use of a rhymed and rhythmical prose, the origin of which it is not difficult to imagine. The Arabic language consists for the most part of triliteral roots, *i.e.* the single words expressing individual ideas consist generally of three consonants each, and the derivative forms expressing modifications of the original idea are not made by affixes and terminations alone, but also by the insertion of letters in the root. Thus *ẓaraba* means 'he struck,' and *qatala*, 'he killed,' while *maẓrûb* and *maqtûl* signify 'one struck' and 'one killed.' A sentence, therefore, consists of a series of words which would each require to be expressed in clauses of several words in other languages, and it is easy to see how a next following sentence, explanatory of or completing the first, would be much more clear and forcible if it consisted of words of a similar shape and implying similar modifications of other ideas. It follows then that the two sentences would be necessarily symmetrical, and the presence of rhythm would not only please the ear but contribute to the better understanding of the sense, while the rhyme would mark the pause in the sense and emphasize the proposition.

"The Qur'ān is written in this rhetorical style, in which the clauses are rhythmical though not symmetrically so, and for the most part end in the same rhyme throughout the chapter.

"The Arabic language lends itself very readily to this species of composition, and the Arabs of the desert in the present day employ it to a great extent in their more formal orations, while the literary men of the towns adopt it as the recognised correct style, deliberately imitating the Qur'ān.

"That the best of Arab writers has never succeeded in producing anything equal in merit to the Qur'ān itself is not surprising.

"In the first place, they have agreed beforehand that it is unapproachable, and they have adopted its style as the perfect standard; any deviation from it therefore must of necessity be a defect. Again, with them this style is not spontaneous as with Mohammed and his contemporaries, but is as artificial as though Englishmen should still continue to follow Chaucer as their model, in spite of the changes which their language has undergone. With the prophet the style was natural, and the words were those used in every-day ordinary life, while with the later Arabic authors the style is imitative and the ancient words are introduced as a literary embellishment. The natural consequence is that their attempts look laboured and unreal by the side of his impromptu and forcible eloquence.

"That Mohammed, though, should have been able to challenge even his contemporaries to produce anything like the Qur'ān, 'And if ye are in doubt of what we have revealed unto our servant, then bring a chapter like it. . . . But if ye do it not, and ye surely shall do it not, &c.,' is at first sight surprising, but, as Nöldeke has pointed out, this challenge really refers much more to the subject than to the mere style,—to the originality of the conception of the unity of God and of a revelation supposed to be couched in God's own words. Any attempt at such a work must of necessity have had all the weakness and want of prestige which attaches to an imitation. This idea is by no means foreign to the genius of the old Arabs.

* * * * *

"Amongst a people who believed firmly in witchcraft and soothsaying, and who, though passionately fond of poetry, believed that every poet had his familiar spirit who inspired his utterances, it was no wonder that the prophet should be taken for 'a soothsayer, for 'one possessed with an evil spirit,' or for 'an infatuated poet.'"

Mr. Stanley Lane Poole, in his Introduction to Lane's *Selections from the Ḳur-án*, remarks:—

"It is confused in its progression and strangely mixed in its contents; but the development of Moḥammad's faith can be traced in it, and we can see dimly into the workings of his mind, as it struggles with the deep things of God, wrestles with the doubts which echoed the cavils of the unbelievers, soars upwards on the wings of ecstatic faith, till at last it gains the repose of fruition. Studied thus, the Ḳur-án is no longer dull reading to one who cares to look upon the working of a passionate troubled human soul, and who can enter into its trials and share in the joy of its triumphs.

"In the soorahs revealed at Mekka, Moḥammad has but one theme—God; and one object—to draw his people away from their idols and bring them to the feet of that God. He tells them of Him in glowing language, that comes from the heart's white heat. He points to the glories of nature, and tells them these are God's works. With all the brilliant imagery of the Arab, he tries to show them what God is, to convince them of His power and His wisdom and His justice. The soorahs of this period are short, for they are pitched in too high a key to be long sustained. The language has the ring of poetry, though no part of the Ḳur-án complies with the demands of Arab metre. The sentences are short and full of half-restrained energy, yet with a musical cadence. The thought is often only half expressed; one feels the speaker has essayed a thing beyond words, and has suddenly discovered the impotence of language, and broken off with the sentence unfinished. There is the fascination of true poetry about these earliest soorahs; as we read them we understand the enthusiasm of the Prophet's followers, though we cannot fully realise the beauty and the power, inasmuch as we cannot hear them hurled forth with Moḥammad's fiery eloquence. From first to last the Ḳur-án is essentially a book to be heard, not read, but this is especially the case with the earliest chapters.

"In the soorahs of the second period of Mekka, we begin to trace the decline of the Prophet's eloquence. There are still the same earnest appeals to the people, the same gorgeous pictures of the Last Day and the world to come; but the language begins to approach the quiet of prose, the sentences become longer, the same words and phrases are frequently repeated, and the wearisome stories of the Jewish prophets and patriarchs, which fill so large a space in the later portion of the Ḳur-án, now make their appearance. The fierce passion of the earliest soorahs, that could not out save in short burning verses, gives place to a calmer more argumentative style. Moḥammad appeals less to the works of God as proofs of his teaching, and more to the history of former teachers, and the punishments of the people who would not hear them. And the characteristic oaths of the first period, when Moḥammad swears by all the varied sights of nature as they mirrored themselves in his imagination, have gone, and in their place we find only the weaker oath 'by the Ḳur-án.' And this declension is carried still further in the last group of the soorahs revealed at Mekka. The style becomes more involved and the sentences longer, and though the old enthusiasm bursts forth ever and anon, it is rather an echo of former things than a new and present intoxication of faith. The fables and repetitions become more and more dreary, and but for the rich eloquence of the old Arabic tongue, which gives some charm even to inextricable sentences and dull stories, the Ḳur-án at this period would be unreadable. As it is, we feel we have fallen the whole depth from poetry to prose, and the matter of the prose is not so superlative as to give us amends for the loss of the poetic thought of the earlier time and the musical fall of the sentences.

"In the soorahs of the Medina period these faults reach their climax. We read a singularly varied collection of criminal laws, social regulations, orders for battle, harangues to the Jews, first conciliatory, then denunciatory, and exhortations to spread the faith, and such-like heterogeneous matters. Happily the Jewish stories disappear in the latest soorahs, but their place is filled by scarcely more palatable materials. The chapters of this period are interesting chiefly as containing the laws which have guided every Muslim state, regulated every Muslim society, and directed in their smallest acts every Mohammadan man and woman in all parts of the world from the Prophet's time till now. The Medina part of the Ḳur-án is the most important part for Islám, considered as a scheme of ritual and a system of manners; the earliest Mekka revelations are those which contain what is highest in a great religion and what was purest in a great man."

Mr. Rodwell, in his Introduction to his Qur'ān, says :—

"The contrast between the earlier, middle, and later Suras is very striking and interesting, and will be at once apparent from the arrangement here adopted. In the Suras as far as the 54th, we cannot but notice the entire predominance of the poetical element, a deep appreciation (as in Sura xci.) of the beauty of natural objects, brief fragmentary and impassioned utterances, denunciations of woe and punishment, expressed for the most part in lines of extreme brevity. With a change, however, in the position of Muhammad when he openly assumes the office of 'public warner,' the Suras begin to assume a more prosaic and didactic tone, though the poetical ornament of rhyme is preserved throughout. We gradually lose the Poet in the missionary aiming to convert, the warm asserter of dogmatic truths; the descriptions of natural objects, of the judgment, of heaven and hell, make way for gradually increasing historical statements, first from Jewish, and subsequently from Christian histories; while, in the 29 Suras revealed at Medina, we no longer listen to vague words, often as it would seem without positive aim, but to the earnest disputant with the enemies of his faith, the Apostle pleading the cause of what he believes to be the Truth of God. He who at Mecca is the admonisher and persuader, at Medina is the legislator and warrior, who dictates obedience, and uses other weapons than the pen of the Poet and the Scribe. When business pressed, as at Medina, Poetry makes way for prose, and although touches of the Poetical element occasionally break forth, and he has to defend himself up to a very late period against the charge of being merely a Poet, yet this is rarely the case in the Medina Suras; and we are startled by finding obedience to God *and the Apostle*, God's gifts *and the Apostle's*, God's pleasure *and the Apostle's*, spoken of in the same breath, and epithets and attributes elsewhere applied to Allah openly applied to himself, as in Sura ix. 118, 129.

"The Suras, viewed as a whole, strike me as being the work of one who began his career as a thoughtful enquirer after truth, and an earnest asserter of it in such rhetorical and poetical forms as he deemed most likely to win and attract his countrymen, and who gradually proceeded from the dogmatic teacher to the politic founder of a system for which laws and regulations had to be provided as occasions arose. And of all the Suras it must be remarked that they were intended non for *readers* but for *hearers*—that they were all promulgated by public *recital*—and that much was left, as the imperfect sentences shew, to the manner and suggestive action of the reciter. It would be impossible, and indeed it is unnecessary, to attempt a detailed life of Muhammad within the narrow limits of a Preface. The main events thereof with which the Suras of the Koran stand in connection, are—The visions of Gabriel, seen, or said to have been seen, at the outset of his career in his 40th year, during one of his seasons of annual monthly retirement, for devotion and meditation to Mount Hirâ, near Mecca,—the period of mental depression and re-assurance previous to the assumption of the office of public teacher—the Fatrah or pause during which he probably waited for a repetition of the angelic vision—his labours in comparative privacy for three years, issuing in about 40 converts, of whom his wife Chadijah was the first, and Abu Bekr the most important; (for it is to him and to Abu Jahl the Sura xcii. refers)—struggles with Meccan unbelief and idolatry followed by a period during which probably he had the second vision, Sura liii. and was listened to and respected as a person 'possessed' (Sura lxix. 42, lii. 29)—the first emigration to Abyssinia in A.D 616, in consequence of the Meccan persecutions brought on by his now open attacks upon idolatry (Taghout)—

increasing reference to Jewish and Christian histories, shewing that much time had been devoted to their study—the conversion of Omar in 617—the journey to the Thaquifites at Taief in A.D. 620—the intercourse with pilgrims from Medina, who believed in Islam, and spread the knowledge thereof in their native town, in the same year—the vision of the midnight journey to Jerusalem and the Heavens—the meetings by night at Acaba, a mountain near Mecca, in the 11th year of his mission, and the pledges of fealty there given to him—the command given to the believers to emigrate to Yathrib, henceforth Medinat-en-nabi (*the city of the Prophet*), or El-Medina (*the city*), in April of A.D. 622—the escape of Muhammad and Abu Bekr from Mecca to the cave of Thaur—the FLIGHT to Medina in June 20, A.D 622—treaties made with Christian tribes—increasing, but still very imperfect acquaintance with Christian doctrines—the Battle of Bedr in Hej. 2, and of Ohod—the coalition formed against Muhammad by the Jews and idolatrous Arabians, issuing in the siege of Medina, Hej. 5 (A.D. 627)—the convention, with reference to the liberty of making the pilgrimage, of Hudaibiya, Hej. 6—the embassy to Chosroes King of Persia in the same year, to the Governor of Egypt and to the King of Abyssinia, desiring them to embrace Islam—the conquest of several Jewish tribes, the most important of which was that of Chaibar in Hej. 7, a year marked by the embassy sent to Heraclius, then in Syria, on his return from the Persian campaign, and by a solemn and peaceful pilgrimage to Mecca—the triumphant entry into Mecca in Hej. 8 (A.D. 630), and the demolition of the idols of the Caaba—the submission of the Christians of Nedjran, of Aila on the Red Sea, and of Taief, etc., in Hej. 9, called 'the year of embassies or deputations,' from the numerous deputations which flocked to Mecca proffering submission—and lastly in Hej. 10, the submission of Hadramont, Yemen, the greater part of the southern and eastern provinces of Arabia—and the final solemn pilgrimage to Mecca.

"While, however, there is no great difficulty in ascertaining the Suras which stand in connection with the more salient features of Muhammad's life, it is a much more arduous, and often impracticable, task, to point out the precise events to which individual verses refer, and out of which they sprung. It is quite possible that Muhammad himself, in a later period of his career, designedly mixed up later with earlier revelations in the same Suras—not for the sake of producing that mysterious style which seems so pleasing to the mind of those who value truth least when it is most clear and obvious—but for the purpose of softening down some of the earlier statements which represent the last hour and awful judgment as imminent; and thus leading his followers to continue still in the attitude of expectation, and to see in his later successes the truth of his earlier predictions. If after-thoughts of this kind are to be traced, and they will often strike the attentive reader, it then follows that the perplexed state of the text in individual Suras is to be considered as due to Muhammad himself, and we are furnished with a series of constant hints for attaining to chronological accuracy. And it may be remarked in passing, that a belief that the end of all things was at hand, may have tended to promote the earlier successes of Islam at Mecca, as it unquestionably was an argument with the Apostles, to flee from 'the wrath to come.' It must be borne in mind that the allusions to contemporary minor events, and to the local efforts made by the new religion to gain the ascendant are very few, and often couched in terms so vague and general, that we are forced to interpret the Koran solely by the Koran itself. And for this, the frequent repetitions of the same histories and the same sentiments, afford much facility: and the peculiar manner in which the details of each history are increased by fresh traits at each recurrence, enables us to trace their growth in the author's mind, and to ascertain the manner in which a part of the Koran was composed. The absence of the historical element from the Koran as regards the details of Muhammad's daily life, may be judged of by the fact, that only two of his contemporaries are mentioned in the entire volume, and that Muhammad's name occurs but five times, although he is all the way through addressed by the Angel Gabriel as the recipient of the divine revelations, with the word SAY. Perhaps such passages as Sura ii. 15 and v. 246, and the constant mention of *guidance*, *direction*, *wandering*, may have been suggested by reminiscences of his mercantile journeys in his earlier years."

Dr. Steingass, the learned compiler of the *English-Arabic* and *Arabic-English Dictionaries* (W. H. Allen & Co.), has obligingly recorded his opinion as follows:—

Invited to subjoin a few further remarks on the composition and style of the Qur'ān, in addition to the valuable and competent opinions contained in the above extracts, I can scarcely introduce them better than by quoting the striking words of Göthe, which Mr. Rodwell places by way of motto on the reverse of the title page of his Translation. These words seem to me so much the more weighty and worthy of attention, as they are uttered by one who, whatever his merits or demerits in other respects may be deemed to be, indisputably belongs to the greatest masters of language of all times, and stands foremost as a leader of modern thought and the intellectual culture of *modern* times. Speaking of the Qur'ān in his *West-Oestlicher Divan*, he says: "However often we turn to it, at first disgusting us each time afresh, it soon attracts, astounds, and in the end enforces our reverence . . . . Its style, in accordance with its contents and aim, is stern, grand, terrible—ever and anon truly sublime . . . . Thus this book will go on exercising through all ages a most potent influence."

A work, then, which calls forth so powerful

and seemingly incompatible emotions, even in the distant reader—distant as to time, and still more so as to mental development—a work which not only conquers the repugnance with which he may begin its perusal, but changes this adverse feeling into astonishment and admiration, such a work must be a wonderful production of the human mind indeed, and a problem of the highest interest to every thoughtful observer of the destinies of mankind. Much has been said in the preceding pages, to acknowledge, to appreciate, and to explain the literary excellencies of the Qur'ān, and a more or less distinct admission that Buffon's much-quoted saying: "Le style c'est l'homme," is here more justified than ever, underlies all these various verdicts. We may well say the Qur'ān is one of the grandest books ever written, because it faithfully reflects the character and life of one of the greatest men that ever breathed. "Sincerity," writes Carlyle, "sincerity, in all senses, seems to me the merit of the Koran." This same sincerity, this ardour and earnestness in the search for truth, this never-flagging perseverance in trying to impress it, when partly found, again and again upon his unwilling hearers, appears to me as the real and undeniable "seal of prophecy" in Muḥammad.

Truth, and above all religious truth, can only be one. Christianity may duly rejoice in the thought that, at the very moment when the representative of the greatest Empire of the ancient world mockingly or despairingly put forth the question, "What is truth?" this one eternal truth was about to be written down with the blood of the Divine Redeemer in the salvation deed of our race, Christ's glorious and holy Gospel. But the approaches to truth are many, and he who devoted all his powers and energies, with untiring patience and self-denial, to the task of leading a whole nation by one of these approaches, from a coarse and effete idolatry, to the worship of the living God, has certainly a strong claim to our warmest sympathies as a faithful servant and noble champion of truth.

It is, however, not my intention to dwell here any longer upon this side of the question. Praise has been bestowed in this work on the Qur'ān and its author without stint or grudge, and the unanimity of so many distinguished voices in this respect will no doubt impress the general reader in favour of the sacred book of the Muḥammadans, which until now he may have known only by name. At the same time, it will be noticed that no less unanimity prevails in pointing out the inferiority of the later portions of the Qur'ān in comparison with the earlier Sūrahs; a falling off, as it were, from the original poetical grandeur and loftiness of its composition into prose and common-place. Göthe, we have seen, uses such a strong word as disgust, again and again experienced by him at the very outset of its repeated reading.

Not being an Arabic scholar himself, he knew the Qur'ān only through the translations existing at the time, which follow throughout the order of the received text. Thus he was made to pass, roughly speaking, from the later to the earlier Madīnah Sūrahs, and from these again to the Sūrahs given at Makkah at the various stages which mark Muḥammad's ministry, while he was yet staying in his irresponsive parent town. In other words, he would have proceeded from the utterances of the worldly ruler and lawgiver to those of the inspired Divine, who had just succeeded in laying the foundation-stones of a new religion, under fierce struggles and sufferings, but in obedience to a call which, in his innermost heart, he felt had gone out to him, and which he had accepted with awe, humility, and resignation. While, therefore, in the beginning of his studies, Göthe may have met with a number of details in the vast structure raised by Muḥammad which appeared distasteful to the refined scion of the nineteenth century, his interest must have been awakened, his admiration kindled and kept increasing, the more he became acquainted, through the work itself, with the nature and personality of its creator, and with the purity and exalted character of the main-spring of his motives.

Those critics, on the other hand, who view the Qur'ān with regard to the chronological order of its constituents, follow the descending scale in their estimate. Speaking at first highly—nay, frequently with enthusiasm—of the earlier parts, they complain more and more of the growing tediousness and wearisomeness of the Sūrahs of later origin.

Nöldeke, for instance, the learned and ingenious author of *Geschichte des Qorâns*, speaking of the deficiencies in style, language, and treatment of the subject matter, which, in his opinion, characterise the second and third period of the Makkan revelations, and in general the Madīnah Sūrahs, pointedly terminates his indictment by the sentence, "if it were not for the exquisite flexibility and vigour (*die ungemeine Feinheit und Kraft*) of the Arabic language itself, which, however, is to be attributed more to the age in which the author lived than to his individuality, it would scarcely be bearable to read the later portions of the Qur'ān a second time."

But if we consider the variety and heterogeneousness of the topics on which the Qur'ān touches, uniformity of style and diction can scarcely be expected; on the contrary, it would appear to be strangely out of place. Let us not forget that in *the* book, as Muḥammad's newest biographer, Ludolf Krehl (*Das Leben des Muhammed*, Leipzig, 1884), expresses it, "there is given a complete code of creed and morals, as well as of the law based thereupon. There are also the foundations laid for every institution of an extensive commonwealth, for instruction, for the administration of justice, for military organization, for the finances, for a most careful legislation for the poor: all built up on the belief in the *one* God, who holds man's destinies in His hand." Where so many important objects are concerned, the standard of excellence by which we have to gauge the composition of the Qur'ān as a whole must needs vary with the matter treated upon in each particular case. Sublime and chaste, where the supreme truth of God's unity is to be proclaimed; appealing in high-pitched strains to the imagination of a poetically-gifted people, where the eternal consequences of man's submission to God's holy will, or of rebellion against it, are pictured; touching in its simple, almost crude, earnestness, when it seeks again and again encouragement or consolation for God's messenger, and a solemn warning for those to whom he has been sent, in the histories of the prophets of old: the language of the Qur'ān adapts itself to the exigencies of every-day life, when this every-day life, in its private and public bearings, is to be brought in harmony with the fundamental principles of the new dispensation.

Here, therefore, its merits as a literary production should, perhaps, not be measured by some preconceived maxims of subjective and æsthetic taste, but by the effects which it produced in Muḥammad's contemporaries and fellow-countrymen. If it spoke so powerfully and convincingly to the hearts of his hearers as to weld hitherto centrifugal and antagonistic elements into one compact and well-organised body, animated by ideas far beyond those which had until now ruled the Arabian mind, then its eloquence was perfect, simply because it created a civilized nation out of savage tribes, and shot a fresh woof into the old warp of history.

Nöldeke's above-quoted remark, it seems to me, raises, however, a very important question. It must, of course, be admitted that the Arabic language, which is now so greatly and deservedly admired, cannot be attributed to Muḥammad individually, but originated in and was at his time the common property of the Arabic-speaking section of the human race, or, more accurately, of its Semitic branch, who were then living within the Peninsula and in some of the neighbouring countries. But we may well ask ourselves, what would in all probability have become of this language without Muḥammad and his Qur'ān? This is not at all an idle and desultory speculation. It is true the Arabic language had already produced numerous fine specimens of genuine and high-flown poetry, but such poetry was chiefly, if not exclusively, preserved in the memory of the people, for the art of writing was certainly very little known, and still less practised.

Moreover, poetry is not tantamount to literature; it may lead to it, and will always form a most essential part of it; but it will live on, and perhaps die, in solitary isolation, unless it becomes, as it were, as Brahmans say, "twice-born," by participating in a literary development of vaster dimensions and a more general character. Divided among themselves into numerous tribes, who were engaged in a perpetual warfare against each other, the Arabs, and with them their various dialects, would more and more have drifted asunder, poetry would have followed in the wake, and the population of Arabia would have broken up into a multitude of clans, with their particular bards, whose love- and war-songs enterprising travellers of our days might now collect, like the popular songs of the Kosaks of the steppe, or the Kalmuks and similar nationalities, vegetating for centuries in a more or less primitive state of existence.

It seems, then, that it is only a work of the nature of the Qur'ān which could develop ancient Arabic into a literary language, notwithstanding the fact that it had already been admirably handled by local poets. As this book places the national life of the Arabs upon an entirely new basis, giving it at the same time a much-needed centre and a wonderful power of expansion, it became a matter of the utmost importance, nay, of urgent necessity, that the contents of the volume should be preserved with scrupulous accuracy and undisputable conformity. This again was only possible by fixing upon *one* dialect, which by its recognized excellence commended itself to general acceptance, and also by establishing a written text.

But not only by raising a dialect, through its generalization, to the power of a language, and by rendering the adoption of writing indispensable, has the Qur'ān initiated the development of an Arabic literature; its composition itself has contributed two factors absolutely needful to this development: it has added to the existing poetry the origins of rhetoric and prose.

Although the decidedly poetical character of the earlier Sūrahs is obvious, they differ in two important points from the hitherto acknowledged form of poetry, which is that of the Qaṣīdah. This form consists of *baits*, or distichs, measured by some variation of one of the fifteen (or sixteen) principal metres, and each containing two half-lines, the same rhyme running through both hemistichs of the first *bait*, and through every second one of the following. For instance:

1. Qifā nabki min z̲ikrā ḥabībin wa-manzilī
   Bi-siqti 'l-liwā baina 'd-dak̲h̲ūli wa-ḥaumalī
2. Fa-tūẓiḥa fa 'l-maqrāti lam ya'fu rasmuhā
   Li-mā nasajat-hā min junūbin wa-sham'alī

which would scan:

⏑— — ⏑ — — — ⏑ — — ⏑
Qifā nab- | ki min z̲ikrā | ḥabībin | wa-
— ⏑ —
manzilī &c.

and belongs to the first variation of the metre Ṭawīl.

Emancipating himself from the fetters of metre, and gradually also of the uniform rhyme, Muḥammad created what is now called *saj'*, that is to say, a rhythmical prose, in which the component parts of a period are balanced and cadenced by a varying rhyme, and of which *e.g.* the Sūratu 'l-Qiyāmah (lxxv.) offers some fair examples; as (5–10):—

Bal yurīdu 'l-insānu li-yafjura amāmah,
Yas'alu aiyāna yaumu 'l-qiyāmah,

Fa-izā bariqa 'l-baṣar.
Wa-khasafa 'l-qamar
Wa-jumi'a 'sh-shamsu wa 'l-qamar
Yaqūlu 'l-insānu yauma'izin aina 'l-mafarr.

(But man chooseth to go astray as to his future;
He asketh, "When this Day of Resurrection?"
When the eye-sight shall be dazzled,
And the moon shall be darkened,
And the sun and the moon shall be together,
On that day man shall cry, "Where is there a place to flee to?")

And again (22-30):

Wa-wujūhin yauma'izin nāẓirah
Ilā rabbi-hā nāẓirah,
Wa-wujūhin yauma'izin bāsirah
Taẓannu an yuf'ala bi-hā fāqirah.
Kallā izā balaghati 't-tarāqiya
Wa-qīla man rāq
Wa-ẓanna annahu 'l-firāq
Wa 'l-taffati 's-sāqu bi 's-sāq
Ilā rabbi-ka yauma'izini 'l-masāq.

(On that day shall faces beam with light,
Out-looking towards their lord;
And faces on that day shall be dismal,
As if they thought that some calamity would therein befall them.
Assuredly when *the soul* shall come up to the breast-bone,
And there shall be a cry, "Who is the magician *to restore him?*"
And the man feeleth that *the time of his departure is come*,
And when one leg shall be enlaced with the other,
To thy Lord on that day shall he be driven on.)

This kind of rhetorical style, the peculiarity of which Professor Palmer, in the passage quoted, p. 523, aptly explains from the etymological structure of Arabic, has become the favourite model of oratorical and ornate language with the later Arabs. It is frequently employed in ordinary narratives, such as the tales of the *Arabian Nights*, whenever the occasion requires a more elevated form of speech; it is the usual garb of that class of compositions, which is known by the name of Maqāmāt, and even extensive historical works, as the *Life of Timur*, by 'Arab Shāh, are written in it throughout.

But Muḥammad made a still greater and more decisive step towards creating a literature for his people. In those Sūrahs, in which he regulated the private and public life of the Muslim, he originated a prose, which has remained the standard of classical purity ever since.

With regard to this point, however, it has been stated, seemingly in disparagement of the later Arabic authors, that their accepting Muḥammad's language as a perfect standard, from which no deviation is admissible, has led them to adopt an artificial style, as unnatural "as though Englishmen should still continue to follow Chaucer as their model, in spite of the changes which their language has undergone." But is such a parallel justified in facts? In English, as amongst modern nations in general, the written language has always kept in close contact with the spoken language; the changes which the former has undergone are simply the registration and legalisation of the changes which in course of time had taken place in the latter. Not so in Arabic. From the moment when, at the epoch of its fullest and richest growth, it was, through the composition of the Qur'ān, invested with the dignity of a literary language, it was, by its very nature, for many centuries to come, precluded from any essential change, whether this be considered as an advantage or not.

The reason for this lies in the first instance in the triliteral character of the Semitic roots, referred to by Professor Palmer, which allows such a root to form one, two, or three syllables, according to the pronunciation of each letter, with or without a vowel. Let us take as an example once more the root *ẓ-r-b* (ضرب), which conveys the idea of "beating," and serves in Arabic grammars, like the Greek τυπτω, to form paradigms, by way of a wholesome admonition, I suppose, to the youthful student. The first of these three consonants can only remain quiescent, *i.e.* vowel-less, if it is preceded by a vowel, as in the Imperative *i-ẓrib* (اِضْرِبْ), "beat thou," where the root appears as a monosyllable, or in the aorist *ya-ẓribu* (يَضْرِبُ), "he beats or will beat," where it takes together with the final *u* a dissylabic form. If we leave the second consonant quiescent and pronounce the first with *a*, we have *ẓarb*, with the nominative termination *ẓarbun* (ضَرْبٌ), the verbal noun "beating" or infinitive "to beat." Vocalising both the first letters, we may obtain *ẓārib*, the active participle "beating," or *ẓurūb*, plural of the last mentioned *ẓarb*, with the nominative termination *ẓāribun* (ضارِبٌ) and *ẓurūbun* (ضُرُوبٌ). If we read all three consonants with vowels, it may be *ẓaraba* (ضَرَبَ), "he did beat," or *ẓarabū* (ضَرَبُوا), "they did beat." Taking, again, the two forms *ẓaraba*, "he did beat," and *yaẓribu*, "he beats or will beat," a simple change of vowels suffices to transform the active into the passive: *ẓuriba* (ضُرِبَ), "he was beaten," and *yuẓrabu* (يُضْرَبُ), "he is beaten or will be beaten." Lastly, it must be noticed, that the distinction between the two fundamental tenses of the Arabic verb rests on the principle that the affixes, representing the personal pronouns, are in the preterite placed at the end, in the aorist at the beginning of the root: *ẓarab-nā*, "we did beat," but *na-ẓribu*, "we beat or will beat."

From all this it will be easily understood

that any essential change in the written language must deeply affect the whole system of Arabic accidence, and that this language will, therefore, naturally be averse to such changes. But, moreover, this system stands in closest connection with and dependence on the syntactical structure of the language, which is equally "conservative," if I may use this expression, in its fundamental principles. The Arabic syntax knows only two kinds of sentences (*jumlah*), one called nominal (*ismīyah*), because it begins with a noun, the other verbal (*fiʿlīyah*), because it begins with a verb. Reduced to their shortest expression, an example of the first would be: *Zaidun ẓāribun* (زيدٌ ضاربٌ), "Zaid (is) beating"; of the second: *ẓaraba zaidun* (ضرب زيدٌ), "(there) did beat Zaid." The constituent parts of the nominal sentence, which we would call subject and predicate, are termed *mubtada'*, "incipient," and *khabar*, "report," meaning that which is enounced or stated of the subject. The *khabar* need not be an attributive, as in the sentence given above, but it may be another clause, either nominal or verbal, and if it is the former, its own *mubtada'* admits even of a third clause as a second *khabar* for its complement. The subject of the verbal sentence is called agent, or *fāʿil*, and, as mentioned before, follows the verb, or *fiʿl*, in the nominative.

The verb with its agent (*fiʿl* and *fāʿil*), or the subject with its predicate (*mubtada'* and *khabar*), form the essential elements of the Arabic sentence. But there are a great many accidental elements, called *fazlah*, "what is superabundant or in excess," which may enter into the composition of a clause, and expand it to considerable length. Such are additional parts of speech expressing the various objective relations (*mafʿūl*) in which a noun may stand to an active verb, or the condition (*ḥāl*) of the agent at the moment when the action occurred, or circumstances of time and place (*ẓarf*) accompanying the action, or specificative distinctions (*tamyīz*) in explanation of what may be vague in a noun, or the dependence of one noun upon another (*iẓāfah*) or upon a preposition (*khafz*), or the different kinds of apposition (*tawābiʿ*) in which a noun may be joined to another, either in the subject or the predicate, and so on.

All these numerous component parts of a fully-developed sentence are influenced by certain ruling principles (*ʿawāmil*, or "regents"), some merely logical, but most of them expressed in words and particles, which determine the *iʿrāb*, that is, the grammatical inflection of nouns and verbs, and bring into play those various vowel-changes, of which we have above given examples with regard to the interior of roots, and which, we must now add, apply equally to the terminations employed in declension and conjugation.

The subject and predicate, for instance, of the nominal sentence stand originally, as it is natural, both in the nominative. There are, however, certain regents called *nawāsikh*, "effacing ones," which, like the particle *inna*, "behold," change the nominative of the subject into the accusative, while others, like the verb *kāna*, "he was," leave the subject unaltered, but place the predicate in the objective case: *zaid-un ẓārib-un* becomes thus either *inna zaid-an ẓārib-un*, or *kāna zaid-un ẓārib-an*.

Again, we have seen that the aorist proper of the third person singular terminates in *u* (*yaẓrib-u*). But under the influence of one class of regents this vowel changes into *a* (*yaẓrib-a*); under that of others it is dropped altogether, and in both cases the meaning and grammatical status of the verb is thereby considerably modified. If we consider the large number of these governing parts of speech—a well-known book treats of the "hundred regents," but other grammarians count a hundred and fifteen and more—it will be seen what delicate and careful handling the Arabic syntax requires, and how little scope there is left for the experiments of wilful innovators.

At the time of Muḥammad this then was, apart from some slight dialectical differences, the spoken language of his people. He took it, so to say, from the mouth of his interlocutors, but, wielding it with the power of a master-mind, he made in the Qur'ān such a complete and perfect use of all its resources as to create a work that, in the estimation of his hearers, appeared worthy to be thought the word of God Himself.

When a long period of conquests scattered the Arabs to the farthest East and to the farthest West, their spoken language might deviate from its pristine purity, slurring over unaccented syllables and dropping terminations. But the fine idiom of their fore-fathers, as deposited in the Qur'ān, remained the language of their prayer and their pious meditation, and thus lived on with them, as a bond of unity, an object of national love and admiration, and a source of literary development for all times.

AL-QUR'ĀNU 'L-'AẒĪM (القران العظيم). *Lit.* "The Exalted Reading." A title given to the Introductory Chapter of the Qur'ān by Muhammad. (*Mishkāt*, book viii. ch. i. pt. 1.)

QURBĀN (قربان), *Lit.* "Approaching near." Heb. קָרְבָּן *korbān.* A term used in the Qur'ān and in the Traditions for a sacrifice or offering. Sūrah v. 30: "Truly when they (Cain and Abel) offered an *offering.*" [SACRIFICE.]

QURBU 'S-SĀ'AH (قرب الساعة). "An hour which is near." A term used for the Day of Resurrection and Judgment.

QUSṬANṬĪNĪYAH (قسطنطينية). The word used in the Traditions and in Muhammadan history for Constantinople. (See *Ḥadīṣu 't-Tirmiẓī.*) Istambūl (استمبول), is the word generally used by modern Muslims.

QUṬB (قطب). *Lit.* "A stake, an axis, a pivot." The highest stage of sanctity amongst Muslim saints. A higher position than that of *ghauṣ*. According to the *Kashshāfu 'l-Iṣṭilāḥāt*, a *quṭb* is one who has attained to that degree of sanctity which is a reflection of the heart of the Prophet himself. *Quṭbu 'd-Dīn*, "the axis of religion," a title given to eminent Muslim divines. [FAQIR.]

R.

AR-RABB (الرب). "The Lord," "The Sustainer," "The Supporter." A title frequently used in the Qur'ān for the Divine Being, *e.g.*:—

Sūrah iii. 44: "God (*Allāh*) is my Lord (*Rabb*) and your Lord (*Rabb*)."

Sūrah xviii. 13: "Our Lord (*Rabb*) is the Lord (*Rabb*) of the heavens and the earth."

From its frequent occurrence in the Qu'rān, it would seem to occupy the place of the Hebrew יְהוָה Jehovah, the Κύριος of the LXX., the Dominus of the Vulgate, and the LORD of the English Bible; but all Muslim writers say that whilst Allāh is the *Ismu 'z-Ẕāt*, or "Essential name of God," *ar-Rabb*, "the Lord," is but an *Ismu Ṣifah*, or attribute, of the Almighty.

Al-Baiẓāwī, the commentator (p. 6, line 10, of Flügel's edition), says, "*rabb*, in its literal meaning, is 'to bring up,' that is, to bring or educate anything up to its perfect standard, by slow degrees, and inasmuch as the Almighty is He who can bring everything to perfection, the word الرب *ar-Rabb*, is especially applied to God."

It is the Hebrew רַב *Rab*, which enters into the composition of many names of dignity and office in the Bible.

In Muslim works of theology, the word occurs with the following combination:—

Rabbu 'l-ʻIzzah .	Lord of Glory.
Rabbu 'l-ʻĀlamīn .	Lord of the Universe.
Rabbu 'l-Arbāb .	Lord of Lords.
Rabbu 'l-ʻIbād .	Lord of (His) Servants.

The word is also used for a master or owner, *e.g.*:—

Rabbu 'd-Dār .	The Master of the house.
Rabbu 'l-Arẓ .	A landowner.
Rabbu 'l-Māl .	A possessor of property.
Rabbu 's-Salaf .	A person who pays in advance for an article.

RABBU 'N-NAUʻ (رب النوع). The "Lord of the Species." An angel who is said to preside over the animate and inanimate creation, viz.: *nabātāt*, "vegetable"; *ḥaiwānāt*, "animal"; *jamādāt*, "inanimate" (stones, earth, &c.), called *al-ʻālamu 's-suflī*, "the lower creation," as distinguished from *al-ʻālamu 'l-ʻulwī*, "the heavenly world." (See *Ghiyāṣu 'l-Lughah*.)

RABĪʻU 'L-ĀKHIR (ربيع الاخر). "The last spring month." The fourth month of the Muhammadan year. [MONTHS.]

RABĪʻU 'L-AWWAL (ربيع الاول). "The first spring month." The third month of the Muḥammadan year. [MONTHS.]

In India, the word *rabīʻ* is used for spring harvest, or crop sown after the rains.

RACHEL. Arabic *Rāḥīl* (راحيل). Heb. רָחֵל, *Rahel*. The wife of Jacob and the mother of Joseph. Not mentioned in the Qur'ān, but the name occurs in commentaries.

The English form *Rachel* is a strange error on the part of our translators, who almost invariably represent the Hebrew ח by the letter *h*. The correct form, *Rahel*, which is the form familiar to Muslim writers, occurs once in the English Bible, Jer. xxxi. 15.

AR-RAʻD (رعد). "Thunder." The title of the XIIIth Sūrah of the Qur'ān, in the 14th verse of which the word occurs. "The *thunder* celebrates his praise."

RADD (الرد). "Rejection, repulsion, refutation, reply; repeal, abrogation, making null and void; sometimes, erasure. In Muḥammadan law it applies especially to the return or surplus of an inheritance which remains after the legal portions have been distributed among the sharers, and which, in default of a residuary heir, returns, or is to be divided amongst the original sharers.

RADDU 'S-SALĀM (رد السلام). The returning of a salutation which is an incumbent duty upon one Muslim to another. [SALUTATION.]

AR-RĀFIʻ (الرافع). "The Exalter." One of the ninety-nine names or attributes of God. The word occurs in the Qur'ān, Sūrah iii. 48: "When God said, O Jesus! I will make thee die and will *take thee up* again *to myself*" (رافعك الى).

RĀFIʻ IBN KHADĪJ (رافع بن خديج). One of the Ṣaḥābah. He was too young to be present at Badr, but he accompanied Muḥammad at Uḥud and was wounded with an arrow, on which occasion the Prophet said to him, "I will answer for you in the Day of Judgment." He died at al-Madinah, A.H. 73, aged 86.

RĀFIẒĪ (رافضى). *Lit.* "A forsaker." Synonymous with *Rāfiẓah* (pl. *Rawāfiẓ*). A term used for a body of soldiers who have deserted their commander and turned back again, applied to a sect of Shī'ahs who joined Zaid the son of 'Alī, the son of al-Ḥusain, the second son of the Khalīfah 'Alī, who, when they had submitted to Zaid, demanded that he should abuse Abū Bakr and 'Umar, the first two Khalīfahs of the Sunnis; but Zaid refused to do so, for he said, "They were both Wazīrs of my forefather Muḥammad." Upon this they *forsook* the party of Zaid, and were called *Rāfiẓah*. Zaid had then only fourteen faithful companions left, and he was soon surrounded by al-Ḥajjāj ibn Yūsuf, the general of the Imām Ja'far's army, and fell at the head of his brave companions, not one of them surviving him.

(2) The term *Rāfiẓī* is used by Sunnī Muslims for any sect of Shī'ahs.

RAHBĀNĪYAH (رهبانية). [MONASTICISM.]

RĀHIB (راهب), pl. *Ruhbān*. A Christian monk. Mentioned in the Qur'ān, Sūrah v. 85: "Thou wilt find the nearest in love to those who believe to be those who say, 'We are Christians'; that is, because there are amongst them priests (*qissīsūn*) and monks (*ruhbān*), and because they are not proud." [MONASTICISM.]

RAḤĪL (رحيل). *Lit.* "That which is fit for travelling." A small book-stand made so as to fold up for convenience in travelling, but now generally used as a book-

stand in mosques and Muslim schools to support the Qur'ān and other books as the student reads his lesson from them. They are also used in private dwellings.

AR-RAḤĪM (الرحيم). "The Compassionate." One of the ninety-nine names or attributes of God. It generally occurs in conjunction with the attribute *ar-Raḥmān*, *e.g.* Qur'ān, Sūrah ii. 158: "The Merciful, The Compassionate." [RAHMAN.]

RAḤMAH (رحمة), Heb. רִחַם *riham*. "Mercy, compassion." The attribute of mercy is frequently dwelt upon in the Qur'ān, *e.g.*:—

Sūrah vii. 54: "The mercy of God is nigh unto those who do well."

Sūrah x. 58: "A guidance and a mercy to believers."

Sūrah vi. 133: "Thy Lord is the rich one, full of compassion."

Ar-Raḥmān, "The Merciful," is one of the chief attributes of the Almighty.

AR-RAḤMĀN (الرحمان), Heb. רַחוּם *rahūm*. "The Merciful." One of the ninety-nine names or attributes of God. It generally occurs in conjunction with the attribute *ar-Raḥīm*, *e.g.* Qur'ān, Sūrah ii. 159: "Your God is one God. There is no god but He, the Merciful, the Compassionate." It also occurs in the initial formula, placed at the commencement of each Sūrah, with the exception of the IXth, "In the name of God, the Merciful, the Compassionate."

Al-Baiẓāwī says that *ar-Raḥmān* is a more exalted attribute than *ar-Raḥīm*, because it not only contains five letters whilst *Raḥīm* only has four, but it expresses that universal attribute of mercy which the Almighty extends to all mankind, the wicked and the good, believers and unbelievers.

RAHN (رهن). Pledging or pawning. A legal term which signifies the detention of a thing on account of a claim which may be answered by means of that thing; as in the case of debt. This practice of pawning and pledging is lawful in Islām, for it is related that the Prophet, in a bargain with a Jew for grain, gave his coat of mail in pledge for the payment. It is also said in the Qur'ān, Sūrah ii. 283: "Let pledges be taken." The word is used in the Qur'ān in its plural form, *rihān*. (For further information on the subject of Pawning, see Hamilton's *Hidāyah*, vol. iv. p. 188.)

RAIḤĀNAH (ريحانة). A Jewess whose husband had been cruelly murdered in the massacre of the Banū Quraiẓah. Muḥammad offered to marry her if she would embrace Islām; but she refused to forsake the faith of her forefathers, and consented to become his concubine instead of his wife.

RAIN. Arabic *maṭar* (مطر), Heb. מָטָר *mātor*. Mentioned in the Qur'ān as one of God's special mercies. Sūrah vii. 55: "He it is who sends forth the winds as heralds before *His mercy*; until when they left the heavy cloud which We drive to a dead land, and send down thereon water, and bring forth therewith every kind of fruit."

Prayers for rain are called *Ṣalātu 'l-Istisqā'*, and consist of two rak'ah prayers. Anas says that on one occasion they were caught in the rain, and the Prophet took off his garment until he got wet, and they said, "O Prophet, why have you done this?" He replied, "This is fresh rain from our Lord." (*Mishkāt*, book iv. ch. liii.)

RĀ'INĀ (راعنا). A word the use of which is forbidden in the Qur'ān, Sūrah ii. 98: "O ye who believe! say not to the Apostle '*Rā'inā*' (*i.e.* 'Look at us'), but say, '*Unẓurnā*' (*i.e.* 'Regard us')." These two words have both the same signification; but Muḥammad had a great aversion to the use of the word *rā'inā*, because it had also a bad meaning in Hebrew (see al-Baiẓāwī, *in oco*), alluding, perhaps, to the Hebrew verb רוּעַ *rūa'*, which signifies "to be mischievous or bad."

RAINBOW. Arabic *qausu quzaḥ* (قوس قزح), Heb. קֶשֶׁת *kesheth*. *Lit.* "The bow of many colours." Not mentioned in the Qur'ān, but in the Traditions. In the book entitled *an-Nihāyah*, it is said that Muḥammad forbade his people calling the rainbow *qausu quzaḥ*, because *quzaḥ* is one of the names of Satan (one who can assume many characters in order to tempt the sons of men). He enjoined them to call it *Qausu 'llāh*, "God's bow," because by it God has promised to protect the world from a second deluge. (*Majma'u 'l-Biḥār*, vol. ii. p. 142.)

The Persians call it *Kamān-i-Rustum*, "the bow of Rustum." (See *Muntaha 'l-'Arab, in loco.*)

RAIYĀN (ريان). *Lit.* "One whose thirst is quenched" The gate of Paradise through which, it is said, the observers of the month of Ramaẓān will enter. It is mentioned in the Traditions (*Mishkāt*, book vi. ch. vii. pt. 1), but not in the Qur'ān.

RAIYĀN IBN AL-WALĪD (ريان بن الوليد). The King of Egypt in the time of Joseph. (See al-Baiẓāwī on Sūratu Yūsuf in the Qur'ān.

RAJAB (رجب). *Lit.* "The honoured month." The seventh month of the Muḥammadan year. So called because of the honour in which it was held in the "Time of Ignorance," *i.e.* before Islām. It is called *Rajabu Muẓar*, because the Muẓar tribe honoured it more than any other month. [MONTHS.]

RAJ'AH (رجعة). "Restitution." Receiving back a wife who has been divorced, before the time has fully elapsed when the divorce must of necessity take place. In other words, the continuance of the marriage bond. (*Hidāyah*, vol. i. p. 289.)

RAJĪM (رجيم). *Lit.* "One who is stoned." A name given to Satan in the Qur'ān, Sūrah iii. 31: "I have called her Mary, and I seek refuge in Thee for her and for her seed from Satan, the pelted one (*Min ash-Shaiṭāni 'r-Rajīmi*).

Muḥammad taught that the devil and his angels listen at the gates of heaven for scraps of information regarding the things of futurity, and when detected by the angels of heaven they are pelted with shooting stars. Abraham is also said to have driven the devil away by pelting him with stones, which legend is expressed in the throwing stones at the pillars at Minā. [PILGRIMAGE.]

RAJM (رجم). "Lapidation." [STONING TO DEATH.]

RAK'AH (ركعة). From *Rukū'*, "to bow, to prostrate one's self." A section of the Muḥammadan daily prayers. [PRAYERS.]

RAMAẒĀN (رمضان). The ninth month of the Muḥammadan year, which is observed as a strict fast from dawn to sunset of each day in the month. The word *Ramaẓān* is derived from *ramẓ*, "to burn." The month is said to have been so called either because it used (before the change of the calendar) to occur in the hot season, or because the month's fast is supposed to burn away the sins of men. (*Ghiyāṣu 'l-Lughah, in loco.*)

The observance of this month is one of the five pillars of practice in the Muslim religion, and its excellence is much extolled by Muḥammad, who said that during Ramaẓān "the gates of Paradise are open, and the gates of hell are shut, and the devils are chained by the leg, and only those who observe it will be permitted to enter at the gate of heaven called Raiyān." Those who keep the fast "will be pardoned all their past venial sins." (*Mishkāt*, book vii. ch. i. pt. 1.)

The express injunctions regarding the observance of this month are given in the Qur'ān, Sūrah ii. 179–184:—

"O believers! a Fast is prescribed to you as it was prescribed to those before you, that ye may fear God, for certain days. But he among you who shall be sick, or on a journey, *shall fast* that same number of other days: and as for those who are able *to keep it and yet break it*, the expiation of this shall be the maintenance of a poor man. And he who of his own accord performeth a good work, shall derive good from it: and good shall it be for you to fast—if ye knew it. As to the month Ramaẓān in which the Qur'ān was sent down to be man's guidance, and an explanation of that guidance, and of that illumination, as soon as any one of you observeth the moon, let him set about the fast; but he who is sick, or upon a journey, shall fast a like number of other days. God wisheth you ease, but wisheth not your discomfort, and that you fulfil the number *of days*, and that you glorify God for his guidance, and that you be thankful. And when my servants ask thee concerning me, then will I be nigh unto them. I will answer the cry of him that crieth, when he crieth unto me: but let them hearken unto me, and believe in me, that they may proceed aright. You are allowed on the night of the fast to approach your wives: they are your garment and ye are their garment. God knoweth that ye defraud yourselves therein, so He turneth unto you and forgiveth you! Now, therefore, go in unto them with full desire for that which God hath ordained for you; and eat and drink until ye can discern a white thread from a black thread by the daybreak: then fast strictly till night, and go not in unto them, but rather pass the time in the Mosques. These are the bounds set up by God: therefore come not near them. Thus God maketh His signs clear to men that they my fear Him."

From the preceding verses it will be seen that fast does not commence until some Muslim is able to state that he has seen the new moon. If the sky be over-clouded and the moon cannot be seen, the fast begins upon the completion of thirty days from beginning of the previous month.

It must be kept by every Muslim, except the sick, the infirm, and pregnant women, or women who are nursing their children. Young children, who have not reached the age of puberty, are exempt, and also travellers on a journey of more than three days. In the case of a sick person or traveller, the month's fast must be kept as soon as they are able to perform it. This act is called *Qaẓā'*, or expiation.

The fast is extremely rigorous and mortifying, and when the Ramaẓān happens to fall in the summer and the days are long, the prohibition even to drink a drop of water to slake the thirst is a very great hardship. Muḥammad speaks of this religious exercise as "easy" (Qur'ān; Sūrah ii. 181), as most probably it was when compared with the ascetic spirit of the times. Sir William Muir (*Life of Mahomet*, vol. iii. 49) thinks Muḥammad did not foresee that, when he changed the Jewish intercalary year for the lunar year, the fast would become a grievous burden instead of an easy one; but Muḥammadan lexicographers say the fast was established when the month occurred in the hot season (see *G͟hiyāṣu 'l-Lug͟hah*).

During the month of Ramaẓān twenty additional *rak'ahs*, or forms of prayer, are repeated after the night-prayer. These are called *Tarāwīḥ*.

Devout Muslims seclude themselves for some time in the Mosque during this month, and abstain from all worldly conversation, engaging themselves in the reading of the Qur'ān. This seclusion is called *I'tikāf*. Muḥammad is said to have usually observed this custom in the last ten days of Ramaẓān. The *Lailatu 'l-Qadr*, or the "night of power," is said by Muḥammad to be either on the twenty-first, twenty-third, or twenty-fifth, or twenty-seventh, or twenty-ninth of the month of Ramaẓān. The exact date of this solemn night has not been discovered by any but the Prophet himself, and some of the Companions, although the learned doctors believe it to be on the twenty-seventh of this night Muḥammad says in the Qur'ān (Sūratu 'l-Qadr):—

"Verily we have caused it (the Qur'ān) to descend on the night of power.
And who shall teach thee what the night of power is?
The night of power excelleth a thousand months;
Therein descend the angels and the spirit by permission
Of their Lord in every matter;
And all is peace till the breaking of the morn."

By these verses the commentator Ḥusain understands that on this night the Qur'ān came down entire in one volume to the lowest heaven, from whence it was revealed by Gabriel in portions, as the occasion required. The excellences of this night are said to be innumerable, and it is believed that during it the whole animal and vegetable kingdom bow in humble adoration to the Almighty, and the waters of the sea become sweet in a moment of time! This night is frequently confounded with the *Shab-i-Barāt*, but even the Qur'ān itself is not quite clear on the subject, for in Sūrah xliv. 1 it reads, "By this clear book. See on a blessed night have we sent it down, for we would warn mankind, on the night wherein all things are disposed in wisdom." From which it appears that "the blessed night," or the *Lailatu 'l-mubārakah*, is both the night of record and the night upon which the Qur'ān came down from heaven, although the one is the twenty-seventh day of Ramaẓān and the other the fifteenth of Sha'bān.

M. Geiger identifies the Ramaẓān with the fast of the tenth (Leviticus xxiii. 27); but it is probable that the fast of the Tenth is identical with the *'Āshurā'*, not only because the Hebrew *Asūr*, "ten," is retained in the title of that Muḥammadan fast, but also because there is a Jewish tradition that creation began upon the Jewish fast of the Tenth, which coincides with the Muḥammadan day, 'Āshurā' being regarded as the day of creation. Moreover, the Jewish Asūr and the Muslim 'Āshurā' are both fasts and days of affliction. It is more probable that Muḥammad got his idea of a thirty days' fast from the Christian Lent. The observance of Lent in the Eastern Church was exceedingly strict, both with regard to the nights as well as the days of that season of abstinence; but Muḥammad entirely relaxed the rules with regard to the night, and from sunset till the dawn of day the Muslim is permitted to indulge in any lawful pleasures, and to feast with his friends; consequently large evening dinner-parties are usual in the nights of the Ramaẓān amongst the better classes. This would be what Muḥammad meant when he said, "God would make the fast an ease and not a difficulty," for, notwithstanding its rigour in the daytime, it must be an easier observance than the strict fast observed during Lent by the Eastern Christians of Muḥammad's day.

The following sayings of Muḥammad regarding the fast of Ramaẓān are found in the Traditions (see *Mishkāt*, Arabic Ed., *Kitābu 's-Ṣaum*).

"The difference between our fast and that of the people of the book (*i.e.* Jews and Christians) is eating only before the first dawn of day (and not afterwards)."

"Keep not the fast till you see the new moon, and if the moon be hidden from you by clouds, count the days." And in one tradition it is thus:—"A month is twenty-nine nights, then keep not the fast till you see the new moon, which, if she be hid from you by clouds, then complete thirty days."

"When the darkness of the night advances from the west and the day departs from the east, and the sun sets, then the keeper of the fast may begin to eat."

"There are eight doors in Paradise, and

one is called Raiyān, by which only the keepers of the fast shall enter."

"When the month Ramaẓān arrives the doors of Heaven are opened" (in another tradition it is said, the doors of Paradise are opened), "and the doors of hell are shut, and the devils are chained" (in one tradition it is said, the doors of God's mercy are opened).

"The person who fasts in the month of Ramaẓān on account of belief in God and in obedience to His command, shall be pardoned of all his past sins, and the person who says the night prayers of the Ramaẓān shall be pardoned all his past sins, and the person who says the prayers on the Lailatu 'l-Qadr with faith and the hope of reward shall be pardoned of all his past sins."

"If a keeper of fast does not abandon lying, God cares not about his leaving off eating and drinking."

"There are many keepers of fast who gain nothing by fasting but thirst, and there are many risers up at night and performers of prayers who gain nothing by their rising but wakefulness."

RAMYU 'L-JIMĀR (رمى الجمار). The throwing of pebbles at the pillars, or Jumrah, at Makkah. A religious ceremony during the Pilgrimage. [PILGRIMAGE.]

RAQABAH (رقبة). *Lit.* "The Neck"; pl. *riqāb.* A term used in the Qur'ān for a captive slave. Sūrah iv. 94: "Whosoever kills a believer by mistake, then let him free a believing neck."

The word is used in India for an enclosed area of land. (See Wilson's *Glossary of Indian Terms.*)

AR-RAQĪB (الرقيب). "The Watcher over." One of the ninety-nine names or attributes of the Almighty. The word occurs in the Qur'ān, *e.g.* Sūrah iv. 1: "Verily God doth watch over you."

AR-RAQĪM (الرقيم). A word which occurs in the Qur'ān, Sūrah xviii. 8: "Hast thou reckoned that the Fellows of the cave and the *Raqīm* were a wonder amongst our signs?" The commentators are not agreed as to the meaning of this word. The Jalālān say, it was a brass plate or stone-table, on which the names of the Fellows of the Cave were written. The Kamālān say it was either the name of the dog which belonged to the young men, or of the valley in which the cave was situated.

AR-RASHĪD (الرشيد). "The Rightly Directing." One of the ninety-nine names or attributes of God. The word occurs once in the Qur'ān, but it is not there used for the Almighty. See Sūrah xi. 80: "Is there not among you one who *can rightly direct?*"

RASM (رسم), pl. *Rusūm.* *Lit.* "That which is stamped or sealed. According to the *Qāmūs*, it is a very ancient word used in Arabia before the days of the Prophet for custom and law, the ancient records of the people being entitled *Rawasīm* (رواسيم). It is a word which is very common in Hindustan for the customs and usages of the people.

AR-RASS (الرس). A word which occurs twice in the Qur'ān, the meaning of which is uncertain.

Sūrah xxv. 40: "The people of 'Ād, and Ṣamūd, the people of the *Rass.*"

Sūrah l. 12: "Before them the people of Noah and the fellows of the *Rass* and Ṣamūd and 'Ād and Pharaoh, called the Apostles liars."

According to the commentators al-Jalālān, it is the name of a well near Midian. Some take it to be the name of a town in Yamāmah.

RASŪL (رسول), pl. *Rusul.* "An Apostle." A title specially applied to Muḥammad, but used also for all Prophets who brought inspired books. [PROPHET.]

RAṬL, RIṬL (رطل). (1) A certain thing which one weighs. A weight or measure. (See *The Mughrib of al-Muṭarrizī, in loco.* (2) That which is chaste. (See the *Tāju 'l-'Arūs, in loco*).

(1) According to the standard of Baghdad, a weight of 12 ounces, and as a measure of capacity, a pint. (Lane's *Arabic Dictionary.*) Muḥammad used to give a *raṭl* of silver as a marriage present, which has given rise to the expression, *As-sunnatu fī 'n-nikāḥi riṭlun* (السنة فى النكاح رطل). Professor Wilson says that at Bombay the *ratal* is equal to 36 Surat rupees, and in the Red Sea the *rottolo*, as it is corruptly called, varies from 10 to 20 ounces avoirdupois.

(2) A boy not having arrived at puberty.

(3) An aged man.

AR-RA'ŪF (الرؤف). "The Kind." One of the ninety-nine names or attributes of God. It occurs frequently in the Qur'ān, *e.g.* Sūrah ii. 138: "God is *kind* and merciful with mankind."

AR-RAUẒAH (الروضة). *Lit.* "The Garden." The garden in which is situated the tomb of Muḥammad at al-Madīnah. The name is also given to the tomb itself by some writers.

RAVEN. Arabic *ghurāb* (غراب). Heb. עֹרֵב *'oreb.* Mentioned once in the Qur'ān, Sūrah v. 34: "Am I too helpless to become like this raven and hide my brother's shame." The raven is not lawful food according to the Muslim law. (*Durru 'l-Mukhtār*, vol. iv. p. 523.)

RAWĀ (روا). A Persian word for that which is lawful. [LAW.]

AR-RAZZĀQ (الرزاق). "The Provider with Food." One of the ninety-nine names or attributes of God. It occurs in the Qur'ān once. Sūrah li. 58: "Verily God; He is the *Provider.*"

REBEL. Arabic *bāghī* (باغى), pl. *bughāt*. A legal term for a person, or a body of people, who withdraw themselves from obedience to the rightful Imām. In case of rebellion, the Imām must first call the rebels to his allegiance and show them what is right, and if they refuse to obey, he must use force of arms. (*Hidāyah*, vol. ii. 248.)

RECORDING ANGELS, The. [KIRAMU 'L-KATIBIN.]

RED SEA. Arabic *al-Baḥru 'l-Aḥmar* (البحر الاحمر). Mentioned in the Qur'ān as *al-Baḥr*, "the Sea."

Sūrah i. 47: "When we divided for you *the sea*, and saved you and drowned Pharaoh's people."

Sūrah x. 90: "And We brought the Children of Israel across *the sea*."

In Muḥammadan works it is known as the *Baḥru 'l-Qulzum*, or *Qalzam*. Jalālu 'd-Dīn, the commentator, says the town of Qulzum is the same as *Ailah* (the Elath of the Bible, Deut. ii. 8), a town at the head of the Arabian Gulf. The Aἴλανα of Strabo (xvi. p. 768). It is referred to in the Qur'ān, Sūrah vii. 163: "Ask them about the city which stood by the sea." Elath was at one time a place of importance, but it has now become quite insignificant.

RELIGION. The religion of Muḥammadans is called Islām (اسلام), and the laws of God *Sharī'ah* (شريعة). There are three words used by Muslim writers for the word religion, namely, *Dīn*, *Millah*, and *Mazhab*. In the *Kitābu 't-Ta'rīfāt*, the difference between these words is as follows:—

Dīn (دين) is used for religion as it stands in relation to God, *e.g.* *Dīnu 'llāh*, "the religion of God."

Millah (ملة), as it stands in relation to the Prophet or lawgiver, *e.g.* *Millatu Ibrāhīm*, "the religion of Abraham," or *Millatu 'r-Rasūl*, "the Prophet's religion."

Mazhab (مذهب), as it stands in relation to the decisions of the *Mujtahidūn*, *e.g.* *Muzhabu Abī Ḥanīfah*.

The expression *Dīn*, however, is of general application, whilst *Millah* and *Mazhab* are restricted in their use. [ISLAM.]

RELIGIOUS DUTIES, The performance of. Strictly according to Muḥammadan law, it is not lawful to accept any remuneration for the performance of religious duties. But these injunctions are now totally disregarded, and fees are taken for almost every religious duty performed by an Imām. The teaching of the *Hidāyah* on the subject is as follows:—

"It is not lawful to accept a recompense for summoning the people to prayers, or for the performance of a pilgrimage, or of the duties of an Imam, or for teaching the Koran, or the law; for it is a general rule, with our doctors, that no recompense can be received for the performance of any duty purely of a religious nature According to Shafei, it is allowed to receive pay for the performance of any religious duty which is not required of the hireling in virtue of a divine ordinance, as this is only accepting a recompense for a certain service; and as the acts above described are not ordained upon the hireling, it is consequently lawful to receive a recompense for them. The arguments of our doctors upon this point are twofold. First, the prophet has said, 'Read the Koran, but do not receive any recompense for so doing'; and he also directed Othman-bin-Abeeyas, that if he were appointed a Mawzin [a cryer to prayer] he should not take any wages. Secondly, where an act of piety is performed, it springs solely from the performer (whence regard is had to his competency), and consequently he is not entitled to any recompense from another, as in the cases of fasting or prayer. A teacher of the Koran, moreover, is incapable of instructing another in it, but by means of qualities existing in his scholar, namely, capacity and docility, and therefore undertakes a thing the performance of which does not depend upon himself, which is consequently invalid. Some of our modern doctors, however, hold it lawful to receive wages for teaching the Koran in the present age, because an indifference has taken place with respect to religion, whence if people were to withhold from paying a recompense for instruction in the sacred writings, they would in time be disregarded;—and decrees pass accordingly.

"It is not lawful to receive wages for singing or lamentation, or for any other species of public exhibition, as this is taking a recompense for an act which is of a criminal nature, and acts of that nature do not entitle to a recompense in virtue of a contract."

RE-MARRIAGE. Re-marriage may take place with the divorcer before or after the completion of the *'iddah*, provided *only* the first or second sentence of divorce has been pronounced, but it cannot take place after a three-fold divorce until the divorced wife is married to another man and is divorced by him after the second marriage has been consummated. This is both Sunnī and Shī'ah law. (*Tagore Law Lectures.*)

A widow can marry again at the expiration of four months and ten days after the death of her former husband. There is no restriction as to the period for a widower.

RENTAL. Arabic *ijārah* (اجارة). [HIRE.]

REPENTANCE. Arabic *taubah* (توبة). *Lit.* "The turning of the heart from sin." (An-Nawawī's *Commentary on Muslim*, vol. ii. p. 354.) It is frequently enjoined in the Qur'ān, *e.g.*:—

Sūrah iv. 20: "If they repent and amend let them be. Verily God is he who relenteth. He is merciful."

Sūrah xxiv. 32: "Be ye wholly turned to God, O ye believers, and it shall be well with you."

Sūrah xxv. 71: "Whoso hath repented and hath done what is right, he verily it is who turneth to God with a true conversion." [PARDON.]

RESIDUARIES. Arabic *'aṣabah* (عصبة), pl. *'aṣabāt.* According to Muḥammadan law, residuaries in their own right are divided into four classes:—

(1) The offspring of the deceased.

(2) The ascendants (such as father, grandfather, &c.).

(3) The offspring of his father, viz. the brothers and their descendants.

(4) The offspring of his grandfather. (Syed Ameer Ali's *Personal Law*, p. 49.) [INHERITANCE.]

RESIGNATION. The literal meaning of Islām is a state or condition in which a believer becomes "resigned" to the will of God, a "Muslim" being one who is "resigned." But in the Qur'ān, the grace of resignation is more frequently expressed by the word *ṣabr*, "patience," *e.g.* Sūrah ii. 150: "Give good tidings to the *patient*, who when there falls on them a calamity, say, 'Verily we are God's and verily to Him do we return.'"

The word *Taslīm*, which the compiler of the *Kitābu 't-Ta'rīfāt* says means to place one's neck under the commands of God, seems to express the English word "resignation."

It occurs in the Qur'ān, Sūrah iv. 68: "They submit with submission."

The author of the *Akhlāq-i-Jālālī* says *Taslīm* is to "acquiesce in and receive with satisfaction (although, perhaps, repugnant to the inclination) the commands of God," as exemplified in the verse above quoted.

Riẓā', is also a word which expresses resignation, and is defined as being pleased with the inevitable decrees of God, whatever they may be.

RESURRECTION. Belief in *al-yaumu 'l-ākhir* (اليوم الاخر), "the Last Day," is an article of the Muḥammadan Faith. The terms used in the Qur'ān are—

Yaumu 'l-Qiyāmah, "Day of Standing up" (Sūrah ii. 79).

Yaumu 'l-Faṣl, "Day of Separation" (Sūrah lxxvii. 14).

Yaumu 'l-Ḥisāb. "Day of Reckoning" (Sūrah xl. 28).

Yaumu 'l-Ba'ṣ, "Day of Awakening" (Sūrah xxx. 56).

Yaumu 'd-Dīn, "Day of Judgment" (Surah i. 3).

Al-Yaumu 'l-Muḥīṭ, "The Encompassing Day" (Sūrah xi. 85).

As-Sā'ah, "The Hour" (Sūrah viii. 186).

There are very graphic descriptions of the Last Day in the poetical Sūrahs of the Qur'ān. The five following belong to an early period in Muḥammad's mission:—

Sūrah lxxv.:—

"It needeth not that I swear by the day of the Resurrection,
Or that I swear by the self-accusing soul.
Thinketh man that we shall not re-unite his bones?
Aye! his very finger tips are we able evenly to replace.
But man chooseth to deny what is before him:
He asketh, 'When this day of Resurrection?'
But when the eye shall be dazzled,
And when the moon shall be darkened,
And the sun and the moon shall be together,
On that day man shall cry, 'Where is there a place to flee to?'
But in vain—there is no refuge—
With thy Lord on that day shall be the sole asylum.
On that day shall man be told of all that he hath done first and last;
Yea, a man shall be the eye-witness against himself:
And even if he put forth his plea . . .
(Move not thy tongue in haste to *follow and master this revelation*:
For we will see to the collecting and the recital of it;
But when we have recited it, then follow thou the recital,
And, verily, afterwards it shall be ours to make it clear to thee.)
Aye, but ye love the transitory,
And ye neglect the life to come.
On that day shall faces beam with light,
Outlooking towards their Lord;
And faces on that day shall be dismal,
As if they thought that some great calamity would befall them.
Aye, when *the soul* shall come up into the throat,
And there shall be a cry, 'Who hath a charm that can restore him?'
And the man feeleth that the time of his departure is come,
And when one leg shall be laid over the other,
To thy Lord on that day shall he be driven on;
For he believed not, and he did not pray,
But he called the truth a lie and turned his back,
Then, walking with haughty mien, rejoined his people.
That Hour is nearer to thee and nearer,
It is ever nearer to thee and nearer still.
Thinketh man that he shall be left supreme?
Was he not a mere embryo?
Then he became thick blood of which God formed him and fashioned him;
And made him twain, male and female.
Is not He powerful enough to quicken the dead?"

Sūrah lxxxi. 1–19:—

"When the sun shall be folded up,
And when the stars shall fall,
And when the mountains shall be set in motion,
And when the she-camels shall be abandoned,

And when the wild beasts shall be gathered together,
And when the seas shall boil,
And when souls shall be paired *with their bodies*,
And when the female child that had been buried alive shall be asked
For what crime she was put to death,
And when the leaves of the Book shall be unrolled,
And when the Heaven shall be stripped away,
And when Hell shall be made to blaze,
And when Paradise shall be brought near,
Every soul shall know what it hath produced.
It needs not that I swear by the stars of retrograde motion,
Which move swiftly and hide themselves away,
And by the night when it cometh darkening on,
And by the dawn when it brighteneth,
That this is the word of an illustrious Messenger."

Sūrah lxxxii. :—

"When the Heaven shall cleave asunder,
And when the stars shall disperse,
And when the seas shall be commingled,
And when the graves shall be turned upside down,
Each soul shall recognize its earliest and its latest actions.
O man! what hath misled thee against thy generous Lord,
Who hath created thee and moulded thee and shaped thee aright?
In the form which pleased Him hath He fashioned thee.
Even so; but ye treat the Judgment as a lie.
Yet truly there are guardians over you—
Illustrious recorders—
Cognizant of your actions.
Surely amid delights *shall* the righteous *dwell*,
But verily the impure in Hell-fire:
They shall be burned at it on the day of doom,
And they shall not be able to hide themselves from it.
Who shall teach thee what the day of doom is?
Once more Who shall teach thee what the day of doom is?
It is a day when one soul shall be powerless for another soul: all sovereignty on that day shall be with God."

Sūrah lxxxiii. 4–20:—

What! have they no thought that they shall be raised again
For the great day?
The day when mankind shall stand before the Lord of the worlds.
Yes! the register of the wicked is in Sijjīn.
And who shall make thee understand what Sijjīn is?
It is a book distinctly written.
Woe, on that day, to those who treated *our signs* as lies,
Who treated the day of judgment as a lie!
None treat it as a lie, save the transgressor, the criminal,
Who, when our signs are rehearsed to him, saith, 'Tales of the Ancients!'
Yes; but their own works have got the mastery over their hearts.
Yes; they shall be shut out as by a veil from their Lord on that day;
Then shall they be burned in Hell-fire:
Then shall it be said *to them*, 'This is what ye deemed a lie.'
Even so. But the register of the righteous is in 'Illīyūn.
And who shall make thee understand what 'Illīyūn is?
A book distinctly written."

Sūrah lxxxiv. 1–19:—

"When the Heaven shall have split asunder
And duteously obeyed its Lord;
And when Earth shall have been stretched out *as a plain*,
And shall have cast forth what was in her and become empty,
And duteously obeyed its Lord;
Then verily, O man, who desirest to reach thy Lord, shalt thou meet him.
And he into whose right hand his Book shall be given,
Shall be reckoned with in an easy reckoning,
And shall turn, rejoicing, to his kindred.
But he whose Book shall be given him behind his back
Shall invoke destruction:
But in the fire shall he burn,
For that he lived joyously among his kindred,
Without a thought that he should return *to God*.
Yea, but his Lord beheld him.
It needs not therefore that I swear by the sunset redness,
And by the night and its gatherings,
And by the moon when at her full,
That from state to state shall ye be surely carried onward."

The following description belongs to a much later period than the former Sūrahs already quoted, and occurs in Sūrah xxii. 1–7, which was given at Al-Madīnah not long before Muḥammad's death:—

"O men (of Makkah) fear your Lord. Verily the Earthquake of the Hour will be a tremendous thing!

"On the day when *ye* shall behold it, every suckling woman shall forsake her sucking babe; and every woman that hath a burden in her womb shall cast her burden; and thou shalt see men drunken, yet are they not drunken: but it is the mighty chastisement of God!

"There is a man who, without knowledge, wrangleth about God, and followeth every rebellious Satan;

"Concerning whom it is decreed, that he shall surely beguile and guide into the torment of the Flame, whoever shall take him for his lord.

"O men! if ye doubt as to the resurrection, yet, of a truth, have We created you of dust, then of the moist germs of life, then of clots of blood, then of pieces of flesh shapen and unshapen, that We might give you proofs *of our power!* And We cause *one sex or the other,* at our pleasure, to abide in the womb until the appointed time; then We bring you forth infants; then permit you to reach your age of strength; and one of you dieth, and another of you liveth on to an age so abject that all his former knowledge is clean forgotten! And thou hast seen the earth dried up and barren: but when We send down the rain upon it, it stirreth and swelleth, and groweth every kind of luxuriant herb.

"This, for that God is the Truth, and that it is He who quickeneth the dead, and that He hath power over everything:

"And that 'the Hour' will *indeed* come—there is no doubt of it—and that God will wake up to life those who are in the tombs."

Very lengthy accounts of the Day of Resurrection, and of the signs preceding it, are given in all books of tradition, and works on dogmatic theology. (See *Ṣaḥīḥu 'l-Buḵẖāri,* Arabic Ed. *Kitābu 'l-Fitan,* p. 1045; *Ṣaḥīḥu 'l-Muslim,* Arabic Ed. vol. ii. p. 388; *Mishkātu 'l-Maṣābīḥ,* Arabic Ed. *Kitābu 'l-Fitan; Sharḥu 'l-Muwāqif,* p. 579.)

The following, collected by Mr. Sale from various writers, is given, with some alterations, additions, and references.

It is the received opinion amongst Muslims of all sects that at the Resurrection the body will be raised and united to its soul, and that one part of the body, namely, the lower part of the spine, the *os sacrum,* in Arabic called *'Ajbu 'ẓ-Zanab,* "the root of the tail," will be preserved as a basis of the future edifice. (*Mishkāt,* book xxiii. ch. ix.)

This bone, it is said, will remain uncorrupted till the last day, as a germ from whence the whole is to be renewed. This will be effected by a forty days' rain which God will send, and which will cover the earth to the height of twelve cubits, and cause the bodies to sprout forth like plants. For this doctrine Muḥammad is beholden to the Jews, who say the same things of the bone *Lūz,* excepting that what he attributes to a great rain will be effected, according to them, by a dew, impregnating the dust of the earth. (*Bereshit rabbah.*)

The time of the Resurrection the Muḥammadans allow to be a perfect secret to all but God alone; the Angel Gabriel himself acknowledged his ignorance on this point when Muḥammad asked him about it. (*Mishkāt,* book i. ch. i.) However, they say the approach of that day may be known from certain signs which are to precede it. These signs are distinguished into "the lesser" and "the greater."

The lesser signs (*Ishārātu 's-Sāʻah*) are as follows :—

(1.) The decay of faith among men.

(2.) The advancing of the meanest persons to eminent dignity.

(3.) A maid-servant shall become the mother of her mistress (or master); by which is meant either that towards the end of the world men shall be much given to sensuality, or that the Muḥammadans shall then take many captives.

(4.) Tumults and seditions.

(5.) A war with the Greeks or Romans.

(6.) Great distress in the world, so that a man, when he passeth by another's grave, shall say, "Would to God I were in his place!"

(7.) The provinces of al-ʻIrāq and Syria shall refuse to pay their tribute.

(8.) The buildings of al-Madīnah or Yaṣrib shall reach to Makkah. (*Mishkāt,* book xxiii. ch. iii.)

The greater signs (*'Alāmātu 'ṣ-Ṣāʻah*) are as follows :—

(1.) The sun's rising in the west, which some have imagined it originally did.

(2.) The appearance of the *Dābbatu 'l-Arẓ,* or "beast," which shall rise out of the earth, in the temple of Makkah, or on Mount aṣ-Ṣafā. This beast will be sixty cubits high, and will be a compound of various species, having the head of a bull, the eyes of a hog, the ears of an elephant, the horns of a stag, the neck of an ostrich, the breast of a lion, the colour of a tiger, the back of a cat, the tail of a ram, the legs of a camel, and the voice of an ass. She will appear three times in several places, and will bring with her the rod of Moses and the seal of Solomon; and, being so swift that none can overtake her or escape her, will with the first strike all the believers on the face, and mark them with the word *Muʼmin,* "believer," and with the latter will mark the unbelievers on the face likewise with the word *kāfir,* "infidel," that every person may be known for what he really is. The same beast is to demonstrate the vanity of all religions except Islām, and to speak Arabic. [DABBATU 'L-ARZ.]

(3.) War with the Romans or Greeks, and the taking of Constantinople by seventy thousand of the posterity of Isaac, who shall not win that city by force of arms, but the walls shall fall down while they cry out, "There is no deity but God! God is most great!" As they are dividing the spoil, news will come to them of the appearance of Antichrist, whereupon they shall leave all and return back.

(4.) The coming of Antichrist, whom the Muḥammadans call *al-Masīḥu 'd-Dajjāl,* "the false or lying Christ." He is to be one-eyed, and marked on the forehead with the letters ر ف ك K F R, signifying *kāfir,* "infidel." He will appear first between al-ʻIrāq and Syria, or, according to others, in the province of Ḵẖorasān. He is to ride on a white ass, be followed by seventy thousand Jews of Ispahān, and continue on earth forty days, of which one will be equal in length to a year.

another to a month, another to a week, and the rest will be common days. He will lay waste all places, but will not enter Makkah or al-Madīnah, which are to be guarded by angels; and at length he will be slain by Jesus, who is to encounter him at the gate of Lud. [MASIHU 'D-DAJJAL.]

(5.) The descent of Jesus on earth. He is to descend near the white tower to the east of Damascus, when the people have returned from the taking of Constantinople. He is to embrace the Muḥammadan religion, marry a wife, get children, kill Antichrist, and at length die, after forty years'—or, according to others, twenty-four years'—continuance on earth, and be buried at Al-Madinah. Under him there will be great security and plenty in the world, all hatred and malice being laid aside; when lions and camels, bears and sheep, shall live in peace, and a child shall play with serpents unhurt. (See *Ṣaḥiḥu 'l-Bukḥāri*.)

(6.) War with the Jews, of whom the Muḥammadans are to make a prodigious slaughter, the very trees and stones discovering such of them as hide themselves, except only the tree called G̲h̲arqad, which is the tree of the Jews.

(7.) The appearance of Gog and Magog, or, as they are called, Ya'jūj and Ma'jūj. These barbarians, having passed the lake of Tiberias, which the vanguard of their vast army will drink dry, will come to Jerusalem, and there greatly distress Jesus and His companions, till, at His request, God will destroy them, and fill the earth with their carcasses, which after some time God will send birds to carry away, at the prayers of Jesus and His followers. Their bows, arrows and quivers the Muslims will burn seven years together; and at last God will send a rain to cleanse the earth, and to make it fertile. [GOG AND MAGOG.]

(8.) A smoke which shall fill the whole earth.

(9.) An eclipse of the moon. Muḥammad is reported to have said, that there would be three eclipses before the last hour, one to be seen in the east, another in the west, and the third in Arabia.

(10.) The returning of the Arabs to the worship of al-Lāt and al-ʿUzzā, and the rest of their ancient idols, after the decease of every one in whose heart there was faith equal to a grain of mustard-seed, none but the very worst of men being left alive. For God, they say, will send a cold odoriferous wind, blowing from Syria, which shall sweep away the souls of the faithful, and the Qur'ān itself, so that men will remain in the grossest ignorance for a hundred years.

(11.) The discovery of a vast heap of gold and silver by the retreating of the Euphrates, which will be the destruction of many.

(12.) The demolition of the Kaʿbah in the Makkan temple by the Ethiopians.

(13.) The speaking of beasts and inanimate things.

(14.) The breaking out of fire in the province of al-Ḥijāz, or, according to others, in al-Yaman.

(15.) The appearance of a man of the descendants of Kaḥtan, who shall drive men before him with his staff.

(16.) The coming of al-Mahdī, "the director," concerning whom Muḥammad prophesied that the world should not have an end till one of his own family should govern the Arabians, whose name should be the same with his own name, and whose father's name should also be the same with his father's name, and who shall fill the earth with righteousness. This person the Shīʿahs believe to be now alive, and concealed in some secret place, till the time of his manifestation; for they suppose him to be no other than the last of the twelve Imāms, named Muḥammad Abū 'l-Qāsim, as their prophet was. [SHIʿAH, MAHDI.]

(17.) A wind which shall sweep away the souls of all who have but a grain of faith in their hearts, as has been mentioned under the tenth sign. (*Mishkāt*, book xxiii. ch. iv.)

These are the greater signs which, according to Muḥammadan traditions, are to precede the Resurrection, but still leave the hour of it uncertain; for the immediate sign of its being come will be the first blast of the trumpet, which they believe will be sounded three times. The first, "the blast of consternation," at the hearing of which all creatures in heaven and earth shall be struck with terror, except those whom God shall please to exempt from it. The effects attributed to this first sound of the trumpet are very wonderful; for they say the earth will be shaken, and not only all buildings, but the very mountains, levelled; that the heavens shall melt, the sun be darkened, the stars fall on the death of the angels, who, as some imagine, hold them suspended between heaven and earth, and the sea shall be troubled and dried up, or, according to others, turned into flames, the sun, moon, and stars being thrown into it; the Qur'ān, to express the greatness of the terror of that day, adds that women who give suck shall abandon the care of their infants, and even the she-camels which have gone ten months with young (a most valuable part of the substance of that nation) shall be utterly neglected. (Qur'ān, Sūrah lxxxi.) A further effect of this blast will be that concourse of beasts mentioned in the Qur'ān, though some doubt whether it be to precede the Resurrection or not. They who suppose it will precede, think that all kinds of animals, forgetting their respective natural fierceness and timidity, will run together into one place, being terrified by the sound of the trumpet and the sudden shock of nature.

This first blast will be followed by a second, the "blast of examination," when all creatures, both in heaven and earth, shall die or be annihilated, except those which God shall please to exempt from the common fate; and this shall happen in the twinkling of an eye, nay, in an instant, nothing surviving except God alone, with Paradise and Hell, and the inhabitants of those two places, and the throne of Glory. The last who shall die will be the angel of death. (*Malaku 'l-Maut*.) (1 Cor. xv. 26.)

Forty years after this will be heard the "blast of resurrection," when the trumpet shall be sounded the third time by Isrāfīl, who, together with Gabriel and Michael, will be previously restored to life, and, standing on the rock of the temple of Jerusalem (*aṣ-Ṣakhrah*), shall at God's command call together all the dry and rotten bones, and other dispersed parts of the bodies, and the very hairs, to judgment. This angel having, by the Divine order, set the trumpet to his mouth, and called together all the souls from all parts, will throw them into his trumpet, from whence, on his giving the last sound, at the command of God, they shall fly forth like bees, and fill the whole space between heaven and earth, and then repair to their respective bodies, which the opening earth will suffer to arise; and the first who shall so arise, according to a tradition of Muḥammad, will be himself. For this the earth will be prepared by the rain above-mentioned, which is to fall continually for forty years, and will resemble the seed of a man, and be supplied from the water under the throne of God, which is called living water; by the efficacy and virtue of which the dead bodies shall spring forth from their graves, as they did in their mother's womb, or as corn sprouts forth by common rain, till they become perfect; after which breath will be breathed into them, and they will sleep in their sepulchres till they are raised to life at the last trump.

As to the length of the Day of Judgment, the Qur'ān in one place (Sūrah xxxii. 4) tells us that it will last one thousand years, and in another (Sūrah lxx. 4) fifty thousand. To reconcile this apparent contradiction, the commentators use several shifts, some saying they know not what measure of time God intends in those passages; others, that these forms of speaking are figurative, and not to be strictly taken, and were designed only to express the terribleness of that day, it being usual for the Arabs to describe what they dislike as of long continuance, and what they like as the contrary; and others suppose them spoken only in reference to the difficulty of the business of the day, which, if God should commit to any of his creatures, they would not be able to go through it in so many thousand years.

That the resurrection will be general, and extend to all creatures, both angels, genii, men, and animals, is the received opinion, and according to the teaching of the Qur'ān. (See Sūrah lxxxi.)

In the resurrection those who are destined to. be partakers of eternal happiness will arise in honour and security, and those who are doomed to misery, in disgrace and under dismal apprehensions. As to mankind, they will be raised perfect in all their parts and members, and in the same state as they came out of their mother's wombs, that is, barefooted, naked, and uncircumcised; which circumstances, when Muḥammad was telling his wife 'Āyishah, she, fearing the rules of modesty might be thereby violated, objected that it would be very indecent for men and women to look upon one another in that condition; but he answered her, that the business of the day would be too weighty and serious to allow them the making use of that liberty.

Others, however, allege the authority of their Prophet for a contrary opinion as to their nakedness, and say he asserted that the dead should arise dressed in the same clothes in which they died; although some interpret these words, not so much of the outward dress of the body as the inward clothing of the mind; and understand thereby that every person will rise again in the same state as to his faith or infidelity, knowledge or ignorance his good or bad works.

Muḥammad taught (*Mishkāt*, book xxiii. ch. x) that mankind shall be assembled at the last day, and shall be distinguished into three classes. The first, those who go on foot; the second, those who ride; and the third, those who creep, grovelling with their faces on the ground. The first class is to consist of those believers whose good works have been few; the second of those who are in greater honour with God, and more acceptable to Him; whence 'Alī affirmed that the pious, when they come forth from the sepulchres, shall find ready prepared for them white-winged camels, with saddles of gold, wherein are to be observed some footsteps of the doctrine of the ancient Arabians; and the third class will be composed of the infidels, whom God shall cause to make their appearance with their faces on the earth, blind, dumb, and deaf.

But the ungodly will not be thus only distinguished; for, according to the commentator al-Baiẓāwī (vol. ii. p. 480), there will be ten sorts of wicked men on whom God shall on that day fix certain discretory marks. The *first* will appear in the form of apes; these are the backbiters. The *second* in that of swine; these they who have been greedy of filthy lucre, and enriched themselves by public oppression. The *third* will be brought with their heads reversed and their feet distorted; these are the usurers. The *fourth* will wander about blind; these are unjust judges. The *fifth* will be deaf, dumb, and blind, understanding nothing; these are they who glory in their works. The *sixth* will gnaw their tongues, which will hang down upon their breasts, corrupted blood flowing from their mouths like spittle, so that everybody shall detest them; these are the learned men and doctors, whose actions contradict their sayings. The *seventh* will have their hands and feet cut off; these are they who have injured their neighbours. The *eighth* will be fixed to the trunks of palm-trees or stakes of wood; these are the false accusers and informers. The *ninth* will stink worse than a corrupted corpse; these are they who have indulged their passions and voluptuous appetites. The *tenth* will be clothed with garments daubed with pitch; and these are the proud, the vain-glorious, and the arrogant.

In the Traditions, Muḥammad is related to have said:—

"The first person who shall receive sentence on the Day of Resurrection will be a martyr, who will be brought into the presence of the Almighty: then God will make known the benefits which were conferred on him in the world, and the person will be sensible of them and confess them; and God will say, 'What didst thou do in gratitude for them?' He will reply, 'I fought in Thy cause till I was slain.' God will say, 'Thou liest, for thou foughtest in order that people might extol thy courage.' Then God will order them to drag him upon his face to hell. The second, a man who shall have obtained knowledge and instructed others, and read the Qur'ān. He will be brought into the presence of God, and will be given to understand the benefits he had received, which he will be sensible of and acknowledge; and God will say, 'What didst thou do in gratitude thereof?' He will reply, 'I learned knowledge and taught others, and I read the Qur'ān to please Thee.' Then God will say, 'Thou liest, for thou didst study that people might call thee learned, and thou didst read the Qur'ān for the name of the thing.' Then God will order him to be dragged upon his face and precipitated into hell. The third, a man to whom God shall have given abundant wealth; and he shall be called into the presence of God, and will be reminded of the benefits which he received, and he will acknowledge and confess them; and God will say, 'What return didst thou in return for them?' He will say, 'I expended my wealth to please thee, in all those ways which Thou hast approved.' God will say, 'Thou liest, for thou didst it that people might extol thy liberality'; after which he will be drawn upon his face and thrown into the fire."

As to the place where they are to be assembled to Judgment, the Qur'ān and Traditions agree that it will be on the earth, but in what part of the earth is not agreed. Some say their Prophet mentioned Syria for the place; others, a white and even tract of land, without inhabitants or any signs of buildings. Al-G͟hazālī imagines it will be a second earth, which he supposes to be of silver; and others an earth which has nothing in common with ours, but the name; having, it is possible, heard something of the new heavens and new earth, mentioned in Scripture (Rev. xxi. 1); whence the Qur'ān has this expression, "on the day wherein the earth shall be changed into another earth." (Sūrah xiv. 49.)

The end of the Resurrection the Muḥammadans declare to be, that they who are so raised may give an account of their actions, and receive the reward thereof. And that not only mankind, but the genii and irrational animals also shall be judged on this great day; when the unharmed cattle shall take vengeance on the horned, till entire satisfaction shall be given to the injured.

As to mankind, when they are all assembled together, they will not be immediately brought to judgment, but the angels will keep them in their ranks and order while they attend for that purpose; and this attendance, some say, is to last forty years, others seventy, others three hundred; nay, some say no less than fifty thousand years, each of them vouching their Prophet's authority. During this space they will stand looking up to heaven, but without receiving any information or orders thence, and are to suffer grievous torments, both the just and the unjust, though with manifest difference. For the limbs of the former, particularly those parts which they used to wash in making the ceremonial ablution before prayer, shall shine gloriously. And their sufferings shall be light in comparison, and shall last no longer than the time necessary to say the appointed prayers; but the latter will have their faces obscured with blackness, and disfigured with all the marks of sorrow and deformity. What will then occasion not the least of their pain, is a wonderful and incredible sweat, which will even stop their mouths, and in which they will be immersed in various degrees, according to their demerits, some to the ankles only and some to the knees, some to the middle, some so high as their mouth, and others as their ears. And this sweat will be provoked not only by that vast concourse of all sorts of creatures mutually pressing and treading on one another's feet, but by the near and unusual approach of the sun, which will be then no farther from them than the distance of a mile, or (as some translate the word, the signification of which is ambiguous) than the length of a bodkin. So that their skulls will boil like a pot, and they will be all bathed in sweat. From this inconvenience, however, the good will be protected by the shade of God's throne; but the wicked will be so miserably tormented with it, also with hunger and thirst, and a stifling air, that they will cry out, "Lord, deliver us from this anguish, though thou send us into hell-fire!" What they fable of the extraordinary heat of the sun on this occasion, the Muḥammadans certainly borrowed from the Jews, who say that, for the punishment of the wicked in the Last Day, that planet shall be drawn forth from its sheath, in which it is now put up, lest it should destroy all things by its excessive heat.

When those who have risen shall have waited the limited time, the Muḥammadans believe God will at length appear to judge them, Muḥammad undertaking the office of intercessor, after it shall have been declined by Adam, Noah, Abraham, Moses, and Jesus, who shall beg deliverance only for their own souls. (*Mishkāt*, book xxiii. ch. xii.) On this solemn occasion God will come in the clouds, surrounded by angels, and will produce the books wherein the actions of every person are recorded by their guardian angels, and will command the prophets to bear witness against those to whom they have been respectively sent. Then everyone will be examined concerning all his words and actions, uttered and done by him in this life; not as if God needed any information in those respects, but to oblige the person to make public confession and acknowledgment of God's justice. The particulars of which they shall give an account, as Muḥammad himself enumerated them, are: of their *time*, how they spent it; of their *wealth*, by what means they acquired it, and how they employed it; of their *bodies*, wherein they exercised them; of their *knowledge*, what use they made of it. It is said, however, that Muḥammad has affirmed that no less than seventy thousand of his followers should be permitted to enter Paradise without any previous examination; which seems to be contradictory to what is said above. To the questions, it is said, each person shall answer, and make his defence in the best manner he can, endeavouring to excuse himself by casting the blame of his evil deeds on others; so that a dispute shall arise even between the soul and the body, to which of them their guilt ought to be imputed: the soul saying, "O Lord, my body I received from thee; for thou createdst me without a hand to lay hold with, till I came and entered into this body; therefore punish it eternally, but deliver me." The body on the other side will make this apology, "O Lord, thou createdest me like a stock of wood, having neither hand that I could lay hold with, nor foot that I could walk with, till this soul, like a ray of light, entered into me, and my tongue began to speak, my eye to see, and my foot to walk; therefore punish it eternally, but deliver me."

But God will propound to them the following parable of the blind man and the lame man, which, as well as the preceding dispute, was borrowed by the Muḥammadans from the Jews. (*Gemara, Sanhedr.*, ch. xi.)

A certain king having a pleasant garden, in which were ripe fruits, set two persons to keep it. One of them was blind, and the other lame, the former not being able to see the fruit nor the latter to gather it. The lame man, however, seeing the fruit, persuaded the blind man to take him upon his shoulders, and by that means he easily gathered the fruit, which they divided between them. The lord of the garden coming some time after, and inquiring after his fruit, each began to excuse himself: the blind man said he had no eyes to see with, and the lame man that he had no feet to approach the trees. But the king, ordering the lame man to be set on the blind, passed sentence on and punished them both. And in the same manner will God deal with the body and the soul. As these apologies will not avail on that day, so will it also be in vain for anyone to deny his evil actions, since men and angels and his own members, nay, the very earth itself, will be ready to bear witness against him.

Though the Muḥammadans assign so long a space for the attendance of the resuscitated before their trial, yet they tell us the trial itself will be over in much less time, and, according to an expression of Muḥammad, familiar enough to the Arabs, will last no longer than while one may milk an ewe, or than the space between two milkings of a she-camel. Some, explaining those words so frequently used in the Qur'ān, "God will be swift in taking an account," say that he will judge all creatures in the space of half a day, and others that it will be done in less time than the twinkling of an eye.

At this examination they also believe that each person will have the book wherein all the actions of his life are written delivered to him, which books the righteous will receive in their right hand, and read with great pleasure and satisfaction; but the ungodly will be obliged to take them against their wills in their left, which will be bound behind their backs, their right hand being tied up to their necks.

To show the exact Justice which will be observed on this great day of trial, the next thing they describe is the *mīzān* or "balance," wherein all things shall be weighed. They say it will be held by Gabriel, and that it is of so vast a size that its two scales, one of which hangs over Paradise, and the other over hell, are capacious enough to contain both heaven and earth. Though some are willing to understand what is said in the Qur'ān concerning this balance allegorically, and only as a figurative representation of God's equity, yet the more ancient and orthodox opinion is that it is to be taken literally; and since words and actions, being mere accidents, are not capable of being themselves weighed, they say that the books wherein they are written will be thrown into the scales, and according as those wherein the good or the evil actions are recorded shall preponderate, sentence will be given; those whose balances laden with their good works shall be heavy will be saved, but those whose balances are light will be condemned. Nor will anyone have cause to complain that God suffers any good action to pass unrewarded, because the wicked for the good they do have their reward in this life, and therefore can expect no favour in the next.

The old Jewish writers make mention as well of the books to be produced at the last day, wherein men's actions are registered, as of the balance wherein they shall be weighed, and the Scripture itself seems to have given the first notion of both. But what the Persian Magi believe of the balance comes nearest to the Muḥammadan opinion. They hold that on the day of judgment two angels, named Mihr and Surush, will stand on the bridge aṣ-Ṣirāṭ, to examine every person as he passes; that the former, who represents the divine mercy, will hold a balance in his hand, to weigh the actions of men; that according to the report he shall make thereof to God, sentence will be pronounced, and those whose good works are found more ponderous, if they turn the scale but by the weight of a hair, will be permitted to pass forward to Paradise; but those whose good works shall be found light will be by the other angel, who represents God's Justice, precipitated from the bridge into hell.

This examination being past, and everyone's works weighed in a just balance, that mutual retaliation will follow, according to which every creature will take vengeance one of another, or have satisfaction made them for the injuries which they have suffered. And since there will be no other way of returning like for like, the manner of giving this satisfaction will be by taking away a proportionable part of the good works of him who offered the injury, and adding it to those of him who suffered it. Which being done, if the angels (by whose ministry this is to be performed) say, "Lord, we have given to every one his due, and there remaineth of this person's good works so much as equalleth the weight of an ant," God will of his mercy cause it to be doubled unto him, that he may be admitted into Paradise. But if, on the contrary, his good works be exhausted, and there remain evil works only, and there be any who have not yet received satisfaction from him, God will order that an equal weight of their sins be added unto his, that he may be punished for them in their stead, and he will be sent to hell laden with both. This will be the method of God's dealing with mankind.

As to brutes, after they shall have likewise taken vengeance of one another, as we have mentioned above, He will command them to be changed into dust, wicked men being reserved to more grievous punishment, so that they shall cry out, on hearing this sentence pronounced on the brutes, "Would to God that we were dust also!"

As to the genii, many Muḥammadans are of opinion that such of them as are true believers will undergo the same fate as the irrational animals, and have no other reward than the favour of being converted into dust, and for this they quote the authority of their Prophet. But this, however, is judged not so very reasonable, since the genii, being capable of putting themselves in the state of believers as well as men, must consequently deserve, as it seems, to be rewarded for their faith, as well as to be punished for their infidelity. Wherefore some entertain a more favourable opinion, and assign the believing genii a place near the confines of Paradise, where they will enjoy sufficient felicity, though they be not admitted into that delightful mansion. But the unbelieving genii, it is universally agreed, will be punished eternally, and be thrown into hell with the infidels of mortal race. It may not be improper to observe that under the denomination of unbelieving genii the Muḥammadans comprehend also the devil and his companions.

The trials being over and the assembly dissolved, the Muḥammadans hold that those who are to be admitted into Paradise will take the right-hand way, and those who are destined to hell-fire will take the left, but both of them must first pass the bridge, called in Arabic *aṣ-Ṣirāṭ*, which they say is laid over the midst of hell, and described to be finer than a hair and sharper than the edge of a sword; so that it seems very difficult to conceive how anyone shall be able to stand upon it, for which reason most of the sect of the Muʿtazilites reject it as a fable, though the orthodox think it a sufficient proof of the truth of this article that it was seriously affirmed by him who never asserted a falsehood, meaning their Prophet; who, to add to the difficulty of the passage, has likewise declared that this bridge is beset on each side with briars and hooked thorns, which will, however, be no impediment to the good, for they shall pass with wonderful ease and swiftness, like lightning, or the wind, Muḥammad and his Muslims leading the way whereas the wicked, what with the slipperiness and extreme narrowness of the path the entangling of the thorns, and the extinction of the light which directed the former to Paradise, will soon miss their footing, and fall down headlong into hell, which is gaping beneath them.

RETALIATION. [QISAS.]

REUBEN. Heb. רְאוּבֵן *Reubain.*

Jacob's first-born son. Referred to in the Qur'ān, Sūrah xii. 10: "A speaker from amongst them said, 'Slay not Joseph, but throw him into the bottom of the pit: some of the travellers may pick him up."

Al-Baiẓāwī, the commentator, says the name of Joseph's eldest brother was either *Yahūẕā*, or *Rūbīl*. Josephus gives the name as *Roubel*, and explains it as the "pity of God." (*Ant.* i. 19, s. 8.)

REVELATION. [INSPIRATION PROPHETS.]

REVENGE. [QISAS.]

RIBĀ (ربا). "Usury." A term

in Muslim law defined as "an excess according to a legal standard of measurement or weight, in one or two homogeneous articles opposed to each other in a contract of exchange, and in which such excess is stipulated as an obligatory condition on one of the parties without any return."

The word *ribā* appears to have the same meaning as the Hebrew נֶשֶׁךְ *neshec*, which included gain, whether from the loan of money, or goods, or property of any kind. In the Mosaic law, conditions of gain for the loan of money or goods were rigorously prohibited. See Exod. xxii. 25; Lev. xxv. 36. [USURY.]

RIBĀṬ (رباط). A station or fort

on the frontier of an enemy's country, erected for the accommodation of Muslim warriors (Hamilton's *Hidāyah*, vol. ii. p. 357.)

RICHES. Arabic *daulah* (دولة), Qur'ān lix. 7, *māl* (مال), *kaṣratu 'l-māl* (كثرة المال), "Great wealth."

Muḥammad is related to have said, "Whoever desires the world and its riches in a lawful manner, in order to withhold himself from begging, or to provide a livelihood for his family, or to be kind to his neighbours, will appear before God in the Last Day with his face as bright as a full moon. But whoever seeks the riches of the world for the sake of ostentation, will appear before God in his anger. (*Mishkāt*, book xxii. ch. xxiii.)

In the Qur'ān it is said :—

Sūrah xviii. 44: "Wealth (*māl*) and children are an adornment of this world, but enduring good works are better with thy Lord as a recompense, and better as a hope."

Sūrah viii. 28: "Know that your wealth and your children are but a temptation."

In the IIIrd Sūrah, 12, 13, the possessions of this world are contrasted with those of the world to come in the following language: "Seemly unto men is a life of lusts, of women, and children, and hoarded talents of gold and silver, and of horses well-bred, and cattle, and tilth:—that is the provision for the life of this world; but God, with Him is the best resort. Say, 'But shall we tell you of a better thing than this?' For those who fear are gardens with their Lord, beneath which rivers flow; they shall dwell therein for aye, and pure wives and grace from God; the Lord looks on His servants, who say, 'Lord, we believe; pardon Thou our sins and keep us from the torment of the fire,'—upon the patient, the truthful, the devout, and those who ask for pardon at the dawn."

RIKĀZ (ركاز). Treasures buried in the earth, particularly those treasures which have been buried at some remote period.

In the *Hidāyah*, the word *rikāz* includes *kanz*, "treasure," or other property buried in the earth, and *ma'din*, "mines." Such treasures are subject to a *zakāt* of a fifth. (Hamilton's *Hidāyah*, vol. i. p. 39.)

RINGS. Arabic *khātim* (خاتم), pl. *khawātim* Silver signet-rings are lawful, but a gold ring is not allowed. (See *Ṣaḥīḥu 'l-Bukhārī*, p. 871.)

Ibn 'Umar says, "The Prophet took a gold ring and put it on his right hand, but he afterwards threw it away, and took a silver ring, on which was engraved *Muhammadun Rasūlu 'llāh*, *i.e.* 'Muḥammad the Messenger of God,' and he said, 'Let none of you engrave on your ring like mine.' And when he wore the ring he used to have the signet under his finger and close to the palm of his hand." 'Alī says the ring was on the little finger of the left hand, and that Muḥammad forbade a ring being worn upon the fore or middle finger.

Anas says the Prophet's ring was of silver and on his right hand!

Modern Muslims usually wear a silver ring on the little finger of the right hand, with a signet of cornelian or other stone, upon which is engraved the wearer's name, with the addition of the word *'abdu* (عبد), "His servant," meaning the servant or worshipper of God. This signet-ring is used for signing documents, letters, &c. A little ink is daubed upon it with one of the fingers, and it is pressed upon the paper—the person who uses the ring having first touched the paper with his tongue and moistened the place upon which the impression is to be made. There is no restriction in Muslim law regarding rings for women. They are generally of gold, and are worn on the fingers, in the ears, and in the nose.

RIQQ (رق). The servitude of a slave. [SLAVERY.]

RISĀLAH (رسالة). Apostleship. The office of an apostle or prophet. [PROPHETS.]

RISING UP. Arabic *qiyām* (قيام). It is a subject of discussion amongst students of the Traditions, as to whether or not it is incumbent on a Muslim to rise up when a visitor or stranger approaches.

Abū Umāmah says: "The Prophet came out of his house leaning on a stick, and we stood up to meet him, and he said, 'Do not stand up like the Gentiles who give honour to others.'"

Anas says: "There was no one more beloved by the Companions than the Prophet; but when they saw him, they used not to rise, for they knew he disliked it."

Abū Hurairah says: "The Prophet used to sit with us in the mosque and talk, and when he rose up, we also rose, and remained standing till we saw him enter his house."

The general practice amongst Muḥammadans is according to the last tradition, but it is held to be very overbearing for a person to require others to rise for him.

Mu'āwiyah says that "the Prophet said, 'He who is pleased at other people rising for him, does but prepare a place for himself in the fire of hell." (*Mishkāt*, book xxii. ch. iv.) [SALUTATION.]

RITES. Arabic *mansak*, *mansik* (منسك), pl. *manāsik*. The rites and ceremonies attending religious worship in general. Qur'ān, Sūrah xxii. 35: "To every nation we appointed *rites* (*mansak*) to mention the name of God over the brute beasts which he has provided for them.

The term *mansik* is more frequently used for a place of sacrifice, while *mansak* applies to religious observances, but the plural *manāsik* is common to both, and rendered by Professor Palmer and Mr. Rodwell in their translations of the Qur'ān, "rites."

The principal rites of the Muslim religion are the *Hajj*, or Pilgrimage to Makkah, with the ceremonies at the Makkan Temple [HAJJ]; the daily ritual of the liturgical prayers [PRAYER]; the marriage and funeral ceremonies; and, with the Shī'ahs, the ceremonies of the Muḥarram. The sacrifice on the great festival, although primarily part of the Makkan Pilgrimage ceremonies, is celebrated in all parts of Islām on the 'Idu l-Azhā, or Feast of Sacrifice. [IDU 'L-AZHA.] The ceremony of Zikr can hardly be said to be one of the rites of orthodox Islām, although it is common in all parts of the Muslim world; it belongs rather to the mystic side of the Muḥammadan religion. [SUFI, ZIKR.]

RIVER. Arabic *nahr* (نهر), pl. *anhār*; Heb. נָהָר *nahar*. The word بحر *baḥr*, "sea," being also used for a large river. [SEA.]

According to Muḥammadan law rivers are of three descriptions:

1. Those which are not the property of any, and of which the waters have not been divided, like the Tigris and the Euphrates. The care of these rivers, being the duty of the State, and the charge of keeping them in order must be defrayed from the public treasury, but these expenses must be disbursed from the funds of tribute and capitation-tax, and not from those of tithe and alms.

2. Rivers which are appropriated and divided, and yet at the same time public rivers on which boats sail. The clearing of such rivers must be done at the expense of the proprietors, although its waters are used for the public benefit.

3. Water-courses which are held in property and divided, and on which no boats sail. The keeping of such streams rests entirely with the proprietors.

In countries where much of the cultivation of land depends upon irrigation, the right to water, or as it is called in Arabic *shirb*, is a subject of much litigation, and chapters are devoted to the consideration of the subject in the *Hidāyah*, *Fatāwā-i-'Alamgīrī*, *Duru 'l-Mukhtār*, and other works on Muslim law.

For the Rivers of Paradise, see EDEN.

RIWĀYAH (رواية). Relating the words of another. A word used for both an ordinary narrative, and also for an authoritative tradition. [TRADITION.]

RIYĀ' (رياء). "Hypocrisy; dissimulation." Condemned in the Qur'ān.

Sūrah ii. 266: "O ye who believe! make not your alms void by reproaches and injury, like him who spendeth his substance to be seen of men, and believeth not in God, and in the Last Day, for the likeness of such an one is that of a rock with a thin soil upon it, on which rain falleth, but leaveth it hard."

Sūrah iv. 41, 42: "We have made ready a shameful chastisement for the unbelievers, and for those who bestow their substance in alms to be seen of men, and believe not in God and in the Last Day."

RIẒĀ' (رضاع). A legal term, which means sucking milk from the breast of a woman for a certain time. The period of fosterage. [FOSTERAGE.]

RIẒWĀN (رضوان). The name of the gardener or keeper of Paradise.

ROAD OF GOD. Arabic *sabīlu 'llāh* (سبيل الله). An expression used in the Qur'ān and Traditions for any good act, but especially for engaging in a religious war. [SABILU 'LLAH.]

ROMAN. [GREEKS.]

ROSARY. Arabic *subḥah* (سبحة). The rosary amongst Muḥammadans consists of 100 beads, and is used by them for counting the ninety-nine attributes of God, together with the essential name *Allāh* [GOD]; or the repetition of the *Tasbīḥ* ("O Holy God!"), the *Taḥmīd* ("Praised be God!"), and the *Takbīr* ("God is Great!"), or for the recital of any act of devotion. It is called in Persian and in Hindūstānī the *Tasbīḥ* (تسبيح).

The introduction of the rosary into Christendom is ascribed by Pope Pius V., in a Bull, A.D. 1596, to Dominic, the founder of the Black Friars (A.D. 1221), and it is related that Paul of Pherma, an Egyptian ascetic of the fourth century, being ordered to recite 300 prayers, collected as many pebbles which he kept in his bosom, and threw out one by one at every prayer, which shows that the rosary was probably not in use at that period.

'Abdu 'l-Ḥaqq, the commentator on the *Mishkātu l'-Maṣābiḥ*, says that in the early days of Islām the Muḥammadans counted God's praises on small pebbles, or on the fingers, from which the Wahhābīs maintain that their Prophet did not use a rosary. It seems probable that the Muslims borrowed the rosary from the Buddhists, and that the Crusaders copied their Muslim opponents and introduced it into Christendom.

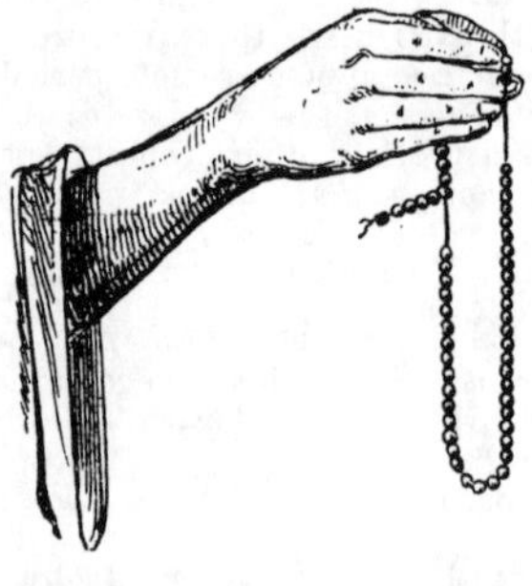

ROZAH (روزه). The Persian word for the Arabic *ṣaum*, or fasting. [FASTING, RAMAZAN.]

RUB' (ربع). A fourth. A legal term used in Muḥammadan law, *e.g.* "a fourth," or the wife's portion when her husband dies without issue.

RUḤ (روح), pl. *arwāḥ*; Heb. רוּחַ *ruakh*, "spirit; soul; life." *Ibnu 'l-Aṡīr*, author of the *Nihāyah*, says it is the nervous fluid or animal spirit. A vaporous substance, which is the principle of vitality and of sensation, and of voluntary motion.

In the *Kitābu 't-Ta'rīfāt*, it is defined as a subtle body, the source of which is the hollow of the corporeal heart, and which diffuses itself into all the other parts of the body by means of the pulsing veins and arteries. See also Gen. ix. 4: "Flesh with the life thereof, which is the blood thereof." Many of the ancients believed the soul to reside in the blood. (See Virgil's *Æn.*, ix. p. 349.) The breath which a man breathes and which pervades the whole body. Called in Persian *jān* (جان). The philosophers say it is the blood, by the exhausting of which life ceases. The word is generally rendered in Hindūstānī as of the feminine gender, but Arabic authors render it as often masculine as feminine. (See Lane's *Arabic Dictionary*, *in loco.*)

In the Qur'ān the word is sometimes used for Jesus, who is known as *Ruḥu 'llāh* ("the Spirit of God"), for the angel Gabriel, and also for life, grace, soul, and the Spirit of Prophecy. (A complete list of texts is given in the article SPIRIT.)

According to the *Kitābu 't-Ta'rīfāt*, p. 76, spirit is of three kinds:—

(1) *Ar-Rūḥu 'l-Insānī* (الروح الانسانى), "the human spirit," by which is understood the mind of man, which distinguishes him from the animal, and which is given to him, by the decree of God, from heaven, of the true essence of which we know nothing. It is this spirit which is sometimes united to the body and sometimes separated from it, as in sleep or death.

(2) *Ar-Ruḥu 'l-Ḥaiwānī* (الروح الحيوانى) "the animal spirit," by which is understood the life, the seat of which is in the heart, and which moves in the veins with the pulsations of the body.

(3) *Ar-Ruḥu 'l-A'ẓam*, (الروح الاعظم) "the exalted spirit," that human spirit which is connected with the existence of God, but the essence of which is unknown to all but the Almighty. The spiritual faculty in man. It is called also *al-'Aqlu 'l-Awwal*, "the first intelligence"; *al-Ḥaqīqatu 'l-Muḥammadīyah*, "the essence of Muḥammad"; *an-Nafsu 'l-Wāḥidah*, "the single essence"; *al-Ḥaqīqatu 'l-Samāwiyāh*, "The original spirit of man first created by God."

The following terms are also found in Muslim works:—

Ar-Ruḥu 'n-Nabātī (الروح النباتى), "the vegetable spirit."

Ar-Rūḥu 't-Ṭabi'ī (الروح الطبعى), "the animal spirit."

Ar-Rūḥu 'l-Ilāhī (الروح اللهى), "the divine spirit."

Ar-Rūḥu 's-Suflī (الروح السفلى), "the lower spirit," which is said to belong merely to animal life.

Ar-Rūḥu 'l-'Ulwī (الروح العلوى), "the lofty or heavenly spirit."

Ar-Rūḥu 'l-Jārī (الروح الجارى), "the travelling spirit," or that which leaves the body in sleep and gives rise to dreams.

Ar-Rūḥu 'l-Muḥkam (الروح المحكم), "the resident spirit," which is said never to leave the body, even after death.

Rūḥu 'l-Ilqā' (روح الالقاء), "the spirit of casting into." Used for Gabriel and the spirit of prophecy. [SPIRIT.]

AR-RŪḤU 'L-AMĪN (الروح الامين). "The faithful spirit." Occurs in the Qur'ān. Sūrah xxvi. 193: "Verily from the Lord of the Worlds hath this book come down; the *faithful spirit* hath come down with it upon thy heart, that thou mayest become a warner in the clear Arabic tongue." It is supposed to refer to the Angel Gabriel. [SPIRIT.]

RUḤU 'LLAH (روح الله). "The Spirit of God." According to Muḥammad, it is the special *Kalimah*, or title of Jesus. See the Qur'ān.

Sūratu 'n-Nisā' (iv.), 169: "The Messiah, Jesus, the son of Mary, is only an Apostle of God, and His Word, which He conveyed into Mary and a *spirit* proceeding from Himself." (*Rūḥun min-hu*).

Sūratu 'l-Ambyā' (xxi.), 91: "Into whom (Mary) we breathed of *our spirit*."

Sūratu 't-Taḥrīm (lxvi), 12: "Into whose womb we breathed of *our spirit*."

It is also used in the Qur'ān for Adam, Sūratu 's-Sajdah (xxxii.), 8; Sūratu 'l-Ḥijr (xv.), 29; and Sūratu Ṣād (xxxviii.), 72; where it is said that God breathed *his spirit* into Adam, but Adam is never called *Rūḥu 'llāh* in any Muḥammadan book. [SPIRIT, JESUS.]

RUḤU 'L-QUDUS (روح القدس). "The Holy Spirit" (*lit.* "Spirit of Holiness"). The expression only occurs three times in the Qur'ān:—

Sūrah ii. 81: "We gave Jesus the Son of Mary manifest signs and aided him with the *Holy Spirit*."

Sūrah ii. 254: "Of them is one to whom God spoke (*i.e.* Moses); and we have raised some of them degrees; and we have given Jesus the son of Mary manifest signs, and strengthened him by the *Holy Spirit*."

Sūrah v. 109: "When God said, 'O Jesus, son of Mary! remember my favours towards thee and towards thy mother, when I aided thee with the *Holy Spirit*, till thou didst speak to men in the cradle, and when grown up."

Al-Baiẓāwī says the meaning of the expression *Rūḥu 'l-Quduṣ* is the Angel Gabriel, although some understand it to refer to the spirit of Jesus, and others to the Gospel of Jesus, whilst some think it is the *Ismu 'l-A'ẓam*, or "the exalted name of God," whereby Jesus raised the dead. (See *Tafsīru 'l-Baiẓāwī*, p. 65.) [SPIRIT. HOLY SPIRIT.]

RUINOUS BUILDINGS. The owner of a ruinous wall in any building is responsible for any accident occasioned by its fall, after having received due warning and requisition to pull it down, and a person building a crooked wall is responsible for the damage occasioned by its falling. But the owner of a ruinous house is not responsible for accidents occasioned by the fall of any article from it, unless such article belong to him. (*Hidāyah*, Grady's Ed., pp. 664, 665.)

RUKH (رخ). The name of a monstrous bird, which is said to have power sufficient to carry off a live elephant. (*Ghiyaṣu 'l-Lughah*, *in loco.*)

AR-RUKNU 'L-YAMĀNĪ (الركن اليمانى). The Yamānī pillar. The south corner of the Ka'bah, said to be one of the most ancient parts of the temple. [MASJIDU 'L-HARAM.]

Burkhardt says: "In the south-east corner of the Ka'bah, or as the Arabs call it, Rokn el Yamany, there is another stone about five feet from the ground; it is one foot and a half in length, and two inches in breadth, placed upright, and of the common Meccah stone. This the people walking round the Ka'bah touch only with the right hand; they do not kiss it." (Captain Burton says he had frequently seen it kissed by men and women.)

Burton remarks: "The Rukn el Yamani is a corner facing the south. The part alluded to (by Burkhardt) is the wall of the Ka'bah, between the Shami and Yemani angles, distant about three feet from the latter, and near the site of the old western door, long since closed. The stone is darker and redder than the rest of the wall. It is called El Mustajab (or Mustajab min el Zunub, or Mustajab el Dua, "where prayer is granted"). Pilgrims here extend their arms, press their bodies against the building, and beg pardon for their sins." (*El Medinah and Mecca*, vol. ii. p. 160.)

RUKŪ' (ركوع). A posture in the daily prayers. An inclination of the head with the palms of the hands resting upon the knees. [PRAYERS.]

THE RUKU'.

RULE OF FAITH. The Muḥammadan rule of faith is based upon what are called the four foundations of orthodoxy, namely, the *Qur'ān*, or, as it is called, *Kalāmu 'llāh*, "the Word of God; the *Ḥadīs̤* (pl. *Aḥādīs̤*), or the traditions of the sayings and practice of Muḥammad; *Ijmā'*, or the consent of the Mujtahidūn, or learned doctors; and *Qiyās*, or the analogical reasoning of the learned.

In studying the Muḥammadan religious system, it must be well understood that Islām is not simply the religion of the Qur'ān, but that all Muḥammadans, whether Sunnī, Shī'ah, or Wahhābī, receive the Traditions as an authority in matters of faith and practice. The *Sunnī* Muḥammadans arrogate to themselves the title of traditionists; but the Shī'ahs also receive the Ḥadīs̤ as binding upon them, although they do do not acknowledge the same collection of traditions as those received by their opponents. [QUR'AN, TRADITIONS, IJMA', QIYAS, RELIGION, ISLAM.]

RULERS. The ideal administration of the Muslim world, as laid down in the Traditions, is that the whole of Islām shall be under the dominion of one Imām or leader, who is the *Khalīfah* (خليفة), or vicegerent, of the Prophet on earth. The rulers of provinces under this Imām are called *Amīr* (امير) (pl. *Umarā'*). The Eastern titles of Sulṭān and Shāh are not established in the Muḥammadan religion. The word *Malik*, Heb. מֶלֶךְ *Melekh*, occurs in the Qūr'ān for a "king," and is used for King Saul (Sūrah ii. 248). The word is still retained in Asia for the chiefs of villages.

In the Qur'ān (Sūrah iv. 62), believers are enjoined to "obey the Apostle and those in authority," but the chief injunctions are found in the Traditions.

In the *Mishkātu 'l-Maṣābiḥ*, book xvi. ch. i., the following sayings of Muḥammad regarding rulers are recorded:—

"Whoever obeys me obeys God, and whoever disobeys me disobeys God. Whoever obeys the Amīr obeys me. An Imām is nothing but a shield to fight behind, by which calamities are avoided; and if he orders you to abstain from that which is unlawful, he will have great regard; but if he enjoins that which God has forbidden, he will bear the punishment of his own acts."

"If God appoints as your Amīr a man who is a slave, with his ears and nose cut off, and who puts people to death according to God's book, then you must listen and obey him in all things."

"If a negro slave is appointed to rule over you, you must listen to him and obey him, even though his head be like a dried grape."

"It is indispensable for every Muslim to listen to and approve the orders of the Imām, whether he likes or dislikes, so long as he is not ordered to sin and act contrary to law. When he is ordered to sin, he must neither attend to it nor obey it."

"There is no obedience due to sinful commands, nor to any order but what is lawful."

"He who shall see a thing in his ruler which he dislikes, let him be patient, for verily there is not one who shall separate a body of Muslims the breadth of a span, and he dies, but he dies like the people of ignorance."

"The best Imāms are those you love, and those who love you, and those who pray for compassion on you, and you on them; and the worst of Imāms are those you hate, and those who hate you; and those whom you curse, and who curse you." Auf said, "O Prophet of God! when they are our enemies and we theirs, may we not fight against them?" He said, "No, so long as they keep on foot the prayers amongst you." This he repeated. "Beware, he who shall be constituted your ruler, see if he does anything in disobedience to God, and if he does, hold it in displeasure, but do not withdraw yourselves from his obedience."

"There will be Amīrs among you, some of whose actions you will find conformable to law, and some contrary thereto; then when anyone who shall say to their faces, 'These acts are contrary to law,' verily he shall be pure; and he who has known their actions to be bad, and has not told them so to their faces, has certainly not remained free from responsibility, and he who has seen a bad act and obeyed it, is their companion in it." The Companions said, "May we not fight them?" The Prophet said, "No, so long as they perform prayers."

"He who is disobedient to the Imām will come before God on the Day of Resurrection without a proof of his faith, and he who dies without having obeyed the Imām, dies as the people of ignorance."

"Prophets were the governors of the children of Israel, and when one died, another supplied his place; and verily there is no prophet after me, and the time is near when there will be after me a great many Khalīfahs." The Companions said, "Then what do you order us?" The Prophet said, "Obey the Khalīfah, and give him his due; for verily God will ask about the duty of the subject."

"When two Khalīfahs have been set up, put the last of them to death, and preserve the other, because the second is a rebel."

"Whoever wishes to make divisions amongst my people, kill with a sword."

"He who acknowledges an Imām must obey him as far as in his power, and if another pretender comes, kill him."

"Verily the time is near that you will be ambitious of ruling; and it is at hand that this love of rule will be a cause of sorrow at the Resurrection, although the possession of it appears pleasant, and its departure unpleasant."

"That is the best of men who dislikes power."

"Beware! you are all guardians of the subject, and you will all be asked about your obedience. The Imām is the guardian of the subject, and he will be asked respecting this. A man is as a shepherd to his own family, and will be asked how they behaved, and about his conduct to them; and a wife is a guardian to her husband's house and children and will be interrogated about them; and a slave is a shepherd to his master's property, and will be asked about it, whether he took good care of it or not."

"There is no Amīr who oppresses the subject and dies, but God forbids Paradise to him."

"Verily the very worst of Amīrs are those who oppress the subject."

"O God! he who shall be ruler over my people and shall throw them into misery, O God! cast him into misery; and he who shall be chief of my people and be kind to them, then be kind to him."

"Verily, just princes will be upon splendid pulpits on the right hand of God; and both God's hands are right."

"God never sent any Prophet, nor ever made any Khalīfah, but had two counsellors with him, one of them directing lawful deeds (that is, a good angel), and the other sin (that is, the devil). He is guarded from sin whom God has guarded." [KHALIFAH.]

AR-RŪM (الروم). The Arabic form of the Latin *Roma*, or *Romanus*. The ancient Byzantine, or Eastern Roman Empire. Still used in Eastern countries as a name for the Turkish Empire.

The title of the xxxth Sūrah of the Qur'ān, which opens with the word. "The *Greeks* are overcome in the highest parts of the land; but after being overcome they shall overcome in a few years." [GREEKS.]

RUQAIYAH (رقية). A daughter of Muḥammad by his wife Khadījah. She was married to 'Utbah, the son of Abū Lahab, but being divorced by her husband, she was married to 'Us̤mān, the third Khalīfah.

RUQBĀ (رقبى). *Lit.* "Waiting." Giving a thing on condition that if the donor die before the receiver it shall become the property of the receiver and his heirs; but if the receiver die first, the property given shall return to the donor. It is forbidden in Muslim law, because it exposes each of the parties to the temptation of wishing for the other's death.

RUQYAH (رقية). "Enchanting." The use of spells. The word used in the Ḥadīs̤ for exorcism and incantation. [EXORCISM.]

RU'YA' (روياء). "A dream; a vision. A term used in the Qur'ān for the visions of the Prophets. It occurs five times. Once for the vision of Joseph (Sūrah xii. 5); twice for the dream of the Egyptian king (Sūrah v. 43); once for the vision of Abraham (Sūrah xxxvii. 105); once for Muḥammad's vision (Sūrah xvii. 62.). [DREAMS.]

S.

ṢĀ' (صاع) or **ṢUWĀ'** (صواع). A certain measure used for measuring corn, and upon which depend the decisions of Muslims relating to measures of capacity. It occurs in the Qur'ān, Sūrah xii. 72, for the drinking-cup placed by Joseph in his brother's pack.

The compiler of the *Tāju 'l-'Arūs*, says that according to five different readers of the Qur'ān, it is given *ṣuwā'* in that verse, but in the majority of texts it is *ṣā'*.

The *Qāmūs* explains *ṣuwā'* as a certain vessel from which one drinks, and *ṣā'*, a measure of capacity. Its invariable measure being, according to ancient authorities, four times the quantity of corn that fills two hands of a man of moderate size.

Al-Baiẓāwī records, besides *ṣuwā'* and *ṣā'*, the reading *ṣau'* and *ṣuwāgh*.

SABA' (سبا). (1) A tribe of Yaman, whose dwelling-places are called Ma'rib, mentioned in the xxxivth Sūrah of the Qur'ān (entitled the Sūratu Saba'), verse 14:—

"A sign there was to Saba' in their dwelling places:—two gardens, the one on the right hand and the other on the left:—'Eat ye of your Lord's supplies, and give thanks to him: Goodly is the country, and gracious is the Lord!'

"But they turned aside: so we sent upon them the flood of Iram; and we changed them their gardens into two gardens of bitter fruit and tamarisk and some few jujube trees.

"Such was our retribution on them for their ingratitude."

M. Caussin de Perceval, *Hist. des Arabes*, vol. iii., as well as M. de Sacy, fix this event in the second century of the Christian era.

(2) Also the name of a province referred to in the Qur'ān, Sūrah xxvii. 21, where it seems to be identical with the Sheba שְׁבָא of the Bible, or the country of the Queen of Sheba:—

"Nor tarried it (the lapwing) long ere it came and said, 'I have gained the knowledge that thou knowest not, and with sure tidings have I come to thee from Saba':

"'I found a woman reigning over them, gifted with everything, and she hath a splendid throne;

"And I found her and her people worshipping the sun instead of God; and Satan hath made their works fair seeming to them, so that he hath turned them from the Way: wherefore they are not guided,

"To the worship of God, who bringeth to light the secret things of heaven and earth, and knoweth what *men* conceal and what they manifest:

"God: there is no god but He! the lord of the glorious throne!"

For a discussion of the identity of the *Saba'* of Arabia with the *Sheba* of the Bible, refer to the word Sheba in Smith's *Dictionary of the Bible.*

SAB'ATU-AḤRUF (سبعة احرف). [SEVEN DIALECTS.]

SABA'U 'L-MAṢĀNI (سبع المثانى). *Lit.* "The Seven Repetitions." A title given to the Introductory Chapter of the Qur'ān by Muhammad himself. (*Mishkāt*, book viii. ch. i.) There are three reasons assigned for this title:—

(1) Because it is a chapter of seven verses, which is said to have been revealed twice over.

(2) Because it contains seven words twice repeated, namely, *Allāh*, God; *Raḥmān*, Compassionate; *Raḥīm*, Merciful; *Iyākā*, Thee and to Thee; *Ṣirāṭ*, Way; *'Alaihim*, to whom and with whom; *Ghair*, Not, and *Lā*, Not.

(3) Because the seven verses are generally recited twice during an ordinary prayer. (See *Majma'u 'l-Biḥār*, *in loco*; and Abdu 'l-Ḥaqq.)

SABBATH. The term used in the Qur'ān for the Jewish Sabbath is *Sabt* (سبت), a corruption of the Hebrew שַׁבָּת *Shabbāth.* It occurs five times in the Qur'ān:—

Sūrah ii. 61: "Ye know, too, those of you who transgressed on the Sabbath, and to whom We (God) said, 'Become scouted apes.'"

Sūrah iv. 50: "Or curse you as We (God) cursed the Sabbath breakers."

Sūrah iv. 153: "We (God) said to them (Israel), 'Break not the Sabbath.'"

Sūrah vii. 163: "And ask them (the Jews) about the city that stood by the sea when its inhabitants broke the Sabbath; when their fish came to them appearing openly on their Sabbath-day, but not to them on the day when they kept no Sabbath."

Sūrah xvi. 125: "The Sabbath was only ordained for those who differed about it."

In explanation of these verses, the commentator, al-Baiẓāwī relates the following traditions. Moses gave orders for the observance of the Day of Rest on Friday; but the Jews would not obey, and declared that they would observe Saturday, as it was on that day that God rested from creation, so it came to pass that "the Sabbath was ordained for those who differed about it." But in the time of King David, certain people began to break the Sabbath by fishing in the Red Sea near the town of Ailah (Elath), and as a punishment they were turned into apes.

For an account of the Muḥammadan Sabbath, see FRIDAY.

SABEANS. Arabic *Ṣābi'* (صابىء), pl. *Ṣābi'ūn.* Probably from the Hebrew צָבָא *tsābā,* "a host." Gen. ii. 1, *i.e.* "Those who worship the hosts of heaven." According to some Arabic writers, the *Ṣābi'ūn* were a certain sect of unbelievers who worshipped the stars secretly, and openly professed to be Christians. According to others, they are of the religion of Sābi', the son of Seth, the son of Adam; whilst others say their religion resembled that of the Christians, except that their *qiblah* was towards the south, from whence the wind blows. In the *Qāmūs* it is said they were of the religion of Noah. The word *ṣābi'* also means one who has departed from one religion to another religion, and the Arabs used to call the Prophet *as-Ṣābi'*, because he departed from the religion of the Quraish to al-Islām. (See Lane's *Dict. in loco.*) Al-Baiẓāwī says some assert they were worshippers of angels, others that they were the worshippers of the stars.

They are mentioned three times in the Qur'ān, and from the following verses it would appear that Muḥammad regarded them as believers in the true God.

Sūrah ii. 50: "They who believe and they who are Jews, and the Christians, and the *Sabeans*—whoever believeth in God and the Last Day, and doeth that which is right, shall have their reward with their Lord."

Sūrah v. 73: "They who believe, and the Jews and the *Sabeans*, and the Christians—whoever of them believeth in God, and in the Last Day, and doeth what is right, on them shall no fear come; neither shall they be put to grief."

Sūrah xxii. 17: "They who believe, and the Jews, and the *Sabeans*, and the Christians, and the Magians, and those who join other gods with God, verily God shall decide between them on the Day of Resurrection."

ṢĀBI' (صابىء). [SABAEANS.]

SABĪLU 'LLĀH (سبيل الله). "The road of God." A term used for religious warfare and other meritorious deeds; *e.g.* Qur'ān, Sūrah ii.:—

Verse 149: "And say not of those who are slain in *the road of God* that they are dead, but rather that they are living."

Verse 263: "Those who expend their wealth in the *road of God.*" [JIHAD.]

SABT (سبت). [SABBATH.]

SACRAMENTS, CHRISTIAN. [EUCHARIST, BAPTISM.]

SACRIFICE. There are six words used in the Muḥammadan religion to express the idea of sacrifice.

(1) ذبح *ẕabḥ*, Hebrew זֶבַח *zebach.* Like the Hebrew word (Gen. xxxi. 54), the Arabic is used generally for slaughtering animals, whether on the Great Festival of Sacrifice ['IDU 'L-AZHA], or, at ordinary times, for food. In the *Qāmūs*, the word *ẕabḥ* is defined "to split or pierce; to cut the throat of any creature." In the Qur'ān, the word is used for the slaughtering of the heifer by Moses (Sūrah ii. 63), for the slaying of the sons of Israel by Pharaoh (Sūrah ii. 46), for sacrificing to idols (Sūrah v. 4); and for the intention of Abraham to sacrifice his son (Sūrah xxxvii. 101).

(2) قربان *qurbān*, Hebrew קָרְבָּן *korbān* (Lev. ii. 14), *Lit.* "Approaching near." It occurs twice in the Qur'ān, for the sacrifice to be devoured by fire from heaven, which the Jews demanded of Muḥammad (Sūrah iii. 179), and for the offering of the sons of Adam (Sūrah v. 30). It is a word frequently employed in Islām to express the ordinary sacrifice, and the great festival is called in Persia the *'Īd-i-Qurbān*, or "Feast of Sacrifice."

(3) نحر *naḥr. Lit.* "To injure the jugular vein." Used for stabbing the breast of a camel, as in sacrifice, hence the sacrifice itself. It occurs once in the Qur'ān, Sūrah cviii. 1, 2: "Verily we have given thee *al-Kauṣar*, so pray to thy Lord and *sacrifice*," which al-Baiẓāwī says means to sacrifice a camel, the most costly victim of the Arabians. The *'Idu 'l-Aẓḥā* is called the *Yaumu 'n-Naḥr.* [IDU' L-AZHA.]

(4) اضحية *uẓḥīyah.* A word which does not occur in the Qur'ān, but in the Traditions it is the subject of a Chapter in *Mishkātu 'l-Maṣabīḥ* (book iv. ch. xlix.). According to the *Qāmūs*, it is derived from *ẓaḥw, ẓuḥā*, a word which expresses that time of the day when the sun has risen to a considerable height, about 10 A.M. (*Ṣalātu 'z-Ẓuḥā*, being a voluntary prayer at that hour). *Uẓhīyah* is therefore the sacrifice offered about 10 o'clock on the day of the Great Festival.

(5) هدى *Hady*, or, according to another reading, *Hadī.* Occurs four times in the Qur'ān, Sūrahs ii. 193, v. 2, 96, 98, for offering of an animal for sacrifice sent to the temple at Makkah, when the pilgrim is not able to reach in time. The *Qāmūs* defines it as that "which is presented." Al-Baiẓāwī (*Tafsīr*, p. 100) gives *Hady* as the plural form of *Hadyah* and *Hadī* as that of *Hadīyah.* The latter occurs in the Qur'ān, Sūrah xxvii. 35, for an offering or gift, and seems to have the same meaning as the Hebrew מִנְחָה *minchah*, which is used in the Old Testament for a gift or tribute (Gen. iv. 3), and also for the unbloody sacrifice or "meat offering" (Lev. ii. 1).

(6) منسك *mansak.* Occurs in the Qur'ān, Sūrah xxii. 35: "We have appointed to every nation a rite (*mansak*)." Sūrah ii. 122: "Show us our rites" (*manāsik*): also verse 196. Al-Baiẓāwī (*Tafsīr*, p. 91), to the first passage, says the word means a place of devotion, or a sacrifice which draws a man near to God, and mentions another reading, *mansik*, a place of worship, of which *manāsik* is likewise the plural. The word, as quoted above, as well as the plural form, is translated by the late Professor Palmer "rites." [RITES.]

II. There are only two occasions upon which Muḥammadans sacrifice, namely, on the Great Festival held on the 10th day of Ẕū 'l-Ḥijjah ['IDU 'L-AZHA] and on the birth of a child [AQIQAH].

(1) The great sacrifice recognised by the Muslim faith is that on the Great Festival, called the *'Īdu 'l-Aẓḥā*, or "Feast of Sacrifice." This sacrifice is not only offered by the pilgrims at Makkah, but in all parts of Islām, upon the day of sacrifice. In the first place, this sacrifice is said to have been established in commemoration of Abraham having consented to sacrifice his son (most Muslims say it was Ishmael), as recorded in the Qur'ān, when it is said God "ransomed his (Abraham's) son with a costly victim" (Sūrah xxxvii. 107); but Shaikh 'Abdu 'l-Ḥaqq, in his commentary on the *Mishkāt*, also says that *al-Uẓḥīyah*, "the sacrifice," is that which at the special time (*i.e.* on the festival) is slaughtered with the object of obtaining nearness to God.

(2) The teaching of the Qur'ān on the subject of sacrifice is conveyed in the following verses (Sūrah xxii. 37):—

"The bulky (camels) we made for you one of the symbols of God (*Sha'ā'iri 'llāhi*), therein have ye good. So mention the name of God over them as they stand in a row (for sacrifice), and when they fall down (dead), eat of them and feed the easily contented and him who begs. Thus have we subjected them to you: haply ye may give thanks. Their flesh will never reach to God, nor yet their blood, but the piety from you will reach Him."

Al-Baiẓāwī on this verse says, "It, the flesh of the sacrifice, does not reach unto God, nor its blood, but the piety (*taqwā*) that is the sincerity and intention of your heart." (*Tafsīru 'l-Baiẓāwī*, vol. ii. p. 52.)

(3) In the Traditions (*Mishkāt*, book iv. ch. xlix.) we have the following:—

Anas says: "The prophet sacrificed two rams, one was black, and the other was white, and he put his foot on their sides as he killed them, and cried out, '*Bi'-smi 'llāhi, Allāhu akbar!* In the name of God! God is most great!'"

'Āyishah says: "The Prophet ordered a ram with horns to be brought to him, and one that should walk in blackness, sleep in blackness, and look in blackness" (by which he meant with black legs, black breast and belly, and black eyes), "and he said, 'O 'Āyishah, give me a knife and sharpen it!' And I did so. Then the Prophet took hold of the ram and threw him on his side and slew it. And when he was killing it he said, 'In the name of God! O God accept this from Muḥammad, and from his children, and from his tribe!' Afterwards he gave to the people their morning meal from the slaughtered ram."

Jābir says: "The Prophet sacrificed two rams on the day of the Festival of Sacrifice, which were black or white, and had horns, and were castrated; and when he turned their heads towards the Qiblah, he said, 'Verily I have turned my face to Him who brought the heavens and the earth into existence from nothing, according to the religion of Abraham, and I am not of the polytheists. Verily my prayers, my worshipping, my life, and my death, are for God, the Lord of the universe, who hath no partner; and I have been ordered to believe in one God, and to abandon associating any other god with Him; and I am one of the Muslims. O God! this sacrifice is of Thee, and for Thee; accept it then from Muḥammad and his people!' And he added, 'In the name of God! the Great God!' and then killed them."

'Alī said: "The Prophet has ordered me to see that there be no blemish in the animal to be sacrificed; and not to sacrifice one with the ears cut, either at the top or the bottom, or split lengthways, or with holes made in them. The Prophet prohibited sacrificing a ram with broken horns, or slit ears."

'Āyishah relates that the Prophet said: "Man hath not done anything, on the day of sacrifice, more pleasing to God than spilling blood; for verily the animal sacrificed will come on the Day of Resurrection, with its horns, its hair, its hoofs, and will make the scales of his actions heavy; and verily its blood reacheth the acceptance of God before it falleth upon the ground; therefore be joyful in it."

Zaid Ibn Arqam relates: "The Companions said, 'O messenger of God! what are these sacrifices, and whence is their origin?' He said, 'These sacrifices are conformable to the laws of your father Abraham.' They said, 'O Prophet! what are our rewards therefrom?' He said, 'There is a reward annexed to every hair.' The Companions then said, 'O Prophet! what are the rewards from the sacrifices of camels and sheep, that have wool?' He said, 'There is a good reward also for every hair of their wool.'"

(4) The following is the teaching of the *Hidāyah* regarding the nature and conditions of the sacrifice:—

It is the duty of every free Muslim arrived at the age of maturity to offer a sacrifice, on the 'Īdu 'l-Aẓḥā, or "Festival of the Sacrifice," provided he be then possessed of a *Niṣāb* (*i.e.* sufficient property), and be not a traveller. This is the opinion of Abū Ḥanīfah, Muḥammad, Zufar, and Ḥasan, and likewise of Abū Yūsuf, according to one tradition. According to another tradition, and also according to ash-Shāfi'ī, sacrifice is not an indispensable duty, but only laudable. At-Tahāwī reports that, in the opinion of Abū Ḥanīfah, it is indispensable, whilst the disciples hold it to be in a strong degree laudable. The offering of a sacrifice is incumbent on a man on account of himself, and on account of his infant child. This is the opinion of Abū Ḥanīfah in one tradition. In another he has said that it is not incumbent on a man to offer a sacrifice for his child. In fact, according to Abū Ḥanīfah and Abū Yūsuf, a father or guardian is to offer a sacrifice at the expense of the child (when he is possessed of property), eating what parts of it are eatable, and selling the remaining parts that are valuable in their substance, such as the skin, &c. Muḥammad, Zufar, and ash-Shāfiʿī have said that a father is to sacrifice on account of his child at his own expense, and not at that of the child. The sacrifice established for one person is a goat; and that for seven, a cow or a camel. If a cow be sacrificed for any number of people fewer than seven, it is lawful; but it is otherwise if sacrificed on account of eight. If for a party of seven people the contribution of any one of them should be less than a seventh share, the sacrifice is not valid on the part of any one of them. If a camel that is jointly and in an equal degree the property of two men should be sacrificed by them on their own account, it is lawful; and in this case they must divide the flesh by weight, as flesh is an article of weight. If, on the contrary, they distribute it from conjectural estimation, it is not lawful, unless they add to each share of the flesh part of the head, neck, and joints. If a person purchase a cow, with an intent to sacrifice it on his own account, and he afterwards admit six others to join with him in the sacrifice, it is lawful. It is, however, most advisable that he associate with the others at the time of purchase, in order that the sacrifice may be valid in the opinion of all our doctors, as otherwise there is a difference of opinion. It is related from Abū Ḥanifah that it is abominable to admit others to share in a sacrifice after purchasing the animal, for, as the purchase was made with a view to devotion, the sale of it is therefore an abomination.

The time of offering the sacrifice is on the morning of the day of the festival, but it is not lawful for the inhabitants of a city to begin the sacrifice until their Imām shall have finished the stated prayers for the day. Villagers, however, may begin after break of day. The place, in fact, must regulate the time. Thus, where the place of celebration is in the country, and the performers of it reside in the city, it is lawful to begin in the morning; but if otherwise, it must be deferred until the stated prayers be ended. If the victim be slain after the prayers of the Mosque, and prior to those offered at the place of sacrifice [IDGAH), it is lawful, as is likewise the reverse of this. Sacrifice is lawful during three days—that is, on the day of the festival, and on the two ensuing days. Ash-Shāfiʿī is of opinion that it is lawful on the *three* ensuing days. The sacrifice of the day of the festival is far superior to any of the others. It is also lawful to sacrifice on the nights of those days, although it be considered as undesirable. Moreover, the offering of sacrifices on these days is more laudable than the custom of omitting them, and afterwards bestowing an adequate sum of money upon the poor. If a person neglect the performance of a sacrifice during the stated days, and have previously determined upon the offering of any particular goat, for instance; or, being poor, have purchased a goat for that purpose,—in either of these cases it is incumbent on him to bestow it alive in charity. But if he be rich, it is in that case incumbent on him to bestow in charity a sum adequate to the price, whether he have purchased a goat with an intent to sacrifice it or not. It is not lawful to sacrifice animals that are blemished, such as those that are blind, or lame, or so lean as to have no marrow in their bones, or having a great part of their ears or tail cut off. Such, however, as have a great part of their ears or tail remaining may lawfully be sacrificed. Concerning the determination of a great part of any member, there are, indeed, various opinions reported from Abū Ḥanīfah. In some animals he has determined it to be the third; in others more than the third; and in others, again, only the fourth. In the opinion of the two disciples, if more than the half should remain, the sacrifice is valid, and this opinion has been adopted by the learned Abū 'l-Laiṣ. If an animal have lost the third of its tail, or the third of its ears or eye-sight, it may be lawfully sacrificed; but if, in either of these cases, it should have lost more than a third, the offering of it is not lawful. The rule which our doctors have laid down to discover in what degree the eye-sight is impaired is as follows. The animal must first be deprived of its food for a day or two that it may be rendered hungry, and having then covered the eye that is impaired, food must be gradually brought towards it from a distance, until it indicate by some emotion that it has discovered it. Having marked the particular spot at which it observed the food, and uncovered the weak eye, the perfect eye must then be bound, and the same process carried on, until it indicate that it has observed it with the defective eye. If, then, the particular distance from those parts to where the animal stood be measured, it may be known, from the proportion they bear to each other, in what degree the sight is impaired.

It is not lawful to offer a sacrifice of any animal except a camel, a cow, or a goat; for it is not recorded that the Prophet, or any of his companions, ever sacrificed others. Buffaloes, however, are lawful as being of the species of a cow. Every animal of a mixed breed, moreover, is considered as of the same species with the mother.

If a Christian or any person whose object is the flesh, and not the sacrifice, be a sharer with six others, the sacrifice is not lawful on the part of any. It is lawful for a person who offers a sacrifice either to eat the flesh or to bestow it on whomsoever he pleases, whether rich or poor, and he may also lay it up in store. It is most advisable that the third part of the flesh of a sacrifice be bestowed in charity. It is not lawful to give a part of the sacrifice in payment to the butcher. It is abominable to take the wool of the victim and sell it before the sacrifice be performed, but not after the sacrifice. In the same manner, it is abominable to milk the victim and sell the milk. It is most advisable that the person who offers the sacrifice should himself perform it, provided he be well acquainted with the method, but if he should not be expert at it, it is then advisable that he take the assistance of another, and be present at the operation. It is abominable to commit the slaying of the victim to a Kitābī (a Jew or Christian). If, however, a person order a Kitābī to slay his victim, it is lawful. It is otherwise where a person orders a Magian, or worshipper of fire, to slay his victim, for this is inadmissible. (Hamilton's *Hidāyah*, vol. iv. 76.)

(5) From the foregoing references to the Qur'ān, the Traditions, 'Abdu 'l-Ḥaqq, al-Baiẓāwī, it will appear that whilst the Muḥammadan sacrifice is (1) *Commemorative*, having been instituted in commemoration of Abraham's willingness to offer his son; (2) *Self Dedicatory*, as expressed in the Traditional sayings of Muḥammad; and (3) *Eucharistic*, according to the verse in the Qur'ān already quoted, "Haply ye may give thanks"; that the *expiatory* character of the sacrifice is not clearly established, for there is no offering for, or acknowledgment of, sin, connected with the institution. Muḥammadanism, true to its anti-Christian character, ignores the doctrine that "without shedding of blood there is no remission." (Lev. xvii. 11; Heb. ix. 22.)

(6) At the birth of a child it is incumbent upon the Muslim father to sacrifice a goat (one for a girl and two for a boy) at the ceremony called *'Aqīqah*, which is celebrated on either the seventh, fourteenth, twenty-first, twenty-eighth, or thirty-fifth day after birth, when the hair is first shaved and its weight in silver given to the poor. 'Abdu 'l-Ḥaqq says *'Aqīqah* comes from *'aqq*, "to cut," and refers to cutting the throat of the animal. Others refer it to cutting the hair. The idea of the sacrifice on this occasion is dedicatory and eucharistic. Buraidah says, "We used, in the time of ignorance, when children were born to us, to slay sheep and rub the child's head with the blood; but when Islām came we sacrificed a sheep on the seventh day, and shaved the child's head and rubbed saffron on it."

ṢĀD (صاد). The fourteenth letter of the Arabic alphabet. The title of the XXXVIIIth Sūrah of the Qur'ān, which begins with the letter.

ṢADAQAH (صدقة), pl. *ṣadaqāt*. From *ṣadq*, "to be righteous, truthful"; Hebrew צדק *tsedek*. A term used in the Qur'ān for "Almsgiving," *e.g.* Sūrah ii. 265: "Kind speech and pardon are better than almsgiving (*ṣadaqah*) followed by annoyance, for God is rich and clement."

Ṣadaqatu 'l-Fiṭr is the alms given on the lesser Festival, called the *'Idu 'l-Fiṭr*, which consists of half a *ṣā'* of wheat, flour, or fruits, or one *ṣā'* of barley. This should be distributed to the poor before the prayers of the festival are said. (*Hidāyah*, vol. i. p. 62.) [IDU 'L-FITR]

SA'D IBN ABĪ WAQQĀS (سعد بن ابی وقاص). Called also Sa'd ibn Malik ibn Wahb az-Zuhrī. He was the seventh person who embraced Islām, and was present with Muḥammad in all his battles. He died at 'Atīq A.H. 55, at the age of 79, and was buried at al-Madīnah.

SA'D IBN MU'ĀẔ (سعد بن معاز). The chief of the Banū Aus. He embraced Islām at al-Madīnah after the first pledge at 'Aqabah. He died of wounds received at the battle of the Ditch, A.H. 5. (See Muir's *Life of Mahomet*, vol. iii. 282.)

SA'D IBN 'UBĀDAH (سعد بن عبادة). One of the Companions, and an Anṣārī of great reputation. He carried the standard at the conquest of Makkah. Died A.H. 15.

ṢADR (صدر), or *Ṣadru 'ṣ-Ṣudūr*. The chief judge. Under Muḥammadan rule, he was especially charged with the settlement of religious grants and the appointment of law officers.

SADŪM (سدوم). [SODOM.]

AS-ṢAFĀ (الصفا). A hill near Makkah. One of the sacred places visited by the pilgrims during the Ḥajj. [PILGRIMAGE.]

ṢAFAR (صفر). *Lit.* "The void month." The second month of the Muḥammadan year. So called because in it the ancient Arabs went forth on their predatory expeditions and left their houses *ṣifr*, or empty; or, according to some, because when it was first named it occurred in the autumn, when the leaves of the trees were *ṣufr*, or "yellow." (*Ghiyāṣu 'l-Lughah, in loco.*) [MONTHS.]

ṢAFF (صف). An even row or line of things.

(1) A term used for a row of persons standing up for prayers.

(2) *Aṣ-Ṣaff*, the title of the LXIth Sūrah of the Qur'ān, in the 6th verse of which the word occurs for the close unbroken line of an army.

AS-ṢĀFFĀT (الصافات), pl. of *ṣāffah*, "Ranged in ranks." The title of the XXXVIIth Sūrah of the Qur'ān, in the first verse of which the angels are mentioned as being ranged in ranks.

ṢAFĪYAH (صفية). One of the wives of Muḥammad. She was the widow of Kinānah, the Jewish chief of Khaibar, who was cruelly put to death. In after years it is said Muḥammad wished to divorce her, but she begged to continue his wife, and requested that her turn might be given to 'Āyishah, as she wished to be one of the Prophet's "pure wives" in Paradise.

ṢAFĪYU 'LLAH (صفی الله). *Lit.* "The Chosen of God." A title given in the Traditions to Adam, the father of mankind. [ADAM.]

ṢAFŪRĀʼ (صفوراء). The Zipporah of the Bible. The wife of Moses. According to Muslim Lexicons, she was the daughter of Shuʻaib. [MOSES.]

ṢAFWĀN IBN UMAIYAH (صفوان بن امية). A Ṣaḥābī of reputation. A native of Makkah. He was slain the same day as the Khalīfah ʻUs̤mān.

ṢAḤĀBĪ (صحابى), fem. *Ṣaḥābīyah.* "An associate." One of the Companions of Muḥammad. The number of persons entitled to this distinction at the time of Muḥammad's death is said to have been 144,000, the number including all persons who had ever served as followers of the Prophet, and who had actually seen him. The general opinion being that one who embraced Islām, saw the Prophet and accompanied him, even for a short time, is a *Ṣaḥābī*, or "associate." [ASHAB.]

ṢĀḤIBU 'N-NIṢĀB (صاحب النصاب). A legal term for one possessed of a certain estate upon which *zakāt*, or "legal alms," must be paid. Also for one who has sufficient means to enable him to offer the sacrifice on the great festival, or to make the pilgrimage to Makkah. The possessor of 200 dirhems, or five camels, is held to be a *Sāhibu 'n-Nisāb*, as regards *zakāt*.

ṢĀḤIBU 'Z-ZAMĀN (صاحب الزمان). "Lord of the Age." A title given by the Shīʻahs to the Imām Mahdī. (*Ghiyās̤u 'l-Lughah, in loco.*)

ṢAḤĪFAH (صحيفة), pl. *ṣuḥuf. Lit.* "A small book or pamphlet." A term generally used for the one hundred portions of scripture said to have been given to Adam, Seth, Enoch, and Abraham, although it is used in the Qur'ān (Sūrah lxxxvii. 19) for the books of Abraham and Moses: "This is truly written in the books (*ṣuḥuf*) of old, the books (*ṣuḥuf*) of Abraham and Moses." [PROPHETS.]

ṢAḤĪFATU 'L-AʻMĀL (صحيفة الاعمال). The "Book of Actions," which is said to be made by the recording angels (*Kirāmu 'l-Kātibīn*) of the deeds of men, and kept until the Day of Judgment, when the books are opened. See Qur'ān:—

Sūrah l. 16: "When two (angels) charged with taking account shall take it, one sitting on the right hand and another on the left."

Sūrah xvii. 14, 15: "And every man's fate have We (God) fastened about his neck; and on the Day of Resurrection will We bring forth to him a book, which shall be proffered to him wide open: Read thy Book: There needeth none but thyself to make out an account against thee this day." [KIRAMU 'L-KATIBIN, RESURRECTION.]

ṢAḤĪḤU 'L-BUKHĀRĪ (صحيح البخارى). The title of the first of the *Kutubu 's-Sittah*, or "six correct" books of traditions received by the Sunnīs. It was compiled by Abū ʻAbd 'llāh Muḥammad ibn Ismāʻīl al-Bukhārī, who was born at Bukhārah, A.H. 194, and died at Khartang, near Samarkand, A.H. 256. It contains 9,882 traditions, of which 2,623 are held to be of undisputed authority. They are arranged into 160 books and 3,450 chapters. [TRADITIONS.]

ṢAḤĪḤU MUSLIM (صحيح مسلم). The title of the second of the *Kutubu 's-Sittah*, or "six correct" books of the traditions received by the Sunnīs. It was compiled by Abū 'l-Ḥusain Muslim ibn al-Ḥajjāj al-Qushairī, who was born at Naishāpūr, A.H. 204, and died A.H. 261. The collection contains 7,275 traditions, of which, it is said, 4,000 are of undisputed authority. The books and chapters of the work were not arranged by the compiler, but by his disciples. The most celebrated edition of this work is that with a commentary by Muḥyiyu 'd-dīn Yaḥya an-Nawawī, who died A.H. 676. [TRADITIONS.]

SAHM (سهم). *Lit.* "An arrow used for drawing lots." A term in Muhammadan law for a portion of an estate allotted to an heir. (Hamilton's *Hidāyah*, vol. iv. p. 487.)

SAḤŪR (سحور). The meal which is taken before the dawn of day during the Ramaẓān. It is called in Persian *Ṭaʻām-i-Saḥarī*. In Hindūstānī, *Sahārqāhī*. In Pushto *Peshmani*. [RAMAZAN.]

SĀʼIBAH (سائبة). Anything set at liberty, as a slave, or she-camel, and devoted to an idol. Mentioned once in the Qur'ān, Sūrah v. 102: "God hath not ordained anything on the subject of *sāʼibah*, but the unbelievers have invented it."

SAʻĪD IBN ZAID (سعيد بن زيد). A Ṣaḥābī who embraced Islām in his youth. He was present with Muḥammad in all his engagements except at Badr. He is held to be one of the *ʻAsharah Mubashsharah*, or ten patriarchs of the Muslim faith. Died at ʻAqīq, A.H. 51, aged 79.

SAIFU 'LLĀH (سيف الله). "The Sword of God." A title given by Muḥammad to the celebrated General Khalīd ibn al-Walīd. (*Mishkāt*, book xxiv. ch. viii.)

SAIḤŪN (سيحون). The river Jaxartes. Said to have been one of the rivers of Eden. [EDEN.]

SAINTS. In Muḥammadan countries, reputed saints are very numerous. Very many religious leaders obtain a great reputation for sanctity even before their deaths, but after death it is usual for the followers of any well-known religious teacher to erect a shrine over his grave, to light it up on Thursdays, and thus establish a saintly reputation for their departed guide. Very disreputable persons are thus often reckoned to have died in the "odour of sanctity." At Hasan Abdal in the Punjab (celebrated in the story of Lala Rookh), there is a shrine erected over a departed cook, who for many years lived on his peculations as keeper of the staging bungalow. When he died, about ten years ago, his family erected over his remains a shrine of some pretensions, which even in the present generation is an object of devout reverence, but which, in the next, will be the scene of reputed miracles. This is but an example of many thousands of shrines and saintly reputations easily gained throughout Islām.

It is generally asserted that according to the teachings of Islām, the Prophets (*ambiyā'*) were without sin, but there is a tradition, related by Anas, which distinctly asserts the contrary, and states that Muḥammad not only admitted his own sinfulness, but also the fall of Adam, the murder committed by Moses, and the three lies told by Abraham. (See *Mishkāt*, book xxiii. ch. xii.) But it is very remarkable that, according to this Ḥadīs̤, Muḥammad does not charge Jesus Christ with having committed sin. The immaculate conception and the sinlessness of Christ are admitted doctrines of Islām. [JESUS CHRIST.]

The terms *pīr* and *walī* are common titles for those who, by reputed miracles and an ascetic life, have established a reputation for sanctity, for whom in Persian the title *buzurg* is generally used. The titles *quṭb* and *g͟haus̤* are very high orders of sanctity, whilst *zāhid* and *'ābid* are employed for persons who devote their lives to religious contemplation and worship

The Ṣūfīs use the word *sālik*, "pilgrim" or "traveller," for one who has renounced the world for the "path" of mysticism, whilst *faqīr* is a title of more general application to one who is poor in the sight of God. *Shaik͟h* and *mīr*, used for old men, also express a degree of reputation in the religious world; *shaik͟h* (in India) being a title generally conferred on a convert from Hinduism to Islām. *Saiyid*, or "lord," is a title always given to the descendants of Muḥammad, *mīr* being sometimes used for the same. *Miyān*, "master" or "friend," is generally used for the descendants of celebrated saints, or as a mere title of respect.

SA'ĪR (سعير). "A flaming fire." The special place of torment appointed for the Sabeans. (See al-Bag͟hawī's *Commentary on the Qur'ān.*) It occurs sixteen times in the Qur'ān (Sūrah iv. 11, and fifteen other places), where it does not seem to be applied to any special class.

ṢAIYIBAH (ثيبة). A legal term for a woman who departs from her husband, whether through divorce or the death of her husband, after the first connection.

SAIYID (سيد). A term used for the descendants of Muḥammad from his daughter Fāṭimah by 'Alī. The word only occurs twice in the Qur'ān—in Sūrah iii. 34, where it is used for John Baptist; and in Sūrah xii. 25, where it stands for the husband of Zalīk͟hah. According to the *Majmu 'l-Biḥār*, p. 151. it means "lord, king, exalted, saint, merciful, meek, husband," &c.

There are two branches of Saiyids—those descended from al-Ḥasan and those descended from al-Ḥusain (both the sons of 'Alī.)

These descendants of Muḥammad are prayed for at every period of the daily prayers [PRAYERS], and they are held in all Muḥammadan countries in the highest respect, however poor or degraded their position may be.

The term Saiyid is also given as a name to persons who are not descended from Muḥammad, *e.g.* Saiyid Shāh, Saiyid Amīn, &c., although it is a mere assumption. In addition to the term *Saiyid*, the term *Bādshāh*, *Shāh*, *Mīr*, and *Sharīf*, are applied to those descended from Bībī Fāṭimah.

The author of the *Ak͟hlāq-i-Jalālī* estimated in his day the descendants of Muḥammad to be not less than 200,000.

SAJDAH (سجدة), vulg. *sijdah*. *Lit.* "Prostration."

(1) The act of worship in which the person's forehead touches the ground in prostration. [PRAYER.]

(2) *As-Sajdah*, the title of the XXXIInd Sūrah of the Qur'ān, in the 15th verse of which the word occurs: "They only believe in our signs who, when they are reminded of them, *fall down adoring* and celebrate the praises of their Lord."

SAJDATU 'S-SAHW (سجدة السهو). "The prostrations of forgetfulness." Two prostrations made on account of forgetfulness or inattention in prayer. Muḥammad said, "When any of you stand up for prayer, and the devil comes to you and casts doubt and perplexity into your mind, so that you do not know how many rak'ahs you have recited, then prostrate yourself twice.

SAJDATU 'SH-SHUKR (سجدة الشكر). "A prostration of thanksgiving." When a Muslim has received some benefit or blessing, he is enjoined to make a prostration in the direction of Makkah, and say, "Holiness to God! and Praise be to God. There is no deity but God! God is most Great!" (*Raddu 'l-Muḥtār*, vol i. p. 816.)

SAJJĀDAH (سجادة). The small carpet, mat, or cloth, on which the Muslim prays. [JAI-NAMAZ, MUSALLA.]

ṢAK͟HR (صخر). The jinn or devil who is said to have obtained possession of

Solomon's magic ring, and to have personated the King for forty days, when Ṣakhr flew away and threw the ring into the sea, where it was swallowed by a fish, which was afterwards caught and brought to Solomon, who by this means recovered his kingdom.

AS-ṢAKHRAH (الصخرة). "The Rock." The sacred rock at Jerusalem on which the Temple was erected, and on which now stands the *Qubbatu 's-Ṣakhrah*, the "Dome of the Rock," known to English readers as the Mosque of 'Umar. This rock is said to have come from Paradise, and to be the foundation-stone of the world, to have been the place of prayer of all prophets, and, next to the Ka'bah, the most sacred spot in the universe. Imām Jalālu 'd-dīn as-Suyūṭī, in his history of the Temple of Jerusalem (Reynolds' edition, p. 44), gives the following traditional account of the glorious *Ṣakhrah.*

"We are informed by Ibn al-Manṣūr that the Rock of the Baitu 'l-Muqaddas, in the days of Solomon, was of the height of twelve thousand cubits; each cubit at that time being the full cubit, viz. one modern cubit, one span and one hand-breadth. Upon it also was a chapel, formed of aloes (or sandal) wood, in height twelve miles (*sic*); also above this was a network of gold, between two eyelet-beads of pearl and ruby, netted by the women of Balka in the night, which net was to serve for three days; also the people of Emmaus were under the shadow of the chapel when the sun rose and the people of

THE DOME OF THE ROCK. (*Conder.*)

Baitu 'r-Raḥmah when it set, and even others of the valleys were under its shadow; also upon it was a jacinth (or ruby), which shone in the night like the light of the sun; but when the light began to dawn its brilliancy was obscured; nor did all these cease until Nebuchadnezzar laid all waste, and seized whatever he found there, and carried it into Greece.

"Again, by a tradition we learn that the Ṣakhrah of Baitu 'l-Muqaddas was raised aloft into the sky, to the height of twelve miles, and the space between it and heaven was no more than twelve miles. All this remained in the same state until Greece (or Rome) obtained the mastery over it, subsequent to its devastation by Nebuchadnezzar. But when the Greeks obtained possession of it, they said, "Let us build thereupon a building far excelling that which was there before." Therefore they built upon it a building as broad at the base as it was high in the sky, and gilded it with gold, and silvered it with silver. Then, entering therein, they began to practise their associating Paganism, upon which it turned upside-down over them, so that not one of them came out.

"Therefore, when the Grecian (king) saw this, he summoned the Patriarch and his ministers (deacons), and the chiefs of Greece, and said, 'What think ye?' who replied, 'We are of opinion that our idol-gods are not well pleased, and therefore will not receive us favourably.' Hereupon he commanded a second temple to be built, which they did, spending a great sum thereon, and having finished the second building, seventy thousand entered it as they had entered the first. But it happened to them as it had happened to the first; when they began their Paganism it turned over upon them. Now their king was not with them. Therefore, when he saw this, he assembled them a third time, and said unto them, 'What think ye?' who said, 'We think that our Lord is not well pleased with us, because we have not offered unto him abundantly; therefore he has destroyed what we have done, therefore we should greatly wish to build a third.' They then built a third, until they thought they had carried it to the greatest possible height, which having done, he assembled the Christians, and said unto them, 'Do ye observe any defect?' who said, 'None, except that we must surround it with crosses of gold and silver.' Then all the people entered it, to read and cite (sacred things). Having bathed and perfumed themselves, and having entered it, they began to practise their associating Paganism, as the others had done before them; whereupon down fell the third building upon them. Hereupon the king again summoned them together, and asked their counsel about what he should do. But their dread was very great; and whilst they were deliberating, there came up to them a very old man, in a white robe and a black turban; his back was bent double and he was leaning upon a staff. So he said, 'O Christian people, listen to me! listen to me! for I am the oldest of any of you in years, and have now come forth from among the retired votaries of religion, in order to inform you that, with respect to this place, all its possessors are accursed, and all holiness hath departed from it, and hath been transferred to this (other) place. I will therefore point out this as the place wherein to build the Church of the Resurrection. I will show you the spot, but you will never see me after this day, for ever. Do, therefore, with a good will that which I shall tell you.' Thus he cheated them, and augmented their accursed state, and commanded them to cut up the rock, and to build with its stones upon the place which he commended them.

"So whilst he was talking with them he became concealed; and they saw him no more. Thereupon they increased in their infidelity, and said, 'This is the Great Word. Then they demolished the Mosques, and carried away the columns and the stones, and all the rest, and built therewith the Church of the Resurrection, and the church which is in the valley of Hinnon. Moreover, this cursed old man commanded them, 'When ye have finished their building upon this place, then take that place whose owners are accursed, and whence all holiness hath departed, to be a common sewer to receive your dung.' By this they gratified their Lord. Also they did this, as follows: At certain seasons, all the filth and excrement was sent in vessels from Constantinople, and was at a certain time all thrown upon the Rock, until God awoke our Prophet Muḥammad (the peace and blessing of God be with him!), and brought him by night thereunto; which he did on account of its peculiar consecration, and on account of the greatness of its super-excellence. We learn, also, that God, on the Day of Judgment, will change the Ṣakhrah into white coral, enlarging it to extend over heaven and earth. Then shall men go from that Rock to heaven or hell, according to that great word, 'There shall be a time when this earth shall change into another earth, and the heaven shall turn white; the soil shall be of silver; no pollution shall ever dwell thereon.' Now from 'Ā'ish (may the satisfying favour of God rest upon him!), I said, 'O apostle of God, on that day when this earth shall become another earth, and this sky shall change, where shall men be on that day?' He replied, 'Upon the bridge aṣ-Ṣirāṭ.' Again, a certain divine says, 'that in the Law, God says to the Rock of the Holy Abode, "Thou art my seat; thou art near to me; from thy foundation have I raised up the heavens, and from beneath thee have I stretched forth the earth, and all the distant inaccessible mountains are beneath thee. Who dies within thee is as if he died within the world of heaven, and who dies around thee is as if he died within thee. Days and nights shall not cease to succeed, until I send down upon thee a Light of Heaven, which shall obliterate all the (traces) of the infidels of the sons of Adam, and all their footsteps. Also I will send upon thee the hierarchy of angels and prophets; and I will wash thee until I leave thee like milk; and I will fix upon thee a wall twelve miles above the thick-gathering clouds of earth, and also a hedge of light. By my hand will I insure to thee thy support and thy virtue; upon thee will I cause to descend my spirits and my angels, to worship within thee; nor shall any one of the sons of Adam enter within thee until the Day of Judgment. And whosoever shall look upon this chapel from afar shall say, 'Blessed be the face of him who devoutly worships and adores in thee!' Upon thee will I place walls of light and a hedge of thick clouds—five walls of ruby and pearl."' Also from the Book of Psalms, 'Great and glorious art thou, thou threshing-floor! Unto thee shall be the general assemblage: from thee shall all men rise from death.' Moreover, from the same author, God says to the Rock of the Holy Abode, 'Who loveth thee, him will

I love; who loveth thee, loveth me; who hateth thee, him will I hate. From year to year my eyes are upon thee, nor will I forget thee until I forget my eyes. Whoso prayeth within thee two rak'ahs, him will I cause to cast off all his sins, and to be as guiltless as I brought him from his mother's womb, unless he return to his sins, beginning them afresh.' This is also a tradition of old standing: 'I solemnly engage and promise to everyone who dwells therein, that all the days of his life the bread of corn and olive-oil never shall fail him; nor shall the days and the nights fail to bring that time, when, out of the supremacy of my bounty, I will cause to descend upon thee the assemblage of man for judgment—the whole company of risen mortals.' There is a tradition that 'Muqātil Ibn Sulaiman came to this Temple to pray, and sat by the gate looking towards the Rock; and we had assembled there in great numbers; he was reading and we were listening. Then came forward 'Alī Ibn al-Badawī, stamping terribly with his slippers upon the pavement. This greatly afflicted him, and he said to those around him, "Make an opening for me." Then the people opened on each side, and he made a threatening motion with his hand to warn him and prevent this stamping, saying, "Tread more gently! That place at which Muqātil is"—pointing with his hand—"and on which thou art stamping, is the very place redolent of Heaven's breezes; and there is not a spot all around it—not a spot within its precincts a hand's-breadth square—wherein some commissioned prophet, some near angel, hath not prayed."' Now from the mother of 'Abdu 'llāh, daughter of Khālid, from her mother, 'the moment is surely fixed, when the Ka'bah shall be led as a bride to the Ṣakhrah, and shall hang upon her all her pilgrimage merits, and become her turban.' Also it is said that the Ṣakhrah is the middle of the Mosque; it is cut off from every touching substance on all sides. No one supports it but He who supports and holds up the sky; so that nothing falls thence but by His good permission; also upon the upper part of the west side stood the Prophet (the blessing and peace of God be with him!) on the night when he rode al-Burāq. This side began to shake about, from veneration of him; and upon the other side are the marks of the angels' fingers, who held it up when it shook; beneath it is a deep hole cut out on each side, over which is the gate opened to men for prayer and devotion. 'I resolved,' says a certain author, 'one day to enter it, in great fear lest it should fall upon me, on account of the sins I had contracted; then, however, I looked, and saw its darkness, and some holy pilgrims entering it at the darkest part, who came forth therefrom quite free from sin. Then I began to reflect upon entering. Then I said, "Perhaps they entered very slowly and leisurely, and I was too much in a hurry; a little delay may facilitate the matter." So I made up my mind to enter; and entering, I saw the Wonder of Wonders, the Rock supported in its position or course on every side; for I saw it separated from the earth, so that no point of the earth touched it. Some of the sides were separated by a wider interval than others; also, the mark of the glorious Foot is at present in a stone divided from the Rock, right over against it, on the other side, west of the Qiblah; it is upon a pillar. Also the Rock is now almost abutting upon the side of the crypt, only divided from it by that space which allows room for the gate of the crypt, on the side of the Qiblah. This gate, also, is disjointed from the base of the Qiblah; it is between the two. Below the gate of the crypt is a stone staircase, whereby one may descend into the crypt. In the midst of this crypt is a dark-brown leather carpet, upon which pilgrims stand when they visit the foundation of the Rock; it is upon the eastern side. There are also columns of marble abutting on the lower side upon the path of the rows of trees upon the side of the Qiblah, and on the other side forming buttresses to the extremity of the Rock; these are to hinder it from shaking on the side of the Qiblah. There are buildings besides these. There is a building in the Chapel of the Rock. Beneath the chapel, the spot marked by the angels' fingers is in the Rock, on the western side, divided from the print of the glorious Foot above-mentioned, very near to it, over against the western gate, at the end.'" (*Hist. Jerusalem*, from the Arabic MS. of Jalālu 'd-dīn as-Suyūṭī, Reynolds' ed. 1835.)

Dr. Robinson (*Biblical Researches*, vol. i. p. 297) says the followers of Muḥammad under 'Umar took possession of the Holy City A.D. 636, and the Khalīfah determined to erect a mosque upon the site of the Jewish Temple. An account of this undertaking, as given by Muslim historians, will be found in the article on JERUSALEM. The historians of the crusades all speak of this great Ṣakhrah as the *Templum Domini*, and describe its form and the rock within it. (*Will. Tyr.*, 8, 2, ib. 12, 7. *Jac. de Vitriac*, c. 62.)

Lieut. E. R. Conder, R.E., remarks that the Dome of the Rock belongs to that obscure period of Saracenic art, when the Arabs had not yet created an architectural style of their own, and when they were in the habit of employing Byzantine architects to build their mosques. The Dome of the Rock, Lieut. Conder says, is not a mosque, as it is sometimes wrongly called, but a "station" in the outer court of the Masjidu 'l-Aqṣā.

We are indebted to this writer for the following account of the gradual growth of the present building (*Tent Work in Palestine*, vol. ii. p. 320):—

"In A.D. 831 the Caliph El Mamûn restored the Dome of the Rock, and, if I am correct, enclosed it with an outer wall, and gave it its present appearance. The beams in the roof of the arcade bear, as above-stated, the date 913 A.D.; a well-carved wooden cornice, hidden by the present ceiling, must then have been visible beneath them.

"In 1016 A.D. the building was partly destroyed by earthquake. To this date belong restorations of the original mosaics in the dome, as evidenced by inscriptions. The present wood-work of the cupola was erected by Husein, son of the Sultan Hakem, as shown by an inscription dated 1022 A.D.

"The place next fell into the hands of the Crusaders, who christened it *Templum Domini*, and established in 1112 A.D. a chapter of Canons.

"The Holy Rock was then cut into its present shape and covered with marble slabs, an altar being erected on it. The works were carried on from 1115 A.D. to 1136 A.D. The beautiful iron grille between the pillars of the dome and various fragments of carved work are of this date, including small altars with sculptured capitals, having heads upon them—abominations to the Moslem, yet still preserved within the precincts. The interior of the outer wall was decorated in the twelfth century with frescoes, traces of which still remain. The exterior of the same wall is surmounted by a parapet, with dwarf pillars and arches, which is first mentioned by John of Wurtzburg, but must be as old as the round arches of the windows below. The Crusaders would seem to have filled up the parapet arches, and to have ornamented the whole with glass mosaic, as at Bethlehem.

"In 1187 A.D. Saladin won the city, tore up the altar, and once more exposed the bare rock, covered up the frescoes with marble slabs, and restored and regilded the dome, as evidenced by an inscription in it dating 1189 A.D.

"In 1318 A.D. the lead outside and the gilding within were restored by Nakr ed Din, as evidenced by an inscription.

"In 1520 A.D. the Sultan Soliman cased the bases and upper blocks of the columns with marble. The wooden cornice, attached to the beam between the pillars, seems to be of this period, and the slightly-pointed marble casing of the arches under the dome is probably of the same date. The windows bear inscriptions of 1528 A.D. The whole exterior was at this time covered with Kishâni tiles, attached by copper hooks, as evidenced by inscriptions dated 1561 A.D. The doors were restored in 1564 A.D., as also shown by inscriptions.

"The date of the beautiful wooden ceiling of the cloisters is not known, but it partly covers the Cufic inscription, and this dates 72 A.H. (688 A.D.), and it hides the wooden cornice, dating probably 913 A.D. The ceiling is therefore probably of the time of Soliman.

"In 1830 A.D. the Sultan Mahmud, and in 1873–75 A.D. the late Abdu 'l-Aziz, repaired the Dome, and the latter period was one specially valuable for those who wished to study the history of the place.

"Such is a plain statement of the gradual growth of the building. The dates of the various inscriptions on the walls fully agree with the circumstantial accounts of the Arab writers who describe the Dome of the Rock." [JERUSALEM.]

SAKĪNAH (سكينة).

A word which occurs in the Qur'ān five times. (1) For that which was in the Ark of the Covenant, Sūrah ii. 249: "The sign of his (Saul's) kingdom is that there shall come to you the Ark (*Tābūt*) with the *sakīnah* in it from your Lord, and the relics that the family of Moses and the family of Aaron left, and the angels bear it." With reference to this verse, al-Baiẓāwī, the great Muslim commentator, says: "The ark here mentioned is the box containing the Books of Moses (Arabic *Taurāt*, namely, *the Torah*, or Law), which was made of box-wood and gilded over with gold, and was three cubits long and two wide, and in it was 'the *sakīnah* from your Lord.' The meaning of which is, that with the Ark there was *tranquillity* and *peace*, namely, the *Taurāt* (Books of Moses), because when Moses went forth to war he always took the Ark with him, which gave repose to the hearts of the children of Israel. But some say that within that Ark there was an idol made either of emerald or sapphire, with the head and tail of a cat, and with two wings; and that this creature made a noise when the Ark was carried forth to war. But others say that the Ark contained images of the prophets, from Adam to Moses. Others assert that the meaning of *sakīnah* is 'knowledge and sincerity.' Others, that the Ark contained the tables of the Law, the rod of Moses, and Aaron's turban." (*Tafsīru 'l-Baiẓāwī*, Fleischer's ed., vol. ii. p. 128.)

(2) It is also used in the Qur'ān for help and confidence or grace. Sūrah xlviii. 26: "When those who misbelieved put in their hearts pique—the pique of ignorance—and God sent down His *Sakīnah* upon His Apostle and upon the believers, and obliged them to keep to the word of piety." Al-Baiẓāwī says that in this verse the word *sakīnah* means the tranquillity and repose of soul, which is the meaning given in all Arabic dictionaries.

The word occurs in three other places in a similar sense:—

Sūrah ix. 26: "God sent down His *Sakīnah* upon His Apostle and upon the believers, and sent down armies which ye could not see, and punished those who did not believe."

Sūrah ix. 40: "God sent down His *Sakīnah* upon him, and aided him with hosts."

Sūrah xlviii. 2: "It is He who sent down the *sakīnah* into the hearts of believers, that they might have faith added to faith."

None of the Muslim commentators seem to understand that the Arabic سكينة *Sakīnah* is identical with the Hebrew שְׁכִינָה *Shechinah*, a term which, although not found in the Bible, has been used by the later Jews, and borrowed by the Christians from them, to express the visible Majesty of the Divine Presence, especially when *resting* or *dwelling* between the Cherubin on the Mercy Seat in the Tabernacle, and in the Temple of Solomon. Rabbinical writers identify the

Shechinah with the Holy Spirit, and some Christian writers have thought that the threefold expression for the Deity—the Lord, the Word of the Lord, and the *Shechinah*—indicates the knowledge of a trinity of persons in the God-head.

For the Talmudic views regarding the *Shechinah*, the English reader can refer to Dr. Hershon's *Talmudic Miscellany* (Trübner & Co., London).

SALAF (سلف). (1) Ancestors; men of repute for piety and faith in past generations.

(2) Money lent without interest. [SALAM.]

SALAM (سلم). A contract involving an immediate payment of the price, and admitting a delay in the delivery of the articles purchased. The word used in the Hadīs is generally *salaf*. In a sale of this kind, the seller is called *musallam ilai-hi*; the purchaser, *rabbu 's-salam*, and the goods purchased, *musallam-fī-hi*. (*Kitābu 't-Ta'rīfāt.*)

AS-SALĀM (السلام). "The Peace(ful) one. (1) One of the ninety-nine names or attributes of God. It occurs once in the Qur'ān, Sūrah lix. 20: "He is God, than whom there is no other . . . the Peaceful." Al-Baiẓāwī explains the word as "He who is free from all loss or harm" (ذو السلامة من كل نقص و آفة).

(2) *As-Salāmu 'alai-kum* (السلام عليكم), "The peace be on you," the common salutation amongst Muslims. [SALUTATION].

AS-ṢALĀT (الصلوة, in construction frequently spelled صلاة), pl. *ṣalawāt*. The term used in the Qur'ān, as well as amongst all Muslims in every part of the world, for the liturgical form of prayer, which is recited five times a day, an account of which is given in the article on PRAYER. Its equivalent in Persian and Urdū is *namāz*, which has been corrupted into *nmūz* by the Afghāns. The word occurs with this meaning in the Qur'ān, Sūrah ii. 239: "Observe the *prayers*," and in very many other places. It has also the meaning of *prayer* or *supplication* in its general sense, *e.g.* Sūrah ix. 104: "Pray for them, of a truth thy prayers shall assure their minds." Also *blessing*, *e.g.* Sūrah xxxiii. 56: "Verily God and His Angels *bless* (not "pray for," as rendered by Palmer) the Prophet." (See Lane's *Dictionary*, *in loco*.)

The word *ṣalāt* occurs with various combinations used to express different periods, and also special occasions of prayer.

The five stated liturgical prayers which are held to be of divine institution:—

(1) *Ṣalātu 'l-Ẓuhr*, the meridian prayer.
(2) *Ṣalātu 'l-'Aṣr*, the afternoon prayer.
(3) *Ṣalātu 'l-Maghrib*, the sunset prayer.
(4) *Ṣalātu 'l-'Ishā'*, the night prayer.
(5) *Ṣalātu 'l-Fajr*, the prayer at dawn.

(*Obs.* The midday prayer is reckoned the first in order.)

Also for the three voluntary daily liturgical prayers:—

(1) *Salātu 'l-Ishrāq*, when the sun has well risen.
(2) *Ṣalātu 'l-Zuḥā*, about 11 A.M.
(3) *Ṣalātu 'l-Tahajjud*, after midnight.

Liturgical prayers said on special occasions are given below. [PRAYER.]

ṢALĀTU 'L-ḤĀJAH (صلاة الحاجة). "Prayer of necessity." Four rak'ah prayers, or, according to some, twelve rak'ahs recited after the night prayer in times of necessity, or trouble. (*Raddu 'l-Muḥtar*, vol. i. p. 719.)

ṢALĀTU 'L-'ĪDAIN (صلاة العيدين). "Prayers of the two festivals." The two rak'ah prayers recited on the two Muhammadan festivals, the 'Īdu 'l-Fiṭr and the 'Īdu 'l-Aẓḥā.

ṢALĀTU 'L-ISTIKHĀRAH (صلاة الاستخارة). *Lit.* "Prayer for conciliating favour." Two rak'ahs recited for success in an undertaking. Jābir relates that Muḥammad taught him *Istikhārah*, and that after reciting two rak'ahs he should thus supplicate God: "O God, I seek Thy good help in Thy great wisdom. I pray for ability to act through Thy power. I ask this thing of thy goodness. Thou knowest, but I know not. Thou art powerful, but I am not. Thou art knower of secrets. O God, if Thou knowest that the matter which I am about to undertake is good for my religion, for my life, for my future, then make it easy, and prosper me in it. But if it is bad for my religion, my life, and my future, then put it away from me, and show me what is good." (*Mishkāt*, book iv. 40.)

ṢALĀTU 'L-ISTISQĀ' (صلاة الاستسقاء), from *saqy*, "Watering." Two rak'ah prayers recited in the time of dearth.

ṢALĀTU 'L-JINĀZAH (صلاة الجنازة). The funeral service. [BURIAL OF THE DEAD, JINAZAH.]

ṢALĀTU 'L-JUM'AH (صلاة الجمعة). *Lit.* "The prayer of assembly." The Friday Prayer. It consists of two rak'ahs recited at the time of *ẓuhr*, or midday prayer on Friday. [FRIDAY, KHUTBAH.]

ṢALĀTU 'L-KHAUF (صلاة الخوف). The "Prayers of Fear." Two rak'ahs of prayers recited first by one regiment and then by another in time of war, when the usual prayers cannot be recited for fear of the enemy. These prayers are founded upon an injunction in the Qur'ān, Sūrah iv. 102: "And when ye go to war in the land, it shall be no sin for you to curtail your prayers, if ye fear that the enemy come upon you." This was also the Talmudic law (*Tr. Berachoth* iv. 4): "He that goeth in a dangerous place may pray a short prayer."

ṢALĀTU 'L-KHUSŪF (صلاة الخسوف). Prayers said at an eclipse of the moon, consisting of two rak'ahs of prayer (*Mishkāt*, book iv. ch. li.)

ṢALĀTU 'L-KUSŪF (صلاة الكسوف). Prayers at an eclipse of the sun, consisting of two rak'ahs of prayer. (*Mishkāt*, book iv. ch. li.)

ṢALĀTU 'L-MARĪẒ (صلاة المريض). "Prayer of the sick." When a person is too sick to stand up in the usual prayers, he is allowed to recite them either in a reclining or sitting posture, provided he performs the usual ablutions. It is ruled that he shall in such a case make the prostrations, &c., mentally. (*Raddu 'l-Muḥtār*, vol. i. p. 891.)

ṢALĀTU 'L-WITR (صلاة الوتر). The Witr prayers. The word *witr* means either a unit, or an odd number, and is used for either a single or odd number of rak'ah prayers recited after the evening prayer (*'ishā'*). (*Mishkāt*, book iv. ch. xxxvi.)

There is considerable controversy amongst the learned doctors as to whether it is *farẓ*, *wājib*, or *sunnah*, but it is generally held to be *sunnah*, *i.e.* founded on the example of the Prophet, but with no divine command. Amongst the Ḥanafī sect, it is also known as *Qunūtu 'l-Witr*, but the Shāfi'īs recite the *Qunūt* separately.

ṢALĀTU 'R-RAGHĀ'IB (صلاة الرغائب). "A prayer for things desired." Two rak'ah prayers recited by one who desires some object in this world. According to the orthodox, it is forbidden in Islām. (*Raddu 'l-Muḥtār*, vol. i. p. 717.) It is recited by some persons in the first week of the month Rajab.

ṢALĀTU 'S-SAFAR (صلاة السفر). "Prayers of travel." A shortened recital of prayer allowed to travellers. It is founded on a tradition by Ya'la ibn Umaiyah, who says, "I said to 'Umar, 'God hath said, "When ye go to war in the land, it shall be no sin for you to shorten your prayers if ye fear that the infidels may attack you"; but now verily we are safe in this journey, and yet we shorten our prayers.' 'Umar replied, 'I also wondered at the thing that astonished you; but the Prophet said, God hath done you a kindness in curtailing your prayers, therefore accept it, Ibn 'Umar says, 'I travelled with the Prophet, and he did not say more than two rak'ahs of prayer, and Abū Bakr and 'Umar and 'Usmān did the same.' Ibn 'Abbās says, 'The Prophet used to say on a journey the noon and afternoon prayer together, and the sunset and evening prayer together.'" (*Mishkāt*, book iv. ch. xlii.)

The established prayers for a traveller are, therefore, two rak'ahs instead of the four *farẓ* rak'ahs at the noon and afternoon and evening prayers, and the usual two *farẓ* at the morning and the usual three *farẓ* at the sunset prayers; all voluntary prayers being omitted. (*Raddu 'l-Muḥtār*, vol. i. p. 821.)

ṢALĀTU 'T-TARĀWĪḤ (صلاة التراويح). "Prayer of rest." So called because of the pause or rest made for ejaculations between every four rak'ahs. (*'Abdu l'-Ḥaqq.*)

Twenty rak'ah prayers recited after the night prayer during the month of Ramaẓān. They are often followed with recitations known as *ẓikrs* [ZIKR], and form an exciting service of devotion. The Imām recites the *Tarāwīḥ* prayers with a loud voice.

Abū Hurairah says: "The Prophet used to encourage people to say night prayers in Ramaẓān without ordering them positively, and would say, 'He who stands up in prayer at night, for the purpose of obtaining reward, will have all his sins pardoned'; then the Prophet died, leaving the prayers of Ramaẓān in this way." It is said 'Umar instituted the present custom of reciting the twenty rak'ahs." (*Mishkāt*, book iv. ch. xxxviii.) [RAMAZAN.]

ṢALĀTU 'T-TASBĪḤ (صلاة التسبيح). "Prayer of praise." A form of prayer founded on the following tradition related by Ibn 'Abbas, who says:—

"Verily the Prophet said to my father, 'O 'Abbās! O my uncle! shall I not give to you, shall I not present unto you, shall I not inform you of a thing which covers acts of sin? When you perform it, God will forgive your sins, your former sins, and your latter sins, and those sins which you did unknowingly, and those which you did knowingly, your great sins, and your small sins, your disclosed sins and your concealed sins? It is this, namely, that you recite four rak'ahs of prayer, and in each rak'ah recite the *Fātiḥatu 'l-Kitāb* (*i.e.* the Introductory chapter of the Qur'ān), and some other Sūrah of the Qur'ān; and when you have recited these portions of the Qur'ān in the position of Qiyām, then say, "Holiness to God!" (*Subḥāna 'llāhi*), and "Praise be to God!" (*Wa 'l-Ḥamdu li-'llāhi*), and "There is no deity but God!" (*Wa lā Ilāha illā huwa*), and "God is most great!" (*Wa 'llāhu Akbar*), fifteen times. Then perform a rukū' and recite it ten times; then raise up your head and say it ten times, then make the sajdah and say it ten times; then raise your head and say it ten times; then make another sajdah, and say it ten times, then raise your head again and say it ten times; altogether seventy-five times in every rak'ah; and do this in each of the rak'ah. If you are able to say this form of prayer every day, then do so, but if not, do it once every Friday, and if not each week, then say it once a month, and if not once a month, then say it once a year, and if not once a year, then do it once in your lifetime.'" (*Mishkāt*, book iv. ch. xli.)

The foregoing is a striking illustration of the mechanical character of the Muslim religion as regards its system of devotion [ZIKR.]

SALE, The Law of. [BAI'.]

ṢALĪB (صليب). "A crucifix; a cross." [CROSS.]

ṢĀLIḤ (صالح). A prophet mentioned in the Qur'ān (Sūrah vii. 71), who was sent to the tribes 'Ād and Ṣamūd. Al-

Baiẕāwī says he was the son of 'Ubaid, the son of Asaf, the son of Māsih, the son of 'Ubaid, the son of Ḥāẕir, the son of Ṣamūd. Bochart thinks he must be the Pileg of Genesis xi. 16. D'Herbelot makes him the Salah of Genesis xi. 13.

The following is the account of him in the Qur'ān, with the commentators' remarks in *italics* (see Lane's *Selections* 2nd ed., by Mr. Stanley Lane Poole):—

"And *We sent* unto *the tribe of* Thamood their brother Ṣáliḥ. He said, O my people, worship God. Ye have no other deity than Him. A *miraculous* proof *of my veracity* hath come unto you from your Lord, this she-camel of God being a sign unto you. [*He had caused her, at their demand, to come forth from the heart of a rock.*] Therefore let her feed in God's earth, and do her no harm, lest a painful punishment seize you. And remember how He hath appointed you vicegerents *in the earth* after [the tribe of] 'A'd, and given you a habitation in the earth: ye make yourselves, on its plains, pavilions *wherein ye dwell in summer*, and cut the mountains into houses *wherein ye dwell in winter*. Remember then the benefits of God, and do not evil in the earth, acting corruptly.—The chiefs who were elated with pride, among his people, said unto those who were esteemed weak, *namely*, to those who had believed among them, Do ye know that Ṣáliḥ hath been sent *unto this?* And they hamstrung the she-camel (*Ḳudár* [the son of Sálif] *doing so by their order and slaying her with the sword*); and they impiously transgressed the command of their Lord, and said, O Ṣáliḥ, bring upon us that *punishment* with which thou threatenest us *for killing her*, if thou be [one] of the apostles. And the violent convulsion (*a great earthquake, and a cry from heaven*) assailed them, and in the morning they were in their dwellings prostrate *and dead*. So he turned away from them, and said, O my people, I have brought unto you the message of my Lord and given you faithful counsel; but ye loved not faithful counsellors." (Sūrah vii. 71–77.)

SĀLIK (سالك). *Lit.* "A traveller." A term used by the mystics for a devotee, or one who has started on the heavenly journey. [SUFI.]

SALSABĪL (سلسبيل). *Lit.* "The softly flowing. A fountain in Paradise, mentioned in the Qur'ān in Sūrah lxxvi. 19, and from which the Muslims in heaven are said to drink. "A spring therein named *Salsabīl*, and there shall go round about them immortal boys."

SALUTATIONS. Arabic *as-salām* (السلام), "peace." *Taslīm* (تسليم), Heb. שָׁלוֹם *shalom*, the act of giving the prayer of peace; pl. *taslīmāt*. The duty of giving and returning a salutation is founded on express injunctions in the Qur'ān.

Sūrah xxiv. 61: "When ye enter houses, then greet each other with a salutation from God, the Blessed and the Good."

Sūrah iv. 88: "When ye are saluted with a salutation, salute ye with a better than it, or return the same salutation."

'Alī says that Muḥammad established it as an incumbent duty that one Muslim should salute another. [FITRAH.] The ordinary salutations of the Muslim is "*as-Salāmu 'alai-kum*," *i.e.* "The peace be on you." And the usual reply is "*Wa 'alai-kum as-salām*," *i.e.* "And on you also be the peace."

The supposed origin of this salutation is given in a tradition by Abū Hurairah, who relates that the Prophet said:—

"God created Adam in his own likeness, and his stature was sixty cubits; and God said to Adam, 'Go and salute that party of angels who are sitting down, and listen to their answer; for verily it shall be the salutation and reply for you and your children.' Adam then went and said to the angels, '*as-Salāmu 'alai-kum*,' *i.e.* 'The peace be on you,' and the angels replied, '*as-Salāmu 'alaika wa raḥmatu 'llāhi*,' *i.e.* 'The peace be on thee, and the mercy of God.'"

This form is now usually given in reply by devout persons. (*Ṣaḥīḥu 'l-Buk͟hārī*, p. 919.)

Muḥammad instructed his people as follows regarding the use of the salutation:—

"The person riding must salute one on foot, and he who is walking must salute those who are sitting, and the small must salute the larger, and the person of higher degree the lower. It is therefore a religious duty for the person of high degree, when meeting one of a lower degree; the giving of the Salām being regarded as a benediction. For," says Muḥammad, "the nearest people to God are those who salute first. When a party is passing, it is sufficient if one of them give the salutation, and, in like manner, it is sufficient if one of the party return it of those sitting down."

The Jews in the time of Muḥammad seem to have made the salutation a subject of annoyance to Muḥammad; for it is related when they went to the Prophet they used to say, "*As-sammu 'alai-ka*," "On you be poison." To which the Prophet always replied, "*Wa 'alai-ka*," "And on you."

Usāmah ibn Zaid says: "The Prophet once passed a mixed assembly of Muslim polytheists, idolaters, and Jews, and he gave the salutation, but he meant it only for the Muslims."

Jarīr relates that on one occasion the Prophet met a party of women, and gave them the salutation. But this is contrary to the usual practice of Muḥammadans; and 'Abdu 'l-Ḥaqq, in his commentary on this tradition, says: "This practice was peculiar to the Prophet, for the laws of Islām forbid a man saluting a woman unless she is old."

In the East it is usual to raise the right hand (the raising of the left hand being disrespectful, as it is the hand used for legal ablutions) when giving the Salām, but this custom, common though it be, is not in accordance with the traditions. For 'Amr ibn Shu'aib relates, from his fore-fathers, that the Prophet said, "He is not of us who likens himself to another. Do not copy the Jews or the Christians in your salutation. For a Jew's salutation is by raising his fingers, and the Christians salute with the palm of the hand. (*Mishkāt*, book xxii. ch. i.)

In Central Asia, the salutation is generally given without any motion of the body, in accordance with the above tradition.

SALVATION. The Arabic word *najāt* (نجاة), "salvation," only occurs once in the Qur'ān, namely, Sūrah xl. 44: "O my people! how is it that I bid you to *salvation*, but that ye bid me to the fire?" Nor is the word generally used in Muslim works of divinity, although the orthodox sect of Muslims claims for itself the title of *Nājiyah*, or those who are being saved.

The word *maghfirah*, "forgiveness," is frequently used in the Qur'ān to express what Christians understand by "salvation"; also *Islām*, *Īmān*, and *Dīn*, words which express the idea of a state of salvation.

According to Islām, a man obtains salvation by a recital of the *Kalimah*, or creed; but if he be an evil doer, he will suffer the pains of a purgatorial fire until his sins are atoned for; whilst he who has not accepted the Muslim creed will endure the pains of everlasting punishment. [HELL.]

AS-ṢAMAD (الصمد). "The Eternal." One of the ninety-nine names or attributes of God. It occurs once in the Qur'ān, Sūrah cxii.: "God the Eternal."

In its original meaning, it implies a lord, because one repairs to him in exigencies; or when applied to God, because affairs are stayed or rested on Him. Hence, according to *al-Muḥkam*, *in loco*, and the *Liṣānu 'l-'Arab*, it signifies the Being that continues for ever—the Eternal One.

SAMĀḤAH (سماحة). [BENEFICENCE.]

SAMARITAN. [AS-SAMIRI.]

AS-SAMĪ' (السميع). "The Hearer." One of the ninety-nine names or attributes of God. The word frequently occurs in the Qur'ān.

AS-SĀMIRĪ (السامرى). Mentioned in the Qur'ān (Sūrah xx. 87: "As-Sāmirī has led them astray") as the person who made the golden calf for the Children of Israel. In Professor Palmer's translation, it is rendered "the Samaritan," which is according to al-Baiẓāwī, who says his name was Mūsā ibn Ẓafar, of the tribe of Samaritans. [MOSES.]

SAMUEL. Arabic *Ishmawīl* (اشمويل), or *Shamwīl*; Heb. שְׁמוּאֵל, referred to in the Qur'ān (Sūrah ii. 247) as "the prophet" to whom the Children of Israel said, "Raise for us a King, and we will fight for him in God's way."

Ḥusain, the commentator, says it is not quite certain who he was. He was either Yūsha' ibn Nūn, or Sham'ūn ibn Ṣafīyā, or Ishmawīl. (*Tafsīr-i-Ḥusainī*, p. 65.)

The Kamālān give his name as *Shamwil*, but say it was originally *Ismā'īl*, and that the meaning is the same.

ṢAN'Ā' (صنعاء). A city in al-Yaman, the Viceroy of which, Abrahatu 'l-Ashram, an Abyssinian Christian, marched with a large army and some elephants upon Makkah, with the intention of destroying the Temple (see Qur'ān, Sūrah cv.) in the year Muḥammad was born. Hence the year was known as that of the Elephant.

SANAD (سند). *Lit.* "That on which one rests, as a pillar or cushion." An authority; a document; a warrant. A term used in Muslim law.

ṢANAM (صنم), pl. *aṣnām*. The word used in the Qur'ān for an idol, *e.g.* Sūrah xiv. 38: "Turn me and my sons away from serving *idols*." [IDOLS.]

SANCTUARY. The Prophet forbade putting a murderer to death in a mosque, but he may be taken by force from the mosque and slain outside the building. The same rule applies to persons guilty of theft. (*Mishkāt*, book iv. ch. viii.)

The custom of sanctuary was derived from the Levitical law of refuge. The six cities being established as cities of refuge for the involuntary manslayer. The altar of burnt offerings was also a place of refuge for those who had undesignedly committed smaller offences. (Deut. xix. 11, 12; Joshua xx.) According to Lecky (*European Morals*, vol. ii. p. 42), the right of sanctuary was possessed by the Imperial statues and by the Pagan temples. Bingham (*Antiquities*, vol. ii. p. 554) says it seems to have been introduced into the Christian Church by Constantine.

SANDALS. [SHOES.]

SAQAR (سقر). "A scorching heat." According to the commentator, al-Baghawī it is the special division of hell set apart for the Magi. It is mentioned thus in the Qur'ān:—

Sūrah liv. 48: "Taste ye the touch of *saqar*."

Sūrah lxxiv. 26: "I will broil him in *saqar*! And what shall make thee know what *saqar* is?" It leaveth nought and spareth nought, blackening the skin of man.

SARACEN. A term used by Christian writers for the follower of Muḥammad, and applied not only to the Arabs, but to the Turks and other Muslim nations.

There is much uncertainty as to the origin of this word. The word Σαρακηνός was used by Ptolemy and Pliny, and also by Ammianus and Procopius, for certain Oriental tribes, long before the death of Muḥammad (see Gibbon). Some etymologists derive it from the Arabic *sharq*, "the rising sun, the East" (see Wedgwood's *Dict*). Others from *ṣaḥrā'*, "a desert,"—the people of the desert (see Webster). Gibbon thinks it may be from the Arabic *saraqah*, "theft," denoting the thievish character of the nation; whilst some have even thought it may be derived from Sarah the wife of the Patriarch Abraham.

SARAH. Arabic *Sārah* (سارة), Heb. שָׂרָה, Greek Σάῤῥα. Abraham's wife. Not mentioned by name in the Qur'ān, but referred to in Sūrah xi. 74: "And his wife was standing by laughing, and We gave her the glad tidings of Isaac, and of Jacob after Isaac."

SARAQAH (سرقة). [THEFT.]

ṢARF (صرف). (1) A term used for a special kind of sale or exchange. According to the *Hidāyah*, *bai'u 'ṣ-ṣarf*, or *ṣarf* sale, means a pure sale, of which the articles opposed to each other in exchange are both representatives of price, as gold for gold or silver for silver. (See Hamilton's *Hidāyah*, vol. ii. p. 551.)

(2) That part of grammar which relates to the declining of nouns and the conjugating of verbs.

ṢARĪḤ (صريح). Explicit or clear. A term used in Muslim law for that which is express in contradistinction to that which is *kināyah*, or implied. For example, the *Ṭalāqu 'ṣ-ṣarīḥ*, is an explicit form of divorce, whilst *Ṭalāqu 'l-kināyah* is an implied form of divorce, as when a man says to his wife, "Thou art free."

ṢĀRIQ (صارق). A thief. [THEFT.]

SATAN. Arabic *Shaiṭan* (شيطن). [DEVIL.]

SATR (ستر). A curtain or veil. A term used for the seclusion of women, called also *ḥijāb*. In the Traditions it is used for necessary and decent attire, *bābu 's-satr* being a special chapter in the *Mishkātu 'l-Maṣābīḥ* (book iv. ch. ix.). The *satr* for a man being from the waist to the knee, and for a free woman from the neck to the feet; but for a slave girl from the waist to the knee as in the case of a man. That part of the body which must be so covered is called *'aurah* or *'aurat*, "shame or modesty," from which the Hindustani word, *'aurat*, "a woman," is derived. [HARIM, WOMEN.]

SATTŪQAH (ستوقة). Base coin. The term is used for a coin which is current amongst merchants, but is not received at the public treasury. Coins in which the pure metal predominates are not considered base. (See Hamilton's *Hidāyah*, vol. ii. p. 560.)

SAUDAH (سودة). One of the wives of Muḥammad. She was the widow of Sakrān, a Quraish, and one of the early companions of the Prophet. Muḥammad married her within two months of the death of Khadījah. (Muir's *Life of Mahomet*, new ed. p. 117.) She died A.H. 55.

SAUL. Arabic *Ṭālūt* (طالوت). Heb. שָׁאוּל *Shaool.* King of Israel. Mentioned in the Qur'ān as a king raised up of God to reign over Israel, to whom was given an excellent degree of knowledge and personal appearance.

The following is the account given of Saul in the Qur'ān, with Mr. Lane's rendering of the commentator's remarks in *italics*. (Mr. Stanley Lane Poole's 2nd Ed.)

"Hast thou not considered the assembly of the children of Israel after *the death of* Moses, when they said unto a prophet of theirs, *namely Samuel*, Set up for us a king, *under whom* we will fight in the way of God? He said *unto them*, If fighting be prescribed as incumbent on you, will ye, peradventure, abstain from fighting? They replied, And wherefore should we not fight in the way of God, since we have been expelled from our habitations and our children *by their having been taken prisoners and slain?—The people of Goliath* [Jáloot] *had done thus unto them.*— But when fighting was commanded them, they turned back, excepting a few of them, *who crossed the river with Saul.* And God knoweth the offenders. *And the prophet begged his Lord to send a king; whereupon he consented to send Saul.* And their prophet said unto them, Verily God hath set up Saul as your king. They said, How shall he have the dominion over us, when we are more worthy of the dominion than he, (*for he was not of the royal lineage, nor of the prophetic, and he was a tanner, or a tender of flocks or herds,*) and he hath not been endowed with ample wealth? He replied, Verily God hath chosen him *as king* over you, and increased him in largeness of knowledge and of body, (*for he was the wisest of the children of Israel at that time, and the most comely of them, and the most perfect of them in make,*) and God giveth his kingdom unto whom He pleaseth; and God is ample *in His beneficence*, knowing *with respect to him who is worthy of the kingdom.*—And their prophet said unto them, *when they demanded of him a sign in proof of his kingship*, Verily the sign of his kingship *shall be* that the ark shall come unto you (*in it were the images of the prophets: God sent it down unto Adam, and it passed into their possession; but the Amalekites took it from them by force: and they used to seek victory thereby over their enemy, and to advance it in the fight, and to trust in it, as He—whose name be exalted!—hath said*); therein is tranquillity [SAKINAH] from your Lord, and relics of what the family of Moses and the family of Aaron have left: *namely, the two shoes (or sandals) of Moses, and his rod, and the turban of Aaron, and a measure of the manna that used to descend upon them, and the fragments of the tables* [of the Law]: the angels shall bear it. Verily in this shall be a sign unto you *of his kingship*, if ye be believers. *Accord-*

ingly the angels bore it between heaven and earth, while they looked at it, until they placed it by Saul; whereupon they acknowledged his kingship, and hastened to the holy war; and he chose of their young men seventy thousand.

"And when Saul went forth with the troops *from Jerusalem, and it was violently hot weather, aud they demanded of him water,* he said, Verily God will try you by a river, *that the obedient among you, and the disobedient, may appear, (and it was between the Jordan and Palestine),* and whoso drinketh thereof, he is not of my party (but he who tasteth not thereof, he is of my party), excepting him who takes forth a draught in his hand, *and is satisfied therewith, not adding to it; for he is of my party;*—then they drank thereof *ahundantly*, excepting a few of them, *who were content only with the handful of water. It is related that it sufficed them for their own drinking and for their beasts, and they were three hundred and somewhat more than ten.* And when he had passed over it, he and those who believed with him, they said, We have no power to-day *to contend* against Goliath and his troops. *And they were cowardly, and passed not over it.* They who held it as certain that they should meet God *at the resurrection (and they were those who had passed over it)* said, How many a small body of men hath overcome a great body by the permission (*or will*) of God! And God is with the patient, *to defend and aid.*—And when they went forth to battle against Goliath and his troops, they said, O our Lord, pour upon us patience, and make firm our feet, *by strengthening our hearts for the holy war,* and help us against the unbelieving people!—And they routed them by the permission (*or will*) of God, and David, *who was in the army of Saul,* slew Goliath." (Sūrah ii. 247–252.)

ṢAUM (صوم). "Fasting." The usual Arabic term used for this religious act whether during the Ramaẓān or at any other time. Its equivalent in Persian is *rozah.* [FASTING, RAMAZAN.]

ṢAUMU 'T-TAṬAWWU' (صوم التطوع). A voluntary fast other than the month of Ramaẓān.

SAUṬ (سوط). [DIRRAH.]

ṢAWĀB (ثواب). "Recompense; reward"; *e.g.* Qur'ān, Sūrah iii. 195: "*A reward* from God; for God, with Him are the best *rewards.*"

AS-SAWĀDU 'L-A'ẒAM (السواد الاعظم). *Lit.* "The exalted multitude." A term used in the Traditions and in Muslim theology for the Assembly of God, or the congregation of faithful men, or for a large majority.

SAWĀ'ĪM (سوايم), pl. of *Sā'imah.* Flocks and herds which are grazing and for which *zakāt* must be collected. [ZAZAT.]

SCHOOLS. Arabic *maktab* (مكتب), pl. *makātib*; *madrasah* (مدرسة), pl. *madāris.* According to Muslim law, all education should be carried on in connection with religious instruction, and consequently schools are generally attached to mosques [EDUCATION.]

SCRIPTURE, HOLY. The expression, "Holy Scripture," is rendered in Persian by *Pāk Nawishtah* (پاك نوشته), "the Holy Writing," its equivalent in Arabic being *al-Kitābu 'l-Muqaddas* (الكتاب المقدس), "the Holy Book," or *Kalāmu 'llāh* (كلام الله), "the Word of God." These terms, whilst they are generally understood by Muslims to refer to the Qur'ān, more correctly include all books acknowledged by Muḥammadans to be the Word of God. They profess to receive all the Jewish Scripture and the New Testament as well as the Qur'ān as the revealed Word of God. [PROPHETS, INSPIRATION.]

SCULPTURE. Arabic *anṣāb* (انصاب). The making of carved, graven, or sculptured figures, is understood to be forbidden in the Qur'ān under the term *ṣanam* (صنم), "an idol" (see Sūrah xiv. 38); also in Sūrah v. 92: "Verily wine, and games of chance, and statues (*anṣāb*), and divining arrows, are an abomination of Satan's device."

Consequently sculpture is not allowed according to Muslim law, although ar-Rāghib says a *ṣanam* is that which diverts the mind from God.

SEA. Arabic *baḥr* (بحر). "The sea," *al-baḥr*, is a term applied in the Qur'ān to the Red Sea, known amongst Muḥammadans as the *Baḥru 'l-Qulzum.* [RED SEA.] Sūrahs ii. 47; vii. 134. "The ships that sail like mountains in the sea," are amongst the "signs" of God. (See Sūrah xlii. 31.) In Sūrah lii. 6, Muḥammad swears by "the swelling sea." In Sūrah xvii. 68: "It is the Lord who drives the ships for you in the sea, that ye may seek after plenty from Him." In Sūrah xviii. 109, it occurs as an illustration of the boundless character of the Word of God. "Were the sea ink for the words of my Lord, the sea would surely fail before the words of my Lord fail; aye, though we brought as much ink again."

In Muḥammadan works, in the Traditions and commentaries, the Arabic *baḥr* is used for large rivers, as the Euphrates and the Nile, in the same sense as the Hebrew יָם *yām* (but the word *nahr*, Hebrew נָהָר *nāhar*, occurs in the Qur'ān for "rivers").

It is related that Muḥammad said, "Let none but three classes of people cross the sea (for it has fire under it which causes its troubled motion), namely, (1) those who perform the *Ḥajj*, or 'Pilgrimage'; (2) those who make the *'umrah*, or 'visitation'; (3) those who go forth to war." (*Majma'u 'l-Biḥār*, vol. i. p. 76.)

The following are the names of the seas as current in Muḥammadan literature :—

Al-Baḥru 'l-Akhẓar, the Green or Indian Ocean.

Al-Baḥru 'l-Abyaẓ, the White or Mediterranean Sea.

Al-Baḥru l'-Aswad, the Black, or Euxine Sea.

Al-Baḥru 'l-Azraq, the Blue or Persian Sea.

Al-Baḥru 'l-Qulzum, or *al-Baḥru 'l-Aḥmar*, the Red Sea.

Al-Baḥru 'l-Lūṭ, the Sea of Lot or Dead Sea.

Al-Baḥru 'l-Khiẓr, the sea of Khizr, the Caspian Sea.

SEAL OF PROPHECY. *Khātimu 'n-Nubūwah* (خاتم النبوة). A mole of an unusual size on the Prophet's back, which is said to have been the divine seal which, according to the predictions of the Scriptures, marked Muḥammad as the "Seal of the Prophets," *Khātimu 'n-Nabiyīn*.

According to a tradition recorded in the *Mishkātu 'l-Maṣābiḥ*, book iii. ch. 7, it was the size of the knob of a bridal canopy. Others say it was the size of a pigeon's egg, or even the size of a closed fist.

Shaikh 'Abdu 'l-Ḥaqq says "it was a piece of flesh, very brilliant in appearance, and according to some traditions it had secretly inscribed *within* it, 'God is one and has no Associate.'"

Abū Ramṣā', whose family were skilled in surgery, offered to remove it, but Muḥammad refused, saying, "The Physician thereof is He who placed it where it is."

According to another tradition, Muḥammad said to Abū Ramṣā', "Come hither and touch my back"; which he did, drawing his fingers over the prophetical seal, and, behold! there was a collection of hairs upon the spot. (See Muir, new ed. p. 542.)

'Abdu 'l-Ḥaqq also says it disappeared from the Prophet's back shortly before his death.

It is not clear how far Muḥammad encouraged the belief in this supernatural sign of his prophetic mission, but from his reply to Abū Ramṣā', it would not appear that he really attributed any special power to its existence. [MUHAMMAD.]

SECTS OF ISLĀM. Arabic *firqah* (فرقة), pl. *firaq*. Muḥammad is related to have prophesied that his followers would be divided into numerous religious sects.

'Abdu 'llāh ibn 'Umar relates that the Prophet said: "Verily it will happen to my people even as it did to the Children of Israel. The Children of Israel were divided into seventy-two sects, and my people will be divided into seventy-three. Every one of these sects will go to Hell except one sect." The Companions said, "O Prophet, which is that?" He said, "The religion which is professed by me and my Companions." (*Mishkāt*, book i. ch. vi. pt. 2.)

The number has, however, far exceeded the Prophet's predictions, for the sects of Islām even exceed in number and variety those of the Christian religion.

The Sunnīs arrogate to themselves the title of the *Nājiyah*, or those who are "being saved" (as, indeed, do the other sects), but within the limits of the Sunnī section of Muḥammadans there are four which are esteemed "orthodox," their differences consisting chiefly in minor differences of ritual, and in varied interpretations of Muslim law. These four orthodox sects or schools of interpretation amongst the Sunnīs, are the Ḥanafīyah, the Shāfi'īyah, the Malakīyah, and the Ḥambalīyah.

1. The Ḥanafīyahs are found in Turkey, Central Asia, and North India. The founder of this sect was the Imām Abū Ḥanīfah, who was born at al-Kūfah, the capital of al-'Irāq, A.D. 702, or A.H. 80, at which time four of the Prophet's companions were still alive. He is the great oracle of jurisprudence, and (with his two pupils, the Imāms Abū Yūsuf and Muḥammad) was the founder of the Hanafīyah Code of Law.

2. The Shāfi'īyahs are found in South India and Egypt. The founder of this school of interpretation was Imām Muḥammad ibn Idrīs as-Shāfi'ī', who was born at Asqalon, in Palestine, A.D. 767 (A.H. 150).

3. The Malakīyahs prevail in Morocco, Barbary, and other parts of Africa, and were founded by Imām Mālik, who was born at al-Madīnah, A.D. 714 (A.H. 95). He enjoyed the personal acquaintance of Abū Ḥanīfah, and he was considered the most learned man of his time.

4. The Ḥambalīyahs were founded by Imām Abū 'Abdi 'llāh Aḥmad ibn Muḥammad ibn Ḥambal, who was born at Baghdād, A.D. 780 (A.H. 164). He attended the lectures delivered by ash-Shāfi'ī, by whom he was instructed in the Traditions. His followers are found in Eastern Arabia, and in some parts of Africa, but it is the least popular of the four schools of interpretation. They have no Muftī at Makkah, whilst the other three sects are represented there. The Wahhābīs rose from this sect. [WAHHABI.]

From the disciples of these four great Imāms have proceeded an immense number of commentaries and other works, all differing on a variety of points in their constructions, although coinciding in their general principles.

The *Ghiyāṣu 'l-Lughāt* gives the following particulars of the seventy-three sects, spoken of in the Traditions, arranging them in six divisions of twelve sects each, and concluding with the *Nājiyah*, or "Orthodox" Sunnīs.

I.—The *Rāfiẓīyah*, "the Separatists," who are divided into—

1. *'Alawīyah*, who esteem the Khalīfah 'Alī to have been a prophet.

2. *Abadīyah*, who hold that 'Alī is divine.

3 *Shu'aibīyah*, who say 'Alī was the first and best of the Khalīfahs.

4. *Isḥāqīyah*, who say the age of prophecy is not yet completed.

5. *Zaidīyah*, who hold that prayers can only be led by a descendant of 'Alī.

6. *'Abbāsiyah*, who say al-'Abbās, the uncle of Muḥammad, was the only rightful Imām.

7. *Imāmīyah*, who state that the world is never left without an Imām of the Banū Hāshim to lead the prayers.

8. *Nārisīyah*, who say it is blasphemy for one person to say he is better than another.

9. *Tanāsukhīyah*, who believe in the transmigration of souls.

10. *Lā'inīyah*, those who curse the names of Ṭalḥah, Zubair, and 'Āyishah.

11. *Rāji'iyah*, who believe that 'Alī is hidden in the clouds and will return again to this earth.

12. *Murtaẓiyah*, who say it is lawful for a Muslim to fight against his Imām.

II.—The *Khārijīyah*, "the Aliens," who are divided into—

1. *Azraqīyah*, who say there is no holy vision now to be obtained by the sons of men, as the days of inspiration are past.

2. *Riyāẓiyah*, who say a man is saved by good works, and not by faith.

3. *Ṣa'labīyah*, who say God is indifferent to the actions of men, as though He were in a state of sleep.

4. *Jāzimīyah*, who hold true faith has not yet been made evident.

5. *Khalfīyah*, who say to run away even from double the number of infidels is a mortal sin for Muslims.

6. *Kūzīyah*, who say that the human body is not made ready for prayer unless the ablutions be such as entirely cleanse the body.

7. *Kanzīyah*, who do not regard the giving of *zakāt* as necessary.

8. *Mu'tazilah*, who maintain that evil actions are not according to the decree of God, and that the prayers of a sinful man are not acceptable to God, and that faith is of man's free will, and that the Qur'ān is created, and that almsgiving and prayer do not benefit the dead, and that there is no *mīzān* or *kitāb*, &c., at the Day of Judgment.

9. *Maimūnīyah*, who hold that belief in the unseen is absurd.

10. *Muḥkamiyah*, who say God has not revealed His will to mankind.

11. *Sirājīyah*, who believe the example of the saints is of no importance.

12. *Akhnasīyah*, who hold that there is no punishment for sin.

III.—The *Jabarīyah*, the "Deniers of Free Will," who are divided into—

1. *Muẓṭariyah*, who hold that both good and evil are entirely from God, and man is not responsible for his actions.

2. *Af'ālīyah*, who say man is responsible for his actions although the power to do and to act is alone from God.

3. *Ma'iyah*, who believe that man possesses an entirely free will.

4. *Ṭarīqīyah*, who say faith without works will save a man.

5. *Bakhtīyah*, who believe that as every mortal receives according to God's special gift, it is not therefore lawful for one to give to another.

6. *Mutamannīyah*, who hold that good works are those from which comfort and happiness are derived in this world.

7. *Kāslānīyah*, they who say punishment and reward is inflicted by God only according to the actions of man.

8. *Ḥabībīyah*, who hold that as one friend never injures another, so God, who is a God of love, does not punish his own creation.

9. *Khaufīyah*, who say that just as a friend does not terrify his friend, so God does not terrify his people by judgments.

10. *Fikrīyah*, who say contemplation is better than worship, and more pleasing to God.

11. *Ḥasabīyah*, who hold that in the world there is no such a thing as fate or predestination.

12. *Ḥujjatīyah*, who say that inasmuch as God doeth everything and everything is of God, man cannot be made responsible for either good or evil.

IV.—The *Qadarīyah*, the "Asserters of Free Will," who are divided into—

1. *Aḥadīyah*, who accept the injunctions of God, but not those of the Prophet.

2. *Ṣanawīyah*, who say there are two eternal principles, good and evil; good being of Yazdān and evil being of Ahraman.

3. *Kaisanīyah*, who say our actions are either the creation of God or they are not.

4. *Shaiṭānīyah*, who deny the personality of Satan.

5. *Sharīkīyah*, who say faith is *ghair makhlūq*, or "uncreated."

6. *Wahmīyah*, who say the actions of man are of no consequence, whether they be good or evil.

7. *Ruwaidīyah*, who maintain that the world has an eternal existence.

8. *Nākisīyah*, who say it is lawful to fight against the Imām or Khalīfah.

9. *Mutabarrīyah*, who say the repentance of sinners is not accepted by God.

10. *Qāsiṭīyah*, who hold that the acquirement of wealth and learning is a religious duty ordered by God.

11. *Naẓāmīyah*, who maintain that it is lawful to speak of the Almighty as a thing (*shai'*).

12. *Mutawallifīyah*, who say it is not evident whether evil is by God's decree or not.

V.—The *Jahimīyah*, the followers of Jahim ibn Ṣafwān, who are divided into—

1. *Mu'aṭṭalīyah*, who say the names and attributes of God are created

2. *Mutarābiṣīyah*, who hold that the power, knowledge, and purpose of God are created.

3. *Mutarāqibiyah*, who say God has a place.

4. *Wāridīyah*, who state that those who enter hell will never escape from it, and that a *mu'min*, or "believer," will never enter hell.

5. *Harqīyah*, who say the inhabitants of hell will so burn, that in time they will be annihilated.

6. *Makhlūqīyah*, who believe that the Qur'ān, the Taurāt, the Injīl, and the Zubūr are created.

7. *'Ibarīyah*, who say Muḥammad was a learned man, and a philosopher, but not a prophet.

8. *Fānīyah*, who say both Paradise and Hell will be annihilated.

9. *Zanādiqīyah*, who say the *Mi'rāj*, or "ascent of Muḥammad to heaven," was only in the spirit, and that the world is eternal, and that there is no Day of Judgment.

10. *Lafẓīyah*, who hold that the Qur'ān is not an inspired writing, but that its instructions are of God.

11. *Qabrīyah*, who say there is no punishment in the grave.

12. *Wāqifīyah*, who state that it is not certain whether the Qur'ān is create or uncreate.

VI.—The *Murjīyah*, or "Procrastinators," who are divided into—

1. *Ṭārīqīyah*, who say nothing is necessary but faith.

2. *Shā'īyah*, who maintain that when once a person has repeated the Muḥammadan creed he is saved.

3. *Rājīyah*, who believe that the worship of God is not necessary to piety, nor are good works necessary.

4. *Shākkīyah*, who say a man cannot be certain if he has faith or not, for faith is spirit.

5. *Nāhīyah*, who say faith is knowledge, and those who do not know the commandments of God have not faith.

6. *'Amalīyah*, who say faith is but good works.

7. *Manqūṣīyah*, who say faith is sometimes less and sometimes more.

8. *Mustaṣnīyah*, who deprecate assurance in religion, but say, "we are believers if God wills it."

9. *Ash'arīyah*, who say *qiyās*, or "analogical reasoning, in matters of faith is unlawful.

10. *Bid'īyah*, who hold that it is a duty to obey a ruler, even if he give orders which are evil.

11. *Mushabbihīyah*, who say God did literally make Adam in his own image.

12. *Hashawīyah*, who consider that in Muslim law there is no difference between *wājib*, *sunnah*, and *mustaḥab*.

VII.—The *Nājiyah*, or "Saved Ones," make up the complete number of seventy-three.

Mr. Sale traces all the Muḥammadan sects to four sources :—

1. The *Mu'tazilīyahs*, the followers of Wāṣil ibn 'Aṭā, who may be said to have been the first inventor of scholastic divinity in Islām.

2. The *Ṣifātīyahs*, or Attributists, who hold the contrary opinions of the *Mu'tazilīyahs*.

3. The *Khārijīyahs*, or Aliens. Those who revolted from 'Alī.

4 The *Shī'ahs*, or the followers of 'Alī

The author of the *Sharḥu 'l-Muwāqif* says there are eight leading divisions of the sects of Islām:—

1. The Mu'tazilah.
2. The Shī'ahs.
3. The Khawārij.
4. The Murjīyah.
5. The Najjārīyah.
6. The Jabarīyah.
7. The Mushabbihīyah.
8. The Nājiyah.

For an account of these leading sects, the reader is referred to the articles under their respective titles.

Shaikh 'Abdu 'l-Qādir says there are not less than 150 sects in Islām.

SERMON. The oration delivered at the Friday midday prayer is called the *khuṭbah* (خطبة); exhortations at any other time are termed *wa'ẓ* (وعظ). The former is an established custom in Islām, and the discourse is always delivered at the *Masjidu 'l-Jāmi'*, or principal mosque, on Fridays, but sermons on other occasions although they are in accordance with the practice of Muḥammad, are not common. Very few Maulawis preach except on Fridays. [KHUTBAH.]

SERPENT, Arabic *ḥaiyah* (حية), occurs in the Qur'ān once for the serpent made from Moses' rod (Sūrah ii. 21). The word used in another place (Sūrah vii. 104) is *ṡu'bān* (ثعبان). The Hebrew תַּנִּין *tanneen* is also used for a large serpent in Muslim books, but it does not occur in the Qur'ān.

In the Qur'ān, Sūrah ii. 34, it is said Satan made Adam and Eve to backslide and "drove them out from what they were in," but no mention is made of the serpent.

The commentators say that when the devil attempted to get into Eden to tempt Adam, he was stopped by the angelic guard at the gates of Paradise, whereupon he begged of the animals to carry him in to speak to Adam and his wife, but they all refused except the serpent, who took him between his teeth and so introduced him to our first parents. (*Tafsiru 'l-'Azīzī*, p. 124.)

SETH. Arabic *Shīṡ* (شيث); Heb. שֵׁת *Sheth*. The third son of Adam. A prophet to whom it is said God revealed fifty small portions of scripture. [PROPHETS.] In the fourth century there existed in Egypt a sect of gnostics, calling themselves Sethians, who regarded Seth as a divine emanation. (Neander's *Ch. Hist.*, vol. ii. p. 115), which will account for Muḥammad classing him as an inspired prophet with a revelation.

SEVEN DIALECTS. Arabic *Sab'atu Aḥruf* (سبعة احرف). The Prophet is related to have said that the Qur'ān was revealed in seven dialects (*Mishkāt*, book ii. ch. ii.). The word *aḥruf*, translated "dialects," may admit of two interpretations Some understand it to mean that the Qur'ān contains seven kinds of revelation: Commandment (*amr*), prohibition (*nahy*), history (*qiṣṣah*), parable (*miṣāl*), exhortation (*wa'ẓ*), promises (*wa'dah*), and threatening (*wa'īd*). But the more common interpretation of *aḥruf* is "dialects," by which is understood that by changing the inflections and accentuations of words, the text of the Qur'ān may be read in the then existing "seven dialects" of Arabia, namely, Quraish, Ṭaiy, Hawāzin, Yaman, Ṣaqīf, Huẕail, Tamīm. [QUR'AN.]

SEVEN SALĀMS. Seven verses of the Qur'ān, in which the word *salām* (سلام), "peace," occurs:—

Sūrah xxxvi. 58: "*Peace* shall be the word spoken unto the righteous by a merciful God."

Sūrah xxxvii. 77: "*Peace* be on Noah and on all creatures."

Sūrah xxxvii. 109: "*Peace* be on Abraham."

Sūrah xxxvii. 120: "*Peace* be on Moses and Aaron."

Sūrah xxxvii. 130: "*Peace* be on Elias."

Sūrah xxxvii. 181: "*Peace* be on His apostles."

Sūrah xcvii. 5: "It is *peace* until the breaking of the morn."

These verses are recited by the religious Muslim during sickness, or in seasons of danger or distress. In some parts of Islām it is customary to write these seven verses of the Qur'ān on paper and then to wash off the ink and drink it as a charm against evil.

SHA'BĀN (شعبان). *Lit.* "The month of separation." The eighth month of the Muḥammadan year. So-called because the Arabs used to separate themselves in search of water during this month.

SHAB-I-BARĀT (شب برات). The Persian title for the fifteenth day of the month Sha'bān, which is called in Arabic *Lailatu 'n-niṣf min Sha'bān*, or "the night of the middle of Sha'bān."

On this night, Muḥammad said, God registers annually all the actions of mankind which they are to perform during the year; and that all the children of men, who are to be born and to die in the year, are recorded. Muḥammad, it is said, enjoined his followers to keep awake the whole night, to repeat one hundred rak'ah prayers, and to fast the next day; but there are generally great rejoicings instead of a fast, and large sums of money are spent in fireworks. It is the "Guy Fawkes Day" of India, being the night for display of fireworks.

The *Shab-i-Barāt* is said to be referred to in the XLIVth Sūrah of the Qur'ān, verse 2, as "the night on which all things are disposed in wisdom," although the commentators are not agreed as to whether the verse alludes to this night or the *Shab-i-Qadr*, on the 27th of the month of Ramaẓān.

The *Shab-i-Barāt* is frequently confounded with the *Lailatu 'l-Qadr*, or, as it is called in India, the *Shab-i-Qadr*

SHAB-I-QADR (شب قدر). [LAILATU 'L-QADR.]

SHĀDI (شادی). Persian. *Lit.* "Festivity." The ordinary term used for weddings amongst Persian and Urdu-speaking peoples. In Arabic the term is *'urs* (عرس). [MARRIAGE.]

SHADĪDU 'L-QUWĀ (شديد القوى). *Lit.* "One terrible in power." A title given to the agent of inspiration in the Sūratu 'l-Najm (liii.), verse 5: "Verily the Qur'ān is no other than a revelation revealed to him: one terrible in power (*shadīdu 'l-quwā*) taught it him."

Commentators are unanimous in assigning this title to the angel Gabriel.

SHAF' (شفع). A term used for *rak'ahs* of prayer when recited in pairs.

SHAFĀ'AH (شفاعة). [INTERCESSION.]

ASH-SHĀFI'Ī (الشافعی). Imām Muḥammad ibn Idrīs ash-Shāfi'ī, the founder of one of the four orthodox sects of Sunnīs, was born at Askalon in Palestine A.H. 150. He was of the same tribe as the Prophet, and is distinguished by the appellation of al-Imāmu 'l-Muṭṭalibī, or Quraish Muṭṭalibī, because of his descent from the Prophet's grandfather, 'Abdu 'l-Muṭṭalib. He derived his patronymic ash-Shāfi'ī from his grandfather, Shāfi'ī Ibn as-Sā'ib. His family were at first among the most inveterate of Muḥammad's enemies. His father, carrying the standard of the tribe of Hāshim at the battle of Badr, was taken prisoner by the Muslims, but released on ransom, and afterwards became a convert to Islām. Ash-Shafi'ī is reported by Muslim writers to be the most accurate of all the traditionists, and, if their accounts be well founded, nature had indeed endowed him with extraordinary talents for excelling in that species of literature. It is said that at seven years of age he had got the whole Qur'ān by rote, at ten he had committed to memory the *Muwaṭṭa'* of Mālik, and at fifteen he obtained the rank of Muftī. He passed the earlier part of his life at Gaza, in Palestine (which has occasioned many to think he was born in that place); there he completed his education and afterwards removed to Makkah. He came to Baghdād A.H. 195, where he gave lectures on the traditions, and composed his first work, entitled *al-Uṣūl*. From Baghdād he went on a pilgrimage to Makkah, and from thence afterwards passed into Egypt, where he met with Imām Mālik It does not appear that he ever returned from that country, but spent the remainder of his life there, dividing his time between the exercises of religion, the instruction of the ignorant, and the composition of his later works. He died at Cairo A.H. 204. Although he was forty-seven years of age before he began to publish, and died at fifty-four, his works are more voluminous than those of any other Muslim doctor. He was a great enemy to the scholastic divines, and most of his productions (especially upon theology), were written with a view to controvert their absurdities. He is said to have been the first who reduced the science of Jurisprudence into a regular system, and to have made a systematic collection of traditions. Imām Ḥambal remarks that until the time of ash-Shāfiʿī men did not know how to distinguish between the traditions that were in force and those that were cancelled. His first work was, as before-mentioned, the *Uṣūl*, or "fundamentals," containing all the principles of the Muslim civil and canon law. His next literary productions were the *Sunan* and *Masnad*, both works on the traditional law, which are held in high estimation among the Sunnīs. His works upon practical divinity are various, and those upon theology consist of fourteen volumes. His tomb is still to be seen at Cairo, where the famous Ṣalāhu 'd-dīn afterwards (A.H. 587) founded a college for the preservation of his works and the propagation of his doctrines. The mosque at Ḥīrah was built by Sultān G͟hiyāṣu 'd-Dīn for the same purpose. Imām ash-Shāfiʿī is said to have been a person of acute discernment and agreeable conversation. His reverence for God was such that he never was heard to mention his name except in prayer. His manners were mild and ingratiating, and he reprobated all unnecessary moroseness or severity in a teacher, it being a saying of his that whoever advised his brother tenderly and in private did him a service, but that public reproof could only operate as a reproach. His principal pupils were Imām Aḥmad ibn Ḥambal and az-Zuhairī, the former of whom afterwards founded a sect [HANBAL].

The Shāfiʿī sect of Sunnīs is chiefly met with in Egypt and Arabia.

SHAG͟HĀR (شغار). A double treaty of marriage common amongst the pagan Arabs, viz. the man marrying the sister or daughter of another, and in return giving his sister or daughter in order to avoid paying the usual dower. It is strictly forbidden by the Muḥammadan religion (see *Mishkāt*, book xii. ch. 11), although it is even now practised by the people of Central Asia

SHĀH (شاه). Persian. "A King." A title usually given to members of the Ascetic order, and to Saiyids, as Faqīr Shāh, Akbar Shāh. It has, however, become a common addition to surnames, both in India and other countries, and no longer denotes a position of dignity.

SHAHĀDAH (شهادة). "Evidence." [WITNESSES.] Martyrdom. [MARTYRS.]

SHAHĪD (شهيد). [MARTYRS, WITNESS.]

ASH-SHAHĪD (الشهيد). "The Witness." One of the ninety-nine names or attributes of God. It frequently occurs in the Qur'ān for the Almighty (*e.g.* Sūrah iii. 93) as one who seeth all things.

SHĀHINSHĀH (شاهنشاه). A Persian title given to the King of Persia—"King of Kings." It is a title strictly forbidden in Traditions, in which it is related that Muḥammad said "'King of Kings' is the vilest name you can call a man, for there is no other King of Kings but God." (*Mishkāt*, book xxii. ch. viii.)

SHAIK͟H (شيخ), pl. *shuyūk͟h*, *ash-yāk͟h*, or *mashāyik͟h*. A venerable old man. A man above fifty years of age. A man of authority. A superior of an order of Darweshes. *Shayk͟hu 'l-Islām*, a title given to the chief Maulawī or Qāẓī of the cities of Constantinople, Cairo, Damascus, &c.

SHAIṬĀN (شيطان). [DEVIL.]

SHAJJAH (شجة), pl. *shijāj*. [WOUNDS.]

SHAKING HANDS. Arabic *muṣāfaḥah* (مصافحة). Is enjoined in the Traditions, and is founded upon the express example of Muḥammad himself.

Al-Barā' ibn ʿĀzib says the Prophet said, "There are no two Muslims who meet and shake hands but their sins will be forgiven them before they separate." (*Mishkāt*, book xxii. ch. iii.)

ASH-SHAKŪR (الشكور). "The Acknowledger of Thanksgiving." One of the ninety-nine special attributes of the Almighty. Qur'ān, Sūrah xxxv. 27: "Verily He (God) is forgiving, and an acknowledger of thanksgiving." When used for anyone but God it means one who is grateful, *e.g* Qur'ān, Sūrah xxxiv. 12: "Few of my servants are grateful."

ASH-SHA'M (الشام). *Lit.* "That which is on the left-hand (looking to the rising sun)," *i.e.* the northern country to Makkah. Syria.

ASH-SHAMS (الشمس). "The Sun." The title of the XCIst Sūrah of the Qur'ān, which begins with the word.

SHAQQU 'Ṣ-ṢADR (شق الصدر). *Lit.* "The splitting open of the heart." Anas relates that "the Angel Gabriel came to the Prophet, when he was playing with boys, and took hold of him, and laid him on the ground, and split open his heart, and brought out a little bag of blood, and said to Muḥammad, 'This is the devil's part of you. After this, Gabriel washed the Prophet's heart with *zamzam* water, then sewed it up and replaced it. Then the boys who were with the Prophet came running to his nurse, saying, 'Verily Muḥammad is killed.'" Anas also says that he "had seen the marks of the sewing in the Prophet's breast." (*Mishkāt*, book xxiv. ch. vi.)

According to the commentators al-Baizāwī, al-Kamālān, and Ḥusain, the first verse of the xcivth Sūrah of the Qur'ān refers to this event: "Have we not opened thy breast for thee, and taken off from thee thy burden, which galled thy back?" But it seems probable that this simple verse of one of the earliest chapters of the Qur'ān refers merely to the enlightenment of Muḥammad's heart, and that his followers afterwards invented the miracle in order to give a supernatural turn to the passage. [MUHAMMAD.]

SHAR' (شرع). [LAW.]

SHARĀB (شراب). In its original meaning, "that which is drunk." A drink. Always applied to wine and intoxicating drinks. In mystic writings, *sharāb*, "wine," signifies the dominion of Divine love over the heart of man.

SHARḤ (شرح). *Lit.* "Expounding." A term used for a commentary written in explanation of any book or treatise, as distinguished from *tafsīr*, which is used only for a commentary of the Qur'ān. These expositions are written either in the text, or on the side of the book or treatise they attempt to expound. The term, however, generally used for marginal notes is *ḥāshiyah*. For example, the *Tanwīru 'l-Abṣār* is the *matn*, or text, of a great work on Muhammadan laws, written by Shamsu 'd-Dīn Muḥammad A.H. 995; the *Durru 'l-Mukhtār* is a *sharḥ*, or commentary written on that work by 'Alā 'd-Dīn Muḥammad, A.H. 1088; and the *Ḥāshiyah*, or marginal notes on these two works, is the *Raddu 'l-Muḥtār*, by Muḥammad Amīn.

SHARĪ'AH (شريعة). The law, including both the teaching of the Qur'ān and of the traditional sayings of Muḥammad. [LAW.]

SHARṬ (شرط). The conditions of marriage, of contracts, &c.

SHAVING. The shaving of the beard is forbidden in the Traditions, for Ibn 'Umar relates that the Prophet said: "Do the opposite of the polytheists; let your beards grow long and clip your mustachios." The shaving of the head is allowed, provided the whole and not a part is shaven, for the Prophet said: "Shave off all the hair of the head or let it alone. (*Mishkāt*, xx. ch. iv. pt. 3.)

In Afghanistan it is the custom to shave the head, but not in other parts of Islām.

SHAVING THE HEAD. Arabic *taḥlīq* (تحليق). Forbidden in the Ḥadīs (*Mishkāt*, book xiv. ch. v.), although it is most common amongst the Muhammadans of India and Central Asia.

SHAWWĀL (شوال). *Lit.* "The month of raising the tail." The tenth month of the Muḥammadan year. For a discussion of the meaning of the title of this month, see Lane's *Arabic Dict. in loco.*)

SHA'YĀ' (شعياء). [ISAIAH.]

SHECHINA. [SAKINAH, TABUT.]

SHEM. Arabic *Sām* (سام). A son of Noah. Not mentioned in the Qur'ān, but his name is given in commentaries.

SHĪ'AH (شيعة). *Lit.* "Followers." The *followers* of 'Alī, first cousin of Muḥammand and the husband of his daughter Fāṭimah. The Shī'ahs maintain that 'Alī was the first legitimate *Imām* or Khalīfah, or successor, to the Prophet, and therefore reject Abu Bakr, 'Umar, and 'Uṣmān, the first three Khalīfahs of the Sunnī Muslims, as usurpers. They are also called the *Imāmīyahs*, because they believe the Muslim religion consists in the true knowledge of the Imām or rightful leaders of the faithful. Also the *Iṣnā-'asharīyah*, or the *twelveans*, as followers of the *twelve* Imāms. The Sunnī Muslims call them the *Rāfiẓī*, or the forsakers of the truth. The Shī'ahs strenuously maintain that they are the "orthodox" Muslims, and arrogate to themselves (as do also the Sunnīs) the title of *al-Mu'minūn*, or the "True Believers."

The spirit of division, which appeared among the followers of Muḥammad, even before his death, broke out with greater violence after it; and the rapid strides of his successors to even imperial power, only afforded a wider sphere for ambition. The great and radical difference between the Shī'ahs and Sunnīs, as we have already remarked, arises from the former maintaining the divine and indefeasible right of 'Alī to succeed to the Khalifate on the death of the Prophet. 'Alī's claims, they assert, rested on his nearness of kindred to Muḥammad, of whom he was a cousin, and on his having married Fāṭimah, the only offspring of the Prophet which survived him. They also assert that he was expressly declared his successor by the Prophet himself, under direct guidance from God.

The text quoted in defence of the divine institution of the Khalifate in the Prophet's own family, is the 118th verse of the Sūratu 'l-Baqarah, or the Second Chapter of the Qur'ān, which reads:—

"And when his Lord tried Abraham with words and he fulfilled them, He said, 'I am about to make of thee an IMĀM to mankind'; he said, 'Of my offspring also?' 'My covenant,' said God, 'embraceth not evil doers.'"

According to the Shī'ahs, this passage shows that the Imāmate, or Khalifate, is a divine institution, and the possessor thereof must be of the seed of Abraham. This the Sunnīs would also admit, as they hold that the true Khalīfah can only be one of the Quraish tribe [KHALIFAH], but from the expression, "my covenant embraceth not evil doers," the Shī'ah doctors establish the supernatural character of the Khalifate, and hold that the divinely appointed leader must himself be without spot or blemish or capacity to sin. The primeval creation of 'Alī is therefore a dogma of the Shī'ah faith.

The author of the *Ḥayātu 'l-Qulūb* (Merrick's ed., p. 4), says: "The Prophet declared that the Most High had created him, and 'Alī and Fāṭimah, and Ḥasan and Ḥusain, before the creation of Adam, and when as yet there was neither heaven, nor earth, nor darkness, nor light, nor sun, nor moon, nor paradise, nor hell.' [HAQIQATU 'L-MUHAMMADIYAH.]

The Shī'ah traditions also give very lengthy accounts of the nomination of 'Alī by the Prophet to be his successor. The following is the account given in the *Ḥayātu 'l-Qulūb* (p. 334):—

"When the ceremonies of the pilgrimage were completed, the Prophet, attended by 'Alī, and the Muslims, left Makkah for al-Madīnah. On reaching Ghadīrkhum, the Prophet halted, although that place had never been known as a stopping-place for caravans because it had neither water nor pasturage. The reason for stopping at this place being a direct message from the Almighty. The Prophet had received divine messages on the subject before, but He had not before expressly appointed the time of 'Alī's inauguration."

* * * * *

"As the day was very hot, the Prophet ordered them to take shelter under some thorn trees. Having ordered all the camel-saddles to be piled up for a pulpit, he commanded a herald to summon the people around him. Most of them had bound their cloaks on their feet as a protection from the excessive heat. When all the people were assembled, the Prophet ascended the pulpit made of camel-saddles, and, calling to him the Commander of the Faithful ('Alī), placed him on his right hand. Muḥammad then gave praise to God, and foretold his own death, saying that he had been called to the gate of God. He then said, 'I leave among you the Book of God, to which, while you adhere, you will never go astray. I leave with you the members of my family who cannot be separated from the Book of God until both they and the Book join me at the fountain of al-Kauṣar' [KAUSAR.] He then, with a loud voice, said, 'Am I not dearer to you than your own lives?' And all the people said, 'Yes.' He then took the hands of 'Alī and raised them up so high, that the white of his arm-pits appeared, and said, 'Whosoever from his heart receives me as his master, then let him receive 'Alī. O Lord, befriend 'Alī. Be the enemy of all his enemies. Help all who help him, and forsake all who forsake him."

The writer also says:—

"Certain authorities, both Shī'ah and Sunnī, declare that when the Prophet died, the hypocritical Muhājirs and Anṣars, such as Abū Bakr, 'Umar, and 'Abdu 'r-Rahmān ibnu 'l-'Auf, instead of visiting the family of the Prophet to comfort them at the time of his death, assembled at the abode of the Banū Saudah, and plotted to seize the Khalīfate. Most of them did not perform the prayers at the Prophet's burial, although 'Alī sent to call them for the purpose. This plan was to make Abū Bakr Khalīfah, and for this they had plotted in the Prophet's lifetime. The hypocritical Ansārs, however, wished to make Sa'd ibnu 'l-Abādah Khalīfah, but they were over-ruled by the Muhājirs. A certain man brought the information that Abū Bakr was constituted Khalīfah, when 'Alī was in the act of filling in the earth of the Prophet's grave, and said that the hypocrites had feared that if they waited till the funeral ceremony was over, they would not succeed in their design of depriving 'Alī of his rights. 'Alī laid his spade on the ground and recited the first verses of the XXIXth Sūrah of the Qur'ān: 'A. L. M. Do men reckon that they will be left alone who say, "We believe," and not be tried? We did try those who were before them, and God will surely know those who are truthful, and he will surely know those who are liars.'"

The Shī'ahs believe that at this time God made special revelations to Fāṭimah, the Prophet's daughter, and 'Alī's wife. These revelations are said to have been possessed by the last of the Imāms, al-Mahdī, and to be still in his possession. [MAHDI.]

It need scarcely be added that the Sunnī writers deny every word of these traditions.

The strong hand of the Sunnī Khalifah 'Umar kept the claims of 'Alī in abeyance; but when 'Umar died, the Khalifate was offered to 'Alī, on condition that he would govern according to the Qur'ān, and the traditions as received by the Sunnīs. The answer of 'Alī not being deemed satisfactory, the election devolved upon 'Usmān (Othman). Usmān was assassinated A.H. 35, and 'Alī was elected on his own terms, in spite of the opposition of 'Āyishah, the favourite wife of the Prophet, who had become a great influence in Islām.

One of the first acts of 'Alī was to recall Mu'āwiyah from Syria. Mu'āwiyah refused, and then claimed the Khalīfate for himself. His claims were supported by 'Āyishah. 'Alī was eventually assassinated at Kūfah, A.H. 40, and upon his death his son Ḥasan was elected Khalīfah, but he resigned it in favour of Mu'āwiyah, on the condition that he should resume it on the death of the latter. Mu'āwiyah consented to this arrangement, although secretly determining that his own son Yazīd should be his successor.

Upon the death of Mu'āwiyah, A.H. 60, his son Yazīd, "the Polluted," obtained the position of Imām or Khalīfah, without the form of election, and with this event commenced the great Shī'ah schism, which has divided the forces of Islām until this day.

The leading, or "orthodox" sect of the Shī'ahs, the *Imāmīyahs*, receive the following as the rightful Khalīfahs:—

1. 'Alī, the son-in-law of the Prophet.
2. Al-Ḥasan, the son of 'Alī.
3. Al-Ḥusain, the second son of 'Alī.
4. 'Alī, surnamed Zainu 'l-'Abidīn, the son of al-Ḥusain.
5. Muḥammad al-Bāqir, son of Zainu 'l-'Abidīn.
6. Ja'far aṣ-Ṣādiq, son of Muḥammad al-Bāqir.

7. Mūsā al-Kāẓim, son of Jā'far
8. Ar-Raẓā, son of Mūsā.
9. Muḥammad at-Taqī, son of ar-Raẓā.
10. 'Alī an-Naqī, son of Muḥammad at-Taqī.
11. Al-Ḥasan al-'Askarī, son of 'Alī an-Naqī.
12. Muḥammad, son of al-Ḥasan al-Askarī, or the *Imām al-Mahdī*, who is supposed by the Shī'ahs to be still alive, though he has withdrawn for a time, and they say he will again appear in the last days as the *Mahdī*, or "Director," which the Prophet prophesied would appear before the Day of Judgment. [MAHDI.]

The Imamites trace the descent of this Imām Muḥammad as direct from 'Alī, thus making him the twelfth lawful Imām, on which account they are called the *Isnā-'asharīyah*, or the "Twelveans." They assert that this last Imām, whilst still a boy, being persecuted by the Abbaside Khalīfahs, disappeared down a well in the courtyard of a house at Hillah near Baghdād, and Ibn Khaldun says, so late as even in his day, devout Shī'ahs would assemble every evening after sunset at this well and entreat the absent Imām to appear again on earth.

In the present day, during the absence of the Imām, the Shī'ahs appeal to the *Mujtahidūn*, or "enlightened doctors of the law," whose opinion is final on all matters, both temporal and spiritual.

There have been two great schisms in the succession of the Imāms, the first upon the death of 'Alī Zainu 'l-'Abidīn, when part of the sect adhered to his son Zaid, the founder of the Zaidīyah sect. And the second on the death of aṣ-Ṣādiq, when his father nominated his second son, Musā al-Kāẓim, as his successor, instead of allowing the Khalifate to go in Ismā'īl's family; those who adhered to Ismā'īl's family being called *Ismā'īlīyah.* The great body of the Shī'ahs acknowledge Musā al-Kāẓim and his descendants as the true Imāms.

The Ismā'īlīyah, like the Twelveans, make profession of a loyal attachment to the cause of 'Alī. Their schism was occasioned by a dispute regarding the succession to the Imāmate on the death of Imām Ja'far Ṣādiq. Jafar had four sons, the eldest of whom was Ismā'īl. One day, however, Ismā'īl was seen in a state of inebriety, and his father disinherited him, and appointed his son Mūsā. The greater number of the Shī'ahs accepted this decision, but a small number, who regarded the drunkenness of the Imām as an evidence that he accepted the *hidden* meaning and not the legal precepts of Islām (!), remained attached to Ismā'īl. They say from the time of 'Alī to the death of Muḥammad, the son of Ismā'īl, the Imāms were visible, but from his death commenced the succession of concealed Imāms. The fourth of these "concealed" Imāms was a certain 'Abdu 'llāh, who lived about the third century of the Hijrah.

The contentions of the Shī'ahs regarding the succession have become endless, and of the proverbial seventy-three sects of Islām, not fewer than thirty-two are assigned to the Shī'ahs, and, according to the *Sharḥu 'l-Muwāqif*, there are as many as seventy-three sects of the Shī'ahs alone.

According to the *Sharḥu 'l-Muwāqif*, the three principal sects of the Shī'as are (1) *Ghulāt*, or Zealots, the title generally given to those who, through their excessive zeal for the Imāms, have raised them above the degree of human beings. (2) *Zaidīyah*, those who separated after the appointment of Muḥammad Bāqir to the Khalīfate, and followed Zaid. (3) *Imāmīyah*, or those who acknowledged Ja'far Ṣādiq as the rightful Imām, to the exclusion of Isma'īl, and which appears to be what may be called the *orthodox* sect of the Shī'as. Out of these three great divisions have grown innumerable sects, which it would be tedious to define. All Shī'ah religionists are more or less infected with mysticism.

Many of the Shī'ahs have carried their veneration for 'Alī so far, as to raise him to the position of a divine person, and most of the sects make their Imāms partakers of the divine nature. These views have their foundation in the traditions already quoted, which assert the pre-existence of Muḥammad and 'Alī, and they have undoubtedly been fostered by the gnostic tendencies of all forms of persian belief, especially Ṣufiism. [SUFI.]

Since the accession of Ismā'īl, the first of the Ṣūfī dynasty, A.D. 1499, the Shī'ah faith has been the national religion of Persia. Nādir Shah, when at the summit of his power, attempted to convert the Persians to the Sunnī form of Islām, in order to assist his ambitious designs, but the attempt failed, and the attachment of the Persians to the Shī'ah faith has remained as decided as ever.

Sir Lewis Pelly remarks :—

"Though the personal history of Ali and his sons was the exciting cause of the Shiah schism, its predisposing cause lies far deeper in the impassable ethnological gulf which separates the Aryan and Semitic races. Owing to their strongly centralised form of government, the empire of the Sassanides succumbed at once before the onslaught of the Saracens; still, Persia was never really converted to Islam, and when Mohammed, the son of Ali, the son of Abdullah, the son of Abbas, the uncle of the Prophet Mohammed, proclaimed the Imamate as inherent of divine right, in the descendants of the Caliph Ali, the vanquished Persians rose as one man against their Arab conquerors. The sons of Abbas had all espoused the cause of their cousin Ali against Moawiyah, and when Yezid succeeded to the Caliphate, Abdullah refused to acknowledge him, and retired to Mecca. It was he who tried to dissuade Husain from going to Cufa. His son was Ali, who, by order of the Caliph Walid, was flogged and paraded through the streets of Damascus, mounted on a camel, with his face to its tail, and it was to avenge this insult on his father that Mohammed resolved to overthrow the dynasty of the Ommiades

"The Persians, in their hatred of the

Arabs, had from the first accepted the rights of the sons of Ali and Fatimah to the Imamate; and Mohammed cunningly represented to them that the Imamate had been transmitted to him by Abou Hashim, the son of Mohammed, another son of the Caliph Ali, whose mother was a daughter of the tribe of Hanifah. This was a gross fraud on the descendants of Fatimah, but the Persians cared not so long as they threw off the Arab yoke." (*Miracle Play*, Intro., p. xvi.; W. H. Allen & Co., 1879.)

The Muḥammadans of the province of Oudh in British India are for the most part Shī'ahs, and there are a few in the region of Tīrah, on the frontier of India With the exception of the province of Oudh, the Muḥammadans of India are for the most part Sunnīs of the Ḥanafī sect, but practices peculiar to the Shī'ahs have long prevailed in certain localities. In most parts of India, where the parties are Shī'ahs, the law of this school of jurisprudence is always administered, especially with regard to marriage and inheritance.

It is not correct, as stated by Sale (Introduction to the Koran) and others, that the Shī'ahs reject the *Sunnah*, or Traditions; for although the Shī'ahs do not receive the "six correct books of the Sunnīs," they acknowledge five collections of their own, namely: (1), Al-Kāfī, (2) Manlayastahzirahu 'l-Faqīh, (3) Tahẕīb, (4) Istibṣār, (5) Nahju 'l-Balāg͟hah. [TRADITIONS.] The works written on the traditions are very numerous.

The Rev. James L. Merrick (Boston, 1850) has translated into English portions of the *Ḥayātu 'l-Qulūb*, the most popular book of traditions amongst the Shī'ahs. It was originally compiled by Muḥammad Bāqir, son of Muḥammad Tākī, whose last work was the well-known *Ḥaqqu 'l-Yaqīn*, A.H. 1027 (A.D. 1627).

The Shī'ah school of jurisprudence is of earlier date than that of the Sunnīs, for Abū Ḥanīfah, the father of the Sunnī Code of Muslim law, received his first instructions in jurisprudence from Ja'far aṣ-Ṣādiq, the sixth Imām of the Shī'ahs; but this learned doctor afterwards separated from his teacher, and established a code of laws of his own.

The differences between the Shī'ahs and the Sunnīs are very numerous, but the following are the principal points:—

(1) The discussion as to the office of Imām, already alluded to.

(2) The Shī'ahs have a profound veneration for the K͟halīfah 'Alī, and some of their sects regard him as an incarnation of divinity, whilst they all assert that next to the Prophet, 'Alī is the most perfect and excellent of men.

(3) They still possess *Mujtahids*, or "enlightened doctors," whose opinion is final in matters of Muslim law and doctrine. The Mujtahid is the highest degree amongst Muḥammadan doctors. The Sunnīs say, in the present divided condition of Islām it is impossible to appoint them, but the Shī'ahs still elect them in Persia, and the appointment is confirmed by the king. [MUJTAHID.]

(4) They observe the ceremonies of the Muḥarram in commemoration of al-Ḥasan and al-Ḥusain, whilst the Sunnīs only observe the tenth day of the Muḥarram, or the *'Ashūrā'*, being, they say, the day on which God created Adam. [MUHARRAM.]

(5) They include the *Majūsī*, or fire worshippers, amongst the *Ahlu 'l-Kitāb*, or people who have received an inspired record from God, whilst the Sunnīs only acknowledge the Jews, Christians, and Muslims as such.

(6) They admit the principle of religious compromise called *Taqīyah* (*lit.* "Guarding oneself"). A pious fraud, whereby the Shī'ah Muḥammadan believes he is justified in either smoothing down, or denying, the peculiarities of his religious belief in order to save himself from persecution. [TAQIYAH.]

(7) There are also various minor differences in the liturgical ceremonies of the Shī'ahs, which will be found in the account of the liturgical prayers. [PRAYER.]

(8) The differences between the civil law of the Shī'ahs and Sunnī have been carefully noted in Mr. N. B. E. Baillie's Introduction to his *Digest of the Imameea Code* (London, 1869):—

(*a*) "With regard to the sexes, any connection between them, which is not sanctioned by some relation founded upon contract or upon slavery, is denounced by both the sects as *zinā'*, or fornication. But, according to the Ḥanafīyahs, the contract must be for the lives of the parties, or the woman be the slave of the man, and it is only to a relation founded on a contract for life that they give the name of *nikāḥ*, or marriage. According to the Shī'ahs, the contract may be either temporary, or for life, and it is not necessary that the slave should be the actual property of the man; for it is sufficient if the usufruct of her person be temporarily surrendered to him by her owner. To a relation established in any of these ways they give the name of *nikāḥ*, or marriage, which is thus, according to them, of three kinds, permanent, temporary, and servile. It is only their permanent marriage that admits of any comparison with the marriage of the Ḥanafīyahs. And here there is, in the first place, some difference in the words by which the contract is effected. According to the Ḥanafīyahs, the words may be *ṣarīḥ* (express) or *kināyah* (ambiguous). According to the Shī'ahs, they must always be express; and to the two express terms of the other sect (*nikāḥ* and *tazwīj*) they add a third *mut'ah*, which is rejected by the others as insufficient. [MUT'AH.] Further, while the Ḥanafīyahs regard the presence of witnesses as essential to a valid contract of marriage, the Shī'ahs do not deem it to be in anywise necessary. The causes of prohibition correspond, to some extent, in both schools; but there is this difference between them, that the Ḥanafīyah includes a difference of *dār*, or nationality, among the causes of prohibition, and excludes *li'ān*, or imprecation, from among them; while the Shī'ah excludes the former and includes the latter. There is, also, some difference between them as to the conditions and restrictions under which fosterage becomes a ground of prohibition. And with regard to infidelity, though both schools entirely prohibit any sexual intercourse between a Muslimah or Musalman woman and a man who is not of her own religion, the Ḥanafī allows of such intercourse, under the sanction of marriage or of slavery, between a Muslim and any woman who is a *kitābiyah*, that is, who belongs to any sect that is supposed to have a revealed religion, while the Shī'ah restricts such connection to *mut'ah*, or temporary and servile marriages. Among Kitābīyah both schools include Christians and Jews, but the Ḥanafī rejects Majūsīs, or fire-worshippers, who are included among them by the Shī'ahs. The Shī'ahs do not appear to make any distinction between invalid and valid marriages, all that are forbidden being apparently void according to them. But the distinction is of little importance to the parties themselves, as under neither of the schools does an unlawful marriage confer any inheritable quality upon the parties; and the rights of the children born of such marriages are determined by another consideration, which will be adverted to in the proper place hereafter.

"(*b*) With regard to the servile marriage of the Shī'ahs, it is nothing more than the right of sexual intercourse which every master has with his slaves; but there is the same difference between the two sects, in this case, as in that of marriage by contract. According to the Ḥanafīyahs, the right must be permanent, by the woman's being the actual property of the man. According to the Shī'ahs, the right may be temporary, as when it is conceded for a limited time by the owner of the slave. When a slave has borne a child to her own master, which he acknowledges, she becomes his *umm-ul-walad*, or mother of a child, and cannot be sold, while she is entitled to emancipation at her master's death. According to the Ḥanafīyahs, these privileges are permanent, but, according to the Shī'ahs, the exemption from sale is restricted to the life of her child, and her title to emancipation is at the expense of her child's share in the master's estate. If that be insufficient, her enfranchisement is only *pro tanto*, or so far as the share will go. Where the child's father has only an usufructuary right in the mother, the child is free, though the mother, being the property of another, does not acquire the rights of an *umm-ul-walad*.

"(*c*) With regard to the persons who may be legally slaves, there seems to be little, if any, difference between the two sects. According to the Shī'ahs, slavery is the proper condition of the *ḥarabīs*, or enemies, with the exception only of Christians, Jews, and Majūsīs, or fire-worshippers, so long as they continue in a state of *ẓimmah*, or subjection, to the Mussulman community. If they renounce their *ẓimmah*, they fall back into the condition of ordinary *ḥarabīs*, and if a person should buy from a *ḥarabī* his child, or wife, or any of his consanguineous relations, the person so purchased is to be adjudged a slave. There seems also to be but little difference in the manner in which slaves may be enfranchised, or their bondage qualified. But there is an important difference as to children; for, according to the Ḥanafīyahs, a child follows the conditions of its mother, being free or a slave, as she is the one or the other; while, according to the Shī'ahs, it is free, if either of its parents be so. Both the sects are agreed that marriage may be dissolved by the husband at any time at his pleasure, and to such dissolutions they both give the name of *ṭalāq*.

"(*d*) But there are some important differences between the repudiation of the two sects Thus, while the Ḥanafīyahs recognize two forms, the Sunnī and Bida'ī, or regular and irregular, as being equally efficacious, and subdivide the regular into two other forms, one of which they designate as *aḥsan*, or best, and the other as *ḥasan*, or good, the Shī'ahs reject these distinctions altogether, recognizing only one form of the Sunnī, or regular. So also as to the expressions by which repudiation may be constituted; while the Ḥanafīyahs distinguish between what they call *ṣarīḥ*, or express words, which are inflections of the word *ṭalāq*, and various expressions which they term *kināyah*, or ambiguous, the Shī'ahs admit the former only. Further, the Ḥanafīyahs do not require intention when express words are used; so that, though a man is actually compelled to use them, the repudiation is valid according to them. Nor do they require the presence of witnesses as necessary in any case to the validity of a repudiation; while, according to the Shī'ahs, both intention and the presence of two witnesses in all cases are essential Both sects agree that repudiation may be either *bā'in* (absolute) or *raja'ī* (revocable), and that a repudiation given three times cannot be revoked, nor a woman so repudiated be again married by her husband until she has been intermediately married to another man, and the marriage with him has been consummated. But, according to the Ḥanafīyahs, repudiation may be made irrevocable by an aggravation of the terms, or the addition of a description, and three repudiations may be given in immediate succession, or even *unico contextu*, in one expression; while, according to the Shī'ahs, on the other hand, the irrevocability of a repudiation is dependent on the state in which the woman may be at the time that it is given, and three repudiations, to have their full effect, must have two intervening revocations. To the *bā'in* and *raja'ī* repudiations of both sects, the Shī'ahs add one peculiar to themselves, to which they give the name of the *ṭalāq-u'l-'iddah*, or repudiation of the *'iddah*, and which has the effect of rendering the repudiated woman for ever unlawful to her husband, so that it is impossible for them ever to marry with each other again The power of revocation continues until the expiration of the *ʻiddah*, or probationary period for ascertaining whether a woman is pregnant or not. After it has expired, the repudiation becomes absolute, according to both schools. So long as it is revocable, the parties are still in a manner husband and wife; and if either of them should happen to die, the other has a right of inheritance in the deceased's estate.

"(*e*) With regard to parentage, maternity is established, according to the Ḥanafīyahs, by birth alone, without any regard to the connection of the parents being lawful or not. According to the Shīʻahs, it must in all cases be lawful; for a *waladu 'z-zinā*, or illegitimate child, has no descent, even from its mother, nor are there any mutual rights of inheritance between them. For the establishment of paternity there must have been, at the time of the child's conception, according to both sects, a legal connection between its parents by marriage or slavery, or a semblance of either. According to the Ḥanafīyahs, an invalid marriage is sufficient for that purpose, or even, according to the head of the school, one that is positively unlawful; but, according to the Shīʻahs, the marriage must in all cases be lawful, except when there is error on the part of both or either of the parents. Again, as to the children by slaves, express acknowledgment by the father is required by both the sects, except when the slave is his *ummu 'l-walad*, or has already borne a child to him; for though, according to the Shīʻahs, there are two reports on the subject, yet, by the most generally received of these, a slave does not become the wife of her master by mere coition, and her child is not affiliated to him without his acknowledgment. With regard to children begotten under a semblance of right, the Ḥanafīyahs require some basis for the semblance in the relation of the parties to each other; while, according to the Shīʻahs, *bonâ fide* belief on the part of the man that the woman is his wife or his slave seems to be all that is required; while no relation short of a legal marriage or slavery, without such belief either on the part of the man or the woman, would apparently be sufficient.

"(*f*) On the subject of testimony, both schools require that it shall be direct to the point in issue; and they also seem to be agreed that when two or more witnesses concur in asserting a fact in the same terms, the judge is bound by their testimony, and must give his judgment in conformity with it. They agree in requiring that a witness should in general have full knowledge, by the cognizance of his own senses, of the fact to which he is bearing testimony; but both allow him, in certain exceptional cases, to testify on information received from others, or when he is convinced of the fact by inference from circumstances with which it is connected.

"(*g*) *Nasab*, or descent, is included by both sects among the exceptional facts to which a witness is allowed to testify when they are generally notorious, or when he is credibly informed of them by others But according to the Ḥanafīyahs, it is enough if the information be received from two just men, or one just man and two just women; while the Shīʻahs require that it should have been received from a considerable number of persons in succession, without any suspicion of their having got up the story in concert. The Ḥanafīyahs class marriage among the exceptional facts, together with *Nasab;* but, according to the Shīʻahs, it more properly follows the general rule, which requires that the witness should have the direct evidence of his own senses to the fact to which he is giving his testimony. They seem, however, to admit an exception in its favour; for they reason that as we adjudge K͟hadījah to have been the mother of Fāt̤imah, the daughter of the Prophet, though we know it only by general notoriety and tradition, which is but continued hearsay, so also we may equally decide her to have been the Prophet's wife, for which we have the same evidence, though we were not present at the contract of marriage, nor even heard the Prophet acknowledge it. Both sects are agreed that a witness may lawfully infer and testify that a thing is the property of a particular person when he has seen it in his possession; and so, according to the Ḥanafīyahs, 'When a person has seen a man and woman dwelling in the same house, and behaving familiarly with each other in the manner of married persons, it is lawful for him to testify that she is his wife, in the same way as when he has seen a specific thing in the hands of another.' The Shīʻahs do not apply this principle of inference to the case of marriage, and there is no ground for saying that, according to them, marriage will be presumed in a case of proved continual cohabitation.

"(*h*) There is difference between the two schools as to the person who is entitled to claim a right of *shufʻah*, or pre-emption. According to the Ḥanafīyahs, the right may be claimed, firstly, by a partner in the thing itself; secondly, by a partner in its rights of water and way; and thirdly, by a neighbour. According to the Shīʻahs, the right belongs only to the first of these, with some slight exception in favour of the second. The claim of the third they reject altogether. In gift the principal difference between the schools is, that a gift of an undivided share of a thing, which is rejected by the Ḥanafīyah, is quite lawful according to the Shīʻahs.

"(*i*) In appropriation and alms there do not seem to be any differences of importance between the two schools. And in wills the leading difference seems to be that, while, according to the Ḥanafīyahs, a bequest in favour of an heir is positively illegal, it is quite unobjectionable according to the Shīʻahs

"(*j*) In respect of inheritance, there are many and important differences between the two sects, but they admit of being reduced to a few leading principles, which I now proceed to notice, following the order in which the different branches of the subject are treated of in this volume. The impediments to inheritance are four in number, according to the Ḥanafīyahs, viz. slavery, homicide, difference of religion, and difference of *dār*, or country. Of these the Shīʿahs recognize the first; the second also with some modification, that is, they require that the homicide be intentional, in other words, murder, while with the Ḥanafīyahs it operates equally as an impediment to inheritance, though accidental. For difference of religion the Shīʿahs substitute infidelity, and difference of country they reject entirely. Exclusion from the whole inheritance, according to the Ḥanafīyahs, is founded upon and regulated by two principles. The one is that a person who is related to the deceased through another has no interest in the succession during the life of that other, with the exception of half-brothers and sisters by the mother, who are not excluded by her. The other principle is, that the nearer relative excludes the more remote. The former of these principles is not expressly mentioned by the Shīʿahs, but it is included without the exception in the second, which is adopted by them, and extended, so as to postpone a more remote residuary to a nearer sharer—an effect which is not given to it by the Ḥanafīyahs.

"With regard to partial exclusion or the diminution of a share, there is also some difference between the sects. According to the Ḥanafīyahs, a child, or the child of a son, how low soever, reduces the shares of a husband, a wife, and a mother, from the highest to the lowest appointed for them; while, according to the Shīaʿhs, the reduction is effected by any child, whether male or female, in any stage of descent from the deceased. Further, when the deceased has left a husband or wife, and both parents, the share of the mother is reduced, according to the Ḥanafīyahs, from a third of the whole estate to a third of the remainder, in order that the male may have double the share of the female; but, according to the Shīʿahs, there is no reduction of the mother's third in these circumstances, though, when the deceased has left a husband, the share of the father can only be a sixth. The shares and the person for whom they are appointed being expressly mentioned in the Qur'ān, there is no difference in respect of them between the two schools. But they differ materially as to the relatives who are not sharers. They are divided by the Ḥanafīyahs into residuaries and distant kindred. The residuaries in their own right they define as every male in whose line of relation to the deceased no female enters; 'and the distant kindred,' as 'all relatives who are neither sharers nor residuaries.' The residuaries not only take any surplus that may remain after the sharers have been satisfied, but also the whole estate when there is no sharer, to the entire exclusion of the distant kindred, though these may, in fact, be much nearer in blood to the deceased. This preference of the residuary is rejected with peculiar abhorrence by the Shīʿahs, who found their objection to it, certainly with some appearance of reason, on two passages of the Qur'ān cited below. Instead of the triple division of the Ḥanafīyahs, they mix up the rights of all the relatives together, and then separate them into three classes, according to their proximity to the deceased, each of which in its order is preferred to that which follows; so that while there is a single individual, even a female, of a prior class, there is no room for the succession of any of the others.

"Within the classes operation is given to the doctrine of the return by the Shīʿahs, nearly in the same way as by the Ḥanafīyahs: that is, if there is a surplus over the shares, it reverts to the sharers, with the exception of the husband or wife, and is proportionately divided among them. According to the Ḥanafīyahs, this surplus is always intercepted by the residuary, and it is only when there is no residuary that there is with them any room for the doctrine of the return. When the shares exceed the whole estate, the deficiency is distributed by the Ḥanafīyahs over all the shares by raising the extractor of the case—a process which is termed the *ʿaul*, or increase. This is also rejected by the Shīʿahs, who make the deficiency to fall exclusively upon those among them whose relationship to the deceased is on the father's side. With regard to the computation of shares, there does not appear to be any difference between the schools." *A Digest of Moohummudan Law. Imameea Code.* N. B. E. Baillie, London (1869).

Mr. Wilfrid S. Blunt, in his *Future of Islam*, has the following remarks on the present position of the Shīʿah sect:—

"In theory, I believe the Shias still hold that there is an Imam aud Caliph, but they will not tolerate the pretension of any one now in authority to the title, and leave it in abeyance until the advent of the Mohady (*Mahdī*), or guide, who is to reunite Islam and restore its fortunes. So much is this the case that, sovereign though he be and absolute master in Persia, the Shah is to the present day looked upon by the Persians as a usurper, and he himself acknowledges the fact in a rather curious ceremony. It is a maxim with Mussulmans of all sects that prayer is not valid if made in another man's house without his permission, and this being so, and the Shah admitting that his palaces of right belong not to himself but to the Mohady, he is obliged to lease them according to legal form from an alem (*ʿālim*) or mujtahed, acting for the supposed Mohady, before he can pray in them to his spiritual profit.

"It will be readily understood that, with such an organization and with such tendencies to deductive reasoning, a wide basis is given for divergence of opinion among the Shiites, and that while the more highly educated of their mollahs occasionally preach absolute pantheism, others consult the grosser inclinations of the vulgar, and indulge their hearers with the most extravagant tales of miracle and superstition. These are a constant source of mockery to the Sunites. Among the more respectable Shiite beliefs, however, there seems to be a general conviction in Persia that a reform of Islam is at hand, and that a new leader may be expected at any moment and from any quarter, so that enthusiasts are constantly found simulating the gifts of inspiration and affecting a divine mission. The history of the Babites, so well described by M. de Gobineau in his *Religions of Asia*, is a case in point, and similar occurrences are by no means rare in Persia. I met at Jeddah a highly educated Persian gentleman, who informed me that he had himself been witness, when a boy, to a religious prodigy, notorious, if I remember rightly, at Tabriz. On that occasion, one of these prophets, being condemned to death by the supreme government, was bound to a cross with two of his companions, and, after remaining suspended thus for several hours, was fired at by the royal troops. It then happened that, while the companions were dispatched at the first volley, the prophet himself remained unhurt, and, incredible to relate, the cords which bound him were cut by the bullets, and he fell to the ground on his feet. 'You Christians,' said another Persian gentleman once to me, 'talk of your Christ as the Son of God and think it strange, but with us the occurrence is a common one. Believe me, we have "sons of God" in nearly all our villages.' [SUFI.]

"Thus, with the Shiites, extremes meet. No Moslems more readily adapt themselves to the superficial atheisms of Europe than do the Persians, and none are more ardently devout, as all who have witnessed the miracle play of the two Imams will be obliged to admit. Extremes, too, of morality are seen, fierce asceticisms and gross licentiousnesses. By no sect of Islam is the duty of pilgrimage more religiously observed, or the prayers and ablutions required by their rule performed with a stricter ritual. But the very pilgrims who go on foot to Mecca scruple not to drink wine there, and Persian morality is everywhere a by-word. In all these circumstances there is much to fear as well as to hope on the side of the Shiite sect; but their future only indirectly involves that of Islam proper. Their whole census does not probably exceed fifteen millions, and it shows no tendency to increase. Outside Persia we find about one million Irâki Arabs, a few in Syria and Afghanistan, and at most five millions in India. One small group still maintains itself in the neighbourhood of Medina, where it is tolerated rather than acknowledged, and a few Shiites are to be found in most of the large cities of the west, but everywhere the sect of Ali stands apart from and almost in a hostile attitude to the rest of Islam. It is noticeable, however, that within the last fifty years the religious bitterness of Shiite and Sunite is sensibly in decline."

For information on the History of the Shīʿahs, the English reader can refer to Malcolm's *History of Persia*, 2 vols. (A.D. 1815); Morier's *Travels*, 2 vols. (A.D. 1812); Markham's *History of Persia* (A.D. 1874). A translation of their traditions is found in the *Life and Religion of Mohammad*, by the Rev. James L. Merrick. Boston (1850). For Shīʿah Law, consult *Tagore Lectures*, 1874; *A Digest of Moohummudan Law. The Imameea Code.* N. B. E. Baillie (1869). [MUHARRAM.]

SHIRB (شرب).
The share of water used for tillage. [RIVER.]

SHIRK (شرك).
"Idolatry; paganism; polytheism." Ascribing plurality to the Deity. Associating anything with God.

According to Wahhābī writers, *Shirk* is defined to be of four kinds: *Shirku 'l-ʿilm*, ascribing knowledge to others than God; *Shirku 't-taṣarruf*, ascribing power to others than God; *Shirku 'l-ʿibādah*, offering worship to created things; *Shirku 'l-ʿādah*, the performance of ceremonies which imply reliance on others than God.

(1) *Shirku 'l-ʿilm* is illustrated by the statement that prophets and holy men have no knowledge of secret things unless as revealed to them by God. Thus some wicked persons made a charge against ʿĀyishah. The Prophet was troubled in mind, but knew not the truth of the matter till God made it known to him. To ascribe, then, power to soothsayers, astrologers, and saints is Polytheism. "All who pretend to have a knowledge of hidden things, such as fortune-tellers, soothsayers, and interpreters of dreams, as well as those who profess to be inspired, are all liars." Again, "should anyone take the name of any saint, or invoke his aid in the time of need, instead of calling on God, or use his name in attacking an enemy, or read passages to propitiate him, or make him the object of contemplation—it is *Shirku 'l-ʿilm*."

(2) *Shirku 't-taṣarruf* is to suppose that anyone has power with God. He who looks up to anyone as an intercessor with God commits *Shirk*. Thus: "But they who take others beside Him as lords, saying, 'We only serve them that they may bring us near God,' —God will judge between them (and the Faithful) concerning that wherein they are at variance." (Sūrah xxxix. 4.) Intercession may be of three kinds. For example, a criminal is placed before the King. The Vizier intercedes. The King, having regard to the rank of the Vizier, pardons the offender. This is called *Shafāʿat-i-Wajāhah*, or "intercession from regard." But to suppose that God so esteems the rank of anyone as to pardon a sinner merely on account of it is *Shirk*. Again, the Queen or the Princes intercede for the criminal. The King, from love to them, pardons him. This is called *Shafāʿat-i-maḥabbah*, or "intercession from affection." But to consider that God so loves anyone as to pardon a criminal on his account is to give that loved one power, and this is *Shirk*, for such power is not possible in the Court of God. "God may out of His bounty confer on His favourite servants the

epithets of *Ḥabīb*, 'favourite,' or *Ḵhalīl*, 'friend,' &c.; but a servant is but a servant, no one can put his foot outside the limits of servitude, or rise beyond the rank of a servant." Again, the King may himself wish to pardon the offender, but he fears lest the majesty of the law should be lowered. The Vizier perceives the King's wish, and intercedes. This intercession is lawful. It is called *Shafā'at-i-ba-'iẕn*, "intercession by permission," and such power Muḥammad will have at the Day of Judgment. Wahhābīs hold that he has not that power now, though all other Musalmāns consider that he has, and in consequence (in Wahhābī opinion) commit the sin of *Shirku 't-taṣarruf*. The Wahhābīs quote the following passages in support of their view. "Who is he that can intercede with Him but by *His own permission*." (Sūrah ii. 256) "Say: Intercession is wholly with God! His the kingdoms of the heavens and of the earth." (Sūrah xxxix. 45.) They also say: "Whenever an allusion is made in the Qur'ān, or the Traditions to the intercession of certain prophets or apostles, it is this kind of intercession and no other that is meant."

(3) *Shirku 'l-'Ibādah* is prostration before any created being, with the idea of worshipping it; perambulating the shrines of departed saints. "Prostration, bowing down, standing with folded arms, spending money in the name of an individual, fasting out of respect to his memory, proceeding to a distant shrine in a pilgrim's garb and calling out the name of the saint." It is wrong "to cover the grave with a sheet, to say prayers at the shrine, to kiss any particular stone, to rub the mouth and breast against the walls of the shrine, &c." This is a stern condemnation of the very common practice of visiting the tombs of saints and of some of the special practices of the pilgrimage to Makkah. All such practices as are here condemned are called *Ishrāk fī 'l-'Ibādah*, "association in worship."

(4) *Shirku 'l-'ādah* is the keeping up of superstitious customs, such as the *Istiḵhārah*, seeking guidance from beads, &c., trusting to omens, good or bad, believing in lucky and unlucky days, adopting such names as 'Abdu 'n-Nabī (Slave of the Prophet), and so on. In fact, the denouncing of such practices and calling them *Shirk* brings Wahhābīism into daily contact with the other sects, for scarcely any people in the world are such profound believers in the virtue of charms and the power of astrologers as Musalmāns. The difference between the first and fourth *Shirk*, the *Shirku 'l-'ilm* and the *Shirku 'l-'ādah*, seems to be that the first is the *belief*, say in the knowledge of a soothsayer, and the second the *habit* of consulting him.

To swear by the name of the Prophet, of 'Alī, of the Imāms, or of Pīrs (Leaders) is to give them the honour due to God alone. It is *Ishrāk fi 'l-adab*, "Shirk in association." [WAHHABI.]

SHIRKAH (شركة). "Partnership." The term signifies the union of two or more persons in one concern. It is applied in Muslim law to contracts as well as to partnerships *Shirkah*, or association, with regard to the essence and person of God, is forbidden in Islām.

SHIS̤ (شيث). [SETH.]

SHOES. The removal of the sandals, shoes, or boots, from the feet upon entering either a mosque or house, or during worship, is not enjoined in Muḥammadan law, although it has become a common custom in all Eastern countries, for the modern Muslim uncovers his feet upon entering the Ka'bah at Makkah (Burckhardt's *Arabia*, vol. i. p. 270), the Muḥammadans of Palestine remove the shoes upon entering their places of worship (Robinson's *Researches*, vol. ii. p 36) and it is also the practice to take off the shoes in Egypt (Lane, vol. i. pp. 16, 105; vol. ii. p. 11), and in Hindūstān.

THE SHOES OF THE FAITHFUL. (*A. F. Hole.*)

The number of traditions which prove that Muḥammad allowed his followers to worship with their feet covered, is very numerous, and they are held to be *Aḥādis̤* of good authority, and supported by the *fatwās* of eminent doctors of law.

Shaddād ibn Aus relates that the Prophet

said, "Act the reverse of the Jews in your prayers, for they do not pray in boots or shoes."

Abū Sa'īd al-Khudrī says "the Prophet said his prayers with the Companions, and suddenly took off his shoes, and put them down on his left side; and when the people observed it, they took off theirs also, and when prayers were finished, the Prophet asked why they took their shoes off. The Companions replied, 'We followed your example.' The Prophet then said, 'Verily Gabriel came to me and told me there was a little filth on my shoes. Therefore, when any of you enter a mosque, look well at your shoes, and if you perceive any dirt on them, wipe it off, and then say your prayer in them.'"

'Amr ibn Shu'aib relates that he saw the Prophet saying his prayers sometimes with his shoes and sometimes without. (*Mishkāt*, book iv. ch. 9.)

In the *Hidāyah* it is enjoined that when there is any uncleanness on the shoes, such as dung, blood, &c., they must be rubbed with earth, and then they become legally clean and fit for worship. (Arabic edition, vol. i. p. 26.)

This is confirmed by the *Durru 'l-Mukhtār* (vol. i. pp. 30, 65), and by numerous traditions. (*Mishkāt*, book iii. ch. ii.)

If the dirt cannot be removed from the shoes by rubbing them with earth, the law permits the Muslim to make them ceremonially clean by wetting his three fingers and drawing them once over the upper part of the shoes or boots. [MASAH.]

According to the Traditions, when a Muslim sits down on the floor, he should take off his shoes and place them on one side, and he should take off the right shoe first and then the left. (*Mishkāt*, book xx. ch. iii.)

SHROUD. Arabic *kafan* (كفن). The act of shrouding is called *takfīn*. A wooden coffin is called *tābūt*, the use of which is generally held to be forbidden by Sunnīs, but it is used by the Shī'ahs.

Muḥammad is related to have said:—

"Do not be expensive in your shrouds, for they soon rot."

"Plain white is the best for the shrouds of your dead."

"The best cloth for a shroud is *ḥullah*" (*i.e.* a white striped cloth used in Arabia).

'Āyishah says: "The Prophet was shrouded in three garments, but there was neither a coat nor a turban."

These three garments are still used as shrouds in all parts of Islām.

(1) *Izār*, a piece of cloth which covers from the waist to the feet.

(2) *Ridā'*, covering from the feet to the shoulders.

(3) *Lifāfah*, a large sheet covering the whole body from head to feet, and closed at the ends.

The bodies of martyrs are not shrouded, but are buried in the garments in which they fell, for it is related that Muḥammad so ordered the men who fell in the battle of Uḥud to be buried; their weapons being first removed from their bodies, they were buried in their blood-stained clothes. [BURIAL.]

SHU'AIB (شعيب). The Muslim commentators generally suppose Shu'aib to be the same person with the father-in-law of Moses, who is named in scripture Reuel or Rageul and Jethro But Aḥmad ibn 'Abdi 'l-Ḥalīm charges those who entertain this opinion with ignorance. They say (after the Jews) that he gave his son-in-law [MOSES] that wonder-working rod with which he performed all those miracles in Egypt and the desert, and also gave excellent advice and instruction; whence he had the surname of Khaṭību 'l-Ambiyā' (خطيب الانبياء), the "Preacher to the Prophets."

The account given of him in the Qur'ān, Sūrah vii. 83–91, is as follows:—

"And unto Midian did we send their brother Shu'aib, who said, 'O my people! serve God, ye have no god save Him. There has come to you a manifest sign from your Lord: then give good weight and measure, and be not niggardly of your gifts to men, and do not evil in the earth after it has been righted. That is better for you if ye are believers; and sit not down in every path, threatening and turning from the path of God those who believe in Him, and craving to make it crooked. Remember when ye were few and He multiplied you; and see what was the end of the evil-doers! And if there be a party of you who believe in what I am sent with, and a party who believe not, then wait patiently until God judges between us, for He is the best of judges! Said the crowd of those who were big with pride amongst his people, 'We will of a surety turn thee out, O Shu'aib, and those who believe with thee, from our village; or else thou shalt return unto our faith.' Said he, 'What even if we be averse therefrom? We shall have devised a lie against God if we return unto your faith after God has saved us from it; and what should ail us that we should return thereto, unless that God our Lord should please? Our Lord embraces everything in His knowledge; on God do we rely. O our Lord! open between us and between our people in truth, for Thou art the best of those who open. And the chiefs of those who disbelieved amongst his people said, 'If ye follow Shu'aib, verily, ye shall be the losers.' Then there took them the earthquake, and in the morning they lay in their dwellings prone. Those who called Shu'aib a liar, (were) as though they had not dwelt therein. Those who called Shu'aib a liar, they were the losers then! And he turned away from them and said, 'O my people! I preached to you the messages of my Lord, and I gave you good advice; how should I be vexed for a people who do misbelieve?'"

ASH-SHU'ARĀ (الشعراء). "The Poets." The title of the XXVIth Sūrah of the Qur'ān, so called because at the conclusion of the chapter the Arabian poets are severely censured. [POETS.]

SHUF'AH (شفعة). [PREEMPTION.]

ASH-SHŪRĀ (الشورى). "The Consultation." The title of the XLIInd Sūrah of the Qur'ān. Taken from the 36th verse, in which the believers are commended for taking consultation together.

SHURB (شرب). *Lit.* "Drinking." A term used for wine-drinking, which is forbidden by the Muslim law. [DRUNKENNESS.]

ṢIBG͟HAH (صبغة). *Lit.* "A dye." A word which occurs in the Qur'ān, Sūrah ii. 132: "The *dye* of God! And who is better than God at dyeing? And we are worshippers of Him"; which both Mr. Sale and Mr. Rodwell translate *baptism*, but which Professor Palmer says must be rendered "dye." According to al-Baiẓāwī, it stands in the text for the *Islām of God*, but refers to Christian baptism. [BAPTISM.]

ṢIDDĪQ (صديق). "One who speaks the truth." It occurs in the Qur'ān for Idrīs (generally identified with Enoch), who is described as a man of eminent truthfulness. Professor Palmer translates the word "confessor" (see Sūrah xix. 57.)

Aṣ-Ṣiddīq is a title said to have been given to the first K͟halīfah Abū Bakr by Muḥammad himself.

SIDRATU 'L-MUNTAHĀ (سدرة المنتهى). *Lit.* "The Lote-tree of the extremity." A tree in the seventh heaven, having its roots in the sixth. Its fruits were like water-pots, and its leaves like elephant's ears. (*Mishkāt*, book xxiv. ch. vii. pt. 1.)

It is mentioned twice in the Qur'an, Sūrah liii. 8–18:—

"Then came he (Gabriel or the angel) nearer and approached,
And was at the distance of two bows, or even closer,—
And he revealed to his servant what he revealed.
His heart falsified not what he saw.
What! will ye then dispute with him as to what he saw?
He had seen him also another time,
Near the Sidrah-tree, which marks the boundary.
Near which is the garden of repose.
When the Sidrah-tree was covered with what covered it,
His eye turned not aside, nor did it wander:
For he saw the greatest of the signs of his Lord."

The Sidrah-tree is the *Zizyphus jujuba* of Linnæus, the prickly plum, which is called *Ber* in India. A decoction of its leaves is used in India to wash the dead, on account of the sacredness of the tree.

ṢIFAH (صفة). pl. *Ṣifāt*. An attribute. Used for the attributes of God. The Qur'ān is also said to be a *Ṣifah* of the Almighty.

Ismu 's-Ṣifah, the name of an attribute, is a term applied to any of the ninety-nine names or attributes of God. [GOD.]

ṢIFĀTĪYAH (صفاتية). From *Ṣifāt*, "attributes." A school of thought rather than a sect of Islām, although it is given by Mr. Sale as one of the Muḥammadan sects. The orthodox Sunnī claims to be a *Ṣifātī*, or Attributist (as opposed to the Mu'tazilahs, who reject the idea of God's attributes being eternal), and maintains that the attributes of God are eternally inherent in His essence without separation or change; every attribute being conjoined with Him as life with knowledge, or knowledge with power. With regard to the verses of the Qur'ān which are held to be *Mutashābih*, and assign some resemblance between God and His creatures, the Ṣifātīyahs say the expressions "hands," "face," "sitting," &c., must simply be accepted as they stand, without any attempt at explanation. [MU'TAZILAH, WAHHABI.]

AS-ṢIḤĀḤU 'S-SITTAH (الصحاح الستة), also called *al-Kutubu 's-Sittah* (الكتب الستة). "The six correct (books)." The title given to the six most trustworthy collections of traditions received by Sunnī Muslims, namely, those by—

(1) Abū 'Abdi 'llāh Muḥammad ibn Ismā'īl *al-Buk͟hārī*, born A.H. 194; died A.H. 256.

(2) Abū 'l-Ḥusain *Muslim* ibn al-Ḥajjāj al-Qushairī, born A.H. 204, died A.H. 261.

(3) Abū 'Isā Muḥammad ibn 'Isā 'l-*Tirmiẕī*, born A.H. 209, died A.H. 279.

(4) *Abū Dā'ūd* Sulaimān ibn Ash'aṣ as-Sajastānī, born A.H. 202, died A.H. 275.

(5) Abū 'Abdi 'r-Raḥmān Aḥmad ibn Shu'aib an-Nasā'ī, born A.H. 215, died A.H. 303.

(6) Abū 'Abdi 'llāh Muḥammad ibn Yazīd, *ibn Mājah*, al-Qazwīnī, born A.H. 209, died A.H. 273.

The above are generally esteemed the six authentic collections, but some substitute for the *Sunan Ibn Mājah* the *Muwaṭṭa'* of Abū 'Abdi 'llāh *Mālik* ibn Anas ibn Mālik ibn Abī 'Āmir ibn 'Amr ibn al-Ḥāriṣ al-Aṣbaḥī al-Ḥimyarī, born A.H. 95, died A.H. 179.

(The above words in *italics* denote the popular title of the collection.)

Al-Buk͟hārī and *Muslim* are held in highest reputation, and are called *aṣ-Ṣaḥīḥān*, or "the two authentics."

The collection by Mālik, the founder of the second orthodox sect of the Sunnīs, is the most ancient collection of traditions, and is held in high reputation, but it is sometimes omitted from the list by the Ḥanafīs, because he is the founder of a certain school of jurisprudence. [TRADITIONS.]

SIJDAH. [SAJDAH.]

SIJILL (سجل). A register. The record of a court of justice. The decree of a judge. In the Qur'ān, the word occurs when it is used for the angel which has charge of the register of the fate of mankind, or, according to others, it may mean the roll itself.

Sūrah xxi. 104: "The day when we will roll up the heavens as *as-Sijill* rolls up his books; as We produced it at the first creation, will we bring it back again."

SIJJĪN (سجين). A deep pit in which is kept the register of the actions of the wicked, and hence this register itself. Qur'ān, Sūrah lxxxiii. 7, 8: "The book of the wicked is in Sijjīn, and what shall make thee know what Sijjīn is?—It is an inscribed book." (See also *Mishkāt*, book v. ch. iii. pt. 3.)

SIKANDAR (سكندر). The Persian for Alexander, by which is meant Alexander the Great. [ZU 'L-QARNAIN.]

SIKHISM (from the Panjābī word *sikh* or *sikhā* = Sanskrit *s'ishya*, "a disciple" or "pupil"). The religion of the Sikhs in the Panjāb. Founded by Nānak, who was born in the village of Talvandī (now known as Nankānā), on the banks of the river Rāvī, near Lahore, in A.D. 1469.

The history of the Sikh religion has not yet been subjected to the scrutiny necessary to warrant strong dogmatism as to the ultimate source, or sources, whence the system of Nānak and his followers took its rise. The literature and traditions of Sikhism present a strange intermingling of Hindū and Muḥammadan ideas; and this is so palpably apparent that even superficial inquirers have been led to conclude that Nānak purposely intended his creed to be a compromise between those two great religions. Dr. Trumpp, the able translator of the *Ādi Granth* (the sacred book of the Sikhs), who is the only author that has written with knowledge on the subject, is, however, distinctly of opinion that Sikhism has only an accidental relationship with Muḥammadanism. In the Introduction to his *Translation of the Ādi Granth* (p. ci.), he says:—

"It is a mistake, if Nānak is represented as having endeavoured to unite the Hindū and Muḥammadan ideas about God. Nānak remained a thorough Hindū, according to all his views; and if he had communionship with Musalmāns, and many of these even became his disciples, it was owing to the fact that Sūfism, which all these Muḥammadans were professing, was in reality nothing but a Pantheism, derived directly from Hindū sources, and only outwardly adapted to the forms of the Islām. Hindū and Muslim Pantheists could well unite together, as they entertained essentially the same ideas about the Supreme."

If the foregoing opinion accurately represents the real truth, then Sikhism hardly deserves mention in the present work; but it will soon be seen that the balance of evidence is heavily on the other side. A careful investigation of early Sikh traditions points strongly to the conclusion that the religion of Nānak was really intended as a compromise between Hindūism and Muhammadanism, if it may not even be spoken of as the religion of a Muḥammadan sect. The very little that seems to be known as to the views of the early Sikh teachers, coupled with the decided opinion put forth by Dr. Trumpp, has made it necessary to give here a longer article on Sikhism than its importance with respect to Islām would have otherwise warranted; because it was necessary to establish the relationship which actually existed between the two faiths. It will be seen that the information given in this article is chiefly taken from original Panjābī books, and from manuscripts in the India Office Library; and it is supported by the authority of the *Ādi Granth*, which is the sacred canon of the Sikhs.

The *Janam-Sākhīs*, or biographical sketches of Nānak and his associates, contain a profusion of curious traditions, which throw considerable light on the origin and development of the Sikh religion. From these old books we learn that, in early life, Nānak, although a Hindū by birth, came under Ṣūfī influence, and was strangely attracted by the saintly demeanour of the *faqīrs* who were thickly scattered over Northern India and swarmed in the Panjāb. Now, Ṣūfīism is not, as Dr. Trumpp supposes, due to Hindū pantheism; for it arose in the very earliest days of Muḥammadanism, and is almost certainly due to the influence of Persian Zoroastrianism on the rude faith of Arab Islāmism. Persia has ever been the stronghold of Ṣūfīistic doctrine; and the leading writers who have illustrated that form of Muḥammadanism have been the Persian poets Firdūsī, Niẕāmī, Sa'dī, Jalālu 'd-Dīn, Ḥāfiẕ, and Jāmī.

Ḥāfiẕ, the prince of Ṣūfī poets, boldly declares: "I am a disciple of the old Magian: be not angry with me, O Shaikh! For thou gavest me a promise; he hath brought me the reality." Although this stanza alludes directly to two persons known to Ḥāfiẕ, its almost obvious meaning is: "I, a Persian, adhere to the faith of my ancestors. Do not blame me, O Arab conqueror! that my faith is more sublime than thine." That Ḥāfiẕ meant his readers to take his words in a general sense, may be inferred from the stanza in which he says: "I am the servant of the old man of the tavern (*i.e.* the Magian); because his beneficence is lasting: on the other hand, the beneficence of the Shaikh and of the Saiyid at times is, and at times is not." Indeed, Ḥāfiẕ was fully conscious of the fact that Ṣūfīism was due to the influence of the faith of his ancestors; for, in another ode, he plainly says: "Make fresh again the essence of the creed of Zoroaster, now that the tulip has kindled the fire of Nimrod." And Niẕāmī, also, was aware that his ideas were perilously akin to heterodoxy; for, he says in his *Khusrū wa Shīrīn*: "See not in me the guide to the temple of the Fire-worshippers; see only the hidden meaning which cleaveth to the allegory." These citations, which could be indefinitely multiplied, sufficiently indicate the Zoroastrian origin of the refined spirituality of the Ṣūfīs. The sublimity of the Persian faith lay in its conception of the unity of

Eternal Spirit, and the intimate association of the Divine with all that is manifest. Arab Muḥammadans believe in the unity of a personal God; but mankind and the world were, to them, mere objects upon which the will of God was exercised. The Ṣūfīs approached nearer to the Christian sentiment embodied in the phrase, "Christ in us."

The Persian conquerors of Hindūstān carried with them the mysticism and spirituality of the Islāmo-Magian creed. It was through Persia that India received its flood of Muḥammadanism; and the mysticism and asceticism of the Persian form of Islām found congenial soil for development among the speculative ascetics of northern India. It is, therefore, only reasonable to suppose that any Hindū affected by Muḥammadanism would show some traces of Ṣūfī influence. As a fact we find that the doctrines preached by the Sikh Gurus were distinctly Ṣūfīistic; and, indeed, the early Gurus openly assumed the manners and dress of faqīrs, thus plainly announcing their connection with the Ṣūfīistic side of Muḥammadanism. In pictures they are represented with small rosaries in their hands, quite in Muḥammadan fashion, as though ready to perform *ẕikr*. Guru Arjun, who was fifth in succession from Nānak, was the first to lay aside the dress of a faqīr. The doctrines, however, still held their position; for we find the last Guru dying while making an open confession of Ṣūfīism. His words are: "The Smritis, the S'āstras, and the Vedas, all speak in various ways: I do not acknowledge one (of them). O possessor of happiness, bestow thy mercy (on me). I do not say, 'I,' I recognise all as 'Thee.'"—(*Sikhān de Rāj dī Vithiā*, p. 81.) Here we have not only the ideas, but the very language of Ṣūfīs, implying a pantheistic denial of all else than Deity. The same manner of expression is found in the *Adi Granth* itself, *e.g.* "Thou art I; I am thou. Of what kind is the difference?" (*Translation*, p. 130); and again, "In all the One dwells, the One is contained" (p. 41). Indeed, throughout the whole *Ādi Granth*, a favourite name for Deity is the "True One," that is, that which is truly one—the Absolute Unity. It is hardly possible to find a more complete correspondence of ideas than that furnished by the following sentences, one taken from the *Yūsuf wa Zulaikha* of Jāmī, the Persian Ṣūfī; and the others, from the *Jap-jī* and the *Ādi Granth*. Jāmī says:—

"Dismiss every vain fancy, and abandon every doubt;
Blend into one every spirit, and form, and place;
See One—know One—speak of One—
Desire One—chant of One—and seek One."

In the *Jap-ji*, a formula familiar to every Sikh household, we find:—

"The Guru is Īsar (Siva), the Guru is Gorakh (Vishnu), Brahmā, the Guru is the mother Pārbatī.
If I should know, would I not tell? The story cannot be told.
O Guru, let me know the One; that the One liberal patron of all living beings may not be forgotten by me."

In the *Adi Granth*, we read:—

"Thou recitest the One; thou placest the One in (thy) mind; thou recognizest the One.
The One (is) in eye, in word, in mouth; thou knowest the One in both places (*i.e.* worlds).
In sleeping, the One; in waking, the One; in the One thou art absorbed."
(*India Office MS.*, No. 2484, fol. 568.)

It is not only with respect to the idea of the unity of God that this identity of expression is discernible; for other technical terms of Ṣūfīism are, also, reproduced in Sikhism. Thus the Ṣūfī Farīdu 'd-Dīn Shakrganj calls Deity "the *light* of life," and Jalālu 'd-Dīn speaks of "*flashes* of His love," while Jāmī represents the "light" of the Lord of Angels as animating all parts of the universe; and Nizāmī exclaims, "Then fell a *light*, as of a lamp, into the garden (of my heart)," when he feels that a ray of the Divine has entered into his soul. It is not difficult to collect many such instances from the works of Persian Ṣūfīs. Turning to Sikhism, we find that the *Ādi Granth* is full of similar expressions. It is enough to cite the following exclamation of Nānak himself: "In all (is) light. He (is) light. From His light, there is light in all." (*India Office MS.*, No. 2484, fol. 35.) And in another place he says: "The Luminous One is the mingler of light (with himself)." (fol. 186.) On fol. 51 we find: "There death enters not; light is absorbed in the Luminous One."

Another favourite metaphor of Ṣūfīs for the Deity is "the Beloved"; for example, when Ḥāfiẓ says: "Be thankful that the Assembly is lighted up by the presence of the Beloved." This term is well recognized in Sikhism; thus in the *Ādi Granth*, "If thou call thyself the servant of the Beloved, do not speak despitefully (of Him). (*India Office MS.*, No. 2484, fol. 564.) "Love to the Beloved naturally puts joy into the heart. I long to meet the Lord (*Prabhu*); therefore why should I be slothful." (*India Office MS.*, 2484, fol. 177.) Also, "In my soul and body are excessive pangs of separation, how shall the Beloved come to my house and meet (with me)?" And again: "The Beloved has become my physician." (*India Office MS.*, No. 1728, fol. 87.) The words used in the Panjābī texts are *pirīā*, *prītam*, and *pirī*, "a lover," or "beloved one."

Another remarkable proof of Persian influence is found in the form of the *Ādi Granth* itself. It consists of a collection of short poems, in many of which all the verses composing the poem rhyme together, in singular conformity with the principle regulating the construction of the Persian *ghazal*. This resemblance is rendered more striking by the fact that the name of Nānak is worked into the composition of the last line of each of the poems. This last characteristic is too persistent to be considered the result of accident; and while it is altogether foreign to the practice of Hindū verse, it is in precise accord with the rule for the correct composition of the *ghazal*.

The foregoing facts seem conclusive as to the influence of Persian Ṣūfīism on the origin of the Sikh religion. Dr. Trumpp, when discussing the philosophy of the *Ādi Granth*, admits the intimate connection between Sikhism and Ṣūfīism in the following words :—

"We can distinguish in the Granth a grosser and a finer kind of Pantheism. . . . . In this finer shade of Pantheism, creation assumes the form of *emanation* from the Supreme (as in the system of the Ṣūfīs); the atomic matter is either likewise considered co-eternal with the Absolute and immanent in it, becoming moulded into various, distinct forms by the energizing vigour of the absolute *joti* (light); or, the reality of matter is more or less denied (as by the Ṣūfīs, who call it the عَدَم, τὸ μὴ ὄν) so that the Divine *joti* is the only real essence in all."—(Introduction to *Translation of the Ādi Granth*, pp. c. ci.)

Any doubt that may remain on the question seems to be set at rest by the express statement in the life of Guru Arjun, who was urged by his followers to reduce to writing the genuine utterances of Nānak, because" by reciting the numerous verses and speeches *uttered by other Ṣūfīs*, which have received the name of Bābā Nānak, pride and worldly wisdom are springing up in the hearts of men." (*Sikhān de Rāj dī Vithi̱ā*, p. 29.) And in the *Ādi Granth* itself, we find the following remarkable verses ascribed to Nānak :—

"A ball of intoxication, of delusion, is given by the Giver.
The intoxicated forget death, they enjoy themselves four days.
The True One is found *by the Ṣofīs*, who keep fast his Court."

(*Translation*, p. 23.)

Here we have not only a plain claim of kinship with the Ṣūfīs, but the incorporation of several of their favourite terms.

The traditions of Nānak preserved in the *Janam-Sākhī*, are full of evidences of his alliance with Muḥammadanism. He was a Hindū by birth, of the Vedī Khattrī caste; and was the son of the *patwārī*, or village-accountant, of the place now called Nankānā, in the neighbourhood of Lahore. In his very early days, he sought the society of faqīrs; and used both fair and unfair means of doing them service, more especially in the bestowal of alms. At fifteen years of age, he misappropriated the money which his father had given him for trade; and this induced his parents to send him to a relative at Sultānpur, in order that he might be weaned from his affection for faqīrs (*India Office MS. No. 1728*, fol. 29). His first act in his new home was to join the service of a Muḥammadan Nawāb, named Daulat Khān Loḍi; and, while serving him, he continued to give to faqīrs all his salary, except the bare maintenance he reserved for himself. While in the service of

this Muḥammadan, Nānak received the ecstatic exaltation which he felt to be Divine inspiration. It is stated in the tradition of his life, that Nānak went to the river to perform his ablutions, and that whilst so engaged, he was translated bodily to the gates of Paradise. "Then a goblet of *amrita* (the water of life) was given (to him) by command (of God). The command was : ' This *amrita* is the goblet of my name; drink thou it.' Then the Guru Nānak made salutation, and drank the goblet. The Lord (*Ṣāḥib*) had mercy (and said): ' Nānak, I am with thee; I have made thee happy, and whoever shall take thy name they all shall be rendered happy by me. Go thou, repeat my name, and cause other people to repeat it. Remain uncontaminated from the world. Continue (steadfast) in the name, in alms-giving, in ablutions, in service, and in the remembrance (of me). I have given to thee my own name : do thou this work.'" (fol. 33.) Here we have notions closely akin to those of the Ṣūfīs, who lay much stress on the repetition of the name of God, which they term ZIKR [*q.v.*], on religious ablutions [WAZŪ', *q.v.*], and on meditating on the unity of God [WAHDANIYAH, *q.v.*] No sooner had Nānak recovered from his trance than he uttered the key-note of his future system in the celebrated phrase, "There is no Hindū, and there is no Musalmān." (fol. 36.) The *Janam-Sākhī* then goes on to say that, "The people went to the Khān (his former employer) and said, ' Bābā Nānak is saying, There is no Hindū, there is no Musalmān.' The Khān replied, ' Do not regard his statement; he is a faqīr.' A Qāzī sitting near said: ' O Khān! it is surprising that he is saying there is no Hindū and no Musalmān.' The Khān then told an attendant to call Nānak; but the Guru Nānak said : ' What have I to do with thy Khān ?' Then the people said : ' This stupid is become mad.' . . . . Then the Bābā (Nānak) was silent. When he said anything, he repeated only this statement: ' There is no Hindū, there is no Musalmān.' The Qāzī then said : ' Khān, is it right that he should say, There is no Hindū, there is no Musalmān ?' Then the Khān said : ' Go, fetch him.' The attendant went, and said: ' Sir, the Khān is calling (you). The Khān says: For God's sake give me an interview [Panj. *aj barā Khudā̱ī de tāṉī*=Persian *az barā̱ī Khudā*]; I want to see thee.' The Guru Nānak arose and went, saying: ' Now the summons of my Lord (*Ṣāḥib*) is come, I will go.' He placed a staff upon his neck and went. The Khān said: ' Nānak, for God's sake take the staff from off thy neck, gird up thy waist; thou art a good faqīr.' Then Guru Nānak took the staff from off (his) neck, and girded up his loins. The Khān said : ' O Nānak, it is a misfortune to me that a steward such as thou shouldst become a faqīr.' Then the Khān seated the Guru Nānak near himself and said : ' Qāzī, if thou desirest to ask anything, ask now; otherwise this one will not again utter a word.' The Qāzī becoming friendly, smiled and said : ' Nānak, what dost thou mean by saying, There is no Hindū, there is no Musalmān ?' Nānak replied: . . . 'To be called a Musalmān is difficult; when one (becomes it) then he may be called a Musalmān. First of all, having made religion (*dīn*) sweet, he clears away Musalmān wealth. Having become firm (مُسلّم), religion (*dīn*) in this way brings to an end the revolution of dying and living.'—(*I. O. MS.*, 2484, fol. 84.) When Nānak had uttered this verse, the Qāẓī became amazed. The Khān said: 'O Qāẓī, is not the questioning of him a mistake?' The time of the afternoon prayer had come. All arose and went (to the mosque) to prayers, and the Bābā (Nānak) also went with them." Nānak then demonstrated his supernatural power by reading the thoughts of the Qāẓī. "Then the Qāẓī came and fell down at his feet, exclaiming, 'Wonderful, wonderful! on this one is the favour of God.' Then the Qāẓī believed; and Nānak uttered this stanza: 'A (real) Musalmān clears away self; (he possesses) sincerity, patience, purity of speech: (what is) erect he does not annoy: (what) lies (dead) he does not eat. O Nānak! that Musalmān goes to heaven (*bihisht*).' When the Bābā had uttered this stanza, the Saiyids, the sons of the Shaikhs, the Qāẓī, the Muftī, the Khān, the chiefs and leaders were amazed. The Khān said: 'Qāẓī, Nānak has reached the truth; the additional questioning is a mistake.' Wherever the Bābā looked, there all were saluting him. After the Bābā had recited a few stanzas, the Khān came and fell down at his feet. Then the people, Hindūs and Musalmāns, began to say to the Khān that God (*Khudā*) was speaking in Nānak." (*India Office MS.* 1728, fol. 36–41.)

The foregoing anecdotes are taken from the India Office MS., No. 1728; but the ordinary *Janam-Sākhīs* current in the Panjāb vary the account somewhat by saying that when the Khān reproved Nānak for not coming to him when sent for, the latter replied: "'Hear, O Nawāb, when I was thy servant I came before thee; now I am not thy servant; now I am become the servant of Khudā (God).' The Nawāb said: 'Sir, (if) you have become such, then come with me and say prayers (*niwāj = nimāz*, see PRAYER). It is Friday.' Nānak said: 'Go, Sir.' The Nawāb, with the Qaẓī and Nānak, and a great concourse of people, went into the Jāmi' Masjid and stood there. All the people who came into the Masjid began to say, 'To-day Nānak has entered this sect.' There was a commotion among the respectable Hindūs in Sultānpur; and Jairām, being much grieved, returned home. Nānakī perceiving that her husband came home dejected, rose up and said, 'Why is it that you are to-day so grieved?' Jairām replied, 'Listen, O servant of Paramesur (God), what has thy brother Nānak done! He has gone, with the Nawāb, into the Jāmi' Masjid to pray; and, in the city, there is an outcry among the Hindūs and Musalmāns that Nānak has become a Turk (*Muslim*) to-day.'" (*India Office MS.*, No. 2885, fol. 39.)

From the foregoing it is perfectly clear that the immediate successors of Nānak believed that he went very close to Muhammadanism; and we can scarcely doubt the accuracy of their view of the matter, when we consider the almost contemporaneous character of the record, from which extracts have been given, and the numerous confirmatory evidences contained in the religion itself. It is particularly worthy of remark that a "cup of *amrita*" (*i.e.* immortality) is considered the symbol of inspiration; just as Ḥāfiẓ exclaims, "Art thou searching, O Ḥāfiẓ, to find the waters of eternal life?" And the same poet expresses his own ecstasy in a way almost identical with the reception accorded to Nānak at the gate of Paradise. His words are: "Then he gave into my hand a cup which flashed back the splendour of Heaven so gloriously, that Zuhrah broke out into dancing and the lute-player exclaimed, 'Drink!'" The staff (*muttakā*) that is mentioned is, also, that of a faqīr, on which a devotee supports himself while in meditation. Another significant fact is that when Nānak speaks of himself as the servant of God, he employs the word *Khudā*, a Persian Muhammadan term; but when his brother-in-law Jairām speaks of God, he uses the Hindū word *Paramesur*. It will, also, be noticed that Muhammadans are affected by the logic and piety of Nānak; and to them he shows himself so partial that he openly accompanies them to the mosque, and thereby causes his Hindū neighbours and friends to believe that he is actually converted to the faith of Islām. But, of course, the most remarkable expression of all is the emphatic and repeated announcement that "There is no Hindū; there is no Musalmān." This can mean nothing else than that it was Nānak's settled intention to do away with the differences between those two forms of belief, by instituting a third course which should supersede both of them.

Nānak's whilom employer, in consequence of the foregoing manifestations of wisdom, became his devoted admirer. After this, Nānak undertook a missionary tour; and it is noticeable that the first person he went to and converted was Shaikh Sajan (? ساجن), who showed himself to be a pious Muhammadan. Nānak then proceeded to Pānīpat, and was met by a certain Shaikh Tatīhar, who accosted him with the Muhammadan greeting, "Peace be on thee, O Darvesh!" (*Salām-āleka Darves*); to which Nānak immediately replied, "And upon you be peace, O servant of the Pīr! (*aleka us-salāmu, ho Pīr ke dasta-pes*)." (*India Office MS.*, No. 1728, fol. 48.) Here we find Nānak both receiving and giving the Muhammadan salutation; and also the acknowledgment that he was recognized as a *darvesh*. The Panjābī form of the Arabic salutation is given lest it might be thought that the special character of the words is due to the translation. The disciple then called his master, the Pīr Shaikh Sharaf, who repeated the salutation of peace, and after a long conversation acknowledged the Divine mission of Nānak, kissed his hands and feet, and left him. (fol. 52.) After the departure of this Pīr, the Guru Nānak wandered on to Dehli, where he was introduced to Sultān Ibrahīm Loḍī, who also called him a *darvesh*. The previous conversations and acts are found to have awakened the curiosity of Nānak's attendant Mardānā, who asked in surprise: "Is God, then, one?" To which Nānak firmly replied: "God (*Khudā*) is one." (fol. 55.) This was intended to satisfy Mardānā that there is no difference between the Muḥammadan and the Hindū God.

Nānak is next said to have proceeded to the holy city of Benares, and there he met with a Pandit named Satrudās. The MS. 1728 (fol. 56) says: "He came to this Nānak, and cried, 'Rām! Rām!' Seeing his (Nānak's) disguise (*bhekhu*), he sat down, and said to him, 'O devotee (*bhagat*), thou hast no *sāligrām*; no necklace of *tulsī*; no rosary; no *tikā* of white clay; and thou callest (thyself) a devotee! What devotion hast thou obtained?'" In other words, the Pandit is made to challenge his piety; because he has none of the marks of a Hindū upon him. Nānak explains his peculiar position and views; and is reported to have converted the Hindū Pandit to his own way of thinking. This anecdote, also, shows that the immediate successors of Nānak were aware that their great Guru occupied an intermediate position between Muḥammadanism and Hindūism; for we see that he is made to convert Muḥammadans on the one hand, and Hindūs on the other. After this primary attack on Hindūism, Nānak is said to have converted some Jogīs, Khattrīs, Thags, necromancers, witches, and even the personified Kaliyug, or present age of the world. These conquests over imaginary Hindūs are obviously allegorical; though they clearly point to a well recognized distinction between the teaching of Nānak and that of orthodox Hindūism.

The most significant associate which Nānak found was, undoubtedly, Shaikh Farīd. He was a famous Muḥammadan Pīr, and a strict Ṣūfī, who attracted much attention by his piety, and formed a school of devotees of his own. Shaikh Farīd must have gained considerable notoriety in his day; for his special disciples are still to be found in the Panjāb, who go by the name of Shaikh Farīd's faqīrs. This strict Muḥammadan became the confidential friend and companion of Nānak; and if all other traditions had failed, this alone would have been enough to establish the eclectic character of early Sikhism. The first greeting of these famous men is significant enough. Shaikh Farīd exclaimed, "Allah, Allah, O Darvesh"; to which Nānak replied, "Allah is the object of my efforts, O Farīd! Come, Shaikh Farīd! Allah, Allah (only) is ever my object." The words in the original being *Allah, Farīd, juhdī; hamesa āu, Sekh Farīd, juhdī Allah Allah*. (*India Office MS.*, No. 1728, fol. 86.) The use of the Arabic term *juhd* implies the energy of the purpose with which he sought for Allah; and the whole phrase is forcibly Muḥammadan in tone.

An intimacy at once sprang up between these two remarkable men; and Shaikh Farīd accompanied Nānak in all his wanderings for the next twelve years. The intended compromise between Hindūism and Islām is shown not only in the fact of this friendship, but in the important circumstance that no less than 142 stanzas composed by Shaikh Farīd are admitted into the *Ādi Granth* itself. An examination of these verses still further proves the mingling of the two religions which Nānak effected. They are distinctly Ṣūfīistic in tone, containing such lines as, "Youth is passing, I am not afraid, if love to the Beloved does not pass"; and still more pointedly, "Full of sins I wander about; the world calls me a Darvesh"; while, between these declarations of steady adherence to Islām, comes the remarkable Hindū line, "As by fire the metal becomes purified, so the fear of Hari removes the filth of folly." The fact that the compositions of a genuine Ṣūfī should have been admitted into the canonical book of the Sikhs, and that they should contain such a clear admixture of Hindū and Muḥammadan ideas, is conclusive evidence that Nānak, and his immediate successors, saw no incongruity in the mixture.

As soon as Nānak and his friend Shaikh Farīd begin to travel in company, it is related that they reached a place called Bisī'ār, where the people applied cow-dung to every spot on which they had stood, as soon as they departed. (*I. O. MS.*, No. 1728, fol. 94.) The obvious meaning of this is, that orthodox Hindūs considered every spot polluted which Nānak and his companion had visited. This could never have been related of Nānak had he remained a Hindū by religion.

In his next journey Nānak is said to have visited Patan, and there he met with Shaikh Ibrahīm, who saluted him as a Muslim, and had a conversation with him on the Unity of God. Nānak expressed his views in the following openly Ṣūfīistic manner: "Thou thyself (art) the wooden tablet; thou (art) the pen; thou (art) also the writing upon (it). O Nānak, why should the One be called a second?" (*India Office MS.* 1728, fol. 117.) The Pīr asks an explanation of this verse in these words: "Thou sayest, 'There is One, why a second?' but there is one Lord (*Ṣāḥib*), and two traditions. Which shall I accept, and which reject? Thou sayest, The only One, he alone is one'; but the Hindūs are saying that in (their) faith there is certainty; and the Musalmāns are saying that only in (their) faith is there certainty. Tell me, in which of them is the truth, and in which is there falsity?" Nānak replied, "There is only one Lord (*Ṣāḥib*), and only one tradition." (fol. 119.) This anecdote serves still further to illustrate the intermediate position between the two religions ascribed to Nānak by his immediate followers.

Shortly after the foregoing episode, Nānak was captured among the prisoners taken by the Emperor Bābar, who seems to have been attracted by the Guru's piety, and to have shown him some attentions. The chronicler informs us that "all the people, both Hindūs and Musalmāns, began to salute (Nānak)." (fol. 137.) After his release, Nānak recommenced his missionary work, and is described as meeting a Muḥammadan named Miyān Mithā, who called upon him for the *Kalimah* [see KALIMAH], or Muḥammadan confession of faith (fol. 143); which leads to a long conversation, in which Nānak lays emphasis on the Ṣūfī doctrine of the Unity of God. In this conversation Nānak is made to say, "The book of the Qur'ān should be practised." (fol. 144.) He also acknowledged that "justice is the Qur'ān." (fol. 148.) When the Miyān asked him what is the one great name, Nānak took him aside and whispered in his ear, "Allah" [GOD]. Immediately the great name is uttered, Miyān Mithā is consumed to ashes; but a celestial voice again utters the word "Allah!" and the Miyān regains life, and falls at the feet of Nānak. (fol. 147.)

Nānak then proceeded to convert some Jainas, and even a Rākshasas, or Hindū demon; and next went to Multān, where he converted the famous Pīr, Makhdūm Bahā'u-'d-Dīn. In Kashmīr he met with a Hindū Pandit who recognized him as a *sādhu*, or virtuous person; but asked him why he had abandoned caste usages, why he wore skins, and ate meat and fish. The Pandit's scruples having been satisfied, he flung away his idols, and became a devoted believer in Nānak's doctrines. This anecdote again furnishes us with distinct evidence that Nānak took up an intermediate position between Islām and Hindūism, and sought to bring both under one common system.

In precise conformity with this deduction is the tradition of Nānak's pilgrimage to Makkah. The particulars of his visit to that holy place are fully given, in all accounts of Nānak's life; and although, as Dr. Trumpp reasonably concludes, the whole story is a fabrication, yet the mere invention of the tale is enough to prove that those who most intimately knew Nānak considered his relationship to Muḥammadanism sufficiently close to warrant the belief in such a pilgrimage. In the course of his teaching in Makkah, Nānak is made to say: "Though men, they are like women, who do not obey the Sunnat, and Divine commandment, nor the order of the book (*i.e.* the Qur'ān)." (*I. O. MS.* No. 1728, fol. 212.) He also admitted the intercession of Muḥammad, denounced the drinking of bhang, wine, &c., acknowledged the existence of hell, the punishment of the wicked, and the resurrection of mankind; in fact, the words here ascribed to Nānak contain a full confession of Islām. These tenets are, of course, due to the narrator of the tale; and are only useful as showing how far Nānak's followers thought it possible for him to go.

A curious incident is next related to the effect that Makhdūm Bahā'u 'd-Dīn, the Pīr of Multān, feeling his end approaching, said to his disciples, "O friends, from this time the faith of no one will remain firm; all will become faithless (*be-īmān*)." His disciples asked for an explanation; and in reply he delivered himself of an oracular statement: "O friends, when one Hindū shall come to Heaven (*bihisht*), there will be brilliancy (*ujālā*) in Heaven." To this strange announcement his disciples replied: "Learned people say that Heaven is not decreed for the Hindū; what is this that you have said?" (*I. O. MS.* 1728, fol. 224.) The Pīr told them that he was alluding to Nānak; and sent one of his disciples to ask Nānak if he, also, had received an intimation of his approaching death.

In this anecdote we have the extraordinary admission from a Muḥammadan that Nānak would succeed in breaking up the faith of Islām It is in consequence of a Hindū's having conquered Heaven itself, and vindicated his right to a place in the paradise of Muḥammad, that those who were then in the faith of the Prophet would lose confidence in his teaching. Here again the words employed are useful; for the Pīr is made to say that Muslims will become *be-īmān*, the Arabic term specially applicable to the "faith" of Islām; and Heaven is called in the Panjābī story *bhisat*, that is *bihisht*, the Paradise of Muḥammadans [see PARADISE]; for had the Hindū heaven been intended, some such word as *swarg*, or *paralok*, or *Brahmalok* would have been used.

The final incident in the life of this enlightened teacher is in precise accord with all that has been said of his former career. Nānak came to the bank of the Rāvī to die—in conformity with Hindū custom—by the side of a natural stream of water. It is expressly said that both Hindūs and Muslims accompanied him. He then seated himself at the foot of a Sarīh tree, and his Assembly of the faithful (*Sangat*) stood around him. His sons asked him what their position was to be; and he told them to subordinate themselves to the Guru Angad whom he had appointed as his successor. They were to succeed to no power or dignity merely on the ground of relationship; no hereditary claim was to be recognized; on the contrary, the sons were frankly told to consider themselves nonentities. The words are: "Sons, even the dogs of the Guru are not in want; bread and clothes will be plentiful; and should you mutter 'Guru! Guru!' (your) life will be (properly) adjusted." (*I. O. MS.* 1728, fol. 238.) The anecdote then proceeds in the following remarkable manner: "Then the Hindūs and Musalmāns who were firm in the name (of God), began to express themselves (thus): the Musalmāns said, 'We will bury (him)'; and the Hindūs said, 'We will burn (him).' Then the Bābā said, 'Place flowers on both sides; on the right side those of the Hindūs, on the left side those of the Musalmāns, (that we may perceive) whose will continue green to-morrow. If those of the Hindūs keep green, then burn (me); and if those of the Musalmāns keep green, then bury (me).' Then the Bābā ordered the Assembly to repeat the praises (of God); and the Assembly began to repeat the praises accordingly. [After a few verses had been recited] he laid down his head. When the sheet (which had been stretched over him) was raised, there was nothing (under it); and the flowers of both (sides) remained green. The Hindūs took away theirs; and the Musalmāns took away theirs. The entire Assembly fell to their feet." (*I. O. MS.* 1728, fol. 239, 240.)

The mixture of Hindūism and Muḥammadanism is evident in this tradition. It is obviously intended to summarize the life of Nānak and the object of his teaching. He is not represented as an outcaste and a failure; on the other hand, his purposes are held to have been fully accomplished. The great triumph was the establishment of a common basis of religious truth for both Muḥammadan and Hindū; and this he is shown to have accomplished with such dexterity that at his death no one could say whether he was more inclined to Hindūism or to Muḥammadanism. His friends stood around him at the last moment quite uncertain as to whether they should dispose of his remains as those of a Muḥammadan, or as those of a Hindū. And Nānak is represented as taking care that the matter should ever remain a moot point. The final miraculous disappearance of the corpse is obviously intended to convey the idea that Nānak belonged specially neither to one party nor to the other; while the green and flourishing appearance of the flowers of both parties conveys the lesson that it was his wish that both should live together in harmony and union. The narrator of the life clearly wishes his history to substantiate the prophetic statement recorded at the commencement of his book (*I. O. MS.* 1728, fol. 7) that, at Nānak's birth, "The Hindūs said, 'The manifestation of some God (*Devatā*) has been produced;' and the Musalmāns said, 'Some holy man (*ṣādiq*) of God (*Khudā*) has been born.'"

The most potent cause of the uncertainty as to Nānak's true position in the religious world, arises from the initial fact that he was born a Hindū, and necessarily brought up in that form of belief. He was a perfectly uneducated man, there being no reason to suppose that he could either read or write, or perform any other literary feat, beyond the composition of extemporaneous verses in his mother tongue. Guru Arjun, the fourth successor of Nānak, appears to have been the first chieftain of the fraternity who could read and write. The necessary result of Nānak's early associations was that all his ideas throughout life were substantially Hindū, his mode of thought and expression was Hindū, his illustrations were taken from Hindū sources, and his system was based on Hindū models. It must be borne in mind that Nānak never openly seceded from the pale of Hindūism, or ever contemplated doing so. Thus in the *Sākhī of Mīyān Mithā* it is related that towards the end of Nānak's life a Muḥammadan named Shāh 'Abdu 'r-Raḥmān acknowledged the great advantages he had derived from the teaching of Nānak, and sent his friend Miyān Mithā to the Guru so that he might derive similar benefit. "Then Miyān Mithā said, 'What is his name? Is he a Hindū, or is he a Musalmān?' Shāh 'Abdu 'r-Raḥmān replied, 'He is a Hindū; and his name is Nānak.'—(*Sikhān de Rāj dī Vithiā*, p. 258.) He struck a heavy blow at Hindūism by his rejection of caste distinctions; and on this point there can be no doubt, for his very words, preserved in the *Ādi Granth*, are: "Thou (O Lord) acknowledgest the Light (the ray of the Divine in man), and dost not ask after caste. In the other world there is no caste."—(*Translation of the Ādi Granth*, p. 494.) In consequence of this opinion Nānak admitted to his fraternity men of all castes; his constant companions being spoken of as Saiyids and Sikhs, that is, Muḥammadan and Hindū pupils. Sikhs have ever before them the intermediate character of their religion by the stanza (21) of the *Jap-Jī*, which says, "Pandits do not know that time, though written in a Purāna; Qāẓīs do not know that time, though written in the Qur'ān." Hindū scholars are told in the *Ādi Granth* that they miss the true meaning of their religion through delusion. "Reading and reading the Pandit explains the Veda, (but) the infatuation of Māyā (delusion personified) lulls him to sleep. By reason of dual affection the name of Hari (*i.e*, God) is forgotten." (*Translation*, p. 117.) In the same way Nānak turns to the Musalmān and says,—

> "Thou must die, O Mullā! thou must die! remain in the fear of the Creator!
> Then thou art a Mullā, then thou art a Qāẓī, if thou knowest the name of God (*Khudā*).
> None, though he be very learned, will remain, he hurries onwards.
> He is a Qāẓī by whom his own self is abandoned, and the One Name is made his support.
> He is, and will be, He will not be destroyed, true is the Creator.
> Five times he prays (*niwāj gujarhi*), he reads the book of the Qur'ān."
>
> (*Translation*, p. 37.)

Nānak does not seem to have been fastidious as to the name under which he recognized the Deity; he was more concerned with impressing on his companions a correct understanding of what Deity was. The names Hari, Rām, Govind, Brahma, Parames'war, Khudā, Allah, &c., are used with perfect freedom, and are even mixed up in the same poem. The most common name for God in the *Ādi Granth* is certainly Hari; but that does not seem to have shocked the Muslim friends of Nānak. Thus, in a poem addressed to Hari as "the invisible, inaccessible, and infinite," we are told that, "Pīrs, prophets, sāliks, ṣādiqs, martyrs, shaikhs, mullās, and darveshes; a great blessing has come upon them, who continually recite his salvation." —(*Translation*, p. 75.)

The chief point of Nānak's teaching was unquestionably the Unity of God. He set himself firmly against the idea of associating any other being with the Absolute Supreme. This exalted idea of Divine Majesty enabled Nānak to treat with indifference the crowd of Hindū deities. To such a mind as that of Nānak it would have been sheer waste of time to argue, with any earnestness, about the attributes, powers, or jurisdictions, of a class of beings, the whole of whom were subordinate to one great, almighty, and incomprehensible Ruler. Without any overt attack on the Hindū pantheon, he caused the whole cluster of deities to subside into a condition similar to that of angels in modern Christianity; whose existence and operations may be the subject of conversation, but the whole of whom sink into utter insignificance compared with the central idea of the Divine Majesty. The One God, in Nānak's opinion (and, it may be added, in the opinion of all Ṣūfīs), was the creator of plurality of form, not the creator of matter out of nothing. The phenomenal world is the manifestation of Deity, and it is owing to pure deception that the idea of severalty exists. In the *Ādi Granth* we read—

"The cause of causes is the Creator.
In His hand are the order and reflection.
As He looks upon, so it becomes.
He Himself, Himself is the Lord.
Whatever is made, (is) according to His own pleasure.
He is far from all, and with all.
He comprehends, sees, and makes discrimination.
He Himself is One, and He Himself is many.
He does not die nor perish, He neither comes nor goes.
Nānak says: He is always contained (in all)."—(*Translation*, p. 400.)

Notwithstanding this conception that the Supreme One comprehends both spirit and matter, and therefore *is* what is; He is nevertheless spoken of as in some way different from the creatures He has formed, and has been endowed with moral and intellectual qualities. Thus we find in the *Ādi Granth*—

"Whose body the universe is, He is not in it, the Creator is not in it.
Who is putting (the things) together, He is always aloof (from them), in what can He be said (to be contained)?"
(*Translation*, p. 474.)

The soul of man is held to be a ray of light from the Light Divine; and it necessarily follows that, in its natural state, the soul of man is sinless. The impurity, which is only too apparent in man, is accounted for by the operation of what is called Māyā, or Delusion; and it is this Māyā which deludes creatures into egotism and duality, that is, into self-consciousness or conceit, and into the idea that there can be existence apart from the Divine. This delusion prevents the pure soul from freeing itself from matter, and hence the spirit passes from one combination of matter to another, in a long chain of births and deaths, until the delusion is removed, and the entramelled ray returns to the Divine Light whence it originally emanated. The belief in metempsychosis is thus seen to be the necessary complement of pantheism; and it is essential to the creed of a Hindū, a Buddhist, and a Ṣūfī.

In Sikhism, as in Buddhism, the prime object of attainment is not Paradise, but the total cessation of individual existence. The method by which this release from transmigration is to be accomplished is by the perfect recognition of identity with the Supreme. When the soul fully realizes what is summed up in the formula *so ham*, "I am that," *i.e.* "I am one with that which was, and is, and will be," then emancipation from the bondage of existence is secured. This is declared by Nānak himself in the *Ādi Granth* in these words—

"Should one know his own self as the *so ham*, he believes in the esoteric mystery.
Should the disciple (*Gur-mukhi*) know his own self, what more can he do, or cause to be done?"—(*I. O. MS.* 2484, fol. 53.)

The principles of early Sikhism given above are obviously too recondite for acceptance among masses of men; accordingly we find that the pantheistic idea of Absolute Substance became gradually changed into the more readily apprehended notion of a self-conscious Supreme Being, the Creator and Governor of the universe. Here Dr. Trumpp himself admits the influence of Muḥammadanism, when he says: "It is not improbable that the Islām had a great share in working silently these changes, which are directly opposed to the teaching of the Gurus."—(Introduction to *Translation of the Ādi Granth*, p. cxii.) The teaching of Nānak was, however, very practical. His followers are daily reminded in the *Jap-Jī* that, "Without the practice of virtue there can be no worship."

In all that has preceeded we have confined ourselves strictly to the intimate relationship subsisting between early Sikhism and the Muḥammadan religion. It is, however, needful to allude to the fact that certain surviving relics of Buddhism had no small share in moulding the thoughts of the Founder of the Sikh religion. A full examination of this part of the subject would be out of place in the present work. It must suffice to say that Buddhism held its position in the Panjāb long after it had disappeared from other parts of Northern India; and the abundance of Buddhistic relics, which are continually being unearthed in the district, prove the wide-spread and long-continued influence of the tenets of the gentle-hearted Buddha. Indications of this influence on early Sikhism are seen in its freedom from caste, in the respect for animal life, the special form of metempsychosis accepted, the importance ascribed to meditation, the profuse charity, the reverence paid to the seat of the Guru (like the Buddhistic worship of the throne), Nānak's respect for the lotos, his missionary tours, and the curious union subsisting between the Guru and his Sangat. In the *Travels of Guru Tegh Bahādur*, translated from the original Gurmukhī by an excellent scholar, Sirdār Atar Singh, we find the following remarkable sentence: "The Guru and his Sangat are like the warp and woof in cloth,—there is no difference between them" (p. 37). In the *Ādi Granth* there is an entire Sukhmanī, or poem, by Guru Arjun, wholly devoted to a recitation of the advantages of "the society of the pious," the term employed being, however, in this case, *sādh kai sang.* (*I. O. MS.* 2484, fol. 134.) In addition to these points of resemblance, there is found in early Sikhism a curious veneration for trees, offerings to which were sometimes made, as will be seen by reference to pp. 67, 70, and 83, of the *Travels of Guru Tegh Bahādur*, just cited. In precise conformity with the tradition that Buddha died under a Sāl tree, we have seen that Nānak purposely breathed his last under a Sarīh tree. Anyone familiar with Buddhism will readily recognize the remarkable coincidences stated above; but the most conclusive of all is the positive inculcation of views identical with the crowning doctrine of Buddhism—the Nirvāna itself. The following is what Dr. Trumpp says on the subject:—

"If there could be any doubt on the pantheistic character of the tenets of the Sikh Gurus regarding the Supreme, it would be dissolved by their doctrine of the Nirbān. Where no personal God is taught or believed in, man cannot aspire to a final personal communion with him, his aim can only be absorption in the Absolute Substance, *i.e.* individual annihilation. We find, therefore, no allusion to the joys of a future life in the Granth, as heaven or paradise, though supposed to exist, is not considered a desirable object. The immortality of the soul is only taught so far as the doctrine of transmigration requires it; but when the soul has reached its highest object, it is no more mentioned, because it no longer exists as individual soul.

"The Nirbān, as is well known, is the grand object which Buddha in his preaching held out to the poor people. From his atheistic point of view, he could look out for nothing else; personal existence, with all the concomitant evils of this life, which are not counterbalanced by corresponding pleasures, necessarily appeared to him as the greatest evil. His whole aim was, therefore, to counteract the troubles and pain of this existence by a stoical indifference to pleasure and pain, and to stop individual consciousness to its utmost limit, in order to escape at the point of death from the dreaded transmigration, which he also, even on his atheistic ground, had not ventured to reject. Buddhism is, therefore, in reality, like Sikhism, nothing but unrestricted Pessimism, unable to hold out to man any solace, except that of annihilation.

"In progress of time, Buddhism has been expelled from India, but the restored Brahmanism, with its confused cosmological legends, and gorgeous mythology of the Purānas, was equally unable to satisfy the thinking minds. It is, therefore, very remarkable, that Buddhism in its highest object, the Nirbān, soon emerges again in the popular teachings of the mediæval reformatory movements. Nāmdev, Trilochan, Kabīr, Ravidās, &c., and after these Nānak, take upon themselves to show the way to the Nirbān, as Buddha in his time had promised, and find eager listeners; the difference is only in the *means* which these Bhagats [saints] propose for obtaining the desired end." (Introduction to *Translation of the Ādi Granth*, p. cvi.)

Such, then, was the Sikh religion as founded by Guru Nānak. It is based on Hindūism, modified by Buddhism, and stirred into new life by Ṣūfīism. There seems to be superabundant evidence that Nānak laboured earnestly to reconcile Hindūism with Muḥammadanism, by insisting strongly on the tenets on which both parties could agree, and by subordinating the points of difference. It is impossible to deny that Nānak in his life-time actually did effect a large amount of reconciliation, and left behind him a system designed to carry on the good work. The circumstances which led to the entire reversal of the project, and produced between Muḥammadans and Sikhs the deadliest of feuds, does not come within the purview of the present article. It is enough to state that the process was gradual, and was as much due to political causes as to a steady departure from the teachings of the Founder of Sikhism.

The Sikhs acknowledge ten Gurus, whose names, with the year in which each died, are given in the following list:—

Name.	Date of Death.	Duration of Guru-ship.
	A.D.	Years.
Guru Nānak . .	1538	34
Guru Angad . .	1552	14
Guru Amar-Dās .	1574	22
Guru Rām-Dās .	1581	7
Guru Arjun . .	1606	25
Guru Har-Govind .	1638	32
Guru Har-Rā‚ī .	1660	22
Guru Har-Kisan .	1664	4
Guru Tegh-Bahādur	1675	11
Guru Govind Singh.	1708	33

It is thus seen that the Sikh fraternity was under the guidance of personal Gurus from A.D. 1504, when Nānak received the spiritual impulse which gave birth to the new sect, until A.D. 1708, a total period of 204 years. After the death of Guru Govind Singh, the *Ādi Granth* itself was taken to be the ever-existing impersonal guide.

The first successor of Nānak was appointed on account of his devotion to the cause. Shortly after the supposed visit to Makkah, Nānak met with a devotee named Lahanā, whose faith and earnestness were so fully demonstrated that Nānak named him, in preference to either of his sons, as his successor in the leadership of the new sect. His name was also changed from Lahanā to Angad (=*anga-da*, "body-giving"), implying that he was willing to give his very body to the cause of God. He was a poor and ignorant man, and maintained himself by rope-making. He is said to have heard the whole account of Nānak's life from Bhā,ī Bālā, who had long been with the Founder. It is related that all the counsel which Nānak had given to the Sikhs was sedulously inculcated by him. (*Sikhān de Rāj di Vithi,ā*, p. 19.) Like his predecessor, the Founder, he also named as his successor a devoted servant; although he had sons whom he might have appointed.

Amar-Dās, the third Guru, was a simple-minded and inoffensive man, who was as unlearned as his two predecessors; nevertheless, he composed several verses incorporated in the *Ādi Granth.* It was in his time that we hear of the first differences between the Sikhs and the Muḥammadans. The gentle disposition of Amar-Dās was unsuited to the position of ruler among the strong-willed people of the Panjāb; accordingly, when a difference occurred, he was quite incapable of settling the matter. It is related that Amar-Dās was completely absorbed in the service of *Paramesur* (God). (*Sikhān de Rāj di Vithi,ā*, p. 25.) The use of this word indicates a marked inclination towards the Hindū side of Sikhism; and we may suppose that such an inclination would be resented by the firmer adherents to Islām; for we find that the Muslims began to annoy this Guru's disciples by trivial acts of aggression. The disciples asked their Guru what they had better do; and he suggested various temporising expedients, which only emboldened the aggressors. When again appealed to, he desired his disciples to endure the wrong, as it was more meritorious to submit than to resent an insult. The weak conduct of this Guru left a legacy of ill-will for his successors to deal with. Amar-Dās nominated his son-in-law as his successor; an example which initiated the hereditary Guru-ship which followed.

Rām-Dās was a poor lad, who got a scanty living by selling boiled grain. He was taken into the family of Amar-Dās, and married his daughter. He had acquired the elements of education, and was a peaceful and non-aggressive man. On attaining the Guru-ship, he set himself industriously to the acquisition of disciples; and took large contributions from them in the shape of voluntary offerings. This wealth placed him above his brothers in the faith; and conferred upon him the elements of a royal state. He restored an old tank in magnificent style, for the purpose of religious ablution, and called it *Amritsar*, or the lake of the water of life. This tank enabled the Sikhs to perform their ablutions in a luxurious manner, and necessarily attracted many to the spot. In the course of time, a town grew up round the tank, which gradually increased in importance, and is now one of the most important places in the Panjāb. This assumption of dignity and increasing wealth in all probability awakened the anxiety of the Muḥammadan governors of the country; and the gradual drifting into common Hindūism accentuated the feeling. It is clear that the Muḥammadans who had fought so desperately to overturn the ancient Hindū kingdoms, could not view with indifference the up-growth of a Hindū sovereignty in their very midst. Rām-Dās named his son as his successor in the Guru-ship—an act which sealed the fate of the Sikh attempt at compromise in religious matters; for every Muḥammadan felt his position as a citizen threatened by the establishment of a rallying-point for disaffected Hindūs.

Guru Arjun, the fifth Guru, was an active and ambitious man. He laid aside the dress of a faqīr, which had been worn by all his predecessors, and converted the voluntary offerings of his disciples into a tax. This raised him to some importance, and enabled him to take men into his pay, a proceeding which conferred additional dignity upon him, and, at the same time, intensified the jealousy of his Muḥammadan neighbours. As an additional means of uniting his community into one compact body, he collected the words of Nānak, and those of other saintly personages, into a book, which he called *Granth, i.e.* "*the* book;" and strictly enjoined his followers to accept no speech as authoritative which was not contained in "the book." The spark which lit the torch was, however, a distinct interference in political affairs, which provoked the resentment of the Muḥammadan ruler at Delhi, and occasioned the arrest and, ultimately, the death of the Guru. It is not clear whether the Emperor actually executed him, or whether the Guru committed suicide; but his death was brought about by the ruler of Delhi; and this was enough to inflame the passions of the Sikhs, who were eager to revenge his death.

Har-Govind succeeded his father in the Guru-ship; and at once proceeded to arm his followers, and slay those who had been personally concerned in procuring the death of the late Guru. This did not, however, prevent him from entering the service of the Emperors Jahāngīr and Shāh-Jahān in a military capacity; but his turbulence got him into much trouble, and he spent a predatory, rather than a religious, life. Under his Guru-ship the Sikhs were changed from faqīrs into soldiers; and were freely recruited from the warlike Jat population, who eagerly availed themselves of any opportunity for securing plunder. It is evident that the actions of this Guru must have led him into frequent contests with the Muḥammadan authorities; and provoked the efforts afterwards made to break up what the rulers must have felt to be a dangerous confederation.

Har-Rā,ī was the grandson of the last Guru; and was chosen as successor because Har-Govind distrusted the fitness of his sons for the office. Har-Rā,ī fought against Aurangzīb in the interest of Dārā-Shikoh; and when the latter was defeated he made his submission to the Emperor, and was pardoned.

Har-Kishan was the younger son of the preceding. Nothing eventful occurred during his short tenure of power. He was called to Delhi by the Emperor Aurangzīb, and was there attacked by small-pox, of which disease he died. The succession to the Guru-ship was broken by his death; for he was too weak to appoint a successor, and merely indicated that the next Guru would be found in Bakālā, a village near Anand-pur.

Tegh-Bahādur, who happened to be residing in Bakālā, was the son of Har-Govind, and had been passed over by his father in favour of Har-Rā,ī. He was by nature contemplative, and not particularly anxious to assume the delicate position of leader among the bellicose Sikhs. Aurangzīb was in the full fury of his Islāmizing mania, and was accordingly specially solicitous to suppress the ambitious projects of the Sikhs. The Panjāb appears to have been too carefully guarded to be pleasant to Tegh-Bahādur, and he, therefore, began a wandering life over the north of India. An account of his travels has been translated from Panjābī into English by the learned Sirdār Atar Singh; and the story is singularly interesting to the student of Sikh history. We learn from one anecdote that, even in the time of this ninth Guru, Muḥammadans could feel a certain respect for the Sikhs. The tale relates that a small party of Hindūs and Muḥammadans went to rob the Guru; but at the last moment the Muḥammadans felt remorse, for they said, "he was undoubtedly a prophet."—(*Travels of Guru Tegh Bahādur*, p. 24.) On reaching S'ivarām the Guru met a Saiyid seated under a Sarīh tree (the same kind of tree, be it remarked, as that under which Nānak breathed his last); and the Saiyid saluted the Guru with reverence, saying: "I am really happy now, having seen your divine countenance." — (*Travels*, &c., p. 46.) Still more marked is the friendly feeling shown by the courteous reception which Tegh-Bahādur received from Sharafu 'd-Dīn, a Muḥammadan gentleman residing near Patiālā. This Muslim sent him presents, and then went out to meet him. He conducted him with much ceremony to his own palace, where he entertained him. It is specially mentioned that "the Guru's eyes fell upon a mosque, and Sharafu 'd-Dīn immediately said that that was the house of God."—(*Travels*, &c., p. 2.) Notwithstanding this reverential treatment by pious Muḥammadans, it is certain that Tegh-Bahādur spent his life in violent antagonism to the Muslim rulers of the country. The book of *Travels*, from which we are quoting, gives numerous instances of this, as may be seen by those who care to study the details, in pp. 45, 49, 57, 58, 69, 126, 130, 131. Some desperate fights took place, and after a specially severe engagement it is said on p. 58 that "from that day the Muḥammadans never ventured to fight with the Guru." However, the Guru appears to have been hunted from place to place, and on many occasions he narrowly escaped capture. The apparent contradiction involved in the reverential attitude of pious Muḥammadans, and the skirmishes with Muḥammadan soldiery, finds its explanation in the supposition that the religious aspect of Sikhism was not antagonistic to Muḥammadan ideas, while its political aspect provoked the violence of the Court of Delhi. In the present day much the same state of things is recognizable with respect to the Wahhābīs. The English Government would never dream of interfering with the religious opinions of that, or any other, sect; but when their doctrines find expression in the subversion of civil authority, the leaders soon find themselves in the Andaman islands. Tegh-Bahādur was at length arrested, and the Emperor is stated to have endeavoured earnestly to bring him over to the pure Muslim faith; but when he proved obdurate he was thrown into prison, where long-continued cruelty induced him to command a Sikh, who was with him, to cut off his head.

Govind Singh was the tenth and last Guru, and he succeeded his father Tegh-Bahādur when only 15 years of age. He was brought up under Hindū guidance, and became a staunch devotee of the goddess Durgā; and, by his pronounced preference for Hindūism, he caused a division in the Sikh community. He introduced several important changes into the constitution of Sikh society. The chief among these was the establishment of the *Khālsā*, by which he bound his disciples into an army, and conferred upon each of them the name *Singh*, or lion. He freely admitted all castes to the ranks of his army; and laboured more earnestly over their military than over their religious discipline. The nature of the changes which Govind Singh effected in the fraternity is best shown by the fact that the special followers of Nānak personally, separated themselves from him, and formed a community of their own, rejecting the title of *Singh* In other words, they preferred the religious to the military idea. This Guru fought against the Muḥammadans with determination; and was so incensed against them that he instituted a fine of 25 rupees for saluting a Muḥammadan tomb, however saintly. Towards the end of his Guru-ship an attempt was made to raise this fine to 5,000 rupees; but it was ultimately fixed at 125 rupees (*Travels*, &c., pp. 69 and 130.) The spirit of toleration so marked during the life of Nānak was clearly gone; and in yet later times this hostility gave birth to the maxim that "a true Sikh should always be engaged in war with the Muḥammadans and slay them, fighting them face to face." After a turbulent reign, Guru Govind Singh was treacherously slain by the dagger of a Pathān follower. He refused to name a successor, telling his followers that after his death the *Granth Ṣāḥib*, or "the Lord the Book," was to be their guide in every respect. (*Sikhān de Rāj dī Vithi,ā*, p. 79.)

The foregoing sketch of the relation of the Sikhs to the Muḥammadans is sufficient to show that the religion of Nānak began in large-hearted tolerance; and that political causes operated to convert its adherents into a narrow-minded sect. The Hindūism which Nānak had disciplined, reasserted its superiority under his successors, and ultimately became predominant. While this change was in progress the religious aspect of the movement became gradually converted into a military and political propaganda. No contrast, indeed, could well be greater than that between the inoffensive and gentle-minded Nānak, and the warlike and ambitious Gurus of later times. But while we cannot help being painfully impressed with the apparently undying feud which still subsists between the Sikhs and the Muḥammadans, it seems perfectly clear that the intention of the Founder was to reconcile the differences between those creeds; and that in this excellent work he attained a large measure of success. His pious object was defeated by political causes, and by the warlike nature of the people of the Panjāb The name "Muḥammadan," in the various countries in which it exists, is allowed to cover differences in religious belief quite as great as those between the views of Nānak and those of Muḥammad; and in all probability would have done so in this instance also, but for the reasons pointed out. We cannot, however, concern ourselves with probabilities; it is enough for the purposes of this article to have established the fact that Sikhism, in its inception, was intimately associated with Muḥammadanism; and that it was intended as a means of bridging the gulf which separated the Hindūs from the believers in the Prophet.

There are five leading sects of Sikhs, the names of which need only be mentioned. They are:—

1. The *Udāsis*, or those who are "indifferent" to the world.
2. The *Suthre*, or the "pure."
3. The *Diwāne*, or "mad" saints.
4. The *Nirmale Sādhu*, or "spotless saints."
5. The *Akālis*, or worshippers of the "Eternal One."

[The foregoing able review of the connection between Sikhism and the teachings of Islām has been contributed, specially for the present work, by Mr. Frederic Pincott, M.R.A.S.]

The authorities upon which this article is based are:—Dr. Trumpp's *Translation of the Ādi Granth*; the text of the *Ādi Granth*, *India Office MS.* No. 2484; the *Janam-Sākhī* of Guru Nānak in old Panjābī, *I. O. MS.* No. 1728; the *Janam-Patrī* of Guru Nānak, *I. O. MS.* No. 2885; *Sikhān de Rāj dī Vithi*‚*ā* (an Account of the Rule of the Sikhs, in Panjābī); *The Travels of Guru Tegh-Bahādur and Guru Gobind Singh*, translated from the original Gur-mukhī by Sirdār Atar Singh, Chief of Bhadaur; *Jap-Jī Sāhib*, the Panjābī text with commentary in Urdū, by Sirdār Atar Singh; *Srī Guru Charitra Prabhākar*, by Pandit Gyānī Sant Singh; *Srī Nānak Prakās*, by Bhā‚ī Santokh Singh; *Srī Granth Gur-Pratāp Sūraj Rāsā*, by Bhā‚ī Santokh Singh. [FAQIR, MUHAMMADANISM, SUFI.]

SILSILAH (سلسلة). *Lit.* "A chain." (1) The line of succession in any religious order, traced either to some religious leader of reputation, or to the four rightly directed Khalīfahs, or to the Prophet himself. (2) An unbroken tradition.

SIMON PETER. Arabic *Sham'ūn* (شمعون). Not mentioned by name in the Qur'ān, but al-Baiẓāwī says he is the Apostle who was sent to Antioch to succour the two disciples in prison (said to be John and Jude), and who is referred to in Sūrah xxxvi. 13: "And we strengthened them with a third."

SIMSĀR (سمسار), pl. *samāsirah*. A term used in Muḥammanan law for agents or brokers.

SIN. Arabic *zamb* (ذنب), *khaṭi'ah* (خطئة), *iṣm* (اثم). Heb. אָשָׁם *āshām*, חֵטְא *khēt'*. Muḥammadan doctors divide sin into two classes. *Kabīrah*, "great," and *ṣaghīrah*, "little" sins. *Kabīrah* sins are those great sins of which, if a Musalmān do not repent, he will be sent to the purgatorial hell reserved for sinful Muslims, whilst *ṣaghīrah* are those venial sins which are inherent in our fallen nature.

Muḥammadan writers are not agreed as to the exact number of *kabīrah* sins, but they are generally held to be the following seventeen:—

1. *Kufr*, or infidelity.
2. Constantly committing little sins.
3. Despairing of God's mercy.
4. Considering oneself safe from the wrath of God.
5. False witness.
6. *Qazf*, or falsely charging a Muslim with adultery.
7. Taking a false oath.
8. Magic.
9. Drinking wine.
10. Appropriation of the property of orphans.
11. Usury.
12. Adultery.
13. Unnatural crime.
14. Theft.
15. Murder.
16. Fleeing in battle before the face of an infidel enemy.
17. Disobedience to parents.

The following are sayings of Muḥammad, as given in the Traditions, on the subject of sin (*Mishkāt*, book i. ch. ii.):—

"He is not a believer who commits adultery, or steals, or drinks liquor, or plunders, or embezzles, when entrusted with the plunder of the infidel. Beware! beware!"

"The greatest sin is to associate another with God, or to vex your father and mother, or to murder your own species, or to commit suicide, or to swear, or to lie."

"The greatest of sins before God is that you call any other like unto the God who created you, or that you murder your child from an idea that it will eat your victuals, or that you commit adultery with your neighbour's wife."

"Abstain ye from seven ruinous destructive things, namely, (1) associating anything with God; (2) magic; (3) killing anyone without reason; (4) taking interest on money; (5) taking the property of the orphan; (6) running away on the day of battle; (7) and taxing an innocent woman with adultery."

"Do not associate anything with God, although they kill or burn you. Do not affront your parents, although they should order you to leave your wives, your children, and your property. Do not abandon the divine prayers, for he who does so will not remain in the asylum of God. Never drink wine; for it is the root of all evil. Abstain from vice, for from it descends the anger of God. Refrain from running away in battle, although ye be killed. When a pestilence shall visit mankind, and you are in the midst of it, remain there. Cherish your children, and chastise them in order to teach them good behaviour, and instruct them in the fear of God."

It is related that a Jew once said to his friend, "Take me to this Prophet." He said, "Do not call him a prophet, for if he hears it he will be pleased." And they came to the Prophet and asked him about the *nine* (*sic*) wonders (*i.e.* Ten Commandments), which appeared (from the hands of Moses). He said, "Do not associate anything with God, nor steal, nor commit adultery, nor murder, nor take an inoffensive person before the king to be killed, nor practise magic, nor take interest, nor accuse an innocent woman of adultery, nor turn your backs on the field of battle; and it is proper, particularly for the Jews, not to work on Saturday." The Jews kissed the hands and feet of the Prophet, and said, "We bear witness that you are a Prophet." He said, "What prevented you from being my disciples?" They replied, "David called on God to perpetuate the gift of prophecy in his family, and we fear the Jews will kill us if we become your followers."

SINAI. Arabic *Sainā'* (سيناء), Heb. סִינַי *Sinai*. In the Qur'ān *Ṭūru Sainā'* (طور سيناء), also *Ṭūru Sīnīn* (طور سينين), "Mount Sinai"; and *aṭ-Ṭūr* (الطور), "the Mount"; Chaldee טוּר *Ṭūr*. In Muslim commentaries, *Jabalu Mūsā* (جبل موسى), "the Mount of Moses."

It is referred to in the Qur'ān as the mountain on which God gave the tables of the Law (Sūrah vii. 139), and as the place where God assembled the prophets and took a compact from them (Sūrah iii. 75). In Sūrah xcv. 2, Muḥammad makes the Almighty swear "by Mount Sinai"; and in Sūrah xxiii. 20, we are told that, "a tree growing out of Mount Sinai produces oil and a condiment for those who eat."

Al-Baiẓāwī (Fleischer's ed., vol. i. p. 343), and the author of the *Majma'u 'l-Biḥār* (p. 57), both say that Moses received the tables of the Law on the mountain called *Jabalu Zubair* (جبل زبير).

SINGING. Arabic *ghinā'* (غناء). Among Muslim theologians, singing is generally held to be unlawful, and the objection is founded on a tradition recorded by Jābir, who relates that Muḥammad said, "Singing and hearing songs causeth hypocrisy to grow in the heart, even as rain causeth the corn to grow in the field." (*Mishkāt*, book xxii. ch. ix. pt. 3.)

Shaikh 'Abdu 'l-Ḥaqq, in his commentary, remarking on this tradition, says, it is not a tradition of any authority, and adds, "The traditionists all agree that there is no Ḥadīs of any authority forbidding the practice of singing" (vol. iv. p. 63.)

The Ṣufīs, who engage in the service of song as an act of worship, say Muḥammad only forbade songs of an objectionable character. Still most divines of reputation regard the practice with disfavour.

SĪPĀRAH (سيپاره). The Persian term for the thirty *juz'*, or divisions of the Qur'ān. From *sī*, "thirty," and *pārah*, "a portion."

The Qur'ān is said to have been thus divided to enable the pious Muslim to recite the whole of the Qūr'ān in the month of Ramaẓān. Muḥammadans generally quote the Qur'ān by the *Sīpārah* and not by the *Sūrah*. [QUR'AN.]

ṢIQAH (ثقة). "Worthy of confidence." A term used in the study of the Ḥadīs for a traditionist worthy of confidence.

ṢIRĀṬ (صراط). *Lit.* "A road." The word occurs in the Qur'ān thirty-eight times, in nearly all of which it is used for the *Ṣirāṭu 'l-Mustaqīm*, or the "right way" of religion. In Muslim traditions and other writings it is more commonly used for the *bridge* across the infernal fire, which is described as finer than a hair and sharper than a sword, and is beset on each side with briars and hooked thorns. The righteous will pass over it with the swiftness of the lightning, but the wicked will soon miss their footing and will fall into the fire of hell. (*Mulla 'Alī Qārī*, p. 110.)

Muḥammad appears to have borrowed his idea of the bridge from the Zoroastrian system, according to which the spirits of the departed, both good and bad, proceed along an appointed path to the "bridge of the gatherer" (*chinvat peretu*). This was a narrow road conducting to Heaven or Paradise, over which the souls of the pious alone could pass, whilst the wicked fell into the gulf below. (Rawlinson's *Seventh Oriental Monarchy*, p. 636.)

The Jews, also, believed in the bridge of hell, which is no broader than a thread, over which idolaters must pass. (*Midrash, Yalkut, Reubeni*, sect. *Gehinnom*.)

AS-ṢIRĀṬU 'L-MUSTAQĪM (الصراط المستقيم). "The right way," *i.e.* the Muḥammadan religion; *e.g.* Qur'ān, Sūrah iii. 44: "Fear God and obey me; of a truth God is my Lord and your Lord: Therefore worship Him. This is the *right way*." It occurs in about thirty other places.

SIRIUS. Arabic *ash-Shiʻrā* (الشعرى). "The dog-star." The Almighty is called in the Qur'ān, Sūrah liii. 50, *Rabbu 'sh-Shiʻrā*, the "Lord of the Dog-star."

The Kamālān say that before the time of Muḥammad this star was worshipped by the Banū Khuzāʻah, hence the reference to it in the Qur'ān.

SITTING. Arabic *julūs* (جلوس). The traditionists are very particular in describing the precise position in which Muḥammad used to sit.

Ibn ʻUmar says: "I saw him sit with his knees up and the bottom of his feet on the ground, and his arms round his legs."

Jābir says: "I saw him sitting reclining upon a pillow which was put under his arm."

Kailah says: "I saw him sitting in the mosque upon his buttocks, in the greatest humility and lowliness."

Jābir says, again: "The Prophet used, after he had said morning prayer, to sit with his feet drawn under him, until sun-rise." (*Mishkāt*, book xxii. ch. v.)

Muḥammadans always sit on the ground in their places of public worship. In social gatherings, people of inferior position always sit lower than their superiors.

SIX FOUNDATIONS OF FAITH. *Al-Īmān* (الايمان), or "the Faith," is defined as consisting of the six articles of belief:—

1. *Allāh*, God.
2. *Al-Malā'ikah*, the Angels.
3. *Al-Kutub*, the Books (of the Prophets).
4. *Ar-Rusul*, the Prophets.
5. *Al-Yaumu 'l-Ākhir*, the Last Day.
6. *Al-Qadar*, the Decrees of God.

These Six Articles of Faith are entitled *Ṣifātu 'l-Īmān*, "the Attributes of Faith," or *Arkānu 'l-Īmān*, "the Pillars of Faith." [MUHAMMADANISM.]

SIYAR (سير), pl. of *sīrah*. *Lit.* "Going in any manner or pace." The record of a man's actions and exploits Stories of the ancients.

Kitābu 's-Siyar is the title given to a history of the establishment of Islām, hence *as-Siyar* means an historical work on the life of Muḥammad, or any of his Companions, or of his successors, &c. The earliest book of the kind written in Islām is that by Imām Muḥammad ibn Isḥāq, who died A.H. 51. (*Kashfu 'z-Ẓunūn*, Flügel's edition, vol. iii. p. 634.)

SLANDER. [QAZF.]

SLAUGHTER OF ANIMALS. [FOOD, ZABH.]

SLAVERY. Arabic *ʻUbūdīyah* (عبودية), Heb. עֲבוֹדָה *ʻabōdāh*. A slave, *ʻAbd* (عبد) (Surah ii. 220), Heb. עֶבֶד *ʻebed*; *Mamlūk* (مملوك) (Sūrah xvi. 77); A female slave, *amah* (امة) (Sūrah ii. 220). The term generally used in the Qur'ān for slaves is ما ملكت ايمانكم *mā malakat aimānukum*, "that which your right hands possess."

Muḥammad found slavery an existing institution, both amongst the Jews and the idolaters of Arabia, and therefore it is recognised although not established in the Qur'ān.

I.—The TEACHING OF THE QUR'AN on the subject of slavery is as follows:

(1) *Muslims are allowed to cohabit with any of their female slaves.* Sūrah iv. 3: "Then marry what seems good to you of women, by twos, or threes, or fours; and if ye fear that ye cannot be equitable, then only one, *or what your right hands possess.*" Sūrah iv. 29: "*Take of what your right hands possess of young women.*" Sūrah xxxiii. 49: "O prophet! verily We make lawful for thee wives to whom thou hast given their hire (dowry), *and what thy right hand possesses out of the booty God hath granted thee.*"

(2) *They are allowed to take possession of married women if they are slaves.* Sūrah iv. 28: "Unlawful for you are . . . married women, *save such as your right hands possess.*" (On this verse al-Jalālān the commentators say: "that is, it is lawful for them to cohabit with those women whom you have made captive, even though their husbands be alive in the *Dāru 'l-Ḥarb.*")

(3) *Muslims are excused from strict rules of decorum in the presence of their female slaves, even as in the presence of their wives.* Sūrah xxiii. 5: "Those who are strict in the rules of decorum, except for their wives, *or what their right hands possess.*" See also Sūrah lxx. 29.

(4) *The helpless position of the slave as regards his master* illustrates the helpless position of the false gods of Arabia in the presence of their Creator. Sūrah xvi. 77: "God has struck out a parable, an owned slave, able to do nothing, and one provided with a good provision, and one who expends therefrom in alms secretly and openly, shall they be held equal? Praise be to God, most of them do not know!" See also Sūrah xxx. 27.

(5) *Muslims shall exercise kindness towards their slaves.* Sūrah iv. 40: "Serve God and do not associate aught with Him, and show kindness to your parents and to kindred . . and to *that which your right hands possess.*"

(6) *When slaves can redeem themselves it is the duty of Muslims to grant the emancipation.* Sūrah xxiv. 33: "And such of those whom your right hands possess as crave a writing (*i.e.* a document of freedom), write it out for them if ye know any good in them, and give them of the wealth of God which He has given you. And do not compel your slave-girls to prostitution if they desire to keep continent."

From the teaching of the Qur'ān above quoted

it will be seen that all male and female slaves taken as plunder in war are the lawful property of their master; that the master has power to take to himself any female slave, either married or single; that the position of a slave is as helpless as that of the stone idols of Arabia; but they should be treated with kindness, and be granted their freedom when they are able to ask for and pay for it.

II.—From the TEACHING OF THE TRADITIONS, it appears that it was the custom of Muḥammad either to put to death or take captive those of the enemy who fell into his hands. If a captive embraced Islām on the field of battle he was a free man; but if he were made captive, and afterwards embraced Islām, the change of creed did not emancipate him. 'Aṭīyatu 'l-Quraẓī relates that, after his battle with the Banū Quraiẓah, the Prophet ordered all those who were able to fight to be killed, and the women and children to be enslaved.

Very special blessings are attached to the emancipation of a slave. Abū Hurairah relates that Muḥammad said, "Whosoever frees a slave who is a Muslim, God will redeem every member of his body, limb for limb, from hell fire." Abū Ẕarr asked which slave was the best to emancipate, and the Prophet replied, "That which is of the highest price and most liked by his master." An Arab once asked the Prophet what act would take him to Paradise, and the Prophet said, "Free a slave, or assist one in redeeming a bond of slavery." The following are some of the sayings of Muḥammad regarding the treatment of slaves:

"It is well for a slave who regularly worships God and discharges his master's work properly."

"Whoever buys a slave and does not agree about his property, then no part of it is for the purchaser of the slave."

"When a slave of yours has money to redeem his bond, then you must not allow him to come into your presence afterwards."

"Behaving well to slaves is a means of prosperity, and behaving ill to them is a cause of loss."

"When any one of you is about to beat his slave, and the slave asks pardon in the name of God, then withhold yourself from beating him."

"It is incumbent upon the master of slaves to find them in victuals and clothes, and not order them to do what they are not able to do."

"When a slave-girl has a child by her master she is free at his death."

"Whoever frees a slave, and the slave has property, it is for the master, unless the master shall have agreed that it was the slave's at the time of freeing him." (See *Mishkātu 'l-Maṣābīḥ*, *Ṣaḥīḥu 'l-Bukhārī*, *Ṣaḥīḥu Muslim.*)

III.—With regard to the ENSLAVING OF CAPTIVES, the author of the *Hidāyah* says:

"The Imām, with respect to captives, has it in his choice to slay them, because the Prophet put captives to death, and also because slaying them terminates wickedness; or, if he choose, he may make them slaves, because by enslaving them the wickedness of them is remedied, and at the same time the Muslims reap an advantage; or, if he please, he may release them so as to make them freemen and Ẕimmīs, according to what is recorded of 'Umar; but it is not lawful so to release the idolaters of Arabia, or apostates. It is not lawful for the Imām to return the captives to their own country, as this would be strengthening the infidels against the Muslims. If captives become Muslims, let not the Imām put them to death, because the wickedness of them is hereby remedied without slaying them; but yet he may lawfully make them slaves, after their conversion, because the reason for making them slaves (namely, their being secured within the Muslim territory) had existence previous to their embracing the faith. It is otherwise where infidels become Muslims before their capture, because then the reason for making them slaves did not exist previous to their conversion. It is not lawful to release infidel captives in exchange for the release of Muslim captives from the infidels. According to the two disciples, this is lawful (and such also is the opinion of ash-Shāfi'ī), because this produces the emancipation of Muslims, which is preferable to slaying the infidels or making them slaves. The argument of Imām Abū Ḥanifah is that such an exchange is an assistance to the infidels, because those captives will again return to fight the Muslims, which is a wickedness, and the prevention of this wickedness is preferable to effecting the release of the Muslims, since, as they remain in the hands of the infidels, the injury only affects them, and does not extend to the other Muslims, whereas the injury attending the release of infidel captives extends to the whole body of Muslims. An exchange for property (that is, releasing infidel prisoners in return for property) is also unlawful, as this is assisting the infidels, as was before observed, and the same is mentioned in the *Maẕhabu 'l-Mashhūr*. In the *Sairu 'l-Kabīr* it is asserted that an exchange of prisoners for property may be made where the Muslims are necessitous, because the Prophet released the captives taken at Badr for a ransom. If a captive become a Muslim in the hands of the Muslims, it is not lawful to release and send him back to the infidels in return for their releasing a Muslim who is a captive in their hands, because no advantage can result from the transaction. If, however, the converted captive consent to it, and there be no apprehension of his apostatizing, in this case the releasing of him in exchange for a Muslim captive is a matter of discretion. It is not lawful to confer a favour upon captives by releasing them gratuitously, that is, without receiving anything in return, or their becoming Ẕimmīs, or being made slaves. Ash-Shāfi'ī says that showing favour to captives in this way is lawful, because the Prophet showed favour in this way to some of the captives taken at the battle of Badr. The arguments of the Ḥanafī doctors upon this point are two-fold: First, it is said in the Qur'ān, '*Slay idolaters wherever ye find them*'; secondly, the right of enslaving them is established by their being conquered and captured, and hence it is not lawful to annul that right without receiving some advantage in return, in the same manner as holds with respect to all plunder; and with respect to what ash-Shāfiʿī relates that the Prophet showed favour in this way to some of the captives taken at the battle of Badr, it is abrogated by the text of the Qur'ān already quoted. (Hamilton's *Hidāyah*, vol. ii. p. 160.)

IV.—SLAVE TRAFFIC is not only allowed but legislated for by Muḥammadan law, and is clearly sanctioned by the example of the Prophet as given in the Traditions (see *Ṣaḥīḥu Muslim*, *Kitābu 'l-Buyūʿ*, vol. i. p. 2). In the Law of Sale (see *Raddu 'l-Muḥtār*. *Hidāyah*, Hamilton's ed., vol. ii. p. 458), slaves, male and female, are treated merely as articles of merchandize. In chapters on sale, and option, and wills, the illustrations are generally given as regards slaves, and the same, or very similar, rules apply both to the sale of animals and bondsmen.

The following traditions (*Mishkāt*, book xiii. chap. xx.) with reference to the action of the Prophet in this matter are notable:—

"'Imrān ibn al-Ḥusain said a man freed six slaves at his death, and he had no other property besides; and the Prophet called them, and divided them into three sections, and then cast lots; he then ordered that two of them should be freed, and he retained four in slavery, and spoke severely of the man who had set them free."

"Jābir said we used to sell the mothers of children in the time of the Prophet, and of Abū Bakr; but 'Umar forbade it in his time."

V.—The MANUMISSION OF SLAVES is permitted by Muḥammadan law under the following forms: (1) *'Atāq* (*'Atq*, *I'tāq*); (2) *Kitābah*; (3) *Tadbīr*; and (4) *Istīlād*.

(1) *'Atāq*, in its literal sense, means *power*, and in law expresses the act of the owner of a slave (either male or female) giving immediate and unconditional freedom to his slave. This act is lawful when it proceeds from a person who is free, sane, adult, and the actual owner of the slave in question. If such a person say to his slave, "Thou art free," or "Thou art *mu'taq*," or "Thou art consecrated to God," or make use of any similar expression to his slave, the slave becomes *ipso facto* free, whether the owner really mean emancipation or not.

(2) *Kitābah*, literally "a writing," signifies a bond of freedom granted to a slave (male or female), in return for money paid. It is founded on the teaching of the Qur'ān, Sūrah xxiv. 33: "And such of those as your right hands possess as crave *a writing*, write it out for them if ye know any good in them," which precept is held to be recommendatory, although not injunctive. The slave thus ransomed is called *mukātab*, until the ransom is fully paid. During the interval between the promise of freedom and the payment of the money the *mukātab* enjoys a certain degree of freedom, but is nevertheless placed under certain restrictions. For example, although he is free to move from place to place, he cannot marry, or bestow alms, or become bail, or grant a loan, or make a pilgrimage, &c., without the permission of his master.

(3) *Tadbīr* signifies literally, "arrangement, disposition, plan," but in the language of the law it means a declaration of freedom made to a slave (male or female), to take effect after the master's death. If the owner of a slave say, "Thou art free at my death," or "Thou art a *mudabbir*," or words to that effect, the slave can claim his freedom upon the decease of his master, and any children born to him in the interval are placed in the same position.

(4) *Istīlād*, *Lit.* "the offspring's claim," signifies a man having a child born to him of a female slave, which he claims and acknowledges as his own, which acknowledgment becomes *ipso facto* the cause of the freedom of the female slave. The woman is then called *ummu 'l-walad*, "the mother of offspring," and stands in relation to her master as his wife, the child being also free.

(5) In addition to the above forms of emancipation, it is also established that the manumission of slaves is the legal penalty or expiation (*kaffārah*) for certain sins, *e.g.* for breaking the fast of Ramaẓān the expiation is either the release of a slave or feeding seven poor persons; this expiation is also made for a rash oath [OATH], as also for the rash form of divorce known as ẓihār [ZIHAR]. (See *Raddu 'l-Muḥtār*, vol. ii. p. 175; iii. p. 92; ii. p. 952.)

VI.—MODERN MUSLIM SLAVERY. The slaves of the Arabs are mostly from Abyssinia and negro countries; a few, chiefly in the homes of wealthy individuals, are from Georgia and Circassia.

Mr. Lane says, in Egypt "Abyssinian and white female slaves are kept by many men of the middle and higher classes, and often instead of wives, as requiring less expense, and being more subservient, but they are generally indulged with the same luxuries as free ladies; their vanity is gratified by costly dresses and ornaments, and they rank high above free servants, as do also the male slaves. Those called Abyssinians appear to be a mixed race between negroes and whites, and from the territories of the Gallas. They are mostly kidnapped and sold by their own countrymen. The negro female slaves, as few of them have considerable personal attractions (which is not the case with the Abyssinians, many of whom are very beautiful), are usually employed only in cooking and other menial offices.

"The female slaves of the higher classes are often instructed in plain needlework and embroidery, and sometimes in music and dancing. Formerly many of them possessed sufficient literary accomplishments to quote largely from esteemed poems, or even to compose extemporary verses, which they would often accompany with the lute. The condition of many concubine slaves is happy, and that of many quite the contrary. These, and all other slaves of either sex, are generally treated with kindness, but at first they are usually importuned, and not unfrequently used with much harshness, to induce them to embrace the Muḥammadan faith, which almost all of them do. Their services are commonly light; the usual office of the male white slave, who is called (memlook) *mamlŭk*, is that of a page, or a military guard.

"Eunuchs are employed as guardians of the women, but only in the houses of men of high rank or of great wealth; on account of the important office which they fill, they are generally treated in public with special consideration. I used to remark, in Cairo, that few persons saluted me with a more dignified and consequential air than these pitiable but self-conceited beings. Most of them are Abyssinians or negroes. Indeed, the slaves in general take too much advantage of the countenance of their masters, especially when they belong to men in power." (*Arabian Nights*, vol. i. p 55.)

In Central Asia the great slave-trade is carried on with Kāfiristān. The Kāfirs, inasmuch as they enslave each other in war, sell their own countrymen and countrywomen into slavery, and, when the slave market is dull, the Muḥammadans residing on their borders make inroads upon the Kāfirs and carry them (especially the women who are very fair and pretty) into slavery. Some Kāfir slaves have risen to eminence in Cabul, the late Sher Ali Khān's commander-in-chief, Feramoz Khān, being a Kāfir slave.

In Hindūstān British rule has abolished slavery, but it nevertheless exists in noble families, where the slaves seem willingly to assent to their condition of bondage.

VII.—The TREATMENT OF SLAVES.—It has been already shown that, both according to the teaching of the Qur'ān and also according to the injunctions of Muḥammad, as given in the Traditions, kindness to slaves is strictly enjoined; and it must be admitted that the treatment of slaves in Muḥammadan countries contrasts favourably with that in America, when slavery existed as an institution under a Christian people.

Mr. Lane (*Arabian Nights*, vol. i. p. 55), writing from his personal observations of slavery in Egypt, remarks:—

"The master is bound to afford his slaves proper food and clothing, or to let them work for their own support, or to sell, give away, or liberate them. It is, however, considered disgraceful for him to sell a slave who has been long in his possession; and it seldom happens that a master emancipates a female slave without marrying her to some man able to support her, or otherwise providing for her.

"The Prophet strongly enjoined the duty of kindness to slaves. 'Feed your slaves,' said he, 'with food of that which ye eat, and clothe them with such clothing as ye wear; and command them not to do that which they are unable.' These precepts are generally attended to, either entirely or in a degree."

"Some other sayings of the Prophet on this subject well deserve to be mentioned; as the following :—

"'He who beats his slave without fault, or slaps him on the face, his atonement for this is freeing him.'

"'A man who behaves ill to his slave will not enter into Paradise.'

"'Whoever is the cause of separation between mother and child by selling or giving, God will separate him from his friends on the day of resurrection.'

"'When a slave wishes well to his master, and worships God well, for him are double rewards.'

"It is related of Othman ('Uṣmān), that he twisted the ear of a memlook belonging to him, on account of disobedience, and afterwards, repenting of it, ordered him to twist his ear in like manner; but he would not. Othman urged him, and the slave advanced and began to wring it by little and little. He said to him, 'Wring it hard, for I cannot endure the punishment of the Day of Judgment [on account of this act].' The memlook answered, 'O my master, the day that thou fearest I also fear.'

"It is related also of Zainu 'l-Abidīn, that he had a memlook who seized a sheep and broke its leg; and he said to him, 'Why didst thou this?' He answered, 'To provoke thee to anger.' 'And I,' said he, 'will provoke to anger him who taught thee; and he is *Iblīs* (*i.e.* the Devil): go, and be free, for the sake of God.'

"Many similar anecdotes might be added; but the general assertions of travellers in the East are far more satisfactory evidence in favour of the humane conduct of most Muslims to their slaves."

But although this testimony of Mr. Lane's will be borne out with regard to the treatment of slaves in Islām in all parts of the Muḥammadan world, the power which a Muslim possesses over the persons of his bondsman or bondsmaid is unlimited. For example, according to the *Hidāyah* (vol. iv. p. 282), "A master is not slain for the murder of his slave," nor "if one of two partners in a slave kill the slave is retaliation incurred." In this the law of Muḥammad departs from that of Moses. See Exodus xxi. 20: "And if a man smite his servant, or his maid, with a rod, and he die under his hand, he shall be surely punished. (Heb. avenged.) Notwithstanding, if he continue a day or two, he shall not be punished: for he is his money."

Slaves have no civil liberty, but are entirely under the authority of their owners, whatever may be the religion, sex, or age, of the latter; and can possess no property, unless by the owner's permission. The owner is entire master, while he pleases, of the person and goods of his slave; and of the offspring of his female slave, which, if begotten by him or presumed to be so, he may recognise as his own legitimate child, or not: the child, if recognised by him, enjoys the same privileges as the offspring of a free wife, and if not recognised by him is his slave.

He may give away or sell his slaves, excepting in some cases which have been mentioned, and may marry them to whom he will, but not separate them when married. A slave, however, according to most of the doctors, cannot have more than two wives at the same time. Unemancipated slaves, at the death of their master, become the property of his heirs; and when an emancipated slave dies, leaving no male descendants or collateral relations, the former master is the heir; or, if he be dead, his heirs inherit the slave's property. As a slave enjoys less advantages than a free person, the law, in some cases, ordains that his punishment for an offence shall be half of that to which the free is liable for the same offence, or even less than half: if it be a fine, or pecuniary compensation, it must be paid by the owner, to the amount, if necessary, of the value of the slave, or the slave must be given in compensation.

The owner, but not the part owner, may cohabit with any of his female slaves who is a Muḥammadan, a Christian, or a Jewess, if he has not married her to another man; but not with two or more who are sisters, or who are related to each other in any of the degrees which would prevent their both being his wives at the same time if they were free: after having so lived with one, he must entirely relinquish such intercourse with her before he can do the same with another who is so related to her. He cannot have intercourse with a pagan slave. A Christian or Jew may have slaves, but not enjoy the privilege above mentioned with one who is a Muḥammadan. The master must wait a certain period (generally from a month to three months) after the acquisition of a female slave before he can have such intercourse with her. If he find any fault in her within three days, he is usually allowed to return her.

When a man, from being the husband, becomes the master of a slave, the marriage is dissolved, and he cannot continue to live with her but as her master, enjoying, however, all a master's privileges; unless he emancipates her, in which case he may again take her as his wife, with her consent. In like manner, when a woman, from being the wife, becomes the possessor of a slave, the marriage is dissolved, and cannot be renewed unless she emancipates him, and he consents to the reunion.

There is absolutely no limit to the number of slave-girls with whom a Muḥammadan may cohabit, and it is the *consecration* of this illimitable indulgence which so popularizes the Muḥammadan religion amongst uncivilized nations, and so popularizes slavery in the Muslim religion.

In the *Akhlāq-i-Jilālī*, which is the popular work upon practical philosophy amongst the Muḥammadans, it is said that "for service a slave is preferable to a freeman, inasmuch as he must be more disposed to submit, obey and adopt his patron's habits and pursuits."

Some Muslim writers of the present day (Syed Ameer Ali's *Life of Mohammed*, p. 257) contend that Muḥammad looked upon the custom as temporary in its nature, and held that its extinction was sure to be achieved by the progress of ideas and change of circumstances; but the slavery of Islām is interwoven with the Law of marriage, the Law of sale, and the Law of inheritance, of the system, and its abolition would strike at the very foundations of the code of Muḥammadanism.

Slavery is in complete harmony with the spirit of Islām, while it is abhorrent to that of Christianity. That Muḥammad ameliorated the condition of the slave, as it existed under the heathen laws of Arabia, we cannot doubt; but it is equally certain that the Arabian legislator intended it to be a perpetual institution.

Although slavery has existed side by side with Christianity, it is undoubtedly contrary to the spirit of the teaching of our divine Lord, who has given to the world the grand doctrine of universal brotherhood.

Mr. Lecky believes (*European Morals*, vol. ii. p. 70) that it was the spirit of Christianity which brought about the abolition of slavery in Europe. He says, "The services of Christianity were of three kinds. It supplied a new order of relations, in which the distinction of classes was unknown. It imparted a moral dignity to the servile classes. It gave an unexampled impetus to the movement of enfranchisement."

SLEEPING. Arabic *naum* (نوم). Heb. נוּם *nūm*. It is usual for Muslims to sleep with the head in the direction of Makkah.

Abū Zarr relates that on one occasion he was sleeping on his belly, and the Prophet saw him, and, kicking him, said, "O Jundub! this way of sleeping is the way the devils sleep!"

Abbab says he saw the Prophet sleeping on his back, with one leg lying over the other, but Jābir says the Prophet forbade that way of sleeping. (*Mishkāt*, book xxii. ch. v. pt. 1.)

SNEEZING. Arabic *'uṭās* (عطاس). According to the Muḥammadan religion, it is a sacred duty to reply to a sneeze. For example, if a person sneeze and say immediately afterwards, "God be praised" (*al-ḥamdu li-'llāh*, الحمد لله), it is incumbent upon at least one of the party to exclaim, "God have mercy on you" (*Yarḥamu-ka 'llāh*, يرحمك الله). This custom of replying to a sneeze existed amongst the Jews, whose sneezing formula was "*Tobim khayim!*" *i.e.* "Good life."

There are interesting chapters on saluting after sneezing in Tylor's *Primitive Culture*, and Isaac D'Israeli's *Curiosities of Literature*.

Replying to a sneeze is amongst the duties called *Farẓ Kafā'i*. (*Mishkāt*, book v. ch. i. pt. 1.)

Abū Hurairah relates that Muḥammad said, "Verily God loves sneezing and hates yawning." (*Mishkāt*, book xxii. ch. vi.)

SODOM. Arabic *Sadūm* (سدوم). Heb. סְדוֹם *Sedōm*. "The City of Lot." The *Qāmūs* says it is more correctly *Zaẕūm*. The city is not mentioned by name in the Qur'ān, but it is admitted to be one of the "overturned cities" referred to in Sūrahs ix. 71; lxix. 9. Amongst Muḥammadans, this city is associated with sodomy, or unnatural crime, called in Arabic *liwāṭah*. *Pæderastia*, is held to be forbidden by Muslim law, and the reader will find a discussion on the subject in Hamilton's *Hidāyah*, vol. ii. p. 26. The prevalence of this vice amongst Muḥammadans is but too well known. (See Vambery's *Sketches of Central Asia*, p. 192.)

SOLOMON. Arabic *Sulaimān* (سليمان). Heb. שְׁלֹמֹה *Shelōmōh*. Both according to the Qur'ān and the Muḥammadan commentators, Solomon was celebrated for his skill and wisdom. The following is the account given of him in the Qur'ān, with the commentators' remarks in *italics*, as given in Mr. Lane's *Selections from the Ḳur'án* (2nd ed. by Mr. Stanley Lane-Poole):—

"And *We subjected* unto Solomon the wind, blowing strongly, *and being light at his desire*, which ran at his command to the land that We blessed (*namely Syria*); and We knew all things (*knowing that what We gave him would stimulate him to be submissive to his Lord*). And *We subjected*, of the devils, those who should dive for him *in the sea and bring forth from it jewels for him*, and do other work besides that; *that is, building, and performing other services;* and We watched over them, *that they might not spoil what they executed; for they used, when they had finished a work before night, to spoil it, if they were not employed in something else.*" (Sūrah xxi. 81, 82.)

"We gave unto David Solomon *his son*. How excellent a servant *was he!* For he was one who earnestly turned himself unto God, *glorifying and praising Him at all times*. Remember when, in the latter part of the day, *after the commencement of the declining of the sun*, the *mares* standing on three feet and touching the ground with the edge of the fourth foot, swift in the course, were displayed before him. *They were a thousand mares, which were displayed before him after he had performed the noon-prayers, on the occasion of his desiring to make use of them in a holy war; and when nine hundred of them had been displayed, the sun set, and he had not performed the afternoon prayers. So he was grieved*, and he said, Verily I have preferred the love of earthly goods above the remembrance of my Lord, (*that is, the performance of the afternoon prayers,*) so that *the sun* is concealed by the veil. Bring them (*namely the horses*) back unto me. *Therefore they brought them back*. And he began to sever *with his sword* the legs and the necks, *slaughtering them, and cutting off their legs, as a sacrifice unto God, and gave their flesh in alms; and God gave him in compensation what was better than they were and swifter, namely the wind, which travelled by his command whithersoever he desired.* And We tried Solomon *by depriving him of his kingdom. This was because he married a woman of whom he became enamoured, and she used to worship an idol in his palace without his knowledge. His dominion was in his signet; and he pulled it off once and deposited it with his wife, who was named El-Emeeneh* (*Amīnah*)*; and a jinnee came unto her in the form of Solomon, and took it from her.* And We placed upon his throne a counterfeit body: *namely that jinnee, who was Ṣakhr* (*Ṣakhr*)*, or another. He sat upon the throne of Solomon, and the birds and other creatures surrounded him; and Solomon went forth, with a changed appearance, and saw him upon his throne, and said unto the people, I am Solomon:—but they denied him.* Then he returned *unto his kingdom, after some days, having obtained the signet and put it on, and seated himself upon his throne.* He said, O my Lord, forgive me, and give me a dominion that may not be to anyone after me (*or beside me*); for Thou art the Liberal Giver. So We subjected unto him the wind, which ran gently at his command whithersoever he desired; and the devils also, every builder *of wonderful structures*, and diver *that brought up pearls from the sea*, and others bound in chains *which connected their hands to their necks. And We said unto him*, This is Our gift, and bestow thou *thereof upon whomsoever thou wilt*, or refrain *from bestowing*, without *rendering* an account. And verily for him was ordained a high rank with Us, and an excellent retreat. (Sūrah xxxviii 29–39.)

"We bestowed on David and Solomon knowledge *in judging men and in the language of the birds and other matters;* and they said, Praise be to God who hath made us to excel many of His believing servants, *by the gift of prophecy and by the subjection of the jinn and mankind and the devils.* And Solomon inherited from David *the gift of prophecy and knowledge;* and he said, O men, we have been taught the language of the birds, and have had bestowed on us of everything *wherewith prophets and kings are gifted.* Verily this is manifest excellence. And his armies of jinn and men and birds were gathered together unto Solomon, and they were led on in order, until, when they came unto the valley of ants, (*which was at Eṭ-Ṭáïf* [*aṭ-Ṭā'if*]*, or in Syria, the ants whereof* were *small or great*), an ant (*the queen of the ants*), *having seen the troops of Solomon*, said, O ants, enter your habitations, lest Solomon and his troops crush you violently, while they perceive not. And *Solomon* smiled, *afterwards* laughing at her saying, *which he heard from the distance of three miles, the wind conveying it to him: so he withheld his forces when he came in sight of their valley, until the ants had entered their dwellings: and his troops were on horses and on foot in this expedition.* And he said, O my Lord, inspire me to be thankful for Thy favour which Thou hast bestowed upon me and upon my parents, and to do righteousness which Thou shalt approve, and admit me, in Thy mercy, among Thy servants, the righteous, *the prophets and the saints.*

"And he examined the birds, *that he might see the lap-wing, that saw the water beneath the earth, and directed to it by pecking the earth, whereupon the devils used to draw it forth when Solomon wanted it* to perform the ablution *for prayer; but he saw it not:* and he said, Wherefore do I not see the lapwing? Is it one of the absent? *And when he was certain of the case he said,* I will assuredly punish it with a severe punishment, *by plucking out its feathers and its tail and casting it in the sun so that it shall not be able to guard against excessive thirst;* or I will slaughter it; or it shall bring me a manifest convincing proof *showing its excuse.* And it tarried not long *before it presented itself unto Solomon submissively, and raised its head and relaxed its tail and its wings: so he forgave it; and he asked it what it had met with during its absence;* and it said, I have become acquainted with that wherewith thou hast not become acquainted, and I have come unto thee from Seba (*a tribe of El-Yemen*) with a sure piece of news. I found a woman reigning over them, *named Bilḳees* (*Bilqīs*), and she hath been gifted with everything *that princes require*, and hath a magnificent throne. (*Its length was eighty cubits, and its breadth, forty cubits; and its height, thirty cubits: it was composed of gold and silver set with fine pearls and with rubies and chrysolites, and its legs were of rubies and chrysolites and emeralds: upon it were closed seven doors: to each chamber through which one passed to it was a closed door.*) I found her and her people worshipping the sun instead of God, and the devil hath made their works to seem comely unto them, so that he hath hindered them from the *right* way, wherefore they are not rightly directed to the worship of God, who produceth what is hidden (*namely, the rain and vegetables*) in the heavens and the earth, and knoweth what they [that is, mankind and others] conceal *in their hearts*, and what they reveal *with their tongues.* God: there is no deity but He, the Lord of the magnificent throne, *between which and the throne of Bilḳees is a vast difference.*

"*Solomon* said *to the lapwing,* We will see whether thou hast spoken truth or whether thou art of the liars. *Then the lapwing guided them to the water, and it was drawn forth by the devils; and they quenched their thirst and performed the ablution and prayed. Then Solomon wrote a letter, the form whereof was this:—From the servant of God, Solomon the son of David, to Bilḳees the queen of Seba. In the name of God, the Compassionate, the Merciful, Peace be on whomsoever followeth the right direction. After this salutation, I say,* Act ye not proudly towards me; *but come unto me submitting. He then sealed it with musk, and stamped it with his signet, and said unto the lapwing,* Go with this my letter and throw it down unto them (*namely Bilḳees and her people*): then turn away from them, *but stay near them,* and see what *reply* they will return. *So the lapwing took it, and came unto her, and around her were her forces; and he threw it down into her lap; and when she saw it, she trembled with fear. Then she considered what was in it, and* she said *unto the nobles of her people,* O nobles, an honourable (*sealed*) letter hath been thrown down unto me. It is from Solomon; and it is *this:*— In the name of God, the Compassionate, the Merciful. Act ye not proudly towards me: but come unto me submitting.—She said, O nobles, advise me in mine affair. I will not decide upon a thing unless ye bear me witness.—They replied, We are endowed with strength and endowed with great valour; but the command belongeth to thee; therefore see what thou wilt command *us to do, and we will obey thee.* She said, Verily kings, when they enter a city, waste it, and render the mighty of its inhabitants abject; and thus will they do *who have sent the letter.* But I will send unto them with a gift, and I will see with what the messengers will return, *whether the gift will be accepted, or whether it will be rejected. If he be merely a king, he will accept it; and if he be a prophet, he will not accept it. And she sent male and female servants, a thousand in equal numbers, five hundred of each sex, and five hundred bricks of gold, and a crown set with jewels, and musk and ambergris and other things, by a messenger with a letter. And the lapwing hastened unto Solomon, to tell him the news; on hearing which, he commanded that bricks of gold and silver should be cast, and that a horse-course should be extended to the length of nine leagues from the place where he was, and that they should build around it a wall with battlements, of gold and silver, and that the handsomest of the beasts of the land and of the sea should be brought with the sons of the jinn on the right side of the horse-course and on its left.*

"And when *the messenger* came *with the gift, and with him his attendants,* unto Solomon, he (Solomon) said, Do ye aid me with wealth? But what God hath given me (*namely, the gift of prophecy and the kingdom*) is better than what He hath given you, *of worldly goods;* yet ye rejoice in your gift, *because ye glory in the showy things of this world.* Return unto them *with the gift that thou hast brought;* for we will surely come unto them with forces with which they have not power to contend, and we will surely drive them out from it, (*that is, from their country, Seba, which was named after the father of their tribe,*) abject and contemptible, *if they come not unto us submitting. And when the messenger returned unto her with the gift, she placed her throne within seven doors, within her palace, and her palace was within seven palaces; and she closed the doors, and set guards to them, and prepared to go unto Solomon, that she might see what he would command her to do. She departed with twelve thousand kings, each king having with him many thousands, and proceeded until she came as near to him as a league's distance; when he knew of her approach,* he said, O nobles, which of you will bring unto me her throne before they come unto me submitting? An 'efreet (*'Ifrīt*) of the jinn, answered, I will bring it unto thee before thou shalt arise from thy place *wherein thou sittest to judge from morning until midday;* for I am able to do it, and trustworthy *with respect to the jewels that it compriseth and other matters. Solomon said, I desire it more speedily.* And thereupon he with whom was knowledge of the *revealed* scripture (*namely his Wezeer, Aṣaf the son of Barkhiya, who was a just person, acquainted with the most great name of God, which ensured an answer to him who invoked thereby*) said, I will bring it unto thee before thy glance can be withdrawn *from any object. And he said unto him, Look at the sky. So he looked at it; then he withdrew his glance, and found it placed before him: for during his look towards the sky, Aṣaf prayed, by the most great name, that God would bring it; and it so happened, the throne passing under the ground until it came up before the throne of Solomon.* And when he saw it firmly placed before him, he said, This is the favour of my Lord, that He may try me, whether I shall be thankful or whether I shall be unthankful. And he who is thankful is thankful for *the sake of* his own soul, *which will have the reward of his thankfulness;* and as to him who is ungrateful, my Lord is independent and bountiful.

"Then Solomon said, Alter ye her throne so that it may not be known by her, that we may see whether she be rightly directed *to the knowledge thereof,* or whether she be of those who are not rightly directed *to the knowledge of that which is altered. He desired thereby to try her intelligence. So they altered it, by adding to it, or taking from it, or in some other manner.* And when she came, it was said *unto her,* Is thy throne like this? She answered, As though it were the same. (*She answered them ambiguously like as they had questioned her ambiguously, not saying, Is this thy throne?—and had they so said, she had answered, Yes.*) *And when Solomon saw her knowledge, he said,* And we have had knowledge bestowed on us before her, and have been Muslims. But what she worshipped instead of God hindered her *from worshipping Him;* for she was of an unbelieving people. It was said unto her *also,* Enter the palace. (*It had a floor of white, transparent glass, beneath which was running water, wherein were fish. Solomon had made it on its being said unto him that her legs and feet were hairy, like the legs of an ass.* And when she saw it, she imagined it to be a great water, and she uncovered her legs, *that she might wade through it; and Solomon was on his throne at the upper end of the palace, and he saw that her legs and her feet were handsome.* He said *unto her,* Verily it is a palace evenly spread with glass. *And he invited her to embrace El-Islám,* whereupon she said, O my Lord, verily I have acted unjustly towards mine own soul, *by worshipping another than Thee,* and I resign myself, with Solomon, unto God, the Lord of the worlds. *And he desired to marry her; but he disliked the hair upon her legs; so the devils made for him the depilatory of quicklime, wherewith she removed the hair, and he married her; and he loved her, and confirmed her in her kingdom. He used to visit her every month once, and to remain with her three days; and her reign expired on the expiration of the reign of Solomon. It is related that he began to reign when he was thirteen years of age, and died at the age of three and fifty years. Extolled be the perfection of Him to the duration of whose dominion there is no end!*" (Sūrah xxvii. 15–45.)

We subjected unto Solomon the wind, which travelled in the morning (*unto the period when the sun began to decline*) *the distance of a month's journey,* and in the evening *from the commencement of the declining of the sun into its setting*) a month's *journey.* And We made the fountain of molten brass to flow for him *three days with their nights in every month, as water floweth; and the people worked until the day of its flowing, with that which had been given unto Solomon.* And of the jinn were those who worked in his presence, by the will of his Lord; and such of them as swerved from *obedience to* Our command We will cause to taste of the punishment of hell *in the world to come (or, as it is said by some, We cause to taste of its punishment in the present world, an angel beating them with a scourge from hell, the stripe of which burneth them).* They made for him whatever be pleased, of lofty halls (*with steps whereby to ascend to them*), and images (*for they were not forbidden by his law*), and large dishes, like great tanks for watering camels, *around each of which assembled a thousand men, eating from it,* and cooking-pots *standing firmly on their legs, cut out from the mountains in El-Yemen, and to which they ascended by ladders. And We said,* Work, O family of David, *in the service of God,* with thanksgiving *unto Him for what He hath given you:*—but few of My servants are the thankful. And when We decreed that he (*namely Solomon*) should die, *and he died, and remained standing, and leaning upon his staff for a year, dead, the jinn meanwhile performing those difficult works as they were accustomed to do, not knowing of his death, until the worm ate his staff, whereupon he fell down,* nothing showed them his death but the eating reptile (*the worm*) that ate his staff. And when he fell down, the jinn plainly perceived that if they had known things unseen (*of which things was the death of Solomon*), they had not continued in the ignominious affliction (*that is, in their difficult works*), *imagininy that he was alive, inconsistently with their opinion that they knew things unseen. And that the period was a year was known by calculating what the worm had eaten of his staff since his death in each day and night or other space of time.*" (Sūrah xxxiv. 11–13.)

Mr. Sale, quoting from the commentators al-Jalālān and al-Baiẓāwī, has the following remarks on the foregoing account of Solomon:—

"Some say the spirits made him (Solomon) two lions, which were placed at the foot of his throne; and two eagles, which were set above it; and that when he mounted it, the lions stretched out their paws; and when he sat down, the eagles shaded him with their wings; and that he had a carpet of green silk, on which his throne was placed, being of a prodigious length and breadth, and sufficient for all his forces to stand on, the men placing themselves on his right hand, and the spirits [or jinn] on his left; and that when all were in order, the wind at his command took up the carpet and transported it with all that were upon it wherever he pleased; the army of birds at the same time flying over their heads and forming a kind of canopy to shade them from the sun. The commentators tell us that David, having laid the foundations of the Temple of Jerusalem, which was to be in lieu of the tabernacle of Moses, when he died, left it to be finished by his son Solomon, who employed the genii in the work; that Solomon, before the edifice was quite completed, perceiving his end drew nigh, begged of God that his death might be concealed from the genii till they had entirely finished it; that God therefore so ordered it that Solomon died as he stood at his prayers, leaning on his staff, which supported the body in that posture a full year; and the genii, supposing him to be alive, continued their work during that term, at the expiration whereof, the temple being perfectly completed, a worm, which had gotten into the staff, ate it through, and the corpse fell to the ground and discovered the king's death. That after the space of forty days, which was the time the image had been worshipped in his house, the devil flew away, and threw the signet into the sea: the signet was immediately swallowed by a fish, which being taken and given to Solomon, he found the ring in its belly, and, having by this means recovered the kingdom, took Ṣakhr, and, tying a great stone to his neck, threw him into the Lake of Tiberias. The Arab historians tell us that Solomon, having finished the Temple of Jerusalem, went in pilgrimage to Makkah, where having stayed as long as he pleased, he proceeded towards al-Yaman; and leaving Makkah in the morning he arrived by noon at Ṣan'ā', and being extremely delighted with the country rested there; but wanting water to make the ablution, he looked among the birds for the lapwing which found it for him. Some say that Bilqīs, to try whether Solomon was a prophet or not, drest the boys like girls and the girls like boys, and sent him in a casket a pearl not drilled and an onyx drilled with a crooked hole; and that Solomon distinguished the boys from the girls by the different manner of their taking water, and ordered one worm to bore the pearl, and another to pass a thread through the onyx."

SON. Arabic *ibn* (ابن), pl. *banū*; Heb. בֵּן *bēn*; *walad* (ولد), pl. *aulād*; Heb. יָלָד *wālād*. The evidence of a son in favour of his parents in a court of law is not admissible. A son cannot be the slave of his father. A father can slay his son without punishment being inflicted upon him for the murder.

According to the law of inheritance of both Sunnī and Shī'ah, when there are several sons they divide the property of their deceased father equally, the eldest son being according to Shī'ah law, entitled to take possession of his father's sabre, Qur'ān, signet-ring, and robes of honour. (*Personal Law*, by Syed Ameer Ali, p. 74.)

For the Muslim doctrine regarding the son-ship of Christ, refer to article JESUS CHRIST.

SORCERY. [MAGIC.]

SOUL. There are two words used in the Qur'ān for the soul of man, *rūḥ* (روح), Heb. רוּחַ *rūakh*, and *nafs* (نفس), נֶפֶשׁ *nephesh*; *e.g.*:—

Sūrah xvii. 87: "They will ask thee of the spirit (*rūḥ*). Say, the spirit proceedeth at my Lord's command, but of knowledge only a little to you is given."

Sūrah iii. 24: "Each soul (*nafs*) shall be paid what it has earned."

Muslim theologians do not distinguish between the *rūḥ* and *nafs*, but the philosophers do. *Nafs* seems to answer the Greek ψυχή, "soul or life," human beings being distinguished as *an-nafsu 'n-nāṭiqah*, "the soul which speaks"; animals as *an-nafsu 'l-ḥaiwānīyah*, "the animal life"; and vegetables as *an-nafsu 'n-nabātīyah*; whilst *rūḥ* expresses the Greek πνεῦμα, "spirit." Man thus forming a tripartite nature of جسم *jism*, "body"; نفس *nafs*, "soul"; and روح *rūḥ*, "spirit"; an idea which does not find expression in the Qur'ān, but which is expressed in the New Testament, 1 Thess. v. 23: "And I pray God your whole *spirit* and *soul*, and *body* be preserved blameless until the coming of our Lord Jesus Christ." This tripartite nature of man is used by Dr. Pfander, and other controversialists, as an illustration of the Trinity in Unity. [SPIRIT.]

SPEAKING. [CONVERSATION.]

SPIDER, The. Arabic *al-'Ankabūt* (العنكبوت). The title of the xxixth Sūrah of the Qur'ān, in the 40th verse of which is given the parable of the spider: "The likeness for those who take to themselves guardians instead of God is the likeness of the *spider* who buildeth her a house: But verily, frailest of all houses surely is the house of the spider. Did they but know this!"

SPIRIT. Arabic (روح). The word *rūḥ* (pl. *arwāḥ*), translated "spirit," is the Arabic form corresponding to the Hebrew רוּחַ *rūakh*. It occurs nineteen times in the Qur'ān:—

1. Sūratu 'l-Baqarah (ii.), 81: "We strengthened him (Jesus) by the Holy Spirit (*Rūḥu 'l-Qudus*)."

2. Sūratu 'l-Baqarah (ii.), 254: "We strengthened him (Jesus) by the Holy Spirit (*Rūḥu 'l-Qudus*)."

3. Sūratu 'n-Nisā' (iv.), 169: "The Masīh, Jesus, son of Mary, is only an apostle of God, and His Word which He conveyed into Mary and a Spirit (proceeding) from Himself (*Rūḥun min-hu*)."

4. Sūratu 'l-Māi'dah (v.), 109: "When I strengthened thee (Jesus) with the Holy Spirit (*Rūḥu 'l-Qudus*)."

5. Sūratu 'n-Naḥl (xvi.), 2: "He will cause the angels to descend with the spirit (*Rūḥ*) on whom He pleaseth among his servants, bidding them warn that there be no God but me."

6. Sūratu 'n-Naḥl (xvi.), 104: "The Holy Spirit (*Rūḥu 'l-Qudus*) hath brought it (the Qur'ān) down with truth from thy Lord."

7. Sūratu 'l-Mi'rāj (xvii.), 87: "They will ask thee of the spirit. Say: The spirit (*ar-Rūḥ*) proceedeth at my Lord's command, but of knowledge only a little to you is given."

8. Sūratu 'sh-Shu'arā' (xxvi.), 193: "The faithful Spirit (*ar-Rūḥu 'l-Amīn*) hath come down with it (the Qur'ān)."

9. Sūratu 'l-Mu'min (xl.), 15: "He sendeth forth the Spirit (*ar-Rūḥ*) at His own behest on whomsoever of His servants He pleaseth."

10. Sūratu 'l-Mujādilah (lviii.), 23: "On the hearts of these (the faithful) hath God graven the Faith, and with a spirit (proceeding from Himself (*Rūḥun min-hu*) hath He strengthened them."

11. Sūratu 'l-Ma'ārij (lxx.), 4: "The angels and the Spirit (*ar-Rūḥ*) ascend to Him in a day, whose length is fifty thousand years."

12. Sūratu 'l-Qadr (xcvii.), 4: "Therein descend the angels and the Spirit (*ar-Rūḥ*) by permission of their Lord for every matter."

13. Sūratu 'sh-Shūrā (xlii.), 52: "Thus have we sent the Spirit (*ar-Rūḥ*) to thee with a revelation, by our command."

14. Sūratu Maryam (xix.), 17: "And we sent our spirit (*Rūḥa-nā*) to her, *Mary*, and he took before her the form of a perfect man."

15. Sūratu 'l-Ambiyā' (xxi.), 91: "Into whom (Mary) we breathed of our Spirit (*min Rūḥi-nā*)."

16. Sūratu 't-Taḥrīm (lxvi.), 12: "Into whose womb (*i.e.* Mary's) we breathed of our Spirit (*min Rūḥi-nā*)."

17. Sūratu 's-Sajdah (xxxii.), 8: "And breathed of His Spirit (*min Rūḥi-hi*) into him (Adam)."

18. Sūratu 'l-Ḥijr (xv.), 29: "And when I shall have finished him (Adam) and breathed of my Spirit (*min Rūḥī*) into him."

19. Sūratu Ṣād (xxxviii.), 72: "And when I have formed him (Adam) and breathed of my Spirit (*min-Rūḥī*) into him."

Of the above quotations, all Muslim commentators are agreed in applying Nos. 1, 2, 4, 5, 6, 8, 11, 12, 14, to the angel Gabriel; Nos. 3, 15, 16, are said to be Jesus, the *Rūḥu 'llāh*, or "Spirit of God"; Nos. 17, 18, 19, the *Rūḥ*, or "Life," given to Adam; Nos. 9, 13, "the Spirit of Prophecy"; No. 10 is held to mean God's grace and strength. With reference to No. 7, there is some discussion. The Khalīfah 'Alī is related to have said that it was an angel with 7,000 mouths, in each mouth there being 7,000 tongues, which unceasingly praised God. Ibn 'Abbās held that it meant the angel Gabriel. Mujāhid, that it meant beings of another world.

The Commentators al-Kamālān say the Jews came and asked Muḥammad regarding the spirit of man, and the Prophet replied, "The Spirit proceedeth at my Lord's command, but of knowledge only a little to you is given," from which it is evident that it is impossible for the finite mind to understand the nature of a spirit.

The philosophical bearings of the question are fully discussed, from an Oriental standpoint in the *Kashshāfu 'ṣṭilāḥāti 'l-Funūn, A Dictionary of Technical Terms used in the Sciences of the Mussalmāns*, edited by W. Nassau Lees, LL.D., 1862, vol. i. p. 541; also in the *Sharḥu 'l-Mawāqif*, p. 582.

Muḥammadan writers hold very conflicting views regarding the state of the soul or spirit after death. All agree that the Angel of Death (*Malaku 'l-Maut*), separates the human soul from the body at the time of death, and that he performs his office with ease and gentleness towards the good, and with force and violence towards the wicked, a view which they establish on the testimony of the Qur'ān, Sūrah lxxix. 1, where the Prophet swears by "those who tear out violently and those who gently release." After death the spirits enter a state called *al-Barzakh*, or the interval between death and the Resurrection, the Ἅιδης of the New Testament. The souls of the faithful are said to be divided into three classes: (1) those of the Prophets who are admitted into Paradise immediately after death; (2) those of the martyrs who, according to a tradition of Muḥammad, rest in the crops of green birds, which eat the fruits and drink of the waters of Paradise; those of all other believers, concerning the state of whose souls before the Resurrection there is great diversity of opinion. Some say they stay near the graves, either for a period of only seven days, or, according to others, until the Day of Resurrection. In proof of this, they quote the example of Muḥammad, who always saluted the spirits of the departed when passing a grave-yard. Others say, all the departed spirits of the faithful are in the lowest heaven with Adam, because the Prophet declared he saw them there in his pretended ascent to heaven. [MI'RAJ.] Whilst others say the departed spirits dwell in the forms of white birds under the throne of God (which is a Jewish tradition).

Al-Baiẓāwī says the souls of the wicked are carried down to a pit in hell called Sijjīn [SIJJIN]; and there is a tradition to the effect that Muḥammad said the spirits of the wicked are tormented until the Day of Resurrection, when they are produced with their bodies for judgment.

The author of the *Sharḥu 'l-Mawāqif* (p. 583), says that some Muslim philosophers state that after death the spirit of man will either be in a state of enlightenment or of ignorance. Those who are in a state of ignorance will go on from worse to worse, and those who are in a state of enlightenment will only suffer so far as they have contracted qualities of an undesirable character when in the body, but they will gradually improve until they arrive at a state of perfect enjoyment. This view, however, is not one which is tenable with the views propounded by the Qur'ān, in which there are very decided notions regarding the future state of heaven and hell. [SOUL.]

SPITTING. According to the Traditions, Muslims must spit on the left side, and cover it over with earth. Spitting in mosques is forbidden. (See 'Abdu 'l-Ḥaqq's *Commentary on the Mishkāt*, vol. i. p. 295.)

Muḥammad said: "Spit not in front, for you are in God's presence. Spit not on the right hand, for there standeth the angel who recordeth your good actions."

SPOILS, The. Arabic *al-Anfāl* (الانفال). The title of the VIIIth Sūrah of the Qur'ān, in which are given instructions regarding the division of the spoils taken at the battle of Badr, a dispute having arisen between the young men who had fought and the old men who had stayed under the ensigns; the former insisting they ought to have the whole, and the latter that they deserved a share. [PLUNDER.]

STANDARDS. Arabic *'alam* (علم), pl. *a'lām*. Regarding the standards used by Muḥammad, there are the following traditions:—

Jābir says: "The Prophet came into Makkah with a white standard."

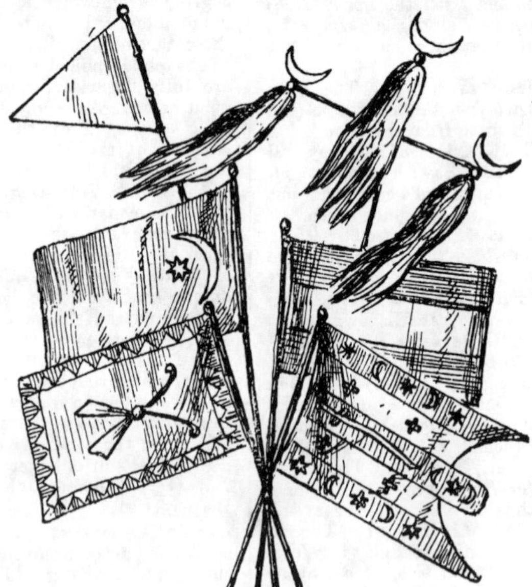

MUHAMMADAN STANDARDS. (*A. F. Hole.*)

1. Muslim Standard of Central Asian Tribes.
2. Standard of the Turkish Empire.
3. Standard of the Empire of Morocco.
4. Horse-tail Standard of Modern Turks
5. Standard of Egypt.
6. Standard of Persia.

Ibn ʻAbbās says: "The Prophet had two standards, a large black one and a small white one."

Al-Barā' ibn ʻĀzib says: "The standard, I remember, was a square one, and black spotted with divers colours."

In the struggle between the Shīʻahs and the Sunnīs, the Fatimides adopted green as the colour of their standard, whilst the Banī Umaiyah assumed white for theirs.

In Central Asia, the ordinary Muslim standards are either black or green, and are triangular. The sign of the crescent, as it appears on Turkish standards, was adopted after the taking of Byzantium; for, long before the conquest of Constantinople, the crescent had been used in the city for an emblem of sovereignty, as may be seen from the medals struck in honour of Augustus and Trajan. [CRESCENT.]

There is a standard still preserved at Constantinople amongst the ancient relics, and called *as-Sinjaqu 'sh-sharīf*, which is held to

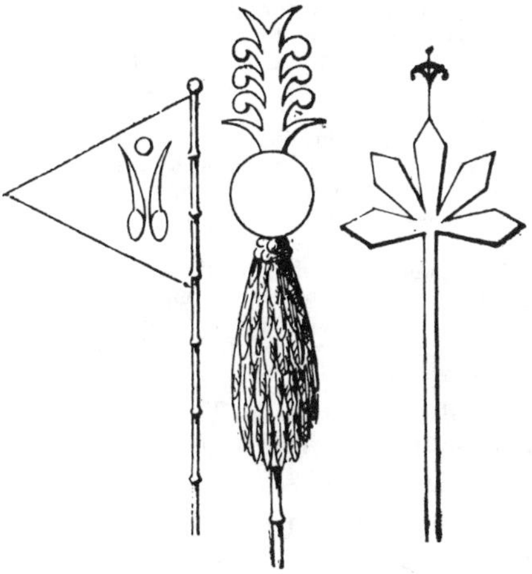

MUHARRAM STANDARDS.

be a most sacred emblem, and is only produced on very special occasions. It is said to be the ancient standard of the Prophet.

A modern writer, describing this flag, says: "It is made of four layers of silk, the topmost of which is green, those below being composed of cloth, embroidered with gold. Its entire length is twelve feet, and from it is suspended the figure of a human hand, which clasps a copy of the Qur'ān, transcribed by the Khalīfah ʻUṣmān. In times of peace, the banner of the Prophet is kept in a chamber appropriated to the purpose, along with the clothes, teeth, the venerable locks, the stirrups, and the bow of the Prophet."

In the Muḥarram, when the martyrdom of al-Ḥasan and al-Ḥusain is celebrated, numerous standards are carried about in the procession.

The origin of the horse-tail standard borne by modern Turks, appears to have been from the people bearing the horse-tail as a distinction of rank, the two ranks of pashas being distinguished respectively by two and three tails, and a further distinction of rank being marked by the elevation of one of the tails above the others.

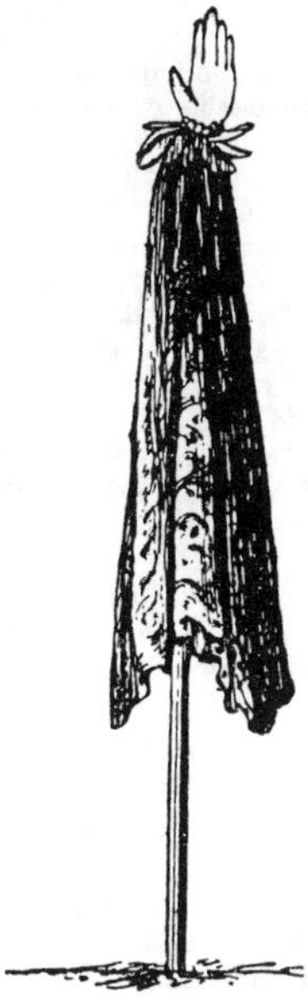

MUHARRAM STANDARD.

According to the Traditions, the Mahdī, in the Last Days, will appear from the direction of Khorosān with black ensigns, and there seems to be every reason to regard the black standard as the primitive ensign of Islām, although the Wahhābīs have generally carried green standards.

STATUES. [SCULPTURE.]

STONING TO DEATH.

Arabic *rajm* (رجم). In Muslim law, the punishment of lapidation is only inflicted for adultery. (Under the Jewish law idolaters and bearers of false witness were also stoned.) It is founded, not upon the Qur'ān, where the only punishment awarded is one hundred stripes (Sūrah xxiv. 2), but upon the Traditions (*Mishkāt*, book xv. ch. 1), where Muḥammad is related to have said, "Verily God hath ordained for a man or woman not married one hundred lashes and expulsion from their town one year, and for a man or woman having been married one hundred lashes and stoning." ʻAbdu 'l-Ḥaqq says the hundred lashes, in addition to the stoning, is abrogated by the express example of the Prophet, who ordered stoning only; for ʻAbdu 'llāh ibn ʻUmar relates the following tradition:—

"A Jew came to the Prophet and said, 'A man and woman of ours have committed adultery.' And the Prophet said, 'What do you meet with in the Book of Moses in the matter of stoning?' The Jew said, 'We do not find stoning in the Bible, but we disgrace adulterers and whip them.' Then 'Abdu 'llāh ibn Salām, who was a learned man of the Jews, and had embraced Islām, said, 'You lie, O Jewish tribe! verily the order for stoning is in the Book of Moses.' Then the book was brought, and opened; and a Jew put his hand upon the revelation for stoning, and read the one above and below it; and 'Abdu 'llāh said, 'Lift up your hand.' And he did so, and behold the revelation for stoning was produced in the book, and the Jews said, ''Abdu 'llāh spoke true, O Muḥammad! the stoning revelation is in the Book of Moses.' Then the Prophet ordered both the man and woman to be stoned." (*Mishkāt*, book xv. ch. i.)

The author of the *Hidāyah* (vol. ii. p. 9) gives the following instructions as to the correct way of carrying out the sentence:—

"It is necessary, when a whoremonger is to be stoned to death, that he should be carried to some barren place void of houses or cultivation, and it is requisite that the stoning be executed—first by the witnesses, and after them by the Imām or Qāẓī, and after those by the rest of the bystanders, because it is so recorded from 'Alī, and also because in the circumstance of the execution being begun by the witnesses there is a precaution, since a person may be very bold in delivering his evidence against a criminal, but afterwards, when directed himself to commence the infliction of that punishment which is a consequence of it, may from compunction retract his testimony; thus, causing the witnesses to begin the punishment may be a means of entirely preventing it. Ash-Shāfi'ī has said that the witnesses beginning the punishment is not a requisite, in a case of lapidation, any more than in a case of scourging. To this our doctors reply that reasoning upon a case of lapidation from a case of scourging is supposing an analogy between things which are essentially different, because all persons are not acquainted with the proper method of inflicting flagellation, and hence, if a witness thus ignorant were to attempt, it might prove fatal to the sufferer, and he would die where death is not his due, contrary to a case of lapidation, as that is of a destructive nature, and what every person is equally capable of executing, wherefore if the witnesses shrink back from the commencement of lapidation the punishment drops, because their reluctance argues their retraction.

"In the same manner punishment is remitted when the witnesses happen to die, or to disappear, as in this case the condition, namely, the commencement of it by the witnesses, is defeated. This is when the whoredom is established upon the testimony of witnesses: but when it is established upon the confession of the offender, it is then requisite that the lapidation be executed, first by the Imām or the Qāẓī, and after them by the rest of the multitude, because it is so recorded from 'Alī. Moreover, the Prophet threw a small stone like a bean at Ghamdīyah who had confessed whoredom. When a woman is to be stoned, a hole or excavation should be dug to receive her, as deep as her waist, because the Prophet ordered such a hole to be dug for Ghamdīyah before mentioned, and 'Alī also ordered a hole to be dug for Shuraha Hamdiānī. It is, however, immaterial whether a hole be dug or not, because the Prophet did not issue any particular ordinance respecting this, and the nakedness of a woman is sufficiently covered by her garments; but yet it is laudable to dig a hole for her, as decency is thus most effectually preserved. There is no manner of necessity to dig a hole for a man, because the prophet did not so in the case of Mā'iz. And observe, it is not lawful to bind a person in order to execute punishment upon him in this case, unless it appears that it cannot otherwise be inflicted.

"The corpse of a person executed by lapidation for whoredom is entitled to the usual ablutions, and to all other funeral ceremonies, because of the declaration of the Prophet with respect to Mā'iz. 'Do by the body as ye do by those of other believers'; and also, because the offender thus put to death is slain in vindication of the laws of God, wherefore ablution is not refused, as in the case of one put to death by a sentence of retaliation; moreover the Prophet allowed the prayers for the dead to Ghamdīyah, after lapidation." (*Hidāyah*, book ii. p. 9.)

This punishment of lapidation for adultery has become almost obsolete in modern times; even in Bukhārah, where the institutes of Muḥammad are supposed to be most strictly observed, it is not inflicted.

SUBḤAH (سبحة). The rosary of ninety-nine beads. [ROSARY.]

SUBḤAN (سبحان). [TASBIH.]

SUBḤĀNA 'LLĀHI (سبحان الله). "Holiness be to God!" An ejaculation which is called the *Tasbīḥ*. It occurs in the liturgical prayer, and is used as an ejaculation of surprise or fear. [TASBIH.]

ṢŪFAH (صوفة). *Banū Ṣūfah.* An ancient tribe of Arabia. The descendants of Tābikha and Elyās (Muir, vol. i. p. cxcix.)

ṢŪFĪ (صوفى), more correctly صوفّى *Ṣūf'īy.* (The Persian form of the plural being صوفيان *Ṣufīyān.*) A man of the people called صوفية *Sufīyah*, who profess the mystic principles of تصوف *Taṣawwuf.* There is considerable discussion as to the origin of this word. It is said to be derived (1) from the Arabic *Ṣūf*, "wool," on account of the woollen dress worn by Eastern ascetics; (2) or from the Arabic *Ṣafū*, "purity," with reference to the effort to attain to metaphysical purity (which is scarcely probable); (3) or from the Greek σοφία, "wisdom"; (4) or, according to the *Ghiyāṣu 'l-Lughāt*, it is derived from the *Ṣūfah*, the name of a tribe of Arabs who in the "time of ignorance," separated themselves from the world, and engaged themselves exclusively in the service of the Makkah Temple.

It might at first sight appear almost an impossibility for mysticism to engraft itself upon the legal system of the Qur'ān, and the Ahādīs̤, with the detailed ritual and cold formality which are so strikingly exemplified in Islām; but it would appear that from the very days of Muḥammad, there have been always those who, whilst they called themselves Muslims, set aside the literal meaning of the words of Muḥammad for a supposed mystic or spiritual interpretation, and it is generally admitted by Ṣūfīs that one of the great founders of their system, as found in Islām, was the adopted son and son-in-law of the Prophet, 'Alī ibn Abī Ṭālib. The Ṣūfīs themselves admit that their religious system has always existed in the world, prior to the mission of Muḥammad, and the unprejudiced student of their system will observe that *Taṣawwuf*, or Ṣūfīism, is but a Muslim adaptation of the Vedānta school of Hindū philosophers, and which also we find in the writings of the old academics of Greece, and Sir William Jones thought Plato learned from the sages of the East.

The Ṣūfīs are divided into innumerable sects, which find expression in the numerous religious orders of Darweshes or Faqīrs [FAQIR]; but although they differ in name and in some of their customs, as dress, meditations and recitations, they are all agreed in their principal tenets, particularly those which inculcate the absolute necessity of blind submission to a *murshid*, or inspired guide. It is generally admitted that, quite irrespective of minor sects, the Ṣūfīs are divided into those who claim to be only the *Ilhāmīyah*, or inspired of God, and those who assert that they are *Ittiḥādīyah*, or unionist with God.

I. The Doctrine of the Ṣūfīs.

The following is a succinct account of the doctrines of the Ṣūfīs:—

1. God only exists. He in all things, and all things in Him.

2. All visible and invisible beings are an emanation from Him, and are not really distinct from Him.

3. Religions are matters of indifference: they however serve as leading to realities. Some for this purpose are more advantageous than others, among which is al-Islām, of which Ṣūfīism is the true philosophy.

4. There does not really exist any difference between good and evil, for all is reduced to Unity, and God is the real Author of the acts of mankind.

5. It is God who fixes the will of man: man therefore is not free in his actions.

6. The soul existed before the body, and is confined within the latter as in a cage. Death, therefore, should be the object of the wishes of the Ṣūfī, for it is then that he returns to the bosom of Divinity.

7. It is by this metempsychosis that souls which have not fulfilled their destination here below are purified and become worthy of reunion with God.

8. Without the grace of God, which the Ṣūfīs call *Fayazānu 'llāh*, or *Faẓlu 'llāh*, no one can attain to this spiritual union, but this, they assert, can be obtained by fervently asking for it.

9. The principal occupation of the Ṣūfī, whilst in the body, is meditation on the *waḥdānīyah*, or Unity of God, the remembrance of God's names [ZIKR], and the progressive advancement in the *Ṭarīqah*, or journey of life, so as to attain unification with God.

II The Ṣūfī Journey.

Human life is likened to a journey (*safar*), and the seeker after God to a traveller (*sālik*).

The great business of the traveller is to exert himself and strive to attain that perfect knowledge (*ma'rifah*) of God which is diffused through all things, for the Soul of man is an exile from its Creator, and human existence is its period of banishment. The sole object of Ṣūfīism is to lead the wandering soul onward, stage by stage, until it reaches the desired goal—perfect union with the Divine Being.

The natural state of every human being is humanity (*nāsūt*), in which state the disciple must observe the Law (*sharī'ah*); but as this is the lowest form of spiritual existence, the performance of the journey is enjoined upon every searcher after true knowledge.

The various stages (*manāzil*) are differently described by Ṣūfī writers, but amongst those of India (and, according to Malcolm, of Persia also,) the following is the usual journey:—

The first stage, as we have already remarked, is humanity (*nāsūt*), in which the disciple must live according to the Law (*sharī'ah*), and observe all the rites, customs, and precepts of his religion. The second is the nature of angels (*malakūt*), for which there is the pathway of purity (*ṭarīqah*). The third is the possession of power (*jabrūt*), for which there is knowledge (*ma'rifah*); and the fourth is extinction (*fanā'*) (*i.e.* absorption into the Deity), for which there is Truth (*ḥaqīqah*).

The following more extended journey is marked out for the traveller by a Ṣūfī writer, 'Azīz ibn Muḥammad Nafasī, in a book called *al-Maqṣadu 'l-Aqṣā*, or the "Remotest Aim," which has been rendered into English by the lamented Professor Palmer (*Oriental Mysticism*, Cambridge, 1867):—

When a man possessing the necessary requirements of fully-developed reasoning powers turns to them for a resolution of his doubts and uncertainties concerning the real nature of the Godhead, he is called a *ṭālib*, "a searcher after God."

If he manifest a further inclination to prosecute his inquiry according to their system, he is called a *murīd*, or "one who inclines."

Placing himself then under the spiritual

instruction of some eminent leader of the sect, he is fairly started upon his journey and becomes a *sālik*, or "traveller," whose whole business in life is devotion, to the end that he may ultimately arrive at the knowledge of God.

1. Here he is exhorted to serve God, as the first step towards a knowledge of Him. This is the *first* stage of his journey, and is called *'ubūdīyah* (عبودية), or "service."

2. When in answer to his prayers the Divine influence or attraction has developed his inclination into the love of God, he is said to have reached the stage called *'Ishq* (عشق) or "love."

3. This Divine Love, expelling all worldly desires from his heart, leads him to the next stage, which is *zuhd* (زهد), or "seclusion."

4. Occupying himself henceforward with contemplations and investigations of metaphysical theories concerning the nature, attributes, and works of God, he reaches *ma'rifah* (معرفة), or "knowledge."

5. This assiduous contemplation of startling metaphysical theories is exceedingly attractive to an oriental mind, and not unfrequently produces a state of mental excitement. Such ecstatic state is considered a sure prognostication of direct illumination of the heart by God, and constitutes the next stage, called *wajd* (وجد), or "ecstasy."

6. During this stage he is supposed to receive a revelation of the true nature of the Godhead, and to have reached the stage called *ḥaqīqah* (حقيقة), or "truth."

7. He then proceeds to the stage of *waṣl* (وصل), or "union with God."

8. Further than this he cannot go, but pursues his habit of self-denial and contemplation until his death, which is looked upon as *fanā'* (فناء), "total absorption into the Deity, extinction."

To develop this quasi "spiritual life" the Ṣūfī leaders have invented various forms of devotion called *ẕikr* (ذكر), or "recitations." These eccentric exercises have generally attracted the notice of travellers in the East, and have been described by Lane, Vambéry, Burton, and other Orientalists. For an account of these ceremonies of *Ẕikr* the reader is referred to the article under that head. [ZIKR.]

III. The Perfect Man in Ṣūfī Spiritualism.

The late Professor E. H. Palmer of Cambridge has in his *Oriental Mysticism*, compiled from native sources, given a very correct idea of what may be considered the spiritual side of Muḥammadanism, as expressed in the teaching of Muslim Ṣūfīs.

"The perfect man is he who has fully comprehended the Law, the Doctrine, and the Truth; or, in other words, he who is endued with four things in perfection, viz. 1. Good words; 2. Good deeds; 3. Good principles; 4. The sciences. It is the business of the Traveller to provide himself with these things in perfection, and by so doing he will provide himself with perfection.

"The Perfect Man has had various other names assigned to him, all equally applicable, viz. Elder, Leader, Guide, Inspired Teacher, Wise, Virtuous, Perfect, Perfecter, Beacon and Mirror of the world, Powerful Antidote, Mighty Elixir, *'Isà* (Jesus) the Raiser of the Dead, *Khizar* the Discoverer of the Water of Life, and *Solomon* who knew the language of Birds.

"The Universe has been likened to a single person, of whom the Perfect Man is the Soul; and again, to a tree, of which mankind is the fruit, and the Perfect Man the pith and essence. Nothing is hidden from the Perfect Man; for after arriving at the knowledge of God, he has attained to that of the nature and properties of material objects, and can henceforth find no better employment than acting mercifully towards mankind. Now there is no mercy better than to devote oneself to the perfection and improvement of others, both by precept and example. Thus the Prophet is called in the Coran 'a mercy to the Universe.' (Cor. cap. 21, v. 107.) But with all his perfection the Perfect Man cannot compass his desires, but passes his life in consistent and unavoidable self-denial: he is perfect in knowledge and principle, but imperfect in faculty and power.

"There have indeed been Perfect Men possessed of power; such power as that which resides in kings and rulers; yet a careful consideration of the poor extent of man's capacities will shew that his weakness is preferable to his power, his want of faculty preferable to his possession of it. Prophets and saints, kings and sultans, have desired many things, and failed to obtain them; they have wished to avoid many things, and have had them forced upon them. Mankind is made up of the Perfect and the Imperfect, of the Wise and the Foolish, of Kings and Subjects, but all are alike weak and helpless, all pass their lives in a manner contrary to their desires; this the Perfect Man recognises and acts upon, and, knowing that nothing is better for man than renunciation, forsakes all and becomes free and at leisure. As before he renounced wealth and dignity, so now he foregoes eldership and teachership, esteeming freedom and rest above everything: the fact is, that though the motive alleged for education and care of others is a feeling of compassion and a regard for discipline, yet the real instigation is the love of dignity: as the Prophet says, 'The last thing that is removed from the chiefs of the righteous is love of dignity.' I have said that the Perfect Man should be endued with four things in perfection: now the Perfectly Free Man should have four additional characteristics, viz. renunciation, retirement, contentment, and leisure. He who has the first four is virtuous, but not free: he who has the whole eight is perfect, liberal, virtuous, and free. Furthermore, there are two grades of the Perfectly Free—those who have renounced wealth and dignity only, and those who have further renounced eldership and teachership, thus becoming free and at leisure. These again are subdivided into two classes; those who, after renunciation, retirement and contentment, make choice of obscurity, and those who, after renunciation, make choice of submission, contemplation, and resignation; but the object of both is the same. Some writers assert that freedom and leisure consists in the former course, while others maintain that it is only to be found in the latter.

"Those who make choice of obscurity are actuated by the knowledge that annoyance and distraction of thought are the invariable concomitants of society; they therefore avoid receiving visits and presents, and fear them as they would venomous beasts. The other class, who adopt submission, resignation and contemplation, do so because they perceive that mankind for the most part are ignorant of what is good for them, being dissatisfied with what is beneficial, and delighted with circumstances that are harmful to them; as the Coran says, 'Perchance ye may dislike what is good for you, and like what is hurtful to you.' (Cor. cap. 2, v. 213.) For this reason they retire from society equally with the other class, caring little what the world may think of them.

"Fellowship has many qualities and effects both of good and evil. The fellowship of the wise is the only thing that can conduct the Traveller safely to the Goal; therefore all the submission, earnestness, and discipline that have been hitherto inculcated are merely in order to render him worthy of such fellowship. Provided he have the capacity, a single day, nay, a single hour, in the society of the wise, tends more to his improvement than years of self-discipline without it. 'Verily one day with thy Lord is better than a thousand years.' (Cor. cap. 22, v. 46.)

"It is, however, possible to frequent the society of the wise without receiving any benefit therefrom, but this must proceed either from want of capacity or want of will. In order then to avoid such a result, the Sufis have laid down the following rules for the conduct of the disciple when in the presence of his teachers.

"Hear, attend, but speak little.

"Never answer a question not addressed to you; but if asked, answer promptly and concisely, never feeling ashamed to say, 'I know not.'

"Do not dispute for disputation's sake.

"Never boast before your elders.

"Never seek the highest place, nor even accept it if it be offered to you.

"Do not be over-ceremonious, for this will compel your elders to act in the same manner towards you, and give them needless annoyance.

"Observe in all cases the etiquette appropriate to the time, place, and persons present.

"In indifferent matters, that is, matters involving no breach of duty by their omission or commission, conform to the practice and wishes of those with whom you are associating.

"Do not make a practice of anything which is not either a duty or calculated to increase the comfort of your associates; otherwise it will become an idol to you; and it is incumbent on every one to break his idols and renounce his habits."

IV. Renunciation.

"This leads us to the subject of Renunciation, which is of two kinds, external and internal. The former is the renunciation of worldly wealth; the latter, the renunciation of worldly desires. Everything that hinders or veils the Traveller's path must be renounced, whether it relate to this world or the next. Wealth and dignity are great hindrances; but too much praying and fasting are often hindrances too. The one is a shroud of darkness, the other a veil of light. The Traveller must renounce idolatry, if he desire to reach the Goal, and everything that bars his progress is an idol. All men have some idol, which they worship; with one it is wealth and dignity, with another overmuch prayer and fasting. If a man sit always upon his prayer-carpet, his prayer-carpet becomes his idol. And so on with a great number of instances.

"Renunciation must not be performed without the advice and permission of an elder. It should be the renunciation of trifles, not of necessaries, such as food, clothing, and dwelling-place, which are indispensable to man; for without them he would be obliged to rely on the aid of others, and this would beget avarice, which is 'the mother of vice.' The renunciation of necessaries produces as corrupting an influence upon the mind as the possession of too much wealth. The greatest of blessings is to have a sufficiency, but to over-step this limit is to gain nought but additional trouble.

"Renunciation is the practice of those who know God, and the characteristic mark of the wise. Every individual fancies that he alone possesses this knowledge, but knowledge is an attribute of the mind, and there is no approach from unaided sense to the attributes of the mind, by which we can discover who is, or who is not, possessed of this knowledge. Qualities however are the sources of action; therefore a man's practice is an infallible indication of the qualities he possesses; if, for instance, a man asserts that he is a baker, a carpenter, or a blacksmith, we can judge at once if he possesses skill in these crafts by the perfection of his handiwork. In a word, theory is internal, and practice external, the presence of the practice, therefore, is a proof that the theory too is there.

"Renunciation is necessary to the real confession of faith; for the formula 'There is no God but God,' involves two things, negation and proof. Negation is the renunciation of other Gods, and proof is the knowledge of God. Wealth and dignity have led many from the right path, they are the gods the people worship; if then you see that one has renounced these, you may be sure that he has expelled the love of this world from his heart, and completed the negation; and whosoever has attained to the knowledge of God has completed the proofs. This is really confessing that 'there is no God but God'; and he who has not attained to the knowledge of God, has never really repeated the confession of faith. Early prejudices are a great stumbling-block to many people; for the first principles of Monotheism are contained in the words of the Hadís: 'Every one is born with a disposition [for the true faith], but his parents make him a Jew, a Christian, or a Magian.' The Unitarians also say, that the real confession of faith consists in negation and proof; but they explain negation by renunciation of self, and proof by acknowledgment of God.

"Thus, according to the Sufis, confession of faith, prayer and fasting contain two distinct features, namely, form and truth; the former being entirely inefficacious without the latter. Renunciation and the knowledge of God are like a tree; the knowledge of God is the root, renunciation the branches, and all good principles and qualities are the fruit. To sum up, the lesson to be learnt is that in repeating the formula the Traveller must acknowledge in his heart that God only always was, God only always will be. This world and the next, nay, the very existence of the Traveller, may vanish, but God alone remains. This is the true confession of faith; and although the Traveller before was blind, the moment he is assured of this his eyes are opened, and he seeth.

V. Helps to Devotion.

"The Sufis hold that there are three aids necessary to conduct the Traveller on his path.

"1. Attraction (*injiẕāb* انجذاب); 2. Devotion (*'ibādah* عبادة); 3. Elevation (*'urūj* عروج).

"Attraction is the act of God, who draws man towards Himself. Man sets his face towards this world, and is entangled in the love of wealth and dignity, until the grace of God steps in and turns his heart towards God. The tendency proceeding from God is called Attraction; that which proceeds from man is called Inclination, Desire and Love. As the inclination increases, its name changes, and it causes the Traveller to renounce everything else becoming a Kiblah, to set his face towards God; when it has become his Kiblah, and made him forget everything but God, it is developed into Love. [QIBLAH.]

"Most men when they have attained this stage are content to pass their lives therein, and leave the world without making further progress. Such a person the Sufis call Attracted (مجذوب *majzūb*).

"Others, however, proceed from this to self-examination, and pass the rest of their lives in devotion. They are then called Devoutly Attracted (مجذوب سالك *majzūb-i-Sālik*). If devotion be first practised, and the attraction of God then step in, such a person is called an Attracted Devotee (سالك مجذوب *Sālik-i-majzūb*). If he practise and complete devotion, but is not influenced by the attraction of God, he is called a Devotee (سالك *Sālik*).

"Sheikh Shehāb-uddín, in his work entitled *'Awárif al Ma'árif*, says that an elder or teacher should be selected from the second class alone: for although many may be estimable and righteous, it is but few who are fit for such offices, or for the education of disciples.

"Devotion is the prosecution of the journey, and that in two ways, to God and in God. The first, the Sufis say, has a limit; the second is boundless; the journey to God is completed when the Traveller has attained to the knowledge of God; and then commences the journey in God, which has for its object the knowledge of the Nature and Attributes of God, a task which they confess is not to be accomplished in so short a space as the lifetime of man.

The knowledge wisest men have shared
Of Thy great power and Thee
Is less, when with Thyself compared,
Than one drop in a sea.

"The Unitarians maintain that the journey to God is completed when the Traveller has acknowledged that there is no existence save that of God; the journey in God they explain to be a subsequent inquiry into the mysteries of nature.

"The term Elevation or ascent (عروج *'urūj*) is almost synonymous with Progress.

VI. The Intellectual and Spiritual Development of Man.

"Every animal possesses a vegetative spirit, a living spirit, and an instinctive spirit; but man has an additional inheritance, namely the Spirit of Humanity. Now this was breathed by God into man directly from Himself, and is therefore of the same character as the Primal Element: 'And when I have fashioned him and breathed My spirit into him.' (Cor. cap, 15. v. 29.) The Sufis do not interpret this of the Life, but of the Spirit of Humanity, and say that it is frequently not attained until a late period of life, thirty or even eighty years. Before man can receive this Spirit of Humanity, he must be furnished with capacity, which is only to be acquired by purifying oneself from all evil and immoral qualities and dispositions, and adorning oneself with the opposite ones. Sheikh Muhíy-uddín ibn ul 'Arabí, in his 'Investigations' (فصوص), says that the words 'and when I have fashioned him,' refer to this preparation, and the rest of the sentence, 'and breathed My spirit into him,' refers to the accession of the Spirit of Humanity.

"Two conditions are therefore imposed upon the Traveller, first, to attain Humanity, second, to acquire capacity.

"There are three developments of character that must be suppressed before man can attain to Humanity; the animal, the brutal, and the fiendish. He who only eats and sleeps, and gives way to lust, is mere animal; if besides these he gives way to anger and cruelty, he is brutal; and if in addition to all these he is crafty, lying, and deceitful, he is fiendish.

"If the Traveller is moderate in his food, rest, and desires, and strives to attain a knowledge of himself and of God, then is the time for acquiring capacity by freeing himself from all that is evil and base, and adorning himself with the opposite qualities; after that by prayer he may obtain the Spirit of Humanity. Some one has truly said that there is none of the perfection, essence, or immortality of man, save only among such as are 'created with a godly disposition.' When the Traveller has once been revivified by the Spirit of Humanity he becomes immortal, and inherits everlasting life. This is why it has been said that 'man has a beginning but no end.'

"If when he has attained this Spirit of Humanity, he is earnest, and does not waste his life in trifling, he soon arrives at the Divine Light itself. For 'God guideth whom He pleaseth unto His Light.' The attainment of this light is the completion of Man's upward progress, but no one can attain to it but those who are pure in spirit and in their lives. Mohammed asserted that he himself had attained it, 'To the light have I reached, and in the light I live;' now this light is the Nature of God; wherefore he said, 'who seeth me seeth God.' [NUR-I-MUHAMMAD.]

"The germ that contains the Primal Element of Man is the lowest of the low, and the Divine Light is the highest of the high; it is between these extremes that the stages of man's upward or downward progress lie. 'We have created man in the fairest of proportions, and then have thrown him back to be the lowest of the low, save only such as believe and act with righteousness; and verily these shall have their reward.' (Cor. cap. 95, v. 4). This reward is said by the Sufis to be defined by the word *ajrat*, 'reward,' itself. This word contains three radical letters ا ج and ر; ا stands for اعادة 'return,' ج for جنة 'paradise,' and ر for روية, that is 'those who have handed down the faith.' Their acting righteously is their return to the Nature of God, for when they have finished their upward progress and reached this they are in Paradise, and in the presence of their God. He therefore is a man, in the true sense of the word, who being sent down upon earth strives upward towards Heaven. These aspirations are indispensable to man; he might by the Almighty Power of God exist without all beside, even had the Heavens and the elements themselves never been; but these things are the aim and want of all.

"It has been said that the Primal Element or constructive spirit as well as the Spirit of Humanity proceed direct from God. They are therefore identical, and are both included by the Sufis in the one term Concomitant Spirit. Now this Spirit, although distinct and individual, comprehends and governs the entire Universe. The Simple Natures are its administrators and exponents; of these the Seven Sires beget, and the Four Mothers conceive from the incarnation of this spirit in them, and their offspring is the triple kingdom, Mineral, Vegetable, and Animal. And so it is with the Lesser World of Man.

"Now this Spirit hath two functions, external and internal; the external is revealed in the material generation just alluded to, the internal abides in the heart of man. Whosoever purifies his heart from worldly impressions and desires, reveals this internal function of the Spirit within him, and illumines and revivifies his soul.

"Thus the Spirit at once comprehends the Universe and dwells in the heart of man.

VII. Of the Upward Progress or Ascent of Man.

"When Man has become assured of the truth of Revelation, he has reached the stage of Belief, and has the name of *Múmin*, 'Believer.' When he further acts in obedience to the will of God, and apportions the night and day for earnest prayer, he has reached the stage of worship, and is called an *'A'bid*, or 'Worshipper.' When he has expelled the love of this world from his heart, and occupies himself with a contemplation of the mighty Whole, he reaches the next stage, and becomes a *Záhid*, or 'Recluse.' When in addition to all this he knows God, and subsequently learns the mysteries of nature, he reaches the stage of Acquaintance, and is called *'A'rif*, 'One who knows.' The next stage is that in which he attains to the love of God, and is called a *Welí*, or 'Saint.' When he is moreover gifted with inspiration and the power of working miracles, he becomes a *Nebí*, 'Prophet'; and when entrusted next with the delivery of God's own message, he is called an 'Apostle,' *Rusúl*. When he is appointed to abrogate a previous dispensation and preach a new one, he is called *Ulu 'l'Azm*, 'One who has a mission.' When this mission is final, he has arrived at the stage called *Khatm*, or 'the Seal.' This is the Upward Progress of Man. The first stage is the 'Believer,' the last the 'Seal.'

"After separation from the body, the soul of Man returns to that Heaven which corresponds to the stage which he has attained; thus the Believer at last dwells in the first or lowest Heaven, and the Seal in the Heaven of Heavens; for it will be noticed that the stages of upward progress correspond to the number of degrees in the Heavenly Spheres, namely, seven inferior and two superior.

"The metaphysicians say that these stages and degrees do not in reality exist, but that the Heavenly Intelligence which corresponds to the degree of intelligence attained by Man, attracts and absorbs his soul into itself after separation from the body. Thus every one who has attained intelligence corresponding to that of the highest sphere, his soul returns thereto; and he who has attained intelligence corresponding to the lowest sphere, his soul in like manner returns to that; those who have not attained intelligence corresponding to any of these will be placed in Hell, which is situate below the lowest sphere.

"As each of the Heavenly Spheres is furnished with knowledge and purity in proportion to its position, the rank of Man's soul in the future state will, according to this last account, be in proportion to his degree of knowledge and purity of life while upon the earth.

"The Unitarians say that man's Upward Progress has no end, for if he strive for a thousand years, each day will teach him something that he knew not before, inasmuch as the knowledge of God has no limit. So Mohammed says, 'He who progresses daily is yet of feeble mind.'

"The religious account says that the soul of every man returns to an individual place after separation from the body. This the metaphysicians deny; for how, say they, can the soul of a man return to a certain place when it has not originally come from a certain place? The soul of man is the Primal Spirit, and if a thousand persons live, it is the same spirit that animates them all; and in like manner if a thousand die, the same spirit returns to itself, and is not lessened or diminished. If a myriad persons build houses and make windows therein, the same sun illumines them all, and though every one of them should be destroyed, the sun would not be lessened or diminished. The sun is the lord of the sensible world, and the exponent of the attributes of the Primal Spirit. The Primal Spirit is the lord of the invisible world and the exponent of the Nature of God.

"When the heart of man has been revivified and illumined by the Primal Spirit, he has arrived at Intelligence; for Intelligence is a light in the heart, distinguishing between truth and vanity. Until he has been so revivified and illumined, it is impossible for him to attain to intelligence at all. But having attained to intelligence, then, and not till then, is the time for the attainment of knowledge, for becoming Wise. Intelligence is a Primal Element, and knowledge the attribute thereof. When from knowledge he has successively proceeded to the attainment of the Divine Light, and acquaintance with the mysteries of nature, his last step will be Perfection, with which his Upward Progress concludes.

"But dive he ever so deeply into the treasury of mysteries and knowledge, unless he examine himself and confess that after all he knows naught, all that he has acquired will slip through his hands, and leave him far poorer than before. His treasure of to-day should as much exceed the treasure of yesterday as an ocean exceeds a drop; but this can never be, unless he, leaving all else for contemplation and self-examination, have freedom and leisure to learn how poor he really is, and how much he needs the saving help of God.

"One class of Unitarians explain the Upward Progress of Man thus. They say that every atom of existent beings is filled with light;

> Arise and look around, for every atom that has birth
> Shines forth a lustrous beacon to illumine all the earth:

but that man walks abroad in darkness, blinded by the lusts of life, and laments the want of light that would, were he but aware of it, involve him in the glorious sheen of brightest day:

> 'Twere well to catch the odours that about our senses play,
> For all the world is full of blasts to bear the sweets away.

What they mean is this, that all existent beings are compounded of two things, darkness and light, which are indistinguishably blended together. The light belongs to the Invisible, and the darkness to the Sensible world; but the two are intimately connected, and the former exercises a paramount influence upon the latter. The object of man, according to them, is to separate the light from the darkness, that its nature and attributes may be understood, and in this consists his Upward Progress.

"Although the light and the darkness can never be entirely separated, for the one is as it were the veil of the other, the light can be made to prevail, so that its attributes may become manifest.

"Now it is possible to separate thus far the light from the darkness in certain cases; in the bodies of men and animals, for instance, there are certain organs always at work, whose sole object is this separation. Thus, when food is introduced into the stomach, the liver receives the cream and essence of it and transmits it to the heart; the heart, in like manner, extracts the essence of this, which is the life, and transmits it to the brain; lastly, the brain extracts the essence of this, and transforms it into the elixir of life, the real light of all.

"The elixir evolved by the brain is the instinctive spirit, and is, as it were, a lamp in a lantern; but it gives forth after all but a flickering and cloudy light, and man's object should therefore be to strengthen and purify it by Renunciation and Contemplation, until it give forth the true light which is the Spirit of Humanity. When man has attained to this he necessarily becomes free from all that is evil, and is adorned instead with every good and noble quality.

"The body of man is like a lantern, the Vegetative Spirit is the lamp, the Animal Spirit is the wick, the Instinctive Spirit the oil, and the Spirit of Humanity the fire that kindles all. 'Verily its oil would almost shine even though no fire kindled it.' (Cor. cap. 24, v. 35.) In other words, the Instinctive Spirit should feed and supply the Spirit of Humanity, as the oil feeds and supplies the flame in a lamp. The Traveller must aim at completing this lamp, so that his heart may be illumined, and he may see things as they really are. When the Spirit of Humanity a 'light upon light' (Cor. cap. 24, v. 35) has thus kindled the Instinctive Spirit, God 'guideth whom He pleaseth to His own light' (idem), that is, to the divine light of His own nature, reaching which the Traveller's Upward Progress is complete; for 'from Him they spring, and unto Him return.'"

VIII. Ṣūfīism adapted to Muhammadanism.

A clear and intelligible exposition of the principles of Ṣūfīism, or Oriental Spiritualism, is given by Muḥammad al-Miṣrī, a Ṣūfī of the Ilhāmīyah school of thought, in the following categorical form (translated by Mr. J. P. Brown, in the *Journal of the American Oriental Society*). It represents more particularly the way in which this form of mysticism is adapted to the stern and dogmatic teaching of Islām.

Question.—What is the beginning of at-Taṣawwuf?

Answer.—*Īmān*, or faith, of which there are six pillars, namely, (1) Belief in God, (2) in His Angels, (3) in His Books, (4) and in His Prophets, (5) in the Last Day, and (6) in His decree of good and evil.

Q.—What is the result of at-Taṣawwuf?

A.—It is not only the reciting with the tongue these pillars of faith, but also establishing them in the heart. This was the reply made by the Murshid Junaidu 'l-Baghdādī, in answer to the same question.

Q.—What is the distinction between a Ṣūfī and an ordinary person?

A.—The knowledge of an ordinary person is but *Īmānu-i-Taqlīdī*, or "a counterfeit faith," whereas that of the Ṣūfī is *Īmān-i-Taḥqīqī*, or "true faith."

Q.—What do you mean by counterfeit faith?

A.—It is that which an ordinary person has derived from his forefathers, or from the teachers and preachers of his own day, without knowing why it is essential that a man should believe in these six articles for his soul's salvation. For example, a person may be walking in the public streets and find a precious jewel which, perhaps, kings had sought for in vain, and rulers who had conquered the whole world had sought for and yet had not found. But in this precious jewel he has found that which is more effulgent than the sun, when it is so bright that it obscures the lesser light of the moon; or even he has found an alchemy which can convert copper into gold. And yet, perhaps, the finder knows not the value of the precious jewel, but thinks it a counterfeit jewel, and one which he would give away even for a drink of water if he were thirsty.

Q.—What is the establishment of faith?

A.—The establishment of faith consists in a search being made for the true origin of each of these six pillars of faith, until the enquirer arrives at *al-Ḥaqīqah*, "the Truth." Many persons pursue the journey for ten, or twenty, or thirty, or even forty years, and, wandering away from the true path, enter upon the path of error, and hence there are known to be seventy-three ways, only one of which is the way of Salvation.' [SECTS.] At last, by a perfect subjection to the teaching of the Murshid, or guide, they find out the value of the lost jewel which they have found, and their faith becomes manifest, and you might say that, with the light of a lamp, they have reached the sun. They then find out that the *Ṭarīqah*, or journey of the Ṣūfī, is consistent with the *Sharīʿah*, or law of Islām.

Q.—In matters of faith and worship, to what sect are the Ṣūfīs attached?

A.—(To this reply the author says, speaking, of course, of his own people, that they are chiefly of the Sunnī sect. But he does not notice that mystic doctrines are more prevalent amongst the Shīʿahs.)

Q.—When Bāyazīd al-Bisṭāmī was asked of what sect he was, he replied, "I am of the sect of Allāh." What did he mean?

A.—The sects of Allāh are the four orthodox sects of Islām. [Here our author departs from true Ṣūfī teaching.]

Q.—Most of the Ṣūfīs, in their poems, use certain words which we hear and understand as showing that they were of the Metempsychosians. They say, "I am sometimes Lot, sometimes a vegetable, sometimes an animal, at other times a man." What does this mean?

A.—Brother! the prophet has said: "My people, in the future life, will rise up in companies"—that is, some as monkeys, others as hogs, or in other forms—as is written in a verse of the Qur'ān, Sūrah lxxviii. 18: "Ye shall come in troops," which has been commented on by al-Baiẓāwī, who cites a tradition to the effect that, at the resurrection, men will rise up in the form of those animals whose chief characteristics resemble their own ruling passions in life: the greedy, avaricious man as a hog; the angry, passionate man as a camel; the tale-bearer or mischief-maker as a monkey. For though these men, while in this life, bore the human form externally, they were internally nothing different from the animals whose characters are in common with their own. The resemblance is not manifest during the life, but becomes so in the other existence, after the resurrection. Let us avoid such traits; repentance before death will free us from these evils. The Prophet said with regard to this: "Sleep is the brother of death. The dying man sees himself in his true character, and so knows whether or not he is, by repentance, freed from his ruling passion of life. In like manner, he will see himself during his slumbers, still following in the path of his passions." For instance, the money-calculator, in sleep, sees himself engaged in his all-absorbing occupation; and this fact is a warning from God not to allow himself to be absorbed in any animal passion or degrading occupation. It is only by prayerful repentance that anyone can hope to see himself, in his sleep, delivered from his ruling carnal passion, and restored to his proper human, intellectual form. If in your slumbers you see a monkey, consider it as a warning to abandon or abstain from the passion of mischief; if a hog, cease to seize upon the goods of others; and so on. Go and give yourself up to an upright *Murshid*, or spiritual guide, who will, through his prayers, show you in your slumbers the evil parts of your character, until one by one they have passed away, and have been replaced by good ones—all through the power of the name of God, whom he will instruct you to invoke [ZIKR]: at length you will only see in your slumbers the forms of holy and pious men, in testimony of that degree of piety to which you will have attained. This is what is meant by that expression of certain poets, referring to one's condition previous to the act of repentance, when the writer says, "I am sometimes an animal, sometimes a vegetable, sometimes a man"; and the same may be said by the Ṣūfīs, in application to themselves, as of any other part of creation, for man is called the *akhiru 'l-maujūdāt*, or "the climax of beings": for in him are comprised all the characteristics of creation. Many mystical books have been written on this subject, all showing that man is the larger part, and the world the smaller part, of God's creation. The human frame is said to comprise all the other parts of creation; and the heart of man is supposed to be even more comprehensive than the rainbow, because, when the eyes are closed, the mental capacity can take in the whole of a vast city; though not seen by the eyes, it is seen by the capacious nature of the mind. Among such books is the *Ḥauẓu 'l-Ḥayāt*, or the "Well of Life," which says that, if a man closes his eyes, ears, and nostrils, he cannot take cold; that the right nostril is called the sun, and the left the moon; that from the former he breathes heat, and from the latter cold air.

Q.—Explain the distinctive opinions of the Ṣūfīs in *at-Tanāsukh*, or the Transmigration of Souls.

A.—O Brother! our teaching regarding *al-Barzakh* (Qur'ān xxiii. 102) has nothing whatever to do with *at-Tanāsukh*. Of all the erring sects in the world, those who believe in Metempsychosis, or Transmigration of Souls, is the very worst.

Q.—The Ṣūfīs regard certain things as lawful which are forbidden. For instance, they enjoin the use of wine, wine-shops, the wine-cup, sweethearts; they speak of the curls of their mistresses, and the moles on their faces, cheeks, &c., and compare the furrows on their brows to verses of the Qur'ān. What does this mean?

A.—The Ṣūfīs often exchange the external features of all things for the internal, the corporeal for the spiritual, and thus give an imaginary signification to outward forms. They behold objects of a precious nature in their natural character and for this reason the greater part of their words have a spiritual and figurative meaning. For instance, when, like Ḥāfiẓ, they mention wine, they mean a knowledge of God, which, figuratively considered, is the love of God. Wine, viewed figuratively, is also love: love and affection are here the same thing. The wine-shop, with them, means the *murshidu 'l-kāmil*, or spiritual director, for his heart is said to be the depository of the love of God; the wine-cup is the *Talqīn*, or the pronunciation of the name of God in a declaration of faith, as: "There is no God but Allāh!" or it signifies the words which flow from the *Murshid's* mouth respecting divine knowledge, and which, when heard by the *Sālik*, or "one who pursues the true path," intoxicates his soul, and divests his heart of passions, giving him pure spiritual delights. The sweetheart means the excellent preceptor, because, when anyone sees his beloved, he admires her perfect proportions, with a heart full of love; the *Sālik* beholds the secret knowledge of God which fills the heart of his spiritual preceptor, or *Murshid*, and through it receives a similar inspiration, and acquires a full perception of all that he possesses, just as the pupil learns from his master. As the lover delights in the presence of his sweetheart, so the *Sālik* rejoices in the company of his beloved *Murshid*, or preceptor. The sweetheart is the object of a worldly affection, but the preceptor of a spiritual attachment. The curls or ringlets of the beloved are the grateful praises of the preceptor, tending to bind the affections of the disciple; the moles on her face signify that when the pupil, at times, beholds the total absence of all worldly wants on the part of the preceptor, he also abandons all the desires of both worlds—he perhaps even goes so far as to desire nothing else in life than his preceptor; the furrows on the brow of the beloved one, which they compare to verses of the Qur'ān, mean the light of the heart of the *Murshid*; they are compared to verses of the Qur'ān, because the attributes of God, in accordance with the injunction of the Prophet: "Be ye endued with divine qualities," are possessed by the *Murshid*.

Q.—The *Murshids* and their disciples often say: "We see God." Is it possible for anyone to see God?

A.—It is not possible. What they mean by this assertion is that they know God, that they see His power; for it is forbidden to mortal eyes to behold Him, as is declared in the Qur'ān, Sūrah vi. 103: "No sight reaches Him; He reaches the sight—the subtle, the knowing." The Prophet commanded us to "adore God, as thou wouldst didst thou see Him; for, if thou dost not see Him, He sees thee." This permission to adore Him is a divine favour, and they say that they are God's servants by divine favour. 'Alī said: "Should the veil fall from my eyes, how would God visit me in truth?" This saying proves that no one really sees God, and that even the sainted 'Alī never saw Him.

Q.—Can it possibly be erroneous to say

that, by seeing the traces of anyone he may be beheld?

A.—One may certainly be thus seen. When any person sees the brightness of the sun, he may safely say that he has seen the sun, though, indeed, he has not really seen it. There is another example, namely: Should you hold a mirror in your hand, you see a figure in it, and you may, therefore, say that you see your own face, which is really an impossibility, for no one has ever seen his own face, and you have asserted what is not strictly correct.

Q.—Since everyone sees the traces of God, as everyone is able to do, how is it that the Ṣūfīs declare that they *only* see Him?

A.—Those who make this statement do not know what they see, for they have never really seen Him. A person who has eaten of a sweet and savoury dish given to him, but of which he knows not the name, seeks for it again with a longing desire after it, and thus wanders about in search of what has given him so much delight, even though he be ignorant of what it really was. So are those who seek after God, without knowing Him, or what He is.

Q.—Some Ṣūfīs declare: "We are neither afraid of Hell, nor do we desire Heaven"—a saying which must be blasphemous. How is this?

A.—They do not really mean that they do not fear Hell, and that they do not wish for Heaven. If they really meant this, it would be blasphemous. Their meaning is not as they express themselves; probably they wish to say: "O Lord, Thou who createdst us, and madest us what we are, Thou hast not made us because we assist Thy workings. We are in duty bound to serve Thee all the more devotedly, wholly in obedience to Thy holy will. We have no bargaining with Thee, and we do not adore Thee with the view of gaining thereby either Heaven or Hell!" As it is written in the Qur'ān, Sūrah ix. 112: "Verily, God hath bought of the believers their persons and their wealth, for the Paradise they are to have," which means that His bounty has no bounds, His mercy no end; and thus it is that He benefits His faithful servants. They would say: "Thou hast no bargaining with anyone; our devotion is from the sincerity of our hearts, and is for love of Thee only. Were there no Heaven, nor any Hell, it would still be our duty to adore Thee. To Thee belongs the perfect right to put us either in Heaven or in Hell, and may Thy commands be executed agreeably to Thy blessed will! If Thou puttest us in Heaven, it is through Thine excellence, not on account of our devotion; if Thou puttest us in Hell, it is from out of Thy great justice, and not from any arbitrary decision on Thy part; so be it for ever and for ever!" This is the true meaning of the Ṣūfīs when they say they do not desire Heaven or fear Hell.

Q.—Thou saidst that there is no conflict between the *Sharī'ah*, "law," and the *Ḥaqīqah*, "truth," and nothing in the latter inconsistent with the former; and yet these two are distinguished from one another by "a something" which the *Ahlu 'l-Ḥaqīqah*, "believers in the truth," conceal. Were there nothing conflicting, why should it be thus hidden?

A.—If it be concealed, it is not because there is a contrariety to the law, but only because the thing hidden is contrary to the human mind; its definition is subtle, and not understood by everyone, for which reason the Prophet said: "Speak to men according to their mental capacities, for if you speak all things to all men, some cannot understand you, and so fall into error." The Ṣūfīs, therefore, hide some things conformably with this precept.

Q.—Should anyone not know the science which is known to the Ṣūfīs, and still do what the law plainly commands, and be satisfied therewith, would his faith and Islām be less than that of the Ṣūfīs?

A.—No. He would not be inferior to the Ṣūfīs; his faith and Islām would be equal even to that of the prophets, because Īmān and Islām are a jewel which admits of no division or separation into parts, and can neither be increased nor diminished, just as the portion of the sun enjoyed by a king and by a *faqīr* is the same, or as the limbs of the poor and the rich are equal in number: just as the members of the body of the king and the subject are precisely alike, so is the faith of the Muslim the same in all and common to all, neither greater nor less in any case.

Q.—Some men are prophets, saints, pure ones, and others *Fāsiqs* (who know God, but perform none of His commands); what difference is there among them?

A.—The difference lies in their *ma'rifah*, or "knowledge of spiritual things"; but in the matter of faith they are all equal; just as, in the case of the ruler and the subject, their limbs are all equal, while they differ in their dress, power, and office.

IX. Ṣūfī Poetry.

The very essence of Ṣūfīism is poetry, and the Eastern Mystics are never tired of expatiating on the *'Ishq*, or "love to God," which is the one distinguishing feature of Ṣūfī mysticism. The Masnawī, which teaches in the sweetest strains that all nature abounds with love divine, that causes even the lowest plant to seek the sublime object of its desire; the works of the celebrated Jāmī, so full of ecstatic rapture; the moral lessons of the eloquent Sa'dī; and the lyric odes of Ḥāfiẓ, may be termed the Scriptures of the Ṣūfī sect; and yet each of these authors contains passages which are unfit for publication in an English dress, and advocate morals at variance with what Christianity teaches us to be the true reflection of God's Holy Will. Whilst propriety demands the suppression of verses of the character alluded to, we give a few odes as specimens of the higher order of Ṣūfī poetry.

Jalālu 'd-dīn ar-Rūmī, the author of the *Maṡnawī* (A.H. 670), thus writes:—

"I am the Gospel, the Psalter, the Qur'ān;
I am 'Uzzā and Lāt—(Arabic deities)—Bell and the Dragon.
Into three and seventy sects is the world divided,
Yet only one God; the faithful who believe in Him am I.
Thou knowest what are fire, water, air and earth;
Fire, water, air, and earth, all am I.
Lies and truth, good, bad, hard and soft,
Knowledge, solitude, virtue, faith,
The deepest ground of hell, the highest torment of the flames,
The highest paradise,
The earth and what is therein,
The angels and the devils, Spirit and man, am I.
What is the goal of speech, O tell it Shams Tabrīzī?
The goal of sense? This:—The world Soul am I."

* * * * *

And again:—

"Are we fools? We are God's captivity.
Are we wise? We are His promenade.
Are we sleeping? We are drunk with God.
Are we waking? Then we are His heralds.
Are we weeping? Then His clouds of wrath.
Are we laughing? Flashes of His love."

* * * * *

"Every night God frees the host of spirits;
Frees them every night from fleshly prison.
Then the soul is neither slave nor master;
Nothing knows the bondsman of his bondage;
Nothing knows the lord of all his lordship.
Gone from such a night, is eating sorrow;
Gone, the thoughts that question good or evil.
Then without distraction, or division,
In this One the spirit sinks and slumbers."

The following is from the mystic poet Maḥmūd:—

"All sects but multiply the I and Thou;
This I and Thou belong to partial being.
When I and Thou, and several being vanish,
Then mosque and church shall find Thee nevermore.
Our individual life is but a phantom;
Make clear thine eye, and see reality."

The following verses are by Farīdu 'd-dīn Shakrgunj (A.H. 662):—

"Man, what thou art is hidden from thyself;
Know'st not that morning, mid-day, and the eve
Are all within Thee? The ninth heaven art Thou;
And from the spheres into the roar of time
Didst fall ere-while, Thou art the brush that painted
The hues of all the world—the light of life
That ranged its glory in the nothingness."
"Joy! joy! I triumph now; no more I know
Myself as simply me. I burn with love.
The centre is within me, and its wonder
Lies as a circle everywhere about me.
Joy! joy! No mortal thought can fathom me.
I am the merchant and the pearl at once.
Lo! time and space lie crouching at my feet.
Joy! joy! When I would revel in a rapture,
I plunge into myself, and all things know."

Mr. Lane, in his *Modern Egyptians*, gives a translation of a Ṣūfī poem recited by an Egyptian Darwesh:—

"With my love my heart is troubled;
And mine eye-lid hind'reth sleep:
My vitals are dissever'd;
While with streaming tears I weep.
My union seems far distant:
Will my love e'er meet mine eye?
Alas! Did not estrangement
Draw my tears, I would not sigh.

By dreary nights I'm wasted:
Absence makes my hope expire:
My tears, like pearls, are dropping;
And my heart is wrapt in fire.
Whose is like my condition?
Scarcely know I remedy.
Alas! Did not estrangement
Draw my tears, I would not sigh.

O turtle-dove! acquaint me
Wherefore thus dost thou lament?
Art thou so stung by absence?
Of thy wings depriv'd and pent?
He saith, 'Our griefs are equal:
Worn away with love, I lie.'
Alas! Did not estrangement
Draw my tears, I would not sigh.

O First, and sole Eternal!
Show thy favour yet to me.
Thy slave, Aḥmad El-Bekree,
Hath no Lord excepting Thee.
By Ṭá-há, the Great Prophet!
Do thou not his wish deny.
Alas! Did not estrangement
Draw my tears, I would not sigh."

Dr. Tholuck quotes this verse from a Darwesh Breviary:—

"Yesterday I beat the kettle-drum of dominion,
I pitched my tent on the highest throne;
I drank, crowned by the Beloved,
The wine of unity from the cup of the Almighty."

One of the most characteristic Sufī poems is the Persian poem by the poet Jāmī, entitled *Salāmān and Absāl*. The whole narrative is supposed to represent the joys of *Love Divine* as compared with the delusive fascinations of a *Life of Sense*. The story is that of a certain King of Ionia, who had a son named Salāmān, who in his infancy was nursed by a young maiden named Absāl, who, as he grew up, fell desperately in love with the youth, and in time ensnared him. Salāmān and Absāl rejoiced together in a life of sense for a full year, and thought their pleasures would never end. A certain sage is then sent by the king to reason with the erring couple. Salāmān confesses that the sage is right, but pleads the weakness of his own will. Salāmān leaves his native land in company with Absāl, and they find themselves on an island of wonderful beauty. Salāmān, unsatisfied with himself and his love, returns once more to his native country, where he and Absāl resolve to destroy themselves. They go to a desert and kindle a pile, and both walk into the fire. Absāl is consumed, but Salāmān is preserved in the fire, and lives to lament the fate of his beloved one. In course of time he is introduced by the sage to a celestial beauty called Zuhrah, with whom he becomes completely enamoured, and Absāl is forgotten.

"· · · · Celestial beauty seen,
He left the earthly; and once come to know
Eternal love, he let the mortal go."

In the epilogue to the poem, the author explains the mystic meaning of the whole story in the following language:—

"Under the outward form of any story
An inner meaning lies—this story now
Completed, do thou of its mystery
(Whereto the wise hath found himself a way)
Have thy desire—no tale of I and Thou,
Though I and Thou be its interpreters.
What signifies the King? and what the Sage?
And what Salāmān not of woman born?
And what Absal who drew him to desire?
And what the Kingdom that awaited him
When he had drawn his garment from her hand?
What means that Fiery Pile? and what the Sea?
And what that heavenly Zuhrah who at last
Clear'd Absāl from the mirror of his soul?
Learn part by part the mystery from me;
All ear from head to foot and understanding be.
The incomparable Creator, when this world
He did create, created first of all
The *first intelligence*—first of a chain
Of ten intelligences, of which the last
Sole Agent is this our Universe,
Active intelligence so call'd, the one
Distributor of evil and of good,
Of joy and sorrow. Himself apart from matter,
In essence and in energy—His treasure
Subject to no such talisman—He yet
Hath fashion'd all that is—material form,
And spiritual sprung from Him—by Him
Directed all, and in His bounty drown'd.
Therefore is He that Firman-issuing King
To whom the world was subject. But because
What he distributes to the Universe
Himself from still higher power receives,
The wise, and all who comprehend aright,
Will recognise that higher in the Sage.

His the Prime Spirit that, spontaneously
Projected by the tenth intelligence,
Was from no womb of matter reproduced
A special essence called the Soul—a Child
Fresh sprung from heaven in raiment undefiled
Of sensual taint, and therefore call'd Salāmān.

And who Absāl?—The lust-adoring body,
Slave to the blood and sense—through whom the Soul,
Although the body's very life it be,
Does yet imbibe the knowledge and desire
Of things of sense; and these united thus
By such a tie God only can unloose,
Body and soul are lovers each of other.

What is the Sea on which they sail'd?—the Sea
Of animal desire—the sensual abyss,
Under whose waters lies a world of being
Swept far from God in that submersion.

And wherefore was Absāl in that Isle
Deceived in her delight, and that Salāmān
Fell short of his desire?—that was to show
How passion tires, and how with time begins
The folding of the carpet of desire.

And what the turning of Salāmān's heart
Back to the King, and looking to the throne
Of pomp and glory? What but the return
Of the lost soul to its true parentage,
And back from carnal error looking up
Repentant to its intellectual throne.

What is the Fire?—Ascetic discipline,
That burns away the animal alloy,
Till all the dross of matter be consumed,
And the essential Soul, its raiment clean
Of mortal taint, be left. But forasmuch
As, any life-long habit so consumed,
May well recur a pang for what is lost,

Therefore the Sage set in Salāmān's eyes.
A soothing fantom of the past, but still
Told of a better Venus, till his soul
She fill'd, and blotted out his mortal love.
For what is Zuhrah?—That divine perfection,
Wherewith the soul inspir'd and all array'd
Its intellectual light is royal blest,
And mounts the throne, and wears the crown, and reigns
Lord of the empire of humanity.

This is the meaning of this mystery,
Which to know wholly ponder in thy heart,
Till all its ancient secret be enlarged.
Enough—the written summary I close,
And set my seal:
THE TRUTH GOD ONLY KNOWS."

X. *The True Character of Ṣufīism.*

It will be seen that the great object of the Ṣūfī Mystic is to lose his own identity. Having effected this, perfection is attained. This ideal conception of the Ṣūfī is thus expressed by Jalālu 'd-dīnu 'r-Rūmī in his book, the *Masnawī* (p. 78). It represents Human Love seeking admission into the Sanctuary of Divinity:—

"One knocked at the door of the Beloved, and a voice from within inquired, 'Who is there?' Then he answered, '*It is I.*' And the voice said, 'This house will not hold me and thee.' So the door remained shut. Then the Lover sped away into the wilderness, and fasted and prayed in solitude. And after a year he returned, and knocked again at the door, and the voice again demanded, 'Who is there?' And the Lover said, '*It is Thou.*' Then the door was opened."

The Ṣūfī doctrines are undoubtedly pantheistic, and are almost identical with those of the Brahmans and Buddhists, the Neo-Platonists, the Beghards and Beguins. There is the same union of man with God, the same emanation of all things from God, and the same final absorption of all things into the Divine Essence. And these doctrines are held in harmony with a Muḥammadan view of predestination, which makes all a necessary evolution of the Divine Essence. The creation of the creature, the fall of those who have departed from God, and their final return, are all events pre-ordained by an absolute necessity.

Bāyazīdu 'l-Bisṭāmī, a mystic of the ninth century, said he was a sea without a bottom, without beginning and without end. Being asked, "What is the throne of God?" he answered, "I am the throne of God." "What is the table on which the divine decrees are written?" "I am that table." "What is the pen of God—the word by which God created all things?" "I am the pen." "What is Abraham, Moses, and Jesus?" "I am Abraham, Moses, and Jesus." "What are the angels Gabriel, Michael, Isrāfīl?" "I am Gabriel, Michael, Isrāfīl, for whatever comes to true being is absorbed into God, and this is God." Again, in another place, al-Bisṭāmī cries, "Praise to me, I am truth. I am the true God. Praise to me, I must be celebrated by divine praise."

The chief school of Arabian philosophy, that of al-Ghazzālī (A.H. 505), passed over to Ṣūfīism by the same reasoning which led Plotinus to his mystical theology. After long inquiries for some ground on which to base the certainty of our knowledge, al-Ghazzālī was led to reject entirely all belief in the senses. He then found it equally difficult to be certified of the accuracy of the conclusions of reason, for there may be, he thought, some faculty higher than reason, which, if we possessed, would show the uncertainty of reason, as reason now shows the uncertainty of the senses. He was left in scepticism, and saw no escape but in the Ṣūfī union with Deity. There alone can man know what is true by becoming *the truth* itself. "I was forced," he said, "to return to the admission of intellectual notions as the bases of all certitude. This, however, was not by systematic reasoning and accumulation of proofs, but by a flash of light which God sent into my soul! For whoever imagines that truth can only be rendered evident by proofs, places narrow limits to the wide compassion of the Creator."

Ṣūfīism (says Mr. Cowell) has arisen from the bosom of Muḥammadanism as a vague protest of the human soul, in its intense longing after a purer creed. On certain tenets of the Qur'ān the Ṣūfīs have erected their own system, professing, indeed, to reverence its authority as a divine revelation, but in reality substituting for it the oral voice of the teacher, or the secret dreams of the Mystic. Dissatisfied with the barren letter of the Qur'ān, Ṣūfīism appeals to human consciousness, and from our nature's felt wants, seeks to set before us nobler hopes than a gross Muḥammadan Paradise can fulfil.

Whilst there are doubtless many amongst the Ṣūfīs who are earnest seekers after truth, it is well known that some of them make their mystical creed a cloak for gross sensual gratification. A sect of Ṣūfīs called the *Muhābīyah*, or "Revered," maintain the doctrine of community of property and women, and the sect known as the *Malāmatīyah*, or "reproached," maintain the doctrine of necessity, and compound all virtue with vice. Many such do not hold themselves in the least responsible for sins committed by the body, which they regard only as the miserable robe of humanity which encircles the pure spirit.

Some of the Sūfī poetry is most objectionable. MacGuckin de Slane, in his Introduction to Ibn Khallikān's Biographical Dictionary, says:—"It often happens that a poet describes his mistress under the attributes of the other sex, lest he should offend that excessive prudery of Oriental feelings which, since the fourth century of Islāmism, scarcely allows an allusion to women, and more particularly in poetry; and this rigidness is still carried so far, that Cairo public singers dare not amuse their auditors with a song in which the beloved is indicated as a female. It cannot, however, be denied that the feelings which inspired poetry of this kind were not always pure, and that polygamy and jealousy have invested the morals of some Eastern nations with the foulest corruption."

The story of the Rev. Dr. 'Imādu 'd-dīn (the eminent native clergyman, a convert from Islām, now residing at Amritsar) is a remarkable testimony to the unsatisfying nature of Ṣūfiistic exercises to meet the spiritual need of anxious soul. The following extract from the printed autobiography of his life will show this :—

"I sought for union with God from travellers and *faqīrs*, and even from the insane people of the city, according to the tenets of the Ṣūfī mystics. The thought of utterly renouncing the world then came into my mind with so much power, that I left everybody, and went out into the desert, and became a *faqīr*, putting on clothes covered with red ochre, and wandered here and there, from city to city and from village to village, step by step, alone, for about 2,000, or (2,500 miles) without plan or baggage. Faith in the Muḥammadan religion will never, indeed, allow true sincerity to be produced in the nature of man; yet I was then, although with many worldly motives, in search only of God. In this state I entered the city of Karuli, where a stream called Cholida flows beneath a mountain, and there I stayed to perform the *Ḥisbu 'l-bahār*. I had a book with me on the doctrines of mysticism and the practice of devotion, which I had received from my religious guide, and held more dear even than the Qur'ān. In my journeys I slept with it at my side at nights, and took comfort in clasping it to my heart whenever my mind was perplexed. My religious guide had forbidden me to show this book, or to speak of its secrets to anyone, for it contained the sum of everlasting happiness; and so this priceless book is even now lying useless on a shelf in my house. I took up the book, and sat down on the bank of the stream, to perform the ceremonies as they were enjoined, according to the following rules :—The celebrant must first perform his ablutions on the bank of the flowing stream, and, wearing an unsewn dress, must sit in a particular manner on one knee for twelve days, and repeat the prayer called *Jugopar* thirty times every day with a loud voice. He must not eat any food with salt, or anything at all, except some barley bread of flour lawfully earned, which he has made with his own hands, and baked with wood that he has brought himself from the jungles. During the day he must fast entirely, after performing his ablutions in the river before daylight; and he must remain barefooted, wearing no shoes; nor must he touch any man, nor, except at an appointed time, even speak to anyone. The object of all this is, that he may meet with God, and from the longing desire to obtain this, I underwent all this pain. In addition to the above, I wrote the name of God on paper 125,000 times, performing a certain portion every day; and I cut out each word separately with scissors, and wrapped them up each in a ball of flour, and fed the fishes of the river with them, in the way the book prescribed. My days were spent in this manner; and during half the night I slept, and the remaining half I sat up, and wrote the name of God mentally on my heart, and saw Him with the eye of thought. When all this toil was over, and I went thence, I had no strength left in my body; my face was wan and pale, and I could not even hold myself up against the wind."

Major Durie Osborn, in his *Islam under the Khalifs of Baghdad* (p. 112), says: "The spread of this Pantheistic spirit has been and is the source of incalculable evil throughout the Muḥammadan world. The true function of religion is to vivify and illuminate all the ordinary relations of life with light from a higher world. The weakness to which religious minds are peculiarly prone is to suppose that this world of working life is an atmosphere too gross and impure for them to live in. They crave for better bread than can be made from wheat. They attempt to fashion a world for themselves, where nothing shall soil the purity of the soul or disturb the serenity of their thoughts. The divorce thus effected between the religious life and the worldly life, is disastrous to both. The ordinary relations of men become emptied of all divine significance. They are considered as the symbols of bondage to the world or to an evil deity. The religious spirit dwindles down to a selfish desire to acquire a felicity from which the children of this world are hopelessly excluded Pre-eminently has this been the result of Muḥammadan mysticism. It has dug a deep gulf between those who can know God and those who must wander in darkness, feeding upon the husks of rites and ceremonies. It has affirmed with emphasis, that only by a complete renunciation of the world is it possible to attain the true end of man's existence. Thus all the best and purest natures—the men who might have put a soul in the decaying Church of Islam—have been drawn off from their proper task to wander about in deserts and solitary places, or expend their lives in idle and profitless passivity disguised under the title of 'spiritual contemplation.' [ZIKR.] But this has only been part of the evil. The logical result of Pantheism is the destruction of a moral law. If God be all in all, and man's apparent individuality a delusion of the perceptive faculty, there exists no will which can act, no conscience which can reprove or applaud. The individual is but a momentary seeming; he comes and goes like 'the snow-flake on the river; a moment seen, then gone for ever.' To reproach such an ephemeral creature for being the slaves of its passions, is to chide the thistledown for yielding to the violence of the wind. Muḥammadans have not been slow to discover these consequences. Thousands of reckless and profligate spirits have entered the orders of the derweshes to enjoy the licence thereby obtained. Their affectation of piety is simply a cloak for the practice of sensuality; their emancipation from the ritual of Islām involves a liberation also from its moral restraints. And thus a movement, animated at its outset by a high and lofty purpose, has degenerated into a fruitful source of ill. The stream which ought to have expanded into a fertilising river, has become a vast swamp, exhaling vapours charged with disease and death." [FAQIR.]

(For further information on the subject of Eastern Mysticism the English reader is referred to the following works : Hunt's *Pantheism*; Tholuck's *Sufismus*; Malcolm's *History of Persia*; Brown's *Darweshes*; *Oxford Essays for 1855*, by E. B. Cowell; Palmer's *Oriental Mysticism*; De Slane's *Introduction to Ibn Ḵẖallikān*; Bicknell's *Translation of Ḥāfiẓ of Shīrāz*; Ouseley's *Persian Poets*; Vaughan's *Hours with the Mystics*. Persian and Arabic books on the subject are too numerous to mention. 'Abdu 'r-Razzāq's *Dictionary of the Technical Terms of the Ṣūfis* was published in Arabic by Dr. Sprenger in Calcutta in 1845.) [FAQIR; ZIKR.]

SUFTAJAH (سفتجة). The delivery
of property by way of loan, and not by way of trust. It is forbidden by the Sunnī law. (Hamilton's *Hidāyah*, vol. iii. p. 244.)

SUHAIL IBN 'AMR (سهيل بن عمرو).
One of the most noble of the Quraish, and one of their leaders on the day of the action of Badr. He was taken prisoner on that occasion. He embraced Islām after the taking of Makkah. He is said to have died A.H. 18.

SUICIDE. Arabic *Qatlu nafsi-hi*
(قتل نفسه). Suicide is not once referred to in the Qur'ān, but it is forbidden in the Traditions, where Muḥammad is related to have said : "Whosoever shall kill himself shall suffer in the fire of hell" (*al-Buḵẖārī*, Arabic ed., p. 984); and "shall be excluded from heaven for ever" (*ibid.* p. 182). It is also related that the Prophet refused the funeral rites to a suicide (*Abū Dā'ūd*, Arabic ed., vol. ii. p. 98), but it is usual in Muḥammadan countries to perform the funeral service, although forbidden by the custom of the Prophet himself.

SUKR (سكر). [DRUNKENNESS.]

SULAIM (سليم). *Banū Sulaim.*
One of the powerful tribes of ancient Arabia, descended from the Banū 'Adwān.

SULAIMĀN (سليمان). [SOLOMON.]

ṢULḤ (صلح). "Concord; reconciliation; peace." It occurs in the Qur'ān, as follows :—
Sūrah iv. 127 : "And if a woman fears

from her husband perverseness or aversion, it is no crime in them both that they should be reconciled to each other, for *reconciliation* is best."

SULS (ثلث). "Three-quarters"
of a Sipārah of the Qur'ān, or of the Qur'ān itself. [QUR'AN.]

SULTĀN (سلطان). A word in
modern times used for a ruler or king, as the Sulṭān of Turkey. Its literal meaning is "strength" or "might," and in this sense it occurs in the Qur'ān :—
Sūrah xvii. 35 : "We have given his next of kin *authority.*"
Sūrah lxix. 29 : "My *authority* has perished from me."
Sūrah li. 38 : "We sent him (Moses) to Pharaoh with a manifest *power* (*miracle*, or *authority*)."

SUNNAH (سنة). *Lit.* "A path or
way; a manner of life." A term used in the religion of the Muslim to express the custom or manner of life. Hence the tradition which records either the sayings or doings of Muḥammad. Consequently all traditional law is divided into (1) *Sunnatu 'l-Fi'l*, or what Muḥammad did; (2) *Sunnatu 'l-Qaul*, or what Muḥammad enjoined; (3) *Sunnatu 't-Taqrīr*, or that which was done or said in the presence of Muḥammad, and which was not forbidden by him,

Those things which the Prophet emphatically enjoined on his followers are called *Sunnatu 'l-Hudā*, "Sunna of Guidance," or *as-Sunnatu 'l-Mu'akkadah* : as, for example, the sounding of the *aẓān* before prayers. Those things which have not been emphatically enjoined, are called *as-Sunnatu 'l-Zā'idah*, or "Superogatory Sunnah."

The Honourable Syed Ahmed Khan, C.S.I., says in his Essay on the Traditions, that "upon examining the sayings (or the *Aḥadīs*), and the deeds (or the *Sunnah*) of the Prophet, we find (1) some of them relating to religion, (2) others connected with the peculiar circumstances of his life, (3) some bearing upon society in general, and (4) others concerning the art of Government." When Muḥammad spoke on the subject of religion, he is held to have been inspired, and also when he performed a religious act he is believed to have been guided by inspiration; but with regard to other matters, the degree to which he was inspired is held to be a subject for investigation as well as for discrimination. In support of this view, the following tradition is related by Rāfi' ibn Ḵẖadīj : "The Prophet came to al-Madīnah when the people were grafting the male bud of a date tree into the female in order to produce greater abundance of fruit, and he said, 'Why do you do this?' They replied, 'It is an ancient custom.' The Prophet said, 'Perhaps it would be better if you did not do it.' And then they left off the custom, and the trees yielded but little fruit. The people complained to the Prophet, and he said, 'I am no more than a man. When I order anything respecting religion, receive it; but when I order you about the affairs of the world, then I speak only as a man.'" (*Mishkāt*, book i. ch. vi. pt. 1.)

'Abdu 'llāh ibn Mas'ūd says: "The Prophet drew a straight line for us, and said, 'This is the *path* of God.' Then he drew several other lines on the right and left of it, and said, There are the paths of those who follow the devil. Verily my *path* (*sunnah*) is straight and you must follow it.'"

It is upon the sayings and customs of Muḥammad that that traditional law is founded which is handed down in the Ḥadīs̤, and which is treated of under the article TRADITION.

SUNNĪ (سنى). *Lit.* "One of the path." A Traditionist. A term generally applied to the large sect of Muslims who acknowledge the first four Khalīfahs to have been the rightful successors of Muḥammad, and who receive the *Kutubu 's-Sittah*, or "six authentic" books of tradition, and who belong to one of the four schools of jurisprudence founded by Imām Abū Ḥanīfah, Imām ash-Shāfi'ī, Imām Mālik, or Imām Aḥmad ibn Ḥambal.

The word *Sunnī* is really a Persian form, with its plural *Sunnīyān*, and stands for that which is expressed by the Arabic *Ahlu 's-Sunnah*, "the People of the Path." The word *sunnah* meaning a "path," but being applied to the example of Muḥammad.

A *Sunnī* is held to be a traditionist, not that any section of Islām rejects the traditions, but merely that the Sunnīs have arrogated to themselves this title, and the rest of the Muslim world has acquiesced in the assumption; hence it comes to pass that although the Shī'ahs, even to a greater degree than the Sunnīs, rest their claims upon traditional evidence, they have allowed their opponents to claim the title of traditionists, and consequently Mr. Sale and many European writers have stated that the Shī'ahs reject the traditions.

The Sunnīs embrace by far the greater portion of the Muḥammadan world. According to Mr. Wilfrid Blunt's census, they are 145 millions, whilst the Shī'ahs are but some 15 millions.

The principal differences between the Sunnīs and the Shī'ahs are treated of in the article SHI'AH.

SUPEREROGATION, ACTS OF. [NAFL.]

SŪRAH (سورة). *Lit.* "A row or series." A term used exclusively for the chapters of the Qur'ān, of which there are one hundred and fourteen in number. These chapters are called after some word which occurs in the text, *e.g.* *Sūratu 'l-Ḥadīd*, the "Chapter of Iron." The ancient Jews divided the whole law of Moses into fifty-four *siderīm*, or "sections," which were named after the same manner as the Sūrahs of the Qur'ān. [QUR'AN.]

SUTRAH (سترة). *Lit.* "That wherewith anything is concealed or covered." Something put up before one engaged in prayer facing Makkah, to prevent others from intruding upon his devotions. It may be a stick, or anything a cubit in height and an inch in thickness. (*Mishkāt*, book iv. ch. x.) [PRAYER.]

SUWĀ' (سواع). An idol mentioned in Sūrah lxxi. 22. Professor Palmer says it was an idol in the form of a woman, and believed to be a relic of antediluvian times. (*Introduction to the Qur'ān*, p. xii.)

SWEARING. [OATH.]

SWINE. Arabic *khinzīr* (خنزير), pl. *khanāzīr*. Heb. חֲזִיר *khazīr*. Swine's flesh is strictly forbidden to Muslims in four different places in the Qur'ān, namely, Sūrahs ii. 168, v. 4, vi. 146, xvi. 116; in which places its use is prohibited with that which dieth of itself and blood.

In the Traditions, it is related that Muḥammad said that "when Jesus the Son of Mary shall descend from the heavens upon your people as a just king, and he will break the cross and *will kill all the swine*. (*Mishkāt*, book xxiii. ch. vi.)

SYNAGOGUES. [CHURCHES.]

SYRIA. [SHAM.]

T.

ṬA'AH (طاعة). *Lit.* "Obedience." A word which occurs once in the Qur'ān, Sūrah iv. 83: "They say 'Obedience!'" It is an old Arabic word used for the worship and service of God.

TA'ALLUQ (تعلق). *Lit.* "That which is suspended." A division or district. A term applied in India to a district including a number of villages, for which a fixed amount of revenue is paid, and the possession of which is hereditary as long as the revenue is paid. These *ta'alluqs*, or, as they are commonly called, *tāluks*, are of two kinds: (1) *Huẓūrī* (from حضور, "the State"), of which the revenue is paid direct to Government; and (2) *Maẕkurī* (from مذكور, "specified"), of which the revenue is paid through a chief, who thus farms the revenue. The term was introduced to India by the Muslim conquerors.

ṬA'ĀM (طعام). [FOOD.]

TA'AWWUẔ (تعوذ). The ejaculation: "I seek refuge from God from the cursed Satan," which forms part of the Muḥammadan daily prayer. It is called also *'auẕun bi-'llāh.* [PRAYER.]

TABARRUK (تبرك). The commutation for an offering incumbent upon a religious medicant holding some endowment (*waqf*).

TABA'U 'T-TĀBI'ĪN (تبع التابعين). *Lit.* "The followers of the followers." Those who conversed with the *Tā'bi'ūn* (which term is used for those who conversed with Companions of Muḥammad). Traditions related by them are received, but are of less authority than those related by persons who had seen the Prophet. [TRADITIONS.]

ṬABĪB (طبيب). A doctor of medicine. One who practises *aṭ-ṭibb*, the "science of medicine." *Ḥakīm* (*lit.* "a philosopher") is also used to express a medical practitioner."

TĀBI'ŪN (تابعون), pl. of *Tābi'*. Those who conversed with the Associates or companions of Muḥammad. The traditions which they related are of high authority and form part of the Sunnah or traditional law. [TRADITIONS.]

TABLES OF THE LAW. Arabic *Alwāḥ* (الواح), pl. of *Lauḥ*. The giving of the Law to Moses on tables is mentioned in the Qur'ān, Sūrah vii. 142: "We wrote for him (Moses) upon tables (*alwāḥ*) a monition concerning every matter." But Muslim doctors are not agreed as to the number of the tables. The commentators al-Jalālān say that there were either seven or ten. [TEN COMMANDMENTS.]

TABŪK (تبوك). A valley in Arabia, celebrated as the scene of one of Muḥammad's military expeditions, and as the place where he made a treaty with John the Christian prince of Ailah. [TREATY.]

TĀBŪT (تابوت). (1) The Ark of the Covenant, mentioned in the Qur'ān, Sūrah ii. 249: "Verily the sign of his (Saul's) kingship shall be that the Ark (*Tābūt*) shall come to you: and in it *Sakīnah* from your Lord, and the relics left by Moses and Aaron; the angels shall bear it."

Tābūt is the Hebrew תֵּבָה *Tēbāh* used for Noah's Ark, and the Ark of bulrushes, Ex. ii. 3, and not אָרוֹן *Ārōn*, the word in the Bible for the Ark of the Covenant.

The commentator, al-Baiẓāwī, says the *Sakīnah* was either the Taurāt, or Books of Moses, or an idol of emeralds or rubies, the head and tail of which was like that of a goat, and the wings of feathers, and which uttered a feeble cry; and when the ark was sent after an enemy, then this was sent. But some say it was a representation of the prophets.

Al-Jalālān say the relics left in the Ark were the fragments of the two tables of the Law, and the rod and robes and shoes of Moses, the mitre of Aaron, and the vase of manna. [ARK OF THE COVENANT, SAKINAH.]

(2) A coffin or bier for the burial of the dead.

(3) The representation of the funeral of al-Ḥusain. [MUHARRAM.]

(4) The box or ark in which the body of the child Moses was placed by his mother for fear of Pharaoh. See Qur'ān, Sūrah xx. 39: "When we spake unto thy mother what was spoken: 'Cast him into the ark: then cast him on the sea [the river], and the sea shall throw him on the shore: and an enemy to me and an enemy to him shall take him up.' And I myself have made thee an object of love, That thou mightest be reared in mine eye."

TADBĪR (تدبير). Post obit manumission of slaves. In its primitive sense it means looking forward to the event of a business. In the language of the law, it means a declaration of a freedom to be established after the master's death. As when the master says to his slave, "Thou art free after my death." The slave so freed is called a *mudabbir*. (Hamilton's *Hidāyah*, vol. i. p. 475.) [SLAVERY.]

TAFAKKUR (تفكر). *Lit.* "Contemplation or thought." According to the *Kitābu 't-Ta'rifāt*, it is the lamp of the heart whereby a man sees his own evils or virtues.

TAFSĪR (تفسير). *Lit.* "Explaining." A term used for a commentary on any book, but especially for a commentary on the Qur'ān. [COMMENTARIES.]

AT-TAGHĀBUN (التغابن). "Mutual deceit." The title of the 64th Sūrah of the Qur'ān, the IXth verse of which begins thus:

"The day when He shall gather you together for the day of the assembly will be the day of *Mutual Deceit*."

That is, when the blessed will deceive or disappoint the damned by taking the places which they would have had in Paradise had they been true believers, and *vice versâ*.

TAGHLIB (تغلب). An Arabian tribe who, on the first spread of Islām, were occupying a province in Mesopotamia and professing the Christian faith. The Banū Taghlib sent an embassy to Muḥammad, formed of sixteen men, some Muslims and some Christians. The latter wore crosses of gold. The Prophet made terms with the Christians, stipulating that they should themselves continue in the profession of their religion, but should not baptize their children into Christian faith. (Sir W. Muir, from *Kātibu 'l-Wāqidī*, p. 61.)

AT-TAGHṬĪS (التغطيس). A term which occurs in the *Kashfu 'z-Ẓunūn* for "baptism." [INJIL, SIGHBAH.]

ṬĀGHŪT (طاغوت). An idol mentioned in the Qur'ān:—

Sūrah iv. 54: "They believe in Jibt and Ṭaghūt."

Sūrah ii. 257: "Whoso disbelieves in Ṭaghūt and believes in God, he has got a firm handle, in which is no breaking off."

Sūrah ii. 259: "But those who misbelieve their patrons are Ṭāghūt, these bring them forth to darkness."

Jalālu 'd-dīn says *Ṭāghūt* was an idol of the Quraish, whom certain renegade Jews honoured in order to please the tribe.

Mr. Lane observes that in the *Arabian Nights* the name is used to express the devil as well as an idol.

ṬĀ HĀ (طه). The title of the xxth Sūrah of the Qur'ān, which begins with these Arabic letters. Their meaning is uncertain. Some fancy the first letter stands for *ṭūbā*, "beatitude," and the second for *Hāwiyah*, the name of the lowest pit of hell. *Ṭah* is also, like *ṣah*, and the English "hush," an interjection commanding silence, and might be here employed to enjoin a silent and reverential listening to the revelation to follow.

TAḤĀLUF (تحالف). The swearing of both plaintiff and defendant. In a civil suit of both seller and purchaser. In a disagreement, if both should take an oath, the Qāẓī must dissolve the sale, or contract. (Hamilton's *Hidāyah*, vol. iii. p. 85.)

TAḤANNUṢ (تحنث). Avoiding and abstaining from sin. Worshipping God for a certain period in seclusion. The word is used in the latter sense for the seclusion of Muḥammad on Mount Ḥirā', when he is supposed to have received his first revelation. (*Mishkāt*, book xxiv. c. v.) [INSPIRATION, QUR'AN].

ṬAHĀRAH (طهارة). "Purification," including *waẓū'*, *tayammum*, *masaḥ*, *ghusl*, and *miswāk*, accounts of which are given under their respective articles. [PURIFICATION.]

ṬĀHIR (طاهر). A woman in a state of purity. [PURIFICATION.]

TAHLĪL (تهليل). The ejaculation, "*Lā ilāha illā 'llāh!*" (لا اله الا الله), "There is no deity but God!" (*Mishkāt*, book x. ch. ii.)

Abū Hurairah relates that the Prophet said, "That person who recites 'There is no deity but God,' one hundred times, shall receive rewards equal to the emancipating of ten slaves, and shall have one hundred good deeds recorded to his account, and one hundred of his sins shall be blotted out, and the words shall be a protection from the devil.' [ZIKR.]

TAḤMĪD (تحميد). The ejaculation, "*al-Ḥamdu li-'llāh!*" (الحمد لله), "God be praised!" (*Mishkāt*, book x. ch. ii.)

'Umar ibn Shu'aib relates from his forefathers that the Prophet said, "He who recites 'God be praised,' a hundred times in the morning and again a hundred times in the evening, shall be like a person who has provided one hundred horsemen for a *jihād*, or 'religious war.'"

TAḤRĪF (تحريف). The word used by Muḥammadan writers for the supposed corruption of the Jewish and Christian scriptures. [CORRUPTION OF THE SCRIPTURES.]

AT-TAḤRĪM (التحريم). "The Prohibition." The title of the 66th Sūrah of the Qur'ān, which begins with the words: "Why O Prophet! dost thou *forbid* that which God hath made lawful to thee, from a desire to please thy wives." The object of this chapter was to free Muḥammad from his obligation to his wife Ḥafṣah, to whom he had recently sworn to separate entirely from the Coptic slave-girl Marīyah.

TAHẔĪB (تهذيب). A book of traditions received by the Shī'ahs, compiled by Shaikh Abū Ja'far Muḥammad, A.H. 466.

AT-ṬĀ'IF (الطائف). The name of a town, the capital of a district of the same name in Arabia, which Muḥammad besieged A.H. 8, but the city was surrounded by strong battlements and was provisioned for some months. The siege was, therefore, raised by Muḥammad, after he had cut down and burned its celebrated vineyards. (Muir's *Life of Mahomet*, new ed. p. 432.)

ṬAIRAH (طيرة). "Lightness; levity of mind." Condemned in the Ḥadīṣ.

ṬAIY (طى). An Arabian tribe who emigrated from al-Yaman to the Najd about the third century. Some of them embraced Judaism and some Christianity, while a portion remained pagans and erected a temple to the idol *Fuls*. The whole tribe eventually embraced Islām, A.D. 632, when 'Alī was sent to destroy the temple of Fuls.

Ḥātim aṭ-Ṭā'īy, a Christian Bedouin Arab, celebrated for his hospitality, is the subject of Eastern poetry. He lived in the "time of ignorance," viz. before Muḥammad, but his son 'Adī became a Muslim, and is numbered among the "Companions." Ḥātim aṭ-Ṭā'īy's most famous act of liberality was that which he showed to an ambassador of the Greek Emperor, sent to demand of him as a present for his master, a horse of very great price. The generous Arab, before he knew the object of this person's mission, slaughtered his horse to regale him, having nothing at the time in his house to serve in its stead. It is also said that he often caused as many as forty camels to be slaughtered for the entertainment of his guests and the poor Arabs of the desert.

TĀJ (تاج). "A crown; a diadem." The Muslim Khalīfahs never wore a crown, the word is therefore not used in Muslim theology, but it is used by the Ṣūfī faqīrs for the cap worn by a leader of a religious order, which is generally of a conical shape. [KULAH.]

AT-TAKĀṢUR (التكاثر). "Multiplying." The title of the CIInd Sūrah of the Qur'ān, the opening verses of which are:

"The desire of *increasing* riches occupieth you
Till you come to the grave."

TAKBĪR (تكبير). The expression, "*Allāhu akbar!*" (الله اكبر), "God is very great!" (*Mishkāt*, book x. ch. ii.)

The ejaculation frequently occurs in the daily liturgy and in the funeral office. [PRAYER.]

TAKBĪRU 'T-TAḤRĪMAH (تكبير التحريمة). The first takbīr in the liturgical prayer, said standing, after the recital of which the worshipper must give himself up entirely to worship. [PRAYER, TAKBIR.]

TAKHĀRUJ (تخارج). An arrangement entered into by some heirs-at-law with others for their share of the inheritance, in consideration of some specific thing which excludes them from inheritance. (Hamilton's *Hidāyah*, vol. iii. p. 201.)

AT-TAKWĪR (التكوير). "The Folding-up." The title of the LXXXIst Sūrah of the Qur'ān, which opens a solemn announcement of the Judgment Day by the words: "When the sun shall be *folded up*."

TAKYAH (تكية). *Lit.* "A pillow; a place of repose." Used in all Muḥammadan countries for—

(1) A place in which some celebrated saint has stayed. In Central Asia, these places are often merely marked by a few stones and a flag, but they are held sacred.

(2) A monastery, or religious house, in which faqīrs and ascetics reside, as the Takyahs at Constantinople and Cairo.

(3) A hostel or rest-house, as the Takyah at Damascus, which is a hostel for pilgrims. Dr. Robinson describes it as a large quadrangular enclosure, divided into two courts, in the southern court of which there is a large mosque. Around the wall of the court runs a row of cells, with a portico or gallery of columns in front. This takyah was founded by Sultan Salīm, A.D. 1516. (*Researches*, vol. iii. p. 459.)

ṬALĀQ (طلاق). (1) The sentence of divorce. [DIVORCE.] (2) The title of the LXVth Sūrah of the Qur'ān which treats of the subject of divorce.

TALBĪYAH (تلبية). *Lit.* "Waiting or standing for orders." The recitation of the following words during the pilgrimage to Makkah: "*Labbaika! Allāhummah! Labbaika! Labbaika! Lā Sharīka laka! Labbaika! Inna 'l-ḥamda wa-ni'amata laka! Wa 'l-mulka! Lā Sharīka-laka!*" "I stand up for Thy service, O God! I stand up! I stand up! There is no partner with Thee! I stand up for Thy service! Verily Thine is the praise, the beneficence, and the kingdom! There is no partner with Thee!"

From the *Mishkāt* (book xi. ch. ii. pt. 1), it appears that this hymn was in use amongst the idolaters of Arabia before Muḥammad's time. [HAJJ.]

ṬALḤAH (طلحة), son of 'Ubaidu 'llāh, the Quraish, was a grand-nephew of Abū Bakr. He was a distinguished Companion, and was honoured with the position of one of the *'Asharah Mubashsharah*, or "ten patriarchs of the Muslim faith." He saved the life of Muḥammad at the battle of Uḥud. He was slain in the fight of the Camel, A.H. 36, aged 64, and was buried at al-Baṣrah.

ṬĀLIB (طالب). *Lit.* "One who seeks." An inquirer. A term generally used for a student of divinity, is *Ṭālibu 'l-'ilm*.

TALISMAN. Arabic (طلسم) *ṭilsam*; pl. *ṭalāsim*. The English word is a corruption of the Arabic. A term applied to mystical characters, and also to seals and stones upon which such characters are engraved or inscribed. The characters are astrological, or of some other magical kind. Talismans are used as charms against evil, for the preserving from enchantment or from accident; they are also sometimes buried with a hidden treasure to protect it. [AMULET, EXORCISM.]

TALKING. [CONVERSATION.]

TALMUD. The traditional law of the Jews. From Heb. לָמַד *lāmad*, "to learn." The learning of the Rabbis. Mr. Emanuel Deutsch says:—

"It seems as if Muḥammad had breathed from his childhood almost the air of contemporary Judaism, as is found by us crystallized in the Talmud, the Targum and the Midrash.

* * * * *

"It is not merely parallelisms, reminiscences, allusions, technical terms, and the like of Judaism, its law and dogma and ceremony, its Halacha and its Haggadah (its law and legend), which we find in the Koran; but we think Islām neither more nor less than Judaism as adapted to Arabia—plus the Apostleship of Jesus and Muḥammad." (*Literary Remains*, p. 64.)

How much Muḥammad was indebted to the Jewish Talmud for his doctrines, ethics, and ceremonial, is shown in an essay by the Jewish Rabbi, Abraham Geiger, in answer to the question put by the University at Bonn: "Inquiratur in fontes Alcorani seu legis Mohammedicæ eos, qui ex Judæismo derivandi sunt," of which a German translation has appeared, *Was hat Mohammed aus dem Judenthume aufgenommen?* (Bonn, 1833), and is treated of in the present work in the article on JUDAISM.

The Talmud consists of two parts: The Mishna, or the text (what is called in Arabic the *Matn*), and the Gemara, or Commentary (Arabic *Sharḥ*). These two form the Talmud.)

The Mishna (from *Shanah*, to "repeat") or the oral law of the Jews, was not committed to writing until about the year A.D. 190, by Rabbi Judah, although it is said it was first commenced by Rabbi Akibah, A.D. 130.

The Gemara (*lit.* "that which is perfect") are two commentaries on the Mishna. The one compiled by Rabbi Jochonam at Jerusalem about the middle of the third century, and the other by Rabbi Ashe at Babylon, about the middle of the sixth.

Canon Farrar (*Life of Christ*, vol. ii. p. 348), says: "Anything more utterly unhistorical than the Talmud, cannot be conceived. It is probable that no human writings ever confounded names, dates, and facts, with more absolute indifference."

And doubtless it is this unsatisfactory feature in the Talmud of the Jews which, to a great extent, accounts for the equally unhistorical character of the Qur'ān.

For information on the Talmud, the English reader can consult the following works: *The Talmud*, by Joseph Barklay, LL.D., Bishop of Jerusalem, 1878; *A Talmudic Miscellany*, by Paul Isaac Hershon, 1880; *Selections from the Talmud*, by H. Polono; *The Talmud*, an article in the *Quarterly Review*, October, 1867, by Emanuel Deutsch; *The Talmud*, a chapter in *The Home and Synagogue of the Modern Jew* (Religious Tract Society). A complete translation of the Talmud is being undertaken by Mr. P. I. Hershon. See Dr. Farrar's Preface to the *Talmudic Miscellany.*

TALQĪN (تلقين). *Lit.* "Instructing." An exhortation or instruction imparted by a religious teacher. It is specially used for the instruction given at the grave of a departed Muslim, at the close of the burial service, when one of the mourners draws near the middle of the grave, addresses the deceased, and says:—

"O servant of God, and child of a female servant of God.

"O son of such an one, remember the faith you professed on earth to the very last; this is your witness that there is no deity but God, and that certainly Muḥammad is His Apostle, and that Paradise and Hell and the Resurrection from the dead are real; that there will be a Day of Judgment; and say: 'I confess that God is my Lord, Islām my religion, Muḥammad (on whom be the mercy and peace of God) my Prophet, the Qur'ān my guide, the Ka'bah my Qiblah, and that Muslims are my brethren.' O God, keep him (the deceased) firm in his faith, and widen his grave, and make his examination (by Munkir and Nakīr) easy, and exalt him and have mercy on him, O Thou most Merciful!" [BURIAL.]

ṬĀLŪT (طالوت). [SAUL.]

TAMATTU' (تمتع). *Lit.* "Reaping advantage." The act of performing the 'Umrah until its completion, and then performing the Ḥajj as a separate ceremony, thus reaping the advantages of both. [HAJJ, UMRAH.]

TAMĪM (تميم). An independent Arab tribe of Makkan origin who occupied the north-eastern desert of Najd. They fought by the side of Muḥammad at Makkah and Ḥunain.

TAMJĪD (تمجيد). The expression, "*La ḥaula wa lā quwwata illā bi-'llāhi 'l 'alīyi 'l-'aẓīm*" (لا حول ولا قوة الا بالله العلى العظيم), "There is no power and strength but in God, the High one, the Great." (*Mishkāt*, book x. ch. ii.)

Abū Hurairah relates that the Prophet said, "Recite very frequently, 'There is no power and strength but in God,' for these words are one of the treasures of Paradise. For there is no escape from God but with God. And God will open for the reciter thereof seventy doors of escape from evil, the least of which is poverty."

TANĀSUKH (تناسخ). (1) In Muḥammadan law, the death of one heir after another before the partition of an inheritance.

(2) *At-Tanāsukh*. The metempsychosis or Pythagorean system of the transmigration of souls, a doctrine held by the Hindus and Buddhists, but forming no part of the Muḥammadan system.

TANFĪL (تنفيل). "Plundering in religious warfare." Commended in the Qur'ān,

Sūrah viii. 1: "They will question thee about the spoils. Say: The spoils are God's and the Apostle's."

TAQARRUB (تقرب). *Lit.* "Seeking admittance or striving to draw near." A term used to express the desire of propitiating the Deity by prayer, almsgiving, or sacrifice.

TAQDĪR (تقدير). *Lit.* "To measure." The doctrine of Fate or Predestination, *al-Qadr*. [PREDESTINATION.]

TAQĪYAH (تقية). *Lit.* "Guarding oneself." A Shīʿah doctrine. A pious fraud whereby the Shīʿah Muslim believes he is justified in either smoothing down or in denying the peculiarities of his religious belief, in order to save himself from religious persecution. A Shīʿah can, therefore, pass himself off as a Sunnī to escape persecution.

The Shīʿah traditionists relate that certain persons inquired of the Imām Ṣādiq if the Prophet had ever practised *taqīyah*, or "religious dissimulation," and the Imām replied, "Not after this verse was sent down to the Prophet, namely, Sūrah v. 71: 'O thou Apostle! publish the whole of what has been revealed to thee from thy Lord; if thou do it not, thou hast not preached His message, and God will not defend thee from wicked men; for God guides not the unbelieving people.' When the Most High became surety for the Prophet against harm, then he no longer dissimulated, although before this revelation appeared he had occasionally done so." (The *Ḥayatu 'l-Qulūb*, Merrick's ed., p. 96.) [SHIʿAH.]

TAQLĪD (تقليد). *Lit.* "Winding round." (1) Putting a wreath round a victim destined to be slain at Makkah. (2) Girding with a sword, as a sign of investiture of a high dignitary. (2) A term used in Muḥammadan law for the following of a religious leader without due inquiry.

TAQWĀ (تقوى). [ABSTINENCE.]

TARĀWĪḤ (تراويح). The plural of *tarwīḥ*, "Rest." The prayers, of usually twenty rakʿahs, recited at night during the month of Ramaẓān; so called because the congregation sit down and *rest* after every fourth rakʿah and every second "*Salām.*" [RAMAZAN.]

TARIKAH (تركة). A legacy, a bequest, an inheritance.

AT-ṬĀRIQ (الطارق). "The night-comer." The title of the LXXXVIth Sūrah of the Qurʾān, beginning thus:

"By the heaven, and by the *night-comer!*
But what shall teach thee
What the night-comer is?
'Tis the star of piercing radiance"

According to al-Wāḥidī, these words were revealed when Abū Ṭālib, at the time of the evening meal, was startled by a shooting star. Nöldeke, however, observes that the three verses seem rather to apply to a planet or a fixed star of particular brightness.

ṬARĪQAH (طريقة). "A path." A term used by the Sūfīs for the religious life. [SUFI.]

TARWIYAH (تروية). *Lit.* "Satisfying thirst," or, according to some, "giving attention." The eighth day of the pilgrimage; so called either because the pilgrims give their camels water on this day, or because Abraham gave attention (*rawwa*) to the vision wherein he was instructed to sacrifice his son Ishmael (?) on this day.

TAṢAWWUF (تصوف). A word used to express the doctrines of the Ṣūfīs or Muḥammadan mystics. Ṣūfiism. The word does not occur in the celebrated Arabic Dictionary, the *Qāmūs*, which was compiled A.H. 817, nor in the *Siḥāḥ*, A.H. 393. [SUFI.]

TASBĪḤ (تسبيح). (1) The ejaculation, "*Subḥāna 'llāh!*" (سبحان الله), "I extol the holiness of God!" or "O Holy God!" A most meritorious ejaculation, which, if recited one hundred times, night and morning, is said by the Prophet to atone for man's sins, however many or great. (*Mishkāt*, book x. ch. ii.)

(2) A Rosary. [ROSARY, ZIKR.]

TASHAHHUD (تشهد). *Lit.* "Testimony." A declaration of the Muslim faith recited during the stated prayers, immediately after the *Taḥīyah*, in the same attitude, but with the first finger of the right hand extended, as a witness to the Unity of God. It is as follows: "I testify that there is no deity but God, and I testify that Muḥammad is the Messenger of God." It is also used as an expression of faith upon a person becoming a Muḥammadan. (*Mishkāt*, book iv. ch. xvi.) [PRAYERS.]

TASHRĪQ (تشريق). *Lit.* "Drying flesh in the sun." A name given to three days after the sacrifice at Makkah during the Pilgrimage, either because the flesh of the victim is then dried, or because they are not slain until sunrise. [HAJJ.]

TASLĪM (تسليم). The benediction at the close of the usual form of prayer, "*As-salāmu ʿalaikum wa raḥmatu 'llāh!*" (السلام

(عليكم ورحمة الله), "The peace and mercy of God be with you." [PRAYERS.]

TASMĪ' (تسميع). The following ejaculation which is recited by the Imām in the daily prayers: "God hears him who praises Him." [PRAYERS.]

TASMIYAH (تسمية). *Lit.* "Giving a name." (1) A title given to the *Basmallah*, or the initial sentence, "In the name of God, the Compassionate, the Merciful." This occurs at the commencement of each chapter or Sūrah of the Qur'ān, with the exception of the IXth Sūrah. [QUR'AN.] (2) Also used at the commencement of any religious act (except sacrifice), such as prayer, ablutions, &c. (3) The usual "grace before meat," amongst Muslims. [BISMILLAH.]

TASNĪM (تسنيم). *Lit.* "Anything convex and shelving at both sides." The name of a fountain in Paradise mentioned in the Qur'ān, Sūrah lxxxiii. 28: "Mingled therewith shall be the waters of *Tasnīm.*"

TAṢWĪB (تثويب). Repeating the phrase, "*Aṣ-ṣalātu khairun mina 'n-nāum*" (*i.e.* "Prayer is better than sleep"), in the Aẕān for the early morning prayer. [AZAN, PRAYER.]

TAṬAWWU' (تطوع). An act of supererogation. A term which includes both the *sunnah* and *nafl* actions of the Muslim (*q.v.*).

AT-TAṬFĪF (التطفيف). "Giving Short Measure." The title of the LXXXIIIrd Sūrah of the Qur'ān, beginning with the words:

"Woe to those who *stint* the measure:
Who when they take by measure from others, exact the full;
But when they mete to them or weigh to them, minish—
Have they no thought that they shall be raised again
For a great day."

We learn from the *Itqān* that some commentators see in this passage allusions to Madīnah circumstances, and consequently think that the Sūrah, or at least part of it, was revealed in that town. But in connection with such obviously Makkan verses, as 30 and following, where it is said:

"The sinners, indeed, laugh the faithful to scorn,
And when they pass by them, they wink at one another,
And when they return to their own people, they return jesting,
And when they see them, they say, 'Verily these are the erring ones'"—

it appears evident, that the pride and arrogance of the Makkans, founded on their ill-gotten wealth, is contrasted with the humble and precarious condition of the followers of Muḥammad, to convey at the same time a solemn warning, that the positions will be reversed on the Great Day of Reckoning.

TAṬHĪR (تطهير). A purifying or cleansing of anything which is ceremonially unclean. For example, if a dog drinks from a vessel, it becomes *najis*, or "impure," but it can be purified (*taṭhīr*) by washing it seven times. A mosque which has been defiled can be cleansed with dry earth or water, and by recitals from the Qur'ān. If the boots on the feet have been defiled, they can be purified by rubbing them on dry earth.

Barā' ibn 'Āzib says that Muḥammad taught that the micturation of an animal lawful for food does not render clothes ceremonially unclean. (*Mishkāt*, book iii. ch. ix.) [PURIFICATION.]

TATTOOING. Muḥammad forbade the custom of the idolaters of Arabia to prick the hands of their women and to rub the punctures over with wood, indigo, and other colours. (*Mishkāt*, book xii. ch. i. pt. 1.)

TAUBAH (توبة). (1) Repentance. (2) *At-Taubah*, a title of the IXth Surah of the Qur'ān. [PARDON, REPENTANCE.]

AT-TAUBATU 'N-NAṢŪḤ (التوبة النصوح). *Lit.* "Sincere repentance." A term used by divines for true repentance of the heart, as distinguished from that only of the lips.

TAUḤĪD (توحيد). A term used to express the unity of the Godhead, which is the great fundamental basis of the religion of Muḥammad. [GOD.]

TAUJĪH (توجيه). Any pious ejaculation recited by the pious before or after the Takbīr. (*Mishkāt*, book iv. ch. xii.) [PRAYER.]

TAURĀT (تورٰة). The title given in the Qur'ān (Sūrah iii. 2), and in all Muḥammadan works, for the Books of Moses. It is the Hebrew תּוֹרָה *Tōrāh*, "the Law."

The author of the *Kashfu 'ẓ-Ẓunūn* (the

bibliographical dictionary of Ḥājī K͟halīfah), says :—

"The Taurāt is the inspired book which God gave to Moses, and of which there are three well-known editions. (1) The *Taurātu 's-Saba'īn,* 'the Torah of the Seventy,' which was translated from the Hebrew into Greek by seventy-two learned Jews. (It is admitted by Christian writers 'that the Law, *i.e.* the Pentateuch, alone was translated first). It has since been translated into Syriac and Arabic. (2) The *Taurātu 'l-Qarrā'īn wa Rab-bānīyīn,* 'the Taurāt of the learned doctors and rabbins.' (3) The *Taurātu 's-Sāmirah,* 'The Samaritan Pentateuch.'"

The same writer says the learned who have examined these editions of the Taurāt, found that although they agreed with each other and taught the unity of God, they do not contain an account of the stated prayers, the fast, the pilgrimage to Jerusalem, and almsgiving, nor anything regarding heaven or hell, which is, he adds, a proof of the Taurāt having been altered by the Jews. (*Kashfu 'ẓ-Ẕunūn,* Flügel's edition, vol. ii. p. 459.)

Although Muḥammad professed to establish the Taurāt of Moses (see Qur'ān, Sūrahs ii. 130; iii. 78; iv. 135), it would appear from the Traditions that he did not view with favour the reading of it in his presence.

It is related that ʻUmar once brought a copy of the Taurāt to the Prophet, and said, "This is a copy of the Taurāt." Muḥammad was silent, and ʻUmar was about to read some portions of it. Then Abū Bakr said, "Your mother weeps for you. Don't you see the Prophet's face look angry." Then ʻUmar looked, and he saw the Prophet was angry, and he said, "God protect me from the anger of God and of His Apostle. I am satisfied with God as my Lord, Islām as my creed, and Muḥammad as my Prophet." Then Muḥammad said, "If Moses were alive and found my prophecy, he would follow me." [OLD TESTAMENT.]

AT-TAUWĀB (التواب). Literally "One who turns frequently," hence "the Relenting." One of the ninety-nine names or attributes of God. Preceded by the article, as a name of God, it occurs four times in the Sūratu 'l-Baqarah (ii. 35, 51, 122, 155), and twice in the Sūratu 't-Taubah (ix. 105, 119). In three of these passages, God's relenting mercy is illustrated by striking instances taken from ancient and contemporaneous history, viz. in the case of Adam, of the Jews after their worshipping the golden calf, and of the three men who did not accompany Muḥammad in the expedition to Tabūk, and who, put under interdiction after his return, were not released from it till after fifty days of penance.

Sūrah ii. 35 : "And words of prayer learned Adam from his Lord : and God relented towards him; verily, He is the *Relenting,* the Merciful."

Sūrah ii. 51 : "And remember when Moses said to his people : 'O my people! verily ye

have sinned to your own hurt, by your taking to yourself the calf to worship it: Be turned then to your Creator, and slay the guilty among you; this will be best for you with your Creator.' So he relented towards you : verily He is *the Relenting,* the Merciful."

Sūrah iv. 119 : "He has also turned in Mercy unto the three who were left behind, so that the earth, spacious as it is, became too strait for them; and their souls became so straitened within them, that there was no refuge from God but unto Himself. Then was He turned to them that they might turn to Him. Verily, God is He that *turneth,* the Merciful."

In the other places, mentioned above, and in two more (Sūrahs xxiv. 10, and xlix. 12), where the word is used as an adjective without the article, it describes God as ever ready to turn in forgiveness to man in general and to the Muslim in particular, if they turn in repentance unto him.

ṬAWĀF (طواف). The ceremony of circumambulating the Kaʻbah seven times, three times in a quick step and four at the ordinary pace. It is enjoined in the Qur'ān, Sūrah xxii. 27. Shaik͟h ʻAbdu 'l-Ḥaqq says it was the custom of the Arabian idolaters to perform the *ṭawāf* naked. [HAJJ.]

TAʻWĪZ (تعويذ). *Lit.* "To flee for refuge." An amulet or charm. A gold or silver case, inclosing quotations from the Qur'ān or Ḥadīs, and worn upon the breast, arm, neck, or waist. [AMULET.]

TAXATION. There are three words used for taxation in Muslim books of law. (1) *ʻUshr* (عشر), "the tenth"; (2) *K͟harāj* (خراج), "land revenue"; (3) *Jizyah* (جزية), "capitation tax."

(1) Lands, the proprietors of which become Muslims, or which the Imām divides among the troops, are *ʻUshrī,* or subject to tithe, because it is necessary that something should be imposed and deducted from the subsistence of Muslims, and a tenth is the proportion most suitable to them, as that admits the construction of an oblation or act of piety; and also, because this is the most equitable method, since in this way the amount of what is levied depends upon the actual product of the lands.

(2) Lands, on the other hand, which the Imām subdues by force of arms and then restores to the people of the conquered territory, are *K͟harājī,* or subject to tribute, because it is necessary that something should be imposed and deducted from the subsistence of infidels, and tribute is the most suitable to their situation, as that bears the construction of a punishment, since it is a sort of hardship, the tax upon tribute land being due from the proprietor, although he should not have cultivated it. It is to be remarked, however, that Makkah is excepted from this rule, as Muḥammad conquered that territory by force of arms, and then restored it to the inhabitants without imposing tribute.

It is written in the *Jāmiʿu 's-Ṣaghīr* that all land subdued by force of arms, if watered by canals cut by the Gentiles, is subject to tribute, whether the Imām have divided it among the troops, or restored it to the original inhabitants; and if there be no canals, but the land be watered by springs, which rise within, it is subject to tithe, in either case, because tithe is peculiar to productive land, that is, land capable of cultivation, and which yields increase, and the increase produced from it is occasioned by water. The standard, therefore, by which tribute is due is the land being watered by tribute water, namely, rivers, and the standard by which tithe is due is the land being watered by tithe water, namely, springs.

If a person cultivate waste lands, the imposition of tithe or tribute upon it (according to Abū Yūsuf) is determined by the neighbouring soils; in other words, if the neighbouring lands be subject to tithe, a tithe is to be imposed upon it, or tribute if they be subject to tribute; because the rule respecting anything is determined by what is nearest to it; as in the case of a house, for instance, the rule with respect to it extends to its court-yard, although it be not the owner's immediate property. The tribute established and imposed by ʿUmar upon the lands of al-ʿIrāq was adjusted as follows:—Upon every *jarīb* of land through which water runs (that is to say, which is capable of cultivation) one *ṣāʿ* and one *dirham*, and upon every *jarīb* of pasture-land five *dirhams*, and upon every *jarīb* of gardens and orchards ten *dirhams*, provided they contain vines and date-trees.

This rule for tribute upon arable and pasture lands, gardens, and orchards, is taken from ʿUmar, who fixed it at the rates above-mentioned, none contradicting him; wherefore it is considered as agreed to by all the Companions. Upon all land of any other description (such as pleasure-grounds, saffron-fields, and so forth) is imposed a tribute according to ability; since, although ʿUmar has not laid down any particular rule with respect to them, yet as he has made ability the standard of tribute upon arable land, so in the same manner, ability is to be regarded in lands of any other description. The learned in the law allege that the utmost extent of tribute is one half of the actual product, nor is it allowable to exact more; but the taking of a half is no more than strict justice, and is not tyrannical, because, as it is lawful to take the whole of the persons and property of infidels, and to distribute them among the Muslims, it follows that taking half their incomes is lawful *a fortiori*.

(3) *Jizyah*, or capitation-tax, is of two kinds. The first species is that which is established voluntarily, and by composition, the rate of which is such as may be agreed upon by both parties. The second is that which the Imām himself imposes, where he conquers infidels, and then confirms them in their possessions, the common rate of which is fixed by his imposing upon every avowedly rich person a tax of forty-eight dirhams per annum, or four dirhams per month; and upon every person in middling circumstances twenty-four dirhams per annum, or two dirhams per month; and upon the labouring poor twelve dirhams per annum, or one dirham per month.

(For further information see *Raddu 'l-Muḥtār*, vol. ii. 7; *Fatāwā-i-ʿAlamgīrī*, ii. 860; *Hidāyah*, vol. i. 102.)

TAYAMMUM (تيمم). *Lit.* "Intending or proposing to do a thing."

The ceremony of ablution performed with sand instead of water, as in the case of *waẓū'*. The permission to use sand for this purpose, when water cannot be obtained, is granted in the Qur'ān, Sūrah v. 9:—

"If ye cannot find water, then take fine surface sand and wipe your faces and your hands therewith. God does not wish to make any hindrance for you."

It is related in the Traditions that Muḥammad said: "God has made me greater than all preceeding prophets, inasmuch as my ranks in worship are like the ranks of angels; and the whole earth is fit for my people to worship on; and the very dust of the earth is fit for purification when water cannot be obtained. (*Mishkāt*, book iii. ch. xi.)

Tayammum, or "purification by sand," is allowable under the following circumstances: (1) When water cannot be procured except at a distance of about two miles; (2) in case of sickness when the use of water might be injurious; (3) when water cannot be obtained without incurring danger from an enemy, a beast, or a reptile; and (4) when on the occasion of the prayers of a Feast day or at a funeral, the worshipper is late and has no time to perform the waẓū'. On ordinary days this substitution of *tayammum* for *waẓū'* is not allowable. [WAZU'.]

TAʿZĪAH (تعزية). *Lit.* "A consolation."

A representation or model of the tomb of Ḥasan and Ḥusain at Karbalā', carried in procession at the Muḥarram by the Shīʿahs. It is usually made of a light frame of wood-work, covered with paper, painted and ornamented, and illuminated within and without. It is sometimes of considerable size and of elaborate execution according to the wealth of the owner. [MUHARRAM.]

A TAʿZIAH. (*A. F. Hole.*)

TA'ZĪR (تعزير). From *'azr*, "to censure or repel." That discretionary correction which is administered for offences, for which *Ḥadd*, or "fixed punishment," has not been appointed.

According to the Sunnī law the following are the leading principles of Ta'zīr:—

Ta'zīr, in its primitive sense, means "prohibition," and also "instruction"; in Law it signifies an infliction undetermined in its degree by the law, on account of the right either of God, or of the individual; and the occasion of it is any offence for which *ḥadd*, or "stated punishment," has not been appointed, whether that offence consist in word or deed.

(1) Chastisement is ordained by the law, the institution of it being established on the authority of the Qur'ān, which enjoins men to chastise their wives, for the purpose of correction and amendment; and the same also occurs in the Traditions. It is, moreover, recorded that the Prophet chastised a person who had called another perjured; and all the Companions agree concerning this. Reason and analogy, moreover, both evince that chastisement ought to be inflicted for acts of an offensive nature, in such a manner that men may not become habituated to the commission of such acts; for if they were, they might by degrees be led into the perpetration of others more atrocious. It is also written in the *Fatāwā-i-Timūr Tashī* of Imām Sirukhsh, that in *ta'zīr*, or "chastisement," nothing is fixed or determined, but that the degree of it is left to the discretion of the Qāẓī, because the design of it is correction, and the dispositions of men with respect to it are different, some being sufficiently corrected by reprimands, whilst others, more obstinate, require confinement, and even blows.

(2) In the *Fatāwā-i-Shāfi'ī* it is said that there are four orders or degrees of chastisement:—First, the chastisement proper to the most noble of the noble (or, in other words, princes and men of learning), which consists merely in admonition, as if the Qāẓī were to say to one of them, "I understand that you have done thus, or thus," so as to make him ashamed. Secondly, the chastisement proper to the noble (namely, commanders of armies, and chiefs of districts), which may be performed in two ways, either by admonition (as above), or by *jarr*, that is, by dragging the offender to the door and exposing him to scorn. Thirdly, the chastisement proper to the middle order (consisting of merchants and shopkeepers), which may be performed by *jarr* (as above), and also by imprisonment; and Fourthly, the chastisement proper to the lowest order in the community, which may be performed by *jarr*, or by imprisonment, and also by blows.

(3) It is recorded from Abū Yūsuf that the ruler of a country may inflict chastisement by means of property, that is, by the exaction of a small sum in the manner of a fine, proportioned to the offence; but this doctrine is rejected by many of the learned.

(4) Imām Timūr Tashī says that chastisement, where it is incurred purely as the right of God, may be inflicted by any person whatever; for Abū Ja'far Hindūānī, being asked whether a man, finding another in the act of adultery with his wife, might slay him, replied, "If the husband know that expostulation and beating will be sufficient to deter the adulterer from a future repetition of his offence, he must not slay him; but if he sees reason to suppose that nothing but death will prevent a repetition of the offence, in such case it is allowed to the husband to slay that man: and if the woman were consenting to his act, it is allowed to her husband to slay her also;" from which it appears that any man is empowered to chastise another by blows, even though there be no magistrate present. He has demonstrated this fully in the *Muntafi'*: and the reason of it is that the chastisement in question is of the class of the removal of evil with the hand, and the Prophet has authorized every person to remove evil with the hand, as he has said: "Whosoever among ye see the evil, let him remedy it with his own hands; but if he be unable so to do, let him forbid it with his tongue." Chastisement, therefore, is evidently contrary to punishment, since authority to inflict the latter does not appertain to any but a magistrate or a judge. This species of chastisement is also contrary to the chastisement which is incurred on account of the right of the individual (such as in cases of slander, and so forth), since that depends upon the complaint of the injured party, whence no person can inflict it but the magistrate, even under a private arbitration, where the plaintiff and defendant may have referred the decision of the matter to any third person.

(5) Chastisement, in any instance in which it is authorized by the law, is to be inflicted where the Imām sees it advisable.

(6) If a person accuse of whoredom a male or female slave, an *ummu 'l-walad*, or an infidel, he is to be chastised, because this accusation is an offensive accusation, and punishment for slander is not incurred by it, as the condition, namely, *Iḥsān* (or marriage in the sense which induces punishment for slander), is not attached to the accused: chastisement, therefore, is to be inflicted. And in the same manner, if any person accuse a Muslim of any other thing than whoredom (that is, abuse him, by calling him a reprobate, or a villain, or an infidel, or a thief), chastisement is incurred, because he injures a Muslim and defames him; and punishment (*ḥadd*) cannot be considered as due from analogy, since analogy has no concern with the necessity of punishment: chastisement, therefore, is to be inflicted. Where the aggrieved party is a slave, or so forth, the chastisement must be inflicted to the extremity of it: but in the case of abuse of a Muslim, the measure of the chastisement is left to the discretion of the magistrate, be it more or less; and whatever he sees proper let him inflict.

(7) If a person abuse a Muslim, by calling him an ass, or a hog, in this case chastisement is not incurred, because these expressions are in no respect defamatory of the person towards whom they are used, it being evident that he is neither an ass nor a hog. Some allege that, in our time, chastisement is inflicted, since, in the modern acceptation, calling a man an ass or a hog is held to be abuse. Others, again, allege that it is esteemed such only where the person towards whom such expressions are used happens to be of dignified rank (such as a prince, or a man of letters), in which case chastisement must be inflicted upon the abuser, as by so speaking he exposes that person of rank to contempt; but if he be only a common person, chastisement is not incurred: and this is the most approved doctrine.

(8) The greatest number of stripes in chastisement is thirty-nine (see 2 Cor. xi. 24), and the smallest number is three. This is according to Abū Ḥanīfah and Imam Muḥammad. Abū Yūsuf says that the greatest number of stripes in chastisement is seventy-five. The restriction to thirty-nine stripes is founded on a saying of the Prophet: "The man who shall inflict scourging to the amount of punishment, in a case where punishment is not established, shall be accounted an aggravator" (meaning a wanton aggravator of punishment), from which saying it is to be inferred that the infliction of a number of stripes in chastisement, to the same amount as in punishment, is unlawful; and this being admitted, Abū Ḥanīfah and Imām Muḥammad, in order to determine the utmost extent of chastisement, consider what is the smallest punishment: and this is punishment for slander with respect to a slave, which is forty stripes; they therefore deduct therefrom one stripe, and establish thirty-nine as the greatest number to be inflicted in chastisement. Abū Yūsuf, on the other hand, has regard to the smallest punishment with respect to freemen (as freedom is the original state of man), which is eighty stripes; he therefore deducts five, and establishes seventy-five as the greatest number to be inflicted in chastisement as aforesaid, because the same is recorded of 'Alī, whose example Abū Yūsuf follows in this instance. It is in one place recorded of Abū Yūsuf that he deducted only one stripe, and declared the utmost number of stripes in chastisement to be seventy-nine. Such, also, is the opinion of Zafr; and this is agreeable to analogy. Imām Muḥammad, in his book, has determined the smallest number of stripes in chastisement to be three, because in fewer there is no chastisement. The more modern doctors assert that the smallest degree of chastisement must be left to the judgment of the Imām or Qāẓī, who is to inflict whatever he may deem sufficient for chastisement, which is different with respect to different men. It is recorded of Abū Yūsuf that he has alleged that the degree thereof is in proportion to the degree of the offence; and it is also recorded from him that the chastisement for petty offences should be inflicted to a degree approaching to the punishment allotted for offences of a similar nature; thus the chastisement for libidinous acts (such as kissing and touching), is to be inflicted to a degree approaching to punishment for whoredom; and the chastisement for abusive language to a degree approaching to punishment for slander.

(9) If the Qāẓī deem it fit in chastisement to unite imprisonment with scourging, it is lawful for him to do both, since imprisonment is of itself capable of constituting chastisement, and has been so employed, for the Prophet once imprisoned a person by way of chastising him. But as imprisonment is thus capable of constituting chastisement, in offences where chastisement is incurred by their being established, imprisonment is not lawful before the offence be proved, merely upon suspicion, since imprisonment is in itself a chastisement: contrary to offences which induce punishment, for there the accused may be lawfully imprisoned upon suspicion, as chastisement is short of punishment (whence the sufficiency of imprisonment alone in chastisement); and such being the case, it is lawful to unite imprisonment with blows.

(10) The severest blows or stripes may be used in chastisement, because, as regard is had to lenity with respect to the number of the stripes, lenity is not to be regarded with respect to the nature of them, for otherwise the design would be defeated; and hence, lenity is not shown in chastisement by inflicting the blows or stripes upon different parts or members of the body. And next to chastisement, the severest blows or stripes are to be inflicted in punishment for whoredom, as that is instituted in the Qur'ān. Whoredom, moreover, is a deadly sin, insomuch that lapidation for it has been ordained by the law. And next to punishment for whoredom, the severest blows or stripes are to be inflicted in punishment for wine-drinking, as the occasion of punishment is there fully certified. And next to punishment for wine-drinking, the severity of the blows or stripes is to be attended to in punishment for slander, because there is a doubt in respect to the occasion of the punishment (namely, the accusation), as an accusation may be either false or true; and also, because severity is here observed, in disqualifying the slanderer from appearing as an evidence: wherefore severity is not also to be observed in the nature of the blows or stripes.

(11) If the magistrate inflict either punishment or chastisement upon a person, and the sufferer should die in consequence of such punishment or chastisement, his blood is *Nadar*, that is to say, nothing whatever is due upon it, because the magistrate is authorized therein, and what he does is done by decree of the law; and an act which is decreed is not restricted to the condition of safety. This is analogous to a case of phlebotomy; that is to say, if any person desire

to be let blood, and should die, the operator is in no respect responsible for his death; and so here also. It is contrary, however, to the case of a husband inflicting chastisement upon his wife, for his act is restricted to safety, as it is only allowed to a husband to chastise his wife; and an act which is only allowed is restricted to the condition of safety, like walking upon the highway. Ash-Shāfiʿī maintains that, in this case, the fine of blood is due from the public treasury; because, although where chastisement or punishment prove destructive, it is homicide by misadventure (as the intention is not the destruction, but the amendment of the sufferer), yet a fine is due from the public treasury, since the advantage of the act of the magistrate extends to the public at large, wherefore the atonement is due from their property, namely, from the public treasury. The Ḥanafī doctors, on the other hand, say that whenever the magistrate inflicts a punishment ordained of God upon any person, and that person dies, it is the same as if he had died by the visitation of God, without any visible cause; wherefore there is no responsibility for it. (See the *Hidāyah*; the *Durru 'l-Mukhtār*; the *Fatāwā-i-ʿĀlamgīrī, in loco.*) [PUNISHMENT.]

TAZKIYAH (تزكية). *Lit.* "Purifying." (1) Giving the legal alms, or *zakāt*.

(2) The purgation of witnesses. (See Hamilton's *Hidāyah*, vol. ii. p. 674.) An institution of inquiry into the character of witnesses.

TAZWĪJ (تزويج). *Lit.* "Joining." A term used for a marriage contract. [MARRIAGE.]

TEMPLE AT MAKKAH, The. [MASJIDU 'L-HARAM.]

TERAH. [AZAR.]

THEFT. [LARCENY.]

THEOLOGY. Arabic *al-ʿIlmu 'l-Ilāhī* (العلم الالهى), "The Science of God." In the Traditions, the term *ʿIlm*, "knowledge," is specially applied to the knowledge of the Qur'ān.

Shaikh ʿAbdu 'l-Ḥaqq, in his remarks on the term *ʿIlm*, says religious knowledge consists in an acquaintance with the Qur'ān and the Traditions of Muḥammad.

Muḥammadan theology may be divided into—

(1) *ʿIlmu 't-Tafsīr*, a knowledge of the Qur'ān and the commentaries thereon.

(2) *ʿIlmu 'l-Hadīs*, a knowledge of the Traditions.

(3) *ʿIlmu 'l-Uṣūl*, a knowledge of the roots, or of the four principles of the foundations of Muslim law, being expositions of the exegesis of the Qur'ān and the Ḥadīs, and the principles of Ijmāʿ and Qiyās.

(4) *ʿIlmu 'l-Fiqh*, Muslim law, whether moral, civil, or ceremonial.

(5) *ʿIlmu 'l-ʿAqāʾid*, scholastic theology, founded on the six articles of the Muslim creed, the Unity of God, the Angels, the Books, the Prophets, the Resurrection, and Predestination. [ʿILM.]

THUNDER. Arabic *Raʿd* (رعد). In the Qur'ān, Surah xiii. 13, 14, it is said: "He (God) it is who shows you the lightning for fear and hope (of rain); and He brings up heavy clouds, and the *thunder* celebrates His praise; and the angels, too, fear him, and He sends the thunder-clap and overtakes therewith whom He will; yet they wrangle about God! But He is strong in might."

AT-ṬIBBU 'R-RŪḤĀNI (الطب الروحانى). *Lit.* "The science (medical) of the heart." A term used by the Ṣūfīs for a knowledge of the heart and of remedies for its health. (See *Kitābu 't-Taʿrīfāt.*)

TILĀWAH (تلاوة). *Lit.* "Reading." The reading of the Qur'ān. [QUR'AN.]

AT-TĪN (التين). "The Fig." The title of the xcvth Sūrah of the Qur'ān, the opening words of which are: "I swear by the *fig* and by the olive."

ṬĪNATU 'L-KHABĀL (طينة الخبال). *Lit.* "The clay of putrid matter." The sweat of the people of hell. An expression used in the Traditions. (*Mishkāt*, book xv. ch. vii. pt. 1.)

AT-TIRMIZĪ (الترمذى). The *Jāmiʿu 't-Tirmizī*, or the "Collection of Tirmizī." One of the six correct books of Sunnī traditions collected by Abū ʿIsā Muḥammad ibn ʿĪsā ibn Saurah at-Tirmizī, who was born at Tirmiz on the banks of the Jaihun, A.H. 209. Died A.H. 279. [TRADITIONS.]

TITHE. [TAXATION.]

TOBACCO. Arabic *dukhān* (دخان) (smoke). In some parts of Syria *tabagh* (تبغ) and *tutun* (تتن); in India and Central Asia, *tamāku*, corruption of the Persian *tambākū* (تنباكو). Tobacco was introduced into Turkey, Arabia, and other parts of Asia soon after the beginning of the seventeeth century of the Christian era, and very soon after it had begun to be regularly imported from America into western Europe. Its lawfulness to the Muslim is warmly disputed. The Wahhābīs have always maintained its unlawfulness, and even other Muslims hardly contend for its lawfulness, but it has become generally used in Muslim countries. In India, smoking is allowed in mosques; but in Afghānistan and Central Asia, it is generally forbidden. The celebrated Muslim leader, the Akhund of Swat, although an opponent of the Wahhābīs, condemned the use of tobacco on account of its exhilarating effects.

TOLERATION, RELIGIOUS. Muḥammadan writers are unanimous in asserting that no religious toleration was extended to the idolaters of Arabia in the time of the Prophet. The only choice given them was death or the reception of Islām

But they are not agreed as to how far idolatry should be tolerated amongst peoples not of Arabia. Still, as a matter of fact, Hindūs professing idolatry are tolerated in all Muslim countries. Jews, Christians, and Majūsīs are tolerated upon the payment of a capitation tax [JIZYAH, TREATY]. Persons paying this tax are called *Ẕimmīs*, and enjoy a certain toleration. (*Fatāwā-i-'Alamgīrī*, vol. i. p. 807.) [ZIMMI.]

According to the Ḥanafīs, the following restrictions are ordained regarding those who do not profess Islām, but enjoy protection on payment of the tax :—

It behoves the Imām to make a distinction between Muslims and Ẕimmīs, in point both of dress and of equipage. It is, therefore, not allowable for Ẕimmīs to ride upon horses, or to use armour, or to use the same saddles and wear the same garments or head-dresses as Muslims, and it is written in the *Jāmi'u 's-Ṣaghīr*, that Ẕimmīs must be directed to wear the *kistīj* openly on the outside of their clothes (the *kistīj* is a woollen cord or belt which Ẕimmīs wear round their waists on the outside of their garments); and also that they must be directed, if they ride upon any animal, to provide themselves a saddle like the panniers of an ass.

The reason for this distinction in point of clothing and so forth, and the direction to wear the *kistīj* openly, is that Muslims are to be held in honour (whence it is they are not saluted first, it being the duty of the highest in rank to salute first [SALUTATION]), and if there were no outward signs to distinguish Muslims from Ẕimmīs, these might be treated with the same respect, which is not allowed. It is to be observed that the insignia incumbent upon them to wear is a woollen rope or cord tied round the waist, and not a silken belt.

It is requisite that the wives of Ẕimmīs be kept separate from the wives of Muslims, both in the public roads, and also in the baths; and it is also requisite that a mark be set upon their dwellings, in order that beggars who come to their doors may not pray for them. The learned have also remarked that it is fit that Ẕimmīs be not permitted to ride at all, except in cases of absolute necessity, and if a Ẕimmī be thus, of necessity, allowed to ride, he must alight wherever he sees any Muslims assembled; and, as mentioned before, if there be a necessity for him to use a saddle, it must be made in the manner of the panniers of an ass. Ẕimmīs of the higher orders must also be prohibited from wearing rich garments.

The construction of churches or synagogues in the Muslim territory is unlawful, this being forbidden in the Traditions; but if places of worship originally belonging to Jews or Christians be destroyed, or fall to decay, they are at liberty to repair them, because buildings cannot endure for ever, and as the Imām has left these people to the exercise of their own religion, it is a necessary inference that he has engaged not to prevent them from rebuilding or repairing their churches and synagogues. If, however, they attempt to remove these, and to build them in a place different from their former situation, the Imām must prevent them, since this is an actual construction; and the places which they use as hermitages are held in the same light as their churches, wherefore the construction of those also is unlawful.

It is otherwise with respect to such places of prayer as are within their dwellings, which they are not prohibited from constructing, because these are an appurtenance to the habitation. What is here said is the rule with respect to cities, but not with respect to villages or hamlets, because, as the tokens of Islām (such as public prayer, festivals, and so forth) appear in cities, Ẕimmīs should not be permitted to celebrate the tokens of infidelity there in the face of them; but as the tokens of Islām do not appear in villages or hamlets, there is no occasion to prevent the construction of synagogues or churches there.

Some allege that Ẕimmīs are to be prohibited from constructing churches or synagogues, not only in cities but also in villages and hamlets, because in the villages various tokens of Islām appear, and what is recorded from Abū Ḥanīfah (that the prohibition against building churches and synagogues is confined to cities, and does not extend to villages and hamlets) relates solely to the villages of al-Kūfah, because the greater part of the inhabitants of villages are Ẕimmīs, there being few Muslims among them, wherefore the tokens of Islām did not there appear; moreover, in the territory of Arabia Ẕimmīs are prohibited from constructing churches or synagogues, either in cities or villages, because the Prophet has said: "Two religions cannot be possessed together in the peninsula of Arabia." (See *Fatāwā-i-'Alamgīrī*, *Durru 'l-Mukhtār*, *Hidāyah*, *in loco.*) [ZIMMI.]

TOMBS. The erection of tombs and monuments over the graves of Muslims is forbidden by the strict laws of Islām. For the teaching of the Traditions on the subject is unmistakable, as will be seen by the following Aḥādīs (*Mishkāt*, book v. ch. vi. pt. 1):—

Jābir says: "The Prophet prohibited building with mortar on graves."

Abū 'l-Haiyāj al-Asadī relates that the Khalīfah 'Alī said to him: "Shall I not give you the orders which the Prophet gave me, namely, to destroy all pictures and images, and not to leave a single lofty tomb without lowering it within a span from the ground."

Sa'd ibn Abī Waqqās said, when he was ill: "Make me a grave towards Makkah, and put unburnt bricks upon it, as was done upon the Prophet's."

The Wahhābīs consequently forbid the erection of monuments, and when they took possession of al-Madīnah, they intended to destroy the handsome building which covers the grave of the Prophet, but were prevented by accident. (See Burton's *Pilgrimage*, vol. i. p. 354.) [WAHHABI.]

But notwithstanding the general consensus of orthodox opinion, that the erection of such buildings is unlawful, domed tombs of substantial structure, similar to the illustration given on this page, are common to all Muḥammadan countries, and masonry tombs are always erected over the graves of persons of respectability.

Some have a head-stone, in which there are recesses for small oil lamps, which are lighted every Thursday evening. Persons of distinction are generally honoured with tombs constructed with domes. The specimens given in the illustrations are common to all parts of the Muslim world.

The most common form of structure is not dissimilar to that which is erected in Christian cemeteries, but it is usual to put a head-stone to the grave of a male on which is a figure representing the turban as a sign of authority. Sometimes there is a cavity in the top of the grave-stone filled with mould, in which flowers are planted.

Writing of the grave-yards of Damascus, Mr. Wellsted says: "I know of nothing which displays the Moslem character to more advantage than the care they bestow on their burial-grounds. On Friday, the Moslem Sunday, those of Damascus afford at once a touching and animated scene. The site selected for the remains of those most cherished in life is generally picturesquely situated, in some lower spot, beneath the lofty cypress or quivering poplar. Here a head-stone of marble, covered with inscriptions, and of a male, surmounted with a turban, mingles with costlier buildings, of an oblong form, very tastefully and elaborately inscribed with sentences from the Koran. The greatest care is observed in preserving these sepulchral monuments. A small aperture is left in some portions, which is filled with earth, and in them the females plant myrtle and other flowers, and not infrequently water them with their tears. On the day I have named, they may be perceived in groups, hastening to perform the sad but pleasing office of mourning for the departed.' (*Travels to the City of the Caliphs*, vol. i. p. 348.)

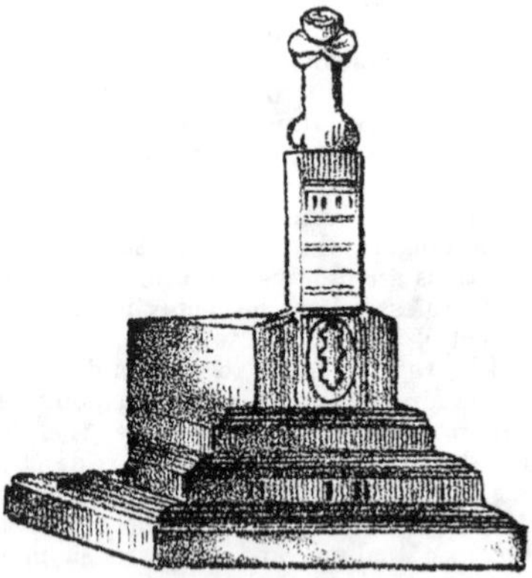

Mr. Lane (*Arabian Nights*, vol. i. p. 433) says the tomb "is a hollow, oblong vault, one side of which faces Mekkeh, generally large enough to contain four or more bodies, and having an oblong monument of stone or brick constructed over it with a stela at the head and foot. Upon the former of these two stelæ (which is often inscribed with a text from the Ḳur-án, and the name of the deceased, with the date of his death), a turban, or other head-dress, is sometimes carved, shewing the rank or class of the person or persons buried beneath; and in many cases, a cupola, supported by four walls, or by columns, &c., is constructed over the smaller monument. The body is laid on its right side, or inclined by means of a few crude bricks, so that the face is turned towards Mekkeh; and a person is generally employed to dictate to the deceased the answers which he should give when he is examined by the two angels Munkir and Nekeer." [TALQIN.]

The tombs of the imperial family of Turkey are amongst the most interesting sights of the city of Constantinople. They are principally erected in the outer courts of mosques and behind the *miḥrāb*. One of the finest of these mausoleums is that of Sultān Sulaiman I., who died A.D. 1566. It is an octagonal building of divers coloured marbles, with cupola and fluted roof; four pillars support the dome, which is elaborately painted in red and delicate arabesque. It contains the remains of three Sultāns, Sulaimān I., Sulaimān II., and Aḥmad II., besides some female members of the family. The biers are decorated with rich embroideries and costly shawls, and with turbans and aigrettes; and that of Sulaimān I. is surrounded by a railing inlaid with mother-of-pearl.

The mausoleum of the Emperor Jahāngīr at Shahdarrah, near Lahore, is one of the finest Muḥammadan tombs in the world. It is situated in a garden 1,600 feet square. There is, first, a fine corridor 233 feet long, from which to the central dome is 108 feet. The passage to the tomb is paved with beautifully streaked marble from Jaipūr and other places. The sarcophagus stands on a white marble platform, 13 feet 5 inches long, from north to south, and 8 feet 9 inches broad. The sarcophagus itself is of white marble, and is 7 feet long. On the east and west sides of it are the ninety-nine names of God. [GOD, NAMES OF] most beautifully carved, and on the south side is inscribed: "The glorious tomb of His High Majesty, the Asylum of Protectors, Nūru 'd-dīn Muḥammad, the Emperor Jihāngīr, A.H. 1037 (A.D. 1627). On the north end of the tomb is in Arabic, "Allah the Living God. There is no deity but God over the invisible world and all things. He is the Merciful and the Compassionate." On the top is a short passage from the Qur'ān, written in beautiful Ṭug͟hra. The central dome of the building is 27 feet square, and on the four sides there are fine screens of trellis work. Just inside the entrance, and to the right of it, is a staircase with twenty-five steps, which leads up to a magnificent tesselated pavement, at each corner of which is a minaret 95 feet high from the platform. This platform is 211 feet 5 inches square, and is truly beautiful. A marble wall ran round the pavement, but it was taken away by the Sikhs, and it has been replaced by a poor substitute of masonry. The minarets are four storeys high, and are built of magnificent blocks of stone 8 feet by 61 feet, and in them are steps leading to the top of the building, from which there is a fine view of Lahore.

The tomb of Aḥmad Shāh Abdalī at Kandahar, is an octagonal structure, overlaid with coloured porcelain bricks, and is surmounted with a gilded dome, surrounded by small minarets. The pavement inside is covered with a carpet, and the sarcophagus of the Afghan king is covered with a shawl. The tomb itself is made of Kandahar stone, inlaid with wreaths of flowers in coloured marble. The interior walls are prettily painted and the windows are of fine trellis work in stone.

The sepulchre of the Taimur, who died A.D. 1405, is at Samarkand in Bukhārah, and is described by M. Vambery as a neat little chapel crowned with a splendid dome, and encircled by a wall in which there is an arched gate. On both sides are two small domes, minature representations of the large one in the centre. The court-yard between the wall and the chapel is filled with trees; the garden being much neglected. Upon entering the dome, there is a vestibule which leads to the chapel itself. This is octagonal, and about ten short paces in diameter. In the middle, under the dome, that is to say, in the place of honour, there are two tombs, placed lengthways, with the head in the direction of Makkah. One of these tombs is covered with a very fine stone of a dark green colour, two and a half spans broad and ten long, and about the thickness of six fingers. It is laid flat in two pieces over the grave of Taimur. The other grave is covered with a black stone. It is the tomb of Mīr Syud Bakar, the teacher and spiritual guide of Taimur, and beside whose grave the great Ameer gratefully desired to be buried. Round about lie other tombstones great and small. The inscriptions are simple, and are in Arabic and Persian.

It has often been the case that Muḥammadan kings have erected their mausoleums during their lifetime, although such acts are strictly contrary to the teachings of their Prophet. A remarkable instance of this is to be seen at Bijapur in India, where the unfinished tomb of ʿAli ʿAdl Shah (A.D. 1557) is still to be seen, having never been completed after his burial. His successor, Ibrahīm (A.D. 1579), warned by the fate of his predecessor's tomb, commenced his own on so small a plan —116 feet square—that, as he was blessed with a long and prosperous reign, it was only by ornament that he could render the place worthy of himself. This he accomplished by covering every part with the most exquisite and elaborate carvings. The ornamental carvings on this tomb are so numerous, that it is said the whole Qur'ān is engraven on its walls. The principal apartment in the tomb is a square of forty feet, covered by a stone roof perfectly flat in the centre, and supported by a cove projecting ten feet from the wall on every side. Mr. Fergusson says: "How the roof is supported is a mystery, which can only be understood by those who are familiar with the use the Indians make of masses of concrete, which, with good mortar, seems capable of infinite applications unknown in Europe." (*Architecture*, vol. iii. p. 562.) The tomb of Maḥmūd, Ibrahīm's successor (A.D. 1626), was also built in his lifetime, and remarkable for its simple grandeur and constructive boldness. It is internally 135 feet each way, and its area is consequently 18,225 square feet, while the Pantheon at Rome has only an area of 15,833 feet.

The tomb of Imām ash-Shāfiʿī, the founder of one of the four orthodox sects of the Sunnīs, and who died A.H. 204, is still to be seen near the city of Cairo. It is surmounted b a large dome, with a weathercock in the form of a boat. It is said to have been erected by Yūsuf Ṣalāḥu 'd-Dīn (Saladin). The interior is cased to a height of eight feet with marble, above which the whole building is coloured in recent and unartistic style. The windows contain coloured glass. There are three niches, with a fourth in the form of a *miḥrāb*, marking the direction of Makkah. The covering of the tomb of the celebrated Muslim doctor is of simple brocade, embroidered with gold. It is enclosed with a wooden railing, inlaid with mother-of-pearl, the corners being clasped with silver fittings. At the head of the tomb is a large turban, partly covered with a Cashmere shawl. Near the head of the tomb is a marble pillar, with sculptured inscriptions, coloured red and gold. From the roof are suspended a few porcelain lamps; and lamps of glass, as well as ostrich eggs, hang in profusion from the canopy of the tomb and from light wooden beams. The walls and tomb-enclosure are adorned with scrolls. Close to the building are four other tombs of the Imām's family.

The tomb of Zubaidah, the beloved wife of the celebrated Khalīfah Hārūnu 'r-Rashīd, the hero of the tales of *The Thousand and One Nights*, is a simple edifice standing on a sloping eminence, within an extensive cemetery outside the city of Baghdad. It is a building of an octagonal shape, thirty feet in diameter, and surmounted by a spire. In the upper part of the building are two ranges of windows, the upper of which presents the flattened and the lower the pointed arch. The spire is a mere sharpened cone, ornamented without with convex divisions corresponding to concave arches within. The interior is occupied by three oblong buildings of masonry, coated with lime. A modern Pacha and his wife have now the honour of reposing beside the remains of the fair Persian, and an inscription over the porch testifies that their remains were deposited nine centuries after the favourite wife of the renowned Khalīfah.

A very interesting specimen of tomb architecture is found at Sultaniah in Persia. It is the sepuchre of one Muḥammad Khudabandia. Texier ascribes the building to Khudabandiah, of the Ṣūfī dynasty, A.D. 1577–85; but Fergusson says its style shows that the monument must be two or three hundred years older than that king. Ker Porter says it is the work of the Tartar Muḥammad Khudabandia, who was the successor of Ghazan Khān, the builder of the celebrated mosque at Tabrīz, who, being seized with as much zeal for his Shīʿite faith as his predecessor had been for the Sunnite, his intention was to lodge in this mausoleum the remains of ʿAlī and his son al-Ḥusain. This intention, however, was not carried into effect, and consequently the bones of the founder repose alone in this splendid shrine, and not under the central dome, but in a side chamber. The general plan of this building is an octagon, with a small chapel opposite the entrance, in

THE TAJ AT AGRA. (*A. F. Hole.*)

which the body lies. Internally, the dome is 81 feet in diameter by 150 feet in height, the octagon being worked (Mr. Fergusson says) into a circle by as elegant a series of brackets as, perhaps, ever were employed for this purpose. The form of the dome is singularly graceful and elegant, and superior to anything of the kind in Persia. The whole is covered with glazed tiles, rivalling in richness those of the celebrated mosque at Tabrīz; and with its general beauty of outline, it affords one of the finest specimens of this style of architecture found in any country.

The grave of the Persian poet Ḥāfiẓ, at Shiraz in Persia, is a single block of beautiful marble from Yezd, of which about eighteen inches appear above the ground. It is a fine slab, is perfectly flat, and is nine feet long by two feet nine inches in width. Raised in low relief, in the centre of the top of the slab, is one of the poet's odes in the beautiful letters of the Persian alphabet, and round the edges, in a band about five inches deep, is another ode. The tomb, which is probably about two hundred years old, is situated in a square enclosure or garden, and the ground around is thickly beset with tombs, mostly flat like that of the poet.

The finest specimen of monumental architecture is the celebrated *Tāj* at Agra, erected over the grave of Urjummad Banu Begum, called *Mumtāz-i-Maḥall*, or the "Exalted One of the Palace," the favourite wife of the Emperor Shāh Jahān, who died about A.D. 1629. The designs and estimates for the building are said to have been prepared by a Venetian named Geronimo Verroneo; but the architect died at Lahore before its completion, and the work is supposed to have been handed over to a Byzantine Turk. Mr. Keene says that it is certain Austin, the French artist, was consulted. Mr. Fergusson gives the following particulars of this remarkable building:—

"The enclosure, including garden and outer court, is a parallelogram of 1,860 feet by more than 1,000 feet. The outer court, surrounded by arcades and adorned by four gateways, is an oblong, occupying in length the whole breadth of the enclosure, and is about 450 feet deep. The principal gateway leads from this court to the garden, where the tomb is seen framed in an avenue of dark cypress trees. The plinth of white marble is 18 feet high, and is an exact square of 313 feet each way. At the four corners stand four columns or towers, each 137 feet high, and crowned with a little pavilion. The mausoleum itself occupies a space of 186 feet square, in the centre of this larger square, and each of the four corners is cut off opposite each of the towers. The central dome is 50 feet in diameter by 80 feet in height. On the platform in front of the *juwab*, or false mosque, is a tracing of the topmost spine, a gilded spike crowning the central dome to the height of 30 feet. The interior is lighted from marble-trellised-screen lights above and below."—*Fergusson's History of Architecture*, vol. ii. p. 693.) [ZIYARAH.]

TRADITION. It is the belief of all Muḥammadans, whether Sunnī, Shī'ah, or Wahhābī, that in addition to the revelation contained in the Qur'ān, the Prophet received the *Waḥy ghair Matlū* (*lit.* "an unread revelation"), whereby he was enabled to give authoritative declarations on religious questions, either moral, ceremonial, or doctrinal. Muḥammad traditions are therefore supposed to be the uninspired record of inspired sayings, and consequently occupy a totally different position to what we understand by traditions in the Christian Church. The Arabic words used for these traditions are *Ḥadīs̤* (حديث), pl. *Aḥādīs̤*, "a saying"; and *Sunnah* (سنة), pl. *Sunan* "a custom." The word Ḥadīs̤, in its singular form, is now generally used by both Muḥammadan and Christian writers for the collections of traditions. They are records of what Muḥammad did (*Sunnatu 'l-fi'l*), what Muḥammad enjoined (*Sunnatu 'l-qaul*), and that which was done in the presence of Muḥammad and which he did not forbid (*Sunnatu 't-taqrīr*). They also include the authoritative sayings and doings of the Companions of the Prophet.

The following quotations from the Traditions as to the sayings of Muḥammad on the subject of this oral law, will explain the position which he intended to assign to it.

"That which the Prophet of God hath made unlawful is like that which God himself hath made so."

"I am no more than a man, but when I enjoin anything respecting religion receive it, and when I order anything about the affairs of the world, then I am nothing more than man."

"Verily the best word is the word of God, and the best rule of life is that delivered by Muḥammad."

"I have left you two things, and you will not stray as long as you hold them fast. The one is the book of God, and the other the law (*sunnah*) of His Prophet."

"My sayings do not abrogate the word of God, but the word of God can abrogate my sayings."

"Some of my injunctions abrogate others." (*Mishkāt*, book i. ch. vi.)

Muḥammad gave very special injunctions respecting the faithful transmission of his sayings, for, according to at-Tirmiẕī, Ibn 'Abbās relates that Muḥammad said: "Convey to other persons none of my words, except those ye know of a surety. Verily he who represents my words wrongly shall find a place for himself in the fire."

But notwithstanding the severe warning given by their Prophet, it is admitted by all Muslim scholars that very many spurious traditions have been handed down. Abū Da'ūd received only four thousand eight hundred traditions out of five hundred thousand, and even in this *careful* selection, he states, that he has given "those which seem to be authentic and those which are nearly so." (*Vide* Ibn Khallikān, vol. i. p. 590.)

Out of forty thousand persons who have

been instrumental in handing down traditions, al Bukhārī only acknowledges two thousand as reliable authorities.

In consequence of the unreliable character of the Traditions, the following canons have been framed for the reception or rejection (*vide Nukhbatu 'l-Faqr*, by Shaikh Shihābu 'd-Dīn Aḥmad, ed. by Captain N. Lees) :—

I. With reference to the character of those who have handed down the tradition :—

(1) *Ḥadīṣu 's-Ṣaḥīḥ*, a *genuine* tradition, is one which has been handed down by truly pious persons who have been distinguished for their integrity.

(2) *Ḥadīṣu 'l-Ḥasan*, a *mediocre* tradition, is one the narrators of which do not approach in moral excellence to those of the Ṣaḥīḥ class.

(3) *Ḥadīṣu 'z-Ẓa'īf*, a *weak* tradition, is one whose narrators are of questionable authority.

The disputed claims of narrators to these three classes have proved a fruitful source of learned discussion, and very numerous are the works written upon the subject.

II. With reference to the original relators of the Ḥadīṣ :—

(1) *Ḥadīṣu 'l-Marfū'*, an *exalted* tradition is a saying, or an act, related or performed by the Prophet himself and handed down in a tradition.

(2) *Ḥadīṣu 'l-Mauqūf*, a *restricted* tradition, is a saying or an act related or performed by one of the *aṣḥāb*, or Companions of the Prophet.

(3) *Ḥadīṣu 'l-Maqṭū'*, an *intersected* tradition, is a saying or an act related or performed by one of the *Tābi'ūn*, or those who conversed with the Companions of the Prophet.

III. With reference to the links in the chain of the narrators of the tradition, a Ḥadīṣ is either *Muttaṣil*, connected, or *Munqaṭi'*, disconnected. If the chain of narrators is complete from the time of the first utterance of the saying or performance of the act recorded to the time that it was written down by the collector of traditions, it is *Muttaṣil*; but if the chain of narrators is incomplete, it is *Munqaṭi'*.

IV. With reference to the manner in which the tradition has been narrated, and transmitted down from the first :—

(1) *Ḥadīṣu 'l-Mutawātir*, an *undoubted* tradition, is one which is handed down by very many distinct chains of narrators, and which has been always accepted as authentic and genuine, no doubt ever having been raised against it. The learned doctors say there are only five such traditions; but the exact number is disputed.

(2) *Ḥadīṣu 'l-Mashhūr*, a *well-known* tradition, is one which has been handed down by at least three distinct lines of narrators. It is called also *Mustafīẓ*, diffused. It is also used for a tradition which was at first recorded by one person, or a few individuals, and afterwards became a popular tradition.

(3) *Ḥadīṣu 'l-'Azīz*, a *rare* tradition, is one related by only two lines of narrators.

(4) *Ḥadīṣu 'l-Gharīb*, a *poor* tradition, is one related by only one line of narrators.

(5) *Khabaru 'l-Wāḥid*, a *single saying*, is a term also used for a tradition related by one person and handed down by one line of narrators. It is a disputed point whether a *Khabar Wāḥid* can form the basis of Muslim doctrine.

(6) *Ḥadīṣu 'l-Mursal* (*lit.* "a tradition let loose"), is a tradition which any collector of traditions, such as al-Bukhārī and others, records with the assertion, "*the Apostle of God said.*"

(7) *Riwāyah*, is a Ḥadīṣ which commences with the words "*it is related,*" without the authority being given.

(8) *Ḥadīṣu 'l-Mauẓū'*, an *invented* tradition, is one the *untruth* of which is beyond dispute.

The following is a specimen of a *ḥadīṣ*, as given in the collection of at-Tirmiẕī, which will exemplify the way in which a tradition is recorded :—

" Abū Kuraib said to us (*ḥaddaṣa-nā*) that Ibrāhīm ibn Yūsuf ibn Abī Isḥāq said to us (*ḥaddaṣa-nā*), from (*'an*) his father, from (*'an*) Abū Isḥāq, from (*'an*) Tulātā ibn Musārif, that he said, I have heard (*sami'tu*), from 'Abdu 'r-Raḥmān ibn Ausajah, that he said (*yaqūlu*), I have heard (*sami'tu*) from Barā ibn 'Āzib that he said (*yaqūlu*) I have heard (*sami'tu*) that the Prophet said, Whoever shall give in charity a milch cow, or silver, or a leathern bottle of water, it shall be equal to the freeing of a slave."

The Honourable Syed Ahmed Khan Bahadur, C.S.I., an educated Muḥammadan gentleman, in an *Essay on Mohammedan Traditions*, gives the following information :—

The Style of Composition employed in the imparting of a Tradition.

For the purpose of expressing how a tradition had been communicated from one person to another, certain introductory verbal forms were selected by duly qualified persons, and it was incumbent upon every one about to narrate a tradition, to commence by that particular form appropriated to the said tradition, and this was done with the view of securing for each tradition the quantum of credit to which it might be justly entitled.

These introductory verbal forms are as follow : (1) حدثنا "He said to me" ; (2) سمعته يقول "I heard him saying" ; (3) قال لنا "He told me" ; (4) ذكر لنا "He related to me" ; (5) اخبرنا "He informed me" ; (6) انبانا "He informed me" ; (7) عن "From."

The first four introductory forms were to be used only in the case of an original narrator communicating the very words of the tradition to the next one below him. The fifth and sixth introductory verbal forms were used when a narrator inquired of the narrator immediately above him whether such or such a fact, or circumstance, was or was not correct. The last form is not sufficiently explicit, and the consequence is that it cannot be decided to which of the two persons the tradition related belongs, so that unless other facts be brought to bear upon it, it cannot be satisfactorily proved whether there be any other persons, one, or more than one, intermediary between the two narrators. As to any external facts that might prove what was required to be known, the learned are divided in their opinions.

First: If it be known of a certainty that the narrator is not notorious for fraudulently omitting the names of other parties forming links in the chain of narration, and who also lived at such a time and in such a locality that it was possible, although not proved, that they visited each other, then it might be taken for granted that there were no other narrators intermediary between these two.

Secondly: Other learned authorities add that it must be proved that they visited each other, at least once in their life-time.

Thirdly: Others assert that it must be proved that they remained together for such a time as would be sufficient to enable them to learn the tradition, one from the other.

Fourthly: Some hold that it must be proved that one of them really learned the tradition from the other.

Degree of Authenticity of the Narrators as judged by their Acquirements.

The associates of the Prophet, and those persons who lived immediately after them, used to relate, with the exception of the Qur'ān, the sense of the Prophet's words in their own language, unless they had to use some phrases containing prayers, or when they had to point out to others the very words of the Prophet. It is natural to suppose that deeply-learned persons would themselves understand and deliver, to others, the sense of the sayings better than persons of inferior parts, and therefore narrators have been divided into seven grades.

First: Persons highly conspicuous for their learning and legal acquirements, as well as for their retentive memory. Such persons are distinguished by the title of ائمة الحديث *A'immatu 'l-Ḥadīs̤*, that is "Leaders in Ḥadīs̤."

Second: Persons who, as to their knowledge, take rank after the first, and who but very rarely committed any mistake.

Third: Persons who have made alterations in the pure religion of the Prophet, without carrying them to extremes by prejudice, but respecting whose integrity and honesty there is no doubt.

Fourth: Persons respecting whom nothing is known.

Fifth: Persons who have made alterations in the pure religion of the Prophet, and, actuated by prejudice, have carried them to extremes.

Sixth: Persons who are pertinaciously sceptical, and have not a retentive memory.

Seventh: Persons who are notorious for inventing spurious traditions. Learned divines are of opinion that the traditions related by persons of the first three classes should be accepted as true, according to their respective merits, and also that traditions related by persons coming under the three last classes should be, at once, entirely rejected; and that the traditions related by persons of the fourth class, should be passed over unnoticed so long as the narrator remained unknown.

Causes of Difference among Traditions.

We should not be justified in concluding that, whenever a difference is met with in traditions, these latter are nothing more than so many mere inventions and fabrications of the narrators, since, besides the fabrication of ḥadīs̤, there are also other natural causes which might occasion such differences; and we shall now consider those natural causes which produce such variety among ḥadīs̤.

(1) A misunderstanding of the real sense of the saying of the Prophet.

(2) Difference of the opinions of two narrators in understanding the true sense of the Prophet's saying.

(3) Inability to enunciate clearly the sense of the Prophet's saying.

(4) Failure of memory on the part of the narrator—in consequence of which he either left out some portion or portions of the Prophet's saying, or mixed up together the meanings of two different ḥadīs̤.

(5) Explanation of any portion of the ḥadīs̤ given by the narrator, with the intention of its being easily understood by the party hearing it, but unfortunately mistaken by the latter for an actual portion of the ḥadīs̤ itself.

(6) Quotations of certain of the Prophet's words by the narrator, for the purpose of supporting his own narration, while the hearers of the narration erroneously took the whole of it as being the Prophet's own words.

(7) Traditions borrowed from the Jews erroneously taken to be the words of the Prophet, and the difference existing between such Jewish traditions was thus transferred to those of the Muhammadans. The stories of ancient persons and early prophets, with which our histories and commentaries are filled, are all derived from these sources.

(8) The difference which is naturally caused in the continual transmission of a tradition by oral communication, as it has been in the case of traditions having miracles for their subject-matter.

(9) The various states and circumstances in which the different narrators saw the Prophet.

Apocryphal Ḥadīs̤.

There exists no doubt respecting the circumstance of certain persons having fabricated some ḥadīs̤ in the Prophet's name. Those who perpetrated so impudent a forgery were men of the following descriptions:—

(1) Persons desirous of introducing some

praiseworthy custom among the public, forged ḥadīs̤ in order to secure success. Such fabrication is restricted exclusively to those ḥadīs̤ which treat of the advantages and benefits which reading the Qur'ān and praying procure to any one, both in this world and the next; which show how reciting passages from the Qur'ān cures every disease, etc.: the real object of such frauds being to lead the public into the habit of reading the Qur'ān and of praying. According to our religion, the perpetrators of such frauds, or of any others, stand in the list of sinners.

(2) Preachers, with a view of collecting large congregations around them, and of amusing their hearers, invented many traditions, such traditions being only those which describe the state and condition of paradise and of hell, as well as the state and condition of the soul after death, etc., in order to awaken the fear of God's wrath and the hope of salvation.

(3) Those persons who made alterations in the religion of the Prophet, and who, urged by their prejudices, carried the same to extremes, and who, for the purpose of successfully confronting their controversial antagonists, forged such traditions in order to favour their own interested views.

(4) Unbelievers who maliciously coined and circulated spurious ḥadīs̤. Learned men, however, have greatly exerted themselves in order to discover such fabricated traditions, and have written many works upon the subject, laying down rules for ascertaining false traditions and for distinguishing them from genuine ones.

The modes of procedure were as follows: Such persons examined the very words employed in such traditions, as well as their style of composition; they compared the contents of each ḥadīs̤ with the commands and injunctions contained in the Qur'ān, with those religious doctrines and dogmas that have been deduced from the Qur'ān, and with those ḥadīs̤ which have been proved to be genuine; they investigated the nature of the import of such traditions, as to whether it was unreasonable, improbable, or impossible.

It will, therefore, be evident that the ḥadīs̤ considered as genuine by Muḥammadans, must indispensably possess the following characters: The narrator must have plainly and distinctly mentioned that such and such a thing was either said or done by the Prophet; the chain of narrators from the last link up to the Prophet, must be unbroken; the subject related must have come under the actual ken of its first narrators; every one of the narrators, from the last up to the Prophet, must have been persons conspicuous for their piety, virtue, and honesty; every narrator must have received more than one ḥadīs̤ from the narrator immediately preceding him; every one of the narrators must be conspicuous for his learning, so that he might be safely presumed to be competent both to understand correctly, and faithfully deliver to others, the sense of the tradition; the import of the tradition must not be contrary to the injunctions contained in the Qur'ān, or to the religious doctrines deduced from that Book, or to the traditions proved to be correct; and the nature of the import of the tradition must not be such as persons might hesitate in accepting.

Any tradition thus proved genuine can be made the basis of any religious doctrine; but notwithstanding this, another objection may be raised against it, which is, that this tradition is the statement of one person only, and therefore, cannot, properly, be believed in implicitly. For obviating this, three grades have been again formed of the ḥadīs̤ proved as genuine. These three grades are the following: متواتر *Mutawātir*, مشهور *Mashhūr*, and خبر احد *Khabar-i-Aḥad*.

Mutawātir is an appellation given to those ḥadīs̤ only that have always been, from the time of the Prophet, ever afterwards recognised and accepted by every associate of the Prophet, and every learned individual, as authentic and genuine, and to which no one has raised any objection. All learned Muḥammadan divines of every period have declared that the Qur'ān only is the Ḥadīs̤ Mutawātir; but some doctors have declared certain other ḥadīs̤ also to be Mutawātir, the number, however, of such ḥadīs̤ not exceeding *five*. Such are the traditions that are implicitly believed and ought to be religiously observed.

Mashhūr is a title given to those traditions that, in every age, have been believed to be genuine, by some learned persons. These are the traditions which are found recorded in the best works that treat of them, and, having been generally accepted as genuine, form the nucleus of some of the Muslim doctrines.

Khabar-i-Aḥad (or ḥadīs̤ related by one person), is an appellation given to traditions that do not possess any of the qualities belonging to the traditions of the first two grades. Opinions of the learned are divided whether or not they can form the basis of any religious doctrine.

Persons who undertook the task of collecting traditions had neither time nor opportunity for examining and investigating all the above particulars, and some of them collected together whatsoever came under their notice, while others collected only those whose narrators were acknowledged to be trustworthy and honest persons, leaving entirely upon their readers the task of investigating and examining all the above-mentioned particulars, as well as of deciding their comparative merits, their genuineness, and the quantum of credit due to them.

There is some difference of opinion as to who first attempted to collect the traditions, and to compile them in a book. Some say 'Abdu 'l-Malik ibn Juraij of Makkah, who died A.H 150, whilst others assert that the collection, which is still extant, by the Imām Mālik, who died A.H. 179, was the first collection. The work by Imām Mālik is still held in very great esteem, and although not generally included among the standard *six*, it is believed by many to be the source from whence a great portion of their materials are derived.

The following are the *Ṣiḥāḥu 's-Sittah*, or "six correct" books, received by Sunnī Muslims :—

(1) Muḥammad Ismā'īl *al-Bukhārī*, A.H. 256.

(2) *Muslim* ibnu 'l-Ḥajjāj, A.H. 261.

(3) Abū 'Īsā Muḥammad, *at-Tirmizī*, A.H. 279.

(4) Abū Da'ūd as-Sajistānī, A.H. 275.

(5) Abū 'Ābdi 'r-Raḥmān *an-Nasā'ī*, A.H. 303.

(6) Abū 'Abdi 'llāh Muḥammad *Ibn Mājah*, A.H. 273.

According to the *Ithāfu 'n-Nubalā'*, there are as many as 1,465 collections of traditions in existence, although the six already recorded are the more generally used amongst the Sunnīs.

It is often stated by European writers that the Shī'ahs reject the Traditions. This is not correct. The Sunnīs arrogate to themselves the title of Traditionists; but the Shī'ahs, although they do not accept the collections of traditions as made by the Sunnīs, receive *five* collections of Aḥādīṣ, upon which their system of law, both civil and religious, is founded.

(1) The *Kāfī*, by Abū Ja'far Muḥammad ibn Ya'qūb, A.H. 329.

(2) The *Man-lā-yastaḥzirahu 'l-Faqīh*, by Shaikh 'Alī, A.H. 381.

(3) The *Tahẕīb*, by Shaikh Abū Ja'far Muḥammad ibn 'Alī ibn Ḥusain, A.H. 466.

(4) The *Istibṣār*, by the same author.

(5) The *Nahju 'l-Balāghah*, by Saiyid ar-Raẓī, A.H. 406.

There are many stories which illustrate the importance the Companions of the Prophet attached to Sunnah. The Khalīfah 'Umar looked towards the black stone at Makkah, and said, "By God, I know that thou art only a stone, and canst grant no benefit, canst do no harm. If I had not known that the Prophet kissed thee, I would not have done so, but on account of that I do it." Abdu 'llāh ibn 'Umar was seen riding his camel round and round a certain place. In answer to an inquiry as to his reason for so doing, he said : "I know not, only I have seen the Prophet do so here." Aḥmad ibn Ḥanbal is said to have been appointed on account of the care with which he observed the Sunnah. One day when sitting in an assembly, he alone of all present observed some formal custom authorised by the practice of the Prophet. Gabriel at once appeared and informed him that now, and on account of his act, he was appointed an Imām. And on another occasion it is said this great traditionist would not even eat water-melons, because, although he knew the Prophet ate them, he could not learn whether he ate them with or without the rind, or whether he broke, bit or cut them : and he forbade a woman, who questioned him as to the propriety of the act, to spin by the light of torches passing in the streets by night, because the Prophet had not mentioned that it was lawful to do so.

The modern Wahhābīs being, for the most part, followers of Ibn Ḥanbal, attach great importance to the teaching of the Traditions, and have therefore caused a revival of this branch of Muslim literature. [WAHHABI.]

We are indebted to Sir William Muir's Introduction to the *Life of Mahomet*, for the following :—

"Mahometan tradition consists of the sayings of the friends and followers of the Prophet, handed down by a real or supposed chain of narrators to the period when they were collected, recorded, and classified. The process of transmission was for the most part oral. It may be sketched as follows.

"After the death of Mahomet, the main employment of his followers was arms. The pursuit of pleasure, and the formal round of religious observances, filled up the interstices of active life, but afforded scanty exercise for the higher faculties of the mind. The tedium of long and irksome marches, and the lazy intervals from one campaign to another, fell listlessly upon a simple and semi-barbarous race. These intervals were occupied, and that tedium beguiled, chiefly by calling up the past in familiar conversation or more formal discourse. On what topic, then, would the early Moslems more enthusiastically descant than on the acts and sayings of that wonderful man who had called them into existence as a conquering nation, and had placed in their hands 'the keys both of this world and of Paradise'?

"Thus the converse of Mahomet's followers would be much about him. The majesty of his character gained greatness by contemplation; and, as time removed him farther and farther from them, the lineaments of the mysterious mortal who was wont to hold familiar intercourse with the messengers of heaven, rose in dimmer, but in more gigantic proportions. The mind was unconsciously led on to think of him as endowed with supernatural power, and ever surrounded by supernatural agency. Here was the material out of which Tradition grew luxuriantly. Whenever there was at hand no standard of fact whereby these recitals may be tested, the memory was aided by the unchecked efforts of the imagination; and as days rolled on, the latter element gained complete ascendancy.

"Such is the result which the lapse of time would naturally have upon the minds and the narratives of the *As-hāb* or 'COMPANIONS' of Mahomet, more especially of those who were young when he died. And then another race sprang up who had never seen the Prophet, who looked up to his contemporaries with a superstitious reverence, and who listened to their stories of him as to the tidings of a messenger from the other world. 'Is it possible, father of Abdallah! that thou hast been with Mahomet?' was the question addressed by a pious Moslem to Hodzeifa, in the mosque of Kufâ; 'didst thou really see the

Prophet, and wert thou on familiar terms with him?'—'Son of my uncle! it is indeed as thou sayest.'—'And how wert thou wont to behave towards the Prophet?'—'Verily, we used to labour hard to please him.'—'Well, by the Lord!' exclaimed the ardent listener, 'had I been but alive in his time, I would not have allowed him to put his blessed foot upon the earth, but would have borne him on my shoulders wherever he listed.' (*Hishâmi*, p. 295.) Upon another occasion, the youthful Obeida listened to a Companion who was reciting before an assembly how the Prophet's head was shaved at the Pilgrimage, and the hair distributed amongst his followers; the eyes of the young man glistened as the speaker proceeded, and he interrupted him with the impatient exclamation,—'Would that I had even a single one of those blessed hairs! I would cherish it for ever, and prize it beyond all the gold and silver in the world.' (*Kâtib al Wâckidi*, p. 279.) Such were the natural feelings of fond devotion with which the Prophet came to be regarded by the followers of the 'Companions.'

"As the tale of the Companions was thus taken up by their followers, distance began to invest it with an increasing charm, while the products of living faith and warm imagination were being fast debased by superstitious credulity. This second generation are termed in the language of the patriotic lore of Arabia, *Tâbiûn*, or 'SUCCESSORS.' Here and there a *Companion* survived till near the end of the first century; but, for all practical purposes, they had passed off the stage before the commencement of its last quarter. Their first *Successors*, who were in some measure also their contemporaries, flourished in the latter half of the same century, though some of the oldest may have survived for a time in the second.

"Meanwhile a new cause was at work, which gave to the tales of Mahomet's companions a fresh and an adventitious importance.

"The Arabs, a simple and unsophisticated race, found in the Coran ample provisions for the regulation of all their affairs, religious, social, and political. But the aspect of Islam soon underwent a mighty change. Scarcely was the Prophet dead when his followers issued forth from their barren peninsula, armed with the warrant of the Coran to impose the faith of Mahomet upon all the nations of the earth. Within a century they had, as a first step to this universal subjugation, conquered every land that intervened between the banks of the Oxus and the farthest shores of Northern Africa and of Spain; and had enrolled the great majority of their peoples under the standard of the Coran. This vast empire differed widely indeed from the Arabia of Mahomet's time; and that which well sufficed for the patriarchal simplicity and limited social system of the early Arabs, became utterly inadequate for the hourly multiplying wants of their descendants. Crowded cities, like Fostât, Kufâ, and Damascus, required an elaborate compilation of laws for the guidance of their courts of justice: new political relations demanded a system of international equity: the speculations of a people before whom literature was preparing to throw open her arena, and the controversies of eager factions upon nice points of Mahometan faith, were impatient of the narrow limits which confined them:—all called loudly for the enlargement of the scanty and naked dogmas of the Coran, and for the development of its defective code of ethics.

"And yet it was the cardinal principle of early Islam, that the standard of Law, of Theology, and of Politics, was the Coran and the Coran alone. By it Mahomet himself ruled; to it in his teaching he always referred; from it he professed to derive his opinions, and upon it to ground his decisions. If he, the Messenger of the Lord, and the Founder of the faith, was thus bound by the Coran, much more were the Caliphs, his uninspired substitutes. New and unforeseen circumstances were continually arising, for which the Coran contained no provision. It no longer sufficed for its original object. How then were its deficiencies to be supplied?

"The difficulty was resolved by adopting the CUSTOM or 'SUNNAT' of Mahomet, that is, his *sayings* and his *practice*, as a supplement to the Coran. The recitals regarding the life of the Prophet now acquired an unlooked-for value. *He* had never held himself to be infallible, except when directly inspired of God; but this new doctrine assumed that a heavenly and unerring guidance pervaded every word and action of his prophetic life. Tradition was thus invested with the force of law, and with some of the authority of inspiration. It was in great measure owing to the rise of this theory, that, during the first century of Islam, the cumbrous recitals of tradition so far outstripped the dimensions of reality. The prerogative now claimed for Tradition stimulated the growth of fabricated evidence, and led to the preservation of every kind of story, spurious or real, touching the Prophet. Before the close of the century it had imparted an almost incredible impulse to the search for traditions, and had in fact given birth to the new profession of *Collectors*. Men devoted their lives to the business. They travelled from city to city, and from tribe to tribe, over the whole Mahometan world; sought out by personal inquiry every vestige of Mahomet's biography yet lingering among the *Companions*, the *Successors*, and their descendants; and committed to writing the tales and reminiscences with which they used to edify their wondering and admiring auditors.

"The work, however, too closely affected the public interests, and the political aspect of the empire, to be left entirely to private and individual zeal. About a hundred years after Mahomet, the Caliph Omar II. issued circular orders for the formal collection of all extant traditions. [He committed to Abu

Bacr ibn Muhammad the task of compiling all the traditions he could meet with. This traditionist died A.H. 120, aged 84. Sprenger's *Mohammed*, p. 67.] The task thus begun continued to be vigorously prosecuted, but we possess no authentic remains of any compilation of an earlier date than the middle or end of the second century. Then, indeed, ample materials had been amassed, and they have been handed down to us both in the shape of *Biographies* and of *general Collections*, which bear upon every imaginable point of Mahomet's character, and detail the minutest incidents of his life.

"It thus appears that the traditions we now possess remained generally in an unrecorded form for at least the greater part of a century. It is not indeed denied that some of Mahomet's sayings may possibly have been noted down in writing during his life-time, and from that source copied and propagated afterwards. We say *possibly*, for the evidence in favour of any such record is meagre, suspicious, and contradictory. The few and uncertain statements of this nature may have owed their origin to the authority which a habit of the kind would impart to the name of a Companion, supposed to have practised it. . . . It is hardly possible that, if the custom had prevailed of writing down Mahomet's sayings during his life, we should not have had frequent intimation of the fact, with notices of the writers, and special references to the nature, contents, and peculiar authority of their records. But no such references or quotations are anywhere to be found. It cannot be objected that the Arabs trusted so implicitly to their memory that they regarded oral to be as authoritative as recorded narratives, and therefore would take no note of the latter; for we see that Omar was afraid lest even the Coran, believed by him to be divine and itself the subject of heavenly care, should become defective if left to the *memory* of man. Just as little weight, on the other hand, should be allowed to the tradition that Mahomet *prohibited* his followers from noting down his words; though it is is not easy to see how that tradition could have gained currency at all, had it been the regular and constant practice of any persons to record his sayings. The truth appears to be that there was in reality no such practice; and that the story of the prohibition, though spurious, embodies the *after-thought* of serious Mahometans as to what Mahomet *would have said*, had he foreseen the loose and fabricated stories that sprang up, and the real danger his people would fall into of allowing *Tradition* to supersede the *Coran*. The evils of Tradition were, in truth, as little thought of as its value was perceived, till many years after Mahomet's death.

"But even were we to admit all that has been advanced, it would prove no more than that *some of the Companions used to keep memoranda* of the Prophet's sayings. Now, unless it be possible to connect such memoranda with extant Tradition, the concession would be useless. But it is not, as far as I know, demonstrable of any single tradition or class of traditions now in existence, that they were copied from such memoranda, or have been derived in any way from them. To prove, therefore, that *some* traditions were at first recorded, will not help us to a knowledge of whether any of these still exist, or to a discrimination of them from others resting on a purely oral basis. The very most that could be urged from the premises is, that our present collections *may* contain *some* traditions founded upon a recorded original, and handed down in writing; but we are unable to single out any individual tradition and make such affirmation regarding it. The entire mass of extant tradition rests in this respect on the same uncertain ground, and the uncertainty of any one portion (apart from internal evidence of probability) attaches equally to the whole. We cannot with confidence, or even with the least show of likelihood, affirm of *any* tradition that it was recorded till nearly the end of the first century of the Hegira.

"We see, then, how entirely tradition, as now possessed by us, rests its authority on the *memory* of those who handed it down; and how dependent therefore it must have been upon their convictions and their prejudices. For, in addition to the common frailty of human recollection which renders traditional evidence notoriously infirm, and to the errors or exaggerations which always distort a narrative transmitted orally through many witnesses, there exist throughout Mahometan Tradition abundant indications of actual fabrication; and there may everywhere be traced the indirect but not less powerful and dangerous influence of a silently working bias, which insensibly gave its colour and its shape to all the stories of their Prophet treasured up in the memories of the believers.

* * * * *

"That the Collectors of Tradition rendered an important service to Islam, and even to history, cannot be doubted. The vast flood of tradition, poured forth from every quarter of the Moslem empire, and daily gathering volume from innumerable tributaries, was composed of the most heterogeneous elements; without the labours of the traditionists it must soon have formed a chaotic sea, in which truth and error, fact and fable, would have mingled together in undistinguishable confusion. It is a legitimate inference from the foregoing sketch, that Tradition, in the second century, embraced a large element of truth. That even respectably derived traditions often contained much that was exaggerated and fabulous, is an equally fair conclusion. It is proved by the testimony of the Collectors themselves, that thousands and tens of thousands were current in their times, which possessed not even a shadow of authority. The mass may be likened to the image in Nebuchadnezzar's dream, formed by the unnatural union of gold, of silver, of the baser metals, and of clay; and here the more valuable parts were fast commingling hopelessly with the bad." (Muir's *Life of Mahomet*, vol. i., Intro. p. xxviii.)

TRANSMIGRATION OF SOULS.

[TANASUKH.]

TREATY. Arabic *'Ahd* (عهد). The observance of treaties is enjoined in the Qur'ān (Sūrah viii. 58; ix. 4); but if peace be made with aliens for a specified term (*e.g.* ten years), and afterwards the Muslim leader shall perceive that it is most advantageous for the Muslim interest to break it, he may in that case lawfully renew the war, after giving the enemy due notice. (*Hidāyah*, vol. ii. p. 151; Arabic edition, vol. ii. p. 423.)

The negotiations between John the Christian prince of Ailah, are an interesting incident in the life of Muḥammad, as indicating the spirit of Islām, in its early history, towards Christianity. In the first place, Muḥammad addressed to John the following letter:—

"To John (*Yaḥya*), the son of Rūbah, and the chiefs of the tribe of Ailah. Peace be unto you! Praise be to God, besides whom there is no God. I will not fight against you until I receive an answer to this letter. Believe, or else pay tribute (*jizyah*). Be obedient unto God and to His Apostle. Receive the embassy of God's Apostle, and honour them, and clothe them with excellent vestments, and not with inferior raiment. Specially honour Ḥāriṣ ibn Zaid, for as long as my messengers are pleased, so am I likewise. Ye know the tribute. If ye desire security by sea and by land, obey God and His Apostle, and you will be defended from every attack, whether by Arab or by foreigner. But if you oppose God and His Apostle, I will not accept a single thing from you until I have fought against you, and have slain your men, and have taken captive your women and children. For, in truth, I am God's Apostle. Believe in God and in His Apostle, as you do in the Messiah the son of Mary; for truly he is the Word of God, and I believe in him as an apostle of God. Submit, then, before trouble reaches you. I commend this embassy to you. Give to Harmalah three measures of barley, for Harmalah hath indeed interceded for you. As for me, if it were not for the Lord and for this intercession, I would not have sent any embassy to you, until you had been brought face to face with my army. But now submit to my embassy, and God will be your protector, as well as Muḥammad and all his followers. This embassy doth consist of Shuraḥbīl, and Ubaiy, and Harmalah, and Ḥāriṣ ibn Zaid. Unto you is the protection of God and of his Apostle. If you submit, then peace be unto you, and convey the people of Maqnah back to their land."

Upon receipt of this message, John hastened to Muḥammad's camp, where he was received with kindness; and having made submission and having agreed to pay tribute of 300 dīnārs a year, the following treaty was ratified:—

"In the name of God, the Merciful, the Gracious. A treaty of Peace from God, and from Muḥammad the Apostle of God, granted unto Yaḥya ibn Rūbah and unto the tribe of Ailah. For them who stay at home and for those who travel abroad, there is the security of God and the security of Muḥammad the Apostle of God, and for all who are with them, whether they belong to Syria, or to al-Yaman, or to the sea-coast. Whoso breaketh this treaty, his wealth shall not save him; it shall be the fair prize of whosoever shall capture him. It shall not be lawful to hinder the men of Ailah from going to the springs which they have hitherto used, nor from any journey they may desire to make, whether by land or by sea. This is the writing of Juhaim and Shuraḥbīl by the command of the Apostle of God." [TOLERATION.]

TRIBUTE. [JIHAD, JIZYAH, TAXATION, TREATY.]

TRINITY. Arabic *Taṣlīṣ* (تثليث), "Holy Trinity," *aṣ-Ṣālūṣu 'l-Aqdas* (الثالوث الاقدس). The references to the doctrine of the Holy Trinity in the Qur'ān occur in two Sūrahs, both of them composed by Muḥammad towards the close of his career at al-Madīnah.

Sūrah iv. 169: "Believe, therefore, in God and His apostles, and say not 'Three.'"

Sūrah v. 77: "They misbelieve who say, 'Verily God is the third of three.' . . . The Messiah, the Son of Mary, is only a prophet, . . . and his mother was a confessor; they both ate food."

Sūrah v. 116: "And when God shall say, 'O Jesus son of Mary, hast thou said unto mankind: Take me and my mother as two Gods besides God?"

Al-Baiẓāwī, in his remarks on Surah iv. 169, says, the Christians made the Trinity consist of *Allāh*, *al-Masīh*, and *Maryam*; and Jalālu 'd-dīn takes the same view. Al-Baiẓāwī, however, refers to a view taken of the Trinity, by some Christians in his day, who explained it to be, *Ab*, Father, or the Essence of God; *Ibn*, Son, or the Knowledge of God; and *Rūḥu 'l-Quds*, the Life of God.

In a work quoted in the *Kashfu 'z-Ẓunūn*, entitled *al-Insānu 'l-Kāmil* (written by the Shaikh 'Abdu 'l-Karīm ibn Ibrahīm al-Jīlī, lived A.H. 767–811) it is said that when the Christians found that there was at the commencement of the *Injīl* the superscription باسم الاب و الابن, *i.e.* 'In the name of the Father and Son,' they took the words in their natural meaning, and [thinking it ought to be *Ab*, father, *Umm*, mother, and *Ibn*, son] understood by *Ab*, the Spirit, by *Umm*, Mary, and by *Ibn*, Jesus; and on this account they said, *Ṣāliṣu Ṣalāṣatin*, *i.e.* '(God is) the third of three.' (Sūrah v. 77.) But they did not understand that by *Ab* is meant God Most High, by *Umm*, the *Māhīyatu 'l-Ḥaqā'iq*, or 'Essence of Truth" (*Quidditas veritatum*), and by *Ibn*, the Book of God, which is called the *Wujūdu 'l-Muṭlaq*, or 'Absolute Existence,' being an emanation of the Essence of Truth, as it is implied in the words of the Qur'ān,

Sūrah xiii. 9: 'And with him is the *Ummu 'l-Kitāb*, or the Mother of the Book.' "

In the *Ghiyāṣu 'l-Lughāt*, *in loco*, it is said the Nazarenes (*Naṣārā*) say there are three *aqānīm*, or principles, namely, *wujūd* (entity), *ḥayāt* (life), and *'ilm* (knowledge); and also *Ab* (Father), *Ibn* (Son), and *Rūḥu 'l-Quds* (Holy Spirit). [INJIL, JESUS, SPIRIT.]

It is evident neither Muḥammad nor his followers (either immediate or remote), had any true conception of the Catholic doctrine of the Trinity, but the elimination of the Holy Spirit from the Trinity is not strange, when we remember that Muḥammad was under the impression that the angel Gabriel was the Holy Ghost.

As the doctrine of the Holy Trinity is one of several stumbling-blocks to the Muslim's reception of Christianity, we cannot refrain from quoting Charles Kingsley's words addressed to Thomas Cooper on the subject (vol. i. p. 311):—

"They will say 'Three in one' is contrary to sense and experience. Answer, 'That is your ignorance.' Every comparative anatomist will tell you the exact contrary, that among the most common, though the most puzzling phenomena, is multiplicity in unity —divided life in the same individual of every extraordinary variety of case. That distinction of persons with unity of individuality (what the old schoolmen properly called substance) is to be met with in some thousand species of animals, *e.g.* all the compound polypes, and that the soundest physiologists, like Huxley, are compelled to talk of these animals in metaphysic terms, just as paradoxical as, and almost identical with, those of the theologian. Ask them then, whether granting one primordial Being who has conceived and made all other beings, it is absurd to suppose in Him, some law of multiplicity in unity, analogous to that on which He has constructed so many millions of His creatures.

* * * * *

"But my heart demands the Trinity, as much as my reason. I want to be sure that God cares for us, that God is our Father, that God has interfered, stooped, sacrificed Himself for us. I do not merely want to love Christ—a Christ, some creation or emanation of God's—whose will and character, for aught I know, may be different from God's. I want to love and honour the absolute, abysmal God Himself, and none other will satisfy me; and in the doctrine of Christ being co-equal and co-eternal, sent by, sacrificed by, His Father, that He might do His Father's will, I find it; and no puzzling texts, like those you quote, shall rob me of that rest for my heart, that Christ is the exact counterpart of Him in whom we live, and move, and have our being."

TROVES, Arabic *luqṭah* (لقطة), signifies property which a person finds on the ground, and takes away for the purpose of preserving it in the manner of a trust. A trove under ten dirhams must be advertised for some days, or as long as he may deem expedient; but if it exceed ten dirhams in value, he must advertise it for a year. (Hamilton's *Hidāyah*, vol. ii. p. 266.)

TRUMPET. Arabic *ṣūr* (صور). According to the Qur'ān, Sūrah xxxix. 68, the trumpet at the Day of Resurrection shall be blown twice. "The trumpet shall be blown (first), and those who are in the heavens and in the earth shall swoon (or die), save whom God pleases. Then it shall be blown again, and, lo! they shall rise again and look on."

Al-Baiẓāwī says there will only be these two blasts, but Traditionists assert there will be three. The blast of *consternation*, the blast of *examination*, and the blast of *resurrection*, for an account of which, see the article on RESURRECTION.

TUBBA' (تبع). A tribe of Ḥimyarite Arabs, whose kings were called *Tubba'*, or "Successors," and who are mentioned in the Qur'ān, Sūrah xliv. 35: "Are they better than the people of *Tubba'* and those before them? Verily, they were sinners, and we destroyed them."

ṬUHR (طهر). The period of purity in a woman. [DIVORCE, PURIFICATION.]

ṬULAIḤAH (طليحة). A chief of the Banū Asad, a warrior of note and influence in Najd, who claimed to have a divine commission in the days of Muḥammad, but who was afterwards subdued by Khālid under the Khalīfate of Abū Bakr, and embraced Islām. (Muir's *Life of Mahomet*, vol. iv. p. 246.)

ṬŪR (طور). Chaldee טוּר. (1) A mount. *Aṭ-Ṭūr*, the mountain mentioned in the Qur'ān, Sūrah ii. 60: "When we took a covenant (*mīṣāq*) with you, and held the mountain (ready to fall) over you." This is generally understood to mean *Ṭūru Sainā'*, or Mount Sinai, but al-Baiẓāwī says it was *Jabal Zubail*. In Persian, the mountain is called *Koh-i-Ṭūr*, or the Mount of Ṭūr. In Arabia, the name is given to the Mount Sinai of Scripture.

(2) The title of the LIInd Sūrah of the Qur'ān.

TURBAN. Arabic *'imāmah* (عمامة), Persian *dastār* (دستار), Hindūstānī *pagṛī* (پگڑی). The turban, which consists of a stiff round cap, occasionally rising to a considerable height, and a long piece of muslin, often as much as twenty-four yards in length, wound round it, is amongst all Muḥammadan nations a sign of authority and honour, and it is held to be disrespectful to stand in the presence of a person of respectability, or to worship God, with the head uncovered. Shaikhs and persons of religious pretensions wear green turbans. The Coptic Christians in Egypt wear a blue turban, having been compelled to do so by an edict published in A.D. 1301. In some parts of Islām, it is usual to set apart a Maulawī, or to appoint a chief or ruler, by placing a turban on his head.

The mitre, bonnet, hood, and diadem of the Old Testament are but varieties of the head-dress known in the East as the turban. Canon Cook, in the *Speaker's Commentary*, on Exodus xxviii. 4, 37, says the *mitznepheth*, or "mitre" of the Hebrew Bible, "according to the derivation of the word, and from the statement in verse 39, was a twisted band of linen coiled into a cap, to which the name *mitre* in its original sense closely answers, but which in modern usage would rather be called a turban."

The term used in the Hebrew Bible for putting on the *tzaniph* or the *peer*, "bonnet," in Ex. xxix. 9, Lev. viii. 13, is חָבַשׁ *khāvash*, "to bind round," and would therefore indicate that even in the earliest periods of Jewish history the head-dress was similar in character to that now seen amongst the different Muslim tribes of the world.

Josephus' account of the high priest's mitre is peculiar; he says (*Antiquities*, book iii. ch. vii. p. 3): "Its make is such that it seems to be a crown, being made of thick swathes, but the contexture is of linen, and it is doubled many times, and sewn together; besides which, a piece of fine linen covers the whole cap from the upper part, and reaches down to the forehead and the seams of the swathes, which would otherwise appear indecently; this adheres closely upon the solid part of the head, and is thereto so firmly fixed that it may not fall off during the sacred service about the sacrifices."

The varieties of turban worn in the East are very great, and their peculiarities are best illustrated by the accompanying drawing, giving seventeen different styles of tying up the turban. In books written upon the subject in Eastern languages, it is said that there are not fewer than a thousand methods of binding the turban. It is in the peculiar method of tying on, and of arranging this head-dress, that not only tribal and religious distinctions are seen, but even peculiarities of disposition. The humility or pride, the virtue or vice, as well as the social standing of the individual, is supposed to be indicated in his method of binding the turban upon his head. And travellers in the East can at once distinguish the different races by their turbans. [DRESS.]

MUSLIM TURBANS. (*A. F. Hole.*)

TURK. Arabic *tark* or *turk* (ترك), pl. *atrāk*. (1) A term applied by European writers to express Muḥammadans of all nationalities. (See *Book of Common Prayer, Collect for Good Friday.*)

(2) An inhabitant of Turkomania, Turkistān or Transoxania, so named from Tur, eldest son of Farīdūn, to whom his father gave it for an inheritance. Also of those numerous races of Tartars who claim to be descended from Turk, a son of Japhet. *Turki chin*, a Chinese Tartar.

(3) A native of European or Asiatic Turkey. Halaku, the Turk, a grandson of Jengiz Khān, took Baghdād A.D. 1258, and about forty years afterwards 'Uṣmān (Othman) founded the 'Uṣmānī or Turk dynasty at Constantinople, A.D. 1299. Hence Muḥammadans were known to the European Christians as Turks.

The word *Turk* is also frequently used by Sikh writers to express Muḥammadans in general. The terms *Turk* and *Musulmān* are employed interchangeably. [KHALIFAH.]

ṬUWĀ (طوى). A sacred valley mentioned in the Qur'ān:—

Sūrah xx. 12: "O Moses! verily I am thy Lord, so take off thy sandals; thou art in the sacred valley of Ṭuwā, and I have chosen thee."

Sūrah lxxix. 16: "Has the story of Moses reached you? when his Lord addressed him in the holy valley of Ṭuwā."

U.

'UBĀDAH IBN AS-ṢĀMIT (عبادة بن الصامت). One of the Anṣārs of al-Madīnah, who was afterwards employed by Abū Bakr to collect the scattered sentences of the Qur'ān.

'UBŪDĪYAH (عبودية). [SLAVERY].

AL-UFUQU 'L-A'LĀ (الافق الاعلى). *Lit.* "The Loftiest Tract." (1) The place in which it is said Gabriel was when he taught Muḥammad, see Sūrah liii. 7: "One mighty in power (*Shadīdu 'l-Quwā*) taught him, endowed with sound understanding, and appeared, he being in the loftiest tract."

(2) According to the Ṣūfīs, it is the highest spiritual state a man can attain in the mystic life.

UḤNŪKH (اخنوخ). The Enoch of the Old Testament, supposed to be the Idrīs of the Qur'ān. A full account of this personage will be found in the article on IDRIS.

UḤUD (احد). Ohod. A hill about three miles distant from al-Madīnah, and described by Burckhardt as a rugged and almost insulated offshoot of the great mountain range. Celebrated for the battle fought by Muḥammad and the victory gained over the Muslims by the Quraish, A.H. 3. (Muir's *Life of Mahomet*, new ed. p. 266 *seqq.*) [MUHAMMAD.]

'ŪJ (عوج). The son of 'Ūq. A giant who is said to have been born in the days of Adam, and lived through the Deluge, as the water only came up to his waist, and to have died in the days of Moses, the great lawgiver having smitten him on the foot with his rod. He lived 3,500 years. (*Ghiyāṣu 'l-Lughāt, in loco.*) The Og of the Bible, concerning whom as-Suyūṭī wrote a long book taken chiefly from Rabbinic traditions. (Ewald, *Gesch.* i. 306.) An apocryphal book of Og was condemned by Pope Gelasius. (Dec. vi. 13.)

UKAIDAR (اكيدر). The Christian chief of Dūmah, who was taken prisoner by Khālid, A.H. 9. (Muir's *Life of Mahomet*, new ed. p. 458.)

In the Traditions it is said: "Khālid took Ukaidar prisoner because the Prophet forbade killing him. And the Prophet did not kill him, but made peace with him, when he paid the poll-tax." (*Mishkāt*, book xvii. ch. ix.)

Sir W. Muir says he became a Muslim, but revolted after the death of Muḥammad.

'UKĀẒ (عكاظ). An annual fair of twenty-one days, which was held between aṭ-Ṭā'if and Nakhlah, and which was opened on the first day of the month of Ẕū 'l-Qa'dah, at the commencement of the three sacred months. It was abolished by Muḥammad.

Mr. Stanley Lane Poole says (*Selections from the Kur-án*):—

"There was one place where, above all others, the Ḳaṣeedehs (Qaṣīdahs) of the ancient Arabs were recited: this was 'Okádh ('Ukāẓ), the Olympia of Arabia, where there was held a great annual Fair, to which not merely the merchants of Mekka and the south, but the poet-heroes of all the land resorted. The Fair of 'Okádh was held during the sacred months,—a sort of 'God's Truce,' when blood could not be shed without a violation of the ancient customs and faiths of the Bedawees. Thither went the poets of rival clans, who had as often locked spears as hurled rhythmical curses. There was little fear of a bloody ending to the poetic contest, for those heroes who might meet there with enemies or blood-avengers are said to have worn masks or veils, and their poems were recited by a public orator at their dictation. That these precautions and the sacredness of the time could not always prevent the ill-feeling evoked by the pointed personalities of rival singers leading to a fray and bloodshed is proved by recorded instances; but such results were uncommon, and as a rule the customs of the time and place were respected. In spite of occasional broils on the spot, and the lasting feuds which these poetic contests must have excited, the Fair of 'Okádh was a grand institution. It served as a focus for the literature of all Arabia: everyone with any pretensions to poetic power came, and if he could not himself gain the applause of the assembled people, at least he could form one of the critical audience on whose verdict rested the fame or the shame of every poet. The Fair of 'Okádh was a literary congress, without formal judges, but with unbounded influence. It was here that the polished heroes of the desert determined points of grammar and prosody; here the seven Golden Songs were recited, although (alas for the charming legend!) they were *not* afterwards 'suspended' on the Kaabeh; and here 'a magical language, the language of the Ḥijáz,' was built out of the dialects of Arabia, and was made ready to the skilful hand of Moḥammad, that he might conquer the world with his Ḳur-án.

"The Fair of 'Okádh was not merely a centre of emulation for Arab poets: it was also an annual review of Bedawee virtues. It was there that the Arab nation once-a-year inspected itself, so to say, and brought forth and criticised its ideals of the noble and the beautiful in life and in poetry. For it was in poetry that the Arab—and for that matter each man all the world over—expressed his highest thoughts, and it was at 'Okádh that these thoughts were measured by the standard of the Bedawee ideal. The Fair not only maintained the highest standard of poetry that the Arabic language has ever reached: it also upheld the noblest idea of life and duty that the Arab nation has yet set forth and obeyed. 'Okádh was the press, the stage, the pulpit, the Parliament, and the Académie Française of the Arab people; and when, in his fear of the infidel poets (whom Imra-el-Keys was to usher to hell), Moḥammad abolished the Fair, he destroyed the Arab nation, even whilst he created his own new nation of Muslims; and the Muslims cannot sit in the places of the old pagan Arabs."

'UKŪF (عکوف). *Lit.* "Remaining behind." A term used to express a life of prayer of one who remains constantly in the mosque.

'ULAMĀ' (علماء), pl. of *'ālim.* "One who knows; learned; a scholar." In this plural form the word is used as the title of those bodies of learned doctors in Muḥammadan divinity and law, who, headed by their Shaikhu 'l-Islām, form the theocratic element of the government in Muslim countries, and who by their *fatwās* or decisions in questions touching private and public matters of importance, regulate the life of the Muḥammadan community. Foremost in influence and authority are naturally reckoned the 'Ulamā' of Constantinople, the seat of the Khalīfah, and of Makkah, the Holy City of Islām. Like the *Aṣḥāb* or Companions of the Prophet under his immediate successors, they correspond in a certain measure to what we would call the representative system of our modern constitutions, in partially limiting and checking the autocratism of an otherwise absolute Oriental ruler.

ULŪHĪYAH (الوهية). "Divinity; godhead"

ULŪ 'L-'AZM (اولو العزم). "The Possessors of Constancy." A title given to certain prophets in the Qur'ān, said by the commentators to have been Noah, Abraham, David, Jacob, Joseph, Job, Moses, Jesus, and Muḥammad. (*Vide Ghiyāṣu 'l-Lughāt.*) See Sūrah xlvi. 34: "Then be thou constant, as the Apostles endowed with a purpose were constant, and hasten not on."

UMANĀ' (امناء), pl. of *amīn.* "Faithful Ones." A title given by the Ṣūfīs to those pious persons who do not make their religious experiences known. They are known also as the *Malāmatīyah*, or those who are willing to undergo misrepresention rather than boast of their piety.

'UMAR (عمر) IBN AL-KHAṬṬĀB. (Omar) the second Khalīfah, who succeeded Abū Bakr, A.H. 13 (A.D. 634), and was assassinated by Fīroz, a Persian slave, A.H. 23 (A.D. 644), after a prosperous reign of ten years. His conversion to Islām took place in the sixth year of Muḥammad's mission, and the Prophet took 'Umar's daughter Ḥafṣah as his third wife.

'Umar is eminent amongst the early Khalīfahs for having chiefly contributed to the spread of Islām. Under him the great generals, Abū 'Ubaidah, Khālid ibn al-Walīd, Yazīd, drove the Greeks out of Syria and Phœnicia; Sa'd ibn Abī Waqqās, Qaqā'ah, Nu'mān, completed the conquest of the two 'Irāqs and the overthrow of the Persian Empire; 'Amr ibn al-'Āṣ (commonly called Amru) subdued Egypt and part of the Libyan coast, after having, as commander in Palestine, prepared by his victories and a severe siege, the surrender of Jerusalem [JERUSALEM] into the Khalīfah's own hands. 'Umar's name is, moreover, intimately connected with the history of Islām, by the initiatory and important share which he took in the first collection of the Qur'ān, under Abū Bakr, by the official introduction of the Muḥammadan era of the Hijrah, and by the first organisation of the *dīwān*, or civil list of the Muḥammadans. The two former subjects have been treated of in this Dictionary in their proper places; the third institution, which laid the foundation to the marvellous successes of the Muslim arms under this and the succeeding Governments, is ably explained in the following extract from Sir W. Muir's *Annals of the Early Caliphate*:—

"The Arabian nation was the champion of Islam, and to fight its battles every Arab was jealously reserved. He must be the soldier, and nothing else. He might not settle down in any conquered province as cultivator of the soil; and for merchandise or other labour, a busy warlike life offered but little leisure. Neither was there any need. The Arabs lived on the fat of the conquered land, and captive natives served them. Of the booty taken in war, four parts were distributed to the army in the field; the fifth was reserved for the State; and even that, after discharging public obligations, was shared among the Arabian people. In the reign of Abu Bakr, this was a simple matter. But in the Caliphate of Omar, the spoil of Syria and of Persia began in ever-increasing volume to pour into the treasury of Medina, where it was distributed almost as soon as received. What was easy in small beginnings, by equal sharing or discretionary preference, became now a heavy task. And there began, also, to arise new sources of revenue in the land assessment, and the poll-tax of subject countries, which, after defraying civil and military charges, had to be accounted for to the Central Government; the surplus being, like the royal fifth, the patrimony of the Arab nation.

"At length, in the second or third year of his Caliphate, Omar determined that the distribution should be regulated on a fixed and systematic scale. The income of the commonwealth was to be divided, as heretofore, amongst the Faithful as their heritage, but upon a rule of precedence befitting the military and theocratic groundwork of Islam. For this end three points only were considered: priority of conversion, affinity to the Prophet, and military service. The widows of Mahomet, 'Mothers of the Faithful,' took the precedence with an annual allowance of 10,000 pieces each; and all his kinsmen were with a corresponding liberality provided for. The famous Three Hundred of Bedr had 5,000 each; presence at Hodeibia (Ḥudaibīyah) and the *Pledge of the Tree*, gave a claim to 4,000; such as took part in quelling the Rebellion (immediately after Muḥammad's death), had 3,000; and those engaged in the great battles of Syria and Irâc, as well as sons of the men of Bedr, 2,000: those taking the field after the actions of Câdesîya and the Yermûk, 1,000. Warriors of distinction received an extra grant of 500. And so they graduated downwards to 200 pieces for the latest levies. Nor were the households forgotten. Women had, as a rule, one-tenth of a man's share. Wives, widows, and children had each their proper stipend; and in the register, every infant, as soon as born, had the title to be entered, with a minimum allowance of ten pieces, rising with advancing age to its proper place. Even Arab slaves (so long as any of that race remained) had, strange to say, their portion.

* * * * *

"The Arabian aristocracy thus created was recognised by the whole Moslem world. The rank and stipend now assigned descended in the direct line of birth. Even rewards given for special gallantry in the field were heritable. By making thus the revenues of Islam the heritage of the nation militant, their martial genius was maintained, and their employment perpetuated as the standing army of the Caliphate.

* * * * *

"To carry out this vast design, a register had to be drawn and kept up of every man, woman and child, entitled to a stipend from the State—in other words, of the whole Arab race employed in the interests of Islam. This was easy enough for the higher grades, but a herculean task for the hundreds and thousands of ordinary fighting men and their families who kept streaming forth from the Peninsula; and who, by the extravagant indulgence of polygamy, were multiplying rapidly. But the task was simplified by the strictly tribal composition and disposition of the forces. Men of a tribe, or branch of a tribe, fought together; and the several corps and brigades being thus territorially arranged in clans, the Register assumed the same form. Every soul was entered under the stock and tribe and class whose lineage it claimed. And to this exhaustive classification we owe in great measure the elaborate genealogies and tribal traditions of Arabia before Islam. The Register itself, as well as the office for its maintenance and for pensionary account was called the Dewân (*Dīwān*), or Department of the Exchequer." (Sir W. Muir, *Annals of the Early Caliphate*, London, 1883, p. 228.)

It was fortunate for Islām, that the reign of Abū Bakr, short in duration, but pregnant with decisive issues, should precede that of 'Umar. During the critical period, immediately after Muḥammad's death, when three false prophets and a prophetess gathered increasing numbers round their rebellious standards, when in the north, east, and south of the Peninsula, tribe after tribe, apostatized from the newly-adopted creed, and when al-Madīnah itself was repeatedly threatened by hostile invasions of the neighbouring clans it needed all the spirit of compromise and conciliation which blended in Abū Bakr's character with penetrating shrewdness and dauntless courage, to steer the bark of the Muslim commonwealth through the dangers which were surrounding it on every side. 'Umar's irrepressible impetuosity would, at that time, probably have caused more harm than good, while, on the other hand, the unprecedented success which crowned Abū Bakr's wise and temporising politics, taught him to temper his own impulses of bold enterprise with prudence and cautiousness, when, in his turn, the reponsibilities of office rested on his shoulders.

The original violent bent of Umar's nature is forcibly illustrated by the history of his conversion, as it is told in various traditions. In his youth and early manhood, a zealous and devoted adherent of the religion of his forefathers, he hated and persecuted Muḥammad as a dangerous innovator, who had come to lead his people astray, and to sow discord between them. Infuriated at some fresh success of the pretended Prophet, he sallied forth one day to kill him, when he met his kinsman, Nu'aim ibn 'Abdi 'llāh, who, seeing him armed and fiercely excited, asked him: "Whither goest thou, and what is thy intent?" "I seek Muḥammad," was 'Umar's reply, "and I will slay him; he has vilified our gods and dishonoured our ancestors." "Passion blinds thee," retorted Nu'aim; "knowest thou not that, if thou killest Muḥammad, thou wilt draw the vengeance of the Hāshimites and the Banū Muṭṭalib upon thy head? Better far it would be for thee, to heed the welfare of thy own family, and to bring back to the right path those members of it who have forsworn their ancestral religion." "And who are they," asked 'Umar. "Thy brother-in-law, Sa'īd ibn Zaid, and Fāṭimah, thy very own sister," answered Nu'aim.

Forthwith the incensed man hurried on to the house of the culprits. Here Khabbāb ibn al-Aratt, a devoted disciple of Muḥammad, the same who had made them acquainted with his teaching and won them over to Islām unknown to 'Umar, was reading with them at that moment a new fragment of the Qur'ān. When he heard 'Umar coming, he concealed himself, and Fāṭimah tried to hide the manuscript in the bosom of her dress. On entering, 'Umar asked: "What have you been reading just now? I heard your voices!" "Nothing," she replied, "thou art mistaken." "You have been reading something, and I am told that you belong to the sect of Muḥammad." With these words he threw himself upon his brother-in-law, and struck him. Fāṭimah rushed in between them. Both husband and wife boldly confessed: "Yes, we are Muslims; we believe that there is no god but God, and that Muḥammad is his sent one; kill us, if thou wilt."

No sooner had 'Umar seen the blood flowing from a wound which he had inflicted on his sister, than shame for his own unmanly act, coupled with admiration of their courageous conduct, brought about a powerful revulsion of his feelings. He asked to be shown the manuscript, and when, after his solemn promise not to destroy it, the fragment was handed over to him, he read :—

"Not to sadden thee have We sent down this Qur'ān to thee,
But as a warning for him who feareth;
A missive from Him who hath made the earth and the lofty heavens,
The God of Mercy who sitteth on His throne!
His, whatsoever is in the heavens and whatsoever is in the earth, and whatsoover is between them both, and whatsoever is beneath the humid soil!
And thou needest not raise thy voice *in prayer*: He verily knoweth the secret *whisper*, and the yet more hidden!
God! there is no God but Him! Most excellent His titles!"
(Sūrah xx. 1–7.)

"How nobly said and how sublime!" exclaimed 'Umar, when he had read the passage. Thereupon Khabbāb came forth from his place of concealment, and summoned him to testify to the teaching of Muḥammad. 'Umar asked where Muḥammad was, went to him, and made his profession of faith to the Prophet himself.

Henceforth 'Umar remained attached to the person of Muḥammad with the most devoted friendship, and embraced the cause of Islām with all the energies of his strong nature. We find 'Umar, immediately after Muhammad's death, unable at first to grasp the reality of the fact. When the news was imparted to him, he exclaimed wildly before the assembly of the faithful: "The Prophet is not dead; he has only swooned away." And, again, when Mughīrah tried to convince him that he was mistaken—"Thou liest!" he cried, "the Prophet of the Lord shall not die, until he have rooted out every hypocrite and unbeliever." At this point Abū Bakr quoted the verses of the Qur'ān, revealed after the defeat at Uḥud: "Muḥammad is no more than an Apostle; verily the other apostles have gone before him. What then! If he were to die or be killed, would you turn back on your heels?" And he added the memorable appeal: "Let him then know, whosoever worshippeth Muḥammad, that Muhammad indeed is dead; but whoso worshippeth God, let him know that the Lord liveth and doth not die."

Then, and only then, on hearing those words, spoken by *the book*, as if he had never heard them before, the truth burst upon 'Umar with crushing force. "By the Lord," he would tell in later days, "it was so that when I heard Abū Bakr reciting those verses, I was horror-struck, my limbs trembled, I dropped down, and I knew of a certainty that Muḥammad indeed was dead."

The paramount ascendency which Muḥammad, during his lifetime, exercised over 'Umar, could not fail to soften his passionate and vehement nature, and to train him to those habits of self-command, which form one of the most essential elements in the character of a good ruler. If it was an act of wise foresight on the part of Muhammad to designate, at the approach of death, the older and sedater Abū Bakr as his successor, by appointing him to conduct the public prayers during his last illness, he could at the same time feel assured that 'Umar, far from contesting the choice of his dying friend, would respect it and make it respected against any defection or rival ambition by his cordial and powerful support. But it was equally natural and wise on the part of Abū Bakr, when the time had come, to fix the choice of his own successor upon 'Umar. It is related that, feeling his end to be near, and willing to fortify his own conviction by the sense of others, he first consulted 'Abdu 'r-Raḥmān, the son of 'Auf, who praised 'Umar "as the fittest man, but withal inclined to be severe." "Which," responded the dying Khalīfah, "is because he saw me soft and tenderhearted, when himself the Master, he will forego much of what thou sayest. I have watched him narrowly. If I were angry with one, he would intercede in his behalf; if overlenient, then he would be severe." 'Us̤mān, too, confirmed Abū Bakr's choice. "What is hidden of 'Umar," he said, "is better than that which doth appear. There is not his equal amongst us all."

And so it was: as in bodily stature 'Umar towered high above his fellow-men, so he excelled in every quality required in an imposing commander of the Faithful (Amīr al-Mu'minīn), this being the title which he adopted in preference to the more cumbersome of "Successor of the Apostle of God" (Khalīfatu 'r-Rasūli 'llāh). It lies outside the scope of the present work to give a complete biography of 'Umar, and we must refer the reader who should wish to make himself acquainted with it, to the above-quoted attractive volume of Sir W. Muir, *Annals of the Early Caliphate*. Our less ambitious object here has merely been to sketch, as it were, in a few salient traits culled from it, the picture of a man, who, as a founder of Islām, was second only to Muḥammad himself. Gifted with a high and penetrating intellect, and possessed of a strong sense of justice, he was impartial, skilful, and fortunate in the choice of his military and civil agents, and had learnt to temper severity with clemency and wise forbearance. While it was he who, in his earlier days, after the battle of Badr, had advised that the prisoners should all be put to death, his later resentment against Khālid, with whose name the cruel fate of Mālik ibn Nuwairah and the gory tale of the "River of Blood" are linked in history, on the contrary, took rise in Khālid's unscrupulous and savage treatment of a fallen foe. And the fanatic intolerance of some of the Muslim captains is favourably contrasted with 'Umar's treatment of the Christianised Arab tribe of the Banū Taghlib. They had tendered their submission to Walīd ibn 'Uqbah, who, solicitous for the adhesion to Islām of this great and famous race, pressed them with some rigour to abjure their ancient faith. 'Umar was much displeased at this—"Leave them," he wrote, "in the profession of the Gospel. It is only within the bounds of the peninsula, where are the Holy Places, that no polytheist tribe is permitted to remain." Walīd was removed from his command; and it was enjoined on his successor to stipulate only that the usual tribute should be paid, that no member of the tribe should be hindered from embracing Islām, and that the children should not be educated in the Christian faith. The last condition can only have been meant as a nominal indication of the supremacy of Islām, for if it had been enforced, we should not read of the Banū Taghlib continuing in the profession of Christianity under the next two dynasties and even later. The tribe, deeming in its pride the payment of tribute (*jazyah*) an indignity, sent a deputation to the Khalīfah, declaring their willingness to pay the tax if only it were levied under the same name as that taken from the Muslims. 'Umar evinced his liberality by allowing the concession; and so the Banū Taghlib enjoyed the singular privilege of being assessed as Christians at a "double tithe" (*'ushr*), instead of paying *jazyah*, the obnoxious badge of subjugation. (Sir W. Muir, *Annals*, p 218.)

As the original asperity of 'Umar's character had been mellowed in the school of life and in close communion with Muḥammad and Abū Bakr, so the same influences, together with the responsibilities of his position, tended to blend his natural boldness and impetuosity with prudence and cautiousness. While his captains in Syria and the 'Irāq were continually urging him to push on his conquests to the north and east, he would not allow any advance to be ventured upon, before the Muslim rule in the occupied provinces was well established and firmly consolidated. In like manner he evinced a singular dread of naval enterprise, ever after an expedition sent to Abyssinia across the Red Sea in the seventh year of his reign had met with a signal disaster; and he was countenanced in this aversion for the treacherous element by a not less daring general than 'Amr, son of al-'Āṣ, who, consulted on the subject, wrote to him:—

"The sea is a boundless expanse, whereon great ships look but tiny specks; there is nought saving the heavens above and the waters beneath. Trust it little, fear it much. Man at sea is an insect floating on a splinter; if the splinter break, the insect perisheth."

When the wily 'Amr wished to raise his people in the estimation of the Egyptians, he had a feast prepared of slaughtered camels, after the Bedouin fashion; and the Egyptians looked on with wonder, while the army satisfied themselves with the rude repast. Next day he commanded a sumptuous banquet to be set before them, with all the dainties of the Egyptian table; and here again the warriors fell to with equal zest. On the third day, there was a grand parade of all the troops in battle array, and the people flocked to see it. Then 'Amr addressed them, saying: "The first day's entertainment was to let you see the plain and simple manner of our life at home; the second, to show you that we can not the less enjoy the good things of the lands we enter; and yet retain, as ye see in the spectacle here before you, our martial vigour notwithstanding."

'Amr gained his end, for the Copts retired, saying one to the other, "See ye not that the Arabs have but to raise their heel upon us, and it is enough!" 'Umar was delighted with his lieutenant's device, and said of him, "Of a truth it is on wisdom and resolve, as well as on mere force, that the success of warfare doth depend."

But, at the same time, 'Umar was much too thoughtful and far-seeing himself not to recognise the danger for the future of Islām, which was lurking in this sudden acquisition of unmeasured riches. On one occasion, when he was about to distribute the fifth of some Persian spoils, he was seen to weep. "What," it was said to him, "a time of joy and thankfulness, and thou sheddest tears." "Yea," replied the simple-minded Khalīfah, "it is not for this I weep; but I foresee that the wealth which the Lord hath bestowed upon us will become a spring of worldliness and envy, and in the end a calamity to my people."

Moreover, the luxury and ostentation which was thus engendered in the enriched leaders, was utterly repulsive to his own frugal habits and homely nature. On his first visit to Syria, Abū 'Ubaidah, Yazīd, and Khālid, met him in state to welcome him. A brilliant cavalcade, robed in Syrian brocade, and mounted on steeds richly caparisoned, they rode forth as he approached. At the sight of all their finery, 'Umar's spirit was stirred within him. He stooped down, and, gathering a handful of gravel, flung it at the astonished chiefs. "Avaunt!" he cried; "is it thus attired that ye come out to meet me? All changed thus in the space of two short years! Verily, had it been after two hundred, ye would have deserved to be degraded."

This primitive simplicity of the Arab chieftain is another grand and highly captivating feature in 'Umar's character. We see in our mind's eye the mighty mover of armies, at the time when the destinies of Islām were trembling in the balance on the battle-field of Qādisīyah, issuing on foot from the gates of al-Medinah in the early morning, if perchance he might meet some messenger from the scene of combat. At last a courier arrived outside the city, who to 'Umar's question replies shortly, "The Lord has discomfited the Persian host." Unrecognised, 'Umar followed the messenger, leading the camel, and with his long strides keeping pace with the high-stepping animal, to glean from him the outline of the great battle. When they entered al-Madīnah, the people crowded round the Khalifah, saluting him, and hearing the happy news, wished him joy of the triumph. The courier, abashed, cried out, "O Commander of the Faithful, why didst thou not tell me?" but his mind was instantly set at rest by the Khalīfah's kindly answer: "It is well, my brother."

Or we may fancy him perambulating, whip in hand, the streets and markets of al-Madīnah, ready to punish the offenders on the spot, may be his own son and his boon companions, who had indulged in the use of wine. For on this head 'Umar did not brook pleasantry. When news of some arch-transgressors on this score was sent from Damascus, and indulgence from the strict enforcement of the law was claimed for them on the plea of their exalted position and military merits, he wrote back: "Gather an assembly and bring them forth. Then ask, *Is wine lawful*, or *is it forbidden*? If they say *forbidden*, lay eighty stripes upon each of them; if they say *lawful*, then behead them every one." The punishment, if inflicted by 'Umar's own hand, was telling, for it became a proverb: 'Umar's whip is more terrible than another's sword.

Or, again, with the groan of repentance of the well-chastised offender still ringing in our ears, we may watch the same 'Umar, as journeying in Arabia in the year of famine, he comes upon a poor woman, seated with her hungry and weeping children round a fire, whereon is an empty pot. He hurries to the next village, procures bread and meat, fills the pot, and cooks an ample meal, leaving the little ones laughing and at play.

Such a man was 'Umar, the great Khalīfah, brave, wise, pious. No fitter epitaph could adorn his tombstone, than his dying words:—"It had gone hard with my soul, if I had not been a Muslim." [DAMASCUS, JERUSALEM, JIHAD, MUHAMMAD.]

(The Editor is indebted to Dr. Steingass, the learned author of the *English-Arabic Dictionary*, A.D. 1882, and *Arabic-English Dictionary*, A.D. 1884 (W. H. Allen & Co., London), for this review of 'Umar's influence on the Muslim religion.)

UMM (ام), pl. *ummāt*, *ummahāt*.

"Mother." Heb. אֵם *ēm*. A word which frequently occurs in combination with other words, *e.g.* *Ummu 'l-Qurā*, "the mother of villages," the metropolis Makkah; *Ummu 'l-'Ulūm*, "the mother of sciences," grammar.

UMMAH (امة). Heb. אֻמָּה *ummāh*.

A people, a nation, a sect. The word occurs about forty times in the Qur'ān.

Ummatu Ibrāhīm, the people of Abraham.

Ummatu 'Isā, the people of Jesus.

Ummatu Muḥammad, the people of Muḥammad.

UMMĪ (امى). The title assumed

by Muḥammad, and which occurs in the Qur'ān, Sūrah viii. 156: "Who shall follow the Apostle, the illiterate Prophet (*ān-Nabīyu 'l-ummī*)"; and in the 158th verse of the same Sūrah.

Commentators are not agreed as to the derivation of this word, the following are the three most common derivations of it:—

(1) From *Umm*, "mother," *i.e.* one just as he came from his mother's womb.

(2) From *Ummah*, "people," *i.e.* a gentile, one who was ignorant; alluding to the time of Muḥammad's ignorance.

(3) From *Ummu 'l-qurā*, "the mother of villages," a name given to Makkah; *i.e.* a native of Makkah.

Muḥammad appears to have wished to be thought ignorant and illiterate, in order to raise the elegance of the Qur'ān into a miracle.

UMMU ḤABĪBAH (ام حبيبة). One

of Muḥammad's wives. She was the daughter of Abū Ṣufyān, and the widow of 'Ubaidu'llāh, one of the "Four Inquirers," who, after emigrating as a Muslim to Abyssinia, embraced Christianity there, and died in profession of that faith.

UMMU KULṢŪM (ام كلثوم). The

youngest daughter of Muḥammad by his wife Khadījah. She had been married to her cousin 'Utaibah, son of Abū Lahab, but separated from him and became, after the death of her sister Ruqaiyah, the second wife of 'Uṣmān, the later Khalīfah. She died a year or two before Muḥammad, who used, after her death, to say he so dearly loved 'Uṣmān, that had there been a third daughter, he would have given her also in marriage to him.

UMMU 'L-KITĀB (ام الكتاب). *Lit.*

"The Mother of the Book."

(1) A title given in the Ḥadīṣ to the first Sūrah of the Qur'ān.

(2) In the Sūratu Ahli 'Imrān (iii.) 5, it is used for the Qur'ān itself.

(3) In the Sūratu 'r-Ra'd (xiii.) 39, it seems to be applied to the preserved tablet, on which were written the decrees of God and the fate of every human being.

UMMU 'L-MU'MINĪN (ام المومنين).

"A mother of the Faithful." A title which English authors restrict either to the Prophet's wife Khadījah, or to 'Āyishah; but it is a title applied to each of the wives of Muḥammad. Qur'ān, Sūrah xxxiii. 6: "His wives are their mothers."

UMMU 'L-QURA (ام القرى). *Lit.* "Mother of Villages." A name given to Makkah. The Metropolis.

UMMU 'L-WALAD (ام الولد). A term used in Muḥammadan law for a female slave who has borne a child to her master, and who is consequently free at his death. [SLAVERY.]

UMMU SALMAH (ام سلمة). One of the wives of the Prophet. The widow of Abū Salmah, to whom she had borne several children. Abū Salmah was killed at Uḥud, and Muḥammad married his widow four months afterwards.

'UMRĀ (عمرى). A life grant, or interest in anything, *e.g.* if the proprietor of a house says to another, "This is yours as long as you live."

'UMRAH (عمرة). A Lesser Pilgrimage, or a visitation to the sacred mosque at Makkah, with the ceremonies of encompassing the Ka'bah and running between al-Marwah and aṣ-Ṣafā, but omitting the sacrifices, &c. It is a meritorious act, but it has not the supposed merit of the *Ḥajj* or Pilgrimage. It can be performed at any time except the eighth, ninth, and tenth days of the month Ẕū 'l-Ḥijjah, these being the days of the *Ḥajj* or Greater Pilgrimage. [HAJJ.]

UMŪMĪYAH (امومية). "Maternity." A term used in Muslim law. (*Hidāyah*, vol. iii. p. 417.)

UNBELIEVERS. There are several terms used in Islām for those who are unbelievers in the mission of Muḥammad, *e.g.*:—

Kāfir (كافر), One who hides the truth. A term generally applied to idolaters, and not to Jews or Christians.

Mushrik (مشرك), One who gives companions to God. Believers in the Blessed Trinity are so called. The term is also applied by the Wahhābīs to any Muslim who observes ceremonies which are not clearly enjoined in the precepts of the Muslim religion, as visiting shrines, &c.

Mulḥid (ملحد), One who has deviated from the truth.

Murtadd (مرتد), An apostate from Islām.

Dahrī (دهرى), An Atheist.

(*For further explanations, refer to the words in their places.*)

UNCLEAN MEATS. [FOOD.]

UNCLEANNESS. [PURIFICATION.]

UNITY OF GOD. [TAUHID.]

UNLAWFUL. Arabic *ḥarām* (حرام). [LAW.]

'UQĀB (عقاب). A black eagle. A celebrated standard belonging to Muḥammad. (See *Ḥayātu 'l-Qulūb*, p. 88, Merrick's edition.) [STANDARDS.]

'UQBĀ (عقبى). *Lit.* "End." A reward or punishment. Hence used to express the life to come either of good or evil. [PARADISE, HELL.]

'UQBAH (عقبة) IBN 'ĀMIR AL-JUHANĪ. A Companion of great celebrity. He was afterwards Governor of Egypt, where he died, A.H. 58.

UQNŪM (اقنوم), pl. *aqānīm*. According to Muslim lexicographers, it is "a word which means the root or principle of a thing, and, according to the Naṣārā (Nazarenes), there are three Aqānīm, namely, *wujūd* (entity or substance), *ḥayāt* (life), and *'ilm* (knowledge); and also, *Ab* (Father), *Ibn* (Son), and *Rūḥu 'l-Quds* (Holy Spirit); and it is also the name of a book amongst the Nazarenes which treats of these three. (See *Ghiyāṣu 'l-Lughāt, in loco.*) [TRINITY.]

'UQŪBAH (عقوبة). "Punishment; chastisement." A legal term for punishment inflicted at the discretion of the magistrate. *'Uqūbah shadīdah* is severe punishment extending to death. [TAZIR.]

AL-'UQŪLU 'L-'ASHARAH (العقول العشرة). *Lit.* "The Ten Intelligences." Ten angels who, according to the philosophers, were created by God in the following manner: First, He created one angel; who then created one heaven and one angel, this second angel then created a second heaven and a third angel; and so on until there were created nine heavens and ten angels. The tenth angel then, by the order of God, created the whole world. (See *Ghiyāṣu 'l-Lughāt, in loco.*)

'URS (عرس). (1) Marriage festivities, as distinguished from *nikāḥ*, "the marriage ceremony." [MARRIAGE.]

(2) A term also used for the ceremonies observed at the anniversary of the death of any celebrated saint or *murshid*.

'USHR (عشر), pl. *a'shār* and *'ushūr*. A tenth or tithe given to the Muslim State or *Baitu 'l-Māl*. [BAITU 'L-MAL.]

'UṢMĀN (عثمان) IBN 'AFFĀN. The third Khalīfah, who succeeded 'Umar A.H. 23 (A.D. 643), and was slain by Muḥammad, son of Abū Bakr and other conspirators on the 18th of Ẕū 'l-Ḥijjah, A.H. 35 (June 17th, A.D. 656), aged eighty-two, and having reigned twelve years. He is known amongst Muslims as Ẕū 'n-Nūrain, "The Possessor of the Two Lights," because he married two of the Prophet's daughters, Ruqaiyah and Ummu Kulṣūm. His chief merit with regard to the cause of Islām was the second and final revision of the sacred book, which he caused to be made, and of which an exhaustive account has been given in our article on the Qur'ān.

Although Muḥammadan historians distinguish the reigns of the first four Khalīfahs as founded on faith (*dīnī*), from those of the later ones, as based on the world and its passions and vanities (*dunyawi*), it must be admitted that worldly motives entered already largely into the politics of 'Uṣmān and 'Ali, as contrasted with Abū Bakr and 'Umar. 'Uṣmān, by his weakness and nepotism, 'Alī by holding aloof with culpable indifference, during the protracted death-struggle of his predecessor, by abetting his murderers in the open field, and by his vacillating spirit, where firmness of purpose was needed, gave rise to those fierce dissensions between rival religious and political parties, which led, for the time being, to the establishment of the Umaiyah dynasty, and eventually caused the division of Islām into the two great sects of the Sunnīs and Shī'ahs.

USŪL (اصول), pl. of *aṣl*. *Lit.* "Roots." The roots or fundamentals of the Muḥammadan religion, as opposed to *furū'* (فروع), "branches," a term used for Muḥammadan law, civil, ceremonial, and religious. The *uṣūl* of Islām are universally held to be four: (1) The *Qur'ān*, (2) The *Ḥadīṣ*, (3) *Ijmā'*, and (4) *Qiyās*, terms which will be found explained under their respective titles.

'Ilmu 'l-Uṣūl is the science of interpretation or exegesis of these four fundamentals

USURY. Arabic *riba'* (ربا). A word which, like the Hebrew נֶשֶׁךְ *neshek*, includes all gain upon loans, whether from the loan of money, or goods, or property of any kind. In the Mosaic law, conditions of gain for the loan of money or goods, were rigorously prohibited: "If thou lend money to any of my people that is poor by thee, thou shalt not be to him as an usurer, neither shalt thou lay upon him usury." (Exodus xxii. 25.) "If thy brother be waxen poor . . . take no usury of him or increase: but fear thy God; that thy brother may live with thee. Thou shalt not give him thy money upon usury, nor lend him thy victuals for increase." (Leviticus xxv. 35-37.)

(1) The teaching of the Qur'ān on the subject is given in Sūrah ii. 276: "They who swallow down usury, shall arise in the Last Day only as he ariseth, whom Satan has infected by his touch. This for that they say, 'Selling is only the like of usury,' and yet God hath allowed selling and forbidden usury; and whosoever receiveth *this* admonition from his Lord, and abstaineth *from it*, shall have *pardon for* the past and his lot shall be with God. But they who return to usury, shall be given over to the Fire,—therein to abide for ever."

(2) In the Traditions, Muḥammad is related to have said:—

"Cursed be the taker of usury, the giver of usury, the writer of usury, and the witness of usury, for they are all equal."

"Verily the wealth that is gained in usury, although it be great, is of small advantage." (*Ṣaḥīḥu Muslim*, *Bābu 'r-Riba'*).

(3) *Riba'*, in the language of the law, signifies "an excess," according to a legal standard of *measurement* or *weight*, in one of two *homogeneous articles* (of weight or measurement of capacity) opposed to each other in a contract of exchange, and in which such excess is stipulated as an obligatory condition on one of the parties, *without any return*, that is, without anything being opposed to it. The sale, therefore, of two loads of barley, for instance, in exchange for one load of wheat, does not constitute usury, since these articles are *not homogeneous*; and, on the other hand, the sale of ten yards of cloth in exchange for five yards of cloth, is not usury, since although these articles be homogeneous, still they are not estimable by *weight* or *measurement* of capacity.

Usury, then, as an illegal transaction, is occasioned (according to most Muḥammadan doctors) by *rate*, united with *species*, where, however, it must be observed, that *rate*, amongst the Musalmāns, applies only to articles of weight or measurement of capacity, and *not* to articles of *longitudinal* measurement, such as cloth, &c., or of tale, such as eggs, dates, walnuts, &c., when exchanged from hand to hand. Ash-Shāfi'ī maintains that usury takes place only in things of an esculent nature, or in money, and according to him, therefore, articles of the last-mentioned description would give occasion to usury. It is, furthermore, to be observed, that superiority or inferiority in the *quality* has no effect in the establishment of the usury; and hence it is lawful to sell a quantity of the better sort of any article in exchange for an equal quantity of an inferior sort. Nor does usury exist where the qualities of an article of weight or measurement by capacity are not ascertained by some *known standard* of measurement. Thus it is lawful to sell one handful of wheat in exchange for two handfuls, or two handfuls for four, because, in such case, the measurement not having been made according to a *legal* standard, the superiority of measurement, establishing usury, has not taken place, and, since the law has fixed no standard of measure beneath half a *ṣā'*, any quantity less than such is considered equivalent to a handful.

Where the quality of being weighable or measureable by capacity, and correspondence of species (being the causes of usury) *both* exist, the stipulation of *inequality* or of suspension of payment to a future period, are both usurious. Thus it is usurious to sell either one measure of wheat in exchange for two measures,—or one measure of wheat for one measure deliverable at a future period. If, on the contrary, *neither* of these circumstances exist (as in the sale of wheat for money), it is lawful, either to stipulate a superiority of rate, or the payment at a future period. If, on the other hand, *one of* these circumstances only exist (as in the sale of wheat for barley, or the sale of one slave for another), then a superiority in the rate may legally be stipulated, but not a suspension in the payment. Thus one measure of wheat may lawfully be sold for two measures of barley, or one slave for two slaves: but it is not lawful to sell one measure of wheat for one measure of barley, payable at a future period; nor one slave for another, deliverable at a future period.

According to the majority of doctors, everything in which the usuriousness of an excess has been established by the Prophet on the ground of measurement of capacity (such as wheat, barley, dates and salt), or on the ground of weight (like gold or silver), is for ever to be considered as of that nature, although mankind should forsake this mode of estimation; because the custom of mankind, which regulates the measurement, is of inferior force to the declaration of the Prophet; and a superior court cannot yield to an inferior. Abū Yūsuf, however, is of opinion that in all things practice or custom ought to prevail, although in opposition to the ordinances of the Prophet; for the ordinance of the Prophet was founded on usage and practice of his own time. In ordinances, therefore, the prevalent customs among mankind are to be regarded; and as these are liable to alter, they must be attended to rather than the letter of an ordinance.

Usury cannot take place between a master and his slave, because whatever is in the possession of the slave is the property of the master, so that no sale can possibly take place between them, and hence the possibility of usury is excluded *à fortiori*. Nor can it take place between a Muslim and a hostile infidel in a hostile country, in accordance with the saying of the Prophet: "There is no usury between a Muslim and a hostile infidel in a foreign land," and on the further ground, that the property of a hostile infidel being free to the Muslim, it follows that it is lawful to take it by whatever mode may be possible, provided there be no deceit used. It is otherwise with respect to a *z̤immī*, or protected alien, as his property is not of a neutral nature, because of the protection that has been accorded to him, and, therefore, usury is as unlawful in his case as in that of a Muslim. Abū Yūsuf and ash-Shāfiʿī conceive an analogy between the case of a hostile infidel, in a hostile country, and that of a *z̤immī*, and hence they hold, contrary to the other Muslim doctors, that usury can take place also between a Muslim and a hostile infidel in a foreign land.

The testimony of a person who receives usury is inadmissible in a court of law. It is recorded in the *Mabsūt̤*, however, that the evidence of a usurer is inadmissible only in case of his being so in a notorious degree; because mankind often make invalid contracts, and these are in some degree usurious. (*Hidāyah*, Grady's edition, p. 362.)

For further information on the subject of usury and for cases, illustrative of the above-stated principles, see *Hidāyah*, Hamilton's translation, vol. ii., p. 489, *seqq.*; Grady's edition, p. 289 *seqq*; the *Durru 'l- Mukhtār*; the *Fatāwā-i-ʿAlamgīrī*, *in loco*.

USWAH, also ISWAH (اسوة).

"An example." The word occurs in the Qur'ān, Sūrah xxxiii. 21: "Ye had in the Apostle of God a good example" (*uṣwatun ḥasanatun*). Ar-Rāghib says it is the condition in which a man is in respect of another's imitating him.

UTERINE RELATIONS.

Arabic *z̤awū 'l-arḥām* (ذوو الارحام), called by the English lawyers "distant kindred."

They are divided into four classes:—

(1) Persons descended from the deceased, how low soever, *i.e.* the children of daughters or of son's daughters.

(2) Those from whom the deceased is descended, how high soever, *i.e. False* grandparents, in contradistinction from the *True*, a true grandfather being one between whom and the deceased no female intervenes; a true grandmother, one between whom and the deceased no false grandfather intervenes.

(3) Those descended from the parents of the deceased, how low soever, *i.e.* the daughters of full-brothers and of half-brothers (by the same father only), the children of half-brothers (by the same mother only), and the children of sisters.

(4) The children of the two grandfathers and two grandmothers of the deceased, *i.e.* father's half-brothers and sisters by the same mother only and their children; the deceased's paternal aunts and their children; maternal uncles and aunts and their children; the daughters of full paternal uncles and half-paternal uncles by the same father only.

This classification, however, does not exhaust the distant kindred, which, in the language of the law, are defined as those relations of a deceased person who are neither sharers nor residuaries. [INHERITANCE.] Thus, cousins who are children of residuaries, but are not residuaries themselves (*e.g.* paternal uncles' daughters) are distant kindred, though not members of any of the foregoing classes, or related through any member of such a class.

When the distant kindred succeed, in consequence of the absence of sharers and residuaries, they are admitted according to the order of their classes. Within the limits of each particular class, it is a general rule that a person nearer in degree succeeds in preference to one more remote; and in all classes, if there be several of an equal degree, the property goes equally among them if they are of the same sex. There is, however, some disagreement as to cases in which persons through whom they are related to the deceased are of different sexes or of different blood; and it is maintained by Muḥammad, against Abū Yūsuf, that regard must be had partly to the "roots" or intermediate relations, and not only to the "branches," or actual claimants. Thus all are agreed that if a man leave a daughter's son and a daughter's daughter, the male will have a double portion, for there is no difference of sex in the intermediate relations; but if there be a daughter's son's daughter and a daughter's daughter's son, it is said by Abū Yūsuf that the male will have a double portion, on account of his sex; but by Muḥammad, that the female, instead of the male, will take the double portion, by reason of her father's sex. And on the other hand, all are agreed that if there be two daughters of different brothers, they will take equally between them; but if there be a daughter of a brother and a daughter of a half-brother by the father only, Muḥammad rules that the latter will take nothing; for having regard to the circumstances that a brother excludes a half-brother by the father only, he considers that there is nothing to be handed down to the descendant of the latter, and that the whole will go to the descendant of the former.

This rule of Muḥammad, which in its application to the different classes of the distant kindred, leads to curious results of a complex character, seems to deserve a particular notice, as resting to a large extent on the principle of representation, which otherwise is all but foreign to the Muḥammadan law of inheritance. (A. Rumsey, *Moohummudan Law of Inheritance*, p. 56; Syed Ameer Ali, *Personal Law*, p. 52; *Durru 'l-Muk̲h̲tār*, p. 873.)

'UZAIR (عزير). [EZRA.]

UZḤĪYAH (اضحية). [SACRIFICE.]

'UZLAH (عزلة). "Retirement." A term used by the Ṣūfīs for a religious life of retirement from the world.

'UZR (عذر). "An excuse." A legal term for a claim or an objection.

AL-'UZZĀ (العزى). An idol mentioned in the Qurʾān. Sūrah liii. 19: "What think ye then of al-Lāt and al-'Uzzā, and Manāt, the third idol besides." According to Husain, it was an idol of the tribe of G̲h̲aṭafān. For a discussion on the subject, see the article on LAT.

V.

VEILS. [DRESS.]

VESSELS.
In the early days of Islām, there were four kinds of drinking-vessels forbidden to Muḥammadans on account of their being used for wine, namely, *ḥantam* (حنتم), a green vessel; *dubbā* (دبا), a large gourd hollowed out; *naqīr* (نقير), a cup made from the hollowed root of a tree; *muzaffat* (مزفت), a vessel covered with a kind of black pitch, or the glutinous substance with which the bottom of boats are payed. (*Mishkāt*, book i. ch. i. pt. i.) But, according to Muslim law, the vessels used by Christians and Jews, and even by idolaters, are lawful, but they must be free from the taste or smell of wine.

VIGIL.
Arabic *'arafah* (عرفة). The only Muḥammadan festival which has a vigil is the *'Īdu 'l-Az̤ḥā*, or "Feast of Sacrifice." ['IDU 'L-AZHA.]

VISITING THE SICK.
Arabic *'iyādah* (عيادة). An incumbent religious duty enjoined by Muḥammad on his followers. The following traditions illustrate his teaching on the subject (*Mishkāt*, book v. ch. i.):—

"When a Muslim visits a sick brother, he gathers the fruits of Paradise from the time he leaves his home until he returns."

"If a Muslim visit a sick person, and say seven times, ' I ask the Almighty God, who is Lord of the great throne, to give thee health,' the prayer shall be granted, unless the appointed time of his death hath surely come."

"Verily God will say at the Day of Resurrection, ' O sons of Adam! I was sick and ye did not visit me.' And the sons of Adam will say, ' O our Defender! how could we visit thee, for Thou art the Lord of the universe and art free from sickness?' And God will say, ' O men! did you not know that such a one of my servants was sick, and you did not visit him? Do you not know that had you visited that servant you would have met me there?' "

'Āyishah says: "When any one of us was sick, the Prophet used to rub his hands upon the sick person's body, after which he would say, ' O Lord of man! take away this pain and give health; for Thou art the giver of health; there is no health but thine, that health which leaveth no sickness."

"When any person complained of being out of order, or having a wound or sore, the Prophet would say, when passing his finger over the part affected, ' In the name of God, the earth of our ground mixed with the spittle of our mouth; we have done this in order to restore the sick to health, by permission of our Lord.' "

VOWS.
Arabic *naz̤r* (نذر), pl. *nuz̤ūr*. Heb. נֶדֶר *neder*. They who fulfil their vows are amongst those who drink of the waters of Kafūr in Paradise (Qurʾān, Sūrah lxxvi. 7); and the non-performance of a vow is sin (*Mishkāt*, book xiii. ch. xxii.). But the Prophet is related to have said, "Do not make a vow for it cannot alter fate; still it does extract something from the wealth of the stingy."

The atonement for a vow which has been not performed is the same as for an oath namely, the freeing of a slave, or clothing ten poor persons, or feeding ten persons, or three days fast. (*Hidāyah*, Arabic ed., vol. i. p. 350.) [OATH.]

W.

WADĪ'AH (وديعة). *Lit.* "A thing put down." The legal term for a deposit. (See Hamilton's *Hidāyah*, vol. iii. p. 259.)

AL-WADŪD (الودود). "The Loving One," or "The Beloved One." One of the the ninety-nine special attributes of God. It occurs twice in the Qur'ān:—

Sūrah xi. 92: "My Lord is Merciful and Loving."

Sūrah lxxxv 14: "He is the Forgiving, the Loving."

Al-Maliku 'l-Wadūd, the "King of Love."

WAḤDANĪYAH (وحدنية). (1) A theological term for the doctrine of the Unity of God. (2) The name of a sect of Ṣūfīs. [GOD, SIKHISM, SUFI.]

WAḤDATU 'L-WUJŪDĪYAH (وحدة الوجودية). A pantheistic sect of Ṣūfīs, who say that everything is God, and of the same essence.

AL-WAHHĀB (الوهاب). "The Bestower of gifts." One of the ninety-nine special attributes of God. It occurs in the Qur'ān, *e.g.* Sūrah iii. 6: "Thou art He who bestoweth gifts."

WAHHĀBĪ (وهابى). A sect of Muslim revivalists founded by Muḥammad, *son* of 'Abdu 'l-Wahhāb, but as their opponents could not call them *Muḥammadans*, they have been distinguished by the name of the father of the founder of their sect, and are called Wahhābīs.

Muḥammad ibn 'Abdu 'l-Wahhāb was born at Ayīnah in Najd in A.D. 1691. Carefully instructed by his father in the tenets of the Muslim faith, according to the Ḥanbalī sect, the strictest of the four great schools of interpretation, the son of 'Abdu 'l-Wahhāb determined to increase his knowledge by visiting the schools of Makkah, al-Baṣrah and Bag͟hdād. The libraries of these celebrated centres of Muḥammadanism placed within the reach of the zealous student those ponderous folios of tradition known as the "six correct books," and also gave him access to numerous manuscript volumes of Muslim law. Having performed the pilgrimage to Makkah with his father, and visited the Prophet's tomb at al-Madīnah, he remained at the latter place to sit at the feet of Shaik͟h 'Abdu 'llāh ibn Ibrāhīm, by whom he was carefully instructed in all the intricacies of the exegetical rules laid down for the exposition of ethics and jurisprudence.

For some years he resided with his father at Horemelah, a place which, according to Palgrave, claims the honour of his birth; but after his father's death, he returned to his native village, Ayīnah, where he assumed the position of a religious leader.

In his various travels, Muḥammad ibn 'Abdu 'l-Wahhāb had observed the laxities and superstitions of those who, whilst they professed to accept the stern unbending precepts of the Prophet of Arabia, had succeeded in stretching the rigid lines of Islām almost to breaking. Omens and auguries, sacred shrines and richly ornamented tombs, the use of intoxicating drugs, the silks and satins of the wealthy, all seemed to the earnest reformer lamentable departures from the first principles of Islām, and unwarrantable concessions to the luxury, idolatry, and superstitions of the age. Having carefully studied the teachings of the Qur'ān and the sacred traditions, he thought he had learned to distinguish between the essential elements of Islām and its recent admixtures, and now once more in the home of his childhood, he determined to teach and to propagate nothing but the "pure faith," as laid down by the precepts and practice of the Prophet himself. The Muslim world had departed from the worship of the Unity, and had yielded a blind allegiance to Walīs, Pīrs, and Saints, and all because the teachings of the sacred traditions had been neglected for that of learned but ambitious teachers.

To accept any doctrine other than that of those "Companions" who received their instructions from the Prophet's lips, was simply the blind leading the blind; and, therefore, the Reformer, refusing to join his faith to the uncertain leading-strings of even the four orthodox doctors, determined to establish the right of private judgment in the interpretation of those two great foundations of Islām—the Qur'ān and the Aḥādīs̤.

His teaching met with acceptance, but his increasing influence excited the opposition of the ruler of his district, and he was compelled to seek an asylum at Deraiah, under the protection of Muḥammad ibn Ṣa'ud, a chief of considerable influence. The protection of the religious teacher was made a pretext for more ambitious designs, and that which the zealous cleric had failed to accomplish by his persuasive eloquence, the warrior chief now sought to attain by the power of the sword; and he thus established in his own person that Wahhābi dynasty which, after a chequered existence of more than a hundred years, still exercises so powerful an influence not only in Central and Eastern Arabia, but wherever the Muḥammadan creed is professed. Like other great men before him, the Chief of Deraiah strengthened his position by a matrimonial alliance, which united the interests of his own family with that of the reformer. He married the daughter of Muḥammad ibn ʿAbdu ʾl-Wahhāb, and she became the mother of the celebrated Wahhābī chief ʿAbdu ʾl-ʿAzīz, who, upon the death of his father (A.D. 1765), led the Wahhābī army to victory, and succeeded in pushing his conquests to the remotest corners of Arabia.

ʿAbdu ʾl-ʿAzīz was not only a brave warrior, but a pious Muslim, and it is said that he fell a victim to the scrupulous regularity with which he performed his devotions in public. A Persian fanatic plunged his sharp Khurasān dagger into his side, just as he was prostrating himself in prayer in the mosque of Deraiah (A.D. 1803).

But the great military champion of the reformed doctrines was Saʿud, the eldest son of ʿAbdu ʾl-ʿAzīz, who during the lifetime of his father led the Wahhābī armies to victory, and threatened even the conquest of the whole Turkish empire. He is said to have been a remarkably handsome man, praised for his wisdom in counsel and skill in war. Having wielded the sword from his youth (for he fought his first battle when a lad of twelve), he was regarded by the wild Arabs of the desert as a fit instrument to effect the conversion of the world, and men from all parts of Arabia flocked round his standard.

Saʿud gained several decisive victories over Sulaimān Pasha, and afterwards, with an army of 20,000 men, marched against Karbalāʾ, the famed city of the East, which contains the tombs of the Shīʿah Khalīfahs. The city was entered with the Wahhābi cry, "Kill and strangle all infidels which give companions to God," and every vestige of supposed idolatry, from the bright golden dome of al-Ḥusain's tomb to the smallest tobacco pipe, was ground to the very dust, whilst the offerings of the numerous devotees, which formed the rich treasure of the sacred shrines, served to replenish the impoverished exchequer of the Wahhābī chief.

The following year the fanatical army effected the conquest of Makkah, and, on the 27th April 1803, Saʿud made his formal entry into the sacred city of the Kaʿbah. The sanctity of the place subdued the barbarous spirit of the conquerors, and not the slightest excesses were committed against the people. The stern principles of the reformed doctrines were, however, strictly enforced. Piles of green ḥuqqas and Persian pipes were collected, rosaries and amulets were forcibly taken from the devotees, silk and satin dresses were demanded from the wealthy and worldly, and the whole, collected into the one heterogeneous mass, was burnt by the infuriated reformers. So strong was the feeling against the pipes, and so necessary did a public example seem to be, that a respectable lady, whose delinquency had well nigh escaped the vigilant eye of the Muḥtasib, was seized and placed on an ass, with a green pipe suspended from her neck, and paraded through the public streets—a terrible warning to all of her sex who may be inclined to indulge in forbidden luxuries. When the usual hours of prayer arrived, the myrmidons of the law sallied forth, and with leathern whips drove all slothful Muslims to their devotions. The mosques were filled. Never since the days of the Prophet had the sacred city witnessed so much piety and devotion. Not one pipe, not a single tobacco-stopper, was to be seen in the streets or found in the houses, and the whole population of Makkah prostrated themselves at least five times a day in solemn adoration. Having carried out his mission with fidelity, Saʿud hastened to convey the news of his success to the Sulṭān of Turkey in the following characteristic letter:—

"Saʿud to Salīm.—I entered Makkah on the fourth day of Muḥarram in the 1218th year of the Hijrah. I kept peace towards the inhabitants, I destroyed all things that were idolatrously worshipped. I abolished all taxes except those required by the law. I confirmed the Qāẓī whom you had appointed agreeably to the commands of the Prophet of God. I desire that you will give orders to the rulers of Damascus and Cairo not to come up to the sacred city with the Maḥmal and with trumpets and drums. Religion is not profited by these things. May the peace and blessing of God be with you." [MAHMAL.]

Before the close of the year, al-Madīnah was added to the Wahhābī conquests, and so thoroughly did Saʿud carry out the work of reform, that even the Ḥujrah, containing the tomb of the Prophet, did not escape. Its richly ornamented dome was destroyed, and the curtain which covered the Prophet's grave would have been removed, had not the Leader of the Faithful been warned in his dreams not to commit so monstrous a sacrilege. [HUJRAH.]

For nine years did the Wahhābī rule exist at Makkah, and so strong was the position occupied by the Wahhābī army, and so rapidly did Wahhābī opinions spread amongst the people, that the Sultan of Turkey began to entertain the worst fears for the safety of his empire. ʿAlī Pasha was therefore ordered by the Sultan of Turkey to collect a strong army to suppress the Wahhābī movement; and eventually, Makkah and al-Madīnah were taken from the fanatics.

Upon the death of Saʿud (A.D. 1814), his son, ʿAbdu ʾllāh, became the Leader of the Faithful. He was even more distinguished than his father for personal bravery, but he lacked that knowledge of men which was so necessary for one called upon to lead the undisciplined nomadic tribes of the Arabian deserts. ʿAbdu ʾllāh and him army met with a series of reverses, and he was at last taken prisoner by Ibrāhīm Pashah and sent to Constantinople. He was executed in the public square of St. Ṣophia, December 19th, 1818. Turkī, the son of ʿAbdu ʾllāh, abandoned all hope of regaining the position, and fled to Riyāẓ, where he was afterwards assassinated. Faizul succeeded his father A.D. 1830, and established the Wahhābī rule in Eastern Arabia, making Riyāẓ the capital of his kingdom. It was this chief who entertained the traveller Palgrave in 1863, and received Lieutenant-Colonel (now Sir Lewis Pelly), as Her Majesty's representative, in 1865. Faizul died in 1866, soon after Sir Lewis Pelly's visit, and was succeeded by his son 'Abdu 'llāh.

But although the great political and military power of the Wahhābīs had been well nigh crushed, and the rule of the dynasty of Sa'ud circumscribed within the limits of the province of Najd, the principles laid down by Muḥammad ibn 'Abdu 'l-Wahhāb were still zealously maintained by certain religious teachers within the sacred mosque itself. And so it came to pass that when a restless spirit from India was endeavouring to redeem a lawless life by performing the pilgrimage to Makkah, he fell in with teachers who had imbibed Wahhābī doctrines and were secretly disseminating them amongst the pilgrims. Saiyid Aḥmad, the freebooter and bandit of Rai Bareli, having performed the sacred rites of the Pilgrimage, returned from Makkah (A.D. 1822), resolved to reclaim the whole of North India to the Faith of Islām. Bing a direct descendant from the Prophet, he possessed (unlike the Wahhābī of Najd) the necessary qualification for a Leader of the Faithful, and the Muslims of India at once hailed him as the true Khalīfah or al-Mahdī. Unheeded by the British Government, he traversed our provinces with a numerous retinue of devoted disciples, and converted the populace to his reformed doctrines by thousands. He appointed deputies at Patna, and then proceeded to Delhi, where he met with a ready listener in Muḥammad Ismā'īl, who became his most devoted disciple, and recorded the sayings of the new Khalīfah in the well-known Wahhābī book, entitled the *Ṣiraṭu 'l-Mustaqīm.*

On the 21st December 1826, Saiyid Aḥmad, the Leader of the Faithful, declared a religious war, or *Jihād*, against the Sikhs, and, hoping to unite the hosts of Islām in Central Asia under his banner, he commenced an insurrection on the Peshawar frontier. A fanatical war of varied successes followed, and lasted for four years; but the Wahhābī army was soon reduced in strength, and its disasters culminated in the death of its chief, who was slain by Sher Singh in an engagement at Balakot in Hazarah, May 1831. The remnant of the Saiyid's army fled across the border and settled at Sattāna, where in 1857, their numbers were augmented by mutineers, who joined their camp. They were eventually displaced by the British Government in the Umbeyla War of 1863, but there are still some three hundred of them residing at Palosi on the banks of the Indus, where they are ruled by Shaikh 'Abdu 'llāh, an old mutineer of 1857, who has recently married his daughter to a former Imām of the Peshawar, Sadar Bāzār, in order to combine the Wahhābi influences of Peshawar with those of the Palosi settlement.

But as in the case of the Wahhābīs of Najd, so with the Wahhābīs of India. The religious tenets of the reformers did not die with their political leader. What Sa'ud of Najd and Aḥmad of Bareli failed to accomplish with the sword, the cheapness of lithographic printing has enabled less daring leaders to accomplish with the pen. The reformed doctrines, as embodied in the *Ṣirāṭu 'l-Mustaqīm* and the *Taqwiyatu 'l-Īmān*, still exercise a powerful influence upon Muḥammadan thought in India.

Wahhābīism has sometimes been designated the Protestantism of Islām, and so it really is, although with this remarkable difference, that whilst Christian Protestantism is the assertion of the paramount authority of sacred scripture to the rejection of traditional teachings, Wahhābīism is the assertion of the paramount authority of the Qur'ān with the Traditions. But both systems contend for first principles, and if there appears to be any incongruity in applying the term Protestant to a sect which receives, instead of rejects, tradition, it arises from the very important fact that what is called "tradition" in Islām occupies a totally different place in the Muḥammadan system from that which it does in the Christian, Tradition in Islām being nothing less than the supposed inspired sayings of the Prophet, recorded and handed down by uninspired writers, and being absolutely necessary to complete the structure of the faith. The daily prayer, the customs of the pilgrimage, and numerous other duties and dogmas held to be of Divine institution, being found not in the Qur'ān but in the Aḥādīs̤, or Traditions. Hence it is that the Wahhābīs of Najd and India call themselves Ahl-i-Ḥadīs̤, or the people of Tradition, and promote in every way they can the study of those records. [TRADITION.]

The Wahhābīs speak of themselves as *Muwaḥḥid*, or "Unitarians," and call all others *Mushrik*, or those who associate another with God; and the following are some of their distinctive religious tenets:—

1. They do not receive the decisions of the four orthodox sects, but say that any man who can read and understand the Qur'ān and the sacred Ḥadīs̤ can judge for himself in matters of doctrine. They, therefore, reject *Ijmā'* after the death of the Companions of the Prophet.

2. That no one but God can know the secrets of men, and that prayers should not be offered to any prophet, walī, pīr, or saint; but that God may be asked to grant a petition for the *sake* of a saint.

3. That at the Last Day, Muḥammad will obtain permission (*iẕn*) of God to intercede for his people. The Sunnīs believe that permission has already been given.

4. That it is unlawful to illuminate the shrines of departed saints, or to prostrate before them, or to perambulate (*ṭawāf*) round them, they do not even perform any act of reverence at the Prophet's tomb at al-Madīnah.

5. That women should not be allowed to visit the graves of the dead, on account of their immoderate weeping.

6. That only four festivals ought to be observed, namely, 'Īdu 'l-Fiṭr, 'Īdu 'l-Azḥā, 'Āshūrā, and al-Lailatu 'l-Mubārakah.

7. They do not observe the ceremonies of *Maulūd*, which are celebrated on the anniversary of Muḥammad's birth.

8. They do not present offerings (*Naẕr*) at any shrine.

9. They count the ninety-nine names of God on their fingers, and not on a rosary.

10. They understand the terms "sitting of God" (Arabic *Istiwā'*), and "hand of God" (*Yadu 'llāh*), which occur in the Qur'ān, in their literal (*Ḥaqīqī*) sense, and not figuratively (*Majāzī*); but, at the same time, they say it is not revealed *how* God sits, or in what sense he has a hand, &c., and on this account the Christian doctrines of the Trinity and the Sonship of Christ do not present the same difficulties to the mind of a Wahhābī which they do to that of a Sunnī.

Mr. Wilfrid Blunt, in his *Future of Islam*, says:—

"I believe it is hardly now recognised by Mohammedans how near Abd el Wahhab was to complete success. Before the close of the eighteenth century, the chiefs of the Ibn Saouds, champions of Unitarian Islam, had established their authority over all Northern Arabia as far as the Euphrates, and in 1808 they took Mecca and Medina. In the meanwhile, the Wahhabite doctrines were gaining ground still further afield. India was at one time very near conversion, and in Egypt, and North Africa, and even in Turkey, many secretly subscribed to the new doctrines. Two things, however, marred the plan of general reform and prevented its full accomplishment. In the first place, the reform was too completely reactive. It took no account whatever of the progress of modern thought, and directly it attempted to leave Arabia it found itself face to face with difficulties which only political as well as religious success could overcome. It was impossible, except by force of arms, to Arabianise the world again, and nothing less than this was in contemplation. Its second mistake, and that was one that a little of the Prophet's prudence which always went hand in hand with his zeal might have avoided, was a too rigid insistance upon trifles. Abd el Wahhab condemned minarets and tombstones because neither were in use during the first years of Islam. The minarets, therefore, were everywhere thrown down, and when the holy places of Hejaz fell into the hands of his followers, the tombs of saints which had for centuries been revered as objects of pilgrimage were levelled to the ground. Even the Prophet's tomb at Medina was laid waste and the treasures it contained distributed among the soldiers of Ibn Saoud. This roused the indignation of all Islam, and turned the tide of the Wahhabite fortunes. Respectable feeling which had hitherto been on their side now declared itself against them, and they never after regained their position as moral and social reformers. Politically, too, it was the cause of their ruin. The outside Musalman world, looking upon them as sacrilegious barbarians, was afraid to visit Mecca, and the pilgrimage declined so rapidly that the Hejazi became alarmed. The source of their revenue they found cut off, and it seemed on the point of ceasing altogether. Then they appealed to Constantinople, urging the Sultan to vindicate his claim to be protector of the holy places. What followed is well known. After the peace of Paris, Sultan Mahmud commissioned Mehemet Ali to deliver Mecca and Medina from the Wahhabite heretics, and this he in time effected. The war was carried into Nejd; Deriyeh, their capital, was sacked, and Ibn Saoud himself taken prisoner and decapitated in front of St. Sophia at Constantinople. The movement of reform in Islam was thus put back for, perhaps, another hundred years.

"Still, the seed cast by Abd el Wahhab has not been entirely without fruit. Wahhabism, as a political regeneration of the world, has failed, but the spirit of reform has remained. Indeed, the present unquiet attitude of expectation in Islam has been its indirect result. Just as the Lutheran reformation in Europe, though it failed to convert the Christian Church, caused its real reform, so Wahhabbism has produced a real desire for reform if not yet reform itself in Mussulmans. Islam is no longer asleep, and were another and a wiser Abd el Wahhab to appear, not as a heretic, but in the body of the orthodox sect, he might play the part of Loyola or Borromeo with success.

"The present condition of the Wahhabites as a sect is one of decline. In India, and I believe in other parts of Southern Asia, their missionaries still make converts and their preachers are held in high esteem. But at home in Arabia, ther zeal has waxed cold, giving place to liberal ideas which in truth are far more congenial to the Arabian mind. The Ibn Saoud dynasty no longer holds the first position in Nejd, and Ibn Rashid who has taken their place, though nominally a Wahhabite, has little of the Wahhabite fanaticism. He is in fact a popular and national rather than a religious leader, and though still designated at Constantinople as a pestilent heretic, is counted as their ally by the more liberal Sunites. It is probable that he would not withhold his allegiance from a Caliph of the legitimate house of Koreysh."

(The following English works may be consulted on the subject of Wahhābīism: Burckhardt's *Bedouins and Wahhabys*; Brydge's *Brief History of the Wahhabis*; Sir Lewis Pelly's *Political Mission to Najd*; Hunter's *Musalmāns of India*; Palgrave's *Central and Eastern Arabia*; Lady Ann Blunt's *Pilgrimage to Najd*; Dr. Badger's *Imāms and Seyyids of 'Omān*; Blunt's *Future of Islam.*)

AL-WĀḤID (الواحد). "The One." One of the ninety-nine special attributes of the Almighty. It occurs frequently in the Qur'ān, *e.g.* Sūrah ii. 158: "Your God is One God."

WAḤY (وحى). [INSPIRATION.]

WĀ'IZ (واعظ). "A preacher." The word *khaṭīb* is generally applied to the Maulawī who recites the *khuṭbah* on Fridays; *wā'iẓ* is of more general application. In the *Qāmūs* dictionary, the *wā'iẓ* is defined as one who reminds mankind of those punishments and rewards which soften the heart. The usual time for preaching is on Fridays, and in the months of Muḥarram and Ramaẓān. [KHUTBAH.]

WAJD (وجد). "Ecstasy." A Ṣūfī term for the fifth stage of the mystic journey, when the spiritual traveller attains to a state of mental excitement which is supposed to indicate a high state of divine illumination. [SUFI.]

WAJH (وجه). *Lit.* "Presence; face." The word occurs in the Qur'ān for the presence of God. Sūrah ii. 109: "Wherever ye turn there is the face of God (*Wajhu 'llah*)."

WĀJIB (واجب). *Lit.* "That which is obligatory." A term used in Muḥammadan law for those injunctions, the non-observance of which constitutes *sin*, but the denial of which does not attain to downright infidelity. For example, that Muslim who does not offer the sacrifice on the day of the Great Festival [IDU 'L-AZHA] commits a sin, and if he says the sacrifice is not a divine institution, he is a sinner, but not an infidel; and he who does not observe the fast [RAMAZAN] is a sinner, but if he deny that the fast is a divine institution, he is an infidel. The sacrifice being *wājib*, whilst the fast is *farẓ*. [LAW.]

(2) A term which frequently occurs in combination with others. For example, *al-Wājibu 'l-wujūd*, "the necessary existence"—God; *Wājibu 'l-ittibā'*, "worthy to be obeyed," as a teacher or prophet; *Wājibu 'l-adā'*, "necessary to be discharged," as a debt or duty.

AL-WĀJID (الواجد). "The Finder, Inventor, or Maker." One of the ninety-nine attributes of God, but the word does not occur in the Qur'ān.

WAKĀLAH, WIKĀLAH (وكالة). The office of substitute. An embassy; an agency; attorneyship. For the Muḥammadan law, with regard to agency for sale, see Hamilton's *Hidāyah*, vol. iii. pp. 1–62. [AGENT, BAIL, SALE.]

WAKĪL (وكيل). An attorney, an agent, an ambassador. [AGENT.]

AL-WAKĪL (الوكيل). "The Guardian." One of the ninety-nine special attributes of God. It occurs in the Qur'ān, Sūrah iv. 83: "For God is all sufficient for a Guardian."

WALĀ' (ولاء). *Lit.* "Proximity, kin, friendship." A peculiar relationship voluntarily established, and which confers a right of inheritance on one or both parties connected. It is of two kinds:—

(1) *Walā'u 'l-'Atāqah* (ولاء العتاقة), Relationship between a master and a manumitted slave, in which the former inherits any property the latter may acquire after emancipation.

(2) *Walā'u 'l-Muwālāt* (ولاء الموالاة), The connection arising out of mutual friendship, especially between a Muḥammadan and a convert. (See *Hidāyah*, Grady's edition, p. 513.)

WALAHĀN (ولهان). The demon who troubles people when they are performing their ablutions. (*Mishkāt*, book ii. ch. 7.) The name signifies grief or distraction of mind. (See *Muntaha 'l-'Arab.*)

WALĪ (ولى), pl. *auliyā'*, "One who is very near." (1) Saints, or holy men, *e.g.* Sūrah x. 63: "Are not, verily, friends (*auliyā'*) of God they on whom there is no fear?" [SAINTS.]

(2) Next of kin or kindred, *e.g.* Sūrah viii. 73: "These shall be next of kin to each other."

Walī 'ahd, an heir, especially to a sovereignty.

Walī ba'īd, a legal guardian of a more remote degree than father, brother, or uncle.

Walī jabīr, an authoritative guardian recognised by law.

Walī ni'mat, a title of respect for a father, a patron, a benefactor.

Walīyu 'd-dam, a relative entitled to exact retaliation.

(3) A benefactor or helper, *e.g.* Sūrah ii. 114: "Thou hast no helper but God."

(4) *Al-Walī*, "the Helper." One of the ninety-nine special attributes of God.

WALĪ (والى), pl. *wulāt*. A prince or governor. A term used for the ruler of a country. It is assumed by the Ameer of Afghanistan in his treaties.

The title implies one who rules a Muslim country as an Amīr, or in behalf of the Khalīfah of Islām.

(2) God. Qur'ān, Sūrah xiii. 12: "Nor have they any *governor* beside Him."

AL-WALĪD IBN 'UQBAH (الوليد بن عقبة). A celebrated Companion. A brother to the Khalīfah 'Usmān, who was Governor of al-Kūfah, and died in the reign of Mu'āwiyah.

WALĪMAH (وليمة). The nuptial feast. *The wedding breakfast*, which is generally given on the morning after the marriage. The custom is founded on the example of Muḥammad, who is related to have given a feast of dates and a meal on the occasion of his marriage with Ṣafīyah.

Ibn Mas'ūd says the Prophet regarded the wedding feast as of divine authority, and he who is invited on such an occasion must accept the invitation. (*Mishkāt*, book xiii. ch. ix. pt. 1.)

WALIYU 'L-'AHD (ولى العهد). Vulg. *Wali'ahd*. The heir to a kingdom or state

WALKING. [DEPORTMENT.]

WAQF (وقف). *Lit.* "Standing, stopping, halting." (1) A term which in the language of the law signifies the appropriation or dedication of property to charitable uses and the service of God. An endowment. The object of such an endowment or appropriation must be of a perpetual nature, and such property or land cannot be sold or transferred. If a person build a mosque his right of property is extinguished as soon as prayers have been recited in the building.

According to the Imām Abū Yūsuf, if the place in which a mosque is situated should become deserted or uninhabited, inasmuch as there is no further use for the mosque, no person coming to worship therein, still the property does not revert to the original owner and founder. But Imām Muḥammad alleges that in such a case the land and the material (bricks, &c.) again become the property of the founder or his heir.

If a person construct a reservoir or well for public use, or a caravansera, for travellers, or a hostel on an infidel frontier for the accommodation of Muslim warriors, or dedicate ground as a burying-place, his right is not extinguished until the magistrate, at his request, issues a decree to that effect. This is the opinion of Imām Abū Ḥanīfah, but Imām Abū Yūsuf maintains that the person's right of property ceases on the instant of his saying: "I have made over this for such and such purposes." Whilst Imām Muḥammad asserts that as soon as the property is used for the purpose to which it is dedicated, it ceases to be the property of the original owner. (See Hamilton's *Hidāyah*, vol. ii. p. 334.)

(2) A term used for a full pause, and particularly for certain pauses in the reading of the Qur'ān, which are marked with the letters قف in the text.

WĀQI'AH (واقعة). *Lit.* The "inevitable." (1) A term generally used for an accident or an unavoidable circumstance in life.

(2) The Day of Judgment. See Qur'ān, Sūrah lvi. 2: "When the inevitable happens none shall call its happening a lie."

(3) The title of the LVIth Sūrah of the Qur'ān.

AL-WĀQIDĪ (الواقدى). His full name: Abū 'Abdi 'llāh Muḥammad ibn 'Umar al-Wāqidī. A celebrated Muslim historian, much quoted by Muir in his *Life of Mahomet*. Born at al-Madīnah A.H. 130, died A.H. 207. He is said to have left a library of 600 boxes of books.

WAQṢ (وقص), pl. *auqāṣ*. Any property under the regulated value or number upon which *zakāt* or legal alms is due.

WAQT (وقت). The present time as distinguished from *al-Waqtu 'd-Dā'im*, or the eternal existence of God.

AL-WAQTU'D-DĀ'IM (الوقت الدائم). *Lit.* "The Everlasting Time." A Ṣūfī term for the extent of the existence of the Eternal One. ('Abdu 'r-Razzāq's *Dictionary of Ṣūfi Terms*.)

WARAQAH (ورقة). Waraqah ibn Naufal ibn Asad ibn 'Abdi 'l-'Uzzā. The cousin of Khadījah; to whom she first made known the supposed revelation, or dream, of Muḥammad, and who is related to have said that the Prophet must have seen the *Nāmūs* which God sent to Moses. (*Mishkāt*, book xxiv. ch. v. pt. 1.)

In the Arabic Dictionary *al-Qāmūs*, it is stated that Waraqah was the son of one of Khadījah's uncles, and that it is not certain if he ever embraced Islām. 'Abdu 'l-Ḥaqq, the commentator on the *Mishkāt*, says he had embraced Christianity and had translated the Gospels into Arabic. There does not seem to be any good authority for the supposition that he was originally a Jew. He appears to have died soon after the incident in the cave at Ḥirā'. [MUHAMMAD.]

WARFARE. There are three terms used in the Traditions for warfare.

(1) *Jihād* (جهاد), warfare carried on by Muslims for the extension of Islām.

(2) *Fitan* (فتن), seditions and commotions which will precede the Resurrection.

(3) *Malāḥim* (ملاحم), pl. of *malḥamah*, warfare carried on between Muslim nations and tribes. These are also signs of the Resurrection. [FITAN, JIHAD, MALAHIM.]

AL-WĀRIṢ (الوارث). "The Heir" (of all things). One of the ninety-nine attributes of the Almighty.

WAṢAN (وثن), pl. *auṣān*. An idol. [IDOLATRY.]

WAṢANĪ (وثنى), from *waṣan*, an idol. An idolater. [IDOLATER.]

WAṢĀYĀ (وصايا), pl. of *waṣīyah*. *Lit.* "Precepts." Used in Muslim law for wills and regulations concerning them [WILLS.]

AL-WĀSI' (الواسع). "The Capacious." One of the ninety-nine attributes of God. It occurs in the Qur'ān, Sūrah ii. 248: "God is the Capacious one and knows."

WASĪLAH (وسيلة). *Lit.* "Nearness." The name of the highest station in Paradise, which Muḥammad said was reserved for one person only, and which he hoped to obtain for himself. (*Mishkāt*, book xxiv. ch. ii. pt. 2.)

It is usual for religious Muhammadans to pray, after the call to prayer (*azān*) has been concluded, that Muḥammad may obtain this station of *Wasīlah*. Hence the place of intercession, and the office of mediator. That which effects nearness to God.

WĀSIṬAH (واسطة). A thing or person intervening; an agent; a broker. Hence, a mediator.

WASL (وصل). "Meeting; union." A Ṣūfi term used for the seventh stage in the spiritual journey, when the mystic, as it were, sees the Divine One face to face. The stage previous to *fanā'*, or extinction in the essence of the Eternal One. [SUFI.]

WASWASAH (وسوسة). *Lit.* "Inspiring," or "suggesting." A suggestion from the devil. The machinations of the devil, to the consideration of which a chapter is devoted in the Traditions. (*Mishkāt*, book i. ch. iii.)

Muḥammad said, "There is not a single child of man, except Mary and her son, who is not touched by the devil at the time of his birth, and hence the child makes a loud cry when he is born, nor is there one human being who has not a devil appointed to attend him. The devil sticks close to the sons of Adam, and also an angel; the business of the devil is to do evil, and that of the angel to guide them unto truth."

WATER. Arabic *mā'* (ماء), pl. *miyāh*, *amwāh*. Heb. מַיִם *mayim*, waters. In the Qur'ān, Sūrah xxi. 31, it is said, "We clave them (the heavens and the earth) asunder, and by means of *water*, We gave life to everything." Which, as Sprenger (vol. i. p. 30*n*) remarks, is one of the principles of the Ebionite doctrine. Al-Baiẓāwī says it means either that God made all animals from water, or that the chief element in animal life is water, or that animal life is supported chiefly by water.

Muḥammadan writers say there are seven kinds of water which are lawful for the purposes of purification and drinking:—

Mā'u 'l-maṭar, rain-water.
Mā'u 'l-'ain, spring-water.
Mā'u 'l-bi'r, well-water.
Mā'u 'l-barad, hail-water.
Mā'u 's-ṡalj, snow-water.
Mā'u 'l-baḥr, sea-water.
Mā'u 'n-nahr, river-water.

Water which is considered lawful for ablution is also lawful for drinking, and *vice versâ*. Ibn 'Umar relates that Muḥammad was asked about the water of the plains in which animals go to drink, &c., and he said, "When the water is equal to two *qullahs*, it is not impure." 'Abdu 'l-Ḥaqq says two *qullahs* are equal to 250 *mans*. (*Mishkāt*, Matthew's ed., vol. i. p. 107.) [WELLS.]

Mr. Sell, in his *Faith of Islam*, says:—

"Minute regulations are laid down with regard to the water which may be used for purification. The following kinds of water are lawful:—rain, sea, river, fountain, well, snow, and ice-water. Ice is not lawful. The first kind is authorised by the Qurán. 'He sent you down water from heaven that He might thereby cleanse you, and cause the pollution of Satan to pass from you.' (Súra viii. 11.) The use of the others is sanctioned by the Traditions. I give one illustration. A man one day came to the Prophet and said: 'I am going on a voyage and shall only have a small supply of fresh water; if I use it for ablutions I shall have none wherewith to quench my thirst, may I use sea-water?' The Prophet replied: 'The water of the sea is pure.' Tirmízí states that this is a Hadís-i-Sahíh. Great difference of opinion exists with regard to what constitutes impurity in water, and so renders it unfit for ablutions. It would be wearisome to the reader to enter into all details, but I may briefly say that, amongst the orthodox, it is generally held that if a dead body or any unclean thing falls into flowing water, or into a reservoir more than 15 feet square, it can be used, provided always that the colour, smell, and taste are not changed. It is for this reason that the pool near a mosque is never less than ten cubits square. If of that size, it is called a *dah dar dah* (literally 10×10). It may be, and commonly is, larger than this. It should be about one foot deep."

Rights regarding water. According to Muḥammadan law, water is of four kinds:—

(1) The water of the ocean, to which every person has a perfect and equal right, for the enjoyment of the ocean is common to everyone, in the same manner as the light of the sun or the air we breathe.

(2) The waters of large rivers, such as the Euphrates, the Tigris, the Indus, or the Oxus, from which every person has an absolute right to drink, and also a conditional right to use it for the purpose of irrigating his lands. For example, if a person desire to cultivate waste land, and dig a watercourse or canal for the purpose of conveying water to it from the river, he may lawfully do so, provided the act be in no sense detrimental to the people. The same law applies to the erection of a water-mill on the banks of a river.

(3) Water in which several have a share; in which case also the right of drinking is common to all, whilst there are certain restrictions regarding its use for the purposes of irrigation, which will be hereafter treated of.

(4) Water which is kept in vessels; which is regarded as property, except in times of scarcity, when it is even lawful to seize it for common use.

The law regarding the division of water for the purposes of irrigation, known as *shirb* (شرب), or "a right to water," is most important in the East, where so much of the cultivation of land depends not upon the fall of rain but upon irrigation. In Afghanistan, there are more disputes and more murders committed over the division of water than with regard to any other question. A claim of *shirb*, or "right of water," is valid, independent of any property in the ground, for a person may become endowed with it, exclusive of the ground, either by inheritance or bequest; and it sometimes happens that when a person sells his lands, he reserves to himself the right of *shirb*. No person can alter or obstruct the course of water running through his ground, and in the case of disputes regarding a rivulet held jointly by several, it is the duty of the judge to make a distribution of the water according to the extent of land which they severally possess; for, as the object of right to water is to moisten the lands, it is but fit that each should receive a just proportion. A rivulet must not be dammed up for the convenience of one partner without the consent of the others; nor can he dig a trench or erect a a mill upon a rivulet used for irrigation, without the general consent of all persons concerned. The same restriction applies, also, to a water-engine or a bridge. One partner cannot alter the mode of partition without the others' consent, nor increase the number of sluices or openings through which he receives his share, nor convey his share into lands not entitled to receive it, nor even to lands which are entitled to receive it, nor can he shut up any of the sluices, or exchange the manner of division in any way, as, for example, by taking the water in rotation instead of division by sluices. A right to water cannot be consigned as a dower, nor given as a consideration in *Khul'*, when a wife bargains for her divorce [KHUL'], nor in composition for a claim, nor sold to discharge the debts of a defunct owner. It is also noted that if a person, by irrigating his lands, should by that means overflow those of his neighbour, he is not liable to make compensation, as he was not guilty of any transgression.

WA'Z (وعظ). A sermon. [KHUTBAH, WAI'Z.]

WAẒĪFAH (وظيفة), from *waẓf*, "a daily ration of food." (1) A term used for a daily lesson, or portion from the Qur'ān which is read by devout Muslims. The Qur'ān is divided into thirty *sipārahs* as the daily *waẓīfah* to be read during the month of Ramaẓān.

(2) A pension or stipend granted to pious persons

(3) Revenue collected at a stipulated rate.

WAZĪR (وزير). A Vezeer. The principal minister in a Muḥammadan country. There are three opinions respecting the etymology of the word. Some derive it from *wizr*, "a burden," because the *wazīr* bears the burden of state; others from *wazar*, "a refuge," because the ruler has recourse to the counsels of the *wazīr*; others from *azr*, "the back, or strength," because the ruler is strengthened by his *wazīr* as the human frame is by the back.

Mr. Lane (*Arabian Nights*, Intro., p. 23), says: "The post of wezeer was the highest that was held by an officer of the pen; and the person who occupied it was properly the next to the Sultān; but the Turkish Sultāns of Egypt made the office of *nāïb*, or "viceroy," to have the pre-eminence. Under them, the post of *wezeer* was sometimes occupied by an officer of the pen, and sometimes by an officer of the sword; and in both cases the *wezeer* was called 'the Ṣāḥeb.'"

Khalīl az-Zāhir relates that Muḥammad said, "Whosoever is in authority over Muslims, if God prosper him, shall be given a virtuous *wazīr*. The *wazīr* shall remind him when he forgetteth his duty, and shall assist him when he doth remember it. But to a bad ruler God giveth an evil-minded *wazīr*, who, when the ruler forgetteth his duty, does not remind him of it, and when he remembereth his duty, doth not assist him to perform it."

WEDDING. [MARRIAGE.]

WEEK. Arabic *usbū'* (اسبوع), *subū'* (سبوع); Heb. שָׁבוּעַ *shāvūa'*. The Muhammadan week (as the Jewish and Christian) begins with Sunday and ends with Saturday. In the Qur'ān, Sūrah vii. 52, it is said "God created the heavens and the earth in six days." In Sūrah xvi. 125, it is said, "the Sabbath was only made for those who dispute thereon," which al-Baiẓāwī says means that the Sabbath was established for the Jews who disputed with Moses regarding it; but there is no injunction in the Qur'ān for the due observance of the Sabbath. [DAY, FRIDAY.]

WEEPING. [BUKA'.]

WELLS. Arabic *bi'r* (بئر), pl. *ab'ār*. Heb. בְּאֵר *Be'ēr*. If a person dig a well for public use, it is held by Imām Muḥammad that his right to the well ceases as soon as the people drink of the well; but Imām Abū Ḥanīfah is of opinion that it does not become common property until the magistrates issue a decree to that effect. (*Hidāyah*, vol. ii. p. 357.)

If a person dig a well in a high road (where no person is entitled to dig a well), he is liable to a fine for any accident which may happen by people falling into it. (*Hidāyah*, vol. ii. p. 719.)

If any animal, or impurity of any kind, fall into a well, all the water must be drawn out before the well can be lawfully used; and if it be impossible to draw the whole of the water, then not less than 300 bucketfuls must be drawn out. If the animal has in any way become putrified in the well, then the water must not be used for three whole days; but in any other case the water can be used after the lapse of a whole day. (*Sharḥu 'l-Wiqāyah*, p. 10.)

WHISTLING. Arabic *mukā'* (مكاء). Mentioned in the Qur'ān, Sūrah viii. 35: "Their (the Quraish) prayer at the House was naught but whistling and clapping hands! Taste, then, the torment, for that ye misbelieve." From which it is understood that whistling was one of the idolatrous ceremonies in the days of ignorance in the Makkan temple. Whistling is therefore generally held to be unlawful for pious Muslims.

WIDOWS. Arabic *armalah* (ارملة). Heb. אַלְמָנָה *almānāh*. Mourning is incumbent upon a widow for a period of four months and ten days after the death of her husband. (Hamilton's *Hidāyah*, vol. i. p. 370.) After this period she may lawfully take another husband, provided she be not pregnant of her first husband. A widow's share of her late husband's property is one-*eighth* when there is a child, or a son's child, how low soever, and a *fourth* when there is no child. Though a man may have as many as four wives, the provision for two or more is the same as that for one: the fourth or eighth, as the case may, being divisible among them equally. (Baillie's *Law of Inheritance*, p. 59.)

If a Muslim, whose wife was once a Christian should die, and his widow appear before a Qāẓī and declare that she is Muslim, and that she embraced the faith prior to the death of her husband, and the heirs assert the contrary, the assertion of the heirs is to be credited to the exclusion of the rights of the widow. And if a Christian die, and his widow appear before the Qāẓī as a Muslim, and the heirs declare the contrary, the assertion of the heirs is to be credited to the exclusion of the widow. (Grady's *Hidāyah*, p. 347.)

WILLS. Arabic *waṣīyah* (وصية), pl. *waṣāyā*, which term is held by Muslim legists to mean "an endowment with the property of anything after death, as if one person should say to another, 'Give this article of mine, after my death, to a particular person.'"

The testator is called *mūṣī*, fem. *mūṣīyah*. The legatee is termed *mūṣa la-hu*. The legacy, *mūṣa bi-hi*. The person appointed to carry out the will, or the executor, is called the *waṣīy*, pl. *auṣīyā*.

It is not necessary that the will of a Muslim should be executed in writing, but it must be certified to by two male witnesses, or one male and two females.

The following are some of the chief points in Muslim law, regarding the making and the execution of wills :—

Wills are lawful and valid to the extent of a third of the testator's property, but not to any further extent unless by consent of the heirs, and it is laudable to avoid making bequests when the heirs are poor.

A bequest to an heir is not valid unless confirmed by the other heirs, and a bequest to a person from whom the testator has received a mortal wound is not valid; and if a legatee slay his testator, the bequest in his favour is void.

A bequest to a part of the heirs is not valid.

Bequests are valid between Muslims and Zimmīs, that is, between Muḥammadans and Jews or Christians under protection. [ZIMMI.]

The acceptance or rejection of bequests is not determined until after the death of the testator.

The legatee becomes proprietor of the legacy by his acceptance of it, which may be either expressed or implied

A bequest by an insolvent person is void, as also that of an infant, or a *mukātab* (a slave who has ransomed himself). A bequest in favour of a fœtus in the womb is also invalid; but ash-Shāfiʿī says it is valid.

A female slave may be bequeathed, with the exception of her progeny. To bequeath the offspring of a female slave is unlawful.

A bequest is rescinded by the express declaration of the testator, or by any act on his part implying his retractation, or which extinguishes his property in the legacy. But the testator's denying his bequest is not a retractation of it, nor his declaring it unlawful or usurious, nor his desiring the execution of it to be deferred. A bequest to one person is annulled by a subsequent bequest of the same article to another, unless that other be not then alive.

A legacy after being divided off by the magistrate, descends to the legatee's heirs in case of his decease.

Concerning the Bequest of a Third of the Estates.

If a person leave a third of his property to one man and a third to another, and the heirs refuse their consent to the execution of the whole, it is then restricted to one third.

If a person bequeath the third of his estate to one, and then a sixth of it to another, and the heirs refuse their consent, in that case one-third of his estate is divided into three shares, of which two are given to the legatee of the third and one to the legatee of the sixth.

A bequest of a son's portion of inheritance is void, but not the bequest of an equivalent to it. For example: If a person say, "I bequeath my son's portion," such a bequest is null; but the bequest will be valid if he say, "I bequeath an equivalent to my son's portion."

A bequest of a "portion" of the estate is executed to the extent of the smallest portion inherited from it, and a bequest of "part of the estate," undefined, may be construed to apply to any part.

A person bequeathing a third of any particular property, if two-thirds of it be lost, and the remainder come within a third of the testator's estate, the legatee is entitled to the whole of such remainder; and a bequest of "the third of" an article, part of which is afterwards destroyed, holds with respect to a third of the remainder

A legacy of money must be paid in full with the property in hand, although all the rest of the estate should be expended in debts.

A legacy left to two persons, one of them being at that time dead, goes entire to the living legatee.

A legacy being bequeathed to two persons indefinitely, if one of them die, a moiety of it only goes to the other.

A bequest made by a poor man is of force if he afterwards become rich.

A bequest of any article, not existing in the possession or disposal of the testator at his decease, is null, unless it was referred to his property, in which case it must be discharged by a payment of the value.

An acknowledgment of debt, upon a death-bed, is efficient to the extent of a third of the estate.

Any accident occasioning uncertainty with respect to the legatees, annuls the bequest.

An heir, after partition of the estate, acknowledging a bequest in favour of another, must pay the acknowledged legatee his proportion of such bequest.

The Period of Making Wills.

As has already been remarked, Muḥammadan wills are not as a rule written documents, and therefore the institutions of the law are entirely made for verbal rather than written bequests.

Gratuitous acts, of immediate operation, if executed upon a death-bed, take effect to the extent of one-third of the property only.

An acknowledgment on a death-bed is valid in favour of the person who afterwards becomes an heir, but not a bequest or gift; neither is an acknowledgment so made valid, if the principle of inheritance had existed in the person previous to the deed.

Such acknowledgment, gift, or bequest, in favour of a son, being a slave, who afterwards becomes free, previous to the father's decease, is nevertheless void.

Rules for Ascertaining a Death-bed Illness.

The following curious paragraph occurs in the *Hidāyah* on this subject:—

"Paralytic, gouty, or consumptive persons, where their disorder has continued for a length of time, and who are in no immediate danger of death, do not fall under the description of *mariẓ* or 'sick,' whence deeds of gift, executed by such, take effect to the extent of their whole property; because, when a long time has elapsed, the patient has become familiarised to his disease, which is not then accounted as sickness. The length of time requisite, by its lapse, to do away with the idea of sickness in those cases, is determined at one year; and if, after that time, the invalid should become bed-ridden, he is then accounted as one recently sick. If, therefore, any of the sick persons thus described make a gift in the beginning of their illness, or after they are bedridden, such gift takes effect from the third of their property, because at such time there is apprehension of death (whence medicine is given to them), and therefore the disorder is then considered as a death-bed illness." (*Hidāyah*, Grady's ed., p. 685.)

Emancipation of Slaves upon a Death-bed.

Emancipation and deeds of gift on a death-bed, take effect to the extent of a third of the property, and emancipation precedes in their execution the actual bequests.

The appropriation of a sum by bequest to the emancipation of a slave is annulled by the subsequent loss or failure of any part of it, but not the appropriation of a sum to the performance of a pilgrimage.

A slave, exceeding one-third of the property, emancipated on death-bed, is exempted from emancipatory labour by the heirs assenting to his freedom.

A bequest of emancipation in favour of a slave is annulled by his being made over in compensation for an offence committed by him.

Where the heir and the legatee agree concerning a slave having been emancipated by the testator, the allegation of the heir is credited with respect to the date of the deed.

Bequests for Pious Purposes.

In the execution of bequests to certain pious purposes, the duties ordained by the command of God precede those which are voluntary, and are then benevolent acts towards mankind.

If a person will that "the pilgrimage which was incumbent upon him be performed on his behalf after his death," the heirs must depute a person for this purpose and pay all his expenses to Makkah.

But when all the purposes mentioned be of equal importance, the arrangement of the testator must be followed.

A legacy, appropriated to pilgrimage, if lost, must be repaired to the extent of a third of the estate.

Wills made by Jews and Christians.

Zimmīs, or Jews and Christians paying tribute for protection, can make bequests, and they are held good in Muslim law, and are subject to the same restrictions with those of Muslims.

A church or synagogue founded during health descends to the founder's heirs, but the bequest of a house to the purpose of an infidel place of worship, is appropriated, whether any particular legatees be mentioned or otherwise.

Abū Hanīfah says the bequests of Zimmīs are of four kinds:—

(1) Those made for purposes held sacred in their belief, but not in that of Muslims, such as the building of a church or synagogue, which according to Hanīfah is valid under certain restrictions.

(2) Those made for purposes held pious by Muslims and not by Zimmīs, such as the building of a mosque, in which case the bequest is invalid.

(3) Those made for a purpose held sacred by both Muslims and Zimmīs, such as an offering to the Temple at Jerusalem, which are valid.

(4) Those made for purposes held to be wrong by both Zimmīs and Muslims, such as the support of singers and dissolute women, which are invalid as being sinful.

The will of a sensualist or innovator is the same as of an orthodox Mussulman, unless he proceed to avowed apostasy. The will of a female apostate is valid, but not that of a male apostate.

A Zimmī may bequeath the whole of his property; but if he bequeath a part only, the residue is transmitted to his heirs.

An emancipation granted by him on his death-bed, takes effect in toto.

Any bequest in favour of a Z̲immī is valid, and he may make a bequest in favour of an unbeliever of a different sect not being a hostile infidel.

Usufructuary Wills.

An article bequeathed in usufruct must be consigned to the legatee; but if it constitute the sole estate, being a slave, he is possessed by the heirs and legatee alternately; or, being a house, it is held among them in their due proportions; nor are the heirs in the latter instance allowed to sell their slaves. The bequest becomes void on the death of the legatee.

A bequest of the produce of an article does not entitle the legatee to the personal use of the article; nor does a bequest of the use entitle him to let it to hire. A bequest of the use of a slave does not entitle the legatee to carry him out of the place, unless his family reside elsewhere. A bequest of a year's product, if the article exceed a third of the estate, does not entitle the legatee to a consignment of it.

In a bequest of the use of an article to one, and the substance of it to another, the legatee of usufruct is exclusively entitled to the use during his term. A bequest of an article to one, and its contents to another, if connectedly expressed, entitles the second legatee to nothing.

A bequest of the fruit of a garden implies the present fruit only, unless it be expressed in perpetuity, and a bequest of the produce of an animal implies the existent produce only in every instance.

The Executors.

An executor having accepted his appointment in presence of the testator, is not afterwards at liberty to reject it, but his silence leaves him an option of rejection; but any act indicative of his acceptance binds him to the execution of the office.

Having rejected the appointment after the testator's decease, he may still accept of it, unless the magistrate appoint an executor in the interim.

Where a slave, a reprobate, or an infidel are appointed, the magistrate must nominate a proper substitute.

The appointment of the testator's slave is invalid if any of the heirs have attained to maturity, but not otherwise.

In case of the executor's incapacity, the magistrate must give him an assistant; but he must not do so on the executor pleading incapacity without due examination; and if he appear perfectly equal to the office, he cannot be removed, not even on the complaint of the heirs, unless his culpability be ascertained.

One of two joint executors cannot act without the concurrence of the other, except in such matters as require immediate execution, or which are of an incumbent nature, or in which the interest or advantage of the estate are concerned.

In case of the death of a joint executor, the magistrate must appoint a substitute, unless the deceased have himself nominated his successor. The executor of an executor is his substitute in office.

An executor is entitled to possess himself of the portions of infant and absent adult heirs on their behalf, but not of the legacies of infant or absent legatees.

An executor may sell a slave of the estate, for the discharge of the debts upon it, in absence of the creditors, unless the slave be involved in debt.

An executor having sold and received the price of an article which afterwards proves to be the property of another, is accountable to the purchaser for the price he had so received; but if this has been lost he may reimburse himself from the person to whom the article had fallen by inheritance.

An executor may accept a transfer for a debt due to his infant ward, or sell or purchase movables on his account. He may also sell movables on account of an absent adult heir, but he cannot trade with his ward's portion. He may sell movable property on account of the infant or absent adult brother of the testator.

The power of a father's executor precedes that of the grandfather. If there be no executor, the grandfather is the father's representative.

Evidence with respect to Wills.

The evidence of two executors to the appointment of a third is not valid, unless he claim or admit it, and the evidence of orphans to the appointment of an executor is not admitted if he deny it.

The testimony of executors with respect to property on behalf of an infant or of an absent adult is not admitted.

The mutual evidence of parties on behalf of each other to debts due to each from an estate is valid, but not their evidence to legacies, unless each legacy respectively consists of a slave.

A mutual evidence of this nature is void where it involves a right of participation in the witnesses.

WINDS.

WINDS. Arabic *riyāḥ* (رياح), pl. of *rīḥ*. Heb. רוּחַ *rūak̲h̲*. There are four special winds mentioned in the Qur'ān: *Ṣarṣar*, a violent hurricane (Sūrah lxix. 6); *'aqīm*, a barren wind (Sūrah li. 42); *lawāqiḥ*, fertilizing winds (Sūrah xv. 22); *mubashshirāt*, harbingers of rain (Sūrah xxx. 47). And it is related that the Prophet said he was assisted by an east wind at the battle of the Ditch, and that the tribe of 'Ād was destroyed by a west wind. A special chapter is devoted to the Prophet's sayings with regard to the wind, as it appears that he had a superstition of it. 'Āyishah said, that when the clouds appeared, the

Prophet used to change colour, and come out of his house and walk to and fro, nor would his alarm cease until the storm had passed away. When she expressed her surprise at his excitement, he said, "O 'Āyishah, peradventure these winds be like those which destroyed the tribe of 'Ād."

WINE. Heb. חֶמֶר *khemer*, Is. i. 22, "old wine." Wine under the term *khamr* (خمر), which is generally held to imply all things which intoxicate, is forbidden in the Qur'ān in the following verses:—

Sūrah ii. 216: "They will ask thee concerning wine and games of chance. Say: In both is great sin, and advantage also, to men; but their sin is greater than their advantage."

Sūrah v. 92: "O believers! surely wine and games of chance, and statues, and the *divining* arrows, are an abomination of Satan's work! Avoid them, that ye may prosper. Only would Satan sow hatred and strife among you, by wine, and games of chance, and turn you aside from the remembrance of God, and from prayer: will ye not, therefore, abstain from them? Obey God and obey the Apostle, and be on your guard: but if ye turn back, know that our Apostle is *only* bound to deliver a plain announcement."

Al-Jalālān, the commentators, on these verses, say, "Only that wine is forbidden which intoxicates the brain and affects the steadiness of the body." But all Muslim doctors hold that wine of any kind is forbidden.

Imām Abū Ḥanīfah says: "This doctrine is founded upon a precept of the Prophet, who said, 'Whoever drinks wine, let him suffer correction by scourging as often as he drinks thereof." (Hamilton's *Hidāyah*, vol. ii. 53.)

If a Musalman drinks wine, and is seized whilst his breath yet smells of wine, or be brought before the Qāẓī whilst he is yet intoxicated, and two witnesses give evidence that he has drunk wine, scourging is to be inflicted. The punishment is eighty lashes for a free man. and forty lashes for a slave.

Mr. Lane says: "Several stories have been told as to the occasion of Muḥammad's prohibiting the drinking of wine. Busbequius says: 'Muḥammad, making a journey to a friend at noon, entered into his house, where there was a marriage feast, and, sitting down with the guests, he observed them to be very merry and jovial, kissing and embracing one another, which was attributed to the cheerfulness of their spirits raised by the wine; so that he blessed it as a sacred thing in being thus an instrument of much love among men. But, returning to the same house the next day, he beheld another face of things, as gore-blood on the ground, a hand cut off, an arm, foot, and other limbs dismembered, which he was told was the effect of the brawls and fightings occasioned by the wine, which made them mad, and inflamed them into a fury, thus to destroy one another. Whereon he changed his mind, and turned his former blessing into a curse, and forbade wine ever after to all his disciples.' Epist. 3. This prohibition of wine hindered many of the Prophet's contemporaries from embracing his religion. Yet several of the most respectable of the pagan Arabs, like certain of the Jews and early Christians, abstained totally from wine, from a feeling of its injurious effects upon moral, and, in their climate, upon health; or, more especially, from the fear of being led by it into the commission of foolish and degrading actions. Thus Keys (Qais), the son of Asim, being one night overcome with wine, attempted to grasp the moon, and swore that he would not quit the spot where he stood until he had laid hold of it. After leaping several times with the view of doing so, he fell flat upon his face; and when he recovered his senses, and was acquainted with the cause of his face being bruised, he made a solemn vow to abstain from wine ever after."—Lane's *Arabian Nights*, vol. i. pp. 217, 218.

WITNESS. Arabic *shahīd* (شهيد), dual *shahīdān*; pl. *shuhadā*, or *shuhūd*.

Terms which are used for witness in legal cases, an account of which is given in the article on EVIDENCE; and also for those who die as martyrs for the Muslim faith, or meet with sudden death from any accidental circumstance. [MARTYR.]

WITR (وتر). *Lit.* "An odd number." *Witr* rak'ahs are an odd number of rak'ahs, 3, 5, or 7, which may be said after the last prayer at night, and before the dawn of day. Usually they are added to the Ṣalātu 'l-'Ishā. Imām Abū Ḥanīfah says they are *wājib*, that is, ordered by God, although they are not authorised by any text in the Qur'ān. But they are instituted by traditions, each of which is generally received as a Ḥadīs̤ Ṣaḥīḥ; and so *witr* rak'ahs are regarded as being of divine authority. Imām Shāfa'ī, however, considers them to be *sunnah* only.

The Traditions referred to are:—

The Prophet said: "God has added to your prayers one prayer more: know that it is *witr*, say it between the Ṣalātu 'l-'Ishā and the dawn."

On the authority of Buzār, it is recorded that the Prophet said: "*Witr* is *wājib* upon Muslims," and in order to enforce the practice, he added: "*Witr* is right; he who does not observe it is not my follower."

The Prophet, the Companions, the Tābi'ūn and the Taba'u 't-Tābi'īn, all observed it.

The word *witr* literally means "odd number," and a tradition says: "God is odd, He loves the odd."

Musalmāns pay the greatest respect to an odd number. It is considered unlucky to begin any work, or to commence a journey on a day, the date of which is an even number.

The number of lines in a page of a book is nearly always an odd number. [SALATU 'L-WITR.]

WIVES. Arabic *zauj* (زوج), pl.
azwāj, also *zaujah*, pl. *zaujāt.* Although
Muḥammad himself claimed the special indulgence of eleven lawful wives, he limited
his followers to four, allowing at the same
time as many female concubines or domestic
slaves as the master's right hand possessed.
See Qur'ān, Sūrah iv. 3 : " Marry what seems
good to you of women, by twos, or threes, or
fours, or what your right hand possesses."
[MARRIAGE.]

According to the Shī'ahs, he also sanctioned temporary marriages, an account of
which will be found in the article on MUT'AH.

Regarding the treatment of wives, the following verse in the Qur'ān (Sūrah iv. 38)
allows the husband absolute power to correct them : " Chide those whose refractoriness you have cause to fear. Remove them
into sleeping chambers apart, and beat
them. But if they are obedient to you, then
seek not occasion against them."

(For other injunctions in the Qur'ān on the
subject, see the article WOMEN.)

The following is Muḥammad's teaching, as
given in the Traditions (see *Mishkāt*, Arabic
edition ; *Bābu 'n-Nikāḥ*) :—

" That is the most perfect Muslim
whose disposition is the best, and the best of
you is he who behaves best to his wives."

" When a man has two wives and does not
treat them equally, he will come on the Day
of Resurrection with half his body fallen
off."

" When a man calls his wife, she must
come, although she be at an oven."

" The Prophet used to divide his time
equally amongst his wives, and he would
say, ' O God, I divide impartially that which
thou hast put in my power.'"

" Admonish your wives with kindness, because women were created from a crooked
bone of the side ; therefore, if you wish to
straighten it, you will break it, and if you let
it alone, it will always be crooked."

" Not one of you must whip his wife like
whipping a slave."

" A Muslim must not hate his wife, for
if he be displeased with one bad quality in
her, then let him be pleased with another that
is good."

" A Muslim cannot obtain anything
better than an amiable and beautiful wife,
such a wife who, when ordered by her husband to do a thing, will obey, and if her husband looks at her will be happy ; and if her
husband swears by her, she will make him a
swearer of truth ; and if he be absent from her,
she will honour him with her own person and
property."

It is related that on one occasion the Prophet said : " Beat not your wives." Then
'Umar came to the Prophet and said, " Our
wives have got the upper hand of their husbands from hearing this." Then the Prophet
permitted beating of wives. Then an immense number of women collected round the
Prophet's family, and complained of their
husbands beating them. And the Prophet
said, " Verily a great number of women are
assembled in my home complaining of their
husbands, and those men who beat their
wives do not behave well. He is not of my
way who teaches a woman to go astray and
who entices a slave from his master."

The legal position of a wife under Sunnī,
and, with some slight differences, under Shī'ah
law also, may be generally stated as follows :—

Her consent to a marriage is necessary.
She cannot legally object to be one of four
wives. Nor can she object to an unlimited
number of hand-maids. She is entitled to a
marriage settlement or dower, which must be
paid to her in case of divorce or separation.
She may, however, remit either whole or part
of the dower. She may refuse to join her
husband until the dower is paid. She may be
at any time, with or without cause, divorced
by her husband. She may seek or claim
divorce (*khul'*) from her husband with her
husband's consent. She may be chastised by
her husband. She cannot give evidence
in a court of law against her husband. According to the Sunnīs, her evidence in favour
of her husband is not admissible, but the
Shī'ahs maintain the opposite view. Her
husband can demand her seclusion from public.
If she becomes a widow, she must observe
ḥidād, or mourning, for the space of four
months and ten days. In the event of her
husband's death, she is entitled to a portion
of her husband's estate, in addition to her
claim of dower, the claim of dower taking
precedence of all other claims on the estate.

There are special arrangements made by
Muslim law for the partition of the husband's
time amongst his wives in case he may have
two or more wives. For it is related that
Muḥammad said, " The man who has two or
more wives, and who, in partition of his time,
inclines particularly to one of them, shall in
the Day of Judgment incline to one side by
being paralytic." And 'Āyishah relates that
the Prophet said, " O God, I make an equal
partition amongst my wives as to what is in
my power ; do not, therefore, bring me to
account for that which is not in my power,
namely, the affections." It is therefore ruled
that the wife of a prior marriage and of a
recent one, are all alike in the matter of the
partition of time spent with them. The husband can, however, arrange and determine
the measure of the partition of his time as
to whether it be one day or more at a time.
But if a man marry two wives, the one a free
woman and the other a bond-maid, he must
divide his time into three portions, giving
two portions to the free woman and one to
the bond-maid. When the husband is on a
journey, his wives can make no claim to accompany him on the journey, and it is entirely
at his option to carry along with him whomsoever he pleases, but it is preferable for him
to cast lots and take with him on the journey
her upon whom the lot may happen to fall.
The time of the journey is not to be counted
against a husband, and he is therefore not
obliged to make up for the partition lost
within that time. It is also allowed by the

law, of one wife to give up her right as regards partition of time to any other of her husband's wives. But if a woman give up her right, she is not at liberty to resume it. *Durru 'l-Mukhtār, in loco.*)

The position of a wife as regards the law of divorce, is treated under the article DIVORCE.

We are indebted to Moulvi Syed Ameer Ali, M.A., LL.B., a Muhammadan Barrister-at-Law, and Presidency Magistrate of Calcutta, for the following able exposition of the position of wives under the Muslim law:—

"Prior to the Islâmic legislation, and especially among the pagan Arabs, women had no *locus standi* in the eye of the law. The pre-Islâmic Arab customs as well as the Rabbinical law, dealt most harshly with them. (3 Caussin de Perceval, *Hist. des. Arabes*, p. 337.)

"The Koran created a thorough revolution in the condition of women. For the first time in the history of Oriental legislation, the principle of equality between the sexes was recognised and practically carried into effect. 'The women,' says the Koran, 'ought to behave towards their husbands in like manner as their husbands should behave towards them, according to what is just.' (Koran, chap. ii., v. 228.) And Mohammed in his discourse on *Jabl-i-Arafât*, emphasised the precept by declaring in eloquent terms, 'Ye men, ye have rights over your wives, and your wives have rights over you.' (Ibn Hishâm.) In accordance with these precepts the Mahommedan law declares *equality* between the married parties to be the regulating principle of all domestic relationship. Fidelity to the marriage bed is inculcated on both sides; and unfaithfulness leads to the same consequences, whether the delinquent be the husband or the wife. Chastity is required equally from man and woman.

"The husband is legally bound to maintain his wife and her domestic servants, whether she and her servants belong to the Moslem faith or not. This obligation of the husband comes into operation when the contract itself comes into operation, and the wife is subjected thereby to the marital control. It continues in force during the conjugal union, and in certain cases even after it is dissolved.

"The maintenance (*nafkah*) of a wife includes everything connected with her support and comfort, such as food, raiment, lodging, &c., and must be provided in accordance with the social position occupied. (1 *Fatâwa-i-Alamgîrî*, p. 737; 1 *Fatâwa-i-Kâzi Khân*; *Jâma-ush-Shattât*; *Fusûl-Imâdiyah*; *Mafâtîh*; 1 *Hed.*, Eng. Trans., p. 392.)

"The wife is not entitled merely to maintenance in the English sense of the word, but has a right to claim a habitation for her own exclusive use, to be provided consistently with the husband's means.

"If the wife, however, is a minor, so that the marriage cannot be consummated, according to the Hanafî and the Shiah doctrines, there is no legal obligation on the husband's part to maintain her. (1 *Fatâwa-i-Alumgîrî*, p. 773; *Kanz-ud-Dakâik*; 1 *Hed.*, Eng. Trans., p. 394; *Jâma-ush-Shattât.*)

"With the Shâfeïs it makes no difference, in the obligation of the husband to maintain his wife, whether the wife be a minor or not. (*Kitâb-ul-Anwâr*; 1 *Hed.*, Eng. Trans., p. 394.)

"Nor is a husband, under the Hanafî and the Shiah law, entitled to the custody of the person of a minor wife whom he is not *bound* to maintain. (In *re* Khatija Bibi, 5 *Bengal Law Reports*, O. C. J. 557.)

"If the husband be a minor and the wife an adult, and the incapacity to complete or consummate the contract be solely on his part, she is entitled to maintenance. (1 *Hed.*, Eng. Trans., p. 395; *Fusûl-i-Imâdiyah*; 1 *Fatâwa-i-Kâzi Khân*, p. 480; *Jâma-ush-Shattât.*)

"It makes no difference in the husband's liability to maintain the wife whether he be in health or suffering from illness, whether he be a prisoner of war or undergoing punishment, 'justly or unjustly,' for some crime, whether he be absent from home on pleasure or business, or gone on a pilgrimage. (1 *Fatâwa-i-Alamgîrî*, p. 733.) In fact, as long as the status of marriage subsists, and as long as the wife is subject to the marital power, so long she is entitled to maintenance from him. Nor does she lose her right by being afflicted with any disease. (1 *Fatâwa-i-Alamgîrî*, p. 734; *Jâma-ush-Shattât.*)

"When the husband has left the place of the conjugal domicil without making any arrangement for his wife's support, the Kazi is authorised by law to make an order that her maintenance shall be paid out of any fund or property which the husband may have left in deposit or in trust, or invested in any trade or business. (1 *Fatâwa-i-Alamgîrî*, p. 750.)

"A wife may contract debts for her support during the husband's absence, and if such debts are legitimate, contracted *bonâ fide* for her support, the creditors have a "right of recovery" against the husband. (*Nail-ul-Marâm.*) In the same way, if the husband be unable for the time being to maintain his wife, 'it would not form a cause for separation,' says the *Hedayah*, 'but the magistrate may direct the woman to pledge her husband's credit and procure necessaries for herself, the husband remaining liable for the debts.' (1 *Hed.*, Eng. Trans., p. 297.)

"When the husband is absent and has left real property either in the possession of his wife or of some other person on her behalf, the wife is not entitled to sell it for her support, though she may raise a temporary loan on it, which the husband will be bound to discharge, provided the mortgage was created *bonâ fide* for her or her children's support, and did not go beyond the actual necessity of the case. Under such circumstances the mortgagee is bound to satisfy himself that the money advanced is applied legitimately to the support of the family of the absent husband. (1 *Fatâwa-i-Alamgîrî*, p. 737.)

"When the woman abandons the conjugal domicil without any valid reason, she is not entitled to maintenance. (1 *Fatâwa-i-Alamgîrî*, p. 733; *Fusûl-i-Imâdiyah*; *Jâma-ush-Shattât*.) Simple refractoriness, as has been popularly supposed, does not lead to a forfeiture of her right. If she live in the house but do not obey the husband's wishes, she would not lose her right to her proper maintenance. If she leave the house against his will without any valid reason, she would lose her right, but would recover it on her return to the conjugal domicil. (*Fatâwa-i-Alamgîrî*; *Jâma-ush-Shattât*; *Kitâb-min lâ-Euhazzar al-Fakîh*.)

" What is a valid and sufficient reason for the abandonment of the conjugal domicil is a matter for the discretion of the Kazi or judge. As a general principle and one which has been adopted and enforced by the Kazis' *mahkamas* in Algeria, a wife who leaves her husband's house on account of his or his relations' continued ill-treatment of her, does not come within the category of *nâshizah* and continues entitled to her maintenance.

" A woman who is imprisoned for some offence, or is undergoing incarceration in the civil jail for non-payment of a debt, or who goes on a voyage or pilgrimage without her husband's consent, has no right to claim any maintenance during her absence. (1 *Fatâwa-i-Alamgîrî*, p. 734.)

" Among the Shiahs, if she goes on an *obligatory* pilgrimage, even without her husband's consent, she is nevertheless entitled to maintenance.

" The husband's liability to support the wife continues during the whole period of probation, if the separation has been caused by any conduct of his, or has taken place in exercise of a right possessed by her. The husband would not, however, be liable to support the wife during the *iddat*, if the separation is caused by her misconduct. (*Fatâwa-i-Alamgîrî*, p. 746; *Jâma-ush-Shattât*: 1 *Fatâwa-i-Kâzi Khân*, p. 481.

" If she is pregnant at the time of separation her right remains intact until she is confined of the child.

" The *Hedâya* seems to imply that a woman is not entitled to maintenance during the period of probation she observes on the death of her husband. (1 *Hed.* p. 407.) As the Koran, however, distinctly says, 'Such of you as shall die and leave wives ought to bequeath to them a year's maintenance,' several jurists have held that a widow has a right to be maintained from the estate of her husband for a year, independently of any share she may obtain in the property left by him. This right would appertain to her whether she be a Moslemah or non-Moslemah.

" In the case of probation (*iddat*) observed by a woman on the death of her husband, the Sunnis calculate the period from the actual date of his decease; the Shiahs from the day on which the wife receives the news of the death.

" According to the Sunnis, the liability of the husband to maintain a pregnant wife from whom he has separated ceases at her confinement. (1 *Hed.* p. 360.) The Shiahs, on the other hand, hold that the liability lasts for the same period after confinement as if the woman was not *enceinte*. (*Jâma-ush-Shattât*.)

" If the husband be insane, the wife is entitled, according to the Shâfeï doctrines and the views of the compilers of the *Fatâwa-i-Alamgîrî*, to maintenance for the period of one year, which is fixed by the Kazi in order to discover whether the insanity is curable or not. The Mâlikis, with whom the author of the *Hedâya* seems to agree, deny to the wife the right of asking for a dissolution of the marriage tie on the ground of the husband's insanity. Among them the wife, therefore, retains the right of maintenance during the insanity of her husband, however long continued. With the Shiahs the wife is entitled to a cancellation of the marriage contract if the husband's insanity be incurable. Should she exercise this right and dissolve the marriage, her right to maintenance ceases.

" The Mahommedan law lays down distinctly (1) that a wife is bound to live with her husband, and to follow him wherever he desires to go; (2) and that on her refusing to do so without sufficient or valid reason, the courts of justice, on a suit for restitution of conjugal rights by the husband, would order her to live with her husband.

" The wife cannot refuse to live with her husband on pretexts like the following:—

" (1.) That she wishes to live with her parents.

" (2.) That the domicil chosen by the husband is distant from the home of her father.

" (3.) That she does not wish to remain away from the place of her birth.

" (4.) That the climate of the place where the husband has established his domicil is likely to be injurious to her health.

" (5.) That she detests her husband.

" (6.) That the husband ill-treats her frequently (unless such ill-treatment is actually proved, which would justify the Kazi to grant a separation).

" The obligation of the woman, however, to live with her husband is not absolute. The law recognises circumstances which justify her refusal to live with him. For instance, if he has habitually ill-treated her, if he has deserted her for a long time, or if he has directed her to leave his house or even connived at her doing so, he cannot require her to re-enter the conjugal domicil or ask the assistance of a court of justice to compel her to live with him. The bad conduct or gross neglect of the husband is, under the Mussulman law, a good defence to a suit brought by him for restitution of conjugal rights.

" In the absence of any conduct on the husband's part justifying an apprehension that, if the wife accompanied him to the place chosen by him for his residence, she would be at his mercy and exposed to his violence, she is bound by law to accompany him wherever he goes. At the same time the law recognises the validity of express stipulations, entered into at the time of marriage, respecting the conjugal domicil. If it be agreed that the husband shall allow his wife to live always with her parents, he cannot afterwards force her to leave her father's house for his own. Such stipulation in order to be practically carried into effect, *must* be entered in the deed of marriage; a mere verbal understanding is not sufficient in the eye of the law.

"If the wife, however, once consent to leave the place of residence agreed upon at the time of marriage, she would be presumed to have waived the right acquired under express stipulation, and to have adopted the domicil chosen by the husband. If a special place be indicated in the deed of marriage as the place where the husband should allow the wife to live, and it appear subsequently that it is not suited for the abode of a respectable woman, or that injury is likely to happen to the wife if she remain there, or that the wife's parents were not of good character, the husband may compel the wife to remove from such place or from the house of such parents.

"The husband may also insist upon his wife accompanying him from one place to another, if the change is occasioned by the requirements of his duty.

"Every case in which the question of conjugal domicil is involved will depend, says De Ménerville, upon its own special features, the general principle of the Mussulman law on the subject being the same as in other systems of law, viz. that the wife is bound to reside with her husband, unless there is any valid reason to justify her refusal to do so. The sufficiency or validity of the reasons is a matter for the consideration of the Kazi or judge, with special regard to the position in life of the parties and the usages and customs of the particular country in which they reside."

Faqīr Jani Muḥammad As'ad, the author of the *Akhlāq-i-Jalālī*, gives the following sage advice, which expresses very much the ordinary Oriental view of the question:—

As regards the Selection of a Wife.

The best of wives would be such an one as is graced with intellect, honour, chastity, good sense, modesty, tenderness of heart, good manners, submission to her husband, and gravity of demeanour. Barren she should not be, but prolific. . . . A free woman is preferable to a bond woman, inasmuch as this supposes the accession of new friends and connections, and the pacification of enemies and the furtherance of temporal interests. Low birth is likewise objectionable on the same account. A young maiden is to be preferred, because she may be expected more readily to attend to her husband's guidance and injunctions; and if she be further graced with the three qualities of family, property, and beauty, she would be the *acmè* of perfection.

To these three qualities, however, sundry dangers may attach; and of these we should accordingly beware. For family engenders conceit; and whereas women are noted for weakness of mind, she will probably be all the slower to submit to the husband's control; nay, at times she will view him in the light of a servant, which must needs prove a perversion of interest, an inversion of relation, and an injury in this world and the next. As to property and beauty, they are liable to the same inconvenience; while in beauty there is this further and peculiar evil, that a beauty is coveted of many; and since women possess less of that judgment which restrains from crime, it may thus lead to mischief without end.

As regards the Management of a Wife.

There are three things to be maintained and three things to be avoided.

Of the three things to be maintained:—

1. *Dignity.*—The husband should constantly preserve a dignified bearing towards her, that she may forbear to slight his commands and prohibitions. This is the primary means of government, and it may be effected by the display of his merits and the concealment of his defects.

2. *Complaisance.*—He is to comply with his wife as far as to assure her of his affection and confidence; otherwise, in the idea of having lost it, she will proceed to set herself in opposition to his will. And this withal, he is to be particular in veiling and secluding her from all persons not of the ḥarīm, in conversing with her in conciliatory terms, and consulting her at the outset of matters in such a manner as to ensure her consent. (*Observe the seclusion and veiling is here put as a compliment rather than a restraint.*)

3. Towards her friends and connections he is to follow the course of deference, politeness, cordiality, and fair dealing, and never, except on proof of her depravity, to take any wife besides her, however superior in family, property and person. For that jealousy and acrimony which, as well as weakness of judgment, is implanted in the nature of women, incites them to misconduct and vice. Excepting, indeed, in the case of kings, who marry to multiply offspring, and to whom the wife has no alternative but obedience, plurality of wives is not defensible. Even in the case of kings, it would be better to be cautious; for husband and wife are like heart and body, and like as one heart cannot supply life to two bodies, one man cannot properly provide for two wives or divide his affection equally between them.

The wife should be empowered to dispose of provisions as occasion may require, and to prescribe to the domestics the duties they are to perform. In order that idleness may not lead her into wrong, her mind should be kept constantly engaged in the transaction of domestic affairs and the superintendence of family interests.

As to the three things to be avoided in a husband towards his wife:—

1. *Excess of affection*, for this gives her the predominance and leads to a state of perversion. When the power is overpowered and the commander commanded, all regularity must infallibly be destroyed. If troubled with redundance of affection, let him at leas conceal it from her.

2. Let him not consult her on matters of paramount importance; let him not make her acquainted with his secrets, nor let her know the amount of his property, or the stores he possesses, beyond those in present consumption, or her weakness of judgment will infallibly set things wrong.

3. Let him allow her no musical instruments, no visiting out of doors, no listening to men's stories, nor intercourse with women noted for such practices; especially where any previous suspicion has been raised.

The particulars which wives should abide by are *five*:—

1. To adhere to chastity.
2. To wear contented demeanour.
3. To consider their husband's dignity and treat them with respect.
4. To submit to their husband's directions.
5. To humour their husbands in their moments of merriment and not to disturb them by captious remarks.

"The Refuge of Revelation (Muḥammad) declared that if the worship of one created thing could be permitted to another, he would have enjoined the worship of husbands. Philosophers have said, 'A good wife is as a mother for affection and tenderness; as a slave-girl for content and attention; as a friend for concord and sincerity. Whilst, on the other hand, a bad wife is as a rebel for unruliness and contumacy; as a foe for contemptuousness and reproach; and as a thief for treacherous designs upon her husband's purse."

The Arab philosophers also say there are five sorts of wives to be avoided: the yearners, the favourers, the deplorers, the backbiters, and the toadstools. The yearner is a widow who has had a child by a former husband, and who will indulge her child out of the property of her present one. The favourer is a woman of property who makes a favour of bestowing it upon her husband. The deplorer is one who is the widow of a former husband whom she will ever aver to be better than her present one. The backbiter is one invested with the robe of continence, and who will ever and anon in his absence brand his blind side by speaking of his faults. The toadstool is an unprincipled beauty, who is like vegetation springing up to corruption. (See *A<u>kh</u>lāq-i-Jalālī*, Thompson's ed., p. 263.)

Mr. Lane, in his *Modern Egyptians*, remarks:—

"Polygamy, which is also attended with very injurious effects upon the morals of the husband and the wives, and only to be defended because it serves to prevent a greater immorality than it occasions, is more rare among the higher and middle classes than it is among the lower orders; and it is not very common among the latter. A poor man may indulge himself with two or more wives, each of whom may be able, by some art or occupation, nearly to provide her own subsistence; but most persons of the middle and higher orders are deterred from doing so by the consideration of the expense and discomfort which they would incur. A man having a wife who has the misfortune to be barren, and being too much attached to her to divorce her, is sometimes induced to take a second wife, merely in the hope of obtaining offspring; and from the same motive, he may take a third, and a fourth; but fickle passion is the most evident and common motive both to polygamy and repeated divorces. They are comparatively very few who gratify this passion by the former practice. I believe that not more than one husband among twenty has two wives.

"When there are two or more wives belonging to one man, the first (that is, the one first married) generally enjoys the highest rank; and is called 'the great lady.' Hence it often happens that, when a man who has already one wife wishes to marry another girl or woman, the father of the latter, or the female herself who is sought in marriage, will not consent to the union unless the first wife be previously divorced. The women, of course, do not approve of a man's marrying more than one wife. Most men of wealth, or of moderate circumstances, and even many men of the lower orders, if they have two or more wives, have, for each, a separate house."

Mrs. Meer Hassan Ali, an Englishwoman who spent twelve years in a Muḥammadan zananah at Lucknow, and who in 1832 published her *Observations on the Musalmans of India*, says:—

"Although he (the Muslim) may be the husband of many wives in the course of time, and some of them prove greater favourites, yet the first wife takes precedence in all matters were dignity is to be preserved. And when several wives meet (each have separate habitations if possible), all the rest pay to the first wife that deference which superiority exacts from inferiors; not only do the secondary wives pay this respect to the first, but the whole circle of relations and friends make the same distinction, as a matter of course; for the first wife takes precedence in every way.

* * * * *

"The latitude allowed by the law preserves the many-wived Musalman from the world's censure; and his conscience rests unaccused when he adds to his numbers, if he cannot reproach himself with having neglected or unkindly treated any of the number bound to him, or their children. But the privilege is not always indulged in by the Musalmans; much depends upon circumstances, and more on the man's disposition. If it be the happy lot of a kind-hearted, good man to be married to a woman of assimilating mind, possessing the needful requirements to render home agreeable, and a prospect of an increasing family, then the husband has no motive to draw him into further engagements, and he is satisfied with one wife. Many such men I have known in Hindustan, particularly among the Sayyuds and religious characters, who deem a plurality of wives a plague to the possessors in proportion to their numbers."

There is a curious work published in Persian, entitled *Kitābi Kulsūm Naneh*, in which are given the maxims regarding wives as they are supposed to exist in Persia. It pretends to be a grave work, compiled under the direction of seven matron law-givers, but is really a specimen of Persian humour, a *jeu d'esprit*, founded upon female customs and superstitions. The work is of little worth as regards its legal value, but shows the popular views of Persian women regarding their own and the opposite sex. The chapter relating to "The Conduct of the Wife to her Husband, Mother-in-Law, and other Relations," is a fair specimen of its character.

"That man is to be praised who confines himself to one wife; for if he takes two it is wrong, and he will certainly repent of his folly. Thus say the seven wise women—

Be that man's life immersed in gloom
  Who weds more wives than one,
With one his cheeks retain their bloom,
  His voice a cheerful tone;
These speak his honest heart at rest,
And he and she are always blest;
But when with two he seeks for joy,
Together they his soul annoy;
With two no sun-beam of delight
Can make his day of misery bright.

"That man, too, must possess an excellent disposition, who never fails to comply with his wife's wishes, since the hearts of women are gentle and tender, and harshness to them would be cruel. If he be angry with her, so great is her sensibility, that she loses her health and becomes weak and delicate. A wife, indeed, is the mirror of her husband, and reflects his character; her joyous and agreeable looks being the best proofs of his temper and goodness of heart. She never of herself departs from the right path, and the colour of her cheeks is like the full-blown rose; but if her husband is continually angry with her, her colour fades, and her complexion becomes yellow as saffron. He should give her money without limit: God forbid that she should die of sorrow and disappointment! in which case her blood would be upon the head of her husband.

"The learned conclave are unanimous in declaring that many instances have occurred of women dying from the barbarous cruelty of their husbands in this respect; and if the husband be even a day-labourer, and he does not give his wages to his wife, she will claim them on the Day of Judgment. It is incumbent on the husband to bestow on the wife a daily allowance in cash, and he must also allow her every expense of feasting, and of excursions, and the bath, and every other kind of recreation. If he has not generosity and pride enough to do this, he will assuredly be punished for all his sins and omissions on the Day of Resurrection. And whenever he goes to the market, he must buy fruit and other little things, and put them in his handkerchief, and take them to his wife, to shew his affection for her, and to please her heart. And if she wishes to undertake a little journey, to go to the house of her friends for a month, to attend the baths, or enjoy any other pastime, it is not fit for the husband to deny those wishes, and distress her mind by refusal. And when she resolves upon giving an entertainment, it is wájib that he should anticipate what she wants, and bring to her all kinds of presents, and food, and wine, required on the festive occasion. And in entertaining her guests, and mixing among them, and doing all that hospitality and cordial friendship demand, she is not to be interrupted or interfered with by her husband saying, 'What have you done? where have you been?' And if her female guests choose to remain all night, they must be allowed to sleep in the woman's room, while the husband sleeps apart and alone. The learned conclave unanimously declare that the woman who possesses such a husband—a man so accommodating and obedient, is truly fortunate; but if he happens to be of an opposite character, morose, disobliging, and irritable, then indeed must she be the most wretched of womankind. In that case she must of necessity sue for a divorce, or make him faithfully promise future obedience and readiness to devote himself wholly to her will and pleasure. If a divorce is denied, she must then pray devoutly to be unburthened of her husband, and that she may soon become a widow. By artifice and manœuvring the spouse may thus be at length induced to say: 'Do, love, whatever you please, for I am your dutiful slave.' Bíbí Ján Afróz says, 'A woman is like a nosegay, always retaining its moisture so as never to wither.' It is not, therefore, proper that such a lovely object should be refused the comfort and felicity of taking pleasant walks in gardens with her friends, and manifesting her hospitality to her guests; nor is it reasonable that she should be prevented from playing on the dyra, and frequently visiting her acquaintance.

"Should her husband, however, maliciously and vexatiously refuse these rights, she cannot remain longer in his house. An old or ugly woman does not lie under the same obligation; she may submit to any privation without infringing the rules of decorum. The conclave also declare that the husband's mother, and other relations, are invariably inimical to the wife: it is therefore wájib that she should maintain her authority when thwarted in her views, by at least once a day using her fists, her teeth, and kicking, and pulling their hair, till tears come into their eyes, and fear prevents further interference with her plans. Kulsúm Naneh says that she must continue this indomitable spirit of independence until she has fully established her power, and on all occasions she must ring in her husband's ears the threat of a divorce. If he still resists, she must redouble all the vexations which she knows from experience irritate his mind, and day and night add to the bitterness and misery of his condition. She must never, whether by day or by night, for a moment relax. For instance, if he condescends to hand her the loaf, she must throw it from her, or at him, with indignation and contempt. She must make his shoe too tight for him, and his pillow a pillow of stone: so that at last he becomes weary of life, and is glad to acknowledge her authority. On the other hand, should these resources fail, the wife may privately convey from her husband's house everything valuable that she can lay her hands upon, and then go to the Kází, and complain that her husband has beaten her with his shoe, and pretend to shew the bruises on her skin. She must state such facts in favour of her case as she knows cannot be refuted by evidence, and pursue every possible plan to escape from the thraldom she endures. For that purpose, every effort of every description is perfectly justifiable, and according to law.

"And the seven learned expounders of the customs regarding the conduct and demeanour of women in Persia declare, that among the forbidden things is that of allowing their features to be seen by men not wearing turbans, unless indeed they are handsome, and have soft and captivating manners; in that case their veils may be drawn aside without the apprehension of incurring blame, or in any degree exceeding the discretionary power with which they are traditionally invested. But they must scrupulously and religiously abstain from all such liberties with Múllahs and Jews; since, respecting them, the prohibition is imperative. It is not necessary, however, to be very particular in the presence of common people; there is nothing criminal in being seen by singers, musicians, hammám-servants, and such persons as go about the streets to sell their wares and trinkets." (Atkinson's *Customs and Manners of the Women of Persia*, p. 54.)

WOMEN. Arabic *nisā'* (نساء).

I.—The Condition of Women before the time of Muḥammad.

Although the condition of women under Muslim law is most unsatisfactory, it must be admitted that Muḥammad effected a vast and marked improvement in the condition of the female population of Arabia.

Amongst the Arabs who inhabited the peninsula of Arabia the condition of women was extremely degraded, for amongst the pagan Arabs a woman was a mere chattel. She formed the integral part of the estate of her husband or father, and the widows of a man descended to his son or sons by right of inheritance, as any other portion of patrimony. Hence the frequent unions between step-sons and mothers-in-law, which were subsequently forbidden by Islām, were branded under the name of *Nikāḥu 'l-Maqt*, or "odious marriages."

The pre-Islāmic Arabs also carried their aversion to women so far as to destroy, by burying alive, many of their female children. This fearful custom was common amongst the tribes of Quraish and Kurdah. For although they used to call the angels "daughters of God," they objected (as do the Badāwī to this day) to female offspring, and used to bury their infant daughters alive. This horrible custom is referred to in the Qur'ān, where it is said, Sūrah vi. 138: "Thus have their associates made seemly to many of the idolaters the killing of their children to destroy them." And, again, Sūrah xvi. 60, 61: "When any one of them has tidings of a female child, his face is overclouded and black, and he has to keep back his wrath. He skulks away from the public for the evil tidings he has heard;—is he to keep it in disgrace, or to bury it in the dust?"

It is said the only time on which Usmān shed a tear, was in the days of ignorance, when his little daughter, whom he was burying alive, wiped the dust of the grave-earth from his beard.

The ancient Arabic proverbs illustrate the ideas of pre-Islāmic Arabia as to the position of women, *e.g.*:—

"A man can bear anything but the mention of his wives."

"Women are the whips of Satan."

"Trust neither a king, a horse, nor a woman."

"Our mother forbids us to err and runs into error."

"What has a woman to do with the councils of a nation?"

"Obedience to a woman will have to be repented of."

II.—The Teaching of the Qur'ān.

It has often been asserted by European writers that the Qur'ān teaches that women have no souls. Such, however, is not the case. What that book does teach on the subject of women will be gathered from the following selections:—

Sūrah xxxiii. 35:—

"Verily the resigned men and the resigned women,
The believing men and the believing women,
The devout men and the devout women,
The truthful men and the truthful women,
The patient men and the patient women,
The humble men and the humble women,
The charitable men and the charitable women,
The fasting men and the fasting women,
The chaste men and the chaste women,
And the men and women who oft remember God,
For them hath God prepared forgiveness and a mighty recompense."

Sūrah xxiv. 31:—

"Speak to the believing women that they refrain their eyes, and observe continence; and that they display not their ornaments, except those which are external; and that they throw their veils over their bosoms, and display not their ornaments, except to their husbands or their fathers, or their husbands' fathers, or their sons, or their husbands' sons, or their brothers, or their brothers' sons, or their sisters' sons, or their women, or their slaves, or male domestics who have no natural force, or to children who note not women's nakedness. And let them not strike their feet together, so as to discover their hidden ornaments. (See Isaiah iii. 16.) And be ye all turned to God, O ye Believers! that it may be well with you."

Sūrah lx. 10–12:—

"O Believers! when believing women come over to you as refugees (Muhājirs), then make trial of them. God best knoweth their faith; but if ye have also ascertained their faith, let them not go back to the infidels; they are not lawful for them, nor are the unbelievers lawful for these women. But give them back what they have spent *for their dowers*. No crime shall it be in you to marry them, provided ye give them their dowers. Do not retain any right in the infidel women, but demand back what you have spent *for their dowers*, and let *the unbelievers* demand back what they have spent *for their wives*. This is the ordinance of God which He ordaineth among you: and God is Knowing, Wise.

"And if any of your wives escape from you to the Infidels from whom ye afterwards take any spoil, then give to those whose wives shall have fled away, the like of what they shall have spent *for their dowers*; and fear God in whom ye believe.

"O Prophet! when believing women come to thee, and pledge themselves that they will not associate aught with God, and that they will not steal or commit adultery, nor kill their children, nor bring scandalous charges, nor disobey thee in what is right, then plight thou thy faith to them, and ask pardon for them of God: for God is Indulgent, Merciful!"

Sūrah iv. 1:—

"O Men! fear your Lord, who hath created you of one man (*nafs*, soul), and of him created his wife, and from these twain hath spread abroad so many men and women. And fear ye God, in whose name ye ask mutual favours—and reverence the wombs that bare you. Verily is God watching you!

* * * * *

"And entrust not to the incapable the substance which God hath placed with you as a means of support; but maintain them therewith, and clothe them, and speak to them with kindly speech."

"Men are superior to women on account of the qualities with which God had gifted the one above the other, and on account of the outlay they make from their substance for them. Virtuous women are obedient, careful during the husband's absence, because God hath of them been careful. But chide those for whose refractoriness ye have cause to fear; remove them into sleeping-chambers apart, and scourge them, but if they are obedient to you, then seek not occasion against them; verily God is High, Great!

* * * * *

"And if a wife fear ill-usage or aversion on the part of her husband, then shall it be no fault in them if they can agree with mutual agreement, for agreement is best. Men's souls are prone to avarice, but if ye act kindly and piously, then, verily, your actions are not unnoticed by God!

"And ye may not have it at all in your power to treat your wives with equal justice, even though you fain would do so; but yield not wholly to disinclination, so that ye leave one of them as it were in suspense; if ye come to an understanding and act in the fear of God, then verily, God is Forgiving, Merciful!

"But if they separate, God can compensate both out of His abundance; for God is Vast, Wise!"

Sūrah xxiv. 4–9:—

"They who defame virtuous women, and bring not four witnesses, scourge them with *fourscore* stripes, and receive ye not their testimony for ever, for these are perverse persons—

"Save those who afterwards repent and live virtuously; for truly God is Lenient, Merciful!

"And they who shall accuse their wives, and have no witnesses but themselves, the testimony of each of them shall be a testimony by God four times repeated, that he is indeed of them that speak the truth.

"And the fifth time that the malison of God be upon him, if he be of them that lie.

"But it shall avert the chastisement from her if she testify a testimony four times repeated, by God, that he is of them that lie;

"And a fifth time *to call down* the wrath of God on her, if he have spoken the truth."

III.—The Teaching of Muḥammad, as given in the Traditions,

will be gathered from the following quotations:—

"I have not left any calamity more detrimental to mankind than women."

"A bad omen is found in a woman, a house, or a horse."

"The best women are those that ride on camels, and the virtuous women of the Quraish are those who are affectionate to young children and who are most careful of their husband's property."

"The world and all things in it are valuable, but more valuable than all is a virtuous woman."

"Look to your actions and abstain from

the world and from women, for verily the first sin which the children of Israel committed was on account of women."

"God will reward the Muslim who, having beheld the beauties of a woman, shuts his eyes."

"Do not visit the houses of men when they are absent from their homes, for the devil circulates within you like the blood in your veins. It was said, 'O Prophet, in your veins also?' He replied, 'My veins also. But God has given me power over the devil and I am free from wickedness.'"

"Two women must not sit together, because the one may describe the other to her husband, so that you might say the husband had seen her himself."

"Do not follow up one look at a woman with another; for verily the first look is excusable, but the next is unlawful."

III.—Muḥammadan law secures the following Rights to Women.

An adult woman may contract herself in marriage without her guardian's consent, and an adult virgin cannot be married against her will. When divorced or a widow, she is at liberty to marry a second husband. She must be treated with respect, and it is not lawful for a judge to see more than her face and the palms of her hands. She should go abroad veiled. She is not required to engage in war, although she may be taken by her husband on a military expedition, but she can have no share in the plunder. She is not to be slain in war.

The fine for a woman is half that of a man, and in evidence the testimony of two women is but equal to that of one man, except in the case of a birth, when the evidence of one woman is to be accepted. Her evidence is not accepted in the case of retaliation. [QISAS.] In the event of a person being found slain in the house or village belonging to a woman, the oath (in the matter of evidence) is administered to her fifty times repeatedly before the fine is imposed. If she apostatize from the faith of Islām, she is not to be put to death, but to be imprisoned until she return to the faith; for although Imām ash-Shāfiʿī maintains that she is to be put to death, Imām Abū Ḥanīfah holds that the Prophet has forbidden the slaying of women, without making any distinction between those who are apostates or those who are original infidels. But, according to an express injunction, they are to be stoned to death for adultery, and beaten for fornication. Women who have no means of subsistence are to be supported by the state.

(The law of divorce is treated under the article DIVORCE.)

It is a curious arrangement of Muslim law, that (according to the *Hidāyah*, Grady's ed., p. 340) a woman may execute the office of a Qāẓī or judge, except in the cases *ḥadd* and *qiṣāṣ*, in conformity with the rule that her evidence is accepted in every legal case except in that of *ḥadd* and *qiṣāṣ*, or "retaliation." There is, in fact, no distinct prohibition against a woman assuming the government of a state. The rulers of the Muḥammadan State of Bhopal in Central India have been women for several generations.

IV.—The Position of Women in Muḥammadan Countries

has been the subject of severe criticism as well as of some controversy. Mr. Stanley Lane-Poole says:—

"The fatal blot in Islām is the degradation of women. . . . Yet it would be hard to lay the blame altogether on Moḥammad. The real roots of the degradation of women lie much deeper. When Islām was instituted, polygamy was almost necessitated by the number of women and their need of support; and the facility of divorce was quite necessitated by the separation of the sexes, and the consequence that a man could not know or even see the woman he was about to marry before the marriage ceremony was accomplished. It is not Moḥammad whom we must blame for these great evils, polygamy and divorce; it is the state of society which demanded the separation of the sexes, and in which it was not safe to allow men and women freely to associate; in other words, it was the sensual constitution of the Arab that lay at the root of the matter. Moḥammad might have done better. He might boldly have swept away the traditions of Arab society, unveiled the women, intermingled the sexes, and punished by the most severe measures any license which such association might at first encourage. With his boundless influence, it is possible that he might have done this, and, the new system once fairly settled, and the people accustomed to it, the good effects of the change would have begun to show themselves. But such an idea could never have occurred to him. We must always remember that we are dealing with a social system of the seventh century, not of the nineteenth. Moḥammad's ideas about women were like those of the rest of his contemporaries. He looked upon them as charming snares to the believer, ornamental articles of furniture difficult to keep in order, pretty playthings; but that a woman should be the counsellor and companion of a man does not seem to have occurred to him. It is to be wondered that the feeling of respect he always entertained for his first wife, Khadeejeh, (which, however, is partly accounted for by the fact that she was old enough to have been his mother,) found no counterpart in his general opinion of womankind: 'Woman was made from a crooked rib, and if you try to bend it straight, it will break; therefore treat your wives kindly.' Moḥammad was not the man to make a social reform affecting women, nor was Arabia the country in which such a change should be made, nor Arab ladies perhaps the best subjects for the experiment.

Still he did something towards bettering the condition of women: he limited the number of wives to four; laid his hand with the utmost severity on the incestuous marriages that were then rife in Arabia; compelled husbands to support their divorced wives during their four months of probation; made irrevocable divorce less common by adding the rough, but deterring, condition that a woman triply divorced could not return to her husband without first being married to some one else—a condition exceedingly disagreeable to the first husband; and required four witnesses to prove a charge of adultery against a wife—a merciful provision, difficult to be fulfilled. The evil permitted by Moḥammad in leaving the number of wives four instead of insisting on monogamy was not great. Without considering the sacrifice of family peace which the possession of a large harem entails, the expense of keeping several wives, each of whom must have a separate suite of apartments or a separate house, is so great, that not more than one in twenty can afford it. It is not so much in the matter of wives as in that of concubines that Moḥammad made an irretrievable mistake. The condition of the female slave in the East is indeed deplorable. She is at the entire mercy of her master, who can do what he pleases with her and her companions; for the Muslim is not restricted in the number of his concubines, as he is in that of his wives. The female white slave is kept solely for the master's sensual gratification, and is sold when he is tired of her, and so she passes from master to master, a very wreck of womanhood. Her condition is a little improved if she bear a son to her tyrant; but even then he is at liberty to refuse to acknowledge the child as his own, though it must be owned he seldom does this. Kind as the Prophet was himself towards bondswomen, one cannot forget the unutterable brutalities which he suffered his followers to inflict upon conquered nations in the taking of slaves. The Muslim soldier was allowed to do as he pleased with any 'infidel' woman he might meet with on his victorious march. When one thinks of the thousands of women, mothers and daughters, who must have suffered untold shame and dishonour by this license, he cannot find words to express his horror, And this cruel indulgence has left its mark on the Muslim character, nay, on the whole character of Eastern life." (*Selections from the Kur-án*, 2nd ed., Preface.)

The strict legislation regarding women as expressed in Muḥammadan law, does not affect their position amongst wild and uncivilized tribes. Amongst them she is as free as the wild goats on the mountain tops. Amongst the Afreedees in the Afghān hills, for example, women roam without protection from hill to hill, and are engaged in tending cattle and other agricultural pursuits. If ill-treated by their husbands, they either demand divorce or run away to some neighbouring tribe. Not a few of the tribal feuds arise from such circumstances.

Amongst the Bedouins (*Badāwīs*), Mr. Palgrave tells us, their armies are led by a maiden of good family, who, mounted amid the fore ranks on a camel, shames the timid and excites the brave by satirical or encomiastic recitations. (*Arabia*, vol. ii. p. 71.)

The influence which Afghān women have exercised upon Central Asian politics has been very great, and, as we have already remarked, the Muḥammadan State of Bhopal in Central India has for several generations past been governed by female sovereigns. [CONCUBINES, DIVORCE, MARRIAGE, WIVES.]

WORD OF GOD. [INSPIRATION, OLD AND NEW TESTAMENTS, PROPHETS, QUR'AN.]

WOUNDS. Arabic *shijāj* (شجاج), pl. of *shajjah*. The Muḥammadan law only treats of wounds on the face and head, all other wounds being compensated for by arbitrary atonement.

According to the *Hidāyah*, *shijāj* are of ten kinds:—

Ḥāriṣah, a scratch, such as does not draw blood.

Dāmi'ah, a scratch which draws blood without causing it to flow.

Dāmiyah, a scratch which causes the blood to flow.

Bāẓi'āh, a cut through the skin.

Mutalāḥimah, a cut into the flesh.

Simḥāq, a wound reaching to the pericranium.

Mūṣiḥah, a wound which lays bare the bone.

Hāshimah, a fracture of the skull.

Munaqqilah, a fracture which requires part of the skull to be removed.

Āmmah, a wound extending to the membrane which encloses the brain.

According to the injunctions of the Prophet, a twentieth of the complete fine for murder is due for *mūṣiḥah*; a tenth for *hāshimah*; three-twentieths for *munaqqilah*; and a third for *āmmah*. All other fines are left to the discretion of the judge.

WRITING. Arabic *'Ilmu 'l-Khaṭṭ* (علم الخط). Sir William Muir, in the Introduction of his *Life of Mahomet*, writes on this subject as follows:—

"De Sacy and Caussin de Perceval concur in fixing the date of the introduction of Arabic writing into Mecca at A.D. 560 (*Mém. de l'Acad.*, vol. l. p. 306; C. de Perc., vol. i. p. 294.) The chief authority is contained in a tradition given by Ibn Khallicân, that the Arabic system was invented by Morâmir at Anbar, whence it spread to Hira. It was thence, shortly after its invention, introduced into Mecca by Harb, father of Abû Sofiân, the great opponent of Mahomet. (*Ibn Khallicân*, by Slane, vol. ii. p. 284.) Other traditions give a later date; but M. C. de Perceval reconciles the discrepancy by referring them rather to the subsequent arrival of some zealous and successful teacher than to the first introduction of the art (vol. i. p. 295). I would observe that either the above traditions are erroneous, or that some sort of writing other than Arabic must have been known long before the date specified, *i.e.* A.D. 560. Abd al Muttalib is described as *writing* from Mecca to his maternal relatives at Medîna for help, in his younger days, *i.e.* about A.D. 520. And still farther back, in the middle of the fifth century, Cussei (*Quṣaiy*) addressed a *written* demand of a similar tenor to his brother in Arabia Petræa. (*Kâtib al Wâckidi*, 11½; *Tabari*, 18, 28.)

"The Himyar or Musnad writing is said by Ibn Khallicân to have been confined to Yemen; but the verses quoted by C. de Perceval (vol. i. p. 295) would seem to imply that it had at one period been known and used by the Meccans, and was in fact *supplanted* by the Arabic. The Syriac and Hebrew were also known and probably extensively used in Medîna and the northern parts of Arabia from a remote period.

"In fine, whatever the system employed may have been, it is evident that writing of some sort was known and practised at Mecca long before A.D. 560. At all events, the frequent notices of written papers leave no room to doubt that Arabic writing was well known, and not uncommonly practised, there in Mahomet's early days. I cannot think, with Weil, that any great 'want of writing materials' could have been felt, even 'by the poorer Moslems in the early days of Islam.' (*Mohammed*, p. 350.) Reeds and palm-leaves would never be wanting." (Muir's *Mahomet*, Intro., p. viii.)

The intimate connection of the Arabic alphabet, as it is now in use, with the Hebrew, or rather Phœnician alphabet, is shown not only by the form of the letters themselves, but by their more ancient numerical arrangement, known by the name of Abjad, and described under that head on page 3 of the present work. This arrangement, it will be remembered, is contained in the six meaningless words :—

أَبْجَدْ هَوَّزْ حُطِّي كَلَمَنْ سَعْفَصْ

1 2 3 4 — 5 6 7 — 8 9 10 — 20 30 40 50 — 60 70 80 90

قَرَشَتْ ثَخَذْ ضَظَغْ

100 200 300 400 — 500 600 700 — 800 900 1000

The first six of these words correspond to the Hebrew alphabet, the last two consist of the letters peculiar to Arabic, and it will be seen that the words *abjad*, *hawwaz*, and *ḥuṭṭī* (as we transcribe them according to our system of transliteration), express the nine units, together with ten, *kalaman* and *sa'faṣ*, the tens from twenty to ninety, and *qaraṣhat*, *ṣakhaẓ*, and *ẓaẓagh*, the hundreds together with one thousand.

The present arrangement of the Arabic alphabet, in the form which the letters take as finals, is the following :—

FINALS.

Order.	Reduced Order.	Separate.	Joined.	Transliteration.
1	1	ا	ـا	a (i, u)
2		ب	ـب	b
3	2	ت	ـت	t
4		ث	ـث	s̤
5		ج	ـج	j
6	3	ح	ـح	ḥ
7		خ	ـخ	kh
8	4	د	ـد	d
9		ذ	ـذ	ẕ
10	5	ر	ـر	r
11		ز	ـز	z
12	6	س	ـس	s
13		ش	ـش	sh
14	7	ص	ـص	ṣ
15		ض	ـض	ẓ
16	8	ط	ـط	ṭ
17		ظ	ـظ	ẓ
18	9	ع	ـع	'
19		غ	ـغ	gh
20	10	ف	ـف	f
21		ق	ـق	q
22	11	ك	ـك	k
23	12	ل	ـل	l
24	13	م	ـم	m
25	14	ن	ـن	n
26	15	ه	ـه	h
27	16	و	ـو	w
28	17	ى	ـى	y

On examining these characters, as represented in the above synopsis, it will at once be seen that, with the exception of the first and the seven last ones, each character stands for two or three sounds, their only distinction consisting in from one to three dots, which are added at the top or bottom of the letter, and that thereby the number of characters is reduced from twenty-eight to seventeen. It will, moreover, be noticed that several of these characters have an appendix or tail, which is well adapted to mark the end of a word, but which would prevent the letter from being readily joined to a following one, and therefore is dispensed with if the letter be initial or connected with others. Suppressing those dots and cutting off these tails, and arranging the characters in their reduced order, and in that form which fits them to appear as initials or medials, we obtain the following simplified schedule :—

INITIALS AND MEDIALS.

Reduced Order.	Final.		Ini-tial.	Me-dial.	Value.
1	ا	ـا	ا	ـا	a (i, u)
2	ٮ	ـٮ	ٮـ	ـٮـ	b, t, s̱
3	ح	ـح	حـ	ـحـ	j, ḥ, kh
4	د	ـد	د	ـد	d, ẕ
5	ر	ـر	ر	ـر	r, z
6	س	ـس	سـ	ـسـ	s, sh
7	ص	ـص	صـ	ـصـ	ṣ, ẓ
8	ط	ـط	طـ	ـطـ	ṭ, ẓ
9	ع	ـع	عـ	ـعـ	‘, gh
10	ڡ	ـڡ	ڡـ	ـڡـ	f, q
11	ك	ـك	كـ	ـكـ	k
12	ل	ـل	لـ	ـلـ	l
13	م	ـم	مـ	ـمـ	m
14	ں	ـں	ٮـ	ـٮـ	n
15	ه	ـه	هـ	ـهـ	h
16	و	ـو	و	ـو	w
17	ى	ـى	ٮـ	ـٮـ	y

A further examination of this reduced list shows, that the characters, 1, 4, 5 and 16, ا, د, ر and و, do not admit of the horizontal prolongation towards the left which serves to connect a letter with a following one, or, in other words, that they can only be joined to a preceding letter, and that the characters 14 and 17, viz. ں and ى, in their initial and medial form, differ from the character *b* only by the superadded dots, and may therefore count for one with it, finally limiting the number of characters to fifteen. Thus the whole Arabic alphabet resolves itself into the four signs

ا د ر و

which can be joined to a preceding letter, but must, even in the middle of a word, remain separate from a following one, and the eleven signs

ٮحسصطعڡكلمه

which can be connected either way.

These, then, are the graphical elements, in their simplest expression, by means of which Arabic, etymologically perhaps the richest language in existence, was originally written, and which were expected to transmit the sacred text of the inspired book to the coming generations. The first in the above series of connectible characters (ٮـ) represents five different sounds, *b*, *t*, *s̱*, *n*, and *y*; the second (حـ) three sounds, *ḥ*, *j*, and *kh*; the next five (سـ, صـ, طـ, عـ, ڡـ), together with د and ر two sounds each, *s* and *sh*, *ṣ* and *ẓ*, *ṭ* and *ẓ*, ‘ and *gh*, *f* and *q*, *d* and *ẕ*, *r* and *z*, respectively, and only five out of the whole number of fifteen (و, مـ, لـ, كـ, ا) are single signs for a single consonantal sound each. As for the vowels, only the long ones, *ā*, *ū*, and *ī*, were in this system of writing graphically expressed, being represented by the so-called weak consonants, ا, و, and ى, which, in this case, act as letters of prolongation. Yet the corresponding short vowels, *a*, *u*, and *i*, were of the utmost importance for the correct reading of a text, for the whole system of Arabic inflection is based upon them, and their faulty employment in the recital of the Qur’ān would frequently lead to grave mistakes, or, at all events, grievously shock the pious and the learned.

So it will be easily understood that the want of additional signs was soon felt, to obviate this double insufficiency of the original alphabet, that is to say, on the one hand to distinguish between letters of the same form but of different sound, and on the other hand to show with what vowel a letter was to be enounced in accordance with the rules of the *I‘rāb* or grammatical inflection.

Accounts differ as to when and by whom these signs were invented and introduced into the sacred as well as the secular writing. We must here at once remark that the form in which they now appear is by no means their oldest form, as we have also, with regard to the characters of the alphabet themselves, to distinguish between two styles of writing, the one called Cufic, used in inscriptions on monuments and coins, in copies of the Qur’ān, and documents of importance, the other of a more cursive character, better adapted to the exigencies of daily life. This latter style, it is true, seems to have existed, like the former, long before Muḥammad, and resembles in a document of the second century of the Hijrah, which has come down to us, already very much the so-called Naskhī character now in use. But the two kept from the first quite apart, and developed independently from each other up to the middle of the fourth century of the Muḥammadan era, when the more popular system began to supplant the older one, which it finally superseded even in the transcriptions of the sacred book.

In tracing the origin of the vowel-marks and the diacritical signs, as we may now call them, in the first instance of the Cufic alphabet, we will follow Ibn Khallikān, whose information on the subject seems the most intelligible and self-consistent that has reached us. In his celebrated biographical dictionary, he relates that Ziyād, a natural brother of the first Umaiyah Khalīfah Mu‘āwiyah, and then Governor of the two ‘Irāqs, directed Abū Aswad ad-Du’ilī, one of the most eminent of the Tābi‘ūn, to compose something to serve as a guide to the public, and enable them to understand "the book of God," meaning thereby a treatise on Grammar, the elements of which Abū Aswad was said to have learned from ‘Alī, the son-in-law of the Prophet himself. He at first asked to be excused, but when he heard a man, on reciting the passage (Sūrah ix. 3): *Anna ’llāha barī’un mina ’l-mushrikīna wa rasūluhu*, pronounce the last word *rasūlihi*, which changes the meaning of the passage from "That God is clear of the idolaters, and His Apostle also," into "That God is clear of the idolators and of His Apostle," he exclaimed, "I never thought that things would have come to such a pass." He then went to Ziyād and said, "I shall do what you ordered; find me an intelligent scribe who will follow my directions." On this a scribe belonging to the tribe of 'Abdu 'l-Qais was brought to him, but did not give him satisfaction: another then came, and 'Abdu 'l-Aswad said to him: "When you see me open (*fataḥ*) my mouth in pronouncing a letter, place a point over it; when I close (*ẓamm*) my mouth, place a point before the letter, and when I pucker up (*kasar*) my mouth, place a point under the letter." Nöldeke, the learned author of *Geschichte des Korans*, rejects this part of the story as a fable, and it is certainly not to be taken in the literal sense, that each time a letter was pronounced, the scribe was supposed to watch the action of the dictater's lips. But it seems reasonable enough to assume that in cases where much depended on the correct vocalisation of a word, and where the reciter would naturally put a particular emphasis on it, Abū Aswad should instruct his amanuensis not to rely upon his ears only in fixing upon the sound, but also call the testimony of his eyes to his aid. At any rate, the name of the vowel-points: *Fatḥah*, "opening," for *a*, *ẓammah*, "contraction," for *u*, and *kasrah*, "fracture" (as the puckering up of the mouth may fitly be called), is well explained, and the notation itself: _•_ for *fatḥah*, •— for *ẓammah* and ‾•‾ for *kasrah*, is that which we still find in some of the old Cufic manuscripts of the Qur'ān marked in red ink or pigment. We refer the reader to the first specimen of Cufic writing given below (p. 687), which he is requested to compare with the transcript in the modern Arabic character and with our Roman transliteration, when he will readily perceive that the points or dots in the Cufic fragment correspond to the short vowels of the transliteration, while, in the Arabic transcript, they serve to distinguish the consonants. Take, for instance, the point above the second letter of the third word, and it will at once be seen that in the Cufic form it expresses the *a* after the *n* of *tanazzalat*, for it recurs again after the *l* in the last syllable, and that in the Naskhī character it distinguishes the *n* (ن) itself from the preceding double-pointed *t* (ت), both which letters remain without a distinctive sign in the Cufic.

To return to Ibn Khallikān: he relates in another place, after Abū Aḥmad al-'Askarī, that in the days of 'Abdu 'l-Malik ibn Marwān, the fifth Khalīfah of the Umaiyah dynasty, the erroneous readings of the Qur'ān had become numerous and spread through 'Irāq. This obliged the governor, al-Ḥajjāj ibn Yūsuf, to have recourse to his *kātibs*, for the purpose of putting distinctive marks on the words of uncertain pronunciation; and it is said that Naṣr ibn 'Āṣim undertook that duty and imagined single and *double* points (*nuqaṭ*, pl. of *nuqṭah*, "drop," "dot"), which he placed in different manners. The people then passed some time without making any copies of the Qur'ān but with points, the usage of which did not, however, prevent some false readings from taking place, and for this reason they invented the I'jām (signs serving to distinguish the letters of the same form from one another), and they thus placed the *i'jām* posteriorly to the *nuqaṭ*.

Primâ facie, this seems to contradict the passage quoted previously, according to which Abū Aswad would be the inventor of the *nuqaṭ* or vowel-points, and the same remark applies to another account of the same author, which we shall adduce presently. Pending our attempt to reconcile the different statements, we notice here two fresh particulars of some importance. For the first time mention is made of *double* points, and we shall scarcely be wrong if we refer this to the way in which the *Nunnation* or *Tanwīn*, that is the sounding of an *n* after the vowels, is expressed in the early writing. It is simply by doubling the vowel-signs in the same position in which the single points are placed: _••_ for *an*, :— for *un*, and ‾••‾ for *in*. Secondly, we meet with the distinct assertion that the invention of the *i'jām* or diacritical signs followed that of the *nuqaṭ* or vowel-points. Nöldeke thinks the reverse more probable, not only because the letter *b* (ب) is found already pointed on coins of 'Abdu 'l-Malik, but also because the diacritical signs are in the ancient manuscripts, like the letters themselves, written with black ink, while the vowel-points are always of a different colour. But the early use of a pointed *b* does not prove that the other letters were similarly marked at the same time. On the contrary, if such a distinction was once established for the *b*, which would be most liable to be confounded with one of its four sister-forms, the other characters of a like shape could for some time dispense with distinctive signs, as for an Arabian reader accustomed to hear, see, and think certain groups of consonants together, and deeply imbued with an instinctive consciousness of the phonetic laws of his language, the danger of mistaking one letter for another would not be by far so great as it appears to us. And as for the argument taken from the different colour of the ink, Nöldeke himself remarks that it was natural to use the same tint for the consonants and their distinctive signs, which form only a part of them, while the vowel-points are an entirely new element.

According to a third tradition, it was Yaḥyā ibn Ya'mar (died A.H. 129) and al-Ḥasan al-Baṣrī (died A.H. 110), by whom al-Ḥajjāj caused the Qur'ān to be pointed, and it is stated that Ibn Shīrīn possessed a copy of it, in which Yaḥyā ibn Ya'mar had marked the vowel points. He was remarkable as a Shī'ah of the primitive class, to use Ibn Khallikān's expression: one of those who, in asserting the superior merit of the *People of the House*, abstained from depreciating the merit of those Companions who did not belong to that family. It is related by 'Āṣim ibn Abī 'n-Najūd, the Qur'ān reader (died A.H. 127), that al-Ḥajjāj summoned Yaḥyā on that account into his presence and thus addressed him:—

"Do you pretend that al-Ḥasan and al-Ḥusain were of the posterity of the Apostle of God? By Allāh, I shall cast to the ground that part of you which has the most hair on it (that is: I shall strike off your head), unless you exculpate yourself." "If I do so," said Yaḥyā, "shall I have amnesty?" "You shall," replied al-Ḥajjāj. "Well," said Yaḥyā, "God, may His praise be exalted! said:

> 'And We gave him (Abraham) Isaac and Jacob, and guided both aright; and We had before guided Noah; and of his posterity, David and Solomon, and Job, and Joseph, and Moses and Aaron: Thus do We reward the righteous: And Zachariah, John, Jesus, and Elias: all were just persons.' (Sūrah vi. 84, 85).

Now, the space of time between Jesus and Abraham is greater than that which separated al-Ḥasan and al-Ḥusain from Muḥammad, on all of whom be the blessing of God and his salvation!" Al-Ḥajjāj answered, "I must admit that you have got out of the difficulty; I read that before, but did not understand it." In the further course of conversation, al-Ḥajjāj said to him: "Tell me if I commit faults in speaking." Yaḥyā remained silent, but as al-Ḥajjāj insisted on having an answer, he at length replied: "O Emir, since you ask me, I must say that you exalt what should be depressed, and depress what should be exalted." This has the *grammatical* meaning: You put in the nominative (*raf'*) what should be in the accusative (*naṣb*), and *vice versâ*; but it is, at the same time an *epigrammatical* stricture on al-Ḥajjāj's arbitrary rulership, which, it is said, won for Yaḥyā the appointment as Qāẓī in Marw, that is to say, a honorary banishment from the former's court.

According to other sources, Yaḥyā had acquired his knowledge of grammar from Abū Aswad ad-Du'ilī. It is related that, when Abū Aswad drew up the chapter on the agent and patient (*fā'il*, subject, and *maf'ūl*, object of the verb), a man of the tribe of Laiṣ made some additions to it, and that Abū Aswad, having found on examination that there existed, in the language of the desert Arabs, some expressions which could not be made to enter into that section, he stopped short and abandoned the work. Ibn Khallikān thinks it possible that this person was Yaḥyā ibn Ya'mar, who, having contracted an alliance by oath with the tribe of Laiṣ, was considered as one of its members. But it is equally possible that the before-mentioned Naṣr ibn 'Āṣim, whose patronymic was al-Laiṣī, may have been that man, and this supposition would enable us to bring the different statements which we have quoted into some harmony. To Abū Aswad the honour can scarcely be contested of having invented the *simple* vowel-points or *nuqaṭ*. Naṣr ibn 'Āṣim, walking in his track, may have added the double points to designate the Tanwīn. Lastly, Yaḥyā would have completed the system by devising the *i'jām*, or diacritical signs of the consonants, and introduced it to a fuller extent into the writing of the Qur'ān, in which task he may have been assisted by al-Ḥasan al-Baṣrī, one of the most learned and accomplished Qur'ān-readers amongst the Tābi'ūn.

But whoever may have been the inventor of the diacritical signs in their earlier form, we must again remark that their shape in Cufic manuscripts, like that of the vowel-points, is essentially different from the dots which are now employed for the same purpose. They have the form of accents (///), or of horizontal lines (═), or of triangular points, either resting on their basis or with their apex turned to the right (▲ ▶). As it cannot be our intention to give here an exhaustive treatise on Arabic writing, we pass over the remaining orthographical signs made use of in the old copies of the Qur'ān, in order to say a few words on the system of notation which is employed in the Naskhī character and our modern Arabic type.

If, with regard to the Cufic alphabet, we have spoken of diacritical signs to distinguish between the consonants, and of vowel-points, we must now reverse these expressions, calling the former diacritical points, the latter vowel-signs. For, as already has been seen from the synopsis of the alphabet on p. 681, the point or dot is there made use of for the distinction of consonants, while the vowels, which in the Greek and Latin alphabets rank as letters equally with the consonants, have no place in that synopsis. As this style of writing was to serve the purposes of daily life, it is probable that the want of some means of fixing the value of the consonants was here more immediately felt, and that therefore the use of points for this end preceded the introduction of the vowel marks, or to speak more accurately, of marks for the short vowels. For the long vowels *ā*, *ī*, and *ū*, were, as in the Cufic writing, also expressed by the weak consonants ا, ى and و taken as letters of prolongation.

When, later on, the necessity arose to represent the short vowels equally in writing, the point or dot, as a distinctive mark, was disposed of, and other signs had to be invented for that purpose. This was accomplished, we are told, by al-Khalīl, the celebrated founder of the Science of Arabic Prosody and Metric. His device was simply to place the abbreviated form of the before-mentioned weak consonants themselves above or beneath the letter after which any short vowel was to be pronounced. The origin of the *ẓammah* or *u* (ـُ) from the و is at once evident. The sign for the *fatḥah* or *a* (ـَ) differs only by its slanting position from the form which the ا assumes frequently in such words as ﷲ for الله; and the *kasrah* or *i* (ـِ) is derived from the bend towards the right which the letter ى takes in its older shape (ے). The Tanwīn was then, as in the Cufic writing, expressed by doubling the signs for the simple vowels: ـً for *an*, ـٌ or ـٌ for *un*, and ـٍ for *in*.

There remains a third set of signs supplementary to the Arabic alphabet, which may be called orthographical signs, and which, in their present form, were probably also invented and introduced by al-Khalīl; at all events, this is distinctly stated with regard to two of them, the Hamzah and the Tashdīd. The Hamzah, to be well understood, must be considered in connection with the letter *'ain* (ع) of which its sign (ء) is the abbreviated form. If the latter assertion needed proof against the erroneous opinion, put forth by some writers, that the Hamzah is derived from the ى, this proof would be afforded by the following anecdote. The Khalīfah Hārūnu 'r-Rashīd was sitting one day with a favourite negro concubine, called Khāliṣah, when the poet Abū Nuwās entered into his presence and recited some verses in his praise. Absorbed in conversation with the fascinating slave-girl, the Khalīfah paid no attention to the poet, who, leaving him in anger, wrote upon ar-Rashīd's door:—

لقد ضاع شعرى على بابكم كما ضاع عقد على خالصة

Laqad ẓā'a shi'rī 'ala bābikum, kamā ẓā'a 'iqdun 'ala Khāliṣah.

"Forsooth, my poetry *is thrown away* at your door, as the jewels are thrown away on the neck of Khāliṣah."

When this was reported to Hārūn, he ordered Abū Nuwās to be called back. On re-entering the room, Abū Nuwās effaced the final stroke of the ع in the word ضاع (*ẓā'a*, "is lost" or "thrown away"), changing it thereby into ضاء (*ẓā'a*), written with the Hamzah and entirely different in meaning. For when the Khalīfah asked: "What have you written upon the door?" the answer was now:

"Truly, my poetry *sparkles* upon your door, as the jewels *sparkle* on the neck of Khāliṣah."

The fact is, that both the letter *'ain* and the Hamzah are different degrees of the distinct effort, which we all make with the muscles of the throat, in endeavouring to pronounce a vowel without a consonant. In the case of the *'ain*, this effort is so strong for the Arabic organ of speech, that it partakes in itself of the nature of a consonant, and found, as such, from the first, a representative in the written alphabet, while the slighter effort, embodied in the Hamzah, was left to the utterance of the speaker. But when their language became the object of a favourite study with the learned Arabs, this difference not only called for a graphical expression, but led even to a further distinction between what is called *Hamzatu 'l-Qaṭ'* or Hamzah of Disjunction, and *Hamzatu 'l-Waṣl* or Hamzah of Conjunction. We will try shortly to explain this difference.

If we take the word امير *amīr*, "a commander or chief," the initial *a* remains the same, whether the word begins the sentence or is preceeded by another word: we say أميرٌ قال *amīrun qāla*, "a commander said" (according to the Arabic construction literally "*as for* a commander, he said"), as well as قال أميرٌ *qāla amīrun*, "there said a commander" (in Arabic literally "he said, *namely*, a commander"). Here the Hamzah (ء), with the *Alif* (ا) as its prop and the *fatḥah* or *a* as its vowel, is called *Hamzatu 'l-Qaṭ'*, because in the latter case it disjoins or cuts off, as it were, the initial *a* of the word *amīrun* from the final *a* of the word *qāla*; and the same holds good if the Hamzah is pronounced with *i*, as in إمارة *imārah*, "commandership," or with *u*, as in أمراء *umarā'*, "commanders," plural of *amīr*. But it would be otherwise with the *a* of the article أل *al*, if joined with the word *amīr*. In الأميرُ قال *al-amīru qāla*, "the commander said," it would preserve its original sound, because it begins the sentence; but if we invert the order of words, we must drop it in pronunciation altogether, and only sound the final *a* of *qāla* instead, thus: *qāla 'l-amīru*, "said the commander," and the same would take place if the preceding word terminated in another vowel, as *yaqūlu 'l-amīru*, "says the commander," or *bi-qauli 'l-amīri*, "by the word of the commander." Here the Hamzah would no longer be written ـَٔ but ـٱ (قال ٱلأمير, etc.), and would be called *Hamzatu 'l-Waṣl* or *Hamzatu 'ṣ-Ṣilah*, because it joins the two words together in closest connection.

In the article, as it has been stated above, and in the word *aimān*, "oath," the original sound of the *Hamzatu 'l-Waṣl* is *fathah*, *a*; it occurs besides in a few nouns, in several derived forms of the verb, and in the Imperative of the primitive triliteral verb, in all of which cases it is sounded with *kasrah* or *i*, except in the Imperative of those triliteral verbs whose aorist takes *ẓammah* or *u* for the vowel of the second radical, where the Hamzah is also pronounced with *ẓammaḥ* (أُسكُتْ *uskut*, "be silent"). But the reader must always keep in mind that it preserves this original pronunciation only at the beginning of a sentence; if it is preceded by any other word, the final vowel of that preceding word takes the place of the Hamzah, and if this word terminates in a consonant, the Hamzah is generally pronounced with *i*. We say *generally*, because the only exceptions are after the preposition مِن *min*, where it is sounded with *a*, and after the pronominal affixes of the second and third person plural, كُمْ *kum* and هُمْ *hum*, where it takes *u*.

We can pass over more rapidly the other signs of this class, which are the Maddah, the Tashdīd, and the Jazmah or Sukūn. If in consequence of any grammatical operation an Alif, as prop of a Hamzah sounded with *fatḥah*, comes to stand before another such Alif, we write آ, pronounced *ā*, instead of أأ, and the upper horizontal sign is called Maddah or Madd, "lengthening," "prolongation." While thus the Maddah is the sign for the doubling of an Alif, the Tashdīd (ـّ is the sign for the doubling of a consonant (بّ=*bb*). If, lastly, a consonant is not to be followed by a vowel, the sign ـْ or ـْ, named Jazmah (cutting off) or Sukūn (rest), is placed above it, and the consonant is called "quiescent" (*sākinah*), in contradistinction from a "moved" consonant (*muḥarrakah*), that is, one sounded with a vowel (*ḥarakah*, "motion").

We have seen that the Hamzatu 'l-Qaṭ' (ـٔ) is an abbreviated form of the letter 'Ain (ع). In similar manner, the sign for the Hamzatu 'l-Waṣl or Hamzatu 's-Ṣilah (ـٱ) is an abbreviated form of the initial ص (*ṣ*) of the word Ṣilah. The sign for the Maddah (ـٓ), as written in old manuscripts, seems to be a stretched out form for the word Madd (مد) itself, and the sign for the Tashdīd (ـّ) represents the initial ش of the word Shiddah, which is the technical term for it. The original sign for the Jazmah (ـْ) is the cypher or zero, employed to indicate the *absence* of a vowel sound. A native Arab scholar of our days, the late Nāṣif al-Yazijī of Beyrout, has combined the vowel marks as well as the last-mentioned orthographical signs in the words:

أَخُطُّ ٱلْهِجَاءَ

Akhuṭṭu 'l-hijā'a.

"I write out the Alphabet,"

and these words, together with the two formulas given on page 682 (ادرو and يحسطمصكلقه), and the dot as a diacritical sign, contain the whole system of Arabic writing, as it were, in a nut-shell.

However indispensable these various supplementary signs may seem to us for fixing the meaning of an Arabic text, educated Arabs themselves look at them in a different light. Although the need for them was from the first most urgently felt for the purpose of securing the correct reading of the Qur'ān, several of the learned doctors of early Islām strongly opposed their introduction into the sacred book as a profane innovation. The great Sunnī traditionist, Mālik ibn Anas (died A.H. 179), prohibited their use in the copies employed at the religious service in the mosque (*ummahātu 'l-maṣāḥif*), and allowed them only in the smaller copies, destined for the instruction of the young in schools. In course of time, however, when even the office of reading the Qur'ān publicly more and more frequently devolved upon persons who had not received a special theological training, the necessity of carefully marking the text with these signs all through went on increasing, and became at last a generally acknowledged principle. In secular literature and in epistolary intercourse amongst the educated, on the contrary, their use should, according to the competent authorities, be limited to those cases where ambiguity is to be apprehended from their omission. If there is no danger of miscomprehension, we are told by Ḥājī Khalīfah, it is preferable to omit them, especially in addressing persons of consequence and refinement, whom it would be impolite not to suppose endued with a perfect knowledge of the written language. Moreover, to a chastened taste, a superabundance of those extraneous signs seems to disfigure the graceful outline of the Arabic character. When a piece of highly elaborate penmanship was presented to 'Abdu 'llāh ibn Ṭāhir, the accomplished governor of Khūrasān under the Abbaside Khalīfah al-Ma'mūn, he exclaimed, "How beautiful this would be if there were not so much coriander seed scattered over it." The diacritical points of the consonants, of course, are now always added, for they have grown to be considered as integral elements of the alphabet itself. Their absence, or their accidental misapplication, gave rise, in former times, to numberless ludicrous or serious perplexities and mistakes, instances of which abound in Muḥammadan history. Al-Balādorī, *e.g.*, relates that the poet al-Farazdaq (died A.H. 110) interceded by letter with Tamīm, governor of the boundaries of Sind, in order to obtain release from military service for the son of a poor woman of the tribe of Ṭaiy. The youth's name was Ḥubaish (حبيش); but as the diaritical points were not marked in al-Farazdaq's letter, Tamīm was at a loss whether to read Ḥubaish or Khunais (خنيس), and solved the difficulty by sending home all soldiers whose names contained the dubious letters. A more tragical event is recorded by Ḥājī Khalīfah, to which we would fain apply the Italian saying: *Sè non è vero, è ben trovato.* The Khalīfah al-Mutawakkil is said to have sent an order to one of his officials to ascertain the number of Zimmīs in his province, and to report the amount. Unfortunately, "a drop fell," as the Arabic original expresses it, upon the second letter of the word احصى (*aḥṣī*, "count"), and the result was, that the officious functionary submitted the ill-fated Zimmīs to a certain painful and degrading operation, in consequence of which they all died but two.

On the other hand, the employment of these signs in the Qur'ān, together with several others, to mark its division into verses, chapters, sections, and portions of sections, to call attention to the pauses that should be observed in reciting it, and to indicate the number of *rukū'* or inclinations with which the recital is to be accompanied, gave occasion for graphical embellishment of various kinds. Brilliantly coloured ink or a solution of gold to write with, delicately tinted and smoothly pressed pergament or paper, frequently overspread with gold or silver dust, highly finished ornamental designs of that fanciful and elegant description which has received the name of arabesques, such are the means which serve to render the copies of the Qur'ān of the halcyon days of Islām gorgeous and oftentimes artistically beautiful. Writing became indeed an art, diligently cultivated, and eloquently treated upon in prose and verse by its possessors, to whom it opened access to the most exalted positions in the State. Amongst the most celebrated calligraphists are mentioned the Wazīr Muḥammad ibn Alī ibn Muqlah (died A.H. 328), 'Alī ibn Hilāl, surnamed al-Bauwāb (died A.H. 413), and Abū 'd-Durr Yāqūt ibn Yāqūt ibn 'Abdi 'llāh ar-Rūmī al-Must'aṣamī (died A.H. 698), whose father and grandfather had excelled in the art before him, but who, according to Ḥājī K͟halīfah, was never surpassed in it by any of his successors.

It was a natural consequence of the general development of the art of writing, that various styles were invented and cultivated independently of each other, and it will now be our task shortly to speak of the principal varieties, trying to describe their distinguishing features by help of a few illustrations chosen from Bresnier's *Cours de Langue Arabe.* Along with the fundamental distinction already mentioned, of the Cufic or monumental, and the Nask͟hī or manuscript style, there runs, in the first instance, that of the Mag͟hrib-Berber or Western, and Mashriq or Eastern style. It must, however be remarked, that the Western Nask͟hī stands in closer connection and has preserved a greater resemblance with the Western Cufic, than is the case with the Eastern Nask͟hī in reference to the Eastern Cufic, as the reader will scarcely fail to perceive on comparing the following specimens.

The first is the before-mentioned fragment of the Qur'ān, written in the Cufic manuscript style, and provided with the vowel-points as invented by Abū Aswad ad-Du'ilī (or Naṣr ibn 'Āṣim, see page 682). Like the remainder of our specimens, we accompany it with a transcript in modern type, a transliteration in Roman character, and a rendering into English.

No. 1.

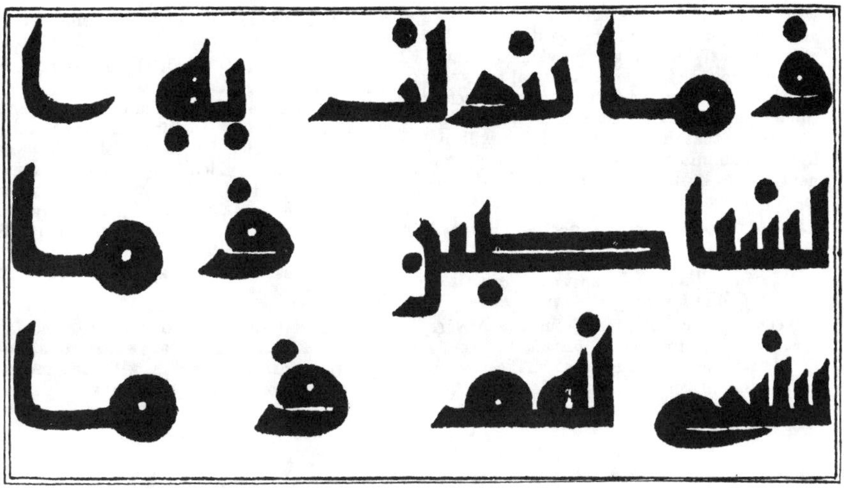

CUFIC MANUSCRIPT CHARACTER.

وَمَا تَنَزَّلَتْ بِهِ آ
لْشَّيَاطِينُ وَمَا
يَنْبَغِى لَهُمْ وَمَا
(يَسْتَطِيعُونَ)

Wa mā tanazzalat bi-hi ash-shayaṭinu wa mā yanbaghī la-hum wa mā (yastaṭī'ūna).

"The Satans were not sent down with it (the Qur'ān): it beseemed them not, and *they had* not *the power.*"

(Sūrah xxvi. 210; the words in italics correspond to the word *yastaṭī'ūna*, which is not contained in the Cufic original.)

The next two specimens illustrate the Cufic style, as it is employed on monuments, and more particularly so its Maghrebian development.

No. 2.

CUFIC MONUMENTAL CHARACTER.

No. 2 is part of an inscription copied from a public building in Tarragona in Spain. It reads :—

بسم الله بركة من الله لعبد الله عبد الرحمن امير المومنين اطال الله (بقاءه)

Bi-smi 'llāhi! barakatun mina 'llāhi li-'abdi 'llāhi 'abdi 'r-raḥmāni amīri 'l-mu'minīna aṭāla 'llāhu (baqā'a-hu).

"In the name of God! May a blessing from God be upon 'Abdillāh 'Abdur-raḥmān, Commander of the Faithful; may God lengthen his life."

No. 3.

MAGHRIB MONUMENTAL CHARACTER.

No. 3, an inscription taken from the Alhambra, exhibits a style of monumental writing which can scarcely be called Cufic any longer, so much resembles it the Naskhī character. While in the previous specimen neither vowel points nor diacritical signs are made use of, here we find them employed in the shape, which they assume in manuscripts written in that hand. The reader will not have much difficulty in tracing the component letters by comparison with the following transcript and transliteration :—

يا وارث الانصار لا عن كلالة تراث جلال تستخف الرواسيا

Yā wāriṣa 'l-anṣāri lā 'an kalālatin turāṣa jalālin tastakhiffu 'r-rawāsiyā.

"O thou who inheritest from the Anṣārs, and not by way of distant kindred, a heirloom of glory that makes every summit of fame appear low."

It will be noticed that the ف (*f*) of the word *tastakhiffu* is left without the diacritical point which distinguishes this letter from the letter ق (*q*). This tallies with a remark of Ḥājī Khalīfah, according to which the diacritical points of these two letters may be put or omitted *ad libitum*; and we seem therefore justified in concluding that the necessity for their distinction was latest felt and provided for. Hence arises one of the peculiarities which at once mark the difference between the Western and Eastern styles of writing, and which the reader will observe in the next three specimens, presenting instances of the Maghrib manuscript character.

The first (No. 4) is written in a bolder hand, and consequently shows more strikingly the close relationship with the monumental style of the Western Arabs.

No. 4.

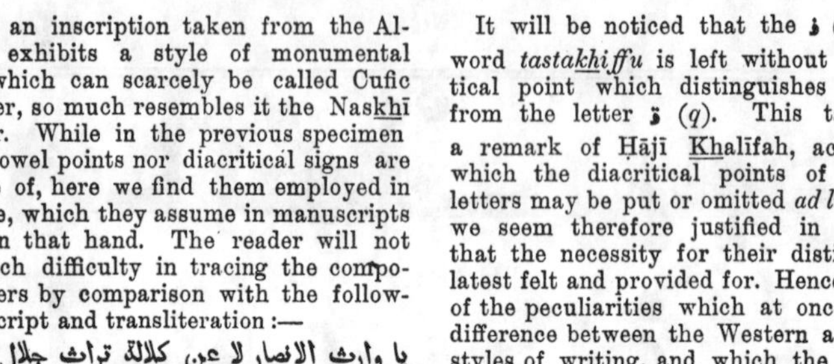

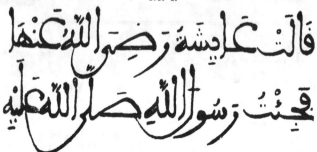

TYPICAL FORM OF THE MAGHRIB MANUSCRIPT CHARACTER

قالت عايشة رضى الله عنها
فجئت رسول الله صلّى الله عليه

Qālat ʻAyishatu raẓiya 'llāhu ʻan-hā
fa-ji'tu rasūla 'llāhi ṣalla 'llāhu ʻalai-hi.

"ʻĀyishah, may God be gracious to her, related:
I went to the Apostle of God, may God's blessing be upon him," &c.

On comparing the initial letter of either line, it will be found that the one is ڧ (in *qālat*), the other ڢ (in *fa-ji'tu*); but in the Maghrebian original, the former is marked by a dot above, the latter by a dot beneath the character, instead of the superscribed double and single point respectively in the transcript. This is the distinguishing feature between the two styles previously alluded to, and it seems to prove that the use of the diacritical points for these two letters is of later origin, and dates from a time when the two great divisions of the nation had definitely separated and followed each their own destinies. Another point to which we draw attention, is the different form of the Tashdīd, as seen in the word *Allāh*. The Maghrib form is ـٚـ instead of ـّـ; and while in the Oriental writing the vowel signs are placed over it, the Western style places the sign for the Tashdid and for the vowel frequently side by side, as it is done here.

No. 5.

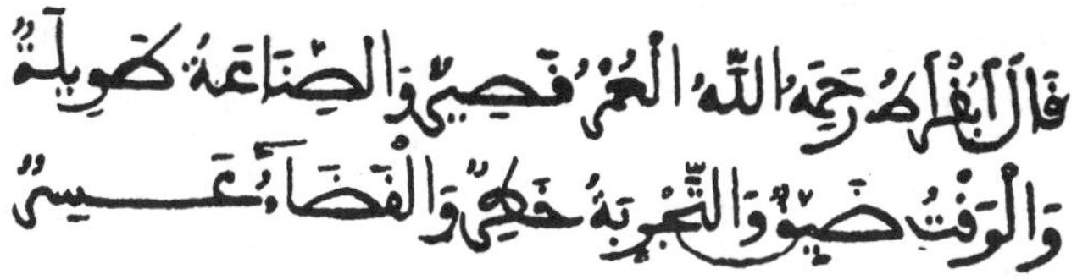

GOOD MAGHRIB WRITING.

قال ابقراط رحمه الله العمر قصير والصناعة طويلة
والوقت ضيق والتجربة خطر والقضاء عسر

Qāla Abuqrāṭu raḥima-hu 'llāhu 'l-ʻumru qaṣīrun wa 'ṣ-ṣināʻatu ṭawīlatun
wa 'l-waqtu ẓaiyiqun wa 't-tajribatu khaṭirun wa 'l-qaẓā'u ʻaṣirun.

"Hippocrates, may God have compassion upon him, said: Life is short, art is long,
Time is narrow, experience dangerous, judgment difficult."

No. 6.

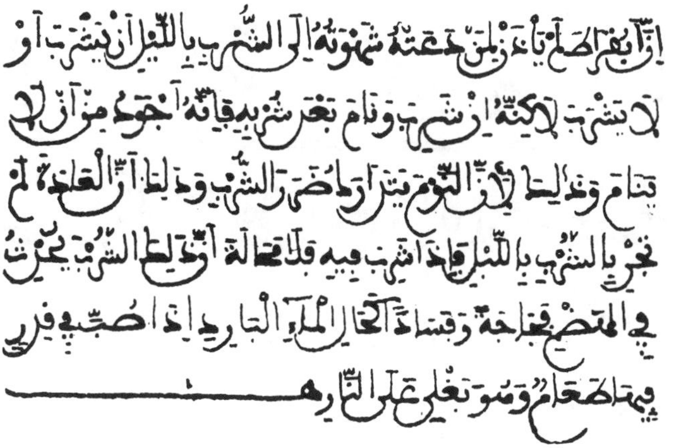

SUPERIOR MAGHRIB WRITING.

ان ابقراط لم ياذن لمن دعته شهوته الى
الشرب بالليل ان يشرب او
لا يشرب لكنه ان شرب ونام بعد شربه فانه
اجود من ان لا
ينام وذلك لان النوم يتدارك ضرر الشرب وذلك
ان العادة لم
تجر بالشرب بالليل فاذا شرب فيه فلا محالة
ان ذلك الشرب يحدث
فى الهضم فجاجة وفسادا كمال الماء البارد
اذا صب فى قدر
فيها طعام وهو يغلى على النار

Inna Abuqrāṭa lam ya'z̤an li-man da'at-hu shahwatu-hu ilā 'sh-shurbi bi-'l-laili an yashraba an
lā yashraba lākinna-hu in shariba wa nāma ba'da shurbi-hi fa'inna-hu ajwadu min an lā
yanāma wa z̤ālika li'anna 'n-nauma yatadāraku ẓarara 'sh-shurbi wa z̤ālika anna 'l-'ādata lam
tajri bi-'sh-shurbi bi-'l-laili fa 'iz̤ā shariba fī-hi fa-lā maḥālata anna z̤ālika 'sh-shurba yuḥdis̤u
fī 'l-haẓmi fajājatan wa fasādan ka-ḥāli 'l-mā'i 'l-bāridi iz̤ā ṣubba fī qadrin
fī-hā ṭa'āmun wa huwa yaghlī 'ala 'n-nāri.

"Hippocrates neither allows nor forbids a man, who has a desire to drink at night-time,
to satisfy his desire. If, however, he drinks, and sleeps after drinking, it is better
than not to sleep, this being so because sleep counteracts, in this case, the evil effect of drinking;
for it is not customary to drink at night-time, and if one does so, this will of necessity produce
a disturbance and derangement in the digestion, just as if cold water were poured into a vessel
containing food that is being boiled."

These two fragments scarcely call forth any further remark, except that in the last both forms of the Tashdīd are employed, the ordinary form even more frequently than the Maghrebian; for the latter occurs only twice, in *bi-'sh-shurbi*, which is the second word in the fourth line, and in *ash-shurba*, which is the last word but one in the same line Moreover, it will be useful to notice the peculiar shape which the letters د (*d*) and ذ (*z̤*) take in the Maghrib character, as in the words *ajwadu* towards the end of the second line, and *ya'z̤an* near the beginning of the first.

Dismissing the Maghrib-Berber style of Arabic writing, with its numerous local varieties, as less interesting for the English reader, we now turn to the Oriental style, where we meet again with a bipartition, viz. into the Eastern Naskhī, as it is written in Arabia itself, Egypt, and Syria, and the Ṭa'līq, current in Persia, India, and Central Asia.

No. 7 is a specimen of the Naskhī in the more limited sense of the word, meaning the style generally employed in manuscripts, and derived from *naskh* or *nuskhah*, "copy."

No 7.

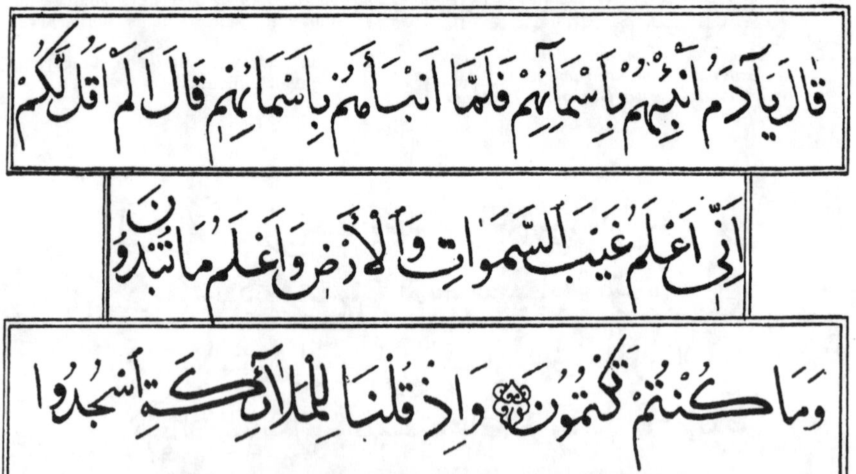

NASKHI CHARACTER FROM A GOOD EGYPTIAN MANUSCRIPT.

قال يا آدم انبئهم باسمائهم فلما انباهم
باسمائهم قال الم اقل لكم
انى اعلم غيب السموات والارض واعلم ما تبدون
وما كنتم تكتمون * واذ قلنا للملائكة اسجدوا

Qāla yā Ādamu 'nbi'-him bi-asmā'i-him fa-lammā anba'a-hum bi-'asmā'i-him qāla alam aqul la-kum
Annī a'lamu ghaiba 's-samawāti wa 'l-arẓi wa a'lamu mā tabdūna
Wa mā kuntum taktumūna. Wa iz̤ qulnā li-'l-malā'i-kati 'sjudū.

"He said: 'O Adam, inform them of their names,' and when he had informed them of their names, He said: 'Did I not say to you,
That I know the hidden things of the heavens and of the earth, and know what ye bring to light,
And what ye hide?' And when we said to the angels: 'Bow down' . . ."

(Sūrah ii. 31, 32.)

From this ordinary Naskhī several more ornate manuscript styles are derived, as the Rīḥānī, Yāqūtī, and Ṣuluṣ. They are distinguished principally by the relative proportions of the characters; and in the Ṣuluṣ in particular, of which we give a specimen under No. 8, the letters are three times the size of the ordinary Naskhī, while the Rīḥānī and Yāqūtī show intermediate proportions between the two.

No. 8.

SULUS STYLE.

كنت نبيا والادم بين الماء والطين

Kuntu nabīyan wa 'l-adamu baina 'l-mā'i wa 't-ṭīni.

"I was a prophet, when man was yet a mixture of water and clay."

It will be observed that beneath the م (*m*) of the words الادم (*al-adamu*) and الما (*al-mā'i*), in the Ṣuluṣ fragment, the letter is written a second time in a smaller character, and that, moreover, in the word الادم it is surmounted by the sign ـٚـ, which in Maghrib writing, as we have seen, generally represents the Tashdīd. This is done in the above-mentioned ornate styles, especially with those letters which admit of diacritical points, viz. ح, د, ر, س, ص, ط, ع, &c. To indicate that no such diacritical point is intended, the sign ـٚـ is placed on the top of the letter, or to make still surer of preventing a mistake, the letter itself is repeated in a minute shape at the bottom. Only the letter ة (*h*), as distinguished from ة (*t*), is, in this case, written above the line, because it frequently occurs as abbreviation of هو *huwa*, "He," or الله *Allāh*, "God," and it would therefore be considered irreverential towards the Deity to write it beneath the other letters. As a feature common to this division of the Eastern Arabic manuscript style, we lastly point out the inclination of the characters from the left to the right, in contradistinction both to the Maghrib and Ṭa'līq writing, where the letters are traced perpendicularly, or even with a slight bend from the right to the left.

Two other deviations from the pure Naskhī style are the Jarī and Dīwānī, officially employed in Turkey, and exhibited in the specimen No. 9:—

No. 9.

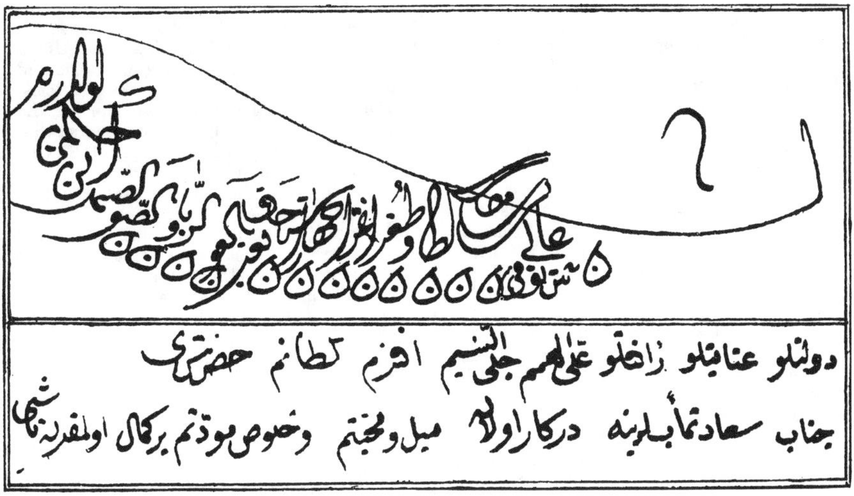

JARI AND DIWANI

The Jarī fragment in the upper division is a facsimile of the formula which accompanies the seal of the Sultān, and runs as follows :—

نشان شریف عالیشان سامی مکان وطغرای
غرای جهان ارای ستان خاقان نفذ بالعون
الربانی والصون الصمدانی حکمی اولدر که

Nishāni sharīfi ʻālīshān sāmī makān va tughrā'i gharrā'i jihān arā'i sitāni khāqān nufiza bi 'l-aun ar-rabbānī wa 'ṣ-ṣaun aṣ-ṣamadānī ḥukmī oldur ki . . .

"This is the noble, exalted, brilliant sign-manual, the world-illuminating and adorning cipher of the Khāqān (may it be made efficient by the aid of the Lord and the protection of the **Eternal**). His order is that, etc."

The beauty of this style is considered to consist in its being written either diagonally from the top to the bottom of the page, or ascending eliptically from the bottom to the top.

The Dīwānī style, of which the lower division gives an example, is used in the official correspondence of the Turkish administration. The final letters, and even words, are placed on the top of one another, and in its more intricate varieties the letters run together in a fanciful manner, which renders the decipherment of this writing frequently very difficult.

Finally, we present in No. 10 a specimen of the Persian Ṭaʻlīq writing :—

No. 10.

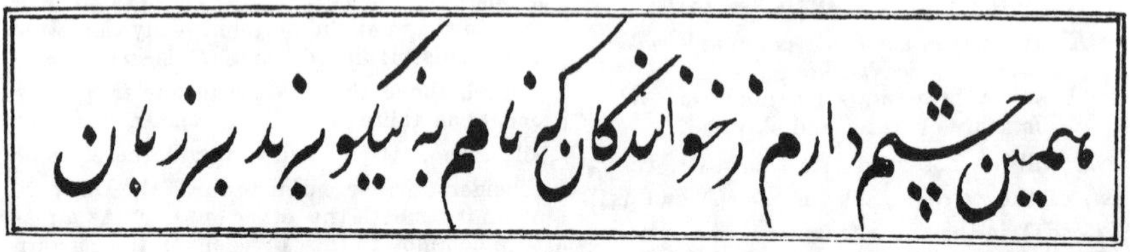

TAʻLIQ CHARACTER.

همین چشم دارم ز خوانندگان
که نامم به نیکو برند بر زبان

Hamīn chashmi dāram zi khwānandagān
Ki nāmam ba nīkū barand bar zabān.

"Such hope I cherish that in minstrel's lay,
With right fair fame my name will live for aye!"

(*Firdausī.*)

From this style of writing the Shikastah is derived, and bears the same relation to it which the Dīwānī bears to Naskhī. While in general preserving the peculiar outline of the Ṭaʻlīq, it superposes finals and words, and joins letters in a similar way to the Dīwānī, with which, however, it contrasts favourably by a far more elegant and graceful delineation of the characters.

It remains now only to add a few words on the writing materials which the Arabs, and Orientals in general, make use of. From the nature of the character and from the direction of the writing from the right to the left, it will be easily understood that our quill and steel pens would answer the purpose rather indifferently. The bolder stroke requires a broader nib, and, at the same time, the edges of the writing instrument should be smooth enough to glide with ease over the paper, so as to enable the hand to give that fine swing and swell to the curved lines, which form one of the chief beauties of the Arabic writing. These conditions are admirably fulfilled by the *qalam* or reed pen. For the same reasons their ink is richer and their paper more glossy than those which we employ ourselves. The best ink is said to be made of lamp-black and vinegar or verjuice, to which red ochre is added, well beaten up and mixed with yellow arsenic and camphor. The paper, before being used for writing, is submitted to the action of the press, or made smooth by placing it on a well-levelled board of chestnut wood, and polishing it with an egg of crystal of about half a pound's weight.

We cannot here enter into further particulars on the subject. The reader who might feel interested in it, will find some curious details in a short poem by Abū 'l-Ḥasan ʻAlī ibn al-Bauwāb, which De Sacy has published and translated in his *Chrestomathie.* As mentioned before, this calligraphist was one of the greatest masters of his art, so much so that when he died, A.H. 413 or 423, the following lines were written in his praise :—

"Thy loss was felt by the writers of former times, and each successive day justifies their grief. The ink-bottles are therefore black with sorrow, and the pens are rent through affliction."

Ibn Khallikān, from whom we quote, finds these verses very fine. Without disparaging his taste, we can happily assure our readers that Ibn al-Bauwābs verses are finer. With regard to the *qalam*, however, he rather mystifies us on the very point which would be most interesting, namely, the manner in which the nib should be cut or made. He says :—

"Give your whole attention to the making of your nib, for on this, verily, all else depends.

"But do not flatter yourself that I am going to reveal this secret; it is a secret which I guard with a miser's jealousy.

"All that I will tell is, that you must observe the golden mean between a too much rounded and too much pointed form."

Disappointed as we are at this oracular saying, we will condone him for his niggardly reticence on account of his final lines, with which we will also terminate our article:—

"Let your hand devote its fingers to writing only useful things that you will leave behind you on quitting this abode of illusion;

"For man will find, when the book of his actions will be unrolled before him, all that he has done during the days of his life."

WUJŪD (وجود). An existence. Philosophers say existences are of three kinds:—

Wājibu 'l-Wujūd, a necessary existence—God.

Mumkinu 'l-Wujūd, a possible existence—Creation.

Mumtaniʿu 'l-Wujūd, an impossible existence—an Associate with God.

WUQŪF (وقوف). "Standing." A name given to those ceremonies of the Pilgrimage which are performed on Mount ʿArafah. (Burton, *Pilgrimage*, vol. ii. p. 383.)

WUẔŪ' (وضوء). The ablution made before saying the appointed prayers. Those which are said to be of divine institution are four in number, namely: to wash (1) the face from the top of the forehead to the chin, and as far as each ear; and (2) the hands and arms up to the elbow; (3) to rub (*masaḥ*) with the wet hand a fourth part of the head; also (4) the feet to the ankles. The authority for these actions is the Qur'ān, Sūrah v. 8: "O Believers! when ye address yourselves to prayer, wash your hands up to the elbow, and wipe your heads, and your feet to the ankles." The Sunnīs wash the feet: the Shīʿahs are apparently more correct, for they only wipe, or rather rub (*masaḥ*) them. In these ablutions, if the least portion of the specified part is left untouched, the whole act becomes useless and the prayer which follows is vain.

The Sunnah regulations (or those established on the example of Muḥammad) regarding it are fourteen in number. (1) to make the intention or *nīyah* of *wuẓū'*, thus: "I make this *wuẓū'* for the purpose of putting away impurity"; (2) to wash the hand up to the wrist, but care must be taken not to put the hands entirely into the water, until each has been rubbed three times with water poured on it; (3) to say one of the names of God at the commencement of the *wuẓū'*, thus: "In the name of the Great God," or "Thanks be to God"; (4) to clean the teeth (*miswāk*); (5) to rinse the mouth three times; (6) to put water into the nostrils three times; (7) to do all the above in proper order; (8) to do all without any delay between the various acts; (9) each part is to be purified three times; (10) the space between the fingers of one hand must be rubbed with the wet fingers of the other; (11) the beard must be combed with the fingers; (12) the whole head must be rubbed once; (13) the ears must be washed with the water remaining on the fingers after the last operation; (14) to rub under and between the toes with the little finger of the left hand, drawing it from the little toe of the right foot and between each toe in succession. [ABLUTION, PRAYER, WATER.]

Y.

YADU 'LLĀH (يد الله). "Hand of God." The expression occurs in the Qur'ān:—

Sūrah xlviii. 10: "God's hand is above their hands."

Sūrah v. 69: "The Jews say, 'God's hand is fettered."

The expression is a subject of controversy amongst the Muḥammadans. The Wahhābīs maintain that it is wrong to hold that it is merely a figurative expression, but rather that God doth possess a hand in such a manner as it exists, without attempting to explain the manner how. On the other hand, some maintain that it is merely a figurative expression for God's power.

YAG͟HŪṢ (يغوث). An idol mentioned in the Qur'ān, Sūrah lxxi. 23. Professor Palmer says it was in the figure of a lion. Al-Baiẓāwī says it was the name of a hero who lived between the days of Adam and Noah, who was afterwards worshipped in an idol of the name.

YĀ HŪ (يا هو). "O He!" that is, "O God." An exclamation often recited by faqīrs or darveshes in their religious ẕikrs. The third personal pronoun singular, *hū* (*huwa*), "He" being a name for God, *i.e.* "He who exists." [ZIKR.]

YAHŪD (يهود), the plural of *Yahūdī*. Heb. יְהוּדִי. Jews. The word used in the Qur'ān (together with *Banū Isrā'īl*) for the Jews. [JEWS, JUDAISM.]

YAḤYĀ (يحيى). John the Baptist. The son of Zachariah, whose birth is mentioned in the Qur'ān, Sūrah xix. 1; iii. 34; and who is said in the latter Sūrah to have been sent with glad tidings "to confirm the Word from God (Jesus), a chief and a chaste one and a prophet from the righteous." And in Sūrah vi. 85, his name occurs with that of Zachariah, Jesus, and Elias, as one of the "righteous ones." [JOHN THE BAPTIST.]

YA'JŪJ WA MA'JŪJ (ياجوج وماجوج). [GOG AND MAGOG.]

YALAMLAM (يلملم). The *mīqāt* or stage where the pilgrims from al-Yaman assume the pilgrim's garb at the pilgrimage. [HAJJ.]

YAMĀMAH (يمامة). A province in the eastern portion of the Ḥijāz frequently mentioned in the history of Muḥammad.

AL-YAMAN (اليمن). The south-western province of Arabia. It is considered the most fertile part of the country, and is called the garden of Arabia.

YAMĪN (يمين). [OATH.]

AL-YAQĪN (اليقين). "The certainty." (1) A term which implies belief, sure knowledge, and which occurs in the Qur'ān to express the hour of death.

Sūrah lxxiv. 43-48: "They shall say, 'We were not of those who prayed, we did not feed the poor; but we did plunge into discussion with those who plunged, and we called the Judgment Day a lie until *the certainty* did come upon us.'"

Sūrah xv. 99: "Serve the Lord until *the certainty* come upon thee."

Muslims say there are three degrees of spiritual knowledge:—

1. *'Ilmu 'l-Yaqīn* (علم اليقين), that which a man apprehends with his intellectual faculties.

2. *'Ainu 'l-Yaqīn* (عين اليقين), that which he sees with the eye.

3. *Ḥaqqu 'l-Yaqīn* (حق اليقين), that which he fully embraces with the heart; the highest form of spiritual knowledge, especially of the Unity of God.

YAQṬĪN (يقطين). Heb. קִיקָיוֹן. The gourd tree under which Jonah sheltered after he escaped from the belly of the fish. Sūrah xxxvii. 145, 146: "We cast him on a barren shore: and he was sick: and we made to grow over him a *gourd tree*."

YA'QŪB (يعقوب). [JACOB.]

YĀ SĪN (يا سين). The two Arabic letters ى and س corresponding to the English *y* and *s*. The title of the xxxvith Sūrah of the Qur'ān, which begins with these two letters, the mystic import of which is said to be unknown. Al-Baiẓāwī says perhaps they mean *Yā Insān!* (يا انسان), "O Man!" Ḥusain suggests that they mean *Yā Saiyid!* (يا سيد), "O Saiyid!" whilst the Jalālān think the meaning is known alone to God. Muḥammad said this chapter was the *Qalbu 'l-Qur'ān*, "the heart of the Qur'ān," and it is consequently held in high estimation. It is usually read to dying persons.

Yā Sīn is a title given to Muḥammad with the belief that he is referred to as "O Saiyid," in the first verse of the Sūrah referred to.

YAS̤RIB (يثرب). The ancient name of al-Madīnah, mentioned once in the Qur'ān, viz. Sūrah xxxiii. 13. According to the traditionist, the Prophet changed the name from Yas̤rib to Madīnatu 'n-Nabī, "the City of the Prophet," because *Yas̤rib* was a name of shame and reproach. (*Majma'u 'l-Biḥār*, vol. iii. p. 499.)

YA'SŪB (يعسوب). *Lit.* "A prince or chief." The King of the Bees. A title given to 'Alī. (*Majma'u 'l-Biḥār*, vol. iii. p. 502.) A name of one of Muḥammad's horses. (Richardson's *Dictionary*.)

YATHRIB. [YASRIB.]

YATĪM (يتيم). [ORPHAN.]

YAUM (يوم). A day of twenty-four hours; pl. *aiyām*. In contradiction to *lail wa nahār*, "night and day."

The seven days of the week are known as:—

Yaumu 'l-aḥad, first day, Sunday.
Yaumu 'l-is̤nain, second day, Monday.
Yaumu 'l-s̤alās̤ā', third day, Tuesday.
Yaumu 'l-arba'ā', fourth day, Wednesday.
Yaumu 'l-khamīs, fifth day, Thursday.
Yaumu 'l-jum'ah, day of Assembly, Friday.
Yaumu 's-sabt, Sabbath day, Saturday.

YAUMU 'D-DĪN (يوم الدين). "Day of Judgment."

Sūrah i.: "The King of the *Day of Judgment*."

Sūrah lxxxiii. 17: "What shall make thee know what the *Day of Judgment* is?"

AL-YAUMU 'L-ĀKHIR (اليوم الاخر). "The Last Day." A name given in the Qur'ān to the Day of Judgment.

YAUMU 'L-'ĀSHŪRA' (يوم العاشوراء). The tenth day of the month of Muḥarram. ['ASHURA'.]

YAUMU 'L-FAṢL (يوم الفصل). "Day of Severing." The Day of Judgment. Sūrah lxxvii. 13, 14: "For the Day of Severing! and who shall teach thee what the Day of Severing is?"

YAUMU 'L-FIṬR (يوم الفطر). "The Day of breaking the fast." ['IDU 'L-FITR.]

YAUMU 'L-ḤARĀ' (يوم الحراء). "The day of the stony country" mentioned in the Traditions. (*Mishkātu 'l-Maṣābiḥ*, book xxiv. ch. ix.) The day on which Yazīd sent an army to al-Madīnah and laid it in ruins. (See Ockley's *Saracens*, p. 425.)

YAUMU 'L-ḤASHR (يوم الحشر). "Day of Assembly." The Day of Judgment.

YAUMU 'L-ḤISĀB (يوم الحساب). "Day of Reckoning." The Day of Judgment. Sūrah xl. 28: "And Moses said, Verily, I will take refuge in my Lord and your Lord from every one who is big with pride, and believes not on the *Day of Reckoning*."

YAUMU 'L-INQIṬĀ' (يوم الانقطاع). "The Day of Cessation." The day on which anything terminates. In law, the last day on which anyone who has become possessed of property illegally may restore it, or make compensation to the owner.

YAUMU 'L-JAM' (يوم الجمع). "Day of Gathering." The Day of Judgment. Sūrah lxiv. 9: "On the day when He shall gather you to the Day of Gathering."

YAUMU 'L-KHULŪD (يوم الخلود). "Day of Eternity." Sūrah l. 34: "Enter into it in peace: this is the Day of Eternity."

YAUMU 'L-KHURŪJ (يوم الخروج). "The Day of Exodus." The Day of Judgment. Sūrah l. 41: "The day when they shall hear the shout in truth; that is, the Day of Coming Forth."

YAUMU 'L-QARR (يوم القر). "The Day of Rest." The day after the sacrifice at the Ḥajj, when the pilgrims rest.

YAUMU 'L-QIYĀMAH (يوم القيامة). "Day of Standing up." The Day of Resurrection." [RESURRECTION.]

YAUMU 'L-WA'ĪD (يوم الوعيد). "The Day of Threatenings." The Day of Judgment. Sūrah l. 19: "And the trumpet shall be blown!—that is the threatened day."

YAUMUN MA'LŪMUN (يوم معلوم). "A Known Day," *i.e.* known to God. The Day of Judgment. Sūrah lvi. 50: "Gathered shall they surely be for the tryst of a known day."

YAUMU 'N-NAḤR (يوم النحر). "Day of Sacrifice." A term used for the Feast of Sacrifice. ['IDU 'L-AZHA.]

YAUMU 'S-SABU' (يوم السبع). The "Day of Sabu'," mentioned in the following tradition (*Mishkātu 'l-Maṣābiḥ*, book xxiv. ch. 16):—

"Abū Hurairah says, 'Whilst a man was with his goats, behold a wolf came in amongst them, and took a goat; and the man released it. And the wolf said to the man, "Who is to guard these goats on the *day of Sabu'*, when there will be no shepherd but me." And the people said, "The wolf speaks." And the Prophet said, "I believe that the wolf did speak." Abū Bakr and 'Umar also said so.'"

'Abdu 'l-Ḥaqq says there is a difference of opinion as to what the Day of Sabu' is, either it is a day of insurrection, or a festival amongst the ancient Arabs, when the flocks were left to themselves.

YAUMU 'T-TAGHĀBUN (يوم التغابن). "Day of Mutual Deceit." The Day of Judgment. Sūrah lxiv. 9: "On that day when he shall gather you to the Day of Gathering, that is the Day of Mutual Deceit."

Al-Baizāwī says: "Both the righteous and the wicked will disappoint each other by reversing their positions, the wicked being punished, while the righteous are in bliss."

YAUMU 'T-TALĀQ (يوم التلاق). "Day of Meeting." The Day of Judgment. Sūrah xl. 15: "He throws the Spirit by his bidding upon whom He will of His servants, to give warning of the *Day of Meeting*."

YAUMU 'T-TANĀD (يوم التناد). "A Day of Mutual Outcry." A name given to the Day of Judgment in the Qur'ān. Sūrah xl. 34: "O my people! verily I fear for you the *day of crying out to one another*."

YA'ŪQ (يعوق). An idol mentioned in the Qur'ān, Sūrah lxxi. 23. Professor Palmer says it was in the figure of a horse. Al-Baizāwī says it is the name of a certain hero who lived between the days of Adam and Noah, and was afterwards worshipped in an idol of the name.

YAWNING. Arabic *taṣāwub* (تثاوب). From the Traditions it appears yawning is regarded as an evil; for Abū Hurairah relates that Muḥammad said, "God loves sneezing and hates yawning. As for yawning, it is of the devil. Therefore, if any of you yawn, let him suppress it as much as possible. If he cannot stop it, let him put the back of his left hand upon his mouth; for, verily, when anyone yawns and opens his mouth, the devil laughs." (*Mishkāt*, book xxii. ch. vi.)

YAZĪD (يزيد). The son of Mu'āwiyah. The second Khalīfah of the house of Umaiyah (Ommiyah), who reigned from A.D. 679 to A.D. 683 (A.H. 60–64). He is celebrated in Muslim history as the opponent of al-Ḥusain. (See Ockley's *Hist. Saracens*, p. 393.)

YEAR. Arabic *sanah* (سنة), pl. *sanūn, sanawāt*; *'ām* (عام), pl. *a'wām*; *ḥaul* (حول), pl. *aḥwāl*; Persian *sāl* (سال), pl. *sālhā*.

The ancient Arabian year is supposed to have consisted of twelve lunar months, as now observed by the Muḥammadans; but about the year A.D. 412, the Arabians introduced a system of intercalation, whereby one month was intercalated into every three years. (See M. de Perceval, vol. i. p. 242). This system of intercalation existed in the time of Muḥammad; but it is related that, at the farewell pilgrimage, the Prophet recited the khuṭbah on the Day of Sacrifice, and said: "A year is twelve months only, as at the time of the creation," and thus again introduced the lunar year. (See *Mishkāt*, book xi. ch. xi.) The Muḥammadan year, therefore, consists of twelve lunar months, without any intercalation to make it correspond with the course of the sun, and amounts very nearly to 354 days and 9 hours. Hence the Muḥammadan New Year's Day, *Nau Roz*, will happen every year about eleven days earlier than in the preceding year.

There also existed amongst the Arabians a system of *commutation* whereby the *Muḥarram*, the last of the three continuous sacred months [MONTHS], became secular, and *Ṣafar* sacred. Some traditions say that the power also existed of commuting the isolated sacred month *Rajab*, for the one succeeding it, *Sha'bān*. When this was done, it became lawful to war in the sacred months of Muḥarram and Rajab; and Ṣafar and Sha'bān acquired the sacredness of the months for which they had been substituted. It is with reference to this custom that Muḥammad says in the Qur'ān (Sūrah ix. 36, 37):—

"Verily, twelve months is the number of months with God, according to God's Book, ever since the day when He created the Heavens and the Earth; of these, four are sacred: this is the right usage. Therefore, wrong not yourselves therein, and attack those who join gods with God, one and all, as they attack you one and all; and know that God is with those who fear Him. To carry over a sacred month to another is only an increase of unbelief. They who do not believe are led in error by it. They allow it one year and forbid it another, that they may make good the number of months which God hath hallowed, and they allow that which God hath prohibited."

This system of commutation is said to have been introduced by Quṣaiy, who wished, by abridging the long three months' cessation of hostilities, to humour the warlike Arabs, as well as to obtain the power of making a sacred month secular when it might best suit his purpose; but Sir William Muir is inclined to think that this system of commutation was an ancient one, and merely restored by Quṣaiy. (Muir's *Mahomet*, vol. i. p. ccviii.)

Both in India and in Egypt, in the present day, the Muḥammadans use the lunar year for their religious observances and the ordinary affairs of life; but for the purposes of agriculture and other calculations, for which the lunar year is inconvenient, they employ the Julian calendar.

To find the number of solar years elapsed *since* any given Muḥammadan date, subtract the given year of the Hijrah from the current year of the Hijrah, and from the remainder deduct three per cent.; the remainder will be the number of solar years which have elapsed. Thus, suppose we see a manuscript written A.H. 681, and wish to know its real age in Christian or solar years, we subtract, in the first place, the number 681 from the current year of the Hijrah, say 1256, and there remains 575; from this last we deduct three per cent, or 17, and there remains 558, which at that period is the real age of the manuscript in solar years.

If the object, however, be to find the precise Christian date corresponding to any given year of the Hijrah, apply the following rule:—From the given number of Musalmān years, deduct three per cent., and to the remainder add the number 621·54; the sum is the period of the Christian era at which the given current Musalmān year ends. For example: from A.H. 942, deduct three per cent., or 28·26, and the remainder is 913·74. To this last add 621·54, and the sum is 1535·28, which shows that A.H. 942 ended in the spring of A.D. 1536. This simple rule is founded on the fact that 100 lunar years are very nearly equal to 97 solar years, there being only eight days of excess in the former period; hence to the result found, as just stated, it will be requisite to add 8 days, as a correction for every century.

The following is a more accurate rule. Express the Muḥammadan date in years and decimals of a year; multiply by ·970225; to the product add 621·54, and the sum will be the precise period of the Christian era. (Dr. Forbes.)

If it is desired to find the year of the Hijrah which comes in in a given year of the Christian era; it is sufficient to subtract 621 from the year given, and to multiply the remainder by 10,307. (Murray.)

YŪḤANNĀ (يوحنا). The Arabic *Christian* name for John the Baptist, and John the Apostle, the corresponding *Muslim* name being *Yaḥyā*. [YAHYA.]

YŪNUS (يونس). [JONAH.]

YŪSHA' (يوشع). [JOSHUA.]

YŪSUF (يوسف). [JOSEPH.]

Z.

ZABḤ (ذبح). Heb. זֶבַח *zebakh*. Arabic lexicographers define the word to mean the act of cutting the throat. In the language of the law, it denotes the act of slaying an animal agreeably to the prescribed forms, without which its flesh is not lawful for the food of man. See Qur'ān, Sūrah ii. 167, 168:—

"Eat of the good things wherewith we have provided you, *and give thanks unto God*, if ye are His worshippers. He has only forbidden for you that which is dead, and blood, and flesh of swine, and whatsoever has been consecrated to other than God; but he who is forced, neither revolting nor transgressing, it is no sin for him: for verily God is forgiving and merciful."

The injunctions in the Traditions are more explicit (*Mishkāt*, book xviii. ch. i.), for example: Abū Ṯufail relates that 'Alī was once asked, "Has the Prophet ever told you anything with regard to religion which he has not told others?" And 'Alī replied, "Nothing, unless it be that which I have in the scabbard of my sword." Then 'Alī brought out of his scabbard a piece of paper, and thereon was written: "May God curse those who slay without repeating the name of God, in the same manner as the polytheists did in the names of their idols; may God curse those who remove their neighbours' landmarks; may God curse those who curse their fathers; may God curse those who harbour innovators in matters of religion."

According to Sunnī law, *ẕabḥ* is of two kinds: (1) *Ikhtiyārī*, of choice; and (2) *Iẓṭirārī*, of necessity.

The first is effected by cutting the throat above the breast and reciting the words *Allāhu akbar*, "God is most great"; and the second by reciting these words upon shooting an arrow or discharging a gun.

The latter act, however, is merely a substitute for the former, and accordingly is not of any account unless the former be impracticable; for the proper *ẕabḥ* is held to be by the shedding of blood, and the former method is most effectual for this purpose.

It is absolutely necessary that the person who slays the animal should be a Muslim or a *kitābī* (*i.e.* a Jew or a Christian), and that he should do it in the name of God alone; it signifies not whether the person be a man or a woman, or an infant, or an idiot, or an uncircumcised person.

An animal slain by a Magian is unlawful, as also that slain by an idolater or a polytheist. *Ẕabḥ* performed by an apostate from the Muslim faith (who is worthy of death) is also unlawful; but, according to Abū Ḥanīfah, if a Jew or a Christian become an apostate from his own creed, his *ẕabḥ* is lawful, for the Muslim law still regards him, with respect to *ẕabḥ*, in the same light as formerly.

If the slayer wilfully omit the invocation, "In the name of the most great God," the flesh of the animal is unlawful; but if he omit the invocation through forgetfulness, it is lawful, although there is some difference of opinion on this subject amongst the Sunnī doctors. Ash-Shāfi'ī is of opinion that the animal is lawful in either case, but the Imām Mālik maintains that it is unlawful in both.

Abū Yūsuf and all the Ḥanafī doctors have declared, that an animal slain under a wilful omission of the invocation is utterly unlawful, and that the magistrate must forbid the sale of meat so killed.

It is a condition of *ẕabḥ ikhtiyārī* that the invocation be pronounced over the animal at the time of slaying it; but in the case of *ẕabḥ iẓṭirārī* (*i.e.* when a person slays an animal, in hunting), the condition is that the invocation be pronounced at the time of letting loose the hound or hawk, or of shooting the arrow or gun, or casting the spear.

It is a condition of *ẕabḥ* that nothing but the invocation *Bismi 'llāhi Allāhi akbar*, "In the name of God, God the most great," should be said. That is, no prayer or other matter must be mentioned.

The place for slaying is betwixt the throat and the head of the breast-bone (Arabic *labbah*), and the vessels it is requisite to cut are four, *al-hulqūm*, "the wind-pipe," *al-marī'*, "the gullet," and *al-warīdan*, or *al-wadajān*, "the two jugular veins."

Ash-Shāfi'ī holds that if a man slay an animal with a nail or horn or teeth, the flesh is unlawful, but this is not the opinion of other doctors. (See *Durru 'l-Mukhtār* and *Hidāyah, in loco.*)

AZ-ZABĀNĪYAH (الزبانية). *Lit.* "Guards." The angels in charge of hell, of whom Mālik is said to be the chief. Sūrah xcvi. 17, 18: "So let him call his council: we will call the *guards* of hell (*az-Zabāniyah*)."

ẔABĪḤAH (ذبيحة). *Lit.* "Cut or divided lengthways." Heb. זֶבַח *zebakh*. An animal slaughtered according to the law; a sacrifice. [LAWFUL FOOD, SACRIFICES.]

ZABĪR (زبير). A name for Mount Sinai. Al-Baiẓāwī says it is the mountain on which the Lord conversed with Moses. [SINAI, TUR.]

ẒABṬ (ضبط). "Occupation, seizure." In Muḥammadan law it means attachment, distraint, or sequestration; taking lands under the management of Government officers.

ZABŪR (زبور), pl. *zubur*. Also *zubūr*, pl. of *zibr*. From the Heb. זִמְרָה *zimrāh*, "a psalm or chant" (Psa. lxxxi. 2, xcviii. 5). The title given to the Psalms of David in the Qur'ān, where it occurs only three times.

Sūratu 'n-Nisā' (iv.) 161: "And to David we gave *Psalms (zabūran)*."

Sūratu 'l-Mir'āj (xvii.) 57: "And Psalms (*zabūran*) we gave to David."

Sūratu 'l-Ambiyā' (xxi.) 105: "And now, since the exhortation (*ẕikr*) was given, have we written in the *Psalms* (*fī 'z-zabūri*) that my servants the righteous shall inherit the earth."

Both Sale and Rodwell take this last to be a quotation from Psa. xxxvii. 29 (it appears to be the only direct quotation from either the Old or New Testament in the whole of the Qur'ān), and they have both translated the Arabic *ẕikr* "the law," meaning, of course, the *Taurāt*. Amongst Muslim commentators, there is considerable difference of opinion as to what is meant in this verse by *ẕikr* and *zabūr*.

The commentator al-Baiẓāwī says there are three views. Said ibn Jubair and Mujaiyid explained the word *zabūr* to mean all inspired books, and that by *ẕikr* was meant the Preserved Tablet (*al-Lauḥu 'l-Maḥfūẓ*). Ibn 'Abbās and aẓ-Ẕaḥḥāk said by *zabūr* was meant the Taurāt, and by *ẕikr* those books which came after. And Sha'bī said the *zabūr* was the Book of David, and the *ẕikr* that of Moses.

Al-Bag͟hawī and al-Jalālān decide in favour of the first interpretation, Ḥusain decides in favour of the third, whilst al-Baiẓāwī leaves it an open question.

Jalālu 'd-dīn aṣ-Ṣuyūṭī gives the word *zabūr* as one of the fifty-five titles of the Qur'ān.

ZACHARIAS. Arabic *Zakarīyā'* (زكرياء). [ZAKARIYA'.]

ZAFĪR (زفير). *Lit.* "Drawing back the breath because of distress; groaning." In the Qur'ān, for the groans of hell. Sūrah xi. 108: "In the Fire, there shall they groan."

ẔA'FIRĀNĪYAH (زعفرانية). A sect of Muslims, who say the Qur'ān is a created thing, the orthodox school maintaining that the Word of God is uncreated. (*Kitābu 't-Ta'rīfāt, in loco.*)

ZAḤF (زحف). *Lit.* "A swarming multitude." An army; a military force arrayed for battle.

Qur'ān, Surah viii. 15: "O ye who believe! when ye meet *the marshalled hosts* of the unbelievers, turn not your backs to them." Hence, battle, combat.

ZĀHID (زاهد). *Lit.* "Abstinent; continent." An ascetic person. *Zāhid-i-k͟hushk*, Persian, "a dissembler, a hypocrite."

ẒĀHIR (ظاهر). "Outward, exterior, manifest." A word much used in Muslim theology to express that which is manifest, as distinguished from *bāṭin*, "interior," or *k͟hafī*, "that which is hidden."

AZ-ẒĀHIR (الظاهر). "The Evident." One of the ninety-nine attributes of God.

Qur'ān, Sūrah lviii. 3: "He is the First and the Last, the *Evident* and the Hidden."

ẒĀHIRU 'L-MAẔHAB (ظاهر المذهب). An expression used by Ḥanafī Muslims for those theological questions which are decided in the four well-known Sunnī books: *al-Mabsūṭ*, *al-Jāmi'u 'l-Kabīr*, *al-Jāmi'u 's-Sag͟hīr*, *as-Sairu 'l-Kabīr*.

ẒĀHIRU 'L-MUMKINĀT (ظاهر الممكنات). An expression used by theologians for the proofs of God's existence, power, and attributes, as exhibited in nature.

ZAID IBN AL-ḤĀRIṢ (زيد بن الحارث). Muḥammad's freedman and adopted son. Muḥammad having seen and admired Zaid's wife Zainab, her husband divorced her. The relations of the ancient Arabs to their adopted children were very strict, and Muḥammad's marriage with the divorced wife of his adopted son occasioned much scandal amongst his contemporaries. A revelation was consequently produced which revoked the inconvenient restrictions.

Sūrah xxxiii. 37: "And when Zaid had settled the necessary matter of her divorce, we did wed her to thee, that it might not be a crime in the faithful to marry the wives of their adopted sons, when they have settled the necessary affair concerning them."

Zaid was slain at the battle of Mūtah, as he carried the standard of Islām, A.H. 8.

ZAIDĪYAH (زيدية). A Shī'ah sect. Those who followed Zaid the son of 'Alī ibn al-Ḥusain instead of the other son Ja'far aṣ-Ṣādiq. [SHI'AH.]

ZAIG͟H (زيغ). *Lit.* "Turned aside" (from the Truth). It occurs in the Qur'ān, Sūrah iii. 5, 6: "In whose hearts is *perversity*. . . . O Lord, *pervert* not our hearts."

ZAINAB (زينب). The daughter of K͟huzaimah and the widow of 'Ubaid, Muḥammad's cousin, who was slain at Badr. She married Muhammad in the third year of the Hijrah. Zainab was renowned for her kindness to the poor, and was called *Ummu 'l-Masākīn*, "the mother of the poor," from her care of destitute converts. She and K͟hadijah were the only wives of the Prophet who died before him.

ZAINAB (زينب). The daughter of Jaḥsh and the divorced wife of Muḥammad's adopted son Zaid. Being the wife of an adopted son, she was unlawful to the Prophet, but a pretended revelation (see Qur'ān, Sūrah xxxiii. 37) settled the difficulty, and Muḥammad married her. [MUHAMMAD.]

ZAINAB BINT MUHAMMAD (زينب بنت محمد). The daughter of Muḥammad by Khadījah. She married Abū 'l-'Āṣ. The story of the conversion of Abū 'l-'Āṣ, through the devotion of his wife, is told by Muir (vol. iv. p. 7). She died A.H. 61.

ZĀ'IR (زائر). A pilgrim to Muḥammad's grave at al-Madīnah, as distinguished from a *ḥājī*, or pilgrim to Makkah. According to Burton, Zā'irs are ordered to visit the tomb perfumed and in their best clothes. The person who conducts the *zā'ir* to the sacred spot, is called a *muzawwir*, who on the occasion of Captain Burton's visit recited the following prayer:—

"In the name of Allah and in the Faith of Allah's Prophet! O Lord, cause me to enter the entering of truth, and cause me to issue forth the issuing of Truth, and permit me to draw near to Thee and make me a King victorious!" (*i.e.* over the world, the flesh, and the devil). Then follow blessings on the Prophet, and afterwards: "O Allah! open to me the doors of Thy mercy, and grant me entrance into it, and protect me from the stoned devil!" (Burton's *El-Medinah and Meccah*, vol. ii. p. 296.)

ZAKARĪYĀ' (زكرياء). Zacharias. The father of John Baptist; the husband of Hannah's sister, and the uncle of the Virgin Mary. Mentioned four times in the Qur'ān:—

Sūrah iii. 32: "So with goodly acceptance did her Lord accept her, with goodly growth did He make her grow, and Zakarīyā' reared her. So oft as Zakarīyā' went in to Mary at the sanctuary, he found her supplied with food. 'Oh Mary!' said he, 'whence hast thou this?' She said, 'It is from God; verily God supplieth whom He will without reckoning!' There did Zakarīyā' call upon his Lord; 'O my Lord!' said he, 'vouchsafe me from Thyself good descendants; Thou verily art the hearer of prayer.' Then did the angels call to him, as he stood praying in the sanctuary: 'God announced John (Yaḥyā) to thee, who shall be a verifier of the Word from God, and a great one, chaste, and a prophet of the number of the just.' He said, 'O my Lord! how shall I have a son now that old age has come upon me and my wife is barren?' He said: 'Thus will God do his pleasure.' He said, 'Lord! give me a token.' He said, 'Thy token is, that not for three days shalt thou speak to man but by signs. But remember thy Lord often, and praise Him at even and at morn.'"

Sūrah vi. 85: "And Zakarīyā', John, Jesus, and Elias: all were just persons."

Sūrah xix. 1-12: "A recital of thy Lord's mercy to His servant Zakarīyā', when he called upon his Lord with secret calling. He said: 'O Lord, verily my bones are weak and the hoar hairs glisten on my head, and never, Lord, have I prayed to Thee with ill success. But now I have fear for my kindred after me; and my wife is barren: Give me, then, a successor as Thy special gift and an heir of the family of Jacob: and make him, Lord, well-pleasing to Thee.' 'O Zakarīyā, verily We announce to Thee a son,—his name Yaḥyā (John): that name We have given to none before him.' He said: 'O my Lord! how when my wife is barren shall I have a son, and when I have now reached old age, failing in my powers?' He said: 'So shall it be. Thy Lord hath said, Easy is this to Me, for I created thee aforetime when thou wast nothing.' He said: 'Vouchsafe me, O my Lord! a sign.' He said: 'Thy sign shall be that for three nights, though sound in health, thou speakest not to man.' And he came forth from the sanctuary to his people, and made signs to them as though he would say, 'Praise God at morn and even.'"

Sūrah xxi. 89: "And Zakarīyā', when he called upon his Lord saying, "O my Lord leave me not childless: but there is no better heir than Thyself.' So We heard him and gave him Yaḥyā (John), and We made his wife fit for child-bearing."

ZAKAT (زكوة). In its primitive sense the word *zakāt* means *purification*, whence it is also used to express a portion of property bestowed in alms, as a sanctification of the remainder to the proprietor. It is an institution of Islām and founded upon an express command in the Qur'ān (*vide* Sūrah ii. 77), being one of the five foundations of practical religion.

It is a religious duty incumbent upon any person who is free, sane, adult, and a Muslim, provided he be possessed in full property of such estate or effects as are termed in the language of the law *niṣāb*, and that he has been in possession of the same for the space of one complete year. The *niṣāb*, or fixed amount of property upon which *zakāt* is due, varies with reference to the different kinds of property in possession, as will be seen in the present article.

The one complete year in which the property is held in possession is termed *ḥaulu 'l-ḥaul*. Zakāt is not incumbent upon a man against whom there are debts equal to or exceeding the amount of his whole property, nor is it due upon the necessaries of life, such as dwelling-houses, or articles of clothing, or household furniture, or cattle kept for immediate use, or slaves employed as actual servants, or armour and weapons designed for present use, or upon books of science and theology used by scholars, or upon tools used by craftsmen.

(1) The zakāt of *camels*. Zakāt is not due upon less than five camels, and upon five camels it is one goat or sheep, provided they subsist upon pasture throughout the year, because *zakāt* is only due upon such camels as live on pasture, and not upon those which are fed in the home with forage. One goat is due upon any number of camels from five to nine; two goats for any number of camels from ten to fourteen; three goats for any number from twenty to twenty-four. Upon any number of camels from twenty-five to thirty-five the

zakāt is a *bint mikhāz*, or a yearling female camel; from thirty-six to forty-five, a *bint labūn*, or a two-year-old female camel; from forty-six to sixty, a *ḥiqqah*, or a three-year-old female camel; from sixty-one to seventy-five, a *jaẕʻah*, or four-year-old female camel; from seventy-five to ninety, two camels' female two-year-old colts; and from ninety-one to one hundred and twenty, two camels' female three-year-old colts. When the number of camels exceeds one hundred and twenty, the zakāt is calculated by the aforesaid rule.

(2) The zakāt of *bulls, cows*, and *buffaloes*. No zakāt is due upon fewer than thirty cattle, and upon thirty cattle which feed on pasture for the greater part of the year, there is due at the end of the year a *tabīʻah*, or a one-year-old calf; and upon forty is due a *musim*, or a calf of two years old; and where the number exceeds forty, the zakāt is to be calculated according to this rule. For example, upon sixty, the zakāt is two yearling calves; upon seventy, one *tabīʻah* and one *musim*; upon eighty, two *musims*; upon ninety, three *tabīʻah*; upon one hundred, two *tabīʻahs* and one *musim*; and thus upon every ten head of cattle a *musim* and a *tabīʻah* alternately. Thus upon one hundred and ten kine, the zakāt is two *musims* and one *tabīʻah*; and upon one hundred and twenty, four *tabīʻahs*. The usual method, however, of calculating the zakāt upon large herds of cattle is by dividing them into thirties and forties, imposing upon every thirty one *tabīʻah*, or upon every forty one *musim*.

(3) Zakāt upon *sheep* and *goats*. No zakāt is due upon less than forty, which have fed the greater part of the year upon pasture, upon which is due one goat, until the number reaches one hundred and twenty; for one hundred and twenty-one to two hundred, it is two goats or sheep; and above this, one for every hundred. The same rules apply to both sheep and goats, because in the Traditions the original word *ghanam* applies to both species.

(4) Zakāt upon *horses*. When horses and mares are kept indiscriminately together, feeding for the greater part of the year on pasture, it is the option of the proprietor to give a zakāt of one dīnār per head for the whole, or to appreciate the whole, and give five per cent. upon the total value. No zakāt whatever is due upon droves of horses consisting entirely of males, or entirely of mares. There is no zakāt due upon horses or mules, unless they are articles of merchandise, nor is it due upon war horses, or upon beasts of burden, or upon cattle kept for drawing ploughs and so forth.

(5) Zakāt upon *silver*. It is not due upon silver of less value than two hundred dirhams, but if one be possessed of this sum for a whole year, the zakāt due upon it is five dirhams. No zakāt is due upon an excess above the two hundred dirhams till such excess amount to forty, upon which the zakāt is one dirham, and for every succeeding forty, one dirham. Those dirhams in which silver predominates are to be accounted silver, and the laws respecting silver apply to them, although they should contain some alloy; and the same rule holds with regard to all articles falling under the denomination of plate, such as cups and goblets.

(6) Zakāt upon *gold*. No zakāt is due upon gold under the value of twenty misqāls, and the zakāt due upon twenty misqāls is half a misqāl. When the quantity of gold exceeds twenty misqāls, on every four misqāls above twenty are due two qirāṭs, and so on in proprotion.

Zakāt is due upon gold and silver bullion, and upon all gold and silver ornaments and utensils.

(7) Zakāt upon articles of *merchandise*. Articles of merchandise should be appraised, and a zakāt of 2½ per cent. paid upon the value, if it exceed two hundred dirhams in value.

(8) Zakāt upon *mines*, or buried treasures. Mines of gold, silver, iron, lead, or copper, are subject to a zakāt of one-fifth (*khums*); but if the mine is discovered within the precincts of a person's own home, nothing is due. And if a person find a deposit of buried treasure, a fifth is due upon it. No zakāt is due upon precious stones.

(9) Zakāt upon the *fruits of the earth*. Upon everything produced from the ground there is a tenth (*ʻāshir* or *ʻushr*), whether the soil be watered by the overflow of rivers or by periodical rains, excepting the articles of wood, bamboo, and grass, which are not subject to the tithe. Land watered by means of buckets, or machinery, or watering camels, is subject to a twentieth. Honey and fruits collected in the wilderness are subject to tithe.

The zakāt is received by a collector duly appointed for the purpose, although it is lawful for the possessor to distribute his alms himself. If a person come to the collector, and make a declaration on oath as to the amount of his property upon which zakāt is due, his statement is to be credited.

There are *seven* descriptions of persons upon whom zakāt may be bestowed.

(1) *Faqīrs*, or persons possessed of property, the whole of which, however, does not amount to a *niṣāb*.

(2) *Miskīns*, or persons who have no property whatever.

(3) The collector of zakāt.

(4) Slaves.

(5) Debtors.

(6) *Fī sabīli 'llāh, i.e.* in the service of God, or religious warfare.

(7) Travellers.

The above laws with reference to zakāt are those according to the Ḥanafīyah sect, but the differences amongst the Imāms of the Sunnīs on this subject are but small. They may be seen upon reference to Hamilton's translation of the *Hidāyah*, vol. i. p. 1.

ẔAKHĀ'IRU 'LLĀH (ذخائر الله).

Lit. "Repositories of God." A Ṣūfī term for

a class of believers who, on account of their spiritual attainments, are the means of preventing troubles in a nation, in the same manner as stores (*z̤aḵẖāʾir*) of grain keep away famines.

Z̤ĀKIR (ذاكر). One who remembers God by reciting His names and praises. The reciter of a *z̤ikr*. [ZIKR.]

Ẓ̤ALĀLAH (ضلالة). "Error." The word frequently occurs in the Qur'ān, *e.g.* Sūrah ii. 15: "These are they who have purchased *error*, at the price of the guidance."

Z̤AMB (ذنب), pl. *z̤unūb*. "A sin; a crime." A charge of such. The word occurs frequently in the Qur'ān, *e.g.*:—

Sūrah xxvi. 13: "They have a *charge* against me (*i.e.* Aaron), and I fear lest they put me to death."

Sūrah xl. 2: [From God] "the forgiver of *sin*."

Sūrah lxxxi. 9: "For what *crime* she was put to death." [SIN.]

ZAMZAM (زمزم). The sacred well within the precincts of the mosque at Makkah. It is supposed to be the identical spring from which Hagar and Ishmael drank in the wilderness (Genesis xvi. 4), but which is stated in the Scriptures to have been between Kadesh and Bared.

The origin of the word *zamzam* is uncertain. According to Johnson's Arabic Dictionary, it means the low buzzing sound, made by the ancient fire-worshippers, and may therefore allude to the murmuring of the water of the well. Some Muslim commentators derive it from *zamm! zamm! i.e.* "fill! fill!" Hagar's words to Ishmael when she saw the water. Sale translates it: "Stay! Stay!" and adds that Hagar called out in the Egyptian language to prevent Ishmael wandering.

The building which encloses the well Zamzam stands close by the Maqām Ḥanbalī, and was erected in A.H. 1072 (A.D. 1661). According to Burckhardt, it is of a square shape, and of massive construction, with an entrance to the north, opening into the room which contains the well. This room is beautifully ornamented with marbles of various colours; and adjoining to it, but having a separate door, is a small room with a stone reservoir, which is always full of Zamzam water. This the pilgrims get to drink by passing their hand, with a cup, through an iron-grated opening which serves as a window, into the reservoir, without entering the room. The mouth of the well is surrounded by a wall five feet in height, and about ten feet in diameter. Upon this the people stand who draw up the water in leathern buckets, an iron railing being so placed as to prevent their falling in. The water is then poured into earthen jars, called *dauraq*, which Captain Burton describes as little amphoræ, each marked with the name of the donor and a peculiar cypher. These jars are placed in long rows on the ground, along the paved causeways which lead up to the Kaʿbah, and between which grass appears growing in several places, produced by the Zamzam water oozing out of the jars.

The Zamzam water is held in great esteem throughout the East. It is used for drinking and ablution, but for no baser purposes; and the Makkans advise pilgrims always to break their fast with it. Captain Burton says: "It is apt to cause diarrhœa and boils, and I never saw a stranger drink it without a wry face. Sale is decidedly correct in his assertion: the flavour is salt-bitter, much resembling an infusion of a teaspoonful of Epsom salts in a large tumbler of tepid water. Moreover, it is exceedingly 'heavy' to the taste; for this reason, Turks and other strangers prefer rain-water collected in cisterns, and sold for five farthings a guglet. The water is transmitted to distant regions in glazed earthen jars covered with basket-work, and sealed by the *Zem Zemis* (*Zamzamīs*, or dispensers of the holy water). Religious men break their lenten fast with it, apply it to their eyes to brighten vision, and imbibe a few drops at the hour of death, when Satan stands by holding a bowl of purest water, the price of the departing soul. The copious supply of the well is considered at Meccah miraculous; in distant countries it facilitates the pronunciation of Arabic to the student; and everywhere the nauseous draught is highly meritorious in a religious point of view."

According to the same author, the name has become generic for a well situated within the walls of a mosque, and amongst these, naturally, the Zamzam of al-Madīnah stands nearest in dignity to the Makkah well, with which it is said to be connected by a subterraneous passage. Others believe that it is filled by a vein of water springing directly under the Prophet's grave, whence it is generally called Bi'ru 'n-Nabī, or the Prophet's well. It stands at the south-east angle of an enclosure within the court of the mosque of al-Madīnah, called the garden of Fāṭimah, under a wooden roof supported by pillars of the same material.

ZANĀNAH (زنانه). A Persian adjective derived from the word *zan*, "a woman." That which belongs to women. It denotes the household of a Muḥammadan, his wives and children, and the apartments in which they reside. For a full account of an Indian zanānah by Mrs. Meer Ali, see HARIM.

"A zanānah mission" is a Christian mission established for the benefit of the wives and daughters of Muḥammadans.

ZANJABĪL (زنجبيل). "Ginger." An aromatic with which the cups of Paradise are flavoured. See Qur'ān, Sūrah lxxvi. 17: "And they shall drink therein a cup tempered with *zanjabīl*."

Z̤ANN (ظن), pl. *z̤unūn*. "Opinion; suspicion." In Muḥammadan law, a presumption that a charge is well-founded, although the evidence is inconclusive. *Az-Zannu 'l-Ghalib*, expresses a strong presumption of truth in a charge, although the evidence does not amount to conviction. The "Not proven" of Scotch law. The word *zann*, in the sense of "suspicion," occurs in the Qur'ān, Sūrah xlix. 12: "O Believers! avoid frequent suspicions, for some suspicions are a crime."

ZAQQŪM (زقوم). An infernal tree described in the Qur'ān.

Sūrah xxxvii. 60–64: "Is this the better repast or the tree az-Zaqqūm? Verily We have made it for a subject of discord to the wicked: Lo, it is a tree which cometh up from the bottom of hell; its fruit is as it were the heads of Satans; and, lo! the damned shall surely eat of it and fill their bellies with it."

Sūrah xliv. 43, 44: "Verily the tree of az-Zaqqūm shall be the sinner's food."

Sūrah lvi. 51–53: "Then verily ye, O ye the erring, the imputers of falsehood, shall surely eat of the tree of Zaqqūm, and fill your bellies with it."

It is a name now given to a thorny tree, whose fruit is sweet and styptic, and from the stone of which oil is extracted. (Richardson's Dictionary.)

ZARĀMĪYAH (زرامية). A sect of Shī'ah Muḥammadans, who say that the next Imāms after 'Alī were Muḥammad ibn Ḥanfiyah, 'Abdullāh, 'Alī ibn 'Abdillāh ibn Abbās, and afterwards his progeny, as far as Manṣūr, until at last the Divine power entered into Abū Muslim, who, they assert, was not really slain. (*Kashfu 'l-Iṣṭilāḥāt, in loco.*)

ZARĀRĪYAH (زرارية). A sect of Muslims founded by one of the Companions, named Zarārah, who say the attributes of God are not eternal. (*Kitābu 't-Ta'rīfāt, in loco.*)

ẒARB (ضرب). *Lit.* "Striking." In arithmetic, "Multiplication." The concluding foot of a line in poetry. A term used by Ṣūfī mystics for the ceremony of *zikr*.

AZ-ẒĀRIYĀT (الذاريات). "The Scatterers." The title of the LIst Sūrah of the Qur'ān which begins with the words "By the Scatterers who scatter." By which is understood the winds of heaven.

AZ-ẒĀRR (الضار). "The Distresser." One of the ninety-nine attributes of God. In the Qur'ān the word is applied to Satan.

Sūrah lviii. 11: "Only of Satan is this clandestine talk, that he may bring the faithful to grief; but, unless by God's permission, not aught shall he *harm* them (*laisa bi-ẓārrihim*)! in God, then, let the faithful trust."

God, therefore, is called the "Distresser," in so far as evil befalls man only by His permission.

ẒARRAH (ذرة). "An atom." The word occurs in the Qur'ān in the following verse:—

Sūrah xcix. 6: "On that day shall men come up in separate bands to behold their works; and whosoever shall have wrought an atom's weight of good shall behold it, and whosoever shall have wrought an atom's weight of evil shall behold it."

ẒĀT (ذات), pl. *zawāt*. From *zū*, "a possessor," of which *zāt* is the feminine. In the Dictionary *al-Mughrab* it is defined as the essence of a thing, meaning that by being which a thing is what it is, or that in being which a thing consists; or the ultimate and radical constituent of a thing. It is used for the nature or essence of God, Allāh being called the *Ismu 'z-Zāt*, or "Essential name of God." *Zātu 'llāh*, the "Essence of God," is a scholastic theological expression. In Muslim law, *zāt* signifies the body connected with the soul, in opposition to *badn*, which means the "material body."

ẒAWŪ 'L-ARḤĀM (ذوو الارحام). [UTERINE RELATIONS.]

ẒAWŪ 'L-FURŪẒ (ذوو الفروض). The Sharers of inheritance whose shares are specified in the Qur'ān itself. [INHERITANCE.]

ZEALOTS. [GHULAT.]

ẒIHAR (ظهار). *Lit.* "Likening to the back." A form of imprecation which involves the separation of husband and wife until expiation is made. According to the *Hidāyah*, *ẓihār* signifies the likening of a woman to a kinswoman within the prohibited degrees, which interpretation is found in the comparison being applied to any of the parts or members of the body improper to be seen. The usual formula is: *Anti 'alaiya ka-ẓahri ummī*, "Thou art unto me as my mother's back."

Before the establishment of Muhammadanism, *ẓihār* stood as a divorce, but Muḥammad changed it to a temporary prohibition, for which expiation must be performed, viz. either freeing a slave, or two months' fast, or feeding sixty persons. Qur'ān, Sūratu 'l-Mujādilah (lviii.), 1–5:—

"God hath heard the words of her who pleaded with thee against her husband, and made her plaint to God; and God hath heard your mutual intercourse: for God Heareth! Beholdeth.

"As to those of you who put away their wives *by saying*, "*Be thou to me as my mother's back*"—their mothers they are not; they only are their mothers who gave them birth! they certainly say a blameworthy thing and an untruth:

"But truly, God is Forgiving, Indulgent.

"And those who *thus* put away their wives, and afterwards would recall their words, must free a captive before they can come together *again*. To this are ye warned to conform: and God is aware of what ye do.

"And he who findeth not *a captive to set free*, shall fast two months in succession before they two come together. And he who shall not be able *to do so*, shall feed sixty poor men. This, that he may believe in God and His Apostle. These are the statutes of God: and for the unbelievers is an afflictive chastisement!"

The above injunction was occasioned by Khaulah, the daughter of Ṣa'labah, having pleaded her case with the Prophet, because she had been divorced by her husband Aus ibn aṣ-Ṣāmit, by the formula above-mentioned, and which was understood by the Arabs to imply perpetual separation. Muḥammad had, in the first instance, decreed the divorce in accordance with ancient Arabic law, but relaxed his order in consequence of the woman's earnest pleadings.

ZIKR (ذكر). *Lit.* "Remembering."

Heb. זָכַר *zākhar*. The religious ceremony, or act of devotion, which is practised by the various religious orders of Faqīrs, or Darweshes. Almost every religious Muḥammadan is a member of some order of Faqīrs, and, consequently, the performance of *zikr* is very common in all Muḥammadan countries; but it does not appear that any one method of performing the religious service of *zikr* is peculiar to any order.

Zikrs, are of two kinds: *zikr jalī*, that which is recited aloud, and *zikr khafī*, that which is performed either with a low voice or mentally.

The Naqshbandīyah order of Faqīrs usually perform the latter, whilst the Chishtīyah and Qādirīyah orders celebrate the former. There are various ways of going through the exercise, but the main features of each are similar in character. The following is a *zikr jalī*, as given in the book *Qaulu 'l-Jamīl*, by Maulawī Shāh Walīyu 'llāh, of Delhi:—

The worshipper sits in the usual sitting posture and shouts the word *Allāh* (God), drawing his voice from his left side and then from his throat.

Sitting as at prayers he repeats the word *Allāh* still louder than before, first from his right knee, and then from his left side.

Folding his legs under him he repeats the word *Allāh* first from his right knee and then from his left side, still louder!

Still remaining in the same position, he shouts the word *Allāh*, first from the left knee, then from the right knee, then from the left side, and lastly in front, still louder!

Sitting as at prayer, with his face towards Makkah, he closes his eyes, says "*Lā*"—drawing the sound as from his navel up to his left shoulder; then he says *ilāha*, drawing out the sound as from his brain; and lastly "*illā 'llāhu*," repeated from his left side with great energy.

Each of these stages is called a *zarb*. They are, of course, recited many hundreds of times over, and the changes we have described account for the variations of sound and motion of the body described by Eastern travellers who have witnessed the performance of a *zikr*.

The following is a *zikr khafī*, or that which is performed in either a low voice or mentally.

Closing his eyes and lips, he says, "with the tongue of the heart,"

Allāhu Samī'un, "God the Hearer."
Allāhu Baṣīrun, "God the Seer."
Allāhu 'Ālimun, "God the Knower."

The first being drawn, as it were, from the navel to the breast; the second, from the breast to the brain; the third, from the brain up the heavens; and then again repeated stage by stage backwards and forwards.

He says in a low voice, "*Allāh*," from the right knee, and then from the left side.

With each exhalation of his breath, he says, "*lā ilāhā*," and with each inhalation, "*illā 'llāhu*."

This third *zarb* is a most exhausting act of devotion, performed, as it is, hundreds or even thousands of times, and is, therefore, considered the most meritorious.

It is related that Maulawī Ḥabību 'llāh, living in the village of Gabāsanri, in the Gadūn country, on the Peshawur frontier, became such an adept in the performance of this *zarb*, that he recited the first part of the *zikr lā ilāha* with the exhalation of his breath after the mid-day prayer; and the second part, *illā 'llāhu*, with the inhalation of his breath before the next time of prayer, thus sustaining his breath for the period of about three hours!

Another act of devotion, which usually accompanies the *zikr*, is that of *Murāqabah*, or meditation.

The worshipper first performs *zikr* of the following:—

Allāho hāzirī, "God who is present with me."
Allāho nāẓirī, "God who sees me."
Allāho shāhidī, "God who witnesses me."
Allāho ma'ī, "God who is with me."

Having recited this *zikr*, either aloud or mentally, the worshipper proceeds to meditate upon some verse or verses of the Qur'ān. Those recommended for the Qādirīyah Faqīrs by Maulavī Shāh Walīyu 'llāh are the following, which we give as indicating the line of thought which is considered most devotional and spiritual by Muslim mystics:—

1. Sūratu 'l-Ḥadīd (lvii.), 3:—

"He (God) is first. He is last. The Manifest, and the Hidden, and who knoweth all things."

2. Sūratu 'l-Ḥadīd (lvii.), 4:—

"He (God) is with you wheresoever ye be."

3. Sūrātu Qāf (l.), 16:—

"We (God) are closer to him (man) than his neck-vein."

4. Sūratu 'l-Baqarah (ii.) 109:—

"Whichever way ye turn, there is the face of God."

5. Sūratu 'n-Nisā' (iv.), 125:—

"God encompasseth all things."

6. Sūratu 'r-Raḥmān (lv.), 26, 27:—

"All on earth shall pass away, but the face of thy God shall abide resplendent with majesty and glory."

Some teachers tell their disciples that the heart has two doors, that which is fleshly, and that which is spiritual; and that the *ẕikr jalī* has been established for the opening of the former, and *ẕikr k͟hafī* for the latter, in order that they may both be enlightened.

To the uninitiated such a ceremony appears but a meaningless rite, but to the Ṣūfī it is one calculated to convey great benefit to his inner man, as will appear from the following instructions which are given by a member of the Order respecting the *ẕikr*, which he says is a union of the heart and the tongue in calling upon God's name. "In the first place, the Shaik͟h, or teacher, must with his heart recite, 'There is no God but Allah, and Muḥammad is the Prophet of Allah,' whilst the *Murid* keeps his attention fixed by placing his heart opposite that of the Shaik͟h; he must close his eyes, keep his mouth firmly shut, and his tongue pressed against the roof of his mouth; his teeth tight against each other, and hold his breath; then, with great force, accompany the Shaik͟h in the *ẕikr*, which he must recite with his heart, and not with his tongue. He must retain his breath patiently, so that within one respiration he shall say the *ẕikr* three times, and by this means allow his heart to be impressed with the meditative *ẕikr*."

"The heart," the same writer continues, "in this manner is kept constantly occupied with the idea of the Most High God; it will be filled with awe, love, and respect for Him; and, if the practiser arrives at the power of continuing to effect this when in the company of a crowd, the *ẕikr* is perfect. If he cannot do this, it is clear that he must continue his efforts. The heart is a subtle part of the human frame, and is apt to wander away after worldly concerns, so that the easier mode of arriving at the proceeding is to compress the breath, and keep the mouth firmly closed with the tongue forced against the lips. The heart is shaped like the cone of a fir-tree; your meditations should be forced upon it, whilst you mentally recite the *ẕikr*. 'Let the "*La*" be upward, the "*Ilaha*" to the right, and the whole phrase "*La ilaha illa 'llahu*" (There is no God but *Allah*) be formed upon the fir-cone, and through it pass to all the members of the whole frame, and they feel its warmth. By this means the world and all its attractions disappear from your vision, and you are enabled to behold the excellence of the Most High. Nothing must be allowed to distract your attention from the *ẕikr*, and ultimately you retain, by its medium, a proper conception of the Tauḥīd, or Unity of God.

"The cone-shaped heart rests in the left breast and contains the whole truth of man. Indeed, it signifies the 'whole truth'; it comprises the whole of man's existence within itself, and is a compendium of man; mankind, great and small, are but an extension of it, and it is to humanity what the seed is to the whole tree which it contains within itself: *in fine*, the essence of the whole of God's book and of all His secrets is the heart of man. Whoever finds a way to the heart obtains his desire; to find a way to the heart is needed by a heartful service, and the heart accepts of the services of the heart. It is only through the fatigues of water and ashes that the Murid reaches the conversation of the heart and the soul; he will be then so drawn towards God that afterwards, without any difficulty, he may without trouble, in case of need, turn his face from all others towards Him. He will then know the real meaning of the *Tark* (the abandonment of the world), the *Haqiqat* (the truth), the *Hurriyat* (the freedom), and the *Zikr* (the recital of God's names and praises)."

As a curious instance of the superstitious character of this devotional exercise, the Chishtīyah order believe that if a man sits cross-legged and seizes the vein called *kaimās*, which is under the leg, with his toes, that it will give peace to his heart, when accompanied by a *ẕikr* of the "*nafī wa is̤bāt*," which is a term used for the Kalimah, namely:—

Lā ilāha illā 'llāhu, "There is no deity but God."

The most common form of *ẕikr* is a recital of the ninety-nine names of God [NAMES OF GOD], for Muḥammad promised those of his followers who recited them a sure entrance to Paradise (*Mishkāt*, book cxi.); and to facilitate the recital of these names, the *ẕākir* (or reciter) uses a *tasbīḥ* (or rosary). [TASBIH.]

In addition to the forms of *ẕikr* already mentioned there are three others, which are even of more common use, and are known as *Tasbīḥ*, *Taḥmīd*, and *Takbīr*. They are used as exclamations of joy and surprise, as well as for the devotional exercise of *ẕikr*.

Tasbīḥ is the expression *Subḥāna 'llāh!* "Holiness be to God!"

Taḥmīd, Alḥamdu li-'llāh! "Praise be to God!"

Takbir, Allahu akbar! "God is great!"

When the *Tasbīḥ* and *Taḥmīd* are recited together it is said thus, *Ṣubḥāna 'llāhi bi-ḥamdi-hi*, *i.e.* "Holiness be to God with His praise." It is related in the Ḥadīs̤ that Muhammad said, "Whoever recites this sentence a hundred times, morning and evening, will have all his sins forgiven."

Muḥammad said, "Repeat the *Tasbīḥ* a hundred times, and a thousand virtues shall be recorded by God for you, ten virtuous deeds for each repetition."

In forming our estimation of Muḥammad and Muḥammadanism, we must take into consideration the important place the devotional exercise of *ẕikr* occupies in the system, not forgetting that it has had the authoritative sanction of "the Prophet" himself.

The following is a graphic description of one of these devotional performances, by Dr. Eugene Schuyler, in his work on Turkistan:—

"At about ten o'clock one Thursday evening, in company with several friends, we went to the mosque, and were at once admitted. Some thirty men, young and old, were on their knees in front of the *qiblah*, reciting prayers with loud cries and violent movements of the body, and around them was a circle, two or three deep, of men standing, who were going through the same motions. We took up a position in one corner and watched the proceedings. For the most part the performers or worshippers had taken off their outside gowns and their turbans, for the night was warm and the exercise was violent. They were reciting the words 'My defence is in God! May Allah be magnified! My light, Muhammad—God bless him! There is no God but God!" These words were chanted to various semi-musical notes in a low voice, and were accompanied by a violent movement of the head over the left shoulder towards the heart, then back, then to the right shoulder, and then down, as if directing all the movements towards the heart. These texts were repeated for hundreds and hundreds of times, and this *zikr* usually lasted for an hour or two. At first the movements were slow, but continually increased in rapidity, until the performers were unable to endure it any longer. If anyone failed in his duty, or was slower, or made less movement than was required, the persons who regulated the enthusiasm went up to him and struck him over the head, or pushed him back out of the circle and called another into it. Occasionally persons got so worn out with their cries, and so wet with perspiration, that it became necessary for them to retire for a few minutes rest, and their places were immediately taken by others. When their voices became entirely hoarse with one cry another was begun, and finally the cry was struck up, 'He lives! He lives! God lives!' at first slowly, with an inclination of the body to the ground: then the rhythm grew faster and in cadence, the body became more vertical, until at last they all stood up: the measure still increased in rapidity, and, each one placing his hand on the shoulder of his neighbour, and then forming several concentric rings, they moved in a mass from side to side of the mosque, leaping about and always crying: 'He lives! God lives!' Hitherto, there had been something wild and unearthly in it, but now to persons of weak nerves it became positively painful, and two of my friends were so much impressed as to be obliged to leave the mosque. Although I was sufficiently cold-blooded to see the ridiculous rather than horrible side of this, I could not help receiving an impression that the devotees were a pack of madmen, whose motions were utterly independent of any volition of their own. . . . . The intonations of the voice were very remarkable, and were often accompanied by most singular gestures, the hands or a book being often held to the side of the mouth in order to throw the voice as far as possible. Often these recitations are merely collections of meaningless words, which always seem to produce the same effect on the hearers, and are constantly interrupted by cries of *Hi*, *ho*, *och*, *och*, *ba*, *ba*, and groans and sobs, and the hearers weep, beat their breasts with their fists, or fall upon the ground."

The dancing and howling darweshes at Constantinople and Cairo have become public sights, and are familiar to those Europeans who have visited those cities.

We are indebted to Mr. Brown's account of *The Dervishes* (Trübner and Co., Ludgate Hill) for the following graphic description of one of these public recitals of *ẕikr*. [FAQIR.]

The ceremony commences by the recital by the Shaikh of the seven first attributes of the Divinity, called by them the seven mysterious words. "He next chants various passages of the Koran, and at each pause the Dervishes, placed in a circle round the hall, respond in chorus by the word 'Allah!' (God) or 'Hoo!' (*Huwa* or *Hū*, He). In some of the societies they sit on their heels, the elbows close to those of each other, and all making simultaneously light movements of the head and body. In others, the movement consists in balancing themselves slowly, from the right to the left, and from the left to the right, or inclining the body methodically forward and aft. There are other societies in which these motions commence seated, in measured cadences, with a staid countenance, the eyes closed or fixed upon the ground, and are continued on foot. These singular exercises are consecrated under the name of Murâkebeh (exaltation of the Divine glory) [*murāqabah*, 'meditation'], and also under that of the Tevheed (celebration of the Divine unity) [*Tauḥīd*], from which comes the name Tevheed khâneh given to the whole of the halls devoted to these religious exercises.

"In some of these institutions, such as the Kâdirees, the Rufâ'ees, the Khalwettees, the Bairâmees, the Gulshenees, and the 'Ushâkees, the exercises are made, each holding the other by the hand, putting forward always the right foot, and increasing at every step the strength of the movement of the body. This is called the *Devr* (*Daur*), which may be translated the 'dance or 'rotation.' The duration of these dances is arbitrary,—each one is free to leave when he pleases. Every one, however, makes it a point to remain as long as possible. The strongest and most robust of the number, and the most enthusiastic, strive to persevere longer than the others; they uncover their heads, take off their turbans, form a second circle within the other, entwine their arms within those of their brethren, lean their shoulders against each other, gradually raise the voice, and without ceasing repeat 'Yâ Allah!' (O God), or 'Yâ Hoo!' (O He), increasing each time the movement of the body, and not stopping until their entire strength is exhausted.

"Those of the order of the Rufâ'ees excel in these exercises. They are, moreover, the only ones who use fire in their devotions. Their practices embrace nearly all those of the other orders; they are ordinarily divided into five different scenes, which last more than three hours, and which are preceded, accompanied, and followed by certain ceremonies peculiar to this order. The first commences with praises which all the Dervishes offer to their sheikhs, seated before the altar. Four of the more ancient come forward the first, and approach their superior, embrace each other as if to give the kiss of peace, and next place themselves two to his right, and two to his left. The remainder of the Dervishes, in a body, press forward in a procession, all having their arms crossed, and their heads inclined. Each one, at first, salutes by a profound bow the tablet on which the name of his founder is inscribed. Afterwards, putting his two hands over his face and his beard, he kneels before the Sheikh, kisses his hand respectfully, and then they all go on with a grave step to take their places on the sheep-skins, which are spread in a half-circle around the interior of the hall. So soon as a circle is formed, the Dervishes together chant the Takbeer (*Takbīr*, the exclamation *Allāhu akbar*, 'God is exalted') and the Fâtiha (*Fātiḥah*, the first chapter of the Qur'ān). Immediately afterwards the shaikh pronounces the words 'Lâ ilâha ill' Allâh' (There is no deity but God), and repeats them incessantly; to which the Dervishes repeat 'Allah!' balancing themselves from side to side, and putting their hands over their faces, on their breasts, and their abdomen, and on their knees.

"The second scene is opened by the Hamdee Mohammedee, a hymn in honour of the Prophet, chanted by one of the elders placed on the right of the sheikh. During this chant the Dervishes continue to repeat the word 'Allah!' moving, however, their bodies forward and aft. A quarter of an hour later they all rise up, approach each other, and press their elbows against each other, balancing from right to left, and afterwards in a reverse motion,—the right foot always firm, and the left in a periodical movement, the reverse of that of the body, all observing great precision of measure and cadence. In the midst of this exercise, they cry out the words 'Yâ Allah!' followed by that of 'Yâ Hoo!' Some of the performers sigh, others sob, some shed tears, others perspire great drops, and all have their eyes closed, their faces pale, and the eyes languishing.

ZIKR. (*A. F. Hole.*)

"A pause of some minutes is followed by a third scene. It is performed in the middle of an Ilâhee, chanted by the two elders on the right of the sheikh. The Ilâhees are spiritual *cantiques*, composed almost exclusively in Persian by sheiks deceased in the odour of sanctity. The Dervishes then hasten their movements, and, to prevent any relaxation, one of the first among them puts himself in their centre, and excites them by his example. If in the assembly there be any strange Dervishes, which often happens, they give them, through politeness, this place of honour; and all fill it successively, the one after the other, shaking themselves as aforesaid. The only exception made is in favour of the Mevlevees; these never perform any other dance than that peculiar to their own order, which consists in turning round on each heel in succession.

"After a new pause commences the fourth scene. Now all the Dervishes take off their turbans, form a circle, bear their arms and shoulders against each other, and thus make the circuit of the hall at a measured pace, striking their feet at intervals against the floor, and all springing up at once. This dance continues during the Ilâhees, chanted alternately by the two elders to the left of the sheikh. In the midst of this chant the cries of 'Yâ Allah!' are increased doubly, as also those of 'Ya Hoo!' with frightful howlings, shrieked by the Dervishes together in the dance. At the moment that they would seem to stop from sheer exhaustion, the sheikh makes a point of exerting them to new efforts by walking through their midst, making also himself most violent movements. He is next replaced by the two elders, who double the quickness of the step and the agitation of the body; they even straighten themselves up from time to time, and excite the envy or emulation of the others in their astonishing efforts to continue the dance, until their strength is entirely exhausted.

"The fourth scene leads to the last, which is the most frightful of all, the wholly prostrated condition of the actors becoming converted into a species of ecstasy which they call *Halet* (*Ḥālah*). It is in the midst of this abandonment of self, or rather of religious delirium, that they make use of red hot irons. Several cutlasses and other instruments of sharp-pointed iron are suspended in the niches of the hall, and upon a part of the wall to the right of the sheikh. Near the close of the fourth scene, two Dervishes take down eight or nine of these instruments, heat them red-hot, and present them to the sheikh. He, after reciting some prayers over them, and invoking the founder of the Order, Ahmed er Rufâ'ee, breathes over them, and raising them slightly to the mouth, gives them to the Dervishes, who ask for them with the greatest eagerness. Then it is that these fanatics, transported by frenzy, seize upon these irons, gloat upon them tenderly, lick them, bite them, hold them between their teeth, and end by cooling them in their mouths! Those who are unable to procure any, seize upon the cutlasses hanging on the wall with fury, and stick them into their sides, arms, and legs.

"Thanks to the fury of their frenzy, and to the amazing boldness which they deem a merit in the eyes of the Divinity, all stoically bear up against the pain which they experience with apparent gaiety. If, however, some of them fall under their sufferings, they throw themselves into the arms of their *confrères*, but without a complaint or the least sign of pain. Some minutes after this the sheikh walks round the hall, visits each one of the performers in turn, breathes upon their wounds, rubs them with saliva, recites prayers over them, and promises them speedy cures. It is said that twenty-four hours afterwards nothing is to be seen of their wounds.

"It is the common opinion among the Rufâ'ees that the origin of these bloody practices can be traced back to the founder of the Order. They pretend that one day, during the transport of his frenzy, Ahmed Rufâ'ee put his legs in a burning basin of coals, and was immediately cured by the breath and saliva and the prayers of 'Abdul Kâdir Ghilânee; they believe that their founder received this same prerogative from heaven, and that at his death he transmitted it to all the sheikhs his successors. It is for this reason that they give to these sharp instruments, and to these red-hot irons, and other objects employed by them in their mysterious frenzy, the name of *Gul*, which signifies 'rose,' wishing to indicate thereby that the use made of them is as agreeable to the soul of the elect Dervishes as the odour of this flower may be to the voluptuary.

"These extraordinary exercises seem to have something prodigious in them, which imposes on common people, but they have not the same effect on the minds of men of good sense and reason. The latter believe less in the sanctity of these pretended thaumaturges than in the virtue of certain secrets which they adroitly use to keep up the illusion and the credulity of the spectators, even among the Dervishes themselves. It is thus, perhaps, that some assemblies of these fanatics have given, in this age of light, and in the heart of the most enlightened nation, the ridiculous spectacle of those pious and barbarous buffooneries known by the name of convulsions. At all times, and amongst every people of the earth, weakness and credulity, enthusiasm and charlatanry, have but too frequently profaned the most holy faith, and objects the most worthy of our veneration.

"After the Rufâ'ees, the Sâ'dees have also the reputation of performing miracles, pretty much of the same sort as the preceding. One reads in the institutes of this Order, that Sâ'd ed Deen Jebâwee, its founder, when cutting wood in the vicinity of Damascus, found three snakes of an enormous length, and that, after having recited some prayers and blown upon them, he caught them alive, and used them as a rope with which to bind his fagot. To this occurrence they ascribe the pretended virtue of the sheikhs and the Dervishes of this society, to find out snakes, to handle them, to bite them, and even to eat them, without any harm to themselves. Their exercises consist, like those of the Rufâ'ees and other Orders, at first in seating themselves, and afterwards in rising upright; but in often changing the attitude, and in redoubling their agitation even until they become overcome with fatigue, when they fall upon the floor motionless and without knowledge. Then the sheikh, aided by his vicars, employs no other means to draw them out of this state of unconsciousness than to rub their arms and legs, and to breathe into their ears the words 'Lâ ilâha ill' Allah.'

"The Mevlevees are distinguished by the singularity of their dance, which has nothing in common with that of the other societies. They call it Sem'a (*Samā'*) in place of Devr (*Daur*), and the halls consecrated to it are called Sem'a khânehs. Their construction is also different. The apartment represents a kind of pavilion, sufficiently light, and sustained by eight columns of wood These Dervishes have also prayers and practices peculiar to themselves. Among them the public exercises are not ordinarily made by more than nine, eleven, or thirteen individuals. They commence by forming a circle, seated on sheep-skin spread upon the floor at equal distances from each other; they remain nearly a half-hour in this position, the arms folded, the eyes closed, the head inclined, and absorbed in profound meditation

"The sheikh, placed on the edge of his seat on a small carpet, breaks silence by a hymn in honour of the Divinity; afterwards he invites the assembly to chant with him the first chapter of the Koran. 'Let us chant the Fâtiha,' he says, in 'glorifying the holy name of God, in honour of the blessed religion of the prophets, but above all, of Mohammed Mustapha, the greatest, the most august, the most magnificent of all the celestial envoys, and in memory of the first four Caliphs, of the sainted Fâtimah, of the chaste Khadeeja, of the Imâms Hasan and Husain, of all the martyrs of the memorable day, of the ten evangelical disciples, the virtuous sponsors of our sainted Prophet, of all his zealous and faithful disciples, of all the Imâms, Mujtahids (sacred interpreters), of all the doctors, of all the holy men and women of Mussulmanism. Let us chant also in honour of Hazreti Mevlânâ, the founder of our Order, of Hazreti Sultan ul 'Ulema (his father), of Sayid Burhân ed Deen (his teacher), of Sheikh Shems ed Din (his consecrator), of Vâlideh Sultan (his mother), of Mohammed 'Allay ed Deen Efendi (his son and vicar), of all the Chelebees (his successors), of all the sheikhs, of all the Dervishes, and all the protectors of our Order, to whom the Supreme Being deigns to give peace and mercy. Let us pray for the constant prosperity of our holy society, for the preservation of the very learned and venerable Chelebee Efendi (the General of the Order), our master and lord, for the preservation of the reigning Sultan, the very majestic and clement Emperor of the Mussulman faith, for the prosperity of the Grand Vizier, and of the Sheikh ul Islâm, and that of all the Mohammedan militia, of all the pilgrims of the holy city of Mekkeh. Let us pray for the repose of the souls of all the institutors, of all the sheikhs, and of all the Dervishes of all other Orders; for all good people, for all those who have been distinguished by their good works, their foundations, and their acts of beneficence. Let us pray also for all the Mussulmans of one and the other sex of the east and the west, for the maintenance of all prosperity, for preventing all adversity, for the accomplishment of all salutary vows, and for the success of all praiseworthy enterprises; finally, let us ask God to deign to preserve in us the gift of His grace, and the fire of holy love.'

"After the Fâtiha, which the assembly chant in a body, the Sheikh recites the Fâtiha and the Salawât, to which the dance of the Dervishes succeeds. Leaving their places all at once, they stand in a file to the left of the superior, and, approaching near him with slow steps, the arms folded, and the head bent to the floor, the first of the Dervishes, arrived nearly opposite the Sheikh, salutes, with a profound inclination, the tablet which is on his seat, on which is the name of Hazreti Mevlânâ, the founder of the Order. Advancing next by two springs forward, to the right side of the superior, he turns toward him, salutes him with reverence, and commences the dance, which consists in turning on the left heel, in advancing slowly, and almost insensibly making the turn of the hall, the eyes closed, and the arms open. He is followed by the second Dervish, he by the third, and so on with all the others, who end by filling up the whole of the hall, each repeating the same exercises separately, and all at a certain distance from each other.

"This dance lasts sometimes for a couple of hours; it is only interrupted by two short pauses, during which the Sheikh recites different prayers. Towards the close of the exercises, he takes a part in them himself, by placing himself in the midst of the Dervishes; then returning to his seat, he recites some Persian verses expressive of good wishes for the prosperity of the religion, and the State. The General of the Order is again named, also the reigning Sultan, in the following terms: 'The Emperor of the Mussalmans, and the most august of monarchs of the house of 'Othman, Sultan, son of a sultan, grandson of a sultan, Sultan ——, son of Sultan ——, Khan,' &c.

"Here the poem mentions all the princes of blood, the Grand Vizier, the Muftee, all the Pashas of the empire, the 'Ulemas, all the Sheikhs, benefactors of the Order, and of all the Mussulman peers, invoking the benediction of heaven on the success of their arms against the enemies of the empire. 'Finally, let us pray for all the Dervishes present and absent, for all the friends of our holy society, and generally for all the faithful, dead and living, in the east and in the west.

"The ceremony terminates by chanting the Fâtiha, or first chapter of the Koran."

(John P. Brown, *The Dervishes, or Oriental Spiritualism*, p. 218 *seqq.*)

These ceremonies of *ẕikr* would at first sight appear to have little in common with original Muḥammadanism, but there appears to be little doubt that the practice of reciting the word *Allāh* and other similar expressions, commenced in the days of Muḥammad himself, and this even the Wahhābīs admit, who at the same time condemn the extravagances of the Howling and Dancing Darveshes of Turkistan, Turkey, and Egypt.

A chapter is devoted to the Prophet's injunctions on the subject in all large books of traditions, called *Bābu 'ẕ-Ẕikr*, from which the following sayings of Muḥammad have been selected:—

Whenever people sit and remember God, they are surrounded by angels which cover them with God's favour, and peace descends upon them, and God remembers them in that assembly which is near him.

Verily there are angels who move to and fro on the roads and seek for the rememberers of God, and when they find an assembly remembering God, they say to one another, "Come ye to that which ye were seeking." Then the angels cover them with their wings as far as the lowest heaven, called the region of the world. The Prophet said:—When the angels go to the court of God, God asks them, while knowing better than they, "What do my servants say and do?" Then the angels say, "They are reciting the Tasbīḥ, the Takbīr, the Taḥmīd, and the Tamjīd for Thee." And God says, "Have they seen Me?" The angels say, "No, by God, they have not seen Thee." Then God says, "What would their condition be if they had seen Me?" The angels say, "If they had seen Thee, they would be more energetic in worshipping Thee and in reciting the Tamjīd, and they would be more excessive in repeating the Tasbīḥ." God says, "Then what do they want?" The angels say, "Paradise." Then God says, "Have they seen Paradise?" The angels say, "We swear by God they have not." Then God says, "What would their state have been had they seen Paradise?" The angels say, "If they had seen Paradise, they would be very ambitious for it, and would be excessive wishers of it, and very great desirers of it." God says, "What thing is it they seek protection from?" The angels say, "From hell fire." God says, "Have they seen the fire?" The angels say, "No, by God, if they had seen the fire——" God says, "How would they have been had they seen the fire?" The angels say, "If they had seen the fire, they would be great runners from it, and would be great fearers of it." Then God says, "I take ye as witnesses that verily I have pardoned them." One of the angels said, "There is a person amongst them who is not a rememberer of Thee, and is only come on account of his own needs."

There is a polish for everything that takes rust, and the polish for the heart is the remembrance of God, and there is no act that redeems from God's punishments so much as the remembrance of Him. The Companions said, "Is not fighting with the infidels also like this?" He said, "No, although he fights until his sword be broken."

"Shall I not inform you of an action which is better for you than fighting with infidels and cutting off their heads, and their cutting off yours?" The Companions said, "Yes, inform us." The Prophet said, "These actions are remembering God."

'Abdullāh ibn Aus said:—An 'Arabī came to the Prophet and asked, "Which is the best of men?" The Prophet said, "Blessed is the person whose life is long and whose actions are good." The 'Arabī said, "O Prophet! which is the best of actions, and the most rewarded?" He said, "The best of actions is this, that you separate from the world, and die whilst your tongue is moist in repeating the name of God."

A man said, "O Prophet of God, really the rules of Islām are many, tell me a thing by which I may lay hold of rewards." The Prophet said, "Let your tongue be always moist in the remembrance of God."

"Verily there are ninety-nine names of God; whosoever counts them up shall enter into Paradise." And in another tradition it is added, "God is *Witr* and like *Witr*."

When Ẕū 'n-Nūn (Jonah) the prophet prayed his Lord, when he was in the fish's belly, he said, "There is no Deity but Thee. I extol Thy holiness. Verily I am of the unjust ones." And a Mussalman who supplicates God with this petition will have his prayer granted.

The best expressions are these four: Subhāna Allahi, al-Hamdu Lillāhi, La ilāha illā 'llāhu, and Allāhu akbar; and it does not matter with which of them you begin.

Verily I like repeating these four expressions: O Holy God! Praise be to God! There is no deity but God! and God is Great! better than anything upon which the sun shines.

No one can bring a better deed on the Day of Resurrection (unless he shall have said the like or added to it) than he who has recited, "O Holy God! Praise be to Thee!" one hundred times every morning and evening.

There are two expressions light upon the tongue and heavy in the scale of good works, and they are, "O Holy God! Praise be to Thee!" and "O Holy God! the Mighty One!"

That person who shall say, "There is no deity but God, who has no partner, to whom is dominion and praise and power," one hundred times, shall receive rewards equal to the emancipating of ten slaves; and one hundred good actions shall be written for him, and one hundred of his sins shall be blotted out; and those words shall be a protection to him from the devil and his wickedness, in that day in which he shall have repeated them, until the night. Nor can anyone perform a better deed for the Day of Resurrection than this, unless he has done even more.

Moses said, "O my Lord, teach me how I am to call upon Thee." And God said, "O Moses, recite 'There is no deity but God!'" Then Moses said, "O my Lord, every one of Thy people say this." And God said, "O Moses, if the seven heavens and their inhabitants and the seven earths were put into one scale, and this expression, 'There is no deity but God,' into another, these words would exceed in weight."

Reciting "O Holy God" is half the scale of good works, and reciting "God be praised," fills the scale. The recital of "There is no deity but one," removes the curtain between the worshipper and his God.

He who recites with an unsullied heart "There is no deity but God," shall have the doors of heaven open for him until he reaches the throne of God, as long as he abstains from great sins.

The ejaculation, "There is no power and strength but in God," is medicine for ninety-nine pains, the least of which is melancholy.

"There are two qualities which, being practised by anyone, shall cause him to enter Paradise; they are small and easy, and it is easy for anyone to practise them. One of them is this: saying 'God is holy' ten times after every prayer, 'Praised be God' ten times, and 'God is great' ten times." And verily I saw the Prophet counting these words on his hand, and he would say, "Then these words are one hundred and fifty with the tongue in the day and night, but they are one thousand and five hundred in the scale of actions, reckoning ten for one. And the second is this: when he goes to his bed-chamber, let him say, 'God is holy,' and 'God be praised,' and 'God is great,' then that is one hundred on the tongue and a thousand in the scales. Then which of you is it that commits two thousand five hundred vices in the day and night, so that these words may cover them?" The Companions said, "If when we repeat these words we have so many rewards, why should we not say them?" The Prophet said, "The Devil comes to one of you when at prayers and says to him, 'Remember so-and-so,' till you have finished your prayers; and the Devil comes to you in your bed-chamber, and is always making you sleep."

AZ-ZILLU 'L-AUWAL (الظل الاول). "The first shade." A Ṣūfī term for *al-'Aqlu 'l-Auwal.* [SUFI.]

ZILLU 'LLĀH (ظل الله). "The Shade of God." A Ṣūfī term for the *Insānu 'l-Kāmil*, or the "perfect man." [SUFI.]

AZ-ZILZĀL (الزلزال). "The Earthquake." The title of the XCIXth Sūrah of the Qur'ān, beginning with the words "When the earth shall quake with its quaking."

ZIMMAH (ذمة), pl. *zimam*, from the root *zamm*, "to blame." A compact, covenant, or contract, a league or treaty, any engagement or obligation, because the breaking thereof necessitates blame; and a right or due, for the neglect of which one is to be blamed. The word is also synonymous with *amān*, in the sense of security of life and property, protection or safeguard, and promise of such; hence *ahlu 'z-zimmah*, or, with suppression of the noun *ahlu*, simply *az-zimmah*, the people with whom a compact or covenant has been made, and particularly the Kitābīs, or the people of the book, *i.e.* Jews and Christians, and the Majūsī or Sabeans, who pay the poll-tax called *jazyah.* [JAZYAH.] An individual of this class—namely, a free non-Muslim subject of a Muslim Government, who pays a poll- or capitation-tax, for which the Muslims are responsible for his security, personal freedom, and religious toleration—is called *zimmī* (see the following article).

In the Qur'ān, the word *zimmah* occurs once, in the sense of clientship, or good faith, as oppposed to ties of blood. Sūrah ix. 7-10:—

"How can they who add gods to God be in league with God and with His Apostle, save those with whom ye made a league at the sacred temple? So long as they are true to you, be ye true to them: verily, God loveth those who fear Him.

"How can they? since if they prevail against you, they will not regard, in their dealing with you, either ties of blood or *good faith*: With their mouths they content you, but their hearts are averse, and most of them are perverse doers.

"They sell the signs of God for a mean price, and turn others aside from his way: of a truth, evil is it that they do!

"They respect not with a believer either ties of blood or *good faith*; and these are the transgressors."

In modern language, the word *zimmah* has frequently the meaning of conscience. (Compare Lane's *Arabic Dictionary, in loco.*)

ZIMMĪ (ذمى), a member of the Ahlu 'z-Zimmah, a non-Muslim subject of a Muslim Government, belonging to the Jewish, Christian, or Sabean creed, who, for the payment of a poll- or capitation-tax, enjoys security of his person and property in a Muḥammadan country.

One of the most urgent duties enjoined by Muḥammad upon the Muslim or true believer, was the Jihād fī Sabīli 'llāhi, or exertion in the road of God, *i.e.* warfare for the spread of Islām, amongst the infidels within and without Arabia [JIHAD]; thus the whole world came to be regarded as divided into two great portions, the Dāru 'l-Ḥarb and Dāru 'l-Islām [DARU 'L-HARB, DARU 'L-ISLAM]—the territories of War and the territories of Peace. These two divisions, one of which represented the land of infidelity and darkness, the other that of light and faith, were supposed to be in a continual state of open or latent belligerency, until the Dāru 'l-Islām should have absorbed the Dāru 'l-Ḥarb and faith conquered unbelief. Infidelity, however, admits of degrees. Its worst shape is idolatry, that is, the worship of idols instead of or besides the *one* true God; and this, again, is a crime most abominable on the part of Arabs, "since the Prophet was sent amongst them, and manifested himself in the midst of them, and the Qur'ān was delivered down in their language." Of an equally atrocious character is the infidelity of apostates, "because they have become infidels, after having been led into the way of faith, and made acquainted with its excellence." In the case of neither, therefore, is a compromise admissible; they must accept or re-embrace the faith, or pay with their lives the full penalty of their crime.

With regard to the idolaters of a non-Arabic or 'Ajam country, which latter expression in the times of early Islām particularly applied to the Persian Empire, ash-Shāfi'ī maintains that destruction is incurred by them also; but the other learned doctors agree that it is lawful to reduce them to slavery, thus allowing them, as it were, a respite during which it may please God to direct them into the right path, but making, at the same time, their persons and substance subservient to the cause of Islām.

The least objectionable form of infidelity in the eyes of Muhammad and his followers, is that of the Kitābīs or people of the Book (*ahlu 'l-kitāb*), *i.e.* the Jews, as possesssors of the Old Testament, or Taurāt, and the Christians, to whom, moreover, the Injīl (Gospel) was revealed. As they are not guilty of an absolute denial, but only of a partial perversion of the truth, only part of the punishment for disbelief is their due, and it is imposed upon them in the shape of a tribute, called poll- or capitation- tax [JAZYAH], by means of which they secure protection for their property, personal freedom, and religious toleration from the Muslim Government. The same privilege is extended to the Majūsī or Sabeans, whose particular form of worship was more leniently judged by Muḥammad and the Traditionists than that of the idolaters of Persia.

This is the state of things if a country inhabited by such infidels be conquered by a Muslim army: theoretically, the inhabitants, together with their wives and children, are considered as plunder and property of the State, and it would be lawful to reduce them to slavery. In practice, however, the milder course prevails, and by paying the stipulated capitation-tax, the subdued people become, in the quality of Ẕimmīs, free subjects of the conquering power, whose condition is but little inferior to that of their Muslim fellow-subjects.

The relations of an alien or Ḥarbī—that is, one who belongs to the people of the Dāru 'l-ḥarb—to a Muslim community which he visits, in time of peace, for the sake of traffic or any other legitimate purpose, are regulated by that high conception of the duties of hospitality, which was innate with the ancient Arab, and which prompted him to defend and honour even a mortal enemy, as soon as he might have crossed as a chance guest the threshold of his tent.

On entering the territory, an alien can claim a guest's protection from the first met Muslim, be it even the lowest peasant, and having obtained this protection, he is entitled to remain in the country unmolested for the term of a whole year. The authorities, however, must within the year give him notice that, if he should remain until its completion, capitation-tax will be imposed upon him, and in such notice the permission for his stay may be limited to some months only, if for some reason or other it should appear advisable or necessary to do so. If the alien continue in the country beyond the full or limited time prescribed, he becomes *ipso facto* liable to the capitation-tax, and if, after thus becoming a Ẕimmī, he be desirous of returning to his own country, he may be prevented, as now being bound to the Muslim Government by a contract of fealty. In similar manner an alien becomes a Ẕimmī upon purchasing tribute land and paying the impost on it, and is then liable to captitation-tax for the ensuing year. An alien woman turns Ẕimmīyah by marrying a Ẕimmī, because thereby she undertakes to reside in the Muḥammadan state. (See Hamilton's *Hidāyah*, vol. ii. p. 196.)

Ẕimmīs do not subject themselves to the laws of Islām, either with respect to things which are merely of a religious nature, such as fasting and prayer, or with respect to those temporal acts which, though contrary to the Muḥammadan religion, may be legal by their own, such as the sale of wine or swine's flesh. The construction of places of worship in the Muslim territory is unlawful for them, unless within their own houses, but if churches and synagogues originally belonging to Christians and Jews be destroyed or fall to decay, they are at liberty to rebuild and repair them. This is the rule with regard to cities, because, as the tokens of Islām, such as public prayer, festivals, &c., appear there, Ẕimmīs should not be permitted to exhibit the tokens of infidelity in the face of them; in villages and hamlets, on the other hand, where the tokens of Islām do not appear, there is no occasion to prevent the construction of Christian and Jewish places of worship. (See Hamilton's *Hidāyah*, vol. ii. p. 219.)

Save some slight restrictions with regard to dress and equipage, Ẕimmīs are held in all transactions of daily life pretty much on a footing of equality with Muslims. Like children, women and slaves, a Ẕimmī has no legal share in the booty, but only a discretionary allowance out of it, if he has taken part in the fight. If he has acted as a guide, and his services as such have been attended with any eminent advantage, he may, however, receive even a larger share than a Muḥammadan combatant. (Hamilton's *Hidāyah*, vol. ii., p. 178.)

Every marriage that is lawful between two Muslims, is lawful between two Ẕimmīs. Marriages that are not lawful between two Muslims are of several kinds. Of these there is the marriage without witnesses. When a Ẕimmī marries a Ẕimmīyah without witnesses, and such marriages are sanctioned by their religion, the marriage is lawful. So that, if they should afterwards embrace the Muslim faith, the marriage would still be established. And in like manner, if they should not embrace that faith, but should both claim from the judge the application of the rules of Islām, or one of them should make such a claim, the judge is not to separate them. There is also the marriage of a woman during her *'iddah* on account of another man ['IDDAH]. When a Ẕimmī marries a woman in her *'iddah* for another man, that man being a Muslim, the marriage is invalid, and may be objected to before their adoption of the Muḥammadan religion, even though their own religion should recognise the legality of marriage in the state of *'iddah*; but if the *'iddah* were rendered incumbent on the woman on account of an infidel, and marriages in a state of *'iddah* are accounted lawful in the religion of the parties, it cannot be objected to while they remain in a state of infidelity, according to general agreement. If under these circumstances they afterwards adopt the Muslim faith, the marriage remains fixed and established, according to Abū Ḥanīfah, whose decision is considered valid in spite of the different opinions of Abū Yūsuf and Muḥammad, and the judge is not to separate them, though both of them or only one of them should adopt the faith, or both or only one of them should bring the matter before the judge. In the Mabsūṭ it is stated that the difference between the masters was only when the reference to the judge, or the adoption of the faith, takes place during the subsistence of the *'iddah*; but where it does not take place till after the *'iddah* has expired, the parties are not to be separated, according to all their opinions. (Baillie's *Digest of Moohummudan Law, Hanifeea*, p. 178.)

If a Z̲immī marry a Z̲immīyah, making the dower consist of wine or pork, and one or both should afterwards embrace the faith before the wife has obtained seisin, according to Abū Ḥanīfah, the woman is entitled to receive the actual article, if it has been "identically specified," but if not, the estimated value of the wine, or her proper dower in lieu of the pork, as the case may be. Abū Yūsuf maintains that she is to have her proper dower, and Muḥammad the estimated value in all cases. If a Christian Z̲immī marry a Christian Z̲immīyah, without specifying any dower, or on a specified dower consisting of carrion (flesh of an animal not lawfully slain), such as may be deemed lawful by members of their profession, and have sexual intercourse with her, or divorce her without consummation, or die without consummation, according to Abū Ḥanīfah, she is not entitled to any dower, although both parties may have embraced the faith in the interim; but according to Abū Yūsuf and Muḥammad, she will take her proper dower if the husband consummate the marriage, or die without consummation, and will be entitled to a present if she be divorced without consummation. (A. Rumsey, *Moohummudan Law of Inheritance*, p. 373.)

When one of an infidel married couple embraces the Muḥammadan faith, Islām is to be presented to the other, and if the other adopt it, good and well; if not, they are to be separated. If the party is silent and says nothing, the judge is to present Islām to him time after time, till the completion of three, by way of caution. And there is no difference between a discerning youth and one who is adult; so that a separation is to be made equally on the refusal of the former as of the latter, according to Abū Ḥanīfah and the Imām Muḥammad. But if one of the parties be young and without sufficient discernment, it is necessary to wait till he has understanding; and when he has understanding, Islām is then to be presented to him; and if he adopt it, well; if not, a separation is to be made without waiting for his arriving at puberty. And if he be mad, Islām is to be presented to his parents; and if they, or one of them, should embrace it, good and well; if not, a separation is to be made between the married parties. If the husband should embrace the faith and the wife refuse, the separation is not accounted repudiation; but if the wife should embrace the faith and the husband decline, the separation in consequence is considered a repudiation, since the cause of separation proceeds from him. When a separation takes place between them by reason of refusal, and it is after consummation, she is entitled to the whole dower; and if it is before consummation and through his refusal, she is entitled to half the dower; but if through her own refusal, she has no dower at all. If, however, the husband of a Kitābīyah adopt the faith, their marriage remains unaffected in accordance with the general principle, that the marriage between a Muslim and a Kitābīyah is originally lawful. (Bailley, *Hanifeea Code*, p. 180.)

When a Z̲immī has repudiated his Z̲immīyah wife three times, and then behaves to her as he had done before the repudiation, without marrying her again, or saying the words of the contract over her; or when his wife has obtained a *k̲h̲ul'* or release [KHUL'], and he then acts to her as before without renewing the contact—they are to be separated, even though they should not bring the matter to the judge. But if he repudiates her three times, and then renews the contract of marriage with her without her being married to another, they are not to be separated. (*Ib.*)

The child follows the religion of the better of its parents. Hence, if one of them be a Muslim, the child is of the Muslim religion. The mother could not be so *ab initio*, but only in consequence of conversion to the Muḥammadan faith, for a Muslim woman cannot lawfully be the wife of any other than a man of her own religion. So also, if one of them should subsequently embrace Islām, having an infant child, the infant would become Muslim by virtue of the parent's conversion, that is, when there is no difference of *dār*, by both of the parents being either within the Dāru 'l-Islām or the Dāru 'l-Ḥarb, or by the child being in the former at the time that its parent embraces the Muslim faith in the foreign country, for he then becomes constructively one of the Muslim people; but when the child is in the foreign country, and the parent within the Muslim territory, and he adopt the faith there, the child does not follow him, and is not a Muslim. A Majūsī is worse than a Kitābī; and if one of the parents be a Majūsī and the other Kitābī, the child is a Kitābī, and may be lawfully married by a Muslim, to whom also things slaughtered by the child would be lawful.

Generally, an infidel cannot *inherit* from a believer, nor, on the other hand, can a believer inherit from an infidel; but infidel subjects of a Muslim state can inherit from one another. And it is immaterial, for such a purpose, whether they be of the same religion or not; all unbelievers being, in this respect, considered as of one class. A Muslim may, however, make a *bequest* to a Z̲immī, and a Z̲immī to a Muslim, as well as to another infidel, whether of the same or of a different religion, not being a hostile alien. The testamentary power of a Z̲immī is subject to the same limitations as that of a Muslim, so that bequests to a person entitled by inheritance are invalid, and bequests to any other person are invalid so far as they exceed one-third of the testator's property. This for the reason that, on entering into the compact of Zimmah, he has agreed to conform to the laws of Islām in all temporal concerns. (See A. Rumsey, *Moohummudan Law of Inheritance*, p. 222.)

The will of a Zimmī for secular purposes is valid, according to all opinions. Other than secular purposes are of four different kinds. First, there are purposes which are *qurbah*, or a means of approach to Almighty God, both with Zimmīs and Muslims; and bequests for these purposes are valid, whether they be to a set of particular persons or not. Thus, when a Kitābī has directed, by his will, that slaves be purchased and emancipated on his account, whether with or without a specification of individuals, or that a third of his property be bestowed in charity on beggars and the indigent, or expended in lighting a lamp in the Baitu 'l-Muqaddas or Holy Temple of Jerusalem, or in making war against the infidel Tartars, the bequest is valid.

Second, there are purposes which are sinful, both with the Zimmīs and the Muslims; and bequests for these purposes are valid, if they are to a set of particular persons, and the bequest is a gift without regard to the purposes; but if the persons are not particularised, the bequest is void. If, therefore, a Zimmī should bequeath, for instance, a third of his property for the support of dissolute women, singers, and the like, the bequest is valid, if such persons are particularised and it is a gift to them; but if they are not particularised, it is void.

Third, there are purposes which are *qurbah* with the Muslims, but sinful with the Zimmīs. In this, as in the previous case, the bequest is a gift and valid if in favour of a set of particular persons; but it is void, if the persons are not particularised. Hence, if the third of a man's property is to be expended in sending a set of Muslims on pilgrimage, or building a masjid, and the persons are particularised, the bequest or gift is valid, and considered to be coupled with a counsel to accomplish the stated purpose, leaving them at liberty to perform the pilgrimage, or erect the mosque, or not, as they please.

Fourth and last, there are purposes which are sinful with a Muslim, but *qurbah* or meritorious with a Zimmī; and bequests for these are valid, according to Abū Ḥanīfah, whether the persons be particularised or not; but void, according to Abū Yūsuf and the Imām Muḥammad, when they are not specified. If, for instance, a Kitābī bequeath a third of his property for the erection of a church or synagogue; or bequeath his mansion to be converted into a place of worship of his religion, the bequest, according to the two disciples, is void, as sinful in the eyes of a Muslim, unless it is for a particular class of persons, when it is a gift to them; but, according to Abū Ḥanīfah, it is valid under all circumstances. This, however, subject to the condition stated above, that the erection of such buildings takes place in villages and not in towns, the bequest in the latter case being inoperative. (See Bailley, *Hanifeea Code*, p. 673.)

If a Jew or a Christian, being in sound health, build a church or a synagogue, and then die, such building is an inheritance, according to all the doctors, and therefore descends to the heirs in the same manner as any other of the founder's property. From the point of view taken by the two disciples this is evident enough. But with regard to Abū Ḥanīfah's doctrine, the question may be raised: What is the difference between the building of a church or synagogue in the time of health, and the bequeathing it by will, that Abū Hanīfah should hold it inheritable in the former instance, and not in the latter. This "objection" is met in the *Hidāyah* with the "reply": "that it is not the mere erecting (of the church, &c.) which extinguishes the builder's property, but the exclusive dedication of the building to the service of God, as in the case of mosques erected by Mussulmāns; and as an infidel place of worship is not dedicated to God indisputably, it therefore still remains the property of the founder, and is consequently inheritable (in common with his other effects); whereas a bequest, on the contrary, is used for the very purpose of destroying a right of property." (*Hidāyah*, Grady's Translation, p. 696.)

ZINA' (زناء). [ADULTERY.]

ZINDĪQ (زنديق).

A term now used to express a person in a hopeless state of infidelity. Some say the word is derived from the Persian *Zan-dīn*, *i.e.* a woman's religion. Others assert that it is a term of relation to the word *Zand* or *Zend*, which means "explanation," *i.e.* the explanation of the book of Zardusht or Zoroaster. (See Lane's *Arabic Dictionary, in loco.*)

ZIPPORAH. [SAFURA'.]

ZIYĀRAH (زيارة),

from the root *zaur*, "to visit," visitation, particularly of the tomb of the Prophet, and of the grave of any martyr or saint of the Muḥammadan faith. In India and Central Asia, the word, always pronounced *ziyārat*, is, by way of abbreviation, used for *ziyārat-gāh*, *i.e.* for the place of such visitation, or the shrine connected with it.

Although it is held by Wahhābīs and other Muslim puritans that the Prophet forbade the visitation of graves for the purposes of devotion, the custom has become so common, that it may be considered part of the Muḥammadan religion. And, indeed, it is difficult to believe that a religious teacher of Muḥammad's cast of mind should have in principle opposed a practice which is so natural to the human heart. However much he may have objected to the clamorous wailings and lamentations over the dead, in which the pagan Arabs of the ignorance, especially the women, indulged, he was not likely to be insensible to the solemn lesson which the resting-place of the departed teaches the living, or to stifle in his followers the pious remembrance of beloved friends and kindred who have gone before. We see, therefore, no reason to doubt the genuineness of the following traditions, which we translate from a manuscript of the *Mishkāt*, belonging to the Library of the India Office (Arabic MSS., No. 2143, New Catalogue, 154), and which the compiler of that work has taken from such authorities as Muslim, Ibn Mājah, at-Tirmizī, &c.

Buraidah related, the Apostle of God said: "(Formerly) I forbade you to visit the graves, but you may visit them now. . . ." (Muslim.) Abū Hurairah related: the Prophet visited the grave of his mother, and he wept and caused those who were around him to weep also. Then he said: "I begged leave from my Lord to ask forgiveness for her, but it was not granted me; then I begged leave to visit her grave, and it was granted me; visit therefore the graves, for they remind you of death." (Muslim.)

Buraidah related: The Apostle of God used to instruct them, when they issued forth to the burial-places, to pronounce the words: "Peace be upon you, O ye people of these abodes from amongst the Believers and the Resigned; and we, if God please, are surely overtaking you to ask salvation from God for us and you." (Muslim.)

Ibn 'Abbās related: The Prophet passed by some graves in al-Madīnah, and he turned his face towards them and said: "Peace be upon you, O ye people of the graves; may God forgive us and you; ye are the van of us and we (following) in your steps."

'Āyishah related that when the turn of her night had come on the Prophet's part, he used to step out towards the end of the night into al-Baqī' (the burial-ground of al-Madīnah) and to say: "Peace be with the abode of a believing people; and the time that has been promised you as your appointed term may come to you on the morrow (speedily); and we, if please God, are overtaking you. O God, grant forgiveness to the people of Baqī'u 'l-Garqad." She asked: "What shall I say, O Apostle of God, to wit, on visiting the graves?" He replied: "Say, Peace be upon the people of these abodes from amongst the Believers and the Resigned, and God have compassion on those of us that go before and those that follow; and we, if please God, are overtaking you." (Muslim.)

Muḥammad ibn Nu'ām related, the Prophet said: "He who visits the grave of his father and mother, or of either of them, on every Friday, his sins are forgiven, and he is written down as one pious." (Baihaqī).

Ibn Mas'ūd related, the Apostle of God said: "I had forbidden you to visit the graves, but now ye may visit them, for they detach from this world and remind of the world to come." (Ibn Mājah.)

Abū Hurairah related: "The Apostle of God cursed women visiting the graves." To this the compiler of the *Mishkāt* adds: At-Tirmizī calls this tradition a well-supported and genuine one, and says: "Some of the learned are of opinion that this happened before the Prophet permitted the visitation of the graves, but that when he did so, both men and women were included in the permission; and some again allege, that he only disapproved of women visiting the graves, because they are but little given to patience and much to fear."

In the face of these texts we cannot wonder that the practice of visiting the graves forms a marked feature in the religious life of the Muḥammadans, and that the tomb of the founder of Islām and the burial-places of its chief confessors have become the objects of great devotional reverence. Pilgrims to Makkah (except the Wahhābīs) always proceed to al-Madīnah to visit the Prophet's shrine and to claim an interest in his intercessions, and in all Muḥammadan countries there are *ziyārats* or "shrines," which are visited by devotees in order to obtain the intercessions of the departed saint. Such a *ziyārat* is the grave of Khwājah 'Abdu 'llāh Anṣārī, who flourished about the time of our King John, A.D. 1200, and who established such a reputation for sanctity that even to this day his tomb, at Gazarghaiah near Herat, is visited by pilgrims from all parts of the province. This tomb is an exceedingly fine piece of Oriental sculpture. Upon its marble slabs are inscribed, in the finest *ṣuluṣ* writing, verses from the Qur'ān. But the chief historic interest in the shrine of this saint is found in the fact that Dost Muḥammad Khān, the great Afghān Ameer of Cabul (A.D. 1863), requested that his bones should be interred at the feet of Khwājah 'Abdu 'llāh, in order that his dark deeds of blood may obtain forgiveness through the potent intercession of this ancient saint. Such is one of the many instances of the great importance which Eastern rulers have attached to the sanctity of the very ground in which have been buried the remains of some great teacher or ascetic.

In towns and in great centres of population, the tombs which are visited as *ziyārats* are usually substantial structures; but in villages they are often the most simple graves, marked by a few flags, and surrounded by a low wall to keep the sacred spot free from defilement. Oftentimes the Eastern traveller will find a *ziyārat* on the road-side of some desert highway. Probably it is the resting-place of some pilgrim who, returning from Makkah, died of disease or was slain by highway robbers, in either case, according to the doctrines of Islām, suffering a martyr's death. [MARTYR.] Such a *ziyārat* will be taken charge of by some poor darwesh or faqīr, who will erect a shed near the sacred spot, and supply the weary traveller with a cup of cold water, as he stops and raises his hands in supplication at the shrine of the martyred saint.

The cures performed at *ziyārats* are diversified. Some will be celebrated as the place where rheumatism can be cured, others are suitable for small-pox patients, whilst some have even gained a reputation as places of healing for those who are bitten by mad dogs. The grave of Khushhal Khān Khatak the warrior poet of the Afghāns, in the Peshawar

A ZIYARAT IN CENTRAL ASIA. (*A. F. Hole.*)

valley, is visited by thousands of childless women.

The *ziyārats* are always visited with the feet uncovered, and when the grave is covered with stones or pebbles, these are used to rub upon the afflicted limbs. Some more substantial monuments are supplied with brushes, which are used for the double purpose of cleaning up the court-yard and for rubbing upon the diseased body of the devotee.

These *ziyārats* are always lighted up with small lamps on Thursday evening, which is the beginning of the Eastern Friday. But Sunday is held to be a propitious day for visiting shrines.

Adjoining many *ziyārats* of eminence, there will be mosques supported by large endowments, in which will be found a large number of students. Such is the renowned *ziyārat* of Kaka Ṣāhib in the Khatak hills on the Afghān frontier. Many *ziyārats* are very largely endowed by princes and nobles, who have believed that they have obtained assistance from the intercessions of the departed saint. There is, however, no proof that Muḥammad ever encouraged the belief that the prayers of departed saints were of any avail in the presence of the Almighty. Indeed, it is a distinctive teaching of Islām that even the Prophet himself cannot intercede for his own people until the Day of Judgment. [INTERCESSION.]

A ROAD-SIDE ZIYARAT IN CENTRAL ASIA. (*E. S. Jukes.*)

ZODIAC, The signs of. Arabic *minṭaqatu 'l-burūj* (منطقة البروج). "The girdle or zone of towers." Greek πύργοι. Mentioned three times in the Qur'ān.

Sūrah lxxxv. 1:

"By the heaven with its *Towers*!" (*Burūj.*)

Sūrah xxv. 62:

"Blessed be He who hath placed in the Heaven the sign of the Zodiac! who hath placed in it the Lamp *of the Sun*, and the light-giving Moon!"

Sūrah xv. 16:

"We have set the signs of the zodiac in the Heavens, and adorned and decked them forth for the beholders.

"And We guard them from every stoned Satan,

"Save such as steal a hearing: and him doth a visible flame pursue."

In explanation of the last verses, commentators tell us that the devils listen at the gate of heaven for scraps of the knowledge of futurity, and when detected by the angels, are pelted with shooting stars (see Sūrah iii. 31: "the *pelted devil*"; also Sūrah xxxvii. 8: "hurled at from every side").

So in the Talmud, in Chagiya xvi. 1, the *shadeem*, or "demons," are said to learn the secrets of the future by listening behind the *pargōd* or "veil."

The names of the signs are:

1. *Ḥamal*, Ram.
2. *Ṣaur*, Bull.
3. *Jauzā'*, Twins.
4. *Sarṭān*, Crab.
5. *Asad*, Lion.
6. *Sumbalah*, *lit.* an "ear of corn," Virgin.
7. *Mīzān*, Scales.
8. *'Aqrab*, Scorpion.
9. *Qaus*, Archer.
10. *Jadī*, He-goat.
11. *Dalw*, Watering-pot.
12. *Ḥūt*, Fish.

ZOROASTRIANISM. The ancient religion of Persia is only referred to once in the Qur'ān, Sūrah xxii. 17, as the religion of the *Majūs* (المجوس), the Magians. Most Muḥammadan writers, especially amongst the Shī'ahs, believe them to have formerly possessed a revelation from God which they have since lost. [AL-MAJUS.]

ZUBAIR IBN AL-'AUWĀM (زبير بن العوام). Cousin german to Muḥammad, and one of the first who embraced his religion. He is one of the ten, called al-'Asharah al-Mubashsharah, to whom the Prophet gave certain assurances of Paradise. He was slain by 'Amr ibn Jurmūz on the day of the battle of the Camel (*waq'atu 'l-Jamal*), A.H. 6.

ẒUḤĀ (ضحى). (1) That part of the day about half-way between sunrise and noon.

(2) A period of voluntary prayer. [PRAYER.]

(3) *Aẓ-Ẓuḥā*, the title of the XCIIIrd Sūrah of the Qur'ān, which begins with the words, "By the noon-day brightness" (*ẓuḥā*).

ZUHD (زهد). Abstinence; a religious life. Exercising oneself in the service of God; especially being abstinent in respect of eating; subduing the passions.

AZ-ZUKHRUF (الزخرف). "Gilding." The name of the XLIIIrd Sūrah of the Qur'ān, in the 34th verse of which the word occurs: "And but that men would then have been one nation, we would have made for those who misbelieve in the Merciful, one roof of silver for their houses, and steps up thereto which they might mount; and to their houses doors, and bedsteads on which they might recline; and *gilding*."

ZULAIKHĀ', more correctly **ZALĪKHĀ** (زليخاء). The wife of Potiphar (*Qiṭfīr*). Al-Baiẓāwī says she was also called Rā'īl. An account of her tempting Joseph is found in the XIIth Sūrah of the Qūr'ān, 23–25:—

"And she in whose house he was, conceived a passion for him, and she shut the doors and said, 'Come hither.' He said, 'God keep me! Verily my lord hath given me a good home: verily the injurious shall not prosper.'

"But she longed for him; and he had longed for her had he not seen a token from his Lord (the apparition of his father, who said, 'Hereafter shall the names of thy brethren, engraven on precious stones, shine on the breast of the High Priest. Shall thine be blotted out?') Thus we averted evil and defilement from him; verily he was one of our sincere servants.

"And they both made for the door, and she rent his shirt from behind; and at the door they met her lord. 'What,' said she, 'shall be the recompense of him who intended evil to my family, but a prison or a sore punishment?'

"He said, 'She solicited me to evil.' And a witness in her own family (an infant in the cradle) witnessed: 'If his shirt be rent in front, then hath she spoken truth, and he is a liar:

"'But if his shirt be rent from behind, then she hath lied and he is a man of truth.'

"And when his lord saw his shirt torn from behind, he said, 'This verily is one of your devices! verily your devices are great!

"'Joseph! turn away from this; and thou *O wife*, ask pardon for thy crime: verily thou hast sinned.'

"And in the city the women said, 'The wife of the Prince hath solicited her servant: he hath fired her with love: verily we perceive her to be in a manifest error.'

"And when she heard of their cabal, she sent to them and got ready a banquet for them, and gave each one of them a knife, and said, '*Joseph*, come forth to them.' And when they saw him they extolled him, and cut their hands (instead of their food, through surprise at his beauty), and said, 'God keep us! This is no man! This is none other than a noble angel!'

"She said, 'This, then, is he about whom ye blamed me. And I wished him indeed to yield to my desires, but he stood firm. But if he obey not my command, he shall surely be cast into prison, and become one of the contemptible.'

"He said, 'O my Lord! I prefer the prison to compliance with her bidding: but unless Thou turn away their snares from me, I shall play the youth with them, and become one of the unwise':

"So his Lord heard him and turned aside their snares from him: verily He is the Hearer, the Knower.

"Then resolved they, *even* after they had seen the signs *of his innocence*, to imprison him for a time."

The explanations put into parentheses are notes of Mr. Rodwell's, in whose translation the passage is given, and who quotes the corresponding Talmudic legends.

This story of Yūsuf wa Zulaikhā' has been celebrated in a well-known Persian poem by 'Abdu 'r-Raḥmān Jāmī, and hence Joseph has become the Adonis of the East.

ZŪ 'L-FIQĀR (ذو الفقار). *Lit.* "The Lord of the Vertebræ of the Back." The name of the celebrated sword which Muḥammad gave to his son-in-law 'Alī.

ZŪ 'L-ḤIJJAH (ذو الحجة). *Lit.* "The Lord of the Pilgrimage." The twelfth month of the Muḥammadan year; so called because it is the month appointed for the Makkan pilgrimage.

ZŪ 'L-JALĀL (ذو الجلال). "Lord of Majesty." One of the ninety-nine attributes of God. See Qur'ān, Sūrah lv. 78: "Blessed be the name of thy Lord possessed of *majesty* and glory."

ZŪ 'L-KIFL (ذو الكفل). *Lit.* "Lord of a portion." A worthy mentioned in the Qur'ān, Sūrah xxi. 85: "And Ishmael, and Idris, and Zū 'l-Kifl, all of these were patient, and we made them enter into our mercy; verily they were among the righteous." Al-Baiẓāwī says he was so called because he had a portion with God the Most High, and guaranteed his people, or because he had double the work of the prophets of his time, and their reward. According to some writers, he was either Elias, or Joshua, or Zachariah.

The root *kafl*, having also the meaning of "care," "support," other interpreters identify him with the Obadiah of 1 Kings xviii. 4, who *supported* one hundred prophets in the cave; or Ezekiel, who is called *Kāfil* by the Arabs. See Niebuhr, *Travels*, vol. ii. p. 265.

ẒULM (ظلم). *Lit.* "Putting a thing not in its proper place." (*Ar-Raghib, in loco.*) Wrong-doing; acting tyranically. Muḥammad ibn aṭ-Ṭaiyib, the author of *Annotations on the Qāmūs*, says *ẓulm* is of three kinds: (1) between man and God, (2) between man and man, (3) between man and himself. In the Qur'ān—

Sūrah iii. 50: "God loves not the *tyrants* (*aẓ-ẓālimīna*)."

Sūrah iii. 104: "God desires not *tyranny* (*ẓulman*) unto the worlds."

Sūrah xxxi. 12: "Associating (with God) is a mighty *wrong* (*ẓulmun 'aẓīmun*)."

Sūrah ii. 54: "It was themselves they were *wronging* (*kānū anfusa-hum yaẓlimūna*)."

ẒULMAH (ظلمة), pl. *ẓulamāt.* "Darkness." A term used in theology for (1) Ignorance, (2) Belief in a plurality of gods, (3) Transgressions, (4) Afflictions.

Qur'ān, Sūrah xxiv. 40: "Or like darkness (*ka-ẓulumātin*) on a deep sea, there covers it a wave above which is a wave, above which is a cloud,—darkness one above another,—when one puts out his hand he can scarcely see it; for he to whom God has given no light, he has no light."

ZŪ 'L-QA'DAH (ذو القعدة). *Lit.* The "Master of Truce." The eleventh month of the Muḥammadan year, so called because it was the month in which the ancient Arabs abstained from warfare. [MONTHS.]

ZŪ 'L-QARNAIN (ذو القرنين). *Lit.* "He of the two horns." A celebrated personage mentioned in the 18th chapter of the Qu'rān, who is generally considered to be Alexander the Great, although Muslim writers hold him to have been contemporary with Abraham.

Al-Qasṭalānī, the commentator on al-Bukhārī, says: "Zū 'l-qarnain was a king named Sakandar, whose *wazīr*, or chancellor, was Khiẓr [KHIZR], and was contemporary with Abraham, the Friend of God, with whom he visited the Ka'bah at Makkah. There is some difference of opinion as to his being a prophet, but all learned men are agreed that he was a man of faith and piety."

Al-Baiẓāwī says: "He was Sakandar ar-Rūmī, King of Persia and Greece."

Al-Kamālain say: "He was Sakandar ar-Rūmī, but was contemporary with Abraham, and not the Sakandar who lived about three hundred years before Christ, who was an infidel."

Muḥammad, in his Qur'ān, whilst professing to give an inspired account of Zū'l-qarnain, supplies us with but a confused description, as follows:—

"They will ask thee of Zū'l-qarnain. Say: I will recite to you an account of him. Verily We (God) established his power upon the earth, and We gave him a means to accomplish every end; so he followed his way, until when he reached the setting of the sun, he found it to set in a miry fount; and hard by he found a people. We (God) said, 'O Zū'l-qarnain! whether thou chastise or whether thou treat them generously'—'As for him who is impious,' he said, 'we will chastise him;' then shall he be taken back to his Lord, and He will chastise him with a grievous chastisement. But as to him who believeth, and doeth that which is right, he shall have a generous recompense, and We will lay on them our easy behests. Then followed he a route, until when he reached the rising of the sun, he found it to rise on a people to whom We had given no shelter from it. Thus it was. And We had a full knowledge of the forces that were with him. Then followed he a route, until he came between the two mountains, beneath which he found a people who scarce understood a language. They said, 'O Zū'l-qarnain! Verily Gog and Magog (*i.e.* the barbarous people of Eastern Asia) waste this land; shall we then pay thee tribute, so thou build a rampart between us and them?' He said, 'Better than your tribute is the might wherewith my Lord hath strengthened me; but help me strenuously, and I will set a barrier between you and them. Bring me blocks of iron'—until when it filled the space between the mountain sides; 'Blow,' said he, 'upon it'—until when he had set it on fire he said,' 'Bring me molten brass that I may pour upon it.' And Gog and Magog were not able to scale it, neither were they able to dig through it. 'This,' said he, 'is a mercy from my Lord.'" (Qur'ān, Sūrah xviii. 82–96.)

There are different opinions as to the reason of the surname, "two-horned." Some think it was given him because he was King of the East and of the West, or because he had made expeditions to both those extreme parts of the earth; or else because he had two horns on his diadem, or two curls of hair, like horns, on his forehead. Perhaps there is some allusion to the he-goat of Daniel, although he is represented with but one horn. (Dan. viii. 5.)

AZ-ZUMAR (الزمر). "Troops." The title of the xxxixth Sūrah of the Qur'ān, in the 73rd verse of which the word occurs: "But those who fear God shall be driven to Paradise in *troops*."

ZUNNĀR (زنار). In Persia, the belt worn by Christians and Jews. In India, the Brahmanical thread. A term used amongst the Ṣūfīs for sincerity in the path of religion. (*Kashfu 'l-Iṣṭilāḥāt, in loco.*)

ZŪ 'N-NŪN (ذو النون). *Lit.* "Man of the fish." A title given to the Prophet Jonah, in Qur'ān, Sūrah xxi. 87. [JONAH.]

ẒURĀḤ (ضراح). *Lit.* "That which is very distant." A term used by al-Baiẓāwī the commentator for the *Baitu 'l-Ma'mūr*, or the model of the Ka'bah, which is said to be in the fourth heaven, and is referred to in the Qur'ān, Sūrah lii. 4: "By the visited home (*i.e. Baitu 'l-Ma'mūr*)." (See *al-Baiẓāwī, in loco.*)

ZŪ 'R-RAḤIM (ذو الرحم), pl. *zawū 'l-arḥām*, or *ūlū 'l-arḥām*. *Lit.* "A possessor of the womb." A uterine relation. The plural form *ūlū 'l-arḥam* occurs twice in the Qur'ān.

Sūrah viii. 76: "And they who have believed and have since fled their country, and fought at your side, these also are of you. Those who are united by ties of blood (*ūlū 'l-arḥām*), are the nearest of kin to each other according to the Book of God. Verily God knoweth all things."

Sūrah xxxiii. 6: "Nearer of kin to the faithful is the Prophet, than they are to their own selves. His wives are their mothers. According to the Book of God, they who are related by blood (*ūlū 'l-arḥām*) are nearer the one to the other than other believers, and than those who have fled their country for the cause of God: but whatever kindness ye show to your kindred, shall be noted down in the Book."

INDEX.

ث

ج

ح

خ

د

ذ

س

ش

غ

ف

ق

ل

م

ن

ه